Wayne Hampton holds a Ph.D. in political science from the University of Tennessee, Knoxville. He plays guitar and banjo and lectures on popular culture.

Guerrilla Minstrels

Wayne Hampton

Guerrilla Minstrels

John Lennon
Joe Hill
Woody Guthrie
Bob Dylan

The
University of
Tennessee Press
KNOXVILLE

Publication of this book has been aided by a grant
from the American Council of Learned Societies
from funds provided by the Andrew W. Mellon Foundation.

Manufactured in the United States of America.
First Edition.

The paper used in this book meets the minimum requirements
of the American National Standard for Permanence of Paper
for Printed Library Materials, Z39.48-1984.
Binding materials have been chosen for durability.

Library of Congress Cataloging-in-Publication Data

Hampton, Wayne, 1947-
Guerrilla minstrels.

Bibliography: p.
Discographies: p.
Includes index.
1. Protest songs—United States—History and criticism. 2. Lennon, John, 1940-1980. 3. Hill, Joe, 1879-1915. 4. Guthrie, Woody, 1912-1967. 5. Dylan, Bob, 1941- . 6. Musicians—United States—Biography. 7. United States—Popular culture. I. Title.
ML3477.H36 1986 784.6'836123'0973 85-31508
ISBN 0-87049-489-9 (alk. paper)

To Lisa and Abigail Rose

Contents

Illustrations

Photo section follows page 148

Woody Guthrie

Bob Dylan

Preface

This book discusses the protest song culture of America and the role of heroism and hero-worship in this tradition over time. I believe that heroism is a fundamental factor in the equation of protest. My interest in protest culture is partly the result of my Appalachian origins and partly a result of my exposure to, and participation in, the popular music and culture of the 1960s. Some of my most vivid childhood memories are of banjo and fiddle players passing the time in the parlors of those little country stores with the sloping floors sanded smooth from the shuffling feet of generations of familiar customers. I grew to love this music and its culture, but my earliest heroes came from the popular "folk" music groups of the early 1960s: Dave Guard of the Kingston Trio, Lou Gotlieb of the Limelighters, John Phillips of the Journeymen, and Chad Mitchell of the trio of the same name. Although they represented an apolitical and nontraditional music culture, I cannot deny the significance of these "button-down" folk heroes. They introduced me to the more authentic protest heroes from the 1940s, particularly Woody Guthrie and Pete Seeger. In time I was also drawn to the more cerebral sounds of the urban protest coffee house singers, more directly in the lineage of Guthrie and Seeger: Joan Baez, Bob Dylan, Phil Ochs, and Tom Paxton. But they soon proved too intellectual for those changing times, and I found myself following Dylan, through the spell cast by the Beatles, into the realm of folk-rock: the Byrds, the Lovin' Spoonful, Simon and Garfunkel, Crosby, Stills, Nash, and Young. And as the names of the groups became more personalized, I became more deeply immersed in the popular cultism of the hippie era.

Looking back on it now it seems silly, but seeing Bob Dylan and Neil Young performing at the recent political cultural events, Live Aid and Farm Aid, ignited a spark inside me, rekindling the old flames of hero-worship. Watching the symbiotic relationship of popular music culture and political idealism mature or degenerate (depending on one's perspective) for almost thirty years now, I have seen the popular personality, or star system, completely devour the tradition of protest singing. I have written this book to struggle with the implications of these developments. I am not convinced that these changes are necessarily bad or good, but only that they are a reality in need of assessment.

I believe that the single most important variable in the protest song tradition is the cult of the singer-songwriter. Although this cult is perhaps the result of the special nature of the protest song—that such songs were written by known authors in response to specific historical circumstances—I think it is true that all cultures are the product of human action, being mediated through the agency of heroism. The phenomenon of the heroic molding and shaping history through the force of idolatry is of fundamental importance in my understanding of culture. Protest song culture is but one example.

When I refer to the "protest song tradition," the "culture of protest," or simply "protest," I mean a specific unfolding historical-cultural movement that has used songs and singing, as well as a variety of other dramatic and symbolic practices, to serve political ends, specifically, the cause of social justice. The heroes of protest have also served these ends. I will discuss heroism and the culture of protest as integral components in a "cultural guerrilla" process, which uses cultural and artistic items in a symbolic and conceptual approach to revolutionary politics and whose primary objective is consciousness (as opposed to institutional) change. I will use the terms "cultural guerrilla" and "mind guerrilla" interchangeably to refer to both the process of consciousness change and those who participate in this process. The political practices that have sustained the culture of protest over time, as well as the performers, promoters, writers, critics, record producers, and fans of the culture of protest, are referred to as cultural or mind guerrillas. They are both the dance and the dancers, doing John Lennon's mind guerrilla.

I have structured my thoughts around certain key personalities

(John Lennon, Joe Hill, Woody Guthrie, and Bob Dylan), who I believe are representative of eras and genres of protest. I call these performer-activists "guerrilla minstrels." I may also at points use the terms "singing heroes" and "protest heroes." This is the story of the guerrilla minstrel in the culture of protest and the cultural guerrilla he has served. It is told from the point of view of a participant. It is my sincere wish that this story itself will become a part of the cultural guerrilla.

The first chapter is a general introduction to heroism and the cultural guerrilla. Chapter II is a brief discussion of the life and works of John Lennon. It is not intended to be an exhaustive analysis but rather to prepare the reader for the chapters on Hill, Guthrie, and Dylan (Chapters IV, V, and VI). Much of the terminology employed here (mind games, mind guerrilla, and the like) was derived from Lennon's songs. The example of his life and death will serve as an ideal type and a point of reference from which to discuss the other heroes of this study. In chapter III, I delve into the political philosophy behind the cultural guerrilla, discussing it as a "utopian sensibility" supporting a "totalization" process that brings together people, ideas, ideals, and practices to form a common community of protest. My intention is to integrate these two concepts into a further discussion of heroism. The theoretical faint of heart might want to skip lightly over this chapter and move on to those about the heroes. The final chapter is a critique of heroism, focusing on problems it creates for the utopian sensibility.

In writing any book, one of necessity incurs debts to friends, colleagues, and family. Because this project has taken almost seven years, my list is long. I must begin with an expression of my grateful thanks to the late Arnett Elliott, who first accepted this work in the form of a rather unorthodox Ph.D. dissertation in political science at the University of Tennessee at Knoxville. I would also especially like to thank Richard Penner of the Department of English for his invaluable encouragement, editing, and assistance throughout the entire period of the conception, preparation, and publication of this manuscript. I am also extremely indebted to the tireless precision of the editing skills of Susan Becker of the Department of History. I must express my warm appreciation to Bob Gorman of the Department of Political Science for his unceasing efforts to keep this project on track. I would also like to thank Mavis Bryant, Cynthia Maude-Gembler, Katherine Holloway, and Jennifer Siler of the University of Tennessee Press for their support as well as their patience. The copyediting of Trudie Calvert was also exceptional. Special thanks are extended to my dear friend Scott Conrad of Asheville, North Carolina, who lent precious books and recordings from his private collection. Finally, I owe a substantial debt to Margaret Garret of Knoxville for her skillful, expert preparation of the original manuscript. And I am always indebted to Lisa and Abbey for putting up with me through the entire process.

November 3, 1985 — Wayne Hampton, Ph.D.
Knoxville, Tennessee

1 Introduction: *The Working-Class Hero and the Cultural Guerrilla*

A working class hero is something to be.
—John Lennon, 1970

On the morning of December 9, 1980, I awoke around 7:30, flipped on the TV on the night stand, and was immediately jarred into total wakefulness by a full-screen image of the name JOHN LENNON with the parenthetic dates 1940–1980. I had just missed the "Today" show's news segment and story on the death of John Lennon. As the Beatle music faded into an American Express commercial, I felt a dull ache deep within me, in some unknown region where I had not felt pain for many years. How could this be? John Lennon is dead? Who would want to kill a former Beatle? It had been more than ten years since he had done anything outrageous enough to provoke a scornful public. I thought that America had long since lost its obsession with the Beatles. How could so much passion remain after all those years?

But on that cold December morning it all came flooding back: February 1964, wondering what all the fuss was about as I watched that funny English band sing "I Wanna Hold Your Hand" on the "Ed Sullivan Show" on a quiet Sunday evening after church with my older sisters; later that summer, listening to *Meet the Beatles* at a girl friend's house, still wondering; and finally being caught by *Rubber Soul* and then stunned by *Sgt. Pepper.* I also remembered watching *Magical Mystery Tour* on TV and later the "Hey Jude" video and then "Imagine," in which Yoko Ono, slowly, ritualistically opens the room-length drapes, while the morning sun floods in on Lennon singing, "Imagine all the people sharing all the world." And I remembered seeing *Help!* in a home-town theater and then *Yel-*

low Submarine in an elegant old theater in Waukeegan, Illinois. I remembered how shocked I was when I stumbled onto the infamous *Two Virgins* LP in a head shop in Old Town, Chicago. I was dismayed by how normal these two heroic figures looked with their saggy bodies and how unkempt their bedroom was. I remembered weird little things, like how I was too embarrassed to buy that album, even though it was packaged in a brown paper bag, and how I thought the line in the "Ballad of John and Yoko" was "we're only trying to get us a piece." I remembered singing along to "Oh Darlin' " on the mess decks of the destroyer on which I was sailing across the Atlantic in the service of God and country and of slowly awakening to the irony of harmonizing with some of my guitar-playing shipmates, singing, "all we are saying is give peace a chance." I also remembered watching Joe Cocker sing "With a Little Help from My Friends" in the movie *Woodstock* in a plush theater in London. There was a bar in the lobby, and later I rode all over the city in a taxi with my drunken sailor friends looking for Abbey Road. And I remembered about hearing that Paul McCartney was dead.

On that awful winter morning in 1980, I thought maybe this was just another Paul-is-dead hoax. But this time it was real. The TV interrupted my youthful reveries with the full, grim details of what was to be perhaps the single most sobering moment in the history of rock music and the counterculture.

As Tom Brokaw began to line out the now familiar tale of Mark David Chapman and the tragedy outside the Dakota, I was struck not only by a genuine, numbing grief and disgust but also by that curious fascination one feels when in the experiential midst of a great historical event. Not since the assassinations of the 1960s had I been so emotionally connected to the mass media. The comparison with the assassination of John F. Kennedy was obvious but misleading. I got that news over the school intercom during a tenth grade biology class. It was a very powerful event, as was the murder of Lee Harvey Oswald by Jack Ruby, which I saw live on national television, but I was too young to appreciate fully what was happening.

Of course I had never experienced John Kennedy in the same way, or at the same level, that I had experienced John Lennon. JFK was not *just* a politician, but he was nevertheless a politician. John Lennon was far more important to my psyche, for he was a rock star and a poet. His words, his deeds, and his image were a part of me in a way that no politician's could ever be. Anyway, a rock star had never before been the target of an assassin's bullet. People have been killing their political leaders for centuries. Although the act is always shocking, it is somehow expected and at some level understood. But though many rock stars had died public deaths, they had either died accidentally in car wrecks or plane crashes or from drug overdoses. Why had John Lennon attracted the assassin?

As a graduate student in political science studying politics and popular culture, already embarked on a scholarly study of the great American protest singers Joe Hill, Woody Guthrie, and Bob Dylan, and using a title suggested by one of Lennon's lesser-known but undeniably significant songs, "Working Class Hero," I could not resist the political questions. Was Lennon not also in the protest tradition? Was Lennon's music—especially songs like "Give Peace a Chance," "Power to the People," "Imagine," and "Woman Is the Nigger of the World"—not also in the topical-political tradition? Did not many people, especially the generation of the 1960s, look to such singers as Pete Seeger, Holly Near, and Arlo Guthrie as political figures? Was John Lennon not one of the most significant, or perhaps the most significant (next to Bob Dylan), of the singer-activists of that decade? Was it not therefore conceivable that Lennon's death, however unprecedented, was more similar to those of John Kennedy, Robert Kennedy, or Martin Luther King, Jr., than I might first have realized? Was Lennon not a political figure in much the same sense as these leaders? Could his assassin have been politically motivated in the same sense that Oswald had been? Was Lennon's death, then, like that of JFK, a political event?

My mind was racing as I slipped into my clothes and headed out the door. My ear stayed glued to the local rock station as I drove to school. My mind was numb with all these questions but hungry for more information to enable me to come to grips with what was happening. I remained glued to the media for the next few weeks. I tapped reels and reels of the Beatle specials and interviews that filled the airwaves. I tapped the memorial service and the ceremonial meditation on December 14. And I bought every newstand publication—from *Rolling Stone* to *TV Guide* to the *National Enquirer*—that featured a story on the tragedy. Every exploitive, trashy exposé that emerged in the aftermath of Lennon's death ended up on my night stand. This book is in many ways the result of my heartfelt yet macabre fascination and obsession with the Lennon assassination.

As the news of the assassination began to sink in, a certainty and confidence about what I was thinking crystallized in my mind. I had finally grasped the significance of my work on Hill, Guthrie, and Dylan. It is not just the music he produces that makes a protest singer. It is also the human image behind the music. It is not just polemical songs but also heroes and hero-worship that make up the culture of protest singing. I came to see not only the importance of the hero to the political process generally but also the overwhelming significance of the hero to the cultural politics of the 1960s.

All the questions I had been struggling with in relation to the protest song tradition in America seem to have been answered, unfortunately, by Mark David Chapman. How is a song culture political? What kind of politics is it? How do Hill, Guthrie, and Dylan represent a continuity of this strange political tradition? What tactics are shared by these three public personages and the historical and political eras they personify? What was political about their lives and their works? Did they share a common purpose and philosophy?

With the death of John Lennon a set of answers fell into place within my mind. I soon came to realize that I was dealing with a form of symbolic politics that involved cultural tactics: the assault of art and image upon the mind. I have come to know this politics of consciousness development as the "cultural guerrilla."

As the years have passed, I have been stunned by the public reaction to Lennon's death. As the memorials, pilgrimages, vigils, memorabilia, tabloid journalism, books, recordings, music videos, and films continue to pour out, my amazement grows along with my bewilderment. The power of this deceased individual to generate public interest and social unity on such a mass scale has been staggering and unbelievable, even eerie, but also puzzling and more than a bit mysterious. I wrote this book to wrestle with this morbid puzzle.

This puzzle, as I have come to terms with it, can be resolved only through a discussion of heroism.[1] In this book I will attempt to make a case for the fundamental importance of heroism and hero-worship in the bonding process which attempts to forge unity out of the rich variety of causes, movements, organizations, and institutions that make up the protest song culture of America. Heroism and hero-worship are the superglue that bonds the music and the protests to the cultural skin of the countless and diverse individuals who make up the mass audience.

Protest song culture is, therefore, to a significant degree, a composite of the cult followings of a narrow plurality of heroes and heroines in the popular music industry and the ideals and symbols with which they are associated. Through the vehicle of hero-worship, protest song culture becomes more than a musical genre to which a complex of abstract principles and partisan polemics has been attached. As these abstractions are embodied in the mythos of the hero, the culture attains its historicity—its life. Musical styles, social values, and political ideals adhere to an actual—though dramaticized—life story. In the process, a biography comes to support political abstractions, and an ideology is humanized. This is all part of a dialectical process that Jean-Paul Sartre and others have called totalization: the process whereby social unity is synthesized out of diversity and chaos.[2]

The hero is thus more than a thinker, spokesman, or activist speculating in song on the problems of the world. He is more than a mere source of propaganda and doctrine. The hero is a human being and, as such, he is a source of identity and allegiance. The hero is a power, a leader, and a source of authority. He is a totalizer.

The hero is a totalizer in that he or she is a public personage and a mythos around whom social unity and action crystallize. This unity takes the form of a cult following and is totalized out of a shared identity with the ideals the hero exemplifies. Hero-worship is our attempt to emulate this heroic example. When the many identify with the ways of one, a collectivity results. Heroism therefore presupposes totalization. In other words, there is a personality (or perhaps a set of personalities) behind our ideological dispositions and associations, even though it may take the death of the individual behind that personality to shock us into realizing the importance that such a public image may hold for us. Whether we acknowledge it or not, we are all hero-worshipers at some level.

Heroism

Foremost among the characteristics of heroism is power. The hero is believed to possess a special genius, a great talent, a magnetic personality, a charisma, and a disarming charm and appeal, which capture and sweep away the follower. Perhaps the hero's greater power is what Thomas Carlyle, in his 1840 *Lectures on Heroes, Hero-Worship, and the Heroic in History*, called "original insight."[3] The hero is a seer, one who is gifted with the ability to comprehend the reality behind the facade. Through his words and deeds these fresh insights into the hidden inner workings of reality are revealed to "ordinary" men and women who constitute the hero's cult following. The visions of the hero, revealed to the chosen ones, become their world view, their "consciousness." In this way the hero puts his stamp on a generation.

Heroism also has a messianic quality.[4] At some level the followers perceive the hero is a savior, one whose insights, teachings, example, and leadership will deliver them from perceived evils, such as oppressive and/or exploitive socioeconomic conditions, the meaninglessness of their empty lives, or the political injustices they perceive. The hero and the ideals he represents are a source of hope and inspiration for the followers. Hero-worship is thus a means of transcending alienation and despair by following a Moses to the Promised Land, or a Karl Marx to the communist utopia, or even a John Lennon to Newtopia. The hero is often perceived as a divine representative, and his or her powers are often believed to be spiritual and sacred. The followers are devotees to the religion of cultural protest.

Though imbued with divinity, the hero is mortal. He, too, suffers. A large part of his mystique is that he sacrifices to defend the principles he represents. Heroes like Socrates, Christ, Gandhi, and Martin Luther King, Jr., have died for their principles; John Lennon's death came to represent such principles. But it is important that the hero is often destined to pass through mortal suffering and the martyr's death to achieve the immortality of legend and myth.

And finally, through such legend and myth, the hero is connected to a cult, or a loose, amorphous collective following formed in his name. The cult first mythologizes the hero, embodying within his image the ideals to which the collectively aspires, and then attempts to gloss over or ignore those aspects of the individual that do not fit neatly into the mold of the myth. It struck me as very odd, for example, that in all the radio and television tributes to Lennon in the immediate aftermath of his death, the headlining songs were almost without exception "Imagine" and "Give Peace a Chance." Not once did I hear "Working Class Hero" and rarely did I hear "Mind Games," the two songs I thought most captured the essence of John Lennon. One of these overused the word "fuck," and the other was perhaps too politically explicit. But, for whatever reasons, the latter two songs do not have the public appeal that the former do. The point is that the hero is not the individual behind the image. He or she is a collective idealization that is associated with that individual.

Another way to look at this concept is that the hero is imaginary. He or she is a transcendental nonobject with the paradoxical capacity to affect real people in the real world in an objective manner. This contradiction is at the heart of what I will later discuss as the problem of hero-worship. For although heroism may be a positive unifying force, it also has a darker side that presents the possibility of a society of blind followers. Such are the dialectics of heroism.

The Guerrilla Minstrel

As the events of December 8, 1980, have passed into rock history, it has become increasingly clear to me that the public image of John Lennon was essentially that of a protest singer in the tradition of Hill, Guthrie, and Dylan.[5] Moreover, as a self-described working-class hero and mind guerrilla, John Lennon was perhaps the epitome of the protest singer, linked in spirit to such performers as Phil Ochs, Joan Baez, or Paul Robeson. Lennon's protest image is so typical that I have chosen him as the first guerrilla minstrel to consider in this book. His story provides a window into the culture of protest from which the discussion of Hill, Guthrie, and Dylan will follow.

In John Lennon the image of the working-class hero and the guerrilla minstrel are one and the same. The totality of his image and of all the life images contained in this book consists of these two complementary elements. In some sense there is a direct line of descent from John Lennon back to Bob Dylan to Woody Guthrie and to Joe Hill. As I will show, Lennon listened to and was deeply influenced by the songs of Bob Dylan, Guthrie was the major formative influence upon the early Dylan, and Guthrie was a product of the union singing movement with which Hill is closely associated. All are heroes in a tradition of protest allied with the popular music culture of America. And all fancied themselves as "working class," though this concept had different meanings for each.

Some people might be uncomfortable with my use of the term "working class" because heroes of the popular music culture, even those whose careers are mediocre, become affluently bourgeois by almost any standard. Moreover, what I refer to as "working-class music"—social protest music- and protest culture generally—has appealed primarily to left-wing intellectuals, artists, and bohemians and has been either ignored or scorned by blue-collar workers. Nevertheless, the proletarian ideal looms large in protest culture. Though they may rarely be exposed to manual labor, these minstrel mind guerrillas often wear work shirts and overalls. Those who are successful may be embarrassed by their wealth and fame. Although they may not take a vow of poverty, they tend to romanticize that condition and at least avoid the most conspicuous of bourgeois comforts. They once were fond of Marxist rhetoric, and their voices have sustained the message and symbolism of working-class revolution, with or without the workers. It is in this sense only that guerrilla minstrels are working-class heroes. They are heroes in the name of the working class, champions of the poor and oppressed.

"Working class" is, of course, an elastic concept. It may be applied in seemingly contradictory ways. Among the heroes considered here it appears to apply more to Hill and Guthrie than to Dylan and Lennon. And yet, as we will see, Lennon, under the influence of Dylan, described himself as working class, and Dylan went out of his way to cultivate a working-class image. Perhaps none were working class in the socioeconomic sense, with the possible exception of Joe Hill, but even for him there is room for doubt. At least three of the four came from what can only be described as middle-class backgrounds. And three of the four were to amass vast fortunes from the sale of their copyrighted music. Their "working classness" was therefore not to be found in their social origins or their economic stations in life but in their social consciousness, their political idealism, and their dedication to some form of revolutionary change.

The other common element shared by all the heroic personalities discussed in this book is a common approach to politics. They all viewed politics from a cultural and symbolic perspective, for in many ways, in the politics of a protest singer, the medium is the message. The means of protest seems to determine the nature of the protest. In blending voices and sustained harmonies, these heroes' political values and ideals were formed. Out of heavily syncopated rhythms or peaceful, lilting melodies, their political world view was constructed. Protesting against the world of discord and strife, they sang the politics of harmony and peace. They were idealists and utopians. And although Dylan in particular has flirted with dark, dystopic visions and totalitarian premonitions, even his pessimism is utopian in the sense that it is imaginary, dramaticized, and romanticized when set to music. All were therefore utopians in some sense. Perhaps Lennon and Dylan are best described by Lennon's concept of "Newtopia." They were representatives of a new utopianism, distinct musically as well as ideologically from the topical-protest Old Left tradition of Hill and Guthrie. All, however, were variations on the utopian theme of the cultural guerrilla.

All the singers discussed in this book were guerrilla minstrels. All saw music, art, and image as political weapons. All felt a responsibility to use their art and notoriety to further the cause, generally speaking, of the working class. All were symbolic politicians abhorring violence on principle, preferring instead to play "mind games." This is a book about the heroes of the cultural guerrilla and the mind games they have played. It is the story of the guerrilla minstrel. It begins with John Lennon.

2 John Lennon: *The Mind Games of Newtopia*

We're playin' those mind games together.
—John Lennon, 1973

The story of John Lennon is a potent symbol of and for the generation of the 1960s.[1] Because he was a creative giant, former Beatle, rock superstar, and international celebrity, his life story is a source of nostalgia and inspiration for millions of young people in search of personal identity. It takes them back to another time and place, to a golden age when flower power, long hair, psychedelics, Oriental mysticism, and mass politics were the rage. It is the hippie version of JFK and Camelot. One stimulates the liberal's imagination, and the other warms the hearts of once young radicals.

The story has all the key dramatic ingredients: excitement, passion, scandal, romance, comedy, tragedy, and pathos. It could be a classic heroic tale from any era, but it is the story of one man's struggle with personal, political, and artistic commitment and responsibility. It is a story of rags-to-riches success and of the disillusionment, rage, and self-destructiveness of sudden, overwhelming fame. It is a story of salvation achieved through public political conversion, commitment, and change and of dedication to love, altruism, and social conscience. But it is also a story of the ridicule, persecution, social isolation, and government repression that were to be the price of that commitment and of the resulting mental, marital, and professional breakdown and depoliticization. And finally, it is the story of perseverance, reunion, and revitalization and of sudden, senseless, tragic death.

The Lennon legend totalizes a system of values and lifestyle. For like few other popular artists of his era, John Lennon was able to capture, articulate, and embody the fleeting essence of his generation and his era: its madness as well as its brilliance and the inherent contradictions of its dark, nihilistic pessimism and its exuberant, euphoric quest for an impossible utopian ideal.

The political impact of such a life and legend is probably impossible to measure. Lennon's impact was more symbolic than institutional, but changes did occur, attitudes were revolutionized, and lifestyles were altered. For the purposes of this book, John Lennon's major contribution to the history of the protest song movement in America was his role, following Bob Dylan's lead, in the politicization of the already inherently revolutionary pop music culture of the 1960s.

Lennon and the Beatles

John Lennon's public character contains all the heroic qualities of greatness and all the prerequisites of immortality: superstar-activist, prophet-seer, martyr, and saint. His outlandish manner, his bizarre stage antics, and his generally anarchic demeanor set the tone for two generations of punk rock and youth rebellion.[2] His creative powers, fresh insights, and uncanny ability to sense and exploit the latest pop cultural trends bordered on the mystical. His outlandish public statements and his repartee with the world press are now legends in the folklore of the world counterculture. Memorable incidents, such as his 1966 remark that the "Beatles are now more popular than Christ," got the blood boiling in the generation gap and brought into sharp focus the cracks in the superstructure of Western civilization.[3] Such a remark also reveals the arrogance and self-assurance that came from riding the crest of the cultural revolution of the 1960s.

Lennon was abandoned by his working-class parents and raised by his Aunt Mimi in a lower-middle-class suburb in Liverpool and therefore carried a burden of pain, resentment, and bitterness throughout his life. And yet he always felt he possessed a special genius and was destined for greatness but that he was being held back and beaten down by an insidious system of institutionalized oppression. In *Lennon Remembers,* he said:

> People like me are aware of their so-called genius at ten, eight, nine. . . . I always wondered, "Why has nobody discovered me?" In school, didn't they see that I'm cleverer than anybody in this school? That the teachers are stupid, too? That all they had was information that I didn't need.

It was obvious to me. . . . Why didn't anybody notice me. . . . A couple of teachers would notice me, encourage me to be something or other, to draw or to paint—express myself. But most of the time they were trying to beat me into being a fuckin' dentist or a teacher. And then the fuckin' fans tried to beat me into being a fuckin' Beatle or an Engelbert Humperdink, and the critics tried to beat me into being Paul McCartney.[4]

For the Beatles, discovery, success, and fame came at a very high price: the loss of personal identity and integrity. Lennon always resented the artificial packaging and commercialization of the Fab Four. He told Jann Wenner:

If I could be a fuckin' fisherman, I would, you know. If I had the capabilities to be something other than I am, I would. It's no fun being an artist. You know what it's like, writing, it isn't fun, it's torture. . . . And these fuckin' bastards there just sucking us to death, that's about all we can do, is do it like circus animals. I resent being an artist, in that respect, I resent performing for fuckin' idiots who don't know anything. They can't feel; I'm the one that's feeling, because I'm the one expressing. They live vicariously through me and other artists.[5]

He became disillusioned by the unreality of the Beatles' unprecedented fame. It was impossible fully to comprehend the incredible mystique that surrounded them. Lennon told Wenner of cripples:

Whenever we went on tour . . . [there were] always a few seats laid aside for cripples and people in wheelchairs. . . . Because we were famous, we were supposed to have . . . [supernatural powers]. And they were in our dressing room all the time. . . . And it's always the mother or nurse pushing them on you. They would just say hello and go away but [the mothers] would push them at you like you were Christ or something, as if there were some aura about you which will rub off on them. . . . and when we would go through corridors they would be all touching us. It got like that, it was horrifying.[6]

In 1971, looking back across the decade, Lennon felt that in spite of the Beatles' supposed supernatural powers and phenomenal mass impact, nothing of substance in the society had changed:

The people who were in control and in power and the class system and the whole bullshit bourgeois scene is exactly the same except that there is a lot of middle-class kids with long hair walking around London in trendy clothes. . . . The same bastards are in control, the same people are running everything, its exactly the same. They hyped the kids and the generation.

We've grown up a little, all of us, and there has been a change and we are a bit freer and all that, but it's the same game, nothin's really changed. They're doing exactly the same things, selling arms to South Africa, killing blacks on the street, people are living in fuckin' poverty with rats crawling over them, it's the same.[7]

After 1966, Lennon became increasingly cynical about his role as Beatle John. He began to see through the artificial reality of his superstardom. A young American folk idol, Bobby Dylan, had shown him a more responsible way to use his medium and introduced him to an illegal substance (marijuana) that promised to open his mind and release his most sensitive creative powers and insights.[8] In 1965, "Help!" had been a desperate plea for someone to rescue him from the emptiness of his existence, and "Nowhere Man" at the beginning of 1966 was a pessimistic view of his numbing sense of powerlessness and despair. "Rain," released that spring, was the first of the metaphorical drug songs that would become common in the pop music culture of the late 1960s. And if we are to believe the right-wing Christian press, "Rain" is not the only Beatle drug metaphor. "Norwegian Wood," from the 1965 LP *Rubber Soul,* is a pseudonym for marijuana imported from Norway, "Yellow Submarine" is a slang term for an amphetamine capsule, and "Lucy in the Sky with Diamonds" stands for LSD.[9] Clearly, the Beatles were an important part of the drug culture. Lennon in particular seemed to be resolving some of his despair and hopelessness through the euphoria of the marijuana high and LSD trip, and he called out to a new generation of the disaffected to follow him out of the tedium of their boring and meaningless lives. No longer content merely to hold his public's hand, John Lennon felt increasingly compelled to take the role of countercultural leader.

Lennon and the Counterculture

The year 1966 was a time of bewildering social and political turbulence.[10] The Johnson administration's War on Poverty and the 1964 Civil Rights Act had not resolved the racial tension in America. In fact, the civil rights struggle was taking a turn toward increased violence, with the black ghettos in many of America's major urban areas exploding in riots. The anger of the separatists and black power advocates was replacing the passive resistance of Martin Luther King, Jr. The administration's escalation of the war in Vietnam only fed the flames of domestic unrest because blacks were dying in disproportionate numbers to whites and white middle-class students were losing their 2-S deferments.

Although the rise of the new radicalism of the mid-1960s had many causes, the war in Southeast Asia served as the major catalyst to mass protest. United States troop strength had risen suddenly and dramatically to almost 400,000 by the end of 1966, and combat losses mounted. In just one week in September there were 970 United States casualties and 145 combat deaths. More than 5,000 United States soldiers were killed in action in 1966.[11]

The world press—and the world—became increasingly fixated on the war. With daily monotony, war news interrupted evening meals around the country and around the world with body counts and films of bloody combat. The Vietnam War was the first truly mass media war, and it reached out through the airwaves to touch more people more dramatically than any previous war in the history of the United States. The domestic impact was predictably unpredictable.[12]

Opposition to the war took two broad forms: radical activism and cultural dissent. One was called the "movement" and the other the "counterculture," and they became the twin pillars of what became known as the New Left.[13] The Old Left had practically vanished in the communist paranoia of the Cold War and the McCarthy era. It had survived the 1950s only as the bare but resilient thread of the peace movement against the spread of the new atomic weapons and as the white appendage of the black civil rights movement.[14] The Vietnam War gave the Left a renewed vitality and sense of purpose unmatched since the Great Depression.[15]

Much had changed since the 1930s. Franklin D. Roosevelt's New Deal and the social security system, World War II and the defeat of fascism, postwar economic prosperity and suburban affluence, atomic power and the superpower stalemate, television and the electric guitar all conspired to alter irrevocably the structure and format of the American Left. Its support base, its institutions and organizations, as well as its tactics and philosophy, underwent dramatic change.

By 1960, the Communist and Socialist parties in America were practically extinct, the victims of Cold War hysteria and government repression. The unions and the working classes had become contented and conservative, the victims of affluence and bourgeios acculturation. A New Left was emerging from America's universities and college campuses instead of from her mines and factories. The new working class consisted of white middle-class students, professors, draftees, and dropouts. This New Left was built on a foundation of student organizations such as the Students for a Democratic Society (SDS) and Student Nonviolent Coordinating Committee (SNCC), and it only loosely followed the blueprints of movement fathers such as Herbert Marcuse, C. Wright Mills, Paul Goodman, and Norman O. Brown, who had begun to analyze the changed conditions and the new revolutionary possibilities.[16]

The new radicals dropped the Marxist-Leninist politics of class conflict, consciousness development, and worker revolution to embrace the Gandhian politics of love, confrontation of conscience, and conversion through example and dignity.[17] They adopted a new bohemianism based on a cultlike devotion to pacifism, mind-altering drugs, Oriental mysticism, uninhibited sexual experimentation, and rock 'n' roll music.[18]

At first, the young radicals preferred folk music.[19] Bob Dylan had passed the old proletarian topical-folksinging tradition of the Wobblies, Woody Guthrie, and the Almanac Singers to a new generation of radicals. Dylan, along with Joan Baez, Phil Ochs, and Pete Seeger, had been a major populizer of this music and its message in the early 1960s.[20] But all that had changed in 1964 with the arrival of the Beatles onto American soil. The young radicals came to find their own distinctive sound in a revival of rock 'n' roll from the 1950s.[21] Even Bob Dylan would be swept up in the phenomenon of Beatlemania and the invasion of the British rockers. Folk music was too low key and square—too intellectual—for the new generation of dissent, who were in search of excitement, ecstasy, and existential fulfillment, instead of propaganda and polemics.

John Lennon can thus be understood as a working-class hero and cultural guerrilla only as an extension of the counterculture and the youth movement in America and the West. The Beatles, along with Dylan, the Rolling Stones, the Who, the Kinks, Jimmi Hendrix, Janis Joplin, the Jefferson Airplane, and the Doors, would become hip heroes and countercultural institutions. Psychedelic music (or acid rock) became the cultural bedcovers in the hallucinogenic dream world of the flower children and freaks who, in the spring of 1967, seemed to flood out of the American heartland by the thousands. Accompanied by the strains of *Sergeant Pepper's Lonely Hearts Club Band*, young runaways, outcasts, and dropouts flocked into San Francisco's Haight Ashbury district, New York City's East Village, and similar hippie enclaves in major cities around the nation and the world.[22] They were literally fleeing from the "good life," rejecting the materialistic values and mores of their mostly middle-class parents, fleeing the boredom and madness of suburban living, seeking adventure and purpose, and finding it in the brotherhood and oneness of the hippie lifestyle,[23] getting by with a little help from their friends.

Long hair, which the Beatles had made a symbol of nonconformity and youth rebellion, became the identity badge of the hippie subculture. Long hair had great symbolic significance. Earlier radicals were less conspicuous in their radicalism and able to ease in and out of the mainstream and avoid confrontation with parents, bosses, and authority figures in everyday situations. As Abbie Hoffman said, growing long hair was the "coming out of the closet for the counterculture."[24] The harassment it generated from parents, teachers, and cops, along with the jeers from "straights," only reinforced the primitive tribal solidarity of the hippies.

The hippies further enhanced their outcast status by consuming large quantities of illegal drugs and were thus always subject to arrest for possession. As a result, many lived in a constant state of paranoia, existing literally as outlaws. But drug use also served an important political function by helping to break down the rational barriers, so as to allow the individual to transcend the fetters of social conditioning. After the mind-altering experiences of the marijuana high, or more particularly the LSD trip, the devotee who had seen through the hypocrisy of his parents' all-consuming materialism could never (so it was thought) return to the plastic lifestyles of the middle class.

Rock music was another important extension of the drug experience and the drug culture. Rock was another vehicle designed to explode one's preconceived notions by setting free one's repressed feelings. The Beatles' psychedelic sound was meant to be listened to when one was stoned, and the combination of drugs and music was supposed to lead the listener to a new sense of awareness.[25]

This inherently antirational and anti-intellectual experimentation with drug-induced mysticism and the frenzied abandon of acid rock went hand in hand with a less inhibited sexuality. The hippies worshiped love and sexual freedom as a further extension of the process of freeing the pent-up passions of the oppressive Puritan morality of the American mainstream.[26]

After 1967, the hippie phenomenon swept suddenly and dramatically throughout the West like an out-of-control brush fire fed by the winds of the mass media. Although the hard-core activists never fully accepted the flower power, long hair, and lifestyle politics of the counterculture, they came to appreciate the political possibilities of cultural rebellion. After the onslaught of the hippies, New Left politics began to shift toward more dramatic publicity-seeking stunts or "events," as they came to be known. The traditional marches, rallies, and sit-ins gained more color and symbolic significance as teach-ins, be-ins, live-ins, love-ins, and smoke-ins evolved.[27]

By 1968, the antics of the Yippies were eclipsing the more sober SDS, which was beginning to suffer from internal disputes that would usher forth the more extremist Weathermen, who took their name and spirit from a Bob Dylan aphorism ("You don't need a weatherman to know which way the wind blows"),[28] taking the New Left in new and more violent directions.[29]

But back in the spring of 1967, as if to launch the summer of love and the birth of the hippies, the Beatles appeared on the international satellite television program *"Our World,"* which was broadcast in twenty-four countries and seen by more than 40 million people, singing a new anthem of countercultural innocence: "All You Need Is Love."[30] It was fitting testimony to the world's alienated youth, in search of belonging and discovering it in the camaraderie of the drug culture.

Lennon and Ono

The message of love would remain constant throughout the career of John Lennon after he left the Beatles and teamed up with the Japanese-American avant-garde artist Yoko Ono. Love was all that could rescue him and the millions he represented from a grim nihilism and total despair. For the message of love was aimed at the young radicals as well as the Cold Warriors. To the generals and politicians, the message was to stop the killing of young boys, the butchering of Asian civilians, and the napalming of primitives' villages. To the youth, Lennon's message was to lighten up a little; burning oneself on the steps of the Pentagon to stop the war was going too far. Pouring pigs' blood or one's own excrement over draft records was not only in bad taste but also provocatively illegal.[31]

Lennon felt that such confrontational politics was counterproductive and would only alienate the public and push the authorities into a corner, leaving them no choice but to come down hard on the protesters. He argued that it was more appropriate to confront the issues in ways that confused and frustrated the police and the court system. If everyone were in jail or dead, where would the revolution be? Instead, Lennon argued that the protesters should play politics at an existential level and in imaginary ways. If they concentrated on changing minds and lifestyles, politics and socioeconomics would then follow.[32]

Lennon was advocating a symbolic approach to politics. To him it was revolutionary to grow one's hair long as a symbol of one's rejection of the more conventional lifestyle. In a 1969 interview with British rock columnist David Wigg, he said, "All we are saying is symbolically, instead of kickin' in a shop window, say, do something like grow your hair . . . or stay in bed . . . Do something like that . . . something that can't be got, can't be smashed."[33] The same message was conveyed in the controversial line in the 1968 Beatle single "Revolution": "If you go carrying pictures of Chairman Mao, you ain't gonna make it with anyone any how."[34] Regardless of the issues he would face, Lennon's message in its essence would be consistently pacifistic, tempered almost always with a touch of humor.

When asked by Wigg if he took his politics seriously, Lennon replied: "I don't take it all too seriously, because I think that's the trouble with art, quote, music, quote, the peace movement, quote, and the world, quote, you know. I take everything with a pinch of salt. But I take life seriously, the serious job of being happy." When pressed by Wigg, who said that people were jeering and not taking him seriously, Lennon continued: "That's good, that's part of our policy, not to be taken seriously. Because I think our opposition, whoever they might be, in all their manifest forms, don't know how to handle humor. . . . We stand a better chance under that guise, because all the serious people, like Martin Luther King and Kennedy and Gandhi, got shot!"[35]

By 1969, the philosophy of love, nonviolence, symbolic radicalism, and the politics of humor had inevitably collided with the Vietnam War. "Love and Peace," along with "Drugs, Sex, and Rock 'n' Roll," had embarked on an imaginary crusade to end, or at least disrupt, the war in Southeast Asia. Lennon and Ono, along with the greater counterculture, came to focus their political energies on the war and a campaign for world peace. Lennon summed up their ambitions in 1969: "We are both artists. Peace is our art. . . . We stand a chance of influencing other young people. And it is they who will rule the world tomorrow."[36]

Lennon's career after he left the Beatles became decidedly political, advocating peace but also the entire countercultural package of personal freedom, worldwide participatory democracy, feminism, and cultural revolution. Within the confines of the Beatles, Lennon's political consciousness was held in check by Paul McCartney's more commercial pen. But in Yoko Ono, Lennon found someone who shared his eccentric approach to revolution. If anything, she was an even more seasoned cultural activist, having come from the art underground of New York City's Greenwich Village. She had also been much more eccentric and absurdist in her approach to politics. Her 1967 film *Bottoms,* for example, was publicized as a peace petition that 365 people had signed with their butts.[37] It was far more irreverent, farcical, and provocative than the boldest of Lennon's Beatle compositions such as "Revolution," "Happiness Is a Warm Gun," or "Why Don't We Do It in the Road?"

Their professional and personal partnership, though always controversial, seemed to be a good match by relieving the political and artistic inhibitions of each. John's celebrity status was so secure that he could take risks, and Yoko had nothing to lose but her anonymity and a great deal to gain from her association with a former Beatle. Both had been flirting with radicalism for years. The catalyst was a long and passionate letter from filmmaker Peter Watkins, who, after spelling out the world's troubles and problems, asked them what they were going to do about it. In a 1969 Canadian interview, Lennon recounted the story: "He [Watkins] said people in our position and his position have a responsibility to use the media for world peace. And we sat on the letter for three weeks and thought it over and figured at first we were doing our best with songs like 'All You Need is Love.' Finally we came up with the bed event and that was what sparked it off. It was like getting your call-up papers for peace. Then we did the bed event."[38]

The first bed event occurred in Amsterdam in March 1969 during the honeymoon of newlyweds John and Yoko. Knowing that the press would be out in full force, they decided to take advantage of the publicity, so they concocted the famous "Bed-in for Peace," inviting the press into the bedroom of the presidential suite of the Amsterdam Hilton for a week of peace talk. They intended it as an advertisement for peace, to counteract the publicity the war was getting. The Lennons repeated the bed event twice in May, first in the Bahamas and then in Toronto, where they recorded their first post-Beatle single, "Give

Peace a Chance."[39] In the 1980 *Playboy* interview, Lennon explained their motives:

> When we got married, we knew our honeymoon was going to be public anyway, so we decided to use it to make a statement. Our life is our art. That's what the bed-in was. We sat in bed and talked to reporters for seven days. It was hilarious. In effect, we were doing a commercial for peace instead of a commercial for war. The reporters were going "un-huh, yea, sure," but it didn't matter because our commercial went out irrespective. As I've said, everybody puts down TV commercials, but they go around singing them.[40]

But although they dedicated their lives and their art to the peace movement and to the counterculture generally, Lennon and Ono steadfastly shunned any notion of leadership, refusing to wear the hippie crown. To do so would have violated a fundamental countercultural tenet, set down in 1965 by Bob Dylan in "Highway 61 Revisited": "Don't follow leaders, watch the parking meters."[41] Again, in the 1980 *Playboy* interview Lennon said: "That's what I'm saying (still). Produce your own dream. If you want to save Peru, go save Peru. It's quite possible to do anything, but not if you put it on the leaders and parking meters. Don't expect Carter or Reagan or John Lennon or Yoko Ono or Bob Dylan or Jesus Christ to come do it for you. . . . I can't wake you up. YOU can wake you up. I can't cure you. YOU can cure you."[42]

Thus with the message of love and peace came a new utopian anarchism. The concept of leadership was in direct violation of the concept of oneness. Even the Beatle Lennon had been saying "Come Together"—form the tribal one—but form it "over me," not behind or under me. He was willing to totalize but not to dictate. Was it not the lesson of the Old Left, watching and witnessing Lenin and Stalin, Mao and Castro, that leaders become dictators? According to Lennon:

> The idea of leadership is a false god. If you want to use the Beatles or John and Yoko or whoever, people are expecting them to do something for them. That's not what's going to happen. But they [the followers] are the ones who didn't understand any message that came before anyway. And they are the ones that will follow Hitler or follow Reverend Moon or whoever. Following is not what it's all about, but leaving messages of "This is what's happening to us. Hey, what's happening to you?" We're sending postcards and letters. That's what we do. And that's the difference. Do you see?[43]

In spite of all his efforts and arguments to the contrary, Lennon, after leaving the Beatles, was retained in the countercultural aristocracy as a combination court jester and guru. Like it or not, Lennon and Ono became a source of vicarious politics for many of the disaffected and rebellious, as symbols of revolutionary consciousness and the utopian values of the tribal one as it rushed confidently into the 1970s. Not unlike the Maharishi Mahesh Yogi, who in 1968 had become the personal guru for the Beatles and a few other pop stars (Donovan, Mia Farrow, and Mike Love of the Beach Boys) who attended a six-week course in transcendental meditation in India, the Lennons became a guru couple to the youth culture in the West. When Lennon later demystified and satirized the Maharishi in "Sexie Sadie" from the Beatles' "White Album," as a seductress who had made "a fool of everyone," he was playing his own fool's game.[44]

This leaderless one, to which the Lennons gave their public allegiance but which they could never accommodate in their private lives, was ultimately an imaginary construct, a utopia. As Lennon put it to *Playboy* in 1980, "We can have examples, but leaders is what we DON'T need. It's the utopian bit again. We're all members of the conceptual utopia. So let's not go round and round it: It's one world, one people, and it's a statement as well as a wish."[45]

But before this countercultural oneness could materialize and revolutionize the world, individuals had to break out of the conventional society's "bag" (to use a favorite Ono metaphor) and seek the real, the genuine "bag," which we humans are all in together. From an egalitarian perspective much older than John Lennon or Yoko Ono, it was being argued that the name of the game was not just to belong, "but to belong to the whole thing, not to one little section of it."[46]

This theme runs deep in Lennon's solo work: the need to break out of the narrow "bag" of class or race or sex or nation and seek the universal bag or what the early Diggers called the Common Treasury and the Wobblies called the Commonwealth of Toil or the One Big Union. Lennon's imaginary construct is the same as John Steinbeck's One Big Soul or what the Communist International was all about.[47] Lennon's idea, his notion of the conceptual country, came to be known simply as Newtopia.

Unforfunately, most people—even newtopians—find it very difficult, if not impossible, to abandon their own narrow bag.

One must be forced out through the rips in the seams, and this is what the Lennons attempted to do with their music and their public image. In his first solo album, Lennon berates his followers, characterizing them as passive sheep, sadly apathetic, trapped inside their bag, with "cock in hand," wallowing in sex, doped with religion, and numbed by TV. He condescendingly refers to them as "fuckin' peasants" and challenges them to break the chains of alienation and apathy, to stand up for and by themselves, and not to follow dictators, idols, and gurus, sheepishly.[48] For, as he would later say in "Freeda People" from the *Mind Games* LP (1973), "We don't want no Big Brother scene" because "a million heads are better than one."[49] He felt that everyone was responsible for the current state of the world. For the Canadian interview of 1970, Lennon summed up his political ideals: "As soon as people realize that they have the power [we will reach a state of world peace]. The power doesn't belong with Mr. Trudeau, Mr. Wilson, or Mr. Nixon. We are the power. The people are the power. As soon as people are aware that they have the power, then they can do what they want. And if it's a case of they don't know what to do, let's advertise to them and tell them they have an option."[50]

But the power he refers to is conceptual power, the power of awareness, of consciousness, and of imagination. This notion of power is clearly utopian. It has never claimed to be anything else. And yet it is very real in the sense that it is a truly awesome force capable of changing the perceptions and attitudes of people toward the reality in which they live. It is the philosophy behind the cultural guerrilla, the symbolic approach to revolution, and the mind games politics of the imagination. Its basis is that if the way people perceive their world is changed, their world will be changed. In the radical politics of the mind guerrilla sensibilities are manipulated. John and Yoko neatly summed up their approach to politics in their "Declaration of Newtopia" of April 1, 1973: "We announce the birth of a conceptual country, Newtopia. Citizenship of the country can be obtained by a declaration of your awareness of Newtopia. Newtopia has no land, no boundaries, no passports, only people. Newtopia has no laws other than cosmic. All people of Newtopia are ambassadors of the country. As two ambassadors of Newtopia, we ask for diplomatic immunity and recognition in the United Nations of our country and its people."[51] This is the April fool's language behind the Lennon-Ono mind guerrilla.

Sometime in New York City

With the 1971 release of the single "Power to the People," the Lennons' career moved into its most politically active phase. They had just moved to New York City's Greenwich Village, where they became associated with the local radical underground, befriending, among others, Jerry Rubin and Abbie Hoffman, who had gained national attention and underground notoriety as a result of their trial for conspiracy in conjunction with the student riots at the 1968 Democratic National Convention in Chicago. During the course of their stay in the Village, the Lennons joined in a protest march by native Americans in Syracuse, played a benefit at the Apollo Theater for the prisoners at Attica State Prison, and performed at a benefit concert for an Ann Arbor, Michigan, political figure, John Sinclair, who had been sentenced to ten years for possession of two marijuana cigarettes.[52]

Three years earlier the Lennons had had firsthand experience with the marijuana laws and the use by public officials of the drug bust as a form of political harassment when they had been publicly arrested and fined £150 for possession of hashish in London.[53] Thus they could relate personally to Sinclair's case.

While the Lennons were becoming more heavily involved in the New York underground and radical activism, their singles released in 1971 continued to reflect the same basic utopian pacifism that had become, and would remain, their political trademark. Perhaps Lennon's most famous song, "Imagine," was released in October 1971. And for the Christmas market, they released "Happy Xmas (War Is Over)," reminiscent of their 1969 Christmas peace campaign, when they had billboards put up in twelve major cities around the world with the slogan "War Is Over if You Want It," an early experiment in collective wish fulfillment.[54] Attaching a political message to a Christmas song was a stroke of advertising genius. The song was intended to play every season, perhaps to replace "White Christmas." And because there was sure to be a war somewhere each Christmas, the song's political significance should be retained over the years.

The Lennons' activism was not without its problems. A fundamental gap separated the pop cultural radicals from such movement activists as Rubin and Hoffman. They agreed on the need for peace and the end of American involvement in Vietnam but not on the tactical means of achieving peace or stopping the American war machine. The conflict centered on the issue of violence, which the Lennons emphatically rejected on principle. They had no intention of overthrowing the government or disrupting the Pentagon. They wished only to overthrow the people's view of the government and the American war machine. Their conception of revolution remained imaginary and symbolic, they were still doing the mind guerrilla.[55] This is not to imply that the Lennons' conception of revolution was not genuine, or that it was held in bad faith, but only that it was utopian. They felt that revolution should originate and occur within people's heads and hearts, not in the streets or with violence. The validity of this concept was to be affirmed by the Nixon administration. Although the activists might have thought the Lennons politically naive, to the administration they were a subversive threat, and they were subjected to a barrage of Richard Nixon's "dirty tricks": phone taps, surveillance, and a long, exhaustive court battle over John's immigration status.[56]

Release of the most politically radical LP of their career, *Sometime in New York City,* a journalistic parody of their adventures in the radical underground over the past year,[57] surely must have confounded the situation. The album's cover art was intended to simulate newsprint, with song titles as headlines, song lyrics arranged in newsblock columns, and black and white news-style photos as illustrations. It is one of the few rock albums ever to contain 1930s-style topical-political songs, as opposed to abstract protest songs in the tradition of "Blowing in the Wind."

The songs of *Sometime in New York City* took the listener on a tour through the revolutionary news of the day. There was a song about the Irish home rule movement, an ode to Angela Davis, the black activist who had just been indicted in connection with the kidnapping and murder of a judge in California, and a song about the uprising at Attica State Prison, which ended when a thousand state troopers stormed the prison, killing twenty-eight inmates and nine hostages. The album also included a song for John Sinclair and two anthems to the feminist movement ("Woman Is the Nigger of the World" and "Sisters, Oh Sisters"), which were also released as a single.

In addition, the LP contained a second record featuring a live performance of John and Yoko along with Frank Zappa at the Filmore East and a version of John's 1969 song "Cold Turkey," about his withdrawal from heroin. Although most of the album's material was morally provocative or blatantly radical, the cover art created the most controversy. Like their first LP, *Two Virgins* (1968),[58] with the notorious cover photo of John and Yoko standing nude staring into the camera, much of the reaction to *Sometime in New York City* came from the album's cover, which featured a faked photograph of Richard Nixon dancing with Chairman Mao in the nude. Also like *Two Virgins,*much of the criticism was directed at Yoko Ono for corrupting "our Johnny" into a pervert and a wild-eyed radical. Needless to say, the album was not a commercial success, and the Lennons gave up coproduction until 1980, when their final LP together, *Double Fantasy,* was issued.

But the high point of the Lennons' radical phase was the week of February 21–25, 1972, when they cohosted the "Mike Douglas Show." To stunned housewives and shut-ins around the country, the gurus of the youth counterculture talked radical politics and performed many of the most inflammatory songs from *Sometime in New York City.*[59]

Lennon Domesticated and Depoliticized

The immigration battle went on for three years (1972–75), and during this period Lennon seemed to be toning down his politics and trying to maintain a lower public profile. A great deal of his time and energy was spent on legal maneuvers, trying to stay in the United States. The couple's artistic partnership as well as marriage began to suffer under the strain. Because Yoko's contributions seemed to enrage the public, Lennon began to perform and record alone. But his projects from this period—*Mind Games* (October 1973), *Walls and Bridges* (September 1974), and *Rock 'n Roll* (March 1975)—received a lukewarm public reception. His career was finally on the downswing.

In October 1973, John and Yoko began an eighteen-month separation. John took a lover, May Pang, and moved to Los Angeles, where he joined Harry Nilsson, Ringo Starr, and Keith Moon (drummer for the Who) and began a drinking and carousing binge that cost him a great deal of adverse publicity. He would later refer to this period as his "lost weekend."[60]

But in November 1974 John and Yoko were reunited. The reunion ultimately resulted in the birth of a son, Sean, on John's birthday, October 9, 1975. The arrival of their first child had a calming effect on the Lennons. They settled into domestic life and dropped out of sight, living "underground" in the splendor of their compound in the Dakota, a fashionable, aristocratic apartment building opposite New York City's Central Park.[61]

In an interview with Barbara Graustark of *Newsweek* in September 1980, Lennon revealed that during the period of seclusion he and Yoko had reversed roles. She went to the office every morning and John stayed home and took care of the baby. He described this as a Zen experiment in housewifery and the beginning of his feminist education.[62]

The *Newsweek* interview was part of the Lennons' coming-out-of-seclusion campaign, part of the hype accompanying a new LP collaboration, their first since *Sometime in New York City.* The birth of Sean had rekindled the flames of the great Lennon-Ono romance. Their latest LP was a tribute to their renewed love. Called *Double Fantasy,* it was released in conjunction with a new single "(Just Like) Starting Over." It was John Lennon's last recording venture. He was murdered just one month after its release.

Double Fantasy

Double Fantasy used a newtopian symbolism consistent with *Imagine* and *Mind Games,* but it was totally devoid of social or political commentary. In this sense, the new LP was a departure from the Lennons' earlier works, which had a consistent, if diminishing, political tone. *Double Fantasy* was a dialogue between two lovers who had quarreled and gone their separate ways and then had reunited in a much tighter bond formed by the birth of a son, causing them to retreat into the security of the self-contained and isolated family unit. In an interview with David Sheff of *Playboy* two months before his death, Lennon explained their withdrawal from the public and from politics: "We got back together and we decided that this was our life, that having a baby was important to us and that everything else was subsidiary to that, and therefore everything else had to be abandoned." *Double Fantasy* was the vehicle of their public resurfacing. The five years of seclusion, Lennon continued, had allowed them "the space to breathe and think and re-establish our dreams."[63] *Double Fantasy* was to be an expression of these revived, shared dreams.

The LP reveals some of the seamier sides of their great romance. Some of the fantasies have an almost nightmarish cast. Yoko sings, "Give me something that's not cold" and "I'm moving on . . . it's getting phony," while John screams back, "I know I hurt you then . . . / . . . do you still have to carry that cross?"[64] These lyrics are vivid indications that all was not happiness and bliss in the Lennon household.

But most of the album has a positive tone. Their reunion and the birth of Sean are celebrated as the fulfillment of their romance. Now the gods were back in the heavens, the oracle had spoken, and there were "no rats aboard the magic ship of perfect harmony."[65] After five years of self-imposed seclusion to get their marriage in order, five years away from the merry-go-round of superstardom, they were ready to spread their professional wings and make a new beginning at recording.

But the tone of this album has a disturbing, almost reactionary quality in the Lennons' remarks that "hard times are over" and it was now "clean-up time." For the first time in their career they focused almost entirely on their personal relationship and family, with no words about the utopian One. Was the mature Lennon, now approaching middle age, suddenly deradicalized and apolitical? Had politics for the Lennons, as for so many of their generation, been merely the expression of the idealistic passions of youth? Had fame and success finally worked a counterrevolution upon the Two Virgins?

Of course, because of the publicity surrounding such celebrities, it is difficult to answer these questions. Yet in press releases from this period, the Lennons discussed *Double Fantasy* as a political fantasy in the tradition of *Imagine* and *Mind Games.* In the *Playboy* interview they said they intended to end the album with the chant, "one world, one people." And in the *Rolling Stone* interview Lennon said the inner vinyl label contained the same slogan, which was evidence of his continuing political concern. In both interviews, Lennon seems to be describing *Double Fantasy* as a shared dream with a positive political purpose. When David Sheff attempted to interpret the album as the next step after *Imagine,* saying that now the hard times were over, the world was ready to become one, Lennon quickly corrected him: "No, no, no. We're one world, one people whether we like it or not. Aren't we? I mean, we can PRETEND we're divided into races and countries and we can carry on pretending that until we stop doin' it. But the reality is that it is one world and it is one people."[66] The album as finally released, however, does not contain the "one world, one people" chant and as a result, it makes almost no political statement.

The only possible political significance of this record is in its form, not its content. In the lyrics of *Double Fantasy,* only in the whispered introduction to Lennon's song "Woman"—Chairman Mao's aphorism "Woman is the other half of the sky"—is there even a hint of social consciousness.[67] All else is romantic sentimentalism: "Let's take a chance and fly away somewhere . . . ALONE."[68] Focusing on the narrow love of two individuals for each other, the LP is dedicated to the imaginary orgasm instead of the imaginary utopia.

Nevertheless, *Double Fantasy* does carry the symbolism of the new feminist concept of love and relationships, and therein lies its political significance. The LP is a genuine coproduction; Lennon and Ono each contributed seven songs in an alternating sequence that forms a dialogue. In discussing the album with the Lennons, *Rolling Stone*'s Jonathan Cott said that "no rock & roll star I can think of has made a record with his wife (or girl friend) and given her fifty percent of the disc."[69] But this was actually the fifth such Lennon-Ono coproduction. The first three—*Unfinished Music No. 1: Two Virgins* (November 1968), *Unfinished Music No. 2: Life with the Lions* (May 1969), and *Wedding Album* (October 1969)—were perceived as so eccentric and self-indulgent that they are practically unknown, except by the most ardent and devoted fans and collectors. The fourth, *Sometime in New York City* (June 1972), was only somewhat more commercial. Thus the Lennons had a long history of coproduction, but the results had always been highly controversial and the public reaction so bewildered and hostile that the Lennons had given up working together, until *Double Fantasy.*

Double Fantasy was a reaffirmation of the public image of John and Yoko. But it was also a reaffirmation of John Lennon's feminist conversion. His concept of relationship had always been the traditional male-dominant one. On the *Sergeant Pepper* LP he had confessed: "I used to be cruel to my woman / I beat her and kept her apart from the things that she loved."[70] This natural machoism—learned in the street culture of 1950s Liverpool—was, of course, greatly exacerbated by his rise to superstardom. The head Beatle, the king of British rock, was used to having girls as sexual playthings and servants. In his Beatle wit, he had once said that women should be "obscene and not heard."[71]

Yoko's demand for equality filled him with both awe and perplexity. She insisted on being treated as an artist and a person in her own right. She would not cower to the famous John Lennon. Lennon explained: "I was a working-class macho guy that didn't know any better. Yoko taught me about women. I was used to being served, like Elvis and a lot of the other stars were. And Yoko didn't buy that. She didn't give a shit about the Beatles—what the fuck are the Beatles? . . . From the day

I met her, she demanded equal time, equal space, equal rights. I didn't know what she was talking about." [72] The Lennon-Ono relationship was probably not so much a feminist experiment as a test of wills that formed the central tension in their romance and was responsible for a great deal of pain and struggle and ultimately for their breakup in 1973. John would have cited his experiment in househusbandry as the most visible manifestation of his feminism,[73] but his learning to bake bread and his determination to take an active part in his son's upbringing must be put into perspective. Househusbandry with a staff of full-time servants and a nanny is only imaginary feminism.

Robert Christgau has commented that Yoko's feminism lacked of a spirit of sisterliness. She may have imagined her sisterhood in public, but in private she had very few women friends and associates. She always tended toward the aggressive competitiveness of the traditional ambitious male.[74] Yoko's feminist image—like John's working-class image—suffered from the egoism of the artist and a life of wealthy isolation. But here politics is not as important as imagery. The politics is buried in the public image. The Lennon-Ono ego battle, the test of wills, the public split and reunion, turned the story of John and Yoko into a great romance, to which the symbolism of feminism adhered, along with that of love and peace and the utopian One. Especially after the Vietnam War, they seemed consciously to pursue a feminist public identification, which enabled them to maintain a radical edge to their public image.

But one need only consider the many failed show business romances in the field of popular music—Ike and Tina Turner, Sonny and Cher, Delaney and Bonnie, Kris Kristofferson and Rita Coolidge, Leon and Mary Russell—to grasp the significance of John and Yoko's romantic-professional achievement. To have survived as a couple for more than ten years was an extraordinary feat, but to do so within the context of superstardom and to have maintained a reciprocity of respect and an egalitarian public face was beyond both public expectations and the norms of their peers. John and Yoko's marriage became a bright and hopeful symbol of the possibilities of the merger of feminist consciousness with the more traditional countercultural notions of love, romance, and marriage. *Double Fantasy* thus takes its political significance from its representation of, and testament to, a new revolutionary concept of romance, breaking from the male dominance practiced by the revolutionaries of the largely patriarchal movements of the 1960s. It was a sharing in which "the two of us are really one."[75]

Martyrdom and Canonization

On the night of December 8, 1980, John Lennon was gunned down outside the entrance to his New York apartment complex by a deranged fan, who, just twenty-four hours earlier and at the same location, had received his idol's autograph on a copy of *Double Fantasy.*[76] In this single act Mark David Chapman made a name for himself by adding the final chapter to the Lennon legend. The widow, Yoko Ono Lennon, would lead the canonization process.

Although in "The Ballad of John and Yoko" Lennon may have indicated a vague premonition about being crucified by an angry public, his newtopianism and sense of humor had usually prevented such dark visions and death wishes. When asked about death in an interview during this period, he had said that he was prepared for death because he did not believe in it. In the language and imagery of pop art mysticism, Lennon had compared death to getting out of one car and into another.[77]

By 1980, Lennon had long forsaken his more offensive public image. He had dropped his anarchic demeanor, his political radicalism, and his abuse of alcohol and hallucinogenic drugs. His outrageous public antics were part of another era. He and Yoko had chosen the cleaner lifestyle and public image symbolized by love and family, which he described in a story that is told almost as a parable in his last interview with *Rolling Stone:*

> I get truly affected by letters from Brazil or Poland or Austria—places I'm not conscious of all the time—just to know somebody is there, listening. One kid living up in Yorkshire (in England) wrote this heartfelt letter about being both Oriental and English and identifying with John and Yoko. The odd kid in the class. There are a lot of those kids who identify with us. They don't need the history of rock & roll. They identify with us as a couple, a bi-racial couple, who stand for love, peace, feminism and the positive things of the world.[78]

And Lennon was no longer combative and condescending with his public. He was more mature and calm. He had seemingly come to terms with his mystique.

Lennon's death was unique in the history of popular music. It was not the result of a drug-crazed life-in-the-fast-lane self-destructiveness which seems to be the norm, as exemplified by Hank Williams, Janis Joplin, Jimmi Hendrix, Jim Morrison, and Elvis Presley. Nor was it a lingering or tragic illness, as in the cases of Woody Guthrie and Bob Marley, nor a tragic plane or car crash such as caused the deaths of Buddy Holly, Jim Croce, and Harry Chapin. John Lennon's death was unique in that it was an assassination.

Death at the hands of an assassin is usually reserved in history for great political leaders: Julius Caesar, Abraham Lincoln, John and Robert Kennedy, and Anwar Sadat, or for great political revolutionaries: Rosa Luxemburg, Pancho Villa, Mohandas Gandhi, Che Guevara, Martin Luther King, Jr., and Malcolm X. Assassination is an inherently political phenomenon and has historically been part of the struggle for power among competing conceptions and symbols of social order, community, and government. Assassination is the murder of a public figure because of the political ideals the person may have represented.[79]

It is thus more than a metaphor to say that John Lennon's assassination was linked to his position as an elder statesman in the 1960s counterculture, or what Abbie Hoffman called the Woodstock Nation.[80] Lennon died in the fashion and style of kings and presidents. And in countercultural circles around the world, his death had the same impact as did the deaths of John F. Kennedy or Martin Luther King, Jr. One of the more respectable journalistic tributes that followed his death summed up the public reaction:

> A fuse had blown out in our lives, and we stumbled around in the dark, bumping into each other in ways we had almost forgotten. For a while, in that global village of the sixties we seemed to breathe with the Beatles, and by virtue of their very existence, we all seemed to breathe the same breath. Within an hour of the release of a new Beatles song, everyone in the world, or in a particular world, heard it, knew it, and assimilated it. We all listened to the same radio. Monday night [the night of Lennon's assassination] we all listened to the same radio again: the community that had fragmented and disintegrated was suddenly reunited, but this time the radio was playing a different song.[81]

But the motives of the assassin seemed to have been more confused and delusionary than political. No conspiracy theory was suggested. Mark David Chapman reported hearing voices and being driven to this action by the devil. The press portrayed Chapman as a mixed-up druggie turned Jesus freak with an excessive identification with John Lennon that even included his marriage to an Onoesque Japanese-American woman in Hawaii. For some unknown reason, the identification had gone sour. Robert Christgau of the *Village Voice* posited:

> John Lennon held out hope. He imagined, and however quietistic he became, he never lost that Utopian identification. But when you hold out hope people get real disappointed if you can't deliver. You're famous and they're not—that's the crux of your relationship. You command the power they crave—the power to make one's identity felt in the world, to be known. No matter that you're even further from resolving anyone's perplexities than the next bohemian, artist, or intellectual. You're denying your most desperate admirers the release they need, and a certain percentage of them will resent or hate you for it. From there, it only takes one to kill.[82]

Chapman's possessions at the time of his arrest consisted of fourteen hours worth of Beatle music on tape, a copy of the Bible, two thousand dollars in cash which he had evidently borrowed from his mother for the trip to New York, and a copy of J. D. Salinger's *Catcher in the Rye,* which he was casually reading while awaiting the arrival of the police after dropping the gun he had used to kill John Lennon.[83]

How could a Beatle fan kill John Lennon? The assassination defied explanation and left the public bewildered. And because rational explanation seemed futile, those who felt they had lost a part of their own souls looked for spiritual explanations and mystical solutions. Ritual pilgrimages brought masses of the faithful to New York City and the Dakota, which became an instant shrine to the memory of John Lennon. There the mourners began a long, sad vigil, standing reverently in the rain, placing flowers, poems, and pictures on the gate of the building and periodically breaking into spontaneous singing: "All we are saying, is give peace a chance."[84]

Despite the extreme stress of shock and grief, Yoko Ono gathered the strength to face the situation. Reports of two suicides by fans unable to cope with Lennon's death and of riots in his home town of Liverpool convinced her that she had to face the public and plead for calm, restraint, and optimism. She was determined to continue the double fantasy and the positive vision of "Starting Over." The mind games had to go on. Information dispersal had always been her speciality, and her public relations and image management in the aftermath of her husband's death were a masterful performance carried out with all the finesse of a veteran practitioner of popular cultural-guerrilla events and mass ritual.[85]

Lennon had once said that Yoko was as important to him as Paul McCartney and Bob Dylan together.[86] During the period of public mourning, her image management was consistent with the utopian politics that she and John had come to represent. Although from the perspective of the political activists, their symbolic politics had been, in the words of Robert Christgau, "short on dialectics and long on yin-and-yang," it was nevertheless a valid statement of the countercultural consciousness of the 1960s.[87]

Yoko made secret arrangements to have the body cremated and the ashes privately interred in England. Instead of a funeral, she asked the public to join her in a ten-minute silent prayer in John's memory the following Sunday, December 14, at 2:00 P.M. In announcing the silent vigil, she included the statement: "John loved and prayed for the human race, please pray the same for him. Please remember that he had a deep faith and concern for life and, though he has now joined the greater force, he is still with us here."[88] On the day following the assassination, Yoko released the following letter to the press:

> I told Sean what happened. I showed him the picture of his father on the cover of the paper and explained the situation. I took Sean to the spot where John lay after he was shot. Sean wanted to know why the person had shot John if he liked John. I explained that he was probably a confused person. Sean said we should find out if he was confused or if he really had meant to kill John. I said that was up to the court. He asked what court—a tennis court or a basketball court? That's how Sean used to talk with his father. They were buddies. John would have been proud of Sean if he had heard this. Sean cried later. He also said "Now Daddy is part of God. I guess when you die you become more bigger because you're part of everything."
>
> I don't have much more to add to Sean's statement. The silent vigil will take place December 14th at 2 p.m. for ten minutes.
>
> Our thoughts will be with you.
>
> Love, Yoko & Sean.[89]

That Sunday, by 2:00 P.M. New York time (7:00 P.M. London time), thirty thousand people had gathered in front of St. George's Hall in Liverpool and thousands more at London's Hyde Park and Trafalgar Square. Formal and informal vigils were held in major cities across America: Seattle, Chicago, Boston, Los Angeles, and Philadelphia, as well as in many smaller cities (including Knoxville, Tennessee). Many millions more participated via radio in the privacy of their homes and apartments. The largest gathering was in New York City, where one hundred thousand people massed in Central Park. *Rolling Stone* correspondent Chet Flippo described the New York vigil. It was a "grey afternoon";

> The band shell was empty except for some garlands of evergreen, a wreath and a picture of Lennon. Two stacks of speakers were playing some of his quieter music: "In My Life," "You've Got to Hide Your Love Away," "Norwegian Wood." The sun broke through during "All You Need is Love," and most of the crowd responded by singing along and flashing the V sign—a reminder of an era that suddenly seemed long ago. The clouds reappeared at the end of "Give Peace a Chance," the final song before the ten-minute silence.
>
> At two sharp, every radio shut off, every hot-dog vender shut down, every button peddler shut up. As a body, the crowd seemed to freeze. The meditation ended with the playing "Imagine," leaving the crowd with "I hope someday you'll join us / And the world will live as one" as Lennon's last words of the afternoon. Bach's "Jesu, Joy of Man's Desiring" accompanied the people out of the park, as the clouds grew more threatening. And then, for a few minutes on an otherwise dry afternoon, snow fell on New York City.[90]

Later that afternoon, the crowd drifted back to the Dakota to continue the vigil. Yoko sent down a message in verse: "I saw John smiling in the sky . . . I saw all of us becoming one mind."[91]

Undoubtedly, this had been another great—if melancholy—moment in the history of the counterculture. It was probably the largest mass experiment in collective telepathy in the history of humanity. Mass communications technology was used for an exercise in mass shamanism, literally a spiritual coming together of a mass conscience and consciousness. Perhaps only the death of Elvis Presley had caused a similar public outpouring of emotion and sorrow on behalf of a popular singer.

The Legacy

Since her husband's death, Yoko Ono has tirelessly pursued a series of projects designed to keep his memory alive and vital. As *Rolling Stone*'s Christopher Connelly has commented, her identity has shifted decisively from "that of Yoko Ono, Avant-Garde Artist, to Mrs. Lennon, Keeper of the Flame."[92] She has released several albums of her own mournful songs. First was *Seasons of Glass* (1981), the cover of which has a photograph of Lennon's bloody glasses lying on what appears to be a windowsill in their Dakota apartment, against the out-of-focus New York skyline. Next to the glasses sits a half-empty glass of water. The cover art of *It's Alright* (1982) is less effective, with a photograph of Yoko and Sean in Central Park accompanied by the ghostly, translucent figure of John Lennon. The songs on these two LPs present a touching glimpse of Yoko's private struggle with grief and sadness: "I Don't Know Why," "Never Say Goodbye," "Loneliness," and "Let the Tears Dry."

In 1983 Yoko released the already planned sequel to *Double Fantasy, Milk and Honey: A Heart Play.* It uses the same alternating song dialogue that was the format of *Double Fantasy.* There are some effectively sentimental pieces such as Yoko's "Your Hands" and John's "Grow Old with Me," but there are also more objective traces of the cracks in the illustrious romance in John's "I'm Stepping Out" and Yoko's "Sleepless Night." It is a relatively balanced work, which discusses the joy and hope of romance as well as the disappointment and fear. And once again, its political significance lies only in the feminism it exhibits. If anything, the political content is reactionary. In "I Don't Wanna Face It," for example, Lennon seems to be rejecting the politics of love and peace, singing cynically (perhaps to Yoko): "You wanna save humanity / But it's people that you just can't stand."[93] Sadly, these are probably Lennon's last comments on the mind guerrilla.

Yet the mind games have continued. Yoko released several music videos from the final Lennon-Ono LPs: "Woman," from *Double Fantasy,* produced before Lennon's death; "Borrowed Time," from *Milk and Honey,* featuring film clips from the Beatle days to evoke a powerful nostalgia; and "Every Man Has a Woman Who Loves Him," from *Double Fantasy,* which uses young actors in a boy-meets-girl story that resolves into an old photograph of Lennon leaning in the doorway of a bar in Hamburg in the early 1960s.

In 1984, an album of Yoko's songs recorded by various artists—Elvis Costello, Roberta Flack, Rosanne Cash, Harry Nilssen, and Eddie Monday—was released under the title *Every Man Has a Woman* and produced by Sam Havadtoy. The idea for the project originated with John, who was planning it as a present for Yoko's fiftieth birthday and as a means of displaying her songwriting talents in a form that could be appreciated by a wider audience. John and Yoko's son Sean also makes his musical debut on this LP, singing "It's Alright." A music video of Sean's song was also released.[94]

Yoko's projects have also included a variety of nonmusical productions. She was the inspiration behind the Sotheby auction of Lennon memorabilia in London in 1984. She is working to establish a John Lennon Museum in New York City and a fully endowed Lennon scholarship to enable American students to study overseas. Perhaps her greatest accomplishment so far is Strawberry Fields, the John Lennon memorial on a tear-shaped two-acre plot in New York City's Central Park, located at Seventy-Second Street and Central Park West, just across the street from the Dakota. The site was chosen for sentimental reasons, as the place where John and Yoko had gone for walks. The memorial was officially dedicated on October 9, 1985, and opened to the public the next day.[95]

The New York City Department of Parks made the plot available at the request of city councilman Henry Stern. Yoko donated one million dollars for development of the site and set up a half-million-dollar endowment for upkeep. With Yoko's advice, architect Bruce Kelly designed the site as a living memorial featuring trees and plants donated by more than one hundred nations around the world. The theme of the memorial was in keeping with the Lennon-Ono cultural guerrilla. At the March 21, 1984, ceremony that officially began the project, Yoko stated that a public request had been sent to all the world's heads of state to donate a "tree or stone from their country to make this island into a garden of love, an island in which all nations could grow together." The living art forms of the park are thus meant to symbolize world peace and harmony. For example, trees from Jordon and Israel are planted close to each other in hopes that their roots and leaves will intertwine in a symbolic gesture of peace. The Lennons' utopian politics are clearly articulated in the only nonliving exhibit on the site, a starburst sidewalk mosaic, eight to ten feet in diameter, with the word "Imagine" set in tiles donated by Italy and imported from Naples.[96]

In 1984, a sensitive one-hour video documentary, *Yoko Ono (Now and Then),* written, produced, and narrated by Barbara Graustark, was released by Sekhmet Productions for Polygram Music Video. In this film, Yoko discusses her motives for assuming the role of keeper of the Lennon "wishing well" by explaining that when John was killed their working partnership was fully intact and that the loss was like being on a battlefield and losing a comrade-in-arms. All she knew to do was to keep on fighting.[97] As part of this fight, the long-anticipated TV docudrama of Lennon's life with Yoko, "John and Yoko: A Love Story," produced by Carson Productions for NBC, was broadcast in November of 1985. During November Yoko also released her seventh solo album, *Star Peace,* and in April of 1986, a film, and an accompanying LP, *John Lennon: Live in New York City,* of John and Yoko's 1972 Madison Square Garden concert in aid of retarded children and adults, was released.

There is also a second-generation Lennon superstar in the making. John's son from his first marriage, Julian, has recently emerged as a major new rock personality. He has capitalized upon and contributed to his father's legacy with his first LP, *Valotte.*[98] Three music videos have been released from the material on this album. Julian's appearance and voice quality are remarkably like his father's. *Rock Magazine*'s June 1985 issue featured Julian's photograph, alongside David Lee Roth (of Van Halen), George Michael (of Wham!), and Bryan Adams, under the caption, "The Hottest Men in Rock."

The Lennon Legacy and the Cultural Guerrilla

John Lennon thought of himself as a working-class hero, and although he was never socioeconomically working class or disadvantaged, his key values were nevertheless formed in reaction to the bourgeois values of the authority figures in his childhood at home and at school. In "Working Class Hero" he tells us that these authorities, the inevitable "they," hurt you at home and hit you at school, until you become so "fucking crazy" that you can no longer follow "their rules." Lennon's reaction, and that of the youth culture he came to personify, was not one of an ideological activist but of a delinquent: the wild and reckless, drug-crazed abandonment of countercultural bohemia. It was only later that Lennon became class-conscious and ideological and began to see himself intellectually as working class.

Revolutionary consciousness is more than ideology. It also contains the nonrational component of pure, impassioned, undirected rebelliousness. To take an ideological position is an intellectual process, whereas rebelliousness is an all-encompassing lifestyle and attitude. Revolutionary consciousness is the force that turns a common worker or student into an activist-organizer. One must be possessed of such a consciousness before becoming ideological; one has the attitude before one understands or accepts the politics associated with it. Revolutionary consciousness is the force that humanizes revolutionary politics. It is also the force behind the cultural guerrilla.

The guerrilla minstrel is both a product of revolutionary consciousness and a medium through which this consciousness is projected into the community of rebellion. The guerrilla minstrel is a public personage with a larger-than-life image consisting largely of legend and myth. He is a hero, and the hero-worship supporting his public image is a crucial component in the mind games I refer to as the cultural guerrilla.

A dramatic element is, of course, part of this process. Heroism presupposes flair, charisma, and acting ability. A real-life individual plays the part of hero in the public eye. Histrionics are necessary to sustain the public image. The hero's life story becomes a soap opera for his fans and admirers, who follow his ups and downs, ins and outs, failures and successes, and joys and horrors in the press.

At some mystical level, the hero becomes a member of the family. John and Yoko's *Wedding Album,* for example, included a photograph of a piece of cake for all who participated in the wedding vicariously by purchasing the LP. The fan thus became a member of the wedding party, an imaginary cousin in the family of rebellion. Fans follow their hero or heroine's life as they would that of an older brother or sister whom they admire in an irrational way. His life seems romantic and exciting compared to one's own dull, ordinary existence. He does all the wonderfully outrageous things the fan would like to do but cannot because of responsibilities in the real world. Heroes affirm that there is more to life than conventional ordinary existence.

The cultural guerrilla requires a heroic medium to channel the values, beliefs, attitudes, and ideals of revolutionary consciousness into the way of life, the very being of the seemingly unorganized mass that constitutes the following. The guerrilla minstrel is a package, an image, and a symbol. He is more than his songs, though his songs are essential. They are necessary but not sufficient. They are part of the lore supporting the legend. They are his words, his special revelations, scripture mystically revealed to the artist through the creative process.

But the lore of the legend encompasses more than scripture. His deeds are as important as his words. The fact (or fiction) that Lennon smoked a joint in Buckingham Palace before receiving the MBE award from the queen, for example, or that he and Yoko sent acorns to fifty of the world's leaders as part of a campaign for peace, form, along with other such anecdotes, an intrinsic part of the legend.

But the package that is the heroic image is more than legend and lore. It is more than simply a myth. It is permeated by ideology. And ideology is what creates the mind guerrilla. Consciousness, as it were, is conquered through the back door. What the fans admire most in the myth, in the scripture, in the sayings, in the stories, is the hero's "bad attitude," his devil-may-care unconventionality, his eccentricity, his refusal to follow the norms of society. He is true to himself in a way the fan can never be. But the image is not complete until this natural delinquent rebelliousness—the very image of youth culture—finally matures into a responsible idealism and is given legitimacy as social consciousness. A radical now exists where once there was merely a delinquent.

And those who have absorbed the image of this heroic revolutionary rocker—his fans and followers, those who still identify with drugs and sex and rock 'n' roll music (even though they now work soberly for the arms industry, have been married and divorced and married again, have children, and rarely rock or roll)—are imperceptibly yet indelibly touched by this social consciousness.

And so it is that our hero comes with political baggage, which is the mind guerrilla. It is perhaps political only as an afterthought, but it is fundamentally political. The process itself—the unification of juvenile delinquency into a culture of protest—is intrinsically political, but in a utopian sense. It is political in the sense that it is a developing of consciousness, molding the undirected, reckless rebelliousness of the young into a determined, positive idealism.

Perhaps the most important dimension of this totality is the hero's death and canonization. Death gives the heroic image an eerie, morbid legitimacy. This is the hardest part of the package to grasp. Does it become legitimate because the image is capable of attracting fanatical hatred? Or is it because of the bewilderment at why someone so beloved by so many could be the object of intense evil? The assassin must have been crazy. But this craziness is also part of the mind guerrilla, although here it has worked its magic with such vehemence that something has short-circuited.

Clearly, a powerful and mysterious force is at work, evoking equally powerful and mysterious reactions, both positive and negative, from those who fall under its spell. Taken in their entirety, and magnified a million times, these forces create the cultural guerrilla.

During one of those grand and glorious mass countercultural events, the Simon and Garfunkel concert in Central Park on September 19, 1982, which drew a crowd as large and enthusiastic as Woodstock more than a decade earlier, largely a tribute to the force of nostalgia for the 1960s, there occurred an incident of alarming symbolic significance. It was an incident that, when I first witnessed it several years later on an HBO special, filled me with a tidal wave of impressions concerning the riddle of heroism in the traditions of the cultural guerrilla. I have been struggling ever since to articulate these impressions. It is not enough to say that the hero is a larger-than-life, charismatic public personality or that he or she is a talented songwriter, poet, and prophet offering insights into the meaning and purpose of life which serve to activate the cultural guerrilla. There remains a puzzling enigma that eludes explanation. With the exception of Bob Dylan, all of the heroes of this book died dramatically tragic public deaths, and their deaths are a fundamental part of their mystique. Violence and death are as much a part of the mind guerrilla as solidarity and peace.

The incident I am referring to sheds light on this puzzle. It happened more than midway into the concert, following a long string of familiar, truly classical songs ("Mrs. Robinson," "Homeward Bound," "America," "Me and Juilo," "Scarborough Fair," "April Come She Will," "Wake up Little Suzie," "Still Crazy after All These Years" that evoked nostalgia for the 1960s. The music worked those present into a warm, enthusiastic oneness that took them out of themselves into a transcendental state. The sound was technically good, and Simon and Garfunkel's performance was extremely compelling. They periodically reminded the audience of the spirit of true friendship that underlay this reunion with handshakes, hugs, smiles, and pats on each other's backs. The chemistry between the two performers and between the performers and audience was vivid and pure. And the songs, an integral part of a generation, pregnant with meaning for so many, worked their own magic. It was truly a totalizing experience, the cultural guerrilla at its best.

Paul Simon then injected a new song, "The Late Great Johnny Ace," which he had recently written in remembrance of John Lennon. The effect was heartwarming, bringing forth goosebumps, until, in the closing lines of the song, the warmth suddenly froze when a crazed fan charged the stage. He was grabbed by security guards just inches from Simon's face. As he was being carried away kicking, he yelled: "Paul, I've got to talk to you!"

Why did this obviously unstable individual choose that moment to demand an audience with Paul Simon? What force could drive someone to such a bizarre act? It is the same force that fuels the cultural guerrilla. It is evident not only in the swaying of the audience to the beat of the music but also is visible in the eyes of Paul Simon as that deranged fan rushed the stage. It is madness as well as oneness. It is as dangerous as it is sacred. It can heal and soothe the soul, but it can also kill.

In this book I will confront this paradox through a careful examination of the heroism of Joe Hill, Woody Guthrie, and Bob Dylan, and with the example of John Lennon, I will explore the role of heroism in the culture of protest in America in the twentieth century. But first I wish to enter the realm of theory and speculate more closely on the cultural guerrilla as a political process proceeding through the agency of heroism.

3 Doing the Mind Guerrilla: *Totalization, the Utopian Sensibility, and the Protest Singing Hero*

Imagine all the people sharing all the world.
—John Lennon, 1971

Much of my discussion of the cultural guerrilla is centered on the notion of "totalization,"[1] which in this chapter I will relate to the concepts of "heroism" and "utopianism." The notion of totalization has inherent utopian possibilities that are exaggerated through the impact of protest singing heroes such as John Lennon, who have embraced the role of "totalizing agent" by lending their public image to the political task of developing the imaginative constructions that I call social protest (or countercultural) totalizations.

Totalization

A totality is any social whole unified by diverse elements which share some quality among or between themselves.[2] In other words, a totality is a sociocultural community that integrates shared values, beliefs, or practices. This book is concerned with totalities of the American political Left and the extent to which they have been unified by a shared musical culture. To the generation of the 1960s, the music of John Lennon and the Beatles provided a common ground that enabled an otherwise heterogeneous mass to integrate into a shared culture and a social totality. A generation of American youth raised on radio, television, and popular music experienced a togetherness through their common assimilation of Beatle recordings, television appearances, and concert tours. Millions of individuals transcended their individuality by carrying within themselves Beatle memories, music, and values. The impact of the Beatle phenomenon tended to reinforce leftist ideals and practices through a loose association with a generalized nonconformity, the desire for sociopolitical change, and the popularization of anti-establishment attitudes and values.[3]

Sartre refers to the totality as a "synthetic unity" brought together through a process that is ultimately symbolic, that is, the resultant oneness is to a large extent imaginary in that, like Yoko Ono's silent vigil after Lennon's death, it comes together only within the mind of the observer or participant. Sartre uses the example of a painting, through which a "complex of dried pigments" is given oneness, or totalized, only through an act of imagination.[4] The sociocultural totality is likewise subject to differing perceptions. Much of the youth of the 1960s viewed the Beatle-led British invasion and the rock revival as something approaching the Second Coming of Christ, while many (or most) of their parents saw it only as the romanticization of juvenile delinquency, if not the twentieth-century revival of satanism. It is in this sense that the sociocultural totality is an imaginary construct.

Thus the totality, if it is anything at all, is but the fleetingly temporary residue of an ongoing and continuous process of understanding and making sense of one's social situation. It is a process that produces both citizens and revolutionaries. It links the individual to the community—any individual to any community. As I am using it, it is the process of developing a consciousness, that exhilerating feeling of oneness and solidarity with one's oppressed, exploited, alienated, or otherwise dehumanized brothers, locked in a mythic contest to overcome evils, both real and imagined.

This struggle takes place under many guises and at many different levels. For in any actual sense, the totality, in the language of Sartre, is a multiplicity of diverse unifying processes, each distinct within itself, differentiated from the others, yet locked in a dialectical process that ultimately contributes to the unification of all.[5] Thus it makes more sense to use the word "totalization," as opposed to "totality." Totality implies the imagined ideal, the abstraction, but totalization refers to the actual process, or complex of processes, that support and promote the understanding and acceptance of that ideal. In other words, totalization is the process that supports the idea of totality; the activities that maintain the sense and sensibility of community. It is the process that Lennon called "mind games," and it proceeds through the activities of various "totalizing agents," including the cultural revolutionaries Lennon called mind guerrillas.

The totalizing agent is the human agency that mediates totalization. The totalizing agent produces and maintains the connections, actual and imaginary, that bring the totality together.[6] Just as the art professor or museum guide helps a viewer make sense of a painting, the totalizing agent, within a sociopolitical context, helps us make sense of, or understand, our community and our culture. It is in this sense that Yoko Ono was a totalizing agent in the aftermath of her husband's death—she was the human vehicle through which the Beatle totality was brought back together for one last unifying experience. Her silent vigil was the last act in the Beatle mind guerrilla.

The totalizing agent, like the totality, is a symbolic entity, a public personage with a heroic image, who, in effect, humanizes the totalization process by providing a human referent for collective symbols and ideals. The totalizing agent becomes the personification of the ideals he or she is communicating and disseminating among a population of followers. The resulting social totality is formed of shared symbols and ideals, through the force of idolization, hero-worship, and vicarious identification. It is most accurately described as a cult: a totality totalized via a charismatic human agency.

Totalization is thus the continuous process of creating and sustaining a collective sensibility, a view of one's social situation, a political identity, a consciousness. Totalization is an imaginary process in that it proceeds through symbolic and perceptual activities. And whether this totalization is merely a dream or a policy platform, it is orchestrated through a human agency, that is, through the mediation of exceptional individuals, gifted with "original insight" and the charisma and determination to propagate their visions persuasively. It is in this sense that the heroic serve the totality. Totalization is thus the dance of the mind guerrilla in the heroic quest for the imagined and idealized human condition.

Perhaps this quest for the imaginary defines all politics: Left, Right, and Center. But it clearly exists within the political theory of the Left, which has a long and well-established history and cultural tradition of idealism—the utopian tradition.

The Utopian Sensibility

The word "utopia," meaning nowhere, was coined by Thomas More in his famous 1516 depiction of an imaginary society.[7] The utopian writer employs the imaginary fable to project his political ideals. In political theory, the tradition dates back to Plato's *Republic* (c. 370 B.C.), but probably experienced its greatest flowering in the early nineteenth century in writings of Count Claude-Henri de Rouvroy de Saint-Simon, Charles Fourier, and Robert Owen. The modern Left has always had its utopian side. The radical tradition as far back as the Diggers of the English Civil Wars of the 1640s have contained utopian elements. Marx and Engels's view of the classless, stateless communist society is essentially utopian.[8] And in the twentieth century, social protest songwriters have consistently used utopian themes and images.[9]

The term "utopian" may be applied to practically any thoroughgoing idealism—any set of impractical, unrealizable ideals—or as Karl Mannheim states it in *Ideology and Utopia*, any state of mind that is "incongruous with the state of reality within which it occurs."[10] Thus in the most general sense, utopianism refers to any orientation that departs from or transcends the reality of actual situations. This definition may apply to a broad variety of belief and value systems, both religious and ideological. Accordingly, both Platonic idealism and Christian fundamentalism are "utopian." Both Plato's Republic and Christ's Kingdom of Heaven were imagined situations, for which there are no actual historical examples.

In the modern era (when the term "utopia" originated), however, its usage has usually been reserved to connote certain secular ideological beliefs, namely certain beliefs of the political Left. In its modern usage, the term is inherently revolutionary. For Mannheim (who was instrumental in developing the modern sociological conception), an idealism becomes utopian only when specific social groups embody these ideals in their conduct and thereby attempt to realize them in the world.[11] Utopianism is a totalizing wish that is acted on or that becomes a part of one's lifestyle. Utopianism is thus a form of revolutionary consciousness. The utopian embraces a lifestyle at odds with sociopolitical convention.

Perhaps the major characteristic of this left-wing revolutionary idealism is something we might call the "communal ideal."[12] This is the idealization of the totalization process, which is captured within the symbolism of social harmony and brotherhood, and a value system that emphasizes altruism and love. The utopian has a fundamental concern for social unification. He seeks solidarity and oneness with his fellows. Like Lennon, he imagines all the people sharing all the world.

In preferring collective to private ownership and communal rather than individualistic modes of social organization, the utopian is a socialist. And yet, even within the socialist tradition, the utopian is an outsider. Ever since Engels's *Socialism: Utopian and Scientific* (1880) the term "utopian" has had a negative political connotation in radical circles. For Engels, "utopian" was a partisan polemical slur used against essentially all non-Marxist socialists. With all the certainty of the utopian, Engels asserted that among the writers of the Left only Marx's firmly stated, rationally grounded, historically verifiable, and thoroughly systematic works were "scientific" and therefore worthy of the name socialist. He found the works of earlier socialists (Saint-Simon, Owen, and Fourier) and contemporaries such as Pierre Joseph Proudhon to be wildly speculative, unsubstantiated mysticism, which he scored as "utopian."[13]

Although Engels's critique of the utopian socialists was no doubt unfair and highly charged with his own biases, his polemics did draw the major theoretical-ideological boundaries between utopian and Marxist socialism. Engels made three fundamental distinctions that are relevant to this discussion. First, and most general, is the argument that, unlike Marx's historical materialism, the works of the utopians lacked a positive historical referent. As a result, the utopians confused causes and results and failed to understand the economic determinants of the social dissatisfaction that underlies all radical thought. The utopians misplaced their emphasis upon the resulting imaginary ideals and abstract empty speculations of the superstructure without the vital recognition and understanding of the economic substructure which were the source of those ideals.[14]

Second, Engels argued that the utopians did not properly understand the role and purpose of the working class and instead focused their hopes unrealistically upon the imagined brotherhood of all mankind: "One thing is common to all three [Owen, Fourier, and Saint-Simon]. Not one of them appears as a representative of the interests of the proletariat . . . they want to emancipate not a particular class to begin with, but all humanity at once."[15]

Finally, and perhaps most fundamental, there is an important tactical difference. The utopians lacked the Marxists' concrete class-based revolutionary strategy, which was the seizure of the economic means of production and the establishment of the dictatorship of the proletariat. Instead of a positive revolutionary policy, the utopians naively depended on the force of persuasion, education, and example to transform society. Engels assessed the utopians' approach to revolution as follows: "It was a question of inventing a new and more perfect social order and of imposing it on society from without, by propaganda and wherever possible by the example of model experiments. These new social systems were foredoomed to be Utopias; the more they were worked out in detail, the more inevitably they became lost in pure fantasy."[16]

In short, Engels saw in the works of Saint-Simon, Owen, and Fourier a highly speculative, unsubstantiated political philosophy grounded in loose conceptualizations and wish fulfillment. He presented Marxisim as the scientific alternative: a positively formulated radical policy grounded in historical fact and socioeconomic reality. In sum, Engels criticized the utopians as mere idealists and felt himself and Marx to be realists. But in his undying devotion to Karl Marx and his determined faith in dialectical materialism, Engels was guilty of another form of idealism—the idealization of science. And yet the distinctions he made in *Socialism: Utopian and Scientific* remain. In their scorn for abstract speculation, Marx and Engels idealized historically (though not necessarily empirically) verifiable hypotheses, and therefore their idealism differed fundamentally from that of the utopians, who idealized imagined ideals. Revealing a similar deep-seated utopianism, Leo Tolstoy once wrote: "I used to believe that there was a green stick on which words were carved that would destroy all the evil in the hearts of men and bring them everything good, and I still believe today that there is such a truth, that it will be revealed to men, and will fulfill its promise."[17] Marx could never have believed that. History, economics, and the logic of the dialectic were his green stick, and that is the essential difference between Marxism and utopianism.

But the proletarian-based scientific socialism of Marx and Engels has never generated a substantial following in America. The American worker has traditionally possessed a stubborn conservative streak. Perhaps it was the vast frontier—which served as a buffer and a safety valve, slowing the growth of urban populations and bolstering the hopes of the propertyless with the ubiquitous dream of the West—that prevented the increasing misery of the working masses that Engels felt would lead to revolution. Or perhaps America's ethnic mix of a variety of competing immigrant nationalist groups impeded the "normal" development of a broad revolutionary working-class consciousness and solidarity. Or perhaps more than anything else, America's vast and abundant natural resources and untapped wealth perpetuated the myth of the promised land and soothed the revolutionary potential of the American proletarian. Relative to Europe, America did seem to offer a greater chance for social mobility, and because of her lack of a rigid and traditional class system, her people seemed to possess a greater faith in the dream of upward mobility and less confidence in the dream of working-class revolution. In any event, Marxism, though clearly the foundation of all modern radicalism, remains a distinctly European political philosophy.

Utopianism, also distinctly European, has had an uneven history on American soil. America's bourgeois origin—its foundation in the liberal political tradition—entrenched the cult of the individual, private property, and capitalism. Therefore, the American mainstream has viewed the communal ideal with suspicion, as something odd and eccentric, if not subversive.[18] Nevertheless, the American frontier of the nineteenth century saw a flurry of communal experiments. There were the religious communes of the Rappites, the Quakers, and the Shakers; the transcendentalist commune at Brook Farm, Massachusetts; and a variety of socialist communes, inspired by the ideas of Robert Owen and Charles Fourier.[19]

The communal ideal was also an important element in the syndicalism of the early labor movement in the late nineteenth and early twentieth centuries. Especially for the Knights of Labor and the Industrial Workers of the World (IWW) the union was a powerful symbol of working-class solidarity and the brotherhood of labor.[20] But both of these examples lie outside the mainstream of the American labor movement. The American worker and the labor movement traditionally have been much more concerned with wages, working conditions, and benefits than with the imagined syndicalist commonwealth.[21] The labor movement and the American Left generally have never transcended their heritage of liberal individualism sufficiently to embrace the communal ideal with anything but the mildest enthusiasm. The American radical has generally tended to seek the peace and isolation of Walden Pond and to shy away from the totalizing fantasies of Owen's New Harmony.[22]

But there is more to utopianism than the idealization of collective living and the consciousness of brotherhood. The utopian sensibility is more than a particular set of beliefs and values. It is also the manner in which one accepts and holds to these beliefs. The utopian is a zealot. He is a man possessed, one who is smitten by the vision of oneness, who finds his sole purpose in life as a glorious mission, proselytizing for the togetherness he feels the world lacks.[23] Both the Christian missionary and the union organizer possess this utopian mentality. Both are selflessly, perhaps irrationally, dedicated to the communal ideal in one form or another. Both are totalizing agents doing the mind guerrilla with the determined enthusiasm that only the true believer can bring to that "dance."

So the utopian sensibility is a fervent idealism, usually—though not necessarily—associated with the non-Marxist Left. It is characterized by a strong commitment to the communal ideal, in one form or another, and a faith in the brotherhood and equality of all mankind. But only when held by zealots bent on changing the world with the force of their dedication, and according to their ideals, do we find the true utopian mind guerrilla.

The Utopian Conception of Politics

The utopian views politics as collective action, that is, as a process aimed at the generation of group consciousness, solidarity, identity, and allegiance. Working-class radicalism, for example, involves the generation of class consciousness and worker solidarity. In short, the utopian tends to view politics as the totalization process. Utopian politics attempts to actualize the communal ideal. Moreover, the communal ideal is usually conceived in the broadest sense possible. Utopian politics is thus often identified with the quest for the oneness of a universal community of mankind.[24]

Utopianism, like all politics of the Left, begins with an abhorrence of existing socioeconomic and political conditions. There is a fundamental sense of injustice, a deeply held feeling that something is wrong with the world in its present form.[25]. Often this sense of injustice is accompanied by eschatological fantasies—visions of the impending apocalypse. There is, typically, a sense of urgency flowing from the fear that, unless something is done immediately, the world is irreversibly doomed.[26]

The utopian usually perceives this fundamental injustice and impending doom in conjunction with institutions and practices that violate the condition of universal oneness. It is often argued that these institutions and practices frustrate the totalization process by aggravating man's primitive tendencies toward divisiveness.[27] Thus from the perspective of the communal ideal, capitalist institutions such as private property and the profit motive are typically viewed as unjust and exploitive because they foster inequality and therefore violate the oneness of humanity.[28]

The nature of the transcendental oneness which the utopian seeks tends to affect the political strategies put forth to achieve it. This utopian oneness, captured poetically by Charles Fourier as "Harmony," is an idealized condition sustained through noncoercive means. Fourier, for example, felt that his utopian scheme was so obviously superior to the conventional way of life that, in due course, the world would naturally come to accept it.[29]

Persuasion, not force, is the utopian's weapon. The primary social bond in utopia is imagined to be love, sexual as well as altruistic. Utopians have a long history of free-love experimentation. Plato's guardians were to have practiced communal marriage, and Fourier's phalansteries were to have contained special rooms for sexual play.[30] To the utopian, reckless romantic that he is, love is a force sufficient to hold any community together. The utopian is usually a pacifist who practices the politics of love and nonviolence.

Since utopia is an imagined condition, rarely actualized in practice, and more an ideal than a reality, it can best be achieved through perceptual politics, or the politics of persuasion. The utopian thus tends toward symbolic politics and wish fulfillment. Almost all utopian schemes, from Plato's Republic to B.F. Skinner's *Walden II,* place great emphasis upon education. Utopian converts are conditioned noncoercively, through a rigorous and systematic training program, to accept the ways of utopia.[31] Accordingly, it can be argued that the political process of developing group consciousness and solidarity and the imaginary pursuit of the utopian One, are of a nonviolent and symbolic nature. Ironically, however, this aspect of utopianism often invites criticisms of brainwashing and mind-game politics. And to the extent that such criticisms are valid, utopian totalities, though imagined as conditions of peace and harmony, often turn out in practice to be dystopic totalitarian corruptions of the communal ideal.[32]

But regardless of the ultimate consequences of the conditioning of group identification and communal sensibility and the controversy over the methodology of inducing allegiance to the imagined universal totality, the political rationale is almost always the same. If we (the people, the working class, blacks, women, Jews, Poles, and so on) all stick together, if we could at least temporarily discard our differences and form a united front, then we could remake or reorder the world, right its wrongs, stamp out injustice, and thereby perfect the relation of man to man and man to woman in a peaceful and harmonious society and world community. Preacher Casey, in John Steinbeck's *The Grapes of Wrath,* sums up the utopian conception of politics: "An' I got thinkin', only it wasn't thinkin', it was deeper down than thinkin'. I got thinkin' how we was holy when we was one thing, an' mankin' was holy when it was one thing. An' it on'y got unholy when one mis'able little fella got the bit in his teeth an' run off his own way, kickin' an' draggin' an' fightin'. Fella like that bust the holiness. But when they're all workin' together, not one fella for another fella, but one fella kind of harnessed to the whole shebang—that's right, that's holy."[33]

But it often takes a Preacher Casey, a gifted visionary, to perceive and then pass along the utopian vision. The quest for oneness and solidarity almost always involves the mediation of charismatic leadership.[34] Accordingly, the Indian independence movement was dependent upon the charisma of Mahatma Gandhi, the black civil rights movement in America was in many ways a function of the public magnetism of Martin Luther King, Jr., and the Polish Solidarity movement is being guided by the force of Lech Walenza's personality. Those heroic public personages who define, articulate, and proselytize the vision and ideals of utopia have the effect of focusing the confused tangle of disaffection, dissatisfaction, and disillusionment into positive collective action. Social totality and political solidarity crystallize around the heroic image. The hero is thus a totalizing agent. The force of charisma and the power of idolization are important factors in the totalization of the utopian vision. Through hero-worship, the vision of one is transformed into the vision of many. In this way, utopianism and heroism come together to support totalization.

I have defined utopianism as a political sensibility based on an idealization of an imagined social condition in which peace and harmony and love among all men and women form the foundation of social living. These imagined conditions, these perceptual totalizations, these world views, form within the individual as a "political consciousness" and among individuals as "solidarity," "camaraderie," and "brotherhood." The result is a strongly felt sense of community and purpose and a determined sense of mission to extend this community spirit to encompass as broad a community as possible. Such a consciousness, though non-Marxist, is nevertheless revolutionary in the sense that it is held in spite of, and in opposition to, actual or existing social conditions. It is also revolutionary in the sense that it is acted upon and taken directly into the being of the individual. The utopian lives his or her politics and adopts it as a lifestyle.

The sense of solidarity and oneness that sustains the utopian vision must be cultivated, and heroic charismatic visionaries walk behind the plow. Utopian personages (working-class heroes and mind guerrillas) are important, perhaps crucial, totalizing agents. Their agency gives the Left a human quality and a cultlike structure. The utopian sensibility is thus a loose, fluid, and amorphorous formation of idealists, vicariously dreaming the dreams of their heroes.

If the utopian sensibility has any validity as a description of the Left generally, it is even more valid in describing the song culture of the Left.

Utopianism and the Protest Song Hero

American popular artists, especially those in the superstar category, have rarely associated themselves with social causes. Only since the 1960s has political radicalism found its way into the pop culture arena. Woody Guthrie, Pete Seeger, and the Almanac Singers recorded and performed protest material in the 1930s and 1940s but never generated a mass following. Their appeal was confined to narrow left-wing labor circles. Their performances attracted hundreds, not thousands. They were recorded on minor underground labels— Keynote, Disc, Timely, Stinson, and Folkways—and because of their radical politics, they were shunned by the major recording companies.[35]

Truly popular artists—Rudy Vallee, Bing Crosby, Frank Sinatra, and Elvis Presley—have been more likely to view their craft as a vehicle for upward social mobility than as a platform from which to espouse ideological positions. In the popular music business, egoism and greed have always been occupational hazards, which have also tended to negate political expression. Commercial success has an insulating effect. The star system and the hit parade have been incompatible with radical politics. Moreover, access to the mass media has been tightly controlled by businessmen who consider radical politics unsavory and distasteful.[36]

In the early 1960s, however, when the first protest singers began to gain access to the mass media and penetrate America's popular culture, their superstar status tended to give them an exaggerated faith in their ability to remake the world. In 1964, at the height of their fame, Peter, Paul, and Mary bragged to an interviewer: "Do you realize the power of PP and M? We could mobilize the youth of America today in a way that nobody else could. We could conceivably travel with a presidential candidate, and maybe even sway an election."[37] Of course, this remark was made on the eve of the Beatles' arrival in America, which quickly diminished the professional and political effectiveness of PP and M and other folk groups. Only Bob Dylan would survive the transition to rock, carrying the torch of the protest tradition with him.

But even before they gained access to the mass media, protest singers in America, though genuinely committed to the politics of the Left, participated at an abstract and ritualistic level, and their perception of political radicalism was essentially idealistic and utopian. Pete Seeger did not form the Almanac Singers to make money, for they made none. And he did not do it to promote rural folk music to urban audiences, though his impact on them is incalculable. His motivation was, and has always remained, political. In his mind, his musical career and his politics have always been inseparable. Seeger is an idealist and a zealot. From the very beginning, he was determined to use folk music to organize the workers and develop their political consciousness. His goal was nothing short of the utopian One.[38]

In participating in political activities, protest singers dramatize this same utopian vision. At strikes, mass demonstrations, protest marches and rallies, or even on the campaign trail, the singer's role is different from that of the promoters and organizers who have laid the material and legal groundwork for the event or the political speakers who will attempt to rationalize the event and give it the appropriate ideological focus. Joan Baez led the masses in singing "We Shall Overcome" at the Washington Monument not just to lend her celebrity status to promote the cause but to entertain and inspire the audience's political consciousness. Her role was symbolic. She was performing a ritualistic act intended to stir the political imagination of the audience. The tangible effect was the collective swaying of one hundred thousand people, connected by clasped hands, forming a single reified entity, singing in one voice. It was a moving and inspirational scene. At that moment, they all believed they could indeed overcome. This is probably the most tangible evidence of the totalization process one can find. Even if it occurred only momentarily and was confined to a specific one hundred thousand individuals, it had residual effects that, with the aid of the six o'clock news, could reverberate throughout the entire nation. And on that particular afternoon, the utopian One, the Left totality, was in some sense made real.

The utopian vision is reinforced by the nature of the medium itself. The song form, the long-playing record, the radio or music video, or the mass sing described above all exert pressure in a romanticized utopian direction. It is not appropriate or possible for the song form to spell out in detail political platforms and ideological arguments. Rather, a few simple, repetitive symbols are used to project broad, abstract ideals designed to sway the collective consciousness and provide a convenient and ritualized format for the dramatic presentation and expression of the utopian vision.[39]

Changing Conceptions of Utopia

The utopian One has been the goal and the dream of all the great protest writers and singers of twentieth-century America, from Joe Hill to John Lennon. But the conception of the One and the role of the protest singer in the totalization process have undergone significant transformations.

At the beginning of the century, the Wobblies' utopian vision was of the One Big Union, perhaps best represented in Ralph Chaplin's "Commonwealth of Toil!"

> But we have a glowing dream
> Of how fair the world will seem
> When each man can live his life secure and free;
> When the earth is owned by Labor
> And there's joy and peace for all
> In the Commonwealth of Toil that is to be.[40]

Woody Guthrie, Pete Seeger, and the Almanac Singers continued this tradition through midcentury. Among Guthrie's many tributes to the union is the following portrait of the One:

> I can see my union shining like the sun! Like the sun!
> I can see my union shining like the sun! Like the sun!
> Well it draws us all together and melts us into one.
> It's that good old union feeling in my soul![41]

In the 1960s, the working-class conception of the One was almost completely lost and along with it the institutional vehicle and symbol of the union. Bob Dylan did not write a single song about the union until "Sundown on the Union," from *Infidels* (1983), which is a very negative view of the role of the labor movement in the economic crisis of the 1980s. The 1960s conception of the One suffered from either egocentricity and cryptic vagueness, as in Lennon's "I Am the Walrus" ("I am he as you are he as you are me and we are all together"),[42] or mystical nihilism, as in Dylan's "The Gates of Eden." Lennon's vision in "Imagine," of all the people sharing all the world, is perhaps a notable exception, but it suffers from this same lack of social referent and therefore seems too quixotic to be taken seriously.

At the beginning of the century, social protest was undertaken for the sake of all; as the century proceeded, it has been increasingly for the sake of the individual. In almost every case in the union era, the protest singer has presented his utopian visions in the second person plural (we). After the 1960s, the visions are presented in the first person (I, me, or you).

The role of singing hero in the protest cultures of the twentieth century has also undergone a significant transformation. In the union era, the protest singer had firm political convictions. For example, an air of certainty permeates the works of Joe Hill:

> Workers of the World awaken
> Break your chains, demand your rights
> All the wealth you make is taken
> By exploiting parasites.

Hill expressed a deeply held conviction that the One Big Union could be achieved and that it would become a vehicle for social justice:

> Join the Union Fellow Workers
> Men and women side by side
> We will crush the greedy shirkers
> Like a sweeping surging tide.[43]

The lyrics had all the naiveté of religious fanaticism. The problems were presented in black and white, and the solutions were always obvious. The singer was inclined toward the selfless pursuit of the totality and, more important, he felt himself a part of that totality, rather than holding an idolized position above and beyond it.

After the 1960s, certainty gave way to ambivalence. In the lyrics of some of Bob Dylan's songs from this period the problems are buried in deep symbolism and dark imagery. The answers were no longer obvious; they were merely "blowing in the wind." The motives of the protest singer had become increasingly ignoble. Perhaps, as most of the literature suggests, when it entered the realm of pop culture, protest politics was corrupted by commercialism. The protest singer came to value his career and artistic integrity above the utopian One. His purpose had changed. No longer seeking glory in association with the One, the working-class hero had become just "something to be."[44]

Utopianism and Music

The use of music in the gentle art of persuasion has long been associated with the utopian tradition.[45] They mesh well, for harmony is, after all, a musical metaphor, which seems to fit the communal condition. The harmony of the One is a life that is shared in the same way as the notes of a chord are shared frequencies that create a transcendent musical harmony.

The musical metaphor fits in another way. The chord may be sustained for only a brief, beautiful moment. Music, like utopia, has an amorphous, mystical quality. It is almost an imaginary construct, with only a fragile and temporary existence. The age of electronics, however, enables the chord to be sustained indefinitely through artificial means. This kink in the metaphor holds out the promise of the dehumanized totalitarian One, not the dream of the humanistic utopia. Technology has grafted an electromagnetic handle onto music that has taken it out of the control of the people.

But in spite of the controversy over its ultimate effects, music has figured prominently in most utopian educational schemes. As far back as Plato, the awesome power of music and its political significance were well understood and appreciated. Plato's views on music were reactionary and could have come from the right-wing's view of 1960s rock music:

> The introduction of novel fashions in music is a thing to beware of as endangering the whole fabric of society, whose most important conventions are unsettled by any revolution in that quarter. . . .
>
> It would be harmless . . . were it not that, little by little, this lawless spirit gains a lodgement and spreads imperceptibly to manners and pursuits; and from thence with gathering force invades men's dealings with one another, and next goes on to attack the laws and the constitution with wanton recklessness, until it ends by overthrowing the whole structure of public and private life.[46]

As if they had read Plato, the protest singers of twentieth-century America believed they were armed with a weapon more powerful than guns and bombs. And they felt that they had no need to resort to violence. Music cannot be used violently (although the high-decible sounds of a rock band might conceivably cross the threshold of pain). But the tactics of protest singing have remained largely symbolic. The inscription on Pete Seeger's banjo head articulates the utopian philosophy of music: "This Machine Surrounds Hate and Forces it to Surrender."

Singing is ritualized and dramatized speech, and it is only through such ritualized activities that hate may be surrounded and conquered by nonviolent means. In American protest cultures, singing has always been an important part of the ritual of union meetings, strikes, rallies, sit-ins, mass demonstrations, and marches. Musical rituals are designed and intended to instill empathy for the cause at hand and to inspire the participants' political consciousness. Music is used the same way it is used in the chants of primitive cultures to evoke magic and in holiness churches to evoke the "spirit." Radical politics has used music to generate group consciousness and solidarity—to evoke the "utopian spirit."[47]

Singing in the early union meetings, for example, closely resembled church singing. Radical lyrics were often sung to old and familiar hymn tunes, such as Joe Hill's transformation of "Power in the Blood of the Lamb" into "Power in a Band of Working Men."[48] The resulting song was referred to as a "labor hymn" and was likely to be sung at the opening and closing of union meetings. "Solidarity Forever" became a union doxology. The union business meeting was also likely to be punctuated at predetermined intervals by special performances by choral groups that functioned as union choirs.[49]

In the 1930s and 1940s, the Communist and Socialist parties also used group singing and employed "worker choruses" at their official functions. The folk groups of the 1940s, 1950s, and 1960s—the Almanac Singers, the Weavers, the Kingston Trio, Peter, Paul, and Mary—were modeled on these choral groups and carried the union singing tradition into the popular culture.[50]

Similarly, black radical movements in America have politicized spirituals—"Go Down Moses," "Freedom Is a Constant Struggle," "People Get Ready," and "We Shall Overcome"—as nonviolent weapons in the struggle for civil rights.[51] The power of ritualized singing to sustain the utopian inspiration even in the face of horrible defeats can be seen in Gordon Baxter's account of the funeral of Martin Luther King, Jr., on National Public Radio:

I followed the mules from way down in the ghetto where King was, on up the road, on up to the shining city of Atlanta. We walked real slow, and we sang the song to the cadence of it. And it was as beautiful as anything that you've ever heard out of the furl-the-banner legacy of the dying Confederacy, as beautiful as anything you've heard from Lee's march or any other of the grand music played a little too slow. And this song just rose up out of their voices as they came up out of the valley and on to the hillside in Atlanta: "We Shall Overcome . . ."

These words were part of a public radio tribute on the twentieth anniversary of the 1960 sit-ins in Greensboro, North Carolina, which touched off the civil rights movement. Former Student Nonviolent Coordinating Committee head John Lewis spoke more directly to the philosophy of nonviolence and the use of singing when he said: "The movement without songs would have been like birds without wings."[52]

Lewis's analogy captures the essence of the utopian vision from the point of view of protest music. In the protest imagination, birds are a symbol of love and nonviolence. The "snow-white dove" of peace is a folk expression. The dove's only weapon is flight, but she can soar above the madness. But song is also a kind of flight, and singers have wings, like angels and doves. The singer's voice is his wings, and his songs allow him, too, to soar above the madness of nonutopian life, of life as it is. The listener is invited to soar with him vicariously into the realm of what might be.

Within the American Left, the totalizing support of the protest hero, his songs, and the myths surrounding both have been significant, perhaps crucial, factors in the proliferation of working-class political culture. Working-class political culture has been characterized as a form of "utopian sensibility," or a determined political idealism that has become part of the lifestyle of a social group. The guerrilla minstrel—folk and popular singers such as Pete Seeger, Joan Baez, and Phil Ochs—has been the source as well as the inspiration for this continuing utopian sensibility. Their music has nourished revolutionary consciousness, and their public image has provided a vicarious gateway into the norms, customs, and conventions, the manners of dress and speech of the utopian lifestyle. It is in this sense that the guerrilla minstrel is an agent of totalization, serving as an ontological ideal-type and a popular mythos, imbued with utopian symbolism, supporting countercultural unification.

Moreover, the phenomenon of the guerrilla minstrel, by penetrating further and further into the popular culture over the course of the twentieth century, has taken on increasing totalizing significance. Over time, left-wing singing heroes have been instrumental in the development of the protest song as a musical genre in and of itself. Through the work of these guerrilla minstrels, the protest song has evolved into a highly effective and widely accepted political weapon and strategy. As a result, protest singing has become one of the cornerstones of the countercultural tradition in America.

4 Joe Hill: *The Man Who Never Died*

I dreamed I saw Joe Hill last night,
Alive as you or me.
Says I, "But Joe, you're ten years dead."
"I never died," said he.
"I never died," said he.
—Alfred Hayes, ca. 1930

Joe Hill at Woodstock

On a hot Friday night in late August 1969, when the wave of social protest that marked the decade was at its crest, Joan Baez walked out onto the stage at the Woodstock Music and Arts Festival to greet the inhabitants of this new youthful utopia, a sea of nearly half a million faces caught up in the spirit of this historic event, inspired by the ecstasy of their youthful solidarity.[1] It was at that time, the single largest countercultural festival in history. Baez, far past her professional peak, seemed out of place, like someone's older sister. The silver-throated folk singer and peacenik stood in stark contrast to the violent, high-voltage antics of the Who or the pain-wrenching, spasmodic gurglings of Joe Cocker. She represented an intellectual, political-ideological element in an otherwise recklessly antirational, uninhibited revolution-for-the-hell-of-it counterculture.

At the age of twenty-eight, Joan Baez was indeed an elder at Woodstock. Professorial and a bit preachy, she was perhaps more well-versed than any of the other performers that weekend in the history of the American Left and its countercultural traditions. Her contribution to this historic occasion was to resuscitate the legend of Wobbly martyr Joe Hill. In her performance of the classic Alfred Hayes–Earl Robinson ballad about one of the American labor movement's most renowned heroes, she was consciously linking the wild, drug-crazed passions of the summer of 1969 with the class-conscious idealism of the winter of 1915.[2] Baez introduced the Hill legend to the ideologically barren youth of the 1960s as the embodiment of an ageless youth rebellion and an aging idealism: the quest for the oneness of utopia.

The Pageant of Paterson

In the summer of 1913, during the first surge of radicalism in twentieth-century America, the Industrial Workers of the World (IWW), the flamboyant labor formed in 1905 by a coalition of socialists, anarchists, and radical trade unionists, popularly known as the Wobblies,[3] produced the first great countercultural festival and media event of the century: the Pageant of the Paterson Strike.[4] It took place in New York City's Madison Square Garden on the evening of June 7 and was a genuine celebration of love and compassion for the plight of the striking mill workers in nearby Paterson, New Jersey. It was also a grand dramatization of worker solidarity and class-consciousness.

The Wobblies were pioneers in the field of revolutionary art and culture and early practitioners of symbolic politics. Always media-wise and publicity conscious, the Wobblies were the first truly modern, institutionalized cultural guerrilla. In many ways IWW organizers were responsible for the romantic Wobbly image, hyping themselves, for political effect, as defiant, idealistic class warriors. This was part of their mind game.

The anarchosyndicalist IWW was intended as a radical alternative to the mainstream unionism of the American Federation of Labor (AFL).[5] Under the conservative leadership of Samuel Gompers, the American labor movement was being carefully steered in the direction of reformism and compromise with management. The primary goal was limited material gains for a growing aristocracy of skilled workers. Gompers expressed little concern for class-consciousness and worker solidarity. The forces behind the IWW, on the other hand, were more concerned with fundamental changes that would liberate all the workers, regardless of skill level, by humanizing the workplace.[6] To paraphrase a popular slogan from the Lawrence, Massachusetts, strike of 1912, the Wobblies wanted "bread and roses too."[7] They came to represent and attract mostly unskilled, unemployed immigrants, itinerant workers, hoboes, and homeless drifters—the desperate underclass of American society.

Most IWW activities were centered in the Western states and directed toward merchant sailors, dock workers, railroadmen, and lumberjacks. The Wobbly rank and file were recruited from a rough-and-tumble breed. IWW organizer and songwriter Ralph Chaplin characterized them as men who preferred to go down slugging rather than submit to wage slavery.[8] The political organization behind them was in principle nonviolent. Their first national publicity came from their free speech fights in California, Oregon, and Washington between 1908 and 1912. These, in turn, spawned the Wobbly song movement, which I will discuss at some length in this chapter. Their songs were undoubtedly the greatest contribution of the Wobblies to the philosophy and practice of the cultural guerrilla.

The Wobblies' participation in the strikes in the northeastern textile centers of Lawrence, Massachusetts, and later at Paterson, New Jersey (in 1912 and 1913), proved to be the high point in their national activities. These colorful, dramatic, and festive strikes were classic expressions of the emerging cultural guerrilla and an example for all modern media radicalism to follow. The report from an observer at the Lawrence strike gives one a sense of the Wobblies' political style:

> It was the first strike I ever saw which sang. I shall not soon forget the curious lift, the strange sudden fire of the mingled nationalities at the strike meetings when they broke into the universal language of song. And not only at the meetings did they sing, but in the soup houses and in the streets. I saw one group of women strikers who were peeling potatoes at a relief station suddenly break into the swing of the "Internationale."[9]

The strike at Paterson was the result of a complex set of conditions centered around a labor crisis in the silk industry of New Jersey, at a time when doctrines of revolutionary trade unionism were being rapidly disseminated throughout America's working classes. A recent influx of Jewish, Italian, and Polish immigrants had offered enterprising textile entrepreneurs a convenient source of cheap, exploitable labor for the new silk garment industry. Ninety-one percent of the silk workers were women and children, who worked ten-hour shifts for wages as low as five dollars a week to supplement their husbands' and fathers' starvation wages from the mines and factories. They worked in dark, damp, noisy, overcrowded mills that were unheated in the winter, improperly ventilated in the summer, and always choking with suffocating steam and acid fumes. Maimings from accidents were common, and tuberculosis and other respiratory diseases were widespread.[10]

Exacerbating the traditional abuses of improperly measuring worker production, kickbacks to foremen, and the exploitation of child labor, the mills at Paterson had just introduced a new four-loom system that doubled the production load per worker, forcing wages down and contributing to unemployment and hardship. On January 27, 1913, eight hundred employees of the Doherty Silk Mill walked off their jobs after four members of the workers' committee were fired for trying to discuss the elimination of the four-loom system with the management. By the end of February, the strike had spread throughout the entire silk industry of Paterson. More than twenty-five thousand silk workers were out on strike, and almost three hundred mills were idle.[11]

IWW organizers, confident after a major victory the previous winter in the textile mills of Lawrence, Massachusetts, came to Paterson to take charge of the strike. Lawrence had propelled the Wobblies into national prominence, crystallizing their image as defiant and romantic revolutionaries. IWW membership was at its highest levels, and sales of the *I.W.W. Songbook* and other Wobbly literature had risen dramatically. A new militant class-consciousness was spreading throughout the working population that threatened to tear apart the fragile and worn condition of American labor relations.

Although there was a great emotional outpouring of sympathy for the plight of immigrant mill workers, an equally emotional reactionary backlash was directed against labor organizers and union advocates. Factory and mill owners, capitalists, and government authorities had become alarmed at what they perceived as the spread of lawlessness and subversion. Economic polarization was giving way to class warfare.

It was also a time when talented young intellectuals such as author and journalist Walter Lippmann, NAACP founder William Walling, and Max Eastman, editor of the radical arts journal the *Masses,* were becoming infatuated with left-wing politics and working-class causes. Political radicalism had become a fashionable and popular topic.[12] It was a time not unlike the late 1960s, a time ripe for a countercultural happening.

Another young intellectual, John Reed, a recent Harvard graduate, was living in New York City's Greenwich Village and frequenting the home of Mabel Dodge, a wealthy widow, intellectual, and radical, whose apartment in the Village functioned as a salon for the new left-wing intelligentsia.[13] Here the young, idealistic Reed had met "Big Bill" Haywood, the fiery IWW president and labor agitator, and learned of the Paterson strike. Like the thousands of young idealists who flocked south in the freedom rides of the early 1960s, Reed was seeking adventure and political fulfillment in the cause of an oppressed people with whom he had little in common.

Reed's adventure in Paterson resulted in his arrest with some of the strikers, touching off a flood of stories in the New York papers about the Harvard boy jailed with immigrants. Upon his release, Reed solicited the financial assistance of Mrs. Dodge and the backing of the IWW, rented Madison Square Garden, and directed a cast of a thousand strikers in a ritualistic reenactment of the Paterson strike.

The Pageant of Paterson featured the walkout, the confrontation with police, the funeral for the innocent bystander shot down by the police, the sending away of the strikers' children to homes in other cities where they could be properly cared for until the strike ended, the fiery speeches by labor leaders Haywood and Elizabeth Gurley Flynn, who played themselves, and the final establishment of the workers' utopia. Throughout the evening there were periodic outbursts of singing. At times the entire audience of fifteen thousand joined in singing the songs from the Wobblies' "Little Red Songbook." The effect was deeply moving. Mabel Dodge described the pageant: "For a few electric moments there was a terrible unity between all those people. They were one: the workers who had come to show their comrades what was happening across the river and the workers who had come to see it. I have never felt such a high pulsing vibration in any gathering before or since."[14]

Like Woodstock, the Paterson pageant was a financial failure. At Woodstock, the flood of young souls so overwhelmed the logistics of ticket gathering that the promoters gave up trying to collect them. At the Paterson pageant, the price of admission was deliberately kept low so that out-of-work strikers could attend. Those who presented their red IWW membership cards gained free admission. The promoters took deliberate losses so they could fill the arena to capacity.

But like Woodstock, the Paterson Pageant was a publicity success, a grand and lasting experiment in the mind guerrilla. Likewise, as a political movement and as a labor organization, the IWW was an almost complete failure, but as a cultural revolution it was a great success. Although perceived as violent anarchists, the Wobblies were actually pioneers in the tactics of passive resistance and nonviolent symbolic politics. The Paterson pageant is but one example, and yet it points out the distinctiveness of the Wobblies as a revolutionary phenomenon.

The Wobblies—as propaganda specialists and forerunners in the practice of revolutionary drama, ritual, and festival—were the first of the radical organizations in America to fully exploit the arts for political purposes. They were responsible for some of the classic American radical poster art and political cartoons. They were pioneers in guerrilla theater, which they used not just in grand extravaganzas like the Paterson pageant but more often to entertain and bolster the spirits of strikers on the picket line. Their newspapers—*Solidarity,* the *Industrial Worker,* and the *One Big Union Monthly*—were early experiments in radical journalism. Probably their most lasting contribution was in the field of revolutionary singing.

Elizabeth Gurley Flynn, the flamboyant Wobbly organizer, feminist, and later Communist party leader, in an analysis of the Paterson strike, clearly outlines the full dimensions of revolutionary agitation and the role and purpose of symbolic and cultural politics:

> What is a labor victory? I maintain that it is a twofold thing. Workers must gain economic advantage, but they must also gain revolutionary spirit, in order to achieve a complete victory. For the workers to gain a few cents more a day, a few minutes less a day, and go back to work with the same psychology, the same attitude toward society, is to have achieved a temporary gain and not a lasting victory. For workers to go back with a class-conscious spirit, with an organized and determined attitude toward society means that even if they have made no economic gain they have the possibility of gaining in the future.[15]

The revolutionary spirit of which Flynn spoke is the major purpose and by-product of cultural events like the Paterson pageant and the Woodstock Music and Arts Festival. The revolutionary spirit is what keeps the people's causes alive long after the historic confrontations of labor and capital, of segregationists and integrationists, of draftees and draft boards, of chemical waste victims and chemical companies, and of peaceniks and the masters of war have long passed from public consciousness. It is the same spirit that Joe Hill continues to symbolize: the spirit of oneness among all who have suffered from social injustice and economic oppression.

Hill and Lennon

The counterculture of the 1960s was the spiritual grandchild of the Wobblies. John Lennon, symbol of the children of Woodstock, was connected—if only subconsciously—to the spirit of Joe Hill and the Wobblies. In his first solo album, *Plastic Ono Band* (1970), in the song "I Found Out," Lennon could have pilfered the "pie in the sky" line and the watch-out-for-the-false-prophets concept from Hill's 1911 song "The Preacher and the Slave." Hill's original lyric was

Long-haired preachers come out every night,
Try to tell you what's wrong and what's right;
But when asked, "How 'bout something to eat?"
They will answer in voices so sweet:
"You will eat, bye and bye,
In that glorious land above the sky;
Work and pray, live on hay,
You'll get pie in the sky when you die."[16]

Lennon's 1970 verse echoed Hill:

Old Hare Krishna got nothing on you.
Just keep you crazy with nothing to do;
Keep you occupied with pie in the sky,
There ain't no guru who can see through your eyes.[17]

Both songs were popularizations of the famous aphorism of Marx that "religion is the opiate of the people."[18] Hill's rendering was from the perspective of traditional dialectical materialism; Lennon's was from modern existentialism. Hill and Lennon merge, in spite of the differences of half a century, in the gospel of the utopian One. Both dreamed of all the people sharing all the world, and both were daring practitioners of the art of the mind guerrilla.

The Wobbly Bard

By the time of the Paterson pageant, Joe Hill, a young Swedish immigrant seaman and sometime saloon piano player, was becoming recognized as a Wobbly songwriter.[19] His earliest known song, "Casey Jones, the Union Scab," a parody of the popular song, was written in 1911 during a strike by shop workers on the Southern Pacific Railroad in San Pedro, California, where engineers and some other skilled workers continued to operate the trains.[20] It was a satirical and playfully vindictive attack on those workers who violated class solidarity by continuing to work after the strike had been called, a practice referred to in the vernacular of labor as "scabbing." The song had the positive and immediate effect of helping to raise the spirits of strikers on the picket lines and in the jails. It was printed on red cards and sold to aid a strike fund. It quickly became popular among workers in California and then spread throughout the nation with immigrant workers and across the oceans with merchant sailors:

The workers on the S.P. line to strike sent out a call;
But Casey Jones, the engineer, he wouldn't strike at all;

His boiler it was leaking, and its drivers on the bum,
And his engine and its bearings, they were all out of plumb.
Casey Jones, kept his junk pile running,
Casey Jones, was working double time;
Casey Jones, got a wooden medal,
For being good and faithful on the S.P. Line.[21]

Another of Hill's early compositions was the famous "pie in the sky" song, "The Preacher and the Slave," sometimes known as "Long Haired Preachers," which appeared in the 1911 edition of the *I.W.W. Songbook* and was Hill's first contribution to the famous Wobbly songster.[22] It was a parody of the hymn "In the Sweet Bye and Bye" and became a popular satire of the Wobblies' principal adversary in the propaganda battles among California's unemployed immigrants, hoboes, and migrant laborers, the Salvation Army. The preachers promised only salvation, or "pie in the sky," while the unemployed and homeless sought food to eat and shelter from the cold. It is considered Hill's masterpiece, and it retained its popularity well into the 1930s. Twelve years after Hill's death the song was included in Carl Sandburg's collection, *American Songbag,* and from there it passed into America's folk tradition.[23]

Hill's colorful, lampooning, and sardonic songs dominated the fourth and fifth editions of the Wobbly songbook in 1912 and 1913 and have remained an important part of all subsequent issues. In the few short years before his death in 1915, Hill contributed as many as twenty-five songs to the "Little Red Songbook." The thirteenth edition in 1917 was a special Joe Hill Memorial Edition.[24]

The songbook, formally titled *I.W.W. Songs: Songs of the Workers,* and provocatively subtitled *To Fan the Flames of Discontent,* had begun publication in 1909 as a tactical spinoff of the famous Wobbly free speech fights in California.[25] The free speech campaigns were to become one of the Wobblies' greatest contributions to the tactics of passive resistance, and the songbook was a lasting contribution to the history of symbolic politics and the culture of protest. The IWW provoked the so-called "free speech movement" in reaction to the unscrupulous practices of employment agencies that preyed on the unemployed by selling them jobs. These agencies often worked in collusion with employers, who would ensure that the jobs were temporary, lasting only a few days or weeks at most, forcing workers through a cycle of exploitation that profited only the employers and the agencies.[26]

The IWW began to organize street meetings, speaking out against the unjust practices of the "slave market" and the employment "sharks." Many towns, unsympathetic to the problems of the unemployed and fearing the spread of unionism, quickly passed ordinances against street speaking. Such a serious breach of First Amendment rights could not go unchallenged. IWW publications sent out a call for help. In response, Wobblies by the thousands flooded into the affected towns. In an unending procession, each Wob in turn would mount the soapbox in defiance of the ban on street speaking and begin his speech: "My Fellow Workers . . . " He would immediately be arrested for disorderly conduct and taken to jail, only to be replaced by the next speaker. Soon the jails were overflowing with defiant Wobblies, loudly singing their songs and causing as much disruption as possible, paralyzing local court systems in a dramatic test of the Constitution.

The Salvation Army was the Wobblies' greatest competitor for the attention of the street people, and its status as a religious organization often exempted it from the ordinances banning street speaking. According to folklorist John Greenway, this competition with the Salvation Army led the Wobblies to realize the political significance of singing.[27] It seems that one Jack Walsh, an organizer for The Spokane, Washington, chapter of the IWW, was attempting to recruit the unemployed hoboes and migrant workers into the One Big Union when the Salvation Army mounted a challenge.

The Salvation Army's technique was simple and effective. It would simply march its band into the crowd, surrounding Walsh, and drown him in a "cacophony of cornets and tambourines."[28] But Jack Walsh was not one to be easily outwitted. He immediately organized his own brass band, with Mac McClintock (a Wobbly songwriter famous for having written "Hallelujah I'm a Bum!") playing the E-flat baritone horn and a giant lumberjack beating on the bass drum, and beat the Salvation Army at its own game. Wobbly ingenuity eventually proved too much for the marching hymn-singers. The Wobblies would sing their own radical political lyrics to the tunes of the Salvation Army's old standard hymns. The Salvation Army band might play a familiar hymn such as

Hallelujah! Thine the glory,
Hallelujah! amen;
Hallelujah! Thine the glory
Revive us again.[29]

and the Wobbly band would irreverently transfigure the lyrics:

Hallelujah! I'm a bum!
Hallelujah! Bum again!
Hallelujah! Give us a handout
To revive us again.[30]

The Salvation Army was finally defeated, and Walsh and the IWW had discovered a new organizing tool; union singing.

Building upon the foundations laid down by Walsh and McClintock, the Spokane IWW produced the first edition of the "Little Red Songbook" in 1909 to replace a song card containing four parodies of popular Salvation Army tunes. The songbook would become the Wobbly bible.[31] From the very beginning it was conceived of as a political propaganda device through which IWW philosophies could be readily disseminated among politically unsophisticated workers. It was so obviously superior to the traditional leaflets containing "dry-as-dust polemics" that it quickly gained popularity throughout the nation and then made its way across the oceans with merchant seamen and into foreign countries.[32] It was designed to fit easily into the pocket of the worker's overalls for ease of transport among the rambling unemployed, and it contained not only songs but poems and stories as well. Its bright red cover symbolized the radical Left. The inside cover of each edition contained a copy of the IWW Preamble, which began with the stirring and provocative lines: "The working class and the employing class have nothing in common. There can be no peace so long as hunger and want are found among millions of working people and the few, who make up the employing class, have all the good things of life."[33] A copy of the latest edition of the songbook was given out along with each new membership card. In union meetings it served a function similar to that of a hymnal in a religious service. Moreover, its pocket size allowed for a portability that made it an invaluable aid at strikes, demonstrations, and even in the jails, forever fanning the flames of discontent, keeping alive the revolutionary spirit of the Wobblies.

Without a doubt, the single greatest contributor to the "Little Red Songbook" was Joe Hill. In the history of the songbook, Hill's contribution, in quantity as well as quality, is far greater than that of any of the other famous Wobbly songwriters: Ralph ("Solidarity Forever") Chaplin; Richard Brazier, who participated in the original songbook committee and wrote such classics as "Meet Me in the Jungle, Louie," "They Are All Fighters," and "The Eight-Hour Song"; E. S. Nelson, who wrote one of the earliest Wobbly songs, "Workingmen Unite!"; and Jim Connell, who wrote "The Red Flag." In an unpublished study, I found that, out of a sample of eighty-six known Wobbly songs, Joe Hill wrote twenty, or 23.8 percent.[34] The overwhelming majority of the songs either came from unknown workers (30 percent), who might contribute a single song in an entire lifetime, or were of unknown origin (26 percent), many arising spontaneously at strikes or street meetings. Also, although the songbook had an active life of eleven years (from 1909 to 1920), Hill contributed songs from 1911 to 1915, or about four years. Thus Joe Hill was clearly the most prolific Wobbly songwriter and by far the most important protest songwriter in the history of American labor.

The Songs of Joe Hill

Historian Gibbs Smith has found thirty-two songs attributed to Joe Hill. In addition to the twenty-four songs and two poems that have appeared in Wobbly literature, Smith included three fragments from the memory of an old Wobbly organizer, Louis Moreau, interviewed in 1967 by IWW scholar Fred Thompson: "Martin Welch and Stuart," "Skookum Ryan, the Walking Boss," and "We Won't Build No More Railroads for Overalls and Snuff." All three were written for the construction workers' strike against the Canadian Northern Railroad Company in British Columbia in the winter of 1912. Smith also lists three sentimental love songs, two of which were found among Hill's possessions at the time of his arrest. The third was uncovered in the Joe Hill file of the Archives of the Royal Ministry of Foreign Affairs in Stockholm, Sweden. These songs stand in stark contrast to the class-conscious propaganda of Hill's Wobbly verses and his guerrilla minstrel image. Apparently Hill could produce pop verses as trite and sentimental as "I Wanna Hold Your Hand" or "Love Me Do." One example should make the point:

> Come take a joy-ride in my aeroplane tonight,
> Way beyond the clouds, where all the stars are shining
> bright.
> There I'd like to look into your loving eyes of blue,
> And if I should fall, then I'd know I'd fall in love with you.

The artistic quality of Hill's music is not at issue here. Hill's medium was the "Little Red Songbook" and other IWW literature. For print culture, the melody was less important than the lyric. These songs were "airs," written to be sung to the tunes of well-known hymns and popular songs. Although most of Hill's melodies were borrowed from Salvation Army hymns and popular show tunes, he did compose some original melodies, most notably "Workers of the World Awaken!" and "The Rebel Girl."[36]

By today's standards, Hill's lyrics are stiff and ideological. Many, like "Casey Jones," are topical and tied to obscure incidents in labor history. They are products of their era. The 1912 strike in British Columbia, for example, was the inspiration for one of Hill's more well-known songs, "Where the Fraser River Flows":

> Where the Fraser River flows, each fellow worker knows,
> They have bullied and oppressed us, but still our Union grows.
> And we're going to find a way, boys, for shorter hours and better pay, boys!
> And we're going to find a way, boys; where the Fraser River flows.

Hill also wrote a song about the despised AFL leader, John Golden, who attempted to persuade the strikers at Lawrence in 1912 to return to work. Irreverently, it was to the tune of the holiness hymn "A Little Talk with Jesus":

> A little talk with Golden makes it right, all right;
> He'll settle any strike, if there is coin in sight;
> Just take him out to dine and ev'rything is fine,
> A little talk with Golden makes it right, all right.[37]

Hill's outstanding characteristic, which distinguishes him from his fellow songwriters, was his humor. This quality assures his two most enduring songs, "Casey Jones" and "The Preacher and the Slave," a place in the folklore of the American Left.

Hill's humor always had a caustic edge and sometimes a scathing sarcasm. His description of the Salvation Army's "long-haired preachers"—as "holy rollers and jumpers," who "holler, jump and shout" until they get "all your coin on the drum," to deliver only "pie in the sky" in return—is a classic example.[38] Most of his satires are mocking and vicious attacks on the false-conscious worker, oblivious to the oppressive conditions of his station in life. Such bumbling characters as Casey Jones, Scissor Bill, or Mr. Block are portrayed as dimwits too stupid to understand they are victims of class exploitation:

Oh, Mr. Block, you were born by mistake,
You take the cake, you make me ache.
Tie a rock on your block and then jump in the lake,
Kindly do that for Liberty's sake.[39]

Hill's hymn parodies have the same biting humor. He interposed "pie in the sky" for "in the sweet bye and bye," "There's Power in a Band of Workingmen" for "Power in the Blood of the Lamb," and "Nearer My Job to Thee" for "Nearer My God to Thee."

But Joe Hill's lyrics could also be didactic, as preachy as any holy roller hymn. Always doing the mind guerrilla, almost all his songs carried the predictable political message, usually in the last verse. Hill resolved the problem of the "long-haired preachers" in typical Wobbly style and language but with a twist of his unique wit:

Workingmen of all countries unite,
Side by side for freedom we will fight;
When the world and its wealth we have gained
To the grafters we'll sing this refrain:
  You will eat, bye and bye,
  When you've learned how to cook and to fry;
  Chop some wood, 'twill do you good
  And you'll eat in the sweet bye and bye.[40]

Hill's purpose was always "organizational," the goal was always totalization, the quest for the utopian One. In a letter to the editor of *Solidarity* in November 1914, Hill explained his (and the Wobblies') philosophy of song: "A pamphlet, no matter how good, is never read more than once, but a song is learned by heart and repeated over and over; and I maintain that if a person can put a few cold, common sense facts into a song, and dress them up in a cloak of humor to take the dryness off of them, he will succeed in reaching a great number of workers who are too unintelligent or too indifferent to read a pamphlet or an editorial on economic science."[41] Thus Hill's songs were for the purpose of recruiting, imploring the worker to join the noble cause of the One Big Union. With his music, Hill was always seeking the mystical "solidarity," always trying to raise working-class consciousness. His songs possessed a clarity of vision and an air of confidence and destiny. He sang of the inevitability of the worker's commonwealth:

Organize! O, toilers, come organize your might;
Then we'll sing one song of the Worker's Commonwealth,
Full of beauty, full of love and health.[42]

Hill's songs also bring out the controversy over the Wobblies' image as violent anarchists. It is clear that, in principle, the Wobblies advocated nonviolence—the "folded arms" philosophy of "Big Bill" Haywood.[43] The history of the IWW is one of passive resistance. The "direct action" tactics pioneered by the Wobblies—the free speech fights, the colorful strikes, boycotts, and demonstrations, and their cultural and symbolic approaches to politics—are in the tradition of Henry David Thoreau, Gandhi, and Martin Luther King, Jr. They were anarchists, but they were not violent anarchists. The term used in most of the literature is anarchosyndicalist. They were anarchists in their advocacy of a stateless society and syndicalists in the sense that this stateless society would be structured around a network of syndicates or unions.

The folded arms philosophy of direct action did have violent possibilities, but the violence that occurred usually was directed against the Wobblies. The hysteria over radical trade unionism provoked violence, and Wobblies and other radicals suffered many atrocities at the hands of the state police, private security forces hired by factory owners, and vigilantes. The IWW perceived the very conditions of capitalist production, private property, and the wage system as an institutionalized act of violence perpetrated against the mine and mill workers on a daily basis.

The IWW viewed the world as a violent class struggle and the apparatus of government as a major belligerent in that struggle. The state, as IWW founding father Vincent St. John phrased it, "was a committee to look out for the interests of the employers." The Wobblies, therefore, naturally shunned and ridiculed the electoral approach to politics. Many of their constituents were disfranchised immigrants, aliens, women, and southern blacks. Instead of organizing workers at the capitalist ballot box, the Wobblies preferred to go directly to the source: the mines, mills, and factories. This is what they mean by "direct action," which an IWW publication defined as meaning "industrial action directly by, for, and of the workers themselves, without the treacherous aid of labor misleaders or scheming politicians. A strike that is initiated, controlled, and settled by the workers directly effected is direct action. . . . Direct action is combined action, directly on the job to secure better job conditions. Direct action is industrial democracy."[44]

But the philosophy of direct action does not necessarily imply the use of violence. IWW leaders preferred to strike passively with "folded arms." This doctrine was carefully articulated by

Wobbly organizer Joseph Ettor, in an address to the Lawrence strikers in January 1912:

> If the workers of the world want to win, all they have to do is recognize their own solidarity. They have nothing to do but fold their arms and the world will stop. The workers are more powerful with their hands in their pockets than all the property of the capitalists. As long as the workers keep their hands in their pockets, the capitalists cannot put theirs there. With passive resistance, with the workers absolutely refusing to move, lying absolutely silent, they are more powerful than all the weapons and instruments that the other side have for attack.[45]

The most controversial element of the Wobblies' philosophy of direct action was the concept of sabotage. The word and the philosophy are derived from the French syndicalist movement of the late nineteenth century. The word "sabotage" comes from the French *sabot,* meaning "wooden shoe."[46] The first peasants recruited to work in the mills at the beginning of the Industrial Revolution wore such shoes. During speedups, or after years of eighteen-to-twenty-hour work days in the squalid conditions of those early factories, when the abuse of the boss or overseer became too brutal, these *sabots* sometimes found their way into the machinery. A rough English equivalent is "a monkey wrench in the works."

The Wobblies perceived sabotage as another nonviolent weapon in the class struggle. To them, destroying dehumanizing private property was sometimes morally justifiable and tactically expedient. But instead of the violent destruction of property, the Wobblies preferred to think of sabotage as the "conscientious withdrawal of efficiency."[47] In a pamphlet Elizabeth Gurley Flynn explained this theory: "Sabotage means either to slacken up and interfere with the quantity, or to botch in your skill and to interfere with the quality of capitalist production so as to give poor service. It is something that is fought out within the walls of the shop. Sabotage is not physical violence; sabotage is an internal industrial process. It is simply another form of coercion."[48]

In Wobbly songs, poster art, and stickerettes, in the logo of their stationery and the mastheads of their newspapers, one finds the symbols of sabotage: the wooden shoe or the "sabo cat," a crouching black cat baring its claws.[49] And it is not surprising to find a few sabotage songs among the works of Joe Hill. In typical satirical humor, Hill captured the images of Wobbly sabotage in "Ta-ra-ra Boom De-ay":

I had a job once threshing wheat,
Worked sixteen hours with hands and feet.
And when the moon was shining bright,
They kept me working all night.
One moon-light night I hate to tell,
I "accidently" slipped and fell.
My pitch-fork went right in between some cog wheels
Of that thresh machine:
  Ta-ra-ra boom de-ay!
  It made a noise that way,
  And wheels and bolts and hay
  Went flying ev'ry way,
  That stingy rube said,
  "Well! A thousand gone to hell."
  But I did sleep that night,
  I needed it all right.[50]

More to the point is a poem by Hill first printed in *Solidarity* (June 27, 1914), "The Rebel's Toast":

If Freedom's road seems rough and hard,
  And strewn with rocks and thorns,
Then put your wooden shoes on, pard,
  And you won't hurt your corns.
To organize and teach, no doubt,
  Is very good—that's true,
But still we can't succeed without
  The Good Old Wooden Shoe.[51]

Elizabeth Gurley Flynn took an active part in Hill's defense campaign, and they corresponded while he was in prison awaiting execution. One of his last songs, "The Rebel Girl," was written for her from his cell. In a letter to Flynn, on the eve of his execution, he explained the song's inspiration:

Dear Friend Gurley:

I have been saying Goodbye so much now that it is becoming monotonous but I just cannot help to send you a few more lines because you have been more to me than a fellow worker. You have been an inspiration and when I composed The Rebel Girl you was right there and helped me all the time. As you furnished the idea I will now that I am gone give you the credit for that song, and be sure to locate a few more Rebel Girls like yourself, because they are needed and needed badly. . . . With a warm handshake across the continent and a last fond Goodbye to all I remain

Yours as Ever,
Joe Hill[52]

The song's chorus is a lasting tribute to Wobbly women and to radical women everywhere:

> That's the Rebel Girl, that's the Rebel Girl,
> To the Working class she's a precious pearl.
> She brings courage, pride and joy
> To the fighting Rebel Boy.
> We've had girls before but we need some more
> In the Industrial Workers of the World.
> Yes it's great to fight for freedom
> With a Rebel Girl.[53]

Hill's songs were thus an inspiration to working men and women alike. Ralph Chaplin described Hill's songs as being "as coarse as homespun and as fine as silk; full of lilting laughter and keen-edged satire; full of fine rage and finer tenderness; simple, forceful and sublime songs; songs of and for the worker, written in the only language that he can understand and set to the music of Joe Hill's own heart."[54]

Although his songs made him famous, Hill's life remains a mystery. Little is known of his early life, and of his trial and execution for murder, much remains enigmatic.

A Young Swede Named Hillstrom

About all we know about the famous Wobbly troubadour and martyr has been elaborately romanticized, embellished with a shiny coat of bright red symbolism, by the mind guerrillas of the One Big Union. Even in the face of death, Hill, the greatest mind guerrilla of them all, stubbornly clung to the public image of the dedicated revolutionary and idealistic visionary, framed on a murder charge by a corrupt system of justice in an America dominated and controlled by the robber barons of the capitalist industrial establishment. In the statements he made for public consumption during the period he spent in jail awaiting trial and execution, Hill was vague about his past and perhaps overly enthusiastic about his martyred future. To a request for biographical data, he craftily replied: "Biography you say? No. Let's not spoil good writing paper with such nonsense—only the here and now is of concern to me. I am a citizen of the world and I was born on a planet called the earth. The exact spot where I first saw the light of day is of such slight importance that it deserves no comment—I haven't much to say about myself. Will only say that I have done what little I could to bring the flag of freedom closer to its goal."[55] And on the eve of his execution, the Wobbly poet seemed determined to make his death a grand heroic episode in the proletarianization of the planet earth: "Tomorrow I expect to make a trip to the planet Mars and, if so, will immediately commence to organize the Mars canal workers into the I.W.W. and we will sing the good old songs so loud that the learned star-gazers on earth will get positive proof that the planet Mars is really inhabited."[56]

The legend that sprang from Hill's ashes was only partly of is own doing. Others contributed much. The emerging legend was captured in song and story and circulated widely throughout the Western world. One of the more beautiful—and typical—examples appeared in John Dos Passos's novel, *Nineteen Nineteen:*

A young Swede named Hillstrom went to sea, got himself calloused hands on sailingships and tramps, learned English in the fo'c'stle of the steamers that make the run from Stockholn to Hull, dreamed the Swede's dream of the West; when he got to America they gave him a job polishing cuspidors in a Bowery saloon.

He moved west to Chicago and worked in a machineshop.

He moved west and followed the harvest, hung around employment agencies, paid out many a dollar for a job in a construction camp, walked out many a mile when the grub was too bum, or the boss too tough, or too many bugs in the bunkhouse; read Marx and the I.W.W. Preamble and dreamed about forming the structure of the new society within the shell of the old.

He was in California for the S.P. strike ("Casey Jones, two locomotives, Casey Jones"), used to play the concertina outside the bunkhouse door, after supper, evenings ("Long-haired preachers come out every night"), had a knack for setting rebel words to tunes ("And the union makes us strong").

Along the coast in cookshacks flophouses jungles wobblies hoboes bindlestiffs began singing Joe Hill's songs. They sang 'em in the county jails of the State of Washington, Oregon, California, Nevada, Idaho, in the bullpens in Montana and Arizona, sang 'em in Walla Walla, San Quentin, and Leavenworth, forming the structure of the new society within the jails of the old.

At Bingham, Utah, Joe Hill organized the workers of the Utah Construction Company in the One Big Union, won a new wagescale, shorter hours, better grub. (The angel Moroni didn't like labororganizers any better than the Southern Pacific did.)

The angel Moroni moved the hearts of the Mormons to decide it was Joe Hill shot a grocer named Morrison. The Swedish consul and President Wilson tried to get him a new trial, but the angel Moroni moved the hearts of the Supreme

Court of the State of Utah to sustain the verdict of guilty. He was in jail a year, went on making up songs. In November 1915 he was stood up against the wall in the jail yard in Salt Lake City.

"Don't mourn for me, organize," was the last word he sent out to the workingstiffs of the I.W.W. Joe Hill stood up against the wall of the jail yard, looked into the muzzles of the guns, and gave the word to fire.

They put him in a black suit, put a stiff collar around his neck and a bow tie, shipped him to Chicago for a bangup funeral, and photographed his handsome stony mask staring into the future.

The first of May they scattered his ashes to the wind.[57]

Dos Passos's sublime prose, unfortunately, captures only the romanticized edges of Joe Hill's story. Recent research has begun to fill in at least some of the details behind the Hill legend, revealing one of the more interesting and significant mind games of the American Left, a stunning example of the mind guerrilla.

He was born Joel Hägglund on October 7, 1879, in Gävle, Sweden. In his childhood, he learned the skills that would enable him to become the renowned Wobbly minstrel. He grew up in a large and musical family and played the piano and organ to accompany the singing of his eight brothers and sisters. As a youngster, he also learned to play the accordian, the guitar, and his favorite instrument, the violin.[58]

When Joel was only ten years old, his father died of injuries received while working on the railroad. The youth was abruptly forced out into the world to seek employment and to begin the long struggle for survival. With his mother's death ten years later, the family disintegrated. Joel, along with his brother Paul, emigrated to America, arriving in the winter of 1902. Joel remained in New York City for about a year, working at odd jobs and looking for the path to the future. He then moved to Chicago where he may have been fired from a job in a machine shop for attempting to organize the workers there. He may have changed his name to Joe Hill at that time in an effort to avoid an employer's blacklist.[59] He appears to have traveled widely—to Philadelphia, the Dakotas, Spokane, Portland, and San Francisco—searching for employment. In 1905, he sent a Christmas card home to his sisters in Sweden from Cleveland, Ohio.[60] In April 1906 he sent a letter to his home-town newspaper in Sweden describing his experiences during the famous San Francisco earthquake of that year.[61] He had apparently joined the millions of homeless migrants, hoboes, and bindlestiffs who were roaming the country looking for work or a handout if a job could not be found.

In 1910, Joe Hill joined the San Pedro, California, chapter of the IWW.[62] He took an active part in the IWW. He was the secretary of the San Pedro local for several years, and he appears to have participated in many of the union's battles. He may have been involved in the free speech campaigns in Spokane in 1909 and in Fresno in 1911. He was also said to have been captured and beaten by vigilantes in Oceanside, California, while on his way to the San Diego free speech fights sometime in 1912.[63]

Hill's other political activities may have included organizing a sabotage plan in an unnamed factory in 1909 by encouraging the workers to "lubricate" their machines with sand. He may have been involved in the 1912 strike against construction contractors on the Canadian Northern Railroad. We can be fairly certain that he at least visited the strikers' camp near Yale, British Columbia, where he wrote the song "Where the Fraser River Flows."[64] Some say he took part in the San Pedro dock workers' strike of 1912.[65] And although he later denied it, he appears to have been involved in an abortive revolution in Mexico in 1911.[66] But it is difficult to assess the authenticity of such reports because most were based on hearsay and circumstantial evidence.

It is certain, however, that by the time of his arrest in 1913, Hill had become, in his own words, "a true-blue rebel":[67] a dedicated, skilled, and seasoned revolutionary, as well as an experienced mind guerrilla. From the point of view of the authorities of the state of Utah, he had also become a threat to social order and justice.

The Angel Moroni

Joe Hill went to Utah sometime in the fall of 1913. The legend has it that he went there to help organize the workers at the United Construction Company in Bingham, near Salt Lake City.[68] Other reports say that he had gone there to visit a relative.[69] The most recent scholarship indicates that he may have worked for awhile in a mine in the mountains outside Salt Lake City.[70] It was here that he may have met an old friend, Otto Applequist, with whom by the year's end he was apparently staying at the home of some friends, the Eselius brothers, in a suburb of Salt Lake City.[71]

On Saturday, January 10, 1914, Joe Hill left the Eselius home sometime between 6:00 P.M. and 9:00 P.M. He did not return until around 1:00 A.M. His activities during this evening have never been adequately explained. All that is known for certain is that Hill visited the home of a Dr. Frank M. McHugh shortly after 11:30 P.M., suffering from a bullet wound in the chest. He told the doctor that he had been wounded by "a friend" who thought he had "insulted" his wife.[72] He never repudiated this story, and he steadfastly refused to provide further details. It was in the mystery of this evening that the legend was to take root.

Shortly before 10:00 P.M. that same night, as John Morrison and his two sons, Merlin and Arling, were closing their grocery store in downtown Salt Lake City, two masked men entered the store. One was tall, the other short. As they entered the store, one shouted, "We've got you now!" There was an exchange of gunfire. John and Arling Morrison were killed, and one of the attackers was apparently wounded. Merlin Morrison was the only witness who lived. Since the two men fled immediately, without taking anything from the store, their motive appears to have been revenge, not robbery. Morrison had been a policeman for several years before becoming a grocer and has arrested many men during that period. Some may have sought revenge, for he had been attacked on two previous occasions, and it was widely known that he lived in fear of retaliation.[73]

Approximately two hours later, Joe Hill turned up at Dr. McHugh's office, which was only about four blocks from the Morrison store. After dressing the wound, the doctor was helping Hill put his shirt back on when a gun and shoulder holster fell from his clothing. He said that he had wrestled the gun from his assailant and kept it as a souvenir. This was almost certainly a fabrication because, during the trial, evidence was produced that indicated that Hill owned the gun he carried that night. While he was being driven back to the Eselius home, the car developed engine trouble. When the driver got out to crank the engine, Hill threw the gun out of the window. The gun was never found, and Hill never explained why he decided to get rid of it. When he returned home, he awoke Applequist, his shorter companion. They had a brief talk, and then Applequist left the house, never to be seen or heard from again.[74]

Although the accounts conflict, sometime during the next two days Dr. McHugh read about the Morrison murders and decided to report Hill's injuries to the police. Then, on Tuesday, January 13, in cooperation with the police, McHugh returned to the Eselius home, where he had been treating Hill's injuries, to change the dressing and to administer a shot of morphine for pain. The shot rendered Hill unconscious, and the police were able to move in and capture him.[75]

As the police entered his room, Hill made a sudden movement with his hand to reach for his handkerchief. One of the officers, thinking he was reaching for a gun, opened fire, wounding Hill in the right shoulder and right hand.[76] Afterward, the room was searched, but no gun was found. On Tuesday night Joe Hill was taken, wounded and bleeding, to the Salt Lake County jail.[77]

He was formally charged with first degree murder on January 20. It appears that he gave his name as Joseph Hillstrom, for that is the name that appears in the court records and in the press accounts of the trial. He was arraigned on January 27 and entered a plea of not guilty.[78]

The Trial

The trial began on Wednesday, June 17, 1914, six months after his arrest. Since he had no money to hire a lawyer, he requested that he be allowed to conduct his own defense. Shortly after the preliminary hearing, however, a young attorney, E.D. McDougall, went to visit Hill in jail and offered to defend him free of charge. The trial lasted for twenty-one days. It became a media event, attracting the attention of both the national and international press. Hill appears to have put on quite a show. On the third day of the trial, in a dramatic outburst, he discharged his counsel and demanded the right to defend himself.[79]

Although he insisted he was innocent, he refused to testify in his own behalf, saying he would rather die than reveal the details of his activities on the night of the murders. His naive idealism may have led him to believe that in America he would be presumed innocent until proven guilty, with the burden of proof resting on the prosecution and that he did not need to be concerned with the practical problem of his defense. Perhaps his utopian mentality led him to believe that right was on his side and justice would surely prevail. Or perhaps his public statements concerning his belief that "justice would prevail" were merely the ideological ploy of a guilty man who was committed to the union and seeking martyrdom to further the cause of the oppressed and exploited masses.[80]

A lawyer provided by the IWW, O.N. Hilton, took over Hill's defense on June 19. The press began to play up Hill's IWW connections, and the mythmaking process began in earnest.[81]

Although he could not be positively identified as the murderer, he had no known motive, and the bullet that passed through his body could not be found in the Morrison store, the jury was not convinced of his innocence. The circumstantial evidence was too strong: an unexplained gunshot wound received the same night as the murders and in the vicinity of the Morrison store.

On Saturday, June 28, Joe Hill was found guilty of first degree murder. It was probably his unwillingness to cooperate, his defiant attitude, and his courtroom antics that moved the jury to convict him. On July 8, he was sentenced to death. He was given a choice of being hanged or shot to death. He is said to have replied dryly to the judge: "I'll take shooting. I'm used to that."[82]

His attorneys immediately filed a motion for a new trial, and the case was appealed to the Utah State Supreme Court. They argued that the state had failed to establish, beyond a reasonable doubt, that Joe Hill had murdered the Morrisons. The court asked for more evidence. Hill was asked to testify, but he refused. The request for a new trial was denied.[83]

Then they appealed to the Utah Board of Pardons for commutation of the sentence to life in prison, arguing that the evidence was not strong enough to take a man's life. Requests (and demands) to save Joe Hill flooded into the board from union locals, private citizens, and various organizations opposed to capital punishment. The board denied the commutation but offered to free Hill if he would reveal—in confidence to his lawyers only—the circumstances behind his wound. Again, Hill refused to cooperate, saying: "I do not want my death sentence commuted to life imprisonment and I am not clamoring for a pardon; I do, however, want a new trial—a fair trial. If I can not have a new trial, I am willing to give my blood as a martyr that others may be afforded fair trials." His lawyers next appealed directly to Utah's Governor William Spry for executive clemency. Letters poured into the governor's office at the rate of two hundred per day, but he would not submit to public pressure. Next, the Swedish minister to the United States asked President Woodrow Wilson to intervene in Hill's behalf. The president telegraphed the governor and, reluctantly, Spry granted a stay of execution so that the case could be reviewed by the Swedish minister. The Board of Pardons then reconvened to hear the appeal by the Swedish minister. Once again, the motion for a new trial was denied. Again, the board demanded "tangible evidence," and, once more, Hill refused to cooperate. The execution was finally set for November 18, 1915.[84]

The movement for Joe Hill's release then took to the streets. In New York City a huge "Joe Hill Protest Meeting" was held on November 8, and an appeal for help was sent to President Wilson. During the next week, thirty thousand people marched in Minneapolis in protest against Joe Hill's execution. On November 16, Samuel Gompers, the president of the American Federation of Labor, wired a resolution to President Wilson, adopted by the thirty-fifth annual convention of that union, appealing for Joe Hill's life. Even Helen Keller sent a telegram to the president, pleading for the life of Joe Hill. On November 17—just two days before the execution—the president again wired Governor Spry, appealing for Hill's life. The governor, annoyed by Wilson's interference, refused to back down.[85]

The Execution

All through the evening of November 18—the night before the execution—protest demonstrations were held. There was a mass demonstration that evening in downtown Salt Lake City. Speakers eloquently proclaimed Joe Hill's innocence and the injustice of his trial. After the speeches, Joe Hill's songs were sung by the masses in unison. Late into the night the crowd was heard chanting, "and Joe Hill will be shot in the morning," loudly answering themselves: "Not if we can help it." On the eve of his execution, Joe Hill was interviewed by the local press, who found him calm and reserved, showing no signs of nervousness. He was reported to have said: "What do I expect to accomplish by my situation? Well, it won't do the I.W.W. any harm and it won't do the state of Utah any good."[86]

He then wrote his famous farewell message to "Big Bill" Haywood, president of the IWW: "Goodbye Bill: I die like a true-blue rebel. Don't waste time in mourning—organize! Its a hundred miles from here to Wyoming. Could you arrange to have my body hauled to the state line to be buried? I don't want to be found dead in Utah."[87] And around 10:00 P.M., he handed a poem through the bars of his cell to a guard. It was his last will:

> My will is easy to decide,
> For there is nothing to divide.
> My kin don't need to fuss and moan—
> "Moss does not cling to a rolling stone."
>
> My body?—Oh!—If I could choose,
> I would to ashes it reduce,

And let the merry breezes blow
My dust to where some flowers grow.

Perhaps some fading flower then
Would come to life and bloom again,
This is my last and final will.
Good luck to all of you,

Joe Hill.[88]

He woke about 5:00 on the morning of his execution. It was reported that he broke a broom handle to serve as a weapon. Then, using his bedding, he tied the door to his cell shut and put his mattress against the door. When the guards tried to break through his barricade, he fought them off with the sharp end of the broom handle. By the time the executioners came for him he had bloodied one of the guards and taken a night stick from another. He finally gave up, saying simply: "Well, I'm through, but you can't blame a man for fighting for his life."

Then he was taken to the prison yard and strapped into a chair. "I will show you how to die," he said, "I have a clear conscience." A mask was placed over his eyes and a white paper target over his heart. Then the attending guards stepped back. Hill tossed his head back, attempting to see from under his mask. To some of his friends whom he thought were there to witness his execution, he shouted, "I'm going now boys. Good-by!" Although no one was there to listen, he shouted again, "good-by boys!" An officer began the sequence of commands: "Ready, aim . . ." Then Hill called out, "Fire—go on and fire!" A smile spread over his face. The officer commanded, "Fire!" And then the shots rang out. There was a thud in the middle of Joe Hill's chest. The white paper target turned red. The smile faded from his face, his body stiffened, then relaxed and hung limp. At 7:45 A.M., on November 19, 1915, Joseph Hillstrom was pronounced dead.[89] But the legend of Joe Hill, the poet and singer who was "framed and murdered" by the authorities in the state of Utah, had just come to life.

The Funeral

In the weeks leading up to Hill's execution, the IWW organization network had begun to prepare for Hill's canonization. They were determined to see that his last will was carried out. First, a funeral service was held in Salt Lake City on November 21, then another, much bigger one, after the body arrived in Chicago. The service in Chicago was held on November 25, Thanksgiving Day. It was during these services that the mythmaking process and the mind games earnestly got under way. The program covers at the funeral read:

In Memorium Joe Hill
We Never Forget,
Murdered by the Authorities of the State of Utah,
November 19, 1915[90]

Thousands of people turned out to see Joe Hill's remains, to hear him proclaimed a martyr, and to hear his executioners denounced as murderers. In Chicago, there was almost a festive air. Many wore red streamers around their necks. Many more wore buttons which read: "He died a Martyr." After the funeral, the procession flowed through the streets of Chicago like a giant human serpent, the crowd spontaneously singing Hill's songs one after another. At the cemetery, the singing went on long into the night.[91]

The next day, Joe Hill's body was photographed for the final time and then placed on a stone slab and pushed into a blast furnace. His ashes were collected, placed in envelopes, and distributed to IWW locals in every state of the Union—except Utah—and then to many countries throughout the world: from South America to New Zealand, from Russia to South Africa. On the first of May 1916, in fulfillment of his last will, his ashes were ceremoniously released into the winds.[92]

The Decline of the IWW

By the time of Hill's death the IWW was already in a serious decline from which it would never recover. It had peaked as a viable political force in America in the years 1912–13.[93] Joe Hill's execution and the publicity that surrounded it was, in a sense, the last deperate gasp of militant enthusiasm for the Wobblies and the radical Left in America generally. The spirit of patriotism that swept the country during World War I proved fatal to the pacifist and anarchist views of the Wobblies. Many Wobblies fell victim to mass war hysteria and vigilante violence.[94] Joe Hill's execution came to symbolize capitalist terrorism and was but a prelude of things to come.

The IWW was, in principle, opposed to the war in Europe, which it perceived as a war among capitalist industrialists, fought by the disinherited working classes to protect the interests of property. Moreover, the utopian vision of the One Big Union—the industrially united working-class world—simply could not incorporate the images of violent conflict among belligerent national entities. As Wobbly organizer J.P. Thompson put it: "In the broad sense, there is no such thing as a foreigner. We are all native-born members of this planet and for members of it to be divided into groups or units and taught that each nation is better than others leads to clashes and world war. We ought to have in place of national patriotism, the idea that one people is better than another, a broader concept—that of international solidarity."[95]

The IWW's national organization, however, fearing the inevitable repression, prudently decided not formally to oppose the war effort or the reinstitution of the military draft. Bill Haywood stated the organization's carefully chosen stance on the war: "It's true that we think there is only one fight in the world, and that is between capital and labor. It's true that we are not interested in nationalities. We will fight for German workers or French workers or Norwegian workers just as hard as we will fight for American workers. But do you think we want to see the Prussian military system prevail? How would we stand to gain anything from that?"[96] Many rank-and-file Wobblies eventually served in the armed forces or in war-related industries. The more militant, however, did agitate against the draft, and some refused to register or left the country, fleeing across the border to Mexico.

In April 1917, after the United States entered the war, the serious repression began.[97] Throughout the summer, an organized reign of terror, fueled by war hysteria, poured down ruthlessly upon the IWW. Since Wobbly activities were perceived as a threat to national security during a time of war, the War Department quickly moved to suppress them and to destroy their base of organization. The state governments were quick to do the same. Between 1917 and 1920, twenty-one states and two territories passed criminal syndicalist and criminal anarchist laws, declaring open season on Wobblies and all other radicals and undesirable elements.[98] The army, state troopers, local police, private security forces, and, most ruthless of all, armed bands of superpatriotic vigilantes, were simultaneously unleashed upon the IWW.

The nation's press went along with the witch hunts, depicting the IWW as lawless, subversive saboteurs. The *New York Tribune* hinted at a German connection behind the IWW. An editorial in the *Cleveland News* expressed the nation's Wobbly hysteria: "While the country is at war, the only room it can afford I.W.W.'s is behind bars." An editorial in the Tulsa, Oklahoma *Daily World* argued: "The first step in the whipping of Germany is to strangle the I.W.W.'s. Kill them, just like you would kill any other kind of a snake. Don't scotch 'em; kill 'em dead. It is no time to waste money on trial and continuances and things like that. All that is necessary is the evidence and a firing squad."[99] In many parts of the country, this is just about what was happening. Even President Wilson, that reluctant warrior and symbol of America's war conscience, is said to have remarked to his attorney general: "The I.W.W.'s certainly are worthy of being suppressed."[100].

Perhaps the IWW was singled out among radical groups because it had become so visible in its militancy. Its public image as a violent, anarchistic organization made the IWW, symbolically, a perfect target in the war against internal subversion. Throughout the summer of 1917 there were raids on IWW headquarters, halls, and members' homes around the nation. Leaders and organizers were arrested and charged with interfering with the war effort. Truckloads of membership records, Wobbly literature and paraphernalia, minutes of meetings, as well as official and personal correspondence, were hauled away to be used against them in later government trials.[101]

By December, all of the IWW's major and secondary leaders were incarcerated, including Vincent St. John, Bill Haywood, Elizabeth Gurley Flynn, Carlo Tressca, Auturo Giovannitti, Joseph Ettor, and Ben Williams.[102] Throughout the country, IWW property had been confiscated or destroyed. The union's organizational and communications network was severely damaged, if not completely destroyed. Of those arrested and tried, fifteen got twenty-year sentences, thirty-five were sentenced to ten years, thirty-three got five years, and twelve received sentences of a year and a day. They were fined a total of $2.3 million.[103] For all practical purposes, the repression wiped out the IWW.

After the war, the Harding administration finally gave in to public pressure and released all political prisoners by the end of 1923.[104] But by this time, the IWW in particular, and the American Left generally, had been dealt a severe blow. Yet though the IWW as an ongoing political movement was almost completely destroyed in the Red Scare of World War I, it persists to this day, its headquarters on North Sheffield Street in Chicago a pitiful shell of the once militant and glorious One Big Union. But the anarchist spirit and the syndicalist vision of the Wobblies have lived on and even prospered in twentieth-century America's emerging culture of protest. Through the turmoil of the 1930s and on into the 1960s, the spirit of the Wobblies thrived. And the songs of Joe Hill and the legend of his martyrdom were to form an essential part of that culture and vision

Why Joe Hill?

Why did the mind guerrillas of the IWW single out Joe Hill to carry their message into the future? This is a very difficult question upon which we may only speculate. There were other public personages and living legends who could have carried the red flag into the 1930s. Bill Haywood or Elizabeth Gurley Flynn, for example, were fine Wobbly specimens and selflessly dedicated organizers, soapboxers, and lecturers for the cause of the One Big Union. Flynn had a long and distinguished radical career, first as the foremost woman organizer of the IWW, then as an officer in the American Communist party.[105] She died in 1964, one of the last veterans of the Wobbly era.[106] Haywood's story is more tragic. In 1921, he and eight other Wobbly defendants in criminal syndicalism trials jumped bail and fled to Soviet Russia, where he died, disillusioned and broken, in May of 1928.[107] Both Haywood and Flynn were great Wobbly statesmen, prominent and respected radical politicians. But their lives lacked the drama of Hill's, and the circumstances of their deaths did not make them martyrs.

But the reactionary terror of the repression during the Great War gave the world two more IWW martyrs. Frank Little, a veteran Wobbly activist, was attacked and beaten by vigilantes after delivering a speech in Butte, Montana, in July 1917. Little was abducted at gunpoint from his boardinghouse room in the middle of the night. His assailants tied a rope around his neck and dragged him behind their car to the outskirts of town, where he was lynched. His body was left hanging from a railroad trestle, tagged with a card bearing the vigilante symbol "3-7-77" (the dimensions of a grave) and the initials "D-D-C-S-S-W," which referred to other Wobbly organizers on their hit list.[108]

And on November 11, 1918, Armistice Day, in the lumber town of Centralia, Washington, Wesley Everest, a war veteran in uniform, was among a group of Wobblies attacked by a mob disguised as an American Legion parade. Everest escaped capture at first and held off his pursuers in a gun battle, but was finally forced to surrender. He was knocked unconscious and dragged to the jail by a strap around his neck. Later that night a lynch mob kidnapped him from his cell. According to legend, he shouted to his fellow prisoners: "Tell the boys I died for my class." He was then driven out of town, and before they hanged him, one of the superpatriots castrated him.[109]

Although the labor movement in America still remembers Little and Everest, they are clearly overshadowed by the image of Joe Hill. In the popular histories of the Wobblies by Joyce L. Kornbluh, Philip S. Foner, and Len De Caux, for example, entire chapters are devoted to Joe Hill, but the stories of Little and Everest are told in a few lines. And the great body of literature and folklore that has grown up around Hill surpasses by far any of the tributes to Little or Everest. How are we to explain this discrepancy?

Hill was not a great political leader and activist, as were Haywood and Flynn. Like Little and Everest, Hill became famous because he was a casualty of America's violent class struggle in the first decade of the twentieth century. Public death for a cause is the ultimate revolutionary act, and, as a result, martyrs are remembered over activists. But, unlike Little and Everest, Hill had not been on union business when he fell into the trap of American class justice. Although the mythmakers of the Joe Hill Defense Committee made a gallant effort to make his IWW connection an issue, it was only an irritant to a criminal prosecution. Moreover, Hill may have been guilty of the criminal offense with which he was charged. Perhaps Hill was unjustly sentenced, but at least he was afforded the pretense of due process. Hill was not ritualistically tortured by vigilantes, nor was his body brutally mutilated by a lynch mob. When compared to the atrocities committed in the cases of Little and Everest, Joe Hill was treated with respect and compassion. The deaths of Little and Everest are by far more convincing examples of Wobbly martyrdom. Why was Joe Hill the one who was remembered?

Joe Hill was a symbol of all that the Wobblies stood for: the exuberant, revolutionary zeal, the naive faith in the mission of the class struggle, and the quest for the proletarian utopia. Hill also embodied the rough, violent edge of the Wobbly image. And the controversy over his guilt or innocence became the central mystery that fuels the drama of his story. Above all, Hill was a showman, with a flair for the dramatic, and the publicity of his trial gave him an international stage upon which to perform his last act. His public statements during the course of his trial read like a Hollywood script: "I have lived like an artist, and I shall die like an artist"; "I'll take shooting. I'm used to that"; "I'm going to get a new trial or die trying"; "I will die like a true-blue rebel"; "I don't want to be found dead in Utah"; "Don't waste time in mourning—organize!" His final stroke on the canvas of his martyrdom was to give the command to fire at his execution. Frank Little and Wesley Everest had no chance to learn their lines or to promote the last scenes of their lives. And, in the end, this histrionic component may have made the difference.

Perhaps the most important reason for Hill's preeminence was that by the time of his arrest, Hill—unlike Little and Everest—was already established as a poet and songster: he was the Wobblies' troubadour. The story of Joe Hill is thus the story of a singer whose voice was stilled but whose songs live on, on the lips of his brothers and sisters in the struggle for social justice in America. For that reason Hill's martyred image most closely captures the spirit and impact of the Wobblies.

The Body of Lore after Hill's Death

After Hill's death, others added to the body of lore. First, other Wobblies wrote poems (Ralph Chaplin's "Joe Hill") and songs (John Nordquist's "November 19.")[110] And then leftist intellectuals took over. Sometime in the early 1930s, Alfred Hayes wrote the poem that, perhaps more than any other single work, has given the legend its endurance.[111] In 1924, Upton Sinclair published a short play, *Singing Jailbirds,* based on Hill's life and songs. In 1927, Carl Sandburg included some of Hill's songs in a collection of folk songs, *American Songbag.*[112]

In the 1930s a short mythical biography of Joe Hill was included in Dos Passos's *Nineteen Nineteen* (1932), and another long poem appeared, Kenneth Patchen's "Joe Hill Listens to the Praying." Archie Binns's novel *Timber Beast* (1944) revived the legend but accepted Hill's guilt and presented a character who would take by force what he needed. When he ran out of money in Salt Lake City, the grocer, unfortunately, got in his way. A more objective view of Joe Hill was emerging.[113]

In 1950, Wallace Stegner's novel *The Preacher and the Slave* appeared. It was the first serious, book-length work on the Hill legend. That same year a play by Barrie Stavis, *The Man Who Never Died,* was released. The Hill character also appeared in several other novels during this period: James Stevens's *Big Jim Turner,* Alexander Saxton's *The Great Midland,* Margaret Graham's *Swing Shift,* James Jones's *From Here to Eternity,* and Eugene Burdick's *The Ninth Wave.*[114]

In the early 1960s, Woody Guthrie, the Joe Hill of the 1930s, published a poem in Hill's honor. In 1966, Phil Ochs, one of Guthrie's disciples, wrote a long narrative ballad, "Joe Hill." In 1964, the Canadian Broadcasting Company produced a film for television about Hill's prison life. And in 1969, Joan Baez sang the Hayes-Robinson song at Woodstock, ensuring a place for the Hill legend in the counterculture of the 1960s and 1970s. And most recently, in 1980 there was a play produced on Broadway about Hill's life: Thomas Babe's *Salt Lake City Skyline*.[115] It can indeed be said that Joe Hill has never died.

With Joe Hill's martyrdom, the working-class subculture in America found its first heroic guerrilla minstrel. Joe Hill is a symbol of the Wobbly mind guerrilla. Revolutionaries of any generation can identify with and emulate this selflessly dedicated poet and singer, true to the cause of the One Big Union even in the face of death. In this sense, the Hill legend is one of the great and lasting working-class totalizers.

In spite of the controversy surrounding his guilt or innocence, Hill's behavior before, during, and after his highly publicized trial was dramatic and heroic. His melodramatic public statements and his calculated selflessness, though perhaps overplayed, were effective before the footlights of the American labor movement. Hill played his role convincingly. He was scorned and feared by the propertied classes, but he became a hero to the toiling masses and their intellectual sympathizers.

With the death of Joe Hill, a pattern of cultural politics was established and a mind guerrilla tradition was born. Woody Guthrie would inherit this tradition in the 1930s and pass it on to Bob Dylan in the 1960s. The mind guerrilla process surrounding the singing hero may be tentatively outlined as follows. Myth and legend naturally follow the mystery and drama surrounding the life and death of a public personage. The myth is then used to further the cause for which the hero stood, in this case the union. The hero need only to have been truly heroic, greatly loved, and genuinely lost. Glorification and embellishment, in the pathos of the aftermath of his death, further the mythmaking process. Of course, media publicity is crucial. And in the case of the singing hero, his songs are quickly absorbed into the folklore of his people. Aphorisms attributed to the hero (like "don't mourn—organize!") take on the force of scripture. Rituals, rites, and pilgrimages occur in his honor. Memorial journalism, souvenirs, trinkets, and other memorabilia circulate widely. Monuments and shrines are erected in his name. All this supports a canonization process that deifies the hero and reveres his name and work. Finally, a cult emerges looking back to a golden, heroic age and forward to a utopian dream world.

By focusing dissent into a convenient set of symbols embodied by a superhero, the cultural guerrilla carries the revolutionary spirit beyond its historic setting, projecting the culture of protest into the future. It is in this sense that the guerrilla minstrel has promoted the cause of the working class, as a totalizing agent in the mind games of social protest.

5 Woody Guthrie: *The Dust Bowl Balladeer*

I've been doin' some hard travelin',
  I thought you knowed.
I've been doin' some hard travelin',
  Way down the road.
I've been doin' some hard travelin',
  Hard ramblin', hard gamblin',
I've been doin' some hard travelin', Lord.
—Woody Guthrie, 1940

Hillbilly Mind Guerrilla

In the early 1960s, as Woody Guthrie lay dying—his body constantly jerking and trembling in the pitiful, spasmodic dance of Huntington's chorea—a cult was forming around him.[1] Suddenly, his songs were heard everywhere. No longer confined to the left-wing bohemian circles of New York's Greenwich Village, they were being sung in the grade schools and on the nation's college campuses and at folk festivals and hootenannies. Some were even making the pop music charts. For the first time in his life, he was making money. To an increasingly fervent following, Woody Guthrie had become a living legend.

His romantic, wandering life as a singing hobo had been mythologized. It was widely believed that he was dying from the hard-drinking, hard-traveling, hard-gambling life on the road and that he was suffering from alcoholism or perhaps syphilis. Some, who knew nothing of his illness, believed he was still rambling on down that long, dusty road, searching for that place where the water tastes like wine. Partly because of the force of the Guthrie legend, folk music—the music of rural America—had become an important part of urban popular music culture. Folk artists from Ramblin' Jack Elliot to Country Joe McDonald, and folk groups from the Weavers to the Kingston Trio, had begun to perform and record his songs. And young Robert Zimmerman was beginning to model himself and his image on the Guthrie myth.

Guthrie's wild, rough-and-tumble, unkempt manner; his dusty, baggy, drab Okie attire; his weathered, crackling voice;

his wry, childlike sense of humor, coupled with his heartfelt dedication to and sense of oneness with "his people," America's "working folks," all merged to transform this wiry little drifter into a genuine folk hero, a symbol of the American working class.

Of his relationship to the people, Guthrie wrote:

> The worst thing that can happen to you is to cut yourself loose from the people. And the best thing is to sort of vaccinate yourself right into the big streams and blood of the people. To feel like you know the best and the worst of folks that you see everywhere and never to feel weak, or lost, or even lonesome anywhere.
>
> There is just one thing that can cut you to drifting from the people, and that's any brand or style of greed. There is just one way to save yourself, and that's to get together and work and fight for everybody.[2]

But perhaps, over and above his selfless dedication to the people, it was his sparkling vitality and energy, his unquenchable sense of wonderment, his determined optimism and naive but genuine faith in the future of his people—the mischievous smile and silly giggle that he always seemed to be able to project even in the face of tragedy after tragedy—that won the hearts of so many. Woody Guthrie was the epitome of the working-class mind guerrilla. John Steinbeck described him in the liner notes to one of Guthrie's early recordings:

> Woody is just Woody. Thousands of people do not know he had any other name. He is just a voice and a guitar. He sings the songs of a people and I suspect that he is, in a way, that people. Harsh voiced and nasal, his guitar hanging like a tire iron on a rusty rim, there is nothing sweet about Woody, and there is nothing sweet about the songs he sings. But there is something more important for those who will listen. There is the will of a people to endure and fight against oppression. I think we call this the American spirit.[3]

What Steinbeck refers to as the American spirit is the same thing Elizabeth Gurley Flynn had called the revolutionary spirit, and Woody Guthrie, like Joe Hill before him, was the embodiment of worker solidarity. And although Woody did not die a martyr's death in the same sense as Joe Hill, he did die tragically after suffering a lingering, humiliating illness. Huntington's disease took him in his prime, reducing the great balladeer and visionary into a pitiful, institutionalized invalid.[4] Perhaps it was this public suffering, the slowly fading light that had once shown with such brilliance and purpose, that gained him the sympathy of the American public.

There has never been a more eloquent spokesman for the utopian One than Woody Guthrie. Although he often used the language of the Wobblies (employing the characteristic expression "One Big Union"), his conception of utopia was a little different. By One Big Union, he was not necessarily referring to industrial workers. He meant specifically the uprooted Okie farmers, reduced to the level of migrant farm laborers after the dust storms and the depression ran them off their farms, and more generally to the rural folk community, or what sociologists refer to as the *gemeinschaft*.[5] He was not a syndicalist in any strict sense.

Woody came to be closely associated with the American communist movement, but he was a political eccentric and would never have been able to follow the party line. When asked if he was a communist, he was fond of saying: "Some people say I'm a Communist. That ain't necessarily so, but it is true that I've always been in the red."[6] Guthrie did apparently eventually join the party. According to Gordon Friesen, who knew Guthrie in New York in the 1940s, he was indeed a card-carrying party member. Friesen has claimed that "when I knew him he was a full-fledged member of the Village branch of the Communist Cultural Section, and proud of it."[7]

Guthrie's Marxism was instinctual and not rational, inbred and not learned. He was class-conscious before he ever heard the term. He had experienced and lived the class struggle, which he was inclined to view as a fight between the rich and the "pore." Because he had always been "pore," he knew which side he was on. Talk about dialectical materialism and economic determinism was to him mere bourgeois intellectualism that could only distract from the issues and interfere with one's ability to reach the uneducated poor. Here he was at one with the tradition of the Wobblies.

Ed Robbin, the radical journalist who introduced the young hillbilly singer into California's left-wing political circles in the late 1930s, described Woody's politics: "He didn't bother to read what Karl Marx had written, or Lenin. Woody believed that what is important is the struggle of the working people to win back the earth, which is rightfully theirs. He believed that people should love one another and organize into one big union. That's the way he saw politics and world affairs."[8] He was thus an excellent utopian specimen: a child of the Wobblies, an unpolished rebel outcast, a rugged and whiskery mind guerrilla.

In discussing what he called the "utopian mentality," or the radical's famed "consciousness," Karl Mannheim observed that the utopian perceives his world—and the events, experiences, and episodes that constitute it—as if it were ordered and arranged in such a way as to "take on the character of destiny."[9] This is clearly how Woody Guthrie saw his world and his place in it. He perceived his life and his work as a calling: he was bound for glory, it was his fate to change the world, and his goal was nothing short of the One Big Union. Marjorie Guthrie, his second wife, described Woody's sense of destiny: "I can only say that he had a tremendous feeling about himself. It's as though he felt he had a mission. He'd say, 'We're poor now, but one day our kids will be rich.' We made a joke of it and talked about what the kids would do with all the money that would be coming in. And then he would say that his one hope was that the kids would be aware of the need to change the world they lived in and become part of the struggle."[10]

In his productive lifetime—before the disease robbed him of his capacity to communicate—he wrote more than a thousand songs and mountains of typed prose: poems, short stories, novels, flights of fantasy and erotica, as well as homespun social commentary and front-porch editorials.[11] Words seemed to gush out of him, like a wild mountain stream after the spring thaw. He wrote long, rambling, intoxicated outpourings in an uninhibited stream-of-consciousness style. He was a man possessed by a sense of destiny and purpose and a burning desire to change the world,

Utopian themes run throughout Guthrie's songs, and among his scattered prose are some of the finest expressions of the utopian soul:

> Our wants, needs, backgrounds, false weaknesses, fears, dreams, hopes, our desires and passions and cravings, all these things, and a million others, drift across the hills of my mind while I think of all of it. And all these things are one, all mixed and blended like colors into a pattern, and like patterns into a big, big picture of life. All of our tangles and mix-ups are the only reason for livin' and workin'.and goin' on. Our loves and kisses and passions and flights of mind, they give us the gas and the juice to keep goin' on. The world I've seen is alive and interesting, not because its perfect and pretty and eternal, but because it needs my fixin', I need fixin', so does the land. And when I let my mind dwell on such truths, I seem to float up like a balloon, way up high somewhere. And the world and the work and the trouble and the people, seem to be goin' as a bunch in such a good

direction, that my own little personal lead weights and drawbacks, miscues, mistakes, and flounderin' around seem to fade away; rubbed out like a big finger rubbin' out a wild pastel color.[12]

Woody Guthrie perceived his life as a holy crusade, part of the eternal quest for the communion of the utopian One. His consciousness was that of a holy man, a prophet on a mission from the gods. His mission was to listen to the people's cries of hunger and oppression and to inspire in them the songs of hope, brotherhood, and change.

Guthrie, in the shadow of the Wobblies, saw his songs as a weapon in the class struggle, but he saw in them much more. The real difference between his music and that of the Wobblies was his use of the rural genre of "folk" music, as opposed to the hymns and urban pop tunes used by Joe Hill and the Wobblies.[13] To Guthrie, the folk song was the special property of the people, or the "folk," and he used the people's music to capture and express their concerns and hopes. In his mind, the music, himself, and the people were all one. Whereas the Wobblies used songs to "fan the flames of discontent," Woody used them as a holy sacrament.

From Guthrie's inspiration, a singing Left, in the spirit of the Wobblies, would differentiate from the main body of the Progressive movement in America to organize itself around the principle of "song power." Beginning with the Almanac Singers, then People's Songs, Inc., and the popular folk group, the Weavers, the social protest song tradition became a radical force.[14] The ideology, philosophy, and values behind this movement were those of Woody Guthrie. He wrote with great conviction on the power of song in the struggles of the mind guerrilla, stressing its ability to evoke community and solidarity, to bring back the past and to capture nostalgia, and to cure the soul and generate hope:

Somewhere, way back in my mind, I can hear the boys in the PX singing their old nickel beer songs at night, 'till the lonesome tears from home rolled down out of their eyes. Their songs are not war songs, they're not gunner songs and they're not shootin' songs. Their songs are back-home songs, songs about brown eyes and blue eyes, eyes of all colors. And every man around those old beer tables sings with his head low and his eyes closed, and he sees home while he sings. I remember seein' my old self back home, I could hear the kids in their club next door to us singing and gruntin', huggin' and kissin', laughin' in the light of their youth club juke-box. Oh I love to hear houses sing, I love to hear windows yell. I remember livin' in the hope that when I got out of those old pesky Army camps, I'd hear every door and every window, just for one night, sing all night long, 'til a new day cracked. I ask ya Mr. President, please, let everybody everywhere, for just one night, sing all night long: Love songs, work songs, new hope songs. That would cure every soul in our jails and asylums, and most of the sick in our hospitals. Try it and see. I know, I'm a Prophet singer.[15]

Woody was indeed a prophet singer, and the folk were his chosen people. His scripture was the great body of American folklore, but his songs—his original adaptations and reworkings of traditional songs—have become a holy grail for the social protest tradition. This prophet singer was also a folk politician, a hillbilly Marxist, a statesman of the folk. In the following parable, Woody explains the role of the singing hero in the mind games of the social protest tradition in America through the analogy of the singing cricket. He could be describing the life of Joe Hill or John Lennon, but he is talking about himself:

I wanna tell ya about a singing cricket I knew once. You know, singing helps keep you going. It might not be all that keeps you going, but it's a mighty powerful way a tellin' somebody you aim to keep going. . . . Now just off hand you might think that us humans is the only outfits that can sing, but I recollect that old cricket was about the best singer for his size that I ever heard.

Crickets always sing under old chunks a rotten wood, old stuffy apartment houses where the stair steps are creaky and liable t'throw ya; anywhere where there's anything bad is a good place for this kinda singin': mold, rot, decay, crooked work, lies, profit-snatchin'. When you hear a cricket singing, you can just look around and find a rotten board or plank that needs to be jacked up and a new one run under it. Crickets don't help bring the house down, he just hangs around to sing that the damn thing's fallin' down. But them other bugs that really brought the house down, they run off somewhere and holler: "That cricket was there all the time, he's the one, he lives in rotten filth, he causes it, he believes in it, get him!"

And finally one day somebody squashed the cricket under their shoe. But the cricket's brothers and sisters heard about it and they started singin' about that. Then all the other relatives heard that singin' and now they're singin' about it. They're all just sittin' around old rotten houses singin' about the death of that one cricket. And you know what they call the song they're all singin'? They call it the song of the singing cricket.[16]

Woody considered singing a source of hope. To him, folk

song was inherently a source of protest and a weapon in the class struggle, and it possessed the power to liberate the folk. Folk song is the embodiment of the folk community and a source of solidarity in the struggle of the working folks and the common man to recapture the world. Folk songs are a channel through which the people vent their anger, frustration, and discontent. And yet, as former Almanac and Weaver Lee Hays has said, folk songs are dangerous.[17] The singer runs the risk of repression, reprisal, alienation, and even death at the hands of the enemies of the folk community. But the singer's songs will live on, on the lips of the singer's brothers and sisters in the family of mankind. In the folk, Woody saw the Wobblies' One Big Union and, to him, folk songs were union songs.

Woody Guthrie was a poet, saloon singer, visionary, prophet, martyr, and saint. He was a hillbilly mind guerrilla and a folk hero. His story begins in Oklahoma in the 1930s, the dust bowl of America's Great Depression. It was a perfect breeding ground for singing crickets.

Dust Bowl Refugee

Woody Guthrie's life was filled to the brim with suffering. He lived life's other side, the dark side, full of failures, tragedies, and disasters. He was born in Okema, Oklahoma, in the summer of 1912. Some years later, he set the stage of his birthing with these words: "It was in the quicksands and muds of the river's rising, the wind that blew and whipped from east to west in a split second, the lightning that splintered the barn loft, the snakey tailed cyclone, prairie cloudbursts, the months of fiery drouth [sic] that crippled the leaves, in the timber fires, prairie fires that took more than it could build back, in the fights of men against all this, that I was born, the third child in our family, and heard my mother sing to my brother Roy, and to my sister, Clara."[18] He was born of suffering, raised in song, and pursued by relentless tragedies. Mysterious fires killed his older sister, Clara, and later, his little daughter, Cathy. Both Woody and his father were seriously burned in similar incidents. Early in his childhood, he watched in horror as his mother slowly withdrew into insanity and had to be committed to the state mental hospital. It was much later in life that he came to realize that his mother had suffered from the same tragic disease that she would pass on to him and he to his children.[19]

Before his fourteenth birthday, his family had disintegrated: his mother institutionalized, his father crippled and broke, his sister dead and buried. Woody and his brother Roy were left to fend for themselves. Roy got a job in a grocery store,[20] and Woody, for the first of countless times, hit the road:

> I hit the road down south to Houston, Galveston, the Gulf, and back, doing all kind of odd jobs, hoeing figs, orchards, pickin grapes, hauling wood, helping carpenters and cement men, working with water well drillers. I was thirteen or fourteen. I carried my harmonica and played in barber shops, at shine stands, in front of shows, around the pool halls, and rattled the bones, done jig dances, sang and played with Negroes, Indians, whites, farmers, town folks, truck drivers, and with every kind of singer you can think of. I learned all of the tricks of strings and music and all of the songs that I could remember and learn by ear. [Then] I struck back up across Texas to the wheat [sic] farm where my dad was.

He stayed around the Texas panhandle town of Pampa for a few years, working at odd jobs and singing in a hillbilly band with his father's brother, Jeff. He married a local girl named Mary Jennings and "lived in the ricketiest of the oil town shacks long enough to have no clothes, no money, no groceries, and two children, both girls, Sue and Teeny."[21]

Woody and Lefty Lou

In the mid-1930s, he left his family and set out to seek his fortune elsewhere. He joined the great migration of homeless dust bowl refugees, victims of the drought and economic depression in the American Southwest, on the long trek across the deserts and into California. He stayed for awhile with relatives, bummed around the migrant camps and hobo jungles, worked in fields and orchards, sang in bars and passed the hat, until he found his way onto the radio as part of a hillbilly act. Eventually he had a half-hour show of his own on progressive station KFVD, with a friend of his cousin Jack, Maxine Crissman, to whom he gave the unglorious nickname "Lefty Lou."[22]

"The Woody and Lefty Lou Show" became popular among the newly arrived Okies and other migrant farm laborers homesick for the rural culture they had left behind. Every evening, after a back-breaking day in the fields and factories, the home folks welcomed these friendly blending voices singing the old songs from back home. Woody came on strong:

> Drop whatever you are doing
> Stop your work and worry too;
> Sit right down and take it easy,
> Here comes Woody and Lefty Lou.[23]

Woody was still naive politically. He was yet to see the connection between the eastern banking interests and the farm failures back home. He was as green as California's fields and orchards when he wrote the first of many self-portraits. It appeared on one of the back pages of *Woody and Left Lou's Favorite Collection [of] Old Time Hill Country Songs: Being Sung for Ages, Still Going Strong.* Entitled simply "Woody," it reflects the cornball country humor he fed the dusty Okies between songs:

Well, when I go to write about myself, I can't say much, 'cause I ain't got no material to work on. I've been around the country for years, a Hobo Hillbilly, eating about twice a week whether I was hungry or not. I've worked in a lot of places, but never did have anybody write and tell me that my work was a bright spot in their day till I got on the airwaves in front of a Microbephone. I never did drink anything stronger than water for a chaser, and never spend my money foolish unless I'm by myself or with somebody. I am a believer in everybody and everything, extry modern, and extry old fashioned. My contract at KFVD don't give me enough money to get the big head, but it gives me enough that I don't care what other people think about me. I'm just a pore boy tryin' to get along. The dust run me out of Texas, and the Officers run me in at Lincoln Heights. But they was nice to me. They had bars fixed up over the windows so nobody could get in and steal my guitar. I was hijacking on credit till I got on the radio. Now I plan to put in a second hand bank. I am never surprised or disappointed, for I have no regret or future ambitions. I am a lazy man, and can't help it. Ugly and can't fix it. The Universe is my home, and Los Angeles is just a vase in my parlor. I like pore people because they'll come out a winner in the long run. And I like rich people because they need friendship.[24]

Woody called these rambling digressions his "cornpone philosophy," and they became a fixed element in his radio act.[25] Here he first began to develop the famous Guthrie humor and easy-talking, friendly style. Here also, for the first time, his class-consciousness began to emerge, intermingled with a relaxed, naive utopianism. KFVD was not only Woody's channel into the public, it became his steppingstone into California's left-wing politics.

The Popular Front

In the 1930s, radicalism in America came to be centered in the Communist party; it was the only time in American history that communist ideology made any significant headway into the American heartland.[26] To Woody, the communists seemed to be the group that was fighting the hardest for the things he believed in, and he became an ardent supporter. He claimed to have "always read the radical (i.e., communist) papers over my program and took sides with the workers all I knew how." It was the communists who led the drive to organize the migrant farm laborers—Woody's special people—into labor unions. Woody was impressed by their zeal and commitment and particularly by their idealism and their utopian vision of a society based on complete equality, a brotherhood of man, in which each would contribute according to his abilities and receive according to his needs.[27]

The Communist party in America had developed in the aftermath of the Russian Revolution, attracting militant unionists and old Wobblies such as Elizabeth Gurley Flynn. The Red Scare after World War I and the Palmer raids of 1920 had forced the communists underground. But the Great Depression of the 1930s brought them vigorously to the surface.[28] Woody Guthrie, like the thousands of victims of Old Man Depression, was attracted to the communists by their carefully thought-out and well-argued assurances that poverty and injustice in America could be overcome by the simple application of Marxist principles.[29]

The stock market crash of 1929 seemed to fulfill the Marxian predictions of the inevitable demise of capitalism. As unemployment soared, farm foreclosures and business failures mounted, and banks closed, the Marxian interpretation of history seemed to make more and more sense in America. The rise of Adolf Hitler and the spread of fascism in the mid-1930s seemed to give the communist movement even greater strength. To the average American, the international lines between good and evil were being sharply drawn, and communism was at the opposite end of the political spectrum from the evil of fascism.[30] From this perspective, communism was on the side of right and justice.

In 1934, at the Seventh World Congress of the Communist International, the delegates vowed to cease the factual bickering that plagued the movement and unite in what came to be known as the Popular Front. Soon a spirit of unity swept the entire radical movement in a desperate bid to check the threat of world fascism. To this end, the communists expressed a willingness to put aside the class struggle and to cooperate with the liberal bourgeoisie as well as with socialists and trade unionists. They even supported Franklin D. Roosevelt's New Deal as an example of enlightened and progressive legislation.[31]

American communists were also leaders in the massive union organizing drive made possible by Roosevelt's encouragement. In 1935, under the leadership of the fiery labor organizer John L. Lewis, the militant Congress of Industrial Organizations (CIO) separated from the parent American Federation of Labor. In the tradition of the IWW, Lewis wanted to unite whole industries as a radical alternative to the craft unionism of the AFL. It was felt that a large industrywide union of construction workers, for example, would be more effective than organization according to individual craft skills such as carpenters, bricklayers, and painters and decorators. Such an ambitious scheme required the cooperation of diverse organizations, however, and the pragmatic Lewis was all too happy to accept the support of the communists, who had long advocated industrial unionism and were experienced as labor organizers.[32] In America in the 1930s, a broad progressive movement was reaching out again, with much joy and great hope, to the One Big Union.

Left-Wing, Right-Wing, Chicken Wing . . .

J. Frank Burke, the owner of station KFVD, was deeply involved in liberal politics in Los Angeles. In 1938, in the spirit of the Popular Front, Burke had hired Ed Robbin, a correspondent for the communist daily newspaper *People's World,* to appear on KFVD three times a week as a radical news commentator. Robbin's show immediately followed Woody's, and Woody would often remain in the studio to listen. A friendship soon developed between the two, and it was through this relationship that Woody was introduced into California's left-wing circles.[33]

Ed Robbin became Woody's informal booking agent. He began by featuring Woody at various party functions as an entertainer and radio personality to lighten up these sometimes dry meetings. The first political function that Woody performed at was a rally to celebrate the freedom of an old labor organizer, Tom Mooney, a victim of the Red Scare of the 1920s, who had served twenty-two years at San Quentin on a charge that most now agreed was unjust. Woody took a great interest in the case and wrote a song about it called "Mr. Tom Mooney Is Free." After hearing him sing it on the air, Robbin decided to ask Woody to sing at the rally for Mooney. Woody replied, "Sure, why not?" Not wanting to drag the naive Okie into a situation he did not fully understand, Robbin explained the situation: "I would like you to know, Woody, that this is sponsored by the Communist party, and it's a politically left-wing gathering." According to Robbin, Woody's response was: "Left-wing, right-wing, chicken-wing—it's all the same thing to me. I sing my songs wherever I can sing 'em. So if you'll have me, I'll be glad to go."[34]

After all the speakers had given their tributes to Mooney and Mooney himself had exercised his rhetorical skills, Robbin nudged Woody, who had fallen asleep, and he got up and sang his ballad. It brought the house down, especially the last verse, in which Woody suggested that the rest of California should be freed. Woody was a little surprised by such an enthusiastic response. The audience clearly wanted more, so he sang a few of his dust bowl songs, songs about the people's struggles, of the dust storms and the farm foreclosures that had forced them out onto the road to California, and of the police harassment and vigilante beatings they had endured along the way. Both Woody and the crowd were overwhelmed. He had touched a nerve. It was the beginning of his career as a radical singer.[35]

But Woody was always much more than a singer. Through Ed Robbin he broke into radical journalism. In May 1939 he started writing a column for the *People's World,* a Will Rogers–style daily commentary. It was a continuation of his old cornpone philosophy. He called the column "Woody Sez." It was usually no more than a paragraph, but it ran on the bottom of the front page and seemed strangely out of place under the most serious and weighty of the party's partisan polemics. Here is a typical example: "The national debit is one thing I cain't figger out. I heard a senater on a radeo a-saying that we owed somebody 15 jillion dollars. I don't know their name but I remember the price. Called it the national debit. If the nation is the government, and the government is the people, that means I owe me and you owe you, and I forget the regular fee, but if I owe myself something, I would be willing to just call it off rather than have senaters argue about it, and I know you would do the same and then we wouldn't have no national debit."[36]

Woody had enthusiastically jumped into California's radical politics. In the same way he had absorbed the traditions and culture of the folks on the road and in the migrant camps, he now began eagerly to assimilate the Stalinist radicalism of the Great Depression. He later claimed that he learned all he could "from the speeches and debates, forums, picnics, where famous labor leaders spoke" and that he had heard "William Z. Foster, Mother Bloor, Gurley Flynn [and] Blackie Myers" and "played my songs on their platforms."[37] His image as a performer was merging with his image as a radical.

Stalin and Hitler

After he had accumulated some money, Woody sent for Mary and the kids.[38] For Mary, a frustratingly predictable pattern was taking shape. He would welcome them warmly, play with the girls, and seem happily settled and satisfied for a while, until boredom set in and the urge to roam took over. He would then hit the roads and rails looking for adventure. Never bothering to say where he was going or when he would be back, he would travel around the migrant camps or the skid row bars to see firsthand what the people were going through. Eventually, Mary would go back to the Panhandle, only to be persuaded at some later date to return to a "new" Woody, cured of his restlessness and needing a family again.

Through Ed Robbin, Woody also met the actor Will Geer, a determined left-winger, who, like Woody, was an artist-activist. He was involved in agitprop theater in New York City but had come to the West Coast to tour the migrant camps. Earlier, he had toured with a ballad singer named Jack Frost, acting out the ballads while Frost sang. He was looking for another ballad singer when Robbin introduced him to Woody Guthrie. They toured the camps together in the summer of 1939 and became lifelong friends.[39]

In August, the nonaggression treaty between Hitler's Germany and the Soviet Union stunned the Western world, and the Popular Front crumbled and fell apart. Frank Burke, as well as the KFVD audience, quickly lost all respect for the communists. Woody, stubborn as ever, steadfastly supported the Soviet action as a momentary defensive maneuver to maintain the peace. More important, the communists were still the only people organizing the migrant workers in California, and they could not be held responsible for what Stalin and Hitler were doing. In September, after the Red Army swept through eastern Poland, "liberating" the peasants there, the position of the American communists became increasingly isolated. Woody experienced red-baiting for the first time in his career. At KFVD, the two "commies," Woody and Ed Robbin, became objects of scorn. But Woody refused to back down. He wrote and performed a new song about the Russian invasion of Poland, which sent Burke into a rage. It was a talking blues called "More War News":

I see where Hitler is a-talking peace
Since Russia met him face to face—
He just got his war machine a-rollin',
Coasting along, and taking Poland.
Stalin stepped in, took a big strip of Poland
and give the farm lands back to the farmers.

In November, when the Soviets invaded Finland and Woody stubbornly defended the communists, tension at the station reached the breaking point, and his first experiment in radio came to an end.[40]

As 1940 and World War II approached, Woody hit the road again. First, he delivered Mary and the children (there were three now with the birth of a baby boy in October, named Will Rogers Guthrie) back to Texas, and after borrowing thirty-five dollars from his brother Roy, he headed for New York City, alone again, to visit Will Geer.[41]

New York Town

The Woody Guthrie who arrived in New York City in January of 1940 was a seasoned performer. His guitar poured out an amazing repertoire of traditional songs, as well as a profusion of original compositions in the traditional style, reflecting the diversity of his road experiences. After his numerous half-hour radio shows and appearances at political rallies, skid-row bars, and migrant camps, he had perfected an easy, relaxed style. When he stepped in front of a microphone or an audience anywhere—from a large, crowded auditorium to a friendly living room or front porch—he performed effortlessly. His guitar-playing was perhaps only average and his voice only adequate, but his style, the force of his stage personality, his melodic Okie accent, his impeccable sense of timing, and his honest, child-like humor were powerfully captivating.[42] Already a West Coast celebrity, he became a folk hero in New York.

New York City was the radical capital of America. Bohemianism and left-wing activism had long been associated with Greenwich Village. And the Village of the 1930s was a major center of American communism and the accompanying radical cultural apparatus. In the nation's major urban center, the Great Depression had triggered a strange fascination with the plight of the homeless, hungry victims of the worst economic crisis in the country's history.[43]

The nation's leading artists, scholars, and journalists—Thomas Hart Benton in painting, Martha Graham in dance, John Steinbeck in literature, the Farm Security Administration's photo journalists Dorothea Lange, Walker Evans, and Ben Shahn, and the folk song collectors John and Alan Lomax—were searching for the soul of the American people, attempting to capture, for all time, the dignity and strength of character of the great American common man in the heroic struggle against adversity. The Progressive era of the Popular Front and Roosevelt's New Deal saw an unprecedented glorification of the working classes, and a folk music revival was taking shape in the charged atmosphere of Greenwich Village.[44]

In New York, Woody continued to write his column for the *People's World* and started to contribute articles to New York's radical newspaper, the *Daily Worker.* He was as comfortable and confident in his radical persona as he was with his folk balladeer image. Indeed, the two were so tightly intermeshed that they formed a single transcendent character: the guerrilla minstrel. A few years later, in the lucid and fluid prose of his autobiography, *Bound for Glory,* Guthrie captured the imagery of his minstrel–mind guerrilla consciousness, as he meditated upon his life's purpose, while staring out a window, down sixty-five stories to the New York City streets of 1940:

> I begun to pace back and forth, keeping my gaze out the window, way down, watching the diapers and underwear blow from fire escapes and clothes lines on the back sides of the buildings. . . . Limp papers whipped and beat upwards, rose into the air and fell head over heels, curving over backwards and sideways, over and over, loose sheets of newspaper with pictures of people and stories of people printed somewhere on them, turning loops in the air. And it was blow little paper blow! Twist and turn and stay up as long as you can, and when you come down, come down on a pent-house porch, come down easy so's not to hurt your self. Come down and lay there in the rain and the wind and the soot and smoke and the grit that gets in your eyes in the big city—and lay there in the sun and get faded and rotten. But keep on trying to tell your message, and keep on trying to be a picture of a man, because without that story and without that message printed on you there, you wouldn't be much. Remember, it's just maybe someday, some time, somebody will pick you up and look at your picture and read your message, and carry you in his pocket, and lay you on his shelf, and burn you in his stove. But he'll have your message in his head and he'll talk it and it'll get around. I'm blowing, and just as wild and whirling as you are, and lots of times I've been picked up, throwed down, and picked up; but my eyes has been my camera taking pictures of the world and my songs has been messages that I tried to scatter across the back sides and along

the steps of the fire escapes and on the window sills and through the dark halls.[45]

In New York, Woody Guthrie began to refine his craft and his vision. He was starting to believe that he was bound for glory.

The Great American Balladeer

When he first arrived, he slept on Will and Herta Geer's living room couch, never taking his boots off, expropriating Herta's brand new Martin guitar, as he toured the city's bars and dives. He was not an easy house guest and was soon politely asked to seek other quarters. He stayed with other friends and casual acquaintances. He spent some time at Burl Ives's apartment but eventually ended up in a cheap hotel near Times Square.[46]

Through his association with Will Geer, he found his way into New York's left-wing cultural community. He played at parties and various fund-raising events. In February, he sang at a huge benefit for the refugees of the Spanish Civil War and was well received. But a concert organized by Geer for March 3 proved to be far more significant. It was a benefit for the John Steinbeck Committee for Agriculture Workers and was billed as "Grapes of Wrath Evening."[47] That performance would profoundly affect Woody Guthrie's life and career, as well as the development of American popular music. It was the first Paterson-style concert of the urban folk music revival, and it marked the beginning of a proletarian renaissance in American popular music.[48]

Woody shared the bill with, among others, Aunt Molly Jackson, a ballad singer from the mining districts in Harlan County, Kentucky, and Huddie Ledbetter ("Leadbelly"), the Negro blues singer imported from a prison farm in Texas. In the audience a gangly Harvard dropout, Peter Seeger, watched with enthusiasm. And backstage, Alan Lomax, the young curator of the Library of Congress folklore archives, watched with great excitement as this strange little man from Oklahoma wandered onstage, scratched his head with his pick, nodded at the audience, and said, "Howdy." After mumbling something about how happy he was to be a part of a "Rapes of Graft" show, he tilted his head back and started to sing. Lomax could barely contain himself. He knew instantly that he was watching something very special. In his tours with his father, John Lomax, down through the Appalachians and into the Southwest, collecting folklore, mountain ballads, and cowboy songs, he had fallen in love with America's ruggedly authentic traditional music. And as a young idealist with leftist values, he had seen something in this music that his conservative father had not. Alan Lomax realized that these were the songs of America's isolated and dispossessed rural poor, songs of the oppressed and exploited. Young Lomax had quickly grasped the revolutionary significance and potential of America's folk song heritage. And here for the first time, he was witnessing, in its purest form, a great American balladeer, and, astonishingly, one who incorporated an almost intellectual, but native, class-consciousness into his traditional songs.[49]

The Library of Congress

Lomax brought Woody to Washington, D.C., to capture him on record. The Library of Congress recording sessions took place on March 21, 22, and 27, 1940, at the Department of Interior's studio.[50] Lomax recorded a long, rambling casual interview with Woody, trying to get as much color and background information as possible to accompany all the songs Woody could remember "on a pint of pretty cheap whiskey."[51] Although both Woody and Lomax were pleased with the recordings, it would be twenty-five years before they were released to the public. Lomax, however, prepared a radio script based on the Library of Congress interviews for his "Columbia School of the Air" program, which was broadcast on CBS in April. For this thirty-minute program, Woody was paid the unbelievable sum of $200. The program was a great success, eventually winning an award for the best educational program of 1940.[52]

Through Lomax's influence, Woody was booked on a few other radio programs and, more important, Lomax persuaded Victor Records to produce a two-album set, including twelve 78-rpm records, of Woody's dust bowl ballads. In one marathon session on May 3, 1940, at Victor's Camden, New Jersey, studios, Woody recorded these documents of the Great Depression in the American Southwest. Although the records were never successful commercially, they were a recording landmark as the first serious production of social protest material. Clearly, Woody Guthrie's *Dust Bowl Ballads* is one of the most influential recordings in the twentieth century.[53]

For these historic sessions, Woody was paid $300. With all the money that was coming his way, his conscience began to stir. He bought a new Plymouth automobile and decided to visit Mary and the children. But before leaving, he got involved in one more of Alan Lomax's projects, a book of protest songs called *Hard-Hitting Songs for Hard-Hit People.* Lomax provided the songs, Pete Seeger transcribed the music, and Woody wrote the introduction to each song. Although not released until 1962, it became another classic in the social protest song tradition.[54]

Pete and Woody

In the spring of 1940, after completing work on *Hard-Hitting Songs,* Woody, with Pete Seeger as a traveling companion, headed down through Appalachia to Texas. Along the way they stopped for a brief visit at the Highlander Folk School, outside Knoxville, Tennessee, where Miles and Zilpha Horton were experimenting with the use of music as an organizing device. It was an inspirational visit.[55]

Upon reaching Oklahoma, they first paid a brief visit to Woody's brother Roy in Konawa, where his sister, Mary Jo, and his father, Charlie, were staying. Then they were back on the road to Oklahoma City, where they stayed with Communist party organizers Bob and Ina Wood. The Woods put them to work by taking them around to the hobo camp outside of town, to a rally for striking oil workers, and to a meeting of the Unemployed Workers Alliance. Seeger and Guthrie played all the labor songs they knew and generally soaked up the revolutionary spirit. Excited by the camaraderie, Woody decided to try to write a few labor songs of his own. He first playfully transformed an old hymn, "You've Got to Walk That Lonesome Valley," into "You've Got to Go Down and Join the Union," and later, in a more substantial effort, wrote the famous song, "The Union Maid," perhaps inspired by the example of Ina Wood.[56]

In Pampa, Pete Seeger's middle-class sensibilities were shocked at the sight of the broken-down shack in which Woody's wife and children were subsisting. After a few uncomfortable days with Woody's family, Seeger begged off and continued his travels alone. Woody lasted only a few more days himself before he packed up and headed back to New York. Along the way he again visited the Woods, who were preparing to take a group to New York for a Communist party convention. Woody helped by offering the services of his new Plymouth, which, after his arrival in the city, he promptly donated to the Oklahoma City Communist party.[57]

New York Radio Personality

Back in the city, Woody resumed his singing career with a reinvigorated sense of mission and purpose. Before the summer was over, Seeger had returned, and together they began to tour the union halls and Communist party functions. They appeared on WNYC, New York's public radio station, with such other folk protest acts as Leadbelly and Burl Ives and traditional singers Jim Garland and Sara Ogan from Kentucky.[58]

During this period Woody also met a would-be actor friend of Will Geer, Gilbert "Cisco" Houston, and they began to appear together in night clubs and bars around the city. It was the beginning of a long and close personal and professional relationship. During the war, both served with the Merchant Marines, and, between ships, recorded hundreds of songs for Moses Asch, which have since been released in many different packages. His friendship with Cisco was probably the closest of Woody's life.[59]

As 1941 approached, Woody was making some inroads into commercial radio, appearing at various times on NBC's "Cavalcade of America" and CBS's "We, the People" and "Pipe Smoking Time." He was making as much as $350 a week from his radio performances, plus all the small change he could pick up in the bars. Woody Guthrie was becoming a successful New York act and making more money than he had ever made in his life. He wrote to Lomax, "They are giving me money so fast I'm using it to sleep under.[60]

But the further he moved into commercial radio, the more difficult it became for him to maintain his political integrity. His act was being subtly polished for popular consumption. Certain songs were quietly discouraged. He was pressured to ease up on the political cracks between songs. The networks were trying to package him as a cornball hillbilly singer, as an Okie in overalls and a straw hat. And in spite of these and other concessions, the stations received a good deal of red-baiting mail, condemning Woody as un-American, a "fifth columner," and a commie.[61]

He was caught in the dilemma between commercial success and political conscience. The dilemma intensified with the events in Europe. In June, Hitler had invaded and occupied France, and by September the bombing of England was at its terrifying height. The war was deepening, drawing the United States ever closer to the fighting, and war fever was starting to make it difficult for American radicals.

The pressure to conform must have been intense. For the first time in his life, Woody Guthrie seemed to be backing away from his stubborn radical posturing. He stopped writing his column for the *Daily Worker,* and he appeared to be settling down into a more respectable, mainstream, almost bourgeois lifestyle. He sent for Mary and the family. He was ready for domestic comforts again.[62]

It appeared that Woody Guthrie had sold out, compromised all he believed in, for a shot at the big time. But though outwardly he was a successful radio personality and a man of means, on the inside he was seething. During his radio performances his quick, caustic wit no longer slapped out at the "poll-il-TISH-uns" and capitalist thieves. He was just another singing hick who had come up from Texas to entertain the city slickers, with only the blandest of songs, the limpest stories, and in the most self-deprecating style.

One example should make the point. Woody's starring role in CBS's "Pipe Smoking Time," which began in November 1940, called for a bastardized, orchestrated opening number that featured Woody embarrassingly singing an advertising jingle to the tune of "So Long, It's Been Good to Know Ya":

> Howdy friend, well it's sure good to know you
> Howdy friend, well it's been good to know you;
> Load up your pipe and take your life easy,
> With Model Tobacco to light up your way
> We're glad to be with you today.[63]

By the year's end he had taken all he could stand. Without so much as a blink, he quit the radio shows, packed his wife and children in a new Buick he had just made the first payment on, and headed for California. And that was the end of Woody Guthrie's radio career.[64]

California and the BPA

After a long, exhausting ride west, by way of Texas, and after a few weeks of cheap West Coast motels and many nights of drunken soul-searching, Woody dragged an angry and hopelessly frustrated wife and three fitful youngsters out to the Los Angeles home of his old friend Ed Robbin. They moved into an abandoned house next door and tried to settle back into the California life.[65]

Woody tried to get rehired at KFVD, but Frank Burke had not forgotten about the Hilter-Stalin pact. The credit union began to send notices about the Buick, and Woody began to seek the comfort of the skid row bars. But mostly, he hung around the house, playing with the children and fighting with Mary. He continued to correspond with the folks back East. At Alan Lomax's urging, he started to write his autobiography. Pete

Seeger wrote to him about the new singing group he had organized, called the Almanac Singers.[66] He was yearning to return to New York until he got sidetracked by the Bonneville Power Administration.

It seems that an obscure documentary film producer, Gunther Von Fritsen, was planning a film about the BPA's massive dam construction project along the Columbia River, on the border between Oregon and Washington, Fritsen was looking for a folksy, backwoods character to narrate the film, and someone had suggested Woody Guthrie.[67]

In May 1940, as the funds for such projects began to dry up, the prospects for the film grew more doubtful and it was finally abandoned. But through this connection, Woody was able to procure a one-month contract with the BPA, at $266.66 per month, to write and record a series of songs about the Bonneville project.[68] He later claimed he wrote twenty-six songs during that month. He wrote many of his most well-known songs for the BPA: "Roll on Columbia," "Hard Traveling," "Jack Hammer John," and "Pastures of Plenty." It was to be the most productive month of his life.[69]

The Almanac Singers

In the spring of 1941, while Woody Guthrie was busily writing songs about the Columbia River and the Grand Coulee Dam, Pete Seeger's Almanac Singers were preparing for a summer tour. Back in December 1940, Seeger and a friend named Lee Hays had begun to tour the city's radical circles singing labor hymns and peace songs. Both were dedicated radicals, who had been drawn, through different channels, to the idea of using rural musical forms as a weapon in the class struggle. And both saw in the union a grand symbol of worker solidarity and a vision of the future.[70]

Lee Hays had come to New York after leaving Commonwealth Labor College in Arkansas, where he had worked as a teacher, activist, and composer of labor hymns. His repertoire already included the classics "We Shall Not Be Moved" and "Roll the Union On." And he had written one of the earliest Almanac songs, "The Ballad of Bob Wood," about the Oklahoma communist leader whom Seeger and Guthrie had visited in the summer of 1940.[71]

Pete Seeger had been carefully prepared for his mission as the guiding spirit behind the Almanac Singers. Indeed, although the Woody Guthrie mystique looms much larger, Pete Seeger has been the tireless force behind the urban folk music revival and the unyielding marshal of the social protest singing tradition in America since the early 1940s.[72] Young Seeger's conversion to the people's music occurred on a trip with his father, musicologist Charles Seeger, to the 1935 Asheville (North Carolina) Folk Festival. But Charles Seeger was also a Marxist and had had a strong hand in developing the song-as-weapon-in-the-class-struggle thesis that the communists of the 1930s had inherited from the Wobblies. He had been a member of the Communist party's Workers' Music League. The formation of the Almanac Singers was young Seeger's attempt to capture the spirit of the Workers' Music League's "worker choruses."[73] They were a loose group of dedicated young people, using their musical talents to further the propaganda battles of the American Left.

Millard Lampell, a young left-wing intellectual and writer, was Hays's roommate in New York and, together with Seeger, these three formed the original Almanac Singers. The group never had a fixed membership, but this did not matter because the message and the mission were always more important than the group's personnel. Seeger, Hays, and Lampell were the founding members, but they formed only the inner core within a loose and shapeless chorus of mind guerrillas. Other Almanacs included Bess Lomax, Alan's younger sister; Pete Hawes, a friend of Seeger; Allen Slone, a friend of Lampell; Arthur Stern, who replaced Lee Hays as bass singer in the fall of 1941; and Agnes "Sis" Cunningham, who, along with her husband, Gordon Friesen, later founded *Broadside,* the topical song journal of the 1960s.[74]

In the spring of 1941, Woody Guthrie, fresh from an exhilarating month with the BPA, joined the Almanac Singers in New York, toured with them that summer, and moved into Almanac House, their Greenwich Village commune, that fall. There, between club dates and radio spots with the Almanacs, he continued to work on his autobiography.[75] Throughout the fall, the Almanacs performed in union halls and International Workers Order (IWO) lodges, at the Russian War Relief benefit, and at a Meat Cutters union banquet.[76] They started giving regular Sunday afternoon concerts from their basement, which they called "hootenannies," a term they had picked up that summer in Seattle.[77]

The significance of the Almanac Singers to the social protest song tradition in America was underscored that fall by a visit to Almanac House by Elizabeth Gurley Flynn. The former Wobbly organizer was now a prominent Communist party leader. Joe Hill's "Rebel Girl" was there that night officially and ceremoniously to pass on to the Almanacs the Wobbly torch in the form of a briefcase containing Hill's private papers.[78]

In December, after the Japanese attack on Pearl Harbor and the American entry into the war, the Almanacs' fortunes began to suffer. Bookings dropped off drastically in the winter of 1942. They tried to transcend their pacifist past and subversive image by writing and performing antifascist songs like "Round and Round Hitler's Grave," "All You Fascists Bound to Lose," and "The Sinking of the Reuben James."[79] But their patriotism was not convincing.

The Almanacs limped on throughout 1942, crusading against world fascism. Woody, like the others, was caught up in the propaganda struggle against Hitler. During this period his guitar carried the inscription: "This Machine Kills Fascists." Times were changing, and Woody wrote a song about it called "Brand New Situation." And indeed it was. The war turned everything upside down. Throughout 1942, the Almanacs slowly drifted apart. Pete Seeger was drafted. Lee Hays got involved in war relief work. Millard Lampell went into radio as a scriptwriter. Allen Slone became a staff writer for *Parade* magazine, and Arthur Stern went back to teaching art history. And in an attempt to avoid the draft, Woody joined the Merchant Marines.[80]

But the new situation also required some ideological adjustments. As Woody and the others directed their radicalism to the war effort, they began to visualize the war in Marxist, or, more accurately, in Stalinist terms, as part of the larger struggle against capitalist imperialism. In the beginning, like the Wobblies during World War I, they had been opposed to sending working folks across the oceans to fight and die to protect the property of the rich. But after Pearl Harbor, they were forced to try to view Hitler and fascism as examples of international capitalism gone haywire, sick with greed.[81]

But the new situation had much wider implications for Woody. In the winter of 1942 he had fallen in love with a young fan, a dance instructor from New Jersey named Marjorie Greenblatt.[82] The BPA and the Almanac summer had been too much for Mary, who had gone back to Texas for the last time. Woody would later say offhandedly: "She was right from her side and I was right from mine."[83] But after a long courtship, while both he and Marjorie settled their previous marriages, and after the birth of a daughter, Cathy Ann, they were finally married in November 1945.[84]

Woody survived the war, serving convoy duty, ferrying soldiers across the Atlantic. He was torpedoed once and then his ship hit a mine after unloading soldiers during the D-Day invasion. The two ships were extensively damaged, but Woody was not. Then cruelly, at the war's end, on May 7, 1945, the day the Germans surrendered, the draft finally caught up with him. He served in the army until the following December, when he was released on a hardship discharge.[85]

During the war he continued to record material for Moses Asch. In 1943, his autobiography, *Bound for Glory,* was published. His association with Pete Seeger continued after the war, and he became involved in Seeger's postwar efforts to revive the Almanac spirit in People's Songs, Inc., and *Sing Out!* magazine. But slowly and embarrassingly, his public and private behavior became increasingly bizarre and unpredictable as the disease descended upon him. His young daughter, who was very dear to him, was killed in a mysterious fire. As he became increasingly withdrawn, he began to lose friends and his relationship with Marjorie started to deteriorate.[86]

After his second marriage fell apart, he resumed his wanderings for the last time. According to John Greenway, who visited Marjorie Guthrie in 1952, Woody had gone down to the corner store for a newspaper and never came back.[87] He bummed his way out to California, stayed for awhile with Will and Herta Geer, then ran off with the wife of one of Geer's friends, Anya Marshall.[88] They were together long enough to give birth to another child, her first, his eighth. By 1956, after a third divorce, he entered Brooklyn State Hospital, unable to care for himself. He died there in October 1967, after a decade of living death.[89]

The Dust Bowl Balladeer

Woody Guthrie claimed to have written more than a thousand songs. He tended to overwrite and underedit, so that much of his work has been justifiably forgotten. Yet his prolific outpourings include some of the greatest classics in American folklore: "This Land Is Your Land," "So Long, It's Been Good to Know You," "Pastures of Plenty," and "Those Oklahoma Hills." Most fall into the traditional folk song categories: love songs, work songs, hobo songs, and outlaw ballads, documentary descriptions of tragedies and disasters, nonprotest war songs, patriotic national anthems, and nursery rhymes. John Greenway, in *Folksongs of Protest,* estimates that only about 140 of Guthrie's songs are of political significance.[90]

But Guthrie's view of politics was much broader than Greenway's. He was inclined to argue that folk songs were political by definition. To Guthrie, folk songs were the cultural expressions of a political entity, and singing was an indelible part of the process by which that entity was sustained over time. Moreover, for Guthrie, the process by which songs entered the public domain (the folk process) was in itself revolutionary. Songs that became public possessions were community products and therefore potent symbols of the socialist ideal. Since folk songs were authorless, they did not draw royalties for the benefit of the few. The folk song was therefore implicitly also a protest song because it inevitably stood outside of, and in direct opposition to, the capitalist system. The same process that turned a folk song into a hit turned the farmer into a migrant laborer, and Woody Guthrie wanted no part of it.[91]

Ironically, Guthrie's family ultimately made a great deal of money from the royalties on his songs and became economically stable, living as capitalists selling the Woody Guthrie mystique. But there was a strong, stubborn side of Woody Guthrie that always resisted, sometimes irresponsibly, profiting from his songs.[92] This was the utopian side of his character.

Especially in the beginning, Woody refused to (or perhaps did not know to) copyright any of his songs and therefore forfeited the royalties. The royalties for his "Oklahoma Hills," for example, went to his cousin, Jack Guthrie, with whom he had sung the song on KFVD. Woody seemed content to see many of his songs slip into the public domain. In the early 1940s, George Wilhelm, a West Coast radio announcer, disturbed because the profits from Guthrie's "Philadelphia Lawyer" were not reaching Woody, took it upon himself to initiate a suit in behalf of Guthrie for copyright infringement. But the action was eventually dropped when Woody showed no interest.[93]

But later, a more profit-minded Woody Guthrie, after being coached by Alan Lomax, would balk at the Almanac Singers' insistence upon giving their songs a collective authorship. Guthrie claimed copyrights and royalties on several Almanac songs ("The Union Maid," "The Sinking of the Reuben James," and "The Ladies Auxiliary"). He made this claim to authorship because he had furnished the major idea or the majority of the lyrics, whereas the other Almanacs (who he sometimes referred to as his "deputy song writers") had made only secondary contributions.[94] Perhaps there was an entrepreneurial side to Woody Guthrie's character also.

The contradiction of the anticapitalist "folk" songwriter forced into the music industry marketplace to make a living may be resolved in light of Guthrie's utopian character. He was not so much interested in money as in fame. His utopian spirit wanted to be remembered; it wanted immortality. Woody Guthrie wanted to become a part of the folk process, along with his songs. He wanted to enter the public domain.[95]

But the irony deepens when one considers that Woody Guthrie wrote few, if any, original melodies. The Almanac songs mentioned above, for example, were written to familiar folk or country tunes: "The Union Maid" to the tune of "Redwing," "Reuben James" to the Carter Family's "Wildwood Flower," and "The Ladies Auxiliary" to the tune of "The Butcher Boy." (He liked that tune so well that he also used it for one of his children's songs, "Clean-O.") Most of his other famous songs were similarly plagiarized: the melody for "This Land Is Your Land" came from "Little Darlin' Pal of Mine," "Tom Joad" from "John Hardy," "Jesus Christ" from "Jesse James," "Jack Hammer John" from "Brown's Ferry Blues," "The Philadelphia Lawyer" from "The Jealous Lover," "Pastures of Plenty" from "Pretty Polly," and both "Roll on Columbia" and "Rambling Blues" from "Irene Goodnight."[96]

But Guthrie saw nothing unusual about such plagiarism, believing it simply the normal folk process and a further indication of his connections to the people.[97] As we have seen, this was the standard procedure used by the Wobblies and other early labor songsters. Songs have circulated in oral cultures since the beginning of time in this fashion.[98]

The notion of melody ownership was foreign to the folk *gemeinschaft,* and Guthrie felt that borrowing a melody was a natural way to compose a song. And yet, in the degree to which he claimed authorship to songs, and especially songs written to the melodies of other songs, Woody Guthrie was violating the folk process and in a sense, joining forces with the Tin Pan Alley capitalists.[99]

Guthrie's Philosophy of Song

To contend, however, that all of Guthrie's songs are inherently political is inaccurate. In sober moments, Guthrie offered specific criteria for what constitutes a political protest song. In one of his New York *Daily Worker* columns in 1940, he gave the following advice on how to write political songs:

> Poor day today. Didn't write but 3 union songs. Oh well, that'll keep the deputy song writers busy another 6 months. Pete's even taking a wack at song making. He plowed out a couple yesterday. You know you are as good a songwriter as there is, but you might not believe it. If you don't believe it, that's why you're not.

All you have to do is sit down and write up what's wrong and how to fix it. That's all there is to it. Lord knows, there is plenty of matter to work on. All we need is more song writers. You, for instance. Naw, come on, it don't even have to rhyme. Don't even have to be spelt right. All you got to do is cut loose and let her roll out on paper, and when you get something that's haywire and how to fit it, you got a song. Best part is that you don't even have to be able to write. You don't even have to be able to hum, whistle, or sing. You just got to speak it. That's all. Just whale away and yell it right out. Loud as you can. So somebody else can hear what's haywire and how to fix it. Then you got a song. Every word is a music note of some kind, so everything you yell is a song. Geetars and banjos ain't what makes the world go 'round. It's talkin' songs and yellin' songs—and the best song you don't even have to yell it—you just double up your fists, roll up your sleeves, and thump it out on any convenient silk hat.[100]

Woody Guthrie's philosophy of song begins with the premise that we, the people—each of us as individuals and all of us as a community—have a right and a responsibility to sing out when we encounter injustice. And he meant this literally as well as metaphorically. We each have a duty to expose injustice and dehumanization whenever and wherever we encounter it. He argued that anyone can sing in the face of oppression. To do so is as natural as talking. No special skills are necessary. We know instinctively when something is wrong, when something has gone "haywire," and we have a responsibility and a duty to speak out, to stand up to the "silk hat" oppressors.

The oppressors that Guthrie usually associated with the silk hat imagery show up in his songs as fat-cat capitalists, bankers, industrialists, and politicians: those who, in his mind, have removed themselves from the community of the people and shed their "folksiness" for a more materially comfortable lifestyle; the few who live in splendor and isolation from the many who barely cling to existence; those evil individuals who are so filled with greed that they are no longer able to reach out with compassion to their brothers and sisters in the world community; those few who wish only to dictate to, exploit, extort, bribe, or brainwash the "folksiness"—the revolutionary spirit—out of the people.

The solution to this violation of the folk utopia, for Woody Guthrie, seemed to have involved simply standing up to the politicians, landlords, and factory owners of the world with the power of a united and determined people behind him. This is the old "Solidarity Forever" argument of the Wobblies, which could have been made by Joe Hill or John Lennon. But where as Hill would have colored his argument in the direction of the industrial worker and Lennon toward the bohemian counterculture, Guthrie painted his songs in the soft hues of the folk, or the rural *gemeinschaft* of the 1930s.

Although the spirit of this philosophy may indeed permeate all of Guthrie's songs, if one searches his lyrics for evidence of "what's wrong" and "how to fit it," very few of them measure up to Guthrie's own criteria for a political song. Greenway's estimate that less than 1 percent of Guthrie's songs were overtly political seems reasonable.[101] Very few of his songs expose social problems and offer political solutions. Perhaps one or two of his union songs, like "Union Maid," live up to Guthrie's dual-propertied political song. Most of his songs possess one or the other quality, but rarely both together.

Some dwell mostly on what is wrong and are vividly descriptive ballads of disasters and tragedies, tributes to the suffering of the people, but without providing solutions to the problems they portray. I will refer to these as documentary songs, and my examples are taken from the *Dust Bowl Ballads,* the *Ballads of Sacco and Vanzetti,* and a few especially descriptive ballads like "The 1913 Massacre" and "Plane Wreck at Los Gatos (Song of the Deportees)." Some Guthrie songs, however, seem to indulge themselves in solution, the problem being self-evident or unknown. To Guthrie, the typical answer to almost any problem, and the only real hope for the people, was the union. Guthrie's union songs, like "You've Got to Go Down and Join the Union," "Good Old Union Feeling," "The Union Maid," and "Union's My Religion," are classic examples of labor hymns, and they are Guthrie's contribution to the old Wobbly organizing song tradition.

Some of Guthrie's more well-known songs do not seem to fit into either of these two categories. They are neither documentary nor organizational. They do not concern themselves with problems or solutions. They may stem from an exaggerated emphasis on imaginary solutions. They appear in the form of august and stately patriotic nationalistic anthems like "This Land Is Your Land" and many of the Bonneville Power Administration songs. Some of his nonprotest war songs such as "The Sinking of the Reuben James" also seem to fit into this category.

Documentary Songs

Woody Guthrie's *Dust Bowl Ballads,* recorded in 1940 by Victor Records, are among the finest documents in song of the Great Depression in the American Southwest, compelling descriptions of the drought, the dust storms, the farm failures, and the migrations of the homeless out of Texas, Oklahoma, and Arkansas, to California in search of a new life. For Woody Guthrie, these songs not only document the plight of his chosen people, the dispossessed Okies; their authenticity and conviction are attributable to their emergence from his own personal experiences trying to survive the devastation of the dust bowl. The *Dust Bowl Ballads* are probably Woody Guthrie's greatest artistic and political accomplishments. What John Steinbeck did in the novel form and Dorothy Lange in photography, Woody Guthrie did in song.[102]

The ravaging dust storms that blew away the topsoil and reduced once rich farmlands to desert were among the most dramatic episodes in the Great Depression. In "The Great Dust Storm," Guthrie describes what he referred to as "the worst of dust storms that ever filled the sky." The storm occurred on April 14, 1935, and laid waste an enormous area, from Oklahoma to the Dakotas and from New Mexico to Kansas. In describing the destruction, Guthrie effectively centers the narrative upon himself and his family, crowded into the parlor, with the children crying, as the wind and the dust "whistled" through the cracks in the windows and the walls of their "oil boom shack." They all thought it was the end of the world, that the Day of Judgment was at hand. When it was all over, the devastated family was loaded into their "jalopie," and they "rattled down the highway to never come back again."[103]

Guthrie and those he portrayed in these songs were more likely to perceive their plight in religious than in political imagery, and the great dust storms were typically viewed in eschatological terms. In "Dusty Old Dust," the people were sitting around talking about the end of the world when

> the telephone rang and it jumped off the wall,
> That was the Preacher a-making his call.
> He said: "Kind friends this may be the end.
> You've got your last chance at salvation of sin."

But the dust was so bad inside the church that the preacher could not read from his Bible. So he folded his "specs," took up the collection, and said, "So long, it's been good to know you."[104] Typically, Guthrie's solution is escapist, to drift down the road and put your troubles behind you.

But Guthrie did not lose his sense of humor through misfortune. Rather, he used it effectively in the service of protest. Humor is as important a component in Guthrie's songs as it was in the songs of Joe Hill. Some of his deadly serious comments on the side effects of the dust are softened by witticisms. In "Dust Pneumonia Blues" (which he pronounced "NEW-monie"), Guthrie describes one of the more serious consequences of the dust storms, a respiratory disease, pneumoconiosis, caused by dust in the lungs. In the song he takes the role of a pneumoconiosis patient. His doctor tells him: "You got that dust pneumonee and you ain't got long, not long." But Guthrie describes all this with a humor that cuts deep into the nature of such a tragedy. About midway through the song, he apologizes for not including some yodeling, singing: "But I can't yodel, for the rattlin' in my lungs."[105] He also weaves in a love story. His girl loves him because "she's got the dust pneumonee, too." In fact, they are both so accustomed to the dust that one day, when his "good gal" fainted in the rain, he had to throw "a bucket of dirt in her face, just to bring her back again." But before it was over, he was starting to realize that "If you wanta get a mama, you have to sing a California song."[106]

To young Guthrie and the other "dust bowl refugees," California became the Promised Land, where they could escape the devastation and make a new beginning. But California turned out not to be so promising. There was no Moses to lead the migrant children, and besides, in California, money was God. In "Do Re Mi," Woody warns the new Israelites of what lies ahead in California but with a disarming wit. He sings of the people leaving "back East" and rolling across the desert sands out to California, thinking they are going to a "sugar bowl," only to find that "if you ain't got the Do Re Mi," life will not be good in "paradise."[107]

"Talking Dust" is another humorous narrative of the flight to California. It is in the form of a "talking blues," a traditional blues format, which lends itself to humor, with periodic pauses and an unusual metric pattern. It is an almost improvised rambling chatter, woven loosely into a repeating bass line on the guitar.[108] The singer first talks of the idyllic "little farm" he lived on with his family back in 1927, of how the dust storms ruined it, and of the trip to California. His description of the family's situation in California is filled with a sarcasm that is just beginning to have a political edge:

> We got out to the west coast broke
> So dadgum hungry, I thought I'd croak.
> So I bummed up a spud or two,
> And my wife fixed up a 'tater stew.

We poured the kids full of it.
Mighty thin stew though.
You could read a magazine right through it.

I always have figured,
That if it'd been just a little bit thinner
Some of these here pol-i-ticians could've seen through it![109]

Along the road to California and in the "Hoovervilles" or migrant camps outside of the western cities, one of the most dreaded fears was the vigilantes, armed patriots and hired thugs who preyed upon the migrants, fearing for their property and jobs in the onslaught of the homeless and hungry. Reflecting the perplexity of the homeless people around him, living as aliens in their own country, Woody Guthrie could not understand the vigilante phenomena. In "Vigilante Man," he asks why these vigilantes carry sawed-off shotguns and then answers himself rhetorically: "Would he shoot his brother and sister down?"[110] Guthrie's utopian ideology was beginning to bear fruit on the vine that Steinbeck would call the "grapes of wrath."

Woody was so taken by Steinbeck's *Grapes of Wrath* that after seeing the movie version in New York City in 1940, he wrote a long narrative ballad, condensing Steinbeck's five-hundred-page novel into seventeen verses, in a song he was very proud of, called "Tom Joad." Through Steinbeck's Preacher Casey, Woody reflected the growing sense of class-consciousness he imagined and hoped would ultimately spread throughout his people:

"Well, I preached for the Lord a mighty long time,
Preached about the rich and the poor.
Us working folks (has got to) get together
'Cause we ain't got a chance anymore, boys,
We ain't got a chance anymore."[111]

But probably the best reflection of Guthrie's growing class-consciousness, and the most consciously political of the *Dust Bowl Ballads,* was "I Ain't Got No Home in This World Any More." In an abbreviated ideological summation of the politics of the dust bowl, Guthrie wrote:

My brothers and my sisters are stranded on this road,
It's a hot and dusty road that a million feet have trod.
Rich man took my home and drove me from my door,
And I ain't got no home in this world anymore.[112]

The entire concept of the *Dust Bowl Ballads* reflects Woody

Guthrie's utopian consciousness. The songs are grand testaments to the strength and perseverance of his "brothers and sisters," the homeless and hungry, struggling to survive on the road. Most of these songs, however, are the product of a preideological Guthrie. With only a few exceptions, they are devoid of any conscious, positive radicalism. But there is a naive class-consciousness, a growing awareness of the struggle of the poor against the rich, and the innocent hope that the poor will unite in their oppression and overcome the stranglehold of the rich. This perception was to form the solid foundation of Woody Guthrie's political philosophy.

Much later in his career, in 1946, at the urging of the record producer Moses Asch, Guthrie attempted a similar project. But this time the subject matter lay outside Guthrie's experience. He was asked to document the controversial trial and execution of Nicola Sacco and Bartolemeo Vanzetti, two Italian anarchists convicted of murder in conjunction with a payroll robbery in Boston some twenty years earlier. Sacco and Vanzetti were executed in 1927 after a long and well-publicized trial. Their case became a celebrated cause in the American Left. Not since Joe Hill had a public execution attracted so much political controversy. Although never as respected artistically or as convincing politically as the *Dust Bowl Ballads,* Woody Guthrie's *Ballads of Sacco and Vanzetti* are nevertheless great monuments to two of the American Left's most notorious martyrs.[113]

In a typical example, "You Souls of Boston," Guthrie recounts the story of Sacco and Vanzetti, while proclaiming their innocence. He argued that at the time of the alleged crime, Vanzetti, a fish peddler, was with "his fish cart thirty-two miles away." And Sacco had relatives who would testify that he was some forty miles away at the time of the robbery. Moreover, after seeing Sacco's pregnant wife break down in tears, a member of the "Morelli Gang" confessed to the crime. But because Sacco and Vanzetti were "union men," they were found guilty and executed.[114]

The other nine songs on the album retell the same story, but they lack the personal insights or the humor of the *Dust Bowl Ballads.* The *Ballads of Sacco and Vanzetti* are merely a few weak, unenthusiastic, and unconvincing songs with which to remember the martyrs.

One final example of the documentary style, and one of Guthrie's most lyrical and poignant narrative ballads, is "The 1913 Massacre." It is another retrospective account of an event in labor history, a vigilante-style incident that occurred during the Christmas season of 1913 in the copper mining districts of Michigan. The narrative is especially effective because Guthrie skillfully draws the listener into the story, creating a powerful empathy with the victims, the Michigan copper miners and their families:

> I'll take you in a door and up a high stairs,
> Where laughing and singing can be heard everywhere,
> I'll let you shake hands with the people you meet,
> And watch the kids dancing 'round the big Christmas tree.[115]

After the listener is comfortably seated and content in the warm closeness of the miners and their families, while a "little girl" sits down by the Christmas tree to play the piano, the quietude is suddenly interrupted as some of the "copper boss thugs," looking for a little fun, open the door at the foot of the stairs and yell "fire!" In the rush to evacuate the crowded hall, seventy-three children are crushed to death while the thugs hold the door and laugh at their "murderous joke," Woody then resolves the ballad in a quiet but powerful protest against such a horrible and inhumane prank:

> The piano played a slow funeral tune
> And the town was lit up by a cold Christmas
> moon;
> The parents they cried and the miners they moaned,
> "See what your greed for money has done?"[116]

To understand this last line, we must recall Guthrie's utopian consciousness. In his mind, all the complexities of world and domestic politics were conveniently reduced to a mythic contest between love and greed, between an altruistic, compassionate family of man and the blind, amoral, materialistic greed of the wealthy few. Woody Guthrie, the utopian, worked out his politics in black and white, the symbolism of good and evil. To him, greed was embodied in the evil institutions of free enterprise capitalism, and love was the only possible weapon to fight such an insidious evil. In his mind, also, love was synonymous with the union. The union, as a symbol of the people united in the struggle against capitalist greed, was the embodiment of altruistic love, or community, locked in a fight to the death against the plague of blind egoism and materialistic greed. Invariably, greed, in any "brand or style," was the "what's wrong" component in Guthrie's protest song equation, and love, in the form of the union, was "how to fix it."[117]

Many more examples of documentary songs are included in Guthrie's compositions: "The Union Burying Ground," "The Ludlow Massacre," "The Dying Miner," and "The Song of the Deportees" are a few of the most well known. These are among Guthrie's best artistic accomplishments. He was a masterful balladeer, and the narrative documentary song was his most powerful medium. Although few of these songs are overtly political, a subtle social commentary usually accompanies the narrative.

Union Hymns

Guthrie's union songs are far less subtle, and some are clumsily propagandistic. But their purpose was more ideological than narrative, and they are thus more didactic than aesthetic.

In one of his more arrogant moments, Woody Guthrie claimed that among the great protest writers of his day—Aunt Molly Jackson, Sara Ogan, Jim Garland, and Pete Seeger—his work would be remembered as "the most radical, the most militant, and the most topical, of them all."[118] Despite this boast, however, Woody Guthrie's most radical songs amount to only a handful of union songs, and these fall into two distinct categories: the traditional union organizing songs (like "Union Maid" and "You've Got to Go Down and Join the Union") and his own unique union utopian songs ("Good Old Union Feeling" and "On My Way").

Within the protest genre, organizing songs are the most obviously revolutionary, the most blatantly radical. These songs are usually written with specific movement politics in mind. Their most obvious musical-lyrical characteristic is the presence of a repetitive refrain line or chorus. Organizing songs are designed for group singing. Whereas the narrative-documentary format demands the descriptive powers of the balladeer, audience participation is minimal. The major purpose of the organizing song is not descriptive but organizational—they are intended to generate audience participation. Organizing songs thus lend themselves to practical political uses on picket lines and at mass demonstrations. They are great rallying songs, imbued with positive political power, the power to totalize protest into decisive revolutionary action.[119]

The classic organizing songs in the protest tradition include Ralph Chaplin's "Solidarity Forever,"[120] Florence Reece's "Which Side Are You On,"[121] the Negro protest spiritual "We Shall Overcome,"[122] and John Lennon's "Give Peace a Chance.[123] Many of these songs are still heard in the 1980s at mass demonstrations and peace rallies. Only Guthrie's "Union Maid" approaches the caliber of the above songs, but it is rarely heard today.

Guthrie may have written many more organizing songs than have survived. Such songs are often written spontaneously for specific events and then quickly forgotten. "Mr. Tom Mooney Is Free," for example, written by Guthrie on the occasion of Mooney's release from prison, and "Why Do You Stand There in the Rain?" written for the 1940 American Youth Congress Convention in Washington, D.C., are so topical as to be of only academic interest.[124] Probably only the most general and abstract of Guthrie's organizational songs have survived.

Another explanation for Guthrie's low output of organizing songs is that very quickly after he immersed himself in leftist politics in the early 1940s, America entered World War II, which created great turmoil in the American Left. For Guthrie, war fever may have transformed many would-be organizing songs into nationalistic anthems. Songs like "This Land Is Your Land" have a definite militant edge and, like organizing songs, have a choral musical-lyrical structure. But for reasons I will discuss later, these songs underwent a political whitewashing when they entered the popular field, losing much of their revolutionary impact.

Guthrie's earliest (and probably best) explicitly radical movement songs were written in the Wobbly style. This was the only pattern to follow. Thus the favorite Wobbly technique of transforming popular hymns into union songs was, as we have seen, used in Guthrie's first organizing song: "You've Gotta Go Down and Join the Union." It was written at the home of Communist party organizers Bob and Ina Wood, while Guthie was traveling with Pete Seeger in the spring of 1940, and it was what Lee Hays would call a "zipper song."[125] Words could be "zipped" in and out of the song to adapt to new situations.

When performing this song Woody would simply exchange "You've got to" for "My brother's got to," or "My sister's got to," or whatever came to mind at the time. But at some point the song included a final stanza, which used the metaphor of the road to symbolize life's hardships and struggles. It also incorporated a reference to the hope-generating role of singing in the romanticized struggle and alluded to the struggle's ultimate goal (which Wobbly poster art often pictured as a beautiful sunset at the end of the road): the utopian One:

Though the road gets rough and rocky
And the hills get steep and high;
We will sing as we go marching
And we'll win that One Big Union by and by. [126]

"The Union Maid," Guthrie's most famous organizing song, also has Wobbly roots and a Wobbly flavor. It is directly in the tradition of Joe Hill's "Rebel Girl." It was also written while he was with Bob and Ina Wood in the spring of 1940 and was at least partly inspired by the example of Ina Wood. In *The Woody Guthrie Songbook,* however, Guthrie is quoted as saying: "This song was made up in honor of Mrs. Merriweather. She's a woman that was stripped naked and beat up, and then hung to the rafters of the house 'till she was unconscious."[127]

The heroine in the song was never afraid of the "goons and ginks and the company finks" or of the deputies who made raids on the homes of union organizers. She was always "wise to the tricks of the company spies" and could not be misled by the "company stools." She was a dedicated union woman who always got her way when she "struck for higher pay." And when confronted by the company guards, she stood her ground, singing defiantly: "Oh, you can't scare me, I'm stickin' to the union . . . 'till the day I die!"[128]

Guthrie originally wrote only two verses and the chorus, and then a convoluted folk protest process took over the song. When it became part of the Almanac Singers' repertoire, they felt it needed a third verse, so Millard Lampell added the following:

Now you gals who want to be free
Take this little tip from me;
Get you a man who's a union man
And join the Ladies Auxiliary;
Married life ain't hard
When you've got a union card,
And a union man has a happy life
When he's got a union wife.[129]

The song remained in this form until the early 1970s, when Lampell's last verse began to grate on some sensitive feminist nerves. In the thirty-fourth edition of the IWW's "Little Red Songbook" in 1973, Lampell's verse was dropped and a new, feminized verse was added by Nancy Katz:

A woman's struggle is hard
Even with a union card,
She's got to stand on her own two feet,

And not be a servant of the male elite.
It's time to take a stand,
Keep working hand in hand,
There's a job that's got to be done
And a fight that's got to be won.[130]

Because of the elasticity of the symbol "union," this song has been able to adapt and develop with changing times. Unfortunately, however, it has not been able to stretch quite as well in the post–World War II era. The IWW's 1973 feminist verse is not well known. After the war, the union as a symbol lost much of its credibility with the radical Left in America. Especially after the 1955 merger of the AFL and the CIO, the American labor movement has been perceived as increasingly elitist and conservative. Union leaders have become indistinguishable from management executives; both seem to dress, act, and think like politicians and bankers. At a symbolic level, the union leader is no longer a convincing radical.

After America's entry into World War II, Guthrie's union songs became increasingly utopian in character. And in the postwar years, union songs and symbolism disappeared altogether from Guthrie's work and from the social protest song tradition generally. In 1941, Guthrie wrote his last union organizing song, at the request of the CIO's Ladies Auxiliary, which had asked Guthrie and the other Almanac Singers to write them a theme song. When Guthrie reminded them of "The Union Maid," saying it had been written for just that purpose, the women said it was not "dignified enough."[131] So, partly in jest, and partly in contempt, Woody wrote them a theme song:

Oh the Ladies Auxiliary,
It's a good Auxiliary,
'Bout the best Auxiliary
That you ever did see.
If you want an Auxiliary,
See the Ladies Auxiliary,
It's that Ladies Auxiliary.[132]

After America's entry into the war, and Guthrie's into the Merchant Marines, he continued to write union songs. He began to see the war effort as part of a worldwide union struggle, the struggle of the working folks against fascism. In 1947, Guthrie put together another songbook, *American Folksong,* edited by Moses Asch and published by Oak Publications. The collection included two union songs written during the war. But these songs reveal a changing conception of "the union."

In "Good Old Union Feeling," the union is represented as an emotional affect, or perhaps a mystical-spiritual condition. "Union" is now something that Guthrie claims to "feel" in his "soul." His view of the union has changed from participatory to experiential, or at least an experiential component has been added. In "On My Way," Woody pushes the concept of the union in a more utopian direction than in his other union songs. He is traveling on an imaginary "union road" and not looking back, and confidently marching off to a "better place," some mysterious "union town," a utopia where "we'll win our war and peace" and presumably live happily ever after.[133]

Although these later songs possessed many of the characteristics of organizing songs, they were now becoming utopian in spirit in that they had lost their class-based activist referent and had become increasingly mystical and escapist.

Nationalistic Anthems

Woody Guthrie had always romanticized the working-class struggle, using what Joe Klein called "comic-book dialectics."[134] The theme was always the evil rich bankers and politicians against the "pore workin' folks." Radical politics to Guthrie was a religion. It was a way of life, a mission, and a cause. It was the missing ingredient that made his life complete. He once even wrote an unmemorable song called "Union's My Religion," explaining his unorthodox beliefs. His "union religion" was the religion of the people, glorifying the working class, which, for Guthrie, was best represented in the symbolism and imagery of the rural *gemeinschaft* of the American heartland. But he idealized all American workers, who toiled by the sweat of their brow and the muscles in their arms.

Guthrie went so far as to proletarianize Christ as "a carpenter true and brave":

> When Jesus come to town,
> All the workin' folks around
> Believed what he did say.
> The bankers and the preachers,
> They nailed him on a cross,
> And they laid Jesus Christ in his grave.[135]

But Guthrie's politics here are more Steinbeckian than Marxian, reflecting not a revolutionary dialectic but a sentimental exaltation of the working class, which was his interpretation of the Depression era's Popular Front Americanized radicalism.

Perhaps, as R. Serge Denisoff has suggested, Guthrie's politics was opportunist in nature, motivated by the desire to reach an audience that demanded a working-class song culture.[136] I think that this criticism is too harsh. Although, like other performers, Guthrie had the problem of finding and keeping an audience, his politics was never as shallow as Denisoff seems to imply. Actually, in his songs, Guthrie was juggling a strange and eccentric blending of American folk-country musical culture, New Deal-Popular Front radicalism, and World War II patriotism, idealizing the vanishing American peasantry and the emerging working class in a nationalistic manner.

The songs Guthrie wrote for the Bonneville Power Administration in the spring of 1941 were among his first to reflect this utopian working-class romanticism. Because of their apparent nationalist pride and patriotism, they are among his most misunderstood songs. And yet, in Guthrie's imagination, they were meant to be great and lasting tributes to an experiment in American socialism. In the liner notes to *Woody Guthrie,* he explains the political significance of the BPA songs:

> I made up 26 songs about the Columbia and about the dam and about the men, and these songs were recorded by the Department of Interior, Bonneville Power Administration, Portland, Oregon. The records were played at all sorts and sizes of meetings where the people bought bonds to bring the power lines over the fields and hills to their own little places.
>
> But there were reactionary congressmen in back of the people that owned those little private dams and power houses out there, that didn't want to see the Grand Coulee built, because it would make electricity dirt cheap and cut down on their profits. (They fought hard to keep the TVA out of the State of Tennessee, too.) They can always think up a million nice good excellent reasons why it is better for you to go ragged and hungry and down and out and even in the dark, as long as it makes them a profit. But lots of people made speeches on both sides. Movie stars flew up in big airplanes and told the folks how nice it was not to have no electricity. . . . But we made speeches on our side, and we played the records over the loud speakers there in those little towns, and the people shelled out the money and bought the bonds and brought the electricity over the hill to milk the cows, shoe the old mare, light up the saloon, the chili joint window, the ladies' dresses and hats in windows, the schools and churches along the way, to run the factories turning out manganese, chrome, bauxite, aluminum, steel, and flying fortresses by the hundreds to bomb the Japs out of this war with.

That's how things get done. Just people doing it. People can get more done that way than anybody else I ever seen, and I'm a man that's seen a lot of them.[137]

What excited Guthrie about the Bonneville Power Administration, the Tennessee Valley Authority, and other New Deal public works projects was that the government (meaning the people) was building these massive dams and highways. This was a revolutionary slap at the private enterprise system and to Guthrie and many others on both sides of the issue it was an important step toward socialism.[138] His political dreams seemed to be coming true. He described the Grand Coulee Dam as the eighth wonder of the world:

Well, the world has seven wonders,
That the travelers always tell;
Some gardens and some towers,
I guess you know them well.
But now the greater wonder
Is in Uncle Sam's fair land;
It's that King Columbia River,
And the Big Grand Coulee Dam.[139]

And he lavished praise and glory on the hardworking men who tamed the Columbia River, bringing electric light to the people, in epic working-class anthems like "Jack Hammer John," "Hard Travelin," and "Roll On Columbia."

To Guthrie, these dam construction projects would create "green pastures of plenty out of dry desert land." And the strong implication was that the land and its resources belonged to the working people. The people's freedom demands that the government (as opposed to private companies) control the nation's natural resources. In Woody's words: the "pastures of plenty must always be free."[140] Thus, when it came, Guthrie had no trouble justifying America's entry into World War II as the defense of the land and the people's freedom.

His sensitivity to the reactionary, anticommunist sentiments of those who warned of the totalitarian possibilities of these government-owned utility monopolies and his overriding concern for upgrading the standard of living of the American common people on their lands are revealed in the satirical ending to "Talking Columbia":

Yes, Uncle Sam needs wool, and Uncle Sam needs wheat,
Uncle Sam needs houses and stuff to eat,
Uncle Sam needs water and power dams
Uncle Sam needs people, and the people need land.

Of course, I never did like dictators much, myself,
But, I think the whole country ought to be run by
e-lec-tri-ci-ty![141]

In Guthrie's mind, the BPA was a humanitarian experiment and an expression of working-class consciousness and solidarity. It was supplying jobs and electricity to the people and demonstrating the courage, determination, and ingenuity of the hardworking men and women who were the backbone of this nation.

In April 1966, Woody Guthrie, with little more than a year of life left to him, was awarded the Department of Interior's Conservation Service Award for his BPA songs. In conjunction with the award, one of the Bonneville Power Administration's substations was named after him. But the letter from the secretary of the interior demonstrates a complete lack of understanding of the meaning and intent of Guthrie's BPA songs and the nature of his songwriting career: "Yours was not a passing comment on the beauties of nature, but a living, breathing, singing force in our struggle to use our land and save it too. The greatness of this land is that people such as you, worked on it and that you told about that work—told about the power of the Bonneville Dam and the men who harnessed it. . . . You have summarized the struggle and the deeply held convictions of all those who love our land and fight to protect it."[142] The secretary saw this Stalinist mind guerrilla as a conservationist.

But clearly something in Guthrie's work invited such patriotic interpretations. He had glorified and proletarianized Roosevelt and the New Deal in a nationalistic manner. In "The Grand Coulee Dam," for example, Guthrie wrote: "Uncle Sam took up the challenge in the year of 'thirty-three, for the farmer and the factory and all of you and me."[143] And as the war in Europe drew closer, this proletarian nationalism became even more pronounced. In "My Uniform's My Dirty Overalls," he enlisted the American worker in the struggle against fascism.[144] In "The Sinking of the Reuben James," he paid tribute to the "hard fighting men" who died for "the stars and stripes of this land of the free."[145] And he ridiculed the great enemy of the workers in "Talking Hitler's Head Off Blues."[146] In Guthrie's version of World War II, Roosevelt and Stalin were the heroes and the American workers the warriors.

Guthrie's view of Roosevelt, the New Deal, and World War

II was a romanticized utopian socialist view. What passed for nationalism was his native folk consciousness filtering through the working-class ideology he had been exposed to in California and New York. In Guthrie's mind, Roosevelt stood symbolically for the fight against capitalism at home and fascism abroad. His death in 1945 came as a great shock to Guthrie's utopian sensibilities, inspiring one of his classic nationalist anthems, "Dear Mrs. Roosevelt." It took the form of a letter, consoling the widow:

> Dear Mrs. Roosevelt,
> Don't hang your head to cry;
> His mortal clay is laid away,
> But his good work fills the sky . . .

The song continued as a tribute to FDR as the crippled leader who had "learned [Guthrie's] soul to walk." Woody's Christlike Roosevelt ran "the money changin' racket boys" out of office and then helped to build the union movement and find jobs for the unemployed. Woody claimed that on his merchant ship, the captain had hated FDR, but he was loved by "all ship's hands." To Woody, Roosevelt had fought the war "the union way," and the fascist "hate gang all got beat." He went on to say that Roosevelt did not like the capitalist leaders, Winston Churchill, Charles De Gaulle, and Chiang Kai-shek, but that, at Yalta, he had shaken the hand of Joseph Stalin, saying, "There's a man I like." And on and on, through fifteen verses, Guthrie spelled out all of FDR's grand accomplishments, always from a "union" perspective and always punctuating his World War II mythology with the poignant refrain: "This world was lucky to see him born."[147]

World War II was to Guthrie a workers' war. Uncle Sam was fighting on the side of Uncle Joe. American populism and Russian socialism were partners in a struggle to preserve the world for the people. Love was locked in a struggle against greed. His war songs were thus utopian in nature, mythologizing the war as a romantic workers' struggle.

The contradiction between Guthrie's love of the land the people and his radicalism is perhaps nowhere more striking than in his most famous song, "This Land Is Your land." Originally written in 1940, just after Guthrie arrived in New York City, and entitled "God Blessed America for Me,"[148] it was intended as a working-class national anthem, a poor boy's "America the Beautiful." This song went through a folk process after it left Guthrie's pen and entered the public domain.

In a cheap hotel room near Times Square, he wrote six verses in one sitting, to the Carter Family's "Little Darlin' Pal of Mine." The first verse evolved into the familiar chorus about this being "our" land (your's and mine) "from California to the New York Island," "redwood forests," "Gulf Stream waters," and all. Two of the more politically explicit verses were eventually dropped, leaving three standard verses in the popular version. But all six were originally capped with the noble but unimaginative line: "God Blessed America for me." In 1944, Guthrie replaced that line with the refrain we are familiar with today: "This Land was made for you and me."[149]

The standard verses effectively disguise Guthrie's original political tone under a heavy coat of nationalist sentimentality:

> As I went walking that ribbon of highway,
> I saw above me the endless skyway,
> I saw below me that golden valley,
> This land was made for you and me.[150]

The political verses paint a much different, proletarianized picture:

> One bright sunny morning, in the shadow
>   of the steeple,
> By the relief office, I saw my people,
> As they stood there hungry, I started to
>   whistle,
> This land was made for you and me.

Or even more to the point:

> A great high wall there tried to stop me,
> Great big sign said, "Private Property,"
> But on the other side, it didn't say nothing;
> That side was made for you and me.

The song's original intent was to reclaim America for the working class. It was a tribute to public, socialistic ownership and a declaration of contempt for private ownership and free enterprise capitalism. But in the popular version, this socialist tint was carefully whitewashed away, leaving only the sentimental nationalism.

It is easy to see how the nationalist sentiment that simmered below the surface of Guthrie's Popular Front radicalism came to the surface as his songs entered America's popular culture in the 1950s and 1960s. Unfortunately, the process of popularization has led to a serious misunderstanding of the origin and intent of Guthrie's career as a singer and songwriter.

Songs to Grow On

Woody Guthrie wrote more children's songs than any other type, many of them in collaboration with his daughter Cathy, who was later killed in a fire. At first they seem artless, repetitive, and trite, filled with nonrhyming, nonsensical, rubbery, and playful word games:

> Wash-y, wash-y, wash-y,
> Wash-y, wash-y, wash-y,
> Jingle, jangle, ding-a-ling,
> Pincky, pancky, ponk.[151]

Never preachy or condescending like many songs written for children, these are authentic reflections of a child's consciousness and spirit. There are songs for waking up and going to sleep; songs about bottle, breast, and nipple; songs about splashing in the bath tub and brushing one's teeth; songs about momma and daddy, sister and brother; songs about birds, fish, and trees, wind, rain, and mud; songs about soda pop, ice cream, candy, and gum; songs to sing and dance and run to; songs for riding in the car; spelling and counting songs; songs to pick up toys to; and songs about planting seeds:

> Tooky, tooky, tooky, tooky tidal, oh;
> Tooky, tooky, tooky, tooky tidal, oh;
> Tooky, tooky, tooky, tooky tidal, oh;
> We'll all dance around and see my
> little seed grow.[152]

In a surprisingly successful attempt to plant these seeds, Moses Asch, a record producer with a great appreciation for these seemingly insignificant songs, carefully recorded many of them in a series called *Songs to Grow On.* The albums sold better than many of Guthrie's more serious records. They became an important staple in progessive day care centers throughout the nation[153] and are still available today.

Few, if any, of these songs are political in content. But their political significance should not be dismissed. In some sense, Guthrie's children's songs have had a political impact equal to or greater than his more serious political songs. Woody Guthrie's children's songs are a part of the larger mind game. They cast a musical spell when the child is still young and malleable. Music in childhood is a very effective consciousness developer. By establishing very early a love for folk music, children are introduced to a song culture that, as the child advances further into it, becomes increasingly political in form and content. And in

Guthrie's children's songs there is an inherent utopianism that fits into the larger analysis. In many ways, the utopian mentality is a child's mentality. When operating at the child's level, Guthrie's utopianism shines through:

> You stick out your little hand
> To every woman, kid, and man,
> And you wave it up and down,
> Howdja do, howdja do?
> And you wave it up and down,
> Howdja do.[154]

In this innocent faith in the goodness of mankind, we see the utopian's desire for the harmony of the One Big Union. And in Woody Guthrie's songs for children, we see the beginning of the struggle to cultivate within the minds of the very young this faith in the oneness of humankind:

> We all work together with a wiggle
> and a giggle,
> We all work together with a giggle
> and a grin,
> With a wiggle and a giggle and a
> google and a gogle
> A jigger and a jagger and a giggle
> and a grin.[155]

Moreover, Woody intended these songs for parents as well as children. His hope was that, through singing, adults would learn to overcome their intrinsic stuffiness, to reach out and connect with their children's openness. In his mind, the world would be a better place if adults were conditioned to be more like children. In the liner notes to *Songs to Grow On,* he gave the following instructions on how to use these songs:

> Now I don't want to see you use my songs to divide nor split your family all apart. I mean, don't just buy these records and take them home so your kids can play around with them while you go off and do something else. I want to see you join right in, do what your kids do. Let your kids teach you how to play and how to act these songs out. Get your whole family into the fun. Get papa. Get mama. Get brother. Get sister. Get aunty. Get uncle. Get grandma. Grampa. The friends. The neighbors. Everybody. But mostly get your own self into it.
>
> Please, please, please, don't read nor sing my songs like no lesson book, like no text for today. But, let them be a little key to sort of unlock and let down all your old bars.
>
> Watch the kids. Do like they do. Act like they act. Yell like

they yell. Dance the way you see them dance. Sing like they sing. Work and rest the way the kids do.

You'll be healthier. You'll feel wealthier. You'll talk wiser. You'll go higher, do better and live longer here amongst us, if you'll just only jump in here and swim around in these songs and do like the kids do.

I don't want the kids to be grownup. I want to see the grown folks be kids.[156]

In Guthrie's mind, adults were kids who had gone sour with age, and singing with their kids was one way to recapture their lost youth. And it was the youthful spirit that would change the world.

But this childlike warmth, this happiness and zest for life, which comes through so convincingly in Woody's children's songs, actually permeates all of his work. And it is the key to understanding Woody Guthrie as a performer, a thinker, and a public personage. Above all, and through all, Woody Guthrie was an idealist and an optimist. He felt it was his duty, and the purpose of his art, to lift the spirits of the listener. Woody Guthrie never sang the blues:

I hate a song that makes you think you're not any good! I hate a song that makes you think that you are just born to lose. Bound to lose. No good for nobody. No good for nothing. Because you are either too old or too young or too fat or too thin or too this or too that. Songs that run you down or songs that poke fun at you on account of your bad luck or your hard traveling.

I'm out to fight those kinds of songs to my very last breath of air and my last drop of blood.

I'm out to sing songs that will prove to you that this is your world, and that if it has hit you pretty hard and knocked you for a dozen loops, no matter how hard it's run you down and rolled over you, no matter what color, what size you are, how you are built, I am out to sing the songs that make you take pride in yourself and in your work.[157]

The one quality that runs through all of Guthrie's works—from the sincerity and purity of the *Dust Bowl Ballads,* to the grand and glorious Bonneville Power Administration songs, to his simple songs for children—is this basic, unflinching optimism so paradoxical in a man who suffered so much and was rewarded so little. Through it all Woody Guthrie never lost this naive faith in the future or the hope for the One Big Union:

There's a better world a-comin',
I'll tell you why, why, why;

There's a better world a-comin',
I'll tell you why.
When we'll all be union
And we'll all be free;
There's a better world a-comin',
Don't you see.[158]

Woody Guthrie may have romanticized and mythologized the working-class struggle, his radicalism may have turned sentimental and nationalistic over the years, he may have stubbornly clung to ideals long after their time had passed, and he may have tended to get carried away with his words, which seemed to spill out unedited and without much thought, but above all, his passion for living was his ideology and his blind faith in the utopian union was his religion. His character had many flaws—he was sometimes irresponsible, arrogant, and selfish—but he had a vision and a talent for putting that vision into songs that others would sing long after his fingers could no longer strum on his guitar. Through Woody Guthrie, the social protest song tradition and the banner of the working-class hero were passed on to the generation of the 1960s.

Afterlife

In the late 1930s, when Woody Guthrie was performing songs of deep social and political significance, documents of the Great Depression in the American Southwest—"The Great Dust Storm," "Dust Bowl Refugee," and "I Ain't Got No Home in This World Anymore"—popular music in America was dominated by such escapist twaddle as "The Boulevard of Broken Dreams," "Life Is Just a Bowl of Cherries," and "On the Good Ship Lollypop." More serious popular songs were recorded during the Depression, such as "Brother Can You Spare a Dime," but all in all remarkably little social protest was generated by the pop music industry of the 1930s. The American public seemed bent on forgetting all their troubles and believing—against all odds—that Old Man Depression would never get them.[159] But during the 1930s Woody Guthrie and social protest music generally went largely unnoticed by the public at large. It was not until the late 1950s, after Guthrie was well beyond his performing years and beginning his mental and physical deterioration, that his songs and the Guthrie phenomenon began to capture large sectors of the popular imagination.

Perhaps more than any other single individual, Pete Seeger—

first with the Almanac Singers, then with the Weavers, and finally as a solo act on the 1950s campus circuit—was largely responsible for the production and maintenance of the Woody Guthrie cult. Seeger tirelessly and persistently performed Guthrie's songs and seemed determined to preserve the memory of the man he considered his friend and mentor. What the organizational network of the IWW did for Joe Hill, Seeger and company, from People's Songs, Inc., to *Sing Out!* have done for Woody Guthrie.[160]

The Folk Boom

The commercial surge of folk music from 1957 to 1965 and the Woody Guthrie cult were mutually reinforcing sociocultural phenomena. Guthrie, with Seeger and the Almanacs, had been instrumental in laying the groundwork for the so-called "folk boom" by bringing the music and protests of rural America into the major metropolitan centers during the 1940s and 1950s. Guthrie and Seeger became the founding fathers of what came to be known as the urban folk music revival.[161]

One of the Weavers' first commercial successes in the early 1950s was Guthrie's "So Long, It's Been Good to Know You," a revision of "The Great Dust Storm," altered for popular consumption. The original version was about a family driven off their farm by a devastating dust storm, but the popular version was a story of lovers marrying and leaving town.[162]

The 1950s saw the first generation of Guthrie admirers and disciples come into being. Besides Seeger, Millard Lampell, Cisco Houston, and the Almanac Singers, there were younger followers such as Ramblin' Jack Elliot, who traveled for awhile with Guthrie, then began to sing his songs, imitating his twangy voice and guitar style and adapting his dress and mannerisms in an uncanny characterization. Such devotion by a Guthrie pupil would not be matched until Robert Zimmerman did the same in the early 1960s.[163]

Guthrie's first real break into the popular mainstream came in 1958, when the Kingston Trio, a clean-cut, collegiate hybrid singing group, a stylistic mixture of the Weavers, Harry Belafonte, and Elvis Presley, recorded an old North Carolina murder ballad, "Tom Dooley," setting off the commercial boom in folk music. The trio's first album was a greater commercial success than anyone in the earlier folk revival could have imagined. Besides "Tom Dooley," the album contained Guthrie's "Hard Ain't It Hard."[164]

From 1958 to 1964, the Kingston Trio recorded many Guthrie standards ("Hard Travelin'," "Pastures of Plenty," "This Land," "The Sinking of the Reuben James," and "The Song of the Deportees") in a strange but successful blending of traditional (folk or country-western) and popular (rock) musical styles.[165] They were a great success on the campuses of the late 1950s and early 1960s. As folk music moved into the mass market, it became standard practice for the Kingston Trio–style folk groups (the Brothers Four, the Limelighters, the Tarriers, the Chad Mitchell Trio, Peter, Paul, and Mary, and others) to include Guthrie songs in their repertoires. In the early 1960s, everybody in the folk community was recording Guthrie material (Joan Baez, Tom Paxton, Odetta, Judy Collins). This trend continued into the folk-rock period of the late 1960s and early 1970s (Country Joe and the Fish, the Byrds, Jesse Colin Young, Ry Cooder).

By the mid-1960s, Guthrie, who had never been financially stable in his life, was receiving $50,000 per year in royalties. His old materials, recorded in the 1940s for Asch, Stinson, and Victor Records, were being reissued. In 1964, a three-record set of his *Library of Congress Recordings* with Alan Lomax was released by Elektra. In 1965, *Born to Win,* a collection of his poetry and short prose, was published. And shortly after his death, his unfinished novel, *Seeds of Man,* was prepared for publication along with an edited version of his columns for the *Daily Worker* and *People's World,* and given the same name as those columns, *Woody Sez.*[166]

This Land Is Your Land

Thus by the mid-1960s, Woody Guthrie had become a national institution. "This Land Is Your Land" had become as popular as the national anthem. In the late 1960s, the song was used as an advertising jingle by United Airlines and the Ford Motor Company. In 1972, it was the theme song for Senator George McGovern's unsuccessful presidental campaign. In 1975, millions of schoolchildren all across the country sang it simultaneously through a video hookup to open the first annual Music in Our Schools Day. Truly an American classic, "This Land" has been recorded by the Weavers, the Wayfarers, Glen Yarborough, the Kingston Trio, the Limelighters, the Brothers Four, the New Christy Minstrels, Peter, Paul, and Mary, Trini Lopez, Harry Belafonte, Jay and the Americans, Glen Campbell, Bing Crosby, the Staples Singers, Pete Seeger, Tex Ritter, Connie Francis, Country Joe McDonald, Paul Anka, Jim Croce, the Mike Curb

Congregation, and the Mormon Tabernacle Choir. But few were aware that the song was intended as a Marxist alternative to "God Bless America."[167]

In 1976, a motion picture based on Guthrie's autobiography, *Bound for Glory,* produced by Robert F. Blumofe and Harold Leventhal and directed by Hal Ashby, was released through United Artists.[168] Although David Carradine's Kung Fu image was an unconvincing Woody Guthrie, the film was nevertheless at times visually splendid and clearly the most colossal tribute to Guthrie to date. But it did little to convey that the hero had been a communist and father of the 1960s protest song movement.

The disappointments of the *Bound for Glory* movie were more than amended by Woody's son Arlo, who in 1984 released a sensitive and compelling full-length documentary for public television on the life of his famous father: *Woody Guthrie: Hard Travelin'*.[169] This wonderful film features interviews and songs by Pete Seeger, Joan Baez, Holt Axton, Judy Collins, Ramblin' Jack Elliot, Ronnie Gilbert, and Holly Near and includes rare footage of Woody singing with Sonny Terry and Brownie McGhee, an intimate talk with Maxine Crissman ("Lefty Lou") and Guthrie's first wife, Mary, and even an unknown and never before released BPA song: "Roll Columbia." It was truly a timely stroke on the canvas of the Guthrie myth and the mind guerrilla from which its colors flow.

The Guthrie Phenomenon

How is one to account for the Guthrie phenomenon? How did Woody Guthrie become so famous without performing to great masses in outdoor stadiums and without million-selling records? Why did Woody Guthrie cast such a great shadow in America's protest song culture, in spite of the controversy over his politics and even though other radical singer/songwriters were perhaps more deserving of the title "father of the folk protest tradition?"

There were the other original Almanac Singers: Lee Hays, of Commonwealth College and later of the Weavers and Millard Lampell, a gifted songwriter ("The Strange Death of John Doe," "The Ballad of Harry Bridges," and "Talking Union") and a working-class intellectual dedicated to the creation of a proletarian culture for the masses. And there were many performers on the loose periphery of the group: Gordon Friesen and Agnes "Sis" Cunningham, who later started the topical song magazine *Broadside*; Arthur Stern, Josh White, Cisco Houston, Brownie McGhee, Sonny Terry, Bess Lomax, and Earl Robinson (who wrote the music to Alfred Hayes's poem "Joe Hill"). All of these people are virtually unknown by the public at large, yet the name of Woody Guthrie, who joined the Almanacs late and remained for only a relatively short period of time, has found a place in the folklore of America.

The only other popular personage to emerge from this period is Pete Seeger, the organizer of the Almanac Singers, People's Songs, Inc., the Weavers, and *Sing Out!* magazine. Seeger has consistently been the major guiding force behind the folk music revival and the social protest singing tradition in America since the 1940s. Clearly superior to Guthrie as a musician and musicologist and a much more consistent performer, with a more respected image, an impeccable political history, and an uncanny ability to transform seemingly apathetic audiences into singing congregations, Pete Seeger is indeed the undisputed elder and guiding spirit behind America's social protest singing tradition.

Seeger's ideological purity, unflinching political commitment, and active involvement in the various causes of the American Left for almost half a century—from union struggles to integration to anti-Vietnam peace movements to environmentalism—contrasts sharply with Woody Guthrie's unorthodox, eccentric, often halfhearted radicalism, his unpredictable public behavior and his impossibly stubborn egotism.[170] Moreover, Seeger's stable married life of almost forty years is a startling contrast to Guthrie's three failed marriages and nine abandoned children. Thus, when compared to Woody, Seeger's life carries the imagery of the responsible, upstanding, idealistic, strongly principled, committed radical and mind guerrilla. In comparison, Woody Guthrie seems a misfit.

Nevertheless, Guthrie's romantic image as a hard-drinking, hard-traveling, hobo-adventurer and womanizer carries the symbolism of the unrestrained, sensuous, Chaplinesque free spirit, whereas Seeger's image of the principled and determined idealist, clinging steadfastly to his principles, heroically standing up to Joseph McCarthy's House Committee on un-American Activities when lesser men caved in, carries the symbolism of political integrity and Puritan righteousness and responsibility.[171] The 1960s youth culture that canonized Guthrie lusted after freedom and sexuality and developed an aversion to political idealism and altruistic social responsibility. Thus it was perhaps natural that they would embrace the romantic figure of Woody Guthrie and rebel against the fatherly image of Pete Seeger.

Moreover, Guthrie's life was a potent symbol of alienation, pain, and suffering, whereas Seeger's life, in comparison, was materially comfortable and bourgeois. Seeger has also clearly suffered a great deal as an ostracized, blacklisted outcast, who for many years went largely unnoticed and unrewarded in proportion to his contribution to the folk song revival in America. But Seeger has persevered and in the end has become famous and wealthy. Woody Guthrie did not experience the blacklisting of the McCarthy era; he was hospitalized with Huntington's disease and too sick to perform or to be much of a threat to the Federal Bureau of Investigation (FBI) or the House Committee on un-American Activities. But Guthrie did not persevere. In his lifetime, he was never economically or commercially successful. Always the outcast, from the beginning he lived a life of alienation and poverty that Pete Seeger could only romanticize and envy.

Pete Seeger suffered, but not in the same way. Seeger's suffering was symbolic, based on principles and ideals that he had chosen to stand for and that others (some in high places) feared. Woody had experienced similar pain (he had been red-baited and placed under surveillance by the FBI in the 1940s),[172] but his suffering was physical as well as political and economic.

Of course, the other obvious difference between Seeger and Guthrie is that Seeger is still alive and Woody is not. Guthrie's long illness, along with the publicity generated by Seeger and others, turned him into a martyr. So perhaps the Guthrie phenomenon may be explained by his more colorful, romanticized proletarian image, or perhaps, like Hill and Lennon, it is a function of the circumstances surrounding his death.

When the Curfew Blows

Many, but certainly not all, of the differences between Guthrie and Seeger may have been the result of Huntington's chorea, the disease passed on to Guthrie by his mother. Beginning almost unnoticed in his early adult years, Huntington's disease slowly began to consume Guthrie's mind and body. Shortly after he established himself and his career, Guthrie slowly went insane, turning into an erratic, unpredictable, often bizarre, and even sex-crazed imbecile—all symptoms of the early stages of Huntington's disease.[173]

But there is another, less tragic, side to his illness, for the disease also appears to have affected Guthrie's creative powers. Under its influence, he became more childlike, uninhibited, and freely associating, until he was filled with fantasies and visions and overflowing with poetic ramblings that expressed his innermost psychic feelings. What Huntington's disease did for

Woody Guthrie, LSD and other drugs would do for Bob Dylan and John Lennon; break down the barriers of rationality so that the creative energies might flow freely.[174]

Unfortunately, the deterioration brought on by the disease progressively, interfered with Guthrie's physical and mental coordination. While the fantastic outpourings of thoughts, visions, and hallucinations flowed with increasing intensity, Guthrie progressively lost his ability to control the visions and ultimately even to communicate the thoughts. Perhaps it was the pain, the humiliation, and the suffering that Woody Guthrie endured that, more than anything else, captured the sympathy of the public. This argument would be convincing except that the public at large knew very little of Guthrie's years as a victim of Huntington's disease. Primarily, they knew only the Woody Guthrie who overcame the hardships of the Depression and defiantly rambled around the country, riding the rails as a hobo and singing for nickels and dimes. This young Woody Guthrie, the man of *Bound for Glory,* came to represent freedom and hope and the victory of youth over adversity and authority. Perhaps that is why the later image of the hospitalized, trembling choreic was so tragically poignant.

Sometime in the fall of 1967, Harold Leventhal, Guthrie's manager, played a recording of Guthrie's son Arlo for Woody to hear. It was an eighteen-minute, comical, Guthriesque talking blues called "Alice's Restaurant Massacree," about how a conviction for littering had saved Arlo from being drafted. It would become one of the classic statements of protest against the military draft during the Vietnam era. And it would bring Arlo, at age nineteen, more notoriety and commercial success than Woody had achieved during his entire career. A major motion picture was eventually made from Arlo's song.[175]

But Woody never saw that film, and in all likelihood he did not comprehend the significance of the recording played for him that fall day, though Leventhal claimed he caught a smile of recognition and approval on the trembling lips of the dying Guthrie. Woody Guthrie died before he could see his son rise to prominence in the very pop music culture that Guthrie's most famous disciple, Bob Dylan, would, almost singlehandedly, construct from the ashes of the Woody Guthrie cultural tradition.

Woody Guthrie finally gave in to death on October 3, 1967. All three networks announced the news, and radio stations across the country played musical tributes to him. But there were no mass demonstrations or even a funeral service. Marjorie and the children did not believe in ceremonies. Ironically, Woody Guthrie had outlived his fame, to be overshadowed by his pupils and children.[176]

Marjorie Guthrie had the body cremated. Then she and the children (Arlo, Joady, and Nora) took the canister of ashes to one of Woody's favorite spots on the jetty at Coney Island. But they had trouble opening the canister and could not release the ashes—Joe Hill style—to the winds. So in a gesture unconsciously symbolic of the parental disdain of the new cult of youth, Arlo Guthrie tossed the vial containing the ashes of his legendary father out into the ocean, as if it were an empty beer can. And then Woody's children, who had never known anything but a grotesque caricature of the noble dust bowl balladeer, went off to find a hot dog stand.[177]

Woody Guthrie was a great spokesman for the working class in America. He was one of the founding fathers of America's folk music revival. His songs romanticize, and mythologize, the people's struggles during America's greatest economic disaster and the world's second global conflict. His public image was that of a hobo and a rambler, a free spirit unfettered by life's burdens and woes, and a working-class minstrel, singing his way across the country, absorbing and expressing the hopes, fears, and dreams of the American people. He was a prophet singer whose words became the guiding light for future generations of radical culture in America. He was the Will Rogers of America's folk music community.

Guthrie's Popular Front Marxism was tempered by his native folksiness. He expressed his radicalism in hillbilly couplets and folk phraseology, partly because it was his natural tendency to do so, but also in a conscious attempt to reach the common people that this philosophy was supposed to represent. His "cornpone" philosophizing tended to alienate the intellectuals and the hard-core activists but seemed to fit the spirit of the Popular Front, by Americanizing and popularizing left-wing radicalism.

Woody Guthrie was a troubadour who carried a political message. The totality he was associated with—the folk music revival in America—was a hybrid mixture of radical politics and traditional folk song culture. To Guthrie, it was natural to fuse working-class politics with what he saw as working-class song culture. If this seems odd today, it is because "folk" music, especially in its urban guise, has never been popular among the working class in America. Its base of support has been in the major urban centers and college campuses. The workers have preferred country-western music. But, of course, these two forms share the same sources in America's traditional music: folk being a politicized and intellectualized descendant of the traditional forms, and country less cerebral but more commercial cousin. This differentiation was less pronounced in Guthrie's day. He was essentially a country musician—as much influenced by the music of the Carter Family and Jimmy Rogers as by the oral folk traditions of the American peasantry—who blended a radical consciousness into his music. The result was a new musical genre and cultural movement: the urban folk music revival, or what we know today simply as folk music.

Thus Woody Guthrie was not just a musician for the sake of the music. He was a thoroughgoing mind guerrilla. He saw his music as a political tool, a weapon in the class struggle. His purpose as a singer and songwriter was not to preserve the old songs for posterity; his mission was to sing out in protest against the injustices of the world and to rally the people behind revolutionary change. To him a singing people was a powerful revolutionary strategy and force. Moreover, his vision of the future was couched in a musical metaphor. He saw a singing people and a singing world in which one people would live together in harmony.

Perhaps it was naive to hope that the right song, sung loud enough, could change the world. But it was a hope he shared with the Wobblies before him and with an entire generation of folk protest singers after him. Clearly, this was the utopian side of Guthrie and the social protest movement generally. But it is not as naive as it sounds. Musical cultures do play an important role in the transmission of revolutionary ideals and symbols, and, especially in the age of electronics, ideas and ideologies transmitted by song have overtaken the more traditional, literate, and academic means.

The politicization of mass movements and cultures in the future may learn a great deal from the example of Woody Guthrie. Modern totalitarian states, from the Nazis to the Soviets, have used such cultural forms effectively for political and propagandistic purposes. And in the West, a mass counterculture of unprecedented size and impact came into being in the 1960s and 1970s, on the grinding rhythms of rock 'n' roll music. The musical approach to radicalism is utopian in the sense that a society and a world community are not built upon songs alone, but singing is far more practical as a totalizing device and as a source of symbolic politics than many other propaganda strategies that could be undertaken.

In this case, however, the totalizing effect runs much deeper than the music, encompassing the image and the public perception of the man behind the songs. As a source of vicarious political identity, and as a vehicle to embody the values of a revolutionary movement symbolically, Woody Guthrie's public image is every bit as important as the songs he may have written or sung. Obviously, the man cannot be easily divorced from his songs. But through the songs, Guthrie's image transcended the immediate situations in which they were written and even transcended his own death.

The songs of Woody Guthrie were sung after the man fell into the death grip of Huntington's disease. And the human drama behind these songs became as crucial a factor and as important a totalizing force as the songs themselves. The drama and romance behind Woody Guthrie's "bound for glory" life—the images of the hobo troubadour, heroically struggling through the Great Depression, persevering against all odds yet always maintaining his sense of humor and his political ideals until tragically cut down in the prime of his life by a mysterious disease—turned this little man with a guitar and a homespun philosophy into a folk hero in the American protest tradition.

Through his songs a man's life story was told, and the symbolism that adhered to that life-image became one of the important sources behind the rise of the folk protest totality in America. Guthrie's greatest disciple, Bob Dylan, would help turn the folk protest totality into the source of the 1960s counterculture.

1. John Lennon at the Statue of Liberty, October 1974. Photograph by Bob Gruen, Star File Photo Agency; used by permission.

2. John and Yoko at Newtopia press conference, announcing the establishment of a new conceptual country, Newtopia, April 1, 1973. Photograph by Bob Gruen, Star File Photo Agency; used by permission.

3. John and Yoko at Newtopia press conference, waving the "white flags of Newtopia" (facial tissues), April 1, 1973. Photograph by Bob Gruen, Star File Photo Agency; used by permission.

4. John and Yoko at U.S. Immigration Office, New York City, July 28, 1976. Photograph by Bob Gruen, Star File Photo Agency; used by permission.

Joseph Hillstrom

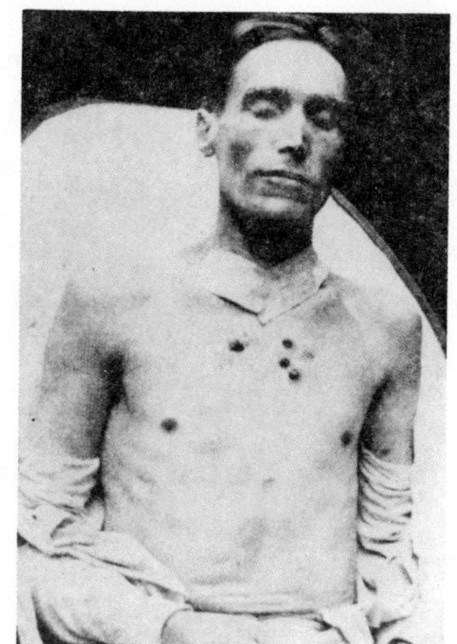

5. Joe Hill in handcuffs. Copied from an issue of the newspaper *Solidarity,* 1915. Archives of Labor and Urban Affairs, Wayne State University; used by permission.

6. Portrait of Joe Hill, 1915. Archives of Labor and Urban Affairs, Wayne State University; used by permission.

7. Post-mortem photograph of Joe Hill following his execution, November 19, 1915. Archives of Labor and Urban Affairs, Wayne State University; used by permission.

8. Cover of a memorial program for Joe Hill, c. 1916. Archives of Labor and Urban Affairs, Wayne State University; used by permission.

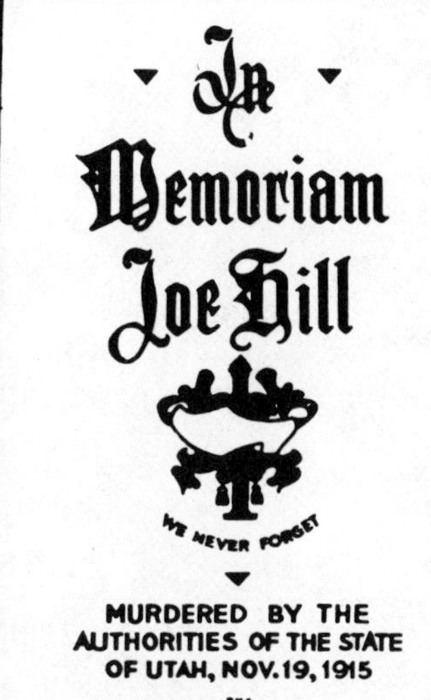

In
Memoriam
Joe Hill
We Never Forget
MURDERED BY THE
AUTHORITIES OF THE STATE
OF UTAH, NOV. 19, 1915

9. Joe Hill's funeral procession in Chicago, November 25, 1915. Archives of Labor and Urban Affairs, Wayne State University; used by permission.

10. Cartoon drawn by Joe Hill. Reproduced from the October 24, 1914, issue of *Solidarity.* Archives of Labor and Urban Affairs, Wayne State University; used by permission.

11. IWW stickerette, c. 1915. Archives of Labor and Urban Affairs, Wayne State University; used by permission.

12. Cover of the twenty-second edition of the "Little Red Songbook," 1926. Archives of Labor and Urban Affairs, Wayne State University; used by permission.

13. Woody Guthrie with Margaret Johnson, CBS radio show for Model Tobacco, 1940. Woody Guthrie Publications, Inc.; used by permission.

14. The Almanac Singers. Woody Guthrie Publications, Inc.; used by permission.

15. Woody Guthrie, Jean Ritchie, Fred Hellerman, and Pete Seeger. Woody Guthrie Publications, Inc.; used by permission.

16. Woody Guthrie and Cisco Houston, New York City, fall 1944. Photographer unknown, from the collection of Jackie Gibson Alper.

17. Woody Guthrie and Lilly May Ledford, New York City, c. 1945. Photographer unknown, from the collection of Jackie Gibson Alper.

18. Woody Guthrie with Lilly May Ledford and Alan Lomax, New York City, c. 1945. Photographer unknown, from the collection of Jackie Gibson Alper.

19. Bob Dylan at San Remo Coffee House, Schenectady, New York, January 13, 1962. Photograph by Joe Alper, from the collection of Jackie Gibson Alper.

20. Bob Dylan at San Remo Coffee House, Schenectady, New York, January 13, 1962. Photograph by Joe Alper, from the collection of Jackie Gibson Alper.

21. Bob Dylan at Gerde's Folk City, New York City, March 23, 1962. Photograph by Joe Alper, from the collection of Jackie Gibson Alper.

22. Bob Dylan with John Hammond, Sr., at Columbia Records recording session. Photograph by Joe Alper, from the collection of Jackie Gibson Alper.

23. Bob Dylan and Joan Baez at the Newport Folk Festival, July 1964. Photograph by Joe Alper, from the collection of Jackie Gibson Alper.

24. Bob Dylan at the Newport Folk Festival, July 1965. Photograph by Joe Alper, from the collection of Jackie Gibson Alper.

6 Bob Dylan: *The Mystery Tramp*

The answer, my friend, is blowin' in the wind.
—Bob Dylan, 1962

Sometime in the bitter cold of late January 1961, an aspiring young folk singer going by the name of Bob Dylan hitchhiked across country from Minnesota to New York City to visit his idol, Woody Guthrie, who lay dying in Greystone Park Hospital in Morristown, New Jersey.[1] It was to be a historic meeting. What Dylan would later describe as the "book of Man"[2] was symbolically passed on to the young singer as he sat at the feet of the dying master. Dylan would fill its pages with so many visions, dreams, flights of fancy, nightmares, and hallucinations that it would literally explode, revolutionizing the popular culture of America and the West.

Beginning as a Guthriesque folk-style performer, he took the folk protest genre to new and unimagined aesthetic heights before scandalizing the folk music community by publicly turning his back on the old topical-protest tradition and embracing the dreaded world of popular rock 'n' roll. But this was only the first of Dylan's many public shifts and image transformations. He would try his hand at nearly every form of American popular music—from folk to rock to country-western to gospel—and likewise cross the full spectrum of politics—from the utopian socialism and pacifism of Guthrie and company, to the radical anarchism and nihilistic existentialism of the rock counterculture, to the right-wing conservatism of Christian fundamentalism.

Bob Dylan's life story and artistic works are thus frustratingly complex, contradictory, and confusing.[3] And because he is still alive and changing daily, it is extremely difficult to summarize and analyze the politics of his songs and poetry. Moreover, he has been staggeringly prolific. In the more than twenty years of his career, he has produced thirty legitimate record albums, and countless bootlegged albums have been produced by pirates from out-takes, informal recording sessions, and concerts.[4] In addition, he has written a novel (*Tarantula*), several films (*Don't Look Back, Renaldo and Clara*), a film score (*Pat Garrett and Billy the Kid*), and an endless flow of poetry.[5] Perhaps more than any other popular artist in America, Bob Dylan came to embody the essence of the 1960s counterculture.

To date, the ever-changing Bob Dylan has given his fans at least six distinct public images: the Guthriesque balladeer (1960–63), the protest poet (1963–64), the punk rocker (1964–67), the moderate man (1967–70), the romantic (1970–78), and the born-again prophet (1979–83). While I have been working on this book, a seventh Bob Dylan has been emerging. Since the 1983 release of *Infidels,* Dylan's Christian fundamentalism has been slowly receding. The 1985 release of *Empire Burlesque* was a further affirmation of this secular trend. His participation in the 1984 "We Are the World" sessions and his appearance at the 1985 political telethons Live Aid and Farm Aid, as well as his participation in Artists United Against Apartheid's music video "Sun City," seem indicative of Dylan's return to protest.

Although protest themes appear throughout all of his works, only the first three phases were explicitly political. Thus I have examined in depth only these first three phases in an attempt to follow Dylan through the transition from the old-style protest of the Guthrie-Seeger era into the new youth-oriented protests of the 1960s counterculture. I then briefly outline Dylan's religiosity and attempt to incorporate his Christianity into the larger discussion of his mind guerrilla politics. Finally, I will offer my impressions on Dylan's most recent changes.

Guthriesque Balladeer, 1960–63

Bobby Zimmerman, who was born in 1941, became musically aware during the mid-1950s through exposure to a wide variety of musical forms, from hillbilly to rock 'n' roll. His first musical idol, when he was in the eighth grade, was country singer Hank Williams. But he was even more strongly influenced by black musical forms: the country blues of Blind Lemon Jefferson and Jesse Fuller; the urban blues of Muddy Waters, Howlin' Wolf, B.B. King, and Jimmy Reed; the gospel-spiritual tradition and its popular derivative, the rhythm and blues of Bo Diddly, Chuck Berry, Fats Domino, and Little Richard. In fact, young Zimmerman was so taken by Little Richard (his second idol) that, while still in junior high school, he had adopted his wild piano style. And in his teen years, Zimmerman got caught up in the first great wave of rock 'n' roll: Bill Haley and the Comets, Elvis Presley, and Buddy Holly.[6]

But it was the radical urban folk revival tradition of Pete Seeger, the Almanac Singers, the Weavers, and the cult of Woody Guthrie, which was popular on American college campuses during the late 1950s as an urbane alternative to the lewd and unintellectual black-based rock musical forms of the top ten, that would serve as Dylan's springboard into the heart of America's popular culture. The irony of this would not be fully appreciated until 1965, when Dylan returned to what he then claimed were his real roots, during the rock music revival brought about by the Beatles and the British invasion. With his discovery of Woody Guthrie, everything came into focus for young Zimmerman. The music, the style, the dress, the mannerisms, and the politics of Woody Guthrie crystallized into an image to emulate for a young man in search of an identity.[7]

From the time of his first trips from his home town of Hibbing, in Minnesota's north country, to the urban centers of Minneapolis and St. Paul, he had been gradually absorbing the culture of the folk revival, the accompanying social consciousness, and the bohemian lifestyle. During his brief stay at the University of Minnesota in the academic year 1959–60, he changed his name to Bob Dylan to disguise his middle-class Jewish background, began performing in folk clubs near the campus, and developed his Guthrie repertoire and image, complete with a mythical past as an orphan, circus hand, hobo and rambler, and encounters with Woody Guthrie. In a typical jive reminiscence, he told a friend: "I was with a carnival when I was about thirteen, and I used to travel with the carnival. All kinds of shows and things. We went all around the Midwest. Gallup and . . . Lasco, Texas, down there. Was a roustabout. And sang around a lot. I didn't sing very much, but I learned a lot of songs in that carnival. A lot of songs people are singing today, I learned those songs in the carnival. That's why I know all these songs I know today." And in an early interview with journalist Studs Terkel, in Chicago, Dylan said: "I saw Woody once, a long, long time ago, in Burbank, California. I was just a little boy. I don't even remember seeing him. I heard him play.

Must have been about ten. My uncle took me there. It stuck in my mind that he was Woody, and everybody else around me was just everybody else."[8]

Thus by 1960, Bobby Zimmerman, a Jewish college student from a small town near the Canadian border in Minnesota, had concocted for himself a completely new, fictitious persona, in the image of Woody Guthrie. He had begun to dress like a 1930s Okie in baggy trousers and work shirts (like Henry Fonda in the *Grapes of Wrath*), and he was particularly proud of his wiry hair, which, when left to grow, resembled the raggedy curls of Woody Guthrie.[9] He frantically searched the campus for a copy of Guthrie's autobiography, *Bound for Glory,* which he greedily devoured in a single afternoon, and then excitedly pursued his friends, reading them passages as if he were quoting from a holy text. He then listened spellbound to all the old Guthrie recordings he could get his hands on, playing them over and over, driving his friends crazy with his Guthrie zeal. He became obsessed with Woody Guthrie and the dream of making a name for himself as a folk singer in the image of his fallen hero.[10]

As his obsession grew, a powerful yearning to meet and talk with Guthrie filled young Dylan. From reading back issues of *Sing Out!* magazine, he learned that Woody was in Greystone Hospital in New Jersey, and he called the hospital but was told that Woody was too sick to come to the phone, although he was allowed to have visitors. It was then he decided to visit Woody Guthrie.[11]

Talking New York

Upon his arrival in New York City, Bob Dylan, like Woody Guthrie twenty years earlier, found his way to Greenwich Village and the folk clubs, bars, and coffee houses. He performed some at the Cafe Wha?, but mostly just hung out, spending nights at the homes of strangers he met in the bars and bumming his meals. After a few days, he thumbed his way to Greystone to visit Guthrie. He immediately sent a postcard back to some of his friends in Minnesota, full of the joy of the pilgrim: "I know Woody. I know Woody . . . I know him and met him and saw him and sang to him. I know Woody . . . Goddamn!"[12]

He began to visit the hospital regularly, hitchhiking out from the city, sometimes as often as four times a week. In another postcard in early February, he wrote: "Woody likes me—he tells me to sing for him—he's the greatest holiest godliest one in the world." And Woody seemed to have taken to him; he started to ask for him: "Is the boy coming today? When is the boy coming back?"[13] A special bond seemed to form between them.

Soon Dylan became a regular at the home of the Gleasons, a family in East Orange, New Jersey, and Guthrie fans from the 1930s, who were keeping Woody in their home on weekends. There the eager young Dylan came into contact with New York City's folk aristocracy, artists like Pete Seeger, Cisco Houston, and Ramblin' Jack Elliot, who congregated at the Gleasons' ritualistically to pay homage to their dying mentor.[14]

After winning Guthrie's confidence, Dylan began to penetrate the Village folk scene. First, he participated in the regular Monday night "hoots" at Gerde's Folk City, and by April he was beginning his first major professional engagement there as the second act behind bluesman John Lee Hooker. Fully aware of the symbolic implications, he wore one of Guthrie's old suits at his debut. Throughout the summer of 1961, he performed in various folk clubs: the Commons, the Gaslight, the Wha?, the Limelight, and the Lion's Head.[15]

In September, he was favorably reviewed by *New York Times* music critic Robert Shelton, and, as a result, he came to the attention of record producer John Hammond, who quickly signed him with Columbia Records. In November, after less than a year in New York, he gave his first formal concert to fifty-three people in Carnegie Recital Hall. Though not an overwhelming success, he had, against all odds, emerged from obscurity to become one of the better-known folk acts under contract with a major record company.[16] Woody Guthrie had never recorded under such a prestigious label. Within less than a year, the student was about to surpass the teacher.

By now Dylan was writing his own material. An unprecedented flood of original songs began to pour from his pen. In a WBAI-FM interview in September 1961, Pete Seeger paid tribute to Dylan's unbelievable songwriting capacity: "Of all the people I've heard in America, he seems to be the most prolific. . . . Bob, do you make up a song before breakfast every day or before supper?" And Dylan, with uncharacteristic humility, replied: "Nah. I don't make up a song like that. In fact, sometimes I could go about two weeks without makin' up songs." "I don't believe you!" Seeger interrupted. Dylan continued:

Oh yea. But then sometimes—well, these are the songs I sing—I might go about two weeks in making' 'em up. I write a lot of stuff, matter a fact I wrote five songs last night [laughter]. But I gave all the papers away. . . . It was in a place called the Bitter End. . . . Some were just about what was happenin' on the stage. . . . I would never sing them anyplace. They were just for myself and some other people. . . .

But I don't sit around . . . with newspapers like a lot of people do . . . and pick something out to write a song about. It's usually right there in my head before I start. That's the way I write, I mean, it might be a bad approach. But I don't even consider it . . . writing songs . . . I just figure that I made it up, or got it someplace. The song was there before me . . . I just sorta came down and . . . took it down with a pencil. But it was all there before I came around. That's the way I feel about it.[17]

Dylan was advocating a nonrational, inspirational approach to songwriting that must have seemed foreign to his peers in the topical songwriting community. Even at this early stage, Dylan seemed to stand out in the topical folk music crowd. His songs from this period include "Hard Times in New York Town," an attempt, similar to Guthrie's "New York Town" (1940), to capture the mood of the big city upon his arrival; "Talking John Birch Society Paranoid Blues," a heavy satire on the red-baiting, anticommunist hysteria that was still prevalent in America; "Baby, I'm in the Mood For You," a tribute to hot teenage lust; "Walking Down the Line," a Guthriesque hobo song; and "Talking Bear Mountain Picnic Massacre Disaster Blues," which demonstrates Dylan's intuitive grasp of Guthrie's talking blues style. It is an exceptionally funny spoof, based on a news account of a tour boat picnic, hastily organized to take advantage of New York tourists. It seems that more tickets were sold than the boat could accommodate. Dylan puts himself (and his fictitious wife and children) in among the six thousand people fighting to get on board as the boat begins to sink. After losing track of his family, he is trampled upon, beaten upon, and left for dead. Understandably, he loses his "picnic spirit." In a final verse, he cuts loose with a humorous, socially conscious moral, reminiscent of Guthrie's best topical comedy in "Talking Dust" or "Talking Columbia." Dylan ruthlessly attacks the unscrupulous businessmen who make their living by exploiting unsuspecting consumers with gimmicks designed to steal their money. His solution to the problem is to put some of these people on a boat and send them to Bear Mountain for a picnic.[18] The words are Bob Dylan's, but the style is that of Woody Guthrie.

At the end of November 1961, Dylan went into Columbia's New York studios to record his first album. He performed alone, with just a harmonica in a wire holder around his neck and his acoustic guitar. The record was released at the end of February 1962; it cost Columbia only $402. It was not a great commercial success, selling five thousand copies in the first year, but it did establish his credentials as a folk virtuoso and song stylist.[19]

Even after more than twenty years of vast changes in popular music, this album remains powerful and exciting. The folk music community had never witnessed such superb renditions of traditional, folk-style material. One is struck immediately by the tremendous energy of the performances, the hard-driving blues guitar style, backed by powerful harmonica riffs. And the voice of this twenty-one-year-old unknown is equally striking and powerful. It is the raspy, gutteral, strained-to-the-limit vocal style of an aged black bluesman. The overall performance is loose, open, sometimes frenzied, but with an impeccable sense of timing, emphasis, and articulation. His performance was miles above those of his contemporaries in the folk field and a striking contrast to his other folk albums in which, to remain in the folk fold, he was forced to tone down his style.

The album *Bob Dylan* is a collection of the best of the folk repertoire he had been performing in the folk clubs over the past several years: his own special treatments of folk standards, "Man of Constant Sorrow," "Pretty Peggy-O," and Dave Van Ronk's version of "House of the Rising Sun." But the meat of the album is Dylanized renditions of some classic gospel and blues numbers from old-time country blues greats: Jesse Fuller's "You're No Good," Bukka White's "Fixin' to Die," and Blind Lemon Jefferson's "See That My Grave Is Kept Clean."[20]

Although black blues may be the strongest musical forms presented in this album, I believe it may be best understood as the fruition of Dylan's obsession with Woody Guthrie. The preoccupation with the romance of death and dying in "In My Time of Dyin'," "Fixin' to Die," and "See That My Grave Is Kept Clean"—and more subtly in "Man of Constant Sorrow" ("I'm a-bound to ride that mornin' railroad, perhaps I'll die on that train"), "Gospel Plow" ("All them prophets are dead and gone"), "Pretty Peggy-O" ("Our Captain, he is dead"), "Highway 51" ("Won't you bury my body out on Highway 51")—may reflect Dylan's subconscious empathy with his dying hero.[21] In songs like "Highway 51" and "Freight Train Blues" there is a much more consciously Guthriesque fixation on highway and railroad themes and the hard-traveling hobo mystique that was identified with Woody Guthrie. Dylan's attempts to manufacture a fictitious hobo background and his various hitchhiking trips back and forth from Minnesota to New York were also part of this attempt to step into Guthrie's ramblin' shoes. In the beginning, hobo and Wobbly songs were also part of Dylan's imaginary role-playing and stage character.[22]

Nowhere is Dylan's attempt to emulate Guthrie more obvious than in the only two original songs of his first album. Both come directly from the rich Guthrie treasury. In "Talking New York," Dylan used Guthrie's talking blues style with finesse in an autobiographical account of his arrival in New York in 1960. More polished and satirical than "Hard Times in New York Town," which Dylan never recorded, it is similar in its picture of New York as cold and uninviting. It is clearly related to another of Guthrie's New York songs from the 1940s, "Talking Subway." Dylan even lifted a line ("I swung onto my old guitar") directly from Guthrie.[23]

According to Dylan's song, he was not received as well as Guthrie had been when he rambled into New York in 1940, offering us a keen insight into the direction the folk song revival had evolved since Guthrie's day. The man at the coffee house where Dylan was playing told him to come back some other day: "You sound like a hillbilly; we want folksingers here." After this initial setback, he got a job playing harmonica, and although the boss said he loved Dylan's sound, it was worth only a dollar a day. But after "weeks and weeks of hangin' around," he finally got a big-time job (a reference to his Gerde's engagement). He was making good money and even joined the musicians' union.[24]

But still Dylan was bitter about his unappreciative reception. So he dropped a few more lines from the Guthrie scripture, to express his frustration, saying that "a very great man" (Guthrie) had once said that "some people rob you with a fountain pen."[25] Dylan goes on to say, "It didn't take too long to find out just what he was talkin' about."[26] He felt he was being robbed by critics and exploited by enterpreneurs.

It seems clear that Dylan did not respond well to the New York cultural climate during the first few months of his stay there. He seemed to feel rejected, having expected a much better reception. So, in frustration, he "rambled out of New York Town," pulled his cap down over his eyes, and headed west, singing: "So long New York, Howdy, East Orange."[27] He wanted no more of the big city, and he needed to spend more time at the Gleasons' communing with the master.

Then late one night, after one of these holy visits, legend has it that Dylan sat down to write his famous tribute to the master: "Song to Woody."[28] In *Sing Out!* he relates the tale:

It was written in the 1960th winter . . . in New York City in the drug store on 8th street. It was on one of them freezing days that I came back from Sid and Bob Gleason's in East Orange, New Jersey. . . . Woody was there and it was a February Sunday night. . . . And I just thought about Woody, I wondered about him, thought harder and wondered harder. . . . I wrote this song in five minutes . . . it's all I got to say. . . . If you know anything at all about Woody then you'll know what I'm a trying to say. . . . If you don't know anything about Woody, then find out.[29]

Again, the song is vintage Guthrie, written to the tune of "The 1913 Massacre." Dylan says he is a thousand miles from home, trying to experience Guthrie's world of the road: "I'm a-seein' your world of people and things, your paupers and peasants and princes and kings." But Guthrie's world seems to be dying, as Guthrie is, when, in fact, it has hardly been born. Dylan senses a new world coming. After paying tribute to his hero and "all the good people" who traveled with him, such as Cisco Houston, Sonny Terry, and Huddie Leadbetter, Dylan rambles on down the road—his road—saying, with a tone of sacrilege: "The very last thing that I'd want to do is to say I've been hittin' some hard travelin' too."[30]

This song is much more than a sentimental idolization of Woody Guthrie. While acknowledging his debt to this great balladeer, Dylan is taking his leave from the Guthrie mystique. He does not intend to be a mere Guthrie imitator—another Jack Elliot. Dylan intends to follow his own road from now on.[31] But disentangling himself from the grip of the Guthrie mystique would prove more difficult than a song.

Protest Poet, 1963–64

After the release of *Bob Dylan* early in 1962, the star syndrome began to descend upon young Dylan, eventually bursting the Guthrie mold to reveal a sensitive yet compelling, socially concerned artist. He would take the social protest genre to unimagined aesthetic heights and in the process become the spokesman for the rising tide of the youth rebellion in America and the West.[32] Dylan moved into the forefront of the topical-protest song movement at precisely the moment that the 1960s youth-student movement was separating itself from the older generation of American radicalism. This group was moving beyond the traditional socialist concerns for the working poor and the faith in the revolutionary potential of the working class. The salient issues now centered around two major concerns: black civil rights, the antisegregation movement, and the accompanying problem of white racist reactionary terrorism in the South; and the Cold War, the arms race, and the ever-present danger of nuclear holocaust. Furthermore, the working class no longer seemed capable of revolution, having grown soft and conservative. The revolutionary potential now seemed to be centered in the concerned youth, as revealed in the dramatic rise of student radicalism and campus revolts and radical organizations such as Students for a Democratic Society.[33]

Carl Oglesby, onetime president and radical theoretician of the SDS, assessed the place of Dylan's music in the rise of the New Left:

> Dylan's early songs appeared so promptly as to seem absolutely contemporary with the civil rights movement. There was no time lag. He wasn't a songwriter who came into an established political mood, he seemed to be a part of it and his songs seemed informative to the Movement as the Movement seemed informative to the song writer. This cross-fertilization was absolutely critical in Dylan's relationship to the Movement and the Movement's relationship to Dylan. He gave character to the sensibilities of the Movement.[34]

As the Cold War reached its terrifying crescendo in the Cuban missle crisis of the fall of 1962, the black civil rights movement was thrust into America's consciousness with the first sit-ins and mass demonstrations in the South, and the first American combat troops were quietly moving into South Vietnam, Bob Dylan unleashed a string of the most powerful and influential songs in the history of American social protest music. He would shatter forever the mold of Guthrie's sentimental idealism with unprecedented anger and vengeance, bitter youthful righteousness, and dark, dystopic visions of Armageddon.

Broadside Ballads

Dylan's protest phase was concurrent with, and thus partly facilitated by, the creation of a new forum for topical-protest songs—a monthly mimeographed radical song sheet published in the Greenwich Village apartment of Old Left activists and former Almanac Singers Gordon Friesen and Agnes Cunningham. They called the publication *Broadside,* and in it Dylan published his first protest songs. The first issue of *Broadside* appeared in February 1962 and featured Dylan's "Talking John Birch Society Paranoid Blues."[35]

Dylan quickly distinguished himself from the other young *Broadside* balladeers, including Tom Paxton, Phil Ochs, Peter La Farge, Mark Spoelstra, and Eric Anderson, who came to be known collectively as "Woody's children."[36] Dylan's songs easily dominated the early issues. Having found a market for political protest songs, he quickly churned them out. Some of his more memorable songs included "I Will Not Go Down under the Ground," expressing his refusal to give in to nuclear terror; "The Death of Emmet Till," the shocking true story of a young black boy from Chicago brutally murdered by the white terror machine in Mississippi in 1955; and "John Brown," about a young man who is sent off to war to the delight of his proud mother and later returns shattered and crippled to present his medals to his horrified mom.[37]

Freewheelin'

From 1962 to 1964, *Broadside* published twenty-three of Bob Dylan's songs and poems, far more than it published of any other protest writer, with the notable exception of Phil Ochs. Some of Dylan's better (and least controversial) *Broadside* ballads found their way onto his two major Columbia recordings of this period: *The Freewheelin' Bob Dylan* (May 1963) and *The Times They Are A-Changin'* (January 1964).[38] These songs became the classic statements of protest of the 1960s. These two discs featured such standards as "Blowin' in the Wind," which became a civil rights anthem second only to "We Shall Overcome"; "Masters of War," Dylan's vicious attack on American militarism; "A Hard Rain's A-Gonna Fall," a dark and mysterious eschatological fantasy, inspired by the nuclear brinkmanship of the Cuban missle crisis; "Talking World War III Blues," a lighthearted farce, likewise inspired by Cold War politics, in the form of a dream about being left alive after a nuclear holocaust; "Oxford Town," about James Meredith's attempt to break the color barrier at the University of Mississippi in 1962; "The Times They Are A-Changing' " and "When the Ship Comes In," prophecies of the coming youth revolution; "With God on Our Side," exposing the hypocrisy of those who use religion to justify violence and war; "The Ballad of

Hollis Brown" and "North Country Blues," portraits of poor people beaten down by the system; "Only a Pawn in Their Game," a comment on the murder of black activist Medgar Evers, pitying the murderer as a victim of the same racist system that killed Evers; and "The Lonesome Death of Hattie Caroll," a hauntingly poignant ballad about the senseless murder of a Negro maid by an aristocratic socialite named William Zantzinger, who attacked the maid with his cane because she was too slow bringing him his drink.[39]

Thus in 1963 and 1964, Bob Dylan led the surge of folk protest into the popular mainstream of American culture, breaking all the rules of the folk idiom in the process. Never before had songs of such stark political intensity reached into the realm of popular culture.[40] Some of the activists were shocked by the poetic vagueness and overt mysticism of his apocalyptic visions in "Hard Rain" and "When the Ship Comes In." Others were stunned by the brilliance of his understated protests, as in "Hollis Brown" and the "Lonesome Death of Hattie Carroll."[41] The times had changed and America was hungry for a voice of protest, and Dylan was just as hungry to rise to the challenge. This politicization of popular music was to be his major contribution to the generation of the 1960s.

Blowin' in the Wind

Bob Dylan had not yet completely disentangled himself from Woody Guthrie's influence. Many of his protest songs still exude Guthrie's idealism, particularly the *Broadside* ballads, as opposed to those he recorded for Columbia. In "Let Me Die in My Footsteps," for example, we find more of Guthrie's lines (from "Pastures of Plenty" again) and a large dose of Guthrie's sentimental nationalism: "Let every state in this union seep down in your souls." And in "Emmett Till" Dylan even flirts with Guthrie's utopian unionism, saying that "this song is just a reminder" to his "fellow man" that the "ghost-robed Ku Klux Klan" is still in existence. He resolves the song in typical Guthriesque fashion, asserting that "if all us folks that thinks alike" could get together, "we could make this great land of ours a greater place to live."[42]

Guthrie's politics is particularly evident in Dylan's most famous protest song, "Blowin' in the Wind." Its theme appears to have been taken (probably subconsciously) from a passage in *Bound for Glory* in which Guthrie compares his mind guerrilla cause to the newspapers blowing in the winds of the New York City streets and alleys. The passage stands out aesthetically, rhetorically, and politically, and it obviously struck a chord deep within young Bob Dylan as he read and reread the book.[43]

When the song first appeared in the pages of *Sing Out!* in the fall of 1962, Dylan explained its meaning:

> There ain't too much I can say about this song except that the answer is blowing in the wind. It ain't in no book or movie or T.V. show or discussion group. Man, it's in the wind—and it's blowing in the wind. Too many of these hip people are telling me where the answer is but oh I won't believe that. I still say it's in the wind and just like a restless piece of paper it's got to come down sometime. . . . But the only trouble is that no one picks up the answer when it comes down so not too many people get to see and know it . . . and then it flies away again.[44]

Dylan, in his own inarticulate fashion, is merely paraphrasing Guthrie here.

But although thematically this song may belong to Guthrie, the poetic form and flair are Bob Dylan's. The song asks nine questions about several of the most important social concerns of the time: racism and social injustice ("how many roads must a man walk down, before you call him a man?"), war and violence ("how many times must the cannon balls fly, before they're forever banned?"), false consciousness ("how many times must a man look up, before he can see the sky?"), political apathy ("how many times can a man turn his head, pretending he just doesn't see?"), and the possibility of social change ("how many years can a mountain exist, before it is washed to the sea?"). All of these concerns are answered with the simple refrain: "The answer, my friend, is blowin' in the wind, the answer is blowin' in the wind."[45]

This enormously popular song, perhaps more than any other, pushed the genre of protest not only beyond the confines of esoteric labor and left-wing circles and into the public domain or mass consciousness, but also beyond the limits of the topical-ideological propaganda song and into the realm of serious art. What Dylan lost in political rhetoric, he gained in public recognition.

Whatcha Gonna Do?

Bob Dylan's politics departs from Woody Guthrie's in the realm of religiosity.[46] Whereas in songs like "Jesus Christ," "Good Old Union Feeling," and "Union's My Religion," Guthrie proletarianized his childhood Christian fundamentalism, Dylan, in songs like "With God on Our Side," "When the Ship Comes In," "I'd Hate to Be You on That Dreadful Day," and "Quit Your

Low Down Ways," Christianizes his radicalism. And whereas Guthrie, in the tradition of the Wobblies, turned religious songs into labor hymns, Dylan produced a hybrid that might be called "gospel protest." In "I'd Hate to Be You on That Dreadful Day" and "Whatcha Gonna Do (When the Shadow Comes under Your Door)," Dylan unleashes the revenge of judgment on those who transgress against their worldly brothers.[47]

Even when the political message is not exclusively housed in a religious vehicle, virtually all of Dylan's protest songs are rich in biblical symbolism and Christian metaphors. In "Blowin' in the Wind" it appears to be Noah's dove that is seeking the sand. In "Masters of War," the warlords are compared to "Judas of old" and are so despicable that "even Jesus" would not forgive them for what they do. In "Talking World War III Blues," Dylan tries to play Adam and Eve with an unwilling young girl, and in "When the Ship Comes In," he compares his defeated foes to the armies of the Pharaoh and to Goliath.[48] Finally, in one of his earliest though little-known protest songs, "Long Ago, Far Away," Dylan uses the life of Christ, who is portrayed as one "they hung on a cross" for preaching peace and brotherhood, to illustrate his point that the inequities and injustices of the past are still with us.[49]

It would be more than twenty years before Dylan's followers would fully appreciate the significance of such songs. Religious concerns were always fundamental to Bob Dylan's utopian sensibilities. Guthrie's utopianism had been a function of his romanticized native class-consciousness, but Dylan's utopianism (as well as his dystopianism) was basically a function of his Judeo-Christian ethics. And herein lies the major difference between Guthrie and his famous disciple: whereas Woody's radicalism took the form of utopian socialism, Dylan's was a nonpolitical Christian-based moralism.

But another side of Dylan's political character was revealed early in this protest phase, taking him in directions Guthrie would never have imagined. As would soon be confirmed in Dylan's punk rock phase, Guthrie's idealism and Christian moralism are but undercurrents in the mainstream of Dylan's juvenile delinquent persona. In "Bob Dylan's Blues," for example, through a sardonic wit, certain un-Christian attitudes come to the surface as Dylan instructs those who wanted to be like him to "pull out your six-shooter and rob every bank you see." He advises them, if caught, to "tell the judge I said it was all right."[50] Dylan playfully, but with violent overtones, rips open the wounds of a new generation gap.

Some of his attacks on the older generation were much less playful and equally violent. Perhaps the most powerful theme is that of nuclear holocaust. There is a "hard rain" in the winds, and the people are being fooled into thinking God is on the side of this terror. Dylan holds the older generation responsible for the impending doom. To the "Masters of War" who hold us all hostage, Dylan vents his anger with a devastating hatred that seem almost to contradict his pacifistic premises. He vehemently condemns them as cowards, who "fasten the triggers for the others to fire" and then hide in their mansions "while young people's blood runs out of their bodies and into the mud." He reminds them that, in the end, all their money will not buy back their souls. He hopes they will die soon and pledges to follow their caskets and watch while their bodies are lowered into the ground to make sure they are dead.[51] Never before had a protest songwriter denounced war so vehemently.

Thus even during his early protest phase, this seemingly idealistic and socially committed young man was expressing very different political views from those of Guthrie's generation. Dylan was sowing the seeds of youthful anger and rebellion that promised to change the times.

The Poet as Activist

Dylan's protest consciousness should not be seen as mere moral posturing. Although Dylan was perceived by many as an opportunist capitalizing on the popularity of folk-protest music to further his career goals, this criticism is almost certainly unfair because Dylan himself was largely responsible for the current popularity of protest music.[52] His social consciousness was genuine.[53] He was sincerely concerned about the arms race and nuclear terror even though he indicated his concern in terms of salvation and judgment rather than secular, proletarian revolution. He was also sincere in his concern for racial justice in America, even though his protests against racism and white terrorism were sometimes expressed in an eclectic manner, as exemplified by "Only a Pawn in Their Game." He had always held blacks in awe and had great respect for Negro music. Moreover, the Negro was a potent symbol of oppression for Dylan.

His social consciousness led Dylan into his only period of serious political activism. In July 1963, he flew to Greenwood, Mississippi, to join Pete Seeger and other northern protest singers in a benefit concert sponsored by the black activist organization Student Non-Violent Coordinating Committee and to assist in a voter registration drive. While Dylan performed to the crowd of about 250 (mostly blacks and a few white newspaper reporters), carloads of angry whites circled the block menacingly.[54]

Then, on August 28, Dylan joined Joan Baez, Peter, Paul, and Mary, Mahalia Jackson, Harry Belafonte, and others at the nation's capitol to entertain and inspire the two hundred thousand protesters of southern segregation at the March on Washington.[55] Dylan sang "Masters of War," "Only a Pawn,"[56] and a few more of his new protest songs. Joan Baez got the entire crowd to sing "We Shall Overcome," and Peter, Paul, and Mary led a mass singing of "Blowin' in the Wind." But it was Martin Luther King, Jr., who captured the message in the winds in his famous "I have a dream" speech. That night the winds blew optimism, but this dream would soon shatter in a wave of public assassinations, urban riots, and national despair.

The Dylan Mystique

Within the year 1963, the Dylan mystique blossomed suddenly and dramatically, breaking out of the confines of the Greenwich Village coffee house scene to reach deep into the national consciousness and to burst forever the Woody Guthrie mold.[57] Dylan quickly and unexpectedly became a classic prophet-hero: a popular seer, inspired with genius, the source of revealed truths, one whose visions take us beyond the facade of reality, Carlyle's "light which enlightens."[58] He had seen through the "masks" of the masters of war, he had seen the horrible and distorted visions of the "hard rain" that was coming, he had realized that the racist assassins were but "pawns" in the game of white terrorism, and he had insisted that the answers to all these problems were blowing in the "wind." And the youth of the West, yearning for a messiah to deliver them from the malaise of life in the nuclear age, turned to Dylan in droves and with unbounded enthusiasm.

Bob Dylan was the first truly popular artist in America to exhibit a social consciousness. He was the first public figure to bring the youth culture a message that went beyond the traditional preoccupation with the boy-meets-girl scenario. His impact on the popular culture of the 1960s is incalculable. Other major pop artists, including John Lennon, were profoundly affected by the scruffy little poet with a guitar. Lennon spent hours listening to Dylan's albums over and over and, inspired by Dylan, would lead the Beatles and the rock community generally in new and more socially concerned directions. Lennon always included Dylan among his major influences.[59]

During the year 1963, Bob Dylan came to be accepted as the spokesman for his peers and his generation. This messiah of protest politicized the popular culture and youthful generation of the 1960s. The effects would reverberate throughout the world in the following decades.[60]

He held his first major concert in New York City's Town Hall on April 12,1963, unleashing a string of powerful protest songs— "Hollis Brown," "Who Killed Davy Moore?" "John Brown," "Hard Rain"—to a stunned audience.[61] To close the concert, he recited a long poem, "Last Thoughts on Woody Guthrie," which seemed to release him from the grip of Woody Guthrie, while acknowledging Guthrie as one of the two influences behind Dylan's mind guerrilla quest for hope. For Bob Dylan, the protest poet, there are only two kinds of roads, two kinds of windows, two kinds of hallways, and two kinds of doors. He states his position here explicitly: "You can either go to the church of your choice" or "to Brooklyn State Hospital." It is either Christ or Woody Guthrie, and, in Dylan's opinion, both emanate from the same source: "You'll find them both in the Grand Canyon at sundown."[62]

Dylan's protests and prophecies were inspired by Christ's morality and Guthrie's idealism. And, although Dylan soon dramatically rejected both, to move beyond hero-worship and religion into the egoism of the star syndrome, this too would be but another phase. And, in the end, Dylan would see the error of his ways and return to working-class idealism and Christian ethics.

Dylan's second album, *The Freewheelin' Bob Dylan,* was released in May 1963. It was a stunning success, selling more than two hundred thousand copies by July.[63] Peter, Paul, and Mary soon recorded two songs from the album ("Blowin' in the Wind" and "Don't Think Twice") as a single, which quickly became the most commercially successful protest single ever released.[64]

On May 12, Dylan was scheduled to appear on the "Ed Sullivan Show," the TV program that had launched the careers of Elvis Presley and the Beatles. But after the CBS decision to censor "Talking John Birch," he refused to appear, a decision Elvis Presley or even John Lennon would have had a hard time understanding. That he would turn down a chance at national television exposure on principle is a good indication of the heroic dimensions to which his social consciousness would lead him.[65]

Later in May he joined Joan Baez at the Monterey Folk Festival in California. Baez fell in love with Dylan and his songs. She took him under her wing, becoming perhaps his most important promoter during this period, recording and performing his songs and taking him on tour with her as her special guest, introducing him to the nation's college campuses and the concerned youth of America. At the Newport Folk Festival at the end of July, Dylan and Baez were the main attractions: the crown prince and princess of folk protest.[66]

When Dylan left Newport, a cult was forming around him. He had become a major figure in the popular consciousness of the Left, a cultural leader and prophet in the rising tide of youth rebellion. He capped off the year with a sellout concert at Carnegie Hall to a tremendously enthusiastic crowd. After the concert, he was mobbed by frenzied, screaming fans. The fame had come suddenly and was overwhelming. He was deathly afraid of being crushed to death by the mobs of fans or smothered by the image of protest poet. Almost immediately he began to retreat from the pressures of the popular prophet mystique.[67]

His last protest album, *The Times They are A-Changin',* was released in January 1964, in the aftermath of the Kennedy assassination,[68] which seemed to make protest idealism futile. Lee Harvey Oswald had also assassinated hope, leaving only cynicism and despair. Dylan quickly lost interest in politics, leaving the realm of active protest forever. He abandoned his Greenwich Village apartment and moved to the serenity and security of the home of his manager, Albert Grossman, in Bearsville, near Woodstock, in upstate New York.[69] In the last song on this album, "Restless Farewell," he bids farewell to movement politics and the protest community. It was too confining. The expectations of fans and critics were too great and burdensome. He was changing so rapidly now that the protest poet image could no longer contain Bob Dylan, and, like the Guthrie image, it too exploded as yet another Bob Dylan began to form.

Punk Rocker, 1964–66

The third Bob Dylan wore the mask of the hip hero and the angry young man. Turning to the revolutionary new medium of rock music, he sent shock waves deep into the heart of the 1960s popular culture, and, although he typically disavowed the titles, he emerged as a teen idol and the cultural leader of what came to be known as the Woodstock Nation: the rebellious hordes of draft-card-burning, antiestablishment students and flower-power, drug-happy hippies and yippies.[70] This would be the most politically influential and commercially successful of Bob Dylan's six phases.

Fame had brought Dylan a self-confidence and an arrogance that assured him he could do no wrong. He became even more daring and innovative artistically and politically, breaking down all barriers, flaunting all conventions and norms, searching for the source of his creative powers: his *real* self, the self beneath the social influences that surrounded him and trapped him within the prison of society. Indeed, the major theme of this period, from *Another Side of Bob Dylan* to *Blonde on Blonde*, is that of personal freedom: the worship of the (transcendental) ego.[71]

But fame had also brought unbearable responsibilities, for it had come through the image of commitment to the cause of social justice. He was now looked to for solutions to all the problems of society in the thermonuclear age. But he had come to realize that there were no answers, at least not in the Old Left—organized protest—tradition. After all, he had only said that the answers were in the wind, implying a great mystery. And the weight of the deep-seated contradiction between the dogma of involvement and the hopelessness of the realities of power became too much for him to bear.

Dylan rejected political involvement in favor of political apathy and radical anarchy. He rejected commitment and cause and sought the inner power of the self, feeling that, in the end, collective egoism and apathy could undermine (or at least weaken) the foundations of social order by withdrawing its popular supports. Dylan's break with society was decisive and complete, and it occurred on several separate levels simultaneously. He rejected not only the established authorities ("the Masters of War"), but also the old-style radicalism (of "Maggie's Farm") that he had come to represent (the *Sing Out!/Broadside*–topical song tradition and the cult of Woody Guthrie). And, in the extremes of his existential binge, he rejected as artificial all social relationships.

In the long run, it was the dark, cynical, revengeful side of Bob Dylan that emerged. Existential soul-searching turned in to paranoia. And in a series of hate-filled, vicious song poems and visions, often using the "love-gone-sour" metaphor, Dylan made his break with social consciousness and political commitment. Asserting the full fury of his brutal poetic daggers, he thrust deeply into the popular consciousness of American (and Western) youth, reflecting symbolically the anger of a new generation of social protest.

The Tom Paine Award Dinner

The first public indication of Dylan's loss of faith came in the wake of the Kennedy assassination on November 22, 1963, and the sense of hopelessness and despair that swept the nation—and Bob Dylan—at that time. A few weeks after the assassination, Dylan spoke at a dinner before the Emergency Civil Liberties Committee, a prominent civil rights organization, in acceptance of its prestigious Tom Paine Award for his work in the desegregation movement.[72]

In his acceptance speech he quickly revealed his hostility and resentment toward this old-fashioned, establishment, black-tie-and-furs audience. His remarks became increasingly insulting, and the audience became uncomfortable. Then, carelessly touching a sensitive nerve, he compared himself to Kennedy's assassin, saying he could understand Oswald's motives, although he could never condone his actions. Dylan had clearly chosen a poor example to illustrate the frustration of the youth culture of America in the face of the entrenchment of the establishment. His hosts were outraged and offended.[73] Unknowingly, Dylan had symbolically drawn what would become the major social battle lines of the 1960s: between the old and the young, between the old and new approaches, not only to politics but to life itself. The old could no longer dictate to the young, for, indeed, the times were changing, and the old had to step aside as the age of youth began.

First English Tour

Even before the release of his last protest album, *The Times They Are A-Changin',* in January 1964, Dylan had become thoroughly disillusioned with the politics of the Old Left and the artistic restraints of the topical-folk idiom. That spring he left for his first concert tour of England. There he came face to face with the rock 'n' roll revival. He was quickly coming under the spell of the revolutionary new developments occurring in the field of popular music, being generated primarily by British groups, especially the Beatles and the Rolling Stones. In anticipation of "folk-rock," Eric Burdon and the Animals had just released a rock version of an old folk standard, "The House of the Rising Sun," which Dylan had recorded on his first album.[74] Dylan was overwhelmed by the excitement of it all.

He spent an evening with John Lennon and Paul McCartney and reportedly introduced them to marijuana, a drug that was to become the symbol of the rising tide of youth rebellion.[75] Dylan's influence would ultimately push the Beatles in a new artistic direction, away from the light pop of "I Wanta Hold Your Hand" and toward more serious compositions, like "Nowhere Man" and "The Fool on the Hill." But their impact on him would be far more dramatic.

Another Side of Bob Dylan

In the summer of 1964, at the Newport Folk Festival, Dylan took the topical-folk establishment by surprise by performing his new nonprotest material, mostly bitter songs of love gone sour. The young people in the audience were captivated by the new Dylan, who seemed to be expressing their own pain, but the professional upholders of the topical tradition were appalled. Reviewers of the festival in *Sing Out!* and *Broadside* accused him of selling out to commercialism.[76]

In August, he released *Another Side of Bob Dylan,* which confirmed his new direction.[77] Gone were the songs of social significance. To the new Bob Dylan, social criticism was a waste of time. During this period, in a conversation with Phil Ochs, who was now the major torchbearer of the protest tradition, Dylan said: "The stuff you're writing is all bullshit, because politics is bullshit. Its all unreal. The only thing that's real is inside you. Your feelings."[78] Bob Dylan, the prophet of protest, had turned his back on politics. His new material was deeply personal, subjective, and existential. This was a stunning reversal, and it sent waves of controversy throughout the topical-protest community.[79]

Eight of the eleven songs on the new album were, outwardly at least, love songs. Some were very clearly about real-life relationships with specific women, such as "Ballad in Plain D," which is a vivid portrait of a lover's quarrel with Suze Rotolo and her "parasite sister" and the resulting disintegration of that romance.[80] Others, however, were couched in a poetic vagueness that allowed more generalized interpretations, transcending the boy-girl theme, to represent Dylan's struggle with the larger world of promoters, fans, and critics who were attempting to trap him within an artificial, stereotypical category (protest singer, radical activist, movement leader, and so on). In "It Ain't Me, Babe," through the metaphor of the lovers' quarrel, he voiced his objections to such type-casting, saying, "I'm not the one you want, babe, I will only let you down." And asserting his humanness above his public image as prophet and leader, he screamed: "No, no, no, It ain't me, babe / It ain't me you're lookin' for, babe."[81]

To the new Dylan, political activism was a trap, which could be symbolized metaphorically by the smothering oppression of an overbearing lover. During this period, almost all of Dylan's lovers and friends were committed, involved radicals, and his public image was that of the artist-activist. But in these seemingly romantic love ballads he often ridiculed his friends and lovers for their blind commitment to the meaningless, utopian charade of Old Left politics, which, in ignorance, overlooked the realities of power and naively overstated the possibilities of change.

> But it grieves my heart, love,
> To see you tryin' to be a part of
> A world that just don't exist.
> It's all just a dream babe,
> A vacuum, a scheme, babe,
> That sucks you into feelin' like this.[82]

The most explicitly political statement on the album is the mystical "Chimes of Freedom" that ring out loudly Dylan's theme of personal freedom. The chimes of freedom are tolling for the underdogs, the refugees, the rebels, the outcasts, and the unfortunate everywhere. They are not ringing for the committed radical activists, but for the alientated, "the abandoned and forsaked"; not for the dogmatic and the ideological, but for the freethinking "guardians and protectors of the mind."[83] Moreover, this is a nonpartisan, apolitical tolling, a simple statement of empathy for those who suffer as outcasts.

Dylan's shift toward existential, transcendent freedom is especially clear in "My Back Pages," the most significant song on the album. Here he exposes the hypocrisy of his old approach, when he followed the path of ideas, believing the lies that life was "black and white" and uncritically accepting empty symbols, such as "equality." He had been a phony prophet, lost in a romantic fantasy world in which the distinction between "good and evil" was clear, unaware that he was destroying his self through his preaching. Attacking the tired old rational world view, he continually repeated the refrain that summed up his new affective attitude and direction: "Ah, but I was so much older then, I'm younger than that now."[84]

The break with the past and with the rationalism of ideology and commitment was complete. The new Bob Dylan was becoming the champion of freedom and feeling and a hero of the rapidly evolving cult of youth.

Bringing It All Back Home

In the fall of 1964 Dylan returned to England. This tour was filmed and later released as a pseudo-documentary entitled *Don't Look Back.*[85] Joan Baez accompanied him, but Dylan was the star now and, cruelly, he never asked her to join him onstage. Their relationship quickly disintegrated, reflecting his broader split with much of what Baez had come to represent politically as well as musically.

Early in 1965, after returning from England, Dylan secretly began to experiment with electric instrumentation. In March he released his epoch-making album, *Bringing It All Back Home.* The title referred to his return to his and the youth culture's rock roots. Coinciding with the rock 'n' roll revival, the album was a tremendous success. It was his first milion-selling album.[86]

Acutely aware that he was risking his career, Dylan cautiously included an all-acoustic side to this album, making it a transitional first step in the inevitable—but highly controversial—direction of rock music. While holding back musically, however, he plunged ahead lyrically, with his new message of rejection and rebellion, aimed directly at the naive idealism of the Left's old guard and the hypocrisy of the folk purists.

Dylan now realized that he had once lived in a utopian dream world in which all the problems of the nuclear age could be overcome by determined collective action. Now he knew there were no easy solutions and no utopian paradise on the horizon. In the album's liner notes he says simply, "I accept chaos," implying that there are no easy solutions to the chaotic absurdity we call reality. But most of all, he rejects his image as the leader of a political or cultural movement: "i would not want to be bach. mozart. tolstoy. joe hill. gertrude stein or james dean / they are all dead."[87]

The quiet, beatless acoustic style of the traditional ballads, square dance tunes, and hymn parodies could not express the new bitterness or the hate within the souls of the new youth cult. So Dylan returned to the original revolutionary medium of the youth revolution in America and Europe: rock 'n' roll music. Only in this strange yet powerful blending of black rhythm and blues and white country and western, with its pounding rhythms and hard-driving electric guitars, would the youth of the West express their pent-up feelings and repressed sexuality.[88]

In "Subterranean Homesick Blues," the driving hard-rock number that opens the album, Dylan wastes no time in getting to the point. In short, biting spurts of paranoid-absurdist lyrics, Dylan expresses powerfully the condition of youth in an age of insanity: the man "wants eleven dollar bills [but] you only got ten." It is a picture of youth alienation; the "heat" is continuous, the phone is always tapped, and "the man in a trench coat" is always watching. Dylan warns his listeners not to trust the authorities: "Stay away from those / that carry around a fire hose." And he forcefully pounds out his message in the famous statement, "You don't need a weatherman to know which way the wind blows," from which the terrorist SDS splinter group, the Weathermen, would take their name. "Subterranean Homesick Blues" sets the tone of the album and reflects the anarchistic-existentialist attitudes that were infecting the popular culture of the West. Distrust of the established authorities and collective disillusionment with the logic and uniformity of life in the age of machinery ring out clearly: "Don't follow leaders / Watch the parkin' meters."[89]

The theme of rejecting authority is further developed in "Maggie's Farm," which is a metaphor for the establishment generally, but specifically the Old Left topical-protest song establishment that had attempted to package Dylan in its own image. Although Dylan had tried his best "to be just like I am," everyone had wanted him "to be just like them." But this only bored him, so now he vows: "I ain't gonna work on Maggie's farm no more."[90]

In "Outlaw Blues," Dylan describes the irony of his persecution at the hands of the dogmatists and purists of the folk community through the metaphor of the outlaw. For, although he was being portrayed in the folk press as the villain who had violated the sacred folk tradition, Dylan feels that the shoe is really on the other foot: "I might look like Robert Ford / but I feel just like Jesse James."[91]

"On the Road Again" is an open letter to Dylan's lost love (symbolizing his break with the topical-folk tradition), explaining why he had to leave. Again, using absurdist imagery, Dylan exposes the insanity of the crusade for the cause, which has driven him onto the road in search of a new place to live. His old home, the house of topical-protest, is characterized by continuous "fist-fights in the kitchen," with everyone, even the mailman and the butler, insisting on taking sides on meaningless issues. Dylan repeatedly screams at his protest sweetheart: "You ask why I don't live here / Honey, how come you don't move?"[92]

"Bob Dylan's 115th Dream" is yet another absurdist, paranoid vision about Captain Kidd (Dylan as the personification of American youth) discovering America (the youth culture) but, like Jesus, being persecuted for his unconventional behavior. Here Dylan goes beyond the simple theme of rejecting authority to a more generalized rejection of political involvement. Here, for the first time, he uses death to symbolize social activism and commitment. In the course of his adventures, Captain Kidd sees a building advertising "Brotherhood" (no doubt a symbol for the "movement"), but when he gets inside he finds out it is a funeral parlor.[93] In other words, by joining in the fellowship of one's brothers and sisters in the struggle (whatever the cause), the self is annihilated: ego is destroyed through commitment.

On the acoustic side there are four long symbolist poems, backed minimally by a single "folk" guitar. Here Dylan reaches a new high as a poet; the music is secondary. He pursues the same themes—rejection of authority and the search for the inner experience—but from a slightly different perspective.

"Mr. Tambourine Man" can be read as a metaphor for the drug trip. Instead of blindly following the dogma of the brotherhood of Maggie's farm, Dylan now wishes only to dance to the song of the tambourine man into the "jingle jangle morning" of chemical ecstasy. Having grown weary under the burden of commitment, Dylan is ready to fade into his own "parade" under the "dancing spell" of the tambourine. In this song Dylan celebrates the drug experience as the major avenue leading out of the rational and ideological and into the realm of feeling and euphoria—"on that magic swirlin' ship"—beyond the reaches of authority and tradition.[94]

He then takes his listeners on "ships with tattoed sails" through "the Gates of Eden," into that mythical land where there is no "relationships of ownership," no sins, no trials, and no kings.[95] Inside these gates there are no false promises of utopia, for this is not "Maggie's farm" but the transcendental dream world within the self. This is the same place where we heard the tambourine man, and it is within this inner world that Dylan now seeks truth.

"It's Alright, Ma (I'm Only Bleeding)" is perhaps the masterpiece of the album and a uniquely poetic achievement for a popular artist. And yet its message is profoundly political, setting new standards for the protest song, politically as well as aesthetically. The theme is vintage 1960s: the generation conflict. "Ma," of course, symbolizes the older generation, the establishment, tradition, and authority. To Ma, Dylan (representing youth) tries to explain himself and the dehumanizing and alienating conditions that have forced him and his peers to reject everything "outside the Gates of Eden." Face it, says Dylan, your world has gone crazy, the system is disintegrating. Darkness now shadows "even the silver spoon." There is no point trying to make sense of anything. The old rationalizations are merely "wasted words" from the "fool's gold mouthpiece," played on the "hollow horn." Such empty reasoning must be seen as a warning: "That he who is not busy being born / Is busy dying."[96] Only the inner experience of feeling and euphoria can lead one out of alienation and pain; rationalism and commitment of traditional ideologies are the paths of the dead.

Dylan's object was to shun the false prophets, the evil preachers and teachers and advertising executives, who try to sell "fake morals" and materialistic values, for, in the end, they will leave you "bent out of shape by society's pliers." The new generation wants to rise above all this and will no longer "gargle in the rat race choir." Intuitively, they seem to have come to a collective understanding of the situation and the only way around it, which is the only way to survive: knowing "that it is not he or she or them or it that you belong to."[97]

Thus the members of the younger generation, after rejecting the morals of their middle-class parents, and with the aid of drugs and a relaxed sensuality, were now attempting to break through the binds of their conditioning so they might transcend the limitations of conventional reason, logic, and ideology. The object is to allow the joy of the drug trip or the sexual encounter to take one beyond the chaos of the unreal world of which we are all a part, but which we cannot accept. This is the only way to transcend the pain and alienation of not belonging.

The struggle to become free of the grip of "Ma," even with the help of the "tambourine man," can be very hard on the psyche. For in transcending reason, one faces the danger of insanity. Dylan shares his experiences of colliding head-on with graveyards, false gods, and a pettiness so insidious that he feels as though he has "walked upside down in hand-cuffs." But he can now kick it off with self-assurance, asking, "What else can you show me?" The message is clear: the times have changed, the world is no longer as rational and orderly as the old would have us believe, and adapting to the changes can be trying. But "It's all right ma"; Dylan concludes, "it's life, and life only."[98]

Dylan brings the album to a dramatic conclusion with "It's All Over Now, Baby Blue." Again, the love theme is metaphoric and the breakup is generational, the rejection by the young of the ways of the old. And because the young represent the path to the future, it is the old who are being asked to leave. There is something in the wind again: the anger of the repressed, alienated, and dissatisfied younger generation. Tradition and authority are breaking down: "All your seasick sailors, they are rowing home." The old order has become fragile: "The sky, too, is folding under you." So it is now time to "strike another match" and "start anew" because "it's all over now, baby blue."[99]

It is hard to exaggerate the profound significance of *Bringing It All Back Home.* It is truly a countercultural classic, bridging the gap between the politics of class conflict and the ideological struggle for the cause of the poor and the economically oppressed, and the generational conflict and the radical anarchistic cult of youth. Moreover, this album also bridged the even greater gap between the old folk-protest song tradition and revolutionary rock music.

Folk-Rock

In April 1965, the Byrds, an innovative group of West Coast folk musicians looking for a way to revitalize their art form, released a soft-rock version of "Mr. Tambourine Man."[100] It was an instant success. The new sound was labeled "folk-rock," and Dylan embraced it enthusiastically. Folk-rock completely transformed popular rock music, softening its mindless sexuality by injecting it with a more serious social conscience flavor. It also temporarily politicized popular music.[101]

This politicization process is evident in the new directions taken by the Beatles, who embodied pop music during this period.[102] In 1964 they had led the British invasion of the American pop charts with such empty boy-girl concepts as "I Want to Hold Your Hand," "Please, Please Me." and "Love Me Do." In 1965 they were still pursuing the boy-girl theme but from a deeper, more thoughtful perspective: "Help! (I need somebody!)." They even softened their sound in the folk-styled "Yesterday." In 1966, they had moved into the social and political realm with "Nowhere Man" and "Eleanor Rigby" ("All the lonely people, where do they all come from?)." In 1967, they became surrealistic in "Strawberry Fields Forever" and downright

Dylanesque in "I Am the Walrus." By 1968, the most popular rock group in the world was reaching into the homes of middle America with a genuine revolutionary message: "You say you want a revolution, well, you know, we all want to change the world." Although criticized as politically naive, this was clearly in the same political tradition as "Maggie's Farm" and "Mr. Tambourine Man": "You tell me it's the institution, well, you know, you better free your mind instead."[103]

Thus in a few short years, the Beatles had effectively merged radical politics with popular music. They could not have done so without the contribution of Bob Dylan. But equally important were the Byrds and later groups in America that flooded into the folk-rock market: the Fugs; the Jefferson Airplane; the Grateful Dead; Moby Grape; Crosby, Stills, Nash, and Young; the Flying Burrito Brothers; the New Riders of the Purple Sage; and the Eagles. These groups radicalized popular music in the late 1960s and early 1970s, pushing the popular culture of the West far to the Left politically, capitalizing upon and aggravating the domestic unrest that was crippling the United States war effort in Vietnam, frustrating the American political leadership, and confusing the authority structure.[104]

At the end of May, Dylan, riding the crest of the folk-rock movement, went into the studio to record his first single, "Like a Rolling Stone," a bitter song of revenge. Backed by a driving rock rhythm, Dylan repeatedly screams at the rejected party (perhaps a friend or lover, perhaps the bourgeois establishment and the older generation, or perhaps the old-style radicalism): "How does it feel, to be on your own . . . like a complete unknown, like a rolling stone?"[105] Released in June, it soared up the charts, reaching the number one position by August. It was Dylan's first popular hit.[106]

Newport 1965

At the Newport Folk Festival in July, Dylan tried out his rock act within the hallowed halls of the folk music establishment.[107] The reaction was predictably hostile as he walked onstage, in British mod attire, carrying an electric solid-body guitar. If his intention was to shake up the folk establishment, he was dramatically successful. The legend is that Pete Seeger, the grandfather of folk, had tears in his eyes as he watched his young protegé and friends (the Paul Butterfield Blues Band) launch into the hard-driving, angry rock sound of "I ain't gonna work on Maggie's Farm no more."[108]

The crowd, taken aback, did not seem to know how to react.

There was scattered applause, mixed with boos and jeers. Then an awkward and strained silence revealed the tension as Dylan tuned his guitar, obviously nervous, before breaking into "Like a Rolling Stone."[109] Relentlessly, he drove his sour, rebellious message deep into the heart of the topical-folk establishment: There once was a time when you used to "dress so fine," and you threw the bums dimes when you were in your prime. But some had warned you, saying: "Beware doll, you're bound to fall," and you thought they were only kidding.[110] Well, they were serious. It may have left its mark, but topical-folk music was finished as a popular cultural form.

Again, the crowd reacted with ambivalence. Some were outraged and insulted, but most were either dazzled or confused. Dylan tried one more rock number, a blues: "Well, I ride on a mailtrain, baby, can't buy a thrill." Within the train imagery, he seemed to be symbolically asking the younger members of the audience to come with him on the inevitable journey into the future. Dylan was, of course, the "brakeman" which was what he wanted to be. But this was not to be confused as a statement of his intent to be the leader of such a journey, for he was just along for the ride. Wanting only to be your "lover" and not your "boss," he screams: "I can't help it if your train gets lost."[111] But in their scattered applause, few accepted his offer. He knew he had pushed them as far as he could safely, so Dylan and the Butterfield Band fled offstage.

But in just a few minutes he was back, alone, with his acoustic guitar. Predictably, the crowd reacted with enthusiasm this time. As he began to sing, folk-style, "You must leave now, take what you need, you think will last," the crowd again broke into spontaneous applause.[112] The irony, of course, was that the message was the same ("It's All Over Now, Baby Blue"); only the instrumentation had changed. The song was followed by impassioned applause. Now that he had clearly won them back, he started to leave, but someone yelled out a request. So he stayed and played "Mr. Tambourine Man" to roaring applause. Still, the message was essentially the same as the electric set: "Take me on a trip upon your magic swirling ship."[113] If anything, this song was even more radical in its advocacy of drug use as a political act. But no one seemed to notice; all that was at issue was the type of guitar accompaniment.

In retrospect, it is easy to understand why Dylan turned his back on such a pretentious and hypocritical crowd. He would no longer follow the dictates of the topical-folk music (or any other) establishment. It was all over; they would have to get along without him. And although topical-folk music may have survived (though primarily at the grass-roots level), the Newport Folk Festival has not. The last concerts at Newport were held in 1968, and folk performances were not held again until the revival of the festival in the summer of 1985.

Highway 61 Revisited

Highway 61 Revisited, Dylan's first all-rock album, was released in August 1965.[114] He continued to pursue the same basic themes of *Bringing It All Back Home.* Highway 61 leads out of Dylan's home country in upper Minnesota, and thus "Highway 61 Revisited" had a connotation very similar to "Bringing It All Back Home." Again, the major themes are youthful alienation, defiance, anger, rebellion, and revenge. This album is perhaps even more powerfully revolutionary than *Bringing It All Back Home.* Musically, it is high-intensity rock from beginning to end. Politically, it is existentially extremist, radically anarchistic, and cynically nihilistic. *Highway 61 Revisited* represents a high-water mark in Dylan's commercial, artistic, and political career. It is perhaps his most well-known album. At the time, it was considered the most important and revolutionary popular music album ever made.[115]

The album's liner notes are by Dylan and offer a general overview of what is to come. They form a long, symbol-filled, absurdist story, taking place on a "slow train," filled with cryptic characters: White Heap, Cream Judge, the Clown, the Inevitables, Savage Rose and Fixable, Autumn, Paul Sargent (a plainclothesman), and the Wipe-out Gang (who run the insanity factor). Into the midst of this chaos and absurdity, Dylan introduces Lifelessness (the Great Enemy), who, we are told, is extremely fond of phrases like "go save the world!" and "involvement! that's the issue." This is Dylan's way of presenting the major theme of this album: the death of the self that results from social commitment and political involvement. The resulting aphorism, "involvement is lifelessness," captures the very essence of the third Bob Dylan.[116]

But then he goes on to tell us—as explicitly as possible for Bob Dylan—that the subject matter of this new album is "the beautiful strangers, Vivaldi's green jacket & the holy slow train."[117] I take this to mean that he will be discussing the alienated condition of youth ("beautiful strangers") in the springtime of their lives (from Vivaldi's "Four Seasons") and the great journey (on the "holy slow train") out of the darkness of their alienated condition, beyond the lifelessness of the activist-ideological world of the past and into the mysterious, experimental, sensuous, and transcendental world of the future.

The album begins with "Like a Rolling Stone," already a hit single, rapidly becoming a classic of the 1960s. Perhaps more than any other popular song of this period, "Like a Rolling Stone" vividly captures the political climate of the counterculture. Coming from an old folk saying ("a rolling stone gathers no moss"), the symbolism has a long cultural tradition.[118] The rolling stone has traditionally been the outcast and the vagabond, the hobo and the free-spirited tramp, unencumbered by material possessions and social conventions. Joe Hill used the phrase in his "Last Will": "My kin don't need to fuss and moan, Moss does not cling to a rolling stone."[119] The rolling stone symbol was very important to the 1960s counterculture. First, there was the British rock band the Rolling Stones, then Dylan's "Like a Rolling Stone," and finally, the rock magazine *Rolling Stone.*

Thus in "Like a Rolling Stone," Dylan chose a potent symbol with a long cultural tradition. But, ironically, he used the symbol in reverse, as a way of expressing the great cultural transformation that was turning the establishment into the outsider, alienating the traditional source of the alienation. In the name of the rising cult of youth, Dylan was saying to the older generation, the traditionalists and the purists, and the established authorities: "How does it feel" to be the outsider, the unknown, and the homeless, on your own, "like a rolling stone?"[120]

Next, Dylan offers the "Tombstone Blues" as a portrait of lifelessness. Here, for the first time, he fully employs the metaphor of death. It is a way of life, a community, and a sensibility that is dying. The strange characters who make up this mythical family are locked into the ugliness and hatred of their life situation. The imagery is generally dark, chaotic, and negative. Life is hard and cold and very dissatisfying: Mama is working barefoot in the factory, while Dad is out in the alley looking for something they can eat. But Dylan, the morbid son, is in the kitchen with death on his mind, singing the "Tombstone Blues."[121]

This song may be interpreted on many levels, but it translates well as a condemnation of the community of folk purists and the orthodox Old Left radicalism of the topical song tradition. For this is the same family-community as "Maggie's Farm," and it is the home of the socially involved and committed activists—it is the "Movement." And Dylan characterizes this as a chaotic place, another meaningless rat race, where the political actor is lost in a charade, fooled into believing that the world may be changed for the better. This is the realm of lifelessness, and it now gives Dylan the "Tombstone Blues." And yet he hates to see old friends trapped in such an unreal world, beside themselves, enveloped in a false consciousness. He would like to help. He would like to show them the light, the path beyond knowledge, to the platform where they are waiting for "the holy slow train."[122]

Dylan follows the "Tombstone Blues" with his train song from Newport. Now entitled "It Takes a Lot to Laugh, It Takes a Train to Cry," and again using a familiar and powerful symbol, the words have been polished, but it is still the song of the slow train. Dylan is still the brakeman, pointing the direction but refusing to lead the way.[123]

Then, in "The Ballad of the Thin Man," Dylan pursues a subject that is thematically similar to "It's All Over Now, Baby Blue," and "Like a Rolling Stone." It is a long symbolist poem about Mr. Jones (the Thin Man), who is the stereotypical bourgeois authoritarian, establishment, organizational man. He is the ugly American, Whiteman, the overbearing parent, teacher, policeman, or judge. Dylan places Mr. Jones in a series of awkward, anxiety-producing situations that confuse and bewilder him, making him feel alienated and threatened. It is Dylan's way of criticizing the rigidity of the older generation, with their pretentious literate, rational, civilized values. Dylan exposes Mr. Jones to the experimental, sensuous, chaotic, and barbaric values of the young. Repeatedly, Dylan, as youth, sarcastically asks poor Mr. Jones: "You know something's happening here, and you don't know what it is, do you, Mr. Jones?"[124]

And in "Queen Jane Approximately," Dylan again uses the love metaphor to attack the old ways. This song could be directed at Joan Baez or the folk establishment and the Old Left. The message is consistent with "Maggie's Farm," "On the Road Again," "It's All Over Now, Baby Blue," "Like a Rolling Stone," and "Tombstone Blues." To his lover, Dylan is saying, when you have tired of the old, worn-out, traditional ways, "won't you come see me, Queen Jane?"[125]

This is followed by Highway 61 Revisited" the title song, which is a caustic comment on middle America. The name is taken from the highway that runs north to south, from Canada, past Dylan's home, all the way down to the Gulf of Mexico, through the heart of America. It is an absurdist glimpse of the circus parade of American life as it passes metaphorically down Highway 61.[126]

"Just Like Tom Thumb's Blues" is perhaps the most revealing song on the album. Thematically, it is a striking departure from the other songs. Is this the first crack in the wall of Dylan's new persona? It is like the flip side to "Like a Rolling Stone." Dylan reveals for the first time that the pressures of the new road he has chosen are beginning to take their toll. He is lost in Juarez in the paradox of a depressing spring rain. I do not feel that here the word "rain" necessarily refers to drugs. I think it may be too simplistic to assume that this is merely a song about an overworked performer, caught in the pressure cooker of fame and fortune, who, in desperation, has turned increasingly to drugs (from burgundy to the harder stuff). It seems more likely that the "shot" he no longer has the strength to get up and take is public criticism. Here the arrogance of "Like a Rolling Stone" has faded into doubt, fatigue, and paranoia. The goddess of gloom has taken his voice and left him howling at the moon. Maybe it is Dylan who is the homeless rolling stone after all, with no one left to call his bluff. Is the joke on him again? Dylan is obviously feeling very small (like Tom Thumb) and is coming to the end of another road. He sings with a pain-choked voice: "I'm going back to New York City, I do believe I've had enough."[127]

Dylan concludes the album with "Desolation Row," another look at the lifelessness of "Maggie's Farm" and "Highway 61." Again, there is the imagery of chaos and cryptic but potently symbolic characters (Cinderella, Bette Davis, Cain and Abel, the hunchback of Notre Dame, the Good Samaritan, Ophelia, Einstein, Casanova, and others). And again, the mood is dark and enigmatic, vaguely constructed symbolic visions of a distorted, confused world with all the lifeless faces going around shouting, "Which side are you on?" It is a frightening maze of hurried, blurred half-images, representing the ugly side of modern life. In the most general sense, Desolation Row is society and the trap of involvement, where the the force of the Other annihilates the self.[128] Indeed, this is the major preoccupation of the third Bob Dylan, the rebellious, paranoid, antiauthority, antisocial "angry young man," who came to represent an angry generation rejecting everything their parents held dear, searching for a new way to live and interrelate, a new level of awareness and openness, a new set of values, and a new world.

Superstardom

By the end of the summer of 1965, Bob Dylan was a superstar. He had fulfilled his lifelong dream of gaining fame greater than that of Elvis Presley. Only the Beatles and the Rolling Stones were capable of causing more public excitement than Dylan. But the fame was overwhelming and destructive, and Bob Dylan would soon retreat from it. Before long, his popularity would wane. And although he would remain a major popular cultural figure and would even periodically shine with brilliance and generate short bursts of enthusiasm, excitement, and record sales, he would never again so dominate Western pop culture as in 1965–66.[129]

On the night of August 27, 1965, fourteen thousand eager fans filled the Forest Hills outdoor stadium in New York City to capacity, anxious with the excitement of what was about to happen: Bob Dylan was changing masks. Careful as always, and with the memory of Newport fresh in his mind, he chose to divide the concert into acoustic and electric sets. Thus in one evening, this crowd of young people was going to be led across the great cultural gap between the old mechanical, rational, ideological world of the past, into the electronic, existential, sensuous world of the future.[130]

He began with just his acoustic guitar, but playing his new, nonfolk material—"Tambourine Man," "It's Alright Ma," "The Chimes of Freedom," "It's All Over Now, Baby Blue," and "Desolation Row." He was carefully preparing the crowd for what was coming, but within a familiar, nonthreatening (acoustic) setting. He ended his first set to thunderous applause.[131]

When he returned after the intermission with his electric guitar and rock backup band, there were scattered boos and some shouts of disapproval. But quickly the music roared back and silenced the audience. Before the night was over the jeering had stopped and the crowd was listening with respect. The following month, Dylan gave another concert at New York's Carnegie Hall, using the Forest Hills format. By now the crowd's reaction was decidedly positive.[132] The tide had changed. Bob Dylan had almost singlehandedly brought about marriage of the traditionally left-wing urban folk music culture with the traditionally apolitical teen-pop music culture. The effect was revolutionary. The "bubble-gum," "teeny-bop" pop music was radicalized, and the urbane, intellectual, left-wing folk music was popularized. The popular culture of the West was creatively alive with excitement. And Bob Dylan—only twenty-four years old—was riding its crest.

World Tour

On November 22, 1965, Dylan was secretly wed to Sara Lowndes.[133] He spent most of the first year of their marriage on a grueling world tour. The first phase took him through Canada and down the American West Coast in the last months of 1965. Then, early in 1966, he and his entourage flew to Nashville to record an outpouring of new material to be released in May as the double album package *Blonde on Blonde*.[134]

Blonde on Blonde would be the last album of Dylan's punk phase. It was intensely personal, almost self-indulgent. Most of the songs were views of romantic entanglements seen from a variety of perspectives: "I'm Pledging My Time (To You)," "(Sooner or Later) One of Us Must Know (I really did try to get close to you)," "I Want You," "Most Likely You'll Go Your Way (And I'll Go Mine)," "Fourth Time Around." Some carried deeper and metaphoric messages: "Stuck Inside of Mobile with the Memphis Blues Again" and "Just Like a Woman," creating images similar to "Like a Rolling Stone" or "It's Alright Ma." There were also some thinly disguised tributes to the two important women in his life during the period: Sara, his wife ("Sad Eyed Lady of the Lowlands"), and Joan Baez, whom he left for Sara ("Visions of Johanna").

But, all in all, this is a shallow album, politically, in comparison to *Bringing It All Back Home* or *Highway 61 Revisited*, and less thematically coherent.[135] Still, it is a further exploration of the same basic themes of personal freedom, the pain of alienation, and the pleasures of drugs and sensuality. Perhaps the most significant philosophical track on the album is "Rainy Day Women #12 & 35 (Everybody Must Get Stoned)," which Dylan uses to open the album and to set the mood. Skillfully using a double entendre, he again plays with the symbol "stone" in a thinly disguised autobiographical sketch, in which the forces of convention and authority are constantly "stoning" Dylan and the youth culture he now represents. But Dylan is unperturbed, for he knows that "everybody must get stoned."[136] Perhaps this song best captures the essence of Dylan's views during this period. The message is to be yourself, even in the face of criticism. This egotistical preoccupation with self—the do-your-own-thing syndrome—filtered down through the youth culture to produce the flower children, the hippies and the Yippies, student riots, LSD experimentation, yoga, meditation, communalism, free love, and the entire counterculture package.

The object was to get beyond, or at least to see past, the trap of society, which only destroyed the natural inner self. Thus the new sensibility abhorred material possessions, deemphasized wealth and glamour, and opted for more natural, simple styles of dress and modes of being. And because of these experimental lifestyles, many young people, including Dylan, were often cruelly and severely ostracized by the society at large for their long hair and strange apparel and mannerisms. They began to experience, as a class, the pain of alienation, and thus came to understand what it was like to be outlaws and outcasts, stoned by society. They responded with glib laughter and flippant attitudes. They turned to drugs—marijuana, LSD, mescaline, amphetamines, tranquilizers—to free them from the trap of their conditioning and the hypocrisy of their elders. They turned apathetic and inward—they got stoned.[137]

By March, before the release of *Blonde on Blonde,* Dylan was back on tour. In April, he went to Honolulu, then to Australia, then on to Stockholm, Copenhagen, Paris, Rome, Ireland, England, Wales, and Scotland. It was a physically and mentally draining experience for Dylan. He was using amphetamines to stay awake and to keep the creative juices flowing. But things were moving so fast that he was rapidly approaching a breaking point. Bob Dylan was riding the crest of a great cultural and social revolution that was flowering within the popular culture of the West, and he was creating much of the lore of the emerging nation of Woodstock. He was becoming a godlike cult figure. His pace of life had become so fast that perhaps it was inevitable that catastrophe would strike. And on July 29, 1966, it did. Dylan had a near-fatal crash on his Triumph 500 motorcycle near his home in Woodstock, New York. He was hospitalized with a concussion and several cracked vertebrae. The accident forced him to remain in bed for more than a month and then to begin a slow, painful recovery, while rumors spread that he was dead or had become a brain-damaged vegetable.[138] But it also gave him time to rest and to rethink his image and, in the long run, to shed his paranoid punk image and to begin the search for a new Bob Dylan.

Moderate Man, 1967–70

On October 3, 1967, while Bob Dylan was recuperating in his upstate New York hideaway, Woody Guthrie, weighing less than one hundred pounds, his jerking reduced to a slow, constant murmur, finally died. As soon as he got word of Guthrie's passing, Dylan agreed to perform at a memorial concert to be held in January.[139] Guthrie's death offered Dylan the opportunity for yet another rebirth.

John Wesley Harding

Later that month, Dylan ended his fifteen months of seclusion, making two short trips down to Nashville to record a new album with country musicians. The new album, *John Wesley Harding,* was released early in January 1968. It was a beautifully simple album musically. Gone were the grinding hard-rock sound. A new mellow, country-style, three-piece combo was backing a soft-voiced, mature balladeer, Bob Dylan.[140]

But *John Wesley Harding* came at a time when the Beatles, at the top of their form, had just caused a sensation with *Sergeant Pepper's Lonely Hearts Club Band,*[141] with its dazzlingly sophisticated, electronically overdubbed sound, its thematic coherency, and its classic psychedelic countercultural themes ("Lucy in the Sky with Diamonds," "She's Leaving Home," "Within You without You," "With a Little Help from My Friends"), innovatively pushing revolutionary rock to its very limits. And Bob Dylan, who in many ways had set this process in motion, was now apparently retreating to the safer territory of country-western music. Many at the time considered this the end of Dylan's career.[142]

But *John Wesley Harding* contained plenty of subtle artistry and a great deal of social and political symbolism. Dylan had once again gone against popular trends (psychedelic electronics) and was pointing in a new direction, anticipating the country-western revival. Dylan admitted that he could not keep up with the high-technology approach of the Beatles, and he no longer wished to play radical politics with his music, but the Dylan phenomenon had not ended. By the end of the decade, the Beatles had disbanded, and during the 1970s country music would seriously challenge rock's hold on the popular music culture of the West.[143] And Bob Dylan was one of the pioneers of the shift toward Nashville.

In the prose parable, "The Three Kings," on the album cover, there are hints of Dylan's new direction. After the visit of the three kings, who had come to ask Frank (a symbol of Christ and Dylan's alter ego) about Dylan's new album, Vera (Frank's wife) asked Frank: "Why didn't you just tell them that you were a moderate man and leave it at that."[144] The latest Dylan was indeed a moderate man. He had left existential egoism behind him and returned to the people and to altruism. Dylan's John Wesley Harding was a friend of the poor and "was always known to lend a helping hand."[145]

In fact, Dylan seemed to be repenting and asking for forgiveness. In an overt reference to the Tom Paine Awards confrontation, Dylan, in "As I Went Out One Morning (To Breathe the Air Around Tom Paine's),"[146] confesses that he has gone astray, that, in his weakness, he gave in to the temptress of the youth revolution. And now, in "I Dreamed I Saw St. Augustine," he has seen a vision of his implication in the death of a martyr.[147] Could this be another "Song to Woody"? Was this vision of the martyr "in the utmost misery" inspired by the death of Guthrie? If so, Dylan now chose to cloak his martyr in the image of the great Christian philosopher of the early middle ages. Thus the two basic threads of Guthrie's folksy idealism and Dylan's Judeo-Christian ethics seem to once again converge in *John Wesley Harding,* after the self-destructive, existential binge of his punk rock phase.

Alan Rinzler points out the similarities between Dylan's lyrics in "I Dreamed I Saw St. Augustine," and those of Alfred Hayes in "Joe Hill." Both melodies and opening lyrics do bear striking resemblances, for example, Dylan's "I dreamed I saw St. Augustine, alive as you or me," and Hayes's "I dreamed I saw Joe Hill last night, alive as you or me." This seems to support the argument that Dylan was repenting for his part in the death of the Joe Hill tradition, the cult of Woody Guthrie, and the positive social values that adhered to them. He was retreating from chaos and was sorry for the damage he had done.[148]

Although it would be impossible to argue seriously that *John Wesley Harding* represents Dylan's return to the Guthrie fold, it does not seem unreasonable to assume that the album was at least partially inspired by the death of Woody Guthrie.[149] And although not exactly a return to "folk" music, there is clearly a conscious attempt to recapture the acoustic simplicity of traditional American folk styles: long narrative ballads (Dylan, like Guthrie, has always been a very effective balladeer), songs of outlaw heroes, hoboes, drifters, fair damsels, jokers, and thieves. Dylan, however, uses these traditional folk symbols and images to achieve poetic effects that go far beyond the folk genre. *John Wesley Harding* is a significant departure from sour punk rock and youthful anarchy and rebellion, but it is by no means a return to folk protest. The sound is "country," not "folk," and the message is decidedly apolitical.

Rather, the message of *John Wesley Harding* is personal and religious. It is Dylan's reaffirmation of faith. Anthony Scaduto refers to it as Dylan's version of the Bible. The songs take the form of parables, which recount Dylan's fall from grace and his rebirth, songs of repentance, salvation, faith, and hope.[150] To the extent to which he touches upon political ideas, he is merely reaffirming the ideals of Christian charity and brotherhood.

Turning against involvement during the punk phase had only led to alienation, despair, and loneliness. He now sees that he was a "lonesome hobo" then, without family or friends. He had not trusted his neighbor and was therefore doomed to "wander off in shame." He now pities those "poor immigrants," like the punk Dylan, whose "visions in the final end must shatter like the glass." He realizes that he was a "wicked messenger" then—a false prophet. But now he has been confronted by those who have opened his heart, saying: "If you can not bring good news, then don't bring any."[151]

In the moral to "The Ballad of Frankie Lee and Judas Priest," Dylan has again come to accept his responsibility to his fellow man, saying: "If you see your neighbor carryin' somethin', help him with his load." He also realizes that he has a responsibility to follow the right path, for one should never be where one does not belong, and one must be careful not to mistake Paradise for the bordello of material success. The new Bob Dylan is even prepared to compromise with the dreaded landlord, the very symbol of authority. Now that he is where he belongs, Dylan is not about to move "to no other place." He asks of the establishment: "If you don't underestimate me, I won't underestimate you."[152]

And in "All Along the Watchtower," taking his imagery and theme directly from the Bible, the reborn Dylan has moved beyond the position that "life is but a joke." He has "been through all that" and no longer wishes to talk falsely or to follow a false prophet. For "two riders" are approaching, the winds are howling, and the apocalypse is at hand.[153] It is time for some soul-searching, time to embrace your fellow man and make your peace with God.

Although he had not necessarily returned to the Guthrie fold, he was clearly back in the mind games arena, offering new advice, enlightening his public with more visions and dreams, full of hidden meanings and moralisms. Dylan had returned to the mind guerrilla. *John Wesley Harding* was a great commercial and artistic success. Within a month of its release, it was number two on *Billboard*'s LP charts, eclipsing the Rolling Stones' *Their*

Satanic Majesties Request and posing a serious threat to the front-running Beatles' *Sergeant Pepper*.[154] It remains among his greatest popular and aesthetic achievements. But it also marks another crucial turning point for Dylan: he is doing the mind guerrilla again, but to a square dance tune, shuffling across the floor of a country church, shaking with the spirit.

The Woody Guthrie Memorial Concert

On January 20, 1968, at the Woody Guthrie Memorial Concert, Dylan gave the public its first view of his new self. It was his first public appearance since the accident seventeen months earlier. When the news of Dylan's appearance got out, ticket prices quadrupled on the black market. It was going to be a truly historic event.[155]

At first it seemed as if Dylan would steal the show. But as the concert opened, Dylan's quiet, unobtrusive posture was reserved and respectful, shoulder to shoulder with the folk aristocracy. The concert also featured Pete Seeger, Guthrie's pal; Arlo Guthrie, his son; Ramblin' Jack Elliot, Guthrie's look-alike, sing-alike double; Tom Paxton, one of many pre-Dylan heirs-apparent; and newcomers Judy Collins, Odetta, and Richie Havens. It was awhile before the audience even noticed Dylan. And although Dylan eventually made his presence felt in a series of rockabilly performances of some well-chosen Guthrie standards—"Dear Mrs. Roosevelt," "Grand Coulee Dam," and "I Ain't Got No Home"—he was clearly there only to pay tribute to his fallen hero. There was much less ego presence and less arrogance. Dylan was all smiles, humbleness, and respect. The concert was a great and moving tribute to Woody Guthrie.[156]

A Few More Protests

The wind had been taken out of Bob Dylan's "tattooed" sails. Perhaps it was the accident, or perhaps he had already lost his nerve and used the accident as a cover. But for whatever the reasons, Bob Dylan backed away from the jarring pace of the star syndrome and the maniacal competition for the latest hit single and the newest musical trend.[157] Instead, he settled into the quiet seclusion of his family life.

He did not produce another album until the April 1969 release of *Nashville Skyline,* which confirmed not only his country-western direction but also his moderate-conservative political learnings. The album began with Dylan harmonizing with Johnny Cash on "Girl from the North Country."[158] *Nashville Skyline* outraged Dylan's political critics, but it clearly helped his career.[159] Its happy songs of love ("Tonight I'll Be Staying Here with You") and passion ("Lay, Lady, Lay") took Dylan into the mainstream of America's popular culture, reaching into the vast blue-collar, Bible-belt sector. But, of course, in the process he was leaving radical politics farther and farther behind.[160]

In 1970, Dylan's career reached an all-time low with the release of *Self-Portrait,* which featured Dylan crooning old pop standards ("Blue Moon") and folk songs ("Copper Kettle," "Gotta Travel On"). There were a few original songs, some old ("Like a Rolling Stone," from the August 1969 Isle of Wight concert), some new ("Quin the Eskimo"), but mostly poorly arranged and badly performed.[161]

The critics had a field day with *Self-Portrait.* Dylan was again accused of selling out to commercial interests, of losing his creative talents, and of deliberately alienating his followers. There were even public calls to boycott him.[162] Dylan fed the fires by showing up at a Princeton University ceremony to receive an honorary doctorate in music.[163] His public image and popularity began to suffer greatly.

Then, in June 1971, as if responding to the overwhelming popular pressure to conform to his old image as a political radical, Dylan released a protest sing, "George Jackson," about the brutal murder by prison guards of the imprisoned Black Panther leader: "Lord, Lord, the cut George Jackson down / Lord, Lord, they laid him in the ground." The song more likely was inspired by feeling for an old friend than as a political protest. His message was ultimately outside of the scope of the traditional Left, far more pessimistic, nihilistic, and despondent:

> Sometimes I think this whole world
> Is one big prison yard.
> Some of us are prisoners,
> Some of us are guards.[164]

The following August, Dylan appeared at former Beatle George Harrison's benefit concert for the refugees of the fighting in Bangladesh, performing acoustically, backed by Harrison's lead guitar and Leon Russell on bass. He sang in a familiar voice a long string of his older protest material: "A Hard Rain's Gonna Fall," "It Takes a Lot to Laugh, It Takes a Train to Cry," "Blowin' in the Wind," "Mr. Tambourine Man," and "Just Like a Woman."[165] This nostalgic journey into the past filled the politicos with the hope that Dylan would return to the protest fold.

Dylan, of course, had not returned to radicalism, but he had returned to the pop culture mainstream, and he remained there throughout the 1970s. In 1975, however, he did return briefly to the protest idiom with the single "Hurricane," about the injustice of the incarceration of boxer Rubin ("Hurricane") Carter. In spite of Dylan's lame radicalism ("he could have been the champion of the world"), Carter was eventually released, largely because of Dylan's involvement.[166] But Dylan spent most of the 1970s sharing his own personal struggles: concentrating on the ups (*New Morning,* 1970) and the downs (*Blood on the Tracks,* 1975), of marriage and the passion (*Desire,* 1975) and freedom (*Street Legal,* 1978) of divorce. Finally, late in 1979, Dylan released *Slow Train Coming,* once again taking the public by surprise and again losing many followers and gaining many more by joining the ranks of the born again.[167] Two more Christian albums followed, *Saved* (1980) and *Shot of Love* (1981). Although some of Dylan's Christian songs were undeniably superb and created out of a deeply felt inspiration (particularly "Gotta Serve Somebody" and "Covenant Woman"), the old guard fans were mortified and inconsolable. As had happened in 1965 when he first used the electric guitar, most fans reacted at the level of image. Not wanting to be identified with the Christian Right, which is probably the most conservative sector of American society, they turned a deaf ear. They could not imagine themselves in company with the likes of Jerry Falwell, Jesse Helms, or Ronald Reagan. They could not tolerate the image of themselves in a Sunday suit shaking hands with the preacher. In true pop culture style, the old guard fans, like those at Newport fifteen years earlier, avoided the content or the substance of this seemingly disappointing image. Clearly, the actual material of Dylan's artistry remained much more subtle and sublime than Jerry Falwell or Jimmy Swaggart could appreciate or accept. Dylan's approach to religion has been more mystical than fundamentalist.

The Christian Phase

Anyone who had been listening to Dylan, even casually, over the years, should have seen this new change coming. Christian themes and biblical symbolism were a part of Dylan's song imagery from the very beginning, in the works of the first three of his public faces. They are clearly visible in such songs as "Gospel Plow," "Dreadful Day," "With God on Our Side," and "Gates of Eden." And as early as *John Wesley Harding* (1967), when for the first time religious themes underlay the overall artistic concept, Christian values figured prominently in Dylan's music. Throughout the 1970s, Dylan offered a long string of Christian songs: "Three Angels," "Father of Night," "Knockin' on Heaven's Door," "Forever Young," "Oh, Sister," and "Senior."

And yet *Slow Train* still caught most of his fans by surprise. Dylan had never been so heavyhanded with his religion. On *Slow Train* he slid out of the pew and took to the pulpit. The old guard fans reacted with dismay. Preaching was preaching, and they did not like it any better coming from born-again Bob Dylan than the punk Dylan had liked it coming from the topical-protest song establishment. So, although he did gain a new generation of Christian fans, he was soon looking for a way to shed his latest public image.

Shot of Love was perhaps a transitional work, containing at least one significant non-Christian masterpiece: "Lenny Bruce." And then, after two years of silence, Dylan gave his old guard fans new reason for hope with the 1983 release of *Infidels*.[168] Musically, it was a superbly crafted album with some of the most exciting and powerful rock music Dylan has ever done. And the title imagery seemed to imply that Dylan was burning his born-again bridges. Was this another "new Dylan"?

There was some reason to believe that Dylan had once more been repoliticized. Songs like "Union Sundown" and "License to Kill" seemed to possess at least some measure of social consciousness. The critics were kind, and the public reception was much more enthusiastic than it had been in years. But though perhaps not religious in the same way as *Slow Train* and *Saved,* Dylan's religiosity is still very much in evidence in "Man of Peace" and "I and I." And though political themes are clearly present, they are just as clearly from a right-wing Christian perspective. "Union Sundown" blames the current economic crisis on the labor movement, and "Neighborhood Bully" is a defense of Israeli militarism. And what are we to make of those bizarre, politically senile lines in "License to Kill: "Man has invented his doom, first step was touchin' the moon."[169]

This is no new Dylan. *Infidels* is but another of the Jokerman's tricks. The title has nothing to do with the album's contents and is in fact misleading. But it does create a mood and an image that will probably allow Dylan to appear to shed another layer of skin.

Dylan's most recent album, *Empire Burlesque* (Columbia, 1985), was released at a time when he was more visible than he had been in more than a decade.[170] His public face was very much that of the "old" Dylan. He quietly reemerged early in 1984 on NBC's "Late Night with David Letterman," stone-faced and nervous, playing songs from *Infidels,* at one point fumbling with a harmonica in the wrong key.[171] This show was rebroadcast several times in 1984. In the spring of 1985, he reappeared, standing meekly, looking out of place and embarrassed, among the chorus in Quincy Jones's "We Are the World" sessions, recorded as the American popular music industry's answer to the December 1984 British Band Aid video "Do They Know It's Christmas," which raised money for famine relief in Ethiopia. Dylan's powerful image as America's foremost protest poet demanded his presence at these historic sessions. Quincy Jones felt so strongly about including Dylan that he edited in a special cameo verse sung by Dylan in his familiar stretched-throat monotone. Jones used Dylan to legitimize the video, to give it a serious political foundation.[172]

Dylan capitalized on his new-found credibility by agreeing to appear at the Live Aid concert on July 13 for the same charity. This media event, which was quickly compared to Woodstock, took place on two continents and was simelcast via satellite from London and Philadelphia around the world to almost half a billion people. Dylan was given a prominent slot in the schedule—the closing act during the prime-time broadcast from JFK Stadium in Philadelphia. Not only did he choose appropriately symbolic selections ("Hollis Brown," "When the Ship Comes In," and "Blowing in the Wind"), but in his mumbled comments between songs about the need to help American farmers, he provided the inspiration for the Farm Aid concert on September 22.[173]

Thus at the very time that Western pop musicians had begun to discover the full potential of their high-technology cultural guerrilla powers, Bob Dylan returned to the public, singing songs from his protest poet phase. His acoustic guitar accompaniment, backed by Rolling Stones Keith Richards and Ron Wood, was unfortunately marred by technical problems. But the image projected was clearly that of the guerrilla minstrel. In the Farm Aid concert, he chose to work with a rock band and an electric guitar. He was again the featured act for the final prime-time performance. Here he elected to showcase his new material from *Empire Burlesque,* offering superb renditions of "I'll Remember You" and "Trust Yourself."[174]

But though *Empire Burlesque* seems to confirm Dylan's return to secular themes, it does not present a new Dylan.[175] The album is overflowing with religious imagery and symbolism, but this typically lies hidden in metaphors and cryptic poetic maneuvers. Some of the love songs are particulary suspicious. "I'll Remember You," for example, has a certain reverent tone that seems odd in song of lost love. His "dear sweet friend" is someone who "cut through to the core," who was true, and who understood. He seems to imply that this was someone he can never forget, though he may have seen the person only "one time or two." And though he may not have approached things the way this mysterious person would have liked him to, he still professes to remember their relationship long after the "roses" have faded and Dylan is all alone in the "great unknown."[176] Admittedly, the image is so vague that one hesitates to draw too many conclusions. But if this is merely a love song, it is sung religiously, as if the love object were sacred.

As in the double entendre songs of another era of transition ("All I Really Want to Do," "It Ain't Me Babe," and "It's All Over Now, Baby Blue"), the love themes of *Empire Burlesque* are subject to a variety of interpretations. "Seeing the Real You at Last," "Never Gonna Be the Same Again," and "Emotionally Yours" also seem less than straightforward. One gets the feeling that Dylan is regretfully rejecting something in his life that goes deeper than any ordinary love relationship. In "Tight Connection to My Heart," he implies that he has gone along with a charade that he now knows was "all a big joke." With typical Dylanesque obtuseness, he says, "I never could learn to drink that blood and call it wine."[177]

There are therefore indications that these love songs may allude to his affair with Christianity. If so, he appears to be saying that he thought the "rain" of mysticism that he brought to gospel music would cool down the obnoxious fundamentalism of the Christian establishment, but this had not occurred. Although at one time Dylan felt that there was nothing wrong with him that Christ could not have fixed, he has now grown tired of the Christian "bag of tricks."[178]

It cannot be denied that Bob Dylan is again in transition. The cultural politics of world hunger has offered him another opportunity for rebirth. He is leaving the Christian phase behind, but with mixed feelings. In the dialectical evolution of Dylan's art, the secular dimensions are, in 1985, slowly overtaking the religious. In the totality of Dylan's works, however, both elements are essential.

The Holy Slow Train

Those who were outraged by Dylan's Christian phase and who are undoubtedly pleased by his recent return to politics harbor a fundamental misunderstanding of their hero. Bob Dylan never abandoned the politics of revolution because he never embraced it. He explicitly stated that the answers were not to be found in rational dialogues in books or discussion groups; rather, they were "blowing in the wind." Dylan was never an ideologue and always a mystic. Likewise, Dylan never abandoned the leadership of a movement, even in the sense of serving as a cultural leader and prophet of the counterculture because he never accepted it. Again, he was explicit. When he said, "Don't follow leaders," he meant himself as well as the establishment authorities because, as he also wrote, "You don't need a weatherman to know which way the wind blows."[179] Dylan has consistently advised his fans not to trust him or anyone else to show them the answers. For, more recently, he has also written, "Look not for answers where no answers can be found." Instead of blindly following vain, ungodly people, he insists only that you must "trust yourself."[180]

Dylan is above leadership, for he is a seer and not a ruler. His involvement in Farm Aid illustrates this point. Although he may have provided the inspiration, he was not actively involved in the physical production. Willie Nelson took on the task of organizing the concert. Dylan did not even help publicize the event with promotional interviews, as did such stars as Arlo Guthrie, Neil Young, and John Cougar Mellencamp. Dylan's aloofness was broken only during his performances.

However presumptuous it may be to seek the "real" Bob Dylan, I must now attempt to draw together the various Dylan phases. We all change by taking the unchanged parts along with us. Dylan is no different. There is a congruence underneath the chaos of Dylan's public images. Despite all the various masks he may have donned, he has abandoned nothing and changed very little. Most of his changes have been superficial—mere theatrics. As Michael Gray has pointed out, Dylan is a self-proclaimed "song and dance man."[181] Like all artists, he must seek an audience. He dramatically switched from acoustic to electric, from folk to rock to country and to gospel, to keep the fans' attention, to give them a show. And yet, through all these surface changes, the underlying message, the means of expressing it, and the images, symbols, and metaphors employed have changed very little.

Throughout his career, in his approach to his art as well as his public image, Bob Dylan has remained true and consistent to two interpenetrating themes. The first is that of the outcast, the rolling-stone drifter freewheeling down life's highway, fleeing conformity and convention. This theme is an extension of the Guthrie cult of the hobo-rambler, expressed by Dylan in his empathy for the misfit and vagabond and his worship of freedom, mediated through the metaphor of the railroad and the highway. The second theme is that of the seer in quest of visions. The philosophical roots of these visions seem to be an eclectic brand of Christianized mysticism, in which social and political concerns are expressed in biblical imagery and enigmatic moral mind games, with an overriding eschatological fascination for the subjects of death and dying, salvation and judgment. The real Bob Dylan is therefore a Bible-toting hobo, a mystery tramp, riding the holy slow train on a transcendental journey in quest of answers in the wind.

These dialectical themes, often seemingly contradictory yet locked in symbiosis, are evident from the very beginning in his "Freight Train Blues," "Highway 51," "Gospel Plow," and "See That My Grave Is Kept Clean" from *Bob Dylan.* These themes continued into his protest phase. For *Broadside* he wrote songs like "Only a Hobo," "This Train A-Travelin'," "Talkin' Devil," and "Dreadful Day." The concern for the cult of the hobo can be seen in the title symbolism of Dylan's second album, *Freewheelin'.* Much of his protest imagery takes place on the road. "Hard Rain" is the tale of a traveler ("Where have you been my blue-eyed son?"), and in "The Times They Are A-Changin'," the "old road" is rapidly aging. Dylan's protest songs are also filled with moral overtones and biblical symbolism. Jesus condemns the warmongers in "Masters of War," and in "With God on Our side," his pacifism is expressed by the words "If God is on our side he'll stop the next war."[182] And finally, the eschatological references in Dylan's protest songs are well known: a "hard rain" is about to fall, and there is a "dreadful day" ahead, when we will all suffer from the "World War III blues."

The punk Dylan continued to use the hobo motif and took the romanticization of freedom to even greater lengths. Included among these absurdist poetics and anarchic revelations are a multitude of hobo images and biblical references. The punk Dylan rides the mail train listening for the "chimes of freedom," heading for the "Gates of Eden," on the run from the lifelessness of "Desolation Row." In his reckless quest for freedom, he abandons the pretentious protest world of "Maggie's farm" and heads down "Highway 61." Throughout his travels, the punk Dylan encounters such potently symbolic characters as Abraham, Cain and Abel, the Good Samaritan, Delilah, and John the Baptist. It was during this period that Dylan's prophecies rang with force and conviction in such classics as "My Back Pages," "It's Alright Ma (I'm Only Bleeding)," and "It's All Over Now, Baby Blue."

During his recovery from the 1966 motorcycle accident, his songwriting seemed more contemplative and less impulsive. But the themes of this material, which later surfaced on one of popular music's most famous bootlegged albums, *The Basement Tapes,* continued to reflect the views of an outsider on a quest for knowledge and transcendental understanding: "Crash on the Levee (Down in the Flood)," "I Shall Be Released," "This Wheel's on Fire," and "Sign on the Cross."[183] *John Wesley Harding* continued to feature Dylan's hobo mysticism. The imagery of "The Drifter's Escape," the "Lonesome Hobo," and the "Poor Immigrant" are by now vintage Dylan. So, too, are the biblical references in "All Along the Watchtower" and "The Ballad of Frankie Lee and Judas Priest."[184]

Dylan pursued these twin themes throughout the 1970s, in his soundtrack for the outlaw movie *Pat Garrett and Billy the Kid,* his epoch-making pain-drenched album, *Blood on the Tracks,* his first major concert album, *Before the Flood,* and his final secular album of the decade, *Street Legal.* "Three Angels," "Father of Night," "Knockin' on Heaven's Door," "Oh Sister," and "Senior (Tales of Yankee Power)" were all songs with strong eschatological content recorded before his Christian phase. And his choice of a setting for his first fundamentalist LP, *Slow Train Coming,* within a hobo metaphor indicates the continued preoccupation with the image of the drifter during Dylan's Christian phase.

The Christian Dylan was still an outsider whose friends and followers had turned against him after his profession of faith. Once again he found himself a rejected and persecuted victim of a godless society, doing the bitter dance of loneliness. His Christian lyrics are filled with social comment, the bitter, cynical critique of the outraged outsider. There is condemnation of all the familiar social problems: child abuse, incest, pornography, water and air pollution, racketeering, and government corruption. Some of his comments, like his reference to Henry Kissinger and Middle Eastern oil sheiks in "When You Gonna Wake Up?" are topical and already sound dated.[185]

The Christian Dylan was also paranoid. His eschatology was sharply focused. The visions of a hard rain were resolved into the stark images of a time when men will beg God to kill them but will not be able to die.[186] But Dylan, the mystical drifter, was still pressing on in rapture, calling out to his fellows to wake up and board the slow train to glory.

The protest, punk, and Christian phases share many common elements. They are preachy. But they have great conviction and high artistic quality and popular appeal. Through all his phases, Dylan has remained controversial. He has always been an outsider, always a mystical seer. The most recent, post-Christian Dylan, is an infidel who has seen through another facade. He now realizes that Satan may come in the form of a man of peace. He is seeing the real face of Christianity at last. He has renewed his faith in himself, but he is still transcendentally seeing the sky falling.

In his dedication to the 1973 compilation of his songs and poems, *Writings and Drawings,* Dylan sums up his influences and the purpose of his art in a prose style reminiscent of Woody Guthrie, with predictable hints of King James:

> Dedicated to the rough riders, ghost poets,
> low-down rounders, sweet lovers,
> desperate characters,
> sad-eyed drifters and rainbow angels—those high
> on life from all ends of
> the wild blue yonder. . . .
>
> To the magnificent Woody Guthrie and
> Robert Johnson
> who sparked it off
> and to the great wondrous
> melodious spirit
> which covereth the oneness
> of us all . . . [187]

Bob Dylan's politics, such as they are, involve the romanticization of freedom, a concern for the social outcast, and the moral condemnation of the alienated conditions of life in the nuclear age, sustained by images of hoboes, outlaws, prophets, and saints on a slow train bound for Glory.

And so, in spite of all his changes, Bob Dylan has continued the tradition of Woody Guthrie, but in a depoliticized form. Both rode the slow train. Both were bound for Glory. Their differences, however, hinge on the connotation of the word "Glory." Guthrie tended to have a secular concept in mind. His destination was the One Big Union, or the communist utopia. Although Guthrie's unionism had a religious component ("Jesus Christ" and "Union's My Religion"), in most of his songs Woody kept this religiosity subordinate to his utopian fantasies. Dylan, on the other hand, played the mystic from beginning to end. The reference to the "oneness" in the dedication to *Writings and Drawings* is one of the few explicit utopian references in Dylan's writings, and it is decidedly religious. But Dylan was rarely so straightforward. More often—as in "The Chimes of Freedom," "Mr. Tambourine Man," and "The Gates of Eden,"—his utopianism is full of mystical vagueness. But in the end, since *Slow Train Coming,* Dylan's conception of glory, has involved the Christian conception of the Kingdom of Heaven.

Thus the differences between Guthrie and Dylan center on the role each gave to religion. Guthrie was by far the more politically radical, and perhaps it was his sensitivity to the atheistic aspects of the left-wing Marxist-based ideologies of his generation that kept his religiosity under control. But Dylan's sensitivities to his generation's Dionysian qualities probably had the opposite effect. The cult of drugs and sex had abandoned the rationalism of Marxian ideologies and sought meaning in transcendental mysticism, which allowed Dylan's eclectic religiosity to surface.

Dylan's major contributions to the social protest tradition, and the areas he parts company with Woody Guthrie, are twofold. First, more than any other protest writer before him, Dylan took the protest genre into the realm of serious art, breaking the confines of the Guthriesque "folk" sound along the way. Second, Dylan took his protest art farther into the mainstream of Western popular culture than anyone at the Paterson pageant or the John Steinbeck Committee for Agricultural Workers Benefit could have ever imagined. But in the process, the music lost its original political contents or was significantly diluted. And yet the new cup of protest was nevertheless a powerful revolutionary brew.

The cult that formed around Bob Dylan, especially before 1968, was indeed revolutionary. His followers did not, however, embrace the politics of their elders. Their politics was contained in their apathy. It was the politics of negation, of hate, revenge, and nihilism induced by the hypnotic effects of drugs and a relaxed sensuality. Unfortunately, the quest for passion and existential freedom involved only a politics of escape, which has been the basis for the youth countercultural punk rocker's politics throughout the 1970s and into the 1980s. It is the politics of Britain's "New Wave" of mid-1970s punk bands (the Sex Pistols, Elvis Costello, the Clash, the Strangers, and others). It is the politics of the character "Pink" in Pink Floyd's

The Wall. Bob Dylan, the mystery tramp, is the father of this punk movement.

It is probably to his credit that Dylan abandoned this form of politics early, for it demonstrates his positive sensibilities. To fall back on Christianized hoboism, though not a complete return to the syndicalism of the Old Left (which by 1970 was, to say the least, an anachronism), was at least socially responsible. It was a return to involvement. The other path, that of existential nihilism, leads, not to self-liberation (annihilating lifelessness), but to despair and negativity (annihilating life itself).

But unfortunately, Dylan's abandonment of nihilism may have cost him his hard-core following. By 1980, seemingly, Dylan was no longer the spokesman of his generation. But though he may no longer be the pop culture Moses leading the children of the technocracy out of the dehumanized void of Maggie's farm across the vast deserts of the industrial wastelands into the pleasures beyond the gates of Eden, his participation in the 1984–85 mass cultural guerrilla projects—USA for Africa, Live Aid, Farm Aid and Artists United Against Apartheid—surely boosted the morale of the counterculturalists. Although Dylan's politics may not now be perceived as political, as in 1966, he remains the most important voice of popular protest in Western civilization.

Among the other guerrilla minstrels discussed in this book, Dylan's greatest lack is not his political religiosity, for this may indeed have served him well. The Bible still has a broad appeal, and in spite of his religious fundamentalism, Bob Dylan is far from finished as a popular singer. Dylan's greatest weakness, ironically, may be his success, his longevity as a popular figure. He is the only singing hero in this study who is still living. What Bob Dylan lacks, through no fault of his own, is the martyr syndrome. Had he died in the 1966 motorcycle crash, his public image would have crystallized in the punk rocker phase, and he would probably possess a stronger cult following than the living Dylan does today. Because his life has continued, so have his changes. He has continued to seek new audiences and to alienate old ones. Unfortunately, the public perception of these constant shifts of position has cost him a great deal of credibility. All of this could have been avoided by his death. Such are the dialectics of martyrdom. A dead man not only evokes the sympathy of the public, but he also possesses the correct dramatic structure of a beginning, a middle, and an end. And the tragedy of his death provides the necessary drama to fuel the mystification process. Thus it may be that a coherent mythos may adhere to the hero's legendary persona only after death has freed him from the confines of his mortal existence. In the aftermath of his death, the hero's crystallized image is deified through a canonization process. The hero becomes a god and the focal point for a cult that arises in his sacred name. Perhaps only after his death will we be able to assess the Bob Dylan phenomenon adequately.

7 Well Just Follow Me: *Some Final Impressions on the Problems of Heroism*

This book has been a study of the heroes of the protest song tradition in twentieth-century America. I have attempted to comment on the role of these heroes in the totalization process that has sustained this culture's utopian sensibility over time. I have explored the utopian dimensions of American radicalism as reflected in the songs and songwriters of the left, focusing on Hill, Guthrie, Dylan, and Lennon, whom I feel to be the most significant and typical protest songwriters in the history of this tradition. This final chapter will be an essay on the politics of heroism, using the examples of the guerrilla minstrels discussed in this book. My overall concern is to reflect on the nature of the relationship of heroism to utopian consciousness and the tradition of the cultural guerrilla. What have we learned about the nature of heroism, its purposes and functions? And because the heroes I have discussed are songwriters, we must also ask how music figures into the equation of protest.

I have discussed heroism as a form of vicarious identity. This interpretation cuts two ways: the hero is the reification of the identities of those he represents, but he is also a model or ideal for the followers to emulate. Although the nature of heroism is such that the hero is by definition an innovator with a unique identity, the hero's public image is in some sense also the result of what he or she perceives to be the public's wishes. The hero is a stage personality whose existence is dependent upon an audience. Heroism presupposes a cult following.

The hero is also an imagined nonentity that exists apart from the real person behind the image. There is a Robert Zimmerman as well as a Bob Dylan. The hero is therefore a transcendental object that is the product of a collective imagination. I like to think of the hero as the head of a transcendental family, although in the case of the rock superstar, it may make more sense to perceive the hero as a transcendental lover. It has been asserted that some young girls had orgasms during Beatle performances. The screaming frenzy of those Beatlemaniacal fans was intensely personal. Whether familial or sensual, the bond between hero and hero-worshiper is personal and emotional. In the case of the protest hero, the bond also has an idealistic dimension; the hero is a source of political identity. The family of protest has an intellectual aspect that makes it unique, but the fundamental forces supporting this political identity are more emotional than rational. Heroism is more crucial to its survival than is ideology.

The presence of the hero excites the follower, who is in awe. And yet one must assume that the hero is also awestruck when encountering the swaying multitudes that fill stadiums in his honor. A mystery and reverence surround such transcendental experiences. And throughout these encounters, the role of the hero is to mediate the totalization process that reifies or gives oneness to that swaying crowd of admirers. Admiration takes the fan out of his or herself, transcending the alienating condition of their individual existences and connecting them in solidarity to a larger social, and perhaps political, existence. The hero is as small and insignificant as the individuals who compose the multitudes and as large as the totality of the multitudes. He understands the feelings and attitudes of the followers and serves as their spokesman. The hero is the voice of a collective consciousness and the channel through which a group expresses its groupness.

The protest song hero is a special case not only because of his or her idealistic properties, but also because of the elements of music. There is still some confusion as to whether it is heroism or music that holds protest song culture together. Songs clearly have a totalizing effect. Audience participation singing is perhaps the most dramatic example of the totalization process. It could have been argued at one time that a good song, such as "We Shall Overcome," could unite great masses of people regardless of who leads the singing. Hymns seem to serve this function for religious totalities. But I would argue that in today's popular culture, the star is clearly more important than the song. At Farm Aid, Neil Young's "Rock and Roll Is Here to Stay" was particularly effective. And it may have worked regardless of who was singing. Elvis Costello's rendition of the Beatles' "All You Need is Love" was an inspirational moment during the Live Aid concerts that could support the case for the power of song to usurp the hero. But these I feel are exceptions to the rule of heroism.

Music is a crucial, but not definitive, component in the equation of protest. Protest song heroes are heroic because of their songs. But the songs are powerful because they are the sacred words of the beloved hero. They are the devotee's bible and the focus of worship. Moreover, the nature of song as ritualized speech facilitates hero-worship by focusing the attention of devotees on familiar repetitive movements (hand clapping, foot stomping, rhythmic swaying, and singing) that allow the totality to exist in collective action. The Protestant church has been aware of this property of song for more than five hundred years. In recent times, advertising executives have applied the well-known secret that a song is more easily internalized than a spoken message in advertising jingles used to sell soft drinks, automobiles, cigarettes, and toilet paper. The guerrilla minstrel emerged in an atmosphere keenly aware of the propagandistic power inherent in the song form. At Live Aid political knowledge gained by the union movement during the first half of the century was applied to the technological conditions of the second half.

I only wish to suggest that the protest song is part of the heroic mythos surrounding the guerrilla minstrel. One may only speculate about the comparative significance of each. The important question remains unanswered: how has the guerrilla minstrel mythos served the utopian sensibility? I have argued that the overall impact of the protest hero mythos has been as an agent of totalization, giving a human quality to the abstractions of utopian consciousness. The hero serves as a reified lifestyle that supports the ideals that serve as a source of vicarious utopian identity, out of which a society of protest has emerged. Without heroes and heroines to serve as models for behavior, the culture of protest would be a lifeless collection of empty ideations and meaningless symbols. Though transcendental, the hero is a point of reference, a human anchor, to which the ship of protest is moored.

But the answer to the question of the impact of the guerrilla minstrel on the cultural guerrilla requires a more thorough explanation. Heroism also has certain dehumanizing properties. It can be argued that the impact of heroism on the utopian sensibility has ultimately been negative, counterrevolutionary, and corrupting. This argument rests on the relationship of the protest singer-songwriter to the protest song and the changing practice of protest singing.

The utopianism of the protest song tradition has ideally been totalized through shared song: the attempt to realize the utopian metaphor of harmony. For utopianism clings to song the way clouds cling to the sky, and the singers are romantics gazing upon those imaginary clouds. But when the heroic image of the singer-songwriter overtakes the songs and the shared singing, those clouds turn gray and the blue sky falls into darkness.

Heroics in the American protest singing tradition have been manifested in the rise of the star syndrome and the cult of originality.[1] The elevation of the protest singer-songwriter to the level of hero, whether folk hero or pop star, is the substance of the star syndrome. The star syndrome thus refers to the transformation of the protest poet into a public personage. The cult of originality flows naturally from the star syndrome and involves the rejection of old familiar songs (songs from the public domain) for newly written ones. The prophets of protest are heroic precisely because of their ability to generate new songs with new messages for newly emerging sensibilities.

Although I agree with Carlyle that great men are important sources of cultural and political leadership,[2] it is the vicarious and elitist qualities of heroic leadership that have been responsible for the corruption of the utopian sensibility of American protest culture. Protest hero-worship (in the form of the star syndrome and the cult of originality) has created a politically apathetic (that is, nonparticipatory) following and an aristocratic leadership (of isolated and unaccountable "stars"). What Carlyle failed to see (or saw but was not concerned by) were the authoritarian and totalitarian possibilities inherent in charismatic leadership.

Hero-worship, in spite of its humanizing qualities, is thus also possessed of despotic and autocratic possibilities. It elevates the few above the many. It is, therefore, from the perspective of the utopian sensibility, essentially dystopic and counterrevolutionary. Just as the cult of Marx and Lenin corrupted the communist utopian ideal into the Stalanist totalitarian state, hero-worship in the culture of protest has corrupted the utopian ideal of union singing into the idolization of the popular protest singer. As the guerrilla minstrel has evolved into the superstar, the grass-roots, generative, and participatory nature of protest singing has steadily declined. As a result, the protest genre, from a political perspective, has become increasingly hierarchic and nondemocratic. Once actively sung together, protest songs are now only listened to alone.

This argument on the nonparticipatory effects of protest heroics runs deep in the scholarly and journalistic accounts of American protest song culture, although it is usually associated only with the post-Dylan era. After the controversial Newport Folk Festival of 1965, the protest press (*Sing Out!* and *Broadside)* was alive with the debate over the rise of the superstar and the cult of originality. It was almost unanimously felt that this was a new and dangerous phenomenon that was destroying forever the collective, participatory ideals of the Old Left topical "folk" protest tradition.[3] I can accept this argument, but only up to a point. I depart from the Old Left in its view of timing. As I have attempted to demonstrate, protest heroics and the cult of originality did not begin with Bob Dylan and folk rock. In twentieth-century America, the cultural guerrilla has always relied upon heroism and idolization for its continuing totalization.

In the creation of the public image of Joe Hill, the IWW and the labor press of the 1910s were every bit as personality-oriented as was the protest culture of the 1960s. And the Guthrie era was no less guilty of succumbing to the lure of heroism. Although the folk revivalists would have argued forcefully for the generative-participatory ideal, as we have seen, Alan Lomax, Pete Seeger, and the People's Songs, Inc., network carried on an extremely effective public relations promotion of the cult of Woody Guthrie. And the idolization of Guthrie was to be an important, perhaps crucial, force in the continuing totalization of the protest tradition. In other words, heroism was an influential element in the protest equation long before Bob Dylan plugged in his electric guitar in Newport.

By far the most ubiquitous explanation for the rise of the star syndrome and the cult of originality is an economic argument. This is the classical Marxian argument that, upon entering the capitalist realm of the commercial music industry (Tin Pan Alley), popular protest singers such as Bob Dylan were corrupted by greed for wealth and bourgeois comforts. The music industry is the culprit that took protest music away from its roots in the American working class. The people (that is, the workers) were thereby alienated from their own music as folk music was cleverly packaged into a popular commodity to be bought and sold in the pop music marketplace. And since one of the more important marketing strategies of the music industry has been to stress the protest singer's public image over and above his or her song's content, the star syndrome quickly infected protest music culture after it entered the popular field. After all, from the point of view of the entrepreneur, stars sell records, and radical politics does not.

Again, although there is obviously much validity to this argument, it is not the full story. The marketing strategies of the music industry have indeed done much to further the cult of originality and the star syndrome in American protest music, but economics is by no means the root cause. The protest hero was in existence long before the modern business practices of the music industry took over protest song culture.

The corruption of protest song culture is also often explained by developments in the technology of communications, which has increasingly emphasized image and personality over substance and content. The heroic image of the protest prophet singer has overtaken the prophet's message; hero-worship has begun to replace revolutionary consciousness; and cultism has triumphed over utopian ideology as the foundation of the protest singing tradition in America and the West.[4] But though media developments have aggravated the trend toward hero-worship, again they are not the fundamental cause, for the protest hero is not a child of mass communications technology.

The origins of the protest hero mythos are to be found in the minstrel traditions of medieval Europe. Long before the introduction of print into the West, these wandering troubadours traveled among feudal kingdoms singing epic ballads of love and romance and chronicling in song the events of the day, often with a partisan flavor that cast them in the role of defenders of the interests of a particular noble family or feudal class.[5] The Robin Hood ballads, for example, which date from as early as 1100, are derived from this tradition (as opposed to the folk tradition) and are among the earliest ballads in the European tradition to express distinct sociopolitical concerns. In almost all versions of this popular English ballad, the class struggle, in one form or another, serves as the central tension fueling the drama of the story. The famous outlaw hero (whom Sir Walter Scott in *Ivanhoe* depicts as a guerrilla leader of the Saxons holding out against the Norman regime) is a champion of the poor and the small landowning yeomanry in their struggle against the villainous tyranny of the nobility and the clergy.[6]

I wish to stress here that the protest singing tradition did not originate out of the folklore of the medieval peasantry but is derived from the minstrel tradition. The wandering troubadour (the medieval equivalent of the modern professional singer-songwriter) and not the authorless folk were the first to use the song form for explicitly political purposes.[7] One early minstrel, for example, Adam of Hale (1240–87), gained widespread notoriety in conjunction with the Robin Hood ballad as the author of an early version ("Jue de Robin et Marion").[8] This is but a single illustration of the point that the star system and the cult of originality were in evidence at the very beginning of the protest tradition in the West. The phenomenon of the protest hero is thus in some sense a function of minstrelsy and not of subsequent developments in the economics of the popular music industry or changes in the technology of communications.

As Europe began to emerge from the darkness of medieval times, political radicalism, as we know it today, began to take shape in the revolt against the Catholic church.[9] It was also a time when the modern song culture of protest, so closely bound in form and function to the Protestant hymn, was also taking shape.[10] Radical preachers such as John Ball of London's Great Revolt of 1381 were becoming the new minstrels of protest. An embryonic secular utopianism was evident in Ball's preaching, which encouraged his followers to persist in "one head."[11] Inspired by the events leading up to the revolt, Ball also gave to protest one of its earliest radical ditties: "When Adam delved and Eve span/who then was the gentleman?"[12]

This early protest against the injustices of feudal class divisions marks the beginning of the modern era in the song literature of the culture of protest. It also illustrates a further development in the star syndrome and the cult of originality. The couplet above attributed to Ball certainly would have been quickly forgotten had its author not been so prominent in this early revolt and died a martyr's death at the hands of the royalist reaction, having been hanged, drawn, and quartered, and his severed head placed on a spike on London Bridge with those of the other leaders of the revolt.[13] John Ball was a hero and a martyr in the protest tradition at a time when mass communications and the recording industry were unimaginable.

But even if discussion is confined to America, there are many examples of protest heroes before Joe Hill and the Wobbly mind guerrillas. Foner in *American Labor Songs of the Nineteenth Century* lists 277 known composers of protest songs in the pre-IWW labor press.[14] Some, like John Siney, a mine union leader, Ira Steward of the eight-hour movement, and John A. Sovereign, grand master workman of the Knights of Labor, were quite famous.[15] A few, like Morris Rosenfeld, gained enough respect to have their works published and widely circulated.[16]

Thus, long before the songwriters of this study came into existence, before the advent of mass communications technology, and before the rise of the pop music industry, a cult of originality and a star system of a sort were already firmly established in the culture of protest in Europe and America.

The song of protest seems to require originality of authorship and to foster the heroic public image of the protest singer-songwriter. Songs of protest arise out of historical-political events. Perhaps, as some have suggested, such songs are simply too dull to survive on their own merit. In contrast to folk songs, the topical nature of protest songs seems to tie them closely to their composers. Such songs rarely outlive their authors because the events they describe quickly lose their significance. Protest songs generally have an ephemeral and anachronistic quality. They are so closely linked to history that they pass quickly in and out of fashion.[17] Perhaps this is why they are so dependent upon their composers for their existence. Since they rarely last long enough to pass through the folk process into the public domain, they may survive only in the mythos of their heroic composers. Thus those that endure do so on the strength of the public personality of their authors and not necessarily because of their melody or message. Their dependence on heroes has a significant impact upon their role in the American culture of protest.

Thus although heroism extends far back into the recesses of protest history and is independent of both economics and changing technologies, the development of mass communications and the emergence of economic incentives through the rise of the recording industry have radically transformed the heroic guerrilla minstrel, dramatically altering his role in the totalization processes of protest culture. The protest song hero thus has played the mind guerrilla through media both hot and cold and through both pre- and postindustrial economics. But although these developments have not been solely responsible for the rise of the guerrilla minstrel mythos, they have been responsible for luring the protest song hero forever out of the remote and esoteric regions of the left-wing labor circles and thrusting him into the mainstream of American (and Western) popular music culture.

In seeking to understand the popularization of the protest hero, we must examine the contribution of each of the four heroes described in this book to the culture of protest in twentieth-century America and particularly their overall effect on the utopian sensibility.

Joe Hill's Will

In America, at the beginning of the twentieth century, the modern notion of the guerrilla minstrel first crystallized in the public image of Joe Hill. Through the Hill myth, the IWW created for America the mythos of the guerrilla minstrel. The publication in 1975 of Foner's *American Labor Songs of the Nineteenth Century,* however, unambiguously established that the American revolutionary song form predates the Wobblies.[18]

The image the IWW created for Hill has stood the test of time. It has subsequently been admired and emulated by several generations of would-be cultural guerrillas, sustaining the chords of protest and the harmonies of the utopian vision throughout the twentieth century. It is the image of a common, ordinary worker ("one of us") full of youth and beauty ("labor's flower"), selflessly dedicated to the cause of the One Big Union ("a rebel true blue"), who is cut down in the prime of his life by a ruthless and insidious injustice perpetrated upon him by the "white-handed lowsome power" of the "Authorities of the State of Utah." To the workers, the loss of one so special (a "singer of Labor's wrongs, joys, hopes, and fears") is devastating, and they vow never to forget it.[19] So determined were the efforts of the Wobbly mythmakers that Joe Hill has indeed never died.

The totalizing impact of the Hill mythos has been a mixed blessing to the song culture of the American Left, however, and in the long run may even have been self-defeating, contradictory, and counterrevolutionary. On the positive side, the Hill mythos has been an extremely effective totalizing agent by personifying the idealized utopian consciousness and creating a revolutionary standard for individuals to identify with and imitate. As a symbolic vehicle, reifying the syndicalist vision of the Wobblies, the Hill mythos has been a focal point for the continuing totalization of the utopian sensibility in the folklore of the American Left.

But on the negative side, the Hill mythos is in many ways an elitist corruption of the Wobblies' union singing ideal. The committee that produced the first edition of the "Little Red Songbook" intended that the songs selected to represent the IWW be communal or "union" products. Rank-and-file workers were encouraged to contribute songs and poems. The Wobbly labor hymn was to reach the ordinary, unsophisticated worker with a message he could understand, appreciate, and find inspirational. In theory, any worker could express himself in song, and all were encouraged to do so. The Wobblies' theory of protest singing was thus inherently democratic and participatory.[20]

But with the rise of the Hill mystique, the "Little Red Songbook" began to lose this democratic-participatory quality, as Hill's songs began to dominate the songbook and overshadow the works of all other Wobbly songwriters.[21] In the process, the generative initiative of the nonprofessional worker-songwriter was delegated to an imaginary and mythical surrogate. Whereas spontaneously generated songs, or songs long in the public domain and therefore familiar to all, were once genuinely shared expressions of a common utopian sensibility, now they were to become akin to tablets handed down from on high. Ever so subtly, as the fiction of the guerrilla minstrel mythos was substituted for the positive participatory experience of spontaneous, worker-generated singing, the communal praxis of union singing was transformed into something artificial and vicarious. The utopian sensibility that was once expressed in a genuinely shared song became an increasingly aristocratic enterprise, induced by the force of idolization upon apathetic sheep and weekend revolutionaries, who, in their aloneness, would listen in awe instead of singing with affection and in solidarity.

Since Joe Hill, the utopian practice of evoking the revolutionary spirit through ritualized singing has substituted a mythical idolization for the goal of oneness. The implications of this shift of emphasis are ultimately dystopic and totalitarian. This dialectic between the positive, participatory, communal totalization and the negative, elitist, vicarious totalization has, over time, produced a protest song culture aggravated by the star syndrome and the cult of originality, and has become decreasingly participatory and increasingly vicarious, increasingly aristocratic and decreasingly communal.

A Picture from Life's Other Side

The Woody Guthrie mythos, though firmly in the tradition of Joe Hill, has had an altogether different impact. It was not part of a union's organizing strategy, nor was it oriented toward the propagation of a specific left-wing ideological system. At least in comparison to Joe Hill, the cult of Woody Guthrie was largely noninstitutional and to a great extent nonideological.

Unlike Joe Hill, Woody Guthrie is respected more for his songwriting talents than for his political activism. Although his reputation as a songwriter was gained through songs that were perceived as political, these songs were more social comment than propaganda. Guthrie took much of the crudeness out of the protest song, shaving off the more sharply ideological edges, adding a more subtle artistry and a more refined and insightful perception. Compared to Joe Hill, Guthrie was an artist rather than a polemicist. His works were intrinsically political, but his class-conscious politics was natural and relaxed, not forced or awkward.

Woody Guthrie began the popularization of the protest song form, using folk songs, rather than labor hymns. The image we have today of the protest singer as a guitar-toting bohemian in blue jeans and work shirts singing folk songs in dark, smoke-filled coffee houses comes directly from Woody Guthrie, not from Joe Hill. Joe Hill did not play the guitar, and, as a Swedish immigrant, he had little or no appreciation for America's traditional music. He wrote his songs either to familiar hymn tunes or to the melodies of pop songs. It was Woody Guthrie (or, more precisely, the network of individuals and organizations behind the Woody Guthrie mythos) who turned the folk song into the protest song and, in the process, infused the utopian sensibility of the protest culture with the values of rural America.[22]

The Guthrie mythos is rooted in the soil of America's folk music revival and has been integral to the spread of folk song into the realm of popular music. The core of the Guthrie mythos is his rural authenticity as a genuine product of the folk community and the embodiment of the great American common man of the 1930s. The mystique of Woody Guthrie thus begins with Guthrie the Okie and refugee of the dust bowl. He is perceived as the classic victim of the Depression in the Southwest, forced onto the road at a tender age by the twin calamities of drought and economic failure. But Guthrie the survivor took to the road naturally. And so the symbolism of the road and the rails—the hobo-rambler mystique—clings tightly to the Guthrie mythos.

Within the Guthrie mythos, hoboing is a political metaphor; the lifestyle of the outcast, homeless, alienated victims of hard times. The boxcar was a haven from oppression, the rails a symbol of freedom. But Guthrie was no ordinary hobo, for he possessed a special gift: he was a ballad-maker. And he packed his road experiences into the songs he wrote and sang. He left behind grand documents in song of the struggles of the children of the Great Depression.

Because his songs portray the plight of the economically disadvantaged, his image is that of a class-conscious troubadour of the people. He was a minstrel with a mission to use his songs as a weapon in the class struggle, as a means of exposing and striking out against the injustices perpetrated upon common, ordinary folks by those sick with greed and the lust for power.

Guthrie's folksy image is therefore infused with a fundamental sense of rebelliousness. His image is that of a defiantly unconventional young man, filled with disdain for the conventions of polite society. His crude, unkempt manner and his undisciplined demeanor were deliberate attempts to affect the behavior of clumsy common folks in the company of city slickers. His politics was unsophisticated and anti-intellectual. Guthrie was a political romantic, reaching out through a sentimental medium to an audience he perceived to be largely uneducated. His is the image of the dedicated cultural guerrilla selflessly committed to the cause of the poor and oppressed.

Guthrie's folk image had great conviction because he was of the folk. He had experienced their poverty, exploitation, and powerlessness. He, too, had suffered. He, too, had lived and therefore understood life's other side. It may well be that the suffering Guthrie endured, the harships and strife he encountered early in life, and the disease that slowly and cruelly robbed him of his life were the forces that ultimately totalized the Guthrie mythos. The despair over Guthrie's fate at the hands of Huntington's disease touched a nerve in the hearts of the mythmakers and torchbearers of the protest song establishment, most notably Pete Seeger and the remains of the Almanac Singers—People's Songs, Inc., network. And through their efforts, the image of Woody Guthrie was canonized in the protest song tradition.

The force of the Guthrie mythos strongly affected the utopian sensibility of protest culture, which began to lose its syndicalist qualities and to take on a populist and nationalist character. A utopian sensibility began to take shape in the image of the American *gemeinschaft*: rural, naturalistic, agrarian, and anti-industrial.

The cumulative effect of all this may have made the utopian vision more acceptable and accessible to the average working-class American, but it also had a depoliticizing effect, especially when contrasted to the Wobbly vision. Americanization would invite certain patriotic misinterpretations of Guthrie's songs (like "This Land") and, in the end, take enough of the radical edge off the folk protest song to prepare it for presentation to a mass audience and a popular culture.

The Guthrie mythos, like that of Joe Hill, also contributed to the further decline and deterioration of the generative and participatory nature of protest singing. Although he would certainly have argued to the contrary, the Guthrie mythos has contributed much to the star syndrome and the cult of originality. Most of Guthrie's better compositions were long, descriptive, narrative ballads, designed for the audience to listen to quietly, without singing along. And by affixing his name to his songs (and often to plagiarized melodies), Guthrie was violating the very folk process and communal ideal he seemed to be espousing. He was accepting exclusive credit for songs that he would have admitted were rightfully the product of the people.

But Guthrie's image as a hobo rambler, traveling from town to town in search of a mythical "union place," has perhaps most damaged the utopian vision and sensibility. Guthrie's hoboism glorified individualism and romanticized freedom. It was, therefore, essentially apolitical and escapist. By drifting on down the road every time something went wrong, the followers of Guthrie lost sight of the community and the communal ideal.

Guthrie's image also contains threads of an out-of-control sensuality, a stubborn egotism, and a notorious social and economic irresponsibility. These qualities admittedly rumble beneath the surface of the Guthrie mythos, but they are there, nevertheless. And they are much closer to the sensibilities of the 1960s counterculture than to the Popular Front Marxism of Guthrie's day.

The Guthrie mythos has thus contributed to the corruption of the communal ideal and the utopian values of altruistic love, which have been replaced by a more banal Dionysian lust for an ego-based ecstasy. The Guthrie mythos elevated an individual above the communal ideal and gave free reign to that individual's eccentric visions. These visions—when compared to those of the Wobblies—were wildly unorthodox and dangerously individualistic.

The Mystery Tramp

Bob Dylan was the first full-fledged superstar in the protest singing tradition. He was the first guerrilla minstrel to transcend the limited and esoteric labor and left-wing circles and enter the realm of mainstream American popular music. But Dylan was also the first antihero in the protest tradition, the first actively to reject the crown of the protest hero. Even while leading the thrust into the arena of popular culture, Dylan was rejecting the political idealism of the Guthrie tradition and repudiating the utopian sensibility of the Old Left. For Dylan there were no kings in utopia, and he had no desire to lead a movement to a place that already existed within us all. Bob Dylan wanted only to express himself through his art and his songs. Aesthetics had become more important than ideology. Through Bob Dylan, the star system and the cult of originality brought to protest culture an unprecedented crisis, seriously challenging the utopian sensibility. The communal ideal was largely abandoned in exchange for the "ecstasy principle," erotica replaced altruism as the basis for utopian consciousness, and transcendental mysticism replaced the ideology of collective action.

In rejecting the folk idiom in favor of rock 'n' roll music, Dylan was rejecting an essentially communal song form for an essentially sensual one. Rock 'n' roll is, after all, a euphemism for sexual intercourse,[23] whereas "folk" implicitly refers to a specific social category.[24] Folk is thus a class concept with natural political overtones, whereas the lustful imagery of rock 'n' roll has no such political connotations. And yet, as a medium of expression, rock music is much more powerfully revolutionary than folk music. Like folk music, rock is a working-class musical form, originating out of Negro folk forms. Rock music is the American folk music of the 1950s and 1960s, the very embodiment of youth rebellion. But, at least before Dylan, rock was an apolitical dance music. Bob Dylan gave rock 'n' roll music its radical sensibility.

But this sensibility was nonutopian, egocentric, and revolutionary. Dylan's rock is a free-flowing antiauthoritarianism, steeped in a paranoid cynicism about politics, both radical and conventional, and a highly pessimistic—even nihilistic—disposition toward the possibilities of social change. Lacking faith in political ideals, antagonistic to social commitment and involvement, the new sensibility was politically apathetic and anarchistic. Bob Dylan gave us the cult of chaos and noninvolvement.

Instead of actively seeking social change, the New Left protestors chose to disassociate themselves from social convention. They withdrew into themselves through psychedelic drugs, promiscuous sexual experimentation, and high-intensity rock music. These child-mystics seeking chemical enlightenment formed vanguard of new barbarians armed with electric guitars.

They sought joy in the practice of shocking the conventional sensibilities with their outrageous dress and manner, reifying their disdain for convention through their appearance and their lifestyles. They were the cultural guerrillas of the new order.[25]

The Dylan mythos is much more complex than that of Guthrie or Hill. The Dylan phenomenon was not only more far-reaching, it was also more dynamic, volatile, and unstable. Bob Dylan is a persona that is always changing. The Bob Dylan of today is not the Bob Dylan of yesterday or tomorrow. Indeed, in many ways the Dylan cult is the cult of change. Thus any generalizations about the Dylan mystique must be qualified carefully as to which Bob Dylan one means. But as we have seen, there are certain traits and qualities that transcend all of Dylan's changes. It is therefore possible (if dangerous) to discuss a single overall Dylan mythos.

First, Bob Dylan's reputation rests upon his image as a popular poet and prophet. He is viewed as a visionary and a seer capable of mystical insights into the ultimate nature of reality. Bob Dylan was, and in a very real sense remains, the spokesman of his generation. At the Live Aid concert, Jack Nicholson introduced him as such, and went on to characterize him with reverence as "the transcendent Bob Dylan." To the generation of the 1960s, his words have all the force of scripture. His albums are treated as holy texts. His words are quoted the way the Bible is quoted: out of context, to back up obscure points, and to justify the peculiarities of one's lifestyle.

Another important element of the Dylan mythos is his image as an innovator and trend-setter, living on the edge of merging sensibilities, perpetually passing across the threshold of the latest musical, political, and philosophical developments. Although his ability to find such thresholds is clearly diminishing (no one can stand in the doorway forever), it is such an important aspect of his legend that it must be mentioned. Only Bob Dylan had the foresight and the nerve (and it took a great deal of both) to make the transition from folk to rock. Eventually even the most stubborn folk purists crossed that great divide in his wake. A similar, though less dramatic, process occurred when Dylan turned to country and western music. Some have even followed his lead into gospel. To this day, the release of a new Dylan LP creates a rumble in the pop music culture of America.

And through all of his various changes—changes that have taken him in a clearly apolitical direction—the image of Bob Dylan as a revolutionary, as a rebellious and unconventional left-wing intellectual, persists. The image of Bob Dylan as the embodiment of youth rebellion has remained an important element in the Dylan mythos. One of the more startling contradictions in the Dylan mythos is his image as a nonleader. It seems to contradict every other part of the mythos. It is a direct refutation of his image as a highly innovative, trend-setting, superstar revolutionary and spokesman for his generation. His stance against cultural leadership, his refusal to play the role of "boss" or "conductor," is perhaps the fundamental flaw in the character of the Dylan mythos.

And finally, the most controversial dimension of the Dylan mystique, his religious nature, is an element that runs deep in Dylan's public character. Dylan, the prophet-seer, is a mystic and a spiritual leader, almost a countercultural preacher. His powers of insight are believed to approach supernatural. And as a poet and singer, Dylan has been consistently preoccupied with the symbolism and imagery of religion, mysticism, and spirituality.

Bob Dylan is a complex and diverse contradictory mythos and one harboring certain functional inconsistencies: the superstar revolutionary who abandoned revolutionary politics, the trend-setting cultural leader who refuses to lead, the nonideological cynic who is deeply religious. Surely it is a confused image, if not fundamentally flawed with inauthenticity. Perhaps this confusion is the natural consequence of the transformation of the protest troubadour into the superstar. Perhaps inauthenticity is the mark of the 1960s sensibility. Dylan's confused image is perhaps but a reflection of the confusion of the 1960s counterculture.

One of the greatest ironies within the Dylan mythos is that it is crystallized directly out of the Guthrie mythos, dramatically exemplifying the power of hero-worship. Young Dylan was a fanatical Guthrie devotee. Bob Dylan's utopian sensibility, revolutionary consciousness, and guerrilla minstrel image were expropriated directly yet vicariously through the worship of the Guthrie mythos. Hero-worship was thus the vehicle that totalized young Dylan's political and artistic sensibilities.

But soon after Dylan's face-to-face encounter with the dying legend he began to grow cynical. The Guthrie mythos was exposed in a horrifying vivid manner, naked and pitiful, before Dylan's impressionable eyes. In "Song to Woody," for example, Dylan seemed to grasp intuitively the unreality of heroism and the artificiality of the vicarious experience of hero-worship. In breaking out of the Guthrie mold, Dylan shattered the idealism of the topical-folk tradition. But the irony is that in refusing to follow Guthrie, Dylan created his own mythos and his own cult following. While preaching the anarchy of "don't follow leaders," Dylan was becoming a superstar and cultural leader of unprecedented scope and magnitude. His refusal to follow in the steps of Woody Guthrie transformed him into Guthrie's replacement as the new prophet singer of the nation. By refusing to follow blindly in the path of the master, Dylan created an independent mythos, but one that would be followed just as blindly as the source of a new brand of vicarious political identity. Rejecting heroism had resulted only in more of the same and at an even more disturbing level.

A further irony is that, while rejecting Guthrie's idealism, Dylan was substituting perhaps an even more abstract and impractical sensibility. Dylan's Christianized protest abandoned rational ideology in favor of mystical spiritualism. His view of utopia (in "Chimes of Freedom" and "Gates of Eden," for example) became vague, dark, and uncertain. The only certainties were existential anxieties. Dylan's utopianism ultimately collapsed into egoism and the worship of freedom, before finally resolving itself into Christian fundamentalism (on *Slow Train Coming*).

But even at the height of his political period (from *Freewheelin'* to *Highway 61*), Dylan's radicalism ignored the communal ideal and scorned the collective sensibility, leaving only political apathy and the ecstasy principle as the fundamental outlines of the new sensibility. And even after returning to community (on *John Wesley Harding*), his embrace of the utopian sensibility was religious and not political. It was a "slow train" utopianism that was ultimately only "pie in the sky" radicalism. Dylan's impact has therefore ultimately been counterrevolutionary, transforming young idealist dreamers and mind guerrillas of the socially conscious Left into apathetic, passive sheep.

Furthermore, the Dylan phenomenon exacerbated the already well-established trends in the protest tradition toward an increasingly nongenerative and nonparticipatory format. After Dylan, practically all political sensibility was dictated from above by specialists. Whereas Guthrie's protest songs could be fairly easily learned and reproduced by the nonprofessional musician, Dylan's more complex electronic sound, his personalized and bitter love songs, and his strange but demanding vocal and lyrical phrasing put much of his music outside the reach of the ordinary protester. Dylan's music, even more than Hill's or

Guthrie's, took on the character of tablets handed down from the mountain, designed to be listened to and mediated upon but never to be shared in a participatory sense.

In giving legitimacy to the star system and the cult of originality, Dylan's ultimate effect on the protest tradition was elitist and authoritarian. Dylan transformed protest into an aristocratic enterprise. Although his music is perhaps complex only in comparison to that of Hill and Guthrie, those who followed in his wake (the Beatles and the other British rock bands like the Stones and the Who; Simon and Garfunkel; the Byrds; the Doors; Jefferson Airplane; Crosby, Stills, Nash, and Young; and so forth) clearly produced a highly sophisticated sound, generated "aristocratically" by talented, technical specialists. It was designed for vicarious participation only.

And yet, at the same time, ironically, it became a social force of unprecedented magnitude and effect. The ultimate result was the mystification of the protest process and the loss of the individual participant, as well as the communal ideal. In the end, the protest tradition has been reduced to the blind cult followings of superheroes.

Just Follow Me

John Lennon's dictum, "If you want to be a hero well just follow me," seems to sum up the evolution of the utopian sensibility within the American protest tradition.[26] He seems to be saying that the listener who wants to live heroically, to live in utopian ecstasy, may do so vicariously through him. Since we are not all capable of heroic deeds because we are too "uptight," "hung-up," afraid to free ourselves from the restrictive "bag" of social convention, we now seem to need the hero. Utopianism has come to mean transcendence. To be utopian is to "shine like the sun," to soar above the madness of social reality, to push oneself daringly beyond one's conditioning to the very limits of rationality and convention and into the realm of pleasure and personal happiness. Since such transcendence is rarely achieved in ordinary life, we have come to depend upon the hero to do it for us.

Yet one detects a note of heavy sarcasm as Lennon sings "well just follow me." The tone is offhand and careless (not "follow me," but "well just follow me"). It is sung with despair and despondency. The imaginary quest for utopia has finally led nowhere. For the listener is not being asked to join the oneness of humanity or the brotherhood of mankind but merely blindly to follow a hero. And, for that matter, he is a doubting hero, one who denies his own heroism, who refuses to lead, and who insists that a working-class hero is just "something to be." Again, there is an annoying hesitation, a sense of uncertainty, in Lennon's voice as he sings the line "a working class hero is something to be." It is almost a question, and especially when viewed within the context of the rest of the album, it seems to imply that the mythos of the hero is an absurdity, playing upon the fears and weaknesses of the public. Lennon admits to being merely a confused kid with a guitar, singing a few coarse words in a flat, uninspired voice, accompanied by a few simple chords. But he is also saying that if it makes the fan happy—if the listener feels heroic vicariously, if he receives some special hope, some meaning—then go ahead, "just follow me."[27]

Utopianism was once a noble, idealistic, and optimistic perspective, one that flowed naturally from the songs of the working class. The act of singing reified the solidarity of the communal ideal. But the utopian ideals are no longer communal, and solidarity comes, not through shared song but through hero-worship. As a result, something has turned sour. Blind faith in show business personalities has replaced the participatory ideal of the mind guerrilla. And when even the leaders have lost faith, utopianism has been lost and cynicism prevails. The dream is over.

Lennon did go on to write "Imagine" and "Mind Games," and he tried to regroup and redirect the mind guerrilla, but the times had changed. The youth of the 1970s could not be easily conned. Things turned so sour that not only did Lennon's record sales drop but he was, in the end, actually gunned down by one of his fans. And though the counterculture and the mind guerrilla network led by Yoko Ono and the rock press attempted to turn Lennon's death into a noble, worthy martyrdom, it remains far removed from the martyrdom of Joe Hill. Hill died defiantly for something; Lennon was assassinated by a demented admirer for nothing.

The protest singer began the century with vision and determination and then quietly lost his way. Although the protest song has been perfected in an artistic and technical sense, and the means of communicating these songs has developed at a rapid rate, offering unlimited possibilities, both the political superstructure of the protest song culture (shared, participatory singing) and its utopian foundations (the communal ideal) have crumbled, leaving only the paranoid search for belonging in a world of increasing alienation and dehumanization.

Heroism is the force behind this souring of protest. Heroism has nurtured the rise of individualism, political apathy, and elitism and in the process has virtually destroyed the communal ideal. The star system and the cult of originality have replaced forever the generative and participatory qualities of American protest song culture. Political idealism has given way to hero-worship, and the objects of this worship have turned increasingly ignoble and unheroic. The solidarity of protest culture now has a vicarious nature and a cultlike structure. Only an artificial totality remains, and it has increasingly dystopic tendencies.

We Are the World

In the 1980s the working-class hero has become more than just something to be, and the politics of the imagination has entered a new era and attained a new level of praxis. In 1984–85, the star system and the cult of originality passed a crucial field test. The British led the way in the 1984 Christmas season, with Bob Geldof's ensemble of English rock stars, Band Aid, and the hit video/single "Do They Know It's Christmas?" The proceeds of the Band Aid effort went to help the victims of famine in northeastern Africa. American rock celebrities followed suit the following January, united under the name USA for Africa, to record "We Are the World" for the same charity. The American and British rock aristocracy then collaborated in the historic Live Aid concert of July 13, simelcast via satellite from London and Philadelphia, taking the message of world hunger to an unprecedented audience of half a billion viewers and raising more than $40 million for famine relief. That September another benefit, Farm Aid, generated only somewhat less dramatic numbers and dollars to aid the American farmer. In November, another group of American rock celebrities, Artists United Against Apartheid, released "Sun City," a powerful protest against racial injustice in South Africa.

This first outpouring of rock protest in the video era generated more than $120 million for various charities and political causes. As Western civilization moved into the Orwellian age, the cult of juvenile delinquency gave a determined legitimacy to the cultural guerrilla in ways no one at the Pageant of Paterson could have imagined. And none of this could have been accomplished without the drawing power of the rock superstars. How can these events be understood in the logic of the dystopic effects of heroism on the culture of protest? Heroism seems to contradict the utopian sensibility, but without the hero to mediate the ideals, surely no utopia, whether real or imagined, can ever exist. We are left with a paradox: heroism is an evil that is necessary. In an age of mass communications, we may as well accept that charisma and star appeal must be present if any message is to reach a significant audience. Yet though this certainly implies aristocracy, it may not necessarily imply autocracy.

The heroes of protest song culture are subject to accountability. To survive in the ultracompetitive world of popular music, even the superstar must perceive and respond to the wishes of fans. The ability to respect and live up to the demands of his or her fans may indeed be the mark of the superhero. Fans may put the superstar on a pedestal, but they are also fickle and capable to turning their idolizing attentions in other directions. For every Beatle there was a Rolling Stone and for every Michael Jackson there is a Prince. The rock music aristocracy is pluralistically structured. Fans have a great many choices. They may switch their loyalties from one artist to another, the way voters jump from one party to another. If by turning to Christian fundamentalism, Bob Dylan is no longer singing my tune, I may turn to Jackson Browne or Bruce Springsteen. If the Stones seem worn out and inauthentic, there are many new groups, such as the Police, the Eurythmics, Duran Duran, Dire Straits, or U2 that may rekindle my excitement.

The fan also now has the option of turning away from rock altogether. In the 1970s country music seriously challanged rock music's supremacy in the field of popular music. Many rock artists, including Dylan, Leon Russell, Neil Young, Dan Fogelberg, and John Fogerty (of Creedence Clearwater Revival), have at some point in their careers taken up country music. Some of us are old enough to remember that Conway Twitty, Johnny Cash, and Waylon Jennings started out as rock musicians. The two music forms have always been very close and have functioned as alternative sources of musical enjoyment. And, at times, both have flirted with protest idealism. Farm Aid was an example of the joining of these two music forms for a common cause. Inspired by the Guthriesque comments of Dylan at Live Aid, Farm Aid was created by Willie Nelson, whose longtime association with country music, long-hair image, captivating voice quality, and rock-based musical style have won him respect in both rock and country camps. Nelson was able to persuade such country greats as Merle Haggart, George Jones, and Roger Miller to perform alongside rock greats Eddie Van Halen, Tom Petty, and Billy Joel.

There are also alternatives to rock and country music, for the fan may decide not to be a pop music fan at all. As the music listener matures, he or she may come to prefer more serious music, such as progessive jazz, urban blues, or the great variety of traditional folk music forms. The technology of magnetic recording has released music fans from the binds of radio and television programming and the tastes of record producers. An almost unlimited supply of musical forms and styles may be tape-recorded for one's listening pleasure, so it is not necessary to turn on the radio or watch television.

And although it may be less true today because of the increased legitimacy of rock music as a serious art form, popular music is still primarily part of youth (or teenage) culture. Many young people still seek alternative heroes as they enter the job market, settle down, get married, and raise families. They may choose movie stars, athletes, politicians, or public figures in business or the professions as examples to guide their lives.

The Orwellian possibilities of pop music hero-worship are therefore severely limited by its pluralistic nature, but the vicarious nature of its social bonds may not be lightly dismissed. Because of the sheer numbers involved in a mass culture, vicarious participation may be the only form that is practical or possible. Utopian protest music culture, in the generative and participatory sense, may be possible only at the grass-roots level, where, indeed, it thrives today in a national network of local folk music organizations. A few examples are the Highlander Center in New Market, Tennessee, the People's Music Network for Songs of Freedom and Struggle in Norwich, Connecticut, and the Delta County Friends of Folk Music in Rapid River, Michigan. This music is recorded on relatively obscure labels—Rounder, June Appal, Greenbriar, and Hogeye—published in national periodicals like *Sing Out!, Broadside,* and the *Black Sheep Review*: and performed in a network of folk clubs such as the Laurel Theater in Knoxville, Tennessee, McDibbs in Black Mountain, North Carolina, and the Cafee Lena in Saratoga Springs, New York. Many of the various groups and organizations hold annual festivals, usually in the summer months. And this grass-roots community also has its heroes: Pete Seeger, Holly Near, John McCutcheon, Happy and Artie Traum, Guy Carawan, Hazel Dickens, Sparky Rucker, Si Kahn, and many more. A discussion of this culture, like that of the larger popular protest music culture, would inevitably include the works and public images of these individuals. Thus a folk music aristocracy functions just as does the aristocracy of the popular music culture as a source of vicarious identity to mediate consciousness and perpetuate utopian values. Although these local enterprises may more resemble union singing, they are every bit as hero-dependent as the larger popular rock-country music culture.

We must face the fact of heroism, accept it as fundamental ingredient in social and political organization, respond to it intelligently, and use it effectively. The purest utopian protest singing may be generated in small, community-based singing organizations that enable participants to sing out in a genuine solidarity against the wrongs affecting family and community, but the technology of mass communications is rapidly creating a global community and a transcendental family. Like it or not, we are now more than ever dependent on familiar faces of people we will never meet in person. The public figure is here to stay. Vicarious interaction is a fact of the information society, and heroes loom larger and larger. They cannot be ignored, but they can and should be cautiously approached. Do not get starstruck or overcome by the glitter of royalty. Maintain your objectivity and your sense of humor. Choose your heroes carefully, listen to the words of their songs, and, if you can accept the message, sing along. Respect the guerrilla minstrel who respects the cultural guerrilla, seek the ideals behind the image, and always be on guard against millionnaire superstars who imagine themselves to be working-class heroes.

Notes

Chapter 1

1. For background on heroism and hero-worship, I have relied on several sources. For the classical conception see C. Kerenyi, *The Heroes of the Greeks,* trans. H.J. Rose (New York: Grove, 1960). The modern conception begins with the work of Thomas Carlyle; see Archibald MacMechan, ed., *Carlyle on Heroes, Hero-Worship, and the Heroic in History* (New York: Ginn, 1901); B.H. Lehman, *Carlyle's Theory of the Hero* (Durham, N.C.: Duke Univ. Press, 1928); and Eric Bentley, *A Century of Hero-Worship* (New York: Beacon, 1944). More recent works include Sidney Hook, *The Hero in History* (Boston: Beacon, 1955); Dixon Wecter, *The Hero in America* (Ann Arbor: Univ. of Michigan Press, 1963); Sidney Kraus and Denis Davis, *The Effects of Mass Communication on Political Behavior* (University Park: Pennsylvania State Univ. Press, 1976); and James Combs, *Dimensions of Political Drama* (Santa Monica, Calif.: Goodyear, 1980).

2. See Jean-Paul Sartre, *Critique of Dialectical Reason,* trans. Alan Sheridan-Smith (London: Atlantic Highlands Humanities, 1976), 45-47.

3. Michael Morgan, "Carlyle, Thomas," in Paul Edwards, ed., *The Encyclopedia of Philosophy* (New York: Macmillan, 1967), 2: 25.

4. MacMechan, *Carlyle,* 28.

5. There is a sizable body of literature on the social protest singing tradition. The first attempt at a broad overview of the left-wing song culture was John Greenway, *American Folksongs of Protest* (Philadelphia: Univ. of Pennsylvania Press, 1953). Another classic work is R. Serge Denisoff, *Great Day Coming: Folk Music and the American Left* (Urbana: Univ. of Illinois Press, 1971). An excellent brief survey may be found in Jerome Rodnitzky, "The Evolution of the American Protest Song," *Journal of Popular Culture* 3 (Summer 1969), 35-45.

Chapter 2

1. The definitive work on the life of John Lennon to date is Ray Coleman's *Lennon* (New York: McGraw-Hill, 1984), although it unfortunately adds little to what has already been written. The first Lennon/Beatle biography to appear was Hunter Davies, *The Beatles: The Authorized Biography* (New York: McGraw-Hill, 1969). Jann Wenner's *Lennon Remembers: The Rolling Stone Interviews* (New York: Fawcett, 1971), provides an insider's retrospective view of life as a Beatle. Cynthia Lennon's *A Twist of Lennon* (New York: Avon, 1978) is interesting only because she was Lennon's first wife. Recordings of Beatle interviews are still available. They are largely commercial Beatlemania hype, for example, *The Beatles' Story* (Capital/EMI, TOB 2222, 1964), and *Hear the Beatles Tell All* (Vee-Jay, Pro-202, c. 1964). For more objective recorded interviews, see *The Beatle Tapes* (Polydor, 2683 068, c. 1971), interviews with British rock columnist David Wigg.

A flood of material appeared in the aftermath of Lennon's assassination. Just two months before his death, Lennon and Yoko Ono were interviewed by David Sheff, and with the help of G. Barry Gibson, this material was later published as *The Playboy Interviews with John Lennon and Yoko Ono* (New York: Playboy, 1981). Philip Norman published an excellent in-depth study, *Shout!: The Beatles in Their Generation* (New York: Warner, 1981). Among the better memorial works are a collection of essays and interviews from *Rolling Stone,* edited by Jonathan Cott and Christine Doudna, *The Ballad of John and Yoko* (Garden City, N.Y.: Doubleday, 1982); Vic Garbarini, Brian Cullman, and Barbara Graustark, *Strawberry Fields Forever: John Lennon Remembered* (New York: Delilah, 1980); and Mike Shatskin, ed., *Tribute to John Lennon* (New York: Proteus, 1981), a print version of a three-hour interview with John and Yoko, conducted by the BBC's Andy Peebles just forty-eight hours before Lennon's death.

A recent trend of exposés includes *Dakota Days: The True Story of John Lennon's Final Years* (New York: St. Martin's, 1983), by John Green, a professional tarot card reader once employed by the Lennons, who exposes the darker, occult side of their life together during Lennon's last five years: Yoko's compulsive quest for supernatural powers, John's bout with a debilitating depression, and the conjuring up of the househusbandry myth to satisfy the inquiries of the press. May Pang, Lennon's lover during his separation from Yoko, has also written a book with Henry Edwards, *Loving John* (New York: Warner, 1983), demystifying the story of John and Yoko's romantic reunion after the 1973 breakup of their marriage. One of Lennon's childhood friends, Pete Shotton, has published an account of his experiences growing up with Lennon, *John Lennon: In My Life* (New York: Stein and Day, 1983), coauthored with Nicholas Shaffner. Peter Brown, once the executive director of NEMS Enterprises, the Beatles' management company, has published his Beatle memoirs, *The Love You Make: An Insider's Story of the Beatles* (New York: McGraw-Hill, 1983), with the help of Steven Gaines, revealing for the first time some of the seamier aspects of the Beatles and Lennon.

Several biographical films are available on video cassette: *John Lennon: Interview* (Karl Video, 1975), an interview with Tom Snyder from

NBC's "Tomorrow Show," focusing on Lennon's immigration battle during the early 1970s; *The Compleat Beatles* (MGM/UA, 1982), a full-length documentary; and *Yoko Ono Lennon: Now and Then* (Polygram Music Video, 1984), which chronicles her childhood as well as her life with Lennon. The interested reader might also look for *The Beatles in Concert* (USA Home Video, c. 1984), a compilation of their personal appearances; and the video releases of the Beatle films of the 1960s: *Hard Day's Night, Help!, Yellow Submarine,* and *Let It Be.* The most recent film/video product is a made-for-TV docudrama, *John and Yoko: A Love Story,* produced and directed by Sandor Stern for NBC, broadcast in December 1985.

2. Lennon's onstage antics, especially during the Hamburg tours before manager Brian Epstein calmed him down and cleaned up the Beatles' image for mass consumption, included shouting "fuckin' Nazis!" at his German audience and walking onstage naked with a toilet seat around his neck; see Norman, *Shout!* 114-16, 191-92.

3. This remark came from an interview with Maureen Cleave of the *London Evening Standard* (Feb. 1966). The full statement was: "Christianity will go. It will vanish and shrink. I needn't argue about that. I'm right and I will be proved right. We are more popular than Jesus now. I don't know which will go first—rock and roll or Christianity. Jesus was all right, but his disciples were thick and ordinary" (Brown and Gaines, *Love You Make,* 191).

4. Wenner, ed., *Lennon Remembers,* 165-66.

5. Ibid., 11.

6. Ibid., 15-16.

7. Ibid., 11-12.

8. See Norman, *Shout!* 330-31, for an account of Dylan's influence on the Beatles. The claim that Dylan introduced them to marijuana was first put forth in Anthony Scaduto's biography *Bob Dylan* (New York: Grosset and Dunlap, 1971), 203-4. For a more detailed account of that infamous evening see Brown and Gaines, *Love You Make,* 141-44.

9. See Bob Larson, *Rock and Roll: The Devil's Diversion* (McCook, Neb.: Bob Larson, 1967).

10. In tracing the historical-political background of the story of John Lennon, a reader edited by Gerald Howard, ed., *The Sixties: The Art, Attitudes, Politics, and Media of Our Most Explosive Decade* (New York: Washington Square Press, 1982), was helpful; it includes articles by such thinkers, scholars, and journalists as Herbert Marcuse, Paul Goodman, Tom Wolfe, and Marshall McLuhan. For a more in-depth study of New Left politics, see Irwin Unger, *The Movement: A History of the American New Left,* 1959–1972 (New York: Dodd, Mead, 1975). For a more specific focus on the peace movement, see Lawrence Wittner, *Rebels against the War: The American Peace Movement,* 1941–1960 (New York: Columbia Univ. Press, 1969), and Michael Ferber and Staughton Lynd, *The Resistance* (Boston: Beacon, 1971). Probably the best work on the counterculture of the 1960s is still Theodore Roszak, *The Making of a Counter Culture: Reflections on the Technocratic Society and Its Youthful Opposition* (Garden City, N.Y.: Doubleday, 1969).

11. See George E. Delury, *The World Almanac and Book of Facts,* 1978 (New York: Newspaper Enterprise Association, 1977), 329, 737.

12. See Michael Arlen, "Television and the Press in Vietnam; Or, Yes I Can Hear You Very Well—Just What Was It You Were Saying," in Howard, *The Sixties,* 425-42.

13. The label "New Left" first appeared in Great Britian during the late 1950s, when a group of young socialists and intellectuals differentiated from the Labour party. In the early 1960s they began to publish the *New Left Review,* which soon found its way into American college communities; see Unger, *The Movement,* 18.

14. See Ferber and Lynd, *The Resistance,* 1-8.

15. See John P. Diggins, *The American Left in the Twentieth Century* (New York: Harcourt Brace Jovanovich, 1973), 177-86.

16. Unger, *The Movement,* 25-50.

17. See Matthew F. Stolz, *Politics of the New Left* (Beverly Hills, Calif.: Glencoe, 1971), 50.

18. See Roszak, *Making of a Counter Culture,* 42-83.

19. Unger, *The Movement,* 41.

20. See R. Serge Denisoff, *Great Day Coming: Folk Music and the American Left* (Urbana: Univ. of Illinois Press, 1971).

21. See Albert Goldman, "The Emergence of Rock," in Howard, ed., *The Sixties,* 343–64.

22. See Warren Hinkle, "A Social History of the Hippies," in ibid., 207–32.

23. See Unger, *The Movement,* 26–35.

24. Abbie Hoffman, *Soon to Be a Major Motion Picture* (New York: Perigee, 1980).

25. See Mike Jahn, *Rock: From Elvis Presley to the Rolling Stones* (New York: Quadrangle, 1973), 209–13.

26. See Rex Weiner and Deanne Stillman, *Woodstock Census: The Nationwide Survey of the Sixties Generation* (New York: Viking, 1979), 163–77.

27. See Unger, *The Movement,* 39–41.

28. Bob Dylan, *Writings and Drawings* (New York: Knopf, 1973), 160.

29. Unger, *The Movement,* 90.

30. See Tony Palmer, *All You Need Is Love: The Story of Popular Music* (New York: Grossman, 1976), 3–4.

31. See Ferber and Lynd, *The Resistance,* 202–3.

32. *The Beatle Tapes,* side I, track 1.

33. Ibid.

34. Copyright © 1968 by Northern Songs Limited.

35. *The Beatle Tapes,* side I, track 1.

36. Cott and Doudna, eds., *Ballad of John and Yoko,* 66.

37. See ibid., 261–71.

38. Ibid., 66.

39. Ibid., 37.

40. Sheff and Golson, *Playboy Interviews,* 91.

41. Copyright © 1965 by M. Witmark & Sons.

42. Sheff and Golson, *Playboy Interviews,* 110.

43. Ibid., 32.

44. See Norman, *Shout!* 374–77, 401–4.

45. Sheff and Golson, *Playboy Interviews,* 17.

46. Ibid., 102.

47. The Diggers' phrase is from Gerrad Winstanley, "The True Levellers' Standard Advanced," in Sheila Delany, ed., *Counter-Tradition: The Literature of Dissent and Alternatives* (New York: Basic Books, 1971), 71. For the Wobbly concept see Joyce L. Kornbluh, ed., *Rebel*

Voices: An I.W.W. Anthology (Ann Arbor: Univ. of Michigan Press, 1964), 1–9. See John Steinbeck, *The Grapes of Wrath* (New York: Viking, 1939), esp. 87–88, 462–64; for the communist concept, see Karl Marx and Frederick Engels, *The Communist Manifesto* (1848) (New York: Simon and Schuster, 1964).

48. From the song "Working Class Hero," copyright © 1970 by Northern Songs Ltd., from the album *John Lennon/Plastic Ono Band* (Apple, SW 3372, 1970).

49. "Freeda People" is the subtitle of "Bring on the Lucie," copyright © 1972 by John Lennon/BMI.

50. Cott and Doudna, eds., *Ballad of John and Yoko,* 67.

51. From an advertisement by Star File photos.

52. Cott and Doudna, eds., *Ballad of John and Yoko,* 40.

53. Ibid., 431–35.

54. The slogan "War Is Over if You Want It" was also used in the song "Happy Xmas (War Is Over)," copyright © 1971 by Northern Songs Ltd.

55. Sheff and Golson, *Playboy Interviews,* 96–97.

56. See Pete Hamill, "Long Night's Journey into Day," in Cott and Doudna, eds., *Ballad of John and Yoko,* 142–55.

57. John Lennon and Yoko Ono and the Elephants Memory Band, *Sometime in New York City* (Apple, SVBB 3392, 1972).

58. Actually, *Sometime in New York City* was the fourth Lennon/Ono collaboration, but the first three were so uncommercial that they have been practically unnoticed by fans and critics alike. Lillian Roxon's *Rock Encyclopedia* (New York: Grosset and Dunlap, 1978) for example, lists only two of the three and confuses them. The first was *Unfinished Music No. 1: Two Virgins,* an Apple product, which, because of the controversy over its nude cover, was released in Great Britain on Track Records and in America on Tetragrammation in 1968. It consisted of an abstract collage of experimental electronic sounds recorded by John and Yoko in his private studio on the night the two "virgins" first got together. The second coproduction, *Unfinished Music No. 2: Life with the Lions* (Apple, 1969), consisted of their performance at an avant-garde "jazz" concert in March 1969, mostly electronic screech, guitar feedback, and a few seconds of the heartbeat of the fetus Yoko later miscarried. Their third joint venture, *Wedding Album* (Zapple, 1969), was intended as a wedding announcement to their fans and included a photo of a piece of wedding cake.

59. Portions of the Mike Douglas performances can be heard on a bootlegged LP, *John Lennon Telecasts* (Buffalo Records, JL 517, 1979).

60. Cott and Doudna, eds., *Ballad of John and Yoko,* 42. May Pang's account of the "lost weekend" period contradicts much of the "official" version released to the press by Lennon and Ono.

61. See Chet Flippo, "The Private Years," in ibid., 158–81, for the official version of Lennon's seclusion and John Green's *Dakota Days* for a contrasting account.

62. "Two Virgins: An Exclusive *Newsweek* Interview" (September 1980). Green has exposed this interview as a mythical construction.

63. Sheff and Golson, *Playboy Interviews,* 14.

64. "Give Me Something" and "I'm Moving On" by Yoko Ono, "I'm Losing You" by John Lennon, are all copyright © 1980 by Lenono Music (BMI).

65. From "Clean Up Time" by John Lennon, copyright © 1980 by Lenono Music (BMI).

66. Sheff and Golson, *Playboy Interviews,* 16–17; Cott and Doudna, eds., *Ballad of John and Yoko,* 190, 16.

67. Lennon credits the introduction to Mao in the 1980 BBC interview with Andy Peebles.

68. From "(Just Like) Starting Over" by John Lennon, copyright © 1980 by Lenono Music (BMI).

69. Cott and Doudna, eds., *Ballad of John and Yoko,* 187.

70. "Getting Better" by John Lennon and Paul McCartney, copyright © 1967 by Northern Songs Ltd.

71. Garbarini, Cullman, and Graustark, *Strawberry Fields Forever,* 100. Lennon did not originate this line.

72. Ibid.

73. *BBC Tribute to John Lennon.*

74. Robert Christgau, "Double Fantasy: Portrait of a Relationship," in Cott and Doudna, eds., *Ballad of John and Yoko,* 302.

75. From "Dear Yoko" by John Lennon, copyright © 1980 by Lenono Music.

76. For a detailed account of the events surrounding John Lennon's death, see Cott and Doudna, eds., *Ballad of John and Yoko,* 196–211; and Garbarini, Cullman, and Graustark, *Strawberry Fields Forever,* 6–26.

77. *The Beatle Tapes,* record I, side 1.

78. Cott and Doudna, eds., *Ballad of John and Yoko,* 190.

79. See H.L. Neiburg, *Political Violence* (New York: St. Martin's Press, 1969), p. 9.

80. From a book by that title: Abbie Hoffman, *Woodstock Nation* (New York: Vintage, 1969).

81. Garbarini, Cullman, and Graustark, *Strawberry Fields Forever,* 2.

82. Ibid., 3.

83. Ibid., 18.

84. "Give Peace a Chance" by John Lennon and Paul McCartney, copyright © 1968 by Northern Songs.

85. See Garbarini, Cullman, and Graustark, *Strawberry Fields Forever;* 6–26.

86. Wenner, ed., *Lennon Remembers,* 167.

87. Cott and Doudna, eds., *Ballad of John and Yoko,* 302.

88. Ibid., 207.

89. Garbarini, Cullman, and Graustark, *Strawberry Fields Forever,* 19.

90. Cott and Doudna, eds., *Ballad of John and Yoko,* 208.

91. Garbarini, Cullman, and Graustark, *Strawberry Fields Forever,* 25–26.

92. Christopher Connelly, "A Survival LP for Yoko Ono: With a Little Help from Some Friends," *Rolling Stone,* No. 434 (November 8, 1984), 62.

93. John Lennon and Yoko Ono, *Milk and Honey,* side I, track 3.

94. Connelly, "A Survival LP for Yoko Ono."

95. This information was obtained through a phone conversation with park ranger Dave Pugh of New York City's Central Park Information service. See also Sue Allison, "Strawberry Fields: John Lennon's Song Becomes a Landmark—Forever," *Life* 8 (Nov. 1985), 61–64.)

96. Allison, "Strawberry Fields."

97. Julian Lennon, *Valotte* (Atlantic 80184-1, 1984).

98. See Tjerk Lammers and Greg Ptacek, "Julian Lennon: A Son Also Rises," *Rock Magazine* 4 (June 1985), 34–39.

Chapter 3

1. Sartre did not originate the concept of totality, but his writings have probably developed this concept more fully than those of any other scholar; see Jean-Paul Sartre, *Critique of Dialectical Reason,* trans. Alan Sheridan-Smith (London: Atlantic Highlands Humanities, 1976), esp. 45–47.

2. Ibid., 45.

3. See Rex Weiner and Deanne Stillman, *Woodstock Census: The Nationwide Survey of the Sixties Generation* (New York: Viking, 1979), 80-81.

4. Sartre, *Critique,* 45.

5. Ibid.

6. Ibid., 57.

7. See Edward Surtz, S.J., ed., *Sir Thomas More: Utopia* (New Haven: Yale Univ. Press, 1964).

8. For a brief summary of the utopian tradition, see George Kateb, "Utopias and Utopianism," in Paul Edwards, ed., *The Encyclopedia of Philosophy* (New York: Macmillan, 1967), 8; 206–15; for a more extensive discussion, see Frank E. Mannuel, ed., *Utopias and Utopian Thought* (Boston: Houghton Mifflin, 1966).

9. For a discussion of protest music and utopianism, see R. Serge Denisoff, *Great Day Coming: Folk Music and the American Left* (Urbana: Univ. of Illinois Press, 1971), 3–17.

10. Karl Mannheim, *Ideology and Utopia: An Introduction to the Sociology of Knowledge* (New York: Harcourt, Brace, and World, 1968), 173.

11. Ibid.

12. See Rosabeth Moss Kanter, *Communes: Creating and Managing the Collective Life* (New York: Harper & Row, 1973), 9.

13. *Socialism: Utopian and Scientific* was taken from a larger work, *Anti-Dühring,* Engels's famous polemic against Dr. E. Dühring of Berlin University (1877), reworked into a separate pamphlet which appeared in 1880. The text I refer to was published in 1975 in Peking by the Foreign Languages Press.

14. Ibid., 61–62.

15. Ibid., 48.

16. Ibid., 52.

17. Henri Troyat, *Tolstoy,* trans. Nancy Amphoux (Garden City, N.Y.: Doubleday, 1967), 16.

18. See John P. Diggins, *The American Left in the Twentieth Century* (New York: Harcourt Brace Jovanovich, 1973), 44–45.

19. See Paul Kagan, *New World Utopias* (New York: Penguin, 1975).

20. See Philip S. Foner, *History of the Labor Movement in the United States,* 4 vols. (New York: International, 1965).

21. See Diggins, *American Left,* 44–48.

22. See David Schuman, *A Preface to Politics,* 3d ed. (Toronto: D.C. Heath, 1981), 150–72.

23. Mannheim, *Ideology and Utopia,* 177; see also Eric Hoffer, *The True Believer* (New York: Harper & Row, 1951).

24. See Hoffer, *True Believer,* 57–60; Mannheim, *Ideology and Utopia,* 215–22.

25. See Margaret Cole, "Socialism," in Edwards, ed., *Encyclopedia of Philosophy,* 7: 467–70.

26. See Paul Goodman, *The Empire City* (New York: Macmillan, 1964); see also Charles A. Reich, *The Greening of America* (New York: Random House, 1970). 4–8.

27. See Kanter, *Communes,* 5–10.

28. This is basically the thesis of *The Communist Manifesto*: see Richard T. De George, *Patterns of Soviet Thought* (Ann Arbor: Univ. of Michigan Press, 1970), 57–63.

29. See Lee Cameron McDonald, *Western Political Theory: Part* 3, Nineteenth and Twentieth Centuries (New York: Harcourt Brace Jovanovich, 1968), 452–53.

30. Kanter, *Communes,* 3–6.

31. Ibid., 5.

32. See W. Cleon Skousen, *The Naked Communist* (Salt Lake City, Utah: Ensign, 1962), 114–15. This book is representative of a body of anti-communist literature from the perspective of Christian fundamentalism.

33. John Steinbeck, *The Grapes of Wrath* (New York: Penguin, 1976), 18.

34. Kanter, *Communes,* 18.

35. See Denisoff, *Great Day Coming,* 77–105.

36. See Tony Palmer, *All You Need Is Love: The Story of Popular Music* (New York: Grossman, 1976), 195–209.

37. Alfred G. Aronowitz and Marshal Blonsky, "Three's Company: Peter, Paul, and Mary," *Saturday Evening Post,* May 30, 1964, p. 32.

38. For the definitive account to date of Seeger's life and politics, see David King Dunaway, *How Can I Keep from Singing: Pete Seeger* (New York: McGraw-Hill, 1981).

39. See Theodore Roszak, *The Making of a Counter Culture: Reflections on the Technocratic Society and Its Youthful Opposition* (Garden City, N.Y.: Doubleday, 1969), 291.

40. *I.W.W. Songs: Songs of the Workers: To Fan the Flames of Discontent,* 4th ed., (Chicago: IWW, 1918), used by permission of the IWW.

41. From "That Good Old Union Feeling," copyright © 1947 by Disc Company of America.

42. Copyright © 1967 by Northern Songs Ltd.

43. "Workers of the World Awaken," *I.W.W. Songs,* 9th ed. (Chicago: IWW, 1916); used by permission of the IWW.

44. John Lennon, "Working Class Hero," copyright © 1970 by Northern Songs Ltd.

45. See Denisoff, *Great Day Coming,* 3–17.

46. Francis MacDonald Cornford, ed., *The Republic of Plato* (London: Oxford Univ. Press, 1976). 115.

47. Denisoff, *Great Day Coming,* 3–17.

48. See *I.W.W. Songs,* 5th ed. (Chicago: IWW, 1913).

49. John Greenway, *American Folksongs of Protest* (Philadelphia: Univ. of Pennsylvania Press, 1953), 12–29.

50. Denisoff, *Great Day Coming,* 41–45, 165–97; see also Oscar Brand, *The Ballad Mongers: The Rise of Modern Folk Song* (New York: Funk and Wagnalls, 1962).

51. See Greenway, *American Folksongs,* 67–120; Guy Carawan and

Candie Carawan, eds., *Freedom Is a Constant Struggle: Songs of the Freedom Movement* (New York: Oak, 1968).

52. "All Things Considered," National Public Radio Broadcast, Feb. 3, 1980.

Chapter 4

1. The Woodstock Music and Arts Festival was filmed and recorded: *Woodstock,* the movie, was produced and directed by Michael Wadleigh and Bob Maurice (Warner Brothers, 1970); the recording was a three-record set, *Woodstock, Music from the Original Soundtrack and More,* produced by Eric Blackstead (Cotillion, SD 3-500, 1970); see also Robert Stephen Spitz, *Barefoot in Babylon: The Creation of the Woodstock Music Festival, 1969* (New York: Viking, 1979); Joseph J. Sia, *Woodstock 69* (New York: Scholastic, 1970); and Abbie Hoffman, *Woodstock Nation: A Talk-Rock Album* (New York: Vintage, 1969).

2. From a poem by Alfred Hayes, "I Dreamed I Saw Joe Hill Last Night," written sometime in the late 1920s or early 1930s; with music added by Earl Robinson it became the song "Joe Hill," copyright © 1938 by Bob Miller, Inc.; see Waldemar Hille, ed., *The People's Song Book* (New York: Boni and Gaer, 1948).

3. The term "wobbly" first entered the IWW vernacular in 1912 during a strike by railroad workers in British Columbia, when a Chinese restaurant keeper accidentally coined the term while attempting to say "IWW." See *I.W.W. Songs,* 34th ed., 2d printing (Chicago: IWW, 1974), 58.

4. See Joyce L. Kornbluh, ed., *Rebel Voices: An I.W.W. Anthology* (Ann Arbor: Univ. of Michigan Press, 1964); also Frederick S. Boyd, *The Pageant of the Paterson Strike* (New York: Success, 1913).

5. There are many excellent histories of the IWW; see Paul F. Brissenden, *The I.W.W.: A Study of American Syndicalism* (New York: Columbia Univ. Press, 1919); Philip S. Foner, *History of the Labor Movement in the United States,* vol. 4, *The Industrial Workers of the World, 1905–1917* (New York: International, 1965); Patrick Renshaw, *The Wobblies: The Story of Syndicalism in the United States* (Garden City, N.Y.: Doubleday, 1967); Joseph Robert Colin, *Bread and Roses Too: Studies of the Wobblies* (Westport, Conn.: Greenwood Press, 1969); and Melvyn Dubofsky, *We Shall Be All: A History of the Industrial Workers of the World* (Chicago: Quadrangle, 1969).

6. Diggins, *The American Left in the Twentieth Century* (New York: Harcourt Brace Jovanovich, 1973), 45–46.

7. Kornbluh, ed., *Rebel Voices,* 164.

8. From an excerpted talk given by Ralph Chaplin on Joe Glazer, *Songs of the Wobblies* (Collector Records, CR 1927, 1977).

9. Kornbluh, ed., *Rebel Voices,* 158.

10. Ibid., 206, 197.

11. Ibid., 198.

12. Diggins, *American Left,* 27–33.

13. See John Reed, "War in Paterson," *International Socialist Review* 14 (July 1913), 43–48; Granville Hicks, *John Reed: The Making of a Revolutionary* (New York: Macmillan, 1936).

14. Mable Dodge Luhan, *Intimate Memories,* vol. 3, *Movers and Shakers* (New York: Harcourt Brace, 1933), 205.

15. Elizabeth G. Flynn, "The Truth about the Paterson Strike," from a speech to the New York Civil Club Forum, Jan. 31, 1914 (Labadie Collection, Univ. of Michigan Library), in Kornbluh, ed., *Rebel Voices,* 215.

16. *I.W.W. Songs,* 3d ed. (Chicago: IWW, 1911); used by permission of the IWW.

17. Copyright © 1970 by Northern Songs Ltd.; from the LP *John Lennon/Plastic Ono Band* (Apple, SW 3372, 1970), side I, track 3.

18. Karl Marx, *Critique of Hegel's "Philosophy of Right"* (London: Cambridge Univ. Press, 1970), 131.

19. Probably the best introduction to Joe Hill is Kornbluh, ed., *Rebel Voices,* chap. 4; see also Gibbs M. Smith, *Labor Martyr: Joe Hill* (New York: Grosset and Dunlap, 1969); Philip S. Foner, *The Case of Joe Hill* (New York: International, 1965); and Wallace Stegner, "Joe Hill: The Wobblies' 'Troubadour,' " *New Republic* 118 (Jan. 5, 1948), 20–24, 38–39.

20. Kornbluh, ed., *Rebel Voices,* 133–34.

21. *I.W.W. Songs,* 4th ed. (Chicago: IWW, 1912); used by permission of the IWW.

22. Kornbluh, ed., *Rebel Voices,* 132–33.

23. Carl Sandburg, *American Songbag* (New York: Harcourt Brace, 1927), 222.

24. See Smith, *Labor Martyr,* Appendix A, "A Joe Hill Song List Compiled by Archie Green," 231–60.

25. See Richard Brazier, "The Story of the I.W.W.'s 'Little Red Songbook,' " *Labor History* 9 (Winter 1968), 91–105.

26. See Kornbluh, ed., *Rebel Voices,* 94–126; see also Theodore Schroeder, *Free Speech for Radicals* (New York: Free Speech League, 1916); and Elizabeth G. Flynn, "The Free Speech Fight at Spokane," *International Socialist Review* 10 (Dec. 1901), 483.

27. John Greenway, *American Folksongs of Protest* (Philadelphia: Univ. of Pennsylvania Press, 1953), 173–77.

28. Ibid., 174.

29. William P. Mackay and John J. Husband, "We Praise Thee, O God" ("Revive Us Again"); see Walter H. Sims, ed., *Baptist Hymnal* (Nashville: Convention, 1956), 205.

30. *I.W.W. Songs,* 34th ed., (Chicago: IWW, 1973), 9; used by permission of the IWW.

31. Greenway, *American Folksongs,* 176.

32. Brazier, "Story of the I.W.W.'s 'Little Red Songbook,' " 96.

33. *I.W.W. Songs,* 34th ed., inside front cover; used by the permission of the IWW.

34. See Charles W. Hampton, "The Politics of Music: A Study of the Political Song as Used by the Industrial Workers of the World" (Master's thesis, Appalachian State Univ., 1977), 84–87.

35. See Smith, *Labor Martyr,* 25–26, 38–39.

36. Other good sources on Hill's songs are Kornbluh, ed., *Rebel Voices,* chap. 5; and Barrie Stavis and Frank Harmon, eds., *The Songs of Joe Hill* (New York: People's Artists, 1955).

37. *I.W.W. Songs,* 4th ed.; used by permission of the IWW.

38. Ibid., 3d ed.; used by permission of the IWW.

39. Ibid., 4th ed.; used by permission of the IWW.

40. Ibid., 3d ed.; used by permission of the IWW.

41. Philip S. Foner, *The Letters of Joe Hill* (New York: Oak, 1965), 167.

42. *I.W.W. Songs,* 5th ed. (Chicago: IWW, 1913); used by permission of the IWW.

43. For a discussion of Wobbly political tactics, see Kornbluh, ed. *Rebel Voices,* 35–64.

44. Ibid., 35.

45. Smith, *Labor Martyr,* 6.

46. Kornbluh, ed., *Rebel Voices,* 37.

47. Ibid.

48. Elizabeth G. Flynn, *Sabotage: The Conscious Withdrawal of the Worker's Industrial Efficiency* (Cleveland: IWW, 1915), 5.

49. Kornbluh includes several examples of sabotage symbolism in IWW graphic as well as literary arts; see *Rebel Voices,* 60–64.

50. *I.W.W. Songs,* 9th ed., (Chicago: IWW, 1916); used by permission of the IWW.

51. Kornbluh, ed., *Rebel Voices,* 57.

52. Smith, *Labor Martyr,* 174.

53. *I.W.W. Songs,* 9th ed. (Chicago: IWW, 1916); used by permission of the IWW.

54. Ralph Chaplin, "Joe Hill: A Biography," *Industrial Pioneer,* Nov. 1923, p. 23.

55. These comments appeared in a letter from Hill to Oscar W. Larson, Sept. 30, 1915, first published in *Revolt,* Dec. 1915, p. 12; also in Foner, *Letters of Joe Hill,* p. 59.

56. Joe Hill to editor Ben Williams, *Solidarity,* Oct. 9, 1915; Kornbluh, ed., *Rebel Voices,* 127.

57. John Dos Passos, *Nineteen Nineteen* (New York: Harcourt Brace, 1932), 456–57; used by permission.

58. The most recent discoveries about Hill's early life come from Ture Nerman, *Arbetarsangaren, Joe Hill: Mordare Eller Martyr*? (Stockholm: Federative Förlag, 1951).

59. This account of Hill's political activities before his arrest is from Nerman. Although in objectivity it may be the most reliable, it is not supported by other sources.

60. Card from Joel to Ester Hägglund, 1905; in a collection of Joe Hill material in Stockholm, Sweden, cited by Smith, *Labor Martyr,* 49.

61. Joel Hägglund to Gefle Dagblad, April 24, 1906, published May 16, 1906. The earthquake occurred April 18, 1906; cited by Nerman, *Arbetarsangaren,* 41; also ibid., 49–50.

62. Most sources agree on this date. See Smith, *Labor Martyr,* 52; Kornbluh, ed., *Rebel Voices,* 127; Foner, *Case of Joe Hill,* 9; and Stavis and Harmon, eds., *Songs of Joe Hill,* 3.

63. Smith, *Labor Martyr,* 52, 55, 53–54.

64. Ibid., 50–52, 55–56.

65. Kornbluh, ed., *Rebel Voices,* 127.

66. Smith, *Labor Martyr,* 53–54.

67. Ibid., 172.

68. Dos Passos, *Nineteen Nineteen,* 456.

69. Chaplin, "Joe Hill: A Biography," 23–26.

70. The most complete scholarly work on Hill's crime, trial, and execution is Smith's *Labor Martyr.* Although I have relied heavily upon this work, whenever possible, I have cited the original sources.

71. Ibid., 63.

72. Ibid., 63–64.
73. Ibid., 71.
74. Ibid., 65–67.
75. Ibid., 75.
76. Smith (p. 75) says only that "the shot, barely missing Hill's chest, struck his hand, shattering the knuckles." Kornbluh, *(Rebel Voices,* 128), says that "one fired a shot which grazed Hill's shoulder and went through his right hand." According to Foner, *Case of Joe Hill,* 21, Hill was reported to have said: "A bullet passed right over my chest, grazing my shoulder and penetrating my right hand through my knuckles, crippling me for life." From this I have inferred that it was Hill's right shoulder that was wounded.
77. Smith, *Labor Martyr,* 75.
78. Ibid., 78.
79. Ibid., 83–86.
80. Ibid., 93, 81.
81. Ibid., 89–91.
82. Ibid., 102.
83. Ibid., 102–13.
84. Ibid., 141, 160–61.
85. Ibid., 164–68.
86. *Salt Lake Herald-Republican,* Nov. 19, 1915; see Smith, *Labor Martyr,* 171.
87. Telegram, Hill to William D. Haywood, Nov. 18, 1915; first published in *Salt Lake Herald-Republican,* Nov. 19, 1915; see Smith, *Labor Martyr,* 171; also in Foner, *Letters of Joe Hill,* 84.
88. According to Barrie Stavis, *The Man Who Never Died* (New York: Haven, 1954), Hill wrote "My Last Will" during an interview in his cell with a reporter from the *Salt Lake City Herald Tribune* on the afternoon of November 18, 1915. The reporter asked how Hill would dispose of his effects. Hill replied: "I have nothing to dispose of. . . . But I have a will to make and I'll scribble it. I'll send it to the world care of Ed Rowan and my I.W.W. friends." According to Kornbluh, ed., *Rebel Voices,* 146, "My Last Will" was first published in the *International Socialist Review* in December 1915 and then in the ninth edition of the *I.W.W. Song Book* (March 1916). Bill Haywood included it in a letter sent to all IWW locals with instructions about scattering Hill's ashes on the following May 1; used by permission of the IWW.
89. *Salt Lake Herald-Republican,* Nov. 20, 1915; Smith, *Labor Martyr,* 175–77.
90. Ibid., 183.
91. Ibid., 84–87.
92. Ibid., 187.
93. See Brissenden, *I.W.W.,* 283.
94. See Kornbluh, ed., *Rebel Voices,* 316–25; also Len De Caux, *The Living Spirit of the Wobblies* (New York: International, 1978), 129–38.
95. Walker C. Smith, *The Everett Massacre: A History of Class Struggle in the Lumber Industry* (Chicago: N.d., c. 1920), cited in Kornbluh, ed., *Rebel Voices,* 316.
96. "What Haywood Says of the I.W.W.," *Survey* 38 (Aug. 11, 1917), 429.
97. See De Caux, *Living Spirit,* 129.

98. Kornbluh, ed., *Rebel Voices,* 321.
99. Ibid., 317.
100. De Caux, *Living Spirit,* 131.
101. Ibid., 129.
102. Ibid., 136.
103. Kornbluh, ed., *Rebel Voices,* 320.
104. Ibid., 325.
105. Ibid., 214; see also Flynn's autobiography, *I Speak My Own Piece* (New York: Masses and Mainstream, 1955).
106. Smith, *Labor Martyr,* 125.
107. Kornbluh, ed., *Rebel Voices,* 324; see also Haywood's memoirs, *Bill Haywood's Book: The Autobiography of Big Bill Haywood* (New York: International, 1929).
108. Kornbluh, ed., *Rebel Voices,* 306; also De Caux, *Living Spirit,* 126–28.
109. De Caux, *Living Spirit,* 137.
110. Chaplin's poem is in *I.W.W. Songs,* 9th ed.; Nordquist's is in *Solidarity,* Nov. 27, 1915, p. 3.
111. Hille, ed., *People's Song Book,* 35.
112. Upton Sinclair, *Singing Jailbirds* (Long Beach, Calif.: By the author, 1924); Carl Sandburg, *American Songbag* (New York: Harcourt Brace, 1927), "The Tramp," 185, "The Preacher and the Slave," 222.
113. Granville Hicks et al., ed., *Proletarian Literature in the United States: An Anthology* (New York: International, 1935); also in Smith, *Labor Martyr,* 196–99; Archie Binns, *The Timber Beast* (New York: Scribner's, 1944).
114. Wallace Stegner, *The Preacher and the Slave* (Boston: Houghton Mifflin, 1950), Barrie Stavis, *The Man Who Never Died* (New York: Haven, 1954); James Stevens, *Big Jim Turner* (Garden City, N.Y.: Doubleday, 1948), 85–89, 92–95, 157–73; Alexander Saxton, *The Great Midland* (New York: Appleton-Century-Crofts, 1948); Margaret Graham, *Swing Shift* (New York: Citadel, 1951); James Jones, *From Here to Eternity* (New York: Scribner's, 1951), 640–42; Eugene Burdick, *The Ninth Wave* (Boston: Houghton Mifflin, 1956), 22–23.
115. Woody Guthrie, "Joe Hillstrom," in Guthrie, *American Folksong,* ed. Moses Asch (New York: Oak, 1961), 22; Phil Ochs, "Joe Hill," *Broadside,* No. 76 (Nov. 1966), 5; *The Man Who Never Died* (Canadian Broadcasting Company, 1964); *Woodstock, Music from the Original Soundtrack and More; Newsweek,* Feb. 4, 1980.

Chapter 5

1. For biographical information, I have relied heavily upon the most recent and definitive work on Guthrie's life: Joe Klein, *Woody Guthrie: A Life* (New York: Knopf, 1980). Other Guthrie biographies include Ed Robbin, *Woody Guthrie and Me* (New York: Lancaster-Miller, 1980); Henrietta Yurchenco, *A Might Hard Road: The Life of Woody Guthrie* (New York: McGraw-Hill, 1970); see also Guthrie's autobiography, *Bound for Glory* (New York: Dutton, 1943). The following works also include chapters on Guthrie: R. Serge Denisoff, *Great Day Coming: Folk Music and the American Left* (Urbana: Univ. of Illinois Press, 1971); John Greenway, *American Folksongs of Protest* (Philadelphia: Univ. of Pennsylvania

Press, 1953); and Pete Seeger, *The Incompleat Folk Singer,* ed. Jo Metcalf Schwartz (New York: Simon and Schuster, 1972). Finally, the interested reader should also see Guthrie's autobiographical introduction to his *American Folksong,* ed. Moses Asch (New York: Oak, 1961).

2. This quote was taken from the notebook kept by the Almanac Singers during their tour of the summer of 1941; see Seeger, *Incompleat Folk Singer,* 59.

3. Quoted in Greenway, *American Folksongs,* 288.

4. Huntington's chorea is a rare hereditary disease marked by chronic and progressive chorea (the ceaseless occurrence of rapid, jerky, involuntary movements) and mental deterioration terminating in dementia. The age of onset is variable but usually occurs in the fourth decade of life. Death usually follows within fifteen years. See *Dorland's Illustrated Medical Dictionary,* 25th ed. (Philadelphia: W.B. Saunders, 1974), 311-12.

5. The term *gemeinschaft* was introduced by Ferdinand Tonnies as an ideal society in which social bonds are based primarily upon the close personal ties of friendship and kinship. He used the term to distinguish two basic types of societies: *gemeinschaft* and *gesellschaft. Gesellschaft* refers to societies in which social relationships are primarily formal, contractual, and impersonal, the urban industrial society Woody Guthrie abhorred. Guthrie's ideal community, his "working class," is best characterized as *gemeinschaft,* meaning rural agricultural, folk or peasant societies. See George A. Theodorson and Achilles G. Theodorson, eds., *A Dictionary of Sociology* (New York: Barnes and Noble, 1979), 170, 173.

6. Robbin, *Woody Guthrie and Me,* 133.

7. Gordon Friesen, "Bound for Glory," *Broadside,* no. 134 (Jan.-March 1977), 24.

8. Ibid., 41.

9. Karl Mannheim, *Ideology and Utopia: An Introduction to the Sociology of Knowledge* (New York: Harcourt, Brace and World, 1936), 216.

10. Robbin, *Woody Guthrie and Me,* 132.

11. The figure comes from Greenway, *American Folksongs,* 282. My own attempts to count the songs of Woody Guthrie have uncovered only 152. Many of Guthrie's scattered prose works have been published in *Born to Win,* ed. Robert Shelton (New York: Macmillan, 1965).

12. See Woody Guthrie's *We Ain't Down Yet,* a recording (Cream Records, CR-1002, 1976), prose narrated by Jess Pearson; "All of Us," side I, track 4.

13. For a further elaboration of this distinction between the musical culture of the Wobblies and the urban folk-music revival which Guthrie came to represent, see Denisoff, *Great Day Coming;* 41–76.

14. Ibid., chaps. 4–5.

15. Woody Guthrie, *We Ain't Down Yet,* "The Prophet Singer," side I, track 1.

16. Ibid., "The Singing Cricket," side II, track 6.

17. PBS, "The Weavers: Wasn't That a Time," March 19, 1983, a rebroadcast of a video documentary of the history of the Weavers, centering on their December 1980 reunion concert at Carnegie Hall, written and produced by Lee Hays.

18. Guthrie, *American Folksong,* 1.

19. Klein, *Woody Guthrie,* 5–40.

20. Ibid., 35.

21. Guthrie, *American Folksong,* 3.
22. Klein, *Woody Guthrie,* 87–99.
23. Ibid., 91.
24. Robbin, *Woody Guthrie and Me,* 55.
25. Klein, *Woody Guthrie,* 91.
26. See John P. Diggins, *The American Left in the Twentieth Century* (New York: Harcourt Brace Jovanovich, 1973), 108–21.
27. Klein, *Woody Guthrie,* 118–19; the quote is from Guthrie, *American Folksong,* 4.
28. Diggins, *American Left,* 110–11.
29. Klein, *Woody Guthrie,* 119.
30. Diggins, *American Left,* 112–14.
31. Ibid., 128–29.
32. See George Charney, *A Long Journey* (Chicago: Quadrangle, 1968), 61–62.
33. Klein, *Woody Guthrie,* 122.
34. Robbin, *Woody Guthrie and Me,* 29–34.
35. Klein, *Woody Guthrie,* 123.
36. Quoted in ibid., 126.
37. Guthrie, *American Folksong,* 4.
38. Klein, *Woody Guthrie,* 99.
39. Ibid., 126–29.
40. Ibid., 129–34.
41. Ibid., 136.
42. For an assessment of Guthrie's performing abilities in 1940, see ibid., 128–29.
43. Diggins, *American Left,* 111.
44. Denisoff, *Great Day Coming,* 41–60.
45. Guthrie, *Bound for Glory,* 295.
46. Klein, *Woody Guthrie,* 141.
47. Ibid., 142.
48. Denisoff, *Great Day Coming,* 80.
49. Klein, *Woody Guthrie,* 143.
50. Ibid., 153.
51. Guthrie, *American Folksong,* 5.
52. Klein, *Woody Guthrie,* 155.
53. Ibid., 158–60.
54. Ibid., 160.
55. Ibid., 160–63; for an account of this trip from Pete Seeger's perspective, see David King Dunaway, *How Can I Keep from Singing*: *Pete Seeger* (New York: McGraw-Hill, 1981), 65–70.
56. Klein, *Woody Guthrie,* 161–62.
57. Ibid.
58. Ibid., 165.
59. Ibid., 166.
60. Ibid., 167.
61. Ibid.
62. Ibid., 169.
63. Ibid., 171.
64. Ibid., 173.
65. Robbin, *Woody Guthrie and Me,* 58.
66. Klein, *Woody Guthrie,* 176–87.

67. Ibid., 189–90.

68. Ibid.

69. Guthrie, *American Folksong,* 5.

70. Denisoff, *Great Day Coming,* 80.

71. Ibid., 81; see also Klein, *Woody Guthrie,* 184.

72. For a detailed and moving account of Seeger's career, see Dunaway, *How Can I Keep from Singing.*

73. Denisoff, *Great Day Coming,* 42, 80.

74. Ibid., 82; also Dunaway, *How Can I Keep from Singing,* 77.

75. See Gordon Friesen, "Woody Works on His Books," *Broadside,* nos. 9–10 (July 1962).

76. Klein, *Woody Guthrie,* 213.

77. Denisoff, *Great Day Coming,* 86.

78. Klein, *Woody Guthrie,* 206.

79. Denisoff, *Great Day Coming,* 95–99.

80. Klein, *Woody Guthrie,* 265, 217; Denisoff, *Great Day Coming,* 101–2.

81. Ibid., 98.

82. Klein, *Woody Guthrie,* 224.

83. Guthrie, *American Folksong,* 6. Bob Dylan would later use this line in his song "One Too Many Mornings," from *The Times They Are A-Changin'* (Columbia, CS 8905, 1964).

84. Klein, *Woody Guthrie,* 253, 302.

85. Ibid., 302–4; see also Guthrie, *American Folksong,* 7–8.

86. Ibid., 276, 255, 332–34.

87. Greenway, *American Folksongs,* 280.

88. Robbin, *Woody Guthrie and Me,* 116–17.

89. Klein, *Woody Guthrie,* 406, 443.

90. Greenway, *American Folksongs,* 282.

91. This assessment comes from many sources. Some of Woody's views on politics and music can be found in an article, "Woody," consisting of a collection of his writings, drawings, and songs published in tribute just after his death in *Sing Out!* 17 (Dec./Jan. 1967–68), 5.

92. See Greenway, *American Folksongs,* 275.

93. Greenway, *American Folksongs,* 283; Klein, *Woody Guthrie,* 297.

94. This comment is from a "Woody Sez" column in *New York Daily Worker,* June 24, 1940; it was reprinted in *Broadside,* No. 21 (Feb. 1963); see also Klein, *Woody Guthrie,* 208–9.

95. Robbin, *Woody Guthrie and Me,* 132.

96. Greenway, *American Folksongs,* 299–301; Klein, *Woody Guthrie,* 209, 141, 195; Irwin Silber, ed., *Reprints from Sing Out!* 7 (New York: Oak, 1964), 19; Seeger, *Incompleat Folksinger,* 52, 54; Harold Leventhal and Marorie Guthrie, eds., *The Woody Guthrie Songbook* (New York: Grosset and Dunlap, 1976), 196, 188.

97. Pete Seeger introducing "Quite Early Morning" (in reference to the preious song, Guthrie's version of "Lonesome Valley"), on Seeger and Arlo Guthie, *Together in Concert* (Warner Brothers, 1975), side IV, track 4.

98. See Jan Harold Brunvand, *The Study of American Folklore: An Introuction,* 2d ed. (New York: Norton, 1978), 165.

99. "Tin Pan Alley" is a derogatory term used to refer to New York City's (and therefore America's) popular music industry. See Tony Palmer, *All You Need Is Love: The Story of Popular Music* (New York: Grossman, 1976), 97–115.

100. Quoted in *Broadside,* no. 21 (Feb. 1963).

101. Greenway, *American Folksong,* 282.

102. These are still available: *Dust Bowl Ballads Sung by Woody Guthrie* (Folkways, FH 5212, 1964).

103. TRO—© copyright 1960 and 1963 by Ludlow Music, Inc.

104. Words and music by Woody Guthrie. TRO—© copyright 1940 (renewed 1968), 1950 (renewed 1978), and 1951 (renewed 1979) by Folkways Music Publishers, Inc., New York; used by permission.

105. TRO—© copyright 1963 by Ludlow Music, Inc.

106. Ibid.

107. TRO—© copyright 1961 and 1963 by Ludlow Music, Inc.

108. See Brunvand, *Study of American Folklore,* 159.

109. By Woody Guthrie. TRO—© copyright 1960 and 1963 by Ludlow Music, Inc., New York; used by permission.

110. TRO, copyright © 1961 and 1963 by Ludlow Music, Inc.

111. Words and music by Woody Guthrie. TRO—© copyright 1960 and 1963 by Ludlow Music Inc., New York; used by permission.

112. Words and music by Woody Guthrie. TRO—© copyright 1961 and 1963 by Ludlow Music, Inc., New York; used by permission.

113. Woody Guthrie, *Ballads of Sacco and Vanzetti* (Folkways, FH 5485, 1947); also issued by Oak in the form of a songbook, c. 1960.

114. Copyright © 1960 by Sing Out, Inc.

115. TRO—© copyright 1961 and 1975 by Sanga Music, Inc.; used by permission.

116. Ibid.

117. See Klein, *Woody Guthrie,* 270.

118. "Woody," *Sing Out–* 17 (Dec.-Jan. 1967–68), 5.

119. The concept of the organizing song is similar to what Denisoff called the "magnetic song," which he distinguished from the more descriptive "rhetorical song"; see his *Sing a Song of Social Significance* (Bowling Green: Bowling Green State Univ. Press, 1971).

120. *I.W.W. Songs,* 34th ed. (Chicago: IWW, 1973), 4; originally published in the 9th ed. (1916).

121. Originally written in Harlan County, Kentucky, in 1931, copyright © 1947, by Stormking Music, Inc.; see Pete Seeger, *American Favorite Ballads* (New York: Oak, 1961), 94.

122. For a discussion of the background of "We Shall Overcome," see Dunaway, *How Can I Keep from Singing,* 222–23; the text has been reproduced in many songbooks, see Maynard Solomon, ed., *The Joan Baez Songbook* (New York: Ryerson, 1964), 144–45.

123. Although written by Lennon, this song is credited to John Lennon and Paul McCartney. It was recorded at the 1969 Montreal "Bed-in," copyright © Maclen Music, Inc., BMI; first released as a single (1969), then on the LP *Shaved Fish* (Apple, SW 3421, 1975).

124. See Klein, *Woody Guthrie,* 122–23, 143.

125. See Denisoff, *Great Day Coming,* 6; Pete Seeger credits Lee Hays with having originated the term "zipper song" on Pete Seeger and Arlo Guthrie, *Precious Friend* (Warner Brothers, 2BSK 3644, 1982), side IV, track 4. Denisoff, however, does not mention Hays in this connection.

126. Words and new music adaptation by Woody Guthrie. TRO—© copyright 1963 by Ludlow Music, Inc., New York; used by permission.

127. Leventhal and Guthrie, *Woody Guthrie Songbook,* 236.

128. Words and music by Woody Guthrie. TRO— © copyright 1961 and 1963 by Ludlow Music, Inc., New York; used by permission.

129. Ibid.

130. *I.W.W. Songs,* 34th ed., p. 46; copyright © 1973 by the IWW; used by permission.

131. See *Reprints from Sing Out!* 7: 19.

132. Words and music by Woody Guthrie. TRO—© copyright 1961 and 1963 by Ludlow Music, Inc., New York; used by permission.

133. See Guthrie, *American Folksong,* 33, 31.

134. Klein, *Woody Guthrie,* 271.

135. Words and music by Woody Guthrie. TRO—© copyright 1961 and 1963 Ludlow Music, Inc., New York; used by permission.

136. Denisoff, *Great Day Coming,* 137.

137. Greenway, *American Folksongs;* 291–92.

138. Klein, *Woody Guthrie;* 195.

139. "Grand Coulee Dam," words and music by Woody Guthrie. TRO—© copyright 1958, 1963, and 1976 by Ludlow Music, Inc., New York; used by permission.

140. From "Pastures of Plenty," copyright © 1960 by Ludlow Music, Inc.

141. Words and music by Woody Guthrie. TRO—© copyright 1961 and 1963 by Ludlow Music, Inc., New York; used by permission.

142. Leventhal and Guthrie, *Woody Guthrie Songbook,* 48.

143. Words and music by Woody Guthrie. TRO—© copyright 1958, 1963, and 1976 by Ludlow Music, Inc., New York; used by permission.

144. TRO, copyright © 1971 and 1976 by Ludlow Music, Inc.

145. Copyright © 1942 by MCA Music.

146. See Klein, *Woody Guthrie,* 235.

147. Words and new music adaptation by Woody Guthrie. TRO—© copyright 1962 and 1963 by Ludlow Music, Inc.; used by permission.

148. See Klein, *Woody Guthrie,* 140–141.

149. Ibid., 276.

150. Words and music by Woody Guthrie. TRO—© copyright 1956 (renewed 1984), 1958, and 1970 by Ludlow Music, Inc., New York; used by permission.

151. "Wish-y Wash, Wash," words and music by Woody Guthrie; TRO—© copyright 1964 by Ludlow Music, Inc., New York; used by permission.

152. "My Little Seed," words and music by Woody Guthrie. TRO—© copyright 1956 (renewed 1984) and 1963 by Folkways Music Publishers, Inc., New York; used by permission.

153. See Klein, *Woody Guthrie,* 312–13.

154. "Howdido," words and music by Woody Guthrie. TRO—© copyright 1961 and 1963 by Ludlow Music, Inc., New York; used by permission.

155. "All Work Together," words and music by Woody Guthrie, TRO—© copyright 1956 (renewed 1984) and 1963 by Folkways Music Publishers, Inc., New York, NY; used by permission.

156. Guthrie, *Songs to Grow On: For Mother and Child* (Folkways, FC 7015, 1956).

157. Seeger, *Incompleat Folksinger;* 41.

158. "Better World," words and music by Woody Guthrie. TRO— © copyright 1963 and 1976 by Ludlow Music, Inc., New York; used by permission.

159. Charles Hamm, "American Song during the Great Depression," liner notes to *Brother Can You Spare a Dime: American Song during the Great Depression* (Washington, D.C.: Recorded Anthology of American Music, NW 270, 1977).

160. See Seeger, *Incompleat Folksinger,* 41–61.

161. An excellent discussion of the folk boom may be found in Mike Jahn, *The Story of Rock: From Elvis Presley to the Rolling Stones* (New York: Quadrangle/New York Times Book Co., 1973), 70–81; for a more specific discussion of Guthrie's role, see Palmer, *All You Need Is Love,* 195–209; see also Klein, *Woody Guthrie,* 421–35.

162. See the Weavers (Lee Hays, Ronnie Gilbert, Fred Hellerman, and Eric Darling), eds., *The Weavers' Song Book* (New York: Harper & Row, 1960), 85–87.

163. See Klein, 363–65.

164. The Kingston Trio (Nick Reynolds, Dave Guard, and Bob Shane), *The Kingston Trio* (Capital, T996, 1958); for an excellent survey of the career of the Kingston Trio, see William J. Bush, "The Kingston Trio," *Frets* 6 (June 1984), 24–31; and "The Kingston Trio, Part II: The John Stewart Trio, the X-Factor, and the '80s," *Frets* 6 (July 1984), 31–43.

165. The Kingston Trio, *Make Way* (Capital, T 1474, 1960); the Kingston Trio, *Goin' Places* (Capital, T 1564, 1961), side I, track 1; ibid., side II, track 2; the Kingston Trio (Bob Shane, Nick Reynolds, and John Stewart), *Close Up* (Capital, ST 2011, 1961), side II, track 6; the Kingston Trio, *Time to Think* (Capital, ST 2011, 1964), Side II, track 1.

166. *The Library of Congress Recordings* (Elektra, EKL-271/2, 1964); *Born to Win,* ed. Robert Shelton (New York: Macmillan, 1965); *Seeds of Man* (New York: Dutton, 1968); *Woody Sez* (New York: Woody Guthrie Publications, 1975).

167. See Klein, *Woody Guthrie,* 433–34; I have recently heard "This Land" on national radio and television advertisements for the National Wildlife Federation, sung by Loretta Lynn, the country singer.

168. *Bound for Glory,* screenplay by Robert Getchell (United Artists, 1976).

169. *Woody Guthrie: Hard Travelin'* (A Ginger Group Production, with Harold Leventhal Management, Inc., 1984).

170. Klein was the first author to gain access to Marjorie Guthrie's personal file of Woody's unpublished writings (including many explicitly erotic letters) and has uncovered some accounts of Guthrie's sexual escapades. Sadly, Guthrie's sexuality evidently grew increasingly out of control as the disease progressed. Before it was over, he had been prosecuted and convicted on a charge of writing obscene letters to a young woman in California and served 180 days in jail. See Klein, *Woody Guthrie,* 350–55).

171. See Dunaway, *How Can I Keep from Singing*; 137–68.

172. See Denisoff, *Great Day Coming,* 138.

173. See Klein, *Woody Guthrie,* 439–42.

174. Will Geer told Ed Robbin of a conversation with Guthrie in which he compared the effects of Huntington's disease to a marijuana high, saying: "I sometimes get the same feeling as with the drug when the sickness comes on me. I think several things at the same time" (Robbin, *Woody Guthrie and Me,* 113).

175. Arlo Guthrie, "Alice's Restaurant Massacree," *Alice's Restaurant* (Reprise, RS 6267, 1967), side I.

176. Klein, *Woody Guthrie,* 444–45.
177. Ibid.

Chapter 6

1. There are few good sources on Dylan's life, for most are seriously biased. A running account can be found in *Sing Out!* and *Broadside* and, later, *Rolling Stone* magazines. *Sing Out!* and *Broadside* consistently favor the early folk-protest Dylan and find the later rock Dylan somewhat repugnant. In *Rolling Stone* it is the other way around. A reader edited by Craig McGregor, *Bob Dylan: A Retrospective* (New York: Morrow, 1972,), is a good source for other press articles on Dylan, but it needs to be updated. There are several interesting pseudo-biographical works on Dylan: Daniel Kramer's *Bob Dylan* (New York: Citadel, 1967) is a photographic essay on Dylan's early career; Toby Thompson's *Positively Main Street* (New York: Coward, McCann, and Geoghegan, 1971) is a shallow, hip-journalistic exploration of Dylan's early life, focusing on interviews with one of his high school sweethearts, Echo Hilstrom ("The Girl from the North Country"). To date, Anthony Scaduto's *Bob Dylan* (New York: Grosset and Dunlap, 1971) remains the most comprehensive biography of Dylan, but it lacks a great deal. The puzzling phenomenon of Dylan's religious conversion is the subject of Steven Pickering's *Bob Dylan Approximately: A Portrait of the Jewish Poet in Search of God* (New York: David McKay, 1975) and Paul Williams's *Dylan—What Happened?* (Glen Ellen, Calif.: Entwhistle, 1979). The inquisitive reader might also want to look at *Rolling Stone*'s *Knockin' on Dylan's Door* (New York: Pocket Books, 1974), and Sam Shephard's *Rolling Thunder Logbook* (New York: Viking, 1977). The most recent work is Jonathan Cott's *Dylan* (Garden City, N.Y.: Doubleday, 1984).

2. From "11 Outlined Epitaphs," a poem by Dylan, used as the liner notes to the LP *The Times They Are A-Changin'* (Columbia, CS 8905, 1964).

3. I have relied on the following works to help in interpreting Dylan's songs, poems, and public phases: Alan Rinzler, *Bob Dylan: The Illustrated Record* (New York: Harmony, 1978), a record-by-record summation of Dylan's works; John Herdman, *Voice without Restraint: Bob Dylan's Lyrics and Their Background* (New York: Delilah, 1982), a substantial analysis of Dylan's lyrics; and Michael Gray, *Song and Dance Man: The Art of Bob Dylan* (New York: Dutton, 1973, 2d ed., 1981), a serious, in-depth examination of Dylan's works as art. None of these works address themselves explicitly to the politics of Dylan's works. Most of the assessments in this chapter are my own.

4. For a listing of Dylan bootlegs, see the latest edition of *Hot Wax Quarterly* (Kitchener, Ontario, Canada: Blue Flake Productions, 1980).

5. Bob Dylan, *Tarantula* (New York: Macmillan, 1971). *Don't Look Back* is a film of Dylan's 1965 English tour, by D.A. Pennerbaker, also published in book form (New York: Ballantine, 1968). *Renaldo and Clara* was made during Dylan's "Rolling Thunder Revues," his tours of 1976–77; see Shepard, *Rolling Thunder Logbook. Pat Garrett* was a Metro-Goldwyn-Meyer production, written by Rudolph Wurlitzer, produced by Gordon Carroll, and directed by Sam Peckinpah. Dylan's musical score was released by Columbia, *Pat Garrett and Billy the Kid: Original Sound Track Recording* (PC 32460, 1973). The film starred Kris Kristofferson, James Coburn, and Jason Robards. Dylan also appeared in a small role as Alisa, a friend

and sidekick of Billy. Dylan's poetry before 1973 has been published along with his song lyrics and some drawings in Bob Dylan, *Writings and Drawings* (New York: Knopf, 1973).

6. Scaduto, *Bob Dylan,* 5–7.

7. Ibid., 26–51.

8. Ibid., 27, 67–69, 41.

9. Joe Klein, *Woody Guthrie: A Life* (New York: Knopf, 1980), 424.

10. Scaduto, *Bob Dylan,* 39–40.

11. Ibid., 43–47.

12. Ibid., 51–53.

13. Ibid., 56.

14. Ibid., 56–57.

15. Ibid., 64–66, 74–75, 59, 71.

16. Ibid., 97–100; the article by Shelton, "Bob Dylan: A Distinctive Folk-Song Stylist," *New York Times,* Sept. 29, 1961, is reprinted in McGregor, ed., *Bob Dylan,* 17–18.

17. This interview was taped but never broadcast by WBAI; see ibid., 119–20. Scaduto quotes only a small portion of this interview, which was reproduced in full on an early bootlegged LP, *The Great White Wonder* (TMOQ 72001, c. 1968).

18. See Dylan, *Writings and Drawings,* 6–7, 17–18, 22, 28, 8–9.

19. *Bob Dylan,* produced by John Hammond (Columbia, CS 8579, 1962); see Scaduto, *Bob Dylan,* 104–5.

20. See Rinzler, *Bob Dylan,* 11–13.

21. *Bob Dylan,* side I, track 4; side II, track 2; side I, track 6; side II, track 1.

22. Scaduto, *Bob Dylan,* 57.

23. See Dylan, *Writings and Drawings,* 3–4; and Woody Guthrie, *American Folksong,* ed. Moses Asch (New York: Oak, 1947), 20.

24. Dylan, *Writings and Drawings,* 3.

25. This line is from Guthrie's "Pretty Boy Floyd," see Harold Leventhal and Marjorie Guthrie, eds., *Woody Guthrie Songbook,* (New York: Grosset & Dunlap, 1976) 186–87.

26. Dylan, "Talking New York," from *Bob Dylan.*

27. Ibid.

28. Dylan, *Writings and Drawings,* 5.

29. *Sing Out!* 12 (Oct.-Nov. 1962), 7.

30. Dylan, "Song to Woody," from *Bob Dylan.*

31. This interpretation was first suggested to be by Richard Penner of the Department of English at the University of Tennessee at Knoxville, after reading an early draft of this chapter. Scaduto does not make this argument. But it is crucial to an understanding of the Dylan-Guthrie relationship. Later works—Rinzler, *Bob Dylan,* 13, and Gray, *Song and Dance Man,* 21—develop similar arguments.

32. Scaduto, *Bob Dylan,* 111–17; Rinzler, *Bob Dylan,* 15–28.

33. See John P. Diggins, *The American Left in the Twentieth Century* (New York: Harcourt Brace Jovanovich, 1973, 155–72.

34. Quoted in Scaduto, *Bob Dylan,* 137–38.

35. On the founding and development of *Broadside,* see Jim Capaldi, "Broadside: The Struggle Continues," *Folk Scene* 4 (Feb. 1977), 16–23; see also R. Serge Denisoff, *Great Day Coming: Folk Music and the American Left* (Urbana: Univ. of Illinois Press, 1971), 170–84; Josh Dunson, *Freedom*

in the Air: Song Movements of the Sixties (New York: International, 1965), 72–77.

36. Dunson, *Freedom in the Air,* 78–98.

37. *Broadside,* no. 3 (April 1962); ibid., no. 16 (Nov. 1962); ibid., no. 22 (March 1963).

38. Columbia, CS 8786 and CS 8905.

39. See Dylan, *Writings and Drawings,* 33–44, 85–97.

40. Denisoff, *Great Day Coming,* 176–84.

41. Dylan, *Writings and Drawings,* 38–39, 96–97.

42. Ibid., 20–21, 19.

43. Woody Guthrie, *Bound for Glory* (New York: Dutton, 1943), 295; quoted above, Chapter V, at n.45. This conclusion is mine, based on my reading of the Guthrie passage, which immediately brought to mind Dylan's "Blowin' in the Wind." None of the Dylan literature to which I have been exposed makes the connection.

44. *Sing Out!* 12 (Oct.-Nov. 1962), 4.

45. Dylan, *Writings and Drawings,* 33.

46. See Gray, *Song and Dance Man,* 48–49.

47. Dylan, *Writings and Drawings,* 62–57.

48. Ibid., 33, 36, 43–44, 94–95.

49. Ibid., 23.

50. Ibid., 37.

51. Ibid., 36.

52. See Denisoff, *Great Day Coming,* 174.

53. See Scaduto, *Bob Dylan,* 132–47.

54. Ibid., 146; see also McGregor, ed., *Bob Dylan,* 38–39.

55. Scaduto, *Bob Dylan,* 151; see also Denisoff, *Great Day Coming,* 176–77 (Denisoff estimates the number of demonstrators at Washington at "nearly a million").

56. According to Rinzler, *Bob Dylan,* 16; Scaduto, *Bob Dylan,* 151.

57. Scaduto, *Bob Dylan,* 172.

58. B.H. Lehman, *Carlyle's Theory of the Hero* (Durham, N.C.: Duke Univ. Press, 1928), 45.

59. See Rinzler, *Bob Dylan,* 23; Philip Norman, *Shout! The Beatles in Their Generation* (New York: Warner, 1981), 300; and Jann Wenner, ed., *Lennon Remembers: The Rolling Stone Interviews* (New York: Fawcett, 1971), 167, 186–89.

60. See Rinzler, *Bob Dylan,* 15–23; Gray, *Song and Dance Man,* 7–10.

61. Scaduto, *Bob Dylan,* 162.

62. Dylan, *Writings and Drawings,* 56.

63. Columbia, CS 8786 (1963); see Rinzler, *Bob Dylan,* 19.

64. Scaduto, *Bob Dylan,* 171.

65. See ibid., 163–65.

66. Ibid., 170–75, 221–43.

67. Ibid., 184–85.

68. Columbia, CS 8905.

69. Scaduto, *Bob Dylan,* 177–79.

70. See Rinzler, *Bob Dylan,* 31–53.

71. See Scaduto, *Bob Dylan,* 203–8; Rinzler, *Bob Dylan,* 36; also Denisoff, *Great Day Coming,* 185–97.

72. Scaduto, *Bob Dylan,* 161–63.

73. Ibid.

74. Ibid., 203–4.

75. Ibid., 204; for a detailed account of this evening, see Peter Brown and Steve Gaines, *The Love You Make: An Insider's Story of the Beatles* (New York: McGraw-Hill, 1983).

76. Ibid., 208–9; see also Denisoff, *Great Day Coming*; 182–84; Irwin Silber, "An Open Letter to Bob Dylan," *Sing Out!* 14 (Nov. 1964),reprinted in McGregor, ed., *Bob Dylan,* 66–68; and Josh Dunson, "Newport: Two Workshops of Our Times," *Broadside,* no. 49 (August 1964).

77. Columbia, CS 8993, 1964.

78. Scaduto, *Bob Dylan,* 205.

79. See Gray, *Song and Dance Man,* 10; Denisoff, *Great Day Coming,* 184.

80. Dylan, *Writings and Drawings,* 136–37.

81. "It Ain't Me Babe," ibid., 138.

82. "To Ramona," copyright 1964 by M. Witmark & Songs, used by permission.

83. Ibid., 126–27.

84. Ibid., 133.

85. See Pennebaker, *Don't Look Back.*

86. Columbia, CS, 9128; see Rinzler, *Bob Dylan,* 39–45.

87. "Notes by Bob Dylan," *Bringing It All Back Home;* see also Dylan, *Writings and Drawings,* 158.

88. See Albert Goldman, "The Emergence of Rock," *New American Review* 3 (April 1968); reprinted in Gerald Howard, ed., *The Sixties: The Art, Attitudes, Politics, and Media of Our Most Explosive Decade* (New York: Washington Square Press, 1982), 343–64.

89. Dylan, *Writings and Drawings,* 160.

90. Ibid., 161.

91. Ibid., 163.

92. Ibid., 164.

93. Ibid., 165–66.

94. Ibid., 167–68.

95. Ibid., 169–70.

96. bid., 171–73.

97. Ibid.

98. Ibid.

99. Ibid., 174.

100. See Bud Scoppa, "The Byrds," in Jim Miller, ed., *The Rolling Stone Illustrated History of Rock and Roll* (New York: Random House, 1976), 214–15.

101. See Paul Nelson, "Folk-Rock," in ibid., 216–21.

102. See Greil Marcus, "The Beatles," ibid., 172–81; also Carl Belz, *The Story of Rock* (New York: Oxford Univ. Press, 1969), 126–57.

103. All the songs listed here can be conveniently found in *Beatles Complete* (New York: Warner Brothers, 1976), 40–43, 9–11, 12–13, 158–59, 206–7, 184–85, 224–25, 300–301, 280–83, 383–85.

104. See Nelson, "Folk-Rock," in Miller, ed., *Rolling Stone Illustrated History,* 216–21.

105. Dylan, *Writings and Drawings,* 183–84.

106. Rinzler, *Bob Dylan,* 40.

107. See Scaduto, *Bob Dylan,* 245–49; there are also recordings of Dylan's 1965 Newport appearance on various bootlegged albums; see Bob Dylan, *Passed Over and Rolling Thunder* (Phoenix, 44770, 1979), side I.

108. Another rumor is that Seeger was so agitated that he threatened to take an ax to the power cables; see David K. Dunaway, *How Can I Keep from Singing: Pete Seeger* (New York: McGraw-Hill, 1981), 246–48.

109. My comments come from listening many times to the version of Dylan at Newport on *Passed Over and Rolling Thunder.* Although not a complete transcript—Peter Yarrow's attempt to calm the crowd between Dylan's electric and acoustic sets, for example, has been edited out—it does preserve Dylan's complete performances along with the audience's immediate reaction.

110. Dylan, *Writings and Drawings,* 183.

111. On the LP *Highway 61 Revisited* (Columbia, CS 9189, 1965), this song appears as "It Takes a Lot to Laugh, It Takes a Train to Cry." The lyrics used at Newport were modified and polished before being recorded.

112. "It's All Over Now, Baby Blue," in Dylan, *Writings and Drawings,* 174.

113. Ibid., 167–68.

114. Columbia, CS 9189.

115. Scaduto, *Bob Dylan,* 225.

116. Dylan, *Writings and Drawings,* 182.

117. Ibid.

118. Although there is a similar saying in the Old Testament: "He that rollest the stone, it will return upon him" (Proverbs 26:27, c. 700 B.C.), the earliest reference to "a rolling stone gathers no moss" is *Pubilius Syrus* by Pliny, in his *Natural History,* 35, sec. 199, from the first century B.C.; see John Bartlett, *Bartlett's Familiar Quotations*, 24th ed. (Boston: Little, Brown, 1968), 26.

119. *I.W.W. Songs,* 34th ed. (Chicago: IWW, 1973), 35.

120. Dylan, *Writings and Drawings,* 183.

121. Ibid., 185–87.

122. Ibid., 182.

123. Ibid., 188.

124. Ibid., 190–91.

125. Ibid., 192.

126. Ibid., 196.

127. Ibid., 197–98.

128. Ibid., 193–95.

129. Scaduto, *Bob Dylan,* 129; Gray, *Song and Dance Man,* 12.

130. See Kramer, *Bob Dylan,* 171–77, 179–212 (photos).

131. Ibid.

132. Ibid.

133. Scaduto, *Bob Dylan,* 266.

134. Columbia, C2S 841, released in May 1966.

135. See Rinzler, *Bob Dylan,* 51–55.

136. *Blonde on Blonde,* side I, track 1; named for two women, aged twelve and thirty-five, who came into the studio during the recording session to get out of the rain.

137. See Rex Weiner and Deanne Stillman, *Woodstock Census: The Nationwide Survey of the Sixties Generation* (New York: Viking, 1979), 105–31.

138. Scaduto, *Bob Dylan,* 245–48.

139. See Klein, *Woody Guthrie,* 444; Lillian Roxon, "The Guthrie Memorial Concert," in McGregor, ed., *Bob Dylan,* 210–17.

140. Columbia, PC 9604, 1968.

141. Capital/EMI, SMAS 2653, 1967.

142. See Scaduto, *Bob Dylan,* 249–57.

143. See Kaye Northcott, "The Life and Death of the Cosmic Cowboy," *Mother Jones* 6 (June 1981), 14–21, 48.

144. Dylan, *Writings and Drawings,* 255–56.

145. Ibid., 257.

146. Ibid., 258.

147. Ibid., 260.

148. Rinzler, *Bob Dylan,* 59; Gray, *Song and Dance Man,* 32, 216–17.

149. See Jon Landau, "John Wesley Harding," in McGregor, ed., *Bob Dylan,* 264.

150. See Scaduto, *Bob Dylan,* 249–57.

151. "I Am a Lonesome Hobo," in Dylan, *Writings and Drawings,* 266; "I Pity the Poor Immigrant," ibid., 267; "The Wicked Messenger," ibid., 268.

152. Ibid., 261–63; see also Scaduto, *Bob Dylan,* 254–55; "Dear Landlord," Dylan, *Writings and Drawings,* 265.

153. Dylan, *Writings and Drawings,* 259; it is taken from Isaiah 21, see Herdman, *Voice without Restraint,* 102.

154. See Hubert Saal, "Dylan is Back," in McGregor, ed., *Bob Dylan,* 243.

155. See Lillian Roxon, "The Guthrie Concert," in ibid., 210–17.

156. Ibid.

157. Scaduto, *Bob Dylan,* 257–58.

158. Columbia, KCS 9825, side I, track 1; ibid., 258–61.

159. See Hubert Saal, "Dylan's Country Pie," in McGregor, ed., *Bob Dylan,* 295–97.

160. See Tom Smucker, "Bob Dylan Meets the Revolution," in ibid., 299–305.

161. Columbia, C2X 30050; see Scaduto, *Bob Dylan,* 266–77.

162. Robert Christgau, "Consumer Guide: Self-Portrait," in McGregor, ed., *Bob Dylan,* 359.

163. Rinzler, *Bob Dylan,* 67; Scaduto, *Bob Dylan,* 267.

164. See Bob Dylan, *The Songs of Bob Dylan: From* 1966 *through* 1975 (New York: Knopf, 1976), 192.

165. George Harrison and Phil Spector, producers, *The Concert for Bangla Desh* (Apple, 1971).

166. Dylan, *Songs of Bob Dylan,* 335–39. For background on Dylan's involvement in the Carter case, see Shephard, *Rolling Thunder Logbook,* 49.

167. See Williams, *Dylan—What Happened?*

168. Columbia, QC 38819.

169. Ibid., side I, track 3.

170. Columbia Records (FC 40110), 1985; see also Kurt Loder, "Bob Dylan Rocks Again," *Rolling Stone,* no. 451 (July 4, 1985), 48–49.

171. Dylan appeared on "Late Night with David Letterman" on March 22, 1984; see Kurt Loder, "The Rolling Stone Interview with Bob Dylan," *Rolling Stone,* no. 424 (June 21, 1984), 14.

172. USA For Africa (video), "We Are The World" (Columbia/CBS, 1985).

173. See Michael Goldberg, "The Day the World Rocked," *Rolling Stone,* no. 454 (August 15, 1985), 22–34.

174. *Farm Aid,* The Nashville Network, September 22, 1985; produced by Willie Nelson for Farm Aid, Inc.; for a edited version, from the perspective of rock music culture, see "MTV Presents Farm Aid: Made in America," written by Michael Dugan and David Felton and produced by Liz Nealon, MTV Networks, Inc., 1985.

175. Dylan, *Empire Burlesque* (Columbia FC 40110), 1985.

176. Ibid., side I, track 3.

177. Ibid., side I, track 1.

178. "Seeing the Real You at Last," ibid., side I, track 2.

179. From "Subterranean Homesick Blues," *Bringing It All Back Home,* side I, track 2.

180. "Trust Yourself," *Empire Burlesque,* side II, track 1.

181. Gray, *Art of Bob Dylan,* 6.

182. Dylan, *Writings and Drawings,* 38, 85, 87.

183. Columbia finally released this as a legitimate LP (C2 33682) of the same name in 1975.

184. Columbia (PC 9604), 1967.

185. From *Slow Train Coming,* side II, track 3.

186. Ibid., "Precious Angel," side I, track 2.

187. Dylan, *Writings and Drawings,* dedication page.

Chapter 7

1. See R. Serge Denisoff, *Great Day Coming: Folk Music and the American Left* (Urbana: Univ. of Illinois Press, 1971), 167–97.

2. See Archibald MacMechan, ed., *Carlyle on Heroes, Hero-Worship, and the Heroic in History* (New York: Ginn, 1901).

3. Denisoff, *Great Day Coming,* 185–97, gives an excellent summary of this debate with full biographical information.

4. Ibid., 185–86.

5. Albert B. Friedman, ed., *The Penguin Book of Folk Ballads of the English Speaking World* (New York: Penguin, 1977), xxv-xxvi.

6. Ibid., 325–47.

7. See John Greenway, *American Folksongs of Protest* (Philadelphia: Univ. of Pennsylvania Press, 1953), 2.

8. Arthur Elson, *The Book of Musical Knowledge* (New York: Tudor, 1927), 35.

9. George H. Sabine and Thomasa L. Thorson, *A History of Political Theory* (Hinsdale, Ill.: Dryden, 1973), 294–96; see also Michael Walzer, *The Revolution of the Saints: A Study in the Origins of Radical Politics* (New York: Atheneum, 1971), 1–21.

10. Greenway, *American Folksongs,* 12–13.

11. Ibid., 2.

12. In other words, when Adam plowed the fields and Eve spun wool for their clothing, there were no class divisions in Eden. Greenway (*American Folksongs,* 2) includes this quote but does not attribute it to John Ball. Sabine and Thorson *(History,* 296) also use this quote, but mention no author. The connection to John Ball is made by Will Durant in *The Story of Civilization: Part VI, The Reformation* (New York: Simon and Schuster,

1957), 41. His source is Charles Oman, *The Great Revolt of* 1381 (Oxford, 1906), 51.

13. Durant, *Story of Civilization,* 45.

14. Philip S. Foner, *American Labor Songs of the Nineteenth Century* (Urbana: Univ. of Illinois, 1975), 347–49.

15. Ibid., xv.

16. Ibid., 321.

17. See Greenway, *American Folksongs,* 5–10.

18. Foner, *American Labor Songs,* xi.

19. The quotations are taken from "Joe Hill," a poem by Ralph Chaplin that appeared in the ninth edition of the IWW songbook in 1916; reprinted in Joyce L. Kornbluh, ed., *Rebel Voices: An I.W.W. Anthology* (Ann Arbor: Univ. of Michigan Press, 1964), 156.

20. See Richard Brazier, "The Story of the I.W.W.'s 'Little Red Songbook,' " *Labor History* 9 (Winter 1968), 91–105.

21. See Charles Wayne Hampton, "The Politics of Music: A Study of the Political Song as Used by the I.W.W." (Master's thesis, Appalachian State Univ., 1977), 84–86.

22. See Nat Hentoff, "The Odyssey of Woody Guthrie: The Rebel Who Started the Folk-Song Craze," *Pageant,* March 1964.

23. See Mike Jahn, *The Story of Rock: From Elvis Presley to the Rolling Stones* (New York: Quadrangle/New York Times Book Co., 1973), 8.

24. See Jan Harold Brunvand, *The Study of American Folklore*: An Introduction, 2d ed. (New York: Norton, 1978), 1–4.

25. See Paul Jacobs and Saul Landau, *The New Radicals* (New York: Random House, 1966).

26. John Lennon, *John Lennon/Plastic Ono Band* (Apple, SW 3372, 1970), side I, track 4.

27. Ibid.

Selected Bibliography

John Lennon

Allison, Sue. "Strawberry Fields: John Lennon's Song Becomes a Landmark—Forever." *Life* 8 (Nov. 1985), 61–64.

Beatles Complete. New York: Warner Brothers, 1976.

The Beatles Lyrics Illustrated. New York: Dell, 1975.

Blackburn, Robin, and Tariq Ali. "Power to the People" (An interview with John Lennon and Yoko Ono). In David Horowitz, Michael P. Lerner, and Craig Pyes, eds., *Counterculture and Revolution.* New York: Random House, 1972.

Cameron, Gail. "The Cool Brain behind the Bonfire." *Life* 57 (Aug. 28, 1964), 58–66.

Coleman, Ray. *Lennon.* New York: McGraw-Hill, 1984.

Connelly, Christopher. "A Survival LP for Yoko Ono: With a Little Help from Some Friends." *Rolling Stone,* Nov. 8, 1984, pp. 53, 62.

Cott, Jonathan, and Christine Doudna, eds. *The Ballad of John and Yoko.* Garden City, N.Y.: Doubleday, 1982.

Davies, Hunter. *The Beatles: The Authorized Biography.* New York: Dell, 1968.

Flippo, Chet. "John Lennon: The Private Years." *Rolling Stone,* Oct. 14, 1982, pp. 38–46.

Gambaccini, Paul, "A Conversation with Paul McCartney." *Rolling Stone,* no. 295 (July 12, 1979), 39–46.

Garbarini, Vic, Bryan Cullman, and Barbara Graustark. *Strawberry Fields Forever: John Lennon Remembered.* New York: Delilah, 1980.

Graustark, Barbara. "Two Virgins." *Newsweek,* Sept. 29, 1980, pp. 76–78; "An Ex-Beatle 'Starting Over.'" *Newsweek,* Dec. 22, 1980, pp. 45–46.

Green, John. *Dakota Days: The True Story of John Lennon's Final Years.* New York: St. Martin's Press, 1983.

Harry, Bill, ed. *Mersey Beat: The Beginnings of the Beatles.* London: Book Sales Limited, 1977.

Kroll, Jack. "Strawberry Fields Forever." *Newsweek,* Dec. 22, 1980, pp. 41–44.

Lennon, Cynthia. *A Twist of Lennon.* New York: Avon Books, 1978.
Lennon, John. *In His Own Write.* New York: Simon and Schuster, 1964.
———. *A Spaniard in the Works.* New York: New American Library, 1967.
Marcus, Greil. "The Beatles." In *The Rolling Stone Illustrated History of Rock and Roll,* edited by Jim Miller. New York: Random House, 1976. Pp. 172–81.
Mathews, Tom. et al. "Lennon's Alter Ego." *Newsweek,* Dec. 22, 1980, pp. 33–35.
Mayer, Allan J. "Death of a Beatle." *Newsweek,* Dec. 22, 1980, pp. 31–36.
Meryman, Richard. "Paul McCartney on the Beatle Breakup." *Life* 70 (April 16, 1971), 52–58.
Naha, Ed. ed. *John Lennon and the Beatles Forever.* New York: Tower Books, 1980.
Norman, Philip. *Shout! The Beatles in Their Generation.* New York: Warner, 1981.
Okum, Milton. *Pocket Beatles: For Guitar.* Greenwich, Conn.: Cherry Lane Music Co., 1980.
Polskin, Howard. "John Lennon's Murder: Did TV Go Too Far?" *TV Guide* 29 (Nov. 21, 1981), 2–8.
Reinhart, Charles. *You Can't Do That! Beatle Bootlegs and Novelty Records,* 1963–80. Ann Arbor: Pierian Press, 1981.
Rollin, Betty, "Top Pop Merger: Lennon/Ono Inc." *Look* 33 (March 18, 1969), 36–42.
Sheff, David. *The Playboy Interviews with John Lennon and Yoko Ono.* Edited by G. Barry Golson. New York: Playboy, 1980.
———. "Yoko and Sean: Starting Over." *People Weekly* 18 (Dec. 13, 1982), 42–45.
Wenner, Jann, ed. *Lennon Remembers: The Rolling Stone Interviews.* New York: Fawcett, 1971.

Rock Era: Politics and Culture

Alper, Jane. *Growing Up Underground.* New York: Morrow, 1981.
Anson, Robert Sam. *Gone Crazy and Back Again: The Rise and Fall of the "Rolling Stone" Generation.* Garden City, N.Y.: Doubleday, 1981.
Anthony, Gene. *Summer of Love.* New York: Celestial Arts, 1980.
Brown, Norman O. *Love's Body.* New York: Random House, 1966.
Brustein, Robert. *Revolution as Theatre: Essays on Radial Style.* New York: Liveright, 1970.
Calas, Nicolas, and Elena Calsa. *Icons and Images of the Sixties.* New York: Dutton, 1971.
Castaneda, Carlos. *Tales of Power.* New York: Simon and Schuster, 1974.
Charters, Ann. *Kerouac.* San Francisco: Straight Arrow, 1973.
Cleaver, Eldridge. *Soul on Ice.* New York: McGraw-Hill, 1968.
Christgau, Robert. *Any Old Way You Choose It.* New York: Penguin, 1973.
Cohn, Mitchel, and Dennis Hale, eds. *The New Student Left.* Rev. ed. Boston: Beacon, 1967.
Cohn, Nik. *Rock from the Beginning.* New York: Stein and Day, 1969.
Dane, Barbara, and Irwin Silber, eds. *The Viet Nam Songbook.* New York: Guardian Books, 1969.
Davidson, Sara. *Loose Change.* New York: Pocket Books, 1978.
De Bell, Garrett, ed. *The Environmental Handbook.* New York: Ballantine, 1970.

Denisoff, R. Serge. *Solid Gold: The Popular Record Industry.* New Brunswick, N.J.: Transaction Books, 1975.
Dickstein, Morris. *Gates of Eden: American Culture in the Sixties.* New York: Basic Books, 1977.
Didion, Joan. *Slouching towards Bethlehem.* New York: Farrar, Straus, and Giroux, 1968.
Diner, Pierre. *The Living Theatre.* New York: Horizon Press, 1972.
Eisen, Jonthan, ed. *The Age of Rock: Sounds of the American Cultural Revolution.* New York: Vintage, 1970.
Ephron, Nora. *Wallflower at the Orgy.* New York: Viking, 1971.
Farina, Richard. *Been Down So Long It Looks Like Up to Me.* New York: Random House, 1966.
Feigelson, Naomi. *The Underground Revolution: Hippies, Yippies, and Others.* New York: Funk and Wagnalls, 1970.
Felton, David, ed. *Mindfuckers.* San Francisco: Straight Arrow, 1972.
Ferber, Michael, and Staughton, Lynd. *The Resistance.* Boston: Beacon, 1971.
Forcade, Thomas King, ed. *Underground Press Anthology.* New York: Ace Books, 1972.
Franklin, Bruce. *From the Movement toward Revolution.* New York: Van Nostrand Reinhold, 1971.
Friedan, Betty. *The Feminine Mystique.* New York: Dell, 1963.
Friedman, Myra. *Buried Alive: The Biography of Janis Joplin.* New York: Morrow, 1973.
Fuller, Buckminster. *Operating Manual for Spaceship Earth.* New York: Pocket Books, 1970.
Ginsberg, Allen. *Howl and Other Poems.* San Francisco: City Lights, 1960.
Gitlin, Todd. *The Whole World Is Watching: Mass Media in the Making and Unmaking of the New Left.* Berkeley and Los Angeles: Univ. of California Press, 1980.
Glessing, Robert J. *The Underground Press in America.* Bloomington: Indiana Univ. Press, 1970.
Goldman, Albert. *Elvis.* New York: Avon Books, 1981.
Goldstein, Richard. *The Poetry of Rock.* New York: Bantam, 1968.
Goldstein, Stewart, and Alan Jacobson. *Oldies but Goodies: The Rock 'n' Roll Years.* New York: Mason/Charter, 1977.
Goodman, Paul. *Compulsory Mis-Education.* New York: Random House, 1964.
———. *Drawing the Line: The Political Essays of Paul Goodman.* Edited by Taylor Stoehr. New York: Free Life, 1977.
———. *Growing Up Absurd.* New York: Random House, 1960.
Harrington, Michael. *The Other America: Poverty in the United States.* New York: Macmillan, 1962.
———. *Toward a Democratic Left.* New York: Macmillan, 1968.
Hodgson, Godfrey. *America in Our Time: From World War II to Nixon—What Happened and Why.* New York: Doubleday, 1976.
Hoffman, Abbie. *Revolution for the Hell of It.* New York: Dial, 1968.
———. *Steal This Book.* New York: Grove, 1971.
———. *Soon to Be a Major Motion Picture.* New York: Perigee, 1980.
———. *Woodstock Nation: A Talk-Rock Album.* New York: Vintage, 1969.
Hopkins, Jerry, and Danny Sugerman. *No One Here Gets Out Alive.* New York: Warner Books, 1980.

Horowitz, David, Michael P. Lerner, and Craig Pyles, eds. *Counterculture and Revolution.* New York: Random House, 1972.

Jackson, George. *Soldad Brothers.* New York: Bantam, 1970.

Jahn, Mike. *Rock: From Elvis Presley to the Rolling Stones.* New York: Quadrangle/New York Times Book Co., 1973.

Keniston, Kenneth. *Young Radicals: Notes on Committed Youth.* New York: Harcourt, Brace and World, 1968.

Kerouac, Jack. *On the Road.* New York: New American Library, 1957.

King, Martin Luther, Jr. *Why We Can't Wait.* New York: Harper & Row, 1967.

Kunen, James Simon. *The Strawberry Statement: Notes of a College Revolutionary.* New York: Random House, 1969.

Kupferberg, Tuli, and Robert Bashlow. *1001 Ways to Beat the Draft.* New York: Grove, 1967.

Laing, R.D. *The Politics of Experience.* New York: Pantheon, 1967.

Larson, Bob. *Hippies, Hindus, and Rock and Roll.* McCook, Neb.: Bob Larson, 1970.

———. *Rock and Roll: The Devil's Diversion.* McCook, Neb.: Bob Larson, 1967.

Lewis, Roger. *Outlaws of America: The Underground Press and Its Context: Notes on a Cultural Revolution.* New York: Penguin, 1972.

Lora, Ronald, ed. *America in the Sixties: Cultural Authorities in Transition.* New York: Wiley, 1974.

Lukas, J. Anthony. *Don't Shoot, We Are Your Children.* New York: Delta, 1972.

Marcus, Greil. *Mystery Train: Images of America in Rock 'n' Roll Music.* New York: Dutton, 1975.

Marsh, Dave, *Born to Run: The Bruce Springsteen Story.* New York: Dell, 1981.

McLuhan, Marshall. *Understanding Media: The Extensions of Man.* New York: McGraw-Hill, 1964.

Mellers, Wilfred. *Twilight of the Gods: The Music of the Beatles.* New York: Viking, 1973.

Miller, Jim, ed. *The Rolling Stone Illustrated History of Rock and Roll.* New York: Random House, 1976.

Morgan, Robin, ed. *Sisterhood Is Powerful: An Anthology of Writings from the Women's Liberation Movement.* New York: Vintage, 1970.

Mungo, Raymond, ed. *Famous Long Ago: My Life and Hard Times with Liberation News Service.* Boston: Beacon Press, 1970.

Nevile, Richard. *Play Power: Exploring the International Underground.* New York: Random House, 1970.

Noebel, David A. *Communism, Hypnotism, and the Beatles.* Tulsa, Okla.: Christian Crusade Publications, 1965.

Nowlis, Helen H. *Drugs on the College Campus.* Garden City: Doubleday, 1969.

Obst, Lynda Rosen, ed. *The Sixties.* New York: Random House/Rolling Stone Press, 1977.

Oglesby, Carl. *The New Left Reader.* New York: Grove, 1969.

O.M. Collective. *The Organizer's Manual.* New York: Bantam, 1971.

Palmer, Tony. *All You Need Is Love: The Story of Popular Music.* New York: Grossman, 1976.

Reaske, Christopher R., and Robert F. Wilson. *Student Voices/One: On Political Action, Culture, and the University.* New York: Random House, 1971.

Reich, Charles A. *The Greening of America.* New York: Random House, 1970.

Rogers, Mick. *Freakout on Sunset Strip.* San Diego: Greenleaf Classics, 1967.

Rosenthal, Raymond, ed. *McLuhan Pro and Con.* New York: Funk and Wagnalls, 1968.

Roszak, Theodore. *The Making of a Counter Culture: Reflections on the Technocratic Society and Its Youthful Opposition.* Garden City, N.Y.: Doubleday, 1969.

Roxon, Lillian. *Rock Encyclopedia.* New York: Grosset and Dunlap, 1978.

Rubin, Jerry. *Do It!* New York: Ballantine, 1970.

———. *We Are Everywhere.* New York: Harper & Row, 1971.

Sale, Kirkpatrick. *SDS.* New York: Vintage, 1974.

Sayre, Nora. *Sixties Going on Seventies.* New York: Arbor House, 1973.

Sia, Joseph J. *Woodstock* 69. New York: Scholastic, 1970.

Sinclair, John. *Guitar Army: Street Writings/Prison Writings.* New York: Douglas Book Corporation, 1972.

Skolnick, Jerome H. *The Politics of Protest.* New York: Ballantine, 1969.

Spitz, Robert Stephen. *Barefoot in Babylon: The Creation of the Woodstock Music Festival, 1969.* New York: Viking, 1979.

Stearns, Gerald, ed. *McLuhan Hot and Cold.* New York: Dial, 1967.

Unger, Irwin. *The Movement: A History of the American New Left, 1959–1972.* New York: Dodd, Mead, 1975.

Weiner, Rex, and Deanne Stillman. *Woodstock Census: The Nationwide Survey of the Sixties Generation.* New York: Viking, 1979.

Wheeler, Richard S. *The Children of Darkness: Some Heretical Reflections on the Kid Cult.* New Rochelle, N.Y.: Arlington House, 1973.

Wolfe, Tom. *The Electric Kool-Aid Acid Test.* New York: Bantam Books, 1969.

Wuthnow, Robert. *The Consciousness Reformation.* Berkeley and Los Angeles: Univ. of California Press, 1976.

Yablonsky, Lewis. *The Hippie Trip.* New York: Penguin, 1973.

Joe Hill: Life and Times

Anderson, Nels. *The Hobo: The Sociology of the Homeless Man.* Chicago: Univ. of Chicago Press, 1923.

Brissenden, Paul F. *The I.W.W.: A Study of American Syndicalism.* New York: Columbia Univ. Press, 1919.

Chaplin, Ralph. "Casey Jones." *New Masses* Jan. 1929, p. 14.

———. "Joe Hill." *Labor Defender* 1 (Nov. 1926), 187–90.

———. "Joe Hill: A Biography." *Industrial Pioneer,* Nov. 1923, pp. 23–26.

———. "Joe Hill's Funeral." *International Socialist Review* 16 (Jan. 1916), 400-405.

———. *Wobbly: The Rough and Tumble Story of an American Radical.* Chicago: Univ. of Chicago Press, 1948.

Commons, John R. *History of Labor in the United States.* 4 vols. New York: Macmillan, 1918–35.

Conlin, Joseph Robert. *Bread and Roses Too: Studies of the Wobblies:* Westport, Conn.: Greenwood Press, 1969.

Dubofsky, Melvyn. *We Shall Be All: A History of the Industrial Workers of the World.* Chicago: Quadrangle, 1969.

Egbert, Donald Drew, and Stow Parsons, eds. *Socialism in American Life.* Vol. 2. Princeton: Princeton Univ. Press, 1952.

Filler, Louis. *A Dictionary of American Social Reform.* New York: Philosophical Library, 1963.

Flynn, Elizabeth Gurley. *I Speak My Own Piece.* New York: Masses and Mainstream, 1955.

Foner, Philip S. *The Case of Joe Hill.* New York: International, 1965.

———. *History of the Labor Movement in the United States.* Vol. 4: *The Industrial Workers of the World,* 1905–1917. New York: International, 1965.

———. *The Letters of Joe Hill.* New York: Oak, 1965.

Friends of Joe Hill Committee. "Joe Hill: I.W.W. Martyr." *New Republic* 15 (Nov. 1948), 18–20.

Haywood, William D. *Bill Haywood's Book: The Autobiography of Big Bill Haywood.* New York: International, 1927.

———. "Sentenced to be Shot—Act Quick!" *International Socialist Review* 16 (Aug. 1915), 110.

Kornbluh, Joyce L., ed., *Rebel Voice: An I.W.W. Anthology.* Ann Arbor: Univ. of Michigan Press, 1964.

Jensen, Vernon H. "The Legend of Joe Hill." *Industrial and Labor Relations Review* 4 (April 1951), 356–66.

Nerman, Ture. *Arbetarsangaren, Joe Hill: Mördare Eller Martyr?* Stockholm: Federative Förlag, 1951.

Renshaw, Patrick. *The Wobblies: The Story of Syndicalism in the United States.* Garden City, N.Y.: Doubleday, 1967.

Smith, Gibbs, M. *Labor Martyr: Joe Hill.* New York: Grosset and Dunlap, 1969.

Stavis, Barrie. *The Man Who Never Died.* New York: Haven, 1954.

Thompson, Fred. *The I.W.W.: Its First Fifty Years.* Chicago: Industrial Workers of the World, 1955.

Tyler, Robert S. *Rebels of the Woods: The I.W.W. in the Pacific Northwest.* Eugene: Univ. of Oregon Books, 1968.

Warrum, Noble, ed. *Utah since Statehood* "The Hilstrom Case," pp. 686–90. Chicago: S.J. Clarke, 1919.

Joe Hill: Legend and Lore

Binns, Archie. *The Timber Beast.* New York: Scribner's, 1944.

Burdick, Eugene. *The Ninth Wave.* Boston: Houghton Mifflin, 1956.

Dos Passos, John. *Nineteen Nineteen.* New York: Random House,

Graham, Marcus, ed. *An Anthology of Revolutionary Poetry.* New York: Active Press, 1929.

Green, Archie. "American Labor Lore: Its Meanings and Uses." *Industrial Relations* 4 (Feb. 1965), 51–68.

Hill, Joe. "How to Make Work for the Unemployed." *International Socialist Review* 15 (Dec. 1914), 335–36.

Holbrook, Stewart H. *Holy Old Mackinaw.* New York: Macmillan, 1938.

Jones, James. *From Here to Eternity.* New York: Scribner's, 1951.

Sinclair, Upton. *Singing Jailbirds.* Long Beach, Calif.: By the author, 1924. (Play).

Stegner, Wallace. *The Preacher and the Slave.* Boston: Houghton Mifflin, 1950.

Stevens, James. *Big Jim Turner.* Garden City, N.Y.: Doubleday, 1948.

Joe Hill: Songs

Balch, Elizabeth. "Songs for Labor." *Survey* 31 (Jan. 3, 1914), 408–12.
Boni, Margaret Bradford, and Norman Lloyd. *Fireside Book of Folksongs.* New York: Simon and Schuster, 1947.
Botkin, B.A., ed. *A Treasury of American Folklore.* New York: Crown, 1944.
———. *A Treasury of Western Folklore.* New York: Crown, 1951.
Brazier, Richard. "The Story of the I.W.W.'s 'Little Red Songbook.' " *Labor History* 9 (Winter 1968), 91–105.
Denisoff, R. Serge. *Great Day Coming: Folk Music and the American Left.* Urbana: Univ. of Illinois Press, 1971.
Dunson, Josh. *Freedom in the Air.* New York: International, 1965.
Fowke, Edith Fulton, and Joe Glazer, eds. *Songs of Work and Freedom.* Garden City, N.Y.: Doubleday, 1960.
Greenway, John. *American Folksongs of Protest.* Philadelphia: Univ. of Pennsylvania Press, 1953.
Guthrie, Woody. "Joe Hill." In *American Folksong,* ed. Moses Asch. New York: Oak, 1961.
Hille, Waldemar, ed. *The People's Song Book.* New York: Boni and Gaer, 1948.
Hobo Ballads. Cincinnati: Hobo College Press Committee, n.d.
I.W.W. Songs: Songs of the Workers: To Fan the Flames of Discontent. 1st–35th eds. Chicago: IWW, 1909–76.
Lingenfelter, Richard E., Richard A. Dwyer, and David Cohen, eds. *Songs of the American West,* Berkeley and Los Angeles: Univ. of California Press, 1968.
Lomax, Alan, ed. *The Folk Songs of North America in the English Language.* Garden City, N.Y.: Doubleday, 1960.
Milburn, George. *The Hobo's Hornbook.* New York: Ives Washburn, 1930.
Reuss, Richard A. "The Ballad of 'Joe Hill' Revisited." *Western Folklore* 22 (July 1967), 187–88.
Sandburg, Carl. *American Songbag.* New York: Harcourt, Brace, 1927.
Seeger, Pete. "Whatever Happened to Singing in the Unions?" *Sing Out*! 15 (May 1965), 28–31.
Silber, Irwin. *Lift Every Voice.* New York: Oak, 1953.
Stavis, Barrie, and Frank Harmon, eds. *The Songs of Joe Hill.* New York: People's Artists, 1955.
Stegner, Wallace. "Joe Hill, The Wobblies' Troubadour." *New Republic* 118 (Jan. 1948), 20–24, 38–39.

Woody Guthrie

Adams, Camilla. "Woody Guthrie: Man or Myth." *Broadside,* no. 71 (June 1966), 7–9, 10.
Friesen, Gordon. "Woody Guthrie: Hard Travlin'." *Mainstream,* Aug. 1963, pp. 4–11.
———. "Woody Works on His Book." *Broadside,* nos. 9, 10 (July 1962), n.p.
"Geer, Woody, in Anti-War Songs Tonight." *Sunday Worker,* Nov. 10, 1940, p. 7.
Gilman, R. "Autobiography of Woody Guthrie." *New Republic* 159 (Oct. 5, 1968), pp. 19–21.

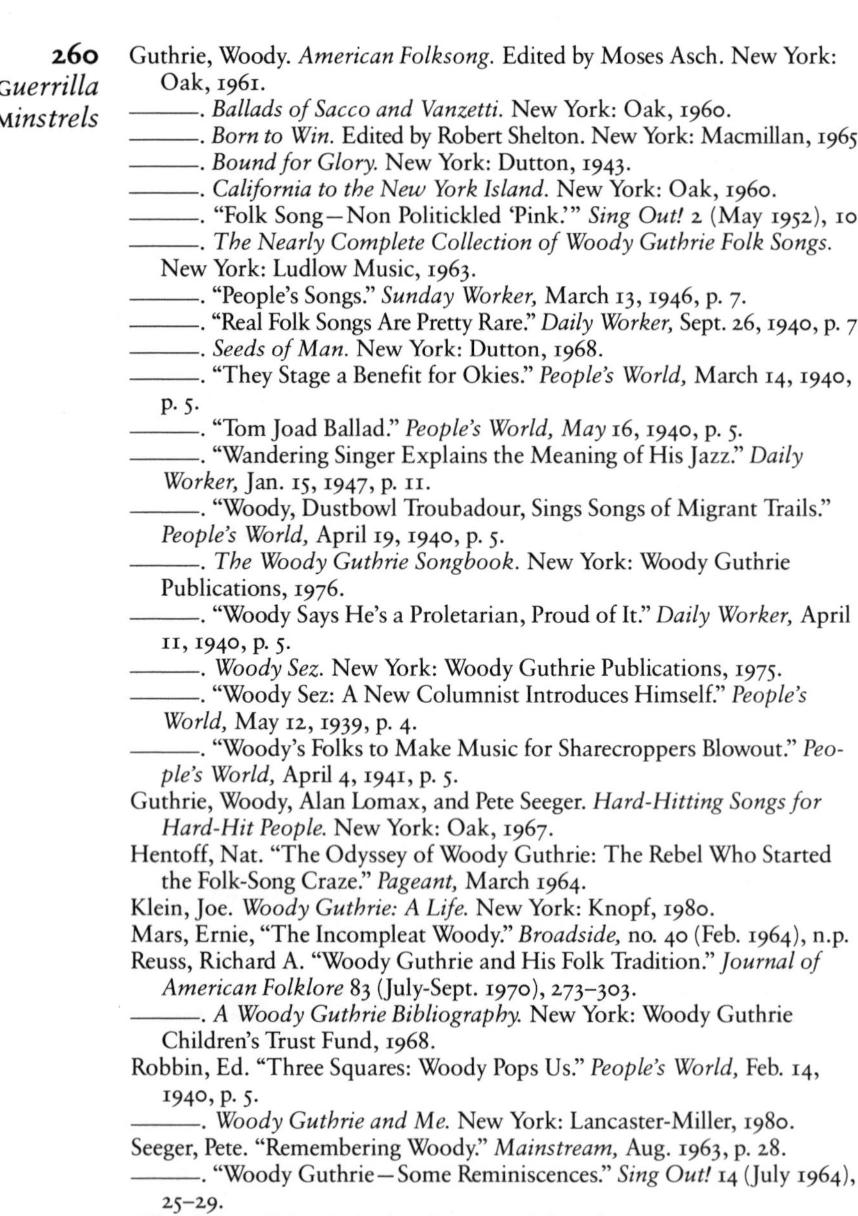

Guthrie, Woody. *American Folksong.* Edited by Moses Asch. New York: Oak, 1961.

———. *Ballads of Sacco and Vanzetti.* New York: Oak, 1960.

———. *Born to Win.* Edited by Robert Shelton. New York: Macmillan, 1965.

———. *Bound for Glory.* New York: Dutton, 1943.

———. *California to the New York Island.* New York: Oak, 1960.

———. "Folk Song—Non Politickled 'Pink.'" *Sing Out!* 2 (May 1952), 10.

———. *The Nearly Complete Collection of Woody Guthrie Folk Songs.* New York: Ludlow Music, 1963.

———. "People's Songs." *Sunday Worker,* March 13, 1946, p. 7.

———. "Real Folk Songs Are Pretty Rare." *Daily Worker,* Sept. 26, 1940, p. 7.

———. *Seeds of Man.* New York: Dutton, 1968.

———. "They Stage a Benefit for Okies." *People's World,* March 14, 1940, p. 5.

———. "Tom Joad Ballad." *People's World, May* 16, 1940, p. 5.

———. "Wandering Singer Explains the Meaning of His Jazz." *Daily Worker,* Jan. 15, 1947, p. 11.

———. "Woody, Dustbowl Troubadour, Sings Songs of Migrant Trails." *People's World,* April 19, 1940, p. 5.

———. *The Woody Guthrie Songbook.* New York: Woody Guthrie Publications, 1976.

———. "Woody Says He's a Proletarian, Proud of It." *Daily Worker,* April 11, 1940, p. 5.

———. *Woody Sez.* New York: Woody Guthrie Publications, 1975.

———. "Woody Sez: A New Columnist Introduces Himself." *People's World,* May 12, 1939, p. 4.

———. "Woody's Folks to Make Music for Sharecroppers Blowout." *People's World,* April 4, 1941, p. 5.

Guthrie, Woody, Alan Lomax, and Pete Seeger. *Hard-Hitting Songs for Hard-Hit People.* New York: Oak, 1967.

Hentoff, Nat. "The Odyssey of Woody Guthrie: The Rebel Who Started the Folk-Song Craze." *Pageant,* March 1964.

Klein, Joe. *Woody Guthrie: A Life.* New York: Knopf, 1980.

Mars, Ernie, "The Incompleat Woody." *Broadside,* no. 40 (Feb. 1964), n.p.

Reuss, Richard A. "Woody Guthrie and His Folk Tradition." *Journal of American Folklore* 83 (July-Sept. 1970), 273–303.

———. *A Woody Guthrie Bibliography.* New York: Woody Guthrie Children's Trust Fund, 1968.

Robbin, Ed. "Three Squares: Woody Pops Us." *People's World,* Feb. 14, 1940, p. 5.

———. *Woody Guthrie and Me.* New York: Lancaster-Miller, 1980.

Seeger, Pete. "Remembering Woody." *Mainstream,* Aug. 1963, p. 28.

———. "Woody Guthrie—Some Reminiscences." *Sing Out!* 14 (July 1964), 25–29.

Silber, Irwin. "Woody Guthrie." *National Guardian,* Oct. 14, 1967, p. 6.

"Woody." *Sing Out!* 17 (Dec.-Jan. 1967–68), 5.

Yurchenco, Henrietta. *A Mighty Hard Road: The Life of Woody Guthrie:* New York: McGraw-Hill, 1970.

Folk Revival: Politics and Culture

Aaron, Daniel, *Writers on the Left.* New York: Harcourt, Brace, and World, 1961.

Ames, Russell. *The Story of American Folk Song.* New York: Grosset and Dunlap, 1955.
Arvon, Henri. *Marxist Esthetics.* Translated from the French by Helen R. Lane. Ithaca: Cornell Univ. Press, 1973.
Baggelaar, Kristin, and Donald Milton. *Folk Music: More Than a Song.* New York: Crowell, 1977.
Brand, Oscar. *The Ballad Mongers: The Rise of the Modern Folk Song.* New York: Funk and Wagnalls, 1962.
Brink, Carol. *Harps in the Wind.* New York: Macmillan, 1947.
Browder, Earl. *Communism and Culture.* New York: International, 1941.
Brunvand, Jan Harold. *The Study of American Folklore: An Introduction.* 2d ed. New York: Norton, 1978.
Chandler, Lester V. *America's Greatest Depression,* 1929–41. New York: Harper & Row, 1970.
Chase, Gilbert. *America's Music.* New York: McGraw-Hill, 1955.
Communist Seeger Sings. Los Angeles: Citizens Committee of California, 1964.
Denisoff, R. Serge. *Great Day Coming: Folk Music and the American Left.* Urbana: Univ. of Illinois Press, 1971.
———. *Sing a Song of Social Significance.* Bowling Green, Ohio: Bowling Green Univ. Press, 1972.
———. *Songs of Protest, War, and Peace.* Santa Barbara, Calif.: ABC–CLIO, 1973.
DeTurk, David, and A. Poulin, eds. *The American Folk Scene: Dimensions of the Folksong Revival.* New York: Dell, 1967.
Dorson, Richard M. *American Folklore.* Chicago: Univ. of Chicago Press, 1959.
Draper, Theodore. *The Roots of American Communism.* New York: Viking, 1957.
Drieser, Theodore. *Harlan Miners Speak.* New York: Harcourt Brace, 1932.
Dunaway, David King. *How Can I Keep from Singing: Pete Seeger.* New York: McGraw-Hill, 1981.
Dunson, Josh. *Freedom in the Air: Song Movements of the Sixties.* New York: International, 1965.
Egbert, Donald Drew. *Socialism and American Art: In the Light of European Utopianism, Marxism and Anarchism.* Princeton: Princeton Univ. Press, 1967.
———, and Stow Persons, eds. *Socialism and American Life.* Vols. I and II. Princeton: Princeton Univ. Press, 1952.
Fast, Howard. *Peekskill, USA.* New York: Civil Rights Congress, 1951.
Finkelstein, Sidney. *Art and Society.* New York: International, 1947.
———. *The Composer and the Nation.* New York: International, 1960.
———. *How Music Expresses Ideas.* New York: International, 1952.
Fitzgerald, Richard. *Art and Politics: Cartoonists of the "Masses" and "Liberator."* Westport, Conn.: Greenwood Press, 1973.
Foster, William Z. *History of the Communist Party of the United States.* New York: International, 1952.
Gates, John. *The Story of an American Communist.* New York: Thomas Nelson and Sons, 1958.
Glazer, Nathan. *The Social Basis of American Communism.* New York: Harcourt, Brace, and World, 1961.

Goldston, Robert. *The Great Depression: The United States in the Thirties.* Indianapolis: Bobbs-Merrill, 1968.

Gordon, Max. *Live at the Village Vanguard.* New York: St. Martin's Press, 1980.

Green, Archie. *Only a Miner: Studies in Recorded Coal Mining Songs.* Urbana: Univ. of Illinois Press, 1972.

Greenway, John. *American Folksongs of Protest.* Philadelphia: Univ. of Pennsylvania Press, 1953.

Gulick, Charles A., Roy A. Ockert, and R.J. Wallace. *History and Theories of Working-Class Movements: A Select Bibliography.* Berkeley: University of California, Bureau of Business and Economic Research and Institute of Industrial Relations, 1955.

Harp, Louis. *Social Roots of the Arts.* New York: International, 1949.

Harris, Herbert. *American Labor.* New Haven: Yale Univ. Press, 1940.

Himelstein, Morgan. *Drama Was a Weapon.* New Brunswick, N.J.: Rutgers Univ. Press, 1963.

Howe, Irving, and Lewis Coser. *The American Communist Party: A Critical History.* Boston: Beacon, 1958.

Ives, Burl. *Song in America.* New York: Duell, Sloan, and Pearce, 1962.

———. *Wayfaring Stranger.* New York: McGraw-Hill, 1948.

Jackson, Bruce, ed. *Folklore and Society.* Hatboro, Pa.: Folklore Associates, 1966.

Jones, Mary Harris. *Autobiography of Mother Jones.* Edited by Mary Field Parton. 1925; rpr. New York: Arno Press, 1969.

Landis, Arthur H. *The Abraham Lincoln Brigade.* New York: Citadel, 1967.

Lang, Berel, and Forrest Williams, eds. *Marxism and Art: Writings in Aesthetics and Criticism.* New York: David McKay, 1972.

Lasswell, Harold, and Dorothy Blumenstock. *World Revolutionary Propaganda.* New York: Knopf, 1939.

Lawless, Roy M. *Folksingers and Folksongs in America.* New York: Duell, Sloan, and Pearce, 1960.

Laws, C. Malcolm, Jr. *American Balladry from British Broadsides.* Philadelphia: American Folklore Society, 1957.

Lens, Sidney. *Radicalism in America.* New York: Crowell, 1966.

Lomax, Alan. *Folksong Style and Culture.* Washington, D.C.: American Association for the Advancement of Science, 1968.

Lowenthal, Leo, and Norbert Guterman. *Prophets of Deceit: A Study of the Techniques of the American Agitator.* New York: Harcourt Brace, 1937.

Lyons, Eugene. *The Red Decade.* Indianapolis: Bobbs-Merrill, 1941.

Marothy, Janus. *Music and the Bourgeois, Music and the Proletarian.* Translated from the Hungarian by Eva Rona. Budapest: Akademiaikado, 1974.

Marsh, J.B.T. *The Story of the Jubilee Singers.* Boston: Houghton Mifflin, 1880.

Noebel, David A. *The Marxist Minstrels: A Handbook on Communist Subversion of Music.* Tulka, Okla.: Christian Crusade, 1974.

Pope, Liston. *Millhands and Preachers.* New Haven: Yale Univ. Press, 1942.

Poulin, A., Jr., and David A. DeTurk, eds. *The American Folk Scene.* New York: Dell, 1967.

Qualtar, Terence H. *Propaganda and Psychological Warfare.* New York: Random House, 1962.

Rolfe, Edwin. *The Lincoln Battalion.* New York: Random House, 1939
Salzman, Jack, ed. *Years of Protest: A Collection of American Writings of the 1930's.* New York: Pegasus, 1967.
Sandberg, Larry, and Dick Weissman. *The Folkmusic Sourcebook.* New York: Knopf, 1976.
Schmidt, Karl M. *Henry A. Wallace: Quixotic Crusade.* Syracuse, N.Y.: Syracuse University Press, 1960.
Seeger, Pete. *The Incompleat Folksinger.* Edited by Jo Metcalf Schwartz. New York: Simon and Schuster, 1972.
Selznick, Philip. *The Organizational Weapon: A Study of Bolshevik Strategy and Tactics:* New York: Free Press, 1960.
Shannon, David A. *The Decline of American Communism.* New York: Harcourt, Brace, 1959.
Shelton, Robert: *The Face of Folk Music.* Photographs by David Gahr. New York: Citadel, 1968.
Siegmeister, Elie. *Music and Society.* New York: Critics Group Press, 1938.
Warren, Frank A. *Liberals and Communism: "The Red Decade" Revisited.* Bloomington: Indiana Univ. Press, 1966.

Folk Revival: Songbooks and Song Collections

AFL-CIO Department of Education, eds. *Songs for Labor.* Washington, D.C.: AFL-CIO, 1983.
Amalgamated Song Book. New York: Amalgamated Clothing Workers of America, CIO, c. 1948.
Arnett, Hazel. *I Hear America Singing! Great Folk Songs from the Revolution to Rock.* New York: Praeger, 1977.
Asch, Moses, Ethel Raim, and Josh Dunson, eds. *Anthology of American Folk Music.* New York: Oak, 1973.
———. 104 *Folk Songs.* New York: Robbins Music Corp., 1964.
———. 124 *Folk Songs.* New York: Robbins Music Corp., 1965.
Carawan, Guy, and Candie Carawan, eds. *Freedom Is a Constant Struggle: Songs of the Freedom Movement.* New York: Oak, 1968.
———. *Voices from the Mountains.* New York: Knopf, 1975.
———. *We Shall Overcome.* New York: Oak, 1964.
Chase, Gilbert. *America's Music.* New York: McGraw-Hill, 1955.
Cohen, Mike, ed. 105 *Plus* 5 *Folk Songs for Camp.* New York: Oak, 1966.
Colcord, James C. *Songs of American Sailormen.* New York: Norton, 1938.
Collins, Judy. *The Judy Collins Songbook.* New York: Grosset and Dunlap, 1969.
Commonwealth Labor Hymnal. Mena, Ark.: Commonwealth College, 1983.
Commonwealth Labor Songs. Mena, Ark.: Commonwealth College, 1938.
Cothran, Kay. *In My Hand: Songs for the Vietnam War.* Atlanta, Ga.: Atlanta Committee to End the War in Vietnam, 1966.
Croce, Jim. *Photographs and Memories: His Greatest Hits.* New York: Blendingwell Music, 1974.
Edwards, Jay. *The Coffee House Songbook.* New York: Oak, n.d.
Eight Union Songs of the Almanacs. New York: New Theatre League, 1941.
Everybody Sings. New York: Education Department, International Ladies Garment Workers Union, 1947.

Fitch, Thomas. *Ballads of Western Miners and Others.* New York: Cochrane, 1910.

Gardner, Emelyn Elizabeth, and Geraldine Jencks Chickering. *Ballads and Songs of Southern Michigan.* Ann Arbor: Univ. of Michigan Press, 1939.

Gellert, Lawrence. *Negro Songs of Protest.* New York: Carl Fischer, 1936.

Glazer, Joe, and Edith Fowke, eds. *Songs of Work and Freedom.* Chicago: Roosevelt Univ. Press, 1960.

Gray, Roland Palmer. *Songs and Ballads of the Maine Lumberjacks.* Cambridge, Mass.: Harvard Univ. Press, 1924.

Hille, Waldemar, ed. *How Can I Keep from Singing.* Los Angeles: Hodgin Press, 1977.

———. *The People's Song Book.* New York: Boni and Gaer, 1948.

Horton, Zilphia. *Labor Songs.* Atlanta, Ga.: Textile Workers Union of America, Southeastern Regional Office, 1939.

Kennedy, R. Emmet. *Mellows.* New York: Boni, 1925.

———. *More Mellows.* New York: Dodd, Mead, 1931.

The Kingston Trio. *Deluxe Souvenir Vocal Album.* New York: Highridge Music Corp., 1962.

Kolb, Sylvia, and John Kolb. *Frankie and Johnnie: A Treasury of Folk Songs.* New York: Bantam Books, 1948.

Korson, George. *Coal Dust on the Fiddle.* Philadelphia: Univ. of Pennsylvania Press, 1943.

———. *The Miner Sings.* New York: J. Fischer and Bros., 1936.

———. *Minstrels of the Mine Patch.* Philadelphia: Univ. of Pennsylvania Press, 1938.

———. *Songs and Ballads of the Anthracite Miner.* New York: Grafton, 1927.

Labor Sings. New York: International Ladies Garment Workers' Union, Combined Locals, 1940.

Labor Songs for All Occasions. Madison: Univ. of Wisconsin Songbooks for Summer Sessions, 1938, 1940.

Landeck, Beatrice, ed. *Songs to Grow On.* New York: Edward Marks Music Publishers–William Sloane, n.d.

Larkin, Margaret. "Ella May's Songs." *Nation* 129 (Oct. 9, 1929).

Let the People Sing. Madison: Univ. of Wisconsin Summer School for Workers, 1941.

Let's Sing. New York: Education Department, International Ladies Garment Workers' Union, n.d.

Lomax, Alan, ed. *The Folksongs of North America in the English Language.* Garden City, N.Y.: Doubleday, 1960.

Lomax, John A., and Alan Lomax. *American Ballads and Folksongs.* New York: Macmillan, 1934.

———. *Negro Folk Songs as Sung by Leadbelly.* New York: Macmillan, 1936.

———. *Our Singing Country.* New York: Macmillan, 1941.

———. *Folk Song, U.S.A.* New York: Duell, Sloan, and Pierce, 1947.

March and Sing. New York: American Music League, 1937.

Melanie's Good Book. New York: Amelanie Music/Sama Rippa Music, 1971.

Milburn, George. *The Hobo's Hornbook.* New York: Ives, Washburn, 1930.

Morse, Jim, and Nancy Mathews, eds. *The Sierra Club Survival Songbook*. San Francisco: Sierra Club, 1971.
Neece, A.C. *The Union Songster*. Sunset, Tex.: Neece, 1923.
New Workers Song Book. New York: Workers Music League, 1933.
Niles, John Jacob. *Singing Soldiers*. New York: Scribner's, 1927.
Ochs, Phil. *The Complete Phil Ochs: Chords of Flame*. Hollywood: Almo Publications, 1978.
———. *The Songs of Phil Ochs*. New York: Appleseed Music, 1974.
Okum, Milton. *Something to Sing About: The Personal Choices of America's Folk Singers*. New York: Macmillan, 1970.
Paxton, Tom. *Ramblin' Boy and Other Songs*. New York: Oak, n.d.
People's Songs. New York: People's Songs, Inc., Feb. 1946–Feb. 1949.
A People's Song Wordbook. New York: People's Songs, Inc., 1947.
Peter, Paul, and Mary: A Collection. New York: Pepamar Music Corp., 1968.
Potamkin, Harry Alan, and Gertrude Rady. *Songs for Workers' and Farmers' Children*. New York: New Pioneer, 1933.
Prison and Mountain Songs. New York: Shapiro, Bernstein, 1959.
Randolf, Vance. *Ozark Folksongs*. Columbia, Mo.: State Historical Society of Missouri, 1946.
Rebel Song Book. New York: Rand School Press, 1935.
Red Song Book. New York: Worker's Library Publishers, 1932
Reprints from Sing Out! Vols. 1–12. New York: Oak, 1962–73.
Reynolds, Malvina. *Little Boxes and Other Handmade Songs*. New York: Oak, 1964.
Richardson, Ethel. *American Mountain Folksongs*. New York: Greenberg, 1927.
Ritchie, Jean. *Singing Family of the Cumberlands*. New York: Oxford Univ. Press, 1955.
Robinson, Earl, ed. *Young Folk Song Book*. New York: Simon and Schuster, n.d.
Sales, Grover, and Larry Shayne, eds. *Cheek in Our Tongue: Twelve Songs of the Limelighters*. Hollywood: Amadeo-Brio, 1959.
Sandburg, Carl. *American Songbag*. New York: Harcourt, Brace, 1927.
School for Workers' Songs. Madison: Univ. of Wisconsin School for Workers, 1945.
The New Lost City Ramblers Songbook. New York: Oak, n.d.
Seeger, Mike, and John Cohen.
———. *Old-Time String Band Songbook*. New York: Oak, 1964.
Seeger, Peggy, and Ewan MacCollm. *Songs for the Sixties*. New York: Hargail Music Press, 1962.
Seeger, Pete. *American Favorite Ballads*. New York: Oak, 1961.
———. *The Bells of Rhymney*. New York: Oak, 1964.
———. *Bits and Pieces*. New York: Ludlow Music, 1965.
———. *The Caroler's Songbag*. New York: Folkways, 1952.
———. *The Goofing Off Suite*. New York: Hargail, 1961.
———. *Oh Had I a Golden Thread*. New York: Sanga Music, 1968.
———. *Pete Seeger on Record*. New York: Ludlow Music, 1971.
———. *Songs for Peace*. New York: Oak, 1968.
———. *We Make Our Tomorrow*. Beacon, N.Y.: Glasco Press, 1965.
Seeger, Ruth Crawford, ed. *American Folksongs for Children*. Garden City, N.Y.: Doubleday, n.d.

———. ed. *Animal Songs for Children*. Garden City, N.Y.: Doubleday, n.d.

Sharp, Cecil. *English Songs from the Southern Appalachians*. 2 vols. London: Oxford Univ. Press, 1932.

Shellans, Herbert. *Folk Songs of the Blue Ridge Mountains*. New York: Oak, 1968.

Shelton, Robert. *The Josh White Song Book*. Chicago: Quadrangle, 1963.

Shneerson, Grigory, ed. *Pete Seeger Sings Popular American Songs*. Translated into Russian by Samuel Bolotin and Tatiana Sikorskaya. Moscow: Music Press, 1965.

Siegmeister, Elie. *Work and Sing*. New York: W.R. Scott, 1944.

———, and Olin Downs. *A Treasury of American Song*. New York: Knopf, 1943.

Silber, Irwin, ed. *Hootenanny Song Book*. New York: Consolidated Music Publishers, 1964.

———. *Lift Every Voice: The Second People's Song Book*. New York: People's Artists, 1953.

———. *Reprints from the People's Song Bulletin* (1946–49). New York: Oak, n.d.

Sing a Labor Song. New York: Gerald Marks Music, 1950.

Sing Along the Way. New York: Woman's Press, c. 1948.

Sing Amalgamated. New York: Amalgamated Clothing Workers of America, 1944.

Singing Farmers. Chicago: National Farmer's Union, 1947.

Sing, Sing, Sing. Allentown, Pa.: International Ladies Garment Workers' Union, Cotton Garment Department, 1946.

Sing While You Fight. New York: Recreation Department, Wholesale and Warehouse Employees Local 65, n.d.

Sizemore, Asher. *Fireside Treasures*. Louisville, Ky.: Asher Sizemore, 1935.

———. *Hearth and Home Songs*. Louisville, Ky.: Asher Sizemore, 1934.

Solomon, Maynard, ed. *The Joan Baez Songbook*. New York: Ryerson, 1964.

Song Book of the I.L.G.W.U. Los Angeles: Educational Department, International Ladies Garment Workers' Union, n.d.

Songs for America. New York: Workers' Library Publishers, n.d.

Songs for Labor. Denver, Colo.: Research and Educational Department, Oil Workers International Union, CIO, n.d.

Songs for Southern Workers. Lexington, Ky.: Kentucky Workers' Alliance, 1937.

Songs of the People: New York: Workers' Library Publishers, 1937.

Songs of Workers: New York: Workers' Educational Division, Adult Educational Department, WPA, 1938.

Songs Our Union Sings. New York: Junior Guards of Local 362, ILGWU, n.d.

Songs Our Union Taught Us. New York: Educational Department, ILGWU, n.d.

"Sowing on the Mountain." An 11–page mimeographed songbook. Knoxville, Tenn.: Highlander Research and Education Center, Nov. 1967.

Station I.L.G.W.U. Calling All Union Songsters. New York: International Ladies Garment Workers' Union, n.d.

The War Is Over. New York: Barricade Music, 1968.

The Weavers, Ronnie Gilbert, editorial supervisor. *Travelin' with the Weavers*. New York: Harper & Row, 1966.

———. *The Weavers' Song Book.* New York: Harper & Row, 1960.
UAW-CIO Sings. Detroit, Mich.: United Auto Workers–CIO Educational Department, 1943.
Union Songs. Atlanta, Ga.: Dressmakers' Union, ILGWU, n.d.
Van Ronk, Dave, and Richard Ellington, eds. *The Bosses' Songbook.* New York: Richard Ellington, 1959.
Warner, Frank. *Folk Songs and Ballads of the Eastern Seaboard: From a Collector's Notebook.* Macon, Ga.: Southern Press, n.d.
West, Hedy. *Hedy West Songbook.* Erlangen, West Germany: Rolf Gekeler, 1969.
Winn, Marie, ed. *The Fireside Book of Children's Songs.* New York: Simon and Schuster, n.d.
Workers Music League. *Red Song Book.* New York: Workers Library, 1932.
Workers' Song Book. Nos. I and II. New York: Workers' Music League, 1935.

Bob Dylan

Bowden, Betty, ed. *Performed Literature: Words and Music by Bob Dylan.* Bloomington: Indiana Univ. Press, 1982.
Cable, Paul. *Bob Dylan: His Unreleased Recordings.* New York: Schirmer, 1980.
Cott, Jonathan. *Dylan.* Garden City, N.Y.: Doubleday, 1984.
Dylan, Bob. *The Songs of Bob Dylan: From 1966 through 1975.* New York: Knopf, 1976.
———. *Tarantula.* New York: Macmillan, 1971.
———. *Writings and Drawings.* New York: Knopf, 1973.
Gray, Michael. *Song and Dance Man: The Art of Bob Dylan.* London: Hart-Davis, MacGibbon, 1972.
Gross, Michael. *Bob Dylan: An Illustrated History.* New York: Grosset and Dunlap, 1978.
Herdman, John. *Voice without Restraint: Bob Dylan's Lyrics and Their Background.* New York: Delilah, 1981.
Hoggard, Stuart, and Jim Shields. *Bob Dylan: An Illustrated Discography.* Oxford: Transmedia Express, 1977.
Kramer, Daniel. *Bob Dylan.* New York: Citadel, 1967.
Loder, Kurt. "Bob Dylan Rocks Again." *Rolling Stone* (July 4, 1985), 48–49.
———. "Bob Dylan: The Rolling Stone Interview." *Rolling Stone* (June 12, 1984), 14–24, 78.
McGregor, Craig, ed. *Bob Dylan: A Retrospective.* New York: Morrow, 1972.
Miles. *Bob Dylan.* London: Big O Publishing, 1978.
———. ed. *Bob Dylan in His Own Words.* London: Omnibus Press, 1978.
Pennebaker, D.A. *Don't Look Back.* New York: Ballantine, 1968.
Pickering, Stephen. *Bob Dylan Approximately: A Portrait of the Jewish Poet in Search of God.* New York: David McKay, 1975.
Ribakove, Sy, and Barbara Ribakove. *Folk-Rock: The Bob Dylan Story.* New York: Dell, 1966.
Rinzler, Alan. *Bob Dylan: The Illustrated Record.* New York: Harmony, 1978.

Rolling Stone, the editors of. *Knockin' on Dylan's Door.* New York: Pocket Books, 1974.
Sarlin, Bob. *Turn It Up! (I Can't Hear the Words).* New York: Simon and Schuster, 1973.
Scaduto, Anthony. *Bob Dylan.* New York: Grosset and Dunlap, 1971.
Shepard, Sam. *Rolling Thunder Logbook.* New York: Viking, 1977.
Thompson, Toby. *Positively Main Street.* New York: Coward, McCann, and Geoghegan, 1971.
Williams, Paul. *Dylan—What Happened*? Glen Ellen, Calif.: Entwistle, 1979.

Selected Discography

John Lennon

Lennon, John. *Imagine.* Apple (3379), 1971.
———. *The John Lennon Collection.* Geffen (GHSP-2023), 1982.
———. *John Lennon/Plastic Ono Band.* Apple (SW 3372), 1970.
———. *Mind Games.* Apple (3414), 1973.
———. *Rock 'n' Roll.* Apple (3419), 1975.
———. *Shaved Fish.* Apple (3421), 1975.
———. *Walls and Bridges.* Apple (3416), 1974.
Lennon, John, and Yoko Ono. *Double Fantasy.* Geffen (GHS-20001), 1980.
———. *Live in New York City.* EMI-Capitol, (SV-12451), 1986.
———. *Live Peace in Toronto 1969.* Apple (3362), 1970.
———. *Milk and Honey: A Heart Play.* Polydor (817 160-1 Y-1), 1983.
———. *Sometime in New York City.* Apple (SVBB 3392), 1972.
———. *Unfinished Music No. 1: Two Virgins.* Tetragrammaton (5001), 1968.
———. *Unfinished Music No. 2: Life with the Lions.* Zapple (3357), 1969.
———. *Wedding Album.* Zapple (3361), 1969.
Ono, Yoko. *Approximately Infinite Universe.* Apple (SVBB 3399), 1973.
———. *Feeling the Space.* Apple (SW 3412), 1973.
———. *Fly.* Apple (SVBB 3380), 1971.
———. *It's Alright (I See Rainbows).* Polydor (PD 1-6364), 1982.
———. *Seasons of Glass.* Geffen (GHS 2004), 1981.
———. *Starpeace.* Polydor (827 530-1 Y-1), 1985.
———. *Yoko Ono/Plastic Ono Band.* Apple (SW 3374), 1970.

Joe Hill

Friedland, Bill, and Joe Glazer. *Songs of the Wobblies.* Labor Arts (3), 1953.
Glazer, Joe. *Songs of Joe Hill.* Folkways Records (FA 2039), n.d.
———. *Songs of the Wobblies.* Collector Records (CR 1927), 1977.

Greenway, John. *American Industrial Folksongs.* Riverside Records (RLP 12-607), n.d.
———. *Great American Bum.* Riverside Records (RLP 12-619), n.d.
Seeger, Pete, and Chorus (the Almanac Singers: Lee Hays, Millard Lampell, Bess Lomax, Peter Hawes; also features Mary Travers and Eric Darling). *Talking Union and Other Union Songs.* Folkways (5285), 1955; originally released as Keynote 106 in May 1941.

Woody Guthrie

Almanac Singers, including Woody Guthrie. *Dear Mr. President.* Keynote Records (III), 1942.
———. *Deep Sea Shanties.* General Records/Commodore Records (BA 21), 1941.
———. *Sod Buster Ballads.* General Records/Commodore Records (BA 20), 1941.
———. *The Soil and the Sea.* A reissue of *Deep Sea Shanties* and *Sod Buster Ballads.* Fontana Mainstream Records (TL 5299), 1964.
Elliot, Jack. *Songs of Woody Guthrie.* Prestige Records (13016), n.d.
———. *Woody Guthrie's Songs to Grow On.* Folkways Records (FC 7501), 1961.
Guthrie, Woody. *American Folkway: Ballads and Dances.* Asch Records (A 432), n.d.
———. *Ballads from the Dust Bowl.* Disc Records (610), n.d.
———. *Ballads of Sacco and Vanzetti.* Folkways Records (FH 5485A), n.d.
———. *Bed on the Floor.* Verve Folkways (FV 9007), n.d.
———. *Bound for Glory.* Folkways Records (FP 78-1), 1956.
———. *Chain Gang.* Stinson Records (SLP-7, SLP-9), two discs, n.d.
———. *Dust Bowl Ballads.* Victor Records, two discs (P-28, P-27), 1940; RCA Victor (LPV 502), n.d.; Folkways (FH 5212), 1964.
———. *The Greatest Songs of Woody Guthrie.* Vanguard Records (VSD 35-36), two discs, 1972.
———. *Immortal Woody Guthrie.* Olympic Records (OL 7101), 1973.
———. *The Legendary Woody Guthrie—In Memorium.* Tradition Records (2058), 1967.
———. *The Library of Congress Recordings.* Archive of American Folk Song (AAFS 3412), n.d.; Elektra Records (EKL-271/2), three discs, 1964.
———. *Original Recordings, 1940–46.* Warner Brothers Records (BS 2999), 1977.
———. *Poor Boy.* Folkways Records (FTS 31010), 1968.
———. *Songs to Grow On: For Mother and Child.* Folkways (FC 7015), 1956.
———. *Songs to Grow On: Nursery Days.* Folkways (FC 7005), 1951.
———. *Sing Out.* Sing Out Records (1A and B), n.d.
———. *Struggle.* Disc Records (360), 1945; Folkways (FA 2481), 1976.
———. *Talking Dust Bowl.* Folkways Records (FA 2011), n.d.
———. *This Land Is My Land.* Folkways Records (FC 7027), n.d.
———. *This Land Is Your Land.* Folkways Records (FT 1001, FTS 31001), 1967.
———. *A Tribute to Woody Guthrie, Part I.* Columbia Records (KC 31171), 1972.
———. *A Tribute to Woody Guthrie, Part II.* Columbia (BS 2586), 1972.
———. *Woody Guthrie.* Asch (347), n.d.

———. *Woody Guthrie.* Disc (40), n.d.
———. *Woody Guthrie.* Stinson (716), n.d.
———. *Woody Guthrie Sings Folk Songs.* Vol. I. Folkways (FA 2483), 1962.
———. *Woody Guthrie Sings Folk Songs.* Vol. II. Folkways (FA 2484), 1962.
Houston, Cisco. *Songs of Woody Guthrie.* Vanguard Records (VRS 9089), n.d.
McDonald, Country Joe. *Thinking of Woody.* Vanguard Records (VDS 6546), 1969.
Seeger, Pete. *Pete Seeger Sings Woody Guthrie.* Folkways Records (FTS 31002), 1968.
We Ain't Down Yet. Cream Records (CR 1002), 1976.
Various Artists. *Woody Guthrie: Hard Travelin'.* New York: Arloco Records 284, 1985.

Bob Dylan

Dylan, Bob. *Another Side of Bob Dylan.* Columbia Records (CS 8993), 1964.
———. *The Basement Tapes.* Columbia (C2 33682), 1975.
———. *Before the Flood.* Asylum (AB 201), 1974.
———. *Biograph.* Columbia (C5X 38830), 1985.
———. *Blonde on Blonde.* Columbia (C2S 841), 1966.
———. *Blood on the Tracks.* Columbia (PC 33235), 1975.
———. *Bob Dylan.* Columbia (CS 8579), 1962.
———. *Bob Dylan's Greatest Hits.* Columbia (KCS 9463), 1967.
———. *Bob Dylan's Greatest Hits.* Vol. II. Columbia (KG 31120), 1971.
———. *Bringing It All Back Home.* Columbia (CS 9128), 1965.
———. *At Budokan.* Columbia (PC2 36067), 1978.
———. *Desire.* Columbia (PC 33893), 1975.
———. *Dylan.* Columbia (PC 32747), 1973.
———. *Empire Burlesque.* Columbia (FC 40110), 1985.
———. *The Freewheelin' Bob Dylan.* Columbia (CS 8786), 1963.
———. *Hard Rain.* Columbia (PC 34349), 1976.
———. *Highway 61 Revisited.* Columbia (CS 9189), 1965.
———. *Infidels.* Columbia (QC 38819), 1983.
———. *John Wesley Harding.* Columbia (PC 9604), 1967.
———. *Nashville Skyline.* Columbia (KCS 9825), 1969.
———. *New Morning.* Columbia (KC 30290), 1970.
———. *Pat Garrett and Billy the Kid.* Columbia (PC 332460), 1973.
———. *Planet Waves.* Asylum (7E 1003), 1974.
———. *Real Live.* Columbia (FC 39944), 1984.
———. *Saved.* Columbia (FC 36553), 1980.
———. *Self Portrait.* Columbia (C2X 30050), 1970.
———. *Shot of Love.* Columbia (TC 37496), 1981.
———. *Slow Train Coming.* Columbia (FC 36120), 1979.
———. *Street Legal.* Columbia (JC 35453), 1978.
———. *The Times They Are A-Changin'.* Columbia (CS 8905), 1964.

Song Lists

John Lennon Song List

I have listed here only Lennon's post-Beatle material. Where possible, I have cited albums, using the dates of the LPs to date the songs. Where there is a discrepancy, I have given the song's copyright date. An asterisk will be used to indicate songs *with* social or political content. The following sources have been helpful in putting this list together:

Coleman, Ray. *Lennon* (McGraw-Hill, 1984).
Naha, Ed., ed. *John Lennon and the Beatles Forever* (Tower, 1980).
———, ed. *Lillian Roxon's Rock Encyclopedia* (Grosset & Dunlap, 1978).

"Aisumasen (I'm Sorry)," *Mind Games* (1973).
*"Angela" (with Yoko Ono), *Sometime in New York, City* (1972).
*"Attica State" (with Yoko Ono), *Sometime in New York City* (1972).
"Aü," *Sometime in New York City* (1972).

"Beautiful Boy (Darling Boy)," *Double Fantasy* (1980).
"Beef Jerky," *Walls and Bridges* (1974).
"Bless You," *Walls and Bridges* (1974).
"Borrowed Time," *Milk and Honey* (1983).
*"Bring on the Lucie (Freda Peeple)," *Mind Games* (1973).

"Cleanup Time," *Double Fantasy* (1980).
*"Cold Turkey," *Live Peace in Toronto* (1969).
*"Crippled Inside," *Imagine* (1971).

"Dear Yoko," *Double Fantasy* (1980).

"(Forgive Me) My Little Flower Princess," *Milk and Honey* (1983).
*"Freda Peeple"; *see* "Bring on the Lucie (Freda Peeple)."

*"Give Me Some Truth," *Imagine* (1971).
*"God," *Plastic Ono Band* (1970).
"Going Down on Love," *Walls and Bridges* (1974).
"Grow Old With Me," *Milk and Honey* (1983).

*"Happy Xmas (War is Over)" (single, 12/71).
*"Hold on John," *Plastic Ono Band* (1970).
*"How?," *Imagine* (1971).
"How Do You Sleep at Night," *Imagine* (1971).

*"I Don't Want to Be a Soldier," *Imagine* (1971).
*"I Don't Wanna Face It," *Milk and Honey* (1983).
*"I Found Out," *Plastic Ono Band* (1970).
"I Know (I Know)," *Mind Games* (1973).
*"Imagine," *Imagine* (1971).
"I'm Losing You," *Double Fantasy* (1980).
"I'm Sorry"; *see* "Aisumasen (I'm Sorry)."
"I'm Stepping Out," *Milk and Honey* (1983).
*"Instant Karma" (single, 3/70), *Shaved Fish* (1975).
"Intuition," *Mind Games* (1973).
*"Isolation," *Plastic Ono Band* (1970).
"It's So Hard," *Imagine* (1971).

"Jealous Guy," *Imagine* (1971).
*"John Sinclair," *Sometime in New York City* (1972).
"(Just Like) Starting Over," *Double Fantasy* (1980).

"Let's Go on Flying" (with Yoko Ono), *Unfinished Music No. 1: Two Virgins* (1969).
"Look at Me," *Plastic Ono Band* (1970).
"Love," *Plastic Ono Band* (1970).
*"The Luck of the Irish" (with Yoko Ono), *Sometime in New York City* (1972).

*"Meat City," *Mind Games* (1973).
*"Mind Games," *Mind Games* (1973).
*"Mother," *Plastic Ono Band* (1970).
"Move Over Mrs. L." (single, 3/75).
"My Mummy's Dead," *Plastic Ono Band* (1970).

*"New York City," *Sometime in New York City* (1972).
"No Bed for Beatle John" (with Yoko Ono), *Unfinished Music No. 2: Life with the Lions* (1969).
"Nobody Loves You (When You're Down and Out)," *Walls and Bridges* (1974).
"Nobody Told Me" (1982), *Milk and Honey* (1983).
"#9 Dream," *Walls and Bridges* (1974).
*"Nutopian International Anthem," *Mind Games* (1973).

"Oh My Love" (with Yoko Ono), *Imagine* (1971).
"Oh Yoko!," *Imagine* (1971).
"Old Dirt Road" (with Harry Nilsson), *Walls and Bridges* (1974).
*"Only People," *Mind Games* (1973).
"One Day (at a Time)," *Mind Games* (1973).
"Out of the Blue," *Mind Games* (1973).

*"Power to the People" (single, 4/71), *Shaved Fish* (1975).

*"Remember," *Plastic Ono Band* (1970).

"Scared," *Walls and Bridges* (1974).
*"Scumbag" (with Yoko Ono and Frank Zappa), *Sometime in New York City* (1972).
"Snow is Falling All The Time" (with Yoko Ono), *Unfinished Music No. 1: Two Virgins* (1960).
"Son for John" (with Yoko Ono), *Unfinished Music No. 1: Two Virgins* (1969).
*"Steel and Glass," *Walls and Bridges* (1974).
*"Sunday Bloody Sunday" (with Yoko Ono), *Sometime in New York City* (1972).
"Surprise, Surprise (Sweet Bird of Paradox)," *Walls and Bridges* (1974).

*"Tight A$," *Mind Games* (1973).

"You Are Here," *Mind Games* (1973).

"Watching the Wheels," *Double Fantasy* (1980).
*"Well, Well, Well," *Plastic Ono Band* (1970).

"What Ever Gets You through the Night," *Walls and Bridges* (1974).
"What You Got," *Walls and Bridges* (1974).
*"Woman," *Double Fantasy* (1980).
*"Working Class Hero," *Plastic Ono Band* (1970).

Joe Hill Song List

The original publication is cited where possible. Two asterisks indicate nonpolitical songs. This list has been compiled after crosschecking song information in the following sources:

Green, Archie. "A Joe Hill Song Checklist." in Gibs M. Smith, *Labor Martyr: Joe Hill* (New York: Grosset and Dunlap, 1969), pp. 231–60.
Hampton, Charles W. "The Politics of Music: A Study of the Political Song as Used by the Industrial Workers of the World" (unpublished master's thesis, Appalachian State Univ., 1977), pp. 110–15.
IWW. Songs: Songs of the Workers, to Fan the Flames of Discontent. 34th ed. (Chicago: I.W.W., 1973).
Kornbluh, Joyce L., ed. *Rebel Voices: An IWW Anthology* (Ann Arbor: Univ. of Michigan Press, 1964), pp. 127–57.
Stavies, Barrie, and Harmon, Frank, eds. *The Songs of Joe Hill* (New York: Oak, 1960).

**"Bronco Buster Flynn," Stavies and Harmon, pp. 38–39.

"Casey Jones (the Union Scab)," *IWW Songs,* 4th ed., 1912, p. 1.
"Coffee An'," *IWW Songs,* 5th ed., 1912, p. 42.
**"Come and Take a Joy Ride in My Aeroplane," Smith, p. 38.

"Don't Take My Poppa Away from Me," Stavies and Harmon, pp. 44–45.
"Down in the Old Dark Mill," *IWW Songs*, 7th ed., 1914, p. 18.

"Everybody's Joining It," *IWW Songs,* 4th ed., 1912, p. 33.

"The Girl Question," *IWW Songs*, 7th ed., 1914, p. 35.

"It's a Long Way Down to the Soupline," *IWW Songs,* 13th ed., p. 28.

"Joe Hill's Farewell Message" (aphorism), *IWW Songs,* 9th ed., 1916, p. 56.
"Joe Hill's Last Will," *IWW Songs*, 9th ed., p. 56.
"John Golden and the Lawrence Strike," *IWW Songs*, 4th ed., p. 43.

"Let Bill Do It" (poem), *The Industrial Worker*, 10 Oct. 1912, p. 2.
"Long Haired Preachers"; *see* "The Preacher and the Slave."

"Martin Welch and Stewart," Smith, p. 25.
"Mister Block," *IWW Songs*, 5th ed., pp. 18–19.
"The Mucker's Dream," Smith, p. 25.
**"My Dreamland Girl," Smith, p. 39.
"My Last Will"; *see* "Joe Hill's Last Will."

"Nearer My Job to Thee," *IWW Songs*, 7th ed., p. 1.

**"Oh, Please Let Me Dance This Waltz with You," Smith, p. 39.

"The Old Toiler's Message," *IWW Songs*, 7th ed., pp. 28–29.

"The Preacher and the Slave," *IWW Songs*, 3rd ed., 1911, p. 26.

"The Rebel Girl," *IWW Songs*, 9th ed., p. 35.
"The Rebel Toast" (poem), *IWW Songs*, 8th ed., Dec. 1914, p. 52.

"Scissor Bill," *IWW Songs*, 5th ed., 1913, p. 17.
"Should I Ever Be a Soldier," *IWW Songs*, 5th ed., p. 4.
"Skookum Ryan the Walking Boss," Smith, p. 25.
"Strung Right," Smith, p. 23.
"Ta-ra-ra Boom De-ay!," *IWW Songs*, 9th ed., pp. 17–18.
"There is Power," *IWW Songs*, 5th ed., p. 27.
"The Tramp," *IWW Songs*, 5th ed., p. 42.

"We Will Sing One More Song," *IWW Songs*, 5th ed., p. 35.
"We Won't Build No More Railroads for Overalls and Snuff," Smith, p. 26.
"What We Want," Smith, p. 9.
"Where the Frazer River Flows," *IWW Songs*, 4th ed., p. 39.
"The White Slave," *IWW Songs*, 5th ed., p. 32.
"Workers of the World, Awaken," *IWW Songs*, 9th ed., pp. 1–2.

Woody Guthrie Song List

This list, which is surely incomplete, has been compiled from a variety of sources which are listed below. Guthrie's recordings are scattered among many different labels, with a great deal of redundancy. Therefore, this was a particularly difficult list to put together. Where possible, the original source is cited. Two asterisks indicate nonpolitical songs. My sources include the following:

Friesen, Gordon, and Cunningham, Agnes, eds. *Broadside* (xeroxed topical song periodical published in New York City since Feb. 1962).
Greenway, John. *American Folksongs of Protest* (Philadelphia: Univ. of Pennsylvania Press, 1953).
Guthrie, Woody. *American Folksong* (New York: Oak, 1961).
———. *Ballads of Sacco and Vanzetti* (Folkways Records, FH 5485A), n.d., originally recorded for Asch, 1946.
———. *Dust Bowl Ballads* (Folkways Records FH5212, 1964).
———. *Library of Congress Recordings* (Electra, EKL 271/272, 1960; original recordings March 21, 22, 27, 1940).
———. *Songs to Grow on for Mother and Child*, vol. 2 (Folkways Records, FC 7015, 1956).
———. *Songs to Grow on: Nursery Days*, vol. 1, (Folkways Records, FC 7675, 1951).
———. *Songs to Grow on Sung by Jack Elliot* (Folkways FC 7501, 1961).
Klein, Joe. *Woody Guthrie: A Life* (New York: Knopf, 1980).
Leventhal, Harold, and Guthrie, Marjorie, eds. *The Woody Guthrie Songbook* (New York: Grosset and Dunlap, 1976).
Silber, Irwin, ed. *Reprints from Sing Out!* (14 volumes of songs excerpted from *Sing Out!*).
———. *Sing Out! The Folk Song Magazine* (published in New York City since 1950).

"Ain't A-Gonna Do," *American Folksong*, p. 38.
"All You Facists Bound to Lose," Klein, 251, 282.
"All Work Together," *Songs to Grow on,* FC 7501.
**"At My Window," *American Folksongs*, p. 34.
"Ballad of Chanukan," *Sing Out!*, vol. 17, no. 6, 1967–68, p. 13.
"Ballad of Isaac Woodward," Klein, pp. 314–15.
"Ballad of Pretty Boy Floyd," *Library of Congress Recordings.*
"Belle Starr," *Woody Guthrie Songbook*, p. 53.
"Been in Jail," *American Folksongs*, pp. 19–20.
"Better World," *Woody Guthrie Songbook*, pp. 56–58.
"Biggest Thing That Man Has Ever Done," *Woody Guthrie Songbook*, p. 59.
"Billy the Kid," *American Folksong*, p. 29.
"Blowin' Down This Road," *Dust Bowl Ballads.*
"Boomtown Bill," *American Folksong*, pp. 23–24.
"Brand New Situation," Klein, p. 217.
**"Bubble My Gum," *Sing Out!*, vol. 17, no. 6 (Dec/Jan 1967/68), p. 9.
**"Build a House," *Songs to Grow on, Sung by Jack Elliot.*
"Business Ain't Dead," *Broadside*, #16 (Nov. 1962).

**"Car Song," *Songs to Grow on*, vol. 1.
"Chain Around My Leg," Greenway, p. 312.
"Chinese and the Japs," Klein, pp. 95–96, 105.
**"Clean-O," *Songs to Grow on*, vol. 1.
**"Come See," *Songs to Grow on*, vol. 1.
"Cowboy's Philosophy," Klein, p. 68.
**"Curly Headed Baby," Klein, p. 72.
**"Dance Around," *Songs to Grow on*, vol. 1.
"Dead from the Dust," Greenway, pp. 295–96.
"Dead or Alive," *Woody Guthrie Songbook*, p. 66–69.
"Dear Mrs. Roosevelt," *Woody Guthrie Songbook*, pp. 70–71.
"Deportees," *Woody Guthrie Songbook*, pp. 72–74.
**"Don't Push Me," *Songs to Grow on*, vol. 1.
"Do Re Mi," *Dust Bowl Ballads.*
"Dust Bowl Refugee," *Dust Bowl Ballads.*
"Dust Can't Kill Me," *Dust Bowl Ballads.*
"Dust Pneumonia Blues," *Dust Bowl Ballads.*
"Dusty Old Dust," *Dust Bowl Ballads.*
**"Dry Bed," *Broadside*, # 44 (April 1964).
"The Dying Miner," *Woody Guthrie Songbook*, pp. 95–97.

"East Texas Red," *Woody Guthrie Songbook*, pp. 98–100.
"Electricity and All," *American Folksong*, p. 40.
"End of My Line," *Woody Guthrie Songbook*, pp. 101–3.

**"Go and Leave Me," *American Folksong*, p. 43.
"God Blessed America,"; *see* "This Land is Your Land."
"Going Down the Road"; see "Blowin' Down This Road."
**"Goodnight Little Arlo," *Woody Guthrie Songbook*, pp. 106–8.
"Good Old Union Feeling," *American Folksong*, p. 33.
"Gotta Get to Boston," *Ballads of Sacco and Vanzetti.*
"Grand Coulee Dam," *Woody Guthrie Songbook*, pp. 109–11.
"Great Dust Storm," *Dust Bowl Ballads.*
"Great Historical Bum"; *see* "Biggest Thing That Man Has Ever Done."

"Greenback Dollar," Klein, pp. 132–33.
**"Grow Grow Grow Grass Grass Grass," *Songs to Grow on*, vol. II.
"Gypsy Davy," *Woody Guthrie Songbook*, pp. 112–14.

"Hangout, Slipknot," *Woody Guthrie Songbook,* pp. 115–18.
**"Hard Ain't it Hard," *Woody Guthrie Songbook*, pp. 123–25.
"Hard Travelin'," *Woody Guthrie Songbook*, pp. 132–34.
**"Here Comes Woody and Lefty Lou," Klein, p. 103.
"Highway 66," *Library of Congress.*
"Hooverville," *American Folksong*, p. 39.
"How Di Do" (also "How Doo Do"), *Songs to Grow on*, vol. 1.

"I Ain't Got No Home in This World Anymore," *Dust Bowl Ballads.*
"I Don't Feel at Home on the Bowery No More," Klein, p. 140.
**"I'll Eat You, I'll Drink You," *Songs to Grow on*, vol. II.
**"I'll Spell You a Word," *Songs to Grow on*, vol. II.
"I Just Want to Sing Your Name," *Ballads of Sacco and Vanzetti.*
"I'm A-Goin' Back to the Farm," Klein, pp. 134–35.
"I'm A-Takin' It Easy"; *see* "Taking It Easy."
"I'm Blowin' Down That Old Dusty Road"; *see* "Blowin' Down This Road."
**"I'm Living in Coney Island 'till I Die," *Woody Guthrie Songbook*, pp. 140–43.
**"It Takes a Married Man to Sing a Worried Song," Klein, p. 172.
"I've Got to Know," *Woody Guthrie Songbook*, pp. 144–46.

"Jackhammer Blues," *Woody Guthrie Songbook*, pp. 147–48.
"Jackhammer John," *Woody Guthrie Songbook*, pp. 150–52.
"Jesus Christ," *Woody Guthrie Songbook*, pp. 153–55.
**"Jig Along," *Songs to Grow on, Sung by Jack Elliot.*
"Joe Hillstrom" (poem), *American Folksong*, pp. 22–23.
"The Jolly Banker," Klein, p. 123.

"The Ladies Auxiliary," *Woody Guthrie Songbook*, pp. 157–59.
"Lonesome Valley," Klein, pp. 78, 216.
"Ludlow Massacre," *Reprints from Sing Out!* vol. 1, pp. 40–41.

**"Mail Myself to You," *Woody Guthrie Songbook*, pp. 160–61.
**"Make a Bubble," *Songs to Grow on*, vol II.
"Matthew Kimes," *Broadside* #120 (July/Aug 1972).
**"Merry Go 'Round," *Songs to Grow on*, vol. 1.
"Miss Pavilichenko," *Broadside* # 84 (Sept. 1967).
"Moneyless Children," *American Folksong* , p. 36.
**"More Pretty Girls Than One," Klein, p. 276.
"More War News," Klein, pp. 131, 134.
"The Mound of Your Grave," Greenway, p. 298.
"My Daddy," *Woody Guthrie Songbook*, pp. 162–65.
**"My Dolly," *Songs to Grow on*, vol. 1.
**"My Little Seed," *Songs to Grow on* (Elliot).
"My Uniform's My Dirty Overhalls," Klein, p. 195.
**"My Wild Woman," Klein, p. 332.

**"Needle Song," *Songs to Grow on* (Elliot).
"Nineteen Thirteen Massacre," *Woody Guthrie Songbook*, pp. 174–76.
"New Found Land," *Woody Guthrie Songbook*, pp. 166–68.
"New York Town," *Woody Guthrie Songbook*, pp. 169–73.

"Oklahoma Hills" (with Jack Guthrie), ibid., pp. 177–80.

"Old Army Mule," *American Folksong*, p. 42.
"On My Way," *American Folksong*, p. 31.
**"1, 2, 3, 4, 5, 6, 7, 8," *Songs to Grow on*, vol. II.

"Pastures of Plenty," *Woody Guthrie Songbook*, pp. 181–82.
"The Philadelphia Lawyer," *Woody Guthrie Songbook*, pp. 183–85.
**"Pick It Up," *Songs to Grow on* (Elliot).
**"Pretty and Shinny-Oh," *Songs to Grow on* (Elliot).
**"Put Your Finger in the Air," *Songs to Grow on* , vol. 1.

**"Race You Down the Mountain," *Songs to Grow on*, vol. 1.
"Ramblin' Blues"; *see* "Ramblin' 'Round."
"Ramblin' 'Round," *Woody Guthrie Songbook*, pp. 188–90.
"Ranger's Command," *Woody Guthrie Songbook*, 191–92.
**"Rattle My Rattle," *Songs to Grow on*, vol. II.
"The Relativity Song," Greenway, p. 282.
"Reuben James"; *see* "The Sinking of the Reuben James."
**"Riding in My Car"; *see* "Car Song."
"The Rio Grande Valley," Klein, p. 170.
"Roll Columbia," *Woody Guthrie Hard Travelin'* [film].
"Roll on Columbia," *Woody Guthrie Songbook*, pp. 196–98.

"Sacco's Letter to His Son," *Sing Out!*, vol. 17, no. 6 (Dec/Jan 1967–68), p. 48.
"Sally Don't You Grieve," *Woody Guthrie Songbook*, pp. 199–203.
"Sharecropper Song," *American Folksong.*
"The Sinking of the Reuben James" (with the Almanac Singers), *Woody Guthrie Songbook*, pp. 204–7.
**"Sleepy Eyes," *Songs to Grow on*, vol. II.
"So Long, It's Been Good to Know You"; *see* "Dusty Old Dust."
"Song of the Deportees"; *see* "Deportees."
**"Stackabones Own Song," *American Folksong*, p. 16.
"Stepstone," *Sing Out!*, vol. 26, no. 1 (May/June 1977), p. 7.
**"Swimmy Swim," *Songs to Grow on*, vol. II.

"Taking It Easy," *Woody Guthrie Songbook*, pp. 212–14.
"Talking Columbia," *Woody Guthrie Songbook*, pp. 215–17.
"Talking Dust Blues," *Dust Bowl Ballads.*
"Talking Dust Bowl"; *see* "Talking Dust Blues."
"Talking Hard Luck Blues," *Woody Guthrie Sings Folksongs* Folkways FA 2484, 1964.
"Talking Hitler's Head Off Blues," Klein, p. 235.
"Talking Sailor," *Woody Guthrie Songbook*, pp. 221–22.
"Talking Subway Blues," *American Folksong*, p. 20.
"This Land Is Your Land," *Woody Guthrie Songbook*, pp. 223–25.
"This World Is Not My Home," Klein, p. 117.
"Tom Joad," *Dust Bowl Ballads.*
**"Turkey in the Corn," *American Folksong* p. 41.

"Union Burying Ground," *Reprints from Sing Out!*, vol. 8.
"Union Maid," *Woody Guthrie Songbook*, pp. 233–36.
"Union's My Religion," Klein, pp. 270–71.

"Vigilante Man," *Dust Bowl Ballads.*

**"Wake Up," *Songs to Grow on*, vol. 1.
**"We All Work Together," *Songs to Grow on* (Elliot).

"When I Get Home," Klein, p. 288.
"When You're Down and Out," *Broadside* #120 (July/Aug) 1972.
**"Wish-y, Wash Wash," *Songs to Grow on*, vol. II.
**"Who's My Pretty Baby," *Songs to Grow on*, vol. II.
"Why Do You Stand There in the Rain?," Klein, p. 142.
**"Why Oh Why," *Songs to Grow on* (Elliott).
"Willy Rogers Highway," *Woody Guthrie Songbook*, pp. 244–47.
"You Gotta Go Down and Join the Union," *Woody Guthrie Songbook*, pp. 248–49.
"You Low Life Son of a Bitch," *Broadside* #111 (Jan/Feb 1971).
"You're on the Last Go 'Round," *Broadside* #40 (Feb 1964).
"You Souls of Boston," *Ballads of Sacco and Vanzetti.*
"Vanzetti's Rock," *Ballads of Saco and Vanzetti.*

Bob Dylan Song List

Most of Dylan's written material has been conveniently published in two volumes *(Writings and Drawings*, Knopf, 1973; *The Songs of Bob Dylan from 1966 through 1975*, Knopf, 1976. Since 1976, however, Dylan has released eight albums. Where possible, the original LP source will be cited, otherwise one of the above written sources will be cited. The first time an LP is cited I have included its date. Unreleased recordings will be followed by the song's copyright date. Where there is a discrepancy, I have included the dates for the song and the LP. For complete information on the LP's cited, see discography. An asterisk indicates songs *with* social or political content. I am fully aware that some of these choices will be controversial (metaphoric love songs, for example), but I went with choices I was comfortable with and that I felt had been supported in the text of this book.

"Abandoned Love" (1975), *Biography* (1985).
"Absolutely Sweet Marie," *Blonde on Blonde* (1966).
"Ain't Gonna Grieve" (1963), *Writings and Drawings*, p. 24.
*"All Along the Watchtower," *John Wesley Harding* (1967).
*"All I Really Want to Do," *Another Side of Bob Dylan* (1964).
"All Over You" (1968), *Writings and Drawings*, p. 68.
"All the Tired Horses," *Self Portrait* (1970).
"Apple Suckling Tree" (1970), *The Basement Tapes* (originally recorded 1967 and circulated for many years as a bootleg until released by Columbia Records in 1975).
"Are You Ready?" *Saved* (1980).
"As I Went Out One Morning," *John Wesley Harding* (1967).
"Baby, I'm in the Mood for You" (1963), *Writings and Drawings*, p. 22.
"Baby Stop Crying," *Street Legal* (1978).
"Ballad for a Friend" (1962) *Writings and Drawings*, p. 15.
"Ballad in Plain D," *Another Side of Bob Dylan* (1964).
*"Ballad of a Thin Man," *Highway 61 Revisited* (1965).
*"Ballad of Donald White" (1972), *Writings*, p. 29.
*"Ballad of Frankie Lee and Judas Priest," *John Wesley Harding* (1967).
*"Ballad of Hollis Brown," *The Times They Are A-Changin'* (1967).
*"Band of the Hand," *Band of the Hand* (1986).
*"Billy," *Pat Garrett and Billy the Kid* (1973).

"Black Crow Blues," *Another Side of Bob Dylan* (1964).
"Black Diamond Bay," *Desire* (1975).
*"Blowin' in the Wind," *The Freewheelin' Bob Dylan* (1963).
*"Bob Dylan's Blues," *Freewheelin'.*
"Bob Dylan's Dream," *Freewheelin'.*
"Bob Dylan's New Orleans Rag" (1970), *Writings*, p. 67.
*"Bob Dylan's 115th Dream," *Bringing It All Back Home* (1965).
"Boots of Spanish Leather," *The Times They Are A-Changin'* (1964).
"Buckets of Rain," *Blood on the Tracks* (1975).

"California" (1972), *Writings*, p. 175.
"Can You Please Crawl out Your Window?" (single, 12/65), *Biography* (1985).
*"Caribbean Wind" (1981), *Biography.*
"Catfish," with Jacques Levy (1975), *Songs of Bob Dylan*, p. 370.
"Changing of the Guards," *Street Legal.*
*"Chimes of Freedom," *Another Side.*
*"Clean Cut Kid" (1984), *Empire Burlesque* (1985).
"Clothes Line Saga" (1970), *Basement Tapes.*
"Corrina, Corrina," *Freewheelin'.*
"Country Pie," *Nashville Skyline* (1969).
"Covenant Woman," *Saved* (1980).
"Crash on the Levee (Down in the Flood)," *Basement Tapes.*

*"Dark Eyes," *Empire Burlesque.*
"Day of the Locusts," *New Morning* (1970).
"Dead Man, Dead Man," *Shot of Love* (1981).
*"Dear Landlord," *John Wesley Harding.*
*"The Death of Emmett Till" (1963), *Writings*, p. 19.
"Denise" (1970), *Writings*, p. 151.
*"Desolation Row," *Highway 61 Revisited.*
"Dirge," *Planet Waves* (1974).
"Don't Fall Apart on Me Tonight," *Infidels* (1983).
"Don't Think Twice, It's All Right," *Freewheelin'.*
"Don't Ya Tell Henry (1971), *Basement Tapes.*
"Do Right to Me Baby (Do Unto Others)," *Slow Train Coming* (1979).
"Down Along the Cove," *John Wesley Harding.*
"Down in the Flood"; *see Crash on the Levee."*
"Down the Highway," *Freewheelin'.*
*"Drifter's Escape," *John Wesley Harding.*

"Emotionally Yours," *Empire Burlesque.*
*"Eternal Circle" (1963), *Writings*, p. 111.
"Every Grain of Sand," *Shot of Love.*

"Farewell" (1963), *Writings*, p. 73.
"Farewell Angelina" (1965), *Writings*, p. 176.
"Father of Night," *New Morning.*
"Forever Young," *Planet Waves.*
"Fourth Time Around," *Blonde on Blonde.*
"From a Buick 6," *Highway 61 Revisited.*
*"Gates of Eden," *Bringing It All Back Home.*
*"George Jackson" (single, 11/71), *Songs of Bob Dylan*, p. 192.
"Get Your Rocks Off! (1968), *Basement Tapes.*
"Girl of the North Country," *Freewheelin'.*
"Goin' to Acapulco" (1975), *Basement Tapes.*
"Going, Going, Gone," Planet Waves.
"Golden Loom" (1975), *Songs of Bob Dylan,* p. 355.
"Gonna Change My Way of Thinking," *Slow Train Coming.*

"Gotta Serve Somebody," *Slow Train Coming.*
*"Groom's Still Waiting at the Altar" (1981), *Biography.*
"Guess I'm Doin' Fine" (1964), *Writings*, p. 117.
"Gypsy Lou" (1963), *Writings*, p. 25

*"A Hard Rain's A-Gonna Fall," *Freewheelin'.*
"Hard Times in New York Town" (1962), *Writings*, p. 6.
"Hazel," *Planet Waves.*
"Heart of Mine," *Shot of Love* (1981).
"Hero Blues" (1963), *Writings*. p. 61.
"Highway 61 Revisited," *Highway 61 Revisisted.*
"Honey Just Allow Me One More Chance," *Freewheelin'.*
*"Hurricane," *Desire.*

*"I Am a Lonesome Hobo," *John Wesley Harding.*
"I Believe in You," *Slow Train Coming.*
"I Don't Believe You (She Acts Like We Never Have Met)," *Another Side of Bob Dylan.*
*"I Dreamed I Saw St. Augustine," *John Wesley Harding.*
*"I and I," *Infidels.*
"I'll Remember You," *Empire Burlesque.*
"In the Garden," *Saved.*
"In the Summertime," *Shot of Love.*
*"I Pity the Poor Immigrant," *John Wesley Harding.*
*"I Shall Be Free, *Freehweelin'.*
*"I Shall Be Free No. 10," *Another Side.*
*"I Shall Be Released" (1967), *Greatest Hits*, vol. 2 (1971).
"I Threw It All Away," *Nashville Skyline.*
"I Wanna Be Your Lover" (1971), *Writings*, p. 225.
"I Want You," *Blonde on Blonde.*
*"I'd Hate to Be You on That Dreadful Day" (1964), *Writings*, p. 57.
"I'd Have You Any Time" (with George Harrison, 1970), *Writings*, p. 297.
"Idiot Wind," *Blood on the Tracks* (1975).
*"If Dogs Run Free," *New Morning.*
"If Not For You," *New Morning.*
"If You Gotta Go, Go Now" (1965), *Writings*, p. 152.
"If You See Her, Say Hello," *Blood on the Tracks.*
"I'll Be Your Baby Tonight," *John Wesley Harding.*
"I'll Keep It With Mine" (1965), *Writings*, p. 224.
"Isis," *Blood on the Tracks.*
"Is Your Love in Vain?," *Street Legal.*
*"It Ain't Me, Babe," *Another Side.*
*"It Takes a Lot to Laugh, It Takes a Train to Cry," *Highway 61 Revisited.*
*"It's All Over Now, Baby Blue," *Bringing It All Back Home.*
*"It's All Right, Ma (I'm Only Bleeding)," *Bringing It All Back Home.*
*"It's Hard to be Poor," *Reprise* (a bootleg released by Toasted Records, 2S 910, 1980).

"Jack of Hearts"; *see* "Lilly, Rosemary, and the Jack of Hearts."
*"Joey," *Desire.*
*"John Brown" (1963), *Writings*, p. 70.
*"John Wesley Harding," *John Wesley Harding.*
*"Jokerman," *Infidels.*
"Just Like a Woman," *Blonde on Blonde.*
*"Just Like Tom Thumb's Blues," *Highway 61 Revisted.*

"Killing Me Alive," *Reprise.*
"Knockin' on Heaven's Door," *Pat Garrett and Billy the Kid.*

*"Last Thoughts on Woody Guthrie" (poem, 1972), *Writings*, p. 52.

*"Lay Down Your Weary Tune" (1964), *Biography.*
"Lay, Lady, Lay," *Nashville Skyline.*
*"Lenny Bruce," *Shot of Love.*
"Leopard Skin Pill-Box Hat," *Blonde on Blonde.*
*"Let Me Die in My Foosteps" (1963), *Writings*, p. 20.
*License to Kill," *Infidels.*
*"Like a Rolling Stone," *Highway 61 Revisited.*
"Lilly, Rosemary, and the Jack of Hearts," *Blood on the Tracks.*
"Living the Blues," *Self-Portrait* (1970).
"Lo and Behold" (1967) *Basement Tapes.*
*"The Lonesome Death of Hattie Carroll," *The Times They Are A-Changin'.*
*"Long Ago and Far Away" (1962), *Writings*, p. 23.
"Long Distance Operator" (1971), *Basement Tapes.*
"Long Time Gone" (1963), *Writings*, p. 26.
"Love is Just a Four Letter Word" (1967), *Writings*, p. 177.
"Love Minus Zero / No Limit," *Bringing It All Back Home.*

*"Maggie's Farm," *Bringing It All Back Home.*
"Mama, You've Been on My Mind" (1964), *Writings*, p. 153.
"Man Gave Names to All the Animals," *Slow Train Coming.*
"The Man in Me," *New Morning.*
*"Man of Peace," *Infidels.*
*"Man on the Street" (1962), *Writings*, p. 16.
"Masterpiece"; *See* "When I Paint My Masterpiece."
*"Masters of War," *Freewheelin'.*
"Meet Me in the Morning," *Blood on the Tracks.*
*"The Mighty Quinn"; *see* "Quin the Eskimo."
"Million Dollar Bash" (1967), *Basement Tapes).*
"Minstrel Boy," *Self-Portrait.*
*"Mister Tambourine Man," *Bringing It All Back Home.*
*"Mixed up Confusion" (1962), *Writings*, p. 60.
*"Money Blues" (with Jacques Levy, 1975), *Songs of Bob Dylan*, p. 372.
"Most Likely You Go Your Way (and I'll Go Mine)," *Blonde on Blonde.*
*"Motorpsycho Nightmare," *Another Side.*
"Mozambique," *Desire.*
"My Back Pages," *Another Side.*
*"Neighborhood Bully," *Infidels.*
"Never Gonna Be the Same Again," *Empire Burlesque.*
"Never Say Goodbye," *Planet Waves.*
"New Morning," *New Morning.*
"New Pony," *Street Legal.*
"Nobody 'Cept You" (1973), *Songs of Bob Dylan*, p. 229.
*"North Country Blues," *The Times They Are A-Changin'.*
"Nothing Was Delivered" (1968), *Basement Tapes.*
"No Time to Think," *Street Legal.*
"Obviously Five Believers," *Blonde on Blonde.*
"Odds and Ends" (1970), *Basement Tapes.*
*"Oh Sister" (with J. Levy), *Desire.*
"On a Night Like This," *Planet Waves.*
"One More Cup of Coffee (Valley Below)," *Desire.*
"One More Night," *Nashville Skyline.*
"One More Weekend," *New Morning.*
"One of Us Must Know (Sooner or Later), *Blonde on Blonde.*
"One Too Many Mornings," *The Times They Are A-Changin'.*
*"Only a Hobo" (1963), *Writings*, p. 113.
*"Only a Pawn in Their Game," *The Times They Are A-Changin'.*
"Open the Door, Homer" (1968), *Basement Tapes.*

*"Outlaw Blues," *Bringing It All Back Home.*
*"Oxford Town," *Freewheelin'.*

*"Paths of Victory" (1964), *Writings*, p. 112.
"Peggy Day," *Nashville Skyline.*
*"Percy's Song" (1963), *Biography.*
*"Playboys and Playgirls" (1964), *Writings*, p. 154.
"Please, Mrs. Henry" (1967), *Basement Tapes.*
"Pledging My Time," *Blonde on Blonde.*
*"Poor Boy Blues" (1962), *Writings*, p. 14.
"Positively 4th Street" (single, 9/65), *Writings*, p. 199.
"Precious Angel," *Slow Train Coming.*
"Pressing On," *Saved.*
"Property of Jesus," *Shot of Love.*
"Queen Jane Approximately," *Highway 61 Revisited.*
*"Quinn the Eskimo," *Self Portrait.*

*"Rainy Day Women #12 and 35," *Blonde on Blonde.*
*"Rambling, Gambling Willie" (1962), *Writings*, p. 10.
*"Restless Farewell," *The Times They Are A-Changin'.*
"Rita May" (with J. Levy, 1975), *Songs of Bob Dylan*, p. 374.
"Romance In Durango" (with J. Levy), *Desire.*

"Sad Eyed Lady of the Lowlands," *Blonde on Blonde.*
"Sara," *Desire.*
"Saved" (with T. Drummond), *Saved.*
"Saving Grace," *Saved.*
"Seeing the Real You at Last," *Empire Burlesque.*
*"Senor (Tales of Yankee Power)," *Street Legal.*
*"Seven Curses" (1963), *Writings*, p. 72.
"She Belongs to Me," *Bringing It All Back Home.*
"Shelter from the Storm," *Blood on the Tracks.*
"She's Your Lover Now" (1971), *Writings*, p. 227.
"Shot of Love," *Shot of Love.*
"Sign on the Cross" (1971), *Writings*, 251.
"Sign on the Window," *New Morning.*
"Silent Weekend" (1973), *Songs of Bob Dylan*, p. 315.
"Simple Twist of Fate," *Blood on the Tracks.*
"Sitting on a Barbed-Wire Fence" (1970), *Writings*, p. 201.
"Solid Rock," *Saved.*
*"Something's Burning, Baby," *Empire Burlesque.*
"Something There Is About You," *Planet Waves.*
"Song to Woody," *Bob Dylan* (1962).
"Spanish Harlem Incident," *Another Side.*
*"Standing on the Highway" (1962), *Writings,* p. 12.
"Stuck Inside Mobile with the Memphis Blues Again," *Blonde on Blonde.*
*"Subterranean Homesick Blues," *Bringing It All Back Home.*
"Sweetheart Like You," *Infidels.*
*"Talking Bear Mountain Picnic Massacre Blues" (1962), *Writings*, p. 8.
*"Talking Devil," *Broadside Ballads*, vol I, Folkways FH 5301, 1964.
*"Talkin' John Birch Paranoid Blues" (1970), *Writings*, p. 17.
*"Talking New York," *Bob Dylan.*
*"Talkin' World War III Blues," *Freewheelin'.*
"Tangled Up In Blue," *Blood on the Tracks.*
*"Tears of Rage" (with music by Richard Manuel, 1968), *Basement Tapes.*
"Tell Me, Momma" (1971), *Writings*, p. 226.
"Tell Me That It Isn't True," *Nashville Skyline.*

"Temporary Like Achilles," *Blonde on Blonde.*
"This Wheel's on Fire" (music by Rick Danko, 1967), *Basement Tapes.*
"Three Angels," *New Morning.*
"Tight Connection to My Heart (Has Anybody Seen My Love?), *Empire Burlesque.*
"Time Passes Slowly," *New Morning.*
*"The Times They Are A-Changin'," *The Times They Are A-Changin'.*
"Tiny Montgomery" (1970), *Basement Tapes.*
"To Be Alone with You," *Nashville Skyline.*
*"To Ramona," *Another Side.*
*"Tombstone Blues," *Highway 61 Revisited.*
"Tomorrow is a Long Time" (1963), *Greatest Hits,* vol. II (1971).
"Tonight I'll Be Staying Here With You," *Nashville Skyline.*
*"Too Much of Nothing" (1967), *Basement Tapes.*
"Tough Mama," *Planet Waves.*
*"Train A-Travelin'" (1968), *Writings*, p. 27.
"Trouble," *Shot of Love.*
"Trouble in Mind," single, 1979.
"True Love Tends to Forget," *Street Legal.*
*"Trust Yourself," *Empire Burlesque.*

*"Union Sundown," *Infidels.*
"Up to Me" (1974), *Biography.*

"Valley Below"; *see* "One More Cup of Coffee."
"Visions of Johanna," *Blonde on Blonde.*

"Walking Down the Line" (1963), *Writings*, p. 28.
"Wall Flower" (1971), *Songs of Bob Dylan*, p. 194.
*"Walls of Red Wing" (1963), *Writings*, p. 64.
*"Wanted Man" (1969), *Writings*, p. 282.
*"Watching the River Flow" (1971), *Greatest Hits*, vol. II.
"Watered-Down Love," *Shot of Love.*
"We Better Talk This Over," *Street Legal.*
"Wedding Song," *Planet Waves.*
"Went to See the Gypsy," *New Morning.*
"What Can I Do For You?," *Saved.*
*"Whatcha Gonna Do" (1963), *Writings*, p. 62.
"Wheels on Fire"; *see* "This Wheel's on Fire."
"When I Paint My Masterpiece" (1971), *Greatest Hits*, vol. II.
*"When the Night Comes Falling from the Sky," *Empire Burlesque.*
*"When the Ship Comes In," *The Times They Are A-Changin'.*
"Where are You Tonight? (Journey through Dark Heat)," *Street Legal.*
*"Who Killed Davey Moore?" (1964), *Writings*, p. 65.
*"The Wicked Messenger," *John Wesley Harding.*
"Winterlude," *New Morning.*
*"With God on Our Side," *The Times They Are A-Changin'.*

"Yey! Heavy and a Bottle of Bread" (1967), *Basement Tapes.*
"You Ain't Goin' Nowhere" (1968), *Greatest Hits*, vol. II; *Basement Tapes.*
"You Angel You," *Planet Waves.*
"You'll Go Your Way and I'll Go Mine"; *see* "Most Likely You'll Go Your Way and I'll Go Mine."
"You're a Big Girl Now," *Blood on the Tracks.*
"You're Gonna Make Me Lonesome When You Go," *Blood on the Tracks.*

Index

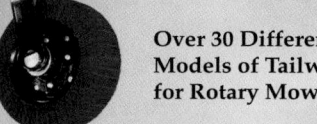

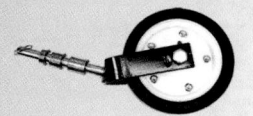

HALLER MOTORWORX, L.L.C.
6261 E. STATE HIGHWAY 10 • MAGAZINE, AR 72943
479-969-6464 • 888-285-3646
www.theloaderdepot.com

AGTECK REPAIR, INC.
18921 US HWY 6 • STERLING, CO 80751
970-522-7849 • 888-871-9197
www.agteckrepair.com

CMR TRACTORS INC.
(MILLINGTON, MI)
7530 STATE RD • MILLINGTON, MI 48746
989-871-9300 • Fax: 989-871-2909
www.cmrtractors.com

MICHIGAN IRON & EQUIPMENT
10231 ROSE BLVD. • MORRICE, MI 48857
517-625-4590 • 855-265-4590
www.michironandequip.com

SWARTZ TRACTOR SALES & SERVICE
12483 HWY. 59 • NEOSHO, MO 64850
417-451-2224

ELLISVILLE AUTO SUPPLY, INC.
704 HILL ST. • ELLISVILLE, MS 39437
601-477-8577 • 866-960-0825
www.ellisvilleautosupply.com

BURR FARMS MACHINERY, INC.
3999 HWY. 2 STE. A • DUNBAR, NE 68346
402-259-3805
www.burrfarms.com

THE TRACTOR PLACE INC
1920 MIZE RD • KNIGHTDALE, NC 27545
919-266-5846
www.thetractorplace.com

DICKSON TRACTOR, INC.
303 E. NORTH AVE. • WESTMINSTER, SC 29693
864-647-0791
www.dicksontractorsc.com

TRI-COUNTY SUPPLY, INC.
12069 OLEAN RD. (RT 16) • CHAFFEE, NY 14030
716-496-8859 • 866-496-8859
www.tricountysupply.com

KLEIS EQUIPMENT LLC
1837 STATE RTE 49 • CONSTANTIA, NY 13044
315-623-2111
217 S. ALBANY RD. • SELKIRK, NY 12158
518-588-4827
www.kleisequipment.com

MOORE'S CORNERS, INC.
8626 STATE ROUTE 22 • GRANVILLE, NY 12832
518-642-1720
www.moorescorners.com

JOYNER'S INC
2506 U.S RT. 11 • MANNSVILLE, NY 13661
315-465-6661

4 SEASONS AG & LAWN
14150 S HWY 169 • OOLOGAH, OK 74053
918-371-5774
www.4seasonsag-lawn.com
4seasonsag.lawn@gmail.com

JOHN'S TRACTOR WORKS & EQUIPMENT
444934 EAST HWY. 60 • VINITA, OK 74301
918-256-5774
www.johnstractorworks.com
johnstractorworks@junct.com

ADDISON FARM & INDUSTRIAL EQUIPMENT
7008 NATIONAL PIKE • ADDISON, PA 15411
814-395-5193
www.addisonfarm.com

R & S EQUIPMENT REPAIR
917 CHERRY LANE • NEWTOWN, PA 18940
215-598-8129
www.randsequipment.com
SEE US ON FACEBOOK

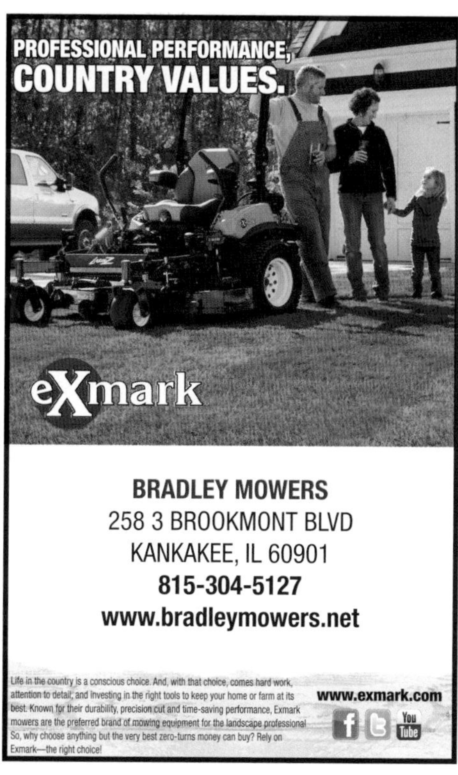
PROFESSIONAL PERFORMANCE,
COUNTRY VALUES.
eXmark
BRADLEY MOWERS
258 3 BROOKMONT BLVD
KANKAKEE, IL 60901
815-304-5127
www.bradleymowers.net
Life in the country is a conscious choice. And, with that choice, comes hard work, attention to detail, and investing in the right tools to keep your home or farm at its best. Known for their durability, precision cut and time-saving performance, Exmark mowers are the preferred brand of mowing equipment for the landscape professional. So, why choose anything but the very best zero-turns money can buy? Rely on Exmark—the right choice!
www.exmark.com

Owning land will forever change you.
Every acre becomes your own piece of heaven. An escape from the outside world. A front row seat to watch God paint the sky with sunsets.
Caring for your land becomes your refuge.
Once you climb into the seat of a Mahindra tractor, stress flutters away with every rumble of the engine and every blade of grass you cut.
Mahindra is honored to help hardworking folks in communities across America rise to meet every challenge from Mother Nature and beyond.
Discover why we're the world's #1 selling tractor at MahindraUSA.com.
Mahindra
Rise.
AGRI-ENTERPRISES FARM EQUIPMENT
P.O BOX 358 • 11929 S. HWY 63
LICKING, MO 65542
573-674-2203 • 800-653-7152
www.agri-enterprises.com
48 EQUIPMENT SALES, LLC
1365 21ST AVE. • RICE LAKE, WI 54868
715-234-6788
www.hwy48farmservice.com

DICKSON
TRACTOR, INC.
303 E. NORTH AVE.
WESTMINSTER, SC 29693
864-647-0791
www.dicksontractorsc.com
HEAVY DUTY
PERFORMANCE
HUSTLER

GEA Houle
Contact your local GEA Manure Equipment Dealer today for more information about manure spreaders, scrapers and agitators.
GEA
engineering for a better world
KOMRO SALES & SERVICE, INC.
W4666 STATE HWY. 85 • DURAND, WI 54736
715-672-4263 • www.komrosales.com
gea.com

REDEFINE
YOUR MOWING
EXPERIENCE
with the new BlackHawk HP from Dixie Chopper
BLACKHAWK HP
A mower built to give you an unparalleled mowing experience is coming to a Dixie Chopper dealer near you. Elevate your ride with the smoothest steering, intuitive controls, and a deep 7-gauge deck for heavy-duty mowing. See the new BlackHawk HP online or at your local Dixie Chopper dealer today.
dixiechopper.com | 765.246.7737
DIXIE CHOPPER
The World's Fastest Lawn Mower.
WALT'S DIXIE CHOPPER
539 WATSON'S MILL RD.
WOODSTOWN, NJ 08098
856-769-3962
www.facebook.com/waltsdixiechopper/

ROSS TRACTOR SALES, INC.
40 S. WOODLAND AVE.
WAYNESBURG, PA 15370
724-627-6966
www.rosstractor.com

NEW & USED

OLDER CRAWLER PARTS

CAT D2, D-3-B-G, D4-C-D-E-H, D5-B-C, D6-B-C, D7-E, D8H, 931, 933, 941B, 943B, 951C, 953-B-C, 955-H-K-L, 963-B, 977-H-K-L **IH:** T5, TD6, TD9-B, TD14, TD15-C, TD18, 150, 175, T340, 500, 500-C-E **JD:** 40, 350-B-C, 420, 440, 450-B-C-D-G, 550, 555-B-G, 750, 755, 1010, 2010 **A-C:** FL9, FL14C, H3, HD4, HD5, HD6, HD7, HD10, HD11, EP, 6G, 7G, 653, 655 M-F: 200, 400, 500, 2244 CASE: 450, 850, 855-D, 1150-B, 1450 **KOMATSU:** D45A, D65A **LIEHBERR:** L631B **CASE:** 1850K **LAMBORGHINI:** 553, 663

Other Models Available
Also Complete Bulldozers & Crawler Loaders of all Types For Sale
New Wheel Tractor Parts

ZIMMERMAN TRACTOR
573-378-7210 • www.crawlerbulldozer.com
13874 Hwy. 5 • Versailles, MO 65084
Closed Sundays • Hrs. 8:00 - 5:00

TMS USED TRACTOR & COMBINE PARTS

8310 Blough Road • Sterling, OH 44276
8-5:30 M-F • 8-12 Sat.

Buying Salvage Tractors & Combines
330-669-3676 • 800-806-3676

SKIDLOADER PARTS

New - Used - Rebuilt for most makes & models

GD Equipment
414 Rowe Rd. Shippensburg, PA 17257
MasterCard **717-530-0170** VISA
Fax: 717-530-7798
UPS Daily
Call to Save on Kubota, Perkins & Ford Engine Parts
New & Remanuf. Hydrostatic Parts & Units

Mike Archibeque, Owner

Clovis Hwy. 70
Portales, NM 88130
Website: www.bjayucca.net

575-356-5982
FAX 575-356-2695
CELL 575-760-6195
email: bja@yucca.net

Nineteenth Edition

2021
Volume XIX

HOT LINE®

COMPACT TRACTOR GUIDE

A QUICK REFERENCE GUIDE
for serial numbers, specifications, and pricing information on Compact Tractors and Riding Mowers.

COMPILED BY

1003 Central Avenue • P.O. Box 1115
Fort Dodge, Iowa 50501
www.HotLineGuides.com
subs@hotlineguides.com
800-673-4763

HOT LINE®
COMPACT TRACTOR GUIDE

2021, Volume XIX

PUBLISHER
Barbara Benton

ADVERTISING SALES MANAGER
Carol Harrison

SUBSCRIPTION SALES MANAGER
Tammy Stein

RESEARCH MANAGER
Donna Hogan

RESEARCH & DEVELOPMENT
Wendy Zurn

RETAIL & AUCTION COORDINATOR
Tammie Littzen

PRODUCTION
Sheila Davis
Becky Rasmussen

Advertising Rates, Deadlines, and Mechanical Requirements
Call 800-673-4763
www.HotLineGuides.com

Subscription Information
(US Only – Call for Foreign Rates)

$30 Print ___ or Online ___ Compact Tractor Guide
$50 Print ___ or Online ___ Hot Line Farm Equipment Guide®
$25 Print ___ or Online ___ Hot Line Antique Tractor Guide®
$140 Print ___ or Online ___ Hot Line® Construction Equipment Guide
(CEG Online includes Cranes)
$35 Print ___ Crane Guide

Call for specials and package prices!
800-673-4763 • Fax 515-574-2182
Heartland Communications Group, Inc.
PO Box 1115 • Fort Dodge, IA 50501
www.HotLineGuides.com • subs@hotlineguides.com

LOOKING FOR PRODUCTS FOR NEW SALES IDEAS?
Multiple orders of **Hot Line Guides** are available for branch locations, educators, fundraisers, gift buyers, and marketing managers.
Hot Line Guides are available at a special discount when purchased in quantities. For details, contact the subscription department at 800-673-4763 or email subs@hotlineguides.com.

Published by

Heartland
Communications Group, Inc.

Publishers of:

Hot Line® Construction Equipment Guide

Crane Guide

Farm Equipment Guide

Compact Tractor Guide

Antique Tractor Guide

ISSN 1541-0013 ISBN 978-0-9702411-4-6

PREFACE

This nineteenth Edition of ***Hot Line® Compact Tractor Guide*** is published alphabetically by manufacturer and then by model. This aids in a faster and easier ability to look up a particular model by the novice or the pro.

Each manufacturer's section has specifications, serial numbers, and retail and auction pricing on crawler tractors and riding mowers from 1990 through 2020. Tractors are 45 HP and less.

The information provided in this annual quick reference guide includes:

- **New & Used Model Data** – Locate hard-to-find specifications on models of equipment that are no longer being produced, plus the newest models on the market.
- **Serial Number Data** – Discover the actual year the equipment was manufactured, or where to locate the serial number on the equipment.
- **Pricing Information** – Discover what equipment is worth on the auction block and what the dealer is asking for it. (Auction Results and Retail Pricing are located at the back of the book.)
- **Option/Value Tables** – These charts show additional values that should be added to the base price of the equipment. The values are based on hours on the machine, and additional option pricing.

Review the following pages for a more detailed description of how to locate this information. Taking a moment now will assist you in reaping the full benefits of this ***Hot Line® Compact Tractor Guide***.

Hot Line Guides Division has attempted to assemble the most accurate information available to us. Some of the models are not complete because the information that is missing is not available, or very little is known about some of the models. Dates will vary depending upon who interprets the data. We are aware that some of our readers are experts on their specific equipment or brand. If and when mistakes or omissions are found, we would greatly appreciate the help of our readers' knowledge to correct our data. Please call **800-673-4763** or email **subs@hotlineguides.com** to inform us of any incorrect or missing information. This book will be re-evaluated, updated and will become better with your help. We hope you will mention ***Hot Line® Compact Tractor Guide*** as your source for specifications and pricing.

TABLE OF CONTENTS

HELPFUL TOOLS

Using the Primary Listings

Compact Tractor Guide is formatted so you can search manufacturers alphabetically. Models are listed under each manufacturer in alphabetical order first and numerically second.

How To Locate Information In This Guide:

SPECIFICATIONS

Step 1 - Go to the section of the manufacturer desired.

Step 2 - Look up the model number.

All information available will be listed. In most cases, when no cutting width appears in the riding garden tractor sections, the deck is an attachment and the M.S.R.P. and pricing will reflect only the price of the tractor.

SERIAL NUMBERS

When available, serial numbers are located after the tractor model specifications and options. Serial numbers are listed by year and location of serial number, if available. A beginning serial number is given for each year that a tractor is produced. The actual year that the tractor was manufactured can be determined by comparing the tractors serial number to the serial numbers given for your particular model number. *Example - If your John Deere 4400 tractor serial number is S336021, it would be a 2000 model...see example to the right.*

PRICING

MSRP - This is the manufacturer's suggested retail price of that particular model and year obtained from dealers nationwide.

RETAIL PRICING - This is a high and low estimated retail price of that particular model and year. These pricing level estimates were computed based upon depreciation formulas used in accepted accounting practices. Tractor condition, geographic location and other factors must be considered.

OPTIONS

Option pricing is located above the retail pricing. To get an accurate value of your tractor, add the option price of each option your tractor has to the retail price.

JOHN DEERE

4400

SPECIFICATIONS

YEARS MFRD	1998-2001
ENGINE	YANMAR
NUM CYLINDERS	3
CID	101
HP: PTO	30
HP: ENGINE	35.7
COOLING	LIQUID
FUEL	D
SPEEDS	12/12
TRANSMISSION	SHUTTLE SHIFT
STEERING	STANDARD
HITCH	CAT. I
BLADE CLUTCH	MANUAL
PTO	YES
DRIVE TYPE	4WD
ROPS/CAB	ROPS
WEIGHT (LBS)	2,850
MSRP	$18,775

OPTIONS

2 HYD	$400
60" DECK	$1,400
72" DECK	$1,850
HYDRO	$600
LDR	$2,050
MID PTO	$200

SERIAL NUMBERS

RH SIDE IMMEDIATELY UP FROM FRONT AXLE ON MAIN FRAME

YEAR	BEGINNING NO.
1999	S140001-SYNC
1999	H140001-HYDRO
2000	S336001-SYNC
2000	H340001-HYDRO
2001	S445001-SYNC
2001	H440001-HYDRO

RETAIL PRICING

YEAR	HIGH	LOW
1998	$6,331	$4,748
1999	$6,745	$5,058
2000	$7,205	$5,404
2001	$7,896	$5,922

EXAMPLE

USING THE TABLES

The tables shown have been provided to help assess a more specific value based on certain factors of the actual machine.

*Below is an example of how to utilize and apply the tables. The example shows a **2001 John Deere tractor, model 4400, with 4500 hours.***

EXAMPLE

Step 1 - Find the model of your tractor in the book.

Step 2 - Determine the horsepower of your tractor.

Step 3 - Find where the horsepower and year of your tractor bi-sect in the table below. (FIG. 1)

Step 4 - Subtract the actual hours of the machine from the number you found in STEP 3.

6300** (from step 3) - **4500** (actual) = **1800 hours

Step 5 - Multiply the difference from Step 4 (1800) by your tractor's coinciding factor in the hourly adjustment table. (FIG. 2)

1800** (from step 4) x **1.4** (Fig 2)) = **$2,520

Step 6 - Add the amount from STEP 5 to the Retail Price for the 2001 tractor.*

$2,520** (from step 5) + **$18,775** = **$21,295

***NOTE: If the hours of your tractor are greater** than those shown in the table, subtract this final calculated figure from the retail pricing shown. **If the hours are less,** add this value to the pricing.*

FIG. 1 - TRACTOR STANDARD HOURS TABLE SAMPLE

Yr. Mfd.	00	01	02	03	04
20-100HP	6650	6300	5950	5600	5250

***STEP 3** →*

STEP 4

FIG. 2 - HOURLY ADJUSTMENT TABLE SAMPLE

Yr. Mfd.	00	01	02	03	04
20-40 HP	1.3	1.4	1.5	1.6	1.7
41-60 HP	1.4	1.5	1.6	1.7	1.8

JOHN DEERE

4400 — ***STEP 1***

SPECIFICATIONS

YEARS MFRD 1998-2001
ENGINE . . . . . YANMAR
NUM CYLINDERS 3
CID 101
HP: PTO 30
STEP 2 — HP: ENGINE 35.7
COOLING . . . . . LIQUID
FUEL . . . . . D
SPEEDS 12/12
TRANSMISSION . . . . . SHUTTLE SHIFT
STEERING . . . . . STANDARD
HITCH . . . . . CAT. I
BLADE CLUTCH . . . . . MANUAL
PTO . . . . . YES
DRIVE TYPE 4WD
ROPS/CAB . . . . . ROPS
WEIGHT (LBS) 2,850
MSRP $18,775

OPTIONS

2 HYD $400
60" DECK $1,400
72" DECK $1,850
HYDRO $600
LDR $2,050
MID PTO $200

SERIAL NUMBERS

RH SIDE IMMEDIATELY UP FROM FRONT AXLE ON MAIN FRAME

YEAR	BEGINNING NO.
1999	S140001-SYNC
1999	H140001-HYDRO
2000	S336001-SYNC
2000	H340001-HYDRO
2001	S445001-SYNC
2001	H440001-HYDRO

RETAIL PRICING

YEAR	HIGH	LOW
1998	$6,331	$4,748
1999	$6,745	$5,058
2000	$7,205	$5,404
2001	$7,896	$5,922

Does Your Tractor have any extra options not listed in the Specifications?

If your tractor has any of the extra options listed, add that amount to the Retail Price to figure the value of the equipment.

OPTION / VALUE TABLES

AT NO TIME SHOULD ANY TOTAL HOURS ADJUSTMENT EXCEED 20% OF THE EXISTING RETAIL VALUES.

TRACTOR STANDARD HOURS TABLE

Yr Mfd	95	96	97	98	99	00	01	02	03	04	05	06	07
20-100HP	9100	8750	8400	8050	7700	7350	7000	6650	6300	5950	5600	5250	4900
Yr Mfd	**08**	**09**	**10**	**11**	**12**	**13**	**14**	**15**	**16**	**17**	**18**	**19**	**20**
20-100HP	4550	4200	3850	3500	3150	2800	2450	2100	1750	1400	1050	700	350

TRACTOR HOURLY ADJUSTMENT

Yr Mfd	95	96	97	98	99	00	01	02	03	04	05	06	07
20-40 HP	0.6	0.7	0.8	0.9	1.0	1.1	1.2	1.3	1.4	1.5	1.6	1.7	1.8
41-60 HP	0.7	0.8	0.9	1.0	1.1	1.2	1.3	1.4	1.5	1.6	1.7	1.8	1.9
Yr Mfd	**08**	**09**	**10**	**11**	**12**	**13**	**14**	**15**	**16**	**17**	**18**	**19**	**20**
20-40 HP	1.9	2.0	2.1	2.2	2.3	2.4	2.5	2.6	2.7	2.8	2.9	3.0	3.1
41-60 HP	2.0	2.1	2.2	2.3	2.4	2.5	2.6	2.7	2.8	2.9	3.0	3.1	3.2

COMPACT TRACTOR FRONT END LOADER OPTION

USE OF THIS TABLE

Step 1 - Find where the horsepower and year of your tractor bi-sect in the specific front end loader option table below.

Step 2 - Add this value to the specific retail pricing under your tractor model in the book and this gives total value.

FRONT END LOADER OPTION

Year Mfd.	91-95	96-00	01-05	06-10	11-15	16-20
20-40 hp	$1175	$1470	$1765	$2060	$2355	$2650
41-60 hp	$1250	$1475	$1700	$1925	$2300	$3400

ABBREVIATIONS

3 pt .... 3 Point Hitch
AWD .... All Wheel Drive
AWS .... All Wheel Steer
BLD .... Blade
CID .... Cubic Inch Displacement
CS .... Case
CVT .... Continuously Variable Transmission
CYL .... Cylinder
D .... Diesel
E .... Engine
ELE .... Electric
EO .... Engine Overhauled
EST .... Estimated

FD .... Ford
FH .... Fast-Hitch
FM .... Front Mounted
FRT .... Front
G .... Gasoline
HP .... Horsepower
HRS .... Hours
HYD .... Hydraulic
HYDRO .... Hydrostatic
IN .... Inch
JD .... John Deere
LDR .... Loader
M.S.R.P ... Manufacturers Suggested Retail Price

MTD .... Mount
MTR .... Mot
N/A .... Not Availab
OH .... Overhaul
OR .... Origin
PS .... Power Sh
PTO .... Power Take O
SPD .... Spe
STD .... Standa
TRANS ...... Transmissi
WD .... Wheel Dri
WHL .... Whee

AGCO

BARON

YEARS MFRD 2000-2001
ENGINE .... B&S
ENGINE HP 18
FUEL .... G
TRANSMISSION .... HYDRO
STEERING .... STANDARD
MSRP $4,849

RETAIL PRICING

YEAR	HIGH	LOW
2000	$1,494	$1,120
2001	$1,655	$1,241

GT45A

YEARS MFRD 2004-2007
ENGINE .... SAME 183CI 3CYL
CYLINDERS 3
CID 183
PTO HP 45
COOLING .... LIQUID
FUEL .... D
SPEEDS 16/8
TRANSMISSION .... GEAR
STEERING .... STANDARD
HYDRAULIC .... YES
PTO .... YES
DRIVE TYPE 2WD
ROPS/CAB .... ROPS
WEIGHT .... 5,035 LBS.
MSRP $26,412

OPTIONS

4WD
CAB

SERIAL NUMBERS

YEAR	BEGINNING NO.
2004	TN
2005	TP
2006	TR
2007	TS

RETAIL PRICING

YEAR	HIGH	LOW
2004	$6,429	$4,822
2005	$6,773	$5,080
2006	$7,152	$5,364
2007	$7,569	$5,676

ST22A

YEARS MFRD 2005-2008
ENGINE .... ISEKI
CYLINDERS 3
CID 68.5
PTO HP 18.7
ENGINE HP 22.5
COOLING .... LIQUID
FUEL .... D
SPEEDS .... VARIABLE
TRANSMISSION .... HYDRO
STEERING .... STANDARD
HITCH .... CAT. I
HYDRAULIC .... YES
PTO .... YES
DRIVE TYPE 4WD
ROPS/CAB .... ROPS
WEIGHT .... 1,367 LBS.
MSRP $10,614

SERIAL NUMBERS

YEAR	BEGINNING NO.
2005	JP
2006	JR
2007	JS
2008	JT

RETAIL PRICING

YEAR	HIGH	LOW
2005	$3,195	$2,396
2006	$3,513	$2,634
2007	$3,845	$2,884
2008	$3,999	$3,000

ST24A

YEARS MFRD 2005-2009
ENGINE .... ISEKI
CYLINDERS 3
CID 68.5
PTO HP 19
ENGINE HP 22.5
COOLING .... LIQUID
FUEL .... D
SPEEDS 6/2
TRANSMISSION .... GEAR
STEERING .... STANDARD
HITCH .... CAT. I
HYDRAULIC .... YES
PTO .... YES
DRIVE TYPE 4WD
ROPS/CAB .... ROPS
WEIGHT .... 1,565 LBS.
MSRP $11,933

OPTIONS

HYDRO

SERIAL NUMBERS

YEAR	BEGINNING NO.
2005	JP
2006	JR
2007	JS
2008	JT
2009	JU

RETAIL PRICING

YEAR	HIGH	LOW
2005	$3,125	$2,344
2006	$3,443	$2,582
2007	$3,772	$2,829
2008	$4,115	$3,086
2009	$4,495	$3,371

ST25

YEARS MFRD 2000-2005
SERIES .... ST SERIES
ENGINE .... ISEKI
CYLINDERS 3
CID 68.5
PTO HP 19.5
ENGINE HP 23.3
COOLING .... LIQUID
FUEL .... D
SPEEDS 6/2
TRANSMISSION .... GEAR
STEERING .... STANDARD
DRIVE TYPE 4WD
ROPS/CAB .... ROPS
WEIGHT .... 1,500 LBS.
MSRP $11,982

OPTIONS

2 HYD
HYDRO

SERIAL NUMBERS

OPERATOR'S PLATFORM, BELOW SEAT

YEAR	BEGINNING NO.
2000	JJ
2001	JK
2002	JL
2003	JM
2004	JN
2005	JP

RETAIL PRICING

YEAR	HIGH	LOW
2000	$2,159	$1,619
2001	$2,328	$1,746
2002	$2,607	$1,956
2003	$2,900	$2,175
2004	$3,203	$2,402
2005	$3,482	$2,611

ST28A

YEARS MFRD 2005-2009
ENGINE .... ISEKI
CYLINDERS 3
CID 89.3
PTO HP 24.5
ENGINE HP 28
COOLING .... LIQUID
FUEL .... D
SPEEDS 9/3
TRANSMISSION .... GEAR
STEERING .... STANDARD
HITCH .... CAT. I
HYDRAULIC .... YES
PTO .... YES
DRIVE TYPE 4WD
ROPS/CAB .... ROPS
WEIGHT .... 2,205 LBS.
MSRP $15,823

OPTIONS

HYDRO

SERIAL NUMBERS

YEAR	BEGINNING NO.
2005	JP
2006	JR
2007	JS
2008	JT
2009	JU

RETAIL PRICING

YEAR	HIGH	LOW
2005	$4,365	$3,274
2006	$4,709	$3,532
2007	$5,069	$3,802
2008	$5,437	$4,078
2009	$5,852	$4,389

ST30

YEARS MFRD 2001-2003
SERIES .... ST SERIES
ENGINE .... ISEKI
CYLINDERS 3
CID 91.4
PTO HP 24.3
ENGINE HP 30.3
FUEL .... D
SPEEDS .... VARIABLE
TRANSMISSION .... HYDRO
STEERING .... STANDARD
PTO .... YES
DRIVE TYPE 4WD
ROPS/CAB .... ROPS
WEIGHT .... 2,469 LBS.
MSRP $16,310

OPTIONS

2 HYD
SOFT CAB

SERIAL NUMBERS

OPERATOR'S PLATFORM, BELOW SEAT

YEAR	BEGINNING NO.
2001	JK30101
2002	JL30101
2003	JM30701

RETAIL PRICING

YEAR	HIGH	LOW
2001	$3,750	$2,812
2002	$4,053	$3,040
2003	$4,368	$3,276

ST30X

YEARS MFRD 2000-2005
SERIES .... ST SERIES
ENGINE .... ISEKI
CYLINDERS 3
CID 89.3
PTO HP 24.2
ENGINE HP 28.4
COOLING .... LIQUID
FUEL .... D
SPEEDS 9/3
TRANSMISSION .... GEAR
STEERING .... STANDARD
WEIGHT .... 2,403 LBS.
MSRP $13,000

OPTIONS

2 HYD
LDR

SERIAL NUMBERS

YEAR	BEGINNING NO.
2000	JJ
2001	JK
2002	JL
2003	JM
2004	JN
2005	JP

RETAIL PRICING

YEAR	HIGH	LOW
2000	$3,181	$2,386
2001	$3,299	$2,474
2002	$3,596	$2,697
2003	$3,900	$2,925
2004	$4,217	$3,163
2005	$4,546	$3,409

AGCO

ST32

YEARS MFRD 2004-2005
SERIES. . . . . ST SERIES
CYLINDERS. 3
CID 91.4
PTO HP 25.9
ENGINE HP 33
COOLING . . . . LIQUID
FUEL . . . . D
SPEEDS . . . . VARIABLE
TRANSMISSION . . . . HYDRO
STEERING. . . . . STANDARD
DRIVE TYPE 4WD
ROPS/CAB . . . . ROPS
WEIGHT . . . . 2,356 LBS.
MSRP. $16,580

OPTIONS

60" DECK
72" DECK

SERIAL NUMBERS

YEAR . . . . BEGINNING NO.
2004 . . . . JN
2005 . . . . JP

RETAIL PRICING

YEAR	HIGH	LOW
2004	$4,841	$3,631
2005	$5,088	$3,816

ST33A

YEARS MFRD 2005-2009
ENGINE . . . . ISEKI
CYLINDERS. 3
CID 91.4
PTO HP 25.9
ENGINE HP 33
COOLING . . . . LIQUID
FUEL . . . . D
SPEEDS . . . . VARIABLE
TRANSMISSION . . . . HYDRO
STEERING. . . . . STANDARD
HITCH . . . . CAT. I
HYDRAULIC . . . . YES
PTO . . . . YES
DRIVE TYPE 4WD
ROPS/CAB . . . . ROPS
WEIGHT . . . . 2,205 LBS.
MSRP. $17,148

SERIAL NUMBERS

YEAR . . . . BEGINNING NO.
2005 . . . . JP
2006 . . . . JR
2007 . . . . JS
2008 . . . . JT
2009 . . . . JU

RETAIL PRICING

YEAR	HIGH	LOW
2005	$4,731	$3,548
2006	$5,084	$3,813
2007	$5,452	$4,089
2008	$5,832	$4,374
2009	$6,252	$4,689

ST34A

YEARS MFRD 2005-2009
ENGINE . . . . ISEKI
CYLINDERS. 3
CID 91.4
PTO HP 26
ENGINE HP 33
COOLING . . . . LIQUID
FUEL . . . . D
SPEEDS . . . . 8/8~12/12
TRANSMISSION . . . . . POWER SHIFT
STEERING. . . . . STANDARD
HITCH . . . . CAT. I
HYDRAULIC . . . . YES
PTO . . . . YES
DRIVE TYPE 4WD
ROPS/CAB . . . . ROPS
WEIGHT . . . . 2,844 LBS.
MSRP. $17,547

OPTIONS

HYDRO
LDR

SERIAL NUMBERS

YEAR . . . . BEGINNING NO.
2005 . . . . JP
2006 . . . . JR
2007 . . . . JS
2008 . . . . JT
2009 . . . . JU

RETAIL PRICING

YEAR	HIGH	LOW
2005	$4,971	$3,728
2006	$5,317	$3,988
2007	$5,706	$4,280
2008	$6,051	$4,538
2009	$6,464	$4,848

ST35

YEARS MFRD 2000-2005
SERIES. . . . . ST SERIES
ENGINE . . . . ISEKI
CYLINDERS. 3
CID 91.4
PTO HP 27
ENGINE HP 33
COOLING . . . . LIQUID
FUEL . . . . D
SPEEDS 16/16
TRANSMISSION . . . . . POWER SHIFT
STEERING. . . . . STANDARD
PTO . . . . YES
WEIGHT . . . . 2,630 LBS.
MSRP. $17,182

OPTIONS

HYDRO
SOFT CAB

SERIAL NUMBERS

OPERATOR'S PLATFORM, BELOW SEAT

YEAR . . . . BEGINNING NO.
2001 . . . . JK
2002 . . . . JL
2003 . . . . JM
2004 . . . . JN
2005 . . . . JP

RETAIL PRICING

YEAR	HIGH	LOW
2000	$3,846	$2,884
2001	$4,018	$3,013
2002	$4,331	$3,248
2003	$4,649	$3,487
2004	$4,984	$3,738
2005	$5,163	$3,872

ST35X

YEARS MFRD 2002-2005
SERIES. . . . . ST SERIES
CYLINDERS. 3
CID 91.4
PTO HP 27
ENGINE HP 33
COOLING . . . . LIQUID
FUEL . . . . D
SPEEDS 8/8
TRANSMISSION . . . . GEAR
STEERING. . . . . STANDARD
PTO . . . . YES
DRIVE TYPE 4WD
ROPS/CAB . . . . ROPS
WEIGHT . . . . 2,788 LBS.
MSRP. $15,477

OPTIONS

2 HYD
LDR

SERIAL NUMBERS

OPERATOR'S PLATFORM, BELOW SEAT

YEAR . . . . BEGINNING NO.
2002 . . . . JL
2003 . . . . JM
2004 . . . . JN
2005 . . . . JP

RETAIL PRICING

YEAR	HIGH	LOW
2002	$3,900	$2,925
2003	$4,211	$3,158
2004	$4,535	$3,401
2005	$4,700	$3,525

ST40

YEARS MFRD 2001-2004
SERIES. . . . . ST SERIES
ENGINE . . . . ISEKI
CYLINDERS. 3
CID 91.4
PTO HP 31
ENGINE HP 40.1
COOLING . . . . LIQUID
FUEL . . . . D
SPEEDS 16/16
TRANSMISSION . . . . . POWER SHIFT
STEERING. . . . . STANDARD
DRIVE TYPE 4WD
ROPS/CAB . . . . ROPS
WEIGHT . . . . 2,688 LBS.
MSRP. $19,519

OPTIONS

2 HYD
HYDRO

SERIAL NUMBERS

OPERATOR'S PLATFORM, BELOW SEAT

YEAR . . . . BEGINNING NO.
2001 . . . . JK
2002 . . . . JL
2003 . . . . JM
2004 . . . . JN

RETAIL PRICING

YEAR	HIGH	LOW
2001	$4,526	$3,395
2002	$4,851	$3,638
2003	$5,190	$3,892
2004	$5,536	$4,152

ST40X

YEARS MFRD 2002-2004
SERIES. . . . . ST SERIES
ENGINE . . . . ISEKI
CYLINDERS. 3
CID 91.4
PTO HP 32.4
ENGINE HP 40.1
COOLING. . . . . LIQUID
FUEL . . . . D
SPEEDS 8/8
TRANSMISSION . . . SHUTTLE SHIFT
STEERING. . . . . STANDARD
PTO . . . . YES
DRIVE TYPE 4WD
ROPS/CAB . . . . ROPS
WEIGHT . . . . 2,590 LBS.
MSRP. $17,774

OPTIONS

2 HYD
LDR

SERIAL NUMBERS

OPERATOR'S PLATFORM, BELOW SEAT

YEAR . . . . BEGINNING NO.
2002 . . . . JL
2003 . . . . JM
2004 . . . . JN

RETAIL PRICING

YEAR	HIGH	LOW
2002	$4,523	$3,392
2003	$4,851	$3,638
2004	$5,192	$3,894

ST41A

YEARS MFRD 2005-2009
ENGINE . . . . ISEKI
CYLINDERS. 3
CID 91.4
PTO HP 31
ENGINE HP 40.1
COOLING . . . . LIQUID
FUEL . . . . D
SPEEDS . . . . 8/8~12/12
TRANSMISSION . . . SHUTTLE SHIFT
STEERING. . . . . STANDARD
HITCH . . . . CAT. I
HYDRAULIC . . . . YES
PTO . . . . YES
DRIVE TYPE 4WD
ROPS/CAB . . . . ROPS
WEIGHT . . . . 2,888 LBS.
MSRP. $20,161

OPTIONS

HYDRO
POWER SHUTTLE

SERIAL NUMBERS

YEAR	BEGINNING NO.
2005	JP
2006	JR
2007	JS
2008	JT
2009	JU

RETAIL PRICING

YEAR	HIGH	LOW
2005	$5,723	$4,292
2006	$6,091	$4,568
2007	$6,473	$4,855
2008	$6,871	$5,153
2009	$7,307	$5,480

ST45

YEARS MFRD	2001-2004
SERIES	ST SERIES
ENGINE	ISEKI
CYLINDERS	3
CID	134.1
PTO HP	37
ENGINE HP	44.2
COOLING	LIQUID
FUEL	D
SPEEDS	16/16
TRANSMISSION	POWER SHIFT
STEERING	STANDARD
DRIVE TYPE	4WD
ROPS/CAB	ROPS
WEIGHT	3,740 LBS.
MSRP	$24,075

OPTIONS

2 HYD
HYDRO

SERIAL NUMBERS

OPERATOR'S PLATFORM, BELOW SEAT

YEAR	BEGINNING NO.
2001	JK80101
2002	JL60101
2003	JM60101
2004	JN

RETAIL PRICING

YEAR	HIGH	LOW
2001	$5,683	$4,262
2002	$6,035	$4,526
2003	$6,398	$4,799
2004	$6,773	$5,080

ST47A

YEARS MFRD	2005-2009
ENGINE	ISEKI
CYLINDERS	4
CID	134
PTO HP	38
ENGINE HP	46
COOLING	LIQUID
FUEL	D
SPEEDS	8/8~12/12
TRANSMISSION	SHUTTLE SHIFT
STEERING	STANDARD
HITCH	CAT. I
HYDRAULIC	YES
PTO	YES
DRIVE TYPE	4WD
ROPS/CAB	ROPS
WEIGHT	3,494 LBS.
MSRP	$24,074

OPTIONS

HYDRO
POWER SHUTTLE

SERIAL NUMBERS

YEAR	BEGINNING NO.
2005	JP
2006	JR
2007	JS
2008	JT
2009	JU

RETAIL PRICING

YEAR	HIGH	LOW
2005	$6,906	$5,180
2006	$7,344	$5,508
2007	$7,752	$5,814
2008	$8,177	$6,133
2009	$8,641	$6,481

ST52A

YEARS MFRD	2005-2009
ENGINE	ISEKI
CYLINDERS	4
CID	180
PTO HP	41
ENGINE HP	52.1
COOLING	AIR
FUEL	D
SPEEDS	8/8
TRANSMISSION	POWER SHIFT
STEERING	STANDARD
HITCH	CAT. I
HYDRAULIC	YES
PTO	YES
DRIVE TYPE	4WD
ROPS/CAB	ROPS
WEIGHT	3,582 LBS.
MSRP	$25,109

OPTIONS

2 HYD
LDR

SERIAL NUMBERS

YEAR	BEGINNING NO.
2005	JP
2006	JR
2007	JS
2008	JT
2009	JU

RETAIL PRICING

YEAR	HIGH	LOW
2005	$7,098	$5,324
2006	$7,512	$5,634
2007	$7,963	$5,972
2008	$8,455	$6,341
2009	$8,992	$6,744

ST55

YEARS MFRD	2003-2005
SERIES	ST SERIES
ENGINE	ISEKI
CYLINDERS	4
CID	173
PTO HP	45.6
ENGINE HP	55.3
FUEL	D
SPEEDS	12/12
TRANSMISSION	POWER SHIFT
STEERING	STANDARD
HYDRAULIC	YES
PTO	YES
DRIVE TYPE	4WD
ROPS/CAB	ROPS
MSRP	$22,610

SERIAL NUMBERS

YEAR	BEGINNING NO.
2003	JM
2004	JN
2005	JP

RETAIL PRICING

YEAR	HIGH	LOW
2003	$6,546	$4,910
2004	$6,925	$5,194
2005	$7,312	$5,484

TW2061

YEARS MFRD	2001-2002
SERIES	DERBY SERIES
ENGINE	B&S
ENGINE HP	20
COOLING	AIR
FUEL	G
TRANSMISSION	HYDRO
STEERING	ZERO
STANDARD DECK	61"
MSRP	$6,099

OPTIONS

50" SNOW BLOWER
60" BLADE
60" BROOM

RETAIL PRICING

YEAR	HIGH	LOW
2001	$866	$649
2002	$956	$717

ZT1638

YEARS MFRD	2002-2002
SERIES	ZT SERIES
ENGINE	B&S
ENGINE HP	16
TRANSMISSION	HYDRO
STEERING	ZERO
STANDARD DECK	38"
MSRP	$3,299

OPTIONS

2 BAG

RETAIL PRICING

YEAR	HIGH	LOW
2002	$517	$388

ZT1644

YEARS MFRD	1998-2003
SERIES	ZT SERIES
ENGINE	KOHLER
ENGINE HP	16
COOLING	AIR
FUEL	G
TRANSMISSION	DUAL HYDRO
STEERING	ZERO
STANDARD DECK	44"
MSRP	$4,075

OPTIONS

2 BAG
4 BAG

RETAIL PRICING

YEAR	HIGH	LOW
1998	$466	$349
1999	$514	$385
2000	$567	$426
2001	$625	$469
2002	$690	$518
2003	$762	$572

ZT1850

YEARS MFRD	1999-2002
SERIES	ZT SERIES
ENGINE	KOHLER
ENGINE HP	18
COOLING	AIR
FUEL	G
SPEEDS	VARIABLE
TRANSMISSION	HYDRO
STEERING	ZERO
STANDARD DECK	50"
MSRP	$4,749

OPTIONS

2 BAG
4 BAG

RETAIL PRICING

YEAR	HIGH	LOW
1999	$553	$415
2000	$612	$459
2001	$675	$506
2002	$745	$559

ZT2148

YEARS MFRD	2002-2003
SERIES	ZT SERIES
ENGINE	B&S
ENGINE HP	21
COOLING	AIR
FUEL	G
SPEEDS	VARIABLE
TRANSMISSION	HYDRO
STEERING	ZERO
STANDARD DECK	48"
MSRP	$6,299

OPTIONS

3 BAG

RETAIL PRICING

YEAR	HIGH	LOW
2002	$1,068	$801
2003	$1,180	$885

ZT2352

YEARS MFRD	2002-2003
SERIES	DERBY SERIES
ENGINE	B&S
ENGINE HP	23
COOLING	AIR

AGCO

SPEEDS . . . VARIABLE
TRANSMISSION . . . HYDRO
STEERING . . . ZERO
STANDARD DECK . . . 52"
MSRP . . . $6,699

OPTIONS

3 BAG

RETAIL PRICING

YEAR	HIGH	LOW
2002	$1,136	$852
2003	$1,254	$940

ZT2354

YEARS MFRD . . . 2001-2002
SERIES . . . DERBY SERIES
ENGINE . . . KOHLER
ENGINE HP . . . 23
COOLING . . . AIR
FUEL . . . G
SPEEDS . . . VARIABLE
TRANSMISSION . . . DUAL HYDRO
STEERING . . . ZERO
STANDARD DECK . . . 54"
MSRP . . . $7,299

OPTIONS

3 BAG

RETAIL PRICING

YEAR	HIGH	LOW
2001	$1,037	$778
2002	$1,144	$858

ZT2561

YEARS MFRD . . . 2001-2003
SERIES . . . DERBY SERIES
ENGINE . . . B&S
ENGINE HP . . . 25
COOLING . . . AIR
FUEL . . . G
SPEEDS . . . VARIABLE
TRANSMISSION . . . DUAL HYDRO
STEERING . . . ZERO
STANDARD DECK . . . 61"
MSRP . . . $7,999

OPTIONS

3 BAG
ROPS

RETAIL PRICING

YEAR	HIGH	LOW
2001	$1,228	$921
2002	$1,356	$1,017
2003	$1,497	$1,122

14.5

YEARS MFRD . . . 2001-2001
SERIES . . . EXPRESS SERIES
ENGINE . . . B&S
ENGINE HP . . . 14.5
FUEL . . . G
TRANSMISSION . . . GEAR
STEERING . . . STANDARD
STANDARD DECK . . . 38"
MSRP . . . $1,599

OPTIONS

2 BAG
42" BLADE
SNOCAB

RETAIL PRICING

YEAR	HIGH	LOW
2001	$233	$175

15.5

YEARS MFRD . . . 2001-2001
SERIES . . . EXPRESS SERIES
ENGINE . . . B&S
ENGINE HP . . . 15.5
FUEL . . . G
TRANSMISSION . . . HYDRO
STEERING . . . STANDARD
STANDARD DECK . . . 38"
MSRP . . . $1,899

OPTIONS

2 BAG
42" BLADE
SNOCAB

RETAIL PRICING

YEAR	HIGH	LOW
2001	$278	$209

15G

YEARS MFRD . . . 1994-1994
ENGINE . . . B&S
ENGINE HP . . . 15
FUEL . . . G
TRANSMISSION . . . GEAR
STEERING . . . STANDARD
STANDARD DECK . . . 44"
MSRP . . . $3,200

RETAIL PRICING

YEAR	HIGH	LOW
1994	$651	$488

16CFC

YEARS MFRD . . . 1993-1994
ENGINE . . . B&S
ENGINE HP . . . 16
FUEL . . . G
SPEEDS . . . VARIABLE
TRANSMISSION . . . HYDRO
STEERING . . . STANDARD
STANDARD DECK . . . 46"
WEIGHT . . . 1,085 LBS.
MSRP . . . $6,900

RETAIL PRICING

YEAR	HIGH	LOW
1993	$1,313	$985
1994	$1,403	$1,052

16G

YEARS MFRD . . . 1993-1994
ENGINE . . . B&S
ENGINE HP . . . 16
FUEL . . . G
SPEEDS . . . VARIABLE
TRANSMISSION . . . HYDRO
STEERING . . . STANDARD
STANDARD DECK . . . 50"
MSRP . . . $4,500

RETAIL PRICING

YEAR	HIGH	LOW
1994	$916	$687

16H

YEARS MFRD . . . 1993-1994
ENGINE . . . B&S
ENGINE HP . . . 16
FUEL . . . G
SPEEDS . . . VARIABLE
TRANSMISSION . . . HYDRO
STEERING . . . STANDARD
STANDARD DECK . . . 48"
WEIGHT . . . 633 LBS.
MSRP . . . $4,600

RETAIL PRICING

YEAR	HIGH	LOW
1993	$869	$652
1994	$936	$702

17

YEARS MFRD . . . 2001-2001
SERIES . . . EXPRESS SERIES
ENGINE . . . B&S
ENGINE HP . . . 17
COOLING . . . AIR
FUEL . . . G
TRANSMISSION . . . HYDRO
STEERING . . . STANDARD
STANDARD DECK . . . 44"
MSRP . . . $2,299

OPTIONS

42" BLADE
SNOCAB

RETAIL PRICING

YEAR	HIGH	LOW
2001	$282	$212

18

YEARS MFRD . . . 2001-2001
SERIES . . . BARON SERIES
ENGINE . . . B&S
ENGINE HP . . . 18
COOLING . . . AIR
FUEL . . . G
TRANSMISSION . . . HYDRO
STEERING . . . STANDARD
STANDARD DECK . . . 40"
MSRP . . . $4,849

OPTIONS

36" SNOW BLOWER
40" SNOW BLOWER
42" BLADE

RETAIL PRICING

YEAR	HIGH	LOW
2001	$596	$447

18CFC

YEARS MFRD . . . 1993-1994
ENGINE . . . KOHLER
ENGINE HP . . . 18
COOLING . . . AIR
FUEL . . . G
SPEEDS . . . VARIABLE
TRANSMISSION . . . HYDRO
STEERING . . . STANDARD
STANDARD DECK . . . 54"
WEIGHT . . . 1,080 LBS.
MSRP . . . $7,700

OPTIONS

BAG & FAN

RETAIL PRICING

YEAR	HIGH	LOW
1993	$445	$334
1994	$493	$370

18H

YEARS MFRD . . . 1994-1994
ENGINE . . . B&S
ENGINE HP . . . 18
FUEL . . . G
SPEEDS . . . VARIABLE
TRANSMISSION . . . HYDRO
STEERING . . . STANDARD
DRIVE TYPE . . . 2WD
STANDARD DECK . . . 48"
MSRP . . . $5,600

OPTIONS

50" DECK

RETAIL PRICING

YEAR	HIGH	LOW
1994	$955	$716

20CFC

YEARS MFRD . . . 1993-1994
ENGINE . . . KOHLER
ENGINE HP . . . 20
COOLING . . . AIR
FUEL . . . G
SPEEDS . . . 0-7
TRANSMISSION . . . HYDRO
STEERING . . . STANDARD
STANDARD DECK . . . 60"
WEIGHT . . . 1,133 LBS.
MSRP . . . $8,100

OPTIONS

BAG & FAN

RETAIL PRICING

YEAR	HIGH	LOW
1993	$469	$352
1994	$519	$390

20CFC PACER

YEARS MFRD . . . 1993-1994
SERIES . . . 3000 SERIES
ENGINE . . . KOHLER
ENGINE HP . . . 20
COOLING . . . AIR
FUEL . . . G
TRANSMISSION . . . HYDRO
STEERING . . . ZERO
STANDARD DECK . . . 60"
MSRP . . . $8,100

RETAIL PRICING

YEAR	HIGH	LOW
1993	$1,563	$1,172
1994	$1,647	$1,236

20H

YEARS MFRD 1994-1994
ENGINE KOHLER
ENGINE HP 20
FUEL G
SPEEDS VARIABLE
TRANSMISSION HYDRO
STEERING STANDARD
DRIVE TYPE 2WD
STANDARD DECK 48"
MSRP $8,400

OPTIONS

60" DECK

RETAIL PRICING

YEAR	HIGH	LOW
1994	$1,403	$1,052

409G

YEARS MFRD 1993-1996
SERIES 400 SERIES
ENGINE B&S
ENGINE HP 8.5
COOLING AIR
FUEL G
TRANSMISSION GEAR
STEERING STANDARD
STANDARD DECK 30"
MSRP $1,995

RETAIL PRICING

YEAR	HIGH	LOW
1996	$429	$322

411G

YEARS MFRD 1996-2002
SERIES 400 SERIES
ENGINE B&S
CYLINDERS 1
ENGINE HP 10.5
COOLING AIR
FUEL G
TRANSMISSION GEAR
STEERING STANDARD
STANDARD DECK 30"
MSRP $1,899

OPTIONS

2 BAG
CART

RETAIL PRICING

YEAR	HIGH	LOW
1996	$144	$108
1997	$160	$120
1998	$178	$133
1999	$197	$148
2000	$218	$163
2001	$242	$181
2002	$268	$201

412G

YEARS MFRD 1993-1995
SERIES 400 SERIES
ENGINE B&S
ENGINE HP 12.5
COOLING AIR
FUEL G
TRANSMISSION GEAR
STEERING STANDARD
STANDARD DECK 34"
MSRP $2,300

RETAIL PRICING

YEAR	HIGH	LOW
1995	$481	$361

412H

YEARS MFRD 1993-1997
SERIES 400 SERIES
ENGINE HP 13
COOLING AIR
FUEL G
TRANSMISSION HYDRO
STEERING STANDARD
STANDARD DECK 34"
MSRP $2,595

RETAIL PRICING

YEAR	HIGH	LOW
1997	$571	$428

413H

YEARS MFRD 1995-2003
SERIES 400 SERIES
ENGINE B&S
ENGINE HP 12.5
COOLING AIR
FUEL G
TRANSMISSION HYDRO
STEERING STANDARD
STANDARD DECK 30"
MSRP $1,999

OPTIONS

2 BAG
CART

RETAIL PRICING

YEAR	HIGH	LOW
1995	$140	$105
1996	$155	$116
1997	$171	$128
1998	$188	$141
1999	$209	$157
2000	$232	$174
2001	$257	$193
2002	$285	$214
2003	$316	$237

414H

YEARS MFRD 1998-2001
SERIES 400 SERIES
ENGINE KOHLER
CYLINDERS 1
ENGINE HP 14
COOLING AIR
FUEL G
TRANSMISSION HYDRO
STEERING STANDARD
STANDARD DECK 24"
MSRP $2,865

OPTIONS

BAGGER

RETAIL PRICING

YEAR	HIGH	LOW
1998	$260	$195
1999	$289	$217
2000	$319	$239
2001	$353	$265

416H

YEARS MFRD 2002-2003
SERIES 400 SERIES
ENGINE HP 16
COOLING AIR
FUEL G
TRANSMISSION HYDRO
STEERING STANDARD
STANDARD DECK 34"
MSRP $2,499

OPTIONS

BAGGER
CART

RETAIL PRICING

YEAR	HIGH	LOW
2002	$357	$268
2003	$396	$297

512G

YEARS MFRD 1992-1996
SERIES 500 SERIES
ENGINE B&S
ENGINE HP 12.5
COOLING AIR
FUEL G
TRANSMISSION GEAR
STEERING STANDARD
STANDARD DECK 38"
MSRP $2,295

RETAIL PRICING

YEAR	HIGH	LOW
1996	$492	$369

514G

YEARS MFRD 1996-1999
SERIES 500 SERIES
ENGINE B&S
ENGINE HP 12.5
COOLING AIR
FUEL G
TRANSMISSION GEAR
STEERING STANDARD
STANDARD DECK 38"
MSRP $2,450

OPTIONS

42" BLADE
42" SNOW BLOWER
BAG & FAN
SNOCAB

RETAIL PRICING

YEAR	HIGH	LOW
1996	$213	$160
1997	$235	$176
1998	$260	$195
1999	$289	$217

514H

YEARS MFRD 1993-1999
SERIES 500 SERIES
ENGINE B&S
ENGINE HP 14
COOLING AIR
FUEL G
TRANSMISSION HYDRO
STEERING STANDARD
STANDARD DECK 38"
MSRP $2,865

OPTIONS

42" BLADE
42" SNOW BLOWER
BAG & FAN
SNOCAB

RETAIL PRICING

YEAR	HIGH	LOW
1993	$150	$112
1994	$166	$125
1995	$184	$138
1996	$204	$153
1997	$227	$170
1998	$250	$187
1999	$278	$209

515G

YEARS MFRD 2000-2002
SERIES 500 SERIES
ENGINE KOHLER
ENGINE HP 15
FUEL G
TRANSMISSION GEAR
STEERING STANDARD
STANDARD DECK 38"
MSRP $1,999

RETAIL PRICING

YEAR	HIGH	LOW
2000	$625	$469
2001	$658	$493
2002	$669	$502

515H

YEARS MFRD 2000-2004
SERIES 500 SERIES
ENGINE KOHLER
ENGINE HP 15
COOLING AIR
FUEL G
SPEEDS VARIABLE
TRANSMISSION HYDRO
STEERING STANDARD
STANDARD DECK 38"
MSRP $1,999

OPTIONS

24" BLADE
36" SNOW THROWER
BAGGER
GEAR

AGCO

RETAIL PRICING

YEAR	HIGH	LOW
2000	$231	$174
2001	$256	$192
2002	$285	$214
2003	$315	$236
2004	$350	$263

516

YEARS MFRD 2004-2004
SERIES .... 500 SERIES
ENGINE .... KOHLER
ENGINE HP 16
COOLING .... AIR
FUEL .... G
SPEEDS .... VARIABLE
TRANSMISSION .... HYDRO
STEERING .... STANDARD
STANDARD DECK .... 38"
MSRP $2,499

RETAIL PRICING

YEAR	HIGH	LOW
2004	$438	$328

516G

YEARS MFRD 1996-1997
SERIES .... 500 SERIES
ENGINE .... B&S
ENGINE HP 16
COOLING .... AIR
FUEL .... G
TRANSMISSION .... GEAR
STEERING .... STANDARD
STANDARD DECK .... 44"
MSRP $2,795

OPTIONS

BAG & FAN

RETAIL PRICING

YEAR	HIGH	LOW
1996	$203	$152
1997	$228	$171

516H

YEARS MFRD 1996-2004
SERIES .... 500 SERIES
ENGINE .... B&S
ENGINE HP 16
COOLING .... AIR
FUEL .... G
SPEEDS .... VARIABLE
TRANSMISSION .... HYDRO
STEERING .... STANDARD
STANDARD DECK .... 44"
MSRP $2,799

OPTIONS

42" BLADE
42" SNOW THROWER
BAG & FAN
SNOCAB

RETAIL PRICING

YEAR	HIGH	LOW
1996	$215	$161
1997	$238	$179
1998	$264	$198
1999	$293	$220
2000	$324	$243
2001	$359	$269
2002	$398	$299
2003	$443	$332
2004	$489	$366

517H

YEARS MFRD 2000-2002
SERIES .... 500 SERIES
ENGINE .... B&S
ENGINE HP 17
COOLING .... AIR
FUEL .... G
SPEEDS .... VARIABLE
TRANSMISSION .... HYDRO
STEERING .... STANDARD
STANDARD DECK .... 40"
MSRP $2,899

OPTIONS

36" SNOW THROWER
42" BLADE
42" SNOW BLOWER
SNOCAB

RETAIL PRICING

YEAR	HIGH	LOW
2000	$321	$240
2001	$356	$267
2002	$395	$296

520H

YEARS MFRD 2006-2011
ENGINE .... B&S
ENGINE HP 20
COOLING .... AIR
FUEL .... G
SPEEDS .... VARIABLE
TRANSMISSION .... HYDRO
STEERING .... STANDARD
STANDARD DECK .... 38"
MSRP $2,600

OPTIONS

2 BAG & FAN
42" BLADE
42" SNOW THROWER
SNOCAB

RETAIL PRICING

YEAR	HIGH	LOW
2006	$567	$426
2007	$629	$472
2008	$698	$523
2009	$774	$580
2010	$857	$643
2011	$950	$713

522H

YEARS MFRD 2006-2011
ENGINE .... B&S
ENGINE HP 22
COOLING .... AIR
FUEL .... G
SPEEDS .... VARIABLE
TRANSMISSION .... HYDRO
STEERING .... STANDARD
STANDARD DECK .... 44"
MSRP $2,799

OPTIONS

3 BAG & FAN
42" BLADE
42" SNOW THROWER
SNOCAB

RETAIL PRICING

YEAR	HIGH	LOW
2006	$611	$458
2007	$678	$508
2008	$751	$563
2009	$833	$625
2010	$923	$692
2011	$1,023	$768

524H

YEARS MFRD 2006-2011
ENGINE .... B&S
ENGINE HP 24
COOLING .... AIR
FUEL .... G
SPEEDS .... VARIABLE
TRANSMISSION .... HYDRO
STEERING .... STANDARD
STANDARD DECK .... 50"
MSRP $3,250

OPTIONS

3 BAG & FAN
42" BLADE
42" SNOW THROWER
SNOCAB

RETAIL PRICING

YEAR	HIGH	LOW
2006	$709	$532
2007	$787	$590
2008	$873	$654
2009	$967	$725
2010	$1,072	$804
2011	$1,188	$891

918H

YEARS MFRD 1993-2000
ENGINE .... KOHLER
ENGINE HP 18
COOLING .... AIR
FUEL .... G
SPEEDS .... VARIABLE
TRANSMISSION .... HYDRO
STEERING .... STANDARD
STANDARD DECK .... 48"
WEIGHT .... 724 LBS.
MSRP $6,925

OPTIONS

36" SNOW THROWER
36"TILLER
42" BLADE
POWER STEERING

RETAIL PRICING

YEAR	HIGH	LOW
1993	$500	$375
1994	$553	$415
1995	$612	$459
1996	$678	$508
1997	$749	$562
1998	$828	$621
1999	$917	$688
2000	$1,014	$760

1316H

YEARS MFRD 1993-1997
ENGINE .... B&S
ENGINE HP 16
COOLING .... AIR
FUEL .... G
SPEEDS .... VARIABLE
TRANSMISSION .... HYDRO
STEERING .... STANDARD
STANDARD DECK .... 42"
MSRP $4,850

OPTIONS

2 BAG & FAN

RETAIL PRICING

YEAR	HIGH	LOW
1993	$293	$220
1994	$324	$243
1995	$357	$268
1996	$396	$297
1997	$437	$328

1606

YEARS MFRD 2003-2004
SERIES .... 1600 SERIES
ENGINE .... KOHLER
ENGINE HP 18
FUEL .... G
STANDARD DECK .... 44"
MSRP $3,550

OPTIONS

2BAG
42" BLADE
42" SNOW BLOWER

RETAIL PRICING

YEAR	HIGH	LOW
2003	$561	$420
2004	$621	$466

1612

YEARS MFRD 1994-1994
SERIES .... 1600 SERIES
ENGINE .... B&S
ENGINE HP 12.5
COOLING .... AIR
FUEL .... G
TRANSMISSION .... HYDRO
STEERING .... STANDARD
STANDARD DECK .... 38"
MSRP $3,500

RETAIL PRICING

YEAR	HIGH	LOW
1994	$712	$534

1613G

YEARS MFRD 1993-1993
SERIES .... 1600 SERIES
ENGINE .... B&S
ENGINE HP 12.5

COOLING . . . . AIR
FUEL . . . . G
TRANSMISSION . . . . GEAR
STEERING. . . . . .STANDARD
STANDARD DECK . . . . 38"
MSRP. $2,950

RETAIL PRICING

YEAR	HIGH	LOW
1993	$569	$427

1613H

YEARS MFRD 1993-1993
SERIES. . . . . 1600 SERIES
ENGINE . . . . B&S
ENGINE HP 12.5
COOLING . . . . AIR
FUEL . . . . G
TRANSMISSION . . . . HYDRO
STEERING. . . . . .STANDARD

1614H

YEARS MFRD 1993-1996
SERIES. . . . . 1600 SERIES
ENGINE . . . . KOHLER
ENGINE HP 14
COOLING . . . . AIR
FUEL . . . . G
SPEEDS . . . . VARIABLE
TRANSMISSION . . . . HYDRO
STEERING. . . . . .STANDARD
STANDARD DECK . . . . 38"
MSRP. $3,295

OPTIONS

2 BAG
36" SNOW THROWER
42" BLADE

RETAIL PRICING

YEAR	HIGH	LOW
1993	$203	$152
1994	$224	$168
1995	$246	$184
1996	$278	$209

1614VH

YEARS MFRD 1995-1999
SERIES. . . . . 1600 SERIES
ENGINE . . . . B&S
ENGINE HP 14
COOLING . . . . AIR
FUEL . . . . G
SPEEDS . . . . VARIABLE
TRANSMISSION . . . . HYDRO
STEERING. . . . . .STANDARD
STANDARD DECK . . . . 38"
MSRP. $4,150

OPTIONS

2 BAG
36" SNOW THROWER
42" BLADE
SNOCAB

RETAIL PRICING

YEAR	HIGH	LOW
1995	$267	$200
1996	$295	$221
1997	$327	$246
1998	$363	$272
1999	$402	$302

1615G

YEARS MFRD 1994-1995
SERIES. . . . . 1600 SERIES
ENGINE . . . . B&S
ENGINE HP 15
COOLING . . . . AIR
FUEL . . . . G
TRANSMISSION . . . . GEAR
STEERING. . . . . .STANDARD
STANDARD DECK . . . . 44"
MSRP. $3,250

RETAIL PRICING

YEAR	HIGH	LOW
1994	$660	$495
1995	$679	$509

1615H

YEARS MFRD 1995-2002
SERIES. . . . . 1600 SERIES
ENGINE . . . . KOHLER
ENGINE HP 15
FUEL . . . . G
SPEEDS . . . . VARIABLE
TRANSMISSION . . . . HYDRO
STEERING. . . . . .STANDARD
STANDARD DECK . . . . 44"
MSRP. $3,099

OPTIONS

2 BAG
36" SNOW THROWER
42" BLADE
SNOCAB

RETAIL PRICING

YEAR	HIGH	LOW
1995	$211	$158
1996	$233	$175
1997	$260	$195
1998	$288	$216
1999	$319	$239
2000	$353	$265
2001	$393	$294
2002	$435	$326

1616H

YEARS MFRD 1993-2004
SERIES. . . . . 1600 SERIES
ENGINE . . . . B&S
ENGINE HP 16
COOLING . . . . AIR
FUEL . . . . G
SPEEDS . . . . VARIABLE
TRANSMISSION . . . . HYDRO
STEERING. . . . . .STANDARD
STANDARD DECK . . . . 44"
WEIGHT . . . . 570 LBS.
MSRP. $3,850

OPTIONS

38" DECK
42" SNOW THROWER
BAG & FAN
SNOCAB

RETAIL PRICING

YEAR	HIGH	LOW
1993	$270	$202
1994	$281	$211
1995	$290	$217
1996	$295	$221
1997	$327	$246
1998	$363	$272
1999	$401	$301
2000	$445	$334
2001	$494	$371
2002	$549	$412
2003	$608	$456
2004	$674	$505

1616VH

YEARS MFRD 2001-2002
SERIES. . . . . 1600 SERIES
ENGINE . . . . B&S
ENGINE HP 16
FUEL . . . . G
TRANSMISSION . . . . HYDRO
STEERING. . . . . .STANDARD
STANDARD DECK . . . . 38"
MSRP. $2,999

OPTIONS

44" DECK

RETAIL PRICING

YEAR	HIGH	LOW
2001	$1,022	$767
2002	$1,115	$836

1617HC

YEARS MFRD 2000-2001
SERIES. . . . . 1600 SERIES
ENGINE . . . . B&S
ENGINE HP 17
COOLING . . . . AIR
FUEL . . . . G
SPEEDS . . . . VARIABLE
TRANSMISSION . . . . HYDRO
STEERING. . . . . .STANDARD
STANDARD DECK . . . . 44"
MSRP. $3,525

OPTIONS

2 BAG
36" SNOW THROWER
42" BLADE
SNOCAB

RETAIL PRICING

YEAR	HIGH	LOW
2000	$398	$299
2001	$441	$330

1618

YEARS MFRD 2004-2004
SERIES. . . . . 1600 SERIES
ENGINE . . . . VANGUARD
ENGINE HP 18
COOLING . . . . AIR
FUEL . . . . G
SPEEDS . . . . VARIABLE
TRANSMISSION . . . . HYDRO
STEERING. . . . . .STANDARD
STANDARD DECK . . . . 50"
MSRP. $4,275

RETAIL PRICING

YEAR	HIGH	LOW
2004	$748	$561

1618H

YEARS MFRD 1999-2001
SERIES. . . . . 1600 SERIES
ENGINE . . . . B&S
ENGINE HP 18
COOLING . . . . AIR
FUEL . . . . G
SPEEDS . . . . VARIABLE
TRANSMISSION . . . . HYDRO
STEERING. . . . . .STANDARD
STANDARD DECK . . . . 50"
MSRP. $5,225

OPTIONS

42" BLADE
42" SNOW THROWER
BAG & FAN
SNOCAB

RETAIL PRICING

YEAR	HIGH	LOW
1999	$523	$392
2000	$579	$434
2001	$642	$482

1620H

YEARS MFRD 2005-2011
ENGINE . . . . VANGUARD
ENGINE HP 20
COOLING . . . . AIR
FUEL . . . . G
SPEEDS . . . . VARIABLE
TRANSMISSION . . . . HYDRO
STEERING. . . . . .STANDARD
STANDARD DECK . . . . 44"
MSRP. $4,650

OPTIONS

3 BAG & FAN
42" BLADE
42" SNOW BLOWER
50" DECK

RETAIL PRICING

YEAR	HIGH	LOW
2005	$916	$687
2006	$1,016	$762
2007	$1,125	$844
2008	$1,247	$935
2009	$1,383	$1,038
2010	$1,533	$1,150
2011	$1,700	$1,275

1714G

YEARS MFRD 1992-1993
SERIES. . . . . 1700 SERIES
ENGINE . . . . KOHLER
ENGINE HP 14
COOLING . . . . AIR
FUEL . . . . G
TRANSMISSION . . . . GEAR
STEERING. . . . . .STANDARD
STANDARD DECK . . . . 44"
MSRP. $4,200

AGCO

OPTIONS
2 BAG & FAN
36" TILLER
4 BAG & FAN
42" SNOW THROWER

RETAIL PRICING

YEAR	HIGH	LOW
1992	$260	$195
1993	$288	$216

1716G

YEARS MFRD 1994-1996
SERIES .... 1700 SERIES
ENGINE .... B&S
ENGINE HP 16
COOLING .... AIR
FUEL .... G
TRANSMISSION .... GEAR
STEERING .... STANDARD
STANDARD DECK .... 50"
MSRP $4,900

OPTIONS
2 BAG & FAN
36" TILLER
4 BAG & FAN
42" SNOW THROWER

RETAIL PRICING

YEAR	HIGH	LOW
1994	$343	$257
1995	$380	$285
1996	$420	$315

1716H

YEARS MFRD 1992-2003
SERIES .... 1700 SERIES
ENGINE .... B&S
ENGINE HP 16
COOLING .... AIR
FUEL .... G
SPEEDS .... VARIABLE
TRANSMISSION .... HYDRO
STEERING .... STANDARD
STANDARD DECK .... 44"
MSRP $4,399

OPTIONS
2 BAG & FAN
36" TILLER
4 BAG & FAN
40" SNOW BLOWER

RETAIL PRICING

YEAR	HIGH	LOW
1993	$327	$246
1994	$349	$262
1995	$364	$273
1996	$401	$301
1997	$444	$333
1998	$492	$369
1999	$545	$409
2000	$602	$451
2001	$666	$500
2002	$815	$611
2003	$815	$611

1717H

YEARS MFRD 1996-2000
SERIES .... 1700 SERIES
ENGINE .... KAWASAKI
ENGINE HP 17
COOLING .... LIQUID
FUEL .... G
SPEEDS .... VARIABLE
TRANSMISSION .... HYDRO
STEERING .... STANDARD
STANDARD DECK .... 50"
MSRP $6,800

OPTIONS
2 BAG
36" TILLER
40" SNOW BLOWER
BAG & FAN

RETAIL PRICING

YEAR	HIGH	LOW
1996	$637	$478
1997	$705	$528
1998	$780	$585
1999	$863	$647
2000	$954	$716

1718H

YEARS MFRD 1993-2004
SERIES .... 1700 SERIES
ENGINE .... B&S
ENGINE HP 18
COOLING .... AIR
FUEL .... G
SPEEDS .... VARIABLE
TRANSMISSION .... HYDRO
STEERING .... STANDARD
STANDARD DECK .... 44"
WEIGHT .... 670 LBS.
MSRP $4,525

OPTIONS
2 BAG
3 BAG & FAN
36" TILLER
40" SNOW BLOWER

RETAIL PRICING

YEAR	HIGH	LOW
1993	$371	$278
1994	$381	$286
1995	$397	$298
1996	$409	$307
1997	$452	$339
1998	$501	$376
1999	$553	$415
2000	$612	$459
2001	$678	$508
2002	$749	$562
2003	$829	$622
2004	$918	$688

1720

YEARS MFRD 2004-2005
SERIES .... 1700 SERIES
ENGINE .... VANGUARD
ENGINE HP 20
COOLING .... AIR
FUEL .... G
SPEEDS .... VARIABLE
TRANSMISSION .... HYDRO
STEERING .... STANDARD
STANDARD DECK .... 44"
MSRP $4,695

OPTIONS
3 BAG
36" TILLER
42" BLADE
42" SNOW BLOWER

RETAIL PRICING

YEAR	HIGH	LOW
2004	$934	$701
2005	$1,033	$775

1720H

YEARS MFRD 1999-2002
SERIES .... 1700 SERIES
ENGINE .... B&S
ENGINE HP 20
COOLING .... AIR
FUEL .... G
SPEEDS .... VARIABLE
TRANSMISSION .... HYDRO
STEERING .... STANDARD
STANDARD DECK .... 54"
MSRP $5,199

OPTIONS
2 BAG
36" TILLER
42" BLADE
42" SNOW THROWER

RETAIL PRICING

YEAR	HIGH	LOW
1999	$645	$484
2000	$714	$536
2001	$790	$593
2002	$875	$656

1721

YEARS MFRD 2006-2006
ENGINE .... VANGUARD
ENGINE HP 21
COOLING .... AIR
FUEL .... G
SPEEDS .... VARIABLE
TRANSMISSION .... HYDRO
STEERING .... STANDARD
STANDARD DECK .... 44"
MSRP $4,825

OPTIONS
3 BAG & FAN
40" SNOW BLOWER
42" BLADE
42" SNOW THROWER

RETAIL PRICING

YEAR	HIGH	LOW
2006	$1,165	$874

1723

YEARS MFRD 2006-2011
ENGINE .... VANGUARD
ENGINE HP 23
COOLING .... AIR
FUEL .... G
SPEEDS .... VARIABLE
TRANSMISSION .... HYDRO
STEERING .... STANDARD
STANDARD DECK .... 50"
MSRP $5,900

OPTIONS
3 BAG & FAN
42" BLADE
42" SNOW BLOWER
42" SNOW THROWER

RETAIL PRICING

YEAR	HIGH	LOW
2006	$1,339	$1,004
2007	$1,481	$1,111
2008	$1,639	$1,229
2009	$1,812	$1,359
2010	$2,005	$1,504
2011	$2,219	$1,664

1723H

YEARS MFRD 2001-2001
ENGINE .... KOHLER
ENGINE HP 23
COOLING .... AIR
FUEL .... G
SPEEDS .... VARIABLE
TRANSMISSION .... HYDRO
STEERING .... STANDARD
STANDARD DECK .... 54"
MSRP $7,099

OPTIONS
3 BAG
36" TILLER
42" BLADE
42" SNOW BLOWER

RETAIL PRICING

YEAR	HIGH	LOW
2001	$885	$664

1820H

YEARS MFRD 2002-2004
SERIES .... 1800 SERIES
ENGINE .... KOHLER
ENGINE HP 20
COOLING .... AIR
FUEL .... G
SPEEDS .... VARIABLE
TRANSMISSION .... HYDRO
STEERING .... STANDARD
STANDARD DECK .... 50"
MSRP $6,095

OPTIONS
2 BAG
40" SNOW BLOWER
42" BLADE

RETAIL PRICING

YEAR	HIGH	LOW
2002	$1,010	$757
2003	$1,116	$837
2004	$1,236	$927

1823

YEARS MFRD 2006-2006
ENGINE . . . . KOHLER
ENGINE HP 23
COOLING . . . . AIR
FUEL . . . . G
SPEEDS . . . . VARIABLE
TRANSMISSION . . . . HYDRO
STEERING. . . . . STANDARD
STANDARD DECK . . . . 50"
MSRP. $6,425

OPTIONS

54" DECK

RETAIL PRICING

YEAR	HIGH	LOW
2006	$3,326	$2,495

1823H

YEARS MFRD 2002-2006
SERIES. . . . . 1800 SERIES
ENGINE . . . . KOHLER
ENGINE HP 23
COOLING . . . . AIR
FUEL . . . . G
SPEEDS . . . . VARIABLE
TRANSMISSION . . . . HYDRO
STEERING. . . . . STANDARD
STANDARD DECK . . . . 54"
MSRP. $6,795

OPTIONS

3 BAG
36" TILLER
40" SNOW BLOWER
42" BLADE

RETAIL PRICING

YEAR	HIGH	LOW
2002	$1,096	$822
2003	$1,213	$910
2004	$1,342	$1,007
2005	$1,484	$1,113
2006	$1,652	$1,239

1825H

YEARS MFRD 2007-2009
ENGINE . . . . . . KOHLER COMMAND
CYLINDERS. 2
ENGINE HP 25
COOLING . . . . AIR
FUEL . . . . G
SPEEDS . . . . VARIABLE
TRANSMISSION . . . . HYDRO
STEERING. . . . . STANDARD
STANDARD DECK . . . . 50"
WEIGHT . . . . 791 LBS.
MSRP. $7,550

OPTIONS

36" TILLER
42" BLADE
42" SNOW BLOWER

RETAIL PRICING

YEAR	HIGH	LOW
2007	$2,000	$1,500
2008	$2,212	$1,659
2009	$2,446	$1,835

1827H

YEARS MFRD 2007-2009
ENGINE . . . . . . KOHLER COMMAND
CYLINDERS. 2
ENGINE HP 27
COOLING . . . . AIR
FUEL . . . . G
SPEEDS . . . . VARIABLE
TRANSMISSION . . . . HYDRO
STEERING. . . . . STANDARD
STANDARD DECK . . . . 54"
WEIGHT . . . . 858 LBS.
MSRP. $7,850

OPTIONS

3 BAG
36" TILLER
42" BLADE
42" SNOW BLOWER

RETAIL PRICING

YEAR	HIGH	LOW
2007	$2,078	$1,559
2008	$2,299	$1,724
2009	$2,544	$1,908

1918H

YEARS MFRD 1993-1997
SERIES. . . . . 1900 SERIES
ENGINE . . . . B&S
ENGINE HP 18
COOLING . . . . AIR
FUEL . . . . G
SPEEDS . . . . VARIABLE
TRANSMISSION . . . . HYDRO
STEERING. . . . . STANDARD
STANDARD DECK . . . . 48"
WEIGHT . . . . 1,003 LBS.
MSRP. $7,950

OPTIONS

38" TILLER
47" SNOW BLOWER
CART

RETAIL PRICING

YEAR	HIGH	LOW
1993	$478	$359
1994	$530	$397
1995	$586	$439
1996	$647	$485
1997	$716	$537

1920H

YEARS MFRD 1995-1997
SERIES. . . . . 1900 SERIES
ENGINE . . . . KOHLER
ENGINE HP 20
COOLING . . . . AIR
FUEL . . . . G
SPEEDS . . . . VARIABLE
TRANSMISSION . . . . HYDRO
STEERING. . . . . STANDARD
STANDARD DECK . . . . 48"
WEIGHT . . . . 1,070 LBS.
MSRP. $9,000

OPTIONS

38" TILLER
46" BLADE
47" SNOW BLOWER
60" DECK

RETAIL PRICING

YEAR	HIGH	LOW
1995	$662	$497
1996	$732	$549
1997	$811	$608

2020H

YEARS MFRD 1998-2002
SERIES. . . . . 2000 SERIES
ENGINE . . . . KOHLER
ENGINE HP 20
COOLING . . . . AIR
FUEL . . . . G
SPEEDS . . . . VARIABLE
TRANSMISSION . . . . HYDRO
STEERING. . . . . STANDARD
STANDARD DECK . . . . 48"
MSRP. $8,250

OPTIONS

3 BAG
47" SNOW BLOWER
50" TILLER
54" DECK

RETAIL PRICING

YEAR	HIGH	LOW
1998	$925	$694
1999	$1,024	$768
2000	$1,134	$850
2001	$1,254	$940
2002	$1,387	$1,040

2020LC

YEARS MFRD 1998-2002
SERIES. . . . . 2000 SERIES
ENGINE . . . . KAWASAKI
ENGINE HP 20
COOLING . . . . LIQUID
FUEL . . . . G
SPEEDS . . . . VARIABLE
TRANSMISSION . . . . HYDRO
STEERING. . . . . STANDARD
STANDARD DECK . . . . 54"
MSRP. $9,799

OPTIONS

3 BAG
47" SNOW BLOWER
50" TILLER
60" BLADE

RETAIL PRICING

YEAR	HIGH	LOW
1998	$1,100	$825
1999	$1,216	$912
2000	$1,346	$1,009
2001	$1,489	$1,117
2002	$1,647	$1,236

2023H

YEARS MFRD 2001-2003
SERIES. . . . . 2000 SERIES
ENGINE . . . . KOHLER
ENGINE HP 23
FUEL . . . . G
SPEEDS . . . . VARIABLE
TRANSMISSION . . . . HYDRO
STEERING. . . . . STANDARD
STANDARD DECK . . . . 54"
MSRP. $9,075

OPTIONS

3 BAG
47" SNOW BLOWER
50" TILLER
60" BLADE

RETAIL PRICING

YEAR	HIGH	LOW
2001	$1,439	$1,079
2002	$1,592	$1,194
2003	$1,762	$1,321

2024D

YEARS MFRD 1999-2002
SERIES. . . . . 2000 SERIES
ENGINE . . . . B&S
ENGINE HP 24.5
COOLING . . . . LIQUID
FUEL . . . . D
SPEEDS . . . . VARIABLE
TRANSMISSION . . . . HYDRO
STEERING. . . . . STANDARD
STANDARD DECK . . . . 60"
MSRP. $11,550

OPTIONS

3 BAG
47" SNOW BLOWER
50" TILLER

RETAIL PRICING

YEAR	HIGH	LOW
1999	$1,434	$1,076
2000	$1,587	$1,190
2001	$1,755	$1,316
2002	$1,941	$1,456

2025FH

YEARS MFRD 2000-2000
SERIES. . . . . 2000 SERIES
ENGINE . . . . KOHLER
ENGINE HP 25
COOLING . . . . AIR
SPEEDS . . . . VARIABLE
TRANSMISSION . . . . HYDRO
STANDARD DECK . . . . 60"
MSRP. $10,550

OPTIONS

3 BAG
47" SNOW BLOWER
50" TILLER
60" BLADE

RETAIL PRICING

YEAR	HIGH	LOW
2000	$1,591	$1,193

2025H

YEARS MFRD 1998-2003
SERIES. . . . . 2000 SERIES
ENGINE . . . . KOHLER
ENGINE HP 25
COOLING . . . . AIR

AGCO

FUEL . . . . . G
SPEEDS . . . . . VARIABLE
TRANSMISSION . . . . . HYDRO
STEERING. . . . . STANDARD
STANDARD DECK . . . . . 60"
MSRP. $9,750

OPTIONS

3 BAG
47" SNOW BLOWER
50" TILLER
60" BLADE

RETAIL PRICING

YEAR	HIGH	LOW
1998	$1,142	$857
1999	$1,264	$948
2000	$1,397	$1,048
2001	$1,547	$1,160
2002	$1,710	$1,282
2003	$1,892	$1,419

2027H

YEARS MFRD 2006-2006
ENGINE . . . . . KOHLER
ENGINE HP 27
COOLING . . . . . AIR
FUEL . . . . . G
SPEEDS . . . . . VARIABLE
TRANSMISSION . . . . . HYDRO
STEERING. . . . . STANDARD
DRIVE TYPE 2WD
STANDARD DECK . . . . . 60"
MSRP. $8,650

OPTIONS

3 BAG
46" SNOW THROWER
47" SNOW BLOWER
50" TILLER

RETAIL PRICING

YEAR	HIGH	LOW
2006	$2,584	$1,938

2027LC

YEARS MFRD 2006-2006
ENGINE . . . . . KAWASAKI
ENGINE HP 27
COOLING . . . . . LIQUID
FUEL . . . . . G
SPEEDS . . . . . VARIABLE
TRANSMISSION . . . . . HYDRO
STEERING. . . . . STANDARD
DRIVE TYPE 4WD
STANDARD DECK . . . . . 60"
MSRP. $10,750

OPTIONS

3 BAG
46" SNOW THROWER
47" SNOW BLOWER
50" TILLER

RETAIL PRICING

YEAR	HIGH	LOW
2006	$3,207	$2,406

1694501

YEARS MFRD 2004-2004
SERIES. . . . . LEGACY XL SERIES
ENGINE . . . . . KOHLER
ENGINE HP 27
COOLING . . . . . AIR
FUEL . . . . . G
SPEEDS . . . . . VARIABLE
TRANSMISSION . . . . . HYDRO
STEERING. . . . . STANDARD
STANDARD DECK . . . . . 48"
MSRP. $8,275

OPTIONS

54" DECK
60" DECK
LDR

RETAIL PRICING

YEAR	HIGH	LOW
2004	$1,677	$1,258

1694502

YEARS MFRD 2004-2004
SERIES. . . . . LEGACY XL SERIES
ENGINE . . . . . KAWASAKI
ENGINE HP 27
COOLING . . . . . AIR
FUEL . . . . . G
SPEEDS . . . . . VARIABLE
TRANSMISSION . . . . . HYDRO
STEERING. . . . . STANDARD
STANDARD DECK . . . . . 48"
MSRP. $9,625

OPTIONS

54" DECK
60" DECK
LDR

RETAIL PRICING

YEAR	HIGH	LOW
2004	$1,951	$1,463

1694503

YEARS MFRD 2004-2004
SERIES. . . . . LEGACY XL SERIES
ENGINE . . . . . KAWASAKI
ENGINE HP 27
COOLING . . . . . AIR
FUEL . . . . . G
SPEEDS . . . . . VARIABLE
TRANSMISSION . . . . . HYDRO
STEERING. . . . . STANDARD
STANDARD DECK . . . . . 48"
MSRP. $10,495

OPTIONS

54" DECK
60" DECK
LDR

RETAIL PRICING

YEAR	HIGH	LOW
2004	$2,128	$1,596

ALLIS-CHALMERS

AC130 23/42

YEARS MFRD 2011-2012
ENGINE . . . . . B&S
ENGINE HP 23
COOLING . . . . . AIR
FUEL . . . . . G
SPEEDS . . . . . VARIABLE
TRANSMISSION . . . . . HYDRO
STEERING. . . . . STANDARD
STANDARD DECK . . . . . 42"
WEIGHT . . . . . 532 LBS.
MSRP. $1,999

OPTIONS

2 BAG
42" BLADE
42" SNOW BLOWER
AWS
B&S 24HP
SNO CAB

RETAIL PRICING

YEAR	HIGH	LOW
2011	$760	$570
2012	$842	$631

5015

YEARS MFRD 1982-1985
ENGINE . . . . . TOYOSHA
CYLINDERS. 3
CID 61.3
PTO HP 15
ENGINE HP 18
FUEL . . . . . D
SPEEDS 9/3
TRANSMISSION . . . . . GEAR
STEERING. . . . . STANDARD
DRIVE TYPE 2WD
WEIGHT . . . . . 1,387 LBS.
MSRP. $6,549

OPTIONS

4WD
LDR

SERIAL NUMBERS

PLATE ABOVE GEARSHIFT LEVER

YEAR	BEGINNING NO.
1982	1001
1983	1727
1984	3277
1985	4236

RETAIL PRICING

YEAR	HIGH	LOW
1982	$741	$556
1983	$908	$681
1984	$1,080	$810
1985	$1,263	$947

5040

YEARS MFRD 1976-1980
ENGINE . . . . . UZINA
CYLINDERS. 3
CID 143
PTO HP 40
COOLING . . . . . LIQUID
FUEL . . . . . D
SPEEDS 12/3 9/3
TRANSMISSION . . . . . GEAR
STEERING. . . . . STANDARD
HYDRAULIC . . . . . YES
PTO . . . . . YES
WEIGHT . . . . . 3,850 LBS.
MSRP. $8,455

SERIAL NUMBERS

REAR OF CONSOLE UNDER STEERING WHEEL

YEAR	BEGINNING NO.
1976	408445
1977	410384
1978	462148
1979	473000
1980	474000

RETAIL PRICING

YEAR	HIGH	LOW
1977	$3,735	$2,801
1978	$3,833	$2,875
1979	$4,262	$3,197
1980	$4,317	$3,238

5050

YEARS MFRD 1977-1983
ENGINE . . . . . FIAT
CYLINDERS. 3
CID 167.8
PTO HP 51
COOLING . . . . . LIQUID
FUEL . . . . . D
SPEEDS 8/2
TRANSMISSION . . . . . GEAR
STEERING. . . . . STANDARD
HYDRAULIC . . . . . YES
PTO . . . . . YES
WEIGHT . . . . . 4,280 LBS.
MSRP. $20,720

SERIAL NUMBERS

PLATE ON CONSOLE UNDER STEERING WHEEL

YEAR	BEGINNING NO.
1977	573461
1978	579632
1979	584000
1980	591000
1981	596014
1982	597730
1983	599191

RETAIL PRICING

YEAR	HIGH	LOW
1983	$6,059	$4,545

6140

YEARS MFRD 1982-1985
ENGINE . . . . . TOYOSHA
CYLINDERS. 3
CID 142
PTO HP 41
FUEL . . . . . D
SPEEDS 10/2
WEIGHT . . . . . 4,200 LBS.
MSRP. $15,900

SERIAL NUMBERS
LEFT HAND SIDE,LEFT SIDE OF FUEL TANK

YEAR	BEGINNING NO.
1982	1001
1983	1447
1984	1851
1985	2711

RETAIL PRICING

YEAR	HIGH	LOW
1985	$5,384	$4,038

6140FWA
YEARS MFRD 1982-1985
ENGINE .... TOYOSHA
CYLINDERS 3
CID 142
PTO HP 41
COOLING .... LIQUID
FUEL .... D
SPEEDS 10/2
TRANSMISSION .... GEAR
STEERING .... STANDARD
HYDRAULIC .... YES
PTO .... YES
WEIGHT .... 4,628 LBS.
MSRP $19,545

SERIAL NUMBERS

YEAR	BEGINNING NO.
1982	1001
1983	1447
1984	1851
1985	2711

RETAIL PRICING

YEAR	HIGH	LOW
1985	$6,615	$4,961

ALTOZ

TRX354
YEARS MFRD 2019-2020
SERIES .... TRX SERIES
ENGINE .... KAWASAKI FX
CID 852
ENGINE HP 27
FUEL .... G
TRANSMISSION .... HYDRO
STEERING .... ZERO
STANDARD DECK .... 54"
WEIGHT .... 1,200 LBS.

TRX561
YEARS MFRD 2019-2020
SERIES .... TRX SERIES
ENGINE .... KAWASAKI FX
CID 999
ENGINE HP 31
FUEL .... G
TRANSMISSION .... HYDRO
STEERING .... ZERO
STANDARD DECK .... 61"
WEIGHT .... 1,540 LBS.

TRX610I
YEARS MFRD 2017-2018
SERIES .... TRX SERIES
ENGINE KOHLER COMMAND PRO EFI
CYLINDERS 2
CID 824CC
ENGINE HP 33
FUEL .... G
TRANSMISSION .... HYDRO
STEERING .... ZERO
BLADE CLUTCH .... ELECTRIC
STANDARD DECK .... 61"
WEIGHT .... 1,560 LBS.

TRX660I
YEARS MFRD 2017-2018
SERIES .... TRX SERIES
ENGINE .... VANGUARD EFI
CYLINDERS 2
CID 993CC
ENGINE HP 37
FUEL .... G
TRANSMISSION .... HYDRO
STEERING .... ZERO
BLADE CLUTCH .... ELECTRIC
STANDARD DECK .... 66"
WEIGHT .... 1,570 LBS.

TRX766
YEARS MFRD 2019-2019
SERIES .... TRX SERIES
ENGINE .... VANGUARD EFI
CID 993
ENGINE HP 37
FUEL .... G
TRANSMISSION .... HYDRO
STEERING .... ZERO
STANDARD DECK .... 66"
WEIGHT .... 1,600 LBS.

TRX766I
YEARS MFRD 2020-2020
SERIES .... TRX SERIES
ENGINE .... VANGUARD EFI
CID 993CC
ENGINE HP 37
TRANSMISSION .... HYDRO
STEERING .... ZERO
STANDARD DECK .... 66"
WEIGHT .... 1,600 LBS.

XC540S
YEARS MFRD 2016-2017
SERIES .... XC S SERIES
ENGINE .... KAWASAKI FX
CID 852CC
ENGINE HP 27
FUEL .... G
TRANSMISSION .... HYDRO
STEERING .... ZERO
STANDARD DECK .... 54"
WEIGHT .... 1,350 LBS.

XC540S
YEARS MFRD 2017-2017
SERIES .... XP HS SERIES
ENGINE .... KAWASAKI FX
ENGINE HP 27
FUEL .... G
TRANSMISSION .... HYDRO
STEERING .... ZERO
BLADE CLUTCH .... ELECTRIC
STANDARD DECK .... 54"

XC540SI
YEARS MFRD 2016-2017
SERIES .... XC S SERIES
ENGINE KOHLER COMMAND PRO EFI
CID 824CC
ENGINE HP 27
FUEL .... G
TRANSMISSION .... HYDRO
STEERING .... ZERO
STANDARD DECK .... 54"
WEIGHT .... 1,350 LBS.

OPTIONS
B&S VANGUARD EFI

XC540Z
YEARS MFRD 2017-2017
SERIES .... XC SERIES
ENGINE .... KAWASAKI FX
ENGINE HP 27
FUEL .... G
TRANSMISSION .... HYDRO
STEERING .... ZERO
BLADE CLUTCH .... ELECTRIC
STANDARD DECK .... 54"

XC540Z
YEARS MFRD 2016-2017
SERIES .... XC Z SERIES
ENGINE .... KAWASAKI FX
CID 852CC
ENGINE HP 27
FUEL .... G
TRANSMISSION .... HYDRO
STEERING .... ZERO
STANDARD DECK .... 54"
WEIGHT .... 1,370 LBS.

XC540ZI
YEARS MFRD 2016-2017
SERIES .... XC Z SERIES
ENGINE KOHLER COMMAND PRO EFI
CID 824CC
ENGINE HP 27
FUEL .... G
TRANSMISSION .... HYDRO
STEERING .... ZERO
STANDARD DECK .... 54"
WEIGHT .... 1,370 LBS.

XC540ZI
YEARS MFRD 2017-2017
SERIES .... XC SERIES
ENGINE KOHLER COMMAND PRO EFI
ENGINE HP 27
FUEL .... G
TRANSMISSION .... HYDRO
STEERING .... ZERO
BLADE CLUTCH .... ELECTRIC
STANDARD DECK .... 54"

XC610S
YEARS MFRD 2016-2017
SERIES .... XC S SERIES
ENGINE .... KAWASAKI FX
CID 852CC
ENGINE HP 27
FUEL .... G
TRANSMISSION .... HYDRO
STEERING .... ZERO
STANDARD DECK .... 61"
WEIGHT .... 1,400 LBS.

OPTIONS
KAWASAKI 31HP

XC610SI
YEARS MFRD 2016-2017
SERIES .... XC S SERIES
ENGINE .... B&S VANGUARD
CID 810CC
ENGINE HP 28
FUEL .... G
TRANSMISSION .... HYDRO
STEERING .... ZERO
STANDARD DECK .... 61"
WEIGHT .... 1,400 LBS.

OPTIONS
KOHLER COMMAND PRO EFI 27

XC610SI
YEARS MFRD 2017-2017
SERIES .... XC SERIES
ENGINE KOHLER COMMAND PRO EFI
CID 824CC
ENGINE HP 33
FUEL .... G
TRANSMISSION .... HYDRO
STEERING .... ZERO
BLADE CLUTCH .... ELECTRIC
STANDARD DECK .... 61"

XC610Z
YEARS MFRD 2017-2017
SERIES .... XC SERIES
ENGINE .... KAWASAKI FX
ENGINE HP 31
FUEL .... G
TRANSMISSION .... HYDRO
STEERING .... ZERO
BLADE CLUTCH .... ELECTRIC
STANDARD DECK .... 61"

ALTOZ

XC610Z
YEARS MFRD 2016-2020
SERIES. . . . . XC Z SERIES
ENGINE . . . . KAWASAKI FX
CYLINDERS. 2
CID 921CC
ENGINE HP 31
TRANSMISSION . . . . HYDRO
STEERING. . . . . ZERO
STANDARD DECK . . . . 61"
WEIGHT . . . . 1,420 LBS.

OPTIONS

KAWASAKI 35HP

XC610ZI
YEARS MFRD 2017-2018
SERIES. . . . . XC SERIES
ENGINE KOHLER COMMAND PRO EFI
ENGINE HP 33
FUEL . . . . G
TRANSMISSION . . . . HYDRO
STEERING. . . . . ZERO
BLADE CLUTCH . . . . ELECTRIC
STANDARD DECK . . . . 61"

OPTIONS

VANGUARD EFI 33HP

XC610ZI
YEARS MFRD 2016-2019
SERIES. . . . . XC Z SERIES
ENGINE KOHLER COMMAND PRO EFI
CYLINDERS. 2
CID 824CC
ENGINE HP 33
FUEL . . . . G
TRANSMISSION . . . . HYDRO
STEERING. . . . . ZERO
STANDARD DECK . . . . 61"
WEIGHT . . . . 1,420 LBS.

OPTIONS

B&S VANGUARD EFI 33HP

XC720S
YEARS MFRD 2017-2017
SERIES. . . . . XC SERIES
ENGINE . . . . KAWASAKI FX
ENGINE HP 35
FUEL . . . . G
TRANSMISSION . . . . HYDRO
STEERING. . . . . ZERO
BLADE CLUTCH . . . . ELECTRIC
STANDARD DECK . . . . 72"

XC720SI
YEARS MFRD 2016-2017
SERIES. . . . . XC Z SERIES
ENGINE . . . . KAWASAKI FX
CID 999CC
ENGINE HP 35
FUEL . . . . G
TRANSMISSION . . . . HYDRO
STEERING. . . . . ZERO
STANDARD DECK . . . . 72"
WEIGHT . . . . 1,500 LBS.

OPTIONS

B&S VANGUARD EFI 37HP

XC720Z
YEARS MFRD 2017-2017
SERIES. . . . . XC SERIES
ENGINE . . . . KAWASAKI FX
ENGINE HP 35
FUEL . . . . G
TRANSMISSION . . . . HYDRO
STEERING. . . . . ZERO
BLADE CLUTCH . . . . ELECTRIC
STANDARD DECK . . . . 72"

XC720ZI
YEARS MFRD 2017-2020
SERIES. . . . . XC SERIES
ENGINE . . . . VANGUARD EFI
CYLINDERS. 2
CID 993CC
ENGINE HP 37
FUEL . . . . G
TRANSMISSION . . . . HYDRO
STEERING. . . . . ZERO
BLADE CLUTCH . . . . ELECTRIC
STANDARD DECK . . . . 72"
WEIGHT . . . . 1,500 LBS.

XE480
YEARS MFRD 2017-2019
SERIES. . . . . XE SERIES
ENGINE . . . . KAWASAKI FS
CYLINDERS. 2
CID 726CC
ENGINE HP 24
FUEL . . . . G
TRANSMISSION . . . . HYDRO
STEERING. . . . . ZERO
BLADE CLUTCH . . . . ELECTRIC
STANDARD DECK . . . . 48"
WEIGHT . . . . 920 LBS.

OPTIONS

B&S COMMERCIAL 24HP
HONDA GVX390 22HP
KOHLER CONFIDANT 23HP

XE480HD
YEARS MFRD 2017-2017
SERIES. . . . . XE HD SERIES
ENGINE . . . . KAWASAKI FX
CYLINDERS. 2
CID 852CC
ENGINE HP 27
FUEL . . . . G
TRANSMISSION . . . . HYDRO
STEERING. . . . . ZERO
BLADE CLUTCH . . . . ELECTRIC
STANDARD DECK . . . . 48"

XE540
YEARS MFRD 2016-2020
SERIES. . . . . XE SERIES
ENGINE . . . . KAWASAKI FS
CYLINDERS. 2
CID 726CC
ENGINE HP 24
FUEL . . . . G
TRANSMISSION . . . . HYDRO
STEERING. . . . . ZERO
BLADE CLUTCH . . . . ELECTRIC
STANDARD DECK . . . . 54"
WEIGHT . . . . 930 LBS.

OPTIONS

B&S COMMERCIAL 26HP
HONDA GXV690 22HP
KOHLER CONFIDANT 25HP

XE540HD
YEARS MFRD 2017-2017
SERIES. . . . . XE HD SERIES
ENGINE . . . . KAWASAKI FX
CYLINDERS. 2
CID 852CC
ENGINE HP 27
FUEL . . . . G
TRANSMISSION . . . . HYDRO
STEERING. . . . . ZERO
BLADE CLUTCH . . . . ELECTRIC
STANDARD DECK . . . . 54"
WEIGHT . . . . 1,020 LBS.

XE610
YEARS MFRD 2018-2020
SERIES. . . . . XE SERIES
ENGINE . . . . KAWASAKI FS
CID 726CC
ENGINE HP 24
FUEL . . . . G
TRANSMISSION . . . . HYDRO
STEERING. . . . . ZERO
STANDARD DECK . . . . 61"
WEIGHT . . . . 960 LBS.

OPTIONS

SS

XE610HD
YEARS MFRD 2017-2018
SERIES. . . . . XE HD SERIES
ENGINE . . . . KAWASAKI FX
CYLINDERS. 2
CID 852CC
ENGINE HP 27
FUEL . . . . G
TRANSMISSION . . . . HYDRO
STEERING. . . . . ZERO
BLADE CLUTCH . . . . ELECTRIC
STANDARD DECK . . . . 61"
WEIGHT . . . . 1,040 LBS.

XP540HD
YEARS MFRD 2017-2020
SERIES. . . . . XP HD SERIES
ENGINE . . . . KAWASAKI FX
CID 852CC
ENGINE HP 27
FUEL . . . . G
TRANSMISSION . . . . HYDRO
STEERING. . . . . ZERO
STANDARD DECK . . . . 54"
WEIGHT . . . . 1,330 LBS.

XP540Z
YEARS MFRD 2016-2017
SERIES. . . . . XP Z SERIES
ENGINE . . . . B&S VANGUARD
CID 810CC
ENGINE HP 26
FUEL . . . . G
TRANSMISSION . . . . HYDRO
STEERING. . . . . ZERO
STANDARD DECK . . . . 54"
WEIGHT . . . . 1,040 LBS.

OPTIONS

KAWASAKI FX 27HP

XP610HD
YEARS MFRD 2017-2020
SERIES. . . . . XP HD SERIES
ENGINE . . . . KAWASAKI FX
CYLINDERS. 2
CID 921CC
ENGINE HP 31
FUEL . . . . G
TRANSMISSION . . . . HYDRO
STEERING. . . . . ZERO
BLADE CLUTCH . . . . ELECTRIC
STANDARD DECK . . . . 61"
WEIGHT . . . . 1,360 LBS.

XP610HDI
YEARS MFRD 2017-2020
SERIES. . . . . XP HD SERIES
ENGINE . . . . VANGUARD EFI
ENGINE HP 28
FUEL . . . . G
TRANSMISSION . . . . HYDRO
STEERING. . . . . ZERO
BLADE CLUTCH . . . . ELECTRIC
STANDARD DECK . . . . 61"

OPTIONS

KOHLER COMMAND PRO 33HP

XP610Z
YEARS MFRD 2016-2017
SERIES. . . . . XP Z SERIES
ENGINE . . . . B&S VANGUARD
CID 810CC
ENGINE HP 26
FUEL . . . . G
TRANSMISSION . . . . HYDRO
STEERING. . . . . ZERO
STANDARD DECK . . . . 61"
WEIGHT . . . . 1,060 LBS.

OPTIONS

KAWASAKI FX 27HP

XP660HD
YEARS MFRD 2017-2020
SERIES. . . . . XP HD SERIES

ENGINE .... KAWASAKI FX
CYLINDERS 2
CID 921CC
ENGINE HP 31.4
FUEL .... G
TRANSMISSION .... HYDRO
STEERING .... ZERO
BLADE CLUTCH .... ELECTRIC
STANDARD DECK .... 66"
WEIGHT .... 1,400 LBS.

OPTIONS

KOHLER COMMAND PRO 33HP

XP660HDI

YEARS MFRD 2017-2019
SERIES .... XP HD SERIES
ENGINE .... VANGUARD EFI
CYLINDERS 2
CID 824CC
ENGINE HP 28
FUEL .... G
TRANSMISSION .... HYDRO
STEERING .... ZERO
BLADE CLUTCH .... ELECTRIC
STANDARD DECK .... 66"
WEIGHT .... 1,400 LBS.

OPTIONS

KOHLER COMMAND PRO 28HP

XP720HD

YEARS MFRD 2019-2020
SERIES .... XP HD SERIES
ENGINE .... KAWASAKI FX
CID 999
ENGINE HP 35
TRANSMISSION .... HYDRO
STEERING .... ZERO
STANDARD DECK .... 72"
WEIGHT .... 1,410 LBS.

XR480

YEARS MFRD 2016-2020
SERIES .... XR SERIES
ENGINE .... KAWASAKI FR
CYLINDERS 2
CID 725CC
ENGINE HP 23
FUEL .... G
TRANSMISSION .... HYDRO
STEERING .... ZERO
BLADE CLUTCH .... ELECTRIC
STANDARD DECK .... 48"
WEIGHT .... 800 LBS.

OPTIONS

HONDA GVX690 22HP
KOHLER 7000 22HP

XR540

YEARS MFRD 2016-2020
SERIES .... XR SERIES
ENGINE .... KAWASAKI FR
CYLINDERS 2
CID 726CC
ENGINE HP 23
FUEL .... G
TRANSMISSION .... HYDRO
STEERING .... ZERO
BLADE CLUTCH .... ELECTRIC
STANDARD DECK .... 54"
WEIGHT .... 820 LBS.

OPTIONS

HONDA GVX690 22HP
KOHLER 7000 22HP
SS

ZC720S

YEARS MFRD 2016-2017
SERIES .... XC S SERIES
ENGINE .... KAWASAKI FX
CID 999CC
ENGINE HP 35
FUEL .... G
TRANSMISSION .... HYDRO
STEERING .... ZERO
STANDARD DECK .... 72"
WEIGHT .... 1,500 LBS.

ANTONIO CARRARO AMERICA INC.

RONDO K.327

YEARS MFRD 2012-2013
ENGINE .... INDIRECT INJECTION
CYLINDERS 3
CID 1006CC
ENGINE HP 16
COOLING .... LIQUID
FUEL .... D
SPEEDS .... VARIABLE
TRANSMISSION .... HYDRO
STEERING .... STANDARD
WEIGHT .... 1,720 LBS.

RONDO K.333

YEARS MFRD 2012-2013
ENGINE .... DIRECT INJECTION
CYLINDERS 3
CID 1331CC
ENGINE HP 22
COOLING .... LIQUID
FUEL .... D
SPEEDS .... VARIABLE
TRANSMISSION .... HYDRO
STEERING .... STANDARD
WEIGHT .... 1,764 LBS.

SP 4400 HST

YEARS MFRD 2012-2013
SERIES .... 32 SERIES
ENGINE .... DIRECT INJECTION
CYLINDERS 3
CID 1642CC
ENGINE HP 38
COOLING .... LIQUID
FUEL .... D
SPEEDS .... VARIABLE
TRANSMISSION .... HYDRO
STEERING .... STANDARD
WEIGHT .... 2,690 LBS.

SUPERTIGRE 5400

YEARS MFRD 2007-2011
SERIES .... 21 SERIES
ENGINE .... DIRECT INJECTION
CYLINDERS 3
ENGINE HP 48
COOLING .... LIQUID
FUEL .... D
SPEEDS 12/8
TRANSMISSION .... GEAR
STEERING .... STANDARD
HITCH .... CAT. I
HYDRAULIC .... YES
PTO .... YES
WEIGHT .... 3,090 LBS.

TIGRE 3100

YEARS MFRD 2007-2007
SERIES .... 15 SERIES
ENGINE .... 4 STROKE
CYLINDERS 2
ENGINE HP 23
COOLING .... AIR
FUEL .... D
SPEEDS 8/4
TRANSMISSION .... GEAR
STEERING .... STANDARD
HITCH .... CAT. I
HYDRAULIC .... YES
PTO .... YES
WEIGHT .... 1,940 LBS.

TIGRE 3200

YEARS MFRD 2012-2013
ENGINE .... YANMAR
CYLINDERS 3
CID 1116CC
ENGINE HP 26
COOLING .... AIR
FUEL .... D
SPEEDS 8/4
TRANSMISSION .... GEAR
STEERING .... STANDARD
WEIGHT .... 1,000 LBS.

TIGRE 4000

YEARS MFRD 2012-2013
ENGINE .... YANMAR
CYLINDERS 3
CID 1331CC
ENGINE HP 31
COOLING .... AIR
FUEL .... D
SPEEDS 8/4
TRANSMISSION .... GEAR
STEERING .... STANDARD
WEIGHT .... 1,050 LBS.

TIGRE 4400F

YEARS MFRD 2012-2013
ENGINE .... YANMAR
CYLINDERS 3
CID 1642CC
ENGINE HP 38
COOLING .... AIR
FUEL .... D
SPEEDS 8/4
TRANSMISSION .... GEAR
STEERING .... STANDARD
WEIGHT .... 1,250 LBS.

TIGRE COUNTRY 3700

YEARS MFRD 2007-2007
SERIES .... 17 SERIES
ENGINE .... 4 STROKE
CYLINDERS 2
ENGINE HP 26
COOLING .... AIR
FUEL .... D
SPEEDS 8/4
TRANSMISSION .... GEAR
STEERING .... STANDARD
HITCH .... CAT. I
HYDRAULIC .... YES
PTO .... YES
WEIGHT .... 2,300 LBS.

TIGRE COUNTRY 4300

YEARS MFRD 2007-2007
SERIES .... 17 SERIES
ENGINE .... 4 STROKE
CYLINDERS 3
ENGINE HP 33
COOLING .... LIQUID
FUEL .... D
SPEEDS 8/4
TRANSMISSION .... GEAR
STEERING .... STANDARD
HITCH .... CAT. I
HYDRAULIC .... YES
PTO .... YES
WEIGHT .... 2,460 LBS.

TIGRE COUNTRY 4400

YEARS MFRD 2012-2013
ENGINE .... YANMAR
CYLINDERS 3
CID 1642CC

ANTONIO CARRARO AMERICA INC.

ENGINE HP . . . 38
COOLING . . . AIR
FUEL . . . D
SPEEDS . . . 8/4
TRANSMISSION . . . GEAR
STEERING. . . STANDARD
WEIGHT . . . 1,150 LBS.

TIGRETRAC 2500 HST

YEARS MFRD . . . 2000-2002
SERIES. . . 30 SERIES
ENGINE . . . 4 STROKE
CYLINDERS. . . 3
ENGINE HP . . . 21
COOLING . . . LIQUID
FUEL . . . D
SPEEDS . . . VARIABLE
TRANSMISSION . . . HYDRO
STEERING. . . ALL WHEEL
HITCH . . . CAT. I
HYDRAULIC . . . YES
PTO . . . YES
WEIGHT . . . 1,080 LBS.

TIGRETRAC 3800 HST

YEARS MFRD . . . 2000-2002
SERIES. . . 30 SERIES
ENGINE . . . 4 STROKE
CYLINDERS. . . 3
ENGINE HP . . . 36
COOLING . . . LIQUID
FUEL . . . D
SPEEDS . . . VARIABLE
TRANSMISSION . . . HYDRO
STEERING. . . ALL WHEEL
HYDRAULIC . . . YES
PTO . . . YES
WEIGHT . . . 1,290 LBS.

TIGRONE NORMAL

YEARS MFRD . . . 2007-2007
SERIES. . . 21 SERIES
ENGINE . . . DIRECT INJECTION
CYLINDERS. . . 3
ENGINE HP . . . 48
COOLING . . . LIQUID
FUEL . . . D
SPEEDS . . . 8/4
TRANSMISSION . . . GEAR
STEERING. . . STANDARD
HITCH . . . CAT. I
HYDRAULIC . . . YES
PTO . . . YES
WEIGHT . . . 3,380 LBS.

TTR 4400 HST

YEARS MFRD . . . 2012-2014
ENGINE . . . YANMAR
CYLINDERS. . . 3
CID . . . 1642CC
ENGINE HP . . . 38
FUEL . . . D
SPEEDS . . . VARIABLE
TRANSMISSION . . . HYDRO
STEERING. . . STANDARD
WEIGHT . . . 1,275 LBS.

TTR MOUNTAIN 4400 HST

YEARS MFRD . . . 2007-2012
SERIES. . . 30 SERIES
ENGINE . . . DIRECT INJECTION
CYLINDERS. . . 3
ENGINE HP . . . 35
COOLING . . . LIQUID
FUEL . . . D
SPEEDS . . . 3 SPEED
TRANSMISSION . . . HYDRO
STEERING. . . STANDARD
HITCH . . . CAT. I
HYDRAULIC . . . YES
PTO . . . YES
WEIGHT . . . 2,790 LBS.

ARIENS

A25-50HE

YEARS MFRD . . . 2017-2017
ENGINE . . . KAWASAKI
CYLINDERS. . . 2
CID . . . 726CC
ENGINE HP . . . 25
COOLING . . . AIR
FUEL . . . G
SPEEDS . . . VARIABLE
TRANSMISSION . . . HYDRO
STEERING. . . STANDARD
STANDARD DECK . . . 50"

A230D

YEARS MFRD . . . 2017-2017
ENGINE . . . YANMAR
CYLINDERS. . . 3
CID . . . 784CC
FUEL . . . D
SPEEDS . . . VARIABLE
TRANSMISSION . . . HYDRO

AMP RIDER

YEARS MFRD . . . 2010-2012
ENGINE . . . 48V 75 AH BATTERY
ENGINE HP . . . 4
SPEEDS . . . VARIABLE
TRANSMISSION . . . HYDRO
STEERING. . . STANDARD
STANDARD DECK . . . 34"
WEIGHT . . . 530 LBS.
MSRP. . . $1,999

RETAIL PRICING

YEAR	HIGH	LOW
2010	$663	$498
2011	$735	$551
2012	$814	$610

APEX 48

YEARS MFRD . . . 2017-2019
ENGINE . . . KOHLER
ENGINE HP . . . 23
COOLING . . . AIR
FUEL . . . G
SPEEDS . . . VARIABLE
TRANSMISSION . . . HYDRO
STEERING. . . ZERO
STANDARD DECK . . . 48"
WEIGHT . . . 823 LBS.
MSRP. . . $4,899

RETAIL PRICING

YEAR	HIGH	LOW
2017	$2,785	$2,089
2018	$3,263	$2,447
2019	$3,977	$2,983

APEX 48 991161

YEARS MFRD . . . 2020-2020
ENGINE . . . KOHLER 7000 SERIES
CYLINDERS. . . 2
CID . . . 725CC
ENGINE HP . . . 23
FUEL . . . G
SPEEDS . . . VARIABLE
TRANSMISSION . . . HYDRO
STEERING. . . ZERO
BLADE CLUTCH . . . ELECTRIC
STANDARD DECK . . . 48"
WEIGHT . . . 825 LBS.

APEX 52

YEARS MFRD . . . 2017-2019
ENGINE . . . KOHLER
ENGINE HP . . . 23
COOLING . . . AIR
FUEL . . . G
SPEEDS . . . VARIABLE
TRANSMISSION . . . HYDRO
STEERING. . . ZERO
STANDARD DECK . . . 52"
WEIGHT . . . 832 LBS.
MSRP. . . $4,999

RETAIL PRICING

YEAR	HIGH	LOW
2017	$2,880	$2,160
2018	$3,335	$2,501
2019	$3,992	$2,994

APEX 52 991159

YEARS MFRD . . . 2020-2020
ENGINE . . . KAWASAKI FR691
CID . . . 726CC
ENGINE HP . . . 23
FUEL . . . G
SPEEDS . . . VARIABLE
TRANSMISSION . . . HYDRO
STEERING. . . ZERO
BLADE CLUTCH . . . ELECTRIC
STANDARD DECK . . . 52"
WEIGHT . . . 850 LBS.

APEX 60

YEARS MFRD . . . 2017-2019
ENGINE . . . KOHLER
ENGINE HP . . . 25
COOLING . . . AIR
FUEL . . . G
SPEEDS . . . VARIABLE
TRANSMISSION . . . HYDRO
STEERING. . . ZERO
STANDARD DECK . . . 60"
WEIGHT . . . 853 LBS.
MSRP. . . $5,099

OPTIONS

KAWASAKI

RETAIL PRICING

YEAR	HIGH	LOW
2017	$3,478	$2,609
2018	$3,736	$2,802
2019	$4,200	$3,150

APEX 60 991163

YEARS MFRD . . . 2020-2020
ENGINE . . . KAWASAKI FR730
CID . . . 726CC
ENGINE HP . . . 24
FUEL . . . G
SPEEDS . . . VARIABLE
TRANSMISSION . . . HYDRO
STEERING. . . ZERO
BLADE CLUTCH . . . ELECTRIC
STANDARD DECK . . . 60"
WEIGHT . . . 870 LBS.

B60 4TRAC

YEARS MFRD . . . 2017-2017
ENGINE . . . KAWASAKI
CYLINDERS. . . 2
CID . . . 603CC
FUEL . . . G
SPEEDS . . . VARIABLE
TRANSMISSION . . . HYDRO
STEERING. . . STANDARD

B250 4TRAC

YEARS MFRD . . . 2017-2017
ENGINE . . . KAWASAKI
CYLINDERS. . . 2
CID . . . 726CC
FUEL . . . G
SPEEDS . . . VARIABLE
TRANSMISSION . . . HYDRO
STEERING. . . STANDARD

C50

YEARS MFRD 2017-2017
ENGINE .... B&S
CYLINDERS.................. 1
CID 500CC
COOLING .... AIR
FUEL .... G
SPEEDS .... VARIABLE
TRANSMISSION .... HYDRO
STANDARD DECK .... 38"

C60

YEARS MFRD 2017-2017
ENGINE .... KAWASAKI
CYLINDERS.................. 2
CID 603CC
FUEL .... G
SPEEDS .... VARIABLE
TRANSMISSION .... HYDRO
STEERING............ STANDARD
STANDARD DECK .... 42"

EDGE 34 915243

YEARS MFRD 2020-2020
ENGINE .... KOHLER 6000 SERIES
CID 660CC
ENGINE HP 19
FUEL .... G
SPEEDS .... VARIABLE
TRANSMISSION .... HYDRO
STEERING................ ZERO
BLADE CLUTCH .... ELECTRIC
STANDARD DECK .... 34"
WEIGHT .... 464 LBS.

EDGE 34 915251

YEARS MFRD 2020-2020
ENGINE .... BRIGGS INTEK
CID 656CC
ENGINE HP 20
FUEL .... G
SPEEDS .... VARIABLE
TRANSMISSION .... HYDRO
STEERING................ ZERO
BLADE CLUTCH .... ELECTRIC
STANDARD DECK .... 34"
WEIGHT .... 447 LBS.

EDGE 42 915245

YEARS MFRD 2020-2020
ENGINE ..... KOHLER 6000 SERIES
CID 660CC
ENGINE HP 19
FUEL .... G
SPEEDS .... VARIABLE
TRANSMISSION .... HYDRO
STEERING................ ZERO
BLADE CLUTCH .... ELECTRIC
STANDARD DECK .... 42"
WEIGHT .... 497 LBS.

EDGE 42 915253

YEARS MFRD 2020-2020
ENGINE .... BRIGGS INTEK
CID 656CC
ENGINE HP 20
FUEL .... G
SPEEDS .... VARIABLE
TRANSMISSION .... HYDRO
STEERING................ ZERO
BLADE CLUTCH .... ELECTRIC
STANDARD DECK .... 42"
WEIGHT .... 510 LBS.

EDGE 52 915254

YEARS MFRD 2020-2020
ENGINE .... KAWASAKI FR651
CID 726CC
ENGINE HP 21.5
FUEL .... G
SPEEDS .... VARIABLE
TRANSMISSION .... HYDRO
STEERING................ ZERO
BLADE CLUTCH .... ELECTRIC
STANDARD DECK .... 52"
WEIGHT .... 560 LBS.

EZR1540

YEARS MFRD 2002-2002
SERIES.......... EZ RIDER SERIES
ENGINE .... B&S
ENGINE HP 15
COOLING .... AIR
FUEL .... G
SPEEDS .... VARIABLE
TRANSMISSION .... HYDRO
STEERING................ ZERO
STANDARD DECK .... 40"
MSRP................. $2,999

OPTIONS

2 BAG
40" SNOW BLOWER
42" BLADE

SERIAL NUMBERS

YEAR	BEGINNING NO.
2002	000101

RETAIL PRICING

YEAR	HIGH	LOW
2002	$488	$366

EZR1542

YEARS MFRD 2001-2001
SERIES.......... EZ RIDER SERIES
ENGINE .... B&S
ENGINE HP 15
COOLING .... AIR
FUEL .... G
SPEEDS .... VARIABLE
TRANSMISSION .... HYDRO
STEERING................ ZERO
STANDARD DECK .... 42"
MSRP................. $3,059

OPTIONS

2 BAG
40" SNOW BLOWER
42" BLADE

RETAIL PRICING

YEAR	HIGH	LOW
2001	$456	$342

EZR1640

YEARS MFRD 1997-1998
SERIES.......... EZ RIDER SERIES
ENGINE .... TECUMSEH
ENGINE HP 16
COOLING .... AIR
FUEL .... G
SPEEDS .... VARIABLE
TRANSMISSION .... HYDRO
STEERING................ ZERO
STANDARD DECK .... 40"
MSRP................. $3,549

OPTIONS

2 BAG

RETAIL PRICING

YEAR	HIGH	LOW
1997	$393	$295
1998	$434	$325

EZR1648

YEARS MFRD 1996-1999
SERIES.......... EZ RIDER SERIES
ENGINE .... B&S
ENGINE HP 16
COOLING .... AIR
FUEL .... G
SPEEDS .... VARIABLE
TRANSMISSION ..... DUAL HYDRO
STEERING................ ZERO
STANDARD DECK .... 48"
MSRP................. $4,149

OPTIONS

2 BAG

RETAIL PRICING

YEAR	HIGH	LOW
1996	$377	$283
1997	$416	$312
1998	$459	$344
1999	$507	$380

EZR1740

YEARS MFRD 2002-2002
SERIES.......... EZ RIDER SERIES
ENGINE .... B&S
ENGINE HP 17
COOLING .... AIR
FUEL .... G
SPEEDS .... VARIABLE
TRANSMISSION .... HYDRO
STEERING................ ZERO
STANDARD DECK .... 40"
MSRP................. $3,199

OPTIONS

2 BAG
40" SNOW BLOWER
42" BLADE

RETAIL PRICING

YEAR	HIGH	LOW
2002	$534	$401

EZR1742

YEARS MFRD 2000-2002
SERIES.......... EZ RIDER SERIES
ENGINE .... B&S
ENGINE HP 17
COOLING .... AIR
FUEL .... G
SPEEDS .... VARIABLE
TRANSMISSION .... HYDRO
STEERING................ ZERO
STANDARD DECK .... 42"
MSRP................. $3,199

OPTIONS

2 BAG
40" SNOW BLOWER
42" BLADE

SERIAL NUMBERS

YEAR	BEGINNING NO.
2001	000101

RETAIL PRICING

YEAR	HIGH	LOW
2000	$438	$329
2001	$484	$363
2002	$534	$401

EZR1842

YEARS MFRD 2001-2001
SERIES.......... EZ RIDER SERIES
ENGINE .... B&S
ENGINE HP 18
COOLING .... AIR
FUEL .... G
SPEEDS .... VARIABLE
TRANSMISSION .... HYDRO
STEERING................ ZERO
STANDARD DECK .... 42"
MSRP................. $3,839

OPTIONS

2 BAG
40" SNOW BLOWER
42" BLADE

RETAIL PRICING

YEAR	HIGH	LOW
2001	$572	$429

EZR2048

YEARS MFRD 2000-2002
SERIES.......... EZ RIDER SERIES
ENGINE .... B&S
ENGINE HP 20
COOLING .... AIR
FUEL .... G
SPEEDS .... VARIABLE
TRANSMISSION .... HYDRO
STEERING................ ZERO
STANDARD DECK .... 48"
MSRP................. $4,399

OPTIONS

2 BAG
40" SNOW BLOWER
42" BLADE

SERIAL NUMBERS

YEAR	BEGINNING NO.
2001	000101

RETAIL PRICING

YEAR	HIGH	LOW
2000	$588	$441
2001	$648	$486
2002	$715	$536

GT18

YEARS MFRD........ 1980-1993
ENGINE........ KOHLER
CYLINDERS........ 2
ENGINE HP........ 18
COOLING........ AIR
FUEL........ G
SPEEDS........ VARIABLE
TRANSMISSION........ HYDRO
STEERING........ STANDARD
STANDARD DECK........ 48"
WEIGHT........ 925 LBS.
MSRP........ $6,629

OPTIONS

40" SNOW BLOWER
TILLER

RETAIL PRICING

YEAR	HIGH	LOW
1985	$126	$95
1986	$139	$104
1987	$153	$115
1988	$170	$127
1989	$188	$141
1990	$208	$156
1991	$229	$172
1992	$254	$191
1993	$281	$211

GT20

YEARS MFRD........ 1988-1993
ENGINE........ KOHLER
ENGINE HP........ 20
COOLING........ AIR
FUEL........ G
SPEEDS........ VARIABLE
TRANSMISSION........ HYDRO
STEERING........ STANDARD
STANDARD DECK........ 60"
WEIGHT........ 925 LBS.
MSRP........ $7,069

OPTIONS

REAR PTO
TILLER

RETAIL PRICING

YEAR	HIGH	LOW
1988	$188	$141
1989	$208	$156
1990	$230	$172
1991	$254	$191
1992	$281	$211
1993	$311	$234

GT20H

YEARS MFRD........ 1994-1995
ENGINE........ KOHLER
ENGINE HP........ 20
COOLING........ AIR
FUEL........ G
SPEEDS........ VARIABLE
TRANSMISSION........ HYDRO
STEERING........ STANDARD
STANDARD DECK........ 60"
MSRP........ $7,945

OPTIONS

40" SNOW BLOWER
TILLER

RETAIL PRICING

YEAR	HIGH	LOW
1994	$477	$358
1995	$528	$396

HT16

YEARS MFRD........ 1982-1992
ENGINE........ KOHLER
ENGINE HP........ 16
FUEL........ G
TRANSMISSION........ GEAR
STEERING........ STANDARD

HT16 B&S

YEARS MFRD........ 1984-1990
ENGINE........ B&S
ENGINE HP........ 16
FUEL........ G
TRANSMISSION........ GEAR
STEERING........ STANDARD
WEIGHT........ 640 LBS.

HT18

YEARS MFRD........ 1984-1992
ENGINE........ KOHLER
ENGINE HP........ 18
COOLING........ AIR
FUEL........ G
SPEEDS........ VARIABLE
TRANSMISSION........ HYDRO
STEERING........ STANDARD
WEIGHT........ 657 LBS.

HT1442

YEARS MFRD........ 1992-1992
ENGINE........ B&S
ENGINE HP........ 14
COOLING........ AIR
FUEL........ G
TRANSMISSION........ HYDRO
STEERING........ STANDARD

HT1642H

YEARS MFRD........ 1992-1994
ENGINE........ KOHLER
ENGINE HP........ 16
COOLING........ AIR
FUEL........ G
SPEEDS........ VARIABLE
TRANSMISSION........ HYDRO
STEERING........ STANDARD
STANDARD DECK........ 42"
MSRP........ $4,549

OPTIONS

40" SNOW BLOWER
42" BLADE
BAGGER

RETAIL PRICING

YEAR	HIGH	LOW
1992	$307	$230
1993	$340	$255
1994	$376	$282

HT1648

YEARS MFRD........ 1992-1992
ENGINE........ KOHLER
CYLINDERS........ 2
ENGINE HP........ 16
COOLING........ AIR
FUEL........ G
SPEEDS........ VARIABLE
TRANSMISSION........ HYDRO
STEERING........ STANDARD
STANDARD DECK........ 48"
MSRP........ $4,979

OPTIONS

40" SNOW BLOWER
42" BLADE
BAGGER

RETAIL PRICING

YEAR	HIGH	LOW
1992	$310	$233

HT1848H

YEARS MFRD........ 1994-1995
SERIES........ YARD TRACTOR SERIES
ENGINE........ KOHLER
ENGINE HP........ 18
COOLING........ AIR
FUEL........ G
SPEEDS........ VARIABLE
TRANSMISSION........ HYDRO
STEERING........ STANDARD
STANDARD DECK........ 48"
MSRP........ $4,610

OPTIONS

40" SNOW BLOWER
42" BLADE
BAGGER

RETAIL PRICING

YEAR	HIGH	LOW
1994	$276	$207
1995	$307	$230

IKON X 42

YEARS MFRD........ 2016-2019
SERIES........ IKON X SERIES
ENGINE........ KOHLER
ENGINE HP........ 22
COOLING........ AIR
FUEL........ G
SPEEDS........ VARIABLE
TRANSMISSION........ HYDRO
STEERING........ ZERO
STANDARD DECK........ 42"
WEIGHT........ 605 LBS.
MSRP........ $2,899

OPTIONS

KAWASAKI

RETAIL PRICING

YEAR	HIGH	LOW
2016	$1,721	$1,291
2017	$2,078	$1,558
2018	$2,208	$1,656
2019	$2,424	$1,818

IKON X 52

YEARS MFRD........ 2016-2019
SERIES........ IKON X SERIES
ENGINE........ KOHLER
ENGINE HP........ 24
COOLING........ AIR
FUEL........ G
SPEEDS........ VARIABLE
TRANSMISSION........ HYDRO
STEERING........ ZERO
STANDARD DECK........ 52"
WEIGHT........ 635 LBS.
MSRP........ $3,099

OPTIONS

15 GAL
2 BAG
CART
KAWASAKI
SPREADER

RETAIL PRICING

YEAR	HIGH	LOW
2016	$1,779	$1,334
2017	$1,974	$1,480
2018	$2,239	$1,679
2019	$2,556	$1,917

IKON XD 42 915265

YEARS MFRD........ 2020-2020
ENGINE........ KOHLER 7000 SERIES
CID........ 725CC
ENGINE HP........ 22
FUEL........ G
SPEEDS........ VARIABLE
TRANSMISSION........ HYDRO
STEERING........ ZERO
BLADE CLUTCH........ ELECTRIC
STANDARD DECK........ 42"
WEIGHT........ 592 LBS.

IKON XD 42 915268

YEARS MFRD........ 2020-2020
ENGINE........ KAWASAKI FR600
CID........ 603CC
ENGINE HP........ 18
FUEL........ G
SPEEDS........ VARIABLE
TRANSMISSION........ HYDRO

STEERING................ZERO
BLADE CLUTCH ....ELECTRIC
STANDARD DECK........... 42"
WEIGHT.............. 594 LBS.

IKON XD 52 915266

YEARS MFRD 2020-2020
ENGINE .....KOHLER 7000 SERIES
CID 725CC
ENGINE HP................ 24
FUEL .... G
SPEEDS ....VARIABLE
TRANSMISSION ....HYDRO
STEERING................ZERO
BLADE CLUTCH ....ELECTRIC
STANDARD DECK........... 52"
WEIGHT.............. 637 LBS.

IKON XD 52 915267

YEARS MFRD 2020-2020
ENGINE ....KAWASAKI FR691
CID 726CC
ENGINE HP................ 23
FUEL .... G
SPEEDS ....VARIABLE
TRANSMISSION ....HYDRO
STEERING................ZERO
BLADE CLUTCH ....ELECTRIC
STANDARD DECK........... 52"
WEIGHT.............. 639 LBS.

IKON XD 60 915273

YEARS MFRD 2020-2020
ENGINE ....KAWASAKI FR691
CID 726CC
ENGINE HP................ 23
FUEL .... G
SPEEDS ....VARIABLE
TRANSMISSION ....HYDRO
STEERING................ZERO
BLADE CLUTCH ....ELECTRIC
STANDARD DECK........... 60"
WEIGHT.............. 671 LBS.

IKON XL 42

YEARS MFRD 2016-2019
SERIES..........IKON XL SERIES
ENGINE ....KOHLER
ENGINE HP................ 22
COOLING ....AIR
FUEL .... G
SPEEDS ....VARIABLE
TRANSMISSION ....HYDRO
STEERING................ZERO
STANDARD DECK........... 42"
WEIGHT.............. 661 LBS.
MSRP................. $3,899

OPTIONS

15 GAL
2 BAG
CART
SPREADER

RETAIL PRICING

YEAR	HIGH	LOW
2016	$2,329	$1,747
2017	$2,611	$1,958
2018	$3,006	$2,255
2019	$3,273	$2,455

IKON XL 52

YEARS MFRD 2016-2019
SERIES..........IKON XL SERIES
ENGINE ....KOHLER
ENGINE HP................ 24
COOLING ....AIR
FUEL .... G
SPEEDS ....VARIABLE
TRANSMISSION ....HYDRO
STEERING................ZERO
STANDARD DECK........... 52"
WEIGHT.............. 679 LBS.
MSRP................. $4,099

OPTIONS

15 GAL
2 BAG
CART
SPREADER

RETAIL PRICING

YEAR	HIGH	LOW
2016	$2,350	$1,763
2017	$2,663	$1,997
2018	$3,265	$2,449
2019	$3,532	$2,649

IKON XL 60

YEARS MFRD 2017-2019
SERIES..........IKON XL SERIES
ENGINE ....KOHLER
ENGINE HP................ 25
COOLING ....AIR
FUEL .... G
SPEEDS ....VARIABLE
TRANSMISSION ....HYDRO
STEERING................ZERO
STANDARD DECK........... 60"
WEIGHT.............. 694 LBS.
MSRP................. $4,299

OPTIONS

15 GAL
2 BAG
KAWASAKI
SPREADER

RETAIL PRICING

YEAR	HIGH	LOW
2017	$2,767	$2,076
2018	$3,440	$2,580
2019	$3,770	$2,828

LAWN TRACTOR 42

YEARS MFRD 2010-2012
ENGINE ....KOHLER
ENGINE HP................ 19
COOLING ....AIR
FUEL .... G
SPEEDS ....VARIABLE
TRANSMISSION ....HYDRO
STEERING............STANDARD
STANDARD DECK........... 42"
MSRP................. $1,399

RETAIL PRICING

YEAR	HIGH	LOW
2010	$517	$388
2011	$599	$450
2012	$645	$484

LAWN TRACTOR 46

YEARS MFRD 2010-2013
ENGINE ....KOHLER
ENGINE HP................ 22
COOLING ....AIR
FUEL .... G
SPEEDS ....VARIABLE
TRANSMISSION ....HYDRO
STEERING............STANDARD
STANDARD DECK........... 46"
MSRP................. $1,499

RETAIL PRICING

YEAR	HIGH	LOW
2010	$547	$410
2011	$655	$491
2012	$634	$476
2013	$780	$585

LT1232

YEARS MFRD 1994-1994
ENGINE ....B&S
ENGINE HP................ 12
COOLING ....AIR
FUEL .... G
TRANSMISSION ....HYDRO
STEERING............STANDARD
STANDARD DECK........... 32"
MSRP................. $2,159

RETAIL PRICING

YEAR	HIGH	LOW
1994	$675	$506

MAX ZOOM 48

YEARS MFRD 2010-2016
ENGINE ....KOHLER
ENGINE HP................ 22
COOLING ....AIR
FUEL .... G
SPEEDS ....VARIABLE
TRANSMISSION ....HYDRO
STEERING................ZERO
STANDARD DECK........... 48"
MSRP................. $5,425

OPTIONS

2 BAG HD
3 BAG
54" BLADE
SNOW BLOWER

RETAIL PRICING

YEAR	HIGH	LOW
2010	$1,689	$1,267
2011	$1,864	$1,398
2012	$2,058	$1,544
2013	$2,271	$1,703
2014	$2,506	$1,880
2015	$2,766	$2,075
2016	$3,055	$2,291

MAX ZOOM 52

YEARS MFRD 2010-2016
ENGINE ....KOHLER
ENGINE HP................ 23
COOLING ....AIR
FUEL .... G
SPEEDS ....VARIABLE
TRANSMISSION ....HYDRO
STEERING................ZERO
STANDARD DECK........... 52"
MSRP................. $5,539

OPTIONS

2 BAG HD
3 BAG
54" BLADE
SNOW BLOWER

RETAIL PRICING

YEAR	HIGH	LOW
2010	$1,724	$1,293
2011	$1,902	$1,427
2012	$2,099	$1,574
2013	$2,317	$1,738
2014	$2,557	$1,918
2015	$2,823	$2,117
2016	$3,116	$2,337

MAX ZOOM 60

YEARS MFRD 2010-2016
ENGINE ....KOHLER
ENGINE HP................ 25
COOLING ....AIR
FUEL .... G
SPEEDS ....VARIABLE
TRANSMISSION ....HYDRO
STEERING................ZERO
STANDARD DECK........... 60"
MSRP................. $5,649

OPTIONS

2 BAG HD
3 BAG
54" BLADE
SNOW BLOWER

RETAIL PRICING

YEAR	HIGH	LOW
2010	$1,758	$1,318
2011	$1,940	$1,455
2012	$2,142	$1,606
2013	$2,363	$1,772
2014	$2,608	$1,956
2015	$2,879	$2,159
2016	$3,178	$2,383

ARIENS

MAX ZOOM 2552

YEARS MFRD 2009-2009
ENGINE .... KOHLER COURAGE
CYLINDERS.................. 2
ENGINE HP.................. 25
COOLING .... AIR
FUEL .... G
SPEEDS .... VARIABLE
TRANSMISSION .... HYDRO
STEERING................ ZERO
STANDARD DECK .... 52"
WEIGHT .... 810 LBS.
MSRP................. $5,959

OPTIONS

3 BAG & FAN

RETAIL PRICING

YEAR	HIGH	LOW
2009	$2,482	$1,862

MAX ZOOM 2560

YEARS MFRD 2009-2009
ENGINE .... KOHLER COURAGE
CYLINDERS.................. 2
ENGINE HP.................. 25
COOLING .... AIR
FUEL .... G
SPEEDS .... VARIABLE
TRANSMISSION .... HYDRO
STEERING................ ZERO
STANDARD DECK .... 60"
WEIGHT .... 830 LBS.
MSRP................. $6,059

OPTIONS

3 BAG & FAN

RETAIL PRICING

YEAR	HIGH	LOW
2009	$2,524	$1,893

MZ ZOOM 1434

YEARS MFRD 2005-2005
SERIES........ MINI ZOOM SERIES
ENGINE .... B&S INTEK
ENGINE HP.................. 14
COOLING .... AIR
FUEL .... G
SPEEDS .... VARIABLE
TRANSMISSION .... HYDRO
STEERING................ ZERO
STANDARD DECK .... 34"
WEIGHT .... 500 LBS.
MSRP................. $2,299

OPTIONS

15 GAL

RETAIL PRICING

YEAR	HIGH	LOW
2005	$560	$420

MZ ZOOM 1534

YEARS MFRD 2005-2007
SERIES........ MINI ZOOM SERIES
ENGINE .... KOHLER COURAGE
ENGINE HP.................. 15
COOLING .... AIR
FUEL .... G
SPEEDS .... VARIABLE
TRANSMISSION .... HYDRO
STEERING................ ZERO
STANDARD DECK .... 34"
WEIGHT .... 500 LBS.
MSRP................. $2,799

OPTIONS

2 BAG & FAN
B&S
BAGGER

RETAIL PRICING

YEAR	HIGH	LOW
2005	$611	$458
2006	$676	$507
2007	$745	$559

MZ ZOOM 1540

YEARS MFRD 2005-2006
SERIES........ MINI ZOOM SERIES
ENGINE .... KOHLER COURAGE
ENGINE HP.................. 15
COOLING .... AIR
FUEL .... G
SPEEDS .... VARIABLE
TRANSMISSION .... HYDRO
STEERING................ ZERO
STANDARD DECK .... 40"
WEIGHT .... 525 LBS.
MSRP................. $3,099

OPTIONS

2 BAG & FAN
BAGGER

RETAIL PRICING

YEAR	HIGH	LOW
2005	$747	$560
2006	$825	$618

PRO ZOOM 54

YEARS MFRD 2012-2013
ENGINE .... KAWASAKI
ENGINE HP................ 24.5
COOLING .... AIR
FUEL .... G
SPEEDS .... VARIABLE
TRANSMISSION .... HYDRO
STEERING................ ZERO
STANDARD DECK .... 54"
MSRP................ $10,899

OPTIONS

3CU BAG

RETAIL PRICING

YEAR	HIGH	LOW
2012	$4,489	$3,367
2013	$4,956	$3,717

PRO ZOOM 60

YEARS MFRD 2012-2013
ENGINE .... KAWASAKI
ENGINE HP................ 24.5
COOLING .... AIR
FUEL .... G
SPEEDS .... VARIABLE
TRANSMISSION .... HYDRO
STEERING................ ZERO
STANDARD DECK .... 60"
MSRP................ $11,099

OPTIONS

3CU BAG

RETAIL PRICING

YEAR	HIGH	LOW
2012	$4,573	$3,429
2013	$5,046	$3,784

RER1028 HYDRO

YEARS MFRD 2004-2005
SERIES REAR ENGINE RIDERS SERIES
ENGINE .... B&S
ENGINE HP.................. 10
COOLING .... AIR
FUEL .... G
SPEEDS 1/1
TRANSMISSION .... HYDRO
STEERING........... STANDARD
STANDARD DECK .... 28"
WEIGHT .... 475 LBS.
MSRP................. $1,871

RETAIL PRICING

YEAR	HIGH	LOW
2004	$860	$645
2005	$1,008	$756

RER1232 HYDRO

YEARS MFRD 2004-2005
SERIES REAR ENGINE RIDERS SERIES
ENGINE .... B&S
ENGINE HP.................. 12
COOLING .... AIR
FUEL .... G
SPEEDS 1/1
TRANSMISSION .... HYDRO
STEERING........... STANDARD
STANDARD DECK .... 32"
WEIGHT .... 485 LBS.
MSRP................. $2,092

RETAIL PRICING

YEAR	HIGH	LOW
2004	$964	$723
2005	$1,125	$844

RER1440 HYDRO

YEARS MFRD 2004-2005
SERIES REAR ENGINE RIDERS SERIES
ENGINE .... B&S
ENGINE HP.................. 14
COOLING .... AIR
FUEL .... G
SPEEDS 1/1
TRANSMISSION .... HYDRO
STEERING........... STANDARD
STANDARD DECK .... 40"
WEIGHT .... 495 LBS.
MSRP................. $2,422

RETAIL PRICING

YEAR	HIGH	LOW
2004	$1,115	$836
2005	$1,304	$978

RER10528 HYDRO

YEARS MFRD 2006-2006
SERIES REAR ENGINE RIDERS SERIES
ENGINE .... B&S
ENGINE HP................ 10.5
COOLING .... AIR
FUEL .... G
SPEEDS .... VARIABLE
TRANSMISSION .... HYDRO
STEERING........... STANDARD
STANDARD DECK .... 28"
WEIGHT .... 475 LBS.
MSRP................. $1,799

RETAIL PRICING

YEAR	HIGH	LOW
2006	$1,022	$767

RER14532 HYDRO

YEARS MFRD 2005-2006
ENGINE .... B&S
CYLINDERS.................. 1
ENGINE HP................ 14.5
COOLING .... AIR
FUEL .... G
SPEEDS .... VARIABLE
TRANSMISSION .... HYDRO
STEERING........... STANDARD
STANDARD DECK .... 32"
WEIGHT .... 485 LBS.
MSRP................. $1,999

RETAIL PRICING

YEAR	HIGH	LOW
2005	$1,076	$807
2006	$1,136	$852

RM128H

YEARS MFRD 2003-2004
ENGINE .... B&S
ENGINE HP.................. 10
COOLING .... AIR
FUEL .... G
TRANSMISSION .... HYDRO
STEERING........... STANDARD
STANDARD DECK .... 28"
MSRP................. $1,699

RETAIL PRICING

YEAR	HIGH	LOW
2003	$809	$607
2004	$860	$645

RM828E

YEARS MFRD 1987-1993
ENGINE . . . . .TECUMSEH
ENGINE HP 8
COOLING . . . . .AIR
FUEL . . . . G
STEERING. . . . . .STANDARD
STANDARD DECK . . . . 28"
MSRP. $1,529

RETAIL PRICING

YEAR	HIGH	LOW
1993	$452	$339

RM1028

YEARS MFRD 2001-2002
ENGINE . . . . B&S
ENGINE HP 10
COOLING . . . . .AIR
FUEL . . . . G
TRANSMISSION . . . . DISC
STEERING. . . . . .STANDARD
STANDARD DECK . . . . 28"
MSRP. $1,449

OPTIONS

BAGGER

RETAIL PRICING

YEAR	HIGH	LOW
2001	$185	$139
2002	$205	$154

RM1132

YEARS MFRD 2003-2003
ENGINE . . . . B&S
ENGINE HP 12
COOLING . . . . .AIR
FUEL . . . . G
TRANSMISSION . . . . .HYDRO
STEERING. . . . . .STANDARD
STANDARD DECK . . . . 32"
MSRP. $1,899

OPTIONS

BAG & VAC

RETAIL PRICING

YEAR	HIGH	LOW
2003	$329	$247

RM1232H

YEARS MFRD 2004-2004
ENGINE . . . . B&S
ENGINE HP 12
COOLING . . . . .AIR
FUEL . . . . G
STEERING. . . . . .STANDARD
STANDARD DECK . . . . 32"
MSRP. $1,899

OPTIONS

BAG & VAC

RETAIL PRICING

YEAR	HIGH	LOW
2004	$312	$234

RM1330

YEARS MFRD 1996-2002
SERIES. . . . . IMPERIAL SERIES
ENGINE . . . . B&S
CYLINDERS. 1
ENGINE HP 13
COOLING . . . . .AIR
FUEL . . . . G
TRANSMISSION . . . . DISC
STEERING. . . . . .STANDARD
STANDARD DECK . . . . 30"
MSRP. $1,769

OPTIONS

2 BAG

RETAIL PRICING

YEAR	HIGH	LOW
1996	$136	$102
1997	$150	$113
1998	$167	$125
1999	$184	$138
2000	$204	$153
2001	$225	$169
2002	$250	$188

RM1340

YEARS MFRD 2003-2003
ENGINE . . . . B&S
ENGINE HP 14
COOLING . . . . .AIR
FUEL . . . . G
SPEEDS . . . . VARIABLE
TRANSMISSION . . . . .HYDRO
STEERING. . . . . .STANDARD
STANDARD DECK . . . . 40"
MSRP. $2,199

OPTIONS

BAG & VAC

RETAIL PRICING

YEAR	HIGH	LOW
2003	$380	$285

RM1440H

YEARS MFRD 2004-2004
ENGINE . . . . B&S
ENGINE HP 14
COOLING . . . . .AIR
FUEL . . . . G
STEERING. . . . . .STANDARD
STANDARD DECK . . . . 40"
MSRP. $2,199

OPTIONS

BAG & VAC

RETAIL PRICING

YEAR	HIGH	LOW
2004	$361	$271

RM8030

YEARS MFRD 1994-1999
SERIES. . . . . IMPERIAL SERIES
ENGINE . . . . B&S
CYLINDERS. 1
ENGINE HP 9
COOLING . . . . .AIR
SPEEDS 5/1
TRANSMISSION . . . . .GEAR
STEERING. . . . . .STANDARD
WEIGHT . . . . 340 LBS.

SPORT ZOOM 1232

YEARS MFRD 2003-2004
SERIES. . . . . . SPORT ZOOM SERIES
ENGINE . . . . B&S
ENGINE HP 12
COOLING . . . . LIQUID
FUEL . . . . G
SPEEDS 1/1
TRANSMISSION . . . . .HYDRO
STEERING. . . . . .STANDARD
STANDARD DECK . . . . 32"
WEIGHT . . . . 500 LBS.
MSRP. $2,299

RETAIL PRICING

YEAR	HIGH	LOW
2003	$1,105	$829
2004	$1,166	$874

SPORT ZOOM 1440

YEARS MFRD 2003-2003
SERIES. . . . . . SPORT ZOOM SERIES
ENGINE . . . . B&S
TRANSMISSION . . . . .HYDRO
WEIGHT . . . . 495 LBS.

WB12.5

YEARS MFRD 1990-1991
SERIES. . . . . . COMMERCIAL SERIES
ENGINE . . . . KOHLER
ENGINE HP 12.5
COOLING . . . . .AIR
FUEL . . . . G
STEERING. . . . . .STANDARD

WB14

YEARS MFRD 1990-1991
SERIES. . . . . . COMMERCIAL SERIES
ENGINE . . . . KOHLER
ENGINE HP 14
COOLING . . . . .AIR
FUEL . . . . G
STEERING. . . . . .STANDARD

WB16

YEARS MFRD 1990-1991
SERIES. . . . . . COMMERCIAL SERIES
ENGINE . . . . KOHLER
ENGINE HP 16
COOLING . . . . .AIR
FUEL . . . . G
STEERING. . . . . .STANDARD

WB18

YEARS MFRD 1990-1991
SERIES. . . . . . COMMERCIAL SERIES
ENGINE . . . . KOHLER
ENGINE HP 18
COOLING . . . . .AIR
FUEL . . . . G
STEERING. . . . . .STANDARD

YT120G

YEARS MFRD 1994-1995
SERIES. . . . . YT SERIES
ENGINE . . . . ARIENS
ENGINE HP 12
COOLING . . . . .AIR
FUEL . . . . G
TRANSMISSION . . . . .GEAR
STEERING. . . . . .STANDARD

YT130G

YEARS MFRD 1994-1995
SERIES. . . . . YT SERIES
ENGINE . . . . ARIENS
ENGINE HP 13
COOLING . . . . .AIR
FUEL . . . . G
TRANSMISSION . . . . .GEAR
STEERING. . . . . .STANDARD

YT130H

YEARS MFRD 1994-1995
SERIES. . . . . YT SERIES
ENGINE . . . . ARIENS
ENGINE HP 13
COOLING . . . . .AIR
FUEL . . . . G
TRANSMISSION . . . . .HYDRO
STEERING. . . . . .STANDARD

YT150H

YEARS MFRD 1994-1995
SERIES. . . . . YT SERIES
ENGINE . . . . ARIENS
ENGINE HP 15
COOLING . . . . .AIR
FUEL . . . . G
TRANSMISSION . . . . .HYDRO
STEERING. . . . . .STANDARD

YT1232GB

YEARS MFRD 1988-1991
SERIES. . . . . YT SERIES
ENGINE . . . . B&S
ENGINE HP 12.5
COOLING . . . . .AIR
FUEL . . . . G
TRANSMISSION . . . . .GEAR
STEERING. . . . . .STANDARD

YT1232HB

YEARS MFRD 1988-1990
SERIES. . . . . YT SERIES
ENGINE . . . . B&S
ENGINE HP 12
COOLING . . . . .AIR
FUEL . . . . G
TRANSMISSION . . . . .HYDRO
STEERING. . . . . .STANDARD

ARIENS

YT1232HK

YEARS MFRD 1990-1991
SERIES .... YT SERIES
ENGINE .... KOHLER
ENGINE HP 12.5
COOLING .... AIR
FUEL .... G
TRANSMISSION .... HYDRO
STEERING .... STANDARD

YT1238GB

YEARS MFRD 1988-1991
ENGINE .... B&S
ENGINE HP 12.5
COOLING .... AIR
FUEL .... G
TRANSMISSION .... GEAR
STEERING .... STANDARD

YT1238HB

YEARS MFRD 1988-1991
SERIES .... YT SERIES
ENGINE .... B&S
ENGINE HP 12.5
COOLING .... AIR
FUEL .... G
TRANSMISSION .... HYDRO
STEERING .... STANDARD

YT1238HK

YEARS MFRD 1988-1991
SERIES .... YT SERIES
ENGINE .... KAWASAKI
ENGINE HP 12
COOLING .... AIR
FUEL .... G
TRANSMISSION .... HYDRO
STEERING .... STANDARD

YT1240G

YEARS MFRD 1992-1993
SERIES .... YT SERIES
ENGINE .... ARIENS
ENGINE HP 12.5
COOLING .... AIR
FUEL .... G
TRANSMISSION .... GEAR
STEERING .... STANDARD

YT1240H

YEARS MFRD 1992-1993
SERIES .... YT SERIES
ENGINE .... ARIENS
ENGINE HP 12.5
COOLING .... AIR
FUEL .... G
TRANSMISSION .... HYDRO
STEERING .... STANDARD

YT1340

YEARS MFRD 1992-1994
SERIES .... YT SERIES
ENGINE .... ARIENS
ENGINE HP 13
COOLING .... AIR
FUEL .... G
TRANSMISSION .... GEAR
STEERING .... STANDARD

YT1340H

YEARS MFRD 1992-1992
SERIES .... YT SERIES
ENGINE .... ARIENS
ENGINE HP 13
COOLING .... AIR
FUEL .... G
TRANSMISSION .... HYDRO
STEERING .... STANDARD

YT1438HK

YEARS MFRD 1990-1991
SERIES .... YT SERIES
ENGINE .... KOHLER
ENGINE HP 14
COOLING .... AIR
FUEL .... G
TRANSMISSION .... HYDRO
STEERING .... STANDARD

YT1540

YEARS MFRD 1993-1993
SERIES .... YT SERIES
ENGINE .... ARIENS
ENGINE HP 15
COOLING .... AIR
FUEL .... G
TRANSMISSION .... GEAR
STEERING .... STANDARD

YT1540H

YEARS MFRD 1993-1993
SERIES .... YT SERIES
ENGINE .... ARIENS
ENGINE HP 15
COOLING .... AIR
FUEL .... G
TRANSMISSION .... HYDRO
STEERING .... STANDARD

YT XS

YEARS MFRD 1994-1995
SERIES .... YT SERIES
ENGINE .... TECUMSEH
ENGINE HP 16.5
COOLING .... AIR
FUEL .... G
SPEEDS 0-4
TRANSMISSION .... HYDRO
STEERING .... STANDARD
WEIGHT .... 465 LBS.

ZENITH 60

YEARS MFRD 2020-2020
ENGINE .... KAWASAKI FX730V
CYLINDERS 2
CID 726CC
ENGINE HP 24
FUEL .... G
SPEEDS .... VARIABLE
TRANSMISSION .... HYDRO
STEERING .... ZERO
BLADE CLUTCH .... ELECTRIC
STANDARD DECK .... 60"
WEIGHT .... 953 LBS.

ZOOM 34

YEARS MFRD 2009-2019
SERIES .... ZOOM SERIES
ENGINE .... KOHLER
ENGINE HP 19
COOLING .... AIR
FUEL .... G
SPEEDS 1/1
TRANSMISSION .... HYDRO
STEERING .... ZERO
STANDARD DECK .... 34"
WEIGHT .... 425 LBS.
MSRP $2,599

OPTIONS

15 GAL
BAGGER
SPREADER

RETAIL PRICING

YEAR	HIGH	LOW
2009	$699	$525
2010	$777	$583
2011	$865	$649
2012	$922	$691
2013	$1,006	$754
2014	$1,124	$843
2015	$1,408	$1,056
2016	$1,554	$1,165
2017	$1,719	$1,289
2018	$1,868	$1,401
2019	$2,076	$1,557

ZOOM 34-16

YEARS MFRD 2015-2015
ENGINE .... B&S
ENGINE HP 16
COOLING .... AIR
FUEL .... G
SPEEDS .... VARIABLE
TRANSMISSION .... HYDRO
STEERING .... ZERO
STANDARD DECK .... 34"
MSRP $2,860

RETAIL PRICING

YEAR	HIGH	LOW
2015	$1,505	$1,129

ZOOM 42

YEARS MFRD 2010-2019
ENGINE .... KOHLER
ENGINE HP 19
COOLING .... AIR
FUEL .... G
SPEEDS .... VARIABLE
TRANSMISSION .... HYDRO
STEERING .... ZERO
STANDARD DECK .... 42"
WEIGHT .... 440 LBS.
MSRP $2,699

OPTIONS

BAGGER
SPRAYER
SPREADER

RETAIL PRICING

YEAR	HIGH	LOW
2010	$849	$637
2011	$1,042	$781
2012	$1,051	$789
2013	$1,163	$872
2014	$1,282	$962
2015	$1,430	$1,072
2016	$1,576	$1,182
2017	$1,752	$1,314
2018	$1,901	$1,426
2019	$2,138	$1,603

ZOOM 50

YEARS MFRD 2010-2017
ENGINE .... KOHLER
ENGINE HP 21
COOLING .... AIR
FUEL .... G
SPEEDS .... VARIABLE
TRANSMISSION .... HYDRO
STEERING .... ZERO
STANDARD DECK .... 50"
MSRP $3,245

OPTIONS

BAGGER
SPRAYER
SPREADER

RETAIL PRICING

YEAR	HIGH	LOW
2010	$1,002	$752
2011	$1,106	$829
2012	$1,221	$916
2013	$1,352	$1,014
2014	$1,487	$1,115
2015	$1,641	$1,231
2016	$1,820	$1,365
2017	$2,000	$1,500

ZOOM 1534

YEARS MFRD 2007-2007
SERIES .... MINI ZOOM
ENGINE .... B&S
ENGINE HP 15
COOLING .... AIR
FUEL .... G
SPEEDS .... VARIABLE
TRANSMISSION .... HYDRO
STEERING .... ZERO
BLADE CLUTCH .... ELECTRIC
STANDARD DECK .... 34"
MSRP $2,699

OPTIONS

KOHLER

RETAIL PRICING

YEAR	HIGH	LOW
2007	$847	$635

ZOOM 1540

YEARS MFRD . . . 2004-2005
SERIES . . . ZOOM SERIES
ENGINE . . . KOHLER
ENGINE HP . . . 15
COOLING . . . AIR
FUEL . . . G
SPEEDS . . . VARIABLE
TRANSMISSION . . . HYDRO
STEERING . . . ZERO
STANDARD DECK . . . 40"
WEIGHT . . . 730 LBS.
MSRP . . . $2,799

OPTIONS

3 BAG
46" SNOW BLOWER
54" BLADE
BAGGER

RETAIL PRICING

YEAR	HIGH	LOW
2004	$617	$463
2005	$682	$511

ZOOM 1634

YEARS MFRD . . . 2007-2008
SERIES . . . ZOOM SERIES
ENGINE . . . B&S INTEK
CYLINDERS . . . 1
ENGINE HP . . . 16
COOLING . . . AIR
FUEL . . . G
SPEEDS . . . VARIABLE
TRANSMISSION . . . HYDRO
STEERING . . . ZERO
BLADE CLUTCH . . . ELECTRIC
STANDARD DECK . . . 34"
WEIGHT . . . 515 LBS.
MSRP . . . $2,799

OPTIONS

3 BAG
CART
SPRAYER

RETAIL PRICING

YEAR	HIGH	LOW
2007	$743	$557
2008	$822	$616

ZOOM 1640

YEARS MFRD . . . 2003-2004
SERIES . . . ZOOM SERIES
ENGINE . . . B&S
ENGINE HP . . . 16
COOLING . . . AIR
FUEL . . . G
SPEEDS . . . VARIABLE
TRANSMISSION . . . HYDRO
STEERING . . . ZERO
STANDARD DECK . . . 40"
WEIGHT . . . 710 LBS.
MSRP . . . $3,299

OPTIONS

3 BAG
46" SNOW BLOWER
54" BLADE

RETAIL PRICING

YEAR	HIGH	LOW
2003	$594	$445
2004	$655	$491

ZOOM 1734XL

YEARS MFRD . . . 2008-2009
SERIES . . . ZOOM SERIES
ENGINE . . . KOHLER COURAGE
CYLINDERS . . . 1
ENGINE HP . . . 17
COOLING . . . AIR
FUEL . . . G
SPEEDS . . . VARIABLE
TRANSMISSION . . . HYDRO
STEERING . . . ZERO
BLADE CLUTCH . . . ELECTRIC
WEIGHT . . . 525 LBS.

ZOOM 1740

YEARS MFRD . . . 2005-2005
SERIES . . . ZOOM SERIES
ENGINE . . . KOHLER COURAGE
CYLINDERS . . . 1
ENGINE HP . . . 17
COOLING . . . AIR
FUEL . . . G
SPEEDS . . . VARIABLE
TRANSMISSION . . . HYDRO
STEERING . . . ZERO
STANDARD DECK . . . 40"
WEIGHT . . . 740 LBS.
MSRP . . . $3,499

OPTIONS

3 BAG
46" SNOW THROWER
54" BLADE
BAGGER

RETAIL PRICING

YEAR	HIGH	LOW
2005	$836	$627

ZOOM 1840

YEARS MFRD . . . 2006-2008
SERIES . . . ZOOM SERIES
ENGINE . . . B&S
CYLINDERS . . . 1
ENGINE HP . . . 18.5
COOLING . . . AIR
FUEL . . . G
SPEEDS . . . VARIABLE
TRANSMISSION . . . HYDRO
STEERING . . . ZERO
BLADE CLUTCH . . . ELECTRIC
STANDARD DECK . . . 40"
MSRP . . . $3,099

OPTIONS

3 BAG & FAN
46" SNOW BLOWER
54" BLADE

RETAIL PRICING

YEAR	HIGH	LOW
2006	$745	$559
2007	$823	$617
2008	$908	$681

ZOOM 1842XL

YEARS MFRD . . . 2008-2008
SERIES . . . ZOOM SERIES
ENGINE . . . B&S ELS
CYLINDERS . . . 2
ENGINE HP . . . 18
COOLING . . . AIR
FUEL . . . G
SPEEDS . . . VARIABLE
TRANSMISSION . . . HYDRO
STEERING . . . ZERO
BLADE CLUTCH . . . ELECTRIC
STANDARD DECK . . . 42"
WEIGHT . . . 615 LBS.
MSRP . . . $4,199

OPTIONS

15 GAL
3 BAG
SPREADER

RETAIL PRICING

YEAR	HIGH	LOW
2008	$1,230	$922

ZOOM 1844

YEARS MFRD . . . 2003-2003
SERIES . . . ZOOM SERIES
ENGINE . . . B&S
ENGINE HP . . . 18
COOLING . . . AIR
FUEL . . . G
SPEEDS . . . VARIABLE
TRANSMISSION . . . HYDRO
STEERING . . . ZERO
STANDARD DECK . . . 44"
WEIGHT . . . 720 LBS.
MSRP . . . $3,899

OPTIONS

3 BAG
46" SNOW BLOWER
54" BLADE

RETAIL PRICING

YEAR	HIGH	LOW
2003	$722	$541

ZOOM 1844XL

YEARS MFRD . . . 2005-2005
SERIES . . . ZOOM SERIES
ENGINE . . . KOHLER COURAGE
ENGINE HP . . . 18
COOLING . . . AIR
FUEL . . . G
SPEEDS . . . VARIABLE
TRANSMISSION . . . HYDRO
STEERING . . . ZERO
STANDARD DECK . . . 44"
WEIGHT . . . 725 LBS.
MSRP . . . $4,599

OPTIONS

3 BAG
BAGGER

RETAIL PRICING

YEAR	HIGH	LOW
2005	$1,119	$840

ZOOM 1944

YEARS MFRD . . . 2004-2005
SERIES . . . ZOOM SERIES
ENGINE . . . KOHLER
CYLINDERS . . . 2
ENGINE HP . . . 19
COOLING . . . AIR
FUEL . . . G
SPEEDS . . . VARIABLE
TRANSMISSION . . . HYDRO
STEERING . . . ZERO
STANDARD DECK . . . 44"
WEIGHT . . . 720 LBS.
MSRP . . . $4,199

OPTIONS

3 BAG
46" SNOW BLOWER
54" BLADE
BAGGER

RETAIL PRICING

YEAR	HIGH	LOW
2004	$926	$695
2005	$1,022	$767

ZOOM 2040

YEARS MFRD . . . 2009-2009
SERIES . . . ZOOM SERIES
ENGINE . . . KOHLER COURAGE
CYLINDERS . . . 1
ENGINE HP . . . 20
COOLING . . . AIR
FUEL . . . G
SPEEDS . . . 1/1
TRANSMISSION . . . GEAR
STEERING . . . ZERO
BLADE CLUTCH . . . ELECTRIC
STANDARD DECK . . . 40"
WEIGHT . . . 520 LBS.
MSRP . . . $3,245

OPTIONS

3 BAG

RETAIL PRICING

YEAR	HIGH	LOW
2009	$1,038	$778

ZOOM 2042XL

YEARS MFRD . . . 2009-2009
ENGINE . . . KOHLER COURAGE
CYLINDERS . . . 2
ENGINE HP . . . 20
COOLING . . . AIR
FUEL . . . G
SPEEDS . . . VARIABLE
TRANSMISSION . . . HYDRO
STEERING . . . ZERO
STANDARD DECK . . . 42"
WEIGHT . . . 615 LBS.
MSRP . . . $4,745

ARIENS

OPTIONS

3 BAG & FAN

RETAIL PRICING

YEAR	HIGH	LOW
2009	$1,518	$1,139

ZOOM 2048

YEARS MFRD 2003-2003
SERIES .... ZOOM SERIES
ENGINE .... B&S
ENGINE HP 20
COOLING .... AIR
FUEL .... G
SPEEDS .... VARIABLE
TRANSMISSION .... HYDRO
STEERING .... ZERO
STANDARD DECK .... 48"
WEIGHT .... 730 LBS.
MSRP $4,199

OPTIONS

3 BAG
46" SNOW BLOWER
54" BLADE

RETAIL PRICING

YEAR	HIGH	LOW
2003	$778	$583

ZOOM 2050

YEARS MFRD 2001-2001
SERIES .... EZ RIDER SERIES
ENGINE .... B&S
ENGINE HP 20
FUEL .... G
SPEEDS .... VARIABLE
TRANSMISSION .... HYDRO
STEERING .... ZERO
STANDARD DECK .... 50"
MSRP $6,399

OPTIONS

ROPS

RETAIL PRICING

YEAR	HIGH	LOW
2001	$896	$672

ZOOM 2148

YEARS MFRD 2004-2005
SERIES .... ZOOM SERIES
ENGINE .... KOHLER
CYLINDERS 2
ENGINE HP 21
COOLING .... AIR
FUEL .... G
SPEEDS .... VARIABLE
TRANSMISSION .... HYDRO
STEERING .... ZERO
STANDARD DECK .... 48"
WEIGHT .... 730 LBS.
MSRP $4,499

OPTIONS

3 BAG
46" SNOW BLOWER
54" BLADE
BAGGER

RETAIL PRICING

YEAR	HIGH	LOW
2004	$937	$703
2005	$1,036	$777

ZOOM 2148XL

YEARS MFRD 2005-2005
SERIES .... ZOOM SERIES
ENGINE ...... KOHLER COMMAND
CYLINDERS 2
ENGINE HP 21
COOLING .... AIR
FUEL .... G
SPEEDS .... VARIABLE
TRANSMISSION .... HYDRO
STEERING .... ZERO
STANDARD DECK .... 48"
WEIGHT .... 740 LBS.
MSRP $4,999

OPTIONS

3 BAG
BAGGER

RETAIL PRICING

YEAR	HIGH	LOW
2005	$1,152	$864

ZOOM 2150

YEARS MFRD 2008-2008
SERIES .... ZOOM SERIES
ENGINE .... B&S INTEK
CYLINDERS 1
ENGINE HP 21
COOLING .... AIR
FUEL .... G
SPEEDS .... VARIABLE
TRANSMISSION .... HYDRO
STEERING .... ZERO
BLADE CLUTCH .... ELECTRIC
STANDARD DECK .... 50"
WEIGHT .... 525 LBS.
MSRP $3,199

OPTIONS

15 GAL
3 BAG
SPREADER

RETAIL PRICING

YEAR	HIGH	LOW
2008	$937	$703

ZOOM 2250

YEARS MFRD 2002-2002
SERIES .... EZ RIDER SERIES
ENGINE .... B&S
ENGINE HP 22
COOLING .... AIR
FUEL .... G
SPEEDS .... VARIABLE
TRANSMISSION .... HYDRO
STEERING .... ZERO
STANDARD DECK .... 50"
MSRP $6,499

OPTIONS

3 BAG

RETAIL PRICING

YEAR	HIGH	LOW
2002	$1,057	$793

ZOOM 2252

YEARS MFRD 2003-2003
SERIES .... ZOOM SERIES
ENGINE .... B&S
ENGINE HP 22
COOLING .... AIR
FUEL .... G
SPEEDS .... VARIABLE
TRANSMISSION .... HYDRO
STEERING .... ZERO
STANDARD DECK .... 52"
WEIGHT .... 740 LBS.
MSRP $4,599

OPTIONS

3 BAG
46" SNOW BLOWER
54" BLADE

RETAIL PRICING

YEAR	HIGH	LOW
2003	$851	$638

ZOOM 2350

YEARS MFRD 2007-2009
SERIES .... ZOOM SERIES
ENGINE .... KOHLER COURAGE
ENGINE HP 23
COOLING .... AIR
FUEL .... G
SPEEDS .... VARIABLE
TRANSMISSION .... HYDRO
STEERING .... ZERO
BLADE CLUTCH .... ELECTRIC
STANDARD DECK .... 50"
MSRP $3,649

OPTIONS

3 BAG

RETAIL PRICING

YEAR	HIGH	LOW
2007	$958	$719
2008	$1,058	$794
2009	$1,168	$876

ZOOM 2352

YEARS MFRD 2004-2005
SERIES .... ZOOM SERIES
ENGINE .... KOHLER
CYLINDERS 2
ENGINE HP 23
COOLING .... AIR
FUEL .... G
SPEEDS .... VARIABLE
TRANSMISSION .... HYDRO
STEERING .... ZERO
STANDARD DECK .... 52"
WEIGHT .... 740 LBS.
MSRP $5,099

OPTIONS

3 BAG
46" SNOW BLOWER
54" BLADE
BAG

RETAIL PRICING

YEAR	HIGH	LOW
2004	$1,063	$797
2005	$1,173	$880

ZOOM 2448XL

YEARS MFRD 2008-2008
SERIES .... ZOOM SERIES
ENGINE .... B&S ELS
CYLINDERS 2
ENGINE HP 24
COOLING .... AIR
FUEL .... G
SPEEDS .... VARIABLE
TRANSMISSION .... HYDRO
STEERING .... ZERO
BLADE CLUTCH .... ELECTRIC
STANDARD DECK .... 48"
WEIGHT .... 630 LBS.
MSRP $4,399

OPTIONS

15 GAL
3 BAG
SPREADER

RETAIL PRICING

YEAR	HIGH	LOW
2008	$1,289	$967

ZOOM 2450

YEARS MFRD 2008-2008
SERIES .... ZOOM SERIES
ENGINE .... B&S ELS
CYLINDERS 2
ENGINE HP 24
COOLING .... AIR
FUEL .... G
SPEEDS .... VARIABLE
TRANSMISSION .... HYDRO
STEERING .... ZERO
BLADE CLUTCH .... ELECTRIC
STANDARD DECK .... 50"
WEIGHT .... 540 LBS.
MSRP $3,489

OPTIONS

15 GAL
3 BAG
SPREADER

RETAIL PRICING

YEAR	HIGH	LOW
2008	$1,021	$766

ZOOM 2452 HD

YEARS MFRD 2008-2008
SERIES .... ZOOM SERIES
ENGINE .... B&S ELS
CYLINDERS 2
ENGINE HP 24
COOLING .... AIR
FUEL .... G
SPEEDS .... VARIABLE
TRANSMISSION .... HYDRO
STEERING .... ZERO
BLADE CLUTCH .... ELECTRIC

STANDARD DECK . . . . 52"
WEIGHT . . . . 830 LBS.
MSRP. $5,449

RETAIL PRICING

YEAR	HIGH	LOW
2008	$1,596	$1,197

ZOOM 2548XL

YEARS MFRD 2009-2009
ENGINE . . . . KOHLER COURAGE
CYLINDERS. 2
ENGINE HP 25
COOLING . . . . AIR
FUEL . . . . G
SPEEDS . . . . VARIABLE
TRANSMISSION . . . . HYDRO
STEERING. . . . . ZERO
STANDARD DECK . . . . 48"
WEIGHT . . . . 630 LBS.
MSRP. $4,949

OPTIONS

3 BAG & FAN

RETAIL PRICING

YEAR	HIGH	LOW
2009	$1,583	$1,187

ZOOM 2552XL

YEARS MFRD 2004-2004
SERIES. . . . . ZOOM SERIES
ENGINE . . . . KOHLER
ENGINE HP 25
COOLING . . . . AIR
FUEL . . . . G
SPEEDS . . . . VARIABLE
TRANSMISSION . . . . HYDRO
STEERING. . . . . ZERO
STANDARD DECK . . . . 52"
WEIGHT . . . . 960 LBS.
MSRP. $6,999

OPTIONS

3 BAG
ROPS

RETAIL PRICING

YEAR	HIGH	LOW
2004	$1,390	$1,043

ZOOM 2560XL

YEARS MFRD 2004-2004
SERIES. . . . . ZOOM SERIES
ENGINE . . . . KOHLER
ENGINE HP 25
COOLING . . . . AIR
FUEL . . . . G
SPEEDS . . . . VARIABLE
TRANSMISSION . . . . HYDRO
STEERING. . . . . ZERO
STANDARD DECK . . . . 60"
WEIGHT . . . . 1,040 LBS.
MSRP. $7,599

OPTIONS

3 BAG
ROPS

RETAIL PRICING

YEAR	HIGH	LOW
2004	$1,508	$1,131

ZOOM 2660 HD

YEARS MFRD 2008-2008
SERIES. . . . . ZOOM SERIES
ENGINE . . . . B&S ELS
CYLINDERS. 2
ENGINE HP 26
COOLING . . . . AIR
FUEL . . . . G
SPEEDS . . . . VARIABLE
TRANSMISSION . . . . HYDRO
STEERING. . . . . ZERO
BLADE CLUTCH . . . . ELECTRIC
STANDARD DECK . . . . 60"
WEIGHT . . . . 830 LBS.
MSRP. $5,649

RETAIL PRICING

YEAR	HIGH	LOW
2008	$1,656	$1,242

ZOOM XL42

YEARS MFRD 2010-2015
ENGINE . . . . KOHLER
ENGINE HP 22
COOLING . . . . AIR
FUEL . . . . G
SPEEDS . . . . VARIABLE
TRANSMISSION . . . . HYDRO
STEERING. . . . . ZERO
STANDARD DECK . . . . 42"
MSRP. $4,405

OPTIONS

3 BAG
54" BLADE
SPRAYER
SPREADER

RETAIL PRICING

YEAR	HIGH	LOW
2010	$1,416	$1,062
2011	$1,563	$1,172
2012	$1,726	$1,294
2013	$1,904	$1,428
2014	$2,102	$1,576
2015	$2,319	$1,739

ZOOM XL48

YEARS MFRD 2010-2015
ENGINE . . . . KOHLER
ENGINE HP 23
COOLING . . . . AIR
FUEL . . . . G
SPEEDS . . . . VARIABLE
TRANSMISSION . . . . HYDRO
STEERING. . . . . ZERO
STANDARD DECK . . . . 48"
MSRP. $4,539

OPTIONS

3 BAG
54" BLADE
SPRAYER
SPREADER

RETAIL PRICING

YEAR	HIGH	LOW
2010	$1,459	$1,094
2011	$1,610	$1,208
2012	$1,778	$1,334
2013	$1,962	$1,472
2014	$2,166	$1,625
2015	$2,390	$1,793

ZOOM XL54

YEARS MFRD 2010-2015
ENGINE . . . . KOHLER
ENGINE HP 24
COOLING . . . . AIR
FUEL . . . . G
SPEEDS . . . . VARIABLE
TRANSMISSION . . . . HYDRO
STEERING. . . . . ZERO
STANDARD DECK . . . . 54"
MSRP. $4,625

OPTIONS

3 BAG
54" BLADE
SPREADER

RETAIL PRICING

YEAR	HIGH	LOW
2010	$1,489	$1,117
2011	$1,641	$1,231
2012	$1,811	$1,358
2013	$1,999	$1,499
2014	$2,206	$1,654
2015	$2,435	$1,826

18.0

YEARS MFRD 1990-1990
SERIES. . . . . . COMMERCIAL SERIES
ENGINE . . . . KOHLER
ENGINE HP 18
COOLING . . . . AIR
FUEL . . . . G
TRANSMISSION . . . . HYDRO
STEERING. . . . . STANDARD

20.0

YEARS MFRD 1990-1990
SERIES. . . . . . COMMERCIAL SERIES
ENGINE . . . . KOHLER
ENGINE HP 20
COOLING . . . . AIR
FUEL . . . . G
SPEEDS . . . . VARIABLE
TRANSMISSION . . . . HYDRO
STEERING. . . . . STANDARD
STANDARD DECK . . . . 60"
MSRP. $5,829

OPTIONS

40" SNOW BLOWER
42" BLADE
BAGGER

RETAIL PRICING

YEAR	HIGH	LOW
1990	$257	$193

42LT

YEARS MFRD 2011-2015
ENGINE . . . . KOHLER
ENGINE HP 20
COOLING . . . . AIR
FUEL . . . . G
SPEEDS . . . . VARIABLE
TRANSMISSION . . . . HYDRO
STEERING. . . . . STANDARD
STANDARD DECK . . . . 42"
MSRP. $1,820

OPTIONS

42" SNOW THROWER
48" BLADE
BAGGER
KOHLER 17HP

RETAIL PRICING

YEAR	HIGH	LOW
2011	$630	$472
2012	$698	$524
2013	$775	$581
2014	$858	$644
2015	$952	$714

46LT

YEARS MFRD 2011-2015
ENGINE . . . . KOHLER
ENGINE HP 22
COOLING . . . . AIR
FUEL . . . . G
SPEEDS . . . . VARIABLE
TRANSMISSION . . . . HYDRO
STEERING. . . . . STANDARD
STANDARD DECK . . . . 46"
MSRP. $2,069

OPTIONS

42"SNOW THROWER
48" BLADE
BAGGER
SOFT CAB

RETAIL PRICING

YEAR	HIGH	LOW
2011	$716	$537
2012	$794	$596
2013	$881	$661
2014	$976	$732
2015	$1,083	$812

48LT

YEARS MFRD 2012-2015
ENGINE . . . . KOHLER
ENGINE HP 22
COOLING . . . . AIR
FUEL . . . . G
SPEEDS . . . . VARIABLE
TRANSMISSION . . . . HYDRO
STEERING. . . . . STANDARD
STANDARD DECK . . . . 48"
MSRP. $2,269

OPTIONS

42" SNOW THROWER
48" BLADE
BAGGER
SOFT CAB

RETAIL PRICING

YEAR	HIGH	LOW
2012	$871	$653
2013	$965	$724
2014	$1,070	$802
2015	$1,187	$890

ARIENS

54GT

YEARS MFRD 2011-2015
ENGINE . . . . KOHLER
ENGINE HP 25
COOLING . . . . AIR
FUEL . . . . G
SPEEDS . . . . VARIABLE
TRANSMISSION . . . . HYDRO
STEERING. . . . . STANDARD
STANDARD DECK . . . . 54"
MSRP. $3,179

OPTIONS

42" SNOW THROWER
BAGGER
BLADE
SNOCAB

RETAIL PRICING

YEAR	HIGH	LOW
2011	$1,177	$882
2012	$1,301	$976
2013	$1,439	$1,079
2014	$1,592	$1,194
2015	$1,761	$1,320

54LT

YEARS MFRD 2012-2015
ENGINE . . . . KOHLER
ENGINE HP 25
COOLING . . . . AIR
FUEL . . . . G
SPEEDS . . . . VARIABLE
TRANSMISSION . . . . HYDRO
STEERING. . . . . STANDARD
STANDARD DECK . . . . 54"
MSRP. $2,375

OPTIONS

42" SNOW THROWER
48" BLADE
BAGGER
SNOCAB

RETAIL PRICING

YEAR	HIGH	LOW
2012	$963	$722
2013	$1,067	$800
2014	$1,183	$888
2015	$1,312	$984

1340G

YEARS MFRD 1996-2001
SERIES. . . . . SIERRA SERIES
ENGINE . . . . TECUMSEH
ENGINE HP 13
COOLING . . . . AIR
FUEL . . . . G
SPEEDS 6/1
TRANSMISSION . . . . GEAR
STEERING. . . . . STANDARD
STANDARD DECK . . . . 40"
WEIGHT . . . . 535 LBS.
MSRP. $2,159

OPTIONS

1 BAG
3 BAG
36" SNOW BLOWER
42" BLADE

SERIAL NUMBERS

YEAR . . . . BEGINNING NO.
2000 000570

RETAIL PRICING

YEAR	HIGH	LOW
1996	$165	$124
1997	$182	$137
1998	$202	$151
1999	$223	$167
2000	$248	$186
2001	$275	$207

1340H

YEARS MFRD 1996-1997
SERIES. . . . . SIERRA SERIES
ENGINE . . . . TECUMSEH
ENGINE HP 13
COOLING . . . . AIR
FUEL . . . . G
SPEEDS . . . . VARIABLE
TRANSMISSION . . . . HYDRO
STEERING. . . . . STANDARD
STANDARD DECK . . . . 40"
WEIGHT . . . . 475 LBS.
MSRP. $2,649

OPTIONS

1 BAG
3 BAG
36" SNOW BLOWER
42" BLADE

RETAIL PRICING

YEAR	HIGH	LOW
1996	$240	$180
1997	$267	$200

1440H

YEARS MFRD 1996-1997
SERIES. . . . . SIERRA SERIES
ENGINE . . . . B&S
ENGINE HP 14
COOLING . . . . AIR
FUEL . . . . G
SPEEDS . . . . VARIABLE
TRANSMISSION . . . . HYDRO
STEERING. . . . . STANDARD
STANDARD DECK . . . . 40"
MSRP. $2,799

OPTIONS

1 BAG
3 BAG
36" SNOW BLOWER
42" BLADE

RETAIL PRICING

YEAR	HIGH	LOW
1996	$315	$236
1997	$351	$263

1540

YEARS MFRD 2002-2003
SERIES. . . . . YARD TRACTOR SERIES
ENGINE . . . . B&S
ENGINE HP 15
FUEL . . . . G
SPEEDS . . . . VARIABLE
TRANSMISSION . . . . HYDRO
STEERING. . . . . STANDARD
STANDARD DECK . . . . 40"
WEIGHT . . . . 442 LBS.
MSRP. $2,599

OPTIONS

3 BAG
36" SNOW BLOWER
42" BLADE

RETAIL PRICING

YEAR	HIGH	LOW
2002	$341	$256
2003	$378	$284

1540H

YEARS MFRD 1996-2000
SERIES. . . . . SIERRA SERIES
ENGINE . . . . B&S
ENGINE HP 15
COOLING . . . . AIR
FUEL . . . . G
SPEEDS . . . . VARIABLE
TRANSMISSION . . . . HYDRO
STEERING. . . . . STANDARD
STANDARD DECK . . . . 40"
MSRP. $2,699

OPTIONS

3 BAG
36" SNOW BLOWER
42" BLADE
KOHLER

SERIAL NUMBERS

YEAR . . . . BEGINNING NO.
2000 . . . . 002000-BS
2000 . . . . 001000-K

RETAIL PRICING

YEAR	HIGH	LOW
1996	$228	$171
1997	$252	$189
1998	$280	$210
1999	$311	$234
2000	$344	$258

1542

YEARS MFRD 2001-2001
SERIES. . . . . YARD TRACTOR SERIES
ENGINE . . . . B&S
ENGINE HP 15
FUEL . . . . G
SPEEDS . . . . VARIABLE
TRANSMISSION . . . . HYDRO
STEERING. . . . . STANDARD
STANDARD DECK . . . . 42"
MSRP. $2,599

OPTIONS

3 BAG
36" SNOW BLOWER
54" BLADE

RETAIL PRICING

YEAR	HIGH	LOW
2001	$333	$250

1548H

YEARS MFRD 1998-2000
SERIES. . . . . SIERRA SERIES
ENGINE . . . . KOHLER
ENGINE HP 15
COOLING . . . . AIR
FUEL . . . . G
SPEEDS . . . . VARIABLE
TRANSMISSION . . . . HYDRO
STEERING. . . . . STANDARD
STANDARD DECK . . . . 48"
MSRP. $3,299

OPTIONS

3 BAG
36" SNOW BLOWER
42" BLADE

SERIAL NUMBERS

YEAR . . . . BEGINNING NO.
2000 000850

RETAIL PRICING

YEAR	HIGH	LOW
1998	$300	$225
1999	$333	$250
2000	$369	$276

1640H

YEARS MFRD 1996-2000
SERIES. . . . . SIERRA SERIES
ENGINE . . . . TECUMSEH
ENGINE HP 16
COOLING . . . . AIR
FUEL . . . . G
SPEEDS . . . . VARIABLE
TRANSMISSION . . . . HYDRO
STEERING. . . . . STANDARD
STANDARD DECK . . . . 40"
MSRP. $2,899

OPTIONS

1 BAG
3 BAG
36" SNOW BLOWER
42" BLADE

SERIAL NUMBERS

YEAR . . . . BEGINNING NO.
2000 000900

RETAIL PRICING

YEAR	HIGH	LOW
1996	$238	$178
1997	$264	$198
1998	$292	$219

1648H

YEARS MFRD 1997-2000
SERIES. . . . . SIERRA SERIES
ENGINE . . . . B&S
ENGINE HP 16
COOLING . . . . LIQUID
FUEL . . . . G
SPEEDS . . . . VARIABLE
TRANSMISSION . . . . HYDRO
STEERING. . . . . STANDARD
STANDARD DECK . . . . 48"
WEIGHT . . . . 505 LBS.
MSRP. $3,499

OPTIONS
3 BAG
36" SNOW BLOWER
42" BLADE

SERIAL NUMBERS

YEAR	BEGINNING NO.
2000	000900

RETAIL PRICING

YEAR	HIGH	LOW
1997	$328	$246
1998	$363	$272
1999	$403	$302
2000	$447	$335

1742

YEARS MFRD 2001-2002
SERIES.... YARD TRACTOR SERIES
ENGINE .... B&S
ENGINE HP 17
COOLING .... LIQUID
FUEL .... G
SPEEDS .... VARIABLE
TRANSMISSION .... HYDRO
STEERING............ STANDARD
STANDARD DECK .... 42"
MSRP.................. $2,949

OPTIONS
3 BAG
36" SNOW BLOWER
42" BLADE
54" BLADE

RETAIL PRICING

YEAR	HIGH	LOW
2001	$416	$312
2002	$375	$282

1848

YEARS MFRD 1996-1999
SERIES....... HIGH SIERRA SERIES
ENGINE .... B&S
ENGINE HP 18
COOLING ....AIR
FUEL .... G
SPEEDS .... VARIABLE
TRANSMISSION .... HYDRO
STEERING............ STANDARD
STANDARD DECK .... 48"
MSRP.................. $4,999

OPTIONS
3 BAG
40" SNOW BLOWER
42" BLADE

RETAIL PRICING

YEAR	HIGH	LOW
1996	$461	$346
1997	$510	$383
1998	$565	$423
1999	$625	$469

2046

YEARS MFRD 2010-2010
ENGINE .... KOHLER COURAGE
CYLINDERS.................. 1
ENGINE HP 20
COOLING ....AIR
FUEL .... G
SPEEDS .... VARIABLE
TRANSMISSION .... HYDRO
STEERING............ STANDARD

2048

YEARS MFRD 1996-1996
SERIES....... HIGH SIERRA SERIES
ENGINE .... KOHLER
ENGINE HP 20
COOLING ....AIR
FUEL .... G
SPEEDS .... VARIABLE
TRANSMISSION .... HYDRO
STEERING............ STANDARD
STANDARD DECK .... 48"
WEIGHT .... 550 LBS.
MSRP.................. $4,699

OPTIONS
3 BAG
40" SNOW BLOWER
42" BLADE

RETAIL PRICING

YEAR	HIGH	LOW
1996	$313	$235

2048

YEARS MFRD 1996-1996
SERIES..... YARD TRACTOR SERIES
ENGINE .... B&S
CYLINDERS.................. 2
ENGINE HP 20
COOLING ....AIR
FUEL .... G
SPEEDS .... VARIABLE
TRANSMISSION .... HYDRO
STEERING............ STANDARD
STANDARD DECK .... 48"
WEIGHT .... 550 LBS.
MSRP.................. $3,839

OPTIONS
36" SNOW BLOWER
42" BLADE

RETAIL PRICING

YEAR	HIGH	LOW
2001	$524	$393

2200

YEARS MFRD 1996-2001
SERIES..... GRAND SIERRA SERIES
ENGINE .... KOHLER
ENGINE HP 22
COOLING ....AIR
FUEL .... G
SPEEDS .... VARIABLE
TRANSMISSION .... HYDRO
STEERING............ STANDARD
STANDARD DECK .... 60"
MSRP.................. $8,868

OPTIONS
42" TILLER
48" SNOW BLOWER
54" BLADE
BAG & FAN

SERIAL NUMBERS

YEAR	BEGINNING NO.
2000	000525

RETAIL PRICING

YEAR	HIGH	LOW
1996	$813	$610
1997	$899	$674
1998	$994	$746
1999	$1,101	$826
2000	$1,218	$914
2001	$1,347	$1,010

2248

YEARS MFRD 2002-2002
SERIES..... YARD TRACTOR SERIES
ENGINE .... B&S
ENGINE HP 22
FUEL .... G
TRANSMISSION .... HYDRO
STEERING............ STANDARD
STANDARD DECK .... 48"
MSRP.................. $5,302

RETAIL PRICING

YEAR	HIGH	LOW
2002	$2,329	$1,747

2248H

YEARS MFRD 2000-2001
SERIES....... HIGH SIERRA SERIES
ENGINE .... B&S
ENGINE HP 22
COOLING ....AIR
FUEL .... G
SPEEDS .... VARIABLE
TRANSMISSION .... HYDRO
STEERING............ STANDARD
STANDARD DECK .... 48"
MSRP.................. $4,909

OPTIONS
40" SNOW BLOWER
42" BLADE

SERIAL NUMBERS

YEAR	BEGINNING NO.
2000	000101

RETAIL PRICING

YEAR	HIGH	LOW
2000	$674	$506
2001	$746	$559

2548

YEARS MFRD 2002-2003
SERIES..... YARD TRACTOR SERIES
ENGINE .... B&S
ENGINE HP 25
FUEL .... G
SPEEDS .... VARIABLE
TRANSMISSION .... HYDRO
STEERING............ STANDARD
STANDARD DECK .... 48"
WEIGHT .... 620 LBS.
MSRP.................. $4,199

OPTIONS
3 BAG
36" SNOW BLOWER
42" BLADE

RETAIL PRICING

YEAR	HIGH	LOW
2002	$765	$574
2003	$846	$634

2554

YEARS MFRD 2010-2010
ENGINE .... KOHLER COURAGE
CYLINDERS.................. 2
ENGINE HP 25
COOLING ....AIR
FUEL .... G
SPEEDS .... VARIABLE
TRANSMISSION .... HYDRO
STEERING............ STANDARD

915005

YEARS MFRD 1997-1997
SERIES.. IMPERIAL RM8530 SERIES
ENGINE .... KOHLER
ENGINE HP 15
FUEL .... G
TRANSMISSION .... HYDRO
STEERING............ STANDARD

915006

YEARS MFRD 1997-1997
SERIES.. IMPERIAL RM8530 SERIES
ENGINE .... TECUMSEH
ENGINE HP 16
FUEL .... G
SPEEDS 0-5
TRANSMISSION .... HYDRO
STEERING............ STANDARD

915007

YEARS MFRD 1997-1997
SERIES.. IMPERIAL RM8530 SERIES
ENGINE .... B&S
ENGINE HP 16
FUEL .... G
TRANSMISSION .... HYDRO
STEERING............ STANDARD

915157

YEARS MFRD 2010-2011
SERIES............ ZOOM SERIES
ENGINE .... B&S
CYLINDERS.................. 1
CID 500CC
ENGINE HP 14.5
COOLING ....AIR
FUEL .... G
SPEEDS .... VARIABLE
TRANSMISSION .... HYDRO
STEERING................ ZERO
BLADE CLUTCH .... ELECTRIC
WEIGHT .... 425 LBS.

ARIENS

915159
YEARS MFRD 2010-2011
SERIES .... ZOOM SERIES
ENGINE .... KOHLER COURAGE
CYLINDERS 2
CID 725CC
ENGINE HP 22
COOLING .... AIR
FUEL .... G
SPEEDS .... VARIABLE
TRANSMISSION .... HYDRO
STEERING .... ZERO
BLADE CLUTCH .... ELECTRIC
WEIGHT .... 440 LBS.

915161
YEARS MFRD 2010-2011
SERIES .... ZOOM SERIES
ENGINE .... KOHLER
CYLINDERS 2
CID 725CC
ENGINE HP 25
COOLING .... AIR
FUEL .... G
SPEEDS .... VARIABLE
TRANSMISSION .... HYDRO
STEERING .... ZERO
BLADE CLUTCH .... ELECTRIC
WEIGHT .... 475 LBS.

915163
YEARS MFRD 2010-2011
SERIES .... ZOOM SERIES
ENGINE .... KAWASAKI
CYLINDERS 2
CID 726CC
ENGINE HP 22
COOLING .... AIR
FUEL .... G
SPEEDS .... VARIABLE
TRANSMISSION .... HYDRO
STEERING .... ZERO
BLADE CLUTCH .... ELECTRIC
WEIGHT .... 615 LBS.

915165
YEARS MFRD 2010-2011
SERIES .... ZOOM XL SERIES
ENGINE .... KAWASAKI
CYLINDERS 2
CID 726CC
ENGINE HP 24
COOLING .... AIR
FUEL .... G
SPEEDS .... VARIABLE
TRANSMISSION .... HYDRO
STEERING .... ZERO
BLADE CLUTCH .... ELECTRIC
WEIGHT .... 630 LBS.

915167
YEARS MFRD 2010-2011
SERIES .... ZOOM XL SERIES
ENGINE .... KAWASAKI
CYLINDERS 2
CID 726CC
ENGINE HP 24
COOLING .... AIR
FUEL .... G
SPEEDS .... VARIABLE
TRANSMISSION .... HYDRO
STEERING .... ZERO
BLADE CLUTCH .... ELECTRIC
WEIGHT .... 645 LBS.

936021
YEARS MFRD 1997-1997
SERIES .. IMPERIAL RM8530 SERIES
ENGINE .... B&S
ENGINE HP 16
FUEL .... G
TRANSMISSION .... HYDRO
STEERING .... STANDARD
STANDARD DECK .... 48"
MSRP $3,699

RETAIL PRICING

YEAR	HIGH	LOW
1997	$1,292	$969

936039
YEARS MFRD 2010-2010
ENGINE .... KOHLER COURAGE
CYLINDERS 1
ENGINE HP 20
COOLING .... AIR
FUEL .... G
SPEEDS .... VARIABLE
TRANSMISSION .... HYDRO
STEERING .... STANDARD
WEIGHT .... 615 LBS.

936040
YEARS MFRD 2010-2010
ENGINE .... KOHLER COURAGE
CYLINDERS 2
ENGINE HP 25
COOLING .... AIR
FUEL .... G
SPEEDS .... VARIABLE
TRANSMISSION .... HYDRO
STEERING .... STANDARD
WEIGHT .... 728 LBS.

936051
YEARS MFRD 2010-2011
ENGINE .... KOHLER COURAGE
CYLINDERS 1
CID 597CC
ENGINE HP 19
COOLING .... AIR
FUEL .... G
SPEEDS .... VARIABLE
TRANSMISSION .... HYDRO
STEERING .... STANDARD
BLADE CLUTCH .... ELECTRIC
WEIGHT .... 472 LBS.

936053
YEARS MFRD 2010-2011
ENGINE .... B&S
CYLINDERS 2
CID 656CC
ENGINE HP 22
COOLING .... AIR
FUEL .... G
SPEEDS .... VARIABLE
TRANSMISSION .... HYDRO
STEERING .... STANDARD
BLADE CLUTCH .... ELECTRIC
WEIGHT .... 493 LBS.

936055
YEARS MFRD 2010-2011
ENGINE .... KOHLER COURAGE
CYLINDERS 2
CID 725CC
ENGINE HP 25
COOLING .... AIR
FUEL .... G
SPEEDS .... VARIABLE
TRANSMISSION .... HYDRO
STEERING .... STANDARD
BLADE CLUTCH .... ELECTRIC
WEIGHT .... 698 LBS.

991085
YEARS MFRD 2010-2011
SERIES .... MAX ZOOM SERIES
ENGINE .... KAWASAKI
CYLINDERS 2
CID 726CC
ENGINE HP 24
COOLING .... AIR
FUEL .... G
SPEEDS .... VARIABLE
TRANSMISSION .... HYDRO
STEERING .... ZERO
BLADE CLUTCH .... ELECTRIC
WEIGHT .... 823 LBS.

991086
YEARS MFRD 2010-2011
SERIES .... MAX ZOOM SERIES
ENGINE .... KAWASAKI
CYLINDERS 2
CID 726CC
ENGINE HP 24
COOLING .... AIR
FUEL .... G
SPEEDS .... VARIABLE
TRANSMISSION .... HYDRO
STEERING .... ZERO
BLADE CLUTCH .... ELECTRIC
WEIGHT .... 832 LBS.

991087
YEARS MFRD 2011-2011
SERIES .... MAX ZOOM SERIES
ENGINE .... KAWASAKI
CYLINDERS 2
CID 726CC
ENGINE HP 26
COOLING .... AIR
FUEL .... G
SPEEDS .... VARIABLE
TRANSMISSION .... HYDRO
STEERING .... ZERO
BLADE CLUTCH .... ELECTRIC
WEIGHT .... 853 LBS.

992806
YEARS MFRD 2010-2011
SERIES .... PRO ZOOM SERIES
ENGINE .... KAWASAKI FX
CID 852CC
ENGINE HP 27
COOLING .... AIR
FUEL .... G
SPEEDS .... VARIABLE
TRANSMISSION .... HYDRO
STEERING .... ZERO
BLADE CLUTCH .... ELECTRIC
WEIGHT .... 1,173 LBS.

992807
YEARS MFRD 2010-2011
SERIES .... PRO ZOOM SERIES
ENGINE .... KAWASAKI
CID 852CC
ENGINE HP 27
COOLING .... AIR
FUEL .... G
SPEEDS .... VARIABLE
TRANSMISSION .... HYDRO
STEERING .... ZERO
BLADE CLUTCH .... ELECTRIC
WEIGHT .... 1,201 LBS.

994806
YEARS MFRD 2010-2011
SERIES .... PRO ZOOM SERIES
ENGINE .... KAWASAKI FX
CID 603CC
ENGINE HP 20
COOLING .... AIR
FUEL .... G
SPEEDS .... VARIABLE
TRANSMISSION .... HYDRO
STEERING .... ZERO
BLADE CLUTCH .... ELECTRIC
WEIGHT .... 860 LBS.

BAD BOY

COMPACT DIESEL 28HP

YEARS MFRD 2010-2013
SERIES. . . COMPACT DIESEL SERIES
ENGINE . . . . CAT
CYLINDERS. 3
ENGINE HP 28
COOLING . . . . LIQUID
FUEL . . . . D
SPEEDS . . . . VARIABLE
TRANSMISSION . . . . HYDRO
STEERING. . . . . ZERO
STANDARD DECK . . . . 60"
WEIGHT . . . . 1,607 LBS.
MSRP. $9,999

RETAIL PRICING

YEAR	HIGH	LOW
2010	$5,423	$4,067
2011	$5,649	$4,236
2012	$6,106	$4,579
2013	$6,340	$4,755

COMPACT OUTLAW 4200

YEARS MFRD 2017-2020
ENGINE . . . . VANGUARD
CID 810CC
COOLING . . . . AIR
FUEL . . . . G
TRANSMISSION . . . . HYDRO
STEERING. . . . . ZERO
STANDARD DECK . . . . 42"
WEIGHT . . . . 990 LBS.
MSRP. $6,299

OPTIONS

KAWASAKI FX691 . . . . $200

COMPACT OUTLAW 4800

YEARS MFRD 2017-2020
ENGINE . . . . VANGUARD
CID 810CC
COOLING . . . . AIR
FUEL . . . . G
TRANSMISSION . . . . HYDRO
STEERING. . . . . ZERO
STANDARD DECK . . . . 48"
WEIGHT . . . . 1,005 LBS.
MSRP. $6,499

OPTIONS

KAWASAKI FX691 . . . . $200

CZT 23HP

YEARS MFRD 2010-2013
SERIES. . . . . CZT SERIES
ENGINE . . . . VANGUARD
CYLINDERS. 2
ENGINE HP 23
COOLING . . . . AIR
FUEL . . . . G
SPEEDS . . . . VARIABLE
TRANSMISSION . . . . HYDRO
STEERING. . . . . ZERO
BLADE CLUTCH . . . . ELECTRIC
STANDARD DECK . . . . 42"
WEIGHT . . . . 862 LBS.
MSRP. $5,299

RETAIL PRICING

YEAR	HIGH	LOW
2010	$2,152	$1,614
2011	$2,683	$2,012
2012	$2,950	$2,213
2013	$3,224	$2,418

CZT 24HP

YEARS MFRD 2010-2013
SERIES. . . . . CZT SERIES
ENGINE . . . . VANGUARD
CYLINDERS. 2
ENGINE HP 24
COOLING . . . . AIR
FUEL . . . . G
SPEEDS . . . . VARIABLE
TRANSMISSION . . . . HYDRO
STEERING. . . . . ZERO
BLADE CLUTCH . . . . ELECTRIC
STANDARD DECK . . . . 50"
WEIGHT . . . . 871 LBS.
MSRP. $5,399

RETAIL PRICING

YEAR	HIGH	LOW
2010	$2,222	$1,667
2011	$2,728	$2,046
2012	$3,014	$2,261
2013	$3,289	$2,467

CZT 25HP

YEARS MFRD 2010-2013
SERIES. . . . . CZT SERIES
ENGINE . . . . VANGUARD
CYLINDERS. 2
ENGINE HP 25
COOLING . . . . AIR
FUEL . . . . G
SPEEDS . . . . VARIABLE
TRANSMISSION . . . . HYDRO
STEERING. . . . . ZERO
BLADE CLUTCH . . . . ELECTRIC
STANDARD DECK . . . . 60"
WEIGHT . . . . 871 LBS.
MSRP. $5,499

RETAIL PRICING

YEAR	HIGH	LOW
2010	$2,326	$1,745
2011	$2,797	$2,098
2012	$3,087	$2,316
2013	$3,435	$2,576

MAVERICK 4800

YEARS MFRD 2018-2020
ENGINE . . . . . . KOHLER CONFIDANT
CID 747CC
COOLING . . . . AIR
FUEL . . . . G
TRANSMISSION . . . . HYDRO
STEERING. . . . . ZERO
STANDARD DECK . . . . 48"
WEIGHT . . . . 862 LBS.
MSRP. $5,899

OPTIONS

HONDA 688CC $900
KAWASAKI FS730 . . . . $300

MAVERICK 5400

YEARS MFRD 2018-2020
ENGINE . . . . . . KOHLER CONFIDANT
CID 747CC
COOLING . . . . AIR
FUEL . . . . G
TRANSMISSION . . . . HYDRO
STEERING. . . . . ZERO
STANDARD DECK . . . . 54"
WEIGHT . . . . 871 LBS.
MSRP. $5,949

OPTIONS

HONDA 688CC $900
KAWASAKI FS730 . . . . $350

MAVERICK 6000

YEARS MFRD 2018-2020
ENGINE . . . . . . KOHLER CONFIDANT
CID 747CC
COOLING . . . . AIR
FUEL . . . . G
TRANSMISSION . . . . HYDRO
STEERING. . . . . ZERO
STANDARD DECK . . . . 60"
WEIGHT . . . . 925 LBS.
MSRP. $5,999

OPTIONS

HONDA 688CC $950
KAWASAKI FS730 . . . . $400

MZ 21HP

YEARS MFRD 2010-2013
SERIES. . . . . MZ SERIES
ENGINE . . . . BRIGGS
CYLINDERS. 1
ENGINE HP 21
COOLING . . . . AIR
FUEL . . . . G
SPEEDS . . . . VARIABLE
TRANSMISSION . . . . HYDRO
STEERING. . . . . ZERO
STANDARD DECK . . . . 42"
WEIGHT . . . . 470 LBS.
MSRP. $2,799

RETAIL PRICING

YEAR	HIGH	LOW
2010	$871	$653
2011	$1,174	$881
2012	$1,406	$1,055
2013	$1,575	$1,182

MZ 26HP

YEARS MFRD 2010-2013
SERIES. . . . . MZ SERIES
ENGINE . . . . BRIGGS
CYLINDERS. 2
ENGINE HP 26
COOLING . . . . LIQUID
FUEL . . . . G
SPEEDS . . . . VARIABLE
TRANSMISSION . . . . HYDRO
STEERING. . . . . ZERO
BLADE CLUTCH . . . . ELECTRIC
STANDARD DECK . . . . 48"
WEIGHT . . . . 470 LBS.
MSRP. $2,999

RETAIL PRICING

YEAR	HIGH	LOW
2010	$983	$737
2011	$1,233	$924
2012	$1,502	$1,127
2013	$1,654	$1,241

OUTLAW 5400

YEARS MFRD 2015-2018
ENGINE . . . . YAMAHA
CID 824CC
COOLING . . . . AIR
FUEL . . . . G
TRANSMISSION . . . . HYDRO
STEERING. . . . . ZERO
STANDARD DECK . . . . 54"
WEIGHT . . . . 1,180 LBS.

OPTIONS

KAWASAKI FX751
KOHLER 747CC

OUTLAW EXTREME 824

YEARS MFRD 2015-2015
ENGINE . . . . KOHLER EFI
CYLINDERS. 2
CID 824CC
COOLING . . . . AIR
FUEL . . . . G
SPEEDS . . . . VARIABLE
TRANSMISSION . . . . HYDRO
STEERING. . . . . ZERO
STANDARD DECK . . . . 54"

OPTIONS

61" DECK

OUTLAW EXTREME 852

YEARS MFRD 2015-2015
ENGINE . . . . KAWASAKI
CYLINDERS. 2

BAD BOY

CID 852
COOLING .... AIR
FUEL .... G
SPEEDS .... VARIABLE
TRANSMISSION .... HYDRO
STEERING................ ZERO
STANDARD DECK .... 54"

OPTIONS

61" DECK
72" DECK

OUTLAW EXTREME 993

YEARS MFRD 2015-2015
ENGINE .... VANGUARD
CYLINDERS.................. 2
CID 993
COOLING .... AIR
FUEL .... G
SPEEDS .... VARIABLE
TRANSMISSION .... HYDRO
STEERING................ ZERO
STANDARD DECK .... 61"

OPTIONS

72" DECK

OUTLAW EXTREME 5400

YEARS MFRD 2015-2018
ENGINE .... KAWASAKI FX850V
CID 852CC
COOLING .... AIR
FUEL .... G
TRANSMISSION .... HYDRO
STEERING................ ZERO
STANDARD DECK .... 54"
WEIGHT .... 1,180 LBS.

OUTLAW EXTREME 6100

YEARS MFRD 2015-2018
ENGINE .... VANGUARD
CID 993CC
COOLING .... AIR
FUEL .... G
TRANSMISSION .... HYDRO
STEERING................ ZERO
STANDARD DECK .... 61"
WEIGHT .... 1,230 LBS.

OPTIONS

KAWASAKI FX850V

OUTLAW EXTREME 7200

YEARS MFRD 2015-2018
ENGINE .... VANGUARD
CID 993CC
COOLING .... AIR
FUEL .... G
TRANSMISSION .... HYDRO
STEERING................ ZERO
STANDARD DECK .... 72"
WEIGHT .... 1,310 LBS.

OPTIONS

KAWASAKI FX850V

OUTLAW REBEL 5400

YEARS MFRD 2019-2020
ENGINE .... KOHLER CV752
CYLINDERS.................. 2
CID 747
ENGINE HP 27
COOLING .... AIR
FUEL .... G
SPEEDS .... VARIABLE
TRANSMISSION .... HYDRO
STEERING................ ZERO
STANDARD DECK .... 54"
WEIGHT .... 1,270 LBS.
MSRP................. $7,499

OPTIONS

KAWASAKI 27HP........... $400
YAMAHA 27.5HP........... $400

OUTLAW REBEL 6100

YEARS MFRD 2019-2020
ENGINE .... KOHLER CV752
CYLINDERS.................. 2
CID 747
ENGINE HP 27
COOLING .... AIR
FUEL .... G
SPEEDS .... VARIABLE
TRANSMISSION .... HYDRO
STEERING................ ZERO
STANDARD DECK .... 61"
WEIGHT .... 1,325 LBS.
MSRP................. $7,599

OPTIONS

KAW 35HP/SUS SEAT $1,300
KAWASAKI 27HP........... $400
VANGUARD 36HP $600
YAMAHA 27.5HP........... $400

OUTLAW REBEL 7200

YEARS MFRD 2019-2020
ENGINE .... VANGUARD
CYLINDERS.................. 2
CID 993
ENGINE HP 36
COOLING .... AIR
FUEL .... G
SPEEDS .... VARIABLE
TRANSMISSION .... HYDRO
STEERING................ ZERO
STANDARD DECK .... 72"
WEIGHT .... 1,375 LBS.
MSRP................. $8,299

OPTIONS

KAW 35HP/SUS SEAT $700

OUTLAW RENEGADE 6100

YEARS MFRD 2019-2020
ENGINE .... VANGUARD EFI
CYLINDERS.................. 2
CID 993
ENGINE HP 37
COOLING .... LIQUID
FUEL .... G
SPEEDS .... VARIABLE
TRANSMISSION ...... DUAL HYDRO
STEERING................ ZERO
STANDARD DECK .... 61"
WEIGHT .... 1,535 LBS.
MSRP................ $11,599

OPTIONS

72" DECK
PERKINS 24.7HP DSL $2,000
VANGUARD 35HP NON EFI .. $-400

OUTLAW REVOLT 4800

YEARS MFRD 2019-2020
ENGINE .... KAWASAKI FX
CYLINDERS.................. 2
CID 726
ENGINE HP 23.5
COOLING .... AIR
FUEL .... G
SPEEDS .... VARIABLE
TRANSMISSION ..... DUAL HYDRO
STEERING................ ZERO
STANDARD DECK .... 48"
WEIGHT .... 905 LBS.
MSRP................. $6,699

OPTIONS

36" DECK............... $-200

OUTLAW REVOLT 5400

YEARS MFRD 2019-2020
ENGINE .... KAWASAKI FX
CYLINDERS.................. 2
CID 726
ENGINE HP 23.5
COOLING .... AIR
FUEL .... G
SPEEDS .... VARIABLE
TRANSMISSION ..... DUAL HYDRO
STEERING................ ZERO
STANDARD DECK .... 54"
WEIGHT .... 925 LBS.
MSRP................. $6,799

OPTIONS

VANGUARD EFI............ $100

OUTLAW REVOLT 6100

YEARS MFRD 2020-2020
ENGINE .... KAWASAKI FX
CYLINDERS.................. 2
CID 852CC
COOLING .... AIR
FUEL .... G
SPEEDS .... VARIABLE
TRANSMISSION .... HYDRO
STEERING................ ZERO
STANDARD DECK .... 61"
WEIGHT .... 945 LBS.
MSRP................. $6,999

OPTIONS

VANGUARD EFI............ $-50

OUTLAW ROGUE 5400

YEARS MFRD 2019-2020
ENGINE .... KAWASAKI FX
CYLINDERS.................. 2
CID 852
ENGINE HP 27
COOLING .... AIR
FUEL .... G
SPEEDS .... VARIABLE
TRANSMISSION ..... DUAL HYDRO
STEERING................ ZERO
STANDARD DECK .... 54"
WEIGHT .... 1,410 LBS.
MSRP................. $9,599

OUTLAW ROGUE 6100

YEARS MFRD 2019-2020
ENGINE .... KAWASAKI FX
CYLINDERS.................. 2
CID 852
ENGINE HP 27
COOLING .... AIR
FUEL .... G
SPEEDS .... VARIABLE
TRANSMISSION ..... DUAL HYDRO
STEERING................ ZERO
STANDARD DECK .... 61"
WEIGHT .... 1,445 LBS.
MSRP................. $9,699

OPTIONS

KAWASAKI 35HP........... $300
KOHLER 33HP $500
VANGUARD 37HP $800
YAMAHA 33HP $400

OUTLAW ROGUE 7200

YEARS MFRD 2019-2020
ENGINE .... YAMAHA EFI
CYLINDERS.................. 2
CID 824
ENGINE HP 33

COOLING . . . . . AIR
FUEL . . . . . G
SPEEDS . . . . . VARIABLE
TRANSMISSION . . . . . DUAL HYDRO
STEERING . . . . . ZERO
STANDARD DECK . . . . . 72"
WEIGHT . . . . . 1,480 LBS.
MSRP $10,199

OPTIONS

KAWASAKI 35HP
KOHLER 33HP $300
VANGUARD 37HP $500

OUTLAW XP852

YEARS MFRD 2015-2015
ENGINE . . . . . KAWASAKI
CYLINDERS 2
CID 852
COOLING . . . . . AIR
FUEL . . . . . G
SPEEDS . . . . . VARIABLE
TRANSMISSION . . . . . HYDRO
STEERING . . . . . ZERO
STANDARD DECK . . . . . 54"

OPTIONS

61" DECK
72" DECK

OUTLAW XP933

YEARS MFRD 2015-2015
ENGINE . . . . . VANGUARD
CYLINDERS 2
CID 933CC
COOLING . . . . . AIR
FUEL . . . . . G
SPEEDS . . . . . VARIABLE
TRANSMISSION . . . . . GEAR
STEERING . . . . . ZERO
STANDARD DECK . . . . . 61"

OPTIONS

72" DECK

OUTLAW XP 5400

YEARS MFRD 2015-2018
ENGINE . . . . . KAWASAKI FX850
CYLINDERS 2
CID 852CC
COOLING . . . . . AIR
FUEL . . . . . G
TRANSMISSION . . . . . DUAL HYDRO
STEERING . . . . . ZERO
STANDARD DECK . . . . . 54"
WEIGHT . . . . . 1,180 LBS.

OUTLAW XP 6100

YEARS MFRD 2015-2018
ENGINE . . . . . KAWASAKI FX850
CID 852CC
COOLING . . . . . AIR
FUEL . . . . . G
TRANSMISSION . . . . . DUAL HYDRO
STEERING . . . . . ZERO
STANDARD DECK . . . . . 61"
WEIGHT . . . . . 1,230 LBS.

OPTIONS

VANGUARD 993CC
YAMAHA EFI 824CC

OUTLAW XP 7200

YEARS MFRD 2015-2018
ENGINE . . . . . KAWASAKI FX850
CID 852CC
COOLING . . . . . AIR
FUEL . . . . . G
TRANSMISSION . . . . . DUAL HYDRO
STEERING . . . . . ZERO
STANDARD DECK . . . . . 72"
WEIGHT . . . . . 1,310 LBS.

OPTIONS

VANGUARD 933CC
YAMAHA EFI 824CC

PUP 4800

YEARS MFRD 2004-2009
ENGINE . . . . . B&S INTEK
CYLINDERS 2
CID 44
ENGINE HP 25
COOLING . . . . . AIR
FUEL . . . . . G
SPEEDS . . . . . VARIABLE
TRANSMISSION . . . . . HYDRO
STEERING . . . . . ZERO
BLADE CLUTCH . . . . . ELECTRIC
STANDARD DECK . . . . . 48"
MSRP $6,145

OPTIONS

KOHLER 27E

RETAIL PRICING

YEAR	HIGH	LOW
2004	$838	$629
2005	$935	$701
2006	$1,316	$987
2007	$1,516	$1,137
2008	$1,785	$1,338
2009	$2,141	$1,606

PUP 5200

YEARS MFRD 2004-2009
ENGINE . . . . . B&S INTEK
CYLINDERS 2
CID 44
ENGINE HP 25
COOLING . . . . . AIR
FUEL . . . . . G
SPEEDS . . . . . VARIABLE
TRANSMISSION . . . . . HYDRO
STEERING . . . . . ZERO
BLADE CLUTCH . . . . . ELECTRIC
STANDARD DECK . . . . . 52"
MSRP $6,345

OPTIONS

KOHLER 27E

RETAIL PRICING

YEAR	HIGH	LOW
2004	$922	$691
2005	$1,025	$769
2006	$1,288	$966
2007	$1,489	$1,117
2008	$1,844	$1,383
2009	$2,211	$1,658

PUP 6000

YEARS MFRD 2004-2009
ENGINE . . . . . B&S INTEX
CYLINDERS 2
CID 44
ENGINE HP 25
COOLING . . . . . AIR
FUEL . . . . . G
SPEEDS . . . . . VARIABLE
TRANSMISSION . . . . . HYDRO
STEERING . . . . . ZERO
BLADE CLUTCH . . . . . ELECTRIC
STANDARD DECK . . . . . 60"
MSRP $6,645

OPTIONS

KOHLER 27E

RETAIL PRICING

YEAR	HIGH	LOW
2004	$1,005	$754
2005	$1,120	$840
2006	$1,232	$924
2007	$1,379	$1,034
2008	$1,928	$1,446
2009	$2,314	$1,735

PUP 7200

YEARS MFRD 2005-2006
ENGINE . . . . . KOHLER
ENGINE HP 27
COOLING . . . . . AIR
FUEL . . . . . G
SPEEDS . . . . . VARIABLE
TRANSMISSION . . . . . HYDRO
STEERING . . . . . ZERO
STANDARD DECK . . . . . 72"
MSRP $8,045

RETAIL PRICING

YEAR	HIGH	LOW
2005	$4,390	$3,293
2006	$4,757	$3,568

23HP VANGUARD

YEARS MFRD 2010-2011
SERIES . . . . . PUP SERIES
ENGINE . . . . . VANGUARD
CYLINDERS 2
ENGINE HP 23
COOLING . . . . . AIR
FUEL . . . . . G
SPEEDS . . . . . VARIABLE
TRANSMISSION . . . . . HYDRO
STEERING . . . . . ZERO
STANDARD DECK . . . . . 48"
WEIGHT . . . . . 1,050 LBS.
MSRP $5,499

RETAIL PRICING

YEAR	HIGH	LOW
2010	$2,964	$2,223
2011	$3,012	$2,259

26HP B&S ELS

YEARS MFRD 2010-2011
SERIES . . . . . ZT SERIES
ENGINE . . . . . B&S INTEK ELS
CYLINDERS 2
ENGINE HP 26
COOLING . . . . . AIR
FUEL . . . . . G
SPEEDS . . . . . VARIABLE
TRANSMISSION . . . . . HYDRO
STEERING . . . . . ZERO
BLADE CLUTCH . . . . . ELECTRIC
STANDARD DECK . . . . . 50"
WEIGHT . . . . . 750 LBS.
MSRP $4,195

RETAIL PRICING

YEAR	HIGH	LOW
2010	$2,262	$1,696
2011	$2,297	$1,723

26HP KAWASAKI

YEARS MFRD 2005-2011
SERIES . . . . . LIGHTNING Z SERIES
ENGINE . . . . . KAWASAKI
CYLINDERS 2
ENGINE HP 26
COOLING . . . . . LIQUID
FUEL . . . . . G
SPEEDS . . . . . VARIABLE
TRANSMISSION . . . . . HYDRO
STEERING . . . . . ZERO
BLADE CLUTCH . . . . . ELECTRIC
STANDARD DECK . . . . . 60"
WEIGHT . . . . . 1,085 LBS.
MSRP $7,295

RETAIL PRICING

YEAR	HIGH	LOW
2005	$4,175	$3,131
2006	$4,250	$3,187
2007	$4,316	$3,237
2008	$4,376	$3,282
2009	$4,401	$3,300
2010	$4,504	$3,378
2011	$4,548	$3,411

27HP KAWASAKI

YEARS MFRD 2010-2011
SERIES . . . . . AOS SERIES
ENGINE . . . . . KAWASAKI
CYLINDERS 2
ENGINE HP 27
COOLING . . . . . LIQUID
FUEL . . . . . G

SPEEDS . . . . VARIABLE
TRANSMISSION . . . . HYDRO
STEERING. . . . . ZERO
BLADE CLUTCH . . . . ELECTRIC
STANDARD DECK . . . . 60"
WEIGHT . . . . 1,278 LBS.
MSRP. $7,995

RETAIL PRICING

YEAR	HIGH	LOW
2010	$4,309	$3,232
2011	$4,379	$3,284

27HP KOHLER

YEARS MFRD 2010-2011
SERIES. . . . . ZT SERIES
ENGINE . . . . KOHLER COURAGE
CYLINDERS. 2
ENGINE HP 27
COOLING . . . . AIR
FUEL . . . . G
SPEEDS . . . . VARIABLE
TRANSMISSION . . . . HYDRO
STEERING. . . . . ZERO
BLADE CLUTCH . . . . ELECTRIC
STANDARD DECK . . . . 60"
WEIGHT . . . . 775 LBS.
MSRP. $4,495

RETAIL PRICING

YEAR	HIGH	LOW
2010	$2,423	$1,817
2011	$2,461	$1,846

28HP CAT DIESEL

YEARS MFRD 2005-2010
ENGINE . . . . CAT
CYLINDERS. 3
ENGINE HP 28
COOLING . . . . LIQUID
FUEL . . . . D
SPEEDS . . . . VARIABLE
TRANSMISSION . . . . HYDRO
STEERING. . . . . ZERO
BLADE CLUTCH . . . . ELECTRIC
STANDARD DECK . . . . 60"
WEIGHT . . . . 1,522 LBS.
MSRP. $11,895

RETAIL PRICING

YEAR	HIGH	LOW
2005	$6,439	$4,829
2006	$6,650	$4,987
2007	$6,710	$5,033
2008	$6,805	$5,104
2009	$6,817	$5,113
2010	$7,041	$5,280

30HP KOHLER

YEARS MFRD 2010-2011
SERIES. . . . . PUP SERIES
ENGINE . . . . . . KOHLER COMMAND
CYLINDERS. 2
ENGINE HP 30
COOLING . . . . AIR
FUEL . . . . G

SPEEDS . . . . VARIABLE
TRANSMISSION . . . . HYDRO
STEERING. . . . . ZERO
BLADE CLUTCH . . . . ELECTRIC
STANDARD DECK . . . . 52"
WEIGHT . . . . 1,066 LBS.
MSRP. $5,999

RETAIL PRICING

YEAR	HIGH	LOW
2010	$3,233	$2,425
2011	$3,285	$2,464

31HP

YEARS MFRD 2010-2011
SERIES. . . . . PUP SERIES
ENGINE . . . . KAWASAKI
CYLINDERS. 2
ENGINE HP 31
COOLING . . . . AIR
FUEL . . . . G
SPEEDS . . . . VARIABLE
TRANSMISSION . . . . HYDRO
STEERING. . . . . ZERO
STANDARD DECK . . . . 60"
WEIGHT . . . . 1,107 LBS.
MSRP. $6,199

RETAIL PRICING

YEAR	HIGH	LOW
2010	$3,342	$2,506
2011	$3,394	$2,545

31HP

YEARS MFRD 2010-2011
SERIES. . . . . . LIGHTNING Z SERIES
ENGINE . . . . KAWASAKI
CYLINDERS. 2
CID 852CC
ENGINE HP 31
COOLING . . . . AIR
FUEL . . . . G
SPEEDS . . . . VARIABLE
TRANSMISSION . . . . HYDRO
STEERING. . . . . ZERO
BLADE CLUTCH . . . . ELECTRIC
STANDARD DECK . . . . 60"
WEIGHT . . . . 1,217 LBS.
MSRP. $7,699

RETAIL PRICING

YEAR	HIGH	LOW
2010	$4,216	$3,162
2011	$4,776	$3,582

31HP

YEARS MFRD 2011-2011
SERIES. . . . . OUTLAW SERIES
ENGINE . . . . KAWASAKI
CYLINDERS. 2
CID 850CC
ENGINE HP 31
FUEL . . . . G
SPEEDS . . . . VARIABLE
TRANSMISSION . . . . HYDRO
STEERING. . . . . ZERO
BLADE CLUTCH . . . . ELECTRIC
STANDARD DECK . . . . 61"

WEIGHT . . . . 1,263 LBS.
MSRP. $7,499

RETAIL PRICING

YEAR	HIGH	LOW
2011	$4,106	$3,079

31HP AOS VANGUARD

YEARS MFRD 2005-2006
ENGINE . . . . B&S VANGUARD
CYLINDERS. 2
CID 54.6
ENGINE HP 31
COOLING . . . . AIR
FUEL . . . . G
SPEEDS . . . . VARIABLE
TRANSMISSION . . . . HYDRO
STEERING. . . . . ZERO
STANDARD DECK . . . . 60"
MSRP. $8,995

RETAIL PRICING

YEAR	HIGH	LOW
2005	$5,268	$3,951
2006	$5,568	$4,176

32HP

YEARS MFRD 2009-2010
SERIES. . . . . PROPANE SERIES
ENGINE . . . . VANGUARD
CYLINDERS. 2
ENGINE HP 32
COOLING . . . . AIR
SPEEDS . . . . VARIABLE
TRANSMISSION . . . . HYDRO
STEERING. . . . . ZERO
BLADE CLUTCH . . . . ELECTRIC
STANDARD DECK . . . . 60"
WEIGHT . . . . 1,100 LBS.
MSRP. $11,879

RETAIL PRICING

YEAR	HIGH	LOW
2009	$6,817	$5,113
2010	$7,031	$5,273

32HP

YEARS MFRD 2010-2011
SERIES. . . . . . LIGHTNING Z SERIES
ENGINE . . . . VANGUARD
CYLINDERS. 2
ENGINE HP 32
COOLING . . . . AIR
FUEL . . . . G
SPEEDS . . . . VARIABLE
TRANSMISSION . . . . HYDRO
STEERING. . . . . ZERO
BLADE CLUTCH . . . . ELECTRIC
STANDARD DECK . . . . 60"
WEIGHT . . . . 1,272 LBS.
MSRP. $7,699

RETAIL PRICING

YEAR	HIGH	LOW
2010	$4,150	$3,113
2011	$4,216	$3,162

35HP CAT DIESEL

YEARS MFRD 2008-2013
SERIES. . . . . AOS SERIES
ENGINE . . . . CAT
CYLINDERS. 4
ENGINE HP 35
COOLING . . . . LIQUID
FUEL . . . . D
SPEEDS . . . . VARIABLE
TRANSMISSION . . . . HYDRO
STEERING. . . . . ZERO
BLADE CLUTCH . . . . ELECTRIC
STANDARD DECK . . . . 60"
WEIGHT . . . . 1,540 LBS.
MSRP. $12,599

RETAIL PRICING

YEAR	HIGH	LOW
2008	$7,022	$5,267
2009	$7,324	$5,493
2010	$7,738	$5,803
2011	$8,012	$6,009
2012	$8,129	$6,097
2013	$8,291	$6,218

35HP VANGUARD

YEARS MFRD 2010-2011
SERIES. . . . . AOS SERIES
ENGINE . . . . VANGUARD
CYLINDERS. 2
ENGINE HP 35
COOLING . . . . LIQUID
FUEL . . . . G
SPEEDS . . . . VARIABLE
TRANSMISSION . . . . HYDRO
STEERING. . . . . ZERO
BLADE CLUTCH . . . . ELECTRIC
STANDARD DECK . . . . 60"
WEIGHT . . . . 1,469 LBS.
MSRP. $8,899

RETAIL PRICING

YEAR	HIGH	LOW
2010	$4,798	$3,599
2011	$4,874	$3,655

2300 ZT 36

YEARS MFRD 2008-2009
SERIES. . . . . ZT SERIES
ENGINE . . . . B&S
CYLINDERS. 2
CID 725CC
ENGINE HP 26
COOLING . . . . AIR
FUEL . . . . G
SPEEDS . . . . VARIABLE
TRANSMISSION . . . . HYDRO
STEERING. . . . . ZERO
BLADE CLUTCH . . . . ELECTRIC
WEIGHT . . . . 750 LBS.

OPTIONS

VANGUARD 23E

2300 ZT 50

YEARS MFRD 2008-2008
SERIES .... ZT SERIES
ENGINE .... B&S
CYLINDERS 2
CID 725CC
ENGINE HP 26
COOLING .... AIR
FUEL .... G
SPEEDS .... VARIABLE
TRANSMISSION .... HYDRO
STEERING .... ZERO
BLADE CLUTCH .... ELECTRIC
WEIGHT .... 775 LBS.

OPTIONS

VANGUARD 23E

2300 ZT 60

YEARS MFRD 2008-2009
SERIES .... ZT SERIES
ENGINE .... B&S
CYLINDERS 2
CID 725CC
ENGINE HP 26
COOLING .... AIR
FUEL .... G
SPEEDS .... VARIABLE
TRANSMISSION .... HYDRO
STEERING .... ZERO
BLADE CLUTCH .... ELECTRIC
WEIGHT .... 800 LBS.

OPTIONS

VANGUARD 23E

2600 ZT 36

YEARS MFRD 2008-2008
SERIES .... ZT SERIES
ENGINE .... B&S ELS
CYLINDERS 2
CID 725CC
ENGINE HP 26
COOLING .... AIR
FUEL .... G
SPEEDS .... VARIABLE
TRANSMISSION .... HYDRO
STEERING .... ZERO
BLADE CLUTCH .... ELECTRIC
WEIGHT .... 750 LBS.

OPTIONS

VANGUARD 23E

2600 ZT 50

YEARS MFRD 2008-2009
SERIES .... ZT SERIES
ENGINE .... B&S
CYLINDERS 2
CID 725CC
ENGINE HP 26
COOLING .... AIR
FUEL .... G
SPEEDS .... VARIABLE
TRANSMISSION .... HYDRO
STEERING .... ZERO
BLADE CLUTCH .... ELECTRIC
WEIGHT .... 775 LBS.

OPTIONS

VANGUARD 23E

2600 ZT 60

YEARS MFRD 2008-2008
SERIES .... ZT SERIES
ENGINE .... B&S
CYLINDERS 2
CID 725CC
ENGINE HP 26
COOLING .... AIR
FUEL .... G
SPEEDS .... VARIABLE
TRANSMISSION .... HYDRO
STEERING .... ZERO
BLADE CLUTCH .... ELECTRIC
WEIGHT .... 800 LBS.

OPTIONS

VANGUARD 23E

4200MZ

YEARS MFRD 2013-2020
ENGINE .... KOHLER
ENGINE HP 21
COOLING .... AIR
FUEL .... G
SPEEDS .... VARIABLE
TRANSMISSION .... HYDRO
STEERING .... ZERO
STANDARD DECK .... 42"
WEIGHT .... 585 LBS.
MSRP $2,999

OPTIONS

KOHLER PRO $300

RETAIL PRICING

YEAR	HIGH	LOW
2013	$1,049	$786
2014	$1,172	$879
2015	$1,317	$988
2016	$1,537	$1,152
2017	$1,798	$1,349
2018	$1,958	$1,469
2019	$2,209	$1,656
2020	$2,413	$1,902

4800

YEARS MFRD 2005-2006
SERIES .... LIGHTNING Z SERIES
ENGINE .... KAWASAKI
CYLINDERS 2
CID 41.1
ENGINE HP 26
COOLING .... LIQUID
FUEL .... G
SPEEDS .... VARIABLE
TRANSMISSION .... HYDRO
STEERING .... ZERO
STANDARD DECK .... 48"
MSRP $6,995

RETAIL PRICING

YEAR	HIGH	LOW
2005	$4,038	$3,028
2006	$4,331	$3,248

4800 STAND-ON

YEARS MFRD 2012-2014
ENGINE .... B&S CYCLONIC
CYLINDERS 2
CID 810CC
ENGINE HP 30
COOLING .... AIR
FUEL .... G
SPEEDS .... VARIABLE
TRANSMISSION .... HYDRO
STEERING .... ZERO
STANDARD DECK .... 48"
WEIGHT .... 862 LBS.
MSRP $5,799

RETAIL PRICING

YEAR	HIGH	LOW
2012	$3,427	$2,570
2013	$3,602	$2,701
2014	$3,786	$2,840

4800MZ MAGNUM

YEARS MFRD 2012-2020
ENGINE .... KOHLER
CID 725CC
ENGINE HP 27
COOLING .... AIR
FUEL .... G
SPEEDS .... VARIABLE
TRANSMISSION .... HYDRO
STEERING .... ZERO
STANDARD DECK .... 48"
WEIGHT .... 661 LBS.
MSRP $3,399

OPTIONS

KAWASAKI 26HP $500

RETAIL PRICING

YEAR	HIGH	LOW
2012	$1,082	$811
2013	$1,186	$890
2014	$1,422	$1,066
2015	$1,513	$1,135
2016	$1,724	$1,292
2017	$2,129	$1,596
2018	$2,213	$1,660
2019	$2,452	$1,840
2020	$2,699	$2,149

4800ZT ELITE

YEARS MFRD 2013-2020
ENGINE .... KOHLER
CID 725CC
ENGINE HP 27
COOLING .... AIR
FUEL .... G
SPEEDS .... VARIABLE
TRANSMISSION .... HYDRO
STEERING .... ZERO
STANDARD DECK .... 48"
WEIGHT .... 783 LBS.
MSRP $4,499

OPTIONS

KAWASAKI $700

RETAIL PRICING

YEAR	HIGH	LOW
2013	$1,579	$1,184
2014	$1,644	$1,233
2015	$1,832	$1,374
2016	$2,197	$1,648
2017	$2,890	$2,167
2018	$3,081	$2,311
2019	$3,464	$2,598
2020	$3,793	$3,026

5200

YEARS MFRD 2004-2004
ENGINE .... KAWASAKI
CYLINDERS 2
CID 45
ENGINE HP 27
COOLING .... LIQUID
FUEL .... G
SPEEDS .... VARIABLE
TRANSMISSION .... HYDRO
STEERING .... ZERO
BLADE CLUTCH .... ELECTRIC
STANDARD DECK .... 52"
MSRP $6,995

RETAIL PRICING

YEAR	HIGH	LOW
2004	$3,862	$2,897

5200 LIGHTNING Z

YEARS MFRD 2005-2009
ENGINE .... KAWASAKI
ENGINE HP 27
COOLING .... AIR
FUEL .... G
SPEEDS .... VARIABLE
TRANSMISSION .... HYDRO
STEERING .... ZERO
STANDARD DECK .... 52"
MSRP $6,995

RETAIL PRICING

YEAR	HIGH	LOW
2005	$4,097	$3,073

5400MZ MAGNUM

YEARS MFRD 2013-2020
ENGINE .... KOHLER
CYLINDERS 2
CID 725CC
ENGINE HP 27
COOLING .... AIR
FUEL .... G
SPEEDS .... VARIABLE
TRANSMISSION .... HYDRO
STEERING .... ZERO
STANDARD DECK .... 54"
WEIGHT .... 1,180 LBS.
MSRP $3,499

OPTIONS

KAWASAKI 27HP $500

BAD BOY

RETAIL PRICING

YEAR	HIGH	LOW
2013	$1,230	$922
2014	$1,562	$1,172
2015	$1,628	$1,220
2016	$1,791	$1,343
2017	$2,166	$1,624
2018	$2,320	$1,740
2019	$2,630	$1,973
2020	$2,891	$2,221

5400ZT AVENGER

YEARS MFRD 2020-2020
ENGINE . . . . KOHLER 7000
CID 725CC
COOLING . . . . AIR
FUEL . . . . G
SPEEDS . . . . VARIABLE
TRANSMISSION . . . . HYDRO
STEERING . . . . ZERO
STANDARD DECK . . . . 54"
WEIGHT . . . . 823 LBS.
MSRP $4,199

5400ZT ELITE

YEARS MFRD 2014-2020
ENGINE . . . . KOHLER
CID 747CC
COOLING . . . . AIR
FUEL . . . . G
SPEEDS . . . . VARIABLE
TRANSMISSION . . . . HYDRO
STEERING . . . . ZERO
STANDARD DECK . . . . 54"
WEIGHT . . . . 823 LBS.
MSRP $4,899

OPTIONS

KAWASAKI $350

RETAIL PRICING

YEAR	HIGH	LOW
2014	$1,595	$1,196
2015	$2,303	$1,728
2016	$2,873	$2,155
2017	$3,223	$2,417
2018	$3,398	$2,548
2019	$3,721	$2,791
2020	$4,069	$3,125

6000

YEARS MFRD 2004-2005
ENGINE . . . . KAWASAKI
CYLINDERS 2
CID 45
ENGINE HP 27
COOLING . . . . LIQUID
FUEL . . . . G
SPEEDS . . . . VARIABLE
TRANSMISSION . . . . HYDRO
STEERING . . . . ZERO
BLADE CLUTCH . . . . ELECTRIC
STANDARD DECK . . . . 60"
MSRP $8,695

RETAIL PRICING

YEAR	HIGH	LOW
2004	$4,136	$3,102
2005	$5,091	$3,818

6000 AOS

YEARS MFRD 2004-2009
ENGINE . . . . VANGUARD
CYLINDERS 2
CID 54
PTO HP 27
ENGINE HP 31
COOLING . . . . AIR
FUEL . . . . G
SPEEDS . . . . VARIABLE
TRANSMISSION . . . . HYDRO
STEERING . . . . ZERO
BLADE CLUTCH . . . . ELECTRIC
STANDARD DECK . . . . 60"
MSRP $8,695

OPTIONS

CAT DIESEL 26E
VANGUARD 31E

RETAIL PRICING

YEAR	HIGH	LOW
2005	$5,091	$3,818

6000ZT AVENGER

YEARS MFRD 2020-2020
ENGINE . . . . KOHLER 7000
CID 725CC
COOLING . . . . AIR
FUEL . . . . G
SPEEDS . . . . VARIABLE
TRANSMISSION . . . . HYDRO
STEERING . . . . ZERO
STANDARD DECK . . . . 60"
WEIGHT . . . . 841 LBS.
MSRP $4,299

6000ZT ELITE

YEARS MFRD 2014-2020
ENGINE . . . . KOHLER
CID 747CC
COOLING . . . . AIR
FUEL . . . . G
SPEEDS . . . . VARIABLE
TRANSMISSION . . . . HYDRO
STEERING . . . . ZERO
STANDARD DECK . . . . 60"
MSRP $4,999

OPTIONS

KAWASAKI $300

RETAIL PRICING

YEAR	HIGH	LOW
2014	$1,628	$1,220
2015	$2,034	$1,526
2016	$2,442	$1,831
2017	$3,077	$2,307
2018	$3,369	$2,527
2019	$3,739	$2,804
2020	$4,090	$3,276

6100

YEARS MFRD 2012-2013
ENGINE . . . . CAT
CYLINDERS 3
ENGINE HP 28
COOLING . . . . LIQUID
FUEL . . . . D
SPEEDS . . . . VARIABLE
TRANSMISSION . . . . HYDRO
STEERING . . . . ZERO
STANDARD DECK . . . . 61"
WEIGHT . . . . 1,607 LBS.
MSRP $11,499

RETAIL PRICING

YEAR	HIGH	LOW
2012	$6,991	$5,243
2013	$7,524	$5,643

6100 COMPACT DIESEL

YEARS MFRD 2017-2018
ENGINE . . . . CAT 1100CC
CYLINDERS 3
COOLING . . . . LIQUID
FUEL . . . . D
TRANSMISSION . . . . . DUAL HYDRO
STEERING . . . . ZERO
STANDARD DECK . . . . 61"
WEIGHT . . . . 1,607 LBS.

OPTIONS

PERKINS DIESEL

6100 DIESEL

YEARS MFRD 2017-2018
ENGINE . . . . PERKINS 1500CC
CYLINDERS 4
COOLING . . . . LIQUID
FUEL . . . . D
TRANSMISSION . . . . HYDRO
STEERING . . . . ZERO
STANDARD DECK . . . . 61"
WEIGHT . . . . 1,895 LBS.

7200

YEARS MFRD 2006-2006
SERIES . . . . . . LIGHTNING Z SERIES
ENGINE . . . . KAWASAKI
ENGINE HP 26
COOLING . . . . AIR
FUEL . . . . G
SPEEDS . . . . VARIABLE
TRANSMISSION . . . . HYDRO
STEERING . . . . ZERO
STANDARD DECK . . . . 72"
MSRP $7,995

RETAIL PRICING

YEAR	HIGH	LOW
2006	$4,682	$3,511

7200 DIESEL

YEARS MFRD 2017-2018
ENGINE . . . . PERKINS 1500CC
CYLINDERS 4
COOLING . . . . LIQUID
FUEL . . . . D
TRANSMISSION . . . . HYDRO
STEERING . . . . ZERO
STANDARD DECK . . . . 72"
WEIGHT . . . . 1,935 LBS.

7200AOS

YEARS MFRD 2004-2009
ENGINE . . . . KAWASAKI
CYLINDERS 2
ENGINE HP 27
COOLING . . . . LIQUID
FUEL . . . . G
SPEEDS . . . . VARIABLE
TRANSMISSION . . . . HYDRO
STEERING . . . . ZERO
BLADE CLUTCH . . . . ELECTRIC
STANDARD DECK . . . . 72"
MSRP $8,995

OPTIONS

CAT DIESEL 26E
VANGUARD 31E

RETAIL PRICING

YEAR	HIGH	LOW
2005	$3,882	$2,912

BELARUS

FS254

YEARS MFRD 1998-1999
ENGINE . . . . BELARUS
CYLINDERS 3
PTO HP 25
FUEL . . . . G
TRANSMISSION . . . . GEAR
STEERING . . . . STANDARD
MSRP $8,480

RETAIL PRICING

YEAR	HIGH	LOW
1998	$4,323	$3,242
1999	$4,613	$3,460

GOLFMASTER

YEARS MFRD 2003-2007
SERIES . . . . 250 SERIES
CYLINDERS 2
CID 127
PTO HP 24
ENGINE HP 31
COOLING . . . . AIR
FUEL . . . . D
SPEEDS 8/6
TRANSMISSION . . . . GEAR
STEERING . . . . STANDARD
WEIGHT . . . . 5,155 LBS.

T25B

YEARS MFRD	1986-1992
ENGINE	OWN
CYLINDERS	2
CID	127
PTO HP	24
FUEL	D
SPEEDS	8/6
WEIGHT	7,055 LBS.

T25LB

YEARS MFRD	2003-2007
SERIES	250 SERIES
CYLINDERS	2
CID	127
PTO HP	24
ENGINE HP	31
COOLING	AIR
FUEL	D
SPEEDS	8/6
TRANSMISSION	GEAR
STEERING	STANDARD
HITCH	CAT. I
WEIGHT	7,055 LBS.

VTZ-30 SCH

YEARS MFRD	2005-2005
ENGINE	D120
CYLINDERS	2
ENGINE HP	36
COOLING	AIR
FUEL	D
SPEEDS	8/8
TRANSMISSION	POWER SHIFT
STEERING	STANDARD
WEIGHT	5,379 LBS.

VTZ-2027

YEARS MFRD	2005-2005
ENGINE	D120
CYLINDERS	2
ENGINE HP	30
COOLING	AIR
FUEL	D
SPEEDS	8/6
TRANSMISSION	GEAR
STEERING	STANDARD
HYDRAULIC	YES
PTO	YES
WEIGHT	4,453 LBS.

VTZ-2032A

YEARS MFRD	2005-2005
ENGINE	D130
ENGINE HP	36
COOLING	AIR
FUEL	D
SPEEDS	8/6
TRANSMISSION	GEAR
STEERING	STANDARD
WEIGHT	5,490 LBS.

VTZ-T30-69

YEARS MFRD	2005-2005
ENGINE	D120
CYLINDERS	2
ENGINE HP	30
COOLING	AIR
FUEL	D
SPEEDS	8/6
TRANSMISSION	GEAR
STEERING	STANDARD
WEIGHT	4,453 LBS.

082

YEARS MFRD	2003-2005
CYLINDERS	2
ENGINE HP	12.5
COOLING	AIR
SPEEDS	4/3
TRANSMISSION	GEAR
STEERING	STANDARD
HITCH	CAT. I
PTO	YES
WEIGHT	882 LBS.

102TD

YEARS MFRD	2004-2005
ENGINE HP	10.7
COOLING	AIR
FUEL	D
SPEEDS	4/3
TRANSMISSION	GEAR
STEERING	STANDARD
WEIGHT	882 LBS.

132H

YEARS MFRD	2005-2005
ENGINE	HONDA 13K
ENGINE HP	13
COOLING	AIR
FUEL	G
SPEEDS	4/3
TRANSMISSION	GEAR
STEERING	STANDARD
HITCH	CAT. II

180D

YEARS MFRD	1998-1999
SERIES	VST SERIES
ENGINE	BELARUS
CYLINDERS	3
PTO HP	18.5
FUEL	G
TRANSMISSION	GEAR
STEERING	STANDARD
MSRP	$8,830

RETAIL PRICING

YEAR	HIGH	LOW
1998	$4,501	$3,376
1999	$4,804	$3,603

200

YEARS MFRD	1995-2006
SERIES	2000 SERIES
ENGINE	SLAVIA 2S90A
CYLINDERS	2
CID	69.9
PTO HP	19
ENGINE HP	22
COOLING	AIR
FUEL	D
SPEEDS	16/8
TRANSMISSION	GEAR
STEERING	STANDARD
HITCH	CAT. I
PTO	YES
WEIGHT	2,602 LBS.
MSRP	$6,950

RETAIL PRICING

YEAR	HIGH	LOW
1995	$3,279	$2,459
1996	$3,400	$2,550
1997	$3,526	$2,644
1998	$3,702	$2,776
1999	$3,948	$2,961
2002	$4,248	$3,186

220

YEARS MFRD	1995-1996
SERIES	2000 SERIES
ENGINE	SLAVIA 2S90A
CYLINDERS	2
CID	69.9
PTO HP	19
ENGINE HP	22
COOLING	AIR
FUEL	D
SPEEDS	16/8
STEERING	STANDARD
HITCH	CAT. I
PTO	YES
WEIGHT	2,712 LBS.
MSRP	$8,500

RETAIL PRICING

YEAR	HIGH	LOW
1995	$3,839	$2,879
1996	$3,979	$2,984

250

YEARS MFRD	1976-1995
ENGINE	OWN D21A
CYLINDERS	4
CID	127
PTO HP	24.95
ENGINE HP	31
COOLING	AIR
FUEL	D
SPEEDS	8/6
STEERING	ALL WHEEL
WEIGHT	4,300 LBS.
MSRP	$6,500

SERIAL NUMBERS

YEAR	BEGINNING NO.
1976	065878
1977	117980
1978	170093
1979	170443
1980	188367
1981	225075
1982	259978
1983	294881
1984	327125
1985	343247
1986	359369
1987	375491
1988	391610
1989	407730
1990	423845
1991	439960
1992	456073
1993	472183

RETAIL PRICING

YEAR	HIGH	LOW
1990	$2,337	$1,753
1991	$2,494	$1,870
1992	$2,596	$1,947
1993	$2,678	$2,009
1994	$2,828	$2,121
1995	$2,935	$2,201

250AS

YEARS MFRD	1985-2007
ENGINE	VLADIMIR D21A
CYLINDERS	2
CID	127
PTO HP	24
ENGINE HP	31
COOLING	AIR
FUEL	D
SPEEDS	8/6
TRANSMISSION	GEAR
STEERING	STANDARD
HITCH	CAT. I
WEIGHT	4,300 LBS.

SERIAL NUMBERS

YEAR	BEGINNING NO.
1985	303878
1986	348925
1987	434067
1988	473738
1989	512751
1990	532228
1991	551705
1992	571174
1993	590619
1994	610063
1995	629507

300

YEARS MFRD	1995-2007
SERIES	300 SERIES
ENGINE	OWN D120
CYLINDERS	2
CID	127
PTO HP	28.5
ENGINE HP	36
COOLING	AIR
FUEL	D
SPEEDS	8/6
TRANSMISSION	GEAR
STEERING	STANDARD
HITCH	CAT. I
WEIGHT	4,500 LBS.
MSRP	$9,645

RETAIL PRICING

YEAR	HIGH	LOW
1995	$4,356	$3,267
1996	$4,515	$3,387

BELARUS

305

YEARS MFRD 1993-1995
SERIES. . . . . 300 SERIES
ENGINE . . . . OWN
CYLINDERS. 2
CID 127
PTO HP 28.5
ENGINE HP 36
COOLING . . . . AIR
FUEL . . . . D
STEERING. . . . . STANDARD
WEIGHT . . . . 4,550 LBS.

310

YEARS MFRD 1989-2007
SERIES. . . . . 300 SERIES
ENGINE . . . . OWN D120
CYLINDERS. 2
CID 127
PTO HP 28.5
ENGINE HP 36
COOLING . . . . AIR
FUEL . . . . D
SPEEDS 8/6
TRANSMISSION . . . . GEAR
STEERING. . . . . STANDARD
HITCH . . . . CAT. I
WEIGHT . . . . 4,750 LBS.

SERIAL NUMBERS

YEAR	BEGINNING NO.
1989	000145
1990	000290
1991	000435
1992	000579
1993	000718
1994	000856
1995	000994

310/320

YEARS MFRD 2004-2004
CYLINDERS. 3
CID 94.6
ENGINE HP 33.5
COOLING . . . . LIQUID
FUEL . . . . D
SPEEDS 4/2
TRANSMISSION . . . . GEAR
STEERING. . . . . STANDARD
HYDRAULIC . . . . YES
PTO . . . . YES

320

YEARS MFRD 2003-2005
CYLINDERS. 3
ENGINE HP 35
COOLING . . . . LIQUID
FUEL . . . . D
SPEEDS 4/2
TRANSMISSION . . . . GEAR
STEERING. . . . . STANDARD
HITCH . . . . CAT. I
WEIGHT . . . . 3,682 LBS.

320A

YEARS MFRD 2003-2005
ENGINE LDW1503CHD
CYLINDERS. 3
ENGINE HP 35
COOLING . . . . LIQUID
FUEL . . . . D
SPEEDS 4/2
TRANSMISSION . . . . GEAR
STEERING. . . . . STANDARD
HITCH . . . . CAT. I
HYDRAULIC . . . . YES
PTO . . . . YES
WEIGHT . . . . 3,682 LBS.

320R

YEARS MFRD 2004-2004
ENGINE . . . . OWN
CYLINDERS. 3
CID 94.6
ENGINE HP 33.5
COOLING . . . . LIQUID
FUEL . . . . D
SPEEDS 16/8
TRANSMISSION . . . . GEAR
STEERING. . . . . STANDARD
HITCH . . . . CAT. I
PTO . . . . YES
WEIGHT . . . . 3,682 LBS.

321

YEARS MFRD 2004-2004
ENGINE . . . . OWN
CYLINDERS. 3
CID 69.8
ENGINE HP 33.5
COOLING . . . . LIQUID
FUEL . . . . D
SPEEDS 16/8
TRANSMISSION . . . . GEAR
STEERING. . . . . STANDARD
HYDRAULIC . . . . YES
PTO . . . . YES
WEIGHT . . . . 2,756 LBS.

2011

YEARS MFRD 1996-2007
SERIES. . . . . 2000 SERIES
ENGINE . . . . SLAVIA 2S90A
CYLINDERS. 2
CID 69.9
PTO HP 19
ENGINE HP 22
FUEL . . . . D
SPEEDS 16/8
TRANSMISSION . . . . GEAR
STEERING. . . . . STANDARD
HITCH . . . . CAT. I
HYDRAULIC . . . . YES
PTO . . . . YES
WEIGHT . . . . 2,602 LBS.
MSRP. $8,595

RETAIL PRICING

YEAR	HIGH	LOW
1996	$3,975	$2,981
1997	$4,124	$3,093
1998	$4,279	$3,209
1999	$4,369	$3,277
2000	$4,797	$3,597
2002	$5,254	$3,940

2045

YEARS MFRD 1996-2007
SERIES. . . . . 2000 SERIES
ENGINE . . . . SLAVIA 2S90A
CYLINDERS. 2
CID 69.9
PTO HP 19
ENGINE HP 22
COOLING . . . . AIR
FUEL . . . . D
SPEEDS 16/8
TRANSMISSION . . . . GEAR
STEERING. . . . . STANDARD
HITCH . . . . CAT. I
HYDRAULIC . . . . YES
PTO . . . . YES
WEIGHT . . . . 2,712 LBS.
MSRP. $9,060

RETAIL PRICING

YEAR	HIGH	LOW
1996	$4,240	$3,180
1997	$4,399	$3,299
1998	$4,620	$3,465
1999	$4,929	$3,696

2145

YEARS MFRD 1998-2007
SERIES. . . . . 2000 SERIES
ENGINE . . . . SLAVIA 2S90A
CYLINDERS. 2
CID 70
PTO HP 19
ENGINE HP 22
COOLING . . . . AIR
FUEL . . . . D
SPEEDS 16/8
TRANSMISSION . . . . GEAR
STEERING. . . . . STANDARD
HITCH . . . . CAT. I
PTO . . . . YES
WEIGHT . . . . 2,685 LBS.
MSRP. $9,360

SERIAL NUMBERS

YEAR	BEGINNING NO.
2002	D500001
2003	D500379
2004	D500700
2005	D501301
2006	D501761
2007	D501981

RETAIL PRICING

YEAR	HIGH	LOW
1998	$3,151	$2,363
1999	$3,591	$2,693

3011

YEARS MFRD 1998-2007
SERIES. . . . . 3000 SERIES
ENGINE . . . . OWN D120.3
CYLINDERS. 2
CID 127
PTO HP 29
ENGINE HP 36
COOLING . . . . AIR
FUEL . . . . D
SPEEDS 8/6
TRANSMISSION . . . . GEAR
STEERING. . . . . STANDARD
WEIGHT . . . . 4,425 LBS.
MSRP. $8,850

RETAIL PRICING

YEAR	HIGH	LOW
1998	$4,786	$3,589
1999	$5,106	$3,830
2002	$5,409	$4,057

3021

YEARS MFRD 1998-2007
SERIES. . . . . 3000 SERIES
ENGINE . . . . OWN D120.3
CYLINDERS. 2
CID 127
PTO HP 29
ENGINE HP 36
COOLING . . . . AIR
FUEL . . . . D
SPEEDS 8/6
TRANSMISSION . . . . GEAR
STEERING. . . . . STANDARD
WEIGHT . . . . 4,500 LBS.
MSRP. $9,560

RETAIL PRICING

YEAR	HIGH	LOW
1998	$5,399	$4,049
1999	$5,758	$4,318
2002	$5,843	$4,382

3045

YEARS MFRD 1996-2007
SERIES. . . . . 3000 SERIES
ENGINE . . . . OWN D120.3
CYLINDERS. 2
CID 127
PTO HP 29
ENGINE HP 36
COOLING . . . . AIR
FUEL . . . . D
SPEEDS 6/6
TRANSMISSION . . . . GEAR
STEERING. . . . . STANDARD
WEIGHT . . . . 4,750 LBS.
MSRP. $11,135

RETAIL PRICING

YEAR	HIGH	LOW
1996	$5,500	$4,125
1997	$5,705	$4,278
1998	$5,993	$4,494
1999	$6,391	$4,793
2002	$6,806	$5,104

3055

YEARS MFRD 2003-2007
SERIES. . . . . 3000 SERIES
CYLINDERS. 2
CID 127

PTO HP 27.8
ENGINE HP 34
COOLING .... AIR
FUEL .... D
SPEEDS 6/6
TRANSMISSION .... HYDRO
STEERING .... STANDARD
HITCH .... CAT. II
WEIGHT .... 4,500 LBS.

3145

YEARS MFRD 1999-2007
SERIES .... 3000 SERIES
ENGINE .... LDW
CYLINDERS 3
PTO HP 27.8
ENGINE HP 33.5
COOLING .... LIQUID
FUEL .... D
SPEEDS 8/8
TRANSMISSION .... GEAR
STEERING .... STANDARD
HITCH .... CAT. I
WEIGHT .... 3,100 LBS.

BOBCAT

CT1021

YEARS MFRD 2020-2020
CYLINDERS 3
CID 69.01
PTO HP 16.7
ENGINE HP 21.1
FUEL .... D
SPEEDS .... VARIABLE
TRANSMISSION .... HYDRO
STEERING .... STANDARD
HITCH .... CAT. I
DRIVE TYPE 4WD
ROPS/CAB .... ROPS
WEIGHT .... 1,488 LBS.
MSRP $11,500

OPTIONS

LOADER $3,530

CT1025

YEARS MFRD 2020-2020
CYLINDERS 3
CID 69.01
PTO HP 19.4
ENGINE HP 24.5
FUEL .... D
SPEEDS .... VARIABLE
TRANSMISSION .... HYDRO
STEERING .... STANDARD
HITCH .... CAT. I
DRIVE TYPE 4WD
ROPS/CAB .... ROPS
WEIGHT .... 1,488 LBS.
MSRP $12,900

OPTIONS

LOADER $3,530

CT2025

YEARS MFRD 2020-2020
ENGINE .... DAEDONG
CYLINDERS 3
CID 100.5
PTO HP 22.2
ENGINE HP 24.5
FUEL .... D
SPEEDS 9/3
TRANSMISSION .... GEAR
STEERING .... STANDARD
HITCH .... CAT. I
DRIVE TYPE 4WD
ROPS/CAB .... ROPS
WEIGHT .... 2,646 LBS.
MSRP $15,300

OPTIONS

HYDRO
LOADER $5,179

CT2035

YEARS MFRD 2020-2020
ENGINE .... DAEDONG
CYLINDERS 3
CID 111.4
PTO HP 30.8
ENGINE HP 34.9
FUEL .... D
SPEEDS 9/3
TRANSMISSION .... GEAR
STEERING .... STANDARD
DRIVE TYPE 4WD
ROPS/CAB .... ROPS
WEIGHT .... 2,679 LBS.
MSRP $19,500

OPTIONS

HYDRO
LOADER $5,179

CT2040

YEARS MFRD 2020-2020
ENGINE .... DAEDONG
CYLINDERS 3
CID 111.4
PTO HP 34.9
ENGINE HP 39.6
FUEL .... D
SPEEDS 9/3
TRANSMISSION .... GEAR
STEERING .... STANDARD
HITCH .... CAT. I
DRIVE TYPE 4WD
ROPS/CAB .... ROPS
WEIGHT .... 2,679 LBS.
MSRP $20,000

OPTIONS

HYDRO
LOADER $5,179

CT2535

YEARS MFRD 2020-2020
ENGINE .... DAEDONG
CYLINDERS 3
CID 111.4
PTO HP 29.4
ENGINE HP 34.9
FUEL .... D
SPEEDS .... VARIABLE
TRANSMISSION .... HYDRO
STEERING .... STANDARD
HITCH .... CAT. I
DRIVE TYPE 4WD
ROPS/CAB .... CAB
WEIGHT .... 3,415 LBS.
MSRP $30,800

OPTIONS

LOADER $5,179

CT2540

YEARS MFRD 2020-2020
ENGINE .... DAEDONG
CYLINDERS 3
CID 111.4
PTO HP 31.9
ENGINE HP 39.6
FUEL .... D
SPEEDS .... VARIABLE
TRANSMISSION .... HYDRO
STEERING .... STANDARD
HITCH .... CAT. I
DRIVE TYPE 4WD
ROPS/CAB .... CAB
WEIGHT .... 3,415 LBS.

OPTIONS

LOADER $5,179

CT4045

YEARS MFRD 2020-2020
ENGINE .... DAEDONG
CYLINDERS 3
CID 111.4
PTO HP 41.6
ENGINE HP 44.9
FUEL .... D
SPEEDS 8/8
TRANSMISSION SYNCHRO SHUTTLE
STEERING .... STANDARD
HITCH .... CAT. I
DRIVE TYPE 4WD
ROPS/CAB .... ROPS
WEIGHT .... 3,373 LBS.
MSRP $23,900

OPTIONS

HYDRO
LOADER $6,704

CT5545

YEARS MFRD 2020-2020
ENGINE .... DAEDONG
CYLINDERS 3
CID 111.4
PTO HP 4533.9
ENGINE HP 45
FUEL .... D
SPEEDS .... VARIABLE
TRANSMISSION .... HYDRO
STEERING .... STANDARD
HITCH .... CAT. I
DRIVE TYPE 4WD
ROPS/CAB .... CAB
WEIGHT .... 4,685 LBS.
MSRP $35,900

OPTIONS

LOADER $7,239

CT5550

YEARS MFRD 2020-2020
ENGINE .... DAEDONG
CYLINDERS 3
CID 111.4
PTO HP 38.9
ENGINE HP 50
FUEL .... D
SPEEDS .... VARIABLE
TRANSMISSION .... HYDRO
STEERING .... STANDARD
HITCH .... CAT. I
DRIVE TYPE 4WD
ROPS/CAB .... CAB
WEIGHT .... 4,685 LBS.
MSRP $37,700

OPTIONS

LOADER $7,239

CT5555

YEARS MFRD 2020-2020
ENGINE .... DAEDONG
CYLINDERS 3
CID 111.4
PTO HP 43.1
ENGINE HP 55
FUEL .... D
SPEEDS .... VARIABLE
TRANSMISSION .... HYDRO
STEERING .... STANDARD
HITCH .... CAT. I
DRIVE TYPE 4WD
ROPS/CAB .... CAB
WEIGHT .... 4,685 LBS.
MSRP $39,700

OPTIONS

LOADER $7,239

BOB-CAT BY JACOBSEN

CRZ 942600

YEARS MFRD 2015-2016
ENGINE .... KAWASAKI FR600V
CID 36.8
COOLING .... AIR
FUEL .... G
SPEEDS .... VARIABLE
TRANSMISSION .... HYDRO
STEERING .... ZERO
STANDARD DECK .... 48"

BOB-CAT BY JACOBSEN

CRZ 942601

YEARS MFRD 2015-2016
ENGINE .... KAWASAKI FR651V
CID 44.3
COOLING .... AIR
FUEL .... G
SPEEDS .... VARIABLE
TRANSMISSION .... HYDRO
STEERING .... ZERO
STANDARD DECK .... 52"

CRZ 942602

YEARS MFRD 2015-2016
ENGINE .... KAWASAKI FR691V
CID 44.3
COOLING .... AIR
FUEL .... G
SPEEDS .... VARIABLE
TRANSMISSION .... HYDRO
STEERING .... ZERO
STANDARD DECK .... 61"

CRZ 942604

YEARS MFRD 2016-2020
ENGINE .... KAWASAKI FR651V
CID 36.8
ENGINE HP 21.5
FUEL .... G
SPEEDS .... VARIABLE
TRANSMISSION .... HYDRO
STEERING .... ZERO
BLADE CLUTCH .... ELECTRIC
STANDARD DECK .... 48"
WEIGHT .... 736 LBS.
MSRP $5,299

CRZ 942605

YEARS MFRD 2017-2020
ENGINE .... KAWASAKI FR651V
ENGINE HP 21.5
FUEL .... G
TRANSMISSION .... HYDRO
STEERING .... ZERO
STANDARD DECK .... 52"
WEIGHT .... 752 LBS.
MSRP $5,499

CRZ 942606

YEARS MFRD 2016-2020
ENGINE .... KAWASAKI FR691V
CID 44.3
ENGINE HP 23
FUEL .... G
SPEEDS .... VARIABLE
TRANSMISSION .... HYDRO
STEERING .... ZERO
BLADE CLUTCH .... ELECTRIC
STANDARD DECK .... 61"
WEIGHT .... 795 LBS.
MSRP $5,799

CRZ 942607

YEARS MFRD 2016-2020
ENGINE .... KAWASAKI FR651V
CID 36.8
ENGINE HP 21.5
FUEL .... G
SPEEDS .... VARIABLE
TRANSMISSION .... HYDRO
STEERING .... ZERO
BLADE CLUTCH .... ELECTRIC
STANDARD DECK .... 42"
WEIGHT .... 684 LBS.
MSRP $4,999

CT120

YEARS MFRD 2008-2009
ENGINE .... DAEDONG TIER 4
CYLINDERS 3
CID 56.6
ENGINE HP 20
COOLING .... LIQUID
FUEL .... D
SPEEDS .... VARIABLE
TRANSMISSION .... HYDRO
STEERING .... STANDARD
HITCH .... CAT. I
HYDRAULIC .... YES
PTO .... YES
WEIGHT .... 1,969 LBS.
MSRP $11,600

RETAIL PRICING

YEAR	HIGH	LOW
2008	$4,509	$3,382
2009	$4,841	$3,631

CT122

YEARS MFRD 2008-2014
ENGINE .... DAEDONG TIER 4
CYLINDERS 3
CID 61
PTO HP 16.2
ENGINE HP 22
FUEL .... D
SPEEDS .... VARIABLE
TRANSMISSION .... HYDRO
STEERING .... STANDARD
HITCH .... CAT. I
DRIVE TYPE 2WD
ROPS/CAB .... ROPS
WEIGHT .... 2,056 LBS.
MSRP $12,557

RETAIL PRICING

YEAR	HIGH	LOW
2008	$4,160	$3,120
2009	$4,303	$3,227
2010	$4,661	$3,496
2011	$5,200	$3,900
2012	$5,880	$4,410
2013	$6,204	$4,653
2014	$7,745	$5,809

CT225

YEARS MFRD 2008-2014
ENGINE .... DAEDONG TIER 4
CYLINDERS 3
CID 85.4
PTO HP 19.5
ENGINE HP 27
COOLING .... LIQUID
FUEL .... D
SPEEDS .... VARIABLE
TRANSMISSION .... HYDRO
STEERING .... STANDARD
HITCH .... CAT. I
DRIVE TYPE 2WD
ROPS/CAB .... ROPS
WEIGHT .... 3,028 LBS.
MSRP $15,282

RETAIL PRICING

YEAR	HIGH	LOW
2008	$4,983	$3,737
2009	$5,271	$3,954
2010	$5,594	$4,195
2011	$6,382	$4,786
2012	$6,920	$5,190
2013	$7,567	$5,675
2014	$9,094	$6,821

CT230

YEARS MFRD 2008-2014
ENGINE .... DAEDONG TIER 4
CYLINDERS 3
CID 91.5
PTO HP 22
ENGINE HP 30
COOLING .... LIQUID
FUEL .... D
SPEEDS .... VARIABLE
TRANSMISSION .... HYDRO
STEERING .... STANDARD
HITCH .... CAT. I
HYDRAULIC .... YES
PTO .... YES
WEIGHT .... 3,056 LBS.
MSRP $16,115

RETAIL PRICING

YEAR	HIGH	LOW
2008	$5,271	$3,954
2009	$5,486	$4,115
2010	$5,916	$4,437
2011	$6,670	$5,002
2012	$7,458	$5,593
2013	$7,961	$5,970
2014	$10,470	$7,853

CT235

YEARS MFRD 2008-2014
ENGINE .... DAEDONG
CYLINDERS 3
CID 97
PTO HP 26.5
ENGINE HP 34
COOLING .... LIQUID
FUEL .... D
SPEEDS .... VARIABLE
TRANSMISSION .... HYDRO
STEERING .... STANDARD
HITCH .... CAT. I
DRIVE TYPE 2WD
ROPS/CAB .... ROPS
WEIGHT .... 3,056 LBS.
MSRP $17,209

RETAIL PRICING

YEAR	HIGH	LOW
2008	$5,559	$4,169
2009	$5,809	$4,357
2010	$6,240	$4,680
2011	$7,136	$5,352
2012	$7,961	$5,970
2013	$8,499	$6,374
2014	$10,828	$8,121

CT335

YEARS MFRD 2008-2014
ENGINE .... DAEDONG TIER 4
CYLINDERS 3
ENGINE HP 38
FUEL .... D
SPEEDS .... VARIABLE
TRANSMISSION .... HYDRO
STEERING .... STANDARD
HITCH .... CAT. I
DRIVE TYPE 2WD
ROPS/CAB .... ROPS
WEIGHT .... 3,668 LBS.
MSRP $18,570

OPTIONS

CAB

RETAIL PRICING

YEAR	HIGH	LOW
2008	$6,275	$4,706
2009	$6,527	$4,895
2010	$7,064	$5,298
2011	$8,104	$6,078
2012	$8,569	$6,427
2013	$9,180	$6,885
2014	$11,402	$8,552

CT335SST

YEARS MFRD 2010-2014
ENGINE .... DAEDONG TIER 4
CYLINDERS 3
CID 111
PTO HP 28.5
ENGINE HP 38
FUEL .... D
SPEEDS .... VARIABLE
TRANSMISSION .... HYDRO
STEERING .... STANDARD
DRIVE TYPE 2WD
ROPS/CAB .... ROPS
WEIGHT .... 3,701 LBS.
MSRP $17,200

RETAIL PRICING

YEAR	HIGH	LOW
2010	$6,885	$5,163
2011	$7,530	$5,648
2012	$7,997	$5,998
2013	$9,215	$6,911
2014	$11,223	$8,417

CT440

YEARS MFRD 2008-2014
ENGINE . . . . DAEDONG TIER 4
CYLINDERS. 4
PTO HP 30
ENGINE HP 41
FUEL . . . . D
SPEEDS . . . . VARIABLE
TRANSMISSION . . . . HYDRO
STEERING. . . . . STANDARD
HITCH . . . . CAT. I
DRIVE TYPE 2WD
ROPS/CAB . . . . ROPS
WEIGHT . . . . 3,847 LBS.
MSRP. $20,820

OPTIONS

CAB

RETAIL PRICING

YEAR	HIGH	LOW
2008	$6,813	$5,110
2009	$7,100	$5,325
2010	$7,673	$5,755
2011	$8,786	$6,589
2012	$9,503	$7,127
2013	$10,290	$7,718
2014	$12,765	$9,573

CT445

YEARS MFRD 2008-2014
ENGINE . . . . DAEDONG TIER 4
CYLINDERS. 4
CID 134
PTO HP 34
ENGINE HP 45
FUEL . . . . D
SPEEDS . . . . VARIABLE
TRANSMISSION . . . . HYDRO
STEERING. . . . . STANDARD
HITCH . . . . CAT. I
DRIVE TYPE 2WD
ROPS/CAB . . . . ROPS
WEIGHT . . . . 3,881 LBS.
MSRP. $23,241

OPTIONS

CAB

RETAIL PRICING

YEAR	HIGH	LOW
2008	$7,458	$5,593
2009	$7,781	$5,836
2010	$8,390	$6,292
2011	$9,609	$7,207
2012	$10,613	$7,960
2013	$11,510	$8,633
2014	$14,486	$10,865

AVG. AUCTION PRICING

LOW	HIGH	AVG
$13,000	$14,200	$13,800

CT445SST

YEARS MFRD 2010-2014
ENGINE . . . . DAEDONG TIER 4
CYLINDERS. 4
CID 134
PTO HP 36.5
ENGINE HP 45
FUEL . . . . D
SPEEDS . . . . VARIABLE
TRANSMISSION . . . . HYDRO
STEERING. . . . . STANDARD
DRIVE TYPE 2WD
ROPS/CAB . . . . ROPS
WEIGHT . . . . 3,914 LBS.
MSRP. $21,771

RETAIL PRICING

YEAR	HIGH	LOW
2010	$8,211	$6,159
2011	$9,000	$6,750
2012	$9,861	$7,396
2013	$10,756	$8,067
2014	$13,697	$10,273

CT450

YEARS MFRD 2008-2014
ENGINE . . . . DAEDONG TIER 4
CYLINDERS. 4
PTO HP 38
ENGINE HP 49
FUEL . . . . D
SPEEDS . . . . VARIABLE
TRANSMISSION . . . . HYDRO
STEERING. . . . . STANDARD
HITCH . . . . CAT. I
DRIVE TYPE 2WD
ROPS/CAB . . . . ROPS
WEIGHT . . . . 3,935 LBS.
MSRP. $25,317

OPTIONS

CAB

RETAIL PRICING

YEAR	HIGH	LOW
2008	$8,104	$6,078
2009	$8,426	$6,320
2010	$9,108	$6,831
2011	$10,400	$7,800
2012	$11,474	$8,605
2013	$12,515	$9,386
2014	$16,601	$12,451

CT450SST

YEARS MFRD 2010-2014
ENGINE . . . . DAEDONG TIER 4
CYLINDERS. 4
CID 146
PTO HP 41
ENGINE HP 49
FUEL . . . . D
SPEEDS . . . . VARIABLE
TRANSMISSION . . . . HYDRO
STEERING. . . . . STANDARD
DRIVE TYPE 2WD
ROPS/CAB . . . . ROPS
WEIGHT . . . . 3,935 LBS.
MSRP. $23,766

RETAIL PRICING

YEAR	HIGH	LOW
2010	$8,929	$6,697
2011	$9,752	$7,314
2012	$10,865	$8,149
2013	$11,761	$8,821
2014	$14,199	$10,649

FAST CAT

YEARS MFRD 2007-2009
CID 725CC
COOLING . . . . AIR
FUEL . . . . G
SPEEDS . . . . VARIABLE
TRANSMISSION . . . . HYDRO
STEERING. . . . . ZERO

FAST CAT PRO

YEARS MFRD 2009-2012
ENGINE . . . . KAWASAKI
CYLINDERS. 2
ENGINE HP 18
COOLING . . . . AIR
FUEL . . . . G
SPEEDS . . . . VARIABLE
TRANSMISSION . . . . HYDRO
STEERING. . . . . ZERO
BLADE CLUTCH . . . . ELECTRIC
STANDARD DECK . . . . 36"
MSRP. $6,049

OPTIONS

KAWASAKI 19E

RETAIL PRICING

YEAR	HIGH	LOW
2009	$1,211	$908
2010	$1,543	$1,157
2011	$1,909	$1,432
2012	$2,278	$1,708

FAST CAT PRO 942406H

YEARS MFRD 2013-2017
ENGINE . . . . KAWASAKI FX691V
CID 726CC
ENGINE HP 22
COOLING . . . . AIR
FUEL . . . . G
SPEEDS . . . . VARIABLE
TRANSMISSION . . . . HYDRO
STEERING. . . . . ZERO
STANDARD DECK . . . . 52"
WEIGHT . . . . 840 LBS.

FAST CAT PRO 942407J

YEARS MFRD 2013-2017
ENGINE . . . . KAWASAKI FX730V
CID 726CC
ENGINE HP 23.5
COOLING . . . . AIR
FUEL . . . . G
SPEEDS . . . . VARIABLE
TRANSMISSION . . . . HYDRO
STEERING. . . . . ZERO
STANDARD DECK . . . . 61"
WEIGHT . . . . 905 LBS.

FAST CAT PRO 942408H

YEARS MFRD 2013-2016
ENGINE . . . . . . KOHLER ECV730EFI
CID 730CC
ENGINE HP 25
COOLING . . . . AIR
FUEL . . . . G
SPEEDS . . . . VARIABLE
TRANSMISSION . . . . HYDRO
STEERING. . . . . ZERO
STANDARD DECK . . . . 52"
WEIGHT . . . . 840 LBS.

FAST CAT PRO 942409J

YEARS MFRD 2013-2016
ENGINE . . . . . . KOHLER ECV749EFI
CID 749CC
ENGINE HP 29
COOLING . . . . AIR
FUEL . . . . G
SPEEDS . . . . VARIABLE
TRANSMISSION . . . . HYDRO
STEERING. . . . . ZERO
STANDARD DECK . . . . 61"
WEIGHT . . . . 905 LBS.

FAST CAT PRO RS 942411

YEARS MFRD 2018-2018
ENGINE . . . . KAWASAKI FX850V
TRANSMISSION . . . . HYDRO
STEERING. . . . . ZERO
STANDARD DECK . . . . 52"
WEIGHT . . . . 840 LBS.
MSRP. $10,239

FAST CAT PRO RS 942412

YEARS MFRD 2018-2018
ENGINE . . . . KAWASAKI FX850V
FUEL . . . . G
TRANSMISSION . . . . HYDRO
STEERING. . . . . ZERO
STANDARD DECK . . . . 61"
WEIGHT . . . . 905 LBS.
MSRP. $10,779

FAST CAT PRO SE 942297H

YEARS MFRD 2013-2020
ENGINE . . . . KAWASAKI FX541V
CID 603CC
ENGINE HP 15
COOLING . . . . AIR
FUEL . . . . G
SPEEDS . . . . VARIABLE
TRANSMISSION . . . . HYDRO
STEERING. . . . . ZERO
STANDARD DECK . . . . 36"
WEIGHT . . . . 705 LBS.

BOB-CAT BY JACOBSEN

FAST CAT PRO SE 942298H

YEARS MFRD	2013-2016
ENGINE	KAWASAKI FX600V
CID	603CC
ENGINE HP	19
COOLING	AIR
FUEL	G
SPEEDS	VARIABLE
TRANSMISSION	HYDRO
STEERING	ZERO
STANDARD DECK	48"
WEIGHT	766 LBS.

FAST CAT PRO SE 942299H

YEARS MFRD	2013-2016
ENGINE	KAWASAKI FX651V
CID	726CC
ENGINE HP	20.5
COOLING	AIR
FUEL	G
SPEEDS	VARIABLE
TRANSMISSION	HYDRO
STEERING	ZERO
STANDARD DECK	52"
WEIGHT	840 LBS.

FAST CAT PRO SE 942302H

YEARS MFRD	2013-2020
ENGINE	KAWASAKI FX600V
CID	603CC
ENGINE HP	19
COOLING	AIR
FUEL	G
SPEEDS	VARIABLE
TRANSMISSION	HYDRO
STEERING	ZERO
STANDARD DECK	19"
WEIGHT	744 LBS.

FAST CAT RZ

YEARS MFRD	2009-2013
ENGINE	B&S
CYLINDERS	2
ENGINE HP	22
COOLING	AIR
FUEL	G
SPEEDS	VARIABLE
TRANSMISSION	HYDRO
STEERING	ZERO
BLADE CLUTCH	ELECTRIC
STANDARD DECK	48"
WEIGHT	744 LBS.
MSRP	$6,500

OPTIONS

KAWASAKI 17E
KAWASAKI 19E

RETAIL PRICING

YEAR	HIGH	LOW
2009	$1,004	$753
2010	$1,280	$960
2011	$1,585	$1,188
2012	$1,889	$1,417
2013	$2,540	$1,905

LEO

YEARS MFRD	2004-2005
ENGINE	B&S ELS
ENGINE HP	17.5
COOLING	AIR
FUEL	G
SPEEDS	VARIABLE
TRANSMISSION	HYDRO
STEERING	ZERO

OPTIONS

B&S INTEK 20E

PREDATOR PRO

YEARS MFRD	2006-2009
ENGINE	GENERAC
ENGINE HP	33
FUEL	G
SPEEDS	VARIABLE
TRANSMISSION	HYDRO
STEERING	ZERO
BLADE CLUTCH	ELECTRIC

OPTIONS

GENERAC 26E
KAWASAKI 26E
KAWASAKI 37E

PREDATOR PRO 942514J

YEARS MFRD	2013-2013
ENGINE	KAWASAKI FX921V
CID	999CC
ENGINE HP	31
COOLING	AIR
FUEL	G
SPEEDS	VARIABLE
TRANSMISSION	HYDRO
STEERING	ZERO
STANDARD DECK	61"
WEIGHT	1,293 LBS.
MSRP	$11,999

RETAIL PRICING

YEAR	HIGH	LOW
2013	$5,943	$4,457

PREDATOR PRO 942515

YEARS MFRD	2016-2016
ENGINE	KAWASAKI FX1000V-DFI
CID	61
COOLING	AIR
FUEL	G
SPEEDS	VARIABLE
TRANSMISSION	HYDRO
STEERING	ZERO
STANDARD DECK	61"

PREDATOR PRO 942519

YEARS MFRD	2016-2017
ENGINE	KAWASAKI FX921V
CID	61
COOLING	AIR
FUEL	G
SPEEDS	VARIABLE
TRANSMISSION	HYDRO
STEERING	ZERO
STANDARD DECK	72"

PREDATOR PRO 942519J

YEARS MFRD	2013-2013
ENGINE	KAWASAKI FX921V
CID	999CC
COOLING	AIR
FUEL	G
SPEEDS	VARIABLE
TRANSMISSION	HYDRO
STEERING	ZERO
STANDARD DECK	72"
MSRP	$12,919

RETAIL PRICING

YEAR	HIGH	LOW
2013	$5,931	$4,448

PREDATOR PRO 942529

YEARS MFRD	2016-2016
ENGINE	KAWASAKI FX921V
CID	61
COOLING	AIR
FUEL	G
SPEEDS	VARIABLE
TRANSMISSION	HYDRO
STEERING	ZERO
STANDARD DECK	52"

PREDATOR PRO 942545

YEARS MFRD	2016-2017
ENGINE	KAWASAKI FX1000V
CID	61
COOLING	AIR
FUEL	G
SPEEDS	VARIABLE
TRANSMISSION	HYDRO
STEERING	ZERO
STANDARD DECK	52"

PREDATOR PRO 9997001

YEARS MFRD	2019-2020
SERIES	PREDATOR-PRO 7000
ENGINE	KAWASAKI FX1000V
CID	999CC
FUEL	G
SPEEDS	VARIABLE
TRANSMISSION	HYDRO
STEERING	ZERO
STANDARD DECK	61"
WEIGHT	1,500 LBS.
MSRP	$15,290

PREDATOR PRO 9997002

YEARS MFRD	2019-2020
SERIES	PREDATOR-PRO 7000
ENGINE	KAWASAKI FX1000V
CID	999CC
FUEL	G
SPEEDS	VARIABLE
STEERING	ZERO
STANDARD DECK	61"
WEIGHT	1,618 LBS.
MSRP	$15,570

PREDATOR PRO 9997003

YEARS MFRD	2019-2020
SERIES	PREDATOR-PRO 7000
ENGINE	KAWASAKI FX1000V
CID	999CC
FUEL	G
SPEEDS	VARIABLE
STEERING	ZERO
STANDARD DECK	72"
WEIGHT	1,659 LBS.
MSRP	$16,350

PREDATOR PRO 9997004

YEARS MFRD	2019-2020
SERIES	PREDATOR-PRO 7000
ENGINE	KAWASAKI FX1000V
CID	999CC
FUEL	G
TRANSMISSION	HYDRO
STEERING	ZERO
STANDARD DECK	72"
WEIGHT	1,541 LBS.
MSRP	$16,100

PREDATOR PRO 9997005

YEARS MFRD	2020-2020
SERIES	PREDATOR-PRO 7000
ENGINE	B&S VANGUARD EFI
CID	993CC
FUEL	G

SPEEDS . . . . VARIABLE
TRANSMISSION . . . . HYDRO
STEERING. . . . . ZERO
STANDARD DECK . . . . 61"
WEIGHT . . . . 1,500 LBS.
MSRP. $16,300

PREDATOR PRO 9997006

YEARS MFRD 2020-2020
SERIES. . . . . PREDATOR-PRO 7000
ENGINE . . . . . . B&S VANGUARD EFI
CID 993CC
SPEEDS . . . . VARIABLE
TRANSMISSION . . . . HYDRO
STEERING. . . . . ZERO
STANDARD DECK . . . . 72"
WEIGHT . . . . 1,541 LBS.
MSRP. $16,500

PREDATOR PRO DFI 942515J

YEARS MFRD 2013-2013
ENGINE . . . . . . KAWASAKI FX1000V
CID 999CC
ENGINE HP 37
COOLING . . . . AIR
FUEL . . . . G
SPEEDS . . . . VARIABLE
TRANSMISSION . . . . HYDRO
STEERING. . . . . ZERO
STANDARD DECK . . . . 61"
WEIGHT . . . . 1,293 LBS.
MSRP. $12,352

RETAIL PRICING

YEAR	HIGH	LOW
2013	$6,091	$4,568

PREDATOR PRO DFI 942516J

YEARS MFRD 2013-2013
ENGINE . . . . . . KAWASAKI FX1000V
CID 999CC
ENGINE HP 37
COOLING . . . . AIR
FUEL . . . . G
SPEEDS . . . . VARIABLE
TRANSMISSION . . . . HYDRO
STEERING. . . . . ZERO
STANDARD DECK . . . . 72"
WEIGHT . . . . 1,404 LBS.
MSRP. $12,466

RETAIL PRICING

YEAR	HIGH	LOW
2013	$6,171	$4,628

PREDATOR PRO LP RD 942510J

YEARS MFRD 2013-2017
ENGINE . . . . GENERAC IND
CID 992CC
COOLING . . . . AIR
SPEEDS . . . . VARIABLE
TRANSMISSION . . . . HYDRO
STEERING. . . . . ZERO

PREDATOR PRO LP RD 942511J

YEARS MFRD 2013-2017
ENGINE . . . . GENERAC IND
CID 992CC
COOLING . . . . AIR
SPEEDS . . . . VARIABLE
TRANSMISSION . . . . HYDRO
STEERING. . . . . ZERO

PREDATOR PRO LP RD 942524J

YEARS MFRD 2013-2014
ENGINE . . . . GENERAC IND
CID 992CC
COOLING . . . . AIR
SPEEDS . . . . VARIABLE
TRANSMISSION . . . . HYDRO
STEERING. . . . . ZERO

PREDATOR PRO LP SD 942509

YEARS MFRD 2011-2017
ENGINE . . . . GENERAC
ENGINE HP 33
COOLING . . . . AIR
SPEEDS . . . . VARIABLE
TRANSMISSION . . . . HYDRO
STEERING. . . . . ZERO
STANDARD DECK . . . . 61"
MSRP. $13,330

RETAIL PRICING

YEAR	HIGH	LOW
2011	$3,531	$2,648
2012	$5,025	$3,769
2013	$5,976	$4,482
2014	$6,572	$4,929
2015	$7,549	$5,662
2016	$8,525	$6,394
2017	$9,864	$7,398

PREDATOR PRO RS 942519

YEARS MFRD 2018-2018
ENGINE . . . . . . KAWASAKI FX1000V
CID 999CC
TRANSMISSION . . . . HYDRO
STEERING. . . . . ZERO
STANDARD DECK . . . . 72"
WEIGHT . . . . 1,404 LBS.

PREDATOR PRO RS 942545

YEARS MFRD 2018-2018
ENGINE . . . . . . KAWASAKI FX1000V
CID 999CC
FUEL . . . . G
TRANSMISSION . . . . HYDRO
STEERING. . . . . ZERO
STANDARD DECK . . . . 61"
WEIGHT . . . . 1,293 LBS.

PRO CAT

YEARS MFRD 2009-2009
ENGINE . . . . KOHLER
CYLINDERS. 2
ENGINE HP 27
COOLING . . . . AIR
FUEL . . . . G
SPEEDS . . . . VARIABLE
TRANSMISSION . . . . HYDRO
STEERING. . . . . ZERO
BLADE CLUTCH . . . . ELECTRIC

OPTIONS

KAWASAKI 19E

PRO CAT 942501J

YEARS MFRD 2013-2016
ENGINE . . . . KAWASAKI FX730V
CID 726CC
COOLING . . . . AIR
FUEL . . . . G
SPEEDS . . . . VARIABLE
TRANSMISSION . . . . HYDRO
STEERING. . . . . ZERO

PRO CAT 942502J

YEARS MFRD 2013-2014
ENGINE . . . . KAWASAKI FX730V
CID 726CC
COOLING . . . . AIR
FUEL . . . . G
SPEEDS . . . . VARIABLE
TRANSMISSION . . . . HYDRO
STEERING. . . . . ZERO

PRO CAT 942504J

YEARS MFRD 2013-2016
ENGINE . . . . KAWASAKI FX801V
CID 852CC
COOLING . . . . AIR
FUEL . . . . G
SPEEDS . . . . VARIABLE
TRANSMISSION . . . . HYDRO
STEERING. . . . . ZERO

PRO CAT 942506J

YEARS MFRD 2013-2016
ENGINE . . . . KAWASAKI FX801V
CID 852CC
COOLING . . . . AIR
FUEL . . . . G
SPEEDS . . . . VARIABLE
TRANSMISSION . . . . HYDRO
STEERING. . . . . ZERO

PRO CAT 942507J

YEARS MFRD 2013-2016
ENGINE . . . . KAWASAKI FX801V
CID 852CC
COOLING . . . . AIR
FUEL . . . . G
SPEEDS . . . . VARIABLE
TRANSMISSION . . . . HYDRO
STEERING. . . . . ZERO

PRO CAT 942508J

YEARS MFRD 2013-2016
ENGINE . . . . KAWASAKI FX801V
CID 852CC
COOLING . . . . AIR
FUEL . . . . G
SPEEDS . . . . VARIABLE
TRANSMISSION . . . . HYDRO
STEERING. . . . . ZERO

PRO CAT 942517J

YEARS MFRD 2013-2016
ENGINE . . . . KAWASAKI FX651V
CID 726
COOLING . . . . AIR
FUEL . . . . G
SPEEDS . . . . VARIABLE
TRANSMISSION . . . . HYDRO
STEERING. . . . . ZERO

BOB-CAT BY JACOBSEN

PRO CAT 942525J

YEARS MFRD 2013-2016
ENGINE . . . . KOHLER EC730EFI
CID 725CC
COOLING . . . . AIR
FUEL . . . . G
SPEEDS . . . . VARIABLE
TRANSMISSION . . . . HYDRO
STEERING . . . . ZERO

PRO CAT 942526J

YEARS MFRD 2013-2016
ENGINE . . . . KAWASAKI FX801V
CID 852CC
COOLING . . . . AIR
FUEL . . . . G
SPEEDS . . . . VARIABLE
TRANSMISSION . . . . HYDRO
STEERING . . . . ZERO

PRO CAT 942532

YEARS MFRD 2016-2017
ENGINE . . . . KAWASAKI FX691V
CID 44.3
FUEL . . . . G
SPEEDS . . . . VARIABLE
TRANSMISSION . . . . HYDRO
STEERING . . . . ZERO
STANDARD DECK . . . . 52"

PRO CAT 942535

YEARS MFRD 2016-2017
ENGINE . . . . KAWASAKI FX801V
CID 51.9
FUEL . . . . G
SPEEDS . . . . VARIABLE
TRANSMISSION . . . . HYDRO
STEERING . . . . ZERO
BLADE CLUTCH . . . . ELECTRIC
STANDARD DECK . . . . 52"

PRO CAT 942542

YEARS MFRD 2016-2017
ENGINE . . . . KAWASAKI FX730V
CID 44.3
FUEL . . . . G
SPEEDS . . . . VARIABLE
TRANSMISSION . . . . HYDRO
STEERING . . . . ZERO
BLADE CLUTCH . . . . ELECTRIC
STANDARD DECK . . . . 61"

PRO CAT 942543

YEARS MFRD 2016-2017
ENGINE . . . . KAWASAKI FX801V
CID 51.9
FUEL . . . . G
SPEEDS . . . . VARIABLE
TRANSMISSION . . . . HYDRO
STEERING . . . . ZERO
BLADE CLUTCH . . . . ELECTRIC
STANDARD DECK . . . . 61"

PRO CAT 9995008

YEARS MFRD 2019-2020
SERIES . . . . PROCAT 5000
ENGINE . . . . KAWASAKI FX730V
CID 726CC
FUEL . . . . G
TRANSMISSION . . . . HYDRO
STEERING . . . . ZERO
STANDARD DECK . . . . 52"
WEIGHT . . . . 1,267 LBS.
MSRP $11,299

PRO CAT 9995009

YEARS MFRD 2019-2020
SERIES . . . . PROCAT 5000
ENGINE . . . . KAWASAKI FX801V
CID 852CC
FUEL . . . . G
SPEEDS . . . . VARIABLE
TRANSMISSION . . . . HYDRO
STEERING . . . . ZERO
STANDARD DECK . . . . 61"
WEIGHT . . . . 1,318 LBS.
MSRP $11,599

PRO CAT 9995010

YEARS MFRD 2019-2020
SERIES . . . . PROCAT 5000
ENGINE . . . . VANGUARD
CID 724CC
ENGINE HP 24
FUEL . . . . G
SPEEDS . . . . VARIABLE
TRANSMISSION . . . . HYDRO
STEERING . . . . ZERO
STANDARD DECK . . . . 48"
WEIGHT . . . . 1,253 LBS.
MSRP $10,699

PRO CAT 9995011

YEARS MFRD 2019-2020
SERIES . . . . PROCAT 5000
ENGINE . . . . VANGUARD
CID 810CC
ENGINE HP 24
FUEL . . . . G
SPEEDS . . . . VARIABLE
TRANSMISSION . . . . HYDRO
STEERING . . . . ZERO
STANDARD DECK . . . . 52"
WEIGHT . . . . 1,287 LBS.
MSRP $10,799

PRO CAT 9995012

YEARS MFRD 2019-2020
SERIES . . . . PROCAT 5000
ENGINE . . . . VANGUARD
CID 810CC
ENGINE HP 26
FUEL . . . . G
SPEEDS . . . . VARIABLE
TRANSMISSION . . . . HYDRO
STEERING . . . . ZERO
STANDARD DECK . . . . 61"
WEIGHT . . . . 1,318 LBS.
MSRP $11,299

PRO CAT 9996001

YEARS MFRD 2019-2019
SERIES . . . . PROCAT 6000
ENGINE . . . . KAWASAKI FX730V
CID 726CC
FUEL . . . . G
SPEEDS . . . . VARIABLE
STEERING . . . . ZERO
STANDARD DECK . . . . 52"
WEIGHT . . . . 1,427 LBS.
MSRP $12,573

PRO CAT 9996002

YEARS MFRD 2019-2019
SERIES . . . . PROCAT 6000
ENGINE . . . . KAWASAKI FX801V
CID 852CC
FUEL . . . . G
SPEEDS . . . . VARIABLE
STEERING . . . . ZERO
STANDARD DECK . . . . 61"
WEIGHT . . . . 1,477 LBS.
MSRP $13,395

PRO CAT 9996003

YEARS MFRD 2019-2019
SERIES . . . . PROCAT 6000
ENGINE . . . . KAWASAKI FX730V
CID 726CC
FUEL . . . . G
SPEEDS . . . . VARIABLE
TRANSMISSION . . . . HYDRO
STEERING . . . . ZERO
STANDARD DECK . . . . 11,920"
WEIGHT . . . . 1,371 LBS.
MSRP $11,920

PRO CAT 9996004

YEARS MFRD 2019-2020
SERIES . . . . PROCAT 6000
ENGINE . . . . KAWASAKI FX810V
CID 852CC
FUEL . . . . G
SPEEDS . . . . VARIABLE
TRANSMISSION . . . . HYDRO
STEERING . . . . ZERO
STANDARD DECK . . . . 61"
WEIGHT . . . . 1,421 LBS.
MSRP $11,999

PRO CAT 9996005

YEARS MFRD 2019-2020
SERIES . . . . PROCAT 6000MX
ENGINE . . . . KAWASAKI FX850V
CID 852CC
FUEL . . . . G
SPEEDS . . . . VARIABLE
TRANSMISSION . . . . HYDRO
STEERING . . . . ZERO
STANDARD DECK . . . . 61"
WEIGHT . . . . 1,464 LBS.
MSRP $12,599

PRO CAT 9996006

YEARS MFRD 2019-2019
SERIES . . . . PROCAT 6000MX
ENGINE . . . . KAWASAKI FX850V
CID 852CC
FUEL . . . . G
SPEEDS . . . . VARIABLE
STEERING . . . . ZERO
STANDARD DECK . . . . 61"
WEIGHT . . . . 1,517 LBS.
MSRP $13,713

PRO CAT 9996007

YEARS MFRD 2020-2020
SERIES . . . . PROCAT 6000MX
ENGINE . . . . KAWASAKI FX850V EFI
CID 852CC
FUEL . . . . G
SPEEDS . . . . VARIABLE
TRANSMISSION . . . . HYDRO
STEERING . . . . ZERO
STANDARD DECK . . . . 61"
WEIGHT . . . . 1,464 LBS.
MSRP $13,999

PRO CAT 9996008

YEARS MFRD 2020-2020
SERIES . . . . PROCAT 6000
ENGINE . . . . KAWASAKI FX801V
CID 852CC

FUEL . . . G
SPEEDS . . . VARIABLE
TRANSMISSION . . . HYDRO
STEERING . . . ZERO
STANDARD DECK . . . 52"
WEIGHT . . . 1,371 LBS.
MSRP . . . $11,595

PRO CAT CV740

YEARS MFRD . . . 2008-2008
ENGINE . . KOHLER COMMAND PRO
CYLINDERS . . . 2
CID . . . 725CC
ENGINE HP . . . 27
COOLING . . . AIR
FUEL . . . G
SPEEDS . . . VARIABLE
TRANSMISSION . . . HYDRO
STEERING . . . ZERO
BLADE CLUTCH . . . ELECTRIC

PRO CAT DX

YEARS MFRD . . . 2009-2009
ENGINE . . . KAWASAKI
ENGINE HP . . . 19
COOLING . . . AIR
FUEL . . . G
SPEEDS . . . VARIABLE
TRANSMISSION . . . HYDRO
STEERING . . . ZERO
BLADE CLUTCH . . . ELECTRIC

OPTIONS

B&S 26E

PRO CAT ESTATE

YEARS MFRD . . . 2008-2008
ENGINE . . . B&S
CYLINDERS . . . 2
ENGINE HP . . . 20
COOLING . . . AIR
FUEL . . . G
SPEEDS . . . VARIABLE
TRANSMISSION . . . HYDRO
STEERING . . . ZERO
BLADE CLUTCH . . . ELECTRIC

PRO CAT FH601V

YEARS MFRD . . . 2008-2008
ENGINE . . . KAWASAKI
CYLINDERS . . . 2
CID . . . 675CC
ENGINE HP . . . 19
COOLING . . . AIR
FUEL . . . G
SPEEDS . . . VARIABLE
TRANSMISSION . . . HYDRO
STEERING . . . ZERO
BLADE CLUTCH . . . ELECTRIC

PRO CAT FH641V

YEARS MFRD . . . 2008-2008
ENGINE . . . KAWASAKI
CYLINDERS . . . 2
CID . . . 675CC
ENGINE HP . . . 21
COOLING . . . AIR
FUEL . . . G
SPEEDS . . . VARIABLE
TRANSMISSION . . . HYDRO
STEERING . . . ZERO
BLADE CLUTCH . . . ELECTRIC

PRO CAT FH721V

YEARS MFRD . . . 2008-2008
ENGINE . . . KAWASAKI
CYLINDERS . . . 2
CID . . . 675CC
ENGINE HP . . . 25
COOLING . . . AIR
FUEL . . . G
SPEEDS . . . VARIABLE
TRANSMISSION . . . HYDRO
STEERING . . . ZERO
BLADE CLUTCH . . . ELECTRIC

PRO CAT FX751V

YEARS MFRD . . . 2008-2008
ENGINE . . . KAWASAKI
CYLINDERS . . . 2
CID . . . 852CC
ENGINE HP . . . 27
COOLING . . . AIR
FUEL . . . G
SPEEDS . . . VARIABLE
TRANSMISSION . . . HYDRO
STEERING . . . ZERO
BLADE CLUTCH . . . ELECTRIC

PRO CAT RS 942542

YEARS MFRD . . . 2018-2018
ENGINE . . . KAWASAKI FX801V
TRANSMISSION . . . HYDRO
STEERING . . . ZERO
STANDARD DECK . . . 61"
WEIGHT . . . 1,293 LBS.

PRO CAT RS 942543

YEARS MFRD . . . 2018-2018
ENGINE . . . KAWASAKI FX850V
TRANSMISSION . . . HYDRO
STEERING . . . ZERO
STANDARD DECK . . . 61"
WEIGHT . . . 1,293 LBS.

PRO CAT RS 942546

YEARS MFRD . . . 2018-2018
ENGINE . . . KAWASAKI FX730V
TRANSMISSION . . . HYDRO
STEERING . . . ZERO
STANDARD DECK . . . 52"
WEIGHT . . . 1,256 LBS.

PRO CAT RS 942547

YEARS MFRD . . . 2018-2018
ENGINE . . . KAWASAKI FX850V
TRANSMISSION . . . HYDRO
STEERING . . . ZERO
STANDARD DECK . . . 52"
WEIGHT . . . 1,256 LBS.

PRO CAT VENGEANCE 750

YEARS MFRD . . . 2008-2008
ENGINE . . . YANMAR
CYLINDERS . . . 2
CID . . . 750CC
ENGINE HP . . . 20
COOLING . . . LIQUID
FUEL . . . D
SPEEDS . . . VARIABLE
TRANSMISSION . . . HYDRO
STEERING . . . ZERO
BLADE CLUTCH . . . ELECTRIC

QUICKCAT 912360

YEARS MFRD . . . 2019-2020
SERIES . . . QUICKCAT 4000
ENGINE . . . KAWASAKI FX600V
CID . . . 603CC
ENGINE HP . . . 19
FUEL . . . G
SPEEDS . . . VARIABLE
TRANSMISSION . . . HYDRO
STEERING . . . ZERO
STANDARD DECK . . . 36"
WEIGHT . . . 800 LBS.
MSRP . . . $8,599

QUICKCAT 912480

YEARS MFRD . . . 2019-2020
SERIES . . . QUICKCAT 4000
ENGINE . . . KAWASAKI FX651V
CID . . . 726CC
ENGINE HP . . . 20.5
FUEL . . . G
SPEEDS . . . VARIABLE
TRANSMISSION . . . HYDRO
STEERING . . . ZERO
STANDARD DECK . . . 48"
WEIGHT . . . 961 LBS.
MSRP . . . $8,999

QUICKCAT 912520

YEARS MFRD . . . 2019-2020
SERIES . . . QUICKCAT 4000
ENGINE . . . KAWASAKI FX691V
CID . . . 726CC
ENGINE HP . . . 22
FUEL . . . G
SPEEDS . . . VARIABLE
TRANSMISSION . . . HYDRO
STEERING . . . ZERO
STANDARD DECK . . . 52"
WEIGHT . . . 991 LBS.
MSRP . . . $9,199

QUICKCAT 912521

YEARS MFRD . . . 2020-2020
SERIES . . . QUICKCAT 4000
ENGINE . . . KAWASAKI FX651V
CID . . . 726CC
ENGINE HP . . . 26
FUEL . . . G
SPEEDS . . . VARIABLE
TRANSMISSION . . . HYDRO
STEERING . . . ZERO
STANDARD DECK . . . 52"
WEIGHT . . . 991 LBS.
MSRP . . . $9,699

QUICKCAT 912610

YEARS MFRD . . . 2019-2020
SERIES . . . QUICKCAT 4000
ENGINE . . . KAWASAKI FX730V
CID . . . 726CC
ENGINE HP . . . 23.5
FUEL . . . G
SPEEDS . . . VARIABLE
TRANSMISSION . . . HYDRO
STEERING . . . ZERO
STANDARD DECK . . . 61"
WEIGHT . . . 1,028 LBS.
MSRP . . . $9,499

QUICKCAT 912611

YEARS MFRD . . . 2020-2020
SERIES . . . QUICKCAT 4000
ENGINE . . . KAWASAKI FT730
CID . . . 726CC
ENGINE HP . . . 26
FUEL . . . G
SPEEDS . . . VARIABLE
TRANSMISSION . . . HYDRO
STEERING . . . ZERO
STANDARD DECK . . . 61"

BOB-CAT BY JACOBSEN

WEIGHT ....1,028 LBS.
MSRP................ $9,999

XRZ 942610

YEARS MFRD 2015-2020
ENGINE .... KAWASAKI FR651V
CID 44.3
ENGINE HP 21.5
COOLING .... AIR
FUEL .... G
SPEEDS .... VARIABLE
TRANSMISSION .... HYDRO
STEERING................ ZERO
STANDARD DECK .... 48"
WEIGHT .... 736 LBS.
MSRP................ $5,799

XRZ 942611

YEARS MFRD 2015-2020
ENGINE .... KAWASAKI FR691V
CID 44.3
ENGINE HP 23
COOLING .... AIR
FUEL .... G
SPEEDS .... VARIABLE
TRANSMISSION .... HYDRO
STEERING................ ZERO
STANDARD DECK .... 52"
WEIGHT .... 752 LBS.
MSRP................ $5,899

XRZ 942612

YEARS MFRD 2015-2020
ENGINE .... KAWASAKI FR730V
CID 44.3
ENGINE HP 24
COOLING .... AIR
FUEL .... G
SPEEDS .... VARIABLE
TRANSMISSION .... HYDRO
STEERING................ ZERO
STANDARD DECK .... 61"
WEIGHT .... 795 LBS.
MSRP................ $6,199

XRZ PRO 942620

YEARS MFRD 2017-2020
ENGINE .... KAWASAKI FX691V
CID 44.3
ENGINE HP 20.5
FUEL .... G
SPEEDS .... VARIABLE
TRANSMISSION .... HYDRO
STEERING................ ZERO
BLADE CLUTCH .... ELECTRIC
STANDARD DECK .... 48"
WEIGHT .... 758 LBS.

XRZ PRO 942621

YEARS MFRD 2016-2020
ENGINE .... KAWASAKI FX691V
CID 44.3
ENGINE HP 22
COOLING .... AIR
FUEL .... G
SPEEDS .... VARIABLE
TRANSMISSION .... HYDRO
STEERING................ ZERO
STANDARD DECK .... 52"
WEIGHT .... 774 LBS.

XRZ PRO 942622

YEARS MFRD 2017-2020
ENGINE .... KAWASAKI FX730V
CID 44.3
ENGINE HP 23.5
FUEL .... G
SPEEDS .... VARIABLE
TRANSMISSION .... HYDRO
STEERING................ ZERO
BLADE CLUTCH .... ELECTRIC
STANDARD DECK .... 61"
WEIGHT .... 817 LBS.

XRZ PRO RS 942630

YEARS MFRD 2018-2020
ENGINE .... KAWASAKI FX651V
ENGINE HP 20.5
TRANSMISSION .... HYDRO
STEERING................ ZERO
STANDARD DECK .... 48"
WEIGHT .... 773 LBS.

XRZ PRO RS 942631

YEARS MFRD 2018-2020
ENGINE .... KAWASAKI FX691V
ENGINE HP 22
TRANSMISSION .... HYDRO
STEERING................ ZERO
STANDARD DECK .... 52"
WEIGHT .... 789 LBS.

XRZ PRO RS 942632

YEARS MFRD 2018-2020
ENGINE .... KAWASAKI FX730V
ENGINE HP 23.5
TRANSMISSION .... HYDRO
STEERING................ ZERO
STANDARD DECK .... 61"
WEIGHT .... 832 LBS.

XRZ PRO RS 942633

YEARS MFRD 2020-2020
ENGINE .... KAWASAKI FX850
CID 852CC
FUEL .... G
SPEEDS .... VARIABLE
TRANSMISSION .... HYDRO
STEERING................ ZERO
STANDARD DECK .... 52"
WEIGHT .... 789 LBS.

XRZ PRO RS 942634

YEARS MFRD 2020-2020
ENGINE .... KAWASAKI FX850
CID 852CC
FUEL .... G
SPEEDS .... VARIABLE
TRANSMISSION .... HYDRO
STEERING................ ZERO
STANDARD DECK .... 61"
WEIGHT .... 832 LBS.

ZT120

YEARS MFRD 1999-2000
ENGINE .... KOHLER
ENGINE HP 20
FUEL .... G
TRANSMISSION .... HYDRO
STEERING............ STANDARD
STANDARD DECK .... 42"
MSRP................ $9,625

RETAIL PRICING

YEAR	HIGH	LOW
1999	$2,936	$2,202
2000	$3,270	$2,453

ZT125

YEARS MFRD 1999-2007
ENGINE ...... KOHLER COMMAND
CYLINDERS................... 2
CID 44
ENGINE HP 25
FUEL .... G
SPEEDS .... VARIABLE
TRANSMISSION .... HYDRO
STEERING................ ZERO
BLADE CLUTCH .... ELECTRIC
STANDARD DECK .... 48"
MSRP............... $11,275

RETAIL PRICING

YEAR	HIGH	LOW
1999	$3,104	$2,328
2000	$3,200	$2,400
2001	$3,210	$2,407
2002	$3,406	$2,554
2003	$5,027	$3,771
2004	$5,477	$4,108

ZT218ES

YEARS MFRD 2001-2004
ENGINE .... B&S INTEK V-TWIN
ENGINE HP 18
COOLING .... AIR
FUEL .... G
SPEEDS .... VARIABLE
TRANSMISSION .... HYDRO
STEERING................ ZERO
STANDARD DECK .... 52"
MSRP................ $7,200

RETAIL PRICING

YEAR	HIGH	LOW
2001	$2,386	$1,790
2002	$2,816	$2,112
2003	$3,212	$2,409
2004	$3,624	$2,718

ZT219

YEARS MFRD 2001-2007
SERIES............ 200 SERIES
ENGINE ... KAWASAKI V-TWIN OHV
CYLINDERS................... 2
ENGINE HP 19
COOLING .... AIR
FUEL .... G
SPEEDS .... VARIABLE
TRANSMISSION .... HYDRO
STEERING................ ZERO
STANDARD DECK .... 52"
MSRP................ $7,957

RETAIL PRICING

YEAR	HIGH	LOW
2001	$2,535	$1,901
2002	$2,991	$2,243
2003	$3,548	$2,661

ZT220D

YEARS MFRD 2001-2002
ENGINE .... YANMAR
ENGINE HP 20
FUEL .... D
TRANSMISSION .... HYDRO
STEERING............ STANDARD
STANDARD DECK .... 52"
MSRP............... $10,737

OPTIONS

62" DECK

RETAIL PRICING

YEAR	HIGH	LOW
2001	$3,696	$2,772
2002	$4,360	$3,270

ZT220ES

YEARS MFRD 2005-2007
SERIES.......... ESTATE SERIES
ENGINE .... B&S INTEK
CYLINDERS................... 2
ENGINE HP 18
COOLING .... AIR
FUEL .... G
SPEEDS .... VARIABLE
TRANSMISSION .... HYDRO
STEERING................ ZERO
BLADE CLUTCH .... ELECTRIC

ZT222

YEARS MFRD 1996-1999
ENGINE . . . . KOHLER
ENGINE HP 22
FUEL . . . . G
TRANSMISSION . . . . HYDRO
STEERING. . . . . .STANDARD
STANDARD DECK . . . . 61"
MSRP. $8,400

RETAIL PRICING

YEAR	HIGH	LOW
1996	$1,897	$1,423
1997	$1,966	$1,474
1998	$2,312	$1,734
1999	$2,368	$1,776

ZT223

YEARS MFRD 2000-2007
SERIES. . . . . 200 SERIES
ENGINE . . . KAWASAKI V-TWIN OHV
ENGINE HP 23
COOLING . . . . AIR
FUEL . . . . G
SPEEDS . . . . VARIABLE
TRANSMISSION . . . . HYDRO
STEERING. . . . . ZERO
STANDARD DECK . . . . 52"
MSRP. $8,088

OPTIONS

61" DECK

RETAIL PRICING

YEAR	HIGH	LOW
2000	$2,208	$1,656
2001	$2,227	$1,670
2002	$2,752	$2,064
2003	$2,815	$2,111
2004	$2,949	$2,212
2005	$3,019	$2,265
2006	$3,026	$2,270
2007	$3,063	$2,298

ZT223LC

YEARS MFRD 2001-2004
ENGINE . . . . . KOHLER AEGIS OHV
ENGINE HP 23
COOLING . . . . LIQUID
FUEL . . . . G
SPEEDS . . . . VARIABLE
TRANSMISSION . . . . HYDRO
STEERING. . . . . ZERO
STANDARD DECK . . . . 52"
MSRP. $9,555

OPTIONS

62" DECK

RETAIL PRICING

YEAR	HIGH	LOW
2001	$3,251	$2,438
2002	$3,836	$2,877
2003	$4,261	$3,196
2004	$4,383	$3,287

ZT225

YEARS MFRD 1998-2007
SERIES. . . . . 200 SERIES
ENGINE . . KOHLER COMMAND OHV
CYLINDERS. 2
ENGINE HP 25
FUEL . . . . G
SPEEDS . . . . VARIABLE
TRANSMISSION . . . . HYDRO
STEERING. . . . . ZERO
STANDARD DECK . . . . 61"
MSRP. $9,500

OPTIONS

KAWASAKI 25E

RETAIL PRICING

YEAR	HIGH	LOW
1998	$2,298	$1,724
1999	$2,704	$2,028
2000	$3,084	$2,313
2001	$3,392	$2,544
2002	$3,696	$2,772
2003	$4,237	$3,177

ZT226

YEARS MFRD 2001-2003
ENGINE . . . . KOHLER
ENGINE HP 25
FUEL . . . . G
TRANSMISSION . . . . HYDRO
STEERING. . . . . .STANDARD
STANDARD DECK . . . . 61"
MSRP. $10,751

OPTIONS

72" DECK

RETAIL PRICING

YEAR	HIGH	LOW
2001	$3,493	$2,620
2002	$4,122	$3,091
2003	$4,795	$3,596

ZT226EFI

YEARS MFRD 2004-2004
ENGINE . . KOHLER COMMAND OHV
CYLINDERS. 2
ENGINE HP 26
FUEL . . . . G
SPEEDS . . . . VARIABLE
TRANSMISSION . . . . HYDRO
STEERING. . . . . ZERO

ZT228EFI

YEARS MFRD 2004-2007
SERIES. . . . . 200 SERIES
ENGINE . . . . KOHLER
CYLINDERS. 2
ENGINE HP 26
COOLING . . . . AIR
FUEL . . . . G
SPEEDS . . . . VARIABLE
TRANSMISSION . . . . HYDRO
STEERING. . . . . ZERO
STANDARD DECK . . . . 61"
MSRP. $10,970

OPTIONS

72" DECK

RETAIL PRICING

YEAR	HIGH	LOW
2004	$3,788	$2,841
2005	$3,822	$2,867
2006	$3,904	$2,928
2007	$4,094	$3,071

ZT331

YEARS MFRD 2000-2002
ENGINE . . . . DAIHATSU
ENGINE HP 31
FUEL . . . . G
TRANSMISSION . . . . HYDRO
STEERING. . . . . .STANDARD
STANDARD DECK . . . . 72"
MSRP. $14,452

RETAIL PRICING

YEAR	HIGH	LOW
2000	$4,581	$3,435
2001	$5,032	$3,774
2002	$5,867	$4,400

BOLENS

B1468

YEARS MFRD 1992-1992
ENGINE . . . . B&S
ENGINE HP 14
COOLING . . . . AIR
FUEL . . . . G
TRANSMISSION . . . . GEAR
STEERING. . . . . .STANDARD
STANDARD DECK . . . . 42"
MSRP. $4,200

RETAIL PRICING

YEAR	HIGH	LOW
1992	$353	$265

B2136

YEARS MFRD 1987-1991
ENGINE . . . . B&S
ENGINE HP 12
COOLING . . . . AIR
FUEL . . . . G
TRANSMISSION . . . . GEAR
STEERING. . . . . .STANDARD
STANDARD DECK . . . . 36"
MSRP. $1,830

RETAIL PRICING

YEAR	HIGH	LOW
1991	$571	$428

DGT1700H

YEARS MFRD 1988-1990
ENGINE . . . . MITSUBISHI
ENGINE HP 17
FUEL . . . . D
TRANSMISSION . . . . HYDRO

SERIAL NUMBERS

YEAR	BEGINNING NO.
1988	5117H-01
1989	5117H-02
1990	5117H-03

G152

YEARS MFRD 1978-1990
ENGINE . . . . MITSUBISHI
CID 47.4
ENGINE HP 15
FUEL . . . . D
SPEEDS 6/2
TRANSMISSION . . . . GEAR
WEIGHT . . . . 1,078 LBS.

SERIAL NUMBERS

YEAR	BEGINNING NO.
1978	TX1300-01
1979	TX1300-02
1980	TX1300-03
1981	TX1502-01
1981	TX1300-04
1982	TX1502-02
1983	TX1502-03
1984	TX1502-04
1985	TX1502-05
1986	TX1502-06
1987	TX1502-07
1988	TX1502-08
1989	TX1502-09
1990	TX1502-10

G154

YEARS MFRD 1978-1986
ENGINE . . . . MITSUBISHI
ENGINE HP 15
FUEL . . . . D
TRANSMISSION . . . . GEAR
STEERING. . . . . .STANDARD

G174

YEARS MFRD 1978-1990
ENGINE . . . . MITSUBISHI
CID 51.8
ENGINE HP 17
FUEL . . . . D
SPEEDS 6/2
TRANSMISSION . . . . GEAR
STEERING. . . . . .STANDARD
WEIGHT . . . . 1,178 LBS.
MSRP. $5,800

SERIAL NUMBERS

YEAR	BEGINNING NO.
1978	TX1500F-01
1979	TX1500F-02
1980	TX1500F-03
1981	TX1500F-04
1981	TX1704-01
1982	TX1704-02
1983	TX1704-03
1984	TX1704-04
1985	TX1704-05
1986	TX1704-06
1987	TX1704-07
1988	TX1704-08

BOLENS

1989 .... TX1704-09
1990 .... TX1704-10

RETAIL PRICING

YEAR	HIGH	LOW
1990	$1,701	$1,276

G192

YEARS MFRD 1979-1986
ENGINE .... ISUZU
ENGINE HP 19
FUEL .... D
TRANSMISSION .... GEAR
STEERING .... STANDARD
MSRP $5,819

RETAIL PRICING

YEAR	HIGH	LOW
1986	$1,540	$1,155

G194

YEARS MFRD 1979-1986
ENGINE .... ISUZU
ENGINE HP 19
FUEL .... D
TRANSMISSION .... GEAR
STEERING .... STANDARD

G242

YEARS MFRD 1979-1986
ENGINE .... ISUZU
ENGINE HP 24
FUEL .... D
TRANSMISSION .... GEAR
STEERING .... STANDARD
MSRP $5,995

RETAIL PRICING

YEAR	HIGH	LOW
1986	$1,585	$1,189

G244

YEARS MFRD 1979-1986
ENGINE .... ISUZU
ENGINE HP 24
FUEL .... D
TRANSMISSION .... GEAR
STEERING .... STANDARD
MSRP $6,495

RETAIL PRICING

YEAR	HIGH	LOW
1986	$1,719	$1,289

G616H

YEARS MFRD 2006-2006
ENGINE .... B&S
CYLINDERS 2
ENGINE HP 20
COOLING .... AIR
FUEL .... G
SPEEDS .... VARIABLE
TRANSMISSION .... HYDRO
STEERING .... STANDARD
STANDARD DECK .... 46"
MSRP $2,899

RETAIL PRICING

YEAR	HIGH	LOW
2006	$1,872	$1,404

G3214

YEARS MFRD 1989-1991
ENGINE .... B&S
ENGINE HP 14
COOLING .... AIR
FUEL .... G
SPEEDS 8/2
TRANSMISSION .... GEAR
STEERING .... STANDARD
WEIGHT .... 515 LBS.

GT1800

YEARS MFRD 1986-1991
ENGINE .... B&S
ENGINE HP 18
FUEL .... G
TRANSMISSION .... HYDRO
WEIGHT .... 888 LBS.
MSRP $4,750

SERIAL NUMBERS

YEAR	BEGINNING NO.
1986	1800-01
1987	1800-02
1988	1800-03
1989	1800-04
1990	1800-05
1991	1800-06

RETAIL PRICING

YEAR	HIGH	LOW
1990	$1,393	$1,045
1991	$1,487	$1,115

GT2000

YEARS MFRD 1986-1991
ENGINE .... B&S
ENGINE HP 20
FUEL .... G
TRANSMISSION .... HYDRO
WEIGHT .... 982 LBS.
MSRP $5,125

SERIAL NUMBERS

YEAR	BEGINNING NO.
1986	2000-01
1987	2000-02
1988	2000-03
1989	2000-04
1990	2000-05
1991	2000-06

RETAIL PRICING

YEAR	HIGH	LOW
1990	$1,504	$1,128
1991	$1,603	$1,203

H152H

YEARS MFRD 1986-1991
ENGINE .... MITSUBISHI
ENGINE HP 15
FUEL .... D
TRANSMISSION .... HYDRO

SERIAL NUMBERS

YEAR	BEGINNING NO.
1986	1502H-01
1987	1502H-02
1988	1502H-03
1989	1502H-04
1990	1502H-05
1991	1502H-06

M662F765

YEARS MFRD 2004-2004
SERIES MTD LAWN TRACTOR SERIES
ENGINE .... B&S IC
ENGINE HP 15.5
COOLING .... AIR
FUEL .... G
SPEEDS 6
TRANSMISSION .... HYDRO
STEERING .... STANDARD
PTO .... YES
STANDARD DECK .... 38"
MSRP $869

RETAIL PRICING

YEAR	HIGH	LOW
2004	$501	$375

M762F

YEARS MFRD 2007-2009
ENGINE .... B&S
CYLINDERS 1
ENGINE HP 15.5
COOLING .... AIR
FUEL .... G
SPEEDS 6/1
TRANSMISSION .... DISC
STEERING .... STANDARD

M762F765

YEARS MFRD 2005-2005
ENGINE .... B&S
ENGINE HP 15.5
COOLING .... AIR
FUEL .... G
SPEEDS .... VARIBLE
TRANSMISSION .... HYDRO
STEERING .... STANDARD

N606G

YEARS MFRD 2006-2006
ENGINE .... B&S
CYLINDERS 1
ENGINE HP 17.5
COOLING .... AIR
FUEL .... G
SPEEDS .... VARIABLE
TRANSMISSION .... HYDRO
STEERING .... STANDARD
STANDARD DECK .... 42"
MSRP $2,099

RETAIL PRICING

YEAR	HIGH	LOW
2006	$1,354	$1,016

ST125

YEARS MFRD 2003-2003
ENGINE .... KOHLER
ENGINE HP 12.5
SPEEDS 5

ST160G

YEARS MFRD 1984-1991
ENGINE .... B&S
ENGINE HP 16
FUEL .... G
SPEEDS 3/1
WEIGHT .... 462 LBS.
MSRP $1,800

SERIAL NUMBERS

YEAR	BEGINNING NO.
1984	3016G-01
1985	3016G-02
1986	3016G-03
1987	3016G-04
1988	3016G-05
1989	3016G-06
1990	3016G-07
1991	3016G-08

RETAIL PRICING

YEAR	HIGH	LOW
1990	$527	$395
1991	$564	$423

ST160H

YEARS MFRD 1984-1991
ENGINE .... B&S
ENGINE HP 16
FUEL .... G
TRANSMISSION .... HYDRO
WEIGHT .... 515 LBS.
MSRP $3,000

SERIAL NUMBERS

YEAR	BEGINNING NO.
1984	3016H-01
1985	3016H-02
1986	3016H-03
1987	3016H-04
1988	3016H-05
1990	3216H-01
1991	3216H-02

RETAIL PRICING

YEAR	HIGH	LOW
1990	$880	$660
1991	$938	$703

ST180G

YEARS MFRD 1988-1991
ENGINE .... B&S
CID 42.3
ENGINE HP 18
FUEL .... G
SPEEDS 5/1
WEIGHT .... 515 LBS.
MSRP $3,500

SERIAL NUMBERS

YEAR	BEGINNING NO.
1988	3018G-01
1989	3108G-02
1990	3218G-01
1991	3218G-02

RETAIL PRICING

YEAR	HIGH	LOW
1990	$1,026	$770
1991	$1,095	$821

ST180H

YEARS MFRD	1988-1991
ENGINE	B&S
ENGINE HP	18
FUEL	G
TRANSMISSION	HYDRO
WEIGHT	582 LBS.
MSRP	$3,450

SERIAL NUMBERS

YEAR	BEGINNING NO.
1988	3018H-01
1989	3018H-02
1990	3218H-01
1991	3218H-02

RETAIL PRICING

YEAR	HIGH	LOW
1990	$1,012	$759
1991	$1,081	$810

U616H

YEARS MFRD	2006-2006
ENGINE	B&S
CYLINDERS	2
ENGINE HP	22
COOLING	AIR
FUEL	G
SPEEDS	VARIABLE
TRANSMISSION	HYDRO
STEERING	STANDARD
STANDARD DECK	46"
MSRP	$3,099

RETAIL PRICING

YEAR	HIGH	LOW
2006	$1,999	$1,499

Z816K

YEARS MFRD	2006-2006
ENGINE	B&S
CYLINDERS	2
ENGINE HP	26
FUEL	G
SPEEDS	VARIABLE
TRANSMISSION	HYDRO
STEERING	STANDARD
BLADE CLUTCH	ELECTRIC

13W1762F065

YEARS MFRD	2011-2014
ENGINE	B&S
ENGINE HP	13.5
COOLING	AIR
FUEL	G
SPEEDS	6/1
TRANSMISSION	GEAR
STEERING	STANDARD
STANDARD DECK	38"
MSRP	$949

RETAIL PRICING

YEAR	HIGH	LOW
2011	$269	$202
2012	$359	$269
2013	$427	$320
2014	$517	$388

13W1762F265

YEARS MFRD	2013-2014
ENGINE	B&S
CYLINDERS	1
ENGINE HP	13.5
COOLING	AIR
FUEL	G
SPEEDS	6/1
TRANSMISSION	GEAR
STEERING	STANDARD
STANDARD DECK	38"
MSRP	$1,049

RETAIL PRICING

YEAR	HIGH	LOW
2013	$471	$354
2014	$635	$477

13WC762F065

YEARS MFRD	2011-2012
ENGINE	B&S
ENGINE HP	13.5
COOLING	AIR
FUEL	G
SPEEDS	6/1
TRANSMISSION	GEAR
STEERING	STANDARD
STANDARD DECK	38"
MSRP	$999

RETAIL PRICING

YEAR	HIGH	LOW
2011	$432	$324
2012	$501	$376

762F752

YEARS MFRD	2005-2006
ENGINE	B&S
ENGINE HP	15.5
COOLING	AIR
FUEL	G
SPEEDS	VARIABLE
TRANSMISSION	HYDRO
STEERING	STANDARD
STANDARD DECK	38"
MSRP	$799

RETAIL PRICING

YEAR	HIGH	LOW
2005	$488	$366
2006	$516	$387

944M

YEARS MFRD	1990-1991
ENGINE	B&S
ENGINE HP	12
COOLING	AIR
FUEL	G
TRANSMISSION	GEAR
STEERING	STANDARD
MSRP	$3,145

RETAIL PRICING

YEAR	HIGH	LOW
1991	$760	$570

966M

YEARS MFRD	1991-1993
ENGINE	B&S
ENGINE HP	16
COOLING	AIR
FUEL	G
SPEEDS	VARIABLE
TRANSMISSION	HYDRO
STEERING	STANDARD
STANDARD DECK	42"
MSRP	$4,755

RETAIL PRICING

YEAR	HIGH	LOW
1991	$224	$168
1992	$251	$188
1993	$278	$209

1467

YEARS MFRD	1987-1990
ENGINE	B&S
ENGINE HP	14
COOLING	AIR
FUEL	G
TRANSMISSION	GEAR
STEERING	STANDARD
MSRP	$4,117

RETAIL PRICING

YEAR	HIGH	LOW
1990	$758	$568

1468

YEARS MFRD	1991-1991
ENGINE	B&S
ENGINE HP	14
COOLING	AIR
FUEL	G
TRANSMISSION	GEAR
STEERING	STANDARD
STANDARD DECK	42"
MSRP	$4,206

RETAIL PRICING

YEAR	HIGH	LOW
1991	$568	$426

1502

YEARS MFRD	1984-1993
ENGINE	MITSUBISHI
CID	47.3
PTO HP	13
ENGINE HP	15
FUEL	D
SPEEDS	6/2
TRANSMISSION	GEAR
WEIGHT	1,190 LBS.
MSRP	$7,830

OPTIONS

HYDRO

SERIAL NUMBERS

YEAR	BEGINNING NO.
1984	1502H-01
1985	1502H-02
1986	1502H-03
1987	1502H-04
1988	1502H-05
1989	1502H-06
1990	1502H-07
1991	1504H-08
1992	1504H-09
1993	1504H-10

RETAIL PRICING

YEAR	HIGH	LOW
1990	$1,256	$942
1991	$1,429	$1,072
1992	$1,706	$1,280
1993	$1,882	$1,411

1504

YEARS MFRD	1984-1991
ENGINE	MITSUBISHI
CID	47.3
PTO HP	13
COOLING	AIR
FUEL	D
SPEEDS	6/2
TRANSMISSION	GEAR
STEERING	STANDARD
WEIGHT	1,177 LBS.

SERIAL NUMBERS

YEAR	BEGINNING NO.
1984	1504-01
1985	1504-02
1986	1504-03
1987	1504-04
1988	1504-05
1989	1504-06
1990	1504-07
1991	1504-08

1668

YEARS MFRD	1983-1991
ENGINE	B&S TWIN
ENGINE HP	16
COOLING	AIR
FUEL	G
SPEEDS	4/1
TRANSMISSION	GEAR
STEERING	STANDARD
STANDARD DECK	42"
WEIGHT	737 LBS.
MSRP	$4,621

OPTIONS

HYDRO

SERIAL NUMBERS

YEAR	BEGINNING NO.
1987	1668-01
1988	1668-02
1989	1668-03
1990	1668-04
1991	1668-05

RETAIL PRICING

YEAR	HIGH	LOW
1991	$699	$525

BOLENS

1669

YEARS MFRD 1990-1993
ENGINE .... B&S TWIN
ENGINE HP 16
FUEL .... G
SPEEDS 11/2
WEIGHT .... 737 LBS.
MSRP $5,210

SERIAL NUMBERS

YEAR	BEGINNING NO.
1990	1669-01
1991	1669-02
1992	1669-03
1993	1669-04

RETAIL PRICING

YEAR	HIGH	LOW
1991	$802	$602
1992	$865	$649
1993	$1,002	$752

1669L

YEARS MFRD 1990-1993
ENGINE .... B&S
ENGINE HP 16
COOLING .... AIR
FUEL .... G
SPEEDS .... VARIABLE
TRANSMISSION .... HYDRO
STEERING .... STANDARD
STANDARD DECK .... 48"
MSRP $5,210

RETAIL PRICING

YEAR	HIGH	LOW
1990	$266	$199
1991	$296	$222
1992	$328	$246
1993	$365	$274

1704

YEARS MFRD 1984-1993
ENGINE .... MITSUBISHI
CID 51.8
ENGINE HP 17
FUEL .... D
SPEEDS 6/2
TRANSMISSION .... HYDRO
WEIGHT .... 1,268 LBS.
MSRP $9,950

OPTIONS

TECUMSEH

SERIAL NUMBERS

YEAR	BEGINNING NO.
1984	1704-01
1985	1704-02
1986	1704-03
1987	1704-04
1988	1704-05
1989	1704-06
1990	1704-07
1991	1704-08
1992	1704-09
1993	1704-10

RETAIL PRICING

YEAR	HIGH	LOW
1990	$2,171	$1,628
1991	$2,305	$1,729
1992	$2,428	$1,821
1993	$2,596	$1,947

2102

YEARS MFRD 1984-1991
ENGINE .... ISUZU
CID 71.4
ENGINE HP 21
FUEL .... D
SPEEDS 12/4
WEIGHT .... 1,580 LBS.
MSRP $10,250

SERIAL NUMBERS

YEAR	BEGINNING NO.
1984	2102-01
1985	2102-02
1986	2102-03
1987	2102-04
1988	2102-05
1989	2102-06
1990	2102-07
1991	2102-08

RETAIL PRICING

YEAR	HIGH	LOW
1987	$1,387	$1,040
1988	$1,939	$1,454
1990	$2,259	$1,694
1991	$2,461	$1,846

2104

YEARS MFRD 1984-1991
ENGINE .... ISUZU
CID 71.4
ENGINE HP 21
FUEL .... D
SPEEDS 12/4
WEIGHT .... 1,657 LBS.
MSRP $11,220

SERIAL NUMBERS

YEAR	BEGINNING NO.
1984	2204-01
1985	2204-02
1986	2204-03
1987	2204-04
1988	2204-05
1989	2204-06
1990	2204-07
1991	2204-08

RETAIL PRICING

YEAR	HIGH	LOW
1987	$1,610	$1,208
1988	$2,169	$1,627
1990	$2,543	$1,908
1991	$2,764	$2,073

2702

YEARS MFRD 1984-1991
ENGINE .... ISUZU
CID 79.1
ENGINE HP 27
FUEL .... D
SPEEDS 18/6
WEIGHT .... 2,250 LBS.
MSRP $11,990

SERIAL NUMBERS

YEAR	BEGINNING NO.
1984	2702-01
1985	2702-02
1986	2702-03
1987	2702-04
1988	2702-05
1989	2702-06
1990	2702-07
1991	2702-08

RETAIL PRICING

YEAR	HIGH	LOW
1987	$1,747	$1,310
1988	$2,352	$1,764
1990	$2,770	$2,078
1991	$3,006	$2,255

2704

YEARS MFRD 1984-1991
ENGINE .... ISUZU
CID 79.1
ENGINE HP 27
FUEL .... D
SPEEDS 18/6
WEIGHT .... 2,440 LBS.
MSRP $14,520

SERIAL NUMBERS

YEAR	BEGINNING NO.
1984	2804-01
1985	2804-02
1986	2804-03
1987	2804-04
1988	2804-05
1989	2804-06
1990	2804-07
1991	2804-08

RETAIL PRICING

YEAR	HIGH	LOW
1987	$2,277	$1,707
1988	$3,076	$2,307
1990	$3,512	$2,634
1991	$3,798	$2,848

3010G

YEARS MFRD 1989-1990
ENGINE .... B&S
ENGINE HP 10
COOLING .... AIR
FUEL .... G
SPEEDS 5/1
TRANSMISSION .... GEAR
STEERING .... STANDARD
WEIGHT .... 447 LBS.

3018G

YEARS MFRD 1987-1991
ENGINE .... B&S TWIN
ENGINE HP 18
COOLING .... AIR
FUEL .... G
SPEEDS 5/1
TRANSMISSION .... GEAR
STEERING .... STANDARD
STANDARD DECK .... 48"
WEIGHT .... 555 LBS.
MSRP $2,999

OPTIONS

KOHLER

SERIAL NUMBERS

YEAR	BEGINNING NO.
1987	3018G-01
1988	3018G-02
1989	3018G-03
1990	3018G-04
1991	3018G-05

RETAIL PRICING

YEAR	HIGH	LOW
1990	$793	$595
1991	$938	$703

3018H

YEARS MFRD 1987-1991
ENGINE .... B&S TWIN
ENGINE HP 18
FUEL .... G
TRANSMISSION .... HYDRO
STEERING .... STANDARD
WEIGHT .... 630 LBS.
MSRP $3,450

SERIAL NUMBERS

YEAR	BEGINNING NO.
1987	3018H-01
1988	3018H-02
1989	3018H-03
1990	3018H-04
1991	3018H-05

RETAIL PRICING

YEAR	HIGH	LOW
1990	$803	$602
1991	$857	$643

3114G

YEARS MFRD 1989-1991
ENGINE .... B&S
ENGINE HP 14
COOLING .... AIR
FUEL .... G
TRANSMISSION .... GEAR
STEERING .... STANDARD
STANDARD DECK .... 42"
MSRP $3,375

RETAIL PRICING

YEAR	HIGH	LOW
1991	$832	$624

3212G

YEARS MFRD 1987-1992
ENGINE .... B&S
ENGINE HP 12
COOLING .... AIR
FUEL .... G
TRANSMISSION .... GEAR
STEERING .... STANDARD
STANDARD DECK .... 36"
MSRP $2,980

RETAIL PRICING

YEAR	HIGH	LOW
1992	$671	$503

3214H

YEARS MFRD 1990-1992
ENGINE . . . . B&S
ENGINE HP 14
COOLING . . . . AIR
FUEL . . . . G
TRANSMISSION . . . . GEAR
STEERING . . . . STANDARD
STANDARD DECK . . . . 42"
MSRP $3,299

RETAIL PRICING

YEAR	HIGH	LOW
1990	$471	$354
1991	$538	$404
1992	$605	$454

3216

YEARS MFRD 1990-1992
ENGINE . . . . B&S
ENGINE HP 16
COOLING . . . . AIR
FUEL . . . . G
TRANSMISSION . . . . HYDRO
STEERING . . . . STANDARD
WEIGHT . . . . 535 LBS.
MSRP $3,800

SERIAL NUMBERS

YEAR	BEGINNING NO.
1990	3216H-01
1991	3216H-02
1992	3216H-03

RETAIL PRICING

YEAR	HIGH	LOW
1990	$758	$568
1991	$823	$617
1992	$939	$704

3216H

YEARS MFRD 1990-1992
ENGINE . . . . B&S
ENGINE HP 16
COOLING . . . . AIR
FUEL . . . . G
TRANSMISSION . . . . HYDRO
STEERING . . . . STANDARD
STANDARD DECK . . . . 42"
MSRP $3,775

RETAIL PRICING

YEAR	HIGH	LOW
1992	$781	$586

5117

YEARS MFRD 1987-1991
ENGINE . . . . MITSUBISHI
ENGINE HP 17
COOLING . . . . LIQUID
FUEL . . . . D
TRANSMISSION . . . . HYDRO
STEERING . . . . STANDARD
WEIGHT . . . . 830 LBS.
MSRP $6,900

SERIAL NUMBERS

YEAR	BEGINNING NO.
1987	5117H-01
1988	5117H-02
1989	5117H-03
1990	5217H-01
1991	5217H-02

RETAIL PRICING

YEAR	HIGH	LOW
1990	$1,277	$957
1991	$1,412	$1,059

5117H

YEARS MFRD 1987-1991
ENGINE . . . . MITSUBISHI
ENGINE HP 17
COOLING . . . . LIQUID
FUEL . . . . D
SPEEDS . . . . VARIABLE
TRANSMISSION . . . . HYDRO
STEERING . . . . STANDARD
STANDARD DECK . . . . 48"
MSRP $8,257

RETAIL PRICING

YEAR	HIGH	LOW
1987	$277	$208
1988	$307	$231
1989	$340	$255
1990	$376	$282
1991	$421	$316

5118H

YEARS MFRD 1987-1993
ENGINE . . . . KOHLER
ENGINE HP 18
COOLING . . . . AIR
FUEL . . . . G
SPEEDS . . . . VARIABLE
TRANSMISSION . . . . HYDRO
STEERING . . . . STANDARD
STANDARD DECK . . . . 48"
MSRP $6,430

SERIAL NUMBERS

YEAR	BEGINNING NO.
1987	5118H-01
1988	5118H-02
1989	5118H-03
1990	5218H-01
1991	5218H-02
1992	5218H-03
1993	5218H-04

RETAIL PRICING

YEAR	HIGH	LOW
1987	$240	$180
1988	$266	$199
1989	$296	$222
1990	$328	$246
1991	$362	$271
1992	$402	$301
1993	$445	$334

5118HS

YEARS MFRD 1987-1993
ENGINE . . . . KOHLER TWIN
CYLINDERS 2
ENGINE HP 18
FUEL . . . . G
TRANSMISSION . . . . HYDRO
STEERING . . . . STANDARD
STANDARD DECK . . . . 48"
WEIGHT . . . . 830 LBS.
MSRP $7,300

SERIAL NUMBERS

YEAR	BEGINNING NO.
1987	5118HS-01
1988	5118HS-02
1989	5118HS-03
1990	5218HS-01
1991	5218HS-02
1992	5218HS-03
1993	5218HS-04

RETAIL PRICING

YEAR	HIGH	LOW
1990	$1,043	$782
1991	$1,162	$872
1992	$1,500	$1,125
1993	$1,705	$1,279

5120

YEARS MFRD 1987-1993
ENGINE . . . . KOHLER TWIN
ENGINE HP 20
FUEL . . . . G
TRANSMISSION . . . . HYDRO
STEERING . . . . STANDARD
STANDARD DECK . . . . 60"
WEIGHT . . . . 914 LBS.
MSRP $8,500

SERIAL NUMBERS

YEAR	BEGINNING NO.
1987	5120H-01
1988	5120H-01
1988	5120H-02
1989	5120H-03
1990	5220H-01
1991	5220H-02
1992	5220H-03
1993	5220H-04

RETAIL PRICING

YEAR	HIGH	LOW
1990	$1,131	$848
1991	$1,256	$942
1992	$1,924	$1,443
1993	$2,110	$1,582

5120H

YEARS MFRD 1987-1993
ENGINE . . . . KOHLER
ENGINE HP 20
COOLING . . . . AIR
FUEL . . . . G
SPEEDS . . . . VARIABLE
TRANSMISSION . . . . HYDRO
STEERING . . . . STANDARD
STANDARD DECK . . . . 60"
MSRP $8,513

RETAIL PRICING

YEAR	HIGH	LOW
1987	$319	$239
1988	$351	$263
1989	$391	$293
1990	$434	$325
1991	$479	$359
1992	$533	$399
1993	$589	$442

13003

YEARS MFRD 1992-1992
ENGINE . . . . B&S
ENGINE HP 12.5
COOLING . . . . AIR
FUEL . . . . G
TRANSMISSION . . . . GEAR
STEERING . . . . STANDARD
STANDARD DECK . . . . 33"
MSRP $1,751

RETAIL PRICING

YEAR	HIGH	LOW
1992	$569	$427

13007

YEARS MFRD 1993-1993
ENGINE . . . . B&S
ENGINE HP 12.5
COOLING . . . . AIR
FUEL . . . . G
TRANSMISSION . . . . GEAR
STEERING . . . . STANDARD
STANDARD DECK . . . . 33"
MSRP $1,735

RETAIL PRICING

YEAR	HIGH	LOW
1993	$583	$437

13014

YEARS MFRD 1993-1993
ENGINE . . . . B&S
ENGINE HP 14
COOLING . . . . AIR
FUEL . . . . G
TRANSMISSION . . . . HYDRO
STEERING . . . . STANDARD
STANDARD DECK . . . . 42"
MSRP $3,285

RETAIL PRICING

YEAR	HIGH	LOW
1993	$1,105	$829

13016

YEARS MFRD 1992-1993
ENGINE . . . . B&S
ENGINE HP 16
COOLING . . . . AIR
FUEL . . . . G
TRANSMISSION . . . . HYDRO
STEERING . . . . STANDARD
STANDARD DECK . . . . 42"
MSRP $3,799

BOLENS

RETAIL PRICING

YEAR	HIGH	LOW
1992	$1,238	$928
1993	$1,277	$957

13023

YEARS MFRD 1993-1993
ENGINE .... KOHLER
ENGINE HP 12.5
COOLING .... AIR
FUEL .... G
TRANSMISSION .... GEAR
STEERING .... STANDARD
STANDARD DECK .... 36"
MSRP $2,300

RETAIL PRICING

YEAR	HIGH	LOW
1993	$774	$581

13024

YEARS MFRD 1993-1993
ENGINE .... KOHLER
ENGINE HP 12.5
COOLING .... AIR
FUEL .... G
TRANSMISSION .... HYDRO
STEERING .... STANDARD
STANDARD DECK .... 36"
MSRP $2,799

RETAIL PRICING

YEAR	HIGH	LOW
1993	$940	$705

13055

YEARS MFRD 1994-1995
ENGINE .... B&S
ENGINE HP 8
COOLING .... AIR
FUEL .... G
TRANSMISSION .... GEAR
STEERING .... STANDARD
STANDARD DECK .... 36"
MSRP $1,359

RETAIL PRICING

YEAR	HIGH	LOW
1995	$501	$376

13056

YEARS MFRD 1994-1994
ENGINE .... B&S
ENGINE HP 12.5
COOLING .... AIR
FUEL .... G
STEERING .... STANDARD
STANDARD DECK .... 33"
MSRP $1,706

RETAIL PRICING

YEAR	HIGH	LOW
1994	$605	$454

13058

YEARS MFRD 1994-1994
ENGINE .... B&S
ENGINE HP 12.5
COOLING .... AIR
FUEL .... G
TRANSMISSION .... GEAR
STEERING .... STANDARD
STANDARD DECK .... 39"
MSRP $1,599

RETAIL PRICING

YEAR	HIGH	LOW
1994	$566	$425

13059

YEARS MFRD 1994-1995
ENGINE .... B&S
ENGINE HP 12.5
COOLING .... AIR
FUEL .... G
TRANSMISSION .... HYDRO
STEERING .... STANDARD

13067

YEARS MFRD 1995-1995
ENGINE .... B&S
CYLINDERS 1
ENGINE HP 12.5
COOLING .... AIR
FUEL .... G
TRANSMISSION .... GEAR
STEERING .... STANDARD
STANDARD DECK .... 33"
MSRP $1,799

RETAIL PRICING

YEAR	HIGH	LOW
1995	$664	$498

13070

YEARS MFRD 1995-1995
ENGINE .... B&S
ENGINE HP 12.5
COOLING .... AIR
FUEL .... G
TRANSMISSION .... GEAR
STEERING .... STANDARD
STANDARD DECK .... 40"
MSRP $1,599

RETAIL PRICING

YEAR	HIGH	LOW
1995	$589	$442

13072

YEARS MFRD 1996-1996
ENGINE .... B&S
ENGINE HP 12.5
COOLING .... AIR
FUEL .... G
TRANSMISSION .... GEAR
STEERING .... STANDARD
STANDARD DECK .... 40"
MSRP $1,699

RETAIL PRICING

YEAR	HIGH	LOW
1996	$648	$486

13073

YEARS MFRD 1996-1996
ENGINE .... B&S
ENGINE HP 12.5
COOLING .... AIR
FUEL .... G
TRANSMISSION .... GEAR
STEERING .... STANDARD
STANDARD DECK .... 40"
MSRP $2,149

RETAIL PRICING

YEAR	HIGH	LOW
1996	$820	$615

BRANSON

F3550

YEARS MFRD 1999-2001
ENGINE .... MITSUBISHI
CYLINDERS 4
CID 107.24
PTO HP 30.5
ENGINE HP 35.5
FUEL .... D
SPEEDS 12/12
TRANSMISSION ... SHUTTLE SHIFT
STEERING .... STANDARD
DRIVE TYPE 2WD
ROPS/CAB .... ROPS
WEIGHT .... 3,530 LBS.
MSRP $15,947

RETAIL PRICING

YEAR	HIGH	LOW
1999	$7,149	$5,362
2000	$7,495	$5,621
2001	$7,816	$5,862

F4350

YEARS MFRD 1999-2001
ENGINE .... YANMAR
CYLINDERS 4
CID 133.5
PTO HP 37
ENGINE HP 43
FUEL .... D
SPEEDS 12/12
TRANSMISSION ... SHUTTLE SHIFT
DRIVE TYPE 2WD
ROPS/CAB .... ROPS
WEIGHT .... 3,891 LBS.

1905HST

YEARS MFRD 2017-2020
SERIES .... 05 SERIES
ENGINE ...... YANMAR 3TNV74F
CYLINDERS 3
CID 993CC
PTO HP 13.4
ENGINE HP 19
FUEL .... G
TRANSMISSION .... HYDRO
HITCH .... CAT. I
WEIGHT .... 1,433 LBS.

2100

YEARS MFRD 2008-2010
SERIES .... 00 SERIES
ENGINE .... 4 CYCLE
CYLINDERS 3
CID 65.4
PTO HP 18
ENGINE HP 21
COOLING .... LIQUID
FUEL .... D
SPEEDS 6/2
TRANSMISSION .... GEAR
STEERING .... STANDARD
HITCH .... CAT. I
HYDRAULIC .... YES
PTO .... YES
WEIGHT .... 1,791 LBS.
MSRP $11,975

RETAIL PRICING

YEAR	HIGH	LOW
2010	$7,466	$5,599

2400

YEARS MFRD 2008-2020
SERIES .... 00 SERIES
ENGINE A1100N2
CYLINDERS 3
CID 71.7
PTO HP 18
ENGINE HP 24
FUEL .... D
SPEEDS 6/2
TRANSMISSION .... GEAR
STEERING .... STANDARD
HITCH .... CAT. I
HYDRAULIC .... YES
PTO .... YES
DRIVE TYPE 2WD
ROPS/CAB .... ROPS
WEIGHT .... 1,810 LBS.

RETAIL PRICING

YEAR	HIGH	LOW
2010	$5,362	$4,021
2011	$6,142	$4,606
2012	$6,729	$5,047
2013	$7,214	$5,410
2014	$7,695	$5,771
2015	$8,307	$6,231
2016	$8,565	$6,424
2017	$9,045	$6,784
2018	$10,312	$7,734
2019	$11,388	$8,541
2020	$12,076	$9,057

2400H

YEARS MFRD 2008-2020
SERIES .... 00 SERIES
ENGINE A1100N2
CYLINDERS 3
CID 65.4

ENGINE HP 21
FUEL . . . . D
SPEEDS . . . . 2 SPEED
TRANSMISSION . . . . HYDRO
STEERING . . . . STANDARD
HYDRAULIC . . . . YES
PTO . . . . YES
WEIGHT . . . . 1,810 LBS.

RETAIL PRICING

YEAR	HIGH	LOW
2010	$5,553	$4,165
2011	$6,457	$4,843
2012	$7,675	$5,757
2013	$7,820	$5,865
2014	$8,369	$6,277
2015	$8,763	$6,572
2016	$9,660	$7,245
2017	$10,314	$7,735
2018	$10,910	$8,183
2019	$12,163	$9,122
2020	$12,776	$9,582

2510H

YEARS MFRD 2018-2020
SERIES . . . . 10 SERIES
ENGINE A1100N2
CYLINDERS 3
CID 1175CC
PTO HP 18
ENGINE HP 25
COOLING . . . . LIQUID
FUEL . . . . D
TRANSMISSION . . . . HYDRO
STEERING . . . . STANDARD
HITCH . . . . CAT. I
PTO . . . . YES
DRIVE TYPE 4WD
ROPS/CAB . . . . ROPS
WEIGHT . . . . 1,810 LBS.

2515H

YEARS MFRD 2020-2020
SERIES . . . . 15 SERIES
ENGINE A1700N6-UTR3
CYLINDERS 3
CID 1714CC
PTO HP 19
ENGINE HP 24
COOLING . . . . LIQUID
FUEL . . . . D
SPEEDS . . . . 3 RANGE
TRANSMISSION . . . . HYDRO
STEERING . . . . STANDARD
HITCH . . . . CAT. I
DRIVE TYPE 4WD
ROPS/CAB . . . . ROPS
WEIGHT . . . . 3,014 LBS.

2515R

YEARS MFRD 2020-2020
SERIES . . . . 15 SERIES
ENGINE A1700N6-UTR3
CYLINDERS 3
PTO HP 19
ENGINE HP 24.5
COOLING . . . . LIQUID
FUEL . . . . D
SPEEDS 12/12
TRANSMISSION SYNCHRO SHUTTLE
STEERING . . . . STANDARD
HITCH . . . . CAT. I
DRIVE TYPE 4WD
ROPS/CAB . . . . ROPS
WEIGHT . . . . 3,014 LBS.

2800

YEARS MFRD 2008-2014
SERIES . . . . 00 SERIES
ENGINE A1100T1
CYLINDERS 3
CID 65.4
PTO HP 25
ENGINE HP 28
FUEL . . . . D
SPEEDS 6/2
TRANSMISSION . . . . GEAR
STEERING . . . . STANDARD
HITCH . . . . CAT. I
HYDRAULIC . . . . YES
PTO . . . . YES
WEIGHT . . . . 1,815 LBS.
MSRP $14,676

RETAIL PRICING

YEAR	HIGH	LOW
2010	$6,582	$4,936
2011	$8,091	$6,068
2012	$8,512	$6,384
2013	$9,048	$6,786
2014	$9,324	$6,993

2800H

YEARS MFRD 2008-2014
SERIES . . . . 00 SERIES
CYLINDERS 3
CID 65.4
PTO HP 25
ENGINE HP 28
FUEL . . . . D
SPEEDS 2SPEED
TRANSMISSION . . . . HYDRO
STEERING . . . . STANDARD
HITCH . . . . CAT. I
HYDRAULIC . . . . YES
PTO . . . . YES
WEIGHT . . . . 1,815 LBS.
MSRP $15,570

RETAIL PRICING

YEAR	HIGH	LOW
2010	$6,856	$5,142
2011	$8,307	$6,231
2012	$8,831	$6,623
2013	$9,462	$7,096
2014	$9,850	$7,387

2810

YEARS MFRD 2000-2004
SERIES . . . . 10 SERIES
ENGINE 3T84L-ATC
CYLINDERS 3
CID 95.28
PTO HP 25
ENGINE HP 28
COOLING . . . . LIQUID
FUEL . . . . D
SPEEDS 12/12
TRANSMISSION . . . . GEAR
STEERING . . . . STANDARD
HITCH . . . . CAT. I
PTO . . . . YES
WEIGHT . . . . 3,330 LBS.

2910

YEARS MFRD 2005-2007
SERIES . . . . 10 SERIES
ENGINE A1400N3
CYLINDERS 3
CID 89.1
ENGINE HP 29
COOLING . . . . LIQUID
FUEL . . . . D
SPEEDS 12/12
TRANSMISSION . . . . POWER SHIFT
STEERING . . . . STANDARD
HITCH . . . . CAT. I
PTO . . . . YES
WEIGHT . . . . 3,708 LBS.

2910I

YEARS MFRD 2008-2009
SERIES . . . . 10 SERIES
CYLINDERS 3
CID 1461CC
ENGINE HP 29
COOLING . . . . LIQUID
FUEL . . . . D
SPEEDS 12/12
TRANSMISSION . . . SHUTTLE SHIFT
STEERING . . . . STANDARD
HITCH . . . . CAT. I
HYDRAULIC . . . . YES
PTO . . . . YES
WEIGHT . . . . 3,715 LBS.
MSRP $14,580

RETAIL PRICING

YEAR	HIGH	LOW
2009	$8,129	$6,097

3015H

YEARS MFRD 2016-2020
SERIES . . . . 15 SERIES
ENGINE A1700N5
CYLINDERS 3
CID 1714CC
ENGINE HP 30
COOLING . . . . LIQUID
FUEL . . . . D
TRANSMISSION . . . . HYDRO
HITCH . . . . CAT. I
DRIVE TYPE 4WD
WEIGHT . . . . 3,014 LBS.

3015R

YEARS MFRD 2016-2020
SERIES . . . . 15 SERIES
ENGINE A1700N5
CYLINDERS 3
CID 1714CC
PTO HP 28
ENGINE HP 30
COOLING . . . . LIQUID
FUEL . . . . D
SPEEDS 12/12
TRANSMISSION . . . SHUTTLE SHIFT
STEERING . . . . STANDARD
HITCH . . . . CAT. I
DRIVE TYPE 4WD
ROPS/CAB . . . . ROPS
WEIGHT . . . . 3,014 LBS.

3110I

YEARS MFRD 2010-2014
SERIES . . . . 10 SERIES
ENGINE A1500N2
CYLINDERS 3
ENGINE HP 31
COOLING . . . . LIQUID
FUEL . . . . D
SPEEDS 12/12
TRANSMISSION . . . SHUTTLE SHIFT
STEERING . . . . STANDARD
WEIGHT . . . . 3,735 LBS.
MSRP $16,980

RETAIL PRICING

YEAR	HIGH	LOW
2010	$7,068	$5,301
2011	$8,764	$6,573
2012	$9,935	$7,451
2013	$10,288	$7,716
2014	$10,703	$8,027

3120R

YEARS MFRD 2011-2017
ENGINE A1500N2-R
CYLINDERS 3
CID 1562CC
ENGINE HP 31
COOLING . . . . LIQUID
FUEL . . . . D
SPEEDS 12/12
TRANSMISSION . . . SHUTTLE SHIFT
STEERING . . . . STANDARD
HITCH . . . . CAT. I
WEIGHT . . . . 4,053 LBS.

3510

YEARS MFRD 2001-2007
SERIES . . . . 10 SERIES
ENGINE . . . . YANMAR 4TNE-88
CYLINDERS 3
CID 109.43
PTO HP 31
ENGINE HP 35
COOLING . . . . LIQUID
FUEL . . . . D
SPEEDS 12/12
TRANSMISSION . . . . GEAR

BRANSON

STEERING............STANDARD
HITCH..................CAT. I
PTO.....................YES
WEIGHT............3,756 LBS.

OPTIONS

HYDRO

3510HST

YEARS MFRD........2008-2011
SERIES..............10 SERIES
ENGINE..............A1700N2
CYLINDERS..................3
CID..................1714CC
ENGINE HP..................35
COOLING..................AIR
FUEL........................D
SPEEDS..............3SPEED
TRANSMISSION..........HYDRO
STEERING............STANDARD
HITCH..................CAT. I
HYDRAULIC...............YES
PTO.....................YES
WEIGHT............3,695 LBS.
MSRP................$18,731

RETAIL PRICING

YEAR	HIGH	LOW
2010	$10,805	$8,103
2011	$11,889	$8,917

3510I

YEARS MFRD........2008-2014
SERIES..............10 SERIES
ENGINE..............A1700N2
CYLINDERS..................3
CID..................1741CC
ENGINE HP..................35
COOLING...............LIQUID
FUEL........................D
SPEEDS...................12/12
TRANSMISSION ... SHUTTLE SHIFT
STEERING............STANDARD
HITCH..................CAT. I
HYDRAULIC...............YES
PTO.....................YES
WEIGHT............3,760 LBS.
MSRP................$18,520

RETAIL PRICING

YEAR	HIGH	LOW
2010	$8,252	$6,189
2011	$9,296	$6,972
2012	$11,077	$8,308
2013	$11,475	$8,606
2014	$12,127	$9,095

3515H

YEARS MFRD........2017-2020
SERIES..............15 SERIES
ENGINE..............A1700N4
CYLINDERS..................3
CID..................1714CC
PTO HP.....................30
ENGINE HP..................35
COOLING...............LIQUID
FUEL........................D
TRANSMISSION..........HYDRO
HITCH..................CAT. I
DRIVE TYPE...............4WD
WEIGHT............3,014 LBS.

3515R

YEARS MFRD........2016-2020
SERIES..............15 SERIES
ENGINE..............A1700N4
CYLINDERS..................3
CID..................1714CC
PTO HP.....................30
ENGINE HP..................35
COOLING...............LIQUID
FUEL........................D
SPEEDS...................12/12
TRANSMISSION ... SHUTTLE SHIFT
STEERING............STANDARD
HITCH..................CAT. I
WEIGHT............3,014 LBS.

3520

YEARS MFRD........2001-2004
SERIES..............20 SERIES
ENGINE.......KUKJE 3T90L-ATC
CYLINDERS..................4
CID...................109.43
ENGINE HP..................35
COOLING...............LIQUID
FUEL........................D
SPEEDS...................12/12
TRANSMISSION............GEAR
STEERING............STANDARD
HITCH..................CAT. I
WEIGHT............3,762 LBS.

3520H

YEARS MFRD........2016-2020
SERIES..............20 SERIES
ENGINE..............A1700N2
CYLINDERS..................3
CID..................2286CC
PTO HP.....................29
ENGINE HP..................35
COOLING...............LIQUID
FUEL........................D
SPEEDS...............VARIABLE
TRANSMISSION..........HYDRO
STEERING............STANDARD
HITCH..................CAT. I
DRIVE TYPE...............4WD
ROPS/CAB................ROPS
WEIGHT............4,053 LBS.

3520R

YEARS MFRD........2011-2020
ENGINE............A1700N2-R
CYLINDERS..................3
CID..................1714CC
ENGINE HP..................35
COOLING...............LIQUID
FUEL........................D
SPEEDS...................12/12
TRANSMISSION ... SHUTTLE SHIFT
STEERING............STANDARD
HITCH..................CAT. I
WEIGHT............4,053 LBS.

3725C

YEARS MFRD........2017-2020
ENGINE........A2000N3-UTC-4
CYLINDERS..................4
CID..................2084CC
PTO HP.....................33
ENGINE HP..................37
COOLING...............LIQUID
FUEL........................D
SPEEDS...................12/12
STEERING............STANDARD
HITCH..................CAT. I
DRIVE TYPE...............4WD
ROPS/CAB..................CAB
WEIGHT............4,210 LBS.

3725CH

YEARS MFRD........2017-2020
ENGINE........A1700N3-UTC-4
CYLINDERS..................4
CID..................2084CC
PTO HP.....................32
ENGINE HP..................37
COOLING...............LIQUID
FUEL........................D
SPEEDS...................12/12
STEERING............STANDARD
HITCH..................CAT. I
DRIVE TYPE...............4WD
ROPS/CAB..................CAB
WEIGHT............4,195 LBS.

3725H

YEARS MFRD........2017-2020
SERIES..............25 SERIES
ENGINE..............A2000N3
PTO HP.....................32
ENGINE HP..................37
COOLING...............LIQUID
FUEL........................D
TRANSMISSION..........HYDRO
HITCH..................CAT. I
DRIVE TYPE...............4WD
WEIGHT............3,716 LBS.

3725R

YEARS MFRD........2017-2020
ENGINE........A2000N3-UTR-4
CYLINDERS..................4
CID..................2084CC
PTO HP.....................33
ENGINE HP..................37
COOLING...............LIQUID
FUEL........................D
SPEEDS...................12/12
STEERING............STANDARD
HITCH..................CAT. I
DRIVE TYPE...............4WD
ROPS/CAB................ROPS
WEIGHT............3,677 LBS.

3820

YEARS MFRD........2005-2007
SERIES..............20 SERIES
ENGINE..................KUKJE
CYLINDERS..................4
CID...................127.2
ENGINE HP..................38
COOLING...............LIQUID
FUEL........................D
SPEEDS...................12/12
TRANSMISSION............GEAR
STEERING............STANDARD
HITCH..................CAT. I
HYDRAULIC...............YES
PTO.....................YES
WEIGHT............4,087 LBS.

3820I

YEARS MFRD........2008-2014
SERIES..............20 SERIES
ENGINE..............A2000N3
CYLINDERS..................4
CID..................2084CC
ENGINE HP..................38
COOLING...............LIQUID
FUEL........................D
SPEEDS...................12/12
TRANSMISSION ... SHUTTLE SHIFT
STEERING............STANDARD
HITCH..................CAT. I
HYDRAULIC...............YES
PTO.....................YES
WEIGHT............4,090 LBS.
MSRP................$19,437

RETAIL PRICING

YEAR	HIGH	LOW
2010	$9,090	$6,817
2011	$10,215	$7,661
2012	$11,327	$8,495
2013	$11,746	$8,810
2014	$12,791	$9,593

4015H

YEARS MFRD........2017-2020
SERIES..............15 SERIES
ENGINE..............A1700T2
CYLINDERS..................3
CID..................1714CC
PTO HP.....................35
ENGINE HP..................40
FUEL........................D
TRANSMISSION..........HYDRO
HITCH..................CAT. I
DRIVE TYPE...............4WD
WEIGHT............3,014 LBS.

4015R

YEARS MFRD........2016-2020
SERIES..............15 SERIES
ENGINE..............A1700T2
CYLINDERS..................3
CID..................1714CC
PTO HP.....................35
ENGINE HP..................40
COOLING...............LIQUID

FUEL . . . . D
SPEEDS 12/12
TRANSMISSION . . . SHUTTLE SHIFT
STEERING. . . . . STANDARD
HITCH . . . . CAT. I
DRIVE TYPE 4WD
ROPS/CAB . . . . ROPS
WEIGHT . . . . 3,014 LBS.

4020

YEARS MFRD 2001-2004
SERIES. . . . . 20 SERIES
ENGINE . . . . KUKJE 3T90LT-ATC
CYLINDERS. 4
CID 109.43
ENGINE HP 40
COOLING . . . . LIQUID
FUEL . . . . D
SPEEDS 12/12
TRANSMISSION . . . . HYDRO
STEERING. . . . . STANDARD
HITCH . . . . CAT. I
PTO . . . . YES
WEIGHT . . . . 3,795 LBS.

4020R

YEARS MFRD 2011-2020
ENGINE A1700T1
CYLINDERS. 3
CID 1714CC
ENGINE HP 40
COOLING . . . . LIQUID
FUEL . . . . D
SPEEDS 12/12
TRANSMISSION . . . SHUTTLE SHIFT
STEERING. . . . . STANDARD
HITCH . . . . CAT. I
HYDRAULIC . . . . YES
PTO . . . . YES
WEIGHT . . . . 4,063 LBS.

4220

YEARS MFRD 2005-2007
SERIES. . . . . 20 SERIES
ENGINE . . . . KUKJE
CYLINDERS. 4
CID 127.2
ENGINE HP 42
COOLING . . . . LIQUID
FUEL . . . . D
SPEEDS 12/12
TRANSMISSION . . . . GEAR
STEERING. . . . . STANDARD
HITCH . . . . CAT. I
HYDRAULIC . . . . YES
PTO . . . . YES
WEIGHT . . . . 4,105 LBS.

4220I

YEARS MFRD 2008-2011
SERIES. . . . . 20 SERIES
ENGINE A2000N2
CYLINDERS. 4
CID 2084
PTO HP 35
ENGINE HP 42
COOLING . . . . LIQUID
FUEL . . . . D
SPEEDS 12/12
TRANSMISSION . . . SHUTTLE SHIFT
STEERING. . . . . STANDARD
HITCH . . . . CAT. I
HYDRAULIC . . . . YES
PTO . . . . YES
WEIGHT . . . . 4,106 LBS.
MSRP. $19,244

RETAIL PRICING

YEAR	HIGH	LOW
2010	$11,502	$8,627
2011	$12,658	$9,493

4225C

YEARS MFRD 2017-2020
ENGINE A2000N2-UTC-4
CYLINDERS. 4
CID 2084CC
PTO HP 36
ENGINE HP 42
COOLING . . . . LIQUID
FUEL . . . . D
SPEEDS 12/12
STEERING. . . . . STANDARD
HITCH . . . . CAT. I
DRIVE TYPE 4WD
ROPS/CAB . . . . CAB

4225CH

YEARS MFRD 2017-2020
ENGINE A1700N2-UYC-4
CYLINDERS. 4
CID 2084CC
PTO HP 34.5
ENGINE HP 42
COOLING . . . . LIQUID
FUEL . . . . D
SPEEDS 12/12
STEERING. . . . . STANDARD
HITCH . . . . CAT. I
DRIVE TYPE 4WD
ROPS/CAB . . . . CAB
WEIGHT . . . . 4,195 LBS.

4225H

YEARS MFRD 2017-2020
SERIES. . . . . 25 SERIES
ENGINE A2000N2
CYLINDERS. 4
CID 2084CC
PTO HP 34.5
ENGINE HP 42
COOLING . . . . LIQUID
FUEL . . . . D
TRANSMISSION . . . . HYDRO
HITCH . . . . CAT. I
DRIVE TYPE 4WD
WEIGHT . . . . 3,716 LBS.

4225R

YEARS MFRD 2017-2020
SERIES. . . . . 25 SERIES
ENGINE A2000N2
CYLINDERS. 4
CID 2084CC
PTO HP 36
ENGINE HP 42
COOLING . . . . LIQUID
FUEL . . . . D
TRANSMISSION . . . SHUTTLE SHIFT
HITCH . . . . CAT. I
DRIVE TYPE 4WD
WEIGHT . . . . 3,677 LBS.

4520

YEARS MFRD 2001-2004
SERIES. . . . . 20 SERIES
ENGINE . . . . YANMAR 4TNE-88
CYLINDERS. 4
CID 133.53
ENGINE HP 45
COOLING . . . . LIQUID
FUEL . . . . D
SPEEDS 12/12
TRANSMISSION . . . . GEAR
STEERING. . . . . STANDARD
HITCH . . . . CAT. I
PTO . . . . YES
WEIGHT . . . . 3,883 LBS.

4520C

YEARS MFRD 2013-2020
SERIES. . . . . 20C SERIES
ENGINE . . . . KUKJE A2300N2-R
CYLINDERS. 4
CID 2286CC
PTO HP 42
ENGINE HP 47
COOLING . . . . LIQUID
FUEL . . . . D
SPEEDS 12/12
TRANSMISSION . . . SHUTTLE SHIFT
STEERING. . . . . STANDARD
HITCH . . . . CAT. I
WEIGHT . . . . 4,118 LBS.

4520R

YEARS MFRD 2013-2015
SERIES. . . . . 20R SERIES
ENGINE . . . . KUKJE A2300N2-R
CYLINDERS. 4
CID 2286CC
PTO HP 42
ENGINE HP 47
COOLING . . . . LIQUID
FUEL . . . . D
SPEEDS 12/12
TRANSMISSION . . . SHUTTLE SHIFT
STEERING. . . . . STANDARD
HITCH . . . . CAT. I
HYDRAULIC . . . . YES
PTO . . . . YES
WEIGHT . . . . 4,118 LBS.

4720

YEARS MFRD 2005-2007
SERIES. . . . . 20 SERIES
ENGINE . . . . KUKJE
CYLINDERS. 4
CID 139.5
ENGINE HP 47
COOLING . . . . LIQUID
FUEL . . . . D
SPEEDS 12/12
TRANSMISSION . . . . GEAR
STEERING. . . . . STANDARD
HITCH . . . . CAT. I
HYDRAULIC . . . . YES
PTO . . . . YES
WEIGHT . . . . 4,116 LBS.

4720CH

YEARS MFRD 2017-2020
SERIES. . . . . 20 SERIES
ENGINE A2300N2
CYLINDERS. 4
CID 2286CC
PTO HP 42
ENGINE HP 47
COOLING . . . . LIQUID
FUEL . . . . D
TRANSMISSION . . . . HYDRO
HITCH . . . . CAT. I
DRIVE TYPE 4WD
WEIGHT . . . . 4,219 LBS.

4720H

YEARS MFRD 2008-2011
SERIES. . . . . 20 SERIES
ENGINE . . . . KUKJE A2300N2
CYLINDERS. 4
CID 2286CC
ENGINE HP 47
COOLING . . . . LIQUID
FUEL . . . . D
SPEEDS 3SPEED
TRANSMISSION . . . . HYDRO
STEERING. . . . . STANDARD
HITCH . . . . CAT. I
HYDRAULIC . . . . YES
PTO . . . . YES
WEIGHT . . . . 4,015 LBS.
MSRP. $22,408

RETAIL PRICING

YEAR	HIGH	LOW
2010	$14,224	$10,668
2011	$14,326	$10,744

4720I

YEARS MFRD 2008-2011
SERIES. . . . . 20 SERIES
ENGINE . . . . KUKJE A2300N2
CYLINDERS. 4
CID 2286CC
PTO HP 42
ENGINE HP 47
COOLING . . . . LIQUID
FUEL . . . . D
SPEEDS 12/12
TRANSMISSION . . . SHUTTLE SHIFT

BRANSON

STEERING. . . . . .STANDARD
HITCH . . . . CAT. I
HYDRAULIC . . . . YES
PTO . . . . YES
WEIGHT . . . . .4,117 LBS.
MSRP. $21,216

RETAIL PRICING

YEAR	HIGH	LOW
2010	$13,468	$10,101
2011	$13,525	$10,144

BUSH HOG

CZ2149

YEARS MFRD 2007-2009
SERIES. . . . . .COMMERCIAL SERIES
ENGINE . . . . KAWASAKI
CYLINDERS. 2
ENGINE HP 21
COOLING . . . . .AIR
FUEL . . . . G
SPEEDS . . . . VARIABLE
TRANSMISSION . . . . .HYDRO
STEERING. . . . . ZERO
BLADE CLUTCH . . . . ELECTRIC
STANDARD DECK . . . . 49"
WEIGHT . . . . .1,230 LBS.
MSRP. $8,229

OPTIONS

10 BU BAG
CANOPY
SUS SEAT

RETAIL PRICING

YEAR	HIGH	LOW
2007	$2,127	$1,595
2008	$2,347	$1,760
2009	$2,590	$1,943

CZ2349

YEARS MFRD 2007-2009
SERIES. . . . . .COMMERCIAL SERIES
ENGINE . . KOHLER COMMAND PRO
CYLINDERS. 2
ENGINE HP 23
COOLING . . . . .AIR
FUEL . . . . G
SPEEDS . . . . VARIABLE
TRANSMISSION . . . . .HYDRO
STEERING. . . . . ZERO
BLADE CLUTCH . . . . ELECTRIC
STANDARD DECK . . . . 49"
WEIGHT . . . . .1,230 LBS.
MSRP. $8,629

OPTIONS

10 BU BAG
CANOPY
SUS SEAT

RETAIL PRICING

YEAR	HIGH	LOW
2007	$2,230	$1,673
2008	$2,461	$1,846
2009	$2,716	$2,037

CZ2355

YEARS MFRD 2007-2011
SERIES. . . . . .COMMERCIAL SERIES
ENGINE . . KOHLER COMMAND PRO
CYLINDERS. 2
ENGINE HP 23
COOLING . . . . .AIR
FUEL . . . . G
SPEEDS . . . . VARIABLE
TRANSMISSION . . . . .HYDRO
STEERING. . . . . ZERO
BLADE CLUTCH . . . . ELECTRIC
STANDARD DECK . . . . 55"
WEIGHT . . . . .1,270 LBS.
MSRP. $8,582

OPTIONS

10 BU BAG
CANOPY
SUS SEAT

RETAIL PRICING

YEAR	HIGH	LOW
2007	$2,178	$1,633
2008	$2,404	$1,803
2009	$2,654	$1,990
2010	$2,928	$2,196
2011	$3,233	$2,425

CZ2555

YEARS MFRD 2007-2011
SERIES. . . . . .COMMERCIAL SERIES
ENGINE . . . . KAWASAKI FH72IV
CYLINDERS. 2
ENGINE HP 25
COOLING . . . . .AIR
FUEL . . . . G
SPEEDS . . . . VARIABLE
TRANSMISSION . . . . .HYDRO
STEERING. . . . . ZERO
BLADE CLUTCH . . . . ELECTRIC
STANDARD DECK . . . . 55"
WEIGHT . . . . .1,270 LBS.
MSRP. $8,582

OPTIONS

10 BU BAG
CANOPY
SUS SEAT

RETAIL PRICING

YEAR	HIGH	LOW
2007	$2,178	$1,633
2008	$2,404	$1,803
2009	$2,654	$1,990
2010	$2,928	$2,196
2011	$3,233	$2,425

CZ2561

YEARS MFRD 2007-2011
SERIES. . . . . .COMMERCIAL SERIES
ENGINE . . . . KAWASAKI FH72IV
CYLINDERS. 2
ENGINE HP 25
COOLING . . . . .AIR
FUEL . . . . G
SPEEDS . . . . VARIABLE
TRANSMISSION . . . . .HYDRO
STEERING. . . . . ZERO
BLADE CLUTCH . . . . ELECTRIC
STANDARD DECK . . . . 61"
WEIGHT . . . . .1,295 LBS.
MSRP. $8,872

OPTIONS

10 BU BAG
CANOPY
SUS SEAT

RETAIL PRICING

YEAR	HIGH	LOW
2007	$2,252	$1,689
2008	$2,486	$1,865
2009	$2,742	$2,057
2010	$3,027	$2,270
2011	$3,342	$2,506

EC2555

YEARS MFRD 2013-2016
ENGINE . . . . KOHLER
ENGINE HP 25
COOLING . . . . .AIR
FUEL . . . . G
SPEEDS . . . . VARIABLE
TRANSMISSION . . . . .HYDRO
STEERING. . . . . ZERO
STANDARD DECK . . . . 55"
MSRP. $8,556

OPTIONS

BAR TIRES
CANOPY
SUSPENSION SEAT

RETAIL PRICING

YEAR	HIGH	LOW
2013	$3,469	$2,602
2014	$3,828	$2,871
2015	$4,226	$3,169
2016	$4,664	$3,498

EC2561

YEARS MFRD 2011-2014
ENGINE . . . . KOHLER
ENGINE HP 25
COOLING . . . . .AIR
FUEL . . . . G
SPEEDS . . . . VARIABLE
TRANSMISSION . . . . .HYDRO
STEERING. . . . . ZERO
STANDARD DECK . . . . 61"
MSRP. $8,660

OPTIONS

CANOPY
SUSPENSION SEAT

RETAIL PRICING

YEAR	HIGH	LOW
2011	$3,560	$2,670
2012	$3,369	$2,527
2013	$3,718	$2,789
2014	$4,105	$3,079

EC2655

YEARS MFRD 2011-2012
ENGINE . . . . KAWASAKI
ENGINE HP 26
COOLING . . . . .AIR
FUEL . . . . G
SPEEDS . . . . VARIABLE
TRANSMISSION . . . . . DUAL HYDRO
STEERING. . . . . ZERO
STANDARD DECK . . . . 55"
MSRP. $8,115

OPTIONS

SUS SEAT

RETAIL PRICING

YEAR	HIGH	LOW
2011	$3,029	$2,272
2012	$3,345	$2,509

EC2661

YEARS MFRD 2011-2012
ENGINE . . . . KAWASAKI
ENGINE HP 26
COOLING . . . . .AIR
FUEL . . . . G
SPEEDS . . . . VARIABLE
TRANSMISSION . . . . . DUAL HYDRO
STEERING. . . . . ZERO
STANDARD DECK . . . . 61"
MSRP. $8,208

OPTIONS

SUS SEAT

RETAIL PRICING

YEAR	HIGH	LOW
2011	$3,064	$2,298
2012	$3,382	$2,536

EC2761

YEARS MFRD 2013-2016
ENGINE . . . . KOHLER
ENGINE HP 27
COOLING . . . . .AIR
FUEL . . . . G
SPEEDS . . . . VARIABLE
TRANSMISSION . . . . . DUAL HYDRO
STEERING. . . . . ZERO
STANDARD DECK . . . . 61"
MSRP. $8,730

OPTIONS

BAR TIRES
CANOPY
SUSPENSION SEAT

RETAIL PRICING

YEAR	HIGH	LOW
2013	$3,597	$2,697
2014	$3,969	$2,977
2015	$4,382	$3,286
2016	$4,836	$3,627

ES1644

YEARS MFRD 2009-2009
SERIES. . . . . .ESTATE SERIES
ENGINE . . . . HONDA GXV530
CYLINDERS. 2

ENGINE HP 16
COOLING . . . . . AIR
FUEL . . . . . G
SPEEDS . . . . . VARIABLE
TRANSMISSION . . . . . HYDRO
STEERING . . . . . ZERO
BLADE CLUTCH . . . . . ELECTRIC

ES1744B2

YEARS MFRD 2007-2009
SERIES . . . . . ESTATE SERIES
ENGINE . . . . B&S INTEK OHV 500CC
ENGINE HP 17
COOLING . . . . . AIR
FUEL . . . . . G
SPEEDS . . . . . VARIABLE
TRANSMISSION . . . . . HYDRO
STEERING . . . . . ZERO
PTO . . . . . YES
STANDARD DECK . . . . . 44"
MSRP $4,999

OPTIONS

2P ROPS
CANOPY
SUS SEAT

RETAIL PRICING

YEAR	HIGH	LOW
2007	$1,292	$969
2008	$1,426	$1,069
2009	$1,574	$1,180

ES1844

YEARS MFRD 2004-2006
SERIES . . . . . ESTATE SERIES
ENGINE . . . . . B&S INTEK OHV
CYLINDERS 2
CID 656CC
ENGINE HP 18
COOLING . . . . . AIR
FUEL . . . . . G
SPEEDS . . . . . VARIABLE
TRANSMISSION . . . . . HYDRO
STEERING . . . . . ZERO

ES1852

YEARS MFRD 2004-2006
SERIES . . . . . ESTATE SERIES
ENGINE . . . . . B&S INTEK OHV
CYLINDERS 2
CID 656CC
ENGINE HP 18
COOLING . . . . . AIR
FUEL . . . . . G
SPEEDS . . . . . VARIABLE
TRANSMISSION . . . . . HYDRO
STEERING . . . . . ZERO

ES2044B2

YEARS MFRD 2007-2016
SERIES . . . . . ESTATE SERIES
ENGINE . . . . . KOHLER
CYLINDERS 2
CID 725CC
ENGINE HP 20
COOLING . . . . . AIR
FUEL . . . . . G
SPEEDS . . . . . VARIABLE
TRANSMISSION . . . . . DUAL HYDRO
STEERING . . . . . ZERO
STANDARD DECK . . . . . 44"
WEIGHT . . . . . 725 LBS.
MSRP $6,163

OPTIONS

2 POST ROPS
CANOPY
SUSPENSION SEAT

RETAIL PRICING

YEAR	HIGH	LOW
2007	$1,398	$1,049
2008	$1,548	$1,161
2009	$1,709	$1,282
2010	$1,887	$1,415
2011	$2,084	$1,563
2012	$2,298	$1,724
2013	$2,537	$1,903
2014	$2,800	$2,100
2015	$3,091	$2,318
2016	$3,411	$2,559

ES2044KH3

YEARS MFRD 2012-2014
ENGINE . . . . . KOHLER
ENGINE HP 20
COOLING . . . . . AIR
FUEL . . . . . G
SPEEDS . . . . . VARIABLE
TRANSMISSION . . . . . HYDRO
STEERING . . . . . STANDARD
STANDARD DECK . . . . . 44"
WEIGHT . . . . . 725 LBS.
MSRP $5,695

RETAIL PRICING

YEAR	HIGH	LOW
2012	$2,046	$1,535
2013	$2,465	$1,849
2014	$3,183	$2,387

ES2052B2

YEARS MFRD 2007-2016
SERIES . . . . . ESTATE SERIES
ENGINE . . . . . KOHLER
CYLINDERS 2
ENGINE HP 20
COOLING . . . . . AIR
FUEL . . . . . G
SPEEDS . . . . . VARIABLE
TRANSMISSION . . . . . DUAL HYDRO
STEERING . . . . . ZERO
STANDARD DECK . . . . . 52"
WEIGHT . . . . . 750 LBS.
MSRP $6,828

OPTIONS

2 POST ROPS
7 BU BAG
HONDA
SUSPENSION SEAT

RETAIL PRICING

YEAR	HIGH	LOW
2007	$1,591	$1,193
2008	$1,720	$1,290
2009	$1,898	$1,424
2010	$2,093	$1,570
2011	$2,310	$1,732
2012	$2,546	$1,910
2013	$2,813	$2,109
2014	$3,103	$2,327
2015	$3,424	$2,568
2016	$3,779	$2,834

ES2052KH3

YEARS MFRD 2012-2014
ENGINE . . . . . KOHLER
ENGINE HP 20
COOLING . . . . . AIR
FUEL . . . . . G
SPEEDS . . . . . VARIABLE
TRANSMISSION . . . . . HYDRO
STANDARD DECK . . . . . 52"
WEIGHT . . . . . 750 LBS.
MSRP $5,829

RETAIL PRICING

YEAR	HIGH	LOW
2012	$2,098	$1,574
2013	$2,587	$1,940
2014	$3,410	$2,558

ES2244

YEARS MFRD 2008-2008
SERIES . . . . . ESTATE SERIES
ENGINE . . . . . B&S ELS
CYLINDERS 2
ENGINE HP 22
COOLING . . . . . AIR
FUEL . . . . . G
SPEEDS . . . . . VARIABLE
TRANSMISSION . . . . . DUAL HYDRO
STEERING . . . . . ZERO
BLADE CLUTCH . . . . . ELECTRIC
STANDARD DECK . . . . . 44"
MSRP $5,319

RETAIL PRICING

YEAR	HIGH	LOW
2008	$1,628	$1,221

ES2252

YEARS MFRD 2008-2008
ENGINE . . . . . B&S
CYLINDERS 2
ENGINE HP 22
COOLING . . . . . AIR
FUEL . . . . . G
SPEEDS . . . . . VARIABLE
TRANSMISSION . . . . . HYDRO
STEERING . . . . . ZERO
BLADE CLUTCH . . . . . ELECTRIC
STANDARD DECK . . . . . 52"
MSRP $5,519

RETAIL PRICING

YEAR	HIGH	LOW
2008	$1,689	$1,266

ES2344

YEARS MFRD 2009-2009
SERIES . . . . . ESTATE SERIES
ENGINE . . . . . B&S
CYLINDERS 2
ENGINE HP 23
COOLING . . . . . AIR
FUEL . . . . . G
SPEEDS . . . . . VARIABLE
TRANSMISSION . . . . . DUAL HYDRO
STEERING . . . . . ZERO
STANDARD DECK . . . . . 44"
MSRP $5,639

RETAIL PRICING

YEAR	HIGH	LOW
2009	$1,775	$1,331

ES2352K2

YEARS MFRD 2007-2013
SERIES . . . . . ESTATE SERIES
ENGINE . . . . . KOHLER
CYLINDERS 2
CID 725CC
ENGINE HP 23
COOLING . . . . . AIR
FUEL . . . . . G
SPEEDS . . . . . VARIABLE
TRANSMISSION . . . . . DUAL HYDRO
STEERING . . . . . ZERO
BLADE CLUTCH . . . . . ELECTRIC
STANDARD DECK . . . . . 52"
WEIGHT . . . . . 750 LBS.
MSRP $6,562

OPTIONS

2P ROPS
B&S
CANOPY
SUS SEAT

RETAIL PRICING

YEAR	HIGH	LOW
2007	$1,624	$1,218
2008	$1,792	$1,344
2009	$1,979	$1,484
2010	$2,183	$1,638
2011	$2,410	$1,807
2012	$2,660	$1,995
2013	$2,936	$2,202

ES2452

YEARS MFRD 2011-2012
ENGINE . . . . . KAWASAKI
ENGINE HP 24
COOLING . . . . . AIR
FUEL . . . . . G
SPEEDS . . . . . VARIABLE
TRANSMISSION . . . . . DUAL HYDRO
STEERING . . . . . ZERO
STANDARD DECK . . . . . 52"
MSRP $6,232

OPTIONS

2P ROPS
BAGGER
CANOPY
SUS SEAT

RETAIL PRICING

YEAR	HIGH	LOW
2011	$2,327	$1,745
2012	$2,568	$1,926

BUSH HOG

ES2552

YEARS MFRD 2013-2016
ENGINE . . . . KOHLER
ENGINE HP 25
COOLING . . . . AIR
FUEL . . . . G
SPEEDS . . . . VARIABLE
TRANSMISSION . . . . HYDRO
STEERING . . . . ZERO
STANDARD DECK . . . . 52"
MSRP $6,649

OPTIONS

CANOPY
SUSPENSION SEAT

RETAIL PRICING

YEAR	HIGH	LOW
2013	$2,737	$2,053
2014	$3,021	$2,266
2015	$3,334	$2,500
2016	$3,680	$2,760

HDC2355FS2

YEARS MFRD 2018-2019
SERIES . . . . HDC 2 SERIES
ENGINE . . . . KAWASAKI FS691
ENGINE HP 23
FUEL . . . . G
SPEEDS . . . . VARIABLE
TRANSMISSION . . . . . DUAL HYDRO
STEERING . . . . ZERO
STANDARD DECK . . . . 55"
MSRP $8,784

HDC2361

YEARS MFRD 2017-2018
ENGINE . . . . KAWASAKI
ENGINE HP 23
FUEL . . . . G
SPEEDS . . . . VARIABLE
TRANSMISSION . . . . HYDRO
STEERING . . . . ZERO
STANDARD DECK . . . . 61"
MSRP $8,684

OPTIONS

55" DECK
BAR TIRES
SUS SEAT

RETAIL PRICING

YEAR	HIGH	LOW
2017	$5,113	$3,834
2018	$5,319	$3,990

HDC2361FS2

YEARS MFRD 2018-2019
SERIES . . . . HDC 2 SERIES
ENGINE . . . . KAWASAKI FS691
ENGINE HP 23
FUEL . . . . G
SPEEDS . . . . VARIABLE
TRANSMISSION . . . . . DUAL HYDRO
STEERING . . . . ZERO
STANDARD DECK . . . . 61"
MSRP $9,223

HDC2361FS3

YEARS MFRD 2020-2020
SERIES . . . . HDC 3 SERIES
ENGINE . . . . KAWASAKI FS691
ENGINE HP 23
FUEL . . . . G
SPEEDS . . . . VARIABLE
TRANSMISSION . . . . HYDRO
STEERING . . . . ZERO
ROPS/CAB . . . . ROPS
STANDARD DECK . . . . 61"

HDC2555

YEARS MFRD 2017-2018
ENGINE . . . . B&S
ENGINE HP 25
FUEL . . . . G
SPEEDS . . . . VARIABLE
TRANSMISSION . . . . HYDRO
STEERING . . . . ZERO
STANDARD DECK . . . . 55"
MSRP $8,232

OPTIONS

61" DECK
BAR TIRES
KOHLER 25HP
SUS SEAT

RETAIL PRICING

YEAR	HIGH	LOW
2017	$4,846	$3,635
2018	$5,251	$3,938

HDC2555KP2

YEARS MFRD 2018-2019
SERIES . . . . HDC 2 SERIES
ENGINE . . . . KOHLER KT740
ENGINE HP 25
FUEL . . . . G
SPEEDS . . . . VARIABLE
TRANSMISSION . . . . . DUAL HYDRO
STEERING . . . . ZERO
STANDARD DECK . . . . 55"
MSRP $8,728

HDC2561KP2

YEARS MFRD 2018-2019
SERIES . . . . HDC 2 SERIES
ENGINE . . . . KOHLER KT740
ENGINE HP 25
FUEL . . . . G
SPEEDS . . . . VARIABLE
TRANSMISSION . . . . . DUAL HYDRO
STEERING . . . . ZERO
STANDARD DECK . . . . 61"
MSRP $8,813

HDC2561KP3

YEARS MFRD 2020-2020
SERIES . . . . HDC 3 SERIES
ENGINE . . . . KOHLER KT740
ENGINE HP 25
FUEL . . . . G
SPEEDS . . . . VARIABLE
TRANSMISSION . . . . HYDRO
STEERING . . . . ZERO
ROPS/CAB . . . . ROPS
STANDARD DECK . . . . 61"

HDC2661

YEARS MFRD 2017-2018
ENGINE . . . . KOHLER
ENGINE HP 26
FUEL . . . . G
SPEEDS . . . . VARIABLE
TRANSMISSION . . . . HYDRO
STEERING . . . . ZERO
STANDARD DECK . . . . 61"
MSRP $8,310

OPTIONS

BAR TIRES
SUS SEAT

RETAIL PRICING

YEAR	HIGH	LOW
2017	$4,782	$3,587
2018	$5,348	$4,011

HDC2761

YEARS MFRD 2017-2018
ENGINE . . . . B&S
ENGINE HP 27
FUEL . . . . G
SPEEDS . . . . VARIABLE
TRANSMISSION . . . . HYDRO
STEERING . . . . ZERO
STANDARD DECK . . . . 61"
MSRP $8,121

OPTIONS

BAR TIRES
SUS SEAT

RETAIL PRICING

YEAR	HIGH	LOW
2017	$4,781	$3,586
2018	$5,677	$4,258

HDE2049

YEARS MFRD 2017-2018
ENGINE . . . . B&S
ENGINE HP 20
FUEL . . . . G
SPEEDS . . . . VARIABLE
TRANSMISSION . . . . . DUAL HYDRO
STEERING . . . . ZERO
STANDARD DECK . . . . 49"
MSRP $6,236

OPTIONS

BAR TIRES
KOHLER 20HP
SUS SEAT

RETAIL PRICING

YEAR	HIGH	LOW
2017	$3,672	$2,754
2018	$4,551	$3,413

HDE2049KT2

YEARS MFRD 2018-2019
SERIES . . . . HDE 2 SERIES
ENGINE . . . . KOHLER KT715
ENGINE HP 20
FUEL . . . . G
SPEEDS . . . . VARIABLE
TRANSMISSION . . . . . DUAL HYDRO
STEERING . . . . ZERO
STANDARD DECK . . . . 49"
MSRP $6,718

HDE2049KT3

YEARS MFRD 2020-2020
SERIES . . . . HDE 3 SERIES
ENGINE . . . . KOHLER KT715
ENGINE HP 20
FUEL . . . . G
SPEEDS . . . . VARIABLE
TRANSMISSION . . . . . DUAL HYDRO
STEERING . . . . ZERO
ROPS/CAB . . . . ROPS
STANDARD DECK . . . . 49"

HDE2249

YEARS MFRD 2018-2018
ENGINE . . . . KAWASAKI
ENGINE HP 22
FUEL . . . . G
TRANSMISSION . . . . HYDRO
STEERING . . . . ZERO
MSRP $6,447

OPTIONS

61" DECK
CANOPY
SUS SEAT

HDE2249FS2

YEARS MFRD 2018-2019
SERIES . . . . HDE 2 SERIES
ENGINE . . . . KAWASAKI FS651
ENGINE HP 22
FUEL . . . . G
SPEEDS . . . . VARIABLE
TRANSMISSION . . . . . DUAL HYDRO
STEERING . . . . ZERO
STANDARD DECK . . . . 49"
MSRP $6,874

HDE2249FS3

YEARS MFRD 2020-2020
SERIES . . . . HDE 3 SERIES
ENGINE . . . . KAWASAKI FS651
ENGINE HP 22
FUEL . . . . G
SPEEDS . . . . VARIABLE
TRANSMISSION . . . . . DUAL HYDRO
STEERING . . . . ZERO
ROPS/CAB . . . . ROPS
STANDARD DECK . . . . 49"

HDE2255FS2

YEARS MFRD 2018-2019
SERIES. . . . . .HDE 2 SERIES
ENGINE . . . . KAWASAKI FS651
ENGINE HP 22
FUEL . . . . G
SPEEDS . . . . .VARIABLE
TRANSMISSION . . . . . DUAL HYDRO
STEERING. . . . . ZERO
STANDARD DECK . . . . 55"
MSRP. $6,887

HDE2255FS3

YEARS MFRD 2020-2020
SERIES. . . . . .HDE 3 SERIES
ENGINE . . . . KAWASAKI FS651
ENGINE HP 22
FUEL . . . . G
SPEEDS . . . . .VARIABLE
TRANSMISSION . . . . . DUAL HYDRO
STEERING. . . . . ZERO
ROPS/CAB . . . . ROPS
STANDARD DECK . . . . 55"

HDE2261FS2

YEARS MFRD 2018-2019
SERIES. . . . . .HDE 2 SERIES
ENGINE . . . . KAWASAKI FS651
ENGINE HP 22
SPEEDS . . . . .VARIABLE
TRANSMISSION . . . . . DUAL HYDRO
STEERING. . . . . ZERO
STANDARD DECK . . . . 61"
MSRP. $6,974

HDE2261FS3

YEARS MFRD 2020-2020
SERIES. . . . . .HDE 3 SERIES
ENGINE . . . . KAWASAKI FS651
ENGINE HP 22
FUEL . . . . G
SPEEDS . . . . .VARIABLE
TRANSMISSION . . . . . DUAL HYDRO
STEERING. . . . . ZERO
ROPS/CAB . . . . ROPS
STANDARD DECK . . . . 61"

HDE2361

YEARS MFRD 2017-2018
ENGINE . . . . KAWASAKI FS
ENGINE HP 23
SPEEDS . . . . .VARIABLE
TRANSMISSION . . . . . DUAL HYDRO
STEERING. . . . . ZERO
STANDARD DECK . . . . 61"
MSRP. $6,650

OPTIONS

BAR TIRES
SUS SEAT

RETAIL PRICING

YEAR	HIGH	LOW
2017	$3,826	$2,869
2018	$4,418	$3,313

HDE2549

YEARS MFRD 2018-2018
ENGINE . . . . B&S
ENGINE HP 25
FUEL . . . . G
TRANSMISSION . . . . . DUAL HYDRO
STEERING. . . . . ZERO
STANDARD DECK . . . . 49"
MSRP. $6,179

OPTIONS

CANOPY
SUS SEAT

HDE2549PS2

YEARS MFRD 2018-2019
SERIES. . . . . .HDE 2 SERIES
ENGINE . . . . . . B&S PROFESSIONAL
ENGINE HP 25
FUEL . . . . G
SPEEDS . . . . .VARIABLE
TRANSMISSION . . . . . DUAL HYDRO
STEERING. . . . . ZERO
STANDARD DECK . . . . 49"

HDE2555

YEARS MFRD 2017-2018
ENGINE . . . . B&S
ENGINE HP 25
FUEL . . . . G
SPEEDS . . . . .VARIABLE
TRANSMISSION . . . . . DUAL HYDRO
STEERING. . . . . ZERO
STANDARD DECK . . . . 55"
MSRP. $6,321

OPTIONS

BAR TIRES
KAWASAKI 25HP
SUS SEAT

RETAIL PRICING

YEAR	HIGH	LOW
2017	$3,637	$2,728
2018	$4,114	$3,086

HDE2555KP2

YEARS MFRD 2018-2019
SERIES. . . . . .HDE 2 SERIES
ENGINE . . . . .KOHLER 7000 SERIES
ENGINE HP 25
FUEL . . . . G
SPEEDS . . . . .VARIABLE
TRANSMISSION . . . . . DUAL HYDRO
STEERING. . . . . ZERO
STANDARD DECK . . . . 55"
MSRP. $6,803

HDE2555KP3

YEARS MFRD 2020-2020
SERIES. . . . . .HDE 3 SERIES
ENGINE . . . . KOHLER KT740
ENGINE HP 25
FUEL . . . . G
SPEEDS . . . . .VARIABLE
TRANSMISSION . . . . . DUAL HYDRO
STEERING. . . . . ZERO
ROPS/CAB . . . . ROPS
STANDARD DECK . . . . 55"

HDE2555PS2

YEARS MFRD 2018-2019
SERIES. . . . . .HDE 2 SERIES
ENGINE . . . . . . B&S PROFESSIONAL
ENGINE HP 25
FUEL . . . . G
SPEEDS . . . . .VARIABLE
TRANSMISSION . . . . . DUAL HYDRO
STEERING. . . . . ZERO
STANDARD DECK . . . . 55"

HDE2561

YEARS MFRD 2017-2018
ENGINE . . . . B&S
ENGINE HP 25
FUEL . . . . G
SPEEDS . . . . .VARIABLE
TRANSMISSION . . . . . DUAL HYDRO
STEERING. . . . . ZERO
STANDARD DECK . . . . 61"
MSRP. $6,365

OPTIONS

BAR TIRES
KOHLER
SUS SEAT

RETAIL PRICING

YEAR	HIGH	LOW
2017	$3,674	$2,756
2018	$4,439	$3,330

HDE2561KP2

YEARS MFRD 2018-2019
SERIES. . . . . .HDE 2 SERIES
ENGINE . . . . .KOHLER 7000 SERIES
ENGINE HP 25
FUEL . . . . G
SPEEDS . . . . .VARIABLE
TRANSMISSION . . . . . DUAL HYDRO
STEERING. . . . . ZERO
STANDARD DECK . . . . 61"
MSRP. $6,890

HDE2561KP3

YEARS MFRD 2020-2020
SERIES. . . . . .HDE 3 SERIES
ENGINE . . . . KOHLER KT740
ENGINE HP 25
FUEL . . . . G
SPEEDS . . . . .VARIABLE
TRANSMISSION . . . . . DUAL HYDRO
STEERING. . . . . ZERO
ROPS/CAB . . . . ROPS
STANDARD DECK . . . . 61"

HDE2561PS2

YEARS MFRD 2018-2019
SERIES. . . . . .HDE 2 SERIES
ENGINE . . . . . . B&S PROFESSIONAL
ENGINE HP 25
FUEL . . . . G
SPEEDS . . . . .VARIABLE
TRANSMISSION . . . . . DUAL HYDRO
STEERING. . . . . ZERO
STANDARD DECK . . . . 61"

HDZ2661

YEARS MFRD 2017-2018
ENGINE . . . . B&S
ENGINE HP 26
FUEL . . . . G
SPEEDS . . . . .VARIABLE
TRANSMISSION . . . . HYDRO
STEERING. . . . . ZERO
STANDARD DECK . . . . 61"
MSRP. $10,025

OPTIONS

BAR TIRES

RETAIL PRICING

YEAR	HIGH	LOW
2017	$5,768	$4,326
2018	$6,733	$5,049

HDZ2761

YEARS MFRD 2017-2018
ENGINE . . . . KOHLER
ENGINE HP 27
FUEL . . . . G
SPEEDS . . . . .VARIABLE
TRANSMISSION . . . . HYDRO
STEERING. . . . . ZERO
STANDARD DECK . . . . 61"
MSRP. $10,581

OPTIONS

73" DECK
BAR TIRES

RETAIL PRICING

YEAR	HIGH	LOW
2017	$6,229	$4,672
2018	$7,404	$5,553

HDZ2761CV2

YEARS MFRD 2018-2019
SERIES. . . . . .HDZ 2 SERIES
ENGINE . . KOHLER COMMAND PRO
ENGINE HP 27
FUEL . . . . G
SPEEDS . . . . .VARIABLE
TRANSMISSION . . . . . DUAL HYDRO
STEERING. . . . . ZERO
STANDARD DECK . . . . 61"
MSRP. $11,501

HDZ2773

YEARS MFRD 2017-2018
ENGINE . . . . KOHLER
ENGINE HP 27
FUEL . . . . G
SPEEDS . . . . .VARIABLE
TRANSMISSION . . . . HYDRO
STEERING. . . . . ZERO
STANDARD DECK . . . . 73"
MSRP. $10,910

BUSH HOG

OPTIONS

BAR TIRES

RETAIL PRICING

YEAR	HIGH	LOW
2017	$6,277	$4,708
2018	$7,453	$5,590

HDZ2773CV2

YEARS MFRD 2018-2019
SERIES . . . . HDZ 2 SERIES
ENGINE . . KOHLER COMMAND PRO
ENGINE HP 27
FUEL . . . . G
SPEEDS . . . . VARIABLE
TRANSMISSION . . . . . DUAL HYDRO
STEERING . . . . ZERO
STANDARD DECK . . . . 73"
MSRP $11,865

HDZ3161

YEARS MFRD 2017-2018
ENGINE . . . . KAWASAKI
ENGINE HP 31
FUEL . . . . G
SPEEDS . . . . VARIABLE
TRANSMISSION . . . . HYDRO
STEERING . . . . ZERO
STANDARD DECK . . . . 61"
MSRP $10,594

OPTIONS

73" DECK
BAR TIRES

RETAIL PRICING

YEAR	HIGH	LOW
2017	$6,237	$4,678
2018	$7,394	$5,546

HDZ3161FX2

YEARS MFRD 2018-2019
SERIES . . . . HDZ 2 SERIES
ENGINE . . . . KAWASAKI FX921
ENGINE HP 31
FUEL . . . . G
SPEEDS . . . . VARIABLE
TRANSMISSION . . . . . DUAL HYDRO
STEERING . . . . ZERO
STANDARD DECK . . . . 61"
MSRP $11,518

HDZ3161FX3

YEARS MFRD 2020-2020
SERIES . . . . HDZ 3 SERIES
ENGINE . . . . KAWASAKI FX921
ENGINE HP 31
FUEL . . . . G
SPEEDS . . . . VARIABLE
TRANSMISSION . . . . HYDRO
STEERING . . . . ZERO
ROPS/CAB . . . . ROPS
STANDARD DECK . . . . 61"

HDZ3173

YEARS MFRD 2017-2018
ENGINE . . . . KAWASAKI FX921V
ENGINE HP 31
STEERING . . . . ZERO
STANDARD DECK . . . . 73"

HDZ3173FX2

YEARS MFRD 2018-2019
SERIES . . . . HDZ 2 SERIES
ENGINE . . . . KAWASAKI FX921
ENGINE HP 31
FUEL . . . . G
SPEEDS . . . . VARIABLE
TRANSMISSION . . . . . DUAL HYDRO
STEERING . . . . ZERO
STANDARD DECK . . . . 73"
MSRP $11,916

HDZ3173FX3

YEARS MFRD 2020-2020
SERIES . . . . HDZ 3 SERIES
ENGINE . . . . KAWASAKI FX921
ENGINE HP 31
FUEL . . . . G
SPEEDS . . . . VARIABLE
TRANSMISSION . . . . HYDRO
STEERING . . . . ZERO
ROPS/CAB . . . . ROPS
STANDARD DECK . . . . 73"

HDZ3273

YEARS MFRD 2017-2018
ENGINE . . . . B&S
ENGINE HP 32
FUEL . . . . G
SPEEDS . . . . VARIABLE
TRANSMISSION . . . . HYDRO
STEERING . . . . ZERO
STANDARD DECK . . . . 73"
MSRP $10,926

OPTIONS

BAR TIRES

RETAIL PRICING

YEAR	HIGH	LOW
2017	$6,433	$4,825
2018	$7,684	$5,763

HDZ3361ECV2

YEARS MFRD 2018-2019
SERIES . . . . HDZ 2 SERIES
ENGINE . . . . KOHLER EFI
ENGINE HP 33
SPEEDS . . . . VARIABLE
TRANSMISSION . . . . . DUAL HYDRO
STEERING . . . . ZERO
STANDARD DECK . . . . 61"
MSRP $12,134

HDZ3361ECV3

YEARS MFRD 2020-2020
SERIES . . . . HDZ 3 SERIES
ENGINE KOHLER EFI COMMAND PRO
ENGINE HP 33
FUEL . . . . G
SPEEDS . . . . VARIABLE
TRANSMISSION . . . . HYDRO
STEERING . . . . ZERO
ROPS/CAB . . . . ROPS
STANDARD DECK . . . . 61"

HDZ3373ECV2

YEARS MFRD 2018-2019
SERIES . . . . HDZ 2 SERIES
ENGINE . . . . KOHLER EFI
ENGINE HP 33
FUEL . . . . G
SPEEDS . . . . VARIABLE
TRANSMISSION . . . . . DUAL HYDRO
STEERING . . . . ZERO
STANDARD DECK . . . . 73"
MSRP $12,531

HDZ3373ECV3

YEARS MFRD 2020-2020
SERIES . . . . HDZ 3 SERIES
ENGINE KOHLER EFI COMMAND PRO
ENGINE HP 33
FUEL . . . . G
SPEEDS . . . . VARIABLE
TRANSMISSION . . . . HYDRO
STEERING . . . . ZERO
ROPS/CAB . . . . ROPS
STANDARD DECK . . . . 73"

HS1642

YEARS MFRD 2009-2009
SERIES . . . . HOME SERIES
ENGINE . . . . HONDA GXV530
CYLINDERS 2
ENGINE HP 16
COOLING . . . . AIR
FUEL . . . . G
SPEEDS . . . . VARIABLE
TRANSMISSION . . . . HYDRO
STEERING . . . . ZERO
BLADE CLUTCH . . . . ELECTRIC

HS1736

YEARS MFRD 2008-2009
SERIES . . . . HOME SERIES
ENGINE . . . . B&S
CID 502CC
ENGINE HP 17.5
COOLING . . . . AIR
FUEL . . . . G
SPEEDS . . . . VARIABLE
TRANSMISSION . . . . . DUAL HYDRO
STEERING . . . . ZERO
BLADE CLUTCH . . . . ELECTRIC
STANDARD DECK . . . . 36"
MSRP $3,999

RETAIL PRICING

YEAR	HIGH	LOW
2008	$1,173	$880
2009	$1,295	$971

HS1742

YEARS MFRD 2008-2009
SERIES . . . . HOME SERIES
ENGINE . . . . B&S
CID 502CC
ENGINE HP 17.5
COOLING . . . . AIR
FUEL . . . . G
SPEEDS . . . . VARIABLE
TRANSMISSION . . . . . DUAL HYDRO
STEERING . . . . ZERO
BLADE CLUTCH . . . . ELECTRIC
STANDARD DECK . . . . 42"
MSRP $4,099

RETAIL PRICING

YEAR	HIGH	LOW
2008	$1,201	$901
2009	$1,327	$995

HS1836

YEARS MFRD 2008-2009
SERIES . . . . HOME SERIES
ENGINE . . . . B&S
CYLINDERS 2
CID 656CC
ENGINE HP 18
COOLING . . . . AIR
FUEL . . . . G
SPEEDS . . . . VARIABLE
TRANSMISSION . . . . . DUAL HYDRO
STEERING . . . . ZERO
BLADE CLUTCH . . . . ELECTRIC
STANDARD DECK . . . . 36"
MSRP $4,369

RETAIL PRICING

YEAR	HIGH	LOW
2008	$1,281	$961
2009	$1,414	$1,061

HS1842

YEARS MFRD 2008-2009
SERIES . . . . HOME SERIES
ENGINE . . . . B&S
CYLINDERS 2
CID 656CC
ENGINE HP 18
COOLING . . . . AIR
FUEL . . . . G
SPEEDS . . . . VARIABLE
TRANSMISSION . . . . . DUAL HYDRO
STEERING . . . . ZERO
BLADE CLUTCH . . . . ELECTRIC
STANDARD DECK . . . . 42"
MSRP $4,469

RETAIL PRICING

YEAR	HIGH	LOW
2008	$1,310	$983
2009	$1,446	$1,085

HS2036K

YEARS MFRD 2011-2011
ENGINE .... KOHLER
ENGINE HP 20
COOLING .... AIR
FUEL .... G
SPEEDS .... VARIABLE
TRANSMISSION .... HYDRO
STEERING .... ZERO
BLADE CLUTCH .... ELECTRIC
STANDARD DECK .... 36"
MSRP $4,626

RETAIL PRICING

YEAR	HIGH	LOW
2011	$1,784	$1,338

HS2042

YEARS MFRD 2008-2011
SERIES .... HOME SERIES
ENGINE .... KOHLER
CYLINDERS 2
CID 725CC
ENGINE HP 20
COOLING .... AIR
FUEL .... G
SPEEDS .... VARIABLE
TRANSMISSION ..... DUAL HYDRO
STEERING .... ZERO
BLADE CLUTCH .... ELECTRIC
STANDARD DECK .... 42"
MSRP $4,859

RETAIL PRICING

YEAR	HIGH	LOW
2008	$1,738	$1,303
2009	$1,927	$1,445

M2254

YEARS MFRD 2001-2001
SERIES .... MID-MOUNT SERIES
ENGINE .... KOHLER
ENGINE HP 22
FUEL .... G
SPEEDS .... VARIABLE
TRANSMISSION ..... DUAL HYDRO
STEERING .... ZERO
STANDARD DECK .... 54"
MSRP $8,350

RETAIL PRICING

YEAR	HIGH	LOW
2001	$1,152	$864

M2260

YEARS MFRD 2001-2001
SERIES .... MID-MOUNT SERIES
ENGINE .... KOHLER
ENGINE HP 22
FUEL .... G
SPEEDS .... VARIABLE
TRANSMISSION ..... DUAL HYDRO
STEERING .... ZERO
STANDARD DECK .... 60"
MSRP $8,500

RETAIL PRICING

YEAR	HIGH	LOW
2001	$1,173	$880

M2354

YEARS MFRD 2001-2001
SERIES .... MID-MOUNT SERIES
ENGINE .... KOHLER
ENGINE HP 23
COOLING .... LIQUID
FUEL .... G
SPEEDS .... VARIABLE
TRANSMISSION ..... DUAL HYDRO
STEERING .... ZERO
STANDARD DECK .... 54"
MSRP $9,000

RETAIL PRICING

YEAR	HIGH	LOW
2001	$1,197	$897

M2355A

YEARS MFRD 2005-2006
SERIES .... M2000 SERIES
ENGINE .. KOHLER COMMAND PRO
ENGINE HP 23
COOLING .... AIR
FUEL .... G
SPEEDS .... VARIABLE
TRANSMISSION ..... DUAL HYDRO
STEERING .... ZERO
BLADE CLUTCH .... ELECTRIC
STANDARD DECK .... 55"
WEIGHT .... 1,170 LBS.
MSRP $9,973

OPTIONS

2P FROPS
2P ROPS
BAGGER
STRIPER

RETAIL PRICING

YEAR	HIGH	LOW
2005	$2,206	$1,654
2006	$2,434	$1,826

M2360

YEARS MFRD 2001-2001
SERIES .... MID-MOUNT SERIES
ENGINE .... KOHLER
ENGINE HP 23
COOLING .... LIQUID
FUEL .... G
SPEEDS .... VARIABLE
TRANSMISSION ..... DUAL HYDRO
STEERING .... ZERO
STANDARD DECK .... 60"
MSRP $9,150

RETAIL PRICING

YEAR	HIGH	LOW
2001	$1,261	$946

M2554

YEARS MFRD 2001-2001
SERIES .... MID-MOUNT SERIES
ENGINE .... KOHLER
ENGINE HP 25
SPEEDS .... VARIABLE
TRANSMISSION ..... DUAL HYDRO
STEERING .... ZERO
STANDARD DECK .... 54"
MSRP $8,600

RETAIL PRICING

YEAR	HIGH	LOW
2001	$1,187	$890

M2555K

YEARS MFRD 2005-2006
SERIES .... M2000 SERIES
ENGINE ...... KAWASAKI FH721V
ENGINE HP 25
COOLING .... AIR
FUEL .... G
SPEEDS .... VARIABLE
TRANSMISSION ..... DUAL HYDRO
STEERING .... ZERO
BLADE CLUTCH .... ELECTRIC
STANDARD DECK .... 55"
WEIGHT .... 1,170 LBS.
MSRP $10,375

OPTIONS

2P FROPS
2P ROPS
BAGGER
STRIPER

RETAIL PRICING

YEAR	HIGH	LOW
2005	$2,293	$1,720
2006	$2,532	$1,899

M2560

YEARS MFRD 2001-2001
SERIES .... MID-MOUNT SERIES
ENGINE .... KOHLER
ENGINE HP 25
SPEEDS .... VARIABLE
TRANSMISSION ..... DUAL HYDRO
STEERING .... ZERO
STANDARD DECK .... 60"
MSRP $8,750

RETAIL PRICING

YEAR	HIGH	LOW
2001	$1,214	$911

M2561

YEARS MFRD 2004-2006
SERIES .... M2000 SERIES
ENGINE .. KOHLER COMMAND PRO
ENGINE HP 25
COOLING .... AIR
FUEL .... G
SPEEDS .... VARAIBLE
TRANSMISSION .... HYDRO
STEERING .... ZERO
STANDARD DECK .... 61"
WEIGHT .... 1,225 LBS.
MSRP $10,625

RETAIL PRICING

YEAR	HIGH	LOW
2004	$4,661	$3,496
2005	$5,666	$4,250
2006	$5,991	$4,493

M2561K

YEARS MFRD 2005-2006
SERIES .... M2000 SERIES
ENGINE ...... KAWASAKI FH721V
ENGINE HP 25
COOLING .... AIR
FUEL .... G
SPEEDS .... VARIABLE
TRANSMISSION ..... DUAL HYDRO
STEERING .... ZERO
BLADE CLUTCH .... ELECTRIC
STANDARD DECK .... 61"
WEIGHT .... 1,220 LBS.
MSRP $10,505

OPTIONS

2P FROPS
2P ROPS
BAGGER
KOHLER

RETAIL PRICING

YEAR	HIGH	LOW
2005	$2,330	$1,748
2006	$2,564	$1,923

M2661

YEARS MFRD 2005-2006
SERIES .... M2000 SERIES
ENGINE KOHLER COMMAND-PRO EFI
ENGINE HP 26
COOLING .... AIR
FUEL .... G
SPEEDS .... VARIABLE
TRANSMISSION ..... DUAL HYDRO
STEERING .... ZERO
BLADE CLUTCH .... ELECTRIC
STANDARD DECK .... 61"
WEIGHT .... 1,225 LBS.
MSRP $11,690

OPTIONS

2P FROPS
2P ROPS
BAGGER
STRIPER

RETAIL PRICING

YEAR	HIGH	LOW
2005	$2,585	$1,939
2006	$2,853	$2,140

M2672

YEARS MFRD 2001-2001
SERIES .... MID-MOUNT SERIES
ENGINE .... KOHLER
ENGINE HP 26
SPEEDS .... VARIABLE
TRANSMISSION ..... DUAL HYDRO
STEERING .... ZERO
STANDARD DECK .... 72"
MSRP $9,250

RETAIL PRICING

YEAR	HIGH	LOW
2001	$1,276	$957

BUSH HOG

M2673

YEARS MFRD 2005-2005
SERIES. . . . . M2000 SERIES
ENGINE KOHLER COMMAND-PRO EFI
ENGINE HP 26
COOLING . . . . AIR
FUEL . . . . G
SPEEDS . . . . VARIABLE
TRANSMISSION . . . . . DUAL HYDRO
STEERING. . . . . ZERO
BLADE CLUTCH . . . . ELECTRIC
STANDARD DECK . . . . 73"
WEIGHT . . . . 1,300 LBS.
MSRP. $11,777

OPTIONS

2P FROPS
2P ROPS
BAGGER

RETAIL PRICING

YEAR	HIGH	LOW
2005	$2,873	$2,155

M2761

YEARS MFRD 2005-2006
SERIES. . . . . M2000 SERIES
ENGINE . . KOHLER COMMAND-PRO
ENGINE HP 27
COOLING . . . . AIR
FUEL . . . . G
SPEEDS . . . . VARIABLE
TRANSMISSION . . . . . DUAL HYDRO
STEERING. . . . . ZERO
BLADE CLUTCH . . . . ELECTRIC
STANDARD DECK . . . . 61"
WEIGHT . . . . 1,225 LBS.
MSRP. $10,994

OPTIONS

2P FROPS
2P ROPS
BAGGER
STRIPER

RETAIL PRICING

YEAR	HIGH	LOW
2005	$2,431	$1,824
2006	$2,683	$2,012

M4420

YEARS MFRD 2017-2017
ENGINE . . . . B&S PRO
ENGINE HP 20
COOLING . . . . AIR
FUEL . . . . G
SPEEDS . . . . VARIABLE
TRANSMISSION . . . . HYDRO
STEERING. . . . . ZERO
STANDARD DECK . . . . 44"
MSRP. $7,334

OPTIONS

CANOPY
SUS SEAT

RETAIL PRICING

YEAR	HIGH	LOW
2017	$4,513	$3,385

M5220

YEARS MFRD 2017-2017
ENGINE . . . . KOHLER
ENGINE HP 20
COOLING . . . . AIR
FUEL . . . . G
SPEEDS . . . . VARIABLE
TRANSMISSION . . . . HYDRO
STEERING. . . . . ZERO
STANDARD DECK . . . . 52"
MSRP. $7,454

OPTIONS

CANOPY
SUS SEAT

RETAIL PRICING

YEAR	HIGH	LOW
2017	$4,587	$3,441

M5225

YEARS MFRD 2017-2017
ENGINE . . . . B&S
ENGINE HP 25
COOLING . . . . AIR
FUEL . . . . G
SPEEDS . . . . VARIABLE
TRANSMISSION . . . . HYDRO
STEERING. . . . . ZERO
STANDARD DECK . . . . 52"
MSRP. $7,475

OPTIONS

CANOPY
SUS SEAT

RETAIL PRICING

YEAR	HIGH	LOW
2017	$4,601	$3,451

P5525

YEARS MFRD 2017-2017
ENGINE . . . . B&S
ENGINE HP 25
COOLING . . . . AIR
FUEL . . . . G
SPEEDS . . . . VARIABLE
TRANSMISSION . . . . HYDRO
STEERING. . . . . ZERO
STANDARD DECK . . . . 55"
MSRP. $8,414

OPTIONS

CANOPY
SUS SEAT

RETAIL PRICING

YEAR	HIGH	LOW
2017	$5,178	$3,884

P6124

YEARS MFRD 2017-2017
ENGINE . . . . KAWASAKI
ENGINE HP 24
COOLING . . . . AIR
FUEL . . . . G
SPEEDS . . . . VARIABLE
TRANSMISSION . . . . HYDRO
STEERING. . . . . ZERO
STANDARD DECK . . . . 61"
MSRP. $8,786

OPTIONS

CANOPY
SUS SEAT

RETAIL PRICING

YEAR	HIGH	LOW
2017	$5,407	$4,055

P6126

YEARS MFRD 2017-2017
ENGINE . . . . KOHLER
ENGINE HP 26
COOLING . . . . AIR
FUEL . . . . G
SPEEDS . . . . VARIABLE
TRANSMISSION . . . . HYDRO
STEERING. . . . . ZERO
STANDARD DECK . . . . 61"
MSRP. $8,666

OPTIONS

CANOPY
SUS SEAT

RETAIL PRICING

YEAR	HIGH	LOW
2017	$5,334	$4,001

P6127

YEARS MFRD 2017-2017
ENGINE . . . . B&S
ENGINE HP 27
COOLING . . . . AIR
FUEL . . . . G
SPEEDS . . . . VARIABLE
TRANSMISSION . . . . HYDRO
STEERING. . . . . ZERO
STANDARD DECK . . . . 61"
MSRP. $8,414

OPTIONS

CANOPY
SUS SEAT

RETAIL PRICING

YEAR	HIGH	LOW
2017	$5,178	$3,884

PZ2555

YEARS MFRD 2007-2011
SERIES. . . . . PROFESSIONAL SERIES
ENGINE . . . . KAWASAKI FH721V
CYLINDERS. 2
ENGINE HP 25
COOLING . . . . AIR
FUEL . . . . G
SPEEDS . . . . VARIABLE
TRANSMISSION . . . . HYDRO
STEERING. . . . . ZERO
BLADE CLUTCH . . . . ELECTRIC
STANDARD DECK . . . . 55"
WEIGHT . . . . 1,300 LBS.
MSRP. $9,469

OPTIONS

10 BU BAG
CANOPY
PWR LIFT

RETAIL PRICING

YEAR	HIGH	LOW
2007	$2,460	$1,845
2008	$2,715	$2,036
2009	$2,996	$2,247
2010	$3,307	$2,480
2011	$3,651	$2,738

PZ2561

YEARS MFRD 2007-2011
SERIES. . . . . PROFESSIONAL SERIES
ENGINE . . . . KAWASAKI FH721V
CYLINDERS. 2
ENGINE HP 25
COOLING . . . . AIR
FUEL . . . . G
SPEEDS . . . . VARIABLE
TRANSMISSION . . . . HYDRO
STEERING. . . . . ZERO
BLADE CLUTCH . . . . ELECTRIC
STANDARD DECK . . . . 61"
WEIGHT . . . . 1,400 LBS.
MSRP. $9,799

OPTIONS

10 BU BAG
CANOPY
PWR LIFT

RETAIL PRICING

YEAR	HIGH	LOW
2007	$2,545	$1,909
2008	$2,810	$2,107
2009	$3,101	$2,326
2010	$3,423	$2,567
2011	$3,777	$2,833

PZ2661

YEARS MFRD 2011-2012
ENGINE . . . . KAWASAKI
ENGINE HP 26
COOLING . . . . AIR
FUEL . . . . G
SPEEDS . . . . VARIABLE
TRANSMISSION . . . . . DUAL HYDRO
STEERING. . . . . ZERO
BLADE CLUTCH . . . . ELECTRIC
STANDARD DECK . . . . 61"
MSRP. $10,094

OPTIONS

10 BU BAG
CANOPY
E-ACTUATOR

RETAIL PRICING

YEAR	HIGH	LOW
2011	$3,769	$2,827
2012	$4,159	$3,119

PZ2755

YEARS MFRD 2007-2011
SERIES. . . . . PROFESSIONAL SERIES
ENGINE . . KOHLER COMMAND PRO
CYLINDERS. 2
ENGINE HP 27
COOLING . . . . AIR
FUEL . . . . G

SPEEDS . . . VARIABLE
TRANSMISSION . . . HYDRO
STEERING . . . ZERO
BLADE CLUTCH . . . ELECTRIC
STANDARD DECK . . . 55"
WEIGHT . . . 1,300 LBS.
MSRP . . . $9,519

OPTIONS

10 BU BAG
CANOPY
PWR LIFT

RETAIL PRICING

YEAR	HIGH	LOW
2007	$2,473	$1,854
2008	$2,728	$2,046
2009	$3,013	$2,259
2010	$3,324	$2,493
2011	$3,670	$2,753

PZ2761

YEARS MFRD . . . 2013-2016
ENGINE . . . KOHLER
ENGINE HP . . . 27
COOLING . . . AIR
FUEL . . . G
SPEEDS . . . VARIABLE
TRANSMISSION . . . HYDRO
STEERING . . . ZERO
STANDARD DECK . . . 61"
MSRP . . . $10,774

OPTIONS

BAR TIRES
CANOPY
E-ACTUATOR

RETAIL PRICING

YEAR	HIGH	LOW
2013	$4,435	$3,327
2014	$4,897	$3,673
2015	$5,405	$4,054
2016	$5,965	$4,474

PZ2861

YEARS MFRD . . . 2007-2011
SERIES . . . PROFESSIONAL SERIES
ENGINE . . KOHLER COMMAND PRO
CYLINDERS . . . 2
ENGINE HP . . . 28
COOLING . . . AIR
FUEL . . . G
SPEEDS . . . VARIABLE
TRANSMISSION . . . HYDRO
STEERING . . . ZERO
BLADE CLUTCH . . . ELECTRIC
STANDARD DECK . . . 61"
WEIGHT . . . 1,410 LBS.
MSRP . . . $11,199

OPTIONS

10 BU BAG
CANOPY
PWR LIFT

RETAIL PRICING

YEAR	HIGH	LOW
2007	$2,804	$2,103
2008	$3,094	$2,320
2009	$3,415	$2,561
2010	$3,770	$2,828
2011	$4,161	$3,121

PZ2873

YEARS MFRD . . . 2007-2011
SERIES . . . PROFESSIONAL SERIES
ENGINE . . KOHLER COMMAND PRO
CYLINDERS . . . 2
ENGINE HP . . . 28
COOLING . . . AIR
FUEL . . . G
SPEEDS . . . VARIABLE
TRANSMISSION . . . HYDRO
STEERING . . . ZERO
BLADE CLUTCH . . . ELECTRIC
STANDARD DECK . . . 73"
WEIGHT . . . 1,550 LBS.
MSRP . . . $11,739

OPTIONS

CANOPY
PWR LIFT

RETAIL PRICING

YEAR	HIGH	LOW
2007	$3,050	$2,287
2008	$3,365	$2,524
2009	$3,714	$2,786
2010	$4,100	$3,075
2011	$4,526	$3,394

PZ3061

YEARS MFRD . . . 2007-2016
SERIES . . . PROFESSIONAL SERIES
ENGINE . . KOHLER COMMAND PRO
CYLINDERS . . . 2
ENGINE HP . . . 30
COOLING . . . AIR
FUEL . . . G
SPEEDS . . . VARIABLE
TRANSMISSION . . . HYDRO
STEERING . . . ZERO
BLADE CLUTCH . . . ELECTRIC
STANDARD DECK . . . 61"
WEIGHT . . . 1,400 LBS.
MSRP . . . $11,144

OPTIONS

10 BU BAG
CANOPY
E-ACTUATOR
POWER LIFT

RETAIL PRICING

YEAR	HIGH	LOW
2007	$2,483	$1,862
2008	$2,800	$2,100
2009	$3,094	$2,320
2010	$3,411	$2,559
2011	$3,765	$2,824
2012	$4,156	$3,117
2013	$4,587	$3,441
2014	$5,064	$3,798
2015	$5,589	$4,192
2016	$6,168	$4,626

PZ3061KH2

YEARS MFRD . . . 2011-2011
ENGINE . . . KOHLER
ENGINE HP . . . 30
COOLING . . . AIR
FUEL . . . G
SPEEDS . . . VARIABLE
TRANSMISSION . . . DUAL HYDRO
STEERING . . . ZERO
BLADE CLUTCH . . . ELECTRIC
STANDARD DECK . . . 61"
MSRP . . . $10,239

OPTIONS

10 BU BAG
E-ACTUATOR

RETAIL PRICING

YEAR	HIGH	LOW
2011	$3,947	$2,961

PZ3073

YEARS MFRD . . . 2007-2016
SERIES . . . PROFESSIONAL SERIES
ENGINE . . KOHLER COMMAND PRO
CYLINDERS . . . 2
ENGINE HP . . . 30
COOLING . . . AIR
FUEL . . . G
SPEEDS . . . VARIABLE
TRANSMISSION . . . HYDRO
STEERING . . . ZERO
BLADE CLUTCH . . . ELECTRIC
STANDARD DECK . . . 73"
WEIGHT . . . 1,550 LBS.
MSRP . . . $11,717

OPTIONS

CANOPY
E-ACTUATOR
POWER LIFT
REAR WT KIT

RETAIL PRICING

YEAR	HIGH	LOW
2007	$2,643	$1,982
2008	$2,945	$2,209
2009	$3,250	$2,437
2010	$3,588	$2,691
2011	$3,960	$2,970
2012	$4,371	$3,278
2013	$4,825	$3,618
2014	$5,324	$3,993
2015	$5,877	$4,408
2016	$6,488	$4,866

PZ3073KH2

YEARS MFRD . . . 2011-2011
ENGINE . . . KOHLER
ENGINE HP . . . 30
COOLING . . . AIR
FUEL . . . G
SPEEDS . . . VARIABLE
TRANSMISSION . . . DUAL HYDRO
STEERING . . . ZERO
BLADE CLUTCH . . . ELECTRIC
STANDARD DECK . . . 73"
MSRP . . . $10,769

OPTIONS

E-ACTUATOR

RETAIL PRICING

YEAR	HIGH	LOW
2011	$4,151	$3,113

PZ6126

YEARS MFRD . . . 2017-2017
ENGINE . . . B&S
ENGINE HP . . . 26
FUEL . . . G
SPEEDS . . . VARIABLE
TRANSMISSION . . . HYDRO
STEERING . . . ZERO
STANDARD DECK . . . 61"
MSRP . . . $11,183

OPTIONS

CANOPY

RETAIL PRICING

YEAR	HIGH	LOW
2017	$6,883	$5,162

PZ6127

YEARS MFRD . . . 2017-2017
ENGINE . . . KAWASAKI
ENGINE HP . . . 27
FUEL . . . G
SPEEDS . . . VARIABLE
TRANSMISSION . . . HYDRO
STEERING . . . ZERO
STANDARD DECK . . . 61"
MSRP . . . $10,891

OPTIONS

CANOPY
KOHLER

RETAIL PRICING

YEAR	HIGH	LOW
2017	$6,703	$5,027

PZ7327

YEARS MFRD . . . 2017-2017
ENGINE . . . KAWASAKI
ENGINE HP . . . 27
FUEL . . . G
SPEEDS . . . VARIABLE
TRANSMISSION . . . HYDRO
STEERING . . . ZERO
STANDARD DECK . . . 73"
MSRP . . . $11,077

OPTIONS

CANOPY

RETAIL PRICING

YEAR	HIGH	LOW
2017	$6,817	$5,113

RS2650

YEARS MFRD . . . 2013-2016
ENGINE . . . B&S
ENGINE HP . . . 26
COOLING . . . AIR
FUEL . . . G
SPEEDS . . . VARIABLE
TRANSMISSION . . . HYDRO

BUSH HOG

STEERING . . . . ZERO
STANDARD DECK . . . . 50"
MSRP. $4,035

OPTIONS

BAGGER

RETAIL PRICING

YEAR	HIGH	LOW
2013	$1,660	$1,245
2014	$1,833	$1,374
2015	$2,023	$1,517
2016	$2,234	$1,676

RS2650B

YEARS MFRD 2013-2014
ENGINE . . . . B&S
ENGINE HP 26
COOLING . . . . AIR
FUEL . . . . G
SPEEDS . . . . VARIABLE
TRANSMISSION . . . . HYDRO
STEERING. . . . . STANDARD
STANDARD DECK . . . . 50"
WEIGHT . . . . 750 LBS.
MSRP. $6,395

RETAIL PRICING

YEAR	HIGH	LOW
2013	$2,672	$2,004
2014	$3,828	$2,871

TC180

YEARS MFRD 1997-1998
SERIES. . . . . . TURF CHAMP SERIES
ENGINE . . . . B&S
ENGINE HP 18
COOLING . . . . AIR
FUEL . . . . G
SPEEDS . . . . VARIABLE
TRANSMISSION . . . . . DUAL HYDRO
STEERING. . . . . ZERO
STANDARD DECK . . . . 48"
WEIGHT . . . . 980 LBS.
MSRP. $7,775

OPTIONS

61" DECK

SERIAL NUMBERS

YEAR	BEGINNING NO.
1997	0001

RETAIL PRICING

YEAR	HIGH	LOW
1997	$754	$565
1998	$832	$624

TC200

YEARS MFRD 1997-1998
SERIES. . . . . . TURF CHAMP SERIES
ENGINE . . . . KAWASAKI
ENGINE HP 20
COOLING . . . . LIQUID
FUEL . . . . G
SPEEDS . . . . VARIABLE
TRANSMISSION . . . . . DUAL HYDRO
STEERING. . . . . ZERO
STANDARD DECK . . . . 52"
WEIGHT . . . . 1,060 LBS.
MSRP. $8,338

OPTIONS

61" DECK

SERIAL NUMBERS

YEAR	BEGINNING NO.
1997	0001

RETAIL PRICING

YEAR	HIGH	LOW
1997	$809	$606
1998	$893	$670

TC220

YEARS MFRD 1997-1998
SERIES. . . . . . TURF CHAMP SERIES
ENGINE . . . . KOHLER
ENGINE HP 22
COOLING . . . . AIR
FUEL . . . . G
SPEEDS . . . . VARIABLE
TRANSMISSION . . . . . DUAL HYDRO
STEERING. . . . . ZERO
STANDARD DECK . . . . 61"
WEIGHT . . . . 1,110 LBS.
MSRP. $9,128

OPTIONS

52" DECK

SERIAL NUMBERS

YEAR	BEGINNING NO.
1997	0001

RETAIL PRICING

YEAR	HIGH	LOW
1997	$885	$664
1998	$976	$732

ZT18

YEARS MFRD 1999-2001
ENGINE . . . . KOHLER
ENGINE HP 18
COOLING . . . . AIR
FUEL . . . . G
SPEEDS . . . . VARIABLE
TRANSMISSION . . . . . DUAL HYDRO
STEERING. . . . . ZERO
STANDARD DECK . . . . 48"
WEIGHT . . . . 640 LBS.
MSRP. $7,799

OPTIONS

54" DECK
BAGGER
ROPS
WTS

RETAIL PRICING

YEAR	HIGH	LOW
1999	$855	$641
2000	$944	$708
2001	$1,042	$781

ZT22

YEARS MFRD 1999-2001
ENGINE . . . . KOHLER
ENGINE HP 22
COOLING . . . . AIR
FUEL . . . . G
SPEEDS . . . . VARIABLE
TRANSMISSION . . . . . DUAL HYDRO
STEERING. . . . . ZERO
STANDARD DECK . . . . 48"
WEIGHT . . . . 640 LBS.
MSRP. $8,281

OPTIONS

54" DECK
60" DECK
ROPS
WTS

RETAIL PRICING

YEAR	HIGH	LOW
1999	$938	$703
2000	$1,042	$781
2001	$1,143	$857

AVG. AUCTION PRICING

LOW	HIGH	AVG
$741	$1,436	$1,074

ZT22W

YEARS MFRD 1999-2001
ENGINE . . . . KAWASAKI
ENGINE HP 22
COOLING . . . . LIQUID
FUEL . . . . G
SPEEDS . . . . VARIABLE
TRANSMISSION . . . . . DUAL HYDRO
STEERING. . . . . ZERO
STANDARD DECK . . . . 48"
WEIGHT . . . . 710 LBS.
MSRP. $9,309

OPTIONS

54" DECK
60" DECK
ROPS
WTS

RETAIL PRICING

YEAR	HIGH	LOW
1999	$1,054	$790
2000	$1,163	$872
2001	$1,284	$963

ZT25

YEARS MFRD 1999-2001
ENGINE . . . . KOHLER
ENGINE HP 25
COOLING . . . . AIR
FUEL . . . . G
SPEEDS . . . . VARIABLE
TRANSMISSION . . . . . DUAL HYDRO
STEERING. . . . . ZERO
STANDARD DECK . . . . 54"
WEIGHT . . . . 640 LBS.
MSRP. $8,917

OPTIONS

60" DECK
ROPS
WTS

RETAIL PRICING

YEAR	HIGH	LOW
1999	$1,009	$757
2000	$1,114	$836
2001	$1,230	$922

ZT30D

YEARS MFRD 2000-2002
ENGINE . . . . LISTER PETTER
ENGINE HP 30
FUEL . . . . D
SPEEDS . . . . VARIABLE
TRANSMISSION . . . . HYDRO
STEERING. . . . . STANDARD
WEIGHT . . . . 1,250 LBS.
MSRP. $11,783

RETAIL PRICING

YEAR	HIGH	LOW
2000	$4,516	$3,387
2001	$4,709	$3,532
2002	$5,134	$3,851

ZT180

YEARS MFRD 2005-2005
SERIES. . . . . FRONT MOUNT SERIES
ENGINE . . KOHLER COMMAND-PRO
ENGINE HP 18
COOLING . . . . AIR
FUEL . . . . G
SPEEDS . . . . VARIABLE
TRANSMISSION . . . . . DUAL HYDRO
STEERING. . . . . ZERO
STANDARD DECK . . . . 48"
MSRP. $9,090

OPTIONS

54" DECK
60" DECK
BAGGER
FULL SUSP

RETAIL PRICING

YEAR	HIGH	LOW
2005	$2,268	$1,701

ZT230

YEARS MFRD 2005-2005
SERIES. . . . . FRONT MOUNT SERIES
ENGINE . . KOHLER COMMAND-PRO
ENGINE HP 23
COOLING . . . . AIR
FUEL . . . . G
SPEEDS . . . . VARIABLE
TRANSMISSION . . . . HYDRO
STEERING. . . . . ZERO
STANDARD DECK . . . . 54"
MSRP. $10,111

OPTIONS

48" DECK
60" DECK
BAGGER
FULL SUSP

RETAIL PRICING

YEAR	HIGH	LOW
2005	$2,288	$1,716

ZT250

YEARS MFRD 2005-2005
SERIES. . . . . FRONT MOUNT SERIES
ENGINE . . KOHLER COMMAND-PRO
ENGINE HP 25
COOLING . . . . AIR
FUEL . . . . G
SPEEDS . . . . VARIABLE
TRANSMISSION . . . . HYDRO
STEERING. . . . . ZERO
STANDARD DECK . . . . 60"
MSRP. $10,651

OPTIONS

48" DECK
54" DECK
BAGGER
FULL SUSP

RETAIL PRICING

YEAR	HIGH	LOW
2005	$2,426	$1,820

ZT1800

YEARS MFRD........ 1995-1996
ENGINE................KOHLER
ENGINE HP..................18
COOLING...................AIR
FUEL.........................G
SPEEDS..............VARIABLE
TRANSMISSION..........HYDRO
STEERING................ZERO
STANDARD DECK........... 48"
MSRP................. $7,592

OPTIONS

60" DECK

RETAIL PRICING

YEAR	HIGH	LOW
1995	$523	$392
1996	$577	$433

ZT2200

YEARS MFRD........ 1995-1996
ENGINE................KOHLER
ENGINE HP..................22
COOLING...................AIR
FUEL.........................G
SPEEDS..............VARIABLE
TRANSMISSION..........HYDRO
STEERING................ZERO
STANDARD DECK........... 48"
MSRP................. $7,899

OPTIONS

60" DECK

RETAIL PRICING

YEAR	HIGH	LOW
1995	$543	$407
1996	$600	$450

NOTES

CASE

480C

YEARS MFRD 1976-1981
ENGINE .... CASE
CID 188
ENGINE HP 43
COOLING .... LIQUID
FUEL .... D
SPEEDS 8/2
TRANSMISSION .... GEAR
STEERING............ STANDARD
WEIGHT .... 5,345 LBS.

SERIAL NUMBERS

YEAR	BEGINNING NO.
1976	8956701
1977	8967001
1978	8967820
1979	8987016
1980	9001090

AVG. AUCTION PRICING

LOW	HIGH	AVG
$3,560	$7,077	$5,707

484

YEARS MFRD 1978-1984
ENGINE .... IH
CID 179
PTO HP 42
FUEL .... D
SPEEDS 8/4
WEIGHT .... 4,853 LBS.

SERIAL NUMBERS

YEAR	BEGINNING NO.
1978	501
1979	1325
1980	2754
1981	5619
1984	9165

1190

YEARS MFRD 1980-1983
ENGINE .... CASE
CYLINDERS.................. 3
CID 164.4
PTO HP 43.09
FUEL .... D
SPEEDS 12/4
WEIGHT .... 4,400 LBS.

SERIAL NUMBERS

RIGHT HAND SIDE OF ENGINE MAIN FRAME

YEAR	BEGINNING NO.
1980	11030101
1981	11031792
1982	11033166
1983	11035592

1194

YEARS MFRD 1983-1985
ENGINE .... CASE
CYLINDERS.................. 3
CID 164.4
PTO HP 43
FUEL .... D
SPEEDS 12/4
WEIGHT .... 4,620 LBS.

SERIAL NUMBERS

RIGHT HAND SIDE OF ENGINE MAIN FRAME

YEAR	BEGINNING NO.
1983	11038050
1984	11038494
1985	11480000

CASE-IH

C50

YEARS MFRD 1997-2002
ENGINE .... CASE 903.27
CYLINDERS.................. 3
CID 165
PTO HP 40
ENGINE HP 53
COOLING .... LIQUID
FUEL .... D
SPEEDS 8/4
TRANSMISSION .... GEAR
STEERING............ STANDARD
HYDRAULIC .... YES
PTO .... YES
DRIVE TYPE 2WD
ROPS/CAB .... ROPS
WEIGHT .... 5,335 LBS.
MSRP................ $19,450

OPTIONS

2 SPEED POWER SHIFT
4WD
8/8 SHUTTLE SHIFT
LOADER

SERIAL NUMBERS

YEAR	BEGINNING NO.
1998	JJE1000056
1999	JJE1008492
2000	JJE1013490
2001	JJE1017672
2002	JJE1019985

RETAIL PRICING

YEAR	HIGH	LOW
2002	$10,272	$7,704

CX50

YEARS MFRD 1997-2002
ENGINE .... CASE 903.27
CYLINDERS.................. 3
CID 165
PTO HP 40
ENGINE HP 53
FUEL .... D
SPEEDS 8/8
TRANSMISSION ... SHUTTLE SHIFT
STEERING............ STANDARD
HYDRAULIC .... YES
PTO .... YES
DRIVE TYPE 2WD
ROPS/CAB .... CAB
MSRP................ $22,600

OPTIONS

2 SPD POWER SHIFT
4WD
CAB W/AIR
LOADER

SERIAL NUMBERS

YEAR	BEGINNING NO.
1998	JJE1000056
1999	JJE1008492
2000	JJE1013490
2001	JJE1017672
2002	JJE1019985

RETAIL PRICING

YEAR	HIGH	LOW
2002	$11,333	$8,500

D25

YEARS MFRD 2001-2003
SERIES.............. DX SERIES
ENGINE .... SHIBAURA
CYLINDERS.................. 3
CID 81.2
PTO HP 21.7
ENGINE HP 25
FUEL .... G
SPEEDS 9/3
TRANSMISSION .... GEAR
STEERING............ STANDARD
HITCH .... CAT. I
DRIVE TYPE 2WD
ROPS/CAB .... ROPS
WEIGHT .... 2,334 LBS.
MSRP................ $11,805

OPTIONS

2 HYD
4WD
60" MID-MOUNT MOWER
72" MID-MOUNT MOWER
HYDRO
LOADER

SERIAL NUMBERS

YEAR	BEGINNING NO.
2003	HBA0001721

RETAIL PRICING

YEAR	HIGH	LOW
2001	$4,363	$3,272
2002	$4,800	$3,600
2003	$5,256	$3,942

D29

YEARS MFRD 2001-2003
SERIES.............. DX SERIES
ENGINE .... SHIBAURA
CYLINDERS.................. 3
CID 81.2
PTO HP 25.1
ENGINE HP 29
FUEL .... D
SPEEDS 9/3
TRANSMISSION .... GEAR
STEERING............ STANDARD
HITCH .... CAT. I
DRIVE TYPE 2WD
ROPS/CAB .... ROPS
WEIGHT .... 2,334 LBS.
MSRP................ $12,557

OPTIONS

2 HYD
4WD
HYDRO
LOADER

SERIAL NUMBERS

YEAR	BEGINNING NO.
2003	HBA0001721

RETAIL PRICING

YEAR	HIGH	LOW
2001	$4,663	$3,498
2002	$5,105	$3,829
2003	$5,569	$4,177

D33

YEARS MFRD 2001-2003
SERIES.............. DX SERIES
ENGINE .... SHIBAURA
CYLINDERS.................. 3
CID 91.3
PTO HP 26.9
ENGINE HP 33
FUEL .... D
SPEEDS 9/3
TRANSMISSION .... GEAR
STEERING............ STANDARD
HITCH .... CAT. I
DRIVE TYPE 2WD
ROPS/CAB .... ROPS
WEIGHT .... 2,334 LBS.
MSRP................ $13,346

OPTIONS

2 HYD
4WD
72" MID-MOUNT MOWER
HYDRO
LOADER

SERIAL NUMBERS

YEAR	BEGINNING NO.
2003	HBA0001721

RETAIL PRICING

YEAR	HIGH	LOW
2001	$4,640	$3,480
2002	$5,130	$3,847
2003	$5,639	$4,229

D35

YEARS MFRD 2001-2003
SERIES............... D SERIES
ENGINE .... SHIBAURA
CYLINDERS.................. 3
CID 101.1
PTO HP 29.6
ENGINE HP 35
FUEL .... D

CASE-IH

SPEEDS 12/12
TRANSMISSION . . . SHUTTLE SHIFT
STEERING. . . . . STANDARD
HITCH . . . . . CAT. I
DRIVE TYPE 2WD
ROPS/CAB . . . . . ROPS
WEIGHT . . . . . 2,947 LBS.
MSRP. $13,637

OPTIONS

2 HYD
HYDRO
LOADER
MFWD
SOFT CAB

SERIAL NUMBERS

YEAR . . . . . BEGINNING NO.
2003 . . . . . HBA006321
2004 . . . . . HBA015001

RETAIL PRICING

YEAR	HIGH	LOW
2001	$4,983	$3,737
2002	$5,474	$4,106
2003	$5,988	$4,491

D40

YEARS MFRD 2001-2003
SERIES. . . . . DX SERIES
ENGINE . . . . . SHIBAURA
CYLINDERS. 4
CID 121.7
PTO HP 35
ENGINE HP 40
FUEL . . . . . D
SPEEDS 12/12
TRANSMISSION . . . SHUTTLE SHIFT
STEERING. . . . . STANDARD
HITCH . . . . . CAT. I
DRIVE TYPE 2WD
ROPS/CAB . . . . . ROPS
WEIGHT . . . . . 2,998 LBS.
MSRP. $15,230

OPTIONS

2 HYD
4WD
HYDRO
LOADER
SOFT CAB

SERIAL NUMBERS

YEAR . . . . . BEGINNING NO.
2003 . . . . . HBA006321

RETAIL PRICING

YEAR	HIGH	LOW
2001	$6,017	$4,513
2002	$6,563	$4,922
2003	$7,132	$5,349

D45

YEARS MFRD 2001-2003
SERIES. . . . . DX SERIES
ENGINE . . . . . FORD
CYLINDERS. 4
CID 135.2
PTO HP 39.6
ENGINE HP 45
FUEL . . . . . D

SPEEDS 12/12
TRANSMISSION . . . SHUTTLE SHIFT
STEERING. . . . . STANDARD
HITCH . . . . . CAT. I
DRIVE TYPE 2WD
ROPS/CAB . . . . . ROPS
WEIGHT . . . . . 3,200 LBS.
MSRP. $17,291

OPTIONS

4WD
HYDRO
LOADER
SOFT CAB

SERIAL NUMBERS

YEAR . . . . . BEGINNING NO.
2003 . . . . . HBA0006321

RETAIL PRICING

YEAR	HIGH	LOW
2001	$6,455	$4,841
2002	$7,036	$5,277
2003	$7,646	$5,734

DX18E

YEARS MFRD 2004-2006
SERIES. . . . . DX SERIES
ENGINE . . . . . ISHI-SHIBAURA
CYLINDERS. 3
CID 58.2
ENGINE HP 18
FUEL . . . . . G
SPEEDS . . . . . VARIABLE
TRANSMISSION . . . . . HYDRO
STEERING. . . . . STANDARD
HITCH . . . . . CAT. I
PTO . . . . . YES
WEIGHT . . . . . 1,314 LBS.
MSRP. $9,802

OPTIONS

2 HYD
SOFT CAB

SERIAL NUMBERS

YEAR . . . . . BEGINNING NO.
2004 . . . . . CB10001

RETAIL PRICING

YEAR	HIGH	LOW
2004	$4,577	$3,433
2005	$5,055	$3,791
2006	$5,583	$4,188

DX21

YEARS MFRD 2004-2004
SERIES. . . . . DX SERIES
ENGINE . . . . . ISHI-SHIBAURA
CYLINDERS. 3
CID 61.3
PTO HP 16
ENGINE HP 21
FUEL . . . . . D
SPEEDS 9/3
TRANSMISSION . . . . . GEAR
STEERING. . . . . STANDARD
HYDRAULIC . . . . . YES
PTO . . . . . YES
WEIGHT . . . . . 1,592 LBS.
MSRP. $12,574

OPTIONS

2 HYD
HYDRO

SERIAL NUMBERS

YEAR . . . . . BEGINNING NO.
2005 . . . . . CF10001

RETAIL PRICING

YEAR	HIGH	LOW
2004	$4,272	$3,204

DX22E

YEARS MFRD 2005-2006
SERIES. . . . . DX SERIES
CYLINDERS. 3
CID 58.2
PTO HP 17
ENGINE HP 22
FUEL . . . . . D
SPEEDS . . . . . VARIABLE
TRANSMISSION . . . . . HYDRO
STEERING. . . . . STANDARD
HITCH . . . . . CAT. I
PTO . . . . . YES
WEIGHT . . . . . 1,314 LBS.
MSRP. $10,313

OPTIONS

2 HYD
54" MID-MOUNT MOWER
60" MID-MOUNT MOWER
LOADER

RETAIL PRICING

YEAR	HIGH	LOW
2005	$5,514	$4,136
2006	$6,053	$4,540

DX23

YEARS MFRD 2005-2006
SERIES. . . . . DX SERIES
CYLINDERS. 3
CID 61.3
PTO HP 17.5
ENGINE HP 23
COOLING . . . . . LIQUID
FUEL . . . . . D
SPEEDS 9/3
TRANSMISSION . . . . . GEAR
STEERING. . . . . STANDARD
HITCH . . . . . CAT. I
HYDRAULIC . . . . . YES
PTO . . . . . YES
DRIVE TYPE 4WD
ROPS/CAB . . . . . ROPS
WEIGHT . . . . . 1,592 LBS.
MSRP. $13,336

OPTIONS

2 HYD
54" MID-MOUNT MOWER
60" MID-MOUNT MOWER
HYDRO
LOADER

SERIAL NUMBERS

YEAR . . . . . BEGINNING NO.
2005 . . . . . HDG310002
2006 . . . . . HDG310064

RETAIL PRICING

YEAR	HIGH	LOW
2005	$6,057	$4,543
2006	$6,676	$5,007

DX24

YEARS MFRD 2004-2004
SERIES. . . . . DX SERIES
ENGINE . . . . . ISHI-SHIBAURA
CYLINDERS. 3
CID 69
PTO HP 18.5
ENGINE HP 24
FUEL . . . . . D
SPEEDS 9/3
TRANSMISSION . . . . . GEAR
STEERING. . . . . STANDARD
HYDRAULIC . . . . . YES
PTO . . . . . YES
DRIVE TYPE 4WD
ROPS/CAB . . . . . ROPS
WEIGHT . . . . . 1,600 LBS.
MSRP. $12,852

OPTIONS

2 HYD
HYDRO

SERIAL NUMBERS

YEAR . . . . . BEGINNING NO.
2004 . . . . . CG10001

RETAIL PRICING

YEAR	HIGH	LOW
2004	$5,824	$4,368

DX24E

YEARS MFRD 2004-2004
SERIES. . . . . DX SERIES
ENGINE . . . . . ISHI-SHIBAURA
CYLINDERS. 3
CID 61.3
PTO HP 18.3
ENGINE HP 24
FUEL . . . . . D
SPEEDS . . . . . VARIABLE
TRANSMISSION . . . . . HYDRO
STEERING. . . . . STANDARD
HYDRAULIC . . . . . YES
PTO . . . . . YES
DRIVE TYPE 4WD
ROPS/CAB . . . . . ROPS
WEIGHT . . . . . 1,323 LBS.
MSRP. $9,989

OPTIONS

2 HYD
SOFT CAB

SERIAL NUMBERS

YEAR . . . . . BEGINNING NO.
2004 . . . . . CC10001

RETAIL PRICING

YEAR	HIGH	LOW
2004	$5,373	$4,030

DX25

YEARS MFRD 2001-2003
SERIES. . . . . DX SERIES
ENGINE . . . . . SHIBAURA

CYLINDERS 3
CID 81.2
PTO HP 20.3
ENGINE HP 25
FUEL . . . . D
SPEEDS . . . . VARIABLE
TRANSMISSION . . . . HYDRO
STEERING . . . . STANDARD
HITCH . . . . CAT. I
DRIVE TYPE 4WD
ROPS/CAB . . . . ROPS
WEIGHT . . . . 2,474 LBS.
MSRP $15,551

RETAIL PRICING

YEAR	HIGH	LOW
2001	$7,304	$5,478
2002	$7,349	$5,512
2003	$7,499	$5,624

DX25E

YEARS MFRD 2005-2006
SERIES . . . . DX SERIES
CYLINDERS 3
CID 61.3
PTO HP 19
ENGINE HP 25
FUEL . . . . G
SPEEDS . . . . VARIABLE
TRANSMISSION . . . . HYDRO
STEERING . . . . STANDARD
HITCH . . . . CAT. I
DRIVE TYPE 4WD
ROPS/CAB . . . . ROPS
WEIGHT . . . . 1,323 LBS.
MSRP $10,694

OPTIONS

2 HYD
54" MIDMOUNT MOWER
60" MIDMOUNT MOWER
LOADER

RETAIL PRICING

YEAR	HIGH	LOW
2005	$5,738	$4,303
2006	$6,284	$4,713

DX26

YEARS MFRD 2005-2006
SERIES . . . . DX SERIES
CYLINDERS 3
CID 69.0
PTO HP 19.7
ENGINE HP 26
COOLING . . . . LIQUID
FUEL . . . . D
SPEEDS . . . . VARIABLE
TRANSMISSION . . . . HYDRO
STEERING . . . . STANDARD
HITCH . . . . CAT. I
DRIVE TYPE 4WD
ROPS/CAB . . . . ROPS
WEIGHT . . . . 1,600 LBS.
MSRP $15,222

OPTIONS

2 HYD
60" MID-MOUNT MOWER
LDR

SERIAL NUMBERS

YEAR	BEGINNING NO.
2005	HDG410005
2006	HDG4101183

RETAIL PRICING

YEAR	HIGH	LOW
2005	$7,049	$5,287
2006	$7,697	$5,773

DX29

YEARS MFRD 2004-2006
SERIES . . . . DX SERIES
ENGINE . . . . ISHI-SHIBAURA
CYLINDERS 3
CID 81.2
PTO HP 23.6
ENGINE HP 29
FUEL . . . . D
SPEEDS 9/3
TRANSMISSION . . . . GEAR
STEERING . . . . STANDARD
HITCH . . . . CAT. I
DRIVE TYPE 4WD
ROPS/CAB . . . . ROPS
WEIGHT . . . . 2,474 LBS.
MSRP $16,159

OPTIONS

2 HYD
60" MID-MOUNT MOWER
72" MID-MOUNT MOWER
HYDRO
LOADER

SERIAL NUMBERS

YEAR	BEGINNING NO.
2004	HBA010001
2005	HBA011319
2006	HBA012248

RETAIL PRICING

YEAR	HIGH	LOW
2004	$6,940	$5,205
2005	$7,496	$5,622
2006	$8,043	$6,032

DX31

YEARS MFRD 2006-2007
SERIES . . . . DX SERIES
ENGINE N843
CYLINDERS 3
CID 91.3
PTO HP 24.9
ENGINE HP 31
COOLING . . . . LIQUID
FUEL . . . . D
SPEEDS 9/3
TRANSMISSION . . . . GEAR
STEERING . . . . STANDARD
HITCH . . . . CAT. I
HYDRAULIC . . . . YES
PTO . . . . YES
DRIVE TYPE 4WD
ROPS/CAB . . . . ROPS
WEIGHT . . . . 2,544 LBS.
MSRP $17,381

OPTIONS

2 HYD
HYDRO
LOADER

SERIAL NUMBERS

YEAR	BEGINNING NO.
2006	Z6DD00103
2007	Z7DE01820

RETAIL PRICING

YEAR	HIGH	LOW
2006	$8,693	$6,520
2007	$9,272	$6,954

DX33

YEARS MFRD 2004-2006
SERIES . . . . DX SERIES
ENGINE . . . . ISHI-SHIBAURA
CYLINDERS 3
CID 91.3
PTO HP 26.9
ENGINE HP 33
FUEL . . . . D
SPEEDS 9/3
TRANSMISSION . . . . GEAR
STEERING . . . . STANDARD
HITCH . . . . CAT. I
DRIVE TYPE 4WD
ROPS/CAB . . . . ROPS
WEIGHT . . . . 2,474 LBS.
MSRP $16,826

OPTIONS

2 HYD
72" MID-MOUNT MOWER
HYDRO
LOADER

SERIAL NUMBERS

YEAR	BEGINNING NO.
2004	HBA010001
2005	HBA011316

RETAIL PRICING

YEAR	HIGH	LOW
2004	$7,123	$5,342
2005	$7,591	$5,693
2006	$8,357	$6,268

DX34

YEARS MFRD 2006-2007
SERIES . . . . DX SERIES
ENGINE N843L
CYLINDERS 3
CID 101.4
PTO HP 28.9
ENGINE HP 35
COOLING . . . . LIQUID
FUEL . . . . D
SPEEDS . . . . VARIABLE
TRANSMISSION . . . . HYDRO
STEERING . . . . STANDARD
HITCH . . . . CAT. I
HYDRAULIC . . . . YES
PTO . . . . YES
DRIVE TYPE 4WD
ROPS/CAB . . . . ROPS
MSRP $19,621

OPTIONS

72" MID MOUNT MOWER
LOADER

SERIAL NUMBERS

YEAR	BEGINNING NO.
2006	Z6DD00104
2007	Z7DE01820

RETAIL PRICING

YEAR	HIGH	LOW
2006	$9,331	$6,998
2007	$9,792	$7,344

DX35

YEARS MFRD 2004-2007
SERIES . . . . DX SERIES
ENGINE . . . . SHIBAURA
CYLINDERS 3
CID 101.1
PTO HP 29.1
ENGINE HP 35
FUEL . . . . D
SPEEDS . . . . VARIABLE
TRANSMISSION . . . . HYDRO
STEERING . . . . STANDARD
HITCH . . . . CAT. I
DRIVE TYPE 4WD
ROPS/CAB . . . . ROPS
WEIGHT . . . . 3,252 LBS.
MSRP $21,657

OPTIONS

12/12 SHUTTLE SHIFT
2 HYD
2WD
LDR
SOFT CAB

SERIAL NUMBERS

YEAR	BEGINNING NO.
2005	HBA016547
2006	HBA018191
2007	Z7DE01820

RETAIL PRICING

YEAR	HIGH	LOW
2004	$8,348	$6,261
2005	$9,066	$6,799
2006	$9,719	$7,289
2007	$10,397	$7,798

DX40

YEARS MFRD 2004-2007
SERIES . . . . DX SERIES
ENGINE . . . . SHIBAURA
CYLINDERS 4
CID 121.7
PTO HP 33.2
ENGINE HP 40
COOLING . . . . LIQUID
FUEL . . . . D
SPEEDS . . . . VARIABLE
TRANSMISSION . . . . HYDRO
STEERING . . . . STANDARD
HITCH . . . . CAT. I
HYDRAULIC . . . . YES
PTO . . . . YES
DRIVE TYPE 4WD
ROPS/CAB . . . . ROPS
WEIGHT . . . . 3,328 LBS.
MSRP $23,466

OPTIONS

12/12 SHUTTLE SHIFT
2 HYD
2WD
CAB W/AIR
LDR

CASE-IH

SERIAL NUMBERS

YEAR	BEGINNING NO.
2004	HBA015001
2005	HBA016549
2006	HBA018197
2007	Z7DE01820

RETAIL PRICING

YEAR	HIGH	LOW
2004	$9,878	$7,408
2005	$10,578	$7,934
2006	$11,312	$8,484
2007	$12,209	$9,157

DX45

YEARS MFRD 2004-2007
SERIES . . . . DX SERIES
ENGINE . . . . FORD
CYLINDERS 4
CID 135.2
PTO HP 37.8
ENGINE HP 45
COOLING . . . . LIQUID
FUEL . . . . D
SPEEDS . . . . VARIABLE
TRANSMISSION . . . . HYDRO
STEERING . . . . STANDARD
HITCH . . . . CAT. I
PTO . . . . YES
DRIVE TYPE 4WD
ROPS/CAB . . . . ROPS
WEIGHT . . . . 3,417 LBS.
MSRP $25,428

OPTIONS

2 HYD
2WD
CAB W/AIR
LDR

SERIAL NUMBERS

YEAR	BEGINNING NO.
2005	HBA016552
2006	HBA018200
2007	Z7DE01820

RETAIL PRICING

YEAR	HIGH	LOW
2004	$10,669	$8,002
2005	$11,435	$8,576
2006	$12,273	$9,204
2007	$13,503	$10,127

DX48

YEARS MFRD 2004-2007
SERIES . . . . DX SERIES
ENGINE . . . . CASE
CYLINDERS 4
CID 135.2
PTO HP 40
ENGINE HP 48
FUEL . . . . D
SPEEDS 12/12
TRANSMISSION . . . SHUTTLE SHIFT
STEERING . . . . STANDARD
HYDRAULIC . . . . YES
PTO . . . . YES
DRIVE TYPE 4WD
ROPS/CAB . . . . ROPS
WEIGHT . . . . 3,700 LBS.
MSRP $24,729

OPTIONS

2WD
LDR

SERIAL NUMBERS

YEAR	BEGINNING NO.
2004	CV10001
2005	HDG500101
2006	HDG500166
2007	Z7DE01820

RETAIL PRICING

YEAR	HIGH	LOW
2004	$9,946	$7,460
2005	$10,739	$8,054
2006	$11,572	$8,679
2007	$12,450	$9,338

DX55

YEARS MFRD 2004-2007
SERIES . . . . DX SERIES
ENGINE . . . . CASE TURBO
CYLINDERS 4
CID 135.3
PTO HP 46
ENGINE HP 55
FUEL . . . . D
SPEEDS 12/12
TRANSMISSION . . . . . POWER SHIFT
STEERING . . . . STANDARD
HYDRAULIC . . . . YES
PTO . . . . YES
DRIVE TYPE 4WD
ROPS/CAB . . . . ROPS
WEIGHT . . . . 4,300 LBS.
MSRP $27,621

OPTIONS

2WD
LDR

SERIAL NUMBERS

YEAR	BEGINNING NO.
2004	CX10001
2005	HDG600154
2006	HDG600457
2007	Z7DE01820

RETAIL PRICING

YEAR	HIGH	LOW
2004	$9,800	$7,350
2005	$10,555	$7,916
2006	$11,558	$8,668
2007	$12,188	$9,141

AVG. AUCTION PRICING

LOW	HIGH	AVG
$10,710	$14,127	$13,005

DX60

YEARS MFRD 2007-2007
SERIES . . . . DX SERIES
ENGINE N844L-T
CYLINDERS 4
CID 135.2
PTO HP 51
ENGINE HP 60
COOLING . . . . LIQUID
FUEL . . . . D
SPEEDS 12/12
TRANSMISSION . . . SHUTTLE SHIFT
STEERING . . . . STANDARD
HITCH . . . . CAT. I
HYDRAULIC . . . . YES
PTO . . . . YES
DRIVE TYPE 4WD
ROPS/CAB . . . . ROPS
MSRP $29,350

OPTIONS

BALLAST BOX
FROPS/CANOPY

SERIAL NUMBERS

YEAR	BEGINNING NO.
2007	Z7DE01820

RETAIL PRICING

YEAR	HIGH	LOW
2007	$14,085	$10,564

FARMALL 30A

YEARS MFRD 2016-2016
ENGINE . . . . ISM
CYLINDERS 3
CID 92
PTO HP 27.4
ENGINE HP 32.2
COOLING . . . . LIQUID
FUEL . . . . D
SPEEDS . . . . VARIABLE
TRANSMISSION . . . SHUTTLE SHIFT
STEERING . . . . STANDARD
DRIVE TYPE 4WD
ROPS/CAB . . . . ROPS
MSRP $21,197

SERIAL NUMBERS

YEAR	BEGINNING NO.
2016	227000

RETAIL PRICING

YEAR	HIGH	LOW
2016	$19,460	$14,595

FARMALL 30B

YEARS MFRD 2012-2013
ENGINE . . . . MITSUBISHI
CYLINDERS 4
CID 92
PTO HP 23.9
ENGINE HP 28.1
COOLING . . . . LIQUID
FUEL . . . . D
SPEEDS 12/12
TRANSMISSION . . . SHUTTLE SHIFT
STEERING . . . . STANDARD
HITCH . . . . CAT. I
PTO . . . . YES
DRIVE TYPE 4WD
ROPS/CAB . . . . ROPS
WEIGHT . . . . 3,121 LBS.
MSRP $17,881

OPTIONS

1 HYD
HYDRO
LDR

SERIAL NUMBERS

YEAR	BEGINNING NO.
2012	2103012481
2013	2103014523

RETAIL PRICING

YEAR	HIGH	LOW
2012	$12,935	$9,701
2013	$13,700	$10,275

FARMALL 30C

YEARS MFRD 2014-2016
ENGINE . . . . ISM
CYLINDERS 3
CID 92
PTO HP 26
ENGINE HP 32.2
COOLING . . . . LIQUID
FUEL . . . . D
SPEEDS 12/12
TRANSMISSION . . . SHUTTLE SHIFT
STEERING . . . . STANDARD
DRIVE TYPE 4WD
ROPS/CAB . . . . ROPS
MSRP $22,872

OPTIONS

1 HYD
2 HYD
72" MID MOUNT MOWER
HYDRO
LOADER

SERIAL NUMBERS

YEAR	BEGINNING NO.
2014	ZEJV00000
2016	224201XXXX

RETAIL PRICING

YEAR	HIGH	LOW
2014	$15,616	$11,712
2015	$16,901	$12,676
2016	$19,141	$14,356

FARMALL 31

YEARS MFRD 2008-2011
SERIES . . . . FARMALL SERIES
ENGINE . . . . CASE IH
CYLINDERS 3
CID 91.3
ENGINE HP 31
COOLING . . . . LIQUID
FUEL . . . . D
SPEEDS 9/3
TRANSMISSION . . . . GEAR
STEERING . . . . STANDARD
HITCH . . . . CAT. I
HYDRAULIC . . . . YES
PTO . . . . YES
DRIVE TYPE 4WD
ROPS/CAB . . . . ROPS
WEIGHT . . . . 2,544 LBS.
MSRP $19,642

OPTIONS

72" MID MOUNT MOWER
HYDRO
LOADER
SOFT CAB

SERIAL NUMBERS

YEAR	BEGINNING NO.
2008	Z8DD04417
2009	Z9DE02675
2010	Z0DE01001
2011	ZBDE01004

RETAIL PRICING

YEAR	HIGH	LOW
2008	$10,406	$7,805
2009	$11,043	$8,282
2010	$11,705	$8,778
2011	$12,424	$9,318

FARMALL 35

YEARS MFRD 2008-2011
SERIES . . . . FARMALL SERIES
ENGINE . . . . CASE IH
CYLINDERS 3
CID 101.1
PTO HP 28.1
ENGINE HP 35
COOLING . . . . LIQUID
FUEL . . . . G
SPEEDS . . . . VARIABLE
TRANSMISSION . . . . HYDRO
STEERING . . . . STANDARD
HITCH . . . . CAT. I
HYDRAULIC . . . . YES
PTO . . . . YES
DRIVE TYPE 2WD
ROPS/CAB . . . . ROPS
WEIGHT . . . . 2,526 LBS.
MSRP $22,257

OPTIONS

72" MID MOUNT MOWER
MFWD
SOFT CAB

SERIAL NUMBERS

YEAR	BEGINNING NO.
2008	Z8DD04417
2009	Z9DE02675
2010	Z0DE01001
2011	ZBDE01004

RETAIL PRICING

YEAR	HIGH	LOW
2008	$10,843	$8,132
2009	$11,562	$8,671
2010	$12,306	$9,230
2011	$13,182	$9,887

FARMALL 35A

YEARS MFRD 2016-2016
ENGINE . . . . ISM
CYLINDERS 3
CID 92
PTO HP 30.8
ENGINE HP 36.2
COOLING . . . . LIQUID
FUEL . . . . D
SPEEDS 12/12
TRANSMISSION . . . SHUTTLE SHIFT
STEERING . . . . STANDARD
HYDRAULIC . . . . YES
PTO . . . . YES
DRIVE TYPE 4WD
ROPS/CAB . . . . ROPS
WEIGHT . . . . 3,530 LBS.
MSRP $22,859

SERIAL NUMBERS

YEAR	BEGINNING NO.
2016	227100

RETAIL PRICING

YEAR	HIGH	LOW
2016	$20,579	$15,434

FARMALL 35A SERIES II

YEARS MFRD 2017-2020
ENGINE . . . . CASE IH
CYLINDERS 3
CID 1.9L
PTO HP 29.7
ENGINE HP 35
COOLING . . . . LIQUID
FUEL . . . . D
SPEEDS 12/12
TRANSMISSION . . . SHUTTLE SHIFT
STEERING . . . . STANDARD
WEIGHT . . . . 2,563 LBS.
MSRP $19,811

OPTIONS

1 HYD OUTLET $664
BACKHOE $9,007
HYDRO TRANS $1,331
LOADER $5,316

SERIAL NUMBERS

YEAR	BEGINNING NO.
2017	AXVG0010001

RETAIL PRICING

YEAR	HIGH	LOW
2017	$15,362	$11,521
2018	$17,011	$13,302
2019	$18,813	$14,541
2020	$19,992	$15,293

FARMALL 35B

YEARS MFRD 2012-2013
ENGINE . . . . MITSUBISHI
CYLINDERS 4
CID 107
PTO HP 32.2
ENGINE HP 38
COOLING . . . . LIQUID
FUEL . . . . D
SPEEDS 12/12
TRANSMISSION . . . SHUTTLE SHIFT
STEERING . . . . STANDARD
HYDRAULIC . . . . YES
PTO . . . . YES
DRIVE TYPE 4WD
ROPS/CAB . . . . ROPS
WEIGHT . . . . 3,200 LBS.
MSRP $20,905

OPTIONS

72" MID MOUNT MOWER
HYDRO
LDR

SERIAL NUMBERS

YEAR	BEGINNING NO.
2012	2103012481
2013	2103014523

RETAIL PRICING

YEAR	HIGH	LOW
2012	$14,696	$11,022
2013	$15,738	$11,803

FARMALL 35C

YEARS MFRD 2014-2016
ENGINE . . . . ISM
CYLINDERS 3
CID 92
PTO HP 29.6
ENGINE HP 36.2
COOLING . . . . LIQUID
FUEL . . . . D
SPEEDS . . . . VARIABLE
TRANSMISSION . . . SHUTTLE SHIFT
STEERING . . . . STANDARD
DRIVE TYPE 4WD
ROPS/CAB . . . . ROPS
MSRP $24,691

OPTIONS

1 HYD
CAB (2016)
HYDRO
LOADER

SERIAL NUMBERS

YEAR	BEGINNING NO.
2014	ZEJV00000
2015	2230011356
2016	2230011980

RETAIL PRICING

YEAR	HIGH	LOW
2014	$16,910	$12,682
2015	$18,205	$13,654
2016	$21,206	$15,904

FARMALL 35C SERIES II

YEARS MFRD 2017-2020
ENGINE . . . . CASE IH
CYLINDERS 3
CID 1.9L
PTO HP 29.7
ENGINE HP 35
COOLING . . . . LIQUID
FUEL . . . . D
SPEEDS 12/12
TRANSMISSION . . . SHUTTLE SHIFT
STEERING . . . . STANDARD
WEIGHT . . . . 3,218 LBS.
MSRP $24,056

OPTIONS

2 HYD OUTLETS $406
HYDRO TRANS $1,511
LOADER $5,316

SERIAL NUMBERS

YEAR	BEGINNING NO.
2017	CXVG0010001

RETAIL PRICING

YEAR	HIGH	LOW
2017	$18,444	$13,833
2018	$20,350	$15,893
2019	$22,289	$17,431
2020	$24,079	$18,408

FARMALL 40

YEARS MFRD 2008-2011
SERIES . . . . FARMALL SERIES
ENGINE . . . . SHIBAURA
CYLINDERS 4
CID 121.7
ENGINE HP 40
COOLING . . . . LIQUID
FUEL . . . . D
SPEEDS 12/12
TRANSMISSION . . . SHUTTLE SHIFT
STEERING . . . . STANDARD
HITCH . . . . CAT. I
HYDRAULIC . . . . YES
PTO . . . . YES
DRIVE TYPE 2WD
ROPS/CAB . . . . ROPS
WEIGHT . . . . 3,433 LBS.
MSRP $27,124

OPTIONS

2 HYD
CAB W/AIR
HYDRO
LDR

SERIAL NUMBERS

YEAR	BEGINNING NO.
2008	Z8DD04417
2009	Z9DE02675
2010	Z0DE01001
2011	ZBDE01004

RETAIL PRICING

YEAR	HIGH	LOW
2008	$13,294	$9,970
2009	$14,182	$10,637
2010	$15,069	$11,302
2011	$16,203	$12,152

FARMALL 40A SERIES II

YEARS MFRD 2017-2020
ENGINE . . . . CASE IH
CYLINDERS 3
CID 1.9L
PTO HP 34
ENGINE HP 40
COOLING . . . . LIQUID
FUEL . . . . D
SPEEDS 12/12
TRANSMISSION . . . SHUTTLE SHIFT
STEERING . . . . STANDARD
DRIVE TYPE 4WD
WEIGHT . . . . 2,563 LBS.
MSRP $21,389

OPTIONS

1 HYD OUTLET $664
BACKHOE $9,007
HYDRO $1,331
LOADER $5,316

SERIAL NUMBERS

YEAR	BEGINNING NO.
2017	AXVG0010001

RETAIL PRICING

YEAR	HIGH	LOW
2017	$16,531	$12,398
2018	$18,317	$14,222
2019	$19,898	$15,406
2020	$21,249	$16,283

CASE-IH

FARMALL 40B

YEARS MFRD 2012-2014
ENGINE . . . . MITSUBISHI
CYLINDERS. 4
CID 153
PTO HP 34.3
ENGINE HP 41
COOLING . . . . LIQUID
FUEL . . . . D
SPEEDS 16/16
TRANSMISSION . . . SHUTTLE SHIFT
STEERING. . . . . STANDARD
HITCH . . . . CAT. I
DRIVE TYPE 4WD
ROPS/CAB . . . . ROPS
WEIGHT . . . . 3,325 LBS.
MSRP. $23,729

OPTIONS

1 HYD
72" MOWER
CVT (2013)
HYDRO
LOADER

SERIAL NUMBERS

YEAR	BEGINNING NO.
2012	2103012481
2013	2103014523
2013	ZCME21137-CVT
2014	ZDME21995-CVT

RETAIL PRICING

YEAR	HIGH	LOW
2012	$16,171	$12,128
2013	$16,456	$12,342
2014	$17,851	$13,388

FARMALL 40C

YEARS MFRD 2014-2016
ENGINE . . . . MITSUBISHI
CYLINDERS. 4
CID 135
PTO HP 32.4
ENGINE HP 40.7
COOLING . . . . LIQUID
FUEL . . . . D
SPEEDS . . . . VARIABLE
TRANSMISSION . . . SHUTTLE SHIFT
STEERING. . . . . STANDARD
MSRP. $28,238

OPTIONS

1 HYD
2 HYD
72" MOWER
CAB (2016)
HYDRO
LOADER

SERIAL NUMBERS

YEAR	BEGINNING NO.
2014	2231010257
2015	2231011773
2016	2231012263

RETAIL PRICING

YEAR	HIGH	LOW
2014	$19,067	$14,300
2015	$20,358	$15,269
2016	$25,467	$19,101

FARMALL 40C SERIES II

YEARS MFRD 2017-2020
ENGINE . . . . CASE IH
CYLINDERS. 3
CID 1.9L
PTO HP 34
ENGINE HP 40
COOLING . . . . LIQUID
FUEL . . . . D
SPEEDS 12/12
TRANSMISSION . . . SHUTTLE SHIFT
STEERING. . . . . STANDARD
DRIVE TYPE 4WD
ROPS/CAB . . . . CAB
WEIGHT . . . . 3,218 LBS.
MSRP. $31,437

OPTIONS

2 HYD OUTLETS $406
BACKHOE. $9,007
HYDRO TRANS $1,511
LOADER. $5,316

SERIAL NUMBERS

YEAR	BEGINNING NO.
2017	CXVG0010001

RETAIL PRICING

YEAR	HIGH	LOW
2017	$23,187	$17,391
2018	$25,464	$19,897
2019	$28,080	$21,866
2020	$31,189	$23,868

FARMALL 45

YEARS MFRD 2008-2011
SERIES. . . . . FARMALL SERIES
ENGINE . . . . SHIBAURA
CYLINDERS. 4
CID 135.2
ENGINE HP 45
COOLING . . . . LIQUID
FUEL . . . . G
SPEEDS 12/12
TRANSMISSION . . . SHUTTLE SHIFT
STEERING. . . . . STANDARD
HITCH . . . . CAT. I
HYDRAULIC . . . . YES
PTO . . . . YES
DRIVE TYPE 4WD
ROPS/CAB . . . . ROPS
WEIGHT . . . . 4,491 LBS.
MSRP. $29,404

OPTIONS

2 HYD
CAB W/AIR
HYDRO
LDR

SERIAL NUMBERS

YEAR	BEGINNING NO.
2008	Z8DD04417
2009	Z9DE02675
2010	Z0DE01001
2011	ZBDE01004

RETAIL PRICING

YEAR	HIGH	LOW
2008	$14,341	$10,756
2009	$15,507	$11,630
2010	$16,449	$12,336
2011	$17,770	$13,328

FARMALL 45A

YEARS MFRD 2010-2014
SERIES. . . . . A SERIES
ENGINE . . . . CASE TIER III
CYLINDERS. 4
PTO HP 39
ENGINE HP 45
COOLING . . . . LIQUID
FUEL . . . . D
SPEEDS 8/8
TRANSMISSION . . . . GEAR
STEERING. . . . . STANDARD
HYDRAULIC . . . . YES
PTO . . . . YES
DRIVE TYPE 2WD
ROPS/CAB . . . . ROPS
WEIGHT . . . . 3,527 LBS.
MSRP. $21,086

OPTIONS

4WD
LDR

SERIAL NUMBERS

YEAR	BEGINNING NO.
2011	6163145
2012	6198141
2013	6231921
2014	FR6271538

RETAIL PRICING

YEAR	HIGH	LOW
2010	$14,223	$10,667
2011	$15,294	$11,470
2012	$16,459	$12,344
2013	$16,803	$12,603
2014	$18,168	$13,626

FARMALL 45B CVT

YEARS MFRD 2013-2014
ENGINE . . . . CASE IH
CYLINDERS. 4
CID 135.2
PTO HP 36
ENGINE HP 45
COOLING . . . . LIQUID
FUEL . . . . D
SPEEDS . . . . VARIABLE
TRANSMISSION . . . . CVT
STEERING. . . . . STANDARD
HYDRAULIC . . . . YES
PTO . . . . YES
DRIVE TYPE 4WD
ROPS/CAB . . . . CAB
WEIGHT . . . . 4,046 LBS.
MSRP. $41,386

OPTIONS

72" MOWER
LDR

SERIAL NUMBERS

YEAR	BEGINNING NO.
2013	ZCME21137
2014	ZDME21995

RETAIL PRICING

YEAR	HIGH	LOW
2013	$29,436	$22,077
2014	$32,697	$24,523

FARMALL 45C CVT

YEARS MFRD 2015-2018
SERIES. . . . . CVT SERIES
ENGINE . . . . CASE IH FPT
CYLINDERS. 3
CID 135.9
PTO HP 36
ENGINE HP 45.1
FUEL . . . . D
SPEEDS . . . . VARIABLE
TRANSMISSION . . . . CVT
STEERING. . . . . STANDARD
HITCH . . . . CAT. I
DRIVE TYPE 4WD
ROPS/CAB . . . . CAB
WEIGHT . . . . 3,479 LBS.
MSRP. $41,424

OPTIONS

1 HYD OUTLET
2 HYD OUTLETS
LOADER

SERIAL NUMBERS

YEAR	BEGINNING NO.
2015	ZGMFA1017
2016	ZGMFA1624
2017	ZHMFA1919
2018	ZIMFC2151

RETAIL PRICING

YEAR	HIGH	LOW
2015	$26,422	$19,817
2016	$28,514	$21,386
2017	$31,532	$23,649
2018	$35,594	$26,695

FARMALL 45C SERIES II

YEARS MFRD 2017-2020
ENGINE . . . . CASE IH
CYLINDERS. 3
CID 1.9L
PTO HP 38
ENGINE HP 45
COOLING . . . . LIQUID
FUEL . . . . D
SPEEDS 16/16
TRANSMISSION . . . SHUTTLE SHIFT
STEERING. . . . . STANDARD
DRIVE TYPE 4WD
ROPS/CAB . . . . ROPS
WEIGHT . . . . 3,218 LBS.
MSRP. $30,061

OPTIONS

2 HYD OUTLETS $406
CAB W/AIR $5,541
HYDRO TRANS $1,511
LOADER. $6,536

SERIAL NUMBERS

YEAR	BEGINNING NO.
2017	CXVG0010001

RETAIL PRICING

YEAR	HIGH	LOW
2017	$22,560	$16,920
2018	$24,911	$19,337
2019	$27,483	$21,361
2020	$29,679	$22,674

FARMALL 50

YEARS MFRD . . . 2008-2011
SERIES . . . FARMALL SERIES
ENGINE . . . SHIBAURA
CYLINDERS . . . 4
CID . . . 135.2
ENGINE HP . . . 50
COOLING . . . LIQUID
FUEL . . . G
SPEEDS . . . 12/12
TRANSMISSION . . . SHUTTLE SHIFT
STEERING . . . STANDARD
HITCH . . . CAT. I
HYDRAULIC . . . YES
PTO . . . YES
DRIVE TYPE . . . 4WD
ROPS/CAB . . . ROPS
WEIGHT . . . 3,454 LBS.
MSRP . . . $27,768

OPTIONS

CVT
FOPS
LDR
SOFT CAB

SERIAL NUMBERS

YEAR	BEGINNING NO.
2008	Z8DD04417
2009	Z9DE02675
2010	Z0DE01001
2011	ZBDE01004

RETAIL PRICING

YEAR	HIGH	LOW
2008	$13,849	$10,386
2009	$14,919	$11,189
2010	$16,089	$12,067
2011	$17,369	$13,026

FARMALL 50A

YEARS MFRD . . . 2015-2020
ENGINE . . . CASE IH
CYLINDERS . . . 3
CID . . . 136
PTO HP . . . 46
ENGINE HP . . . 53
FUEL . . . D
SPEEDS . . . 16/16
TRANSMISSION . . . SHUTTLE SHIFT
STEERING . . . STANDARD
HITCH . . . CAT. I
DRIVE TYPE . . . 4WD
ROPS/CAB . . . ROPS
MSRP . . . $29,381

OPTIONS

2 HYD . . . $517
2WD . . . $-3,533
LOADER RDY . . . $3,115

SERIAL NUMBERS

YEAR	BEGINNING NO.
2015	FR5322437
2016	FR5333272

RETAIL PRICING

YEAR	HIGH	LOW
2015	$17,606	$13,203
2016	$19,258	$14,443
2017	$21,285	$15,963
2018	$24,502	$19,185
2019	$26,499	$20,457
2020	$29,119	$22,582

FARMALL 50B

YEARS MFRD . . . 2012-2014
ENGINE . . . MITSUBISHI
CYLINDERS . . . 4
CID . . . 107
PTO HP . . . 32.2
ENGINE HP . . . 38
COOLING . . . LIQUID
FUEL . . . D
SPEEDS . . . 12/12
TRANSMISSION . . . SHUTTLE SHIFT
STEERING . . . STANDARD
HITCH . . . CAT. I
DRIVE TYPE . . . 4WD
ROPS/CAB . . . CAB
WEIGHT . . . 3,400 LBS.
MSRP . . . $20,905

OPTIONS

1 HYD
72" MOWER
CVT (2013-2014)
HYDRO
LDR

SERIAL NUMBERS

YEAR	BEGINNING NO.
2013	ZCME21137
2014	ZDME21995

RETAIL PRICING

YEAR	HIGH	LOW
2012	$12,811	$9,608
2013	$13,630	$10,223

FARMALL 50C

YEARS MFRD . . . 2014-2016
ENGINE . . . IH
CYLINDERS . . . 4
CID . . . 135
PTO HP . . . 37.3
ENGINE HP . . . 45.6
COOLING . . . LIQUID
FUEL . . . D
SPEEDS . . . 16/16
TRANSMISSION . . . SHUTTLE SHIFT
STEERING . . . STANDARD
DRIVE TYPE . . . 4WD
ROPS/CAB . . . ROPS
MSRP . . . $27,530

OPTIONS

2 HYD
72" MOWER
CAB (2016)
HYDRO
LOADER

SERIAL NUMBERS

YEAR	BEGINNING NO.
2014	2229010260
2015	2229012243
2016	2229012778

RETAIL PRICING

YEAR	HIGH	LOW
2014	$20,621	$15,466
2015	$21,535	$16,151
2016	$24,393	$18,295

FARMALL 55C CVT

YEARS MFRD . . . 2015-2018
SERIES . . . CVT SERIES
ENGINE . . . CASE IH FPT
CYLINDERS . . . 3
CID . . . 135.9
PTO HP . . . 43
ENGINE HP . . . 53
FUEL . . . D
SPEEDS . . . VARIABLE
TRANSMISSION . . . CVT
STEERING . . . STANDARD
HITCH . . . CAT. I
DRIVE TYPE . . . 4WD
ROPS/CAB . . . CAB
WEIGHT . . . 3,218 LBS.
MSRP . . . $43,594

OPTIONS

1 HYD
2 HYD
LOADER

SERIAL NUMBERS

YEAR	BEGINNING NO.
2015	ZGMFB1019
2016	ZGMFB1626
2017	ZHMFB1910
2018	ZIMFB2153

RETAIL PRICING

YEAR	HIGH	LOW
2015	$28,163	$21,122
2016	$30,753	$23,065
2017	$33,418	$25,064
2018	$37,946	$28,460

FARMALL 55C SERIES II

YEARS MFRD . . . 2017-2020
ENGINE . . . CASE IH
CYLINDERS . . . 3
CID . . . 1.9L
PTO HP . . . 42.5
ENGINE HP . . . 55
COOLING . . . LIQUID
FUEL . . . D
SPEEDS . . . 16/16
TRANSMISSION . . . SHUTTLE SHIFT
STEERING . . . STANDARD
DRIVE TYPE . . . 4WD
ROPS/CAB . . . ROPS
WEIGHT . . . 3,218 LBS.
MSRP . . . $36,310

OPTIONS

2 HYD OUTLETS . . . $406
CAB W/AIR . . . $5,541
HYDRO TRANS . . . $1,511
LOADER . . . $6,536

SERIAL NUMBERS

YEAR	BEGINNING NO.
2017	CXVG0010001

RETAIL PRICING

YEAR	HIGH	LOW
2017	$26,794	$20,095
2018	$29,366	$22,967
2019	$33,060	$25,211
2020	$36,091	$27,584

JX55

YEARS MFRD . . . 2002-2006
SERIES . . . JX SERIES
ENGINE . . . CASE
CYLINDERS . . . 3
CID . . . 165
PTO HP . . . 45
ENGINE HP . . . 58
FUEL . . . D
SPEEDS . . . 12/12
TRANSMISSION . . . POWER SHIFT
STEERING . . . STANDARD
HYDRAULIC . . . YES
PTO . . . YES
DRIVE TYPE . . . 2WD
ROPS/CAB . . . ROPS
WEIGHT . . . 5,813 LBS.
MSRP . . . $19,988

OPTIONS

4WD
CAB W/AIR
LDR

SERIAL NUMBERS

YEAR	BEGINNING NO.
2003	HFJ000001
2004	HFJ013982
2005	HFJ025393
2006	HFJ034575

RETAIL PRICING

YEAR	HIGH	LOW
2002	$9,501	$7,126
2003	$9,796	$7,347
2004	$10,511	$7,883
2005	$11,681	$8,761
2006	$12,009	$9,007

JX1060C

YEARS MFRD . . . 2004-2007
ENGINE . . . CASE
CYLINDERS . . . 3
CID . . . 179
PTO HP . . . 45
ENGINE HP . . . 57
COOLING . . . LIQUID
FUEL . . . D
SPEEDS . . . 16/16
TRANSMISSION . . . POWER SHIFT
STEERING . . . STANDARD
HYDRAULIC . . . YES
PTO . . . YES
DRIVE TYPE . . . 2WD
ROPS/CAB . . . ROPS
WEIGHT . . . 5,588 LBS.
MSRP . . . $23,028

OPTIONS
16/16 POWER SHUTTLE
CAB W/AIR
LDR

SERIAL NUMBERS
YEAR	BEGINNING NO.
2004	1317364
2005	HJH021881
2006	HJH051488
2007	HJH080554

RETAIL PRICING
YEAR	HIGH	LOW
2004	$10,736	$8,052
2005	$11,381	$8,536
2006	$12,160	$9,120
2007	$13,111	$9,833

234
YEARS MFRD 1982-1986
ENGINE .... MITSUBISHI
CID 51.8
ENGINE HP 15.2
COOLING .... LIQUID
FUEL .... D
SPEEDS 6/1
TRANSMISSION .... GEAR
STEERING .... STANDARD
DRIVE TYPE 2WD
ROPS/CAB .... ROPS
WEIGHT .... 1,360 LBS.
MSRP $7,046

OPTIONS
4WD
HYDRO

SERIAL NUMBERS
RIGHT SIDE OF ENGINE MAIN FRAME

YEAR	BEGINNING NO.
1982	8001
1983	8683
1983	8122-HYDRO
1984	8383-HYDRO
1984	8844
1985	09406
1986	10454

RETAIL PRICING
YEAR	HIGH	LOW
1982	$589	$441
1983	$796	$597
1984	$1,011	$758
1985	$1,231	$923
1986	$1,459	$1,094

235
YEARS MFRD 1986-1990
ENGINE .... MITSUBISHI
CYLINDERS 3
CID 51.8
PTO HP 15.2
ENGINE HP 18
FUEL .... D
SPEEDS 6/2
TRANSMISSION .... HYDRO
STEERING .... STANDARD
PTO .... YES
DRIVE TYPE 2WD
ROPS/CAB .... ROPS
WEIGHT .... 1,350 LBS.
MSRP $9,410

OPTIONS
1 HYD
4WD

SERIAL NUMBERS
RIGHT FRONT FRAME

YEAR	BEGINNING NO.
1986	17626500
1987	17627429
1988	CCJ0001501
1989	CCJ0002370
1990	CCJ0031120

RETAIL PRICING
YEAR	HIGH	LOW
1986	$1,359	$1,019
1987	$1,595	$1,196
1988	$1,832	$1,374
1989	$2,081	$1,561
1990	$2,330	$1,747

AVG. AUCTION PRICING
LOW	HIGH	AVG
$1,020	$2,142	$1,785

244
YEARS MFRD 1982-1986
ENGINE .... MITSUBISHI
ENGINE HP 18
COOLING .... LIQUID
FUEL .... D
SPEEDS 9/3
TRANSMISSION .... GEAR
STEERING .... STANDARD
DRIVE TYPE 2WD
WEIGHT .... 1,865 LBS.
MSRP $7,535

OPTIONS
4WD
HYDRO

SERIAL NUMBERS
RIGHT SIDE OF ENGINE MAIN FRAME

YEAR	BEGINNING NO.
1982	8001
1983	8460
1984	9089
1985	09805
1986	11180

RETAIL PRICING
YEAR	HIGH	LOW
1982	$592	$444
1983	$800	$600
1984	$1,011	$758
1985	$1,231	$923
1986	$1,459	$1,094

245
YEARS MFRD 1986-1990
ENGINE .... MITSUBISHI
CYLINDERS 3
CID 59.7
PTO HP 18
ENGINE HP 21
FUEL .... D
SPEEDS .... 9/3 SYN
TRANSMISSION .... GEAR
STEERING .... STANDARD
DRIVE TYPE 2WD
ROPS/CAB .... ROPS
WEIGHT .... 1,910 LBS.
MSRP $10,295

OPTIONS
4WD
SYNCHRO

SERIAL NUMBERS
RIGHT FRONT FRAME

YEAR	BEGINNING NO.
1986	17636500
1987	17637276
1988	CCJ0009001
1989	CCJ0009993
1990	CCJ0010844

RETAIL PRICING
YEAR	HIGH	LOW
1986	$1,475	$1,106
1987	$1,711	$1,283
1988	$1,952	$1,464
1989	$2,196	$1,647
1990	$2,465	$1,849

254
YEARS MFRD 1982-1986
ENGINE .... MITSUBISHI
CID 64.7
PTO HP 21
COOLING .... LIQUID
FUEL .... D
SPEEDS 9/3
TRANSMISSION .... GEAR
STEERING .... STANDARD
WEIGHT .... 2,075 LBS.
MSRP $8,274

OPTIONS
4WD
PS

SERIAL NUMBERS
RIGHT SIDE OF ENGINE MAIN FRAME

YEAR	BEGINNING NO.
1982	8001
1983	8386
1984	8811
1985	09451
1986	11464

RETAIL PRICING
YEAR	HIGH	LOW
1982	$762	$571
1983	$990	$743
1984	$1,206	$904
1985	$1,438	$1,079
1986	$1,682	$1,261

255
YEARS MFRD 1986-1990
ENGINE .... MITSUBISHI
CYLINDERS 3
CID 64.7
PTO HP 21
ENGINE HP 24
FUEL .... D
SPEEDS 9/3
TRANSMISSION .... GEAR
STEERING .... STANDARD
PTO .... YES
DRIVE TYPE 2WD
ROPS/CAB .... ROPS
WEIGHT .... 1,762 LBS.
MSRP $10,841

OPTIONS
4WD
SYNCHRO

SERIAL NUMBERS
RIGHT FRONT FRAME

YEAR	BEGINNING NO.
1986	17646500
1987	17647066
1988	CCJ0018001
1989	CCJ0018787
1990	CCJ0019378

RETAIL PRICING
YEAR	HIGH	LOW
1986	$1,993	$1,495
1987	$2,250	$1,688
1988	$2,515	$1,886
1989	$2,795	$2,096
1990	$3,075	$2,306

265
YEARS MFRD 1987-1992
ENGINE .... MITSUBISHI
CYLINDERS 3
PTO HP 24
FUEL .... G
TRANSMISSION .... GEAR
STEERING .... STANDARD
WEIGHT .... 2,523 LBS.
MSRP $12,340

SERIAL NUMBERS
RIGHT FRONT FRAME

YEAR	BEGINNING NO.
1987	17666500
1988	CCJ0025001
1989	CCJ0025194
1990	CCJ0059281
1991	CCJ0089368
1992	CCJ0119455

RETAIL PRICING
YEAR	HIGH	LOW
1987	$2,204	$1,653
1988	$2,430	$1,822
1989	$2,825	$2,119
1990	$3,579	$2,684
1991	$3,691	$2,769
1992	$3,802	$2,851

265 OFFSET
YEARS MFRD 1987-1991
ENGINE .... MITSUBISHI
CYLINDERS 3
CID 78.7
PTO HP 24
ENGINE HP 27
FUEL .... D
SPEEDS .... 8/2 GEAR 9/3 SYN
WEIGHT .... 2,810 LBS.
MSRP $12,340

SERIAL NUMBERS

RIGHT SIDE OF FRAME

YEAR	BEGINNING NO.
1987	17666500
1988	CCJ0025001
1989	CCJ0025194
1990	CCJ0059281
1991	CCJ0069487

RETAIL PRICING

YEAR	HIGH	LOW
1987	$4,781	$3,586
1988	$4,928	$3,696
1989	$5,202	$3,902
1990	$5,721	$4,291
1991	$5,885	$4,414

274

YEARS MFRD 1979-1988
ENGINE .... NISSAN
CID 99
PTO HP 27
COOLING .... LIQUID
FUEL .... D
SPEEDS 8/2
TRANSMISSION .... GEAR
STEERING .... STANDARD
WEIGHT .... 3,150 LBS.

SERIAL NUMBERS

RIGHT SIDE OF ENGINE MAIN FRAME

YEAR	BEGINNING NO.
1979	502
1980	670
1981	1836
1982	8948
1983	9556
1984	12000
1985	15000
1986	18000
1987	21000
1988	24000

275

YEARS MFRD 1986-1991
ENGINE .... MITSUBISHI
CYLINDERS 3
CID 91.3
PTO HP 27
ENGINE HP 31
FUEL .... D
SPEEDS 9/3
TRANSMISSION .... GEAR
STEERING .... STANDARD
PTO .... YES
DRIVE TYPE 2WD
ROPS/CAB .... ROPS
WEIGHT .... 2,512 LBS.
MSRP $13,072

OPTIONS

2 HYD
4WD

SERIAL NUMBERS

RIGHT FRONT FRAME

YEAR	BEGINNING NO.
1986	17656500
1987	17656510
1988	CCJ0028001
1989	CCJ0028614
1990	CCJ0029303
1991	CCJ0019378

RETAIL PRICING

YEAR	HIGH	LOW
1986	$2,419	$1,815
1987	$2,688	$2,016
1988	$2,969	$2,227
1989	$3,260	$2,445
1990	$3,559	$2,669
1991	$3,871	$2,903

AVG. AUCTION PRICING

LOW	HIGH	AVG
$2,520	$4,349	$3,865

284

YEARS MFRD 1985-1987
ENGINE .... NISSAN
CYLINDERS 3
CID 99
PTO HP 27.47
COOLING .... LIQUID
FUEL .... D
SPEEDS 8/2
TRANSMISSION .... GEAR
STEERING .... STANDARD
DRIVE TYPE 2WD
ROPS/CAB .... ROPS
MSRP $11,185

SERIAL NUMBERS

RIGHT FRONT FRAME

YEAR	BEGINNING NO.
1985	4031
1986	4371
1987	4716

RETAIL PRICING

YEAR	HIGH	LOW
1985	$3,158	$2,368
1986	$3,663	$2,747
1987	$3,755	$2,816

385

YEARS MFRD 1985-1990
ENGINE .... CASE IH
CYLINDERS 3
CID 155
PTO HP 35
FUEL .... D
SPEEDS .... 8/4 SYN 16/8 8/8
TRANSMISSION .... GEAR
STEERING .... STANDARD
PTO .... YES
DRIVE TYPE 2WD
ROPS/CAB .... ROPS
WEIGHT .... 4,929 LBS.
MSRP $13,831

OPTIONS

2 HYD
4WD
LOADER

SERIAL NUMBERS

YEAR	BEGINNING NO.
1985	15000
1986	18000
1987	18806
1988	19454
1989	20881
1990	22231

RETAIL PRICING

YEAR	HIGH	LOW
1985	$2,468	$1,851
1986	$2,746	$2,059
1987	$3,028	$2,271
1988	$3,325	$2,494
1989	$3,629	$2,722
1990	$3,947	$2,961

395

YEARS MFRD 1991-1993
ENGINE .... CASE
CYLINDERS 3
CID 155
PTO HP 35
FUEL .... D
SPEEDS 8/4-16/8
TRANSMISSION .... GEAR
STEERING .... STANDARD
PTO .... YES
DRIVE TYPE 2WD
ROPS/CAB .... ROPS
WEIGHT .... 5,680 LBS.
MSRP $16,744

OPTIONS

2 HYD
4WD
LOADER

SERIAL NUMBERS

YEAR	BEGINNING NO.
1991	JJE0001501
1992	JJE0018291
1993	JJE0025736

RETAIL PRICING

YEAR	HIGH	LOW
1991	$4,349	$3,262
1992	$4,686	$3,514
1993	$5,037	$3,778

484

YEARS MFRD 1985-1986
ENGINE .... OWN
CYLINDERS 3
CID 179
PTO HP 42.4
COOLING .... LIQUID
FUEL .... G
SPEEDS 8/4
TRANSMISSION .... GEAR
STEERING .... STANDARD
HYDRAULIC .... YES
PTO .... YES
DRIVE TYPE 2WD
ROPS/CAB .... ROPS
WEIGHT .... 4,540 LBS.

484 MFWD

YEARS MFRD 1985-1986
ENGINE .... CASE
CYLINDERS 3
CID 179
PTO HP 42.4
COOLING .... LIQUID
FUEL .... G
SPEEDS 8/4
TRANSMISSION .... GEAR
STEERING .... STANDARD
HYDRAULIC .... YES
PTO .... YES
WEIGHT .... 4,940 LBS.

485

YEARS MFRD 1985-1991
ENGINE .... CASE
CYLINDERS 3
CID 179
PTO HP 43
COOLING .... LIQUID
FUEL .... G
SPEEDS 8/4 16/8 8/8
TRANSMISSION .... GEAR
STEERING .... STANDARD
HYDRAULIC .... YES
PTO .... YES
DRIVE TYPE 2WD
ROPS/CAB .... ROPS
WEIGHT .... 4,960 LBS.

OPTIONS

LDR

SERIAL NUMBERS

RIGHT FRONT BOLSTER

YEAR	BEGINNING NO.
1985	E0015000
1986	E0018000
1987	E0019057
1988	E0021250
1989	E0023490
1990	E0024938
1991	E0026386

RETAIL PRICING

YEAR	HIGH	LOW
1985	$2,204	$1,653
1986	$2,493	$1,870
1987	$2,780	$2,085
1988	$3,164	$2,373
1989	$3,451	$2,588
1990	$3,739	$2,804
1991	$3,931	$2,948

AVG. AUCTION PRICING

LOW	HIGH	AVG
$4,080	$7,446	$5,610

495

YEARS MFRD 1991-1994
ENGINE .... CASE
CYLINDERS 3
CID 179
PTO HP 43
ENGINE HP 53
COOLING .... LIQUID
FUEL .... D
SPEEDS 8/4 16/8 8/8
TRANSMISSION .... GEAR
STEERING .... STANDARD
HITCH .... CAT. I
HYDRAULIC .... YES
PTO .... YES
DRIVE TYPE 2WD
ROPS/CAB .... ROPS
WEIGHT .... 4,960 LBS.

OPTIONS
4WD
LDR

SERIAL NUMBERS

YEAR	BEGINNING NO.
1991	JJE0001501
1992	JJE0018291
1993	JJE0025736
1994	JJE0033230

RETAIL PRICING

YEAR	HIGH	LOW
1991	$4,315	$3,236
1992	$4,697	$3,523
1993	$5,082	$3,811
1994	$5,465	$4,099

1120

YEARS MFRD 1991-1991
ENGINE .... MITSUBISHI
CYLINDERS 3
CID 64.7
PTO HP 16.5
ENGINE HP 19
FUEL .... D
TRANSMISSION .... GEAR
STEERING .... STANDARD
DRIVE TYPE 2WD
ROPS/CAB .... ROPS
WEIGHT .... 1,680 LBS.
MSRP $11,500

OPTIONS
1 HYD
4WD
HYDRO

SERIAL NUMBERS

YEAR	BEGINNING NO.
1991	CCJ0069001-CA
1991	CCJ0106501-RO

RETAIL PRICING

YEAR	HIGH	LOW
1991	$2,686	$2,014

1120 UTILITY

YEARS MFRD 1991-1991
ENGINE .... MITSUBISHI K3E
CYLINDERS 3
CID 64.7
PTO HP 16.5
ENGINE HP 19
FUEL .... D
SPEEDS .... 6/2 SYN
DRIVE TYPE 2WD
ROPS/CAB .... ROPS
WEIGHT .... 1,350 LBS.
MSRP $10,500

OPTIONS
4WD

RETAIL PRICING

YEAR	HIGH	LOW
1991	$4,704	$3,528

1130

YEARS MFRD 1991-1991
ENGINE .... MITSUBISHI
CYLINDERS 3
CID 75.4
PTO HP 20
FUEL .... D
TRANSMISSION .... GEAR
STEERING .... STANDARD
PTO .... YES
DRIVE TYPE 2WD
ROPS/CAB .... ROPS
WEIGHT .... 2,062 LBS.
MSRP $12,629

OPTIONS
1 HYD
4WD

SERIAL NUMBERS

YEAR	BEGINNING NO.
1991	CCJ0119001-CA
1991	CCJ0081501-RO

RETAIL PRICING

YEAR	HIGH	LOW
1991	$2,905	$2,179

1130 UTILITY

YEARS MFRD 1991-1991
ENGINE .... MITSUBISHI K3G
CYLINDERS 3
CID 75.4
PTO HP 18
ENGINE HP 23
FUEL .... D
SPEEDS 9/3
TRANSMISSION .... HYDRO
DRIVE TYPE 2WD
ROPS/CAB .... ROPS
WEIGHT .... 1,900 LBS.
MSRP $11,500

OPTIONS
4WD

RETAIL PRICING

YEAR	HIGH	LOW
1991	$4,939	$3,704

1140

YEARS MFRD 1991-1991
ENGINE .... MITSUBISHI
CYLINDERS 3
CID 91.3
PTO HP 23
FUEL .... D
TRANSMISSION .... GEAR
STEERING .... STANDARD
PTO .... YES
DRIVE TYPE 2WD
ROPS/CAB .... ROPS
WEIGHT .... 2,062 LBS.
MSRP $13,350

OPTIONS
1 HYD
4WD

SERIAL NUMBERS

YEAR	BEGINNING NO.
1991	CCJ0094001

RETAIL PRICING

YEAR	HIGH	LOW
1991	$3,178	$2,384

1140 UTILITY

YEARS MFRD 1991-1991
ENGINE .... MITSUBISHI K3M
CYLINDERS 3
CID 91.3
PTO HP 23
ENGINE HP 27
COOLING .... LIQUID
FUEL .... D
SPEEDS .... VARIABLE
TRANSMISSION .... HYDRO
STEERING .... STANDARD
DRIVE TYPE 2WD
ROPS/CAB .... ROPS
WEIGHT .... 1,950 LBS.
MSRP $12,000

OPTIONS
4WD

RETAIL PRICING

YEAR	HIGH	LOW
1991	$5,290	$3,967

1194

YEARS MFRD 1983-1985
ENGINE .... CASE
CID 165
PTO HP 43
COOLING .... LIQUID
FUEL .... D
SPEEDS 12/4
TRANSMISSION .... GEAR
STEERING .... STANDARD
WEIGHT .... 4,516 LBS.

SERIAL NUMBERS
ON PLATE INSIDE CAB ABOVE DOOR

YEAR	BEGINNING NO.
1983	11038050
1984	11038494
1985	11480001

2120 MFWD

YEARS MFRD 1990-1992
ENGINE .... SAME
CID 183
PTO HP 40
FUEL .... D
SPEEDS 8/8
TRANSMISSION .... HYDRO
STEERING .... STANDARD
PTO .... YES
WEIGHT .... 4,500 LBS.

3210

YEARS MFRD 1994-1995
ENGINE .... CASE
CID 155
PTO HP 36
FUEL .... D
SPEEDS 8/4
TRANSMISSION .... GEAR
STEERING .... STANDARD
PTO .... YES
WEIGHT .... 5,100 LBS.

3220

YEARS MFRD 1994-1997
ENGINE .... CASE
CYLINDERS 3
CID 179
PTO HP 42
COOLING .... LIQUID
FUEL .... D
SPEEDS 8/4
TRANSMISSION .... GEAR
STEERING .... STANDARD
HYDRAULIC .... YES
PTO .... YES
DRIVE TYPE 2WD
ROPS/CAB .... ROPS
WEIGHT .... 5,590 LBS.

OPTIONS
8/8 SHUTTLE SHIFT
LOADER
MFWD

SERIAL NUMBERS

YEAR	BEGINNING NO.
1994	JJE0900062
1995	JJE0904337
1996	JJE0915555
1997	JJE0923921

RETAIL PRICING

YEAR	HIGH	LOW
1994	$5,368	$4,026
1995	$5,848	$4,386
1996	$6,136	$4,602
1997	$6,519	$4,889

3230

YEARS MFRD 1994-1997
ENGINE .... CASE
CYLINDERS 4
CID 206
PTO HP 52
COOLING .... LIQUID
FUEL .... D
SPEEDS 16/8
TRANSMISSION .... GEAR
STEERING .... STANDARD
HYDRAULIC .... YES
PTO .... YES
DRIVE TYPE 4WD
ROPS/CAB .... ROPS
WEIGHT .... 5,660 LBS.
MSRP $20,350

SERIAL NUMBERS

YEAR	BEGINNING NO.
1994	JJE0900062
1995	JJE0904337
1996	JJE0915556
1997	JJE0923921

RETAIL PRICING

YEAR	HIGH	LOW
1997	$12,542	$9,406

CHALLENGER

MT225
YEARS MFRD 2002-2004
SERIES. . . . . MT200 SERIES
ENGINE . . . . ISEKI
PTO HP 19
ENGINE HP. 23.3
COOLING . . . . AIR
FUEL . . . . D
SPEEDS . . . . VARIABLE
TRANSMISSION . . . . HYDRO
STEERING. . . . . STANDARD
HITCH . . . . CAT. I
HYDRAULIC . . . . YES
PTO. YES
WEIGHT . . . . 1,499 LBS.
MSRP. $15,050

SERIAL NUMBERS

OPERATORS PLATFORM, BELOW SEAT

YEAR	BEGINNING NO.
2002	JCL1
2003	JCM1
2004	JCN1

RETAIL PRICING

YEAR	HIGH	LOW
2002	$3,643	$2,732
2003	$4,039	$3,029
2004	$4,448	$3,336

MT225B
YEARS MFRD 2005-2008
SERIES. . . . . MT200B SERIES
ENGINE . . . . ISEKI TIER II
CYLINDERS. 3
ENGINE HP. 22.5
FUEL . . . . D
SPEEDS . . . . VARIABLE
TRANSMISSION . . . . HYDRO
STEERING. . . . . STANDARD
HITCH . . . . CAT. I
HYDRAULIC . . . . YES
PTO. YES
WEIGHT . . . . 1,520 LBS.
MSRP. $13,095

OPTIONS

2 HYD

SERIAL NUMBERS

YEAR	BEGINNING NO.
2005	JP
2006	JR
2007	JS
2008	JT

RETAIL PRICING

YEAR	HIGH	LOW
2005	$4,683	$3,512
2006	$5,129	$3,847
2007	$5,592	$4,194
2008	$6,111	$4,583

MT255
YEARS MFRD 2002-2004
SERIES. . . . . MT200 SERIES
ENGINE . . . . ISEKI
PTO HP 24.2
ENGINE HP. 28.4
FUEL . . . . D
SPEEDS 9/3
TRANSMISSION . . . . GEAR
STEERING. . . . . STANDARD
HITCH . . . . CAT. I
HYDRAULIC . . . . YES
PTO. YES
WEIGHT . . . . 2,100 LBS.
MSRP. $14,344

OPTIONS

2 HYD
LDR

SERIAL NUMBERS

OPERATORS PLATFORM BELOW SEAT

YEAR	BEGINNING NO.
2002	JCL2
2003	JCM2
2004	JCN2

RETAIL PRICING

YEAR	HIGH	LOW
2002	$3,508	$2,631
2003	$3,915	$2,936
2004	$4,339	$3,254

MT255B
YEARS MFRD 2005-2008
SERIES. . . . . MT200B SERIES
ENGINE . . . . TIER II
CYLINDERS. 3
ENGINE HP. 28.4
COOLING . . . . LIQUID
FUEL . . . . D
SPEEDS 9/3
TRANSMISSION . . . . . POWER SHIFT
STEERING. . . . . STANDARD
HITCH . . . . CAT. I
PTO. YES
WEIGHT . . . . 1,665 LBS.
MSRP. $15,471

OPTIONS

2 HYD

SERIAL NUMBERS

YEAR	BEGINNING NO.
2005	JP
2006	JR
2007	JS

RETAIL PRICING

YEAR	HIGH	LOW
2005	$4,936	$3,702
2006	$5,412	$4,059
2007	$5,907	$4,430
2008	$6,431	$4,823

MT265
YEARS MFRD 2002-2004
SERIES. . . . . MT200 SERIES
ENGINE . . . . ISEKI
PTO HP 26.8
ENGINE HP. 33
FUEL . . . . D
SPEEDS 16/16
TRANSMISSION . . . . . POWER SHIFT
STEERING. . . . . STANDARD
PTO. YES
WEIGHT . . . . 2,746 LBS.
MSRP. $19,079

OPTIONS

2 HYD
HYDRO

SERIAL NUMBERS

OPERATORS PLATFORM BELOW SEAT

YEAR	BEGINNING NO.
2002	JCL3
2003	JCM3
2004	JCN3

RETAIL PRICING

YEAR	HIGH	LOW
2002	$5,180	$3,885
2003	$5,644	$4,233
2004	$6,133	$4,600

MT265B
YEARS MFRD 2005-2009
SERIES. . . . . MT200B SERIES
CYLINDERS. 3
CID 91.4
PTO HP 24.5
ENGINE HP. 33
COOLING . . . . AIR
FUEL . . . . D
SPEEDS 8/8
TRANSMISSION . . . SHUTTLE SHIFT
STEERING. . . . . STANDARD
HITCH . . . . CAT. II
HYDRAULIC . . . . YES
PTO. YES
WEIGHT . . . . 3,136 LBS.
MSRP. $17,757

OPTIONS

12/12 POWER SHIFT
2 HYD
HYDRO

SERIAL NUMBERS

YEAR	BEGINNING NO.
2005	JP
2006	JR
2007	JS
2008	JT

RETAIL PRICING

YEAR	HIGH	LOW
2005	$6,579	$4,934
2006	$7,115	$5,336
2007	$7,677	$5,757
2008	$8,268	$6,201
2009	$8,916	$6,687

MT275
YEARS MFRD 2002-2004
SERIES. . . . . MT200 SERIES
ENGINE . . . . ISEKI
PTO HP 31
ENGINE HP. 40.1
FUEL . . . . D
SPEEDS 8/8
TRANSMISSION . . . . . POWER SHIFT
STEERING. . . . . STANDARD
HITCH . . . . CAT. I
HYDRAULIC . . . . YES
PTO. YES
WEIGHT . . . . 2,788 LBS.
MSRP. $19,734

OPTIONS

2 HYD
SOFT CAB

SERIAL NUMBERS

OPERATOR'S PLATFORM BELOW SEAT

YEAR	BEGINNING NO.
2002	JCL4
2003	JCM4
2004	JCN4
2005	JCP4

RETAIL PRICING

YEAR	HIGH	LOW
2002	$5,865	$4,398
2003	$6,358	$4,769
2004	$6,876	$5,157

MT275B
YEARS MFRD 2005-2009
SERIES. . . . . MT200B SERIES
ENGINE . . . . TIER II TURBO
CYLINDERS. 3
PTO HP 31
ENGINE HP. 40.1
COOLING . . . . LIQUID
FUEL . . . . D
SPEEDS 8/8
TRANSMISSION . . . SHUTTLE SHIFT
STEERING. . . . . STANDARD
HITCH . . . . CAT. I
WEIGHT . . . . 3,169 LBS.
MSRP. $20,371

OPTIONS

2 HYD
HYDRO

SERIAL NUMBERS

YEAR	BEGINNING NO.
2005	JP
2006	JR
2007	JS
2008	JT

RETAIL PRICING

YEAR	HIGH	LOW
2005	$7,654	$5,741
2006	$8,230	$6,173
2007	$8,834	$6,625
2008	$9,467	$7,100
2009	$10,161	$7,621

MT285
YEARS MFRD 2003-2004
SERIES. . . . . MT200 SERIES
ENGINE . . . . ISEKI
CYLINDERS. 3
PTO HP 32.4
ENGINE HP. 40.1
FUEL . . . . D
SPEEDS 16/16
TRANSMISSION . . . . . POWER SHIFT

CHALLENGER

STEERING............STANDARD
HITCH..................CAT. I
HYDRAULIC...............YES
PTO.....................YES
WEIGHT............3,174 LBS.
MSRP...............$21,649

OPTIONS

HYDRO

SERIAL NUMBERS

OPERATOR'S PLATFORM BELOW SEAT

YEAR	BEGINNING NO.
2003	JCM6
2004	JCN6

RETAIL PRICING

YEAR	HIGH	LOW
2003	$7,658	$5,744
2004	$8,308	$6,231

MT285B

YEARS MFRD........2005-2009
SERIES..........MT200B SERIES
CYLINDERS..................4
CID....................134.1
PTO HP....................38
ENGINE HP...............47.5
FUEL.......................D
SPEEDS...................8/8
TRANSMISSION...SHUTTLE SHIFT
STEERING............STANDARD
HITCH..................CAT. I
HYDRAULIC...............YES
PTO.....................YES
ROPS/CAB...............ROPS
WEIGHT............3,660 LBS.
MSRP...............$25,376

OPTIONS

12/12 POWER SHIFT
HYDRO
LDR

SERIAL NUMBERS

YEAR	BEGINNING NO.
2005	JP
2006	JR
2007	JS
2008	JT

RETAIL PRICING

YEAR	HIGH	LOW
2005	$9,286	$6,964
2006	$9,960	$7,470
2007	$10,804	$8,103
2008	$11,631	$8,723
2009	$12,531	$9,399

AVG. AUCTION PRICING

LOW	HIGH	AVG
$8,152	$11,156	$9,440

MT295

YEARS MFRD........2002-2004
SERIES...........MT200 SERIES
ENGINE.................ISEKI
PTO HP....................37
ENGINE HP...............44.2
FUEL.......................D
SPEEDS.................12/12
TRANSMISSION.....POWER SHIFT
STEERING............STANDARD
HITCH..................CAT. I
HYDRAULIC...............YES
PTO.....................YES
WEIGHT............3,733 LBS.
MSRP...............$26,659

OPTIONS

2 HYD
HYDRO

SERIAL NUMBERS

OPERATOR'S PLATFORM BELOW SEAT

YEAR	BEGINNING NO.
2002	JCL5
2003	JCM50601
2004	JCN5

RETAIL PRICING

YEAR	HIGH	LOW
2002	$7,736	$5,802
2003	$8,380	$6,285
2004	$9,066	$6,799

MT295B

YEARS MFRD........2005-2009
SERIES..........MT200B SERIES
CYLINDERS..................4
CID......................180
PTO HP....................41
ENGINE HP...............52.1
FUEL.......................D
SPEEDS...................8/8
TRANSMISSION...SHUTTLE SHIFT
STEERING............STANDARD
HITCH.................CAT. II
HYDRAULIC...............YES
PTO.....................YES
WEIGHT............3,726 LBS.
MSRP...............$26,408

OPTIONS

12/12 POWER SHIFT
2 HYD
LDR

SERIAL NUMBERS

YEAR	BEGINNING NO.
2005	JP
2006	JR
2007	JS
2008	JT

RETAIL PRICING

YEAR	HIGH	LOW
2005	$9,685	$7,264
2006	$10,442	$7,832
2007	$11,244	$8,433
2008	$12,088	$9,066
2009	$13,013	$9,759

MT297B

YEARS MFRD........2007-2009
SERIES............200B SERIES
ENGINE.................ISEKI
CYLINDERS..................4
CID......................180
PTO HP..................46.4
ENGINE HP...............59.1
COOLING...............LIQUID
FUEL.......................D
SPEEDS.................12/12
TRANSMISSION.....POWER SHIFT
STEERING............STANDARD
HITCH..................CAT. I
HYDRAULIC...............YES
PTO.....................YES
DRIVE TYPE..............4WD
ROPS/CAB...............ROPS
WEIGHT............4,078 LBS.
MSRP...............$29,772

OPTIONS

2 HYD
LDR

SERIAL NUMBERS

YEAR	BEGINNING NO.
2007	S
2008	T

RETAIL PRICING

YEAR	HIGH	LOW
2007	$12,672	$9,504
2008	$13,584	$10,188
2009	$14,582	$10,937

MT315B

YEARS MFRD........2006-2007
ENGINE............CHALLENGER
CYLINDERS..................3
CID......................201
PTO HP....................45
ENGINE HP.................58
COOLING...............LIQUID
FUEL.......................D
SPEEDS.................12/12
TRANSMISSION...SHUTTLE SHIFT
STEERING............STANDARD
DRIVE TYPE..............2WD
WEIGHT............5,291 LBS.
MSRP...............$24,930

OPTIONS

4WD
FRT FENDERS

SERIAL NUMBERS

YEAR	BEGINNING NO.
2006	CR
2007	CS

RETAIL PRICING

YEAR	HIGH	LOW
2006	$10,776	$8,082
2007	$11,733	$8,800

COUNTRY CLIPPER

1536KAH-SR10

YEARS MFRD........2011-2012
SERIES...........TREK SERIES
ENGINE..............KAWASAKI
CYLINDERS..................2
ENGINE HP.................15
COOLING..................AIR
FUEL.......................G
SPEEDS.............VARIABLE
TRANSMISSION...........HYDRO
STEERING................ZERO
BLADE CLUTCH........ELECTRIC
WEIGHT..............550 LBS.

1548KAH-SR10

YEARS MFRD........2011-2012
SERIES...........TREK SERIES
ENGINE..............KAWASAKI
CYLINDERS..................2
ENGINE HP.................15
COOLING..................AIR
FUEL.......................G
SPEEDS.............VARIABLE
TRANSMISSION...........HYDRO
STEERING................ZERO
BLADE CLUTCH........ELECTRIC
WEIGHT..............575 LBS.

1638KOJI

YEARS MFRD........2004-2004
SERIES..........JAZEE SERIES
ENGINE............KOHLER OHV
CYLINDERS..................1
ENGINE HP.................16
FUEL.......................G
SPEEDS.............VARIABLE
TRANSMISSION...........HYDRO
STEERING................ZERO
BLADE CLUTCH........ELECTRIC
STANDARD DECK............38"
WEIGHT..............600 LBS.
MSRP.................$3,395

OPTIONS

BAGGER

RETAIL PRICING

YEAR	HIGH	LOW
2004	$866	$650

1642KOJI

YEARS MFRD........2004-2004
SERIES..........JAZEE SERIES
ENGINE............KOHLER OHV
CYLINDERS..................1
ENGINE HP.................16
COOLING..................AIR
FUEL.......................G
SPEEDS.............VARIABLE
TRANSMISSION...........HYDRO
STEERING................ZERO
BLADE CLUTCH........ELECTRIC
STANDARD DECK............42"
WEIGHT..............613 LBS.
MSRP.................$3,595

OPTIONS

BAGGER

RETAIL PRICING

YEAR	HIGH	LOW
2004	$930	$698

1706KAJ
YEARS MFRD 2004-2004
SERIES .... ZETON BRAT SERIES
ENGINE .... KAWASAKI
CYLINDERS 2
CID 30.1
ENGINE HP 17
COOLING .... AIR
FUEL .... G
SPEEDS .... VARIABLE
TRANSMISSION .... HYDRO
STEERING .... ZERO
BLADE CLUTCH .... ELECTRIC
STANDARD DECK .... 42"
MSRP $7,040

OPTIONS

48" DECK
DIX SEAT

RETAIL PRICING

YEAR	HIGH	LOW
2004	$1,799	$1,349

1738KOJI
YEARS MFRD 2005-2005
SERIES .... JAZEE ONE SERIES
ENGINE .... KOHLER COURAGE
CYLINDERS 1
ENGINE HP 17
COOLING .... AIR
FUEL .... G
SPEEDS .... VARIABLE
TRANSMISSION .... HYDRO
STEERING .... ZERO
BLADE CLUTCH .... ELECTRIC
WEIGHT .... 600 LBS.

1742KOJ
YEARS MFRD 2004-2004
SERIES .... JAZEE SERIES
ENGINE .. KOHLER COMMAND PRO
CYLINDERS 1
ENGINE HP 17
COOLING .... AIR
FUEL .... G
SPEEDS .... VARIABLE
TRANSMISSION .... HYDRO
STEERING .... ZERO
BLADE CLUTCH .... MANUAL
STANDARD DECK .... 42"
MSRP $4,769

OPTIONS

BAGGER

RETAIL PRICING

YEAR	HIGH	LOW
2004	$1,218	$914

1742KOJI
YEARS MFRD 2005-2005
SERIES .... JAZEE ONE SERIES
ENGINE .... KOHLER COURAGE
CYLINDERS 1
ENGINE HP 17
COOLING .... AIR
FUEL .... G
SPEEDS .... VARIABLE
TRANSMISSION .... HYDRO
STEERING .... ZERO
BLADE CLUTCH .... ELECTRIC
WEIGHT .... 613 LBS.

1748KOJ
YEARS MFRD 2004-2004
SERIES .... JAZEE SERIES
ENGINE .. KOHLER COMMAND PRO
CYLINDERS 1
ENGINE HP 17
COOLING .... AIR
SPEEDS .... VARIABLE
TRANSMISSION .... HYDRO
STEERING .... ZERO
BLADE CLUTCH .... ELECTRIC
STANDARD DECK .... 48"
MSRP $4,849

OPTIONS

BAGGER

RETAIL PRICING

YEAR	HIGH	LOW
2004	$1,239	$929

1752KOJ
YEARS MFRD 2004-2004
SERIES .... JAZEE SERIES
ENGINE .. KOHLER COMMAND PRO
CYLINDERS 1
ENGINE HP 17
FUEL .... G
SPEEDS .... 1/1 VARIABLE
TRANSMISSION .... HYDRO
STEERING .... ZERO
BLADE CLUTCH .... ELECTRIC

1800F
YEARS MFRD 1996-1997
ENGINE .... KOHLER
ENGINE HP 18
COOLING .... AIR
FUEL .... G
SPEEDS .... VARIABLE
TRANSMISSION ..... DUAL HYDRO
STEERING .... ZERO
STANDARD DECK .... 48"
MSRP $7,904

SERIAL NUMBERS

YEAR	BEGINNING NO.
1996	1700
1997	1973

RETAIL PRICING

YEAR	HIGH	LOW
1996	$938	$703
1997	$1,038	$778

1800M
YEARS MFRD 1996-1997
ENGINE .... KOHLER
ENGINE HP 18
FUEL .... G
SPEEDS .... VARIABLE
TRANSMISSION ..... DUAL HYDRO
STEERING .... ZERO
STANDARD DECK .... 48"
MSRP $7,100

SERIAL NUMBERS

YEAR	BEGINNING NO.
1996	1848
1997	1894

RETAIL PRICING

YEAR	HIGH	LOW
1996	$841	$631
1997	$934	$700

1841KOJ-SR125
YEARS MFRD 2012-2013
SERIES .... WRANGLER SERIES
ENGINE .... KOHLER COURAGE
CYLINDERS 1
ENGINE HP 18
COOLING .... AIR
FUEL .... G
SPEEDS .... VARIABLE
TRANSMISSION .... HYDRO
STEERING .... ZERO
BLADE CLUTCH .... ELECTRIC
WEIGHT .... 660 LBS.

1842KAJ-A105
YEARS MFRD 2016-2017
SERIES .... AVENUE SERIES
ENGINE .... KAWASAKI
ENGINE HP 18
FUEL .... G
SPEEDS .... VARIABLE
TRANSMISSION .... HYDRO
STEERING .... ZERO
STANDARD DECK .... 42"
WEIGHT .... 587 LBS.
MSRP $3,599

RETAIL PRICING

YEAR	HIGH	LOW
2016	$1,965	$1,474
2017	$2,303	$1,727

1842KAJ-A110
YEARS MFRD 2018-2020
SERIES .... AVENUE SERIES
ENGINE .... KAWASAKI FR600V
CYLINDERS 2
ENGINE HP 18
FUEL .... G
SPEEDS .... VARIABLE
TRANSMISSION .... HYDRO
STEERING .... ZERO
BLADE CLUTCH .... ELECTRIC
STANDARD DECK .... 42"
WEIGHT .... 587 LBS.

1906KAJ
YEARS MFRD 2004-2004
SERIES .... ZETON BRAT SERIES
ENGINE .... KAWASAKI
CYLINDERS 2
CID 41.2
ENGINE HP 19
COOLING .... AIR
FUEL .... G
SPEEDS .... VARIABLE
TRANSMISSION .... HYDRO
STEERING .... ZERO
BLADE CLUTCH .... ELECTRIC
STANDARD DECK .... 48"
MSRP $7,499

RETAIL PRICING

YEAR	HIGH	LOW
2004	$1,916	$1,437

1948KAJ-SR1000
YEARS MFRD 2006-2006
SERIES .... CHARGER SERIES
ENGINE .... KAWASAKI
CYLINDERS 2
CID 41.2
ENGINE HP 19
COOLING .... AIR
FUEL .... G
SPEEDS .... VARIABLE
TRANSMISSION .... HYDRO
STEERING .... ZERO
BLADE CLUTCH .... ELECTRIC
WEIGHT .... 840 LBS.
MSRP $6,575

RETAIL PRICING

YEAR	HIGH	LOW
2006	$4,025	$3,019

1948KAJ-SR350
YEARS MFRD 2006-2007
SERIES .... JAZEE PRO SERIES
ENGINE .... KAWASAKI
CYLINDERS 2
ENGINE HP 19
COOLING .... AIR
FUEL .... G
SPEEDS .... VARIABLE
TRANSMISSION .... HYDRO
STEERING .... ZERO
STANDARD DECK .... 48"
WEIGHT .... 675 LBS.
MSRP $5,495

RETAIL PRICING

YEAR	HIGH	LOW
2006	$3,365	$2,524
2007	$3,432	$2,574

1948KAJC
YEARS MFRD 2005-2005
SERIES .... CHARGER SERIES
ENGINE .... KAWASAKI

COUNTRY CLIPPER

ENGINE HP 19
COOLING . . . . . AIR
FUEL . . . . . G
SPEEDS . . . . . VARIABLE
TRANSMISSION . . . . . HYDRO
STEERING. . . . . ZERO
STANDARD DECK . . . . . 48"
WEIGHT . . . . . 840 LBS.
MSRP. $6,295

RETAIL PRICING

YEAR	HIGH	LOW
2005	$3,646	$2,734

1948KAJII

YEARS MFRD 2005-2005
SERIES. . . . . JAZZEE TWO SERIES
ENGINE . . . . . KAWASAKI
CYLINDERS. 2
ENGINE HP 19
COOLING . . . . . AIR
FUEL . . . . . G
SPEEDS . . . . . VARIABLE
TRANSMISSION . . . . . HYDRO
STEERING. . . . . ZERO
BLADE CLUTCH . . . . . ELECTRIC
WEIGHT . . . . . 675 LBS.

1948KAT-SR1000

YEARS MFRD 2006-2006
SERIES. . . . . CHARGER SERIES
ENGINE . . . . . KAWASAKI
CYLINDERS. 2
CID 41.2
ENGINE HP 19
COOLING . . . . . AIR
FUEL . . . . . G
SPEEDS . . . . . VARIABLE
TRANSMISSION . . . . . HYDRO
STEERING. . . . . ZERO
STANDARD DECK . . . . . 48"
WEIGHT . . . . . 840 LBS.
MSRP. $6,575

RETAIL PRICING

YEAR	HIGH	LOW
2006	$4,025	$3,019

1948KAT-SR350

YEARS MFRD 2006-2007
SERIES. . . . . JAZEE PRO SERIES
ENGINE . . . . . KAWASAKI
CYLINDERS. 2
ENGINE HP 19
COOLING . . . . . AIR
FUEL . . . . . G
SPEEDS . . . . . VARIABLE
TRANSMISSION . . . . . HYDRO
STEERING. . . . . ZERO
STANDARD DECK . . . . . 48"
WEIGHT . . . . . 675 LBS.
MSRP. $5,495

RETAIL PRICING

YEAR	HIGH	LOW
2006	$3,365	$2,524
2007	$3,444	$2,583

1948KATC

YEARS MFRD 2005-2005
SERIES. . . . . CHARGER SERIES
ENGINE . . . . . KAWASAKI
ENGINE HP 19
COOLING . . . . . AIR
FUEL . . . . . G
SPEEDS . . . . . VARIABLE
TRANSMISSION . . . . . HYDRO
STEERING. . . . . ZERO
STANDARD DECK . . . . . 48"
WEIGHT . . . . . 840 LBS.
MSRP. $6,295

RETAIL PRICING

YEAR	HIGH	LOW
2005	$3,646	$2,734

1948KATII

YEARS MFRD 2005-2005
SERIES. . . . . JAZEE TWO SERIES
ENGINE . . . . . KAWASAKI
CYLINDERS. 2
ENGINE HP 19
COOLING . . . . . AIR
FUEL . . . . . G
SPEEDS . . . . . VARIABLE
TRANSMISSION . . . . . HYDRO
STEERING. . . . . ZERO
BLADE CLUTCH . . . . . ELECTRIC
WEIGHT . . . . . 675 LBS.

1952KAJ-SR350

YEARS MFRD 2006-2007
SERIES. . . . . JAZEE PRO SERIES
ENGINE . . . . . KAWASAKI
CYLINDERS. 2
ENGINE HP 19
COOLING . . . . . AIR
FUEL . . . . . G
SPEEDS . . . . . VARIABLE
TRANSMISSION . . . . . HYDRO
STEERING. . . . . ZERO
STANDARD DECK . . . . . 52"
WEIGHT . . . . . 690 LBS.
MSRP. $5,645

RETAIL PRICING

YEAR	HIGH	LOW
2006	$2,747	$2,060
2007	$2,806	$2,104

1952KAT-SR350

YEARS MFRD 2006-2007
SERIES. . . . . JAZEE PRO SERIES
ENGINE . . . . . KAWASAKI
CYLINDERS. 2
ENGINE HP 19
COOLING . . . . . AIR
FUEL . . . . . G
SPEEDS . . . . . VARIABLE
TRANSMISSION . . . . . HYDRO
STEERING. . . . . ZERO
STANDARD DECK . . . . . 52"
WEIGHT . . . . . 690 LBS.
MSRP. $5,645

RETAIL PRICING

YEAR	HIGH	LOW
2006	$2,747	$2,060
2007	$2,821	$2,116

2038BSJ-SR110

YEARS MFRD 2010-2011
SERIES. . . . . JAZEE ONE SERIES
ENGINE . . . . . B&S PRO
CYLINDERS. 1
ENGINE HP 20
COOLING . . . . . AIR
FUEL . . . . . G
SPEEDS . . . . . VARIABLE
TRANSMISSION . . . . . HYDRO
STEERING. . . . . ZERO
BLADE CLUTCH . . . . . ELECTRIC
WEIGHT . . . . . 600 LBS.

2041KOJ135

YEARS MFRD 2014-2014
SERIES. . . . . WRANGLER SERIES
ENGINE . . . . . KOHLER COURAGE
CYLINDERS. 1
ENGINE HP 20
COOLING . . . . . AIR
FUEL . . . . . G
SPEEDS . . . . . VARIABLE
TRANSMISSION . . . . . HYDRO
STEERING. . . . . ZERO
BLADE CLUTCH . . . . . ELECTRIC
STANDARD DECK . . . . . 41"
WEIGHT . . . . . 665 LBS.

2041KOT135

YEARS MFRD 2014-2014
SERIES. . . . . WRANGLER SERIES
ENGINE . . . . . KOHLER COURAGE
CYLINDERS. 1
ENGINE HP 20
COOLING . . . . . AIR
FUEL . . . . . G
SPEEDS . . . . . VARIABLE
TRANSMISSION . . . . . HYDRO
STEERING. . . . . ZERO
BLADE CLUTCH . . . . . ELECTRIC
STANDARD DECK . . . . . 41"
WEIGHT . . . . . 660 LBS.

2042BSJ

YEARS MFRD 2005-2005
SERIES. . . . . JAZEE SERIES
ENGINE . . . . . B&S ELS
CYLINDERS. 2
ENGINE HP 20
COOLING . . . . . AIR
FUEL . . . . . G
SPEEDS . . . . . VARIABLE
TRANSMISSION . . . . . HYDRO
STEERING. . . . . ZERO
BLADE CLUTCH . . . . . ELECTRIC

2042BSJ-SR110

YEARS MFRD 2010-2011
SERIES. . . . . JAZEE ONE SERIES
ENGINE . . . . . B&S PRO
CYLINDERS. 1
ENGINE HP 20
COOLING . . . . . AIR
FUEL . . . . . G
SPEEDS . . . . . VARIABLE
TRANSMISSION . . . . . HYDRO
STEERING. . . . . ZERO
BLADE CLUTCH . . . . . ELECTRIC
WEIGHT . . . . . 600 LBS.

2042BSJ-SR200

YEARS MFRD 2006-2007
SERIES. . . . . JAZEE SERIES
ENGINE . . . . . B&S ELS
CYLINDERS. 2
ENGINE HP 20
COOLING . . . . . AIR
FUEL . . . . . G
SPEEDS . . . . . VARIABLE
TRANSMISSION . . . . . HYDRO
STEERING. . . . . ZERO
STANDARD DECK . . . . . 42"
MSRP. $4,649

RETAIL PRICING

YEAR	HIGH	LOW
2006	$2,137	$1,603
2007	$2,174	$1,630

2042BSJ-SR215

YEARS MFRD 2010-2011
SERIES. . . . . JAZEE SERIES
ENGINE . . . . . B&S PRO
CYLINDERS. 1
ENGINE HP 20
COOLING . . . . . AIR
FUEL . . . . . G
SPEEDS . . . . . VARIABLE
TRANSMISSION . . . . . HYDRO
STEERING. . . . . ZERO
BLADE CLUTCH . . . . . ELECTRIC
STANDARD DECK . . . . . 48"
WEIGHT . . . . . 650 LBS.
MSRP. $4,350

RETAIL PRICING

YEAR	HIGH	LOW
2010	$1,810	$1,358
2011	$2,356	$1,767

2042KOJ

YEARS MFRD 2004-2004
SERIES. . . . . JAZEE SERIES
ENGINE . . KOHLER COMMAND PRO
CYLINDERS. 2
ENGINE HP 20
FUEL . . . . G
SPEEDS 1/1
TRANSMISSION . . . . HYDRO
STEERING. . . . . ZERO
BLADE CLUTCH . . . . ELECTRIC

2048BSJ

YEARS MFRD 2005-2005
SERIES. . . . . JAZEE SERIES
ENGINE . . . . B&S ELS
CYLINDERS. 2
ENGINE HP 20
COOLING . . . . AIR
FUEL . . . . G
SPEEDS . . . . VARIABLE
TRANSMISSION . . . . HYDRO
STEERING. . . . . ZERO
BLADE CLUTCH . . . . ELECTRIC

2048BSJ-SR200

YEARS MFRD 2006-2007
SERIES. . . . . JAZEE SERIES
ENGINE . . . . B&S
ENGINE HP 20
COOLING . . . . AIR
FUEL . . . . G
SPEEDS . . . . VARIABLE
TRANSMISSION . . . . HYDRO
STEERING. . . . . ZERO
STANDARD DECK . . . . 48"
MSRP. $4,999

RETAIL PRICING

YEAR	HIGH	LOW
2006	$2,260	$1,695
2007	$2,297	$1,723

2048BSJ-SR215

YEARS MFRD 2010-2011
SERIES. . . . . JAZEE SERIES
ENGINE . . . . B&S PRO
CYLINDERS. 1
ENGINE HP 20
COOLING . . . . AIR
FUEL . . . . G
SPEEDS . . . . VARIABLE
TRANSMISSION . . . . HYDRO
STEERING. . . . . ZERO
BLADE CLUTCH . . . . ELECTRIC
STANDARD DECK . . . . 48"
WEIGHT . . . . 675 LBS.
MSRP. $4,595

RETAIL PRICING

YEAR	HIGH	LOW
2010	$1,917	$1,438
2011	$2,488	$1,866

2048BST-SR215

YEARS MFRD 2010-2011
SERIES. . . . . JAZEE SERIES
ENGINE . . . . B&S PRO
CYLINDERS. 1
ENGINE HP 20
COOLING . . . . AIR
FUEL . . . . G
SPEEDS . . . . VARIABLE
TRANSMISSION . . . . HYDRO
STEERING. . . . . ZERO
BLADE CLUTCH . . . . ELECTRIC
STANDARD DECK . . . . 48"
WEIGHT . . . . 650 LBS.
MSRP. $4,595

RETAIL PRICING

YEAR	HIGH	LOW
2010	$1,917	$1,438
2011	$2,488	$1,866

2048KOJ

YEARS MFRD 2004-2004
SERIES. . . . . JAZEE SERIES
ENGINE . . KOHLER COMMAND PRO
CYLINDERS. 2
ENGINE HP 20
FUEL . . . . G
SPEEDS 1/1
TRANSMISSION . . . . HYDRO
STEERING. . . . . ZERO
BLADE CLUTCH . . . . ELECTRIC
STANDARD DECK . . . . 48"
MSRP. $5,299

RETAIL PRICING

YEAR	HIGH	LOW
2004	$2,185	$1,639

2048KOJ-SR1000

YEARS MFRD 2006-2006
SERIES. . . . . CHARGER SERIES
ENGINE . . . . KOHLER
CYLINDERS. 2
CID 38
ENGINE HP 20
COOLING . . . . AIR
FUEL . . . . G
SPEEDS . . . . VARIABLE
TRANSMISSION . . . . HYDRO
STEERING. . . . . ZERO
BLADE CLUTCH . . . . ELECTRIC
STANDARD DECK . . . . 48"
WEIGHT . . . . 840 LBS.
MSRP. $6,695

RETAIL PRICING

YEAR	HIGH	LOW
2006	$4,100	$3,075

2048KOJ-SR350

YEARS MFRD 2006-2007
SERIES. . . . . JAZEE PRO SERIES
ENGINE . . . . KOHLER
CYLINDERS. 2
ENGINE HP 20
COOLING . . . . AIR
FUEL . . . . G
SPEEDS . . . . VARIABLE
TRANSMISSION . . . . HYDRO
STEERING. . . . . ZERO
STANDARD DECK . . . . 48"
WEIGHT . . . . 675 LBS.
MSRP. $5,875

RETAIL PRICING

YEAR	HIGH	LOW
2006	$2,717	$2,037
2007	$2,771	$2,079

2048KOJ135

YEARS MFRD 2014-2014
SERIES. . . . . WRANGLER SERIES
ENGINE . . . . KOHLER COURAGE
CYLINDERS. 1
ENGINE HP 20
COOLING . . . . AIR
FUEL . . . . G
SPEEDS . . . . VARIABLE
TRANSMISSION . . . . HYDRO
STEERING. . . . . ZERO
BLADE CLUTCH . . . . ELECTRIC
STANDARD DECK . . . . 48"
WEIGHT . . . . 685 LBS.

2048KOJC

YEARS MFRD 2005-2005
SERIES. . . . . CHARGER SERIES
ENGINE . . KOHLER COMMAND PRO
CYLINDERS. 2
ENGINE HP 20
COOLING . . . . AIR
FUEL . . . . G
SPEEDS . . . . VARIABLE
TRANSMISSION . . . . HYDRO
STEERING. . . . . ZERO
STANDARD DECK . . . . 48"
WEIGHT . . . . 852 LBS.
MSRP. $6,295

RETAIL PRICING

YEAR	HIGH	LOW
2005	$2,936	$2,202

2048KOJII

YEARS MFRD 2004-2004
SERIES. . . . . JAZEE TWO SERIES
ENGINE . . . . KOHLER COMMAND
CYLINDERS. 2
ENGINE HP 20
COOLING . . . . AIR
FUEL . . . . G
SPEEDS . . . . VARIABLE
TRANSMISSION . . . . HYDRO
STEERING. . . . . ZERO
BLADE CLUTCH . . . . ELECTRIC
STANDARD DECK . . . . 48"
WEIGHT . . . . 690 LBS.
MSRP. $5,499

OPTIONS

BAGGER

RETAIL PRICING

YEAR	HIGH	LOW
2004	$1,404	$1,053

2048KOT-SR350

YEARS MFRD 2006-2007
SERIES. . . . . JAZEE PRO SERIES
ENGINE . . . . KOHLER
CYLINDERS. 2
ENGINE HP 20
COOLING . . . . AIR
FUEL . . . . G
SPEEDS . . . . VARIABLE
TRANSMISSION . . . . HYDRO
STEERING. . . . . ZERO
STANDARD DECK . . . . 48"
WEIGHT . . . . 675 LBS.
MSRP. $5,820

RETAIL PRICING

YEAR	HIGH	LOW
2006	$2,930	$2,198
2007	$3,056	$2,292

2048KOT135

YEARS MFRD 2014-2014
SERIES. . . . . WRANGLER SERIES
ENGINE . . . . KOHLER COURAGE
CYLINDERS. 1
ENGINE HP 20
COOLING . . . . AIR
FUEL . . . . G
SPEEDS . . . . VARIABLE
TRANSMISSION . . . . HYDRO
STEERING. . . . . ZERO
BLADE CLUTCH . . . . ELECTRIC
STANDARD DECK . . . . 48"
WEIGHT . . . . 680 LBS.

2048KOTII

YEARS MFRD 2004-2004
ENGINE . . . . KOHLER
ENGINE HP 20
COOLING . . . . AIR
FUEL . . . . G
SPEEDS . . . . VARIABLE
TRANSMISSION . . . . HYDRO
STEERING. . . . . ZERO
STANDARD DECK . . . . 48"
MSRP. $5,499

RETAIL PRICING

YEAR	HIGH	LOW
2004	$2,293	$1,720

2052BSJ-SR200

YEARS MFRD 2006-2006
SERIES. . . . . JAZEE SERIES
ENGINE . . . . B&S
ENGINE HP 20
COOLING . . . . AIR
FUEL . . . . G

SPEEDS . . . . VARIABLE
TRANSMISSION . . . . HYDRO
STEERING. . . . . ZERO
STANDARD DECK . . . . 52"
MSRP. $4,999

RETAIL PRICING

YEAR	HIGH	LOW
2006	$2,352	$1,764

2052KOJ

YEARS MFRD 2003-2004
ENGINE . . . . KOHLER
ENGINE HP 20
COOLING . . . . AIR
FUEL . . . . G
SPEEDS . . . . VARIABLE
TRANSMISSION . . . . HYDRO
STEERING. . . . . ZERO
STANDARD DECK . . . . 52"
MSRP. $5,429

RETAIL PRICING

YEAR	HIGH	LOW
2003	$2,025	$1,519
2004	$2,255	$1,691

2052KOJ-SR350

YEARS MFRD 2006-2007
SERIES. . . . . JAZEE SERIES
ENGINE . . . . KOHLER
ENGINE HP 20
COOLING . . . . AIR
FUEL . . . . G
SPEEDS . . . . VARIABLE
TRANSMISSION . . . . HYDRO
STEERING. . . . . ZERO
STANDARD DECK . . . . 52"
MSRP. $5,745

RETAIL PRICING

YEAR	HIGH	LOW
2006	$2,808	$2,106
2007	$2,865	$2,148

2052KOJII

YEARS MFRD 2004-2004
SERIES. . . . . JAZEE TWO SERIES
ENGINE . . . . . . KOHLER COMMAND
CYLINDERS. 2
ENGINE HP 20
COOLING . . . . AIR
FUEL . . . . G
SPEEDS . . . . VARIABLE
TRANSMISSION . . . . HYDRO
STEERING. . . . . ZERO
STANDARD DECK . . . . 52"
WEIGHT . . . . 690 LBS.
MSRP. $5,629

RETAIL PRICING

YEAR	HIGH	LOW
2004	$1,438	$1,078

2052KOT-SR350

YEARS MFRD 2006-2007
SERIES. . . . . JAZEE SERIES
ENGINE . . . . KOHLER
ENGINE HP 20
COOLING . . . . AIR
FUEL . . . . G
SPEEDS . . . . VARIABLE
TRANSMISSION . . . . HYDRO
STEERING. . . . . ZERO
STANDARD DECK . . . . 52"
MSRP. $5,850

RETAIL PRICING

YEAR	HIGH	LOW
2006	$2,808	$2,106
2007	$2,880	$2,160

2052KOTII

YEARS MFRD 2003-2004
ENGINE . . . . KOHLER
ENGINE HP 20
COOLING . . . . AIR
FUEL . . . . G
SPEEDS . . . . VARIABLE
TRANSMISSION . . . . HYDRO
STEERING. . . . . ZERO
STANDARD DECK . . . . 52"
MSRP. $5,529

RETAIL PRICING

YEAR	HIGH	LOW
2003	$2,127	$1,595
2004	$2,208	$1,656

2148KAJ-SR355

YEARS MFRD 2008-2009
SERIES. . . . . JAZEE PRO SERIES
ENGINE . . . . KAWASAKI
CYLINDERS. 2
ENGINE HP 21
COOLING . . . . AIR
FUEL . . . . G
SPEEDS . . . . VARIABLE
TRANSMISSION . . . . HYDRO
STEERING. . . . . ZERO
BLADE CLUTCH . . . . ELECTRIC
STANDARD DECK . . . . 48"
WEIGHT . . . . 760 LBS.
MSRP. $5,950

RETAIL PRICING

YEAR	HIGH	LOW
2008	$2,567	$1,925
2009	$2,722	$2,042

2148KAT-SR355

YEARS MFRD 2008-2009
SERIES. . . . . JAZEE PRO SERIES
ENGINE . . . . KAWASAKI
CYLINDERS. 2
ENGINE HP 21
COOLING . . . . AIR
FUEL . . . . G
SPEEDS . . . . VARIABLE
TRANSMISSION . . . . HYDRO
STEERING. . . . . ZERO
BLADE CLUTCH . . . . ELECTRIC
STANDARD DECK . . . . 46"
WEIGHT . . . . 760 LBS.
MSRP. $5,950

RETAIL PRICING

YEAR	HIGH	LOW
2008	$2,567	$1,925
2009	$2,722	$2,042

2152KAJ-SR355

YEARS MFRD 2008-2009
SERIES. . . . . JAZEE PRO SERIES
ENGINE . . . . KAWASAKI
CYLINDERS. 2
ENGINE HP 21
COOLING . . . . AIR
FUEL . . . . G
SPEEDS . . . . VARIABLE
TRANSMISSION . . . . HYDRO
STEERING. . . . . ZERO
STANDARD DECK . . . . 49"
WEIGHT . . . . 775 LBS.
MSRP. $6,150

RETAIL PRICING

YEAR	HIGH	LOW
2008	$2,684	$2,013
2009	$2,837	$2,128

2152KAT-SR355

YEARS MFRD 2008-2009
SERIES. . . . . JAZEE PRO SERIES
ENGINE . . . . KAWASAKI
CYLINDERS. 2
ENGINE HP 21
COOLING . . . . AIR
FUEL . . . . G
SPEEDS . . . . VARIABLE
TRANSMISSION . . . . HYDRO
STEERING. . . . . ZERO
BLADE CLUTCH . . . . ELECTRIC
STANDARD DECK . . . . 49"
WEIGHT . . . . 775 LBS.
MSRP. $6,150

RETAIL PRICING

YEAR	HIGH	LOW
2008	$2,684	$2,013
2009	$2,837	$2,128

2200F

YEARS MFRD 1996-1997
ENGINE . . . . KOHLER
ENGINE HP 22
COOLING . . . . AIR
FUEL . . . . G
SPEEDS . . . . VARIABLE
TRANSMISSION . . . . . DUAL HYDRO
STEERING. . . . . ZERO
STANDARD DECK . . . . 60"
MSRP. $8,652

SERIAL NUMBERS

YEAR	BEGINNING NO.
1996	10016
1997	1983

RETAIL PRICING

YEAR	HIGH	LOW
1996	$1,025	$769
1997	$1,139	$854

2200M

YEARS MFRD 1996-1997
ENGINE . . . . KOHLER
ENGINE HP 22
FUEL . . . . G
SPEEDS . . . . VARIABLE
TRANSMISSION . . . . . DUAL HYDRO
STEERING. . . . . ZERO
STANDARD DECK . . . . 60"
MSRP. $7,750

SERIAL NUMBERS

YEAR	BEGINNING NO.
1996	1842
1997	1908

RETAIL PRICING

YEAR	HIGH	LOW
1996	$919	$689
1997	$1,018	$764

2201M

YEARS MFRD 1998-1998
ENGINE . . . . KOHLER
ENGINE HP 22
FUEL . . . . G
SPEEDS . . . . VARIABLE
TRANSMISSION . . . . . DUAL HYDRO
STEERING. . . . . ZERO
STANDARD DECK . . . . 48"
MSRP. $7,200

SERIAL NUMBERS

YEAR	BEGINNING NO.
1998	6144

RETAIL PRICING

YEAR	HIGH	LOW
1998	$1,075	$806

2203F

YEARS MFRD 1998-2000
ENGINE . . . . KOHLER
ENGINE HP 22
FUEL . . . . G
SPEEDS . . . . VARIABLE
TRANSMISSION . . . . . DUAL HYDRO
STEERING. . . . . ZERO
STANDARD DECK . . . . 48"
MSRP. $8,222

SERIAL NUMBERS

YEAR	BEGINNING NO.
1998	6545

RETAIL PRICING

YEAR	HIGH	LOW
1998	$1,302	$977
1999	$1,446	$1,085
2000	$1,607	$1,205

2203M

YEARS MFRD 1998-1999
ENGINE . . . . KOHLER
ENGINE HP 22
COOLING . . . . AIR
FUEL . . . . G
SPEEDS . . . . VARIABLE
TRANSMISSION . . . . . DUAL HYDRO
STEERING. . . . . ZERO
STANDARD DECK . . . . 48"
MSRP. $7,329

OPTIONS

60" DECK

SERIAL NUMBERS

YEAR	BEGINNING NO.
1998	6346-MT
1998	6238

RETAIL PRICING

YEAR	HIGH	LOW
1998	$1,100	$825
1999	$1,223	$917

2204M

YEARS MFRD 1999-2000
ENGINE . . . . KOHLER
ENGINE HP 22
FUEL . . . . G
SPEEDS . . . . VARIABLE
TRANSMISSION . . . . . DUAL HYDRO
STEERING. . . . . ZERO
STANDARD DECK . . . . 48"
MSRP. $7,540

OPTIONS

60" DECK

RETAIL PRICING

YEAR	HIGH	LOW
1999	$1,341	$1,005
2000	$1,472	$1,104

2248BST-SR205

YEARS MFRD 2008-2009
SERIES. . . . . JAZEE SERIES
ENGINE . . . . B&S ELS
CYLINDERS. 1
ENGINE HP 22
COOLING . . . . AIR
FUEL . . . . G
SPEEDS . . . . VARIABLE
TRANSMISSION . . . . HYDRO
STEERING. . . . . ZERO
BLADE CLUTCH . . . . ELECTRIC
WEIGHT . . . . 675 LBS.

2248KAJ-SR365

YEARS MFRD 2010-2011
SERIES. . . . . JAZEE PRO SERIES
ENGINE . . . . KAWASAKI
CYLINDERS. 2
ENGINE HP 22
COOLING . . . . AIR
FUEL . . . . G
SPEEDS . . . . VARIABLE
TRANSMISSION . . . . HYDRO
STEERING. . . . . ZERO
BLADE CLUTCH . . . . ELECTRIC
WEIGHT . . . . 760 LBS.

2248KAJ-SR375

YEARS MFRD 2011-2013
SERIES. . . . . JAZEE PRO SERIES
ENGINE . . . . KAWASAKI
CYLINDERS. 2
ENGINE HP 22
COOLING . . . . AIR
FUEL . . . . G
SPEEDS . . . . VARIABLE
TRANSMISSION . . . . HYDRO
STEERING. . . . . ZERO
BLADE CLUTCH . . . . ELECTRIC
WEIGHT . . . . 760 LBS.

2248KAT-SR365

YEARS MFRD 2010-2011
SERIES. . . . . JAZEE PRO SERIES
ENGINE . . . . KAWASAKI
CYLINDERS. 2
ENGINE HP 22
COOLING . . . . AIR
FUEL . . . . G
SPEEDS . . . . VARIABLE
TRANSMISSION . . . . HYDRO
STEERING. . . . . ZERO
BLADE CLUTCH . . . . ELECTRIC
WEIGHT . . . . 760 LBS.

2248KAT-SR375

YEARS MFRD 2011-2013
SERIES. . . . . JAZEE PRO SERIES
ENGINE . . . . KAWASAKI
CYLINDERS. 2
ENGINE HP 22
COOLING . . . . AIR
FUEL . . . . G
SPEEDS . . . . VARIABLE
TRANSMISSION . . . . HYDRO
STEERING. . . . . ZERO
BLADE CLUTCH . . . . ELECTRIC
WEIGHT . . . . 760 LBS.

2248KOJ-SR125

YEARS MFRD 2012-2013
SERIES. . . . . WANGLER SERIES
ENGINE . . . . KOHLER COURAGE
CYLINDERS. 1
ENGINE HP 22
COOLING . . . . AIR
FUEL . . . . G
SPEEDS . . . . VARIABLE
TRANSMISSION . . . . HYDRO
STEERING. . . . . ZERO
BLADE CLUTCH . . . . ELECTRIC
WEIGHT . . . . 680 LBS.

2248KOT-SR225

YEARS MFRD 2011-2013
SERIES. . . . . JAZEE SERIES
ENGINE . . . . KOHLER COURAGE
CYLINDERS. 1
ENGINE HP 22
COOLING . . . . AIR
FUEL . . . . G
SPEEDS . . . . VARIABLE
TRANSMISSION . . . . HYDRO
STEERING. . . . . ZERO
BLADE CLUTCH . . . . ELECTRIC
WEIGHT . . . . 675 LBS.

2252KAJ-SR365

YEARS MFRD 2010-2011
SERIES. . . . . JAZEE PRO SERIES
ENGINE . . . . KAWASAKI
CYLINDERS. 2
ENGINE HP 22
COOLING . . . . AIR
FUEL . . . . G
SPEEDS . . . . VARIABLE
TRANSMISSION . . . . HYDRO
STEERING. . . . . ZERO
BLADE CLUTCH . . . . ELECTRIC
WEIGHT . . . . 775 LBS.

2252KAJ-SR375

YEARS MFRD 2011-2013
SERIES. . . . . JAZEE PRO SERIES
ENGINE . . . . KAWASAKI
CYLINDERS. 2
ENGINE HP 22
COOLING . . . . AIR
FUEL . . . . G
SPEEDS . . . . VARIABLE
TRANSMISSION . . . . HYDRO
STEERING. . . . . ZERO
BLADE CLUTCH . . . . ELECTRIC
WEIGHT . . . . 775 LBS.

2252KAT-SR365

YEARS MFRD 2010-2011
SERIES. . . . . JAZEE PRO SERIES
ENGINE . . . . KAWASAKI
CYLINDERS. 2
ENGINE HP 22
COOLING . . . . AIR
FUEL . . . . G
SPEEDS . . . . VARIABLE
TRANSMISSION . . . . HYDRO
STEERING. . . . . ZERO
BLADE CLUTCH . . . . ELECTRIC
WEIGHT . . . . 775 LBS.

2252KAT-SR375

YEARS MFRD 2011-2013
SERIES. . . . . JAZEE PRO SERIES
ENGINE . . . . KAWASAKI
CYLINDERS. 2
ENGINE HP 22
COOLING . . . . AIR
FUEL . . . . G
SPEEDS . . . . VARIABLE
TRANSMISSION . . . . HYDRO
STEERING. . . . . ZERO
BLADE CLUTCH . . . . ELECTRIC
WEIGHT . . . . 775 LBS.

2304KA

YEARS MFRD 2003-2004
SERIES. . . . . . . MID MOUNT SERIES
ENGINE . . . . KAWASAKI
ENGINE HP 23
FUEL . . . . G
TRANSMISSION . . . . HYDRO
STEERING. . . . . ZERO
STANDARD DECK . . . . 52"
MSRP. $6,355

RETAIL PRICING

YEAR	HIGH	LOW
2003	$3,259	$2,445
2004	$3,389	$2,542

2304M

YEARS MFRD 2003-2004
SERIES. . . . . . . MID MOUNT SERIES
ENGINE . . KOHLER COMMAND PRO
ENGINE HP 23
COOLING . . . . AIR
FUEL . . . . G
SPEEDS . . . . VARIABLE
TRANSMISSION . . . . HYDRO
STEERING. . . . . ZERO
STANDARD DECK . . . . 52"
MSRP. $7,831

OPTIONS

60" DECK

RETAIL PRICING

YEAR	HIGH	LOW
2004	$2,002	$1,502

COUNTRY CLIPPER

2304MT

YEARS MFRD 2001-2004
SERIES . . . . . . MID MOUNT SERIES
ENGINE . . KOHLER COMMAND PRO
ENGINE HP 23
FUEL . . . . G
TRANSMISSION . . . . HYDRO
STEERING. . . . . ZERO
STANDARD DECK . . . . 52"
WEIGHT . . . . 670 LBS.
MSRP. $6,355

RETAIL PRICING

YEAR	HIGH	LOW
2001	$2,980	$2,235
2002	$3,094	$2,320
2003	$3,259	$2,445
2004	$3,397	$2,548

2348BVJ-SR355

YEARS MFRD 2008-2009
SERIES . . . . JAZEE PRO SERIES
ENGINE . . . . B&S VANGUARD
CYLINDERS. 2
ENGINE HP 23
COOLING . . . . AIR
FUEL . . . . G
SPEEDS . . . . VARIABLE
TRANSMISSION . . . . HYDRO
STEERING. . . . . ZERO
BLADE CLUTCH . . . . ELECTRIC
STANDARD DECK . . . . 52"
WEIGHT . . . . 775 LBS.
MSRP. $5,795

RETAIL PRICING

YEAR	HIGH	LOW
2008	$2,415	$1,811
2009	$2,632	$1,974

2348KOJ-B205

YEARS MFRD 2016-2017
SERIES . . . . BOULEVARD SERIES
ENGINE . . . . KOHLER
ENGINE HP 23
COOLING . . . . AIR
FUEL . . . . G
SPEEDS . . . . VARIABLE
TRANSMISSION . . . . HYDRO
STEERING. . . . . ZERO
STANDARD DECK . . . . 48"
WEIGHT . . . . 688 LBS.
MSRP. $4,299

RETAIL PRICING

YEAR	HIGH	LOW
2016	$2,346	$1,760
2017	$2,805	$2,104

2348KOJ-B210

YEARS MFRD 2018-2020
SERIES . . . . BOULEVARD SERIES
ENGINE . . . . KOHLER KT730
CYLINDERS. 2
ENGINE HP 23
FUEL . . . . G
SPEEDS . . . . VARIABLE
TRANSMISSION . . . . HYDRO
STEERING. . . . . ZERO
BLADE CLUTCH . . . . ELECTRIC
STANDARD DECK . . . . 48"
WEIGHT . . . . 688 LBS.

2348KOJ-SR300

YEARS MFRD 2006-2007
SERIES . . . . JAZEE TWO SERIES
ENGINE . . . . KOHLER COURAGE
CYLINDERS. 2
ENGINE HP 23
COOLING . . . . AIR
FUEL . . . . G
SPEEDS . . . . VARIABLE
TRANSMISSION . . . . HYDRO
STEERING. . . . . ZERO
STANDARD DECK . . . . 48"
WEIGHT . . . . 675 LBS.
MSRP. $5,424

RETAIL PRICING

YEAR	HIGH	LOW
2006	$2,471	$1,853
2007	$2,489	$1,867

2348KOJ-SR355

YEARS MFRD 2008-2009
SERIES . . . . JAZEE PRO SERIES
ENGINE . . . . KOHLER
CYLINDERS. 2
ENGINE HP 23
COOLING . . . . AIR
FUEL . . . . G
SPEEDS . . . . VARIABLE
TRANSMISSION . . . . HYDRO
STEERING. . . . . ZERO
BLADE CLUTCH . . . . ELECTRIC
STANDARD DECK . . . . 46"
WEIGHT . . . . 760 LBS.
MSRP. $5,995

RETAIL PRICING

YEAR	HIGH	LOW
2008	$2,530	$1,898
2009	$2,747	$2,060

2348KOJ140

YEARS MFRD 2015-2015
SERIES . . . . WRANGLER SERIES
ENGINE . . . . KOHLER
ENGINE HP 23
FUEL . . . . G
SPEEDS . . . . VARIABLE
TRANSMISSION . . . . HYDRO
STEERING. . . . . ZERO
STANDARD DECK . . . . 48"
MSRP. $4,595

RETAIL PRICING

YEAR	HIGH	LOW
2015	$2,895	$2,171

2348KOJ8-SR1005

YEARS MFRD 2008-2009
SERIES . . . . CHARGER SERIES
ENGINE . . . . KOHLER
CYLINDERS. 2
ENGINE HP 23
COOLING . . . . AIR
FUEL . . . . G
SPEEDS . . . . VARIABLE
TRANSMISSION . . . . HYDRO
STEERING. . . . . ZERO
BLADE CLUTCH . . . . ELECTRIC
STANDARD DECK . . . . 48"
WEIGHT . . . . 1,100 LBS.
MSRP. $6,995

RETAIL PRICING

YEAR	HIGH	LOW
2008	$3,762	$2,822
2009	$4,034	$3,025

2348KOT-SR355

YEARS MFRD 2008-2009
SERIES . . . . JAZEE PRO SERIES
ENGINE . . . . KOHLER
CYLINDERS. 2
ENGINE HP 23
COOLING . . . . AIR
FUEL . . . . G
SPEEDS . . . . VARIABLE
TRANSMISSION . . . . HYDRO
STEERING. . . . . ZERO
BLADE CLUTCH . . . . ELECTRIC
STANDARD DECK . . . . 46"
WEIGHT . . . . 760 LBS.
MSRP. $5,995

RETAIL PRICING

YEAR	HIGH	LOW
2008	$3,240	$2,430
2009	$3,456	$2,592

2348KOT8-SR1005

YEARS MFRD 2008-2009
SERIES . . . . CHARGER SERIES
ENGINE . . . . KOHLER
CYLINDERS. 2
ENGINE HP 23
COOLING . . . . AIR
FUEL . . . . G
SPEEDS . . . . VARIABLE
TRANSMISSION . . . . HYDRO
STEERING. . . . . ZERO
BLADE CLUTCH . . . . ELECTRIC
STANDARD DECK . . . . 48"
WEIGHT . . . . 1,100 LBS.
MSRP. $6,995

RETAIL PRICING

YEAR	HIGH	LOW
2008	$3,762	$2,822
2009	$4,034	$3,025

2352BVJ-SR355

YEARS MFRD 2008-2009
SERIES . . . . JAZEE PRO SERIES
ENGINE . . . . B&S VANGUARD
CYLINDERS. 2
ENGINE HP 23
COOLING . . . . AIR
FUEL . . . . G
SPEEDS . . . . VARIABLE
TRANSMISSION . . . . HYDRO
STEERING. . . . . ZERO
BLADE CLUTCH . . . . ELECTRIC
STANDARD DECK . . . . 49"
WEIGHT . . . . 775 LBS.
MSRP. $5,995

RETAIL PRICING

YEAR	HIGH	LOW
2008	$3,240	$2,430
2009	$3,456	$2,592

2352KAJC

YEARS MFRD 2005-2005
SERIES . . . . CHARGER SERIES
ENGINE . . . . . . KOHLER COMMAND
CYLINDERS. 2
ENGINE HP 23
COOLING . . . . AIR
FUEL . . . . G
SPEEDS . . . . VARIABLE
TRANSMISSION . . . . HYDRO
STEERING. . . . . ZERO
STANDARD DECK . . . . 52"
WEIGHT . . . . 852 LBS.
MSRP. $6,695

OPTIONS

KAWASAKI 23E

RETAIL PRICING

YEAR	HIGH	LOW
2005	$3,878	$2,908

2352KOJ-SR1000

YEARS MFRD 2006-2006
SERIES . . . . CHARGER SERIES
ENGINE . . . . KOHLER
CYLINDERS. 2
CID 38
ENGINE HP 23
COOLING . . . . AIR
FUEL . . . . G
SPEEDS . . . . VARIABLE
TRANSMISSION . . . . HYDRO
STEERING. . . . . ZERO
BLADE CLUTCH . . . . ELECTRIC
STANDARD DECK . . . . 52"
WEIGHT . . . . 852 LBS.
MSRP. $7,150

RETAIL PRICING

YEAR	HIGH	LOW
2006	$4,379	$3,284

2352KOJ-SR1015

YEARS MFRD 2010-2011
SERIES .... CHARGER SERIES
ENGINE .. KOHLER COMMAND PRO
CYLINDERS 2
ENGINE HP 23
COOLING .... AIR
FUEL .... G
SPEEDS .... VARIABLE
TRANSMISSION .... HYDRO
STEERING .... ZERO
BLADE CLUTCH .... ELECTRIC
WEIGHT .... 1,100 LBS.

2352KOJ-SR300

YEARS MFRD 2006-2007
SERIES .... JAZEE TWO SERIES
ENGINE .... KOHLER COURAGE
CYLINDERS 2
ENGINE HP 23
COOLING .... AIR
FUEL .... G
SPEEDS .... VARIABLE
TRANSMISSION .... HYDRO
STEERING .... ZERO
STANDARD DECK .... 52"
WEIGHT .... 690 LBS.
MSRP $5,550

RETAIL PRICING

YEAR	HIGH	LOW
2006	$1,857	$1,393
2007	$1,899	$1,424

2352KOJ-SR355

YEARS MFRD 2008-2009
SERIES .... JAZEE PRO SERIES
ENGINE .... KOHLER
CYLINDERS 2
ENGINE HP 23
COOLING .... AIR
FUEL .... G
SPEEDS .... VARIABLE
TRANSMISSION .... HYDRO
STEERING .... ZERO
BLADE CLUTCH .... ELECTRIC
STANDARD DECK .... 49"
WEIGHT .... 775 LBS.
MSRP $6,195

RETAIL PRICING

YEAR	HIGH	LOW
2008	$3,482	$2,611
2009	$3,571	$2,678

2352KOJ8-SR1005

YEARS MFRD 2008-2009
SERIES .... CHARGER SERIES
ENGINE ...... KOHLER COMMAND
CYLINDERS 2
ENGINE HP 23
COOLING .... AIR
FUEL .... G
SPEEDS .... VARIABLE
TRANSMISSION .... HYDRO
STEERING .... ZERO
BLADE CLUTCH .... ELECTRIC
STANDARD DECK .... 52"
WEIGHT .... 1,100 LBS.
MSRP $7,495

RETAIL PRICING

YEAR	HIGH	LOW
2008	$3,468	$2,601
2009	$3,613	$2,710

2352KOT-SR1000

YEARS MFRD 2006-2006
SERIES .... CHARGER SERIES
ENGINE .... KOHLER
CYLINDERS 2
CID 38
ENGINE HP 23
COOLING .... AIR
FUEL .... G
SPEEDS .... VARIABLE
TRANSMISSION .... HYDRO
STEERING .... ZERO
BLADE CLUTCH .... ELECTRIC
STANDARD DECK .... 52"
WEIGHT .... 852 LBS.
MSRP $7,150

RETAIL PRICING

YEAR	HIGH	LOW
2006	$3,668	$2,751

2352KOT-SR1015

YEARS MFRD 2010-2011
SERIES .... CHARGER SERIES
ENGINE .. KOHLER COMMAND PRO
CYLINDERS 2
ENGINE HP 23
COOLING .... AIR
FUEL .... G
SPEEDS .... VARIABLE
TRANSMISSION .... HYDRO
STEERING .... ZERO
BLADE CLUTCH .... ELECTRIC
WEIGHT .... 1,100 LBS.

2352KOT-SR355

YEARS MFRD 2008-2009
SERIES .... JAZEE PRO SERIES
ENGINE .... KOHLER
CYLINDERS 2
ENGINE HP 23
COOLING .... AIR
FUEL .... G
SPEEDS .... VARIABLE
TRANSMISSION .... HYDRO
STEERING .... ZERO
BLADE CLUTCH .... ELECTRIC
STANDARD DECK .... 49"
WEIGHT .... 775 LBS.
MSRP $6,195

RETAIL PRICING

YEAR	HIGH	LOW
2008	$3,482	$2,611
2009	$3,571	$2,678

2352KOT8-SR1005

YEARS MFRD 2008-2009
SERIES .... CHARGER SERIES
ENGINE ...... KOHLER COMMAND
CYLINDERS 2
ENGINE HP 23
COOLING .... AIR
FUEL .... G
SPEEDS .... VARIABLE
TRANSMISSION .... HYDRO
STEERING .... ZERO
BLADE CLUTCH .... ELECTRIC
STANDARD DECK .... 52"
WEIGHT .... 1,100 LBS.
MSRP $7,495

RETAIL PRICING

YEAR	HIGH	LOW
2008	$3,468	$2,601
2009	$3,613	$2,710

2354KOJ-A105

YEARS MFRD 2016-2017
SERIES .... AVENUE SERIES
ENGINE .... KOHLER
ENGINE HP 23
COOLING .... AIR
FUEL .... G
SPEEDS .... VARIABLE
TRANSMISSION .... HYDRO
STEERING .... ZERO
STANDARD DECK .... 54"
WEIGHT .... 635 LBS.
MSRP $3,699

RETAIL PRICING

YEAR	HIGH	LOW
2016	$2,018	$1,513
2017	$2,432	$1,824

2354KOJ-A110

YEARS MFRD 2018-2020
SERIES .... AVENUE SERIES
ENGINE .... KOHLER KT730
CYLINDERS 2
ENGINE HP 23
FUEL .... G
SPEEDS .... VARIABLE
TRANSMISSION .... HYDRO
STEERING .... ZERO
STANDARD DECK .... 54"
WEIGHT .... 635 LBS.

2354KOJ-B205

YEARS MFRD 2016-2017
ENGINE .... KOHLER
ENGINE HP 23
FUEL .... G
SPEEDS .... VARIABLE
TRANSMISSION .... HYDRO
STEERING .... ZERO
STANDARD DECK .... 54"
WEIGHT .... 700 LBS.
MSRP $4,399

RETAIL PRICING

YEAR	HIGH	LOW
2016	$2,398	$1,799
2017	$2,866	$2,149

2354KOJ-B210

YEARS MFRD 2018-2020
SERIES .... BOULEVARD SERIES
ENGINE .... KOHLER KT730
CYLINDERS 2
ENGINE HP 23
FUEL .... G
SPEEDS .... VARIABLE
TRANSMISSION .... HYDRO
STEERING .... ZERO
BLADE CLUTCH .... ELECTRIC
STANDARD DECK .... 54"
WEIGHT .... 700 LBS.

2360KOJ-B200

YEARS MFRD 2016-2017
SERIES .... BOULEVARD SERIES
ENGINE .... KOHLER
ENGINE HP 23
FUEL .... G
SPEEDS .... VARIABLE
TRANSMISSION .... HYDRO
STEERING .... ZERO
STANDARD DECK .... 60"
WEIGHT .... 722 LBS.
MSRP $4,499

RETAIL PRICING

YEAR	HIGH	LOW
2016	$2,450	$1,838
2017	$2,996	$2,247

2360KOJ-B210

YEARS MFRD 2018-2020
SERIES .... BOULEVARD SERIES
ENGINE .... KOHLER KT730

COUNTRY CLIPPER

CYLINDERS. 2
ENGINE HP 23
FUEL . . . . G
SPEEDS . . . . VARIABLE
TRANSMISSION . . . . .HYDRO
STEERING. . . . . ZERO
BLADE CLUTCH . . . . .ELECTRIC
STANDARD DECK . . . . 60"
WEIGHT . . . . 722 LBS.

2360KOJ-SR1000

YEARS MFRD 2006-2006
SERIES. . . . . CHARGER SERIES
ENGINE . . . . KOHLER
CYLINDERS. 2
CID 38
ENGINE HP 23
FUEL . . . . G
SPEEDS . . . . VARIABLE
TRANSMISSION . . . . .HYDRO
STEERING. . . . . ZERO
BLADE CLUTCH . . . . .ELECTRIC
STANDARD DECK . . . . 60"
WEIGHT . . . . 852 LBS.
MSRP. $7,565

RETAIL PRICING

YEAR	HIGH	LOW
2006	$3,922	$2,941

2360KOJ-SR355

YEARS MFRD 2008-2009
SERIES. . . . . JAZEE PRO SERIES
ENGINE . . . . KOHLER
CYLINDERS. 2
ENGINE HP 23
COOLING . . . . AIR
FUEL . . . . G
SPEEDS . . . . VARIABLE
TRANSMISSION . . . . .HYDRO
STEERING. . . . . ZERO
BLADE CLUTCH . . . . .ELECTRIC
STANDARD DECK . . . . 49"
WEIGHT . . . . 775 LBS.
MSRP. $6,595

RETAIL PRICING

YEAR	HIGH	LOW
2008	$3,592	$2,694
2009	$3,803	$2,853

2360KOT-SR355

YEARS MFRD 2008-2009
SERIES. . . . . JAZEE PRO SERIES
ENGINE . . . . KOHLER
CYLINDERS. 2
ENGINE HP 23
COOLING . . . . AIR
FUEL . . . . G
SPEEDS . . . . VARIABLE
TRANSMISSION . . . . .HYDRO
STEERING. . . . . ZERO
BLADE CLUTCH . . . . .ELECTRIC
STANDARD DECK . . . . 49"
WEIGHT . . . . 800 LBS.
MSRP. $6,595

RETAIL PRICING

YEAR	HIGH	LOW
2008	$3,592	$2,694
2009	$3,803	$2,853

2448KAJ-460

YEARS MFRD 2016-2017
SERIES. . . . . EDGE XLT SERIES
ENGINE . . . . KAWASAKI
ENGINE HP 24
FUEL . . . . G
SPEEDS . . . . VARIABLE
TRANSMISSION . . . . .HYDRO
STEERING. . . . . ZERO
STANDARD DECK . . . . 48"
WEIGHT . . . . 818 LBS.
MSRP. $6,195

RETAIL PRICING

YEAR	HIGH	LOW
2016	$3,377	$2,533
2017	$3,862	$2,897

2448KAJ-C300

YEARS MFRD 2018-2019
SERIES. . . . . XLT SERIES
ENGINE . . . . KAWASAKI FR730V
CYLINDERS. 2
ENGINE HP 24
FUEL . . . . G
SPEEDS . . . . VARIABLE
TRANSMISSION . . . . .HYDRO
STEERING. . . . . ZERO
BLADE CLUTCH . . . . .ELECTRIC
STANDARD DECK . . . . 48"
WEIGHT . . . . 798 LBS.

2448KAJ-C305

YEARS MFRD 2020-2020
SERIES. . . . . XLT SERIES
ENGINE . . . . KAWASAKI FR730V
CYLINDERS. 2
ENGINE HP 24
FUEL . . . . G
SPEEDS . . . . VARIABLE
TRANSMISSION . . . . . DUAL HYDRO
STEERING. . . . . ZERO
BLADE CLUTCH . . . . .ELECTRIC
STANDARD DECK . . . . 48"
WEIGHT . . . . 814 LBS.

2448KAJ450

YEARS MFRD 2014-2014
SERIES. . . . . EDGE XLT SERIES
ENGINE . . . . KAWASAKI FR730
CYLINDERS. 2
ENGINE HP 24
COOLING . . . . AIR
FUEL . . . . G
SPEEDS . . . . VARIABLE
TRANSMISSION . . . . .HYDRO
STEERING. . . . . ZERO
BLADE CLUTCH . . . . .ELECTRIC
STANDARD DECK . . . . 48"
WEIGHT . . . . 818 LBS.

2448KAJ455

YEARS MFRD 2015-2015
SERIES. . . . . EDGE XLT SERIES
ENGINE . . . . KAWASAKI
ENGINE HP 24
FUEL . . . . G
SPEEDS . . . . VARIABLE
TRANSMISSION . . . . .HYDRO
STEERING. . . . . ZERO
STANDARD DECK . . . . 48"
MSRP. $6,195

RETAIL PRICING

YEAR	HIGH	LOW
2015	$3,757	$2,818

2448KOJ-SR215

YEARS MFRD 2010-2011
SERIES. . . . . JAZEE SERIES
ENGINE . . . KOHLER COURAGE PRO
CYLINDERS. 2
ENGINE HP 24
COOLING . . . . AIR
FUEL . . . . G
SPEEDS . . . . VARIABLE
TRANSMISSION . . . . .HYDRO
STEERING. . . . . ZERO
BLADE CLUTCH . . . . .ELECTRIC
STANDARD DECK . . . . 48"
WEIGHT . . . . 675 LBS.
MSRP. $5,395

RETAIL PRICING

YEAR	HIGH	LOW
2010	$2,246	$1,685
2011	$2,923	$2,193

2452KA-D500

YEARS MFRD 2018-2019
SERIES. . . . . . CHALLENGER SERIES
ENGINE . . . . KAWASAKI FS730V
CYLINDERS. 2
ENGINE HP 24
FUEL . . . . G
SPEEDS . . . . VARIABLE
TRANSMISSION . . . . .HYDRO
STEERING. . . . . ZERO
BLADE CLUTCH . . . . .ELECTRIC
STANDARD DECK . . . . 52"
WEIGHT . . . . 861 LBS.

OPTIONS

TWIN LEVER

2452KAJ-465

YEARS MFRD 2016-2017
SERIES. . . . . EDGE XLT SERIES
ENGINE . . . . KAWASAKI
ENGINE HP 24
FUEL . . . . G
SPEEDS . . . . VARIABLE
TRANSMISSION . . . . .HYDRO
STEERING. . . . . ZERO
STANDARD DECK . . . . 52"
WEIGHT . . . . 700 LBS.
MSRP. $6,395

RETAIL PRICING

YEAR	HIGH	LOW
2016	$3,490	$2,617
2017	$3,983	$2,987

2452KAJ-C305

YEARS MFRD 2020-2020
SERIES. . . . . XLT SERIES
ENGINE . . . . KAWASAKI FR730V
CYLINDERS. 2
ENGINE HP 24
FUEL . . . . G
SPEEDS . . . . VARIABLE
TRANSMISSION . . . . . DUAL HYDRO
STEERING. . . . . ZERO
BLADE CLUTCH . . . . .ELECTRIC
STANDARD DECK . . . . 52"
WEIGHT . . . . 823 LBS.

2452KAJ-D505

YEARS MFRD 2020-2020
SERIES. . . . . . CHALLENGER SERIES
ENGINE . . . . KAWASAKI FS730V
CYLINDERS. 2
ENGINE HP 24
FUEL . . . . G
SPEEDS . . . . VARIABLE
TRANSMISSION . . . . . DUAL HYDRO
STEERING. . . . . ZERO
BLADE CLUTCH . . . . .ELECTRIC
STANDARD DECK . . . . 52"
WEIGHT . . . . 829 LBS.

2452KAJ405

YEARS MFRD 2014-2014
SERIES. . . . . EDGE SERIES
ENGINE . . . . KAWASAKI FR730
CYLINDERS. 2
ENGINE HP 24
COOLING . . . . AIR
FUEL . . . . G
SPEEDS . . . . VARIABLE
TRANSMISSION . . . . .HYDRO
STEERING. . . . . ZERO
BLADE CLUTCH . . . . .ELECTRIC
STANDARD DECK . . . . 52"
WEIGHT . . . . 776 LBS.

2452KAJ450
YEARS MFRD........ 2014-2014
SERIES......... EDGE XLT SERIES
ENGINE ....KAWASAKI FR730
CYLINDERS.................. 2
ENGINE HP.................. 24
COOLING....................AIR
FUEL.......................G
SPEEDS.............VARIABLE
TRANSMISSION ....HYDRO
STEERING................ZERO
BLADE CLUTCH ....ELECTRIC
STANDARD DECK........... 52"
WEIGHT.............. 822 LBS.

2452KAJ455
YEARS MFRD........ 2015-2015
SERIES......... EDGE XLT SERIES
ENGINE .... KAWASAKI
ENGINE HP.................. 24
FUEL.......................G
SPEEDS.............VARIABLE
TRANSMISSION ....HYDRO
STEERING................ZERO
STANDARD DECK........... 52"
MSRP................ $6,395

RETAIL PRICING

YEAR	HIGH	LOW
2015	$4,200	$3,150

2452KAJ505
YEARS MFRD........ 2014-2014
SERIES...... CHALLENGER SERIES
ENGINE ....KAWASAKI FS730
CYLINDERS.................. 2
ENGINE HP.................. 24
COOLING....................AIR
FUEL.......................G
SPEEDS.............VARIABLE
TRANSMISSION ....HYDRO
STEERING................ZERO
BLADE CLUTCH ....ELECTRIC
STANDARD DECK........... 52"
WEIGHT.............. 895 LBS.

2452KAT-465
YEARS MFRD........ 2016-2017
SERIES......... EDGE XLT SERIES
ENGINE .... KAWASAKI
ENGINE HP.................. 24
FUEL.......................G
SPEEDS.............VARIABLE
TRANSMISSION ....HYDRO
STEERING................ZERO
STANDARD DECK........... 52"
WEIGHT.............. 822 LBS.
MSRP................ $6,395

RETAIL PRICING

YEAR	HIGH	LOW
2016	$3,490	$2,617
2017	$3,983	$2,987

2452KAT405
YEARS MFRD........ 2014-2014
SERIES............ EDGE SERIES
ENGINE ....KAWASAKI FR730
CYLINDERS.................. 2
ENGINE HP.................. 24
COOLING....................AIR
FUEL.......................G
SPEEDS.............VARIABLE
TRANSMISSION ....HYDRO
STEERING................ZERO
BLADE CLUTCH ....ELECTRIC
STANDARD DECK........... 52"
WEIGHT.............. 776 LBS.

2452KAT450
YEARS MFRD........ 2014-2014
SERIES......... EDGE XLT SERIES
ENGINE ....KAWASAKI FR730
CYLINDERS.................. 2
ENGINE HP.................. 24
COOLING....................AIR
FUEL.......................G
SPEEDS.............VARIABLE
TRANSMISSION ....HYDRO
STEERING................ZERO
BLADE CLUTCH ....ELECTRIC
STANDARD DECK........... 52"
WEIGHT.............. 822 LBS.

2452KAT455
YEARS MFRD........ 2015-2015
SERIES......... EDGE XLT SERIES
ENGINE .... KAWASAKI
ENGINE HP.................. 24
FUEL.......................G
SPEEDS.............VARIABLE
TRANSMISSION ....HYDRO
STEERING................ZERO
STANDARD DECK........... 52"
MSRP................ $6,395

RETAIL PRICING

YEAR	HIGH	LOW
2015	$4,200	$3,150

2452KAT505
YEARS MFRD........ 2014-2014
SERIES...... CHALLENGER SERIES
ENGINE ....KAWASAKI FS730
CYLINDERS.................. 2
ENGINE HP.................. 24
COOLING....................AIR
FUEL.......................G
SPEEDS.............VARIABLE
TRANSMISSION ....HYDRO
STEERING................ZERO
BLADE CLUTCH ....ELECTRIC
STANDARD DECK........... 52"
WEIGHT.............. 895 LBS.

2452KOJ-SR215
YEARS MFRD........ 2010-2011
SERIES............ JAZEE SERIES
ENGINE .... KOHLER COURAGE PRO
CYLINDERS.................. 2
ENGINE HP.................. 24
COOLING....................AIR
FUEL.......................G
SPEEDS.............VARIABLE
TRANSMISSION ....HYDRO
STEERING................ZERO
BLADE CLUTCH ....ELECTRIC
STANDARD DECK........... 52"
WEIGHT.............. 675 LBS.
MSRP................ $5,595

RETAIL PRICING

YEAR	HIGH	LOW
2010	$2,250	$1,688
2011	$3,030	$2,273

2452KOT-SR215
YEARS MFRD........ 2010-2011
SERIES........... JAZZEE SERIES
ENGINE .... KOHLER
CYLINDERS.................. 2
ENGINE HP.................. 24
COOLING....................AIR
FUEL.......................G
SPEEDS.............VARIABLE
TRANSMISSION ....HYDRO
STEERING................ZERO
BLADE CLUTCH ....ELECTRIC
STANDARD DECK........... 52"
WEIGHT.............. 675 LBS.
MSRP................ $5,595

RETAIL PRICING

YEAR	HIGH	LOW
2010	$2,332	$1,749
2011	$3,030	$2,273

2454KAJ-C300
YEARS MFRD........ 2018-2019
SERIES............... XLT SERIES
ENGINE ....KAWASAKI FR730V
CYLINDERS.................. 2
ENGINE HP.................. 24
FUEL.......................G
SPEEDS.............VARIABLE
TRANSMISSION ....HYDRO
STEERING................ZERO
BLADE CLUTCH ....ELECTRIC
STANDARD DECK........... 54"
WEIGHT.............. 803 LBS.

OPTIONS

TWIN LEVER

2460KAJ-465
YEARS MFRD........ 2016-2017
SERIES......... EDGE XLT SERIES
ENGINE .... KAWASAKI
ENGINE HP.................. 24
FUEL.......................G
SPEEDS.............VARIABLE
TRANSMISSION ....HYDRO
STEERING................ZERO
STANDARD DECK........... 60"
WEIGHT.............. 853 LBS.
MSRP................ $6,595

RETAIL PRICING

YEAR	HIGH	LOW
2016	$3,602	$2,702
2017	$4,113	$3,085

2460KAJ-C300
YEARS MFRD........ 2018-2019
SERIES............... XLT SERIES
ENGINE ....KAWASAKI FR730V
CYLINDERS.................. 2
ENGINE HP.................. 24
FUEL.......................G
SPEEDS.............VARIABLE
TRANSMISSION ....HYDRO
STEERING................ZERO
BLADE CLUTCH ....ELECTRIC
STANDARD DECK........... 60"
WEIGHT.............. 846 LBS.

OPTIONS

TWIN LEVER

2460KAJ-C305
YEARS MFRD........ 2020-2020
SERIES............... XLT SERIES
ENGINE ....KAWASAKI FR730V
CYLINDERS.................. 2
ENGINE HP.................. 24
FUEL.......................G
SPEEDS.............VARIABLE
TRANSMISSION ..... DUAL HYDRO
STEERING................ZERO
BLADE CLUTCH ....ELECTRIC
STANDARD DECK........... 60"
WEIGHT.............. 838 LBS.

2460KAJ-D500
YEARS MFRD........ 2018-2019
SERIES...... CHALLENGER SERIES
ENGINE ....KAWASAKI FS730V
CYLINDERS.................. 2
ENGINE HP.................. 24
FUEL.......................G
SPEEDS.............VARIABLE
TRANSMISSION ....HYDRO
STEERING................ZERO
BLADE CLUTCH ....ELECTRIC
STANDARD DECK........... 60"
WEIGHT.............. 875 LBS.

OPTIONS

TWIN LEVER

COUNTRY CLIPPER

2460KAJ-D505

YEARS MFRD 2020-2020
SERIES ...... CHALLENGER SERIES
ENGINE .... KAWASAKI FS730V
CYLINDERS 2
ENGINE HP 24
FUEL .... G
SPEEDS .... VARIABLE
TRANSMISSION ..... DUAL HYDRO
STEERING .... ZERO
BLADE CLUTCH .... ELECTRIC
STANDARD DECK .... 60"
WEIGHT .... 839 LBS.

2460KAJ405

YEARS MFRD 2014-2014
SERIES .... EDGE SERIES
ENGINE .... KAWASAKI FR730
CYLINDERS 2
ENGINE HP 24
COOLING .... AIR
FUEL .... G
SPEEDS .... VARIABLE
TRANSMISSION .... HYDRO
STEERING .... ZERO
BLADE CLUTCH .... ELECTRIC
STANDARD DECK .... 60"
WEIGHT .... 807 LBS.

2460KAJ450

YEARS MFRD 2014-2014
SERIES .... EDGE XLT SERIES
ENGINE .... KAWASAKI FR730
CYLINDERS 2
ENGINE HP 24
COOLING .... AIR
FUEL .... G
SPEEDS .... VARIABLE
TRANSMISSION .... HYDRO
STEERING .... ZERO
BLADE CLUTCH .... ELECTRIC
STANDARD DECK .... 60"
WEIGHT .... 853 LBS.

2460KAJ455

YEARS MFRD 2015-2015
SERIES .... EDGE XLT SERIES
ENGINE .... KAWASAKI
ENGINE HP 24
FUEL .... G
SPEEDS .... VARIABLE
TRANSMISSION .... HYDRO
STEERING .... ZERO
STANDARD DECK .... 60"
MSRP $6,595

RETAIL PRICING

YEAR	HIGH	LOW
2015	$4,286	$3,214

2460KAJ505

YEARS MFRD 2014-2014
SERIES ...... CHALLENGER SERIES
ENGINE .... KAWASAKI FS730
CYLINDERS 2
ENGINE HP 24
COOLING .... AIR
FUEL .... G
SPEEDS .... VARIABLE
TRANSMISSION .... HYDRO
STEERING .... ZERO
BLADE CLUTCH .... ELECTRIC
STANDARD DECK .... 60"
WEIGHT .... 906 LBS.

2460KAT-465

YEARS MFRD 2016-2017
SERIES .... EDGE XLT SERIES
ENGINE .... KAWASAKI
ENGINE HP 24
FUEL .... G
SPEEDS .... VARIABLE
TRANSMISSION .... HYDRO
STEERING .... ZERO
STANDARD DECK .... 60"
WEIGHT .... 853 LBS.
MSRP $6,595

RETAIL PRICING

YEAR	HIGH	LOW
2016	$3,602	$2,702
2017	$4,113	$3,085

2460KAT405

YEARS MFRD 2014-2014
SERIES .... EDGE SERIES
ENGINE .... KAWASAKI FR730
CYLINDERS 2
ENGINE HP 24
COOLING .... AIR
FUEL .... G
SPEEDS .... VARIABLE
TRANSMISSION .... HYDRO
STEERING .... ZERO
BLADE CLUTCH .... ELECTRIC
STANDARD DECK .... 60"
WEIGHT .... 807 LBS.

2460KAT450

YEARS MFRD 2014-2014
SERIES .... EDGE XLT SERIES
ENGINE .... KAWASAKI FR730
CYLINDERS 2
ENGINE HP 24
COOLING .... AIR
FUEL .... G
SPEEDS .... VARIABLE
TRANSMISSION .... HYDRO
STEERING .... ZERO
BLADE CLUTCH .... ELECTRIC
STANDARD DECK .... 60"
WEIGHT .... 853 LBS.

2460KAT455

YEARS MFRD 2015-2015
SERIES .... EDGE XLT SERIES
ENGINE .... KAWASAKI
ENGINE HP 24
FUEL .... G
SPEEDS .... VARIABLE
TRANSMISSION .... HYDRO
STEERING .... ZERO
STANDARD DECK .... 60"
MSRP $6,595

RETAIL PRICING

YEAR	HIGH	LOW
2015	$4,286	$3,214

2460KAT505

YEARS MFRD 2014-2014
SERIES ...... CHALLENGER SERIES
ENGINE .... KAWASAKI FS730
CYLINDERS 2
ENGINE HP 24
COOLING .... AIR
FUEL .... G
SPEEDS .... VARIABLE
TRANSMISSION .... HYDRO
STEERING .... ZERO
BLADE CLUTCH .... ELECTRIC
STANDARD DECK .... 60"
WEIGHT .... 906 LBS.

2500F

YEARS MFRD 1997-1997
ENGINE .... KOHLER
ENGINE HP 25
COOLING .... AIR
FUEL .... G
SPEEDS .... VARIABLE
TRANSMISSION ..... DUAL HYDRO
STEERING .... ZERO
STANDARD DECK .... 60"
MSRP $9,047

SERIAL NUMBERS

YEAR	BEGINNING NO.
1997	3074

RETAIL PRICING

YEAR	HIGH	LOW
1997	$1,189	$892

2500M

YEARS MFRD 1997-1998
ENGINE .... KOHLER
ENGINE HP 25
FUEL .... G
TRANSMISSION .... HYDRO
STEERING .... STANDARD
STANDARD DECK .... 60"
MSRP $7,774

RETAIL PRICING

YEAR	HIGH	LOW
1997	$2,212	$1,659
1998	$2,360	$1,770

2501M

YEARS MFRD 1998-1998
ENGINE .... KOHLER
ENGINE HP 25
FUEL .... G
SPEEDS .... VARIABLE
TRANSMISSION ..... DUAL HYDRO
STEERING .... ZERO
STANDARD DECK .... 60"
MSRP $7,800

SERIAL NUMBERS

YEAR	BEGINNING NO.
1998	6201

RETAIL PRICING

YEAR	HIGH	LOW
1998	$1,163	$872

2503F

YEARS MFRD 1998-2000
ENGINE .... KOHLER
ENGINE HP 25
FUEL .... G
SPEEDS .... VARIABLE
TRANSMISSION .... HYDRO
STEERING .... ZERO
STANDARD DECK .... 60"
MSRP $9,047

SERIAL NUMBERS

YEAR	BEGINNING NO.
1998	6555

RETAIL PRICING

YEAR	HIGH	LOW
1998	$1,434	$1,075
1999	$1,590	$1,192
2000	$1,766	$1,324

2503M

YEARS MFRD 1998-1999
ENGINE .... KOHLER
ENGINE HP 25
COOLING .... AIR
FUEL .... G
SPEEDS .... VARIABLE
TRANSMISSION ..... DUAL HYDRO
STEERING .... ZERO
STANDARD DECK .... 60"
MSRP $7,924

SERIAL NUMBERS

YEAR	BEGINNING NO.
1998	6361-MT
1998	6260

RETAIL PRICING

YEAR	HIGH	LOW
1998	$1,218	$914
1999	$1,351	$1,014

2504M

YEARS MFRD 1999-2004
SERIES .... MID MOUNT SERIES
ENGINE .... KOHLER
ENGINE HP 25
COOLING .... AIR
FUEL .... G
SPEEDS .... VARIABLE
TRANSMISSION .... HYDRO
STEERING .... ZERO
STANDARD DECK .... 60"
MSRP $8,448

RETAIL PRICING

YEAR	HIGH	LOW
1999	$1,348	$1,011
2000	$1,498	$1,124

2001............$1,664..........$1,248
2002............$1,848..........$1,386
2003............$2,055..........$1,541
2004............$2,279..........$1,709

2504MT

YEARS MFRD 2001-2004
SERIES....... MID MOUNT SERIES
ENGINE .. KOHLER COMMAND PRO
ENGINE HP.................. 25
FUEL .... G
TRANSMISSION ....HYDRO
STEERING................ZERO
WEIGHT .... 710 LBS.
MSRP.................. $6,740

RETAIL PRICING

YEAR	HIGH	LOW
2001	$2,442	$1,832
2002	$2,563	$1,922
2003	$2,747	$2,060
2004	$3,130	$2,348

2505KAJ

YEARS MFRD 2004-2004
SERIES. .ZETON MID MOUNT SERIES
ENGINE .... KAWASAKI
ENGINE HP.................. 25
COOLING ....AIR
FUEL .... G
SPEEDS .... VARIABLE
TRANSMISSION ....HYDRO
STEERING................ZERO
STANDARD DECK .... 52"
MSRP.................. $8,651

OPTIONS

60" DECK
DIX SEAT

RETAIL PRICING

YEAR	HIGH	LOW
2004	$2,209	$1,657

2505KAT

YEARS MFRD 2001-2005
SERIES. .ZETON MID MOUNT SERIES
ENGINE .... KAWASAKI
ENGINE HP.................. 25
FUEL .... G
SPEEDS .... VARIABLE
TRANSMISSION ....HYDRO
STEERING................ZERO
MSRP.................. $7,485

RETAIL PRICING

YEAR	HIGH	LOW
2001	$2,489	$1,867
2002	$2,612	$1,959
2003	$2,970	$2,228
2004	$3,194	$2,395
2005	$3,274	$2,456

2505KOJ

YEARS MFRD 2004-2004
SERIES. .ZETON MID MOUNT SERIES
ENGINE .... KOHLER
CID 44.1
ENGINE HP.................. 25
COOLING ....AIR
FUEL .... G
SPEEDS .... VARIABLE
TRANSMISSION ....HYDRO
STEERING................ZERO
STANDARD DECK .... 52"
WEIGHT .... 763 LBS.
MSRP.................. $8,651

OPTIONS

60" DECK
DIX SEAT

RETAIL PRICING

YEAR	HIGH	LOW
2004	$2,209	$1,657

2505KOT

YEARS MFRD 2001-2005
SERIES. .ZETON MID MOUNT SERIES
ENGINE .... KOHLER
CID 44.1
ENGINE HP.................. 25
COOLING ....AIR
FUEL .... G
SPEEDS .... VARIABLE
TRANSMISSION ....HYDRO
STEERING................ZERO
WEIGHT .... 763 LBS.
MSRP.................. $7,485

RETAIL PRICING

YEAR	HIGH	LOW
2001	$2,489	$1,867
2002	$2,612	$1,959
2003	$2,968	$2,226
2004	$3,194	$2,395
2005	$3,276	$2,457

2552KAJ-SR1000

YEARS MFRD 2006-2006
SERIES.......... CHARGER SERIES
ENGINE .... KAWASAKI
CYLINDERS.................. 2
CID 41.2
ENGINE HP.................. 25
COOLING ....AIR
FUEL .... G
SPEEDS .... VARIABLE
TRANSMISSION ....HYDRO
STEERING................ZERO
BLADE CLUTCH ....ELECTRIC
STANDARD DECK .... 52"
WEIGHT .... 852 LBS.
MSRP.................. $7,425

RETAIL PRICING

YEAR	HIGH	LOW
2006	$3,838	$2,878

2552KAJ-SR1200

YEARS MFRD 2006-2006
SERIES............ BOSS SERIES
ENGINE .... KAWASAKI
CYLINDERS.................. 2
CID 41.2
ENGINE HP.................. 25
COOLING ....AIR
FUEL .... G
SPEEDS .... VARIABLE
TRANSMISSION ....HYDRO
STEERING................ZERO
STANDARD DECK .... 52"
WEIGHT .... 1,040 LBS.
MSRP.................. $8,445

RETAIL PRICING

YEAR	HIGH	LOW
2006	$4,461	$3,346

2552KAJ8-SR1005

YEARS MFRD 2008-2009
SERIES.......... CHARGER SERIES
ENGINE .... KAWASAKI
CYLINDERS.................. 2
ENGINE HP.................. 25
COOLING ....AIR
FUEL .... G
SPEEDS .... VARIABLE
TRANSMISSION ....HYDRO
STEERING................ZERO
BLADE CLUTCH ....ELECTRIC
STANDARD DECK .... 48"
WEIGHT .... 1,100 LBS.
MSRP.................. $7,795

RETAIL PRICING

YEAR	HIGH	LOW
2008	$4,289	$3,217
2009	$4,494	$3,371

2552KAJ8-SR1205

YEARS MFRD 2008-2009
SERIES............ BOSS SERIES
ENGINE .... KAWASAKI
CYLINDERS.................. 2
ENGINE HP.................. 25
COOLING ....AIR
FUEL .... G
SPEEDS .... VARIABLE
TRANSMISSION ....HYDRO
STEERING................ZERO
BLADE CLUTCH ....ELECTRIC
STANDARD DECK .... 52"
WEIGHT .... 1,100 LBS.
MSRP.................. $8,495

RETAIL PRICING

YEAR	HIGH	LOW
2008	$4,696	$3,522
2009	$4,899	$3,674

2552KAT-SR1000

YEARS MFRD 2006-2006
SERIES.......... CHARGER SERIES
ENGINE .... KAWASAKI
CYLINDERS.................. 2
CID 41.2
ENGINE HP.................. 25
COOLING ....AIR
FUEL .... G
SPEEDS .... VARIABLE
TRANSMISSION ....HYDRO
STEERING................ZERO
BLADE CLUTCH ....ELECTRIC
STANDARD DECK .... 52"
WEIGHT .... 852 LBS.
MSRP.................. $7,425

RETAIL PRICING

YEAR	HIGH	LOW
2006	$3,838	$2,878

2552KAT-SR1200

YEARS MFRD 2006-2006
SERIES............ BOSS SERIES
ENGINE .... KAWASAKI
CYLINDERS.................. 2
ENGINE HP.................. 26
COOLING ....AIR
FUEL .... G
SPEEDS .... VARIABLE
TRANSMISSION ....HYDRO
STEERING................ZERO
STANDARD DECK .... 52"
WEIGHT .... 1,040 LBS.
MSRP.................. $8,445

RETAIL PRICING

YEAR	HIGH	LOW
2006	$4,461	$3,346

2552KAT8-SR1005

YEARS MFRD 2008-2009
SERIES.......... CHARGER SERIES
ENGINE .... KAWASAKI
CYLINDERS.................. 2
ENGINE HP.................. 25
COOLING ....AIR
FUEL .... G
SPEEDS .... VARIABLE
TRANSMISSION ....HYDRO
STEERING................ZERO
BLADE CLUTCH ....ELECTRIC
STANDARD DECK .... 48"
WEIGHT .... 1,100 LBS.
MSRP.................. $7,795

RETAIL PRICING

YEAR	HIGH	LOW
2008	$4,289	$3,217
2009	$4,494	$3,371

2552KAT8-SR1205

YEARS MFRD 2008-2009
SERIES............ BOSS SERIES
ENGINE .... KAWASAKI
CYLINDERS.................. 2
ENGINE HP.................. 25
COOLING ....AIR

FUEL .... G
SPEEDS .... VARIABLE
TRANSMISSION .... HYDRO
STEERING .... ZERO
BLADE CLUTCH .... ELECTRIC
STANDARD DECK .... 52"
WEIGHT .... 1,100 LBS.
MSRP $8,495

RETAIL PRICING

YEAR	HIGH	LOW
2008	$4,696	$3,522
2009	$4,899	$3,674

2552KOJ-D500

YEARS MFRD 2018-2019
SERIES .... CHALLENGER SERIES
ENGINE .... KOHLER ZT740
CYLINDERS 2
ENGINE HP 25
FUEL .... G
SPEEDS .... VARIABLE
TRANSMISSION .... HYDRO
STEERING .... ZERO
BLADE CLUTCH .... ELECTRIC
STANDARD DECK .... 52"
WEIGHT .... 861 LBS.

2552KOJ-D505

YEARS MFRD 2020-2020
SERIES .... CHALLENGER SERIES
ENGINE .... KOHLER ZT740
CYLINDERS 2
ENGINE HP 25
FUEL .... G
SPEEDS .... VARIABLE
TRANSMISSION .... DUAL HYDRO
STEERING .... ZERO
BLADE CLUTCH .... ELECTRIC
STANDARD DECK .... 52"
WEIGHT .... 829 LBS.

2552TKAT-SR1025

YEARS MFRD 2011-2013
SERIES .... CHARGER SERIES
ENGINE .... KAWASAKI
CYLINDERS 2
ENGINE HP 25.5
COOLING .... AIR
FUEL .... G
SPEEDS .... VARIABLE
TRANSMISSION .... HYDRO
STEERING .... ZERO
BLADE CLUTCH .... ELECTRIC
WEIGHT .... 1,040 LBS.

2560KAJ-SR1000

YEARS MFRD 2006-2006
SERIES .... CHARGER SERIES
ENGINE .... KAWASAKI
CYLINDERS 2
CID 41.2
ENGINE HP 25
FUEL .... G
SPEEDS .... VARIABLE
TRANSMISSION .... HYDRO
STEERING .... ZERO
BLADE CLUTCH .... ELECTRIC
STANDARD DECK .... 60"
WEIGHT .... 852 LBS.
MSRP $7,799

RETAIL PRICING

YEAR	HIGH	LOW
2006	$4,065	$3,049

2560KAJ8-SR1005

YEARS MFRD 2008-2009
SERIES .... CHARGER SERIES
ENGINE .... KAWASAKI
CYLINDERS 2
ENGINE HP 25
COOLING .... AIR
FUEL .... G
SPEEDS .... VARIABLE
TRANSMISSION .... HYDRO
STEERING .... ZERO
BLADE CLUTCH .... ELECTRIC
STANDARD DECK .... 52"
WEIGHT .... 1,100 LBS.
MSRP $8,150

RETAIL PRICING

YEAR	HIGH	LOW
2008	$4,558	$3,418
2009	$4,700	$3,525

2560KAT-SR1000

YEARS MFRD 2006-2006
SERIES .... CHARGER SERIES
ENGINE .... KAWASAKI
CYLINDERS 2
CID 41.2
ENGINE HP 25
FUEL .... G
SPEEDS .... VARIABLE
TRANSMISSION .... HYDRO
STEERING .... ZERO
BLADE CLUTCH .... ELECTRIC
STANDARD DECK .... 60"
WEIGHT .... 852 LBS.
MSRP $7,799

RETAIL PRICING

YEAR	HIGH	LOW
2006	$4,065	$3,049

2560KAT8-SR1005

YEARS MFRD 2008-2009
SERIES .... CHARGER SERIES
ENGINE .... KAWASAKI
CYLINDERS 2
ENGINE HP 25
COOLING .... AIR
FUEL .... G
SPEEDS .... VARIABLE
TRANSMISSION .... HYDRO
STEERING .... ZERO
BLADE CLUTCH .... ELECTRIC
STANDARD DECK .... 52"
WEIGHT .... 1,100 LBS.
MSRP $8,150

RETAIL PRICING

YEAR	HIGH	LOW
2008	$4,558	$3,418
2009	$4,700	$3,525

2560KOJ-D500

YEARS MFRD 2018-2019
SERIES .... CHALLENGER SERIES
ENGINE .... KOHLER ZT740
CYLINDERS 2
ENGINE HP 25
FUEL .... G
SPEEDS .... VARIABLE
TRANSMISSION .... HYDRO
STEERING .... ZERO
BLADE CLUTCH .... ELECTRIC
STANDARD DECK .... 60"
WEIGHT .... 875 LBS.

2560KOJ-D505

YEARS MFRD 2020-2020
SERIES .... CHALLENGER SERIES
ENGINE .... KOHLER ZT740
CYLINDERS 2
ENGINE HP 25
FUEL .... G
SPEEDS .... VARIABLE
TRANSMISSION .... DUAL HYDRO
STEERING .... ZERO
BLADE CLUTCH .... ELECTRIC
STANDARD DECK .... 60"
WEIGHT .... 839 LBS.

2605KOJ

YEARS MFRD 2001-2004
SERIES .... ZETON MID MOUNT SERIES
ENGINE .... KOHLER
ENGINE HP 25
FUEL .... G
TRANSMISSION .... HYDRO
STEERING .... ZERO
MSRP $7,200

RETAIL PRICING

YEAR	HIGH	LOW
2001	$3,198	$2,398
2002	$3,321	$2,491
2003	$3,574	$2,681
2004	$3,952	$2,964

2605KOT

YEARS MFRD 2001-2004
SERIES .... ZETON MID MOUNT SERIES
ENGINE .... KOHLER
ENGINE HP 25
FUEL .... G
TRANSMISSION .... HYDRO
STEERING .... ZERO
MSRP $7,200

RETAIL PRICING

YEAR	HIGH	LOW
2001	$3,198	$2,398
2002	$3,321	$2,491
2003	$3,574	$2,681
2004	$3,952	$2,964

2648KOJ-C300

YEARS MFRD 2018-2019
SERIES .... XLT SERIES
ENGINE .... KOHLER KT745
CYLINDERS 2
ENGINE HP 26
FUEL .... G
SPEEDS .... VARIABLE
TRANSMISSION .... HYDRO
STEERING .... ZERO
BLADE CLUTCH .... ELECTRIC
STANDARD DECK .... 48"
WEIGHT .... 798 LBS.

2648KOJ-C305

YEARS MFRD 2020-2020
SERIES .... XLT SERIES
ENGINE .... KOHLER KT745
CYLINDERS 2
ENGINE HP 26
FUEL .... G
SPEEDS .... VARIABLE
TRANSMISSION .... DUAL HYDRO
STEERING .... ZERO
BLADE CLUTCH .... ELECTRIC
STANDARD DECK .... 48"
WEIGHT .... 814 LBS.

2652BSJ-SR205

YEARS MFRD 2008-2009
SERIES .... JAZEE SERIES
ENGINE .... B&S ELS
CYLINDERS 2
ENGINE HP 26
COOLING .... AIR
FUEL .... G

SPEEDS . . . VARIABLE
TRANSMISSION . . . HYDRO
BLADE CLUTCH . . . ELECTRIC
WEIGHT . . . 675 LBS.

2652KALJ-SR1200

YEARS MFRD . . . 2006-2006
SERIES . . . BOSS SERIES
ENGINE . . . KAWASAKI
CYLINDERS . . . 2
ENGINE HP . . . 26
COOLING . . . LIQUID
FUEL . . . G
SPEEDS . . . VARIABLE
TRANSMISSION . . . HYDRO
STEERING . . . ZERO
STANDARD DECK . . . 52"
WEIGHT . . . 1,040 LBS.
MSRP . . . $8,725

RETAIL PRICING

YEAR	HIGH	LOW
2006	$5,342	$4,006

2652KALJ8-SR1205

YEARS MFRD . . . 2008-2009
SERIES . . . BOSS SERIES
ENGINE . . . KAWASAKI
CYLINDERS . . . 2
ENGINE HP . . . 26
COOLING . . . LIQUID
FUEL . . . G
SPEEDS . . . VARIABLE
TRANSMISSION . . . HYDRO
STEERING . . . ZERO
BLADE CLUTCH . . . ELECTRIC
STANDARD DECK . . . 52"
WEIGHT . . . 1,100 LBS.
MSRP . . . $8,895

RETAIL PRICING

YEAR	HIGH	LOW
2008	$4,993	$3,745
2009	$5,129	$3,847

2652KALT-SR1200

YEARS MFRD . . . 2006-2006
SERIES . . . BOSS SERIES
ENGINE . . . KAWASAKI
CYLINDERS . . . 2
CID . . . 42
ENGINE HP . . . 26
COOLING . . . LIQUID
FUEL . . . G
SPEEDS . . . VARIABLE
TRANSMISSION . . . HYDRO
STEERING . . . ZERO
STANDARD DECK . . . 52"
WEIGHT . . . 1,040 LBS.
MSRP . . . $8,725

RETAIL PRICING

YEAR	HIGH	LOW
2006	$5,342	$4,006

2652KALT8-SR1205

YEARS MFRD . . . 2008-2009
SERIES . . . BOSS SERIES
ENGINE . . . KAWASAKI
CYLINDERS . . . 2
ENGINE HP . . . 26
COOLING . . . LIQUID
FUEL . . . G
SPEEDS . . . VARIABLE
TRANSMISSION . . . HYDRO
STEERING . . . ZERO
BLADE CLUTCH . . . ELECTRIC
STANDARD DECK . . . 52"
WEIGHT . . . 1,100 LBS.
MSRP . . . $8,895

RETAIL PRICING

YEAR	HIGH	LOW
2008	$4,993	$3,745
2009	$5,129	$3,847

2652KOJ-C305

YEARS MFRD . . . 2020-2020
SERIES . . . XLT SERIES
ENGINE . . . KOHLER KT745
CYLINDERS . . . 2
ENGINE HP . . . 26
FUEL . . . G
SPEEDS . . . VARIABLE
TRANSMISSION . . . DUAL HYDRO
STEERING . . . ZERO
BLADE CLUTCH . . . ELECTRIC
STANDARD DECK . . . 52"
WEIGHT . . . 823 LBS.

2652TKAJ-SR1015

YEARS MFRD . . . 2010-2011
SERIES . . . CHARGER SERIES
ENGINE . . . KAWASAKI
CYLINDERS . . . 2
ENGINE HP . . . 26
COOLING . . . AIR
FUEL . . . G
SPEEDS . . . VARIABLE
TRANSMISSION . . . HYDRO
STEERING . . . ZERO
BLADE CLUTCH . . . ELECTRIC
WEIGHT . . . 1,100 LBS.

2652TKAT-SR1015

YEARS MFRD . . . 2010-2011
SERIES . . . CHARGER SERIES
ENGINE . . . KAWASAKI
CYLINDERS . . . 2
ENGINE HP . . . 26
COOLING . . . AIR
FUEL . . . G
SPEEDS . . . VARIABLE
TRANSMISSION . . . HYDRO
STEERING . . . ZERO
BLADE CLUTCH . . . ELECTRIC
WEIGHT . . . 1,100 LBS.

2654KOJ-C300

YEARS MFRD . . . 2018-2019
SERIES . . . XLT SERIES
ENGINE . . . KOHLER KT745
CYLINDERS . . . 2
ENGINE HP . . . 26
FUEL . . . G
SPEEDS . . . VARIABLE
TRANSMISSION . . . HYDRO
STEERING . . . ZERO
BLADE CLUTCH . . . ELECTRIC
STANDARD DECK . . . 54"
WEIGHT . . . 803 LBS.

2660KAJ-SR1015

YEARS MFRD . . . 2010-2011
SERIES . . . CHARGER SERIES
ENGINE . . . KAWASAKI
CYLINDERS . . . 2
ENGINE HP . . . 26
COOLING . . . AIR
FUEL . . . G
TRANSMISSION . . . HYDRO
STEERING . . . ZERO
BLADE CLUTCH . . . ELECTRIC
WEIGHT . . . 1,100 LBS.

2660KALJ-SR1200

YEARS MFRD . . . 2006-2006
SERIES . . . BOSS SERIES
ENGINE . . . KAWASAKI
CYLINDERS . . . 2
CID . . . 42
ENGINE HP . . . 26
COOLING . . . LIQUID
FUEL . . . G
SPEEDS . . . VARIABLE
TRANSMISSION . . . HYDRO
STEERING . . . ZERO
STANDARD DECK . . . 52"
WEIGHT . . . 1,040 LBS.
MSRP . . . $8,995

RETAIL PRICING

YEAR	HIGH	LOW
2006	$4,798	$3,599

2660KALJ-SR1210

YEARS MFRD . . . 2010-2011
SERIES . . . BOSS SERIES
ENGINE . . . KAWASAKI
CYLINDERS . . . 2
ENGINE HP . . . 26
COOLING . . . LIQUID
FUEL . . . G
SPEEDS . . . VARIABLE
TRANSMISSION . . . HYDRO
STEERING . . . ZERO
BLADE CLUTCH . . . ELECTRIC
WEIGHT . . . 1,120 LBS.

2660KALJ-SR1210L

YEARS MFRD . . . 2010-2011
SERIES . . . BOSS SERIES
ENGINE . . . KAWASAKI
CYLINDERS . . . 2
ENGINE HP . . . 26
COOLING . . . LIQUID
FUEL . . . G
SPEEDS . . . VARIABLE
TRANSMISSION . . . HYDRO
STEERING . . . ZERO
BLADE CLUTCH . . . ELECTRIC
WEIGHT . . . 1,120 LBS.

2660KALJ8-SR1205

YEARS MFRD . . . 2008-2009
SERIES . . . BOSS SERIES
ENGINE . . . KAWASAKI
CYLINDERS . . . 2
ENGINE HP . . . 26
COOLING . . . LIQUID
FUEL . . . G
SPEEDS . . . VARIABLE
TRANSMISSION . . . HYDRO
STEERING . . . ZERO
BLADE CLUTCH . . . ELECTRIC
STANDARD DECK . . . 60"
WEIGHT . . . 1,120 LBS.
MSRP . . . $9,295

RETAIL PRICING

YEAR	HIGH	LOW
2008	$5,165	$3,873
2009	$5,361	$4,020

2660KALT-SR1200

YEARS MFRD . . . 2006-2006
SERIES . . . BOSS SERIES
ENGINE . . . KAWASAKI
CYLINDERS . . . 2
CID . . . 42
ENGINE HP . . . 26
COOLING . . . LIQUID
FUEL . . . G
SPEEDS . . . VARIABLE
TRANSMISSION . . . HYDRO
STEERING . . . ZERO
STANDARD DECK . . . 60"
WEIGHT . . . 1,040 LBS.
MSRP . . . $8,995

RETAIL PRICING

YEAR	HIGH	LOW
2006	$4,798	$3,599

COUNTRY CLIPPER

2660KALT-SR1210

YEARS MFRD........2010-2011
SERIES............BOSS SERIES
ENGINE............KAWASAKI
CYLINDERS..................2
ENGINE HP.................26
COOLING...............LIQUID
FUEL.......................G
SPEEDS.............VARIABLE
TRANSMISSION..........HYDRO
STEERING................ZERO
BLADE CLUTCH........ELECTRIC
WEIGHT............1,120 LBS.

2660KALT8-SR1205

YEARS MFRD........2008-2009
SERIES............BOSS SERIES
ENGINE............KAWASAKI
CYLINDERS..................2
ENGINE HP.................26
COOLING...............LIQUID
FUEL.......................G
SPEEDS.............VARIABLE
TRANSMISSION..........HYDRO
STEERING................ZERO
BLADE CLUTCH........ELECTRIC
STANDARD DECK............60"
WEIGHT............1,120 LBS.
MSRP...................$9,295

RETAIL PRICING

YEAR	HIGH	LOW
2008	$5,165	$3,873
2009	$5,361	$4,020

2660KAT-SR1015

YEARS MFRD........2010-2011
SERIES.........CHARGER SERIES
ENGINE............KAWASAKI
CYLINDERS..................2
ENGINE HP.................26
COOLING..................AIR
FUEL.......................G
SPEEDS.............VARIABLE
TRANSMISSION..........HYDRO
STEERING................ZERO
BLADE CLUTCH........ELECTRIC
WEIGHT............1,100 LBS.

2660KOJ-C300

YEARS MFRD........2018-2019
SERIES.............XLT SERIES
ENGINE.........KOHLER KT745
CYLINDERS..................2
ENGINE HP.................26
FUEL.......................G
SPEEDS.............VARIABLE
TRANSMISSION..........HYDRO
STEERING................ZERO
BLADE CLUTCH........ELECTRIC
STANDARD DECK............60"
WEIGHT..............846 LBS.

2660KOJ-C305

YEARS MFRD........2020-2020
SERIES.............XLT SERIES
ENGINE.........KOHLER KT745
CYLINDERS..................2
ENGINE HP.................26
FUEL.......................G
SPEEDS.............VARIABLE
TRANSMISSION.....DUAL HYDRO
STEERING................ZERO
BLADE CLUTCH........ELECTRIC
STANDARD DECK............60"
WEIGHT..............838 LBS.

2660KOJ8-SR1205

YEARS MFRD........2008-2008
SERIES............BOSS SERIES
ENGINE............KOHLER EFI
CYLINDERS..................2
ENGINE HP.................28
COOLING..................AIR
FUEL.......................G
SPEEDS.............VARIABLE
TRANSMISSION..........HYDRO
STEERING................ZERO
BLADE CLUTCH........ELECTRIC
STANDARD DECK............60"
WEIGHT............1,120 LBS.
MSRP...................$9,895

RETAIL PRICING

YEAR	HIGH	LOW
2008	$5,761	$4,321

2672KALJ-SR1200

YEARS MFRD........2006-2006
SERIES............BOSS SERIES
ENGINE............KAWASAKI
ENGINE HP.................26
FUEL.......................G
SPEEDS.............VARIABLE
TRANSMISSION..........HYDRO
STEERING................ZERO
STANDARD DECK............72"
MSRP...................$9,525

RETAIL PRICING

YEAR	HIGH	LOW
2006	$5,123	$3,843

2672KALJ8-SR1205

YEARS MFRD........2008-2009
SERIES............BOSS SERIES
ENGINE............KAWASAKI
CYLINDERS..................2
ENGINE HP.................26
COOLING...............LIQUID
FUEL.......................G
SPEEDS.............VARIABLE
TRANSMISSION..........HYDRO
STEERING................ZERO
BLADE CLUTCH........ELECTRIC
STANDARD DECK............72"
WEIGHT............1,120 LBS.
MSRP...................$9,850

RETAIL PRICING

YEAR	HIGH	LOW
2008	$5,734	$4,300
2009	$5,867	$4,400

2672KALT-SR1200

YEARS MFRD........2006-2006
SERIES............BOSS SERIES
ENGINE............KAWASAKI
ENGINE HP.................26
FUEL.......................G
SPEEDS.............VARIABLE
TRANSMISSION..........HYDRO
STEERING................ZERO
STANDARD DECK............72"
MSRP...................$9,525

RETAIL PRICING

YEAR	HIGH	LOW
2006	$5,123	$3,843

2672KALT8-SR1205

YEARS MFRD........2008-2009
SERIES............BOSS SERIES
ENGINE............KAWASAKI
CYLINDERS..................2
ENGINE HP.................26
COOLING...............LIQUID
FUEL.......................G
SPEEDS.............VARIABLE
TRANSMISSION..........HYDRO
STEERING................ZERO
BLADE CLUTCH........ELECTRIC
STANDARD DECK............72"
WEIGHT............1,220 LBS.
MSRP...................$9,850

RETAIL PRICING

YEAR	HIGH	LOW
2008	$5,734	$4,300
2009	$5,867	$4,400

2707KOJ

YEARS MFRD........2004-2004
SERIES.....ZETON BOSS SERIES
ENGINE..KOHLER COMMAND PRO
CYLINDERS..................2
CID.......................44
ENGINE HP.................27
COOLING..................AIR
FUEL.......................G
SPEEDS.............VARIABLE
TRANSMISSION..........HYDRO
STEERING................ZERO
BLADE CLUTCH........ELECTRIC
STANDARD DECK............72"
MSRP...................$9,381

OPTIONS

DIX SEAT

RETAIL PRICING

YEAR	HIGH	LOW
2004	$2,397	$1,798

2707KOT

YEARS MFRD........2004-2005
SERIES.....ZETON BOSS SERIES
ENGINE..KOHLER COMMAND PRO
CYLINDERS..................2
CID.......................44
ENGINE HP.................27
COOLING..................AIR
FUEL.......................G
SPEEDS.............VARIABLE
TRANSMISSION..........HYDRO
STEERING................ZERO
BLADE CLUTCH........ELECTRIC
WEIGHT..............775 LBS.

2748KOJ-SR225

YEARS MFRD........2011-2013
SERIES...........JAZEE SERIES
ENGINE.......KOHLER COURAGE
CYLINDERS..................2
ENGINE HP.................27
COOLING..................AIR
FUEL.......................G
SPEEDS.............VARIABLE
TRANSMISSION..........HYDRO
STEERING................ZERO
BLADE CLUTCH........ELECTRIC
WEIGHT..............675 LBS.

2748KOJ-SR365

YEARS MFRD........2011-2011
SERIES.......JAZEE PRO SERIES
ENGINE...KOHLER COURAGE PRO
CYLINDERS..................2
ENGINE HP.................27
COOLING..................AIR
FUEL.......................G
SPEEDS.............VARIABLE
TRANSMISSION..........HYDRO
STEERING................ZERO
BLADE CLUTCH........ELECTRIC
WEIGHT..............775 LBS.

2748KOJ-SR375

YEARS MFRD........2011-2012
SERIES.......JAZEE PRO SERIES
ENGINE.......KOHLER COURAGE

CYLINDERS. 2
ENGINE HP 27
COOLING . . . . AIR
FUEL . . . . G
SPEEDS . . . . VARIABLE
TRANSMISSION . . . . HYDRO
STEERING. . . . . ZERO
BLADE CLUTCH . . . . ELECTRIC
WEIGHT . . . . 760 LBS.

2748KOT-SR225

YEARS MFRD 2011-2013
SERIES. . . . . JAZEE SERIES
ENGINE . . . . KOHLER COURAGE
CYLINDERS. 2
ENGINE HP 27
COOLING . . . . AIR
FUEL . . . . G
SPEEDS . . . . VARIABLE
TRANSMISSION . . . . HYDRO
STEERING. . . . . ZERO
BLADE CLUTCH . . . . ELECTRIC
WEIGHT . . . . 675 LBS.

2752KOJ-SR225

YEARS MFRD 2011-2013
SERIES. . . . . JAZEE SERIES
ENGINE . . . . KOHLER COURAGE
CYLINDERS. 2
ENGINE HP 27
COOLING . . . . AIR
FUEL . . . . G
SPEEDS . . . . VARIABLE
TRANSMISSION . . . . HYDRO
STEERING. . . . . ZERO
BLADE CLUTCH . . . . ELECTRIC
WEIGHT . . . . 675 LBS.

2752KOJ-SR365

YEARS MFRD 2010-2011
SERIES. . . . . JAZEE PRO SERIES
ENGINE . . . . KOHLER
CYLINDERS. 2
ENGINE HP 27
COOLING . . . . AIR
FUEL . . . . G
SPEEDS . . . . VARIABLE
TRANSMISSION . . . . HYDRO
STEERING. . . . . ZERO
BLADE CLUTCH . . . . ELECTRIC
WEIGHT . . . . 775 LBS.

2752KOJ-SR375

YEARS MFRD 2011-2012
SERIES. . . . . JAZEE PRO SERIES
ENGINE . . . . KOHLER COURAGE
CYLINDERS. 2
ENGINE HP 27
COOLING . . . . AIR
FUEL . . . . G
SPEEDS . . . . VARIABLE
TRANSMISSION . . . . HYDRO
STEERING. . . . . ZERO
BLADE CLUTCH . . . . ELECTRIC
WEIGHT . . . . 775 LBS.

2752KOJ505

YEARS MFRD 2014-2014
SERIES. . . . . . CHALLENGER SERIES
ENGINE . . . . . . KOHLER COMMAND
CYLINDERS. 2
ENGINE HP 27
COOLING . . . . AIR
FUEL . . . . G
SPEEDS . . . . VARIABLE
TRANSMISSION . . . . HYDRO
STEERING. . . . . ZERO
BLADE CLUTCH . . . . ELECTRIC
STANDARD DECK . . . . 52"
WEIGHT . . . . 895 LBS.

2752KOJL-SR365

YEARS MFRD 2010-2011
SERIES. . . . . JAZEE PRO SERIES
ENGINE . . . . KOHLER
CYLINDERS. 2
ENGINE HP 27
COOLING . . . . AIR
FUEL . . . . G
SPEEDS . . . . VARIABLE
TRANSMISSION . . . . HYDRO
STEERING. . . . . ZERO
BLADE CLUTCH . . . . ELECTRIC
WEIGHT . . . . 775 LBS.

2752KOJL-SR375

YEARS MFRD 2011-2012
SERIES. . . . . JAZEE PRO SERIES
ENGINE . . . . KOHLER COURAGE
CYLINDERS. 2
ENGINE HP 27
COOLING . . . . AIR
FUEL . . . . G
SPEEDS . . . . VARIABLE
TRANSMISSION . . . . HYDRO
STEERING. . . . . ZERO
BLADE CLUTCH . . . . ELECTRIC
WEIGHT . . . . 775 LBS.

2752KOT-SR225

YEARS MFRD 2011-2013
SERIES. . . . . JAZEE SERIES
ENGINE . . . . KOHLER COURAGE
CYLINDERS. 2
ENGINE HP 27
COOLING . . . . AIR
FUEL . . . . G
SPEEDS . . . . VARIABLE
TRANSMISSION . . . . HYDRO
STEERING. . . . . ZERO
BLADE CLUTCH . . . . ELECTRIC
WEIGHT . . . . 675 LBS.

2752KOT-SR365

YEARS MFRD 2010-2011
SERIES. . . . . JAZEE PRO SERIES
ENGINE . . . . KOHLER COURAGE PRO
CYLINDERS. 2
ENGINE HP 27
COOLING . . . . AIR
FUEL . . . . G
SPEEDS . . . . VARIABLE
TRANSMISSION . . . . HYDRO
STEERING. . . . . ZERO
BLADE CLUTCH . . . . ELECTRIC
WEIGHT . . . . 775 LBS.

2752KOT-SR375

YEARS MFRD 2011-2012
SERIES. . . . . JAZEE PRO SERIES
ENGINE . . . . KOHLER COURAGE
CYLINDERS. 2
ENGINE HP 27
COOLING . . . . AIR
FUEL . . . . G
SPEEDS . . . . VARIABLE
TRANSMISSION . . . . HYDRO
STEERING. . . . . ZERO
BLADE CLUTCH . . . . ELECTRIC
WEIGHT . . . . 775 LBS.

2760KAT-SR1015

YEARS MFRD 2010-2010
SERIES. . . . . CHARGER SERIES
ENGINE . . . . KOHLER
CYLINDERS. 2
ENGINE HP 27
COOLING . . . . AIR
FUEL . . . . G
SPEEDS . . . . VARIABLE
TRANSMISSION . . . . HYDRO
STEERING. . . . . ZERO
BLADE CLUTCH . . . . ELECTRIC
WEIGHT . . . . 1,100 LBS.

2760KOHJ-SR375

YEARS MFRD 2012-2013
SERIES. . . . JAZEE PRO DLX SERIES
ENGINE . . . . KOHLER
CYLINDERS. 2
ENGINE HP 27
COOLING . . . . AIR
FUEL . . . . G
SPEEDS . . . . VARIABLE
TRANSMISSION . . . . HYDRO
STEERING. . . . . ZERO
BLADE CLUTCH . . . . ELECTRIC
WEIGHT . . . . 837 LBS.

2760KOHT-SR375

YEARS MFRD 2012-2013
SERIES. . . . JAZEE PRO DLX SERIES
ENGINE . . . . . . KOHLER COMMAND
CYLINDERS. 2
ENGINE HP 27
COOLING . . . . AIR
FUEL . . . . G
SPEEDS . . . . VARIABLE
TRANSMISSION . . . . HYDRO
STEERING. . . . . ZERO
BLADE CLUTCH . . . . ELECTRIC
WEIGHT . . . . 837 LBS.

2760KOJ-1525

YEARS MFRD 2018-2020
SERIES. . . . . BOSS XL SERIES
ENGINE . . . . KOHLER CV752
CYLINDERS. 2
ENGINE HP 27
FUEL . . . . G
SPEEDS . . . . VARIABLE
TRANSMISSION . . . . HYDRO
STEERING. . . . . ZERO
BLADE CLUTCH . . . . ELECTRIC
STANDARD DECK . . . . 60"
WEIGHT . . . . 1,258 LBS.

2760KOJ-SR1000

YEARS MFRD 2006-2006
SERIES. . . . . CHARGER SERIES
ENGINE . . . . KOHLER
ENGINE HP 27
FUEL . . . . G
SPEEDS . . . . VARIABLE
TRANSMISSION . . . . HYDRO
STEERING. . . . . ZERO
STANDARD DECK . . . . 60"
MSRP. $7,950

RETAIL PRICING

YEAR	HIGH	LOW
2006	$4,158	$3,119

2760KOJ-SR1015

YEARS MFRD 2011-2011
SERIES. . . . . CHARGER SERIES
ENGINE . . KOHLER COMMAND PRO
CYLINDERS. 2
ENGINE HP 27
COOLING . . . . AIR
FUEL . . . . G

COUNTRY CLIPPER

SPEEDS .... VARIABLE
TRANSMISSION .... HYDRO
STEERING................ ZERO
BLADE CLUTCH .... ELECTRIC
WEIGHT .... 1,100 LBS.

2760KOJ-SR1025

YEARS MFRD 2011-2013
SERIES......... CHARGER SERIES
ENGINE .. KOHLER COMMAND PRO
CYLINDERS.................. 2
ENGINE HP.................. 27
COOLING .... AIR
FUEL .... G
SPEEDS .... VARIABLE
TRANSMISSION .... HYDRO
STEERING................ ZERO
BLADE CLUTCH .... ELECTRIC
WEIGHT .... 1,020 LBS.

2760KOJ-SR1200

YEARS MFRD 2006-2006
SERIES............ BOSS SERIES
ENGINE ...... KOHLER COMMAND
CYLINDERS.................. 2
CID 44
ENGINE HP.................. 27
COOLING .... AIR
FUEL .... G
SPEEDS .... VARIABLE
TRANSMISSION .... HYDRO
STEERING................ ZERO
STANDARD DECK .... 60"
WEIGHT .... 1,035 LBS.
MSRP................ $8,600

RETAIL PRICING

YEAR	HIGH	LOW
2006	$4,556	$3,417

2760KOJ-SR1210

YEARS MFRD 2010-2011
SERIES............ BOSS SERIES
ENGINE .. KOHLER COMMAND PRO
CYLINDERS.................. 2
ENGINE HP.................. 27
COOLING .... AIR
FUEL .... G
SPEEDS .... VARIABLE
TRANSMISSION .... HYDRO
STEERING................ ZERO
BLADE CLUTCH .... ELECTRIC
WEIGHT .... 1,120 LBS.

2760KOJ-SR1210L

YEARS MFRD 2010-2011
SERIES............ BOSS SERIES
ENGINE .. KOHLER COMMAND PRO
CYLINDERS.................. 2
ENGINE HP.................. 27
COOLING .... LIQUID
FUEL .... G
SPEEDS .... VARIABLE
TRANSMISSION .... HYDRO
STEERING................ ZERO
BLADE CLUTCH .... ELECTRIC
WEIGHT .... 1,120 LBS.

2760KOJ-SR1220

YEARS MFRD 2011-2013
SERIES............ BOSS SERIES
ENGINE .... KOHLER
CYLINDERS.................. 2
ENGINE HP.................. 27
COOLING .... AIR
FUEL .... G
SPEEDS .... VARIABLE
TRANSMISSION .... HYDRO
STEERING................ ZERO
WEIGHT .... 1,190 LBS.

2760KOJ-SR1220L

YEARS MFRD 2011-2012
SERIES... BOSS POWERLIFT SERIES
ENGINE .... KOHLER
CYLINDERS.................. 2
ENGINE HP.................. 27
COOLING .... AIR
FUEL .... G
SPEEDS .... VARIABLE
TRANSMISSION .... HYDRO
STEERING................ ZERO
BLADE CLUTCH .... ELECTRIC
WEIGHT .... 1,230 LBS.

2760KOJ-SR365

YEARS MFRD 2011-2011
SERIES........ JAZEE PRO SERIES
ENGINE ... KOHLER COURAGE PRO
CYLINDERS.................. 2
ENGINE HP.................. 27
COOLING .... AIR
FUEL .... G
SPEEDS .... VARIABLE
TRANSMISSION .... HYDRO
STEERING................ ZERO
BLADE CLUTCH .... ELECTRIC
WEIGHT .... 800 LBS.

2760KOJ-SR375

YEARS MFRD 2011-2012
SERIES........ JAZEE PRO SERIES
ENGINE .... KOHLER COURAGE
CYLINDERS.................. 2
ENGINE HP.................. 27
COOLING .... AIR
FUEL .... G
SPEEDS .... VARIABLE
TRANSMISSION .... HYDRO
STEERING................ ZERO
BLADE CLUTCH .... ELECTRIC
WEIGHT .... 800 LBS.

2760KOJ1505

YEARS MFRD 2014-2014
SERIES........ DEFENDER SERIES
ENGINE ...... KOHLER COMMAND
CYLINDERS.................. 2
ENGINE HP.................. 27
COOLING .... AIR
FUEL .... G
SPEEDS .... VARIABLE
TRANSMISSION .... HYDRO
STEERING................ ZERO
BLADE CLUTCH .... ELECTRIC
STANDARD DECK .... 60"
WEIGHT .... 1,257 LBS.

2760KOJ505

YEARS MFRD 2014-2014
SERIES...... CHALLENGER SERIES
ENGINE ...... KOHLER COMMAND
CYLINDERS.................. 2
ENGINE HP.................. 27
COOLING .... AIR
FUEL .... G
SPEEDS .... VARIABLE
TRANSMISSION .... HYDRO
STEERING................ ZERO
BLADE CLUTCH .... ELECTRIC
STANDARD DECK .... 60"
WEIGHT .... 906 LBS.

2760KOJ8-SR1005

YEARS MFRD 2008-2009
SERIES......... CHARGER SERIES
ENGINE .. KOHLER COMMAND PRO
CYLINDERS.................. 2
ENGINE HP.................. 27
COOLING .... AIR
FUEL .... G
SPEEDS .... VARIABLE
TRANSMISSION .... HYDRO
STEERING................ ZERO
BLADE CLUTCH .... ELECTRIC
STANDARD DECK .... 60"
WEIGHT .... 1,100 LBS.
MSRP................ $8,295

RETAIL PRICING

YEAR	HIGH	LOW
2008	$4,830	$3,623
2009	$4,970	$3,727

2760KOJ8-SR2105

YEARS MFRD 2008-2009
SERIES............ BOSS SERIES
ENGINE .... KOHLER
CYLINDERS.................. 2
ENGINE HP.................. 27
COOLING .... AIR
FUEL .... G
SPEEDS .... VARIABLE
TRANSMISSION .... HYDRO
STEERING................ ZERO
BLADE CLUTCH .... ELECTRIC
STANDARD DECK .... 60"
WEIGHT .... 1,120 LBS.
MSRP................ $8,950

RETAIL PRICING

YEAR	HIGH	LOW
2008	$5,212	$3,909
2009	$5,410	$4,057

2760KOT-1220

YEARS MFRD 2011-2013
SERIES............ BOSS SERIES
ENGINE .... KOHLER
CYLINDERS.................. 2
ENGINE HP.................. 27
COOLING .... AIR
FUEL .... G
SPEEDS .... VARIABLE
TRANSMISSION .... HYDRO
STEERING................ ZERO
BLADE CLUTCH .... ELECTRIC
WEIGHT .... 1,190 LBS.

2760KOT-SR1000

YEARS MFRD 2006-2006
SERIES......... CHARGER SERIES
ENGINE .... KOHLER
ENGINE HP.................. 27
FUEL .... G
SPEEDS .... VARIABLE
TRANSMISSION .... HYDRO
STEERING................ ZERO
STANDARD DECK .... 60"
MSRP................ $7,950

RETAIL PRICING

YEAR	HIGH	LOW
2006	$4,158	$3,119

2760KOT-SR1015

YEARS MFRD 2010-2011
SERIES......... CHARGER SERIES
ENGINE .. KOHLER COMMAND PRO
CYLINDERS.................. 2
ENGINE HP.................. 27
COOLING .... AIR
FUEL .... G
SPEEDS .... VARIABLE
TRANSMISSION .... HYDRO

STEERING . . . ZERO
BLADE CLUTCH . . . ELECTRIC
WEIGHT . . . 1,100 LBS.

2760KOT-SR1025

YEARS MFRD . . . 2011-2013
SERIES . . . CHARGER SERIES
ENGINE . . KOHLER COMMAND PRO
CYLINDERS . . . 2
ENGINE HP . . . 27
COOLING . . . AIR
FUEL . . . G
SPEEDS . . . VARIABLE
TRANSMISSION . . . HYDRO
STEERING . . . ZERO
BLADE CLUTCH . . . ELECTRIC
WEIGHT . . . 1,020 LBS.

2760KOT-SR1200

YEARS MFRD . . . 2006-2006
SERIES . . . BOSS SERIES
ENGINE . . . KOHLER COMMAND
CYLINDERS . . . 2
CID . . . 44
ENGINE HP . . . 27
COOLING . . . AIR
FUEL . . . G
SPEEDS . . . VARIABLE
TRANSMISSION . . . HYDRO
STEERING . . . ZERO
STANDARD DECK . . . 52"
WEIGHT . . . 1,035 LBS.
MSRP . . . $8,600

RETAIL PRICING

YEAR	HIGH	LOW
2006	$4,556	$3,417

2760KOT-SR1210

YEARS MFRD . . . 2010-2011
SERIES . . . BOSS SERIES
ENGINE . . KOHLER COMMAND PRO
CYLINDERS . . . 2
ENGINE HP . . . 27
COOLING . . . AIR
FUEL . . . G
SPEEDS . . . VARIABLE
TRANSMISSION . . . HYDRO
STEERING . . . ZERO
BLADE CLUTCH . . . ELECTRIC
WEIGHT . . . 1,120 LBS.

2760KOT-SR365

YEARS MFRD . . . 2010-2011
SERIES . . . JAZEE PRO SERIES
ENGINE . . . KOHLER COURAGE PRO
CYLINDERS . . . 2
ENGINE HP . . . 27
COOLING . . . AIR
FUEL . . . G
SPEEDS . . . VARIABLE
TRANSMISSION . . . HYDRO
STEERING . . . ZERO
BLADE CLUTCH . . . ELECTRIC
WEIGHT . . . 775 LBS.

2760KOT-SR375

YEARS MFRD . . . 2011-2012
SERIES . . . JAZEE PRO SERIES
ENGINE . . . KOHLER COURAGE
CYLINDERS . . . 2
ENGINE HP . . . 27
COOLING . . . AIR
FUEL . . . G
SPEEDS . . . VARIABLE
TRANSMISSION . . . HYDRO
STEERING . . . ZERO
BLADE CLUTCH . . . ELECTRIC
WEIGHT . . . 800 LBS.

2760KOT1505

YEARS MFRD . . . 2014-2014
SERIES . . . DEFENDER SERIES
ENGINE . . . KOHLER COMMAND
CYLINDERS . . . 2
ENGINE HP . . . 27
COOLING . . . AIR
FUEL . . . G
SPEEDS . . . VARIABLE
TRANSMISSION . . . HYDRO
STEERING . . . ZERO
BLADE CLUTCH . . . ELECTRIC
STANDARD DECK . . . 60"
WEIGHT . . . 1,258 LBS.

2760KOT505

YEARS MFRD . . . 2014-2014
SERIES . . . CHALLENGER SERIES
ENGINE . . . KOHLER COMMAND
CYLINDERS . . . 2
ENGINE HP . . . 27
COOLING . . . AIR
FUEL . . . G
SPEEDS . . . VARIABLE
TRANSMISSION . . . HYDRO
STEERING . . . ZERO
BLADE CLUTCH . . . ELECTRIC
STANDARD DECK . . . 60"
WEIGHT . . . 906 LBS.

2760KOT8-SR1005

YEARS MFRD . . . 2008-2009
SERIES . . . CHARGER SERIES
ENGINE . . KOHLER COMMAND PRO
CYLINDERS . . . 2
ENGINE HP . . . 27
COOLING . . . AIR
FUEL . . . G
SPEEDS . . . VARIABLE
TRANSMISSION . . . HYDRO
STEERING . . . ZERO
BLADE CLUTCH . . . ELECTRIC
STANDARD DECK . . . 60"
WEIGHT . . . 1,100 LBS.
MSRP . . . $8,295

RETAIL PRICING

YEAR	HIGH	LOW
2008	$4,830	$3,623
2009	$5,033	$3,775

2760KOT8-SR1205

YEARS MFRD . . . 2008-2008
SERIES . . . BOSS SERIES
ENGINE . . . KOHLER
CYLINDERS . . . 2
ENGINE HP . . . 27
COOLING . . . AIR
FUEL . . . G
SPEEDS . . . VARIABLE
TRANSMISSION . . . HYDRO
STEERING . . . ZERO
BLADE CLUTCH . . . ELECTRIC
STANDARD DECK . . . 60"
WEIGHT . . . 1,120 LBS.
MSRP . . . $8,950

RETAIL PRICING

YEAR	HIGH	LOW
2008	$5,212	$3,909

2852KOJ8-SR1205

YEARS MFRD . . . 2008-2009
SERIES . . . BOSS SERIES
ENGINE . . . KOHLER EFI
CYLINDERS . . . 2
ENGINE HP . . . 28
COOLING . . . AIR
FUEL . . . G
SPEEDS . . . VARIABLE
TRANSMISSION . . . HYDRO
STEERING . . . ZERO
BLADE CLUTCH . . . ELECTRIC
STANDARD DECK . . . 52"
WEIGHT . . . 1,100 LBS.
MSRP . . . $9,395

RETAIL PRICING

YEAR	HIGH	LOW
2008	$5,471	$4,104
2009	$5,605	$4,203

2852KOT8-SR1205

YEARS MFRD . . . 2008-2009
SERIES . . . BOSS SERIES
ENGINE . . . KOHLER EFI
CYLINDERS . . . 2
ENGINE HP . . . 28
COOLING . . . AIR
FUEL . . . G
SPEEDS . . . VARIABLE
TRANSMISSION . . . HYDRO
STEERING . . . ZERO
BLADE CLUTCH . . . ELECTRIC
STANDARD DECK . . . 52"
WEIGHT . . . 1,100 LBS.
MSRP . . . $9,395

RETAIL PRICING

YEAR	HIGH	LOW
2008	$5,471	$4,104
2009	$5,605	$4,203

2860KOT8-SR1205

YEARS MFRD . . . 2008-2009
SERIES . . . BOSS SERIES
ENGINE . . . KOHLER EFI
CYLINDERS . . . 2
ENGINE HP . . . 28
COOLING . . . AIR
FUEL . . . G
SPEEDS . . . VARIABLE
TRANSMISSION . . . HYDRO
STEERING . . . ZERO
BLADE CLUTCH . . . ELECTRIC
STANDARD DECK . . . 60"
WEIGHT . . . 1,120 LBS.
MSRP . . . $9,895

RETAIL PRICING

YEAR	HIGH	LOW
2008	$5,761	$4,321
2009	$5,894	$4,420

2872KOT8-SR1205

YEARS MFRD . . . 2008-2009
SERIES . . . BOSS SERIES
ENGINE . . . KOHLER EFI
CYLINDERS . . . 2
ENGINE HP . . . 28
COOLING . . . AIR
FUEL . . . G
SPEEDS . . . VARIABLE
TRANSMISSION . . . HYDRO
STEERING . . . ZERO
BLADE CLUTCH . . . ELECTRIC
STANDARD DECK . . . 72"
WEIGHT . . . 1,220 LBS.
MSRP . . . $10,695

RETAIL PRICING

YEAR	HIGH	LOW
2008	$6,228	$4,671
2009	$6,353	$4,765

3052BSJ505

YEARS MFRD . . . 2014-2014
SERIES . . . CHALLENGER SERIES
ENGINE . . . B&S
CYLINDERS . . . 3
ENGINE HP . . . 30
COOLING . . . AIR
FUEL . . . G
SPEEDS . . . VARIABLE
TRANSMISSION . . . HYDRO
STEERING . . . ZERO

COUNTRY CLIPPER

BLADE CLUTCH ....ELECTRIC
STANDARD DECK .... 52"
WEIGHT .... 895 LBS.

3052BST505

YEARS MFRD 2014-2014
SERIES...... CHALLENGER SERIES
ENGINE ....B&S
CYLINDERS..................2
ENGINE HP.................30
COOLING...................AIR
FUEL ....G
SPEEDS ....VARIABLE
TRANSMISSION ....HYDRO
STEERING................ZERO
BLADE CLUTCH ....ELECTRIC
STANDARD DECK .... 52"
WEIGHT .... 895 LBS.

3060BSJ505

YEARS MFRD 2014-2014
SERIES...... CHALLENGER SERIES
ENGINE ....B&S
CYLINDERS..................2
ENGINE HP.................30
COOLING...................AIR
FUEL ....G
SPEEDS ....VARIABLE
TRANSMISSION ....HYDRO
STEERING................ZERO
BLADE CLUTCH ....ELECTRIC
STANDARD DECK .... 60"
WEIGHT .... 906 LBS.

3060BST505

YEARS MFRD 2014-2014
SERIES...... CHALLENGER SERIES
ENGINE ....B&S
CYLINDERS..................2
ENGINE HP.................30
COOLING...................AIR
FUEL ....G
SPEEDS ....VARIABLE
TRANSMISSION ....HYDRO
STEERING................ZERO
BLADE CLUTCH ....ELECTRIC
STANDARD DECK .... 60"
WEIGHT .... 906 LBS.

3060KOJ-SR1200

YEARS MFRD 2006-2006
SERIES............ BOSS SERIES
ENGINE ...... KOHLER COMMAND
CYLINDERS..................2
CID 44
ENGINE HP.................30
COOLING...................AIR
FUEL ....G
SPEEDS ....VARIABLE
TRANSMISSION ....HYDRO
STEERING................ZERO
STANDARD DECK .... 60"
WEIGHT .... 1,035 LBS.
MSRP.................. $8,999

RETAIL PRICING

YEAR	HIGH	LOW
2006	$4,801	$3,601

3060KOJ8-SR1005

YEARS MFRD 2008-2009
SERIES......... CHARGER SERIES
ENGINE .. KOHLER COMMAND PRO
CYLINDERS..................2
ENGINE HP.................30
COOLING...................AIR
FUEL ....G
SPEEDS ....VARIABLE
TRANSMISSION ....HYDRO
STEERING................ZERO
STANDARD DECK .... 60"
WEIGHT .... 1,100 LBS.
MSRP.................. $8,550

RETAIL PRICING

YEAR	HIGH	LOW
2008	$4,979	$3,735
2009	$5,180	$3,885

3060KOT-SR1200

YEARS MFRD 2006-2006
SERIES............ BOSS SERIES
ENGINE ...... KOHLER COMMAND
CYLINDERS..................2
CID 44
ENGINE HP.................30
COOLING...................AIR
FUEL ....G
SPEEDS ....VARIABLE
TRANSMISSION ....HYDRO
STEERING................ZERO
STANDARD DECK .... 60"
WEIGHT .... 1,035 LBS.
MSRP.................. $8,999

RETAIL PRICING

YEAR	HIGH	LOW
2006	$4,801	$3,601

3060KOT8-SR1005

YEARS MFRD 2008-2009
SERIES......... CHARGER SERIES
ENGINE .. KOHLER COMMAND PRO
CYLINDERS..................2
ENGINE HP.................30
COOLING...................AIR
FUEL ....G
SPEEDS ....VARIABLE
TRANSMISSION ....HYDRO
STEERING................ZERO
BLADE CLUTCH ....ELECTRIC
STANDARD DECK .... 60"
WEIGHT .... 1,100 LBS.
MSRP.................. $8,550

RETAIL PRICING

YEAR	HIGH	LOW
2008	$4,979	$3,735
2009	$5,180	$3,885

3072KOJ-SR1200

YEARS MFRD 2006-2006
SERIES............ BOSS SERIES
ENGINE ....KOHLER
ENGINE HP.................30
FUEL ....G
SPEEDS ....VARIABLE
TRANSMISSION ....HYDRO
STEERING................ZERO
STANDARD DECK .... 60"
MSRP.................. $9,550

RETAIL PRICING

YEAR	HIGH	LOW
2006	$5,137	$3,853

3072KOT-SR1200

YEARS MFRD 2006-2006
SERIES............ BOSS SERIES
ENGINE ....KOHLER
ENGINE HP.................30
FUEL ....G
SPEEDS ....VARIABLE
TRANSMISSION ....HYDRO
STEERING................ZERO
STANDARD DECK .... 72"
MSRP.................. $9,550

RETAIL PRICING

YEAR	HIGH	LOW
2006	$5,137	$3,853

3160KAJ8-SR1205

YEARS MFRD 2008-2009
SERIES............ BOSS SERIES
ENGINE .... KAWASAKI
CYLINDERS..................2
ENGINE HP.................31
COOLING...................AIR
FUEL ....G
SPEEDS ....VARIABLE
TRANSMISSION ....HYDRO
STEERING................ZERO
BLADE CLUTCH ....ELECTRIC
STANDARD DECK .... 60"
WEIGHT .... 1,120 LBS.
MSRP.................. $9,350

RETAIL PRICING

YEAR	HIGH	LOW
2008	$5,445	$4,084
2009	$5,641	$4,231

3160KAT8-SR1205

YEARS MFRD 2008-2009
SERIES............ BOSS SERIES
ENGINE .... KAWASAKI
CYLINDERS..................2
ENGINE HP.................31
COOLING...................AIR
FUEL ....G
SPEEDS ....VARIABLE
TRANSMISSION ....HYDRO
STEERING................ZERO
BLADE CLUTCH ....ELECTRIC
STANDARD DECK .... 60"
WEIGHT .... 1,120 LBS.
MSRP.................. $9,350

RETAIL PRICING

YEAR	HIGH	LOW
2008	$5,445	$4,084
2009	$5,641	$4,231

3172KAJ8-SR1205

YEARS MFRD 2008-2009
SERIES............ BOSS SERIES
ENGINE .... KAWASAKI
CYLINDERS..................2
ENGINE HP.................31
COOLING...................AIR
FUEL ....G
SPEEDS ....VARIABLE
TRANSMISSION ....HYDRO
STEERING................ZERO
BLADE CLUTCH ....ELECTRIC
STANDARD DECK .... 72"
WEIGHT .... 1,220 LBS.
MSRP.................. $9,895

RETAIL PRICING

YEAR	HIGH	LOW
2008	$5,761	$4,321
2009	$5,955	$4,467

3172KAT8-SR1205

YEARS MFRD 2008-2009
SERIES............ BOSS SERIES
ENGINE .... KAWASAKI
CYLINDERS..................2
ENGINE HP.................31
COOLING...................AIR
FUEL ....G
SPEEDS ....VARIABLE
TRANSMISSION ....HYDRO
STEERING................ZERO
BLADE CLUTCH ....ELECTRIC
STANDARD DECK .... 72"
WEIGHT .... 1,220 LBS.
MSRP.................. $9,895

RETAIL PRICING

YEAR	HIGH	LOW
2008	$5,761	$4,321
2009	$5,955	$4,467

3560KAJ-1525
YEARS MFRD........2018-2020
SERIES..........BOSS XL SERIES
ENGINE......KAWASAKI FX1000V
CYLINDERS..................2
ENGINE HP..................35
FUEL.......................G
SPEEDS.............VARIABLE
TRANSMISSION..........HYDRO
STEERING................ZERO
BLADE CLUTCH........ELECTRIC
STANDARD DECK..............60"
WEIGHT.............1,311 LBS.

OPTIONS

TWIN LEVER

3560KAJ-SR1220
YEARS MFRD........2011-2013
SERIES............BOSS SERIES
ENGINE.............KAWASAKI
CYLINDERS..................2
ENGINE HP..................35
COOLING..................AIR
FUEL.......................G
SPEEDS.............VARIABLE
TRANSMISSION..........HYDRO
STEERING................ZERO
BLADE CLUTCH........ELECTRIC
WEIGHT.............1,217 LBS.

3560KAJ-SR1220L
YEARS MFRD........2011-2012
SERIES...BOSS POWERLIFT SERIES
ENGINE.............KAWASAKI
CYLINDERS..................2
ENGINE HP..................35
COOLING..................AIR
FUEL.......................G
SPEEDS.............VARIABLE
TRANSMISSION..........HYDRO
STEERING................ZERO
BLADE CLUTCH........ELECTRIC
WEIGHT.............1,270 LBS.

3560KAJ1505
YEARS MFRD........2014-2014
SERIES........DEFENDER SERIES
ENGINE.......KAWASAKI FX1000
CYLINDERS..................2
ENGINE HP..................35
COOLING..................AIR
FUEL.......................G
SPEEDS.............VARIABLE
TRANSMISSION..........HYDRO
STEERING................ZERO
BLADE CLUTCH........ELECTRIC
STANDARD DECK..............60"
WEIGHT.............1,310 LBS.

3560KAT-SR1220
YEARS MFRD........2011-2013
SERIES............BOSS SERIES
ENGINE.............KAWASAKI
CYLINDERS..................2
ENGINE HP..................35
COOLING..................AIR
FUEL.......................G
SPEEDS.............VARIABLE
TRANSMISSION..........HYDRO
STEERING................ZERO
BLADE CLUTCH........ELECTRIC
WEIGHT.............1,217 LBS.

3560KAT1505
YEARS MFRD........2014-2014
SERIES........DEFENDER SERIES
ENGINE.......KAWASAKI FX1000
CYLINDERS..................2
ENGINE HP..................35
COOLING..................AIR
FUEL.......................G
SPEEDS.............VARIABLE
TRANSMISSION..........HYDRO
STEERING................ZERO
BLADE CLUTCH........ELECTRIC
STANDARD DECK..............60"
WEIGHT.............1,311 LBS.

3572KAJ-1525
YEARS MFRD........2018-2020
SERIES..........BOSS XL SERIES
ENGINE......KAWASAKI FX1000V
CYLINDERS..................2
ENGINE HP..................35
FUEL.......................G
SPEEDS.............VARIABLE
TRANSMISSION..........HYDRO
STEERING................ZERO
BLADE CLUTCH........ELECTRIC
STANDARD DECK..............72"
WEIGHT.............1,372 LBS.

OPTIONS

TWIN LEVER

3572KAJ-SR1220
YEARS MFRD........2011-2012
SERIES............BOSS SERIES
ENGINE.............KAWASAKI
CYLINDERS..................2
ENGINE HP..................35
COOLING..................AIR
FUEL.......................G
SPEEDS.............VARIABLE
TRANSMISSION..........HYDRO
STEERING................ZERO
BLADE CLUTCH........ELECTRIC
WEIGHT.............1,260 LBS.

3572KAJ-SR1220L
YEARS MFRD........2011-2012
SERIES...BOSS POWERLIFT SERIES
ENGINE.............KAWASAKI
CYLINDERS..................2
ENGINE HP..................35
COOLING..................AIR
FUEL.......................G
SPEEDS.............VARIABLE
TRANSMISSION..........HYDRO
STEERING................ZERO
BLADE CLUTCH........ELECTRIC
WEIGHT.............1,300 LBS.

3572KAJ1505
YEARS MFRD........2014-2014
SERIES........DEFENDER SERIES
ENGINE........KAWASAKIFX1000
CYLINDERS..................2
ENGINE HP..................35
COOLING..................AIR
FUEL.......................G
SPEEDS.............VARIABLE
TRANSMISSION..........HYDRO
STEERING................ZERO
BLADE CLUTCH........ELECTRIC
STANDARD DECK..............72"
WEIGHT.............1,371 LBS.

3572KAT-SR1220
YEARS MFRD........2011-2012
SERIES............BOSS SERIES
ENGINE.............KAWASAKI
CYLINDERS..................2
ENGINE HP..................35
COOLING..................AIR
FUEL.......................G
SPEEDS.............VARIABLE
TRANSMISSION..........HYDRO
STEERING................ZERO
BLADE CLUTCH........ELECTRIC
WEIGHT.............1,260 LBS.

3572KAT-SR1220L
YEARS MFRD........2011-2012
SERIES...BOSS POWERLIFT SERIES
ENGINE.............KAWASAKI
CYLINDERS..................2
ENGINE HP..................35
COOLING..................AIR
FUEL.......................G
SPEEDS.............VARIABLE
TRANSMISSION..........HYDRO
STEERING................ZERO
BLADE CLUTCH........ELECTRIC
WEIGHT.............1,300 LBS.

3572KAT1505
YEARS MFRD........2014-2014
SERIES........DEFENDER SERIES
ENGINE.......KAWASAKI FX1000
CYLINDERS..................2
ENGINE HP..................35
COOLING..................AIR
FUEL.......................G
SPEEDS.............VARIABLE
TRANSMISSION..........HYDRO
STEERING................ZERO
BLADE CLUTCH........ELECTRIC
STANDARD DECK..............72"
WEIGHT.............1,372 LBS.

3760KADJ-SR1210
YEARS MFRD........2010-2011
SERIES............BOSS SERIES
ENGINE.............KAWASAKI
CYLINDERS..................2
ENGINE HP..................37
COOLING...............LIQUID
FUEL.......................G
SPEEDS.............VARIABLE
TRANSMISSION..........HYDRO
STEERING................ZERO
BLADE CLUTCH........ELECTRIC
WEIGHT.............1,120 LBS.

3760KADT-SR1220
YEARS MFRD........2011-2012
SERIES............BOSS SERIES
ENGINE.............KAWASAKI
CYLINDERS..................2
ENGINE HP..................37
COOLING..................AIR
FUEL.......................G
SPEEDS.............VARIABLE
TRANSMISSION..........HYDRO
STEERING................ZERO
BLADE CLUTCH........ELECTRIC
WEIGHT.............1,230 LBS.

3760KAJ-SR1210
YEARS MFRD........2010-2011
SERIES............BOSS SERIES
CYLINDERS..................2
ENGINE HP..................37
COOLING...............LIQUID
FUEL.......................G
SPEEDS.............VARIABLE
TRANSMISSION..........HYDRO
STEERING................ZERO
BLADE CLUTCH........ELECTRIC
WEIGHT.............1,120 LBS.

COUNTRY CLIPPER

3760KAT-SR1210
YEARS MFRD 2010-2011
SERIES . . . . BOSS SERIES
ENGINE . . . . KAWASAKI
CYLINDERS 2
ENGINE HP 37
COOLING . . . . LIQUID
FUEL . . . . G
SPEEDS . . . . VARIABLE
TRANSMISSION . . . . HYDRO
STEERING . . . . ZERO
BLADE CLUTCH . . . . ELECTRIC
WEIGHT . . . . 1,120 LBS.

3760KAT8-SR1205
YEARS MFRD 2008-2009
SERIES . . . . BOSS SERIES
ENGINE . . . . KAWASAKI
CYLINDERS 2
ENGINE HP 37
COOLING . . . . AIR
FUEL . . . . G
SPEEDS . . . . VARIABLE
TRANSMISSION . . . . HYDRO
STEERING . . . . ZERO
BLADE CLUTCH . . . . ELECTRIC
STANDARD DECK . . . . 60"
WEIGHT . . . . 1,120 LBS.
MSRP $9,595

RETAIL PRICING

YEAR	HIGH	LOW
2008	$5,585	$4,189
2009	$5,782	$4,337

3760KSJ8-SR1205
YEARS MFRD 2008-2009
SERIES . . . . BOSS SERIES
ENGINE . . . . KAWASAKI
CYLINDERS 2
ENGINE HP 37
COOLING . . . . AIR
FUEL . . . . G
SPEEDS . . . . VARIABLE
TRANSMISSION . . . . HYDRO
STEERING . . . . ZERO
BLADE CLUTCH . . . . ELECTRIC
STANDARD DECK . . . . 60"
WEIGHT . . . . 1,120 LBS.
MSRP $9,595

RETAIL PRICING

YEAR	HIGH	LOW
2008	$5,585	$4,189
2009	$5,782	$4,337

3772KADJ-SR1210
YEARS MFRD 2010-2011
SERIES . . . . BOSS SERIES
ENGINE . . . . KAWASAKI
CYLINDERS 2
ENGINE HP 37
COOLING . . . . LIQUID
FUEL . . . . G
SPEEDS . . . . VARIABLE
TRANSMISSION . . . . HYDRO
STEERING . . . . ZERO
BLADE CLUTCH . . . . ELECTRIC
WEIGHT . . . . 1,220 LBS.

3772KADJ-SR1220
YEARS MFRD 2011-2012
SERIES . . . . BOSS SERIES
ENGINE . . . . KAWASAKI
CYLINDERS 2
ENGINE HP 37
COOLING . . . . AIR
FUEL . . . . G
SPEEDS . . . . VARIABLE
TRANSMISSION . . . . HYDRO
STEERING . . . . ZERO
BLADE CLUTCH . . . . ELECTRIC
WEIGHT . . . . 1,260 LBS.

3772KADT-SR1210
YEARS MFRD 2011-2011
SERIES . . . . BOSS SERIES
ENGINE . . . . KAWASAKI
CYLINDERS 2
ENGINE HP 37
COOLING . . . . AIR
FUEL . . . . G
SPEEDS . . . . VARIABLE
TRANSMISSION . . . . HYDRO
STEERING . . . . ZERO
BLADE CLUTCH . . . . ELECTRIC
WEIGHT . . . . 1,220 LBS.

3772KADT-SR1210L
YEARS MFRD 2010-2011
SERIES . . . . BOSS SERIES
ENGINE . . . . KAWASAKI
CYLINDERS 2
ENGINE HP 37
COOLING . . . . LIQUID
FUEL . . . . G
SPEEDS . . . . VARIABLE
TRANSMISSION . . . . HYDRO
STEERING . . . . ZERO
BLADE CLUTCH . . . . ELECTRIC
WEIGHT . . . . 1,220 LBS.

3772KAJ-SR1210
YEARS MFRD 2010-2011
SERIES . . . . BOSS SERIES
ENGINE . . . . KAWASAKI
CYLINDERS 2
ENGINE HP 37
COOLING . . . . LIQUID
FUEL . . . . G
SPEEDS . . . . VARIABLE
TRANSMISSION . . . . HYDRO
STEERING . . . . ZERO
BLADE CLUTCH . . . . ELECTRIC
WEIGHT . . . . 1,220 LBS.

3772KAJ-SR1210L
YEARS MFRD 2010-2011
SERIES . . . . BOSS SERIES
ENGINE . . . . KAWASAKI
CYLINDERS 2
ENGINE HP 37
COOLING . . . . LIQUID
FUEL . . . . G
SPEEDS . . . . VARIABLE
TRANSMISSION . . . . HYDRO
STEERING . . . . ZERO
BLADE CLUTCH . . . . ELECTRIC
WEIGHT . . . . 1,220 LBS.

3772KAJ8-SR1205
YEARS MFRD 2008-2009
SERIES . . . . BOSS SERIES
ENGINE . . . . KAWASAKI
CYLINDERS 2
ENGINE HP 37
COOLING . . . . AIR
FUEL . . . . G
SPEEDS . . . . VARIABLE
TRANSMISSION . . . . HYDRO
STEERING . . . . ZERO
BLADE CLUTCH . . . . ELECTRIC
STANDARD DECK . . . . 72"
WEIGHT . . . . 1,220 LBS.
MSRP $10,095

RETAIL PRICING

YEAR	HIGH	LOW
2008	$5,878	$4,409
2009	$6,070	$4,553

3772KAT8-SR1205
YEARS MFRD 2008-2009
SERIES . . . . BOSS SERIES
ENGINE . . . . KAWASAKI
CYLINDERS 2
ENGINE HP 37
COOLING . . . . AIR
FUEL . . . . G
SPEEDS . . . . VARIABLE
TRANSMISSION . . . . HYDRO
STEERING . . . . ZERO
BLADE CLUTCH . . . . ELECTRIC
STANDARD DECK . . . . 72"
WEIGHT . . . . 1,220 LBS.
MSRP $10,095

RETAIL PRICING

YEAR	HIGH	LOW
2008	$5,878	$4,409
2009	$6,070	$4,553

15538BSJ-SR100
YEARS MFRD 2006-2007
SERIES . . . . JAZEE ONE SERIES
ENGINE . . . . B&S ELS
CYLINDERS 1
ENGINE HP 15.5
COOLING . . . . AIR
FUEL . . . . G
SPEEDS . . . . VARIABLE
TRANSMISSION . . . . HYDRO
STEERING . . . . ZERO
WEIGHT . . . . 600 LBS.

15538KOJ-SR100
YEARS MFRD 2006-2006
SERIES . . . . JAZEE SERIES
ENGINE . . . . B&S
ENGINE HP 15.5
COOLING . . . . AIR
FUEL . . . . G
SPEEDS . . . . VARIABLE
TRANSMISSION . . . . HYDRO
STEERING . . . . ZERO
STANDARD DECK . . . . 38"
MSRP $3,350

RETAIL PRICING

YEAR	HIGH	LOW
2006	$1,341	$1,005

18418KAJ140
YEARS MFRD 2015-2015
SERIES . . . . WRANGLER SERIES
ENGINE . . . . KAWASAKI
ENGINE HP 18
FUEL . . . . G
SPEEDS . . . . VARIABLE
TRANSMISSION . . . . HYDRO
STEERING . . . . ZERO
STANDARD DECK . . . . 41"
MSRP $4,075

RETAIL PRICING

YEAR	HIGH	LOW
2015	$2,519	$1,889

18538BSJ-SR105
YEARS MFRD 2008-2009
SERIES . . . . JAZEE ONE SERIES
ENGINE . . . . B&S ELS
CYLINDERS 1
ENGINE HP 18.5
COOLING . . . . AIR
FUEL . . . . G
SPEEDS . . . . VARIABLE
TRANSMISSION . . . . HYDRO
STEERING . . . . ZERO
BLADE CLUTCH . . . . ELECTRIC
WEIGHT . . . . 600 LBS.

18542BSJ-SR100

YEARS MFRD........2006-2007
SERIES........JAZEE ONE SERIES
ENGINE...............B&S ELS
CYLINDERS..................1
ENGINE HP...............18.5
COOLING..................AIR
FUEL.......................G
SPEEDS.............VARIABLE
TRANSMISSION..........HYDRO
STEERING................ZERO
STANDARD DECK...........42"
WEIGHT.............613 LBS.
MSRP.................$3,750

RETAIL PRICING

YEAR	HIGH	LOW
2006	$1,433	$1,075
2007	$1,508	$1,131

18542BSJ-SR105

YEARS MFRD........2008-2009
SERIES........JAZEE ONE SERIES
ENGINE...............B&S ELS
CYLINDERS..................1
ENGINE HP...............18.5
COOLING..................AIR
FUEL.......................G
SPEEDS.............VARIABLE
TRANSMISSION..........HYDRO
STEERING................ZERO
BLADE CLUTCH........ELECTRIC
WEIGHT.............600 LBS.

18542BSJ-SR200

YEARS MFRD........2006-2007
SERIES............JAZEE SERIES
ENGINE...............B&S ELS
CYLINDERS..................1
ENGINE HP...............18.5
COOLING..................AIR
FUEL.......................G
SPEEDS.............VARIABLE
TRANSMISSION..........HYDRO
STEERING................ZERO
STANDARD DECK...........42"
MSRP.................$4,100

RETAIL PRICING

YEAR	HIGH	LOW
2006	$2,418	$1,813
2007	$2,484	$1,863

18542BSJ-SR205

YEARS MFRD........2008-2008
SERIES............JAZEE SERIES
ENGINE...................B&S
CYLINDERS..................1
ENGINE HP...............18.5
COOLING..................AIR
FUEL.......................G
SPEEDS.............VARIABLE
TRANSMISSION..........HYDRO
STEERING................ZERO
BLADE CLUTCH........ELECTRIC
WEIGHT.............650 LBS.

18548BSJ-SR200

YEARS MFRD........2006-2007
SERIES............JAZEE SERIES
ENGINE...............B&S ELS
CYLINDERS..................1
ENGINE HP...............18.5
COOLING..................AIR
FUEL.......................G
SPEEDS.............VARIABLE
TRANSMISSION..........HYDRO
STEERING................ZERO
STANDARD DECK...........48"
MSRP.................$4,220

RETAIL PRICING

YEAR	HIGH	LOW
2006	$1,800	$1,350
2007	$1,860	$1,395

18548BSJ-SR205

YEARS MFRD........2008-2009
SERIES............JAZEE SERIES
ENGINE...............B&S ELS
CYLINDERS..................1
ENGINE HP...............18.5
COOLING..................AIR
FUEL.......................G
SPEEDS.............VARIABLE
TRANSMISSION..........HYDRO
STEERING................ZERO
BLADE CLUTCH........ELECTRIC
WEIGHT.............675 LBS.

21548KAJ135

YEARS MFRD........2014-2014
SERIES........WRANGLER SERIES
ENGINE........KAWASAKI FR651
CYLINDERS..................2
ENGINE HP...............21.5
COOLING..................AIR
FUEL.......................G
SPEEDS.............VARIABLE
TRANSMISSION..........HYDRO
STEERING................ZERO
BLADE CLUTCH........ELECTRIC
STANDARD DECK...........48"
WEIGHT.............730 LBS.

21548KAJ140

YEARS MFRD........2015-2015
SERIES........WRANGLER SERIES
ENGINE..............KAWASAKI
ENGINE HP...............21.5
FUEL.......................G
SPEEDS.............VARIABLE
TRANSMISSION..........HYDRO
STEERING................ZERO
STANDARD DECK...........48"
MSRP.................$4,795

RETAIL PRICING

YEAR	HIGH	LOW
2015	$3,023	$2,267

21548KAJ405

YEARS MFRD........2014-2014
SERIES............EDGE SERIES
ENGINE........KAWASAKI FR651
CYLINDERS..................2
ENGINE HP...............21.5
COOLING..................AIR
FUEL.......................G
SPEEDS.............VARIABLE
TRANSMISSION..........HYDRO
STEERING................ZERO
BLADE CLUTCH........ELECTRIC
STANDARD DECK...........48"
WEIGHT.............772 LBS.

21548KAJ410

YEARS MFRD........2015-2015
SERIES............EDGE SERIES
ENGINE..............KAWASAKI
ENGINE HP...............21.5
COOLING..................AIR
FUEL.......................G
SPEEDS.............VARIABLE
TRANSMISSION..........HYDRO
STEERING................ZERO
STANDARD DECK...........48"
MSRP.................$5,545

OPTIONS

52" DECK
KAWASAKI 24HP

RETAIL PRICING

YEAR	HIGH	LOW
2015	$3,643	$2,732

21548KAT135

YEARS MFRD........2014-2014
SERIES........WRANGLER SERIES
ENGINE........KAWASAKI FR651
CYLINDERS..................2
ENGINE HP...............21.5
COOLING..................AIR
FUEL.......................G
SPEEDS.............VARIABLE
TRANSMISSION..........HYDRO
STEERING................ZERO
BLADE CLUTCH........ELECTRIC
STANDARD DECK...........48"
WEIGHT.............725 LBS.

21548KAT405

YEARS MFRD........2014-2014
SERIES............EDGE SERIES
ENGINE........KAWASAKI FR651
CYLINDERS..................2
ENGINE HP...............21.5
COOLING..................AIR
FUEL.......................G
SPEEDS.............VARIABLE
TRANSMISSION..........HYDRO
STEERING................ZERO
BLADE CLUTCH........ELECTRIC
STANDARD DECK...........48"
WEIGHT.............772 LBS.

21552KAJ135

YEARS MFRD........2014-2014
SERIES........WRANGLER SERIES
ENGINE........KAWASAKI FR651
CYLINDERS..................2
ENGINE HP...............21.5
COOLING..................AIR
FUEL.......................G
SPEEDS.............VARIABLE
TRANSMISSION..........HYDRO
STEERING................ZERO
BLADE CLUTCH........ELECTRIC
STANDARD DECK...........52"
WEIGHT.............745 LBS.

21552KAJ140

YEARS MFRD........2015-2015
SERIES........WRANGLER SERIES
ENGINE..............KAWASAKI
ENGINE HP...............21.5
FUEL.......................G
SPEEDS.............VARIABLE
TRANSMISSION..........HYDRO
STEERING................ZERO
STANDARD DECK...........52"
MSRP.................$5,195

RETAIL PRICING

YEAR	HIGH	LOW
2015	$3,392	$2,544

21552KAT135

YEARS MFRD........2014-2014
SERIES........WRANGLER SERIES
ENGINE........KAWASAKI FR651
CYLINDERS..................2
ENGINE HP...............21.5
COOLING..................AIR
FUEL.......................G
SPEEDS.............VARIABLE
TRANSMISSION..........HYDRO
STEERING................ZERO
BLADE CLUTCH........ELECTRIC
STANDARD DECK...........52"
WEIGHT.............740 LBS.

25552KAJ-1055

YEARS MFRD........2018-2020
SERIES.........CHARGER SERIES
ENGINE.......KAWASAKI FX801V
CYLINDERS..................2
ENGINE HP...............25.5
FUEL.......................G
SPEEDS.............VARIABLE

COUNTRY CLIPPER

TRANSMISSION ....HYDRO
STEERING................ZERO
BLADE CLUTCH ....ELECTRIC
STANDARD DECK .... 52"
WEIGHT ....1,081 LBS.

OPTIONS

TWIN LEVER

25552KAJ-SR1025

YEARS MFRD 2011-2013
SERIES.........CHARGER SERIES
ENGINE ....KAWASAKI
CYLINDERS..................2
ENGINE HP............... 25.5
COOLING ....AIR
FUEL ....G
SPEEDS ....VARIABLE
TRANSMISSION ....HYDRO
STEERING................ZERO
BLADE CLUTCH ....ELECTRIC
WEIGHT ....1,015 LBS.

25552KAJ-1035

YEARS MFRD 2014-2014
SERIES.........CHARGER SERIES
ENGINE ....KAWASAKI FX801
CYLINDERS..................2
ENGINE HP............... 25.5
COOLING ....AIR
FUEL ....G
SPEEDS ....VARIABLE
TRANSMISSION ....HYDRO
STEERING................ZERO
BLADE CLUTCH ....ELECTRIC
STANDARD DECK .... 52"
WEIGHT ....1,081 LBS.

25552KAT-SR1025

YEARS MFRD 2011-2013
SERIES.........CHARGER SERIES
ENGINE ....KAWASAKI
CYLINDERS..................2
ENGINE HP............... 25.5
COOLING ....AIR
FUEL ....G
SPEEDS ....VARIABLE
TRANSMISSION ....HYDRO
STEERING................ZERO
BLADE CLUTCH ....ELECTRIC
WEIGHT ....1,015 LBS.

25552KAT 1035

YEARS MFRD 2014-2014
SERIES.........CHARGER SERIES
ENGINE ....KAWASAKI FX801
CYLINDERS..................2
ENGINE HP............... 25.5

COOLING ....AIR
FUEL ....G
SPEEDS ....VARIABLE
TRANSMISSION ....HYDRO
STEERING................ZERO
BLADE CLUTCH ....ELECTRIC
STANDARD DECK .... 52"
WEIGHT ....1,081 LBS.

25552TKAJ-SR1025

YEARS MFRD 2011-2013
SERIES.........CHARGER SERIES
ENGINE ....KAWASAKI
CYLINDERS..................2
ENGINE HP............... 25.5
COOLING ....AIR
FUEL ....G
SPEEDS ....VARIABLE
TRANSMISSION ....HYDRO
STEERING................ZERO
BLADE CLUTCH ....ELECTRIC
WEIGHT ....1,040 LBS.

25560KAJ-1055

YEARS MFRD 2018-2020
SERIES.........CHARGER SERIES
ENGINE ....KAWASAKI FX801V
CYLINDERS..................2
ENGINE HP............... 25.5
FUEL ....G
SPEEDS ....VARIABLE
TRANSMISSION ....HYDRO
STEERING................ZERO
BLADE CLUTCH ....ELECTRIC
STANDARD DECK .... 60"
WEIGHT ....1,096 LBS.

OPTIONS

TWIN LEVER

25560KAJ-SR1025

YEARS MFRD 2011-2013
SERIES.........CHARGER SERIES
ENGINE ....KAWASAKI
CYLINDERS..................2
ENGINE HP............... 25.5
COOLING ....AIR
FUEL ....G
SPEEDS ....VARIABLE
TRANSMISSION ....HYDRO
STEERING................ZERO
BLADE CLUTCH ....ELECTRIC
WEIGHT ....1,030 LBS.

25560KAJ-SR1220

YEARS MFRD 2011-2013
SERIES............BOSS SERIES
ENGINE ....KAWASAKI
CYLINDERS..................2

ENGINE HP............... 25.5
COOLING ....AIR
FUEL ....G
SPEEDS ....VARIABLE
TRANSMISSION ....HYDRO
STEERING................ZERO
BLADE CLUTCH ....ELECTRIC
WEIGHT ....1,200 LBS.

25560KAJ-SR1220L

YEARS MFRD 2011-2012
SERIES.. BOSS POWER LIFT SERIES
ENGINE ....KAWASAKI
CYLINDERS..................2
ENGINE HP............... 25.5
COOLING ....AIR
FUEL ....G
SPEEDS ....VARIABLE
TRANSMISSION ....HYDRO
STEERING................ZERO
BLADE CLUTCH ....ELECTRIC
WEIGHT ....1,240 LBS.

25560KAJ 1035

YEARS MFRD 2014-2014
SERIES.........CHARGER SERIES
ENGINE ....KAWASAKI FX801
CYLINDERS..................2
ENGINE HP............... 25.5
COOLING ....AIR
FUEL ....G
SPEEDS ....VARIABLE
TRANSMISSION ....HYDRO
STEERING................ZERO
BLADE CLUTCH ....ELECTRIC
STANDARD DECK .... 60"
WEIGHT ....1,096 LBS.

25560KAJ 1505

YEARS MFRD 2014-2014
SERIES........DEFENDER SERIES
ENGINE ....KAWASAKI FX801
CYLINDERS..................2
ENGINE HP............... 25.5
COOLING ....AIR
FUEL ....G
SPEEDS ....VARIABLE
TRANSMISSION ....HYDRO
STEERING................ZERO
BLADE CLUTCH ....ELECTRIC
STANDARD DECK .... 60"
WEIGHT ....1,268 LBS.

25560KAT-SR1025

YEARS MFRD 2011-2013
SERIES.........CHARGER SERIES
ENGINE ....KAWASAKI

CYLINDERS..................2
ENGINE HP............... 25.5
COOLING ....AIR
FUEL ....G
SPEEDS ....VARIABLE
TRANSMISSION ....HYDRO
STEERING................ZERO
BLADE CLUTCH ....ELECTRIC
WEIGHT ....1,030 LBS.

25560KAT-SR1220

YEARS MFRD 2011-2013
SERIES............BOSS SERIES
ENGINE ....KAWASAKI
CYLINDERS..................2
ENGINE HP............... 25.5
COOLING ....AIR
FUEL ....G
SPEEDS ....VARIABLE
TRANSMISSION ....HYDRO
STEERING................ZERO
BLADE CLUTCH ....ELECTRIC
WEIGHT ....1,200 LBS.

25560KAT 1035

YEARS MFRD 2014-2014
SERIES.........CHARGER SERIES
ENGINE ....KAWASAKI FX801
CYLINDERS..................2
ENGINE HP............... 25.5
COOLING ....AIR
FUEL ....G
SPEEDS ....VARIABLE
TRANSMISSION ....HYDRO
STEERING................ZERO
BLADE CLUTCH ....ELECTRIC
STANDARD DECK .... 60"
WEIGHT ....1,096 LBS.

25560KAT 1505

YEARS MFRD 2014-2014
SERIES........DEFENDER SERIES
ENGINE ....KAWASAKI FX801
CYLINDERS..................2
ENGINE HP............... 25.5
COOLING ....AIR
FUEL ....G
SPEEDS ....VARIABLE
TRANSMISSION ....HYDRO
STEERING................ZERO
BLADE CLUTCH ....ELECTRIC
STANDARD DECK .... 60"
WEIGHT ....1,269 LBS.

27484KOJ-SR365

YEARS MFRD 2010-2010
SERIES........JAZEE PRO SERIES
ENGINE ... KOHLER COURAGE PRO

CYLINDERS . . . 2
ENGINE HP . . . 27
COOLING . . . AIR
FUEL . . . G
SPEEDS . . . VARIABLE
TRANSMISSION . . . HYDRO
STEERING . . . ZERO
BLADE CLUTCH . . . ELECTRIC
WEIGHT . . . 775 LBS.

CRAFTSMAN

CTX9000

YEARS MFRD . . . 2013-2014
ENGINE . . . B&S
ENGINE HP . . . 22
COOLING . . . AIR
FUEL . . . G
SPEEDS . . . VARIABLE
TRANSMISSION . . . HYDRO
STEERING . . . STANDARD
STANDARD DECK . . . 46"
MSRP . . . $4,849

RETAIL PRICING

YEAR	HIGH	LOW
2013	$1,475	$1,107
2014	$2,214	$1,660

CTX9500

YEARS MFRD . . . 2012-2012
ENGINE . . . B&S
CYLINDERS . . . 2
ENGINE HP . . . 26
COOLING . . . AIR
FUEL . . . G
SPEEDS . . . VARIABLE
TRANSMISSION . . . HYDRO
STEERING . . . STANDARD
BLADE CLUTCH . . . ELECTRIC
STANDARD DECK . . . 52"
MSRP . . . $5,499

RETAIL PRICING

YEAR	HIGH	LOW
2012	$2,945	$2,209

GT6000

YEARS MFRD . . . 2012-2012
ENGINE . . . KOHLER COURAGE
CYLINDERS . . . 2
ENGINE HP . . . 26
COOLING . . . AIR
FUEL . . . G
SPEEDS . . . VARIABLE
TRANSMISSION . . . HYDRO
STEERING . . . STANDARD
STANDARD DECK . . . 54"
WEIGHT . . . 596 LBS.
MSRP . . . $2,999

RETAIL PRICING

YEAR	HIGH	LOW
2012	$1,606	$1,204

LT2000

YEARS MFRD . . . 2012-2012
ENGINE . . . B&S
CYLINDERS . . . 1
ENGINE HP . . . 19.5
COOLING . . . AIR
FUEL . . . G
SPEEDS . . . VARIABLE
TRANSMISSION . . . HYDRO
STEERING . . . STANDARD
STANDARD DECK . . . 42"
MSRP . . . $1,199

RETAIL PRICING

YEAR	HIGH	LOW
2012	$643	$482

R110 1130035

YEARS MFRD . . . 2019-2020
ENGINE . . . B&S
CYLINDERS . . . 1
ENGINE HP . . . 10.5
FUEL . . . G
SPEEDS . . . 6 SPD
TRANSMISSION . . . GEAR
STEERING . . . STANDARD
STANDARD DECK . . . 30"

R140 1130040

YEARS MFRD . . . 2019-2020
ENGINE . . . B&S
CYLINDERS . . . 1
ENGINE HP . . . 10.5
FUEL . . . G
TRANSMISSION . . . HYDRO
STEERING . . . STANDARD
BLADE CLUTCH . . . MANUAL
STANDARD DECK . . . 30"
WEIGHT . . . 330 LBS.

T110 1130036

YEARS MFRD . . . 2019-2020
ENGINE . . . B&S
CYLINDERS . . . 1
ENGINE HP . . . 17.5
FUEL . . . G
SPEEDS . . . 7 SPD
TRANSMISSION . . . GEAR
STEERING . . . STANDARD
STANDARD DECK . . . 42"

T130 1130038

YEARS MFRD . . . 2019-2020
ENGINE . . . B&S READYSTART
ENGINE HP . . . 18.5
FUEL . . . G
STEERING . . . STANDARD
STANDARD DECK . . . 24"

T130 1130039

YEARS MFRD . . . 2019-2019
ENGINE . . . B&S READY START
ENGINE HP . . . 18.5
FUEL . . . G
STEERING . . . STANDARD
BLADE CLUTCH . . . MANUAL
STANDARD DECK . . . 42"
WEIGHT . . . 510 LBS.

T150 1130041

YEARS MFRD . . . 2019-2020
ENGINE . . . B&S READY START
ENGINE HP . . . 19
FUEL . . . G
TRANSMISSION . . . HYDRO
STEERING . . . STANDARD
BLADE CLUTCH . . . MANUAL
STANDARD DECK . . . 46"
WEIGHT . . . 520 LBS.

T210 1130043

YEARS MFRD . . . 2019-2020
ENGINE . . . KOHLER 5400 SERIES
CYLINDERS . . . 1
ENGINE HP . . . 18
FUEL . . . G
TRANSMISSION . . . HYDRO
STEERING . . . STANDARD
BLADE CLUTCH . . . MANUAL
STANDARD DECK . . . 42"
WEIGHT . . . 510 LBS.

T240 1130044

YEARS MFRD . . . 2019-2020
ENGINE . . . KOHLER 7000 SERIES
CYLINDERS . . . 2
ENGINE HP . . . 22
FUEL . . . G
TRANSMISSION . . . HYDRO
STEERING . . . STANDARD
BLADE CLUTCH . . . MANUAL
STANDARD DECK . . . 46"
WEIGHT . . . 590 LBS.

T260 1130045

YEARS MFRD . . . 2019-2020
ENGINE . . . KOHLER 700 SERIES
CYLINDERS . . . 2
ENGINE HP . . . 23
FUEL . . . G
TRANSMISSION . . . HYDRO
STEERING . . . STANDARD
BLADE CLUTCH . . . ELECTRIC
STANDARD DECK . . . 50"
WEIGHT . . . 630 LBS.

T310 1130047

YEARS MFRD . . . 2019-2020
ENGINE . . . KOHLER 7000 SERIES
CYLINDERS . . . 2
ENGINE HP . . . 24
FUEL . . . G
TRANSMISSION . . . HYDRO
STEERING . . . STANDARD
BLADE CLUTCH . . . ELECTRIC
STANDARD DECK . . . 54"
WEIGHT . . . 650 LBS.

13A7A1ZW099

YEARS MFRD . . . 2015-2015
ENGINE . . . KOHLER
CYLINDERS . . . 2
CID . . . 747CC
ENGINE HP . . . 26
COOLING . . . AIR
FUEL . . . G
SPEEDS . . . VARIABLE
TRANSMISSION . . . HYDRO
STEERING . . . STANDARD
STANDARD DECK . . . 54"
MSRP . . . $2,499

RETAIL PRICING

YEAR	HIGH	LOW
2015	$1,387	$1,040

13AP71XT099

YEARS MFRD . . . 2015-2015
ENGINE . . . KOHLER
CYLINDERS . . . 2
CID . . . 725CC
ENGINE HP . . . 22
COOLING . . . AIR
FUEL . . . G
SPEEDS . . . VARIABLE
TRANSMISSION . . . HYDRO
STEERING . . . STANDARD
BLADE CLUTCH . . . ELECTRIC
STANDARD DECK . . . 46"
MSRP . . . $1,712

RETAIL PRICING

YEAR	HIGH	LOW
2015	$903	$678

13AP78XS099

YEARS MFRD . . . 2015-2015
ENGINE . . . KOHLER
CYLINDERS . . . 2
CID . . . 725CC
ENGINE HP . . . 20
COOLING . . . AIR
FUEL . . . G
SPEEDS . . . VARIABLE
TRANSMISSION . . . HYDRO
STEERING . . . STANDARD
BLADE CLUTCH . . . MANUAL
STANDARD DECK . . . 42"
MSRP . . . $1,516

RETAIL PRICING

YEAR	HIGH	LOW
2015	$769	$576

13APA1ZS099

YEARS MFRD . . . 2015-2015
ENGINE . . . KOHLER
CYLINDERS . . . 2
CID . . . 725CC
ENGINE HP . . . 22
COOLING . . . AIR
FUEL . . . G
SPEEDS . . . VARIABLE
TRANSMISSION . . . HYDRO
STEERING . . . STANDARD

BLADE CLUTCH . . . . MANUAL
STANDARD DECK . . . . 42"
MSRP. $1,999

RETAIL PRICING

YEAR	HIGH	LOW
2015	$989	$742

13AQA1ZT099

YEARS MFRD 2015-2015
ENGINE . . . . KOHLER
CYLINDERS. 2
CID 725CC
ENGINE HP 24
COOLING . . . . AIR
FUEL . . . . G
SPEEDS . . . . VARIABLE
TRANSMISSION . . . . HYDRO
STEERING. . . . . STANDARD
BLADE CLUTCH . . . . ELECTRIC
STANDARD DECK . . . . 46"
MSRP. $2,199

RETAIL PRICING

YEAR	HIGH	LOW
2015	$1,182	$886

13AR91PT299

YEARS MFRD 2012-2012
ENGINE . . . . B&S
CYLINDERS. 2
ENGINE HP 26
COOLING . . . . AIR
FUEL . . . . G
SPEEDS . . . . VARIABLE
TRANSMISSION . . . . HYDRO
STEERING. . . . . STANDARD
STANDARD DECK . . . . 46"
MSRP. $1,948

RETAIL PRICING

YEAR	HIGH	LOW
2012	$1,044	$783

13B226JD299

YEARS MFRD 2016-2016
CYLINDERS. 1
CID 420CC
COOLING . . . . AIR
FUEL . . . . G
SPEEDS 6/1
TRANSMISSION . . . . GEAR
STEERING. . . . . STANDARD
BLADE CLUTCH . . . . MANUAL
STANDARD DECK . . . . 30"
WEIGHT . . . . 340 LBS.
MSRP. $1,099

RETAIL PRICING

YEAR	HIGH	LOW
2016	$553	$415

17AKCACS299

YEARS MFRD 2016-2016
ENGINE . . . . B&S
CID 724CC
ENGINE HP 22
COOLING . . . . AIR
FUEL . . . . G
SPEEDS . . . . VARIABLE
TRANSMISSION . . . . HYDRO
STEERING. . . . . ZERO
BLADE CLUTCH . . . . ELECTRIC
STANDARD DECK . . . . 42"
WEIGHT . . . . 600 LBS.
MSRP. $2,899

RETAIL PRICING

YEAR	HIGH	LOW
2016	$1,883	$1,412

17ARCACA099

YEARS MFRD 2017-2017
ENGINE . . . . KOHLER
CYLINDERS. 2
ENGINE HP 24
COOLING . . . . AIR
FUEL . . . . G
SPEEDS . . . . VARIABLE
TRANSMISSION . . . . HYDRO
STEERING. . . . . ZERO
BLADE CLUTCH . . . . ELECTRIC
STANDARD DECK . . . . 54"
WEIGHT . . . . 829 LBS.
MSRP. $3,199

RETAIL PRICING

YEAR	HIGH	LOW
2017	$2,123	$1,592

17ARCAC W099

YEARS MFRD 2015-2015
ENGINE . . . . KOHLER
CYLINDERS. 2
CID 725CC
ENGINE HP 24
COOLING . . . . AIR
FUEL . . . . G
SPEEDS . . . . VARIABLE
TRANSMISSION . . . . HYDRO
STEERING. . . . . ZERO
BLADE CLUTCH . . . . ELECTRIC
STANDARD DECK . . . . 54"
MSRP. $2,935

RETAIL PRICING

YEAR	HIGH	LOW
2015	$1,665	$1,249

17ASDALB099

YEARS MFRD 2015-2015
ENGINE . . . . KOHLER
CYLINDERS. 2
CID 725CC
ENGINE HP 24
COOLING . . . . AIR
FUEL . . . . G
SPEEDS . . . . VARIABLE
TRANSMISSION . . . . HYDRO
STEERING. . . . . ZERO
BLADE CLUTCH . . . . ELECTRIC
STANDARD DECK . . . . 48"
MSRP. $3,899

RETAIL PRICING

YEAR	HIGH	LOW
2015	$2,278	$1,709

17ASDALC099

YEARS MFRD 2015-2015
ENGINE . . . . KOHLER
CYLINDERS. 2
CID 725CC
ENGINE HP 25
COOLING . . . . AIR
FUEL . . . . G
SPEEDS . . . . VARIABLE
TRANSMISSION . . . . HYDRO
STEERING. . . . . ZERO
BLADE CLUTCH . . . . ELECTRIC
STANDARD DECK . . . . 54"
MSRP. $4,299

RETAIL PRICING

YEAR	HIGH	LOW
2015	$2,613	$1,960

17ASDALD099

YEARS MFRD 2015-2015
ENGINE . . . . KOHLER
CYLINDERS. 2
CID 725CC
ENGINE HP 25
COOLING . . . . AIR
FUEL . . . . G
SPEEDS . . . . VARIABLE
TRANSMISSION . . . . HYDRO
STEERING. . . . . ZERO
BLADE CLUTCH . . . . ELECTRIC
STANDARD DECK . . . . 60"
MSRP. $4,999

RETAIL PRICING

YEAR	HIGH	LOW
2015	$3,063	$2,297

17BRCACT099

YEARS MFRD 2015-2015
ENGINE . . . . KOHLER
CYLINDERS. 2
CID 725CC
ENGINE HP 22
COOLING . . . . AIR
FUEL . . . . G
SPEEDS . . . . VARIABLE
TRANSMISSION . . . . HYDRO
STEERING. . . . . STANDARD
BLADE CLUTCH . . . . ELECTRIC
STANDARD DECK . . . . 46"
MSRP. $2,544

RETAIL PRICING

YEAR	HIGH	LOW
2015	$1,391	$1,043

17BSDALB099

YEARS MFRD 2017-2017
ENGINE . . . . KOHLER
CYLINDERS. 2
CID 725CC
ENGINE HP 24
COOLING . . . . AIR
FUEL . . . . G
SPEEDS . . . . VARIABLE
TRANSMISSION . . . . HYDRO
STEERING. . . . . ZERO
BLADE CLUTCH . . . . ELECTRIC
STANDARD DECK . . . . 48"
WEIGHT . . . . 800 LBS.
MSRP. $3,899

RETAIL PRICING

YEAR	HIGH	LOW
2017	$2,767	$2,076

17BSDALD099

YEARS MFRD 2017-2017
ENGINE . . . . KOHLER
CYLINDERS. 2
CID 725CC
ENGINE HP 25
COOLING . . . . AIR
FUEL . . . . G
SPEEDS . . . . VARIABLE
TRANSMISSION . . . . HYDRO
STEERING. . . . . ZERO
BLADE CLUTCH . . . . ELECTRIC
STANDARD DECK . . . . 60"
WEIGHT . . . . 900 LBS.
MSRP. $4,999

RETAIL PRICING

YEAR	HIGH	LOW
2017	$3,573	$2,680

536.270320

YEARS MFRD 2010-2010
SERIES. . . . . RER SERIES
ENGINE . . . . B&S
CYLINDERS. 1
ENGINE HP 13.5
COOLING . . . . AIR
FUEL . . . . G
SPEEDS . . . . VARIABLE
TRANSMISSION . . . . HYDRO
STEERING. . . . . STANDARD
BLADE CLUTCH . . . . MANUAL
WEIGHT . . . . 353 LBS.

2499

YEARS MFRD 2016-2016
ENGINE . . . . KOHLER ELITE
CYLINDERS. 2
CID 747CC
ENGINE HP 26
COOLING . . . . AIR
FUEL . . . . G
SPEEDS . . . . VARIABLE
TRANSMISSION . . . . HYDRO
STEERING. . . . . STANDARD
BLADE CLUTCH . . . . ELECTRIC
STANDARD DECK . . . . 54"
WEIGHT . . . . 660 LBS.
MSRP. $2,499

RETAIL PRICING

YEAR	HIGH	LOW
2016	$1,594	$1,196

20242
YEARS MFRD 2016-2016
ENGINE . . . . KOHLER
CYLINDERS. 2
CID 725CC
ENGINE HP 24
COOLING . . . . AIR
FUEL . . . . G
SPEEDS . . . . VAIABLE
TRANSMISSION . . . . HYDRO
STEERING. . . . . STANDARD
BLADE CLUTCH . . . . ELECTRIC
STANDARD DECK . . . . 46"
MSRP. $2,299

RETAIL PRICING

YEAR	HIGH	LOW
2016	$1,434	$1,075

20370
YEARS MFRD 2016-2016
ENGINE . . . . CRAFTSMAN
CYLINDERS. 1
CID 420CC
COOLING . . . . AIR
FUEL . . . . G
SPEEDS 7/1
TRANSMISSION . . . . GEAR
STEERING. . . . . STANDARD
BLADE CLUTCH . . . . MANUAL
STANDARD DECK . . . . 42"
WEIGHT . . . . 520 LBS.
MSRP. $999

RETAIL PRICING

YEAR	HIGH	LOW
2016	$497	$373

20371
YEARS MFRD 2016-2016
ENGINE . . . . CRAFTSMAN
CYLINDERS. 1
CID 420CC
COOLING . . . . AIR
FUEL . . . . G
SPEEDS 7/1
TRANSMISSION . . . . GEAR
STEERING. . . . . STANDARD
BLADE CLUTCH . . . . MANUAL
STANDARD DECK . . . . 42"
WEIGHT . . . . 520 LBS.
MSRP. $1,099

RETAIL PRICING

YEAR	HIGH	LOW
2016	$553	$415

20372
YEARS MFRD 2016-2018
ENGINE . . . . CRAFTSMAN
CYLINDERS. 1
CID 420CC
COOLING . . . . AIR
FUEL . . . . G
SPEEDS . . . . VARIABLE
TRANSMISSION . . . . HYDRO
BLADE CLUTCH . . . . MANUAL
STANDARD DECK . . . . 42"
WEIGHT . . . . 530 LBS.

RETAIL PRICING

YEAR	HIGH	LOW
2016	$455	$341
2017	$533	$400
2018	$625	$469

20373
YEARS MFRD 2016-2016
ENGINE . . . . B&S
CYLINDERS. 1
CID 500CC
COOLING . . . . AIR
FUEL . . . . G
SPEEDS . . . . VARIABLE
TRANSMISSION . . . . HYDRO
STEERING. . . . . STANDARD
BLADE CLUTCH . . . . MANUAL
STANDARD DECK . . . . 42"
WEIGHT . . . . 518 LBS.
MSRP. $1,199

RETAIL PRICING

YEAR	HIGH	LOW
2016	$641	$481

20374
YEARS MFRD 2016-2016
ENGINE . . . . B&S
CYLINDERS. 1
CID 540CC
ENGINE HP 19
COOLING . . . . AIR
FUEL . . . . G
SPEEDS . . . . VARIABLE
TRANSMISSION . . . . HYDRO
STEERING. . . . . STANDARD
BLADE CLUTCH . . . . MANUAL
STANDARD DECK . . . . 46"
WEIGHT . . . . 530 LBS.
MSRP. $1,299

RETAIL PRICING

YEAR	HIGH	LOW
2016	$721	$541

20375
YEARS MFRD 2016-2016
ENGINE . . . . B&S
CID 540CC
ENGINE HP 19
COOLING . . . . AIR
FUEL . . . . G
SPEEDS . . . . VARIABLE
TRANSMISSION . . . . HYDRO
STEERING. . . . . STANDARD
BLADE CLUTCH . . . . MANUAL
STANDARD DECK . . . . 46"
WEIGHT . . . . 530 LBS.
MSRP. $1,399

RETAIL PRICING

YEAR	HIGH	LOW
2016	$800	$600

20376
YEARS MFRD 2016-2016
ENGINE . . . . KOHLER
CYLINDERS. 2
CID 725CC
ENGINE HP 20
COOLING . . . . AIR
FUEL . . . . G
SPEEDS . . . . VARIABLE
TRANSMISSION . . . . HYDRO
STEERING. . . . . STANDARD
BLADE CLUTCH . . . . MANUAL
STANDARD DECK . . . . 42"
WEIGHT . . . . 520 LBS.
MSRP. $1,449

RETAIL PRICING

YEAR	HIGH	LOW
2016	$826	$619

20379
YEARS MFRD 2016-2016
ENGINE . . . . KOHLER
CYLINDERS. 2
CID 725CC
ENGINE HP 22
COOLING . . . . AIR
FUEL . . . . G
SPEEDS . . . . VARIABLE
TRANSMISSION . . . . HYDRO
BLADE CLUTCH . . . . MANUAL
STANDARD DECK . . . . 46"
WEIGHT . . . . 530 LBS.
MSRP. $1,699

RETAIL PRICING

YEAR	HIGH	LOW
2016	$1,026	$770

20380
YEARS MFRD 2016-2017
ENGINE . . . . B&S
CYLINDERS. 1
CID 540CC
ENGINE HP 19
COOLING . . . . AIR
FUEL . . . . G
SPEEDS 6/1
TRANSMISSION . . . . GEAR
STEERING. . . . . STANDARD
BLADE CLUTCH . . . . MANUAL
STANDARD DECK . . . . 42"
WEIGHT . . . . 490 LBS.
MSRP. $1,499

RETAIL PRICING

YEAR	HIGH	LOW
2016	$822	$616
2017	$904	$678

20381
YEARS MFRD 2016-2017
ENGINE . . . . B&S
CYLINDERS. 1
CID 540CC
ENGINE HP 19
COOLING . . . . AIR
FUEL . . . . G
SPEEDS . . . . VARIABLE
TRANSMISSION . . . . HYDRO
STEERING. . . . . STANDARD
BLADE CLUTCH . . . . MANUAL
STANDARD DECK . . . . 42"
MSRP. $1,549

RETAIL PRICING

YEAR	HIGH	LOW
2016	$864	$648
2017	$946	$710

20381X
YEARS MFRD 2015-2015
ENGINE . . . . B&S
CYLINDERS. 1
CID 540CC
ENGINE HP 19
COOLING . . . . AIR
FUEL . . . . G
SPEEDS . . . . VARIABLE
TRANSMISSION . . . . HYDRO
STEERING. . . . . STANDARD
BLADE CLUTCH . . . . MANUAL
STANDARD DECK . . . . 42"
MSRP. $1,516

RETAIL PRICING

YEAR	HIGH	LOW
2015	$761	$571

20382X
YEARS MFRD 2015-2015
ENGINE . . . . B&S
CYLINDERS. 1
CID 540CC
ENGINE HP 19
COOLING . . . . AIR
FUEL . . . . G
SPEEDS . . . . VARIABLE
TRANSMISSION . . . . HYDRO
STEERING. . . . . STANDARD
BLADE CLUTCH . . . . MANUAL
STANDARD DECK . . . . 42"
MSRP. $1,614

RETAIL PRICING

YEAR	HIGH	LOW
2015	$850	$638

20383
YEARS MFRD 2016-2017
ENGINE . . . . B&S
CYLINDERS. 1
CID 540CC
ENGINE HP 19
COOLING . . . . AIR
FUEL . . . . G
SPEEDS . . . . VARIABLE
TRANSMISSION . . . . HYDRO
STEERING. . . . . STANDARD
BLADE CLUTCH . . . . MANUAL
STANDARD DECK . . . . 46"
MSRP. $1,599

RETAIL PRICING

YEAR	HIGH	LOW
2016	$904	$678
2017	$987	$740

CRAFTSMAN

20384X

YEARS MFRD 2015-2015
ENGINE . . . . B&S
CYLINDERS. 1
CID 540CC
ENGINE HP 19
COOLING . . . . AIR
FUEL . . . . G
SPEEDS . . . . VARIABLE
TRANSMISSION . . . . HYDRO
STEERING. . . . . STANDARD
BLADE CLUTCH . . . . MANUAL
STANDARD DECK . . . . 46"
MSRP. $1,663

RETAIL PRICING

YEAR	HIGH	LOW
2015	$798	$599

20390

YEARS MFRD 2016-2016
ENGINE . . . . B&S
CYLINDERS. 2
CID 724CC
ENGINE HP 22
COOLING . . . . AIR
FUEL . . . . G
SPEEDS . . . . VARIABLE
TRANSMISSION . . . . HYDRO
STEERING. . . . . STANDARD
BLADE CLUTCH . . . . MANUAL
STANDARD DECK . . . . 42"
WEIGHT . . . . 532 LBS.
MSRP. $1,699

RETAIL PRICING

YEAR	HIGH	LOW
2016	$958	$718

20391

YEARS MFRD 2016-2016
ENGINE . . . . B&S
CYLINDERS. 2
CID 724CC
ENGINE HP 22
COOLING . . . . AIR
FUEL . . . . G
SPEEDS . . . . VARIABLE
TRANSMISSION . . . . HYDRO
STEERING. . . . . STANDARD
BLADE CLUTCH . . . . ELECTRIC
STANDARD DECK . . . . 48"
WEIGHT . . . . 584 LBS.
MSRP. $1,899

RETAIL PRICING

YEAR	HIGH	LOW
2016	$1,188	$891

20400

YEARS MFRD 2016-2017
ENGINE . . . . KOHLER
CID 725CC
ENGINE HP 22
COOLING . . . . AIR
FUEL . . . . G
SPEEDS . . . . VARIABLE
TRANSMISSION . . . . HYDRO
STEERING. . . . . ZERO
BLADE CLUTCH . . . . ELECTRIC
STANDARD DECK . . . . 42"
MSRP. $2,799

RETAIL PRICING

YEAR	HIGH	LOW
2016	$1,816	$1,362
2017	$1,899	$1,424

20401X

YEARS MFRD 2016-2016
ENGINE . . . . B&S
CYLINDERS. 2
CID 724CC
ENGINE HP 24
COOLING . . . . AIR
FUEL . . . . G
SPEEDS . . . . VARIABLE
TRANSMISSION . . . . HYDRO
STEERING. . . . . STANDARD
BLADE CLUTCH . . . . ELECTRIC
STANDARD DECK . . . . 48"
WEIGHT . . . . 536 LBS.
MSRP. $2,599

RETAIL PRICING

YEAR	HIGH	LOW
2016	$1,667	$1,250

20407

YEARS MFRD 2017-2017
ENGINE . . . . B&S PLATINUM
CYLINDERS. 2
CID 724CC
ENGINE HP 24
COOLING . . . . AIR
FUEL . . . . G
SPEEDS . . . . VARIABLE
TRANSMISSION . . . . HYDRO
STEERING. . . . . STANDARD
BLADE CLUTCH . . . . ELECTRIC
STANDARD DECK . . . . 48"
WEIGHT . . . . 536 LBS.
MSRP. $2,599

RETAIL PRICING

YEAR	HIGH	LOW
2017	$1,694	$1,270

20408

YEARS MFRD 2016-2017
ENGINE . . . . B&S
CYLINDERS. 2
CID 724
ENGINE HP 24
COOLING . . . . AIR
FUEL . . . . G
SPEEDS . . . . VARIABLE
TRANSMISSION . . . . HYDRO
STEERING. . . . . STANDARD
BLADE CLUTCH . . . . ELECTRIC
STANDARD DECK . . . . 54"
WEIGHT . . . . 569 LBS.
MSRP. $2,799

RETAIL PRICING

YEAR	HIGH	LOW
2016	$1,743	$1,307
2017	$1,826	$1,369

20409

YEARS MFRD 2016-2017
ENGINE . . . . B&S
CYLINDERS. 2
CID 724CC
ENGINE HP 24
COOLING . . . . AIR
FUEL . . . . G
SPEEDS . . . . VARIABLE
TRANSMISSION . . . . HYDRO
STEERING. . . . . STANDARD
BLADE CLUTCH . . . . ELECTRIC
STANDARD DECK . . . . 54"
WEIGHT . . . . 570 LBS.
MSRP. $2,899

RETAIL PRICING

YEAR	HIGH	LOW
2016	$1,883	$1,412
2017	$1,966	$1,474

20410

YEARS MFRD 2016-2017
ENGINE . . . . KOHLER
CID 725CC
ENGINE HP 23
COOLING . . . . AIR
FUEL . . . . G
SPEEDS . . . . VARIABLE
TRANSMISSION . . . . HYDRO
STEERING. . . . . ZERO
BLADE CLUTCH . . . . ELECTRIC
STANDARD DECK . . . . 50"
MSRP. $3,199

RETAIL PRICING

YEAR	HIGH	LOW
2016	$2,064	$1,548
2017	$2,230	$1,672

20411

YEARS MFRD 2016-2017
ENGINE . . . . B&S
CID 724
ENGINE HP 22
COOLING . . . . AIR
FUEL . . . . G
SPEEDS . . . . VARIABLE
TRANSMISSION . . . . HYDRO
STEERING. . . . . ZERO
BLADE CLUTCH . . . . ELECTRIC
STANDARD DECK . . . . 42"
WEIGHT . . . . 600 LBS.
MSRP. $2,299

RETAIL PRICING

YEAR	HIGH	LOW
2016	$1,321	$990
2017	$1,486	$1,114

20418

YEARS MFRD 2016-2016
ENGINE . . . . KOHLER
CID 725
ENGINE HP 22
COOLING . . . . AIR
FUEL . . . . G
SPEEDS . . . . VARIABLE
TRANSMISSION . . . . HYDRO
STEERING. . . . . ZERO
BLADE CLUTCH . . . . ELECTRIC
STANDARD DECK . . . . 46"
WEIGHT . . . . 650 LBS.
MSRP. $2,699

RETAIL PRICING

YEAR	HIGH	LOW
2016	$1,762	$1,322

20419

YEARS MFRD 2016-2016
ENGINE . . . . KOHLER
CID 725CC
ENGINE HP 24
COOLING . . . . AIR
FUEL . . . . G
SPEEDS . . . . VARIABLE
TRANSMISSION . . . . HYDRO
STEERING. . . . . ZERO
BLADE CLUTCH . . . . ELECTRIC
STANDARD DECK . . . . 54"
WEIGHT . . . . 712 LBS.
MSRP. $2,999

RETAIL PRICING

YEAR	HIGH	LOW
2016	$2,002	$1,501

20424

YEARS MFRD 2017-2017
ENGINE . . . . KOHLER
CYLINDERS. 2
ENGINE HP 25
COOLING . . . . AIR
FUEL . . . . G
SPEEDS . . . . VARIABLE
TRANSMISSION . . . . HYDRO
STEERING. . . . . ZERO
BLADE CLUTCH . . . . ELECTRIC
STANDARD DECK . . . . 60"
WEIGHT . . . . 900 LBS.
MSRP. $4,899

RETAIL PRICING

YEAR	HIGH	LOW
2017	$3,503	$2,627

20438

YEARS MFRD 2016-2016
ENGINE . . . . KOHLER ELITE
CYLINDERS. 2
CID 725CC
ENGINE HP 20
COOLING . . . . AIR
FUEL . . . . G
SPEEDS . . . . VARIABLE
TRANSMISSION . . . . HYDRO

STEERING............STANDARD
BLADE CLUTCH........MANUAL
STANDARD DECK..........42"
MSRP..................$1,699

RETAIL PRICING

YEAR	HIGH	LOW
2016	$950	$713

20439

YEARS MFRD........2016-2016
ENGINE..........KOHLER ELITE
CYLINDERS..................2
CID....................725CC
ENGINE HP.................24
COOLING.................AIR
FUEL.......................G
SPEEDS............VARIABLE
TRANSMISSION..........HYDRO
STEERING............STANDARD
BLADE CLUTCH........ELECTRIC
STANDARD DECK..........46"
MSRP..................$2,699

RETAIL PRICING

YEAR	HIGH	LOW
2016	$1,742	$1,307

20440

YEARS MFRD........2016-2016
ENGINE..........KOHLER ELITE
CYLINDERS..................2
CID....................725CC
ENGINE HP.................24
COOLING.................AIR
FUEL.......................G
SPEEDS............VARIABLE
TRANSMISSION..........HYDRO
STEERING............STANDARD
BLADE CLUTCH........MANUAL
STANDARD DECK..........46"
WEIGHT..............580 LBS.
MSRP..................$1,999

RETAIL PRICING

YEAR	HIGH	LOW
2016	$1,202	$901

20442

YEARS MFRD........2016-2016
ENGINE..........KOHLER ELITE
CYLINDERS..................2
CID....................725CC
ENGINE HP.................24
COOLING.................AIR
FUEL.......................G
SPEEDS............VARIABLE
TRANSMISSION..........HYDRO
STEERING............STANDARD
BLADE CLUTCH........ELECTRIC
STANDARD DECK..........46"
WEIGHT..............600 LBS.
MSRP..................$2,199

RETAIL PRICING

YEAR	HIGH	LOW
2016	$1,366	$1,025

20443

YEARS MFRD........2016-2016
ENGINE..............KOHLER
CYLINDERS..................2
CID....................747CC
ENGINE HP.................26
COOLING.................AIR
FUEL.......................G
SPEEDS............VARIABLE
TRANSMISSION..........HYDRO
STEERING............STANDARD
BLADE CLUTCH........ELECTRIC
STANDARD DECK..........50"
WEIGHT..............640 LBS.
MSRP..................$2,799

RETAIL PRICING

YEAR	HIGH	LOW
2016	$1,824	$1,368

20445

YEARS MFRD........2016-2016
ENGINE..............KOHLER
CYLINDERS..................2
CID....................747CC
ENGINE HP.................26
COOLING.................AIR
FUEL.......................G
SPEEDS............VARIABLE
TRANSMISSION..........HYDRO
STEERING............STANDARD
BLADE CLUTCH........ELECTRIC
STANDARD DECK..........54"
WEIGHT..............685 LBS.
MSRP..................$3,199

RETAIL PRICING

YEAR	HIGH	LOW
2016	$2,152	$1,614

20447

YEARS MFRD........2016-2016
ENGINE..............KOHLER
CYLINDERS..................2
CID....................747CC
ENGINE HP.................26
COOLING.................AIR
FUEL.......................G
SPEEDS............VARIABLE
TRANSMISSION..........HYDRO
STEERING............STANDARD
BLADE CLUTCH........ELECTRIC
STANDARD DECK..........54"
WEIGHT..............685 LBS.
MSRP..................$3,999

RETAIL PRICING

YEAR	HIGH	LOW
2016	$2,814	$2,110

25000

YEARS MFRD........2012-2012
ENGINE...........CRAFTSMAN
CID....................420CC
COOLING.................AIR
FUEL.......................G
SPEEDS...................6/1
TRANSMISSION...........DISC
STEERING............STANDARD
STANDARD DECK..........30"
MSRP....................$999

RETAIL PRICING

YEAR	HIGH	LOW
2012	$535	$401

25001

YEARS MFRD........2012-2014
ENGINE.....................B&S
CYLINDERS..................2
ENGINE HP.................24
COOLING.................AIR
FUEL.......................G
SPEEDS............VARIABLE
TRANSMISSION..........HYDRO
STEERING...............ZERO
BLADE CLUTCH........ELECTRIC
STANDARD DECK..........42"
MSRP..................$2,869

RETAIL PRICING

YEAR	HIGH	LOW
2012	$813	$610
2013	$941	$705
2014	$1,116	$837

25002

YEARS MFRD........2012-2014
ENGINE..........B&S PLATINUM
CYLINDERS..................2
ENGINE HP.................26
COOLING.................AIR
FUEL.......................G
SPEEDS............VARIABLE
TRANSMISSION..........HYDRO
STEERING...............ZERO
BLADE CLUTCH........ELECTRIC
STANDARD DECK..........50"
MSRP..................$3,434

RETAIL PRICING

YEAR	HIGH	LOW
2012	$934	$700
2013	$1,049	$787
2014	$1,861	$1,396

25003

YEARS MFRD........2012-2014
ENGINE..............KOHLER
ENGINE HP.................27
COOLING.................AIR
FUEL.......................G
SPEEDS............VARIABLE
TRANSMISSION..........HYDRO
STEERING...............ZERO
STANDARD DECK..........48"
WEIGHT..............760 LBS.
MSRP..................$5,299

RETAIL PRICING

YEAR	HIGH	LOW
2012	$1,442	$1,082
2013	$1,922	$1,441
2014	$2,632	$1,974

25004

YEARS MFRD........2012-2012
ENGINE.....................B&S
CYLINDERS..................2
ENGINE HP.................20
COOLING.................AIR
FUEL.......................G
SPEEDS............VARIABLE
TRANSMISSION..........HYDRO
STEERING............STANDARD
STANDARD DECK..........42"
MSRP..................$2,999

RETAIL PRICING

YEAR	HIGH	LOW
2012	$1,606	$1,204

25005

YEARS MFRD........2012-2012
ENGINE.....................B&S
CYLINDERS..................2
ENGINE HP.................22
COOLING.................AIR
FUEL.......................G
SPEEDS............VARIABLE
TRANSMISSION..........HYDRO
STEERING............STANDARD
STANDARD DECK..........46"
MSRP..................$3,999

RETAIL PRICING

YEAR	HIGH	LOW
2012	$2,141	$1,606

25006

YEARS MFRD........1990-1990
ENGINE HP.................20
FUEL.......................G
STEERING............STANDARD
STANDARD DECK..........50"
WEIGHT..............758 LBS.
MSRP..................$3,299

RETAIL PRICING

YEAR	HIGH	LOW
1990	$877	$658

25007

YEARS MFRD........2012-2012
ENGINE.....................B&S
CYLINDERS..................2
ENGINE HP.................30
COOLING.................AIR
FUEL.......................G
SPEEDS............VARIABLE
TRANSMISSION..........HYDRO
STEERING............STANDARD
STANDARD DECK..........54"
MSRP..................$6,499

RETAIL PRICING

YEAR	HIGH	LOW
2012	$3,481	$2,611

25022

YEARS MFRD........2012-2014
ENGINE.....................B&S
ENGINE HP.................21

CRAFTSMAN

COOLING .... AIR
FUEL .... G
SPEEDS 6/1
TRANSMISSION .... GEAR
STEERING............ STANDARD
STANDARD DECK .... 42"
MSRP................. $1,749

RETAIL PRICING

YEAR	HIGH	LOW
2012	$481	$361
2013	$602	$452
2014	$813	$610

25023

YEARS MFRD 2012-2012
ENGINE .... B&S PLATINUM
CYLINDERS.................. 2
ENGINE HP 24
COOLING .... AIR
FUEL .... G
SPEEDS 6/1
TRANSMISSION .... GEAR
STEERING............ STANDARD
STANDARD DECK .... 42"
MSRP................. $1,649

RETAIL PRICING

YEAR	HIGH	LOW
2012	$883	$662

25024

YEARS MFRD 2012-2012
ENGINE ... KOHLER COURAGE PLUS
CYLINDERS.................. 2
ENGINE HP 26
COOLING .... AIR
FUEL .... G
SPEEDS 6/1
TRANSMISSION .... GEAR
STEERING............ STANDARD
STANDARD DECK .... 54"
MSRP................. $2,599

RETAIL PRICING

YEAR	HIGH	LOW
2012	$1,392	$1,044

25025

YEARS MFRD 2012-2012
ENGINE .... KOHLER COURAGE
CYLINDERS.................. 2
ENGINE HP 26
COOLING .... AIR
FUEL .... G
SPEEDS 6/1
TRANSMISSION .... GEAR
STEERING............ STANDARD
STANDARD DECK .... 54"
MSRP................. $2,699

RETAIL PRICING

YEAR	HIGH	LOW
2012	$1,446	$1,084

25026

YEARS MFRD 1995-1995
ENGINE .... KOHLER
ENGINE HP 20
COOLING .... AIR
FUEL .... G
SPEEDS 6
TRANSMISSION .... GEAR
STEERING............ STANDARD
STANDARD DECK .... 50"
MSRP................. $2,999

RETAIL PRICING

YEAR	HIGH	LOW
1995	$662	$497

25048

YEARS MFRD 1995-1995
ENGINE .... KOHLER
ENGINE HP 18
COOLING .... AIR
FUEL .... G
SPEEDS 6
TRANSMISSION .... GEAR
STEERING............ STANDARD
STANDARD DECK .... 44"
WEIGHT .... 562 LBS.
MSRP................. $2,499

RETAIL PRICING

YEAR	HIGH	LOW
1995	$630	$472

25049

YEARS MFRD 1995-1995
ENGINE .... KOHLER
ENGINE HP 18
COOLING .... AIR
FUEL .... G
SPEEDS .... VARIABLE
TRANSMISSION .... HYDRO
STEERING............ STANDARD
STANDARD DECK .... 44"
WEIGHT .... 562 LBS.
MSRP................. $2,799

RETAIL PRICING

YEAR	HIGH	LOW
1995	$663	$497

25051

YEARS MFRD 1995-1995
ENGINE .... KOHLER
ENGINE HP 19.5
COOLING .... AIR
FUEL .... G
SPEEDS 6
TRANSMISSION .... GEAR
STEERING............ STANDARD
STANDARD DECK .... 46"
WEIGHT .... 603 LBS.
MSRP................. $2,499

RETAIL PRICING

YEAR	HIGH	LOW
1995	$630	$472

25052

YEARS MFRD 1995-1995
ENGINE .... KOHLER
ENGINE HP 19.5
COOLING .... AIR
FUEL .... G
SPEEDS .... VARIABLE
TRANSMISSION .... HYDRO
STEERING............ STANDARD
STANDARD DECK .... 46"
WEIGHT .... 603 LBS.
MSRP................. $2,799

RETAIL PRICING

YEAR	HIGH	LOW
1995	$663	$497

25054

YEARS MFRD 1995-1995
ENGINE .... KOHLER
ENGINE HP 20
COOLING .... AIR
FUEL .... G
SPEEDS 6
TRANSMISSION .... GEAR
STEERING............ STANDARD
STANDARD DECK .... 50"
WEIGHT .... 613 LBS.
MSRP................. $2,999

RETAIL PRICING

YEAR	HIGH	LOW
1995	$662	$497

25055

YEARS MFRD 1995-1995
ENGINE .... KOHLER
ENGINE HP 22.5
COOLING .... AIR
FUEL .... G
SPEEDS 6
TRANSMISSION .... GEAR
STEERING............ STANDARD
STANDARD DECK .... 50"
WEIGHT .... 613 LBS.
MSRP................. $2,999

RETAIL PRICING

YEAR	HIGH	LOW
1995	$662	$497

25056

YEARS MFRD 1995-1995
ENGINE .... KOHLER
ENGINE HP 22.5
COOLING .... AIR
FUEL .... G
SPEEDS .... VARIABLE
TRANSMISSION .... HYDRO
STEERING............ STANDARD
STANDARD DECK .... 50"
WEIGHT .... 613 LBS.
MSRP................. $3,299

RETAIL PRICING

YEAR	HIGH	LOW
1995	$626	$470

25122

YEARS MFRD 1995-1995
ENGINE .... TECUMSEH
ENGINE HP 10
COOLING .... AIR
FUEL .... G
SPEEDS 5
TRANSMISSION .... GEAR
STEERING............ STANDARD
STANDARD DECK .... 30"
WEIGHT .... 357 LBS.
MSRP................... $899

RETAIL PRICING

YEAR	HIGH	LOW
1995	$300	$225

25125

YEARS MFRD 1995-1995
ENGINE .... B&S
ENGINE HP 13
COOLING .... AIR
FUEL .... G
SPEEDS 5
TRANSMISSION .... GEAR
STEERING............ STANDARD
STANDARD DECK .... 30"
WEIGHT .... 365 LBS.
MSRP................. $1,299

RETAIL PRICING

YEAR	HIGH	LOW
1995	$432	$324

25147

YEARS MFRD 1996-1996
ENGINE .... B&S
ENGINE HP 20
COOLING .... AIR
FUEL .... G
SPEEDS 6
TRANSMISSION .... GEAR
STEERING............ STANDARD
STANDARD DECK .... 44"
MSRP................. $2,099

RETAIL PRICING

YEAR	HIGH	LOW
1996	$726	$544

25148

YEARS MFRD 1996-1996
ENGINE .... KOHLER
ENGINE HP 18.5
COOLING .... AIR
FUEL .... G
SPEEDS 6
TRANSMISSION .... GEAR
STEERING............ STANDARD
STANDARD DECK .... 46"
MSRP................. $2,299

RETAIL PRICING

YEAR	HIGH	LOW
1996	$794	$596

25149

YEARS MFRD 1996-1996
ENGINE .... KOHLER
ENGINE HP 18.5
COOLING .... AIR
FUEL .... G
SPEEDS .... VARIABLE
TRANSMISSION .... HYDRO
STEERING. .... STANDARD
STANDARD DECK .... 46"
MSRP. $2,599

RETAIL PRICING

YEAR	HIGH	LOW
1996	$763	$572

25151

YEARS MFRD 1996-1996
ENGINE .... KOHLER
ENGINE HP 20.5
COOLING .... AIR
FUEL .... G
SPEEDS 6
TRANSMISSION .... GEAR
STEERING. .... STANDARD
STANDARD DECK .... 46"
MSRP. $2,799

RETAIL PRICING

YEAR	HIGH	LOW
1996	$764	$573

25155

YEARS MFRD 1996-1996
ENGINE .... KOHLER
ENGINE HP 22.5
COOLING .... AIR
FUEL .... G
SPEEDS 6
TRANSMISSION .... GEAR
STEERING. .... STANDARD
STANDARD DECK .... 50"
MSRP. $3,299

RETAIL PRICING

YEAR	HIGH	LOW
1996	$802	$601

25156

YEARS MFRD 1996-1996
ENGINE .... KOHLER
ENGINE HP 22.5
COOLING .... AIR
FUEL .... G
SPEEDS .... VARIABLE
TRANSMISSION .... HYDRO
STEERING. .... STANDARD
STANDARD DECK .... 50"
MSRP. $3,599

RETAIL PRICING

YEAR	HIGH	LOW
1996	$838	$628

25157

YEARS MFRD 1996-1996
ENGINE .... KOHLER
ENGINE HP 25
COOLING .... AIR
FUEL .... G
SPEEDS .... VARIABLE
TRANSMISSION .... HYDRO
STEERING. .... STANDARD
STANDARD DECK .... 50"
MSRP. $3,799

RETAIL PRICING

YEAR	HIGH	LOW
1996	$839	$629

25245

YEARS MFRD 1995-1995
ENGINE .... B&S
ENGINE HP 12.5
COOLING .... AIR
FUEL .... G
SPEEDS 5
TRANSMISSION .... GEAR
STEERING. .... STANDARD
STANDARD DECK .... 38"
WEIGHT .... 370 LBS.
MSRP. $1,099

RETAIL PRICING

YEAR	HIGH	LOW
1995	$367	$275

25250

YEARS MFRD 1995-1995
ENGINE .... B&S
ENGINE HP 13
COOLING .... AIR
FUEL .... G
SPEEDS 6
TRANSMISSION .... GEAR
STEERING. .... STANDARD
STANDARD DECK .... 42"
WEIGHT .... 380 LBS.
MSRP. $1,199

RETAIL PRICING

YEAR	HIGH	LOW
1995	$400	$300

25251

YEARS MFRD 1995-1995
ENGINE .... B&S
ENGINE HP 15
COOLING .... AIR
FUEL .... G
SPEEDS 6
TRANSMISSION .... GEAR
STEERING. .... STANDARD
STANDARD DECK .... 42"
WEIGHT .... 392 LBS.
MSRP. $1,299

RETAIL PRICING

YEAR	HIGH	LOW
1995	$432	$324

25252

YEARS MFRD 1996-1996
ENGINE .... KOHLER
ENGINE HP 20.5
COOLING .... AIR
FUEL .... G
SPEEDS .... VARIABLE
TRANSMISSION .... HYDRO
STEERING. .... STANDARD
STANDARD DECK .... 46"
MSRP. $3,099

RETAIL PRICING

YEAR	HIGH	LOW
1996	$868	$651

25253

YEARS MFRD 1995-1995
ENGINE .... B&S
ENGINE HP 15
COOLING .... AIR
FUEL .... G
SPEEDS .... VARIABLE
TRANSMISSION .... HYDRO
STEERING. .... STANDARD
STANDARD DECK .... 42"
WEIGHT .... 405 LBS.
MSRP. $1,599

RETAIL PRICING

YEAR	HIGH	LOW
1995	$533	$400

25254

YEARS MFRD 1995-1995
ENGINE .... KOHLER
ENGINE HP 14.5
COOLING .... AIR
FUEL .... G
SPEEDS 6
TRANSMISSION .... GEAR
STEERING. .... STANDARD
STANDARD DECK .... 42"
WEIGHT .... 422 LBS.
MSRP. $1,699

RETAIL PRICING

YEAR	HIGH	LOW
1995	$567	$425

25255

YEARS MFRD 1995-1995
ENGINE .... KOHLER
ENGINE HP 14
COOLING .... AIR
FUEL .... G
SPEEDS 5
TRANSMISSION .... GEAR
STEERING. .... STANDARD
STANDARD DECK .... 38"
WEIGHT .... 369 LBS.
MSRP. $1,599

RETAIL PRICING

YEAR	HIGH	LOW
1995	$533	$400

25256

YEARS MFRD 1995-1995
ENGINE .... B&S
ENGINE HP 19
COOLING .... AIR
FUEL .... G
SPEEDS 6
TRANSMISSION .... GEAR
STEERING. .... STANDARD
STANDARD DECK .... 42"
WEIGHT .... 435 LBS.
MSRP. $1,699

RETAIL PRICING

YEAR	HIGH	LOW
1995	$567	$425

25258

YEARS MFRD 1995-1995
ENGINE .... KOHLER
ENGINE HP 15.5
COOLING .... AIR
FUEL .... G
SPEEDS 6
TRANSMISSION .... GEAR
STEERING. .... STANDARD
STANDARD DECK .... 42"
WEIGHT .... 427 LBS.
MSRP. $1,699

RETAIL PRICING

YEAR	HIGH	LOW
1995	$567	$425

25259

YEARS MFRD 1995-1995
ENGINE .... KOHLER
ENGINE HP 15.5
COOLING .... AIR
FUEL .... G
SPEEDS .... VARIABLE
TRANSMISSION .... HYDRO
STEERING. .... STANDARD
STANDARD DECK .... 42"
WEIGHT .... 441 LBS.
MSRP. $1,899

RETAIL PRICING

YEAR	HIGH	LOW
1995	$635	$476

25260

YEARS MFRD 1995-1995
ENGINE .... KOHLER
ENGINE HP 15
COOLING .... AIR
FUEL .... G
SPEEDS 6
TRANSMISSION .... GEAR
STEERING. .... STANDARD
STANDARD DECK .... 42"
WEIGHT .... 446 LBS.
MSRP. $1,699

RETAIL PRICING

YEAR	HIGH	LOW
1995	$567	$425

25261

YEARS MFRD 1995-1995
ENGINE .... KOHLER
ENGINE HP 15

COOLING . . . AIR
FUEL . . . G
SPEEDS . . . VARIABLE
TRANSMISSION . . . HYDRO
STEERING. . . STANDARD
STANDARD DECK . . . 42"
WEIGHT . . . 490 LBS.
MSRP. . . $1,699

RETAIL PRICING

YEAR	HIGH	LOW
1995	$567	$425

25270

YEARS MFRD . . . 1995-1995
ENGINE . . . KOHLER
ENGINE HP . . . 18
COOLING . . . AIR
FUEL . . . G
SPEEDS . . . 6
TRANSMISSION . . . GEAR
STEERING. . . STANDARD
STANDARD DECK . . . 42"
WEIGHT . . . 535 LBS.
MSRP. . . $2,199

RETAIL PRICING

YEAR	HIGH	LOW
1995	$734	$551

25271

YEARS MFRD . . . 1995-1995
ENGINE . . . KOHLER
ENGINE HP . . . 18
COOLING . . . AIR
FUEL . . . G
SPEEDS . . . VARIABLE
TRANSMISSION . . . GEAR
STEERING. . . STANDARD
STANDARD DECK . . . 42"
WEIGHT . . . 548 LBS.
MSRP. . . $2,399

RETAIL PRICING

YEAR	HIGH	LOW
1995	$799	$599

25411

YEARS MFRD . . . 1990-1992
ENGINE . . . B&S
ENGINE HP . . . 5
FUEL . . . G
SPEEDS . . . 3
STEERING. . . STANDARD
STANDARD DECK . . . 25"
WEIGHT . . . 278 LBS.
MSRP. . . $669

RETAIL PRICING

YEAR	HIGH	LOW
1990	$171	$128
1991	$189	$142
1992	$197	$147

25416

YEARS MFRD . . . 1990-1991
ENGINE . . . B&S
ENGINE HP . . . 10
FUEL . . . G
SPEEDS . . . 5
STEERING. . . STANDARD
STANDARD DECK . . . 30"
WEIGHT . . . 327 LBS.
MSRP. . . $948

RETAIL PRICING

YEAR	HIGH	LOW
1990	$252	$189
1991	$269	$202

25445

YEARS MFRD . . . 1990-1990
ENGINE HP . . . 18
FUEL . . . G
STEERING. . . STANDARD
STANDARD DECK . . . 44"
WEIGHT . . . 650 LBS.
MSRP. . . $1,993

RETAIL PRICING

YEAR	HIGH	LOW
1990	$528	$396

25492

YEARS MFRD . . . 1990-1990
ENGINE . . . B&S
ENGINE HP . . . 12
FUEL . . . G
SPEEDS . . . 6
STEERING. . . STANDARD
STANDARD DECK . . . 38"
WEIGHT . . . 522 LBS.
MSRP. . . $1,197

RETAIL PRICING

YEAR	HIGH	LOW
1990	$317	$238

25494

YEARS MFRD . . . 1990-1990
ENGINE . . . B&S
ENGINE HP . . . 14
FUEL . . . G
STEERING. . . STANDARD
STANDARD DECK . . . 38"
WEIGHT . . . 570 LBS.
MSRP. . . $1,497

RETAIL PRICING

YEAR	HIGH	LOW
1990	$397	$298

25496

YEARS MFRD . . . 1990-1990
ENGINE . . . B&S
ENGINE HP . . . 11
FUEL . . . G
SPEEDS . . . 4
STEERING. . . STANDARD
STANDARD DECK . . . 38"
WEIGHT . . . 515 LBS.
MSRP. . . $994

RETAIL PRICING

YEAR	HIGH	LOW
1990	$264	$198

25502

YEARS MFRD . . . 1992-1992
ENGINE . . . TECUMSEH
ENGINE HP . . . 10
COOLING . . . AIR
FUEL . . . G
SPEEDS . . . 5
TRANSMISSION . . . GEAR
STEERING. . . STANDARD
STANDARD DECK . . . 30"
WEIGHT . . . 370 LBS.
MSRP. . . $999

RETAIL PRICING

YEAR	HIGH	LOW
1992	$295	$221

25503

YEARS MFRD . . . 1994-1994
ENGINE . . . TECUMSEH
ENGINE HP . . . 10
COOLING . . . AIR
FUEL . . . G
SPEEDS . . . 5
TRANSMISSION . . . GEAR
STEERING. . . STANDARD
STANDARD DECK . . . 30"
MSRP. . . $1,099

RETAIL PRICING

YEAR	HIGH	LOW
1994	$353	$265

25506

YEARS MFRD . . . 1992-1992
ENGINE . . . TECUMSEH
ENGINE HP . . . 10
COOLING . . . AIR
FUEL . . . G
SPEEDS . . . 5
TRANSMISSION . . . GEAR
STEERING. . . STANDARD
STANDARD DECK . . . 30"
WEIGHT . . . 406 LBS.
MSRP. . . $1,099

RETAIL PRICING

YEAR	HIGH	LOW
1992	$324	$243

25512

YEARS MFRD . . . 1994-1994
ENGINE . . . TECUMSEH
ENGINE HP . . . 12
COOLING . . . AIR
FUEL . . . G
SPEEDS . . . 5
TRANSMISSION . . . GEAR
STEERING. . . STANDARD
STANDARD DECK . . . 38"
MSRP. . . $899

RETAIL PRICING

YEAR	HIGH	LOW
1994	$290	$217

25517

YEARS MFRD . . . 1992-1992
ENGINE . . . TECHMSEH
ENGINE HP . . . 8
COOLING . . . AIR
FUEL . . . G
SPEEDS . . . 5
TRANSMISSION . . . GEAR
STEERING. . . STANDARD
STANDARD DECK . . . 30"
WEIGHT . . . 355 LBS.
MSRP. . . $899

RETAIL PRICING

YEAR	HIGH	LOW
1992	$266	$200

25552

YEARS MFRD . . . 1991-1991
ENGINE . . . B&S
ENGINE HP . . . 12.5
FUEL . . . G
TRANSMISSION . . . GEAR
STEERING. . . STANDARD
STANDARD DECK . . . 38"
WEIGHT . . . 496 LBS.
MSRP. . . $1,197

RETAIL PRICING

YEAR	HIGH	LOW
1991	$338	$254

25554

YEARS MFRD . . . 1991-1991
ENGINE . . . B&S
ENGINE HP . . . 14
FUEL . . . G
TRANSMISSION . . . GEAR
STEERING. . . STANDARD
STANDARD DECK . . . 38"
WEIGHT . . . 559 LBS.
MSRP. . . $1,597

RETAIL PRICING

YEAR	HIGH	LOW
1991	$453	$340

25557

YEARS MFRD . . . 1992-1992
ENGINE . . . B&S
ENGINE HP . . . 12.5
COOLING . . . AIR
FUEL . . . G
SPEEDS . . . 6
TRANSMISSION . . . GEAR
STEERING. . . STANDARD
STANDARD DECK . . . 38"
WEIGHT . . . 496 LBS.
MSRP. . . $1,299

RETAIL PRICING

YEAR	HIGH	LOW
1992	$384	$288

25558

YEARS MFRD . . . 1992-1992
ENGINE . . . B&S
ENGINE HP . . . 12.5

COOLING . . . . AIR
FUEL . . . . G
SPEEDS 6
TRANSMISSION . . . . GEAR
STEERING. . . . STANDARD
STANDARD DECK . . . . 42"
WEIGHT . . . . 466 LBS.
MSRP. . . . $1,399

RETAIL PRICING

YEAR	HIGH	LOW
1992	$414	$311

25559

YEARS MFRD 1992-1992
ENGINE . . . . B&S
ENGINE HP 12.5
COOLING . . . . AIR
FUEL . . . . G
SPEEDS . . . . VARIABLE
TRANSMISSION . . . . HYDRO
STEERING. . . . STANDARD
STANDARD DECK . . . . 38"
WEIGHT . . . . 541 LBS.
MSRP. . . . $1,699

RETAIL PRICING

YEAR	HIGH	LOW
1992	$500	$375

25569

YEARS MFRD 1992-1992
ENGINE . . . . KOHLER
ENGINE HP 14
FUEL . . . . G
SPEEDS 6
TRANSMISSION . . . . GEAR
STEERING. . . . STANDARD
STANDARD DECK . . . . 42"
WEIGHT . . . . 559 LBS.
MSRP. . . . $1,799

RETAIL PRICING

YEAR	HIGH	LOW
1992	$530	$398

25581

YEARS MFRD 2017-2017
ENGINE . . . . B&S PLATINUM
CYLINDERS. . . . 1
CID 540CC
ENGINE HP 14
COOLING . . . . AIR
FUEL . . . . G
SPEEDS . . . . VARIABLE
TRANSMISSION . . . . HYDRO
STEERING. . . . STANDARD
STANDARD DECK . . . . 42"
WEIGHT . . . . 495 LBS.
MSRP. . . . $1,399

RETAIL PRICING

YEAR	HIGH	LOW
2017	$772	$579

25583

YEARS MFRD 2016-2017
ENGINE . . . . B&S
CYLINDERS. . . . 1
CID 540CC
ENGINE HP 19
COOLING . . . . AIR
FUEL . . . . G
SPEEDS . . . . VARIABLE
TRANSMISSION . . . . HYDRO
STEERING. . . . STANDARD
BLADE CLUTCH . . . . MANUAL
STANDARD DECK . . . . 46"
WEIGHT . . . . 425 LBS.
MSRP. . . . $1,499

RETAIL PRICING

YEAR	HIGH	LOW
2016	$827	$620
2017	$909	$682

25584

YEARS MFRD 2016-2017
ENGINE . . . . B&S
CYLINDERS. . . . 1
CID 540CC
ENGINE HP 19
COOLING . . . . AIR
FUEL . . . . G
SPEEDS . . . . VARIABLE
TRANSMISSION . . . . HYDRO
STEERING. . . . STANDARD
BLADE CLUTCH . . . . MANUAL
STANDARD DECK . . . . 46"
WEIGHT . . . . 428 LBS.
MSRP. . . . $1,599

RETAIL PRICING

YEAR	HIGH	LOW
2016	$827	$620
2017	$975	$731

25587

YEARS MFRD 2018-2019
ENGINE . . . . B&S PLATINUM
CYLINDERS. . . . 1
CID 540CC
ENGINE HP 19
FUEL . . . . G
TRANSMISSION . . . . HYDRO
STEERING. . . . STANDARD
BLADE CLUTCH . . . . MANUAL
STANDARD DECK . . . . 42"
WEIGHT . . . . 520 LBS.

25588

YEARS MFRD 1992-1992
ENGINE . . . . B&S
ENGINE HP 14
FUEL . . . . G
SPEEDS 6
TRANSMISSION . . . . GEAR
STEERING. . . . STANDARD
STANDARD DECK . . . . 43"
MSRP. . . . $2,199

RETAIL PRICING

YEAR	HIGH	LOW
1992	$648	$486

25593

YEARS MFRD 1992-1992
ENGINE . . . . B&S
ENGINE HP 18
FUEL . . . . G
SPEEDS 6
TRANSMISSION . . . . GEAR
STEERING. . . . STANDARD
STANDARD DECK . . . . 44"
WEIGHT . . . . 740 LBS.
MSRP. . . . $2,299

RETAIL PRICING

YEAR	HIGH	LOW
1992	$678	$509

25594

YEARS MFRD 1992-1992
ENGINE . . . . B&S
ENGINE HP 18
FUEL . . . . G
SPEEDS 6
TRANSMISSION . . . . GEAR
STEERING. . . . STANDARD
STANDARD DECK . . . . 44"
WEIGHT . . . . 655 LBS.
MSRP. . . . $2,099

RETAIL PRICING

YEAR	HIGH	LOW
1992	$619	$465

25595

YEARS MFRD 1991-1991
ENGINE . . . . KOHLER
ENGINE HP 18
FUEL . . . . G
TRANSMISSION . . . . GEAR
STEERING. . . . STANDARD
STANDARD DECK . . . . 44"
WEIGHT . . . . 750 LBS.
MSRP. . . . $2,299

RETAIL PRICING

YEAR	HIGH	LOW
1991	$652	$489

25596

YEARS MFRD 1992-1992
ENGINE . . . . KOHLER
ENGINE HP 18
FUEL . . . . G
SPEEDS 6
TRANSMISSION . . . . GEAR
STEERING. . . . STANDARD
STANDARD DECK . . . . 44"
WEIGHT . . . . 752 LBS.
MSRP. . . . $2,499

RETAIL PRICING

YEAR	HIGH	LOW
1992	$737	$553

25621

YEARS MFRD 1997-1997
ENGINE . . . . CRAFTSMAN
ENGINE HP 13.5
COOLING . . . . AIR
FUEL . . . . G
SPEEDS 5
TRANSMISSION . . . . GEAR
STEERING. . . . STANDARD
STANDARD DECK . . . . 30"
MSRP. . . . $1,099

RETAIL PRICING

YEAR	HIGH	LOW
1997	$394	$296

25622

YEARS MFRD 1996-1996
ENGINE . . . . CRAFTSMAN
ENGINE HP 13
COOLING . . . . AIR
FUEL . . . . G
SPEEDS 5
TRANSMISSION . . . . GEAR
STEERING. . . . STANDARD
STANDARD DECK . . . . 30"
MSRP. . . . $1,199

RETAIL PRICING

YEAR	HIGH	LOW
1996	$414	$311

25623

YEARS MFRD 1991-1991
ENGINE . . . . B&S
ENGINE HP 11
FUEL . . . . G
SPEEDS 4
STEERING. . . . STANDARD
STANDARD DECK . . . . 36"
WEIGHT . . . . 439 LBS.
MSRP. . . . $897

RETAIL PRICING

YEAR	HIGH	LOW
1991	$254	$190

25645

YEARS MFRD 1996-1996
ENGINE . . . . B&S
ENGINE HP 12.5
COOLING . . . . AIR
FUEL . . . . G
SPEEDS 5
TRANSMISSION . . . . GEAR
STEERING. . . . STANDARD
STANDARD DECK . . . . 38"
MSRP. . . . $949

RETAIL PRICING

YEAR	HIGH	LOW
1996	$329	$247

25649

YEARS MFRD 1996-1996
ENGINE . . . . B&S
ENGINE HP 15.5

COOLING . . . AIR
FUEL . . . G
SPEEDS . . . 5
TRANSMISSION . . . GEAR
STEERING . . . STANDARD
STANDARD DECK . . . 42"
MSRP . . . $1,399

RETAIL PRICING

YEAR	HIGH	LOW
1996	$483	$362

25650

YEARS MFRD . . . 1996-1996
ENGINE . . . B&S
ENGINE HP . . . 13.5
FUEL . . . G
SPEEDS . . . 6
TRANSMISSION . . . GEAR
STEERING . . . STANDARD
STANDARD DECK . . . 42"
MSRP . . . $1,049

RETAIL PRICING

YEAR	HIGH	LOW
1996	$362	$271

25651

YEARS MFRD . . . 1996-1996
ENGINE . . . B&S
ENGINE HP . . . 15.5
COOLING . . . AIR
FUEL . . . G
SPEEDS . . . 6
TRANSMISSION . . . GEAR
STEERING . . . STANDARD
STANDARD DECK . . . 42"
MSRP . . . $1,199

RETAIL PRICING

YEAR	HIGH	LOW
1996	$414	$311

25652

YEARS MFRD . . . 1996-1996
ENGINE . . . B&S
ENGINE HP . . . 15.5
COOLING . . . AIR
FUEL . . . G
SPEEDS . . . 6
TRANSMISSION . . . GEAR
STEERING . . . STANDARD
STANDARD DECK . . . 42"
MSRP . . . $1,299

RETAIL PRICING

YEAR	HIGH	LOW
1996	$449	$337

25653

YEARS MFRD . . . 1996-1996
ENGINE . . . B&S
ENGINE HP . . . 15.5
COOLING . . . AIR
FUEL . . . G
SPEEDS . . . VARIABLE
TRANSMISSION . . . HYDRO
STEERING . . . STANDARD
MSRP . . . $1,499

RETAIL PRICING

YEAR	HIGH	LOW
1996	$517	$388

25654

YEARS MFRD . . . 1996-1996
ENGINE . . . KOHLER
ENGINE HP . . . 15
COOLING . . . AIR
FUEL . . . G
SPEEDS . . . 6
TRANSMISSION . . . GEAR
STEERING . . . STANDARD
MSRP . . . $1,399

RETAIL PRICING

YEAR	HIGH	LOW
1996	$483	$362

25655

YEARS MFRD . . . 1996-1996
ENGINE . . . KOHLER
ENGINE HP . . . 15
COOLING . . . AIR
FUEL . . . G
SPEEDS . . . VARIABLE
TRANSMISSION . . . HYDRO
STEERING . . . STANDARD
MSRP . . . $1,599

RETAIL PRICING

YEAR	HIGH	LOW
1996	$550	$413

25656

YEARS MFRD . . . 1996-1996
ENGINE . . . KOHLER
ENGINE HP . . . 15
COOLING . . . AIR
FUEL . . . G
SPEEDS . . . VARIABLE
TRANSMISSION . . . HYDRO
STEERING . . . STANDARD
STANDARD DECK . . . 42"
MSRP . . . $1,499

RETAIL PRICING

YEAR	HIGH	LOW
1996	$517	$388

25657

YEARS MFRD . . . 1996-1996
ENGINE . . . B&S
ENGINE HP . . . 19
COOLING . . . AIR
FUEL . . . G
SPEEDS . . . VARIABLE
TRANSMISSION . . . HYDRO
STEERING . . . STANDARD
STANDARD DECK . . . 42"
MSRP . . . $1,699

RETAIL PRICING

YEAR	HIGH	LOW
1996	$586	$440

25658

YEARS MFRD . . . 1996-1996
ENGINE . . . KOHLER
ENGINE HP . . . 15.5
COOLING . . . AIR
FUEL . . . G
SPEEDS . . . 6
TRANSMISSION . . . GEAR
STEERING . . . STANDARD
STANDARD DECK . . . 42"
MSRP . . . $1,699

RETAIL PRICING

YEAR	HIGH	LOW
1996	$586	$440

25659

YEARS MFRD . . . 1996-1996
ENGINE . . . KOHLER
ENGINE HP . . . 15.5
COOLING . . . AIR
FUEL . . . G
SPEEDS . . . VARIABLE
TRANSMISSION . . . HYDRO
STEERING . . . STANDARD
STANDARD DECK . . . 42"
MSRP . . . $1,899

RETAIL PRICING

YEAR	HIGH	LOW
1996	$656	$492

25660

YEARS MFRD . . . 1996-1996
ENGINE . . . KOHLER
ENGINE HP . . . 15.5
COOLING . . . AIR
FUEL . . . G
SPEEDS . . . 6
TRANSMISSION . . . GEAR
STEERING . . . STANDARD
STANDARD DECK . . . 46"
MSRP . . . $1,899

RETAIL PRICING

YEAR	HIGH	LOW
1996	$656	$492

25661

YEARS MFRD . . . 1996-1996
ENGINE . . . KOHLER
ENGINE HP . . . 15.5
COOLING . . . AIR
FUEL . . . G
SPEEDS . . . VARIABLE
TRANSMISSION . . . HYDRO
STEERING . . . STANDARD
STANDARD DECK . . . 46"
MSRP . . . $2,099

RETAIL PRICING

YEAR	HIGH	LOW
1996	$726	$544

25670

YEARS MFRD . . . 1996-1996
ENGINE . . . KOHLER
ENGINE HP . . . 18
COOLING . . . AIR
FUEL . . . G
SPEEDS . . . 6
TRANSMISSION . . . GEAR
STEERING . . . STANDARD
WEIGHT . . . 46 LBS.
MSRP . . . $2,199

RETAIL PRICING

YEAR	HIGH	LOW
1996	$760	$570

25671

YEARS MFRD . . . 1996-1996
ENGINE . . . KOHLER
ENGINE HP . . . 18
COOLING . . . AIR
FUEL . . . G
SPEEDS . . . VARIABLE
TRANSMISSION . . . HYDRO
STEERING . . . STANDARD
STANDARD DECK . . . 46"
MSRP . . . $2,399

RETAIL PRICING

YEAR	HIGH	LOW
1996	$828	$621

25685

YEARS MFRD . . . 1992-1992
ENGINE . . . B&S
ENGINE HP . . . 12
FUEL . . . G
SPEEDS . . . 5
TRANSMISSION . . . GEAR
STEERING . . . STANDARD
STANDARD DECK . . . 38"
WEIGHT . . . 436 LBS.
MSRP . . . $999

RETAIL PRICING

YEAR	HIGH	LOW
1992	$295	$221

25688

YEARS MFRD . . . 1992-1992
ENGINE . . . B&S
ENGINE HP . . . 12.5
FUEL . . . G
SPEEDS . . . 5
TRANSMISSION . . . GEAR
STEERING . . . STANDARD
STANDARD DECK . . . 38"
WEIGHT . . . 433 LBS.
MSRP . . . $1,099

RETAIL PRICING

YEAR	HIGH	LOW
1992	$324	$243

25728

YEARS MFRD . . . 1992-1992
ENGINE . . . B&S
ENGINE HP . . . 12
COOLING . . . AIR
FUEL . . . G
SPEEDS . . . 5
TRANSMISSION . . . GEAR

STEERING............STANDARD
STANDARD DECK........... 38"
WEIGHT.............. 500 LBS.
MSRP................. $1,199

RETAIL PRICING

YEAR	HIGH	LOW
1992	$354	$266

25735

YEARS MFRD........ 1991-1991
ENGINE..................B&S
ENGINE HP.............. 12.5
FUEL......................G
TRANSMISSION...........GEAR
STEERING............STANDARD
STANDARD DECK........... 38"
WEIGHT.............. 496 LBS.
MSRP................. $1,299

RETAIL PRICING

YEAR	HIGH	LOW
1991	$369	$276

25736

YEARS MFRD........ 1991-1991
ENGINE..................B&S
ENGINE HP.................12
FUEL......................G
SPEEDS..............VARIABLE
TRANSMISSION..........HYDRO
STEERING............STANDARD
STANDARD DECK........... 38"
WEIGHT.............. 541 LBS.
MSRP................. $1,597

RETAIL PRICING

YEAR	HIGH	LOW
1991	$453	$340

25746

YEARS MFRD........ 1991-1991
ENGINE..................B&S
ENGINE HP.................12
FUEL......................G
SPEEDS....................5
STEERING............STANDARD
STANDARD DECK........... 36"
WEIGHT.............. 433 LBS.
MSRP................... $997

RETAIL PRICING

YEAR	HIGH	LOW
1991	$281	$211

25748

YEARS MFRD........ 1991-1991
ENGINE..................B&S
ENGINE HP.................18
FUEL......................G
TRANSMISSION...........GEAR
STEERING............STANDARD
STANDARD DECK........... 38"
WEIGHT.............. 548 LBS.
MSRP................. $1,687

RETAIL PRICING

YEAR	HIGH	LOW
1991	$477	$358

25755

YEARS MFRD........ 1995-1995
ENGINE...............KOHLER
ENGINE HP.................14
COOLING.................AIR
FUEL......................G
SPEEDS....................6
TRANSMISSION...........GEAR
STEERING............STANDARD
STANDARD DECK........... 42"
MSRP................. $1,599

RETAIL PRICING

YEAR	HIGH	LOW
1995	$533	$400

25762

YEARS MFRD........ 1994-1994
ENGINE..................B&S
ENGINE HP.............. 12.5
COOLING.................AIR
FUEL......................G
SPEEDS....................5
TRANSMISSION...........GEAR
STEERING............STANDARD
STANDARD DECK........... 38"
MSRP................... $999

RETAIL PRICING

YEAR	HIGH	LOW
1994	$321	$241

25763

YEARS MFRD........ 1994-1994
ENGINE..................B&S
ENGINE HP.................13
COOLING.................AIR
FUEL......................G
SPEEDS....................6
TRANSMISSION...........GEAR
STEERING............STANDARD
STANDARD DECK........... 42"
MSRP................. $1,199

RETAIL PRICING

YEAR	HIGH	LOW
1994	$387	$290

25764

YEARS MFRD........ 1994-1994
ENGINE..................B&S
ENGINE HP.................15
COOLING.................AIR
FUEL......................G
SPEEDS....................6
TRANSMISSION...........GEAR
STEERING............STANDARD
STANDARD DECK........... 42"
MSRP................. $1,399

RETAIL PRICING

YEAR	HIGH	LOW
1994	$449	$337

25765

YEARS MFRD........ 1994-1994
ENGINE...............KOHLER
ENGINE HP.............. 15.5
COOLING.................AIR
FUEL......................G
SPEEDS....................6
TRANSMISSION...........GEAR
STEERING............STANDARD
STANDARD DECK........... 42"
MSRP................. $1,799

RETAIL PRICING

YEAR	HIGH	LOW
1994	$579	$434

25766

YEARS MFRD........ 1994-1994
ENGINE...............KOHLER
ENGINE HP.............. 15.5
COOLING.................AIR
FUEL......................G
SPEEDS..............VARIABLE
TRANSMISSION..........HYDRO
STEERING............STANDARD
STANDARD DECK........... 42"
MSRP................. $1,999

RETAIL PRICING

YEAR	HIGH	LOW
1994	$643	$482

25767

YEARS MFRD........ 1994-1995
ENGINE..................B&S
ENGINE HP.................15
COOLING.................AIR
FUEL......................G
SPEEDS....................6
TRANSMISSION...........GEAR
STEERING............STANDARD
STANDARD DECK........... 43"
MSRP................. $1,799

RETAIL PRICING

YEAR	HIGH	LOW
1994	$579	$434
1995	$601	$451

25769

YEARS MFRD........ 1994-1994
ENGINE..................B&S
ENGINE HP.............. 12.5
COOLING.................AIR
FUEL......................G
SPEEDS..............VARIABLE
TRANSMISSION..........HYDRO
STEERING............STANDARD
STANDARD DECK........... 42"
MSRP................. $1,399

RETAIL PRICING

YEAR	HIGH	LOW
1994	$449	$337

25771

YEARS MFRD........ 1994-1994
ENGINE..................B&S
ENGINE HP.................18
COOLING.................AIR
FUEL......................G
SPEEDS....................6
TRANSMISSION...........GEAR
STEERING............STANDARD
STANDARD DECK........... 44"
MSRP................. $2,099

RETAIL PRICING

YEAR	HIGH	LOW
1994	$675	$507

25772

YEARS MFRD........ 1994-1995
ENGINE...............KOHLER
ENGINE HP.................18
COOLING.................AIR
FUEL......................G
SPEEDS....................6
TRANSMISSION...........GEAR
STEERING............STANDARD
STANDARD DECK........... 44"
MSRP................. $2,499

RETAIL PRICING

YEAR	HIGH	LOW
1994	$867	$651
1995	$951	$713

25773

YEARS MFRD........ 1994-1994
ENGINE..................B&S
ENGINE HP.................18
COOLING.................AIR
FUEL......................G
SPEEDS..............VARIABLE
TRANSMISSION..........HYDRO
STEERING............STANDARD
STANDARD DECK........... 44"
MSRP................. $2,899

RETAIL PRICING

YEAR	HIGH	LOW
1994	$932	$699

25774

YEARS MFRD........ 1994-1994
ENGINE...............KOHLER
ENGINE HP.................22
COOLING.................AIR
FUEL......................G
SPEEDS....................6
TRANSMISSION...........GEAR
STEERING............STANDARD
STANDARD DECK........... 50"
MSRP................. $2,999

RETAIL PRICING

YEAR	HIGH	LOW
1994	$963	$722

25848

YEARS MFRD........ 1997-1997
ENGINE..................B&S
ENGINE HP.............. 15.5
COOLING.................AIR
FUEL......................G
SPEEDS..............VARIABLE
TRANSMISSION..........HYDRO

CRAFTSMAN

STEERING............STANDARD
STANDARD DECK........... 42"
MSRP................ $1,349

RETAIL PRICING

YEAR	HIGH	LOW
1997	$483	$362

25849

YEARS MFRD........ 1992-1992
ENGINE................ B&S
ENGINE HP................. 18
FUEL..................... G
SPEEDS.................... 5
TRANSMISSION........... GEAR
STEERING............STANDARD
STANDARD DECK........... 38"
WEIGHT.............. 552 LBS.
MSRP................ $1,699

RETAIL PRICING

YEAR	HIGH	LOW
1992	$500	$375

25850

YEARS MFRD........ 1997-1997
ENGINE................ B&S
ENGINE HP............... 13.5
COOLING.................. AIR
FUEL..................... G
SPEEDS.................... 6
TRANSMISSION........... GEAR
STEERING............STANDARD
STANDARD DECK........... 42"
MSRP.................. $899

RETAIL PRICING

YEAR	HIGH	LOW
1997	$322	$242

25851

YEARS MFRD........ 1997-1997
ENGINE................ B&S
ENGINE HP............... 14.5
COOLING.................. AIR
FUEL..................... G
SPEEDS.................... 6
TRANSMISSION........... GEAR
STEERING............STANDARD
STANDARD DECK........... 42"
MSRP................ $1,099

RETAIL PRICING

YEAR	HIGH	LOW
1997	$394	$296

25853

YEARS MFRD........ 1997-1997
ENGINE................ B&S
ENGINE HP............... 15.5
COOLING.................. AIR
FUEL..................... G
SPEEDS.............. VARIABLE
TRANSMISSION.......... HYDRO
STEERING............STANDARD
STANDARD DECK........... 42"
MSRP................ $1,499

RETAIL PRICING

YEAR	HIGH	LOW
1997	$538	$403

25855

YEARS MFRD........ 1997-1997
ENGINE............... KOHLER
ENGINE HP................. 15
COOLING.................. AIR
FUEL..................... G
SPEEDS.............. VARIABLE
TRANSMISSION.......... HYDRO
STEERING............STANDARD
STANDARD DECK........... 42"
MSRP................ $1,599

RETAIL PRICING

YEAR	HIGH	LOW
1997	$572	$429

25857

YEARS MFRD........ 1997-1997
ENGINE................ B&S
ENGINE HP................. 19
COOLING.................. AIR
FUEL..................... G
SPEEDS.............. VARIABLE
TRANSMISSION.......... HYDRO
STEERING............STANDARD
STANDARD DECK........... 42"
MSRP................ $1,699

RETAIL PRICING

YEAR	HIGH	LOW
1997	$608	$456

25859

YEARS MFRD........ 1997-1997
ENGINE............... KOHLER
ENGINE HP................. 16
COOLING.................. AIR
FUEL..................... G
SPEEDS.............. VARIABLE
TRANSMISSION.......... HYDRO
STEERING............STANDARD
STANDARD DECK........... 46"
MSRP................ $1,899

RETAIL PRICING

YEAR	HIGH	LOW
1997	$680	$510

25869

YEARS MFRD........ 1997-1997
ENGINE............... KOHLER
ENGINE HP................. 18
COOLING.................. AIR
FUEL..................... G
SPEEDS.............. VARIABLE
TRANSMISSION.......... HYDRO
STEERING............STANDARD
STANDARD DECK........... 46"
MSRP................ $1,999

RETAIL PRICING

YEAR	HIGH	LOW
1997	$717	$538

25886

YEARS MFRD........ 1997-1997
ENGINE............... KOHLER
ENGINE HP............... 18.5
COOLING.................. AIR
FUEL..................... G
SPEEDS.................... 6
TRANSMISSION........... GEAR
STEERING............STANDARD
STANDARD DECK........... 46"
MSRP................ $2,399

RETAIL PRICING

YEAR	HIGH	LOW
1997	$860	$645

25887

YEARS MFRD........ 1997-1997
ENGINE............... KOHLER
ENGINE HP............... 18.5
COOLING.................. AIR
FUEL..................... G
SPEEDS.............. VARIABLE
TRANSMISSION.......... HYDRO
STEERING............STANDARD
STANDARD DECK........... 46"
MSRP................ $2,699

RETAIL PRICING

YEAR	HIGH	LOW
1997	$968	$726

25889

YEARS MFRD........ 1997-1997
ENGINE............... KOHLER
ENGINE HP............... 20.5
COOLING.................. AIR
FUEL..................... G
SPEEDS.............. VARIABLE
TRANSMISSION.......... HYDRO
STEERING............STANDARD
STANDARD DECK........... 46"
MSRP................ $2,899

RETAIL PRICING

YEAR	HIGH	LOW
1997	$1,039	$779

25891

YEARS MFRD........ 1997-1997
ENGINE............... KOHLER
ENGINE HP............... 22.5
COOLING.................. AIR
FUEL..................... G
SPEEDS.............. VARIABLE
TRANSMISSION.......... HYDRO
STEERING............STANDARD
STANDARD DECK........... 50"
MSRP................ $3,799

RETAIL PRICING

YEAR	HIGH	LOW
1997	$1,362	$1,022

25892

YEARS MFRD........ 1997-1997
ENGINE............... KOHLER
ENGINE HP................. 25
COOLING.................. AIR
FUEL..................... G
SPEEDS.............. VARIABLE
TRANSMISSION.......... HYDRO
STEERING............STANDARD
STANDARD DECK........... 50"
MSRP................ $3,999

RETAIL PRICING

YEAR	HIGH	LOW
1997	$1,433	$1,074

25927

YEARS MFRD........ 1991-1991
ENGINE................ B&S
ENGINE HP................. 12
FUEL..................... G
TRANSMISSION........... GEAR
STEERING............STANDARD
STANDARD DECK........... 38"
WEIGHT.............. 492 LBS.
MSRP.................. $949

RETAIL PRICING

YEAR	HIGH	LOW
1991	$269	$202

25954

YEARS MFRD........ 1997-1997
ENGINE............... KOHLER
ENGINE HP............... 15.5
COOLING.................. AIR
FUEL..................... G
TRANSMISSION........... GEAR
STEERING............STANDARD
STANDARD DECK........... 42"
MSRP................ $1,399

RETAIL PRICING

YEAR	HIGH	LOW
1997	$502	$376

25955

YEARS MFRD........ 1997-1997
ENGINE............... KOHLER
ENGINE HP............... 15.5
COOLING.................. AIR
FUEL..................... G
SPEEDS.............. VARIABLE
TRANSMISSION.......... HYDRO
STEERING............STANDARD
STANDARD DECK........... 42"
MSRP................ $1,579

RETAIL PRICING

YEAR	HIGH	LOW
1997	$567	$425

26522

YEARS MFRD........ 1990-1990
ENGINE................ B&S
ENGINE HP................. 12
FUEL..................... G
SPEEDS.................... 5
STEERING............STANDARD
STANDARD DECK........... 36"
WEIGHT.............. 440 LBS.
MSRP.................. $997

RETAIL PRICING

YEAR	HIGH	LOW
1990	$266	$200

26786

YEARS MFRD 2007-2009
ENGINE .... B&S
CYLINDERS 1
CID 502CC
ENGINE HP 21
COOLING .... AIR
FUEL .... G
SPEEDS .... VARIABLE
TRANSMISSION .... HYDRO
STEERING .... ZERO
BLADE CLUTCH .... ELECTRIC
STANDARD DECK .... 42"
MSRP $2,999

RETAIL PRICING

YEAR	HIGH	LOW
2008	$1,721	$1,291
2009	$1,769	$1,327

27011

YEARS MFRD 1998-2001
ENGINE .... CRAFTSMAN
ENGINE HP 10
FUEL .... G
SPEEDS 5
TRANSMISSION .... GEAR
STEERING .... STANDARD
STANDARD DECK .... 30"
MSRP $979

RETAIL PRICING

YEAR	HIGH	LOW
1998	$334	$251
1999	$361	$271
2000	$378	$284
2001	$430	$323

27021

YEARS MFRD 1998-2000
ENGINE .... CRAFTSMAN
ENGINE HP 13.5
COOLING .... AIR
FUEL .... G
SPEEDS 5
TRANSMISSION .... GEAR
STEERING .... STANDARD
STANDARD DECK .... 30"
MSRP $1,099

RETAIL PRICING

YEAR	HIGH	LOW
1998	$361	$271
1999	$443	$332
2000	$463	$347

27022

YEARS MFRD 2003-2003
ENGINE .... B&S
ENGINE HP 10
FUEL .... G
SPEEDS .... VARIABLE
TRANSMISSION .... HYDRO
STEERING .... STANDARD
STANDARD DECK .... 27"
MSRP $1,399

RETAIL PRICING

YEAR	HIGH	LOW
2003	$685	$514

27025

YEARS MFRD 2002-2002
ENGINE .... B&S
ENGINE HP 6.75
FUEL .... G
SPEEDS .... VARIABLE
TRANSMISSION .... HYDRO
STEERING .... STANDARD
STANDARD DECK .... 24"
MSRP $999

RETAIL PRICING

YEAR	HIGH	LOW
2002	$451	$338

27027

YEARS MFRD 2002-2002
ENGINE .... B&S
ENGINE HP 13.5
FUEL .... G
SPEEDS .... VARIABLE
TRANSMISSION .... HYDRO
STEERING .... STANDARD
STANDARD DECK .... 30"
MSRP $1,199

RETAIL PRICING

YEAR	HIGH	LOW
2002	$542	$406

27028

YEARS MFRD 2003-2003
ENGINE .... B&S
ENGINE HP 13.5
FUEL .... G
SPEEDS .... VARIABLE
TRANSMISSION .... HYDRO
STEERING .... STANDARD
STANDARD DECK .... 30"
MSRP $1,399

RETAIL PRICING

YEAR	HIGH	LOW
2003	$685	$514

27030

YEARS MFRD 2005-2006
ENGINE .... B&S
ENGINE HP 13.5
COOLING .... AIR
FUEL .... G
SPEEDS .... VARIABLE
TRANSMISSION .... HYDRO
STEERING .... STANDARD
STANDARD DECK .... 30"
MSRP $1,799

RETAIL PRICING

YEAR	HIGH	LOW
2005	$996	$747

27031

YEARS MFRD 1998-1998
ENGINE .... CRAFTSMAN
ENGINE HP 12.5
COOLING .... AIR
FUEL .... G
SPEEDS 5
TRANSMISSION .... GEAR
STEERING .... STANDARD
STANDARD DECK .... 38"
MSRP $859

RETAIL PRICING

YEAR	HIGH	LOW
1998	$324	$243

27038

YEARS MFRD 2017-2019
ENGINE .... KOHLER
CYLINDERS 2
CID 725CC
ENGINE HP 20
COOLING .... AIR
FUEL .... G
SPEEDS .... VARIABLE
TRANSMISSION .... HYDRO
STEERING .... STANDARD
BLADE CLUTCH .... ELECTRIC
STANDARD DECK .... 42"

RETAIL PRICING

YEAR	HIGH	LOW
2017	$944	$708
2018	$1,039	$779
2019	$1,112	$834

27039

YEARS MFRD 2017-2017
ENGINE .... KOHLER
CYLINDERS 2
CID 725CC
ENGINE HP 24
COOLING .... AIR
FUEL .... G
SPEEDS .... VARIABLE
TRANSMISSION .... HYDRO
STEERING .... STANDARD
BLADE CLUTCH .... ELECTRIC
STANDARD DECK .... 46"
MSRP $2,699

RETAIL PRICING

YEAR	HIGH	LOW
2017	$1,759	$1,320

27040

YEARS MFRD 2018-2018
ENGINE .... CRAFTSMAN
CYLINDERS 2
CID 679CC
COOLING .... AIR
FUEL .... G
TRANSMISSION .... HYDRO
STEERING .... STANDARD
BLADE CLUTCH .... MANUAL
STANDARD DECK .... 423"
WEIGHT .... 650 LBS.

27041

YEARS MFRD 1998-1998
ENGINE .... B&S
ENGINE HP 13.5
FUEL .... G
SPEEDS 6
TRANSMISSION .... GEAR
STEERING .... STANDARD
STANDARD DECK .... 42"
MSRP $899

RETAIL PRICING

YEAR	HIGH	LOW
1998	$338	$254

27042

YEARS MFRD 2017-2019
ENGINE .... KOHLER
CYLINDERS 2
CID 725CC
ENGINE HP 24
COOLING .... AIR
FUEL .... G
SPEEDS .... VARIABLE
TRANSMISSION .... HYDRO
STEERING .... STANDARD
BLADE CLUTCH .... ELECTRIC
STANDARD DECK .... 46"

RETAIL PRICING

YEAR	HIGH	LOW
2017	$1,347	$1,010
2018	$1,453	$1,089
2019	$1,583	$1,187

27043

YEARS MFRD 1999-1999
ENGINE .... B&S
ENGINE HP 13.5
COOLING .... AIR
FUEL .... G
SPEEDS 5
TRANSMISSION .... GEAR
STEERING .... STANDARD
STANDARD DECK .... 38"
MSRP $949

RETAIL PRICING

YEAR	HIGH	LOW
1999	$382	$286

27044

YEARS MFRD 2017-2019
ENGINE .... KOHLER
CYLINDERS 2
CID 747CC
ENGINE HP 26
COOLING .... AIR
FUEL .... G
SPEEDS .... VARIABLE
TRANSMISSION .... HYDRO
STEERING .... STANDARD
BLADE CLUTCH .... ELECTRIC
STANDARD DECK .... 54"

RETAIL PRICING

YEAR	HIGH	LOW
2017	$1,545	$1,159
2018	$1,686	$1,265
2019	$1,838	$1,379

CRAFTSMAN

27045

YEARS MFRD........2000-2000
ENGINE..................B&S
ENGINE HP.............. 13.5
COOLING...................AIR
FUEL..........................G
SPEEDS.........................6
TRANSMISSION...........GEAR
STEERING............STANDARD
STANDARD DECK........... 38"
MSRP.....................$949

RETAIL PRICING

YEAR	HIGH	LOW
2000	$400	$300

27046

YEARS MFRD........2018-2018
ENGINE................KOHLER
CYLINDERS..................2
CID....................747CC
ENGINE HP.................26
COOLING...................AIR
FUEL..........................G
TRANSMISSION..........HYDRO
STEERING............STANDARD
BLADE CLUTCH........ELECTRIC
STANDARD DECK........... 50"
WEIGHT..............740 LBS.

27047

YEARS MFRD........2017-2017
ENGINE................KOHLER
CYLINDERS..................2
CID....................747CC
ENGINE HP.................26
COOLING...................AIR
FUEL..........................G
SPEEDS..............VARIABLE
TRANSMISSION..........HYDRO
STEERING............STANDARD
BLADE CLUTCH........ELECTRIC
STANDARD DECK........... 54"
WEIGHT..............750 LBS.
MSRP...................$3,999

RETAIL PRICING

YEAR	HIGH	LOW
2017	$2,767	$2,076

27048

YEARS MFRD........2017-2017
ENGINE................KOHLER
CYLINDERS..................2
CID....................747CC
ENGINE HP.................26
COOLING...................AIR
FUEL..........................G
SPEEDS..............VARIABLE
TRANSMISSION..........HYDRO
STEERING............STANDARD
BLADE CLUTCH........ELECTRIC
STANDARD DECK........... 50"
MSRP...................$3,499

RETAIL PRICING

YEAR	HIGH	LOW
2017	$2,445	$1,834

27049

YEARS MFRD........2017-2017
ENGINE................KOHLER
CYLINDERS..................2
CID....................725CC
ENGINE HP.................24
COOLING...................AIR
FUEL..........................G
SPEEDS..............VARIABLE
TRANSMISSION..........HYDRO
STEERING............STANDARD
BLADE CLUTCH........ELECTRIC
STANDARD DECK........... 46"
MSRP...................$2,299

RETAIL PRICING

YEAR	HIGH	LOW
2017	$2,272	$1,704

27051

YEARS MFRD........1998-2000
ENGINE..................B&S
ENGINE HP.............. 14.5
COOLING...................AIR
FUEL..........................G
SPEEDS.........................6
TRANSMISSION...........GEAR
STEERING............STANDARD
STANDARD DECK........... 42"
MSRP.....................$999

RETAIL PRICING

YEAR	HIGH	LOW
1998	$376	$282
1999	$402	$301
2000	$420	$315

27052

YEARS MFRD........2017-2017
ENGINE................KOHLER
CID....................725CC
ENGINE HP.................25
COOLING...................AIR
FUEL..........................G
SPEEDS..............VARIABLE
TRANSMISSION..........HYDRO
STEERING...................ZERO
BLADE CLUTCH........ELECTRIC
STANDARD DECK........... 54"
WEIGHT..............850 LBS.
MSRP...................$4,299

RETAIL PRICING

YEAR	HIGH	LOW
2017	$2,716	$2,037

27053

YEARS MFRD........2000-2000
ENGINE..................B&S
ENGINE HP.............. 14.5
COOLING...................AIR
FUEL..........................G
SPEEDS.........................6
TRANSMISSION...........GEAR
STEERING............STANDARD
STANDARD DECK........... 42"
MSRP.....................$999

RETAIL PRICING

YEAR	HIGH	LOW
2000	$420	$315

27054

YEARS MFRD........2000-2000
ENGINE................KOHLER
ENGINE HP.................23
COOLING...................AIR
FUEL..........................G
SPEEDS..............VARIABLE
TRANSMISSION..........HYDRO
STEERING............STANDARD
STANDARD DECK........... 50"
MSRP...................$3,099

RETAIL PRICING

YEAR	HIGH	LOW
2000	$1,305	$979

27055

YEARS MFRD........2017-2018
ENGINE................KOHLER
CYLINDERS..................2
CID....................747CC
ENGINE HP.................26
COOLING...................AIR
FUEL..........................G
SPEEDS..............VARIABLE
TRANSMISSION..........HYDRO
STEERING............STANDARD
BLADE CLUTCH........ELECTRIC
STANDARD DECK........... 54"
WEIGHT..............750 LBS.
MSRP...................$3,199

RETAIL PRICING

YEAR	HIGH	LOW
2017	$2,238	$1,679

27061

YEARS MFRD........1998-1998
ENGINE..................B&S
ENGINE HP.............. 15.5
COOLING...................AIR
FUEL..........................G
SPEEDS.........................6
TRANSMISSION...........GEAR
STEERING............STANDARD
STANDARD DECK........... 42"
MSRP...................$1,199

RETAIL PRICING

YEAR	HIGH	LOW
1998	$452	$339

27062

YEARS MFRD........1998-1998
ENGINE..................B&S
ENGINE HP.............. 15.5
COOLING...................AIR
FUEL..........................G
SPEEDS..............VARIABLE
TRANSMISSION..........HYDRO
STEERING............STANDARD
STANDARD DECK........... 42"
MSRP...................$1,349

RETAIL PRICING

YEAR	HIGH	LOW
1998	$509	$382

27063

YEARS MFRD........1998-1998
ENGINE..................B&S
ENGINE HP.................16
COOLING...................AIR
FUEL..........................G
SPEEDS.........................6
TRANSMISSION...........GEAR
STEERING............STANDARD
STANDARD DECK........... 42"
MSRP...................$1,299

RETAIL PRICING

YEAR	HIGH	LOW
1998	$489	$367

27064

YEARS MFRD........1998-1998
ENGINE..................B&S
ENGINE HP.................16
COOLING...................AIR
FUEL..........................G
SPEEDS..............VARIABLE
TRANSMISSION..........HYDRO
STEERING............STANDARD
STANDARD DECK........... 42"
MSRP...................$1,479

RETAIL PRICING

YEAR	HIGH	LOW
1998	$556	$417

27065

YEARS MFRD........1999-2000
ENGINE..................B&S
ENGINE HP.............. 15.5
COOLING...................AIR
FUEL..........................G
SPEEDS.........................6
TRANSMISSION...........GEAR
STEERING............STANDARD
STANDARD DECK........... 42"
MSRP...................$1,199

RETAIL PRICING

YEAR	HIGH	LOW
1999	$481	$361
2000	$504	$378

27066

YEARS MFRD........1999-2000
ENGINE..................B&S
ENGINE HP.............. 15.5
COOLING...................AIR
FUEL..........................G
SPEEDS..............VARIABLE
TRANSMISSION..........HYDRO
STEERING............STANDARD
STANDARD DECK........... 42"
MSRP...................$1,399

RETAIL PRICING

YEAR	HIGH	LOW
1999	$561	$421
2000	$588	$441

27067
YEARS MFRD........ 2000-2000
ENGINE.................. B&S
ENGINE HP................ 16
COOLING.................. AIR
FUEL..................... G
SPEEDS................... 6
TRANSMISSION........... GEAR
STEERING............ STANDARD
STANDARD DECK........... 42"
MSRP.................. $1,249

RETAIL PRICING

YEAR	HIGH	LOW
2000	$526	$395

27071
YEARS MFRD........ 1998-1999
ENGINE.................. B&S
ENGINE HP................ 17
COOLING.................. AIR
FUEL..................... G
SPEEDS................... 6
TRANSMISSION........... GEAR
STEERING............ STANDARD
STANDARD DECK........... 42"
MSRP.................. $1,349

RETAIL PRICING

YEAR	HIGH	LOW
1998	$526	$395
1999	$542	$407

27072
YEARS MFRD........ 1998-1999
ENGINE.................. B&S
ENGINE HP................ 17
COOLING.................. AIR
FUEL..................... G
SPEEDS.............. VARIABLE
TRANSMISSION.......... HYDRO
STEERING............ STANDARD
STANDARD DECK........... 42"
MSRP.................. $1,549

RETAIL PRICING

YEAR	HIGH	LOW
1998	$583	$437
1999	$622	$467

27073
YEARS MFRD........ 2000-2000
ENGINE.................. B&S
ENGINE HP................ 17
COOLING.................. AIR
FUEL..................... G
SPEEDS................... 6
TRANSMISSION........... GEAR
STEERING............ STANDARD
STANDARD DECK........... 42"
MSRP.................. $1,399

RETAIL PRICING

YEAR	HIGH	LOW
2000	$588	$441

27074
YEARS MFRD........ 2000-2000
ENGINE.................. B&S
ENGINE HP................ 17
COOLING.................. AIR
FUEL..................... G
SPEEDS.............. VARIABLE
TRANSMISSION.......... HYDRO
STEERING............ STANDARD
STANDARD DECK........... 42"
MSRP.................. $1,599

RETAIL PRICING

YEAR	HIGH	LOW
2000	$675	$506

27075
YEARS MFRD........ 2000-2000
ENGINE.................. B&S
ENGINE HP.............. 18.5
COOLING.................. AIR
FUEL..................... G
SPEEDS................... 6
TRANSMISSION........... GEAR
STEERING............ STANDARD
STANDARD DECK........... 42"
MSRP.................. $1,399

RETAIL PRICING

YEAR	HIGH	LOW
2000	$588	$441

27077
YEARS MFRD........ 1999-2000
ENGINE.................. B&S
ENGINE HP................ 19
COOLING.................. AIR
FUEL..................... G
SPEEDS................... 6
TRANSMISSION........... GEAR
STEERING............ STANDARD
STANDARD DECK........... 42"
MSRP.................. $1,449

RETAIL PRICING

YEAR	HIGH	LOW
1999	$582	$437
2000	$609	$457

27078
YEARS MFRD........ 1999-2000
ENGINE.................. B&S
ENGINE HP................ 19
COOLING.................. AIR
FUEL..................... G
SPEEDS.............. VARIABLE
TRANSMISSION.......... HYDRO
STEERING............ STANDARD
STANDARD DECK........... 42"
MSRP.................. $1,649

RETAIL PRICING

YEAR	HIGH	LOW
1999	$663	$497
2000	$694	$521

27081
YEARS MFRD........ 1998-1999
ENGINE.................. B&S
ENGINE HP.............. 19.5
COOLING.................. AIR
FUEL..................... G
SPEEDS................... 6
TRANSMISSION........... GEAR
STEERING............ STANDARD
STANDARD DECK........... 42"
MSRP.................. $1,549

RETAIL PRICING

YEAR	HIGH	LOW
1998	$526	$395
1999	$622	$467

27082
YEARS MFRD........ 1998-1999
ENGINE.................. B&S
ENGINE HP.............. 19.5
COOLING.................. AIR
FUEL..................... G
SPEEDS.............. VARIABLE
TRANSMISSION.......... HYDRO
STEERING............ STANDARD
STANDARD DECK........... 42"
MSRP.................. $1,749

RETAIL PRICING

YEAR	HIGH	LOW
1998	$602	$452
1999	$703	$527

27083
YEARS MFRD........ 1999-2000
ENGINE.................. B&S
ENGINE HP................ 20
COOLING.................. AIR
FUEL..................... G
SPEEDS................... 6
TRANSMISSION........... GEAR
STEERING............ STANDARD
STANDARD DECK........... 46"
MSRP.................. $1,499

RETAIL PRICING

YEAR	HIGH	LOW
1999	$602	$452
2000	$632	$474

27084
YEARS MFRD........ 1999-2000
ENGINE.................. B&S
ENGINE HP................ 20
COOLING.................. AIR
FUEL..................... G
SPEEDS.............. VARIABLE
TRANSMISSION.......... HYDRO
STEERING............ STANDARD
STANDARD DECK........... 46"
MSRP.................. $1,699

RETAIL PRICING

YEAR	HIGH	LOW
1999	$682	$512
2000	$716	$537

27085
YEARS MFRD........ 1999-2000
ENGINE.................. B&S
ENGINE HP.............. 20.5
COOLING.................. AIR
FUEL..................... G
SPEEDS................... 6
TRANSMISSION........... GEAR
STEERING............ STANDARD
STANDARD DECK........... 42"
MSRP.................. $1,599

RETAIL PRICING

YEAR	HIGH	LOW
1999	$643	$482
2000	$675	$506

27086
YEARS MFRD........ 1999-2000
ENGINE.................. B&S
ENGINE HP.............. 20.5
COOLING.................. AIR
FUEL..................... G
SPEEDS.............. VARIABLE
TRANSMISSION.......... HYDRO
STEERING............ STANDARD
STANDARD DECK........... 42"
MSRP.................. $1,799

RETAIL PRICING

YEAR	HIGH	LOW
1999	$722	$542
2000	$758	$569

27091
YEARS MFRD........ 2000-2000
ENGINE.................. B&S
ENGINE HP.............. 19.5
COOLING.................. AIR
FUEL..................... G
SPEEDS................... 6
TRANSMISSION........... GEAR
STEERING............ STANDARD
STANDARD DECK........... 42"
MSRP.................. $1,549

RETAIL PRICING

YEAR	HIGH	LOW
2000	$652	$489

27092
YEARS MFRD........ 2000-2000
ENGINE.................. B&S
ENGINE HP.............. 19.5
COOLING.................. AIR
FUEL..................... G
SPEEDS.............. VARIABLE
TRANSMISSION.......... HYDRO
STEERING............ STANDARD
STANDARD DECK........... 42"
MSRP.................. $1,749

RETAIL PRICING

YEAR	HIGH	LOW
2000	$737	$553

CRAFTSMAN

27101

YEARS MFRD........1998-1999
ENGINE........KOHLER
ENGINE HP........15.5
COOLING........AIR
FUEL........G
SPEEDS........6
TRANSMISSION........GEAR
STEERING........STANDARD
STANDARD DECK........42"
MSRP........$1,399

RETAIL PRICING

YEAR	HIGH	LOW
1998	$526	$395
1999	$561	$421

27102

YEARS MFRD........1998-1999
ENGINE........KOHLER
ENGINE HP........15.5
FUEL........G
SPEEDS........VARIABLE
TRANSMISSION........HYDRO
STEERING........STANDARD
STANDARD DECK........42"
MSRP........$1,599

RETAIL PRICING

YEAR	HIGH	LOW
1998	$602	$452
1999	$643	$482

27103

YEARS MFRD........1998-1998
ENGINE........KOHLER
ENGINE HP........16
COOLING........AIR
FUEL........G
SPEEDS........6
TRANSMISSION........GEAR
STEERING........STANDARD
STANDARD DECK........42"
MSRP........$1,449

RETAIL PRICING

YEAR	HIGH	LOW
1998	$548	$411

27104

YEARS MFRD........1998-1998
ENGINE........KOHLER
ENGINE HP........16
COOLING........AIR
FUEL........G
SPEEDS........VARIABLE
TRANSMISSION........HYDRO
STEERING........STANDARD
STANDARD DECK........42"
MSRP........$1,649

RETAIL PRICING

YEAR	HIGH	LOW
1998	$621	$466

27105

YEARS MFRD........2000-2000
ENGINE........KOHLER
ENGINE HP........15.5
COOLING........AIR
FUEL........G
TRANSMISSION........GEAR
STEERING........STANDARD
STANDARD DECK........42"
MSRP........$1,399

RETAIL PRICING

YEAR	HIGH	LOW
2000	$588	$441

27106

YEARS MFRD........2000-2000
ENGINE........KOHLER
ENGINE HP........15.5
COOLING........AIR
FUEL........G
TRANSMISSION........HYDRO
STEERING........STANDARD
STANDARD DECK........42"
MSRP........$1,599

RETAIL PRICING

YEAR	HIGH	LOW
2000	$675	$506

27107

YEARS MFRD........1999-1999
ENGINE........KOHLER
ENGINE HP........16
COOLING........AIR
FUEL........G
SPEEDS........6
TRANSMISSION........GEAR
STEERING........STANDARD
STANDARD DECK........42"
MSRP........$1,499

RETAIL PRICING

YEAR	HIGH	LOW
1999	$602	$452

27108

YEARS MFRD........1999-2000
ENGINE........KOHLER
ENGINE HP........16
COOLING........AIR
FUEL........G
SPEEDS........VARIABLE
TRANSMISSION........HYDRO
STEERING........STANDARD
STANDARD DECK........42"
MSRP........$1,699

RETAIL PRICING

YEAR	HIGH	LOW
1999	$682	$512
2000	$716	$537

27109

YEARS MFRD........1999-2000
ENGINE........KOHLER
ENGINE HP........16.5
COOLING........AIR
FUEL........G
SPEEDS........6
TRANSMISSION........GEAR
STEERING........STANDARD
STANDARD DECK........42"
MSRP........$1,449

RETAIL PRICING

YEAR	HIGH	LOW
1999	$582	$437
2000	$609	$457

27110

YEARS MFRD........1999-2000
ENGINE........KOHLER
ENGINE HP........16.5
COOLING........AIR
FUEL........G
SPEEDS........VARIABLE
TRANSMISSION........HYDRO
STEERING........STANDARD
STANDARD DECK........42"
MSRP........$1,649

RETAIL PRICING

YEAR	HIGH	LOW
1999	$663	$497
2000	$694	$521

27111

YEARS MFRD........1998-1998
ENGINE........KOHLER
ENGINE HP........16.5
FUEL........G
SPEEDS........6
TRANSMISSION........GEAR
STEERING........STANDARD
STANDARD DECK........42"
MSRP........$1,499

RETAIL PRICING

YEAR	HIGH	LOW
1998	$566	$425

27112

YEARS MFRD........1998-1998
ENGINE........KOHLER
ENGINE HP........16.5
COOLING........AIR
FUEL........G
SPEEDS........VARIABLE
TRANSMISSION........HYDRO
STEERING........STANDARD
STANDARD DECK........42"
MSRP........$1,699

RETAIL PRICING

YEAR	HIGH	LOW
1998	$640	$480

27113

YEARS MFRD........2000-2000
ENGINE........KOHLER
ENGINE HP........16.5
COOLING........AIR
FUEL........G
SPEEDS........VARIABLE
TRANSMISSION........HYDRO
STEERING........STANDARD
STANDARD DECK........42"
MSRP........$1,549

RETAIL PRICING

YEAR	HIGH	LOW
2000	$652	$489

27153

YEARS MFRD........2000-2000
ENGINE........B&S
ENGINE HP........14.5
COOLING........AIR
FUEL........G
SPEEDS........6
TRANSMISSION........GEAR
STEERING........STANDARD
STANDARD DECK........42"
MSRP........$1,049

RETAIL PRICING

YEAR	HIGH	LOW
2000	$443	$332

27155

YEARS MFRD........2002-2002
ENGINE........B&S
ENGINE HP........15.5
FUEL........G
SPEEDS........6
TRANSMISSION........GEAR
STEERING........STANDARD
STANDARD DECK........42"
MSRP........$1,049

RETAIL PRICING

YEAR	HIGH	LOW
2002	$474	$356

27163

YEARS MFRD........2000-2000
ENGINE........B&S
ENGINE HP........16.5
COOLING........AIR
FUEL........G
SPEEDS........VARIABLE
TRANSMISSION........HYDRO
STEERING........STANDARD
STANDARD DECK........42"
MSRP........$1,449

RETAIL PRICING

YEAR	HIGH	LOW
2000	$609	$457

27175

YEARS MFRD........2002-2002
ENGINE........B&S
ENGINE HP........18
FUEL........G
SPEEDS........6
TRANSMISSION........GEAR
STEERING........STANDARD
STANDARD DECK........42"
MSRP........$1,399

RETAIL PRICING

YEAR	HIGH	LOW
2002	$632	$474

27176

YEARS MFRD . . . 2002-2002
ENGINE . . . B&S
ENGINE HP . . . 18
FUEL . . . G
SPEEDS . . . VARIABLE
TRANSMISSION . . . HYDRO
STEERING . . . STANDARD
STANDARD DECK . . . 42"
MSRP . . . $1,599

RETAIL PRICING

YEAR	HIGH	LOW
2002	$721	$541

27183

YEARS MFRD . . . 2000-2000
ENGINE . . . B&S
ENGINE HP . . . 21
COOLING . . . AIR
FUEL . . . G
SPEEDS . . . 6
TRANSMISSION . . . GEAR
STEERING . . . STANDARD
STANDARD DECK . . . 42"
MSRP . . . $1,599

RETAIL PRICING

YEAR	HIGH	LOW
2000	$675	$506

27184

YEARS MFRD . . . 2000-2000
ENGINE . . . B&S
ENGINE HP . . . 21
COOLING . . . AIR
FUEL . . . G
SPEEDS . . . VARIABLE
TRANSMISSION . . . HYDRO
STEERING . . . STANDARD
STANDARD DECK . . . 42"
MSRP . . . $1,799

RETAIL PRICING

YEAR	HIGH	LOW
2000	$758	$569

27191

YEARS MFRD . . . 2002-2002
ENGINE . . . B&S
ENGINE HP . . . 20
FUEL . . . G
SPEEDS . . . 6
TRANSMISSION . . . GEAR
STEERING . . . STANDARD
STANDARD DECK . . . 42"
MSRP . . . $1,549

RETAIL PRICING

YEAR	HIGH	LOW
2002	$701	$526

27192

YEARS MFRD . . . 2002-2002
ENGINE . . . B&S
ENGINE HP . . . 20
FUEL . . . G
SPEEDS . . . VARIABLE
TRANSMISSION . . . HYDRO
STEERING . . . STANDARD
STANDARD DECK . . . 42"
MSRP . . . $1,749

RETAIL PRICING

YEAR	HIGH	LOW
2002	$789	$592

27201

YEARS MFRD . . . 1998-1998
ENGINE . . . KOHLER
ENGINE HP . . . 16.5
COOLING . . . AIR
FUEL . . . G
SPEEDS . . . 6
TRANSMISSION . . . GEAR
STEERING . . . STANDARD
STANDARD DECK . . . 46"
MSRP . . . $1,699

RETAIL PRICING

YEAR	HIGH	LOW
1998	$640	$480

27202

YEARS MFRD . . . 1998-1998
ENGINE . . . KOHLER
ENGINE HP . . . 16.5
COOLING . . . AIR
FUEL . . . G
SPEEDS . . . VARIABLE
TRANSMISSION . . . HYDRO
STEERING . . . STANDARD
STANDARD DECK . . . 46"
MSRP . . . $1,899

RETAIL PRICING

YEAR	HIGH	LOW
1998	$715	$537

27203

YEARS MFRD . . . 1999-2000
ENGINE . . . B&S
ENGINE HP . . . 18
COOLING . . . AIR
FUEL . . . G
SPEEDS . . . 6
TRANSMISSION . . . GEAR
STEERING . . . STANDARD
STANDARD DECK . . . 46"
MSRP . . . $1,899

RETAIL PRICING

YEAR	HIGH	LOW
1999	$762	$571
2000	$798	$599

27204

YEARS MFRD . . . 1999-2000
ENGINE . . . B&S
ENGINE HP . . . 18
COOLING . . . AIR
FUEL . . . G
SPEEDS . . . VARIABLE
TRANSMISSION . . . HYDRO
STEERING . . . STANDARD
STANDARD DECK . . . 46"
MSRP . . . $2,099

RETAIL PRICING

YEAR	HIGH	LOW
1999	$843	$632
2000	$883	$662

27205

YEARS MFRD . . . 2000-2002
ENGINE . . . KOHLER
ENGINE HP . . . 16
COOLING . . . AIR
FUEL . . . G
SPEEDS . . . 6
TRANSMISSION . . . GEAR
STEERING . . . STANDARD
STANDARD DECK . . . 42"
MSRP . . . $1,449

RETAIL PRICING

YEAR	HIGH	LOW
2000	$609	$457
2002	$655	$491

27206

YEARS MFRD . . . 2000-2000
ENGINE . . . KOHLER
ENGINE HP . . . 16
COOLING . . . AIR
FUEL . . . G
SPEEDS . . . VARIABLE
TRANSMISSION . . . HYDRO
STEERING . . . STANDARD
STANDARD DECK . . . 42"
MSRP . . . $1,649

RETAIL PRICING

YEAR	HIGH	LOW
2000	$694	$521

27207

YEARS MFRD . . . 2002-2002
ENGINE . . . KOHLER
ENGINE HP . . . 16
FUEL . . . G
SPEEDS . . . 6
TRANSMISSION . . . GEAR
STEERING . . . STANDARD
STANDARD DECK . . . 42"
MSRP . . . $1,549

RETAIL PRICING

YEAR	HIGH	LOW
2002	$701	$526

27212

YEARS MFRD . . . 1998-1998
ENGINE . . . KOHLER
ENGINE HP . . . 18.5
COOLING . . . AIR
FUEL . . . G
SPEEDS . . . VARIABLE
TRANSMISSION . . . HYDRO
STEERING . . . STANDARD
STANDARD DECK . . . 46"
MSRP . . . $2,599

RETAIL PRICING

YEAR	HIGH	LOW
1998	$979	$734

27213

YEARS MFRD . . . 1999-2000
ENGINE . . . B&S
ENGINE HP . . . 20
COOLING . . . AIR
FUEL . . . G
SPEEDS . . . 6
TRANSMISSION . . . GEAR
STEERING . . . STANDARD
STANDARD DECK . . . 46"
MSRP . . . $1,999

RETAIL PRICING

YEAR	HIGH	LOW
1999	$803	$602
2000	$842	$631

27214

YEARS MFRD . . . 1999-2000
ENGINE . . . B&S
ENGINE HP . . . 20
COOLING . . . AIR
FUEL . . . G
SPEEDS . . . VARIABLE
TRANSMISSION . . . HYDRO
STEERING . . . STANDARD
STANDARD DECK . . . 46"
MSRP . . . $2,199

RETAIL PRICING

YEAR	HIGH	LOW
1999	$883	$662
2000	$925	$694

27220

YEARS MFRD . . . 2000-2000
ENGINE . . . B&S
ENGINE HP . . . 25
COOLING . . . AIR
FUEL . . . G
SPEEDS . . . VARIABLE
TRANSMISSION . . . HYDRO
STEERING . . . STANDARD
STANDARD DECK . . . 46"
MSRP . . . $2,499

RETAIL PRICING

YEAR	HIGH	LOW
2000	$1,053	$789

27222

YEARS MFRD . . . 2000-2000
ENGINE . . . KOHLER
ENGINE HP . . . 17.5
COOLING . . . AIR
FUEL . . . G
SPEEDS . . . VARIABLE

TRANSMISSION .... HYDRO
STEERING............ STANDARD
STANDARD DECK .... 42"
MSRP................. $1,999

RETAIL PRICING

YEAR	HIGH	LOW
2000	$842	$631

27223

YEARS MFRD 2000-2000
ENGINE .... KOHLER
ENGINE HP 20
COOLING .... AIR
FUEL .... G
SPEEDS 6
TRANSMISSION .... GEAR
STEERING............ STANDARD
STANDARD DECK .... 42"
MSRP................. $2,299

RETAIL PRICING

YEAR	HIGH	LOW
2000	$968	$726

27224

YEARS MFRD 2000-2002
ENGINE .... KOHLER
ENGINE HP 20
COOLING .... AIR
FUEL .... G
SPEEDS .... VARIABLE
TRANSMISSION .... HYDRO
STEERING............ STANDARD
STANDARD DECK .... 42"
MSRP................. $2,599

RETAIL PRICING

YEAR	HIGH	LOW
2000	$1,053	$789
2002	$1,173	$880

27226

YEARS MFRD 2000-2000
ENGINE .... B&S
ENGINE HP 25
COOLING .... AIR
FUEL .... G
SPEEDS .... VARIABLE
TRANSMISSION .... HYDRO
STEERING............ STANDARD
STANDARD DECK .... 42"
MSRP................. $2,599

RETAIL PRICING

YEAR	HIGH	LOW
2000	$1,093	$820

27235

YEARS MFRD 2003-2004
ENGINE .... B&S OHV
CYLINDERS.................. 1
CID 465CC
ENGINE HP 15.5
COOLING .... AIR
FUEL .... G
SPEEDS 6/1
TRANSMISSION .... GEAR
STEERING............ STANDARD
STANDARD DECK .... 42"
WEIGHT .... 480 LBS.
MSRP................. $1,099

RETAIL PRICING

YEAR	HIGH	LOW
2003	$538	$403
2004	$572	$429

27267

YEARS MFRD 2003-2004
ENGINE .... B&S IC OHV
CYLINDERS.................. 1
CID 502CC
ENGINE HP 17.5
COOLING .... AIR
FUEL .... G
SPEEDS 6/1
TRANSMISSION .... GEAR
STEERING............ STANDARD
STANDARD DECK .... 42"
WEIGHT .... 480 LBS.
MSRP................. $1,299

RETAIL PRICING

YEAR	HIGH	LOW
2003	$636	$477
2004	$677	$508

27268

YEARS MFRD 2003-2004
ENGINE .... B&S IC OHV
CYLINDERS.................. 1
CID 502CC
ENGINE HP 17.5
COOLING .... AIR
FUEL .... G
SPEEDS .... VARIABLE
TRANSMISSION .... HYDRO
STEERING............ STANDARD
STANDARD DECK .... 42"
WEIGHT .... 485 LBS.
MSRP................. $1,499

RETAIL PRICING

YEAR	HIGH	LOW
2003	$734	$551
2004	$781	$586

27272

YEARS MFRD 2005-2006
ENGINE .... KOHLER
ENGINE HP 20
COOLING .... AIR
FUEL .... G
SPEEDS .... VARIABLE
TRANSMISSION .... HYDRO
STEERING............ STANDARD
STANDARD DECK .... 44"
MSRP................. $2,999

RETAIL PRICING

YEAR	HIGH	LOW
2005	$1,659	$1,244

27275

YEARS MFRD 2003-2004
ENGINE .... B&S INTEK IC OHV
CYLINDERS.................. 1
CID 502CC
ENGINE HP 18
COOLING .... AIR
FUEL .... G
SPEEDS 6/1
TRANSMISSION .... GEAR
STEERING............ STANDARD
STANDARD DECK .... 42"
WEIGHT .... 500 LBS.
MSRP................. $1,399

RETAIL PRICING

YEAR	HIGH	LOW
2003	$685	$514
2004	$731	$548

27276

YEARS MFRD 2003-2004
ENGINE .... B&S INTEK IC OHV
CYLINDERS.................. 1
CID 502CC
ENGINE HP 18
COOLING .... AIR
FUEL .... G
SPEEDS .... VARIABLE
TRANSMISSION .... HYDRO
STEERING............ STANDARD
STANDARD DECK .... 42"
WEIGHT .... 503 LBS.
MSRP................. $1,599

RETAIL PRICING

YEAR	HIGH	LOW
2003	$783	$587
2004	$832	$624

27291

YEARS MFRD 2003-2003
ENGINE .... B&S
ENGINE HP 20
FUEL .... G
SPEEDS 6
TRANSMISSION .... GEAR
STEERING............ STANDARD
STANDARD DECK .... 42"
MSRP................. $1,599

RETAIL PRICING

YEAR	HIGH	LOW
2003	$783	$587

27292

YEARS MFRD 2003-2003
ENGINE .... B&S
ENGINE HP 20
FUEL .... G
SPEEDS .... VARIABLE
TRANSMISSION .... HYDRO
STEERING............ STANDARD
STANDARD DECK .... 42"
MSRP................. $1,799

RETAIL PRICING

YEAR	HIGH	LOW
2003	$880	$660

27295

YEARS MFRD 2000-2000
ENGINE .... KOHLER
ENGINE HP 20
COOLING .... AIR
FUEL .... G
SPEEDS 6
TRANSMISSION .... GEAR
STEERING............ STANDARD
STANDARD DECK .... 46"
MSRP................. $2,399

RETAIL PRICING

YEAR	HIGH	LOW
2000	$1,010	$757

27301

YEARS MFRD 1998-1999
ENGINE .... KOHLER
ENGINE HP 20
COOLING .... AIR
FUEL .... G
SPEEDS 6
TRANSMISSION .... GEAR
STEERING............ STANDARD
STANDARD DECK .... 46"
MSRP................. $2,699

RETAIL PRICING

YEAR	HIGH	LOW
1998	$1,018	$764
1999	$1,086	$814

27302

YEARS MFRD 1998-2000
ENGINE .... KOHLER
ENGINE HP 20
COOLING .... AIR
FUEL .... G
SPEEDS .... VARIABLE
TRANSMISSION .... HYDRO
STEERING............ STANDARD
STANDARD DECK .... 46"
MSRP................. $2,999

RETAIL PRICING

YEAR	HIGH	LOW
1998	$1,129	$846
1999	$1,205	$903
2000	$1,264	$948

27303

YEARS MFRD 1998-1998
ENGINE .... B&S
ENGINE HP 20
COOLING .... AIR
FUEL .... G
SPEEDS 6
TRANSMISSION .... GEAR
STEERING............ STANDARD
STANDARD DECK .... 46"
MSRP................. $2,499

RETAIL PRICING

YEAR	HIGH	LOW
1998	$942	$707

27304

YEARS MFRD 1998-1998
ENGINE .... B&S
ENGINE HP 20
COOLING .... AIR
FUEL .... G
SPEEDS .... VARIABLE
TRANSMISSION .... GEAR
STEERING .... STANDARD
STANDARD DECK .... 46"
MSRP $2,699

RETAIL PRICING

YEAR	HIGH	LOW
1998	$1,018	$764

27305

YEARS MFRD 1999-1999
ENGINE .... KOHLER
ENGINE HP 20
COOLING .... AIR
FUEL .... G
SPEEDS 6
TRANSMISSION .... GEAR
STEERING .... STANDARD
STANDARD DECK .... 50"
MSRP $2,699

RETAIL PRICING

YEAR	HIGH	LOW
1999	$1,086	$814

27306

YEARS MFRD 1999-1999
ENGINE .... KOHLER
ENGINE HP 20
COOLING .... AIR
FUEL .... G
SPEEDS .... VARIABLE
TRANSMISSION .... HYDRO
STEERING .... STANDARD
STANDARD DECK .... 50"
MSRP $2,999

RETAIL PRICING

YEAR	HIGH	LOW
1999	$1,205	$903

27307

YEARS MFRD 2000-2000
ENGINE .... KOHLER
ENGINE HP 22
COOLING .... AIR
FUEL .... G
SPEEDS 6
TRANSMISSION .... GEAR
STEERING .... STANDARD
STANDARD DECK .... 46"
MSRP $2,799

RETAIL PRICING

YEAR	HIGH	LOW
2000	$1,179	$884

27308

YEARS MFRD 2000-2000
ENGINE .... KOHLER
ENGINE HP 22
COOLING .... AIR
FUEL .... G
SPEEDS .... VARIABLE
TRANSMISSION .... HYDRO
STEERING .... STANDARD
STANDARD DECK .... 46"
MSRP $3,099

RETAIL PRICING

YEAR	HIGH	LOW
2000	$1,305	$979

27309

YEARS MFRD 2000-2000
ENGINE .... KOHLER
ENGINE HP 22
COOLING .... AIR
FUEL .... G
SPEEDS .... VARIABLE
TRANSMISSION .... HYDRO
STEERING .... STANDARD
STANDARD DECK .... 50"
MSRP $2,799

RETAIL PRICING

YEAR	HIGH	LOW
2000	$1,179	$884

27311

YEARS MFRD 1998-1998
ENGINE .... KOHLER
ENGINE HP 22
COOLING .... AIR
FUEL .... G
SPEEDS 6
TRANSMISSION .... GEAR
STEERING .... STANDARD
STANDARD DECK .... 46"
MSRP $2,899

RETAIL PRICING

YEAR	HIGH	LOW
1998	$1,092	$819

27312

YEARS MFRD 1998-1998
ENGINE .... KOHLER
ENGINE HP 22
COOLING .... AIR
FUEL .... G
SPEEDS .... VARIABLE
TRANSMISSION .... HYDRO
STEERING .... STANDARD
STANDARD DECK .... 46"
MSRP $3,199

RETAIL PRICING

YEAR	HIGH	LOW
1998	$1,205	$903

27313

YEARS MFRD 2003-2004
ENGINE .... KOHLER
CYLINDERS 1
CID 29.9
ENGINE HP 17
COOLING .... AIR
FUEL .... G
SPEEDS 6/1
TRANSMISSION .... GEAR
STEERING .... STANDARD
STANDARD DECK .... 42"
WEIGHT .... 511 LBS.
MSRP $1,399

RETAIL PRICING

YEAR	HIGH	LOW
2003	$685	$514
2004	$731	$548

27314

YEARS MFRD 2003-2004
ENGINE .... KOHLER PRO
CYLINDERS 1
CID 29.9
ENGINE HP 17
COOLING .... AIR
FUEL .... G
SPEEDS .... VARIABLE
TRANSMISSION .... HYDRO
STEERING .... STANDARD
STANDARD DECK .... 42"
WEIGHT .... 516 LBS.
MSRP $1,599

RETAIL PRICING

YEAR	HIGH	LOW
2003	$783	$587
2004	$832	$624

27318

YEARS MFRD 2004-2004
ENGINE .... KOHLER PRO
CYLINDERS 1
CID 29.9
ENGINE HP 17.5
COOLING .... AIR
SPEEDS .... VARIABLE
TRANSMISSION .... HYDRO
STEERING .... STANDARD
STANDARD DECK .... 42"
WEIGHT .... 511 LBS.
MSRP $1,549

RETAIL PRICING

YEAR	HIGH	LOW
2004	$808	$606

27320

YEARS MFRD 1999-2000
ENGINE .... KOHLER
ENGINE HP 24
COOLING .... AIR
FUEL .... G
SPEEDS .... VARIABLE
TRANSMISSION .... HYDRO
STEERING .... STANDARD
STANDARD DECK .... 46"
MSRP $3,299

RETAIL PRICING

YEAR	HIGH	LOW
1999	$1,325	$994
2000	$1,390	$1,042

27322

YEARS MFRD 1998-2000
ENGINE .... KOHLER
ENGINE HP 24
COOLING .... AIR
FUEL .... G
SPEEDS .... VARIABLE
TRANSMISSION .... HYDRO
STEERING .... STANDARD
STANDARD DECK .... 50"
MSRP $3,399

RETAIL PRICING

YEAR	HIGH	LOW
1998	$1,279	$959
1999	$1,365	$1,024
2000	$1,431	$1,073

27324

YEARS MFRD 2003-2004
ENGINE .... KOHLER
CYLINDERS 2
ENGINE HP 25
COOLING .... AIR
FUEL .... G
SPEEDS .... VARIABLE
TRANSMISSION .... HYDRO
STEERING .... STANDARD
STANDARD DECK .... 48"
WEIGHT .... 581 LBS.
MSRP $2,699

RETAIL PRICING

YEAR	HIGH	LOW
2003	$1,321	$990
2004	$1,406	$1,055

27327

YEARS MFRD 2018-2018
ENGINE .... CRAFTSMAN
CID 420CC
COOLING .... AIR
FUEL .... G
STEERING .... STANDARD
BLADE CLUTCH .... MANUAL
STANDARD DECK .... 42"
WEIGHT .... 520 LBS.

27332

YEARS MFRD 1998-2000
ENGINE .... KOHLER
ENGINE HP 25
COOLING .... AIR
FUEL .... G
SPEEDS .... VARIABLE
TRANSMISSION .... HYDRO
STEERING .... STANDARD
STANDARD DECK .... 50"
MSRP $3,699

RETAIL PRICING

YEAR	HIGH	LOW
1998	$1,356	$1,017
1999	$1,486	$1,114
2000	$1,558	$1,169

CRAFTSMAN

27333
YEARS MFRD 2018-2019
ENGINE . . . . B&S PLATINUM
CYLINDERS. 2
CID 656CC
ENGINE HP 20
COOLING . . . . AIR
FUEL . . . . G
TRANSMISSION . . . . HYDRO
STEERING. . . . . STANDARD
STANDARD DECK . . . . 46"
WEIGHT . . . . 600 LBS.

27334
YEARS MFRD 2018-2019
ENGINE . . . . B&S PLATINUM
CYLINDERS. 2
CID 724CC
ENGINE HP 24
FUEL . . . . G
TRANSMISSION . . . . HYDRO
STEERING. . . . . STANDARD
BLADE CLUTCH . . . . ELECTRIC
STANDARD DECK . . . . 54"
WEIGHT . . . . 660 LBS.

27335
YEARS MFRD 2003-2004
ENGINE . . . . B&S IC OHV
CYLINDERS. 1
CID 502CC
ENGINE HP 16
COOLING . . . . AIR
FUEL . . . . G
SPEEDS 6/1
TRANSMISSION . . . . GEAR
STEERING. . . . . STANDARD
STANDARD DECK . . . . 42"
WEIGHT . . . . 480 LBS.
MSRP. $899

RETAIL PRICING

YEAR	HIGH	LOW
2003	$442	$331
2004	$468	$351

27336
YEARS MFRD 2004-2004
ENGINE . . . . B&S IC OHV
CYLINDERS. 1
CID 502CC
ENGINE HP 16
COOLING . . . . AIR
FUEL . . . . G
SPEEDS . . . . VARIABLE
TRANSMISSION . . . . HYDRO
STEERING. . . . . STANDARD
STANDARD DECK . . . . 42"
WEIGHT . . . . 485 LBS.
MSRP. $1,099

RETAIL PRICING

YEAR	HIGH	LOW
2004	$572	$429

27338
YEARS MFRD 2004-2004
ENGINE . . . . B&S
CYLINDERS. 1
CID 30.6
ENGINE HP 17.5
COOLING . . . . AIR
FUEL . . . . G
SPEEDS . . . . VARIABLE
TRANSMISSION . . . . HYDRO
STEERING. . . . . STANDARD
STANDARD DECK . . . . 42"
WEIGHT . . . . 485 LBS.
MSRP. $1,299

RETAIL PRICING

YEAR	HIGH	LOW
2004	$677	$508

27339
YEARS MFRD 2004-2004
ENGINE . . . . B&S INTEK
CID 30.6
ENGINE HP 18
COOLING . . . . AIR
FUEL . . . . G
SPEEDS 6/1
TRANSMISSION . . . . GEAR
STEERING. . . . . STANDARD
STANDARD DECK . . . . 42"
WEIGHT . . . . 480 LBS.
MSRP. $1,149

RETAIL PRICING

YEAR	HIGH	LOW
2004	$600	$450

27340
YEARS MFRD 2004-2004
ENGINE . . . . B&S
CYLINDERS. 1
ENGINE HP 18
COOLING . . . . AIR
FUEL . . . . G
SPEEDS . . . . VARIABLE
TRANSMISSION . . . . HYDRO
STEERING. . . . . STANDARD
STANDARD DECK . . . . 42"
WEIGHT . . . . 485 LBS.
MSRP. $1,399

RETAIL PRICING

YEAR	HIGH	LOW
2004	$731	$548

27342
YEARS MFRD 1998-2000
ENGINE . . . . KAWASAKI
ENGINE HP 18
FUEL . . . . G
SPEEDS . . . . VARIABLE
TRANSMISSION . . . . HYDRO
STEERING. . . . . STANDARD
STANDARD DECK . . . . 46"
MSRP. $4,199

RETAIL PRICING

YEAR	HIGH	LOW
1998	$1,243	$932
1999	$1,687	$1,265
2000	$1,769	$1,327

27343
YEARS MFRD 2018-2019
ENGINE . . . . B&S
CID 540CC
ENGINE HP 19
COOLING . . . . AIR
FUEL . . . . G
STEERING. . . . . STANDARD
BLADE CLUTCH . . . . MANUAL
STANDARD DECK . . . . 46"
WEIGHT . . . . 525 LBS.

27347
YEARS MFRD 2003-2004
ENGINE . . . . KOHLER PRO
CYLINDERS. 2
CID 38
ENGINE HP 20
COOLING . . . . AIR
FUEL . . . . G
SPEEDS 6/1
TRANSMISSION . . . . GEAR
STEERING. . . . . STANDARD
STANDARD DECK . . . . 42"
WEIGHT . . . . 513 LBS.
MSRP. $1,799

RETAIL PRICING

YEAR	HIGH	LOW
2003	$880	$660
2004	$938	$703

27348
YEARS MFRD 2003-2004
ENGINE . . . . KOHLER PRO
CYLINDERS. 2
CID 38
ENGINE HP 20
COOLING . . . . AIR
FUEL . . . . G
SPEEDS . . . . VARIABLE
TRANSMISSION . . . . HYDRO
STEERING. . . . . STANDARD
STANDARD DECK . . . . 42"
WEIGHT . . . . 518 LBS.
MSRP. $2,049

RETAIL PRICING

YEAR	HIGH	LOW
2003	$1,002	$752
2004	$1,068	$801

27349
YEARS MFRD 2004-2004
ENGINE . . . . HONDA OHC
CYLINDERS. 2
CID 32.3
ENGINE HP 16.5
COOLING . . . . AIR
FUEL . . . . G
SPEEDS 6/1
TRANSMISSION . . . . GEAR
STEERING. . . . . STANDARD
STANDARD DECK . . . . 42"
WEIGHT . . . . 526 LBS.
MSRP. $1,949

RETAIL PRICING

YEAR	HIGH	LOW
2004	$1,017	$762

27350
YEARS MFRD 2004-2004
ENGINE . . . . HONDA OHV
CYLINDERS. 2
ENGINE HP 16.5
COOLING . . . . AIR
FUEL . . . . G
SPEEDS . . . . VARIABLE
TRANSMISSION . . . . HYDRO
STEERING. . . . . STANDARD
STANDARD DECK . . . . 42"
WEIGHT . . . . 518 LBS.
MSRP. $2,149

RETAIL PRICING

YEAR	HIGH	LOW
2004	$1,120	$840

27351
YEARS MFRD 2004-2004
ENGINE . . . . B&S
CYLINDERS. 2
CID 40
ENGINE HP 21
COOLING . . . . AIR
FUEL . . . . G
SPEEDS 6/1
TRANSMISSION . . . . GEAR
STEERING. . . . . STANDARD
BLADE CLUTCH . . . . MANUAL
STANDARD DECK . . . . 42"
WEIGHT . . . . 523 LBS.
MSRP. $1,349

RETAIL PRICING

YEAR	HIGH	LOW
2004	$703	$527

27361
YEARS MFRD 2003-2004
ENGINE . . . . B&S V TWIN OHV
CYLINDERS. 2
CID 44.2
ENGINE HP 24
COOLING . . . . AIR
FUEL . . . . G
SPEEDS 6/1
TRANSMISSION . . . . GEAR
STEERING. . . . . STANDARD
STANDARD DECK . . . . 48"
WEIGHT . . . . 575 LBS.
MSRP. $1,999

RETAIL PRICING

YEAR	HIGH	LOW
2003	$979	$734
2004	$1,042	$782

27362
YEARS MFRD 2003-2004
ENGINE .... B&S
CYLINDERS.................. 2
CID 44.2
ENGINE HP 24
COOLING .... AIR
FUEL .... G
SPEEDS .... VARIABLE
TRANSMISSION .... HYDRO
STEERING............ STANDARD
STANDARD DECK .... 48"
WEIGHT .... 581 LBS.
MSRP................. $2,199

RETAIL PRICING

YEAR	HIGH	LOW
2003	$1,075	$807
2004	$1,145	$859

27363
YEARS MFRD 2004-2004
ENGINE .... B&S
CYLINDERS.................. 1
CID 30.6
ENGINE HP 18.5
COOLING .... AIR
FUEL .... G
SPEEDS 6/1
TRANSMISSION .... GEAR
STEERING............ STANDARD
STANDARD DECK .... 42"
WEIGHT .... 535 LBS.
MSRP................. $1,499

RETAIL PRICING

YEAR	HIGH	LOW
2004	$781	$586

27364
YEARS MFRD 2004-2004
ENGINE .... B&S INTEK PLUS
CYLINDERS.................. 1
CID 30.6
ENGINE HP 18.5
COOLING .... AIR
SPEEDS .... VARIABLE
TRANSMISSION .... HYDRO
STEERING............ STANDARD
STANDARD DECK .... 42"
WEIGHT .... 540 LBS.
MSRP................. $1,699

RETAIL PRICING

YEAR	HIGH	LOW
2004	$884	$663

27373
YEARS MFRD 2017-2018
ENGINE .... CRAFTSMAN
CID 547CC
COOLING .... AIR
FUEL .... G
SPEEDS .... VARIABLE
TRANSMISSION .... HYDRO
STEERING............ STANDARD
BLADE CLUTCH .... MANUAL
STANDARD DECK .... 42"
MSRP................. $1,199

RETAIL PRICING

YEAR	HIGH	LOW
2017	$645	$484
2018	$708	$531

27374
YEARS MFRD 2017-2018
ENGINE .... CRAFTSMAN
CID 547CC
COOLING .... AIR
FUEL .... G
SPEEDS .... VARIABLE
TRANSMISSION .... HYDRO
STEERING............ STANDARD
BLADE CLUTCH .... MANUAL
STANDARD DECK .... 46"
MSRP................. $1,299

RETAIL PRICING

YEAR	HIGH	LOW
2017	$660	$495
2018	$720	$540

27375
YEARS MFRD 2004-2004
ENGINE .... B&S INTEK
CYLINDERS.................. 1
CID 30.6
ENGINE HP 18
COOLING .... AIR
FUEL .... G
SPEEDS 6/1
TRANSMISSION .... GEAR
STEERING............ STANDARD
STANDARD DECK .... 42"
WEIGHT .... 495 LBS.
MSRP................. $1,199

RETAIL PRICING

YEAR	HIGH	LOW
2004	$625	$469

27376
YEARS MFRD 2004-2004
ENGINE .... B&S
CYLINDERS.................. 1
CID 30.6
ENGINE HP 18
COOLING .... AIR
FUEL .... G
SPEEDS .... VARIABLE
TRANSMISSION .... HYDRO
STEERING............ STANDARD
STANDARD DECK .... 42"
WEIGHT .... 505 LBS.
MSRP................. $1,349

RETAIL PRICING

YEAR	HIGH	LOW
2004	$703	$527

27377
YEARS MFRD 2004-2004
ENGINE .... B&S
CYLINDERS.................. 2
CID 40
ENGINE HP 22
COOLING .... AIR
FUEL .... G
SPEEDS 6/1
TRANSMISSION .... GEAR
STEERING............ STANDARD
STANDARD DECK .... 42"
WEIGHT .... 525 LBS.
MSRP................. $1,449

RETAIL PRICING

YEAR	HIGH	LOW
2004	$756	$567

27378
YEARS MFRD 2004-2004
ENGINE .... B&S INTEK V TWIN
CYLINDERS.................. 2
CID 40
ENGINE HP 22
COOLING .... AIR
FUEL .... G
SPEEDS .... VARIABLE
TRANSMISSION .... HYDRO
STEERING............ STANDARD
STANDARD DECK .... 42"
WEIGHT .... 530 LBS.
MSRP................. $1,649

RETAIL PRICING

YEAR	HIGH	LOW
2004	$859	$644

27379
YEARS MFRD 2004-2004
ENGINE .... HONDA OHC
CYLINDERS.................. 2
CID 32.3
ENGINE HP 16
COOLING .... AIR
FUEL .... G
SPEEDS 6/1
TRANSMISSION .... GEAR
STEERING............ STANDARD
STANDARD DECK .... 42"
WEIGHT .... 518 LBS.
MSRP................. $1,849

RETAIL PRICING

YEAR	HIGH	LOW
2004	$963	$722

27381
YEARS MFRD 2004-2004
ENGINE .... B&S
CYLINDERS.................. 1
CID 30.6
ENGINE HP 18.5
COOLING .... AIR
FUEL .... G
SPEEDS 6/1
TRANSMISSION .... GEAR
STEERING............ STANDARD
BLADE CLUTCH .... MANUAL
STANDARD DECK .... 42"
WEIGHT .... 513 LBS.
MSRP................. $1,349

RETAIL PRICING

YEAR	HIGH	LOW
2004	$703	$527

27382
YEARS MFRD 2004-2004
ENGINE .... B&S INTEK PLUS
CYLINDERS.................. 1
CID 30.6
ENGINE HP 18.5
COOLING .... AIR
FUEL .... G
SPEEDS .... VARIABLE
TRANSMISSION .... HYDRO
STEERING............ STANDARD
STANDARD DECK .... 42"
WEIGHT .... 531 LBS.
MSRP................. $1,549

RETAIL PRICING

YEAR	HIGH	LOW
2004	$808	$606

27390
YEARS MFRD 2017-2017
ENGINE .... B&S PLATINUM
CYLINDERS.................. 2
CID 656CC
ENGINE HP 20
COOLING .... AIR
FUEL .... G
SPEEDS .... VARIABLE
TRANSMISSION .... HYDRO
STEERING............ STANDARD
BLADE CLUTCH .... ELECTRIC
STANDARD DECK .... 46"
MSRP................. $1,699

RETAIL PRICING

YEAR	HIGH	LOW
2017	$950	$713

27392
YEARS MFRD 1999-2000
ENGINE .... KOHLER
ENGINE HP 15.5
COOLING .... AIR
FUEL .... G
SPEEDS .... VARIABLE
TRANSMISSION .... HYDRO
STEERING............ STANDARD
STANDARD DECK .... 40"
MSRP................. $3,699

RETAIL PRICING

YEAR	HIGH	LOW
1999	$1,486	$1,114
2000	$1,558	$1,169

27394
YEARS MFRD 2017-2017
ENGINE .... B&S PLATINUM
CYLINDERS.................. 2
CID 724CC
ENGINE HP 24
COOLING .... AIR
FUEL .... G
SPEEDS .... VARIABLE
TRANSMISSION .... HYDRO
STEERING............ STANDARD
BLADE CLUTCH .... ELECTRIC
STANDARD DECK .... 54"
MSRP................. $1,999

CRAFTSMAN

RETAIL PRICING

YEAR	HIGH	LOW
2017	$1,248	$936

27398

YEARS MFRD........ 2017-2017
ENGINE.................. B&S
CYLINDERS.................. 2
CID.................. 656CC
ENGINE HP.................. 20
COOLING.................. AIR
FUEL.................. G
SPEEDS.................. VARIABLE
TRANSMISSION.................. HYDRO
STEERING.................. STANDARD
BLADE CLUTCH.................. MANUAL
STANDARD DECK.................. 42"
WEIGHT.................. 459 LBS.
MSRP.................. $1,399

RETAIL PRICING

YEAR	HIGH	LOW
2017	$826	$619

27435

YEARS MFRD........ 2005-2006
ENGINE.................. B&S
ENGINE HP.................. 16
COOLING.................. AIR
FUEL.................. G
SPEEDS.................. 6/1
TRANSMISSION.................. GEAR
STEERING.................. STANDARD
STANDARD DECK.................. 42"
MSRP.................. $999

RETAIL PRICING

YEAR	HIGH	LOW
2005	$549	$412

27440

YEARS MFRD........ 2005-2006
ENGINE.................. B&S
ENGINE HP.................. 18
COOLING.................. AIR
FUEL.................. G
SPEEDS.................. VARIABLE
TRANSMISSION.................. HYDRO
STEERING.................. STANDARD
STANDARD DECK.................. 42"
MSRP.................. $1,399

RETAIL PRICING

YEAR	HIGH	LOW
2005	$773	$580

27463

YEARS MFRD........ 2005-2006
ENGINE.................. B&S
CYLINDERS.................. 1
CID.................. 30.6
ENGINE HP.................. 18.5
COOLING.................. AIR
FUEL.................. G
SPEEDS.................. 6/1
TRANSMISSION.................. GEAR
STEERING.................. STANDARD
BLADE CLUTCH.................. ELECTRIC
STANDARD DECK.................. 42"
WEIGHT.................. 535 LBS.
MSRP.................. $1,599

RETAIL PRICING

YEAR	HIGH	LOW
2005	$883	$662
2006	$934	$700

27464

YEARS MFRD........ 2005-2006
ENGINE.................. B&S
CYLINDERS.................. 1
CID.................. 30.6
ENGINE HP.................. 18.5
COOLING.................. AIR
FUEL.................. G
SPEEDS.................. VARIABLE
TRANSMISSION.................. HYDRO
STEERING.................. STANDARD
BLADE CLUTCH.................. ELECTRIC
STANDARD DECK.................. 42"
WEIGHT.................. 540 LBS.
MSRP.................. $1,799

RETAIL PRICING

YEAR	HIGH	LOW
2005	$996	$747
2006	$1,053	$789

27476

YEARS MFRD........ 2005-2005
ENGINE.................. B&S
CYLINDERS.................. 1
ENGINE HP.................. 18.5
COOLING.................. AIR
FUEL.................. G
SPEEDS.................. VARIABLE
TRANSMISSION.................. HYDRO
STEERING.................. STANDARD
BLADE CLUTCH.................. ELECTRIC
STANDARD DECK.................. 42"
MSRP.................. $1,199

RETAIL PRICING

YEAR	HIGH	LOW
2005	$663	$497

27482

YEARS MFRD........ 2005-2006
ENGINE.................. B&S
CYLINDERS.................. 1
ENGINE HP.................. 18.5
COOLING.................. AIR
FUEL.................. G
SPEEDS.................. VARIABLE
TRANSMISSION.................. HYDRO
STEERING.................. STANDARD
BLADE CLUTCH.................. ELECTRIC
STANDARD DECK.................. 42"
WEIGHT.................. 531 LBS.
MSRP.................. $1,649

RETAIL PRICING

YEAR	HIGH	LOW
2005	$719	$539
2006	$963	$722

27495

YEARS MFRD........ 2000-2000
ENGINE.................. KOHLER
ENGINE HP.................. 21
COOLING.................. AIR
FUEL.................. G
SPEEDS.................. 6
TRANSMISSION.................. GEAR
STEERING.................. STANDARD
STANDARD DECK.................. 46"
MSRP.................. $2,399

RETAIL PRICING

YEAR	HIGH	LOW
2000	$1,010	$757

27497

YEARS MFRD........ 2002-2002
ENGINE.................. B&S
ENGINE HP.................. 22
FUEL.................. G
SPEEDS.................. 6
TRANSMISSION.................. GEAR
STEERING.................. STANDARD
STANDARD DECK.................. 46"
MSRP.................. $2,399

RETAIL PRICING

YEAR	HIGH	LOW
2002	$1,084	$813

27499

YEARS MFRD........ 2000-2000
ENGINE.................. KOHLER
ENGINE HP.................. 23
COOLING.................. AIR
FUEL.................. G
SPEEDS.................. 6
TRANSMISSION.................. GEAR
STEERING.................. STANDARD
MSRP.................. $2,199

RETAIL PRICING

YEAR	HIGH	LOW
2000	$925	$694

27500

YEARS MFRD........ 2000-2000
ENGINE.................. KOHLER
ENGINE HP.................. 23
COOLING.................. AIR
FUEL.................. G
SPEEDS.................. VARIABLE
TRANSMISSION.................. HYDRO
STEERING.................. STANDARD
MSRP.................. $2,499

RETAIL PRICING

YEAR	HIGH	LOW
2000	$1,053	$789

27501

YEARS MFRD........ 2000-2002
ENGINE.................. KOHLER
ENGINE HP.................. 23
COOLING.................. AIR
FUEL.................. G
SPEEDS.................. 6
TRANSMISSION.................. GEAR
STEERING.................. STANDARD
STANDARD DECK.................. 48"
MSRP.................. $2,799

RETAIL PRICING

YEAR	HIGH	LOW
2000	$1,179	$884
2002	$1,264	$948

27502

YEARS MFRD........ 2000-2002
ENGINE.................. KOHLER
ENGINE HP.................. 23
COOLING.................. AIR
FUEL.................. G
SPEEDS.................. VARIABLE
TRANSMISSION.................. HYDRO
STEERING.................. STANDARD
STANDARD DECK.................. 48"
MSRP.................. $3,099

RETAIL PRICING

YEAR	HIGH	LOW
2000	$1,305	$979
2002	$1,399	$1,050

27503

YEARS MFRD........ 2000-2000
ENGINE.................. KOHLER
ENGINE HP.................. 23
COOLING.................. AIR
FUEL.................. G
SPEEDS.................. 6
TRANSMISSION.................. GEAR
STEERING.................. STANDARD
STANDARD DECK.................. 50"
MSRP.................. $2,799

RETAIL PRICING

YEAR	HIGH	LOW
2000	$1,179	$884

27518

YEARS MFRD........ 2005-2005
ENGINE.................. KOHLER
CYLINDERS.................. 1
ENGINE HP.................. 19
COOLING.................. AIR
FUEL.................. G
SPEEDS.................. VARIABLE
TRANSMISSION.................. HYDRO
STEERING.................. STANDARD
BLADE CLUTCH.................. ELECTRIC
STANDARD DECK.................. 42"
WEIGHT.................. 510 LBS.
MSRP.................. $1,299

RETAIL PRICING

YEAR	HIGH	LOW
2005	$719	$539

27528

YEARS MFRD........ 2002-2002
ENGINE.................. KOHLER
ENGINE HP.................. 27

FUEL . . . . G
SPEEDS . . . . VARIABLE
TRANSMISSION . . . . HYDRO
STEERING. . . . . STANDARD
STANDARD DECK . . . . 48"
MSRP. $3,999

RETAIL PRICING

YEAR	HIGH	LOW
2002	$1,128	$846

27530

YEARS MFRD 2005-2006
ENGINE . . . . B&S
ENGINE HP 18
COOLING . . . . AIR
FUEL . . . . G
SPEEDS 6/1
TRANSMISSION . . . . GEAR
STEERING. . . . . STANDARD
STANDARD DECK . . . . 42"
MSRP. $1,149

RETAIL PRICING

YEAR	HIGH	LOW
2005	$635	$476

27537

YEARS MFRD 2005-2006
ENGINE . . . . B&S
ENGINE HP 17.5
COOLING . . . . AIR
FUEL . . . . G
SPEEDS 6/1
TRANSMISSION . . . . GEAR
STEERING. . . . . STANDARD
STANDARD DECK . . . . 42"
MSRP. $1,099

RETAIL PRICING

YEAR	HIGH	LOW
2005	$607	$455

27539

YEARS MFRD 2006-2006
ENGINE . . . . B&S
CYLINDERS. 1
ENGINE HP 18
COOLING . . . . AIR
FUEL . . . . G
SPEEDS 6/1
TRANSMISSION . . . . GEAR
STEERING. . . . . STANDARD
BLADE CLUTCH . . . . MANUAL
STANDARD DECK . . . . 42"
WEIGHT . . . . 478 LBS.
MSRP. $1,149

RETAIL PRICING

YEAR	HIGH	LOW
2006	$671	$503

27540

YEARS MFRD 2005-2006
ENGINE . . . . B&S
CYLINDERS. 1
CID 30.6
ENGINE HP 18
COOLING . . . . AIR
FUEL . . . . G
SPEEDS . . . . VARIABLE
TRANSMISSION . . . . HYDRO
STEERING. . . . . STANDARD
BLADE CLUTCH . . . . ELECTRIC
STANDARD DECK . . . . 42"
WEIGHT . . . . 482 LBS.
MSRP. $1,349

RETAIL PRICING

YEAR	HIGH	LOW
2005	$624	$468
2006	$787	$590

27552

YEARS MFRD 2005-2005
ENGINE . . . . B&S
CYLINDERS. 2
CID 44.2
ENGINE HP 23
COOLING . . . . AIR
FUEL . . . . G
SPEEDS . . . . VARIABLE
TRANSMISSION . . . . HYDRO
STEERING. . . . . STANDARD
BLADE CLUTCH . . . . ELECTRIC
STANDARD DECK . . . . 42"
WEIGHT . . . . 528 LBS.
MSRP. $1,599

RETAIL PRICING

YEAR	HIGH	LOW
2005	$883	$662

27562

YEARS MFRD 2005-2006
ENGINE . . . . B&S
CYLINDERS. 1
CID 30.6
ENGINE HP 18.5
COOLING . . . . AIR
FUEL . . . . G
SPEEDS . . . . VARIABLE
TRANSMISSION . . . . HYDRO
STEERING. . . . . STANDARD
BLADE CLUTCH . . . . ELECTRIC
STANDARD DECK . . . . 42"
WEIGHT . . . . 527 LBS.
MSRP. $1,499

RETAIL PRICING

YEAR	HIGH	LOW
2005	$773	$580
2006	$875	$656

27563

YEARS MFRD 2005-2006
ENGINE . . . . B&S
CYLINDERS. 1
CID 30.6
ENGINE HP 18.5
COOLING . . . . AIR
FUEL . . . . G
SPEEDS 6/1
TRANSMISSION . . . . GEAR
STEERING. . . . . STANDARD
BLADE CLUTCH . . . . ELECTRIC
STANDARD DECK . . . . 42"
WEIGHT . . . . 542 LBS.
MSRP. $1,499

RETAIL PRICING

YEAR	HIGH	LOW
2005	$827	$621
2006	$875	$656

27564

YEARS MFRD 2005-2006
ENGINE . . . . B&S
CYLINDERS. 1
CID 30.6
ENGINE HP 18.5
COOLING . . . . AIR
FUEL . . . . G
SPEEDS . . . . VARIABLE
TRANSMISSION . . . . HYDRO
STEERING. . . . . STANDARD
BLADE CLUTCH . . . . ELECTRIC
STANDARD DECK . . . . 42"
WEIGHT . . . . 547 LBS.
MSRP. $1,699

RETAIL PRICING

YEAR	HIGH	LOW
2005	$939	$704
2006	$993	$745

27566

YEARS MFRD 2005-2006
ENGINE . . . . KOHLER
CYLINDERS. 1
CID 36.4
ENGINE HP 20
COOLING . . . . AIR
FUEL . . . . G
SPEEDS . . . . VARIABLE
TRANSMISSION . . . . HYDRO
STEERING. . . . . STANDARD
BLADE CLUTCH . . . . ELECTRIC
STANDARD DECK . . . . 42"
WEIGHT . . . . 550 LBS.
MSRP. $1,799

RETAIL PRICING

YEAR	HIGH	LOW
2005	$996	$747
2006	$1,053	$789

27567

YEARS MFRD 2005-2005
ENGINE . . . . B&S
CYLINDERS. 2
CID 44.2
ENGINE HP 24
COOLING . . . . AIR
FUEL . . . . G
SPEEDS 6/1
TRANSMISSION . . . . GEAR
STEERING. . . . . STANDARD
BLADE CLUTCH . . . . ELECTRIC
STANDARD DECK . . . . 42"
WEIGHT . . . . 552 LBS.
MSRP. $1,699

RETAIL PRICING

YEAR	HIGH	LOW
2005	$939	$704

27568

YEARS MFRD 2005-2006
ENGINE . . . . B&S
CYLINDERS. 2
CID 44.2
ENGINE HP 24
COOLING . . . . AIR
FUEL . . . . G
SPEEDS . . . . VARIABLE
TRANSMISSION . . . . HYDRO
STEERING. . . . . STANDARD
BLADE CLUTCH . . . . ELECTRIC
STANDARD DECK . . . . 42"
MSRP. $1,899

RETAIL PRICING

YEAR	HIGH	LOW
2005	$1,051	$788
2006	$1,109	$831

27570

YEARS MFRD 2005-2006
ENGINE . . . . B&S
CYLINDERS. 2
CID 44.2
ENGINE HP 24
COOLING . . . . AIR
FUEL . . . . G
SPEEDS . . . . VARIABLE
TRANSMISSION . . . . HYDRO
STEERING. . . . . STANDARD
BLADE CLUTCH . . . . ELECTRIC
STANDARD DECK . . . . 48"
WEIGHT . . . . 558 LBS.
MSRP. $1,999

RETAIL PRICING

YEAR	HIGH	LOW
2005	$902	$676
2006	$963	$722

27574

YEARS MFRD 2005-2005
ENGINE . . . . B&S
CYLINDERS. 2
CID 44.2
ENGINE HP 27
COOLING . . . . AIR
FUEL . . . . G
SPEEDS . . . . VARIABLE
TRANSMISSION . . . . HYDRO
STEERING. . . . . STANDARD
BLADE CLUTCH . . . . ELECTRIC
STANDARD DECK . . . . 48"
WEIGHT . . . . 558 LBS.
MSRP. $2,199

RETAIL PRICING

YEAR	HIGH	LOW
2005	$1,215	$911

CRAFTSMAN

27575

YEARS MFRD	2005-2006
ENGINE	B&S
CYLINDERS	1
ENGINE HP	18.5
COOLING	AIR
FUEL	G
SPEEDS	6/1
TRANSMISSION	GEAR
STEERING	STANDARD
BLADE CLUTCH	MANUAL
STANDARD DECK	42"
WEIGHT	488 LBS.
MSRP	$1,249

RETAIL PRICING

YEAR	HIGH	LOW
2005	$690	$517
2006	$731	$548

27576

YEARS MFRD	2005-2006
ENGINE	B&S
CYLINDERS	1
CID	30.6
ENGINE HP	18.5
COOLING	AIR
FUEL	G
SPEEDS	VARIABLE
TRANSMISSION	HYDRO
STEERING	STANDARD
BLADE CLUTCH	ELECTRIC
STANDARD DECK	42"
WEIGHT	492 LBS.
MSRP	$1,449

RETAIL PRICING

YEAR	HIGH	LOW
2005	$800	$600
2006	$846	$634

27581

YEARS MFRD	2005-2006
ENGINE	B&S
CYLINDERS	1
CID	30.6
ENGINE HP	18.5
COOLING	AIR
FUEL	G
SPEEDS	6/1
TRANSMISSION	GEAR
STEERING	STANDARD
BLADE CLUTCH	MANUAL
STANDARD DECK	42"
WEIGHT	504 LBS.
MSRP	$1,299

RETAIL PRICING

YEAR	HIGH	LOW
2005	$719	$539
2006	$759	$569

27582

YEARS MFRD	2005-2006
ENGINE	B&S
CYLINDERS	1
CID	30.6
ENGINE HP	18.5
COOLING	AIR
FUEL	G
SPEEDS	VARIABLE
TRANSMISSION	HYDRO
STEERING	STANDARD
BLADE CLUTCH	MANUAL
STANDARD DECK	42"
WEIGHT	516 LBS.
MSRP	$1,499

RETAIL PRICING

YEAR	HIGH	LOW
2005	$827	$621
2006	$875	$656

27590

YEARS MFRD	2005-2006
ENGINE	KOHLER
CYLINDERS	2
CID	44.2
ENGINE HP	26
COOLING	AIR
FUEL	G
SPEEDS	VARIABLE
TRANSMISSION	HYDRO
STEERING	STANDARD
BLADE CLUTCH	ELECTRIC
STANDARD DECK	48"
WEIGHT	571 LBS.
MSRP	$2,299

RETAIL PRICING

YEAR	HIGH	LOW
2005	$1,270	$953
2006	$1,343	$1,007

27597

YEARS MFRD	2002-2003
ENGINE	B&S
ENGINE HP	22
FUEL	G
SPEEDS	VARIABLE
TRANSMISSION	GEAR
STEERING	STANDARD
STANDARD DECK	50"
MSRP	$2,399

RETAIL PRICING

YEAR	HIGH	LOW
2002	$1,084	$813
2003	$1,174	$881

27601

YEARS MFRD	2003-2003
ENGINE	KOHLER
ENGINE HP	25
FUEL	G
SPEEDS	6
TRANSMISSION	GEAR
STEERING	STANDARD
STANDARD DECK	48"
MSRP	$2,799

RETAIL PRICING

YEAR	HIGH	LOW
2003	$1,372	$1,029

27602

YEARS MFRD	2003-2003
ENGINE	KOHLER
ENGINE HP	25
FUEL	G
SPEEDS	VARIABLE
TRANSMISSION	HYDRO
STEERING	STANDARD
STANDARD DECK	48"
MSRP	$3,099

RETAIL PRICING

YEAR	HIGH	LOW
2003	$1,516	$1,137

27605

YEARS MFRD	2003-2003
ENGINE	B&S
ENGINE HP	22
FUEL	G
SPEEDS	VARIABLE
TRANSMISSION	HYDRO
STEERING	STANDARD
STANDARD DECK	50"
MSRP	$2,249

RETAIL PRICING

YEAR	HIGH	LOW
2003	$1,100	$825

27609

YEARS MFRD	2005-2005
ENGINE	KOHLER PRO
CYLINDERS	2
CID	44.2
ENGINE HP	25
COOLING	AIR
FUEL	G
SPEEDS	6/2
TRANSMISSION	GEAR
STEERING	STANDARD
BLADE CLUTCH	ELECTRIC
STANDARD DECK	54"
WEIGHT	705 LBS.
MSRP	$2,699

RETAIL PRICING

YEAR	HIGH	LOW
2005	$1,153	$865

27621

YEARS MFRD	2005-2006
ENGINE	B&S
CYLINDERS	2
CID	40
ENGINE HP	22
COOLING	AIR
FUEL	G
SPEEDS	6/2
TRANSMISSION	GEAR
STEERING	STANDARD
BLADE CLUTCH	ELECTRIC
STANDARD DECK	54"
WEIGHT	680 LBS.
MSRP	$2,299

RETAIL PRICING

YEAR	HIGH	LOW
2005	$1,270	$953
2006	$1,343	$1,007

27622

YEARS MFRD	2005-2006
ENGINE	B&S
CYLINDERS	2
CID	40
ENGINE HP	22
COOLING	AIR
FUEL	G
SPEEDS	VARIABLE
TRANSMISSION	HYDRO
STEERING	STANDARD
BLADE CLUTCH	ELECTRIC
STANDARD DECK	54"
WEIGHT	689 LBS.
MSRP	$2,599

RETAIL PRICING

YEAR	HIGH	LOW
2005	$1,435	$1,076
2006	$1,518	$1,139

27623

YEARS MFRD	2005-2005
ENGINE	KOHLER PRO
CYLINDERS	2
CID	44.2
ENGINE HP	25
COOLING	AIR
FUEL	G
SPEEDS	6/2
TRANSMISSION	GEAR
STEERING	STANDARD
BLADE CLUTCH	ELECTRIC
STANDARD DECK	54"
WEIGHT	705 LBS.
MSRP	$2,699

RETAIL PRICING

YEAR	HIGH	LOW
2005	$1,356	$1,017

27624

YEARS MFRD	2005-2005
ENGINE	KOHLER PRO
CYLINDERS	2
CID	44.2
ENGINE HP	25
COOLING	AIR
FUEL	G
SPEEDS	VARIABLE
TRANSMISSION	HYDRO
STEERING	STANDARD
BLADE CLUTCH	ELECTRIC
STANDARD DECK	54"
WEIGHT	714 LBS.
MSRP	$2,999

RETAIL PRICING

YEAR	HIGH	LOW
2005	$1,387	$1,040

27630

YEARS MFRD 2009-2009
ENGINE .... B&S
CYLINDERS 1
ENGINE HP 13.5
COOLING .... AIR
FUEL .... G
SPEEDS .... VARIABLE
TRANSMISSION .... HYDRO
STEERING .... STANDARD
BLADE CLUTCH .... MANUAL
STANDARD DECK .... 30"
WEIGHT .... 353 LBS.
MSRP $1,549

RETAIL PRICING

YEAR	HIGH	LOW
2009	$852	$639

27631

YEARS MFRD 2005-2005
ENGINE .... B&S
CYLINDERS 2
CID 44.2
ENGINE HP 24
COOLING .... AIR
FUEL .... G
SPEEDS 6/2
TRANSMISSION .... GEAR
STEERING .... STANDARD
BLADE CLUTCH .... ELECTRIC
STANDARD DECK .... 48"
WEIGHT .... 680 LBS.
MSRP $2,299

RETAIL PRICING

YEAR	HIGH	LOW
2005	$933	$700

27632

YEARS MFRD 2005-2005
ENGINE .... B&S
CYLINDERS 2
CID 44.2
ENGINE HP 24
COOLING .... AIR
FUEL .... G
SPEEDS .... VARIABLE
TRANSMISSION .... HYDRO
STEERING .... STANDARD
BLADE CLUTCH .... ELECTRIC
STANDARD DECK .... 48"
WEIGHT .... 689 LBS.
MSRP $2,599

RETAIL PRICING

YEAR	HIGH	LOW
2005	$1,233	$925

27633

YEARS MFRD 2005-2005
ENGINE .... B&S
CYLINDERS 2
CID 44.2
ENGINE HP 27
COOLING .... AIR
FUEL .... G
SPEEDS 6/2
TRANSMISSION .... GEAR
STEERING .... STANDARD
BLADE CLUTCH .... ELECTRIC
STANDARD DECK .... 54"
WEIGHT .... 705 LBS.
MSRP $2,599

RETAIL PRICING

YEAR	HIGH	LOW
2005	$1,233	$925

27634

YEARS MFRD 2005-2005
ENGINE .... B&S
CYLINDERS 2
CID 44.2
ENGINE HP 27
COOLING .... AIR
FUEL .... G
SPEEDS .... VARIABLE
TRANSMISSION .... HYDRO
STEERING .... STANDARD
BLADE CLUTCH .... ELECTRIC
STANDARD DECK .... 54"
WEIGHT .... 714 LBS.
MSRP $2,899

RETAIL PRICING

YEAR	HIGH	LOW
2005	$1,264	$948

27635

YEARS MFRD 2005-2005
ENGINE .... KOHLER
CYLINDERS 2
CID 44.2
ENGINE HP 25
COOLING .... AIR
FUEL .... G
SPEEDS 6/2
TRANSMISSION .... GEAR
STEERING .... STANDARD
BLADE CLUTCH .... ELECTRIC
STANDARD DECK .... 48"
WEIGHT .... 685 LBS.
MSRP $2,564

RETAIL PRICING

YEAR	HIGH	LOW
2005	$1,078	$809

27636

YEARS MFRD 2005-2006
ENGINE .... KOHLER
CYLINDERS 2
CID 44.2
ENGINE HP 25
COOLING .... AIR
FUEL .... G
SPEEDS .... VARIABLE
TRANSMISSION .... HYDRO
STEERING .... STANDARD
BLADE CLUTCH .... ELECTRIC
STANDARD DECK .... 48"
WEIGHT .... 694 LBS.
MSRP $2,999

RETAIL PRICING

YEAR	HIGH	LOW
2005	$1,387	$1,040
2006	$1,481	$1,111

27638

YEARS MFRD 2005-2006
ENGINE .... KOHLER
CYLINDERS 2
CID 44.2
ENGINE HP 26
COOLING .... AIR
FUEL .... G
SPEEDS .... VARIABLE
TRANSMISSION .... HYDRO
STEERING .... STANDARD
BLADE CLUTCH .... ELECTRIC
STANDARD DECK .... 54"
WEIGHT .... 717 LBS.
MSRP $3,099

RETAIL PRICING

YEAR	HIGH	LOW
2005	$1,375	$1,031
2006	$1,471	$1,103

27639

YEARS MFRD 2005-2006
ENGINE .... B&S INTEK
CYLINDERS 1
ENGINE HP 18
COOLING .... AIR
FUEL .... G
SPEEDS 6/1
TRANSMISSION .... GEAR
STEERING .... STANDARD
BLADE CLUTCH .... MANUAL

27690

YEARS MFRD 2007-2009
ENGINE .... KOHLER PRO
CYLINDERS 2
CID 725CC
ENGINE HP 26
COOLING .... AIR
FUEL .... G
SPEEDS .... VARIABLE
TRANSMISSION .... HYDRO
STEERING .... STANDARD
BLADE CLUTCH .... ELECTRIC
STANDARD DECK .... 54"
WEIGHT .... 561 LBS.
MSRP $2,499

RETAIL PRICING

YEAR	HIGH	LOW
2008	$1,111	$833
2009	$1,307	$980

27770

YEARS MFRD 2004-2004
ENGINE .. KOHLER COMMAND OHV
CYLINDERS 1
ENGINE HP 18
COOLING .... AIR
FUEL .... G
SPEEDS .... VARIABLE
TRANSMISSION .... HYDRO
STEERING .... ZERO
STANDARD DECK .... 50"
WEIGHT .... 670 LBS.
MSRP $3,599

RETAIL PRICING

YEAR	HIGH	LOW
2004	$1,875	$1,406

27771

YEARS MFRD 2017-2017
ENGINE .... KAWASAKI
CYLINDERS 2
CID 726CC
ENGINE HP 21.5
COOLING .... AIR
FUEL .... G
SPEEDS .... VARIABLE
TRANSMISSION .... HYDRO
STEERING .... ZERO
BLADE CLUTCH .... ELECTRIC
STANDARD DECK .... 42"
WEIGHT .... 695 LBS.
MSRP $2,899

RETAIL PRICING

YEAR	HIGH	LOW
2017	$1,942	$1,456

27772

YEARS MFRD 2005-2006
ENGINE .... KOHLER
CYLINDERS 1
CID 36.4
ENGINE HP 20
COOLING .... AIR
FUEL .... G
SPEEDS .... VARIABLE
TRANSMISSION .... HYDRO
STEERING .... ZERO
BLADE CLUTCH .... ELECTRIC
STANDARD DECK .... 44"
WEIGHT .... 590 LBS.
MSRP $2,999

RETAIL PRICING

YEAR	HIGH	LOW
2005	$1,659	$1,244
2006	$1,752	$1,314

27773

YEARS MFRD 2017-2017
ENGINE .... KOHLER
CYLINDERS 2
CID 724CC
ENGINE HP 24
COOLING .... AIR
FUEL .... G
SPEEDS .... VARIABLE
TRANSMISSION .... HYDRO
STEERING .... ZERO
BLADE CLUTCH .... ELECTRIC
STANDARD DECK .... 42"
WEIGHT .... 695 LBS.
MSRP $2,849

RETAIL PRICING

YEAR	HIGH	LOW
2017	$1,908	$1,431

27774

YEARS MFRD . . . 2005-2006
ENGINE . . . B&S
CYLINDERS. . . 2
CID . . . 40
ENGINE HP . . . 22
COOLING . . . AIR
FUEL . . . G
SPEEDS . . . VARIABLE
TRANSMISSION . . . HYDRO
STEERING. . . ZERO
BLADE CLUTCH . . . ELECTRIC
STANDARD DECK . . . 50"
WEIGHT . . . 618 LBS.
MSRP. . . $3,399

RETAIL PRICING

YEAR	HIGH	LOW
2005	$1,675	$1,256
2006	$1,716	$1,287

27778

YEARS MFRD . . . 2017-2017
ENGINE . . . B&S PLATINUM
CYLINDERS. . . 2
CID . . . 724CC
ENGINE HP . . . 22
COOLING . . . AIR
FUEL . . . G
SPEEDS . . . VARIABLE
TRANSMISSION . . . HYDRO
STEERING. . . ZERO
BLADE CLUTCH . . . ELECTRIC
STANDARD DECK . . . 46"
WEIGHT . . . 720 LBS.
MSRP. . . $2,599

RETAIL PRICING

YEAR	HIGH	LOW
2017	$1,694	$1,270

27779

YEARS MFRD . . . 2017-2017
ENGINE . . . KAWASAKI
CYLINDERS. . . 2
CID . . . 726CC
ENGINE HP . . . 23
COOLING . . . AIR
FUEL . . . G
SPEEDS . . . VARIABLE
TRANSMISSION . . . HYDRO
STEERING. . . ZERO
BLADE CLUTCH . . . ELECTRIC
STANDARD DECK . . . 54"
WEIGHT . . . 780 LBS.
MSRP. . . $2,999

RETAIL PRICING

YEAR	HIGH	LOW
2017	$2,024	$1,518

27830

YEARS MFRD . . . 2004-2004
ENGINE . . . HONDA OHC
CYLINDERS. . . 2
CID . . . 32.3
ENGINE HP . . . 16
COOLING . . . AIR
FUEL . . . G
SPEEDS . . . VARIABLE
TRANSMISSION . . . HYDRO
STEERING. . . STANDARD
STANDARD DECK . . . 42"
WEIGHT . . . 528 LBS.
MSRP. . . $2,049

RETAIL PRICING

YEAR	HIGH	LOW
2004	$1,068	$801

28008

YEARS MFRD . . . 2012-2012
ENGINE . . . KOHLER COURAGE PLUS
CYLINDERS. . . 2
ENGINE HP . . . 26
COOLING . . . AIR
FUEL . . . G
SPEEDS . . . VARIABLE
TRANSMISSION . . . HYDRO
STEERING. . . STANDARD
STANDARD DECK . . . 54"
WEIGHT . . . 520 LBS.
MSRP. . . $2,199

RETAIL PRICING

YEAR	HIGH	LOW
2012	$1,178	$884

28033

YEARS MFRD . . . 2009-2009
ENGINE . . . B&S
CYLINDERS. . . 1
ENGINE HP . . . 17.5
COOLING . . . AIR
FUEL . . . G
SPEEDS . . . VARIABLE
TRANSMISSION . . . HYDRO
STEERING. . . STANDARD
BLADE CLUTCH . . . MANUAL
STANDARD DECK . . . 30"
WEIGHT . . . 495 LBS.
MSRP. . . $1,969

RETAIL PRICING

YEAR	HIGH	LOW
2009	$1,084	$813

28601

YEARS MFRD . . . 2009-2009
ENGINE . . . B&S
CYLINDERS. . . 1
ENGINE HP . . . 15.5
COOLING . . . AIR
FUEL . . . G
SPEEDS . . . 6/1
TRANSMISSION . . . GEAR
STEERING. . . STANDARD
BLADE CLUTCH . . . MANUAL
STANDARD DECK . . . 38"
WEIGHT . . . 492 LBS.
MSRP. . . $899

RETAIL PRICING

YEAR	HIGH	LOW
2009	$494	$371

28603

YEARS MFRD . . . 2009-2009
ENGINE . . . B&S
CYLINDERS. . . 1
ENGINE HP . . . 17.5
COOLING . . . AIR
FUEL . . . G
SPEEDS . . . 6/1
TRANSMISSION . . . GEAR
STEERING. . . STANDARD
BLADE CLUTCH . . . MANUAL
STANDARD DECK . . . 42"
WEIGHT . . . 495 LBS.
MSRP. . . $1,249

RETAIL PRICING

YEAR	HIGH	LOW
2009	$686	$514

28605

YEARS MFRD . . . 2009-2009
ENGINE . . . B&S
CYLINDERS. . . 1
ENGINE HP . . . 17.5
COOLING . . . AIR
FUEL . . . G
SPEEDS . . . 6/1
TRANSMISSION . . . GEAR
STEERING. . . STANDARD
BLADE CLUTCH . . . MANUAL
STANDARD DECK . . . 42"
WEIGHT . . . 495 LBS.
MSRP. . . $1,249

RETAIL PRICING

YEAR	HIGH	LOW
2009	$686	$514

28607

YEARS MFRD . . . 2009-2009
ENGINE . . . B&S
CYLINDERS. . . 1
ENGINE HP . . . 20
COOLING . . . AIR
FUEL . . . G
SPEEDS . . . 6/1
TRANSMISSION . . . GEAR
STEERING. . . STANDARD
BLADE CLUTCH . . . MANUAL
STANDARD DECK . . . 42"
WEIGHT . . . 495 LBS.
MSRP. . . $1,499

RETAIL PRICING

YEAR	HIGH	LOW
2009	$825	$618

28608

YEARS MFRD . . . 2009-2009
ENGINE . . . B&S
CYLINDERS. . . 1
ENGINE HP . . . 20
COOLING . . . AIR
FUEL . . . G
SPEEDS . . . VARIABLE
TRANSMISSION . . . HYDRO
STEERING. . . STANDARD
BLADE CLUTCH . . . MANUAL
STANDARD DECK . . . 42"
WEIGHT . . . 507 LBS.
MSRP. . . $1,649

RETAIL PRICING

YEAR	HIGH	LOW
2009	$908	$681

28612

YEARS MFRD . . . 2009-2009
ENGINE . . . B&S
CYLINDERS. . . 1
ENGINE HP . . . 20
COOLING . . . AIR
FUEL . . . G
SPEEDS . . . VARIABLE
TRANSMISSION . . . HYDRO
STEERING. . . STANDARD
BLADE CLUTCH . . . MANUAL
STANDARD DECK . . . 42"
WEIGHT . . . 493 LBS.
MSRP. . . $1,749

RETAIL PRICING

YEAR	HIGH	LOW
2009	$962	$722

28614

YEARS MFRD . . . 2009-2009
ENGINE . . . B&S
CYLINDERS. . . 1
ENGINE HP . . . 20
COOLING . . . AIR
FUEL . . . G
SPEEDS . . . VARIABLE
TRANSMISSION . . . HYDRO
STEERING. . . STANDARD
BLADE CLUTCH . . . MANUAL
STANDARD DECK . . . 46"
WEIGHT . . . 513 LBS.
MSRP. . . $1,799

RETAIL PRICING

YEAR	HIGH	LOW
2009	$991	$743

28621

YEARS MFRD . . . 2009-2009
ENGINE . . . B&S
CYLINDERS. . . 1
ENGINE HP . . . 21
COOLING . . . AIR
FUEL . . . G
SPEEDS . . . 6/1
TRANSMISSION . . . HYDRO
STEERING. . . STANDARD

BLADE CLUTCH .... MANUAL
STANDARD DECK .... 42"
WEIGHT .... 498 LBS.
MSRP................. $1,649

RETAIL PRICING

YEAR	HIGH	LOW
2009	$908	$681

28622

YEARS MFRD 2009-2009
ENGINE .... B&S
CYLINDERS.................. 1
ENGINE HP 21
COOLING .... AIR
FUEL .... G
SPEEDS .... VARIABLE
TRANSMISSION .... HYDRO
STEERING............ STANDARD
BLADE CLUTCH .... MANUAL
STANDARD DECK .... 42"
WEIGHT .... 505 LBS.
MSRP................. $1,849

RETAIL PRICING

YEAR	HIGH	LOW
2009	$1,018	$764

28626

YEARS MFRD 2009-2009
ENGINE .... B&S
CYLINDERS.................. 2
ENGINE HP 24
COOLING .... AIR
FUEL .... G
SPEEDS .... VARIABLE
TRANSMISSION .... HYDRO
STEERING............ STANDARD
BLADE CLUTCH .... MANUAL
STANDARD DECK .... 42"
WEIGHT .... 516 LBS.
MSRP................. $1,999

RETAIL PRICING

YEAR	HIGH	LOW
2009	$1,100	$825

28634

YEARS MFRD 2007-2009
ENGINE .... KOHLER PRO
CYLINDERS.................. 1
ENGINE HP 20
COOLING .... AIR
FUEL .... G
SPEEDS .... VARIABLE
TRANSMISSION .... HYDRO
STEERING............ STANDARD
STANDARD DECK .... 42"
WEIGHT .... 506 LBS.
MSRP................. $1,999

RETAIL PRICING

YEAR	HIGH	LOW
2008	$889	$667
2009	$1,100	$825

28638

YEARS MFRD 2007-2009
ENGINE .... B&S
CYLINDERS.................. 2
CID 725CC
ENGINE HP 22
COOLING .... AIR
FUEL .... G
SPEEDS .... VARIABLE
TRANSMISSION .... HYDRO
STEERING............ STANDARD
STANDARD DECK .... 42"
WEIGHT .... 516 LBS.
MSRP................. $1,999

RETAIL PRICING

YEAR	HIGH	LOW
2008	$991	$743
2009	$1,100	$825

28642

YEARS MFRD 2009-2009
ENGINE .... B&S
CYLINDERS.................. 2
ENGINE HP 26
COOLING .... AIR
FUEL .... G
SPEEDS .... VARIABLE
TRANSMISSION .... HYDRO
STEERING............ STANDARD
BLADE CLUTCH .... ELECTRIC
STANDARD DECK .... 48"
WEIGHT .... 561 LBS.
MSRP................. $2,549

RETAIL PRICING

YEAR	HIGH	LOW
2009	$1,402	$1,052

28645

YEARS MFRD 2009-2009
ENGINE .... KOHLER PRO
CYLINDERS.................. 2
ENGINE HP 26
COOLING .... AIR
FUEL .... G
SPEEDS 6/1
TRANSMISSION .... GEAR
STEERING............ STANDARD
BLADE CLUTCH .... ELECTRIC
STANDARD DECK .... 54"
WEIGHT .... 589 LBS.
MSRP................. $2,999

RETAIL PRICING

YEAR	HIGH	LOW
2009	$1,649	$1,237

28646

YEARS MFRD 2007-2009
ENGINE .... KOHLER PRO
CYLINDERS.................. 2
CID 725CC
ENGINE HP 26
COOLING .... AIR
FUEL .... G
SPEEDS .... VARIABLE
TRANSMISSION .... HYDRO
STEERING............ STANDARD
STANDARD DECK .... 54"
WEIGHT .... 596 LBS.
MSRP................. $3,249

RETAIL PRICING

YEAR	HIGH	LOW
2008	$1,625	$1,219
2009	$1,787	$1,340

28672

YEARS MFRD 2011-2011
ENGINE .... B&S OHV
CYLINDERS.................. 2
ENGINE HP 24
COOLING .... AIR
FUEL .... G
SPEEDS .... VARIABLE
TRANSMISSION .... HYDRO
STEERING............ STANDARD
STANDARD DECK .... 42"
WEIGHT .... 594 LBS.
MSRP................. $1,956

RETAIL PRICING

YEAR	HIGH	LOW
2011	$1,011	$758

28690

YEARS MFRD 2009-2009
ENGINE .... KOHLER PRO
CYLINDERS.................. 2
ENGINE HP 26
FUEL .... G
SPEEDS .... VARIABLE
TRANSMISSION .... HYDRO
STEERING............ STANDARD
BLADE CLUTCH .... ELECTRIC
STANDARD DECK .... 54"
MSRP................. $2,499

RETAIL PRICING

YEAR	HIGH	LOW
2009	$1,375	$1,031

28724

YEARS MFRD 2009-2009
ENGINE .... B&S
CYLINDERS.................. 1
ENGINE HP 21
COOLING .... AIR
FUEL .... G
SPEEDS .... VARIABLE
TRANSMISSION .... HYDRO
STEERING............ STANDARD
BLADE CLUTCH .... MANUAL
STANDARD DECK .... 46"
MSRP................. $1,899

RETAIL PRICING

YEAR	HIGH	LOW
2009	$1,045	$784

28744

YEARS MFRD 2007-2008
ENGINE .... B&S
CYLINDERS.................. 2
CID 725CC
ENGINE HP 26
COOLING .... AIR
FUEL .... G
SPEEDS .... VARIABLE
TRANSMISSION .... HYDRO
STEERING............ STANDARD
BLADE CLUTCH .... ELECTRIC
STANDARD DECK .... 54"
WEIGHT .... 576 LBS.
MSRP................. $2,099

RETAIL PRICING

YEAR	HIGH	LOW
2008	$1,165	$874

28745

YEARS MFRD 2007-2008
ENGINE .... KOHLER
CYLINDERS.................. 2
CID 725CC
ENGINE HP 26
COOLING .... AIR
FUEL .... G
SPEEDS 6/1
TRANSMISSION .... GEAR
STEERING............ STANDARD
BLADE CLUTCH .... ELECTRIC
STANDARD DECK .... 54"
MSRP................. $2,299

RETAIL PRICING

YEAR	HIGH	LOW
2008	$1,278	$958

28746

YEARS MFRD 2007-2008
ENGINE .... KOHLER
CYLINDERS.................. 2
CID 725CC
ENGINE HP 26
COOLING .... AIR
FUEL .... G
SPEEDS .... VARIABLE
TRANSMISSION .... HYDRO
STEERING............ STANDARD
BLADE CLUTCH .... ELECTRIC
STANDARD DECK .... 54"
WEIGHT .... 596 LBS.
MSRP................. $2,499

RETAIL PRICING

YEAR	HIGH	LOW
2008	$1,389	$1,042

28786

YEARS MFRD 2007-2009
ENGINE .... B&S
CYLINDERS.................. 1
CID 502CC
ENGINE HP 21
COOLING .... AIR
FUEL .... G
SPEEDS .... VARIABLE
TRANSMISSION .... HYDRO
STEERING................ ZERO
BLADE CLUTCH .... ELECTRIC
STANDARD DECK .... 42"
MSRP................. $3,099

CRAFTSMAN

RETAIL PRICING

YEAR	HIGH	LOW
2008	$1,604	$1,203
2009	$1,705	$1,279

28790

YEARS MFRD 2009-2009
ENGINE .... B&S
CYLINDERS.................. 2
ENGINE HP.................. 26
COOLING .... AIR
FUEL .... G
SPEEDS .... VARIABLE
TRANSMISSION .... HYDRO
STEERING.............. ZERO
BLADE CLUTCH .... ELECTRIC
STANDARD DECK .... 50"
WEIGHT .... 775 LBS.
MSRP................. $3,699

RETAIL PRICING

YEAR	HIGH	LOW
2009	$2,035	$1,526

28791

YEARS MFRD 2007-2009
ENGINE .... KOHLER
CYLINDERS.................. 2
ENGINE HP.................. 26
COOLING .... AIR
FUEL .... G
SPEEDS .... VARIABLE
TRANSMISSION .... HYDRO
STEERING.............. ZERO
BLADE CLUTCH .... ELECTRIC
STANDARD DECK .... 50"
MSRP................. $3,699

RETAIL PRICING

YEAR	HIGH	LOW
2008	$1,667	$1,250
2009	$2,035	$1,526

28803

YEARS MFRD 2009-2009
ENGINE .... B&S
CYLINDERS.................. 1
ENGINE HP.............. 17.5
COOLING .... AIR
FUEL .... G
SPEEDS 6/1
TRANSMISSION .... GEAR
STEERING........... STANDARD
BLADE CLUTCH .... MANUAL
STANDARD DECK .... 42"
WEIGHT .... 495 LBS.
MSRP................. $1,249

RETAIL PRICING

YEAR	HIGH	LOW
2009	$686	$514

28807

YEARS MFRD 2009-2009
ENGINE .... B%S
CYLINDERS.................. 1
ENGINE HP.............. 19.5
COOLING .... AIR
FUEL .... G
SPEEDS 6/1
TRANSMISSION .... GEAR
STEERING........... STANDARD
BLADE CLUTCH .... MANUAL
STANDARD DECK .... 42"
WEIGHT .... 495 LBS.
MSRP................. $1,449

RETAIL PRICING

YEAR	HIGH	LOW
2009	$797	$598

28809

YEARS MFRD 2009-2009
ENGINE .... B&S
CYLINDERS.................. 1
ENGINE HP.................. 20
COOLING .... AIR
FUEL .... G
SPEEDS 6/1
TRANSMISSION .... GEAR
STEERING........... STANDARD
BLADE CLUTCH .... MANUAL
STANDARD DECK .... 42"
WEIGHT .... 495 LBS.
MSRP................. $1,499

RETAIL PRICING

YEAR	HIGH	LOW
2009	$825	$618

28811

YEARS MFRD 2009-2009
ENGINE .... B&S
CYLINDERS.................. 2
ENGINE HP.................. 20
COOLING .... AIR
FUEL .... G
SPEEDS 6/1
TRANSMISSION .... GEAR
STEERING........... STANDARD
BLADE CLUTCH .... MANUAL
STANDARD DECK .... 42"
MSRP................. $1,549

RETAIL PRICING

YEAR	HIGH	LOW
2009	$852	$639

28813

YEARS MFRD 2009-2009
ENGINE .... B&S
CYLINDERS.................. 2
ENGINE HP.................. 20
COOLING .... AIR
FUEL .... G
SPEEDS 6/1
TRANSMISSION .... GEAR
STEERING........... STANDARD
BLADE CLUTCH .... MANUAL
STANDARD DECK .... 46"
MSRP................. $1,649

RETAIL PRICING

YEAR	HIGH	LOW
2009	$908	$681

28814

YEARS MFRD 2009-2009
ENGINE .... B&S
CYLINDERS.................. 2
ENGINE HP.................. 20
COOLING .... AIR
FUEL .... G
SPEEDS .... VARIABLE
TRANSMISSION .... HYDRO
STEERING........... STANDARD
BLADE CLUTCH .... MANUAL
STANDARD DECK .... 46"
MSRP................. $1,799

RETAIL PRICING

YEAR	HIGH	LOW
2009	$991	$743

28821

YEARS MFRD 2009-2009
ENGINE .... B&S
CYLINDERS.................. 1
ENGINE HP.................. 20
COOLING .... AIR
FUEL .... G
SPEEDS 6/1
TRANSMISSION .... GEAR
STEERING........... STANDARD
BLADE CLUTCH .... MANUAL
STANDARD DECK .... 42"
WEIGHT .... 498 LBS.
MSRP................. $1,649

RETAIL PRICING

YEAR	HIGH	LOW
2009	$908	$681

28822

YEARS MFRD 2009-2009
ENGINE .... B&S
CYLINDERS.................. 1
ENGINE HP.................. 20
COOLING .... AIR
FUEL .... G
SPEEDS .... VARIABLE
TRANSMISSION .... HYDRO
STEERING........... STANDARD
BLADE CLUTCH .... MANUAL
STANDARD DECK .... 42"
WEIGHT .... 1,849 LBS.
MSRP................. $1,849

RETAIL PRICING

YEAR	HIGH	LOW
2009	$1,018	$764

28825

YEARS MFRD 2009-2009
ENGINE .... B&S
CYLINDERS.................. 2
ENGINE HP.................. 24
COOLING .... AIR
FUEL .... G
SPEEDS 6/1
TRANSMISSION .... GEAR
STEERING........... STANDARD
BLADE CLUTCH .... MANUAL
STANDARD DECK .... 42"
WEIGHT .... 506 LBS.
MSRP................. $1,799

RETAIL PRICING

YEAR	HIGH	LOW
2009	$991	$743

28826

YEARS MFRD 2009-2009
ENGINE .... B&S
CYLINDERS.................. 2
ENGINE HP.................. 24
COOLING .... AIR
FUEL .... G
SPEEDS .... VARIABLE
TRANSMISSION .... HYDRO
STEERING........... STANDARD
BLADE CLUTCH .... MANUAL
STANDARD DECK .... 42"
WEIGHT .... 516 LBS.
MSRP................. $1,999

RETAIL PRICING

YEAR	HIGH	LOW
2009	$1,100	$825

28827

YEARS MFRD 2009-2009
ENGINE .... B&S
CYLINDERS.................. 2
ENGINE HP.................. 24
COOLING .... AIR
FUEL .... G
SPEEDS 6/1
TRANSMISSION .... GEAR
STEERING........... STANDARD
STANDARD DECK .... 46"
WEIGHT .... 518 LBS.
MSRP................. $1,899

RETAIL PRICING

YEAR	HIGH	LOW
2009	$1,045	$784

28828

YEARS MFRD 2007-2009
ENGINE .... B&S
CYLINDERS.................. 2
CID 725CC
ENGINE HP.................. 24
COOLING .... AIR
FUEL .... G
SPEEDS .... VARIABLE
TRANSMISSION .... HYDRO
STEERING........... STANDARD
STANDARD DECK .... 46"
WEIGHT .... 526 LBS.
MSRP................. $2,049

RETAIL PRICING

YEAR	HIGH	LOW
2008	$889	$667
2009	$1,128	$846

28832

YEARS MFRD 2009-2009
ENGINE .... B&S
CYLINDERS.................. 2
ENGINE HP 24
COOLING .... AIR
FUEL .... G
SPEEDS .... VARIABLE
TRANSMISSION .... HYDRO
STEERING............ STANDARD
BLADE CLUTCH .... ELECTRIC
STANDARD DECK .... 54"
WEIGHT .... 556 LBS.
MSRP................. $2,249

RETAIL PRICING

YEAR	HIGH	LOW
2009	$1,238	$928

28833

YEARS MFRD 2007-2009
ENGINE .... KOHLER
CYLINDERS.................. 1
CID 597CC
ENGINE HP 20
COOLING .... AIR
FUEL .... G
SPEEDS 6/1
TRANSMISSION .... GEAR
STEERING............ STANDARD
STANDARD DECK .... 42"
WEIGHT .... 498 LBS.
MSRP................. $1,799

RETAIL PRICING

YEAR	HIGH	LOW
2008	$805	$603
2009	$991	$743

28834

YEARS MFRD 2009-2009
ENGINE .... KOHLER
CYLINDERS.................. 1
ENGINE HP 20
COOLING .... AIR
FUEL .... G
SPEEDS .... VARIABLE
TRANSMISSION .... HYDRO
STEERING............ STANDARD
BLADE CLUTCH .... MANUAL
STANDARD DECK .... 42"
WEIGHT .... 506 LBS.
MSRP................. $1,999

RETAIL PRICING

YEAR	HIGH	LOW
2009	$1,100	$825

28836

YEARS MFRD 2007-2009
ENGINE .... KOHLER
CYLINDERS.................. 1
CID 597CC
ENGINE HP 22
COOLING .... AIR
FUEL .... G
SPEEDS .... VARIABLE
TRANSMISSION .... HYDRO
STEERING............ STANDARD
STANDARD DECK .... 46"
WEIGHT .... 514 LBS.
MSRP................. $2,099

RETAIL PRICING

YEAR	HIGH	LOW
2008	$1,046	$784
2009	$1,155	$866

28842

YEARS MFRD 2009-2009
ENGINE .... B&S
CYLINDERS.................. 2
ENGINE HP 24
COOLING .... AIR
FUEL .... G
SPEEDS .... VARIABLE
TRANSMISSION .... HYDRO
STEERING............ STANDARD
STANDARD DECK .... 48"
WEIGHT .... 561 LBS.
MSRP................. $2,549

RETAIL PRICING

YEAR	HIGH	LOW
2009	$1,402	$1,052

28845

YEARS MFRD 2009-2009
ENGINE .... KOHLER
CYLINDERS.................. 2
ENGINE HP 26
COOLING .... AIR
FUEL .... G
SPEEDS 6/1
TRANSMISSION .... GEAR
STEERING............ STANDARD
BLADE CLUTCH .... ELECTRIC
STANDARD DECK .... 54"
WEIGHT .... 589 LBS.
MSRP................. $2,999

RETAIL PRICING

YEAR	HIGH	LOW
2009	$1,649	$1,237

28846

YEARS MFRD 2007-2009
ENGINE .... KOHLER
CYLINDERS.................. 2
CID 725CC
ENGINE HP 26
COOLING .... AIR
FUEL .... G
SPEEDS .... VARIABLE
TRANSMISSION .... HYDRO
STEERING............ STANDARD
STANDARD DECK .... 54"
WEIGHT .... 596 LBS.
MSRP................. $3,249

RETAIL PRICING

YEAR	HIGH	LOW
2008	$1,625	$1,219
2009	$1,787	$1,340

28848

YEARS MFRD 2007-2009
ENGINE .... KOHLER
CYLINDERS.................. 2
CID 725CC
ENGINE HP 24
COOLING .... AIR
FUEL .... G
SPEEDS .... VARIABLE
TRANSMISSION .... HYDRO
STEERING............ STANDARD
BLADE CLUTCH .... ELECTRIC
STANDARD DECK .... 48"
WEIGHT .... 596 LBS.
MSRP................. $3,099

RETAIL PRICING

YEAR	HIGH	LOW
2008	$1,389	$1,042
2009	$1,705	$1,279

28851

YEARS MFRD 2012-2014
ENGINE .... B&S
CYLINDERS.................. 1
ENGINE HP 21
COOLING .... AIR
FUEL .... G
SPEEDS .... VARIABLE
TRANSMISSION .... HYDRO
STEERING............ STANDARD
STANDARD DECK .... 42"
WEIGHT .... 505 LBS.
MSRP................. $1,779

RETAIL PRICING

YEAR	HIGH	LOW
2012	$481	$361
2013	$608	$456
2014	$840	$630

28852

YEARS MFRD 2012-2014
ENGINE .... B&S PLATINUM
ENGINE HP 21
COOLING .... AIR
FUEL .... G
SPEEDS .... VARIABLE
TRANSMISSION .... HYDRO
STEERING............ STANDARD
STANDARD DECK .... 46"
WEIGHT .... 515 LBS.
MSRP................. $1,899

RETAIL PRICING

YEAR	HIGH	LOW
2012	$514	$385
2013	$650	$487
2014	$895	$671

28853

YEARS MFRD 2012-2014
ENGINE .... KOHLER COURAGE
ENGINE HP 22
COOLING .... AIR
FUEL .... G
SPEEDS .... VARIABLE
TRANSMISSION .... HYDRO
STEERING............ STANDARD
STANDARD DECK .... 46"
WEIGHT .... 514 LBS.
MSRP................. $2,029

RETAIL PRICING

YEAR	HIGH	LOW
2012	$548	$411
2013	$732	$549
2014	$1,043	$782

28856

YEARS MFRD 2011-2014
ENGINE .... B&S PLATINUM
CYLINDERS.................. 2
ENGINE HP 24
COOLING .... AIR
FUEL .... G
SPEEDS .... VARIABLE
TRANSMISSION .... HYDRO
STEERING............ STANDARD
STANDARD DECK .... 42"
WEIGHT .... 518 LBS.
MSRP................. $1,989

RETAIL PRICING

YEAR	HIGH	LOW
2011	$432	$324
2012	$561	$421
2013	$697	$523
2014	$1,029	$772

28857

YEARS MFRD 2011-2014
ENGINE .... B&S PLATINUM
CYLINDERS.................. 2
ENGINE HP 24
COOLING .... AIR
FUEL .... G
SPEEDS .... VARIABLE
TRANSMISSION .... HYDRO
STEERING............ STANDARD
STANDARD DECK .... 46"
WEIGHT .... 526 LBS.
MSRP................. $2,119

RETAIL PRICING

YEAR	HIGH	LOW
2011	$460	$345
2012	$575	$431
2013	$711	$533
2014	$1,063	$797

28857CAX

YEARS MFRD 2016-2016
ENGINE .... B&S
CYLINDERS.................. 2
CID 724CC
ENGINE HP 22
COOLING .... AIR
FUEL .... G
SPEEDS .... VARIABLE
TRANSMISSION .... HYDRO
STEERING............ STANDARD
BLADE CLUTCH .... ELECTRIC
STANDARD DECK .... 48"
MSRP................. $1,999

CRAFTSMAN

RETAIL PRICING

YEAR	HIGH	LOW
2016	$1,184	$888

28858

YEARS MFRD 2011-2014
ENGINE .... B&S
CYLINDERS 2
ENGINE HP 26
COOLING .... AIR
FUEL .... G
SPEEDS .... VARIABLE
TRANSMISSION .... HYDRO
STEERING .... STANDARD
STANDARD DECK .... 54"
WEIGHT .... 556 LBS.
MSRP $2,559

RETAIL PRICING

YEAR	HIGH	LOW
2011	$542	$406
2012	$697	$523
2013	$914	$685
2014	$1,327	$995

28860

YEARS MFRD 2007-2009
ENGINE .... KOHLER
CYLINDERS 2
CID 725CC
ENGINE HP 26
COOLING .... AIR
FUEL .... G
SPEEDS .... VARIABLE
TRANSMISSION .... HYDRO
STEERING .... STANDARD
BLADE CLUTCH .... ELECTRIC
STANDARD DECK .... 54"
WEIGHT .... 596 LBS.
MSRP $3,249

RETAIL PRICING

YEAR	HIGH	LOW
2008	$1,444	$1,083
2009	$1,787	$1,340

28861

YEARS MFRD 2011-2014
ENGINE .... KOHLER
ENGINE HP 26
COOLING .... AIR
FUEL .... G
SPEEDS .... VARIABLE
TRANSMISSION .... HYDRO
STEERING .... STANDARD
STANDARD DECK .... 54"
MSRP $3,659

RETAIL PRICING

YEAR	HIGH	LOW
2011	$786	$589
2012	$996	$747
2013	$1,320	$990
2014	$1,949	$1,462

28862

YEARS MFRD 2012-2014
ENGINE .... B&S PLATINUM
ENGINE HP 21
COOLING .... AIR
FUEL .... G
SPEEDS .... VARIABLE
TRANSMISSION .... HYDRO
STEERING .... STANDARD
STANDARD DECK .... 46"
WEIGHT .... 421 LBS.
MSRP $2,009

RETAIL PRICING

YEAR	HIGH	LOW
2012	$542	$406
2013	$683	$512
2014	$1,035	$776

28863

YEARS MFRD 2012-2012
ENGINE .... B&S PLATINUM
CYLINDERS 2
ENGINE HP 26
COOLING .... AIR
FUEL .... G
SPEEDS .... VARIABLE
TRANSMISSION .... HYDRO
STEERING .... STANDARD
STANDARD DECK .... 54"
WEIGHT .... 520 LBS.
MSRP $2,199

RETAIL PRICING

YEAR	HIGH	LOW
2012	$1,178	$884

28866

YEARS MFRD 2013-2014
ENGINE .... B&S
CYLINDERS 2
ENGINE HP 24
COOLING .... AIR
FUEL .... G
SPEEDS .... VARIABLE
TRANSMISSION .... HYDRO
STEERING .... STANDARD
STANDARD DECK .... 42"
WEIGHT .... 518 LBS.
MSRP $2,239

RETAIL PRICING

YEAR	HIGH	LOW
2013	$819	$614
2014	$1,056	$792

28867

YEARS MFRD 2012-2012
ENGINE ... KOHLER COURAGE PLUS
CYLINDERS 2
ENGINE HP 26
COOLING .... AIR
FUEL .... G
SPEEDS .... VARIABLE
TRANSMISSION .... HYDRO
STEERING .... STANDARD
STANDARD DECK .... 54"
WEIGHT .... 548 LBS.
MSRP $2,999

RETAIL PRICING

YEAR	HIGH	LOW
2012	$1,606	$1,204

28870

YEARS MFRD 2007-2009
ENGINE .... B&S
CYLINDERS 2
CID 725CC
ENGINE HP 24
COOLING .... AIR
FUEL .... G
SPEEDS .... VARIABLE
TRANSMISSION .... HYDRO
STEERING .... STANDARD
STANDARD DECK .... 42"
WEIGHT .... 529 LBS.
MSRP $2,249

RETAIL PRICING

YEAR	HIGH	LOW
2008	$999	$750
2009	$1,238	$928

28872

YEARS MFRD 2007-2008
ENGINE .... KOHLER
CYLINDERS 2
CID 725CC
ENGINE HP 25
COOLING .... AIR
FUEL .... G
SPEEDS .... VARIABLE
TRANSMISSION .... HYDRO
STEERING .... STANDARD
STANDARD DECK .... 46"
WEIGHT .... 541 LBS.
MSRP $2,499

RETAIL PRICING

YEAR	HIGH	LOW
2008	$1,389	$1,042

28874

YEARS MFRD 2007-2009
ENGINE .... KOHLER
CYLINDERS 2
CID 725CC
ENGINE HP 27
COOLING .... AIR
FUEL .... G
SPEEDS .... VARIABLE
TRANSMISSION .... HYDRO
STEERING .... STANDARD
STANDARD DECK .... 54"
WEIGHT .... 613 LBS.
MSRP $3,499

RETAIL PRICING

YEAR	HIGH	LOW
2008	$1,824	$1,368
2009	$1,926	$1,444

28875

YEARS MFRD 2007-2010
ENGINE .... B&S
ENGINE HP 26
COOLING .... AIR
FUEL .... G
SPEEDS .... VARIABLE
TRANSMISSION .... HYDRO
STEERING .... ZERO
BLADE CLUTCH .... ELECTRIC
STANDARD DECK .... 52"
MSRP $7,124

RETAIL PRICING

YEAR	HIGH	LOW
2008	$3,553	$2,665
2009	$3,850	$2,888
2010	$3,980	$2,985

28876

YEARS MFRD 2009-2009
ENGINE .... B&S
CYLINDERS 2
ENGINE HP 22
COOLING .... AIR
FUEL .... G
SPEEDS .... VARIABLE
TRANSMISSION .... HYDRO
STEERING .... ZERO
BLADE CLUTCH .... ELECTRIC
STANDARD DECK .... 42"
WEIGHT .... 738 LBS.
MSRP $6,459

RETAIL PRICING

YEAR	HIGH	LOW
2009	$3,555	$2,666

28881

YEARS MFRD 2011-2014
ENGINE .... B&S
CYLINDERS 1
ENGINE HP 17.5
COOLING .... AIR
FUEL .... G
SPEEDS 7/1
TRANSMISSION .... DISC
STEERING .... STANDARD
STANDARD DECK .... 42"
MSRP $1,312

RETAIL PRICING

YEAR	HIGH	LOW
2011	$337	$253
2012	$514	$385
2013	$568	$426
2014	$670	$502

28883

YEARS MFRD 2013-2014
ENGINE .... B&S
CYLINDERS 1
ENGINE HP 17.5
COOLING .... AIR
FUEL .... G
SPEEDS 7/1
TRANSMISSION .... DISC

STEERING...........STANDARD
STANDARD DECK........... 42"
MSRP................. $1,374

RETAIL PRICING

YEAR	HIGH	LOW
2013	$514	$385
2014	$670	$502

28884

YEARS MFRD........ 2013-2014
ENGINE.................B&S
ENGINE HP.............. 19.5
COOLING..................AIR
FUEL.......................G
SPEEDS..............VARIABLE
TRANSMISSION........... DISC
STEERING...........STANDARD
STANDARD DECK........... 42"
MSRP................. $1,489

RETAIL PRICING

YEAR	HIGH	LOW
2013	$589	$442
2014	$732	$549

28885

YEARS MFRD........ 2012-2014
ENGINE.................B&S
ENGINE HP................ 21
COOLING..................AIR
FUEL.......................G
SPEEDS..............VARIABLE
TRANSMISSION........... DISC
STEERING...........STANDARD
STANDARD DECK........... 46"
MSRP................. $1,639

RETAIL PRICING

YEAR	HIGH	LOW
2012	$648	$486
2013	$751	$564
2014	$900	$675

28886

YEARS MFRD........ 2013-2014
ENGINE.................B&S
CYLINDERS..................1
ENGINE HP................ 21
COOLING..................AIR
FUEL.......................G
SPEEDS..............VARIABLE
TRANSMISSION..........HYDRO
STEERING...............ZERO
STANDARD DECK........... 46"
MSRP................. $1,739

RETAIL PRICING

YEAR	HIGH	LOW
2013	$704	$528
2014	$900	$675

28890

YEARS MFRD........ 2007-2009
ENGINE...............KOHLER
CYLINDERS..................2
CID...................725CC
ENGINE HP................ 25
COOLING..................AIR
FUEL.......................G
SPEEDS..............VARIABLE
TRANSMISSION..........HYDRO
STEERING...........STANDARD
STANDARD DECK........... 48"
WEIGHT.............. 556 LBS.
MSRP................. $2,449

RETAIL PRICING

YEAR	HIGH	LOW
2008	$1,242	$931
2009	$1,347	$1,010

28901

YEARS MFRD........ 2011-2011
ENGINE.............B&S OHV
CYLINDERS..................1
ENGINE HP.............. 17.5
COOLING..................AIR
FUEL.......................G
SPEEDS.................. 7/1
TRANSMISSION........... DISC
STEERING...........STANDARD
STANDARD DECK........... 42"
MSRP...................$930

RETAIL PRICING

YEAR	HIGH	LOW
2011	$480	$360

28902

YEARS MFRD........ 2011-2011
ENGINE.............B&S OHV
ENGINE HP.............. 19.5
COOLING..................AIR
FUEL.......................G
SPEEDS.................. 7/1
TRANSMISSION........... DISC
STEERING...........STANDARD
STANDARD DECK........... 42"
MSRP................. $1,022

RETAIL PRICING

YEAR	HIGH	LOW
2011	$528	$396

28903

YEARS MFRD........ 2009-2010
ENGINE.................B&S
CYLINDERS..................1
ENGINE HP.............. 17.5
COOLING..................AIR
FUEL.......................G
SPEEDS.................. 6/1
TRANSMISSION...........GEAR
STEERING...........STANDARD
BLADE CLUTCH........ MANUAL
STANDARD DECK........... 42"
WEIGHT.............. 495 LBS.
MSRP................. $1,229

RETAIL PRICING

YEAR	HIGH	LOW
2009	$676	$507
2010	$686	$514

28904

YEARS MFRD........ 2011-2011
ENGINE.............B&S OHV
ENGINE HP................ 20
COOLING..................AIR
FUEL.......................G
SPEEDS..............VARIABLE
TRANSMISSION..........HYDRO
STEERING...........STANDARD
STANDARD DECK........... 42"
WEIGHT.............. 520 LBS.
MSRP................. $1,116

RETAIL PRICING

YEAR	HIGH	LOW
2011	$577	$432

28905

YEARS MFRD........ 2011-2011
ENGINE.............B&S OHV
ENGINE HP................ 20
COOLING..................AIR
FUEL.......................G
SPEEDS..............VARIABLE
TRANSMISSION..........HYDRO
STEERING...........STANDARD
STANDARD DECK........... 42"
WEIGHT.............. 520 LBS.
MSRP................. $1,210

RETAIL PRICING

YEAR	HIGH	LOW
2011	$625	$469

28907

YEARS MFRD........ 2009-2010
ENGINE.................B&S
CYLINDERS..................1
ENGINE HP.............. 19.5
COOLING..................AIR
FUEL.......................G
SPEEDS.................. 6/1
TRANSMISSION...........GEAR
STEERING...........STANDARD
BLADE CLUTCH........ MANUAL
STANDARD DECK........... 42"
WEIGHT.............. 495 LBS.
MSRP................. $1,359

RETAIL PRICING

YEAR	HIGH	LOW
2009	$748	$561
2010	$759	$569

28908

YEARS MFRD........ 2009-2010
ENGINE.................B&S
CYLINDERS..................1
ENGINE HP.............. 19.5
COOLING..................AIR
FUEL.......................G
SPEEDS..............VARIABLE
TRANSMISSION..........HYDRO
STEERING...........STANDARD
BLADE CLUTCH........ MANUAL
STANDARD DECK........... 42"
WEIGHT.............. 507 LBS.
MSRP................. $1,479

RETAIL PRICING

YEAR	HIGH	LOW
2009	$813	$610
2010	$827	$620

28910

YEARS MFRD........ 2009-2009
ENGINE.................B&S
CYLINDERS..................1
ENGINE HP................ 20
COOLING..................AIR
FUEL.......................G
SPEEDS..............VARIABLE
TRANSMISSION..........HYDRO
STEERING...........STANDARD
BLADE CLUTCH........ MANUAL
STANDARD DECK........... 42"
WEIGHT.............. 507 LBS.
MSRP................. $1,599

RETAIL PRICING

YEAR	HIGH	LOW
2009	$880	$660

28911

YEARS MFRD........ 2011-2011
ENGINE.............B&S OHV
ENGINE HP.............. 17.5
COOLING..................AIR
FUEL.......................G
SPEEDS.................. 7/1
TRANSMISSION........... DISC
STEERING...........STANDARD
STANDARD DECK........... 42"
WEIGHT.............. 520 LBS.
MSRP................. $1,022

RETAIL PRICING

YEAR	HIGH	LOW
2011	$528	$396

28913

YEARS MFRD........ 2009-2009
ENGINE.................B&S
CYLINDERS..................1
ENGINE HP.............. 17.5
COOLING..................AIR
FUEL.......................G
SPEEDS.................. 6/1
TRANSMISSION...........GEAR
STEERING...........STANDARD
BLADE CLUTCH........ MANUAL
STANDARD DECK........... 42"
WEIGHT.............. 495 LBS.
MSRP................. $1,349

RETAIL PRICING

YEAR	HIGH	LOW
2009	$742	$556

28914

YEARS MFRD........ 2011-2011
ENGINE.........B&S PLATINUM
ENGINE HP................ 21
COOLING..................AIR
FUEL.......................G
SPEEDS..............VARIABLE

CRAFTSMAN

- TRANSMISSION ... HYDRO
- STEERING ... STANDARD
- STANDARD DECK ... 46"
- MSRP ... $1,398

RETAIL PRICING

YEAR	HIGH	LOW
2011	$722	$542

28919

- YEARS MFRD ... 2011-2011
- ENGINE ... B&S OV
- ENGINE HP ... 20
- COOLING ... AIR
- FUEL ... G
- SPEEDS ... VARIABLE
- TRANSMISSION ... HYDRO
- STEERING ... STANDARD
- STANDARD DECK ... 42"
- WEIGHT ... 520 LBS.
- MSRP ... $1,210

RETAIL PRICING

YEAR	HIGH	LOW
2011	$625	$469

28922

- YEARS MFRD ... 2009-2011
- ENGINE ... B&S
- CYLINDERS ... 1
- ENGINE HP ... 21
- COOLING ... AIR
- FUEL ... G
- SPEEDS ... VARIABLE
- TRANSMISSION ... HYDRO
- STEERING ... STANDARD
- BLADE CLUTCH ... MANUAL
- STANDARD DECK ... 42"
- WEIGHT ... 505 LBS.
- MSRP ... $1,304

RETAIL PRICING

YEAR	HIGH	LOW
2009	$428	$321
2010	$581	$436
2011	$675	$506

28924

- YEARS MFRD ... 2009-2011
- ENGINE ... B&S
- CYLINDERS ... 1
- ENGINE HP ... 21
- COOLING ... AIR
- FUEL ... G
- SPEEDS ... VARIABLE
- TRANSMISSION ... HYDRO
- STEERING ... STANDARD
- BLADE CLUTCH ... MANUAL
- STANDARD DECK ... 46"
- WEIGHT ... 513 LBS.
- MSRP ... $1,305

RETAIL PRICING

YEAR	HIGH	LOW
2009	$428	$321
2010	$584	$438
2011	$675	$507

28925

- YEARS MFRD ... 2009-2010
- ENGINE ... B&S
- CYLINDERS ... 2
- ENGINE HP ... 22
- COOLING ... AIR
- FUEL ... G
- SPEEDS ... 6/1
- TRANSMISSION ... GEAR
- STEERING ... STANDARD
- BLADE CLUTCH ... MANUAL
- STANDARD DECK ... 42"
- WEIGHT ... 506 LBS.
- MSRP ... $1,864

RETAIL PRICING

YEAR	HIGH	LOW
2009	$1,018	$764
2010	$1,041	$781

28926

- YEARS MFRD ... 2009-2009
- ENGINE ... B&S
- CYLINDERS ... 2
- ENGINE HP ... 24
- COOLING ... AIR
- FUEL ... G
- SPEEDS ... VARIABLE
- TRANSMISSION ... HYDRO
- STEERING ... STANDARD
- BLADE CLUTCH ... MANUAL
- STANDARD DECK ... 42"
- WEIGHT ... 506 LBS.
- MSRP ... $2,099

RETAIL PRICING

YEAR	HIGH	LOW
2009	$1,155	$866

28927

- YEARS MFRD ... 2009-2011
- ENGINE ... B&S
- CYLINDERS ... 2
- ENGINE HP ... 24
- COOLING ... AIR
- FUEL ... G
- SPEEDS ... VARIABLE
- TRANSMISSION ... HYDRO
- STEERING ... STANDARD
- BLADE CLUTCH ... MANUAL
- STANDARD DECK ... 42"
- WEIGHT ... 518 LBS.
- MSRP ... $1,491

RETAIL PRICING

YEAR	HIGH	LOW
2009	$516	$387
2010	$594	$445
2011	$771	$579

28928

- YEARS MFRD ... 2009-2010
- ENGINE ... B&S
- CYLINDERS ... 2
- ENGINE HP ... 24
- COOLING ... AIR
- FUEL ... G
- SPEEDS ... VARIABLE
- TRANSMISSION ... HYDRO
- STEERING ... STANDARD
- BLADE CLUTCH ... MANUAL
- STANDARD DECK ... 46"
- WEIGHT ... 526 LBS.
- MSRP ... $2,099

RETAIL PRICING

YEAR	HIGH	LOW
2009	$1,155	$866
2010	$1,173	$880

28933

- YEARS MFRD ... 2009-2010
- ENGINE ... B&S
- CYLINDERS ... 2
- ENGINE HP ... 22
- COOLING ... AIR
- FUEL ... G
- SPEEDS ... VARIABLE
- TRANSMISSION ... HYDRO
- STEERING ... ZERO
- BLADE CLUTCH ... ELECTRIC
- STANDARD DECK ... 42"
- WEIGHT ... 600 LBS.
- MSRP ... $3,799

RETAIL PRICING

YEAR	HIGH	LOW
2009	$2,035	$1,526
2010	$2,122	$1,592

28934

- YEARS MFRD ... 2009-2009
- ENGINE ... KOHLER
- CYLINDERS ... 1
- ENGINE HP ... 22
- COOLING ... AIR
- FUEL ... G
- SPEEDS ... VARIABLE
- TRANSMISSION ... HYDRO
- STEERING ... STANDARD
- BLADE CLUTCH ... MANUAL
- STANDARD DECK ... 42"
- WEIGHT ... 514 LBS.
- MSRP ... $1,969

RETAIL PRICING

YEAR	HIGH	LOW
2009	$1,084	$813

28936

- YEARS MFRD ... 2009-2009
- ENGINE ... B&S
- CYLINDERS ... 2
- ENGINE HP ... 24
- COOLING ... AIR
- FUEL ... G
- SPEEDS ... VARIABLE
- TRANSMISSION ... HYDRO
- STEERING ... STANDARD
- BLADE CLUTCH ... MANUAL
- STANDARD DECK ... 42"
- WEIGHT ... 506 LBS.
- MSRP ... $2,219

RETAIL PRICING

YEAR	HIGH	LOW
2009	$1,222	$916

28945

- YEARS MFRD ... 2009-2009
- ENGINE ... KOHLER
- CYLINDERS ... 2
- ENGINE HP ... 26
- COOLING ... AIR
- FUEL ... G
- SPEEDS ... 6/1
- TRANSMISSION ... HYDRO
- STEERING ... STANDARD
- BLADE CLUTCH ... ELECTRIC
- STANDARD DECK ... 54"
- WEIGHT ... 589 LBS.
- MSRP ... $3,099

RETAIL PRICING

YEAR	HIGH	LOW
2009	$1,705	$1,279

28947

- YEARS MFRD ... 2009-2011
- ENGINE ... KOHLER COURAGE
- CYLINDERS ... 2
- ENGINE HP ... 26
- COOLING ... AIR
- FUEL ... G
- SPEEDS ... VARIABLE
- TRANSMISSION ... HYDRO
- STEERING ... STANDARD
- BLADE CLUTCH ... ELECTRIC
- STANDARD DECK ... 54"
- WEIGHT ... 596 LBS.
- MSRP ... $2,520

RETAIL PRICING

YEAR	HIGH	LOW
2009	$1,087	$815
2010	$1,153	$865
2011	$1,302	$977

28955

- YEARS MFRD ... 2010-2010
- ENGINE ... KOHLER COURAGE
- CYLINDERS ... 2
- ENGINE HP ... 26
- COOLING ... AIR
- FUEL ... G
- SPEEDS ... 6/1
- TRANSMISSION ... GEAR
- STEERING ... STANDARD
- WEIGHT ... 644 LBS.

28956

- YEARS MFRD ... 2009-2009
- ENGINE ... B&S
- CYLINDERS ... 2
- ENGINE HP ... 23
- COOLING ... AIR
- FUEL ... G
- SPEEDS ... VARIABLE
- TRANSMISSION ... HYDRO
- STEERING ... STANDARD

BLADE CLUTCH ....ELECTRIC
STANDARD DECK .... 48"
WEIGHT .... 560 LBS.
MSRP.................. $2,349

RETAIL PRICING

YEAR	HIGH	LOW
2009	$1,292	$969

28970

YEARS MFRD 2009-2010
ENGINE ....B&S
CYLINDERS.................2
ENGINE HP.................24
COOLING ....AIR
FUEL ....G
SPEEDS ....VARIABLE
TRANSMISSION ....HYDRO
STEERING............STANDARD
BLADE CLUTCH ....ELECTRIC
STANDARD DECK .... 42"
WEIGHT .... 529 LBS.
MSRP.................. $2,599

RETAIL PRICING

YEAR	HIGH	LOW
2009	$1,359	$1,019
2010	$1,452	$1,089

28972

YEARS MFRD 2009-2009
ENGINE ....B&S
CYLINDERS.................2
ENGINE HP.................26
COOLING ....AIR
FUEL ....G
SPEEDS ....VARIABLE
TRANSMISSION ....HYDRO
STEERING............STANDARD
BLADE CLUTCH ....ELECTRIC
STANDARD DECK .... 48"
WEIGHT .... 541 LBS.
MSRP.................. $2,839

RETAIL PRICING

YEAR	HIGH	LOW
2009	$1,563	$1,172

28973

YEARS MFRD 2009-2009
ENGINE ....B&S
CYLINDERS.................2
ENGINE HP.................28
COOLING ....AIR
FUEL ....G
SPEEDS ....VARIABLE
TRANSMISSION ....HYDRO
STEERING............STANDARD
BLADE CLUTCH ....ELECTRIC
STANDARD DECK .... 54"
WEIGHT .... 613 LBS.
MSRP.................. $3,099

RETAIL PRICING

YEAR	HIGH	LOW
2009	$1,705	$1,279

28974

YEARS MFRD 2009-2009
ENGINE ....B&S
CYLINDERS.................2
ENGINE HP.................28
COOLING ....AIR
FUEL ....G
SPEEDS ....VARIABLE
TRANSMISSION ....HYDRO
STEERING............STANDARD
BLADE CLUTCH ....ELECTRIC
STANDARD DECK .... 54"
WEIGHT .... 613 LBS.
MSRP.................. $3,599

RETAIL PRICING

YEAR	HIGH	LOW
2009	$1,980	$1,485

28980

YEARS MFRD 2011-2011
ENGINE .... B&S OHV
ENGINE HP.................24
COOLING ....AIR
FUEL ....G
SPEEDS ....VARIABLE
TRANSMISSION ....HYDRO
STEERING............STANDARD
STANDARD DECK .... 42"
WEIGHT .... 594 LBS.
MSRP.................. $1,862

RETAIL PRICING

YEAR	HIGH	LOW
2011	$962	$722

28981

YEARS MFRD 2011-2011
ENGINE .... B&S OHV
ENGINE HP.................26
COOLING ....AIR
FUEL ....G
SPEEDS ....VARIABLE
TRANSMISSION ....HYDRO
STEERING............STANDARD
STANDARD DECK .... 50"
MSRP.................. $2,238

RETAIL PRICING

YEAR	HIGH	LOW
2011	$1,156	$867

28984

YEARS MFRD 2011-2011
ENGINE .... B&S OHV
CYLINDERS.................2
ENGINE HP.................28
COOLING ....AIR
FUEL ....G
SPEEDS ....VARIABLE
TRANSMISSION ....HYDRO
STEERING............STANDARD
STANDARD DECK .... 54"
MSRP.................. $2,797

RETAIL PRICING

YEAR	HIGH	LOW
2011	$1,446	$1,084

28986

YEARS MFRD 2009-2011
ENGINE ....B&S
CYLINDERS.................1
ENGINE HP.................21
COOLING ....AIR
FUEL ....G
SPEEDS ....VARIABLE
TRANSMISSION ....HYDRO
STEERING................ZERO
BLADE CLUTCH ....ELECTRIC
STANDARD DECK .... 42"
WEIGHT .... 750 LBS.
MSRP.................. $1,999

RETAIL PRICING

YEAR	HIGH	LOW
2009	$844	$633
2010	$909	$682
2011	$1,033	$774

28990

YEARS MFRD 2009-2011
ENGINE ....KOHLER
CYLINDERS.................2
ENGINE HP.................26
COOLING ....AIR
FUEL ....G
SPEEDS ....VARIABLE
TRANSMISSION ....HYDRO
STEERING............STANDARD
BLADE CLUTCH ....ELECTRIC
STANDARD DECK .... 54"
WEIGHT .... 556 LBS.
MSRP.................. $1,866

RETAIL PRICING

YEAR	HIGH	LOW
2009	$895	$671
2010	$962	$722
2011	$963	$722

28992

YEARS MFRD 2009-2011
ENGINE ....B&S
CYLINDERS.................2
ENGINE HP.................26
COOLING ....AIR
FUEL ....G
SPEEDS ....VARIABLE
TRANSMISSION ....HYDRO
STEERING................ZERO
BLADE CLUTCH ....ELECTRIC
STANDARD DECK .... 52"
WEIGHT .... 780 LBS.
MSRP.................. $2,499

RETAIL PRICING

YEAR	HIGH	LOW
2009	$1,194	$896
2010	$1,293	$970
2011	$1,322	$992

29000

YEARS MFRD 2016-2017
ENGINE .... CRAFTSMAN
CYLINDERS.................1
CID 420CC
COOLING ....AIR
FUEL ....G
SPEEDS 6/1
TRANSMISSION ....GEAR
STEERING............STANDARD
BLADE CLUTCH .... MANUAL
STANDARD DECK .... 30"
WEIGHT .... 335 LBS.
MSRP.................... $999

RETAIL PRICING

YEAR	HIGH	LOW
2016	$475	$356
2017	$558	$418

29900

YEARS MFRD 2018-2019
ENGINE .... CRAFTSMAN
CYLINDERS.................1
CID 382CC
FUEL ....G
SPEEDS 6
TRANSMISSION ....GEAR
STEERING............STANDARD
STANDARD DECK .... 30"
WEIGHT .... 340 LBS.

309602X1

YEARS MFRD 2006-2006
ENGINE ....B&S
CYLINDERS.................1
ENGINE HP...............13.5
COOLING ....AIR
FUEL ....G
SPEEDS ....VARIABLE
TRANSMISSION ....HYDRO
STEERING............STANDARD
STANDARD DECK .... 30"
WEIGHT .... 353 LBS.
MSRP.................. $1,399

RETAIL PRICING

YEAR	HIGH	LOW
2006	$817	$613

2690639

YEARS MFRD 2007-2008
ENGINE ....B&S
CYLINDERS.................1
CID 502CC
ENGINE HP.................20
COOLING ....AIR
FUEL ....G
SPEEDS ....VARIABLE
TRANSMISSION ....HYDRO
STEERING................ZERO
BLADE CLUTCH ....ELECTRIC
STANDARD DECK .... 42"
MSRP.................. $2,499

RETAIL PRICING

YEAR	HIGH	LOW
2008	$1,389	$1,042

CRAFTSMAN

2690640

YEARS MFRD 2007-2008
ENGINE .... KOHLER
CYLINDERS.................. 1
CID 502CC
ENGINE HP 20
COOLING .... AIR
FUEL .... G
SPEEDS .... VARIABLE
TRANSMISSION .... HYDRO
STEERING.................ZERO
BLADE CLUTCH .... ELECTRIC
STANDARD DECK .... 44"
MSRP................. $2,699

RETAIL PRICING

YEAR	HIGH	LOW
2008	$1,500	$1,125

CUB CADET

ALL ZERO TURN MOWERS AND COMPACT TRACTORS

SERIAL NUMBERS

5TH DIGIT IN SERIAL NUMBER IS YEAR MFG.

AGS2130

YEARS MFRD 1994-1999
SERIES............ 2000 SERIES
ENGINE .... KOHLER
ENGINE HP 20
COOLING .... AIR
FUEL .... G
TRANSMISSION .... GEAR
STEERING............ STANDARD
STANDARD DECK .... 38"
MSRP................. $2,399

SERIAL NUMBERS

YEAR	BEGINNING NO.
1994	239301
1995	272501
1996	328136
1997	359000
1998	XXXX8XXXXXX
1999	XXXX9XXXXXX

RETAIL PRICING

YEAR	HIGH	LOW
1994	$193	$145
1995	$218	$164
1996	$238	$178
1997	$261	$196
1998	$294	$221
1999	$330	$248

AGS2135

YEARS MFRD 1994-1999
SERIES............ 2000 SERIES
ENGINE .... KOHLER
ENGINE HP 13
COOLING .... AIR
FUEL .... G
TRANSMISSION .... HYDRO
STEERING............ STANDARD
STANDARD DECK .... 38"
MSRP................. $2,599

RETAIL PRICING

YEAR	HIGH	LOW
1999	$374	$281

AGS2140

YEARS MFRD 1994-1995
SERIES............ 2000 SERIES
ENGINE .... ONAN
ENGINE HP 14
COOLING .... AIR
FUEL .... G
TRANSMISSION .... GEAR
STEERING............ STANDARD
STANDARD DECK .... 42"
MSRP................. $3,029

SERIAL NUMBERS

YEAR	BEGINNING NO.
1994	239301
1995	272501

RETAIL PRICING

YEAR	HIGH	LOW
1994	$338	$254
1995	$367	$275

AGS2150

YEARS MFRD 1996-1999
SERIES............ 2000 SERIES
ENGINE .... KOHLER
ENGINE HP 15
COOLING .... AIR
FUEL .... G
TRANSMISSION .... GEAR
STEERING............ STANDARD
STANDARD DECK .... 42"
MSRP................. $2,799

OPTIONS

2 BAG
28" TILLER
40" SNOW THROWER
42" BLADE

SERIAL NUMBERS

YEAR	BEGINNING NO.
1996	328136
1997	359000
1998	XXXX8XXXXX
1999	XXXX9XXXXX

RETAIL PRICING

YEAR	HIGH	LOW
1996	$222	$167
1997	$247	$185
1998	$274	$205
1999	$303	$228

AGS2160

YEARS MFRD 1994-1997
SERIES............ 2000 SERIES
ENGINE .... B&S
ENGINE HP 16
COOLING .... AIR
FUEL .... G
TRANSMISSION .... GEAR
STEERING............ STANDARD
STANDARD DECK .... 48"
MSRP................. $3,499

OPTIONS

28" TILLER
3 BAG
40" SNOW THROWER
42" BLADE

SERIAL NUMBERS

YEAR	BEGINNING NO.
1994	239301
1995	272501
1996	328136
1997	359000

RETAIL PRICING

YEAR	HIGH	LOW
1994	$254	$191
1995	$281	$211
1996	$313	$234
1997	$346	$260

CC30

YEARS MFRD 2014-2017
CID 420CC
COOLING .... AIR
FUEL .... G
TRANSMISSION .... GEAR
STEERING............ STANDARD
STANDARD DECK .... 30"
MSRP................. $1,199

OPTIONS

BAGGER

RETAIL PRICING

YEAR	HIGH	LOW
2014	$591	$444
2015	$658	$494
2016	$726	$544
2017	$805	$603

CC30 H

YEARS MFRD 2016-2020
ENGINE CC
CYLINDERS.................. 1
CID 382CC
COOLING .... AIR
FUEL .... G
SPEEDS .... VARIABLE
TRANSMISSION .... HYDRO
STEERING............ STANDARD
STANDARD DECK .... 30"
WEIGHT .... 340 LBS.
MSRP................. $1,499

OPTIONS

BAGGER................. $250

RETAIL PRICING

YEAR	HIGH	LOW
2016	$815	$612
2017	$903	$677
2018	$1,003	$752
2019	$1,106	$829
2020	$1,227	$937

FMZ50

YEARS MFRD 2009-2009
ENGINE ...... KOHLER COURAGE
CYLINDERS.................. 2
ENGINE HP 22
COOLING .... AIR
FUEL .... G
SPEEDS .... VARIABLE
TRANSMISSION .... HYDRO
STEERING.................ZERO
BLADE CLUTCH .... ELECTRIC
STANDARD DECK .... 50"
WEIGHT .... 680 LBS.
MSRP................. $4,999

RETAIL PRICING

YEAR	HIGH	LOW
2009	$3,086	$2,315

GS

YEARS MFRD 2015-2020
SERIES...... XT3 ENDURO SERIES
ENGINE .... KOHLER
CYLINDERS.................. 2
ENGINE HP 22.5
COOLING .... AIR
FUEL .... G
SPEEDS .... VARIABLE
TRANSMISSION .... HYDRO
STEERING............ STANDARD
STANDARD DECK .... 50"
MSRP................. $5,299

OPTIONS

42" DECK............... $-200
48" FAB DECK............ $200
54" DECK................ $100
60" FAB DECK $500

RETAIL PRICING

YEAR	HIGH	LOW
2015	$2,467	$1,850
2016	$2,729	$2,047
2017	$3,019	$2,264
2018	$3,313	$2,485
2019	$3,940	$2,956
2020	$4,562	$3,403

GSE

YEARS MFRD 2015-2017
SERIES...... XT2 ENDURO SERIES
ENGINE .... KOHLER
ENGINE HP 22.5
COOLING .... AIR
FUEL .... G
SPEEDS .... VARIABLE
TRANSMISSION .... HYDRO
STEERING............ STANDARD
STANDARD DECK .... 50"
MSRP................. $5,099

OPTIONS

42" DECK
42" SNOW THROWER
46" BLADE

RETAIL PRICING

YEAR	HIGH	LOW
2015	$2,843	$2,133
2016	$3,146	$2,359
2017	$3,480	$2,610

GSX

YEARS MFRD 2015-2020
SERIES ...... XT3 ENDURO SERIES
ENGINE ...... KOHLER COMMAND
ENGINE HP 25
COOLING .... AIR
FUEL .... G
SPEEDS .... VARIABLE
TRANSMISSION .... HYDRO
STEERING .... STANDARD
STANDARD DECK .... 50"
WEIGHT .... 800 LBS.
MSRP $6,299

OPTIONS

42" DECK
46" BLADE $880
54" DECK
SNOW BLOWER $1,485

RETAIL PRICING

YEAR	HIGH	LOW
2015	$2,897	$2,173
2016	$3,224	$2,418
2017	$3,545	$2,658
2018	$4,001	$3,001
2019	$4,696	$3,522
2020	$5,387	$4,197

GT50

YEARS MFRD 2015-2020
SERIES ...... XT1 ENDURO SERIES
ENGINE .... KOHLER
CYLINDERS 2
ENGINE HP 25
COOLING .... AIR
FUEL .... G
SPEEDS .... VARIABLE
TRANSMISSION .... HYDRO
STEERING .... STANDARD
STANDARD DECK .... 50"
WEIGHT .... 530 LBS.
MSRP $2,999

OPTIONS

42" SNOW THROWER $1,350
46" BLADE $340
SNOW CAB $418

RETAIL PRICING

YEAR	HIGH	LOW
2015	$1,505	$1,128
2016	$1,665	$1,249
2017	$1,734	$1,300
2018	$1,878	$1,409
2019	$2,120	$1,589
2020	$2,240	$1,684

GT54

YEARS MFRD 2015-2020
SERIES ...... XT1 ENDURO SERIES
ENGINE .... KOHLER
CYLINDERS 2
ENGINE HP 25
FUEL .... G
TRANSMISSION .... HYDRO
STEERING .... STANDARD
STANDARD DECK .... 54"
WEIGHT .... 530 LBS.
MSRP $3,299

OPTIONS

42" SNOW BLOWER $1,350
46" BLADE $340
SPREADER $250

GT1222

YEARS MFRD 2004-2004
SERIES .... 1000 SERIES
ENGINE .... B&S INTEK ELS
CYLINDERS 2
ENGINE HP 22
COOLING .... AIR
FUEL .... G
SPEEDS .... VARIABLE
TRANSMISSION .... HYDRO
STEERING .... STANDARD
PTO .... YES
STANDARD DECK .... 46"
WEIGHT .... 529 LBS.
MSRP $2,799

OPTIONS

2 BAG
42" SNOW THROWER
46" BLADE
46" SWEEP

RETAIL PRICING

YEAR	HIGH	LOW
2004	$636	$477

GT1554

YEARS MFRD 2005-2008
SERIES .... 1500 SERIES
ENGINE .... KOHLER
CYLINDERS 2
ENGINE HP 27
COOLING .... AIR
FUEL .... G
SPEEDS .... VARIABLE
TRANSMISSION .... HYDRO
STEERING .... STANDARD
BLADE CLUTCH .... ELECTRIC
STANDARD DECK .... 54"
WEIGHT .... 587 LBS.
MSRP $3,299

OPTIONS

3 BAG
42" SNOW THROWER
46" BLADE
46" SWEEP

RETAIL PRICING

YEAR	HIGH	LOW
2005	$815	$611
2006	$898	$673
2007	$997	$748
2008	$1,107	$830

GT1554 VT

YEARS MFRD 2009-2009
ENGINE .... B&S PRO
CYLINDERS 2
ENGINE HP 26
COOLING .... AIR
FUEL .... G
SPEEDS .... VARIABLE
TRANSMISSION .... HYDRO
STEERING .... STANDARD
BLADE CLUTCH .... ELECTRIC
STANDARD DECK .... 54"
WEIGHT .... 587 LBS.
MSRP $3,299

OPTIONS

3 BAG
42" SNOW THROWER
46" BLADE

RETAIL PRICING

YEAR	HIGH	LOW
2009	$1,164	$873

GT2000

YEARS MFRD 2011-2013
ENGINE .... KOHLER
ENGINE HP 20
COOLING .... AIR
FUEL .... G
SPEEDS .... VARIABLE
TRANSMISSION .... HYDRO
STEERING .... STANDARD
STANDARD DECK .... 50"
MSRP $4,399

OPTIONS

3 BAG
42" DECK
44" SNOW THROWER
46" BLADE

RETAIL PRICING

YEAR	HIGH	LOW
2011	$1,792	$1,344
2012	$1,981	$1,486
2013	$2,190	$1,643

GT2042

YEARS MFRD 2005-2006
ENGINE .... KOHLER
ENGINE HP 18
COOLING .... AIR
FUEL .... G
SPEEDS .... VARIABLE
TRANSMISSION .... HYDRO
STEERING .... ZERO
STANDARD DECK .... 42"
MSRP $2,699

RETAIL PRICING

YEAR	HIGH	LOW
2005	$966	$724
2006	$988	$741

GT2042

YEARS MFRD 2014-2014
SERIES .... 2000 SERIES
ENGINE .... KOHLER
ENGINE HP 20.5
COOLING .... AIR
FUEL .... G
SPEEDS .... VARIABLE
TRANSMISSION .... HYDRO
STEERING .... STANDARD
STANDARD DECK .... 42"
MSRP $4,699

OPTIONS

2 BAG
44" SNOW THROWER
46" BLADE

RETAIL PRICING

YEAR	HIGH	LOW
2014	$2,479	$1,860

GT2050

YEARS MFRD 2014-2014
SERIES .... 2000 SERIES
ENGINE .... KOHLER
ENGINE HP 22.5
COOLING .... AIR
FUEL .... G
SPEEDS .... VARIABLE
TRANSMISSION .... HYDRO
STEERING .... STANDARD
STANDARD DECK .... 50"
MSRP $5,299

OPTIONS

2 BAG
44" SNOW BLOWER
46" BLADE

RETAIL PRICING

YEAR	HIGH	LOW
2014	$2,776	$2,082

GT2100

YEARS MFRD 2011-2013
ENGINE .... KOHLER
ENGINE HP 23
COOLING .... AIR
FUEL .... G
SPEEDS .... VARIABLE
TRANSMISSION .... HYDRO
STEERING .... STANDARD
STANDARD DECK .... 48"
MSRP $4,899

OPTIONS

3 BAG
44" SNOW THROWER
46" BLADE

RETAIL PRICING

YEAR	HIGH	LOW
2011	$2,004	$1,503
2012	$2,206	$1,654
2013	$2,445	$1,833

CUB CADET

GT2148

YEARS MFRD 2014-2014
SERIES. . . . . 2000 SERIES
ENGINE . . . . KOHLER
ENGINE HP 22.5
COOLING . . . . AIR
FUEL . . . . G
SPEEDS . . . . VARIABLE
TRANSMISSION . . . . HYDRO
STEERING. . . . . STANDARD
STANDARD DECK . . . . 48"
MSRP. $5,899

OPTIONS

2 BAG
44" SNOW BLOWER
46" BLADE

RETAIL PRICING

YEAR	HIGH	LOW
2014	$3,111	$2,333

GT2186

YEARS MFRD 2004-2004
SERIES. . . . . 2000 SERIES
ENGINE . . . . KOHLER
CYLINDERS. 2
ENGINE HP 20
COOLING . . . . AIR
FUEL . . . . G
SPEEDS . . . . VARIABLE
TRANSMISSION . . . . HYDRO
STEERING. . . . . STANDARD
PTO . . . . YES
STANDARD DECK . . . . 44"
WEIGHT . . . . 635 LBS.
MSRP. $3,349

OPTIONS

3 BAG
30" TILLER
42" SNOW BLOWER
BAG&FAN

RETAIL PRICING

YEAR	HIGH	LOW
2004	$760	$570

GT2348

YEARS MFRD 2014-2014
SERIES. . . . . 2000 SERIES
ENGINE . . . . KOHLER
ENGINE HP 22.5
COOLING . . . . AIR
FUEL . . . . G
SPEEDS . . . . VARIABLE
TRANSMISSION . . . . HYDRO
STEERING. . . . . STANDARD
STANDARD DECK . . . . 48"
MSRP. $4,999

OPTIONS

2 BAG
44" SNOW BLOWER
46" BLADE

RETAIL PRICING

YEAR	HIGH	LOW
2014	$2,491	$1,868

GT2521

YEARS MFRD 2004-2004
SERIES. . . . . 2500 SERIES
ENGINE . . . . B&S VANGUARD
CYLINDERS. 2
ENGINE HP 21
COOLING . . . . AIR
FUEL . . . . G
SPEEDS . . . . VARIABLE
TRANSMISSION . . . . HYDRO
STEERING. . . . . STANDARD
PTO . . . . YES
STANDARD DECK . . . . 48"
WEIGHT . . . . 720 LBS.
MSRP. $3,899

OPTIONS

30" TILLER
42" BLADE
42" SNOW BLOWER
BAG & FAN

RETAIL PRICING

YEAR	HIGH	LOW
2004	$885	$663

GT2523

YEARS MFRD 2004-2004
SERIES. . . . . 2500 SERIES
ENGINE . . . . KOHLER
CYLINDERS. 2
ENGINE HP 23
COOLING . . . . AIR
FUEL . . . . G
SPEEDS . . . . VARIABLE
TRANSMISSION . . . . HYDRO
STEERING. . . . . STANDARD
PTO . . . . YES
STANDARD DECK . . . . 54"
WEIGHT . . . . 735 LBS.
MSRP. $4,299

OPTIONS

30" TILLER
42" BLADE
42" SNOW BLOWER
BAG & FAN

RETAIL PRICING

YEAR	HIGH	LOW
2004	$975	$731

GT2542

YEARS MFRD 2006-2010
SERIES. . . . . 2500 SERIES
ENGINE . . . . . . KOHLER COMMAND
CYLINDERS. 2
ENGINE HP 20
COOLING . . . . AIR
FUEL . . . . G
SPEEDS . . . . VARIABLE
TRANSMISSION . . . . HYDRO
STEERING. . . . . STANDARD
STANDARD DECK . . . . 42"
WEIGHT . . . . 735 LBS.
MSRP. $4,049

OPTIONS

3 BAG
32 VAC
42" BLADE
42" SNOW THROWER

RETAIL PRICING

YEAR	HIGH	LOW
2006	$1,059	$794
2007	$1,177	$883
2008	$1,296	$972
2009	$1,433	$1,075
2010	$1,596	$1,197

GT2544

YEARS MFRD 2005-2010
SERIES. . . . . 2500 SERIES
ENGINE . . . . KOHLER
CYLINDERS. 2
ENGINE HP 20
COOLING . . . . AIR
FUEL . . . . G
SPEEDS . . . . VARIABLE
TRANSMISSION . . . . HYDRO
STEERING. . . . . STANDARD
BLADE CLUTCH . . . . ELECTRIC
STANDARD DECK . . . . 44"
WEIGHT . . . . 800 LBS.
MSRP. $3,699

OPTIONS

3 BAG
32 VAC
42" BLADE
42" SNOW THROWER

RETAIL PRICING

YEAR	HIGH	LOW
2005	$874	$656
2006	$968	$726
2007	$1,070	$803
2008	$1,184	$888
2009	$1,310	$982
2010	$1,448	$1,086

GT2550

YEARS MFRD 2005-2010
SERIES. . . . . 2500 SERIES
ENGINE . . . . KOHLER
CYLINDERS. 2
ENGINE HP 22
COOLING . . . . AIR
FUEL . . . . G
SPEEDS . . . . VARIABLE
TRANSMISSION . . . . HYDRO
STEERING. . . . . STANDARD
BLADE CLUTCH . . . . ELECTRIC
STANDARD DECK . . . . 50"
WEIGHT . . . . 841 LBS.
MSRP. $4,349

OPTIONS

3 BAG
32 VAC
42" BLADE
42" SNOW THROWER

RETAIL PRICING

YEAR	HIGH	LOW
2005	$1,029	$772
2006	$1,140	$855
2007	$1,261	$946
2008	$1,392	$1,044
2009	$1,540	$1,155
2010	$1,704	$1,278

GT2554

YEARS MFRD 2005-2010
SERIES. . . . . 2500 SERIES
ENGINE . . . . KOHLER
CYLINDERS. 2
ENGINE HP 23
COOLING . . . . AIR
FUEL . . . . G
SPEEDS . . . . VARIABLE
TRANSMISSION . . . . HYDRO
STEERING. . . . . STANDARD
BLADE CLUTCH . . . . ELECTRIC
STANDARD DECK . . . . 54"
WEIGHT . . . . 846 LBS.
MSRP. $4,749

OPTIONS

3 BAG
32 VAC
42" BLADE
42" SNOW THROWER

RETAIL PRICING

YEAR	HIGH	LOW
2005	$1,130	$847
2006	$1,241	$931
2007	$1,382	$1,036
2008	$1,520	$1,140
2009	$1,681	$1,261
2010	$1,860	$1,395

GT3100

YEARS MFRD 2005-2010
SERIES. . . . . 3000 SERIES
ENGINE . . . . . . KOHLER COMMAND
CYLINDERS. 2
ENGINE HP 23
COOLING . . . . AIR
FUEL . . . . G
SPEEDS . . . . VARIABLE
TRANSMISSION . . . . HYDRO
STEERING. . . . . ZERO
BLADE CLUTCH . . . . ELECTRIC
STANDARD DECK . . . . 50"
WEIGHT . . . . 950 LBS.
MSRP. $6,648

OPTIONS

3 BAG
32 VAC
45" SNOW THROWER
54" DECK

RETAIL PRICING

YEAR	HIGH	LOW
2005	$1,573	$1,180
2006	$1,738	$1,304
2007	$1,923	$1,442
2008	$2,128	$1,596
2009	$2,353	$1,765
2010	$2,604	$1,953

GT3200

YEARS MFRD 2005-2010
SERIES. . . . . 3000 SERIES
ENGINE . . . . KOHLER
CYLINDERS. 2
ENGINE HP 25
COOLING . . . . AIR

FUEL . . . . G
SPEEDS . . . . VARIABLE
TRANSMISSION . . . . HYDRO
STEERING. . . . . STANDARD
BLADE CLUTCH . . . . ELECTRIC
STANDARD DECK . . . . 50"
WEIGHT . . . . 950 LBS.
MSRP. $7,748

OPTIONS

3 BAG
32 VAC
45" SNOW THROWER
60" DECK

RETAIL PRICING

YEAR	HIGH	LOW
2005	$1,832	$1,374
2006	$2,030	$1,522
2007	$2,240	$1,680
2008	$2,479	$1,860
2009	$2,743	$2,057
2010	$3,040	$2,280

GT3204

YEARS MFRD 2004-2004
SERIES. . . . . 3000 SERIES
ENGINE . . . . KOHLER
CYLINDERS. 2
ENGINE HP 23
COOLING . . . . AIR
FUEL . . . . G
SPEEDS . . . . VARIABLE
TRANSMISSION . . . . HYDRO
STEERING. . . . . STANDARD
PTO . . . . YES
STANDARD DECK . . . . 48"
WEIGHT . . . . 950 LBS.
MSRP. $5,928

OPTIONS

42" TILLER
45" SNOW BLOWER
54" BLADE
BAG & FAN

RETAIL PRICING

YEAR	HIGH	LOW
2004	$1,286	$965

GT3235

YEARS MFRD 2004-2004
SERIES. . . . . 3000 SERIES
ENGINE . . . . KOHLER
CYLINDERS. 2
ENGINE HP 25
COOLING . . . . AIR
FUEL . . . . G
SPEEDS . . . . VARIABLE
TRANSMISSION . . . . HYDRO
STEERING. . . . . STANDARD
PTO . . . . YES
STANDARD DECK . . . . 54"
WEIGHT . . . . 950 LBS.
MSRP. $7,128

OPTIONS

42" TILLER
45" SNOW BLOWER
54" BLADE
BAG & FAN

RETAIL PRICING

YEAR	HIGH	LOW
2004	$1,548	$1,161

GTH200

YEARS MFRD 1993-1999
ENGINE . . . . KOHLER
ENGINE HP 20
COOLING . . . . AIR
FUEL . . . . G
STEERING. . . . . STANDARD
STANDARD DECK . . . . 46"
MSRP. $3,199

RETAIL PRICING

YEAR	HIGH	LOW
1993	$769	$577
1994	$835	$627
1995	$883	$662
1996	$996	$747
1997	$1,038	$779
1998	$1,198	$899
1999	$1,338	$1,003

GTX1054

YEARS MFRD 2010-2014
ENGINE . . . . KOHLER COURAGE
CYLINDERS. 2
ENGINE HP 27
COOLING . . . . AIR
FUEL . . . . G
SPEEDS . . . . VARIABLE
TRANSMISSION . . . . HYDRO
STEERING. . . . . STANDARD
BLADE CLUTCH . . . . ELECTRIC
STANDARD DECK . . . . 54"
WEIGHT . . . . 587 LBS.
MSRP. $3,299

OPTIONS

3 BAG
42" SNOW THROWER
46" BLADE

RETAIL PRICING

YEAR	HIGH	LOW
2010	$1,141	$856
2011	$1,261	$946
2012	$1,396	$1,047
2013	$1,544	$1,158
2014	$1,714	$1,285

GTX2000

YEARS MFRD 2012-2014
ENGINE . . . . KOHLER
ENGINE HP 20
COOLING . . . . AIR
FUEL . . . . G
SPEEDS . . . . VARIABLE
TRANSMISSION . . . . HYDRO
STEERING. . . . . STANDARD
STANDARD DECK . . . . 48"
MSRP. $5,399

OPTIONS

3 BAG
44" SNOW THROWER
46" BLADE

RETAIL PRICING

YEAR	HIGH	LOW
2012	$2,284	$1,713
2013	$2,527	$1,895
2014	$2,799	$2,099

GTX2100

YEARS MFRD 2012-2013
ENGINE . . . . KOHLER
ENGINE HP 20
COOLING . . . . AIR
FUEL . . . . G
SPEEDS . . . . VARIABLE
TRANSMISSION . . . . HYDRO
STEERING. . . . . STANDARD
STANDARD DECK . . . . 48"
MSRP. $5,299

OPTIONS

3 BAG
44" SNOW THROWER
46" BLADE

RETAIL PRICING

YEAR	HIGH	LOW
2012	$2,344	$1,758
2013	$2,593	$1,945

GTX2154

YEARS MFRD 2014-2014
SERIES. . . . . 2000 SERIES
ENGINE . . . . KOHLER
ENGINE HP 22.5
COOLING . . . . AIR
FUEL . . . . G
SPEEDS . . . . VARIABLE
TRANSMISSION . . . . HYDRO
STEERING. . . . . STANDARD
STANDARD DECK . . . . 54"
MSRP. $6,399

OPTIONS

2 BAG
44" SNOW THROWER
46" BLADE

RETAIL PRICING

YEAR	HIGH	LOW
2014	$3,321	$2,491

GTX2354

YEARS MFRD 2014-2014
SERIES. . . . . 2000 SERIES
ENGINE . . . . KOHLER
ENGINE HP 22.5
COOLING . . . . AIR
FUEL . . . . G
SPEEDS . . . . VARIABLE
TRANSMISSION . . . . HYDRO
STEERING. . . . . STANDARD
STANDARD DECK . . . . 54"
MSRP. $5,499

OPTIONS

2 BAG
44" SNOW BLOWER
46" BLADE

RETAIL PRICING

YEAR	HIGH	LOW
2014	$2,845	$2,134

GX50

YEARS MFRD 2019-2020
SERIES. . . . . . XT2 ENDURO SERIES
ENGINE . . . . .KOHLER 7000 SERIES
CYLINDERS. 2
CID 679CC
ENGINE HP 25
FUEL . . . . G
TRANSMISSION . . . . HYDRO
STEERING. . . . . STANDARD
BLADE CLUTCH . . . . ELECTRIC
STANDARD DECK . . . . 50"
WEIGHT . . . . 700 LBS.
MSRP. $3,599

OPTIONS

42" SNOW BLOWER $1,350
SNOW CAB. $418

GX54 FAB

YEARS MFRD 2017-2018
SERIES. . . . . . XT2 ENDURO SERIES
ENGINE . . . . KOHLER
ENGINE HP 25
COOLING . . . . AIR
FUEL . . . . G
SPEEDS . . . . VARIABLE
TRANSMISSION . . . . HYDRO
STEERING. . . . . STANDARD
STANDARD DECK . . . . 54"
MSRP. $3,299

OPTIONS

MULCH KIT

RETAIL PRICING

YEAR	HIGH	LOW
2017	$1,781	$1,336
2018	$2,256	$1,692

GX54 FAB D

YEARS MFRD 2017-2020
SERIES. . . . . . XT2 ENDURO SERIES
ENGINE . . . . KOHLER
CYLINDERS. 2
CID 747CC
ENGINE HP 25
SPEEDS . . . . VARIABLE
TRANSMISSION . . . . HYDRO
STEERING. . . . . STANDARD
STANDARD DECK . . . . 54"
WEIGHT . . . . 700 LBS.
MSRP. $3,899

OPTIONS

MULCH KIT. $110
SLEEVE HITCH $275
SNOW CAB. $418

RETAIL PRICING

YEAR	HIGH	LOW
2017	$2,361	$1,771
2018	$2,617	$1,963
2019	$2,977	$2,233
2020	$3,349	$2,521

CUB CADET

GX54 FAB KH

YEARS MFRD 2015-2016
SERIES. . . . . . XT2 ENDURO SERIES
ENGINE . . . . KOHLER
ENGINE HP 26
COOLING . . . . AIR
FUEL . . . . G
SPEEDS . . . . VARIABLE
TRANSMISSION . . . . HYDRO
STEERING. . . . . STANDARD
STANDARD DECK . . . . 54"
MSRP. $3,299

OPTIONS

42" SNOW THROWER
46" BLADE
6 BU BAG

RETAIL PRICING

YEAR	HIGH	LOW
2015	$1,910	$1,432
2016	$2,117	$1,587

HDS2145

YEARS MFRD 1994-1995
SERIES. . . . . 2000 SERIES
ENGINE . . . . ONAN
ENGINE HP 14
COOLING . . . . AIR
FUEL . . . . G
TRANSMISSION . . . . HYDRO
STEERING. . . . . STANDARD
STANDARD DECK . . . . 42"
MSRP. $3,499

SERIAL NUMBERS

YEAR	BEGINNING NO.
1994	239301
1995	272501

RETAIL PRICING

YEAR	HIGH	LOW
1994	$322	$241
1995	$366	$274

HDS2146

YEARS MFRD 2000-2000
SERIES. . . . . 2000 SERIES
ENGINE . . . . CUB CADET
ENGINE HP 14
COOLING . . . . AIR
FUEL . . . . G
SPEEDS . . . . VARIABLE
TRANSMISSION . . . . HYDRO
STEERING. . . . . STANDARD
STANDARD DECK . . . . 38"
MSRP. $2,899

OPTIONS

2 BAG
40" SNOW THROWER
42" BLADE

RETAIL PRICING

YEAR	HIGH	LOW
2000	$433	$324

HDS2155

YEARS MFRD 1996-1999
SERIES. . . . . 2000 SERIES
ENGINE . . . . KOHLER
ENGINE HP 15
COOLING . . . . AIR
FUEL . . . . G
SPEEDS . . . . VARIABLE
TRANSMISSION . . . . HYDRO
STEERING. . . . . STANDARD
STANDARD DECK . . . . 42"
MSRP. $2,999

OPTIONS

2 BAG
28" TILLER
40" SNOW THROWER
42" BLADE

SERIAL NUMBERS

YEAR	BEGINNING NO.
1996	328136
1997	359000
1998	XXXX8XXXXX
1999	XXXX9XXXXX

RETAIL PRICING

YEAR	HIGH	LOW
1996	$239	$179
1997	$265	$199
1998	$294	$221
1999	$325	$244

HDS2164

YEARS MFRD 1999-2000
SERIES. . . . . 2000 SERIES
ENGINE . . . . B&S
ENGINE HP 16
COOLING . . . . AIR
FUEL . . . . G
SPEEDS . . . . VARIABLE
TRANSMISSION . . . . HYDRO
STEERING. . . . . STANDARD
STANDARD DECK . . . . 42"
MSRP. $3,799

OPTIONS

2 BAG
28" TILLER
40" SNOW BLOWER
42" BLADE

SERIAL NUMBERS

YEAR	BEGINNING NO.
1999	XXXX9XXXXX

RETAIL PRICING

YEAR	HIGH	LOW
1999	$472	$354
2000	$523	$392

HDS2165

YEARS MFRD 1994-1999
SERIES. . . . . 2000 SERIES
ENGINE . . . . B&S
ENGINE HP 16
COOLING . . . . AIR
FUEL . . . . G
TRANSMISSION . . . . HYDRO
STEERING. . . . . STANDARD
STANDARD DECK . . . . 48"
MSRP. $3,099

OPTIONS

28" TILLER
3 BAG
40" SNOW THROWER
42" BLADE

SERIAL NUMBERS

YEAR	BEGINNING NO.
1994	239301
1995	272501
1996	328136
1997	359000
1998	XXXX8XXXXX
1999	XXXX9XXXXX

RETAIL PRICING

YEAR	HIGH	LOW
1994	$245	$184
1995	$272	$204
1996	$302	$227
1997	$334	$251
1998	$371	$278
1999	$412	$309

HDS2185

YEARS MFRD 1994-1999
SERIES. . . . . 2000 SERIES
ENGINE . . . . KOHLER
ENGINE HP 18
COOLING . . . . AIR
FUEL . . . . G
SPEEDS . . . . VARIABLE
TRANSMISSION . . . . HYDRO
STEERING. . . . . STANDARD
STANDARD DECK . . . . 48"
MSRP. $3,499

OPTIONS

28" TILLER
3 BAG
40" SNOW THROWER
42" BLADE

SERIAL NUMBERS

YEAR	BEGINNING NO.
1994	239301
1995	272501
1996	328136
1997	359000
1998	XXXX8XXXXX
1999	XXXX9XXXXX

RETAIL PRICING

YEAR	HIGH	LOW
1994	$277	$208
1995	$308	$231
1996	$341	$256
1997	$378	$284
1998	$418	$314
1999	$466	$350

I 1042

YEARS MFRD 2008-2010
SERIES. . . . . I 1000 SERIES
ENGINE . . . . KOHLER
ENGINE HP 18
COOLING . . . . AIR
FUEL . . . . G
SPEEDS . . . . VARIABLE
TRANSMISSION . . . . . DUAL HYDRO
STEERING. . . . . STANDARD
STANDARD DECK . . . . 42"
MSRP. $2,949

OPTIONS

2 BAG
42" SNOW BLOWER

RETAIL PRICING

YEAR	HIGH	LOW
2008	$936	$702
2009	$1,038	$779
2010	$1,148	$861

I 1046

YEARS MFRD 2007-2009
SERIES. . . . . I 1000 SERIES
ENGINE . . . . KOHLER COURAGE
CYLINDERS. 2
ENGINE HP 20
COOLING . . . . AIR
FUEL . . . . G
SPEEDS . . . . VARIABLE
TRANSMISSION . . . . HYDRO
STEERING. . . . . STANDARD
STANDARD DECK . . . . 46"
WEIGHT . . . . 550 LBS.
MSRP. $3,249

OPTIONS

2 BAG
42" SNOW BLOWER
46" BLADE

RETAIL PRICING

YEAR	HIGH	LOW
2007	$941	$706
2008	$1,042	$782
2009	$1,155	$866

I 1050

YEARS MFRD 2007-2010
SERIES. . . . . I 1000 SERIES
ENGINE . . . . KOHLER COURAGE
CYLINDERS. 2
ENGINE HP 25
COOLING . . . . AIR
FUEL . . . . G
SPEEDS . . . . VARIABLE
TRANSMISSION . . . . HYDRO
STEERING. . . . . ZERO
STANDARD DECK . . . . 50"
WEIGHT . . . . 590 LBS.
MSRP. $3,899

OPTIONS

2 BAG
42" SNOW BLOWER
46" BLADE

RETAIL PRICING

YEAR	HIGH	LOW
2007	$1,115	$836
2008	$1,236	$927
2009	$1,370	$1,028
2010	$1,524	$1,143

L48

YEARS MFRD 2010-2011
SERIES .... TANK SERIES
ENGINE ..... KOHLER COMMMAND
CYLINDERS 2
CID 724CC
ENGINE HP 25
COOLING .... AIR
FUEL .... G
SPEEDS .... VARIABLE
TRANSMISSION .... HYDRO
STEERING .... ZERO
BLADE CLUTCH .... ELECTRIC
STANDARD DECK .... 48"
WEIGHT .... 1,080 LBS.
MSRP $7,799

RETAIL PRICING

YEAR	HIGH	LOW
2010	$3,250	$2,438
2011	$3,513	$2,635

L48KW PRO

YEARS MFRD 2014-2014
SERIES .... ZF SERIES
ENGINE .... KAWASAKI
ENGINE HP 24
COOLING .... AIR
FUEL .... G
SPEEDS .... VARIABLE
TRANSMISSION .... HYDRO
STEERING .... ZERO
STANDARD DECK .... 48"
MSRP $4,399

OPTIONS

2 BAG
58" BLADE
POWER LIFT

RETAIL PRICING

YEAR	HIGH	LOW
2014	$2,244	$1,683

L54 FAB

YEARS MFRD 2017-2017
ENGINE .... KOHLER
ENGINE HP 24
COOLING .... AIR
FUEL .... G
SPEEDS .... VARIABLE
TRANSMISSION ..... DUAL HYDRO
STEERING .... ZERO
STANDARD DECK .... 54"
MSRP $2,999

RETAIL PRICING

YEAR	HIGH	LOW
2017	$1,994	$1,495

L54KW PRO

YEARS MFRD 2014-2014
SERIES .... ZF SERIES
ENGINE .... KAWASAKI
ENGINE HP 24
COOLING .... AIR
FUEL .... G
SPEEDS .... VARIABLE
TRANSMISSION .... HYDRO
STEERING .... ZERO
STANDARD DECK .... 54"
MSRP $4,999

OPTIONS

2 BAG
58" BLADE
POWER LIFT

RETAIL PRICING

YEAR	HIGH	LOW
2014	$2,548	$1,911

L60

YEARS MFRD 2010-2011
SERIES .... TANK SERIES
ENGINE ...... KOHLER COMMAND
CYLINDERS 2
CID 725CC
ENGINE HP 27
COOLING .... AIR
FUEL .... G
SPEEDS .... VARIABLE
TRANSMISSION .... HYDRO
STEERING .... ZERO
BLADE CLUTCH .... ELECTRIC
STANDARD DECK .... 60"
WEIGHT .... 1,100 LBS.
MSRP $8,199

RETAIL PRICING

YEAR	HIGH	LOW
2010	$3,462	$2,597
2011	$3,949	$2,962

L60KW PRO

YEARS MFRD 2014-2014
SERIES .... ZF SERIES
ENGINE .... KAWASAKI
ENGINE HP 24
COOLING .... AIR
FUEL .... G
SPEEDS .... VARIABLE
TRANSMISSION .... HYDRO
STEERING .... ZERO
STANDARD DECK .... 60"
MSRP $5,499

OPTIONS

2 BAG
58" BLADE
POWER LIFT

RETAIL PRICING

YEAR	HIGH	LOW
2014	$2,803	$2,103

LGT1050

YEARS MFRD 2013-2014
ENGINE .... KOHLER
ENGINE HP 25
COOLING .... AIR
FUEL .... G
SPEEDS .... VARIABLE
TRANSMISSION .... HYDRO
STEERING .... STANDARD
STANDARD DECK .... 50"
MSRP $2,499

OPTIONS

3 BAG
42" SNOW THROWER
46" BLADE

RETAIL PRICING

YEAR	HIGH	LOW
2013	$1,141	$856
2014	$1,271	$953

LGT1054

YEARS MFRD 2012-2014
ENGINE .... KOHLER
ENGINE HP 26
COOLING .... AIR
FUEL .... G
SPEEDS .... VARIABLE
TRANSMISSION .... HYDRO
STEERING .... STANDARD
STANDARD DECK .... 54"
MSRP $2,899

OPTIONS

3 BAG
42" SNOW BLOWER
46" BLADE

RETAIL PRICING

YEAR	HIGH	LOW
2012	$1,194	$896
2013	$1,323	$992
2014	$1,467	$1,100

LGTX1050

YEARS MFRD 2012-2014
ENGINE .... KOHLER
ENGINE HP 25
COOLING .... AIR
FUEL .... G
SPEEDS .... VARIABLE
TRANSMISSION .... HYDRO
STEERING .... STANDARD
STANDARD DECK .... 50"
MSRP $2,999

OPTIONS

3 BAG
42" SNOW BLOWER
46" BLADE

RETAIL PRICING

YEAR	HIGH	LOW
2012	$1,243	$932
2013	$1,375	$1,031
2014	$1,517	$1,138

LGTX1054

YEARS MFRD 2012-2014
ENGINE .... KOHLER
ENGINE HP 27
COOLING .... AIR
FUEL .... G
SPEEDS .... VARIABLE
TRANSMISSION .... HYDRO
STEERING .... STANDARD
STANDARD DECK .... 54"
MSRP $3,299

OPTIONS

3 BAG
42" SNOW BLOWER
46" BLADE

RETAIL PRICING

YEAR	HIGH	LOW
2012	$1,362	$1,022
2013	$1,506	$1,129
2014	$1,670	$1,252

LT42

YEARS MFRD 2015-2019
SERIES ...... XT1 ENDURO SERIES
ENGINE .... KOHLER
ENGINE HP 18
COOLING .... AIR
FUEL .... G
SPEEDS .... VARIABLE
TRANSMISSION .... HYDRO
STEERING .... STANDARD
STANDARD DECK .... 42"
MSRP $1,699

OPTIONS

42" SNOW THROWER
46" BLADE
RR SPREADER

RETAIL PRICING

YEAR	HIGH	LOW
2015	$801	$600
2016	$885	$663
2017	$983	$737
2018	$1,080	$810
2019	$1,207	$906

LT42 EFI

YEARS MFRD 2017-2020
SERIES ...... XT1 ENDURO SERIES
ENGINE .... CUB CADET
CYLINDERS 1
CID 547CC
COOLING .... AIR
FUEL .... G
SPEEDS .... VARIABLE
TRANSMISSION .... HYDRO
STEERING .... STANDARD
STANDARD DECK .... 42"
MSRP $1,949

OPTIONS

46" SNOW BLADE $340
INTELLIPOWER .... $-250
SPREADER $250

RETAIL PRICING

YEAR	HIGH	LOW
2017	$1,146	$861
2018	$1,261	$947
2019	$1,401	$1,051
2020	$1,549	$1,192

LT42C

YEARS MFRD 2016-2017
SERIES ...... XT1 ENDURO SERIES
ENGINE CC
CID 547CC
COOLING .... AIR
FUEL .... G
SPEEDS .... VARIABLE
TRANSMISSION .... HYDRO
STEERING .... STANDARD
STANDARD DECK .... 42"
MSRP $1,499

CUB CADET

OPTIONS

4 BU BAG
42" SNOW THROWER
46" BLADE

RETAIL PRICING

YEAR	HIGH	LOW
2016	$919	$690
2017	$1,022	$766

LT46

YEARS MFRD 2015-2020
SERIES...... XT1 ENDURO SERIES
ENGINE .... KOHLER
CYLINDERS................. 2
ENGINE HP................ 22
COOLING .... AIR
FUEL .... G
SPEEDS .... VARIABLE
TRANSMISSION .... HYDRO
STEERING............ STANDARD
STANDARD DECK .... 46"
MSRP................. $1,899

OPTIONS

42" SNOW BLOWER $1,350
46" BLADE............... $340
INTELLIPOWER............ $-100

RETAIL PRICING

YEAR	HIGH	LOW
2015	$904	$678
2016	$1,006	$754
2017	$1,111	$833
2018	$1,222	$917
2019	$1,367	$1,024
2020	$1,471	$1,113

LT46 EFI

YEARS MFRD 2017-2020
SERIES...... XT1 ENDURO SERIES
ENGINE .... CUB CADET
CYLINDERS.................. 1
CID 547CC
COOLING .... AIR
FUEL .... G
SPEEDS .... VARIABLE
TRANSMISSION .... HYDRO
STEERING............ STANDARD
STANDARD DECK .... 46"
WEIGHT .... 420 LBS.
MSRP................. $2,199

OPTIONS

46" BLADE............... $340
SNOW CAB................ $418

RETAIL PRICING

YEAR	HIGH	LOW
2017	$1,306	$979
2018	$1,440	$1,080
2019	$1,637	$1,228
2020	$1,783	$1,324

LT50

YEARS MFRD 2015-2020
SERIES...... XT1 ENDURO SERIES
ENGINE .... KOHLER
CYLINDERS................. 2
ENGINE HP................ 24
COOLING .... AIR
FUEL .... G
SPEEDS .... VARIABLE
TRANSMISSION .... HYDRO
STEERING............ STANDARD
STANDARD DECK .... 50"
WEIGHT .... 500 LBS.
MSRP................. $2,099

OPTIONS

42" SNOW BLOWER $1,350
46" BLADE............... $340

RETAIL PRICING

YEAR	HIGH	LOW
2015	$1,065	$789
2016	$1,180	$885
2017	$1,308	$981
2018	$1,443	$1,082
2019	$1,617	$1,212
2020	$1,755	$1,321

LT54

YEARS MFRD 2015-2015
SERIES....... XT1 ENDURE SERIES
ENGINE .... KOHLER
ENGINE HP................ 24
COOLING .... AIR
FUEL .... G
SPEEDS .... VARIABLE
TRANSMISSION .... HYDRO
STEERING............ STANDARD
STANDARD DECK .... 54"
MSRP................. $2,299

OPTIONS

42" SNOW THROWER
46" BLADE
6 BU BAG

RETAIL PRICING

YEAR	HIGH	LOW
2015	$1,342	$1,006

LT54 FAB

YEARS MFRD 2015-2015
SERIES....... XT1 ENDURE SERIES
ENGINE .... KOHLER
ENGINE HP................ 24
COOLING .... AIR
FUEL .... G
SPEEDS .... VARIABLE
TRANSMISSION .... HYDRO
STEERING............ STANDARD
STANDARD DECK .... 54"
MSRP................. $2,499

OPTIONS

42" SNOW THROWER
46" BLADE
6 BU BAG

RETAIL PRICING

YEAR	HIGH	LOW
2015	$1,458	$1,093

LT1018

YEARS MFRD 2004-2004
SERIES............ 1000 SERIES
ENGINE .... B&S INTEK ELS
CYLINDERS.................. 1
ENGINE HP.............. 18.5
COOLING .... AIR
FUEL .... G
SPEEDS .... 1/1 VARIABLE
TRANSMISSION .... HYDRO
STEERING............ STANDARD
PTO .... YES
STANDARD DECK .... 42"
WEIGHT .... 498 LBS.
MSRP................. $1,799

OPTIONS

2 BAG
42" SNOW THROWER
46" BLADE
46" SWEEP

RETAIL PRICING

YEAR	HIGH	LOW
2004	$386	$290

LT1022

YEARS MFRD 2004-2004
SERIES............ 1000 SERIES
ENGINE .... B&S INTEK ELS
CYLINDERS.................. 2
ENGINE HP................ 22
COOLING .... AIR
FUEL .... G
SPEEDS .... 1/1 VARIABLE
TRANSMISSION .... HYDRO
STEERING............ STANDARD
PTO .... YES
STANDARD DECK .... 46"
WEIGHT .... 501 LBS.
MSRP................. $1,999

OPTIONS

2 BAG
42" SNOW THROWER
46" BLADE
46" SWEEP

RETAIL PRICING

YEAR	HIGH	LOW
2004	$431	$323

LT1024

YEARS MFRD 2004-2004
SERIES............ 1000 SERIES
ENGINE .... B&S INTEK ELS
CYLINDERS.................. 2
ENGINE HP................ 24
COOLING .... AIR
FUEL .... G
SPEEDS .... 1/1 VARIABLE
TRANSMISSION .... HYDRO
STEERING............ STANDARD
PTO .... YES
STANDARD DECK .... 46"
WEIGHT .... 525 LBS.
MSRP................. $2,249

OPTIONS

2 BAG
42" SNOW THROWER
46" BLADE
46" SWEEP

RETAIL PRICING

YEAR	HIGH	LOW
2004	$490	$367

LT1040

YEARS MFRD 2006-2008
SERIES............ 1000 SERIES
ENGINE .... KOHLER COURAGE
CYLINDERS.................. 1
ENGINE HP................ 18
COOLING .... AIR
FUEL .... G
SPEEDS .... VARIABLE
TRANSMISSION .... HYDRO
STEERING............ STANDARD
STANDARD DECK .... 42"
WEIGHT .... 468 LBS.
MSRP................. $1,499

OPTIONS

2 BAG
42" SNOW THROWER
46" BLADE
46" SWEEP

RETAIL PRICING

YEAR	HIGH	LOW
2006	$415	$311
2007	$461	$346
2008	$514	$385

LT1042

YEARS MFRD 2005-2008
SERIES............ 1000 SERIES
ENGINE .... KOHLER COURAGE
CYLINDERS.................. 1
ENGINE HP................ 19
COOLING .... AIR
FUEL .... G
SPEEDS .... VARIABLE
TRANSMISSION .... HYDRO
STEERING............ STANDARD
STANDARD DECK .... 42"
WEIGHT .... 498 LBS.
MSRP................. $1,699

OPTIONS

2 BAG
42" SNOW THROWER
46" BLADE
46" SWEEP

RETAIL PRICING

YEAR	HIGH	LOW
2005	$425	$319
2006	$476	$357
2007	$524	$393
2008	$583	$437

LT1045

YEARS MFRD 2005-2008
SERIES............ 1000 SERIES
ENGINE .... KOHLER COURAGE
CYLINDERS.................. 1
ENGINE HP................ 20
COOLING .... AIR
FUEL .... G
SPEEDS .... VARIABLE

TRANSMISSION .... HYDRO
STEERING............ STANDARD
BLADE CLUTCH .... ELECTRIC
STANDARD DECK .... 46"
WEIGHT .... 510 LBS.
MSRP................. $1,799

OPTIONS

2 BAG
42" SNOW THROWER
46" BLADE
46" SWEEP

RETAIL PRICING

YEAR	HIGH	LOW
2005	$451	$338
2006	$501	$376
2007	$555	$416
2008	$619	$464

LT1046

YEARS MFRD 2005-2008
SERIES............ 1000 SERIES
ENGINE .... KOHLER COMMAND
CYLINDERS................... 2
ENGINE HP 23
COOLING .... AIR
FUEL .... G
SPEEDS .... VARIABLE
TRANSMISSION .... HYDRO
STEERING............ STANDARD
BLADE CLUTCH .... ELECTRIC
STANDARD DECK .... 46"
WEIGHT .... 513 LBS.
MSRP................. $2,099

OPTIONS

2 BAG
42" SNOW THROWER
46" BLADE
46" SWEEP

RETAIL PRICING

YEAR	HIGH	LOW
2005	$526	$394
2006	$585	$439
2007	$646	$484
2008	$721	$540

LT1050

YEARS MFRD 2005-2008
SERIES............ 1000 SERIES
ENGINE .... KOHLER
CYLINDERS................... 2
ENGINE HP 26
COOLING .... AIR
FUEL .... G
SPEEDS .... VARIABLE
TRANSMISSION .... HYDRO
STEERING............ STANDARD
BLADE CLUTCH .... ELECTRIC
STANDARD DECK .... 50"
WEIGHT .... 548 LBS.
MSRP................. $2,199

OPTIONS

3 BAG
42" SNOW THROWER
46" BLADE
46" SWEEP

RETAIL PRICING

YEAR	HIGH	LOW
2005	$552	$414
2006	$613	$460
2007	$677	$507
2008	$751	$563

LT2042

YEARS MFRD 2005-2005
SERIES............ 2000 SERIES
ENGINE .... KOHLER
CYLINDERS................... 2
ENGINE HP 18
COOLING .... AIR
FUEL .... G
SPEEDS .... VARIABLE
TRANSMISSION .... HYDRO
STEERING............ STANDARD
BLADE CLUTCH .... ELECTRIC
STANDARD DECK .... 42"
MSRP................. $2,899

OPTIONS

2 BAG
42" SNOW THROWER
46" BLADE
46" SWEEP

RETAIL PRICING

YEAR	HIGH	LOW
2005	$653	$490

LT2138

YEARS MFRD 2004-2004
SERIES............ 2000 SERIES
ENGINE .... KOHLER
CYLINDERS................... 1
ENGINE HP 16
COOLING .... AIR
FUEL .... G
SPEEDS .... VARIABLE
TRANSMISSION .... HYDRO
STEERING............ STANDARD
PTO .... YES
STANDARD DECK .... 38"
WEIGHT .... 565 LBS.
MSRP................. $2,749

OPTIONS

2 BAG
42" BLADE
42" SNOW BLOWER
BAG & FAN

RETAIL PRICING

YEAR	HIGH	LOW
2004	$565	$424

LT2180

YEARS MFRD 2004-2004
SERIES............ 2000 SERIES
ENGINE .... B&S VANGUARD
CYLINDERS................... 2
ENGINE HP 18
COOLING .... AIR
FUEL .... G
SPEEDS .... VARIABLE
TRANSMISSION .... HYDRO
STEERING............ STANDARD
PTO .... YES
STANDARD DECK .... 42"
WEIGHT .... 600 LBS.
MSRP................. $2,899

OPTIONS

2 BAG
42" BLADE
42" SNOW BLOWER
BAG & VAC

RETAIL PRICING

YEAR	HIGH	LOW
2004	$601	$450

LTX1040

YEARS MFRD 2009-2014
ENGINE .... KOHLER COURAGE
CYLINDERS................... 1
ENGINE HP 19
COOLING .... AIR
FUEL .... G
SPEEDS .... VARIABLE
TRANSMISSION .... BELT
STEERING............ STANDARD
BLADE CLUTCH .... ELECTRIC
STANDARD DECK .... 42"
WEIGHT .... 468 LBS.
MSRP................. $1,699

OPTIONS

2 BAG
42" SNOW THROWER
46" BLADE

RETAIL PRICING

YEAR	HIGH	LOW
2009	$497	$373
2010	$548	$411
2011	$613	$460
2012	$673	$505
2013	$749	$562
2014	$829	$622

AVG. AUCTION PRICING

LOW	HIGH	AVG
$258	$421	$367

LTX1042

YEARS MFRD 2009-2011
ENGINE .... KOHLER COURAGE
CYLINDERS................... 1
ENGINE HP 19
COOLING .... AIR
FUEL .... G
SPEEDS .... VARIABLE
TRANSMISSION .... HYDRO
STEERING............ STANDARD
BLADE CLUTCH .... ELECTRIC
STANDARD DECK .... 42"
WEIGHT .... 498 LBS.
MSRP................. $1,849

OPTIONS

2 BAG
42" SNOW THROWER
46" BLADE

RETAIL PRICING

YEAR	HIGH	LOW
2009	$617	$463
2010	$688	$516
2011	$764	$573

LTX1042KW

YEARS MFRD 2012-2014
ENGINE .... KAWASAKI
ENGINE HP 18
COOLING .... AIR
FUEL .... G
SPEEDS .... VARIABLE
TRANSMISSION .... HYDRO
STEERING............ STANDARD
STANDARD DECK .... 42"
MSRP................. $1,999

OPTIONS

2 BAG
42" SNOW THROWER
46" BLADE

RETAIL PRICING

YEAR	HIGH	LOW
2012	$824	$618
2013	$912	$684
2014	$1,012	$759

LTX1045

YEARS MFRD 2009-2014
ENGINE .... KOHLER COURAGE
CYLINDERS................... 1
ENGINE HP 20
COOLING .... AIR
FUEL .... G
SPEEDS .... VARIABLE
TRANSMISSION .... HYDRO
STEERING............ STANDARD
BLADE CLUTCH .... ELECTRIC
STANDARD DECK .... 46"
WEIGHT .... 510 LBS.
MSRP................. $1,899

OPTIONS

2 BAG
42" SNOW THROWER
46" BLADE

RETAIL PRICING

YEAR	HIGH	LOW
2009	$575	$431
2010	$636	$477
2011	$704	$528
2012	$782	$587
2013	$866	$650
2014	$964	$723

LTX1045M

YEARS MFRD 2012-2012
ENGINE .... KOHLER
ENGINE HP 22
COOLING .... AIR
FUEL .... G
SPEEDS .... VARIABLE
TRANSMISSION .... HYDRO
STEERING............ STANDARD
STANDARD DECK .... 46"
MSRP................. $1,999

OPTIONS

2 BAG
42" SNOW THROWER
46" BLADE

RETAIL PRICING

YEAR	HIGH	LOW
2012	$935	$701

CUB CADET

LTX1046

YEARS MFRD 2009-2010
ENGINE . . . . KOHLER COURAGE
CYLINDERS. 2
ENGINE HP 22
COOLING . . . . AIR
FUEL . . . . G
SPEEDS . . . . VARIABLE
TRANSMISSION . . . . HYDRO
STEERING. . . . . STANDARD
STANDARD DECK . . . . 46"
WEIGHT . . . . 513 LBS.
MSRP. $2,099

OPTIONS

2 BAG
42" SNOW THROWER
46" BLADE

RETAIL PRICING

YEAR	HIGH	LOW
2009	$745	$559
2010	$826	$620

LTX1046 VT

YEARS MFRD 2009-2010
ENGINE . . . . B&S
CYLINDERS. 2
ENGINE HP 23
COOLING . . . . AIR
FUEL . . . . G
SPEEDS . . . . VARIABLE
TRANSMISSION . . . . HYDRO
STEERING. . . . . STANDARD
BLADE CLUTCH . . . . ELECTRIC
STANDARD DECK . . . . 46"
WEIGHT . . . . 513 LBS.
MSRP. $1,999

OPTIONS

2 BAG
42" SNOW THROWER
46" BLADE

RETAIL PRICING

YEAR	HIGH	LOW
2009	$704	$528
2010	$779	$584

LTX1046KW

YEARS MFRD 2012-2014
ENGINE . . . . KAWASAKI
ENGINE HP 21.5
COOLING . . . . AIR
FUEL . . . . G
SPEEDS . . . . VARIABLE
TRANSMISSION . . . . HYDRO
STEERING. . . . . STANDARD
STANDARD DECK . . . . 46"
MSRP. $2,199

OPTIONS

2 BAG
42" SNOW THROWER
46" BLADE

RETAIL PRICING

YEAR	HIGH	LOW
2012	$870	$653
2013	$966	$724
2014	$1,075	$806

LTX1046M

YEARS MFRD 2013-2014
ENGINE . . . . KOHLER
ENGINE HP 22
COOLING . . . . AIR
FUEL . . . . G
SPEEDS . . . . VARIABLE
TRANSMISSION . . . . HYDRO
STEERING. . . . . STANDARD
STANDARD DECK . . . . 46"
MSRP. $1,999

OPTIONS

2 BAG
42" SNOW THROWER
46" BLADE

RETAIL PRICING

YEAR	HIGH	LOW
2013	$877	$658
2014	$973	$730

LTX1050

YEARS MFRD 2009-2014
ENGINE . . . . KOHLER
ENGINE HP 24
COOLING . . . . AIR
FUEL . . . . G
SPEEDS . . . . VARIABLE
TRANSMISSION . . . . HYDRO
STEERING. . . . . STANDARD
STANDARD DECK . . . . 50"
MSRP. $2,199

OPTIONS

3 BAG
42" SNOW THROWER
46" BLADE

RETAIL PRICING

YEAR	HIGH	LOW
2009	$643	$482
2010	$708	$531
2011	$786	$590
2012	$877	$658
2013	$973	$730
2014	$1,084	$813

AVG. AUCTION PRICING

LOW	HIGH	AVG
$544	$989	$791

LTX1050 VT

YEARS MFRD 2009-2010
ENGINE . . . . B&S PRO
CYLINDERS. 2
ENGINE HP 24
COOLING . . . . AIR
FUEL . . . . G
SPEEDS . . . . VARIABLE
TRANSMISSION . . . . HYDRO
STEERING. . . . . STANDARD
BLADE CLUTCH . . . . ELECTRIC
STANDARD DECK . . . . 50"
WEIGHT . . . . 548 LBS.
MSRP. $2,249

OPTIONS

3 BAG
42" SNOW THROWER
46" BLADE

RETAIL PRICING

YEAR	HIGH	LOW
2009	$790	$593
2010	$880	$660

LTX1050KW

YEARS MFRD 2010-2014
ENGINE . . . . KAWASAKI
CYLINDERS. 2
ENGINE HP 22
COOLING . . . . AIR
FUEL . . . . G
SPEEDS . . . . VARIABLE
TRANSMISSION . . . . HYDRO
STEERING. . . . . STANDARD
BLADE CLUTCH . . . . ELECTRIC
STANDARD DECK . . . . 50"
WEIGHT . . . . 548 LBS.
MSRP. $2,399

OPTIONS

3 BAG
42" SNOW THROWER
46" BLADE

RETAIL PRICING

YEAR	HIGH	LOW
2010	$774	$580
2011	$857	$643
2012	$955	$716
2013	$1,053	$790
2014	$1,167	$876

LX42 EFI

YEARS MFRD 2016-2020
SERIES. . . . . . XT2 ENDURO SERIES
ENGINE . . . . CUB CADET
CYLINDERS. 2
CID 679CC
COOLING . . . . AIR
FUEL . . . . G
SPEEDS . . . . VARIABLE
TRANSMISSION . . . . HYDRO
STEERING. . . . . STANDARD
STANDARD DECK . . . . 42"
MSRP. $2,099

RETAIL PRICING

YEAR	HIGH	LOW
2016	$1,164	$873
2017	$1,287	$965
2018	$1,395	$1,047
2019	$1,448	$1,122
2020	$1,518	$1,188

LX42 KH

YEARS MFRD 2015-2019
SERIES. . . . . . XT2 ENDURO SERIES
ENGINE . . . . KOHLER
ENGINE HP 22
COOLING . . . . AIR
FUEL . . . . G
SPEEDS . . . . VARIABLE
TRANSMISSION . . . . HYDRO
STEERING. . . . . STANDARD
STANDARD DECK . . . . 42"
MSRP. $1,999

OPTIONS

42" SNOW THROWER
46" BLADE
BAGGER

RETAIL PRICING

YEAR	HIGH	LOW
2015	$947	$710
2016	$1,051	$788
2017	$1,164	$873
2018	$1,284	$963
2019	$1,409	$1,057

LX46

YEARS MFRD 2015-2018
SERIES. . . . . . XT2 ENDURO SERIES
ENGINE . . . . KAWASAKI
ENGINE HP 21.5
COOLING . . . . AIR
FUEL . . . . G
SPEEDS . . . . VARIABLE
TRANSMISSION . . . . HYDRO
STEERING. . . . . STANDARD
STANDARD DECK . . . . 46"
MSRP. $1,999

OPTIONS

42" SNOW THROWER
46" BLADE
BAGGER

RETAIL PRICING

YEAR	HIGH	LOW
2015	$1,053	$790
2016	$1,167	$876
2017	$1,293	$969
2018	$1,427	$1,070

LX46 FAB

YEARS MFRD 2015-2017
SERIES. . . . . . XT2 ENDURO SERIES
ENGINE . . . . KAWASAKI
ENGINE HP 23
COOLING . . . . AIR
FUEL . . . . G
SPEEDS . . . . VARIABLE
TRANSMISSION . . . . HYDRO
STEERING. . . . . STANDARD
STANDARD DECK . . . . 46"
MSRP. $2,499

OPTIONS

42" SNOW THROWER
46" BLADE
6 BU BAG

RETAIL PRICING

YEAR	HIGH	LOW
2015	$1,364	$1,023
2016	$1,512	$1,134
2017	$1,676	$1,257

LX46 KH

YEARS MFRD 2015-2020
SERIES. . . . . . XT2 ENDURO SERIES
ENGINE . . . . KOHLER
CYLINDERS. 2
CID 679CC
ENGINE HP 24

COOLING . . . . . . AIR
FUEL . . . . . . G
SPEEDS . . . . . . VARIABLE
TRANSMISSION . . . . . . HYDRO
STEERING . . . . . . STANDARD
STANDARD DECK . . . . . . 46"
MSRP $2,299

OPTIONS

42" SNOW BLOWER $1,350
46" BLADE $340
BAGGER $400
CUB CADET EFI $300

RETAIL PRICING

YEAR	HIGH	LOW
2015	$1,113	$835
2016	$1,234	$925
2017	$1,361	$1,021
2018	$1,502	$1,126
2019	$1,657	$1,243
2020	$1,773	$1,351

LX46 LE FAB

YEARS MFRD 2017-2017
SERIES . . . . . . XT2 ENDURO SERIES
COOLING . . . . . . AIR
FUEL . . . . . . G
SPEEDS . . . . . . VARIABLE
TRANSMISSION . . . . . . HYDRO
STEERING . . . . . . STANDARD
STANDARD DECK . . . . . . 46"
MSRP $2,599

RETAIL PRICING

YEAR	HIGH	LOW
2017	$1,744	$1,308

LX50

YEARS MFRD 2015-2017
SERIES . . . . . . XT2 ENDURO SERIES
ENGINE . . . . . . KAWASAKI
ENGINE HP 23
COOLING . . . . . . AIR
FUEL . . . . . . G
SPEEDS . . . . . . VARIABLE
TRANSMISSION . . . . . . HYDRO
STEERING . . . . . . STANDARD
STANDARD DECK . . . . . . 50"
MSRP $2,299

OPTIONS

42" SNOW THROWER
46" BLADE
6 BU BAG

RETAIL PRICING

YEAR	HIGH	LOW
2015	$1,259	$944
2016	$1,391	$1,043
2017	$1,542	$1,156

LX50 FAB KW

YEARS MFRD 2017-2017
ENGINE . . . . . . KAWASAKI
ENGINE HP 23
COOLING . . . . . . AIR
FUEL . . . . . . G
SPEEDS . . . . . . VARIABLE
TRANSMISSION . . . . . . DUAL HYDRO
STEERING . . . . . . ZERO
STANDARD DECK . . . . . . 50"
MSRP $2,999

OPTIONS

54" DECK

RETAIL PRICING

YEAR	HIGH	LOW
2017	$1,994	$1,495

LX54 FAB

YEARS MFRD 2015-2017
SERIES . . . . . . XT2 ENDURO SERIES
ENGINE . . . . . . KAWASAKI
ENGINE HP 23
COOLING . . . . . . AIR
FUEL . . . . . . G
SPEEDS . . . . . . VARIABLE
TRANSMISSION . . . . . . HYDRO
STEERING . . . . . . STANDARD
STANDARD DECK . . . . . . 54"
MSRP $2,999

OPTIONS

42" SNOW THROWER
46" BLADE
6 BU BAG

RETAIL PRICING

YEAR	HIGH	LOW
2015	$1,645	$1,234
2016	$1,818	$1,364
2017	$2,012	$1,509

LZ48

YEARS MFRD 2014-2014
SERIES . . . . . . TANK SERIES
ENGINE . . . . . . KOHLER
ENGINE HP 22.5
COOLING . . . . . . AIR
FUEL . . . . . . G
SPEEDS . . . . . . VARIABLE
TRANSMISSION . . . . . . HYDRO
STEERING . . . . . . ZERO
STANDARD DECK . . . . . . 48"
MSRP $8,499

OPTIONS

72" BLADE
BAGGER
POWER LIFT

RETAIL PRICING

YEAR	HIGH	LOW
2014	$4,375	$3,281

LZ54KW

YEARS MFRD 2014-2015
SERIES . . . . . . TANK SERIES
ENGINE . . . . . . KAWASAKI
ENGINE HP 23.5
COOLING . . . . . . AIR
FUEL . . . . . . G
SPEEDS . . . . . . VARIABLE
TRANSMISSION . . . . . . DUAL HYDRO
STEERING . . . . . . ZERO
STANDARD DECK . . . . . . 54"
MSRP $9,499

OPTIONS

72" BLADE
BAGGER
POWER LIFT

RETAIL PRICING

YEAR	HIGH	LOW
2014	$4,722	$3,542
2015	$5,211	$3,908

LZ54KW PRO

YEARS MFRD 2014-2014
SERIES . . . . . . TANK SERIES
ENGINE . . . . . . KAWASAKI
ENGINE HP 27
COOLING . . . . . . AIR
SPEEDS . . . . . . VARIABLE
TRANSMISSION . . . . . . HYDRO
STEERING . . . . . . ZERO
STANDARD DECK . . . . . . 54"
MSRP $12,499

OPTIONS

72" BLADE
BAGGER
POWER LIFT

RETAIL PRICING

YEAR	HIGH	LOW
2014	$6,372	$4,779

LZ60

YEARS MFRD 2014-2014
SERIES . . . . . . TANK SERIES
ENGINE . . . . . . KOHLER
ENGINE HP 23.5
COOLING . . . . . . AIR
FUEL . . . . . . G
SPEEDS . . . . . . VARIABLE
TRANSMISSION . . . . . . HYDRO
STEERING . . . . . . ZERO
STANDARD DECK . . . . . . 60"
MSRP $9,199

OPTIONS

72" BLADE
BAGGER
POWER LIFT

RETAIL PRICING

YEAR	HIGH	LOW
2014	$4,690	$3,518

LZ60KW

YEARS MFRD 2014-2015
SERIES . . . . . . TANK SERIES
ENGINE . . . . . . KAWASAKI
ENGINE HP 27
COOLING . . . . . . AIR
FUEL . . . . . . G
SPEEDS . . . . . . VARIABLE
TRANSMISSION . . . . . . DUAL HYDRO
STEERING . . . . . . ZERO
STANDARD DECK . . . . . . 60"
MSRP $10,000

OPTIONS

72" BLADE
BAGGER
POWER LIFT

RETAIL PRICING

YEAR	HIGH	LOW
2014	$4,970	$3,728
2015	$5,487	$4,115

LZ60KW PRO

YEARS MFRD 2014-2014
SERIES . . . . . . TANK SERIES
ENGINE . . . . . . KAWASAKI
ENGINE HP 27
COOLING . . . . . . AIR
FUEL . . . . . . G
SPEEDS . . . . . . VARIABLE
TRANSMISSION . . . . . . HYDRO
STEERING . . . . . . ZERO
STANDARD DECK . . . . . . 60"
MSRP $12,999

OPTIONS

72" BLADE
BAGGER
POWER LIFT

RETAIL PRICING

YEAR	HIGH	LOW
2014	$6,628	$4,971

M48HN

YEARS MFRD 2004-2005
SERIES . . . . . . MID-MOUNT SERIES
ENGINE . . . . . . HONDA V TWIN OHV
CYLINDERS 2
ENGINE HP 20
COOLING . . . . . . AIR
FUEL . . . . . . G
SPEEDS . . . . . . VARIABLE
TRANSMISSION . . . . . . DUAL HYDRO
STEERING . . . . . . ZERO
PTO . . . . . . YES
STANDARD DECK . . . . . . 48"
WEIGHT . . . . . . 1,040 LBS.
MSRP $6,699

OPTIONS

3 BAG
54" BLADE
BAG & FAN
SUS SEAT

RETAIL PRICING

YEAR	HIGH	LOW
2004	$1,507	$1,130
2005	$1,663	$1,247

M48KHS

YEARS MFRD 2004-2004
SERIES . . . . . . MID-MOUNT SERIES
ENGINE . . . . . . KOHLER V TWIN OHV
CYLINDERS 2
ENGINE HP 18
COOLING . . . . . . AIR
FUEL . . . . . . G
SPEEDS . . . . . . VARIABLE
TRANSMISSION . . . . . . DUAL HYDRO
STEERING . . . . . . ZERO
PTO . . . . . . YES
STANDARD DECK . . . . . . 48"
WEIGHT . . . . . . 850 LBS.
MSRP $5,999

CUB CADET

OPTIONS

3 BAG
54" BLADE
BAG & FAN
SUS SEAT

RETAIL PRICING

YEAR	HIGH	LOW
2004	$1,318	$989

M48KW

YEARS MFRD 2004-2010
SERIES .... MID-MOUNT SERIES
ENGINE .... KAWASAKI V-TWIN
CYLINDERS 2
ENGINE HP 23
COOLING .... AIR
FUEL .... G
SPEEDS .... VARIABLE
TRANSMISSION ..... DUAL HYDRO
STEERING .... ZERO
PTO .... YES
STANDARD DECK .... 48"
WEIGHT .... 1,040 LBS.
MSRP $8,849

OPTIONS

12 BU BAG
3 BAG
54" BLADE
SUS SEAT

RETAIL PRICING

YEAR	HIGH	LOW
2004	$1,879	$1,409
2005	$2,074	$1,555
2006	$2,289	$1,717
2007	$2,527	$1,895
2008	$2,787	$2,090
2009	$3,078	$2,309
2010	$3,397	$2,548

M48KWS

YEARS MFRD 2002-2003
SERIES .... MID-MOUNT SERIES
ENGINE .... KAWASAKI V-TWIN
CYLINDERS 2
ENGINE HP 17
COOLING .... AIR
FUEL .... G
STEERING .... ZERO
PTO .... YES
STANDARD DECK .... 48"
MSRP $6,100

RETAIL PRICING

YEAR	HIGH	LOW
2002	$2,112	$1,584
2003	$2,352	$1,764

M54HN

YEARS MFRD 2004-2005
SERIES .... MID-MOUNT SERIES
ENGINE ...... HONDA V TWIN OHV
CYLINDERS 2
ENGINE HP 24
COOLING .... AIR
FUEL .... G
SPEEDS .... VARIABLE
TRANSMISSION ..... DUAL HYDRO
STEERING .... ZERO
PTO .... YES
STANDARD DECK .... 54"
WEIGHT .... 1,055 LBS.
MSRP $8,499

OPTIONS

54" BLADE
BAG & FAN
SUS SEAT

RETAIL PRICING

YEAR	HIGH	LOW
2004	$1,911	$1,433
2005	$2,108	$1,581

M54KH

YEARS MFRD 2004-2004
SERIES .... TANK SERIES
ENGINE ...... KOHLER COMMAND
CYLINDERS 2
ENGINE HP 25
COOLING .... AIR
FUEL .... G
SPEEDS .... VARIABLE
TRANSMISSION ..... DUAL HYDRO
STEERING .... ZERO
BLADE CLUTCH .... ELECTRIC
STANDARD DECK .... 54"
WEIGHT .... 1,100 LBS.
MSRP $7,899

OPTIONS

54" BLADE
BAG & FAN
SUS SEAT

RETAIL PRICING

YEAR	HIGH	LOW
2004	$1,730	$1,298

M54KH

YEARS MFRD 2008-2010
SERIES .... MID-MOUNT SERIES
ENGINE ..... KOHLER V TWIN OHV
CYLINDERS 2
ENGINE HP 27
COOLING .... AIR
FUEL .... G
SPEEDS .... VARIABLE
TRANSMISSION ..... DUAL HYDRO
STEERING .... ZERO
PTO .... YES
STANDARD DECK .... 54"
MSRP $9,299

OPTIONS

12 BU BAG
3 BAG
54" BLADE
SUS SEAT

RETAIL PRICING

YEAR	HIGH	LOW
2008	$2,930	$2,198
2009	$3,234	$2,425
2010	$3,569	$2,677

M54KW

YEARS MFRD 2004-2009
SERIES .... MID-MOUNT SERIES
ENGINE .... KAWASAKI V-TWIN
CYLINDERS 2
ENGINE HP 25
COOLING .... AIR
FUEL .... G
SPEEDS .... VARIABLE
TRANSMISSION ..... DUAL HYDRO
STEERING .... ZERO
PTO .... YES
STANDARD DECK .... 54"
MSRP $9,549

OPTIONS

12 BU BAG
27HP KOHLER
54" BLADE
SUS SEAT

RETAIL PRICING

YEAR	HIGH	LOW
2004	$2,067	$1,551
2005	$2,283	$1,712
2006	$2,519	$1,890
2007	$2,782	$2,086
2008	$3,069	$2,302
2009	$3,388	$2,541

M60 ROPS

YEARS MFRD 2004-2006
SERIES .... MID-MOUNT SERIES
ENGINE .... KAWASAKI V TWIN OHV
CYLINDERS 2
ENGINE HP 25
FUEL .... G
SPEEDS .... VARIABLE
TRANSMISSION .... HYDRO
STEERING .... ZERO
PTO .... YES
STANDARD DECK .... 60"
WEIGHT .... 1,120 LBS.
MSRP $8,999

RETAIL PRICING

YEAR	HIGH	LOW
2004	$4,753	$3,565
2005	$5,080	$3,810
2006	$5,471	$4,104

M60KH

YEARS MFRD 2001-2006
SERIES .... MID-MOUNT SERIES
ENGINE .... KOHLER V-TWIN
CYLINDERS 2
ENGINE HP 25
COOLING .... AIR
FUEL .... G
SPEEDS .... VARIABLE
TRANSMISSION .... HYDRO
STEERING .... ZERO
PTO .... YES
STANDARD DECK .... 60"
MSRP $8,999

RETAIL PRICING

YEAR	HIGH	LOW
2001	$3,839	$2,879
2002	$3,946	$2,960
2003	$4,279	$3,210
2004	$4,608	$3,456
2005	$5,175	$3,881
2006	$5,471	$4,104

M60KH EFI

YEARS MFRD 2004-2005
SERIES .... MID-MOUNT SERIES
ENGINE ..... KOHLER V TWIN OHV
CYLINDERS 2
ENGINE HP 28
COOLING .... AIR
FUEL .... G
SPEEDS .... VARIABLE
TRANSMISSION ..... DUAL HYDRO
STEERING .... ZERO
PTO .... YES
STANDARD DECK .... 60"
WEIGHT .... 1,075 LBS.
MSRP $9,999

OPTIONS

54" BLADE
BAG & FAN
SUS SEAT

RETAIL PRICING

YEAR	HIGH	LOW
2004	$2,248	$1,686
2005	$2,482	$1,861

M60KH27

YEARS MFRD 2009-2010
SERIES .... TANK SERIES
ENGINE ...... KOHLER COMMAND
CYLINDERS 2
CID 725CC
ENGINE HP 27
COOLING .... AIR
FUEL .... G
SPEEDS .... VARIABLE
TRANSMISSION .... HYDRO
STEERING .... ZERO
BLADE CLUTCH .... ELECTRIC
STANDARD DECK .... 60"
WEIGHT .... 1,150 LBS.
MSRP $9,749

OPTIONS

12 BU BAG
54" BLADE

RETAIL PRICING

YEAR	HIGH	LOW
2009	$3,391	$2,543
2010	$3,743	$2,807

M60KO ROPS

YEARS MFRD 2004-2004
SERIES .... MID-MOUNT SERIES
ENGINE ..... KOHLER V TWIN OHV
CYLINDERS 2
ENGINE HP 27
COOLING .... AIR
FUEL .... G
SPEEDS .... VARIABLE
TRANSMISSION .... HYDRO
STEERING .... ZERO
PTO .... YES

STANDARD DECK . . . . 60"
WEIGHT . . . . 1,120 LBS.
MSRP. $9,999

RETAIL PRICING

YEAR	HIGH	LOW
2004	$5,422	$4,067

M60KW

YEARS MFRD 2004-2010
SERIES . . . . TANK SERIES
ENGINE . . . . KAWASAKI
CYLINDERS. 2
CID 852CC
ENGINE HP 31
COOLING . . . . AIR
FUEL . . . . G
SPEEDS . . . . VARIABLE
TRANSMISSION . . . . . DUAL HYDRO
STEERING. . . . . ZERO
BLADE CLUTCH . . . . ELECTRIC
STANDARD DECK . . . . 60"
WEIGHT . . . . 1,150 LBS.
MSRP. $10,149

OPTIONS

12 BU BAG
54" BLADE
SUS SEAT

RETAIL PRICING

YEAR	HIGH	LOW
2004	$2,156	$1,617
2005	$2,378	$1,784
2006	$2,625	$1,969
2007	$2,897	$2,172
2008	$3,198	$2,399
2009	$3,529	$2,647
2010	$3,896	$2,922

M60KW

YEARS MFRD 2001-2006
SERIES . . . . MID-MOUNT SERIES
ENGINE . . . . KAWASAKI V-TWIN
CYLINDERS. 2
ENGINE HP 25
COOLING . . . . AIR
FUEL . . . . G
SPEEDS . . . . VARIABLE
TRANSMISSION . . . . HYDRO
STEERING. . . . . ZERO
PTO . . . . YES
STANDARD DECK . . . . 60"
WEIGHT . . . . 1,070 LBS.
MSRP. $7,999

RETAIL PRICING

YEAR	HIGH	LOW
2001	$3,886	$2,914
2002	$4,128	$3,096
2003	$4,330	$3,247
2004	$4,608	$3,456
2005	$4,706	$3,529
2006	$4,865	$3,648

M60KW LC

YEARS MFRD 2004-2009
SERIES . . . . MID-MOUNT SERIES
ENGINE . . . . . KAWASAKI V TWIN EFI
CYLINDERS. 2
ENGINE HP 29
COOLING . . . . LIQUID
FUEL . . . . G
SPEEDS . . . . VARIABLE
TRANSMISSION . . . . . DUAL HYDRO
STEERING. . . . . ZERO
PTO . . . . YES
STANDARD DECK . . . . 60"
WEIGHT . . . . 1,200 LBS.
MSRP. $12,149

OPTIONS

12 BU BAG
54" BLADE
SUS SEAT

RETAIL PRICING

YEAR	HIGH	LOW
2004	$2,631	$1,973
2005	$2,904	$2,178
2006	$3,206	$2,405
2007	$3,538	$2,654
2008	$3,905	$2,929
2009	$4,310	$3,233

M72GN

YEARS MFRD 2004-2006
SERIES . . . . MID-MOUNT SERIES
ENGINE . . . . . GUARDIAN (GENERAC)
CYLINDERS. 2
ENGINE HP 33
COOLING . . . . AIR
FUEL . . . . G
SPEEDS . . . . VARIABLE
TRANSMISSION . . . . HYDRO
STEERING. . . . . ZERO
PTO . . . . YES
STANDARD DECK . . . . 72"
WEIGHT . . . . 1,330 LBS.
MSRP. $8,999

OPTIONS

54" BLADE
SUS SEAT

RETAIL PRICING

YEAR	HIGH	LOW
2004	$2,049	$1,537
2005	$2,260	$1,695
2006	$2,496	$1,872

M72KW

YEARS MFRD 2009-2011
SERIES . . . . TANK SERIES
ENGINE . . . . KAWASAKI
CYLINDERS. 2
CID 999CC
ENGINE HP 37
COOLING . . . . AIR
FUEL . . . . G
SPEEDS . . . . VARIABLE
TRANSMISSION . . . . HYDRO
STEERING. . . . . ZERO
BLADE CLUTCH . . . . ELECTRIC
STANDARD DECK . . . . 72"
WEIGHT . . . . 1,380 LBS.
MSRP. $11,699

RETAIL PRICING

YEAR	HIGH	LOW
2009	$4,169	$3,127
2010	$4,550	$3,412
2011	$5,182	$3,887

M72KW LC

YEARS MFRD 2005-2010
SERIES . . . . MID MOUNT SERIES
ENGINE . . . . KAWASAKI
ENGINE HP 37
COOLING . . . . LIQUID
FUEL . . . . G
SPEEDS . . . . VARIABLE
TRANSMISSION . . . . HYDRO
STEERING. . . . . ZERO
STANDARD DECK . . . . 72"
MSRP. $11,749

OPTIONS

12 BU BAG
54" BLADE
SUS SEAT

RETAIL PRICING

YEAR	HIGH	LOW
2005	$2,730	$2,047
2006	$3,038	$2,279
2007	$3,354	$2,515
2008	$3,702	$2,777
2009	$4,086	$3,064
2010	$4,510	$3,383

PRO X 648

YEARS MFRD 2020-2020
ENGINE . . . . KAWASAKI FX691V
CID 726CC
ENGINE HP 22
FUEL . . . . G
SPEEDS . . . . VARIABLE
TRANSMISSION . . . . HYDRO
BLADE CLUTCH . . . . ELECTRIC
STANDARD DECK . . . . 48"
WEIGHT . . . . 1,015 LBS.
MSRP. $8,499

PRO X 654

YEARS MFRD 2020-2020
ENGINE . . . . KAWASAKI FX801V
CID 852CC
ENGINE HP 25.5
FUEL . . . . G
SPEEDS . . . . VARIABLE
TRANSMISSION . . . . HYDRO
BLADE CLUTCH . . . . ELECTRIC
STANDARD DECK . . . . 54"
WEIGHT . . . . 1,080 LBS.
MSRP. $8,999

PRO X 660

YEARS MFRD 2020-2020
ENGINE . . . . KAWASAKI FX801V
CID 852CC
ENGINE HP 25.5
FUEL . . . . G
SPEEDS . . . . VARIABLE
TRANSMISSION . . . . HYDRO
BLADE CLUTCH . . . . ELECTRIC
STANDARD DECK . . . . 60"
WEIGHT . . . . 1,115 LBS.
MSRP. $9,499

PRO Z 548L

YEARS MFRD 2018-2020
ENGINE . . . . KAWASAKI FX730V
CID 726CC
ENGINE HP 23.5
FUEL . . . . G
TRANSMISSION . . . . . DUAL HYDRO
STEERING. . . . . ZERO
STANDARD DECK . . . . 48"
WEIGHT . . . . 1,272 LBS.
MSRP. $8,799

OPTIONS

ELEC DECK LIFT $803

PRO Z 554L

YEARS MFRD 2017-2020
ENGINE . . . . KAWASAKI FX850V
CID 852CC
ENGINE HP 27
COOLING . . . . AIR
FUEL . . . . G
SPEEDS . . . . VARIABLE
TRANSMISSION . . . . . DUAL HYDRO
STEERING. . . . . ZERO
STANDARD DECK . . . . 54"
WEIGHT . . . . 1,300 LBS.
MSRP. $9,799

OPTIONS

3 BAG & FAN $3,200
ELEC DECK LIFT $803

RETAIL PRICING

YEAR	HIGH	LOW
2017	$5,902	$4,426
2018	$6,492	$4,869
2019	$7,175	$5,381
2020	$8,017	$6,261

PRO Z 554S

YEARS MFRD 2017-2020
ENGINE . . . . KAWASAKI FX850V
CID 852
ENGINE HP 27
COOLING . . . . AIR
FUEL . . . . G
SPEEDS . . . . VARIABLE
TRANSMISSION . . . . . DUAL HYDRO
STEERING. . . . . ZERO
STANDARD DECK . . . . 54"
WEIGHT . . . . 1,424 LBS.
MSRP. $10,999

OPTIONS

3 BAG & FAN $3,200
ELEC DECK LIFT $803

RETAIL PRICING

YEAR	HIGH	LOW
2017	$6,415	$4,811
2018	$7,050	$5,287
2019	$8,192	$6,144
2020	$9,096	$7,131

CUB CADET

PRO Z 560L

YEARS MFRD 2017-2020
ENGINE . . . . KAWASAKI FX850V
CID 852CC
ENGINE HP 27
COOLING . . . . AIR
FUEL . . . . G
SPEEDS . . . . VARIABLE
TRANSMISSION . . . . . DUAL HYDRO
STEERING . . . . ZERO
STANDARD DECK . . . . 60"
WEIGHT . . . . 1,324 LBS.
MSRP $10,149

OPTIONS

3 BAG & FAN $3,200
ELEC DECK LIFT $803

RETAIL PRICING

YEAR	HIGH	LOW
2017	$6,094	$4,571
2018	$6,840	$5,130
2019	$7,513	$5,635
2020	$8,515	$6,326

PRO Z 560S

YEARS MFRD 2017-2020
ENGINE . . . . KAWASAKI FX850V
CID 852CC
ENGINE HP 27
COOLING . . . . AIR
FUEL . . . . G
SPEEDS . . . . VARIABLE
TRANSMISSION . . . . . DUAL HYDRO
STEERING . . . . ZERO
STANDARD DECK . . . . 60"
WEIGHT . . . . 1,424 LBS.
MSRP $11,199

OPTIONS

3 BAG & FAN $3,200
ELEC DECK LIFT $803

RETAIL PRICING

YEAR	HIGH	LOW
2017	$6,544	$4,908
2018	$7,220	$5,415
2019	$7,933	$5,950
2020	$9,087	$6,651

PRO Z 760L

YEARS MFRD 2017-2020
ENGINE . . . . KAWASAKI FX921V
CID 999CC
ENGINE HP 31
COOLING . . . . AIR
FUEL . . . . G
SPEEDS . . . . VARIABLE
TRANSMISSION . . . . . DUAL HYDRO
STEERING . . . . ZERO
STANDARD DECK . . . . 60"
WEIGHT . . . . 1,424 LBS.
MSRP $10,999

OPTIONS

EFI $300
LIGHT KIT $160
PWR TRIPLE BAGGER $3,200

RETAIL PRICING

YEAR	HIGH	LOW
2017	$6,544	$4,908
2018	$7,227	$5,420
2019	$8,089	$6,066
2020	$8,987	$6,850

PRO Z 760S

YEARS MFRD 2017-2020
ENGINE . . . . KAWASAKI FX921V
CID 999CC
ENGINE HP 31
TRANSMISSION . . . . . DUAL HYDRO
STEERING . . . . ZERO
STANDARD DECK . . . . 60"
WEIGHT . . . . 1,562 LBS.
MSRP $12,199

OPTIONS

ELIFT $803
PWR TRIPLE BAGGER $3,200

RETAIL PRICING

YEAR	HIGH	LOW
2017	$7,186	$5,389
2018	$7,936	$5,952
2019	$8,761	$6,571
2020	$10,045	$7,353

PRO Z 772L

YEARS MFRD 2017-2020
ENGINE . . . . KAWASAKI FX921V
CID 999CC
ENGINE HP 31
COOLING . . . . AIR
FUEL . . . . G
SPEEDS . . . . VARIABLE
TRANSMISSION . . . . . DUAL HYDRO
STEERING . . . . ZERO
STANDARD DECK . . . . 72"
WEIGHT . . . . 1,424 LBS.
MSRP $11,999

OPTIONS

ELEC DECK LIFT $803
LIGHT KIT $160

RETAIL PRICING

YEAR	HIGH	LOW
2017	$7,057	$5,293
2018	$7,791	$5,843
2019	$8,555	$6,416
2020	$9,698	$7,375

PRO Z 772S

YEARS MFRD 2017-2017
ENGINE . . . . KAWASAKI
ENGINE HP 31
COOLING . . . . AIR
FUEL . . . . G
SPEEDS . . . . VARIABLE
TRANSMISSION . . . . . DUAL HYDRO
STEERING . . . . ZERO
STANDARD DECK . . . . 72"
MSRP $11,999

OPTIONS

3 BAG & FAN
ELIFT

RETAIL PRICING

YEAR	HIGH	LOW
2017	$7,979	$5,984

PRO Z 960L

YEARS MFRD 2017-2020
ENGINE . . . . . . KAWASAKI FX1000V
CID 999CC
ENGINE HP 35
COOLING . . . . AIR
FUEL . . . . G
SPEEDS . . . . VARIABLE
TRANSMISSION . . . . . DUAL HYDRO
STEERING . . . . ZERO
STANDARD DECK . . . . 60"
WEIGHT . . . . 1,591 LBS.
MSRP $11,999

OPTIONS

3 BAG & FAN $3,200
ELEC DECK LIFT $803

RETAIL PRICING

YEAR	HIGH	LOW
2017	$7,057	$5,293
2018	$7,778	$5,834
2019	$8,445	$6,408
2020	$9,268	$7,162

PRO Z 960S

YEARS MFRD 2017-2020
ENGINE . . . . . . KAWASAKI FX1000V
CID 999CC
ENGINE HP 35
COOLING . . . . AIR
FUEL . . . . G
SPEEDS . . . . VARIABLE
TRANSMISSION . . . . . DUAL HYDRO
STEERING . . . . ZERO
STANDARD DECK . . . . 60"
WEIGHT . . . . 1,580 LBS.
MSRP $12,999

OPTIONS

3 BAG & FAN $3,200
ELEC DECK LIFT $803

RETAIL PRICING

YEAR	HIGH	LOW
2017	$7,698	$5,773
2018	$8,515	$6,386
2019	$9,519	$7,139
2020	$10,667	$8,273

PRO Z 972L

YEARS MFRD 2017-2020
ENGINE . . . . . . KAWASAKI FX1000V
CID 999CC
ENGINE HP 35
COOLING . . . . AIR
FUEL . . . . G
SPEEDS . . . . VARIABLE
TRANSMISSION . . . . . DUAL HYDRO
STEERING . . . . ZERO
STANDARD DECK . . . . 72"
WEIGHT . . . . 1,591 LBS.
MSRP $12,899

OPTIONS

ELEC DECK LIFT $803

RETAIL PRICING

YEAR	HIGH	LOW
2017	$8,341	$6,255
2018	$9,228	$6,921
2019	$10,071	$7,553
2020	$11,406	$8,728

PRO Z 972S

YEARS MFRD 2017-2020
ENGINE . . . . . . KAWASAKI FX1000V
CID 999CC
ENGINE HP 35
COOLING . . . . AIR
FUEL . . . . G
TRANSMISSION . . . . . DUAL HYDRO
STANDARD DECK . . . . 72"
WEIGHT . . . . 1,631 LBS.
MSRP $13,999

OPTIONS

ELEC DECK LIFT $803
MULCH KIT $200

PRO Z 972SD

YEARS MFRD 2019-2020
ENGINE . . . . . . KAWASAKI FX1000V
CID 999CC
ENGINE HP 35
SPEEDS . . . . VARIABLE
TRANSMISSION . . . . . DUAL HYDRO
STEERING . . . . ZERO
STANDARD DECK . . . . 72"
WEIGHT . . . . 1,850 LBS.
MSRP $17,499

OPTIONS

ELEC DECK LIFT $803
LIGHT KIT $160
MULCH KIT $200

PRO Z 972SDL

YEARS MFRD 2020-2020
ENGINE . . . . . . KAWASAKI FX1000V
CID 999CC
ENGINE HP 35
FUEL . . . . G
SPEEDS . . . . VARIABLE
TRANSMISSION . . . . HYDRO
STEERING . . . . ZERO
BLADE CLUTCH . . . . ELECTRIC
ROPS/CAB . . . . ROPS
STANDARD DECK . . . . 72"
WEIGHT . . . . 1,885 LBS.
MSRP $20,999

RZT42

YEARS MFRD 2005-2012
ENGINE . . . . KOHLER
CYLINDERS 1
ENGINE HP 22
COOLING . . . . AIR
FUEL . . . . G
SPEEDS . . . . VARIABLE
TRANSMISSION . . . . HYDRO
STEERING . . . . ZERO
BLADE CLUTCH . . . . ELECTRIC

STANDARD DECK . . . . 42"
WEIGHT . . . . 480 LBS.
MSRP. $2,649

OPTIONS

2 BAG
REAR SPREADER

RETAIL PRICING

YEAR	HIGH	LOW
2005	$612	$459
2006	$678	$508
2007	$748	$561
2008	$825	$619
2009	$909	$682
2010	$1,003	$753
2011	$1,110	$833
2012	$1,223	$917

RZT50

YEARS MFRD 2005-2010
ENGINE . . . . KAWASAKI
CYLINDERS. 2
ENGINE HP 22
COOLING . . . . AIR
FUEL . . . . G
SPEEDS . . . . VARIABLE
TRANSMISSION . . . . . DUAL HYDRO
STEERING. . . . . ZERO
BLADE CLUTCH . . . . ELECTRIC
STANDARD DECK . . . . 50"
WEIGHT . . . . 527 LBS.
MSRP. $3,249

OPTIONS

3 BAG

RETAIL PRICING

YEAR	HIGH	LOW
2005	$780	$585
2006	$862	$647
2007	$950	$713
2008	$1,054	$790
2009	$1,159	$869
2010	$1,300	$975

RZT50KH

YEARS MFRD 2011-2012
ENGINE . . . . KOHLER
ENGINE HP 24
COOLING . . . . AIR
FUEL . . . . G
SPEEDS . . . . VARIABLE
TRANSMISSION . . . . . DUAL HYDRO
STEERING. . . . . ZERO
STANDARD DECK . . . . 50"
MSRP. $3,299

OPTIONS

3BAG
REAR SPREADER

RETAIL PRICING

YEAR	HIGH	LOW
2011	$1,380	$1,035
2012	$1,522	$1,142

RZT50KW

YEARS MFRD 2011-2012
ENGINE . . . . KAWASAKI
ENGINE HP 23
COOLING . . . . AIR
FUEL . . . . G
SPEEDS . . . . VARIABLE
TRANSMISSION . . . . . DUAL HYDRO
STEERING. . . . . ZERO
STANDARD DECK . . . . 50"
MSRP. $3,299

OPTIONS

3 BAG
REAR SPREADER

RETAIL PRICING

YEAR	HIGH	LOW
2011	$1,380	$1,035
2012	$1,522	$1,142

RZT50VT

YEARS MFRD 2009-2010
ENGINE . . . . B&S
CYLINDERS. 2
ENGINE HP 24
COOLING . . . . AIR
FUEL . . . . G
SPEEDS . . . . VARIABLE
TRANSMISSION . . . . . DUAL HYDRO
STEERING. . . . . ZERO
BLADE CLUTCH . . . . ELECTRIC
STANDARD DECK . . . . 50"
WEIGHT . . . . 527 LBS.
MSRP. $3,249

OPTIONS

3 BAG

RETAIL PRICING

YEAR	HIGH	LOW
2009	$1,161	$871
2010	$1,279	$959

RZT54

YEARS MFRD 2007-2010
ENGINE . . . . KAWASAKI
CYLINDERS. 2
ENGINE HP 25
COOLING . . . . AIR
FUEL . . . . G
SPEEDS . . . . VARIABLE
TRANSMISSION . . . . . DUAL HYDRO
STEERING. . . . . ZERO
STANDARD DECK . . . . 54"
WEIGHT . . . . 557 LBS.
MSRP. $3,849

OPTIONS

3 BAG

RETAIL PRICING

YEAR	HIGH	LOW
2007	$1,126	$845
2008	$1,243	$932
2009	$1,372	$1,029
2010	$1,515	$1,136

RZT54KW

YEARS MFRD 2011-2012
ENGINE . . . . KAWASAKI
ENGINE HP 23
COOLING . . . . AIR
FUEL . . . . G
SPEEDS . . . . VARIABLE

TRANSMISSION . . . . . DUAL HYDRO
STEERING. . . . . ZERO
STANDARD DECK . . . . 54"
MSRP. $3,299

OPTIONS

3 BAG
REAR SPREADER

RETAIL PRICING

YEAR	HIGH	LOW
2011	$1,380	$1,035
2012	$1,527	$1,145

RZT L34

YEARS MFRD 2017-2019
COOLING . . . . AIR
FUEL . . . . G
SPEEDS . . . . VARIABLE
TRANSMISSION . . . . . DUAL HYDRO
STANDARD DECK . . . . 34"
MSRP. $2,449

RETAIL PRICING

YEAR	HIGH	LOW
2017	$1,472	$1,104
2018	$1,623	$1,217
2019	$1,788	$1,341

RZT L42

YEARS MFRD 2013-2018
ENGINE . . . . KOHLER
ENGINE HP 23
COOLING . . . . AIR
FUEL . . . . G
SPEEDS . . . . VARIABLE
TRANSMISSION . . . . . DUAL HYDRO
STEERING. . . . . ZERO
STANDARD DECK . . . . 42"
MSRP. $2,399

OPTIONS

2 BAG
52" BLADE
REAR SPREADER

RETAIL PRICING

YEAR	HIGH	LOW
2013	$1,036	$777
2014	$1,145	$859
2015	$1,268	$951
2016	$1,394	$1,046
2017	$1,540	$1,155
2018	$1,696	$1,272

RZT L46

YEARS MFRD 2014-2018
ENGINE . . . . KAWASAKI
ENGINE HP 23
COOLING . . . . AIR
FUEL . . . . G
SPEEDS . . . . VARIABLE
TRANSMISSION . . . . . DUAL HYDRO
STEERING. . . . . ZERO
STANDARD DECK . . . . 46"
MSRP. $2,799

OPTIONS

2 BAG
52" BLADE
HONDA

RETAIL PRICING

YEAR	HIGH	LOW
2014	$1,339	$1,004
2015	$1,473	$1,105
2016	$1,635	$1,226
2017	$1,796	$1,347
2018	$1,981	$1,486

RZT L50 KH

YEARS MFRD 2013-2016
ENGINE . . . . KOHLER
ENGINE HP 23
COOLING . . . . AIR
FUEL . . . . G
SPEEDS . . . . VARIABLE
TRANSMISSION . . . . . DUAL HYDRO
STEERING. . . . . ZERO
STANDARD DECK . . . . 50"
MSRP. $3,199

OPTIONS

2 BAG
SPREADER

RETAIL PRICING

YEAR	HIGH	LOW
2013	$1,443	$1,082
2014	$1,594	$1,195
2015	$1,759	$1,319
2016	$1,941	$1,456

RZT L50 KW

YEARS MFRD 2013-2014
ENGINE . . . . KAWASAKI
ENGINE HP 23
COOLING . . . . AIR
FUEL . . . . G
SPEEDS . . . . VARIABLE
TRANSMISSION . . . . HYDRO
STEERING. . . . . ZERO
STANDARD DECK . . . . 50"
MSRP. $3,299

OPTIONS

2 BAG
SPREADER

RETAIL PRICING

YEAR	HIGH	LOW
2013	$1,524	$1,143
2014	$1,682	$1,262

RZT L54 KH

YEARS MFRD 2013-2018
ENGINE . . . . KOHLER
ENGINE HP 24
COOLING . . . . AIR
FUEL . . . . G
SPEEDS . . . . VARIABLE
TRANSMISSION . . . . . DUAL HYDRO
STEERING. . . . . ZERO
STANDARD DECK . . . . 54"
MSRP. $2,999

OPTIONS

BAGGER
MULCH KIT

RETAIL PRICING

YEAR	HIGH	LOW
2013	$1,310	$982
2014	$1,441	$1,081

YEAR	HIGH	LOW
2015	$1,599	$1,199
2016	$1,755	$1,316
2017	$1,937	$1,453
2018	$2,139	$1,604

RZT L54 KW

YEARS MFRD 2013-2015
ENGINE HP 23
COOLING . . . . AIR
FUEL . . . . G
SPEEDS . . . . VARIABLE
TRANSMISSION . . . . . DUAL HYDRO
STEERING. . . . . ZERO
STANDARD DECK . . . . 54"
MSRP. $3,199

OPTIONS

2 BAG
52" BLADE
REAR SPREADER

RETAIL PRICING

YEAR	HIGH	LOW
2013	$1,491	$1,119
2014	$1,646	$1,235
2015	$1,818	$1,364

RZT S46 FAB KW

YEARS MFRD 2017-2017
ENGINE . . . . KAWASAKI
COOLING . . . . AIR
FUEL . . . . G
SPEEDS . . . . VARIABLE
TRANSMISSION . . . . . DUAL HYDRO
STEERING. . . . . ZERO
STANDARD DECK . . . . 46"
MSRP. $3,199

RETAIL PRICING

YEAR	HIGH	LOW
2017	$2,128	$1,596

RZT S54 FAB KW

YEARS MFRD 2017-2017
ENGINE . . . . KAWASAKI
COOLING . . . . AIR
FUEL . . . . G
SPEEDS . . . . VARIABLE
TRANSMISSION . . . . . DUAL HYDRO
STEERING. . . . . ZERO
STANDARD DECK . . . . 54"
MSRP. $3,499

RETAIL PRICING

YEAR	HIGH	LOW
2017	$2,327	$1,745

RZT SX42 KH

YEARS MFRD 2018-2020
ENGINE . . . . KOHLER
CYLINDERS. 2
ENGINE HP 22
FUEL . . . . G
TRANSMISSION . . . . . DUAL HYDRO
STEERING. . . . . ZERO
STANDARD DECK . . . . 42"
WEIGHT . . . . 546 LBS.
MSRP. $3,499

RZT SX46 KH

YEARS MFRD 2018-2020
ENGINE . . . . KOHLER
CYLINDERS. 2
CID 679CC
ENGINE HP 23
FUEL . . . . G
TRANSMISSION . . . . . DUAL HYDRO
STEERING. . . . . ZERO
STANDARD DECK . . . . 46"
WEIGHT . . . . 565 LBS.
MSRP. $3,699

RZT SX50

YEARS MFRD 2018-2020
ENGINE . . . . CUB CADET
CID 679CC
FUEL . . . . G
TRANSMISSION . . . . . DUAL HYDRO
STEERING. . . . . ZERO
STANDARD DECK . . . . 50"
WEIGHT . . . . 620 LBS.
MSRP. $3,799

RZT SX54

YEARS MFRD 2018-2020
ENGINE . . . . KAWASAKI
ENGINE HP 21.5
FUEL . . . . G
TRANSMISSION . . . . . DUAL HYDRO
STEERING. . . . . ZERO
STANDARD DECK . . . . 54"
WEIGHT . . . . 635 LBS.
MSRP. $3,999

RZTS42

YEARS MFRD 2012-2018
ENGINE . . . . KOHLER
ENGINE HP 22
COOLING . . . . AIR
FUEL . . . . G
SPEEDS . . . . VARIABLE
TRANSMISSION . . . . . DUAL HYDRO
STEERING. . . . . ZERO
STANDARD DECK . . . . 42"
MSRP. $2,699

OPTIONS

2 BAG
52" BLADE
SPREADER

RETAIL PRICING

YEAR	HIGH	LOW
2012	$1,059	$794
2013	$1,166	$875
2014	$1,293	$969
2015	$1,422	$1,066
2016	$1,569	$1,177
2017	$1,732	$1,299
2018	$1,911	$1,433

RZTS46

YEARS MFRD 2013-2016
ENGINE . . . . KOHLER
ENGINE HP 23
COOLING . . . . AIR
FUEL . . . . G
SPEEDS . . . . VARIABLE
TRANSMISSION . . . . HYDRO
STEERING. . . . . ZERO
STANDARD DECK . . . . 46"
MSRP. $3,199

OPTIONS

2 BAG
52" BLADE
SPREADER

RETAIL PRICING

YEAR	HIGH	LOW
2013	$1,458	$1,093
2014	$1,595	$1,196
2015	$1,759	$1,319
2016	$1,949	$1,461

RZTS48

YEARS MFRD 2012-2012
ENGINE . . . . KOHLER
ENGINE HP 23
COOLING . . . . AIR
FUEL . . . . G
SPEEDS . . . . VARIABLE
TRANSMISSION . . . . . DUAL HYDRO
STEERING. . . . . ZERO
STANDARD DECK . . . . 46"
MSRP. $3,199

OPTIONS

2 BAG
REAR SPREADER

RETAIL PRICING

YEAR	HIGH	LOW
2012	$1,445	$1,084

RZTS50

YEARS MFRD 2012-2017
ENGINE . . . . KOHLER
ENGINE HP 23
COOLING . . . . AIR
FUEL . . . . G
SPEEDS . . . . VARIABLE
TRANSMISSION . . . . . DUAL HYDRO
STEERING. . . . . ZERO
STANDARD DECK . . . . 50"
MSRP. $2,999

OPTIONS

2 BAG
52" BLADE
SPREADER

RETAIL PRICING

YEAR	HIGH	LOW
2012	$1,224	$918
2013	$1,343	$1,007
2014	$1,485	$1,114
2015	$1,641	$1,231
2016	$1,807	$1,355
2017	$1,994	$1,495

RZTS54

YEARS MFRD 2013-2017
ENGINE . . . . KAWASAKI
ENGINE HP 23
COOLING . . . . AIR
FUEL . . . . G
SPEEDS . . . . VARIABLE
TRANSMISSION . . . . . DUAL HYDRO
STEERING. . . . . ZERO
STANDARD DECK . . . . 54"
MSRP. $3,399

OPTIONS

2 BAG
52" BLADE
SPREADER

RETAIL PRICING

YEAR	HIGH	LOW
2013	$1,526	$1,145
2014	$1,681	$1,261
2015	$1,855	$1,391
2016	$2,049	$1,537
2017	$2,260	$1,695

RZTS54 KH

YEARS MFRD 2015-2017
ENGINE . . . . KOHLER
ENGINE HP 25
COOLING . . . . AIR
FUEL . . . . G
SPEEDS . . . . VARIABLE
TRANSMISSION . . . . . DUAL HYDRO
STEERING. . . . . ZERO
STANDARD DECK . . . . 54"
MSRP. $3,399

OPTIONS

2 BAG
52" BLADE
SPREADER

RETAIL PRICING

YEAR	HIGH	LOW
2015	$1,855	$1,391
2016	$2,049	$1,537
2017	$2,260	$1,695

S48KW PRO

YEARS MFRD 2014-2014
SERIES. . . . . ZF SERIES
ENGINE . . . . KAWASAKI
ENGINE HP 24
COOLING . . . . AIR
FUEL . . . . G
SPEEDS . . . . VARIABLE
TRANSMISSION . . . . HYDRO
STEERING. . . . . ZERO
STANDARD DECK . . . . 48"
MSRP. $4,999

OPTIONS

2 BAG
58" BLADE
POWER LIFT

RETAIL PRICING

YEAR	HIGH	LOW
2014	$2,548	$1,911

S54KW PRO

YEARS MFRD 2014-2014
SERIES. . . . . ZF SERIES
ENGINE . . . . KAWASAKI
ENGINE HP 24
COOLING . . . . AIR
FUEL . . . . G
SPEEDS . . . . VARIABLE
TRANSMISSION . . . . HYDRO
STEERING. . . . . ZERO
STANDARD DECK . . . . 54"
MSRP. $5,499

OPTIONS

2 BAG
58" BLADE
POWER LIFT

RETAIL PRICING

YEAR	HIGH	LOW
2014	$2,803	$2,103

S60KW PRO

YEARS MFRD 2014-2014
SERIES. . . . . ZF SERIES
ENGINE . . . . KAWASAKI
ENGINE HP 24
COOLING . . . . AIR
FUEL . . . . G
SPEEDS . . . . VARIABLE
TRANSMISSION . . . . HYDRO
STEERING. . . . . ZERO
STANDARD DECK . . . . 60"
MSRP. $5,999

OPTIONS

2 BAG
58" BLADE
POWER LIFT

RETAIL PRICING

YEAR	HIGH	LOW
2014	$3,059	$2,294

S6031

YEARS MFRD 2009-2012
SERIES. . . . . TANK SERIES
ENGINE . . . . KAWASAKI
CYLINDERS. 2
CID 852CC
ENGINE HP 31
COOLING . . . . AIR
FUEL . . . . G
SPEEDS . . . . VARIABLE
TRANSMISSION . . . . . DUAL HYDRO
STEERING. . . . . ZERO
BLADE CLUTCH . . . . ELECTRIC
STANDARD DECK . . . . 60"
WEIGHT . . . . 1,470 LBS.
MSRP. $17,999

OPTIONS

BLADE
CAB ENCL
LP SERIES
SPREADER

RETAIL PRICING

YEAR	HIGH	LOW
2009	$6,046	$4,535
2010	$6,674	$5,005
2011	$7,366	$5,524
2012	$8,130	$6,098

S6032 D

YEARS MFRD 2010-2012
SERIES. . . . . TANK SERIES
ENGINE . . . . YANMAR
CYLINDERS. 3
CID 1.33L
ENGINE HP 31.2
COOLING . . . . LIQUID
FUEL . . . . D
SPEEDS . . . . VARIABLE
TRANSMISSION . . . . . DUAL HYDRO
STEERING. . . . . ZERO
BLADE CLUTCH . . . . ELECTRIC
STANDARD DECK . . . . 60"
WEIGHT . . . . 1,850 LBS.
MSRP. $20,399

OPTIONS

72" BLADE
CAB ENCL
SPREADER

RETAIL PRICING

YEAR	HIGH	LOW
2010	$7,563	$5,673
2011	$8,349	$6,261
2012	$9,215	$6,911

S7232 D

YEARS MFRD 2010-2012
SERIES. . . . . TANK SERIES
ENGINE . . . . YANMAR
CYLINDERS. 3
CID 1.33L
ENGINE HP 31.2
COOLING . . . . LIQUID
FUEL . . . . D
SPEEDS . . . . VARIABLE
TRANSMISSION . . . . . DUAL HYDRO
STEERING. . . . . ZERO
BLADE CLUTCH . . . . ELECTRIC
STANDARD DECK . . . . 72"
WEIGHT . . . . 1,890 LBS.
MSRP. $20,999

OPTIONS

72" BLADE
CAB ENCL
SPREADER

RETAIL PRICING

YEAR	HIGH	LOW
2010	$7,786	$5,839
2011	$8,595	$6,446
2012	$9,487	$7,116

S7237

YEARS MFRD 2009-2012
SERIES. . . . . TANK SERIES
ENGINE . . . . KAWASAKI
CYLINDERS. 2
CID 999CC
ENGINE HP 37
COOLING . . . . AIR
FUEL . . . . G
SPEEDS . . . . VARIABLE
TRANSMISSION . . . . . DUAL HYDRO
STEERING. . . . . ZERO
BLADE CLUTCH . . . . ELECTRIC
STANDARD DECK . . . . 72"
WEIGHT . . . . 1,540 LBS.
MSRP. $18,749

OPTIONS

BLADE
CAB ENCL
LP SERIES
SPREADER

RETAIL PRICING

YEAR	HIGH	LOW
2009	$6,299	$4,724
2010	$6,953	$5,214
2011	$7,673	$5,755
2012	$8,469	$6,351

SLT1550

YEARS MFRD 2006-2008
SERIES. . . . . 1500 SERIES
ENGINE . . . . KOHLER COURAGE
CYLINDERS. 2
ENGINE HP 25
COOLING . . . . AIR
FUEL . . . . G
SPEEDS . . . . VARIABLE
TRANSMISSION . . . . HYDRO
STEERING. . . . . STANDARD
BLADE CLUTCH . . . . ELECTRIC
STANDARD DECK . . . . 60"
WEIGHT . . . . 529 LBS.
MSRP. $2,699

OPTIONS

3 BAG
42" SNOW THROWER
46" BLADE
46" SWEEP

RETAIL PRICING

YEAR	HIGH	LOW
2006	$730	$547
2007	$807	$605
2008	$895	$671

SLT1554

YEARS MFRD 2005-2008
SERIES. . . . . 1500 SERIES
ENGINE . . . . KOHLER
CYLINDERS. 2
ENGINE HP 27
COOLING . . . . AIR
FUEL . . . . G
SPEEDS . . . . VARIABLE
TRANSMISSION . . . . HYDRO
STEERING. . . . . STANDARD
BLADE CLUTCH . . . . ELECTRIC
STANDARD DECK . . . . 54"
WEIGHT . . . . 567 LBS.
MSRP. $2,899

OPTIONS

3 BAG
42" SNOW THROWER
46" BLADE
46" SWEEP

RETAIL PRICING

YEAR	HIGH	LOW
2005	$705	$529
2006	$788	$591
2007	$868	$651
2008	$962	$722

SLTX1050

YEARS MFRD 2009-2012
ENGINE . . . . KOHLER COURAGE
CYLINDERS. 2
ENGINE HP 25
COOLING . . . . AIR
FUEL . . . . G
SPEEDS . . . . VARIABLE
TRANSMISSION . . . . HYDRO
STEERING. . . . . STANDARD
BLADE CLUTCH . . . . ELECTRIC
STANDARD DECK . . . . 50"
WEIGHT . . . . 548 LBS.
MSRP. $2,599

OPTIONS

3 BAG
42" SNOW THROWER
46" BLADE

RETAIL PRICING

YEAR	HIGH	LOW
2009	$891	$668
2010	$990	$743
2011	$1,095	$821
2012	$1,217	$913

SLTX1054

YEARS MFRD 2009-2010
ENGINE . . . . KOHLER COURAGE
CYLINDERS. 2
ENGINE HP 26
COOLING . . . . AIR
FUEL . . . . G
SPEEDS . . . . VARIABLE
TRANSMISSION . . . . HYDRO
STEERING. . . . . STANDARD
BLADE CLUTCH . . . . ELECTRIC
STANDARD DECK . . . . 54"
WEIGHT . . . . 567 LBS.
MSRP. $2,849

OPTIONS

3 BAG
42" SNOW THROWER
46" BLADE

RETAIL PRICING

YEAR	HIGH	LOW
2009	$1,003	$753
2010	$1,119	$839

SLTX1054VT

YEARS MFRD 2010-2010
ENGINE . . . . B&S
CYLINDERS. 2
ENGINE HP 26
COOLING . . . . AIR
FUEL . . . . G
SPEEDS . . . . VARIABLE
TRANSMISSION . . . . HYDRO
STEERING. . . . . STANDARD

CUB CADET

BLADE CLUTCH . . . . ELECTRIC
STANDARD DECK . . . . 54"
WEIGHT . . . . 567 LBS.
MSRP. $2,775

OPTIONS

3 BAG
42" SNOW THROWER
46" BLADE

RETAIL PRICING

YEAR	HIGH	LOW
2010	$1,082	$812

SLX50

YEARS MFRD 2018-2020
SERIES. . . . . . ZT2 ENDURO SERIES
ENGINE . . . . CUB CADET EFI
CYLINDERS. 2
CID 679CC
TRANSMISSION . . . . HYDRO
STEERING. . . . . STANDARD
STANDARD DECK . . . . 50"
WEIGHT . . . . 470 LBS.
MSRP. $2,999

OPTIONS

42" SNOW BLOWER $1,350
46" BLADE. $340
SNOW CAB. $418

SLX54

YEARS MFRD 2018-2020
SERIES. . . . . . XT2 ENDURO SERIES
ENGINE . . . . KOHLER 7000
CYLINDERS. 2
CID 725CC
ENGINE HP 25
FUEL . . . . G
TRANSMISSION . . . . HYDRO
STEERING. . . . . STANDARD
STANDARD DECK . . . . 54"
WEIGHT . . . . 470 LBS.
MSRP. $3,299

OPTIONS

42" SNOW BLOWER $1,350
46" BLADE. $340
SNOW CAB. $418

ST54 FAB

YEARS MFRD 2016-2020
SERIES. . . . . . XT1 ENDURO SERIES
ENGINE . . . . KOHLER
CYLINDERS. 2
CID 725CC
ENGINE HP 24
COOLING . . . . AIR
FUEL . . . . G
SPEEDS . . . . VARIABLE
TRANSMISSION . . . . HYDRO
STEERING. . . . . STANDARD
STANDARD DECK . . . . 54"
WEIGHT . . . . 520 LBS.
MSRP. $2,699

OPTIONS

42" SNOW BLOWER $1,350
46" BLADE. $340
SPREADER $250

RETAIL PRICING

YEAR	HIGH	LOW
2016	$1,455	$1,092
2017	$1,612	$1,209
2018	$1,780	$1,335
2019	$1,965	$1,474
2020	$2,214	$1,657

SZ54KW PRO

YEARS MFRD 2014-2015
SERIES. . . . . TANK SERIES
ENGINE . . . . KAWASAKI
ENGINE HP 27
COOLING . . . . AIR
FUEL . . . . G
SPEEDS . . . . VARIABLE
TRANSMISSION . . . . . DUAL HYDRO
STEERING. . . . . ZERO
STANDARD DECK . . . . 54"
MSRP. $10,500

OPTIONS

72" BLADE
BAGGER
POWER LIFT

RETAIL PRICING

YEAR	HIGH	LOW
2014	$5,405	$4,054
2015	$5,964	$4,473

SZ60KW PRO

YEARS MFRD 2014-2015
SERIES. . . . . TANK SERIES
ENGINE . . . . KAWASAKI
ENGINE HP 27
COOLING . . . . AIR
FUEL . . . . G
SPEEDS . . . . VARIABLE
TRANSMISSION . . . . . DUAL HYDRO
STEERING. . . . . ZERO
STANDARD DECK . . . . 60"
MSRP. $11,000

OPTIONS

72" BLADE
BAGGER
POWER LIFT

RETAIL PRICING

YEAR	HIGH	LOW
2014	$5,661	$4,246
2015	$6,255	$4,691

TANK L60 KW

YEARS MFRD 2015-2016
SERIES. . . . . TANK SERIES
ENGINE . . . . KAWASAKI
ENGINE HP 27
COOLING . . . . AIR
FUEL . . . . G
SPEEDS . . . . VARIABLE
TRANSMISSION . . . . . DUAL HYDRO
STEERING. . . . . ZERO
STANDARD DECK . . . . 60"
MSRP. $8,499

OPTIONS

72" BLADE
BAGGER
PWR LIFT

RETAIL PRICING

YEAR	HIGH	LOW
2015	$4,673	$3,505
2016	$5,158	$3,868

TANK LZ48

YEARS MFRD 2012-2013
ENGINE . . . . B&S
ENGINE HP 24
COOLING . . . . AIR
FUEL . . . . G
SPEEDS . . . . VARIABLE
TRANSMISSION . . . . . DUAL HYDRO
STEERING. . . . . ZERO
STANDARD DECK . . . . 48"
MSRP. $8,899

OPTIONS

3 BAG
72" BLADE
PWR LIFT

RETAIL PRICING

YEAR	HIGH	LOW
2012	$3,877	$2,907
2013	$4,279	$3,210

TANK LZ54

YEARS MFRD 2012-2013
ENGINE . . . . KOHLER
ENGINE HP 25
COOLING . . . . AIR
FUEL . . . . G
SPEEDS . . . . VARIABLE
TRANSMISSION . . . . . DUAL HYDRO
STEERING. . . . . ZERO
STANDARD DECK . . . . 54"
MSRP. $9,899

OPTIONS

3 BAG
72" BLADE
PWR LIFT

RETAIL PRICING

YEAR	HIGH	LOW
2012	$4,311	$3,233
2013	$4,760	$3,570

TANK LZ54 KW

YEARS MFRD 2016-2016
SERIES. . . . . TANK SERIES
ENGINE . . . . KAWASAKI
ENGINE HP 27
COOLING . . . . AIR
FUEL . . . . G
SPEEDS . . . . VARIABLE
TRANSMISSION . . . . . DUAL HYDRO
STEERING. . . . . ZERO
STANDARD DECK . . . . 54"
MSRP. $9,499

OPTIONS

72" BLADE
BAG
PWR LIFT

RETAIL PRICING

YEAR	HIGH	LOW
2016	$5,953	$4,465

TANK LZ60

YEARS MFRD 2012-2013
ENGINE . . . . KOHLER
ENGINE HP 27
COOLING . . . . AIR
FUEL . . . . G
SPEEDS . . . . VARIABLE
TRANSMISSION . . . . . DUAL HYDRO
STEERING. . . . . ZERO
STANDARD DECK . . . . 60"
MSRP. $10,199

OPTIONS

3 BAG
72" BLADE
KAWASAKI
PWR LIFT

RETAIL PRICING

YEAR	HIGH	LOW
2012	$4,442	$3,332
2013	$4,917	$3,688

TANK LZ60 KW

YEARS MFRD 2016-2016
SERIES. . . . . TANK SERIES
ENGINE . . . . KAWASAKI
ENGINE HP 27
COOLING . . . . AIR
FUEL . . . . G
SPEEDS . . . . VARIABLE
TRANSMISSION . . . . . DUAL HYDRO
STEERING. . . . . ZERO
STANDARD DECK . . . . 60"
MSRP. $9,999

OPTIONS

72" BLADE
BAG
PWR LIFT

RETAIL PRICING

YEAR	HIGH	LOW
2016	$6,255	$4,691

TANK M72 KW

YEARS MFRD 2012-2013
ENGINE . . . . KAWASAKI
ENGINE HP 37
COOLING . . . . AIR
FUEL . . . . G
SPEEDS . . . . VARIABLE
TRANSMISSION . . . . . DUAL HYDRO
STEERING. . . . . ZERO
STANDARD DECK . . . . 72"
MSRP. $12,599

OPTIONS

72" BLADE

RETAIL PRICING

YEAR	HIGH	LOW
2012	$5,497	$4,123
2013	$6,058	$4,543

TANK S60

YEARS MFRD 2015-2016
SERIES. . . . . TANK SERIES
ENGINE . . . . KOHLER

ENGINE HP 23.5
COOLING . . . . . AIR
FUEL . . . . . G
SPEEDS . . . . . VARIABLE
TRANSMISSION . . . . . DUAL HYDRO
STEERING . . . . . ZERO
STANDARD DECK . . . . . 60"
MSRP $8,999

OPTIONS

72" BLADE
BAGGER
PWR LIFT

RETAIL PRICING

YEAR	HIGH	LOW
2015	$4,948	$3,711
2016	$5,460	$4,095

TANK SZ48

YEARS MFRD 2012-2013
ENGINE . . . . . KOHLER
ENGINE HP 23
COOLING . . . . . AIR
FUEL . . . . . G
SPEEDS . . . . . VARIABLE
TRANSMISSION . . . . . DUAL HYDRO
STEERING . . . . . ZERO
STANDARD DECK . . . . . 48"
MSRP $10,199

OPTIONS

3 BAG
72" BLADE
PWR LIFT

RETAIL PRICING

YEAR	HIGH	LOW
2012	$4,442	$3,332
2013	$4,904	$3,678

TANK SZ54 KW

YEARS MFRD 2016-2016
SERIES . . . . . TANK SERIES
ENGINE . . . . . KAWASAKI
ENGINE HP 27
COOLING . . . . . AIR
FUEL . . . . . G
SPEEDS . . . . . VARIABLE
TRANSMISSION . . . . . DUAL HYDRO
STEERING . . . . . ZERO
STANDARD DECK . . . . . 54"
MSRP $10,499

OPTIONS

72" BLADE
BAG
PWR LIFT

RETAIL PRICING

YEAR	HIGH	LOW
2016	$9,090	$6,817

TANK SZ60

YEARS MFRD 2012-2013
ENGINE . . . . . KAWASAKI
ENGINE HP 27
COOLING . . . . . AIR
FUEL . . . . . G
SPEEDS . . . . . VARIABLE
TRANSMISSION . . . . . DUAL HYDRO
STEERING . . . . . ZERO
STANDARD DECK . . . . . 60"
MSRP $12,999

OPTIONS

3 BAG
72" BLADE
PWR LIFT

RETAIL PRICING

YEAR	HIGH	LOW
2012	$5,665	$4,249
2013	$6,250	$4,688

AVG. AUCTION PRICING

LOW	HIGH	AVG
$4,254	$5,045	$4,517

TANK SZ60 EFI

YEARS MFRD 2015-2016
SERIES . . . . . TANK SERIES
ENGINE . . . . . KAWASAKI EFI
ENGINE HP 33
COOLING . . . . . AIR
FUEL . . . . . G
SPEEDS . . . . . VARIABLE
TRANSMISSION . . . . . DUAL HYDRO
STEERING . . . . . ZERO
STANDARD DECK . . . . . 60"
MSRP $12,500

OPTIONS

72" BLADE
BAGGER
PWR LIFT

RETAIL PRICING

YEAR	HIGH	LOW
2015	$6,872	$5,154
2016	$7,586	$5,690

TANK SZ60 KW

YEARS MFRD 2016-2016
SERIES . . . . . TANK SERIES
ENGINE . . . . . KAWASAKI
ENGINE HP 27
COOLING . . . . . AIR
FUEL . . . . . G
SPEEDS . . . . . VARIABLE
TRANSMISSION . . . . . DUAL HYDRO
STEERING . . . . . ZERO
STANDARD DECK . . . . . 54"
MSRP $10,999

OPTIONS

72" BLADE
BAG
PWR LIFT

RETAIL PRICING

YEAR	HIGH	LOW
2016	$6,674	$5,005

YARD BUG

YEARS MFRD 1999-1999
ENGINE . . . . . B&S
ENGINE HP 8.5
COOLING . . . . . AIR
FUEL . . . . . G
TRANSMISSION . . . . . HYDRO
STANDARD DECK . . . . . 27"
MSRP $1,199

RETAIL PRICING

YEAR	HIGH	LOW
1999	$502	$377

YTH150

YEARS MFRD 1996-1999
ENGINE . . . . . KOHLER
ENGINE HP 15
COOLING . . . . . AIR
FUEL . . . . . G
STEERING . . . . . STANDARD
STANDARD DECK . . . . . 42"
MSRP $2,299

RETAIL PRICING

YEAR	HIGH	LOW
1996	$760	$570
1997	$820	$615
1998	$930	$697
1999	$962	$722

Z42

YEARS MFRD 1997-1999
SERIES . . . . . Z SERIES
ENGINE . . . . . KOHLER
ENGINE HP 15
COOLING . . . . . AIR
FUEL . . . . . G
SPEEDS . . . . . VARIABLE
TRANSMISSION . . . . . DUAL HYDRO
STEERING . . . . . ZERO
STANDARD DECK . . . . . 42"
MSRP $3,799

RETAIL PRICING

YEAR	HIGH	LOW
1997	$397	$298
1998	$438	$328
1999	$483	$362

Z48

YEARS MFRD 1997-1999
SERIES . . . . . Z SERIES
ENGINE . . . . . KOHLER
ENGINE HP 18
COOLING . . . . . AIR
FUEL . . . . . G
TRANSMISSION . . . . . DUAL HYDRO
STEERING . . . . . ZERO
STANDARD DECK . . . . . 48"
MSRP $4,899

RETAIL PRICING

YEAR	HIGH	LOW
1997	$510	$383
1998	$563	$422
1999	$622	$467

Z48L

YEARS MFRD 1997-1998
SERIES . . . . . Z SERIES
ENGINE . . . . . KAWASAKI
ENGINE HP 18
COOLING . . . . . LIQUID
FUEL . . . . . G
TRANSMISSION . . . . . DUAL HYDRO
STEERING . . . . . ZERO
STANDARD DECK . . . . . 48"
MSRP $5,499

RETAIL PRICING

YEAR	HIGH	LOW
1997	$608	$456
1998	$671	$504

Z54

YEARS MFRD 1997-1999
SERIES . . . . . Z SERIES
ENGINE . . . . . KOHLER
ENGINE HP 22
COOLING . . . . . AIR
FUEL . . . . . G
SPEEDS . . . . . VARIABLE
TRANSMISSION . . . . . DUAL HYDRO
STEERING . . . . . ZERO
STANDARD DECK . . . . . 54"
MSRP $5,099

RETAIL PRICING

YEAR	HIGH	LOW
1997	$531	$398
1998	$586	$440
1999	$648	$486

Z54L

YEARS MFRD 1997-1998
SERIES . . . . . Z SERIES
ENGINE . . . . . KAWASAKI
ENGINE HP 18
COOLING . . . . . LIQUID
FUEL . . . . . G
SPEEDS . . . . . VARIABLE
TRANSMISSION . . . . . DUAL HYDRO
STEERING . . . . . ZERO
STANDARD DECK . . . . . 54"
MSRP $5,599

RETAIL PRICING

YEAR	HIGH	LOW
1997	$619	$464
1998	$684	$513

Z FORCE 42

YEARS MFRD 2004-2004
SERIES . . . . . Z-FORCE SERIES
ENGINE . . . . . B&S INTEK
CYLINDERS 1
ENGINE HP 18.5
COOLING . . . . . AIR
FUEL . . . . . G
SPEEDS . . . . . VARIABLE
TRANSMISSION . . . . . HYDRO
STEERING . . . . . ZERO
PTO . . . . . YES
STANDARD DECK . . . . . 42"
MSRP $3,699

OPTIONS

2 BAG

RETAIL PRICING

YEAR	HIGH	LOW
2004	$847	$635

CUB CADET

Z FORCE 44

YEARS MFRD 2003-2010
SERIES . . . . Z FORCE SERIES
ENGINE . . . . B&S INTEK
CYLINDERS 2
ENGINE HP 20
COOLING . . . . AIR
FUEL . . . . G
SPEEDS . . . . VARIABLE
TRANSMISSION . . . . . DUAL HYDRO
STEERING . . . . ZERO
BLADE CLUTCH . . . . ELECTRIC
PTO . . . . YES
STANDARD DECK . . . . 44"
WEIGHT . . . . 602 LBS.
MSRP $4,249

OPTIONS

2 BAG

RETAIL PRICING

YEAR	HIGH	LOW
2003	$817	$613
2004	$902	$677
2005	$995	$746
2006	$1,099	$824
2007	$1,213	$909
2008	$1,339	$1,004
2009	$1,482	$1,112
2010	$1,633	$1,225

Z FORCE 48

YEARS MFRD 2009-2011
ENGINE . . . . KOHLER COURAGE
CYLINDERS 2
ENGINE HP 22
COOLING . . . . AIR
FUEL . . . . G
SPEEDS . . . . VARIABLE
TRANSMISSION . . . . HYDRO
STEERING . . . . ZERO
STANDARD DECK . . . . 48"
WEIGHT . . . . 722 LBS.
MSRP $4,849

RETAIL PRICING

YEAR	HIGH	LOW
2009	$1,540	$1,155
2010	$1,756	$1,317
2011	$2,891	$2,168

Z FORCE 48

YEARS MFRD 2004-2006
SERIES . . . . Z FORCE SERIES
ENGINE . . . . B&S INTEK
CYLINDERS 2
ENGINE HP 22
COOLING . . . . AIR
FUEL . . . . G
SPEEDS . . . . VARIABLE
TRANSMISSION . . . . . DUAL HYDRO
STEERING . . . . ZERO
PTO . . . . YES
STANDARD DECK . . . . 48"
WEIGHT . . . . 648 LBS.
MSRP $4,599

OPTIONS

2 BAG

RETAIL PRICING

YEAR	HIGH	LOW
2004	$1,048	$786
2005	$1,155	$866
2006	$1,275	$956

Z FORCE 48 FAB

YEARS MFRD 2008-2013
ENGINE . . . KOHLER COURAGE PRO
CYLINDERS 2
ENGINE HP 22
COOLING . . . . AIR
FUEL . . . . G
SPEEDS . . . . VARIABLE
TRANSMISSION . . . . . DUAL HYDRO
STEERING . . . . ZERO
BLADE CLUTCH . . . . ELECTRIC
STANDARD DECK . . . . 48"
WEIGHT . . . . 648 LBS.
MSRP $4,849

OPTIONS

2 BAG
58" BLADE

RETAIL PRICING

YEAR	HIGH	LOW
2008	$1,452	$1,089
2009	$1,603	$1,202
2010	$1,769	$1,327
2011	$1,953	$1,464
2012	$2,156	$1,617
2013	$2,377	$1,783

Z FORCE 50

YEARS MFRD 2005-2009
SERIES . . . . Z FORCE SERIES
ENGINE . . . . KOHLER
CYLINDERS 2
ENGINE HP 23
COOLING . . . . AIR
FUEL . . . . G
SPEEDS . . . . VARIABLE
TRANSMISSION . . . . . DUAL HYDRO
STEERING . . . . ZERO
BLADE CLUTCH . . . . ELECTRIC
STANDARD DECK . . . . 50"
WEIGHT . . . . 622 LBS.
MSRP $4,649

OPTIONS

2 BAG

RETAIL PRICING

YEAR	HIGH	LOW
2005	$1,116	$837
2006	$1,227	$920
2007	$1,360	$1,020
2008	$1,501	$1,125
2009	$1,650	$1,238

Z FORCE 54

YEARS MFRD 2010-2011
ENGINE . . . . KOHLER COURAGE
CYLINDERS 2
ENGINE HP 23
COOLING . . . . AIR
FUEL . . . . G
SPEEDS . . . . VARIABLE
TRANSMISSION . . . . HYDRO
STEERING . . . . ZERO
BLADE CLUTCH . . . . ELECTRIC
STANDARD DECK . . . . 50"
WEIGHT . . . . 740 LBS.
MSRP $5,799

RETAIL PRICING

YEAR	HIGH	LOW
2010	$2,764	$2,073
2011	$3,456	$2,592

Z FORCE 54 FAB

YEARS MFRD 2010-2013
ENGINE . . . . KOHLER
ENGINE HP 24
COOLING . . . . AIR
FUEL . . . . G
SPEEDS . . . . VARIABLE
TRANSMISSION . . . . . DUAL HYDRO
STEERING . . . . ZERO
STANDARD DECK . . . . 54"
MSRP $5,599

OPTIONS

2 BAG
58" BLADE

RETAIL PRICING

YEAR	HIGH	LOW
2010	$2,043	$1,532
2011	$2,254	$1,690
2012	$2,489	$1,867
2013	$2,746	$2,059

Z FORCE 60

YEARS MFRD 2007-2008
SERIES . . . . Z-FORCE SERIES
ENGINE . . . . . . KOHLER COMMAND
CYLINDERS 2
ENGINE HP 23
COOLING . . . . AIR
FUEL . . . . G
SPEEDS . . . . VARIABLE
TRANSMISSION . . . . . DUAL HYDRO
STEERING . . . . ZERO
BLADE CLUTCH . . . . ELECTRIC
STANDARD DECK . . . . 60"
WEIGHT . . . . 843 LBS.
MSRP $5,199

OPTIONS

2 BAG

RETAIL PRICING

YEAR	HIGH	LOW
2007	$1,648	$1,236
2008	$1,830	$1,372

Z FORCE 60KH

YEARS MFRD 2006-2006
SERIES . . . . Z FORCE SERIES
ENGINE . . . . KAWASAKI
CYLINDERS 2
ENGINE HP 23
COOLING . . . . AIR
FUEL . . . . G
SPEEDS . . . . VARIABLE
TRANSMISSION . . . . HYDRO
STEERING . . . . ZERO
STANDARD DECK . . . . 60"
WEIGHT . . . . 679 LBS.
MSRP $5,699

RETAIL PRICING

YEAR	HIGH	LOW
2006	$1,635	$1,226

Z FORCE S 46

YEARS MFRD 2011-2012
ENGINE . . . . KOHLER
ENGINE HP 20
COOLING . . . . AIR
FUEL . . . . G
SPEEDS . . . . VARIABLE
TRANSMISSION . . . . . DUAL HYDRO
STEERING . . . . ZERO
STANDARD DECK . . . . 46"
MSRP $3,999

OPTIONS

2 BAG
58" BLADE

RETAIL PRICING

YEAR	HIGH	LOW
2011	$1,601	$1,201
2012	$1,768	$1,326

Z FORCE S 48

YEARS MFRD 2010-2013
SERIES . . . . FR SERIES
ENGINE . . . . KAWASAKI
CYLINDERS 2
ENGINE HP 21.5
COOLING . . . . AIR
FUEL . . . . G
SPEEDS . . . . VARIABLE
TRANSMISSION . . . . HYDRO
STEERING . . . . ZERO
BLADE CLUTCH . . . . ELECTRIC
STANDARD DECK . . . . 48"
WEIGHT . . . . 602 LBS.
MSRP $4,699

OPTIONS

2 BAG
58" BLADE
LP SERIES

RETAIL PRICING

YEAR	HIGH	LOW
2010	$1,714	$1,285
2011	$1,893	$1,420
2012	$2,088	$1,566
2013	$2,303	$1,727

Z FORCE S 54

YEARS MFRD 2011-2013
ENGINE . . . . KAWASAKI
ENGINE HP 23
COOLING . . . . AIR
FUEL . . . . G
SPEEDS . . . . VARIABLE

TRANSMISSION . . . . . DUAL HYDRO
STEERING. . . . . ZERO
STANDARD DECK . . . . 54"
MSRP. $5,799

OPTIONS

3 BAG
58" BLADE

RETAIL PRICING

YEAR	HIGH	LOW
2011	$2,335	$1,751
2012	$2,577	$1,933
2013	$2,853	$2,139

Z FORCE S 60

YEARS MFRD 2010-2013
SERIES. . . . . FR SERIES
ENGINE . . . . KAWASAKI
CYLINDERS. 2
ENGINE HP 24
COOLING . . . . AIR
FUEL . . . . G
SPEEDS . . . . VARIABLE
TRANSMISSION . . . . . DUAL HYDRO
STEERING. . . . . ZERO
BLADE CLUTCH . . . . ELECTRIC
STANDARD DECK . . . . 60"
WEIGHT . . . . 722 LBS.
MSRP. $5,999

OPTIONS

2 BAG
58" BLADE
E LIFT
LP SERIES

RETAIL PRICING

YEAR	HIGH	LOW
2010	$2,190	$1,643
2011	$2,416	$1,812
2012	$2,680	$2,010
2013	$2,966	$2,225

ZF COM L60

YEARS MFRD 2014-2015
ENGINE . . . . KOHLER
ENGINE HP 23.5
COOLING . . . . AIR
FUEL . . . . G
SPEEDS . . . . VARIABLE
TRANSMISSION . . . . . DUAL HYDRO
STEERING. . . . . ZERO
STANDARD DECK . . . . 60"
MSRP. $5,999

OPTIONS

58" BLADE
BAGGER
FAB BAGGER
PWR LIFT

RETAIL PRICING

YEAR	HIGH	LOW
2014	$3,087	$2,315
2015	$3,407	$2,555

ZF COM S48

YEARS MFRD 2014-2015
ENGINE . . . . KOHLER
ENGINE HP 23
COOLING . . . . AIR
FUEL . . . . G
SPEEDS . . . . VARIABLE
TRANSMISSION . . . . . DUAL HYDRO
STEERING. . . . . ZERO
STANDARD DECK . . . . 48"
MSRP. $5,499

OPTIONS

58" BLADE
BAGGER
FAB BAGGER
PWR LIFT

RETAIL PRICING

YEAR	HIGH	LOW
2014	$2,831	$2,123
2015	$3,123	$2,342

ZF COM S54

YEARS MFRD 2015-2015
SERIES. . . . . Z FORCE SERIES
ENGINE . . . . KOHLER
ENGINE HP 23.5
COOLING . . . . AIR
FUEL . . . . G
SPEEDS . . . . VARIABLE
TRANSMISSION . . . . . DUAL HYDRO
STEERING. . . . . ZERO
STANDARD DECK . . . . 54"
MSRP. $5,999

OPTIONS

58" BLADE
BAGGER
FAB BAGGER
PWR LIFT

RETAIL PRICING

YEAR	HIGH	LOW
2015	$3,407	$2,555

ZF COM S60

YEARS MFRD 2014-2015
ENGINE . . . . KOHLER
ENGINE HP 23.5
COOLING . . . . AIR
FUEL . . . . G
SPEEDS . . . . VARIABLE
TRANSMISSION . . . . . DUAL HYDRO
STEERING. . . . . ZERO
STANDARD DECK . . . . 60"
MSRP. $6,500

OPTIONS

58" BLADE
BAGGER

RETAIL PRICING

YEAR	HIGH	LOW
2014	$3,346	$2,509
2015	$3,692	$2,769

ZFL48

YEARS MFRD 2014-2018
SERIES. . . . . Z FORCE SERIES
ENGINE . . . . KOHLER
ENGINE HP 24
COOLING . . . . AIR
FUEL . . . . G
SPEEDS . . . . VARIABLE
TRANSMISSION . . . . . DUAL HYDRO
STEERING. . . . . ZERO
STANDARD DECK . . . . 48"
MSRP. $3,599

OPTIONS

3 BAG
58" BLADE
POWER LIFT

RETAIL PRICING

YEAR	HIGH	LOW
2014	$1,717	$1,288
2015	$1,895	$1,421
2016	$2,094	$1,571
2017	$2,309	$1,732
2018	$2,547	$1,910

ZFL54

YEARS MFRD 2014-2018
SERIES. . . . . Z FORCE SERIES
ENGINE . . . . KOHLER
ENGINE HP 25
COOLING . . . . AIR
FUEL . . . . G
SPEEDS . . . . VARIABLE
TRANSMISSION . . . . . DUAL HYDRO
STEERING. . . . . ZERO
STANDARD DECK . . . . 54"
MSRP. $3,899

OPTIONS

2 BAG
58" BLADE
POWER LIFT

RETAIL PRICING

YEAR	HIGH	LOW
2014	$1,859	$1,395
2015	$2,053	$1,540
2016	$2,268	$1,701
2017	$2,502	$1,877
2018	$2,764	$2,073

ZFL60

YEARS MFRD 2014-2018
SERIES. . . . . Z FORCE SERIES
ENGINE . . . . KOHLER
ENGINE HP 25
COOLING . . . . AIR
FUEL . . . . G
SPEEDS . . . . VARIABLE
TRANSMISSION . . . . . DUAL HYDRO
STEERING. . . . . ZERO
STANDARD DECK . . . . 60"
MSRP. $3,999

OPTIONS

2 BAG
58" BLADE
POWER LIFT

RETAIL PRICING

YEAR	HIGH	LOW
2014	$1,908	$1,431
2015	$2,105	$1,579
2016	$2,324	$1,743
2017	$2,565	$1,923
2018	$2,840	$2,130

ZFL60 LE

YEARS MFRD 2017-2017
ENGINE . . . . KOHLER
ENGINE HP 25
COOLING . . . . AIR
FUEL . . . . G
SPEEDS . . . . VARIABLE
TRANSMISSION . . . . . DUAL HYDRO
STEERING. . . . . ZERO
STANDARD DECK . . . . 60"
MSRP. $4,099

RETAIL PRICING

YEAR	HIGH	LOW
2017	$2,727	$2,045

ZFLX48

YEARS MFRD 2016-2019
SERIES. . . . . Z FORCE SERIES
ENGINE . . . . KAWASAKI
ENGINE HP 24
COOLING . . . . AIR
FUEL . . . . G
SPEEDS . . . . VARIABLE
TRANSMISSION . . . . . DUAL HYDRO
STEERING. . . . . ZERO
STANDARD DECK . . . . 48"
MSRP. $5,199

OPTIONS

BAGGER
POWERLIFT DECK KIT

RETAIL PRICING

YEAR	HIGH	LOW
2016	$2,906	$2,179
2017	$3,207	$2,405
2018	$3,544	$2,658
2019	$4,012	$3,009

ZFLX54

YEARS MFRD 2016-2019
SERIES. . . . . Z FORCE SERIES
ENGINE . . . . KAWASAKI
ENGINE HP 24
COOLING . . . . AIR
FUEL . . . . G
SPEEDS . . . . VARIABLE
TRANSMISSION . . . . . DUAL HYDRO
STEERING. . . . . ZERO
STANDARD DECK . . . . 54"
MSRP. $5,499

OPTIONS

BAGGER
POWERLIFT DECK KIT

RETAIL PRICING

YEAR	HIGH	LOW
2016	$3,080	$2,310
2017	$3,400	$2,550
2018	$3,736	$2,802
2019	$4,103	$3,077

ZFLX60

YEARS MFRD 2016-2019
SERIES. . . . . Z FORCE SERIES
ENGINE . . . . KAWASAKI
ENGINE HP 24

CUB CADET

COOLING ... AIR
FUEL ... G
SPEEDS ... VARIABLE
TRANSMISSION ... DUAL HYDRO
STEERING ... ZERO
STANDARD DECK ... 60"
MSRP ... $5,699

OPTIONS

BAGGER
POWERLIFT DECK KIT

RETAIL PRICING

YEAR	HIGH	LOW
2016	$3,197	$2,398
2017	$3,528	$2,646
2018	$3,886	$2,914
2019	$4,276	$3,207

ZFLZ48 KW

YEARS MFRD ... 2015-2015
SERIES ... Z FORCE SERIES
ENGINE ... KAWASAKI
ENGINE HP ... 24
COOLING ... AIR
FUEL ... G
SPEEDS ... VARIABLE
TRANSMISSION ... DUAL HYDRO
STEERING ... ZERO
STANDARD DECK ... 48"
MSRP ... $3,999

OPTIONS

58" BLADE
BAGGER
PWR LIFT

RETAIL PRICING

YEAR	HIGH	LOW
2015	$2,271	$1,704

ZFLZ60 KW

YEARS MFRD ... 2015-2015
SERIES ... Z FORCE SERIES
ENGINE ... KAWASAKI
ENGINE HP ... 60
COOLING ... AIR
FUEL ... G
SPEEDS ... VARIABLE
TRANSMISSION ... DUAL HYDRO
STEERING ... ZERO
STANDARD DECK ... 60"
MSRP ... $4,999

OPTIONS

58" BLADE
BAGGER
PWR LIFT

RETAIL PRICING

YEAR	HIGH	LOW
2015	$2,839	$2,129

ZFS48

YEARS MFRD ... 2016-2020
SERIES ... Z FORCE SERIES
ENGINE ... KOHLER
ENGINE HP ... 24
COOLING ... AIR
FUEL ... G
SPEEDS ... VARIABLE
TRANSMISSION ... DUAL HYDRO
STEERING ... ZERO
STANDARD DECK ... 48"
MSRP ... $4,399

OPTIONS

58" BLADE ... $1,089
BAGGER ... $550

RETAIL PRICING

YEAR	HIGH	LOW
2016	$2,383	$1,787
2017	$2,630	$1,972
2018	$2,897	$2,174
2019	$3,200	$2,399
2020	$3,466	$2,703

ZFS48 COMM

YEARS MFRD ... 2011-2014
SERIES ...
ENGINE ... KOHLER
ENGINE HP ... 23
COOLING ... AIR
FUEL ... G
SPEEDS ... VARIABLE
TRANSMISSION ... HYDRO
STEERING ... ZERO
STANDARD DECK ... 48"
MSRP ... $6,999

OPTIONS

2 BAG
58" BLADE
POWER ASST

RETAIL PRICING

YEAR	HIGH	LOW
2011	$2,654	$1,990
2012	$2,935	$2,201
2013	$3,233	$2,425
2014	$3,568	$2,676

ZFS54

YEARS MFRD ... 2016-2020
SERIES ... Z FORCE SERIES
ENGINE ... KOHLER
ENGINE HP ... 25
COOLING ... AIR
FUEL ... G
SPEEDS ... VARIABLE
TRANSMISSION ... DUAL HYDRO
STEERING ... ZERO
STANDARD DECK ... 54"
MSRP ... $4,699

OPTIONS

58" BLADE ... $1,089
BAGGER ... $550

RETAIL PRICING

YEAR	HIGH	LOW
2016	$2,557	$1,917
2017	$2,822	$2,117
2018	$3,100	$2,325
2019	$3,477	$2,608
2020	$3,722	$2,914

ZFS60

YEARS MFRD ... 2016-2020
SERIES ... Z FORCE SERIES
ENGINE ... KOHLER
ENGINE HP ... 25
COOLING ... AIR
FUEL ... G
SPEEDS ... VARIABLE
TRANSMISSION ... DUAL HYDRO
STEERING ... ZERO
STANDARD DECK ... 60"
MSRP ... $4,799

OPTIONS

58" BLADE ... $1,089
BAGGER ... $550

RETAIL PRICING

YEAR	HIGH	LOW
2016	$2,614	$1,961
2017	$2,886	$2,164
2018	$3,178	$2,383
2019	$3,517	$2,638
2020	$3,808	$3,026

ZFS60 COMM

YEARS MFRD ... 2011-2013
ENGINE ... KOHLER
ENGINE HP ... 25
COOLING ... AIR
FUEL ... G
SPEEDS ... VARIABLE
TRANSMISSION ... HYDRO
STEERING ... ZERO
STANDARD DECK ... 60"
MSRP ... $7,999

OPTIONS

2BAG
58" BLADE
PWR ASST

RETAIL PRICING

YEAR	HIGH	LOW
2011	$3,221	$2,415
2012	$3,555	$2,666
2013	$3,923	$2,942

ZFSX48

YEARS MFRD ... 2016-2020
SERIES ... Z FORCE SERIES
ENGINE ... KAWASAKI
ENGINE HP ... 24
COOLING ... AIR
FUEL ... G
SPEEDS ... VARIABLE
TRANSMISSION ... DUAL HYDRO
STEERING ... ZERO
STANDARD DECK ... 48"
MSRP ... $5,799

OPTIONS

58" BLADE ... $1,089
BAGGER ... $550

RETAIL PRICING

YEAR	HIGH	LOW
2016	$3,195	$2,396
2017	$3,528	$2,646
2018	$3,887	$2,916
2019	$4,319	$3,240
2020	$4,687	$3,702

ZFSX54

YEARS MFRD ... 2016-2020
SERIES ... Z FORCE SERIES
ENGINE ... KAWASAKI
ENGINE HP ... 24
COOLING ... AIR
FUEL ... G
SPEEDS ... VARIABLE
TRANSMISSION ... DUAL HYDRO
STEERING ... ZERO
STANDARD DECK ... 54"
MSRP ... $6,099

OPTIONS

58" BLADE ... $1,089
BAGGER ... $550

RETAIL PRICING

YEAR	HIGH	LOW
2016	$3,379	$2,534
2017	$3,719	$2,790
2018	$4,122	$3,092
2019	$4,563	$3,422
2020	$4,833	$3,818

ZFSX60

YEARS MFRD ... 2016-2020
SERIES ... Z FORCE SERIES
ENGINE ... KAWASAKI
ENGINE HP ... 24
COOLING ... AIR
FUEL ... G
SPEEDS ... VARIABLE
TRANSMISSION ... DUAL HYDRO
STEERING ... ZERO
STANDARD DECK ... 60"
MSRP ... $6,299

OPTIONS

58" BLADE ... $1,089
BAGGER ... $550

RETAIL PRICING

YEAR	HIGH	LOW
2016	$3,487	$2,614
2017	$3,848	$2,886
2018	$4,231	$3,173
2019	$4,671	$3,503
2020	$5,052	$3,992

ZFSZ48 KH

YEARS MFRD ... 2015-2015
SERIES ... Z FORCE SERIES
ENGINE ... KOHLER
ENGINE HP ... 48
COOLING ... AIR
FUEL ... G
SPEEDS ... VARIABLE
TRANSMISSION ... DUAL HYDRO
STEERING ... ZERO
STANDARD DECK ... 48"
MSRP ... $4,299

OPTIONS

58" BLADE
BAGGER
PWR LIFT

RETAIL PRICING

YEAR	HIGH	LOW
2015	$2,443	$1,832

ZFSZ48 KW

YEARS MFRD 2015-2015
SERIES .... Z FORCE SERIES
ENGINE .... KAWASAKI
ENGINE HP 24
COOLING .... AIR
FUEL .... G
SPEEDS .... VARIABLE
TRANSMISSION ..... DUAL HYDRO
STEERING .... ZERO
STANDARD DECK .... 48"
MSRP $4,499

OPTIONS

58" BLADE
BAGGER
PWR LIFT

RETAIL PRICING

YEAR	HIGH	LOW
2015	$2,557	$1,918

ZFSZ54 KH

YEARS MFRD 2015-2015
SERIES .... Z FORCE SERIES
ENGINE .... KOHLER
ENGINE HP 24
COOLING .... AIR
FUEL .... G
SPEEDS .... VARIABLE
TRANSMISSION ..... DUAL HYDRO
STEERING .... ZERO
STANDARD DECK .... 54"
MSRP $4,599

OPTIONS

58" BLADE
BAGGER
PWR LIFT

RETAIL PRICING

YEAR	HIGH	LOW
2015	$2,613	$1,960

ZFSZ54 KW

YEARS MFRD 2015-2015
SERIES .... Z FORCE SERIES
ENGINE .... KAWASAKI
ENGINE HP 24
COOLING .... AIR
FUEL .... G
SPEEDS .... VARIABLE
TRANSMISSION ..... DUAL HYDRO
STEERING .... ZERO
STANDARD DECK .... 54"
MSRP $4,999

OPTIONS

58" BLADE
BAGGER
PWR LIFT

RETAIL PRICING

YEAR	HIGH	LOW
2015	$2,839	$2,129

ZFSZ60 KH

YEARS MFRD 2015-2015
SERIES .... Z FORCE SERIES
ENGINE .... KOHLER
ENGINE HP 24
COOLING .... AIR
FUEL .... G
SPEEDS .... VARIABLE
TRANSMISSION ..... DUAL HYDRO
STEERING .... ZERO
STANDARD DECK .... 60"
MSRP $4,999

OPTIONS

58" BLADE
BAGGER
PWR LIFT

RETAIL PRICING

YEAR	HIGH	LOW
2015	$2,857	$2,143

ZFSZ60 KW

YEARS MFRD 2015-2015
SERIES .... Z FORCE SERIES
ENGINE .... KAWASAKI
ENGINE HP 24
COOLING .... AIR
FUEL .... G
SPEEDS .... VARIABLE
TRANSMISSION ..... DUAL HYDRO
STEERING .... ZERO
STANDARD DECK .... 60"
MSRP $5,499

OPTIONS

58" BLADE
BAGGER
PWR LIFT

RETAIL PRICING

YEAR	HIGH	LOW
2015	$3,126	$2,345

ZT1 42

YEARS MFRD 2019-2020
SERIES .... ULTIMA SERIES
ENGINE .... KOHLER
CID 725CC
ENGINE HP 22
FUEL .... G
TRANSMISSION ..... DUAL HYDRO
STEERING .... ZERO
STANDARD DECK .... 42"
WEIGHT .... 500 LBS.
MSRP $2,699

ZT1 46

YEARS MFRD 2019-2020
SERIES .... ULTIMA SERIES
ENGINE .... KOHLER
CYLINDERS 2
CID 725CC
ENGINE HP 22
FUEL .... G
TRANSMISSION ..... DUAL HYDRO
STEERING .... ZERO
STANDARD DECK .... 46"
WEIGHT .... 570 LBS.
MSRP $2,899

ZT1 50

YEARS MFRD 2019-2020
SERIES .... ULTIMA SERIES
ENGINE .... KAWASAKI
CYLINDERS 2
CID 726CC
ENGINE HP 23
FUEL .... G
TRANSMISSION ..... DUAL HYDRO
STEERING .... ZERO
STANDARD DECK .... 50"
WEIGHT .... 585 LBS.
MSRP $3,099

ZT1 54

YEARS MFRD 2019-2020
SERIES .... ULTIMA SERIES
ENGINE .... KOHLER
CYLINDERS 2
CID 725CC
ENGINE HP 24
FUEL .... G
TRANSMISSION ..... DUAL HYDRO
STEERING .... ZERO
STANDARD DECK .... 54"
WEIGHT .... 600 LBS.
MSRP $3,099

ZT2 50

YEARS MFRD 2019-2020
SERIES .... ULTIMA SERIES
ENGINE .... KAWASAKI FR691
CYLINDERS 2
CID 726CC
ENGINE HP 23
FUEL .... G
TRANSMISSION ..... DUAL HYDRO
STEERING .... ZERO
STANDARD DECK .... 50"
WEIGHT .... 600 LBS.
MSRP $3,699

ZT2 54

YEARS MFRD 2019-2020
SERIES .... ULTIMA SERIES
ENGINE .... KAWASAKI FR691
CYLINDERS 2
CID 726CC
ENGINE HP 23
FUEL .... G
TRANSMISSION ..... DUAL HYDRO
STEERING .... ZERO
STANDARD DECK .... 54"
WEIGHT .... 615 LBS.
MSRP $3,899

ZT2 60

YEARS MFRD 2019-2020
SERIES .... ULTIMA SERIES
ENGINE ..... KAWASAKI FR SERIES
CYLINDERS 2
CID 726CC
ENGINE HP 24
FUEL .... G
TRANSMISSION ..... DUAL HYDRO
STEERING .... ZERO
STANDARD DECK .... 60"
WEIGHT .... 640 LBS.
MSRP $4,199

ZT3 60

YEARS MFRD 2020-2020
SERIES .... ULTIMA SERIES
ENGINE .... KAWASAKI FS
CYLINDERS 2
CID 725CC
ENGINE HP 24
FUEL .... G
SPEEDS .... VARIABLE
TRANSMISSION ..... DUAL HYDRO
STEERING .... ZERO
BLADE CLUTCH .... ELECTRIC
STANDARD DECK .... 60"
MSRP $4,999

ZTT42

YEARS MFRD 2008-2011
SERIES .... I SERIES
ENGINE ... KOHLER COURAGE OHV
CYLINDERS 2
ENGINE HP 18
COOLING .... AIR
FUEL .... G
SPEEDS .... VARIABLE
TRANSMISSION .... HYDRO
STEERING .... ZERO
BLADE CLUTCH .... ELECTRIC
STANDARD DECK .... 42"
WEIGHT .... 535 LBS.
MSRP $2,799

RETAIL PRICING

YEAR	HIGH	LOW
2008	$869	$652
2009	$889	$667
2010	$1,012	$759
2011	$1,669	$1,252

ZTT46

YEARS MFRD 2008-2009
SERIES .... I SERIES
ENGINE .... KOHLER COURAGE
CYLINDERS 2
ENGINE HP 20
COOLING .... AIR
FUEL .... G
SPEEDS .... VARIABLE
TRANSMISSION .... HYDRO
STEERING .... ZERO
BLADE CLUTCH .... ELECTRIC
STANDARD DECK .... 46"
WEIGHT .... 550 LBS.
MSRP $2,999

RETAIL PRICING

YEAR	HIGH	LOW
2008	$970	$727
2009	$1,000	$750

CUB CADET

ZTT50

YEARS MFRD 2008-2011
SERIES .... I SERIES
ENGINE .... KOHLER COURAGE
CYLINDERS 2
ENGINE HP 25
COOLING .... AIR
FUEL .... G
SPEEDS .... VARIABLE
TRANSMISSION .... HYDRO
STEERING .... ZERO
BLADE CLUTCH .... ELECTRIC
STANDARD DECK .... 50"
WEIGHT .... 590 LBS.
MSRP $3,299

RETAIL PRICING

YEAR	HIGH	LOW
2008	$1,051	$788
2009	$1,094	$820
2010	$1,219	$914
2011	$1,965	$1,474

ZTX4 48

YEARS MFRD 2020-2020
SERIES .... ULTIMA SERIES
ENGINE .... KOHLER PRO 7000
CYLINDERS 2
CID 725CC
ENGINE HP 23
FUEL .... G
SPEEDS .... VARIABLE
TRANSMISSION ..... DUAL HYDRO
STEERING .... ZERO
BLADE CLUTCH .... ELECTRIC
ROPS/CAB .... ROPS
STANDARD DECK .... 48"
MSRP $5,499

ZTX4 54

YEARS MFRD 2020-2020
SERIES .... ULTIMA SERIES
ENGINE .... KOHLER PRO 7000
CYLINDERS 2
CID 725CC
ENGINE HP 24
FUEL .... G
SPEEDS .... VARIABLE
TRANSMISSION ..... DUAL HYDRO
STEERING .... ZERO
BLADE CLUTCH .... ELECTRIC
ROPS/CAB .... ROPS
STANDARD DECK .... 54"
MSRP $5,699

ZTX4 60

YEARS MFRD 2020-2020
SERIES .... ULTIMA SERIES
ENGINE .... KOHLER PRO 7000
CYLINDERS 2
CID 725CC
ENGINE HP 24
FUEL .... G
SPEEDS .... VARIABLE
TRANSMISSION ..... DUAL HYDRO
STEERING .... ZERO
BLADE CLUTCH .... ELECTRIC
ROPS/CAB .... ROPS
STANDARD DECK .... 60"
MSRP $5,899

ZTX5 48

YEARS MFRD 2020-2020
SERIES .... ULTIMA SERIES
ENGINE .... KAWASAKI FR
CYLINDERS 2
CID 726CC
ENGINE HP 23
SPEEDS .... VARIABLE
TRANSMISSION ..... DUAL HYDRO
STEERING .... ZERO
BLADE CLUTCH .... ELECTRIC
ROPS/CAB .... ROPS
STANDARD DECK .... 48"
MSRP $6,499

ZTX5 54

YEARS MFRD 2020-2020
SERIES .... ULTIMA SERIES
ENGINE .... KAWASAKI FR
CYLINDERS 2
CID 726CC
ENGINE HP 24
FUEL .... G
SPEEDS .... VARIABLE
TRANSMISSION ..... DUAL HYDRO
STEERING .... ZERO
BLADE CLUTCH .... ELECTRIC
ROPS/CAB .... ROPS
STANDARD DECK .... 54"
MSRP $6,699

ZTX5 60

YEARS MFRD 2020-2020
SERIES .... ULTIMA SERIES
ENGINE .... KAWASAKI FR
CYLINDERS 2
CID 726CC
ENGINE HP 24
FUEL .... G
SPEEDS .... VARIABLE
TRANSMISSION ..... DUAL HYDRO
STEERING .... ZERO
BLADE CLUTCH .... ELECTRIC
ROPS/CAB .... ROPS
STANDARD DECK .... 60"
MSRP $6,899

ZTX6 48

YEARS MFRD 2020-2020
SERIES .... ULTIMA SERIES
ENGINE .... KAWASAKI FX730
CYLINDERS 2
CID 726CC
ENGINE HP 23.5
FUEL .... G
SPEEDS .... VARIABLE
TRANSMISSION ..... DUAL HYDRO
STEERING .... ZERO
BLADE CLUTCH .... ELECTRIC
ROPS/CAB .... ROPS
STANDARD DECK .... 48"
MSRP $7,599

ZTX6 54

YEARS MFRD 2020-2020
SERIES .... ULTIMA SERIES
ENGINE .... KAWASAKI FX801
CYLINDERS 2
CID 852CC
ENGINE HP 25.5
FUEL .... G
SPEEDS .... VARIABLE
TRANSMISSION ..... DUAL HYDRO
STEERING .... ZERO
BLADE CLUTCH .... ELECTRIC
ROPS/CAB .... ROPS
STANDARD DECK .... 54"
MSRP $7,899

ZTX6 60

YEARS MFRD 2020-2020
SERIES .... ULTIMA SERIES
ENGINE .... KAWASAKI FX801
CYLINDERS 2
CID 852CC
ENGINE HP 25.5
FUEL .... G
SPEEDS .... VARIABLE
TRANSMISSION ..... DUAL HYDRO
STEERING .... ZERO
BLADE CLUTCH .... ELECTRIC
ROPS/CAB .... ROPS
STANDARD DECK .... 60"
MSRP $8,199

ZTX6 60 EFI

YEARS MFRD 2020-2020
SERIES .... ULTIMA SERIES
ENGINEKOHLER CONFIDANT EZT750
CYLINDERS 2
CID 747CC
ENGINE HP 27
FUEL .... G
SPEEDS .... VARIABLE
TRANSMISSION ..... DUAL HYDRO
STEERING .... ZERO
BLADE CLUTCH .... ELECTRIC
ROPS/CAB .... ROPS
STANDARD DECK .... 60"
MSRP $8,199

148L EFI

YEARS MFRD 2016-2019
SERIES .... PRO Z SERIES
ENGINE .... KOHLER
ENGINE HP 25
COOLING .... AIR
FUEL .... G
SPEEDS .... VARIABLE
TRANSMISSION ..... DUAL HYDRO
STEERING .... ZERO
STANDARD DECK .... 48"
MSRP $6,849

OPTIONS

POWERLIFT DECK KIT
PWR TWIN BAGGER

RETAIL PRICING

YEAR	HIGH	LOW
2016	$3,777	$2,833
2017	$4,170	$3,127
2018	$4,591	$3,443
2019	$5,096	$3,822

148S EFI

YEARS MFRD 2016-2020
SERIES .... PRO Z SERIES
ENGINE .... KOHLER
CID 747CC
ENGINE HP 25
COOLING .... AIR
FUEL .... G
SPEEDS .... VARIABLE
TRANSMISSION ..... DUAL HYDRO
STEERING .... ZERO
STANDARD DECK .... 48"
WEIGHT .... 1,000 LBS.
MSRP $7,399

OPTIONS

POWERLIFT DECK KIT $700

RETAIL PRICING

YEAR	HIGH	LOW
2016	$3,952	$2,964
2017	$4,363	$3,271
2018	$4,803	$3,602
2019	$5,383	$4,037
2020	$6,099	$4,643

154L EFI

YEARS MFRD 2016-2020
SERIES .... PRO Z SERIES
ENGINE .... KOHLER
CID 747CC
ENGINE HP 27
COOLING .... AIR
FUEL .... G
SPEEDS .... VARIABLE
TRANSMISSION ..... DUAL HYDRO
STEERING .... ZERO
STANDARD DECK .... 54"
WEIGHT .... 1,000 LBS.
MSRP $7,149

OPTIONS

POWERLIFT DECK KIT $700
PWR ASSIST BAGGER $2,300

RETAIL PRICING

YEAR	HIGH	LOW
2016	$3,952	$2,964
2017	$4,363	$3,271
2018	$4,801	$3,600
2019	$5,494	$4,120
2020	$6,124	$4,615

154S EFI

YEARS MFRD 2016-2020
SERIES .... PRO Z SERIES
ENGINE .... KOHLER
CID 747CC

ENGINE HP 27
COOLING . . . . . AIR
FUEL . . . . . G
SPEEDS . . . . . VARIABLE
TRANSMISSION . . . . . DUAL HYDRO
STEERING. . . . . ZERO
STANDARD DECK . . . . . 54"
WEIGHT . . . . . 1,000 LBS.
MSRP. $7,599

OPTIONS

POWERLIFT DECK KIT $700

RETAIL PRICING

YEAR	HIGH	LOW
2016	$4,068	$3,051
2017	$4,490	$3,368
2018	$4,941	$3,706
2019	$5,516	$4,136
2020	$6,257	$4,780

160L EFI

YEARS MFRD 2016-2020
SERIES. . . . . PRO Z SERIES
ENGINE . . . . . KOHLER
ENGINE HP 27
COOLING . . . . . AIR
FUEL . . . . . G
SPEEDS . . . . . VARIABLE
TRANSMISSION . . . . . DUAL HYDRO
STEERING. . . . . ZERO
STANDARD DECK . . . . . 60"
MSRP. $7,549

OPTIONS

POWERLIFT DECK KIT $700

RETAIL PRICING

YEAR	HIGH	LOW
2016	$4,185	$3,137
2017	$4,619	$3,464
2018	$5,128	$3,845
2019	$5,689	$4,267
2020	$6,424	$4,837

160L KW

YEARS MFRD 2016-2020
SERIES. . . . . PRO Z SERIES
ENGINE . . . . . KAWASAKI
CID 726CC
ENGINE HP 23.5
COOLING . . . . . AIR
FUEL . . . . . G
SPEEDS . . . . . VARIABLE
TRANSMISSION . . . . . DUAL HYDRO
STEERING. . . . . ZERO
STANDARD DECK . . . . . 60"
WEIGHT . . . . . 1,030 LBS.
MSRP. $7,549

OPTIONS

POWERLIFT DECK. $700
PWR ASSIST BAGEGR $2,300

RETAIL PRICING

YEAR	HIGH	LOW
2016	$4,185	$3,138
2017	$4,619	$3,464
2018	$5,128	$3,845
2019	$5,688	$4,266
2020	$6,417	$4,832

160S EFI

YEARS MFRD 2016-2020
SERIES. . . . . PRO Z SERIES
ENGINE . . . . . KOHLER
ENGINE HP 27
COOLING . . . . . AIR
FUEL . . . . . G
SPEEDS . . . . . VARIABLE
TRANSMISSION . . . . . DUAL HYDRO
STEERING. . . . . ZERO
STANDARD DECK . . . . . 60"
MSRP. $7,999

OPTIONS

POWERLIFT DECK. $700

RETAIL PRICING

YEAR	HIGH	LOW
2016	$4,314	$3,235
2017	$4,746	$3,559
2018	$5,283	$3,962
2019	$5,863	$4,397
2020	$6,371	$4,888

160S KW

YEARS MFRD 2016-2020
SERIES. . . . . PRO Z SERIES
ENGINE . . . . . KAWASAKI FX730V
CID 726CC
ENGINE HP 24
COOLING . . . . . AIR
FUEL . . . . . G
SPEEDS . . . . . VARIABLE
TRANSMISSION . . . . . DUAL HYDRO
STEERING. . . . . ZERO
STANDARD DECK . . . . . 60"
WEIGHT . . . . . 1,000 LBS.
MSRP. $7,999

OPTIONS

POWERLIFT DECK. $700

RETAIL PRICING

YEAR	HIGH	LOW
2016	$4,317	$3,237
2017	$4,746	$3,559
2018	$5,241	$3,930
2019	$5,967	$4,475
2020	$6,718	$5,113

364

YEARS MFRD 2000-2002
SERIES. . . . . 360 SERIES
ENGINE . . . . . B&S
ENGINE HP 18
COOLING . . . . . AIR
FUEL . . . . . G
SPEEDS . . . . . VARIABLE
TRANSMISSION . . . . . DUAL HYDRO
STEERING. . . . . ZERO
STANDARD DECK . . . . . 44"
MSRP. $4,499

OPTIONS

BAGGER

RETAIL PRICING

YEAR	HIGH	LOW
2000	$665	$499
2001	$735	$551
2002	$811	$608

365

YEARS MFRD 2000-2002
SERIES. . . . . 360 SERIES
ENGINE . . . . . KOHLER
ENGINE HP 20
COOLING . . . . . AIR
FUEL . . . . . G
SPEEDS . . . . . VARIABLE
TRANSMISSION . . . . . DUAL HYDRO
STEERING. . . . . ZERO
STANDARD DECK . . . . . 54"
MSRP. $5,499

OPTIONS

MULCHER

RETAIL PRICING

YEAR	HIGH	LOW
2000	$814	$610
2001	$898	$673
2002	$992	$744

365L

YEARS MFRD 2000-2002
SERIES. . . . . 360 SERIES
ENGINE . . . . . KAWASAKI
ENGINE HP 18
COOLING . . . . . LIQUID
FUEL . . . . . G
SPEEDS . . . . . VARIABLE
TRANSMISSION . . . . . DUAL HYDRO
STEERING. . . . . ZERO
STANDARD DECK . . . . . 44"
MSRP. $5,499

OPTIONS

BAGGER
MULCHER

RETAIL PRICING

YEAR	HIGH	LOW
2000	$814	$610
2001	$898	$673
2002	$992	$744

1000/1600

YEARS MFRD 1999-1999
ENGINE . . . . . B&S
ENGINE HP 16.5
COOLING . . . . . AIR
FUEL . . . . . G
TRANSMISSION . . . . . HYDRO
STEERING. . . . . STANDARD
STANDARD DECK . . . . . 42"
MSRP. $1,699

RETAIL PRICING

YEAR	HIGH	LOW
1999	$710	$533

1000/1800

YEARS MFRD 1999-1999
ENGINE . . . . . B&S
ENGINE HP 18
COOLING . . . . . AIR
FUEL . . . . . G
TRANSMISSION . . . . . HYDRO
STEERING. . . . . STANDARD
STANDARD DECK . . . . . 46"
MSRP. $2,199

RETAIL PRICING

YEAR	HIGH	LOW
1999	$918	$689

1002

YEARS MFRD 1990-1991
ENGINE . . . . . B&S
ENGINE HP 10
COOLING . . . . . AIR
FUEL . . . . . G
TRANSMISSION . . . . . GEAR
STEERING. . . . . STANDARD
STANDARD DECK . . . . . 32"
MSRP. $1,710

RETAIL PRICING

YEAR	HIGH	LOW
1990	$470	$353

1015

YEARS MFRD 1988-1991
ENGINE . . . . . B&S
ENGINE HP 10
COOLING . . . . . AIR
FUEL . . . . . G
TRANSMISSION . . . . . GEAR
STEERING. . . . . STANDARD
STANDARD DECK . . . . . 32"
MSRP. $2,060

SERIAL NUMBERS

YEAR	BEGINNING NO.
1988	126001
1989	147088
1990	169002
1991	192201

RETAIL PRICING

YEAR	HIGH	LOW
1988	$543	$407

1020

YEARS MFRD 1988-1991
ENGINE . . . . . B&S
ENGINE HP 10
COOLING . . . . . AIR
FUEL . . . . . G
TRANSMISSION . . . . . HYDRO
STEERING. . . . . STANDARD
STANDARD DECK . . . . . 32"
MSRP. $2,400

SERIAL NUMBERS

YEAR	BEGINNING NO.
1988	126001
1989	147088
1990	169002
1991	192201

RETAIL PRICING

YEAR	HIGH	LOW
1988	$630	$473

1027

YEARS MFRD 2000-2002
SERIES. . . . . 1000 SERIES
ENGINE . . . . . B&S
ENGINE HP 9

CUB CADET

COOLING.....AIR
FUEL.....G
TRANSMISSION.....GEAR
STEERING.....STANDARD
STANDARD DECK.....27"
MSRP.....$1,499

RETAIL PRICING

YEAR	HIGH	LOW
2000	$179	$135
2001	$200	$150
2002	$220	$165

1030

YEARS MFRD.....1992-1996
ENGINE.....B&S
ENGINE HP.....10.5
COOLING.....AIR
FUEL.....G
TRANSMISSION.....GEAR
STEERING.....STANDARD
STANDARD DECK.....30"
MSRP.....$1,699

RETAIL PRICING

YEAR	HIGH	LOW
1992	$522	$391

1170

YEARS MFRD.....2000-2002
SERIES.....1000 SERIES
ENGINE.....B&S
ENGINE HP.....17
COOLING.....AIR
FUEL.....G
SPEEDS.....VARIABLE
TRANSMISSION.....HYDRO
STEERING.....STANDARD
STANDARD DECK.....42"
MSRP.....$1,999

OPTIONS

2 BAG
42" SNOW THROWER
46" BLADE

RETAIL PRICING

YEAR	HIGH	LOW
2000	$260	$195
2001	$287	$215
2002	$318	$238

1180

YEARS MFRD.....2000-2000
SERIES.....1000 SERIES
ENGINE.....B&S
ENGINE HP.....18
FUEL.....G
SPEEDS.....VARIABLE
TRANSMISSION.....HYDRO
STEERING.....STANDARD
STANDARD DECK.....46"
MSRP.....$2,399

OPTIONS

2 BAG
42" SNOW THROWER
46" BLADE

RETAIL PRICING

YEAR	HIGH	LOW
2000	$371	$278

1204

YEARS MFRD.....1986-1990
ENGINE.....KOHLER
CID.....35.9
ENGINE HP.....12
COOLING.....AIR
FUEL.....G
SPEEDS.....4/1
TRANSMISSION.....GEAR
STEERING.....STANDARD
WEIGHT.....736 LBS.

SERIAL NUMBERS

YEAR	BEGINNING NO.
1987	756300
1988	767352
1989	779097

1208

YEARS MFRD.....1990-1991
ENGINE.....B&S
ENGINE HP.....12
COOLING.....AIR
FUEL.....G
TRANSMISSION.....GEAR
STEERING.....STANDARD
STANDARD DECK.....38"
MSRP.....$1,900

RETAIL PRICING

YEAR	HIGH	LOW
1990	$525	$394

1212

YEARS MFRD.....2000-2000
ENGINE.....B&S
ENGINE HP.....21
FUEL.....G
SPEEDS.....VARIABLE
TRANSMISSION.....HYDRO
STEERING.....STANDARD
STANDARD DECK.....46"
MSRP.....$3,099

OPTIONS

2 BAG
3 BAG
42" SNOW THROWER
46" BLADE

RETAIL PRICING

YEAR	HIGH	LOW
2000	$403	$302

1225

YEARS MFRD.....1992-1993
ENGINE.....B&S
ENGINE HP.....12
COOLING.....AIR
FUEL.....G
TRANSMISSION.....HYDRO
STEERING.....STANDARD
STANDARD DECK.....38"
MSRP.....$2,299

SERIAL NUMBERS

YEAR	BEGINNING NO.
1992	207401
1993	224001

RETAIL PRICING

YEAR	HIGH	LOW
1992	$706	$530

1238

YEARS MFRD.....1992-1993
ENGINE.....B&S
ENGINE HP.....12
COOLING.....AIR
FUEL.....G
TRANSMISSION.....HYDRO
STEERING.....STANDARD
STANDARD DECK.....38"
MSRP.....$1,949

RETAIL PRICING

YEAR	HIGH	LOW
1992	$600	$450

1315

YEARS MFRD.....1989-1991
ENGINE.....KOHLER
ENGINE HP.....12.5
COOLING.....AIR
FUEL.....G
TRANSMISSION.....GEAR
STEERING.....STANDARD

SERIAL NUMBERS

YEAR	BEGINNING NO.
1989	147088
1990	169002
1991	192001

1320

YEARS MFRD.....1989-1991
ENGINE.....KOHLER
ENGINE HP.....12.5
COOLING.....AIR
FUEL.....G
TRANSMISSION.....HYDRO
STEERING.....STANDARD
STANDARD DECK.....38"
MSRP.....$2,779

SERIAL NUMBERS

YEAR	BEGINNING NO.
1989	147088
1990	169002
1991	192001

RETAIL PRICING

YEAR	HIGH	LOW
1989	$762	$571

1325

YEARS MFRD.....1992-1993
ENGINE.....KOHLER
ENGINE HP.....12.5
COOLING.....AIR
FUEL.....G
TRANSMISSION.....GEAR
STEERING.....STANDARD
STANDARD DECK.....38"
MSRP.....$2,649

SERIAL NUMBERS

YEAR	BEGINNING NO.
1992	207401
1993	224001

RETAIL PRICING

YEAR	HIGH	LOW
1992	$813	$610

1330

YEARS MFRD.....1992-1993
ENGINE.....KOHLER
ENGINE HP.....12.5
COOLING.....AIR
FUEL.....G
SPEEDS.....VARIABLE
TRANSMISSION.....HYDRO
STEERING.....STANDARD
STANDARD DECK.....38"
MSRP.....$2,999

SERIAL NUMBERS

YEAR	BEGINNING NO.
1992	207401
1993	224001

RETAIL PRICING

YEAR	HIGH	LOW
1992	$918	$689

1335

YEARS MFRD.....1990-1990
ENGINE.....KOHLER
ENGINE HP.....12.5
COOLING.....AIR
FUEL.....G
TRANSMISSION.....GEAR
STEERING.....STANDARD
STANDARD DECK.....38"
MSRP.....$3,599

RETAIL PRICING

YEAR	HIGH	LOW
1990	$994	$746

1340

YEARS MFRD.....1990-1991
ENGINE.....KOHLER
ENGINE HP.....12.5
COOLING.....AIR
FUEL.....G
SPEEDS.....VARIABLE
TRANSMISSION.....HYDRO
STANDARD DECK.....38"
MSRP.....$4,199

SERIAL NUMBERS

YEAR	BEGINNING NO.
1990	800000
1991	811672

RETAIL PRICING

YEAR	HIGH	LOW
1990	$317	$238
1991	$363	$272

1405

YEARS MFRD	1990-1991
ENGINE	KOHLER
ENGINE HP	14
COOLING	AIR
FUEL	G
TRANSMISSION	GEAR
STEERING	STANDARD
STANDARD DECK	38"
MSRP	$2,479

SERIAL NUMBERS

YEAR	BEGINNING NO.
1990	169002
1991	192001

RETAIL PRICING

YEAR	HIGH	LOW
1990	$686	$514
1991	$731	$548

1420

YEARS MFRD	1988-1991
ENGINE	KOHLER
ENGINE HP	14
COOLING	AIR
FUEL	G
TRANSMISSION	HYDRO
STEERING	STANDARD
STANDARD DECK	38"
MSRP	$2,585

SERIAL NUMBERS

YEAR	BEGINNING NO.
1988	126001
1989	147088
1990	169002
1991	192001

RETAIL PRICING

YEAR	HIGH	LOW
1988	$681	$510
1989	$708	$531

1430

YEARS MFRD	1992-1993
ENGINE	KOHLER
ENGINE HP	14
COOLING	AIR
FUEL	G
SPEEDS	VARIABLE
TRANSMISSION	HYDRO
STEERING	STANDARD
STANDARD DECK	38"
MSRP	$3,738

SERIAL NUMBERS

YEAR	BEGINNING NO.
1992	207401
1993	224001

RETAIL PRICING

YEAR	HIGH	LOW
1992	$260	$195
1993	$295	$221

1440

YEARS MFRD	1992-1997
ENGINE	B&S
ENGINE HP	14
COOLING	AIR
FUEL	G
TRANSMISSION	GEAR
STEERING	STANDARD
STANDARD DECK	42"
MSRP	$4,579

OPTIONS

3 BAG
38" TILLER
45" SNOW BLOWER
46" DECK

SERIAL NUMBERS

YEAR	BEGINNING NO.
1992	821001
1993	836001
1994	851001
1995	864501
1996	880015
1997	889001

RETAIL PRICING

YEAR	HIGH	LOW
1992	$332	$249
1993	$367	$275
1994	$407	$305
1995	$450	$337
1996	$497	$373
1997	$551	$414

1515

YEARS MFRD	2002-2002
SERIES	1500 SERIES
ENGINE	KOHLER
ENGINE HP	15
FUEL	G
TRANSMISSION	HYDRO
STEERING	STANDARD
STANDARD DECK	38"
MSRP	$2,499

OPTIONS

42" SNOW BLOWER
46" BLADE

RETAIL PRICING

YEAR	HIGH	LOW
2002	$398	$298

1517

YEARS MFRD	2002-2002
SERIES	1500 SERIES
ENGINE	KOHLER
ENGINE HP	17
FUEL	G
SPEEDS	VARIABLE
TRANSMISSION	HYDRO
STEERING	STANDARD
STANDARD DECK	42"
MSRP	$2,899

OPTIONS

2 BAG
42" SNOW BLOWER
46" BLADE

RETAIL PRICING

YEAR	HIGH	LOW
2002	$461	$346

1525

YEARS MFRD	2003-2003
SERIES	1500 SERIES
ENGINE	KAWASAKI
ENGINE HP	15
COOLING	AIR
FUEL	G
SPEEDS	VARIABLE
TRANSMISSION	HYDRO
STEERING	STANDARD
STANDARD DECK	38"
MSRP	$2,299

RETAIL PRICING

YEAR	HIGH	LOW
2003	$409	$307

1527

YEARS MFRD	2003-2003
SERIES	1500 SERIES
ENGINE	KOHLER
ENGINE HP	17
COOLING	AIR
FUEL	G
SPEEDS	VARIABLE
TRANSMISSION	HYDRO
STEERING	STANDARD
STANDARD DECK	42"
MSRP	$2,699

RETAIL PRICING

YEAR	HIGH	LOW
2003	$476	$357

1529

YEARS MFRD	2003-2003
SERIES	1500 SERIES
ENGINE	KAWASAKI
ENGINE HP	19
COOLING	AIR
FUEL	G
SPEEDS	VARIABLE
TRANSMISSION	HYDRO
STEERING	STANDARD
STANDARD DECK	46"
MSRP	$3,099

RETAIL PRICING

YEAR	HIGH	LOW
2003	$547	$411

1535

YEARS MFRD	1990-1991
SERIES	1500 SERIES
ENGINE	KOHLER
ENGINE HP	15
FUEL	G
TRANSMISSION	GEAR
STEERING	STANDARD
STANDARD DECK	44"
MSRP	$4,671

SERIAL NUMBERS

YEAR	BEGINNING NO.
1990	800000
1991	811672

RETAIL PRICING

YEAR	HIGH	LOW
1990	$1,180	$885
1991	$1,289	$967

1541

YEARS MFRD	1990-1991
SERIES	1500 SERIES
ENGINE	KOHLER
ENGINE HP	15
COOLING	AIR
FUEL	G
TRANSMISSION	HYDRO
STEERING	STANDARD
STANDARD DECK	44"
MSRP	$4,599

SERIAL NUMBERS

YEAR	BEGINNING NO.
1990	800000
1991	811672

RETAIL PRICING

YEAR	HIGH	LOW
1990	$422	$317
1991	$482	$361

1600

YEARS MFRD	1999-1999
ENGINE	B&S
ENGINE HP	16.5
FUEL	G
SPEEDS	VARIABLE
TRANSMISSION	HYDRO
STEERING	STANDARD
STANDARD DECK	42"
WEIGHT	690 LBS.
MSRP	$1,699

RETAIL PRICING

YEAR	HIGH	LOW
1999	$710	$533

1641

YEARS MFRD	1992-1997
ENGINE	VANGUARD
ENGINE HP	16
COOLING	AIR
FUEL	G
TRANSMISSION	GEAR
STEERING	STANDARD
STANDARD DECK	46"
MSRP	$5,289

OPTIONS

3 BAG
38" TILLER
45" SNOW BLOWER
BAG & FAN

SERIAL NUMBERS

YEAR	BEGINNING NO.
1992	821101
1993	836001
1994	851001
1995	864501
1996	880015
1997	889001

RETAIL PRICING

YEAR	HIGH	LOW
1992	$385	$289
1993	$425	$319
1994	$469	$352
1995	$520	$390
1996	$575	$431
1997	$636	$477

CUB CADET

1715

YEARS MFRD 1988-1990
ENGINE . . . . KOHLER
ENGINE HP 17
COOLING . . . . AIR
FUEL . . . . G
TRANSMISSION . . . . GEAR
STEERING. . . . . STANDARD
STANDARD DECK . . . . 46"
MSRP. $3,495

SERIAL NUMBERS

YEAR	BEGINNING NO.
1988	126001
1989	147088

RETAIL PRICING

YEAR	HIGH	LOW
1988	$696	$522
1989	$779	$584
1990	$968	$726

1720

YEARS MFRD 1988-1991
ENGINE . . . . KOHLER
ENGINE HP 17
COOLING . . . . AIR
FUEL . . . . G
TRANSMISSION . . . . HYDRO
STEERING. . . . . STANDARD
STANDARD DECK . . . . 46"
MSRP. $3,915

SERIAL NUMBERS

YEAR	BEGINNING NO.
1988	126001
1989	147088
1990	170601
1991	192001

RETAIL PRICING

YEAR	HIGH	LOW
1988	$788	$591
1989	$875	$657
1990	$974	$730
1991	$1,082	$812

1730

YEARS MFRD 1992-1993
ENGINE . . . . KOHLER
ENGINE HP 17
COOLING . . . . AIR
FUEL . . . . G
TRANSMISSION . . . . HYDRO
STEERING. . . . . STANDARD
STANDARD DECK . . . . 46"
MSRP. $4,238

SERIAL NUMBERS

YEAR	BEGINNING NO.
1992	207401
1993	224001

RETAIL PRICING

YEAR	HIGH	LOW
1992	$1,295	$971
1993	$1,341	$1,006

1782

YEARS MFRD 1990-1996
SERIES. . . . . SUPER GT SERIES
ENGINE . . . . KUBOTA
ENGINE HP 17
COOLING . . . . LIQUID
FUEL . . . . D
SPEEDS . . . . VARIABLE
TRANSMISSION . . . . HYDRO
STEERING. . . . . STANDARD
STANDARD DECK . . . . 48"
MSRP. $9,518

OPTIONS

38" TILLER
45" SNOW BLOWER
54" BLADE
60" DECK

SERIAL NUMBERS

YEAR	BEGINNING NO.
1990	800000
1991	811672
1992	821101
1993	836001
1994	851001
1995	864501
1996	880015

RETAIL PRICING

YEAR	HIGH	LOW
1990	$549	$412
1991	$607	$455
1992	$671	$504
1993	$743	$557
1994	$822	$617
1995	$909	$682
1996	$1,005	$753

1800

YEARS MFRD 1999-1999
ENGINE . . . . B&S
ENGINE HP 18
FUEL . . . . G
TRANSMISSION . . . . CVT
STEERING. . . . . STANDARD
STANDARD DECK . . . . 46"
MSRP. $2,199

RETAIL PRICING

YEAR	HIGH	LOW
1999	$918	$689

1860

YEARS MFRD 1990-1991
ENGINE . . . . KOHLER
ENGINE HP 18
COOLING . . . . AIR
FUEL . . . . G
SPEEDS . . . . VARIABLE
TRANSMISSION . . . . HYDRO
STEERING. . . . . STANDARD
STANDARD DECK . . . . 46"
MSRP. $4,899

OPTIONS

3 BAG
45" SNOW BLOWER
54" BLADE

SERIAL NUMBERS

YEAR	BEGINNING NO.
1990	800000
1991	811672

RETAIL PRICING

YEAR	HIGH	LOW
1990	$297	$223
1991	$327	$245

1861

YEARS MFRD 1990-1992
ENGINE . . . . KOHLER
ENGINE HP 18
COOLING . . . . AIR
FUEL . . . . G
SPEEDS . . . . VARIABLE
TRANSMISSION . . . . HYDRO
STEERING. . . . . STANDARD
STANDARD DECK . . . . 54"
MSRP. $5,978

OPTIONS

3 BAG
45" SNOW BLOWER
54" BLADE

SERIAL NUMBERS

YEAR	BEGINNING NO.
1990	800000
1992	821101

RETAIL PRICING

YEAR	HIGH	LOW
1990	$398	$298
1991	$440	$330
1992	$487	$365

1862

YEARS MFRD 1990-1992
ENGINE . . . . KOHLER
ENGINE HP 18
COOLING . . . . AIR
FUEL . . . . G
SPEEDS . . . . VARIABLE
TRANSMISSION . . . . HYDRO
STEERING. . . . . STANDARD
STANDARD DECK . . . . 50"
MSRP. $6,878

OPTIONS

3 BAG
45" SNOW BLOWER
54" BLADE

SERIAL NUMBERS

YEAR	BEGINNING NO.
1990	800000
1991	811672
1992	821101

RETAIL PRICING

YEAR	HIGH	LOW
1990	$458	$344
1991	$506	$380
1992	$560	$420

1863

YEARS MFRD 1993-1997
ENGINE . . . . KOHLER
ENGINE HP 18
COOLING . . . . AIR
FUEL . . . . G
STEERING. . . . . STANDARD
STANDARD DECK . . . . 46"
MSRP. $5,799

OPTIONS

3 BAG
38" TILLER
45" SNOW BLOWER
60" DECK

SERIAL NUMBERS

YEAR	BEGINNING NO.
1993	836001
1994	851001
1995	864501
1996	880015
1997	889001

RETAIL PRICING

YEAR	HIGH	LOW
1993	$465	$349
1994	$515	$386
1995	$570	$427
1996	$630	$473
1997	$697	$523

1864

YEARS MFRD 1993-1997
ENGINE . . . . KOHLER
ENGINE HP 18
COOLING . . . . AIR
FUEL . . . . G
SPEEDS . . . . VARIABLE
TRANSMISSION . . . . HYDRO
STEERING. . . . . STANDARD
STANDARD DECK . . . . 48"
MSRP. $6,599

OPTIONS

3 BAG
38" TILLER
45" SNOW BLOWER
54" DECK

SERIAL NUMBERS

YEAR	BEGINNING NO.
1993	836001
1994	851001
1995	864501
1996	880015
1997	889001

RETAIL PRICING

YEAR	HIGH	LOW
1993	$530	$397
1994	$586	$440
1995	$649	$487
1996	$718	$538
1997	$793	$595

1882

YEARS MFRD 1990-1991
ENGINE . . . . KOHLER
ENGINE HP 18
COOLING . . . . AIR
FUEL . . . . G
SPEEDS . . . . VARIABLE
TRANSMISSION . . . . HYDRO
STEERING. . . . . STANDARD
STANDARD DECK . . . . 50"
MSRP. $6,199

OPTIONS

3 BAG
40" TILLER
45" SNOW BLOWER
54" BLADE

SERIAL NUMBERS

YEAR	BEGINNING NO.
1990	800000
1991	811672

RETAIL PRICING

YEAR	HIGH	LOW
1990	$375	$281
1991	$414	$311

2082

YEARS MFRD	1990-1992
SERIES	SUPER GT SERIES
ENGINE	KOHLER
ENGINE HP	20
COOLING	AIR
FUEL	G
SPEEDS	VARIABLE
TRANSMISSION	HYDRO
STEERING	STANDARD
STANDARD DECK	54"
MSRP	$7,988

OPTIONS

3 BAG
40" TILLER
45" SNOW BLOWER
54" BLADE
60" DECK

SERIAL NUMBERS

YEAR	BEGINNING NO.
1990	800000
1991	811672
1992	821101

RETAIL PRICING

YEAR	HIGH	LOW
1990	$467	$351
1991	$518	$388
1992	$573	$430

2084

YEARS MFRD	1993-1994
SERIES	SUPER GT SERIES
ENGINE	KOHLER OHV
ENGINE HP	20
COOLING	LIQUID
FUEL	G
SPEEDS	VARIABLE
TRANSMISSION	HYDRO
STEERING	STANDARD
STANDARD DECK	60"
MSRP	$8,388

OPTIONS

3 BAG
40" TILLER
45" SNOW BLOWER
54" BLADE

SERIAL NUMBERS

YEAR	BEGINNING NO.
1993	836001
1994	851001

RETAIL PRICING

YEAR	HIGH	LOW
1993	$728	$546
1994	$805	$603

2086

YEARS MFRD	1996-1997
SERIES	SUPER GT SERIES
ENGINE	KAWASAKI
ENGINE HP	20
COOLING	LIQUID
FUEL	G
TRANSMISSION	HYDRO
STEERING	STANDARD
STANDARD DECK	54"
MSRP	$7,829

OPTIONS

40" TILLER
45" SNOW BLOWER
54" BLADE
60" DECK

SERIAL NUMBERS

YEAR	BEGINNING NO.
1996	880015
1997	889001

RETAIL PRICING

YEAR	HIGH	LOW
1996	$1,091	$818
1997	$1,206	$905

2135

YEARS MFRD	1994-1999
ENGINE	KOHLER
CYLINDERS	1
CID	398CC
ENGINE HP	12.5
COOLING	AIR
FUEL	G
SPEEDS	VARIABLE
TRANSMISSION	HYDRO
STEERING	STANDARD

2146

YEARS MFRD	2000-2000
SERIES	2000 SERIES
ENGINE	CUB CADET
ENGINE HP	14
COOLING	AIR
FUEL	G
SPEEDS	VARIABLE
TRANSMISSION	HYDRO
STEERING	STANDARD
STANDARD DECK	38"
MSRP	$2,899

OPTIONS

2 BAG
40" SNOW THROWER
42" BLADE

RETAIL PRICING

YEAR	HIGH	LOW
2000	$343	$258

2164

YEARS MFRD	2000-2000
SERIES	2000 SERIES
ENGINE	B&S
ENGINE HP	16
FUEL	G
TRANSMISSION	HYDRO
STEERING	STANDARD
STANDARD DECK	42"
MSRP	$3,799

RETAIL PRICING

YEAR	HIGH	LOW
2000	$832	$624

2166

YEARS MFRD	2000-2003
SERIES	2000 SERIES
ENGINE	KOHLER
ENGINE HP	16
COOLING	AIR
FUEL	G
SPEEDS	VARIABLE
TRANSMISSION	HYDRO
STEERING	STANDARD
PTO	YES
STANDARD DECK	42"
MSRP	$3,499

OPTIONS

30" TILLER
40" SNOW THROWER
42" BLADE
BAGGER

RETAIL PRICING

YEAR	HIGH	LOW
2000	$505	$379
2001	$558	$418
2002	$618	$464
2003	$693	$520

2176

YEARS MFRD	2000-2001
SERIES	2000 SERIES
ENGINE	KOHLER
ENGINE HP	17
COOLING	AIR
FUEL	G
TRANSMISSION	HYDRO
STEERING	STANDARD
PTO	YES
STANDARD DECK	42"
MSRP	$3,999

OPTIONS

40" SNOW THROWER
42" BLADE
BAGGER

RETAIL PRICING

YEAR	HIGH	LOW
2000	$602	$451
2001	$666	$500

2182

YEARS MFRD	1990-1995
SERIES	SUPER GT SERIES
ENGINE	KUBOTA
ENGINE HP	21
COOLING	LIQUID
FUEL	G
SPEEDS	VARIABLE
TRANSMISSION	HYDRO
STEERING	STANDARD
STANDARD DECK	54"
MSRP	$9,508

OPTIONS

40" TILLER
45" SNOW BLOWER
54" BLADE

SERIAL NUMBERS

YEAR	BEGINNING NO.
1990	800000
1991	811672
1992	821101
1993	836001
1994	851001
1995	864501

RETAIL PRICING

YEAR	HIGH	LOW
1990	$634	$476
1991	$702	$527
1992	$777	$583
1993	$859	$644
1994	$949	$712
1995	$1,051	$788

2186GT

YEARS MFRD	2005-2006
SERIES	2000 SERIES
ENGINE	B&S
ENGINE HP	10.5
COOLING	AIR
FUEL	G
SPEEDS	VARIABLE
TRANSMISSION	HYDRO
STANDARD DECK	28"
MSRP	$2,099

RETAIL PRICING

YEAR	HIGH	LOW
2005	$503	$377
2005	$503	$377
2006	$557	$417
2006	$557	$417

2186LT

YEARS MFRD	2003-2003
SERIES	2000 SERIES
ENGINE	KOHLER
ENGINE HP	18
COOLING	AIR
FUEL	G
TRANSMISSION	HYDRO
STEERING	STANDARD
PTO	YES
STANDARD DECK	44"
MSRP	$4,199

OPTIONS

48" DECK

RETAIL PRICING

YEAR	HIGH	LOW
2003	$822	$617

CUB CADET

2206

YEARS MFRD 2000-2001
SERIES............ 2000 SERIES
ENGINE .... KOHLER
ENGINE HP................. 20
FUEL .... G
SPEEDS .... VARIABLE
TRANSMISSION .... HYDRO
STEERING........... STANDARD
PTO .... YES
STANDARD DECK .... 48"
MSRP................ $4,899

OPTIONS

3 BAG
40" SNOW THROWER
42" BLADE
BAG & FAN

RETAIL PRICING

YEAR	HIGH	LOW
2000	$683	$512
2001	$754	$566

2284

YEARS MFRD 1995-1997
SERIES.......... SUPER GT SERIES
ENGINE .... KOHLER
ENGINE HP................. 22
COOLING .... AIR
FUEL .... G
SPEEDS .... VARIABLE
TRANSMISSION .... HYDRO
STEERING........... STANDARD
STANDARD DECK .... 54"
MSRP................ $7,798

OPTIONS

42" TILLER
45" SNOW BLOWER
54" BLADE
BAG & FAN

SERIAL NUMBERS

YEAR	BEGINNING NO.
1995	864501
1996	880015
1997	889001

RETAIL PRICING

YEAR	HIGH	LOW
1995	$859	$644
1996	$949	$712
1997	$1,051	$788

2518

YEARS MFRD 2003-2003
SERIES............ 2000 SERIES
ENGINE .... KOHLER
ENGINE HP................. 18
COOLING .... AIR
FUEL .... G
TRANSMISSION .... HYDRO
STEERING........... STANDARD
PTO .... YES
STANDARD DECK .... 44"
MSRP................ $4,499

OPTIONS

48" DECK

RETAIL PRICING

YEAR	HIGH	LOW
2003	$885	$663

3165

YEARS MFRD 1998-1999
SERIES............ 3000 SERIES
ENGINE .... B&S
ENGINE HP................. 16
COOLING .... AIR
FUEL .... G
SPEEDS .... VARIABLE
TRANSMISSION .... HYDRO
STEERING........... STANDARD
STANDARD DECK .... 48"
MSRP................ $6,099

OPTIONS

45" SNOW BLOWER
54" BLADE
BAG & FAN
TILLER

SERIAL NUMBERS

YEAR	BEGINNING NO.
1998	XXXX8XXXXXX
1999	XXXX9XXXXXX

RETAIL PRICING

YEAR	HIGH	LOW
1998	$770	$577
1999	$851	$638

3184

YEARS MFRD 2000-2000
SERIES............ 3000 SERIES
ENGINE .... KOHLER
ENGINE HP................. 18
FUEL .... G
SPEEDS .... VARIABLE
TRANSMISSION .... HYDRO
STEERING........... STANDARD
STANDARD DECK .... 44"
MSRP................ $5,499

OPTIONS

3 BAG
42" TILLER
45" SNOW THROWER
54" BLADE

RETAIL PRICING

YEAR	HIGH	LOW
2000	$797	$598

3185

YEARS MFRD 1998-1999
SERIES............ 3000 SERIES
ENGINE .... B&S
ENGINE HP................. 18
COOLING .... AIR
FUEL .... G
SPEEDS .... VARIABLE
TRANSMISSION .... HYDRO
STEERING........... STANDARD
STANDARD DECK .... 54"
MSRP................ $6,509

OPTIONS

45" SNOW BLOWER
54" BLADE
BAG & FAN
TILLER

SERIAL NUMBERS

YEAR	BEGINNING NO.
1998	XXXX8XXXXXX
1999	XXXX9XXXXXX

RETAIL PRICING

YEAR	HIGH	LOW
1998	$821	$616
1999	$908	$681

3186

YEARS MFRD 1999-1999
SERIES............ 3000 SERIES
ENGINE .... B&S
ENGINE HP................. 18
COOLING .... AIR
FUEL .... G
SPEEDS .... VARIABLE
TRANSMISSION .... HYDRO
STEERING........... STANDARD
STANDARD DECK .... 54"
MSRP................ $6,709

OPTIONS

45" SNOW BLOWER
54" BLADE
BAG & FAN
TILLER

SERIAL NUMBERS

YEAR	BEGINNING NO.
1999	XXXX9XXXXXX

RETAIL PRICING

YEAR	HIGH	LOW
1999	$845	$633

3204

YEARS MFRD 2002-2003
SERIES............ 3000 SERIES
ENGINE .... KOHLER
ENGINE HP................. 20
FUEL .... G
SPEEDS .... VARIABLE
TRANSMISSION .... HYDRO
STEERING........... STANDARD
HYDRAULIC .... YES
PTO .... YES
STANDARD DECK .... 48"
MSRP................ $6,198

OPTIONS

45" SNOW THROWER
54" BLADE
BAG & FAN

RETAIL PRICING

YEAR	HIGH	LOW
2002	$1,001	$751
2003	$1,109	$832

3205

YEARS MFRD 1998-1999
SERIES............ 3000 SERIES
ENGINE .... KAWASAKI
ENGINE HP................. 20
COOLING .... LIQUID
FUEL .... G
SPEEDS .... VARIABLE
TRANSMISSION .... HYDRO
STEERING........... STANDARD
STANDARD DECK .... 60"
MSRP................ $8,449

OPTIONS

45" SNOW BLOWER
54" BLADE
BAGGER
TILLER

SERIAL NUMBERS

YEAR	BEGINNING NO.
1998	XXXX8XXXXXX
1999	XXXX9XXXXXX

RETAIL PRICING

YEAR	HIGH	LOW
1998	$1,104	$828
1999	$1,221	$916

3206

YEARS MFRD 2000-2002
SERIES............ 3000 SERIES
ENGINE .... KOHLER
ENGINE HP................. 22
FUEL .... G
SPEEDS .... VARIABLE
TRANSMISSION .... HYDRO
STEERING........... STANDARD
HYDRAULIC .... YES
PTO .... YES
STANDARD DECK .... 48"
MSRP................ $7,428

OPTIONS

45" SNOW THROWER
54" BLADE
54" DECK
BAG & FAN

RETAIL PRICING

YEAR	HIGH	LOW
2000	$1,083	$813
2001	$1,198	$899
2002	$1,325	$994

3208

YEARS MFRD 2000-2000
SERIES............ 3000 SERIES
ENGINE .... KAWASAKI
ENGINE HP................. 20
COOLING .... LIQUID
FUEL .... G
SPEEDS .... VARIABLE
TRANSMISSION .... HYDRO
STEERING........... STANDARD
STANDARD DECK .... 54"
MSRP................ $8,798

OPTIONS

42" TILLER
45" SNOW THROWER
54" BLADE
60" DECK

RETAIL PRICING

YEAR	HIGH	LOW
2000	$1,271	$953

3225

YEARS MFRD 1998-1999
SERIES .... 3000 SERIES
ENGINE .... KOHLER
ENGINE HP 22
COOLING .... AIR
FUEL .... G
TRANSMISSION .... HYDRO
STEERING .... STANDARD
STANDARD DECK .... 60"
MSRP $7,549

OPTIONS

45" SNOW BLOWER
54" BLADE
BAGGER
TILLER

SERIAL NUMBERS

YEAR	BEGINNING NO.
1998	XXXX8XXXXXX
1999	XXXX9XXXXXX

RETAIL PRICING

YEAR	HIGH	LOW
1998	$986	$740
1999	$1,091	$818

3235

YEARS MFRD 2000-2003
SERIES .... 3000 SERIES
ENGINE .... KOHLER
ENGINE HP 25
FUEL .... G
SPEEDS .... VARIABLE
TRANSMISSION .... HYDRO
STEERING .... STANDARD
HYDRAULIC .... YES
PTO .... YES
STANDARD DECK .... 54"
MSRP $8,028

OPTIONS

45" SNOW THROWER
54" BLADE
60" DECK
BAG & FAN

RETAIL PRICING

YEAR	HIGH	LOW
2000	$1,058	$793
2001	$1,171	$878
2002	$1,294	$970
2003	$1,431	$1,073

3240

YEARS MFRD 2001-2001
SERIES .... 3000 SERIES
ENGINE .... KOHLER
ENGINE HP 20
FUEL .... G
TRANSMISSION .... HYDRO
STEERING .... STANDARD
MSRP $5,999

RETAIL PRICING

YEAR	HIGH	LOW
2001	$2,742	$2,056

3435

YEARS MFRD 2000-2000
SERIES .... 3000 SERIES
ENGINE .... KOHLER
ENGINE HP 23
FUEL .... G
TRANSMISSION .... HYDRO
STEERING .... STANDARD
MSRP $6,699

RETAIL PRICING

YEAR	HIGH	LOW
2000	$2,937	$2,202

3654

YEARS MFRD 2000-2000
SERIES .... 360 SERIES
ENGINE .... KOHLER
ENGINE HP 25
COOLING .... LIQUID
FUEL .... G
SPEEDS .... VARIABLE
TRANSMISSION .... DUAL HYDRO
STEERING .... ZERO
STANDARD DECK .... 54"
MSRP $7,499

OPTIONS

VAC & BAG

RETAIL PRICING

YEAR	HIGH	LOW
2000	$1,025	$769

3660

YEARS MFRD 2000-2000
SERIES .... 360 SERIES
ENGINE .... KOHLER
ENGINE HP 25
FUEL .... G
SPEEDS .... VARIABLE
TRANSMISSION .... DUAL HYDRO
STEERING .... ZERO
STANDARD DECK .... 60"
MSRP $7,999

OPTIONS

VAC & BAG

RETAIL PRICING

YEAR	HIGH	LOW
2000	$1,100	$825

5234D

YEARS MFRD 2004-2006
SERIES .... 5000 SERIES
ENGINE .... DAIHATSU
CYLINDERS 3
CID 51.8
PTO HP 17
ENGINE HP 23
COOLING .... LIQUID
FUEL .... D
SPEEDS .... VARIABLE
TRANSMISSION .... HYDRO
STEERING .... STANDARD
HYDRAULIC .... YES
PTO .... YES
STANDARD DECK .... 60"
WEIGHT .... 1,350 LBS.
MSRP $9,299

OPTIONS

48" SNOW THROWER
60" DECK

RETAIL PRICING

YEAR	HIGH	LOW
2004	$4,153	$3,115
2005	$4,235	$3,176
2006	$4,483	$3,363

AVG. AUCTION PRICING

LOW	HIGH	AVG
$3,660	$6,133	$4,772

5252

YEARS MFRD 2004-2007
SERIES .... 5000 SERIES
ENGINE .... KOHLER
CYLINDERS 2
CID 45.6
PTO HP 16.3
ENGINE HP 25
COOLING .... AIR
FUEL .... G
SPEEDS .... VARIABLE
TRANSMISSION .... HYDRO
STEERING .... STANDARD
HITCH .... CAT. I
HYDRAULIC .... YES
PTO .... YES
STANDARD DECK .... 60"
WEIGHT .... 1,350 LBS.
MSRP $9,299

OPTIONS

48" SNOW THROWER

RETAIL PRICING

YEAR	HIGH	LOW
2004	$3,882	$2,911
2005	$4,064	$3,048
2006	$4,308	$3,231
2007	$4,533	$3,399

5254

YEARS MFRD 2004-2007
SERIES .... 5000 SERIES
ENGINE .... KAWASAKI
CYLINDERS 2
CID 45.6
PTO HP 17
ENGINE HP 25
COOLING .... LIQUID
FUEL .... G
SPEEDS .... VARIABLE
TRANSMISSION .... HYDRO
STEERING .... STANDARD
HITCH .... CAT. I
HYDRAULIC .... YES
PTO .... YES
STANDARD DECK .... 60"
WEIGHT .... 1,267 LBS.
MSRP $9,699

OPTIONS

48" SNOW THROWER

RETAIL PRICING

YEAR	HIGH	LOW
2004	$4,052	$3,039
2005	$4,231	$3,173
2006	$4,491	$3,368
2007	$4,726	$3,545

5264

YEARS MFRD 2006-2007
SERIES .... 5000 SERIES
ENGINE .... DAIHATSU
CYLINDERS 3
PTO HP 16
ENGINE HP 26
COOLING .... LIQUID
FUEL .... D
SPEEDS .... VARIABLE
TRANSMISSION .... HYDRO
STEERING .... STANDARD
HITCH .... CAT. I
PTO .... YES
DRIVE TYPE 4WD
ROPS/CAB .... ROPS
STANDARD DECK .... 54"
WEIGHT .... 1,350 LBS.
MSRP $10,899

OPTIONS

48" SNOW THROWER
60" DECK

RETAIL PRICING

YEAR	HIGH	LOW
2006	$5,048	$3,786
2007	$5,312	$3,984

6284D

YEARS MFRD 2005-2007
SERIES .... 6000 SERIES
ENGINE .... CAT
CYLINDERS 3
CID 69.01
PTO HP 21
ENGINE HP 28
COOLING .... LIQUID
FUEL .... D
SPEEDS .... VARIABLE
TRANSMISSION .... HYDRO
STEERING .... STANDARD
HITCH .... CAT. I
HYDRAULIC .... YES
PTO .... YES
WEIGHT .... 1,953 LBS.
MSRP $14,995

OPTIONS

LDR

RETAIL PRICING

YEAR	HIGH	LOW
2005	$6,600	$4,950
2006	$6,946	$5,210
2007	$7,311	$5,483

CUB CADET

7000

YEARS MFRD 1998-1999
SERIES .... 7000 SERIES
ENGINE .... MITSUBISHI
CYLINDERS 3
CID 69
PTO HP 17.5
ENGINE HP 20
FUEL .... D
TRANSMISSION .... GEAR
STEERING .... STANDARD
HITCH .... CAT. I
PTO .... YES
DRIVE TYPE 2WD
ROPS/CAB .... ROPS
WEIGHT .... 1,746 LBS.
MSRP $11,689

SERIAL NUMBERS

YEAR	BEGINNING NO.
1998	XXXX8XXXXXX

RETAIL PRICING

YEAR	HIGH	LOW
1998	$2,980	$2,235
1999	$3,132	$2,349

7192

YEARS MFRD 1995-1997
SERIES .... 7000 SERIES
CYLINDERS 3
CID 64.7
PTO HP 17
ENGINE HP 19
FUEL .... D
TRANSMISSION .... GEAR
STEERING .... STANDARD
PTO .... YES
WEIGHT .... 1,822 LBS.
MSRP $12,599

RETAIL PRICING

YEAR	HIGH	LOW
1995	$2,586	$1,940
1996	$2,724	$2,043
1997	$2,906	$2,179

7193

YEARS MFRD 1996-1997
SERIES .... 7000 SERIES
ENGINE .... MITSUBISHI
CYLINDERS 3
CID 64.7
PTO HP 15
ENGINE HP 19
FUEL .... D
SPEEDS .... VARIABLE
TRANSMISSION .... HYDRO
STEERING .... STANDARD
PTO .... YES
WEIGHT .... 1,865 LBS.
MSRP $14,229

RETAIL PRICING

YEAR	HIGH	LOW
1996	$3,077	$2,308
1997	$3,236	$2,427

7194

YEARS MFRD 1995-1997
SERIES .... 7000 SERIES
ENGINE .... MITSUBISHI
CYLINDERS 3
CID 64.7
PTO HP 17
ENGINE HP 19
FUEL .... D
TRANSMISSION .... GEAR
STEERING .... STANDARD
PTO .... YES
DRIVE TYPE 4WD
ROPS/CAB .... ROPS
MSRP $13,729

RETAIL PRICING

YEAR	HIGH	LOW
1995	$2,817	$2,113
1996	$2,967	$2,226
1997	$3,123	$2,342

7195

YEARS MFRD 1995-1997
SERIES .... 7000 SERIES
ENGINE .... MITSUBISHI
CYLINDERS 3
CID 64.7
PTO HP 19
ENGINE HP 15
FUEL .... D
TRANSMISSION .... HYDRO
STEERING .... STANDARD
PTO .... YES
DRIVE TYPE 4WD
ROPS/CAB .... ROPS
WEIGHT .... 1,992 LBS.
MSRP $15,429

RETAIL PRICING

YEAR	HIGH	LOW
1995	$3,166	$2,375
1996	$3,332	$2,499
1997	$3,512	$2,634

7200

YEARS MFRD 1998-1999
SERIES .... 7000 SERIES
ENGINE .... MITSUBISHI
CYLINDERS 3
CID 69
PTO HP 17.5
ENGINE HP 20
COOLING .... LIQUID
FUEL .... D
TRANSMISSION .... GEAR
STEERING .... STANDARD
HITCH .... CAT. I
PTO .... YES
DRIVE TYPE 4WD
ROPS/CAB .... ROPS
WEIGHT .... 1,882 LBS.
MSRP $12,749

SERIAL NUMBERS

YEAR	BEGINNING NO.
1998	XXXX8XXXXXX

RETAIL PRICING

YEAR	HIGH	LOW
1998	$3,353	$2,515
1999	$3,524	$2,643

7205

YEARS MFRD 1998-1999
SERIES .... 7000 SERIES
ENGINE .... MITSUBISHI
CYLINDERS 3
CID 69
PTO HP 16
ENGINE HP 20
FUEL .... D
TRANSMISSION .... HYDRO
STEERING .... STANDARD
HITCH .... CAT. I
PTO .... YES
DRIVE TYPE 4WD
ROPS/CAB .... ROPS
WEIGHT .... 1,910 LBS.
MSRP $14,309

SERIAL NUMBERS

YEAR	BEGINNING NO.
1998	XXXX8XXXXXX

RETAIL PRICING

YEAR	HIGH	LOW
1998	$3,759	$2,819
1999	$3,953	$2,965

7232

YEARS MFRD 1995-1997
SERIES .... 7000 SERIES
ENGINE .... MITSUBISHI
CYLINDERS 3
CID 75.4
PTO HP 20
ENGINE HP 23
FUEL .... D
TRANSMISSION .... GEAR
STEERING .... STANDARD
PTO .... YES
DRIVE TYPE 2WD
ROPS/CAB .... ROPS
WEIGHT .... 2,391 LBS.
MSRP $13,939

RETAIL PRICING

YEAR	HIGH	LOW
1995	$3,272	$2,454
1996	$3,442	$2,581
1997	$3,655	$2,741

7233

YEARS MFRD 1996-1997
SERIES .... 7000 SERIES
ENGINE .... MITSUBISHI
CYLINDERS 3
CID 75.4
PTO HP 18
ENGINE HP 23
FUEL .... D
TRANSMISSION .... HYDRO
STEERING .... STANDARD
PTO .... YES
DRIVE TYPE 2WD
ROPS/CAB .... ROPS
WEIGHT .... 2,422 LBS.
MSRP $15,869

RETAIL PRICING

YEAR	HIGH	LOW
1996	$3,917	$2,937
1997	$4,134	$3,100

7234

YEARS MFRD 1995-1997
SERIES .... 7000 SERIES
ENGINE .... MITSUBISHI
CYLINDERS 3
CID 75.4
PTO HP 20
ENGINE HP 23
FUEL .... D
TRANSMISSION .... GEAR
STEERING .... STANDARD
PTO .... YES
DRIVE TYPE 4WD
ROPS/CAB .... ROPS
WEIGHT .... 2,510 LBS.
MSRP $15,159

RETAIL PRICING

YEAR	HIGH	LOW
1995	$3,557	$2,668
1996	$3,744	$2,808
1997	$3,943	$2,957

7235

YEARS MFRD 1995-1997
SERIES .... 7000 SERIES
ENGINE .... MITSUBISHI
CYLINDERS 3
CID 75.4
PTO HP 18
ENGINE HP 23
FUEL .... D
TRANSMISSION .... HYDRO
STEERING .... STANDARD
PTO .... YES
DRIVE TYPE 4WD
ROPS/CAB .... ROPS
WEIGHT .... 2,538 LBS.
MSRP $16,999

RETAIL PRICING

YEAR	HIGH	LOW
1995	$3,991	$2,994
1996	$4,197	$3,148
1997	$4,495	$3,371

7252

YEARS MFRD 2002-2002
SERIES .... 7000 SERIES
ENGINE .... KAWASAKI
PTO HP 20
ENGINE HP 25
COOLING .... LIQUID
FUEL .... G
TRANSMISSION .... HYDRO
STEERING .... STANDARD
HITCH .... CAT. I
DRIVE TYPE 2WD
MSRP $9,999

RETAIL PRICING

YEAR	HIGH	LOW
2002	$4,304	$3,228

7254

YEARS MFRD 2002-2002
SERIES . . . . 7000 SERIES
ENGINE . . . . KAWASAKI
PTO HP 20
ENGINE HP 25
COOLING . . . . LIQUID
FUEL . . . . G
TRANSMISSION . . . . HYDRO
STEERING . . . . STANDARD
HITCH . . . . CAT. I
DRIVE TYPE 4WD
MSRP $11,749

RETAIL PRICING

YEAR	HIGH	LOW
2002	$5,080	$3,810

7260

YEARS MFRD 1998-1999
SERIES . . . . 7000 SERIES
CYLINDERS 3
CID 80.4
PTO HP 23
ENGINE HP 26
FUEL . . . . D
TRANSMISSION . . . . GEAR
STEERING . . . . STANDARD
HITCH . . . . CAT. I
PTO . . . . YES
DRIVE TYPE 4WD
ROPS/CAB . . . . ROPS
WEIGHT . . . . 2,520 LBS.
MSRP $14,429

SERIAL NUMBERS

YEAR	BEGINNING NO.
1998	XXXX8XXXXXX

RETAIL PRICING

YEAR	HIGH	LOW
1998	$4,231	$3,173
1999	$4,455	$3,341

7264

YEARS MFRD 2004-2004
SERIES . . . . 7000 SERIES
ENGINE . . . . DAIHATSU
PTO HP 21
ENGINE HP 26
COOLING . . . . LIQUID
FUEL . . . . D
TRANSMISSION . . . . HYDRO
STEERING . . . . STANDARD
HITCH . . . . CAT. I
PTO . . . . YES
DRIVE TYPE 4WD
MSRP $13,199

OPTIONS

60" DECK

RETAIL PRICING

YEAR	HIGH	LOW
2004	$6,092	$4,569

7265

YEARS MFRD 1998-1999
SERIES . . . . 7000 SERIES
ENGINE . . . . MITSUBISHI
CYLINDERS 3
CID 80.4
PTO HP 21
ENGINE HP 26
COOLING . . . . LIQUID
FUEL . . . . D
TRANSMISSION . . . . HYDRO
STEERING . . . . STANDARD
HITCH . . . . CAT. I
PTO . . . . YES
DRIVE TYPE 4WD
ROPS/CAB . . . . ROPS
WEIGHT . . . . 2,552 LBS.
MSRP $15,820

SERIAL NUMBERS

YEAR	BEGINNING NO.
1998	XXXX8XXXXXX

RETAIL PRICING

YEAR	HIGH	LOW
1998	$4,641	$3,481
1999	$4,885	$3,664

7272

YEARS MFRD 1995-1997
SERIES . . . . 7000 SERIES
ENGINE . . . . MITSUBISHI
CYLINDERS 3
CID 91.3
PTO HP 23
ENGINE HP 27
FUEL . . . . D
TRANSMISSION . . . . GEAR
STEERING . . . . STANDARD
PTO . . . . YES
DRIVE TYPE 2WD
ROPS/CAB . . . . ROPS
WEIGHT . . . . 2,433 LBS.
MSRP $15,749

RETAIL PRICING

YEAR	HIGH	LOW
1995	$3,694	$2,771
1996	$3,889	$2,917
1997	$4,097	$3,073

7273

YEARS MFRD 1996-1997
SERIES . . . . 7000 SERIES
ENGINE . . . . MITSUBISHI
CYLINDERS 3
CID 91.3
PTO HP 21
ENGINE HP 27
FUEL . . . . D
TRANSMISSION . . . . HYDRO
STEERING . . . . STANDARD
PTO . . . . YES
DRIVE TYPE 2WD
ROPS/CAB . . . . ROPS
WEIGHT . . . . 2,472 LBS.
MSRP $17,149

RETAIL PRICING

YEAR	HIGH	LOW
1996	$4,235	$3,176
1997	$4,491	$3,368

7274

YEARS MFRD 1995-1997
SERIES . . . . 7000 SERIES
ENGINE . . . . MITSUBISHI
CYLINDERS 3
CID 91.3
PTO HP 23
ENGINE HP 27
FUEL . . . . D
TRANSMISSION . . . . GEAR
STEERING . . . . STANDARD
PTO . . . . YES
DRIVE TYPE 4WD
ROPS/CAB . . . . ROPS
WEIGHT . . . . 2,566 LBS.
MSRP $17,389

RETAIL PRICING

YEAR	HIGH	LOW
1995	$4,207	$3,155
1996	$4,430	$3,323
1997	$4,665	$3,499

7275

YEARS MFRD 1995-1997
SERIES . . . . 7000 SERIES
ENGINE . . . . MITSUBISHI
CYLINDERS 3
CID 91.3
PTO HP 21
ENGINE HP 27
FUEL . . . . D
TRANSMISSION . . . . HYDRO
STEERING . . . . STANDARD
PTO . . . . YES
DRIVE TYPE 4WD
ROPS/CAB . . . . ROPS
WEIGHT . . . . 2,595 LBS.
MSRP $18,799

RETAIL PRICING

YEAR	HIGH	LOW
1995	$4,410	$3,307
1996	$4,646	$3,485
1997	$4,967	$3,725

7284

YEARS MFRD 2004-2004
SERIES . . . . 7000 SERIES
ENGINE . . . . CAT
CYLINDERS 3
CID 69
PTO HP 21
ENGINE HP 28
COOLING . . . . LIQUID
FUEL . . . . D
SPEEDS . . . . VARIABLE
TRANSMISSION . . . . HYDRO
STEERING . . . . STANDARD
HYDRAULIC . . . . YES
PTO . . . . YES
DRIVE TYPE 4WD
ROPS/CAB . . . . ROPS
WEIGHT . . . . 1,953 LBS.

7300

YEARS MFRD 1998-1999
SERIES . . . . 7000 SERIES
ENGINE . . . . MITSUBISHI
CYLINDERS 3
CID 91.3
PTO HP 26
ENGINE HP 30
FUEL . . . . D
TRANSMISSION . . . . GEAR
STEERING . . . . STANDARD
HITCH . . . . CAT. I
PTO . . . . YES
DRIVE TYPE 4WD
ROPS/CAB . . . . ROPS
WEIGHT . . . . 2,576 LBS.
MSRP $15,839

SERIAL NUMBERS

YEAR	BEGINNING NO.
1998	XXXX8XXXXXX

RETAIL PRICING

YEAR	HIGH	LOW
1998	$4,646	$3,485
1999	$4,890	$3,668

7305

YEARS MFRD 1998-1999
SERIES . . . . 7000 SERIES
ENGINE . . . . MITSUBISHI
CYLINDERS 3
CID 91.3
PTO HP 24
ENGINE HP 30
COOLING . . . . LIQUID
FUEL . . . . D
TRANSMISSION . . . . HYDRO
STEERING . . . . STANDARD
HITCH . . . . CAT. I
PTO . . . . YES
DRIVE TYPE 4WD
ROPS/CAB . . . . ROPS
WEIGHT . . . . 2,605 LBS.
MSRP $17,139

SERIAL NUMBERS

YEAR	BEGINNING NO.
1998	XXXX8XXXXXX

RETAIL PRICING

YEAR	HIGH	LOW
1998	$5,027	$3,770
1999	$5,293	$3,970

AVG. AUCTION PRICING

LOW	HIGH	AVG
$3,462	$6,924	$5,193

7360

YEARS MFRD 1999-1999
SERIES . . . . 7000 SERIES
ENGINE . . . . MITSUBISHI
CYLINDERS 4
CID 107.3
PTO HP 29.5

CUB CADET

ENGINE HP . . . 36
FUEL . . . D
SPEEDS . . . 8/8
TRANSMISSION . . . GEAR
STEERING . . . STANDARD
HITCH . . . CAT. I
PTO . . . YES
DRIVE TYPE . . . 4WD
ROPS/CAB . . . ROPS
WEIGHT . . . 3,197 LBS.
MSRP . . . $18,854

RETAIL PRICING

YEAR	HIGH	LOW
1999	$5,825	$4,369

7530

YEARS MFRD . . . 2004-2006
SERIES . . . 7500 SERIES
ENGINE . . . MITSUBISHI TURBO
CYLINDERS . . . 3
CID . . . 91.3
PTO HP . . . 26
ENGINE HP . . . 30
COOLING . . . LIQUID
FUEL . . . D
SPEEDS . . . 8/8
TRANSMISSION . . . SHUTTLE SHIFT
STEERING . . . STANDARD
HITCH . . . CAT. I
HYDRAULIC . . . YES
PTO . . . YES
DRIVE TYPE . . . 4WD
ROPS/CAB . . . ROPS
STANDARD DECK . . . 60"
WEIGHT . . . 2,121 LBS.
MSRP . . . $12,799

OPTIONS

BACKHOE
LDR

RETAIL PRICING

YEAR	HIGH	LOW
2004	$5,540	$4,155
2005	$5,829	$4,372
2006	$6,138	$4,603

7532

YEARS MFRD . . . 2004-2006
SERIES . . . 7500 SERIES
ENGINE . . . MITSUBISHI TURBO
CYLINDERS . . . 3
CID . . . 91.3
PTO HP . . . 25.5
ENGINE HP . . . 32
COOLING . . . LIQUID
FUEL . . . D
SPEEDS . . . 3 RANGES
TRANSMISSION . . . HYDRO
STEERING . . . STANDARD
HITCH . . . CAT. I
HYDRAULIC . . . YES
PTO . . . YES
DRIVE TYPE . . . 4WD
ROPS/CAB . . . ROPS
STANDARD DECK . . . 60"
WEIGHT . . . 2,275 LBS.
MSRP . . . $13,799

OPTIONS

LDR

RETAIL PRICING

YEAR	HIGH	LOW
2004	$5,972	$4,479
2005	$6,283	$4,712
2006	$6,616	$4,962

8354

YEARS MFRD . . . 2004-2006
SERIES . . . 8000 SERIES
ENGINE . . . DAEDONG
CYLINDERS . . . 3
CID . . . 100.5
PTO HP . . . 23.8
ENGINE HP . . . 35
COOLING . . . LIQUID
FUEL . . . D
SPEEDS . . . 8/8
TRANSMISSION . . . SHUTTLE SHIFT
STEERING . . . STANDARD
HITCH . . . CAT. I
HYDRAULIC . . . YES
PTO . . . YES
DRIVE TYPE . . . 4WD
ROPS/CAB . . . ROPS
WEIGHT . . . 3,872 LBS.
MSRP . . . $15,999

OPTIONS

BACKHOE
LDR

RETAIL PRICING

YEAR	HIGH	LOW
2004	$6,922	$5,191
2005	$7,287	$5,465
2006	$7,670	$5,753

8404

YEARS MFRD . . . 2004-2004
SERIES . . . 8000 SERIES
ENGINE . . . DAEDONG
CYLINDERS . . . 4
CID . . . 121.9
PTO HP . . . 33.4
ENGINE HP . . . 41
COOLING . . . LIQUID
FUEL . . . D
SPEEDS . . . 8/8
TRANSMISSION . . . HYDRO
STEERING . . . STANDARD
HITCH . . . CAT. I
HYDRAULIC . . . YES
PTO . . . YES
DRIVE TYPE . . . 4WD
ROPS/CAB . . . ROPS
WEIGHT . . . 4,182 LBS.
MSRP . . . $19,999

OPTIONS

BACKHOE
LDR

RETAIL PRICING

YEAR	HIGH	LOW
2004	$9,425	$7,069

8454

YEARS MFRD . . . 2004-2006
SERIES . . . 8000 SERIES
ENGINE . . . DAEDONG
CYLINDERS . . . 4
CID . . . 134
PTO HP . . . 38
ENGINE HP . . . 45
COOLING . . . LIQUID
FUEL . . . D
SPEEDS . . . 12/12
TRANSMISSION . . . HYDRO
STEERING . . . STANDARD
HITCH . . . CAT. II
HYDRAULIC . . . YES
PTO . . . YES
DRIVE TYPE . . . 4WD
ROPS/CAB . . . ROPS
WEIGHT . . . 4,468 LBS.
MSRP . . . $17,999

OPTIONS

BACKHOE
LDR

RETAIL PRICING

YEAR	HIGH	LOW
2004	$7,787	$5,840
2005	$8,198	$6,148
2006	$8,629	$6,472

CUB CADET YANMAR

EX450

YEARS MFRD . . . 2009-2010
ENGINE . . . YANMAR
CYLINDERS . . . 4
CID . . . 133
PTO HP . . . 37.5
ENGINE HP . . . 45
COOLING . . . LIQUID
FUEL . . . D
SPEEDS . . . 9/9
TRANSMISSION . . . GEAR
STEERING . . . STANDARD
HYDRAULIC . . . YES
PTO . . . YES
WEIGHT . . . 3,464 LBS.
MSRP . . . $21,299

OPTIONS

LDR

RETAIL PRICING

YEAR	HIGH	LOW
2009	$10,052	$7,539
2010	$10,632	$7,974

EX450 TL

YEARS MFRD . . . 2009-2010
ENGINE . . . YANMAR
CYLINDERS . . . 4
CID . . . 133.6
PTO HP . . . 37.5
ENGINE HP . . . 45
COOLING . . . LIQUID
FUEL . . . D
SPEEDS . . . 9/9
TRANSMISSION . . . SHUTTLE SHIFT
STEERING . . . STANDARD
WEIGHT . . . 2,464 LBS.
MSRP . . . $23,939

RETAIL PRICING

YEAR	HIGH	LOW
2009	$11,643	$8,732
2010	$12,165	$9,124

EX450 TLB

YEARS MFRD . . . 2009-2012
ENGINE . . . YANMAR
CYLINDERS . . . 4
CID . . . 133.6
PTO HP . . . 37.5
ENGINE HP . . . 45
COOLING . . . LIQUID
FUEL . . . D
SPEEDS . . . 9/9
TRANSMISSION . . . SHUTTLE SHIFT
STEERING . . . STANDARD
HITCH . . . CAT. I
HYDRAULIC . . . YES
PTO . . . YES
MSRP . . . $37,999

RETAIL PRICING

YEAR	HIGH	LOW
2009	$13,485	$10,114
2010	$14,741	$11,056
2011	$17,317	$12,988
2012	$19,334	$14,501

EX2900

YEARS MFRD . . . 2008-2010
ENGINE . . . YANMAR
CYLINDERS . . . 3
ENGINE HP . . . 28.7
COOLING . . . LIQUID
FUEL . . . D
SPEEDS . . . VARIABLE
TRANSMISSION . . . HYDRO
STEERING . . . STANDARD
HITCH . . . CAT. I
HYDRAULIC . . . YES
PTO . . . YES
WEIGHT . . . 2,540 LBS.
MSRP . . . $15,599

OPTIONS

60" DECK
LDR

RETAIL PRICING

YEAR	HIGH	LOW
2008	$7,112	$5,334
2009	$7,361	$5,521
2010	$7,788	$5,841

EX2900 TL

YEARS MFRD . . . 2008-2010
ENGINE . . . YANMAR
CYLINDERS . . . 3

CID	100.2
ENGINE HP	28.7
COOLING	LIQUID
FUEL	D
SPEEDS	VARIABLE
TRANSMISSION	HYDRO
STEERING	STANDARD
HITCH	CAT. I
WEIGHT	3,355 LBS.
MSRP	$17,414

RETAIL PRICING

YEAR	HIGH	LOW
2008	$8,086	$6,064
2009	$8,448	$6,336
2010	$8,829	$6,622

EX2900 TLB

YEARS MFRD	2011-2012
ENGINE	YANMAR
CYLINDERS	3
CID	100.2
ENGINE HP	27.4
COOLING	LIQUID
FUEL	D
SPEEDS	VARIABLE
TRANSMISSION	HYDRO
STEERING	STANDARD
HITCH	CAT. I
WEIGHT	4,504 LBS.
MSRP	$28,399

RETAIL PRICING

YEAR	HIGH	LOW
2011	$12,955	$9,716
2012	$14,442	$10,832

EX3200

YEARS MFRD	2008-2009
ENGINE	YANMAR
CYLINDERS	3
CID	100.1
ENGINE HP	32
COOLING	LIQUID
FUEL	D
SPEEDS	VARIABLE
TRANSMISSION	HYDRO
STEERING	STANDARD
HITCH	CAT. I
HYDRAULIC	YES
PTO	YES
WEIGHT	2,550 LBS.
MSRP	$16,599

OPTIONS

60" DECK
LDR

RETAIL PRICING

YEAR	HIGH	LOW
2008	$7,610	$5,707
2009	$8,038	$6,029

AVG. AUCTION PRICING

LOW	HIGH	AVG
$8,822	$9,662	$9,191

EX3200 TL

YEARS MFRD	2008-2009
ENGINE	YANMAR
CYLINDERS	3
ENGINE HP	32
COOLING	LIQUID
FUEL	D
SPEEDS	VARIABLE
TRANSMISSION	HYDRO
STEERING	STANDARD
HITCH	CAT. I
HYDRAULIC	YES
PTO	YES
WEIGHT	3,365 LBS.
MSRP	$18,414

RETAIL PRICING

YEAR	HIGH	LOW
2008	$8,913	$6,685
2009	$9,320	$6,990

AVG. AUCTION PRICING

LOW	HIGH	AVG
$8,470	$9,277	$8,822

EX3200 TLB

YEARS MFRD	2011-2012
ENGINE	YANMAR
CYLINDERS	3
CID	100.1
PTO HP	25.5
ENGINE HP	32
COOLING	LIQUID
FUEL	D
SPEEDS	VARIABLE
TRANSMISSION	HYDRO
STEERING	STANDARD
HITCH	CAT. I
HYDRAULIC	YES
PTO	YES
WEIGHT	4,511 LBS.
MSRP	$31,299

RETAIL PRICING

YEAR	HIGH	LOW
2011	$14,277	$10,708
2012	$15,930	$11,948

LX410

YEARS MFRD	2011-2012
ENGINE	YANMAR
CYLINDERS	4
CID	133
PTO HP	32.5
COOLING	LIQUID
FUEL	D
SPEEDS	12/12
TRANSMISSION	SHUTTLE SHIFT
STEERING	STANDARD
WEIGHT	3,464 LBS.
MSRP	$25,399

RETAIL PRICING

YEAR	HIGH	LOW
2011	$11,601	$8,701
2012	$12,923	$9,692

LX410TL

YEARS MFRD	2011-2012
ENGINE	YANMAR
CYLINDERS	4
CID	133
PTO HP	32.5
FUEL	D
SPEEDS	12/12
TRANSMISSION	SHUTTLE SHIFT
STEERING	STANDARD
HYDRAULIC	YES
PTO	YES
WEIGHT	3,664 LBS.
MSRP	$30,799

RETAIL PRICING

YEAR	HIGH	LOW
2011	$14,046	$10,534
2012	$15,666	$11,750

LX410TLB

YEARS MFRD	2011-2012
ENGINE	YANMAR
CYLINDERS	4
CID	133
PTO HP	32.5
FUEL	D
SPEEDS	12/12
TRANSMISSION	SHUTTLE SHIFT
STEERING	STANDARD
WEIGHT	3,710 LBS.
MSRP	$40,999

RETAIL PRICING

YEAR	HIGH	LOW
2011	$18,706	$14,030
2012	$20,854	$15,641

LX450

YEARS MFRD	2011-2012
ENGINE	YANMAR
CYLINDERS	4
CID	133
PTO HP	36
FUEL	D
SPEEDS	12/12
TRANSMISSION	SHUTTLE SHIFT
STEERING	STANDARD
WEIGHT	3,464 LBS.
MSRP	$27,399

RETAIL PRICING

YEAR	HIGH	LOW
2011	$12,494	$9,370
2012	$13,947	$10,460

LX450TL

YEARS MFRD	2011-2012
ENGINE	YANMAR
CYLINDERS	4
CID	133
PTO HP	36
FUEL	D
SPEEDS	12/12
TRANSMISSION	SHUTTLE SHIFT
STEERING	STANDARD
WEIGHT	3,464 LBS.
MSRP	$32,799

RETAIL PRICING

YEAR	HIGH	LOW
2011	$14,972	$11,229
2012	$16,690	$12,517

LX450TLB

YEARS MFRD	2011-2012
ENGINE	YANMAR
CYLINDERS	4
CID	133
PTO HP	36
FUEL	D
SPEEDS	12/12
TRANSMISSION	SHUTTLE SHIFT
STEERING	STANDARD
HYDRAULIC	YES
PTO	YES
WEIGHT	3,464 LBS.
MSRP	$42,999

RETAIL PRICING

YEAR	HIGH	LOW
2011	$19,599	$14,699
2012	$21,879	$16,409

LX490

YEARS MFRD	2011-2012
ENGINE	YANMAR TURBO
CYLINDERS	4
CID	119
PTO HP	39
COOLING	LIQUID
FUEL	D
SPEEDS	12/12
TRANSMISSION	SHUTTLE SHIFT
STEERING	STANDARD
HYDRAULIC	YES
PTO	YES
WEIGHT	3,464 LBS.
MSRP	$29,499

RETAIL PRICING

YEAR	HIGH	LOW
2011	$13,453	$10,090
2012	$15,005	$11,254

LX490TL

YEARS MFRD	2011-2012
ENGINE	YANMAR TURBO
CYLINDERS	4
CID	119
PTO HP	39
COOLING	LIQUID
FUEL	D
SPEEDS	12/12
TRANSMISSION	SHUTTLE SHIFT
STEERING	STANDARD
HYDRAULIC	YES
PTO	YES
WEIGHT	3,464 LBS.
MSRP	$34,999

RETAIL PRICING

YEAR	HIGH	LOW
2011	$15,963	$11,972
2012	$17,815	$13,361

CUB CADET YANMAR

LX490TLB

YEARS MFRD 2011-2012
ENGINE . . . . YANMAR TURBO
CYLINDERS. 4
CID 119
PTO HP 39
COOLING . . . . LIQUID
FUEL . . . . D
SPEEDS 12/12
TRANSMISSION . . . SHUTTLE SHIFT
STEERING. . . . . STANDARD
HYDRAULIC . . . . YES
PTO . . . . YES
WEIGHT . . . . 3,464 LBS.
MSRP. $44,999

RETAIL PRICING

YEAR	HIGH	LOW
2011	$20,523	$15,392
2012	$22,904	$17,178

SC2400

YEARS MFRD 2008-2010
ENGINE . . . . YANMAR
CYLINDERS. 3
CID 55.1
PTO HP 16.5
ENGINE HP 24
COOLING . . . . LIQUID
FUEL . . . . D
SPEEDS . . . . VARIABLE
TRANSMISSION . . . . HYDRO
STEERING. . . . . STANDARD
HITCH . . . . CAT. I
HYDRAULIC . . . . YES
PTO . . . . YES
WEIGHT . . . . 1,280 LBS.
MSRP. $10,999

OPTIONS

60" DECK
LDR

RETAIL PRICING

YEAR	HIGH	LOW
2008	$4,931	$3,698
2009	$5,190	$3,892
2010	$5,463	$4,097

SC2400 TD

YEARS MFRD 2009-2012
ENGINE . . . . YANMAR
CYLINDERS. 3
CID 55.1
PTO HP 16.5
ENGINE HP 24
COOLING . . . . LIQUID
FUEL . . . . D
SPEEDS . . . . VARIABLE
TRANSMISSION . . . . HYDRO
STEERING. . . . . STANDARD
HITCH . . . . CAT. I
HYDRAULIC . . . . YES
PTO . . . . YES
STANDARD DECK . . . . 60"
WEIGHT . . . . 1,516 LBS.
MSRP. $14,699

RETAIL PRICING

YEAR	HIGH	LOW
2009	$5,024	$3,768
2010	$5,717	$4,288
2011	$6,709	$5,032
2012	$7,469	$5,602

SC2400 TL

YEARS MFRD 2008-2010
ENGINE . . . . YANMAR
CYLINDERS. 3
CID 55.1
ENGINE HP 24
COOLING . . . . LIQUID
FUEL . . . . D
SPEEDS . . . . VARIABLE
TRANSMISSION . . . . HYDRO
STEERING. . . . . STANDARD
HITCH . . . . CAT. I
HYDRAULIC . . . . YES
PTO . . . . YES
WEIGHT . . . . 1,725 LBS.
MSRP. $12,449

RETAIL PRICING

YEAR	HIGH	LOW
2008	$5,813	$4,360
2009	$6,070	$4,553
2010	$6,339	$4,754

SC2400 TLD

YEARS MFRD 2009-2012
ENGINE . . . . YANMAR
CYLINDERS. 3
CID 55.1
PTO HP 16.5
ENGINE HP 24
COOLING . . . . LIQUID
FUEL . . . . D
SPEEDS . . . . VARIABLE
TRANSMISSION . . . . HYDRO
STEERING. . . . . STANDARD
HITCH . . . . CAT. I
HYDRAULIC . . . . YES
PTO . . . . YES
STANDARD DECK . . . . 60"
WEIGHT . . . . 1,961 LBS.
MSRP. $18,399

RETAIL PRICING

YEAR	HIGH	LOW
2009	$6,246	$4,684
2010	$7,172	$5,379
2011	$8,395	$6,297
2012	$9,354	$7,015

SC2450

YEARS MFRD 2010-2012
ENGINE . . . . YANMAR
CYLINDERS. 3
CID 55.1
ENGINE HP 20.4
COOLING . . . . LIQUID
FUEL . . . . D
SPEEDS . . . . VARIABLE
TRANSMISSION . . . . HYDRO
STEERING. . . . . STANDARD
HYDRAULIC . . . . YES
PTO . . . . YES
WEIGHT . . . . 2,525 LBS.
MSRP. $21,799

RETAIL PRICING

YEAR	HIGH	LOW
2010	$8,494	$6,371
2011	$9,948	$7,461
2012	$11,105	$8,328

SX3100

YEARS MFRD 2010-2010
ENGINE . . . . YANMAR
CYLINDERS. 3
CID 100.2
ENGINE HP 31
COOLING . . . . LIQUID
FUEL . . . . D
SPEEDS . . . . VARIABLE
TRANSMISSION . . . . HYDRO
STEERING. . . . . STANDARD
HITCH . . . . CAT. I
HYDRAULIC . . . . YES
PTO . . . . YES
WEIGHT . . . . 1,973 LBS.
MSRP. $19,165

OPTIONS

61" DECK
LDR

RETAIL PRICING

YEAR	HIGH	LOW
2010	$9,522	$7,141

SX3100 TD

YEARS MFRD 2010-2012
ENGINE . . . . YANMAR
CYLINDERS. 3
CID 100.2
ENGINE HP 30
COOLING . . . . LIQUID
FUEL . . . . D
SPEEDS . . . . VARIABLE
TRANSMISSION . . . . HYDRO
STEERING. . . . . STANDARD
HITCH . . . . CAT. I
HYDRAULIC . . . . YES
PTO . . . . YES
WEIGHT . . . . 2,544 LBS.
MSRP. $22,899

RETAIL PRICING

YEAR	HIGH	LOW
2010	$8,923	$6,692
2011	$10,443	$7,832
2012	$11,666	$8,750

SX3100 TL

YEARS MFRD 2010-2010
ENGINE . . . . YANMAR
CYLINDERS. 3
CID 100.2
ENGINE HP 30
COOLING . . . . LIQUID
FUEL . . . . D
SPEEDS . . . . VARIABLE
TRANSMISSION . . . . HYDRO
STEERING. . . . . STANDARD
HITCH . . . . CAT. I
HYDRAULIC . . . . YES
PTO . . . . YES
WEIGHT . . . . 2,580 LBS.
MSRP. $20,410

RETAIL PRICING

YEAR	HIGH	LOW
2010	$10,197	$7,647

SX3100 TLB

YEARS MFRD 2010-2012
ENGINE . . . . YANMAR
CYLINDERS. 3
CID 100.2
ENGINE HP 30
COOLING . . . . LIQUID
FUEL . . . . D
SPEEDS . . . . VARIABLE
TRANSMISSION . . . . HYDRO
STEERING. . . . . STANDARD
HITCH . . . . CAT. I
HYDRAULIC . . . . YES
PTO . . . . YES
WEIGHT . . . . 3,986 LBS.
MSRP. $31,299

RETAIL PRICING

YEAR	HIGH	LOW
2010	$12,229	$9,172
2011	$14,277	$10,708
2012	$15,930	$11,948

SX3100 TLD

YEARS MFRD 2010-2012
ENGINE . . . . YANMAR
CYLINDERS. 3
CID 100.2
ENGINE HP 30
COOLING . . . . LIQUID
FUEL . . . . D
SPEEDS . . . . VARIABLE
TRANSMISSION . . . . HYDRO
STEERING. . . . . STANDARD
HITCH . . . . CAT. I
HYDRAULIC . . . . YES
PTO . . . . YES
WEIGHT . . . . 3,030 LBS.
MSRP. $26,699

RETAIL PRICING

YEAR	HIGH	LOW
2010	$10,411	$7,808
2011	$12,164	$9,123
2012	$13,584	$10,188

DEINES

ALL MODELS

SERIAL NUMBERS

FIRST TWO # OF SERIAL # REVERSE AND THAT IS THE YEAR MFG.

D1840

YEARS MFRD 2011-2017
ENGINE . . . . KOHLER
ENGINE HP 18
COOLING . . . . AIR
FUEL . . . . G
SPEEDS . . . . VARIABLE
TRANSMISSION . . . . HYDRO
STEERING. . . . . ZERO
STANDARD DECK . . . . 39"
MSRP. $11,310

RETAIL PRICING

YEAR	HIGH	LOW
2011	$3,378	$2,534
2012	$4,157	$3,118
2013	$5,432	$4,074
2014	$5,772	$4,329
2015	$6,666	$4,999
2016	$7,801	$5,851
2017	$8,584	$6,438

D1848

YEARS MFRD 2011-2017
ENGINE . . . . KOHLER
ENGINE HP 18
COOLING . . . . AIR
FUEL . . . . G
SPEEDS . . . . VARIABLE
TRANSMISSION . . . . HYDRO
STEERING. . . . . ZERO
STANDARD DECK . . . . 47"
MSRP. $11,715

RETAIL PRICING

YEAR	HIGH	LOW
2011	$3,535	$2,651
2012	$4,331	$3,248
2013	$5,733	$4,300
2014	$6,831	$5,123
2015	$7,284	$5,463
2016	$7,990	$5,992
2017	$9,045	$6,784

D1850

YEARS MFRD 2011-2017
ENGINE . . . . KOHLER
ENGINE HP 18
COOLING . . . . AIR
FUEL . . . . G
SPEEDS . . . . VARIABLE
TRANSMISSION . . . . HYDRO
STEERING. . . . . ZERO
STANDARD DECK . . . . 49"
MSRP. $11,525

RETAIL PRICING

YEAR	HIGH	LOW
2011	$3,453	$2,589
2012	$4,239	$3,180
2013	$5,633	$4,225
2014	$6,683	$5,012
2015	$7,905	$5,929
2016	$8,531	$6,398
2017	$8,628	$6,471

D1850 HT

YEARS MFRD 2011-2017
ENGINE . . . . KOHLER
ENGINE HP 18
COOLING . . . . AIR
FUEL . . . . G
SPEEDS . . . . VARIABLE
TRANSMISSION . . . . HYDRO
STEERING. . . . . ZERO
STANDARD DECK . . . . 49"
MSRP. $12,165

RETAIL PRICING

YEAR	HIGH	LOW
2011	$3,973	$2,980
2012	$4,866	$3,649
2013	$6,052	$4,539
2014	$7,202	$5,402
2015	$7,926	$5,945
2016	$8,856	$6,642
2017	$9,714	$7,285

D1860

YEARS MFRD 2011-2017
ENGINE . . . . KOHLER
ENGINE HP 18
COOLING . . . . AIR
FUEL . . . . G
SPEEDS . . . . VARIABLE
TRANSMISSION . . . . HYDRO
STEERING. . . . . ZERO
STANDARD DECK . . . . 58"
MSRP. $12,045

RETAIL PRICING

YEAR	HIGH	LOW
2011	$3,704	$2,778
2012	$4,405	$3,304
2013	$5,772	$4,329
2014	$6,898	$5,174
2015	$8,405	$6,304
2016	$9,053	$6,790
2017	$9,704	$7,278

D1860 HT

YEARS MFRD 2011-2017
ENGINE . . . . KOHLER
ENGINE HP 18
COOLING . . . . AIR
FUEL . . . . G
SPEEDS . . . . VARIABLE
TRANSMISSION . . . . HYDRO
STEERING. . . . . ZERO
STANDARD DECK . . . . 58"
MSRP. $12,615

RETAIL PRICING

YEAR	HIGH	LOW
2011	$3,942	$2,956
2012	$4,852	$3,639
2013	$6,095	$4,571
2014	$7,254	$5,440
2015	$8,734	$6,550
2016	$8,697	$6,522
2017	$10,051	$7,538

D2060

YEARS MFRD 2011-2017
ENGINE . . . . KOHLER
ENGINE HP 20
COOLING . . . . AIR
FUEL . . . . G
SPEEDS . . . . VARIABLE
TRANSMISSION . . . . HYDRO
STEERING. . . . . ZERO
STANDARD DECK . . . . 58"
WEIGHT . . . . 1,030 LBS.
MSRP. $13,200

RETAIL PRICING

YEAR	HIGH	LOW
2011	$4,066	$3,050
2012	$5,692	$4,269
2013	$6,385	$4,789
2014	$7,602	$5,701
2015	$8,906	$6,680
2016	$9,449	$7,087
2017	$10,739	$8,054

D2060 HT

YEARS MFRD 2011-2017
ENGINE . . . . KOHLER
ENGINE HP 20
COOLING . . . . AIR
FUEL . . . . G
SPEEDS . . . . VARIABLE
TRANSMISSION . . . . HYDRO
STEERING. . . . . ZERO
STANDARD DECK . . . . 58"
MSRP. $14,255

RETAIL PRICING

YEAR	HIGH	LOW
2011	$4,504	$3,378
2012	$5,609	$4,206
2013	$6,992	$5,244
2014	$8,215	$6,162
2015	$9,961	$7,471
2016	$10,662	$7,997
2017	$11,397	$8,548

D2072

YEARS MFRD 2011-2017
ENGINE . . . . KOHLER
ENGINE HP 20
COOLING . . . . AIR
FUEL . . . . G
SPEEDS . . . . VARIABLE
TRANSMISSION . . . . HYDRO
STEERING. . . . . ZERO
STANDARD DECK . . . . 70"
WEIGHT . . . . 1,079 LBS.
MSRP. $13,490

RETAIL PRICING

YEAR	HIGH	LOW
2011	$4,140	$3,105
2012	$5,035	$3,776
2013	$6,552	$4,914
2014	$7,760	$5,820
2015	$9,128	$6,846
2016	$10,333	$7,750
2017	$11,388	$8,541

D2072 HT

YEARS MFRD 2011-2017
ENGINE . . . . KOHLER
ENGINE HP 20
COOLING . . . . AIR
FUEL . . . . G
SPEEDS . . . . VARIABLE
TRANSMISSION . . . . HYDRO
STEERING. . . . . ZERO
STANDARD DECK . . . . 70"
MSRP. $14,520

RETAIL PRICING

YEAR	HIGH	LOW
2011	$4,674	$3,505
2012	$5,692	$4,269
2013	$6,964	$5,223
2014	$8,466	$6,350
2015	$9,822	$7,366
2016	$11,322	$8,491
2017	$12,547	$9,410

D2360 HT

YEARS MFRD 2011-2017
ENGINE . . . . KOHLER
ENGINE HP 23
COOLING . . . . AIR
FUEL . . . . G
SPEEDS . . . . VARIABLE
TRANSMISSION . . . . HYDRO
STEERING. . . . . STANDARD
STANDARD DECK . . . . 58"
WEIGHT . . . . 1,030 LBS.
MSRP. $14,460

RETAIL PRICING

YEAR	HIGH	LOW
2011	$4,698	$3,524
2012	$5,724	$4,293
2013	$6,982	$5,236
2014	$8,433	$6,325
2015	$9,945	$7,459
2016	$11,449	$8,587
2017	$12,432	$9,324

D2372 HT

YEARS MFRD 2011-2017
ENGINE . . . . KOHLER
ENGINE HP 23
COOLING . . . . AIR
FUEL . . . . G
SPEEDS . . . . VARIABLE
TRANSMISSION . . . . HYDRO
STEERING. . . . . STANDARD
STANDARD DECK . . . . 70"
WEIGHT , ... 1,079 LBS.
MSRP. $14,675

DEINES

RETAIL PRICING

YEAR	HIGH	LOW
2011	$4,764	$3,573
2012	$5,721	$4,291
2013	$7,047	$5,285
2014	$8,472	$6,354
2015	$9,242	$6,932
2016	$10,986	$8,239
2017	$12,121	$9,090

1840

YEARS MFRD 1998-1999
SERIES .... OHV SERIES
ENGINE .... KOHLER OHV
CYLINDERS 2
ENGINE HP 18
FUEL .... G
SPEEDS .... VARIABLE
TRANSMISSION .... HYDRO
STEERING .... STANDARD
STANDARD DECK .... 40"
WEIGHT .... 905 LBS.
MSRP $7,160

SERIAL NUMBERS

YEAR	BEGINNING NO.
1998	L1151

RETAIL PRICING

YEAR	HIGH	LOW
1998	$1,025	$769
1999	$1,138	$853

1848

YEARS MFRD 1971-1999
SERIES .... OHV SERIES
ENGINE .... KOHLER OHV
CYLINDERS 2
ENGINE HP 18
COOLING .... AIR
FUEL .... G
SPEEDS .... VARIABLE
TRANSMISSION .... HYDRO
STEERING .... STANDARD
STANDARD DECK .... 48"
WEIGHT .... 990 LBS.
MSRP $7,655

SERIAL NUMBERS

YEAR	BEGINNING NO.
1998	L1151

RETAIL PRICING

YEAR	HIGH	LOW
1991	$559	$419
1992	$620	$465
1993	$686	$515
1994	$763	$573
1995	$848	$636
1996	$941	$706
1997	$1,041	$781
1998	$1,156	$867
1999	$1,284	$963

1850

YEARS MFRD 1978-1999
SERIES .... OHV SERIES
ENGINE .... KOHLER OHV
CYLINDERS 2
ENGINE HP 18
COOLING .... AIR
FUEL .... G
SPEEDS .... VARIABLE
TRANSMISSION .... HYDRO
STEERING .... STANDARD
STANDARD DECK .... 50"
WEIGHT .... 922 LBS.
MSRP $7,555

SERIAL NUMBERS

YEAR	BEGINNING NO.
1998	L1151

RETAIL PRICING

YEAR	HIGH	LOW
1991	$552	$414
1992	$613	$460
1993	$679	$509
1994	$752	$564
1995	$837	$628
1996	$926	$695
1997	$1,030	$772
1998	$1,142	$856
1999	$1,264	$948

1860

YEARS MFRD 1971-1999
SERIES .... OHV SERIES
ENGINE .... KOHLER OHV
CYLINDERS 2
ENGINE HP 18
COOLING .... AIR
FUEL .... G
SPEEDS .... VARIABLE
TRANSMISSION .... HYDRO
STEERING .... STANDARD
STANDARD DECK .... 60"
WEIGHT .... 1,005 LBS.
MSRP $7,850

SERIAL NUMBERS

YEAR	BEGINNING NO.
1998	L1151

RETAIL PRICING

YEAR	HIGH	LOW
1991	$575	$431
1992	$636	$477
1993	$707	$530
1994	$782	$587
1995	$868	$651
1996	$964	$723
1997	$1,068	$801
1998	$1,184	$888
1999	$1,315	$986

2060

YEARS MFRD 1982-1999
SERIES .... OHV SERIES
ENGINE .... KOHLER OHV
CYLINDERS 2
ENGINE HP 20
COOLING .... AIR
FUEL .... G
SPEEDS .... VARIABLE
TRANSMISSION .... HYDRO
STEERING .... STANDARD
STANDARD DECK .... 60"
WEIGHT .... 1,030 LBS.
MSRP $9,300

SERIAL NUMBERS

YEAR	BEGINNING NO.
1998	L1707

RETAIL PRICING

YEAR	HIGH	LOW
1991	$679	$509
1992	$752	$564
1993	$837	$628
1994	$926	$695
1995	$1,030	$772
1996	$1,142	$856
1997	$1,264	$948
1998	$1,404	$1,053
1999	$1,558	$1,169

2072

YEARS MFRD 1982-1999
SERIES .... OHV SERIES
ENGINE .... KOHLER OHV
CYLINDERS 2
ENGINE HP 20
COOLING .... AIR
FUEL .... G
SPEEDS .... VARIABLE
TRANSMISSION .... HYDRO
STEERING .... ZERO
STANDARD DECK .... 72"
WEIGHT .... 1,079 LBS.
MSRP $9,500

SERIAL NUMBERS

YEAR	BEGINNING NO.
1998	L1707

RETAIL PRICING

YEAR	HIGH	LOW
1991	$707	$530
1992	$782	$587
1993	$871	$653
1994	$964	$723
1995	$1,072	$804
1996	$1,188	$891
1997	$1,319	$989
1998	$1,461	$1,096
1999	$1,620	$1,215

2260HT

YEARS MFRD 2004-2010
SERIES .... OHV SERIES
ENGINE .... KOHLER OHV
ENGINE HP 23
COOLING .... AIR
FUEL .... G
SPEEDS .... VARIABLE
TRANSMISSION .... HYDRO
STEERING .... ZERO
STANDARD DECK .... 58"
WEIGHT .... 1,050 LBS.
MSRP $13,170

RETAIL PRICING

YEAR	HIGH	LOW
2004	$1,972	$1,479
2005	$2,158	$1,618
2006	$2,352	$1,764
2007	$2,619	$1,964
2008	$3,036	$2,277
2009	$3,625	$2,719
2010	$4,413	$3,310

2272HT

YEARS MFRD 2004-2010
SERIES .... OHV SERIES
ENGINE .... KOHLER OHV
ENGINE HP 23
COOLING .... AIR
FUEL .... G
SPEEDS .... VARIABLE
TRANSMISSION .... HYDRO
STEERING .... STANDARD
STANDARD DECK .... 70"
WEIGHT .... 1,100 LBS.
MSRP $13,367

RETAIL PRICING

YEAR	HIGH	LOW
2004	$2,010	$1,507
2005	$2,196	$1,647
2006	$2,389	$1,792
2007	$2,664	$1,998
2008	$3,089	$2,317
2009	$3,685	$2,764
2010	$4,481	$3,360

DERBY BY SIMPLICITY

TW2061

YEARS MFRD 2001-2004
SERIES .... MORGAN SERIES
ENGINE .... B&S
CYLINDERS 2
ENGINE HP 20
COOLING .... AIR
FUEL .... G
SPEEDS .... VARIABLE
TRANSMISSION .... HYDRO
STEERING .... ZERO
STANDARD DECK .... 61"
WEIGHT .... 1,200 LBS.
MSRP $6,399

RETAIL PRICING

YEAR	HIGH	LOW
2001	$2,822	$2,117
2002	$2,949	$2,212
2003	$3,197	$2,398
2004	$3,571	$2,678

ZT2148K

YEARS MFRD 2001-2004
SERIES .... COLT SERIES
ENGINE .... B&S
CYLINDERS 2
ENGINE HP 21
FUEL .... G
TRANSMISSION .... HYDRO
STEERING .... ZERO

STANDARD DECK . . . . 48"
WEIGHT . . . . 950 LBS.
MSRP. $6,699

OPTIONS

KOHLER COMMAND 21E

RETAIL PRICING

YEAR	HIGH	LOW
2001	$2,822	$2,117
2002	$2,899	$2,174
2003	$3,303	$2,478
2004	$3,738	$2,804

ZT2348

YEARS MFRD 2004-2004
SERIES. . . . . COLT SERIES
ENGINE . . . . . . KOHLER COMMAND
CYLINDERS. 2
ENGINE HP 23
COOLING . . . . AIR
FUEL . . . . G
SPEEDS . . . . VARIABLE
TRANSMISSION . . . . HYDRO
STEERING. . . . . ZERO
STANDARD DECK . . . . 48"
WEIGHT . . . . 1,300 LBS.
MSRP. $6,399

RETAIL PRICING

YEAR	HIGH	LOW
2004	$3,571	$2,678

ZT2352K

YEARS MFRD 2001-2004
SERIES. . . . . COLT SERIES
ENGINE . . . . B&S
ENGINE HP 23
FUEL . . . . G
TRANSMISSION . . . . HYDRO
STEERING. . . . . ZERO
STANDARD DECK . . . . 52"
WEIGHT . . . . 1,300 LBS.
MSRP. $7,099

OPTIONS

KOHLER COMMAND 23E

RETAIL PRICING

YEAR	HIGH	LOW
2001	$3,058	$2,293
2002	$3,142	$2,357
2003	$3,511	$2,633
2004	$3,962	$2,971

ZT2354

YEARS MFRD 2001-2003
SERIES. . . . . STALLION SERIES
ENGINE . . . . KOHLER
ENGINE HP 23
FUEL . . . . G
STEERING. . . . . ZERO
STANDARD DECK . . . . 54"
MSRP. $7,300

RETAIL PRICING

YEAR	HIGH	LOW
2001	$3,432	$2,574
2002	$3,528	$2,646
2003	$3,828	$2,871

ZT2561

YEARS MFRD 2001-2004
SERIES. . . . . STALLION SERIES
ENGINE . . . . . . KOHLER COMMAND
CYLINDERS. 2
ENGINE HP 25
FUEL . . . . G
SPEEDS . . . . VARIABLE
TRANSMISSION . . . . HYDRO
STEERING. . . . . ZERO
STANDARD DECK . . . . 61"
MSRP. $8,299

OPTIONS

KOHLER COMMAND 27E

RETAIL PRICING

YEAR	HIGH	LOW
2001	$3,620	$2,715
2002	$3,721	$2,791
2003	$4,191	$3,144
2004	$4,630	$3,473

ZT2761

YEARS MFRD 2004-2004
SERIES. . . . . STALLION SERIES
ENGINE . . . . . . KOHLER COMMAND
CYLINDERS. 2
ENGINE HP 27
COOLING . . . . AIR
FUEL . . . . G
SPEEDS . . . . VARIABLE
TRANSMISSION . . . . HYDRO
STEERING. . . . . ZERO
STANDARD DECK . . . . 61"
MSRP. $8,299

RETAIL PRICING

YEAR	HIGH	LOW
2004	$4,630	$3,473

DEUTZ-ALLIS

FC1316

YEARS MFRD 1990-1992
ENGINE . . . . B&S
ENGINE HP 16
COOLING . . . . AIR
FUEL . . . . G
TRANSMISSION . . . . HYDRO
STEERING. . . . . ZERO
STANDARD DECK . . . . 48"
MSRP. $4,400

RETAIL PRICING

YEAR	HIGH	LOW
1990	$219	$164
1991	$242	$182
1992	$268	$201

FC1316H48

YEARS MFRD 1991-1992
ENGINE . . . . B&S
ENGINE HP 16
FUEL . . . . G
TRANSMISSION . . . . HYDRO
STEERING. . . . . STANDARD
STANDARD DECK . . . . 48"
MSRP. $4,400

RETAIL PRICING

YEAR	HIGH	LOW
1991	$572	$429
1992	$694	$520

512G

YEARS MFRD 1992-1992
ENGINE . . . . B&S
ENGINE HP 12
FUEL . . . . G
SPEEDS 5
TRANSMISSION . . . . GEAR
STEERING. . . . . STANDARD
STANDARD DECK . . . . 36"
WEIGHT . . . . 538 LBS.
MSRP. $1,699

RETAIL PRICING

YEAR	HIGH	LOW
1992	$558	$418

512H

YEARS MFRD 1992-1992
ENGINE . . . . B&S
ENGINE HP 12
FUEL . . . . G
SPEEDS . . . . VARIABLE
TRANSMISSION . . . . HYDRO
STEERING. . . . . STANDARD
STANDARD DECK . . . . 36"
WEIGHT . . . . 552 LBS.
MSRP. $1,999

RETAIL PRICING

YEAR	HIGH	LOW
1992	$657	$492

612G

YEARS MFRD 1991-1991
ENGINE . . . . B&S
ENGINE HP 12
COOLING . . . . AIR
FUEL . . . . G
TRANSMISSION . . . . GEAR
STEERING. . . . . STANDARD
STANDARD DECK . . . . 36"
WEIGHT . . . . 538 LBS.
MSRP. $2,250

RETAIL PRICING

YEAR	HIGH	LOW
1991	$711	$534

612H

YEARS MFRD 1989-1991
ENGINE . . . . B&S
ENGINE HP 12
COOLING . . . . AIR
FUEL . . . . G
SPEEDS . . . . VARIABLE
TRANSMISSION . . . . HYDRO
STEERING. . . . . STANDARD
STANDARD DECK . . . . 36"
WEIGHT . . . . 550 LBS.
MSRP. $2,600

SERIAL NUMBERS

YEAR	BEGINNING NO.
1989	12001
1990	12601

RETAIL PRICING

YEAR	HIGH	LOW
1989	$779	$584
1991	$822	$617

612HST

YEARS MFRD 1987-1990
ENGINE . . . . B&S
ENGINE HP 12
COOLING . . . . AIR
FUEL . . . . G
TRANSMISSION . . . . HYDRO
STEERING. . . . . STANDARD
STANDARD DECK . . . . 36"
WEIGHT . . . . 516 LBS.
MSRP. $2,649

RETAIL PRICING

YEAR	HIGH	LOW
1987	$736	$552
1988	$771	$578
1989	$779	$584
1990	$785	$589

612LTD

YEARS MFRD 1987-1990
ENGINE . . . . B&S
ENGINE HP 12
COOLING . . . . AIR
FUEL . . . . G
SPEEDS 5
TRANSMISSION . . . . GEAR
STEERING. . . . . STANDARD
STANDARD DECK . . . . 36"
WEIGHT . . . . 538 LBS.
MSRP. $2,359

SERIAL NUMBERS

YEAR	BEGINNING NO.
1989	12051
1990	12501

RETAIL PRICING

YEAR	HIGH	LOW
1987	$626	$470
1988	$704	$528
1989	$711	$533
1990	$733	$550

613HST

YEARS MFRD 1987-1990
ENGINE . . . . B&S
ENGINE HP 12.5
COOLING . . . . AIR
FUEL . . . . G

DEUTZ-ALLIS

TRANSMISSION . . . . HYDRO
STEERING. . . . . STANDARD
STANDARD DECK . . . . 42"
WEIGHT . . . . 655 LBS.
MSRP. $3,399

RETAIL PRICING

YEAR	HIGH	LOW
1987	$839	$629
1988	$990	$742
1989	$999	$749
1990	$1,007	$756

613SPL

YEARS MFRD 1987-1990
ENGINE . . . . B&S
ENGINE HP 12.5
COOLING . . . . AIR
FUEL . . . . G
SPEEDS 5
TRANSMISSION . . . . GEAR
STEERING. . . . . STANDARD
STANDARD DECK . . . . 36"
WEIGHT . . . . 604 LBS.
MSRP. $2,849

OPTIONS

HYDRO

SERIAL NUMBERS

YEAR	BEGINNING NO.
1989	11251

RETAIL PRICING

YEAR	HIGH	LOW
1987	$727	$545
1988	$765	$574
1989	$839	$629
1990	$844	$633

616HST

YEARS MFRD 1987-1990
ENGINE . . . . B&S
ENGINE HP 16
FUEL . . . . G
SPEEDS . . . . VARIABLE
TRANSMISSION . . . . HYDRO
STEERING. . . . . STANDARD
STANDARD DECK . . . . 42"
WEIGHT . . . . 655 LBS.
MSRP. $3,639

RETAIL PRICING

YEAR	HIGH	LOW
1987	$934	$700
1988	$1,005	$754
1989	$1,071	$803
1990	$1,079	$809

830

YEARS MFRD 1985-1990
SERIES. . . . . SPRINT SERIES
ENGINE . . . . B&S
ENGINE HP 8
COOLING . . . . AIR
FUEL . . . . G
SPEEDS 5
TRANSMISSION . . . . GEAR
STEERING. . . . . STANDARD
STANDARD DECK . . . . 30"
WEIGHT . . . . 426 LBS.
MSRP. $1,749

SERIAL NUMBERS

YEAR	BEGINNING NO.
1985	10001
1986	10501
1988	11901

RETAIL PRICING

YEAR	HIGH	LOW
1986	$444	$333
1987	$462	$346
1988	$463	$347
1989	$495	$371
1990	$518	$389

917H

YEARS MFRD 1986-1992
ENGINE . . . . KOHLER
ENGINE HP 17
FUEL . . . . G
SPEEDS . . . . VARIABLE
TRANSMISSION . . . . HYDRO
STEERING. . . . . STANDARD
STANDARD DECK . . . . 48"
WEIGHT . . . . 949 LBS.
MSRP. $5,520

RETAIL PRICING

YEAR	HIGH	LOW
1986	$1,389	$1,041
1989	$1,724	$1,293
1990	$1,740	$1,305
1991	$1,760	$1,320
1992	$1,799	$1,349

1030

YEARS MFRD 1991-1992
ENGINE . . . . B&S
ENGINE HP 10
FUEL . . . . G
SPEEDS 5
TRANSMISSION . . . . GEAR
STEERING. . . . . STANDARD
STANDARD DECK . . . . 30"
WEIGHT . . . . 447 LBS.
MSRP. $1,499

RETAIL PRICING

YEAR	HIGH	LOW
1991	$552	$414
1992	$495	$371

1030M

YEARS MFRD 1991-1992
ENGINE . . . . B&S
ENGINE HP 10.5
FUEL . . . . G
SPEEDS 5
TRANSMISSION . . . . GEAR
STEERING. . . . . STANDARD
STANDARD DECK . . . . 30"
WEIGHT . . . . 459 LBS.
MSRP. $2,000

RETAIL PRICING

YEAR	HIGH	LOW
1991	$601	$451
1992	$657	$492

1036

YEARS MFRD 1985-1992
SERIES. . . . . SPRINT SERIES
ENGINE . . . . B&S
ENGINE HP 10.5
COOLING . . . . LIQUID
FUEL . . . . G
SPEEDS 5
TRANSMISSION . . . . GEAR
STEERING. . . . . STANDARD
STANDARD DECK . . . . 36"
WEIGHT . . . . 459 LBS.
MSRP. $2,075

SERIAL NUMBERS

YEAR	BEGINNING NO.
1985	10001
1986	10601
1988	11551

RETAIL PRICING

YEAR	HIGH	LOW
1986	$497	$373
1987	$515	$387
1988	$535	$401
1989	$588	$441
1990	$592	$444
1991	$624	$468
1992	$683	$512

1236H

YEARS MFRD 1986-1990
SERIES. . . . . VANGUARD SERIES
ENGINE . . . . B&S
CYLINDERS. 1
ENGINE HP 12
COOLING . . . . AIR
FUEL . . . . G
SPEEDS . . . . VARIABLE
TRANSMISSION . . . . HYDRO
STEERING. . . . . STANDARD
STANDARD DECK . . . . 36"
WEIGHT . . . . 450 LBS.
MSRP. $2,749

SERIAL NUMBERS

YEAR	BEGINNING NO.
1988	32951

RETAIL PRICING

YEAR	HIGH	LOW
1987	$700	$525
1988	$719	$539
1989	$808	$606
1990	$815	$612

1242G

YEARS MFRD 1987-1990
SERIES. . . . . VANGUARD SERIES
ENGINE . . . . B&S
CYLINDERS. 1
ENGINE HP 12
COOLING . . . . AIR
FUEL . . . . G
SPEEDS 5
TRANSMISSION . . . . GEAR
STEERING. . . . . STANDARD
STANDARD DECK . . . . 42"
WEIGHT . . . . 570 LBS.
MSRP. $2,599

SERIAL NUMBERS

YEAR	BEGINNING NO.
1988	32951

RETAIL PRICING

YEAR	HIGH	LOW
1987	$646	$484
1988	$676	$507
1989	$764	$573
1990	$771	$578

1242H

YEARS MFRD 1986-1990
SERIES. . . . . VANGUARD SERIES
ENGINE . . . . B&S
CYLINDERS. 1
ENGINE HP 12
COOLING . . . . AIR
FUEL . . . . G
TRANSMISSION . . . . GEAR
STEERING. . . . . STANDARD
STANDARD DECK . . . . 42"
MSRP. $2,999

OPTIONS

HYDRO

SERIAL NUMBERS

YEAR	BEGINNING NO.
1988	32951

RETAIL PRICING

YEAR	HIGH	LOW
1986	$682	$512
1987	$768	$576
1988	$791	$593
1989	$830	$623
1990	$888	$666

1613

YEARS MFRD 1989-1991
SERIES . . . . 1600 SERIES
ENGINE . . . . B&S
CYLINDERS. 1
ENGINE HP 12.5
COOLING . . . . AIR
FUEL . . . . G
SPEEDS . . . . VARIABLE
TRANSMISSION . . . . HYDRO
STEERING. . . . . STANDARD
STANDARD DECK . . . . 38"
WEIGHT . . . . 660 LBS.
MSRP. $3,079

RETAIL PRICING

YEAR	HIGH	LOW
1990	$894	$670
1991	$974	$731

1613G

YEARS MFRD 1991-1992
ENGINE . . . . KOHLER
ENGINE HP 12.5

COOLING ... AIR
FUEL ... G
SPEEDS ... 5
TRANSMISSION ... GEAR
STEERING ... STANDARD
STANDARD DECK ... 38"
WEIGHT ... 663 LBS.
MSRP ... $2,850

RETAIL PRICING

YEAR	HIGH	LOW
1991	$870	$653
1992	$938	$703

1613H

YEARS MFRD ... 1991-1992
ENGINE ... B&S
ENGINE HP ... 12.5
COOLING ... AIR
FUEL ... G
SPEEDS ... VARIABLE
TRANSMISSION ... HYDRO
STEERING ... STANDARD
STANDARD DECK ... 38"
WEIGHT ... 675 LBS.
MSRP ... $3,290

RETAIL PRICING

YEAR	HIGH	LOW
1991	$1,011	$759
1992	$1,083	$812

1616

YEARS MFRD ... 1990-1992
SERIES ... 1600 SERIES
ENGINE ... B&S
ENGINE HP ... 16
COOLING ... AIR
FUEL ... G
SPEEDS ... VARIABLE
TRANSMISSION ... HYDRO
STEERING ... STANDARD
STANDARD DECK ... 44"
WEIGHT ... 690 LBS.
MSRP ... $3,990

RETAIL PRICING

YEAR	HIGH	LOW
1990	$1,144	$858
1991	$1,250	$937
1992	$1,314	$986

1616H

YEARS MFRD ... 1992-1992
ENGINE ... B&S
ENGINE HP ... 16
COOLING ... AIR
FUEL ... G
SPEEDS ... VARIABLE
TRANSMISSION ... HYDRO
STEERING ... STANDARD
STANDARD DECK ... 44"
WEIGHT ... 715 LBS.
MSRP ... $3,990

RETAIL PRICING

YEAR	HIGH	LOW
1992	$1,314	$986

1617

YEARS MFRD ... 1991-1991
SERIES ... 1600 SERIES
ENGINE ... B&S
ENGINE HP ... 16
COOLING ... AIR
FUEL ... G
TRANSMISSION ... HYDRO
STEERING ... STANDARD
STANDARD DECK ... 44"
MSRP ... $3,900

RETAIL PRICING

YEAR	HIGH	LOW
1991	$1,233	$925

1617H

YEARS MFRD ... 1991-1991
ENGINE ... B&S
ENGINE HP ... 16
COOLING ... AIR
FUEL ... G
SPEEDS ... VARIABLE
TRANSMISSION ... HYDRO
STEERING ... STANDARD
STANDARD DECK ... 44"
WEIGHT ... 715 LBS.
MSRP ... $3,900

RETAIL PRICING

YEAR	HIGH	LOW
1991	$1,233	$925

1714G

YEARS MFRD ... 1992-1992
ENGINE ... KOHLER
ENGINE HP ... 14
COOLING ... AIR
FUEL ... G
SPEEDS ... 5
TRANSMISSION ... GEAR
STEERING ... STANDARD
STANDARD DECK ... 44"
WEIGHT ... 813 LBS.
MSRP ... $4,190

RETAIL PRICING

YEAR	HIGH	LOW
1992	$1,380	$1,035

1716H

YEARS MFRD ... 1992-1992
ENGINE ... B&S
ENGINE HP ... 16
FUEL ... G
TRANSMISSION ... HYDRO
STEERING ... STANDARD
STANDARD DECK ... 50"
MSRP ... $5,190

RETAIL PRICING

YEAR	HIGH	LOW
1992	$1,707	$1,280

1814

YEARS MFRD ... 1988-1990
SERIES ... SIGMA SERIES
ENGINE ... B&S
ENGINE HP ... 14
COOLING ... AIR
FUEL ... G
SPEEDS ... VARIABLE
TRANSMISSION ... HYDRO
STANDARD DECK ... 42"
WEIGHT ... 730 LBS.
MSRP ... $5,950

SERIAL NUMBERS

YEAR	BEGINNING NO.
1989	11451

RETAIL PRICING

YEAR	HIGH	LOW
1988	$1,015	$761
1989	$1,117	$838
1990	$1,158	$869

1816

YEARS MFRD ... 1988-1991
SERIES ... SIGMA SERIES
ENGINE ... B&S
ENGINE HP ... 16
COOLING ... AIR
FUEL ... G
SPEEDS ... VARIABLE
TRANSMISSION ... HYDRO
STEERING ... STANDARD
STANDARD DECK ... 48"
WEIGHT ... 745 LBS.
MSRP ... $4,475

SERIAL NUMBERS

YEAR	BEGINNING NO.
1988	10901
1989	13501

RETAIL PRICING

YEAR	HIGH	LOW
1988	$944	$708
1989	$1,234	$925
1990	$1,275	$956
1991	$1,417	$1,063

1816V

YEARS MFRD ... 1990-1990
ENGINE ... B&S
ENGINE HP ... 16
COOLING ... AIR
FUEL ... G
SPEEDS ... VARIABLE
TRANSMISSION ... HYDRO
STEERING ... STANDARD
STANDARD DECK ... 48"
WEIGHT ... 745 LBS.
MSRP ... $4,569

RETAIL PRICING

YEAR	HIGH	LOW
1990	$1,354	$1,016

1816VH

YEARS MFRD ... 1991-1991
ENGINE ... B&S
ENGINE HP ... 16
COOLING ... AIR
FUEL ... G
SPEEDS ... VARIABLE
TRANSMISSION ... HYDRO
STEERING ... STANDARD
STANDARD DECK ... 42"
WEIGHT ... 727 LBS.
MSRP ... $4,500

RETAIL PRICING

YEAR	HIGH	LOW
1991	$1,424	$1,068

1817

YEARS MFRD ... 1988-1991
SERIES ... SIGMA SERIES
ENGINE ... KOHLER
ENGINE HP ... 17
COOLING ... AIR
FUEL ... G
SPEEDS ... VARIABLE
TRANSMISSION ... HYDRO
STEERING ... STANDARD
STANDARD DECK ... 48"
WEIGHT ... 745 LBS.
MSRP ... $4,875

SERIAL NUMBERS

YEAR	BEGINNING NO.
1988	10004
1989	10801

RETAIL PRICING

YEAR	HIGH	LOW
1988	$212	$159
1989	$225	$169
1990	$271	$204
1991	$312	$234

1914

YEARS MFRD ... 1988-1990
SERIES ... ULTIMA SERIES
ENGINE ... KOHLER
ENGINE HP ... 14
COOLING ... AIR
FUEL ... G
SPEEDS ... VARIABLE
TRANSMISSION ... HYDRO
STEERING ... STANDARD
STANDARD DECK ... 42"
WEIGHT ... 955 LBS.
MSRP ... $5,799

SERIAL NUMBERS

YEAR	BEGINNING NO.
1988	10451

RETAIL PRICING

YEAR	HIGH	LOW
1988	$1,356	$1,017
1989	$1,510	$1,133
1990	$1,704	$1,278

1916

YEARS MFRD ... 1988-1990
SERIES ... ULTIMA SERIES
ENGINE ... KOHLER
ENGINE HP ... 16
COOLING ... AIR
FUEL ... G
SPEEDS ... VARIABLE
TRANSMISSION ... HYDRO

DEUTZ-ALLIS

STEERING............STANDARD
STANDARD DECK........... 48"
WEIGHT.............. 980 LBS.
MSRP................ $5,999

SERIAL NUMBERS

YEAR	BEGINNING NO.
1988	10451
1989	10701

RETAIL PRICING

YEAR	HIGH	LOW
1988	$249	$187
1989	$271	$204
1990	$317	$237

1918

YEARS MFRD........ 1985-1992
SERIES..........ULTIMA SERIES
ENGINE....... KOHLER MAGNUM
CYLINDERS................. 2
ENGINE HP................ 18
COOLING.................AIR
FUEL.....................G
SPEEDS..............VARIABLE
TRANSMISSION..........HYDRO
STEERING............STANDARD
STANDARD DECK........... 48"
WEIGHT............1,018 LBS.
MSRP................ $6,479

SERIAL NUMBERS

YEAR	BEGINNING NO.
1987	10001
1988	10401
1989	11251
1990	21301

RETAIL PRICING

YEAR	HIGH	LOW
1987	$242	$182
1988	$268	$201
1989	$297	$223
1990	$329	$247
1991	$367	$275
1992	$416	$312

1918H

YEARS MFRD........ 1991-1992
ENGINE...............KOHLER
ENGINE HP................ 18
COOLING.................AIR
SPEEDS..............VARIABLE
TRANSMISSION..........HYDRO
STEERING............STANDARD
STANDARD DECK........... 48"
WEIGHT............1,176 LBS.
MSRP................ $7,750

RETAIL PRICING

YEAR	HIGH	LOW
1991	$1,992	$1,494
1992	$2,551	$1,913

1920

YEARS MFRD........ 1985-1991
SERIES..........ULTIMA SERIES
ENGINE....... KOHLER MAGNUM
CYLINDERS................. 2
ENGINE HP................ 20
COOLING.................AIR
FUEL.....................G
SPEEDS..............VARIABLE
TRANSMISSION..........HYDRO
STEERING............STANDARD
STANDARD DECK........... 48"
WEIGHT............1,036 LBS.
MSRP................ $7,199

OPTIONS

60" DECK

SERIAL NUMBERS

YEAR	BEGINNING NO.
1985	10001
1986	10601
1987	12551
1988	20851
1989	13301

RETAIL PRICING

YEAR	HIGH	LOW
1985	$257	$193
1986	$285	$214
1987	$317	$237
1988	$352	$264
1989	$389	$292
1990	$431	$323
1991	$483	$362

1920H

YEARS MFRD........ 1991-1992
ENGINE...............KOHLER
ENGINE HP................ 20
COOLING.................AIR
FUEL.....................G
SPEEDS..............VARIABLE
TRANSMISSION..........HYDRO
STEERING............STANDARD
STANDARD DECK........... 48"
WEIGHT............1,197 LBS.
MSRP................ $8,250

OPTIONS

60" DECK

RETAIL PRICING

YEAR	HIGH	LOW
1991	$2,451	$1,838
1992	$2,715	$2,036

3016

YEARS MFRD........ 1989-1992
SERIES............ 3000 SERIES
ENGINE...................B&S
ENGINE HP................ 16
COOLING.................AIR
FUEL.....................G
TRANSMISSION..........HYDRO
STEERING............STANDARD
STANDARD DECK........... 46"
MSRP................ $6,275

SERIAL NUMBERS

YEAR	BEGINNING NO.
1990	10001

RETAIL PRICING

YEAR	HIGH	LOW
1989	$283	$212
1990	$313	$234
1991	$348	$261
1992	$385	$289

3016L

YEARS MFRD........ 1991-1992
ENGINE...................B&S
ENGINE HP................ 16
FUEL.....................G
TRANSMISSION..........HYDRO
STEERING............STANDARD
STANDARD DECK........... 46"
MSRP................ $6,290

RETAIL PRICING

YEAR	HIGH	LOW
1991	$1,819	$1,364
1992	$2,072	$1,554

3016S

YEARS MFRD........ 1991-1992
ENGINE...................B&S
ENGINE HP................ 16
FUEL.....................G
TRANSMISSION..........HYDRO
STEERING............STANDARD
STANDARD DECK........... 46"
MSRP................ $6,490

RETAIL PRICING

YEAR	HIGH	LOW
1991	$1,881	$1,410
1992	$2,135	$1,602

3018

YEARS MFRD........ 1991-1992
SERIES............ 3000 SERIES
ENGINE...............KOHLER
ENGINE HP................ 18
COOLING.................AIR
FUEL.....................G
TRANSMISSION..........HYDRO
STEERING................ZERO
STANDARD DECK........... 54"
MSRP................ $7,275

SERIAL NUMBERS

YEAR	BEGINNING NO.
1991	10001

RETAIL PRICING

YEAR	HIGH	LOW
1991	$404	$303
1992	$446	$334

3018L

YEARS MFRD........ 1991-1992
ENGINE...............KOHLER
ENGINE HP................ 18
FUEL.....................G
TRANSMISSION..........HYDRO
STEERING............STANDARD
STANDARD DECK........... 54"
MSRP................ $7,290

RETAIL PRICING

YEAR	HIGH	LOW
1991	$2,087	$1,566
1992	$2,400	$1,800

3018S

YEARS MFRD........ 1991-1992
ENGINE...............KOHLER
ENGINE HP................ 18
FUEL.....................G
TRANSMISSION..........HYDRO
STEERING............STANDARD
STANDARD DECK........... 54"
MSRP................ $7,490

RETAIL PRICING

YEAR	HIGH	LOW
1991	$2,150	$1,613
1992	$2,466	$1,849

3020

YEARS MFRD........ 1991-1992
SERIES............ 3000 SERIES
ENGINE...............KOHLER
ENGINE HP................ 20
COOLING.................AIR
FUEL.....................G
TRANSMISSION..........HYDRO
STEERING................ZERO
MSRP................ $6,895

RETAIL PRICING

YEAR	HIGH	LOW
1991	$380	$285
1992	$423	$318

3020L

YEARS MFRD........ 1991-1992
ENGINE...............KOHLER
ENGINE HP................ 20
FUEL.....................G
TRANSMISSION..........HYDRO
STEERING............STANDARD
STANDARD DECK........... 60"
MSRP................ $7,590

RETAIL PRICING

YEAR	HIGH	LOW
1991	$2,181	$1,636
1992	$2,499	$1,874

3020S

YEARS MFRD........ 1991-1992
ENGINE...............KOHLER
ENGINE HP................ 20
FUEL.....................G
TRANSMISSION..........HYDRO
STEERING............STANDARD
STANDARD DECK........... 60"
MSRP................ $7,790

RETAIL PRICING

YEAR	HIGH	LOW
1991	$2,244	$1,683
1992	$2,566	$1,924

5220

YEARS MFRD........ 1986-1990
ENGINE..............TOYOSHA
CYLINDERS................. 3
CID...................... 87

PTO HP . . . 21
ENGINE HP . . . 26
COOLING . . . LIQUID
FUEL . . . D
SPEEDS . . . 12/4
TRANSMISSION . . . SHUTTLE SHIFT
STEERING . . . STANDARD
DRIVE TYPE . . . 2WD
ROPS/CAB . . . ROPS
WEIGHT . . . 2,433 LBS.
MSRP . . . $9,899

OPTIONS

4WD
HYDRO
REAR HYD

SERIAL NUMBERS

YEAR	BEGINNING NO.
1986	1001 GEAR
1987	1919 GEAR
1988	2170 GEAR
1989	2341 GEAR
1989	2182 HYDRO

RETAIL PRICING

YEAR	HIGH	LOW
1986	$2,119	$1,589
1987	$2,358	$1,768
1988	$2,595	$1,946
1989	$2,887	$2,165

AVG. AUCTION PRICING

LOW	HIGH	AVG
$984	$5,232	$2,937

6035

YEARS MFRD . . . 1985-1986
ENGINE . . . DEUTZ
CYLINDERS . . . 2
CID . . . 115
PTO HP . . . 33
FUEL . . . D
SPEEDS . . . 8/2
TRANSMISSION . . . GEAR
STEERING . . . STANDARD
HYDRAULIC . . . YES
PTO . . . YES
WEIGHT . . . 4,310 LBS.
MSRP . . . $11,700

SERIAL NUMBERS

RIGHT SIDE LOWER FRONT OF HOOD

YEAR	BEGINNING NO.
1985	1301
1986	7866

RETAIL PRICING

YEAR	HIGH	LOW
1986	$3,128	$2,346

6140

YEARS MFRD . . . 1985-1987
ENGINE . . . HINOMOTO
CID . . . 142
PTO HP . . . 41
FUEL . . . D
SPEEDS . . . 10/2
TRANSMISSION . . . GEAR
STEERING . . . STANDARD
HYDRAULIC . . . YES
PTO . . . YES
DRIVE TYPE . . . 2WD
ROPS/CAB . . . ROPS
WEIGHT . . . 4,228 LBS.
MSRP . . . $15,890

OPTIONS

4WD

SERIAL NUMBERS

YEAR	BEGINNING NO.
1985	2711
1986	2836
1987	3061

RETAIL PRICING

YEAR	HIGH	LOW
1987	$4,365	$3,274

6240

YEARS MFRD . . . 1985-1992
ENGINE . . . DEUTZ
CYLINDERS . . . 3
CID . . . 172.5
PTO HP . . . 43
FUEL . . . D
SPEEDS . . . 8/4 SYN
TRANSMISSION . . . SHUTTLE SHIFT
STEERING . . . STANDARD
HYDRAULIC . . . YES
PTO . . . YES
DRIVE TYPE . . . 2WD
ROPS/CAB . . . ROPS
WEIGHT . . . 5,776 LBS.
MSRP . . . $18,015

OPTIONS

4WD

SERIAL NUMBERS

YEAR	BEGINNING NO.
1985	7722-0001-2WD
1985	7726-0001-4WD
1986	7726-0201-4WD
1986	7722-0489-2WD
1987	7726-0573-4WD
1987	7722-1427-2WD
1988	7726-0711-4WD
1988	7722-1746-2WD
1989	7722-3129-2WD
1989	7726-3122-4WD
1990	7722-3400-2WD
1990	7726-3252-4WD
1991	7726-6916-4WD
1991	7722-3671-2WD
1992	7722-3943-2WD
1992	7726-8301-4WD

RETAIL PRICING

YEAR	HIGH	LOW
1992	$5,931	$4,448

DEUTZ-FAHR

AGROKID 30 4WD

YEARS MFRD . . . 2005-2010
ENGINE . . . MITSUBISHI S4L-61ST
CYLINDERS . . . 4
ENGINE HP . . . 35
COOLING . . . LIQUID
FUEL . . . D
SPEEDS . . . 12/12
TRANSMISSION . . . SHUTTLE SHIFT
STEERING . . . STANDARD
HITCH . . . CAT. I
HYDRAULIC . . . YES
PTO . . . YES
WEIGHT . . . 2,756 LBS.

AGROKID 40 4WD

YEARS MFRD . . . 2005-2010
ENGINE . . . MITSUBISHI S4L-T61ST
CYLINDERS . . . 4
ENGINE HP . . . 41
COOLING . . . LIQUID
FUEL . . . D
SPEEDS . . . 12/12
TRANSMISSION . . . SHUTTLE SHIFT
STEERING . . . STANDARD
HITCH . . . CAT. I
HYDRAULIC . . . YES
PTO . . . YES
WEIGHT . . . 2,866 LBS.

AGROKID 50 4WD

YEARS MFRD . . . 2005-2010
ENGINE . . MITSUBISHI S4L2-T61ST
CYLINDERS . . . 4
ENGINE HP . . . 47
COOLING . . . LIQUID
FUEL . . . D
SPEEDS . . . 12/12
TRANSMISSION . . . SHUTTLE SHIFT
STEERING . . . STANDARD
HITCH . . . CAT. I
HYDRAULIC . . . YES
PTO . . . YES
WEIGHT . . . 2,910 LBS.

AGROKID 210

YEARS MFRD . . . 2008-2013
ENGINE . . . MITSUBISHI S4L-62ST
CYLINDERS . . . 4
CID . . . 91.5
ENGINE HP . . . 39
COOLING . . . LIQUID
FUEL . . . D
SPEEDS . . . 7/1
TRANSMISSION . . . GEAR
STEERING . . . STANDARD
HYDRAULIC . . . YES
PTO . . . YES
WEIGHT . . . 2,750 LBS.

AGROKID 220

YEARS MFRD . . . 2008-2013
ENGINE . . . MITSUBISHI S4L-T62ST TURBO
CYLINDERS . . . 4
CID . . . 91.5
ENGINE HP . . . 43
COOLING . . . LIQUID
FUEL . . . D
SPEEDS . . . 7/1
TRANSMISSION . . . GEAR
STEERING . . . STANDARD
HYDRAULIC . . . YES
PTO . . . YES
WEIGHT . . . 2,900 LBS.

AGROKID 230

YEARS MFRD . . . 2008-2013
ENGINE . . . MITSUBISHI S4L2-T
CYLINDERS . . . 4
CID . . . 107.2
ENGINE HP . . . 50
COOLING . . . LIQUID
FUEL . . . D
SPEEDS . . . 7/1
TRANSMISSION . . . GEAR
STEERING . . . STANDARD
HYDRAULIC . . . YES
PTO . . . YES
WEIGHT . . . 2,900 LBS.

D25-06

YEARS MFRD . . . 1970-1972
ENGINE . . . DEUTZ
CYLINDERS . . . 2
CID . . . 115
PTO HP . . . 23
FUEL . . . D
SPEEDS . . . 8/2
WEIGHT . . . 3,700 LBS.

SERIAL NUMBERS

YEAR	BEGINNING NO.
1970	7900001
1971	7911844
1972	7923688

D30-06

YEARS MFRD . . . 1969-1980
ENGINE . . . DEUTZ
CYLINDERS . . . 2
CID . . . 115
PTO HP . . . 30
FUEL . . . D
SPEEDS . . . 8/2
WEIGHT . . . 3,930 LBS.

DEUTZ-FAHR

SERIAL NUMBERS

YEAR	BEGINNING NO.
1969	7900010
1970	7915277
1971	7938965
1972	7961327
1973	7984657
1974	79130850
1975	79177187
1976	79225795
1977	79324737
1978	79375933
1979	79427534
1980	79480092

D36-07

YEARS MFRD	1985-1985
ENGINE	DEUTZ
CYLINDERS	2
CID	115
PTO HP	33
FUEL	D
SPEEDS	8/2
TRANSMISSION	GEAR
STEERING	STANDARD
HYDRAULIC	YES
PTO	YES
WEIGHT	4,120 LBS.
MSRP	$11,890

SERIAL NUMBERS

YEAR	BEGINNING NO.
1985	7866-0001

RETAIL PRICING

YEAR	HIGH	LOW
1985	$3,007	$2,255

D40-06

YEARS MFRD	1969-1978
ENGINE	DEUTZ
CYLINDERS	3
CID	172.5
PTO HP	36
FUEL	D
SPEEDS	8/2
TRANSMISSION	GEAR
STEERING	STANDARD
PTO	YES
WEIGHT	4,100 LBS.
MSRP	$7,165

SERIAL NUMBERS

YEAR	BEGINNING NO.
1969	7900010
1970	7915277
1971	7938965
1972	7961327
1973	7984657
1974	79130850
1975	79177187
1976	79225795
1977	79324737
1978	79375933

RETAIL PRICING

YEAR	HIGH	LOW
1978	$1,298	$973

D40-06A 4WD

YEARS MFRD	1972-1978
ENGINE	DEUTZ F3L912
CYLINDERS	3
CID	172.5
PTO HP	36
FUEL	D
SPEEDS	8/2-12/4
TRANSMISSION	GEAR
STEERING	STANDARD
PTO	YES
WEIGHT	5,005 LBS.
MSRP	$9,905

RETAIL PRICING

YEAR	HIGH	LOW
1978	$1,795	$1,347

D45-06 2WD

YEARS MFRD	1972-1980
ENGINE	DEUTZ
CYLINDERS	3
CID	172.5
PTO HP	43.1
FUEL	D
SPEEDS	8/2
TRANSMISSION	GEAR
STEERING	STANDARD
PTO	YES
WEIGHT	4,200 LBS.
MSRP	$11,890

SERIAL NUMBERS

YEAR	BEGINNING NO.
1972	7961327
1973	7984657
1974	79130850
1975	79177187
1976	79225795
1977	79324737
1978	79375933
1979	79427534
1980	79480092

RETAIL PRICING

YEAR	HIGH	LOW
1980	$2,155	$1,616

D45-06A 4WD

YEARS MFRD	1972-1980
ENGINE	DEUTZ
CYLINDERS	3
CID	172.5
PTO HP	43.1
FUEL	D
SPEEDS	8/2
TRANSMISSION	GEAR
STEERING	STANDARD
PTO	YES
WEIGHT	5,080 LBS.
MSRP	$16,115

RETAIL PRICING

YEAR	HIGH	LOW
1980	$2,919	$2,190

D45-07 2WD

YEARS MFRD	1980-1985
ENGINE	DEUTZ
CYLINDERS	3
CID	172.5
PTO HP	43.1
FUEL	D
SPEEDS	8/2
TRANSMISSION	GEAR
STEERING	STANDARD
PTO	YES
WEIGHT	4,670 LBS.
MSRP	$16,065

SERIAL NUMBERS

RIGHT HAND SIDE OF LOWER FRONT PORTION OF HOOD

YEAR	BEGINNING NO.
1980	7548-1862
1981	7548-2317
1982	7548-3047
1983	7548-3779
1984	7548-5422
1985	7548-7055

RETAIL PRICING

YEAR	HIGH	LOW
1985	$4,064	$3,048

D45-07A 4WD

YEARS MFRD	1981-1986
ENGINE	DEUTZ
CYLINDERS	3
CID	172.5
PTO HP	43.1
FUEL	D
SPEEDS	8/2
TRANSMISSION	GEAR
STEERING	STANDARD
PTO	YES
WEIGHT	5,300 LBS.
MSRP	$21,080

SERIAL NUMBERS

RIGHT HAND SIDE OF LOWER FRONT PORTION OF THE HOOD

YEAR	BEGINNING NO.
1981	7868-1797
1982	7868-1856
1983	7868-1995
1984	7868-2141

RETAIL PRICING

YEAR	HIGH	LOW
1986	$5,636	$4,227

DX3.10 2WD

YEARS MFRD	1985-1985
ENGINE	DEUTZ
CYLINDERS	3
CID	172
PTO HP	44
FUEL	D
SPEEDS	8/4
TRANSMISSION	GEAR
STEERING	STANDARD
PTO	YES
WEIGHT	5,776 LBS.
MSRP	$16,885

SERIAL NUMBERS

RIGHT SIDE LOWER FRONT OF HOOD

YEAR	BEGINNING NO.
1985	7722-0001

RETAIL PRICING

YEAR	HIGH	LOW
1985	$4,272	$3,204

DX3.10A 4WD

YEARS MFRD	1985-1985
ENGINE	DEUTZ
CYLINDERS	3
CID	172
PTO HP	44
FUEL	D
SPEEDS	8/4
TRANSMISSION	GEAR
STEERING	STANDARD
PTO	YES
WEIGHT	6,251 LBS.
MSRP	$21,100

SERIAL NUMBERS

YEAR	BEGINNING NO.
1985	7726-0001

RETAIL PRICING

YEAR	HIGH	LOW
1985	$5,336	$4,002

DEWEZE

ATM72LC

YEARS MFRD	2005-2015
ENGINE	YANMAR
CYLINDERS	3
ENGINE HP	30.2
COOLING	LIQUID
FUEL	D
SPEEDS	VARIABLE
TRANSMISSION	HYDRO
STEERING	STANDARD
WEIGHT	2,250 LBS.

ATM162

YEARS MFRD	2008-2015
ENGINE	CUMMINS
CID	275
ENGINE HP	99
COOLING	LIQUID
FUEL	D
SPEEDS	VARIABLE
TRANSMISSION	HYDRO
STEERING	STANDARD
WEIGHT	8,250 LBS.

DIXIE CHOPPER

ALL MODELS

SERIAL NUMBERS

REVERSE FIRST 2 DIGITS FOR YEAR MFG.

BURB'N'TURF

YEARS MFRD 1997-1997
ENGINE .... KOHLER
ENGINE HP 20
COOLING .... AIR
FUEL .... G
SPEEDS .... VARIABLE
TRANSMISSION .... HYDRO
STEERING .... ZERO
STANDARD DECK .... 72"
MSRP $12,700

RETAIL PRICING

YEAR	HIGH	LOW
1997	$3,986	$2,989

CCE4000

YEARS MFRD 1997-1997
ENGINE .... KOHLER
ENGINE HP 20
COOLING .... AIR
FUEL .... G
TRANSMISSION .... HYDRO
STEERING .... ZERO
STANDARD DECK .... 72"
MSRP $12,700

RETAIL PRICING

YEAR	HIGH	LOW
1997	$1,017	$763

CNG66

YEARS MFRD 2010-2010
SERIES .... NATURAL GAS SERIES
ENGINE .... GENERAC
CID 990CC
COOLING .... AIR
SPEEDS .... VARIABLE
TRANSMISSION .... HYDRO
STEERING .... ZERO

DOMINATOR

YEARS MFRD 2011-2011
ENGINE .... GENERAC
ENGINE HP 33
FUEL .... G
SPEEDS .... VARIABLE
TRANSMISSION .... HYDRO
STEERING .... ZERO
WEIGHT .... 1,725 LBS.

ECO-EAGLE

YEARS MFRD 2010-2012
SERIES .... XCALIBER SERIES
ENGINE .... GENERAC
CID 990CC
ENGINE HP 30
FUEL .... G
SPEEDS .... VARIABLE
TRANSMISSION .... HYDRO
STEERING .... ZERO
STANDARD DECK .... 66"
WEIGHT .... 1,686 LBS.
MSRP $20,599

RETAIL PRICING

YEAR	HIGH	LOW
2010	$7,340	$5,505
2011	$8,102	$6,076
2012	$8,943	$6,707

FLATLAND 50,60

YEARS MFRD 1994-2000
SERIES .... XF SERIES
ENGINE .... KOHLER
ENGINE HP 22
COOLING .... AIR
FUEL .... G
SPEEDS .... VARIABLE
TRANSMISSION .... HYDRO
STEERING .... ZERO
STANDARD DECK .... 50"
MSRP $9,830

OPTIONS

60" DECK

SERIAL NUMBERS

YEAR	BEGINNING NO.
1994	49XXXXX
1995	59XXXXX
1996	69XXXXX
1997	79XXXXX
1998	89XXXXX
1999	99XXXXX
2000	00XXXXX

RETAIL PRICING

YEAR	HIGH	LOW
1994	$866	$650
1995	$956	$717
1996	$1,055	$792
1997	$1,165	$874
1998	$1,286	$964
1999	$1,418	$1,064
2000	$1,566	$1,175

LP3000

YEARS MFRD 2007-2010
SERIES .... PROPANE SERIES
ENGINE .... GENERAC
SPEEDS .... VARIABLE
TRANSMISSION .... HYDRO
STEERING .... ZERO
STANDARD DECK .... 60"
MSRP $12,250

OPTIONS

72"DECK

RETAIL PRICING

YEAR	HIGH	LOW
2007	$5,343	$4,007
2008	$5,836	$4,377
2009	$6,728	$5,046
2010	$6,824	$5,118

LT1800

YEARS MFRD 2007-2007
SERIES .... SILVER EAGLE SERIES
ENGINE .... KOHLER
ENGINE HP 18
COOLING .... AIR
FUEL .... G
SPEEDS .... VARIABLE
TRANSMISSION .... HYDRO
STEERING .... ZERO
BLADE CLUTCH .... ELECTRIC
STANDARD DECK .... 34"
MSRP $4,999

OPTIONS

44" DECK

RETAIL PRICING

YEAR	HIGH	LOW
2007	$1,379	$1,034

LT2000

YEARS MFRD 2004-2004
SERIES .... SILVER EAGLE SERIES
ENGINE .... KOHLER
FUEL .... G
SPEEDS .... VARIABLE
TRANSMISSION .... HYDRO
STEERING .... ZERO

LT2000-34

YEARS MFRD 2006-2006
SERIES .... SILVER EAGLE SERIES
ENGINE .... KOHLER
ENGINE HP 20
COOLING .... AIR
FUEL .... G
SPEEDS .... VARIABLE
TRANSMISSION .... HYDRO
STEERING .... ZERO
BLADE CLUTCH .... ELECTRIC

LT2000-36

YEARS MFRD 2005-2005
SERIES .... SILVER EAGLE SERIES
ENGINE .... KOHLER
ENGINE HP 20
COOLING .... AIR
FUEL .... G
SPEEDS .... VARIABLE
TRANSMISSION .... HYDRO
STEERING .... ZERO
BLADE CLUTCH .... ELECTRIC
STANDARD DECK .... 36"
MSRP $5,199

RETAIL PRICING

YEAR	HIGH	LOW
2005	$1,216	$912

LT2000-44

YEARS MFRD 2005-2006
SERIES .... SILVER EAGLE SERIES
ENGINE .... KOHLER
ENGINE HP 20
COOLING .... AIR
FUEL .... G
SPEEDS .... VARIABLE
TRANSMISSION .... HYDRO
STEERING .... ZERO
BLADE CLUTCH .... ELECTRIC
STANDARD DECK .... 44"
MSRP $5,799

SERIAL NUMBERS

YEAR	BEGINNING NO.
2006	60XXXX

RETAIL PRICING

YEAR	HIGH	LOW
2005	$1,351	$1,014
2006	$1,492	$1,119

LT2000-50D

YEARS MFRD 2006-2006
SERIES .... SILVER EAGLE SERIES
ENGINE .... KOHLER
ENGINE HP 20
COOLING .... AIR
FUEL .... G
SPEEDS .... VARIABLE
TRANSMISSION .... HYDRO
STEERING .... ZERO
BLADE CLUTCH .... ELECTRIC
STANDARD DECK .... 50"
MSRP $6,399

RETAIL PRICING

YEAR	HIGH	LOW
2006	$1,645	$1,234

LT2200-34

YEARS MFRD 2006-2007
SERIES .... SILVER EAGLE SERIES
ENGINE .... GENERAC
ENGINE HP 22
COOLING .... AIR
FUEL .... G
SPEEDS .... VARIABLE
TRANSMISSION .... HYDRO
STEERING .... ZERO
STANDARD DECK .... 34"
MSRP $5,399

SERIAL NUMBERS

YEAR	BEGINNING NO.
2006	60XXXX

RETAIL PRICING

YEAR	HIGH	LOW
2006	$1,349	$1,012
2007	$1,489	$1,116

LT2300-50D

YEARS MFRD 2007-2007
ENGINE .... KOHLER
ENGINE HP 23
COOLING .... AIR
FUEL .... G

DIXIE CHOPPER

SPEEDS . . . . VARIABLE
TRANSMISSION . . . . HYDRO
STEERING . . . . ZERO
BLADE CLUTCH . . . . ELECTRIC
STANDARD DECK . . . . 50"
MSRP $6,499

RETAIL PRICING

YEAR	HIGH	LOW
2007	$1,792	$1,344

LT2400-44D

YEARS MFRD 2005-2005
SERIES . . . . . . SILVER EAGLE SERIES
ENGINE . . . . GUARDIAN
ENGINE HP 24
COOLING . . . . AIR
FUEL . . . . G
SPEEDS . . . . VARIABLE
TRANSMISSION . . . . HYDRO
STEERING . . . . ZERO
BLADE CLUTCH . . . . ELECTRIC
STANDARD DECK . . . . 44"
MSRP $5,799

RETAIL PRICING

YEAR	HIGH	LOW
2005	$1,356	$1,017

LT2400-50D

YEARS MFRD 2005-2005
SERIES . . . . . . SILVER EAGLE SERIES
ENGINE . . . . GUARDIAN
ENGINE HP 24
COOLING . . . . AIR
FUEL . . . . G
SPEEDS . . . . VARIABLE
TRANSMISSION . . . . HYDRO
STEERING . . . . ZERO
BLADE CLUTCH . . . . ELECTRIC
STANDARD DECK . . . . 50"
MSRP $6,299

RETAIL PRICING

YEAR	HIGH	LOW
2005	$1,473	$1,105

LT2500-44D

YEARS MFRD 2006-2007
SERIES . . . . . . SILVER EAGLE SERIES
ENGINE . . . . GENERAC
ENGINE HP 25
FUEL . . . . G
SPEEDS . . . . VARIABLE
TRANSMISSION . . . . HYDRO
STEERING . . . . ZERO
STANDARD DECK . . . . 44"
MSRP $6,499

OPTIONS

50" DECK

SERIAL NUMBERS

YEAR	BEGINNING NO.
2006	60XXXX

RETAIL PRICING

YEAR	HIGH	LOW
2006	$1,624	$1,218
2007	$1,801	$1,351

LT2700-60D

YEARS MFRD 2005-2007
SERIES . . . . . . SILVER EAGLE SERIES
ENGINE . . . . GUARDIAN
ENGINE HP 27
COOLING . . . . AIR
FUEL . . . . G
SPEEDS . . . . VARIABLE
TRANSMISSION . . . . HYDRO
STEERING . . . . ZERO
BLADE CLUTCH . . . . ELECTRIC
STANDARD DECK . . . . 60"
MSRP $7,799

SERIAL NUMBERS

YEAR	BEGINNING NO.
2006	60XXXX

RETAIL PRICING

YEAR	HIGH	LOW
2005	$1,765	$1,324
2006	$1,951	$1,463
2007	$2,151	$1,613

LX1901

YEARS MFRD 2000-2001
SERIES . . . . LX SERIES
ENGINE . . . . KAWASAKI
ENGINE HP 19
FUEL . . . . G
SPEEDS . . . . VARIABLE
TRANSMISSION . . . . HYDRO
STEERING . . . . STANDARD
STANDARD DECK . . . . 42"
MSRP $6,495

RETAIL PRICING

YEAR	HIGH	LOW
2000	$2,394	$1,796
2001	$2,497	$1,873

LX2000

YEARS MFRD 1994-1995
SERIES . . . . LX SERIES
ENGINE . . . . KOHLER
ENGINE HP 20
COOLING . . . . AIR
FUEL . . . . G
SPEEDS . . . . VARIABLE
TRANSMISSION . . . . HYDRO
STEERING . . . . ZERO
STANDARD DECK . . . . 42"
MSRP $7,725

OPTIONS

50" DECK
60" DECK

SERIAL NUMBERS

YEAR	BEGINNING NO.
1994	49XXXXX
1995	59XXXXX

RETAIL PRICING

YEAR	HIGH	LOW
1994	$496	$372
1995	$547	$410

LX2001

YEARS MFRD 1991-2004
SERIES . . . . LX SERIES
ENGINE . . . . KOHLER
ENGINE HP 20
COOLING . . . . AIR
FUEL . . . . G
SPEEDS . . . . VARIABLE
TRANSMISSION . . . . HYDRO
STEERING . . . . ZERO
STANDARD DECK . . . . 42"
MSRP $6,999

OPTIONS

50" DECK
60" DECK
BAGGER
BLADE

RETAIL PRICING

YEAR	HIGH	LOW
1996	$654	$490
1997	$722	$542
1998	$824	$618
1999	$880	$660
2000	$971	$728
2001	$1,072	$804
2002	$1,183	$887
2003	$1,305	$979
2004	$1,442	$1,081

LX2002

YEARS MFRD 1997-2000
SERIES . . . . LX SERIES
ENGINE . . . . KOHLER
ENGINE HP 20
COOLING . . . . AIR
FUEL . . . . G
TRANSMISSION . . . . HYDRO
STEERING . . . . ZERO
STANDARD DECK . . . . 42"
MSRP $7,425

OPTIONS

60" BLADE
BAGGER

RETAIL PRICING

YEAR	HIGH	LOW
1997	$802	$601
1998	$886	$664
1999	$978	$734
2000	$1,079	$809

LX2400

YEARS MFRD 1991-1992
SERIES . . . . LX SERIES
ENGINE . . . . KOHLER
ENGINE HP 24
COOLING . . . . AIR
FUEL . . . . G
TRANSMISSION . . . . HYDRO
STEERING . . . . ZERO
STANDARD DECK . . . . 42"
MSRP $8,295

OPTIONS

50" DECK
60" DECK

RETAIL PRICING

YEAR	HIGH	LOW
1991	$388	$291
1992	$433	$325

LX2401

YEARS MFRD 1991-1992
SERIES . . . . LX SERIES
ENGINE . . . . KOHLER
ENGINE HP 24
COOLING . . . . AIR
FUEL . . . . G
TRANSMISSION . . . . HYDRO
STEERING . . . . ZERO
STANDARD DECK . . . . 42"
MSRP $7,095

OPTIONS

50" DECK
60" DECK

RETAIL PRICING

YEAR	HIGH	LOW
1991	$335	$251
1992	$369	$277

LX4218

YEARS MFRD 1990-1990
SERIES . . . . LX SERIES
ENGINE . . . . KOHLER
ENGINE HP 18
COOLING . . . . AIR
FUEL . . . . G
TRANSMISSION . . . . HYDRO
STEERING . . . . ZERO
STANDARD DECK . . . . 42"
MSRP $5,975

SERIAL NUMBERS

YEAR	BEGINNING NO.
1990	09XXXXX

RETAIL PRICING

YEAR	HIGH	LOW
1990	$295	$221

LX4220

YEARS MFRD 1990-1990
SERIES . . . . LX SERIES
ENGINE . . . . KOHLER
ENGINE HP 20
COOLING . . . . AIR
FUEL . . . . G
TRANSMISSION . . . . HYDRO
STEERING . . . . ZERO
STANDARD DECK . . . . 42"
MSRP $6,395

RETAIL PRICING

YEAR	HIGH	LOW
1990	$314	$235

LX5018

YEARS MFRD 1990-1990
SERIES . . . . LX SERIES
ENGINE . . . . KOHLER
ENGINE HP 18
COOLING . . . . AIR

FUEL . . . . . G
TRANSMISSION . . . . . HYDRO
STEERING . . . . . ZERO
STANDARD DECK . . . . . 50"
MSRP $6,195

RETAIL PRICING

YEAR	HIGH	LOW
1990	$782	$587

LX5020

YEARS MFRD 1990-1990
SERIES . . . . . LX SERIES
ENGINE . . . . . KOHLER
ENGINE HP 20
COOLING . . . . . AIR
FUEL . . . . . G
TRANSMISSION . . . . . HYDRO
STEERING . . . . . ZERO
STANDARD DECK . . . . . 50"
MSRP $6,695

RETAIL PRICING

YEAR	HIGH	LOW
1990	$898	$673

N5020

YEARS MFRD 1990-1990
SERIES . . . . . N SERIES
ENGINE . . . . . KOHLER
ENGINE HP 20
COOLING . . . . . AIR
FUEL . . . . . G
SPEEDS . . . . . VARIABLE
TRANSMISSION . . . . . HYDRO
STEERING . . . . . ZERO
STANDARD DECK . . . . . 50"
WEIGHT . . . . . 755 LBS.
MSRP $7,995

RETAIL PRICING

YEAR	HIGH	LOW
1990	$397	$298

N5024

YEARS MFRD 1988-1990
SERIES . . . . . N SERIES
ENGINE . . . . . ONAN
ENGINE HP 24
FUEL . . . . . G
TRANSMISSION . . . . . HYDRO
STEERING . . . . . ZERO
STANDARD DECK . . . . . 50"
WEIGHT . . . . . 755 LBS.
MSRP $8,795

RETAIL PRICING

YEAR	HIGH	LOW
1988	$242	$182
1989	$267	$200
1990	$295	$221

N6020

YEARS MFRD 1990-1990
SERIES . . . . . N SERIES
ENGINE . . . . . KOHLER
ENGINE HP 20
COOLING . . . . . AIR
FUEL . . . . . G
TRANSMISSION . . . . . HYDRO
STEERING . . . . . ZERO
STANDARD DECK . . . . . 60"
WEIGHT . . . . . 775 LBS.
MSRP $8,395

RETAIL PRICING

YEAR	HIGH	LOW
1990	$281	$211

N6024

YEARS MFRD 1988-1990
SERIES . . . . . N SERIES
ENGINE . . . . . ONAN
ENGINE HP 24
TRANSMISSION . . . . . HYDRO
STEERING . . . . . ZERO
STANDARD DECK . . . . . 60"
MSRP $8,995

RETAIL PRICING

YEAR	HIGH	LOW
1988	$248	$186
1989	$272	$204
1990	$302	$226

NX2000

YEARS MFRD 1992-1992
SERIES . . . . . NX SERIES
ENGINE . . . . . KOHLER
ENGINE HP 20
COOLING . . . . . AIR
FUEL . . . . . G
TRANSMISSION . . . . . HYDRO
STEERING . . . . . ZERO
STANDARD DECK . . . . . 36"
MSRP $7,595

RETAIL PRICING

YEAR	HIGH	LOW
1992	$396	$297

NX2001

YEARS MFRD 1992-1992
SERIES . . . . . NX SERIES
ENGINE . . . . . KOHLER
ENGINE HP 20
COOLING . . . . . AIR
FUEL . . . . . G
TRANSMISSION . . . . . HYDRO
STEERING . . . . . ZERO
STANDARD DECK . . . . . 36"
MSRP $6,595

RETAIL PRICING

YEAR	HIGH	LOW
1992	$344	$258

NX2400

YEARS MFRD 1992-1992
SERIES . . . . . NX SERIES
ENGINE . . . . . KOHLER
ENGINE HP 24
COOLING . . . . . AIR
FUEL . . . . . G
TRANSMISSION . . . . . HYDRO
STEERING . . . . . ZERO
STANDARD DECK . . . . . 36"
MSRP $8,995

RETAIL PRICING

YEAR	HIGH	LOW
1992	$469	$352

NX2401

YEARS MFRD 1992-1992
SERIES . . . . . NX SERIES
ENGINE . . . . . KOHLER
ENGINE HP 24
COOLING . . . . . AIR
FUEL . . . . . G
SPEEDS . . . . . VARIABLE
TRANSMISSION . . . . . HYDRO
STEERING . . . . . ZERO
STANDARD DECK . . . . . 36"
WEIGHT . . . . . 835 LBS.
MSRP $7,595

RETAIL PRICING

YEAR	HIGH	LOW
1992	$396	$297

RT270360

YEARS MFRD 2009-2009
SERIES . . . . . REALTREE SERIES
ENGINE . . . . . GENERAC
CYLINDERS 2
ENGINE HP 27
COOLING . . . . . AIR
FUEL . . . . . G
SPEEDS . . . . . VARIABLE
TRANSMISSION . . . . . HYDRO
STEERING . . . . . ZERO
BLADE CLUTCH . . . . . ELECTRIC
STANDARD DECK . . . . . 60"
MSRP $8,399

RETAIL PRICING

YEAR	HIGH	LOW
2009	$4,045	$3,034

SP2800

YEARS MFRD 2004-2004
SERIES . . . . . SUPREME SERIES
ENGINE . . . . . KOHLER EFI
ENGINE HP 28
COOLING . . . . . AIR
FUEL . . . . . G
SPEEDS . . . . . VARIABLE
TRANSMISSION . . . . . HYDRO
STEERING . . . . . ZERO
STANDARD DECK . . . . . 60"
MSRP $9,999

OPTIONS

70" DECK
GENERAC 32E

RETAIL PRICING

YEAR	HIGH	LOW
2004	$3,902	$2,927

SP2800-60

YEARS MFRD 2004-2007
SERIES . . . . .
. . . . . SUPREME MOWCHINE SERIES
ENGINE . . . . . KOHLER
ENGINE HP 28
COOLING . . . . . AIR
FUEL . . . . . G
SPEEDS . . . . . VARIABLE
TRANSMISSION . . . . . HYDRO
STEERING . . . . . ZERO
BLADE CLUTCH . . . . . ELECTRIC
STANDARD DECK . . . . . 60"
MSRP $9,999

RETAIL PRICING

YEAR	HIGH	LOW
2004	$1,982	$1,486
2005	$2,186	$1,640
2006	$2,414	$1,810
2007	$2,665	$1,998

SP3000

YEARS MFRD 2004-2004
SERIES . . . . . SUPREME SERIES
ENGINE . . . . . GERERAC
ENGINE HP 30
COOLING . . . . . AIR
FUEL . . . . . G
SPEEDS . . . . . VARIABLE
TRANSMISSION . . . . . HYDRO
STEERING . . . . . ZERO
STANDARD DECK . . . . . 72"
MSRP $10,499

RETAIL PRICING

YEAR	HIGH	LOW
2004	$2,211	$1,658

WXF2300

YEARS MFRD 2003-2003
ENGINE . . . . . KOHLER
ENGINE HP 23
COOLING . . . . . AIR
FUEL . . . . . G
SPEEDS . . . . . VARIABLE
TRANSMISSION . . . . . HYDRO
STEERING . . . . . ZERO
STANDARD DECK . . . . . 60"
MSRP $9,165

RETAIL PRICING

YEAR	HIGH	LOW
2003	$3,269	$2,452

X1701

YEARS MFRD 2002-2002
SERIES . . . . . X SERIES
ENGINE . . . . . KOHLER
ENGINE HP 17
FUEL . . . . . G
SPEEDS . . . . . VARIABLE
TRANSMISSION . . . . . HYDRO
STEERING . . . . . STANDARD
STANDARD DECK . . . . . 42"
MSRP $6,495

DIXIE CHOPPER

OPTIONS

50" DECK

RETAIL PRICING

YEAR	HIGH	LOW
2002	$1,134	$850

X2000

YEARS MFRD 1991-2000
SERIES . . . . X SERIES
ENGINE . . . . KOHLER
ENGINE HP 20
COOLING . . . . AIR
FUEL . . . . G
SPEEDS . . . . VARIABLE
TRANSMISSION . . . . HYDRO
STEERING . . . . ZERO
STANDARD DECK . . . . 50"
WEIGHT . . . . 950 LBS.
MSRP $9,125

OPTIONS

60" DECK

RETAIL PRICING

YEAR	HIGH	LOW
1992	$715	$537
1993	$795	$596
1994	$886	$664
1995	$981	$736
1996	$1,091	$818
1997	$1,212	$909
1998	$1,349	$1,012
1999	$1,496	$1,122
2000	$1,661	$1,246

X2001

YEARS MFRD 1992-2004
SERIES . . . . . . COATESVILLE SERIES
ENGINE . . . . KOHLER
ENGINE HP 20
COOLING . . . . AIR
FUEL . . . . G
TRANSMISSION . . . . HYDRO
STEERING . . . . ZERO
STANDARD DECK . . . . 50"
MSRP $5,999

OPTIONS

60" DECK
BAGGER
BLADE

RETAIL PRICING

YEAR	HIGH	LOW
1996	$686	$515
1997	$764	$573
1998	$848	$636
1999	$942	$706
2000	$1,045	$784
2001	$1,162	$872
2002	$1,292	$969
2003	$1,432	$1,074
2004	$1,591	$1,193

X2002

YEARS MFRD 1998-2001
SERIES . . . . X SERIES
ENGINE . . . . KOHLER
ENGINE HP 20
COOLING . . . . AIR
FUEL . . . . G
TRANSMISSION . . . . HYDRO
STEERING . . . . ZERO
STANDARD DECK . . . . 50"
MSRP $7,770

RETAIL PRICING

YEAR	HIGH	LOW
1998	$1,449	$1,087
1999	$1,627	$1,220
2000	$2,206	$1,654
2001	$2,328	$1,746

X2002-50HD

YEARS MFRD 1997-2000
SERIES . . . . X SERIES
ENGINE . . . . KOHLER
ENGINE HP 20
COOLING . . . . AIR
FUEL . . . . G
TRANSMISSION . . . . HYDRO
STEERING . . . . ZERO
STANDARD DECK . . . . 50"
WEIGHT . . . . 935 LBS.
MSRP $7,770

OPTIONS

60" BLADE
BAGGER

RETAIL PRICING

YEAR	HIGH	LOW
1997	$840	$630
1998	$927	$695
1999	$1,023	$767
2000	$1,129	$847

X2002-50STD

YEARS MFRD 1997-1997
SERIES . . . . X SERIES
ENGINE . . . . KOHLER
ENGINE HP 20
COOLING . . . . AIR
FUEL . . . . G
TRANSMISSION . . . . HYDRO
STEERING . . . . ZERO
STANDARD DECK . . . . 50"
MSRP $7,270

RETAIL PRICING

YEAR	HIGH	LOW
1997	$752	$564

X2003-50

YEARS MFRD 2005-2005
SERIES . . . .
. . . . COATESVILLE CLASSIC SERIES
ENGINE . . . . KOHLER
ENGINE HP 20
COOLING . . . . AIR
FUEL . . . . G
SPEEDS . . . . VARIABLE
TRANSMISSION . . . . HYDRO
STEERING . . . . ZERO
BLADE CLUTCH . . . . ELECTRIC
STANDARD DECK . . . . 50"
MSRP $6,599

RETAIL PRICING

YEAR	HIGH	LOW
2005	$1,512	$1,134

X2200

YEARS MFRD 1999-1999
SERIES . . . . X SERIES
ENGINE . . . . KOHLER
ENGINE HP 22
FUEL . . . . G
TRANSMISSION . . . . HYDRO
STEERING . . . . STANDARD
STANDARD DECK . . . . 50"
MSRP $9,830

RETAIL PRICING

YEAR	HIGH	LOW
1999	$2,140	$1,605

X2200-50HD

YEARS MFRD 1997-2000
SERIES . . . . X SERIES
ENGINE . . . . KOHLER
ENGINE HP 22
COOLING . . . . AIR
FUEL . . . . G
TRANSMISSION . . . . HYDRO
STEERING . . . . ZERO
STANDARD DECK . . . . 50"
MSRP $9,830

OPTIONS

60" BLADE
BAGGER

RETAIL PRICING

YEAR	HIGH	LOW
1997	$1,062	$797
1998	$1,173	$880
1999	$1,294	$970
2000	$1,428	$1,071

X2202-50HD

YEARS MFRD 1997-1999
SERIES . . . . X SERIES
ENGINE . . . . KOHLER
ENGINE HP 22
COOLING . . . . AIR
FUEL . . . . G
TRANSMISSION . . . . HYDRO
STEERING . . . . ZERO
STANDARD DECK . . . . 50"
MSRP $7,935

OPTIONS

60" BLADE
BAGGER

SERIAL NUMBERS

YEAR	BEGINNING NO.
1997	79
1998	89
1999	99

RETAIL PRICING

YEAR	HIGH	LOW
1997	$794	$595
1998	$878	$659
1999	$968	$726

X2203-50

YEARS MFRD 2000-2000
SERIES . . . . X SERIES
ENGINE . . . . KOHLER
ENGINE HP 22
FUEL . . . . G
STEERING . . . . ZERO
STANDARD DECK . . . . 50"
MSRP $8,595

RETAIL PRICING

YEAR	HIGH	LOW
2000	$1,250	$937

X2300

YEARS MFRD 2000-2001
SERIES . . . . X SERIES
ENGINE . . . . KAWASAKI
ENGINE HP 23
FUEL . . . . G
TRANSMISSION . . . . HYDRO
STEERING . . . . STANDARD
STANDARD DECK . . . . 50"
MSRP $9,830

RETAIL PRICING

YEAR	HIGH	LOW
2000	$2,965	$2,224
2001	$3,121	$2,341

X2303

YEARS MFRD 2000-2001
SERIES . . . . X SERIES
ENGINE . . . . KAWASAKI
ENGINE HP 23
FUEL . . . . G
TRANSMISSION . . . . HYDRO
STEERING . . . . STANDARD
STANDARD DECK . . . . 50"
MSRP $8,595

RETAIL PRICING

YEAR	HIGH	LOW
2000	$2,510	$1,882
2001	$2,646	$1,985

X2303-50

YEARS MFRD 2007-2007
SERIES . . . . X SERIES
ENGINE . . . . KOHLER
ENGINE HP 23
COOLING . . . . AIR
FUEL . . . . G
SPEEDS . . . . VARIABLE
TRANSMISSION . . . . HYDRO
STEERING . . . . ZERO
BLADE CLUTCH . . . . ELECTRIC
STANDARD DECK . . . . 50"
MSRP $6,999

RETAIL PRICING

YEAR	HIGH	LOW
2007	$1,865	$1,399

X2400-50

YEARS MFRD 1991-1995
SERIES. . . . . X SERIES
ENGINE . . . . KOHLER
ENGINE HP 23
COOLING . . . . AIR
FUEL . . . . G
TRANSMISSION . . . . HYDRO
STEERING. . . . . ZERO
STANDARD DECK . . . . 50"
MSRP. $8,595

OPTIONS

60" DECK
BAGGER
BLADE

SERIAL NUMBERS

YEAR	BEGINNING NO.
1991	19
1992	29
1993	39
1994	49
1995	59

RETAIL PRICING

YEAR	HIGH	LOW
1991	$491	$368
1992	$543	$407
1993	$599	$449
1994	$661	$495
1995	$729	$547

X2401-50

YEARS MFRD 1992-1996
SERIES. . . . . X SERIES
ENGINE . . . . KOHLER
ENGINE HP 22
FUEL . . . . G
TRANSMISSION . . . . HYDRO
STEERING. . . . . ZERO
STANDARD DECK . . . . 50"
MSRP. $7,375

OPTIONS

60" DECK
BAGGER
BLADE

RETAIL PRICING

YEAR	HIGH	LOW
1992	$467	$351
1993	$515	$387
1994	$569	$427
1995	$629	$472
1996	$695	$521

X2500-50

YEARS MFRD 1998-2000
SERIES. . . . . X SERIES
ENGINE . . . . KOHLER
ENGINE HP 25
FUEL . . . . G
TRANSMISSION . . . . HYDRO
STEERING. . . . . ZERO
STANDARD DECK . . . . 50"
MSRP. $10,080

OPTIONS

60" BLADE
BAGGER

RETAIL PRICING

YEAR	HIGH	LOW
1998	$1,202	$902
1999	$1,327	$995
2000	$1,465	$1,099

X2502-50

YEARS MFRD 1998-1999
SERIES. . . . . X SERIES
ENGINE . . . . KOHLER
ENGINE HP 25
FUEL . . . . G
TRANSMISSION . . . . HYDRO
STEERING. . . . . ZERO
STANDARD DECK . . . . 50"
MSRP. $8,185

OPTIONS

60" BLADE
60" DECK
BAGGER

RETAIL PRICING

YEAR	HIGH	LOW
1998	$905	$678
1999	$999	$749

X2503

YEARS MFRD 2000-2006
SERIES. . . . . . COATESVILLE SERIES
ENGINE . . . . KOHLER
ENGINE HP 25
FUEL . . . . G
SPEEDS . . . . VARIABLE
TRANSMISSION . . . . HYDRO
STEERING. . . . . ZERO
STANDARD DECK . . . . 60"
MSRP. $7,599

RETAIL PRICING

YEAR	HIGH	LOW
2000	$3,225	$2,419
2002	$3,477	$2,608
2003	$3,528	$2,646
2004	$3,547	$2,660
2005	$3,725	$2,794
2006	$3,776	$2,832

X2503-50

YEARS MFRD 2000-2005
SERIES. . . . . X SERIES
ENGINE . . . . KOHLER
ENGINE HP 25
COOLING . . . . AIR
FUEL . . . . G
SPEEDS . . . . VARIABLE
TRANSMISSION . . . . HYDRO
STEERING. . . . . ZERO
BLADE CLUTCH . . . . ELECTRIC
STANDARD DECK . . . . 50"
MSRP. $7,699

OPTIONS

60" DECK (2003-2005)

SERIAL NUMBERS

YEAR	BEGINNING NO.
2004	04XXXXX

RETAIL PRICING

YEAR	HIGH	LOW
2000	$1,077	$808
2001	$1,189	$892
2002	$1,312	$984
2003	$1,448	$1,086
2004	$1,604	$1,203
2005	$1,764	$1,323

X2503-60

YEARS MFRD 2005-2006
SERIES. . . . .
. . . . COATESVILLE CLASSIC SERIES
ENGINE . . . . KOHLER
ENGINE HP 25
COOLING . . . . AIR
FUEL . . . . G
SPEEDS . . . . VARIABLE
TRANSMISSION . . . . HYDRO
STEERING. . . . . ZERO
BLADE CLUTCH . . . . ELECTRIC
STANDARD DECK . . . . 60"
MSRP. $7,699

RETAIL PRICING

YEAR	HIGH	LOW
2005	$3,725	$2,794

X2600

YEARS MFRD 1999-1999
SERIES. . . . . X SERIES
ENGINE . . . . YANMAR
ENGINE HP 26
FUEL . . . . D
TRANSMISSION . . . . HYDRO
STEERING. . . . . STANDARD
STANDARD DECK . . . . 60"
MSRP. $12,995

OPTIONS

72" DECK

RETAIL PRICING

YEAR	HIGH	LOW
1999	$3,912	$2,934

X2703-60

YEARS MFRD 2006-2007
SERIES COATSVILLE CLASSIC SERIES
ENGINE . . . . KOHLER
ENGINE HP 27
COOLING . . . . AIR
FUEL . . . . G
SPEEDS . . . . VARIABLE
TRANSMISSION . . . . HYDRO
STEERING. . . . . ZERO
STANDARD DECK . . . . 60"
MSRP. $8,499

RETAIL PRICING

YEAR	HIGH	LOW
2006	$2,051	$1,538
2007	$2,265	$1,699

X5018

YEARS MFRD 1990-1990
SERIES. . . . . X SERIES
ENGINE . . . . KOHLER
ENGINE HP 18
COOLING . . . . AIR
FUEL . . . . G
TRANSMISSION . . . . HYDRO
STEERING. . . . . ZERO
STANDARD DECK . . . . 50"
MSRP. $6,395

RETAIL PRICING

YEAR	HIGH	LOW
1990	$828	$621

X5020

YEARS MFRD 1990-1990
SERIES. . . . . X SERIES
ENGINE . . . . KOHLER
ENGINE HP 20
COOLING . . . . AIR
FUEL . . . . G
TRANSMISSION . . . . HYDRO
STEERING. . . . . ZERO
STANDARD DECK . . . . 50"
MSRP. $6,895

RETAIL PRICING

YEAR	HIGH	LOW
1990	$944	$708

X5024

YEARS MFRD 1990-1990
SERIES. . . . . X SERIES
ENGINE . . . . ONAN
ENGINE HP 24
FUEL . . . . G
TRANSMISSION . . . . HYDRO
STEERING. . . . . ZERO
STANDARD DECK . . . . 50"
MSRP. $7,795

RETAIL PRICING

YEAR	HIGH	LOW
1990	$1,154	$866

X6020

YEARS MFRD 1990-1990
SERIES. . . . . X SERIES
ENGINE . . . . KOHLER
ENGINE HP 20
FUEL . . . . G
TRANSMISSION . . . . HYDRO
STEERING. . . . . STANDARD
STANDARD DECK . . . . 60"
MSRP. $7,095

RETAIL PRICING

YEAR	HIGH	LOW
1990	$990	$742

X6024

YEARS MFRD 1990-1990
SERIES. . . . . X SERIES
ENGINE . . . . ONAN
ENGINE HP 24
COOLING . . . . AIR
FUEL . . . . G
TRANSMISSION . . . . HYDRO
STEERING. . . . . ZERO
STANDARD DECK . . . . 60"
MSRP. $7,995

DIXIE CHOPPER

RETAIL PRICING

YEAR	HIGH	LOW
1990	$1,201	$900

XC3300-74

YEARS MFRD 2007-2007
SERIES . . . . X XCALIBER SERIES
ENGINE . . . . GENERAC
ENGINE HP 33
COOLING . . . . AIR
FUEL . . . . G
SPEEDS . . . . VARIABLE
TRANSMISSION . . . . HYDRO
STEERING . . . . ZERO
BLADE CLUTCH . . . . ELECTRIC
STANDARD DECK . . . . 74"
MSRP $11,599

RETAIL PRICING

YEAR	HIGH	LOW
2007	$3,090	$2,317

XCALIBER 4X4

YEARS MFRD 2012-2012
SERIES . . . . XCALIBER SERIES
ENGINE . . . . GENERAC
ENGINE HP 33
COOLING . . . . AIR
FUEL . . . . G
SPEEDS . . . . VARIABLE
TRANSMISSION . . . . HYDRO
STEERING . . . . ZERO
STANDARD DECK . . . . 56"
MSRP $18,799

RETAIL PRICING

YEAR	HIGH	LOW
2012	$8,160	$6,120

XCALIBER TWIN

YEARS MFRD 2014-2014
ENGINE . . . . GENERAC (2)
ENGINE HP 54
COOLING . . . . LIQUID
FUEL . . . . G
SPEEDS . . . . VARIABLE
TRANSMISSION . . . . HYDRO
STEERING . . . . ZERO
STANDARD DECK . . . . 74"
MSRP $15,999

RETAIL PRICING

YEAR	HIGH	LOW
2014	$7,989	$5,992

XF2200

YEARS MFRD 1999-1999
SERIES . . . . XF SERIES
ENGINE . . . . KOHLER
ENGINE HP 22
FUEL . . . . G
TRANSMISSION . . . . HYDRO
STEERING . . . . STANDARD
STANDARD DECK . . . . 50"
MSRP $9,830

RETAIL PRICING

YEAR	HIGH	LOW
1999	$2,800	$2,100

XF2300-50

YEARS MFRD 2002-2003
SERIES . . . . . . FLATLANDER SERIES
ENGINE . . . . KOHLER
ENGINE HP 23
FUEL . . . . G
TRANSMISSION . . . . HYDRO
STEERING . . . . STANDARD
STANDARD DECK . . . . 50"
MSRP $9,165

RETAIL PRICING

YEAR	HIGH	LOW
2002	$1,671	$1,253
2003	$1,845	$1,384

XF2500-60

YEARS MFRD 2002-2002
SERIES . . . . . . FLATLANDER SERIES
ENGINE . . . . KOHLER
ENGINE HP 25
FUEL . . . . G
TRANSMISSION . . . . HYDRO
STEERING . . . . STANDARD
STANDARD DECK . . . . 60"
MSRP $9,695

RETAIL PRICING

YEAR	HIGH	LOW
2002	$1,770	$1,327

XF2600-60EFI

YEARS MFRD 2002-2003
SERIES . . . . . . FLATLANDER SERIES
ENGINE . . . . KOHLER EFI
ENGINE HP 26
COOLING . . . . AIR
FUEL . . . . G
SPEEDS . . . . VARIABLE
TRANSMISSION . . . . HYDRO
STEERING . . . . ZERO
STANDARD DECK . . . . 60"
MSRP $9,895

RETAIL PRICING

YEAR	HIGH	LOW
2002	$1,803	$1,352
2003	$1,991	$1,494

XF2700

YEARS MFRD 2004-2005
SERIES . . . . XF SERIES
ENGINE . . . . KOHLER
ENGINE HP 27
COOLING . . . . AIR
FUEL . . . . G
SPEEDS . . . . VARIABLE
TRANSMISSION . . . . HYDRO
STEERING . . . . ZERO
STANDARD DECK . . . . 50"
MSRP $9,895

RETAIL PRICING

YEAR	HIGH	LOW
2004	$2,260	$1,695
2005	$2,511	$1,883

XF2700 FLATLANDER

YEARS MFRD 1994-1998
SERIES . . . . XF SERIES
ENGINE . . . . KOHLER
ENGINE HP 20
COOLING . . . . AIR
FUEL . . . . G
TRANSMISSION . . . . HYDRO
STEERING . . . . ZERO
STANDARD DECK . . . . 50"
MSRP $9,730

OPTIONS

60" DECK

RETAIL PRICING

YEAR	HIGH	LOW
1994	$886	$664
1995	$981	$736
1996	$1,091	$818
1997	$1,212	$909
1998	$1,349	$1,012

XFG2700

YEARS MFRD 2006-2007
SERIES . . . . . . FLATLANDER SERIES
ENGINE . . . . GENERAC
ENGINE HP 27
COOLING . . . . AIR
FUEL . . . . G
SPEEDS . . . . VARIABLE
TRANSMISSION . . . . HYDRO
STEERING . . . . ZERO
STANDARD DECK . . . . 50"
MSRP $8,499

OPTIONS

60" DECK

RETAIL PRICING

YEAR	HIGH	LOW
2006	$2,088	$1,566
2007	$2,304	$1,728

XG2503-50

YEARS MFRD 2006-2007
SERIES COATSVILLE CLASSIC SERIES
ENGINE . . . . GENERAC
ENGINE HP 25
COOLING . . . . AIR
FUEL . . . . G
SPEEDS . . . . VARIABLE
TRANSMISSION . . . . HYDRO
STEERING . . . . ZERO
BLADE CLUTCH . . . . ELECTRIC
STANDARD DECK . . . . 50"
MSRP $7,799

SERIAL NUMBERS

YEAR	BEGINNING NO.
2006	60XXXX

RETAIL PRICING

YEAR	HIGH	LOW
2006	$1,915	$1,436
2007	$2,115	$1,586

XG2703

YEARS MFRD 2004-2007
SERIES . . . .
. . . . COATESVILLE SERIES
ENGINE . . . . GENERAC
SPEEDS . . . . VARIABLE
TRANSMISSION . . . . HYDRO
STEERING . . . . ZERO
STANDARD DECK . . . . 60"
MSRP $8,499

RETAIL PRICING

YEAR	HIGH	LOW
2004	$3,375	$2,531
2007	$3,784	$2,838

XG2703-60

YEARS MFRD 2004-2007
SERIES . . . .
. . . . COATESVILLE CLASSIC SERIES
ENGINE . . . . GUARDIAN
ENGINE HP 27
COOLING . . . . AIR
FUEL . . . . G
SPEEDS . . . . VARIABLE
TRANSMISSION . . . . HYDRO
STEERING . . . . ZERO
BLADE CLUTCH . . . . ELECTRIC
STANDARD DECK . . . . 60"
MSRP $8,499

SERIAL NUMBERS

YEAR	BEGINNING NO.
2004	04XXXXX
2006	60XXXX

RETAIL PRICING

YEAR	HIGH	LOW
2004	$1,713	$1,285
2005	$1,891	$1,419
2006	$2,088	$1,566
2007	$2,304	$1,728

XK2303

YEARS MFRD 2000-2001
SERIES . . . . XK SERIES
ENGINE . . . . KAWASAKI
ENGINE HP 23
FUEL . . . . G
TRANSMISSION . . . . HYDRO
STEERING . . . . STANDARD
STANDARD DECK . . . . 50"
MSRP $8,595

RETAIL PRICING

YEAR	HIGH	LOW
2000	$2,510	$1,882
2001	$2,646	$1,985

XK2501-60

YEARS MFRD 2002-2002
SERIES . . . . XK SERIES

ENGINE . . . . KAWASAKI
ENGINE HP 25
FUEL . . . . G
TRANSMISSION . . . . HYDRO
STEERING. . . . . ZERO
STANDARD DECK . . . . 60"
MSRP. $8,395

RETAIL PRICING

YEAR	HIGH	LOW
2002	$1,533	$1,150

XK2503-50

YEARS MFRD 2002-2003
SERIES. . . . . XK SERIES
ENGINE . . . . KAWASAKI
ENGINE HP 25
FUEL . . . . G
SPEEDS . . . . VARIABLE
TRANSMISSION . . . . HYDRO
STEERING. . . . . ZERO
STANDARD DECK . . . . 50"
MSRP. $8,795

OPTIONS

60" DECK

RETAIL PRICING

YEAR	HIGH	LOW
2002	$1,529	$1,147
2003	$1,689	$1,266

XT2800

YEARS MFRD 2003-2003
SERIES. . . . . XT SERIES
ENGINE . . . . KOHLER EFI
ENGINE HP 28
COOLING . . . . AIR
FUEL . . . . G
SPEEDS . . . . VARIABLE
TRANSMISSION . . . . HYDRO
STEERING. . . . . ZERO
STANDARD DECK . . . . 60"
MSRP. $9,895

OPTIONS

72" DECK

RETAIL PRICING

YEAR	HIGH	LOW
2003	$1,898	$1,424

XT3000

YEARS MFRD 2003-2004
SERIES. . . . . XT SERIES
ENGINE . . . . GENERAC
ENGINE HP 30
FUEL . . . . G
TRANSMISSION . . . . HYDRO
STEERING. . . . . ZERO
STANDARD DECK . . . . 60"
MSRP. $9,999

OPTIONS

72" DECK
80" DECK

SERIAL NUMBERS

YEAR	BEGINNING NO.
2004	04XXXXX

RETAIL PRICING

YEAR	HIGH	LOW
2003	$1,907	$1,430
2004	$2,105	$1,579

XT3200

YEARS MFRD 2005-2005
SERIES XTREME MOWCHINE SERIES
ENGINE . . . . GENERAC OHV
ENGINE HP 32
COOLING . . . . AIR
SPEEDS . . . . VARIABLE
TRANSMISSION . . . . HYDRO
STEERING. . . . . ZERO
STANDARD DECK . . . . 60"
MSRP. $9,999

OPTIONS

72" DECK

RETAIL PRICING

YEAR	HIGH	LOW
2005	$2,968	$2,226

XT3200-60

YEARS MFRD 2005-2006
SERIES XTREME MOWCHINE SERIES
ENGINE . . . . GUARDIAN
ENGINE HP 32
COOLING . . . . AIR
FUEL . . . . G
SPEEDS . . . . VARIABLE
TRANSMISSION . . . . HYDRO
STEERING. . . . . ZERO
BLADE CLUTCH . . . . ELECTRIC
STANDARD DECK . . . . 60"
MSRP. $9,999

RETAIL PRICING

YEAR	HIGH	LOW
2005	$2,384	$1,788

XT3200-72

YEARS MFRD 2005-2005
SERIES XTREME MOWCHINE SERIES
ENGINE . . . . GUARDIAN
ENGINE HP 32
COOLING . . . . AIR
FUEL . . . . G
SPEEDS . . . . VARIABLE
TRANSMISSION . . . . HYDRO
STEERING. . . . . ZERO
BLADE CLUTCH . . . . ELECTRIC
STANDARD DECK . . . . 72"
MSRP. $10,499

RETAIL PRICING

YEAR	HIGH	LOW
2005	$2,506	$1,879

XT3300

YEARS MFRD 2006-2007
SERIES. . . . . XTREME SERIES
ENGINE . . . . GENERAC
ENGINE HP 33
COOLING . . . . AIR
FUEL . . . . G
SPEEDS . . . . VARIABLE
TRANSMISSION . . . . HYDRO
STEERING. . . . . ZERO
STANDARD DECK . . . . 60"
MSRP. $9,999

OPTIONS

72" DECK

RETAIL PRICING

YEAR	HIGH	LOW
2006	$2,456	$1,842
2007	$2,712	$2,034

XW2000

YEARS MFRD 1994-2000
SERIES. . . . . XW SERIES
ENGINE . . . . KOHLER
ENGINE HP 20
COOLING . . . . AIR
FUEL . . . . G
SPEEDS . . . . VARIABLE
TRANSMISSION . . . . HYDRO
STEERING. . . . . ZERO
STANDARD DECK . . . . 60"
WEIGHT . . . . 950 LBS.
MSRP. $9,125

OPTIONS

60" BLADE
BAGGER

RETAIL PRICING

YEAR	HIGH	LOW
1994	$781	$586
1995	$861	$646
1996	$951	$713
1997	$1,049	$786
1998	$1,158	$869
1999	$1,278	$958
2000	$1,412	$1,059

XW2001

YEARS MFRD 1994-1996
SERIES. . . . . XW SERIES
ENGINE . . . . KOHLER
ENGINE HP 20
COOLING . . . . AIR
FUEL . . . . G
TRANSMISSION . . . . HYDRO
STEERING. . . . . ZERO
STANDARD DECK . . . . 60"
MSRP. $7,495

OPTIONS

BAGGER
BLADE

SERIAL NUMBERS

YEAR	BEGINNING NO.
1994	49XXXXX
1995	59XXXXX
1996	69XXXXX

RETAIL PRICING

YEAR	HIGH	LOW
1994	$665	$499
1995	$734	$551
1996	$809	$607

XW2002

YEARS MFRD 1997-2000
SERIES. . . . . XW SERIES
ENGINE . . . . KOHLER
ENGINE HP 20
COOLING . . . . AIR
FUEL . . . . G
TRANSMISSION . . . . HYDRO
STEERING. . . . . ZERO
STANDARD DECK . . . . 50"
WEIGHT . . . . 915 LBS.
MSRP. $8,000

OPTIONS

60" BLADE
BAGGER

RETAIL PRICING

YEAR	HIGH	LOW
1997	$920	$690
1998	$1,015	$761
1999	$1,121	$841
2000	$1,237	$928

XW2200

YEARS MFRD 1997-2000
SERIES. . . . . XW SERIES
ENGINE . . . . KOHLER
ENGINE HP 22
COOLING . . . . AIR
FUEL . . . . G
TRANSMISSION . . . . HYDRO
STEERING. . . . . ZERO
STANDARD DECK . . . . 60"
MSRP. $9,830

OPTIONS

60" BLADE
BAGGER

RETAIL PRICING

YEAR	HIGH	LOW
1997	$1,131	$848
1998	$1,248	$936
1999	$1,377	$1,033
2000	$1,520	$1,140

XW2202

YEARS MFRD 1997-1999
SERIES. . . . . XW SERIES
ENGINE . . . . KOHLER
ENGINE HP 22
COOLING . . . . AIR
FUEL . . . . G
TRANSMISSION . . . . HYDRO
STEERING. . . . . ZERO
STANDARD DECK . . . . 60"
MSRP. $7,935

OPTIONS

60" BLADE
BAGGER

RETAIL PRICING

YEAR	HIGH	LOW
1997	$886	$664
1998	$979	$734
1999	$1,080	$810

DIXIE CHOPPER

XW2203

YEARS MFRD........2000-2000
SERIES..............XW SERIES
ENGINE..............KOHLER
ENGINE HP..............22
FUEL..............G
STEERING..............ZERO
STANDARD DECK..............60"
MSRP..............$8,595

RETAIL PRICING

YEAR	HIGH	LOW
2000	$1,329	$997

XW2300

YEARS MFRD........2002-2002
SERIES..............XW SERIES
ENGINE..............KOHLER
ENGINE HP..............23
COOLING..............AIR
FUEL..............G
TRANSMISSION..............HYDRO
STEERING..............ZERO
STANDARD DECK..............60"
MSRP..............$9,165

RETAIL PRICING

YEAR	HIGH	LOW
2002	$1,673	$1,255

XW2303

YEARS MFRD........2000-2001
SERIES..............XW SERIES
ENGINE..............KAWASAKI
ENGINE HP..............23
FUEL..............G
TRANSMISSION..............HYDRO
STEERING..............STANDARD
STANDARD DECK..............60"
MSRP..............$8,595

RETAIL PRICING

YEAR	HIGH	LOW
2000	$2,510	$1,882
2001	$2,646	$1,985

XW2400

YEARS MFRD........1994-1996
SERIES..............XW SERIES
ENGINE..............KOHLER
ENGINE HP..............24
COOLING..............AIR
FUEL..............G
TRANSMISSION..............HYDRO
STEERING..............ZERO
STANDARD DECK..............60"
MSRP..............$9,495

OPTIONS

BAGGER
BLADE

RETAIL PRICING

YEAR	HIGH	LOW
1994	$842	$631
1995	$930	$698
1996	$1,026	$770

XW2401

YEARS MFRD........1994-1996
SERIES..............XW SERIES
ENGINE..............KOHLER
ENGINE HP..............24
COOLING..............AIR
FUEL..............G
TRANSMISSION..............HYDRO
STEERING..............ZERO
STANDARD DECK..............60"
MSRP..............$8,595

OPTIONS

BAGGER
BLADE

RETAIL PRICING

YEAR	HIGH	LOW
1994	$761	$571
1995	$841	$631
1996	$929	$697

XW2500

YEARS MFRD........1998-2002
SERIES..............XW SERIES
ENGINE..............KOHLER
ENGINE HP..............25
COOLING..............AIR
FUEL..............G
TRANSMISSION..............HYDRO
STEERING..............ZERO
STANDARD DECK..............60"
MSRP..............$10,080

OPTIONS

60" BLADE
BAGGER

SERIAL NUMBERS

YEAR	BEGINNING NO.
1998	89XXXXX
1999	99XXXXX
2000	00XXXXX
2001	10XXXXX
2002	20XXXXX

RETAIL PRICING

YEAR	HIGH	LOW
1998	$1,245	$933
1999	$1,369	$1,027
2000	$1,511	$1,133
2001	$1,667	$1,250
2002	$1,841	$1,381

XW2502

YEARS MFRD........1998-1999
SERIES..............XW SERIES
ENGINE..............KOHLER
ENGINE HP..............25
FUEL..............G
TRANSMISSION..............HYDRO
STEERING..............ZERO
STANDARD DECK..............60"
MSRP..............$8,185

OPTIONS

60" BLADE
BAGGER

RETAIL PRICING

YEAR	HIGH	LOW
1998	$1,009	$757
1999	$1,113	$835

XW2503

YEARS MFRD........2000-2000
SERIES..............XW SERIES
ENGINE..............KOHLER
ENGINE HP..............25
FUEL..............G
STEERING..............ZERO
STANDARD DECK..............60"
MSRP..............$8,750

RETAIL PRICING

YEAR	HIGH	LOW
2000	$1,353	$1,015

XW2600

YEARS MFRD........2002-2003
SERIES..............XW SERIES
ENGINE..............KOHLER EFI
ENGINE HP..............26
FUEL..............G
SPEEDS..............VARIABLE
TRANSMISSION..............HYDRO
STEERING..............STANDARD
STANDARD DECK..............60"
MSRP..............$9,895

RETAIL PRICING

YEAR	HIGH	LOW
2002	$1,721	$1,291
2003	$1,898	$1,424

XWD2600

YEARS MFRD........2002-2002
ENGINE..............YANMAR
ENGINE HP..............26
COOLING..............AIR
FUEL..............D
TRANSMISSION..............HYDRO
STEERING..............ZERO
STANDARD DECK..............60"
MSRP..............$12,995

OPTIONS

72" DECK

RETAIL PRICING

YEAR	HIGH	LOW
2002	$2,374	$1,780

XWD3500

YEARS MFRD........2007-2007
ENGINE..............YANMAR
ENGINE HP..............35
COOLING..............LIQUID
FUEL..............D
SPEEDS..............VARIABLE
TRANSMISSION..............HYDRO
STEERING..............ZERO
STANDARD DECK..............60"
MSRP..............$13,199

OPTIONS

72" DECK

RETAIL PRICING

YEAR	HIGH	LOW
2007	$3,578	$2,683

XWF2400

YEARS MFRD........2003-2003
SERIES..............XWF SERIES
ENGINE..............HONDA
ENGINE HP..............24
COOLING..............AIR
FUEL..............G
SPEEDS..............VARIABLE
TRANSMISSION..............HYDRO
STEERING..............ZERO
STANDARD DECK..............60"
MSRP..............$9,695

RETAIL PRICING

YEAR	HIGH	LOW
2003	$1,860	$1,395

XWF2700

YEARS MFRD........2003-2006
SERIES..............XWF SERIES
ENGINE..............KOHLER
ENGINE HP..............27
COOLING..............AIR
FUEL..............G
SPEEDS..............VARIABLE
TRANSMISSION..............HYDRO
STEERING..............ZERO
BLADE CLUTCH..............ELECTRIC
STANDARD DECK..............60"
MSRP..............$8,999

RETAIL PRICING

YEAR	HIGH	LOW
2003	$1,784	$1,338
2004	$1,969	$1,477
2005	$2,173	$1,629
2006	$2,398	$1,799

XWK2303

YEARS MFRD........2000-2001
ENGINE..............KAWASAKI
ENGINE HP..............23
FUEL..............G
TRANSMISSION..............HYDRO
STEERING..............STANDARD
STANDARD DECK..............60"
MSRP..............$8,595

RETAIL PRICING

YEAR	HIGH	LOW
2000	$3,168	$2,376
2001	$3,305	$2,478

XWK2503

YEARS MFRD........2002-2002
SERIES..............XWK SERIES
ENGINE..............KAWASAKI
ENGINE HP..............25
FUEL..............G
TRANSMISSION..............HYDRO
STEERING..............STANDARD
STANDARD DECK..............60"
MSRP..............$8,795

RETAIL PRICING

YEAR	HIGH	LOW
2002	$1,527	$1,145

XWL2300

YEARS MFRD 2001-2001
ENGINE . . . . KOHLER
ENGINE HP 23
FUEL . . . . G
TRANSMISSION . . . . .HYDRO
STEERING. . . . . .STANDARD
STANDARD DECK . . . . 60"
MSRP. $9,250

RETAIL PRICING

YEAR	HIGH	LOW
2001	$3,555	$2,667

XXG2703

YEARS MFRD 2005-2007
SERIES. . . . .
. . . . COATESVILLE CLASSIC SERIES
ENGINE . . . . GUARDIAN
ENGINE HP 27
COOLING . . . . .AIR
FUEL . . . . G
SPEEDS . . . . .VARIABLE
TRANSMISSION . . . . .HYDRO
STEERING. . . . . .ZERO
BLADE CLUTCH . . . . .ELECTRIC
STANDARD DECK . . . . 72"
MSRP. $9,499

RETAIL PRICING

YEAR	HIGH	LOW
2005	$2,684	$2,013
2006	$2,980	$2,235
2007	$3,308	$2,481

XXG5400-72

YEARS MFRD 2005-2006
ENGINE . . . . GUARDIAN
ENGINE HP 54
COOLING . . . . .AIR
FUEL . . . . G
SPEEDS . . . . .VARIABLE
TRANSMISSION . . . . .HYDRO
STEERING. . . . . .ZERO
BLADE CLUTCH . . . . .ELECTRIC
STANDARD DECK . . . . 72"
MSRP. $12,999

SERIAL NUMBERS

YEAR	BEGINNING NO.
2006	60XXXX

RETAIL PRICING

YEAR	HIGH	LOW
2005	$3,813	$2,860
2006	$4,238	$3,178

XXW2500

YEARS MFRD 1997-2000
SERIES. . . . . XXW SERIES
ENGINE . . . . KOHLER
ENGINE HP 25
COOLING . . . . .AIR
FUEL . . . . G
TRANSMISSION . . . . .HYDRO
STEERING. . . . . .ZERO
STANDARD DECK . . . . 72"
MSRP. $10,900

OPTIONS

60" BLADE
BAGGER

RETAIL PRICING

YEAR	HIGH	LOW
1997	$1,216	$912
1998	$1,342	$1,006
1999	$1,481	$1,111
2000	$1,635	$1,226

XXW2503

YEARS MFRD 2000-2000
SERIES. . . . . XXW SERIES
ENGINE . . . . KOHLER
ENGINE HP 25
FUEL . . . . G
TRANSMISSION . . . . .HYDRO
STEERING. . . . . .STANDARD
STANDARD DECK . . . . 72"
MSRP. $10,100

RETAIL PRICING

YEAR	HIGH	LOW
2000	$3,723	$2,792

XXW2600EFI

YEARS MFRD 2002-2003
SERIES. . . . . XXW SERIES
ENGINE . . . . KOHLER
ENGINE HP 26
FUEL . . . . G
TRANSMISSION . . . . .HYDRO
STEERING. . . . . .STANDARD
STANDARD DECK . . . . 72"
MSRP. $10,499

RETAIL PRICING

YEAR	HIGH	LOW
2002	$2,401	$1,801
2003	$2,666	$1,999

XXW4000

YEARS MFRD 1998-2000
SERIES. . . . . XXW SERIES
ENGINE . . . . KOHLER
ENGINE HP 40
SPEEDS . . . . .VARIABLE
TRANSMISSION . . . . .HYDRO
STEERING. . . . . .ZERO
STANDARD DECK . . . . 72"
MSRP. $12,800

OPTIONS

60" BLADE
BAGGER

RETAIL PRICING

YEAR	HIGH	LOW
1998	$1,576	$1,182
1999	$1,740	$1,305
2000	$1,920	$1,440

XXW4600

YEARS MFRD 2002-2005
SERIES. . . . . XXW SERIES
ENGINE . . . . KOHLER
ENGINE HP 46
SPEEDS . . . . .VARIABLE
TRANSMISSION . . . . .HYDRO
STEERING. . . . . .ZERO
STANDARD DECK . . . . 72"
MSRP. $12,599

RETAIL PRICING

YEAR	HIGH	LOW
2002	$2,409	$1,807
2003	$2,659	$1,994
2004	$2,935	$2,201
2005	$3,240	$2,430

XXWD2600

YEARS MFRD 2001-2003
ENGINE . . . . YANMAR
ENGINE HP 26
FUEL . . . . D
TRANSMISSION . . . . .HYDRO
STEERING. . . . . .STANDARD
STANDARD DECK . . . . 60"
MSRP. $14,300

OPTIONS

72" DECK

RETAIL PRICING

YEAR	HIGH	LOW
2001	$3,913	$2,935
2002	$5,498	$4,123

XXWD3500

YEARS MFRD 2007-2007
SERIES. . . . . XXWD SERIES
ENGINE . . . . YANMAR
ENGINE HP 35
COOLING . . . . LIQUID
FUEL . . . . D
SPEEDS . . . . .VARIABLE
TRANSMISSION . . . . .HYDRO
STEERING. . . . . .ZERO
STANDARD DECK . . . . 72"
MSRP. $14,399

RETAIL PRICING

YEAR	HIGH	LOW
2007	$3,903	$2,928

XXWD5000

YEARS MFRD 2003-2006
SERIES. . . . . XXWD SERIES
ENGINE . . . . YANMAR
ENGINE HP 41
COOLING . . . . LIQUID
FUEL . . . . D
SPEEDS 0-13
TRANSMISSION . . . . .HYDRO
STEERING. . . . . .ZERO
STANDARD DECK . . . . 72"
MSRP. $15,899

RETAIL PRICING

YEAR	HIGH	LOW
2003	$3,151	$2,363
2004	$3,477	$2,608
2005	$3,838	$2,878
2006	$4,237	$3,177

ZEE 1 1942

YEARS MFRD 2012-2014
ENGINE . . . . B&S
ENGINE HP 19
COOLING . . . . .AIR
FUEL . . . . G
SPEEDS . . . . .VARIABLE
TRANSMISSION . . . . .HYDRO
STEERING. . . . . .ZERO
STANDARD DECK . . . . 42"
MSRP. $3,599

RETAIL PRICING

YEAR	HIGH	LOW
2012	$1,475	$1,106
2013	$1,629	$1,222
2014	$1,797	$1,348

ZEE 1 2342

YEARS MFRD 2012-2014
ENGINE . . . . B&S
ENGINE HP 23
COOLING . . . . .AIR
FUEL . . . . G
SPEEDS . . . . .VARIABLE
TRANSMISSION . . . . .HYDRO
STEERING. . . . . .ZERO
STANDARD DECK . . . . 42"
MSRP. $3,799

RETAIL PRICING

YEAR	HIGH	LOW
2012	$1,557	$1,168
2013	$1,719	$1,289
2014	$1,897	$1,423

ZEE 1 2348

YEARS MFRD 2012-2014
ENGINE . . . . B&S
ENGINE HP 23
COOLING . . . . .AIR
FUEL . . . . G
SPEEDS . . . . .VARIABLE
TRANSMISSION . . . . .HYDRO
STEERING. . . . . .ZERO
STANDARD DECK . . . . 48"
MSRP. $3,999

RETAIL PRICING

YEAR	HIGH	LOW
2012	$1,639	$1,229
2013	$1,809	$1,357
2014	$1,996	$1,497

ZEE 2 2142

YEARS MFRD 2013-2014
ENGINE . . . . KAWASAKI
ENGINE HP 21
COOLING . . . . .AIR
FUEL . . . . G
SPEEDS . . . . .VARIABLE
TRANSMISSION . . . . .HYDRO
STEERING. . . . . .ZERO
STANDARD DECK . . . . 42"
MSRP. $4,799

DIXIE CHOPPER

RETAIL PRICING

YEAR	HIGH	LOW
2013	$2,180	$1,635
2014	$2,396	$1,797

ZEE 2 2342KO

YEARS MFRD 2016-2017
ENGINE .... KOHLER
ENGINE HP 23
COOLING .... AIR
FUEL .... G
SPEEDS .... VARIABLE
TRANSMISSION .... HYDRO
STEERING .... ZERO
STANDARD DECK .... 42"
MSRP $4,049

RETAIL PRICING

YEAR	HIGH	LOW
2016	$2,858	$2,143
2017	$3,102	$2,326

ZEE 2 2348

YEARS MFRD 2013-2016
ENGINE .... KAWASAKI
ENGINE HP 23
COOLING .... AIR
FUEL .... G
SPEEDS .... VARIABLE
TRANSMISSION .... HYDRO
STEERING .... ZERO
STANDARD DECK .... 48"
MSRP $4,299

RETAIL PRICING

YEAR	HIGH	LOW
2013	$1,864	$1,398
2014	$2,058	$1,544
2015	$2,272	$1,704
2016	$2,507	$1,880

ZEE 2 2348BR

YEARS MFRD 2016-2017
ENGINE .... B&S
ENGINE HP 23
COOLING .... AIR
FUEL .... G
SPEEDS .... VARIABLE
TRANSMISSION .... HYDRO
STEERING .... ZERO
STANDARD DECK .... 48"
MSRP $4,199

RETAIL PRICING

YEAR	HIGH	LOW
2016	$2,431	$1,824
2017	$2,684	$2,013

ZEE 2 2348HP

YEARS MFRD 2014-2014
ENGINE .... KAWASAKI FS
ENGINE HP 23
COOLING .... AIR
FUEL .... G
SPEEDS .... VARIABLE
TRANSMISSION .... HYDRO
STEERING .... ZERO
STANDARD DECK .... 48"
MSRP $5,699

RETAIL PRICING

YEAR	HIGH	LOW
2014	$2,846	$2,134

ZEE 2 2348KO

YEARS MFRD 2016-2017
ENGINE .... KOHLER
ENGINE HP 23
COOLING .... AIR
FUEL .... G
SPEEDS .... VARIABLE
TRANSMISSION .... HYDRO
STEERING .... ZERO
STANDARD DECK .... 48"
MSRP $4,099

RETAIL PRICING

YEAR	HIGH	LOW
2016	$2,893	$2,170
2017	$3,270	$2,453

ZEE 2 2348KW

YEARS MFRD 2017-2017
ENGINE .... KAWASAKI FR
ENGINE HP 23
COOLING .... AIR
FUEL .... G
SPEEDS .... VARAIBLE
TRANSMISSION .... HYDRO
STEERING .... ZERO
STANDARD DECK .... 48"

ZEE 2 2354

YEARS MFRD 2013-2017
ENGINE .... KAWASAKI
ENGINE HP 23
COOLING .... AIR
FUEL .... G
SPEEDS .... VARIABLE
TRANSMISSION .... HYDRO
STEERING .... ZERO
STANDARD DECK .... 54"
MSRP $4,699

RETAIL PRICING

YEAR	HIGH	LOW
2013	$2,467	$1,850
2014	$2,722	$2,042
2015	$3,004	$2,253
2016	$3,315	$2,487
2017	$3,736	$2,802

ZEE 2 2354BR

YEARS MFRD 2016-2017
ENGINE .... B&S
ENGINE HP 23
COOLING .... AIR
FUEL .... G
SPEEDS .... VARIABLE
TRANSMISSION .... HYDRO
STEERING .... ZERO
STANDARD DECK .... 54"
MSRP $4,499

RETAIL PRICING

YEAR	HIGH	LOW
2016	$2,605	$1,954
2017	$2,874	$2,156

ZEE 2 2354HP

YEARS MFRD 2014-2014
ENGINE .... KAWASAKI FS
ENGINE HP 23
COOLING .... AIR
FUEL .... G
SPEEDS .... VARIABLE
TRANSMISSION .... HYDRO
STEERING .... ZERO
STANDARD DECK .... 54"
MSRP $5,999

RETAIL PRICING

YEAR	HIGH	LOW
2014	$2,360	$1,770

ZEE 2 2354KO

YEARS MFRD 2016-2017
ENGINE .... KOHLER
ENGINE HP 23
COOLING .... AIR
FUEL .... G
SPEEDS .... VARIABLE
TRANSMISSION .... HYDRO
STEERING .... ZERO
STANDARD DECK .... 54"
MSRP $4,399

RETAIL PRICING

YEAR	HIGH	LOW
2016	$3,104	$2,328
2017	$3,457	$2,593

ZEE 3 2344

YEARS MFRD 2012-2012
ENGINE .... B&S
ENGINE HP 23
COOLING .... AIR
FUEL .... G
SPEEDS .... VARIABLE
TRANSMISSION .... HYDRO
STEERING .... ZERO
STANDARD DECK .... 44"
MSRP $5,299

RETAIL PRICING

YEAR	HIGH	LOW
2012	$2,349	$1,762

ZEE 3 2650

YEARS MFRD 2012-2012
ENGINE .... B&S
ENGINE HP 26
COOLING .... AIR
FUEL .... G
SPEEDS .... VARIABLE
TRANSMISSION .... HYDRO
STEERING .... ZERO
STANDARD DECK .... 50"
MSRP $5,499

RETAIL PRICING

YEAR	HIGH	LOW
2012	$2,438	$1,829

ZWF2700

YEARS MFRD 2003-2004
SERIES .... XWF SERIES
ENGINE .... KOHLER
ENGINE HP 27
COOLING .... AIR
FUEL .... G
SPEEDS .... VARIABLE
TRANSMISSION .... HYDRO
STEERING .... ZERO
STANDARD DECK .... 60"
MSRP $8,999

RETAIL PRICING

YEAR	HIGH	LOW
2003	$3,856	$2,892
2004	$4,105	$3,079

2044

YEARS MFRD 2008-2008
SERIES .... IRON EAGLE SERIES
ENGINE .... KOHLER
ENGINE HP 20
COOLING .... AIR
FUEL .... G
SPEEDS .... VARIABLE
TRANSMISSION .... HYDRO
STEERING .... ZERO
BLADE CLUTCH .... ELECTRIC
STANDARD DECK .... 44"
MSRP $4,699

RETAIL PRICING

YEAR	HIGH	LOW
2008	$1,493	$1,119

2244

YEARS MFRD 2013-2017
SERIES .... MAGNUM SERIES
ENGINE .... KAWASAKI FS
ENGINE HP 22
COOLING .... AIR
FUEL .... G
SPEEDS .... VARIABLE
TRANSMISSION .... HYDRO
STEERING .... ZERO
STANDARD DECK .... 44"
MSRP $6,699

RETAIL PRICING

YEAR	HIGH	LOW
2013	$2,774	$2,081
2014	$3,062	$2,296
2015	$3,514	$2,636
2016	$3,879	$2,909
2017	$4,282	$3,211

2248KW

YEARS MFRD 2017-2019
SERIES .... BLACKHAWK HP SERIES
ENGINE .... KAWASAKI
ENGINE HP 22

COOLING . . . AIR
FUEL . . . G
SPEEDS . . . VARIABLE
TRANSMISSION . . . DUAL HYDRO
STEERING . . . ZERO
STANDARD DECK . . . 48"
WEIGHT . . . 1,116 LBS.

RETAIL PRICING

YEAR	HIGH	LOW
2017	$5,646	$4,235
2018	$6,278	$4,709

2248KW

YEARS MFRD . . . 2017-2020
SERIES . . . BLACKHAWK SERIES
ENGINE . . . KAWASAKI
ENGINE HP . . . 22
COOLING . . . AIR
FUEL . . . G
TRANSMISSION . . . DUAL HYDRO
STEERING . . . ZERO
PTO . . . YES
STANDARD DECK . . . 48"
WEIGHT . . . 1,116 LBS.

RETAIL PRICING

YEAR	HIGH	LOW
2017	$4,906	$3,679
2018	$5,428	$4,071

2250

YEARS MFRD . . . 2014-2014
SERIES . . . MAGNUM HP SERIES
ENGINE . . . KAWASAKI FX
ENGINE HP . . . 22
COOLING . . . AIR
FUEL . . . G
SPEEDS . . . VARIABLE
TRANSMISSION . . . HYDRO
STEERING . . . ZERO
STANDARD DECK . . . 50"
MSRP . . . $6,999

RETAIL PRICING

YEAR	HIGH	LOW
2014	$3,430	$2,573

2250

YEARS MFRD . . . 2012-2017
SERIES . . . MAGNUM SERIES
ENGINE . . . KAWASAKI FS
ENGINE HP . . . 22
COOLING . . . AIR
FUEL . . . G
SPEEDS . . . VARIABLE
TRANSMISSION . . . HYDRO
STEERING . . . ZERO
STANDARD DECK . . . 50"
MSRP . . . $6,999

RETAIL PRICING

YEAR	HIGH	LOW
2012	$2,554	$1,915
2013	$2,818	$2,114
2014	$3,112	$2,334
2015	$3,672	$2,754
2016	$4,053	$3,040
2017	$4,473	$3,355

2250R

YEARS MFRD . . . 2015-2016
SERIES . . . MAGNUM SERIES
ENGINE . . . KAWASAKI
ENGINE HP . . . 22
COOLING . . . AIR
FUEL . . . G
SPEEDS . . . VARIABLE
TRANSMISSION . . . HYDRO
STEERING . . . ZERO
STANDARD DECK . . . 50"
MSRP . . . $5,399

RETAIL PRICING

YEAR	HIGH	LOW
2015	$2,853	$2,140
2016	$3,149	$2,362

2342BR

YEARS MFRD . . . 2015-2015
SERIES . . . ZEE 2 SERIES
ENGINE . . . B&S CYCLONIC
ENGINE HP . . . 23
COOLING . . . AIR
FUEL . . . G
SPEEDS . . . VARIABLE
TRANSMISSION . . . HYDRO
STEERING . . . ZERO
STANDARD DECK . . . 42"
MSRP . . . $3,699

RETAIL PRICING

YEAR	HIGH	LOW
2015	$2,002	$1,502

2342KO

YEARS MFRD . . . 2016-2020
SERIES . . . ZEE 2 SERIES
ENGINE . . . KOHLER 7000
ENGINE HP . . . 23
COOLING . . . AIR
FUEL . . . G
TRANSMISSION . . . HYDRO
STEERING . . . ZERO
STANDARD DECK . . . 42"
WEIGHT . . . 730 LBS.

RETAIL PRICING

YEAR	HIGH	LOW
2016	$2,571	$1,928
2017	$2,838	$2,129
2018	$3,149	$2,361

2344

YEARS MFRD . . . 2009-2011
SERIES . . . IRON EAGLE SERIES
ENGINE . . . B&S
ENGINE HP . . . 23
COOLING . . . AIR
FUEL . . . G
SPEEDS . . . VARIABLE
TRANSMISSION . . . HYDRO
STEERING . . . ZERO
BLADE CLUTCH . . . ELECTRIC
STANDARD DECK . . . 44"
WEIGHT . . . 834 LBS.
MSRP . . . $5,699

RETAIL PRICING

YEAR	HIGH	LOW
2009	$1,900	$1,425
2010	$2,096	$1,572
2011	$2,315	$1,736

2348BR

YEARS MFRD . . . 2015-2015
SERIES . . . ZEE 2 SERIES
ENGINE . . . B&S CYCLONIC
ENGINE HP . . . 23
COOLING . . . AIR
FUEL . . . G
SPEEDS . . . VARIABLE
TRANSMISSION . . . HYDRO
STEERING . . . ZERO
STANDARD DECK . . . 48"
MSRP . . . $3,999

RETAIL PRICING

YEAR	HIGH	LOW
2015	$2,164	$1,623

2348KO

YEARS MFRD . . . 2016-2019
SERIES . . . ZEE 2 SERIES
ENGINE . . . KOHLER 7000
ENGINE HP . . . 23
COOLING . . . AIR
FUEL . . . G
TRANSMISSION . . . HYDRO
STEERING . . . ZERO
STANDARD DECK . . . 48"
WEIGHT . . . 750 LBS.

RETAIL PRICING

YEAR	HIGH	LOW
2016	$2,627	$1,971
2017	$2,900	$2,174
2018	$3,214	$2,411

2348KW

YEARS MFRD . . . 2017-2020
SERIES . . . ZEE 2 SERIES
ENGINE . . . KAWASAKI FR
ENGINE HP . . . 23
COOLING . . . AIR
FUEL . . . G
TRANSMISSION . . . HYDRO
STEERING . . . ZERO
STANDARD DECK . . . 48"
WEIGHT . . . 750 LBS.

RETAIL PRICING

YEAR	HIGH	LOW
2017	$3,282	$2,461

2350

YEARS MFRD . . . 2013-2014
SERIES . . . MAGNUM EFI SERIES
ENGINE . . . KOHLER EFI
ENGINE HP . . . 23
COOLING . . . AIR
FUEL . . . G
SPEEDS . . . VARIABLE
TRANSMISSION . . . HYDRO
STEERING . . . ZERO
STANDARD DECK . . . 50"
MSRP . . . $7,349

RETAIL PRICING

YEAR	HIGH	LOW
2013	$3,262	$2,447
2014	$3,624	$2,718

2350

YEARS MFRD . . . 2008-2009
SERIES . . . IRON EAGLE SERIES
ENGINE . . . KOHLER
ENGINE HP . . . 23
COOLING . . . AIR
FUEL . . . G
SPEEDS . . . VARIABLE
TRANSMISSION . . . HYDRO
STEERING . . . STANDARD
BLADE CLUTCH . . . ELECTRIC
STANDARD DECK . . . 50"
MSRP . . . $4,999

SERIAL NUMBERS

YEAR	BEGINNING NO.
2008	80XXXX

RETAIL PRICING

YEAR	HIGH	LOW
2008	$1,502	$1,127
2009	$1,658	$1,244

2354

YEARS MFRD . . . 2013-2020
SERIES . . . ZEE 2 SERIES
ENGINE . . . KAWASAKI
ENGINE HP . . . 23
COOLING . . . AIR
FUEL . . . G
TRANSMISSION . . . HYDRO
STEERING . . . ZERO
STANDARD DECK . . . 54"
WEIGHT . . . 763 LBS.

RETAIL PRICING

YEAR	HIGH	LOW
2013	$2,203	$1,652
2014	$2,431	$1,823
2015	$2,683	$2,012
2016	$2,963	$2,222
2017	$3,270	$2,453
2018	$3,682	$2,761

2354BR

YEARS MFRD . . . 2015-2015
SERIES . . . ZEE 2 SERIES
ENGINE . . . B&S CYCLONIC
ENGINE HP . . . 23
COOLING . . . AIR
FUEL . . . G
SPEEDS . . . VARIABLE
TRANSMISSION . . . HYDRO
STEERING . . . ZERO
STANDARD DECK . . . 54"
MSRP . . . $4,199

RETAIL PRICING

YEAR	HIGH	LOW
2015	$2,274	$1,705

DIXIE CHOPPER

2354KO

- YEARS MFRD: 2016-2019
- SERIES: ZEE 2 SERIES
- ENGINE: KOHLER 7000
- ENGINE HP: 23
- COOLING: AIR
- FUEL: G
- TRANSMISSION: HYDRO
- STEERING: ZERO
- STANDARD DECK: 54"
- WEIGHT: 763 LBS.

RETAIL PRICING

YEAR	HIGH	LOW
2016	$2,767	$2,075
2017	$3,053	$2,290
2018	$3,379	$2,534

2450KW

- YEARS MFRD: 2017-2018
- SERIES: MAGNUM HP SERIES
- ENGINE HP: 24
- COOLING: AIR
- FUEL: G
- SPEEDS: VARIABLE
- TRANSMISSION: HYDRO
- STEERING: ZERO
- STANDARD DECK: 50"
- MSRP: $6,099

RETAIL PRICING

YEAR	HIGH	LOW
2017	$4,046	$3,035
2018	$4,825	$3,618

2454KW

- YEARS MFRD: 2017-2020
- SERIES: BLACKHAWK SERIES
- ENGINE: KAWASAKI
- ENGINE HP: 24
- COOLING: AIR
- FUEL: G
- SPEEDS: VARIABLE
- TRANSMISSION: DUAL HYDRO
- STEERING: ZERO
- STANDARD DECK: 54"

RETAIL PRICING

YEAR	HIGH	LOW
2017	$5,213	$3,910
2018	$5,792	$4,344

2454KW

- YEARS MFRD: 2017-2020
- SERIES: BLACKHAWK HP SERIES
- ENGINE: KAWASAKI
- ENGINE HP: 24
- COOLING: AIR
- FUEL: G
- SPEEDS: VARIABLE
- TRANSMISSION: DUAL HYDRO
- STEERING: ZERO
- STANDARD DECK: 54"
- WEIGHT: 1,132 LBS.

RETAIL PRICING

YEAR	HIGH	LOW
2017	$5,862	$4,397
2018	$6,499	$4,875

2460

- YEARS MFRD: 2012-2017
- SERIES: MAGNUM HP SERIES
- ENGINE: KAWASAKI FS
- ENGINE HP: 24
- COOLING: AIR
- FUEL: G
- SPEEDS: VARIABLE
- TRANSMISSION: HYDRO
- STEERING: ZERO
- STANDARD DECK: 60"
- MSRP: $7,199

RETAIL PRICING

YEAR	HIGH	LOW
2012	$2,705	$2,029
2013	$2,986	$2,240
2014	$3,295	$2,471
2015	$3,780	$2,835
2016	$4,168	$3,126
2017	$4,601	$3,451

2460

- YEARS MFRD: 2014-2014
- SERIES: MAGNUM SERIES
- ENGINE: KAWASAKI FX
- ENGINE HP: 23.5
- COOLING: AIR
- FUEL: G
- SPEEDS: VARIABLE
- TRANSMISSION: HYDRO
- STEERING: ZERO
- STANDARD DECK: 60"
- MSRP: $7,249

RETAIL PRICING

YEAR	HIGH	LOW
2014	$3,643	$2,732

2460KW

- YEARS MFRD: 2017-2020
- SERIES: BLACKHAWK HP SERIES
- ENGINE: KAWASAKI
- ENGINE HP: 24
- COOLING: AIR
- FUEL: G
- SPEEDS: VARIABLE
- TRANSMISSION: DUAL HYDRO
- STEERING: ZERO
- STANDARD DECK: 60"
- WEIGHT: 1,140 LBS.

RETAIL PRICING

YEAR	HIGH	LOW
2017	$6,015	$4,512
2018	$6,668	$5,001

2460KW

- YEARS MFRD: 2017-2020
- SERIES: BLACKHAWK SERIES
- ENGINE: KAWASAKI
- ENGINE HP: 24
- COOLING: AIR
- FUEL: G
- SPEEDS: VARIABLE
- TRANSMISSION: DUAL HYDRO
- STEERING: ZERO
- STANDARD DECK: 60"

RETAIL PRICING

YEAR	HIGH	LOW
2017	$5,275	$3,956
2018	$5,932	$4,449

2460R

- YEARS MFRD: 2015-2018
- SERIES: MAGNUM SERIES
- ENGINE: KAWASAKI
- ENGINE HP: 24
- COOLING: AIR
- FUEL: G
- SPEEDS: VARIABLE
- TRANSMISSION: HYDRO
- STEERING: ZERO
- STANDARD DECK: 60"
- MSRP: $6,349

RETAIL PRICING

YEAR	HIGH	LOW
2015	$3,457	$2,593
2016	$3,816	$2,862
2017	$4,211	$3,158

2548KOE

- YEARS MFRD: 2017-2019
- SERIES: BLACKHAWK HP SERIES
- ENGINE: KOHLER EFI
- ENGINE HP: 25
- COOLING: AIR
- FUEL: G
- SPEEDS: VARIABLE
- TRANSMISSION: DUAL HYDRO
- STEERING: ZERO
- STANDARD DECK: 48"
- WEIGHT: 1,116 LBS.

RETAIL PRICING

YEAR	HIGH	LOW
2017	$5,585	$4,188
2018	$6,214	$4,660

2550

- YEARS MFRD: 2008-2013
- SERIES: SILVER EAGLE SERIES
- ENGINE: KOHLER
- ENGINE HP: 25
- COOLING: AIR
- FUEL: G
- SPEEDS: VARIABLE
- TRANSMISSION: HYDRO
- STEERING: ZERO
- BLADE CLUTCH: ELECTRIC
- STANDARD DECK: 50"
- MSRP: $8,999

SERIAL NUMBERS

YEAR	BEGINNING NO.
2008	80XXXX

RETAIL PRICING

YEAR	HIGH	LOW
2008	$2,596	$1,947
2009	$2,858	$2,143
2010	$3,154	$2,365
2011	$3,482	$2,611
2012	$3,843	$2,882
2013	$4,241	$3,181

2550

- YEARS MFRD: 2008-2009
- SERIES: CLASSIC SERIES
- ENGINE: KOHLER
- ENGINE HP: 25
- COOLING: AIR
- FUEL: G
- SPEEDS: VARIABLE
- TRANSMISSION: HYDRO
- STEERING: ZERO
- BLADE CLUTCH: ELECTRIC
- STANDARD DECK: 50"
- MSRP: $8,799

SERIAL NUMBERS

YEAR	BEGINNING NO.
2008	80XXXX

RETAIL PRICING

YEAR	HIGH	LOW
2008	$2,941	$2,206
2009	$3,245	$2,434

2550

- YEARS MFRD: 2010-2010
- SERIES: IRON EAGLE SERIES
- ENGINE: KOHLER
- ENGINE HP: 25
- COOLING: AIR
- FUEL: G
- SPEEDS: VARIABLE
- TRANSMISSION: HYDRO
- STEERING: ZERO
- BLADE CLUTCH: ELECTRIC
- STANDARD DECK: 50"
- MSRP: $5,999

RETAIL PRICING

YEAR	HIGH	LOW
2010	$2,214	$1,660

2550BR

- YEARS MFRD: 2015-2016
- SERIES: MAGNUM SERIES
- ENGINE: B&S CYCLONIC
- ENGINE HP: 25
- COOLING: AIR
- FUEL: G
- SPEEDS: VARIABLE
- TRANSMISSION: HYDRO
- STEERING: ZERO
- STANDARD DECK: 50"
- MSRP: $5,199

RETAIL PRICING

YEAR	HIGH	LOW
2015	$2,748	$2,061
2016	$3,032	$2,274

2550KO

- YEARS MFRD: 2016-2018
- SERIES: MAGNUM SERIES
- ENGINE: KOHLER EFI
- ENGINE HP: 25
- COOLING: AIR
- FUEL: G
- SPEEDS: VARIABLE
- TRANSMISSION: HYDRO

STEERING................ZERO
STANDARD DECK.......... 50"
MSRP................. $6,099

RETAIL PRICING

YEAR	HIGH	LOW
2016	$3,666	$2,750
2017	$4,046	$3,035
2018	$4,876	$3,657

2550KW

YEARS MFRD........ 2015-2017
SERIES...... SILVER EAGLE SERIES
ENGINE............. KAWASAKI
ENGINE HP................ 25
COOLING.................AIR
FUEL......................G
SPEEDS.............VARIABLE
TRANSMISSION..........HYDRO
STEERING................ZERO
STANDARD DECK.......... 50"
MSRP................. $9,499

OPTIONS

KOHLER EFI 27HP

RETAIL PRICING

YEAR	HIGH	LOW
2015	$4,983	$3,737
2016	$5,500	$4,125
2017	$6,071	$4,553

2554BR

YEARS MFRD........ 2017-2017
SERIES....... BLACKHAWK SERIES
ENGINE.................. B&S
ENGINE HP................ 25
COOLING.................AIR
FUEL......................G
SPEEDS.............VARIABLE
TRANSMISSION..... DUAL HYDRO
STEERING................ZERO
STANDARD DECK.......... 54"
MSRP................. $7,299

RETAIL PRICING

YEAR	HIGH	LOW
2017	$4,665	$3,499

2554KOE

YEARS MFRD........ 2017-2019
SERIES.... BLACKHAWK HP SERIES
ENGINE............ KOHLER EFI
ENGINE HP................ 25
COOLING.................AIR
FUEL......................G
SPEEDS.............VARIABLE
TRANSMISSION..... DUAL HYDRO
STEERING................ZERO
STANDARD DECK.......... 54"
WEIGHT............. 1,132 LBS.

RETAIL PRICING

YEAR	HIGH	LOW
2017	$5,862	$4,397
2018	$6,508	$4,882

2560

YEARS MFRD........ 2008-2009
SERIES....... IRON EAGLE SERIES
ENGINE................ KOHLER
ENGINE HP................ 25
COOLING.................AIR
FUEL......................G
SPEEDS.............VARIABLE
TRANSMISSION..........HYDRO
STEERING................ZERO
BLADE CLUTCH........ ELECTRIC
STANDARD DECK.......... 60"
MSRP................. $5,599

SERIAL NUMBERS

YEAR	BEGINNING NO.
2008	80XXXX

RETAIL PRICING

YEAR	HIGH	LOW
2008	$1,683	$1,262
2009	$1,856	$1,392

2560BR

YEARS MFRD........ 2017-2017
SERIES....... BLACKHAWK SERIES
ENGINE.................. B&S
ENGINE HP................ 25
COOLING.................AIR
FUEL......................G
SPEEDS.............VARIABLE
TRANSMISSION..... DUAL HYDRO
STEERING................ZERO
STANDARD DECK.......... 60"
MSRP................. $7,499

RETAIL PRICING

YEAR	HIGH	LOW
2017	$4,792	$3,594

2560BR

YEARS MFRD........ 2015-2016
SERIES......... MAGNUM SERIES
ENGINE.......... B&S CYCLONIC
ENGINE HP................ 25
COOLING.................AIR
FUEL......................G
SPEEDS.............VARIABLE
TRANSMISSION..........HYDRO
STEERING................ZERO
STANDARD DECK.......... 60"
MSRP................. $5,399

RETAIL PRICING

YEAR	HIGH	LOW
2015	$2,853	$2,140
2016	$3,149	$2,362

2560KO

YEARS MFRD........ 2016-2018
SERIES......... MAGNUM SERIES
ENGINE............ KOHLER EFI
ENGINE HP................ 25
COOLING.................AIR
FUEL......................G
SPEEDS.............VARIABLE
TRANSMISSION..........HYDRO
STEERING................ZERO
STANDARD DECK.......... 60"
MSRP................. $6,349

RETAIL PRICING

YEAR	HIGH	LOW
2016	$3,816	$2,862
2017	$4,211	$3,158
2018	$4,974	$3,730

2560KOE

YEARS MFRD........ 2017-2019
SERIES.... BLACKHAWK HP SERIES
ENGINE............ KOHLER EFI
ENGINE HP................ 25
COOLING.................AIR
FUEL......................G
SPEEDS.............VARIABLE
TRANSMISSION..... DUAL HYDRO
STEERING................ZERO
STANDARD DECK.......... 60"
WEIGHT............. 1,144 LBS.

RETAIL PRICING

YEAR	HIGH	LOW
2017	$5,955	$4,466
2018	$6,630	$4,973

2600

YEARS MFRD........ 2002-2003
SERIES............. XXW SERIES
ENGINE............ KOHLER EFI
ENGINE HP................ 26
COOLING.................AIR
FUEL......................G
SPEEDS.............VARIABLE
TRANSMISSION..........HYDRO
STEERING................ZERO
STANDARD DECK.......... 72"
MSRP................ $10,499

RETAIL PRICING

YEAR	HIGH	LOW
2002	$3,277	$2,458
2003	$3,553	$2,665

2650

YEARS MFRD........ 2011-2011
SERIES....... IRON EAGLE SERIES
ENGINE.................. B&S
ENGINE HP................ 26
COOLING.................AIR
FUEL......................G
SPEEDS.............VARIABLE
TRANSMISSION..........HYDRO
STEERING................ZERO
BLADE CLUTCH........ ELECTRIC
STANDARD DECK.......... 50"
WEIGHT............... 845 LBS.
MSRP................. $5,999

RETAIL PRICING

YEAR	HIGH	LOW
2011	$2,437	$1,828

2660 EFI

YEARS MFRD........ 2014-2014
SERIES...... SILVER EAGLE SERIES
ENGINE............ KOHLER EFI
ENGINE HP................ 26
COOLING.................AIR
FUEL......................G
SPEEDS.............VARIABLE
TRANSMISSION..........HYDRO
STEERING................ZERO
STANDARD DECK.......... 60"
MSRP................ $10,699

RETAIL PRICING

YEAR	HIGH	LOW
2014	$5,443	$4,082

2734

YEARS MFRD........ 2008-2013
SERIES...... SILVER EAGLE SERIES
ENGINE............... GENERAC
ENGINE HP................ 27
COOLING.................AIR
FUEL......................G
SPEEDS.............VARIABLE
TRANSMISSION..........HYDRO
STEERING................ZERO
BLADE CLUTCH........ ELECTRIC
STANDARD DECK.......... 34"
MSRP................. $7,799

SERIAL NUMBERS

YEAR	BEGINNING NO.
2008	80XXXX

RETAIL PRICING

YEAR	HIGH	LOW
2008	$2,244	$1,683
2009	$2,476	$1,857
2010	$2,734	$2,051
2011	$3,017	$2,263
2012	$3,331	$2,498
2013	$3,676	$2,757

2744

YEARS MFRD........ 2008-2014
SERIES...... SILVER EAGLE SERIES
ENGINE............... GENERAC
ENGINE HP................ 27
COOLING.................AIR
FUEL......................G
SPEEDS.............VARIABLE
TRANSMISSION..........HYDRO
STEERING................ZERO
BLADE CLUTCH........ ELECTRIC
STANDARD DECK.......... 44"
MSRP................. $8,999

SERIAL NUMBERS

YEAR	BEGINNING NO.
2008	80XXXX

RETAIL PRICING

YEAR	HIGH	LOW
2008	$2,530	$1,898
2009	$2,794	$2,095
2010	$3,085	$2,314
2011	$3,404	$2,553
2012	$3,757	$2,818
2013	$4,147	$3,111
2014	$4,578	$3,433

DIXIE CHOPPER

2750

YEARS MFRD 2008-2014
SERIES...... SILVER EAGLE SERIES
ENGINE .... GENERAC
ENGINE HP.................. 27
COOLING .... AIR
FUEL .... G
SPEEDS .... VARIABLE
TRANSMISSION .... HYDRO
STEERING................ ZERO
BLADE CLUTCH .... ELECTRIC
STANDARD DECK .... 50"
MSRP................. $9,199

SERIAL NUMBERS

YEAR	BEGINNING NO.
2008	80XXXX

RETAIL PRICING

YEAR	HIGH	LOW
2008	$2,588	$1,941
2009	$2,857	$2,143
2010	$3,152	$2,364
2011	$3,480	$2,610
2012	$3,841	$2,880
2013	$4,239	$3,180
2014	$4,680	$3,510

2750

YEARS MFRD 2008-2011
SERIES.......... CLASSIC SERIES
ENGINE .... GENERAC
ENGINE HP.................. 27
COOLING .... AIR
FUEL .... G
SPEEDS .... VARIABLE
TRANSMISSION .... HYDRO
STEERING................ ZERO
BLADE CLUTCH .... ELECTRIC
STANDARD DECK .... 50"
MSRP................. $9,199

SERIAL NUMBERS

YEAR	BEGINNING NO.
2008	80XXXX

RETAIL PRICING

YEAR	HIGH	LOW
2008	$2,842	$2,132
2009	$3,138	$2,353
2010	$3,462	$2,597
2011	$3,822	$2,867

2750

YEARS MFRD 2013-2013
SERIES.... GOLDEN EAGLE SERIES
ENGINE .... KAWASAKI
ENGINE HP.................. 27
COOLING .... AIR
FUEL .... G
SPEEDS .... VARIABLE
TRANSMISSION .... HYDRO
STEERING................ ZERO
STANDARD DECK .... 50"
MSRP................. $10,399

RETAIL PRICING

YEAR	HIGH	LOW
2013	$4,902	$3,676

2750

YEARS MFRD 2010-2012
SERIES......... MAGNUM SERIES
ENGINE .... B&S
ENGINE HP.................. 27
COOLING .... AIR
FUEL .... G
SPEEDS .... VARIABLE
TRANSMISSION .... HYDRO
STEERING................ ZERO
BLADE CLUTCH .... ELECTRIC
STANDARD DECK .... 50"
WEIGHT .... 863 LBS.
MSRP................. $7,699

RETAIL PRICING

YEAR	HIGH	LOW
2010	$2,744	$2,058
2011	$3,028	$2,271
2012	$3,342	$2,506

2750 EFI

YEARS MFRD 2016-2017
SERIES...... MAGNUM HP SERIES
ENGINE .... KOHLER EFI
ENGINE HP.................. 27
COOLING .... AIR
FUEL .... G
SPEEDS .... VARIABLE
TRANSMISSION .... HYDRO
STEERING................ ZERO
STANDARD DECK .... 50"
MSRP................. $7,199

RETAIL PRICING

YEAR	HIGH	LOW
2016	$3,776	$2,832
2017	$4,601	$3,451

2750HP

YEARS MFRD 2008-2010
SERIES.......... CLASSIC SERIES
ENGINE .... GENERAC
ENGINE HP.................. 27
COOLING .... AIR
FUEL .... G
SPEEDS .... VARIABLE
TRANSMISSION .... HYDRO
STEERING................ ZERO
BLADE CLUTCH .... ELECTRIC
STANDARD DECK .... 50"
MSRP................. $10,295

SERIAL NUMBERS

YEAR	BEGINNING NO.
2008	80XXXX

RETAIL PRICING

YEAR	HIGH	LOW
2008	$3,196	$2,397
2009	$3,528	$2,646
2010	$3,895	$2,921

2750KW

YEARS MFRD 2015-2020
SERIES.......... CLASSIC SERIES
ENGINE .... KAWASAKI
ENGINE HP.................. 27
COOLING .... AIR
FUEL .... G
SPEEDS .... VARIABLE
TRANSMISSION .... HYDRO
STEERING................ ZERO
STANDARD DECK .... 50"

RETAIL PRICING

YEAR	HIGH	LOW
2015	$5,623	$4,217
2016	$6,206	$4,655
2017	$6,850	$5,137
2018	$7,624	$5,718

2750T

YEARS MFRD 2012-2012
SERIES.......... CLASSIC SERIES
ENGINE .... KAWASAKI
ENGINE HP.................. 27
COOLING .... AIR
FUEL .... G
SPEEDS .... VARIABLE
TRANSMISSION .... HYDRO
STEERING................ ZERO
STANDARD DECK .... 50"
MSRP................. $10,399

RETAIL PRICING

YEAR	HIGH	LOW
2012	$4,563	$3,422

2750W

YEARS MFRD 2012-2014
SERIES.......... CLASSIC SERIES
ENGINE .... GENERAC
ENGINE HP.................. 27
COOLING .... AIR
FUEL .... G
SPEEDS .... VARIABLE
TRANSMISSION .... HYDRO
STEERING................ ZERO
STANDARD DECK .... 50"
MSRP................. $9,899

RETAIL PRICING

YEAR	HIGH	LOW
2012	$4,057	$3,043
2013	$4,479	$3,359
2014	$4,943	$3,707

2754

YEARS MFRD 2018-2020
SERIES.......... EAGLE SERIES
ENGINE .... KAWASAKI FX
ENGINE HP.................. 27
COOLING .... AIR
FUEL .... G
TRANSMISSION ..... DUAL HYDRO
STEERING................ ZERO
STANDARD DECK .... 54"
WEIGHT .... 1,306 LBS.

OPTIONS

KOHLER 27HP

2760

YEARS MFRD 2018-2020
SERIES............ EAGLE SERIES
ENGINE .... KAWASAKI
ENGINE HP.................. 27
COOLING .... AIR
FUEL .... G
TRANSMISSION ..... DUAL HYDRO
STEERING................ ZERO
WEIGHT .... 1,322 LBS.

OPTIONS

KOHLER 27HP

2760

YEARS MFRD 2010-2012
SERIES......... MAGNUM SERIES
ENGINE .... B&S
ENGINE HP.................. 27
COOLING .... AIR
FUEL .... G
SPEEDS .... VARIABLE
TRANSMISSION .... HYDRO
STEERING................ ZERO
BLADE CLUTCH .... ELECTRIC
STANDARD DECK .... 60"
MSRP................. $8,199

RETAIL PRICING

YEAR	HIGH	LOW
2010	$2,921	$2,191
2011	$3,225	$2,419
2012	$3,572	$2,679

2760

YEARS MFRD 2013-2013
SERIES.... GOLDEN EAGLE SERIES
ENGINE .... KAWASAKI
ENGINE HP.................. 27
COOLING .... AIR
FUEL .... G
SPEEDS .... VARIABLE
TRANSMISSION .... HYDRO
STEERING................ ZERO
STANDARD DECK .... 60"
MSRP................. $11,099

RETAIL PRICING

YEAR	HIGH	LOW
2013	$5,232	$3,924

2760

YEARS MFRD 2008-2014
SERIES...... SILVER EAGLE SERIES
ENGINE .... GENERAC
ENGINE HP.................. 27
COOLING .... AIR
FUEL .... G
SPEEDS .... VARIABLE
TRANSMISSION .... HYDRO
STEERING................ ZERO
STANDARD DECK .... 60"
MSRP................. $9,599

SERIAL NUMBERS

YEAR	BEGINNING NO.
2008	80XXXX

RETAIL PRICING

YEAR	HIGH	LOW
2008	$2,701	$2,026
2009	$2,980	$2,235
2010	$3,290	$2,467
2011	$3,631	$2,723
2012	$4,008	$3,006
2013	$4,424	$3,318
2014	$4,882	$3,662

2760

YEARS MFRD 2008-2014
SERIES .... CLASSIC SERIES
ENGINE .... GENERAC
ENGINE HP 27
COOLING .... AIR
FUEL .... G
SPEEDS .... VARIABLE
TRANSMISSION .... HYDRO
STEERING .... ZERO
BLADE CLUTCH .... ELECTRIC
STANDARD DECK .... 60"
MSRP $9,999

SERIAL NUMBERS

YEAR	BEGINNING NO.
2008	80XXXX

RETAIL PRICING

YEAR	HIGH	LOW
2008	$2,762	$2,071
2009	$3,059	$2,294
2010	$3,364	$2,523
2011	$3,713	$2,785
2012	$4,098	$3,074
2013	$4,524	$3,393
2014	$4,992	$3,744

2760 EFI

YEARS MFRD 2015-2016
SERIES ...... SILVER EAGLE SERIES
ENGINE .... KOHLER EFI
ENGINE HP 27
COOLING .... AIR
FUEL .... G
SPEEDS .... VARIABLE
TRANSMISSION .... HYDRO
STEERING .... ZERO
STANDARD DECK .... 60"
MSRP $10,899

RETAIL PRICING

YEAR	HIGH	LOW
2015	$5,758	$4,319
2016	$6,356	$4,767

2760 EFI

YEARS MFRD 2016-2017
SERIES ...... MAGNUM HP SERIES
ENGINE .... KOHLER EFI
ENGINE HP 27
COOLING .... AIR
FUEL .... G
SPEEDS .... VARIABLE
TRANSMISSION .... HYDRO
STEERING .... ZERO
STANDARD DECK .... 60"
MSRP $7,399

RETAIL PRICING

YEAR	HIGH	LOW
2016	$4,285	$3,213
2017	$4,729	$3,547

2760HP

YEARS MFRD 2008-2011
SERIES ...... SILVER EAGLE SERIES
ENGINE .... GENERAC
ENGINE HP 27
COOLING .... AIR
FUEL .... G
SPEEDS .... VARIABLE
TRANSMISSION .... HYDRO
STEERING .... ZERO
BLADE CLUTCH .... ELECTRIC
STANDARD DECK .... 60"
MSRP $9,475

RETAIL PRICING

YEAR	HIGH	LOW
2008	$4,159	$3,119
2009	$4,445	$3,334
2010	$4,582	$3,436
2011	$4,713	$3,535

2760KW

YEARS MFRD 2015-2020
SERIES .... CLASSIC SERIES
ENGINE .... KAWASAKI
ENGINE HP 27
FUEL .... G
SPEEDS .... VARIABLE
TRANSMISSION .... HYDRO
STEERING .... ZERO
STANDARD DECK .... 60"

RETAIL PRICING

YEAR	HIGH	LOW
2015	$6,170	$4,627
2016	$6,828	$5,121
2017	$7,517	$5,637

2760KW

YEARS MFRD 2013-2017
SERIES ...... SILVER EAGLE SERIES
ENGINE .... KAWASAKI
ENGINE HP 27
COOLING .... AIR
FUEL .... G
SPEEDS .... VARIABLE
TRANSMISSION .... HYDRO
STEERING .... ZERO
STANDARD DECK .... 60"
MSRP $10,499

OPTIONS

KOHLER EFI

RETAIL PRICING

YEAR	HIGH	LOW
2013	$4,535	$3,402
2014	$4,989	$3,742
2015	$5,508	$4,131
2016	$6,078	$4,558
2017	$6,709	$5,032

2760T

YEARS MFRD 2012-2012
SERIES .... CLASSIC SERIES
ENGINE .... KAWASAKI
ENGINE HP 27
COOLING .... AIR
FUEL .... G
SPEEDS .... VARIABLE
TRANSMISSION .... HYDRO
STEERING .... ZERO
STANDARD DECK .... 60"
MSRP $11,099

RETAIL PRICING

YEAR	HIGH	LOW
2012	$4,871	$3,653

2760W

YEARS MFRD 2012-2012
SERIES .... CLASSIC SERIES
ENGINE .... GENERAC
ENGINE HP 27
COOLING .... AIR
FUEL .... G
SPEEDS .... VARIABLE
TRANSMISSION .... HYDRO
STEERING .... ZERO
STANDARD DECK .... 60"
MSRP $10,899

RETAIL PRICING

YEAR	HIGH	LOW
2012	$4,781	$3,586

2772KW

YEARS MFRD 2016-2016
SERIES ...... SILVER EAGLE SERIES
ENGINE .... KAWASAKI
ENGINE HP 27
COOLING .... AIR
FUEL .... G
SPEEDS .... VARIABLE
TRANSMISSION .... HYDRO
STEERING .... ZERO
STANDARD DECK .... 72"
MSRP $10,899

OPTIONS

KOHLER EFI

RETAIL PRICING

YEAR	HIGH	LOW
2016	$6,381	$4,786

2960

YEARS MFRD 2013-2013
SERIES .... CLASSIC EFI SERIES
ENGINE .... KOHLER EFI
ENGINE HP 29
COOLING .... AIR
FUEL .... G
SPEEDS .... VARIABLE
TRANSMISSION .... HYDRO
STEERING .... ZERO
STANDARD DECK .... 60"
MSRP $11,499

RETAIL PRICING

YEAR	HIGH	LOW
2013	$5,527	$4,145

2960 EFI

YEARS MFRD 2013-2013
SERIES ...... SILVER EAGLE SERIES
ENGINE .... KOHLER
ENGINE HP 29
COOLING .... AIR
FUEL .... G
SPEEDS .... VARIABLE
TRANSMISSION .... HYDRO
STEERING .... ZERO
STANDARD DECK .... 60"
MSRP $10,699

RETAIL PRICING

YEAR	HIGH	LOW
2013	$5,044	$3,783

3060

YEARS MFRD 2008-2008
SERIES .... CLASSIC SERIES
ENGINE .... KOHLER
ENGINE HP 30
COOLING .... AIR
FUEL .... G
SPEEDS .... VARIABLE
TRANSMISSION .... HYDRO
STEERING .... ZERO
BLADE CLUTCH .... ELECTRIC
STANDARD DECK .... 60"
MSRP $9,998

RETAIL PRICING

YEAR	HIGH	LOW
2008	$4,864	$3,648

3060HP

YEARS MFRD 2008-2012
SERIES .... CLASSIC SERIES
ENGINE .... KOHLER
CYLINDERS 2
ENGINE HP 30
COOLING .... AIR
FUEL .... G
SPEEDS .... VARIABLE
TRANSMISSION .... HYDRO
STEERING .... ZERO
BLADE CLUTCH .... ELECTRIC
STANDARD DECK .... 60"
MSRP $11,599

SERIAL NUMBERS

YEAR	BEGINNING NO.
2008	80XXXX

RETAIL PRICING

YEAR	HIGH	LOW
2008	$3,430	$2,573
2009	$3,785	$2,839
2010	$4,177	$3,133
2011	$4,612	$3,459
2012	$5,089	$3,817

3060LP

YEARS MFRD 2009-2009
SERIES .... PROPANE SERIES
ENGINE .... GENERAC
CYLINDERS 2
ENGINE HP 30

DIXIE CHOPPER

COOLING . . . . . AIR
SPEEDS . . . . . VARIABLE
TRANSMISSION . . . . . HYDRO
STEERING. . . . . ZERO
BLADE CLUTCH . . . . . ELECTRIC
STANDARD DECK . . . . . 66"
MSRP. $11,499

RETAIL PRICING

YEAR	HIGH	LOW
2009	$5,538	$4,153

3066LP

YEARS MFRD 2009-2014
SERIES. . . . . XCALIBER SERIES
ENGINE . . . . . GENERAC
CYLINDERS. 2
ENGINE HP 30
SPEEDS . . . . . VARIABLE
TRANSMISSION . . . . . HYDRO
STEERING. . . . . ZERO
BLADE CLUTCH . . . . . ELECTRIC
STANDARD DECK . . . . . 66"
MSRP. $14,199

RETAIL PRICING

YEAR	HIGH	LOW
2009	$4,329	$3,246
2010	$4,778	$3,583
2011	$5,272	$3,954
2012	$5,820	$4,365
2013	$6,423	$4,817
2014	$7,090	$5,318

3072LP

YEARS MFRD 2009-2009
SERIES. . . . . PROPANE SERIES
ENGINE . . . . . GENERAC
CYLINDERS. 3
ENGINE HP 30
COOLING . . . . . AIR
SPEEDS . . . . . VARIABLE
TRANSMISSION . . . . . HYDRO
STEERING. . . . . ZERO
BLADE CLUTCH . . . . . ELECTRIC
STANDARD DECK . . . . . 74"
MSRP. $11,499

RETAIL PRICING

YEAR	HIGH	LOW
2009	$5,538	$4,153

3074LP

YEARS MFRD 2009-2014
SERIES. . . . . XCALIBER SERIES
ENGINE . . . . . GENERAC
CYLINDERS. 2
ENGINE HP 30
SPEEDS . . . . . VARIABLE
TRANSMISSION . . . . . HYDRO
STEERING. . . . . ZERO
BLADE CLUTCH . . . . . ELECTRIC
STANDARD DECK . . . . . 74"
MSRP. $14,299

RETAIL PRICING

YEAR	HIGH	LOW
2009	$4,359	$3,269
2010	$4,811	$3,608
2011	$5,310	$3,982
2012	$5,860	$4,395
2013	$6,469	$4,852
2014	$7,139	$5,354

3160

YEARS MFRD 2015-2019
SERIES. . . . . XCALIBER SERIES
ENGINE . . . . . KAWASAKI
ENGINE HP 31
COOLING . . . . . AIR
FUEL . . . . . G
SPEEDS . . . . . VARIABLE
TRANSMISSION . . . . . HYDRO
STEERING. . . . . ZERO
STANDARD DECK . . . . . 60"

RETAIL PRICING

YEAR	HIGH	LOW
2015	$7,066	$5,300
2016	$7,800	$5,850
2017	$8,608	$6,456
2018	$9,557	$7,168

3160

YEARS MFRD 2018-2020
SERIES. . . . . EAGLE HP SERIES
ENGINE . . . . . KAWASAKI FX
ENGINE HP 31
COOLING . . . . . AIR
FUEL . . . . . G
TRANSMISSION . . . . . DUAL HYDRO
STEERING. . . . . ZERO
STANDARD DECK . . . . . 60"
WEIGHT . . . . . 1,386 LBS.

OPTIONS

KOHLER 31HP

3160HP

YEARS MFRD 2015-2020
SERIES. . . . . CLASSIC SERIES
ENGINE . . . . . KAWASAKI
ENGINE HP 31
FUEL . . . . . G
SPEEDS . . . . . VARIABLE
TRANSMISSION . . . . . HYDRO
STEERING. . . . . ZERO
STANDARD DECK . . . . . 60"

OPTIONS

KOHLER EFI 33HP

RETAIL PRICING

YEAR	HIGH	LOW
2015	$6,407	$4,806
2016	$7,073	$5,304
2017	$7,807	$5,855
2018	$8,659	$6,494

3356

YEARS MFRD 2008-2011
SERIES. . . . . XCALIBER SERIES
ENGINE . . . . . GENERAC
ENGINE HP 33
COOLING . . . . . AIR
FUEL . . . . . G
SPEEDS . . . . . VARIABLE
TRANSMISSION . . . . . HYDRO
STEERING. . . . . ZERO
BLADE CLUTCH . . . . . ELECTRIC
STANDARD DECK . . . . . 56"
MSRP. $11,732

SERIAL NUMBERS

YEAR	BEGINNING NO.
2008	80XXXX

RETAIL PRICING

YEAR	HIGH	LOW
2008	$3,462	$2,597
2009	$3,821	$2,866
2010	$4,218	$3,163
2011	$4,656	$3,492

3360

YEARS MFRD 2008-2008
SERIES. . . . . XTREME SERIES
ENGINE . . . . . GENERAC
ENGINE HP 33
COOLING . . . . . AIR
FUEL . . . . . G
SPEEDS . . . . . VARIABLE
TRANSMISSION . . . . . HYDRO
STEERING. . . . . ZERO
BLADE CLUTCH . . . . . ELECTRIC
STANDARD DECK . . . . . 60"
MSRP. $10,932

RETAIL PRICING

YEAR	HIGH	LOW
2008	$3,422	$2,567

3360 EFI

YEARS MFRD 2015-2020
SERIES. . . . . XCALIBER SERIES
ENGINE . . . . . KOHLER
ENGINE HP 33
COOLING . . . . . AIR
FUEL . . . . . G
SPEEDS . . . . . VARIABLE
TRANSMISSION . . . . . HYDRO
STEERING. . . . . ZERO
STANDARD DECK . . . . . 60"

RETAIL PRICING

YEAR	HIGH	LOW
2015	$7,268	$5,451
2016	$8,023	$6,017
2017	$8,856	$6,641
2018	$9,818	$7,364

3360HP

YEARS MFRD 2008-2014
SERIES. . . . . CLASSIC SERIES
ENGINE . . . . . GENERAC
ENGINE HP 33
COOLING . . . . . AIR
FUEL . . . . . G
SPEEDS . . . . . VARIABLE
TRANSMISSION . . . . . HYDRO
STEERING. . . . . ZERO
BLADE CLUTCH . . . . . ELECTRIC
STANDARD DECK . . . . . 60"
MSRP. $11,199

SERIAL NUMBERS

YEAR	BEGINNING NO.
2008	80XXXX

RETAIL PRICING

YEAR	HIGH	LOW
2008	$3,093	$2,320
2009	$3,413	$2,560
2010	$3,768	$2,826
2011	$4,158	$3,119
2012	$4,589	$3,442
2013	$5,067	$3,800
2014	$5,593	$4,195

3360W

YEARS MFRD 2012-2012
SERIES. . . . . CLASSIC SERIES
ENGINE . . . . . GENERAC
ENGINE HP 33
COOLING . . . . . AIR
FUEL . . . . . G
SPEEDS . . . . . VARIABLE
TRANSMISSION . . . . . HYDRO
STEERING. . . . . ZERO
STANDARD DECK . . . . . 60"
MSRP. $12,399

RETAIL PRICING

YEAR	HIGH	LOW
2012	$5,441	$4,081

3366

YEARS MFRD 2018-2019
SERIES. . . . . EAGLE HP SERIES
ENGINE . . . . . KOHLER EFI
ENGINE HP 33
COOLING . . . . . AIR
TRANSMISSION . . . . . DUAL HYDRO
STEERING. . . . . ZERO
STANDARD DECK . . . . . 66"
WEIGHT . . . . . 1,403 LBS.

3366

YEARS MFRD 2008-2014
SERIES. . . . . XCALIBER SERIES
ENGINE . . . . . GENERAC
ENGINE HP 33
COOLING . . . . . AIR
FUEL . . . . . G
SPEEDS . . . . . VARIABLE
TRANSMISSION . . . . . HYDRO
STEERING. . . . . ZERO
BLADE CLUTCH . . . . . ELECTRIC
STANDARD DECK . . . . . 66"
MSRP. $13,299

SERIAL NUMBERS

YEAR	BEGINNING NO.
2008	80XXXX

RETAIL PRICING

YEAR	HIGH	LOW
2008	$3,673	$2,755
2009	$4,053	$3,040
2010	$4,475	$3,356
2011	$4,938	$3,704
2012	$5,451	$4,088
2013	$6,016	$4,512
2014	$6,640	$4,980

3366 EFI

YEARS MFRD 2016-2019
SERIES .... XCALIBER SERIES
ENGINE .... KOHLER EFI
ENGINE HP 33
COOLING .... AIR
FUEL .... G
SPEEDS .... VARIABLE
TRANSMISSION .... HYDRO
STEERING .... ZERO
STANDARD DECK .... 66"

RETAIL PRICING

YEAR	HIGH	LOW
2016	$8,079	$6,059
2017	$8,917	$6,688
2018	$9,887	$7,415

3372

YEARS MFRD 2008-2008
SERIES .... XTREME SERIES
ENGINE .... GENERAC
ENGINE HP 33
COOLING .... AIR
FUEL .... G
SPEEDS .... VARIABLE
TRANSMISSION .... HYDRO
STEERING .... ZERO
BLADE CLUTCH .... ELECTRIC
STANDARD DECK .... 72"
MSRP $11,198

RETAIL PRICING

YEAR	HIGH	LOW
2008	$3,517	$2,638

3372

YEARS MFRD 2018-2019
SERIES .... EAGLE HP SERIES
ENGINE .... KOHLER EFI
ENGINE HP 33
COOLING .... AIR
FUEL .... G
TRANSMISSION ..... DUAL HYDRO
STEERING .... ZERO
STANDARD DECK .... 72"
WEIGHT .... 1,442 LBS.

3372HP

YEARS MFRD 2009-2014
SERIES .... CLASSIC SERIES
ENGINE .... GENERAC
CYLINDERS 2
ENGINE HP 33
COOLING .... AIR
FUEL .... G
SPEEDS .... VARIABLE
TRANSMISSION .... HYDRO
STEERING .... ZERO
BLADE CLUTCH .... ELECTRIC
STANDARD DECK .... 60"
MSRP $12,599

RETAIL PRICING

YEAR	HIGH	LOW
2009	$3,840	$2,880
2010	$4,239	$3,180
2011	$4,679	$3,509
2012	$5,164	$3,873
2013	$5,699	$4,274
2014	$6,291	$4,718

3374

YEARS MFRD 2008-2014
SERIES .... XCALIBER SERIES
ENGINE .... GENERAC
ENGINE HP 33
COOLING .... AIR
FUEL .... G
SPEEDS .... VARIABLE
TRANSMISSION .... HYDRO
STEERING .... ZERO
BLADE CLUTCH .... ELECTRIC
STANDARD DECK .... 74"
MSRP $13,699

SERIAL NUMBERS

YEAR	BEGINNING NO.
2008	80XXXX

RETAIL PRICING

YEAR	HIGH	LOW
2008	$3,792	$2,844
2009	$4,176	$3,132
2010	$4,609	$3,457
2011	$5,107	$3,830
2012	$5,614	$4,211
2013	$6,197	$4,647
2014	$6,841	$5,131

3560

YEARS MFRD 2013-2013
SERIES .... GOLDEN EAGLE SERIES
ENGINE .... KAWASAKI
ENGINE HP 35
COOLING .... AIR
FUEL .... G
SPEEDS .... VARIABLE
TRANSMISSION .... HYDRO
STEERING .... ZERO
STANDARD DECK .... 60"
MSRP $12,599

RETAIL PRICING

YEAR	HIGH	LOW
2013	$5,939	$4,454

3560T

YEARS MFRD 2012-2012
SERIES .... CLASSIC SERIES
ENGINE .... KAWASAKI
ENGINE HP 35
COOLING .... AIR
FUEL .... G
SPEEDS .... VARIABLE
TRANSMISSION .... HYDRO
STEERING .... ZERO
STANDARD DECK .... 60"
MSRP $11,099

RETAIL PRICING

YEAR	HIGH	LOW
2012	$4,871	$3,653

3566

YEARS MFRD 2015-2020
SERIES .... XCALIBER SERIES
ENGINE .... KAWASAKI
ENGINE HP 35
COOLING .... AIR
FUEL .... G
SPEEDS .... VARIABLE
TRANSMISSION .... HYDRO
STEERING .... ZERO
STANDARD DECK .... 66"

RETAIL PRICING

YEAR	HIGH	LOW
2015	$7,320	$5,490
2016	$8,079	$6,059
2017	$8,917	$6,688
2018	$9,981	$7,486

3566

YEARS MFRD 2018-2019
SERIES .... EAGLE HP SERIES
ENGINE .... KAWASAKI FX
ENGINE HP 35
COOLING .... AIR
FUEL .... G
TRANSMISSION ..... DUAL HYDRO
STEERING .... ZERO
STANDARD DECK .... 66"
WEIGHT .... 1,409 LBS.

3566D

YEARS MFRD 2008-2009
SERIES .... XCALIBER SERIES
ENGINE .... YANMAR
ENGINE HP 35
COOLING .... LIQUID
FUEL .... D
SPEEDS .... VARIABLE
TRANSMISSION .... HYDRO
STEERING .... STANDARD
BLADE CLUTCH .... ELECTRIC
STANDARD DECK .... 66"
MSRP $15,465

SERIAL NUMBERS

YEAR	BEGINNING NO.
2008	80XXXX

RETAIL PRICING

YEAR	HIGH	LOW
2008	$4,646	$3,485
2009	$5,129	$3,847

3572

YEARS MFRD 2018-2020
SERIES .... EAGLE HP SERIES
ENGINE .... KAWASAKI FX
ENGINE HP 35
COOLING .... AIR
FUEL .... G
TRANSMISSION ..... DUAL HYDRO
STEERING .... ZERO
STANDARD DECK .... 72"
WEIGHT .... 1,426 LBS.

3572 EFI

YEARS MFRD 2015-2019
SERIES .... CLASSIC SERIES
ENGINE .... KOHLER EFI
ENGINE HP 34
FUEL .... G
SPEEDS .... VARIABLE
TRANSMISSION .... HYDRO
STEERING .... ZERO
STANDARD DECK .... 72"

RETAIL PRICING

YEAR	HIGH	LOW
2015	$6,584	$4,938
2016	$7,268	$5,451
2017	$8,022	$6,016
2018	$8,833	$6,625

3572HP

YEARS MFRD 2015-2020
SERIES .... CLASSIC SERIES
ENGINE .... KAWASAKI
ENGINE HP 35
FUEL .... G
SPEEDS .... VARIABLE
TRANSMISSION .... HYDRO
STEERING .... ZERO
STANDARD DECK .... 72"

RETAIL PRICING

YEAR	HIGH	LOW
2015	$6,712	$5,034
2016	$7,408	$5,557
2017	$8,177	$6,132
2018	$9,010	$6,657

3574

YEARS MFRD 2015-2020
SERIES .... XCALIBER SERIES
ENGINE .... KAWASAKI
ENGINE HP 35
COOLING .... AIR
FUEL .... G
SPEEDS .... VARIABLE
TRANSMISSION .... HYDRO
STEERING .... ZERO
STANDARD DECK .... 74"

RETAIL PRICING

YEAR	HIGH	LOW
2015	$7,497	$5,623
2016	$8,276	$6,207
2017	$9,134	$6,851
2018	$10,049	$7,536

3574 EFI

YEARS MFRD 2015-2019
SERIES .... XCALIBER SERIES
ENGINE .... KOHLER EFI
ENGINE HP 34
COOLING .... AIR
FUEL .... G
SPEEDS .... VARIABLE
TRANSMISSION .... HYDRO
STEERING .... ZERO
STANDARD DECK .... 74"

DIXIE CHOPPER

RETAIL PRICING

YEAR	HIGH	LOW
2015	$7,625	$5,718
2016	$8,409	$6,307
2017	$9,288	$6,966
2018	$10,434	$7,825

3574D

YEARS MFRD 2008-2009
SERIES .... XCALIBER SERIES
ENGINE .... YANMAR
ENGINE HP 35
COOLING .... LIQUID
FUEL .... D
SPEEDS .... VARIABLE
TRANSMISSION .... HYDRO
STEERING .... ZERO
BLADE CLUTCH .... ELECTRIC
STANDARD DECK .... 74"
MSRP $15,999

SERIAL NUMBERS

YEAR .... BEGINNING NO.
2008 .... 80XXX

RETAIL PRICING

YEAR	HIGH	LOW
2008	$4,807	$3,605
2009	$5,307	$3,980

3666D

YEARS MFRD 2010-2012
SERIES .... XCALIBER DIESEL
ENGINE .... CAT
ENGINE HP 36
COOLING .... LIQUID
FUEL .... D
SPEEDS .... VARIBLE
TRANSMISSION .... HYDRO
STEERING .... ZERO
BLADE CLUTCH .... ELECTRIC
STANDARD DECK .... 66"
MSRP $18,799

RETAIL PRICING

YEAR	HIGH	LOW
2010	$6,699	$5,024
2011	$7,394	$5,546
2012	$8,160	$6,120

3672BR

YEARS MFRD 2015-2019
SERIES .... CLASSIC SERIES
ENGINE .... VANGUARD
ENGINE HP 36
COOLING .... AIR
FUEL .... G
SPEEDS .... VARIABLE
TRANSMISSION .... HYDRO
STEERING .... ZERO
STANDARD DECK .... 72"

RETAIL PRICING

YEAR	HIGH	LOW
2015	$6,712	$5,034
2016	$7,408	$5,557
2017	$8,177	$6,132
2018	$9,263	$6,948

3674

YEARS MFRD 2015-2019
SERIES .... XCALIBER SERIES
ENGINE .... VANGUARD
ENGINE HP 36
COOLING .... AIR
FUEL .... G
SPEEDS .... VARIABLE
TRANSMISSION .... HYDRO
STEERING .... ZERO
STANDARD DECK .... 74"

RETAIL PRICING

YEAR	HIGH	LOW
2015	$7,445	$5,584
2016	$8,219	$6,165
2017	$9,071	$6,803
2018	$10,153	$7,615

3674D

YEARS MFRD 2010-2012
SERIES .... XCALIBER DIESEL
ENGINE .... CAT
CYLINDERS 4
ENGINE HP 36
COOLING .... LIQUID
FUEL .... D
SPEEDS .... VARIABLE
TRANSMISSION .... HYDRO
STEERING .... ZERO
BLADE CLUTCH .... ELECTRIC
STANDARD DECK .... 74"
MSRP $19,399

RETAIL PRICING

YEAR	HIGH	LOW
2010	$6,912	$5,184
2011	$7,629	$5,722
2012	$8,422	$6,317

3874

YEARS MFRD 2008-2008
SERIES .... XCALIBER SERIES
ENGINE .... KOHLER
ENGINE HP 38
COOLING .... AIR
FUEL .... G
SPEEDS .... VARIABLE
TRANSMISSION .... HYDRO
STEERING .... ZERO
BLADE CLUTCH .... ELECTRIC
STANDARD DECK .... 74"
MSRP $12,665

RETAIL PRICING

YEAR	HIGH	LOW
2008	$4,318	$3,238

4074

YEARS MFRD 2009-2013
SERIES .... XCALIBER SERIES
ENGINE .... KOHLER
ENGINE HP 40
FUEL .... G
SPEEDS .... VARIABLE
TRANSMISSION .... HYDRO
STEERING .... ZERO
BLADE CLUTCH .... ELECTRIC
STANDARD DECK .... 74"
MSRP $14,499

RETAIL PRICING

YEAR	HIGH	LOW
2009	$4,514	$3,385
2010	$4,982	$3,737
2011	$5,499	$4,124
2012	$6,071	$4,553
2013	$6,699	$5,024

6020

YEARS MFRD 1990-1990
ENGINE .... KOHLER
ENGINE HP 20
COOLING .... AIR
FUEL .... G
TRANSMISSION .... HYDRO
STEERING .... ZERO
STANDARD DECK .... 60"
MSRP $6,995

RETAIL PRICING

YEAR	HIGH	LOW
1990	$292	$219

DIXON

ALL MODELS 30 INCHES

YEARS MFRD NA-1997

SERIAL NUMBERS

YEAR	BEGINNING NO.
1977	00001
1978	01030
1979	01722
1980	03364
1981	05315
1982	07506
1983	09454
1984	12014
1985	15167
1986	18198
1987	20935
1988	23253
1989	26663
1990	29801
1991	32688
1992	34916
1993	37684
1994	40543
1995	43714
1996	47251
1997	50914

ALL MODELS 36 INCHES

YEARS MFRD NA-1997

SERIAL NUMBERS

YEAR	BEGINNING NO.
1989	00001
1990	01372
1991	02418
1992	03412
1993	04377
1994	05540
1995	07219
1996	09594
1997	12001

ALL MODELS 42 INCHES

YEARS MFRD NA-1997

SERIAL NUMBERS

YEAR	BEGINNING NO.
1974	00454
1975	00826
1976	01687
1977	03301
1978	04742
1979	07148
1980	11875
1981	15227
1982	17739
1983	20709
1984	23723
1985	26971
1986	30160
1987	33296
1988	36324
1989	41000
1990	44355
1991	48253
1992	52842
1993	57030
1994	61583
1995	67779
1996	74456
1997	81254

ALL MODELS 50 INCHES

YEARS MFRD NA-1997

SERIAL NUMBERS

YEAR	BEGINNING NO.
1987	00001
1988	01087
1989	01780
1990	02365
1991	03101
1992	03788
1993	04338
1994	04870
1995	05475
1996	06263
1997	07575

BLACK BEAR 34

YEARS MFRD 2006-2009
ENGINE .... KAWASAKI
CYLINDERS 2
CID 28.8
ENGINE HP 17
COOLING .... AIR
FUEL .... G
SPEEDS .... VARIABLE
TRANSMISSION .... HYDRO
STEERING .... ZERO
BLADE CLUTCH .... ELECTRIC
STANDARD DECK .... 34"
WEIGHT .... 640 LBS.
MSRP $5,599

OPTIONS

2BAG & FAN
KOHLER 18E

RETAIL PRICING

YEAR	HIGH	LOW
2006	$1,391	$1,043
2007	$1,535	$1,151
2008	$1,694	$1,270
2009	$1,870	$1,403

BLACK BEAR 44

YEARS MFRD 2006-2009
ENGINE .... KOHLER
CYLINDERS 1
CID 29.9
ENGINE HP 19
COOLING .... AIR
FUEL .... G
SPEEDS .... VARIABLE
TRANSMISSION .... HYDRO
STEERING .... ZERO
BLADE CLUTCH .... ELECTRIC
STANDARD DECK .... 44"
WEIGHT .... 735 LBS.
MSRP $5,899

OPTIONS

2 BAG & FAN

RETAIL PRICING

YEAR	HIGH	LOW
2006	$1,465	$1,099
2007	$1,617	$1,213
2008	$1,784	$1,338
2009	$1,969	$1,477

D20KH42

YEARS MFRD 2014-2014
ENGINE .... KOHLER COURAGE
CYLINDERS 1
ENGINE HP 20
COOLING .... AIR
FUEL .... G
SPEEDS .... VARIABLE
TRANSMISSION .... HYDRO
STEERING .... STANDARD
BLADE CLUTCH .... ELECTRIC
STANDARD DECK .... 42"
WEIGHT .... 424 LBS.

D22KH46

YEARS MFRD 2011-2011
ENGINE .... KOHLER COURAGE
CYLINDERS 2
ENGINE HP 22
COOLING .... AIR
FUEL .... G
SPEEDS .... VARIABLE
TRANSMISSION .... HYDRO
STEERING .... STANDARD
BLADE CLUTCH .... ELECTRIC
WEIGHT .... 468 LBS.

D24KH54

YEARS MFRD 2014-2014
ENGINE .... KAWASAKI
CYLINDERS 2
CID 44.3
ENGINE HP 24
COOLING .... AIR
FUEL .... G
SPEEDS .... VARIABLE
TRANSMISSION .... HYDRO
STEERING .... STANDARD
BLADE CLUTCH .... ELECTRIC
STANDARD DECK .... 54"
WEIGHT .... 593 LBS.

D25KH48

YEARS MFRD 2011-2011
ENGINE .... KOHLER COURAGE
CYLINDERS 2
ENGINE HP 25
COOLING .... AIR
FUEL .... G
SPEEDS .... VARIABLE
TRANSMISSION .... HYDRO
STEERING .... STANDARD
BLADE CLUTCH .... ELECTRIC
WEIGHT .... 492 LBS.

D26KH48

YEARS MFRD 2014-2014
ENGINE .... KOHLER
CYLINDERS 2
CID 44.2
ENGINE HP 26
COOLING .... AIR
FUEL .... G
SPEEDS .... VARIABLE
TRANSMISSION .... HYDRO
STEERING .... STANDARD
BLADE CLUTCH .... ELECTRIC
STANDARD DECK .... 48"
WEIGHT .... 489 LBS.

D26KH54

YEARS MFRD 2011-2011
ENGINE .... KAWASAKI
CYLINDERS 2
ENGINE HP 26
COOLING .... AIR
FUEL .... G
SPEEDS .... VARIABLE
TRANSMISSION .... HYDRO
STEERING .... STANDARD
BLADE CLUTCH .... ELECTRIC
WEIGHT .... 642 LBS.

DX148

YEARS MFRD 2011-2013
ENGINE .... KAWASAKI FX
CYLINDERS 2
CID 44.3
ENGINE HP 20.5
COOLING .... AIR
FUEL .... G
SPEEDS .... VARIABLE
TRANSMISSION .... HYDRO
STEERING .... ZERO
BLADE CLUTCH .... ELECTRIC
STANDARD DECK .... 48"
WEIGHT .... 880 LBS.
MSRP $6,899

OPTIONS

BAGGER

RETAIL PRICING

YEAR	HIGH	LOW
2011	$2,614	$1,960
2012	$2,886	$2,164
2013	$3,185	$2,389

DX152

YEARS MFRD 2011-2013
ENGINE .... KAWASAKI FS
CYLINDERS 2
CID 44.3
ENGINE HP 22
COOLING .... AIR
FUEL .... G
SPEEDS .... VARIABLE
TRANSMISSION .... HYDRO
STEERING .... ZERO
BLADE CLUTCH .... ELECTRIC
STANDARD DECK .... 52"
WEIGHT .... 900 LBS.
MSRP $7,199

OPTIONS

BAGGER

RETAIL PRICING

YEAR	HIGH	LOW
2011	$2,728	$2,046
2012	$3,011	$2,258
2013	$3,323	$2,493

DX161

YEARS MFRD 2011-2013
ENGINE .... B&S
CYLINDERS 2
CID 49.43
ENGINE HP 28
COOLING .... AIR
FUEL .... G
SPEEDS .... VARIABLE
TRANSMISSION .... HYDRO
STEERING .... ZERO
BLADE CLUTCH .... ELECTRIC
STANDARD DECK .... 61"
WEIGHT .... 955 LBS.
MSRP $6,999

OPTIONS

BAGGER

RETAIL PRICING

YEAR	HIGH	LOW
2011	$2,652	$1,989
2012	$2,928	$2,196
2013	$3,230	$2,423

DX161KAW

YEARS MFRD 2011-2013
ENGINE .... KAWASAKI
ENGINE HP 23.5
COOLING .... AIR
FUEL .... G
SPEEDS .... VARIABLE
TRANSMISSION .... HYDRO
STEERING .... ZERO
STANDARD DECK .... 61"
MSRP $7,399

OPTIONS

BAGGER

RETAIL PRICING

YEAR	HIGH	LOW
2011	$2,803	$2,102
2012	$3,094	$2,320
2013	$3,416	$2,562

DX254

YEARS MFRD 2011-2013
ENGINE .... KAWASAKI FX
CYLINDERS 2
CID 44.3
ENGINE HP 24.5
COOLING .... AIR
FUEL .... G
SPEEDS .... VARIABLE
TRANSMISSION .... HYDRO
STEERING .... ZERO
BLADE CLUTCH .... ELECTRIC
STANDARD DECK .... 54"
WEIGHT .... 1,260 LBS.
MSRP $9,399

OPTIONS

BAGGER

RETAIL PRICING

YEAR	HIGH	LOW
2011	$3,562	$2,672
2012	$3,931	$2,948
2013	$4,338	$3,254

DX260

YEARS MFRD 2011-2013
ENGINE .... KAWASAKI FX
CYLINDERS 2
ENGINE HP 25.5
COOLING .... AIR
FUEL .... G
SPEEDS .... VARIABLE
TRANSMISSION .... HYDRO
STEERING .... ZERO
BLADE CLUTCH .... ELECTRIC
STANDARD DECK .... 60"
WEIGHT .... 1,320 LBS.
MSRP $9,999

DIXON

OPTIONS

KAWASAKI 34HP

RETAIL PRICING

YEAR	HIGH	LOW
2011	$3,789	$2,842
2012	$4,182	$3,136
2013	$4,615	$3,462

DX260D

YEARS MFRD 2011-2012
ENGINE . . . . KUBOTA
CYLINDERS. 3
CID 76.95
ENGINE HP 29
COOLING . . . . LIQUID
FUEL . . . . D
SPEEDS . . . . VARIABLE
TRANSMISSION . . . . .HYDRO
STEERING. . . . . ZERO
BLADE CLUTCH . . . . ELECTRIC
STANDARD DECK . . . . 60"
WEIGHT . . . . 1,600 LBS.
MSRP. $15,299

RETAIL PRICING

YEAR	HIGH	LOW
2011	$6,398	$4,799
2012	$7,062	$5,296

DX260KAW

YEARS MFRD 2011-2013
ENGINE . . . . KAWASAKI
ENGINE HP 31
COOLING . . . . AIR
FUEL . . . . G
SPEEDS . . . . VARIABLE
TRANSMISSION . . . . .HYDRO
STEERING. . . . . ZERO
STANDARD DECK . . . . 60"
MSRP. $10,499

RETAIL PRICING

YEAR	HIGH	LOW
2011	$3,979	$2,984
2012	$4,391	$3,293
2013	$4,846	$3,635

DX272

YEARS MFRD 2011-2013
ENGINE . . . . KAWASAKI FX
CYLINDERS. 2
CID 60.96
ENGINE HP 31
COOLING . . . . AIR
FUEL . . . . G
SPEEDS . . . . VARIABLE
TRANSMISSION . . . . .HYDRO
STEERING. . . . . ZERO
BLADE CLUTCH . . . . ELECTRIC
STANDARD DECK . . . . 72"
WEIGHT . . . . 1,650 LBS.
MSRP. $10,799

RETAIL PRICING

YEAR	HIGH	LOW
2011	$4,092	$3,069
2012	$4,516	$3,387
2013	$4,988	$3,741

GRIZZLY 50

YEARS MFRD 2006-2006
ENGINE . . KOHLER COMMAND PRO
CYLINDERS. 2
CID 41
ENGINE HP 23
COOLING . . . . AIR
FUEL . . . . G
SPEEDS . . . . VARIABLE
TRANSMISSION . . . . .HYDRO
STEERING. . . . . ZERO
BLADE CLUTCH . . . . ELECTRIC
STANDARD DECK . . . . 50"
WEIGHT . . . . 737 LBS.
MSRP. $6,995

RETAIL PRICING

YEAR	HIGH	LOW
2006	$3,217	$2,412

GRIZZLY 52

YEARS MFRD 2006-2009
ENGINE . . KOHLER COMMAND PRO
CYLINDERS. 2
CID 44
ENGINE HP 25
COOLING . . . . AIR
FUEL . . . . G
SPEEDS . . . . VARIABLE
TRANSMISSION . . . . .HYDRO
STEERING. . . . . ZERO
BLADE CLUTCH . . . . ELECTRIC
STANDARD DECK . . . . 52"
WEIGHT . . . . 884 LBS.
MSRP. $7,395

OPTIONS

HONDA 24E
KOHLER 27E

RETAIL PRICING

YEAR	HIGH	LOW
2006	$3,600	$2,700
2007	$3,647	$2,735

GRIZZLY 60

YEARS MFRD 2006-2009
ENGINE . . KOHLER COMMAND PRO
CYLINDERS. 2
CID 44
ENGINE HP 25
COOLING . . . . AIR
FUEL . . . . G
SPEEDS . . . . VARIABLE
TRANSMISSION . . . . .HYDRO
STEERING. . . . . ZERO
BLADE CLUTCH . . . . ELECTRIC
STANDARD DECK . . . . 60"
WEIGHT . . . . 917 LBS.
MSRP. $7,725

OPTIONS

HONDA 24E
KOHLER 27E

RETAIL PRICING

YEAR	HIGH	LOW
2006	$3,630	$2,723

GRIZZLY 60SE

YEARS MFRD 2010-2010
ENGINE . . . . KAWASAKI
ENGINE HP 29
COOLING . . . . AIR
FUEL . . . . G
SPEEDS . . . . VARIABLE
TRANSMISSION . . . . .HYDRO
STEERING. . . . . ZERO
BLADE CLUTCH . . . . ELECTRIC
STANDARD DECK . . . . 60"
MSRP. $9,299

OPTIONS

BAGGER

RETAIL PRICING

YEAR	HIGH	LOW
2010	$3,275	$2,456

GRIZZLY 72

YEARS MFRD 2006-2008
ENGINE . . KOHLER COMMAND PRO
CYLINDERS. 2
ENGINE HP 30
FUEL . . . . G
SPEEDS . . . . VARIABLE
TRANSMISSION . . . . .HYDRO
STEERING. . . . . ZERO

GRIZZLY 72SE

YEARS MFRD 2010-2010
ENGINE . . . . KAWASAKI
ENGINE HP 34
COOLING . . . . AIR
FUEL . . . . G
SPEEDS . . . . VARIABLE
TRANSMISSION . . . . .HYDRO
STEERING. . . . . ZERO
BLADE CLUTCH . . . . ELECTRIC
STANDARD DECK . . . . 72"
MSRP. $9,999

RETAIL PRICING

YEAR	HIGH	LOW
2010	$3,533	$2,650

GRIZZLY ZTR

YEARS MFRD 2005-2006
ENGINE . . . . . . KOHLER COMMAND
CYLINDERS. 2
ENGINE HP 23
COOLING . . . . AIR
FUEL . . . . G
SPEEDS . . . . VARIABLE
TRANSMISSION . . . . .HYDRO
STEERING. . . . . ZERO
BLADE CLUTCH . . . . ELECTRIC
STANDARD DECK . . . . 50"
MSRP. $7,011

OPTIONS

HONDA 24E
KOHLER 23E
KOHLER 25E

RETAIL PRICING

YEAR	HIGH	LOW
2005	$3,125	$2,344
2006	$3,170	$2,377

KODIAK 52

YEARS MFRD 2008-2009
SERIES. . . . . KODIAK SERIES
ENGINE . . . . KOHLER
ENGINE HP 25
COOLING . . . . AIR
FUEL . . . . G
SPEEDS . . . . VARIABLE
TRANSMISSION . . . . .HYDRO
STEERING. . . . . ZERO
BLADE CLUTCH . . . . ELECTRIC
WEIGHT . . . . 966 LBS.

OPTIONS

HONDA 20E
KAWASAKI 21E
KOHLER 20E

KODIAK 60

YEARS MFRD 2008-2008
SERIES. . . . . KODIAK SERIES
ENGINE . . . . KOHLER
CYLINDERS. 2
ENGINE HP 25
COOLING . . . . AIR
FUEL . . . . G
SPEEDS . . . . VARIABLE
TRANSMISSION . . . . .HYDRO
STEERING. . . . . ZERO
BLADE CLUTCH . . . . ELECTRIC
WEIGHT . . . . 986 LBS.

OPTIONS

B&S 26E

KODIAK 907

YEARS MFRD 2006-2006
ENGINE . . . . KAWASAKI FH
CYLINDERS. 2
CID 41.2
ENGINE HP 19
COOLING . . . . AIR
FUEL . . . . G
SPEEDS . . . . VARIABLE
TRANSMISSION . . . . .HYDRO
STEERING. . . . . ZERO
BLADE CLUTCH . . . . ELECTRIC
STANDARD DECK . . . . 50"
WEIGHT . . . . 737 LBS.
MSRP. $6,245

RETAIL PRICING

YEAR	HIGH	LOW
2006	$3,538	$2,654

KODIAK 908

YEARS MFRD 2006-2006
ENGINE . . KOHLER COMMAND PRO
CYLINDERS. 2
CID 41
ENGINE HP 20
COOLING . . . . AIR
FUEL . . . . G
SPEEDS . . . . VARIABLE
TRANSMISSION . . . . .HYDRO
STEERING. . . . . ZERO
BLADE CLUTCH . . . . ELECTRIC

STANDARD DECK . . . . 50"
WEIGHT . . . . 737 LBS.
MSRP. $6,245

RETAIL PRICING

YEAR	HIGH	LOW
2006	$3,538	$2,654

KODIAK 909

YEARS MFRD 2006-2006
ENGINE . . . . HONDA GXV
CYLINDERS. 2
ENGINE HP 20
COOLING . . . . AIR
FUEL . . . . G
SPEEDS . . . . VARIABLE
TRANSMISSION . . . . HYDRO
STEERING. . . . . ZERO
BLADE CLUTCH . . . . ELECTRIC
STANDARD DECK . . . . 50"
WEIGHT . . . . 737 LBS.
MSRP. $6,445

RETAIL PRICING

YEAR	HIGH	LOW
2006	$3,651	$2,738

KODIAK 910

YEARS MFRD 2006-2006
ENGINE . . . . B&S VANGUARD
CYLINDERS. 2
CID 38.26
ENGINE HP 21
COOLING . . . . AIR
FUEL . . . . G
SPEEDS . . . . VARIABLE
TRANSMISSION . . . . HYDRO
STEERING. . . . . ZERO
BLADE CLUTCH . . . . ELECTRIC
STANDARD DECK . . . . 50"
WEIGHT . . . . 737 LBS.
MSRP. $6,045

RETAIL PRICING

YEAR	HIGH	LOW
2006	$3,426	$2,570

KODIAK 90053

YEARS MFRD 2006-2006
ENGINE . . . . YANMAR
CYLINDERS. 2
CID 45.7
ENGINE HP 20
COOLING . . . . LIQUID
FUEL . . . . D
SPEEDS . . . . VARIABLE
TRANSMISSION . . . . HYDRO
STEERING. . . . . ZERO
BLADE CLUTCH . . . . ELECTRIC
STANDARD DECK . . . . 52"
WEIGHT . . . . 1,046 LBS.
MSRP. $9,295

RETAIL PRICING

YEAR	HIGH	LOW
2006	$4,519	$3,390

KODIAK ELS 60

YEARS MFRD 2006-2007
ENGINE . . . . B&S
CYLINDERS. 2
CID 44
ENGINE HP 26
COOLING . . . . AIR
FUEL . . . . G
SPEEDS . . . . VARIABLE
TRANSMISSION . . . . HYDRO
STEERING. . . . . ZERO
BLADE CLUTCH . . . . ELECTRIC
STANDARD DECK . . . . 60"
WEIGHT . . . . 770 LBS.
MSRP. $5,995

RETAIL PRICING

YEAR	HIGH	LOW
2006	$3,398	$2,548

KODIAK SE 52

YEARS MFRD 2010-2010
ENGINE . . . . VANGUARD
ENGINE HP 23
COOLING . . . . AIR
FUEL . . . . G
SPEEDS . . . . VARIABLE
TRANSMISSION . . . . HYDRO
STEERING. . . . . ZERO
BLADE CLUTCH . . . . ELECTRIC
STANDARD DECK . . . . 52"
WEIGHT . . . . 900 LBS.
MSRP. $5,999

OPTIONS

BAGGER

RETAIL PRICING

YEAR	HIGH	LOW
2010	$2,113	$1,584

KODIAK SE 61

YEARS MFRD 2010-2010
ENGINE . . . . KOHLER
ENGINE HP 25
COOLING . . . . AIR
FUEL . . . . G
SPEEDS . . . . VARIABLE
TRANSMISSION . . . . HYDRO
STEERING. . . . . ZERO
BLADE CLUTCH . . . . ELECTRIC
STANDARD DECK . . . . 61"
WEIGHT . . . . 930 LBS.
MSRP. $6,499

OPTIONS

BAGGER

RETAIL PRICING

YEAR	HIGH	LOW
2010	$2,289	$1,717

KODIAK ZTR

YEARS MFRD 2005-2006
ENGINE . . . . B&S
CYLINDERS. 2
ENGINE HP 21
COOLING . . . . AIR
FUEL . . . . G
SPEEDS . . . . VARIABLE
TRANSMISSION . . . . HYDRO
STEERING. . . . . ZERO
BLADE CLUTCH . . . . ELECTRIC
STANDARD DECK . . . . 50"
MSRP. $6,045

OPTIONS

HONDA 20E
KAWASAKI 19E
KOHLER 20E

RETAIL PRICING

YEAR	HIGH	LOW
2005	$3,136	$2,352
2006	$3,426	$2,570

MOUNTAIN KODIAK

YEARS MFRD 2006-2006
ENGINE . . KOHLER COMMAND PRO
CYLINDERS. 2
CID 44
ENGINE HP 25
COOLING . . . . AIR
FUEL . . . . G
SPEEDS . . . . VARIABLE
TRANSMISSION . . . . HYDRO
STEERING. . . . . ZERO
BLADE CLUTCH . . . . ELECTRIC
STANDARD DECK . . . . 50"
WEIGHT . . . . 737 LBS.
MSRP. $6,545

OPTIONS

60" DECK

RETAIL PRICING

YEAR	HIGH	LOW
2006	$3,709	$2,781

RAM 44

YEARS MFRD 2005-2009
SERIES. . . . . RAM SERIES
ENGINE . . . . B&S ELS
CYLINDERS. 2
ENGINE HP 26
COOLING . . . . AIR
FUEL . . . . G
SPEEDS . . . . VARIABLE
TRANSMISSION . . . . HYDRO
STEERING. . . . . ZERO
BLADE CLUTCH . . . . ELECTRIC
STANDARD DECK . . . . 44"
WEIGHT . . . . 652 LBS.
MSRP. $4,999

OPTIONS

48" BLADE
BAG & FAN
SNOW BLOWER

SERIAL NUMBERS

YEAR . . . . BEGINNING NO.
2005 101000
2007 64000000

RETAIL PRICING

YEAR	HIGH	LOW
2005	$1,127	$845
2006	$1,241	$931
2007	$1,370	$1,028
2008	$1,513	$1,135
2009	$1,670	$1,253

RAM 44 MAG

YEARS MFRD 2005-2009
SERIES. . . . . MAG SERIES
ENGINE . . . . . . KOHLER COMMAND
CYLINDERS. 2
ENGINE HP 24
COOLING . . . . AIR
FUEL . . . . G
SPEEDS . . . . VARIABLE
TRANSMISSION . . . . HYDRO
STEERING. . . . . ZERO
BLADE CLUTCH . . . . ELECTRIC
STANDARD DECK . . . . 44"
MSRP. $5,399

OPTIONS

48" BLADE
BAG & FAN
HONDA 20E
KAWASAKI 19E
SNOW BLOWER

SERIAL NUMBERS

YEAR . . . . BEGINNING NO.
2005 101000
2007 64000000

RETAIL PRICING

YEAR	HIGH	LOW
2005	$1,214	$910
2006	$1,341	$1,006
2007	$1,480	$1,110
2008	$1,634	$1,225
2009	$1,803	$1,352

RAM 48 ZT

YEARS MFRD 2010-2013
ENGINE . . . . B&S PRO
CYLINDERS. 2
CID 44.18
ENGINE HP 26
COOLING . . . . AIR
FUEL . . . . G
SPEEDS . . . . VARIABLE
TRANSMISSION . . . . HYDRO
STEERING. . . . . ZERO
BLADE CLUTCH . . . . ELECTRIC
STANDARD DECK . . . . 48"
WEIGHT . . . . 660 LBS.
MSRP. $4,399

OPTIONS

BAGGER

RETAIL PRICING

YEAR	HIGH	LOW
2010	$1,481	$1,111
2011	$1,634	$1,225
2012	$1,804	$1,353
2013	$1,991	$1,493

DIXON

RAM 50

YEARS MFRD 2005-2009
SERIES. . . . . .RAM SERIES
ENGINE . . . . B&S
CYLINDERS. 2
ENGINE HP. 26
COOLING . . . . .AIR
FUEL . . . . G
SPEEDS . . . . .VARIABLE
TRANSMISSION . . . . .HYDRO
STEERING. . . . . .ZERO
BLADE CLUTCH . . . . .ELECTRIC
STANDARD DECK . . . . 50"
WEIGHT . . . . 665 LBS.
MSRP. $5,179

OPTIONS

48" BLADE
BAG & FAN
SNOW BLOWER

SERIAL NUMBERS

YEAR	BEGINNING NO.
2005	101000
2007	64000000

RETAIL PRICING

YEAR	HIGH	LOW
2005	$1,165	$874
2006	$1,287	$965
2007	$1,419	$1,064
2008	$1,569	$1,177
2009	$1,735	$1,302

RAM 50 MAG

YEARS MFRD 2005-2009
SERIES. . . . . .MAG SERIES
ENGINE . . . . KOHLER
CYLINDERS. 2
ENGINE HP 20
COOLING . . . . .AIR
FUEL . . . . G
SPEEDS . . . . .VARIABLE
TRANSMISSION . . . . .HYDRO
STEERING. . . . . .ZERO
BLADE CLUTCH . . . . .ELECTRIC
STANDARD DECK . . . . 50"
MSRP. $5,599

OPTIONS

48" BLADE
BAG & FAN
HONDA 20E
KAWASAKI 19E
SNOW BLOWER

SERIAL NUMBERS

YEAR	BEGINNING NO.
2005	101000
2007	64000000

RETAIL PRICING

YEAR	HIGH	LOW
2005	$1,260	$945
2006	$1,391	$1,043
2007	$1,535	$1,152
2008	$1,694	$1,270
2009	$1,870	$1,403

RAM 52 ZT

YEARS MFRD 2010-2010
ENGINE . . . . KOHLER COURAGE
ENGINE HP 26
COOLING . . . . .AIR
FUEL . . . . G
SPEEDS . . . . .VARIABLE
TRANSMISSION . . . . .HYDRO
STEERING. . . . . .ZERO
BLADE CLUTCH . . . . .ELECTRIC
STANDARD DECK . . . . 52"
MSRP. $4,599

OPTIONS

BAGGER

RETAIL PRICING

YEAR	HIGH	LOW
2010	$1,619	$1,214

RAM ULTRA 50

YEARS MFRD 2008-2009
ENGINE . . . . KOHLER
CYLINDERS. 2
ENGINE HP 25
COOLING . . . . .AIR
FUEL . . . . G
SPEEDS . . . . .VARIABLE
TRANSMISSION . . . . .HYDRO
STEERING. . . . . .ZERO
BLADE CLUTCH . . . . .ELECTRIC
STANDARD DECK . . . . 50"
WEIGHT . . . . 760 LBS.
MSRP. $6,299

OPTIONS

48" BLADE
BAG & FAN

RETAIL PRICING

YEAR	HIGH	LOW
2008	$1,906	$1,429
2009	$2,103	$1,577

RAM ULTRA 52

YEARS MFRD 2011-2013
ENGINE . . KOHLER COMMAND PRO
CYLINDERS. 2
CID 44.24
ENGINE HP 25
COOLING . . . . .AIR
FUEL . . . . G
SPEEDS . . . . .VARIABLE
TRANSMISSION . . . . .HYDRO
STEERING. . . . . .ZERO
STANDARD DECK . . . . 52"
WEIGHT . . . . 885 LBS.
MSRP. $4,899

OPTIONS

BAGGER

RETAIL PRICING

YEAR	HIGH	LOW
2011	$1,820	$1,365
2012	$2,008	$1,506
2013	$2,223	$1,667

RAM ULTRA 60

YEARS MFRD 2008-2009
ENGINE . . . . KOHLER COURAGE
CYLINDERS. 2
ENGINE HP 25
COOLING . . . . .AIR
FUEL . . . . G
SPEEDS . . . . .VARIABLE
TRANSMISSION . . . . .HYDRO
STEERING. . . . . .ZERO
BLADE CLUTCH . . . . .ELECTRIC
STANDARD DECK . . . . 60"
WEIGHT . . . . 775 LBS.
MSRP. $6,599

OPTIONS

48" BLADE
BAG & FAN

RETAIL PRICING

YEAR	HIGH	LOW
2008	$1,997	$1,498
2009	$2,203	$1,652

RAM ULTRA 61

YEARS MFRD 2010-2013
ENGINE . . . KOHLER COURAGE PRO
CYLINDERS. 2
ENGINE HP 27
COOLING . . . . .AIR
FUEL . . . . G
SPEEDS . . . . .VARIABLE
TRANSMISSION . . . . .HYDRO
STEERING. . . . . .ZERO
BLADE CLUTCH . . . . .ELECTRIC
STANDARD DECK . . . . 61"
WEIGHT . . . . 760 LBS.
MSRP. $5,499

OPTIONS

BAGGER

RETAIL PRICING

YEAR	HIGH	LOW
2010	$1,856	$1,392
2011	$2,042	$1,532
2012	$2,254	$1,691
2013	$2,500	$1,875

RAM ULTRA 72

YEARS MFRD 2008-2009
ENGINE . . . . KOHLER
CYLINDERS. 2
ENGINE HP 27
COOLING . . . . .AIR
FUEL . . . . G
SPEEDS . . . . .VARIABLE
TRANSMISSION . . . . .HYDRO
STEERING. . . . . .ZERO
BLADE CLUTCH . . . . .ELECTRIC
STANDARD DECK . . . . 72"
WEIGHT . . . . 795 LBS.
MSRP. $7,199

OPTIONS

48" BLADE
BAG & FAN

RETAIL PRICING

YEAR	HIGH	LOW
2008	$2,178	$1,634
2009	$2,417	$1,812

RAM ZTR 42

YEARS MFRD 2005-2006
ENGINE . . . . B&S
CYLINDERS. 1
ENGINE HP 18
COOLING . . . . .AIR
FUEL . . . . G
SPEEDS . . . . .VARIABLE
TRANSMISSION . . . . .HYDRO
STEERING. . . . . .ZERO
STANDARD DECK . . . . 42"
MSRP. $4,320

SERIAL NUMBERS

YEAR	BEGINNING NO.
2005	101000

RETAIL PRICING

YEAR	HIGH	LOW
2005	$1,958	$1,469
2006	$2,448	$1,836

RAM ZTR 44

YEARS MFRD 2004-2007
SERIES. . . . . .RAM SERIES
ENGINE . . . . KAWASAKI
CYLINDERS. 1
CID 30.6
ENGINE HP 19
COOLING . . . . .AIR
FUEL . . . . G
SPEEDS . . . . .VARIABLE
TRANSMISSION . . . . .HYDRO
STEERING. . . . . .ZERO
BLADE CLUTCH . . . . .ELECTRIC
STANDARD DECK . . . . 44"
WEIGHT . . . . 545 LBS.
MSRP. $4,875

SERIAL NUMBERS

YEAR	BEGINNING NO.
2005	101000
2007	64000000

RETAIL PRICING

YEAR	HIGH	LOW
2004	$2,123	$1,592
2005	$2,582	$1,936
2006	$2,763	$2,072

RAM ZTR 50

YEARS MFRD 2004-2007
SERIES. . . . . .RAM SERIES
ENGINE . . . . B&S
CYLINDERS. 2
CID 44
ENGINE HP 25
COOLING . . . . .AIR
FUEL . . . . G
SPEEDS . . . . .VARIABLE
TRANSMISSION . . . . .HYDRO
STEERING. . . . . .ZERO
BLADE CLUTCH . . . . .ELECTRIC

STANDARD DECK .... 50"
WEIGHT .... 650 LBS.
MSRP.................. $5,020

SERIAL NUMBERS

YEAR	BEGINNING NO.
2005	101000
2007	64000000

RETAIL PRICING

YEAR	HIGH	LOW
2004	$2,375	$1,781
2005	$2,691	$2,018
2006	$2,844	$2,133

SILVERTIP 60

YEARS MFRD 2006-2007
ENGINE .. KOHLER COMMAND PRO
CYLINDERS.................. 2
CID 44
ENGINE HP 27
COOLING .... AIR
FUEL .... G
SPEEDS .... VARIABLE
TRANSMISSION .... HYDRO
STEERING................ ZERO
BLADE CLUTCH .... ELECTRIC
STANDARD DECK .... 60"
WEIGHT .... 1,317 LBS.
MSRP.................. $9,595

RETAIL PRICING

YEAR	HIGH	LOW
2006	$4,733	$3,550
2007	$5,437	$4,078

SILVERTIP 72

YEARS MFRD 2006-2007
ENGINE .... KAWASAKI
CYLINDERS.................. 2
CID 45.5
ENGINE HP 27
COOLING .... AIR
FUEL .... G
SPEEDS .... VARIABLE
TRANSMISSION .... HYDRO
STEERING................ ZERO
BLADE CLUTCH .... ELECTRIC
STANDARD DECK .... 72"
WEIGHT .... 1,317 LBS.
MSRP................. $10,195

RETAIL PRICING

YEAR	HIGH	LOW
2006	$4,882	$3,661
2007	$5,777	$4,332

SILVERTIP ZTR

YEARS MFRD 2005-2005
ENGINE .... KOHLER
CYLINDERS.................. 2
ENGINE HP 27
COOLING .... AIR
FUEL .... G
SPEEDS .... VARIABLE
TRANSMISSION .... HYDRO
STEERING................ ZERO
BLADE CLUTCH .... ELECTRIC
STANDARD DECK .... 60"
MSRP.................. $9,300

OPTIONS

72" DECK
KAWASAKI 27E

RETAIL PRICING

YEAR	HIGH	LOW
2005	$4,985	$3,738

SPEEDZTR 30

YEARS MFRD 2005-2013
ENGINE .... B&S
CYLINDERS.................. 1
ENGINE HP 16.5
COOLING .... AIR
FUEL .... G
SPEEDS .... VARIABLE
TRANSMISSION .... HYDRO
STEERING................ ZERO
STANDARD DECK .... 30"
MSRP.................. $2,399

OPTIONS

2 BAG
36" BLADE

SERIAL NUMBERS

YEAR	BEGINNING NO.
2005	101000
2007	64000000

RETAIL PRICING

YEAR	HIGH	LOW
2005	$493	$370
2006	$544	$408
2007	$600	$450
2008	$662	$497
2009	$732	$549
2010	$808	$606
2011	$891	$668
2012	$983	$737
2013	$1,086	$815

SPEEDZTR 36

YEARS MFRD 2004-2009
SERIES........ SPEEDZTR SERIES
ENGINE .... B&S INTEK
CYLINDERS.................. 1
CID 28.4
ENGINE HP 16
COOLING .... AIR
FUEL .... G
SPEEDS .... VARIABLE
TRANSMISSION .... HYDRO
STEERING................ ZERO
STANDARD DECK .... 36"
WEIGHT .... 574 LBS.
MSRP.................. $3,699

OPTIONS

2 BAG & FAN
36" BLADE

SERIAL NUMBERS

YEAR	BEGINNING NO.
2004	73075
2007	64000000

RETAIL PRICING

YEAR	HIGH	LOW
2004	$753	$565
2005	$832	$624
2006	$919	$689
2007	$1,013	$760
2008	$1,120	$840
2009	$1,235	$926

SPEEDZTR 38

YEARS MFRD 2005-2006
ENGINE .... B&S
ENGINE HP 15
COOLING .... AIR
FUEL .... G
SPEEDS .... VARIABLE
TRANSMISSION .... HYDRO
STEERING................ ZERO
BLADE CLUTCH .... ELECTRIC
STANDARD DECK .... 38"
MSRP.................. $3,400

OPTIONS

2 BAG
36" BLADE

SERIAL NUMBERS

YEAR	BEGINNING NO.
2005	101000

RETAIL PRICING

YEAR	HIGH	LOW
2005	$776	$582
2006	$855	$642

SPEEDZTR 42

YEARS MFRD 2004-2013
SERIES........ SPEEDZTR SERIES
ENGINE .... B&S INTEK
CYLINDERS.................. 1
CID 28.4
ENGINE HP 19.5
COOLING .... AIR
FUEL .... G
SPEEDS .... VARIABLE
TRANSMISSION .... HYDRO
STEERING................ ZERO
BLADE CLUTCH .... ELECTRIC
STANDARD DECK .... 42"
WEIGHT .... 471 LBS.
MSRP.................. $2,449

OPTIONS

2 BAG
42" BLADE

SERIAL NUMBERS

YEAR	BEGINNING NO.
2004	73075
2005	101000
2007	64000000

RETAIL PRICING

YEAR	HIGH	LOW
2004	$457	$343
2005	$502	$376
2006	$556	$417
2007	$613	$460
2008	$677	$508
2009	$746	$560
2010	$824	$618
2011	$912	$684
2012	$1,005	$754
2013	$1,108	$831

SPEEDZTR 42 SE

YEARS MFRD 2010-2013
ENGINE .... B&S
CYLINDERS.................. 2
ENGINE HP 21.5
COOLING .... AIR
FUEL .... G
SPEEDS .... VARIABLE
TRANSMISSION .... HYDRO
STEERING................ ZERO
BLADE CLUTCH .... ELECTRIC
STANDARD DECK .... 42"
WEIGHT .... 590 LBS.
MSRP.................. $3,499

OPTIONS

BAGGER

RETAIL PRICING

YEAR	HIGH	LOW
2010	$1,177	$883
2011	$1,300	$975
2012	$1,434	$1,075
2013	$1,584	$1,188

SPEEDZTR 44

YEARS MFRD 2006-2009
ENGINE .... B&S
CYLINDERS.................. 2
ENGINE HP 22
COOLING .... AIR
FUEL .... G
SPEEDS .... VARIABLE
TRANSMISSION .... HYDRO
STEERING................ ZERO
BLADE CLUTCH .... ELECTRIC
STANDARD DECK .... 44"
MSRP.................. $4,349

OPTIONS

2 BAG & FAN
BLADE
HONDA 16HP

SERIAL NUMBERS

YEAR	BEGINNING NO.
2007	64000000

RETAIL PRICING

YEAR	HIGH	LOW
2006	$1,080	$810
2007	$1,193	$895
2008	$1,316	$987
2009	$1,452	$1,089

SPEEDZTR 46

YEARS MFRD 2010-2013
ENGINE .... B&S
ENGINE HP 22
COOLING .... AIR
FUEL .... G
SPEEDS .... VARIABLE
TRANSMISSION .... HYDRO
STEERING................ ZERO
BLADE CLUTCH .... ELECTRIC
STANDARD DECK .... 46"
WEIGHT .... 525 LBS.
MSRP.................. $2,749

DIXON

OPTIONS
2 BAG

RETAIL PRICING

YEAR	HIGH	LOW
2010	$931	$698
2011	$1,021	$766
2012	$1,127	$845
2013	$1,244	$933

SPEEDZTR 48

YEARS MFRD 2011-2012
ENGINE . . . . KOHLER
CYLINDERS. 2
CID 44.24
ENGINE HP 24
COOLING . . . . AIR
FUEL . . . . G
SPEEDS . . . . VARIABLE
TRANSMISSION . . . . HYDRO
STEERING. . . . . ZERO
BLADE CLUTCH . . . . ELECTRIC
STANDARD DECK . . . . 48"
WEIGHT . . . . 620 LBS.
MSRP. $3,599

RETAIL PRICING

YEAR	HIGH	LOW
2011	$1,550	$1,163
2012	$1,711	$1,283

SPEEDZTR 48 SE

YEARS MFRD 2013-2013
ENGINE . . . . KAWASAKI
ENGINE HP 24
COOLING . . . . AIR
FUEL . . . . G
SPEEDS . . . . VARIABLE
TRANSMISSION . . . . HYDRO
STEERING. . . . . ZERO
STANDARD DECK . . . . 48"
MSRP. $3,899

OPTIONS
BAGGER

RETAIL PRICING

YEAR	HIGH	LOW
2013	$1,764	$1,323

SPEEDZTR 54

YEARS MFRD 2010-2013
ENGINE . . . . KAWASAKI
ENGINE HP 24
COOLING . . . . AIR
FUEL . . . . G
SPEEDS . . . . VARIABLE
TRANSMISSION . . . . HYDRO
STEERING. . . . . ZERO
BLADE CLUTCH . . . . ELECTRIC
STANDARD DECK . . . . 54"
WEIGHT . . . . 539 LBS.
MSRP. $3,299

OPTIONS
BAGGER

RETAIL PRICING

YEAR	HIGH	LOW
2010	$1,110	$832
2011	$1,226	$919
2012	$1,360	$1,020
2013	$1,492	$1,119

ULTRA 52

YEARS MFRD 2014-2014
ENGINE . . . . KOHLER
CYLINDERS. 2
CID 44.18
ENGINE HP 25
COOLING . . . . AIR
FUEL . . . . G
SPEEDS . . . . VARIABLE
TRANSMISSION . . . . HYDRO
STEERING. . . . . ZERO
BLADE CLUTCH . . . . ELECTRIC
STANDARD DECK . . . . 52"
WEIGHT . . . . 740 LBS.

ULTRA 52SE

YEARS MFRD 2014-2014
ENGINE . . . . KAWASAKI
CYLINDERS. 2
CID 44.3
ENGINE HP 24
COOLING . . . . AIR
FUEL . . . . G
SPEEDS . . . . VARIABLE
TRANSMISSION . . . . HYDRO
STEERING. . . . . ZERO
BLADE CLUTCH . . . . ELECTRIC
STANDARD DECK . . . . 52"
WEIGHT . . . . 740 LBS.

ULTRA 61

YEARS MFRD 2014-2014
ENGINE . . . . KOHLER
CYLINDERS. 2
CID 45.58
ENGINE HP 26
COOLING . . . . AIR
FUEL . . . . G
SPEEDS . . . . VARIABLE
TRANSMISSION . . . . HYDRO
STEERING. . . . . ZERO
BLADE CLUTCH . . . . ELECTRIC
STANDARD DECK . . . . 61"
WEIGHT . . . . 770 LBS.

ZEETER

YEARS MFRD 2005-2006
ENGINE . . . . B&S
CYLINDERS. 1
ENGINE HP 11.5
COOLING . . . . AIR
FUEL . . . . G
SPEEDS . . . . VARIABLE
TRANSMISSION . . . . HYDRO
STEERING. . . . . ZERO
STANDARD DECK . . . . 30"
MSRP. $2,295

OPTIONS
CATCHER

SERIAL NUMBERS

YEAR	BEGINNING NO.
2003	69713

RETAIL PRICING

YEAR	HIGH	LOW
2005	$514	$385
2006	$567	$425

ZEETER 30

YEARS MFRD 2004-2004
SERIES. . . . . ZEETER SERIES
ENGINE . . . . B&S
ENGINE HP 11.5
COOLING . . . . AIR
FUEL . . . . G
SPEEDS . . . . VARIABLE
TRANSMISSION . . . . GEAR
STEERING. . . . . ZERO
STANDARD DECK . . . . 30"
WEIGHT . . . . 368 LBS.
MSRP. $2,099

OPTIONS
BAGGER

SERIAL NUMBERS

YEAR	BEGINNING NO.
2004	73075

RETAIL PRICING

YEAR	HIGH	LOW
2004	$413	$310

ZEETER 36

YEARS MFRD 2004-2004
SERIES. . . . . ZEETER SERIES
ENGINE . . . . B&S
ENGINE HP 11
COOLING . . . . AIR
FUEL . . . . G
SPEEDS . . . . VARIABLE
STEERING. . . . . ZERO
STANDARD DECK . . . . 36"
WEIGHT . . . . 400 LBS.
MSRP. $2,599

OPTIONS
BAG & FAN

SERIAL NUMBERS

YEAR	BEGINNING NO.
2004	73075

RETAIL PRICING

YEAR	HIGH	LOW
2004	$512	$384

ZEETER 42

YEARS MFRD 2004-2004
SERIES. . . . . ZEETER SERIES
ENGINE . . . . B&S
ENGINE HP 13
COOLING . . . . AIR
FUEL . . . . G
SPEEDS . . . . VARIABLE
STEERING. . . . . ZERO
STANDARD DECK . . . . 42"
WEIGHT . . . . 430 LBS.
MSRP. $2,799

OPTIONS
BAG & FAN

SERIAL NUMBERS

YEAR	BEGINNING NO.
2004	73075

RETAIL PRICING

YEAR	HIGH	LOW
2004	$552	$414

ZEETER HL30

YEARS MFRD 2004-2004
SERIES. . . . . ZEETER SERIES
ENGINE . . . . B&S IC
ENGINE HP 11
COOLING . . . . AIR
FUEL . . . . G
SPEEDS . . . . VARIABLE
TRANSMISSION . . . . HYDRO
STEERING. . . . . ZERO
STANDARD DECK . . . . 30"
WEIGHT . . . . 440 LBS.
MSRP. $2,799

OPTIONS
36" BLADE
BAGGER

SERIAL NUMBERS

YEAR	BEGINNING NO.
2004	73075

RETAIL PRICING

YEAR	HIGH	LOW
2004	$552	$414

ZEETER HL36

YEARS MFRD 2004-2004
SERIES. . . . . ZEETER SERIES
ENGINE . . . . B&S IC
ENGINE HP 13
COOLING . . . . AIR
FUEL . . . . G
SPEEDS . . . . VARIABLE
TRANSMISSION . . . . HYDRO
STEERING. . . . . ZERO
STANDARD DECK . . . . 36"
WEIGHT . . . . 450 LBS.
MSRP. $3,299

OPTIONS
36" BLADE
BAG & FAN

SERIAL NUMBERS

YEAR	BEGINNING NO.
2004	73075

RETAIL PRICING

YEAR	HIGH	LOW
2004	$650	$488

ZEETER HL42

YEARS MFRD 2004-2004
SERIES. . . . . ZEETER SERIES
ENGINE . . . . B&S IC
ENGINE HP 14.5
COOLING . . . . AIR

FUEL . . . . . G
SPEEDS . . . . . VARIABLE
TRANSMISSION . . . . . HYDRO
STEERING . . . . . ZERO
STANDARD DECK . . . . . 42"
WEIGHT . . . . . 465 LBS.
MSRP $3,399

OPTIONS

48" BLADE
BAG & FAN

SERIAL NUMBERS

YEAR	BEGINNING NO.
2004	73075

RETAIL PRICING

YEAR	HIGH	LOW
2004	$669	$502

ZTR304

YEARS MFRD 1989-1993
ENGINE . . . . . B&S
ENGINE HP 10
COOLING . . . . . AIR
FUEL . . . . . G
SPEEDS . . . . . VARIABLE
STEERING . . . . . ZERO
STANDARD DECK . . . . . 30"
WEIGHT . . . . . 390 LBS.
MSRP $2,095

RETAIL PRICING

YEAR	HIGH	LOW
1989	$484	$363
1990	$514	$385
1991	$548	$411
1992	$572	$429
1993	$619	$464

ZTR312

YEARS MFRD 1989-1993
ENGINE . . . . . B&S
ENGINE HP 12
COOLING . . . . . AIR
FUEL . . . . . G
SPEEDS . . . . . VARIABLE
STEERING . . . . . ZERO
STANDARD DECK . . . . . 30"
WEIGHT . . . . . 390 LBS.
MSRP $2,495

RETAIL PRICING

YEAR	HIGH	LOW
1989	$587	$440
1990	$618	$463
1991	$657	$493
1992	$701	$526
1993	$737	$552

ZTR361

YEARS MFRD 1989-1993
ENGINE . . . . . B&S
ENGINE HP 12
COOLING . . . . . AIR
FUEL . . . . . G
SPEEDS . . . . . VARIABLE
STEERING . . . . . ZERO
STANDARD DECK . . . . . 36"
WEIGHT . . . . . 400 LBS.
MSRP $2,745

RETAIL PRICING

YEAR	HIGH	LOW
1990	$693	$520
1991	$740	$555
1992	$771	$578
1993	$811	$608

ZTR428

YEARS MFRD 1987-1993
ENGINE . . . . . B&S
ENGINE HP 12
COOLING . . . . . AIR
FUEL . . . . . G
SPEEDS . . . . . VARIABLE
STEERING . . . . . ZERO
STANDARD DECK . . . . . 42"
WEIGHT . . . . . 450 LBS.
MSRP $3,195

RETAIL PRICING

YEAR	HIGH	LOW
1987	$153	$115
1988	$168	$126
1989	$187	$140
1990	$209	$157
1991	$232	$174
1992	$258	$194
1993	$287	$215

ZTR429

YEARS MFRD 1989-1993
ENGINE . . . . . KAWASAKI
ENGINE HP 14
COOLING . . . . . AIR
FUEL . . . . . G
SPEEDS . . . . . VARIABLE
STEERING . . . . . ZERO
STANDARD DECK . . . . . 42"
WEIGHT . . . . . 565 LBS.
MSRP $3,625

RETAIL PRICING

YEAR	HIGH	LOW
1989	$213	$160
1990	$236	$177
1991	$262	$197
1992	$291	$218
1993	$326	$244

ZTR502

YEARS MFRD 1989-1991
ENGINE . . . . . KOHLER
ENGINE HP 18
COOLING . . . . . AIR
FUEL . . . . . G
SPEEDS . . . . . VARIABLE
TRANSMISSION . . . . . HYDRO
STEERING . . . . . ZERO
STANDARD DECK . . . . . 50"
WEIGHT . . . . . 630 LBS.
MSRP $5,495

OPTIONS

48" BLADE
BAGGER

SERIAL NUMBERS

YEAR	BEGINNING NO.
1989	1780
1990	2365
1991	3101

RETAIL PRICING

YEAR	HIGH	LOW
1989	$272	$204
1990	$301	$226
1991	$332	$249

ZTR503

YEARS MFRD 1990-1991
ENGINE . . . . . ONAN
ENGINE HP 20
COOLING . . . . . AIR
FUEL . . . . . G
STEERING . . . . . ZERO
STANDARD DECK . . . . . 50"
MSRP $6,045

OPTIONS

48" BLADE
BAGGER

SERIAL NUMBERS

YEAR	BEGINNING NO.
1990	2365
1991	3101

RETAIL PRICING

YEAR	HIGH	LOW
1990	$330	$247
1991	$364	$273

ZTR503HG

YEARS MFRD 1992-1993
ENGINE . . . . . KOHLER
ENGINE HP 20
COOLING . . . . . AIR
FUEL . . . . . G
SPEEDS . . . . . VARIABLE
TRANSMISSION . . . . . HYDRO
STEERING . . . . . ZERO
STANDARD DECK . . . . . 50"
WEIGHT . . . . . 645 LBS.
MSRP $6,195

OPTIONS

48" BLADE
BAGGER

RETAIL PRICING

YEAR	HIGH	LOW
1992	$441	$330
1993	$486	$365

ZTR542HG

YEARS MFRD 1992-1993
ENGINE . . . . . KOHLER
ENGINE HP 16
COOLING . . . . . AIR
FUEL . . . . . G
TRANSMISSION . . . . . HYDRO
STEERING . . . . . ZERO
STANDARD DECK . . . . . 42"
MSRP $5,295

OPTIONS

48" BLADE
BAGGER

RETAIL PRICING

YEAR	HIGH	LOW
1992	$376	$282
1993	$415	$311

ZTR560HG

YEARS MFRD 1993-1993
ENGINE . . . . . KOHLER
ENGINE HP 20
COOLING . . . . . AIR
FUEL . . . . . G
TRANSMISSION . . . . . HYDRO
STEERING . . . . . ZERO
STANDARD DECK . . . . . 60"
MSRP $6,995

OPTIONS

48" BLADE
BAGGER

RETAIL PRICING

YEAR	HIGH	LOW
1993	$681	$511

ZTR1950

YEARS MFRD 2004-2004
ENGINE . . . . . KAWASAKI
ENGINE HP 19
COOLING . . . . . AIR
FUEL . . . . . G
SPEEDS . . . . . VARIABLE
TRANSMISSION . . . . . HYDRO
STEERING . . . . . ZERO
STANDARD DECK . . . . . 50"
WEIGHT . . . . . 737 LBS.
MSRP $6,099

OPTIONS

48" BLADE
BAG & FAN
SNOW BLOWER

SERIAL NUMBERS

YEAR	BEGINNING NO.
2004	3116

RETAIL PRICING

YEAR	HIGH	LOW
2004	$1,201	$901

ZTR2300

YEARS MFRD 2004-2004
ENGINE . . . . . KOHLER
ENGINE HP 19
COOLING . . . . . AIR
FUEL . . . . . G
SPEEDS . . . . . VARIABLE
TRANSMISSION . . . . . HYDRO
STEERING . . . . . ZERO
STANDARD DECK . . . . . 50"
WEIGHT . . . . . 737 LBS.
MSRP $6,499

OPTIONS

48" BLADE
60" DECK
BAG & FAN
SNOW BLOWER

DIXON

SERIAL NUMBERS

YEAR .... BEGINNING NO.
2004 3116

RETAIL PRICING

YEAR	HIGH	LOW
2004	$1,281	$961

ZTR2301

YEARS MFRD 1994-1997
ENGINE .... KOHLER
ENGINE HP 14
COOLING .... AIR
FUEL .... G
SPEEDS .... VARIABLE
TRANSMISSION .... HYDRO
STEERING .... ZERO
STANDARD DECK .... 30"
MSRP $3,245

OPTIONS

36" BLADE
BAGGER

SERIAL NUMBERS

YEAR .... BEGINNING NO.
1994 00001
1995 01128
1996 01861

RETAIL PRICING

YEAR	HIGH	LOW
1994	$277	$208
1995	$306	$229
1996	$338	$253
1997	$373	$280

ZTR2560

YEARS MFRD 2004-2004
ENGINE .... KOHLER
ENGINE HP 25
COOLING .... AIR
FUEL .... G
SPEEDS .... VARIABLE
TRANSMISSION .... HYDRO
STEERING .... ZERO
STANDARD DECK .... 60"
WEIGHT .... 1,130 LBS.
MSRP $8,499

OPTIONS

BAGGER
BLADE
SNOW BLOWER

SERIAL NUMBERS

YEAR .... BEGINNING NO.
2004 2943

RETAIL PRICING

YEAR	HIGH	LOW
2004	$1,675	$1,256

ZTR3014

YEARS MFRD 1998-2002
ENGINE .... B&S
ENGINE HP 13.5
COOLING .... AIR
FUEL .... G
SPEEDS .... VARIABLE
TRANSMISSION .... HYDRO
STEERING .... ZERO
STANDARD DECK .... 36"
WEIGHT .... 510 LBS.
MSRP $3,095

OPTIONS

36" BLADE
42" DECK
BAG & FAN
BAGGER

SERIAL NUMBERS

YEAR .... BEGINNING NO.
1998 14116
1999 17500
2000 20011
2001 22510
2002 24455

RETAIL PRICING

YEAR	HIGH	LOW
1998	$354	$266
1999	$391	$293
2000	$432	$324
2001	$476	$357
2002	$526	$394

ZTR3301

YEARS MFRD 1994-1994
ENGINE .... B&S
ENGINE HP 10
COOLING .... AIR
FUEL .... G
SPEEDS .... VARIABLE
TRANSMISSION .... GEAR
STEERING .... ZERO
STANDARD DECK .... 30"
WEIGHT .... 380 LBS.
MSRP $2,195

RETAIL PRICING

YEAR	HIGH	LOW
1994	$247	$185

ZTR3302

YEARS MFRD 1994-1994
ENGINE .... B&S
ENGINE HP 12
COOLING .... AIR
FUEL .... G
SPEEDS .... VARIABLE
STEERING .... ZERO
STANDARD DECK .... 30"
WEIGHT .... 390 LBS.
MSRP $2,545

RETAIL PRICING

YEAR	HIGH	LOW
1994	$283	$212

ZTR3303

YEARS MFRD 1995-2003
ENGINE .... B&S
ENGINE HP 10.5
COOLING .... AIR
FUEL .... G
SPEEDS .... VARAIBLE
TRANSMISSION .... HYDRO
STEERING .... ZERO
STANDARD DECK .... 30"
WEIGHT .... 430 LBS.
MSRP $2,495

OPTIONS

36" BLADE
BAGGER
BROOM

SERIAL NUMBERS

YEAR .... BEGINNING NO.
1998 54246
1999 57482
2000 60676
2001 64507
2002 67182
2003 69457

RETAIL PRICING

YEAR	HIGH	LOW
1995	$212	$159
1996	$236	$177
1997	$259	$195
1998	$286	$215
1999	$316	$237
2000	$348	$261
2001	$385	$289
2002	$426	$319
2003	$468	$351

ZTR3304

YEARS MFRD 1995-2003
ENGINE .... B&S
ENGINE HP 14.5
COOLING .... AIR
FUEL .... G
SPEEDS .... VARIABLE
TRANSMISSION .... DISC
STEERING .... ZERO
STANDARD DECK .... 30"
WEIGHT .... 440 LBS.
MSRP $2,795

OPTIONS

36" BLADE
BAGGER
BROOM

SERIAL NUMBERS

YEAR .... BEGINNING NO.
1998 54241
1999 57482
2000 60675
2001 64499
2002 67419
2003 69455

RETAIL PRICING

YEAR	HIGH	LOW
1995	$228	$171
1996	$249	$187
1997	$276	$207
1998	$304	$228
1999	$337	$252
2000	$371	$278
2001	$411	$308
2002	$452	$339
2003	$500	$375

ZTR3361

YEARS MFRD 1994-1994
ENGINE .... B&S
ENGINE HP 13
COOLING .... AIR
FUEL .... G
SPEEDS .... VARIABLE
STEERING .... ZERO
STANDARD DECK .... 36"
WEIGHT .... 400 LBS.
MSRP $2,795

RETAIL PRICING

YEAR	HIGH	LOW
1994	$303	$227

ZTR3362

YEARS MFRD 1995-1997
ENGINE .... B&S
ENGINE HP 13
COOLING .... AIR
FUEL .... G
SPEEDS .... VARIABLE
STEERING .... ZERO
STANDARD DECK .... 36"
WEIGHT .... 500 LBS.
MSRP $2,945

OPTIONS

36" BLADE
BAGGER

RETAIL PRICING

YEAR	HIGH	LOW
1995	$301	$226
1996	$332	$249
1997	$366	$275

ZTR3363

YEARS MFRD 2003-2003
ENGINE .... B&S
ENGINE HP 14.5
COOLING .... AIR
FUEL .... G
SPEEDS .... VARIABLE
TRANSMISSION .... HYDRO
STEERING .... ZERO
STANDARD DECK .... 42"
WEIGHT .... 510 LBS.
MSRP $3,095

OPTIONS

BAG & FAN
BAGGER
BROOM

SERIAL NUMBERS

YEAR .... BEGINNING NO.
2003 25807

RETAIL PRICING

YEAR	HIGH	LOW
2003	$582	$437

ZTR3530

YEARS MFRD 2003-2003
SERIES .... ESTATE SERIES
ENGINE .... B&S
ENGINE HP 13.5

COOLING . . . AIR
FUEL . . . G
SPEEDS . . . VARIABLE
TRANSMISSION . . . HYDRO
STEERING . . . ZERO
STANDARD DECK . . . 30"
WEIGHT . . . 465 LBS.
MSRP . . . $3,495

OPTIONS

2 BAG

RETAIL PRICING

YEAR	HIGH	LOW
2003	$656	$492

ZTR3536

YEARS MFRD . . . 2003-2003
SERIES . . . ESTATE SERIES
ENGINE . . . B&S
ENGINE HP . . . 14.5
COOLING . . . AIR
FUEL . . . G
SPEEDS . . . VARIABLE
TRANSMISSION . . . HYDRO
STEERING . . . ZERO
STANDARD DECK . . . 36"
WEIGHT . . . 470 LBS.
MSRP . . . $3,795

OPTIONS

BAG & FAN
BAGGER

RETAIL PRICING

YEAR	HIGH	LOW
2003	$714	$535

ZTR4421

YEARS MFRD . . . 1994-1997
ENGINE . . . B&S
ENGINE HP . . . 13
COOLING . . . AIR
FUEL . . . G
SPEEDS . . . VARIABLE
STEERING . . . ZERO
STANDARD DECK . . . 42"
WEIGHT . . . 480 LBS.
MSRP . . . $3,395

OPTIONS

48" BLADE
BAGGER

RETAIL PRICING

YEAR	HIGH	LOW
1994	$290	$218
1995	$320	$240
1996	$354	$266
1997	$391	$293

ZTR4422

YEARS MFRD . . . 1994-1996
ENGINE . . . KOHLER
ENGINE HP . . . 14
COOLING . . . AIR
FUEL . . . G
SPEEDS . . . VARIABLE
STEERING . . . ZERO
STANDARD DECK . . . 42"
WEIGHT . . . 480 LBS.
MSRP . . . $3,795

OPTIONS

48" BLADE
BAGGER

RETAIL PRICING

YEAR	HIGH	LOW
1994	$272	$204
1995	$302	$226
1996	$333	$249

ZTR4423

YEARS MFRD . . . 1997-2003
SERIES . . . 4000 SERIES
ENGINE . . . B&S
ENGINE HP . . . 15.5
FUEL . . . G
SPEEDS . . . VARIABLE
STEERING . . . ZERO
STANDARD DECK . . . 42"
WEIGHT . . . 547 LBS.
MSRP . . . $3,595

OPTIONS

48" BLADE
BAG & FAN
BROOM

SERIAL NUMBERS

YEAR	BEGINNING NO.
1998	88340
1999	91152
2000	92849
2001	95343
2002	97144
2003	98825

RETAIL PRICING

YEAR	HIGH	LOW
1997	$374	$281
1998	$412	$309
1999	$455	$342
2000	$503	$377
2001	$555	$417
2002	$612	$459
2003	$676	$507

ZTR4424

YEARS MFRD . . . 1997-1998
ENGINE . . . KOHLER
ENGINE HP . . . 15
FUEL . . . G
TRANSMISSION . . . HYDRO
STEERING . . . STANDARD
STANDARD DECK . . . 42"
WEIGHT . . . 670 LBS.
MSRP . . . $3,995

OPTIONS

48" BLADE
BAGGER

SERIAL NUMBERS

YEAR	BEGINNING NO.
1998	88275

RETAIL PRICING

YEAR	HIGH	LOW
1997	$416	$312
1998	$459	$345

ZTR4425

YEARS MFRD . . . 1999-1999
SERIES . . . 4000 SERIES
ENGINE . . . B&S
ENGINE HP . . . 15
FUEL . . . G
SPEEDS . . . VARIABLE
STEERING . . . ZERO
STANDARD DECK . . . 42"
WEIGHT . . . 520 LBS.
MSRP . . . $3,995

OPTIONS

48" BLADE
BAG & FAN

SERIAL NUMBERS

YEAR	BEGINNING NO.
1999	00001

RETAIL PRICING

YEAR	HIGH	LOW
1999	$496	$372

ZTR4426

YEARS MFRD . . . 1999-1999
SERIES . . . 4000 SERIES
ENGINE . . . KOHLER
ENGINE HP . . . 16
FUEL . . . G
SPEEDS . . . VARIABLE
STEERING . . . ZERO
STANDARD DECK . . . 42"
WEIGHT . . . 520 LBS.
MSRP . . . $3,995

OPTIONS

48" BLADE
BAG & FAN

SERIAL NUMBERS

YEAR	BEGINNING NO.
1999	91174

RETAIL PRICING

YEAR	HIGH	LOW
1999	$496	$372

ZTR4515B

YEARS MFRD . . . 1998-2004
SERIES . . . 4500 SERIES
ENGINE . . . B&S VANGUARD
CYLINDERS . . . 1
CID . . . 28.4
ENGINE HP . . . 15.5
COOLING . . . AIR
FUEL . . . G
SPEEDS . . . VARIABLE
TRANSMISSION . . . HYDRO
STEERING . . . ZERO
STANDARD DECK . . . 42"
WEIGHT . . . 615 LBS.
MSRP . . . $4,199

OPTIONS

48" BLADE
50" DECK
BAG & FAN
BROOM

SERIAL NUMBERS

YEAR	BEGINNING NO.
1998	100
1999	3915
2000	9462
2001	16007
2002	21630
2003	27200
2004	31000

RETAIL PRICING

YEAR	HIGH	LOW
1998	$479	$359
1999	$529	$396
2000	$583	$437
2001	$644	$483
2002	$711	$533
2003	$784	$588
2004	$866	$650

ZTR4516K

YEARS MFRD . . . 1999-2004
SERIES . . . 4500 SERIES
ENGINE . . KOHLER COMMAND PRO
CYLINDERS . . . 1
CID . . . 28.1
ENGINE HP . . . 16
COOLING . . . AIR
FUEL . . . G
SPEEDS . . . VARIABLE
TRANSMISSION . . . HYDRO
STEERING . . . ZERO
STANDARD DECK . . . 42"
WEIGHT . . . 615 LBS.
MSRP . . . $4,545

OPTIONS

48" BLADE
50" DECK
BAG & FAN
BAGGER

SERIAL NUMBERS

YEAR	BEGINNING NO.
1999	4058
2000	9462
2001	16020
2002	21824
2003	27191
2004	31000

RETAIL PRICING

YEAR	HIGH	LOW
1999	$572	$429
2000	$631	$473
2001	$698	$523
2002	$771	$578
2003	$848	$636
2004	$938	$703

ZTR4518

YEARS MFRD . . . 2002-2004
SERIES . . . ZTR SERIES
ENGINE . . KOHLER COMMAND PRO
CYLINDERS . . . 2
CID . . . 38
ENGINE HP . . . 18
COOLING . . . AIR
FUEL . . . G
SPEEDS . . . VARIABLE

DIXON

TRANSMISSION .... HYDRO
STEERING .... ZERO
STANDARD DECK .... 42"
WEIGHT .... 618 LBS.
MSRP $4,899

OPTIONS

48" BLADE
50" DECK
BAG & FAN
BAGGER

SERIAL NUMBERS

YEAR .... BEGINNING NO.
2002 23419
2003 27182
2004 31000

RETAIL PRICING

YEAR	HIGH	LOW
2002	$830	$622
2003	$915	$686
2004	$1,010	$757

ZTR5004

YEARS MFRD 2003-2003
ENGINE .... KAWASAKI
ENGINE HP 19
COOLING .... AIR
FUEL .... G
SPEEDS .... VARIABLE
TRANSMISSION .... HYDRO
STEERING .... ZERO
STANDARD DECK .... 42"
WEIGHT .... 820 LBS.
MSRP $6,295

OPTIONS

48" BLADE
BAG & FAN
BAGGER
SNOW BLOWER

SERIAL NUMBERS

YEAR .... BEGINNING NO.
2003 6967

RETAIL PRICING

YEAR	HIGH	LOW
2003	$1,268	$951

ZTR5017

YEARS MFRD 1999-2001
SERIES .... 5000 SERIES
ENGINE .... B&S
ENGINE HP 17
FUEL .... G
SPEEDS .... VARIABLE
TRANSMISSION .... HYDRO
STEERING .... ZERO
STANDARD DECK .... 42"
WEIGHT .... 796 LBS.
MSRP $5,945

OPTIONS

48" BLADE
50" DECK
BAG & FAN

SERIAL NUMBERS

YEAR .... BEGINNING NO.
1999 5327
2001 5836

RETAIL PRICING

YEAR	HIGH	LOW
1999	$694	$520
2000	$766	$575
2001	$846	$635

ZTR5020

YEARS MFRD 1998-2002
SERIES .... 5000 SERIES
ENGINE .... B&S
ENGINE HP 20
FUEL .... G
SPEEDS .... VARIABLE
TRANSMISSION .... HYDRO
STEERING .... ZERO
STANDARD DECK .... 50"
WEIGHT .... 853 LBS.
MSRP $6,610

OPTIONS

60" DECK
BAG & FAN
BAGGER
SNOW BLOWER

SERIAL NUMBERS

YEAR .... BEGINNING NO.
1998 1000
1999 2478
2000 4024
2001 5391
2002 6127

RETAIL PRICING

YEAR	HIGH	LOW
1998	$796	$597
1999	$879	$659
2000	$970	$728
2001	$1,071	$803
2002	$1,182	$887

ZTR5022

YEARS MFRD 1998-1999
SERIES .... 5000 SERIES
ENGINE .... KOHLER
ENGINE HP 22
FUEL .... G
TRANSMISSION .... HYDRO
STEERING .... ZERO
STANDARD DECK .... 42"
MSRP $7,095

OPTIONS

50" DECK
60" DECK
BAGGER

SERIAL NUMBERS

YEAR .... BEGINNING NO.
1998 1000
1999 2478

RETAIL PRICING

YEAR	HIGH	LOW
1998	$797	$598
1999	$880	$660

ZTR5023

YEARS MFRD 2000-2003
SERIES .... ESTATE SERIES
ENGINE .... KOHLER
ENGINE HP 23
COOLING .... AIR
FUEL .... G
SPEEDS .... VARIABLE
TRANSMISSION .... HYDRO
STEERING .... ZERO
STANDARD DECK .... 50"
WEIGHT .... 865 LBS.
MSRP $7,095

OPTIONS

48" BLADE
60" DECK
BAG & FAN
SNOW BLOWER

SERIAL NUMBERS

YEAR .... BEGINNING NO.
2000 4024
2001 5383
2002 6146
2003 6960

RETAIL PRICING

YEAR	HIGH	LOW
2000	$1,064	$798
2001	$1,174	$881
2002	$1,297	$973
2003	$1,431	$1,073

ZTR5421

YEARS MFRD 1994-1995
ENGINE .... KOHLER
ENGINE HP 16
COOLING .... AIR
FUEL .... G
TRANSMISSION .... HYDRO
STEERING .... ZERO
STANDARD DECK .... 42"
MSRP $5,495

OPTIONS

48" BLADE
BAGGER

SERIAL NUMBERS

YEAR .... BEGINNING NO.
1994 01465
1995 02210

RETAIL PRICING

YEAR	HIGH	LOW
1994	$482	$362
1995	$531	$398

ZTR5422

YEARS MFRD 1996-1996
ENGINE .... KOHLER
ENGINE HP 16
COOLING .... AIR
FUEL .... G
TRANSMISSION .... HYDRO
STEERING .... ZERO
STANDARD DECK .... 42"
MSRP $5,695

OPTIONS

48" BLADE
BAGGER

SERIAL NUMBERS

YEAR .... BEGINNING NO.
1996 3035

RETAIL PRICING

YEAR	HIGH	LOW
1996	$603	$452

ZTR5423

YEARS MFRD 1997-1997
ENGINE .... KOHLER
ENGINE HP 18
FUEL .... G
TRANSMISSION .... HYDRO
STEERING .... ZERO
STANDARD DECK .... 42"
MSRP $5,895

OPTIONS

48" BLADE
BAGGER

SERIAL NUMBERS

YEAR .... BEGINNING NO.
1997 3998

RETAIL PRICING

YEAR	HIGH	LOW
1997	$678	$509

ZTR5424

YEARS MFRD 1998-1998
SERIES .... ESTATE SERIES
ENGINE .... B&S
ENGINE HP 17
FUEL .... G
TRANSMISSION .... HYDRO
STEERING .... ZERO
STANDARD DECK .... 42"
MSRP $5,295

OPTIONS

48" BLADE
BAGGER

SERIAL NUMBERS

YEAR .... BEGINNING NO.
1998 4635

RETAIL PRICING

YEAR	HIGH	LOW
1998	$656	$492

ZTR5425

YEARS MFRD 2000-2000
SERIES .... ESTATE SERIES
ENGINE .... B&S
ENGINE HP 17
COOLING .... AIR
FUEL .... G
SPEEDS .... VARIABLE
TRANSMISSION .... HYDRO
STEERING .... ZERO
STANDARD DECK .... 42"
WEIGHT .... 780 LBS.
MSRP $5,745

OPTIONS

48" BLADE
BAG & FAN
SNOW BLOWER

SERIAL NUMBERS

YEAR .... BEGINNING NO.
2000 5618

RETAIL PRICING

YEAR	HIGH	LOW
2000	$791	$593

ZTR5501

YEARS MFRD 1994-1995
ENGINE .... KOHLER
ENGINE HP 20
COOLING .... AIR
FUEL .... G
TRANSMISSION .... HYDRO
STEERING.............. ZERO
STANDARD DECK .... 50"
MSRP.................. $6,295

OPTIONS

48" BLADE
BAGGER

RETAIL PRICING

YEAR	HIGH	LOW
1994	$552	$414
1995	$609	$457

ZTR5502

YEARS MFRD 1996-1997
ENGINE .... KOHLER
ENGINE HP 20
COOLING .... AIR
FUEL .... G
TRANSMISSION .... HYDRO
STEERING.......... STANDARD
STANDARD DECK .... 50"
MSRP.................. $6,695

OPTIONS

48" BLADE
BAGGER

RETAIL PRICING

YEAR	HIGH	LOW
1996	$697	$523
1997	$770	$578

ZTR5601

YEARS MFRD 1993-1997
ENGINE .... KOHLER
ENGINE HP 22
COOLING .... AIR
FUEL .... G
TRANSMISSION .... HYDRO
STEERING.............. ZERO
STANDARD DECK .... 60"
MSRP.................. $7,295

OPTIONS

48" BLADE
BAGGER

SERIAL NUMBERS

YEAR	BEGINNING NO.
1993	00001
1994	00302
1995	00679
1996	01306
1997	01779

RETAIL PRICING

YEAR	HIGH	LOW
1993	$585	$439
1994	$625	$469
1995	$688	$516
1996	$759	$569
1997	$839	$629

ZTR6022

YEARS MFRD 1998-1998
SERIES .... 6000 SERIES
ENGINE .... KOHLER
ENGINE HP 22
FUEL .... G
TRANSMISSION .... HYDRO
STEERING.............. ZERO
STANDARD DECK .... 48"
MSRP.................. $8,645

OPTIONS

48" BLADE
60" DECK
BAGGER

SERIAL NUMBERS

YEAR	BEGINNING NO.
1998	1801

RETAIL PRICING

YEAR	HIGH	LOW
1998	$994	$745

ZTR6023

YEARS MFRD 2002-2002
SERIES .... ZTR SERIES
ENGINE .... KOHLER
ENGINE HP 23
FUEL .... G
TRANSMISSION .... HYDRO
STEERING.............. ZERO
STANDARD DECK .... 60"
MSRP.................. $9,190

OPTIONS

BAGGER

SERIAL NUMBERS

YEAR	BEGINNING NO.
2002	2827

RETAIL PRICING

YEAR	HIGH	LOW
2002	$1,643	$1,233

ZTR6025

YEARS MFRD 1999-2001
SERIES .... 6000 SERIES
ENGINE .... KOHLER
ENGINE HP 25
FUEL .... G
TRANSMISSION .... HYDRO
STEERING.............. ZERO
STANDARD DECK .... 60"
MSRP.................. $9,605

OPTIONS

48" DECK
BLOWER

SERIAL NUMBERS

YEAR	BEGINNING NO.
1999	2409
2000	2634
2001	2781

RETAIL PRICING

YEAR	HIGH	LOW
1999	$1,123	$842
2000	$1,238	$929
2001	$1,366	$1,025

ZTR6601

YEARS MFRD 1995-1997
ENGINE .... KOHLER
ENGINE HP 22
COOLING .... AIR
FUEL .... G
TRANSMISSION .... HYDRO
STEERING.............. ZERO
STANDARD DECK .... 60"
MSRP.................. $7,795

OPTIONS

48" BLADE
BAGGER

SERIAL NUMBERS

YEAR	BEGINNING NO.
1995	1000
1996	1406
1997	1577

RETAIL PRICING

YEAR	HIGH	LOW
1995	$736	$552
1996	$813	$610
1997	$896	$672

ZTR7025

YEARS MFRD 2000-2001
ENGINE .... KOHLER
ENGINE HP 25
FUEL .... G
TRANSMISSION .... HYDRO
STEERING.............. ZERO
STANDARD DECK .... 52"
MSRP.................. $8,405

OPTIONS

BAGGER

SERIAL NUMBERS

YEAR	BEGINNING NO.
2000	2455
2001	5000

RETAIL PRICING

YEAR	HIGH	LOW
2000	$1,084	$813
2001	$1,196	$897

ZTR7523

YEARS MFRD 2002-2002
SERIES .... ZTR SERIES
ENGINE .... KOHLER
ENGINE HP 23
FUEL .... G
TRANSMISSION .... HYDRO
STEERING.............. ZERO
STANDARD DECK .... 52"
MSRP.................. $8,200

OPTIONS

60" DECK
BAGGER
BLADE
SNOW BLOWER

SERIAL NUMBERS

YEAR	BEGINNING NO.
2002	2000

RETAIL PRICING

YEAR	HIGH	LOW
2002	$1,466	$1,100

ZTR7525

YEARS MFRD 2003-2003
ENGINE .... KOHLER
ENGINE HP 25
COOLING .... AIR
FUEL .... G
SPEEDS .... VARIABLE
TRANSMISSION .... HYDRO
STEERING.............. ZERO
STANDARD DECK .... 60"
WEIGHT .... 1,225 LBS.
MSRP.................. $8,600

OPTIONS

48" BLADE
BAGGER
SNOW BLOWER

SERIAL NUMBERS

YEAR	BEGINNING NO.
2003	2489

RETAIL PRICING

YEAR	HIGH	LOW
2003	$1,734	$1,301

ZTR8025

YEARS MFRD 2001-2003
SERIES .... 8000 SERIES
ENGINE .... KOHLER
ENGINE HP 25
FUEL .... G
TRANSMISSION .... HYDRO
STEERING.............. ZERO
STANDARD DECK .... 60"
MSRP.................. $9,560

OPTIONS

48" BLADE
72" DECK
CANOPY
ROPS

SERIAL NUMBERS

YEAR	BEGINNING NO.
2001	2000
2002	2422
2003	2661

RETAIL PRICING

YEAR	HIGH	LOW
2001	$1,582	$1,187
2002	$1,745	$1,309
2003	$1,928	$1,446

DIXON

ZTR8026D

YEARS MFRD 2001-2003
SERIES. . . . . 8000 SERIES
ENGINE . . . . DAIHATSU
ENGINE HP 26.5
FUEL . . . . D
TRANSMISSION . . . . .HYDRO
STEERING. . . . . ZERO
STANDARD DECK . . . . 60"
MSRP. $13,315

OPTIONS

48" BLADE
CANOPY
ROPS

SERIAL NUMBERS

YEAR	BEGINNING NO.
2001	2000
2002	2422
2003	2643

RETAIL PRICING

YEAR	HIGH	LOW
2001	$2,203	$1,652
2002	$2,432	$1,824
2003	$2,685	$2,014

ZTR CLASSIC

YEARS MFRD 2002-2003
ENGINE . . . . B&S
ENGINE HP 15.5
COOLING . . . . AIR
FUEL . . . . G
SPEEDS . . . . VARIABLE
TRANSMISSION . . . . .HYDRO
STEERING. . . . . ZERO
STANDARD DECK . . . . 42"
WEIGHT . . . . 400 LBS.
MSRP. $3,495

SERIAL NUMBERS

YEAR	BEGINNING NO.
2002	97077

RETAIL PRICING

YEAR	HIGH	LOW
2003	$1,659	$1,244

ENCORE

B850PFC POWER TRAIN

YEARS MFRD 2000-2000
ENGINE .... B&S
ENGINE HP 26
FUEL .... D
TRANSMISSION .... HYDRO
STEERING............ STANDARD
MSRP................ $11,173

RETAIL PRICING

YEAR	HIGH	LOW
2000	$2,746	$2,059

B850PFC-WT POWER TRAIN

YEARS MFRD 2000-2003
ENGINE .... B&S
ENGINE HP 26
FUEL .... D
TRANSMISSION .... HYDRO
STEERING............ STANDARD
STANDARD DECK .... 61"
MSRP................ $13,185

OPTIONS

B&S 31E

RETAIL PRICING

YEAR	HIGH	LOW
2000	$4,156	$3,117
2001	$4,343	$3,257
2002	$4,483	$3,362
2003	$5,236	$3,927

B950PFC POWER TRAIN

YEARS MFRD 2000-2003
ENGINE .... B&S
ENGINE HP 31
FUEL .... G
TRANSMISSION .... HYDRO
STEERING............ STANDARD
STANDARD DECK .... 61"
MSRP................ $9,060

RETAIL PRICING

YEAR	HIGH	LOW
2000	$4,503	$3,378
2001	$4,695	$3,522
2002	$4,828	$3,621
2003	$4,860	$3,645

C650PFC POWER TRAIN

YEARS MFRD 2000-2001
ENGINE .... KOHLER
ENGINE HP 22
FUEL .... G
TRANSMISSION .... HYDRO
STEERING............ STANDARD
MSRP................ $6,665

RETAIL PRICING

YEAR	HIGH	LOW
2000	$2,881	$2,161
2001	$3,004	$2,253

C700PFC POWER TRAIN

YEARS MFRD 2002-2002
ENGINE .... KOHLER
ENGINE HP 23
FUEL .... G
TRANSMISSION .... HYDRO
STEERING............ STANDARD
MSRP................ $6,532

RETAIL PRICING

YEAR	HIGH	LOW
2002	$3,027	$2,270

EA46XS22KW

YEARS MFRD 2018-2020
SERIES.......... ARROW SERIES
ENGINE .... KAWASAKI
ENGINE HP 21.5
FUEL .... G
SPEEDS .... VARIABLE
TRANSMISSION .... HYDRO
STEERING................ ZERO
STANDARD DECK .... 46"
WEIGHT .... 544 LBS.

EA50XL24KW

YEARS MFRD 2018-2020
SERIES.......... ARROW SERIES
ENGINE .... KAWASAKI
ENGINE HP 23
FUEL .... G
SPEEDS .... VARIABLE
TRANSMISSION .... HYDRO
STEERING................ ZERO
STANDARD DECK .... 50"
WEIGHT .... 590 LBS.

EA60XL24KW

YEARS MFRD 2018-2020
SERIES.......... ARROW SERIES
ENGINE .... KAWASAKI
ENGINE HP 23
FUEL .... G
SPEEDS .... VARIABLE
TRANSMISSION .... HYDRO
STEERING................ ZERO
STANDARD DECK .... 60"
WEIGHT .... 637 LBS.

EC52FX730V3

YEARS MFRD 2016-2019
SERIES.......... CALIBER SERIES
ENGINE .... KAWASAKI FX730
CID 726CC
ENGINE HP 23.5
FUEL .... G
SPEEDS .... VARIABLE
TRANSMISSION .... HYDRO
STEERING................ ZERO
BLADE CLUTCH .... ELECTRIC
STANDARD DECK .... 52"
WEIGHT .... 1,035 LBS.

EC52FX730V5

YEARS MFRD 2016-2019
SERIES.......... CALIBER SERIES
ENGINE .... KAWASAKI FX801
CID 852CC
ENGINE HP 25.5
COOLING .... AIR
FUEL .... G
SPEEDS .... VARIABLE
TRANSMISSION .... HYDRO
STEERING................ ZERO
BLADE CLUTCH .... ELECTRIC
STANDARD DECK .... 60"
WEIGHT .... 1,050 LBS.

EC52FX801V4

YEARS MFRD 2019-2020
SERIES.......... CALIBER SERIES
ENGINE .... KAWASAKI
ENGINE HP 25.5
FUEL .... G
SPEEDS .... VARIABLE
TRANSMISSION .... HYDRO
STEERING................ ZERO
STANDARD DECK .... 52"
WEIGHT .... 1,050 LBS.

EC60FX730V3

YEARS MFRD 2016-2019
SERIES.......... CALIBER SERIES
ENGINE .... KAWASAKI FX730
CID 726CC
ENGINE HP 23.5
COOLING .... AIR
FUEL .... G
SPEEDS .... VARIABLE
TRANSMISSION .... HYDRO
STEERING................ ZERO
BLADE CLUTCH .... ELECTRIC
STANDARD DECK .... 52"
WEIGHT .... 1,060 LBS.

EC60FX801V5

YEARS MFRD 2016-2019
SERIES.......... CALIBER SERIES
ENGINE .... KAWASAKI FX801
CID 852CC
ENGINE HP 25.5
COOLING .... AIR
FUEL .... G
SPEEDS .... VARIABLE
TRANSMISSION .... HYDRO
STEERING................ ZERO
BLADE CLUTCH .... ELECTRIC
STANDARD DECK .... 60"
WEIGHT .... 1,110 LBS.

EC60FX-850V5X

YEARS MFRD 2019-2020
SERIES.......... CALIBER SERIES
ENGINE .... KAWASAKI
ENGINE HP 27
FUEL .... G
SPEEDS .... VARIABLE
TRANSMISSION .... HYDRO
STEERING................ ZERO
STANDARD DECK .... 60"
WEIGHT .... 1,110 LBS.

ED34FS600V

YEARS MFRD 2016-2020
SERIES.......... DART SERIES
ENGINE .... KAWASAKI FS600V
CID 603CC
ENGINE HP 18.5
COOLING .... AIR
FUEL .... G
SPEEDS .... VARIABLE
TRANSMISSION .... HYDRO
STEERING................ ZERO
BLADE CLUTCH .... ELECTRIC
STANDARD DECK .... 45"
WEIGHT .... 560 LBS.

EE48FR-691V32

YEARS MFRD 2017-2020
SERIES.......... EDGE SERIES
ENGINE .... KAWASAKI FR691V
ENGINE HP 23
COOLING .... AIR
FUEL .... G
SPEEDS .... VARIABLE
TRANSMISSION .... HYDRO
STEERING................ ZERO
BLADE CLUTCH .... ELECTRIC
STANDARD DECK .... 48"
WEIGHT .... 950 LBS.

OPTIONS

SINGLE STICK

EE52FR-691V32

YEARS MFRD 2017-2020
SERIES.......... EDGE SERIES
ENGINE .... KAWASAKI FR691V
ENGINE HP 23
COOLING .... AIR
FUEL .... G
SPEEDS .... VARIABLE
TRANSMISSION .... HYDRO
STEERING................ ZERO
BLADE CLUTCH .... ELECTRIC
STANDARD DECK .... 52"
WEIGHT .... 950 LBS.

OPTIONS

SINGLE STICK

ENCORE

EE52FX-691V34

YEARS MFRD 2019-2020
SERIES. . . . . EDGE SERIES
ENGINE . . . . KAWASAKI FX691
ENGINE HP. 23
FUEL . . . . G
SPEEDS . . . . VARIABLE
TRANSMISSION . . . . HYDRO
STEERING. . . . . ZERO
ROPS/CAB . . . . ROPS
STANDARD DECK . . . . 52"
WEIGHT . . . . 950 LBS.

EE60FR-730V32

YEARS MFRD 2019-2020
SERIES. . . . . EDGE SERIES
ENGINE . . . . KAWASAKI FR730
ENGINE HP. 24
FUEL . . . . G
SPEEDS . . . . VARIABLE
TRANSMISSION . . . . HYDRO
STEERING. . . . . ZERO
ROPS/CAB . . . . ROPS
STANDARD DECK . . . . 60"
WEIGHT . . . . 1,020 LBS.

EE60FX-730V34

YEARS MFRD 2019-2020
SERIES. . . . . EDGE SERIES
ENGINE . . . . KAWASAKI FX730
ENGINE HP. 24
FUEL . . . . G
SPEEDS . . . . VARIABLE
TRANSMISSION . . . . HYDRO
STEERING. . . . . ZERO
ROPS/CAB . . . . ROPS
STANDARD DECK . . . . 60"
WEIGHT . . . . 1,020 LBS.

EP60FX921V5

YEARS MFRD 2019-2020
SERIES. . . . . PROWLER SERIES
ENGINE . . . . KAWASAKI
ENGINE HP. 31
SPEEDS . . . . VARIABLE
TRANSMISSION . . . . HYDRO
STEERING. . . . . ZERO
ROPS/CAB . . . . ROPS
STANDARD DECK . . . . 60"
WEIGHT . . . . 1,410 LBS.

EP60MX-800EV5

YEARS MFRD 2020-2020
SERIES. . . . . PROWLER SERIES
ENGINE . . . . YAMAHA
ENGINE HP. 32
FUEL . . . . G
TRANSMISSION . . . . HYDRO
STEERING. . . . . ZERO
ROPS/CAB . . . . ROPS
STANDARD DECK . . . . 60"
WEIGHT . . . . 1,410 LBS.

EP72BSV-37EV5RD

YEARS MFRD 2020-2020
SERIES. . . . . PROWLER SERIES
ENGINE . . . . B&S
ENGINE HP. 37
FUEL . . . . G
SPEEDS . . . . VARIABLE
TRANSMISSION . . . . HYDRO
STEERING. . . . . ZERO
ROPS/CAB . . . . ROPS
STANDARD DECK . . . . 72"
WEIGHT . . . . 1,570 LBS.

EP72FX-1000V5

YEARS MFRD 2019-2020
SERIES. . . . . PROWLER SERIES
ENGINE . . . . KAWASAKI
ENGINE HP. 35
FUEL . . . . G
SPEEDS . . . . VARIABLE
TRANSMISSION . . . . HYDRO
STEERING. . . . . ZERO
ROPS/CAB . . . . ROPS
STANDARD DECK . . . . 72"
WEIGHT . . . . 1,550 LBS.

EP72MX-825EV5

YEARS MFRD 2020-2020
SERIES. . . . . PROWLER SERIES
ENGINE . . . . YAMAHA
ENGINE HP. 34
FUEL . . . . G
SPEEDS . . . . VARIABLE
TRANSMISSION . . . . HYDRO
STEERING. . . . . ZERO
ROPS/CAB . . . . ROPS
STANDARD DECK . . . . 72"
WEIGHT . . . . 1,550 LBS.

ER32FS600VL

YEARS MFRD 2017-2020
SERIES. . . . . RAGE SERIES
ENGINE . . . . KAWASAKI FS600
ENGINE HP. 18
FUEL . . . . G
SPEEDS . . . . VARIABLE
TRANSMISSION . . . . . DUAL HYDRO
STEERING. . . . . ZERO
STANDARD DECK . . . . 32"
WEIGHT . . . . 690 LBS.

ER36FS600VL

YEARS MFRD 2017-2020
SERIES. . . . . RAGE SERIES
ENGINE . . . . KAWASAKI FS600V
ENGINE HP. 18
COOLING . . . . AIR
FUEL . . . . G
SPEEDS . . . . VARIABLE
TRANSMISSION . . . . HYDRO
STEERING. . . . . ZERO
STANDARD DECK . . . . 36"
WEIGHT . . . . 700 LBS.

ER48FX730VL

YEARS MFRD 2017-2019
SERIES. . . . . RAGE SERIES
ENGINE . . . . KAWASAKI FX730V
ENGINE HP. 23.5
COOLING . . . . AIR
FUEL . . . . G
SPEEDS . . . . VARIABLE
TRANSMISSION . . . . . DUAL HYDRO
STEERING. . . . . ZERO
STANDARD DECK . . . . 48"
WEIGHT . . . . 740 LBS.

ER48FX730VX

YEARS MFRD 2019-2020
SERIES. . . . . RAGE SERIES
ENGINE . . . . KAWASAKI FX730
ENGINE HP. 24
FUEL . . . . G
SPEEDS . . . . VARIABLE
TRANSMISSION . . . . HYDRO
STEERING. . . . . ZERO
STANDARD DECK . . . . 48"
WEIGHT . . . . 880 LBS.

ER52FX730VL

YEARS MFRD 2017-2018
ENGINE . . . . KAWASAKI FX730V
ENGINE HP. 23.5
COOLING . . . . AIR
FUEL . . . . G
SPEEDS . . . . VARIABLE
TRANSMISSION . . . . . DUAL HYDRO
STEERING. . . . . ZERO
STANDARD DECK . . . . 52"
WEIGHT . . . . 750 LBS.

ER52FX730VX

YEARS MFRD 2019-2020
SERIES. . . . . RAGE SERIES
ENGINE . . . . KAWASAKI FX730
ENGINE HP. 24
FUEL . . . . G
SPEEDS . . . . VARIABLE
TRANSMISSION . . . . HYDRO
STEERING. . . . . ZERO
STANDARD DECK . . . . 52"
WEIGHT . . . . 895 LBS.

ER60FX730VX

YEARS MFRD 2019-2020
SERIES. . . . . RAGE SERIES
ENGINE . . . . KAWASAKI FX730
ENGINE HP. 24
FUEL . . . . G
SPEEDS . . . . VARIABLE
TRANSMISSION . . . . HYDRO
STEERING. . . . . ZERO
STANDARD DECK . . . . 60"
WEIGHT . . . . 916 LBS.

FC PROWLER

YEARS MFRD 2005-2005
SERIES. . . . . X34 SERIES
ENGINE . . . . KAWASAKI
ENGINE HP. 15
COOLING . . . . AIR
FUEL . . . . G
SPEEDS . . . . VARIABLE
TRANSMISSION . . . . HYDRO
STEERING. . . . . ZERO
BLADE CLUTCH . . . . ELECTRIC
WEIGHT . . . . 750 LBS.

FD750D

YEARS MFRD 2004-2004
SERIES. . . . . PROWLER SERIES
ENGINE . . . . KAWASAKI OHV
CYLINDERS. 2
CID 45.5
ENGINE HP. 27
COOLING . . . . LIQUID
FUEL . . . . G
SPEEDS . . . . VARIABLE
TRANSMISSION . . . . HYDRO
STEERING. . . . . ZERO
BLADE CLUTCH . . . . ELECTRIC
HYDRAULIC . . . . YES
PTO . . . . YES
WEIGHT . . . . 1,450 LBS.

FH451V

YEARS MFRD 2004-2004
SERIES. . . . . Z34 SERIES
ENGINE . . . . KAWASAKI
CYLINDERS. 2
CID 30.1
ENGINE HP. 15
COOLING . . . . AIR
FUEL . . . . G
SPEEDS . . . . VARIABLE
TRANSMISSION . . . . HYDRO
STEERING. . . . . ZERO
WEIGHT . . . . 600 LBS.

FH500V

YEARS MFRD 2004-2004
SERIES. . . . . Z42 SERIES
ENGINE . . . . KAWASAKI OHV
CYLINDERS. 2
CID 30.5
ENGINE HP. 17

COOLING ... AIR
SPEEDS ... VARIABLE
TRANSMISSION ... HYDRO
STEERING ... ZERO
HYDRAULIC ... YES
WEIGHT ... 755 LBS.

FH601V

YEARS MFRD ... 2004-2004
SERIES ... Z48 SERIES
ENGINE ... KAWASAKI OHV
CYLINDERS ... 2
CID ... 41.2
ENGINE HP ... 19
COOLING ... AIR
FUEL ... G
SPEEDS ... VARIABLE
TRANSMISSION ... HYDRO
HYDRAULIC ... YES
WEIGHT ... 755 LBS.

FH641V

YEARS MFRD ... 2004-2004
SERIES ... Z52 SERIES
ENGINE ... KAWASAKI OHV
CYLINDERS ... 2
CID ... 41.2
ENGINE HP ... 21
COOLING ... AIR
FUEL ... G
SPEEDS ... VARIABLE
TRANSMISSION ... HYDRO
STEERING ... ZERO
BLADE CLUTCH ... ELECTRIC
HYDRAULIC ... YES
WEIGHT ... 805 LBS.

FH680D

YEARS MFRD ... 2004-2004
SERIES ... PROWLER SERIES
ENGINE ... KAWASAKI OHV
CYLINDERS ... 2
CID ... 41.2
ENGINE HP ... 25
COOLING ... AIR
FUEL ... G
SPEEDS ... VARIABLE
TRANSMISSION ... HYDRO
STEERING ... ZERO
HYDRAULIC ... YES
PTO ... YES
WEIGHT ... 1,450 LBS.

FH721V

YEARS MFRD ... 2004-2004
SERIES ... Z60 SERIES
ENGINE ... KAWASAKI OHV
CYLINDERS ... 2
CID ... 41.2
ENGINE HP ... 25
COOLING ... AIR
FUEL ... G
SPEEDS ... VARIABLE
TRANSMISSION ... HYDRO
STEERING ... ZERO
BLADE CLUTCH ... ELECTRIC
HYDRAULIC ... YES

FROWLER 72K28A3

YEARS MFRD ... 2013-2013
ENGINE ... KAWASAKI
ENGINE HP ... 28
COOLING ... AIR
FUEL ... G
SPEEDS ... VARIABLE
TRANSMISSION ... HYDRO
STEERING ... ZERO
BLADE CLUTCH ... ELECTRIC
WEIGHT ... 1,300 LBS.

FUZION F34B24

YEARS MFRD ... 2013-2013
ENGINE ... B&S
CYLINDERS ... 2
CID ... 724CC
ENGINE HP ... 24
COOLING ... AIR
FUEL ... G
SPEEDS ... VARIABLE
TRANSMISSION ... HYDRO
STEERING ... ZERO
BLADE CLUTCH ... ELECTRIC
STANDARD DECK ... 34"
WEIGHT ... 720 LBS.
MSRP ... $2,999

RETAIL PRICING

YEAR	HIGH	LOW
2013	$1,449	$1,086

FUZION F34K15

YEARS MFRD ... 2007-2012
ENGINE ... KAWASAKI
ENGINE HP ... 15
COOLING ... AIR
FUEL ... G
SPEEDS ... VARIABLE
TRANSMISSION ... HYDRO
STEERING ... ZERO
STANDARD DECK ... 34"
WEIGHT ... 720 LBS.
MSRP ... $5,389

OPTIONS

KAWASAKI 17E
KAWASAKI 19E

RETAIL PRICING

YEAR	HIGH	LOW
2007	$1,196	$897
2008	$1,294	$971
2009	$1,923	$1,442
2010	$2,200	$1,650
2011	$2,704	$2,028
2012	$2,926	$2,195

FUZION F34K20

YEARS MFRD ... 2013-2020
ENGINE ... KAWASAKI FS600V
ENGINE HP ... 20
FUEL ... G
SPEEDS ... VARIABLE
TRANSMISSION ... HYDRO
STEERING ... ZERO
BLADE CLUTCH ... ELECTRIC
STANDARD DECK ... 34"
WEIGHT ... 720 LBS.

RETAIL PRICING

YEAR	HIGH	LOW
2013	$1,429	$1,071
2014	$1,637	$1,228
2015	$1,940	$1,454
2016	$2,328	$1,747
2017	$2,892	$2,169
2018	$3,076	$2,307
2019	$3,333	$2,548
2020	$3,545	$2,806

FUZION F42B24

YEARS MFRD ... 2013-2013
ENGINE ... B&S
CID ... 724CC
ENGINE HP ... 24
COOLING ... AIR
FUEL ... G
SPEEDS ... VARIABLE
TRANSMISSION ... HYDRO
STEERING ... ZERO
BLADE CLUTCH ... ELECTRIC
STANDARD DECK ... 42"
WEIGHT ... 750 LBS.
MSRP ... $3,299

RETAIL PRICING

YEAR	HIGH	LOW
2013	$1,596	$1,197

FUZION F42K17

YEARS MFRD ... 2008-2012
ENGINE ... KAWASAKI
ENGINE HP ... 17
COOLING ... AIR
FUEL ... G
SPEEDS ... VARIABLE
TRANSMISSION ... HYDRO
STEERING ... ZERO
STANDARD DECK ... 42"
WEIGHT ... 590 LBS.
MSRP ... $5,999

RETAIL PRICING

YEAR	HIGH	LOW
2008	$1,412	$1,059
2009	$2,149	$1,612
2010	$2,654	$1,991
2011	$2,975	$2,231
2012	$3,318	$2,488

FUZION F42K20

YEARS MFRD ... 2012-2020
ENGINE ... KAWASAKI FS600V
ENGINE HP ... 18
COOLING ... AIR
FUEL ... G
SPEEDS ... VARIABLE
TRANSMISSION ... HYDRO
STEERING ... ZERO
BLADE CLUTCH ... ELECTRIC
STANDARD DECK ... 42"
WEIGHT ... 750 LBS.

RETAIL PRICING

YEAR	HIGH	LOW
2012	$1,420	$1,065
2013	$1,687	$1,266
2014	$1,822	$1,367
2015	$2,148	$1,611
2016	$2,581	$1,936
2017	$3,005	$2,254
2018	$3,256	$2,442
2019	$3,623	$2,845
2020	$3,873	$3,175

FUZION F48B24

YEARS MFRD ... 2013-2013
ENGINE ... B&S
CYLINDERS ... 2
CID ... 724CC
ENGINE HP ... 24
COOLING ... AIR
FUEL ... G
SPEEDS ... VARIABLE
TRANSMISSION ... HYDRO
STEERING ... ZERO
BLADE CLUTCH ... ELECTRIC
STANDARD DECK ... 48"
WEIGHT ... 770 LBS.
MSRP ... $3,499

RETAIL PRICING

YEAR	HIGH	LOW
2013	$1,690	$1,267

FUZION F48K19

YEARS MFRD ... 2008-2012
ENGINE ... KAWASAKI F48K19
ENGINE HP ... 19
COOLING ... AIR
FUEL ... G
SPEEDS ... VARIABLE
TRANSMISSION ... HYDRO
STEERING ... ZERO
STANDARD DECK ... 48"
WEIGHT ... 610 LBS.
MSRP ... $6,479

RETAIL PRICING

YEAR	HIGH	LOW
2008	$1,948	$1,461
2009	$2,323	$1,742
2010	$2,659	$1,994
2011	$3,496	$2,622
2012	$3,847	$2,885

ENCORE

FUZION F48K20

YEARS MFRD 2012-2019
ENGINE .... KAWASAKI
ENGINE HP 18
COOLING .... AIR
FUEL .... G
SPEEDS .... VARIABLE
TRANSMISSION .... HYDRO
STEERING. .... ZERO
BLADE CLUTCH .... ELECTRIC
STANDARD DECK .... 48"
WEIGHT .... 770 LBS.
MSRP. $4,749

RETAIL PRICING

YEAR	HIGH	LOW
2012	$1,546	$1,159
2013	$1,739	$1,304
2014	$1,973	$1,480
2015	$2,357	$1,768
2016	$3,000	$2,250
2017	$3,279	$2,460
2018	$3,548	$2,661
2019	$3,799	$2,849

HYDRO PRO

YEARS MFRD 2010-2010
ENGINE .... KAWASAKI
ENGINE HP 13
COOLING .... AIR
FUEL .... G
SPEEDS .... VARIABLE
TRANSMISSION .... HYDRO
STEERING. .... ZERO
WEIGHT .... 523 LBS.

OPTIONS

KAWASAKI 15E
KAWASAKI 17E

K650PFC POWER TRAIN

YEARS MFRD 2000-2001
ENGINE .... KAWASAKI
ENGINE HP 22
FUEL .... G
TRANSMISSION .... HYDRO
STEERING. .... STANDARD
MSRP. $6,800

RETAIL PRICING

YEAR	HIGH	LOW
2000	$2,940	$2,205
2001	$3,065	$2,299

K850PFC POWER TRAIN

YEARS MFRD 2002-2003
ENGINE .... KAWASAKI
ENGINE HP 22
FUEL .... G
TRANSMISSION .... HYDRO
STEERING. .... STANDARD
STANDARD DECK .... 61"
MSRP. $8,710

RETAIL PRICING

YEAR	HIGH	LOW
2002	$3,152	$2,364
2003	$3,683	$2,762

PREMIER HYDRO PRO

YEARS MFRD 2007-2012
ENGINE .... KAWASAKI
ENGINE HP 13
COOLING .... AIR
FUEL .... G
SPEEDS .... VARIABLE
TRANSMISSION .... HYDRO
STEERING. .... ZERO
WEIGHT .... 523 LBS.

OPTIONS

KAWASAKI 15E
KAWASAKI 17E

PREMIER PRO BELT GEAR

YEARS MFRD 2007-2012
ENGINE .... KAWASAKI
ENGINE HP 13
COOLING .... AIR
FUEL .... G
SPEEDS .... VARIABLE
TRANSMISSION .... HYDRO
STEERING. .... ZERO
WEIGHT .... 432 LBS.

OPTIONS

KAWASAKI 15E
KAWASAKI 17E

PROWLER

YEARS MFRD 1998-1999
ENGINE .... KAWASAKI
ENGINE HP 20
COOLING .... LIQUID
FUEL .... G
SPEEDS .... VARIABLE
TRANSMISSION .... HYDRO
STEERING. .... ZERO
STANDARD DECK .... 52"
MSRP. $8,841

RETAIL PRICING

YEAR	HIGH	LOW
1998	$1,143	$858
1999	$1,268	$951

PROWLER 61K28A3

YEARS MFRD 2012-2019
ENGINE .... KAWASAKI
ENGINE HP 28
COOLING .... AIR
FUEL .... G
SPEEDS .... VARIABLE
TRANSMISSION .... HYDRO
STEERING. .... ZERO
BLADE CLUTCH .... ELECTRIC
STANDARD DECK .... 61"
WEIGHT .... 1,210 LBS.
MSRP. $8,279

RETAIL PRICING

YEAR	HIGH	LOW
2012	$2,771	$2,078
2013	$3,380	$2,535
2014	$4,148	$3,111
2015	$4,832	$3,624
2016	$5,601	$4,200
2017	$6,342	$4,756
2018	$6,824	$5,118
2019	$7,260	$5,445

PROWLER 72K28A3

YEARS MFRD 2012-2019
ENGINE .... KAWASAKI
ENGINE HP 28
COOLING .... AIR
FUEL .... G
SPEEDS .... VARIABLE
TRANSMISSION .... HYDRO
STEERING. .... ZERO
STANDARD DECK .... 72"
MSRP. $8,799

RETAIL PRICING

YEAR	HIGH	LOW
2012	$2,976	$2,232
2013	$3,622	$2,717
2014	$4,331	$3,248
2015	$5,203	$3,902
2016	$6,170	$4,627
2017	$6,687	$5,016
2018	$7,160	$5,370
2019	$7,666	$5,749

PROWLER FRONT CUT 52

YEARS MFRD 2005-2010
ENGINE .... KAWASAKI
CYLINDERS. 2
ENGINE HP 25
COOLING .... AIR
FUEL .... G
SPEEDS .... VARIABLE
TRANSMISSION .... HYDRO
STEERING. .... ZERO
BLADE CLUTCH .... ELECTRIC
STANDARD DECK .... 52"
WEIGHT .... 1,292 LBS.
MSRP. $9,300

RETAIL PRICING

YEAR	HIGH	LOW
2005	$4,453	$3,340
2006	$5,085	$3,814

PROWLER FRONT CUT 61

YEARS MFRD 2005-2011
ENGINE .... DAIHATSU
CYLINDERS. 2
ENGINE HP 27
COOLING .... LIQUID
FUEL .... D
SPEEDS .... VARIABLE
TRANSMISSION .... HYDRO
STEERING. .... ZERO
BLADE CLUTCH .... ELECTRIC
STANDARD DECK .... 61"
WEIGHT .... 1,329 LBS.
MSRP. $13,750

RETAIL PRICING

YEAR	HIGH	LOW
2005	$6,269	$4,702
2006	$7,008	$5,256

PROWLER FRONT CUT 72

YEARS MFRD 2005-2011
ENGINE .... KAWASAKI
CYLINDERS. 2
ENGINE HP 27
COOLING .... AIR
FUEL .... G
SPEEDS .... VARIABLE
TRANSMISSION .... HYDRO
STEERING. .... ZERO
BLADE CLUTCH .... ELECTRIC
STANDARD DECK .... 72"
WEIGHT .... 1,480 LBS.
MSRP. $15,000

RETAIL PRICING

YEAR	HIGH	LOW
2005	$7,598	$5,699
2006	$7,773	$5,830

PROWLER MID CUT 52

YEARS MFRD 2006-2010
ENGINE .... KAWASAKI
ENGINE HP 25
COOLING .... AIR
FUEL .... G
SPEEDS .... VARIABLE
TRANSMISSION .... HYDRO
STEERING. .... ZERO

OPTIONS

DAIHATSU DIESEL 27E
GENERAC 33E
KAWASAKI 27E

PROWLER MID CUT 61

YEARS MFRD 2006-2012
ENGINE .... KAWASAKI
ENGINE HP 25
COOLING .... AIR
FUEL .... G
SPEEDS .... VARIABLE
TRANSMISSION .... HYDRO
STEERING. .... ZERO
BLADE CLUTCH .... ELECTRIC
WEIGHT .... 1,470 LBS.

OPTIONS
DAIHATSU DIESEL 27E
GENERAC 33E
KAWASAKI 27E

PROWLER MID CUT 72

YEARS MFRD . . . 2006-2012
ENGINE . . . KAWASAKI
ENGINE HP . . . 25
COOLING . . . AIR
FUEL . . . G
SPEEDS . . . VARIABLE
TRANSMISSION . . . HYDRO
STEERING . . . ZERO
BLADE CLUTCH . . . ELECTRIC
WEIGHT . . . 1,660 LBS.

OPTIONS
DAIHATSU DIESEL 27E
GENERAC 33E
KAWASAKI 27E

RAGE ER52FX730V

YEARS MFRD . . . 2014-2014
ENGINE . . . KAWASAKI
ENGINE HP . . . 23.5
COOLING . . . AIR
FUEL . . . G
SPEEDS . . . VARIABLE
TRANSMISSION . . . HYDRO
STEERING . . . ZERO
STANDARD DECK . . . 52"
MSRP . . . $5,799

RETAIL PRICING

YEAR	HIGH	LOW
2014	$2,905	$2,179

X-TREME

YEARS MFRD . . . 2010-2012
ENGINE . . . KAWASAKI
CYLINDERS . . . 2
ENGINE HP . . . 19
COOLING . . . AIR
FUEL . . . G
SPEEDS . . . VARIABLE
TRANSMISSION . . . HYDRO
STEERING . . . ZERO
WEIGHT . . . 1,100 LBS.

OPTIONS
B&S 20E
B&S 25E
KAWASAKI 23E
KAWASAKI 25E

X-TREME 52

YEARS MFRD . . . 2005-2009
ENGINE . . . KAWASAKI
CYLINDERS . . . 2
ENGINE HP . . . 23
COOLING . . . AIR
FUEL . . . G
SPEEDS . . . VARIABLE
TRANSMISSION . . . HYDRO
STEERING . . . ZERO
BLADE CLUTCH . . . ELECTRIC
WEIGHT . . . 1,000 LBS.

OPTIONS
B&S 20E
B&S 25E
KAWASAKI 25E

X-TREME 52K26X

YEARS MFRD . . . 2012-2014
ENGINE . . . KAWASAKI
ENGINE HP . . . 23.5
COOLING . . . AIR
FUEL . . . G
SPEEDS . . . VARIABLE
TRANSMISSION . . . HYDRO
STEERING . . . ZERO
BLADE CLUTCH . . . ELECTRIC
STANDARD DECK . . . 52"
WEIGHT . . . 940 LBS.
MSRP . . . $6,799

RETAIL PRICING

YEAR	HIGH	LOW
2012	$2,412	$1,809
2013	$2,885	$2,164
2014	$3,406	$2,555

X-TREME 60K26X

YEARS MFRD . . . 2012-2014
ENGINE . . . KAWASAKI FX730V
ENGINE HP . . . 23.5
COOLING . . . AIR
FUEL . . . G
SPEEDS . . . VARIABLE
TRANSMISSION . . . HYDRO
STEERING . . . ZERO
BLADE CLUTCH . . . ELECTRIC
STANDARD DECK . . . 60"
WEIGHT . . . 1,000 LBS.
MSRP . . . $7,250

RETAIL PRICING

YEAR	HIGH	LOW
2012	$2,572	$1,929
2013	$3,072	$2,304
2014	$3,629	$2,722

Z34

YEARS MFRD . . . 2007-2010
ENGINE . . . KAWASAKI
ENGINE HP . . . 15
COOLING . . . AIR
FUEL . . . G
SPEEDS . . . VARIABLE
TRANSMISSION . . . HYDRO
STEERING . . . ZERO
WEIGHT . . . 750 LBS.

Z42

YEARS MFRD . . . 1998-1999
SERIES . . . Z SERIES
ENGINE . . . VANGUARD V-TWIN
ENGINE HP . . . 16
FUEL . . . G
TRANSMISSION . . . DUAL HYDRO
STEERING . . . ZERO
STANDARD DECK . . . 42"
WEIGHT . . . 805 LBS.
MSRP . . . $4,999

RETAIL PRICING

YEAR	HIGH	LOW
1998	$646	$485
1999	$716	$537

Z48

YEARS MFRD . . . 2003-2003
SERIES . . . Z SERIES
ENGINE . . . VANGUARD
ENGINE HP . . . 18
FUEL . . . G
TRANSMISSION . . . BELT
STEERING . . . ZERO

Z52

YEARS MFRD . . . 1998-1999
SERIES . . . Z SERIES
ENGINE . . . B&S
ENGINE HP . . . 20
FUEL . . . G
TRANSMISSION . . . HYDRO
STEERING . . . ZERO
STANDARD DECK . . . 52"
MSRP . . . $5,938

RETAIL PRICING

YEAR	HIGH	LOW
1998	$768	$576

34B18

YEARS MFRD . . . 2006-2006
SERIES . . . Z SERIES
ENGINE . . . B&S
ENGINE HP . . . 18
COOLING . . . AIR
FUEL . . . G
SPEEDS . . . VARIABLE
TRANSMISSION . . . HYDRO
STEERING . . . ZERO
STANDARD DECK . . . 34"
WEIGHT . . . 750 LBS.
MSRP . . . $4,500

RETAIL PRICING

YEAR	HIGH	LOW
2006	$2,700	$2,025

34K15Z

YEARS MFRD . . . 2006-2006
SERIES . . . Z SERIES
ENGINE . . . KAWASAKI
ENGINE HP . . . 15
COOLING . . . AIR
FUEL . . . G
SPEEDS . . . VARIABLE
TRANSMISSION . . . HYDRO
STEERING . . . STANDARD
STANDARD DECK . . . 34"
WEIGHT . . . 750 LBS.
MSRP . . . $4,999

RETAIL PRICING

YEAR	HIGH	LOW
2006	$2,304	$1,728

42B17

YEARS MFRD . . . 2006-2006
SERIES . . . Z SERIES
ENGINE . . . KAWASAKI
ENGINE HP . . . 17
COOLING . . . AIR
FUEL . . . G
SPEEDS . . . VARIABLE
TRANSMISSION . . . HYDRO
STEERING . . . ZERO
STANDARD DECK . . . 42"
WEIGHT . . . 920 LBS.
MSRP . . . $5,900

RETAIL PRICING

YEAR	HIGH	LOW
2006	$2,844	$2,133

42B18

YEARS MFRD . . . 2006-2006
SERIES . . . Z SERIES
ENGINE . . . B&S
ENGINE HP . . . 18
COOLING . . . AIR
FUEL . . . G
SPEEDS . . . VARIABLE
TRANSMISSION . . . HYDRO
STEERING . . . ZERO
STANDARD DECK . . . 42"
WEIGHT . . . 920 LBS.
MSRP . . . $5,400

RETAIL PRICING

YEAR	HIGH	LOW
2006	$2,544	$1,908

42B350Z

YEARS MFRD . . . 1997-1999
ENGINE . . . B&S
ENGINE HP . . . 16
FUEL . . . G
TRANSMISSION . . . HYDRO
STEERING . . . STANDARD
STANDARD DECK . . . 42"
MSRP . . . $5,109

RETAIL PRICING

YEAR	HIGH	LOW
1997	$1,144	$858
1998	$1,276	$957
1999	$1,412	$1,059

42K17Z

YEARS MFRD . . . 2006-2006
SERIES . . . Z SERIES
ENGINE . . . KAWASAKI

ENCORE

ENGINE HP 17
COOLING . . . . . AIR
FUEL . . . . . G
SPEEDS . . . . . VARIABLE
TRANSMISSION . . . . . HYDRO
STEERING . . . . . ZERO
STANDARD DECK . . . . . 42"
WEIGHT . . . . . 920 LBS.
MSRP $5,900

RETAIL PRICING

YEAR	HIGH	LOW
2006	$2,844	$2,133

42K450Z

YEARS MFRD 2000-2002
ENGINE . . . . . KAWASAKI
ENGINE HP 17
FUEL . . . . . G
TRANSMISSION . . . . . HYDRO
STEERING . . . . . STANDARD
STANDARD DECK . . . . . 42"
MSRP $5,311

RETAIL PRICING

YEAR	HIGH	LOW
2000	$1,533	$1,150
2001	$1,700	$1,275
2002	$1,767	$1,326

48B450Z

YEARS MFRD 1997-1999
ENGINE . . . . . B&S
ENGINE HP 18
FUEL . . . . . G
TRANSMISSION . . . . . HYDRO
STEERING . . . . . STANDARD
STANDARD DECK . . . . . 48"
MSRP $5,695

RETAIL PRICING

YEAR	HIGH	LOW
1997	$1,329	$996
1998	$1,471	$1,103
1999	$1,654	$1,241

48K550Z

YEARS MFRD 2000-2002
ENGINE . . . . . KAWASAKI
ENGINE HP 19
FUEL . . . . . G
TRANSMISSION . . . . . HYDRO
STEERING . . . . . STANDARD
STANDARD DECK . . . . . 48"
MSRP $5,866

RETAIL PRICING

YEAR	HIGH	LOW
2000	$1,781	$1,336
2001	$1,950	$1,462
2002	$2,024	$1,518

52B550Z

YEARS MFRD 1999-1999
ENGINE . . . . . B&S
ENGINE HP 20
FUEL . . . . . G
TRANSMISSION . . . . . HYDRO
STEERING . . . . . STANDARD
STANDARD DECK . . . . . 52"
MSRP $5,935

RETAIL PRICING

YEAR	HIGH	LOW
1999	$1,752	$1,314

52K550R

YEARS MFRD 1994-1995
ENGINE . . . . . KAWASAKI
ENGINE HP 20
FUEL . . . . . G
TRANSMISSION . . . . . HYDRO
STEERING . . . . . STANDARD
STANDARD DECK . . . . . 52"
MSRP $6,999

RETAIL PRICING

YEAR	HIGH	LOW
1994	$1,450	$1,087
1995	$1,703	$1,277

52K555R

YEARS MFRD 1996-1999
ENGINE . . . . . KAWASAKI
ENGINE HP 20
FUEL . . . . . G
TRANSMISSION . . . . . HYDRO
STEERING . . . . . STANDARD
STANDARD DECK . . . . . 52"
MSRP $8,054

RETAIL PRICING

YEAR	HIGH	LOW
1996	$1,270	$953
1997	$1,518	$1,138
1998	$1,724	$1,293
1999	$1,932	$1,449

52K650Z

YEARS MFRD 2000-2002
ENGINE . . . . . KAWASAKI
ENGINE HP 21
FUEL . . . . . G
TRANSMISSION . . . . . HYDRO
STEERING . . . . . STANDARD
STANDARD DECK . . . . . 52"
MSRP $6,352

RETAIL PRICING

YEAR	HIGH	LOW
2000	$1,977	$1,482
2001	$2,169	$1,626
2002	$2,249	$1,687

52K650ZP

YEARS MFRD 2000-2001
ENGINE . . . . . KAWASAKI
ENGINE HP 22
FUEL . . . . . G
TRANSMISSION . . . . . HYDRO
STANDARD DECK . . . . . 52"
MSRP $8,634

RETAIL PRICING

YEAR	HIGH	LOW
2000	$3,002	$2,251
2001	$3,198	$2,398

52K700ZP

YEARS MFRD 2002-2002
ENGINE . . . . . KAWASAKI
ENGINE HP 23
FUEL . . . . . G
TRANSMISSION . . . . . HYDRO
STEERING . . . . . STANDARD
STANDARD DECK . . . . . 52"
MSRP $7,811

RETAIL PRICING

YEAR	HIGH	LOW
2002	$2,925	$2,194

52K850ZP

YEARS MFRD 2002-2003
ENGINE . . . . . KAWASAKI
ENGINE HP 27
FUEL . . . . . G
TRANSMISSION . . . . . HYDRO
STEERING . . . . . STANDARD
STANDARD DECK . . . . . 52"
MSRP $8,795

RETAIL PRICING

YEAR	HIGH	LOW
2002	$3,307	$2,480
2003	$3,724	$2,793

61B27LDML

YEARS MFRD 2006-2006
SERIES . PROWLER MID-CUT SERIES
ENGINE . . . . . DAIHATSU
ENGINE HP 26.5
FUEL . . . . . D
SPEEDS . . . . . VARIABLE
TRANSMISSION . . . . . HYDRO
STEERING . . . . . STANDARD
STANDARD DECK . . . . . 61"
WEIGHT . . . . . 1,520 LBS.
MSRP $14,900

RETAIL PRICING

YEAR	HIGH	LOW
2006	$6,156	$4,617

61B850P

YEARS MFRD 2000-2005
ENGINE . . . . . B&S
ENGINE HP 26
FUEL . . . . . D
TRANSMISSION . . . . . HYDRO
STEERING . . . . . STANDARD
STANDARD DECK . . . . . 61"
MSRP $13,530

RETAIL PRICING

YEAR	HIGH	LOW
2000	$4,918	$3,689
2001	$5,206	$3,905
2002	$5,370	$4,028
2003	$5,911	$4,433
2004	$6,334	$4,751
2005	$6,987	$5,240

61B950P

YEARS MFRD 2000-2003
ENGINE . . . . . B&S
ENGINE HP 31
FUEL . . . . . G
TRANSMISSION . . . . . HYDRO
STEERING . . . . . STANDARD
STANDARD DECK . . . . . 61"
MSRP $12,388

RETAIL PRICING

YEAR	HIGH	LOW
2000	$5,312	$3,984
2001	$5,586	$4,190
2002	$5,741	$4,306
2003	$5,781	$4,336

61G33A

YEARS MFRD 2006-2006
SERIES . PROWLER MID-CUT SERIES
ENGINE . . . . . GENERAC
ENGINE HP 33
FUEL . . . . . G
SPEEDS . . . . . VARIABLE
TRANSMISSION . . . . . HYDRO
STEERING . . . . . STANDARD
STANDARD DECK . . . . . 61"
WEIGHT . . . . . 1,470 LBS.
MSRP $10,300

RETAIL PRICING

YEAR	HIGH	LOW
2006	$6,179	$4,634

61K25A

YEARS MFRD 2006-2006
SERIES . PROWLER MID-CUT SERIES
ENGINE . . . . . KAWASAKI
ENGINE HP 25
FUEL . . . . . G
SPEEDS . . . . . VARIABLE
TRANSMISSION . . . . . HYDRO
STEERING . . . . . STANDARD
STANDARD DECK . . . . . 61"
WEIGHT . . . . . 1,470 LBS.
MSRP $9,300

RETAIL PRICING

YEAR	HIGH	LOW
2006	$5,579	$4,184

61K27L

YEARS MFRD 2006-2006
SERIES . PROWLER MID-CUT SERIES
ENGINE . . . . . KAWASAKI
ENGINE HP 27
FUEL . . . . . G
SPEEDS . . . . . VARIABLE
TRANSMISSION . . . . . HYDRO
STEERING . . . . . STANDARD
STANDARD DECK . . . . . 61"
WEIGHT . . . . . 1,470 LBS.
MSRP $9,600

RETAIL PRICING

YEAR	HIGH	LOW
2006	$5,758	$4,319

61K555R

YEARS MFRD 1996-1999
ENGINE . . . . KAWASAKI
ENGINE HP 20
FUEL . . . . G
TRANSMISSION . . . . HYDRO
STEERING. . . . . STANDARD
STANDARD DECK . . . . 61"
MSRP. $8,286

RETAIL PRICING

YEAR	HIGH	LOW
1996	$2,785	$2,089
1997	$2,991	$2,244
1998	$3,204	$2,403
1999	$3,418	$2,563

61K650ZP

YEARS MFRD 2000-2001
ENGINE . . . . KAWASAKI
ENGINE HP 22
FUEL . . . . G
TRANSMISSION . . . . HYDRO
STEERING. . . . . STANDARD
STANDARD DECK . . . . 61"
MSRP. $8,794

RETAIL PRICING

YEAR	HIGH	LOW
2000	$3,762	$2,822
2001	$3,965	$2,974

61K850ZP

YEARS MFRD 2002-2005
ENGINE . . . . KAWASAKI
ENGINE HP 27
FUEL . . . . G
TRANSMISSION . . . . HYDRO
STEERING. . . . . STANDARD
STANDARD DECK . . . . 61"
MSRP. $9,509

RETAIL PRICING

YEAR	HIGH	LOW
2002	$4,174	$3,131
2003	$4,546	$3,409
2004	$5,043	$3,782
2005	$5,395	$4,046

72B27LD

YEARS MFRD 2006-2006
SERIES. PROWLER MID-CUT SERIES
ENGINE . . . . B&S
ENGINE HP 27
FUEL . . . . D
SPEEDS . . . . VARIABLE
TRANSMISSION . . . . HYDRO
STEERING. . . . . STANDARD
STANDARD DECK . . . . 72"
WEIGHT . . . . 1,710 LBS.
MSRP. $15,500

RETAIL PRICING

YEAR	HIGH	LOW
2006	$7,908	$5,931

72B27LDML

YEARS MFRD 2006-2006
SERIES. PROWLER MID-CUT SERIES
ENGINE . . . . DAIHATSU
ENGINE HP 26.5
FUEL . . . . D
SPEEDS . . . . VARIABLE
TRANSMISSION . . . . HYDRO
STEERING. . . . . STANDARD
STANDARD DECK . . . . 72"
WEIGHT . . . . 1,710 LBS.
MSRP. $15,500

RETAIL PRICING

YEAR	HIGH	LOW
2006	$7,908	$5,931

72B850P

YEARS MFRD 2001-2005
ENGINE . . . . B&S
ENGINE HP 26.5
FUEL . . . . D
TRANSMISSION . . . . HYDRO
STEERING. . . . . STANDARD
STANDARD DECK . . . . 72"
MSRP. $14,449

RETAIL PRICING

YEAR	HIGH	LOW
2001	$6,189	$4,642
2002	$6,362	$4,771
2003	$7,147	$5,360
2004	$7,522	$5,641
2005	$8,198	$6,149

72B950P

YEARS MFRD 2001-2003
ENGINE . . . . B&S
ENGINE HP 31
FUEL . . . . G
TRANSMISSION . . . . HYDRO
STEERING. . . . . STANDARD
STANDARD DECK . . . . 72"
MSRP. $12,966

RETAIL PRICING

YEAR	HIGH	LOW
2001	$5,846	$4,385
2002	$6,010	$4,507
2003	$6,067	$4,550

72G33A

YEARS MFRD 2006-2006
SERIES. . . . . PROWLER
ENGINE . . . . GENERAC
ENGINE HP 33
FUEL . . . . G
SPEEDS . . . . VARIABLE
TRANSMISSION . . . . HYDRO
STEERING. . . . . STANDARD
STANDARD DECK . . . . 72"
WEIGHT . . . . 1,710 LBS.
MSRP. $10,900

RETAIL PRICING

YEAR	HIGH	LOW
2006	$5,844	$4,383

72K27L

YEARS MFRD 2006-2006
SERIES. PROWLER MID-CUT SERIES
ENGINE . . . . KAWASAKI
ENGINE HP 27
FUEL . . . . G
SPEEDS . . . . VARIABLE
TRANSMISSION . . . . HYDRO
STEERING. . . . . STANDARD
STANDARD DECK . . . . 72"
WEIGHT . . . . 1,660 LBS.
MSRP. $10,800

RETAIL PRICING

YEAR	HIGH	LOW
2006	$5,783	$4,337

72K850ZP

YEARS MFRD 2002-2005
ENGINE . . . . KAWASAKI
ENGINE HP 27
FUEL . . . . G
TRANSMISSION . . . . HYDRO
STEERING. . . . . STANDARD
STANDARD DECK . . . . 72"
MSRP. $10,259

RETAIL PRICING

YEAR	HIGH	LOW
2002	$4,512	$3,384
2003	$4,991	$3,743
2004	$5,452	$4,089
2005	$5,820	$4,365

582447 FRONT CUT

YEARS MFRD 2004-2004
SERIES. . . . . PROWLER SERIES
ENGINE . . . . DAIHATSU
CYLINDERS. 3
CID 58.1
ENGINE HP 26.5
COOLING . . . . LIQUID
FUEL . . . . D
SPEEDS . . . . VARIABLE
TRANSMISSION . . . . HYDRO
STEERING. . . . . ZERO
BLADE CLUTCH . . . . ELECTRIC
HYDRAULIC . . . . YES
PTO . . . . YES
WEIGHT . . . . 1,450 LBS.

582447 MID CUT

YEARS MFRD 2004-2004
SERIES. . . . . PROWLER SERIES
ENGINE . . . . B&S OHV
CYLINDERS. 3
CID 58.1
ENGINE HP 27
COOLING . . . . LIQUID
FUEL . . . . G
SPEEDS . . . . VARIABLE
TRANSMISSION . . . . HYDRO
STEERING. . . . . ZERO
BLADE CLUTCH . . . . ELECTRIC
HYDRAULIC . . . . YES
PTO . . . . YES
WEIGHT . . . . 1,660 LBS.

EVERRIDE

BRIGGS HORNET 25HP

YEARS MFRD 2007-2008
ENGINE . . . . B&S OHV
CYLINDERS. 2
ENGINE HP 25
COOLING . . . . AIR
FUEL . . . . G
SPEEDS . . . . VARIABLE
TRANSMISSION . . . . HYDRO
STEERING. . . . . ZERO
BLADE CLUTCH . . . . ELECTRIC

BRIGGS WARRIOR 26HP

YEARS MFRD 2007-2008
ENGINE . . . . B&S OHV
CYLINDERS. 2
ENGINE HP 26
COOLING . . . . AIR
FUEL . . . . G
SPEEDS . . . . VARIABLE
TRANSMISSION . . . . HYDRO
STEERING. . . . . ZERO
BLADE CLUTCH . . . . ELECTRIC
WEIGHT . . . . 959 LBS.

FURY

YEARS MFRD 2010-2014
ENGINE . . . . KAWASAKI
ENGINE HP 19
COOLING . . . . AIR
FUEL . . . . G
SPEEDS . . . . VARIABLE
TRANSMISSION . . . . HYDRO
STEERING. . . . . ZERO
WEIGHT . . . . 1,161 LBS.

OPTIONS

KAWASAKI 23E
KAWASAKI 25E

HORNET 17.85HP

YEARS MFRD 2007-2008
ENGINE . . . . . YANMAR 2V750-CVER
CYLINDERS. 2
ENGINE HP 17.85
COOLING . . . . LIQUID
FUEL . . . . D

EVERRIDE

SPEEDS ... VARIABLE
TRANSMISSION ... HYDRO
STEERING ... ZERO
WEIGHT ... 1,175 LBS.

HORNET 19HP

YEARS MFRD ... 2008-2014
ENGINE ... KAWASAKI FH601V
ENGINE HP ... 19
COOLING ... AIR
FUEL ... G
SPEEDS ... VARIABLE
TRANSMISSION ... HYDRO
STEERING ... ZERO
BLADE CLUTCH ... ELECTRIC
STANDARD DECK ... 48"
MSRP ... $7,449

RETAIL PRICING

YEAR	HIGH	LOW
2008	$1,419	$1,064
2009	$1,841	$1,381
2010	$2,170	$1,627
2011	$3,391	$2,543
2012	$3,807	$2,855
2013	$4,368	$3,276
2014	$4,502	$3,376

HORNET 23HP

YEARS MFRD ... 2008-2014
ENGINE ... KAWASAKI FH680V
ENGINE HP ... 23
COOLING ... AIR
FUEL ... G
SPEEDS ... VARIABLE
TRANSMISSION ... HYDRO
STEERING ... ZERO
BLADE CLUTCH ... ELECTRIC
STANDARD DECK ... 52"
MSRP ... $7,699

RETAIL PRICING

YEAR	HIGH	LOW
2008	$1,510	$1,133
2009	$2,100	$1,575
2010	$2,564	$1,923
2011	$3,048	$2,286
2012	$4,129	$3,097
2013	$4,543	$3,408
2014	$4,854	$3,640

SCORPION 18HP

YEARS MFRD ... 2007-2008
ENGINE ... KOHLER CV18S
ENGINE HP ... 18
COOLING ... AIR
FUEL ... G
SPEEDS ... VARIABLE
TRANSMISSION ... HYDRO
STEERING ... ZERO
BLADE CLUTCH ... ELECTRIC
WEIGHT ... 900 LBS.

SCORPION 19HP

YEARS MFRD ... 2008-2014
ENGINE ... KAWASAKI FH601V
CID ... 41.2
ENGINE HP ... 19
COOLING ... AIR
FUEL ... G
SPEEDS ... VARIABLE
TRANSMISSION ... HYDRO
STEERING ... ZERO
STANDARD DECK ... 48"
WEIGHT ... 900 LBS.
MSRP ... $7,499

RETAIL PRICING

YEAR	HIGH	LOW
2008	$1,342	$1,006
2009	$2,001	$1,501
2010	$2,473	$1,854
2011	$2,859	$2,144
2012	$3,848	$2,886
2013	$4,278	$3,208
2014	$4,585	$3,439

SCORPION 23HP

YEARS MFRD ... 2008-2014
ENGINE ... KOHLER CV23S
CID ... 41.1
ENGINE HP ... 23
COOLING ... AIR
FUEL ... G
SPEEDS ... VARIABLE
TRANSMISSION ... HYDRO
STEERING ... ZERO
STANDARD DECK ... 52"
WEIGHT ... 930 LBS.
MSRP ... $8,299

OPTIONS

KAWASAKI 23E

RETAIL PRICING

YEAR	HIGH	LOW
2008	$1,595	$1,196
2009	$2,121	$1,591
2010	$2,698	$2,023
2011	$3,298	$2,474
2012	$4,090	$3,068
2013	$4,909	$3,682
2014	$5,113	$3,835

SCORPION FX 19HP

YEARS MFRD ... 2008-2011
ENGINE ... KAWASAKI FH580V
ENGINE HP ... 19
COOLING ... AIR
FUEL ... G
SPEEDS ... VARIABLE
TRANSMISSION ... HYDRO
STEERING ... ZERO
BLADE CLUTCH ... ELECTRIC
STANDARD DECK ... 34"
WEIGHT ... 860 LBS.
MSRP ... $5,899

OPTIONS

48" DECK
52" DECK

RETAIL PRICING

YEAR	HIGH	LOW
2008	$1,648	$1,236
2009	$2,086	$1,565
2010	$2,432	$1,824
2011	$3,278	$2,458

SCORPION FX 23HP

YEARS MFRD ... 2008-2014
ENGINE ... KAWASAKI FH680V
ENGINE HP ... 23
COOLING ... AIR
FUEL ... G
SPEEDS ... VARIABLE
TRANSMISSION ... HYDRO
STEERING ... ZERO
BLADE CLUTCH ... ELECTRIC
STANDARD DECK ... 52"
WEIGHT ... 860 LBS.
MSRP ... $7,199

RETAIL PRICING

YEAR	HIGH	LOW
2008	$1,376	$1,032
2009	$1,890	$1,417
2010	$2,344	$1,758
2011	$3,251	$2,439
2012	$3,638	$2,729
2013	$4,267	$3,200
2014	$4,550	$3,413

WARRIOR 25HP

YEARS MFRD ... 2009-2014
ENGINE ... KAWASAKI FH721V
CYLINDERS ... 2
ENGINE HP ... 25
COOLING ... AIR
FUEL ... G
SPEEDS ... VARIABLE
TRANSMISSION ... HYDRO
STEERING ... ZERO
BLADE CLUTCH ... ELECTRIC
STANDARD DECK ... 60"
MSRP ... $9,999

RETAIL PRICING

YEAR	HIGH	LOW
2009	$2,950	$2,212
2010	$3,581	$2,686
2011	$4,280	$3,210
2012	$5,369	$4,027
2013	$6,082	$4,561
2014	$6,229	$4,672

WARRIOR 27HP

YEARS MFRD ... 2008-2014
ENGINE ... KOHLER CV740
CYLINDERS ... 2
ENGINE HP ... 27
COOLING ... AIR
FUEL ... G
SPEEDS ... VARIABLE
TRANSMISSION ... HYDRO
STEERING ... ZERO
BLADE CLUTCH ... ELECTRIC
STANDARD DECK ... 66"
WEIGHT ... 959 LBS.
MSRP ... $10,499

RETAIL PRICING

YEAR	HIGH	LOW
2008	$2,381	$1,786
2009	$3,141	$2,356
2010	$3,800	$2,850
2011	$5,420	$4,065
2012	$5,776	$4,332
2013	$6,135	$4,601
2014	$6,434	$4,826

WARRIOR 31HP

YEARS MFRD ... 2009-2014
ENGINE ... KAWASAKI
CYLINDERS ... 2
CID ... 44
ENGINE HP ... 31
COOLING ... AIR
FUEL ... G
SPEEDS ... VARIABLE
TRANSMISSION ... HYDRO
STEERING ... ZERO
BLADE CLUTCH ... ELECTRIC
STANDARD DECK ... 66"
WEIGHT ... 1,218 LBS.
MSRP ... $10,499

RETAIL PRICING

YEAR	HIGH	LOW
2009	$3,141	$2,356
2010	$3,800	$2,850
2011	$5,420	$4,065
2012	$5,676	$4,257
2013	$6,024	$4,518
2014	$6,296	$4,722

WASP GEAR DRIVE

YEARS MFRD ... 2010-2014
ENGINE ... KAWASAKI
ENGINE HP ... 13
COOLING ... AIR
FUEL ... G
SPEEDS ... 5/1
TRANSMISSION ... GEAR
STEERING ... ZERO
WEIGHT ... 478 LBS.

OPTIONS

KAWASAKI 15E

WASP HYDRO

YEARS MFRD ... 2010-2014
ENGINE ... KAWASAKI
ENGINE HP ... 15
COOLING ... AIR

FUEL . . . . . G
SPEEDS . . . . . VARIABLE
TRANSMISSION . . . . . HYDRO
STEERING . . . . . ZERO
WEIGHT . . . . . 647 LBS.

OPTIONS

KAWASAKI 19E

YJ18HP

YEARS MFRD 2008-2014
ENGINE . . . . . KOHLER COURAGE
CYLINDERS 1
ENGINE HP 18
COOLING . . . . . AIR
FUEL . . . . . G
SPEEDS . . . . . VARIABLE
TRANSMISSION . . . . . HYDRO
STEERING . . . . . ZERO
BLADE CLUTCH . . . . . ELECTRIC
STANDARD DECK . . . . . 40"
MSRP $3,999

RETAIL PRICING

YEAR	HIGH	LOW
2008	$568	$426
2009	$674	$506
2010	$928	$696
2011	$1,191	$893
2012	$1,676	$1,257
2013	$1,994	$1,496
2014	$2,226	$1,670

YJ20HP

YEARS MFRD 2009-2014
ENGINE . . . . . KOHLER
CYLINDERS 2
ENGINE HP 20
COOLING . . . . . AIR
FUEL . . . . . G
SPEEDS . . . . . VARIABLE
TRANSMISSION . . . . . HYDRO
STEERING . . . . . ZERO
BLADE CLUTCH . . . . . ELECTRIC
STANDARD DECK . . . . . 44"
WEIGHT . . . . . 720 LBS.
MSRP $4,799

RETAIL PRICING

YEAR	HIGH	LOW
2009	$1,047	$785
2010	$1,279	$960
2011	$1,951	$1,463
2012	$2,146	$1,609
2013	$2,506	$1,880
2014	$2,766	$2,075

YJ23HP

YEARS MFRD 2009-2014
ENGINE . . . . . KOHLER COURAGE
CYLINDERS 2
ENGINE HP 23
COOLING . . . . . AIR
FUEL . . . . . G
SPEEDS . . . . . VARIABLE
TRANSMISSION . . . . . HYDRO
STEERING . . . . . ZERO
BLADE CLUTCH . . . . . ELECTRIC
STANDARD DECK . . . . . 48"
WEIGHT . . . . . 740 LBS.
MSRP $4,999

RETAIL PRICING

YEAR	HIGH	LOW
2009	$703	$527
2010	$1,300	$975
2011	$2,000	$1,500
2012	$2,190	$1,643
2013	$2,689	$2,017
2014	$2,935	$2,201

EX MARK

ALL MODELS

YEARS MFRD 2012-2020

SERIAL NUMBERS

YEAR	BEGINNING NO.
2012	312000000
2013	313000000
2014	314000000
2015	315000000
2016	316000000
2017	400000000
2018	402082300
2019	404314159
2020	406294354

CD42CD

YEARS MFRD 2013-2013
SERIES . . . . . NAVIGATOR SERIES
ENGINE . . . . . KOHLER
COOLING . . . . . AIR
FUEL . . . . . G
SPEEDS . . . . . VARIABLE
TRANSMISSION . . . . . HYDRO
STEERING . . . . . ZERO
STANDARD DECK . . . . . 42"
MSRP $3,218

RETAIL PRICING

YEAR	HIGH	LOW
2013	$1,398	$1,049

CD48CD

YEARS MFRD 2013-2013
SERIES . . . . . NAVIGATOR SERIES
ENGINE . . . . . KOHLER
COOLING . . . . . AIR
FUEL . . . . . G
SPEEDS . . . . . VARIABLE
TRANSMISSION . . . . . HYDRO
STEERING . . . . . ZERO
STANDARD DECK . . . . . 48"
MSRP $3,329

RETAIL PRICING

YEAR	HIGH	LOW
2013	$1,446	$1,085

EXPLORER (EX) ALL MODELS

YEARS MFRD NA-1997

SERIAL NUMBERS

YEAR	BEGINNING NO.
1992	72000
1993	80000
1994	90000
1995	102000
1996	115000
1997	130000

EX18KO

YEARS MFRD 1991-1991
SERIES . . . . . EXPLORER SERIES
ENGINE . . . . . KOHLER
ENGINE HP 18
COOLING . . . . . AIR
FUEL . . . . . G
TRANSMISSION . . . . . HYDRO
STEERING . . . . . ZERO
STANDARD DECK . . . . . 44"
MSRP $8,308

RETAIL PRICING

YEAR	HIGH	LOW
1991	$584	$438

EX20KC44RD

YEARS MFRD 1997-1998
SERIES . . . . . EXPLORER SERIES
ENGINE . . . . . KOHLER COMMAND
ENGINE HP 20
COOLING . . . . . AIR
FUEL . . . . . G
STEERING . . . . . ZERO
STANDARD DECK . . . . . 44"
MSRP $9,180

RETAIL PRICING

YEAR	HIGH	LOW
1997	$920	$690
1998	$1,017	$763

EX20KC52RD

YEARS MFRD 1997-1999
SERIES . . . . . EXPLORER SERIES
ENGINE . . . . . KOHLER COMMAND
ENGINE HP 20
COOLING . . . . . AIR
FUEL . . . . . G
STEERING . . . . . ZERO
STANDARD DECK . . . . . 52"
MSRP $9,380

RETAIL PRICING

YEAR	HIGH	LOW
1997	$918	$689
1998	$1,015	$761
1999	$1,123	$842

EX20KC52SD

YEARS MFRD 1997-1998
SERIES . . . . . EXPLORER SERIES
ENGINE . . . . . KOHLER COMMAND
ENGINE HP 20
COOLING . . . . . AIR
FUEL . . . . . G
TRANSMISSION . . . . . DUAL HYDRO
STEERING . . . . . ZERO
STANDARD DECK . . . . . 52"
MSRP $9,380

RETAIL PRICING

YEAR	HIGH	LOW
1997	$939	$704
1998	$1,040	$780

EX20KO

YEARS MFRD 1991-1991
SERIES . . . . . EXPLORER SERIES
ENGINE . . . . . KOHLER
ENGINE HP 20
COOLING . . . . . AIR
FUEL . . . . . G
TRANSMISSION . . . . . HYDRO
STEERING . . . . . ZERO
STANDARD DECK . . . . . 44"
MSRP $8,608

OPTIONS

52" DECK

RETAIL PRICING

YEAR	HIGH	LOW
1991	$415	$311

EXS18KO

YEARS MFRD 1992-1993
SERIES . . . . . EXPLORER SERIES
ENGINE . . . . . KOHLER
ENGINE HP 18
COOLING . . . . . AIR
FUEL . . . . . G
TRANSMISSION . . . . . HYDRO
STEERING . . . . . ZERO
STANDARD DECK . . . . . 44"
MSRP $7,358

OPTIONS

52" DECK

RETAIL PRICING

YEAR	HIGH	LOW
1992	$381	$286
1993	$420	$315

EXS20KC

YEARS MFRD 1995-1996
SERIES . . . . . EXPLORER SERIES
ENGINE . . . . . KOHLER COMMAND
ENGINE HP 20
FUEL . . . . . G
TRANSMISSION . . . . . HYDRO
STEERING . . . . . ZERO
STANDARD DECK . . . . . 52"
MSRP $8,620

OPTIONS

60" DECK

RETAIL PRICING

YEAR	HIGH	LOW
1995	$654	$490
1996	$724	$543

EX MARK

EXS20KO

YEARS MFRD 1992-1993
SERIES .... EXPLORER SERIES
ENGINE .... KOHLER
ENGINE HP 20
COOLING .... AIR
FUEL .... G
TRANSMISSION .... HYDRO
STEERING .... ZERO
STANDARD DECK .... 44"
MSRP $7,828

OPTIONS

52" DECK

RETAIL PRICING

YEAR	HIGH	LOW
1992	$436	$327
1993	$482	$362

FR23KC

YEARS MFRD 2006-2008
SERIES ..... FRONTRUNNER SERIES
ENGINE ...... KOHLER COMMAND
CYLINDERS 2
ENGINE HP 23
COOLING .... AIR
FUEL .... G
SPEEDS .... VARIABLE
TRANSMISSION .... HYDRO
STEERING .... ZERO
BLADE CLUTCH .... ELECTRIC
STANDARD DECK .... 52"
WEIGHT .... 930 LBS.
MSRP $11,819

OPTIONS

60" DECK

RETAIL PRICING

YEAR	HIGH	LOW
2006	$3,285	$2,464
2007	$3,658	$2,744
2008	$4,051	$3,038

FR25KD

YEARS MFRD 2006-2009
SERIES ..... FRONTRUNNER SERIES
ENGINE .... KUBOTA
CYLINDERS 3
ENGINE HP 25
COOLING .... AIR
FUEL .... D
SPEEDS .... VARIABLE
TRANSMISSION .... HYDRO
STEERING .... ZERO
BLADE CLUTCH .... ELECTRIC
STANDARD DECK .... 60"
WEIGHT .... 1,165 LBS.
MSRP $19,090

OPTIONS

52" DECK
BAGGER

RETAIL PRICING

YEAR	HIGH	LOW
2006	$5,202	$3,901
2007	$5,773	$4,330
2008	$6,415	$4,811
2009	$7,127	$5,345

FR27KC

YEARS MFRD 2006-2009
SERIES ..... FRONTRUNNER SERIES
ENGINE ...... KOHLER COMMAND
CYLINDERS 2
ENGINE HP 27
COOLING .... AIR
FUEL .... G
SPEEDS .... VARIABLE
TRANSMISSION .... HYDRO
STEERING .... ZERO
BLADE CLUTCH .... ELECTRIC
STANDARD DECK .... 60"
WEIGHT .... 1,010 LBS.
MSRP $14,650

OPTIONS

52" DECK
BAGGER

RETAIL PRICING

YEAR	HIGH	LOW
2006	$3,897	$2,923
2007	$4,328	$3,246
2008	$4,807	$3,605
2009	$5,337	$4,003

FR31BV

YEARS MFRD 2007-2009
SERIES ..... FRONTRUNNER SERIES
ENGINE .... VANGUARD
CYLINDERS 2
ENGINE HP 31
COOLING .... AIR
FUEL .... G
SPEEDS .... VARIABLE
TRANSMISSION .... HYDRO
STEERING .... ZERO
BLADE CLUTCH .... ELECTRIC
STANDARD DECK .... 72"
WEIGHT .... 1,040 LBS.
MSRP $15,649

OPTIONS

52" DECK
60" DECK
BAGGER

RETAIL PRICING

YEAR	HIGH	LOW
2007	$4,623	$3,467
2008	$5,135	$3,851
2009	$5,703	$4,277

LAS23KC524

YEARS MFRD 2006-2006
SERIES LAZER Z ADVANTAGE SERIES
ENGINE ...... KOHLER COMMAND
CYLINDERS 2
ENGINE HP 23
COOLING .... AIR
FUEL .... G
SPEEDS .... VARIABLE
TRANSMISSION .... HYDRO
STEERING .... ZERO
WEIGHT .... 1,085 LBS.

LAS25KC604

YEARS MFRD 2006-2008
SERIES LAZER Z ADVANTAGE SERIES
ENGINE ...... KOHLER COMMAND
CYLINDERS 2
ENGINE HP 25
COOLING .... AIR
FUEL .... G
SPEEDS .... VARIABLE
TRANSMISSION .... HYDRO
STEERING .... ZERO
BLADE CLUTCH .... ELECTRIC
STANDARD DECK .... 60"
WEIGHT .... 1,126 LBS.
MSRP $9,212

RETAIL PRICING

YEAR	HIGH	LOW
2008	$5,236	$3,927

LAS28KA524

YEARS MFRD 2008-2008
SERIES LAZER Z ADVANTAGE SERIES
ENGINE .... KAWASAKI
CYLINDERS 2
ENGINE HP 28
COOLING .... AIR
FUEL .... G
SPEEDS .... VARIABLE
TRANSMISSION .... HYDRO
STEERING .... ZERO
BLADE CLUTCH .... ELECTRIC
STANDARD DECK .... 52"
WEIGHT .... 1,130 LBS.
MSRP $9,434

RETAIL PRICING

YEAR	HIGH	LOW
2008	$5,364	$4,023

LAS28KA604

YEARS MFRD 2008-2008
SERIES LAZER Z ADVANTAGE SERIES
ENGINE .... KAWASAKI
CYLINDERS 2
ENGINE HP 28
COOLING .... AIR
FUEL .... G
SPEEDS .... VARIABLE
TRANSMISSION .... HYDRO
STEERING .... ZERO
BLADE CLUTCH .... ELECTRIC
STANDARD DECK .... 60"
WEIGHT .... 1,160 LBS.
MSRP $9,767

RETAIL PRICING

YEAR	HIGH	LOW
2008	$5,552	$4,164

LAS28KA604 LP

YEARS MFRD 2010-2010
SERIES ....
.... ADVANTAGE SERIES PROPANE
ENGINE .... KAWASAKI
CYLINDERS 2
ENGINE HP 28
COOLING .... AIR
SPEEDS .... VARIABLE
TRANSMISSION .... HYDRO
STEERING .... ZERO
BLADE CLUTCH .... ELECTRIC
WEIGHT .... 1,270 LBS.

LAS28KA724

YEARS MFRD 2008-2008
SERIES LAZER Z ADVANTAGE SERIES
ENGINE .... KAWASAKI
CYLINDERS 2
ENGINE HP 28
COOLING .... AIR
FUEL .... G
SPEEDS .... VARIABLE
TRANSMISSION .... HYDRO
STEERING .... ZERO
BLADE CLUTCH .... ELECTRIC
STANDARD DECK .... 72"
WEIGHT .... 1,220 LBS.
MSRP $10,211

RETAIL PRICING

YEAR	HIGH	LOW
2008	$5,805	$4,353

LCT18BV483

YEARS MFRD 2006-2008
SERIES .... LAZER Z CT SERIES
ENGINE .... B&S VANGUARD
CYLINDERS 2
ENGINE HP 18
COOLING .... AIR
FUEL .... G
SPEEDS .... VARIABLE
TRANSMISSION .... HYDRO
STEERING .... ZERO
BLADE CLUTCH .... ELECTRIC
WEIGHT .... 874 LBS.

OPTIONS

B&S 21E
B&S 23E

LCT21BV523

YEARS MFRD 2008-2008
SERIES .... LAZER Z CT SERIES
ENGINE .... VANGUARD
CYLINDERS 2
ENGINE HP 21
COOLING .... AIR
FUEL .... G
SPEEDS .... VARIABLE
TRANSMISSION .... HYDRO
STEERING .... ZERO
BLADE CLUTCH .... ELECTRIC
WEIGHT .... 887 LBS.

LCT23BV603

YEARS MFRD 2008-2008
SERIES .... LAZER Z CT SERIES
ENGINE .... VANGUARD
CYLINDERS 2

ENGINE HP 23
COOLING . . . . . AIR
FUEL . . . . . G
SPEEDS . . . . . VARIABLE
TRANSMISSION . . . . . HYDRO
STEERING . . . . . ZERO
BLADE CLUTCH . . . . . ELECTRIC
WEIGHT . . . . . 978 LBS.

LCT4418BV

YEARS MFRD 2005-2005
SERIES . . . . . LAZER Z CT SERIES
ENGINE . . . . . B&S
CYLINDERS 2
ENGINE HP 18
COOLING . . . . . AIR
FUEL . . . . . G
SPEEDS . . . . . VARIABLE
TRANSMISSION . . . . . HYDRO
STEERING . . . . . ZERO
BLADE CLUTCH . . . . . ELECTRIC
STANDARD DECK . . . . . 44"
WEIGHT . . . . . 880 LBS.
MSRP $5,993

OPTIONS

2P ROPS
56" BLADE
BAGGER

SERIAL NUMBERS

YEAR	BEGINNING NO.
2005	510000

RETAIL PRICING

YEAR	HIGH	LOW
2005	$1,517	$1,138

LCT4418KC

YEARS MFRD 2004-2004
SERIES . . . . . LAZER Z CT SERIES
ENGINE . . . . . KOHLER COMMAND
CYLINDERS 1
ENGINE HP 18
COOLING . . . . . AIR
FUEL . . . . . G
SPEEDS . . . . . VARIABLE
TRANSMISSION . . . . . HYDRO
STEERING . . . . . ZERO
BLADE CLUTCH . . . . . ELECTRIC
PTO . . . . . YES
STANDARD DECK . . . . . 44"
WEIGHT . . . . . 877 LBS.
MSRP $5,882

OPTIONS

BAGGER

SERIAL NUMBERS

YEAR	BEGINNING NO.
2004	440000

RETAIL PRICING

YEAR	HIGH	LOW
2004	$1,294	$970

LCT4818BV

YEARS MFRD 2005-2008
SERIES . . . . . LAZER Z CT SERIES
ENGINE . . . . . B&S
CYLINDERS 2
ENGINE HP 18
COOLING . . . . . AIR
FUEL . . . . . G
SPEEDS . . . . . VARIABLE
TRANSMISSION . . . . . HYDRO
STEERING . . . . . ZERO
BLADE CLUTCH . . . . . ELECTRIC
STANDARD DECK . . . . . 48"
WEIGHT . . . . . 910 LBS.
MSRP $6,792

OPTIONS

2 POST ROPS
56" BLADE
BAGGER

SERIAL NUMBERS

YEAR	BEGINNING NO.
2005	510000

RETAIL PRICING

YEAR	HIGH	LOW
2005	$1,472	$1,104
2006	$1,624	$1,218
2007	$1,793	$1,345
2008	$1,982	$1,486

LCT4818KC

YEARS MFRD 2004-2004
SERIES . . . . . LAZER Z CT SERIES
ENGINE . . . . . KOHLER
CYLINDERS 1
ENGINE HP 18
COOLING . . . . . AIR
FUEL . . . . . G
SPEEDS . . . . . VARIABLE
TRANSMISSION . . . . . HYDRO
STEERING . . . . . ZERO
BLADE CLUTCH . . . . . ELECTRIC
PTO . . . . . YES
STANDARD DECK . . . . . 48"
WEIGHT . . . . . 907 LBS.
MSRP $6,104

OPTIONS

BAGGER

RETAIL PRICING

YEAR	HIGH	LOW
2004	$1,245	$933

LCT4819KA

YEARS MFRD 2004-2004
SERIES . . . . . LAZER Z CT SERIES
ENGINE . . . . . KAWASAKI V-TWIN
CYLINDERS 2
ENGINE HP 19
COOLING . . . . . AIR
FUEL . . . . . G
SPEEDS . . . . . VARIABLE
TRANSMISSION . . . . . HYDRO
STEERING . . . . . ZERO
BLADE CLUTCH . . . . . ELECTRIC
PTO . . . . . YES
STANDARD DECK . . . . . 48"
WEIGHT . . . . . 907 LBS.
MSRP $6,437

OPTIONS

BAGGER

SERIAL NUMBERS

YEAR	BEGINNING NO.
2004	440000

RETAIL PRICING

YEAR	HIGH	LOW
2004	$1,300	$975

LCT5218BV

YEARS MFRD 2005-2005
SERIES . . . . . LAZER Z CT SERIES
ENGINE . . . . . B&S
CYLINDERS 2
ENGINE HP 18
COOLING . . . . . AIR
FUEL . . . . . G
SPEEDS . . . . . VARIABLE
TRANSMISSION . . . . . HYDRO
STEERING . . . . . ZERO
BLADE CLUTCH . . . . . ELECTRIC
STANDARD DECK . . . . . 52"
WEIGHT . . . . . 970 LBS.
MSRP $6,659

OPTIONS

2P ROPS
56" BLADE
BAGGER

SERIAL NUMBERS

YEAR	BEGINNING NO.
2005	510000

RETAIL PRICING

YEAR	HIGH	LOW
2005	$1,524	$1,143

LCT5219KA

YEARS MFRD 2004-2004
SERIES . . . . . LAZER Z CT SERIES
ENGINE . . . . . KAWASAKI V-TWIN
CYLINDERS 2
ENGINE HP 19
COOLING . . . . . AIR
FUEL . . . . . G
SPEEDS . . . . . VARIABLE
TRANSMISSION . . . . . HYDRO
STEERING . . . . . ZERO
BLADE CLUTCH . . . . . ELECTRIC
STANDARD DECK . . . . . 52"
WEIGHT . . . . . 968 LBS.
MSRP $6,659

OPTIONS

BAGGER

SERIAL NUMBERS

YEAR	BEGINNING NO.
2004	440000

RETAIL PRICING

YEAR	HIGH	LOW
2004	$1,346	$1,009

LHP19KA465

YEARS MFRD 2006-2008
SERIES . . . . . LAZER Z HP SERIES
ENGINE . . . . . KAWASAKI
CYLINDERS 2
ENGINE HP 19
COOLING . . . . . AIR
FUEL . . . . . G
SPEEDS . . . . . VARIABLE
TRANSMISSION . . . . . HYDRO
STEERING . . . . . ZERO
STANDARD DECK . . . . . 46"
WEIGHT . . . . . 1,080 LBS.
MSRP $7,769

OPTIONS

50" DECK

RETAIL PRICING

YEAR	HIGH	LOW
2006	$1,957	$1,468
2007	$2,173	$1,629
2008	$2,413	$1,810

LHP20KC505

YEARS MFRD 2006-2006
SERIES . . . . . LAZER Z HP SERIES
ENGINE . . . . . KOHLER
CYLINDERS 2
ENGINE HP 20
COOLING . . . . . AIR
FUEL . . . . . G
SPEEDS . . . . . VARIABLE
TRANSMISSION . . . . . HYDRO
STEERING . . . . . ZERO
BLADE CLUTCH . . . . . ELECTRIC
STANDARD DECK . . . . . 50"
WEIGHT . . . . . 1,135 LBS.
MSRP $8,324

OPTIONS

KAWASAKI 23E
KOHLER 27E

RETAIL PRICING

YEAR	HIGH	LOW
2006	$2,154	$1,616

LHP23KA465

YEARS MFRD 2008-2008
SERIES . . . . . LAZER Z HP SERIES
ENGINE . . . . . KAWASAKI
CYLINDERS 2
ENGINE HP 23
COOLING . . . . . AIR
FUEL . . . . . G
SPEEDS . . . . . VARIABLE
TRANSMISSION . . . . . HYDRO
STEERING . . . . . ZERO
BLADE CLUTCH . . . . . ELECTRIC
STANDARD DECK . . . . . 46"
WEIGHT . . . . . 1,080 LBS.
MSRP $8,657

RETAIL PRICING

YEAR	HIGH	LOW
2008	$4,922	$3,691

LHP23KA505

YEARS MFRD 2006-2008
SERIES . . . . . LAZER Z HP SERIES
ENGINE . . . . . KAWASAKI
CYLINDERS 2
ENGINE HP 23
COOLING . . . . . AIR
FUEL . . . . . G

EX MARK

SPEEDS ... VARIABLE
TRANSMISSION ... HYDRO
STEERING ... ZERO
BLADE CLUTCH ... ELECTRIC
STANDARD DECK ... 50"
WEIGHT ... 1,135 LBS.
MSRP ... $9,212

RETAIL PRICING

YEAR	HIGH	LOW
2006	$2,319	$1,739
2007	$2,578	$1,934
2008	$2,864	$2,148

LHP23KA565

YEARS MFRD ... 2006-2008
SERIES ... LAZER Z HP SERIES
ENGINE ... KAWASAKI
CYLINDERS ... 2
ENGINE HP ... 23
COOLING ... AIR
FUEL ... G
SPEEDS ... VARIABLE
TRANSMISSION ... HYDRO
STEERING ... ZERO
STANDARD DECK ... 56"
WEIGHT ... 1,190 LBS.
MSRP ... $9,545

OPTIONS

KOHLER 27E

RETAIL PRICING

YEAR	HIGH	LOW
2006	$2,405	$1,804
2007	$2,670	$2,002
2008	$3,005	$2,254

LHP27KC505

YEARS MFRD ... 2006-2008
SERIES ... LAZER Z HP SERIES
ENGINE ... KOHLER
CYLINDERS ... 2
ENGINE HP ... 27
COOLING ... AIR
FUEL ... G
SPEEDS ... VARIABLE
TRANSMISSION ... HYDRO
STEERING ... ZERO
BLADE CLUTCH ... ELECTRIC
STANDARD DECK ... 50"
WEIGHT ... 1,135 LBS.
MSRP ... $9,767

RETAIL PRICING

YEAR	HIGH	LOW
2006	$2,458	$1,843
2007	$2,733	$2,050
2008	$3,034	$2,276

LHP27KC565

YEARS MFRD ... 2006-2008
SERIES ... LAZER Z HP SERIES
ENGINE ... KOHLER COMMAND
CYLINDERS ... 2
ENGINE HP ... 27
COOLING ... AIR
FUEL ... G

SPEEDS ... VARIABLE
TRANSMISSION ... HYDRO
STEERING ... ZERO
BLADE CLUTCH ... ELECTRIC
STANDARD DECK ... 56"
WEIGHT ... 1,190 LBS.
MSRP ... $10,100

RETAIL PRICING

YEAR	HIGH	LOW
2006	$2,545	$1,909
2007	$2,824	$2,118
2008	$3,129	$2,347

LHP4417KA

YEARS MFRD ... 1998-2004
SERIES ... LAZER Z HP SERIES
ENGINE ... KAWASAKI V-TWIN
CYLINDERS ... 2
ENGINE HP ... 17
COOLING ... AIR
FUEL ... G
SPEEDS ... VARIABLE
TRANSMISSION ... HYDRO
STEERING ... ZERO
PTO ... YES
STANDARD DECK ... 44"
WEIGHT ... 963 LBS.
MSRP ... $7,214

OPTIONS

SUS SEAT

SERIAL NUMBERS

YEAR	BEGINNING NO.
1998	160000
1999	190000
2000	220000
2004	440000

RETAIL PRICING

YEAR	HIGH	LOW
1998	$1,034	$775
1999	$1,148	$861
2000	$1,275	$956
2001	$1,417	$1,063
2002	$1,571	$1,178
2003	$1,745	$1,309
2004	$1,940	$1,455

LHP4419KA

YEARS MFRD ... 2000-2005
SERIES ... LAZER Z HP SERIES
ENGINE ... KAWASAKI
CYLINDERS ... 2
ENGINE HP ... 19
COOLING ... AIR
FUEL ... G
SPEEDS ... VARIABLE
TRANSMISSION ... HYDRO
STEERING ... ZERO
BLADE CLUTCH ... ELECTRIC
STANDARD DECK ... 44"
WEIGHT ... 963 LBS.
MSRP ... $7,325

OPTIONS

2 POST ROPS
BAG & FAN
SUS SEAT

SERIAL NUMBERS

YEAR	BEGINNING NO.
2000	220000
2005	510000

RETAIL PRICING

YEAR	HIGH	LOW
2000	$1,152	$864
2001	$1,278	$958
2002	$1,422	$1,066
2003	$1,577	$1,183
2004	$1,753	$1,315
2005	$1,945	$1,459

LHP4420KC

YEARS MFRD ... 2004-2004
SERIES ... LAZER Z HP SERIES
ENGINE ... KOHLER COMMAND SP
CYLINDERS ... 2
ENGINE HP ... 20
COOLING ... AIR
FUEL ... G
SPEEDS ... VARIABLE
TRANSMISSION ... HYDRO
STEERING ... ZERO
PTO ... YES
STANDARD DECK ... 44"
WEIGHT ... 963 LBS.
MSRP ... $7,547

OPTIONS

SUS SEAT

SERIAL NUMBERS

YEAR	BEGINNING NO.
2004	440000

RETAIL PRICING

YEAR	HIGH	LOW
2004	$1,706	$1,280

LHP4819KA

YEARS MFRD ... 1999-2005
SERIES ... LAZER Z HP SERIES
ENGINE ... KAWASAKI
CYLINDERS ... 2
ENGINE HP ... 19
COOLING ... AIR
FUEL ... G
SPEEDS ... VARIABLE
TRANSMISSION ... HYDRO
STEERING ... ZERO
BLADE CLUTCH ... ELECTRIC
STANDARD DECK ... 48"
WEIGHT ... 983 LBS.
MSRP ... $7,658

OPTIONS

2 POST ROPS
BAG & FAN
SUS SEAT

SERIAL NUMBERS

YEAR	BEGINNING NO.
1999	190000
2005	510000

RETAIL PRICING

YEAR	HIGH	LOW
1999	$1,034	$775
2000	$1,148	$861
2001	$1,275	$956
2002	$1,417	$1,063
2003	$1,571	$1,178
2004	$1,745	$1,309
2005	$1,938	$1,454

LHP4820KC

YEARS MFRD ... 2000-2004
SERIES ... LAZER Z HP SERIES
ENGINE ... KOHLER COMMAND SP
CYLINDERS ... 2
ENGINE HP ... 20
COOLING ... AIR
FUEL ... G
SPEEDS ... VARIABLE
TRANSMISSION ... HYDRO
STEERING ... ZERO
PTO ... YES
STANDARD DECK ... 48"
WEIGHT ... 983 LBS.
MSRP ... $7,991

OPTIONS

2 POST ROPS
BAG & FAN
SUS SEAT

SERIAL NUMBERS

YEAR	BEGINNING NO.
2000	220000
2005	510000

RETAIL PRICING

YEAR	HIGH	LOW
2000	$1,281	$961
2001	$1,422	$1,066
2002	$1,581	$1,186
2003	$1,754	$1,316
2004	$1,967	$1,475

LHP4821KA

YEARS MFRD ... 2000-2004
SERIES ... LAZER A HP SERIES
ENGINE ... KAWASAKI V-TWIN
CYLINDERS ... 2
ENGINE HP ... 21
COOLING ... AIR
FUEL ... G
SPEEDS ... VARIABLE
TRANSMISSION ... HYDRO
STEERING ... ZERO
PTO ... YES
STANDARD DECK ... 48"
WEIGHT ... 983 LBS.
MSRP ... $7,991

OPTIONS

SUS SEAT

SERIAL NUMBERS

YEAR	BEGINNING NO.
2000	220000
2004	440000

RETAIL PRICING

YEAR	HIGH	LOW
2000	$1,282	$961
2001	$1,422	$1,066
2002	$1,581	$1,186
2003	$1,754	$1,316
2004	$1,948	$1,461

LHP4823KA

YEARS MFRD 2005-2005
SERIES. . . . . . . LAZER Z HP SERIES
ENGINE . . . . KAWASAKI
CYLINDERS. 2
ENGINE HP 23
COOLING . . . . AIR
FUEL . . . . G
SPEEDS . . . . VARIABLE
TRANSMISSION . . . . .HYDRO
STEERING. . . . . ZERO
BLADE CLUTCH . . . . ELECTRIC
STANDARD DECK . . . . 48"
WEIGHT . . . . 983 LBS.
MSRP. $8,324

OPTIONS

2P ROPS
BAG & FAN

SERIAL NUMBERS

YEAR	BEGINNING NO.
2005	510000

RETAIL PRICING

YEAR	HIGH	LOW
2005	$2,081	$1,560

LHP5220KC

YEARS MFRD 2000-2005
SERIES. . . . . . . LAZER Z HP SERIES
ENGINE . . . . . KOHLER COMMAND
CYLINDERS. 2
ENGINE HP 20
COOLING . . . . AIR
FUEL . . . . G
SPEEDS . . . . VARIABLE
TRANSMISSION . . . . .HYDRO
STEERING. . . . . ZERO
BLADE CLUTCH . . . . ELECTRIC
STANDARD DECK . . . . 52"
WEIGHT . . . . 1,103 LBS.
MSRP. $8,324

OPTIONS

2P ROPS
BAG & FAN
SUS SEAT

SERIAL NUMBERS

YEAR	BEGINNING NO.
2000	220000
2005	510000

RETAIL PRICING

YEAR	HIGH	LOW
2000	$1,230	$922
2001	$1,368	$1,026
2002	$1,517	$1,138
2003	$1,686	$1,264
2004	$1,873	$1,405
2005	$2,081	$1,560

LHP5223KA

YEARS MFRD 2000-2005
SERIES. . . . . . . LAZER Z HP SERIES
ENGINE . . . . KAWASAKI V-TWIN
CYLINDERS. 2
ENGINE HP 23
COOLING . . . . AIR
FUEL . . . . G
SPEEDS . . . . VARIABLE
TRANSMISSION . . . . .HYDRO
STEERING. . . . . ZERO
BLADE CLUTCH . . . . ELECTRIC
PTO . . . . YES
STANDARD DECK . . . . 52"
WEIGHT . . . . 1,103 LBS.
MSRP. $8,879

OPTIONS

2 POST ROPS
BAG & FAN
SUS SEAT

SERIAL NUMBERS

YEAR	BEGINNING NO.
2000	220000
2004	440000
2005	510000

RETAIL PRICING

YEAR	HIGH	LOW
2000	$1,281	$961
2001	$1,422	$1,066
2002	$1,580	$1,185
2003	$1,752	$1,314
2004	$1,954	$1,466
2005	$2,164	$1,623

LHP5223KC

YEARS MFRD 2000-2005
SERIES. . . . . . . LAZER Z HP SERIES
ENGINE . . . .KOHLER COMMAND SP
CYLINDERS. 2
ENGINE HP 23
COOLING . . . . AIR
FUEL . . . . G
SPEEDS . . . . VARIABLE
TRANSMISSION . . . . .HYDRO
STEERING. . . . . ZERO
BLADE CLUTCH . . . . ELECTRIC
PTO . . . . YES
STANDARD DECK . . . . 52"
WEIGHT . . . . 1,103 LBS.
MSRP. $8,546

OPTIONS

2 POST ROPS
BAG & FAN
SUS SEAT

SERIAL NUMBERS

YEAR	BEGINNING NO.
2000	220000
2004	440000
2005	510000

RETAIL PRICING

YEAR	HIGH	LOW
2000	$1,232	$924
2001	$1,367	$1,025
2002	$1,519	$1,139
2003	$1,689	$1,266
2004	$1,887	$1,415
2005	$2,083	$1,562

LXS25KD605

YEARS MFRD 2006-2009
SERIES. . . . . . . LAZER Z XS SERIES
ENGINE . . . . KUBOTA
CYLINDERS. 3
ENGINE HP 25
COOLING . . . . LIQUID
FUEL . . . . D
SPEEDS . . . . VARIABLE
TRANSMISSION . . . . .HYDRO
STEERING. . . . . ZERO
BLADE CLUTCH . . . . ELECTRIC
STANDARD DECK . . . . 60"
WEIGHT . . . . 1,610 LBS.
MSRP. $17,315

RETAIL PRICING

YEAR	HIGH	LOW
2006	$5,551	$4,163
2007	$6,167	$4,625
2008	$6,847	$5,135
2009	$7,603	$5,702

LXS25KD665

YEARS MFRD 2006-2009
SERIES. . . . . . . LAZER Z XS SERIES
ENGINE . . . . KUBOTA
CYLINDERS. 3
ENGINE HP 25
COOLING . . . . LIQUID
FUEL . . . . D
SPEEDS . . . . VARIABLE
TRANSMISSION . . . . .HYDRO
STEERING. . . . . ZERO
BLADE CLUTCH . . . . ELECTRIC
STANDARD DECK . . . . 66"
WEIGHT . . . . 1,660 LBS.
MSRP. $17,648

RETAIL PRICING

YEAR	HIGH	LOW
2006	$5,657	$4,242
2007	$6,287	$4,715
2008	$6,978	$5,233
2009	$7,750	$5,812

LXS25KD725

YEARS MFRD 2006-2009
SERIES. . . . . . . LAZER Z XS SERIES
ENGINE . . . . KUBOTA
CYLINDERS. 3
ENGINE HP 25
COOLING . . . . LIQUID
FUEL . . . . D
SPEEDS . . . . VARIABLE
TRANSMISSION . . . . .HYDRO
STEERING. . . . . ZERO
BLADE CLUTCH . . . . ELECTRIC
STANDARD DECK . . . . 72"
WEIGHT . . . . 1,710 LBS.
MSRP. $18,203

RETAIL PRICING

YEAR	HIGH	LOW
2006	$5,836	$4,377
2007	$6,483	$4,862
2008	$7,199	$5,399
2009	$7,994	$5,995

LXS29LKA605

YEARS MFRD 2006-2008
SERIES. . . . . . . LAZER Z XS SERIES
ENGINE . . . . KAWASAKI
CYLINDERS. 2
ENGINE HP 29
COOLING . . . . LIQUID
FUEL . . . . G
SPEEDS . . . . VARIABLE
TRANSMISSION . . . . .HYDRO
STEERING. . . . . ZERO
STANDARD DECK . . . . 60"
WEIGHT . . . . 1,510 LBS.
MSRP. $13,874

OPTIONS

KUBOTA DIESEL 25E
VANGUARD 31E

RETAIL PRICING

YEAR	HIGH	LOW
2006	$4,538	$3,404
2007	$5,041	$3,781
2008	$5,598	$4,198

LXS29LKA665

YEARS MFRD 2006-2007
SERIES. . . . . . . LAZER Z XS SERIES
ENGINE . . . . KAWASAKI
CYLINDERS. 2
ENGINE HP 29
COOLING . . . . LIQUID
FUEL . . . . G
SPEEDS . . . . VARIABLE
TRANSMISSION . . . . .HYDRO
STEERING. . . . . ZERO
STANDARD DECK . . . . 66"
WEIGHT . . . . 1,560 LBS.
MSRP. $13,763

OPTIONS

B&S VANGUARD 31E
KOHLER DIESEL 25E

RETAIL PRICING

YEAR	HIGH	LOW
2006	$4,610	$3,457
2007	$5,121	$3,840

LXS29LKA725

YEARS MFRD 2006-2008
SERIES. . . . . . . LAZER Z XS SERIES
ENGINE . . . . KAWASAKI
CYLINDERS. 2
ENGINE HP 29
COOLING . . . . LIQUID
FUEL . . . . G
SPEEDS . . . . VARIABLE
TRANSMISSION . . . . .HYDRO
STEERING. . . . . ZERO
STANDARD DECK . . . . 72"
WEIGHT . . . . 1,610 LBS.
MSRP. $14,429

OPTIONS

B&S VANGUARD 31E
KOHLER DIESEL 25E

RETAIL PRICING

YEAR	HIGH	LOW
2006	$4,720	$3,540
2007	$5,242	$3,932
2008	$5,822	$4,367

EX MARK

LXS35BV605

YEARS MFRD	2008-2010
SERIES	LAZER Z XS SERIES
ENGINE	VANGUARD
CYLINDERS	2
ENGINE HP	35
COOLING	AIR
FUEL	G
SPEEDS	VARIABLE
TRANSMISSION	HYDRO
STEERING	ZERO
BLADE CLUTCH	ELECTRIC
STANDARD DECK	60"
WEIGHT	1,510 LBS.
MSRP	$12,810

RETAIL PRICING

YEAR	HIGH	LOW
2008	$7,193	$5,395
2009	$7,303	$5,477
2010	$7,322	$5,491

LXS35BV665

YEARS MFRD	2008-2010
SERIES	LAZER Z XS SERIES
ENGINE	VANGUARD
CYLINDERS	2
ENGINE HP	35
COOLING	AIR
FUEL	G
SPEEDS	VARIABLE
TRANSMISSION	HYDRO
STEERING	ZERO
BLADE CLUTCH	ELECTRIC
STANDARD DECK	66"
WEIGHT	1,560 LBS.
MSRP	$12,920

RETAIL PRICING

YEAR	HIGH	LOW
2008	$7,320	$5,490
2009	$7,413	$5,560
2010	$7,445	$5,584

LXS35BV725

YEARS MFRD	2006-2009
SERIES	LAZER Z XS SERIES
ENGINE	VANGUARD
CYLINDERS	2
ENGINE HP	35
COOLING	AIR
FUEL	G
SPEEDS	VARIABLE
TRANSMISSION	HYDRO
STEERING	ZERO
BLADE CLUTCH	ELECTRIC
STANDARD DECK	72"
WEIGHT	1,610 LBS.
MSRP	$15,539

RETAIL PRICING

YEAR	HIGH	LOW
2006	$4,981	$3,736
2007	$5,534	$4,151
2008	$6,144	$4,608
2009	$6,823	$5,117

LZ18KC523

YEARS MFRD	1997-1999
SERIES	LAZER Z SERIES
ENGINE	KOHLER COMMAND
ENGINE HP	18
COOLING	AIR
FUEL	G
SPEEDS	VARIABLE
TRANSMISSION	DUAL HYDRO
STEERING	ZERO
STANDARD DECK	52"
MSRP	$7,810

SERIAL NUMBERS

YEAR	BEGINNING NO.
1997	130000
1998	160000
1999	190000

RETAIL PRICING

YEAR	HIGH	LOW
1997	$952	$714
1998	$1,050	$787
1999	$1,158	$869

LZ20KC524AS

YEARS MFRD	2004-2004
SERIES	LAZER Z ADVANTAGE SERIES
ENGINE	KOHLER COMMAND SP
CYLINDERS	2
ENGINE HP	20
COOLING	AIR
FUEL	G
SPEEDS	VARIABLE
TRANSMISSION	DUAL HYDRO
STEERING	ZERO
PTO	YES
STANDARD DECK	52"
WEIGHT	1,085 LBS.
MSRP	$7,991

OPTIONS

ROPS

VAC & BAG

SERIAL NUMBERS

YEAR	BEGINNING NO.
2004	440000

RETAIL PRICING

YEAR	HIGH	LOW
2004	$1,771	$1,328

LZ22KC52

YEARS MFRD	1995-1996
SERIES	LAZER Z SERIES
ENGINE	KOHLER COMMAND
ENGINE HP	22
COOLING	AIR
FUEL	G
TRANSMISSION	HYDRO
STEERING	ZERO
STANDARD DECK	52"
MSRP	$8,480

OPTIONS

60" DECK

SERIAL NUMBERS

YEAR	BEGINNING NO.
1996	115000

RETAIL PRICING

YEAR	HIGH	LOW
1995	$796	$597
1996	$895	$671

LZ22KC523

YEARS MFRD	1997-1999
SERIES	LAZER Z SERIES
ENGINE	KOHLER COMMAND
ENGINE HP	22
COOLING	AIR
FUEL	G
TRANSMISSION	DUAL HYDRO
STEERING	ZERO
STANDARD DECK	52"
MSRP	$8,480

SERIAL NUMBERS

YEAR	BEGINNING NO.
1997	130000
1998	160000
1999	190000

RETAIL PRICING

YEAR	HIGH	LOW
1997	$1,032	$774
1998	$1,140	$855
1999	$1,258	$944

LZ22KC603

YEARS MFRD	1995-1996
SERIES	LAZER Z SERIES
ENGINE	KOHLER COMMAND
ENGINE HP	22
COOLING	AIR
FUEL	G
TRANSMISSION	HYDRO
STEERING	ZERO
STANDARD DECK	60"
MSRP	$8,700

SERIAL NUMBERS

YEAR	BEGINNING NO.
1995	130000
1996	160000

RETAIL PRICING

YEAR	HIGH	LOW
1995	$1,055	$792
1996	$1,171	$878

LZ22LKA523

YEARS MFRD	1999-2000
SERIES	LAZER Z SERIES
ENGINE	KAWASAKI
ENGINE HP	22
COOLING	LIQUID
FUEL	G
TRANSMISSION	HYDRO
STEERING	ZERO
STANDARD DECK	52"
MSRP	$9,590

OPTIONS

SUS SEAT

SERIAL NUMBERS

YEAR	BEGINNING NO.
1999	190000
2000	220000

RETAIL PRICING

YEAR	HIGH	LOW
1999	$1,890	$1,418
2000	$2,005	$1,504

LZ22LKA604

YEARS MFRD	1999-2000
SERIES	LAZER Z SERIES
ENGINE	KAWASAKI
ENGINE HP	22
COOLING	LIQUID
FUEL	G
TRANSMISSION	HYDRO
STEERING	ZERO
STANDARD DECK	60"
MSRP	$9,930

OPTIONS

SUS SEAT

SERIAL NUMBERS

YEAR	BEGINNING NO.
1999	190000
2000	220000

RETAIL PRICING

YEAR	HIGH	LOW
1999	$1,975	$1,481
2000	$2,093	$1,570

LZ23KA604

YEARS MFRD	2001-2001
SERIES	LAZER Z SERIES
ENGINE	KAWASAKI
ENGINE HP	23
FUEL	G
TRANSMISSION	HYDRO
STEERING	ZERO
STANDARD DECK	60"
MSRP	$8,920

RETAIL PRICING

YEAR	HIGH	LOW
2001	$1,487	$1,115

LZ23KC523

YEARS MFRD	2000-2000
SERIES	LAZER Z SERIES
ENGINE	KOHLER COMMAND
ENGINE HP	23
COOLING	AIR
FUEL	G
SPEEDS	VARIABLE
TRANSMISSION	HYDRO
STEERING	ZERO
STANDARD DECK	52"
MSRP	$8,480

OPTIONS

60" DECK

SUS SEAT

SERIAL NUMBERS

YEAR	BEGINNING NO.
2000	220000

RETAIL PRICING

YEAR	HIGH	LOW
2000	$1,333	$1,000

LZ23KC524AS
YEARS MFRD 2005-2006
SERIES LAZER Z ADVANTAGE SERIES
ENGINE . . . . . . KOHLER COMMAND
CYLINDERS. 2
ENGINE HP 23
COOLING . . . . AIR
FUEL . . . . G
SPEEDS . . . . VARIABLE
TRANSMISSION . . . . HYDRO
STEERING. . . . . ZERO
BLADE CLUTCH . . . . ELECTRIC
STANDARD DECK . . . . 52"
WEIGHT . . . . 1,097 LBS.
MSRP. $8,768

OPTIONS
2 POST ROPS
BAG & FAN

SERIAL NUMBERS
YEAR	BEGINNING NO.
2005	510000

RETAIL PRICING
YEAR	HIGH	LOW
2005	$1,996	$1,497
2006	$2,217	$1,663

LZ23KC604
YEARS MFRD 2001-2007
SERIES. . . . . LAZER Z SERIES
ENGINE . . . . . . KOHLER COMMAND
CYLINDERS. 2
ENGINE HP 23
COOLING . . . . AIR
FUEL . . . . G
SPEEDS . . . . VARIABLE
TRANSMISSION . . . . HYDRO
STEERING. . . . . ZERO
BLADE CLUTCH . . . . ELECTRIC
STANDARD DECK . . . . 60"
WEIGHT . . . . 1,038 LBS.
MSRP. $10,322

OPTIONS
2 POST ROPS
BAG & FAN
SUS SEAT

SERIAL NUMBERS
YEAR	BEGINNING NO.
2004	440000
2005	510000

RETAIL PRICING
YEAR	HIGH	LOW
2001	$1,637	$1,227
2002	$1,818	$1,363
2003	$2,039	$1,530
2004	$2,242	$1,682
2005	$2,488	$1,866
2006	$2,764	$2,073
2007	$3,070	$2,303

LZ23KC604AS
YEARS MFRD 2004-2004
SERIES LAZER Z ADVANTAGE SERIES
ENGINE . . . KOHLER COMMAND SP
CYLINDERS. 2
ENGINE HP 23
COOLING . . . . AIR
FUEL . . . . G
SPEEDS . . . . VARIABLE
TRANSMISSION . . . . . DUAL HYDRO
STEERING. . . . . STANDARD
PTO . . . . YES
STANDARD DECK . . . . 60"
WEIGHT . . . . 1,126 LBS.
MSRP. $8,546

OPTIONS
ROPS
VAC & BAG

SERIAL NUMBERS
YEAR	BEGINNING NO.
2004	440000

RETAIL PRICING
YEAR	HIGH	LOW
2004	$1,894	$1,421

LZ23KC605
YEARS MFRD 2006-2007
SERIES. . . . . LAZER Z SERIES
ENGINE . . . . . . KOHLER COMMAND
CYLINDERS. 2
ENGINE HP 27
COOLING . . . . AIR
FUEL . . . . G
SPEEDS . . . . VARIABLE
TRANSMISSION . . . . HYDRO
STEERING. . . . . ZERO
WEIGHT . . . . 1,360 LBS.

OPTIONS
KOHLER 30E

LZ23LKA604
YEARS MFRD 2001-2001
SERIES. . . . . . . LAZER Z LIQ SERIES
ENGINE . . . . KAWASAKI
ENGINE HP 23
COOLING . . . . LIQUID
FUEL . . . . G
TRANSMISSION . . . . HYDRO
STEERING. . . . . ZERO
STANDARD DECK . . . . 60"
MSRP. $9,260

RETAIL PRICING
YEAR	HIGH	LOW
2001	$1,612	$1,209

LZ25KA604
YEARS MFRD 2002-2003
SERIES. . . . . LAZER Z SERIES
ENGINE . . . . KAWASAKI
ENGINE HP 25
FUEL . . . . G
TRANSMISSION . . . . HYDRO
STEERING. . . . . STANDARD
STANDARD DECK . . . . 60"
WEIGHT . . . . 1,031 LBS.
MSRP. $9,750

RETAIL PRICING
YEAR	HIGH	LOW
2002	$4,504	$3,378
2003	$4,783	$3,588

LZ25KC52
YEARS MFRD 1995-1996
SERIES. . . . . LAZER Z SERIES
ENGINE . . . . . . KOHLER COMMAND
ENGINE HP 25
COOLING . . . . AIR
FUEL . . . . G
TRANSMISSION . . . . HYDRO
STEERING. . . . . ZERO
STANDARD DECK . . . . 52"
MSRP. $8,920

SERIAL NUMBERS
YEAR	BEGINNING NO.
1996	115000

RETAIL PRICING
YEAR	HIGH	LOW
1995	$788	$591
1996	$876	$657

LZ25KC523
YEARS MFRD 1997-2000
SERIES. . . . . LAZER Z SERIES
ENGINE . . . . . . KOHLER COMMAND
ENGINE HP 25
COOLING . . . . AIR
FUEL . . . . G
TRANSMISSION . . . . . DUAL HYDRO
STEERING. . . . . ZERO
STANDARD DECK . . . . 52"
MSRP. $8,920

OPTIONS
60" DECK
72" DECK
SUS SEAT

SERIAL NUMBERS
YEAR	BEGINNING NO.
1997	130000
1998	160000
1999	190000
2000	220000

RETAIL PRICING
YEAR	HIGH	LOW
1997	$1,176	$882
1998	$1,305	$979
1999	$1,447	$1,086
2000	$1,610	$1,208

LZ25KC524
YEARS MFRD 2001-2005
SERIES. . . . . LAZER Z SERIES
ENGINE . . . . . . KOHLER COMMAND
CYLINDERS. 2
ENGINE HP 25
COOLING . . . . AIR
FUEL . . . . G
SPEEDS . . . . VARIABLE
TRANSMISSION . . . . HYDRO
STEERING. . . . . ZERO
BLADE CLUTCH . . . . ELECTRIC
STANDARD DECK . . . . 52"
WEIGHT . . . . 1,150 LBS.
MSRP. $9,656

OPTIONS
2 POST ROPS
BAG & FAN

SERIAL NUMBERS
YEAR	BEGINNING NO.
2005	510000

RETAIL PRICING
YEAR	HIGH	LOW
2001	$1,546	$1,160
2002	$1,707	$1,280
2003	$1,885	$1,413
2004	$2,081	$1,560
2005	$2,295	$1,721

LZ25KC60
YEARS MFRD 1995-1996
SERIES. . . . . LAZER Z SERIES
ENGINE . . . . . . KOHLER COMMAND
ENGINE HP 25
COOLING . . . . AIR
FUEL . . . . G
TRANSMISSION . . . . HYDRO
STEERING. . . . . ZERO
STANDARD DECK . . . . 60"
MSRP. $9,150

SERIAL NUMBERS
YEAR	BEGINNING NO.
1996	115000

RETAIL PRICING
YEAR	HIGH	LOW
1995	$786	$589
1996	$867	$650

LZ25KC603
YEARS MFRD 1997-1999
SERIES. . . . . LAZER Z SERIES
ENGINE . . . . . . KOHLER COMMAND
ENGINE HP 25
COOLING . . . . AIR
FUEL . . . . G
TRANSMISSION . . . . . DUAL HYDRO
STEERING. . . . . ZERO
STANDARD DECK . . . . 60"
MSRP. $9,260

SERIAL NUMBERS
YEAR	BEGINNING NO.
1997	130000
1998	160000

RETAIL PRICING
YEAR	HIGH	LOW
1997	$1,128	$846
1998	$1,245	$933
1999	$1,374	$1,030

LZ25KC604
YEARS MFRD 2001-2005
SERIES. . . . . LAZER Z SERIES
ENGINE . . . . . . KOHLER COMMAND
ENGINE HP 25
COOLING . . . . AIR
FUEL . . . . G
SPEEDS . . . . VARIABLE
TRANSMISSION . . . . HYDRO
STEERING. . . . . ZERO
BLADE CLUTCH . . . . ELECTRIC
STANDARD DECK . . . . 60"
WEIGHT . . . . 1,138 LBS.
MSRP. $9,767

OPTIONS

2 POST ROPS
BAG & FAN

SERIAL NUMBERS

YEAR	BEGINNING NO.
2005	510000

RETAIL PRICING

YEAR	HIGH	LOW
2001	$1,564	$1,173
2002	$1,727	$1,295
2003	$1,906	$1,430
2004	$2,104	$1,578
2005	$2,322	$1,741

LZ25KC604AS

YEARS MFRD 2005-2008
SERIES LAZER Z ADVANTAGE SERIES
ENGINE KOHLER COMMAND
CYLINDERS 2
ENGINE HP 25
COOLING AIR
FUEL G
SPEEDS VARIABLE
TRANSMISSION HYDRO
STEERING ZERO
BLADE CLUTCH ELECTRIC
STANDARD DECK 60"
WEIGHT 1,098 LBS.
MSRP $9,323

OPTIONS

2P ROPS
BAG & FAN

SERIAL NUMBERS

YEAR	BEGINNING NO.
2005	510000

RETAIL PRICING

YEAR	HIGH	LOW
2005	$2,020	$1,515
2006	$2,230	$1,672
2007	$2,701	$2,026
2008	$2,998	$2,248

LZ25KC724

YEARS MFRD 1999-1999
SERIES LAZER Z SERIES
ENGINE KOHLER COMMAND
ENGINE HP 25
FUEL G
STEERING ZERO
STANDARD DECK 72"
MSRP $9,590

SERIAL NUMBERS

YEAR	BEGINNING NO.
1999	190000

RETAIL PRICING

YEAR	HIGH	LOW
1999	$1,337	$1,003

LZ26KC604

YEARS MFRD 2000-2001
SERIES LAZER Z EFI SERIES
ENGINE KOHLER COMMAND
ENGINE HP 26
FUEL G
TRANSMISSION HYDRO
STEERING ZERO
STANDARD DECK 60"
WEIGHT 1,063 LBS.
MSRP $10,700

SERIAL NUMBERS

YEAR	BEGINNING NO.
2000	220000

RETAIL PRICING

YEAR	HIGH	LOW
2000	$1,568	$1,176
2001	$1,731	$1,298

LZ26KC724

YEARS MFRD 2000-2001
SERIES LAZER Z EFI SERIES
ENGINE KOHLER COMMAND
ENGINE HP 26
FUEL G
TRANSMISSION HYDRO
STEERING ZERO
STANDARD DECK 72"
WEIGHT 1,136 LBS.
MSRP $11,100

SERIAL NUMBERS

YEAR	BEGINNING NO.
2000	220000

RETAIL PRICING

YEAR	HIGH	LOW
2000	$1,627	$1,220
2001	$1,796	$1,347

LZ27DD604

YEARS MFRD 2001-2005
SERIES LAZER Z XP SERIES
ENGINE B&S DAIHATSU
CYLINDERS 3
ENGINE HP 27
COOLING LIQUID
FUEL D
SPEEDS VARIABLE
TRANSMISSION HYDRO
STEERING ZERO
BLADE CLUTCH ELECTRIC
STANDARD DECK 60"
WEIGHT 1,639 LBS.
MSRP $14,429

OPTIONS

2 POST ROPS
72" DECK
BAG & FAN

SERIAL NUMBERS

YEAR	BEGINNING NO.
2004	440000
2005	510000

RETAIL PRICING

YEAR	HIGH	LOW
2001	$2,312	$1,734
2002	$2,551	$1,913
2003	$2,816	$2,112
2004	$3,145	$2,359
2005	$3,440	$2,580

LZ27DD724

YEARS MFRD 2001-2005
SERIES LAZER Z XP SERIES
ENGINE B&S DAIHATSU
CYLINDERS 3
ENGINE HP 27
COOLING LIQUID
FUEL D
SPEEDS VARIABLE
TRANSMISSION HYDRO
STEERING ZERO
BLADE CLUTCH ELECTRIC
STANDARD DECK 72"
WEIGHT 1,657 LBS.
MSRP $13,499

RETAIL PRICING

YEAR	HIGH	LOW
2001	$6,277	$4,708
2002	$6,632	$4,974
2003	$6,910	$5,182
2004	$7,187	$5,390
2005	$7,632	$5,724

LZ27KC524

YEARS MFRD 2004-2005
SERIES LAZER Z SERIES
ENGINE KOHLER COMMAND SP
CYLINDERS 2
ENGINE HP 27
COOLING AIR
FUEL G
SPEEDS VARIABLE
TRANSMISSION HYDRO
STEERING ZERO
BLADE CLUTCH ELECTRIC
HYDRAULIC YES
PTO YES
STANDARD DECK 52"
WEIGHT 1,150 LBS.
MSRP $9,989

OPTIONS

2 POST ROPS
BAG & FAN

SERIAL NUMBERS

YEAR	BEGINNING NO.
2004	440000
2005	510000

RETAIL PRICING

YEAR	HIGH	LOW
2004	$2,152	$1,614
2005	$2,375	$1,781

LZ27KC604

YEARS MFRD 2004-2008
SERIES LAZER Z SERIES
ENGINE KOHLER COMMAND SP
CYLINDERS 2
ENGINE HP 27
COOLING AIR
FUEL G
SPEEDS VARIABLE
TRANSMISSION HYDRO
STEERING ZERO
BLADE CLUTCH ELECTRIC
HYDRAULIC YES
PTO YES
STANDARD DECK 60"
WEIGHT 1,138 LBS.
MSRP $10,988

OPTIONS

2 POST ROPS
BAG & FAN

SERIAL NUMBERS

YEAR	BEGINNING NO.
2004	440000
2005	510000

RETAIL PRICING

YEAR	HIGH	LOW
2004	$2,329	$1,747
2005	$2,580	$1,935
2006	$2,858	$2,143
2007	$3,181	$2,386
2008	$3,533	$2,650

LZ27KC605

YEARS MFRD 2008-2008
SERIES LAZER Z SERIES
ENGINE KOHLER COMMAND
CYLINDERS 2
ENGINE HP 27
COOLING AIR
FUEL G
SPEEDS VARIABLE
TRANSMISSION HYDRO
STEERING ZERO
BLADE CLUTCH ELECTRIC
STANDARD DECK 60"
WEIGHT 1,360 LBS.
MSRP $10,766

RETAIL PRICING

YEAR	HIGH	LOW
2008	$6,122	$4,592

LZ27KC665

YEARS MFRD 2006-2006
SERIES LAZER Z SERIES
ENGINE KOHLER COMMAND
CYLINDERS 2
ENGINE HP 27
COOLING AIR
FUEL G
SPEEDS VARIABLE
TRANSMISSION HYDRO
STEERING ZERO
STANDARD DECK 66"
WEIGHT 1,430 LBS.
MSRP $10,766

OPTIONS

KOHLER COMMAND 28E
KOHLER COMMAND 30E

RETAIL PRICING

YEAR	HIGH	LOW
2006	$3,621	$2,716

LZ27KC724

YEARS MFRD 2004-2005
SERIES LAZER Z SERIES
ENGINE KOHLER COMMAND SP
CYLINDERS 2

ENGINE HP 27
COOLING . . . . AIR
FUEL . . . . G
SPEEDS . . . . VARIABLE
TRANSMISSION . . . . HYDRO
STEERING. . . . . ZERO
BLADE CLUTCH . . . . ELECTRIC
HYDRAULIC . . . . YES
PTO . . . . YES
STANDARD DECK . . . . 72"
WEIGHT . . . . 1,213 LBS.
MSRP. $10,655

OPTIONS

2P ROPS
BAG & FAN

SERIAL NUMBERS

YEAR	BEGINNING NO.
2004	440000
2005	510000

RETAIL PRICING

YEAR	HIGH	LOW
2004	$2,331	$1,749
2005	$2,588	$1,941

LZ27LKA604

YEARS MFRD 2004-2005
SERIES . . . . LAZER Z LIQUID SERIES
ENGINE . . . . KAWASAKI
CYLINDERS. 2
ENGINE HP 27
COOLING . . . . LIQUID
FUEL . . . . G
SPEEDS . . . . VARIABLE
TRANSMISSION . . . . . DUAL HYDRO
STEERING. . . . . ZERO
BLADE CLUTCH . . . . ELECTRIC
STANDARD DECK . . . . 60"
WEIGHT . . . . 1,403 LBS.
MSRP. $11,543

OPTIONS

2 POST ROPS
BAG & FAN

SERIAL NUMBERS

YEAR	BEGINNING NO.
2004	440000
2005	510000

RETAIL PRICING

YEAR	HIGH	LOW
2004	$2,486	$1,865
2005	$2,744	$2,058

LZ27LKA724

YEARS MFRD 2001-2005
SERIES. . . . .
. . LAZER Z LIQUID COOLED SERIES
ENGINE . . . . KAWASAKI
CYLINDERS. 2
ENGINE HP 27
COOLING . . . . LIQUID
FUEL . . . . G
SPEEDS . . . . VARIABLE
TRANSMISSION . . . . HYDRO
STEERING. . . . . ZERO
BLADE CLUTCH . . . . ELECTRIC
HYDRAULIC . . . . YES
PTO . . . . YES
STANDARD DECK . . . . 72"
WEIGHT . . . . 1,408 LBS.
MSRP. $10,899

SERIAL NUMBERS

YEAR	BEGINNING NO.
2004	440000
2005	510000

RETAIL PRICING

YEAR	HIGH	LOW
2001	$4,804	$3,603
2002	$5,035	$3,776
2003	$5,070	$3,802
2004	$5,492	$4,119
2005	$6,164	$4,623

LZ28KA605

YEARS MFRD 2007-2008
SERIES. . . . . LAZER Z SERIES
ENGINE . . . . KOHLER
CYLINDERS. 2
ENGINE HP 28
COOLING . . . . AIR
FUEL . . . . G
SPEEDS . . . . VARIABLE
TRANSMISSION . . . . . DUAL HYDRO
STEERING. . . . . ZERO
BLADE CLUTCH . . . . ELECTRIC
STANDARD DECK . . . . 60"
WEIGHT . . . . 1,360 LBS.
MSRP. $11,099

OPTIONS

66" DECK

RETAIL PRICING

YEAR	HIGH	LOW
2007	$4,230	$3,172
2008	$4,696	$3,522

LZ28KC604

YEARS MFRD 2004-2008
SERIES. . . . . . . LAZER Z EFI SERIES
ENGINE . . . . . . KOHLER COMMAND
CYLINDERS. 2
ENGINE HP 28
COOLING . . . . AIR
FUEL . . . . G
SPEEDS . . . . VARIABLE
TRANSMISSION . . . . . DUAL HYDRO
STEERING. . . . . ZERO
BLADE CLUTCH . . . . ELECTRIC
HYDRAULIC . . . . YES
PTO . . . . YES
STANDARD DECK . . . . 60"
WEIGHT . . . . 1,163 LBS.
MSRP. $11,654

OPTIONS

2 POST ROPS
BAG & FAN

SERIAL NUMBERS

YEAR	BEGINNING NO.
2004	440000
2005	510000

RETAIL PRICING

YEAR	HIGH	LOW
2004	$2,392	$1,794
2005	$2,665	$1,998
2006	$2,952	$2,214
2007	$3,297	$2,473
2008	$3,651	$2,738

LZ28KC605

YEARS MFRD 2006-2008
SERIES. . . . . LAZER Z SERIES
ENGINE . . . . . . KOHLER COMMAND
CYLINDERS. 2
ENGINE HP 28
COOLING . . . . AIR
FUEL . . . . G
SPEEDS . . . . VARIABLE
TRANSMISSION . . . . HYDRO
STEERING. . . . . ZERO
STANDARD DECK . . . . 60"
WEIGHT . . . . 1,380 LBS.
MSRP. $12,209

RETAIL PRICING

YEAR	HIGH	LOW
2008	$6,941	$5,206

LZ28KC724

YEARS MFRD 2004-2005
SERIES. . . . . . . LAZER Z EFI SERIES
ENGINE . . . .KOHLER COMMAND SP
CYLINDERS. 2
ENGINE HP 28
COOLING . . . . AIR
FUEL . . . . G
SPEEDS . . . . VARIABLE
TRANSMISSION . . . . . DUAL HYDRO
STEERING. . . . . ZERO
BLADE CLUTCH . . . . ELECTRIC
HYDRAULIC . . . . YES
PTO . . . . YES
STANDARD DECK . . . . 72"
WEIGHT . . . . 1,230 LBS.
MSRP. $11,876

OPTIONS

2 POST ROPS
BAG & FAN

SERIAL NUMBERS

YEAR	BEGINNING NO.
2004	440000
2005	510000

RETAIL PRICING

YEAR	HIGH	LOW
2004	$2,558	$1,918
2005	$2,839	$2,129

LZ30KC725

YEARS MFRD 2006-2006
SERIES. . . . . LAZER Z SERIES
ENGINE . . . . . . KOHLER COMMAND
CYLINDERS. 2
ENGINE HP 30
COOLING . . . . AIR
FUEL . . . . G
SPEEDS . . . . VARIABLE
TRANSMISSION . . . . HYDRO
STEERING. . . . . ZERO
STANDARD DECK . . . . 72"
WEIGHT . . . . 1,530 LBS.
MSRP. $11,321

RETAIL PRICING

YEAR	HIGH	LOW
2006	$3,807	$2,855

LZ31BV604

YEARS MFRD 2005-2005
SERIES. . . . . . . LAZER Z XS SERIES
ENGINE . . . . B&S
CYLINDERS. 2
ENGINE HP 31
COOLING . . . . AIR
FUEL . . . . G
SPEEDS . . . . VARIABLE
TRANSMISSION . . . . HYDRO
STEERING. . . . . ZERO
BLADE CLUTCH . . . . ELECTRIC
STANDARD DECK . . . . 60"
WEIGHT . . . . 1,450 LBS.
MSRP. $11,543

OPTIONS

2 POST ROPS
BAG & FAN

SERIAL NUMBERS

YEAR	BEGINNING NO.
2005	510000

RETAIL PRICING

YEAR	HIGH	LOW
2005	$2,744	$2,058

LZ31BV605

YEARS MFRD 2008-2008
SERIES. . . . . LAZER Z SERIES
ENGINE . . . . VANGUARD
CYLINDERS. 2
ENGINE HP 31
COOLING . . . . AIR
FUEL . . . . G
SPEEDS . . . . VARIABLE
TRANSMISSION . . . . HYDRO
STEERING. . . . . ZERO
BLADE CLUTCH . . . . ELECTRIC
STANDARD DECK . . . . 60"
WEIGHT . . . . 1,395 LBS.
MSRP. $11,210

RETAIL PRICING

YEAR	HIGH	LOW
2008	$6,373	$4,780

LZ31BV665

YEARS MFRD 2008-2008
SERIES. . . . . LAZER Z SERIES
ENGINE . . . . VANGUARD
CYLINDERS. 2
ENGINE HP 31
COOLING . . . . AIR
FUEL . . . . G
SPEEDS . . . . VARIABLE
TRANSMISSION . . . . HYDRO
STEERING. . . . . ZERO
BLADE CLUTCH . . . . ELECTRIC
STANDARD DECK . . . . 66"
WEIGHT . . . . 1,445 LBS.
MSRP. $11,432

RETAIL PRICING

YEAR	HIGH	LOW
2008	$6,499	$4,875

EX MARK

LZ31BV724

YEARS MFRD 2005-2005
SERIES. . . . . . . LAZER Z XS SERIES
ENGINE . . . . B&S
CYLINDERS. 2
ENGINE HP 31
COOLING . . . . AIR
FUEL . . . . G
SPEEDS . . . . VARIABLE
TRANSMISSION . . . . HYDRO
STEERING. . . . . ZERO
BLADE CLUTCH . . . . ELECTRIC
STANDARD DECK . . . . 72"
WEIGHT . . . . 1,520 LBS.
MSRP. $11,987

OPTIONS

2 POST ROPS
BAG & FAN

SERIAL NUMBERS

YEAR	BEGINNING NO.
2005	510000

RETAIL PRICING

YEAR	HIGH	LOW
2005	$2,851	$2,138

LZ31BV725

YEARS MFRD 2008-2008
SERIES. . . . . LAZER Z SERIES
ENGINE . . . . VANGUARD
CYLINDERS. 2
ENGINE HP 31
COOLING . . . . AIR
FUEL . . . . G
SPEEDS . . . . VARIABLE
TRANSMISSION . . . . HYDRO
STEERING. . . . . ZERO
BLADE CLUTCH . . . . ELECTRIC
STANDARD DECK . . . . 72"
WEIGHT . . . . 1,495 LBS.
MSRP. $11,765

RETAIL PRICING

YEAR	HIGH	LOW
2008	$6,689	$5,016

LZ31DG604

YEARS MFRD 2001-2001
SERIES. . . . . . . LAZER Z XP SERIES
ENGINE . . . . DAIHATSU
ENGINE HP 31
FUEL . . . . G
TRANSMISSION . . . . HYDRO
STEERING. . . . . ZERO
STANDARD DECK . . . . 60"
WEIGHT . . . . 1,565 LBS.
MSRP. $14,200

OPTIONS

72" DECK

RETAIL PRICING

YEAR	HIGH	LOW
2001	$2,297	$1,723

LZ31DG724

YEARS MFRD 2001-2003
SERIES. . . . . . . LAZER Z XP SERIES
ENGINE . . . . DAIHATSU
ENGINE HP 31
FUEL . . . . D
TRANSMISSION . . . . HYDRO
STEERING. . . . . STANDARD
STANDARD DECK . . . . 72"
WEIGHT . . . . 1,583 LBS.
MSRP. $13,700

RETAIL PRICING

YEAR	HIGH	LOW
2001	$5,769	$4,327
2002	$6,230	$4,672
2003	$6,632	$4,974

LZAS20BV484

YEARS MFRD 2009-2009
SERIES LAZER Z ADVANTAGE SERIES
ENGINE . . . . B&S VANGUARD
CYLINDERS. 2
ENGINE HP 20
COOLING . . . . AIR
FUEL . . . . G
SPEEDS . . . . VARIABLE
TRANSMISSION . . . . . DUAL HYDRO
STEERING. . . . . ZERO
BLADE CLUTCH . . . . ELECTRIC
STANDARD DECK . . . . 48"
WEIGHT . . . . 1,062 LBS.
MSRP. $8,879

RETAIL PRICING

YEAR	HIGH	LOW
2009	$2,865	$2,148

LZAS23KC524

YEARS MFRD 2009-2009
ENGINE . . . . . . KOHLER COMMAND
CYLINDERS. 2
ENGINE HP 23
COOLING . . . . AIR
FUEL . . . . G
SPEEDS . . . . VARIABLE
TRANSMISSION . . . . . DUAL HYDRO
STEERING. . . . . ZERO
BLADE CLUTCH . . . . ELECTRIC
STANDARD DECK . . . . 52"
MSRP. $9,878

RETAIL PRICING

YEAR	HIGH	LOW
2009	$3,187	$2,390

LZAS25KC604

YEARS MFRD 2009-2009
ENGINE . . . . . . KOHLER COMMAND
CYLINDERS. 2
ENGINE HP 25
COOLING . . . . AIR
FUEL . . . . G
SPEEDS . . . . VARIABLE
TRANSMISSION . . . . . DUAL HYDRO
STEERING. . . . . ZERO
BLADE CLUTCH . . . . ELECTRIC
STANDARD DECK . . . . 60"
MSRP. $10,766

RETAIL PRICING

YEAR	HIGH	LOW
2009	$3,474	$2,606

LZAS26LKA-604

YEARS MFRD 2009-2009
ENGINE . . . . KAWASAKI
CYLINDERS. 2
ENGINE HP 26
COOLING . . . . LIQUID
FUEL . . . . G
SPEEDS . . . . VARIABLE
TRANSMISSION . . . . . DUAL HYDRO
STEERING. . . . . ZERO
BLADE CLUTCH . . . . ELECTRIC
STANDARD DECK . . . . 60"
MSRP. $11,876

RETAIL PRICING

YEAR	HIGH	LOW
2009	$5,214	$3,910

LZAS27KC524

YEARS MFRD 2009-2009
ENGINE . . . . . . KOHLER COMMAND
CYLINDERS. 2
ENGINE HP 27
COOLING . . . . AIR
FUEL . . . . G
SPEEDS . . . . VARIABLE
TRANSMISSION . . . . . DUAL HYDRO
STEERING. . . . . ZERO
BLADE CLUTCH . . . . ELECTRIC
STANDARD DECK . . . . 52"
MSRP. $10,433

OPTIONS

60" DECK

RETAIL PRICING

YEAR	HIGH	LOW
2009	$3,366	$2,525

LZAS27KC604

YEARS MFRD 2010-2010
SERIES LAZER Z ADVANTAGE SERIES
ENGINE . . . . . . KOHLER COMMAND
CYLINDERS. 2
ENGINE HP 27
COOLING . . . . AIR
FUEL . . . . G
SPEEDS . . . . VARIABLE
TRANSMISSION . . . . HYDRO
STEERING. . . . . ZERO
BLADE CLUTCH . . . . ELECTRIC
WEIGHT . . . . 1,113 LBS.

LZAS29KA724

YEARS MFRD 2009-2009
ENGINE . . . . KAWASAKI
CYLINDERS. 2
ENGINE HP 29
COOLING . . . . LIQUID
FUEL . . . . G
SPEEDS . . . . VARIABLE
TRANSMISSION . . . . . DUAL HYDRO
STEERING. . . . . ZERO
BLADE CLUTCH . . . . ELECTRIC
STANDARD DECK . . . . 72"
MSRP. $11,876

RETAIL PRICING

YEAR	HIGH	LOW
2009	$3,832	$2,874

LZD25KD605

YEARS MFRD 2011-2011
SERIES. . . . . LAZER Z D SERIES
ENGINE . . . . KUBOTA
ENGINE HP 25
COOLING . . . . AIR
FUEL . . . . D
SPEEDS . . . . VARIABLE
TRANSMISSION . . . . HYDRO
STEERING. . . . . ZERO
BLADE CLUTCH . . . . ELECTRIC

LZD25KD725

YEARS MFRD 2011-2011
SERIES. . . . . LAZER Z D SERIES
ENGINE . . . . KUBOTA
ENGINE HP 25
COOLING . . . . AIR
FUEL . . . . D
SPEEDS . . . . VARIABLE
TRANSMISSION . . . . HYDRO
STEERING. . . . . ZERO
BLADE CLUTCH . . . . ELECTRIC

LZDS902K

YEARS MFRD 2013-2013
SERIES. . . . . LAZER DS SERIES
ENGINE . . . . KUBOTA D902
FUEL . . . . D
SPEEDS . . . . VARIABLE
TRANSMISSION . . . . HYDRO
STEERING. . . . . ZERO
BLADE CLUTCH . . . . ELECTRIC
STANDARD DECK . . . . 60"
MSRP. $18,869

SERIAL NUMBERS

YEAR	BEGINNING NO.
2013	313600000

RETAIL PRICING

YEAR	HIGH	LOW
2013	$8,848	$6,636

LZE20KA484

YEARS MFRD 2011-2011
SERIES. . . . . LAZER Z E SERIES
ENGINE . . . . KAWASAKI
CYLINDERS. 2
ENGINE HP 20
COOLING . . . . AIR
FUEL . . . . G
SPEEDS . . . . VARIABLE

TRANSMISSION . . . . .HYDRO
STEERING. . . . . .ZERO
BLADE CLUTCH . . . . .ELECTRIC

LZE22KA484

YEARS MFRD 2011-2011
SERIES. . . . . LAZER Z SERIES
ENGINE . . . . KAWASAKI
CYLINDERS. 2
ENGINE HP 22
COOLING . . . . .AIR
FUEL . . . . G
SPEEDS . . . . VARIABLE
TRANSMISSION . . . . .HYDRO
STEERING. . . . . .ZERO
BLADE CLUTCH . . . . .ELECTRIC

LZE24KA524

YEARS MFRD 2011-2011
SERIES. . . . . LAZER Z SERIES
ENGINE . . . . KAWASAKI
CYLINDERS. 2
ENGINE HP 24
COOLING . . . . .AIR
FUEL . . . . G
SPEEDS . . . . VARIABLE
TRANSMISSION . . . . .HYDRO
STEERING. . . . . .ZERO
BLADE CLUTCH . . . . .ELECTRIC

LZE27KC604

YEARS MFRD 2011-2011
SERIES. . . . . LAZER Z E SERIES
ENGINE . . . . KOHLER COMMAND
CYLINDERS. 2
ENGINE HP 27
COOLING . . . . .AIR
FUEL . . . . G
SPEEDS . . . . VARIABLE
TRANSMISSION . . . . .HYDRO
STEERING. . . . . .ZERO
BLADE CLUTCH . . . . .ELECTRIC

LZE600KA

YEARS MFRD 2013-2013
SERIES. . . . . LAZER E SERIES
ENGINE . . . . KAWASAKI FX600V
COOLING . . . . .AIR
FUEL . . . . G
SPEEDS . . . . VARIABLE
TRANSMISSION . . . . .HYDRO
STEERING. . . . . .ZERO
BLADE CLUTCH . . . . .ELECTRIC
STANDARD DECK . . . . 48"
MSRP. $9,212

RETAIL PRICING

YEAR	HIGH	LOW
2013	$5,610	$4,207

LZE600KA484

YEARS MFRD 2012-2014
ENGINE . . . . KAWASAKI FX600V
COOLING . . . . .AIR
FUEL . . . . G
SPEEDS . . . . VARIABLE
TRANSMISSION . . . . .HYDRO
STEERING. . . . . .ZERO
BLADE CLUTCH . . . . .ELECTRIC
STANDARD DECK . . . . 48"
WEIGHT . . . . .1,035 LBS.
MSRP. $7,999

RETAIL PRICING

YEAR	HIGH	LOW
2012	$3,227	$2,420
2013	$4,000	$3,000
2014	$4,783	$3,588

LZE651CKA

YEARS MFRD 2020-2020
SERIES. . . . . LAZER Z E SERIES
ENGINE . . . . KAWASAKI FX651V
CYLINDERS. 2
CID 726CC
ENGINE HP 21.5
FUEL . . . . G
SPEEDS . . . . VARIABLE
TRANSMISSION . . . . . DUAL HYDRO
STEERING. . . . . .ZERO
ROPS/CAB . . . . .ROPS
STANDARD DECK . . . . 48"
WEIGHT . . . . .1,118 LBS.
MSRP. $10,877

LZE651GKA

YEARS MFRD 2016-2019
SERIES. . . . . LAZER Z E SERIES
ENGINE . . . . KAWASAKI FX651V
ENGINE HP 20.5
COOLING . . . . .AIR
FUEL . . . . G
SPEEDS . . . . VARIABLE
TRANSMISSION . . . . .HYDRO
STEERING. . . . . .ZERO
STANDARD DECK . . . . 48"
MSRP. $9,699

RETAIL PRICING

YEAR	HIGH	LOW
2016	$5,203	$3,902
2017	$5,742	$4,306
2018	$6,303	$4,728
2019	$6,939	$5,205

LZE691KA

YEARS MFRD 2013-2013
SERIES. . . . . LAZER E SERIES
ENGINE . . . . KAWASAKI FX691V
COOLING . . . . .AIR
FUEL . . . . G
SPEEDS . . . . VARIABLE
TRANSMISSION . . . . .HYDRO
STEERING. . . . . .ZERO
BLADE CLUTCH . . . . .ELECTRIC
STANDARD DECK . . . . 52"
MSRP. $9,878

SERIAL NUMBERS

YEAR . . . . BEGINNING NO.
2013 313600000

RETAIL PRICING

YEAR	HIGH	LOW
2013	$6,017	$4,513

LZE691KA524

YEARS MFRD 2012-2014
SERIES. . . . . LAZER Z E SERIES
ENGINE . . . . KAWASAKI FX691V
COOLING . . . . .AIR
FUEL . . . . G
SPEEDS . . . . VARIABLE
TRANSMISSION . . . . .HYDRO
STEERING. . . . . .ZERO
BLADE CLUTCH . . . . .ELECTRIC
STANDARD DECK . . . . 52"
WEIGHT . . . . .1,070 LBS.
MSRP. $8,599

RETAIL PRICING

YEAR	HIGH	LOW
2012	$3,471	$2,603
2013	$4,292	$3,219
2014	$5,123	$3,843

LZE730KA604

YEARS MFRD 2013-2013
SERIES. . . . . LAZER E SERIES
ENGINE . . . . KAWASAKI FX730V
COOLING . . . . .AIR
FUEL . . . . G
SPEEDS . . . . VARIABLE
TRANSMISSION . . . . .HYDRO
STEERING. . . . . .ZERO
BLADE CLUTCH . . . . .ELECTRIC
STANDARD DECK . . . . 60"
MSRP. $10,544

SERIAL NUMBERS

YEAR . . . . BEGINNING NO.
2013 313600000

RETAIL PRICING

YEAR	HIGH	LOW
2013	$6,420	$4,815

LZE740EKC

YEARS MFRD 2014-2020
SERIES. . . . . LAZER Z E SERIES
ENGINE . . . . KOHLER EFI
ENGINE HP 25
COOLING . . . . .AIR
FUEL . . . . G
SPEEDS . . . . VARIABLE
TRANSMISSION . . . . .HYDRO
STEERING. . . . . .ZERO
STANDARD DECK . . . . 60"
MSRP. $12,089

RETAIL PRICING

YEAR	HIGH	LOW
2014	$4,769	$3,577
2015	$5,264	$3,948
2016	$5,808	$4,356
2017	$6,414	$4,810
2018	$7,081	$5,310
2019	$7,834	$5,875
2020	$9,401	$7,007

LZE740KC604

YEARS MFRD 2012-2014
SERIES. . . . . LAZER Z E SERIES
ENGINE . . . . KOHLER CV740
COOLING . . . . .AIR
FUEL . . . . G
SPEEDS . . . . VARIABLE
TRANSMISSION . . . . .HYDRO
STEERING. . . . . .ZERO
BLADE CLUTCH . . . . .ELECTRIC
STANDARD DECK . . . . 60"
WEIGHT . . . . .1,105 LBS.
MSRP. $10,199

RETAIL PRICING

YEAR	HIGH	LOW
2012	$4,278	$3,208
2013	$4,871	$3,653
2014	$5,803	$4,352

LZE742GKC

YEARS MFRD 2017-2020
SERIES. . . . . LAZER Z E SERIES
ENGINE . . . . KOHLER CV742
CID 747CC
ENGINE HP 25
FUEL . . . . G
SPEEDS . . . . VARIABLE
TRANSMISSION . . . . . DUAL HYDRO
STEERING. . . . . .ZERO
ROPS/CAB . . . . .ROPS
STANDARD DECK . . . . 60"
WEIGHT . . . . .1,279 LBS.

LZE751CKA

YEARS MFRD 2017-2020
SERIES. . . . . LAZER Z E SERIES
ENGINE . . . . KAWASAKI FX751V
CYLINDERS. 2
CID 852CC
ENGINE HP 24.5
FUEL . . . . G
SPEEDS . . . . VARIABLE
TRANSMISSION . . . . . DUAL HYDRO
STEERING. . . . . .ZERO
ROPS/CAB . . . . .ROPS
STANDARD DECK . . . . 52"
WEIGHT . . . . .1,136 LBS.

LZE751GKA

YEARS MFRD 2017-2020
SERIES. . . . . LAZER Z E SERIES
ENGINE . . . . KAWASAKI FX751V
CYLINDERS. 2
CID 852CC
ENGINE HP 24.5
COOLING . . . . .AIR
FUEL . . . . G
SPEEDS . . . . VARIABLE
TRANSMISSION . . . . .HYDRO
STEERING. . . . . .ZERO
STANDARD DECK . . . . 52"
MSRP. $11,654

OPTIONS

60" DECK. $555
60" DECK RD
60" SUSP PLATFORM $1,665

EX MARK

72" DECK $1,110
72" DECK RD

RETAIL PRICING

YEAR	HIGH	LOW
2017	$6,108	$4,581
2018	$6,783	$5,087
2019	$7,544	$5,658
2020	$8,945	$6,529

LZHP4417KA

YEARS MFRD 1998-2003
SERIES . . . . LAZER Z HP SERIES
ENGINE . . . . KAWASAKI
ENGINE HP 17
FUEL . . . . G
TRANSMISSION . . . . .HYDRO
STEERING. . . . . ZERO
STANDARD DECK . . . . 44"
WEIGHT . . . . 861 LBS.
MSRP. $7,050

SERIAL NUMBERS

YEAR	BEGINNING NO.
1998	160000
1999	190000
2000	220000

RETAIL PRICING

YEAR	HIGH	LOW
1998	$2,668	$2,001
1999	$2,845	$2,134
2000	$3,029	$2,272
2001	$3,160	$2,370
2002	$3,256	$2,442
2003	$3,387	$2,540

LZHP4418KC

YEARS MFRD 1999-2000
SERIES . . . . LAZER Z SERIES
ENGINE . . . . . . KOHLER COMMAND
ENGINE HP 18
FUEL . . . . G
TRANSMISSION . . . . .HYDRO
STEERING. . . . . ZERO
STANDARD DECK . . . . 44"
MSRP. $7,250

SERIAL NUMBERS

YEAR	BEGINNING NO.
1999	190000
2000	220000

RETAIL PRICING

YEAR	HIGH	LOW
1999	$2,146	$1,610
2000	$2,333	$1,750

LZHP4419KA

YEARS MFRD 2000-2002
SERIES . . . . LAZER Z SERIES
ENGINE . . . . KAWASAKI
ENGINE HP 19
FUEL . . . . G
TRANSMISSION . . . . .HYDRO
STEERING. . . . . ZERO
STANDARD DECK . . . . 44"
MSRP. $7,260

SERIAL NUMBERS

YEAR	BEGINNING NO.
2000	220000

RETAIL PRICING

YEAR	HIGH	LOW
2000	$2,381	$1,786
2001	$2,473	$1,854
2002	$2,563	$1,922

LZHP4420KC

YEARS MFRD 2002-2003
SERIES . . . . LAZER Z HP SERIES
ENGINE . . . . . . KOHLER COMMAND
ENGINE HP 20
FUEL . . . . G
TRANSMISSION . . . . .HYDRO
STEERING. . . . . STANDARD
STANDARD DECK . . . . 44"
WEIGHT . . . . 861 LBS.
MSRP. $7,400

RETAIL PRICING

YEAR	HIGH	LOW
2002	$2,626	$1,970
2003	$2,939	$2,204

LZHP4818KC

YEARS MFRD 1998-2001
SERIES . . . . LAZER Z SERIES
ENGINE . . . . . . KOHLER COMMAND
ENGINE HP 18
FUEL . . . . G
TRANSMISSION . . . . .HYDRO
STEERING. . . . . ZERO
STANDARD DECK . . . . 48"
MSRP. $7,480

SERIAL NUMBERS

YEAR	BEGINNING NO.
1998	160000
1999	190000
2000	220000

RETAIL PRICING

YEAR	HIGH	LOW
1998	$2,003	$1,502
1999	$2,190	$1,643
2000	$2,381	$1,786
2001	$2,571	$1,928

LZHP4819KA

YEARS MFRD 1999-1999
SERIES . . . . LAZER Z SERIES
ENGINE . . . . KAWASAKI
ENGINE HP 19
FUEL . . . . G
TRANSMISSION . . . . BELT
STEERING. . . . . ZERO
STANDARD DECK . . . . 48"
MSRP. $7,360

SERIAL NUMBERS

YEAR	BEGINNING NO.
1999	190000

RETAIL PRICING

YEAR	HIGH	LOW
1999	$2,234	$1,676

LZHP4820KC

YEARS MFRD 2000-2003
SERIES . . . . LAZER Z SERIES
ENGINE . . . . . . KOHLER COMMAND
ENGINE HP 20
FUEL . . . . G
TRANSMISSION . . . . .HYDRO
STEERING. . . . . ZERO
STANDARD DECK . . . . 48"
WEIGHT . . . . 891 LBS.
MSRP. $7,650

SERIAL NUMBERS

YEAR	BEGINNING NO.
2000	220000

RETAIL PRICING

YEAR	HIGH	LOW
2000	$2,479	$1,860
2001	$2,634	$1,976
2002	$2,743	$2,057
2003	$2,913	$2,184

LZHP4821KA

YEARS MFRD 2000-2003
SERIES . . . . LAZER Z SERIES
ENGINE . . . . KAWASAKI
ENGINE HP 21
FUEL . . . . G
TRANSMISSION . . . . .HYDRO
STEERING. . . . . ZERO
STANDARD DECK . . . . 48"
WEIGHT . . . . 891 LBS.
MSRP. $8,200

SERIAL NUMBERS

YEAR	BEGINNING NO.
2000	220000

RETAIL PRICING

YEAR	HIGH	LOW
2000	$2,528	$1,896
2001	$2,732	$2,049
2002	$2,905	$2,179
2003	$3,066	$2,300

LZHP5220KC

YEARS MFRD 2000-2003
SERIES . . . . LAZER Z SERIES
ENGINE . . . . . . KOHLER COMMAND
ENGINE HP 20
FUEL . . . . G
TRANSMISSION . . . . .HYDRO
STEERING. . . . . ZERO
STANDARD DECK . . . . 52"
WEIGHT . . . . 965 LBS.
MSRP. $8,190

SERIAL NUMBERS

YEAR	BEGINNING NO.
2000	220000

RETAIL PRICING

YEAR	HIGH	LOW
2000	$2,573	$1,930
2001	$2,781	$2,086
2002	$2,993	$2,245
2003	$3,267	$2,450

LZHP5223KA

YEARS MFRD 2000-2003
SERIES . . . . LAZER Z SERIES
ENGINE . . . . KAWASAKI
ENGINE HP 23
FUEL . . . . G
SPEEDS . . . . VARIABLE
TRANSMISSION . . . . .HYDRO
STEERING. . . . . ZERO
STANDARD DECK . . . . 52"
WEIGHT . . . . 965 LBS.
MSRP. $7,700

SERIAL NUMBERS

YEAR	BEGINNING NO.
2000	220000

RETAIL PRICING

YEAR	HIGH	LOW
2000	$2,717	$2,037
2001	$2,868	$2,151
2002	$3,090	$2,317
2003	$3,440	$2,580

LZHP5223KC

YEARS MFRD 2000-2003
SERIES . . . . LAZER Z SERIES
ENGINE . . . . . . KOHLER COMMAND
ENGINE HP 23
FUEL . . . . G
TRANSMISSION . . . . .HYDRO
STEERING. . . . . ZERO
STANDARD DECK . . . . 52"
WEIGHT . . . . 965 LBS.
MSRP. $8,200

SERIAL NUMBERS

YEAR	BEGINNING NO.
2000	220000

RETAIL PRICING

YEAR	HIGH	LOW
2000	$2,670	$2,002
2001	$2,818	$2,113
2002	$2,998	$2,248
2003	$3,182	$2,387

LZS22KA484

YEARS MFRD 2011-2011
SERIES . . . . LAZER Z S SERIES
ENGINE . . . . KAWASAKI
CYLINDERS. 2
ENGINE HP 22
COOLING . . . . AIR
FUEL . . . . G
SPEEDS . . . . VARIABLE
TRANSMISSION . . . . .HYDRO
STEERING. . . . . ZERO
BLADE CLUTCH . . . . ELECTRIC

LZS23KC524

YEARS MFRD 2011-2011
SERIES . . . . LAZER Z S SERIES
ENGINE . . . . . . KOHLER COMMAND
CYLINDERS. 2
ENGINE HP 23
COOLING . . . . AIR
FUEL . . . . G

SPEEDS . . . . VARIABLE
TRANSMISSION . . . . HYDRO
STEERING. . . . . ZERO
BLADE CLUTCH . . . . ELECTRIC

LZS25EKC604

YEARS MFRD 2011-2011
SERIES. . . . . LAZER Z S SERIES
ENGINE . . . . . . KOHLER COMMAND
CYLINDERS. 2
ENGINE HP 25
COOLING . . . . AIR
FUEL . . . . G
SPEEDS . . . . VARIABLE
TRANSMISSION . . . . HYDRO
STEERING. . . . . ZERO
BLADE CLUTCH . . . . ELECTRIC

LZS25KC604

YEARS MFRD 2011-2011
SERIES. . . . . LAZER Z S SERIES
ENGINE . . . . . . KOHLER COMMAND
CYLINDERS. 2
ENGINE HP 25
COOLING . . . . AIR
FUEL . . . . G
SPEEDS . . . . VARIABLE
TRANSMISSION . . . . HYDRO
STEERING. . . . . ZERO
BLADE CLUTCH . . . . ELECTRIC

LZS27KC524

YEARS MFRD 2011-2011
SERIES. . . . . LAZER Z S SERIES
ENGINE . . . . . . KOHLER COMMAND
CYLINDERS. 2
ENGINE HP 27
COOLING . . . . AIR
FUEL . . . . G
SPEEDS . . . . VARIABLE
TRANSMISSION . . . . HYDRO
STEERING. . . . . ZERO
BLADE CLUTCH . . . . ELECTRIC

LZS27KC604

YEARS MFRD 2011-2011
SERIES. . . . . LAZER Z S SERIES
ENGINE . . . . . . KOHLER COMMAND
CYLINDERS. 2
ENGINE HP 27
COOLING . . . . AIR
FUEL . . . . G
SPEEDS . . . . VARIABLE
TRANSMISSION . . . . HYDRO
STEERING. . . . . ZERO
BLADE CLUTCH . . . . ELECTRIC

LZS29EKC724

YEARS MFRD 2011-2011
SERIES. . . . . LAZER Z S SERIES
ENGINE . . . . . . KOHLER COMMAND
CYLINDERS. 2
ENGINE HP 29
COOLING . . . . AIR
FUEL . . . . G
SPEEDS . . . . VARIABLE
TRANSMISSION . . . . HYDRO
STEERING. . . . . ZERO
BLADE CLUTCH . . . . ELECTRIC

LZS29KA724

YEARS MFRD 2011-2011
SERIES. . . . . LAZER Z S SERIES
ENGINE . . . . KAWASAKI
CYLINDERS. 2
ENGINE HP 29
COOLING . . . . AIR
FUEL . . . . G
SPEEDS . . . . VARIABLE
TRANSMISSION . . . . HYDRO
STEERING. . . . . ZERO
BLADE CLUTCH . . . . ELECTRIC

LZS80TDYM

YEARS MFRD 2018-2020
SERIES. . . . . LAZER Z SERIES
ENGINE . . . . YANMAR
ENGINE HP 25
FUEL . . . . D
TRANSMISSION . . . . HYDRO
STEERING. . . . . ZERO
STANDARD DECK . . . . 60"
WEIGHT . . . . 1,915 LBS.
MSRP. $23,864

OPTIONS

72" DECK. $555
72" DECK RD $999

LZS88CDYM

YEARS MFRD 2018-2020
SERIES. . . . . LAZER Z SERIES
ENGINE . . . . YANMAR
ENGINE HP 37
FUEL . . . . D
TRANSMISSION . . . . HYDRO
STEERING. . . . . ZERO
STANDARD DECK . . . . 60"
WEIGHT . . . . 2,124 LBS.

OPTIONS

72" DECK
96" DECK RD

LZS651KA

YEARS MFRD 2013-2019
SERIES. . . . . LAZER Z S SERIES
ENGINE . . . . KAWASAKI FX651V
ENGINE HP 20.5
COOLING . . . . AIR
FUEL . . . . G
SPEEDS . . . . VARIABLE
TRANSMISSION . . . . HYDRO
STEERING. . . . . ZERO
BLADE CLUTCH . . . . ELECTRIC
STANDARD DECK . . . . 48"
MSRP. $10,399

SERIAL NUMBERS

YEAR	BEGINNING NO.
2013	313600000

RETAIL PRICING

YEAR	HIGH	LOW
2013	$4,157	$3,118
2014	$4,588	$3,441
2015	$5,065	$3,798
2016	$5,590	$4,192
2017	$6,170	$4,628
2018	$6,823	$5,117
2019	$7,832	$5,874

LZS651KA484

YEARS MFRD 2012-2012
SERIES. . . . . LAZER Z S SERIES
ENGINE . . . . KAWASAKI FX651V
COOLING . . . . AIR
FUEL . . . . G
SPEEDS . . . . VARIABLE
TRANSMISSION . . . . HYDRO
STEERING. . . . . ZERO
BLADE CLUTCH . . . . ELECTRIC
WEIGHT . . . . 1,089 LBS.

LZS651KA484 CA

YEARS MFRD 2012-2012
SERIES. . . . . LAZER Z S SERIES
ENGINE . . . . KAWASAKI FX651V
COOLING . . . . AIR
FUEL . . . . G
SPEEDS . . . . VARIABLE
TRANSMISSION . . . . HYDRO
STEERING. . . . . ZERO
BLADE CLUTCH . . . . ELECTRIC
WEIGHT . . . . 1,089 LBS.

LZS680KC524

YEARS MFRD 2012-2012
SERIES. . . . . LAZER Z S SERIES
ENGINE . . . . KOHLER CV680
COOLING . . . . AIR
FUEL . . . . G
SPEEDS . . . . VARIABLE
TRANSMISSION . . . . HYDRO
STEERING. . . . . ZERO
BLADE CLUTCH . . . . ELECTRIC
WEIGHT . . . . 1,088 LBS.

LZS691KA

YEARS MFRD 2013-2013
SERIES. . . . . LAZER S SERIES
ENGINE . . . . KAWASAKI FX691V
COOLING . . . . AIR
FUEL . . . . G
SPEEDS . . . . VARIABLE
TRANSMISSION . . . . HYDRO
STEERING. . . . . ZERO
BLADE CLUTCH . . . . ELECTRIC
STANDARD DECK . . . . 52"
MSRP. $10,988

SERIAL NUMBERS

YEAR	BEGINNING NO.
2013	313600000

RETAIL PRICING

YEAR	HIGH	LOW
2013	$6,693	$5,020

LZS691KA524 CA

YEARS MFRD 2012-2012
SERIES. . . . . LAZER Z S SERIES
ENGINE . . . . KAWASAKI FX691V
COOLING . . . . AIR
FUEL . . . . G
SPEEDS . . . . VARIABLE
TRANSMISSION . . . . HYDRO
STEERING. . . . . ZERO
BLADE CLUTCH . . . . ELECTRIC
WEIGHT . . . . 1,088 LBS.

LZS730EK

YEARS MFRD 2013-2013
SERIES. . . . . LAZER S SERIES
ENGINE . . . . KAWASAKI ECV730
COOLING . . . . AIR
FUEL . . . . G
SPEEDS . . . . VARIABLE
TRANSMISSION . . . . HYDRO
STEERING. . . . . ZERO
BLADE CLUTCH . . . . ELECTRIC
STANDARD DECK . . . . 52"
MSRP. $11,654

SERIAL NUMBERS

YEAR	BEGINNING NO.
2013	313600000

RETAIL PRICING

YEAR	HIGH	LOW
2013	$5,270	$3,953

LZS730EKC 604

YEARS MFRD 2012-2012
SERIES. . . . . LAZER Z S SERIES
ENGINE . . . . KOHLER ECV730
COOLING . . . . AIR
FUEL . . . . G
SPEEDS . . . . VARIABLE
TRANSMISSION . . . . HYDRO
STEERING. . . . . ZERO
BLADE CLUTCH . . . . ELECTRIC
WEIGHT . . . . 1,133 LBS.

LZS740AKC

YEARS MFRD 2016-2020
SERIES. . . . . LAZER Z S SERIES
ENGINE . . . KOHLER COMMAND EFI
CID 747CC
ENGINE HP 25
FUEL . . . . G
SPEEDS . . . . VARIABLE
TRANSMISSION . . . . . DUAL HYDRO
STEERING. . . . . ZERO

EX MARK

ROPS/CAB . . . . ROPS
STANDARD DECK . . . . 52"
WEIGHT . . . . 1,159 LBS.
MSRP. $13,097

LZS740KC

YEARS MFRD 2013-2019
SERIES . . . . LAZER Z S SERIES
ENGINE . . . . KOHLER EFI
ENGINE HP 25
COOLING . . . . AIR
FUEL . . . . G
SPEEDS . . . . VARIABLE
TRANSMISSION . . . . HYDRO
STEERING. . . . . ZERO
BLADE CLUTCH . . . . ELECTRIC
STANDARD DECK . . . . 52"

SERIAL NUMBERS

YEAR	BEGINNING NO.
2013	313600000

RETAIL PRICING

YEAR	HIGH	LOW
2013	$4,651	$3,488
2014	$5,134	$3,851
2015	$5,667	$4,251
2016	$6,254	$4,691
2017	$6,903	$5,177
2018	$7,634	$5,726
2019	$8,430	$6,322

LZS740KC524

YEARS MFRD 2012-2012
SERIES . . . . LAZER Z S SERIES
ENGINE . . . . KOHLER CV740
COOLING . . . . AIR
FUEL . . . . G
SPEEDS . . . . VARIABLE
TRANSMISSION . . . . HYDRO
STEERING. . . . . ZERO
BLADE CLUTCH . . . . ELECTRIC
WEIGHT . . . . 1,088 LBS.

LZS740KC604

YEARS MFRD 2012-2012
SERIES . . . . LAZER Z S SERIES
ENGINE . . . . KOHLER CV740
COOLING . . . . AIR
FUEL . . . . G
SPEEDS . . . . VARIABLE
TRANSMISSION . . . . HYDRO
STEERING. . . . . ZERO
BLADE CLUTCH . . . . ELECTRIC
WEIGHT . . . . 1,133 LBS.

LZS740KC 604CA

YEARS MFRD 2012-2012
SERIES . . . . LAZER Z S SERIES
ENGINE . . . . KOHLER CV740
COOLING . . . . AIR
FUEL . . . . G
SPEEDS . . . . VARIABLE
TRANSMISSION . . . . HYDRO
STEERING. . . . . ZERO
BLADE CLUTCH . . . . ELECTRIC
WEIGHT . . . . 1,133 LBS.

LZS740PKC

YEARS MFRD 2013-2020
SERIES . . . . LAZER Z S SERIES
ENGINE . . . . KOHLER PCV740
ENGINE HP 24
COOLING . . . . AIR
FUEL . . . . G
SPEEDS . . . . VARIABLE
TRANSMISSION . . . . HYDRO
STEERING. . . . . ZERO
BLADE CLUTCH . . . . ELECTRIC
STANDARD DECK . . . . 60"

OPTIONS

52" DECK THROUGH 2018
72" DECK

SERIAL NUMBERS

YEAR	BEGINNING NO.
2013	313600000

RETAIL PRICING

YEAR	HIGH	LOW
2013	$6,051	$4,538
2014	$6,678	$5,008
2015	$7,337	$5,502
2016	$8,135	$6,102
2017	$8,980	$6,735
2018	$9,935	$7,450
2019	$10,960	$8,220
2020	$12,099	$9,117

LZS742KC604

YEARS MFRD 2014-2014
SERIES . . . . LAZER Z S SERIES
ENGINE . . . . KOHLER CV742
CID 747
COOLING . . . . AIR
FUEL . . . . G
SPEEDS . . . . VARIABLE
TRANSMISSION . . . . HYDRO
STEERING. . . . . ZERO
STANDARD DECK . . . . 60"
MSRP. $10,799

RETAIL PRICING

YEAR	HIGH	LOW
2014	$6,151	$4,614

LZS749AKC

YEARS MFRD 2016-2020
SERIES . . . . LASER Z S SERIES
ENGINE . . . . KOHLER ECV749
CID 747CC
ENGINE HP 26.5
FUEL . . . . G
SPEEDS . . . . VARIABLE
TRANSMISSION . . . . HYDRO
STEERING. . . . . ZERO
STANDARD DECK . . . . 60"
WEIGHT . . . . 1,249 LBS.
MSRP. $14,429

OPTIONS

72" DECK. $444
72" DECK NON SUSP $111

LZS749EKC

YEARS MFRD 2013-2018
SERIES . . . . LAZER Z S SERIES
ENGINE . . . . KOHLER ECV 749
COOLING . . . . AIR
FUEL . . . . G
SPEEDS . . . . VARIABLE
TRANSMISSION . . . . HYDRO
STEERING. . . . . ZERO
BLADE CLUTCH . . . . ELECTRIC
STANDARD DECK . . . . 60"
MSRP. $12,499

OPTIONS

72" DECK
SUS SEAT

SERIAL NUMBERS

YEAR	BEGINNING NO.
2013	313600000

RETAIL PRICING

YEAR	HIGH	LOW
2013	$5,153	$3,865
2014	$5,679	$4,259
2015	$6,268	$4,701
2016	$6,919	$5,189
2017	$7,636	$5,727
2018	$8,481	$6,361

LZS749EKC 724

YEARS MFRD 2012-2014
SERIES . . . . LAZER Z S SERIES
ENGINE . . . . KOHLER ECV749
COOLING . . . . AIR
FUEL . . . . G
SPEEDS . . . . VARIABLE
TRANSMISSION . . . . HYDRO
STEERING. . . . . ZERO
BLADE CLUTCH . . . . ELECTRIC
STANDARD DECK . . . . 72"
WEIGHT . . . . 1,208 LBS.
MSRP. $11,899

RETAIL PRICING

YEAR	HIGH	LOW
2012	$4,760	$3,570
2013	$5,740	$4,305
2014	$6,776	$5,082

LZS801CKA

YEARS MFRD 2020-2020
SERIES . . . . LAZER Z S SERIES
ENGINE . . . . KAWASAKI
CYLINDERS. 2
CID 852CC
ENGINE HP 25.5
FUEL . . . . G
SPEEDS . . . . VARIABLE
TRANSMISSION . . . . . DUAL HYDRO
STEERING. . . . . ZERO
ROPS/CAB . . . . ROPS
STANDARD DECK . . . . 60"
WEIGHT . . . . 1,287 LBS.
MSRP. $14,207

OPTIONS

72" DECK. $555

LZS801GKA

YEARS MFRD 2015-2020
SERIES . . . . LASER Z S SERIES
ENGINE . . . . KAWASAKI FX801V
CYLINDERS. 2
CID 852CC
ENGINE HP 25.5
FUEL . . . . G
SPEEDS . . . . VARIABLE
TRANSMISSION . . . . . DUAL HYDRO
STEERING. . . . . ZERO
STANDARD DECK . . . . 52"
WEIGHT . . . . 1,134 LBS.
MSRP. $13,319

OPTIONS

60" DECK. $444

LZS801KA

YEARS MFRD 2013-2018
SERIES . . . . LAZER Z S SERIES
ENGINE . . . . KAWASAKI FX801V
ENGINE HP 25.5
COOLING . . . . AIR
FUEL . . . . G
SPEEDS . . . . VARIABLE
TRANSMISSION . . . . HYDRO
STEERING. . . . . ZERO
BLADE CLUTCH . . . . ELECTRIC
STANDARD DECK . . . . 52"
MSRP. $11,499

OPTIONS

60" DECK
72" DECK

SERIAL NUMBERS

YEAR	BEGINNING NO.
2013	313600000

RETAIL PRICING

YEAR	HIGH	LOW
2013	$4,930	$3,698
2014	$5,444	$4,083
2015	$6,008	$4,506
2016	$6,631	$4,973
2017	$7,320	$5,490

LZS801KA 724

YEARS MFRD 2012-2012
SERIES . . . . LAZER Z S SERIES
ENGINE . . . . KAWASAKI FX801V
COOLING . . . . AIR
FUEL . . . . G
SPEEDS . . . . VARIABLE
TRANSMISSION . . . . HYDRO
STEERING. . . . . ZERO
BLADE CLUTCH . . . . ELECTRIC
WEIGHT . . . . 1,208 LBS.

LZS801PKA 604

YEARS MFRD 2012-2012
SERIES LAZER Z S SERIES PROPANE
ENGINE . . . . KAWASAKI FX801V
COOLING . . . . AIR

SPEEDS .... VARIABLE
TRANSMISSION .... HYDRO
STEERING................ ZERO
BLADE CLUTCH .... ELECTRIC
WEIGHT .... 1,316 LBS.

LZS801PKA 724

YEARS MFRD 2012-2012
SERIES LAZER Z S SERIES PROPANE
ENGINE .... KAWASAKI FX801V
COOLING .... AIR
SPEEDS .... VARIABLE
TRANSMISSION .... HYDRO
STEERING................ ZERO
BLADE CLUTCH .... ELECTRIC
WEIGHT .... 1,403 LBS.

LZS850EKA

YEARS MFRD 2018-2020
SERIES........ LAZER Z S SERIES
ENGINE .... KAWASAKI EFI
ENGINE HP 29.5
COOLING .... AIR
FUEL .... G
TRANSMISSION .... HYDRO
STEERING................ ZERO
STANDARD DECK .... 60"
MSRP................ $15,317

OPTIONS

72" DECK................ $555

LZX23KC486

YEARS MFRD 2011-2011
SERIES........ LAZER Z X SERIES
ENGINE ...... KOHLER COMMAND
CYLINDERS.................... 2
ENGINE HP 23
COOLING .... AIR
FUEL .... G
SPEEDS .... VARIABLE
TRANSMISSION .... HYDRO
STEERING................ ZERO
BLADE CLUTCH .... ELECTRIC

LZX24KA526

YEARS MFRD 2011-2011
SERIES........ LAZER Z X SERIES
ENGINE .... KAWASAKI
CYLINDERS.................... 2
ENGINE HP 24
COOLING .... AIR
FUEL .... G
SPEEDS .... VARIABLE
TRANSMISSION .... HYDRO
STEERING................ ZERO
BLADE CLUTCH .... ELECTRIC

LZX27KC526

YEARS MFRD 2011-2011
SERIES........ LAZER Z X SERIES
ENGINE ...... KOHLER COMMAND
CYLINDERS.................... 2
ENGINE HP 27
COOLING .... AIR
FUEL .... G
SPEEDS .... VARIABLE
TRANSMISSION .... HYDRO
STEERING................ ZERO
BLADE CLUTCH .... ELECTRIC

LZX27KC606

YEARS MFRD 2011-2011
SERIES........ LAZER Z X SERIES
ENGINE ...... KOHLER COMMAND
CYLINDERS.................... 2
ENGINE HP 27
COOLING .... AIR
FUEL .... G
SPEEDS .... VARIABLE
TRANSMISSION .... HYDRO
STEERING................ ZERO
BLADE CLUTCH .... ELECTRIC

LZX29KA606

YEARS MFRD 2011-2011
SERIES........ LAZER Z X SERIES
ENGINE .... KAWASAKI
CYLINDERS.................... 2
ENGINE HP 29
COOLING .... AIR
FUEL .... G
SPEEDS .... VARIABLE
TRANSMISSION .... HYDRO
STEERING................ ZERO
BLADE CLUTCH .... ELECTRIC

LZX29KA606 SS

YEARS MFRD 2011-2011
SERIES........ LAZER Z X SERIES
ENGINE .... KAWASAKI
CYLINDERS.................... 2
ENGINE HP 29
COOLING .... AIR
FUEL .... G
SPEEDS .... VARIABLE
TRANSMISSION .... HYDRO
STEERING................ ZERO
BLADE CLUTCH .... ELECTRIC

LZX34KC606

YEARS MFRD 2011-2011
SERIES........ LAZER Z X SERIES
ENGINE ...... KOHLER COMMAND
CYLINDERS.................... 2
ENGINE HP 34
COOLING .... AIR
FUEL .... G
SPEEDS .... VARIABLE
TRANSMISSION .... HYDRO
STEERING................ ZERO
BLADE CLUTCH .... ELECTRIC

LZX34KC606 SS

YEARS MFRD 2011-2011
SERIES........ LAZER Z X SERIES
ENGINE ...... KOHLER COMMAND
CYLINDERS.................... 2
ENGINE HP 34
COOLING .... AIR
FUEL .... G
SPEEDS .... VARIABLE
TRANSMISSION .... HYDRO
STEERING................ ZERO
BLADE CLUTCH .... ELECTRIC

LZX34KC726

YEARS MFRD 2011-2011
SERIES........ LAZER Z X SERIES
ENGINE ...... KOHLER COMMAND
CYLINDERS.................... 2
ENGINE HP 34
COOLING .... AIR
FUEL .... G
SPEEDS .... VARIABLE
TRANSMISSION .... HYDRO
STEERING................ ZERO
BLADE CLUTCH .... ELECTRIC

LZX34KC726 SS

YEARS MFRD 2011-2011
SERIES........ LAZER Z X SERIES
ENGINE ...... KOHLER COMMAND
CYLINDERS.................... 2
ENGINE HP 34
COOLING .... AIR
FUEL .... G
SPEEDS .... VARIABLE
TRANSMISSION .... HYDRO
STEERING................ ZERO
BLADE CLUTCH .... ELECTRIC

LZX38KC606 SS

YEARS MFRD 2011-2011
SERIES........ LAZER Z X SERIES
ENGINE ...... KOHLER COMMAND
CYLINDERS.................... 2
ENGINE HP 38
COOLING .... AIR
FUEL .... G
SPEEDS .... VARIABLE
TRANSMISSION .... HYDRO
STEERING................ ZERO
BLADE CLUTCH .... ELECTRIC

LZX38KC726 SS

YEARS MFRD 2011-2011
SERIES........ LAZER Z X SERIES
ENGINE ...... KOHLER COMMAND
CYLINDERS.................... 2
ENGINE HP 38
COOLING .... AIR
FUEL .... G
SPEEDS .... VARIABLE
TRANSMISSION .... HYDRO
STEERING................ ZERO
BLADE CLUTCH .... ELECTRIC

LZX740EKC

YEARS MFRD 2013-2019
SERIES........ LAZER Z X SERIES
ENGINE .... KOHLER ECV740
ENGINE HP 25
COOLING .... AIR
FUEL .... G
SPEEDS .... VARIABLE
TRANSMISSION .... HYDRO
STEERING................ ZERO
BLADE CLUTCH .... ELECTRIC
STANDARD DECK .... 52"

SERIAL NUMBERS

YEAR	BEGINNING NO.
2013	313600000

RETAIL PRICING

YEAR	HIGH	LOW
2013	$5,272	$3,954
2014	$5,815	$4,361
2015	$6,418	$4,814
2016	$7,085	$5,314
2017	$7,819	$5,865
2018	$8,681	$6,511
2019	$9,637	$7,228

LZX740KC526

YEARS MFRD 2014-2014
SERIES........ LAZER Z X SERIES
ENGINE .... KOHLER
COOLING .... AIR
FUEL .... G
SPEEDS .... VARIABLE
TRANSMISSION .... HYDRO
STEERING................ ZERO
BLADE CLUTCH .... ELECTRIC
STANDARD DECK .... 52"
MSRP................ $11,799

RETAIL PRICING

YEAR	HIGH	LOW
2014	$6,720	$5,040

LZX749EKC 606

YEARS MFRD 2012-2012
SERIES........ LAZER Z X SERIES
ENGINE .... KOHLER ECV749
COOLING .... AIR
FUEL .... G
SPEEDS .... VARIABLE
TRANSMISSION .... HYDRO
STEERING................ ZERO
BLADE CLUTCH .... ELECTRIC
WEIGHT .... 1,212 LBS.

EX MARK

LZX801CKA

YEARS MFRD 2017-2020
SERIES. . . . . LASER Z X SERIES
ENGINE . . . . KAWASAKI FX801V
CYLINDERS. 2
CID 852CC
ENGINE HP. 25.5
FUEL . . . . G
SPEEDS . . . . VARIABLE
TRANSMISSION . . . . HYDRO
STEERING. . . . . ZERO
STANDARD DECK . . . . 60"
WEIGHT . . . . 1,215 LBS.
MSRP. $15,539

OPTIONS

72" DECK

RETAIL PRICING

YEAR	HIGH	LOW
2017	$8,430	$6,322
2018	$9,411	$7,058
2019	$10,466	$7,849
2020	$12,175	$9,179

LZX801KA

YEARS MFRD 2013-2019
SERIES. . . . . LAZER Z X SERIES
ENGINE . . . . KAWASAKI FX801V
ENGINE HP. 25.5
COOLING . . . . AIR
FUEL . . . . G
SPEEDS . . . . VARIABLE
TRANSMISSION . . . . HYDRO
STEERING. . . . . ZERO
BLADE CLUTCH . . . . ELECTRIC
STANDARD DECK . . . . 60"
MSRP. $12,999

OPTIONS

72" DECK
SUS PLTFRM

SERIAL NUMBERS

YEAR	BEGINNING NO.
2013	313600000

RETAIL PRICING

YEAR	HIGH	LOW
2013	$5,373	$4,030
2014	$5,915	$4,436
2015	$6,535	$4,901
2016	$7,246	$5,435
2017	$7,956	$5,967
2018	$8,672	$6,768
2019	$9,462	$7,525

AVG. AUCTION PRICING

LOW	HIGH	AVG
$3,920	$4,410	$4,148

LZX921GKA

YEARS MFRD 2017-2020
SERIES. . . . . LAZER Z X SERIES
ENGINE . . . . KAWASAKI FX921V
ENGINE HP. 31
COOLING . . . . AIR
FUEL . . . . G
SPEEDS . . . . VARIABLE
TRANSMISSION . . . . HYDRO
STEERING. . . . . ZERO
STANDARD DECK . . . . 60"
MSRP. $15,983

OPTIONS

72" DECK. $444
72" SUSP PLTFRM $1,554

RETAIL PRICING

YEAR	HIGH	LOW
2017	$8,919	$6,689
2018	$9,952	$7,464
2019	$11,053	$8,290

LZX921KA606

YEARS MFRD 2014-2014
SERIES. . . . . LAZER Z X SERIES
ENGINE . . . . KAWASAKI FX921V
CID 999CC
COOLING . . . . AIR
FUEL . . . . G
SPEEDS . . . . VARIABLE
TRANSMISSION . . . . HYDRO
STEERING. . . . . ZERO
BLADE CLUTCH . . . . ELECTRIC
STANDARD DECK . . . . 60"
MSRP. $13,299

RETAIL PRICING

YEAR	HIGH	LOW
2014	$7,574	$5,681

LZX921KA726

YEARS MFRD 2014-2014
SERIES. . . . . LAZER Z X SERIES
ENGINE . . . . KAWASAKI EX921V
CID 999CC
COOLING . . . . AIR
FUEL . . . . G
SPEEDS . . . . VARIABLE
TRANSMISSION . . . . HYDRO
STEERING. . . . . ZERO
BLADE CLUTCH . . . . ELECTRIC
STANDARD DECK . . . . 72"
MSRP. $13,699

RETAIL PRICING

YEAR	HIGH	LOW
2014	$7,796	$5,847

LZX940EKC

YEARS MFRD 2013-2019
SERIES. . . . . LAZER Z X SERIES
ENGINE . . . . KOHLER ECV940
ENGINE HP. 35
COOLING . . . . AIR
FUEL . . . . G
SPEEDS . . . . VARIABLE
TRANSMISSION . . . . HYDRO
STEERING. . . . . ZERO
BLADE CLUTCH . . . . ELECTRIC
STANDARD DECK . . . . 60"
MSRP. $15,199

OPTIONS

60" DECK RD
72" DECK RD

SERIAL NUMBERS

YEAR	BEGINNING NO.
2013	313600000

RETAIL PRICING

YEAR	HIGH	LOW
2013	$6,000	$4,500
2014	$6,651	$4,988
2015	$7,322	$5,491
2016	$8,081	$6,061
2017	$8,919	$6,689
2018	$9,952	$7,464
2019	$11,053	$8,290

LZX949EKC 606

YEARS MFRD 2014-2014
SERIES. . . . . LAZER Z X SERIES
ENGINE . . . . KOHLER FX921V
CID 999CC
COOLING . . . . AIR
FUEL . . . . G
SPEEDS . . . . VARIABLE
TRANSMISSION . . . . HYDRO
STEERING. . . . . ZERO
BLADE CLUTCH . . . . ELECTRIC
STANDARD DECK . . . . 60"
MSRP. $13,599

RETAIL PRICING

YEAR	HIGH	LOW
2014	$7,740	$5,805

LZX980EKC

YEARS MFRD 2017-2020
SERIES. . . . . LASER Z X SERIES
ENGINE . . . . KOHLER ECV980
CID 999CC
ENGINE HP. 38
FUEL . . . . G
SPEEDS . . . . VARIABLE
TRANSMISSION . . . . . DUAL HYDRO
STEERING. . . . . ZERO
STANDARD DECK . . . . 72"
MSRP. $17,759

OPTIONS

60" DECK. . . . . $-444
96" RD DECK $18,870

LZX980EKC 726

YEARS MFRD 2014-2014
SERIES. . . . . LAZER Z X SERIES
ENGINE . . . . KOHLER ECV980
CID 999CC
COOLING . . . . AIR
FUEL . . . . G
SPEEDS . . . . VARIABLE
TRANSMISSION . . . . HYDRO
STEERING. . . . . ZERO
BLADE CLUTCH . . . . ELECTRIC
STANDARD DECK . . . . 72"
MSRP. $14,999

RETAIL PRICING

YEAR	HIGH	LOW
2014	$8,539	$6,404

LZX980KC

YEARS MFRD 2013-2018
SERIES. . . . . LAZER Z X SERIES
ENGINE . . . . KOHLER ECV980
ENGINE HP. 38
COOLING . . . . AIR
FUEL . . . . G
SPEEDS . . . . VARIABLE
TRANSMISSION . . . . HYDRO
STEERING. . . . . ZERO
BLADE CLUTCH . . . . ELECTRIC
STANDARD DECK . . . . 60"
MSRP. $15,399

OPTIONS

72" DECK

SERIAL NUMBERS

YEAR	BEGINNING NO.
2013	313600000

RETAIL PRICING

YEAR	HIGH	LOW
2013	$6,354	$4,766
2014	$6,997	$5,248
2015	$7,722	$5,792
2016	$8,524	$6,393
2017	$9,409	$7,057
2018	$10,432	$7,824

LZZ23KA526

YEARS MFRD 2009-2009
ENGINE . . . . KAWASAKI
CYLINDERS. 2
ENGINE HP. 23
COOLING . . . . AIR
FUEL . . . . G
SPEEDS . . . . VARIABLE
TRANSMISSION . . . . HYDRO
STEERING. . . . . ZERO
BLADE CLUTCH . . . . ELECTRIC
STANDARD DECK . . . . 52"
MSRP. $10,988

RETAIL PRICING

YEAR	HIGH	LOW
2009	$3,595	$2,696

LZZ23KC486

YEARS MFRD 2009-2009
SERIES. . . . . LAZER Z SERIES
ENGINE . . . . . . KOHLER COMMAND
CYLINDERS. 2
ENGINE HP. 23
COOLING . . . . AIR
FUEL . . . . G
SPEEDS . . . . VARIABLE
TRANSMISSION . . . . HYDRO
STEERING. . . . . ZERO
BLADE CLUTCH . . . . ELECTRIC
STANDARD DECK . . . . 48"
WEIGHT . . . . 1,104 LBS.
MSRP. $10,433

OPTIONS

52" DECK

RETAIL PRICING

YEAR	HIGH	LOW
2009	$3,412	$2,559

LZZ27KC526

YEARS MFRD 2009-2009
ENGINE . . . . . . KOHLER COMMAND
CYLINDERS. 2

ENGINE HP 27
COOLING .... AIR
FUEL .... G
SPEEDS .... VARIABLE
TRANSMISSION .... HYDRO
STEERING .... ZERO
BLADE CLUTCH .... ELECTRIC
STANDARD DECK .... 52"
MSRP $11,210

OPTIONS

60" DECK

RETAIL PRICING

YEAR	HIGH	LOW
2009	$3,667	$2,750

LZZ29KA606

YEARS MFRD 2009-2009
ENGINE .... KAWASAKI
CYLINDERS 2
ENGINE HP 29
COOLING .... AIR
FUEL .... G
SPEEDS .... VARIABLE
TRANSMISSION .... DUAL HYDRO
STEERING .... ZERO
BLADE CLUTCH .... ELECTRIC
STANDARD DECK .... 60"
MSRP $12,209

RETAIL PRICING

YEAR	HIGH	LOW
2009	$4,009	$3,007

LZZ34KA606

YEARS MFRD 2009-2009
ENGINE .... KAWASAKI
CYLINDERS 2
ENGINE HP 34
COOLING .... AIR
FUEL .... G
SPEEDS .... VARIABLE
TRANSMISSION .... DUAL HYDRO
STEERING .... ZERO
BLADE CLUTCH .... ELECTRIC
STANDARD DECK .... 60"
MSRP $12,875

OPTIONS

72" DECK

RETAIL PRICING

YEAR	HIGH	LOW
2009	$4,228	$3,171

NAV20KC

YEARS MFRD 2006-2009
SERIES .... NAVIGATOR SERIES
ENGINE .... KOHLER COMMAND
CYLINDERS 2
ENGINE HP 20
COOLING .... AIR
FUEL .... G
SPEEDS .... VARIABLE
TRANSMISSION .... DUAL HYDRO
STEERING .... ZERO
BLADE CLUTCH .... ELECTRIC
STANDARD DECK .... 42"
WEIGHT .... 1,170 LBS.
MSRP $13,984

RETAIL PRICING

YEAR	HIGH	LOW
2006	$3,402	$2,551
2007	$3,754	$2,816
2008	$4,144	$3,108
2009	$4,575	$3,431

NAV27KC

YEARS MFRD 2006-2009
SERIES .... NAVIGATOR SERIES
ENGINE .... KOHLER COMMAND
CYLINDERS 2
ENGINE HP 27
COOLING .... AIR
FUEL .... G
SPEEDS .... VARIABLE
TRANSMISSION .... HYDRO
STEERING .... ZERO
BLADE CLUTCH .... ELECTRIC
STANDARD DECK .... 48"
WEIGHT .... 1,175 LBS.
MSRP $15,205

RETAIL PRICING

YEAR	HIGH	LOW
2006	$3,702	$2,777
2007	$4,085	$3,063
2008	$4,506	$3,380
2009	$4,974	$3,731

NV640KC42

YEARS MFRD 2013-2013
SERIES .... NAVIGATOR SERIES
ENGINE .... KOHLER CH640
COOLING .... AIR
FUEL .... G
SPEEDS .... VARIABLE
TRANSMISSION .... HYDRO
STEERING .... ZERO
BLADE CLUTCH .... ELECTRIC
STANDARD DECK .... 42"
MSRP $15,208

OPTIONS

48" DECK

SERIAL NUMBERS

YEAR	BEGINNING NO.
2013	313600000

RETAIL PRICING

YEAR	HIGH	LOW
2013	$7,410	$5,557

NV730EKC42

YEARS MFRD 2013-2013
SERIES .... NAVIGATOR SERIES
ENGINE .... KOHLER ECH730
COOLING .... AIR
FUEL .... G
SPEEDS .... VARIABLE
TRANSMISSION .... HYDRO
STEERING .... ZERO
BLADE CLUTCH .... ELECTRIC
STANDARD DECK .... 42"
MSRP $16,649

OPTIONS

48" DECK

SERIAL NUMBERS

YEAR	BEGINNING NO.
2013	313600000

RETAIL PRICING

YEAR	HIGH	LOW
2013	$8,111	$6,084

NV740EKC48

YEARS MFRD 2014-2014
SERIES .... NAVIGATOR SERIES
ENGINE .... KOHLER CH640
CID 624CC
COOLING .... AIR
FUEL .... G
SPEEDS .... VARIABLE
TRANSMISSION .... HYDRO
STEERING .... ZERO
BLADE CLUTCH .... ELECTRIC
STANDARD DECK .... 48"
MSRP $15,199

RETAIL PRICING

YEAR	HIGH	LOW
2014	$8,650	$6,488

NV740KC

YEARS MFRD 2012-2012
SERIES .... NAVIGATOR SERIES
ENGINE .... KOHLER CV740
COOLING .... AIR
FUEL .... G
SPEEDS .... VARIABLE
TRANSMISSION .... HYDRO
STEERING .... ZERO
BLADE CLUTCH .... ELECTRIC
WEIGHT .... 850 LBS.

NVS730AKC

YEARS MFRD 2014-2020
SERIES .... NAVIGATOR SERIES
ENGINE .... KOHLER EFI
CID 725CC
ENGINE HP 23
COOLING .... AIR
FUEL .... G
SPEEDS .... VARIABLE
TRANSMISSION .... DUAL HYDRO
STEERING .... ZERO
STANDARD DECK .... 48"
WEIGHT .... 1,170 LBS.
MSRP $17,759

RETAIL PRICING

YEAR	HIGH	LOW
2014	$7,133	$5,349
2015	$7,873	$5,905
2016	$8,690	$6,517
2017	$9,592	$7,194
2018	$10,650	$7,987
2019	$11,640	$8,730
2020	$13,170	$9,938

NVS740CKC

YEARS MFRD 2014-2020
SERIES .... NAVIGATOR SERIES
ENGINE .... KOHLER CH740
CID 725CC
ENGINE HP 25
COOLING .... AIR
FUEL .... G
SPEEDS .... VARIABLE
TRANSMISSION .... DUAL HYDRO
STEERING .... ZERO
STANDARD DECK .... 42"
WEIGHT .... 1,140 LBS.
MSRP $16,427

OPTIONS

48" DECK

RETAIL PRICING

YEAR	HIGH	LOW
2014	$6,542	$4,906
2015	$7,221	$5,416
2016	$7,970	$5,978
2017	$8,797	$6,598
2018	$9,752	$7,314
2019	$10,846	$8,134
2020	$12,061	$9,163

PHZ19KA343

YEARS MFRD 2007-2009
SERIES .... PHAZER SERIES
ENGINE .... KAWASAKI
CYLINDERS 2
ENGINE HP 19
COOLING .... AIR
FUEL .... G
SPEEDS .... VARIABLE
TRANSMISSION .... HYDRO
STEERING .... ZERO
BLADE CLUTCH .... ELECTRIC
STANDARD DECK .... 34"
WEIGHT .... 570 LBS.
MSRP $6,659

RETAIL PRICING

YEAR	HIGH	LOW
2007	$1,789	$1,341
2008	$1,974	$1,480
2009	$2,178	$1,633

PHZ19KA443

YEARS MFRD 2006-2007
SERIES .... PHAZER SERIES
ENGINE .... KAWASAKI
ENGINE HP 19
FUEL .... G
SPEEDS .... VARIABLE
TRANSMISSION .... HYDRO
STEERING .... STANDARD
WEIGHT .... 610 LBS.

PNE22KA482

YEARS MFRD 2011-2011
SERIES .... PIONEER E SERIES
ENGINE .... KAWASAKI
CYLINDERS 2
ENGINE HP 22

COOLING . . . . AIR
FUEL . . . . G
SPEEDS . . . . VARIABLE
TRANSMISSION . . . . HYDRO
STEERING. . . . . ZERO
BLADE CLUTCH . . . . ELECTRIC

PNE24KA522

YEARS MFRD 2011-2011
SERIES. . . . . PIONEER E SERIES
ENGINE . . . . KAWASAKI
CYLINDERS. 2
ENGINE HP 24
COOLING . . . . AIR
FUEL . . . . G
SPEEDS . . . . VARIABLE
TRANSMISSION . . . . HYDRO
STEERING. . . . . ZERO
BLADE CLUTCH . . . . ELECTRIC

PNE651KA

YEARS MFRD 2013-2013
SERIES. . . . . PIONEER E SERIES
ENGINE . . . . KAWASAKI FR651V
COOLING . . . . AIR
FUEL . . . . G
SPEEDS . . . . VARIABLE
TRANSMISSION . . . . . DUAL HYDRO
STEERING. . . . . ZERO
BLADE CLUTCH . . . . ELECTRIC
STANDARD DECK . . . . 48"
MSRP. $5,599

RETAIL PRICING

YEAR	HIGH	LOW
2013	$3,407	$2,556

PNE651KA482

YEARS MFRD 2012-2012
SERIES. . . . . PIONEER E SERIES
ENGINE . . . . KAWASAKI FR651V
COOLING . . . . AIR
FUEL . . . . G
SPEEDS . . . . VARIABLE
TRANSMISSION . . . . HYDRO
STEERING. . . . . ZERO
BLADE CLUTCH . . . . ELECTRIC
WEIGHT . . . . 799 LBS.

PNE691KA

YEARS MFRD 2013-2013
SERIES. . . . . PIONEER E SERIES
ENGINE . . . . KAWASAKI FR691V
COOLING . . . . AIR
FUEL . . . . G
SPEEDS . . . . VARIABLE
TRANSMISSION . . . . . DUAL HYDRO
STEERING. . . . . ZERO
BLADE CLUTCH . . . . ELECTRIC
STANDARD DECK . . . . 52"
MSRP. $5,999

RETAIL PRICING

YEAR	HIGH	LOW
2013	$3,653	$2,740

PNE691KA522

YEARS MFRD 2012-2012
SERIES. . . . . PIONEER E SERIES
ENGINE . . . . KAWASAKI FR691V
COOLING . . . . AIR
FUEL . . . . G
SPEEDS . . . . VARIABLE
TRANSMISSION . . . . HYDRO
STEERING. . . . . ZERO
BLADE CLUTCH . . . . ELECTRIC
WEIGHT . . . . 805 LBS.

PNS22KA483

YEARS MFRD 2011-2011
SERIES. . . . . PIONEER S SERIES
ENGINE . . . . KAWASAKI
CYLINDERS. 2
ENGINE HP 22
COOLING . . . . AIR
FUEL . . . . G
SPEEDS . . . . VARIABLE
TRANSMISSION . . . . HYDRO
STEERING. . . . . ZERO
BLADE CLUTCH . . . . ELECTRIC

PNS24KA523

YEARS MFRD 2011-2011
SERIES. . . . . PIONEER S SERIES
ENGINE . . . . KAWASAKI
CYLINDERS. 2
ENGINE HP 24
COOLING . . . . AIR
FUEL . . . . G
SPEEDS . . . . VARIABLE
TRANSMISSION . . . . HYDRO
STEERING. . . . . ZERO
BLADE CLUTCH . . . . ELECTRIC

PNS600KA

YEARS MFRD 2013-2013
SERIES. . . . . PIONEER S SERIES
ENGINE . . . . KAWASAKI FX600V
ENGINE HP 23
COOLING . . . . AIR
FUEL . . . . G
SPEEDS . . . . VARIABLE
TRANSMISSION . . . . HYDRO
STEERING. . . . . ZERO
BLADE CLUTCH . . . . ELECTRIC
STANDARD DECK . . . . 44"
MSRP. $7,214

RETAIL PRICING

YEAR	HIGH	LOW
2013	$3,198	$2,398

PNS600KA443

YEARS MFRD 2012-2012
SERIES. . . . . PIONEER S SERIES
ENGINE . . . . KAWASAKI FX600V
COOLING . . . . AIR
FUEL . . . . G
SPEEDS . . . . VARIABLE
TRANSMISSION . . . . HYDRO
STEERING. . . . . ZERO
BLADE CLUTCH . . . . ELECTRIC
WEIGHT . . . . 822 LBS.

PNS651KA

YEARS MFRD 2013-2013
SERIES. . . . . PIONEER S SERIES
ENGINE . . . . KAWASAKI FX651V
COOLING . . . . AIR
FUEL . . . . G
SPEEDS . . . . VARIABLE
TRANSMISSION . . . . . DUAL HYDRO
STEERING. . . . . ZERO
BLADE CLUTCH . . . . ELECTRIC
STANDARD DECK . . . . 48"
MSRP. $7,436

RETAIL PRICING

YEAR	HIGH	LOW
2013	$4,527	$3,395

PNS651KA483

YEARS MFRD 2012-2012
SERIES. . . . . PIONEER S SERIES
ENGINE . . . . KAWASAKI FX651V
COOLING . . . . AIR
FUEL . . . . G
SPEEDS . . . . VARIABLE
TRANSMISSION . . . . HYDRO
STEERING. . . . . ZERO
BLADE CLUTCH . . . . ELECTRIC
WEIGHT . . . . 862 LBS.

PNS680KC

YEARS MFRD 2013-2013
SERIES. . . . . PIONEER S SERIES
ENGINE . . . . KOHLER CV680
COOLING . . . . AIR
FUEL . . . . G
SPEEDS . . . . VARIABLE
TRANSMISSION . . . . . DUAL HYDRO
STEERING. . . . . ZERO
BLADE CLUTCH . . . . ELECTRIC
STANDARD DECK . . . . 48"
MSRP. $7,880

RETAIL PRICING

YEAR	HIGH	LOW
2013	$3,551	$2,663

PNS680KC523

YEARS MFRD 2012-2012
SERIES. . . . . PIONEER S SERIES
ENGINE . . . . KOHLER CV680
COOLING . . . . AIR
FUEL . . . . G
SPEEDS . . . . VARIABLE
TRANSMISSION . . . . HYDRO
STEERING. . . . . ZERO
BLADE CLUTCH . . . . ELECTRIC
WEIGHT . . . . 873 LBS.

PNS691KA523

YEARS MFRD 2014-2014
SERIES. . . . . PIONEER SERIES
ENGINE . . . . KAWASAKI FX691V
CID 691CC
COOLING . . . . AIR
FUEL . . . . G
SPEEDS . . . . VARIABLE
TRANSMISSION . . . . HYDRO
STEERING. . . . . ZERO
BLADE CLUTCH . . . . ELECTRIC
STANDARD DECK . . . . 52"
MSRP. $7,299

RETAIL PRICING

YEAR	HIGH	LOW
2014	$4,158	$3,119

PNS710KC443

YEARS MFRD 2014-2014
SERIES. . . . . PIONEER SERIES
ENGINE . . . . KOHLER ZT710
CID 725CC
COOLING . . . . AIR
FUEL . . . . G
SPEEDS . . . . VARIABLE
TRANSMISSION . . . . HYDRO
STEERING. . . . . ZERO
BLADE CLUTCH . . . . ELECTRIC
STANDARD DECK . . . . 44"
MSRP. $6,499

OPTIONS

48" DECK

RETAIL PRICING

YEAR	HIGH	LOW
2014	$3,700	$2,775

PNS720KC523

YEARS MFRD 2014-2014
SERIES. . . . . PIONEER SERIES
ENGINE . . . . KOHLER FX691V
CID 691CC
COOLING . . . . AIR
FUEL . . . . G
SPEEDS . . . . VARIABLE
TRANSMISSION . . . . HYDRO
STEERING. . . . . ZERO
BLADE CLUTCH . . . . ELECTRIC
STANDARD DECK . . . . 52"
MSRP. $7,099

RETAIL PRICING

YEAR	HIGH	LOW
2014	$4,041	$3,030

PNS730KA604

YEARS MFRD 2014-2014
SERIES. . . . . PIONEER SERIES
ENGINE . . . . KAWASAKI FX730V
CID 747
COOLING . . . . AIR
FUEL . . . . G
SPEEDS . . . . VARIABLE
TRANSMISSION . . . . HYDRO
STEERING. . . . . ZERO
BLADE CLUTCH . . . . ELECTRIC

STANDARD DECK . . . . 60"
MSRP. $7,699

RETAIL PRICING

YEAR	HIGH	LOW
2014	$4,381	$3,285

PNS740KC

YEARS MFRD 2013-2013
SERIES. . . . . PIONEER S SERIES
ENGINE . . . . KOHLER CV740
COOLING . . . . AIR
FUEL . . . . G
SPEEDS . . . . VARIABLE
TRANSMISSION . . . . . DUAL HYDRO
STEERING. . . . . ZERO
BLADE CLUTCH . . . . ELECTRIC
STANDARD DECK . . . . 60"
MSRP. $8,324

RETAIL PRICING

YEAR	HIGH	LOW
2013	$5,069	$3,801

PNS740KC604

YEARS MFRD 2012-2014
SERIES. . . . . PIONEER S SERIES
ENGINE . . . . KOHLER CV740
COOLING . . . . AIR
FUEL . . . . G
SPEEDS . . . . VARIABLE
TRANSMISSION . . . . HYDRO
STEERING. . . . . ZERO
BLADE CLUTCH . . . . ELECTRIC
STANDARD DECK . . . . 60"
WEIGHT . . . . 948 LBS.
MSRP. $7,799

RETAIL PRICING

YEAR	HIGH	LOW
2012	$3,020	$2,265
2013	$3,613	$2,710
2014	$4,442	$3,332

QSS708GEM

YEARS MFRD 2015-2017
SERIES. . . . . QUEST S FRTSTR
ENGINE . . . . EXMARK
COOLING . . . . AIR
FUEL . . . . G
SPEEDS . . . . VARIABLE
TRANSMISSION . . . . . DUAL HYDRO
STEERING. . . . . ZERO
STANDARD DECK . . . . 42"
MSRP. $4,599

OPTIONS

50" DECK

RETAIL PRICING

YEAR	HIGH	LOW
2015	$2,325	$1,743
2016	$2,554	$1,915
2017	$2,819	$2,115

QST20BE422

YEARS MFRD 2009-2009
ENGINE . . . . B&S
ENGINE HP 24
COOLING . . . . AIR
FUEL . . . . G
SPEEDS . . . . VARIABLE
TRANSMISSION . . . . . DUAL HYDRO
STEERING. . . . . ZERO
STANDARD DECK . . . . 52"
WEIGHT . . . . 625 LBS.
MSRP. $4,883

OPTIONS

BAGGER

RETAIL PRICING

YEAR	HIGH	LOW
2009	$1,576	$1,182

QST22BE482

YEARS MFRD 2007-2009
SERIES. . . . . QUEST SERIES
ENGINE . . . . B&S
ENGINE HP 22
COOLING . . . . AIR
FUEL . . . . G
SPEEDS . . . . VARIABLE
TRANSMISSION . . . . HYDRO
STEERING. . . . . ZERO
BLADE CLUTCH . . . . ELECTRIC
STANDARD DECK . . . . 48"
WEIGHT . . . . 645 LBS.
MSRP. $5,549

OPTIONS

BAGGER

RETAIL PRICING

YEAR	HIGH	LOW
2007	$1,470	$1,103
2008	$1,622	$1,216
2009	$1,790	$1,343

QST22BE522

YEARS MFRD 2008-2010
SERIES. . . . . QUEST SERIES
ENGINE . . . . B&S
CYLINDERS. 2
ENGINE HP 22
COOLING . . . . AIR
FUEL . . . . G
SPEEDS . . . . VARIABLE
TRANSMISSION . . . . HYDRO
STEERING. . . . . ZERO
BLADE CLUTCH . . . . ELECTRIC
STANDARD DECK . . . . 52"
WEIGHT . . . . 660 LBS.
MSRP. $5,689

RETAIL PRICING

YEAR	HIGH	LOW
2009	$3,123	$2,342
2010	$3,253	$2,439

QST23KC482

YEARS MFRD 2008-2008
SERIES. . . . . QUEST SERIES
ENGINE . . . . . . KOHLER COMMAND
CYLINDERS. 2
ENGINE HP 23
COOLING . . . . AIR
FUEL . . . . G
SPEEDS . . . . VARIABLE
TRANSMISSION . . . . HYDRO
STEERING. . . . . ZERO
BLADE CLUTCH . . . . ELECTRIC
WEIGHT . . . . 651 LBS.

QST23KC522

YEARS MFRD 2008-2008
SERIES. . . . . QUEST SERIES
ENGINE . . . . . . KOHLER COMMAND
CYLINDERS. 2
ENGINE HP 23
COOLING . . . . AIR
FUEL . . . . G
SPEEDS . . . . VARIABLE
TRANSMISSION . . . . HYDRO
STEERING. . . . . ZERO
BLADE CLUTCH . . . . ELECTRIC
WEIGHT . . . . 666 LBS.

QT22KA421

YEARS MFRD 2011-2011
SERIES. . . . . QUEST SERIES
ENGINE . . . . KAWASAKI
CYLINDERS. 2
ENGINE HP 22
COOLING . . . . AIR
FUEL . . . . G
SPEEDS . . . . VARIABLE
TRANSMISSION . . . . HYDRO
STEERING. . . . . ZERO
BLADE CLUTCH . . . . ELECTRIC

QT24KA501

YEARS MFRD 2011-2011
SERIES. . . . . QUEST SERIES
ENGINE . . . . KAWASAKI
CYLINDERS. 2
ENGINE HP 24
COOLING . . . . AIR
FUEL . . . . G
SPEEDS . . . . VARIABLE
TRANSMISSION . . . . HYDRO
STEERING. . . . . ZERO
BLADE CLUTCH . . . . ELECTRIC

QTE452CEM

YEARS MFRD 2016-2017
SERIES. . . . . QUEST E
ENGINE . . . . EXMARK
COOLING . . . . AIR
FUEL . . . . G
SPEEDS . . . . VARIABLE
TRANSMISSION . . . . . DUAL HYDRO
STEERING. . . . . ZERO
STANDARD DECK . . . . 42"
MSRP. $2,699

OPTIONS

42" FAB

RETAIL PRICING

YEAR	HIGH	LOW
2016	$1,498	$1,124
2017	$1,655	$1,241

QTE651KA

YEARS MFRD 2013-2013
SERIES. . . . . QUEST E SERIES
ENGINE . . . . KAWASAKI FR651V
COOLING . . . . AIR
FUEL . . . . G
SPEEDS . . . . VARIABLE
TRANSMISSION . . . . . DUAL HYDRO
STEERING. . . . . ZERO
BLADE CLUTCH . . . . ELECTRIC
STANDARD DECK . . . . 42"
MSRP. $3,662

SERIAL NUMBERS

YEAR . . . . BEGINNING NO.
2013 313600000

RETAIL PRICING

YEAR	HIGH	LOW
2013	$1,694	$1,271

QTE651KA421

YEARS MFRD 2012-2014
SERIES. . . . . QUEST E SERIES
ENGINE . . . . KAWASAKI FR651V
CID 726CC
COOLING . . . . AIR
FUEL . . . . G
SPEEDS . . . . VARIABLE
TRANSMISSION . . . . HYDRO
STEERING. . . . . ZERO
BLADE CLUTCH . . . . ELECTRIC
STANDARD DECK . . . . 42"
WEIGHT . . . . 551 LBS.
MSRP. $3,662

RETAIL PRICING

YEAR	HIGH	LOW
2012	$1,463	$1,097
2013	$1,644	$1,233
2014	$2,284	$1,713

QTE691KA

YEARS MFRD 2013-2013
SERIES. . . . . QUEST E SERIES
ENGINE . . . . KAWASAKI FR691V
COOLING . . . . AIR
FUEL . . . . G
SPEEDS . . . . VARIABLE
TRANSMISSION . . . . . DUAL HYDRO
STEERING. . . . . ZERO
BLADE CLUTCH . . . . ELECTRIC
STANDARD DECK . . . . 50"
MSRP. $4,106

SERIAL NUMBERS

YEAR . . . . BEGINNING NO.
2013 313600000

RETAIL PRICING

YEAR	HIGH	LOW
2013	$1,915	$1,436

QTE691KA501

YEARS MFRD 2012-2014
SERIES. . . . . QUEST E SERIES
ENGINE . . . . KAWASAKI FR691V
COOLING . . . . AIR
FUEL . . . . G

EX MARK

SPEEDS . . . . VARIABLE
TRANSMISSION . . . . HYDRO
STEERING. . . . . ZERO
BLADE CLUTCH . . . . ELECTRIC
STANDARD DECK . . . . 50"
WEIGHT . . . . 623 LBS.
MSRP. $4,106

RETAIL PRICING

YEAR	HIGH	LOW
2012	$1,573	$1,180
2013	$2,025	$1,519
2014	$2,601	$1,951

QTE708GEM

YEARS MFRD 2015-2017
SERIES. . . . . QUEST E
ENGINE . . . . EXMARK
COOLING . . . . AIR
FUEL . . . . G
SPEEDS . . . . VARIABLE
TRANSMISSION . . . . . DUAL HYDRO
STEERING. . . . . ZERO
STANDARD DECK . . . . 42"
MSRP. $3,299

OPTIONS

50" DECK

RETAIL PRICING

YEAR	HIGH	LOW
2015	$1,660	$1,245
2016	$1,833	$1,374
2017	$2,023	$1,517

QTS691KA FR691V

YEARS MFRD 2013-2013
SERIES. . . . . QUEST S SERIES
ENGINE . . . . . . KAWASAKI FR691V
COOLING . . . . AIR
FUEL . . . . G
SPEEDS . . . . VARIABLE
TRANSMISSION . . . . HYDRO
STEERING. . . . . ZERO
BLADE CLUTCH . . . . ELECTRIC
STANDARD DECK . . . . 42"
MSRP. $4,328

RETAIL PRICING

YEAR	HIGH	LOW
2013	$3,015	$2,262

QTS691KA422

YEARS MFRD 2013-2014
ENGINE . . . . KAWASAKI
CID 726CC
COOLING . . . . AIR
FUEL . . . . G
SPEEDS . . . . VARIABLE
TRANSMISSION . . . . HYDRO
STEERING. . . . . ZERO
BLADE CLUTCH . . . . ELECTRIC
STANDARD DECK . . . . 42"

QTS691KA502

YEARS MFRD 2012-2014
SERIES. . . . . QUEST S SERIES
ENGINE . . . . . . KAWASAKI FR691V
COOLING . . . . AIR
FUEL . . . . G
SPEEDS . . . . VARIABLE
TRANSMISSION . . . . HYDRO
STEERING. . . . . ZERO
BLADE CLUTCH . . . . ELECTRIC
WEIGHT . . . . 681 LBS.

QTS708GEM

YEARS MFRD 2015-2017
SERIES. . . . . QUEST S SERIES
ENGINE . . . . EXMARK
COOLING . . . . AIR
FUEL . . . . G
SPEEDS . . . . VARIABLE
TRANSMISSION . . . . . DUAL HYDRO
STEERING. . . . . ZERO
STANDARD DECK . . . . 42"
MSRP. $3,899

OPTIONS

50" DECK
60" DECK

RETAIL PRICING

YEAR	HIGH	LOW
2015	$1,968	$1,476
2016	$2,166	$1,624
2017	$2,390	$1,793

QTX452CEM

YEARS MFRD 2015-2017
SERIES. . . . . QUEST S
ENGINE . . . . EXMARK
COOLING . . . . AIR
FUEL . . . . G
SPEEDS . . . . VARIABLE
TRANSMISSION . . . . . DUAL HYDRO
STEERING. . . . . ZERO
STANDARD DECK . . . . 34"
MSRP. $3,699

RETAIL PRICING

YEAR	HIGH	LOW
2015	$1,862	$1,397
2016	$2,055	$1,541
2017	$2,269	$1,702

QZE452CEM

YEARS MFRD 2018-2018
SERIES. . . . . QUEST E SERIES
ENGINE . . . . EXMARK
COOLING . . . . AIR
FUEL . . . . G
TRANSMISSION . . . . . DUAL HYDRO
STANDARD DECK . . . . 42"

QZE702GEM

YEARS MFRD 2019-2020
SERIES. . . . . QUEST E SERIES
ENGINE . . . . EXMARK
CYLINDERS. 2
CID 708CC
ENGINE HP 22.5
FUEL . . . . G
SPEEDS . . . . VARIABLE
TRANSMISSION . . . . . DUAL HYDRO
STEERING. . . . . ZERO
STANDARD DECK . . . . 34"
WEIGHT . . . . 547 LBS.

OPTIONS

42" DECK

QZE708GEM

YEARS MFRD 2018-2018
SERIES. . . . . QUEST E SERIES
ENGINE . . . . EXMARK
ENGINE HP 24.5
COOLING . . . . AIR
FUEL . . . . G
SPEEDS . . . . VARIABLE
TRANSMISSION . . . . . DUAL HYDRO
STANDARD DECK . . . . 34"
WEIGHT . . . . 521 LBS.

OPTIONS

42" DECK

QZS708GEM

YEARS MFRD 2018-2020
SERIES. . . . . QUEST S SERIES
ENGINE . . . . EXMARK
CID 708CC
ENGINE HP 24.5
COOLING . . . . AIR
FUEL . . . . G
SPEEDS . . . . VARIABLE
TRANSMISSION . . . . . DUAL HYDRO
STANDARD DECK . . . . 50"
WEIGHT . . . . 681 LBS.
MSRP. $4,499

OPTIONS

60" DECK

RAE702GEM

YEARS MFRD 2019-2020
SERIES. . . . . RADIUS E SERIES
ENGINE . . . . EXMARK
CYLINDERS. 2
CID 708CC
ENGINE HP 22.5
FUEL . . . . G
SPEEDS . . . . VARIABLE
TRANSMISSION . . . . . DUAL HYDRO
STEERING. . . . . ZERO
STANDARD DECK . . . . 44"
WEIGHT . . . . 798 LBS.
MSRP. $6,104

RAE708GEM

YEARS MFRD 2016-2020
SERIES. . . . . RADIUS E SERIES
ENGINE . . . . EXMARK
ENGINE HP 24.5
COOLING . . . . AIR
FUEL . . . . G

SPEEDS . . . . VARIABLE
TRANSMISSION . . . . . DUAL HYDRO
STEERING. . . . . ZERO
STANDARD DECK . . . . 48"
WEIGHT . . . . 849 LBS.

OPTIONS

52" DECK
60" DECK

RETAIL PRICING

YEAR	HIGH	LOW
2016	$3,003	$2,253
2017	$3,313	$2,485
2018	$3,479	$2,609
2019	$3,595	$2,696
2020	$3,806	$2,877

RAE720CKC

YEARS MFRD 2018-2020
SERIES. . . . . RADIUS E SERIES
ENGINE . . . . KOHLER ZT720
CID 725CC
FUEL . . . . G
SPEEDS . . . . VARIABLE
TRANSMISSION . . . . . DUAL HYDRO
STEERING. . . . . ZERO
STANDARD DECK . . . . 48"
WEIGHT . . . . 873 LBS.

RAS708GEM

YEARS MFRD 2018-2020
SERIES. . . . . RADIUS S SERIES
ENGINE . . . . EXMARK
CID 708CC
ENGINE HP 24.5
COOLING . . . . AIR
FUEL . . . . G
SPEEDS . . . . VARIABLE
TRANSMISSION . . . . . DUAL HYDRO
STEERING. . . . . ZERO
STANDARD DECK . . . . 48"
MSRP. $7,769

OPTIONS

52" DECK. $555
60" DECK. $1,110
60" DECK RD $1,554

RAS710CKC

YEARS MFRD 2016-2017
SERIES. . . . . RADIUS S SERIES
ENGINE . . . . KOHLER
COOLING . . . . AIR
FUEL . . . . G
SPEEDS . . . . VARIABLE
TRANSMISSION . . . . . DUAL HYDRO
STEERING. . . . . ZERO
STANDARD DECK . . . . 48"
MSRP. $6,699

RETAIL PRICING

YEAR	HIGH	LOW
2016	$3,722	$2,792
2017	$4,107	$3,080

RAS720CKC

YEARS MFRD........ 2016-2018
SERIES......... RADIUS S SERIES
ENGINE................KOHLER
COOLING..................AIR
FUEL.....................G
SPEEDS.............VARIABLE
TRANSMISSION ..... DUAL HYDRO
STEERING................ZERO
STANDARD DECK........... 52"
MSRP................ $7,099

RETAIL PRICING

YEAR	HIGH	LOW
2016	$3,929	$2,947
2017	$4,337	$3,252
2018	$4,748	$3,561

RAS740CKC

YEARS MFRD........ 2016-2018
SERIES......... RADIUS S SERIES
ENGINE................KOHLER
COOLING..................AIR
FUEL.....................G
SPEEDS.............VARIABLE
TRANSMISSION ..... DUAL HYDRO
STEERING................ZERO
STANDARD DECK........... 60"
MSRP................ $7,599

OPTIONS

60" DECK RD

RETAIL PRICING

YEAR	HIGH	LOW
2016	$4,206	$3,155
2017	$4,642	$3,482
2018	$5,116	$3,837

RAW830CKC

YEARS MFRD........ 2018-2018
SERIES......... RADIUS E SERIES
ENGINE................KOHLER
ENGINE HP................ 21
COOLING..................AIR
FUEL.....................G
TRANSMISSION ..... DUAL HYDRO
STEERING................ZERO
STANDARD DECK........... 48"

RAX651GKA

YEARS MFRD........ 2016-2020
SERIES......... RADIUS X SERIES
ENGINE ....KAWASAKI FX651V
ENGINE HP.............. 20.5
COOLING..................AIR
FUEL.....................G
SPEEDS.............VARIABLE
TRANSMISSION ..... DUAL HYDRO
STEERING................ZERO
STANDARD DECK........... 48"
WEIGHT.............. 937 LBS.
MSRP................ $8,879

RETAIL PRICING

YEAR	HIGH	LOW
2016	$4,262	$3,196
2017	$4,704	$3,528
2018	$5,231	$3,922
2019	$5,797	$4,348
2020	$6,270	$4,784

RAX691GKA

YEARS MFRD........ 2016-2020
SERIES......... RADIUS X SERIES
ENGINE............. KAWASAKI
ENGINE HP................ 22
COOLING..................AIR
FUEL.....................G
SPEEDS.............VARIABLE
TRANSMISSION ..... DUAL HYDRO
STEERING................ZERO
STANDARD DECK........... 52"
WEIGHT.............. 957 LBS.
MSRP................ $9,434

RETAIL PRICING

YEAR	HIGH	LOW
2016	$4,482	$3,362
2017	$4,948	$3,710
2018	$5,485	$4,114
2019	$6,079	$4,559
2020	$6,834	$5,114

RAX730GKA

YEARS MFRD........ 2016-2020
SERIES......... RADIUS X SERIES
ENGINE............. KAWASAKI
ENGINE HP.............. 23.5
COOLING..................AIR
FUEL.....................G
SPEEDS.............VARIABLE
TRANSMISSION ..... DUAL HYDRO
STEERING................ZERO
STANDARD DECK........... 60"
WEIGHT............1,006 LBS.
MSRP................ $9,989

RETAIL PRICING

YEAR	HIGH	LOW
2016	$4,760	$3,570
2017	$5,253	$3,939
2018	$5,825	$4,368
2019	$6,452	$4,839
2020	$7,306	$5,524

STE600CKA

YEARS MFRD........ 2018-2020
SERIES..........STARIS E SERIES
ENGINE ....KAWASAKI FS600V
CID.................603CC
ENGINE HP.............. 18.5
FUEL.....................G
SPEEDS.............VARIABLE
TRANSMISSION ....HYDRO
STEERING................ZERO
STANDARD DECK........... 32"
WEIGHT.............. 712 LBS.
MSRP................ $8,879

OPTIONS

36" DECK.............. $888

STE600GKA

YEARS MFRD........ 2018-2020
SERIES..........STARIS E SERIES
ENGINE ....KAWASAKI FS600V
CYLINDERS..................2
CID.................603CC
ENGINE HP.............. 18.5
FUEL.....................G
SPEEDS.............VARIABLE
TRANSMISSION ..... DUAL HYDRO
STEERING................ZERO
STANDARD DECK........... 44"
WEIGHT.............. 737 LBS.
MSRP................ $9,989

OPTIONS

36" DECK............... $-666
44" DECK SPHOC.......... $444

STS650AKC

YEARS MFRD........ 2019-2020
SERIES......... STARIS S SERIES
ENGINE .... KOHLER CV650
CID.................694CC
FUEL.....................G
SPEEDS.............VARIABLE
TRANSMISSION ....HYDRO
STEERING................ZERO
STANDARD DECK........... 48"
WEIGHT.............. 960 LBS.

OPTIONS

EFI

STS651GKA

YEARS MFRD........ 2018-2020
SERIES......... STARIS S SERIES
ENGINE ....KAWASAKI FX651V
CID.................726CC
ENGINE HP.............. 20.5
FUEL.....................G
SPEEDS.............VARIABLE
TRANSMISSION ....HYDRO
STEERING................ZERO
STANDARD DECK........... 48"
WEIGHT.............. 960 LBS.
MSRP................ $11,099

STS730AKC

YEARS MFRD........ 2018-2020
SERIES......... STARIS S SERIES
ENGINE .... KOHLER ECV730
CID.................747CC
ENGINE HP................ 23
FUEL.....................G
SPEEDS.............VARIABLE
TRANSMISSION ....HYDRO
STEERING................ZERO
STANDARD DECK........... 52"
WEIGHT.............. 990 LBS.
MSRP................ $11,876

OPTIONS

EFI

STS730GKA

YEARS MFRD........ 2018-2020
SERIES......... STARIS S SERIES
ENGINE ....KAWASAKI FX730V
CID.................726CC
ENGINE HP.............. 23.5
FUEL.....................G
SPEEDS.............VARIABLE
TRANSMISSION ....HYDRO
STEERING................ZERO
STANDARD DECK........... 52"
WEIGHT.............. 990 LBS.
MSRP................ $11,432

OPTIONS

60" DECK............... $555

STS740EKC

YEARS MFRD........ 2018-2020
SERIES......... STARIS S SERIES
ENGINE .... KOHLER ECV740
CID.................747CC
ENGINE HP................ 25
FUEL.....................G
SPEEDS.............VARIABLE
TRANSMISSION ....HYDRO
STEERING................ZERO
STANDARD DECK........... 60"
WEIGHT............1,045 LBS.
MSRP................ $12,431

OPTIONS

EFI

TURF RANGER (TR) ALL MODELS

YEARS MFRD........ 1994-1999

SERIAL NUMBERS

YEAR	BEGINNING NO.
1991	61000
1992	70000
1993	80000
1994	90000
1995	102000
1996	115000
1997	130000
1998	160000
1999	190000

TR17KA

YEARS MFRD........ 1991-1991
SERIES......TURF RANGER SERIES
ENGINE............. KAWASAKI
ENGINE HP................ 17
COOLING..................AIR
FUEL.....................G
TRANSMISSION ....HYDRO
STEERING................ZERO
STANDARD DECK........... 52"
MSRP................ $6,978

OPTIONS

60" DECK

EX MARK

RETAIL PRICING

YEAR	HIGH	LOW
1991	$306	$229

TR18KC

YEARS MFRD 1995-1996
SERIES . . . . TURF RANGER SERIES
ENGINE . . . . KOHLER COMMAND
ENGINE HP 18
COOLING . . . . AIR
FUEL . . . . G
TRANSMISSION . . . . HYDRO
STEERING . . . . ZERO
STANDARD DECK . . . . 52"
MSRP $7,910

OPTIONS

60" DECK

RETAIL PRICING

YEAR	HIGH	LOW
1995	$600	$450
1996	$665	$499

TR18KO

YEARS MFRD 1991-1993
SERIES . . . . TURF RANGER SERIES
ENGINE . . . . KOHLER
ENGINE HP 18
COOLING . . . . AIR
FUEL . . . . G
SPEEDS . . . . VARIABLE
TRANSMISSION . . . . HYDRO
STEERING . . . . ZERO
STANDARD DECK . . . . 52"
MSRP $6,678

OPTIONS

60" DECK

SERIAL NUMBERS

YEAR	BEGINNING NO.
1991	61000
1992	70000
1993	80000

RETAIL PRICING

YEAR	HIGH	LOW
1991	$337	$253
1992	$372	$279
1993	$412	$309

TR20BV

YEARS MFRD 1995-1996
SERIES . . . . TURF RANGER SERIES
ENGINE . . . . B&S
ENGINE HP 20
COOLING . . . . AIR
FUEL . . . . G
TRANSMISSION . . . . HYDRO
STEERING . . . . ZERO
STANDARD DECK . . . . 52"
MSRP $8,150

RETAIL PRICING

YEAR	HIGH	LOW
1995	$619	$465
1996	$685	$514

TR20KO

YEARS MFRD 1991-1993
SERIES . . . . TURF RANGER SERIES
ENGINE . . . . KOHLER
ENGINE HP 20
COOLING . . . . AIR
FUEL . . . . G
TRANSMISSION . . . . HYDRO
STEERING . . . . ZERO
STANDARD DECK . . . . 52"
MSRP $6,948

OPTIONS

60" DECK

RETAIL PRICING

YEAR	HIGH	LOW
1991	$350	$262
1992	$387	$290
1993	$428	$321

TR22KC

YEARS MFRD 1995-1996
SERIES . . . . TURF RANGER SERIES
ENGINE . . . . KOHLER
ENGINE HP 22
COOLING . . . . AIR
FUEL . . . . G
TRANSMISSION . . . . HYDRO
STEERING . . . . ZERO
STANDARD DECK . . . . 52"
MSRP $8,320

OPTIONS

60" DECK

RETAIL PRICING

YEAR	HIGH	LOW
1995	$856	$642
1996	$926	$695

TR23KC524

YEARS MFRD 2004-2005
SERIES . . . . TURF RANGER SERIES
ENGINE . . . . KOHLER COMMAND SP
CYLINDERS 2
ENGINE HP 23
COOLING . . . . AIR
FUEL . . . . G
SPEEDS . . . . VARIABLE
TRANSMISSION . . . . HYDRO
STEERING . . . . STANDARD
BLADE CLUTCH . . . . ELECTRIC
PTO . . . . YES
STANDARD DECK . . . . 60"
WEIGHT . . . . 931 LBS.
MSRP $9,323

OPTIONS

BAGGER

RETAIL PRICING

YEAR	HIGH	LOW
2004	$2,534	$1,901
2005	$2,811	$2,108

TR23KC604

YEARS MFRD 2003-2005
SERIES . . . . TURF RANGER SERIES
ENGINE . . KOHLER COMMAND PRO
CYLINDERS 2
ENGINE HP 23
COOLING . . . . AIR
FUEL . . . . G
SPEEDS . . . . VARIABLE
TRANSMISSION . . . . HYDRO
STEERING . . . . STANDARD
BLADE CLUTCH . . . . ELECTRIC
PTO . . . . YES
WEIGHT . . . . 972 LBS.

TX730EKC524

YEARS MFRD 2013-2013
SERIES . . . . VANTAGE X SERIES
ENGINE . . . . KOHLER
COOLING . . . . AIR
FUEL . . . . G
SPEEDS . . . . VARIABLE
TRANSMISSION . . . . HYDRO
STEERING . . . . ZERO
STANDARD DECK . . . . 52"
MSRP $10,655

RETAIL PRICING

YEAR	HIGH	LOW
2013	$5,198	$3,898

TX740EKC604

YEARS MFRD 2013-2013
SERIES . . . . VANTAGE X V SERIES
ENGINE . . . . KAWASAKI
COOLING . . . . AIR
FUEL . . . . G
SPEEDS . . . . VARIABLE
TRANSMISSION . . . . HYDRO
STEERING . . . . ZERO
STANDARD DECK . . . . 60"
MSRP $11,210

RETAIL PRICING

YEAR	HIGH	LOW
2013	$6,433	$4,825

VH481KA362

YEARS MFRD 2013-2013
SERIES . . . . VIKING SERIES
ENGINE . . . . KAWASAKI
COOLING . . . . AIR
FUEL . . . . G
SPEEDS . . . . VARIABLE
TRANSMISSION . . . . HYDRO
STEERING . . . . ZERO
STANDARD DECK . . . . 36"
MSRP $5,882

SERIAL NUMBERS

YEAR	BEGINNING NO.
2013	313600000

RETAIL PRICING

YEAR	HIGH	LOW
2013	$2,941	$2,206

VH481KA483

YEARS MFRD 2013-2013
SERIES . . . . VIKING SERIES
ENGINE . . . . KAWASAKI
COOLING . . . . AIR
FUEL . . . . G
SPEEDS . . . . VARIABLE
TRANSMISSION . . . . HYDRO
STEERING . . . . ZERO
STANDARD DECK . . . . 48"
MSRP $6,104

SERIAL NUMBERS

YEAR	BEGINNING NO.
2013	313600000

RETAIL PRICING

YEAR	HIGH	LOW
2013	$3,049	$2,287

VT18KA363

YEARS MFRD 2011-2011
SERIES . VANTAGE STANDON SERIES
ENGINE . . . . KAWASAKI
CYLINDERS 1
ENGINE HP 18
COOLING . . . . AIR
FUEL . . . . G
SPEEDS . . . . VARIABLE
TRANSMISSION . . . . HYDRO
STEERING . . . . ZERO
BLADE CLUTCH . . . . ELECTRIC

VT24KA484

YEARS MFRD 2011-2011
SERIES . VANTAGE STANDON SERIES
ENGINE . . . . KAWASAKI
CYLINDERS 2
ENGINE HP 24
COOLING . . . . AIR
FUEL . . . . G
SPEEDS . . . . VARIABLE
TRANSMISSION . . . . HYDRO
STEERING . . . . ZERO
BLADE CLUTCH . . . . ELECTRIC

VT24KA524

YEARS MFRD 2011-2011
SERIES . VANTAGE STANDON SERIES
ENGINE . . . . KAWASAKI
CYLINDERS 2
ENGINE HP 24
COOLING . . . . AIR
FUEL . . . . G
SPEEDS . . . . VARIABLE
TRANSMISSION . . . . HYDRO
STEERING . . . . ZERO
BLADE CLUTCH . . . . ELECTRIC

VT541KA363

YEARS MFRD 2012-2012
SERIES . . . . VANTAGE SERIES
ENGINE . . . . KAWASAKI FS541V
COOLING . . . . AIR
FUEL . . . . G
SPEEDS . . . . VARIABLE
TRANSMISSION . . . . HYDRO
STEERING . . . . ZERO
BLADE CLUTCH . . . . ELECTRIC
WEIGHT . . . . 790 LBS.

VT541KA 363CA

YEARS MFRD 2012-2012
SERIES . . . . VANTAGE SERIES
ENGINE . . . . KAWASAKI FS541V
COOLING . . . . AIR
FUEL . . . . G
SPEEDS . . . . VARIABLE
TRANSMISSION . . . . HYDRO
STEERING . . . . ZERO
BLADE CLUTCH . . . . ELECTRIC
WEIGHT . . . . 790 LBS.

VT651KA484

YEARS MFRD 2012-2012
SERIES . . . . VANTAGE SERIES
ENGINE . . . . KAWASAKI FS651V
COOLING . . . . AIR
FUEL . . . . G
SPEEDS . . . . VARIABLE
TRANSMISSION . . . . HYDRO
STEERING . . . . ZERO
BLADE CLUTCH . . . . ELECTRIC
WEIGHT . . . . 855 LBS.

VT691KA 484CA

YEARS MFRD 2012-2012
SERIES . . . . VANTAGE SERIES
ENGINE . . . . KAWASAKI FS691V
COOLING . . . . AIR
FUEL . . . . G
SPEEDS . . . . VARIABLE
TRANSMISSION . . . . HYDRO
STEERING . . . . ZERO
BLADE CLUTCH . . . . ELECTRIC
WEIGHT . . . . 855 LBS.

VT691KA524

YEARS MFRD 2012-2012
SERIES . . . . VANTAGE SERIES
ENGINE . . . . KAWASAKI FS691V
COOLING . . . . AIR
FUEL . . . . G
SPEEDS . . . . VARIABLE
TRANSMISSION . . . . HYDRO
STEERING . . . . ZERO
BLADE CLUTCH . . . . ELECTRIC
WEIGHT . . . . 866 LBS.

VT691KA 524CA

YEARS MFRD 2012-2012
ENGINE . . . . KAWASAKI FX691V
COOLING . . . . AIR
FUEL . . . . G
SPEEDS . . . . VARIABLE
TRANSMISSION . . . . HYDRO
STEERING . . . . ZERO
BLADE CLUTCH . . . . ELECTRIC
WEIGHT . . . . 866 LBS.

VT730EKC524

YEARS MFRD 2012-2012
SERIES . . . . VANTAGE SERIES
ENGINE . . . . KOHLER ECV730
COOLING . . . . AIR
FUEL . . . . G
SPEEDS . . . . VARIABLE
TRANSMISSION . . . . HYDRO
STEERING . . . . ZERO
BLADE CLUTCH . . . . ELECTRIC
WEIGHT . . . . 875 LBS.

VT740EKC604

YEARS MFRD 2012-2012
SERIES . . . . VANTAGE SERIES
ENGINE . . . . KOHLER ECV740
COOLING . . . . AIR
FUEL . . . . G
SPEEDS . . . . VARIABLE
TRANSMISSION . . . . HYDRO
STEERING . . . . ZERO
BLADE CLUTCH . . . . ELECTRIC
WEIGHT . . . . 883 LBS.

VTS541KA363

YEARS MFRD 2013-2013
SERIES . . . . VANTAGE S SERIES
ENGINE . . . . KAWASAKI
COOLING . . . . AIR
SPEEDS . . . . VARIABLE
TRANSMISSION . . . . HYDRO
STEERING . . . . ZERO
STANDARD DECK . . . . 36"
MSRP $8,435

SERIAL NUMBERS

YEAR	BEGINNING NO.
2013	313600000

RETAIL PRICING

YEAR	HIGH	LOW
2013	$4,218	$3,163

VTS651KA484

YEARS MFRD 2013-2013
SERIES . . . . VANTAGE S SERIES
ENGINE . . . . KAWASAKI
COOLING . . . . AIR
FUEL . . . . G
SPEEDS . . . . VARIABLE
TRANSMISSION . . . . HYDRO
STEERING . . . . ZERO
STANDARD DECK . . . . 48"
MSRP $9,434

SERIAL NUMBERS

YEAR	BEGINNING NO.
2013	313600000

RETAIL PRICING

YEAR	HIGH	LOW
2013	$4,716	$3,537

VTS691KA 484CA

YEARS MFRD 2014-2014
SERIES VANTAGE STAND ON SERIES
ENGINE . . . . KAWASAKI FX691V
CID 726CC
COOLING . . . . AIR
FUEL . . . . G
SPEEDS . . . . VARIABLE
TRANSMISSION . . . . HYDRO
STEERING . . . . ZERO
BLADE CLUTCH . . . . ELECTRIC
STANDARD DECK . . . . 48"
MSRP $8,699

RETAIL PRICING

YEAR	HIGH	LOW
2014	$4,950	$3,712

VTS691KA524

YEARS MFRD 2013-2013
SERIES . . . . VANTAGE S SERIES
ENGINE . . . . KAWASAKI
COOLING . . . . AIR
FUEL . . . . G
SPEEDS . . . . VARIABLE
TRANSMISSION . . . . HYDRO
STEERING . . . . ZERO
STANDARD DECK . . . . 52"
MSRP $9,878

RETAIL PRICING

YEAR	HIGH	LOW
2013	$4,939	$3,704

VTS730EKC 524

YEARS MFRD 2014-2014
SERIES VANTAGE STAND ON SERIES
ENGINE . . . . KOHLER ECV730
CID 747CC
COOLING . . . . AIR
FUEL . . . . G
SPEEDS . . . . VARIABLE
TRANSMISSION . . . . HYDRO
STEERING . . . . ZERO
BLADE CLUTCH . . . . ELECTRIC
STANDARD DECK . . . . 52"
MSRP $9,499

RETAIL PRICING

YEAR	HIGH	LOW
2014	$5,409	$4,056

VTS740EKC 604

YEARS MFRD 2014-2014
SERIES VANTAGE STAND ON SERIES
ENGINE . . . . KOHLER ECV740
CID 747
COOLING . . . . AIR
FUEL . . . . G
SPEEDS . . . . VARIABLE
TRANSMISSION . . . . HYDRO
STEERING . . . . ZERO
BLADE CLUTCH . . . . ELECTRIC
STANDARD DECK . . . . 60"
MSRP $9,999

RETAIL PRICING

YEAR	HIGH	LOW
2014	$5,694	$4,270

VTX651KA484

YEARS MFRD 2013-2013
SERIES . . . . VANTAGE X SERIES
ENGINE . . . . KAWASAKI
COOLING . . . . AIR
FUEL . . . . G
SPEEDS . . . . VARIABLE
TRANSMISSION . . . . HYDRO
STEERING . . . . ZERO
STANDARD DECK . . . . 48"
MSRP $9,767

RETAIL PRICING

YEAR	HIGH	LOW
2013	$4,885	$3,664

VTX691KA 524

YEARS MFRD 2013-2013
SERIES . . . . VANTAGE X SERIES
ENGINE . . . . KAWASAKI
COOLING . . . . AIR
FUEL . . . . G
SPEEDS . . . . VARIABLE
TRANSMISSION . . . . HYDRO
STEERING . . . . ZERO
STANDARD DECK . . . . 52"
MSRP $10,100

RETAIL PRICING

YEAR	HIGH	LOW
2013	$5,112	$3,834

VTX730EKC 524

YEARS MFRD 2014-2014
SERIES VANTAGE STAND ON SERIES
ENGINE . . . . KOHLER ECV730
CID 747CC
COOLING . . . . AIR
FUEL . . . . G
SPEEDS . . . . VARIABLE
TRANSMISSION . . . . HYDRO
STEERING . . . . ZERO
BLADE CLUTCH . . . . ELECTRIC
STANDARD DECK . . . . 52"
MSRP $9,695

RETAIL PRICING

YEAR	HIGH	LOW
2014	$5,518	$4,139

EX MARK

VTX740EKC 604

YEARS MFRD 2013-2013
SERIES........VANTAGE X SERIES
ENGINE .... KOHLER ECV740
CID 747CC
COOLING.................. AIR
FUEL........................G
SPEEDS..............VARIABLE
TRANSMISSION ....HYDRO
STEERING.................ZERO
BLADE CLUTCH ....ELECTRIC
STANDARD DECK........... 60"
MSRP................ $11,210

RETAIL PRICING

YEAR	HIGH	LOW
2013	$6,836	$5,127

FARM PRO (HOMIER FARM PRO)

TY395

YEARS MFRD 2004-2004
SERIES. . . . . TRAK KING SERIES
CYLINDERS. 3
CID 136
ENGINE HP 30
COOLING . . . . LIQUID
FUEL . . . . D
SPEEDS 8
TRANSMISSION . . . . GEAR
HYDRAULIC . . . . YES

2010

YEARS MFRD 2005-2012
SERIES. . . . . 10 SERIES
CYLINDERS. 2
CID 73.8
ENGINE HP 20
COOLING . . . . LIQUID
FUEL . . . . D
SPEEDS 12/4
TRANSMISSION . . . . GEAR
STEERING. . . . . STANDARD
HITCH . . . . CAT. I
HYDRAULIC . . . . YES
PTO . . . . YES
WEIGHT . . . . 2,660 LBS.

2420

YEARS MFRD 2004-2004
SERIES. . . . . 2000 SERIES
CYLINDERS. 2
ENGINE HP 20
COOLING . . . . LIQUID
FUEL . . . . D
SPEEDS 12/4
TRANSMISSION . . . . GEAR
STEERING. . . . . STANDARD
HITCH . . . . CAT. I
HYDRAULIC . . . . YES
PTO . . . . YES
DRIVE TYPE 4WD
ROPS/CAB . . . . ROPS
WEIGHT . . . . 2,660 LBS.

RETAIL PRICING

YEAR	HIGH	LOW
2004	$2,466	$1,849

AVG. AUCTION PRICING

LOW	HIGH	AVG
$1,647	$3,200	$2,276

2425

YEARS MFRD 2004-2004
SERIES. . . . . 2000 SERIES
CYLINDERS. 3
ENGINE HP 25
COOLING . . . . LIQUID
FUEL . . . . D
SPEEDS 12/4
TRANSMISSION . . . . GEAR
STEERING. . . . . STANDARD
HITCH . . . . CAT. I
HYDRAULIC . . . . YES
PTO . . . . YES
DRIVE TYPE 4WD
ROPS/CAB . . . . ROPS
WEIGHT . . . . 3,040 LBS.

RETAIL PRICING

YEAR	HIGH	LOW
2004	$4,755	$3,566

2430

YEARS MFRD 2004-2004
SERIES. . . . . 2000 SERIES
CYLINDERS. 3
ENGINE HP 30
COOLING . . . . LIQUID
FUEL . . . . D
SPEEDS 8/2
TRANSMISSION . . . . GEAR
STEERING. . . . . STANDARD
HITCH . . . . CAT. I
HYDRAULIC . . . . YES
PTO . . . . YES
DRIVE TYPE 4WD
ROPS/CAB . . . . ROPS
WEIGHT . . . . 4,380 LBS.

RETAIL PRICING

YEAR	HIGH	LOW
2004	$5,773	$4,330

2510

YEARS MFRD 2005-2012
SERIES. . . . . 10 SERIES
CYLINDERS. 3
CID 86.5
ENGINE HP 25
COOLING . . . . LIQUID
FUEL . . . . D
SPEEDS 12/4
TRANSMISSION . . . . GEAR
STEERING. . . . . STANDARD
HITCH . . . . CAT. I
HYDRAULIC . . . . YES
PTO . . . . YES
WEIGHT . . . . 2,513 LBS.

2520

YEARS MFRD 2006-2006
ENGINE Y385
CYLINDERS. 3
CID 93.4
ENGINE HP 25
COOLING . . . . LIQUID
FUEL . . . . D
SPEEDS 16/8
TRANSMISSION . . . . GEAR
STEERING. . . . . STANDARD
HITCH . . . . CAT. I
HYDRAULIC . . . . YES
PTO . . . . YES

3010

YEARS MFRD 2005-2012
SERIES. . . . . 10 SERIES
CYLINDERS. 3
CID 116.2
ENGINE HP 30
COOLING . . . . LIQUID
FUEL . . . . D
SPEEDS 8/2
TRANSMISSION . . . . GEAR
STEERING. . . . . STANDARD
HITCH . . . . CAT. I
HYDRAULIC . . . . YES
PTO . . . . YES
WEIGHT . . . . 3,858 LBS.

4010

YEARS MFRD 2008-2012
SERIES. . . . . 10 SERIES
CYLINDERS. 3
ENGINE HP 40
COOLING . . . . LIQUID
FUEL . . . . D
SPEEDS 8/4
TRANSMISSION . . . . GEAR
STEERING. . . . . STANDARD
HITCH . . . . CAT. I
HYDRAULIC . . . . YES
PTO . . . . YES
WEIGHT . . . . 4,632 LBS.

4020

YEARS MFRD 2006-2009
ENGINE SL3105BT
CYLINDERS. 3
CID 175.4
ENGINE HP 40
COOLING . . . . LIQUID
FUEL . . . . D
SPEEDS 8/4
TRANSMISSION . . . . GEAR
STEERING. . . . . STANDARD
HITCH . . . . CAT. I

FERRIS

CTR52

YEARS MFRD 1994-1997
ENGINE . . . . KOHLER
ENGINE HP 20
COOLING . . . . AIR
FUEL . . . . G
TRANSMISSION . . . . HYDRO
STEERING. . . . . ZERO
STANDARD DECK . . . . 52"
MSRP. $7,675

RETAIL PRICING

YEAR	HIGH	LOW
1994	$688	$516
1995	$762	$572
1996	$844	$633
1997	$939	$704

CTR61

YEARS MFRD 1994-1997
ENGINE . . . . KOHLER
ENGINE HP 20
COOLING . . . . AIR
FUEL . . . . G
TRANSMISSION . . . . HYDRO
STEERING. . . . . ZERO
STANDARD DECK . . . . 61"
MSRP. $7,775

RETAIL PRICING

YEAR	HIGH	LOW
1994	$696	$522
1995	$770	$578
1996	$857	$642
1997	$950	$712

EVKAV19

YEARS MFRD 2009-2013
SERIES. . . . . EVOLUTION SERIES
ENGINE . . . . KAWASAKI
CYLINDERS. 2
ENGINE HP 19
COOLING . . . . AIR
FUEL . . . . G
SPEEDS . . . . VARIABLE
TRANSMISSION . . . . HYDRO
STEERING. . . . . ZERO
BLADE CLUTCH . . . . ELECTRIC
STANDARD DECK . . . . 36"
WEIGHT . . . . 818 LBS.
MSRP. $6,248

RETAIL PRICING

YEAR	HIGH	LOW
2009	$2,506	$1,879
2010	$2,785	$2,089
2011	$3,089	$2,317
2012	$3,434	$2,575
2013	$3,813	$2,860

EVKAV20

YEARS MFRD 2010-2013
SERIES. . . . . EVOLUTION SERIES
ENGINE . . . . KAWASAKI
CYLINDERS. 2
ENGINE HP 20
COOLING . . . . AIR
FUEL . . . . G
SPEEDS . . . . VARIABLE
TRANSMISSION . . . . HYDRO
STEERING. . . . . ZERO
BLADE CLUTCH . . . . ELECTRIC
STANDARD DECK . . . . 48"
WEIGHT . . . . 978 LBS.
MSRP. $6,248

OPTIONS

52" DECK

RETAIL PRICING

YEAR	HIGH	LOW
2010	$2,785	$2,089
2011	$3,089	$2,317
2012	$3,434	$2,575
2013	$3,813	$2,860

FERRIS

EVKAV26

YEARS MFRD 2010-2013
SERIES. . . . . . . .EVOLUTION SERIES
ENGINE . . . . KAWASAKI
CYLINDERS. 2
ENGINE HP 26
COOLING . . . . .AIR
FUEL . . . . G
SPEEDS . . . . .VARIABLE
TRANSMISSION . . . . .HYDRO
STEERING. . . . . .ZERO
BLADE CLUTCH . . . . ELECTRIC
STANDARD DECK . . . . 52"
WEIGHT . . . . .1,016 LBS.
MSRP. $7,385

RETAIL PRICING

YEAR	HIGH	LOW
2010	$3,289	$2,467
2011	$3,652	$2,739
2012	$4,059	$3,045
2013	$4,505	$3,379

EVKAV27

YEARS MFRD 2009-2013
SERIES. . . . . . . .EVOLUTION SERIES
ENGINE . . . . KAWASAKI
CYLINDERS. 2
ENGINE HP 27
COOLING . . . . .AIR
FUEL . . . . G
SPEEDS . . . . .VARIABLE
TRANSMISSION . . . . .HYDRO
STEERING. . . . . .ZERO
BLADE CLUTCH . . . . ELECTRIC
STANDARD DECK . . . . 48"
WEIGHT . . . . 978 LBS.
MSRP. $6,817

RETAIL PRICING

YEAR	HIGH	LOW
2009	$2,733	$2,050
2010	$3,038	$2,279
2011	$3,375	$2,531
2012	$3,746	$2,810
2013	$4,161	$3,121

F60ZB25

YEARS MFRD 2017-2020
ENGINE . . . . B&S
CYLINDERS. 2
CID .724CC
ENGINE HP 25
COOLING . . . . .AIR
FUEL . . . . G
SPEEDS . . . . .VARIABLE
TRANSMISSION . . . . .HYDRO
STEERING. . . . . .ZERO
STANDARD DECK . . . . 36"
MSRP. $5,249

F60ZKAV19

YEARS MFRD 2017-2020
ENGINE . . . . . . .KAWASAKI FX600V
CYLINDERS. 2
CID .603CC
ENGINE HP 19
COOLING . . . . .AIR
FUEL . . . . G
SPEEDS . . . . .VARIABLE
TRANSMISSION . . . . .HYDRO
STEERING. . . . . .ZERO
STANDARD DECK . . . . 36"
MSRP. $5,899

RETAIL PRICING

YEAR	HIGH	LOW
2017	$3,642	$2,731
2018	$3,949	$2,962
2019	$4,318	$3,238
2020	$4,790	$3,654

F160ZBV26

YEARS MFRD 2016-2020
SERIES. . . . . F160Z SERIES
ENGINE . . . . .VANGUARD
CYLINDERS. 2
CID .810CC
ENGINE HP 26
COOLING . . . . .AIR
FUEL . . . . G
SPEEDS . . . . .VARIABLE
TRANSMISSION . . . . .HYDRO
STEERING. . . . . .ZERO
STANDARD DECK . . . . 48"

RETAIL PRICING

YEAR	HIGH	LOW
2016	$4,543	$3,407
2017	$5,015	$3,761
2018	$5,560	$4,170
2019	$6,173	$4,629
2020	$6,836	$5,215

F160ZBVE28

YEARS MFRD 2016-2020
SERIES. . . . . F160Z SERIES
ENGINE . . . . .VANGUARD EFI
CYLINDERS. 2
CID .810CC
ENGINE HP 28
COOLING . . . . .AIR
FUEL . . . . G
SPEEDS . . . . .VARIABLE
TRANSMISSION . . . . .HYDRO
STEERING. . . . . .ZERO
STANDARD DECK . . . . 52"
MSRP. $8,849

RETAIL PRICING

YEAR	HIGH	LOW
2016	$4,979	$3,735
2017	$5,496	$4,121
2018	$6,087	$4,565
2019	$6,775	$5,081
2020	$7,532	$5,707

F160ZKAV24

YEARS MFRD 2016-2020
SERIES. . . . . F160Z SERIES
ENGINE . . . . KAWASAKI FX730V
CYLINDERS. 2
CID .726CC
ENGINE HP 24
COOLING . . . . .AIR
FUEL . . . . G
SPEEDS . . . . .VARIABLE
TRANSMISSION . . . . .HYDRO
STEERING. . . . . .ZERO
STANDARD DECK . . . . 48"
MSRP. $8,299

OPTIONS

52" DECK. $250

RETAIL PRICING

YEAR	HIGH	LOW
2016	$4,668	$3,501
2017	$5,153	$3,864
2018	$5,707	$4,280
2019	$6,324	$4,743
2020	$7,180	$5,492

F210ZBV26

YEARS MFRD 2018-2019
SERIES. . . . . F210Z SERIES
ENGINE . . . . .VANGUARD
ENGINE HP 26
FUEL . . . . G
TRANSMISSION . . . . .HYDRO
STEERING. . . . . .ZERO
STANDARD DECK . . . . 61"
MSRP. $8,399

F210ZBVE28

YEARS MFRD 2016-2020
SERIES. . . . . F210Z SERIES
ENGINE . . . . .VANGUARD EFI
CYLINDERS. 2
CID .810CC
ENGINE HP 28
COOLING . . . . .AIR
FUEL . . . . G
SPEEDS . . . . .VARIABLE
TRANSMISSION . . . . .HYDRO
STEERING. . . . . .ZERO
STANDARD DECK . . . . 61"
MSRP. $10,099

RETAIL PRICING

YEAR	HIGH	LOW
2016	$5,726	$4,295
2017	$6,321	$4,741
2018	$7,007	$5,255
2019	$7,767	$5,825
2020	$8,591	$6,559

F210ZKAV26

YEARS MFRD 2016-2020
SERIES. . . . . F210Z SERIES
ENGINE . . . . KAWASAKI
CYLINDERS. 2
CID .852CC
ENGINE HP 25.5
COOLING . . . . .AIR
FUEL . . . . G
SPEEDS . . . . .VARIABLE
TRANSMISSION . . . . .HYDRO
STEERING. . . . . .ZERO
STANDARD DECK . . . . 61"
MSRP. $9,599

RETAIL PRICING

YEAR	HIGH	LOW
2016	$5,415	$4,062
2017	$5,977	$4,483
2018	$6,627	$4,970
2019	$7,372	$5,529
2020	$8,179	$6,190

F320ZBV32

YEARS MFRD 2018-2019
ENGINE . . . . .VANGUARD
ENGINE HP 32
FUEL . . . . G
TRANSMISSION . . . . .HYDRO
STEERING. . . . . .ZERO
STANDARD DECK . . . . 61"
MSRP. $10,299

OPTIONS

72" DECK

F320ZBVE37

YEARS MFRD 2016-2020
SERIES. . . . . F320Z SERIES
ENGINE . . . . .VANGUARD EFI
CYLINDERS. 2
CID .993CC
ENGINE HP 37
COOLING . . . . .AIR
FUEL . . . . G
SPEEDS . . . . .VARIABLE
TRANSMISSION . . . . .HYDRO
STEERING. . . . . .ZERO
STANDARD DECK . . . . 61"
MSRP. $12,199

OPTIONS

72" DECK. $650

RETAIL PRICING

YEAR	HIGH	LOW
2016	$6,847	$5,135
2017	$7,557	$5,668
2018	$8,229	$6,172
2019	$8,952	$6,714
2020	$9,898	$7,565

F320ZKAV35

YEARS MFRD 2016-2017
SERIES. . . . . F320Z SERIES
ENGINE . . . . KAWASAKI
ENGINE HP 35
COOLING . . . . .AIR
FUEL . . . . G
SPEEDS . . . . .VARIABLE
TRANSMISSION . . . . .HYDRO
STEERING. . . . . .ZERO
STANDARD DECK . . . . 61"
MSRP. $11,476

OPTIONS

72"DECK

RETAIL PRICING

YEAR	HIGH	LOW
2016	$7,689	$5,767
2017	$8,944	$6,708

F320ZKAVE30

YEARS MFRD 2018-2019
SERIES . . . . F320Z SERIES
ENGINE . . . . KAWASAKI
ENGINE HP 29.5
FUEL . . . . G
TRANSMISSION . . . . HYDRO
STEERING . . . . ZERO
STANDARD DECK . . . . 61"
MSRP $10,799

OPTIONS

72" DECK

F400ZB23

YEARS MFRD 2018-2018
ENGINE . . . . B%S
ENGINE HP 23
FUEL . . . . G
TRANSMISSION . . . . HYDRO
STEERING . . . . ZERO
STANDARD DECK . . . . 48"

F400ZKAV22

YEARS MFRD 2018-2018
ENGINE . . . . KAWASAKI
ENGINE HP 21.5
FUEL . . . . G
TRANSMISSION . . . . HYDRO
STEERING . . . . ZERO
STANDARD DECK . . . . 48"

F800X BV31

YEARS MFRD 2013-2020
ENGINE . . . . VANGUARD
CYLINDERS 2
CID 896CC
ENGINE HP 31
COOLING . . . . LIQUID
FUEL . . . . D
SPEEDS . . . . VARIABLE
TRANSMISSION . . . . HYDRO
STEERING . . . . ZERO
BLADE CLUTCH . . . . ELECTRIC
STANDARD DECK . . . . 61"
MSRP $14,548

OPTIONS

72" DECK $600

RETAIL PRICING

YEAR	HIGH	LOW
2013	$5,604	$4,203
2014	$6,206	$4,655
2015	$6,827	$5,120
2016	$7,534	$5,651
2017	$8,317	$6,238
2018	$9,129	$6,847
2019	$9,928	$7,370
2020	$11,496	$8,758

F800X Y29

YEARS MFRD 2015-2015
ENGINE . . . . YANMAR
ENGINE HP 31
FUEL . . . . D
SPEEDS . . . . VARIABLE
TRANSMISSION . . . . HYDRO
STEERING . . . . ZERO
STANDARD DECK . . . . 61"
MSRP $16,506

OPTIONS

72" DECK

RETAIL PRICING

YEAR	HIGH	LOW
2015	$12,420	$9,315

F800X Y30D

YEARS MFRD 2013-2014
ENGINE . . . . YANMAR
ENGINE HP 30
COOLING . . . . LIQUID
FUEL . . . . D
SPEEDS . . . . VARIABLE
TRANSMISSION . . . . HYDRO
STEERING . . . . ZERO
BLADE CLUTCH . . . . ELECTRIC
STANDARD DECK . . . . 61"
MSRP $15,977

OPTIONS

72" DECK

RETAIL PRICING

YEAR	HIGH	LOW
2013	$8,541	$6,406
2014	$10,633	$7,975

F4020

YEARS MFRD 1994-1995
ENGINE . . . . KAWASAKI
ENGINE HP 20
COOLING . . . . AIR
FUEL . . . . G
TRANSMISSION . . . . HYDRO
STEERING . . . . ZERO
STANDARD DECK . . . . 61"
MSRP $12,495

RETAIL PRICING

YEAR	HIGH	LOW
1994	$1,115	$836
1995	$1,236	$927

H220B

YEARS MFRD 1994-2001
ENGINE . . . . B&S
ENGINE HP 20
COOLING . . . . AIR
FUEL . . . . G
TRANSMISSION . . . . HYDRO
STEERING . . . . ZERO
STANDARD DECK . . . . 52"
MSRP $6,830

RETAIL PRICING

YEAR	HIGH	LOW
1996	$2,299	$1,724
1997	$2,433	$1,825
1998	$2,586	$1,940
1999	$2,810	$2,108
2000	$2,980	$2,235
2001	$3,167	$2,375

H1920B-0F

YEARS MFRD 1994-1995
ENGINE . . . . B&S
ENGINE HP 18
COOLING . . . . AIR
FUEL . . . . G
TRANSMISSION . . . . HYDRO
STEERING . . . . ZERO
STANDARD DECK . . . . 52"
MSRP $6,705

OPTIONS

61" DECK

RETAIL PRICING

YEAR	HIGH	LOW
1994	$598	$448
1995	$662	$496

H1920BV-0F

YEARS MFRD 1995-1995
ENGINE . . . . B&S
ENGINE HP 20
COOLING . . . . AIR
FUEL . . . . G
TRANSMISSION . . . . HYDRO
STEERING . . . . ZERO
STANDARD DECK . . . . 52"
MSRP $6,875

OPTIONS

61" DECK

RETAIL PRICING

YEAR	HIGH	LOW
1995	$681	$511

H2220B

YEARS MFRD 1994-2006
ENGINE . . . . B&S
ENGINE HP 20
FUEL . . . . G
SPEEDS . . . . VARIABLE
TRANSMISSION . . . . HYDRO
STEERING . . . . STANDARD
STANDARD DECK . . . . 52"
MSRP $7,520

OPTIONS

61" DECK

RETAIL PRICING

YEAR	HIGH	LOW
1996	$954	$716
1997	$1,024	$768
1998	$1,068	$801
1999	$1,185	$889
2000	$1,314	$986
2001	$1,458	$1,093
2002	$1,616	$1,212
2003	$1,795	$1,346
2004	$1,990	$1,493
2005	$2,206	$1,654
2006	$2,503	$1,877

H2220K

YEARS MFRD 1994-1997
SERIES . . . . PROCUT 22 SERIES
ENGINE . . . . KOHLER
ENGINE HP 20
COOLING . . . . AIR
FUEL . . . . G
TRANSMISSION . . . . HYDRO
STEERING . . . . ZERO
STANDARD DECK . . . . 52"
MSRP $7,675

RETAIL PRICING

YEAR	HIGH	LOW
1994	$732	$549
1995	$810	$607
1996	$900	$675
1997	$997	$748

H2222K

YEARS MFRD 1995-2000
SERIES . . . . PROCUT 22 SERIES
ENGINE . . . . KOHLER
ENGINE HP 22
COOLING . . . . AIR
FUEL . . . . G
TRANSMISSION . . . . HYDRO
STEERING . . . . ZERO
STANDARD DECK . . . . 52"
MSRP $7,695

OPTIONS

61" DECK

SERIAL NUMBERS

YEAR	BEGINNING NO.
1997	6500
1998	7546
1999	7921

RETAIL PRICING

YEAR	HIGH	LOW
1995	$864	$648
1996	$958	$719
1997	$1,064	$798
1998	$1,180	$885
1999	$1,310	$983
2000	$1,451	$1,088

H2223K

YEARS MFRD 2001-2006
SERIES . . . . PROCUT 22 SERIES
ENGINE . . . . KOHLER
ENGINE HP 23
COOLING . . . . AIR
FUEL . . . . G
SPEEDS . . . . VARIABLE
TRANSMISSION . . . . HYDRO
STEERING . . . . ZERO
STANDARD DECK . . . . 52"
MSRP $8,100

OPTIONS

61" DECK

RETAIL PRICING

YEAR	HIGH	LOW
2001	$1,622	$1,216
2002	$1,803	$1,352
2003	$2,002	$1,502
2004	$2,221	$1,666
2005	$2,464	$1,848
2006	$2,733	$2,050

FERRIS

H2224KAV

YEARS MFRD........ 2012-2020
SERIES.......... PROCUT SERIES
ENGINE .... KAWASAKI FS730V
CYLINDERS.................. 2
CID 726CC
ENGINE HP................. 24
COOLING................. AIR
FUEL...................... G
SPEEDS............ VARIABLE
TRANSMISSION .... HYDRO
STEERING................ ZERO
STANDARD DECK........... 61"
MSRP................ $9,998

OPTIONS

50" SNOW BLOWER
CAB

RETAIL PRICING

YEAR	HIGH	LOW
2012	$3,715	$2,786
2013	$4,109	$3,082
2014	$4,546	$3,409
2015	$5,096	$3,822
2016	$5,563	$4,172
2017	$6,155	$4,616
2018	$6,704	$5,028
2019	$7,266	$5,449
2020	$8,109	$6,205

H2227B

YEARS MFRD........ 2011-2020
SERIES.......... PROCUT SERIES
ENGINE.................. B&S
CYLINDERS.................. 2
CID 810CC
ENGINE HP................. 27
COOLING................. AIR
FUEL...................... G
SPEEDS............ VARIABLE
TRANSMISSION .... HYDRO
STEERING................ ZERO
STANDARD DECK........... 61"
MSRP................ $9,598

OPTIONS

50" SNOWBLOWER
CAB

RETAIL PRICING

YEAR	HIGH	LOW
2011	$3,208	$2,406
2012	$3,550	$2,662
2013	$3,927	$2,945
2014	$4,402	$3,301
2015	$4,805	$3,603
2016	$5,316	$3,986
2017	$5,880	$4,410
2018	$6,417	$4,813
2019	$6,915	$5,186
2020	$7,917	$5,905

H2227B B&S

YEARS MFRD........ 2014-2016
ENGINE.................. B&S
ENGINE HP................. 27
COOLING................. AIR
FUEL...................... G
SPEEDS............ VARIABLE
TRANSMISSION .... HYDRO
STEERING................ ZERO
STANDARD DECK........... 61"
MSRP................ $9,771

OPTIONS

50" SNOW BLOWER
CAB

RETAIL PRICING

YEAR	HIGH	LOW
2014	$5,715	$4,286
2015	$6,321	$4,741
2016	$7,775	$5,831

H2228B

YEARS MFRD........ 2012-2013
SERIES.......... PROCUT SERIES
ENGINE.......... B&S CYCLONIC
ENGINE HP................. 27
COOLING................. AIR
FUEL...................... G
SPEEDS............ VARIABLE
TRANSMISSION .... HYDRO
STEERING................ ZERO
BLADE CLUTCH .... ELECTRIC
STANDARD DECK........... 61"
MSRP................ $9,771

RETAIL PRICING

YEAR	HIGH	LOW
2012	$5,295	$3,971
2013	$5,894	$4,420

H3222K

YEARS MFRD........ 1994-1997
SERIES....... PROCUT 32 SERIES
ENGINE.............. KOHLER
ENGINE HP................. 22
COOLING................. AIR
FUEL...................... G
TRANSMISSION .... HYDRO
STEERING................ ZERO
STANDARD DECK........... 61"
MSRP................ $9,740

OPTIONS

72" DECK

RETAIL PRICING

YEAR	HIGH	LOW
1994	$927	$695
1995	$1,036	$777
1996	$1,142	$856
1997	$1,268	$951

H3225K

YEARS MFRD........ 1997-2004
SERIES....... PROCUT 32 SERIES
ENGINE.............. KOHLER
ENGINE HP................. 25
FUEL...................... G
TRANSMISSION .... HYDRO
STEERING................ ZERO
STANDARD DECK........... 61"
MSRP................ $10,065

OPTIONS

72" DECK

SERIAL NUMBERS

YEAR	BEGINNING NO.
1998	984

RETAIL PRICING

YEAR	HIGH	LOW
1997	$1,491	$1,118
1998	$1,655	$1,241
1999	$1,833	$1,375
2000	$2,034	$1,526
2001	$2,256	$1,692
2002	$2,503	$1,877
2003	$2,777	$2,083
2004	$3,082	$2,311

HUMMER

YEARS MFRD........ 1996-1997
ENGINE.............. KOHLER
ENGINE HP................. 22
FUEL...................... G
TRANSMISSION .... HYDRO
STEERING................ ZERO
STANDARD DECK........... 52"
MSRP................ $8,395

OPTIONS

61" DECK

RETAIL PRICING

YEAR	HIGH	LOW
1996	$979	$734
1997	$1,083	$812

IS500Z24 B44

YEARS MFRD........ 2008-2012
SERIES........ ZERO TURN SERIES
ENGINE.................. B&S
CYLINDERS.................. 2
ENGINE HP................. 24
COOLING................. AIR
FUEL...................... G
SPEEDS............ VARIABLE
TRANSMISSION .... HYDRO
STEERING................ ZERO
BLADE CLUTCH .... ELECTRIC
STANDARD DECK........... 44"
WEIGHT............. 1,065 LBS.
MSRP................ $5,275

RETAIL PRICING

YEAR	HIGH	LOW
2008	$1,952	$1,464
2009	$2,170	$1,627
2010	$2,413	$1,810
2011	$2,674	$2,006
2012	$2,964	$2,223

IS500Z27 B52

YEARS MFRD........ 2011-2012
ENGINE.................. B&S
ENGINE HP................. 27
COOLING................. AIR
FUEL...................... G
SPEEDS............ VARIABLE
TRANSMISSION .... HYDRO
STEERING................ ZERO
STANDARD DECK........... 52"
MSRP................ $6,211

OPTIONS

61" DECK

RETAIL PRICING

YEAR	HIGH	LOW
2011	$3,153	$2,364
2012	$3,501	$2,626

IS600Z KAV23

YEARS MFRD........ 2019-2020
SERIES.......... IS600Z SERIES
ENGINE .... KAWASAKI FS691V
CYLINDERS.................. 2
CID 726CC
ENGINE HP................. 23
FUEL...................... G
SPEEDS............ VARIABLE
TRANSMISSION ..... DUAL HYDRO
STEERING................ ZERO
STANDARD DECK........... 52"
WEIGHT............... 972 LBS.
MSRP................ $6,649

IS600Z19 KAV44

YEARS MFRD........ 2013-2017
ENGINE............ KAWASAKI
ENGINE HP............... 18.5
COOLING................. AIR
FUEL...................... G
SPEEDS............ VARIABLE
TRANSMISSION .... HYDRO
STEERING................ ZERO
BLADE CLUTCH .... ELECTRIC
STANDARD DECK........... 44"
MSRP................ $5,820

OPTIONS

2 BAG HARD
2 BAG SOFT
FROPS

RETAIL PRICING

YEAR	HIGH	LOW
2013	$2,899	$2,174
2014	$3,201	$2,401
2015	$3,533	$2,650
2016	$3,899	$2,925
2017	$4,406	$3,304

IS600Z19 KAV48

YEARS MFRD........ 2013-2020
SERIES.......... IS600Z SERIES
ENGINE............ KAWASAKI
CYLINDERS.................. 2
CID 603CC
ENGINE HP............... 18.5
COOLING................. AIR
FUEL...................... G
SPEEDS............ VARIABLE
TRANSMISSION .... HYDRO
STEERING................ ZERO
BLADE CLUTCH .... ELECTRIC
STANDARD DECK........... 48"
MSRP................ $6,299

OPTIONS
2 BAG HARD
2 BAG SOFT
FROPS

RETAIL PRICING
YEAR	HIGH	LOW
2013	$2,369	$1,777
2014	$2,621	$1,967
2015	$2,887	$2,166
2016	$3,187	$2,391
2017	$3,519	$2,639
2018	$3,833	$2,875
2019	$4,192	$3,143
2020	$4,828	$3,620

IS600Z25 B44
YEARS MFRD 2014-2019
ENGINE .... B&S
ENGINE HP 25
COOLING .... AIR
FUEL .... G
SPEEDS .... VARIABLE
TRANSMISSION .... HYDRO
STEERING .... ZERO
STANDARD DECK .... 44"
MSRP $5,199

OPTIONS
2 BAG HARD
2 BAG SOFT
FROPS

RETAIL PRICING
YEAR	HIGH	LOW
2014	$2,379	$1,785
2015	$2,625	$1,969
2016	$2,898	$2,174
2017	$3,199	$2,399
2018	$3,480	$2,610
2019	$3,755	$2,816

IS600Z25 B48
YEARS MFRD 2014-2020
SERIES .... IS600Z SERIES
ENGINE .... B&S
CYLINDERS 2
CID 724CC
ENGINE HP 25
COOLING .... AIR
FUEL .... G
SPEEDS .... VARIABLE
TRANSMISSION .... HYDRO
STEERING .... ZERO
STANDARD DECK .... 48"
MSRP $5,999

OPTIONS
2 BAG HARD
2 BAG SOFT
FROPS

RETAIL PRICING
YEAR	HIGH	LOW
2014	$2,570	$1,927
2015	$2,835	$2,126
2016	$3,130	$2,347
2017	$3,455	$2,590
2018	$3,754	$2,815
2019	$4,177	$3,133
2020	$4,575	$3,460

IS600Z25 B52
YEARS MFRD 2018-2020
SERIES .... IS600Z SERIES
ENGINE .... B&S
CYLINDERS 2
CID 724CC
ENGINE HP 25
FUEL .... G
TRANSMISSION .... HYDRO
STEERING .... ZERO
STANDARD DECK .... 52"
MSRP $6,099

IS600Z27 B44
YEARS MFRD 2013-2013
ENGINE .... B&S
ENGINE HP 27
COOLING .... AIR
FUEL .... G
SPEEDS .... VARIABLE
TRANSMISSION .... HYDRO
STEERING .... ZERO
BLADE CLUTCH .... ELECTRIC
STANDARD DECK .... 44"
MSRP $5,289

RETAIL PRICING
YEAR	HIGH	LOW
2013	$3,187	$2,391

IS600Z27 B48
YEARS MFRD 2013-2013
ENGINE .... B&S
ENGINE HP 27
COOLING .... AIR
FUEL .... G
SPEEDS .... VARIABLE
TRANSMISSION .... HYDRO
STEERING .... ZERO
BLADE CLUTCH .... ELECTRIC
STANDARD DECK .... 48"
MSRP $5,607

RETAIL PRICING
YEAR	HIGH	LOW
2013	$3,379	$2,535

IS700Z23 KAV52
YEARS MFRD 2013-2018
ENGINE .... KAWASAKI
ENGINE HP 23
COOLING .... AIR
FUEL .... G
SPEEDS .... VARIABLE
TRANSMISSION .... HYDRO
STEERING .... ZERO
BLADE CLUTCH .... ELECTRIC
STANDARD DECK .... 52"
MSRP $7,088

OPTIONS
2 BAG HARD
2 BAG SOFT
3 BAG HARD
3 BAG SOFT

RETAIL PRICING
YEAR	HIGH	LOW
2013	$2,886	$2,164
2014	$3,187	$2,391
2015	$3,527	$2,645
2016	$3,883	$2,912
2017	$4,286	$3,215
2018	$4,695	$3,521

IS700Z24 KAV61
YEARS MFRD 2013-2018
ENGINE .... KAWASAKI
ENGINE HP 23.5
COOLING .... AIR
FUEL .... G
SPEEDS .... VARIABLE
TRANSMISSION .... HYDRO
STEERING .... ZERO
BLADE CLUTCH .... ELECTRIC
STANDARD DECK .... 61"
MSRP $7,617

OPTIONS
2 BAG HARD
2 BAG SOFT
3 BAG HARD
3 BAG SOFT

RETAIL PRICING
YEAR	HIGH	LOW
2013	$3,104	$2,328
2014	$3,425	$2,569
2015	$3,780	$2,835
2016	$4,173	$3,130
2017	$4,606	$3,454
2018	$5,060	$3,795

IS700Z27 B52
YEARS MFRD 2014-2018
ENGINE .... B&S
ENGINE HP 27
COOLING .... AIR
FUEL .... G
SPEEDS .... VARIABLE
TRANSMISSION .... HYDRO
STEERING .... ZERO
STANDARD DECK .... 52"
MSRP $6,559

OPTIONS
2 BAG HARD
2 BAG SOFT
3 BAG HARD
3 BAG SOFT

RETAIL PRICING
YEAR	HIGH	LOW
2014	$2,950	$2,212
2015	$3,255	$2,441
2016	$3,598	$2,698
2017	$3,966	$2,975
2018	$4,342	$3,256

IS700Z27 B61
YEARS MFRD 2014-2018
ENGINE .... B&S
ENGINE HP 27
COOLING .... AIR
FUEL .... G
SPEEDS .... VARIABLE
TRANSMISSION .... HYDRO
STEERING .... ZERO
STANDARD DECK .... 61"
MSRP $6,983

OPTIONS
2 BAG HARD
2 BAG SOFT
3 BAG HARD
3 BAG SOFT

RETAIL PRICING
YEAR	HIGH	LOW
2014	$3,151	$2,363
2015	$3,466	$2,599
2016	$3,826	$2,869
2017	$4,223	$3,168
2018	$4,715	$3,536

IS700Z28 B52
YEARS MFRD 2013-2013
ENGINE .... B&S
ENGINE HP 28
COOLING .... AIR
FUEL .... G
SPEEDS .... VARIABLE
TRANSMISSION .... HYDRO
STEERING .... ZERO
BLADE CLUTCH .... ELECTRIC
STANDARD DECK .... 52"
MSRP $6,348

OPTIONS
61" DECK

RETAIL PRICING
YEAR	HIGH	LOW
2013	$4,123	$3,093

IS700Z28 BV61
YEARS MFRD 2013-2015
ENGINE .... VANGUARD
ENGINE HP 28
COOLING .... AIR
FUEL .... G
SPEEDS .... VARIABLE
TRANSMISSION .... HYDRO
STEERING .... ZERO
BLADE CLUTCH .... ELECTRIC
STANDARD DECK .... 61"
MSRP $7,723

RETAIL PRICING
YEAR	HIGH	LOW
2013	$4,066	$3,050
2014	$4,517	$3,388
2015	$5,151	$3,863

IS700ZB27
YEARS MFRD 2019-2019
ENGINE .... B&S
CYLINDERS 2
CID 810CC
ENGINE HP 27
FUEL .... G

FERRIS

SPEEDS .... VARIABLE
TRANSMISSION ..... DUAL HYDRO
STEERING .... ZERO
STANDARD DECK .... 52"
WEIGHT .... 1,059 LBS.
MSRP $6,399

OPTIONS

61" DECK

IS700ZBV26

YEARS MFRD 2016-2018
ENGINE .... VANGUARD
ENGINE HP 26
COOLING .... AIR
FUEL .... G
SPEEDS .... VARIABLE
TRANSMISSION .... HYDRO
STEERING .... ZERO
STANDARD DECK .... 61"
MSRP $7,617

OPTIONS

2 BAG HARD
2 BAG SOFT
3 BAG HARD
3 BAG SOFT

RETAIL PRICING

YEAR	HIGH	LOW
2016	$4,173	$3,130
2017	$4,606	$3,454
2018	$5,054	$3,790

IS700ZKAVE26

YEARS MFRD 2016-2018
ENGINE .... KAWASAKI EFI
ENGINE HP 26
COOLING .... AIR
FUEL .... G
SPEEDS .... VARIABLE
TRANSMISSION .... HYDRO
STEERING .... ZERO
STANDARD DECK .... 61"
MSRP $8,147

OPTIONS

2 BAG HARD
2 BAG SOFT
3 BAG HARD
3 BAG SOFT

RETAIL PRICING

YEAR	HIGH	LOW
2016	$4,463	$3,347
2017	$4,927	$3,695
2018	$5,763	$4,322

IS1000Z

YEARS MFRD 2004-2005
ENGINE .... KAWASAKI
CYLINDERS 2
ENGINE HP 23
COOLING .... AIR
FUEL .... G
SPEEDS .... VARIABLE
TRANSMISSION .... HYDRO
STEERING .... ZERO
BLADE CLUTCH .... ELECTRIC
PTO .... YES
WEIGHT .... 1,102 LBS.

OPTIONS

KAWASAKI 21E

IS1500Z

YEARS MFRD 2005-2011
ENGINE .... KAWASAKI
ENGINE HP 19
COOLING .... AIR
FUEL .... G
SPEEDS .... VARIABLE
TRANSMISSION .... HYDRO
STEERING .... STANDARD
STANDARD DECK .... 44"
MSRP $6,980

OPTIONS

48" DECK
52" DECK
KAWASAKI 21E
KAWASAKI 25E

RETAIL PRICING

YEAR	HIGH	LOW
2005	$3,411	$2,558
2006	$3,437	$2,578
2007	$3,457	$2,593
2008	$3,476	$2,607
2009	$3,812	$2,859
2010	$4,181	$3,136
2011	$4,201	$3,151

IS2000Z

YEARS MFRD 2007-2011
ENGINE .... B&S VANGUARD
CYLINDERS 2
ENGINE HP 30
FUEL .... G
SPEEDS .... VARIABLE
TRANSMISSION .... HYDRO
BLADE CLUTCH .... ELECTRIC
STANDARD DECK .... 61"
WEIGHT .... 1,200 LBS.
MSRP $10,275

OPTIONS

KAWASAKI 30E
KOHLER 27E

RETAIL PRICING

YEAR	HIGH	LOW
2008	$5,906	$4,430
2009	$6,042	$4,532
2010	$6,070	$4,553
2011	$6,250	$4,687

IS2500Z

YEARS MFRD 2010-2011
SERIES .... ZERO TURN SERIES
ENGINE .... YANMAR
CYLINDERS 2
ENGINE HP 20
COOLING .... AIR
FUEL .... D
SPEEDS .... VARIABLE
TRANSMISSION .... HYDRO
STEERING .... ZERO
BLADE CLUTCH .... ELECTRIC
STANDARD DECK .... 52"
WEIGHT .... 1,582 LBS.
MSRP $12,349

OPTIONS

61" DECK

RETAIL PRICING

YEAR	HIGH	LOW
2010	$5,313	$3,985
2011	$6,739	$5,054

IS2600ZY24

YEARS MFRD 2016-2020
ENGINE .... YANMAR
CYLINDERS 3
CID 904CC
ENGINE HP 24
COOLING .... AIR
FUEL .... D
SPEEDS .... VARIABLE
TRANSMISSION .... HYDRO
STEERING .... ZERO
STANDARD DECK .... 61"
MSRP $17,149

RETAIL PRICING

YEAR	HIGH	LOW
2016	$9,649	$7,237
2017	$10,650	$7,987
2018	$11,680	$8,761
2019	$12,785	$9,589
2020	$14,158	$10,808

IS3000Z K25/61

YEARS MFRD 2001-2005
ENGINE .... KOHLER
ENGINE HP 25
FUEL .... G
SPEEDS .... VARIABLE
TRANSMISSION .... HYDRO
STEERING .... STANDARD
STANDARD DECK .... 61"
MSRP $9,799

RETAIL PRICING

YEAR	HIGH	LOW
2001	$4,265	$3,199
2003	$4,768	$3,576
2004	$5,436	$4,077
2005	$5,717	$4,288

IS3000Z KAV23/61

YEARS MFRD 2001-2001
ENGINE .... KAWASAKI
ENGINE HP 23
FUEL .... G
TRANSMISSION .... HYDRO
STEERING .... STANDARD
STANDARD DECK .... 61"
MSRP $8,995

RETAIL PRICING

YEAR	HIGH	LOW
2001	$4,171	$3,128

IS3000Z KAV25/61

YEARS MFRD 2001-2002
ENGINE .... KAWASAKI
ENGINE HP 23
FUEL .... G
TRANSMISSION .... HYDRO
STEERING .... STANDARD
STANDARD DECK .... 61"
MSRP $9,225

RETAIL PRICING

YEAR	HIGH	LOW
2001	$4,276	$3,207
2002	$4,397	$3,298

IS3000ZF

YEARS MFRD 2004-2005
ENGINE .... KOHLER
CYLINDERS 2
ENGINE HP 27
COOLING .... AIR
FUEL .... G
SPEEDS .... VARIABLE
TRANSMISSION .... HYDRO
STEERING .... ZERO
BLADE CLUTCH .... ELECTRIC
WEIGHT .... 1,246 LBS.

IS3000ZL KAV26/61

YEARS MFRD 2006-2006
ENGINE .... KAWASAKI
ENGINE HP 26
FUEL .... G
SPEEDS .... VARIABLE
TRANSMISSION .... HYDRO
STEERING .... STANDARD
STANDARD DECK .... 61"
MSRP $11,199

RETAIL PRICING

YEAR	HIGH	LOW
2006	$6,908	$5,181

IS3000ZX

YEARS MFRD 2004-2005
ENGINE .... KAWASAKI
CYLINDERS 2
ENGINE HP 25
COOLING .... AIR
FUEL .... G
SPEEDS .... VARIABLE
TRANSMISSION .... HYDRO
STEERING .... ZERO
BLADE CLUTCH .... ELECTRIC
PTO .... YES
WEIGHT .... 1,246 LBS.

IS3000ZX EXTREME

YEARS MFRD 2004-2004
ENGINE .... KOHLER
CYLINDERS 2

ENGINE HP 27
FUEL . . . . . G
SPEEDS 10/6
TRANSMISSION . . . . . HYDRO
STEERING. . . . . ZERO

IS3100Z

YEARS MFRD 2007-2011
ENGINE . . . . . B&S VANGUARD
CYLINDERS. 2
ENGINE HP 32
FUEL . . . . . G
SPEEDS . . . . . VARIABLE
TRANSMISSION . . . . . HYDRO
STEERING. . . . . ZERO
BLADE CLUTCH . . . . . ELECTRIC
STANDARD DECK . . . . . 61"
WEIGHT . . . . . 1,325 LBS.
MSRP. $12,369

OPTIONS

KAWASAKI 26E
KOHLER 30E

RETAIL PRICING

YEAR	HIGH	LOW
2007	$5,449	$4,087
2008	$6,441	$4,831
2009	$7,169	$5,377
2010	$7,339	$5,504
2011	$7,391	$5,544

IS3200Z MIDNIGHT

YEARS MFRD 2019-2019
ENGINE . . . . . VANGUARD EFI
CID 993CC
ENGINE HP 37
FUEL . . . . . G
SPEEDS . . . . . VARIABLE
TRANSMISSION . . . . . DUAL HYDRO
STEERING. . . . . ZERO
STANDARD DECK . . . . . 61"
WEIGHT . . . . . 1,520 LBS.
MSRP. $14,999

IS3200ZBV32

YEARS MFRD 2016-2020
SERIES. . . . . IS3200 SERIES
ENGINE . . . . . VANGUARD
ENGINE HP 32
FUEL . . . . . G
SPEEDS . . . . . VARIABLE
TRANSMISSION . . . . . DUAL HYDRO
STEERING. . . . . ZERO
STANDARD DECK . . . . . 61"
MSRP. $12,599

OPTIONS

3 BAG HARD
3 BAG SOFT
72" DECK. $750

RETAIL PRICING

YEAR	HIGH	LOW
2016	$6,860	$5,145
2017	$7,557	$5,668
2018	$8,270	$6,202
2019	$9,053	$6,790
2020	$10,117	$7,629

IS3200ZBVE37

YEARS MFRD 2016-2020
SERIES. . . . . IS3200 SERIES
ENGINE . . . . . VANGUARD EFI
ENGINE HP 37
FUEL . . . . . G
SPEEDS . . . . . VARIABLE
TRANSMISSION . . . . . DUAL HYDRO
STEERING. . . . . ZERO
STANDARD DECK . . . . . 61"

OPTIONS

3 BAG HARD
3 BAG SOFT
72" DECK

RETAIL PRICING

YEAR	HIGH	LOW
2016	$7,469	$5,602
2017	$8,246	$6,184
2018	$8,983	$6,737
2019	$9,809	$7,356
2020	$11,083	$8,267

IS3200ZKAV35

YEARS MFRD 2016-2020
SERIES. . . . . IS3200 SERIES
ENGINE . . . . . KAWASAKI
ENGINE HP 35
FUEL . . . . . G
SPEEDS . . . . . VARIABLE
TRANSMISSION . . . . . DUAL HYDRO
STEERING. . . . . ZERO
STANDARD DECK . . . . . 72"
MSRP. $13,999

OPTIONS

3 BAG HARD
3 BAG SOFT
61" DECK

RETAIL PRICING

YEAR	HIGH	LOW
2016	$7,303	$5,477
2017	$8,040	$6,029
2018	$8,852	$6,638
2019	$9,725	$7,294
2020	$11,508	$8,800

IS4000Z

YEARS MFRD 2004-2005
ENGINE . . . . . KAWASAKI
CYLINDERS. 2
ENGINE HP 27
COOLING . . . . . LIQUID
FUEL . . . . . G
SPEEDS . . . . . VARIABLE
TRANSMISSION . . . . . HYDRO
STEERING. . . . . ZERO
BLADE CLUTCH . . . . . ELECTRIC
PTO . . . . . YES
STANDARD DECK . . . . . 72"
WEIGHT . . . . . 1,700 LBS.

OPTIONS

DAIHATSU

IS4000Z D31/72

YEARS MFRD 2001-2002
ENGINE . . . . . DAIHATSU
ENGINE HP 31
FUEL . . . . . G
TRANSMISSION . . . . . HYDRO
STEERING. . . . . STANDARD
STANDARD DECK . . . . . 72"
MSRP. $14,995

RETAIL PRICING

YEAR	HIGH	LOW
2001	$6,488	$4,866
2002	$7,146	$5,359

IS4000Z KAV27/61

YEARS MFRD 2001-2002
ENGINE . . . . . KAWASAKI
ENGINE HP 27
FUEL . . . . . G
TRANSMISSION . . . . . HYDRO
STEERING. . . . . STANDARD
STANDARD DECK . . . . . 61"
MSRP. $11,495

RETAIL PRICING

YEAR	HIGH	LOW
2001	$5,102	$3,827
2002	$5,479	$4,109

IS4000Z KAV27/72

YEARS MFRD 2001-2001
ENGINE . . . . . KAWASAKI
ENGINE HP 27
FUEL . . . . . G
TRANSMISSION . . . . . HYDRO
STEERING. . . . . STANDARD
STANDARD DECK . . . . . 72"
MSRP. $11,499

RETAIL PRICING

YEAR	HIGH	LOW
2001	$5,332	$3,999

IS4500Z

YEARS MFRD 2005-2008
ENGINE . . . . . BRIGGS BIG BLOCK
CYLINDERS. 2
ENGINE HP 35
COOLING . . . . . LIQUID
FUEL . . . . . D
SPEEDS . . . . . VARIABLE
TRANSMISSION . . . . . HYDRO
STEERING. . . . . ZERO
BLADE CLUTCH . . . . . ELECTRIC
STANDARD DECK . . . . . 61"
MSRP. $14,592

OPTIONS

72" DECK
CAT DIESEL

RETAIL PRICING

YEAR	HIGH	LOW
2006	$7,485	$5,613
2007	$7,655	$5,741
2008	$8,718	$6,539

IS5000Z

YEARS MFRD 2004-2004
ENGINE . . . . . DAIHATSU
CYLINDERS. 3
ENGINE HP 34
COOLING . . . . . LIQUID
FUEL . . . . . D
SPEEDS . . . . . VARIABLE
TRANSMISSION . . . . . HYDRO
STEERING. . . . . ZERO
BLADE CLUTCH . . . . . MANUAL
PTO . . . . . YES
ROPS/CAB . . . . . ROPS
STANDARD DECK . . . . . 72"
WEIGHT . . . . . 1,908 LBS.
MSRP. $15,499

OPTIONS

CAT DIESEL 31.5
CAT DIESEL 33

RETAIL PRICING

YEAR	HIGH	LOW
2004	$4,048	$3,036

IS5100Z C33D

YEARS MFRD 2007-2011
ENGINE . . . . . CAT
CYLINDERS. 3
ENGINE HP 33.5
COOLING . . . . . AIR
FUEL . . . . . D
SPEEDS . . . . . VARIABLE
TRANSMISSION . . . . . HYDRO
STEERING. . . . . ZERO
BLADE CLUTCH . . . . . ELECTRIC
STANDARD DECK . . . . . 61"
WEIGHT . . . . . 2,218 LBS.
MSRP. $20,789

OPTIONS

72" DECK

RETAIL PRICING

YEAR	HIGH	LOW
2008	$11,277	$8,458
2009	$11,447	$8,585
2010	$11,772	$8,829
2011	$12,010	$9,007

IS20002

YEARS MFRD 2006-2006
ENGINE . . . . . KOHLER
ENGINE HP 27
FUEL . . . . . G
SPEEDS . . . . . VARIABLE
TRANSMISSION . . . . . HYDRO
STEERING. . . . . STANDARD
STANDARD DECK . . . . . 61"
MSRP. $9,915

OPTIONS

KAWASAKI

RETAIL PRICING

YEAR HIGH LOW
2006 $6,115 $4,586

IS30002

YEARS MFRD 2006-2006
ENGINE B&S
ENGINE HP 30
FUEL G
SPEEDS VARIABLE
TRANSMISSION HYDRO
STEERING STANDARD
STANDARD DECK 61"
MSRP $11,199

OPTIONS

KOHLER 30

RETAIL PRICING

YEAR HIGH LOW
2006 $6,908 $5,181

IS50002

YEARS MFRD 2006-2006
ENGINE CAT
ENGINE HP 31.5
FUEL D
SPEEDS VARIABLE
TRANSMISSION HYDRO
STEERING STANDARD
STANDARD DECK 61"
MSRP $18,150

OPTIONS

72" DECK

RETAIL PRICING

YEAR HIGH LOW
2006 $11,197 $8,398

ISX800BE27

YEARS MFRD 2019-2020
ENGINE B&S EFI
CYLINDERS 2
CID 810CC
ENGINE HP 27
FUEL G
SPEEDS VARIABLE
TRANSMISSION DUAL HYDRO
STEERING ZERO
STANDARD DECK 61"
WEIGHT 1,197 LBS.
MSRP $8,649

ISX800ZB27

YEARS MFRD 2019-2020
ENGINE B&S
CYLINDERS 2
CID 724CC
ENGINE HP 27
FUEL G
SPEEDS VARIABLE
TRANSMISSION DUAL HYDRO
STEERING ZERO
STANDARD DECK 52"
WEIGHT 1,119 LBS.
MSRP $7,799

OPTIONS

61" DECK $500

ISX800ZBV26

YEARS MFRD 2019-2020
ENGINE VANGUARD
CYLINDERS 2
CID 810CC
ENGINE HP 26
FUEL G
SPEEDS VARIABLE
TRANSMISSION DUAL HYDRO
STEERING ZERO
STANDARD DECK 61"
WEIGHT 1,197 LBS.
MSRP $9,449

ISX800ZKAV24

YEARS MFRD 2019-2020
ENGINE KAWASAKI FS730V
CYLINDERS 2
CID 726CC
ENGINE HP 24
FUEL G
SPEEDS VARIABLE
TRANSMISSION DUAL HYDRO
STEERING ZERO
STANDARD DECK 52"
WEIGHT 1,119 LBS.
MSRP $7,999

ISX800Z KAVE26

YEARS MFRD 2019-2020
ENGINE KAWASAKI EFI
CYLINDERS 2
CID 726CC
ENGINE HP 26
FUEL G
SPEEDS VARIABLE
TRANSMISSION DUAL HYDRO
STEERING ZERO
STANDARD DECK 61"
WEIGHT 1,197 LBS.
MSRP $8,949

ISX2200 BVE26

YEARS MFRD 2020-2020
SERIES ISX2200 SERIES
ENGINE VANGUARD EFI
CYLINDERS 2
CID 810CC
ENGINE HP 26
FUEL G
SPEEDS VARIABLE
TRANSMISSION DUAL HYDRO
STEERING ZERO
ROPS/CAB ROPS
STANDARD DECK 52"
WEIGHT 1,319 LBS.
MSRP $11,549

ISX2200 BVE28

YEARS MFRD 2020-2020
SERIES ISX2200 SERIES
ENGINE VANGUARD EFI
CYLINDERS 2
CID 810CC
ENGINE HP 28
FUEL G
SPEEDS VARIABLE
TRANSMISSION DUAL HYDRO
STEERING ZERO
ROPS/CAB ROPS
STANDARD DECK 61"
WEIGHT 1,398 LBS.
MSRP $12,099

ISX3300 BVE37

YEARS MFRD 2020-2020
SERIES ISX3300 SERIES
ENGINE VANGUARD BIG BLOCK EFI
CYLINDERS 2
CID 993CC
ENGINE HP 37
FUEL G
SPEEDS VARIABLE
TRANSMISSION DUAL HYDRO
STEERING ZERO
ROPS/CAB ROPS
STANDARD DECK 61"
WEIGHT 1,608 LBS.
MSRP $14,699

OPTIONS

72" DECK $550

ISZ25K

YEARS MFRD 1999-2000
SERIES PROCUT Z IS SERIES
ENGINE KOHLER
ENGINE HP 25
FUEL G
TRANSMISSION HYDRO
STEERING ZERO
STANDARD DECK 52"
MSRP $9,095

OPTIONS

61" DECK

SERIAL NUMBERS

YEAR BEGINNING NO.
1999 281

RETAIL PRICING

YEAR HIGH LOW
1999 $1,504 $1,128
2000 $1,673 $1,255

ISZKAV23

YEARS MFRD 1999-2000
SERIES PROCUT Z IS SERIES
ENGINE KAWASAKI
ENGINE HP 23
FUEL G
TRANSMISSION HYDRO
STEERING ZERO
STANDARD DECK 52"
MSRP $8,895

OPTIONS

61" DECK

SERIAL NUMBERS

YEAR BEGINNING NO.
1999 281
2000 281

RETAIL PRICING

YEAR HIGH LOW
1999 $1,474 $1,106
2000 $1,638 $1,229

PCZ22K

YEARS MFRD 1997-1998
SERIES PROCUT Z SERIES
ENGINE KOHLER
ENGINE HP 22
FUEL G
TRANSMISSION HYDRO
STEERING ZERO
STANDARD DECK 52"
MSRP $8,395

OPTIONS

61" DECK

SERIAL NUMBERS

YEAR BEGINNING NO.
1997 101
1998 749

RETAIL PRICING

YEAR HIGH LOW
1997 $1,245 $933
1998 $1,380 $1,035

PCZ25K

YEARS MFRD 1997-1999
SERIES PROCUT Z SERIES
ENGINE KOHLER
ENGINE HP 25
FUEL G
TRANSMISSION HYDRO
STEERING ZERO
STANDARD DECK 61"
MSRP $8,795

SERIAL NUMBERS

YEAR BEGINNING NO.
1997 275
1998 749

RETAIL PRICING

YEAR HIGH LOW
1997 $1,314 $986
1998 $1,458 $1,093
1999 $1,619 $1,214

PCZ2252

YEARS MFRD 1997-1998
ENGINE KOHLER
ENGINE HP 22
FUEL G
TRANSMISSION HYDRO
STEERING STANDARD
STANDARD DECK 52"
MSRP $8,395

RETAIL PRICING

YEAR	HIGH	LOW
1997	$3,178	$2,383
1998	$3,339	$2,504

PCZ2261

YEARS MFRD 1997-1998
ENGINE KOHLER
ENGINE HP 22
FUEL G
TRANSMISSION HYDRO
STEERING STANDARD
STANDARD DECK 61"
MSRP $8,495

RETAIL PRICING

YEAR	HIGH	LOW
1997	$3,217	$2,413
1998	$3,379	$2,535

PCZ2552

YEARS MFRD 1997-1999
ENGINE KOHLER
ENGINE HP 25
FUEL G
TRANSMISSION HYDRO
STEERING STANDARD
STANDARD DECK 52"
MSRP $8,795

RETAIL PRICING

YEAR	HIGH	LOW
1997	$3,293	$2,470
1998	$3,537	$2,652
1999	$3,733	$2,799

PCZ2561

YEARS MFRD 1997-1999
ENGINE KOHLER
ENGINE HP 25
FUEL G
TRANSMISSION HYDRO
STEERING STANDARD
STANDARD DECK 61"
MSRP $8,795

RETAIL PRICING

YEAR	HIGH	LOW
1997	$3,332	$2,499
1998	$3,497	$2,623
1999	$3,733	$2,799

PROCUT 20

YEARS MFRD 2005-2006
SERIES PROCUT SERIES
ENGINE KOHLER
CYLINDERS 2
ENGINE HP 23
COOLING AIR
FUEL G
SPEEDS VARIABLE
TRANSMISSION HYDRO
STEERING ZERO
WEIGHT 900 LBS.

OPTIONS

B&S 20

PROCUT 30

YEARS MFRD 2005-2005
SERIES PROCUT SERIES
ENGINE KOHLER
CYLINDERS 2
ENGINE HP 25
COOLING AIR
FUEL G
SPEEDS VARIABLE
TRANSMISSION HYDRO
STEERING ZERO
WEIGHT 1,060 LBS.

PROCUT S

YEARS MFRD 2008-2010
ENGINE KAWASAKI
CYLINDERS 2
ENGINE HP 25
FUEL G
SPEEDS VARIABLE
TRANSMISSION HYDRO
STEERING ZERO
BLADE CLUTCH ELECTRIC
STANDARD DECK 61"
MSRP $8,479

OPTIONS

B&S 26

RETAIL PRICING

YEAR	HIGH	LOW
2008	$4,796	$3,597
2009	$4,905	$3,679
2010	$5,000	$3,750

SRSZ1BV23

YEARS MFRD 2017-2020
ENGINE VANGUARD
CYLINDERS 2
CID 627CC
ENGINE HP 23
COOLING AIR
FUEL G
SPEEDS VARIABLE
TRANSMISSION HYDRO
STEERING ZERO
STANDARD DECK 36"
MSRP $7,799

OPTIONS

48" DECK $200

RETAIL PRICING

YEAR	HIGH	LOW
2017	$4,808	$3,606
2018	$5,305	$3,979
2019	$5,829	$4,371
2020	$6,463	$4,849

SRSZ1KAV19

YEARS MFRD 2017-2020
ENGINE KAWASAKI
CYLINDERS 2
CID 603CC
ENGINE HP 19
COOLING AIR
FUEL G
SPEEDS VARIABLE
TRANSMISSION HYDRO
STEERING ZERO
STANDARD DECK 36"
MSRP $7,799

RETAIL PRICING

YEAR	HIGH	LOW
2017	$5,010	$3,757
2018	$5,432	$4,054
2019	$5,949	$4,482
2020	$6,533	$4,923

SRSZ1KAV22

YEARS MFRD 2017-2020
ENGINE KAWASAKI
CYLINDERS 2
CID 726CC
ENGINE HP 22
FUEL G
SPEEDS VARIABLE
TRANSMISSION HYDRO
STEERING ZERO
STANDARD DECK 48"
MSRP $8,099

RETAIL PRICING

YEAR	HIGH	LOW
2017	$5,015	$3,761
2018	$5,507	$4,131
2019	$6,041	$4,530
2020	$6,733	$5,137

SRSZ2BVE28

YEARS MFRD 2016-2020
ENGINE VANGUARD
CYLINDERS 2
CID 810CC
ENGINE HP 28
COOLING AIR
FUEL G
SPEEDS VARIABLE
TRANSMISSION HYDRO
STEERING ZERO
STANDARD DECK 52"
MSRP $9,899

OPTIONS

61" DECK $500

RETAIL PRICING

YEAR	HIGH	LOW
2016	$5,415	$4,062
2017	$5,977	$4,483
2018	$6,537	$4,903
2019	$7,123	$5,342
2020	$7,992	$6,133

SRSZ2KAV26

YEARS MFRD 2016-2020
ENGINE KAWASAKI
CYLINDERS 2
CID 852CC
ENGINE HP 25.5
COOLING AIR
FUEL G
SPEEDS VARIABLE
TRANSMISSION HYDRO
STEERING ZERO
STANDARD DECK 52"
MSRP $9,249

OPTIONS

61" DECK
EFI

RETAIL PRICING

YEAR	HIGH	LOW
2016	$5,042	$3,782
2017	$5,564	$4,173
2018	$6,076	$4,557
2019	$6,656	$4,999
2020	$7,466	$5,699

SRSZ3BVE37

YEARS MFRD 2018-2020
ENGINE VANGUARD
CYLINDERS 2
CID 852CC
ENGINE HP 37
FUEL G
TRANSMISSION HYDRO
STEERING ZERO
STANDARD DECK 61"
MSRP $11,699

OPTIONS

52" DECK $-450
72" DECK $500

SRSZ3KAVE30

YEARS MFRD 2018-2020
ENGINE KAWASAKI FX850V EFI
CYLINDERS 2
CID 852CC
ENGINE HP 29.5
COOLING AIR
FUEL G
TRANSMISSION HYDRO
STEERING ZERO
STANDARD DECK 61"
WEIGHT 1,267 LBS.
MSRP $11,149

OPTIONS

72" DECK

SRSZ3XBVE33

YEARS MFRD 2019-2020
ENGINE VANGUARD EFI
CYLINDERS 2
CID 896CC
ENGINE HP 33
FUEL G
SPEEDS VARIABLE
TRANSMISSION DUAL HYDRO
STEERING ZERO
STANDARD DECK 52"
WEIGHT 1,184 LBS.
MSRP $10,849

OPTIONS

61" DECK

Z100

YEARS MFRD 1999-1999
ENGINE KOHLER
ENGINE HP 25
FUEL G

TRANSMISSION . . . . .HYDRO
STEERING. . . . . ZERO
STANDARD DECK . . . . 61"
MSRP. $8,795

SERIAL NUMBERS

YEAR	BEGINNING NO.
1999	116

RETAIL PRICING

YEAR	HIGH	LOW
1999	$1,619	$1,214

400SB2344

YEARS MFRD 2019-2020
ENGINE . . . . B&S
CYLINDERS. 2
CID 724CC
ENGINE HP 23
FUEL . . . . G
SPEEDS . . . . VARIABLE
TRANSMISSION . . . . . DUAL HYDRO
STEERING. . . . . ZERO
STANDARD DECK . . . . 44"
WEIGHT . . . . 728 LBS.
MSRP. $4,649

400SB2548

YEARS MFRD 2019-2020
ENGINE . . . . B&S
CYLINDERS. 2
CID 724CC
ENGINE HP 25
FUEL . . . . G
SPEEDS . . . . VARIABLE
TRANSMISSION . . . . . DUAL HYDRO
STEERING. . . . . ZERO
STANDARD DECK . . . . 48"
WEIGHT . . . . 753 LBS.
MSRP. $4,849

400SKAV2244

YEARS MFRD 2019-2020
ENGINE . . . . KAWASAKI FR651V
CYLINDERS. 2
CID 726CC
ENGINE HP 22
FUEL . . . . G
SPEEDS . . . . VARIABLE
TRANSMISSION . . . . . DUAL HYDRO
STEERING. . . . . ZERO
STANDARD DECK . . . . 44"
WEIGHT . . . . 728 LBS.
MSRP. $4,749

400SKAV2248

YEARS MFRD 2018-2020
ENGINE . . . . KAWASAKI FR651V
CYLINDERS. 2
CID 651CC
ENGINE HP 21.5
FUEL . . . . G
SPEEDS . . . . VARIABLE
TRANSMISSION . . . . . DUAL HYDRO
STEERING. . . . . ZERO
STANDARD DECK . . . . 48"
WEIGHT . . . . 753 LBS.
MSRP. $4,949

1000Z KAV21/48

YEARS MFRD 2001-2004
SERIES. . . . . .PROCUT Z SERIES
ENGINE . . . . KAWASAKI
ENGINE HP 21
COOLING . . . . .AIR
FUEL . . . . G
SPEEDS . . . . VARIABLE
TRANSMISSION . . . . .HYDRO
STEERING. . . . . ZERO
STANDARD DECK . . . . 48"
MSRP. $7,049

OPTIONS

52" DECK

RETAIL PRICING

YEAR	HIGH	LOW
2001	$1,408	$1,056
2002	$1,565	$1,173
2003	$1,740	$1,305
2004	$1,931	$1,448

1500Z B26

YEARS MFRD 2012-2012
SERIES. . . . . IS RIDERS SERIES
ENGINE . . . . B&S
ENGINE HP 26
COOLING . . . . .AIR
FUEL . . . . G
SPEEDS . . . . VARIABLE
TRANSMISSION . . . . .HYDRO
STEERING. . . . . ZERO
STANDARD DECK . . . . 44"
MSRP. $6,348

OPTIONS

48" DECK

RETAIL PRICING

YEAR	HIGH	LOW
2012	$3,573	$2,680

1500Z KAV19

YEARS MFRD 2005-2012
SERIES. . . . . IS RIDERS SERIES
ENGINE . . . . KAWASAKI
CYLINDERS. 2
ENGINE HP 19
COOLING . . . . .AIR
FUEL . . . . G
SPEEDS . . . . VARIABLE
TRANSMISSION . . . . .HYDRO
STEERING. . . . . ZERO
STANDARD DECK . . . . 44"
MSRP. $6,559

OPTIONS

48" DECK
KAWASAKI 21
KAWASAKI 25

RETAIL PRICING

YEAR	HIGH	LOW
2005	$1,771	$1,328
2006	$1,971	$1,478
2007	$2,185	$1,639
2008	$2,429	$1,822
2009	$2,699	$2,024
2010	$2,995	$2,247
2011	$3,328	$2,496
2012	$3,695	$2,771

1500ZX B26

YEARS MFRD 2012-2012
ENGINE . . . . B&S
ENGINE HP 26
COOLING . . . . .AIR
FUEL . . . . G
SPEEDS . . . . VARIABLE
TRANSMISSION . . . . .HYDRO
STEERING. . . . . ZERO
STANDARD DECK . . . . 52"
MSRP. $7,406

RETAIL PRICING

YEAR	HIGH	LOW
2012	$4,173	$3,130

1500ZX BV28

YEARS MFRD 2010-2012
ENGINE . . . . B&S
ENGINE HP 28
COOLING . . . . .AIR
FUEL . . . . G
SPEEDS . . . . VARIABLE
TRANSMISSION . . . . .HYDRO
STEERING. . . . . ZERO
STANDARD DECK . . . . 61"
MSRP. $7,935

RETAIL PRICING

YEAR	HIGH	LOW
2010	$3,620	$2,715
2011	$4,024	$3,018
2012	$4,470	$3,352

1500ZX KAV23

YEARS MFRD 2012-2012
ENGINE . . . . B&S
ENGINE HP 23
COOLING . . . . .AIR
FUEL . . . . G
SPEEDS . . . . VARIABLE
TRANSMISSION . . . . .HYDRO
STEERING. . . . . ZERO
STANDARD DECK . . . . 52"
MSRP. $7,617

RETAIL PRICING

YEAR	HIGH	LOW
2012	$4,302	$3,226

1500ZX KAV24

YEARS MFRD 2012-2012
ENGINE . . . . KAWASAKI
ENGINE HP 24
COOLING . . . . .AIR
FUEL . . . . G
SPEEDS . . . . VARIABLE
TRANSMISSION . . . . .HYDRO
STEERING. . . . . ZERO
STANDARD DECK . . . . 61"
MSRP. $8,464

RETAIL PRICING

YEAR	HIGH	LOW
2012	$4,767	$3,575

2000Z

YEARS MFRD 2006-2006
ENGINE . . . . KAWASAKI
ENGINE HP 25
COOLING . . . . .AIR
FUEL . . . . G
SPEEDS . . . . VARIABLE
TRANSMISSION . . . . .HYDRO
STEERING. . . . . ZERO

OPTIONS

KOHLER 27

2000Z B28

YEARS MFRD 2007-2013
ENGINE . . . . B&S
ENGINE HP 26
COOLING . . . . .AIR
FUEL . . . . G
SPEEDS . . . . VARIABLE
TRANSMISSION . . . . .HYDRO
STEERING. . . . . ZERO
STANDARD DECK . . . . 52"
MSRP. $9,089

RETAIL PRICING

YEAR	HIGH	LOW
2007	$2,957	$2,217
2008	$3,284	$2,463
2009	$3,652	$2,739
2010	$4,051	$3,038
2011	$4,508	$3,381
2012	$4,994	$3,745
2013	$5,545	$4,159

2000Z B30

YEARS MFRD 2012-2013
ENGINE . . . . B&S
ENGINE HP 30
COOLING . . . . .AIR
FUEL . . . . G
SPEEDS . . . . VARIABLE
TRANSMISSION . . . . .HYDRO
STEERING. . . . . ZERO
STANDARD DECK . . . . 61"
MSRP. $10,226

RETAIL PRICING

YEAR	HIGH	LOW
2012	$5,636	$4,227
2013	$6,241	$4,681

2000Z BV32

YEARS MFRD 2012-2013
SERIES. . . . . IS RIDERS SERIES
ENGINE . . . . B&S
ENGINE HP 32
COOLING . . . . .AIR
FUEL . . . . G
SPEEDS . . . . VARIABLE
TRANSMISSION . . . . .HYDRO
STEERING. . . . . ZERO
STANDARD DECK . . . . 61"
MSRP. $11,930

RETAIL PRICING

YEAR	HIGH	LOW
2012	$6,557	$4,918
2013	$7,281	$5,461

2000Z KAV26

YEARS MFRD ... 2011-2013
ENGINE ... KAWASAKI
ENGINE HP ... 25.5
COOLING ... AIR
FUEL ... G
SPEEDS ... VARIABLE
TRANSMISSION ... HYDRO
STEERING ... ZERO
BLADE CLUTCH ... ELECTRIC
STANDARD DECK ... 52"
MSRP ... $10,226

OPTIONS

61" DECK

RETAIL PRICING

YEAR	HIGH	LOW
2011	$4,994	$3,745
2012	$5,548	$4,161
2013	$6,160	$4,620

2000Z KOH29

YEARS MFRD ... 2013-2013
SERIES ... IS RIDERS SERIES
ENGINE ... B&S
ENGINE HP ... 29
COOLING ... AIR
FUEL ... G
SPEEDS ... VARIABLE
TRANSMISSION ... HYDRO
STEERING ... ZERO
BLADE CLUTCH ... ELECTRIC
STANDARD DECK ... 61"
MSRP ... $11,930

RETAIL PRICING

YEAR	HIGH	LOW
2013	$7,188	$5,391

2100Z BV26

YEARS MFRD ... 2014-2020
SERIES ... IS RIDERS SERIES
ENGINE ... VANGUARD
CYLINDERS ... 2
CID ... 810CC
ENGINE HP ... 26
COOLING ... AIR
FUEL ... G
SPEEDS ... VARIABLE
TRANSMISSION ... HYDRO
STEERING ... ZERO
STANDARD DECK ... 52"
MSRP ... $9,799

OPTIONS

2 BAG HARD
2 BAG SOFT
3 BAG HARD
61" DECK ... $500

RETAIL PRICING

YEAR	HIGH	LOW
2014	$4,464	$3,348
2015	$4,906	$3,680
2016	$5,415	$4,062
2017	$5,977	$4,483
2018	$6,553	$4,914
2019	$7,173	$5,546
2020	$8,032	$6,149

2100Z BV28

YEARS MFRD ... 2015-2020
SERIES ... IS RIDERS SERIES
ENGINE ... VANGUARD EFI
CYLINDERS ... 2
CID ... 810CC
ENGINE HP ... 28
COOLING ... AIR
FUEL ... G
SPEEDS ... VARIABLE
TRANSMISSION ... HYDRO
STEERING ... ZERO
STANDARD DECK ... 61"
MSRP ... $11,349

OPTIONS

2 BAG HARD
2 BAG SOFT
3 BAG HARD
52" DECK ... $-500

RETAIL PRICING

YEAR	HIGH	LOW
2015	$5,639	$4,229
2016	$6,225	$4,668
2017	$6,870	$5,152
2018	$7,520	$5,640
2019	$8,230	$6,173
2020	$9,110	$7,042

2100Z BV32

YEARS MFRD ... 2014-2016
SERIES ... IS RIDERS SERIES
ENGINE ... VANGUARD
ENGINE HP ... 32
COOLING ... AIR
FUEL ... G
SPEEDS ... VARIABLE
TRANSMISSION ... HYDRO
STEERING ... ZERO
STANDARD DECK ... 61"
MSRP ... $11,362

OPTIONS

2BAG HARD
2BAG SOFT
3BAG HARD

RETAIL PRICING

YEAR	HIGH	LOW
2014	$6,600	$4,950
2015	$7,317	$5,488
2016	$8,562	$6,422

2100Z KAV26

YEARS MFRD ... 2014-2020
SERIES ... IS RIDERS SERIES
ENGINE ... KAWASAKI
CYLINDERS ... 2
CID ... 852CC
ENGINE HP ... 25.5
COOLING ... AIR
FUEL ... G
SPEEDS ... VARIABLE
TRANSMISSION ... HYDRO
STEERING ... ZERO
STANDARD DECK ... 52"
MSRP ... $10,749

OPTIONS

2 BAG HARD
2 BAG SOFT
3 BAG HARD
61" DECK ... $400

RETAIL PRICING

YEAR	HIGH	LOW
2014	$4,752	$3,563
2015	$5,245	$3,934
2016	$5,788	$4,341
2017	$6,390	$4,792
2018	$6,995	$5,246
2019	$7,661	$5,745
2020	$8,588	$6,563

2100Z KAVE30

YEARS MFRD ... 2018-2020
SERIES ... IS RIDERS SERIES
ENGINE ... KAWASAKI
CYLINDERS ... 2
CID ... 852CC
ENGINE HP ... 29.5
FUEL ... G
TRANSMISSION ... HYDRO
STEERING ... ZERO
STANDARD DECK ... 61"
MSRP ... $11,799

2100Z KOH29

YEARS MFRD ... 2014-2015
SERIES ... IS RIDERS SERIES
ENGINE ... KOHLER
ENGINE HP ... 29
COOLING ... AIR
FUEL ... G
SPEEDS ... VARIABLE
TRANSMISSION ... HYDRO
STEERING ... ZERO
STANDARD DECK ... 61"
MSRP ... $10,226

RETAIL PRICING

YEAR	HIGH	LOW
2014	$5,979	$4,484
2015	$7,032	$5,274

2500Z Y20D

YEARS MFRD ... 2010-2013
ENGINE ... YANMAR
ENGINE HP ... 20
COOLING ... AIR
FUEL ... D
SPEEDS ... VARIABLE
TRANSMISSION ... HYDRO
STEERING ... ZERO
STANDARD DECK ... 52"
MSRP ... $13,521

RETAIL PRICING

YEAR	HIGH	LOW
2010	$5,984	$4,488
2011	$6,605	$4,954
2012	$7,336	$5,502
2013	$8,145	$6,109

2500Z Y24D

YEARS MFRD ... 2010-2015
SERIES ... IS RIDERS SERIES
ENGINE ... YANMAR
ENGINE HP ... 24
COOLING ... AIR
FUEL ... D
SPEEDS ... VARIABLE
TRANSMISSION ... HYDRO
STEERING ... ZERO
STANDARD DECK ... 61"
MSRP ... $15,339

OPTIONS

52" DECK

RETAIL PRICING

YEAR	HIGH	LOW
2010	$5,955	$4,466
2011	$6,550	$4,913
2012	$7,274	$5,456
2013	$8,079	$6,059
2014	$8,971	$6,728
2015	$10,076	$7,557

3000Z K25

YEARS MFRD ... 2001-2001
SERIES ... IS RIDERS SERIES
ENGINE ... KAWASAKI
ENGINE HP ... 23
COOLING ... AIR
FUEL ... G
TRANSMISSION ... HYDRO
STEERING ... ZERO
STANDARD DECK ... 61"
MSRP ... $9,195

RETAIL PRICING

YEAR	HIGH	LOW
2001	$2,124	$1,593

3000Z KAV23

YEARS MFRD ... 2001-2001
SERIES ... IS RIDERS SERIES
ENGINE ... KAWASAKI
ENGINE HP ... 23
COOLING ... AIR
FUEL ... G
TRANSMISSION ... HYDRO
STEERING ... ZERO
STANDARD DECK ... 61"
MSRP ... $8,995

RETAIL PRICING

YEAR	HIGH	LOW
2001	$2,077	$1,558

3000Z KAV25

YEARS MFRD ... 2001-2002
SERIES ... IS RIDERS SERIES
ENGINE ... KAWASAKI
ENGINE HP ... 25
COOLING ... AIR
FUEL ... G
SPEEDS ... VARIABLE
TRANSMISSION ... HYDRO
STEERING ... ZERO
STANDARD DECK ... 61"
MSRP ... $9,250

FERRIS

RETAIL PRICING

YEAR	HIGH	LOW
2001	$2,053	$1,539
2002	$2,292	$1,719

3100Z

YEARS MFRD 2006-2006
ENGINE .... KAWASAKI
ENGINE HP 26
COOLING .... LIQUID
FUEL .... G
SPEEDS .... VARIABLE
TRANSMISSION .... HYDRO
STEERING .... ZERO

OPTIONS

B&S 32
KOHLER 30

3100Z B30

YEARS MFRD 2012-2013
ENGINE .... B&S
ENGINE HP 30
COOLING .... AIR
FUEL .... G
SPEEDS .... VARIABLE
TRANSMISSION .... HYDRO
STEERING .... ZERO
BLADE CLUTCH .... ELECTRIC
STANDARD DECK .... 61"
MSRP $12,385

RETAIL PRICING

YEAR	HIGH	LOW
2012	$6,717	$5,038
2013	$7,461	$5,596

3100Z BV32

YEARS MFRD 2007-2013
SERIES .... IS RIDERS SERIES
ENGINE .... B&S
ENGINE HP 32
COOLING .... AIR
FUEL .... G
SPEEDS .... VARIABLE
TRANSMISSION .... HYDRO
STEERING .... ZERO
STANDARD DECK .... 61"
MSRP $13,635

OPTIONS

72" DECK

RETAIL PRICING

YEAR	HIGH	LOW
2007	$4,380	$3,285
2008	$4,865	$3,648
2009	$5,413	$4,059
2010	$5,979	$4,484
2011	$6,660	$4,995
2012	$7,406	$5,554
2013	$8,217	$6,163

3100Z BV36

YEARS MFRD 2012-2015
SERIES .... IS RIDERS SERIES
ENGINE .... B&S
ENGINE HP 36
COOLING .... AIR
FUEL .... G
SPEEDS .... VARIABLE
TRANSMISSION .... HYDRO
STEERING .... ZERO
STANDARD DECK .... 61"
MSRP $14,203

OPTIONS

72" DECK

RETAIL PRICING

YEAR	HIGH	LOW
2012	$6,734	$5,050
2013	$7,480	$5,610
2014	$8,306	$6,230
2015	$9,635	$7,226

3100Z BVP32

YEARS MFRD 2009-2015
SERIES .... IS RIDERS SERIES
ENGINE .... B&S
CID 895CC
COOLING .... AIR
FUEL .... G
SPEEDS .... VARIABLE
TRANSMISSION .... HYDRO
STEERING .... ZERO
BLADE CLUTCH .... ELECTRIC
STANDARD DECK .... 61"
MSRP $17,385

OPTIONS

72" DECK

RETAIL PRICING

YEAR	HIGH	LOW
2009	$6,018	$4,513
2010	$6,682	$5,012
2011	$7,422	$5,567
2012	$8,243	$6,182
2013	$9,155	$6,866
2014	$10,167	$7,625
2015	$11,912	$8,934

3100Z KAV37

YEARS MFRD 2010-2015
SERIES .... IS RIDERS SERIES
ENGINE .... KAWASAKI
ENGINE HP 37
COOLING .... AIR
FUEL .... G
SPEEDS .... VARIABLE
TRANSMISSION .... HYDRO
STEERING .... ZERO
STANDARD DECK .... 61"
MSRP $14,544

OPTIONS

72" DECK

RETAIL PRICING

YEAR	HIGH	LOW
2010	$5,592	$4,194
2011	$6,209	$4,657
2012	$6,899	$5,174
2013	$7,660	$5,745
2014	$8,506	$6,379
2015	$10,058	$7,543

4000Z D31

YEARS MFRD 2001-2002
SERIES .... IS RIDERS SERIES
ENGINE .... DAIHATSU
ENGINE HP 31
COOLING .... LIQUID
FUEL .... G
TRANSMISSION .... HYDRO
STEERING .... ZERO
STANDARD DECK .... 72"
MSRP $13,995

RETAIL PRICING

YEAR	HIGH	LOW
2001	$3,108	$2,331
2002	$3,453	$2,590

4000Z KAV27

YEARS MFRD 2001-2002
SERIES .... IS RIDERS SERIES
ENGINE .... KAWASAKI
ENGINE HP 27
COOLING .... LIQUID
FUEL .... G
TRANSMISSION .... HYDRO
STEERING .... ZERO
STANDARD DECK .... 61"
MSRP $11,495

OPTIONS

72" DECK

RETAIL PRICING

YEAR	HIGH	LOW
2001	$2,388	$1,791
2002	$2,655	$1,991

5100Z C33D

YEARS MFRD 2007-2016
SERIES .... IS RIDERS SERIES
ENGINE .... CAT 3013C
ENGINE HP 33.5
COOLING .... AIR
FUEL .... D
SPEEDS .... VARIABLE
TRANSMISSION .... HYDRO
STEERING .... ZERO
STANDARD DECK .... 72"
MSRP $24,704

OPTIONS

61" DECK RR DIS

RETAIL PRICING

YEAR	HIGH	LOW
2007	$6,971	$5,229
2008	$7,761	$5,821
2009	$8,568	$6,426
2010	$9,499	$7,124
2011	$10,531	$7,898
2012	$11,675	$8,756
2013	$12,943	$9,707
2014	$14,350	$10,763
2015	$15,909	$11,932
2016	$19,631	$14,723

FORD

1100

YEARS MFRD 1979-1983
ENGINE .... SHIBAURA
CYLINDERS 2
CID 43
PTO HP 11
ENGINE HP 13
FUEL .... D
SPEEDS 10/2
TRANSMISSION .... GEAR
DRIVE TYPE 2WD
WEIGHT .... 1,131 LBS.
MSRP $5,609

OPTIONS

4WD
HYDRO

SERIAL NUMBERS

LEFT SIDE RAIL ABOVE FRONT AXLE

YEAR	BEGINNING NO.
1979	U125001
1980	U127591
1981	U129066
1982	U130665
1983	U131359

RETAIL PRICING

YEAR	HIGH	LOW
1979	$652	$489
1980	$746	$559
1981	$845	$634
1982	$968	$726
1983	$1,208	$906

1110

YEARS MFRD 1983-1986
ENGINE .... SHIBAURA
CYLINDERS 2
CID 43
PTO HP 11.5
ENGINE HP 13
FUEL .... D
SPEEDS 10/2
TRANSMISSION .... GEAR
DRIVE TYPE 2WD
WEIGHT .... 1,395 LBS.
MSRP $6,231

OPTIONS

4WD
HYDRO

SERIAL NUMBERS

LEFT SIDE OF TRANSMISSION HOUSING

YEAR	BEGINNING NO.
1983	UB00001
1984	UB00785
1985	UB01622
1986	UB02107

RETAIL PRICING

YEAR	HIGH	LOW
1983	$987	$740
1984	$1,107	$831

YEAR	HIGH	LOW
1985	$1,228	$921
1986	$1,356	$1,017

AVG. AUCTION PRICING

LOW	HIGH	AVG
$1,129	$2,823	$1,930

1120H

YEARS MFRD	1989-1994
ENGINE	SHIBAURA
CYLINDERS	3
CID	53.6
PTO HP	12
ENGINE HP	14
FUEL	D
SPEEDS	HYDRO
WEIGHT	1,570 LBS.

1210

YEARS MFRD	1983-1986
ENGINE	SHIBAURA
CYLINDERS	3
CID	54
PTO HP	13.5
ENGINE HP	16
COOLING	LIQUID
FUEL	D
SPEEDS	10/2
TRANSMISSION	GEAR
STEERING	STANDARD
DRIVE TYPE	2WD
WEIGHT	1,329 LBS.
MSRP	$6,952

OPTIONS

4WD
HYDRO

SERIAL NUMBERS

YEAR	BEGINNING NO.
1983	UC00001
1984	UC01417
1985	UC03937
1986	UC07232

RETAIL PRICING

YEAR	HIGH	LOW
1983	$1,374	$1,030
1984	$1,497	$1,123
1985	$1,638	$1,228
1986	$1,738	$1,303

1210H

YEARS MFRD	1983-1986
ENGINE	SHIBAURA
CYLINDERS	3
CID	54
PTO HP	13
ENGINE HP	16
FUEL	D
SPEEDS	VARIABLE
TRANSMISSION	HYDRO
STEERING	STANDARD
DRIVE TYPE	2WD
WEIGHT	1,342 LBS.
MSRP	$7,884

OPTIONS

4WD

SERIAL NUMBERS

LEFT HAND SIDE RAIL
ABOVE FRONT AXLE

YEAR	BEGINNING NO.
1983	UC0001
1984	UC01417-4WD
1984	UC01815
1985	UC03937
1986	UC07232

RETAIL PRICING

YEAR	HIGH	LOW
1983	$1,925	$1,444
1984	$1,981	$1,485
1985	$2,108	$1,581
1986	$2,659	$1,994

1300

YEARS MFRD	1979-1982
ENGINE	SHIBAURA
CYLINDERS	2
CID	49
PTO HP	13.5
ENGINE HP	16
FUEL	D
SPEEDS	12/4
TRANSMISSION	GEAR
STEERING	STANDARD
DRIVE TYPE	2WD
ROPS/CAB	ROPS
WEIGHT	1,984 LBS.
MSRP	$6,257

OPTIONS

2 HYD
4WD

SERIAL NUMBERS

LEFT SIDE OF TRANSMISSION HOUSING

YEAR	BEGINNING NO.
1979	U300001
1980	U302697
1981	U303446
1982	U304962

RETAIL PRICING

YEAR	HIGH	LOW
1979	$1,096	$822
1980	$1,223	$917
1981	$1,290	$967
1982	$1,354	$1,016

1500

YEARS MFRD	1979-1982
ENGINE	SHIBAURA
CYLINDERS	2
CID	68.2
PTO HP	17
ENGINE HP	20
FUEL	D
SPEEDS	12/4
TRANSMISSION	GEAR
STEERING	STANDARD
HITCH	CAT. I
DRIVE TYPE	2WD
WEIGHT	2,044 LBS.
MSRP	$6,745

OPTIONS

4WD

SERIAL NUMBERS

LEFT SIDE OF TRANSMISSION HOUSING

YEAR	BEGINNING NO.
1979	U500001
1980	U503026
1981	U504437
1982	U505813

RETAIL PRICING

YEAR	HIGH	LOW
1979	$1,417	$1,063
1980	$1,534	$1,150
1981	$1,567	$1,175
1982	$1,653	$1,240

1520

YEARS MFRD	1987-1998
ENGINE	SHIBAURA
CYLINDERS	3
CID	81.2
PTO HP	19.5
ENGINE HP	23
FUEL	D
SPEEDS	9/3
TRANSMISSION	GEAR
DRIVE TYPE	2WD
ROPS/CAB	ROPS
WEIGHT	2,156 LBS.
MSRP	$13,005

OPTIONS

4WD
HYDRO

SERIAL NUMBERS

YEAR	BEGINNING NO.
1987	UH06476
1988	UH22102
1989	UH23802
1990	UH25500
1991	UH26935
1992	UH28254
1993	UH29228
1994	UH30029
1995	UH31125
1996	UH31915
1997	UH32546
1998	UH33012

RETAIL PRICING

YEAR	HIGH	LOW
1987	$4,418	$3,313
1988	$6,199	$4,650
1989	$6,974	$5,230
1990	$7,831	$5,873
1991	$8,287	$6,215
1992	$8,389	$6,292
1993	$8,436	$6,327
1994	$8,455	$6,342
1995	$8,487	$6,365
1996	$8,506	$6,380

AVG. AUCTION PRICING

LOW	HIGH	AVG
$3,724	$7,448	$5,324

1710

YEARS MFRD	1983-1986
ENGINE	SHIBAURA
CYLINDERS	3
CID	85.2
PTO HP	23.88
ENGINE HP	26
COOLING	LIQUID
FUEL	D
SPEEDS	12/4
TRANSMISSION	GEAR
STEERING	STANDARD
DRIVE TYPE	2WD
ROPS/CAB	ROPS
WEIGHT	2,560 LBS.
MSRP	$8,859

OPTIONS

4WD

SERIAL NUMBERS

LEFT SIDE OF TRANSMISSION HOUSING

YEAR	BEGINNING NO.
1983	UL00001
1984	UL03489
1985	UL07985
1986	UL13798

RETAIL PRICING

YEAR	HIGH	LOW
1983	$961	$721
1984	$1,138	$853
1985	$1,314	$986
1986	$1,494	$1,120

AVG. AUCTION PRICING

LOW	HIGH	AVG
$2,695	$4,802	$4,329

1710 OFFSET

YEARS MFRD	1985-1988
ENGINE	SHIBAURA
CYLINDERS	3
CID	85
PTO HP	23.8
FUEL	D
SPEEDS	12/4
WEIGHT	3,267 LBS.
MSRP	$11,200

SERIAL NUMBERS

YEAR	BEGINNING NO.
1985	N00010
1986	N00201
1987	UN00421
1988	UN00641

RETAIL PRICING

YEAR	HIGH	LOW
1988	$10,816	$8,112

2310

YEARS MFRD	1982-1985
ENGINE	FORD
CYLINDERS	3
CID	158
PTO HP	32.4
FUEL	D
SPEEDS	8/2
TRANSMISSION	GEAR
STEERING	STANDARD
PTO	YES
WEIGHT	3,859 LBS.
MSRP	$11,890

SERIAL NUMBERS

YEAR	BEGINNING NO.
1982	C682000
1983	C694500

1984 . . . . C707400
1985 . . . . C732600

RETAIL PRICING

YEAR	HIGH	LOW
1985	$3,698	$2,773

2610

YEARS MFRD 1982-1983
ENGINE . . . . FORD
CYLINDERS 3
CID 158
PTO HP 34
FUEL . . . . G
SPEEDS 8/4-8/2
TRANSMISSION . . . . GEAR
STEERING . . . . STANDARD
PTO . . . . YES
WEIGHT . . . . 3,877 LBS.
MSRP $13,542

OPTIONS

FORD DIESEL 36.69PTO HP

SERIAL NUMBERS

YEAR . . . . BEGINNING NO.
1982 . . . . C682000
1983 . . . . C694500

RETAIL PRICING

YEAR	HIGH	LOW
1982	$1,605	$1,204
1983	$1,855	$1,391

3610

YEARS MFRD 1982-1986
ENGINE . . . . FORD
CYLINDERS 3
CID 175
PTO HP 40.6
FUEL . . . . G
SPEEDS 8/4-8/2
TRANSMISSION . . . . GEAR
STEERING . . . . STANDARD
PTO . . . . YES
WEIGHT . . . . 3,715 LBS.
MSRP $15,220

OPTIONS

FORD DIESEL 42PTO HP

SERIAL NUMBERS

YEAR . . . . BEGINNING NO.
1982 . . . . C682000
1983 . . . . C694500

RETAIL PRICING

YEAR	HIGH	LOW
1986	$5,322	$3,992

FORD-NEW HOLLAND

1110H

YEARS MFRD 1983-1989
ENGINE . . . . SHIBAURA
CYLINDERS 2
CID 43
PTO HP 11.5
ENGINE HP 13
FUEL . . . . D
SPEEDS . . . . VARIABLE
TRANSMISSION . . . . HYDRO
DRIVE TYPE 2WD
WEIGHT . . . . 1,403 LBS.
MSRP $6,806

OPTIONS

4WD

RETAIL PRICING

YEAR	HIGH	LOW
1983	$1,027	$770
1984	$1,225	$919
1985	$1,582	$1,186
1986	$1,842	$1,382

1120

YEARS MFRD 1987-1993
ENGINE . . . . SHIBAURA
CYLINDERS 3
CID 53.6
PTO HP 12.5
ENGINE HP 14
FUEL . . . . D
SPEEDS 9/3
TRANSMISSION . . . . GEAR
STEERING . . . . STANDARD
DRIVE TYPE 2WD
WEIGHT . . . . 1,338 LBS.
MSRP $8,800

OPTIONS

4WD
HYDRO

SERIAL NUMBERS

LEFT SIDE OF TRANS HOUSING

YEAR . . . . BEGINNING NO.
1987 . . . . UB02475
1988 . . . . UB21281
1989 . . . . UB21944
1990 . . . . UB22142
1991 . . . . UB22329
1992 . . . . UB22439
1993 . . . . UB22527

RETAIL PRICING

YEAR	HIGH	LOW
1987	$1,010	$758
1988	$1,107	$831
1989	$1,216	$912
1990	$1,323	$992
1991	$1,435	$1,076
1992	$1,553	$1,165
1993	$1,669	$1,252

1215

YEARS MFRD 1993-1998
ENGINE . . . . SHIBAURA
CYLINDERS 3
CID 54
PTO HP 13.5
ENGINE HP 16
FUEL . . . . D
SPEEDS . . . . VARIABLE
TRANSMISSION . . . . HYDRO
STEERING . . . . STANDARD
DRIVE TYPE 2WD
MSRP $8,978

OPTIONS

4WD
HYDRO

SERIAL NUMBERS

LEFT SIDE OF TRANS HOUSING

YEAR . . . . BEGINNING NO.
1993 . . . . UA20001
1994 . . . . UA20462
1995 . . . . UA21150
1996 . . . . UA21632
1997 . . . . UA21874
1998 . . . . UA22187

RETAIL PRICING

YEAR	HIGH	LOW
1993	$1,686	$1,264
1994	$1,860	$1,395
1995	$2,046	$1,535
1996	$2,233	$1,675
1997	$2,427	$1,821
1998	$2,628	$1,971

AVG. AUCTION PRICING

LOW	HIGH	AVG
$2,353	$3,012	$2,729

1220

YEARS MFRD 1987-1999
ENGINE . . . . SHIBAURA
CYLINDERS 3
CID 58.2
PTO HP 14.5
ENGINE HP 16
COOLING . . . . LIQUID
FUEL . . . . D
SPEEDS . . . . VARIABLE
TRANSMISSION . . . . HYDRO
STEERING . . . . STANDARD
DRIVE TYPE 2WD
ROPS/CAB . . . . ROPS
WEIGHT . . . . 1,338 LBS.
MSRP $11,817

OPTIONS

4WD
GEAR

SERIAL NUMBERS

LEFT SIDE OF TRANS HOUSING

YEAR . . . . BEGINNING NO.
1987 . . . . UC10329
1988 . . . . UC21707
1989 . . . . UC23249
1990 . . . . UC24273
1991 . . . . UC25359
1992 . . . . UC26052
1993 . . . . UC26585
1994 . . . . UC27014
1995 . . . . UC27524
1996 . . . . UC27839
1997 . . . . UC28097
1998 . . . . UC28612
1999 . . . . UC28907

RETAIL PRICING

YEAR	HIGH	LOW
1991	$2,100	$1,575
1992	$2,274	$1,705
1993	$2,447	$1,835
1994	$2,628	$1,971
1995	$2,817	$2,112
1996	$3,036	$2,277
1997	$3,259	$2,444
1998	$3,494	$2,620
1999	$3,732	$2,799

AVG. AUCTION PRICING

LOW	HIGH	AVG
$1,813	$2,940	$2,519

1310

YEARS MFRD 1983-1986
ENGINE . . . . SHIBAURA
CYLINDERS 3
CID 58
PTO HP 16.5
ENGINE HP 19
FUEL . . . . D
SPEEDS 12/4
TRANSMISSION . . . . GEAR
STEERING . . . . STANDARD
HITCH . . . . CAT. I
DRIVE TYPE 2WD
ROPS/CAB . . . . ROPS
WEIGHT . . . . 2,063 LBS.
MSRP $7,699

OPTIONS

4WD
HYDRO

SERIAL NUMBERS

LEFT SIDE OF TRANSMISSION HOUSING

YEAR . . . . BEGINNING NO.
1983 . . . . UE00001
1984 . . . . UE01019
1985 . . . . UE02438
1986 . . . . UE04444

RETAIL PRICING

YEAR	HIGH	LOW
1983	$625	$469
1984	$762	$572
1985	$898	$673
1986	$1,038	$778

1320

YEARS MFRD 1987-1998
ENGINE . . . . SHIBAURA
CYLINDERS 3
CID 77.4
PTO HP 17
ENGINE HP 20
FUEL . . . . D
SPEEDS 9/3
TRANSMISSION . . . . GEAR
STEERING . . . . STANDARD
PTO . . . . YES
DRIVE TYPE 2WD
ROPS/CAB . . . . ROPS
WEIGHT . . . . 2,145 LBS.
MSRP $12,145

OPTIONS

4WD
HYDRO

SERIAL NUMBERS

LEFT SIDE OF TRANS HOUSING

YEAR . . . . BEGINNING NO.
1987 . . . . UE06106
1988 . . . . UE22001
1989 . . . . UE23392

YEAR	BEGINNING NO.
1990	UE24511
1991	UE25495
1992	UE26189
1993	UE26960
1994	UE27440
1995	UE28084
1996	UE28490
1997	UE28772
1998	UE29318

RETAIL PRICING

YEAR	HIGH	LOW
1990	$1,735	$1,301
1991	$1,936	$1,452
1992	$2,072	$1,554
1993	$2,279	$1,709
1994	$2,487	$1,865
1995	$2,703	$2,027
1996	$2,925	$2,194
1997	$3,155	$2,366
1998	$3,435	$2,576

1510

YEARS MFRD	1983-1986
ENGINE	SHIBAURA
CYLINDERS	3
CID	68.2
PTO HP	19.72
ENGINE HP	22
FUEL	D
SPEEDS	12/4
TRANSMISSION	GEAR
STEERING	STANDARD
DRIVE TYPE	2WD
ROPS/CAB	ROPS
WEIGHT	2,230 LBS.
MSRP	$7,930

OPTIONS

4WD
HYDRO

SERIAL NUMBERS

LEFT SIDE OF TRANSMISSION HOUSING

YEAR	BEGINNING NO.
1983	UH00001
1984	UH01280
1985	UH02828
1986	UH04797

RETAIL PRICING

YEAR	HIGH	LOW
1983	$1,339	$1,004
1984	$1,503	$1,127
1985	$1,694	$1,271
1986	$1,848	$1,386

AVG. AUCTION PRICING

LOW	HIGH	AVG
$2,588	$3,671	$3,106

1512

YEARS MFRD	1983-1987
ENGINE	SHIBAURA
CYLINDERS	3
CID	68
PTO HP	19.7
ENGINE HP	22
FUEL	D
SPEEDS	12/4
TRANSMISSION	GEAR
STEERING	STANDARD
DRIVE TYPE	2WD
ROPS/CAB	ROPS
WEIGHT	2,000 LBS.

1520

YEARS MFRD	1987-1998
ENGINE	SHIBAURA
CYLINDERS	3
CID	81.2
PTO HP	19.5
ENGINE HP	23
FUEL	D
SPEEDS	9/3
TRANSMISSION	GEAR
STEERING	STANDARD
PTO	YES
DRIVE TYPE	2WD
ROPS/CAB	ROPS
WEIGHT	2,156 LBS.
MSRP	$12,535

OPTIONS

4WD
HYDRO

SERIAL NUMBERS

LEFT SIDE OF TRANS HOUSING

YEAR	BEGINNING NO.
1987	UH06476
1988	UH22102
1989	UH23802
1990	UH25500
1991	UH26935
1992	UH28254
1993	UH29228
1994	UH30029
1995	UH31125
1996	UH31915
1997	UH32546
1998	UH33012

RETAIL PRICING

YEAR	HIGH	LOW
1990	$2,617	$1,962
1991	$2,810	$2,107
1992	$3,012	$2,259
1993	$3,242	$2,431
1994	$3,459	$2,595
1995	$3,728	$2,796
1996	$4,003	$3,002
1997	$4,292	$3,219
1998	$4,592	$3,444

1530

YEARS MFRD	1997-1999
ENGINE	SHIBAURA
CYLINDERS	3
CID	81
PTO HP	21
ENGINE HP	25
FUEL	D
SPEEDS	9/3
TRANSMISSION	GEAR
STEERING	STANDARD
DRIVE TYPE	2WD
ROPS/CAB	ROPS
MSRP	$13,782

OPTIONS

4WD
HYDRO

SERIAL NUMBERS

LEFT SIDE OF TRANS HOUSING

YEAR	BEGINNING NO.
1998	G003354
1999	G009617

RETAIL PRICING

YEAR	HIGH	LOW
1997	$4,371	$3,278
1998	$4,646	$3,485
1999	$4,916	$3,687

1620

YEARS MFRD	1992-1997
ENGINE	SHIBAURA
CYLINDERS	3
CID	81
PTO HP	22
ENGINE HP	27
FUEL	G
TRANSMISSION	HYDRO
STEERING	STANDARD
DRIVE TYPE	2WD
ROPS/CAB	ROPS
WEIGHT	2,233 LBS.
MSRP	$16,701

OPTIONS

2 HYD
4WD

SERIAL NUMBERS

LEFT SIDE OF TRANSMISSION HOUSING

YEAR	BEGINNING NO.
1992	UJ20136
1993	UJ20911
1994	UJ21591
1995	UJ22718
1996	UJ23587
1997	UJ24311

RETAIL PRICING

YEAR	HIGH	LOW
1992	$3,024	$2,268
1993	$3,300	$2,475
1994	$3,736	$2,802
1995	$3,983	$2,987
1996	$4,379	$3,284
1997	$4,691	$3,518

AVG. AUCTION PRICING

LOW	HIGH	AVG
$3,038	$6,762	$4,998

1630

YEARS MFRD	1997-1999
ENGINE	SHIBAURA
CYLINDERS	3
CID	81
PTO HP	24
ENGINE HP	27
FUEL	D
SPEEDS	9/3
TRANSMISSION	GEAR
STEERING	STANDARD
DRIVE TYPE	4WD
ROPS/CAB	ROPS
MSRP	$16,164

OPTIONS

2 HYD
HYDRO

SERIAL NUMBERS

LEFT SIDE OF TRANS HOUSING

YEAR	BEGINNING NO.
1997	G6J0014
1998	G003352
1999	G009615

RETAIL PRICING

YEAR	HIGH	LOW
1997	$4,718	$3,538
1998	$5,073	$3,805
1999	$5,450	$4,087

1715

YEARS MFRD	1992-1997
ENGINE	SHIBAURA
CYLINDERS	3
CID	81.2
PTO HP	23
ENGINE HP	27.3
FUEL	D
SPEEDS	7/3,9/3
TRANSMISSION	GEAR
DRIVE TYPE	2WD
ROPS/CAB	ROPS
WEIGHT	2,630 LBS.
MSRP	$11,124

OPTIONS

2 HYD
4WD

SERIAL NUMBERS

LEFT SIDE OF TRANS HOUSING

YEAR	BEGINNING NO.
1992	UK20001
1993	UK20307
1994	UK22179
1995	UK25017
1996	UK27586
1997	UK29295

RETAIL PRICING

YEAR	HIGH	LOW
1992	$1,669	$1,252
1993	$1,924	$1,443
1994	$2,187	$1,641
1995	$2,577	$1,933
1996	$2,735	$2,051
1997	$3,028	$2,271

AVG. AUCTION PRICING

LOW	HIGH	AVG
$5,782	$7,938	$6,860

1720

YEARS MFRD	1987-2000
ENGINE	SHIBAURA
CYLINDERS	3
CID	91.3
PTO HP	23.5
ENGINE HP	26.5
FUEL	D
SPEEDS	12/4, 12/12
TRANSMISSION	SHUTTLE SHIFT
STEERING	STANDARD
DRIVE TYPE	2WD

FORD-NEW HOLLAND

ROPS/CAB . . . . ROPS
WEIGHT . . . . 2,491 LBS.
MSRP. $13,772

OPTIONS

4WD

SERIAL NUMBERS

LEFT SIDE OF TRANS HOUSING

YEAR	BEGINNING NO.
1987	UL18261
1988	UL22701
1989	UL26556
1990	UL28593
1991	UL30784
1992	UL32230
1993	UL33920
1994	UL35012
1995	UL36435
1996	UL37607
1997	UL38466
1998	UL40069
1999	UL41414
2000	UL42699

RETAIL PRICING

YEAR	HIGH	LOW
1992	$2,714	$2,035
1993	$2,896	$2,172
1994	$3,134	$2,351
1995	$3,334	$2,500
1996	$3,520	$2,640
1997	$3,851	$2,889
1998	$4,132	$3,099
1999	$4,430	$3,322
2000	$4,734	$3,551

AVG. AUCTION PRICING

LOW	HIGH	AVG
$3,250	$6,200	$4,925

1725

YEARS MFRD 1997-1999
ENGINE . . . . SHIBAURA
CYLINDERS. 3
CID 81
PTO HP 25
ENGINE HP 29
FUEL . . . . D
SPEEDS 9/3
TRANSMISSION . . . . GEAR
STEERING. . . . . STANDARD
DRIVE TYPE 2WD
ROPS/CAB . . . . ROPS
MSRP. $12,410

OPTIONS

2 HYD
4WD

SERIAL NUMBERS

LEFT SIDE OF TRANS HOUSING

YEAR	BEGINNING NO.
1997	G6K0028
1998	G003377
1999	G007570

RETAIL PRICING

YEAR	HIGH	LOW
1997	$2,649	$1,987
1998	$2,973	$2,230
1999	$3,308	$2,481

1910

YEARS MFRD 1983-1986
ENGINE . . . . SHIBAURA
CYLINDERS. 3
CID 103.9
PTO HP 28.5
ENGINE HP 32
FUEL . . . . D
SPEEDS 12/4
TRANSMISSION . . . . GEAR
STEERING. . . . . STANDARD
DRIVE TYPE 2WD
ROPS/CAB . . . . ROPS
WEIGHT . . . . 3,070 LBS.
MSRP. $9,742

OPTIONS

2 HYD
4WD

SERIAL NUMBERS

LEFT SIDE OF TRANSMISSION HOUSING

YEAR	BEGINNING NO.
1983	UP0001
1984	UP01089
1985	UP04638
1986	UP08193

RETAIL PRICING

YEAR	HIGH	LOW
1983	$2,055	$1,541
1984	$2,166	$1,624
1985	$2,277	$1,707
1986	$2,447	$1,835

AVG. AUCTION PRICING

LOW	HIGH	AVG
$1,977	$4,800	$4,010

1920

YEARS MFRD 1987-2000
ENGINE . . . . SHIBAURA
CYLINDERS. 4
CID 121.7
PTO HP 28.5
ENGINE HP 33.3
FUEL . . . . D
SPEEDS 12/4
TRANSMISSION . . . . GEAR
STEERING. . . . . STANDARD
DRIVE TYPE 2WD
ROPS/CAB . . . . ROPS
WEIGHT . . . . 3,069 LBS.
MSRP. $15,269

OPTIONS

12/12 SS
4WD

SERIAL NUMBERS

LEFT SIDE OF TRANS HOUSING

YEAR	BEGINNING NO.
1987	UP11426
1988	UP21710
1989	UP24896
1990	UP27219
1991	UP29354
1992	UP30817
1993	UP32448
1994	UP34037
1995	UP35988
1996	UP37672
1997	UP39076
1998	UP41105
1999	UP43277
2000	UP45272

RETAIL PRICING

YEAR	HIGH	LOW
1992	$3,108	$2,331
1993	$3,393	$2,545
1994	$3,687	$2,765
1995	$4,072	$3,054
1996	$4,298	$3,224
1997	$4,612	$3,459
1998	$5,012	$3,759
1999	$5,346	$4,009
2000	$5,810	$4,358

AVG. AUCTION PRICING

LOW	HIGH	AVG
$4,116	$8,722	$5,853

1925

YEARS MFRD 1997-1999
ENGINE . . . . SHIBAURA
CYLINDERS. 3
CID 91
PTO HP 29
ENGINE HP 34
FUEL . . . . D
SPEEDS 9/3
TRANSMISSION . . . . GEAR
STEERING. . . . . STANDARD
DRIVE TYPE 4WD
ROPS/CAB . . . . ROPS
MSRP. $17,257

OPTIONS

HYDRO

SERIAL NUMBERS

LEFT SIDE OF TRANS HOUSING

YEAR	BEGINNING NO.
1998	G003381
1999	G009691

RETAIL PRICING

YEAR	HIGH	LOW
1997	$3,794	$2,845
1998	$4,177	$3,133
1999	$4,578	$3,433

2110

YEARS MFRD 1983-1988
ENGINE . . . . SHIBAURA
CYLINDERS. 4
CID 139
PTO HP 34.5
ENGINE HP 40
FUEL . . . . D
SPEEDS 12/4
DRIVE TYPE 2WD
ROPS/CAB . . . . ROPS
WEIGHT . . . . 3,435 LBS.
MSRP. $13,103

OPTIONS

4WD
SYNCHRO

SERIAL NUMBERS

LEFT SIDE OF TRANSMISSION HOUSING

YEAR	BEGINNING NO.
1983	UV00010
1984	UV00734
1985	UV02153
1986	UV03580
1987	UV04673
1988	UV21003

RETAIL PRICING

YEAR	HIGH	LOW
1983	$1,821	$1,366
1984	$1,848	$1,386
1985	$2,086	$1,565
1986	$2,343	$1,757
1987	$2,590	$1,943
1988	$2,777	$2,083

AVG. AUCTION PRICING

LOW	HIGH	AVG
$1,600	$3,953	$3,075

2110 INDUSTRIAL

YEARS MFRD 1983-1987
ENGINE . . . . FORD
CYLINDERS. 3
CID 158
PTO HP 30.5
FUEL . . . . G
SPEEDS 4/1
TRANSMISSION . . . . GEAR
STEERING. . . . . STANDARD
WEIGHT . . . . 3,230 LBS.
MSRP. $5,935

RETAIL PRICING

YEAR	HIGH	LOW
1985	$1,131	$848

2120

YEARS MFRD 1987-2002
ENGINE . . . . SHIBAURA
CYLINDERS. 4
CID 138.5
PTO HP 35
ENGINE HP 43
COOLING . . . . LIQUID
FUEL . . . . D
TRANSMISSION . . . . GEAR
STEERING. . . . . STANDARD
HITCH . . . . CAT. I
PTO . . . . YES
DRIVE TYPE 2WD
MSRP. $21,507

OPTIONS

4WD 1991-2002

SERIAL NUMBERS

LEFT SIDE OF TRANS HOUSING

YEAR	BEGINNING NO.
1987	UV04693
1988	UV05077
1989	UV22331
1990	UV23589
1991	UV24295
1992	UV25141
1993	UV25891
1994	UV26737
1995	UV27935
1996	UV28911
1997	UV29267
1998	UV30679

YEAR	BEGINNING NO.
1999	UV31770
2000	UV32211
2001	UV33463
2002	UV33674

RETAIL PRICING

YEAR	HIGH	LOW
1994	$5,491	$4,118
1995	$5,750	$4,312
1996	$6,098	$4,573
1997	$6,450	$4,838
1998	$6,885	$5,163
1999	$7,194	$5,396
2000	$7,669	$5,751
2001	$8,154	$6,115
2002	$8,388	$6,291

AVG. AUCTION PRICING

LOW	HIGH	AVG
$3,822	$11,368	$7,497

2810

YEARS MFRD	1983-1990
ENGINE	FORD
CYLINDERS	3
CID	158
PTO HP	32.8
FUEL	D
SPEEDS	8/2
TRANSMISSION	GEAR
DRIVE TYPE	2WD
ROPS/CAB	ROPS
WEIGHT	4,352 LBS.
MSRP	$15,712

OPTIONS

2 HYD
4WD

SERIAL NUMBERS

UPPER RIGHT FRONT CORNER OF TRANS

YEAR	BEGINNING NO.
1983	C695880
1984	C713459
1985	C737800
1986	C754100
1986	BA80100
1987	BB06622
1987	C768000
1988	BB31777
1988	C777683
1989	BB84620
1990	BC26239

RETAIL PRICING

YEAR	HIGH	LOW
1983	$2,195	$1,646
1984	$2,432	$1,824
1985	$2,675	$2,007
1986	$2,922	$2,192
1987	$3,180	$2,385
1988	$3,445	$2,584
1989	$3,720	$2,790
1990	$3,996	$2,997

AVG. AUCTION PRICING

LOW	HIGH	AVG
$3,528	$8,330	$6,804

2910

YEARS MFRD	1983-1989
ENGINE	FORD
CYLINDERS	3
CID	175
PTO HP	36
FUEL	D
SPEEDS	8/2-8/4
TRANSMISSION	GEAR
STEERING	STANDARD
PTO	YES
DRIVE TYPE	2WD
ROPS/CAB	ROPS
WEIGHT	5,200 LBS.
MSRP	$15,701

OPTIONS

4WD

SERIAL NUMBERS

UPPER RIGHT FRONT CORNER OF TRANS

YEAR	BEGINNING NO.
1983	C694500
1984	C707400
1985	C732600
1986	BA74292
1986	C750422
1987	BB05681
1987	C763228
1988	BB31777
1989	BB80620

RETAIL PRICING

YEAR	HIGH	LOW
1983	$2,059	$1,544
1984	$2,286	$1,715
1985	$2,521	$1,890
1986	$2,771	$2,079
1987	$3,012	$2,259
1988	$3,288	$2,466
1989	$3,530	$2,647

3010S

YEARS MFRD	1996-2003
ENGINE	FORD
CYLINDERS	3
CID	165
PTO HP	42
COOLING	LIQUID
FUEL	D
SPEEDS	8/2
TRANSMISSION	GEAR
STEERING	STANDARD
HYDRAULIC	YES
PTO	YES
DRIVE TYPE	2WD
ROPS/CAB	ROPS

OPTIONS

4WD

SERIAL NUMBERS

UPPER RIGHT FRONT CORNER OF TRANS

YEAR	BEGINNING NO.
1996	700000M
1997	700723M
1998	701587M
1999	702358M
2000	703096M
2001	704042M
2002	704537M
2003	705140M

AVG. AUCTION PRICING

LOW	HIGH	AVG
$5,390	$8,085	$6,579

3230

YEARS MFRD	1990-1995
ENGINE	FORD
CYLINDERS	3
CID	192
PTO HP	32
FUEL	D
SPEEDS	8/2
TRANSMISSION	GEAR
STEERING	STANDARD
PTO	YES
DRIVE TYPE	2WD
ROPS/CAB	ROPS
WEIGHT	4,622 LBS.
MSRP	$17,310

OPTIONS

4WD

SERIAL NUMBERS

RH SIDE OF TRANS ON TOP OF UPPER IMPLEMENT MOUNTING BOSS

YEAR	BEGINNING NO.
1990	BC26239
1991	BC68791
1992	BD07628
1993	BD32445
1994	BD60322

RETAIL PRICING

YEAR	HIGH	LOW
1990	$4,082	$3,061
1991	$4,230	$3,172
1992	$4,482	$3,361
1993	$4,597	$3,448
1994	$4,901	$3,676
1995	$4,982	$3,737

3415

YEARS MFRD	1993-2002
ENGINE	SHIBAURA
CYLINDERS	4
CID	135.2
PTO HP	38
ENGINE HP	47.5
COOLING	LIQUID
FUEL	D
SPEEDS	12/4
TRANSMISSION	GEAR
STEERING	STANDARD
HYDRAULIC	YES
PTO	YES
DRIVE TYPE	2WD
ROPS/CAB	ROPS
WEIGHT	3,483 LBS.
MSRP	$17,892

OPTIONS

LDR

SERIAL NUMBERS

LEFT SIDE OF TRANS HOUSING

YEAR	BEGINNING NO.
1993	UX20001
1994	UX20798
1995	UX21715
1996	UX22323
1997	UX22504
1998	UX22858
1999	UX23290
2000	UX23811
2001	UX24232
2002	UX24442

RETAIL PRICING

YEAR	HIGH	LOW
1994	$4,111	$3,083
1995	$4,416	$3,312
1996	$4,728	$3,546
1997	$5,049	$3,787
1998	$5,381	$4,036
1999	$5,720	$4,290
2000	$6,068	$4,551
2001	$6,429	$4,822
2002	$6,799	$5,099

AVG. AUCTION PRICING

LOW	HIGH	AVG
$4,214	$8,330	$5,366

3430

YEARS MFRD	1989-1997
ENGINE	FORD
CYLINDERS	3
CID	192
PTO HP	38
FUEL	D
SPEEDS	8/2-8/8
TRANSMISSION	GEAR
STEERING	STANDARD
PTO	YES
DRIVE TYPE	2WD
ROPS/CAB	ROPS
WEIGHT	4,391 LBS.
MSRP	$20,660

OPTIONS

4WD

SERIAL NUMBERS

RH SIDE OF TRANS ON TOP OF UPPER IMPLEMENT MOUNTING BOSS

YEAR	BEGINNING NO.
1990	BC26239
1991	BC68791
1992	BD03778
1993	BD36144
1994	BD66161
1995	BD77434
1996	021670B
1997	056058B

RETAIL PRICING

YEAR	HIGH	LOW
1996	$6,164	$4,623

3830

YEARS MFRD	1996-2000
CYLINDERS	3
CID	165
PTO HP	45
FUEL	D
SPEEDS	12/12
TRANSMISSION	GEAR
STEERING	STANDARD
PTO	YES
DRIVE TYPE	2WD
ROPS/CAB	ROPS
WEIGHT	3,851 LBS.
MSRP	$23,550

OPTIONS

4WD
CAB

SERIAL NUMBERS

YEAR	BEGINNING NO.
1996	F001436
1997	1105511
1998	1130047

RETAIL PRICING

YEAR	HIGH	LOW
2000	$7,338	$5,504

3830 NARROW

YEARS MFRD . . . 1992-1998
ENGINE . . . IVECO
CYLINDERS . . . 3
CID . . . 165
PTO HP . . . 45
FUEL . . . D
SPEEDS . . . 12/4-12/12
STEERING . . . STANDARD
PTO . . . YES
DRIVE TYPE . . . 2WD
ROPS/CAB . . . ROPS
WEIGHT . . . 3,784 LBS.
MSRP . . . $20,005

OPTIONS

4WD NARROW

SERIAL NUMBERS

YEAR	BEGINNING NO.
1992	F399000
1993	F399354
1994	F022000
1995	F051000
1996	F001436
1997	1105511
1998	1130047

RETAIL PRICING

YEAR	HIGH	LOW
1996	$5,970	$4,478

3910

YEARS MFRD . . . 1982-1990
ENGINE . . . FORD
CYLINDERS . . . 3
CID . . . 192
PTO HP . . . 42.62
FUEL . . . D
SPEEDS . . . 8/2-8/4
TRANSMISSION . . . GEAR
STEERING . . . STANDARD
PTO . . . YES
DRIVE TYPE . . . 2WD
ROPS/CAB . . . ROPS
WEIGHT . . . 5,180 LBS.
MSRP . . . $20,050

OPTIONS

4WD
CAB

SERIAL NUMBERS

UPPER RIGHT FRONT CORNER OF TRANS

YEAR	BEGINNING NO.
1982	C682000
1983	C694500
1984	C707400
1985	C732600
1986	C750422
1987	C763228
1988	BB31777
1989	BB84620

RETAIL PRICING

YEAR	HIGH	LOW
1990	$5,106	$3,829

AVG. AUCTION PRICING

LOW	HIGH	AVG
$3,822	$7,546	$5,488

3930

YEARS MFRD . . . 1996-2002
CYLINDERS . . . 3
CID . . . 192
PTO HP . . . 45
SPEEDS . . . 8/2-8/8
TRANSMISSION . . . SHUTTLE SHIFT
STEERING . . . STANDARD
DRIVE TYPE . . . 2WD
ROPS/CAB . . . ROPS
WEIGHT . . . 5,157 LBS.
MSRP . . . $22,200

OPTIONS

4WD

SERIAL NUMBERS

YEAR	BEGINNING NO.
1996	011128B
1997	056056B
1998	083357B
1999	111612B

RETAIL PRICING

YEAR	HIGH	LOW
2002	$10,445	$7,834

AVG. AUCTION PRICING

LOW	HIGH	AVG
$4,200	$15,000	$7,419

FOTON

FT250

YEARS MFRD . . . 2016-2017
SERIES . . . 2500 SERIES
CYLINDERS . . . 3
CID . . . 1.6
ENGINE HP . . . 25
COOLING . . . LIQUID
FUEL . . . D
SPEEDS . . . 10/10
STEERING . . . STANDARD
HITCH . . . CAT. I
MSRP . . . $7,169

OPTIONS

MFWD

RETAIL PRICING

YEAR	HIGH	LOW
2016	$5,202	$3,902
2017	$5,380	$4,035

FT254

YEARS MFRD . . . 2014-2017
SERIES . . . 2500 SERIES
CYLINDERS . . . 3
CID . . . 1.6L
ENGINE HP . . . 25
COOLING . . . LIQUID
FUEL . . . D
SPEEDS . . . 10/10
STEERING . . . STANDARD
HITCH . . . CAT. I
DRIVE TYPE . . . 2WD
ROPS/CAB . . . ROPS
MSRP . . . $8,366

OPTIONS

MFWD

RETAIL PRICING

YEAR	HIGH	LOW
2016	$6,124	$4,593
2017	$6,291	$4,718

FT254

YEARS MFRD . . . 2016-2017
SERIES . . . 3000 SERIES
CYLINDERS . . . 3
CID . . . 1.6L
ENGINE HP . . . 25
COOLING . . . LIQUID
FUEL . . . D
SPEEDS . . . 10/10
STEERING . . . STANDARD
HITCH . . . CAT. I
MSRP . . . $9,083

OPTIONS

MFWD

RETAIL PRICING

YEAR	HIGH	LOW
2016	$6,862	$5,147
2017	$7,087	$5,315

FT254

YEARS MFRD . . . 2008-2013
ENGINE . . . NATIONAL
CYLINDERS . . . 3
ENGINE HP . . . 25
COOLING . . . LIQUID
FUEL . . . D
SPEEDS . . . 8/8
TRANSMISSION . . . GEAR
STEERING . . . STANDARD
HITCH . . . CAT. I
WEIGHT . . . 2,712 LBS.

FT300

YEARS MFRD . . . 2004-2009
ENGINE . . . TY395T
CYLINDERS . . . 3
CID . . . 136
PTO HP . . . 27.8
ENGINE HP . . . 30
COOLING . . . LIQUID
TRANSMISSION . . . GEAR
STEERING . . . STANDARD
HYDRAULIC . . . YES
PTO . . . YES
WEIGHT . . . 1,785 LBS.

FT304

YEARS MFRD . . . 2007-2013
ENGINE . . . TY395T
CYLINDERS . . . 3
ENGINE HP . . . 22
COOLING . . . LIQUID
FUEL . . . G
SPEEDS . . . 8/4
TRANSMISSION . . . GEAR
STEERING . . . STANDARD
HITCH . . . CAT. I

FT350

YEARS MFRD . . . 2004-2009
ENGINE . . . TY395T
CYLINDERS . . . 3
CID . . . 136.1
PTO HP . . . 23
ENGINE HP . . . 35
COOLING . . . LIQUID
TRANSMISSION . . . GEAR
STEERING . . . STANDARD
HYDRAULIC . . . YES
PTO . . . YES
WEIGHT . . . 1,800 LBS.

FT354

YEARS MFRD . . . 2007-2015
ENGINE . . . TY395T
CYLINDERS . . . 3
ENGINE HP . . . 25.7
COOLING . . . LIQUID
FUEL . . . G
SPEEDS . . . VARIABLE
TRANSMISSION . . . HYDRO
STEERING . . . STANDARD
HITCH . . . CAT. I

FT400

YEARS MFRD . . . 2004-2009
ENGINE . . . SL3105BT
CYLINDERS . . . 3
CID . . . 175
PTO HP . . . 37
ENGINE HP . . . 40
COOLING . . . LIQUID
TRANSMISSION . . . GEAR
STEERING . . . STANDARD
HYDRAULIC . . . YES
PTO . . . YES
DRIVE TYPE . . . 2WD
ROPS/CAB . . . ROPS
WEIGHT . . . 1,785 LBS.

FT404

YEARS MFRD . . . 2004-2011
ENGINE . . . SL3105BT
CYLINDERS . . . 3
CID . . . 175
PTO HP . . . 37

ENGINE HP 40
COOLING . . . . LIQUID
FUEL . . . . D
TRANSMISSION . . . . GEAR
STEERING. . . . . .STANDARD
HYDRAULIC . . . . YES
PTO . . . . YES
DRIVE TYPE 4WD
ROPS/CAB . . . . ROPS
WEIGHT . . . . 4,233 LBS.

NOTES

GRASSHOPPER

120

YEARS MFRD	2007-2007
SERIES	100 SERIES
ENGINE	B&S
CYLINDERS	2
ENGINE HP	20
COOLING	AIR
FUEL	G
SPEEDS	VARIABLE
TRANSMISSION	HYDRO
STEERING	ZERO
STANDARD DECK	41"
WEIGHT	850 LBS.
MSRP	$5,800

OPTIONS

BAGGER

RETAIL PRICING

YEAR	HIGH	LOW
2007	$2,036	$1,527

120K

YEARS MFRD	2007-2011
SERIES	100 SERIES
ENGINE	KOHLER COMMAND
CYLINDERS	2
ENGINE HP	20
COOLING	AIR
FUEL	G
SPEEDS	VARIABLE
TRANSMISSION	HYDRO
STEERING	ZERO
BLADE CLUTCH	ELECTRIC
STANDARD DECK	48"
WEIGHT	930 LBS.
MSRP	$7,120

OPTIONS

BAGGER

RETAIL PRICING

YEAR	HIGH	LOW
2007	$2,373	$1,779
2008	$2,637	$1,978
2009	$2,929	$2,197
2010	$3,249	$2,437
2011	$3,609	$2,707

124

YEARS MFRD	2008-2013
SERIES	100 SERIES
ENGINE	B&S
CYLINDERS	2
ENGINE HP	24
COOLING	AIR
FUEL	G
SPEEDS	VARIABLE
TRANSMISSION	HYDRO
STEERING	ZERO
STANDARD DECK	52"
WEIGHT	750 LBS.
MSRP	$6,705

OPTIONS

BAGGER

RETAIL PRICING

YEAR	HIGH	LOW
2008	$2,431	$1,824
2009	$2,669	$2,001
2010	$2,951	$2,213
2011	$3,276	$2,457
2012	$3,639	$2,729
2013	$4,395	$3,296

124V

YEARS MFRD	2014-2020
SERIES	100 SERIES
ENGINE	B&S
CID	724CC
ENGINE HP	24
COOLING	AIR
FUEL	G
SPEEDS	VARIABLE
TRANSMISSION	HYDRO
STEERING	ZERO
STANDARD DECK	48"
MSRP	$6,995

OPTIONS

41" DECK . . . $-400

POWERVAC SYS

RETAIL PRICING

YEAR	HIGH	LOW
2014	$3,094	$2,321
2015	$3,415	$2,561
2016	$3,771	$2,828
2017	$4,162	$3,121
2018	$4,606	$3,454
2019	$5,086	$3,815
2020	$5,635	$4,299

125V

YEARS MFRD	2016-2020
SERIES	100 SERIES
ENGINE	KOHLER
CID	747CC
ENGINE HP	25
COOLING	AIR
FUEL	G
SPEEDS	VARIABLE
TRANSMISSION	HYDRO
STEERING	ZERO
STANDARD DECK	52"
MSRP	$7,295

OPTIONS

48" DECK . . . $-45

61" DECK . . . $150

POWERVAC SYS

RETAIL PRICING

YEAR	HIGH	LOW
2016	$3,980	$2,986
2017	$4,394	$3,295
2018	$4,843	$3,632
2019	$5,380	$4,035
2020	$5,851	$4,459

126V

YEARS MFRD	2016-2020
SERIES	100 SERIES
ENGINE	B&S
CID	810CC
ENGINE HP	26
COOLING	AIR
FUEL	G
SPEEDS	VARIABLE
TRANSMISSION	HYDRO
STEERING	ZERO
STANDARD DECK	52"
MSRP	$7,160

OPTIONS

61" DECK . . . $135

POWERVAC SYS

RETAIL PRICING

YEAR	HIGH	LOW
2016	$3,873	$2,905
2017	$4,276	$3,207
2018	$4,729	$3,546
2019	$5,227	$3,920
2020	$5,742	$4,345

218

YEARS MFRD	2004-2007
SERIES	MID-MOUNT 200 SERIES
ENGINE	KOHLER COMMAND
CYLINDERS	2
ENGINE HP	18
COOLING	AIR
FUEL	G
SPEEDS	VARIABLE
TRANSMISSION	HYDRO
STEERING	ZERO
STANDARD DECK	48"
WEIGHT	990 LBS.
MSRP	$8,303

OPTIONS

BAGGER

RETAIL PRICING

YEAR	HIGH	LOW
2004	$2,111	$1,583
2005	$2,346	$1,760
2006	$2,603	$1,952
2007	$2,917	$2,188

220

YEARS MFRD	2000-2005
SERIES	MID-MOUNT 200 SERIES
ENGINE	KOHLER COMMAND V-TWIN
CYLINDERS	2
CID	38
ENGINE HP	20
COOLING	AIR
FUEL	G
SPEEDS	VARIABLE
TRANSMISSION	DUAL HYDRO
STEERING	ZERO
STANDARD DECK	52"
WEIGHT	1,010 LBS.
MSRP	$8,750

RETAIL PRICING

YEAR	HIGH	LOW
2000	$1,537	$1,152
2001	$1,698	$1,274
2002	$1,888	$1,416
2003	$2,096	$1,572
2004	$2,328	$1,746
2005	$2,603	$1,952

220/48

YEARS MFRD	2008-2013
ENGINE	KOHLER COMMAND
CYLINDERS	2
ENGINE HP	20
COOLING	AIR
FUEL	G
SPEEDS	VARIABLE
TRANSMISSION	HYDRO
STEERING	ZERO
STANDARD DECK	48"
WEIGHT	1,030 LBS.
MSRP	$9,235

OPTIONS

BAGGER

RETAIL PRICING

YEAR	HIGH	LOW
2008	$3,269	$2,452
2009	$3,632	$2,724
2010	$4,034	$3,025
2011	$4,480	$3,360
2012	$4,972	$3,729
2013	$5,523	$4,142

220/52

YEARS MFRD	2005-2005
ENGINE	KOHLER COMMAND
CYLINDERS	2
ENGINE HP	20
COOLING	AIR
FUEL	G
SPEEDS	VARIABLE
TRANSMISSION	HYDRO
STEERING	ZERO

223

YEARS MFRD	2005-2013
ENGINE	KOHLER COMMAND PRO
CYLINDERS	2
ENGINE HP	23
COOLING	AIR
FUEL	G
SPEEDS	VARIABLE
TRANSMISSION	HYDRO
STEERING	ZERO
STANDARD DECK	52"
WEIGHT	1,380 LBS.
MSRP	$10,075

OPTIONS

61" DECK

BAGGER

RETAIL PRICING

YEAR	HIGH	LOW
2005	$2,660	$1,995
2006	$2,891	$2,168
2007	$3,258	$2,443
2008	$3,567	$2,675
2009	$3,961	$2,971
2010	$4,400	$3,300
2011	$4,884	$3,663
2012	$5,425	$4,069
2013	$6,023	$4,517

GRASSHOPPER

225

YEARS MFRD 2000-2004
SERIES... MID-MOUNT 200 SERIES
ENGINE .. KOHLER COMMAND PRO
CYLINDERS 2
CID 44
ENGINE HP 25
COOLING .... AIR
FUEL .... G
SPEEDS .... VARIABLE
TRANSMISSION ..... DUAL HYDRO
STEERING .... ZERO
STANDARD DECK .... 61"
WEIGHT .... 1,060 LBS.
MSRP $8,815

OPTIONS

72" DECK

RETAIL PRICING

YEAR	HIGH	LOW
2000	$1,778	$1,333
2001	$1,977	$1,482
2002	$2,194	$1,646
2003	$2,438	$1,829
2004	$2,732	$2,049

AVG. AUCTION PRICING

LOW	HIGH	AVG
$1,734	$2,767	$2,182

225K

YEARS MFRD 2014-2020
SERIES .... 200 SERIES
ENGINE .... KOHLER
CYLINDERS 2
CID 747CC
ENGINE HP 25
COOLING .... AIR
FUEL .... G
SPEEDS .... VARIABLE
TRANSMISSION ..... DUAL HYDRO
STEERING .... ZERO
STANDARD DECK .... 61"
MSRP $11,285

OPTIONS

48" DECK .... $-350
52" DECK .... $-270
BAGGER

RETAIL PRICING

YEAR	HIGH	LOW
2014	$5,145	$3,859
2015	$5,680	$4,260
2016	$6,270	$4,703
2017	$6,919	$5,189
2018	$7,652	$5,738
2019	$8,480	$6,361
2020	$9,356	$7,052

225V

YEARS MFRD 2016-2020
SERIES .... 200 V SERIES
ENGINE .... KOHLER
CID 747CC
ENGINE HP 25
COOLING .... AIR
FUEL .... G
SPEEDS .... VARIABLE
TRANSMISSION .... HYDRO
STEERING .... ZERO
STANDARD DECK .... 52"
MSRP $8,415

OPTIONS

61" DECK $150
POWERVAC SYS

RETAIL PRICING

YEAR	HIGH	LOW
2016	$4,760	$3,570
2017	$5,254	$3,941
2018	$5,814	$4,361
2019	$6,418	$4,715
2020	$7,187	$5,435

226V

YEARS MFRD 2011-2020
SERIES .... 200 V SERIES
ENGINE .... B&S
CYLINDERS 2
CID 810CC
ENGINE HP 26
COOLING .... AIR
FUEL .... G
SPEEDS .... VARIABLE
TRANSMISSION .... HYDRO
STEERING .... ZERO
BLADE CLUTCH .... ELECTRIC
STANDARD DECK .... 52"
WEIGHT .... 1,256 LBS.
MSRP $8,610

OPTIONS

48" DECK
61" DECK $150
POWERVAC SYS

RETAIL PRICING

YEAR	HIGH	LOW
2011	$3,820	$2,130
2012	$3,135	$2,351
2013	$3,461	$2,596
2014	$3,819	$2,864
2015	$4,215	$3,161
2016	$4,653	$3,489
2017	$5,136	$3,852
2018	$5,698	$4,273
2019	$6,322	$4,742
2020	$7,099	$5,351

227

YEARS MFRD 2005-2013
ENGINE .. KOHLER COMMAND PRO
CYLINDERS 2
ENGINE HP 27
COOLING .... AIR
FUEL .... G
SPEEDS .... VARIABLE
TRANSMISSION .... HYDRO
STEERING .... ZERO
STANDARD DECK .... 52"
MSRP $10,995

OPTIONS

61" DECK
72" DECK
BAGGER

RETAIL PRICING

YEAR	HIGH	LOW
2005	$2,837	$2,128
2006	$3,155	$2,366
2007	$3,511	$2,634
2008	$3,905	$2,929
2009	$4,325	$3,244
2010	$4,825	$3,618
2011	$5,331	$3,998
2012	$5,890	$4,417
2013	$6,576	$4,932

227V EFI

YEARS MFRD 2017-2020
SERIES .... 200 V SERIES
ENGINE ...... KOHLER CONFIDANT
CID 747CC
COOLING .... AIR
FUEL .... G
SPEEDS .... VARIABLE
TRANSMISSION .... HYDRO
STEERING .... ZERO
STANDARD DECK .... 52"
WEIGHT .... 1,015 LBS.
MSRP $9,065

OPTIONS

61" DECK $150
POWERVAC SYS

321D

YEARS MFRD 2001-2019
SERIES... MID-MOUNT 300 SERIES
ENGINE .... KUBOTA
CYLINDERS 3
CID 44
ENGINE HP 21
COOLING .... LIQUID
FUEL .... D
SPEEDS .... VARIABLE
TRANSMISSION .... HYDRO
STEERING .... ZERO
BLADE CLUTCH .... ELECTRIC
STANDARD DECK .... 48"
WEIGHT .... 1,605 LBS.
MSRP $14,365

OPTIONS

52" DECK
POWERVAC SYS

RETAIL PRICING

YEAR	HIGH	LOW
2006	$3,321	$2,491
2007	$3,429	$2,572
2008	$3,641	$2,731
2009	$4,088	$3,066
2010	$4,513	$3,385
2011	$4,980	$3,735
2012	$5,498	$4,123
2013	$6,067	$4,550
2014	$6,697	$5,023
2015	$7,392	$5,544
2016	$8,159	$6,120
2017	$9,005	$6,754
2018	$9,903	$7,427
2019	$10,984	$8,238

322D

YEARS MFRD 2004-2004
SERIES .... MID-MOUNT SERIES
ENGINE .... KUBOTA OHV
CYLINDERS 3
CID 54.8
ENGINE HP 22
COOLING .... LIQUID
FUEL .... D
SPEEDS .... VARIABLE
TRANSMISSION .... HYDRO
STEERING .... ZERO
BLADE CLUTCH .... MANUAL
WEIGHT .... 1,250 LBS.

322D/61

YEARS MFRD 2005-2008
ENGINE .... KUBOTA
CYLINDERS 3
ENGINE HP 22
COOLING .... LIQUID
FUEL .... D
SPEEDS .... VARIABLE
TRANSMISSION .... HYDRO
STEERING .... ZERO
STANDARD DECK .... 61"
WEIGHT .... 1,710 LBS.
MSRP $12,445

OPTIONS

72" DECK
BAGGER
HYD LIFT

RETAIL PRICING

YEAR	HIGH	LOW
2005	$3,546	$2,659
2006	$3,935	$2,951
2007	$4,370	$3,277
2008	$4,839	$3,629

325

YEARS MFRD 2001-2005
SERIES... MID-MOUNT 300 SERIES
ENGINE .... KUBOTA
CID 45.21
ENGINE HP 24.5
COOLING .... LIQUID
FUEL .... G
SPEEDS .... VARIABLE
TRANSMISSION .... HYDRO
STEERING .... STANDARD
STANDARD DECK .... 52"
WEIGHT .... 1,230 LBS.
MSRP $11,330

OPTIONS

2 BAG
3 BAG
61" DECK
72" DECK

RETAIL PRICING

YEAR	HIGH	LOW
2001	$2,198	$1,649
2002	$2,444	$1,833
2003	$2,713	$2,034
2004	$3,012	$2,259
2005	$3,344	$2,508

325A
YEARS MFRD 2004-2004
SERIES . . . . 300 SERIES
ENGINE . . . . KOHLER
ENGINE HP 24.5
COOLING . . . . LIQUID
FUEL . . . . G
SPEEDS . . . . VARIABLE
TRANSMISSION . . . . HYDRO
STEERING . . . . ZERO
STANDARD DECK . . . . 61"
MSRP $9,935

OPTIONS
72" DECK
BAG & FAN

RETAIL PRICING
YEAR	HIGH	LOW
2004	$2,633	$1,975

325D
YEARS MFRD 2009-2020
SERIES . . . . 300 SERIES
ENGINE . . . . KUBOTA
CYLINDERS 3
CID 898CC
ENGINE HP 25
COOLING . . . . LIQUID
FUEL . . . . D
SPEEDS . . . . VARIABLE
TRANSMISSION . . . . HYDRO
STEERING . . . . ZERO
BLADE CLUTCH . . . . ELECTRIC
STANDARD DECK . . . . 61"
MSRP $15,535

OPTIONS
52" DECK . . . . $-270
72" DECK $415
POWERVAC SYS

RETAIL PRICING
YEAR	HIGH	LOW
2009	$4,331	$3,248
2010	$4,780	$3,585
2011	$5,276	$3,957
2012	$5,824	$4,367
2013	$6,426	$4,820
2014	$7,112	$5,334
2015	$7,833	$5,875
2016	$8,643	$6,482
2017	$9,540	$7,154
2018	$10,595	$7,946
2019	$11,764	$8,823
2020	$13,073	$9,903

327
YEARS MFRD 2004-2004
SERIES . . . . MID-MOUNT SERIES
ENGINE . . . . KAWASAKI OHV
CYLINDERS 2
ENGINE HP 27
COOLING . . . . LIQUID
FUEL . . . . G
SPEEDS . . . . VARAIBLE
TRANSMISSION . . . . HYDRO
STEERING . . . . ZERO
HYDRAULIC . . . . YES
WEIGHT . . . . 1,250 LBS.

327/52
YEARS MFRD 2005-2006
ENGINE . . . . KAWASAKI
CYLINDERS 2
ENGINE HP 27
COOLING . . . . LIQUID
FUEL . . . . G
SPEEDS . . . . VARIABLE
TRANSMISSION . . . . HYDRO
STEERING . . . . ZERO
STANDARD DECK . . . . 52"
MSRP $10,405

OPTIONS
2 BAG
3 BAG
61" DECK
72" DECK

RETAIL PRICING
YEAR	HIGH	LOW
2005	$3,016	$2,262
2006	$3,349	$2,511

327A
YEARS MFRD 2003-2003
ENGINE . . . . KOHLER AEGIS
CID 45.6
ENGINE HP 27
COOLING . . . . LIQUID
FUEL . . . . G
TRANSMISSION . . . . HYDRO
STANDARD DECK . . . . 61"
WEIGHT . . . . 1,250 LBS.
MSRP $9,935

OPTIONS
72" DECK
BAG & FAN
ROPS

RETAIL PRICING
YEAR	HIGH	LOW
2003	$3,130	$2,348

327EFI
YEARS MFRD 2014-2019
ENGINE . . . . KOHLER
ENGINE HP 27
COOLING . . . . AIR
FUEL . . . . G
SPEEDS . . . . VARIABLE
TRANSMISSION . . . . HYDRO
STEERING . . . . ZERO
STANDARD DECK . . . . 61"
MSRP $12,065

OPTIONS
52" DECK
72" DECK
POWERVAC SYS

RETAIL PRICING
YEAR	HIGH	LOW
2014	$5,608	$4,206
2015	$6,190	$4,642
2016	$6,832	$5,124
2017	$7,540	$5,655
2018	$8,366	$6,275
2019	$9,284	$6,963

328G4 EFI
YEARS MFRD 2019-2020
SERIES . . . . 300G SERIES
ENGINE . . . . VANGUARD
CYLINDERS 2
CID 49.4
COOLING . . . . AIR
FUEL . . . . G
SPEEDS . . . . VARIABLE
TRANSMISSION . . . . HYDRO
STEERING . . . . ZERO
STANDARD DECK . . . . 52"
WEIGHT . . . . 1,140 LBS.
MSRP $10,295

OPTIONS
61" DECK $265

329
YEARS MFRD 2006-2020
ENGINE . . . . KUBOTA
CYLINDERS 3
CID 962CC
ENGINE HP 29
COOLING . . . . LIQUID
FUEL . . . . G
SPEEDS . . . . VARIABLE
TRANSMISSION . . . . HYDRO
STEERING . . . . ZERO
BLADE CLUTCH . . . . ELECTRIC
STANDARD DECK . . . . 61"
WEIGHT . . . . 1,630 LBS.
MSRP $14,865

OPTIONS
52" DECK . . . . $-90
72" DECK $390
HYD LIFT
POWERVAC SYS

RETAIL PRICING
YEAR	HIGH	LOW
2006	$3,289	$2,467
2007	$3,561	$2,670
2008	$3,734	$2,800
2009	$4,193	$3,144
2010	$4,629	$3,472
2011	$5,109	$3,831
2012	$5,638	$4,229
2013	$6,224	$4,668
2014	$6,870	$5,152
2015	$7,584	$5,687
2016	$8,369	$6,276
2017	$9,237	$6,928
2018	$10,244	$7,683
2019	$11,348	$8,511
2020	$12,643	$9,659

329B
YEARS MFRD 2009-2020
ENGINE . . . . B&S
CID 896CC
ENGINE HP 29
COOLING . . . . AIR
FUEL . . . . G
SPEEDS . . . . VARIABLE
TRANSMISSION . . . . HYDRO
STEERING . . . . ZERO
BLADE CLUTCH . . . . ELECTRIC
STANDARD DECK . . . . 52"
MSRP $11,720

OPTIONS
61" DECK $75
72" DECK
POWERVAC SYS

RETAIL PRICING
YEAR	HIGH	LOW
2009	$3,240	$2,430
2010	$3,577	$2,683
2011	$3,948	$2,961
2012	$4,369	$3,277
2013	$4,818	$3,614
2014	$5,309	$3,982
2015	$5,860	$4,395
2016	$6,468	$4,851
2017	$7,140	$5,354
2018	$7,924	$5,942
2019	$8,794	$6,596
2020	$9,721	$7,501

329G4 EFI
YEARS MFRD 2019-2020
SERIES . . . . 300G SERIES
ENGINE . . . . KOHLER
CYLINDERS 2
CID 50.3
COOLING . . . . AIR
FUEL . . . . G
TRANSMISSION . . . . HYDRO
STEERING . . . . ZERO
STANDARD DECK . . . . 52"
WEIGHT . . . . 1,140 LBS.
MSRP $10,910

OPTIONS
61" DECK $265

333G5 EFI
YEARS MFRD 2019-2020
SERIES . . . . 300G SERIES
ENGINE . . . . KOHLER
CYLINDERS 2
CID 50.3
COOLING . . . . AIR
FUEL . . . . G
SPEEDS . . . . VARIABLE
TRANSMISSION . . . . HYDRO
STEERING . . . . ZERO
STANDARD DECK . . . . 61"
WEIGHT . . . . 1,250 LBS.
MSRP $12,585

OPTIONS
72" DECK $410

335
YEARS MFRD 2008-2020
ENGINE . . . . B&S VANGUARD
CYLINDERS 2
CID 993CC
ENGINE HP 35
COOLING . . . . AIR
FUEL . . . . G
SPEEDS . . . . VARIABLE
TRANSMISSION . . . . HYDRO
STEERING . . . . ZERO

GRASSHOPPER

BLADE CLUTCH .... ELECTRIC
STANDARD DECK .... 61"
WEIGHT .... 1,692 LBS.
MSRP $12,605

OPTIONS

72" DECK $370
POWERVAC SYS

RETAIL PRICING

YEAR	HIGH	LOW
2008	$3,311	$2,483
2009	$3,663	$2,747
2010	$4,045	$3,034
2011	$4,465	$3,349
2012	$4,929	$3,697
2013	$5,439	$4,079
2014	$6,005	$4,504
2015	$6,629	$4,972
2016	$7,316	$5,488
2017	$8,076	$6,057
2018	$8,969	$6,727
2019	$9,958	$7,468
2020	$11,060	$8,384

337G5 EFI

YEARS MFRD 2019-2020
SERIES .... 300G SERIES
ENGINE .... VANGUARD
CYLINDERS 2
CID 60.6
COOLING .... AIR
FUEL .... G
SPEEDS .... VARIABLE
TRANSMISSION .... HYDRO
STEERING .... ZERO
STANDARD DECK .... 61"
WEIGHT .... 1,260 LBS.
MSRP $12,865

OPTIONS

72" DECK $410

400D

YEARS MFRD 2018-2020
SERIES .... 400 SERIES
ENGINE .... KUBOTA
CYLINDERS 3
CID 1.3L
COOLING .... LIQUID
FUEL .... D
TRANSMISSION .... HYDRO
STEERING .... ZERO
STANDARD DECK .... 61"
WEIGHT .... 1,450 LBS.
MSRP $18,375

OPTIONS

72" DECK $395
POWERVAC SYS

411

YEARS MFRD 1989-1990
ENGINE .... B&S
ENGINE HP 11
COOLING .... AIR
FUEL .... G
SPEEDS .... VARIABLE
TRANSMISSION .... HYDRO
STEERING .... ZERO
STANDARD DECK .... 35"
MSRP $3,900

RETAIL PRICING

YEAR	HIGH	LOW
1989	$283	$212
1990	$315	$236

411R

YEARS MFRD 1991-1992
ENGINE .... WISCONSIN ROBIN
ENGINE HP 11
COOLING .... AIR
FUEL .... G
SPEEDS .... VARIABLE
TRANSMISSION .... HYDRO
STEERING .... ZERO
STANDARD DECK .... 41"
MSRP $4,440

RETAIL PRICING

YEAR	HIGH	LOW
1991	$320	$240
1992	$355	$266

428D

YEARS MFRD 2003-2008
SERIES ... MID-MOUNT 400 SERIES
ENGINE .... KUBOTA
CID 68.58
ENGINE HP 28
COOLING .... LIQUID
FUEL .... D
TRANSMISSION .... HYDRO
STEERING .... ZERO
STANDARD DECK .... 61"
WEIGHT .... 1,360 LBS.
MSRP $14,915

OPTIONS

12 CU BAG
72" DECK
8 CU BAG
ROPS

RETAIL PRICING

YEAR	HIGH	LOW
2003	$3,788	$2,841
2004	$4,208	$3,156
2005	$4,674	$3,505
2006	$5,179	$3,884
2007	$5,763	$4,323
2008	$6,397	$4,798

AVG. AUCTION PRICING

LOW	HIGH	AVG
$1,729	$5,164	$3,127

430D

YEARS MFRD 2009-2014
SERIES .... 400 SERIES
ENGINE .... KUBOTA
CYLINDERS 3
ENGINE HP 30
COOLING .... LIQUID
FUEL .... D
SPEEDS .... VARIABLE
TRANSMISSION .... HYDRO
STEERING .... ZERO
BLADE CLUTCH .... ELECTRIC
STANDARD DECK .... 61"
MSRP $17,095

OPTIONS

12 CU BAG
72" DECK

RETAIL PRICING

YEAR	HIGH	LOW
2009	$6,091	$4,568
2010	$6,764	$5,073
2011	$7,511	$5,633
2012	$8,342	$6,256
2013	$9,264	$6,948
2014	$11,172	$8,379

432

YEARS MFRD 2003-2019
SERIES ... MID-MOUNT 400 SERIES
ENGINE .... KUBOTA
CYLINDERS 3
CID 60.80
ENGINE HP 32
COOLING .... LIQUID
FUEL .... G
SPEEDS .... VARIABLE
TRANSMISSION .... HYDRO
STEERING .... ZERO
BLADE CLUTCH .... ELECTRIC
STANDARD DECK .... 61"
WEIGHT .... 1,360 LBS.
MSRP $15,610

OPTIONS

72" DECK
POWERVAC SYS

RETAIL PRICING

YEAR	HIGH	LOW
2006	$3,485	$2,614
2007	$3,771	$2,828
2008	$3,955	$2,966
2009	$4,441	$3,331
2010	$4,902	$3,676
2011	$5,410	$4,057
2012	$5,972	$4,479
2013	$6,591	$4,944
2014	$7,275	$5,456
2015	$8,030	$6,023
2016	$8,863	$6,647
2017	$9,782	$7,337
2018	$10,870	$8,153
2019	$12,090	$9,068

524V

YEARS MFRD 2018-2020
SERIES .... 500V SERIES
ENGINE .... B&S
CYLINDERS 2
CID 44.2
ENGINE HP 24
COOLING .... AIR
FUEL .... G
SPEEDS .... VARIABLE
TRANSMISSION .... HYDRO
STEERING .... ZERO
STANDARD DECK .... 42"
WEIGHT .... 935 LBS.
MSRP $8,455

OPTIONS

CANOPY $155
MULCH PKG $190

526V

YEARS MFRD 2018-2020
SERIES .... 500V SERIES
ENGINE .... B&S
CYLINDERS 2
CID 49.4
ENGINE HP 26
COOLING .... AIR
FUEL .... G
TRANSMISSION .... HYDRO
STEERING .... ZERO
STANDARD DECK .... 52"
WEIGHT .... 1,025 LBS.
MSRP $9,175

OPTIONS

CANOPY $155
MULCH PKG $200

612

YEARS MFRD 1992-1995
ENGINE .... B&S
ENGINE HP 12.5
COOLING .... AIR
FUEL .... G
SPEEDS .... VARIABLE
TRANSMISSION .... HYDRO
STEERING .... ZERO
STANDARD DECK .... 44"
MSRP $5,425

OPTIONS

48" DECK
BLADE
SNOW THROWER

RETAIL PRICING

YEAR	HIGH	LOW
1992	$494	$370
1993	$554	$415
1994	$612	$459
1995	$680	$510

614

YEARS MFRD 1991-2005
SERIES .... 600 SERIES
ENGINE ... B&S VANGUARD V-TWIN
CYLINDERS 2
CID 23.9
ENGINE HP 14
COOLING .... AIR
FUEL .... G
SPEEDS .... VARIABLE
TRANSMISSION .... HYDRO
STEERING .... ZERO
STANDARD DECK .... 44"
WEIGHT .... 570 LBS.
MSRP $7,275

OPTIONS

2 BAG
3 BAG

48" DECK
MAXTRAX

RETAIL PRICING

YEAR	HIGH	LOW
1997	$988	$741
1998	$1,093	$820
1999	$1,215	$911
2000	$1,347	$1,010
2001	$1,495	$1,121
2002	$1,657	$1,243
2003	$1,838	$1,379
2004	$2,039	$1,530
2005	$2,286	$1,715

616

YEARS MFRD 1993-2006
SERIES .... 600 SERIES
ENGINE ... B&S VANGUARD V-TWIN
CYLINDERS 2
CID 29.3
ENGINE HP 16
COOLING .... AIR
FUEL .... G
SPEEDS .... VARIABLE
TRANSMISSION ...... DUAL HYDRO
STEERING .... ZERO
STANDARD DECK .... 48"
WEIGHT .... 576 LBS.
MSRP $8,285

OPTIONS

2 BAG
3 BAG
MAXTRAX

RETAIL PRICING

YEAR	HIGH	LOW
1998	$1,344	$1,008
1999	$1,491	$1,118
2000	$1,706	$1,280
2001	$1,836	$1,377
2002	$2,036	$1,527
2003	$2,255	$1,691
2004	$2,502	$1,876
2005	$2,777	$2,083
2006	$3,080	$2,310

616SL

YEARS MFRD 1999-2003
ENGINE .... B&S
ENGINE HP 16
FUEL .... G
SPEEDS 0-5.5
TRANSMISSION .... HYDRO
STEERING .... STANDARD
STANDARD DECK .... 44"
MSRP $7,525

OPTIONS

48" DECK

RETAIL PRICING

YEAR	HIGH	LOW
1999	$3,242	$2,431
2000	$3,458	$2,594
2001	$3,675	$2,756
2002	$3,944	$2,958
2003	$4,339	$3,255

616T

YEARS MFRD 2009-2016
ENGINE .... B&S VANGUARD
CYLINDERS 2
ENGINE HP 16
COOLING .... AIR
FUEL .... G
SPEEDS .... VARIABLE
TRANSMISSION ..... DUAL HYDRO
STEERING .... ZERO
BLADE CLUTCH .... ELECTRIC
STANDARD DECK .... 44"
MSRP $9,505

OPTIONS

48" DECK
BAGGER
BLADE
SNOW THROWER

RETAIL PRICING

YEAR	HIGH	LOW
2009	$3,285	$2,464
2010	$3,590	$2,692
2011	$3,972	$2,979
2012	$4,393	$3,295
2013	$4,860	$3,645
2014	$5,375	$4,031
2015	$5,947	$4,460
2016	$7,283	$5,463

616T2

YEARS MFRD 2007-2008
SERIES .... 600 SERIES
ENGINE .... B&S VANGUARD
CYLINDERS 2
ENGINE HP 16
COOLING .... AIR
FUEL .... G
SPEEDS .... VARIABLE
TRANSMISSION .... HYDRO
STEERING .... ZERO
STANDARD DECK .... 44"
MSRP $8,655

OPTIONS

48" DECK

RETAIL PRICING

YEAR	HIGH	LOW
2007	$3,166	$2,375
2008	$3,511	$2,634

618

YEARS MFRD 1998-2006
SERIES .... 600 SERIES
ENGINE .. KOHLER COMMAND OHV
CYLINDERS 2
CID 38
ENGINE HP 18
COOLING .... AIR
FUEL .... G
SPEEDS .... VARIABLE
TRANSMISSION ..... DUAL HYDRO
STEERING .... ZERO
STANDARD DECK .... 44"
WEIGHT .... 685 LBS.
MSRP $8,935

OPTIONS

2 BAG
3 BAG
52" DECK

RETAIL PRICING

YEAR	HIGH	LOW
1998	$1,706	$1,280
1999	$1,895	$1,421
2000	$2,124	$1,593
2001	$2,329	$1,747
2002	$2,585	$1,939
2003	$2,859	$2,144
2004	$3,212	$2,409
2005	$3,565	$2,674
2006	$3,910	$2,933

AVG. AUCTION PRICING

LOW	HIGH	AVG
$830	$2,674	$2,013

618SL

YEARS MFRD 1999-2003
ENGINE .... KOHLER
ENGINE HP 18
FUEL .... G
TRANSMISSION .... HYDRO
STEERING .... STANDARD
STANDARD DECK .... 44"
MSRP $8,015

OPTIONS

48" DECK
52" DECK

RETAIL PRICING

YEAR	HIGH	LOW
1999	$3,536	$2,652
2000	$3,777	$2,833
2001	$4,008	$3,006
2002	$4,198	$3,149
2003	$4,622	$3,466

620T

YEARS MFRD 2009-2013
ENGINE ...... KOHLER COMMAND
CYLINDERS 2
ENGINE HP 20
COOLING .... AIR
FUEL .... G
SPEEDS .... VARIABLE
TRANSMISSION .... HYDRO
STEERING .... ZERO
BLADE CLUTCH .... ELECTRIC
STANDARD DECK .... 48"
MSRP $10,170

OPTIONS

52" DECK
BAGGER
SNOW THROWER

RETAIL PRICING

YEAR	HIGH	LOW
2009	$3,980	$2,985
2010	$4,280	$3,210
2011	$4,760	$3,570
2012	$5,301	$3,976
2013	$5,856	$4,392

620T2

YEARS MFRD 2007-2008
SERIES .... 600 SERIES
ENGINE ...... KOHLER COMMAND
CID 38.1
ENGINE HP 20
COOLING .... AIR
FUEL .... G
SPEEDS .... VARIABLE
TRANSMISSION .... HYDRO
STEERING .... ZERO
STANDARD DECK .... 44"
WEIGHT .... 1,120 LBS.
MSRP $9,210

OPTIONS

48" DECK
52" DECK

RETAIL PRICING

YEAR	HIGH	LOW
2007	$3,439	$2,579
2008	$3,739	$2,804

623T

YEARS MFRD 2014-2020
ENGINE .... KOHLER
CYLINDERS 2
CID 41.1
ENGINE HP 23
COOLING .... AIR
FUEL .... G
SPEEDS .... VARIABLE
TRANSMISSION ..... DUAL HYDRO
STEERING .... ZERO
STANDARD DECK .... 48"
MSRP $11,245

OPTIONS

48" BROOM $2,025
48" DOZER BLADE $1,075
48" SNOW THROWER $1,795
52" DECK $150

RETAIL PRICING

YEAR	HIGH	LOW
2014	$5,433	$4,074
2015	$5,814	$4,360
2016	$6,533	$4,900
2017	$7,114	$5,336
2018	$7,900	$5,925
2019	$8,771	$6,578
2020	$9,809	$7,496

718

YEARS MFRD 1989-2005
SERIES .... 700 SERIES
ENGINE ..... B&S VANGUARD OHV
CYLINDERS 2
CID 34.75
ENGINE HP 18
COOLING .... AIR
FUEL .... G
SPEEDS .... VARIABLE
TRANSMISSION ..... DUAL HYDRO
STEERING .... ZERO
STANDARD DECK .... 48"
WEIGHT .... 720 LBS.
MSRP $9,630

GRASSHOPPER

OPTIONS

2 BAG
3 BAG
61" DECK

RETAIL PRICING

YEAR	HIGH	LOW
1997	$1,714	$1,286
1998	$1,740	$1,305
1999	$1,925	$1,444
2000	$2,131	$1,598
2001	$2,406	$1,804
2002	$2,622	$1,966
2003	$2,909	$2,181
2004	$3,227	$2,420
2005	$3,606	$2,705

718D

YEARS MFRD	1989-1990
ENGINE	KUBOTA
ENGINE HP	16.5
COOLING	LIQUID
FUEL	D
TRANSMISSION	HYDRO
STEERING	ZERO
STANDARD DECK	44"
MSRP	$8,000

OPTIONS

48" SNOW THROWER
52" DECK
61" DECK

RETAIL PRICING

YEAR	HIGH	LOW
1989	$723	$542
1990	$802	$601

718K

YEARS MFRD	1990-1996
ENGINE	KOHLER
ENGINE HP	18
FUEL	G
TRANSMISSION	HYDRO
STEERING	STANDARD
STANDARD DECK	44"
MSRP	$7,555

OPTIONS

52" DECK
61" DECK

RETAIL PRICING

YEAR	HIGH	LOW
1990	$2,012	$1,509
1991	$2,203	$1,652
1992	$2,352	$1,764
1993	$2,494	$1,871
1994	$2,715	$2,036
1995	$2,900	$2,175
1996	$3,076	$2,307

718KH2

YEARS MFRD	2006-2006
SERIES	700 SERIES
ENGINE	KOHLER COMMAND
CYLINDERS	2
ENGINE HP	18
COOLING	AIR
FUEL	G
SPEEDS	VARIABLE
TRANSMISSION	HYDRO
STEERING	ZERO
STANDARD DECK	52"
MSRP	$9,565

RETAIL PRICING

YEAR	HIGH	LOW
2006	$3,556	$2,667

718SL

YEARS MFRD	1999-2003
ENGINE	B&S
ENGINE HP	18
FUEL	G
TRANSMISSION	HYDRO
STEERING	STANDARD
STANDARD DECK	48"
MSRP	$8,700

OPTIONS

52" DECK
61" DECK

RETAIL PRICING

YEAR	HIGH	LOW
1999	$3,860	$2,895
2000	$4,114	$3,086
2001	$4,361	$3,271
2002	$4,559	$3,419
2003	$5,017	$3,762

720

YEARS MFRD	1991-2005
SERIES	700 SERIES
ENGINE	KOHLER COMMAND
CYLINDERS	2
CID	38
ENGINE HP	20
COOLING	AIR
FUEL	G
SPEEDS	VARIABLE
TRANSMISSION	DUAL HYDRO
STEERING	ZERO
STANDARD DECK	61"
WEIGHT	725 LBS.
MSRP	$10,160

OPTIONS

2 BAG
3 BAG
72" DECK

RETAIL PRICING

YEAR	HIGH	LOW
1997	$1,646	$1,235
1998	$1,789	$1,342
1999	$1,986	$1,490
2000	$2,202	$1,652
2001	$2,444	$1,833
2002	$2,723	$2,043
2003	$3,023	$2,267
2004	$3,344	$2,508
2005	$3,700	$2,775

720K

YEARS MFRD	1993-1994
ENGINE	KOHLER
ENGINE HP	20
FUEL	G
TRANSMISSION	HYDRO
STEERING	STANDARD
STANDARD DECK	44"
MSRP	$7,365

OPTIONS

48" DECK
52" DECK
61" DECK
72" DECK

RETAIL PRICING

YEAR	HIGH	LOW
1993	$2,665	$1,998
1994	$2,788	$2,091

720LS

YEARS MFRD	1999-2002
ENGINE	KOHLER
ENGINE HP	20
FUEL	G
TRANSMISSION	HYDRO
STEERING	STANDARD
STANDARD DECK	48"
MSRP	$8,992

OPTIONS

52" DECK

RETAIL PRICING

YEAR	HIGH	LOW
1999	$4,244	$3,183
2000	$4,459	$3,344

720SL

YEARS MFRD	1999-2003
ENGINE	KOHLER
ENGINE HP	20
FUEL	G
TRANSMISSION	HYDRO
STEERING	STANDARD
STANDARD DECK	48"
MSRP	$9,225

OPTIONS

52" DECK
61" DECK

RETAIL PRICING

YEAR	HIGH	LOW
1999	$4,187	$3,140
2000	$4,337	$3,253
2001	$4,631	$3,473
2002	$4,837	$3,628
2003	$5,317	$3,988

721

YEARS MFRD	1989-2001
ENGINE	KUBOTA
ENGINE HP	21
COOLING	LIQUID
FUEL	G
TRANSMISSION	DUAL HYDRO
STEERING	ZERO
STANDARD DECK	61"
MSRP	$10,730

OPTIONS

72" DECK
ROPS
SNOW THROWER

RETAIL PRICING

YEAR	HIGH	LOW
1993	$1,143	$857
1994	$1,268	$951
1995	$1,403	$1,053
1996	$1,561	$1,171
1997	$1,728	$1,296
1998	$1,921	$1,441
1999	$2,128	$1,596
2000	$2,379	$1,785
2001	$2,618	$1,963

721D

YEARS MFRD	1991-2005
SERIES	700 SERIES
ENGINE	KUBOTA OHV
CYLINDERS	3
CID	44
ENGINE HP	20.9
COOLING	LIQUID
FUEL	D
SPEEDS	VARIABLE
TRANSMISSION	HYDRO
STEERING	ZERO
HYDRAULIC	YES
STANDARD DECK	72"
WEIGHT	830 LBS.
MSRP	$12,525

OPTIONS

ROPS
SNOW THROWER

RETAIL PRICING

YEAR	HIGH	LOW
1997	$2,166	$1,624
1998	$2,446	$1,835
1999	$2,708	$2,031
2000	$2,994	$2,245
2001	$3,435	$2,576
2002	$3,632	$2,724
2003	$4,032	$3,024
2004	$4,473	$3,355
2005	$5,040	$3,780

AVG. AUCTION PRICING

LOW	HIGH	AVG
$1,960	$3,528	$2,548

721D2

YEARS MFRD	2000-2004
SERIES	GEMINI 2 SERIES
ENGINE	KUBOTA
CID	44
ENGINE HP	20.9
COOLING	LIQUID
FUEL	G
SPEEDS	VARIABLE
TRANSMISSION	DUAL HYDRO
STEERING	ZERO
STANDARD DECK	72"
WEIGHT	920 LBS.
MSRP	$12,695

OPTIONS

ROPS
SNOW THROWER

RETAIL PRICING

YEAR	HIGH	LOW
2000	$2,818	$2,114
2001	$3,128	$2,346
2002	$3,448	$2,586
2003	$3,858	$2,894
2004	$4,245	$3,184

721D2SL

YEARS MFRD 1999-2003
ENGINE .... KUBOTA
ENGINE HP 20.9
FUEL .... D
TRANSMISSION .... HYDRO
STEERING............ STANDARD
STANDARD DECK .... 48"
MSRP................. $12,255

OPTIONS

52" DECK
61" DECK

RETAIL PRICING

YEAR	HIGH	LOW
1999	$5,620	$4,215
2000	$5,975	$4,481
2001	$6,225	$4,669
2002	$6,505	$4,879
2003	$7,065	$5,299

721DH2

YEARS MFRD 2006-2007
SERIES.............. 700 SERIES
ENGINE .... KUBOTA
CYLINDERS.................... 3
ENGINE HP 22
COOLING .... LIQUID
FUEL .... G
SPEEDS .... VARIABLE
TRANSMISSION .... HYDRO
STEERING.................. ZERO
STANDARD DECK .... 72"
WEIGHT .... 1,442 LBS.
MSRP................. $13,110

OPTIONS

52" DECK
61" DECK

RETAIL PRICING

YEAR	HIGH	LOW
2006	$4,529	$3,396
2007	$4,994	$3,746

721DSL

YEARS MFRD 1999-2003
ENGINE .... KUBOTA
ENGINE HP 20.9
FUEL .... D
TRANSMISSION .... HYDRO
STEERING............ STANDARD
STANDARD DECK .... 48"
MSRP................. $11,469

OPTIONS

52" DECK
61" DECK

RETAIL PRICING

YEAR	HIGH	LOW
1999	$5,241	$3,931
2000	$5,578	$4,184
2001	$5,814	$4,361
2002	$6,086	$4,564
2003	$6,611	$4,958

721DT

YEARS MFRD 2008-2019
ENGINE .... KUBOTA
CYLINDERS.................... 3
ENGINE HP 21
COOLING .... LIQUID
FUEL .... D
SPEEDS .... VARIABLE
TRANSMISSION .... HYDRO
STEERING.................. ZERO
BLADE CLUTCH .... ELECTRIC
STANDARD DECK .... 52"
WEIGHT .... 1,294 LBS.
MSRP................. $15,185

OPTIONS

48" SNOW THROWER
52" RD DECK
60" BLADE
ENCLOSURE

RETAIL PRICING

YEAR	HIGH	LOW
2009	$4,222	$3,166
2010	$4,799	$3,599
2011	$5,244	$3,933
2012	$5,715	$4,287
2013	$6,434	$4,825
2014	$6,993	$5,245
2015	$7,737	$5,803
2016	$8,637	$6,478
2017	$9,466	$7,099
2018	$10,520	$7,890
2019	$11,709	$8,782

721G2

YEARS MFRD 2002-2002
ENGINE .... KUBOTA
ENGINE HP 21
FUEL .... G
TRANSMISSION .... HYDRO
STEERING............ STANDARD
STANDARD DECK .... 48"
MSRP................. $11,665

OPTIONS

52" DECK
61" DECK
72" DECK

RETAIL PRICING

YEAR	HIGH	LOW
2002	$6,202	$4,652

721G2SL

YEARS MFRD 2002-2002
ENGINE .... KUBOTA
ENGINE HP 21
FUEL .... G
TRANSMISSION .... HYDRO
STEERING............ STANDARD
STANDARD DECK .... 48"
MSRP................. $11,915

OPTIONS

52" DECK
61" DECK

RETAIL PRICING

YEAR	HIGH	LOW
2002	$6,335	$4,751

721SL

YEARS MFRD 1999-2001
ENGINE .... KUBOTA
ENGINE HP 21
FUEL .... G
TRANSMISSION .... HYDRO
STEERING............ STANDARD
STANDARD DECK .... 48"
MSRP................. $10,590

OPTIONS

52" DECK
61" DECK

RETAIL PRICING

YEAR	HIGH	LOW
1999	$4,851	$3,638
2000	$5,169	$3,876
2001	$5,478	$4,109

722D2

YEARS MFRD 2005-2007
SERIES.............. 700 SERIES
ENGINE .... KUBOTA OHV
CYLINDERS.................... 3
CID 54.8
ENGINE HP 22
COOLING .... LIQUID
FUEL .... D
SPEEDS .... VARIABLE
TRANSMISSION .... HYDRO
STEERING.................. ZERO
STANDARD DECK .... 72"
MSRP................. $14,485

OPTIONS

52" DECK
61" DECK
BAGGER
SNOW THROWER

RETAIL PRICING

YEAR	HIGH	LOW
2005	$4,665	$3,499
2006	$5,043	$3,782
2007	$5,523	$4,142

723KH2

YEARS MFRD 2006-2007
SERIES.............. 700 SERIES
ENGINE .... KOHLER
CYLINDERS.................... 2
ENGINE HP 23
COOLING .... AIR
FUEL .... G
SPEEDS .... VARIABLE
TRANSMISSION .... HYDRO
STEERING.................. ZERO
STANDARD DECK .... 48"
MSRP................. $10,240

OPTIONS

52" DECK
61" DECK

RETAIL PRICING

YEAR	HIGH	LOW
2006	$3,580	$2,685
2007	$3,946	$2,960

723T

YEARS MFRD 2008-2013
ENGINE .. KOHLER COMMAND PRO
CYLINDERS.................... 2
ENGINE HP 23
COOLING .... AIR
FUEL .... G
SPEEDS .... VARIABLE
TRANSMISSION .... HYDRO
STEERING.................. ZERO
STANDARD DECK .... 48"
WEIGHT .... 1,219 LBS.
MSRP................. $11,305

OPTIONS

52" DECK
61" DECK
BAGGER
SNOW THROWER

RETAIL PRICING

YEAR	HIGH	LOW
2008	$4,072	$3,054
2009	$4,431	$3,323
2010	$4,859	$3,644
2011	$5,407	$4,055
2012	$5,994	$4,495
2013	$6,598	$4,949

725

YEARS MFRD 1991-2002
ENGINE .... KUBOTA
ENGINE HP 24.5
COOLING .... LIQUID
FUEL .... G
SPEEDS .... VARIABLE
TRANSMISSION .... HYDRO
STEERING.................. ZERO
STANDARD DECK .... 72"
MSRP................. $11,685

OPTIONS

BAGGER
BLADE
ROPS
SNOW THROWER

RETAIL PRICING

YEAR	HIGH	LOW
1994	$1,677	$1,258
1995	$1,862	$1,397
1996	$2,064	$1,548
1997	$2,294	$1,721
1998	$2,541	$1,906
1999	$2,820	$2,115
2000	$3,141	$2,356
2001	$3,471	$2,603
2002	$3,994	$2,996

GRASSHOPPER

725A

YEARS MFRD 2004-2004
SERIES............. 700 SERIES
ENGINE ...... KOHLER AEGIS OHV
CYLINDERS.................. 2
ENGINE HP.................. 25
COOLING .... LIQUID
FUEL .... G
SPEEDS .... VARIABLE
TRANSMISSION .... HYDRO
STEERING................ ZERO
STANDARD DECK .... 72"
MSRP................ $11,405

OPTIONS

BAG & FAN
ROPS
SNOW THROWER

RETAIL PRICING

YEAR	HIGH	LOW
2004	$3,450	$2,587

725DT

YEARS MFRD 2009-2020
ENGINE .... KUBOTA MAX
CYLINDERS.................. 3
CID 898CC
ENGINE HP.................. 25
COOLING .... LIQUID
FUEL .... D
SPEEDS .... VARIABLE
TRANSMISSION ..... DUAL HYDRO
STEERING................ ZERO
BLADE CLUTCH .... ELECTRIC
STANDARD DECK .... 52"
MSRP................ $17,165

OPTIONS

48" BLADE............. $1,075
48" SNOW THROWER $1,795
61" DECK................ $330
72" DECK................ $985

RETAIL PRICING

YEAR	HIGH	LOW
2009	$4,932	$3,699
2010	$5,696	$4,186
2011	$5,737	$4,303
2012	$6,499	$4,874
2013	$7,238	$5,428
2014	$8,167	$6,125
2015	$8,762	$6,571
2016	$9,653	$7,240
2017	$10,511	$7,884
2018	$11,684	$8,763
2019	$12,994	$9,746
2020	$14,702	$11,252

725G2

YEARS MFRD 2000-2005
SERIES......... GEMINI 2 SERIES
ENGINE .... KUBOTA
CYLINDERS.................. 3
CID 45.21
ENGINE HP................ 24.5
COOLING .... LIQUID
FUEL .... G
SPEEDS .... VARIABLE
TRANSMISSION .... HYDRO
STEERING................ ZERO
HYDRAULIC .... YES
STANDARD DECK .... 72"
WEIGHT .... 920 LBS.
MSRP................ $13,155

OPTIONS

BLADE
ROPS
SNOW THROWER

RETAIL PRICING

YEAR	HIGH	LOW
2000	$2,793	$2,095
2001	$3,099	$2,324
2002	$3,436	$2,577
2003	$3,814	$2,861
2004	$4,245	$3,184
2005	$4,691	$3,518

725G2SL

YEARS MFRD 1999-2003
ENGINE .... KUBOTA
ENGINE HP................ 24.5
FUEL .... G
TRANSMISSION .... HYDRO
STEERING............ STANDARD
STANDARD DECK .... 48"
MSRP................ $11,945

OPTIONS

52" DECK
61" DECK

RETAIL PRICING

YEAR	HIGH	LOW
1999	$5,467	$4,101
2000	$5,817	$4,363
2001	$6,058	$4,544
2002	$6,335	$4,751
2003	$6,887	$5,166

725K

YEARS MFRD 1997-2001
ENGINE .... KOHLER
ENGINE HP.................. 25
COOLING .... AIR
FUEL .... G
SPEEDS .... VARIABLE
TRANSMISSION ..... DUAL HYDRO
STEERING................ ZERO
STANDARD DECK .... 72"
MSRP................ $10,076

RETAIL PRICING

YEAR	HIGH	LOW
1997	$1,737	$1,302
1998	$1,926	$1,444
1999	$2,137	$1,603
2000	$2,411	$1,808
2001	$2,686	$2,015

725K2

YEARS MFRD 2002-2004
SERIES............. 700 SERIES
ENGINE .... KUBOTA
CYLINDERS.................. 2
CID 44
ENGINE HP.................. 25
COOLING .... AIR
FUEL .... G
SPEEDS .... VARIABLE
TRANSMISSION .... HYDRO
STEERING................ ZERO
STANDARD DECK .... 48"
WEIGHT .... 825 LBS.
MSRP................. $9,765

OPTIONS

52" DECK
61" DECK
72" DECK

RETAIL PRICING

YEAR	HIGH	LOW
2002	$4,319	$3,239
2003	$4,682	$3,512
2004	$5,040	$3,780

725K2LP

YEARS MFRD 2004-2004
SERIES............. 700 SERIES
ENGINE .. KOHLER COMMAND PRO
DUAL FUEL
CYLINDERS.................. 2
ENGINE HP.................. 25
COOLING .... AIR
SPEEDS .... VARIABLE
TRANSMISSION .... HYDRO
STEERING................ ZERO

725K2SL

YEARS MFRD 2002-2003
ENGINE .... KUBOTA
ENGINE HP.................. 25
FUEL .... G
TRANSMISSION .... HYDRO
STEERING............ STANDARD
STANDARD DECK .... 48"
MSRP................. $9,929

OPTIONS

52" DECK
61" DECK

RETAIL PRICING

YEAR	HIGH	LOW
2002	$5,267	$3,950
2003	$5,724	$4,293

725KLP

YEARS MFRD 2002-2003
SERIES............. 700 SERIES
ENGINE ...... KOHLER COMMAND
CYLINDERS.................. 2
CID 44
ENGINE HP.................. 25
COOLING .... AIR
FUEL .... G
SPEEDS .... VARIABLE
TRANSMISSION .... HYDRO
STEERING............ STANDARD
STANDARD DECK .... 48"
WEIGHT .... 800 LBS.
MSRP................ $10,661

OPTIONS

52" DECK
61" DECK
72" DECK

RETAIL PRICING

YEAR	HIGH	LOW
2002	$5,668	$4,251
2003	$6,146	$4,609

725KLPSL

YEARS MFRD 2002-2003
ENGINE .... KOHLER
ENGINE HP.................. 25
FUEL .... G
TRANSMISSION .... HYDRO
STEERING............ STANDARD
STANDARD DECK .... 48"
MSRP................ $10,990

OPTIONS

52" DECK
61" DECK

RETAIL PRICING

YEAR	HIGH	LOW
2002	$5,801	$4,350
2003	$5,906	$4,430

725KSL

YEARS MFRD 1999-2001
ENGINE .... KOHLER
ENGINE HP.................. 25
FUEL .... G
TRANSMISSION .... HYDRO
STEERING............ STANDARD
STANDARD DECK .... 48"
MSRP................. $9,540

OPTIONS

52" DECK
61" DECK

RETAIL PRICING

YEAR	HIGH	LOW
1999	$4,380	$3,285
2000	$4,660	$3,495
2001	$4,933	$3,700

725KT

YEARS MFRD 2014-2020
ENGINE .... KOHLER
CYLINDERS.................. 2
CID 747CC
ENGINE HP.................. 25
COOLING .... AIR
FUEL .... G
SPEEDS .... VARIABLE
TRANSMISSION .... HYDRO
STEERING................ ZERO
STANDARD DECK .... 52"
MSRP................ $13,140

OPTIONS

48" DOZER BLADE $1,075
48" SNOW THROWER $1,795
61" DECK................ $690
72" DECK................ $910

RETAIL PRICING

YEAR	HIGH	LOW
2014	$6,061	$4,546
2015	$6,669	$5,001
2016	$7,294	$5,470
2017	$8,068	$6,051
2018	$8,964	$6,722
2019	$9,968	$7,476
2020	$11,021	$8,334

725SL

YEARS MFRD 1999-2002
ENGINE . . . . KUBOTA
ENGINE HP 24.5
FUEL . . . . G
TRANSMISSION . . . . .HYDRO
STEERING. . . . . .STANDARD
STANDARD DECK . . . . 48"
MSRP. $11,095

OPTIONS

52" DECK
61" DECK

RETAIL PRICING

YEAR	HIGH	LOW
1999	$5,088	$3,816
2000	$5,417	$4,063
2001	$5,644	$4,233
2002	$5,900	$4,425

727A

YEARS MFRD 2003-2003
ENGINE . . . . KOHLER AEGIS
CID 45.6
ENGINE HP 27
COOLING . . . . LIQUID
FUEL . . . . G
TRANSMISSION . . . . .HYDRO
STANDARD DECK . . . . 61"
WEIGHT . . . . 880 LBS.
MSRP. $10,905

OPTIONS

72" DECK

RETAIL PRICING

YEAR	HIGH	LOW
2003	$3,743	$2,807

727K2

YEARS MFRD 2005-2008
SERIES. . . . . 700 SERIES
ENGINE . . . . KOHLER
CYLINDERS. 2
ENGINE HP 27
COOLING . . . . AIR
FUEL . . . . G
SPEEDS . . . . .VARIABLE
TRANSMISSION . . . . .HYDRO
STEERING. . . . . .ZERO
STANDARD DECK . . . . 72"
MSRP. $12,240

OPTIONS

BAGGER
SNOW THROWER

RETAIL PRICING

YEAR	HIGH	LOW
2005	$3,973	$2,980
2006	$4,411	$3,308
2007	$4,790	$3,593
2008	$5,293	$3,970

727KW

YEARS MFRD 2005-2006
ENGINE . . . . KAWASAKI
CYLINDERS. 2
ENGINE HP 27
COOLING . . . . LIQUID
FUEL . . . . G
SPEEDS . . . . .VARIABLE
TRANSMISSION . . . . .HYDRO
STEERING. . . . . .ZERO
STANDARD DECK . . . . 61"
MSRP. $11,825

OPTIONS

3 BAG
72" DECK
SNOW THROWER

RETAIL PRICING

YEAR	HIGH	LOW
2005	$4,004	$3,003
2006	$4,441	$3,331

727T

YEARS MFRD 2009-2020
ENGINE KOHLER COMMAND PRO EFI
CYLINDERS. 2
CID 747CC
ENGINE HP 27
COOLING . . . . AIR
FUEL . . . . G
SPEEDS . . . . .VARIABLE
TRANSMISSION . . . . .HYDRO
STEERING. . . . . .ZERO
BLADE CLUTCH . . . . .ELECTRIC
STANDARD DECK . . . . 52"
MSRP. $14,155

OPTIONS

48" SNOW THROWER $1,795
60" BROOM $2,275
61" DECK. $495
72" DECK. $985

RETAIL PRICING

YEAR	HIGH	LOW
2009	$3,929	$2,946
2010	$4,245	$3,184
2011	$4,801	$3,601
2012	$5,346	$4,010
2013	$5,815	$4,361
2014	$6,375	$4,781
2015	$7,083	$5,312
2016	$7,777	$5,832
2017	$8,604	$6,453
2018	$9,580	$7,185
2019	$10,658	$7,993
2020	$11,941	$9,059

729

YEARS MFRD 2008-2008
SERIES. . . . . 700 SERIES
ENGINE . . . . KUBOTA
CYLINDERS. 3
ENGINE HP 29
COOLING . . . . LIQUID
FUEL . . . . G
SPEEDS . . . . .VARIABLE
TRANSMISSION . . . . .HYDRO
STEERING. . . . . .ZERO
STANDARD DECK . . . . 72"
MSRP. $14,425

OPTIONS

BAGGER
SNOW THROWER

RETAIL PRICING

YEAR	HIGH	LOW
2008	$5,994	$4,495

729BT

YEARS MFRD 2009-2020
ENGINE . . . . B&S
CYLINDERS. 2
CID 896CC
ENGINE HP 29
COOLING . . . . AIR
FUEL . . . . G
SPEEDS . . . . .VARIABLE
TRANSMISSION . . . . . DUAL HYDRO
STEERING. . . . . .ZERO
BLADE CLUTCH . . . . .ELECTRIC
STANDARD DECK . . . . 52"
MSRP. $13,700

OPTIONS

48" BROOM $2,025
48" SNOW THROWER $1,795
61" DECK. $495
72" DECK. $985

RETAIL PRICING

YEAR	HIGH	LOW
2009	$3,715	$2,786
2010	$4,109	$3,082
2011	$4,547	$3,410
2012	$5,027	$3,771
2013	$5,561	$4,171
2014	$6,214	$4,660
2015	$6,807	$5,105
2016	$7,529	$5,647
2017	$8,329	$6,246
2018	$9,254	$6,940
2019	$10,283	$7,712
2020	$11,508	$8,539

729G2

YEARS MFRD 2006-2007
ENGINE . . . . KUBOTA
CYLINDERS. 3
ENGINE HP 29
COOLING . . . . LIQUID
FUEL . . . . G
SPEEDS . . . . .VARIABLE
TRANSMISSION . . . . .HYDRO
STEERING. . . . . .ZERO
BLADE CLUTCH . . . . .ELECTRIC
STANDARD DECK . . . . 61"
MSRP. $13,680

OPTIONS

72" DECK
BLADE
SNOW THROWER

RETAIL PRICING

YEAR	HIGH	LOW
2006	$5,387	$4,040
2007	$6,112	$4,584

729T

YEARS MFRD 2009-2020
ENGINE . . . . KUBOTA
CYLINDERS. 3
CID 962CC
ENGINE HP 29
COOLING . . . . LIQUID
FUEL . . . . G
SPEEDS . . . . .VARIABLE
TRANSMISSION . . . . . DUAL HYDRO
STEERING. . . . . .ZERO
BLADE CLUTCH . . . . .ELECTRIC
STANDARD DECK . . . . 52"
MSRP. $16,675

OPTIONS

48" BROOM $2,025
48" SNOW THROWER $1,795
61" DECK. $330
72" DECK. $985

RETAIL PRICING

YEAR	HIGH	LOW
2009	$4,549	$3,412
2010	$5,222	$3,917
2011	$5,709	$4,281
2012	$6,444	$4,833
2013	$6,812	$5,109
2014	$7,536	$5,652
2015	$8,336	$6,252
2016	$9,222	$6,916
2017	$10,202	$7,651
2018	$11,330	$8,498
2019	$12,590	$9,442
2020	$14,073	$10,654

735BT

YEARS MFRD 2009-2020
ENGINE . . . . B&S
CYLINDERS. 2
CID 993CC
ENGINE HP 35
COOLING . . . . AIR
FUEL . . . . G
SPEEDS . . . . .VARIABLE
TRANSMISSION . . . . . DUAL HYDRO
STEERING. . . . . .ZERO
BLADE CLUTCH . . . . .ELECTRIC
STANDARD DECK . . . . 61"
MSRP. $14,890

OPTIONS

48" BROOM $2,025
48" SNOW THROWER $1,795
52" DECK
72" DECK. $490

RETAIL PRICING

YEAR	HIGH	LOW
2009	$3,911	$2,933
2010	$4,326	$3,245
2011	$4,785	$3,588
2012	$5,293	$3,969
2013	$5,856	$4,392
2014	$6,479	$4,859

GRASSHOPPER

YEAR	HIGH	LOW
2015	$7,166	$5,375
2016	$7,928	$5,945
2017	$8,769	$6,576
2018	$9,732	$7,299
2019	$10,791	$8,093
2020	$12,215	$9,344

900D

YEARS MFRD 2018-2020
ENGINE KUBOTA
CYLINDERS 3
CID 1.3L
COOLING LIQUID
FUEL D
TRANSMISSION HYDRO
STEERING ZERO
STANDARD DECK 61"
WEIGHT 1,595 LBS.
MSRP $21,240

OPTIONS

72" DECK $345
ENCLOSURE $3,450

928D

YEARS MFRD 1995-1999
ENGINE KUBOTA
CID 68.58
ENGINE HP 28
COOLING LIQUID
FUEL D
TRANSMISSION HYDRO
STEERING ZERO
STANDARD DECK 61"
WEIGHT 1,090 LBS.
MSRP $14,860

OPTIONS

72" DECK
ROPS
SNOW THROWER

RETAIL PRICING

YEAR	HIGH	LOW
1995	$2,352	$1,764
1996	$2,609	$1,957
1997	$2,892	$2,169
1998	$3,212	$2,409
1999	$3,607	$2,706

928D2

YEARS MFRD 2000-2008
SERIES GEMINI 2 SERIES
ENGINE KUBOTA OHV
CYLINDERS 3
ENGINE HP 28
COOLING LIQUID
FUEL D
SPEEDS VARIABLE
TRANSMISSION DUAL HYDRO
STEERING ZERO
HYDRAULIC YES
STANDARD DECK 72"
MSRP $17,440

OPTIONS

BLADE
SNOW THROWER

RETAIL PRICING

YEAR	HIGH	LOW
2000	$3,030	$2,273
2001	$3,360	$2,520
2002	$3,727	$2,795
2003	$4,129	$3,097
2004	$4,589	$3,442
2005	$5,062	$3,796
2006	$5,675	$4,256
2007	$6,307	$4,730
2008	$6,875	$5,156

928D2SL

YEARS MFRD 1999-2003
ENGINE KUBOTA
ENGINE HP 28
FUEL D
TRANSMISSION HYDRO
STEERING STANDARD
STANDARD DECK 52"
MSRP $15,400

OPTIONS

61" DECK

RETAIL PRICING

YEAR	HIGH	LOW
1999	$7,068	$5,301
2000	$7,494	$5,621
2001	$7,806	$5,854
2002	$8,172	$6,129
2003	$8,879	$6,659

930D

YEARS MFRD 2009-2014
SERIES 900 SERIES
ENGINE KUBOTA
CYLINDERS 3
ENGINE HP 30
COOLING AIR
FUEL D
SPEEDS VARIABLE
TRANSMISSION HYDRO
STEERING ZERO
BLADE CLUTCH ELECTRIC
STANDARD DECK 52"
MSRP $19,210

OPTIONS

61" DECK
72" DECK
BAGGER
SNOW THROWER

RETAIL PRICING

YEAR	HIGH	LOW
2009	$6,891	$5,169
2010	$7,712	$5,784
2011	$8,610	$6,458
2012	$9,528	$7,146
2013	$10,433	$7,825
2014	$12,954	$9,715

932

YEARS MFRD 2002-2005
SERIES 900 SERIES
ENGINE KUBOTA OHV
CYLINDERS 3
CID 60.80
ENGINE HP 32
COOLING LIQUID
FUEL G
SPEEDS VARIABLE
TRANSMISSION HYDRO
STEERING ZERO
STANDARD DECK 61"
WEIGHT 1,090 LBS.
MSRP $16,025

OPTIONS

72" DECK
ROPS
SNOW THROWER

RETAIL PRICING

YEAR	HIGH	LOW
2002	$3,655	$2,742
2003	$4,052	$3,039
2004	$4,498	$3,374
2005	$4,987	$3,740

932G2

YEARS MFRD 2006-2020
ENGINE KUBOTA
CYLINDERS 3
CID 962CC
ENGINE HP 32
COOLING LIQUID
FUEL G
SPEEDS VARIABLE
TRANSMISSION HYDRO
STEERING ZERO
STANDARD DECK 72"
MSRP $19,460

OPTIONS

48" BLADE $1,075
48" SNOW THROWER $1,795
61" DECK $-345
72" DECK RD $460

RETAIL PRICING

YEAR	HIGH	LOW
2006	$4,199	$3,149
2007	$4,418	$3,313
2008	$4,665	$3,499
2009	$5,298	$3,973
2010	$5,862	$4,396
2011	$6,484	$4,863
2012	$7,173	$5,380
2013	$7,935	$5,950
2014	$8,778	$6,583
2015	$9,771	$7,328
2016	$10,741	$8,056
2017	$11,881	$8,911
2018	$13,210	$9,907
2019	$14,705	$11,028
2020	$16,583	$12,684

932SL

YEARS MFRD 2002-2003
ENGINE KUBOTA
ENGINE HP 32
FUEL G
TRANSMISSION HYDRO
STEERING STANDARD
STANDARD DECK 52"
MSRP $15,310

OPTIONS

61" DECK

RETAIL PRICING

YEAR	HIGH	LOW
2002	$2,890	$2,168
2003	$3,253	$2,439

937 EFI

YEARS MFRD 2020-2020
ENGINE VANGUARD BIG BLOCK
CID 993CC
COOLING AIR
FUEL G
SPEEDS VARIABLE
TRANSMISSION HYDRO
STEERING ZERO
ROPS/CAB ROPS
STANDARD DECK 61"
WEIGHT 1,585 LBS.
MSRP $16,470

OPTIONS

72" DECK

1212

YEARS MFRD 1987-1990
ENGINE KOHLER
ENGINE HP 12
COOLING AIR
FUEL G
TRANSMISSION HYDRO
STEERING ZERO
STANDARD DECK 44"
MSRP $4,800

OPTIONS

BAGGER

RETAIL PRICING

YEAR	HIGH	LOW
1987	$323	$243
1988	$365	$273
1989	$399	$299
1990	$446	$334

GRAVELY

ALL MODELS

YEARS MFRD NA-1991

SERIAL NUMBERS

YEAR	BEGINNING NO.
1975	200000
1976	205039
1977	259009
1978	311672
1979	372211
1979	5001100
1979	1600000
1979	500001
1979	5006751
1980	5005784
1980	1620000

1980	5018442
1980	504959
1980	514751
1980	5000001
1981	510010
1981	5037379
1981	520274
1982	5058285
1982	533769
1983	5071796
1983	543774
1984	5087909
1984	557707
1985	5108709
1985	567266
1986	5126612
1986	578485
1987	5147058
1987	590275
1988	5165160
1988	601532
1989	5182986
1989	611992
1990	5196083
1990	624538
1991	5199998
1991	633888

ATM70C

YEARS MFRD 1996-1997
ENGINE .... KOHLER
ENGINE HP 20
FUEL .... G
TRANSMISSION .... HYDRO
STEERING .... STANDARD
STANDARD DECK .... 70"
MSRP $17,539

RETAIL PRICING

YEAR	HIGH	LOW
1996	$6,087	$4,565
1997	$6,315	$4,736

ATM72

YEARS MFRD 1996-1997
ENGINE HP 27
FUEL .... D
TRANSMISSION .... HYDRO
STEERING .... STANDARD
STANDARD DECK .... 72"
MSRP $25,099

RETAIL PRICING

YEAR	HIGH	LOW
1996	$8,712	$6,534
1997	$9,039	$6,779

COMPACT-PRO 34

YEARS MFRD 2019-2020
ENGINE .... KAWASAKI FX481V
CID 603CC
ENGINE HP 15.5
FUEL .... G
SPEEDS .... VARIABLE
TRANSMISSION .... HYDRO
STEERING .... ZERO
BLADE CLUTCH .... ELECTRIC
STANDARD DECK .... 34"
WEIGHT .... 737 LBS.
MSRP $6,873

COMPACT-PRO 44

YEARS MFRD 2019-2020
ENGINE .... KAWASAKI FX600V
CID 603CC
ENGINE HP 19
FUEL .... G
SPEEDS .... VARIABLE
TRANSMISSION .... HYDRO
STEERING .... ZERO
BLADE CLUTCH .... ELECTRIC
STANDARD DECK .... 44"
WEIGHT .... 789 LBS.
MSRP $7,533

GEM16

YEARS MFRD 1991-1995
SERIES .... ESTATE SERIES
ENGINE .... B&S
ENGINE HP 16
FUEL .... G
TRANSMISSION .... HYDRO
STEERING .... STANDARD
STANDARD DECK .... 50"
MSRP $4,998

RETAIL PRICING

YEAR	HIGH	LOW
1991	$1,095	$821
1992	$1,199	$899
1993	$1,389	$1,041
1994	$1,645	$1,234
1995	$1,675	$1,256

GLT440

YEARS MFRD 2000-2000
SERIES .... GLT SERIES
ENGINE .... KOHLER
ENGINE HP 15
COOLING .... AIR
FUEL .... G
SPEEDS .... VARIABLE
TRANSMISSION .... HYDRO
STEERING .... STANDARD
STANDARD DECK .... 40"
MSRP $2,499

OPTIONS

3 BAG
36" SNOW THROWER
42" BLADE

SERIAL NUMBERS

YEAR	BEGINNING NO.
2000	000270

RETAIL PRICING

YEAR	HIGH	LOW
2000	$315	$236

GLT448

YEARS MFRD 2000-2000
SERIES .... GLT SERIES
ENGINE .... B&S
ENGINE HP 16
FUEL .... G
SPEEDS .... VARIABLE
TRANSMISSION .... HYDRO
STEERING .... STANDARD
STANDARD DECK .... 48"
MSRP $3,499

OPTIONS

3 BAG
36" SNOW THROWER
42" BLADE

SERIAL NUMBERS

YEAR	BEGINNING NO.
2000	000330

RETAIL PRICING

YEAR	HIGH	LOW
2000	$408	$306

GLT548

YEARS MFRD 2000-2000
SERIES .... GLT SERIES
ENGINE .... B&S
ENGINE HP 22
FUEL .... G
SPEEDS .... VARIABLE
TRANSMISSION .... HYDRO
STEERING .... STANDARD
STANDARD DECK .... 48"
MSRP $4,259

OPTIONS

40" SNOW THROWER
42" BLADE

SERIAL NUMBERS

YEAR	BEGINNING NO.
2000	000101

RETAIL PRICING

YEAR	HIGH	LOW
2000	$496	$372

GT600

YEARS MFRD 2000-2000
SERIES .... GT SERIES
ENGINE .... KOHLER
ENGINE HP 22
FUEL .... G
SPEEDS .... VARIABLE
TRANSMISSION .... HYDRO
STEERING .... STANDARD
STANDARD DECK .... 60"
MSRP $8,758

OPTIONS

42" TILLER
48" SNOW THROWER
BAG & VAC

RETAIL PRICING

YEAR	HIGH	LOW
2000	$1,021	$766

HD PRO18

YEARS MFRD 1990-1992
ENGINE .... KOHLER
ENGINE HP 18
FUEL .... G
TRANSMISSION .... GEAR
WEIGHT .... 427 LBS.
MSRP $3,075

RETAIL PRICING

YEAR	HIGH	LOW
1990	$760	$570
1991	$852	$639
1992	$911	$684

MZ1434ZT

YEARS MFRD 2005-2005
ENGINE .... B&S INTEK
ENGINE HP 14
COOLING .... AIR
FUEL .... G
SPEEDS .... VARIABLE
TRANSMISSION .... HYDRO
STEERING .... ZERO
STANDARD DECK .... 34"
MSRP $2,299

OPTIONS

15 GAL
3 BAG

RETAIL PRICING

YEAR	HIGH	LOW
2005	$771	$578

MZ1534ZT

YEARS MFRD 2005-2006
ENGINE .... KOHLER
ENGINE HP 15
COOLING .... AIR
FUEL .... G
SPEEDS .... VARIABLE
TRANSMISSION .... HYDRO
STEERING .... ZERO
STANDARD DECK .... 34"
MSRP $2,699

OPTIONS

15 GAL
2 BAG & FAN
B&S 15HP

RETAIL PRICING

YEAR	HIGH	LOW
2005	$813	$610
2006	$906	$679

MZ1540ZT

YEARS MFRD 2005-2006
ENGINE .... KOHLER
ENGINE HP 15
COOLING .... AIR
FUEL .... G
SPEEDS .... VARIABLE
TRANSMISSION .... HYDRO
STEERING .... ZERO
STANDARD DECK .... 40"
MSRP $3,099

GRAVELY

OPTIONS

15 GAL
3 BAG

RETAIL PRICING

YEAR	HIGH	LOW
2005	$937	$703
2006	$1,039	$779

PM20H

YEARS MFRD 1990-1992
SERIES . . . . PROMASTER SERIES
ENGINE . . . . ONAN TWIN
ENGINE HP 20
FUEL . . . . G
TRANSMISSION . . . . HYDRO
STANDARD DECK . . . . 50"
WEIGHT . . . . 830 LBS.
MSRP. $5,199

OPTIONS

KOHLER MAGNUM 20HP

RETAIL PRICING

YEAR	HIGH	LOW
1990	$1,294	$970
1991	$1,479	$1,109
1992	$1,695	$1,272

PM30H

YEARS MFRD 1990-1992
SERIES . . . . PROMASTER SERIES
ENGINE . . . . YANMAR
ENGINE HP 30
COOLING . . . . LIQUID
FUEL . . . . D
TRANSMISSION . . . . HYDRO
STEERING. . . . . ZERO
STANDARD DECK . . . . 50"
WEIGHT . . . . 1,400 LBS.
MSRP. $12,000

OPTIONS

72" DECK

SERIAL NUMBERS

YEAR	BEGINNING NO.
1990	5196083
1990	624538
1991	6338888
1991	5199998

RETAIL PRICING

YEAR	HIGH	LOW
1990	$3,200	$2,400
1991	$3,612	$2,709
1992	$4,278	$3,208

PM34Z

YEARS MFRD 2004-2006
SERIES . . . . PROMASTER SERIES
ENGINE . . . . KAWASAKI V-TWIN
CYLINDERS. 2
ENGINE HP 15
COOLING . . . . AIR
FUEL . . . . G
SPEEDS . . . . VARIABLE
TRANSMISSION . . . . HYDRO
STEERING. . . . . ZERO
STANDARD DECK . . . . 34"
WEIGHT . . . . 725 LBS.
MSRP. $4,899

RETAIL PRICING

YEAR	HIGH	LOW
2004	$2,301	$1,726
2005	$2,747	$2,060
2006	$2,875	$2,156

PM44Z

YEARS MFRD 2005-2006
SERIES . . . . PROMASTER SERIES
ENGINE . . . . KAWASAKI
CYLINDERS. 2
ENGINE HP 17
COOLING . . . . AIR
FUEL . . . . G
SPEEDS . . . . VARIABLE
TRANSMISSION . . . . HYDRO
STEERING. . . . . ZERO
STANDARD DECK . . . . 44"
MSRP. $5,499

RETAIL PRICING

YEAR	HIGH	LOW
2005	$3,121	$2,341
2006	$3,227	$2,420

PM144Z

YEARS MFRD 2004-2005
SERIES . . . . PROMASTER SERIES
ENGINE . . . . KAWASAKI
CYLINDERS. 2
ENGINE HP 19
FUEL . . . . G
SPEEDS . . . . VARIABLE
TRANSMISSION . . . . HYDRO
STEERING. . . . . ZERO
STANDARD DECK . . . . 44"
MSRP. $6,599

OPTIONS

KAWASAKI 17HP

RETAIL PRICING

YEAR	HIGH	LOW
2004	$3,452	$2,589
2005	$3,617	$2,713

PM148ZHQ

YEARS MFRD 2003-2006
SERIES . . . . PROMASTER SERIES
ENGINE . . . . KAWASAKI V-TWIN
CYLINDERS. 2
ENGINE HP 21
COOLING . . . . AIR
FUEL . . . . G
SPEEDS . . . . VARIABLE
TRANSMISSION . . . . HYDRO
STEERING. . . . . ZERO
HYDRAULIC . . . . YES
STANDARD DECK . . . . 48"
MSRP. $7,399

RETAIL PRICING

YEAR	HIGH	LOW
2003	$3,292	$2,469
2004	$3,681	$2,761
2005	$4,141	$3,105
2006	$4,339	$3,255

PM152Z

YEARS MFRD 2003-2005
SERIES . . . . PROMASTER SERIES
ENGINE . . . . KAWASAKI
CYLINDERS. 2
ENGINE HP 23
COOLING . . . . AIR
FUEL . . . . G
SPEEDS . . . . VARIABLE
TRANSMISSION . . . . HYDRO
STEERING. . . . . ZERO
STANDARD DECK . . . . 52"
MSRP. $7,138

OPTIONS

KOHLER 25HP

RETAIL PRICING

YEAR	HIGH	LOW
2003	$3,538	$2,653
2004	$3,735	$2,801
2005	$4,162	$3,122

PM160Z

YEARS MFRD 2003-2006
SERIES . . . . PROMASTER SERIES
ENGINE . . . . KAWASAKI
CYLINDERS. 2
ENGINE HP 23
COOLING . . . . AIR
FUEL . . . . G
SPEEDS . . . . VARIABLE
TRANSMISSION . . . . HYDRO
STEERING. . . . . ZERO
STANDARD DECK . . . . 60"
MSRP. $8,099

OPTIONS

KOHLER 25HP

RETAIL PRICING

YEAR	HIGH	LOW
2003	$3,736	$2,802
2004	$4,081	$3,061
2005	$4,571	$3,428
2006	$4,751	$3,563

PM250Z

YEARS MFRD 2000-2001
SERIES . . . . PROMASTER SERIES
ENGINE . . . . B&S
ENGINE HP 20
COOLING . . . . AIR
FUEL . . . . G
TRANSMISSION . . . . HYDRO
STEERING. . . . . ZERO
STANDARD DECK . . . . 50"
MSRP. $7,249

OPTIONS

BAGGER
KAWASAKI 19HP
ROPS

SERIAL NUMBERS

YEAR	BEGINNING NO.
2000	000101

RETAIL PRICING

YEAR	HIGH	LOW
2000	$1,418	$1,064
2001	$1,576	$1,182

PM252Z

YEARS MFRD 2003-2005
SERIES . . . . PROMASTER SERIES
ENGINE . . . . KAWASAKI
CYLINDERS. 2
ENGINE HP 25
COOLING . . . . AIR
FUEL . . . . G
SPEEDS . . . . VARIABLE
TRANSMISSION . . . . HYDRO
STEERING. . . . . ZERO
STANDARD DECK . . . . 52"
WEIGHT . . . . 1,050 LBS.
MSRP. $8,199

OPTIONS

KAWASAKI 26HP
KOHLER 27HP

RETAIL PRICING

YEAR	HIGH	LOW
2003	$3,932	$2,949
2004	$4,289	$3,217
2005	$4,742	$3,557

PM260H

YEARS MFRD 2010-2016
SERIES . . . . PROMASTER SERIES
ENGINE . . . . KAWASAKI FX850V
CID 852CC
ENGINE HP 27
COOLING . . . . AIR
FUEL . . . . G
SPEEDS . . . . VARIABLE
TRANSMISSION . . . . HYDRO
STEERING. . . . . ZERO
BLADE CLUTCH . . . . ELECTRIC
STANDARD DECK . . . . 60"
MSRP. $12,299

OPTIONS

3 BAG & FAN
BLADE
HOPPER BAG
SNOW BLOWER

RETAIL PRICING

YEAR	HIGH	LOW
2010	$4,828	$3,621
2011	$5,351	$4,013
2012	$5,935	$4,451
2013	$6,580	$4,935
2014	$7,293	$5,470
2015	$8,086	$6,064
2016	$9,970	$7,477

PM260H DSL

YEARS MFRD 2010-2012
SERIES . . . . PROMASTER SERIES
ENGINE . . . . DAIHATSU
ENGINE HP 27
COOLING . . . . LIQUID
FUEL . . . . D
SPEEDS . . . . VARIABLE
TRANSMISSION . . . . HYDRO
STEERING. . . . . ZERO
STANDARD DECK . . . . 60"
MSRP. $15,299

OPTIONS

3 BAG & FAN
BLADE
HPPR BAG
SNOW BLOWER

RETAIL PRICING

YEAR	HIGH	LOW
2010	$7,062	$5,296
2011	$7,844	$5,883
2012	$8,711	$6,533

PM260Z

YEARS MFRD 1999-2001
SERIES . . . . PROMASTER SERIES
ENGINE . . . . KAWASAKI
CYLINDERS 2
ENGINE HP 25
COOLING . . . . AIR
FUEL . . . . G
SPEEDS . . . . VARIABLE
TRANSMISSION . . . . HYDRO
STEERING . . . . ZERO
STANDARD DECK . . . . 60"
WEIGHT . . . . 1,125 LBS.
MSRP $8,399

OPTIONS

BAGGER
DAIHATSU 27HP
KOHLER 27HP

RETAIL PRICING

YEAR	HIGH	LOW
1999	$1,482	$1,111
2000	$1,643	$1,233
2001	$1,825	$1,369

AVG. AUCTION PRICING

LOW	HIGH	AVG
$4,606	$4,900	$4,736

PM270Z

YEARS MFRD 2000-2000
SERIES . . . . PROMASTER SERIES
ENGINE . . . . YANMAR
ENGINE HP 20
COOLING . . . . LIQUID
FUEL . . . . G
TRANSMISSION . . . . HYDRO
STEERING . . . . ZERO
STANDARD DECK . . . . 60"
MSRP $10,699

OPTIONS

BAGGER

SERIAL NUMBERS

YEAR . . . . BEGINNING NO.
2000 000101

RETAIL PRICING

YEAR	HIGH	LOW
2000	$2,328	$1,746

PM272Z

YEARS MFRD 2002-2006
SERIES . . . . PROMASTER SERIES
ENGINE . . . . . DAIHATSU TURBO LC
CYLINDERS 3
ENGINE HP 31
FUEL . . . . D
SPEEDS . . . . VARIABLE
TRANSMISSION . . . . HYDRO
STEERING . . . . ZERO
HYDRAULIC . . . . YES
STANDARD DECK . . . . 72"
MSRP $14,399

OPTIONS

KAWASAKI 26HP
KOHLER 28HP

RETAIL PRICING

YEAR	HIGH	LOW
2002	$4,079	$3,059
2003	$4,572	$3,429
2004	$7,534	$5,651
2005	$8,078	$6,059
2006	$8,223	$6,167

AVG. AUCTION PRICING

LOW	HIGH	AVG
$4,998	$6,125	$5,520

PM300

YEARS MFRD 2000-2000
SERIES . . . . PM SERIES
ENGINE . . . . B&S
ENGINE HP 20
COOLING . . . . AIR
FUEL . . . . G
SPEEDS . . . . VARIABLE
TRANSMISSION . . . . HYDRO
STEERING . . . . STANDARD
STANDARD DECK . . . . 50"
MSRP $5,329

OPTIONS

BAGGER
KOHLER 25HP

SERIAL NUMBERS

YEAR . . . . BEGINNING NO.
2000 . . . . 000101-B&S
2000 . . . . 0010000-K

RETAIL PRICING

YEAR	HIGH	LOW
2000	$1,101	$825

PM310

YEARS MFRD 2001-2003
SERIES . . . . PM SERIES
ENGINE . . KOHLER COMMAND PRO
ENGINE HP 27
COOLING . . . . AIR
FUEL . . . . G
TRANSMISSION . . . . HYDRO
STEERING . . . . ZERO
STANDARD DECK . . . . 60"
WEIGHT . . . . 684 LBS.
MSRP $8,048

OPTIONS

72" DECK
BAGGER
KAWASAKI 23HP

RETAIL PRICING

YEAR	HIGH	LOW
2001	$1,687	$1,265
2002	$1,869	$1,402
2003	$2,075	$1,556

PM320HD

YEARS MFRD 2004-2007
SERIES . . . . PROMASTER SERIES
ENGINE . . . . KAWASAKI
CYLINDERS 2
ENGINE HP 25
COOLING . . . . AIR
FUEL . . . . G
SPEEDS . . . . VARIABLE
TRANSMISSION . . . . HYDRO
STEERING . . . . ZERO
HYDRAULIC . . . . YES
STANDARD DECK . . . . 60"
MSRP $9,869

OPTIONS

72" DECK
BAGGER

RETAIL PRICING

YEAR	HIGH	LOW
2004	$2,664	$1,998
2005	$2,956	$2,217
2006	$3,281	$2,461
2007	$3,636	$2,727

PM320 HD-24.5

YEARS MFRD 2012-2013
ENGINE . . . . KAWASAKI
ENGINE HP 24.5
COOLING . . . . AIR
FUEL . . . . G
SPEEDS . . . . VARIABLE
TRANSMISSION . . . . HYDRO
STEERING . . . . ZERO
BLADE CLUTCH . . . . ELECTRIC
STANDARD DECK . . . . 60"
MSRP $12,088

OPTIONS

BAGGER

RETAIL PRICING

YEAR	HIGH	LOW
2012	$6,643	$4,983
2013	$7,371	$5,528

PM360D

YEARS MFRD 2000-2000
SERIES . . . . PROMASTER SERIES
ENGINE . . . . YANMAR
ENGINE HP 22
COOLING . . . . LIQUID
FUEL . . . . D
TRANSMISSION . . . . HYDRO
STEERING . . . . ZERO
STANDARD DECK . . . . 60"
MSRP $11,248

SERIAL NUMBERS

YEAR . . . . BEGINNING NO.
2000 000360

RETAIL PRICING

YEAR	HIGH	LOW
2000	$2,304	$1,728

PM360G

YEARS MFRD 2000-2000
SERIES . . . . PROMASTER SERIES
ENGINE . . . . KAWASAKI
ENGINE HP 22
FUEL . . . . G
SPEEDS . . . . VARIABLE
TRANSMISSION . . . . HYDRO
STEERING . . . . ZERO
STANDARD DECK . . . . 60"
MSRP $10,498

SERIAL NUMBERS

YEAR . . . . BEGINNING NO.
2000 000140

RETAIL PRICING

YEAR	HIGH	LOW
2000	$2,150	$1,613

PM400

YEARS MFRD 1995-2000
SERIES . . . . PROMASTER SERIES
ENGINE . . . . KUBOTA
ENGINE HP 30
FUEL . . . . D
TRANSMISSION . . . . HYDRO
STEERING . . . . STANDARD
STANDARD DECK . . . . 60"
MSRP $15,999

OPTIONS

72" DECK
YANMAR 31HP

RETAIL PRICING

YEAR	HIGH	LOW
1995	$5,068	$3,801
1997	$6,143	$4,607
1998	$6,216	$4,662
1999	$6,831	$5,123
2000	$6,765	$5,074

PM460

YEARS MFRD 2000-2002
SERIES . . . . PROMASTER SERIES
ENGINE . . . . KUBOTA
ENGINE HP 30
COOLING . . . . LIQUID
FUEL . . . . D
TRANSMISSION . . . . HYDRO
STEERING . . . . ZERO
STANDARD DECK . . . . 60"
MSRP $16,228

OPTIONS

4 ROPS
4WD
72" DECK
CAB

SERIAL NUMBERS

YEAR . . . . BEGINNING NO.
2000 000101

RETAIL PRICING

YEAR	HIGH	LOW
2000	$2,880	$2,160
2001	$3,197	$2,398
2002	$3,545	$2,658

GRAVELY

PM 252M

YEARS MFRD	2010-2011
SERIES	200 XDZ SERIES
ENGINE	KAWASAKI
CYLINDERS	2
ENGINE HP	27
COOLING	AIR
FUEL	G
SPEEDS	VARIABLE
TRANSMISSION	HYDRO
STEERING	ZERO
STANDARD DECK	52"
MSRP	$9,859

OPTIONS

3 BAG & FAN
BLADE
SNOW BLOWER

RETAIL PRICING

YEAR	HIGH	LOW
2010	$4,668	$3,501
2011	$5,116	$3,837

PM 260H

YEARS MFRD	2010-2011
SERIES	200 XDZ SERIES
ENGINE	KAWASAKI
ENGINE HP	31
COOLING	AIR
FUEL	G
SPEEDS	VARIABLE
TRANSMISSION	HYDRO
STEERING	ZERO
BLADE CLUTCH	ELECTRIC
STANDARD DECK	60"
MSRP	$10,649

RETAIL PRICING

YEAR	HIGH	LOW
2010	$5,042	$3,782
2011	$5,525	$4,144

PM 260H DSL

YEARS MFRD	2010-2011
SERIES	200 XDZ SERIES
ENGINE	DAIHATSU
ENGINE HP	27
COOLING	LIQUID
FUEL	D
SPEEDS	VARIABLE
TRANSMISSION	HYDRO
STEERING	ZERO
BLADE CLUTCH	ELECTRIC
STANDARD DECK	60"
MSRP	$14,599

RETAIL PRICING

YEAR	HIGH	LOW
2010	$6,912	$5,184
2011	$7,577	$5,683

PM 260M

YEARS MFRD	2010-2011
SERIES	200 XDZ SERIES
ENGINE	KAWASAKI
ENGINE HP	27
COOLING	AIR
FUEL	G
SPEEDS	VARIABLE
TRANSMISSION	HYDRO
STEERING	ZERO
BLADE CLUTCH	ELECTRIC
STANDARD DECK	60"
MSRP	$10,059

RETAIL PRICING

YEAR	HIGH	LOW
2010	$4,763	$3,572
2011	$5,220	$3,915

PM 272H

YEARS MFRD	2010-2011
SERIES	200 XDZ SERIES
ENGINE	KAWASAKI
ENGINE HP	31
COOLING	AIR
FUEL	G
SPEEDS	VARIABLE
TRANSMISSION	HYDRO
STEERING	ZERO
BLADE CLUTCH	ELECTRIC
STANDARD DECK	72"
MSRP	$11,499

RETAIL PRICING

YEAR	HIGH	LOW
2010	$5,445	$4,084
2011	$5,967	$4,475

PM 272H DSL

YEARS MFRD	2010-2011
SERIES	200 XDZ SERIES
ENGINE	DAIHATSU
ENGINE HP	31
COOLING	LIQUID
FUEL	D
SPEEDS	VARIABLE
TRANSMISSION	HYDRO
STEERING	ZERO
BLADE CLUTCH	ELECTRIC
STANDARD DECK	72"
MSRP	$18,888

OPTIONS

3 BAG & FAN
BLADE
HPPR BAG
SNOW BLOWER

RETAIL PRICING

YEAR	HIGH	LOW
2010	$9,009	$6,757
2011	$10,006	$7,504

PRO16G

YEARS MFRD	1987-2002
ENGINE	KOHLER
ENGINE HP	16
FUEL	G
TRANSMISSION	GEAR
STEERING	STANDARD
STANDARD DECK	40"
MSRP	$5,449

OPTIONS

50" DECK
60" DECK

RETAIL PRICING

YEAR	HIGH	LOW
1987	$1,101	$825
1988	$1,117	$838
1989	$1,164	$873
1990	$1,212	$909
1991	$1,257	$943
1992	$1,365	$1,024
1993	$1,416	$1,062
1994	$1,521	$1,141
1995	$1,621	$1,216
1996	$1,637	$1,227
1997	$1,690	$1,267
1998	$1,713	$1,285
1999	$1,786	$1,339
2000	$1,870	$1,402
2001	$1,943	$1,458
2002	$1,970	$1,477

PRO16H

YEARS MFRD	1988-1992
ENGINE	B&S TWIN
ENGINE HP	16
FUEL	G
TRANSMISSION	HYDRO
STEERING	STANDARD
WEIGHT	385 LBS.
MSRP	$3,680

RETAIL PRICING

YEAR	HIGH	LOW
1990	$816	$612
1991	$982	$736
1992	$1,241	$931

PRO17

YEARS MFRD	1991-1992
ENGINE	KAWASASKI
ENGINE HP	17
FUEL	G
TRANSMISSION	GEAR
STEERING	STANDARD
WEIGHT	390 LBS.
MSRP	$3,070

RETAIL PRICING

YEAR	HIGH	LOW
1991	$873	$655
1992	$1,051	$788

PRO18

YEARS MFRD	1990-1992
ENGINE	KOHLER
ENGINE HP	18
FUEL	G
TRANSMISSION	GEAR
STEERING	STANDARD
WEIGHT	427 LBS.
MSRP	$3,075

RETAIL PRICING

YEAR	HIGH	LOW
1990	$820	$615
1991	$995	$746
1992	$1,128	$846

PRO18G

YEARS MFRD	1987-1999
ENGINE	KOHLER
ENGINE HP	18
FUEL	G
TRANSMISSION	GEAR
STEERING	STANDARD
MSRP	$7,787

SERIAL NUMBERS

YEAR	BEGINNING NO.
1990	624538
1990	5196083
1991	633888
1991	5199998

RETAIL PRICING

YEAR	HIGH	LOW
1987	$1,399	$1,050
1988	$1,435	$1,076
1989	$1,562	$1,172
1990	$1,645	$1,234
1991	$1,849	$1,387
1995	$2,379	$1,785
1996	$2,544	$1,908
1997	$2,743	$2,057
1998	$2,946	$2,209
1999	$3,141	$2,356

PRO20G

YEARS MFRD	1987-1999
ENGINE	KOHLER
ENGINE HP	20
FUEL	G
TRANSMISSION	GEAR
STEERING	STANDARD
MSRP	$8,181

SERIAL NUMBERS

YEAR	BEGINNING NO.
1990	624538
1990	5196083
1991	533888
1991	5199998

RETAIL PRICING

YEAR	HIGH	LOW
1987	$1,474	$1,105
1988	$1,511	$1,133
1989	$1,640	$1,230
1990	$1,728	$1,296
1991	$1,964	$1,473
1995	$2,513	$1,885
1996	$2,683	$2,012
1997	$2,895	$2,171
1998	$3,094	$2,320
1999	$3,301	$2,475

PRO 34

YEARS MFRD	2010-2018
SERIES	COMPACT SERIES
ENGINE	KAWASAKI
ENGINE HP	15.5
COOLING	AIR
FUEL	G
SPEEDS	VARIABLE
TRANSMISSION	HYDRO
STEERING	ZERO
BLADE CLUTCH	ELECTRIC
STANDARD DECK	34"
MSRP	$7,163

OPTIONS
BAGGER
CART
LEAF COLLECTOR
SUSPENSION SEAT

RETAIL PRICING

YEAR	HIGH	LOW
2010	$2,309	$1,732
2011	$2,548	$1,911
2012	$2,812	$2,109
2013	$3,105	$2,328
2014	$3,425	$2,569
2015	$3,782	$2,836
2016	$4,174	$3,130
2017	$4,607	$3,455
2018	$5,166	$3,874

PRO 44
YEARS MFRD 2010-2016
SERIES .... COMPACT SERIES
ENGINE .... KAWASAKI
ENGINE HP 19
COOLING .... AIR
FUEL .... G
SPEEDS .... VARIABLE
TRANSMISSION .... HYDRO
STEERING .... ZERO
BLADE CLUTCH .... ELECTRIC
STANDARD DECK .... 44"
MSRP $6,969

OPTIONS
2 BAG
3 BAG
CART
SUSPENSION SEAT

RETAIL PRICING

YEAR	HIGH	LOW
2010	$2,736	$2,052
2011	$3,033	$2,275
2012	$3,362	$2,522
2013	$3,728	$2,796
2014	$4,132	$3,099
2015	$4,582	$3,436
2016	$5,451	$4,088

PRO-RIDE 254
YEARS MFRD 2011-2013
SERIES .... 200 SERIES
ENGINE .... KAWASAKI
ENGINE HP 24.5
COOLING .... AIR
FUEL .... G
SPEEDS .... VARIABLE
TRANSMISSION .... HYDRO
STEERING .... ZERO
BLADE CLUTCH .... ELECTRIC
STANDARD DECK .... 54"
MSRP $10,899

OPTIONS
4 BU BAG
RRWT KIT

RETAIL PRICING

YEAR	HIGH	LOW
2011	$5,382	$4,037
2012	$5,974	$4,481
2013	$6,635	$4,976

PRO-RIDE 260
YEARS MFRD 2011-2013
SERIES .... 200 SERIES
ENGINE .... KAWASAKI FX751V
CID 852CC
ENGINE HP 24.5
COOLING .... AIR
FUEL .... G
SPEEDS .... VARIABLE
TRANSMISSION .... HYDRO
STEERING .... ZERO
BLADE CLUTCH .... ELECTRIC
STANDARD DECK .... 60"
MSRP $11,099

OPTIONS
3 BAG & FAN
RRWT KIT

RETAIL PRICING

YEAR	HIGH	LOW
2011	$5,489	$4,117
2012	$6,085	$4,564
2013	$6,758	$5,069

PRO-RIDE 266
YEARS MFRD 2011-2013
SERIES .... 200 SERIES
ENGINE .... KAWASAKI FX850V
CID 852CC
ENGINE HP 27
COOLING .... AIR
FUEL .... G
SPEEDS .... VARIABLE
TRANSMISSION .... HYDRO
STEERING .... ZERO
BLADE CLUTCH .... ELECTRIC
STANDARD DECK .... 66"
MSRP $11,749

OPTIONS
3 BAG & FAN
RRWT KIT

RETAIL PRICING

YEAR	HIGH	LOW
2011	$5,801	$4,350
2012	$6,442	$4,831
2013	$7,152	$5,364

PRO-STANCE 32FL 994157
YEARS MFRD 2020-2020
ENGINE .... KAWASAKI FS600
CYLINDERS 2
CID 603CC
ENGINE HP 18.5
FUEL .... G
SPEEDS .... VARIABLE
TRANSMISSION .... HYDRO
STEERING .... ZERO
BLADE CLUTCH .... ELECTRIC
STANDARD DECK .... 32"
WEIGHT .... 750 LBS.

PRO-STANCE 34
YEARS MFRD 2011-2013
ENGINE .... KAWASAKI
ENGINE HP 15.5
COOLING .... AIR
FUEL .... G
SPEEDS .... VARIABLE
TRANSMISSION .... HYDRO
STEERING .... ZERO
BLADE CLUTCH .... ELECTRIC
STANDARD DECK .... 34"
MSRP $6,299

OPTIONS
BAGGER

RETAIL PRICING

YEAR	HIGH	LOW
2011	$3,150	$2,362
2012	$3,497	$2,622
2013	$3,885	$2,914

PRO-STANCE 36
YEARS MFRD 2015-2016
ENGINE .... KAWASAKI
ENGINE HP 18.5
COOLING .... AIR
FUEL .... G
TRANSMISSION .... GEAR
STEERING .... ZERO
STANDARD DECK .... 36"
MSRP $7,469

OPTIONS
BAGGER

RETAIL PRICING

YEAR	HIGH	LOW
2015	$4,911	$3,683
2016	$6,055	$4,542

PRO-STANCE 36FL
YEARS MFRD 2017-2019
ENGINE .... KAWASAKI FS600V
CID 603CC
ENGINE HP 18.5
TRANSMISSION .... HYDRO
STEERING .... ZERO
BLADE CLUTCH .... ELECTRIC
STANDARD DECK .... 36"
WEIGHT .... 784 LBS.
MSRP $7,672

PRO-STANCE 36FL 994149
YEARS MFRD 2020-2020
ENGINE .... KAWASAKI FS600
CYLINDERS 2
CID 603CC
ENGINE HP 18.5
FUEL .... G
SPEEDS .... VARIABLE
TRANSMISSION .... HYDRO
STEERING .... ZERO
STANDARD DECK .... 36"
WEIGHT .... 760 LBS.

PRO-STANCE 48
YEARS MFRD 2011-2016
ENGINE .... KAWASAKI
ENGINE HP 22
COOLING .... AIR
FUEL .... G
SPEEDS .... VARIABLE
TRANSMISSION .... HYDRO
STEERING .... ZERO
BLADE CLUTCH .... ELECTRIC
STANDARD DECK .... 48"
MSRP $8,689

OPTIONS
BAGGER

RETAIL PRICING

YEAR	HIGH	LOW
2011	$3,782	$2,836
2012	$4,191	$3,144
2013	$4,647	$3,485
2014	$5,154	$3,865
2015	$5,712	$4,284
2016	$6,903	$5,177

PRO-STANCE 48FL
YEARS MFRD 2017-2019
ENGINE .... KAWASAKI FX691V
CID 726CC
ENGINE HP 22
FUEL .... G
TRANSMISSION .... GEAR
STEERING .... ZERO
BLADE CLUTCH .... ELECTRIC
STANDARD DECK .... 48"
WEIGHT .... 995 LBS.
MSRP $8,821

PRO-STANCE 48FL 994150
YEARS MFRD 2020-2020
ENGINE .... KAWASAKI FX730
CYLINDERS 2
CID 726CC
ENGINE HP 23.5
FUEL .... G
SPEEDS .... VARIABLE
TRANSMISSION .... HYDRO
STEERING .... ZERO
STANDARD DECK .... 48"
WEIGHT .... 875 LBS.

PRO-STANCE 52
YEARS MFRD 2011-2016
ENGINE .... KAWASAKI FX691V
ENGINE HP 22

GRAVELY

COOLING .... AIR
FUEL .... G
SPEEDS .... VARIABLE
TRANSMISSION .... HYDRO
STEERING................ ZERO
BLADE CLUTCH .... ELECTRIC
STANDARD DECK .... 52"
MSRP................. $8,889

OPTIONS

BAGGER
KOHLER 23HP

RETAIL PRICING

YEAR	HIGH	LOW
2011	$3,869	$2,902
2012	$4,289	$3,217
2013	$4,754	$3,565
2014	$5,271	$3,954
2015	$5,845	$4,384
2016	$7,105	$5,329

PRO-STANCE 52FL

YEARS MFRD 2017-2019
ENGINE .... KOHLER ZT730
CID 747CC
ENGINE HP 23
FUEL .... G
SPEEDS .... VARIABLE
TRANSMISSION .... HYDRO
STEERING................ ZERO
BLADE CLUTCH .... ELECTRIC
STANDARD DECK .... 52"
WEIGHT .... 1,004 LBS.
MSRP................. $8,372

OPTIONS

KAWASAKI 22HP
KOHLER EFI

PRO-STANCE 52FL 994151

YEARS MFRD 2020-2020
ENGINE .... KAWASAKI FX730
CYLINDERS................... 2
CID 726CC
ENGINE HP 23.5
FUEL .... G
SPEEDS .... VARIABLE
TRANSMISSION .... HYDRO
STEERING................ ZERO
STANDARD DECK .... 52"
WEIGHT .... 910 LBS.

OPTIONS

KAW EFI 26HP 994152

PRO-STANCE 60

YEARS MFRD 2015-2016
ENGINE .... KAWASAKI
ENGINE HP 23.5
COOLING .... AIR
FUEL .... G
TRANSMISSION .... GEAR
STEERING................ ZERO
STANDARD DECK .... 60"
MSRP................. $9,289

OPTIONS

BAGGER
KOHLER 25HP

RETAIL PRICING

YEAR	HIGH	LOW
2015	$6,107	$4,581
2016	$7,632	$5,724

PRO-STANCE 60FL

YEARS MFRD 2017-2019
ENGINE .... KAWASAKI FX730V
CID 726CC
ENGINE HP 23.5
FUEL .... G
SPEEDS .... VARIABLE
TRANSMISSION .... HYDRO
STEERING................ ZERO
BLADE CLUTCH .... ELECTRIC
STANDARD DECK .... 60"
WEIGHT .... 1,043 LBS.
MSRP................. $9,533

OPTIONS

KOHLER EFI

PRO-STANCE 60FL 994153

YEARS MFRD 2020-2020
ENGINE .... KAWASAKI FX730
CYLINDERS................... 2
CID 726CC
ENGINE HP 23.5
FUEL .... G
SPEEDS .... VARIABLE
TRANSMISSION .... HYDRO
STEERING................ ZERO
STANDARD DECK .... 60"
WEIGHT .... 940 LBS.

OPTIONS

KAW EFI 26HP 994154

PRO-STANCE 61

YEARS MFRD 2013-2014
ENGINE .... KAWASAKI FX730V
CID 726CC
ENGINE HP 23.5
COOLING .... AIR
FUEL .... G
SPEEDS .... VARIABLE
TRANSMISSION .... HYDRO
STEERING................ ZERO
STANDARD DECK .... 61"
MSRP................. $8,899

OPTIONS

BAGGER
KOHLER 25HP

RETAIL PRICING

YEAR	HIGH	LOW
2013	$4,876	$3,657
2014	$5,417	$4,063

PRO-STANCE 1934FX

YEARS MFRD 2008-2010
ENGINE .... KAWASAKI
ENGINE HP 19
COOLING .... AIR
FUEL .... G
SPEEDS .... VARIABLE
TRANSMISSION .... HYDRO
STEERING................ ZERO
BLADE CLUTCH .... ELECTRIC
STANDARD DECK .... 34"
WEIGHT .... 830 LBS.
MSRP................. $5,999

OPTIONS

BAGGER

RETAIL PRICING

YEAR	HIGH	LOW
2008	$2,309	$1,732
2009	$2,561	$1,921
2010	$2,846	$2,134

PRO-STANCE 1948FL

YEARS MFRD 2008-2010
ENGINE .... KAWASAKI
CYLINDERS................... 2
ENGINE HP 19
COOLING .... AIR
FUEL .... G
SPEEDS .... VARIABLE
TRANSMISSION .... HYDRO
STEERING................ ZERO
BLADE CLUTCH .... ELECTRIC
STANDARD DECK .... 48"
MSRP................. $7,645

OPTIONS

BAGGER
FLO DECK

RETAIL PRICING

YEAR	HIGH	LOW
2008	$2,940	$2,205
2009	$3,263	$2,448
2010	$3,628	$2,721

PRO-STANCE 1952FX

YEARS MFRD 2008-2010
ENGINE .... KAWASAKI
CYLINDERS................... 2
ENGINE HP 19
COOLING .... AIR
FUEL .... G
SPEEDS .... VARIABLE
TRANSMISSION .... HYDRO
STEERING................ ZERO
BLADE CLUTCH .... ELECTRIC
STANDARD DECK .... 52"
WEIGHT .... 860 LBS.
MSRP................. $6,767

OPTIONS

BAGGER

RETAIL PRICING

YEAR	HIGH	LOW
2008	$2,604	$1,953
2009	$2,888	$2,166
2010	$3,210	$2,407

PRO-STANCE 2352FL

YEARS MFRD 2008-2010
ENGINE .... KAWASAKI
CYLINDERS................... 2
ENGINE HP 23
COOLING .... AIR
FUEL .... G
SPEEDS .... VARIABLE
TRANSMISSION .... HYDRO
STEERING................ ZERO
BLADE CLUTCH .... ELECTRIC
STANDARD DECK .... 52"
MSRP................. $8,299

OPTIONS

BAGGER

RETAIL PRICING

YEAR	HIGH	LOW
2008	$3,193	$2,395
2009	$3,545	$2,658
2010	$3,936	$2,952

PRO-STANCE 2352FX

YEARS MFRD 2008-2009
ENGINE .... KAWASAKI
CYLINDERS................... 2
ENGINE HP 23
COOLING .... AIR
FUEL .... G
SPEEDS .... VARIABLE
TRANSMISSION .... HYDRO
STEERING................ ZERO
BLADE CLUTCH .... ELECTRIC
STANDARD DECK .... 52"
MSRP................. $7,313

OPTIONS

BAGGER

RETAIL PRICING

YEAR	HIGH	LOW
2008	$2,888	$2,166
2009	$3,210	$2,407

PRO-TURN 48

YEARS MFRD 2013-2019
ENGINE .... KAWASAKI FS691
CID 726CC
ENGINE HP 23
COOLING .... AIR
FUEL .... G
SPEEDS .... VARIABLE

TRANSMISSION . . . . HYDRO
STEERING. . . . . ZERO
BLADE CLUTCH . . . . ELECTRIC
STANDARD DECK . . . . 48"

OPTIONS

2 BAG & FAN
KOHLER 23HP
SHADE
SUSPENSION SEAT

RETAIL PRICING

YEAR	HIGH	LOW
2013	$3,041	$2,281
2014	$3,356	$2,517
2015	$3,704	$2,778
2016	$4,088	$3,066
2017	$4,514	$3,385
2018	$5,035	$3,776
2019	$5,573	$4,180

PRO-TURN 52

YEARS MFRD 2013-2019
ENGINE . . . . KAWASAKI FS691
CID 726CC
ENGINE HP 23
COOLING . . . . AIR
FUEL . . . . G
SPEEDS . . . . VARIABLE
TRANSMISSION . . . . HYDRO
STEERING. . . . . ZERO
BLADE CLUTCH . . . . ELECTRIC
STANDARD DECK . . . . 52"
WEIGHT . . . . 977 LBS.

OPTIONS

2 BAG & FAN
KOHLER 23HP
SHADE
SUSPENSION SEAT

RETAIL PRICING

YEAR	HIGH	LOW
2013	$3,134	$2,351
2014	$3,458	$2,594
2015	$3,818	$2,864
2016	$4,215	$3,161
2017	$4,651	$3,488
2018	$5,160	$3,870
2019	$5,725	$4,294

PRO-TURN 60

YEARS MFRD 2013-2019
ENGINE . . . . KAWASAKI FS730
CID 726CC
ENGINE HP 24
COOLING . . . . AIR
FUEL . . . . G
SPEEDS . . . . VARIABLE
TRANSMISSION . . . . HYDRO
STEERING. . . . . ZERO
BLADE CLUTCH . . . . ELECTRIC
STANDARD DECK . . . . 60"
WEIGHT . . . . 1,006 LBS.

OPTIONS

2 BAG & FAN
KOHLER 25HP
SHADE
SUSPENSION SEAT

RETAIL PRICING

YEAR	HIGH	LOW
2013	$3,270	$2,453
2014	$3,615	$2,711
2015	$3,985	$2,989
2016	$4,397	$3,298
2017	$4,855	$3,641
2018	$5,341	$4,006
2019	$5,866	$4,400

PRO-TURN 148

YEARS MFRD 2010-2020
SERIES. . . . . 100 SERIES
ENGINE . . . . KAWASAKI FX691V
CID 726CC
ENGINE HP 22
COOLING . . . . AIR
FUEL . . . . G
SPEEDS . . . . VARIABLE
TRANSMISSION . . . . HYDRO
STEERING. . . . . ZERO
BLADE CLUTCH . . . . ELECTRIC
STANDARD DECK . . . . 48"
WEIGHT . . . . 1,062 LBS.
MSRP. $9,185

OPTIONS

2 BAG
E-LIFT

RETAIL PRICING

YEAR	HIGH	LOW
2010	$2,732	$2,049
2011	$3,015	$2,261
2012	$3,328	$2,496
2013	$3,674	$2,755
2014	$4,055	$3,040
2015	$4,475	$3,356
2016	$4,940	$3,705
2017	$5,451	$4,088
2018	$5,973	$4,479
2019	$6,732	$5,048
2020	$7,612	$5,809

PRO-TURN 152

YEARS MFRD 2010-2020
SERIES. . . . . 100 SERIES
ENGINE . . . . KAWASAKI FX691V
CID 726CC
ENGINE HP 22
COOLING . . . . AIR
FUEL . . . . G
SPEEDS . . . . VARIABLE
TRANSMISSION . . . . HYDRO
STEERING. . . . . ZERO
BLADE CLUTCH . . . . ELECTRIC
STANDARD DECK . . . . 52"
WEIGHT . . . . 1,079 LBS.
MSRP. $9,407

OPTIONS

3 BAG
E-LIFT
KOHLER 23HP
KOHLER EFI

RETAIL PRICING

YEAR	HIGH	LOW
2010	$2,802	$2,102
2011	$3,088	$2,316
2012	$3,409	$2,556
2013	$3,763	$2,744
2014	$4,153	$3,115
2015	$4,583	$3,437
2016	$5,060	$3,795
2017	$5,586	$4,189
2019	$6,131	$4,599
2019	$6,714	$5,036
2020	$7,764	$5,871

PRO-TURN 160

YEARS MFRD 2010-2020
SERIES. . . . . 100 SERIES
ENGINE . . . . KAWASAKI FX730V
CID 726CC
ENGINE HP 23.5
COOLING . . . . AIR
FUEL . . . . G
SPEEDS . . . . VARIABLE
TRANSMISSION . . . . HYDRO
STEERING. . . . . ZERO
BLADE CLUTCH . . . . ELECTRIC
STANDARD DECK . . . . 60"
WEIGHT . . . . 1,121 LBS.
MSRP. $9,458

OPTIONS

2 BAG
3 BAG
KOHLER 25HP
KOHLER EFI
YAMAHA 26HP $284

RETAIL PRICING

YEAR	HIGH	LOW
2010	$2,846	$2,135
2011	$3,141	$2,356
2012	$3,469	$2,601
2013	$3,827	$2,871
2014	$4,224	$3,169
2015	$4,674	$3,506
2016	$5,147	$3,861
2017	$5,682	$4,262
2018	$6,227	$4,670
2019	$6,846	$5,134
2020	$7,787	$5,934

PRO-TURN 252

YEARS MFRD 2010-2020
SERIES. . . . . 200 SERIES
ENGINE . . . . KAWASAKI FX850V
CID 852CC
ENGINE HP 27
COOLING . . . . AIR
FUEL . . . . G
SPEEDS . . . . VARIABLE
TRANSMISSION . . . . HYDRO
STEERING. . . . . ZERO
BLADE CLUTCH . . . . ELECTRIC
STANDARD DECK . . . . 52"
WEIGHT . . . . 1,302 LBS.
MSRP. $11,341

OPTIONS

3 BAG & FAN
E-LIFT
HOPPER BAG
KAWASAKI FX730V

RETAIL PRICING

YEAR	HIGH	LOW
2010	$3,400	$2,550
2011	$3,763	$2,822
2012	$4,143	$3,107
2013	$4,573	$3,430
2014	$5,047	$3,785
2015	$5,571	$4,178
2016	$6,152	$4,611
2017	$6,787	$5,091
2018	$7,453	$5,590
2019	$8,190	$6,142
2020	$9,226	$6,839

PRO-TURN 260

YEARS MFRD 2010-2020
SERIES. . . . . 200 SERIES
ENGINE . . . . KAWASAKI FX850V
CID 852CC
ENGINE HP 27
COOLING . . . . AIR
FUEL . . . . G
SPEEDS . . . . VARIABLE
TRANSMISSION . . . . HYDRO
STEERING. . . . . ZERO
BLADE CLUTCH . . . . ELECTRIC
STANDARD DECK . . . . 60"
WEIGHT . . . . 1,336 LBS.
MSRP. $11,627

OPTIONS

3 BAG & FAN
HOPPER BAG
KOHLER 25HP . . . . $-1,241
KOHLER 29HP $906
YAMAHA 27.5HP. . . . . $-200
YAMAHA 29HP $906

RETAIL PRICING

YEAR	HIGH	LOW
2010	$3,486	$2,614
2011	$3,847	$2,886
2012	$4,247	$3,185
2013	$4,689	$3,516
2014	$5,192	$3,894
2015	$5,727	$4,295
2016	$6,304	$4,728
2017	$6,958	$5,219
2018	$7,623	$5,717
2019	$8,284	$6,213
2020	$9,276	$7,055

AVG. AUCTION PRICING

LOW	HIGH	AVG
$2,058	$3,920	$3,038

PRO-TURN 266

YEARS MFRD 2010-2012
SERIES. . . . . 200 SERIES
ENGINE . . . . KAWASAKI
ENGINE HP 27
COOLING . . . . AIR
FUEL . . . . G
SPEEDS . . . . VARIABLE
TRANSMISSION . . . . HYDRO
STEERING. . . . . ZERO
BLADE CLUTCH . . . . ELECTRIC
STANDARD DECK . . . . 66"
MSRP. $10,499

GRAVELY

OPTIONS
3 BAG & FAN
HPPR BAG

RETAIL PRICING

YEAR	HIGH	LOW
2010	$4,844	$3,633
2011	$5,382	$4,037
2012	$5,978	$4,484

PRO-TURN 272

YEARS MFRD 2013-2020
SERIES . . . . 200 SERIES
ENGINE . . . . . KAWASAKI FX8921V
CID 999CC
ENGINE HP 31
COOLING . . . . AIR
FUEL . . . . G
SPEEDS . . . . VARIABLE
TRANSMISSION . . . . HYDRO
STEERING . . . . ZERO
BLADE CLUTCH . . . . ELECTRIC
STANDARD DECK . . . . 72"
WEIGHT . . . . 1,410 LBS.
MSRP $12,533

OPTIONS
3 BAG & FAN
CART
E-LIFT
HOPPER BAG

RETAIL PRICING

YEAR	HIGH	LOW
2013	$5,025	$3,769
2014	$5,551	$4,164
2015	$6,123	$4,592
2016	$6,759	$5,068
2017	$7,459	$5,594
2018	$8,205	$6,154
2019	$8,980	$6,735
2020	$10,142	$7,445

PRO-TURN 452

YEARS MFRD 2012-2020
SERIES . . . . 400 SERIES
ENGINE . . . . KAWASAKI FX850
CID 852CC
ENGINE HP 27
COOLING . . . . AIR
FUEL . . . . G
SPEEDS . . . . VARIABLE
TRANSMISSION . . . . HYDRO
STEERING . . . . ZERO
STANDARD DECK . . . . 52"
WEIGHT . . . . 1,326 LBS.
MSRP $12,438

OPTIONS
3 BAG & FAN
KOHLER 29HP
POWER LIFT
SUSPENSION SEAT
YAMAHA 29HP $820

RETAIL PRICING

YEAR	HIGH	LOW
2012	$5,557	$4,167
2013	$6,161	$4,620
2014	$6,830	$5,122
2015	$7,573	$5,680
2016	$8,367	$6,275
2017	$9,015	$6,761
2018	$9,569	$7,177
2019	$10,427	$7,820
2020	$11,321	$8,490

PRO-TURN 460

YEARS MFRD 2012-2020
SERIES . . . . 400 SERIES
ENGINE . . . . KOHLER
CID 824CC
ENGINE HP 33
COOLING . . . . AIR
FUEL . . . . G
SPEEDS . . . . VARIABLE
TRANSMISSION . . . . HYDRO
STEERING . . . . ZERO
STANDARD DECK . . . . 60"
WEIGHT . . . . 1,360 LBS.
MSRP $14,064

RETAIL PRICING

YEAR	HIGH	LOW
2012	$5,119	$3,839
2013	$5,649	$4,237
2014	$6,238	$4,678
2015	$6,883	$5,162
2016	$7,596	$5,697
2017	$8,197	$6,148
2018	$9,261	$6,946
2019	$10,303	$7,727
2020	$11,563	$8,811

AVG. AUCTION PRICING

LOW	HIGH	AVG
$2,200	$5,500	$3,225

PRO-TURN 466

YEARS MFRD 2012-2012
SERIES . . . . 400 SERIES
ENGINE . . . . KAWASAKI
ENGINE HP 27
COOLING . . . . AIR
FUEL . . . . G
SPEEDS . . . . VARIABLE
TRANSMISSION . . . . HYDRO
STEERING . . . . ZERO
STANDARD DECK . . . . 66"
MSRP $11,999

RETAIL PRICING

YEAR	HIGH	LOW
2012	$6,833	$5,124

PRO-TURN 472

YEARS MFRD 2012-2020
SERIES . . . . 400 SERIES
ENGINE . . . . . KAWASAKI FX1000V
CID 999CC
ENGINE HP 35
COOLING . . . . AIR
FUEL . . . . G
SPEEDS . . . . VARIABLE
TRANSMISSION . . . . HYDRO
STEERING . . . . ZERO
STANDARD DECK . . . . 72"
WEIGHT . . . . 1,453 LBS.
MSRP $14,290

OPTIONS
3 BAG & FAN
POWER LIFT
YAMAHA 33HP $311

RETAIL PRICING

YEAR	HIGH	LOW
2012	$5,241	$3,930
2013	$5,784	$4,338
2014	$6,385	$4,789
2015	$7,048	$5,286
2016	$7,779	$5,834
2017	$8,586	$6,439
2018	$9,585	$7,189
2019	$10,686	$8,014
2020	$12,056	$9,101

PRO-TURN MACH ONE

YEARS MFRD 2020-2020
ENGINE . . . . . . KAWASAKI FX921V
CID 999C
ENGINE HP 31
FUEL . . . . G
SPEEDS . . . . VARIABLE
TRANSMISSION . . . . HYDRO
STEERING . . . . ZERO
BLADE CLUTCH . . . . ELECTRIC
ROPS/CAB . . . . ROPS
STANDARD DECK . . . . 60"
WEIGHT . . . . 1,375 LBS.
MSRP $12,540

PRO-TURN Z48

YEARS MFRD 2020-2020
ENGINE . . . . GRAVELY
CID 764CC
ENGINE HP 26.5
FUEL . . . . G
SPEEDS . . . . VARIABLE
TRANSMISSION . . . . HYDRO
STEERING . . . . ZERO
BLADE CLUTCH . . . . ELECTRIC
ROPS/CAB . . . . ROPS
STANDARD DECK . . . . 48"
WEIGHT . . . . 923 LBS.
MSRP $6,821

PRO-TURN Z52

YEARS MFRD 2018-2020
ENGINE . . . . GRAVELY
CID 764CC
ENGINE HP 26.5
FUEL . . . . G
SPEEDS . . . . VARIABLE
TRANSMISSION . . . . HYDRO
STEERING . . . . ZERO
BLADE CLUTCH . . . . ELECTRIC
STANDARD DECK . . . . 52"
WEIGHT . . . . 932 LBS.
MSRP $6,963

PRO-TURN Z60

YEARS MFRD 2018-2020
ENGINE . . . . GRAVELY
CID 764CC
ENGINE HP 26.5
FUEL . . . . G
SPEEDS . . . . VARIABLE
TRANSMISSION . . . . HYDRO
STEERING . . . . ZERO
BLADE CLUTCH . . . . ELECTRIC
STANDARD DECK . . . . 60"
WEIGHT . . . . 953 LBS.
MSRP $7,075

PRO-TURN ZX48

YEARS MFRD 2019-2020
ENGINE . . . . KAWASAKI FX691V
CYLINDERS 2
CID 726CC
ENGINE HP 22
COOLING . . . . AIR
FUEL . . . . G
SPEEDS . . . . VARIABLE
TRANSMISSION . . . . HYDRO
STEERING . . . . ZERO
BLADE CLUTCH . . . . ELECTRIC
STANDARD DECK . . . . 48"
WEIGHT . . . . 924 LBS.
MSRP $7,800

PRO-TURN ZX52

YEARS MFRD 2019-2020
ENGINE . . . . KAWASAKI FX691V
CYLINDERS 2
CID 726CC
ENGINE HP 22
COOLING . . . . AIR
FUEL . . . . G
SPEEDS . . . . VARIABLE
TRANSMISSION . . . . HYDRO
STEERING . . . . ZERO
BLADE CLUTCH . . . . ELECTRIC
STANDARD DECK . . . . 52"
WEIGHT . . . . 932 LBS.
MSRP $7,914

PRO-TURN ZX60

YEARS MFRD 2019-2020
ENGINE . . . . KAWASAKI FX730V
CYLINDERS 2
CID 726CC
ENGINE HP 23.5
COOLING . . . . AIR
FUEL . . . . G
SPEEDS . . . . VARIABLE
TRANSMISSION . . . . HYDRO
STEERING . . . . ZERO
BLADE CLUTCH . . . . ELECTRIC
STANDARD DECK . . . . 60"
WEIGHT . . . . 953 LBS.
MSRP $8,029

PROF G

YEARS MFRD 2000-2002
SERIES.....PROFESSIONAL SERIES
ENGINE .... B&S
ENGINE HP 16
FUEL .... G
TRANSMISSION .... GEAR
STEERING............STANDARD
MSRP.................. $6,829

OPTIONS

ROBIN 20.5HP

RETAIL PRICING

YEAR	HIGH	LOW
2000	$2,622	$1,966
2001	$2,820	$2,115
2002	$3,096	$2,322

RAPID XZ

YEARS MFRD 2007-2009
ENGINE .... KOHLER
CYLINDERS.................... 2
ENGINE HP 27
COOLING .... AIR
FUEL .... G
SPEEDS .... VARIABLE
TRANSMISSION .... HYDRO
STEERING.................. ZERO
BLADE CLUTCH .... ELECTRIC
WEIGHT .... 1,650 LBS.

OPTIONS

KOHLER 25HP
KOHLER 30HP

ZT34

YEARS MFRD 2009-2014
SERIES.............. ZT SERIES
ENGINE .... B&S
CID 500CC
ENGINE HP 16.5
COOLING .... AIR
FUEL .... G
SPEEDS .... VARIABLE
TRANSMISSION .... HYDRO
STEERING.................. ZERO
BLADE CLUTCH .... ELECTRIC
STANDARD DECK .... 34"
MSRP.................. $2,695

OPTIONS

BAGGER
CART
SPRAYER

RETAIL PRICING

YEAR	HIGH	LOW
2009	$983	$737
2010	$1,102	$826
2011	$1,212	$909
2012	$1,348	$1,011
2013	$1,494	$1,120
2014	$1,659	$1,244

ZT34 18HP

YEARS MFRD 2015-2015
SERIES.............. ZT SERIES
ENGINE .... B&S
ENGINE HP 18
COOLING .... AIR
FUEL .... G
SPEEDS .... VARIABLE
TRANSMISSION .... HYDRO
STEERING.................. ZERO
STANDARD DECK .... 34"
MSRP.................. $2,965

OPTIONS

BAGGER
CART
SPRAYER

RETAIL PRICING

YEAR	HIGH	LOW
2015	$1,841	$1,381

ZT34 21HP

YEARS MFRD 2016-2018
SERIES.............. ZT SERIES
ENGINE .... KOHLER
CID 660CC
ENGINE HP 21
COOLING .... AIR
FUEL .... G
SPEEDS .... VARIABLE
TRANSMISSION .... HYDRO
STEERING.................. ZERO
STANDARD DECK .... 34"
WEIGHT .... 425 LBS.
MSRP.................. $2,985

OPTIONS

15 GAL
2 BAG
CART

RETAIL PRICING

YEAR	HIGH	LOW
2016	$1,670	$1,252
2017	$1,843	$1,383
2018	$2,178	$1,633

ZT42

YEARS MFRD 2010-2018
SERIES.............. ZT SERIES
ENGINE .... KOHLER
CID 726CC
ENGINE HP 22
COOLING .... AIR
FUEL .... G
SPEEDS .... VARIABLE
TRANSMISSION .... HYDRO
STEERING.................. ZERO
BLADE CLUTCH .... ELECTRIC
STANDARD DECK .... 42"
WEIGHT .... 440 LBS.
MSRP.................. $3,069

OPTIONS

BAGGER
CART
SPRAYER

RETAIL PRICING

YEAR	HIGH	LOW
2010	$952	$714
2011	$1,048	$786
2012	$1,156	$867
2013	$1,280	$960
2014	$1,408	$1,056
2015	$1,555	$1,166
2016	$1,723	$1,292
2017	$1,894	$1,421
2018	$2,082	$1,561

ZT50

YEARS MFRD 2010-2017
SERIES.............. ZT SERIES
ENGINE .... KAWASAKI FR730V
CID 726CC
ENGINE HP 24
COOLING .... AIR
FUEL .... G
SPEEDS .... VARIABLE
TRANSMISSION .... HYDRO
STEERING.................. ZERO
BLADE CLUTCH .... ELECTRIC
STANDARD DECK .... 50"
MSRP.................. $3,275

OPTIONS

15GAL SPRAYER
BAGGER
CART

RETAIL PRICING

YEAR	HIGH	LOW
2010	$1,017	$763
2011	$1,122	$842
2012	$1,238	$928
2013	$1,369	$1,027
2014	$1,509	$1,132
2015	$1,665	$1,249
2016	$1,838	$1,379
2017	$2,030	$1,522

ZT1534

YEARS MFRD 2005-2006
ENGINE .... B&S
ENGINE HP 15
COOLING .... AIR
FUEL .... G
SPEEDS .... VARIABLE
TRANSMISSION .... HYDRO
STEERING.................. ZERO
STANDARD DECK .... 34"
MSRP.................. $2,499

OPTIONS

KOHLER 15HP

RETAIL PRICING

YEAR	HIGH	LOW
2005	$1,388	$1,041
2006	$1,608	$1,206

ZT1540

YEARS MFRD 2004-2005
ENGINE .... KOHLER
ENGINE HP 15
COOLING .... AIR
FUEL .... G
SPEEDS .... VARIABLE
TRANSMISSION .... HYDRO
STEERING.................. ZERO
STANDARD DECK .... 40"
MSRP.................. $3,099

OPTIONS

3 BAG
42" SNOW THROWER
54" BLADE

RETAIL PRICING

YEAR	HIGH	LOW
2004	$861	$646
2005	$956	$717

ZT1640

YEARS MFRD 2006-2006
ENGINE .... KOHLER
ENGINE HP 16
COOLING .... AIR
FUEL .... G
SPEEDS .... VARIABLE
TRANSMISSION ..... DUAL HYDRO
STEERING.................. ZERO
STANDARD DECK .... 40"
MSRP.................. $3,299

OPTIONS

3 BAG & FAN
46" SNOW BLOWER
54" BLADE

RETAIL PRICING

YEAR	HIGH	LOW
2006	$1,106	$830

ZT1734

YEARS MFRD 2008-2009
SERIES.............. ZT SERIES
ENGINE .... KOHLER COURAGE
CYLINDERS.................... 1
ENGINE HP 17
COOLING .... AIR
FUEL .... G
SPEEDS .... VARIABLE
TRANSMISSION .... HYDRO
STEERING.................. ZERO
BLADE CLUTCH .... ELECTRIC
STANDARD DECK .... 34"
WEIGHT .... 515 LBS.
MSRP.................. $3,129

OPTIONS

15 GAL
BAGGER
SPREADER

RETAIL PRICING

YEAR	HIGH	LOW
2008	$1,236	$927
2009	$1,372	$1,029

ZT1734 XL

YEARS MFRD 2008-2009
ENGINE .... KOHLER COURAGE
CYLINDERS.................... 1
ENGINE HP 17
COOLING .... AIR
FUEL .... G

GRAVELY

SPEEDS . . . . VARIABLE
TRANSMISSION . . . . HYDRO
STEERING. . . . . ZERO
BLADE CLUTCH . . . . ELECTRIC
STANDARD DECK . . . . 34"
WEIGHT . . . . 525 LBS.
MSRP. $3,635

OPTIONS

15 GAL
BAGGER
SPREADER

RETAIL PRICING

YEAR	HIGH	LOW
2008	$1,434	$1,075
2009	$1,592	$1,194

ZT1740

YEARS MFRD 2002-2005
SERIES. . . . . ZT RIDER SERIES
ENGINE . . . . KOHLER
ENGINE HP 17
COOLING . . . . AIR
FUEL . . . . G
SPEEDS . . . . VARIABLE
TRANSMISSION . . . . HYDRO
STEERING. . . . . ZERO
STANDARD DECK . . . . 40"
MSRP. $3,499

OPTIONS

3 BAG
42" SNOW BLOWER
54" BLADE

RETAIL PRICING

YEAR	HIGH	LOW
2002	$786	$589
2003	$873	$655
2004	$973	$730
2005	$1,078	$809

ZT1742

YEARS MFRD 2000-2000
SERIES. . . . . EZ RIDER SERIES
ENGINE . . . . B&S
ENGINE HP 17
COOLING . . . . AIR
FUEL . . . . G
TRANSMISSION . . . . HYDRO
STEERING. . . . . ZERO
STANDARD DECK . . . . 42"
MSRP. $3,729

OPTIONS

2 BAG

SERIAL NUMBERS

YEAR . . . . BEGINNING NO.
2000 000101

RETAIL PRICING

YEAR	HIGH	LOW
2000	$708	$531

ZT1840 XL

YEARS MFRD 2006-2007
ENGINE . . . . KOHLER COURAGE
CYLINDERS. 1
ENGINE HP 18
COOLING . . . . AIR
FUEL . . . . G
SPEEDS . . . . VARIABLE
TRANSMISSION . . . . . DUAL HYDRO
STEERING. . . . . ZERO
BLADE CLUTCH . . . . ELECTRIC
STANDARD DECK . . . . 40"
WEIGHT . . . . 700 LBS.
MSRP. $3,899

OPTIONS

3 BAG & FAN
46" SNOW BLOWER
54" BLADE

RETAIL PRICING

YEAR	HIGH	LOW
2006	$1,289	$967
2007	$1,446	$1,085

ZT1842

YEARS MFRD 2001-2002
SERIES. . . . . ZT RIDER SERIES
ENGINE . . . . B&S
ENGINE HP 18
COOLING . . . . AIR
FUEL . . . . G
TRANSMISSION . . . . HYDRO
STEERING. . . . . ZERO
STANDARD DECK . . . . 42"
MSRP. $3,699

OPTIONS

2 BAG
40" SNOW BLOWER
42" BLADE

RETAIL PRICING

YEAR	HIGH	LOW
2001	$854	$640
2002	$950	$712

ZT1842 XL

YEARS MFRD 2008-2008
ENGINE . . . . B&S ELS
CYLINDERS. 2
ENGINE HP 18
COOLING . . . . AIR
FUEL . . . . G
SPEEDS . . . . VARIABLE
TRANSMISSION . . . . HYDRO
STEERING. . . . . ZERO
BLADE CLUTCH . . . . ELECTRIC
STANDARD DECK . . . . 42"
WEIGHT . . . . 615 LBS.
MSRP. $4,199

OPTIONS

15 GAL
BAGGER
SPREADER

RETAIL PRICING

YEAR	HIGH	LOW
2008	$1,659	$1,244

ZT1844 XL

YEARS MFRD 2005-2005
ENGINE . . . . KOHLER COURAGE
ENGINE HP 18
COOLING . . . . AIR
FUEL . . . . G
SPEEDS . . . . VARIABLE
TRANSMISSION . . . . HYDRO
STEERING. . . . . ZERO
STANDARD DECK . . . . 44"
MSRP. $4,599

OPTIONS

3 BAG

RETAIL PRICING

YEAR	HIGH	LOW
2005	$1,418	$1,064

ZT1944

YEARS MFRD 2004-2005
ENGINE . . . . KOHLER
CYLINDERS. 2
ENGINE HP 19
COOLING . . . . AIR
FUEL . . . . G
SPEEDS . . . . VARIABLE
TRANSMISSION . . . . HYDRO
STEERING. . . . . ZERO
STANDARD DECK . . . . 44"
MSRP. $4,199

OPTIONS

3 BAG
46" SNOW BLOWER
54" BLADE

RETAIL PRICING

YEAR	HIGH	LOW
2004	$1,165	$874
2005	$1,297	$972

ZT2040

YEARS MFRD 2008-2009
ENGINE . . . . KOHLER COURAGE
CYLINDERS. 1
ENGINE HP 20
COOLING . . . . AIR
FUEL . . . . G
SPEEDS . . . . VARIABLE
TRANSMISSION . . . . HYDRO
STEERING. . . . . ZERO
BLADE CLUTCH . . . . ELECTRIC
STANDARD DECK . . . . 40"
WEIGHT . . . . 520 LBS.
MSRP. $3,245

OPTIONS

15 GAL
BAGGER
SPREADER

RETAIL PRICING

YEAR	HIGH	LOW
2008	$1,281	$961
2009	$1,423	$1,067

ZT2042 XL

YEARS MFRD 2008-2009
ENGINE . . . . KOHLER COURAGE
CYLINDERS. 1
ENGINE HP 20
COOLING . . . . AIR
FUEL . . . . G
SPEEDS . . . . VARIABLE
TRANSMISSION . . . . HYDRO
STEERING. . . . . ZERO
BLADE CLUTCH . . . . ELECTRIC
STANDARD DECK . . . . 42"
WEIGHT . . . . 615 LBS.
MSRP. $4,645

OPTIONS

15 GAL
2 CYL
3 BAG
SPREADER

RETAIL PRICING

YEAR	HIGH	LOW
2008	$1,834	$1,375
2009	$2,038	$1,529

ZT2044

YEARS MFRD 2006-2007
ENGINE . . . . KOHLER
ENGINE HP 20
COOLING . . . . AIR
FUEL . . . . G
SPEEDS . . . . VARIABLE
TRANSMISSION . . . . . DUAL HYDRO
STEERING. . . . . ZERO
STANDARD DECK . . . . 44"
MSRP. $4,599

OPTIONS

3 BAG & FAN
46" SNOW BLOWER
54" BLADE

RETAIL PRICING

YEAR	HIGH	LOW
2006	$1,521	$1,141
2007	$1,691	$1,268

ZT2044 XL

YEARS MFRD 2006-2007
SERIES. . . . . XL SERIES
ENGINE . . . . KOHLER COURAGE
CYLINDERS. 2
ENGINE HP 20
COOLING . . . . AIR
FUEL . . . . G
SPEEDS . . . . VARIABLE
TRANSMISSION . . . . HYDRO
STEERING. . . . . ZERO
BLADE CLUTCH . . . . ELECTRIC
STANDARD DECK . . . . 44"
WEIGHT . . . . 725 LBS.
MSRP. $5,449

OPTIONS

3 BAG & FAN
46" SNOW BLOWER
54" BLADE

RETAIL PRICING

YEAR	HIGH	LOW
2006	$1,800	$1,350
2007	$2,003	$1,502

ZT2048

YEARS MFRD 2000-2003
SERIES. . . . . EZ RIDER SERIES

ENGINE . . . B&S
ENGINE HP . . . 20
COOLING . . . AIR
FUEL . . . G
SPEEDS . . . VARIABLE
TRANSMISSION . . . HYDRO
STEERING . . . ZERO
STANDARD DECK . . . 48"
MSRP . . . $4,399

OPTIONS

3 BAG
46" SNOW BLOWER
54" BLADE

SERIAL NUMBERS

YEAR	BEGINNING NO.
2000	000101

RETAIL PRICING

YEAR	HIGH	LOW
2000	$826	$620
2001	$917	$688
2002	$1,015	$761
2003	$1,130	$847

ZT2050

YEARS MFRD . . . 2001-2001
SERIES . . . ZT RIDER SERIES
ENGINE . . . B&S
ENGINE HP . . . 20
FUEL . . . G
TRANSMISSION . . . HYDRO
STEERING . . . ZERO
STANDARD DECK . . . 50"
MSRP . . . $6,399

OPTIONS

2P ROPS

RETAIL PRICING

YEAR	HIGH	LOW
2001	$1,418	$1,064

ZT2148

YEARS MFRD . . . 2004-2005
ENGINE . . . KOHLER
CYLINDERS . . . 2
ENGINE HP . . . 21
COOLING . . . AIR
FUEL . . . G
SPEEDS . . . VARIABLE
TRANSMISSION . . . HYDRO
STEERING . . . ZERO
BLADE CLUTCH . . . ELECTRIC
STANDARD DECK . . . 48"
MSRP . . . $4,499

OPTIONS

3 BAG
46" SNOW BLOWER
54" BLADE

RETAIL PRICING

YEAR	HIGH	LOW
2004	$1,249	$936
2005	$1,391	$1,043

ZT2148 XL

YEARS MFRD . . . 2005-2005
ENGINE . . . KOHLER COMMAND
CYLINDERS . . . 2
ENGINE HP . . . 21
COOLING . . . AIR
FUEL . . . G
SPEEDS . . . VARIABLE
TRANSMISSION . . . HYDRO
STEERING . . . ZERO
STANDARD DECK . . . 48"
MSRP . . . $4,999

OPTIONS

3 BAG

RETAIL PRICING

YEAR	HIGH	LOW
2005	$1,621	$1,216

ZT2250

YEARS MFRD . . . 2002-2002
SERIES . . . ZT RIDER SERIES
ENGINE . . . B&S
ENGINE HP . . . 22
FUEL . . . G
TRANSMISSION . . . HYDRO
STEERING . . . ZERO
STANDARD DECK . . . 50"
MSRP . . . $6,499

OPTIONS

BAGGER
ROPS

RETAIL PRICING

YEAR	HIGH	LOW
2002	$1,672	$1,254

ZT2250

YEARS MFRD . . . 2008-2009
SERIES . . . ZT SERIES
ENGINE . . . KOHLER COURAGE
CYLINDERS . . . 1
ENGINE HP . . . 22
COOLING . . . AIR
FUEL . . . G
SPEEDS . . . VARIABLE
TRANSMISSION . . . HYDRO
STEERING . . . ZERO
BLADE CLUTCH . . . ELECTRIC
STANDARD DECK . . . 50"
WEIGHT . . . 525 LBS.
MSRP . . . $3,535

OPTIONS

15 GAL
BAGGER
SPREADER

RETAIL PRICING

YEAR	HIGH	LOW
2008	$1,395	$1,046
2009	$1,548	$1,161

ZT2348

YEARS MFRD . . . 2006-2007
ENGINE . . . KOHLER
ENGINE HP . . . 23
COOLING . . . AIR
FUEL . . . G
SPEEDS . . . VARIABLE
TRANSMISSION . . . DUAL HYDRO
STEERING . . . ZERO
STANDARD DECK . . . 48"
MSRP . . . $5,149

OPTIONS

3 BAG & FAN
46" SNOW BLOWER
54" BLADE

RETAIL PRICING

YEAR	HIGH	LOW
2006	$1,687	$1,265
2007	$1,873	$1,405

ZT2348 HD

YEARS MFRD . . . 2009-2009
SERIES . . . HD SERIES
ENGINE . . . KOHLER COURAGE
CYLINDERS . . . 2
ENGINE HP . . . 23
COOLING . . . AIR
FUEL . . . G
SPEEDS . . . VARIABLE
TRANSMISSION . . . HYDRO
STEERING . . . ZERO
BLADE CLUTCH . . . ELECTRIC
STANDARD DECK . . . 48"
WEIGHT . . . 730 LBS.
MSRP . . . $5,757

OPTIONS

15 GAL
3 BAG
SPREADER

RETAIL PRICING

YEAR	HIGH	LOW
2009	$2,525	$1,894

ZT2348 XL

YEARS MFRD . . . 2006-2007
SERIES . . . XL SERIES
ENGINE . . . KOHLER COURAGE
CYLINDERS . . . 2
ENGINE HP . . . 23
COOLING . . . AIR
FUEL . . . G
SPEEDS . . . VARIABLE
TRANSMISSION . . . HYDRO
STEERING . . . ZERO
BLADE CLUTCH . . . ELECTRIC
STANDARD DECK . . . 48"
WEIGHT . . . 740 LBS.
MSRP . . . $5,899

OPTIONS

3 BAG & FAN
46" SNOW BLOWER
54" BLADE

RETAIL PRICING

YEAR	HIGH	LOW
2006	$1,933	$1,449
2007	$2,146	$1,610

ZT2352

YEARS MFRD . . . 2004-2005
ENGINE . . . KOHLER
CYLINDERS . . . 2
ENGINE HP . . . 23
COOLING . . . AIR
FUEL . . . G
SPEEDS . . . VARIABLE
TRANSMISSION . . . HYDRO
STEERING . . . ZERO
BLADE CLUTCH . . . ELECTRIC
STANDARD DECK . . . 52"
MSRP . . . $5,099

OPTIONS

3 BAG
46" SNOW BLOWER
54" BLADE

RETAIL PRICING

YEAR	HIGH	LOW
2004	$1,415	$1,061
2005	$1,572	$1,179

ZT2444 HD

YEARS MFRD . . . 2009-2009
ENGINE . . . B&S
CYLINDERS . . . 2
ENGINE HP . . . 24
COOLING . . . AIR
FUEL . . . G
SPEEDS . . . VARIABLE
TRANSMISSION . . . HYDRO
STEERING . . . ZERO
BLADE CLUTCH . . . ELECTRIC
WEIGHT . . . 810 LBS.

ZT2448 XL

YEARS MFRD . . . 2008-2008
ENGINE . . . B&S ELS
CYLINDERS . . . 2
ENGINE HP . . . 24
COOLING . . . AIR
FUEL . . . G
SPEEDS . . . VARIABLE
TRANSMISSION . . . HYDRO
STEERING . . . ZERO
BLADE CLUTCH . . . ELECTRIC
STANDARD DECK . . . 48"
WEIGHT . . . 630 LBS.
MSRP . . . $4,399

OPTIONS

15 GAL
BAGGER
SPREADER

RETAIL PRICING

YEAR	HIGH	LOW
2008	$1,929	$1,446

ZT2450

YEARS MFRD . . . 2008-2008
ENGINE . . . B&S ELS
CYLINDERS . . . 2
ENGINE HP . . . 24
COOLING . . . AIR
FUEL . . . G
SPEEDS . . . VARIABLE
TRANSMISSION . . . HYDRO
STEERING . . . ZERO
BLADE CLUTCH . . . ELECTRIC
STANDARD DECK . . . 50"
WEIGHT . . . 540 LBS.
MSRP . . . $3,489

GRAVELY

OPTIONS

15 GAL
BAGGER
SPREADER

RETAIL PRICING

YEAR	HIGH	LOW
2008	$1,530	$1,147

ZT2548 XL

YEARS MFRD 2008-2009
ENGINE .... KOHLER COURAGE
CYLINDERS 2
ENGINE HP 25
COOLING .... AIR
FUEL .... G
SPEEDS .... VARIABLE
TRANSMISSION .... HYDRO
STEERING .... ZERO
BLADE CLUTCH .... ELECTRIC
STANDARD DECK .... 48"
WEIGHT .... 630 LBS.
MSRP $4,949

OPTIONS

15 GAL
BAGGER
SPREADER

RETAIL PRICING

YEAR	HIGH	LOW
2008	$1,996	$1,497
2009	$2,208	$1,656

ZT2550

YEARS MFRD 2008-2009
ENGINE .... KOHLER COURAGE
CYLINDERS 2
ENGINE HP 25
COOLING .... AIR
FUEL .... G
SPEEDS .... VARIABLE
TRANSMISSION .... HYDRO
STEERING .... ZERO
BLADE CLUTCH .... ELECTRIC
STANDARD DECK .... 50"
WEIGHT .... 540 LBS.
MSRP $3,835

OPTIONS

15 GAL
BAGGER
SPREADER

RETAIL PRICING

YEAR	HIGH	LOW
2008	$1,542	$1,156
2009	$1,710	$1,283

ZT2552

YEARS MFRD 2006-2007
ENGINE .... KOHLER
ENGINE HP 25
COOLING .... AIR
FUEL .... G
SPEEDS .... VARIABLE
TRANSMISSION .... HYDRO
STEERING .... ZERO
STANDARD DECK .... 52"
WEIGHT .... 810 LBS.
MSRP $5,449

OPTIONS

3 BAG & FAN
46" SNOW BLOWER
54" BLADE

RETAIL PRICING

YEAR	HIGH	LOW
2006	$1,940	$1,455
2007	$2,153	$1,615

ZT2552 HD

YEARS MFRD 2008-2009
SERIES .... HD SERIES
ENGINE .... KOHLER COURAGE
CYLINDERS 2
ENGINE HP 25
COOLING .... AIR
FUEL .... G
SPEEDS .... VARIABLE
TRANSMISSION .... HYDRO
STEERING .... ZERO
STANDARD DECK .... 52"
WEIGHT .... 740 LBS.
MSRP $5,959

OPTIONS

15 GAL
BAGGER
PRO TWIN
SPREADER

RETAIL PRICING

YEAR	HIGH	LOW
2008	$2,355	$1,766
2009	$2,636	$1,977

ZT2554 XL

YEARS MFRD 2008-2009
SERIES .... XL SERIES
ENGINE .... KOHLER COURAGE
CYLINDERS 2
ENGINE HP 25
COOLING .... AIR
FUEL .... G
SPEEDS .... VARIABLE
TRANSMISSION .... HYDRO
STEERING .... ZERO
BLADE CLUTCH .... ELECTRIC
STANDARD DECK .... 54"
WEIGHT .... 645 LBS.
MSRP $5,454

OPTIONS

15 GAL
BAGGER
SPREADER

RETAIL PRICING

YEAR	HIGH	LOW
2008	$2,153	$1,615
2009	$2,394	$1,796

ZT2648 HD

YEARS MFRD 2009-2009
ENGINE .... B&S
CYLINDERS 2
ENGINE HP 26
COOLING .... AIR
FUEL .... G
SPEEDS .... VARIABLE
TRANSMISSION .... HYDRO
STEERING .... ZERO
BLADE CLUTCH .... ELECTRIC
WEIGHT .... 805 LBS.

ZT2660 HD

YEARS MFRD 2008-2008
ENGINE .... KOHLER
ENGINE HP 25
FUEL .... G
SPEEDS .... VARIABLE
TRANSMISSION .... HYDRO
STEERING .... ZERO
STANDARD DECK .... 52"
WEIGHT .... 830 LBS.
MSRP $5,649

OPTIONS

15 GAL
BAGGER
SPREADER

RETAIL PRICING

YEAR	HIGH	LOW
2008	$2,458	$1,843

ZT2760 HD

YEARS MFRD 2008-2009
ENGINE .... KOHLER COURAGE
ENGINE HP 27
COOLING .... AIR
FUEL .... G
SPEEDS .... VARIABLE
TRANSMISSION .... HYDRO
STEERING .... ZERO
BLADE CLUTCH .... ELECTRIC
STANDARD DECK .... 60"
WEIGHT .... 830 LBS.
MSRP $6,659

OPTIONS

15 GAL
BAGGER
SPREADER

RETAIL PRICING

YEAR	HIGH	LOW
2008	$2,631	$1,973
2009	$2,920	$2,190

ZT HD44

YEARS MFRD 2012-2020
SERIES .... ZT SERIES
ENGINE .... KAWASAKI FR691V
CID 726CC
ENGINE HP 21.5
COOLING .... AIR
FUEL .... G
SPEEDS .... VARIABLE
TRANSMISSION .... HYDRO
STEERING .... ZERO
STANDARD DECK .... 44"
WEIGHT .... 800 LBS.

OPTIONS

15GAL SPRAYER
2 BAG
E-LIFT
SUS SEAT

RETAIL PRICING

YEAR	HIGH	LOW
2012	$2,103	$1,576
2013	$2,320	$1,740
2014	$2,561	$1,921
2015	$2,828	$2,120
2016	$3,120	$2,340
2017	$3,445	$2,584
2018	$3,832	$2,874
2019	$4,507	$3,381
2020	$5,177	$3,926

ZT HD48

YEARS MFRD 2010-2020
SERIES .... ZT SERIES
ENGINE .... KAWASAKI FR730V
CID 726CC
ENGINE HP 23
COOLING .... AIR
FUEL .... G
SPEEDS .... VARIABLE
TRANSMISSION .... HYDRO
STEERING .... ZERO
BLADE CLUTCH .... ELECTRIC
STANDARD DECK .... 48"
WEIGHT .... 823 LBS.

OPTIONS

2 BAG
3 BAG
E-LIFT
KOHLER 25HP

RETAIL PRICING

YEAR	HIGH	LOW
2010	$1,761	$1,321
2011	$1,943	$1,458
2012	$2,146	$1,609
2013	$2,368	$1,776
2014	$2,614	$1,960
2015	$2,886	$2,164
2016	$3,185	$2,388
2017	$3,516	$2,637
2018	$3,939	$2,954
2019	$4,556	$3,417
2020	$5,234	$3,998

ZT HD52

YEARS MFRD 2010-2020
SERIES .... ZT SERIES
ENGINE .... KAWASAKI FR730V
CID 726CC
ENGINE HP 23
COOLING .... AIR
FUEL .... G
SPEEDS .... VARIABLE
TRANSMISSION .... HYDRO
STEERING .... ZERO
BLADE CLUTCH .... ELECTRIC
STANDARD DECK .... 52"
WEIGHT .... 832 LBS.

OPTIONS
2 BAG
3 BAG
E-LIFT
KOHLER 25HP

RETAIL PRICING

YEAR	HIGH	LOW
2010	$1,795	$1,346
2011	$1,982	$1,486
2012	$2,187	$1,640
2013	$2,414	$1,811
2014	$2,664	$1,998
2015	$2,940	$2,205
2016	$3,246	$2,435
2017	$3,584	$2,688
2018	$4,036	$3,028
2019	$4,522	$3,391
2020	$5,289	$4,042

ZT HD60

YEARS MFRD 2010-2020
SERIES . . . . ZT SERIES
ENGINE . . . . KAWASAKI FR730V
CID 726CC
ENGINE HP 24
COOLING . . . . AIR
FUEL . . . . G
SPEEDS . . . . VARIABLE
TRANSMISSION . . . . HYDRO
STEERING . . . . ZERO
BLADE CLUTCH . . . . ELECTRIC
STANDARD DECK . . . . 60"
WEIGHT . . . . 853 LBS.

OPTIONS
2 BAG
3 BAG
KOHLER 26HP
SUS SEAT

RETAIL PRICING

YEAR	HIGH	LOW
2010	$1,795	$1,346
2011	$1,982	$1,486
2012	$2,187	$1,640
2013	$2,414	$1,811
2014	$2,667	$2,000
2015	$2,944	$2,208
2016	$3,246	$2,435
2017	$3,584	$2,688
2018	$3,960	$2,969
2019	$4,362	$3,272
2020	$5,294	$4,023

ZT X42

YEARS MFRD 2016-2020
SERIES . . . . ZT X SERIES
ENGINE . . . . KOHLER
CID 725CC
ENGINE HP 24
COOLING . . . . AIR
FUEL . . . . G
SPEEDS . . . . VARIABLE
TRANSMISSION . . . . HYDRO
STEERING . . . . ZERO
STANDARD DECK . . . . 42"
WEIGHT . . . . 605 LBS.

OPTIONS
2 BAG
CART
SPRAYER
SPREADER

RETAIL PRICING

YEAR	HIGH	LOW
2016	$1,840	$1,379
2017	$2,031	$1,522
2018	$2,249	$1,687
2019	$2,477	$1,858
2020	$2,727	$2,086

ZT X52

YEARS MFRD 2016-2020
SERIES . . . . ZT X SERIES
ENGINE . . . . KOHLER
CID 725CC
ENGINE HP 25
COOLING . . . . AIR
FUEL . . . . G
SPEEDS . . . . VARIABLE
TRANSMISSION . . . . HYDRO
STEERING . . . . ZERO
STANDARD DECK . . . . 52"
WEIGHT . . . . 635 LBS.

OPTIONS
2BAG
CART
KAWASAKI 23HP
SPRAYER

RETAIL PRICING

YEAR	HIGH	LOW
2016	$1,901	$1,425
2017	$2,099	$1,573
2018	$2,326	$1,745
2019	$2,584	$1,938
2020	$2,827	$2,165

ZT X60

YEARS MFRD 2020-2020
SERIES . . . . ZT X SERIES
ENGINE . . . . KAWASAKI FR691
CID 726CC
ENGINE HP 23
FUEL . . . . G
SPEEDS . . . . VARIABLE
TRANSMISSION . . . . HYDRO
STEERING . . . . ZERO
BLADE CLUTCH . . . . ELECTRIC
STANDARD DECK . . . . 60"
WEIGHT . . . . 634 LBS.

ZT XL42

YEARS MFRD 2010-2020
SERIES . . . . ZT XL SERIES
ENGINE . . . . KOHLER
CID 725CC
ENGINE HP 24
COOLING . . . . AIR
FUEL . . . . G
SPEEDS . . . . VARIABLE
TRANSMISSION . . . . HYDRO
STEERING . . . . ZERO
BLADE CLUTCH . . . . ELECTRIC
STANDARD DECK . . . . 42"
WEIGHT . . . . 661 LBS.

OPTIONS
2 BAG
54" BLADE
KAWASAKI 21.5HP
SNOW BLOWER
SPRAYER

RETAIL PRICING

YEAR	HIGH	LOW
2010	$1,328	$996
2011	$1,467	$1,099
2012	$1,617	$1,213
2013	$1,786	$1,339
2014	$1,971	$1,478
2015	$2,176	$1,632
2016	$2,401	$1,801
2017	$2,651	$1,989
2018	$2,959	$2,219
2019	$3,257	$2,443
2020	$3,684	$2,784

ZT XL48

YEARS MFRD 2020-2020
SERIES . . . . ZT XL SERIES
ENGINE . . . . KAWASAKI FR691
CID 726CC
ENGINE HP 23
FUEL . . . . G
SPEEDS . . . . VARIABLE
TRANSMISSION . . . . HYDRO
STEERING . . . . ZERO
BLADE CLUTCH . . . . ELECTRIC
STANDARD DECK . . . . 48"
WEIGHT . . . . 621 LBS.

ZT XL48

YEARS MFRD 2010-2015
SERIES . . . . ZT SERIES
ENGINE . . . . KAWASAKI FR730V
CID 726CC
ENGINE HP 24
COOLING . . . . AIR
FUEL . . . . G
SPEEDS . . . . VARIABLE
TRANSMISSION . . . . HYDRO
STEERING . . . . ZERO
BLADE CLUTCH . . . . ELECTRIC
STANDARD DECK . . . . 48"
MSRP $4,705

OPTIONS
3 BAG
54" BLADE
SNOW BLOWER
SPRAYER

RETAIL PRICING

YEAR	HIGH	LOW
2010	$1,925	$1,444
2011	$2,133	$1,600
2012	$2,365	$1,774
2013	$2,651	$1,988
2014	$2,907	$2,180
2015	$3,223	$2,417

ZT XL52

YEARS MFRD 2016-2020
SERIES . . . . ZT XL SERIES
ENGINE . . . . KOHLER
CID 725CC
ENGINE HP 25
COOLING . . . . AIR
FUEL . . . . G
SPEEDS . . . . VARIABLE
TRANSMISSION . . . . HYDRO
STEERING . . . . ZERO
STANDARD DECK . . . . 52"
WEIGHT . . . . 679 LBS.

OPTIONS
2 BAG
CART
KAWASAKI 23HP
SPRAYER

RETAIL PRICING

YEAR	HIGH	LOW
2016	$2,558	$1,918
2017	$2,824	$2,117
2018	$3,147	$2,360
2019	$3,434	$2,576
2020	$3,865	$2,854

ZT XL54

YEARS MFRD 2010-2015
SERIES . . . . ZT SERIES
ENGINE . . . . KAWASAKI FR730V
CID 726CC
ENGINE HP 24
COOLING . . . . AIR
FUEL . . . . G
SPEEDS . . . . VARIABLE
TRANSMISSION . . . . HYDRO
STEERING . . . . ZERO
BLADE CLUTCH . . . . ELECTRIC
STANDARD DECK . . . . 54"
MSRP $4,799

OPTIONS
3 BAG
54" BLADE
SNOW BLOWER
SPRAYER

RETAIL PRICING

YEAR	HIGH	LOW
2010	$1,909	$1,432
2011	$2,117	$1,588
2012	$2,355	$1,766
2013	$2,616	$1,962
2014	$2,905	$2,179
2015	$3,259	$2,445

ZT XL60

YEARS MFRD 2017-2020
SERIES . . . . ZT XL SERIES
ENGINE . . . . KOHLER
CID 747CC
ENGINE HP 26
COOLING . . . . AIR
FUEL . . . . G
SPEEDS . . . . VARIABLE
TRANSMISSION . . . . HYDRO
STEERING . . . . ZERO
STANDARD DECK . . . . 60"
WEIGHT . . . . 697 LBS.

GRAVELY

OPTIONS

2 BAG
CART
KAWASAKI 24HP
SPRAYER

RETAIL PRICING

YEAR	HIGH	LOW
2017	$2,962	$2,221
2018	$3,269	$2,451
2019	$3,555	$2,666
2020	$4,000	$2,960

12G

YEARS MFRD 1987-1992
SERIES ..... PROFESSIONAL SERIES
ENGINE .... KOHLER
CYLINDERS 1
ENGINE HP 12
COOLING .... AIR
FUEL .... G
TRANSMISSION .... GEAR
STEERING .... STANDARD
STANDARD DECK .... 40"
MSRP $5,589

RETAIL PRICING

YEAR	HIGH	LOW
1992	$1,656	$1,242

14G

YEARS MFRD 1992-1997
SERIES ..... PROFESSIONAL SERIES
ENGINE .... KOHLER
CYLINDERS 1
ENGINE HP 14
COOLING .... AIR
FUEL .... G
TRANSMISSION .... GEAR
STEERING .... STANDARD
STANDARD DECK .... 50"
MSRP $7,098

OPTIONS

40" SNOW BLOWER
48" BLADE
BAG & FAN
HYD LIFT

RETAIL PRICING

YEAR	HIGH	LOW
1992	$355	$266
1993	$394	$295
1994	$436	$327
1995	$483	$362
1996	$535	$401
1997	$594	$445

16G

YEARS MFRD 1987-1998
SERIES .... PROMASTER SERIES
ENGINE .... KOHLER
ENGINE HP 16
FUEL .... G
SPEEDS 0-8
TRANSMISSION .... GEAR
STEERING .... STANDARD
STANDARD DECK .... 50"
WEIGHT .... 970 LBS.
MSRP $7,964

OPTIONS

60" DECK
B&S
BAGGER
HYD LIFT

RETAIL PRICING

YEAR	HIGH	LOW
1989	$294	$221
1990	$321	$241
1991	$357	$268
1992	$395	$296
1993	$438	$329
1994	$485	$364
1995	$538	$404
1996	$598	$448
1997	$662	$497
1998	$734	$551

18G

YEARS MFRD 1987-1998
SERIES .... PROMASTER SERIES
ENGINE .... KOHLER
ENGINE HP 18
COOLING .... AIR
FUEL .... G
TRANSMISSION .... GEAR
STEERING .... STANDARD
STANDARD DECK .... 50"
WEIGHT .... 895 LBS.
MSRP $9,244

OPTIONS

48" BLADE
48" SNOW BLOWER
60" DECK
B&S 18E
BAG & FAN

RETAIL PRICING

YEAR	HIGH	LOW
1987	$294	$221
1988	$320	$240
1989	$358	$268
1990	$372	$279
1991	$414	$310
1992	$459	$344
1993	$508	$381
1994	$564	$423
1995	$624	$468
1996	$693	$520
1997	$767	$576
1998	$852	$639

18H

YEARS MFRD 1987-1992
SERIES ..... PROFESSIONAL SERIES
ENGINE .... KOHLER
ENGINE HP 18
COOLING .... AIR
FUEL .... G
SPEEDS .... VARIABLE
TRANSMISSION .... HYDRO
STEERING .... STANDARD
STANDARD DECK .... 48"
WEIGHT .... 940 LBS.
MSRP $6,869

RETAIL PRICING

YEAR	HIGH	LOW
1987	$231	$173
1988	$259	$194
1989	$285	$214
1990	$317	$237
1991	$350	$262
1992	$388	$291

20G

YEARS MFRD 1987-1998
SERIES ..... PROFESSIONAL SERIES
ENGINE .... KOHLER
ENGINE HP 20
COOLING .... AIR
FUEL .... G
SPEEDS 0-8
TRANSMISSION .... GEAR
STEERING .... STANDARD
STANDARD DECK .... 50"
WEIGHT .... 1,010 LBS.
MSRP $10,108

OPTIONS

48" BLADE
48" SNOW BLOWER
60" DECK
BAG & FAN

RETAIL PRICING

YEAR	HIGH	LOW
1990	$409	$306
1991	$453	$340
1992	$502	$376
1993	$556	$417
1994	$616	$462
1995	$684	$513
1996	$758	$568
1997	$840	$630
1998	$931	$698

20K

YEARS MFRD 1996-1997
SERIES ... PROMASTER 200 SERIES
ENGINE .... KAWASAKI
ENGINE HP 20
COOLING .... LIQUID
FUEL .... G
TRANSMISSION .... HYDRO
STEERING .... ZERO
STANDARD DECK .... 50"
MSRP $8,249

OPTIONS

60" DECK

RETAIL PRICING

YEAR	HIGH	LOW
1996	$929	$697
1997	$1,032	$774

22

YEARS MFRD 1993-1993
SERIES ... PROMASTER 400 SERIES
ENGINE .... YANMAR
ENGINE HP 22
COOLING .... LIQUID
FUEL .... D
TRANSMISSION .... HYDRO
STEERING .... ZERO
STANDARD DECK .... 60"
MSRP $13,328

OPTIONS

72" DECK

RETAIL PRICING

YEAR	HIGH	LOW
1993	$1,067	$800

22H

YEARS MFRD 1991-1992
SERIES .... PROMASTER SERIES
ENGINE .... YANMAR
ENGINE HP 22
FUEL .... D
TRANSMISSION .... HYDRO
WEIGHT .... 1,115 LBS.
MSRP $11,270

RETAIL PRICING

YEAR	HIGH	LOW
1991	$3,208	$2,406

24G

YEARS MFRD 1990-1991
SERIES ..... PROFESSIONAL SERIES
ENGINE .... ONAN
ENGINE HP 24
FUEL .... G
TRANSMISSION .... HYDRO
STEERING .... STANDARD
WEIGHT .... 1,020 LBS.
MSRP $8,000

RETAIL PRICING

YEAR	HIGH	LOW
1990	$2,133	$1,600
1991	$2,191	$1,643

25

YEARS MFRD 1998-1999
SERIES ... PROMASTER 300 SERIES
ENGINE .... KOHLER
ENGINE HP 25
COOLING .... AIR
FUEL .... G
TRANSMISSION .... HYDRO
STEERING .... ZERO
STANDARD DECK .... 60"
MSRP $7,605

OPTIONS

32" SNOW BLOWER
BAGGER

RETAIL PRICING

YEAR	HIGH	LOW
1998	$1,147	$860
1999	$1,269	$952

30

YEARS MFRD 1997-1999
SERIES ... PROMASTER 400 SERIES
ENGINE .... KUBOTA
ENGINE HP 30
COOLING .... LIQUID

FUEL . . . D
TRANSMISSION . . . HYDRO
STEERING. . . ZERO
STANDARD DECK . . . 60"
MSRP. . . $16,813

OPTIONS

72" DECK

RETAIL PRICING

YEAR	HIGH	LOW
1997	$2,284	$1,713
1998	$2,533	$1,900
1999	$2,811	$2,108

31

YEARS MFRD . . . 1996-1996
SERIES. . . PROMASTER 400 SERIES
ENGINE . . . YANMAR
ENGINE HP . . . 31
COOLING . . . LIQUID
FUEL . . . D
TRANSMISSION . . . HYDRO
STEERING. . . ZERO
STANDARD DECK . . . 60"
MSRP. . . $15,383

OPTIONS

4WD
72" DECK

RETAIL PRICING

YEAR	HIGH	LOW
1996	$1,659	$1,244

34Z

YEARS MFRD . . . 2004-2009
ENGINE . . . KAWASAKI
CYLINDERS. . . 2
ENGINE HP . . . 17
COOLING . . . AIR
FUEL . . . G
SPEEDS . . . VARIABLE
TRANSMISSION . . . HYDRO
STEERING. . . ZERO
BLADE CLUTCH . . . ELECTRIC
STANDARD DECK . . . 34"
WEIGHT . . . 725 LBS.
MSRP. . . $5,839

OPTIONS

BAGGER
SUS SEAT

RETAIL PRICING

YEAR	HIGH	LOW
2004	$1,517	$1,138
2005	$1,683	$1,262
2006	$1,869	$1,402
2007	$2,080	$1,560
2008	$2,309	$1,732
2009	$2,561	$1,921

35

YEARS MFRD . . . 1993-1995
SERIES. . . PROMASTER 400 SERIES
ENGINE . . . YANMAR
ENGINE HP . . . 35
COOLING . . . LIQUID
FUEL . . . D
TRANSMISSION . . . HYDRO
STEERING. . . ZERO
STANDARD DECK . . . 60"
MSRP. . . $14,778

OPTIONS

4WD
72" DECK

RETAIL PRICING

YEAR	HIGH	LOW
1993	$1,198	$898
1994	$1,331	$998
1995	$1,474	$1,105

44Z

YEARS MFRD . . . 2005-2009
ENGINE . . . KAWASAKI
CYLINDERS. . . 2
ENGINE HP . . . 19
COOLING . . . AIR
FUEL . . . G
SPEEDS . . . VARIABLE
TRANSMISSION . . . HYDRO
STEERING. . . ZERO
BLADE CLUTCH . . . ELECTRIC
STANDARD DECK . . . 44"
WEIGHT . . . 830 LBS.
MSRP. . . $6,181

OPTIONS

BAGGER
SUS SEAT

RETAIL PRICING

YEAR	HIGH	LOW
2005	$1,782	$1,336
2006	$1,980	$1,485
2007	$2,197	$1,648
2008	$2,442	$1,832
2009	$2,711	$2,033

48Z

YEARS MFRD . . . 2008-2009
ENGINE . . . KAWASAKI
CYLINDERS. . . 2
ENGINE HP . . . 19
COOLING . . . AIR
FUEL . . . G
SPEEDS . . . VARIABLE
TRANSMISSION . . . HYDRO
STEERING. . . ZERO
BLADE CLUTCH . . . ELECTRIC
STANDARD DECK . . . 48"
WEIGHT . . . 805 LBS.
MSRP. . . $6,383

OPTIONS

BAGGER
SUS SEAT

RETAIL PRICING

YEAR	HIGH	LOW
2008	$2,522	$1,891
2009	$2,802	$2,101

100

YEARS MFRD . . . 1994-1998
SERIES. . . PROMASTER SERIES
ENGINE . . . B&S
ENGINE HP . . . 16
FUEL . . . G
TRANSMISSION . . . HYDRO
STEERING. . . STANDARD
STANDARD DECK . . . 40"
MSRP. . . $6,777

OPTIONS

50" DECK
KOHLER 18E

RETAIL PRICING

YEAR	HIGH	LOW
1994	$1,887	$1,416
1995	$1,960	$1,470
1996	$2,083	$1,562
1997	$2,246	$1,685
1998	$2,563	$1,922

144 XDZ

YEARS MFRD . . . 2006-2009
SERIES. . . XDZ 100 SERIES
ENGINE . . . KAWASAKI
CYLINDERS. . . 2
ENGINE HP . . . 21
COOLING . . . AIR
FUEL . . . G
SPEEDS . . . VARIABLE
TRANSMISSION . . . HYDRO
STEERING. . . ZERO
BLADE CLUTCH . . . ELECTRIC
STANDARD DECK . . . 44"
MSRP. . . $7,969

OPTIONS

2 BAG
ROPS
SUS SEAT

RETAIL PRICING

YEAR	HIGH	LOW
2006	$2,553	$1,915
2007	$2,837	$2,128
2008	$3,150	$2,362
2009	$3,497	$2,622

144M

YEARS MFRD . . . 2005-2006
ENGINE . . . KAWASAKI
CYLINDERS. . . 2
ENGINE HP . . . 21
COOLING . . . AIR
FUEL . . . G
SPEEDS . . . VARIABLE
TRANSMISSION . . . HYDRO
STEERING. . . ZERO
STANDARD DECK . . . 44"
WEIGHT . . . 946 LBS.
MSRP. . . $6,799

OPTIONS

3 BAG
ROPS
SUS SEAT

RETAIL PRICING

YEAR	HIGH	LOW
2005	$2,059	$1,544
2006	$2,284	$1,713

148 XDZ

YEARS MFRD . . . 2010-2010
ENGINE . . . KAWASAKI
CYLINDERS. . . 2
ENGINE HP . . . 21
COOLING . . . AIR
FUEL . . . G
SPEEDS . . . VARIABLE
TRANSMISSION . . . HYDRO
STEERING. . . ZERO
BLADE CLUTCH . . . ELECTRIC

148IM XDZ

YEARS MFRD . . . 2009-2009
ENGINE . . . KAWASAKI
CYLINDERS. . . 2
ENGINE HP . . . 23
COOLING . . . AIR
FUEL . . . G
SPEEDS . . . VARIABLE
TRANSMISSION . . . HYDRO
STEERING. . . ZERO
BLADE CLUTCH . . . ELECTRIC
STANDARD DECK . . . 48"
MSRP. . . $7,373

OPTIONS

2 BAG
3 BAG
ROPS

RETAIL PRICING

YEAR	HIGH	LOW
2009	$3,236	$2,427

148M

YEARS MFRD . . . 2005-2008
ENGINE . . . KAWASAKI
CYLINDERS. . . 2
ENGINE HP . . . 19
COOLING . . . AIR
FUEL . . . G
SPEEDS . . . VARIABLE
TRANSMISSION . . . HYDRO
STEERING. . . ZERO
BLADE CLUTCH . . . ELECTRIC
STANDARD DECK . . . 48"
WEIGHT . . . 951 LBS.
MSRP. . . $7,089

OPTIONS

2 BAG
ROPS
SUS SEAT

RETAIL PRICING

YEAR	HIGH	LOW
2005	$2,086	$1,565
2006	$2,320	$1,740
2007	$2,573	$1,929
2008	$2,857	$2,143

148M XDZ

YEARS MFRD . . . 2006-2009
ENGINE . . . KAWASAKI
CYLINDERS. . . 2
ENGINE HP . . . 21
COOLING . . . AIR

FUEL . . . . . G
SPEEDS . . . . . VARIABLE
TRANSMISSION . . . . . HYDRO
STEERING . . . . . ZERO
STANDARD DECK . . . . . 48"
WEIGHT . . . . . 951 LBS.
MSRP $8,399

OPTIONS

2 BAG
52" DECK
ROPS
SUS SEAT

RETAIL PRICING

YEAR	HIGH	LOW
2006	$2,692	$2,019
2007	$2,988	$2,241
2008	$3,319	$2,489
2009	$3,687	$2,765

152 XDZ

YEARS MFRD 2010-2010
ENGINE . . . . . KAWASAKI
CYLINDERS 2
ENGINE HP 23
COOLING . . . . . AIR
FUEL . . . . . G
SPEEDS . . . . . VARIABLE
TRANSMISSION . . . . . HYDRO
STEERING . . . . . ZERO
BLADE CLUTCH . . . . . ELECTRIC

152IM XDZ

YEARS MFRD 2009-2009
ENGINE . . . . . KAWASAKI
CYLINDERS 2
ENGINE HP 23
COOLING . . . . . AIR
FUEL . . . . . G
SPEEDS . . . . . VARIABLE
TRANSMISSION . . . . . HYDRO
STEERING . . . . . ZERO
BLADE CLUTCH . . . . . ELECTRIC
STANDARD DECK . . . . . 52"
MSRP $7,676

OPTIONS

2 BAG
3 BAG
ROPS

RETAIL PRICING

YEAR	HIGH	LOW
2009	$3,367	$2,525

152M

YEARS MFRD 2005-2008
ENGINE . . . . . KAWASAKI
CYLINDERS 2
ENGINE HP 21
COOLING . . . . . AIR
FUEL . . . . . G
SPEEDS . . . . . VARIABLE
TRANSMISSION . . . . . HYDRO
STEERING . . . . . ZERO
BLADE CLUTCH . . . . . ELECTRIC
STANDARD DECK . . . . . 52"
WEIGHT . . . . . 961 LBS.
MSRP $7,399

OPTIONS

2 BAG
KOHLER 25HP
ROPS
SUS SEAT

RETAIL PRICING

YEAR	HIGH	LOW
2005	$2,177	$1,632
2006	$2,419	$1,814
2007	$2,687	$2,015
2008	$2,984	$2,238

152M XDZ

YEARS MFRD 2006-2009
ENGINE . . . . . KAWASAKI
CYLINDERS 2
ENGINE HP 23
COOLING . . . . . AIR
FUEL . . . . . G
SPEEDS . . . . . VARIABLE
TRANSMISSION . . . . . HYDRO
STEERING . . . . . ZERO
STANDARD DECK . . . . . 52"
WEIGHT . . . . . 961 LBS.
MSRP $8,729

OPTIONS

3 BAG
KOHLER 23HP
ROPS
SUS SEAT

RETAIL PRICING

YEAR	HIGH	LOW
2006	$2,797	$2,098
2007	$3,106	$2,329
2008	$3,449	$2,586
2009	$3,829	$2,872

160IM XDZ

YEARS MFRD 2009-2009
ENGINE . . . . . KAWASAKI
CYLINDERS 2
ENGINE HP 25
COOLING . . . . . AIR
FUEL . . . . . G
SPEEDS . . . . . VARIABLE
TRANSMISSION . . . . . HYDRO
STEERING . . . . . ZERO
BLADE CLUTCH . . . . . ELECTRIC
STANDARD DECK . . . . . 60"
MSRP $7,878

OPTIONS

2 BAG
3 BAG
ROPS

RETAIL PRICING

YEAR	HIGH	LOW
2009	$3,458	$2,594

200

YEARS MFRD 1994-1998
SERIES . . . . . PROMASTER SERIES
ENGINE . . . . . KOHLER
ENGINE HP 20
FUEL . . . . . G
TRANSMISSION . . . . . HYDRO
STEERING . . . . . STANDARD
STANDARD DECK . . . . . 50"
MSRP $8,260

OPTIONS

60" DECK
KAWASAKI 20E

RETAIL PRICING

YEAR	HIGH	LOW
1994	$2,419	$1,814
1995	$2,513	$1,885
1996	$2,670	$2,002
1997	$2,970	$2,228
1998	$3,123	$2,342

252H

YEARS MFRD 2005-2006
ENGINE . . . . . KOHLER
CYLINDERS 2
ENGINE HP 23
FUEL . . . . . G
SPEEDS . . . . . VARIABLE
TRANSMISSION . . . . . HYDRO
STEERING . . . . . ZERO
STANDARD DECK . . . . . 52"
MSRP $9,099

OPTIONS

3 BAG
BLADE
ROPS
SNOW BLOWER

RETAIL PRICING

YEAR	HIGH	LOW
2005	$2,722	$2,042
2006	$3,022	$2,267

252M

YEARS MFRD 2005-2005
ENGINE . . . . . KOHLER
CYLINDERS 2
ENGINE HP 27
COOLING . . . . . AIR
FUEL . . . . . G
SPEEDS . . . . . VARIABLE
TRANSMISSION . . . . . HYDRO
STEERING . . . . . ZERO
BLADE CLUTCH . . . . . ELECTRIC
STANDARD DECK . . . . . 52"
WEIGHT . . . . . 1,145 LBS.
MSRP $7,999

OPTIONS

PTO BAG
SNOW BLOWER

RETAIL PRICING

YEAR	HIGH	LOW
2005	$2,536	$1,902

252M XDZ

YEARS MFRD 2005-2006
ENGINE . . . . . KAWASAKI
CYLINDERS 2
ENGINE HP 26
COOLING . . . . . LIQUID
FUEL . . . . . G
SPEEDS . . . . . VARIABLE
TRANSMISSION . . . . . HYDRO
STEERING . . . . . ZERO
STANDARD DECK . . . . . 52"
WEIGHT . . . . . 1,145 LBS.
MSRP $8,699

OPTIONS

3 BAG
HYD LIFT
ROPS
SNOW BLOWER

RETAIL PRICING

YEAR	HIGH	LOW
2005	$2,631	$1,973
2006	$2,924	$2,193

260H RD

YEARS MFRD 2014-2014
SERIES . . . . . 200 SERIES
ENGINE . . . . . KAWASAKI FX850V
CID 852CC
ENGINE HP 27
COOLING . . . . . AIR
FUEL . . . . . G
SPEEDS . . . . . VARIABLE
TRANSMISSION . . . . . HYDRO
STEERING . . . . . ZERO
BLADE CLUTCH . . . . . ELECTRIC

260H-27

YEARS MFRD 2007-2009
SERIES . . . . . XDZ 200 SERIES
ENGINE . . . . . KOHLER
CYLINDERS 2
ENGINE HP 27
COOLING . . . . . AIR
FUEL . . . . . G
SPEEDS . . . . . VARIABLE
TRANSMISSION . . . . . HYDRO
STEERING . . . . . ZERO
BLADE CLUTCH . . . . . ELECTRIC
STANDARD DECK . . . . . 60"
MSRP $10,839

OPTIONS

3 BAG
BLADE
ROPS
SNOW BLOWER

RETAIL PRICING

YEAR	HIGH	LOW
2007	$3,856	$2,892
2008	$4,284	$3,213
2009	$4,758	$3,568

260H-27D

YEARS MFRD 2007-2009
SERIES . . . . . XDZ 200 SERIES
ENGINE . . . . . DAIHATSU
CYLINDERS 2
ENGINE HP 27
COOLING . . . . . LIQUID
FUEL . . . . . D
SPEEDS . . . . . VARIABLE
TRANSMISSION . . . . . HYDRO

STEERING................ZERO
BLADE CLUTCH........ELECTRIC
STANDARD DECK........... 60"
MSRP................ $15,279

OPTIONS

3 BAG
BLADE
ROPS
SNOW BLOWER

RETAIL PRICING

YEAR	HIGH	LOW
2007	$5,437	$4,078
2008	$6,038	$4,528
2009	$6,705	$5,029

260H-28

YEARS MFRD........ 2009-2009
SERIES..........XDZ 200 SERIES
ENGINE .... GENERAC LP
ENGINE HP................28
COOLING..................AIR
FUEL.......................G
SPEEDS.............VARIABLE
TRANSMISSION ....HYDRO
STEERING................ZERO
STANDARD DECK........... 60"
MSRP................ $12,725

OPTIONS

3 BAG
BLADE
DAIHATSU 27HP
KAWASAKI 26HP
KAWASAKI 27HP
KAWASAKI 31HP
ROPS
SNOW BLOWER

RETAIL PRICING

YEAR	HIGH	LOW
2009	$5,584	$4,188

260M

YEARS MFRD........ 2005-2008
ENGINE ....KOHLER
CYLINDERS..................2
ENGINE HP................27
COOLING..................AIR
FUEL.......................G
SPEEDS.............VARIABLE
TRANSMISSION ....HYDRO
STEERING................ZERO
BLADE CLUTCH........ELECTRIC
STANDARD DECK........... 60"
WEIGHT.............1,160 LBS.
MSRP.................. $8,899

OPTIONS

3 BAG
HYD LIFT
ROPS
SNOW BLOWER

RETAIL PRICING

YEAR	HIGH	LOW
2005	$2,621	$1,965
2006	$2,907	$2,180
2007	$3,233	$2,425
2008	$3,587	$2,690

260M XDZ

YEARS MFRD........ 2006-2007
ENGINE ....KAWASAKI LC
CYLINDERS..................2
ENGINE HP................25
COOLING..................AIR
FUEL.......................G
SPEEDS.............VARIABLE
TRANSMISSION ....HYDRO
STEERING................ZERO
STANDARD DECK........... 60"
MSRP.................. $9,415

OPTIONS

3 BAG
HYD LIFT
ROPS

RETAIL PRICING

YEAR	HIGH	LOW
2006	$3,117	$2,338
2007	$3,466	$2,600

266 M/H XDZ

YEARS MFRD........ 2010-2010
SERIES..........200 XDZ SERIES
ENGINE ....KAWASAKI
CYLINDERS..................2
ENGINE HP................30
FUEL.......................G
SPEEDS.............VARIABLE
TRANSMISSION ....HYDRO
STEERING................ZERO
BLADE CLUTCH........ELECTRIC

OPTIONS

KAWASAKI 31HP

266H-30

YEARS MFRD........ 2008-2009
SERIES..........XDZ 200 SERIES
ENGINE ...... KOHLER COMMAND
CYLINDERS..................2
ENGINE HP................30
COOLING..................AIR
FUEL.......................G
SPEEDS.............VARIABLE
TRANSMISSION ....HYDRO
STEERING................ZERO
BLADE CLUTCH........ELECTRIC
STANDARD DECK........... 66"
MSRP................ $11,495

OPTIONS

3 BAG
BLADE
KAWASAKI 31HP
KOHLER 40HP
ROPS
SNOW BLOWER

RETAIL PRICING

YEAR	HIGH	LOW
2008	$4,545	$3,409
2009	$5,046	$3,785

266M-31

YEARS MFRD........ 2008-2009
SERIES..........XDZ 200 SERIES
ENGINE ....KAWASAKI
CYLINDERS..................2
ENGINE HP................31
COOLING..................AIR
FUEL.......................G
SPEEDS.............VARIABLE
TRANSMISSION ....HYDRO
STEERING................ZERO
STANDARD DECK........... 66"
MSRP................ $11,059

OPTIONS

3 BAG
BLADE
KOHLER 30HP
ROPS
SNOW BLOWER

RETAIL PRICING

YEAR	HIGH	LOW
2008	$4,370	$3,277
2009	$4,853	$3,640

272H-26

YEARS MFRD........ 2006-2007
SERIES..........XDZ 200 SERIES
ENGINE ....KAWASAKI LC
CYLINDERS..................2
ENGINE HP................26
COOLING...............LIQUID
FUEL.......................G
SPEEDS.............VARIABLE
TRANSMISSION ....HYDRO
STEERING................ZERO
STANDARD DECK........... 72"
WEIGHT.............1,275 LBS.
MSRP................ $11,349

OPTIONS

3 BAG
DAIHATSU 31HP
DAIHATSU DIESEL 27HP
KAWASAKI 31E
KOHLER 40HP
ROPS

RETAIL PRICING

YEAR	HIGH	LOW
2006	$3,757	$2,818
2007	$4,173	$3,130

272H-31

YEARS MFRD........ 2006-2009
SERIES..........XDZ 200 SERIES
ENGINE .... DAIHATSU
CYLINDERS..................2
ENGINE HP................31
COOLING...............LIQUID
FUEL.......................D
SPEEDS.............VARIABLE
TRANSMISSION ....HYDRO
STEERING................ZERO
BLADE CLUTCH........ELECTRIC
STANDARD DECK........... 72"
MSRP................ $18,888

OPTIONS

3 BAG
KAWASAKI 31HP
ROPS
SNOW BLOWER

RETAIL PRICING

YEAR	HIGH	LOW
2006	$6,054	$4,541
2007	$6,722	$5,041
2008	$7,464	$5,598
2009	$8,291	$6,218

320HD

YEARS MFRD........ 2007-2007
ENGINE ....KOHLER
ENGINE HP................27
COOLING..................AIR
FUEL.......................G
SPEEDS.............VARIABLE
TRANSMISSION ....HYDRO
STEERING................ZERO
BLADE CLUTCH........ELECTRIC
STANDARD DECK........... 60"
WEIGHT.............. 925 LBS.
MSRP.................. $7,199

OPTIONS

KAWASAKI 25HP

RETAIL PRICING

YEAR	HIGH	LOW
2007	$3,676	$2,757

350

YEARS MFRD........ 1996-1998
SERIES.......PROMASTER SERIES
ENGINE ....KAWASAKI
ENGINE HP................20
TRANSMISSION ....HYDRO
STEERING............STANDARD
STANDARD DECK........... 50"
MSRP.................. $9,071

OPTIONS

60" DECK
KUBOTA 21HP

RETAIL PRICING

YEAR	HIGH	LOW
1996	$2,860	$2,145
1997	$3,176	$2,382
1998	$3,430	$2,573

1028

YEARS MFRD........ 2003-2004
ENGINE ....B&S
ENGINE HP................10
COOLING..................AIR
FUEL.......................G
SPEEDS.............VARIABLE
TRANSMISSION ....HYDRO
STEERING............STANDARD
STANDARD DECK........... 28"
MSRP.................. $1,699

OPTIONS

BAG & VAC

RETAIL PRICING

YEAR	HIGH	LOW
2003	$260	$195
2004	$288	$216

GRAVELY

1232

YEARS MFRD 2003-2004
ENGINE . . . . B&S
ENGINE HP 12
COOLING . . . . AIR
FUEL . . . . G
SPEEDS . . . . VARIABLE
TRANSMISSION . . . . HYDRO
STEERING. . . . . ZERO
STANDARD DECK . . . . 32"
MSRP. $1,899

OPTIONS

BAG & VAC

RETAIL PRICING

YEAR	HIGH	LOW
2003	$290	$218
2004	$321	$241

1232G

YEARS MFRD 1988-1991
SERIES. . . . . 1200 SERIES
ENGINE . . . . B&S
ENGINE HP 12
COOLING . . . . AIR
FUEL . . . . G
TRANSMISSION . . . . GEAR
STEERING. . . . . STANDARD

1238G

YEARS MFRD 1988-1991
SERIES. . . . . 1200 SERIES
ENGINE . . . . B&S
ENGINE HP 12
COOLING . . . . AIR
FUEL . . . . G
TRANSMISSION . . . . GEAR
STEERING. . . . . STANDARD

1440

YEARS MFRD 2003-2004
ENGINE . . . . B&S
ENGINE HP 14
COOLING . . . . AIR
FUEL . . . . G
SPEEDS . . . . VARIABLE
TRANSMISSION . . . . HYDRO
STEERING. . . . . STANDARD
STANDARD DECK . . . . 40"
MSRP. $2,199

OPTIONS

BAG & VAC

RETAIL PRICING

YEAR	HIGH	LOW
2003	$336	$252
2004	$372	$279

2186GT

YEARS MFRD 2005-2006
SERIES. . . . . 2000 SERIES
ENGINE . . . . B&S
ENGINE HP 10.5
COOLING . . . . AIR
FUEL . . . . G
SPEEDS . . . . VARIABLE
TRANSMISSION . . . . HYDRO
STANDARD DECK . . . . 28"
MSRP. $2,099

RETAIL PRICING

YEAR	HIGH	LOW
2005	$503	$377
2005	$503	$377
2006	$557	$417
2006	$557	$417

14532

YEARS MFRD 2005-2006
ENGINE . . . . B&S
ENGINE HP 14.5
COOLING . . . . AIR
FUEL . . . . G
SPEEDS . . . . VARIABLE
TRANSMISSION . . . . HYDRO
STEERING. . . . . STANDARD
STANDARD DECK . . . . 32"
MSRP. $2,299

OPTIONS

2 BAG

RETAIL PRICING

YEAR	HIGH	LOW
2005	$435	$326
2006	$483	$362

GRAZER

G209V

YEARS MFRD 1996-1996
ENGINE . . . . B&S
ENGINE HP 20
FUEL . . . . G
TRANSMISSION . . . . HYDRO
STEERING. . . . . STANDARD
STANDARD DECK . . . . 52"
MSRP. $8,629

RETAIL PRICING

YEAR	HIGH	LOW
1996	$3,193	$2,395

G1600

YEARS MFRD 1992-1996
ENGINE . . . . B&S
ENGINE HP 16
COOLING . . . . AIR
FUEL . . . . G
TRANSMISSION . . . . HYDRO
STEERING. . . . . ZERO
STANDARD DECK . . . . 52"
MSRP. $6,595

SERIAL NUMBERS

YEAR	BEGINNING NO.
1992	02-09-0001
1993	953304001
1994	953308001
1995	953408001
1996	953508014

RETAIL PRICING

YEAR	HIGH	LOW
1992	$406	$305
1993	$449	$337
1994	$500	$375
1995	$555	$416
1996	$589	$442

G1800CD

YEARS MFRD 1996-2001
ENGINE . . . . B&S
ENGINE HP 18
COOLING . . . . AIR
FUEL . . . . G
TRANSMISSION . . . . HYDRO
STEERING. . . . . ZERO
STANDARD DECK . . . . 52"
MSRP. $7,399

OPTIONS

52" SNOW BLOWER
62" DECK
BAGGER

SERIAL NUMBERS

YEAR	BEGINNING NO.
1996	953508001
1997	953608016
1998	953707045

RETAIL PRICING

YEAR	HIGH	LOW
1996	$660	$495
1997	$729	$546
1998	$808	$606
1999	$899	$674
2000	$997	$748
2001	$1,105	$829

G1800KSS

YEARS MFRD 1988-1991
ENGINE . . . . KOHLER
ENGINE HP 18
COOLING . . . . AIR
FUEL . . . . G
TRANSMISSION . . . . HYDRO
STEERING. . . . . ZERO
STANDARD DECK . . . . 42"
MSRP. $6,140

OPTIONS

52" DECK
62" DECK

SERIAL NUMBERS

YEAR	BEGINNING NO.
1988	08-08-0001
1989	09-08-0001
1990	00-09-0001

RETAIL PRICING

YEAR	HIGH	LOW
1989	$1,332	$999
1990	$1,746	$1,310
1991	$1,864	$1,398

G1800SS

YEARS MFRD 1988-1991
ENGINE . . . . B&S
ENGINE HP 18
COOLING . . . . AIR
FUEL . . . . G
TRANSMISSION . . . . HYDRO
STEERING. . . . . STANDARD
STANDARD DECK . . . . 42"
MSRP. $6,010

OPTIONS

52" DECK
62" DECK

SERIAL NUMBERS

YEAR	BEGINNING NO.
1988	08-08-0001
1989	09-08-0001
1990	00-09-0001
1991	01-09-0001

RETAIL PRICING

YEAR	HIGH	LOW
1989	$1,301	$976
1990	$1,710	$1,282
1991	$1,823	$1,367

G1890

YEARS MFRD 1990-1995
ENGINE . . . . B&S
ENGINE HP 18
COOLING . . . . AIR
FUEL . . . . G
TRANSMISSION . . . . HYDRO
STEERING. . . . . ZERO
STANDARD DECK . . . . 52"
MSRP. $7,665

OPTIONS

62" DECK

SERIAL NUMBERS

YEAR	BEGINNING NO.
1990	00-09-0001
1991	01-09-0001
1992	02-09-0001
1993	953304001
1994	953308001
1995	953408001

RETAIL PRICING

YEAR	HIGH	LOW
1990	$402	$302
1991	$445	$334
1992	$493	$370
1993	$546	$410
1994	$609	$456
1995	$674	$505

G1890K

YEARS MFRD 1990-1997
ENGINE . . . . KOHLER
ENGINE HP 18
COOLING . . . . AIR
FUEL . . . . G
TRANSMISSION . . . . HYDRO
STEERING. . . . . ZERO
STANDARD DECK . . . . 52"
MSRP. $7,975

OPTIONS
62" DECK

SERIAL NUMBERS

YEAR	BEGINNING NO.
1990	00-09-0001
1991	01-09-0001
1992	02-09-0001
1993	953304001
1994	953308001
1995	953408001
1996	953508001
1997	953608001

RETAIL PRICING

YEAR	HIGH	LOW
1990	$445	$334
1991	$497	$373
1992	$551	$413
1993	$609	$456
1994	$678	$508
1995	$751	$563
1996	$834	$626
1997	$997	$748

G1890V

YEARS MFRD	1993-1996
ENGINE	B&S
ENGINE HP	18
COOLING	AIR
FUEL	G
TRANSMISSION	HYDRO
STEERING	ZERO
STANDARD DECK	52"
MSRP	$8,010

OPTIONS
62" DECK

SERIAL NUMBERS

YEAR	BEGINNING NO.
1993	953304001
1994	953308001
1995	953408801
1996	953505016

RETAIL PRICING

YEAR	HIGH	LOW
1993	$594	$446
1994	$660	$495
1995	$732	$549
1996	$818	$613

G1897V

YEARS MFRD	1997-2003
ENGINE	B&S
ENGINE HP	18
COOLING	AIR
FUEL	G
SPEEDS	VARIABLE
TRANSMISSION	HYDRO
STEERING	ZERO
STANDARD DECK	52"
MSRP	$8,799

OPTIONS
52" SNOW BLOWER
62" DECK
BAGGER

SERIAL NUMBERS

YEAR	BEGINNING NO.
1998	953707045
2002	953209035

RETAIL PRICING

YEAR	HIGH	LOW
1997	$1,084	$813
1998	$1,200	$900
1999	$1,331	$998
2000	$1,478	$1,109
2001	$1,639	$1,229
2002	$1,820	$1,365
2003	$2,019	$1,514

G2000C II

YEARS MFRD	1988-1996
ENGINE	KUBOTA
ENGINE HP	20
COOLING	AIR
FUEL	G
SPEEDS	VARIABLE
TRANSMISSION	HYDRO
STEERING	ZERO
STANDARD DECK	62"
MSRP	$10,699

SERIAL NUMBERS

YEAR	BEGINNING NO.
1988	08-08-0001
1989	09-08-0001
1990	00-09-0001
1991	01-09-0001
1992	02-09-0001
1993	953304001
1994	953308001
1995	953408001
1996	953508001

RETAIL PRICING

YEAR	HIGH	LOW
1988	$504	$378
1989	$559	$419
1990	$619	$464
1991	$689	$517
1992	$764	$573
1993	$849	$636
1994	$942	$706
1995	$1,044	$783
1996	$1,161	$870

G2018D

YEARS MFRD	1993-1996
ENGINE	PERKINS
ENGINE HP	18
COOLING	LIQUID
FUEL	D
TRANSMISSION	HYDRO
STEERING	ZERO
STANDARD DECK	52"
MSRP	$15,779

OPTIONS
62" DECK

SERIAL NUMBERS

YEAR	BEGINNING NO.
1993	953304001
1994	953308001
1995	953408001
1996	953508001

RETAIL PRICING

YEAR	HIGH	LOW
1993	$1,200	$900
1994	$1,333	$1,000
1995	$1,478	$1,109
1996	$1,639	$1,229

G2090V

YEARS MFRD	1996-1996
ENGINE	B&S
ENGINE HP	20
COOLING	AIR
FUEL	G
SPEEDS	VARIABLE
TRANSMISSION	HYDRO
STEERING	ZERO
STANDARD DECK	62"
MSRP	$8,799

SERIAL NUMBERS

YEAR	BEGINNING NO.
1996	953508001

RETAIL PRICING

YEAR	HIGH	LOW
1996	$902	$677

G2097V

YEARS MFRD	1997-2003
ENGINE	B&S
ENGINE HP	20
COOLING	AIR
FUEL	G
SPEEDS	VARIABLE
TRANSMISSION	HYDRO
STEERING	ZERO
STANDARD DECK	52"
MSRP	$9,108

OPTIONS
52" SNOW BLOWER
62" DECK
BAGGER

SERIAL NUMBERS

YEAR	BEGINNING NO.
1998	953707045
2002	953209035

RETAIL PRICING

YEAR	HIGH	LOW
1997	$1,164	$873
1998	$1,290	$968
1999	$1,431	$1,074
2000	$1,588	$1,191
2001	$1,761	$1,320
2002	$1,955	$1,466
2003	$2,168	$1,626

G2297K

YEARS MFRD	1997-2003
ENGINE	KOHLER
ENGINE HP	22
COOLING	AIR
FUEL	G
SPEEDS	VARIABLE
TRANSMISSION	HYDRO
STEERING	ZERO
STANDARD DECK	52"
MSRP	$7,499

OPTIONS
52" SNOW BLOWER
62" DECK
72" DECK
BAGGER

SERIAL NUMBERS

YEAR	BEGINNING NO.
1998	953707045
2002	953209035

RETAIL PRICING

YEAR	HIGH	LOW
1997	$1,229	$922
1998	$1,362	$1,022
1999	$1,512	$1,134
2000	$1,678	$1,259
2001	$1,860	$1,395
2002	$2,067	$1,550
2003	$2,292	$1,719
2004	$3,765	$2,824

G3200C

YEARS MFRD	1987-1992
ENGINE	KUBOTA
ENGINE HP	21
FUEL	D
TRANSMISSION	HYDRO
STEERING	ZERO
STANDARD DECK	52"
MSRP	$13,415

OPTIONS
62" DECK

SERIAL NUMBERS

YEAR	BEGINNING NO.
1987	07-08-0001
1988	08-08-0001
1989	09-08-0001
1990	00-09-0001
1991	01-09-0001
1992	02-09-0001

RETAIL PRICING

YEAR	HIGH	LOW
1987	$461	$346
1988	$507	$380
1989	$564	$423
1990	$628	$471
1991	$697	$523
1992	$772	$579

G3210C

YEARS MFRD	1990-1991
ENGINE	KUBOTA
ENGINE HP	21
COOLING	LIQUID
FUEL	G
TRANSMISSION	HYDRO
STEERING	ZERO
STANDARD DECK	72"
MSRP	$13,750

RETAIL PRICING

YEAR	HIGH	LOW
1990	$668	$501
1991	$740	$555

G4200CD

YEARS MFRD	1987-1992
ENGINE	KUBOTA
ENGINE HP	22

GRAZER

FUEL .... D
TRANSMISSION .... HYDRO
STEERING .... ZERO
STANDARD DECK .... 52"
MSRP $15,345

OPTIONS

62" DECK

SERIAL NUMBERS

YEAR	BEGINNING NO.
1987	07-08-0001
1988	08-08-0001
1989	09-08-0001
1990	00-09-0001
1991	01-09-0001
1992	02-09-0001

RETAIL PRICING

YEAR	HIGH	LOW
1987	$559	$419
1988	$619	$464
1989	$689	$517
1990	$761	$571
1991	$844	$633
1992	$939	$704

G4210CD

YEARS MFRD 1990-1991
ENGINE .... KUBOTA
ENGINE HP 22
COOLING .... LIQUID
FUEL .... G
TRANSMISSION .... HYDRO
STEERING .... ZERO
STANDARD DECK .... 72"
MSRP $15,745

RETAIL PRICING

YEAR	HIGH	LOW
1990	$867	$650
1991	$963	$722

GREAT DANE

GBKH2752S

YEARS MFRD 2008-2009
SERIES .... BRUTUS SERIES
ENGINE .... KOHLER E/S
ENGINE HP 27
COOLING .... AIR
FUEL .... G
SPEEDS .... VARIABLE
TRANSMISSION .... HYDRO
STEERING .... ZERO
STANDARD DECK .... 52"
WEIGHT .... 1,124 LBS.
MSRP $8,599

RETAIL PRICING

YEAR	HIGH	LOW
2008	$2,614	$1,961
2009	$3,449	$2,587

GBKH2761S

YEARS MFRD 2008-2012
SERIES .... BRUTUS SERIES
ENGINE .... KOHLER
ENGINE HP 27
COOLING .... AIR
FUEL .... G
SPEEDS .... VARIABLE
TRANSMISSION .... HYDRO
STEERING .... ZERO
STANDARD DECK .... 61"
WEIGHT .... 1,149 LBS.
MSRP $9,099

RETAIL PRICING

YEAR	HIGH	LOW
2008	$2,640	$1,980
2009	$3,700	$2,775
2010	$3,801	$2,850
2011	$5,083	$3,812
2012	$5,543	$4,157

GBKW2552S

YEARS MFRD 2008-2012
SERIES .... BRUTUS SERIES
ENGINE .... KAWASAKI E/S
ENGINE HP 25
COOLING .... AIR
FUEL .... G
SPEEDS .... VARIABLE
TRANSMISSION .... HYDRO
STEERING .... ZERO
STANDARD DECK .... 52"
WEIGHT .... 1,119 LBS.
MSRP $8,849

RETAIL PRICING

YEAR	HIGH	LOW
2008	$2,221	$1,666
2009	$2,822	$2,117
2010	$3,564	$2,673
2011	$4,806	$3,604
2012	$5,392	$4,044

GBKW2561S

YEARS MFRD 2008-2012
SERIES .... BRUTUS SERIES
ENGINE .... KAWASAKI E/S
ENGINE HP 25
COOLING .... AIR
FUEL .... G
SPEEDS .... VARIABLE
TRANSMISSION .... HYDRO
STEERING .... ZERO
STANDARD DECK .... 61"
WEIGHT .... 1,144 LBS.
MSRP $8,999

RETAIL PRICING

YEAR	HIGH	LOW
2008	$2,518	$1,889
2009	$3,207	$2,406
2010	$3,761	$2,821
2011	$5,095	$3,821
2012	$5,402	$4,051

GCBR2652S

YEARS MFRD 2012-2012
SERIES .... CHARIOT SERIES
ENGINE .... B&S
ENGINE HP 26
COOLING .... AIR
FUEL .... G
SPEEDS .... VARIABLE
TRANSMISSION .... HYDRO
STEERING .... ZERO
BLADE CLUTCH .... ELECTRIC
WEIGHT .... 1,119 LBS.

GCBV2348S

YEARS MFRD 2012-2012
SERIES .... CHARIOT SERIES
ENGINE .... B&S VANGUARD
ENGINE HP 23
COOLING .... AIR
FUEL .... G
SPEEDS .... VARIABLE
TRANSMISSION .... HYDRO
STEERING .... ZERO
BLADE CLUTCH .... ELECTRIC
WEIGHT .... 1,104 LBS.

GCBV2361S

YEARS MFRD 2008-2009
SERIES .... CHARIOT SERIES
ENGINE .... B&S VANGUARD
ENGINE HP 23
COOLING .... AIR
FUEL .... G
SPEEDS .... VARIABLE
TRANSMISSION .... HYDRO
STEERING .... ZERO
BLADE CLUTCH .... ELECTRIC
WEIGHT .... 1,144 LBS.

GCKA1948S

YEARS MFRD 2009-2009
SERIES .... CHARIOT SERIES
ENGINE .... KAWASAKI
ENGINE HP 19
COOLING .... AIR
FUEL .... G
SPEEDS .... VARIABLE
TRANSMISSION .... HYDRO
STEERING .... ZERO
BLADE CLUTCH .... ELECTRIC
STANDARD DECK .... 48"
WEIGHT .... 1,104 LBS.
MSRP $6,929

RETAIL PRICING

YEAR	HIGH	LOW
2009	$3,123	$2,342

GCKH2352S

YEARS MFRD 2008-2008
SERIES .... CHARIOT SERIES
ENGINE .... KOHLER
ENGINE HP 23
COOLING .... AIR
FUEL .... G
SPEEDS .... VARIABLE
TRANSMISSION .... HYDRO
STEERING .... ZERO
BLADE CLUTCH .... ELECTRIC
STANDARD DECK .... 52"
WEIGHT .... 1,119 LBS.
MSRP $7,599

RETAIL PRICING

YEAR	HIGH	LOW
2008	$2,310	$1,732

GCKW2352S

YEARS MFRD 2009-2011
SERIES .... CHARIOT SERIES
ENGINE .... KAWASAKI
CYLINDERS 2
ENGINE HP 23
COOLING .... AIR
FUEL .... G
SPEEDS .... VARIABLE
TRANSMISSION .... HYDRO
STEERING .... ZERO
BLADE CLUTCH .... ELECTRIC
STANDARD DECK .... 52"
WEIGHT .... 1,119 LBS.
MSRP $7,699

RETAIL PRICING

YEAR	HIGH	LOW
2009	$2,709	$2,032
2010	$3,106	$2,329
2011	$4,260	$3,195

GCKW2561S

YEARS MFRD 2008-2009
SERIES .... CHARIOT SERIES
ENGINE .... KAWASAKI
ENGINE HP 25
COOLING .... AIR
FUEL .... G
SPEEDS .... VARIABLE
TRANSMISSION .... HYDRO
STEERING .... ZERO
BLADE CLUTCH .... ELECTRIC
STANDARD DECK .... 61"
WEIGHT .... 1,144 LBS.
MSRP $8,499

RETAIL PRICING

YEAR	HIGH	LOW
2008	$2,496	$1,872
2009	$2,815	$2,111

GLKW1536S

YEARS MFRD 2007-2007
SERIES ... SCAMPER HYDRO SERIES
ENGINE .... KAWASAKI
ENGINE HP 15
COOLING .... AIR
FUEL .... G
SPEEDS .... VARIABLE
TRANSMISSION .... HYDRO
STEERING .... ZERO
WEIGHT .... 560 LBS.

GLKW1748S

YEARS MFRD 2007-2007
SERIES ... SCAMPER HYDRO SERIES
ENGINE .... KAWASAKI
ENGINE HP 17
COOLING .... AIR
FUEL .... G
SPEEDS .... VARIABLE
TRANSMISSION .... HYDRO
STEERING .... ZERO
WEIGHT .... 580 LBS.

GSKA1948S

YEARS MFRD 2008-2012
SERIES ..... SUPER SURFER SERIES
ENGINE .... KAWASAKI
ENGINE HP 19
COOLING .... AIR
FUEL .... G
SPEEDS .... VARIABLE
TRANSMISSION .... HYDRO
STEERING .... ZERO
BLADE CLUTCH .... ELECTRIC
STANDARD DECK .... 48"
WEIGHT .... 735 LBS.
MSRP $7,499

RETAIL PRICING

YEAR	HIGH	LOW
2008	$3,324	$2,493
2009	$3,528	$2,646
2010	$3,973	$2,980
2011	$4,329	$3,246
2012	$4,712	$3,534

GSKH1848S

YEARS MFRD 2008-2009
SERIES ..... SUPER SURFER SERIES
ENGINE .... KOHLER
ENGINE HP 18
COOLING .... AIR
FUEL .... G
SPEEDS .... VARIABLE
TRANSMISSION .... HYDRO
STEERING .... ZERO
BLADE CLUTCH .... ELECTRIC
STANDARD DECK .... 48"
WEIGHT .... 750 LBS.
MSRP $6,599

RETAIL PRICING

YEAR	HIGH	LOW
2008	$3,808	$2,856
2009	$4,207	$3,155

GSKH2352S

YEARS MFRD 2008-2008
SERIES ..... SUPER SURFER SERIES
ENGINE .... KOHLER
ENGINE HP 23
COOLING .... AIR
FUEL .... G
SPEEDS .... VARIABLE
TRANSMISSION .... HYDRO
STEERING .... ZERO
BLADE CLUTCH .... ELECTRIC
STANDARD DECK .... 52"
WEIGHT .... 775 LBS.
MSRP $7,299

RETAIL PRICING

YEAR	HIGH	LOW
2008	$2,144	$1,608

GSKH2561S

YEARS MFRD 2008-2009
SERIES ..... SUPER SURFER SERIES
ENGINE .... KOHLER
ENGINE HP 25
COOLING .... AIR
FUEL .... G
SPEEDS .... VARIABLE
TRANSMISSION .... HYDRO
STEERING .... ZERO
BLADE CLUTCH .... ELECTRIC
STANDARD DECK .... 61"
WEIGHT .... 785 LBS.
MSRP $7,599

RETAIL PRICING

YEAR	HIGH	LOW
2008	$4,523	$3,392
2009	$4,808	$3,606

GSKW1948S

YEARS MFRD 2010-2011
SERIES ..... SUPER SURFER SERIES
ENGINE .... KAWASAKI
ENGINE HP 19
COOLING .... AIR
FUEL .... G
SPEEDS .... VARIABLE
TRANSMISSION .... HYDRO
STEERING .... ZERO
BLADE CLUTCH .... ELECTRIC
STANDARD DECK .... 48"
WEIGHT .... 750 LBS.
MSRP $7,499

RETAIL PRICING

YEAR	HIGH	LOW
2010	$3,187	$2,390
2011	$4,150	$3,113

GSKW2352S

YEARS MFRD 2008-2012
SERIES ..... SUPER SURFER SERIES
ENGINE HP 23
COOLING .... AIR
FUEL .... G
SPEEDS .... VARIABLE
TRANSMISSION .... HYDRO
STEERING .... ZERO
BLADE CLUTCH .... ELECTRIC
STANDARD DECK .... 52"
WEIGHT .... 750 LBS.
MSRP $7,999

RETAIL PRICING

YEAR	HIGH	LOW
2008	$2,148	$1,611
2009	$2,713	$2,035
2010	$3,334	$2,501
2011	$4,386	$3,290
2012	$4,745	$3,559

GSRKA1934S

YEARS MFRD 2008-2012
SERIES .... SURFER SERIES
ENGINE .... KAWASAKI
ENGINE HP 19
COOLING .... AIR
FUEL .... G
SPEEDS .... VARIABLE
TRANSMISSION .... HYDRO
STEERING .... ZERO
BLADE CLUTCH .... ELECTRIC
STANDARD DECK .... 34"
WEIGHT .... 860 LBS.
MSRP $5,899

RETAIL PRICING

YEAR	HIGH	LOW
2008	$1,567	$1,175
2009	$2,087	$1,565
2010	$2,444	$1,833
2011	$3,181	$2,386
2012	$3,444	$2,583

GSRKA1948S

YEARS MFRD 2008-2012
SERIES .... SURFER SERIES
ENGINE .... KAWASAKI
ENGINE HP 19
COOLING .... AIR
FUEL .... G
SPEEDS .... VARIABLE
TRANSMISSION .... HYDRO
STEERING .... ZERO
BLADE CLUTCH .... ELECTRIC
STANDARD DECK .... 48"
WEIGHT .... 860 LBS.
MSRP $6,199

RETAIL PRICING

YEAR	HIGH	LOW
2008	$1,708	$1,281
2009	$2,059	$1,544
2010	$2,572	$1,929
2011	$3,420	$2,565
2012	$3,780	$2,835

GSRKA1952S

YEARS MFRD 2008-2012
SERIES .... SURFER SERIES
ENGINE .... KAWASAKI
ENGINE HP 19
COOLING .... AIR
FUEL .... G
SPEEDS .... VARIABLE
TRANSMISSION .... HYDRO
STEERING .... ZERO
STANDARD DECK .... 52"
WEIGHT .... 860 LBS.
MSRP $6,499

RETAIL PRICING

YEAR	HIGH	LOW
2008	$1,756	$1,317
2009	$2,303	$1,727
2010	$2,828	$2,121
2011	$3,458	$2,593
2012	$3,971	$2,978

GSRKW2352S

YEARS MFRD 2008-2012
SERIES .... SURFER SERIES
ENGINE .... KAWASAKI
ENGINE HP 23
COOLING .... AIR
FUEL .... G
SPEEDS .... VARIABLE
TRANSMISSION .... HYDRO
STEERING .... ZERO
STANDARD DECK .... 52"
WEIGHT .... 860 LBS.
MSRP $7,199

RETAIL PRICING

YEAR	HIGH	LOW
2008	$2,067	$1,550
2009	$2,559	$1,920
2010	$3,005	$2,254
2011	$3,994	$2,995
2012	$4,305	$3,228

HG36-15KA

YEARS MFRD 2007-2007
SERIES ...... SCAMPER HG SERIES
ENGINE .... KAWASAKI
ENGINE HP 15
COOLING .... AIR
FUEL .... G
SPEEDS .... VARIABLE
TRANSMISSION .... HYDRO
STEERING .... ZERO
WEIGHT .... 560 LBS.

HG48-15KA

YEARS MFRD 2007-2007
SERIES ...... SCAMPER HG SERIES
ENGINE .... KAWASAKI
ENGINE HP 15
COOLING .... AIR
FUEL .... G
SPEEDS .... VARIABLE
TRANSMISSION .... HYDRO
STEERING .... ZERO
WEIGHT .... 580 LBS.

HG48-17KA

YEARS MFRD 2007-2007
SERIES ...... SCAMPER HG SERIES
ENGINE .... KAWASAKI
ENGINE HP 17
COOLING .... AIR
FUEL .... G
SPEEDS .... VARIABLE
TRANSMISSION .... HYDRO
STEERING .... ZERO
WEIGHT .... 580 LBS.

HG48-17KAE

YEARS MFRD 2007-2007
SERIES ...... SCAMPER HG SERIES
ENGINE .... KAWASAKI E/S
ENGINE HP 17
COOLING .... AIR
FUEL .... G

SPEEDS . . . . VARIABLE
TRANSMISSION . . . . HYDRO
STEERING . . . . ZERO
WEIGHT . . . . 580 LBS.

HG52-17KA

YEARS MFRD 2007-2007
SERIES . . . . . . SCAMPER HG SERIES
ENGINE . . . . KAWASAKI
ENGINE HP 17
COOLING . . . . AIR
FUEL . . . . G
SPEEDS . . . . VARIABLE
TRANSMISSION . . . . HYDRO
STEERING . . . . ZERO
WEIGHT . . . . 595 LBS.

HG52-17KAE

YEARS MFRD 2007-2007
SERIES . . . . . . SCAMPER HG SERIES
ENGINE . . . . KAWASAKI E/S
ENGINE HP 17
COOLING . . . . AIR
FUEL . . . . G
SPEEDS . . . . VARIABLE
TRANSMISSION . . . . HYDRO
STEERING . . . . ZERO
WEIGHT . . . . 610 LBS.

LX61-25KAE

YEARS MFRD 2002-2007
SERIES . . . . CHARIOT LX SERIES
ENGINE . . . . KAWASAKI
ENGINE HP 25
COOLING . . . . AIR
FUEL . . . . G
SPEEDS . . . . VARIABLE
TRANSMISSION . . . . HYDRO
STEERING . . . . ZERO
STANDARD DECK . . . . 61"
WEIGHT . . . . 1,179 LBS.
MSRP $8,299

RETAIL PRICING

YEAR	HIGH	LOW
2002	$4,350	$3,262
2003	$4,630	$3,473
2004	$4,716	$3,537
2005	$4,782	$3,586
2006	$4,867	$3,650
2007	$5,071	$3,803

LX61-25KHE

YEARS MFRD 2002-2007
SERIES . . . . CHARIOT LX SERIES
ENGINE . . . . KOHLER
ENGINE HP 25
COOLING . . . . AIR
FUEL . . . . G
SPEEDS . . . . VARIABLE
TRANSMISSION . . . . HYDRO
STEERING . . . . ZERO
STANDARD DECK . . . . 61"
WEIGHT . . . . 1,179 LBS.
MSRP $8,199

RETAIL PRICING

YEAR	HIGH	LOW
2005	$4,850	$3,637
2006	$5,130	$3,848
2007	$5,346	$4,010

LX61-27KHE

YEARS MFRD 2002-2007
SERIES . . . . CHARIOT LX SERIES
ENGINE . . . . KOHLER
ENGINE HP 27
COOLING . . . . AIR
FUEL . . . . G
SPEEDS . . . . VARIABLE
TRANSMISSION . . . . HYDRO
STEERING . . . . ZERO
STANDARD DECK . . . . 61"
WEIGHT . . . . 1,182 LBS.
MSRP $8,699

RETAIL PRICING

YEAR	HIGH	LOW
2002	$4,737	$3,552
2003	$4,798	$3,599
2004	$4,853	$3,640
2005	$4,887	$3,666
2006	$4,988	$3,741
2007	$5,219	$3,914

LX72-27KHE

YEARS MFRD 2002-2007
SERIES . . . . CHARIOT LX SERIES
ENGINE . . . . KOHLER
ENGINE HP 27
COOLING . . . . AIR
FUEL . . . . G
SPEEDS . . . . VARIABLE
TRANSMISSION . . . . HYDRO
STEERING . . . . ZERO
STANDARD DECK . . . . 72"
WEIGHT . . . . 1,225 LBS.
MSRP $8,999

RETAIL PRICING

YEAR	HIGH	LOW
2002	$5,439	$4,080
2003	$5,507	$4,130
2004	$5,580	$4,185
2005	$5,656	$4,242
2006	$5,696	$4,272
2007	$5,935	$4,451

LX72-28KHE

YEARS MFRD 2002-2007
SERIES . . . . CHARIOT LX SERIES
ENGINE . . . . KOHLER
ENGINE HP 28
COOLING . . . . AIR
FUEL . . . . G
SPEEDS . . . . VARIABLE
TRANSMISSION . . . . HYDRO
STEERING . . . . ZERO
STANDARD DECK . . . . 72"
WEIGHT . . . . 1,230 LBS.
MSRP $10,600

RETAIL PRICING

YEAR	HIGH	LOW
2002	$5,800	$4,350
2003	$5,842	$4,381
2004	$5,915	$4,436
2005	$5,954	$4,465
2006	$6,067	$4,550
2007	$6,431	$4,823

48-17KAE

YEARS MFRD 2002-2007
SERIES . . . . CHARIOT SERIES
ENGINE . . . . KAWASAKI
ENGINE HP 17
COOLING . . . . AIR
FUEL . . . . G
SPEEDS . . . . VARIABLE
TRANSMISSION . . . . HYDRO
STEERING . . . . ZERO
STANDARD DECK . . . . 48"
WEIGHT . . . . 1,055 LBS.
MSRP $6,629

RETAIL PRICING

YEAR	HIGH	LOW
2002	$3,606	$2,704
2003	$3,654	$2,740
2004	$3,747	$2,810
2005	$3,905	$2,929
2006	$4,001	$3,001
2007	$4,260	$3,195

48-17KAE

YEARS MFRD 2005-2006
SERIES . . . . . SUPER SURFER SERIES
ENGINE . . . . KAWASAKI
ENGINE HP 17
COOLING . . . . AIR
FUEL . . . . G
SPEEDS . . . . VARIABLE
TRANSMISSION . . . . HYDRO
STEERING . . . . ZERO
STANDARD DECK . . . . 48"
MSRP $6,299

RETAIL PRICING

YEAR	HIGH	LOW
2005	$3,728	$2,796
2006	$4,070	$3,053

48-18KAE

YEARS MFRD 2005-2007
SERIES . . . . . SUPER SURFER SERIES
ENGINE . . . . KOHLER
ENGINE HP 18
COOLING . . . . AIR
FUEL . . . . G
SPEEDS . . . . VARIABLE
TRANSMISSION . . . . HYDRO
STEERING . . . . ZERO
STANDARD DECK . . . . 48"
WEIGHT . . . . 735 LBS.
MSRP $6,499

RETAIL PRICING

YEAR	HIGH	LOW
2005	$3,788	$2,841
2006	$3,876	$2,907
2007	$4,178	$3,133

48-19KAE

YEARS MFRD 2002-2007
SERIES . . . . CHARIOT SERIES
ENGINE . . . . KAWASAKI
ENGINE HP 19
COOLING . . . . AIR
FUEL . . . . G
SPEEDS . . . . VARIABLE
TRANSMISSION . . . . HYDRO
STEERING . . . . ZERO
STANDARD DECK . . . . 48"
WEIGHT . . . . 1,055 LBS.
MSRP $6,899

RETAIL PRICING

YEAR	HIGH	LOW
2002	$3,751	$2,813
2003	$3,807	$2,856
2004	$3,849	$2,886
2005	$3,952	$2,964
2006	$3,992	$2,994
2007	$4,186	$3,139

52-17KAE

YEARS MFRD 2002-2007
SERIES . . . . . SUPER SURFER SERIES
ENGINE . . . . KAWASAKI
ENGINE HP 17
COOLING . . . . AIR
FUEL . . . . G
SPEEDS . . . . VARIABLE
TRANSMISSION . . . . HYDRO
STEERING . . . . ZERO
STANDARD DECK . . . . 52"
WEIGHT . . . . 750 LBS.
MSRP $6,299

RETAIL PRICING

YEAR	HIGH	LOW
2002	$3,214	$2,411
2003	$3,486	$2,614
2004	$3,514	$2,635
2005	$3,533	$2,650
2006	$3,615	$2,712
2007	$3,866	$2,899

52-22KHE

YEARS MFRD 2007-2007
SERIES . . . . GATEWAY SERIES
ENGINE . . . . KOHLER E/S
ENGINE HP 22
COOLING . . . . AIR
FUEL . . . . G
SPEEDS . . . . VARIABLE
TRANSMISSION . . . . HYDRO
STEERING . . . . ZERO
WEIGHT . . . . 713 LBS.

52-23KAE

YEARS MFRD 2002-2007
SERIES . . . . . SUPER SURFER SERIES
ENGINE . . . . KAWASAKI
ENGINE HP 23
COOLING . . . . AIR
FUEL . . . . G
SPEEDS . . . . VARIABLE

TRANSMISSION . . . . .HYDRO
STEERING. . . . . ZERO
STANDARD DECK . . . . 52"
WEIGHT . . . . 750 LBS.
MSRP. $6,999

RETAIL PRICING

YEAR	HIGH	LOW
2002	$3,528	$2,646
2003	$3,826	$2,869
2004	$3,905	$2,929
2005	$3,948	$2,961
2006	$3,989	$2,992
2007	$4,276	$3,207

52-23KHE

YEARS MFRD 2005-2007
SERIES. . . . . SUPER SURFER SERIES
ENGINE . . . . KOHLER
ENGINE HP 23
COOLING . . . . .AIR
FUEL . . . . G
SPEEDS . . . . VARIABLE
TRANSMISSION . . . . .HYDRO
STEERING. . . . . ZERO
STANDARD DECK . . . . 52"
WEIGHT . . . . 750 LBS.
MSRP. $7,099

RETAIL PRICING

YEAR	HIGH	LOW
2005	$4,201	$3,151
2006	$4,247	$3,185
2007	$4,452	$3,339

52-25KAE

YEARS MFRD 2005-2007
SERIES. . . . . .CHARIOT SERIES
ENGINE . . . . KAWASAKI
ENGINE HP 25
COOLING . . . . .AIR
FUEL . . . . G
SPEEDS . . . . VARIABLE
TRANSMISSION . . . . .HYDRO
STEERING. . . . . ZERO
STANDARD DECK . . . . 52"
WEIGHT . . . . .1,079 LBS.
MSRP. $7,399

RETAIL PRICING

YEAR	HIGH	LOW
2005	$4,379	$3,284
2006	$4,434	$3,326
2007	$4,651	$3,488

52-25KHE

YEARS MFRD 2002-2007
SERIES. . . . . .CHARIOT SERIES
ENGINE . . . . KOHLER
ENGINE HP 25
COOLING . . . . .AIR
FUEL . . . . G
SPEEDS . . . . VARIABLE
TRANSMISSION . . . . .HYDRO
STEERING. . . . . ZERO
STANDARD DECK . . . . 52"
WEIGHT . . . . .1,079 LBS.
MSRP. $7,399

RETAIL PRICING

YEAR	HIGH	LOW
2002	$3,972	$2,979
2003	$4,130	$3,097
2004	$4,308	$3,231
2005	$4,379	$3,284
2006	$4,434	$3,326
2007	$4,643	$3,482

61-22KHE

YEARS MFRD 2005-2006
SERIES. . . . . SUPER SURFER SERIES
ENGINE . . . . KOHLER
ENGINE HP 22
COOLING . . . . .AIR
FUEL . . . . G
SPEEDS . . . . VARIABLE
TRANSMISSION . . . . .HYDRO
STEERING. . . . . ZERO
STANDARD DECK . . . . 61"
MSRP. $6,999

RETAIL PRICING

YEAR	HIGH	LOW
2005	$4,012	$3,009
2006	$4,179	$3,134

61-23KAE

YEARS MFRD 2002-2007
SERIES. . . . . SUPER SURFER SERIES
ENGINE . . . . KAWASAKI
ENGINE HP 23
COOLING . . . . .AIR
FUEL . . . . G
SPEEDS . . . . VARIABLE
TRANSMISSION . . . . .HYDRO
STEERING. . . . . ZERO
STANDARD DECK . . . . 61"
WEIGHT . . . . 775 LBS.
MSRP. $7,199

RETAIL PRICING

YEAR	HIGH	LOW
2002	$3,577	$2,683
2003	$3,878	$2,909
2004	$3,962	$2,971
2005	$4,201	$3,151
2006	$4,244	$3,183
2007	$4,468	$3,351

61-25KAE

YEARS MFRD 2002-2007
SERIES. . . . . .CHARIOT SERIES
ENGINE . . . . KAWASAKI
ENGINE HP 25
COOLING . . . . .AIR
FUEL . . . . G
SPEEDS . . . . VARIABLE
TRANSMISSION . . . . .HYDRO
STEERING. . . . . ZERO
STANDARD DECK . . . . 61"
WEIGHT . . . . .1,104 LBS.
MSRP. $7,599

RETAIL PRICING

YEAR	HIGH	LOW
2002	$4,012	$3,009
2003	$4,350	$3,262
2004	$4,408	$3,306
2005	$4,479	$3,360
2006	$4,559	$3,419
2007	$4,773	$3,580

61-25KHE

YEARS MFRD 2002-2007
SERIES. . . . . SUPER SURFER SERIES
ENGINE . . . . KOHLER
ENGINE HP 25
COOLING . . . . .AIR
FUEL . . . . G
SPEEDS . . . . VARIABLE
TRANSMISSION . . . . .HYDRO
STEERING. . . . . ZERO
STANDARD DECK . . . . 61"
WEIGHT . . . . 775 LBS.
MSRP. $7,599

RETAIL PRICING

YEAR	HIGH	LOW
2002	$4,302	$3,226
2003	$4,573	$3,430
2004	$4,665	$3,498
2005	$4,698	$3,524
2006	$4,755	$3,566
2007	$4,939	$3,704

61-25KHE

YEARS MFRD 2002-2007
SERIES. . . . . .CHARIOT SERIES
ENGINE . . . . KOHLER
ENGINE HP 25
COOLING . . . . .AIR
FUEL . . . . G
SPEEDS . . . . VARIABLE
TRANSMISSION . . . . .HYDRO
STEERING. . . . . ZERO
STANDARD DECK . . . . 61"
WEIGHT . . . . .1,104 LBS.
MSRP. $7,499

RETAIL PRICING

YEAR	HIGH	LOW
2002	$3,975	$2,982
2003	$4,310	$3,233
2004	$4,352	$3,264
2005	$4,420	$3,315
2006	$4,432	$3,324
2007	$4,706	$3,529

NOTES

HUSKEE

I693H

YEARS MFRD 1999-1999
ENGINE . . . . B&S
ENGINE HP 20
FUEL . . . . G
TRANSMISSION . . . . .HYDRO
STEERING. . . . . .STANDARD
STANDARD DECK . . . . 46"
MSRP. $1,500

RETAIL PRICING

YEAR	HIGH	LOW
1999	$646	$485

I834P

YEARS MFRD 1999-1999
ENGINE . . . . B&S
ENGINE HP 22
FUEL . . . . G
TRANSMISSION . . . . .HYDRO
STEERING. . . . . .STANDARD
STANDARD DECK . . . . 46"
MSRP. $2,800

RETAIL PRICING

YEAR	HIGH	LOW
1999	$1,206	$904

I839H

YEARS MFRD 1999-1999
ENGINE . . . . B&S
ENGINE HP 20
FUEL . . . . G
TRANSMISSION . . . . .HYDRO
STEERING. . . . . .STANDARD
STANDARD DECK . . . . 46"
MSRP. $2,100

RETAIL PRICING

YEAR	HIGH	LOW
1999	$709	$532

I849H

YEARS MFRD 1999-1999
ENGINE . . . . B&S
ENGINE HP 20
FUEL . . . . G
TRANSMISSION . . . . GEAR
STEERING. . . . . .STANDARD
STANDARD DECK . . . . 46"
MSRP. $1,800

RETAIL PRICING

YEAR	HIGH	LOW
1999	$774	$580

J839P

YEARS MFRD 1998-1998
ENGINE . . . . B&S
ENGINE HP 20
FUEL . . . . G
TRANSMISSION . . . . .HYDRO
STEERING. . . . . .STANDARD
STANDARD DECK . . . . 50"
MSRP. $2,699

RETAIL PRICING

YEAR	HIGH	LOW
1998	$1,091	$818

J848H

YEARS MFRD 2000-2000
ENGINE . . . . B&S
ENGINE HP 21
FUEL . . . . G
TRANSMISSION . . . . GEAR
STEERING. . . . . .STANDARD
STANDARD DECK . . . . 46"
MSRP. $1,900

RETAIL PRICING

YEAR	HIGH	LOW
2000	$855	$642

J849P

YEARS MFRD 1998-1998
ENGINE . . . . B&S
ENGINE HP 20
FUEL . . . . G
TRANSMISSION . . . . GEAR
STEERING. . . . . .STANDARD
STANDARD DECK . . . . 50"
MSRP. $2,299

RETAIL PRICING

YEAR	HIGH	LOW
1998	$928	$696

LT38

YEARS MFRD 2010-2014
ENGINE . . . . B&S
ENGINE HP 12.5
COOLING . . . . AIR
FUEL . . . . G
SPEEDS 6/1
TRANSMISSION . . . . GEAR
STEERING. . . . . .STANDARD
STANDARD DECK . . . . 38"
MSRP. $899

RETAIL PRICING

YEAR	HIGH	LOW
2010	$294	$220
2011	$350	$263
2012	$406	$305
2013	$456	$342
2014	$551	$413

LT42

YEARS MFRD 2008-2014
ENGINE . . . . B&S
ENGINE HP 17
COOLING . . . . AIR
FUEL . . . . G
SPEEDS 7/1
TRANSMISSION . . . . GEAR
STEERING. . . . . .STANDARD
STANDARD DECK . . . . 42"
MSRP. $1,099

RETAIL PRICING

YEAR	HIGH	LOW
2008	$224	$168
2009	$294	$220
2010	$364	$273
2011	$433	$325
2012	$504	$378
2013	$528	$396
2014	$608	$456

LT4200

YEARS MFRD 2005-2005
SERIES. . . . CONFIGURATOR SERIES
ENGINE . . . . B&S INTEK
CYLINDERS. 2
ENGINE HP 18
COOLING . . . . AIR
FUEL . . . . G
SPEEDS . . . . VARIABLE
TRANSMISSION . . . . .HYDRO
STEERING. . . . . .STANDARD

N673G

YEARS MFRD 2000-2000
ENGINE . . . . B&S
ENGINE HP 16.5
FUEL . . . . G
TRANSMISSION . . . . GEAR
STEERING. . . . . .STANDARD
STANDARD DECK . . . . 42"
MSRP. $1,100

RETAIL PRICING

YEAR	HIGH	LOW
2000	$496	$372

O673G

YEARS MFRD 1998-1999
ENGINE . . . . TECUMSEH
ENGINE HP 15.5
FUEL . . . . G
TRANSMISSION . . . . GEAR
STEERING. . . . . .STANDARD
STANDARD DECK . . . . 42"
MSRP. $1,000

RETAIL PRICING

YEAR	HIGH	LOW
1998	$403	$302
1999	$430	$323

P849P

YEARS MFRD 1997-1997
ENGINE . . . . B&S
ENGINE HP 20
FUEL . . . . G
TRANSMISSION . . . . GEAR
STEERING. . . . . .STANDARD
STANDARD DECK . . . . 50"
MSRP. $2,199

RETAIL PRICING

YEAR	HIGH	LOW
1997	$844	$633

S608H

YEARS MFRD 2000-2000
ENGINE . . . . B&S
ENGINE HP 18.5
FUEL . . . . G
STEERING. . . . . .STANDARD
STANDARD DECK . . . . 46"
MSRP. $1,900

RETAIL PRICING

YEAR	HIGH	LOW
2000	$855	$642

S673G

YEARS MFRD 1997-1997
ENGINE . . . . B&S
ENGINE HP 18.5
FUEL . . . . G
TRANSMISSION . . . . GEAR
STEERING. . . . . .STANDARD
STANDARD DECK . . . . 42"
MSRP. $1,199

RETAIL PRICING

YEAR	HIGH	LOW
1997	$461	$346

S673H

YEARS MFRD 1999-1999
ENGINE . . . . B&S
ENGINE HP 18.5
FUEL . . . . G
TRANSMISSION . . . . GEAR
STEERING. . . . . .STANDARD
STANDARD DECK . . . . 46"
MSRP. $1,250

RETAIL PRICING

YEAR	HIGH	LOW
1999	$539	$404

S693H

YEARS MFRD 1997-1998
ENGINE . . . . B&S
ENGINE HP 18.5
FUEL . . . . G
TRANSMISSION . . . . .HYDRO
STEERING. . . . . .STANDARD
STANDARD DECK . . . . 42"
MSRP. $1,399

OPTIONS

46" DECK

RETAIL PRICING

YEAR	HIGH	LOW
1997	$461	$346
1998	$564	$423

S833H

YEARS MFRD 1997-1998
ENGINE . . . . B&S
ENGINE HP 18.5
FUEL . . . . G
TRANSMISSION . . . . .HYDRO
STEERING. . . . . .STANDARD
STANDARD DECK . . . . 46"
MSRP. $1,999

HUSKEE

RETAIL PRICING

YEAR	HIGH	LOW
1997	$729	$546
1998	$807	$606

S843H

YEARS MFRD 1997-1998
ENGINE .... B&S
ENGINE HP 18.5
FUEL .... G
TRANSMISSION .... GEAR
STEERING .... STANDARD
STANDARD DECK .... 46"
MSRP $1,699

RETAIL PRICING

YEAR	HIGH	LOW
1997	$653	$490
1998	$685	$514

S6693G

YEARS MFRD 1998-1999
ENGINE .... TECUMSEH
ENGINE HP 17.5
FUEL .... G
TRANSMISSION .... HYDRO
STEERING .... STANDARD
STANDARD DECK .... 42"
MSRP $1,250

RETAIL PRICING

YEAR	HIGH	LOW
1998	$484	$363
1999	$539	$404

SLT4200

YEARS MFRD 2005-2005
SERIES .... CONFIGURATOR SERIES
ENGINE .... B&S
CYLINDERS 1
ENGINE HP 18.5
COOLING .... AIR
FUEL .... G
SPEEDS .... VARIABLE
TRANSMISSION .... HYDRO
STEERING .... STANDARD
BLADE CLUTCH .... MANUAL

SLT4600

YEARS MFRD 2005-2005
SERIES .... CONFIGURATOR SERIES
ENGINE .... B&S
CYLINDERS 2
ENGINE HP 22
COOLING .... AIR
FUEL .... G
SPEEDS .... VARIABLE
TRANSMISSION .... HYDRO
STEERING .... STANDARD
BLADE CLUTCH .... MANUAL

SYT5000

YEARS MFRD 2005-2005
SERIES .... CONFIGURATOR SERIES
ENGINE .... B&S
CYLINDERS 2
ENGINE HP 25
COOLING .... AIR
FUEL .... G
SPEEDS .... VARIABLE
TRANSMISSION .... HYDRO
STEERING .... STANDARD
BLADE CLUTCH ...... ELECTRIC

TS22H50-1996

YEARS MFRD 1996-1996
ENGINE .... ONAN
ENGINE HP 22
FUEL .... G
TRANSMISSION .... HYDRO
STEERING .... STANDARD
STANDARD DECK .... 50"
MSRP $2,999

RETAIL PRICING

YEAR	HIGH	LOW
1996	$1,109	$832

TS1846-1996

YEARS MFRD 1996-1996
ENGINE .... ONAN
ENGINE HP 18
FUEL .... G
TRANSMISSION .... GEAR
STEERING .... STANDARD
STANDARD DECK .... 46"
MSRP $1,999

RETAIL PRICING

YEAR	HIGH	LOW
1996	$740	$555

TS2051-1996

YEARS MFRD 1996-1996
ENGINE .... ONAN
ENGINE HP 20
FUEL .... G
TRANSMISSION .... GEAR
STEERING .... STANDARD
STANDARD DECK .... 50"
MSRP $2,499

RETAIL PRICING

YEAR	HIGH	LOW
1996	$924	$693

TSC4493051

YEARS MFRD 2004-2004
SERIES .. HUSKEE SUPREME SERIES
ENGINE .... B&S ELS
ENGINE HP 26
COOLING .... AIR
FUEL .... G
SPEEDS .... VARIABLE
TRANSMISSION .... HYDRO
STEERING .... STANDARD
STANDARD DECK .... 54"
MSRP $2,599

RETAIL PRICING

YEAR	HIGH	LOW
2004	$1,451	$1,088

TSC4494049

YEARS MFRD 2004-2004
ENGINE .... B&S INTEK OHV
CYLINDERS 2
ENGINE HP 21
COOLING .... AIR
FUEL .... G
SPEEDS 8
TRANSMISSION .... GEAR
STEERING .... STANDARD
STANDARD DECK .... 46"
MSRP $1,199

RETAIL PRICING

YEAR	HIGH	LOW
2004	$670	$503

TSC4494057

YEARS MFRD 2004-2004
ENGINE .... B&S ELS
ENGINE HP 18.5
COOLING .... AIR
FUEL .... G
SPEEDS .... VARIABLE
TRANSMISSION .... HYDRO
STEERING .... STANDARD
STANDARD DECK .... 42"
MSRP $1,299

RETAIL PRICING

YEAR	HIGH	LOW
2004	$726	$544

TSC4494065

YEARS MFRD 2004-2004
SERIES .. HUSKEE SUPREME SERIES
ENGINE .... B&S
CYLINDERS 2
ENGINE HP 23
COOLING .... AIR
FUEL .... G
SPEEDS .... VARIABLE
TRANSMISSION .... HYDRO
STEERING .... STANDARD

TSC4494081

YEARS MFRD 2004-2004
ENGINE .... B&S INTEK
CYLINDERS 2
ENGINE HP 24
COOLING .... AIR
FUEL .... G
SPEEDS .... VARIABLE
TRANSMISSION .... HYDRO
STEERING .... STANDARD
STANDARD DECK .... 46"
MSRP $1,899

RETAIL PRICING

YEAR	HIGH	LOW
2004	$1,061	$796

U607H

YEARS MFRD 2000-2000
ENGINE .... B&S
ENGINE HP 18.5
FUEL .... G
STEERING .... STANDARD
STANDARD DECK .... 46"
MSRP $1,600

RETAIL PRICING

YEAR	HIGH	LOW
2000	$722	$541

V807P

YEARS MFRD 2000-2000
ENGINE .... B&S
ENGINE HP 22
FUEL .... G
TRANSMISSION .... HYDRO
STEERING .... STANDARD
STANDARD DECK .... 46"
MSRP $2,500

RETAIL PRICING

YEAR	HIGH	LOW
2000	$1,128	$846

V844P

YEARS MFRD 1999-1999
ENGINE .... B&S
ENGINE HP 22
FUEL .... G
TRANSMISSION .... GEAR
STEERING .... STANDARD
STANDARD DECK .... 46"
MSRP $2,400

RETAIL PRICING

YEAR	HIGH	LOW
1999	$1,032	$774

13AJ608H131

YEARS MFRD 2002-2002
ENGINE .... B&S V-TWIN
ENGINE HP 21
FUEL .... G
STEERING .... STANDARD
STANDARD DECK .... 46"
WEIGHT .... 500 LBS.
MSRP $1,600

RETAIL PRICING

YEAR	HIGH	LOW
2002	$772	$579

13AN673G131

YEARS MFRD 2002-2002
ENGINE .... B&S U/C OHV
ENGINE HP 16.5
FUEL .... G
TRANSMISSION .... GEAR
STEERING .... STANDARD
STANDARD DECK .... 42"
WEIGHT .... 465 LBS.
MSRP $1,100

RETAIL PRICING

YEAR	HIGH	LOW
2002	$529	$397

13AN698G131

YEARS MFRD 2002-2002

ENGINE .... B&S OHV

ENGINE HP 17.5

FUEL .... G

TRANSMISSION .... HYDRO

STEERING .... STANDARD

STANDARD DECK .... 42"

WEIGHT .... 475 LBS.

MSRP $1,280

RETAIL PRICING

YEAR	HIGH	LOW
2002	$619	$464

13AS698H131

YEARS MFRD 2002-2002

ENGINE .... B&S TWIN II I/C

ENGINE HP 18.5

FUEL .... G

TRANSMISSION .... HYDRO

STEERING .... STANDARD

STANDARD DECK .... 46"

WEIGHT .... 495 LBS.

MSRP $1,400

RETAIL PRICING

YEAR	HIGH	LOW
2002	$677	$508

13AX605H730

YEARS MFRD 2016-2016

ENGINE .... KOHLER 752KSV5911

ENGINE HP 19

COOLING .... AIR

FUEL .... G

SPEEDS .... VARIABLE

TRANSMISSION .... HYDRO

STEERING .... STANDARD

STANDARD DECK .... 46"

14AZ808K131

YEARS MFRD 2002-2002

ENGINE .... B&S V-TWIN

ENGINE HP 24

FUEL .... G

STEERING .... STANDARD

STANDARD DECK .... 54"

WEIGHT .... 690 LBS.

MSRP $2,800

RETAIL PRICING

YEAR	HIGH	LOW
2002	$1,355	$1,016

14BJ848H131

YEARS MFRD 2002-2002

ENGINE .... B&S V-TWIN

ENGINE HP 21

FUEL .... G

TRANSMISSION .... GEAR

STEERING .... STANDARD

STANDARD DECK .... 46"

WEIGHT .... 690 LBS.

MSRP $1,900

RETAIL PRICING

YEAR	HIGH	LOW
2002	$918	$688

44-19879

YEARS MFRD 1995-1995

ENGINE .... TECUMSEH

ENGINE HP 16

FUEL .... G

TRANSMISSION .... HYDRO

STEERING .... STANDARD

STANDARD DECK .... 42"

MSRP $1,149

RETAIL PRICING

YEAR	HIGH	LOW
1995	$411	$308

44-19887

YEARS MFRD 1995-1995

ENGINE .... B&S

ENGINE HP 18

FUEL .... G

TRANSMISSION .... HYDRO

STEERING .... STANDARD

STANDARD DECK .... 46"

MSRP $1,399

RETAIL PRICING

YEAR	HIGH	LOW
1995	$499	$374

44-19895

YEARS MFRD 1995-1995

ENGINE .... KOHLER

ENGINE HP 18

FUEL .... G

TRANSMISSION .... GEAR

STEERING .... STANDARD

STANDARD DECK .... 44"

MSRP $1,999

RETAIL PRICING

YEAR	HIGH	LOW
1995	$714	$536

44-19900

YEARS MFRD 1995-1995

ENGINE .... KOHLER

ENGINE HP 20

FUEL .... G

TRANSMISSION .... HYDRO

STEERING .... STANDARD

STANDARD DECK .... 50"

MSRP $3,199

RETAIL PRICING

YEAR	HIGH	LOW
1995	$1,142	$857

44-20278

YEARS MFRD 1995-1995

ENGINE .... B&S

ENGINE HP 18

FUEL .... G

TRANSMISSION .... GEAR

STEERING .... STANDARD

STANDARD DECK .... 46"

MSRP $1,599

RETAIL PRICING

YEAR	HIGH	LOW
1995	$570	$428

44-20294

YEARS MFRD 1995-1995

ENGINE .... KOHLER

ENGINE HP 20

FUEL .... G

TRANSMISSION .... GEAR

STEERING .... STANDARD

STANDARD DECK .... 50"

MSRP $2,699

RETAIL PRICING

YEAR	HIGH	LOW
1995	$964	$723

136S693H131

YEARS MFRD 1996-1996

ENGINE .... B&S

ENGINE HP 18.5

FUEL .... G

TRANSMISSION .... HYDRO

STEERING .... STANDARD

STANDARD DECK .... 46"

MSRP $1,399

RETAIL PRICING

YEAR	HIGH	LOW
1996	$517	$388

146S843H131

YEARS MFRD 1996-1996

ENGINE .... B&S

ENGINE HP 18.5

FUEL .... G

TRANSMISSION .... GEAR

STEERING .... STANDARD

STANDARD DECK .... 46"

MSRP $1,699

RETAIL PRICING

YEAR	HIGH	LOW
1996	$629	$472

6660G

YEARS MFRD 1997-1997

ENGINE .... TECUMSEH

ENGINE HP 17

FUEL .... G

TRANSMISSION .... GEAR

STEERING .... STANDARD

STANDARD DECK .... 42"

MSRP $999

RETAIL PRICING

YEAR	HIGH	LOW
1997	$384	$288

8693G

YEARS MFRD 2000-2000

ENGINE .... TECUMSEH

ENGINE HP 17.5

FUEL .... G

TRANSMISSION .... HYDRO

STEERING .... STANDARD

STANDARD DECK .... 42"

MSRP $1,250

RETAIL PRICING

YEAR	HIGH	LOW
2000	$564	$423

136693G131

YEARS MFRD 1996-1996

ENGINE .... TECUMSEH

ENGINE HP 16.5

FUEL .... G

TRANSMISSION .... HYDRO

STEERING .... STANDARD

STANDARD DECK .... 42"

MSRP $1,199

RETAIL PRICING

YEAR	HIGH	LOW
1996	$444	$333

4490003SKU

YEARS MFRD 2005-2006

ENGINE .... B&S

ENGINE HP 22

COOLING .... AIR

FUEL .... G

SPEEDS .... VARIABLE

TRANSMISSION .... HYDRO

STEERING .... STANDARD

STANDARD DECK .... 46"

MSRP $1,999

RETAIL PRICING

YEAR	HIGH	LOW
2005	$1,067	$800
2006	$1,133	$850

4490037 SKU

YEARS MFRD 2005-2006

ENGINE .... B&S

ENGINE HP 18

COOLING .... AIR

FUEL .... G

SPEEDS .... VARIABLE

TRANSMISSION .... HYDRO

STEERING .... STANDARD

STANDARD DECK .... 42"

MSRP $1,399

RETAIL PRICING

YEAR	HIGH	LOW
2005	$710	$533
2006	$802	$601

4490045 SKU

YEARS MFRD 2005-2006

ENGINE .... B&S

ENGINE HP 18.5

COOLING .... AIR

HUSKEE

FUEL . . . G
SPEEDS . . . VARIABLE
TRANSMISSION . . . HYDRO
STEERING . . . STANDARD
STANDARD DECK . . . 42"
MSRP . . . $1,599

RETAIL PRICING

YEAR	HIGH	LOW
2005	$829	$622
2006	$909	$682

4490061

YEARS MFRD . . . 2005-2006
ENGINE . . . B&S
ENGINE HP . . . 25
COOLING . . . AIR
FUEL . . . G
SPEEDS . . . VARIABLE
TRANSMISSION . . . HYDRO
STEERING . . . STANDARD
STANDARD DECK . . . 50"
MSRP . . . $2,799

RETAIL PRICING

YEAR	HIGH	LOW
2005	$1,537	$1,153
2006	$1,635	$1,226

HUSQVARNA

BZ6127TD

YEARS MFRD . . . 2007-2009
ENGINE . . . DAIHATSU
CYLINDERS . . . 3
ENGINE HP . . . 27
COOLING . . . LIQUID
FUEL . . . D
SPEEDS . . . VARIABLE
TRANSMISSION . . . HYDRO
STEERING . . . ZERO
STANDARD DECK . . . 61"
WEIGHT . . . 1,540 LBS.
MSRP . . . $14,499

SERIAL NUMBERS

YEAR	BEGINNING NO.
2007	64000000

RETAIL PRICING

YEAR	HIGH	LOW
2007	$4,985	$3,739
2008	$5,534	$4,151
2009	$6,146	$4,609

BZ7234TD

YEARS MFRD . . . 2007-2009
ENGINE . . . DAIHATSU TURBO
CYLINDERS . . . 3
ENGINE HP . . . 34
COOLING . . . LIQUID
FUEL . . . D
SPEEDS . . . VARIABLE
TRANSMISSION . . . HYDRO
STEERING . . . ZERO
STANDARD DECK . . . 72"
WEIGHT . . . 1,540 LBS.
MSRP . . . $15,799

SERIAL NUMBERS

YEAR	BEGINNING NO.
2007	64000000

RETAIL PRICING

YEAR	HIGH	LOW
2007	$5,432	$4,074
2008	$6,032	$4,524
2009	$6,699	$5,024

CTH150

YEARS MFRD . . . 2000-2000
ENGINE . . . KOHLER
ENGINE HP . . . 15
FUEL . . . G
TRANSMISSION . . . HYDRO
STEERING . . . STANDARD
STANDARD DECK . . . 42"
MSRP . . . $2,500

RETAIL PRICING

YEAR	HIGH	LOW
2000	$1,189	$892

CTH151

YEARS MFRD . . . 2004-2004
ENGINE . . KOHLER COURAGE SV470
CYLINDERS . . . 2
CID . . . 29.1
ENGINE HP . . . 15
FUEL . . . G
SPEEDS . . . VARIABLE
TRANSMISSION . . . HYDRO
STEERING . . . STANDARD
BLADE CLUTCH . . . MANUAL
PTO . . . YES
WEIGHT . . . 484 LBS.

CTH180XP

YEARS MFRD . . . 2004-2004
ENGINE . . . KAWASAKI V-TWIN
CYLINDERS . . . 2
CID . . . 30.1
ENGINE HP . . . 18
FUEL . . . G
SPEEDS . . . VARIABLE
TRANSMISSION . . . HYDRO
STEERING . . . STANDARD
BLADE CLUTCH . . . ELECTRIC
WEIGHT . . . 495 LBS.

CZ4817

YEARS MFRD . . . 2004-2004
ENGINE . . . KOHLER
CYLINDERS . . . 1
ENGINE HP . . . 17
COOLING . . . AIR
FUEL . . . G
SPEEDS . . . VARIABLE
TRANSMISSION . . . HYDRO
STEERING . . . ZERO
BLADE CLUTCH . . . ELECTRIC
STANDARD DECK . . . 48"
WEIGHT . . . 140 LBS.
MSRP . . . $3,499

RETAIL PRICING

YEAR	HIGH	LOW
2004	$935	$701

EZ4217

YEARS MFRD . . . 2007-2007
ENGINE . . . KAWASAKI
ENGINE HP . . . 17
COOLING . . . AIR
FUEL . . . G
SPEEDS . . . VARIABLE
TRANSMISSION . . . HYDRO
STEERING . . . ZERO
STANDARD DECK . . . 42"
WEIGHT . . . 630 LBS.
MSRP . . . $4,799

SERIAL NUMBERS

YEAR	BEGINNING NO.
2007	64000000

RETAIL PRICING

YEAR	HIGH	LOW
2007	$1,688	$1,266

EZ4220

YEARS MFRD . . . 2008-2009
ENGINE . . . KOHLER
ENGINE HP . . . 20
COOLING . . . AIR
FUEL . . . G
SPEEDS . . . VARIABLE
TRANSMISSION . . . HYDRO
STEERING . . . ZERO
BLADE CLUTCH . . . ELECTRIC
STANDARD DECK . . . 42"
WEIGHT . . . 630 LBS.
MSRP . . . $4,799

RETAIL PRICING

YEAR	HIGH	LOW
2008	$2,789	$2,092
2009	$2,977	$2,233

EZ4624

YEARS MFRD . . . 2008-2009
ENGINE . . . B&S
ENGINE HP . . . 24
COOLING . . . AIR
FUEL . . . G
SPEEDS . . . VARIABLE
TRANSMISSION . . . HYDRO
STEERING . . . ZERO
BLADE CLUTCH . . . ELECTRIC
STANDARD DECK . . . 46"
WEIGHT . . . 630 LBS.
MSRP . . . $3,999

RETAIL PRICING

YEAR	HIGH	LOW
2008	$2,226	$1,669
2009	$2,482	$1,862

EZ4819

YEARS MFRD . . . 2007-2007
ENGINE . . . KAWASAKI
ENGINE HP . . . 19
COOLING . . . AIR
FUEL . . . G
SPEEDS . . . VARIABLE
TRANSMISSION . . . HYDRO
STEERING . . . ZERO
STANDARD DECK . . . 48"
WEIGHT . . . 645 LBS.
MSRP . . . $4,999

SERIAL NUMBERS

YEAR	BEGINNING NO.
2007	64000000

RETAIL PRICING

YEAR	HIGH	LOW
2007	$1,756	$1,317

EZ4824

YEARS MFRD . . . 2007-2013
ENGINE . . . B&S
CID . . . 724CC
ENGINE HP . . . 24
COOLING . . . AIR
FUEL . . . G
SPEEDS . . . VARIABLE
TRANSMISSION . . . HYDRO
STEERING . . . ZERO
BLADE CLUTCH . . . ELECTRIC
STANDARD DECK . . . 48"
WEIGHT . . . 640 LBS.
MSRP . . . $4,299

OPTIONS

BAGGER

SERIAL NUMBERS

YEAR	BEGINNING NO.
2007	64000000

RETAIL PRICING

YEAR	HIGH	LOW
2007	$1,347	$1,010
2008	$1,496	$1,122
2009	$1,660	$1,245
2010	$1,843	$1,383
2011	$2,049	$1,537
2012	$2,274	$1,705
2013	$2,526	$1,895

EZ5221

YEARS MFRD . . . 2007-2009
ENGINE . . . KAWASAKI
ENGINE HP . . . 21
COOLING . . . AIR
FUEL . . . G
SPEEDS . . . VARIABLE
TRANSMISSION . . . HYDRO
STEERING . . . ZERO
STANDARD DECK . . . 52"
WEIGHT . . . 665 LBS.
MSRP . . . $5,499

SERIAL NUMBERS

YEAR	BEGINNING NO.
2007	64000000

RETAIL PRICING

YEAR	HIGH	LOW
2007	$1,822	$1,366
2007	$1,822	$1,366
2008	$2,024	$1,518
2008	$2,024	$1,518
2009	$2,244	$1,683
2009	$2,244	$1,683

EZ5224

YEARS MFRD 2008-2010
ENGINE . . . . KOHLER
ENGINE HP 24
COOLING . . . . AIR
FUEL . . . . G
SPEEDS . . . . VARIABLE
TRANSMISSION . . . . HYDRO
STEERING. . . . . ZERO
BLADE CLUTCH . . . . ELECTRIC
STANDARD DECK . . . . 52"
WEIGHT . . . . 645 LBS.
MSRP. $4,499

OPTIONS

BAGGER

RETAIL PRICING

YEAR	HIGH	LOW
2008	$1,946	$1,460
2009	$2,165	$1,624
2010	$2,400	$1,800

EZ5226

YEARS MFRD 2008-2009
ENGINE . . . . B&S
ENGINE HP 26
COOLING . . . . AIR
FUEL . . . . G
SPEEDS . . . . VARIABLE
TRANSMISSION . . . . HYDRO
STEERING. . . . . ZERO
BLADE CLUTCH . . . . ELECTRIC
STANDARD DECK . . . . 52"
WEIGHT . . . . 655 LBS.
MSRP. $4,699

RETAIL PRICING

YEAR	HIGH	LOW
2008	$1,793	$1,345
2009	$1,992	$1,494

EZ5426

YEARS MFRD 2007-2007
ENGINE . . . . B&S
ENGINE HP 26
COOLING . . . . AIR
FUEL . . . . G
SPEEDS . . . . VARIABLE
TRANSMISSION . . . . HYDRO
STEERING. . . . . ZERO
STANDARD DECK . . . . 54"
WEIGHT . . . . 645 LBS.
MSRP. $4,599

SERIAL NUMBERS

YEAR	BEGINNING NO.
2007	64000000

RETAIL PRICING

YEAR	HIGH	LOW
2007	$1,879	$1,409

EZ6124

YEARS MFRD 2007-2009
ENGINE . . . . KOHLER
ENGINE HP 24
COOLING . . . . AIR
FUEL . . . . G
SPEEDS . . . . VARIABLE
TRANSMISSION . . . . HYDRO
STEERING. . . . . ZERO
STANDARD DECK . . . . 61"
WEIGHT . . . . 700 LBS.
MSRP. $5,699

SERIAL NUMBERS

YEAR	BEGINNING NO.
2007	64000000

RETAIL PRICING

YEAR	HIGH	LOW
2007	$1,958	$1,469
2008	$2,176	$1,632
2009	$2,417	$1,813

GHT2554XP

YEARS MFRD 2004-2004
ENGINE . . . . KAWASAKI
CYLINDERS. 2
CID 41.2
ENGINE HP 25
FUEL . . . . G
SPEEDS . . . . VARIABLE
TRANSMISSION . . . . HYDRO
STEERING. . . . . STANDARD
BLADE CLUTCH . . . . ELECTRIC

GT48XLS

YEARS MFRD 2014-2015
ENGINE . . . . B&S
ENGINE HP 27
COOLING . . . . AIR
FUEL . . . . G
SPEEDS . . . . VARIABLE
TRANSMISSION . . . . HYDRO
STEERING. . . . . STANDARD
STANDARD DECK . . . . 48"
MSRP. $2,899

RETAIL PRICING

YEAR	HIGH	LOW
2014	$1,689	$1,266
2015	$1,865	$1,399

GT48XLSI

YEARS MFRD 2014-2016
ENGINE . . . . B&S
ENGINE HP 24
COOLING . . . . AIR
SPEEDS . . . . VARIABLE
TRANSMISSION . . . . HYDRO
STEERING. . . . . STANDARD
STANDARD DECK . . . . 48"
MSRP. $3,399

OPTIONS

52" DECK

RETAIL PRICING

YEAR	HIGH	LOW
2014	$1,850	$1,388
2015	$2,255	$1,691
2016	$2,590	$1,943

GT52XLS

YEARS MFRD 2014-2016
ENGINE . . . . KAWASAKI
ENGINE HP 24
COOLING . . . . AIR
FUEL . . . . G
SPEEDS . . . . VARIABLE
TRANSMISSION . . . . HYDRO
STEERING. . . . . STANDARD
STANDARD DECK . . . . 52"
MSRP. $3,299

RETAIL PRICING

YEAR	HIGH	LOW
2014	$1,850	$1,388
2015	$2,190	$1,643
2016	$2,501	$1,876

GT54LS

YEARS MFRD 2014-2016
ENGINE . . . . B&S
ENGINE HP 27
COOLING . . . . AIR
FUEL . . . . G
SPEEDS . . . . VARIABLE
TRANSMISSION . . . . HYDRO
STEERING. . . . . STANDARD
STANDARD DECK . . . . 54"
MSRP. $3,199

RETAIL PRICING

YEAR	HIGH	LOW
2014	$1,739	$1,304
2015	$2,160	$1,620
2016	$2,631	$1,973

GT160

YEARS MFRD 1990-1992
ENGINE . . . . B&S
ENGINE HP 16
COOLING . . . . AIR
FUEL . . . . G
TRANSMISSION . . . . GEAR
STEERING. . . . . STANDARD
STANDARD DECK . . . . 44"
MSRP. $3,099

RETAIL PRICING

YEAR	HIGH	LOW
1990	$899	$674
1991	$973	$730
1992	$1,030	$772

GT180

YEARS MFRD 1990-1993
ENGINE . . . . KOHLER
ENGINE HP 18
COOLING . . . . AIR
FUEL . . . . G
TRANSMISSION . . . . GEAR
STEERING. . . . . STANDARD
STANDARD DECK . . . . 50"
MSRP. $3,799

RETAIL PRICING

YEAR	HIGH	LOW
1990	$1,077	$808
1991	$1,167	$875
1992	$1,231	$923
1993	$1,303	$978

GT200

YEARS MFRD 1994-1997
ENGINE . . . . KOHLER
ENGINE HP 20
COOLING . . . . AIR
FUEL . . . . G
TRANSMISSION . . . . GEAR
STEERING. . . . . STANDARD
STANDARD DECK . . . . 46"
MSRP. $3,599

RETAIL PRICING

YEAR	HIGH	LOW
1994	$221	$165
1995	$244	$183
1996	$270	$202
1997	$299	$224

GT2254

YEARS MFRD 2006-2006
ENGINE . . . . B&S
CYLINDERS. 2
ENGINE HP 22
COOLING . . . . AIR
FUEL . . . . G
SPEEDS . . . . VARIABLE
TRANSMISSION . . . . HYDRO
STEERING. . . . . STANDARD

GTH24K54

YEARS MFRD 2014-2015
ENGINE . . . . KAWASAKI
ENGINE HP 24
COOLING . . . . AIR
FUEL . . . . G
SPEEDS . . . . VARIABLE
TRANSMISSION . . . . HYDRO
STEERING. . . . . STANDARD
STANDARD DECK . . . . 54"
MSRP. $2,899

RETAIL PRICING

YEAR	HIGH	LOW
2014	$1,642	$1,231
2015	$1,896	$1,422

GTH26K54

YEARS MFRD 2007-2007
ENGINE . . . . KOHLER COURAGE
CYLINDERS. 2
ENGINE HP 26
COOLING . . . . AIR
FUEL . . . . G
SPEEDS . . . . VARIABLE
TRANSMISSION . . . . HYDRO
STEERING. . . . . STANDARD

HUSQVARNA

GTH200

YEARS MFRD 1993-1999
ENGINE .... KOHLER
ENGINE HP 20
COOLING .... AIR
FUEL .... G
TRANSMISSION .... HYDRO
STEERING .... STANDARD
STANDARD DECK .... 46"
MSRP $3,199

OPTIONS

3 BAG
BLADE
ELIFT
TILLER

RETAIL PRICING

YEAR	HIGH	LOW
1993	$210	$157
1994	$232	$174
1995	$257	$193
1996	$284	$213
1997	$314	$235
1998	$348	$261
1999	$385	$289

GTH220

YEARS MFRD 1996-1999
ENGINE .... KOHLER
ENGINE HP 22
COOLING .... AIR
FUEL .... G
SPEEDS .... VARIABLE
TRANSMISSION .... HYDRO
STEERING .... STANDARD
STANDARD DECK .... 50"
MSRP $3,429

OPTIONS

BLADE
ELIFT
TILLER

RETAIL PRICING

YEAR	HIGH	LOW
1996	$304	$228
1997	$336	$252
1998	$372	$279
1999	$412	$309

GTH225

YEARS MFRD 2000-2000
ENGINE .... KOHLER
ENGINE HP 22
FUEL .... G
TRANSMISSION .... HYDRO
STEERING .... STANDARD
STANDARD DECK .... 46"
MSRP $3,440

RETAIL PRICING

YEAR	HIGH	LOW
2000	$1,634	$1,225

GTH250

YEARS MFRD 2000-2000
ENGINE .... KOHLER
ENGINE HP 22
FUEL .... G
TRANSMISSION .... HYDRO
STEERING .... STANDARD
STANDARD DECK .... 50"
MSRP $3,600

RETAIL PRICING

YEAR	HIGH	LOW
2000	$1,709	$1,282

GTH2248XP

YEARS MFRD 2001-2003
SERIES .... XP SERIES
ENGINE .... KAWASAKI
ENGINE HP 22
FUEL .... G
STEERING .... STANDARD
STANDARD DECK .... 48"
MSRP $3,700

RETAIL PRICING

YEAR	HIGH	LOW
2001	$1,884	$1,413
2002	$1,885	$1,413
2003	$2,042	$1,532

GTH2250

YEARS MFRD 2001-2001
SERIES .... CROWN SERIES
ENGINE .... OHV
ENGINE HP 22
FUEL .... G
SPEEDS .... VARIABLE
TRANSMISSION .... HYDRO
STEERING .... STANDARD
STANDARD DECK .... 50"
MSRP $2,999

RETAIL PRICING

YEAR	HIGH	LOW
2001	$361	$270

GTH2254XP

YEARS MFRD 2004-2006
SERIES .... XP SERIES
ENGINE ... KAWASAKI V-TWIN OHV
CYLINDERS 2
ENGINE HP 22
COOLING .... AIR
FUEL .... G
SPEEDS .... VARIABLE
TRANSMISSION .... HYDRO
STEERING .... STANDARD
BLADE CLUTCH .... ELECTRIC
PTO .... YES
STANDARD DECK .... 54"
MSRP $2,999

RETAIL PRICING

YEAR	HIGH	LOW
2004	$1,701	$1,276
2005	$1,870	$1,402
2006	$1,976	$1,482

GTH2350

YEARS MFRD 2003-2003
SERIES .... CROWN SERIES
ENGINE ...... B&S TWIN OHV ELS
ENGINE HP 23
FUEL .... G
TRANSMISSION ..... HYDRO/GEAR
STEERING .... STANDARD

GTH2548

YEARS MFRD 2004-2006
ENGINE ..... KOHLER V-TWIN OHV
CYLINDERS 2
ENGINE HP 25
COOLING .... AIR
FUEL .... G
SPEEDS .... VARIABLE
TRANSMISSION .... HYDRO
STEERING .... STANDARD
BLADE CLUTCH .... ELECTRIC
STANDARD DECK .... 48"
MSRP $2,599

RETAIL PRICING

YEAR	HIGH	LOW
2004	$1,528	$1,146
2005	$1,618	$1,213
2006	$1,712	$1,284

GTH2548XP

YEARS MFRD 2003-2003
SERIES .... XP SERIES
ENGINE .... KAWASAKI V-TWIN
ENGINE HP 25
FUEL .... G
STEERING .... STANDARD
STANDARD DECK .... 48"
MSRP $4,300

RETAIL PRICING

YEAR	HIGH	LOW
2003	$2,374	$1,780

GTH2550

YEARS MFRD 2001-2001
SERIES .... CROWN SERIES
ENGINE .... OHV
ENGINE HP 25
FUEL .... G
TRANSMISSION .... HYDRO
STEERING .... STANDARD
STANDARD DECK .... 50"
MSRP $3,499

RETAIL PRICING

YEAR	HIGH	LOW
2001	$420	$315

GTH2550XP

YEARS MFRD 2001-2001
SERIES .... XP SERIES
ENGINE .... KAWASAKI
ENGINE HP 25
FUEL .... G
TRANSMISSION .... HYDRO
STEERING .... STANDARD
STANDARD DECK .... 50"
MSRP $3,999

RETAIL PRICING

YEAR	HIGH	LOW
2001	$481	$361

GTH2554XP

YEARS MFRD 2004-2004
ENGINE .... KAWASAKI V-TWIN
CYLINDERS 2
CID 41.2
ENGINE HP 25
FUEL .... G
SPEEDS .... VARIABLE
TRANSMISSION .... HYDRO
STEERING .... STANDARD
BLADE CLUTCH .... ELECTRIC
WEIGHT .... 539 LBS.

GTH2648

YEARS MFRD 2007-2007
ENGINE .... B&S
CYLINDERS 2
ENGINE HP 26
COOLING .... AIR
FUEL .... G
SPEEDS .... VARIABLE
TRANSMISSION .... HYDRO
STEERING .... STANDARD

GTH2754

YEARS MFRD 2005-2005
ENGINE .... KOHLER OHV
CYLINDERS 2
ENGINE HP 27
COOLING .... AIR
FUEL .... G
SPEEDS .... VARIABLE
TRANSMISSION .... HYDRO
STEERING .... STANDARD
BLADE CLUTCH .... ELECTRIC
STANDARD DECK .... 54"
MSRP $3,599

RETAIL PRICING

YEAR	HIGH	LOW
2005	$2,243	$1,682

GTVH200

YEARS MFRD 1999-1999
ENGINE .... B&S
ENGINE HP 20
FUEL .... G
TRANSMISSION .... HYDRO
STEERING .... STANDARD
STANDARD DECK .... 46"
MSRP $2,199

RETAIL PRICING

YEAR	HIGH	LOW
1999	$288	$216

GTVH205

YEARS MFRD 2000-2000
ENGINE .... KOHLER
ENGINE HP 20
FUEL .... G
TRANSMISSION .... HYDRO
STEERING .... STANDARD
STANDARD DECK .... 46"
MSRP $3,000

RETAIL PRICING

YEAR	HIGH	LOW
2000	$1,425	$1,069

IZ25

YEARS MFRD 2009-2009
SERIES .... IZ SERIES
ENGINE .... KOHLER
CYLINDERS 2
ENGINE HP 25
COOLING .... AIR
FUEL .... G
SPEEDS .... VARIABLE
TRANSMISSION .... HYDRO
STEERING .... ZERO
BLADE CLUTCH .... ELECTRIC
MSRP $6,999

RETAIL PRICING

YEAR	HIGH	LOW
2009	$4,342	$3,257

IZ4217T

YEARS MFRD 2007-2007
ENGINE .... KAWASAKI
CYLINDERS 2
ENGINE HP 17
COOLING .... AIR
FUEL .... G
SPEEDS .... VARIABLE
TRANSMISSION .... HYDRO
STEERING .... ZERO
STANDARD DECK .... 42"
WEIGHT .... 832 LBS.
MSRP $5,999

SERIAL NUMBERS

YEAR	BEGINNING NO.
2007	64000000

RETAIL PRICING

YEAR	HIGH	LOW
2007	$2,107	$1,580

IZ4817T

YEARS MFRD 2007-2007
ENGINE .... KAWASAKI
CYLINDERS 2
ENGINE HP 17
COOLING .... AIR
FUEL .... G
SPEEDS .... VARIABLE
TRANSMISSION .... HYDRO
STEERING .... ZERO
STANDARD DECK .... 48"
WEIGHT .... 870 LBS.
MSRP $6,149

SERIAL NUMBERS

YEAR	BEGINNING NO.
2007	64000000

RETAIL PRICING

YEAR	HIGH	LOW
2007	$2,160	$1,620

IZ4819

YEARS MFRD 2008-2009
SERIES .... IZ SERIES
ENGINE .... KAWASAKI
CYLINDERS 2
ENGINE HP 19
COOLING .... AIR
FUEL .... G
SPEEDS .... VARIABLE
TRANSMISSION .... HYDRO
STEERING .... ZERO
BLADE CLUTCH .... ELECTRIC
STANDARD DECK .... 48"
WEIGHT .... 870 LBS.
MSRP $6,999

RETAIL PRICING

YEAR	HIGH	LOW
2008	$2,672	$2,004
2009	$2,965	$2,224

IZ4819T

YEARS MFRD 2007-2008
ENGINE .... KAWASAKI
CYLINDERS 2
ENGINE HP 19
COOLING .... AIR
FUEL .... G
SPEEDS .... VARIABLE
TRANSMISSION .... HYDRO
STEERING .... ZERO
WEIGHT .... 870 LBS.

IZ4821T

YEARS MFRD 2007-2007
ENGINE .... KAWASAKI
ENGINE HP 21
COOLING .... AIR
FUEL .... G
SPEEDS .... VARIABLE
TRANSMISSION .... HYDRO
STEERING .... ZERO
STANDARD DECK .... 48"
WEIGHT .... 870 LBS.
MSRP $7,299

SERIAL NUMBERS

YEAR	BEGINNING NO.
2007	64000000

RETAIL PRICING

YEAR	HIGH	LOW
2007	$2,566	$1,924

IZ4824

YEARS MFRD 2010-2011
ENGINE .... KAWASAKI
CYLINDERS 2
ENGINE HP 21
COOLING .... AIR
FUEL .... G
SPEEDS .... VARIABLE
TRANSMISSION .... HYDRO
STEERING .... ZERO
BLADE CLUTCH .... ELECTRIC
STANDARD DECK .... 48"
MSRP $6,899

RETAIL PRICING

YEAR	HIGH	LOW
2010	$3,191	$2,393
2011	$3,632	$2,724

IZ5223

YEARS MFRD 2008-2010
ENGINE .... B&S
CYLINDERS 2
ENGINE HP 23
COOLING .... AIR
FUEL .... G
SPEEDS .... VARIABLE
TRANSMISSION .... HYDRO
STEERING .... ZERO
BLADE CLUTCH .... ELECTRIC
STANDARD DECK .... 52"
MSRP $6,799

OPTIONS

KAWASAKI 23HP

RETAIL PRICING

YEAR	HIGH	LOW
2008	$2,570	$1,927
2009	$2,852	$2,139
2010	$3,168	$2,376

IZ5223T

YEARS MFRD 2007-2007
ENGINE .... B&S
ENGINE HP 23
COOLING .... AIR
FUEL .... G
SPEEDS .... VARIABLE
TRANSMISSION .... HYDRO
STEERING .... ZERO
STANDARD DECK .... 52"
WEIGHT .... 880 LBS.
MSRP $7,699

OPTIONS

KOHLER 23HP

SERIAL NUMBERS

YEAR	BEGINNING NO.
2007	64000000

RETAIL PRICING

YEAR	HIGH	LOW
2007	$2,707	$2,030

IZ5225TXP

YEARS MFRD 2007-2007
ENGINE .... KOHLER
CYLINDERS 2
ENGINE HP 25
COOLING .... AIR
FUEL .... G
SPEEDS .... VARIABLE
TRANSMISSION .... HYDRO
STEERING .... ZERO
STANDARD DECK .... 52"
WEIGHT .... 880 LBS.
MSRP $8,199

SERIAL NUMBERS

YEAR	BEGINNING NO.
2007	64000000

RETAIL PRICING

YEAR	HIGH	LOW
2007	$2,881	$2,161

IZ6125T

YEARS MFRD 2007-2007
ENGINE .... KOHLER
ENGINE HP 25
COOLING .... AIR
FUEL .... G
SPEEDS .... VARIABLE
TRANSMISSION .... HYDRO
STEERING .... ZERO
STANDARD DECK .... 61"
WEIGHT .... 920 LBS.
MSRP $8,299

SERIAL NUMBERS

YEAR	BEGINNING NO.
2007	64000000

RETAIL PRICING

YEAR	HIGH	LOW
2007	$2,916	$2,187

LGT48DXL

YEARS MFRD 2018-2020
ENGINE .... KOHLER
CYLINDERS 2
ENGINE HP 25
FUEL .... G
SPEEDS .... VARIABLE
TRANSMISSION .... HYDRO
STEERING .... STANDARD
BLADE CLUTCH .... ELECTRIC
STANDARD DECK .... 48"
MSRP $2,699

LGT54DXL

YEARS MFRD 2018-2020
ENGINE .... KOHLER
CYLINDERS 2
ENGINE HP 25
FUEL .... G
SPEEDS .... VARIABLE
TRANSMISSION .... HYDRO
STEERING .... STANDARD
STANDARD DECK .... 54"
MSRP $2,999

LGT2554

YEARS MFRD 2009-2009
ENGINE .... KOHLER
CYLINDERS 2
CID 44
ENGINE HP 25
COOLING .... AIR
FUEL .... G
SPEEDS .... VARIABLE
TRANSMISSION .... HYDRO
STEERING .... STANDARD
BLADE CLUTCH .... ELECTRIC
STANDARD DECK .... 54"
MSRP $2,299

HUSQVARNA

RETAIL PRICING

YEAR	HIGH	LOW
2009	$689	$517

LGT2654
YEARS MFRD 2014-2016
ENGINE KOHLER
CYLINDERS 2
ENGINE HP 26
COOLING AIR
FUEL G
SPEEDS VARIABLE
TRANSMISSION HYDRO
STEERING STANDARD
STANDARD DECK 54"
MSRP $2,399

RETAIL PRICING

YEAR	HIGH	LOW
2014	$1,284	$963
2015	$1,468	$1,101
2016	$1,795	$1,347

LR100
YEARS MFRD 1993-1993
ENGINE B&S
ENGINE HP 10
COOLING AIR
FUEL G
TRANSMISSION GEAR
STEERING STANDARD

LR110
YEARS MFRD 1994-1996
ENGINE B&S
ENGINE HP 11
COOLING AIR
FUEL G
STEERING STANDARD

LR111
YEARS MFRD 1993-1995
ENGINE B&S
ENGINE HP 11
COOLING AIR
FUEL G
TRANSMISSION GEAR
STEERING STANDARD

LR120
YEARS MFRD 1993-1996
ENGINE B&S
ENGINE HP 12
COOLING AIR
FUEL G
STEERING STANDARD

LR122
YEARS MFRD 1999-1999
ENGINE B&S
ENGINE HP 12
COOLING AIR
FUEL G
TRANSMISSION GEAR
STEERING STANDARD

LR125
YEARS MFRD 1994-1995
ENGINE B&S
ENGINE HP 13
COOLING AIR
FUEL G
TRANSMISSION GEAR
STEERING STANDARD

LRH125
YEARS MFRD 1994-1995
ENGINE KOHLER
ENGINE HP 12.5
COOLING AIR
FUEL G
TRANSMISSION HYDRO
STEERING STANDARD

LT100
YEARS MFRD 1992-1992
ENGINE B&S
ENGINE HP 10
COOLING AIR
FUEL G
TRANSMISSION GEAR
STEERING STANDARD

LT110
YEARS MFRD 1994-1996
ENGINE B&S
ENGINE HP 11
COOLING AIR
FUEL G
STEERING STANDARD

LT120
YEARS MFRD 1997-1997
ENGINE B&S
ENGINE HP 12
COOLING AIR
FUEL G
TRANSMISSION GEAR
STEERING STANDARD

LT121
YEARS MFRD 1997-1997
ENGINE B&S
ENGINE HP 12
COOLING AIR
FUEL G
TRANSMISSION GEAR
STEERING STANDARD

LT125
YEARS MFRD 1992-1992
ENGINE B&S
ENGINE HP 12.5
COOLING AIR
FUEL G
TRANSMISSION GEAR
STEERING STANDARD

LT130
YEARS MFRD 1996-1997
ENGINE B&S
ENGINE HP 13
COOLING AIR
FUEL G
TRANSMISSION GEAR
STEERING STANDARD

LT18542
YEARS MFRD 2004-2005
ENGINE B&S
ENGINE HP 18.5
FUEL G
SPEEDS 6/1
TRANSMISSION GEAR
STEERING STANDARD
BLADE CLUTCH MANUAL
STANDARD DECK 42"
MSRP $1,199

RETAIL PRICING

YEAR	HIGH	LOW
2004	$706	$529
2005	$748	$561

LTA18538
YEARS MFRD 2016-2018
ENGINE B&S INTEK
CYLINDERS 1
ENGINE HP 18.5
FUEL G
TRANSMISSION HYDRO
STEERING STANDARD
STANDARD DECK 38"

LTH120
YEARS MFRD 1997-1999
ENGINE B&S
ENGINE HP 12
COOLING AIR
FUEL G
TRANSMISSION HYDRO
STEERING STANDARD

LTH130
YEARS MFRD 1996-1999
ENGINE KOHLER
ENGINE HP 13
COOLING AIR
FUEL G
TRANSMISSION HYDRO
STEERING STANDARD

LTH140
YEARS MFRD 1994-1995
ENGINE KOHLER
ENGINE HP 14
COOLING AIR
FUEL G
TRANSMISSION HYDRO
STEERING STANDARD

LTH145
YEARS MFRD 1997-1997
ENGINE B&S
ENGINE HP 14.5
COOLING AIR
FUEL G
TRANSMISSION HYDRO
STEERING STANDARD

LTH1438
YEARS MFRD 2009-2009
ENGINE B&S INTEK
CYLINDERS 1
CID 31
ENGINE HP 14
COOLING AIR
FUEL G
SPEEDS VARIABLE
TRANSMISSION HYDRO
STEERING STANDARD
BLADE CLUTCH MANUAL
STANDARD DECK 38"
MSRP $1,499

RETAIL PRICING

YEAR	HIGH	LOW
2009	$450	$337

LTH1536
YEARS MFRD 2004-2004
ENGINE KOHLER COURAGE SV470
CYLINDERS 1
CID 29.1
ENGINE HP 15
FUEL G
SPEEDS VARIABLE
TRANSMISSION HYDRO
STEERING STANDARD
BLADE CLUTCH MANUAL
WEIGHT 407 LBS.

LTH1538
YEARS MFRD 2007-2007
ENGINE B&S INTEK
ENGINE HP 15
COOLING AIR
FUEL G
SPEEDS VARIABLE
TRANSMISSION HYDRO
STEERING STANDARD

LTH1542
YEARS MFRD 2005-2005
ENGINE KOHLER COURAGE
CYLINDERS 1
ENGINE HP 15
COOLING AIR
FUEL G
SPEEDS VARIABLE

TRANSMISSION . . . . HYDRO
STEERING. . . . . STANDARD
STANDARD DECK . . . . 42"
MSRP. $1,399

RETAIL PRICING

YEAR	HIGH	LOW
2005	$872	$654

LTH1738

YEARS MFRD 2018-2019
ENGINE . . . . HUSQVARNA
CYLINDERS. 1
ENGINE HP 17
FUEL . . . . G
TRANSMISSION . . . . HYDRO
STEERING. . . . . STANDARD
STANDARD DECK . . . . 38"
MSRP. $1,599

LTH1742

YEARS MFRD 2004-2004
ENGINE . . . . KOHLER COURAGE
CYLINDERS. 1
CID 32.6
ENGINE HP 17
FUEL . . . . G
SPEEDS . . . . VARIABLE
TRANSMISSION . . . . HYDRO
STEERING. . . . . STANDARD
BLADE CLUTCH . . . . MANUAL
WEIGHT . . . . 425 LBS.

LTH2038

YEARS MFRD 2014-2014
ENGINE . . . . B&S
ENGINE HP 20
COOLING . . . . AIR
FUEL . . . . G
SPEEDS . . . . VARIABLE
TRANSMISSION . . . . HYDRO
STEERING. . . . . STANDARD
STANDARD DECK . . . . 38"
MSRP. $1,499

RETAIL PRICING

YEAR	HIGH	LOW
2014	$824	$618

LTH17538

YEARS MFRD 2019-2020
ENGINE . . . . B&S
CYLINDERS. 1
ENGINE HP 17.5
FUEL . . . . G
SPEEDS . . . . VARIABLE
TRANSMISSION . . . . HYDRO
STEERING. . . . . STANDARD
STANDARD DECK . . . . 38"
MSRP. $1,599

LTH18538

YEARS MFRD 2015-2015
ENGINE . . . . B&S
ENGINE HP 18.5

COOLING . . . . AIR
FUEL . . . . G
SPEEDS . . . . VARIABLE
TRANSMISSION . . . . HYDRO
STEERING. . . . . STANDARD
STANDARD DECK . . . . 38"
MSRP. $1,499

RETAIL PRICING

YEAR	HIGH	LOW
2015	$836	$627

LZ25

YEARS MFRD 2009-2009
SERIES. . . . . LZ SERIES
ENGINE . . . . KOHLER
CYLINDERS. 2
ENGINE HP 25
COOLING . . . . AIR
FUEL . . . . G
SPEEDS . . . . VARIABLE
TRANSMISSION . . . . HYDRO
STEERING. . . . . ZERO
BLADE CLUTCH . . . . ELECTRIC
MSRP. $8,899

RETAIL PRICING

YEAR	HIGH	LOW
2009	$5,520	$4,140

LZ30

YEARS MFRD 2009-2009
SERIES. . . . . LZ SERIES
ENGINE . . . . KOHLER
CYLINDERS. 2
ENGINE HP 30
COOLING . . . . AIR
FUEL . . . . G
SPEEDS . . . . VARIABLE
TRANSMISSION . . . . HYDRO
STEERING. . . . . ZERO
BLADE CLUTCH . . . . ELECTRIC
MSRP. $8,799

RETAIL PRICING

YEAR	HIGH	LOW
2009	$5,460	$4,095

LZ5225T

YEARS MFRD 2007-2007
ENGINE . . . . KAWASAKI
ENGINE HP 25
COOLING . . . . AIR
FUEL . . . . G
SPEEDS . . . . VARIABLE
TRANSMISSION . . . . HYDRO
STEERING. . . . . ZERO
WEIGHT . . . . 1,030 LBS.

LZ5227TXP

YEARS MFRD 2007-2009
ENGINE . . . . KOHLER
ENGINE HP 27
COOLING . . . . AIR
FUEL . . . . G
SPEEDS . . . . VARIABLE
TRANSMISSION . . . . HYDRO

STEERING. . . . . ZERO
STANDARD DECK . . . . 52"
WEIGHT . . . . 1,030 LBS.
MSRP. $9,399

SERIAL NUMBERS

YEAR	BEGINNING NO.
2007	64000000

RETAIL PRICING

YEAR	HIGH	LOW
2007	$3,229	$2,422
2008	$3,589	$2,692
2009	$3,985	$2,989

LZ6125T

YEARS MFRD 2007-2007
ENGINE . . . . KAWASAKI
ENGINE HP 25
COOLING . . . . AIR
FUEL . . . . G
SPEEDS . . . . VARIABLE
TRANSMISSION . . . . HYDRO
STEERING. . . . . ZERO
WEIGHT . . . . 1,060 LBS.

LZ6127T

YEARS MFRD 2007-2009
ENGINE . . . . KOHLER
CYLINDERS. 2
ENGINE HP 27
COOLING . . . . AIR
FUEL . . . . G
SPEEDS . . . . VARIABLE
TRANSMISSION . . . . HYDRO
STEERING. . . . . ZERO
PTO . . . . YES
STANDARD DECK . . . . 61"
WEIGHT . . . . 1,060 LBS.
MSRP. $9,699

SERIAL NUMBERS

YEAR	BEGINNING NO.
2007	64000000

RETAIL PRICING

YEAR	HIGH	LOW
2007	$3,340	$2,505
2008	$3,702	$2,777
2009	$4,111	$3,083

LZ6130TXP

YEARS MFRD 2007-2009
ENGINE . . . . KOHLER
CYLINDERS. 2
ENGINE HP 30
COOLING . . . . AIR
FUEL . . . . G
SPEEDS . . . . VARIABLE
TRANSMISSION . . . . HYDRO
STEERING. . . . . ZERO
STANDARD DECK . . . . 61"
WEIGHT . . . . 1,060 LBS.
MSRP. $9,799

SERIAL NUMBERS

YEAR	BEGINNING NO.
2007	64000000

RETAIL PRICING

YEAR	HIGH	LOW
2007	$3,367	$2,525
2008	$3,742	$2,806
2009	$4,153	$3,115

LZ7230TXP

YEARS MFRD 2007-2009
ENGINE . . . . KOHLER
CYLINDERS. 2
ENGINE HP 30
COOLING . . . . AIR
FUEL . . . . G
SPEEDS . . . . VARIABLE
TRANSMISSION . . . . HYDRO
STEERING. . . . . ZERO
STANDARD DECK . . . . 72"
WEIGHT . . . . 1,140 LBS.
MSRP. $10,499

SERIAL NUMBERS

YEAR	BEGINNING NO.
2007	64000000

RETAIL PRICING

YEAR	HIGH	LOW
2007	$3,607	$2,706
2008	$4,008	$3,006
2009	$4,450	$3,338

LZF5227

YEARS MFRD 2008-2009
SERIES. . . . . LZF SERIES
ENGINE . . . . KOHLER
CYLINDERS. 2
ENGINE HP 27
COOLING . . . . AIR
FUEL . . . . G
SPEEDS . . . . VARIABLE
TRANSMISSION . . . . HYDRO
STEERING. . . . . ZERO
BLADE CLUTCH . . . . ELECTRIC
STANDARD DECK . . . . 52"
WEIGHT . . . . 1,030 LBS.
MSRP. $7,699

RETAIL PRICING

YEAR	HIGH	LOW
2008	$2,938	$2,204
2009	$3,264	$2,448

LZF6127

YEARS MFRD 2010-2010
ENGINE . . . . KOHLER
ENGINE HP 27
COOLING . . . . AIR
FUEL . . . . G
SPEEDS . . . . VARIABLE
TRANSMISSION . . . . HYDRO
STEERING. . . . . ZERO
BLADE CLUTCH . . . . ELECTRIC
STANDARD DECK . . . . 61"
MSRP. $7,899

OPTIONS

BAGGER

RETAIL PRICING

YEAR	HIGH	LOW
2010	$3,920	$2,940

HUSQVARNA

M5225

YEARS MFRD 2008-2008
ENGINE .... KOHLER
ENGINE HP 25
COOLING .... AIR
FUEL .... G
SPEEDS .... VARIABLE
TRANSMISSION .... HYDRO
STEERING .... ZERO
BLADE CLUTCH .... ELECTRIC
WEIGHT .... 760 LBS.

M6125

YEARS MFRD 2008-2008
ENGINE .... KOHLER
ENGINE HP 25
COOLING .... AIR
FUEL .... G
SPEEDS .... VARIABLE
TRANSMISSION .... HYDRO
STEERING .... ZERO
BLADE CLUTCH .... ELECTRIC
WEIGHT .... 790 LBS.

M7227

YEARS MFRD 2008-2008
ENGINE .... KOHLER
ENGINE HP 27
COOLING .... AIR
FUEL .... G
SPEEDS .... VARIABLE
TRANSMISSION .... HYDRO
STEERING .... ZERO
BLADE CLUTCH .... ELECTRIC
WEIGHT .... 820 LBS.

M-ZT52

YEARS MFRD 2013-2020
ENGINE .... KOHLER
CID 44.2
ENGINE HP 23
COOLING .... AIR
FUEL .... G
SPEEDS .... VARIABLE
TRANSMISSION .... HYDRO
STEERING .... ZERO
BLADE CLUTCH .... ELECTRIC
STANDARD DECK .... 52"
WEIGHT .... 760 LBS.
MSRP $6,299

OPTIONS

B&S 30HP
KAWASAKI 22HP $300

RETAIL PRICING

YEAR	HIGH	LOW
2013	$3,084	$2,312
2014	$3,454	$2,591
2015	$3,813	$2,859
2016	$4,119	$3,089
2017	$4,528	$3,396
2018	$5,018	$3,763
2019	$5,421	$4,066
2020	$5,682	$4,324

M-ZT61

YEARS MFRD 2013-2019
ENGINE .... B&S
ENGINE HP 27
COOLING .... AIR
FUEL .... G
SPEEDS .... VARIABLE
TRANSMISSION .... HYDRO
STEERING .... ZERO
BLADE CLUTCH .... ELECTRIC
STANDARD DECK .... 61"
MSRP $6,399

OPTIONS

KAWASAKI 23HP
KOHLER 27HP

RETAIL PRICING

YEAR	HIGH	LOW
2013	$3,638	$2,728
2014	$3,928	$2,946
2015	$4,152	$3,114
2016	$4,446	$3,335
2017	$4,915	$3,686
2018	$5,127	$3,846
2019	$5,464	$4,098

M-ZT61 KOH

YEARS MFRD 2019-2020
ENGINE .... KOHLER KT740
CYLINDERS 2
CID 45.58
ENGINE HP 25
COOLING .... AIR
FUEL .... G
SPEEDS .... VARIABLE
TRANSMISSION .... HYDRO
STEERING .... ZERO
ROPS/CAB .... ROPS
STANDARD DECK .... 61"
WEIGHT .... 790 LBS.
MSRP $6,699

OPTIONS

KAWASAKI 23HP $300

MZ48

YEARS MFRD 2017-2020
ENGINE .... KOHLER KT730
CYLINDERS 2
ENGINE HP 23
COOLING .... AIR
FUEL .... G
TRANSMISSION .... HYDRO
STEERING .... ZERO
BLADE CLUTCH .... ELECTRIC
STANDARD DECK .... 48"
MSRP $4,499

MZ52

YEARS MFRD 2015-2017
ENGINE .... KOHLER
ENGINE HP 25
COOLING .... AIR
FUEL .... G
SPEEDS .... VARIABLE
TRANSMISSION .... HYDRO
STEERING .... STANDARD
STANDARD DECK .... 52"
MSRP $4,799

OPTIONS

KAWASAKI 23HP

RETAIL PRICING

YEAR	HIGH	LOW
2015	$3,470	$2,603
2016	$3,784	$2,838
2017	$4,156	$3,117

MZ52LE

YEARS MFRD 2016-2016
ENGINE .... KAWASAKI
ENGINE HP 23
FUEL .... G
SPEEDS .... VARIABLE
TRANSMISSION .... HYDRO
STEERING .... ZERO
STANDARD DECK .... 52"
MSRP $4,999

RETAIL PRICING

YEAR	HIGH	LOW
2016	$3,253	$2,439

MZ54

YEARS MFRD 2018-2020
ENGINE .... KOHLER ZT730
CYLINDERS 2
CID 45.6
ENGINE HP 23
COOLING .... AIR
FUEL .... G
SPEEDS .... VARIABLE
TRANSMISSION .... HYDRO
STEERING .... ZERO
BLADE CLUTCH .... ELECTRIC
STANDARD DECK .... 54"
WEIGHT .... 740 LBS.
MSRP $4,699

OPTIONS

KAW 24HP FAB DECK $300
KAWASAKI 24HP

MZ54S

YEARS MFRD 2016-2017
ENGINE .... ENDURANCE
ENGINE HP 24
FUEL .... G
SPEEDS .... VARIABLE
TRANSMISSION .... HYDRO
STEERING .... ZERO
STANDARD DECK .... 54"
MSRP $3,999

RETAIL PRICING

YEAR	HIGH	LOW
2016	$2,394	$1,796
2017	$2,682	$2,012

MZ61

YEARS MFRD 2015-2020
ENGINE .... B&S
ENGINE HP 27
COOLING .... AIR
FUEL .... G
SPEEDS .... VARIABLE
TRANSMISSION .... HYDRO
STEERING .... STANDARD
STANDARD DECK .... 61"
MSRP $4,999

OPTIONS

KAWASAKI 24HP $400

RETAIL PRICING

YEAR	HIGH	LOW
2015	$3,488	$2,616
2016	$3,642	$2,732
2017	$3,857	$2,892
2018	$4,008	$3,006
2019	$4,195	$3,145
2020	$4,397	$3,324

MZ5225ZT

YEARS MFRD 2011-2013
ENGINE ... KOHLER COURAGE PRO
CYLINDERS 2
CID 725CC
ENGINE HP 25
COOLING .... AIR
FUEL .... G
SPEEDS .... VARIABLE
TRANSMISSION .... HYDRO
STEERING .... ZERO
BLADE CLUTCH .... ELECTRIC
STANDARD DECK .... 52"
WEIGHT .... 740 LBS.
MSRP $4,699

OPTIONS

BAGGER

RETAIL PRICING

YEAR	HIGH	LOW
2011	$2,267	$1,700
2012	$2,520	$1,890
2013	$2,798	$2,098

MZ5226

YEARS MFRD 2009-2009
SERIES .... MZ SERIES
ENGINE .... B&S ENDURANCE
CYLINDERS 2
ENGINE HP 26
COOLING .... AIR
FUEL .... G
SPEEDS .... VARIABLE
TRANSMISSION .... HYDRO
STEERING .... ZERO
BLADE CLUTCH .... ELECTRIC
STANDARD DECK .... 52"
WEIGHT .... 760 LBS.
MSRP $5,999

RETAIL PRICING

YEAR	HIGH	LOW
2009	$2,542	$1,907

MZ5424S

YEARS MFRD 2011-2013
ENGINE .... KAWASAKI FR
CYLINDERS 2

CID 726CC
ENGINE HP 24
COOLING .... AIR
FUEL .... G
SPEEDS .... VARIABLE
TRANSMISSION .... HYDRO
STEERING .... ZERO
BLADE CLUTCH .... ELECTRIC
STANDARD DECK .... 54"
WEIGHT .... 700 LBS.
MSRP $4,299

OPTIONS

BAGGER

RETAIL PRICING

YEAR	HIGH	LOW
2011	$2,049	$1,537
2012	$2,274	$1,705
2013	$2,526	$1,895

MZ5424SR

YEARS MFRD 2013-2015
ENGINE .... KAWASAKI
ENGINE HP 24
COOLING .... AIR
FUEL .... G
SPEEDS .... VARIABLE
TRANSMISSION .... HYDRO
STEERING .... ZERO
BLADE CLUTCH .... ELECTRIC
STANDARD DECK .... 54"
MSRP $4,499

OPTIONS

BAGGER

RETAIL PRICING

YEAR	HIGH	LOW
2013	$2,722	$2,042
2014	$2,849	$2,137
2015	$3,068	$2,301

MZ6125

YEARS MFRD 2008-2009
SERIES .... MZ SERIES
ENGINE .... KOHLER COURAGE
CYLINDERS 2
ENGINE HP 25
COOLING .... AIR
FUEL .... G
SPEEDS .... VARIABLE
TRANSMISSION .... HYDRO
STEERING .... ZERO
BLADE CLUTCH .... ELECTRIC
STANDARD DECK .... 61"
WEIGHT .... 790 LBS.
MSRP $6,499

RETAIL PRICING

YEAR	HIGH	LOW
2008	$2,482	$1,862
2009	$2,757	$2,068

MZ6128

YEARS MFRD 2011-2015
ENGINE .... B&S ENDURANCE
CYLINDERS 2
CID 810CC
ENGINE HP 28
COOLING .... AIR
FUEL .... G
SPEEDS .... VARIABLE
TRANSMISSION .... HYDRO
STEERING .... ZERO
BLADE CLUTCH .... ELECTRIC
STANDARD DECK .... 61"
WEIGHT .... 770 LBS.
MSRP $4,999

OPTIONS

BAGGER

RETAIL PRICING

YEAR	HIGH	LOW
2011	$2,695	$2,021
2012	$2,986	$2,240
2013	$3,178	$2,384
2014	$3,292	$2,469
2015	$3,462	$2,597

MZ7227

YEARS MFRD 2008-2009
SERIES .... MZ SERIES
ENGINE .... KOHLER COURAGE
CYLINDERS 2
ENGINE HP 27
COOLING .... AIR
FUEL .... G
SPEEDS .... VARIABLE
TRANSMISSION .... HYDRO
STEERING .... ZERO
BLADE CLUTCH .... ELECTRIC
STANDARD DECK .... 72"
WEIGHT .... 820 LBS.
MSRP $7,199

RETAIL PRICING

YEAR	HIGH	LOW
2008	$2,748	$2,061
2009	$3,051	$2,288

P-ZT48

YEARS MFRD 2013-2017
ENGINE .... KAWASAKI FX
ENGINE HP 22
COOLING .... AIR
FUEL .... G
SPEEDS .... VARIABLE
TRANSMISSION .... HYDRO
STEERING .... ZERO
BLADE CLUTCH .... ELECTRIC
STANDARD DECK .... 48"
WEIGHT .... 1,040 LBS.
MSRP $7,599

OPTIONS

B&S 24HP
BAGGER

RETAIL PRICING

YEAR	HIGH	LOW
2013	$3,463	$2,597
2014	$3,822	$2,867
2015	$4,218	$3,163
2016	$4,656	$3,492
2017	$5,140	$3,855

P-ZT54

YEARS MFRD 2013-2013
ENGINE .... KAWASAKI FX
ENGINE HP 23.5
COOLING .... AIR
FUEL .... G
SPEEDS .... VARIABLE
TRANSMISSION .... HYDRO
STEERING .... ZERO
BLADE CLUTCH .... ELECTRIC
STANDARD DECK .... 54"
WEIGHT .... 1,070 LBS.
MSRP $7,699

OPTIONS

BAGGER

RETAIL PRICING

YEAR	HIGH	LOW
2013	$4,527	$3,395

P-ZT60

YEARS MFRD 2013-2017
ENGINE .... KAWASAKI FX
ENGINE HP 24.5
COOLING .... AIR
FUEL .... G
SPEEDS .... VARIABLE
TRANSMISSION .... HYDRO
STEERING .... ZERO
BLADE CLUTCH .... ELECTRIC
STANDARD DECK .... 60"
WEIGHT .... 1,100 LBS.
MSRP $8,299

OPTIONS

BAGGER
VANGUARD 26HP

RETAIL PRICING

YEAR	HIGH	LOW
2013	$3,783	$2,837
2014	$4,174	$3,130
2015	$4,608	$3,456
2016	$5,086	$3,815
2017	$5,613	$4,210

P-ZT5224

YEARS MFRD 2011-2012
ENGINE .... KAWASAKI FX
CYLINDERS 2
CID 726CC
ENGINE HP 22
COOLING .... AIR
FUEL .... G
SPEEDS .... VARIABLE
TRANSMISSION .... HYDRO
STEERING .... ZERO
BLADE CLUTCH .... ELECTRIC
STANDARD DECK .... 52"
WEIGHT .... 1,070 LBS.
MSRP $7,299

OPTIONS

BAGGER

RETAIL PRICING

YEAR	HIGH	LOW
2011	$3,615	$2,711
2012	$4,011	$3,008

P-ZT6126

YEARS MFRD 2011-2012
ENGINE .... KAWASAKI FX
CYLINDERS 2
CID 726
ENGINE HP 23.5
COOLING .... AIR
FUEL .... G
SPEEDS .... VARIABLE
TRANSMISSION .... HYDRO
STEERING .... ZERO
BLADE CLUTCH .... ELECTRIC
STANDARD DECK .... 61"
WEIGHT .... 1,100 LBS.
MSRP $7,499

OPTIONS

BAGGER

RETAIL PRICING

YEAR	HIGH	LOW
2011	$3,714	$2,786
2012	$4,123	$3,092

P-ZT6128

YEARS MFRD 2011-2012
ENGINE .... B&S COMMERCIAL TURF
CYLINDERS 2
CID 810CC
ENGINE HP 28
COOLING .... AIR
FUEL .... G
SPEEDS .... VARIABLE
TRANSMISSION .... HYDRO
STEERING .... ZERO
BLADE CLUTCH .... ELECTRIC
STANDARD DECK .... 61"
WEIGHT .... 1,100 LBS.
MSRP $6,999

OPTIONS

BAGGER

RETAIL PRICING

YEAR	HIGH	LOW
2011	$3,466	$2,600
2012	$3,847	$2,886

PRO15

YEARS MFRD 2001-2003
SERIES .... RIDER SERIES
ENGINE .... KAWASAKI
CID 494
ENGINE HP 15
COOLING .... AIR
FUEL .... G
TRANSMISSION .... HYDRO
STEERING .... STANDARD
STANDARD DECK .... 38"
MSRP $4,500

RETAIL PRICING

YEAR	HIGH	LOW
2001	$2,228	$1,671
2002	$2,290	$1,718
2003	$2,362	$1,771

HUSQVARNA

PROFLEX 21

YEARS MFRD 2001-2003
SERIES .... RIDER SERIES
ENGINE .... KAWASAKI
CID 675
ENGINE HP 21
COOLING .... AIR
FUEL .... G
TRANSMISSION .... HYDRO
STEERING .... STANDARD
STANDARD DECK .... 48"
MSRP $5,000

RETAIL PRICING

YEAR	HIGH	LOW
2001	$2,476	$1,857
2002	$2,545	$1,909
2003	$2,616	$1,962

PZ54

YEARS MFRD 2013-2017
ENGINE .... KAWASAKI FX
ENGINE HP 24.5
COOLING .... AIR
FUEL .... G
SPEEDS .... VARIABLE
TRANSMISSION .... HYDRO
STEERING .... ZERO
BLADE CLUTCH .... ELECTRIC
STANDARD DECK .... 54"
WEIGHT .... 1,260 LBS.
MSRP $10,399

OPTIONS

27HP
BAGGER
MULCHER

RETAIL PRICING

YEAR	HIGH	LOW
2013	$4,738	$3,554
2014	$5,231	$3,923
2015	$5,773	$4,330
2016	$6,372	$4,779
2017	$7,033	$5,275

PZ60

YEARS MFRD 2013-2013
ENGINE .... KAWASAKI FX
ENGINE HP 25.5
COOLING .... AIR
FUEL .... G
SPEEDS .... VARIABLE
TRANSMISSION .... HYDRO
STEERING .... ZERO
BLADE CLUTCH .... ELECTRIC
STANDARD DECK .... 60"
WEIGHT .... 1,320 LBS.
MSRP $10,499

OPTIONS

BAGGER
MULCHER
PROPANE

RETAIL PRICING

YEAR	HIGH	LOW
2013	$6,172	$4,629

PZ72

YEARS MFRD 2013-2017
ENGINE .... KAWASAKI FX
ENGINE HP 31
COOLING .... AIR
FUEL .... G
SPEEDS .... VARIABLE
TRANSMISSION .... HYDRO
STEERING .... ZERO
BLADE CLUTCH .... ELECTRIC
STANDARD DECK .... 72"
WEIGHT .... 1,400 LBS.
MSRP $11,899

OPTIONS

KOHLER 31HP

RETAIL PRICING

YEAR	HIGH	LOW
2013	$5,422	$4,067
2014	$5,985	$4,489
2015	$6,606	$4,955
2016	$7,291	$5,468
2017	$8,048	$6,036

PZ5426FX

YEARS MFRD 2010-2012
ENGINE .... KAWASAKI
CYLINDERS 2
ENGINE HP 23.5
COOLING .... AIR
FUEL .... G
SPEEDS .... VARIABLE
TRANSMISSION .... HYDRO
STEERING .... ZERO
BLADE CLUTCH .... ELECTRIC
STANDARD DECK .... 54"
WEIGHT .... 1,260 LBS.
MSRP $9,499

OPTIONS

BAGGER

RETAIL PRICING

YEAR	HIGH	LOW
2010	$4,237	$3,177
2011	$4,703	$3,527
2012	$5,221	$3,916

PZ5430

YEARS MFRD 2012-2012
ENGINE .... KOHLER
ENGINE HP 30
COOLING .... AIR
FUEL .... G
SPEEDS .... VARIABLE
TRANSMISSION .... HYDRO
STEERING .... ZERO
STANDARD DECK .... 54"
MSRP $9,699

OPTIONS

BAGGER

RETAIL PRICING

YEAR	HIGH	LOW
2012	$5,333	$4,000

PZ6025

YEARS MFRD 2013-2014
ENGINE .... KAWASAKI
ENGINE HP 25.5
COOLING .... AIR
FUEL .... G
SPEEDS .... VARIABLE
TRANSMISSION .... HYDRO
STEERING .... ZERO
STANDARD DECK .... 60"
MSRP $10,499

RETAIL PRICING

YEAR	HIGH	LOW
2013	$5,130	$3,848
2014	$5,932	$4,449

PZ6029D

YEARS MFRD 2011-2012
ENGINE .... KUBOTA 05
CYLINDERS 3
ENGINE HP 29
COOLING .... LIQUID
FUEL .... D
SPEEDS .... VARIABLE
TRANSMISSION .... HYDRO
STEERING .... ZERO
BLADE CLUTCH .... ELECTRIC
STANDARD DECK .... 60"
WEIGHT .... 1,680 LBS.
MSRP $15,499

OPTIONS

BAGGER

RETAIL PRICING

YEAR	HIGH	LOW
2011	$7,675	$5,757
2012	$8,523	$6,392

PZ6029FX

YEARS MFRD 2010-2012
ENGINE .... KAWASAKI
CYLINDERS 2
ENGINE HP 25.5
COOLING .... AIR
FUEL .... G
SPEEDS .... VARIABLE
TRANSMISSION .... HYDRO
STEERING .... ZERO
BLADE CLUTCH .... ELECTRIC
STANDARD DECK .... 60"
WEIGHT .... 1,320 LBS.
MSRP $10,299

OPTIONS

PROPANE

RETAIL PRICING

YEAR	HIGH	LOW
2010	$4,591	$3,443
2011	$5,100	$3,825
2012	$5,664	$4,248

PZ6029PFX

YEARS MFRD 2010-2011
ENGINE .... KAWASAKI PROPANE
CYLINDERS 2
ENGINE HP 29
COOLING .... AIR
SPEEDS .... VARIABLE
TRANSMISSION .... HYDRO
STEERING .... ZERO
BLADE CLUTCH .... ELECTRIC
STANDARD DECK .... 60"
WEIGHT .... 1,320 LBS.
MSRP $11,199

RETAIL PRICING

YEAR	HIGH	LOW
2010	$4,994	$3,746
2011	$5,893	$4,420

PZ6030CV

YEARS MFRD 2010-2011
ENGINE .... KOHLER
CYLINDERS 2
ENGINE HP 30
COOLING .... AIR
FUEL .... G
SPEEDS .... VARIABLE
TRANSMISSION .... HYDRO
STEERING .... ZERO
BLADE CLUTCH .... ELECTRIC
STANDARD DECK .... 60"
WEIGHT .... 1,320 LBS.
MSRP $9,799

OPTIONS

BAGGER
MULCHER

RETAIL PRICING

YEAR	HIGH	LOW
2010	$4,516	$3,387
2011	$5,016	$3,762

PZ6031

YEARS MFRD 2013-2014
ENGINE .... KAWASAKI
ENGINE HP 31
COOLING .... AIR
FUEL .... G
SPEEDS .... VARIABLE
TRANSMISSION .... HYDRO
STEERING .... ZERO
STANDARD DECK .... 60"
MSRP $10,999

RETAIL PRICING

YEAR	HIGH	LOW
2013	$5,374	$4,031
2014	$6,214	$4,661

PZ6034FX

YEARS MFRD 2010-2012
ENGINE .... KAWASAKI
CYLINDERS 2
ENGINE HP 31
COOLING .... AIR
FUEL .... G
SPEEDS .... VARIABLE
TRANSMISSION .... HYDRO
STEERING .... ZERO
BLADE CLUTCH .... ELECTRIC
STANDARD DECK .... 60"
WEIGHT .... 1,320 LBS.
MSRP $10,699

OPTIONS

2 SPD
BAGGER

RETAIL PRICING

YEAR	HIGH	LOW
2010	$4,772	$3,579
2011	$5,298	$3,973
2012	$5,882	$4,411

PZ6034FXZT

YEARS MFRD 2010-2011
ENGINE . . . . KAWASAKI
CYLINDERS. 2
CID 999CC
ENGINE HP 34
COOLING . . . . AIR
FUEL . . . . G
SPEEDS . . . . VARIABLE
TRANSMISSION . . . . HYDRO
STEERING. . . . . ZERO
BLADE CLUTCH . . . . ELECTRIC
STANDARD DECK . . . . 60"
WEIGHT . . . . 1,320 LBS.
MSRP. $10,299

RETAIL PRICING

YEAR	HIGH	LOW
2010	$4,764	$3,573
2011	$5,416	$4,062

PZ7231FX

YEARS MFRD 2013-2014
ENGINE . . . . KAWASAKI
ENGINE HP 31
COOLING . . . . AIR
FUEL . . . . G
SPEEDS . . . . VARIABLE
TRANSMISSION . . . . HYDRO
STEERING. . . . . ZERO
STANDARD DECK . . . . 72"
MSRP. $11,499

RETAIL PRICING

YEAR	HIGH	LOW
2013	$5,618	$4,214
2014	$6,496	$4,872

PZ7234FX

YEARS MFRD 2010-2012
ENGINE . . . . KAWASAKI
CYLINDERS. 2
ENGINE HP 31
COOLING . . . . AIR
FUEL . . . . G
SPEEDS . . . . VARIABLE
TRANSMISSION . . . . HYDRO
STEERING. . . . . ZERO
BLADE CLUTCH . . . . ELECTRIC
STANDARD DECK . . . . 72"
WEIGHT . . . . 1,400 LBS.
MSRP. $11,199

RETAIL PRICING

YEAR	HIGH	LOW
2010	$4,992	$3,744
2011	$5,546	$4,159
2012	$6,157	$4,618

R120S

YEARS MFRD 2013-2015
ENGINE . . . . B&S
ENGINE HP 19.5
COOLING . . . . AIR
FUEL . . . . G
SPEEDS . . . . VARIABLE
TRANSMISSION . . . . HYDRO
STEERING. . . . . ZERO
BLADE CLUTCH . . . . ELECTRIC
STANDARD DECK . . . . 42"
MSRP. $1,999

RETAIL PRICING

YEAR	HIGH	LOW
2013	$923	$692
2014	$1,099	$824
2015	$1,268	$951

R220T

YEARS MFRD 2012-2016
ENGINE . . . . B&S
ENGINE HP 20
COOLING . . . . AIR
FUEL . . . . G
SPEEDS . . . . VARIABLE
TRANSMISSION . . . . HYDRO
STEERING. . . . . ZERO
STANDARD DECK . . . . 48"
MSRP. $3,999

RETAIL PRICING

YEAR	HIGH	LOW
2012	$1,866	$1,399
2013	$2,061	$1,546
2014	$2,347	$1,760
2015	$2,761	$2,070
2016	$3,145	$2,359

R322T

YEARS MFRD 2012-2016
ENGINE . . . . B&S
ENGINE HP 22
COOLING . . . . AIR
FUEL . . . . G
SPEEDS . . . . VARIABLE
TRANSMISSION . . . . HYDRO
STEERING. . . . . ZERO
DRIVE TYPE 4WD
STANDARD DECK . . . . 48"
MSRP. $5,299

RETAIL PRICING

YEAR	HIGH	LOW
2012	$2,943	$2,207
2013	$3,098	$2,323
2014	$3,420	$2,565
2015	$3,744	$2,808
2016	$4,328	$3,246

RER800

YEARS MFRD 1993-1993
ENGINE . . . . B&S
ENGINE HP 8.5
COOLING . . . . AIR
FUEL . . . . G
TRANSMISSION . . . . GEAR
STEERING. . . . . STANDARD

RIDER 155

YEARS MFRD 2007-2007
ENGINE . . . . B&S
ENGINE HP 15
COOLING . . . . AIR
FUEL . . . . G
SPEEDS . . . . VARIABLE
TRANSMISSION . . . . HYDRO
STEERING. . . . . STANDARD
STANDARD DECK . . . . 41"
WEIGHT . . . . 626 LBS.
MSRP. $3,999

OPTIONS

4WD

SERIAL NUMBERS

YEAR	BEGINNING NO.
2007	64000000

RETAIL PRICING

YEAR	HIGH	LOW
2007	$978	$734

RIDER 175

YEARS MFRD 2008-2009
ENGINE . . . . B&S
CYLINDERS. 1
ENGINE HP 17.5
COOLING . . . . AIR
FUEL . . . . G
SPEEDS . . . . VARIABLE
TRANSMISSION . . . . HYDRO
STEERING. . . . . ZERO
BLADE CLUTCH . . . . ELECTRIC
STANDARD DECK . . . . 41"
WEIGHT . . . . 608 LBS.
MSRP. $4,299

OPTIONS

4WD

RETAIL PRICING

YEAR	HIGH	LOW
2008	$1,332	$999
2009	$1,474	$1,105

RZ46I

YEARS MFRD 2015-2015
ENGINE . . . . B&S
ENGINE HP 23
COOLING . . . . AIR
FUEL . . . . G
SPEEDS . . . . VARIABLE
TRANSMISSION . . . . HYDRO
STEERING. . . . . ZERO
STANDARD DECK . . . . 46"
MSRP. $2,499

RETAIL PRICING

YEAR	HIGH	LOW
2015	$1,635	$1,226

RZ3016

YEARS MFRD 2010-2016
ENGINE . . . . B&S INTEK
CYLINDERS. 1
ENGINE HP 16.5
COOLING . . . . AIR
FUEL . . . . G
SPEEDS . . . . VARIABLE
TRANSMISSION . . . . HYDRO
STEERING. . . . . ZERO
BLADE CLUTCH . . . . MANUAL
STANDARD DECK . . . . 30"
WEIGHT . . . . 395 LBS.
MSRP. $2,399

OPTIONS

BAGGER

RETAIL PRICING

YEAR	HIGH	LOW
2010	$801	$600
2011	$996	$747
2012	$1,114	$836
2013	$1,250	$938
2014	$1,397	$1,048
2015	$1,492	$1,119
2016	$1,777	$1,333

RZ4216

YEARS MFRD 2010-2011
ENGINE . . . . B&S INTEK
CYLINDERS. 1
ENGINE HP 16.5
COOLING . . . . AIR
FUEL . . . . G
SPEEDS . . . . VARIABLE
TRANSMISSION . . . . HYDRO
STEERING. . . . . ZERO
BLADE CLUTCH . . . . MANUAL
STANDARD DECK . . . . 42"
MSRP. $2,399

OPTIONS

BAGGER

RETAIL PRICING

YEAR	HIGH	LOW
2010	$1,103	$827
2011	$1,225	$919

RZ4219

YEARS MFRD 2012-2015
ENGINE . . . . B&S ENDURANCE
CYLINDERS. 1
CID 500CC
ENGINE HP 19.5
COOLING . . . . AIR
FUEL . . . . G
SPEEDS . . . . VARIABLE
TRANSMISSION . . . . HYDRO
STEERING. . . . . ZERO
STANDARD DECK . . . . 42"
WEIGHT . . . . 430 LBS.
MSRP. $2,399

OPTIONS

BAGGER

RETAIL PRICING

YEAR	HIGH	LOW
2012	$1,286	$964
2013	$1,428	$1,071
2014	$1,459	$1,094
2015	$1,572	$1,179

HUSQVARNA

RZ4219F

YEARS MFRD 2010-2010
ENGINE . . . . . . B&S PROFESSIONAL
CYLINDERS 1
ENGINE HP 19.5
COOLING . . . . AIR
FUEL . . . . G
SPEEDS . . . . VARIABLE
TRANSMISSION . . . . HYDRO
STEERING . . . . ZERO
BLADE CLUTCH . . . . ELECTRIC
STANDARD DECK . . . . 42"
MSRP $2,999

OPTIONS

BAGGER

RETAIL PRICING

YEAR	HIGH	LOW
2010	$1,397	$1,048

RZ4222F

YEARS MFRD 2012-2015
ENGINE . . . . B&S ENDURANCE
CYLINDERS 2
CID 656CC
ENGINE HP 22
COOLING . . . . AIR
FUEL . . . . G
SPEEDS . . . . VARIABLE
TRANSMISSION . . . . HYDRO
STEERING . . . . ZERO
STANDARD DECK . . . . 42"
WEIGHT . . . . 580 LBS.
MSRP $3,399

OPTIONS

BAGGER

RETAIL PRICING

YEAR	HIGH	LOW
2012	$1,796	$1,347
2013	$1,996	$1,497
2014	$2,122	$1,591
2015	$2,266	$1,699

RZ4619

YEARS MFRD 2008-2010
ENGINE . . . . . . B&S PROFESSIONAL
CYLINDERS 1
ENGINE HP 19
COOLING . . . . AIR
FUEL . . . . G
SPEEDS . . . . VARIABLE
TRANSMISSION . . . . HYDRO
STEERING . . . . ZERO
BLADE CLUTCH . . . . ELECTRIC
STANDARD DECK . . . . 46"
WEIGHT . . . . 580 LBS.
MSRP $2,549

OPTIONS

BAGGER

RETAIL PRICING

YEAR	HIGH	LOW
2008	$1,057	$793
2009	$1,172	$879
2010	$1,301	$976

RZ4621

YEARS MFRD 2011-2013
ENGINE . . . . B&S
CYLINDERS 1
CID 540CC
ENGINE HP 21
COOLING . . . . AIR
FUEL . . . . G
SPEEDS . . . . VARIABLE
TRANSMISSION . . . . HYDRO
STEERING . . . . ZERO
BLADE CLUTCH . . . . ELECTRIC
STANDARD DECK . . . . 46"
WEIGHT . . . . 580 LBS.
MSRP $2,649

OPTIONS

BAGGER

RETAIL PRICING

YEAR	HIGH	LOW
2011	$1,280	$960
2012	$1,423	$1,067
2013	$1,576	$1,182

RZ4623

YEARS MFRD 2011-2013
ENGINE . . . . . . KOHLER COURAGE
CYLINDERS 2
CID 725CC
ENGINE HP 23
COOLING . . . . AIR
FUEL . . . . G
SPEEDS . . . . VARIABLE
TRANSMISSION . . . . HYDRO
STEERING . . . . ZERO
BLADE CLUTCH . . . . ELECTRIC
STANDARD DECK . . . . 46"
WEIGHT . . . . 580 LBS.
MSRP $2,599

OPTIONS

BAGGER

RETAIL PRICING

YEAR	HIGH	LOW
2011	$1,255	$942
2012	$1,394	$1,045
2013	$1,546	$1,160

RZ4824F

YEARS MFRD 2011-2015
ENGINE . . . . B&S
CYLINDERS 2
CID 726CC
ENGINE HP 24
COOLING . . . . AIR
FUEL . . . . G
SPEEDS . . . . VARIABLE
TRANSMISSION . . . . HYDRO
STEERING . . . . ZERO
BLADE CLUTCH . . . . ELECTRIC
STANDARD DECK . . . . 48"
WEIGHT . . . . 595 LBS.
MSRP $3,699

OPTIONS

BAGGER
KAWASAKI 24HP

RETAIL PRICING

YEAR	HIGH	LOW
2012	$1,542	$1,156
2013	$1,897	$1,423
2014	$2,031	$1,523
2015	$2,357	$1,768

RZ5424

YEARS MFRD 2009-2015
ENGINE . . . . B&S
CYLINDERS 2
CID 725CC
ENGINE HP 24
COOLING . . . . AIR
FUEL . . . . G
SPEEDS . . . . VARIABLE
TRANSMISSION . . . . HYDRO
STEERING . . . . ZERO
BLADE CLUTCH . . . . ELECTRIC
STANDARD DECK . . . . 54"
WEIGHT . . . . 640 LBS.
MSRP $2,999

OPTIONS

BAGGER
KAWASAKI 24HP

RETAIL PRICING

YEAR	HIGH	LOW
2009	$1,245	$933
2010	$1,313	$985
2011	$1,446	$1,085
2012	$1,607	$1,205
2013	$2,321	$1,740
2014	$2,568	$1,926
2015	$2,815	$2,111

RZ5426

YEARS MFRD 2013-2015
ENGINE . . . . . . KOHLER COURAGE
CYLINDERS 2
CID 725CC
ENGINE HP 26
COOLING . . . . AIR
FUEL . . . . G
SPEEDS . . . . VARIABLE
TRANSMISSION . . . . HYDRO
STEERING . . . . ZERO
BLADE CLUTCH . . . . ELECTRIC
STANDARD DECK . . . . 54"
WEIGHT . . . . 640 LBS.
MSRP $3,199

OPTIONS

BAGGER

RETAIL PRICING

YEAR	HIGH	LOW
2012	$1,714	$1,286
2013	$1,905	$1,429
2014	$2,072	$1,554
2015	$2,236	$1,677

SRD17530

YEARS MFRD 2014-2014
ENGINE . . . . B&S
ENGINE HP 17.5
COOLING . . . . AIR
FUEL . . . . G
SPEEDS 4/1
TRANSMISSION . . . . GEAR
STEERING . . . . STANDARD
STANDARD DECK . . . . 30"
MSRP $1,499

RETAIL PRICING

YEAR	HIGH	LOW
2014	$824	$618

TS142

YEARS MFRD 2020-2020
SERIES . . . . 100 SERIES
ENGINE . . . . . BRIGGS & STRATTON
CYLINDERS 1
ENGINE HP 18.5
FUEL . . . . G
SPEEDS . . . . VARIABLE
TRANSMISSION . . . . HYDRO
STEERING . . . . STANDARD
BLADE CLUTCH . . . . MANUAL
STANDARD DECK . . . . 42"
MSRP $1,799

TS142X

YEARS MFRD 2020-2020
SERIES . . . . 100 SERIES
ENGINE . . . . . BRIGGS & STRATTON
CYLINDERS 2
ENGINE HP 20
FUEL . . . . G
SPEEDS . . . . VARIABLE
TRANSMISSION . . . . HYDRO
STEERING . . . . STANDARD
BLADE CLUTCH . . . . MANUAL
STANDARD DECK . . . . 42"
MSRP $1,999

TS146X

YEARS MFRD 2020-2020
SERIES . . . . 100 SERIES
ENGINE . . . . . BRIGGS & STRATTON
CYLINDERS 2
ENGINE HP 22
FUEL . . . . G
SPEEDS . . . . VARIABLE
TRANSMISSION . . . . HYDRO
STEERING . . . . STANDARD
STANDARD DECK . . . . 46"
MSRP $1,999

TS146XD

YEARS MFRD 2020-2020
SERIES . . . . 100 SERIES
ENGINE . . . . . BRIGGS & STRATTON
CYLINDERS 2
ENGINE HP 22
FUEL . . . . G
SPEEDS . . . . VARIABLE
TRANSMISSION . . . . HYDRO
STEERING . . . . STANDARD
BLADE CLUTCH . . . . MANUAL
STANDARD DECK . . . . 46"
MSRP $2,299

TS148X
YEARS MFRD 2020-2020
SERIES . . . . 100 SERIES
ENGINE . . . . . BRIGGS & STRATTON
CYLINDERS 2
ENGINE HP 24
FUEL . . . . G
SPEEDS . . . . VARIABLE
TRANSMISSION . . . . HYDRO
STEERING . . . . STANDARD
BLADE CLUTCH . . . . ELECTRIC
STANDARD DECK . . . . 48"
MSRP $2,299

TS242XD
YEARS MFRD 2020-2020
SERIES . . . . 200 SERIES
ENGINE . . . . KAWASAKI FR
CYLINDERS 2
ENGINE HP 21.5
FUEL . . . . G
SPEEDS . . . . VARIABLE
TRANSMISSION . . . . HYDRO
STEERING . . . . STANDARD
BLADE CLUTCH . . . . ELECTRIC
STANDARD DECK . . . . 42"
MSRP $2,799

TS248G
YEARS MFRD 2020-2020
SERIES . . . . 200 SERIES
ENGINE . . . . KAWASAKI FR
CYLINDERS 2
ENGINE HP 24
FUEL . . . . G
SPEEDS . . . . VARIABLE
TRANSMISSION . . . . HYDRO
STEERING . . . . STANDARD
BLADE CLUTCH . . . . ELECTRIC
STANDARD DECK . . . . 48"
MSRP $3,099

TS248XD
YEARS MFRD 2020-2020
SERIES . . . . 200 SERIES
ENGINE . . . . KAWASAKI FR
CYLINDERS 2
ENGINE HP 23
FUEL . . . . G
SPEEDS . . . . VARIABLE
TRANSMISSION . . . . HYDRO
STEERING . . . . STANDARD
BLADE CLUTCH . . . . ELECTRIC
STANDARD DECK . . . . 48"
MSRP $2,999

TS254XG
YEARS MFRD 2020-2020
SERIES . . . . 200 SERIES
ENGINE . . . . KAWASAKI FR
CYLINDERS 2
ENGINE HP 24
FUEL . . . . G
SPEEDS . . . . VARIABLE
TRANSMISSION . . . . HYDRO
STEERING . . . . STANDARD
BLADE CLUTCH . . . . ELECTRIC
STANDARD DECK . . . . 54"
MSRP $3,399

TS348D
YEARS MFRD 2018-2020
SERIES . . . . 300 SERIES
ENGINE . . . . KOHLER
CYLINDERS 2
ENGINE HP 24
FUEL . . . . G
SPEEDS . . . . VARIABLE
TRANSMISSION . . . . HYDRO
STEERING . . . . STANDARD
BLADE CLUTCH . . . . ELECTRIC
STANDARD DECK . . . . 48"
MSRP $3,199

TS348XD
YEARS MFRD 2019-2020
SERIES . . . . 300 SERIES
ENGINE . . . . KOHLER
CYLINDERS 2
ENGINE HP 26
FUEL . . . . G
SPEEDS . . . . VARIABLE
TRANSMISSION . . . . HYDRO
STEERING . . . . STANDARD
BLADE CLUTCH . . . . ELECTRIC
STANDARD DECK . . . . 48"
MSRP $3,499

OPTIONS

KAWASAKI 24HP $100

TS354D
YEARS MFRD 2018-2020
SERIES . . . . 300 SERIES
ENGINE . . . . KOHLER
CYLINDERS 2
ENGINE HP 25
FUEL . . . . G
SPEEDS . . . . VARIABLE
TRANSMISSION . . . . HYDRO
STEERING . . . . STANDARD
BLADE CLUTCH . . . . ELECTRIC
STANDARD DECK . . . . 54"
MSRP $3,699

TS354X
YEARS MFRD 2019-2020
SERIES . . . . 300 SERIES
ENGINE . . . . KOHLER
CYLINDERS 2
ENGINE HP 26
FUEL . . . . G
SPEEDS . . . . VARIABLE
TRANSMISSION . . . . HYDRO
STEERING . . . . STANDARD
STANDARD DECK . . . . 54"
MSRP $3,499

TS354XD
YEARS MFRD 2019-2020
SERIES . . . . 300 SERIES
ENGINE . . . . KOHLER
CYLINDERS 2
ENGINE HP 26
FUEL . . . . G
SPEEDS . . . . VARIABLE
TRANSMISSION . . . . HYDRO
STEERING . . . . STANDARD
BLADE CLUTCH . . . . ELECTRIC
STANDARD DECK . . . . 54"
MSRP $3,599

OPTIONS

KAWASAKI 24HP $300

V548
YEARS MFRD 2018-2020
SERIES . . . . V500 SERIES
ENGINE . . . . KAWASAKI FX
CYLINDERS 2
CID 52
ENGINE HP 24.5
COOLING . . . . AIR
FUEL . . . . G
STEERING . . . . ZERO
BLADE CLUTCH . . . . ELECTRIC
STANDARD DECK . . . . 48"
WEIGHT . . . . 1,164 LBS.
MSRP $8,899

V554
YEARS MFRD 2018-2020
SERIES . . . . V500 SERIES
ENGINE . . . . KAWASAKI FX
CYLINDERS 2
CID 52
ENGINE HP 24.5
COOLING . . . . AIR
FUEL . . . . G
STEERING . . . . ZERO
BLADE CLUTCH . . . . ELECTRIC
STANDARD DECK . . . . 54"
WEIGHT . . . . 1,176 LBS.
MSRP $8,999

YT42DXL
YEARS MFRD 2019-2020
ENGINE . . . . KOHLER
CYLINDERS 2
ENGINE HP 22
FUEL . . . . G
SPEEDS . . . . VARIABLE
TRANSMISSION . . . . HYDRO
STEERING . . . . STANDARD
BLADE CLUTCH . . . . ELECTRIC
STANDARD DECK . . . . 42"
MSRP $2,499

YT42DXLS
YEARS MFRD 2016-2016
ENGINE . . . . KOHLER
ENGINE HP 22
COOLING . . . . AIR
FUEL . . . . G
SPEEDS . . . . VARIABLE
TRANSMISSION . . . . HYDRO
STEERING . . . . STANDARD
STANDARD DECK . . . . 42"
MSRP $2,599

RETAIL PRICING

YEAR	HIGH	LOW
2016	$1,825	$1,369

YT42LS
YEARS MFRD 2015-2016
ENGINE . . . . KAWASAKI
ENGINE HP 18
COOLING . . . . AIR
FUEL . . . . G
SPEEDS . . . . VARIABLE
TRANSMISSION . . . . HYDRO
STEERING . . . . STANDARD
STANDARD DECK . . . . 42"
MSRP $2,099

RETAIL PRICING

YEAR	HIGH	LOW
2015	$1,294	$970
2016	$1,488	$1,116

YT42XLS
YEARS MFRD 2014-2016
ENGINE . . . . KAWASAKI
ENGINE HP 23
COOLING . . . . AIR
FUEL . . . . G
SPEEDS . . . . VARIABLE
TRANSMISSION . . . . HYDRO
STEERING . . . . STANDARD
STANDARD DECK . . . . 42"
MSRP $2,699

RETAIL PRICING

YEAR	HIGH	LOW
2014	$1,452	$1,089
2015	$1,730	$1,297
2016	$2,044	$1,533

YT46LS
YEARS MFRD 2014-2016
ENGINE . . . . KAWASAKI
ENGINE HP 21.5
COOLING . . . . AIR
FUEL . . . . G
SPEEDS . . . . VARIABLE
TRANSMISSION . . . . HYDRO
STEERING . . . . STANDARD
STANDARD DECK . . . . 46"
MSRP $2,299

OPTIONS

KOHLER 24HP

RETAIL PRICING

YEAR	HIGH	LOW
2014	$1,393	$1,044
2015	$1,508	$1,131
2016	$1,674	$1,255

HUSQVARNA

YT48DXLS

YEARS MFRD........ 2017-2020
ENGINE............... KOHLER
CYLINDERS................. 2
ENGINE HP................. 25
FUEL...................... G
SPEEDS............. VARIABLE
TRANSMISSION.......... HYDRO
STEERING........... STANDARD
BLADE CLUTCH........ ELECTRIC
STANDARD DECK............ 48"
MSRP................. $2,799

YT48XLS

YEARS MFRD........ 2014-2016
ENGINE............. KAWASAKI
ENGINE HP................. 24
COOLING.................. AIR
FUEL...................... G
SPEEDS............. VARIABLE
TRANSMISSION.......... HYDRO
STEERING........... STANDARD
STANDARD DECK............ 48"
MSRP................. $2,899

RETAIL PRICING

YEAR	HIGH	LOW
2014	$1,675	$1,256
2015	$1,934	$1,450
2016	$2,118	$1,588

YT52XLS

YEARS MFRD........ 2016-2016
ENGINE............... KOHLER
ENGINE HP................. 26
COOLING.................. AIR
FUEL...................... G
SPEEDS............. VARIABLE
TRANSMISSION.......... HYDRO
STEERING........... STANDARD
STANDARD DECK............ 52"
MSRP................. $3,199

RETAIL PRICING

YEAR	HIGH	LOW
2016	$2,169	$1,627

YT54LS

YEARS MFRD........ 2014-2015
ENGINE............. KAWASAKI
ENGINE HP................. 23
COOLING.................. AIR
FUEL...................... G
SPEEDS............. VARIABLE
TRANSMISSION.......... HYDRO
STEERING........... STANDARD
STANDARD DECK............ 54"
MSRP................. $2,649

RETAIL PRICING

YEAR	HIGH	LOW
2014	$1,434	$1,075
2015	$1,695	$1,272

YT120

YEARS MFRD........ 1990-1991
ENGINE.................. B&S
ENGINE HP................. 12
COOLING.................. AIR
FUEL...................... G
TRANSMISSION........... GEAR
STEERING........... STANDARD

YT125

YEARS MFRD........ 1990-1991
ENGINE............. KAWASAKI
ENGINE HP............... 12.5
COOLING.................. AIR
FUEL...................... G
TRANSMISSION........... GEAR
STEERING........... STANDARD

YT130

YEARS MFRD........ 1992-1992
SERIES......................
ENGINE............... KOHLER
ENGINE HP................. 13
COOLING.................. AIR
FUEL...................... G
TRANSMISSION........... GEAR
STEERING........... STANDARD

YT141H

YEARS MFRD........ 1991-2003
ENGINE............. KAWASAKI
FUEL...................... G
TRANSMISSION.......... HYDRO

YT160

YEARS MFRD........ 1993-1993
ENGINE............. KAWASAKI
ENGINE HP................. 16
COOLING.................. AIR
FUEL...................... G
TRANSMISSION........... GEAR
STEERING........... STANDARD
STANDARD DECK............ 42"
MSRP................. $3,299

RETAIL PRICING

YEAR	HIGH	LOW
1993	$1,130	$847

YT161H

YEARS MFRD........ 1992-1992
ENGINE.................. B&S
ENGINE HP................. 16
COOLING.................. AIR
FUEL...................... G
TRANSMISSION.......... HYDRO
STEERING........... STANDARD
STANDARD DECK............ 44"
MSRP................. $3,199

RETAIL PRICING

YEAR	HIGH	LOW
1992	$1,065	$799

YT180

YEARS MFRD........ 1993-1997
ENGINE............... KOHLER
ENGINE HP................. 18
COOLING.................. AIR
FUEL...................... G
TRANSMISSION........... GEAR
STEERING........... STANDARD
STANDARD DECK............ 46"
MSRP................. $2,599

RETAIL PRICING

YEAR	HIGH	LOW
1993	$754	$565
1994	$798	$598
1995	$828	$621
1996	$935	$701
1997	$1,052	$789

YTA19K42

YEARS MFRD........ 2014-2014
ENGINE............... KOHLER
ENGINE HP................. 19
COOLING.................. AIR
FUEL...................... G
SPEEDS................. AUTO
TRANSMISSION........... BELT
STEERING........... STANDARD
STANDARD DECK............ 42"
MSRP................. $1,499

RETAIL PRICING

YEAR	HIGH	LOW
2014	$824	$618

YTA22V46

YEARS MFRD........ 2016-2018
ENGINE.................. B&S
CYLINDERS................. 2
ENGINE HP................. 22
FUEL...................... G
TRANSMISSION.......... HYDRO
STEERING........... STANDARD
STANDARD DECK............ 46"

YTA18542

YEARS MFRD........ 2016-2018
ENGINE............ B&S INTEK
CYLINDERS................. 1
ENGINE HP............... 18.5
FUEL...................... G
TRANSMISSION............ CVT
STEERING........... STANDARD
STANDARD DECK............ 42"
WEIGHT.............. 419 LBS.

YTH18K46

YEARS MFRD........ 2014-2015
ENGINE............. KAWASAKI
ENGINE HP............... 18.5
COOLING.................. AIR
FUEL...................... G
SPEEDS............. VARIABLE
TRANSMISSION.......... HYDRO
STEERING........... STANDARD
STANDARD DECK............ 46"
MSRP................. $1,799

RETAIL PRICING

YEAR	HIGH	LOW
2014	$901	$675
2015	$1,009	$757

YTH20K42

YEARS MFRD........ 2018-2020
ENGINE............... KOHLER
CYLINDERS................. 2
ENGINE HP................. 20
FUEL...................... G
SPEEDS............. VARIABLE
TRANSMISSION.......... HYDRO
STEERING........... STANDARD
STANDARD DECK............ 42"
MSRP................. $1,799

YTH20K46

YEARS MFRD........ 2009-2009
ENGINE....... KOHLER COURAGE
ENGINE HP................. 20
COOLING.................. AIR
FUEL...................... G
SPEEDS............. VARIABLE
TRANSMISSION.......... HYDRO
STEERING........... STANDARD
STANDARD DECK............ 46"
MSRP................. $1,599

RETAIL PRICING

YEAR	HIGH	LOW
2009	$481	$361

YTH20K46 960 43 02-77

YEARS MFRD........ 2018-2020
ENGINE..... KOHLER 7000 SERIES
CYLINDERS................. 2
ENGINE HP................. 20
FUEL...................... G
SPEEDS............. VARIABLE
TRANSMISSION.......... HYDRO
STEERING........... STANDARD
STANDARD DECK............ 46"
MSRP................. $2,199

YTH20V42

YEARS MFRD........ 2019-2019
ENGINE.................. B&S
CYLINDERS................. 2
ENGINE HP................. 20
FUEL...................... G
TRANSMISSION.......... HYDRO
STEERING........... STANDARD
STANDARD DECK............ 42"
MSRP................. $1,699

YTH22V42

YEARS MFRD........ 2015-2016
ENGINE.................. B&S
ENGINE HP................. 22

COOLING . . . . . . AIR
FUEL . . . . . . G
SPEEDS . . . . . . VARIABLE
TRANSMISSION . . . . . . HYDRO
STEERING. . . . . . STANDARD
STANDARD DECK . . . . . . 42"
MSRP. $1,799

RETAIL PRICING

YEAR	HIGH	LOW
2015	$1,099	$824
2016	$1,311	$983

YTH22V46

YEARS MFRD 2014-2020
ENGINE . . . . . . B&S
ENGINE HP 22
COOLING . . . . . . AIR
FUEL . . . . . . G
SPEEDS . . . . . . VARIABLE
TRANSMISSION . . . . . . HYDRO
STEERING. . . . . . STANDARD
STANDARD DECK . . . . . . 46"
MSRP. $1,899

RETAIL PRICING

YEAR	HIGH	LOW
2014	$870	$653
2015	$1,020	$765
2016	$1,210	$907
2020	$0	$0

YTH23V42

YEARS MFRD 2014-2014
ENGINE . . . . . . B&S
ENGINE HP 23
COOLING . . . . . . AIR
FUEL . . . . . . G
SPEEDS . . . . . . VARIABLE
TRANSMISSION . . . . . . HYDRO
STEERING. . . . . . STANDARD
STANDARD DECK . . . . . . 42"
MSRP. $1,699

RETAIL PRICING

YEAR	HIGH	LOW
2014	$932	$699

YTH23V48

YEARS MFRD 2010-2015
ENGINE . . . . . . B&S
ENGINE HP 23
COOLING . . . . . . AIR
FUEL . . . . . . G
SPEEDS . . . . . . VARIABLE
TRANSMISSION . . . . . . HYDRO
STEERING. . . . . . STANDARD
STANDARD DECK . . . . . . 48"
MSRP. $1,799

RETAIL PRICING

YEAR	HIGH	LOW
2010	$397	$298
2011	$450	$337
2012	$551	$413
2013	$686	$515
2014	$901	$675
2015	$1,069	$802

YTH24K48

YEARS MFRD 2014-2015
ENGINE . . . . . . KOHLER
ENGINE HP 24
COOLING . . . . . . AIR
FUEL . . . . . . G
SPEEDS . . . . . . VARIABLE
TRANSMISSION . . . . . . HYDRO
STEERING. . . . . . STANDARD
STANDARD DECK . . . . . . 48"
MSRP. $2,099

OPTIONS

54" DECK

RETAIL PRICING

YEAR	HIGH	LOW
2014	$1,099	$824
2015	$1,288	$966

YTH24K48 960 43 02-78

YEARS MFRD 2018-2020
ENGINE . . . . KOHLER 7000 SERIES
CYLINDERS. 2
ENGINE HP 24
FUEL . . . . . . G
SPEEDS . . . . . . VARIABLE
TRANSMISSION . . . . . . HYDRO
STEERING. . . . . . STANDARD
BLADE CLUTCH . . . . . . ELECTRIC
STANDARD DECK . . . . . . 48"
MSRP. $2,099

OPTIONS

54" DECK. $200

YTH24V48

YEARS MFRD 2015-2016
ENGINE . . . . . . B&S
ENGINE HP 24
COOLING . . . . . . AIR
FUEL . . . . . . G
SPEEDS . . . . . . VARIABLE
TRANSMISSION . . . . . . HYDRO
STEERING. . . . . . STANDARD
STANDARD DECK . . . . . . 48"
MSRP. $1,999

RETAIL PRICING

YEAR	HIGH	LOW
2015	$1,165	$874
2016	$1,435	$1,076

YTH24V48 960 43 02-58

YEARS MFRD 2018-2020
ENGINE BRIGGS & STRATTON INTEK
CYLINDERS. 2
ENGINE HP 24
FUEL . . . . . . G
SPEEDS . . . . . . VARIABLE
TRANSMISSION . . . . . . HYDRO
STEERING. . . . . . STANDARD
BLADE CLUTCH . . . . . . ELECTRIC
STANDARD DECK . . . . . . 48"
MSRP. $2,099

OPTIONS

54" DECK. $100

YTH24V54

YEARS MFRD 2015-2016
ENGINE . . . . . . B&S
ENGINE HP 24
COOLING . . . . . . AIR
FUEL . . . . . . G
SPEEDS . . . . . . VARIABLE
TRANSMISSION . . . . . . HYDRO
STEERING. . . . . . STANDARD
STANDARD DECK . . . . . . 54"
MSRP. $2,199

RETAIL PRICING

YEAR	HIGH	LOW
2015	$1,246	$934
2016	$1,606	$1,205

YTH26V54

YEARS MFRD 2014-2014
ENGINE . . . . . . B&S
ENGINE HP 26
COOLING . . . . . . AIR
FUEL . . . . . . G
SPEEDS . . . . . . VARIABLE
TRANSMISSION . . . . . . HYDRO
STEERING. . . . . . STANDARD
STANDARD DECK . . . . . . 54"
MSRP. $2,099

RETAIL PRICING

YEAR	HIGH	LOW
2014	$1,153	$865

YTH145

YEARS MFRD 1999-1999
ENGINE . . . . . . KOHLER
ENGINE HP 14.5
COOLING . . . . . . AIR
FUEL . . . . . . G
TRANSMISSION . . . . . . HYDRO
STEERING. . . . . . STANDARD

YTH150

YEARS MFRD 1996-1999
ENGINE . . . . . . KOHLER
ENGINE HP 15
FUEL . . . . . . G
SPEEDS . . . . . . VARIABLE
TRANSMISSION . . . . . . HYDRO
STEERING. . . . . . STANDARD
STANDARD DECK . . . . . . 42"
MSRP. $2,299

RETAIL PRICING

YEAR	HIGH	LOW
1996	$237	$178
1997	$259	$194
1998	$290	$218
1999	$332	$249

YTH160

YEARS MFRD 1997-1998
ENGINE . . . . . . B&S
ENGINE HP 16
COOLING . . . . . . AIR
FUEL . . . . . . G
TRANSMISSION . . . . . . HYDRO
STEERING. . . . . . STANDARD
STANDARD DECK . . . . . . 42"
MSRP. $2,300

RETAIL PRICING

YEAR	HIGH	LOW
1997	$268	$201
1998	$290	$218

YTH161H

YEARS MFRD 1992-1992
ENGINE . . . . . . B&S
ENGINE HP 16
COOLING . . . . . . AIR
FUEL . . . . . . G
TRANSMISSION . . . . . . HYDRO
STEERING. . . . . . STANDARD

YTH180

YEARS MFRD 1994-1999
ENGINE . . . . . . KOHLER
ENGINE HP 18
COOLING . . . . . . AIR
FUEL . . . . . . G
TRANSMISSION . . . . . . HYDRO
STEERING. . . . . . STANDARD
STANDARD DECK . . . . . . 46"
MSRP. $2,199

RETAIL PRICING

YEAR	HIGH	LOW
1994	$203	$152
1995	$228	$171
1996	$252	$189
1997	$278	$209
1998	$314	$235
1999	$347	$260

YTH1542

YEARS MFRD 2001-2001
SERIES. . . . . . CROWN SERIES
ENGINE . . . . . . B&S OHV
ENGINE HP 15.5
COOLING . . . . . . AIR
FUEL . . . . . . G
SPEEDS . . . . . . VARIABLE
TRANSMISSION . . . . . . HYDRO
STEERING. . . . . . STANDARD
STANDARD DECK . . . . . . 42"
MSRP. $1,799

RETAIL PRICING

YEAR	HIGH	LOW
2001	$286	$215

YTH1542XP

YEARS MFRD 2001-2001
SERIES. . . . . . XP SERIES
ENGINE . . . . . . KAWASAKI V-TWIN

HUSQVARNA

CYLINDERS . . . 2
CID . . . 26.3
ENGINE HP . . . 15
COOLING . . . AIR
FUEL . . . G
SPEEDS . . . VARIABLE
TRANSMISSION . . . HYDRO
STEERING . . . STANDARD
BLADE CLUTCH . . . ELECTRIC
STANDARD DECK . . . 42"
WEIGHT . . . 425 LBS.
MSRP . . . $1,999

RETAIL PRICING

YEAR	HIGH	LOW
2001	$347	$260

YTH1746

YEARS MFRD . . . 2001-2001
SERIES . . . CROWN SERIES
ENGINE . . . B&S OHV
ENGINE HP . . . 17.5
COOLING . . . AIR
FUEL . . . G
SPEEDS . . . VARIABLE
TRANSMISSION . . . HYDRO
STEERING . . . STANDARD
STANDARD DECK . . . 46"
MSRP . . . $1,999

RETAIL PRICING

YEAR	HIGH	LOW
2001	$325	$244

YTH1842

YEARS MFRD . . . 2005-2005
ENGINE . . . B&S INTEK
ENGINE HP . . . 18
COOLING . . . AIR
FUEL . . . G
SPEEDS . . . VARIABLE
TRANSMISSION . . . HYDRO
STEERING . . . STANDARD
STANDARD DECK . . . 42"
MSRP . . . $1,699

RETAIL PRICING

YEAR	HIGH	LOW
2005	$1,059	$795

YTH1848XP

YEARS MFRD . . . 2001-2001
SERIES . . . XP SERIES
ENGINE . . . KAWASAKI V-TWIN OHV
CYLINDERS . . . 2
CID . . . 30.1
ENGINE HP . . . 18
COOLING . . . AIR
FUEL . . . G
SPEEDS . . . VARIABLE
TRANSMISSION . . . HYDRO
STEERING . . . STANDARD
BLADE CLUTCH . . . ELECTRIC
STANDARD DECK . . . 48"
WEIGHT . . . 425 LBS.
MSRP . . . $2,499

RETAIL PRICING

YEAR	HIGH	LOW
2001	$284	$213

YTH1942

YEARS MFRD . . . 2018-2019
ENGINE . . . HUSQVARNA
CYLINDERS . . . 1
ENGINE HP . . . 19
FUEL . . . G
TRANSMISSION . . . HYDRO
STEERING . . . STANDARD
STANDARD DECK . . . 42"
MSRP . . . $1,599

YTH2042

YEARS MFRD . . . 2010-2014
ENGINE . . . B&S
ENGINE HP . . . 20
COOLING . . . AIR
FUEL . . . G
SPEEDS . . . VARIABLE
TRANSMISSION . . . HYDRO
STEERING . . . STANDARD
BLADE CLUTCH . . . MANUAL
PTO . . . YES
STANDARD DECK . . . 42"
MSRP . . . $1,499

RETAIL PRICING

YEAR	HIGH	LOW
2010	$428	$321
2011	$504	$378
2012	$587	$440
2013	$704	$528
2014	$824	$618

YTH2042 960 43 03-15

YEARS MFRD . . . 2020-2020
ENGINE . . . BRIGGS & STRATTON
CYLINDERS . . . 2
ENGINE HP . . . 20
FUEL . . . G
SPEEDS . . . VARIABLE
TRANSMISSION . . . HYDRO
STEERING . . . STANDARD
STANDARD DECK . . . 42"

YTH2046

YEARS MFRD . . . 2001-2001
SERIES . . . CROWN SERIES
ENGINE . . . OHV
ENGINE HP . . . 20
FUEL . . . G
SPEEDS . . . VARIABLE
TRANSMISSION . . . HYDRO
STEERING . . . STANDARD
STANDARD DECK . . . 46"
MSRP . . . $2,499

RETAIL PRICING

YEAR	HIGH	LOW
2001	$284	$213

YTH2048

YEARS MFRD . . . 2001-2002
SERIES . . . CROWN SERIES
ENGINE . . . B&S TWIN OHV
ENGINE HP . . . 20
FUEL . . . G
STEERING . . . STANDARD
STANDARD DECK . . . 48"
MSRP . . . $3,000

RETAIL PRICING

YEAR	HIGH	LOW
2001	$1,486	$1,114
2002	$1,528	$1,146

YTH2146XP

YEARS MFRD . . . 2007-2007
ENGINE . . . KAWASAKI
CYLINDERS . . . 2
ENGINE HP . . . 21
COOLING . . . AIR
FUEL . . . G
SPEEDS . . . VARIABLE
TRANSMISSION . . . HYDRO
STEERING . . . STANDARD

YTH2148

YEARS MFRD . . . 2004-2004
ENGINE . . . B&S V-TWIN
CYLINDERS . . . 2
ENGINE HP . . . 21
SPEEDS . . . VARIABLE
TRANSMISSION . . . HYDRO
STEERING . . . STANDARD
BLADE CLUTCH . . . ELECTRIC
PTO . . . YES
STANDARD DECK . . . 48"
MSRP . . . $1,799

RETAIL PRICING

YEAR	HIGH	LOW
2004	$1,057	$793

YTH2242

YEARS MFRD . . . 2009-2009
ENGINE . . . B&S INTEK
CYLINDERS . . . 2
ENGINE HP . . . 22
COOLING . . . AIR
FUEL . . . G
SPEEDS . . . VARIABLE
TRANSMISSION . . . HYDRO
STEERING . . . ZERO
BLADE CLUTCH . . . MANUAL
STANDARD DECK . . . 42"
MSRP . . . $1,599

RETAIL PRICING

YEAR	HIGH	LOW
2009	$480	$360

YTH2246

YEARS MFRD . . . 2007-2007
ENGINE . . . B&S INTEK
CYLINDERS . . . 2
ENGINE HP . . . 22
COOLING . . . AIR
FUEL . . . G
SPEEDS . . . VARIABLE
TRANSMISSION . . . HYDRO
STEERING . . . STANDARD

YTH2248

YEARS MFRD . . . 2004-2004
ENGINE . . . KOHLER V-TWIN OHV
CYLINDERS . . . 2
ENGINE HP . . . 22
FUEL . . . G
SPEEDS . . . VARIABLE
TRANSMISSION . . . HYDRO
STEERING . . . STANDARD
BLADE CLUTCH . . . ELECTRIC
PTO . . . YES
STANDARD DECK . . . 48"
MSRP . . . $1,999

RETAIL PRICING

YEAR	HIGH	LOW
2004	$1,175	$881

YTH2348

YEARS MFRD . . . 2009-2009
ENGINE . . . B&S INTEK
CYLINDERS . . . 2
ENGINE HP . . . 23
COOLING . . . AIR
FUEL . . . G
SPEEDS . . . VARIABLE
TRANSMISSION . . . HYDRO
STEERING . . . STANDARD
STANDARD DECK . . . 48"
MSRP . . . $1,799

RETAIL PRICING

YEAR	HIGH	LOW
2009	$483	$362

AVG. AUCTION PRICING

LOW	HIGH	AVG
$452	$769	$555

YTH2448

YEARS MFRD . . . 2005-2005
ENGINE . . . B&S INTEK
CYLINDERS . . . 2
ENGINE HP . . . 24
COOLING . . . AIR
FUEL . . . G
SPEEDS . . . VARIABLE
TRANSMISSION . . . HYDRO
STEERING . . . STANDARD
BLADE CLUTCH . . . ELECTRIC
STANDARD DECK . . . 48"
MSRP . . . $1,999

RETAIL PRICING

YEAR	HIGH	LOW
2005	$1,247	$935

YTH2454

YEARS MFRD . . . 2009-2009
ENGINE . . . B&S
CYLINDERS . . . 2
ENGINE HP . . . 24

COOLING . . . AIR
FUEL . . . G
SPEEDS . . . VARIABLE
TRANSMISSION . . . HYDRO
STEERING . . . STANDARD
STANDARD DECK . . . 54"
MSRP . . . $1,999

RETAIL PRICING

YEAR	HIGH	LOW
2009	$543	$407

YTH2548

YEARS MFRD . . . 2004-2004
ENGINE . . . KOHLER V-TWIN
CYLINDERS . . . 2
ENGINE HP . . . 25
FUEL . . . G
SPEEDS . . . VARIABLE
TRANSMISSION . . . HYDRO
STEERING . . . STANDARD
BLADE CLUTCH . . . ELECTRIC
PTO . . . YES
STANDARD DECK . . . 48"
MSRP . . . $2,299

RETAIL PRICING

YEAR	HIGH	LOW
2004	$1,350	$1,013

YTH2748

YEARS MFRD . . . 2005-2005
ENGINE . . . KOHLER OHV
ENGINE HP . . . 27
COOLING . . . AIR
FUEL . . . G
SPEEDS . . . VARIABLE
TRANSMISSION . . . HYDRO
STEERING . . . STANDARD
BLADE CLUTCH . . . ELECTRIC
STANDARD DECK . . . 48"
MSRP . . . $2,399

RETAIL PRICING

YEAR	HIGH	LOW
2005	$1,495	$1,121

YTH18542

YEARS MFRD . . . 2015-2016
ENGINE . . . B&S
ENGINE HP . . . 18.5
COOLING . . . AIR
FUEL . . . G
SPEEDS . . . VARIABLE
TRANSMISSION . . . HYDRO
STEERING . . . STANDARD
STANDARD DECK . . . 54"
MSRP . . . $1,499

RETAIL PRICING

YEAR	HIGH	LOW
2015	$828	$621

Z142

YEARS MFRD . . . 2019-2020
ENGINE . . . KOHLER
CYLINDERS . . . 2
CID . . . 40
ENGINE HP . . . 17
FUEL . . . G
SPEEDS . . . VARIABLE
TRANSMISSION . . . HYDRO
STEERING . . . ZERO
BLADE CLUTCH . . . ELECTRIC
STANDARD DECK . . . 42"
WEIGHT . . . 474 LBS.
MSRP . . . $2,599

Z242F

YEARS MFRD . . . 2016-2020
ENGINE . . . B&S
ENGINE HP . . . 22
COOLING . . . AIR
FUEL . . . G
SPEEDS . . . VARIABLE
TRANSMISSION . . . HYDRO
STEERING . . . ZERO
STANDARD DECK . . . 42"
MSRP . . . $2,799

OPTIONS

KAWASAKI 18HP
KAWASAKI 21.5HP
KOHLER 23HP

RETAIL PRICING

YEAR	HIGH	LOW
2016	$1,972	$1,479
2017	$2,202	$1,652
2018	$2,360	$1,770
2019	$2,492	$1,869
2020	$2,607	$1,966

Z246

YEARS MFRD . . . 2016-2020
ENGINE . . . B&S
ENGINE HP . . . 20
COOLING . . . AIR
FUEL . . . G
SPEEDS . . . VARIABLE
TRANSMISSION . . . HYDRO
STEERING . . . ZERO
STANDARD DECK . . . 46"
MSRP . . . $2,699

OPTIONS

KOHLER 23HP

RETAIL PRICING

YEAR	HIGH	LOW
2016	$1,759	$1,320
2017	$1,933	$1,450
2018	$2,175	$1,631
2019	$2,381	$1,785
2020	$2,475	$1,863

Z246I

YEARS MFRD . . . 2016-2017
ENGINE . . . B&S
ENGINE HP . . . 23
COOLING . . . AIR
FUEL . . . G
SPEEDS . . . VARIABLE
TRANSMISSION . . . HYDRO
STEERING . . . ZERO
STANDARD DECK . . . 46"
MSRP . . . $2,799

RETAIL PRICING

YEAR	HIGH	LOW
2016	$1,687	$1,265
2017	$1,976	$1,482

Z248F

YEARS MFRD . . . 2016-2019
ENGINE . . . B&S
ENGINE HP . . . 23.5
COOLING . . . AIR
FUEL . . . G
SPEEDS . . . VARIABLE
TRANSMISSION . . . HYDRO
STEERING . . . ZERO
STANDARD DECK . . . 48"
MSRP . . . $2,999

OPTIONS

KAWASAKI 21.5HP
KAWASAKI 23HP
KOHLER 26HP

RETAIL PRICING

YEAR	HIGH	LOW
2016	$1,997	$1,498
2017	$2,367	$1,775
2018	$2,560	$1,920
2019	$2,740	$2,055

Z248F KAW

YEARS MFRD . . . 2019-2020
ENGINE . . . KAWASAKI FR651V
CYLINDERS . . . 2
CID . . . 44.3
ENGINE HP . . . 21.5
FUEL . . . G
SPEEDS . . . VARIABLE
TRANSMISSION . . . HYDRO
STEERING . . . ZERO
BLADE CLUTCH . . . ELECTRIC
STANDARD DECK . . . 48"
WEIGHT . . . 581 LBS.
MSRP . . . $2,899

OPTIONS

KOHLER 26HP . . . $300

Z254

YEARS MFRD . . . 2016-2020
ENGINE . . . B&S
ENGINE HP . . . 24
COOLING . . . AIR
FUEL . . . G
SPEEDS . . . VARIABLE
TRANSMISSION . . . HYDRO
STEERING . . . ZERO
STANDARD DECK . . . 54"
MSRP . . . $2,799

OPTIONS

KAWASAKI 23HP
KOHLER 26HP . . . $100

RETAIL PRICING

YEAR	HIGH	LOW
2016	$1,695	$1,272
2017	$2,042	$1,531
2018	$2,263	$1,697
2019	$2,473	$1,855
2020	$2,622	$2,026

Z254F

YEARS MFRD . . . 2018-2019
ENGINE . . . B&S 44T8
CYLINDERS . . . 2
CID . . . 44.18
ENGINE HP . . . 24
COOLING . . . AIR
FUEL . . . G
SPEEDS . . . VARIABLE
TRANSMISSION . . . HYDRO
STEERING . . . ZERO
STANDARD DECK . . . 54"
WEIGHT . . . 574 LBS.
MSRP . . . $3,299

OPTIONS

KAWASAKI 23HP
KOHLER 26HP

Z254F KAW

YEARS MFRD . . . 2019-2020
ENGINE . . . KAWASAKI FR691V
CYLINDERS . . . 2
CID . . . 44.3
ENGINE HP . . . 23
FUEL . . . G
SPEEDS . . . VARIABLE
TRANSMISSION . . . HYDRO
STEERING . . . ZERO
BLADE CLUTCH . . . ELECTRIC
STANDARD DECK . . . 54"
WEIGHT . . . 595 LBS.
MSRP . . . $2,999

OPTIONS

KOHLER 26HP . . . $300

Z254I

YEARS MFRD . . . 2016-2016
ENGINE . . . B&S
ENGINE HP . . . 24
COOLING . . . AIR
FUEL . . . G
SPEEDS . . . VARIABLE
TRANSMISSION . . . HYDRO
STEERING . . . ZERO
STANDARD DECK . . . 54"
MSRP . . . $3,199

RETAIL PRICING

YEAR	HIGH	LOW
2016	$2,169	$1,627

Z448

YEARS MFRD . . . 2020-2020
ENGINE . . . KAWASAKI FS
CYLINDERS . . . 2
CID . . . 44.3
ENGINE HP . . . 22
COOLING . . . AIR
FUEL . . . G
SPEEDS . . . VARIABLE
TRANSMISSION . . . HYDRO
STEERING . . . ZERO
BLADE CLUTCH . . . ELECTRIC
STANDARD DECK . . . 48"
WEIGHT . . . 725 LBS.
MSRP . . . $5,999

HUSQVARNA

Z454
YEARS MFRD 2020-2020
ENGINE KAWASAKI FS
CYLINDERS 2
CID 44.3
ENGINE HP 22
FUEL G
SPEEDS VARIABLE
TRANSMISSION HYDRO
STEERING ZERO
BLADE CLUTCH ELECTRIC
STANDARD DECK 54"
WEIGHT 745 LBS.
MSRP $6,499

Z454X
YEARS MFRD 2020-2020
ENGINE KAWASAKI FX
CYLINDERS 2
CID 44.3
ENGINE HP 22
FUEL G
SPEEDS VARIABLE
TRANSMISSION HYDRO
STEERING ZERO
BLADE CLUTCH ELECTRIC
STANDARD DECK 54"
WEIGHT 865 LBS.
MSRP $7,999

Z460
YEARS MFRD 2020-2020
ENGINE KAWASAKI FS
CYLINDERS 2
CID 44.3
ENGINE HP 23
FUEL G
SPEEDS VARIABLE
TRANSMISSION HYDRO
STEERING ZERO
BLADE CLUTCH ELECTRIC
STANDARD DECK 54"
WEIGHT 823 LBS.
MSRP $6,999

Z460X
YEARS MFRD 2020-2020
ENGINE KAWASAKI FX
CYLINDERS 2
CID 44.3
ENGINE HP 23.5
FUEL G
SPEEDS VARIABLE
TRANSMISSION HYDRO
STEERING ZERO
BLADE CLUTCH ELECTRIC
STANDARD DECK 60"
WEIGHT 877 LBS.
MSRP $8,499

Z544 KOH
YEARS MFRD 2018-2018
ENGINE KOHLER ECV740
CYLINDERS 2
CID 45
ENGINE HP 25
FUEL G
TRANSMISSION HYDRO
STEERING ZERO
BLADE CLUTCH ELECTRIC
STANDARD DECK 54"
MSRP $8,599

OPTIONS

KAWASAKI 24.5HP

Z548
YEARS MFRD 2019-2020
ENGINE YAMAHA
CID 50.28
ENGINE HP 26
FUEL G
SPEEDS VARIABLE
TRANSMISSION HYDRO
STEERING ZERO
BLADE CLUTCH ELECTRIC
STANDARD DECK 48"
WEIGHT 1,100 LBS.
MSRP $7,999

Z548 KAW
YEARS MFRD 2018-2018
ENGINE KAWASAKI 691V
CYLINDERS 2
CID 44.3
ENGINE HP 22
COOLING AIR
FUEL G
SPEEDS VARIABLE
TRANSMISSION HYDRO
STEERING ZERO
BLADE CLUTCH ELECTRIC
STANDARD DECK 48"
MSRP $7,799

Z554
YEARS MFRD 2019-2020
ENGINE YAMAHA
CYLINDERS 2
CID 50.28
ENGINE HP 26
FUEL G
SPEEDS VARIABLE
TRANSMISSION HYDRO
STEERING ZERO
BLADE CLUTCH ELECTRIC
STANDARD DECK 54"
WEIGHT 1,215 LBS.
MSRP $8,499

Z554X
YEARS MFRD 2019-2020
ENGINE YAMAHA
CYLINDERS 2
CID 50.28
ENGINE HP 27.5
FUEL G
SPEEDS VARIABLE
TRANSMISSION HYDRO
STEERING ZERO
BLADE CLUTCH ELECTRIC
STANDARD DECK 54"
WEIGHT 1,250 LBS.
MSRP $10,999

Z560
YEARS MFRD 2019-2020
ENGINE YAMAHA
CYLINDERS 2
CID 50.28
ENGINE HP 27.5
FUEL G
SPEEDS VARIABLE
TRANSMISSION HYDRO
STEERING ZERO
BLADE CLUTCH ELECTRIC
STANDARD DECK 60"
WEIGHT 1,250 LBS.
MSRP $8,999

OPTIONS

KOHLER 27HP

Z560X
YEARS MFRD 2018-2020
ENGINE KAWASAKI
CYLINDERS 2
ENGINE HP 31
COOLING AIR
FUEL G
SPEEDS VARIABLE
TRANSMISSION HYDRO
STEERING ZERO
BLADE CLUTCH ELECTRIC
STANDARD DECK 60"
WEIGHT 1,309 LBS.
MSRP $12,499

OPTIONS

YAMAHA 27.5HP $-600

Z572X
YEARS MFRD 2018-2020
ENGINE KOHLER 921V
CYLINDERS 2
ENGINE HP 31
COOLING AIR
FUEL G
SPEEDS VARIABLE
TRANSMISSION HYDRO
STEERING ZERO
BLADE CLUTCH ELECTRIC
STANDARD DECK 72"
WEIGHT 1,359 LBS.
MSRP $13,299

OPTIONS

YAMAHA 33HP $100

Z3815
YEARS MFRD 2005-2005
SERIES ZERO TURN SERIES
ENGINE B&S
ENGINE HP 15
COOLING AIR
FUEL G
SPEEDS VARIABLE
TRANSMISSION HYDRO
STEERING ZERO
STANDARD DECK 38"
MSRP $2,699

RETAIL PRICING

YEAR	HIGH	LOW
2005	$1,682	$1,261

Z4217
YEARS MFRD 2005-2006
SERIES ZERO TURN SERIES
ENGINE KAWASAKI
CYLINDERS 1
ENGINE HP 17.5
COOLING AIR
FUEL G
SPEEDS VARIABLE
TRANSMISSION HYDRO
STEERING ZERO
STANDARD DECK 38"
MSRP $2,899

RETAIL PRICING

YEAR	HIGH	LOW
2005	$1,807	$1,355
2006	$1,841	$1,381

Z4218
YEARS MFRD 2007-2007
SERIES ZERO TURN SERIES
ENGINE KOHLER
ENGINE HP 18
COOLING AIR
FUEL G
SPEEDS VARIABLE
TRANSMISSION HYDRO
STEERING ZERO
STANDARD DECK 42"
MSRP $2,999

SERIAL NUMBERS

YEAR	BEGINNING NO.
2007	64000000

RETAIL PRICING

YEAR	HIGH	LOW
2007	$1,053	$789

Z4219
YEARS MFRD 2007-2009
ENGINE B&S
ENGINE HP 19
COOLING AIR
FUEL G
SPEEDS VARIABLE
TRANSMISSION HYDRO
STEERING ZERO
STANDARD DECK 42"
MSRP $2,699

SERIAL NUMBERS

YEAR	BEGINNING NO.
2007	64000000

RETAIL PRICING

YEAR	HIGH	LOW
2007	$927	$695
2008	$1,030	$772
2009	$1,142	$856

Z4220

YEARS MFRD........ 2008-2009
ENGINE.................B&S
ENGINE HP................20
COOLING.................AIR
FUEL......................G
SPEEDS............VARIABLE
TRANSMISSION..........HYDRO
STEERING.................ZERO
BLADE CLUTCH........ELECTRIC
STANDARD DECK............42"
MSRP.....................$2,999

RETAIL PRICING

YEAR	HIGH	LOW
2008	$1,740	$1,305
2009	$1,860	$1,395

Z4619

YEARS MFRD........ 2008-2009
ENGINE.................B&S
ENGINE HP................19
COOLING.................AIR
FUEL......................G
SPEEDS............VARIABLE
TRANSMISSION..........HYDRO
STEERING.................ZERO
BLADE CLUTCH........ELECTRIC
STANDARD DECK............46"
WEIGHT...............575 LBS.
MSRP.....................$2,849

RETAIL PRICING

YEAR	HIGH	LOW
2008	$1,667	$1,250
2009	$1,767	$1,325

Z4818

YEARS MFRD........ 2005-2006
SERIES........ZERO TURN SERIES
ENGINE.................B&S
CYLINDERS..................1
ENGINE HP................18
COOLING.................AIR
FUEL......................G
SPEEDS............VARIABLE
TRANSMISSION..........HYDRO
STEERING.................ZERO
STANDARD DECK............48"
MSRP.....................$4,439

RETAIL PRICING

YEAR	HIGH	LOW
2005	$2,814	$2,110
2006	$2,924	$2,193

Z4824

YEARS MFRD........ 2007-2007
ENGINE.................B&S
ENGINE HP................24
COOLING.................AIR
FUEL......................G
SPEEDS............VARIABLE
TRANSMISSION..........HYDRO
STEERING.................ZERO
STANDARD DECK............48"
MSRP.....................$2,999

SERIAL NUMBERS

YEAR	BEGINNING NO.
2007	64000000

RETAIL PRICING

YEAR	HIGH	LOW
2007	$1,053	$789

Z5426

YEARS MFRD........ 2007-2007
ENGINE.................B&S
ENGINE HP................26
COOLING.................AIR
FUEL......................G
SPEEDS............VARIABLE
TRANSMISSION..........HYDRO
STEERING.................ZERO
STANDARD DECK............54"
WEIGHT...............600 LBS.
MSRP.....................$3,199

SERIAL NUMBERS

YEAR	BEGINNING NO.
2007	64000000

RETAIL PRICING

YEAR	HIGH	LOW
2007	$1,138	$853

ZTH4217

YEARS MFRD........ 2000-2002
ENGINE..............KAWASAKI
ENGINE HP................17
FUEL......................G
TRANSMISSION..........HYDRO
STEERING............STANDARD
STANDARD DECK............42"
MSRP.....................$3,055

RETAIL PRICING

YEAR	HIGH	LOW
2000	$992	$744
2001	$1,311	$983
2002	$1,554	$1,166

ZTH4218

YEARS MFRD........ 2001-2003
ENGINE..............KAWASAKI
ENGINE HP................18
FUEL......................G
STEERING............STANDARD
STANDARD DECK............42"
MSRP.....................$2,500

RETAIL PRICING

YEAR	HIGH	LOW
2001	$1,237	$928

ZTH4817

YEARS MFRD........ 2000-2002
ENGINE..............KAWASAKI
ENGINE HP................17
FUEL......................G
TRANSMISSION..........HYDRO
STEERING............STANDARD
STANDARD DECK............42"
MSRP.....................$3,230

RETAIL PRICING

YEAR	HIGH	LOW
2000	$1,064	$798
2001	$1,204	$903
2002	$1,644	$1,233

ZTH4818QL

YEARS MFRD........ 2001-2003
ENGINE................KOHLER
ENGINE HP................18
FUEL......................G
STEERING............STANDARD
STANDARD DECK............48"
MSRP.....................$2,550

OPTIONS

KAWASAKI 18HP

RETAIL PRICING

YEAR	HIGH	LOW
2001	$1,263	$947

ZTH4819

YEARS MFRD........ 2000-2002
ENGINE..............KAWASAKI
ENGINE HP................19
FUEL......................G
TRANSMISSION..........HYDRO
STEERING............STANDARD
STANDARD DECK............48"
MSRP.....................$3,540

RETAIL PRICING

YEAR	HIGH	LOW
2000	$1,163	$872
2002	$1,802	$1,352

ZTH4821

YEARS MFRD........ 2001-2003
ENGINE..............KAWASAKI
ENGINE HP................21
FUEL......................G
STEERING............STANDARD
STANDARD DECK............48"
MSRP.....................$2,800

RETAIL PRICING

YEAR	HIGH	LOW
2001	$1,385	$1,039

ZTH5221

YEARS MFRD........ 2001-2003
ENGINE..............KAWASAKI
ENGINE HP................21
FUEL......................G
STEERING............STANDARD
STANDARD DECK............52"
MSRP.....................$3,330

RETAIL PRICING

YEAR	HIGH	LOW
2001	$1,649	$1,237

ZTH5222

YEARS MFRD........ 2000-2002
ENGINE................KOHLER
ENGINE HP................22
FUEL......................G
TRANSMISSION..........HYDRO
STEERING............STANDARD
STANDARD DECK............52"
MSRP.....................$2,800

RETAIL PRICING

YEAR	HIGH	LOW
2000	$1,330	$997

ZTH5223L

YEARS MFRD........ 2001-2003
ENGINE..........KOHLER AEGIS
ENGINE HP................23
COOLING..............LIQUID
FUEL......................G
STEERING............STANDARD
STANDARD DECK............52"
MSRP.....................$4,075

RETAIL PRICING

YEAR	HIGH	LOW
2001	$1,658	$1,244
2002	$2,074	$1,555

ZTH5223XP

YEARS MFRD........ 2001-2003
ENGINE................KOHLER
ENGINE HP................23
FUEL......................G
STEERING............STANDARD

OPTIONS

KAWASAKI 23HP

ZTH5225

YEARS MFRD........ 2000-2003
ENGINE................KOHLER
ENGINE HP................25
FUEL......................G
STEERING............STANDARD
STANDARD DECK............52"
MSRP.....................$4,455

OPTIONS

KAWASAKI 25HP

RETAIL PRICING

YEAR	HIGH	LOW
2000	$1,473	$1,105
2001	$1,783	$1,337
2002	$2,266	$1,699

ZTH6125XP

YEARS MFRD........ 2000-2003
ENGINE................KOHLER
ENGINE HP................25
FUEL......................G
TRANSMISSION.....HYDRO DUAL
STEERING............STANDARD

ZTH6126

YEARS MFRD........ 2001-2001
ENGINE................KOHLER
ENGINE HP................26
FUEL......................G
TRANSMISSION..........HYDRO
STEERING............STANDARD

HUSQVARNA

ZTH7226XP

YEARS MFRD 2001-2003
ENGINE . . . . KOHLER EFI
ENGINE HP 26
FUEL . . . . G
TRANSMISSION . . . . . HYDRO DUAL
STEERING. . . . . STANDARD

16H

YEARS MFRD 2000-2002
SERIES. . . . . RIDER SERIES
ENGINE . . . . B&S
ENGINE HP 16
COOLING . . . . AIR
FUEL . . . . G
TRANSMISSION . . . . HYDRO
STEERING. . . . . STANDARD
STANDARD DECK . . . . 38"
MSRP. $3,600

RETAIL PRICING

YEAR	HIGH	LOW
2000	$1,591	$1,193
2001	$1,783	$1,337
2002	$1,833	$1,374

155

YEARS MFRD 2003-2007
SERIES. . . . . RIDER SERIES
ENGINE . . . . KOHLER OHV
ENGINE HP 15
WEIGHT . . . . 622 LBS.
MSRP. $2,999

SERIAL NUMBERS

YEAR	BEGINNING NO.
2007	64000000

RETAIL PRICING

YEAR	HIGH	LOW
2004	$1,761	$1,321

850 12IC

YEARS MFRD 1989-1990
ENGINE . . . . B&S
ENGINE HP 12
COOLING . . . . AIR
FUEL . . . . G
TRANSMISSION . . . . BELT
STEERING. . . . . STANDARD

970H15

YEARS MFRD 1999-1999
ENGINE . . . . B&S
ENGINE HP 15.5
COOLING . . . . AIR
FUEL . . . . G
TRANSMISSION . . . . HYDRO
STEERING. . . . . ZERO
STANDARD DECK . . . . 38"
MSRP. $3,169

OPTIONS

41" DECK

RETAIL PRICING

YEAR	HIGH	LOW
1999	$515	$387

1200H18

YEARS MFRD 1996-1998
ENGINE . . . . B&S
ENGINE HP 18
COOLING . . . . AIR
FUEL . . . . G
TRANSMISSION . . . . HYDRO
STEERING. . . . . ZERO
STANDARD DECK . . . . 48"
MSRP. $5,999

RETAIL PRICING

YEAR	HIGH	LOW
1996	$657	$492
1997	$728	$546
1998	$806	$604

2042LS

YEARS MFRD 2009-2009
ENGINE . . . . B&S ENDURANCE
CYLINDERS. 2
CID 31
ENGINE HP 20
COOLING . . . . AIR
FUEL . . . . G
SPEEDS . . . . VARIABLE
TRANSMISSION . . . . HYDRO
STEERING. . . . . STANDARD
BLADE CLUTCH . . . . ELECTRIC
STANDARD DECK . . . . 42"
MSRP. $1,999

RETAIL PRICING

YEAR	HIGH	LOW
2009	$600	$450

2146XLS

YEARS MFRD 2009-2009
ENGINE . . . . B&S VANGUARD
CYLINDERS. 2
ENGINE HP 21
COOLING . . . . AIR
FUEL . . . . G
SPEEDS . . . . VARIABLE
TRANSMISSION . . . . HYDRO
STEERING. . . . . STANDARD
BLADE CLUTCH . . . . ELECTRIC
STANDARD DECK . . . . 46"
WEIGHT . . . . 625 LBS.
MSRP. $2,899

RETAIL PRICING

YEAR	HIGH	LOW
2009	$869	$652

2246LS

YEARS MFRD 2009-2009
SERIES. . . . . LS SERIES
ENGINE . . . . B&S ENDURANCE
CYLINDERS. 2
CID 44
ENGINE HP 22
COOLING . . . . AIR
FUEL . . . . G
SPEEDS . . . . VARIABLE
TRANSMISSION . . . . HYDRO
STEERING. . . . . STANDARD
BLADE CLUTCH . . . . ELECTRIC
STANDARD DECK . . . . 46"
MSRP. $2,199

RETAIL PRICING

YEAR	HIGH	LOW
2009	$663	$498

2348LS

YEARS MFRD 2009-2009
SERIES. . . . . LS SERIES
ENGINE . . . . B&S ENDURANCE
CYLINDERS. 2
CID 44
ENGINE HP 23
COOLING . . . . AIR
FUEL . . . . G
SPEEDS . . . . VARIABLE
TRANSMISSION . . . . HYDRO
STEERING. . . . . STANDARD
BLADE CLUTCH . . . . ELECTRIC
STANDARD DECK . . . . 46"
MSRP. $2,299

RETAIL PRICING

YEAR	HIGH	LOW
2009	$691	$518

2354GXLS

YEARS MFRD 2009-2009
ENGINE . . . . B&S VANGUARD
CYLINDERS. 2
ENGINE HP 23
COOLING . . . . AIR
FUEL . . . . G
SPEEDS . . . . VARIABLE
TRANSMISSION . . . . HYDRO
STEERING. . . . . STANDARD
BLADE CLUTCH . . . . ELECTRIC
STANDARD DECK . . . . 54"
MSRP. $3,499

RETAIL PRICING

YEAR	HIGH	LOW
2009	$1,202	$902

2748GLS

YEARS MFRD 2009-2009
SERIES. . . . . LS SERIES
ENGINE . . . . B&S ENDURANCE
CYLINDERS. 2
ENGINE HP 27
COOLING . . . . AIR
FUEL . . . . G
SPEEDS . . . . VARIABLE
TRANSMISSION . . . . HYDRO
STEERING. . . . . STANDARD
BLADE CLUTCH . . . . ELECTRIC
STANDARD DECK . . . . 48"
MSRP. $3,199

RETAIL PRICING

YEAR	HIGH	LOW
2009	$1,099	$824

2754GLS

YEARS MFRD 2009-2009
ENGINE . . . . B&S
CYLINDERS. 2
ENGINE HP 27
COOLING . . . . AIR
FUEL . . . . G
SPEEDS . . . . VARIABLE
TRANSMISSION . . . . HYDRO
STEERING. . . . . STANDARD
BLADE CLUTCH . . . . ELECTRIC
STANDARD DECK . . . . 54"
MSRP. $3,299

RETAIL PRICING

YEAR	HIGH	LOW
2009	$1,134	$850

4125H

YEARS MFRD 1992-1992
ENGINE . . . . B&S
ENGINE HP 12.5
COOLING . . . . AIR
FUEL . . . . G
TRANSMISSION . . . . HYDRO
STEERING. . . . . STANDARD

4140G

YEARS MFRD 1992-1992
ENGINE . . . . B&S
ENGINE HP 18
COOLING . . . . AIR
FUEL . . . . G
TRANSMISSION . . . . HYDRO
STEERING. . . . . STANDARD

4140H

YEARS MFRD 1992-1991
ENGINE . . . . B&S
ENGINE HP 14
COOLING . . . . AIR
FUEL . . . . G
TRANSMISSION . . . . HYDRO
STEERING. . . . . STANDARD

HUSTLER

ATZ35

YEARS MFRD 2014-2014
ENGINE . . . . KAWASAKI
ENGINE HP 35
COOLING . . . . AIR
FUEL . . . . G
SPEEDS . . . . VARIABLE
TRANSMISSION . . . . HYDRO
STEERING. . . . . ZERO
STANDARD DECK . . . . 60"
MSRP. $15,499

RETAIL PRICING

YEAR	HIGH	LOW
2014	$11,093	$8,320

ATZ 27/60

YEARS MFRD 2006-2008
ENGINE .... KOHLER
CYLINDERS 2
CID 44
ENGINE HP 27
COOLING .... AIR
FUEL .... G
SPEEDS .... VARIABLE
TRANSMISSION .... HYDRO
STEERING .... ZERO
STANDARD DECK .... 60"
WEIGHT .... 1,500 LBS.
MSRP $12,349

RETAIL PRICING

YEAR	HIGH	LOW
2006	$2,177	$1,633
2007	$2,862	$2,147
2008	$3,658	$2,744

ATZ 31/60

YEARS MFRD 2009-2011
ENGINE .... KAWASAKI
ENGINE HP 31
COOLING .... AIR
FUEL .... G
SPEEDS .... VARIABLE
TRANSMISSION .... HYDRO
STEERING .... ZERO
BLADE CLUTCH .... ELECTRIC
STANDARD DECK .... 60"
WEIGHT .... 1,240 LBS.
MSRP $13,299

RETAIL PRICING

YEAR	HIGH	LOW
2009	$4,764	$3,573
2010	$5,681	$4,261
2011	$7,686	$5,764

CV742

YEARS MFRD 2019-2020
SERIES .... HUSTLER X-ONE SERIES
ENGINE .. KOHLER COMMAND PRO
CID 742CC
ENGINE HP 25
COOLING .... AIR
FUEL .... G
SPEEDS .... VARIABLE
TRANSMISSION ..... DUAL HYDRO
STEERING .... ZERO
STANDARD DECK .... 52"
WEIGHT .... 1,240 LBS.
MSRP $10,273

OPTIONS

60" DECK

DASH

YEARS MFRD 2019-2020
ENGINE .... B&S
CID 344
ENGINE HP 10.5
COOLING .... AIR
FUEL .... G
SPEEDS .... VARIABLE
TRANSMISSION ..... DUAL HYDRO
STEERING .... ZERO
STANDARD DECK .... 34"
WEIGHT .... 390 LBS.
MSRP $2,449

OPTIONS

42" DECK $100

FASTRAK

YEARS MFRD 2003-2004
SERIES .... FASTRAK SERIES
ENGINE .... B&S
ENGINE HP 17.5
FUEL .... G
SPEEDS .... VARIABLE
TRANSMISSION .... HYDRO
STEERING .... ZERO
STANDARD DECK .... 44"
WEIGHT .... 730 LBS.
MSRP $4,699

RETAIL PRICING

YEAR	HIGH	LOW
2003	$2,571	$1,928
2004	$2,738	$2,054

FASTRAK 16/44

YEARS MFRD 2002-2007
SERIES .... FASTRAK SERIES
ENGINE .... HONDA OHV
CYLINDERS 2
CID 32.3
ENGINE HP 16
COOLING .... AIR
FUEL .... G
SPEEDS .... VARIABLE
TRANSMISSION ..... DUAL HYDRO
STEERING .... ZERO
STANDARD DECK .... 44"
WEIGHT .... 730 LBS.
MSRP $5,249

OPTIONS

2 BAG
48" SNOW BLOWER
BLADE

RETAIL PRICING

YEAR	HIGH	LOW
2002	$1,001	$751
2003	$1,111	$834
2004	$1,236	$927
2005	$1,373	$1,030
2006	$1,523	$1,142
2007	$1,695	$1,271

FASTRAK 18/44

YEARS MFRD 2002-2007
SERIES .... FASTRAK SERIES
ENGINE .... HONDA OHV
CYLINDERS 2
CID 37.5
ENGINE HP 18
COOLING .... AIR
FUEL .... G
SPEEDS .... VARIABLE
TRANSMISSION .... HYDRO
STEERING .... ZERO
STANDARD DECK .... 44"
WEIGHT .... 730 LBS.
MSRP $5,449

OPTIONS

2 BAG
48" SNOW BLOWER
52" DECK
BLADE

RETAIL PRICING

YEAR	HIGH	LOW
2002	$1,026	$770
2003	$1,141	$856
2004	$1,266	$949
2005	$1,407	$1,055
2006	$1,564	$1,173
2007	$1,739	$1,304

FASTRAK 20/52

YEARS MFRD 2002-2007
SERIES .... FASTRAK SERIES
ENGINE .... HONDA OHV
CYLINDERS 2
CID 37.5
ENGINE HP 20
COOLING .... AIR
FUEL .... G
SPEEDS .... VARIABLE
TRANSMISSION ..... DUAL HYDRO
STEERING .... ZERO
STANDARD DECK .... 52"
WEIGHT .... 740 LBS.
MSRP $5,899

OPTIONS

2 BAG
48" SNOW BLOWER
54" DECK
BLADE

RETAIL PRICING

YEAR	HIGH	LOW
2002	$1,111	$834
2003	$1,236	$927
2004	$1,373	$1,030
2005	$1,523	$1,142
2006	$1,692	$1,269
2007	$1,903	$1,427

FASTRAK 21.5

YEARS MFRD 2014-2014
ENGINE .... KAWASAKI
ENGINE HP 21.5
COOLING .... AIR
FUEL .... G
SPEEDS .... VARIABLE
TRANSMISSION .... HYDRO
STEERING .... ZERO
STANDARD DECK .... 48"
MSRP $6,749

OPTIONS

2 BAG

RETAIL PRICING

YEAR	HIGH	LOW
2014	$5,081	$3,811

FASTRAK 22

YEARS MFRD 2012-2013
ENGINE .... KAWASAKI
ENGINE HP 22
COOLING .... AIR
FUEL .... G
SPEEDS .... VARIABLE
TRANSMISSION ..... DUAL HYDRO
STEERING .... ZERO
STANDARD DECK .... 48"
MSRP $6,599

OPTIONS

2 BAG
STRIPER

RETAIL PRICING

YEAR	HIGH	LOW
2012	$3,786	$2,839
2013	$4,207	$3,155

FASTRAK 23

YEARS MFRD 2014-2020
ENGINE .... KAWASAKI
ENGINE HP 23
COOLING .... AIR
FUEL .... G
SPEEDS .... VARIABLE
TRANSMISSION ..... DUAL HYDRO
STEERING .... ZERO
STANDARD DECK .... 54"
MSRP $7,419

OPTIONS

48" DECK .... $-343
48" DECK RD
54" DECK RD $342

RETAIL PRICING

YEAR	HIGH	LOW
2014	$3,419	$2,563
2015	$3,773	$2,830
2016	$4,164	$3,123
2017	$4,597	$3,448
2018	$5,059	$3,795
2019	$5,555	$4,166
2020	$6,157	$4,642

FASTRAK 24

YEARS MFRD 2012-2020
ENGINE .... KAWASAKI FR730
ENGINE HP 24
COOLING .... AIR
FUEL .... G
SPEEDS .... VARIABLE
TRANSMISSION ..... DUAL HYDRO
STEERING .... ZERO
STANDARD DECK .... 60"
WEIGHT .... 835 LBS.
MSRP $7,761

OPTIONS

2 BAG KIT $1,974
FLEX FORKS $311
STRIPER $113

HUSTLER

RETAIL PRICING

YEAR	HIGH	LOW
2012	$2,895	$2,172
2013	$3,197	$2,397
2014	$3,528	$2,646
2015	$3,894	$2,921
2016	$4,299	$3,224
2017	$4,744	$3,558
2018	$5,183	$3,887
2019	$5,739	$4,305
2020	$6,354	$4,895

FASTRAK 26

YEARS MFRD 2012-2013
ENGINE . . . . KAWASAKI
ENGINE HP 26
COOLING . . . . AIR
FUEL . . . . G
SPEEDS . . . . VARIABLE
TRANSMISSION . . . . . DUAL HYDRO
STEERING . . . . ZERO
STANDARD DECK . . . . 60"
MSRP $7,099

OPTIONS

2 BAG
STRIPER

RETAIL PRICING

YEAR	HIGH	LOW
2012	$4,075	$3,056
2013	$4,525	$3,394

FASTRAK 27

YEARS MFRD 2018-2020
ENGINE . . . . KOHLER 7500 EFI
CID 747CC
ENGINE HP 27
COOLING . . . . AIR
FUEL . . . . G
SPEEDS . . . . VARIABLE
TRANSMISSION . . . . . DUAL HYDRO
STEERING . . . . ZERO
STANDARD DECK . . . . 54"
WEIGHT . . . . 845 LBS.
MSRP $7,761

OPTIONS

2 BAG $1,974
60" DECK $343

FASTRAK 36/42

YEARS MFRD 2005-2010
SERIES . . . . FASTRAK SERIES
ENGINE . . . . HONDA
CYLINDERS 2
CID 32.3
ENGINE HP 16
COOLING . . . . AIR
FUEL . . . . G
SPEEDS . . . . VARIABLE
TRANSMISSION . . . . HYDRO
STEERING . . . . ZERO
WEIGHT . . . . 552 LBS.

OPTIONS

KOHLER 15HP
KOHLER 17HP

FASTRAK 44/52

YEARS MFRD 2006-2007
ENGINE . . . . HONDA OHV
CYLINDERS 2
CID 32.3
ENGINE HP 16
COOLING . . . . AIR
FUEL . . . . G
SPEEDS . . . . VARIABLE
TRANSMISSION . . . . HYDRO
STEERING . . . . ZERO
WEIGHT . . . . 740 LBS.

OPTIONS

HONDA 18HP
HONDA 20HP
KOHLER 18HP
KOHLER 20HP

FASTRAK 48

YEARS MFRD 2007-2010
ENGINE . . . . KAWASAKI
CYLINDERS 2
ENGINE HP 19
COOLING . . . . AIR
FUEL . . . . G
SPEEDS . . . . VARIABLE
TRANSMISSION . . . . HYDRO
STEERING . . . . ZERO
WEIGHT . . . . 790 LBS.

OPTIONS

HONDA 18HP
KOHLER 19HP

FASTRAK 54

YEARS MFRD 2007-2010
ENGINE . . . . KAWASAKI
CYLINDERS 2
ENGINE HP 21
COOLING . . . . AIR
FUEL . . . . G
SPEEDS . . . . VARIABLE
TRANSMISSION . . . . HYDRO
STEERING . . . . ZERO
WEIGHT . . . . 815 LBS.

OPTIONS

HONDA 20HP

FASTRAK MINI Z

YEARS MFRD 2004-2004
SERIES . . . . FASTRAK SERIES
ENGINE . . . . KOHLER COURAGE
CYLINDERS 2
ENGINE HP 15
FUEL . . . . G
SPEEDS . . . . VARIABLE
TRANSMISSION . . . . HYDRO
STEERING . . . . ZERO

OPTIONS

HONDA 17HP

FASTRAK SD17

YEARS MFRD 2014-2014
SERIES . . . . SUPER DUTY SERIES
ENGINE . . . . KAWASAKI
ENGINE HP 17
COOLING . . . . AIR
FUEL . . . . G
SPEEDS . . . . VARIABLE
TRANSMISSION . . . . HYDRO
STEERING . . . . ZERO
STANDARD DECK . . . . 36"
MSRP $6,499

OPTIONS

2 BAG
42" DECK

RETAIL PRICING

YEAR	HIGH	LOW
2014	$4,946	$3,710

FASTRAK SD20

YEARS MFRD 2012-2013
SERIES . . . . SUPER DUTY SERIES
ENGINE . . . . KAWASAKI
ENGINE HP 20
COOLING . . . . AIR
FUEL . . . . G
SPEEDS . . . . VARIABLE
TRANSMISSION . . . . . DUAL HYDRO
STEERING . . . . ZERO
STANDARD DECK . . . . 36"
WEIGHT . . . . 680 LBS.
MSRP $6,499

OPTIONS

2 BAG
42" DECK
STRIPER

RETAIL PRICING

YEAR	HIGH	LOW
2012	$3,735	$2,801
2013	$4,141	$3,106

FASTRAK SD22

YEARS MFRD 2014-2014
SERIES . . . . SUPER DUTY SERIES
ENGINE . . . . KAWASAKI
ENGINE HP 22
COOLING . . . . AIR
FUEL . . . . G
SPEEDS . . . . VARIABLE
TRANSMISSION . . . . HYDRO
STEERING . . . . ZERO
STANDARD DECK . . . . 48"
MSRP $7,549

OPTIONS

2 BAG

RETAIL PRICING

YEAR	HIGH	LOW
2014	$5,799	$4,349

FASTRAK SD23.5

YEARS MFRD 2014-2017
SERIES . . . . SUPER DUTY SERIES
ENGINE . . . . KAWASAKI
ENGINE HP 23.5
COOLING . . . . AIR
FUEL . . . . G
SPEEDS . . . . VARIABLE
TRANSMISSION . . . . . DUAL HYDRO
STEERING . . . . ZERO
STANDARD DECK . . . . 54"
MSRP $7,933

OPTIONS

2 BAG
48" DECK
60" DECK

RETAIL PRICING

YEAR	HIGH	LOW
2014	$4,614	$3,461
2015	$5,092	$3,819
2016	$5,621	$4,216
2017	$6,444	$4,833

FASTRAK SD24

YEARS MFRD 2012-2017
SERIES . . . . SUPER DUTY SERIES
ENGINE . . . . KAWASAKI
ENGINE HP 24
COOLING . . . . AIR
FUEL . . . . G
SPEEDS . . . . VARIABLE
TRANSMISSION . . . . . DUAL HYDRO
STEERING . . . . ZERO
STANDARD DECK . . . . 60"
MSRP $8,161

OPTIONS

2 BAG
FLEX FORKS
STRIPER

RETAIL PRICING

YEAR	HIGH	LOW
2012	$3,896	$2,922
2013	$4,300	$3,225
2014	$4,746	$3,560
2015	$5,238	$3,929
2016	$5,782	$4,337
2017	$6,796	$5,097

FASTRAK SD26

YEARS MFRD 2012-2013
SERIES . . . . SUPER DUTY
ENGINE . . . . KAWASAKI
ENGINE HP 26
COOLING . . . . AIR
FUEL . . . . G
SPEEDS . . . . VARIABLE
TRANSMISSION . . . . . DUAL HYDRO
STEERING . . . . ZERO
STANDARD DECK . . . . 54"
WEIGHT . . . . 860 LBS.
MSRP $7,549

OPTIONS

2 BAG
60" DECK
STRIPER

RETAIL PRICING

YEAR	HIGH	LOW
2012	$4,331	$3,248
2013	$4,811	$3,608

FASTRAK SUPER DUTY 23/48

YEARS MFRD 2008-2010
ENGINE . . . . KAWASAKI
CYLINDERS. 2
ENGINE HP 23
COOLING . . . . AIR
FUEL . . . . G
SPEEDS . . . . VARIABLE
TRANSMISSION . . . . HYDRO
STEERING. . . . . ZERO
BLADE CLUTCH . . . . ELECTRIC
STANDARD DECK . . . . 48"
WEIGHT . . . . 835 LBS.
MSRP. $8,959

RETAIL PRICING

YEAR	HIGH	LOW
2009	$4,947	$3,710
2010	$5,595	$4,196

FASTRAK SUPER DUTY 25/54

YEARS MFRD 2008-2010
ENGINE . . . . KAWASAKI
CYLINDERS. 2
ENGINE HP 25
COOLING . . . . AIR
FUEL . . . . G
SPEEDS . . . . VARIABLE
TRANSMISSION . . . . HYDRO
STEERING. . . . . ZERO
BLADE CLUTCH . . . . ELECTRIC
STANDARD DECK . . . . 54"
WEIGHT . . . . 860 LBS.
MSRP. $9,079

RETAIL PRICING

YEAR	HIGH	LOW
2009	$5,015	$3,761
2010	$5,670	$4,252

FASTRAK SUPER DUTY 25/60

YEARS MFRD 2008-2010
ENGINE . . . . KAWASAKI
CYLINDERS. 2
ENGINE HP 25
COOLING . . . . AIR
FUEL . . . . G
SPEEDS . . . . VARIABLE
TRANSMISSION . . . . HYDRO
STEERING. . . . . ZERO
BLADE CLUTCH . . . . ELECTRIC
STANDARD DECK . . . . 60"
WEIGHT . . . . 885 LBS.
MSRP. $9,599

RETAIL PRICING

YEAR	HIGH	LOW
2009	$5,306	$3,980
2010	$5,996	$4,497

FASTRAK SUPER DUTY 48/54/60

YEARS MFRD 2010-2010
ENGINE . . . . HONDA GXV630
COOLING . . . . AIR
FUEL . . . . G
SPEEDS . . . . VARIABLE
TRANSMISSION . . . . HYDRO
STEERING. . . . . ZERO
BLADE CLUTCH . . . . ELECTRIC
WEIGHT . . . . 885 LBS.

FLIPUP25

YEARS MFRD 2016-2018
SERIES. . . . . RAPTOR SERIES
ENGINE . . . . KOHLER
ENGINE HP 25
COOLING . . . . AIR
FUEL . . . . G
SPEEDS . . . . VARIABLE
TRANSMISSION . . . . . DUAL HYDRO
STEERING. . . . . ZERO
STANDARD DECK . . . . 48"
MSRP. $5,399

OPTIONS

2 BAG
54" DECK
FLEX FORKS

RETAIL PRICING

YEAR	HIGH	LOW
2016	$3,128	$2,346
2017	$3,452	$2,589
2018	$3,798	$2,849

FLIPUP 23

YEARS MFRD 2019-2020
SERIES. . . . . RAPTOR SERIES
ENGINE . . . . KAWASAKI FR691
CID 726CC
ENGINE HP 23
COOLING . . . . AIR
FUEL . . . . G
TRANSMISSION . . . . . DUAL HYDRO
STEERING. . . . . ZERO
STANDARD DECK . . . . 48"
WEIGHT . . . . 755 LBS.
MSRP. $5,449

OPTIONS

2 BAG $699
54" DECK. $200

FR541

YEARS MFRD 2013-2013
SERIES. . . . . SPORT SERIES
ENGINE . . . . KAWASAKI
CID 541CC
ENGINE HP 15
COOLING . . . . AIR
FUEL . . . . G
SPEEDS . . . . VARIABLE
TRANSMISSION . . . . HYDRO
STEERING. . . . . ZERO
STANDARD DECK . . . . 42"
MSRP. $2,983

OPTIONS

BAGGER

RETAIL PRICING

YEAR	HIGH	LOW
2013	$1,898	$1,424

FR541 36KAW

YEARS MFRD 2019-2020
SERIES. . . . . RAPTOR SERIES
ENGINE . . . . KAWASAKI FR541
CID 603CC
ENGINE HP 15
COOLING . . . . AIR
FUEL . . . . G
SPEEDS . . . . VARIABLE
TRANSMISSION . . . . . DUAL HYDRO
STEERING. . . . . ZERO
BLADE CLUTCH . . . . ELECTRIC
STANDARD DECK . . . . 36"
WEIGHT . . . . 450 LBS.
MSRP. $3,049

OPTIONS

2 BAG $699

FR600

YEARS MFRD 2013-2013
SERIES. . . . . SPORT SERIES
ENGINE . . . . KAWASAKI
CID 600CC
ENGINE HP 18
COOLING . . . . AIR
FUEL . . . . G
SPEEDS . . . . VARIABLE
TRANSMISSION . . . . HYDRO
STEERING. . . . . ZERO
STANDARD DECK . . . . 48"
MSRP. $3,279

OPTIONS

BAGGER

RETAIL PRICING

YEAR	HIGH	LOW
2013	$2,090	$1,567

FR600 42KAW

YEARS MFRD 2019-2020
SERIES. . . . . RAPTOR SERIES
ENGINE . . . . KAWASAKI
CID 603CC
ENGINE HP 18
COOLING . . . . AIR
FUEL . . . . G
SPEEDS . . . . VARIABLE
TRANSMISSION . . . . . DUAL HYDRO
STEERING. . . . . ZERO
STANDARD DECK . . . . 42"
WEIGHT . . . . 479 LBS.
MSRP. $3,049

OPTIONS

2 BAG $699

FR651

YEARS MFRD 2013-2013
SERIES. . . . . SPORT SERIES
ENGINE . . . . KAWASAKI
ENGINE HP 21.5
COOLING . . . . AIR
FUEL . . . . G
SPEEDS . . . . VARIABLE
TRANSMISSION . . . . HYDRO
STEERING. . . . . ZERO
STANDARD DECK . . . . 54"
MSRP. $3,559

OPTIONS

BAGGER

RETAIL PRICING

YEAR	HIGH	LOW
2013	$2,269	$1,701

FR651

YEARS MFRD 2013-2014
SERIES. . . . . RAPTOR SERIES
ENGINE . . . . KAWASAKI
CID 651CC
ENGINE HP 21.5
COOLING . . . . AIR
FUEL . . . . G
SPEEDS . . . . VARIABLE
TRANSMISSION . . . . HYDRO
STEERING. . . . . ZERO
STANDARD DECK . . . . 42"
MSRP. $2,899

RETAIL PRICING

YEAR	HIGH	LOW
2013	$1,415	$1,061
2014	$1,763	$1,322

FR651 42KAW

YEARS MFRD 2018-2019
SERIES. . . . . RAPTOR SERIES
ENGINE . . . . KAWASAKI
CID 726CC
ENGINE HP 21.5
COOLING . . . . AIR
FUEL . . . . G
TRANSMISSION . . . . . DUAL HYDRO
STEERING. . . . . ZERO
STANDARD DECK . . . . 42"
WEIGHT . . . . 479 LBS.

OPTIONS

2 BAG

FR691

YEARS MFRD 2013-2014
SERIES. . . . . RAPTOR SERIES
ENGINE . . . . KAWASAKI

HUSTLER

ENGINE HP 23
COOLING . . . . AIR
FUEL . . . . G
SPEEDS . . . . VARIABLE
TRANSMISSION . . . . HYDRO
STEERING . . . . ZERO
STANDARD DECK . . . . 52"
MSRP $3,099

RETAIL PRICING

YEAR	HIGH	LOW
2013	$1,363	$1,022
2014	$1,938	$1,453

FR691 52KAW

YEARS MFRD 2018-2020
SERIES . . . . RAPTOR SERIES
ENGINE . . . . KAWASAKI
CID 726CC
ENGINE HP 23
COOLING . . . . AIR
FUEL . . . . G
TRANSMISSION . . . . DUAL HYDRO
STEERING . . . . ZERO
STANDARD DECK . . . . 52"
WEIGHT . . . . 503 LBS.
MSRP $3,249

OPTIONS

2 BAG $699

FS651

YEARS MFRD 2012-2014
SERIES . . . . FASTRAK SERIES
ENGINE . . . . KAWASAKI
ENGINE HP 22
COOLING . . . . AIR
FUEL . . . . G
SPEEDS . . . . VARIABLE
TRANSMISSION . . . . HYDRO
STEERING . . . . ZERO
STANDARD DECK . . . . 48"
MSRP $6,599

RETAIL PRICING

YEAR	HIGH	LOW
2012	$2,241	$1,681
2013	$2,816	$2,112
2014	$3,625	$2,718

FS691

YEARS MFRD 2012-2014
SERIES . . . . FASTRAK SERIES
ENGINE . . . . KAWASAKI
ENGINE HP 23
COOLING . . . . AIR
FUEL . . . . G
SPEEDS . . . . VARIABLE
TRANSMISSION . . . . HYDRO
STEERING . . . . ZERO
STANDARD DECK . . . . 54"
MSRP $6,849

RETAIL PRICING

YEAR	HIGH	LOW
2012	$2,430	$1,822
2013	$2,907	$2,180
2014	$3,777	$2,833

FS730

YEARS MFRD 2012-2014
SERIES . . . . FASTRAK SERIES
ENGINE . . . . KAWASAKI
ENGINE HP 24
COOLING . . . . AIR
FUEL . . . . G
SPEEDS . . . . VARIABLE
TRANSMISSION . . . . HYDRO
STEERING . . . . ZERO
STANDARD DECK . . . . 60"
MSRP $7,099

RETAIL PRICING

YEAR	HIGH	LOW
2012	$2,551	$1,913
2013	$3,051	$2,288
2014	$4,458	$3,343

FX650

YEARS MFRD 2013-2013
SERIES . . . . SUPER Z SERIES
ENGINE . . . . KAWASAKI
COOLING . . . . AIR
FUEL . . . . G
SPEEDS . . . . VARIABLE
TRANSMISSION . . . . HYDRO
STEERING . . . . ZERO
BLADE CLUTCH . . . . ELECTRIC
STANDARD DECK . . . . 60"
MSRP $12,899

OPTIONS

10BU BAG
3 BAG & FAN

RETAIL PRICING

YEAR	HIGH	LOW
2013	$9,016	$6,762

FX691

YEARS MFRD 2013-2017
SERIES . . . . HUSTLER X-ONE SERIES
ENGINE . . . . KAWASAKI
ENGINE HP 22
COOLING . . . . AIR
FUEL . . . . G
SPEEDS . . . . VARIABLE
TRANSMISSION . . . . DUAL HYDRO
STEERING . . . . ZERO
STANDARD DECK . . . . 48"
MSRP $10,749

OPTIONS

3 BAG & VAC
54" DECK

RETAIL PRICING

YEAR	HIGH	LOW
2013	$5,664	$4,248
2014	$6,292	$4,719
2015	$6,900	$5,175
2016	$7,615	$5,711
2017	$8,491	$6,369

FX730

YEARS MFRD 2013-2020
SERIES . . . . HUSTLER X-ONE SERIES
ENGINE . . . . KAWASAKI FX730
CID 726CC
ENGINE HP 23.5
COOLING . . . . AIR
FUEL . . . . G
SPEEDS . . . . VARIABLE
TRANSMISSION . . . . DUAL HYDRO
STEERING . . . . ZERO
STANDARD DECK . . . . 60"
MSRP $10,844

OPTIONS

54" DECK RD $228
60" DECK RD $456

RETAIL PRICING

YEAR	HIGH	LOW
2013	$5,492	$4,118
2014	$6,070	$4,553
2015	$6,711	$5,033
2016	$7,417	$5,563
2017	$8,226	$6,170
2018	$8,942	$6,706
2019	$9,477	$7,108
2020	$9,905	$7,656

FX850

YEARS MFRD 2013-2020
SERIES . . . . HUSTLER X-ONE SERIES
ENGINE . . . . KAWASAKI
CID 852CC
ENGINE HP 27
COOLING . . . . AIR
FUEL . . . . G
SPEEDS . . . . VARIABLE
TRANSMISSION . . . . DUAL HYDRO
STEERING . . . . ZERO
STANDARD DECK . . . . 52"
MSRP $10,958

OPTIONS

60" DECK $456
72" DECK $685

RETAIL PRICING

YEAR	HIGH	LOW
2013	$5,795	$4,347
2014	$6,355	$4,767
2015	$7,012	$5,259
2016	$7,483	$5,612
2017	$7,993	$5,994
2018	$8,585	$6,439
2019	$9,022	$6,765
2020	$9,811	$7,473

FX850

YEARS MFRD 2013-2020
SERIES . . . . SUPER Z SERIES
ENGINE . . . . KAWASAKI
ENGINE HP 27
COOLING . . . . AIR
FUEL . . . . G
SPEEDS . . . . VARIABLE
TRANSMISSION . . . . DUAL HYDRO
STEERING . . . . ZERO
BLADE CLUTCH . . . . ELECTRIC
STANDARD DECK . . . . 60"
MSRP $14,154

OPTIONS

3 BAG & KIT $3,595
54" DECK . . . . $-114
60" RD $685
72" RD $1,427

RETAIL PRICING

YEAR	HIGH	LOW
2013	$5,754	$4,315
2014	$6,347	$4,761
2015	$7,009	$5,257
2016	$7,736	$5,802
2017	$8,539	$6,404
2018	$9,452	$7,089
2019	$11,301	$8,476
2020	$12,513	$9,593

FX1000

YEARS MFRD 2013-2020
SERIES . . . . SUPER Z SERIES
ENGINE . . . . KAWASAKI
CID 999CC
ENGINE HP 35
COOLING . . . . AIR
FUEL . . . . G
SPEEDS . . . . VARIABLE
TRANSMISSION . . . . DUAL HYDRO
STEERING . . . . ZERO
BLADE CLUTCH . . . . ELECTRIC
STANDARD DECK . . . . 60"
MSRP $14,497

OPTIONS

3 BAG & KIT $3,595
66" DECK $342
72" DECK $456

RETAIL PRICING

YEAR	HIGH	LOW
2013	$7,044	$5,283
2014	$7,775	$5,832
2015	$8,582	$6,437
2016	$9,471	$7,103
2017	$10,458	$7,843
2018	$11,476	$8,607
2019	$12,466	$9,350
2020	$13,614	$10,510

GXV690

YEARS MFRD 2013-2013
SERIES . . . . HUSTLER X-ONE SERIES
ENGINE . . . . HONDA
COOLING . . . . AIR
FUEL . . . . G
SPEEDS . . . . VARIABLE
TRANSMISSION . . . . HYDRO
STEERING . . . . ZERO
STANDARD DECK . . . . 48"
MSRP $10,349

OPTIONS

54" DECK
60" DECK
BAG & VAC

RETAIL PRICING

YEAR	HIGH	LOW
2013	$6,593	$4,945

HD 35

YEARS MFRD 2016-2016
SERIES . . . . SUPER Z SERIES
ENGINE . . . . KAWASAKI

ENGINE HP 35
COOLING .... AIR
FUEL .... G
SPEEDS .... VARIABLE
TRANSMISSION ..... DUAL HYDRO
STEERING................ ZERO
STANDARD DECK .... 60"
MSRP................. $15,157

OPTIONS

3 BAG
BAG & FAN
HYD LIFT
STRIPER

RETAIL PRICING

YEAR	HIGH	LOW
2016	$13,171	$9,878

HD 35

YEARS MFRD 2020-2020
SERIESSUPER Z HYPERDRIVE SERIES
ENGINE .... KAWASAKI FX1000
CID 993C
ENGINE HP 35
COOLING .... AIR
FUEL .... G
SPEEDS .... VARIABLE
TRANSMISSION ..... DUAL HYDRO
STEERING................ ZERO
BLADE CLUTCH .... ELECTRIC
STANDARD DECK .... 60"
WEIGHT .... 1,536 LBS.
MSRP................. $16,437

OPTIONS

72" DECK................. $113

HD 36

YEARS MFRD 2016-2020
SERIESSUPER Z HYPERDRIVE SERIES
ENGINE .... VANGUARD
CID 993CC
ENGINE HP 36
COOLING .... AIR
FUEL .... G
SPEEDS .... VARIABLE
TRANSMISSION ..... DUAL HYDRO
STEERING................ ZERO
STANDARD DECK .... 60"
WEIGHT .... 1,536 LBS.
MSRP................. $16,209

OPTIONS

3 BAG & KIT $3,595
72" DECK................. $342
STRIPER.................. $727

RETAIL PRICING

YEAR	HIGH	LOW
2016	$8,954	$6,716
2017	$9,853	$7,390
2018	$10,833	$8,125
2019	$12,136	$9,102
2020	$13,453	$10,385

HD 37

YEARS MFRD 2017-2020
SERIESSUPER Z HYPERDRIVE SERIES
ENGINE .... VANGUARD
CID 993CC
ENGINE HP 37
COOLING .... AIR
FUEL .... G
SPEEDS .... VARIABLE
TRANSMISSION ..... DUAL HYDRO
STEERING................ ZERO
STANDARD DECK .... 60"
WEIGHT .... 1,536 LBS.
MSRP................. $17,008

OPTIONS

3 BAG & KIT $34,583,595
60" DECK OIL GUARD $913
66" DECK................. $228
72" DECK................. $342
72" DECK OIL GUARD $1,256
72" DECK RD $970
DECK RD $628

RETAIL PRICING

YEAR	HIGH	LOW
2017	$10,365	$7,773
2018	$11,404	$8,553
2019	$13,126	$9,845
2020	$14,568	$11,161

HOG

YEARS MFRD 2000-2000
ENGINE .... KOHLER
ENGINE HP 20
FUEL .... G
TRANSMISSION .... HYDRO
STEERING................ ZERO
STANDARD DECK .... 48"
MSRP.................. $2,575

RETAIL PRICING

YEAR	HIGH	LOW
2000	$509	$381

HUSTLER 4600

YEARS MFRD 2007-2008
ENGINE .... KUBOTA VI505
CYLINDERS................... 4
ENGINE HP 38
COOLING .... LIQUID
FUEL .... D
SPEEDS .... VARIABLE
TRANSMISSION .... HYDRO
STEERING................ ZERO
STANDARD DECK .... 72"
WEIGHT .... 1,520 LBS.
MSRP................. $27,551

RETAIL PRICING

YEAR	HIGH	LOW
2008	$17,114	$12,835

HUSTLER MINI Z 36/42

YEARS MFRD 2007-2007
ENGINE .... KAWASAKI
CYLINDERS................... 2
ENGINE HP 17
COOLING .... AIR
FUEL .... G
SPEEDS .... VARIABLE
TRANSMISSION .... HYDRO
STEERING................ ZERO
WEIGHT .... 675 LBS.

OPTIONS

KAWASAKI 19HP

HUSTLER SUPER Z 24/60

YEARS MFRD 2009-2011
ENGINE .... HONDA
ENGINE HP 24
COOLING .... AIR
FUEL .... G
SPEEDS .... VARIABLE
TRANSMISSION .... HYDRO
STEERING................ ZERO
BLADE CLUTCH .... ELECTRIC
STANDARD DECK .... 60"
MSRP................. $11,199

RETAIL PRICING

YEAR	HIGH	LOW
2009	$4,102	$3,076
2010	$4,891	$3,668
2011	$6,471	$4,853

HUSTLER SUPER Z 25/60

YEARS MFRD 2009-2011
ENGINE .... KAWASAKI
ENGINE HP 25
COOLING .... AIR
FUEL .... G
SPEEDS .... VARIABLE
TRANSMISSION .... HYDRO
STEERING................ ZERO
BLADE CLUTCH .... ELECTRIC
STANDARD DECK .... 60"
WEIGHT .... 1,230 LBS.
MSRP................. $11,549

RETAIL PRICING

YEAR	HIGH	LOW
2009	$4,237	$3,177
2010	$5,047	$3,785
2011	$6,675	$5,006

HUSTLER SUPER Z 27/60

YEARS MFRD 2009-2011
ENGINE .... KOHLER
ENGINE HP 27
COOLING .... AIR
FUEL .... G
SPEEDS .... VARIABLE
TRANSMISSION .... HYDRO
STEERING................ ZERO
BLADE CLUTCH .... ELECTRIC
STANDARD DECK .... 60"
WEIGHT .... 1,240 LBS.
MSRP................. $11,649

RETAIL PRICING

YEAR	HIGH	LOW
2009	$4,271	$3,203
2010	$5,089	$3,817
2011	$6,731	$5,049

HUSTLER SUPER Z 28/66

YEARS MFRD 2009-2011
ENGINE .... KOHLER
ENGINE HP 28
COOLING .... AIR
FUEL .... G
SPEEDS .... VARIABLE
TRANSMISSION .... HYDRO
STEERING................ ZERO
BLADE CLUTCH .... ELECTRIC
STANDARD DECK .... 66"
MSRP................. $12,849

RETAIL PRICING

YEAR	HIGH	LOW
2009	$4,709	$3,531
2010	$5,618	$4,214
2011	$7,425	$5,569

HUSTLER SUPER Z 30/66

YEARS MFRD 2009-2011
ENGINE .... KOHLER
ENGINE HP 30
COOLING .... AIR
FUEL .... G
SPEEDS .... VARIABLE
TRANSMISSION .... HYDRO
STEERING................ ZERO
BLADE CLUTCH .... ELECTRIC
STANDARD DECK .... 72"
MSRP................. $12,199

RETAIL PRICING

YEAR	HIGH	LOW
2009	$4,469	$3,352
2010	$5,328	$3,996
2011	$7,049	$5,287

HUSTLER SUPER Z 31/66

YEARS MFRD 2009-2011
ENGINE .... KAWASAKI
ENGINE HP 31
COOLING .... AIR
FUEL .... G
SPEEDS .... VARIABLE
TRANSMISSION .... HYDRO
STEERING................ ZERO
BLADE CLUTCH .... ELECTRIC
STANDARD DECK .... 66"
MSRP................. $12,039

HUSTLER

RETAIL PRICING

YEAR	HIGH	LOW
2009	$4,413	$3,310
2010	$5,258	$3,943
2011	$6,957	$5,218

HUSTLER Z

YEARS MFRD	2002-2010
ENGINE	KAWASAKI
CYLINDERS	2
CID	41.2
ENGINE HP	25
COOLING	AIR
FUEL	G
SPEEDS	VARIABLE
TRANSMISSION	HYDRO
STEERING	ZERO
STANDARD DECK	52"
WEIGHT	1,100 LBS.
MSRP	$10,689

OPTIONS

60" DECK
HONDA 24HP
KAWASAKI 23HP
KOHLER 27HP

RETAIL PRICING

YEAR	HIGH	LOW
2002	$4,179	$3,134
2003	$4,531	$3,398
2004	$4,824	$3,618
2005	$5,371	$4,029
2006	$5,714	$4,286
2007	$5,801	$4,351
2008	$5,810	$4,357
2009	$5,885	$4,414
2010	$6,676	$5,007

HUSTLER Z

YEARS MFRD	2010-2010
ENGINE	SHIBAURA
ENGINE HP	25
COOLING	AIR
FUEL	D
SPEEDS	VARIABLE
TRANSMISSION	HYDRO
STEERING	ZERO
BLADE CLUTCH	ELECTRIC
WEIGHT	1,648 LBS.

HUSTLER Z DSL

YEARS MFRD	2012-2020
ENGINE	SHIBAURA
CID	1131CC
ENGINE HP	25
COOLING	LIQUID
FUEL	D
SPEEDS	VARIABLE
TRANSMISSION	DUAL HYDRO
STEERING	ZERO
STANDARD DECK	60"
WEIGHT	1,656 LBS.
MSRP	$18,834

OPTIONS

60" DECK RD	$628
72" DECK	$343
72" RD	$914

RETAIL PRICING

YEAR	HIGH	LOW
2012	$8,071	$6,053
2013	$8,896	$6,672
2014	$9,820	$7,364
2015	$10,838	$8,129
2016	$11,962	$8,971
2017	$13,353	$10,015
2018	$14,691	$11,017
2019	$16,187	$12,140
2020	$17,648	$13,506

HUSTLER Z XR-7 24/60

YEARS MFRD	2009-2011
ENGINE	HONDA
ENGINE HP	24
COOLING	AIR
FUEL	G
SPEEDS	VARIABLE
TRANSMISSION	HYDRO
STEERING	ZERO
BLADE CLUTCH	ELECTRIC
STANDARD DECK	60"
WEIGHT	1,215 LBS.
MSRP	$10,249

RETAIL PRICING

YEAR	HIGH	LOW
2009	$3,757	$2,817
2010	$4,476	$3,357
2011	$5,923	$4,442

HUSTLER Z XR-7 25/60

YEARS MFRD	2009-2011
ENGINE	KAWASAKI
ENGINE HP	25
COOLING	AIR
FUEL	G
SPEEDS	VARIABLE
TRANSMISSION	HYDRO
STEERING	ZERO
BLADE CLUTCH	ELECTRIC
STANDARD DECK	60"
WEIGHT	1,215 LBS.
MSRP	$10,369

RETAIL PRICING

YEAR	HIGH	LOW
2009	$3,799	$2,849
2010	$4,533	$3,400
2011	$5,993	$4,494

HUSTLER Z XR-7 26/60

YEARS MFRD	2009-2011
ENGINE	KAWASAKI
ENGINE HP	26
COOLING	AIR
FUEL	G
SPEEDS	VARIABLE
TRANSMISSION	HYDRO
STEERING	ZERO
BLADE CLUTCH	ELECTRIC
STANDARD DECK	60"
WEIGHT	1,215 LBS.
MSRP	$11,029

RETAIL PRICING

YEAR	HIGH	LOW
2009	$4,046	$3,034
2010	$4,822	$3,617
2011	$6,372	$4,779

HUSTLER Z XR-7 27/60

YEARS MFRD	2009-2011
ENGINE	KOHLER
ENGINE HP	27
COOLING	AIR
FUEL	G
SPEEDS	VARIABLE
TRANSMISSION	HYDRO
STEERING	ZERO
BLADE CLUTCH	ELECTRIC
STANDARD DECK	60"
WEIGHT	1,215 LBS.
MSRP	$10,249

RETAIL PRICING

YEAR	HIGH	LOW
2009	$3,757	$2,817
2010	$4,476	$3,357
2011	$5,923	$4,442

HUSTLER Z XR-7 29/60

YEARS MFRD	2009-2011
ENGINE	KAWASAKI
ENGINE HP	29
COOLING	AIR
FUEL	G
SPEEDS	VARIABLE
TRANSMISSION	HYDRO
STEERING	ZERO
BLADE CLUTCH	ELECTRIC
STANDARD DECK	60"
MSRP	$10,899

RETAIL PRICING

YEAR	HIGH	LOW
2009	$3,997	$2,998
2010	$4,764	$3,573
2011	$6,297	$4,723

HUSTLER Z-4 23/48

YEARS MFRD	2009-2011
ENGINE	KAWASAKI
ENGINE HP	23
COOLING	AIR
FUEL	G
SPEEDS	VARIABLE
TRANSMISSION	HYDRO
STEERING	ZERO
BLADE CLUTCH	ELECTRIC
STANDARD DECK	48"
MSRP	$8,959

RETAIL PRICING

YEAR	HIGH	LOW
2009	$3,285	$2,463
2010	$3,917	$2,938
2011	$5,178	$3,883

HUSTLER Z-4 25/54

YEARS MFRD	2009-2011
ENGINE	KAWASAKI
ENGINE HP	25
COOLING	AIR
FUEL	G
SPEEDS	VARIABLE
TRANSMISSION	HYDRO
STEERING	ZERO
BLADE CLUTCH	ELECTRIC
STANDARD DECK	54"
MSRP	$9,079

RETAIL PRICING

YEAR	HIGH	LOW
2009	$3,328	$2,496
2010	$3,969	$2,976
2011	$5,248	$3,936

HUSTLER Z-4 25/61

YEARS MFRD	2009-2011
ENGINE	KAWASAKI
ENGINE HP	25
COOLING	AIR
FUEL	G
SPEEDS	VARIABLE
TRANSMISSION	HYDRO
STEERING	ZERO
BLADE CLUTCH	ELECTRIC
STANDARD DECK	61"
MSRP	$9,599

RETAIL PRICING

YEAR	HIGH	LOW
2009	$3,518	$2,638
2010	$4,194	$3,145
2011	$5,547	$4,160

KAWASAKI

YEARS MFRD	2009-2011
ENGINE	KAWASAKI
ENGINE HP	26
COOLING	AIR
FUEL	G
SPEEDS	VARIABLE
TRANSMISSION	HYDRO
STEERING	ZERO
BLADE CLUTCH	ELECTRIC
STANDARD DECK	66"
MSRP	$12,149

RETAIL PRICING

YEAR	HIGH	LOW
2009	$4,455	$3,341
2010	$5,307	$3,981
2011	$7,022	$5,266

MINI FASTRAK 36/42

YEARS MFRD 2006-2010
ENGINE .... HONDA OHV
CYLINDERS.................. 2
CID 32.3
ENGINE HP 16
COOLING .... AIR
FUEL .... G
SPEEDS .... VARIABLE
TRANSMISSION .... HYDRO
STEERING................ ZERO
WEIGHT .... 572 LBS.

OPTIONS

KOHLER 15HP
KOHLER 17HP

MINI FASTRAK Z 15/36

YEARS MFRD 2005-2007
SERIES............. MINI SERIES
ENGINE .... KOHLER
ENGINE HP.................. 15
COOLING .... AIR
FUEL .... G
SPEEDS .... VARIABLE
TRANSMISSION ..... DUAL HYDRO
STEERING................ ZERO
STANDARD DECK .... 36"
WEIGHT .... 730 LBS.
MSRP................. $3,999

OPTIONS

BAGGER
BLADE

RETAIL PRICING

YEAR	HIGH	LOW
2005	$1,045	$784
2006	$1,162	$872
2007	$1,290	$968

MINI FASTRAK Z 16/36

YEARS MFRD 2005-2007
SERIES............. MINI SERIES
ENGINE .... HONDA
ENGINE HP.................. 16
COOLING .... AIR
FUEL .... G
SPEEDS .... VARIABLE
TRANSMISSION .... HYDRO
STEERING................ ZERO
STANDARD DECK .... 36"
WEIGHT .... 730 LBS.
MSRP................. $4,499

OPTIONS

42" DECK
BAGGER
BLADE

RETAIL PRICING

YEAR	HIGH	LOW
2005	$1,180	$885
2006	$1,306	$980
2007	$1,452	$1,089

MINI FASTRAK Z 17/42

YEARS MFRD 2005-2007
SERIES............. MINI SERIES
ENGINE .... KOHLER
ENGINE HP.................. 17
COOLING .... AIR
FUEL .... G
SPEEDS .... VARIABLE
TRANSMISSION .... HYDRO
STEERING................ ZERO
STANDARD DECK .... 42"
WEIGHT .... 730 LBS.
MSRP................. $4,299

OPTIONS

BAGGER
BLADE

RETAIL PRICING

YEAR	HIGH	LOW
2005	$1,131	$848
2006	$1,249	$937
2007	$1,386	$1,040

RAPTOR15

YEARS MFRD 2015-2017
ENGINE .... KAWASAKI
ENGINE HP.................. 15
COOLING .... AIR
FUEL .... G
SPEEDS .... VARIABLE
TRANSMISSION ..... DUAL HYDRO
STEERING................ ZERO
STANDARD DECK .... 36"
MSRP................. $2,899

OPTIONS

2 BAG

RETAIL PRICING

YEAR	HIGH	LOW
2015	$1,860	$1,395
2016	$2,054	$1,541
2017	$2,258	$1,694

RAPTOR19

YEARS MFRD 2018-2019
ENGINE .... KOHLER
ENGINE HP.................. 19
COOLING .... AIR
FUEL .... G
TRANSMISSION ..... DUAL HYDRO
STEERING................ ZERO
STANDARD DECK .... 36"
MSRP................. $3,009

OPTIONS

2 BAG

RAPTOR21.5

YEARS MFRD 2014-2016
ENGINE .... KAWASAKI
ENGINE HP................ 21.5
COOLING .... AIR
FUEL .... G
SPEEDS .... VARIABLE
TRANSMISSION ..... DUAL HYDRO
STEERING................ ZERO
STANDARD DECK .... 42"
MSRP................. $2,899

RETAIL PRICING

YEAR	HIGH	LOW
2014	$1,856	$1,392
2015	$2,057	$1,543
2016	$2,327	$1,746

RAPTOR22

YEARS MFRD 2016-2019
ENGINE .... KOHLER
ENGINE HP.................. 22
COOLING .... AIR
FUEL .... G
SPEEDS .... VARIABLE
TRANSMISSION ..... DUAL HYDRO
STEERING................ ZERO
STANDARD DECK .... 42"
MSRP................. $3,009

OPTIONS

2 BAG

RETAIL PRICING

YEAR	HIGH	LOW
2016	$1,685	$1,264
2017	$1,860	$1,395
2018	$2,029	$1,522
2019	$2,218	$1,663

RAPTOR23

YEARS MFRD 2014-2015
ENGINE .... KAWASAKI
ENGINE HP.................. 23
COOLING .... AIR
FUEL .... G
SPEEDS .... VARIABLE
TRANSMISSION ..... DUAL HYDRO
STEERING................ ZERO
STANDARD DECK .... 52"
MSRP................. $3,099

RETAIL PRICING

YEAR	HIGH	LOW
2014	$1,915	$1,436
2015	$2,132	$1,599

RAPTOR24

YEARS MFRD 2016-2019
ENGINE .... KOHLER
ENGINE HP.................. 24
COOLING .... AIR
FUEL .... G
SPEEDS .... VARIABLE
TRANSMISSION ..... DUAL HYDRO
STEERING................ ZERO
STANDARD DECK .... 52"
MSRP................. $3,209

OPTIONS

2 BAG

RETAIL PRICING

YEAR	HIGH	LOW
2016	$1,801	$1,350
2017	$1,987	$1,491
2018	$2,195	$1,647
2019	$2,423	$1,817

RAPTOR LTD 42

YEARS MFRD 2019-2020
ENGINE .... KAWASAKI FR651
CID 726CC
ENGINE HP................ 21.5
COOLING .... AIR
FUEL .... G
TRANSMISSION ..... DUAL HYDRO
STEERING................ ZERO
STANDARD DECK .... 42"
WEIGHT .... 510 LBS.
MSRP................. $3,549

RAPTOR LTD 52

YEARS MFRD 2018-2020
ENGINE .... KAWASAKI FR691
CID 726CC
ENGINE HP.................. 23
COOLING .... AIR
FUEL .... G
TRANSMISSION ..... DUAL HYDRO
STEERING................ ZERO
STANDARD DECK .... 52"
WEIGHT .... 553 LBS.
MSRP................. $3,649

RAPTOR SD 21.5

YEARS MFRD 2019-2020
ENGINE .... KAWASAKI FR651
CID 726CC
ENGINE HP................ 21.5
COOLING .... AIR
FUEL .... G
TRANSMISSION ..... DUAL HYDRO
STEERING................ ZERO
STANDARD DECK .... 48"
WEIGHT .... 620 LBS.
MSRP................. $4,149

OPTIONS

36" DECK............... $-100
42" DECK............... $-100

RAPTOR SD 22

YEARS MFRD 2016-2019
ENGINE .... KOHLER
ENGINE HP.................. 22
COOLING .... AIR
FUEL .... G
SPEEDS .... VARIABLE
TRANSMISSION ..... DUAL HYDRO
STEERING................ ZERO
STANDARD DECK .... 36"
MSRP................. $4,009

OPTIONS

2 BAG
42" DECK

RETAIL PRICING

YEAR	HIGH	LOW
2016	$2,264	$1,698
2017	$2,500	$1,875

HUSTLER

2018............$2,763 .... $2,072
2019............$3,052 .... $2,289

RAPTOR SD 23

YEARS MFRD 2014-2020
ENGINE ....KAWASAKI FR691
CID 726CC
ENGINE HP 23
COOLING .... AIR
FUEL .... G
SPEEDS .... VARIABLE
TRANSMISSION ..... DUAL HYDRO
STEERING................. ZERO
STANDARD DECK .... 54"
MSRP.................. $4,249

OPTIONS

2 BAG $699

RETAIL PRICING

YEAR	HIGH	LOW
2014	$1,924	$1,443
2015	$2,125	$1,593
2016	$2,345	$1,758
2017	$2,589	$1,941
2018	$2,837	$2,128
2019	$3,116	$2,337
2020	$3,454	$2,616

RAPTOR SD 24

YEARS MFRD 2014-2020
ENGINE ....KAWASAKI FR730
CID 726CC
ENGINE HP 24
COOLING .... AIR
FUEL .... G
SPEEDS .... VARIABLE
TRANSMISSION ..... DUAL HYDRO
STEERING................. ZERO
STANDARD DECK .... 60"
MSRP.................. $4,649

OPTIONS

2 BAG $699

RETAIL PRICING

YEAR	HIGH	LOW
2014	$2,162	$1,621
2015	$2,387	$1,790
2016	$2,635	$1,977
2017	$2,907	$2,180
2018	$3,175	$2,381
2019	$3,464	$2,598
2020	$3,843	$2,855

RAPTOR SD 25

YEARS MFRD 2016-2019
ENGINE .... KOHLER
ENGINE HP 25
COOLING .... AIR
FUEL .... G
SPEEDS .... VARIABLE
TRANSMISSION ..... DUAL HYDRO
STEERING................. ZERO
STANDARD DECK .... 48"
MSRP.................. $4,109

OPTIONS

2 BAG
54" DECK

RETAIL PRICING

YEAR	HIGH	LOW
2016	$2,323	$1,743
2017	$2,564	$1,923
2018	$2,821	$2,116
2019	$3,101	$2,326

RAPTOR SD 26

YEARS MFRD 2016-2019
ENGINE .... KOHLER
ENGINE HP 26
COOLING .... AIR
FUEL .... G
SPEEDS .... VARIABLE
TRANSMISSION ..... DUAL HYDRO
STEERING................. ZERO
STANDARD DECK .... 60"
MSRP.................. $4,609

OPTIONS

2 BAG

RETAIL PRICING

YEAR	HIGH	LOW
2016	$2,613	$1,959
2017	$2,884	$2,163
2018	$3,156	$2,367
2019	$3,451	$2,588

RAPTOR SDX 48

YEARS MFRD 2019-2020
ENGINE ....KAWASAKI FR691
CID 726CC
ENGINE HP 23
COOLING .... AIR
FUEL .... G
TRANSMISSION ..... DUAL HYDRO
STEERING................. ZERO
BLADE CLUTCH .... ELECTRIC
STANDARD DECK .... 48"
WEIGHT .... 620 LBS.
MSRP.................. $5,149

OPTIONS

2 BAG $799

RAPTOR SDX 54

YEARS MFRD 2019-2020
ENGINE ....KAWASAKI FR691
CID 726CC
ENGINE HP 23
COOLING .... AIR
FUEL .... G
TRANSMISSION ..... DUAL HYDRO
STEERING................. ZERO
BLADE CLUTCH .... ELECTRIC
STANDARD DECK .... 54"
WEIGHT .... 666 LBS.
MSRP.................. $5,349

OPTIONS

2 BAG $799

RAPTOR SDX 60

YEARS MFRD 2019-2020
ENGINE ....KAWASAKI FR730
CID 726CC
ENGINE HP 24
COOLING .... AIR
FUEL .... G
TRANSMISSION ..... DUAL HYDRO
STEERING................. ZERO
BLADE CLUTCH .... ELECTRIC
STANDARD DECK .... 60"
WEIGHT .... 671 LBS.
MSRP.................. $5,549

OPTIONS

2 BAG $799

SD GXV630

YEARS MFRD 2012-2013
SERIES....... SD FASTRAK SERIES
ENGINE .... KAWASAKI
ENGINE HP 24
COOLING .... AIR
FUEL .... G
SPEEDS .... VARIABLE
TRANSMISSION ..... DUAL HYDRO
STEERING................. ZERO
STANDARD DECK .... 48"
MSRP.................. $7,249

OPTIONS

2 BAG
54" DECK
60" DECK
STRIPER

RETAIL PRICING

YEAR	HIGH	LOW
2012	$4,160	$3,120
2013	$4,620	$3,465

SDX 22

YEARS MFRD 2016-2017
SERIES......... FASTRAK SERIES
ENGINE .... KAWASAKI
ENGINE HP 22
COOLING .... AIR
FUEL .... G
SPEEDS .... VARIABLE
TRANSMISSION ..... DUAL HYDRO
STEERING................. ZERO
STANDARD DECK .... 48"
MSRP.................. $8,560

OPTIONS

2 BAG
54"DECK

RETAIL PRICING

YEAR	HIGH	LOW
2016	$6,065	$4,548
2017	$7,451	$5,588

SDX 22

YEARS MFRD 2019-2020
SERIES..... FASTRAK SDX SERIES
ENGINE ....KAWASAKI FX691
CID 726CC
ENGINE HP 22
COOLING .... AIR
FUEL .... G
SPEEDS .... VARIABLE
TRANSMISSION ..... DUAL HYDRO
STEERING................. ZERO
STANDARD DECK .... 48"
MSRP.................. $8,903

OPTIONS

2 BAG & KIT $1,974
54" DECK $228

SDX 23

YEARS MFRD 2018-2018
SERIES......... FASTRAK SERIES
ENGINE .... KOHLER
CID 747CC
ENGINE HP 23
COOLING .... AIR
FUEL .... G
TRANSMISSION ..... DUAL HYDRO
STEERING................. ZERO
STANDARD DECK .... 48"
WEIGHT .... 820 LBS.

OPTIONS

2 BAG
54" DECK

SDX 23.5

YEARS MFRD 2016-2017
SERIES......... FASTRAK SERIES
ENGINE .... KAWASAKI
ENGINE HP 23.5
COOLING .... AIR
FUEL .... G
SPEEDS .... VARIABLE
TRANSMISSION ..... DUAL HYDRO
STEERING................. ZERO
STANDARD DECK .... 54"
MSRP.................. $9,131

OPTIONS

2 BAG

RETAIL PRICING

YEAR	HIGH	LOW
2016	$6,469	$4,851
2017	$7,753	$5,814

SDX 23.5

YEARS MFRD 2019-2020
SERIES..... FASTRAK SDX SERIES
ENGINE ....KAWASAKI FX730
CID 726CC
ENGINE HP 23.5
COOLING .... AIR
FUEL .... G
SPEEDS .... VARIABLE
TRANSMISSION ..... DUAL HYDRO
STEERING................. ZERO
STANDARD DECK .... 60"
WEIGHT .... 916 LBS.
MSRP.................. $9,474

OPTIONS

2 BAG & KIT $1,974

SDX 25

YEARS MFRD 2018-2018
SERIES .... FASTRAK SERIES
ENGINE .... KOHLER
CID 747CC
ENGINE HP 25
COOLING .... AIR
FUEL .... G
TRANSMISSION ..... DUAL HYDRO
STEERING................ ZERO
STANDARD DECK .... 60"
WEIGHT .... 870 LBS.

OPTIONS

2 BAG

RETAIL PRICING

YEAR	HIGH	LOW
2016	$17,394	$13,045
2017	$19,199	$14,399
2018	$21,303	$15,978
2019	$23,327	$17,496
2020	$25,549	$19,698

SUPER 88

YEARS MFRD 2020-2020
ENGINE .... VANGUARD
CID 993
ENGINE HP 36
COOLING .... AIR
FUEL .... G
SPEEDS .... VARIABLE
TRANSMISSION ..... DUAL HYDRO
STEERING................ ZERO
BLADE CLUTCH .... ELECTRIC
STANDARD DECK .... 88"
WEIGHT .... 2,057 LBS.
MSRP................. $20,547

OPTIONS

37HP OIL GUARD $1,712

SUPER 104 35

YEARS MFRD 2016-2016
ENGINE .... KAWASAKI
ENGINE HP 35
COOLING .... AIR
FUEL .... G
SPEEDS .... VARIABLE
TRANSMISSION ..... DUAL HYDRO
STEERING................ ZERO
STANDARD DECK .... 104"
MSRP................. $29,000

OPTIONS

ANTI SCALP

RETAIL PRICING

YEAR	HIGH	LOW
2016	$24,317	$18,238

SUPER 104 36

YEARS MFRD 2016-2020
ENGINE .... VANGUARD
CID 993CC
ENGINE HP 36
COOLING .... AIR
FUEL .... G
SPEEDS .... VARIABLE
TRANSMISSION ..... DUAL HYDRO
STEERING................ ZERO
STANDARD DECK .... 104"
WEIGHT .... 2,500 LBS.
MSRP................. $30,936

OPTIONS

ANTI SCALP

SUPER 104 37

YEARS MFRD 2017-2020
ENGINE .... VANGUARD EFI
CID 993CC
ENGINE HP 37
COOLING .... AIR
FUEL .... G
SPEEDS .... VARIABLE
TRANSMISSION ..... DUAL HYDRO
STEERING................ ZERO
STANDARD DECK .... 104"
WEIGHT .... 2,500 LBS.
MSRP................. $32,648

OPTIONS

ANTI SCALP

RETAIL PRICING

YEAR	HIGH	LOW
2017	$19,710	$14,782
2018	$21,604	$16,203
2019	$23,573	$17,680
2020	$26,018	$19,851

SUPER MINI Z

YEARS MFRD 2004-2009
ENGINE .... KAWASAKI
CYLINDERS.................. 2
CID 41.2
ENGINE HP 19
COOLING .... AIR
FUEL .... G
SPEEDS .... VARIABLE
TRANSMISSION .... HYDRO
STEERING................ ZERO
BLADE CLUTCH .... ELECTRIC
WEIGHT .... 985 LBS.

OPTIONS

HONDA 24HP
KAWASAKI 23HP
KAWASAKI 25HP

SUPER Z31

YEARS MFRD 2012-2012
ENGINE .... KAWASAKI
ENGINE HP 31
COOLING .... AIR
FUEL .... G
SPEEDS .... VARIABLE
TRANSMISSION .... HYDRO
STEERING................ ZERO
STANDARD DECK .... 60"
MSRP................. $12,749

OPTIONS

72" DECK
RR DIS 60"
RR DIS 72"
SUS SEAT

RETAIL PRICING

YEAR	HIGH	LOW
2012	$7,587	$5,690

SUPER Z37

YEARS MFRD 2012-2012
ENGINE .... KAWASAKI
ENGINE HP 37
COOLING .... AIR
FUEL .... G
SPEEDS .... VARIABLE
TRANSMISSION ..... DUAL HYDRO
STEERING................ ZERO
STANDARD DECK .... 60"
MSRP................. $13,749

OPTIONS

66" DECK
72" DECK

RETAIL PRICING

YEAR	HIGH	LOW
2012	$8,196	$6,147

SUPER Z

YEARS MFRD 2002-2010
SERIES .... HUSTLER SERIES
ENGINE .... KAWASAKI
CYLINDERS.................. 2
CID 41.2
ENGINE HP 25
COOLING .... AIR
FUEL .... G
SPEEDS .... VARIABLE
TRANSMISSION .... HYDRO
STEERING................ ZERO
HYDRAULIC .... YES
STANDARD DECK .... 60"
WEIGHT .... 1,230 LBS.
MSRP................. $11,550

OPTIONS

72" DECK
HONDA 24HP
KAWASAKI 23HP
KOHLER 27HP

RETAIL PRICING

YEAR	HIGH	LOW
2002	$4,680	$3,510
2003	$5,075	$3,806
2004	$5,342	$4,006
2005	$6,178	$4,634
2006	$6,600	$4,950
2007	$6,675	$5,006
2008	$6,769	$5,077
2009	$6,780	$5,085
2010	$6,910	$5,183

AVG. AUCTION PRICING

LOW	HIGH	AVG
$1,117	$7,866	$4,578

SUPER Z 28 EFI

YEARS MFRD 2016-2016
ENGINE .... VANGUARD
ENGINE HP 28
COOLING .... AIR
FUEL .... G
SPEEDS .... VARIABLE
TRANSMISSION ..... DUAL HYDRO
STEERING................ ZERO
STANDARD DECK .... 60"
MSRP................. $13,557

OPTIONS

10 BU BAG
3 BAG & FAN
HYD LIFT
STRIPER

RETAIL PRICING

YEAR	HIGH	LOW
2016	$11,696	$8,772

SUPER Z DIESEL

YEARS MFRD 2005-2007
ENGINE .... CAT
CYLINDERS.................. 3
CID 91
ENGINE HP 34
FUEL .... D
SPEEDS .... VARIABLE
TRANSMISSION .... HYDRO
STEERING................ ZERO
WEIGHT .... 1,880 LBS.

X ONEI22

YEARS MFRD 2014-2015
SERIES .... HUSTLER X ONE SERIES
ENGINE .... KAWASAKI
ENGINE HP 22
COOLING .... AIR
FUEL .... G
SPEEDS .... VARIABLE
TRANSMISSION ..... DUAL HYDRO
STEERING................ ZERO
STANDARD DECK .... 52"
MSRP.................. $8,863

RETAIL PRICING

YEAR	HIGH	LOW
2014	$5,482	$4,112
2015	$6,353	$4,765

X ONEI23.5

YEARS MFRD 2014-2015
SERIES .... HUSTLER X ONE SERIES
ENGINE .... KAWASAKI
ENGINE HP 23.5
COOLING .... AIR
FUEL .... G
SPEEDS .... VARIABLE
TRANSMISSION ..... DUAL HYDRO
STEERING................ ZERO
STANDARD DECK .... 60"
MSRP.................. $9,106

RETAIL PRICING

YEAR	HIGH	LOW
2014	$5,634	$4,226
2015	$6,593	$4,945

HUSTLER

ZEON

YEARS MFRD 2012-2012
SERIES......... HUSTLER SERIES
ENGINE .... ELECTRIC
SPEEDS .... VARIABLE
TRANSMISSION .... GEAR
STEERING................ ZERO
STANDARD DECK .... 42"
MSRP................ $6,999

OPTIONS

2 BAG

RETAIL PRICING

YEAR	HIGH	LOW
2012	$4,226	$3,170

17

YEARS MFRD 2002-2002
SERIES........ SHORTCUT SERIES
ENGINE .... KAWASAKI
ENGINE HP.................. 17
FUEL .... G
TRANSMISSION .... HYDRO
STEERING............ STANDARD
STANDARD DECK .... 48"
MSRP................ $7,560

RETAIL PRICING

YEAR	HIGH	LOW
2002	$3,816	$2,862

17.5

YEARS MFRD 2012-2013
SERIES.... HUSTLER SPORT SERIES
ENGINE .... B&S
ENGINE HP................ 17.5
COOLING .... AIR
FUEL .... G
SPEEDS .... VARIABLE
TRANSMISSION .... HYDRO
STEERING................ ZERO
STANDARD DECK .... 42"
WEIGHT............... 537 LBS.
MSRP................ $3,199

OPTIONS

BAGGER

RETAIL PRICING

YEAR	HIGH	LOW
2012	$1,836	$1,377
2013	$2,039	$1,529

18

YEARS MFRD 2012-2012
SERIES.... HUSTLER SPORT SERIES
ENGINE .... KAWASAKI
ENGINE HP.................. 18
COOLING .... AIR
FUEL .... G
SPEEDS .... VARIABLE
TRANSMISSION ..... DUAL HYDRO
STEERING................ ZERO
STANDARD DECK .... 42"
MSRP................ $3,729

OPTIONS

BAGGER

RETAIL PRICING

YEAR	HIGH	LOW
2012	$2,222	$1,666

20

YEARS MFRD 2002-2002
SERIES........ SHORTCUT SERIES
ENGINE .... KOHLER
ENGINE HP.................. 20
FUEL .... G
TRANSMISSION .... HYDRO
STEERING............ STANDARD
STANDARD DECK .... 48"
MSRP................ $7,770

RETAIL PRICING

YEAR	HIGH	LOW
2002	$3,920	$2,940

20

YEARS MFRD 2012-2012
SERIES.... HUSTLER SPORT SERIES
ENGINE .... KAWASAKI
ENGINE HP.................. 20
COOLING .... AIR
FUEL .... G
SPEEDS .... VARIABLE
TRANSMISSION ..... DUAL HYDRO
STEERING................ ZERO
STANDARD DECK .... 48"
MSRP................ $4,099

OPTIONS

BAGGER

RETAIL PRICING

YEAR	HIGH	LOW
2012	$2,441	$1,831

21

YEARS MFRD 2012-2013
SERIES.... HUSTLER SPORT SERIES
ENGINE .... B&S
ENGINE HP.................. 21
COOLING .... AIR
FUEL .... G
SPEEDS .... VARUABLE
TRANSMISSION ..... DUAL HYDRO
STEERING................ ZERO
STANDARD DECK .... 48"
MSRP................ $3,699

RETAIL PRICING

YEAR	HIGH	LOW
2012	$2,122	$1,592
2013	$2,358	$1,768

22

YEARS MFRD 2012-2012
SERIES.... HUSTLER SPORT SERIES
ENGINE .... KAWASAKI
ENGINE HP.................. 22
COOLING .... AIR
FUEL .... G
SPEEDS .... VARIABLE
TRANSMISSION ..... DUAL HYDRO
STEERING................ ZERO
STANDARD DECK .... 54"
MSRP................ $4,449

OPTIONS

BAGGER

RETAIL PRICING

YEAR	HIGH	LOW
2012	$2,652	$1,989

23

YEARS MFRD 2002-2002
SERIES........ SHORTCUT SERIES
ENGINE .... KAWASAKI
ENGINE HP.................. 23
FUEL .... G
TRANSMISSION .... HYDRO
STEERING............ STANDARD
STANDARD DECK .... 54"
MSRP................ $8,935

RETAIL PRICING

YEAR	HIGH	LOW
2002	$4,509	$3,381

25

YEARS MFRD 2002-2002
SERIES........ SHORTCUT SERIES
ENGINE .... KOHLER
ENGINE HP.................. 25
FUEL .... G
TRANSMISSION .... HYDRO
STEERING............ STANDARD
STANDARD DECK .... 54"
MSRP................ $8,735

RETAIL PRICING

YEAR	HIGH	LOW
2002	$4,408	$3,306

26

YEARS MFRD 2012-2013
SERIES.... HUSTLER SPORT SERIES
ENGINE .... B&S
ENGINE HP.................. 26
COOLING .... AIR
FUEL .... G
SPEEDS .... VARIABLE
TRANSMISSION ..... DUAL HYDRO
STEERING................ ZERO
STANDARD DECK .... 54"
WEIGHT............... 640 LBS.
MSRP................ $4,349

OPTIONS

BAGGER

RETAIL PRICING

YEAR	HIGH	LOW
2012	$2,495	$1,871
2013	$2,771	$2,078

28

YEARS MFRD 2016-2017
SERIES.... HUSTLER X ONE SERIES
ENGINE .... VANGUARD
ENGINE HP.................. 28
COOLING .... AIR
FUEL .... G
SPEEDS .... VARIABLE
TRANSMISSION ..... DUAL HYDRO
STEERING................ ZERO
STANDARD DECK .... 54"
MSRP................ $12,149

OPTIONS

3 BAG
60"DECK
HYD LIFT
STRIPPER

RETAIL PRICING

YEAR	HIGH	LOW
2016	$8,608	$6,456
2017	$10,365	$7,774

29

YEARS MFRD 2013-2014
SERIES.... HUSTLER X-ONE SERIES
ENGINE .... KOHLER
ENGINE HP.................. 29
COOLING .... AIR
FUEL .... G
SPEEDS .... VARIABLE
TRANSMISSION .... HYDRO
STEERING................ ZERO
STANDARD DECK .... 60"
MSRP................ $11,349

OPTIONS

2 BAG & VAC

RETAIL PRICING

YEAR	HIGH	LOW
2013	$6,425	$4,819
2014	$7,755	$5,816

251

YEARS MFRD 1986-1996
SERIES......... HUSTLER SERIES
ENGINE .... KOHLER
PTO HP..................... 20
ENGINE HP.................. 22
FUEL .... G
SPEEDS .... VARIABLE
TRANSMISSION .... HYDRO
STEERING............ STANDARD

251K

YEARS MFRD 2001-2002
SERIES......... HUSTLER SERIES
ENGINE .... KOHLER
ENGINE HP.................. 22
COOLING .... AIR
FUEL .... G
SPEEDS .... VARIABLE
TRANSMISSION ..... DUAL HYDRO
STEERING................ ZERO
STANDARD DECK .... 51"
MSRP................ $10,685

OPTIONS

48" BLADE
BAGGER

RETAIL PRICING

YEAR	HIGH	LOW
2001	$2,428	$1,821
2002	$2,697	$2,023

260

YEARS MFRD 1993-1996
SERIES .... HUSTLER SERIES
ENGINE .... KOHLER
ENGINE HP 22
FUEL .... G
TRANSMISSION .... HYDRO
STEERING .... STANDARD

260K

YEARS MFRD 1990-2002
SERIES .... HUSTLER SERIES
ENGINE .... KUBOTA
ENGINE HP 22
COOLING .... AIR
FUEL .... G
SPEEDS .... VARIABLE
TRANSMISSION ..... DUAL HYDRO
STEERING .... STANDARD
STANDARD DECK .... 60"
MSRP $11,250

OPTIONS

48" BLADE
BAGGER

RETAIL PRICING

YEAR	HIGH	LOW
1994	$1,228	$921
1995	$1,365	$1,024
1996	$1,513	$1,135
1997	$1,684	$1,263
1998	$1,869	$1,401
1999	$2,076	$1,557
2000	$2,303	$1,727
2001	$2,561	$1,921
2002	$2,841	$2,131

275

YEARS MFRD 1988-1993
SERIES .... HUSTLER SERIES
ENGINE .... KOHLER
ENGINE HP 23
FUEL .... G
TRANSMISSION .... HYDRO
STEERING .... STANDARD
STANDARD DECK .... 72"
MSRP $11,990

OPTIONS

BAGGER

RETAIL PRICING

YEAR	HIGH	LOW
1988	$600	$450
1989	$662	$496
1990	$737	$553
1991	$815	$611
1992	$905	$679
1993	$1,006	$754

320

YEARS MFRD 1986-1993
SERIES .... HUSTLER SERIES
ENGINE .... KUBOTA
ENGINE HP 21.5
FUEL .... D
TRANSMISSION .... HYDRO
STEERING .... STANDARD
STANDARD DECK .... 72"
MSRP $13,995

OPTIONS

60" BLADE

RETAIL PRICING

YEAR	HIGH	LOW
1986	$567	$426
1987	$628	$471
1988	$698	$524
1989	$773	$580
1990	$862	$646
1991	$952	$714
1993	$1,175	$882

340

YEARS MFRD 1986-1993
SERIES .... HUSTLER SERIES
ENGINE .... KUBOTA
ENGINE HP 28.5
COOLING .... LIQUID
FUEL .... D
TRANSMISSION .... HYDRO
STEERING .... STANDARD
STANDARD DECK .... 72"
MSRP $15,250

OPTIONS

HI LIFT
RANGE WING

RETAIL PRICING

YEAR	HIGH	LOW
1986	$617	$463
1987	$687	$515
1988	$761	$571
1989	$843	$633
1990	$935	$701
1991	$1,039	$780
1992	$1,155	$866
1993	$1,278	$958

400

YEARS MFRD 1986-1993
SERIES .... HUSTLER SERIES
ENGINE .... FORD
ENGINE HP 44
COOLING .... LIQUID
FUEL .... G
SPEEDS .... VARIABLE
TRANSMISSION .... HYDRO
STEERING .... ZERO
STANDARD DECK .... 72"
MSRP $13,995

OPTIONS

HI LIFT
RANGE WING

RETAIL PRICING

YEAR	HIGH	LOW
1986	$567	$426
1987	$628	$471
1988	$698	$524
1989	$773	$580
1990	$862	$646
1991	$952	$714
1992	$1,060	$795
1993	$1,175	$882

640 6WD

YEARS MFRD 1989-1992
SERIES .... HUSTLER SERIES
ENGINE .... KUBOTA
ENGINE HP 28.5
COOLING .... LIQUID
FUEL .... D
SPEEDS .... VARIABLE
TRANSMISSION .... HYDRO
STEERING .... ZERO
STANDARD DECK .... 72"
MSRP $25,475

RETAIL PRICING

YEAR	HIGH	LOW
1989	$1,411	$1,058
1990	$1,564	$1,173
1991	$1,739	$1,304
1992	$1,927	$1,446

824 EFI

YEARS MFRD 2017-2017
SERIES .... SUPER Z SERIES
ENGINE .... KOHLER
ENGINE HP 29
COOLING .... AIR
FUEL .... G
SPEEDS .... VARIABLE
TRANSMISSION ..... DUAL HYDRO
STEERING .... ZERO
STANDARD DECK .... 54"
MSRP $13,697

OPTIONS

10 BU BAG
3 BAG & FAN
60" DECK
RR DISCHARGE

RETAIL PRICING

YEAR	HIGH	LOW
2017	$8,661	$6,496

824 EFI

YEARS MFRD 2018-2020
SERIES .... HUSTLER X-ONE SERIES
ENGINE .... KOHLER
CID 824CC
ENGINE HP 29
COOLING .... AIR
FUEL .... G
SPEEDS .... VARIABLE
TRANSMISSION ..... DUAL HYDRO
STEERING .... ZERO
STANDARD DECK .... 60"
WEIGHT .... 1,240 LBS.
MSRP $11,985

OPTIONS

3 BAG & KIT
52" DECK
72" DECK $228

824 EFI 33HP

YEARS MFRD 2017-2020
SERIES .... SUPER Z SERIES
ENGINE .... KOHLER
CID 824CC
ENGINE HP 33
COOLING .... AIR
FUEL .... G
SPEEDS .... VARIABLE
TRANSMISSION ..... DUAL HYDRO
STEERING .... ZERO
STANDARD DECK .... 60"
WEIGHT .... 1,516 LBS.
MSRP $14,839

OPTIONS

66" DECK
72" DECK
72" RD DECK

RETAIL PRICING

YEAR	HIGH	LOW
2017	$9,195	$6,896
2018	$10,048	$7,536
2019	$11,184	$8,387
2020	$12,263	$9,267

1500

YEARS MFRD 1998-2000
SERIES .... SHORTCUT SERIES
ENGINE .... KAWASAKI
ENGINE HP 14
FUEL .... G
SPEEDS 0-7
TRANSMISSION .... HYDRO
STEERING .... STANDARD
STANDARD DECK .... 48"
WEIGHT .... 750 LBS.
MSRP $6,309

OPTIONS

54" DECK
BAGGER
KAWASAKI 17HP
KOHLER 25HP

SERIAL NUMBERS

YEAR	BEGINNING NO.
1998	7125101-17
1998	7125232-22
1998	7125226-20
1999	99063411-22CE
1999	99063412-14
1999	99073709-23
1999	99073713-20
1999	99073717-23KAW
1999	99022314-22
1999	99022288-22
1999	99032396-25

RETAIL PRICING

YEAR	HIGH	LOW
1998	$1,207	$905
1999	$1,341	$1,006
2000	$1,489	$1,117

2500

YEARS MFRD 1994-2000
SERIES .... COMPACT SERIES
ENGINE .... KOHLER
ENGINE HP 25
COOLING .... AIR
FUEL .... G
TRANSMISSION .... HYDRO
STEERING .... STANDARD
STANDARD DECK .... 60"
WEIGHT .... 1,304 LBS.
MSRP $11,550

HUSTLER

OPTIONS
60" BLADE
72" DECK
BAGGER
ROPS

SERIAL NUMBERS
YEAR	BEGINNING NO.
1999	99053243

RETAIL PRICING
YEAR	HIGH	LOW
1994	$1,402	$1,051
1995	$1,555	$1,166
1996	$1,730	$1,297
1997	$1,920	$1,440
1998	$2,134	$1,600
1999	$2,371	$1,778
2000	$2,631	$1,973

2700
YEARS MFRD........1996-1996
SERIES.........COMPACT SERIES
ENGINE...............KOHLER
ENGINE HP.................25
FUEL......................G
SPEEDS..................0-8
TRANSMISSION ....HYDRO
STEERING............STANDARD
STANDARD DECK........... 60"
WEIGHT............1,300 LBS.
MSRP................. $9,600

RETAIL PRICING
YEAR	HIGH	LOW
1996	$3,711	$2,783

3200
YEARS MFRD........1996-2000
SERIES.....HUSTLER 3000 SERIES
ENGINE...............KUBOTA
ENGINE HP.................23
COOLING..............LIQUID
FUEL......................D
SPEEDS..................0-9
TRANSMISSION ....HYDRO
STEERING.................ZERO
STANDARD DECK........... 60"
WEIGHT............1,415 LBS.
MSRP................ $15,830

OPTIONS
72" DECK
BAGGER
SNOW THROWER

SERIAL NUMBERS
YEAR	BEGINNING NO.
1999	99032381-R
1999	99011708-Z

RETAIL PRICING
YEAR	HIGH	LOW
1996	$2,371	$1,778
1997	$2,635	$1,976
1998	$2,924	$2,193
1999	$3,248	$2,436
2000	$3,607	$2,705

3200Z
YEARS MFRD........2002-2004
SERIES............3000 SERIES
ENGINE...............KUBOTA
CYLINDERS..................3
CID....................54.86
ENGINE HP.................23
COOLING..............LIQUID
FUEL......................D
SPEEDS..................0-9
TRANSMISSION ....HYDRO
STEERING.................ZERO
BLADE CLUTCH........ELECTRIC
HYDRAULIC................YES
PTO......................YES
STANDARD DECK........... 72"
WEIGHT............1,415 LBS.
MSRP................ $13,556

RETAIL PRICING
YEAR	HIGH	LOW
2002	$6,842	$5,132

3300
YEARS MFRD........1996-2000
SERIES.........HUSTLER SERIES
ENGINE...............KUBOTA
ENGINE HP.................25
COOLING..................AIR
FUEL......................D
SPEEDS..............VARIABLE
TRANSMISSION ....HYDRO
STEERING............STANDARD
STANDARD DECK........... 60"
MSRP................ $13,105

RETAIL PRICING
YEAR	HIGH	LOW
1996	$2,961	$2,221
1997	$3,289	$2,466
1998	$3,653	$2,740
1999	$4,055	$3,041
2000	$4,504	$3,378

3400
YEARS MFRD........1996-2000
SERIES.....HUSTLER 3000 SERIES
ENGINE........KUBOTA D1105B
CYLINDERS..................3
CID....................68.58
ENGINE HP.................28
COOLING..............LIQUID
FUEL......................D
SPEEDS..............VARIABLE
TRANSMISSION .....DUAL HYDRO
STEERING.................ZERO
BLADE CLUTCH........ELECTRIC
HYDRAULIC................YES
PTO......................YES
STANDARD DECK........... 72"
WEIGHT............1,500 LBS.
MSRP................ $17,585

OPTIONS
AWD
BAGGER
SNOW THROWER

SERIAL NUMBERS
YEAR	BEGINNING NO.
1999	99042914-AWD
1999	99011640-Z

RETAIL PRICING
YEAR	HIGH	LOW
1996	$2,540	$1,905
1997	$2,818	$2,113
1998	$3,130	$2,348
1999	$3,474	$2,606
2000	$3,859	$2,894

3400ZH
YEARS MFRD........2001-2004
SERIES............3000 SERIES
ENGINE...............KUBOTA
ENGINE HP.................28
COOLING..............LIQUID
FUEL......................D
SPEEDS..............VARIABLE
TRANSMISSION ....HYDRO
STEERING............STANDARD
STANDARD DECK........... 60"
MSRP................ $18,345

OPTIONS
72" DECK
HD SEAT
ROPS/CAB
SUS SEAT

RETAIL PRICING
YEAR	HIGH	LOW
2001	$4,129	$3,097
2002	$4,580	$3,435
2003	$5,080	$3,810
2004	$5,639	$4,230

3500
YEARS MFRD........2010-2010
ENGINE.........SHIBAURA N843
CYLINDERS..................3
CID.....................91.3
ENGINE HP.................30
COOLING..............LIQUID
FUEL......................D
SPEEDS..............VARIABLE
TRANSMISSION ....HYDRO
STEERING.................ZERO
WEIGHT............1,653 LBS.

3700
YEARS MFRD........2012-2016
ENGINE........SHIBAURA N843L
CYLINDERS..................3
CID....................101.4
ENGINE HP.................36
COOLING..............LIQUID
FUEL......................D
SPEEDS..............VARIABLE
TRANSMISSION .....DUAL HYDRO
STEERING.................ZERO
BLADE CLUTCH........ELECTRIC
STANDARD DECK........... 72"
WEIGHT............1,653 LBS.
MSRP................ $27,424

OPTIONS
60"DECK
84" DECK
BAG

RETAIL PRICING
YEAR	HIGH	LOW
2012	$13,860	$10,395
2013	$15,332	$11,499
2014	$16,960	$12,720
2015	$18,761	$14,071
2016	$23,015	$17,261

4100
YEARS MFRD........1992-1995
SERIES.........HUSTLER SERIES
ENGINE...............KOHLER
ENGINE HP.................23
COOLING..................AIR
FUEL......................G
SPEEDS..............VARIABLE
TRANSMISSION ....HYDRO
STEERING.................ZERO
STANDARD DECK........... 60"
WEIGHT............1,500 LBS.
MSRP................ $13,470

OPTIONS
54" SNOW THROWER
60" BLADE
BAGGER

RETAIL PRICING
YEAR	HIGH	LOW
1992	$1,071	$803
1993	$1,192	$894
1994	$1,320	$990
1995	$1,465	$1,098

4200
YEARS MFRD........1992-1996
SERIES.........HUSTLER SERIES
ENGINE...............KUBOTA
ENGINE HP...............21.5
COOLING..............LIQUID
FUEL......................D
SPEEDS..............VARIABLE
TRANSMISSION ....HYDRO
STEERING............STANDARD
STANDARD DECK........... 72"
WEIGHT............1,900 LBS.
MSRP................ $16,275

OPTIONS
54" SNOW THROWER
BAGGER
ROPS

RETAIL PRICING
YEAR	HIGH	LOW
1992	$1,365	$1,024
1993	$1,513	$1,135
1994	$1,679	$1,259
1995	$1,862	$1,396
1996	$2,065	$1,548

4300

YEARS MFRD 1992-1997
SERIES......... HUSTLER SERIES
ENGINE .... FORD
ENGINE HP 45
COOLING .... LIQUID
FUEL .... G
SPEEDS .... VARIABLE
TRANSMISSION ..... DUAL HYDRO
STEERING............ STANDARD
STANDARD DECK .... 72"
WEIGHT .... 1,900 LBS.
MSRP................ $17,679

OPTIONS

60" BLADE
BAGGER
ROPS

RETAIL PRICING

YEAR	HIGH	LOW
1992	$1,535	$1,151
1993	$1,704	$1,278
1994	$2,346	$1,759
1995	$2,601	$1,951
1996	$2,448	$1,836
1997	$2,714	$2,036

4400

YEARS MFRD 1992-1995
SERIES......... HUSTLER SERIES
ENGINE .... KUBOTA
ENGINE HP 28.5
COOLING .... LIQUID
FUEL .... D
SPEEDS .... VARIABLE
TRANSMISSION ..... DUAL HYDRO
STEERING............ STANDARD
STANDARD DECK .... 72"
WEIGHT .... 1,900 LBS.
MSRP................ $17,820

OPTIONS

72" BLADE
BAGGER

RETAIL PRICING

YEAR	HIGH	LOW
1992	$1,903	$1,427
1993	$2,114	$1,586
1994	$2,346	$1,759
1995	$2,601	$1,951

4420

YEARS MFRD 1996-1997
SERIES......... HUSTLER SERIES
ENGINE .... KUBOTA
ENGINE HP 28.5
COOLING .... LIQUID
FUEL .... D
SPEEDS 0-10
TRANSMISSION .... HYDRO
STEERING............ STANDARD
STANDARD DECK .... 72"
WEIGHT .... 1,900 LBS.
MSRP................ $19,132

OPTIONS

72" BLADE
BAGGER

4500

YEARS MFRD 1992-2000
SERIES............ 4000 SERIES
ENGINE .... FORD VSG413 IND
CYLINDERS.................. 4
CID 76
ENGINE HP 54
COOLING .... LIQUID
FUEL .... G
SPEEDS .... VARIABLE
TRANSMISSION ..... DUAL HYDRO
STEERING................ ZERO
BLADE CLUTCH .... ELECTRIC
HYDRAULIC .... YES
PTO .... YES
STANDARD DECK .... 72"
WEIGHT .... 1,510 LBS.
MSRP................ $20,510

OPTIONS

BAGGER
SNOW THROWER

SERIAL NUMBERS

YEAR	BEGINNING NO.
1999	99052963

RETAIL PRICING

YEAR	HIGH	LOW
1992	$1,787	$1,341
1993	$1,981	$1,486
1994	$2,196	$1,647
1995	$2,436	$1,827
1996	$2,706	$2,029
1997	$3,000	$2,250
1998	$3,330	$2,498
1999	$3,694	$2,770
2000	$4,096	$3,072

4600

YEARS MFRD 1996-2007
SERIES............ 4000 SERIES
ENGINE .... KUBOTA V1505
CYLINDERS.................. 4
CID 91.4
ENGINE HP 38
COOLING .... LIQUID
FUEL .... D
SPEEDS .... VARIABLE
TRANSMISSION .... HYDRO
STEERING................ ZERO
BLADE CLUTCH .... ELECTRIC
HYDRAULIC .... YES
PTO .... YES
STANDARD DECK .... 72"
WEIGHT .... 1,520 LBS.
MSRP................ $27,551

OPTIONS

ENCLOSED CAB
ROPS
SUS SEAT

SERIAL NUMBERS

YEAR	BEGINNING NO.
1999	99053206

RETAIL PRICING

YEAR	HIGH	LOW
1999	$4,687	$3,515
2000	$5,201	$3,901
2001	$5,765	$4,324
2002	$6,399	$4,799
2003	$7,098	$5,323
2004	$7,872	$5,904
2005	$8,733	$6,550
2006	$9,688	$7,266
2007	$10,748	$8,061

6400 HILLSIDER

YEARS MFRD 1996-2000
SERIES......... HUSTLER SERIES
ENGINE .... KUBOTA V15505
CYLINDERS.................. 4
CID 91.44
ENGINE HP 38
COOLING .... LIQUID
FUEL .... D
SPEEDS .... VARIABLE
TRANSMISSION .... HYDRO
STEERING................ ZERO
BLADE CLUTCH .... ELECTRIC
HYDRAULIC .... YES
PTO .... YES
STANDARD DECK .... 72"
WEIGHT .... 2,175 LBS.
MSRP................ $37,390

SERIAL NUMBERS

YEAR	BEGINNING NO.
1999	99063516

RETAIL PRICING

YEAR	HIGH	LOW
1996	$5,034	$3,776
1997	$5,585	$4,188
1998	$6,198	$4,648
1999	$6,872	$5,154
2000	$7,624	$5,718

NOTES

IMT

536 ORCHARD VINEYARD

YEARS MFRD 1989-2006
ENGINE .... IMR M33T
CID 152
PTO HP 35
ENGINE HP 39.5
FUEL .... D
SPEEDS 6/2
TRANSMISSION .... GEAR
STEERING .... STANDARD
PTO .... YES
DRIVE TYPE 2WD
ROPS/CAB .... ROPS
WEIGHT .... 3,461 LBS.
MSRP $7,200

OPTIONS

4WD

RETAIL PRICING

YEAR	HIGH	LOW
1989	$1,926	$1,444
1990	$2,027	$1,520

539

YEARS MFRD 1985-2006
ENGINE .... IMR M33/T
CYLINDERS 3
CID 152
PTO HP 35
ENGINE HP 39
FUEL .... D
SPEEDS 6/2
WEIGHT .... 3,174 LBS.

OPTIONS

4WD

539 POWER STEERING

YEARS MFRD 1989-2001
ENGINE .... IMR M33/T
CYLINDERS 3
CID 152
PTO HP 35
ENGINE HP 39
FUEL .... D
SPEEDS 6/2
TRANSMISSION .... GEAR
STEERING .... STANDARD
PTO .... YES
WEIGHT .... 3,290 LBS.

542

YEARS MFRD 1986-2006
ENGINE .... IMR M33/T
CYLINDERS 3
CID 152
PTO HP 35.8
ENGINE HP 42
FUEL .... D
SPEEDS 6/2
TRANSMISSION .... GEAR
STEERING .... STANDARD
HYDRAULIC .... YES
PTO .... YES
WEIGHT .... 3,174 LBS.

OPTIONS

4WD

546 ORCHARD/ VINEYARD

YEARS MFRD 2001-2006
ENGINE .... IMT M33T
ENGINE HP 46.2
SPEEDS 10/2
TRANSMISSION .... GEAR
PTO .... YES
DRIVE TYPE 2WD
ROPS/CAB .... ROPS
WEIGHT .... 3,792 LBS.

OPTIONS

4WD

549

YEARS MFRD 2001-2006
ENGINE DM33T
ENGINE HP 46.2
SPEEDS 10/2
TRANSMISSION .... GEAR
STEERING .... STANDARD
HYDRAULIC .... YES
PTO .... YES
DRIVE TYPE 2WD
ROPS/CAB .... ROPS
WEIGHT .... 5,247 LBS.

OPTIONS

4WD

549DV

YEARS MFRD 1990-1993
ENGINE .... IMR D33/T
CYLINDERS 3
CID 152
PTO HP 40
ENGINE HP 44
FUEL .... D
SPEEDS 10/2
WEIGHT .... 4,950 LBS.

INGERSOLL-CASE

6018

YEARS MFRD 1989-2001
ENGINE .... ONAN
CYLINDERS 2
CID 48
PTO HP 18
FUEL .... G
SPEEDS .... VARIABLE
TRANSMISSION .... HYDRO
STEERING .... STANDARD
MSRP $11,049

RETAIL PRICING

YEAR	HIGH	LOW
1989	$2,818	$2,114
1990	$2,859	$2,144
1991	$3,067	$2,301
1992	$3,192	$2,394
1999	$5,059	$3,794
2000	$5,301	$3,976
2001	$5,530	$4,148

6018BH

YEARS MFRD 1997-2001
ENGINE .... ONAN
CYLINDERS 2
CID 48
PTO HP 18
FUEL .... G
SPEEDS .... VARIABLE
TRANSMISSION .... HYDRO
STEERING .... STANDARD
MSRP $20,750

RETAIL PRICING

YEAR	HIGH	LOW
1997	$7,394	$5,546
1998	$8,903	$6,677
1999	$9,496	$7,122
2000	$9,955	$7,466
2001	$10,382	$7,787

6018L

YEARS MFRD 1993-1996
ENGINE .... ONAN
CYLINDERS 2
CID 48
PTO HP 18
FUEL .... G
SPEEDS .... VARIABLE
TRANSMISSION .... HYDRO
STEERING .... STANDARD
MSRP $10,499

RETAIL PRICING

YEAR	HIGH	LOW
1993	$3,395	$2,546
1994	$3,626	$2,720
1995	$3,800	$2,850
1996	$4,136	$3,102

6018LBH

YEARS MFRD 1994-1996
ENGINE .... ONAN
CYLINDERS 2
CID 48
PTO HP 18
FUEL .... G
SPEEDS .... VARIABLE
TRANSMISSION .... HYDRO
STEERING .... STANDARD
MSRP $17,599

RETAIL PRICING

YEAR	HIGH	LOW
1994	$6,077	$4,558
1995	$6,462	$4,847
1996	$6,933	$5,199

6020

YEARS MFRD 1999-2001
ENGINE .... HONDA
CYLINDERS 2
CID 38
PTO HP 20
FUEL .... G
SPEEDS .... VARIABLE
TRANSMISSION .... HYDRO
STEERING .... STANDARD
MSRP $11,799

RETAIL PRICING

YEAR	HIGH	LOW
1999	$5,402	$4,051
2000	$5,660	$4,245
2001	$5,903	$4,427

6020BH

YEARS MFRD 1998-2001
ENGINE .... HONDA
CYLINDERS 2
CID 39
PTO HP 20
FUEL .... G
SPEEDS .... VARIABLE
TRANSMISSION .... HYDRO
STEERING .... STANDARD
MSRP $21,500

RETAIL PRICING

YEAR	HIGH	LOW
1998	$9,225	$6,919
1999	$9,841	$7,381
2000	$10,315	$7,736
2001	$10,757	$8,068

6020L

YEARS MFRD 2002-2002
ENGINE .... KOHLER
CYLINDERS 2
CID 38
PTO HP 20
FUEL .... G
SPEEDS .... VARIABLE
TRANSMISSION .... HYDRO
STEERING .... STANDARD
MSRP $11,910

INGERSOLL-CASE

RETAIL PRICING

YEAR	HIGH	LOW
2002	$6,125	$4,594

6020LBH

YEARS MFRD 2002-2002
ENGINE . . . . KOHLER
CYLINDERS. 2
CID 38
PTO HP 20
FUEL . . . . G
SPEEDS . . . . VARIABLE
TRANSMISSION . . . . HYDRO
STEERING. . . . . STANDARD
MSRP. $20,500

RETAIL PRICING

YEAR	HIGH	LOW
2002	$10,542	$7,906

7020L

YEARS MFRD 2002-2002
ENGINE . . . . KOHLER
CYLINDERS. 2
CID 38
PTO HP 20
FUEL . . . . G
SPEEDS . . . . VARIABLE
TRANSMISSION . . . . HYDRO
STEERING. . . . . STANDARD
MSRP. $14,999

RETAIL PRICING

YEAR	HIGH	LOW
2002	$7,713	$5,784

7020LBH

YEARS MFRD 2002-2002
ENGINE . . . . KOHLER
CYLINDERS. 2
CID 38
PTO HP 20
FUEL . . . . G
SPEEDS . . . . VARIABLE
TRANSMISSION . . . . HYDRO
STEERING. . . . . STANDARD
MSRP. $23,500

RETAIL PRICING

YEAR	HIGH	LOW
2002	$12,085	$9,064

INTERNATIONAL HARVESTER

INTERNATIONAL 140

YEARS MFRD 1958-1981
ENGINE . . . C-123 VERTICAL I HEAD
CID 122.7
PTO HP 23
ENGINE HP 21
COOLING . . . . LIQUID
FUEL . . . . G
SPEEDS 4/1
TRANSMISSION . . . . GEAR
STEERING. . . . . STANDARD
HYDRAULIC . . . . YES
PTO . . . . YES
WEIGHT . . . . 3,031 LBS.

SERIAL NUMBERS

YEAR	BEGINNING NO.
1958	501
1959	2011
1960	8082
1961	11168
1962	16637
1963	21181
1964	25387
1965	28408
1966	31285
1967	34818
1968	37352
1969	39906
1970	42300
1971	44424
1972	46605
1973	48507
1974	50720
1975	54273
1976	57773
1977	60839
1978	63111
1979	64544
1980	65976
1981	67411

AVG. AUCTION PRICING

LOW	HIGH	AVG
$2,413	$3,575	$2,950

INTERNATIONAL CUB 154 LO-BOY

YEARS MFRD 1968-1974
ENGINE . . . . C-60 L HEAD
CYLINDERS. 4
ENGINE HP 15
COOLING . . . . LIQUID
FUEL . . . . G
SPEEDS 3/1
TRANSMISSION . . . . GEAR
STEERING. . . . . STANDARD
PTO . . . . YES

SERIAL NUMBERS

YEAR	BEGINNING NO.
1968	7505
1969	8273
1970	15502
1971	20332
1972	23343
1973	27538
1974	31766

INTERNATIONAL CUB 184 LO-BOY

YEARS MFRD 1977-1980
ENGINE . . . . C-60 L HEAD
CYLINDERS. 4
ENGINE HP 18.5
COOLING . . . . LIQUID
FUEL . . . . G
SPEEDS 3/1
TRANSMISSION . . . . GEAR
STEERING. . . . . STANDARD
PTO . . . . YES
MSRP. $4,185

SERIAL NUMBERS

YEAR	BEGINNING NO.
1977	43802
1978	46163
1979	48030

RETAIL PRICING

YEAR	HIGH	LOW
1977	$772	$579
1978	$813	$610
1979	$858	$643
1980	$906	$679

INTERNATIONAL CUB 185 LO-BOY

YEARS MFRD 1974-1976
ENGINE . . . . C-60 LHEAD
CYLINDERS. 4
ENGINE HP 18.5
COOLING . . . . LIQUID
FUEL . . . . G
SPEEDS 3/1
TRANSMISSION . . . . GEAR
STEERING. . . . . STANDARD
PTO . . . . YES

SERIAL NUMBERS

YEAR	BEGINNING NO.
1974	37001
1975	37316
1976	41241

ISEKI

SF200

YEARS MFRD 2005-2008
SERIES. . . . . SF SERIES
ENGINE . . . . ISEKI
CYLINDERS. 3
ENGINE HP 21
COOLING . . . . LIQUID
FUEL . . . . D
SPEEDS . . . . VARIABLE
TRANSMISSION . . . . HYDRO
STEERING. . . . . ZERO
WEIGHT . . . . 1,080 LBS.

SF230

YEARS MFRD 2005-2008
SERIES. . . . . SF SERIES
ENGINE . . . . ISEKI
CYLINDERS. 3
ENGINE HP 24
COOLING . . . . LIQUID
FUEL . . . . D
SPEEDS . . . . VARIABLE
TRANSMISSION . . . . HYDRO
STEERING. . . . . ZERO
WEIGHT . . . . 1,155 LBS.

SF300

YEARS MFRD 2005-2007
SERIES. . . . . SF SERIES
ENGINE . . . . ISEKI
CYLINDERS. 3
ENGINE HP 28
COOLING . . . . LIQUID
FUEL . . . . D
SPEEDS . . . . VARIABLE
TRANSMISSION . . . . HYDRO
STEERING. . . . . ZERO
WEIGHT . . . . 441 LBS.

SF310

YEARS MFRD 2008-2013
SERIES. . . . . SF300 SERIES
ENGINE E3CD-VG03
CID 1498CC
ENGINE HP 30
COOLING . . . . LIQUID
FUEL . . . . D
SPEEDS . . . . VARIABLE
TRANSMISSION . . . . HYDRO
WEIGHT . . . . 440 LBS.

SF330

YEARS MFRD 2005-2007
SERIES. . . . . SF SERIES
ENGINE . . . . ISEKI
CYLINDERS. 3
ENGINE HP 31
COOLING . . . . LIQUID
FUEL . . . . D
SPEEDS . . . . VARIABLE
TRANSMISSION . . . . HYDRO
STEERING. . . . . ZERO
WEIGHT . . . . 507 LBS.

SF370

YEARS MFRD 2008-2013
SERIES. . . . . SF300 SERIES
ENGINE . . . . E3CD-VTG TURBO
CID 1498CC
ENGINE HP 36
COOLING . . . . LIQUID
FUEL . . . . D
SPEEDS . . . . VARIABLE
TRANSMISSION . . . . HYDRO
STEERING. . . . . STANDARD
WEIGHT . . . . 507 LBS.

SG153H
YEARS MFRD 2005-2007
SERIES. . . . . SG SERIES
ENGINE . . . . ISEKI
CYLINDERS. 3
ENGINE HP 15
COOLING . . . . LIQUID
FUEL . . . . D
SPEEDS . . . . VARIABLE
TRANSMISSION . . . . HYDRO
STEERING. . . . . STANDARD
WEIGHT . . . . 772 LBS.

SG173H
YEARS MFRD 2005-2007
SERIES. . . . . SG SERIES
ENGINE . . . . ISEKI
CYLINDERS. 3
ENGINE HP 17
COOLING . . . . LIQUID
FUEL . . . . D
SPEEDS . . . . VARIABLE
TRANSMISSION . . . . HYDRO
STEERING. . . . . STANDARD
WEIGHT . . . . 870 LBS.

SG173HU
YEARS MFRD 2005-2007
SERIES. . . . . SG SERIES
ENGINE . . . . ISEKI
CYLINDERS. 3
ENGINE HP 17
COOLING . . . . LIQUID
FUEL . . . . D
SPEEDS . . . . VARIABLE
TRANSMISSION . . . . HYDRO
STEERING. . . . . STANDARD
WEIGHT . . . . 870 LBS.

SXG15
YEARS MFRD 2010-2013
ENGINE . . . . ISEKI
CYLINDERS. 2
CID 688CC
ENGINE HP 13.6
COOLING . . . . AIR
FUEL . . . . D
SPEEDS . . . . VARIABLE
TRANSMISSION . . . . HYDRO
STEERING. . . . . STANDARD
WEIGHT . . . . 738 LBS.

SXG19
YEARS MFRD 2005-2008
SERIES. . . . . SXG SERIES
ENGINE . . . . ISEKI
CYLINDERS. 3
ENGINE HP 19.6
COOLING . . . . LIQUID
FUEL . . . . D
SPEEDS . . . . VARIABLE
TRANSMISSION . . . . HYDRO
STEERING. . . . . STANDARD
WEIGHT . . . . 1,124 LBS.

SXG22
YEARS MFRD 2005-2013
SERIES. . . . . SXG SERIES
ENGINE . . . . ISEKI
CYLINDERS. 3
ENGINE HP 21.6
COOLING . . . . LIQUID
FUEL . . . . D
SPEEDS . . . . VARIABLE
TRANSMISSION . . . . HYDRO
STEERING. . . . . STANDARD
WEIGHT . . . . 1,135 LBS.

SZ330
YEARS MFRD 2007-2009
ENGINE . . . . ISEKI E3CD
CYLINDERS. 3
COOLING . . . . LIQUID
FUEL . . . . D
SPEEDS . . . . VARIABLE
TRANSMISSION . . . . HYDRO
STEERING. . . . . ZERO

TF327
YEARS MFRD 2005-2008
SERIES. . . . . TF SERIES
ENGINE . . . . ISEKI
CYLINDERS. 3
ENGINE HP 28
COOLING . . . . LIQUID
FUEL . . . . D
SPEEDS 9/3
TRANSMISSION . . . . GEAR
STEERING. . . . . STANDARD
HITCH . . . . CAT. I
HYDRAULIC . . . . YES
PTO . . . . YES
WEIGHT . . . . 1,973 LBS.

TG5330
YEARS MFRD 2005-2013
SERIES. . . . . TG SERIES
ENGINE . . . . ISEKI
CYLINDERS. 3
ENGINE HP 32
COOLING . . . . LIQUID
FUEL . . . . D
SPEEDS . . . . VARIABLE
TRANSMISSION . . . . HYDRO
STEERING. . . . . STANDARD
HYDRAULIC . . . . YES
PTO . . . . YES
WEIGHT . . . . 2,877 LBS.

TG5390
YEARS MFRD 2005-2013
SERIES. . . . . TG SERIES
ENGINE . . . . ISEKI
CYLINDERS. 3
ENGINE HP 38
COOLING . . . . LIQUID
FUEL . . . . D
SPEEDS . . . . VARIABLE
TRANSMISSION . . . . HYDRO
STEERING. . . . . STANDARD
HYDRAULIC . . . . YES
PTO . . . . YES
WEIGHT . . . . 2,888 LBS.

TG5470
YEARS MFRD 2005-2013
SERIES. . . . . TG SERIES
ENGINE . . . . ISEKI
CYLINDERS. 4
ENGINE HP 46
COOLING . . . . LIQUID
FUEL . . . . D
SPEEDS . . . . VARIABLE
TRANSMISSION . . . . HYDRO
STEERING. . . . . STANDARD
HYDRAULIC . . . . YES
PTO . . . . YES
WEIGHT . . . . 3,494 LBS.

TH4260
YEARS MFRD 2005-2008
SERIES. . . . . TH SERIES
ENGINE . . . . ISEKI
CYLINDERS. 3
ENGINE HP 24
COOLING . . . . LIQUID
FUEL . . . . D
SPEEDS 9/3
TRANSMISSION . . . . GEAR
STEERING. . . . . STANDARD
HITCH . . . . CAT. I
HYDRAULIC . . . . YES
PTO . . . . YES
WEIGHT . . . . 2,105 LBS.

OPTIONS

HYDRO

TH4290
YEARS MFRD 2005-2008
SERIES. . . . . TH SERIES
ENGINE . . . . ISEKI
CYLINDERS. 3
ENGINE HP 28
COOLING . . . . LIQUID
FUEL . . . . D
SPEEDS 9/3
TRANSMISSION . . . . GEAR
STEERING. . . . . STANDARD
HYDRAULIC . . . . YES
PTO . . . . YES
WEIGHT . . . . 2,127 LBS.

OPTIONS

HYDRO

TH4295
YEARS MFRD 2012-2013
ENGINE . . . . ISEKI
CYLINDERS. 3
CID 1498CC
ENGINE HP 27.6
COOLING . . . . LIQUID
FUEL . . . . D
SPEEDS . . . . VARIABLE
TRANSMISSION . . . . HYDRO
STEERING. . . . . STANDARD
HYDRAULIC . . . . YES
PTO . . . . YES
WEIGHT . . . . 2,579 LBS.

TH4330
YEARS MFRD 2007-2012
SERIES. . . . . TH SERIES
ENGINE . . . . ISEKI
CYLINDERS. 3
ENGINE HP 33
COOLING . . . . LIQUID
FUEL . . . . D
SPEEDS 9/3
TRANSMISSION . . . . GEAR
STEERING. . . . . STANDARD
BLADE CLUTCH . . . . ELECTRIC
HYDRAULIC . . . . YES
PTO . . . . YES

TH4335
YEARS MFRD 2012-2013
ENGINE . . . . ISEKI
CYLINDERS. 3
CID 1498CC
ENGINE HP 31.5
COOLING . . . . LIQUID
FUEL . . . . D
SPEEDS . . . . VARIABLE
TRANSMISSION . . . . HYDRO
STEERING. . . . . STANDARD
HITCH . . . . CAT. I
WEIGHT . . . . 2,590 LBS.

TH4365
YEARS MFRD 2012-2013
ENGINE . . . . ISEKI
CYLINDERS. 3
CID 1647CC
ENGINE HP 34.7
COOLING . . . . LIQUID
FUEL . . . . D
SPEEDS . . . . VARIABLE
TRANSMISSION . . . . HYDRO
STEERING. . . . . STANDARD
HITCH . . . . CAT. I
HYDRAULIC . . . . YES
PTO . . . . YES
WEIGHT . . . . 2,668 LBS.

TK527
YEARS MFRD 2005-2006
SERIES. . . . . TK SERIES
ENGINE . . . . ISEKI
CYLINDERS. 3
ENGINE HP 27
COOLING . . . . LIQUID
FUEL . . . . D
SPEEDS 16/16
TRANSMISSION . . . . . POWER SHIFT
STEERING. . . . . STANDARD
HYDRAULIC . . . . YES
PTO . . . . YES
WEIGHT . . . . 2,690 LBS.

ISEKI

TK532
YEARS MFRD........2005-2006
SERIES..............TK SERIES
ENGINE.................ISEKI
CYLINDERS..................3
ENGINE HP.................32
COOLING..............LIQUID
FUEL........................D
SPEEDS...............16/16
TRANSMISSION.....POWER SHIFT
STEERING............STANDARD
HYDRAULIC...............YES
PTO.......................YES
WEIGHT............2,756 LBS.

TK538
YEARS MFRD........2005-2006
SERIES..............TK SERIES
ENGINE.................ISEKI
CYLINDERS..................3
ENGINE HP.................38
COOLING..............LIQUID
FUEL........................D
SPEEDS...............16/16
TRANSMISSION.....POWER SHIFT
STEERING............STANDARD
HYDRAULIC...............YES
PTO.......................YES
WEIGHT............2,778 LBS.

TK546
YEARS MFRD........2005-2006
SERIES..............TK SERIES
ENGINE.................ISEKI
CYLINDERS..................4
ENGINE HP.................46
COOLING..............LIQUID
FUEL........................D
SPEEDS...............16/16
TRANSMISSION.....POWER SHIFT
STEERING............STANDARD
HYDRAULIC...............YES
PTO.......................YES
WEIGHT............4,023 LBS.

TM3160
YEARS MFRD........2005-2008
SERIES..............TM SERIES
ENGINE.................ISEKI
CYLINDERS..................3
ENGINE HP...............15.5
COOLING..............LIQUID
FUEL........................D
SPEEDS....................6/2
TRANSMISSION............GEAR
STEERING............STANDARD
HITCH.....................CAT. I
PTO.......................YES
WEIGHT............1,312 LBS.

TM3200
YEARS MFRD........2005-2008
SERIES..............TM SERIES
ENGINE.................ISEKI
CYLINDERS..................3
ENGINE HP...............19.5
COOLING..............LIQUID
FUEL........................D
SPEEDS....................6/2
TRANSMISSION............GEAR
STEERING............STANDARD
HITCH.....................CAT. I
PTO.......................YES
WEIGHT............1,433 LBS.

OPTIONS

HYDRO

TM3215
YEARS MFRD........2010-2013
ENGINE.................ISEKI
CYLINDERS..................3
CID....................1123CC
ENGINE HP...............19.2
COOLING..............LIQUID
FUEL........................D
SPEEDS...............VARIABLE
TRANSMISSION...........HYDRO
STEERING............STANDARD
HITCH.....................CAT. I
WEIGHT............1,830 LBS.

TM3240
YEARS MFRD........2005-2010
SERIES..............TM SERIES
ENGINE.................ISEKI
CYLINDERS..................3
ENGINE HP.................26
COOLING..............LIQUID
FUEL........................D
SPEEDS....................6/2
TRANSMISSION............GEAR
STEERING............STANDARD
HITCH.....................CAT. I
PTO.......................YES
WEIGHT............1,521 LBS.

TM3245
YEARS MFRD........2010-2013
SERIES..............TM SERIES
ENGINE.................ISEKI
CYLINDERS..................3
CID........................1123
ENGINE HP...............21.6
COOLING..............LIQUID
FUEL........................D
SPEEDS...............VARIABLE
TRANSMISSION...........HYDRO
STEERING............STANDARD
HITCH.....................CAT. I
HYDRAULIC...............YES
PTO.......................YES
WEIGHT............1,819 LBS.

TM3265
YEARS MFRD........2010-2013
ENGINE.................ISEKI
CYLINDERS..................3
CID....................1498CC
ENGINE HP...............25.1
COOLING..............LIQUID
FUEL........................D
SPEEDS...............VARIABLE
TRANSMISSION...........HYDRO
STEERING............STANDARD
HITCH.....................CAT. I
HYDRAULIC...............YES
PTO.......................YES
WEIGHT............1,907 LBS.

TS1610
YEARS MFRD........1981-1981
SERIES..............TS SERIES
CYLINDERS..................2
ENGINE HP.................19
WEIGHT............1,670 LBS.

OPTIONS

4WD

TS1910
SERIES..............TS SERIES
ENGINE.................ISUZU
CYLINDERS..................2
CID........................59.5
ENGINE HP.................19
COOLING..............LIQUID
FUEL........................D
SPEEDS....................9/3
TRANSMISSION............GEAR
STEERING............STANDARD
HITCH.....................CAT. I
PTO.......................YES
WEIGHT............1,672 LBS.

TX1014
YEARS MFRD........1978-1981
SERIES..............TX SERIES
CYLINDERS..................3
ENGINE HP.................17
WEIGHT............1,199 LBS.

OPTIONS

4WD

TX1210
YEARS MFRD........1978-1981
SERIES..............TX SERIES
CYLINDERS..................2
ENGINE HP.................14
WEIGHT............1,089 LBS.

OPTIONS

4WD

TX1500
YEARS MFRD........1978-1981
ENGINE.............MITSUBISHI
CYLINDERS..................2
ENGINE HP.................17
FUEL........................D
STEERING............STANDARD

TX1510
YEARS MFRD........1978-1981
SERIES..............TX SERIES
CYLINDERS..................3
ENGINE HP.................18
WEIGHT............1,331 LBS.

OPTIONS

4WD

TXG23
YEARS MFRD........2005-2008
SERIES.............TXG SERIES
ENGINE.................ISEKI
CYLINDERS..................3
ENGINE HP...............22.5
COOLING..............LIQUID
FUEL........................D
SPEEDS...............VARIABLE
TRANSMISSION...........HYDRO
STEERING............STANDARD
HITCH.....................CAT. I
WEIGHT............1,389 LBS.

TXG237
YEARS MFRD........2010-2013
ENGINE.................ISEKI
CYLINDERS..................3
CID....................1123CC
ENGINE HP...............16.8
COOLING..............LIQUID
FUEL........................D
SPEEDS...............VARIABLE
TRANSMISSION...........HYDRO
STEERING............STANDARD
HITCH.....................CAT. I
WEIGHT............1,477 LBS.

JACOBSEN

AR3

YEARS MFRD 2008-2010
ENGINE . KUBOTA D1105-TE TURBO
CYLINDERS. 3
CID 68.55
ENGINE HP 32.8
COOLING . . . . LIQUID
FUEL . . . . D
SPEEDS . . . . VARIABLE
TRANSMISSION . . . . HYDRO
STEERING. . . . . ZERO
WEIGHT . . . . 2,293 LBS.

AR5

YEARS MFRD 2004-2008
ENGINE . . . . KUBOTA
CYLINDERS. 4
CID 112
ENGINE HP 59
COOLING . . . . LIQUID
FUEL . . . . D
SPEEDS . . . . VARIABLE
TRANSMISSION . . . . HYDRO
STEERING. . . . . STANDARD
HYDRAULIC . . . . YES
STANDARD DECK . . . . 90"
WEIGHT . . . . 3,576 LBS.
MSRP. $50,819

RETAIL PRICING

YEAR	HIGH	LOW
2005	$24,893	$18,670
2006	$25,263	$18,948
2007	$25,700	$19,275
2008	$26,020	$19,515

AR522

YEARS MFRD 2009-2015
ENGINE . . . . . . KUBOTA V2003-M-T
CYLINDERS. 4
CID 112
ENGINE HP 59
COOLING . . . . LIQUID
FUEL . . . . D
SPEEDS . . . . VARIABLE
TRANSMISSION . . . . HYDRO
STEERING. . . . . ZERO
BLADE CLUTCH . . . . ELECTRIC
WEIGHT . . . . 3,805 LBS.

AR2500

YEARS MFRD 2002-2004
ENGINE . . . . KUBOTA TURBO
CYLINDERS. 4
CID 91.44
ENGINE HP 36
COOLING . . . . LIQUID
FUEL . . . . D
SPEEDS . . . . VARIABLE
TRANSMISSION . . . . HYDRO
STEERING. . . . . STANDARD
HYDRAULIC . . . . YES
STANDARD DECK . . . . 98"
WEIGHT . . . . 3,160 LBS.
MSRP. $44,065

RETAIL PRICING

YEAR	HIGH	LOW
2003	$21,448	$16,086

C318G

YEARS MFRD 1988-1995
SERIES. . . . . TURFCAT SERIES
ENGINE . . . . KOHLER
ENGINE HP 18
COOLING . . . . AIR
FUEL . . . . G
TRANSMISSION . . . . HYDRO
STEERING. . . . . STANDARD
STANDARD DECK . . . . 50"
MSRP. $6,528

OPTIONS

B&S 18HP

RETAIL PRICING

YEAR	HIGH	LOW
1988	$256	$192
1989	$286	$214
1990	$316	$237
1991	$351	$263
1992	$390	$293
1993	$435	$326
1994	$482	$361
1995	$531	$398

C417D

YEARS MFRD 1988-1995
SERIES. . . . . TURFCAT SERIES
ENGINE . . . . KUBOTA
ENGINE HP 16.5
FUEL . . . . D
TRANSMISSION . . . . HYDRO
STEERING. . . . . STANDARD
STANDARD DECK . . . . 50"
WEIGHT . . . . 1,350 LBS.
MSRP. $9,720

RETAIL PRICING

YEAR	HIGH	LOW
1988	$2,144	$1,608
1989	$2,284	$1,713
1990	$2,374	$1,781
1991	$2,570	$1,927
1992	$2,733	$2,050
1993	$2,880	$2,160
1994	$3,074	$2,306
1995	$3,224	$2,418

C420G

YEARS MFRD 1988-1995
SERIES. . . . . TURFCAT SERIES
ENGINE . . . . KUBOTA
ENGINE HP 21
COOLING . . . . LIQUID
FUEL . . . . G
TRANSMISSION . . . . HYDRO
STEERING. . . . . STANDARD
STANDARD DECK . . . . 50"
WEIGHT . . . . 1,350 LBS.
MSRP. $8,730

RETAIL PRICING

YEAR	HIGH	LOW
1988	$344	$258
1989	$380	$285
1990	$425	$318
1991	$470	$353
1992	$522	$391
1993	$580	$435
1994	$642	$482
1995	$713	$535

E PLEX II

YEARS MFRD 2004-2011
SERIES . . . ELECTRIC DRIVES SERIES
ENGINE . . . . 48V ELECTRIC MOTOR
SPEEDS . . . . VARIABLE
STEERING. . . . . ZERO
STANDARD DECK . . . . 62"
WEIGHT . . . . 1,464 LBS.
MSRP. $21,695

RETAIL PRICING

YEAR	HIGH	LOW
2004	$9,234	$6,926
2005	$10,012	$7,509
2006	$10,067	$7,550
2007	$10,319	$7,739
2008	$10,685	$8,013
2009	$11,467	$8,600
2010	$12,193	$9,145
2011	$12,663	$9,497

ECLIPSE 322 BATTERY

YEARS MFRD 2010-2012
SPEEDS . . . . VARIABLE
STEERING. . . . . ZERO
WEIGHT . . . . 1,342 LBS.

ECLIPSE 322 HYBRID

YEARS MFRD 2010-2015
ENGINE . . . . B&S VANGUARD
CYLINDERS. 2
CID 29.23
COOLING . . . . AIR
FUEL . . . . G
SPEEDS . . . . VARIABLE
TRANSMISSION . . . . HYDRO
STEERING. . . . . ZERO
BLADE CLUTCH . . . . ELECTRIC
WEIGHT . . . . 1,481 LBS.

OPTIONS

KUBOTA Z482

G PLEX II

YEARS MFRD 2002-2002
ENGINE . . . . B&S
ENGINE HP 18
FUEL . . . . G
TRANSMISSION . . . . HYDRO
STEERING. . . . . STANDARD
DRIVE TYPE 2WD
STANDARD DECK . . . . 62"
MSRP. $11,900

OPTIONS

3WD
KUBOTA 19HP

RETAIL PRICING

YEAR	HIGH	LOW
2002	$5,343	$4,007

G PLEX III (DIESEL)

YEARS MFRD 2004-2014
ENGINE . . . . KUBOTA D722
CYLINDERS. 3
CID 43.88
ENGINE HP 18.8
COOLING . . . . LIQUID
FUEL . . . . D
SPEEDS . . . . VARIABLE
TRANSMISSION . . . . HYDRO
STEERING. . . . . ZERO
STANDARD DECK . . . . 62"
WEIGHT . . . . 1,388 LBS.
MSRP. $27,437

OPTIONS

3WD

RETAIL PRICING

YEAR	HIGH	LOW
2004	$7,131	$5,348
2005	$7,955	$5,966
2006	$8,852	$6,639
2007	$9,607	$7,206
2008	$10,522	$7,892
2009	$12,270	$9,203
2010	$13,353	$10,015
2011	$13,918	$10,439
2012	$14,736	$11,052
2013	$15,327	$11,495
2014	$15,850	$11,887

G PLEX III (GAS)

YEARS MFRD 2003-2010
ENGINE . . . B&S VANGUARD V-TWIN
CYLINDERS. 2
CID 35
ENGINE HP 18
COOLING . . . . AIR
FUEL . . . . G
SPEEDS . . . . VARIABLE
TRANSMISSION . . . . HYDRO
STEERING. . . . . ZERO
STANDARD DECK . . . . 62"
WEIGHT . . . . 1,264 LBS.
MSRP. $22,599

RETAIL PRICING

YEAR	HIGH	LOW
2003	$7,693	$5,770
2004	$7,899	$5,924
2005	$8,652	$6,489
2006	$9,349	$7,012
2007	$10,053	$7,540
2008	$10,324	$7,743
2009	$11,761	$8,821
2010	$12,554	$9,416

JACOBSEN

GK IV TRIPLEX
YEARS MFRD 1992-1994
ENGINE .... KOHLER
ENGINE HP 16
FUEL .... G
TRANSMISSION .... HYDRO
STEERING............ STANDARD

OPTIONS

KUBOTA 16.5HP

GP400 DIESEL
YEARS MFRD 2013-2014
ENGINE .... KUBOTA
CYLINDERS.................... 3
CID 43.88
ENGINE HP 17.7
COOLING .... LIQUID
FUEL .... D
SPEEDS .... VARIABLE
TRANSMISSION .... HYDRO
STEERING................. ZERO
BLADE CLUTCH .... ELECTRIC
WEIGHT .... 1,622 LBS.

GP400 GAS
YEARS MFRD 2013-2014
ENGINE .... B&S VANGUARD
CYLINDERS.................... 2
CID 35
ENGINE HP 17.7
COOLING .... AIR
FUEL .... G
SPEEDS .... VARIABLE
TRANSMISSION .... HYDRO
STEERING................. ZERO
BLADE CLUTCH .... ELECTRIC
WEIGHT .... 1,463 LBS.

GREENS KING IV
YEARS MFRD 2004-2012
ENGINE ... B&S VANGUARD V-TWIN
CYLINDERS.................... 2
CID 29.3
ENGINE HP 16
COOLING .... AIR
FUEL .... G
SPEEDS .... VARIABLE
TRANSMISSION .... HYDRO
STEERING................. ZERO
STANDARD DECK .... 66"
WEIGHT .... 900 LBS.
MSRP................. $21,623

RETAIL PRICING

YEAR	HIGH	LOW
2004	$8,922	$6,692
2007	$9,586	$7,189
2008	$10,178	$7,634
2009	$11,144	$8,358
2010	$11,390	$8,542
2011	$12,043	$9,032
2012	$12,602	$9,451

GREENS KING IV PLUS (DIESEL)
YEARS MFRD 2004-2014
ENGINE .... KUBOTA D662
CYLINDERS.................... 3
CID 40.3
ENGINE HP 19
COOLING .... LIQUID
FUEL .... D
SPEEDS .... VARIABLE
TRANSMISSION .... HYDRO
STEERING................. ZERO
STANDARD DECK .... 62"
WEIGHT .... 1,340 LBS.
MSRP................. $26,820

RETAIL PRICING

YEAR	HIGH	LOW
2004	$9,815	$7,362
2005	$10,275	$7,706
2006	$11,209	$8,407
2007	$11,667	$8,750
2008	$12,441	$9,331
2009	$12,927	$9,695
2010	$13,495	$10,121
2011	$14,233	$10,675
2012	$14,980	$11,235
2013	$16,030	$12,023
2014	$16,323	$12,242

GREENS KING IV PLUS (GAS)
YEARS MFRD 2004-2014
ENGINE ..... B&S VANGUARD OHV
CYLINDERS.................... 2
CID 34.8
ENGINE HP 18
COOLING .... AIR
FUEL .... G
SPEEDS .... VARIABLE
TRANSMISSION .... HYDRO
STEERING................. ZERO
STANDARD DECK .... 62"
WEIGHT .... 1,074 LBS.
MSRP................. $23,410

OPTIONS

B&S VANGUARD OHV 16HP

RETAIL PRICING

YEAR	HIGH	LOW
2004	$8,252	$6,189
2005	$8,929	$6,697
2006	$9,748	$7,311
2007	$10,480	$7,860
2008	$11,429	$8,571
2009	$11,757	$8,818
2010	$12,678	$9,508
2011	$12,912	$9,684
2012	$13,404	$10,053
2013	$13,696	$10,272
2014	$14,055	$10,541

GREENS KING VI
YEARS MFRD 2004-2006
ENGINE .... KUBOTA D662
CYLINDERS.................... 3
CID 40.03
ENGINE HP 19
COOLING .... LIQUID
FUEL .... D
SPEEDS .... VARIABLE
TRANSMISSION .... HYDRO
STEERING................. ZERO
DRIVE TYPE 2WD
STANDARD DECK .... 62"
WEIGHT .... 1,269 LBS.
MSRP................. $27,389

OPTIONS

3WD
B&S 18HP

RETAIL PRICING

YEAR	HIGH	LOW
2004	$14,191	$10,643

GROOM MASTER II
YEARS MFRD 2004-2004
ENGINE ... B&S VANGUARD V-TWIN
CYLINDERS.................... 2
ENGINE HP 16
COOLING .... AIR
FUEL .... G
SPEEDS .... VARIABLE
TRANSMISSION .... HYDRO
STEERING................. ZERO
WEIGHT .... 984 LBS.

OPTIONS

KUBOTA 19.2HP 3CYL

HR4600 TURBO
YEARS MFRD 2003-2007
ENGINE .... KUBOTA
CYLINDERS.................... 4
CID 91.4
ENGINE HP 44.2
COOLING .... LIQUID
FUEL .... D
SPEEDS .... VARIABLE
TRANSMISSION .... HYDRO
STEERING............ STANDARD
HYDRAULIC .... YES
PTO .... YES
DRIVE TYPE 2WD
ROPS/CAB .... ROPS
STANDARD DECK .... 92"
WEIGHT .... 2,930 LBS.
MSRP................. $46,392

OPTIONS

4WD

RETAIL PRICING

YEAR	HIGH	LOW
2003	$20,205	$15,153
2004	$22,696	$17,022
2005	$25,495	$19,121
2006	$26,952	$20,214
2007	$27,929	$20,947

HR5111
YEARS MFRD 2004-2008
ENGINE .... KUBOTA V2203D
CYLINDERS.................... 4
CID 134.1
ENGINE HP 49
COOLING .... LIQUID
FUEL .... D
SPEEDS .... VARIABLE
TRANSMISSION .... HYDRO
STEERING............ STANDARD
HYDRAULIC .... YES
PTO .... YES
STANDARD DECK .... 134"
WEIGHT .... 3,780 LBS.
MSRP................. $55,272

RETAIL PRICING

YEAR	HIGH	LOW
2004	$27,035	$20,276
2005	$30,375	$22,781
2006	$32,111	$24,083
2007	$33,895	$25,421
2008	$35,909	$26,932

HR6010
YEARS MFRD 2004-2014
ENGINE .... PERKINS TURBO
CYLINDERS.................... 4
CID 135.2
ENGINE HP 60
COOLING .... LIQUID
FUEL .... D
SPEEDS .... VARIABLE
TRANSMISSION .... HYDRO
STEERING............ STANDARD
HYDRAULIC .... YES
PTO .... YES
STANDARD DECK .... 127"
WEIGHT .... 3,476 LBS.
MSRP................. $53,650

RETAIL PRICING

YEAR	HIGH	LOW
2004	$22,211	$16,658
2005	$23,074	$17,305
2006	$24,258	$18,194
2007	$25,869	$19,401
2008	$26,648	$19,986
2009	$27,879	$20,909
2010	$29,002	$21,751
2011	$29,689	$22,267
2012	$30,895	$23,171
2013	$31,627	$23,721
2014	$32,900	$24,675

HR9016 TURBO
YEARS MFRD 2004-2015
ENGINE .... DETROIT
CYLINDERS.................... 4
ENGINE HP 87

COOLING . . . . LIQUID
FUEL . . . . D
SPEEDS . . . . VARIABLE
TRANSMISSION . . . . .HYDRO
STEERING. . . . . .STANDARD
HYDRAULIC . . . . YES
STANDARD DECK . . . . 92"
WEIGHT . . . . .6,350 LBS.
MSRP. $87,200

RETAIL PRICING

YEAR	HIGH	LOW
2004	$39,753	$29,815
2005	$40,455	$30,341
2006	$42,787	$32,090
2007	$43,564	$32,673
2008	$45,390	$34,043
2009	$46,901	$35,175
2010	$47,434	$35,575
2011	$48,930	$36,697
2012	$49,752	$37,314
2013	$50,910	$38,182
2014	$53,010	$39,758
2015	$54,440	$40,830

HR9510

YEARS MFRD 2004-2004
ENGINE . . . . .PERKINS
CYLINDERS. 4
ENGINE HP 50
COOLING . . . . LIQUID
FUEL . . . . D
SPEEDS . . . . VARIABLE
TRANSMISSION . . . . .HYDRO
STEERING. . . . . .STANDARD
HYDRAULIC . . . . YES
PTO . . . . YES
WEIGHT . . . . .3,476 LBS.

JZT1250

YEARS MFRD 2003-2005
ENGINE . . KOHLER COMMAND OHV
CYLINDERS. 2
CID 44
ENGINE HP 25
COOLING . . . . .AIR
FUEL . . . . D
SPEEDS . . . . VARIABLE
TRANSMISSION . . . . .HYDRO
STEERING. . . . . ZERO
BLADE CLUTCH . . . . MANUAL
HYDRAULIC . . . . YES
PTO . . . . YES
STANDARD DECK . . . . 48"
MSRP. $11,273

RETAIL PRICING

YEAR	HIGH	LOW
2003	$5,332	$3,999
2004	$5,470	$4,103
2005	$5,653	$4,240

JZT2180ES

YEARS MFRD 2003-2005
SERIES. . . . . ESTATES SERIES
ENGINE . . . . B&S INTEK V-TWIN
CYLINDERS. 2
ENGINE HP 18
COOLING . . . . .AIR
FUEL . . . . G
SPEEDS . . . . VARIABLE
TRANSMISSION . . . . .HYDRO
STEERING. . . . . ZERO
BLADE CLUTCH . . . . .ELECTRIC
HYDRAULIC . . . . YES
PTO . . . . YES

JZT2190

YEARS MFRD 2004-2004
SERIES. . . . . JZT 2000 SERIES
ENGINE . . . . KAWASAKI OHV
ENGINE HP 19
COOLING . . . . .AIR
FUEL . . . . G
SPEEDS . . . . VARIABLE
TRANSMISSION . . . . GEAR
STEERING. . . . . ZERO
BLADE CLUTCH . . . . MANUAL
HYDRAULIC . . . . YES
PTO . . . . YES

JZT2230

YEARS MFRD 2003-2004
SERIES. . . . . JZT 2000 SERIES
ENGINE . . . .KAWASAKI V TWIN OHV
ENGINE HP 23
COOLING . . . . .AIR
FUEL . . . . G
SPEEDS . . . . VARIABLE
TRANSMISSION . . . . .HYDRO
STEERING. . . . . ZERO
BLADE CLUTCH . . . . MANUAL
HYDRAULIC . . . . YES
PTO . . . . YES
STANDARD DECK . . . . 61"
MSRP. $9,335

RETAIL PRICING

YEAR	HIGH	LOW
2003	$4,542	$3,406
2004	$4,721	$3,540

JZT2230LC

YEARS MFRD 2003-2005
SERIES. . . . . JTZ 2000 SERIES
ENGINE . . . . . . KOHLER AEGIS OHV
CYLINDERS. 2
ENGINE HP 23
COOLING . . . . LIQUID
FUEL . . . . G
SPEEDS . . . . VARIABLE
TRANSMISSION . . . . .HYDRO
STEERING. . . . . ZERO
BLADE CLUTCH . . . . MANUAL
HYDRAULIC . . . . YES
PTO . . . . YES
STANDARD DECK . . . . 52"
MSRP. $10,500

OPTIONS

61" DECK

RETAIL PRICING

YEAR	HIGH	LOW
2003	$4,949	$3,711
2004	$5,440	$4,080
2005	$5,769	$4,327

JZT2250

YEARS MFRD 2003-2005
SERIES. . . . . JZY 2000 SERIES
ENGINE . . . .KAWASAKI V TWIN OHV
CYLINDERS. 2
ENGINE HP 25
COOLING . . . . .AIR
FUEL . . . . G
SPEEDS . . . . VARIABLE
TRANSMISSION . . . . .HYDRO
STEERING. . . . . ZERO
BLADE CLUTCH . . . . MANUAL
HYDRAULIC . . . . YES
PTO . . . . YES
STANDARD DECK . . . . 61"
MSRP. $10,140

RETAIL PRICING

YEAR	HIGH	LOW
2003	$4,934	$3,701

LF100

YEARS MFRD 1992-1992
ENGINE . . . . KUBOTA
ENGINE HP 22
FUEL . . . . D
TRANSMISSION . . . . .HYDRO
STEERING. . . . . .STANDARD
STANDARD DECK . . . . 100"
MSRP. $5,120

RETAIL PRICING

YEAR	HIGH	LOW
1992	$1,501	$1,126

LF123

YEARS MFRD 1995-1996
ENGINE . . . . KUBOTA
ENGINE HP 23
FUEL . . . . D
TRANSMISSION . . . . .HYDRO
STEERING. . . . . .STANDARD
DRIVE TYPE 2WD

OPTIONS

4WD

LF128

YEARS MFRD 1995-2001
ENGINE . . . . KUBOTA
ENGINE HP 28
FUEL . . . . D
TRANSMISSION . . . . .HYDRO
STEERING. . . . . .STANDARD
DRIVE TYPE 2WD

OPTIONS

4WD

LF135

YEARS MFRD 1998-1999
ENGINE . . . . KUBOTA
ENGINE HP 35
FUEL . . . . D
TRANSMISSION . . . . .HYDRO
STEERING. . . . . .STANDARD
DRIVE TYPE 4WD

LF510

YEARS MFRD 2013-2014
ENGINE . . . . KUBOTA D1105E
CYLINDERS. 3
CID 68.5
ENGINE HP 24.8
COOLING . . . . LIQUID
FUEL . . . . D
SPEEDS . . . . VARIABLE
TRANSMISSION . . . . .HYDRO
STEERING. . . . . ZERO
BLADE CLUTCH . . . . .ELECTRIC

LF550/570

YEARS MFRD 2013-2014
ENGINE . . . . .KUBOTA V1505E
CYLINDERS. 4
CID 91.4
ENGINE HP 35.5
COOLING . . . . LIQUID
FUEL . . . . D
SPEEDS . . . . VARIABLE
TRANSMISSION . . . . .HYDRO
STEERING. . . . . ZERO

LF2500

YEARS MFRD 2002-2004
ENGINE . . . . KUBOTA
ENGINE HP 31
FUEL . . . . D
TRANSMISSION . . . . .HYDRO
STEERING. . . . . .STANDARD
DRIVE TYPE 2WD
STANDARD DECK . . . . 98"
MSRP. $33,736

OPTIONS

4WD

RETAIL PRICING

YEAR	HIGH	LOW
2003	$16,420	$12,315
2004	$17,480	$13,110

LF3050

YEARS MFRD 2002-2004
ENGINE . . . . KUBOTA
ENGINE HP 36
FUEL . . . . D
SPEEDS . . . . VARIABLE
TRANSMISSION . . . . .HYDRO
STEERING. . . . . .STANDARD
MSRP. $44,946

RETAIL PRICING

YEAR	HIGH	LOW
2002	$18,163	$13,622
2003	$21,876	$16,407
2004	$23,287	$17,466

LF3400

YEARS MFRD 1999-2010
ENGINE . . . . .KUBOTA V1305SE
CYLINDERS. 4
CID 81.5
ENGINE HP 34

JACOBSEN

COOLING . . . . . LIQUID
FUEL . . . . . D
SPEEDS . . . . . VARIABLE
TRANSMISSION . . . . . HYDRO
STEERING. . . . . ZERO
DRIVE TYPE. 2WD
ROPS/CAB. . . . . ROPS
STANDARD DECK . . . . . 100"
WEIGHT . . . . . 2,705 LBS.
MSRP. $43,288

OPTIONS

4WD

RETAIL PRICING

YEAR	HIGH	LOW
2003	$15,769	$11,827
2004	$16,390	$12,293
2005	$17,652	$13,239
2006	$18,407	$13,805
2007	$18,743	$14,057
2008	$19,854	$14,891
2009	$21,456	$16,092
2010	$24,045	$18,034

LF3407

YEARS MFRD 2006-2008
ENGINE . . . . . KUBOTA V1305E
CYLINDERS. 4
CID 81.5
ENGINE HP. 31
COOLING . . . . . LIQUID
FUEL . . . . . D
SPEEDS . . . . . VARIABLE
TRANSMISSION . . . . . HYDRO
STEERING. . . . . ZERO
DRIVE TYPE 2WD
STANDARD DECK . . . . . 98"
WEIGHT . . . . . 2,580 LBS.
MSRP. $46,609

OPTIONS

4WD

RETAIL PRICING

YEAR	HIGH	LOW
2006	$22,327	$16,745
2007	$23,572	$17,679

LF3800

YEARS MFRD 1999-2010
ENGINE . . . . . KUBOTA V1505E
CYLINDERS. 4
CID 91.4
ENGINE HP 36
COOLING . . . . . LIQUID
FUEL . . . . . D
SPEEDS . . . . . VARIABLE
TRANSMISSION . . . . . HYDRO
STEERING. . . . . ZERO
DRIVE TYPE 2WD
STANDARD DECK . . . . . 100"
WEIGHT . . . . . 2,915 LBS.
MSRP. $48,149

OPTIONS

4WD

RETAIL PRICING

YEAR	HIGH	LOW
2003	$17,093	$12,820
2004	$17,870	$13,403
2005	$19,937	$14,953
2006	$20,323	$15,243
2007	$20,929	$15,696
2008	$21,942	$16,457
2009	$23,741	$17,806
2010	$26,747	$20,060

LF3810

YEARS MFRD 1995-2002
ENGINE . . . . . KUBOTA
ENGINE HP 36
FUEL . . . . . D
TRANSMISSION . . . . . HYDRO
STEERING. . . . . STANDARD
DRIVE TYPE 2WD

OPTIONS

4WD

LF4675

YEARS MFRD 2004-2009
ENGINE . . . . . KUBOTA V1505TE
CYLINDERS. 4
ENGINE HP 44.2
COOLING . . . . . LIQUID
FUEL . . . . . D
SPEEDS . . . . . VARIABLE
TRANSMISSION . . . . . HYDRO
STEERING. . . . . ZERO
HYDRAULIC . . . . . YES
DRIVE TYPE 2WD
ROPS/CAB . . . . . ROPS
STANDARD DECK . . . . . 139"
WEIGHT . . . . . 3,180 LBS.
MSRP. $61,247

OPTIONS

4WD

RETAIL PRICING

YEAR	HIGH	LOW
2004	$28,558	$21,418
2005	$29,358	$22,018
2006	$30,095	$22,571
2007	$30,976	$23,232

LF4677

YEARS MFRD 2004-2010
ENGINE . . . . . KUBOTA V1505TE
CYLINDERS. 4
ENGINE HP 44.2
COOLING . . . . . LIQUID
FUEL . . . . . D
SPEEDS . . . . . VARIABLE
TRANSMISSION . . . . . HYDRO
STEERING. . . . . ZERO
HYDRAULIC . . . . . YES
DRIVE TYPE 2WD
ROPS/CAB . . . . . ROPS
STANDARD DECK . . . . . 139"
WEIGHT . . . . . 3,450 LBS.
MSRP. $62,555

OPTIONS

4WD

RETAIL PRICING

YEAR	HIGH	LOW
2004	$23,190	$17,393
2005	$23,954	$17,966
2006	$25,307	$18,980
2007	$26,588	$19,941
2008	$28,743	$21,557
2009	$30,975	$23,231
2010	$34,747	$26,060

R311

YEARS MFRD 2009-2014
ENGINE . . . . . KUBOTA V2203-M
CYLINDERS. 4
CID 134.1
ENGINE HP 44.6
COOLING . . . . . LIQUID
FUEL . . . . . D
SPEEDS . . . . . VARIABLE
TRANSMISSION . . . . . HYDRO
STEERING. . . . . ZERO
BLADE CLUTCH . . . . . ELECTRIC
WEIGHT . . . . . 3,970 LBS.

RZT

YEARS MFRD 2016-2016
SERIES. . . . . PRO SERIES
ENGINE . . . . KAWASAKI FX 2550KW
ENGINE HP 25
FUEL . . . . . G
SPEEDS . . . . . VARIABLE
TRANSMISSION . . . . . HYDRO
STEERING. . . . . ZERO
STANDARD DECK . . . . . 50"

OPTIONS

KAWASAKI 27HP
KAWASAKI 31HP
KOHLER 27HP
KOHLER 31

RZT PRO

YEARS MFRD 2017-2017
ENGINE . . . . . KOHLER
ENGINE HP 31
COOLING . . . . . AIR
FUEL . . . . . G
SPEEDS . . . . . VARIABLE
TRANSMISSION . . . . . HYDRO
STEERING. . . . . ZERO
STANDARD DECK . . . . . 72"
MSRP. $11,199

RETAIL PRICING

YEAR	HIGH	LOW
2017	$6,837	$5,128

SLF530

YEARS MFRD 2017-2018
ENGINE . . . . . KUBOTA D1105
ENGINE HP 24.8
COOLING . . . . . LIQUID
FUEL . . . . . D
STANDARD DECK . . . . . 82"
WEIGHT . . . . . 1,956 LBS.

SLF1880

YEARS MFRD 2004-2010
SERIES. . . FAIRWAY MOWER SERIES
ENGINE . . . . . KUBOTA D1105E
CYLINDERS. 3
ENGINE HP 26
COOLING . . . . . LIQUID
FUEL . . . . . G
SPEEDS . . . . . VARIABLE
TRANSMISSION . . . . . HYDRO
STEERING. . . . . ZERO
HYDRAULIC . . . . . YES
DRIVE TYPE 2WD
STANDARD DECK . . . . . 80"
WEIGHT . . . . . 2,200 LBS.
MSRP. $36,129

OPTIONS

4WD

RETAIL PRICING

YEAR	HIGH	LOW
2004	$13,861	$10,395
2005	$14,821	$11,116
2006	$15,344	$11,508
2007	$15,635	$11,726
2008	$16,488	$12,366
2009	$17,833	$13,375
2010	$20,071	$15,053

SZT PRO

YEARS MFRD 2017-2017
ENGINE . . . . . KAWASAKI
ENGINE HP 25
COOLING . . . . . AIR
FUEL . . . . . G
SPEEDS . . . . . VARIABLE
TRANSMISSION . . . . . HYDRO
STEERING. . . . . ZERO
STANDARD DECK . . . . . 48"

OPTIONS

54" DECK

T422D

YEARS MFRD 1996-1996
SERIES. . . . . TURFCAT SERIES
ENGINE . . . . . KUBOTA
ENGINE HP 22
COOLING . . . . . LIQUID
FUEL . . . . . D
TRANSMISSION . . . . . HYDRO
STEERING. . . . . ZERO
DRIVE TYPE 2WD
STANDARD DECK . . . . . 60"
MSRP. $15,293

OPTIONS

4WD

RETAIL PRICING

YEAR	HIGH	LOW
1996	$1,414	$1,060

T423D

YEARS MFRD 1996-1998
SERIES. . . . . TURFCAT SERIES
ENGINE . . . . . KUBOTA
ENGINE HP 23
COOLING . . . . . LIQUID
FUEL . . . . . D
TRANSMISSION . . . . . HYDRO
STEERING. . . . . ZERO

DRIVE TYPE 2WD
STANDARD DECK . . . . 60"
MSRP. $16,558

OPTIONS

4WD

RETAIL PRICING

YEAR	HIGH	LOW
1996	$1,689	$1,267
1997	$1,872	$1,404
1998	$2,077	$1,558

T425D

YEARS MFRD 1996-1998
SERIES. . . . . TURFCAT SERIES
ENGINE . . . . KUBOTA
ENGINE HP 28
COOLING . . . . LIQUID
FUEL . . . . D
TRANSMISSION . . . . .HYDRO
STEERING. . . . . ZERO
DRIVE TYPE 2WD
STANDARD DECK . . . . 60"
MSRP. $18,702

RETAIL PRICING

YEAR	HIGH	LOW
1998	$7,005	$5,254

T428D

YEARS MFRD 1996-1998
SERIES. . . . . TURFCAT SERIES
ENGINE . . . . KUBOTA
ENGINE HP 28
FUEL . . . . D
TRANSMISSION . . . . .HYDRO
STEERING. . . . . ZERO
DRIVE TYPE 2WD
STANDARD DECK . . . . 60"
MSRP. $18,702

OPTIONS

4WD

RETAIL PRICING

YEAR	HIGH	LOW
1996	$1,909	$1,431
1997	$2,113	$1,585
1998	$2,347	$1,760

T436G

YEARS MFRD 1996-1996
SERIES. . . . . TURFCAT SERIES
ENGINE . . . . CONTINENTAL
ENGINE HP 36
COOLING . . . . LIQUID
FUEL . . . . G
TRANSMISSION . . . . .HYDRO
STEERING. . . . . ZERO
DRIVE TYPE 2WD
STANDARD DECK . . . . 60"
MSRP. $14,855

RETAIL PRICING

YEAR	HIGH	LOW
1996	$1,373	$1,030

T523D

YEARS MFRD 1999-2000
SERIES. . . . . T500 SERIES
ENGINE . . . . KUBOTA
ENGINE HP 23
COOLING . . . . LIQUID
FUEL . . . . D
TRANSMISSION . . . . .HYDRO
STEERING. . . . . ZERO
DRIVE TYPE 2WD
STANDARD DECK . . . . 60"
MSRP. $15,954

OPTIONS

2 POST ROPS
4WD
CANOPY

RETAIL PRICING

YEAR	HIGH	LOW
1999	$2,589	$1,942
2000	$2,873	$2,155

T528D

YEARS MFRD 1999-2000
SERIES. . . . . T500 SERIES
ENGINE . . . . KUBOTA
ENGINE HP 28
COOLING . . . . LIQUID
FUEL . . . . D
TRANSMISSION . . . . .HYDRO
STEERING. . . . . ZERO
DRIVE TYPE 2WD
STANDARD DECK . . . . 72"
MSRP. $18,021

OPTIONS

2 POST ROPS
4WD
CANOPY

RETAIL PRICING

YEAR	HIGH	LOW
1999	$2,803	$2,103
2000	$3,110	$2,333

T531G

YEARS MFRD 1999-2000
SERIES. . . . . T500 SERIES
ENGINE . . . . B&S
ENGINE HP 31
COOLING . . . . LIQUID
FUEL . . . . G
TRANSMISSION . . . . .HYDRO
STEERING. . . . . ZERO
DRIVE TYPE 2WD
STANDARD DECK . . . . 72"
MSRP. $16,894

OPTIONS

4WD

RETAIL PRICING

YEAR	HIGH	LOW
1999	$2,744	$2,058
2000	$3,042	$2,281

T535D

YEARS MFRD 1999-2000
SERIES. . . . . T500 SERIES
ENGINE . . . . KUBOTA
ENGINE HP 35
COOLING . . . . LIQUID
FUEL . . . . D
TRANSMISSION . . . . .HYDRO
STEERING. . . . . ZERO
DRIVE TYPE 4WD
STANDARD DECK . . . . 72"
MSRP. $23,948

OPTIONS

2 POST ROPS

RETAIL PRICING

YEAR	HIGH	LOW
1999	$3,889	$2,917
2000	$4,313	$3,235

TK1671D

YEARS MFRD 1992-1996
ENGINE . . . . KUBOTA
ENGINE HP 16.5
FUEL . . . . D
TRANSMISSION . . . . .HYDRO
STEERING. . . . . STANDARD

TK1671G

YEARS MFRD 1992-1996
ENGINE . . . . KOHLER
ENGINE HP 16
FUEL . . . . G
TRANSMISSION . . . . .HYDRO
STEERING. . . . . STANDARD

TK1684D

YEARS MFRD 1992-1996
ENGINE . . . . KUBOTA
ENGINE HP 16.5
FUEL . . . . D
TRANSMISSION . . . . .HYDRO
STEERING. . . . . STANDARD

TR3

YEARS MFRD 2006-2014
ENGINE . . . . KUBOTA
CYLINDERS. 3
CID 68.55
ENGINE HP 26
COOLING . . . . LIQUID
FUEL . . . . D
SPEEDS . . . . VARIABLE
TRANSMISSION . . . . .HYDRO
STEERING. . . . . ZERO
STANDARD DECK . . . . 72"
WEIGHT . . . . 2,050 LBS.
MSRP. $29,356

RETAIL PRICING

YEAR	HIGH	LOW
2006	$10,486	$7,865
2007	$12,010	$9,007
2008	$13,259	$9,944
2009	$14,489	$10,867
2010	$15,139	$11,354
2011	$15,831	$11,873
2012	$16,773	$12,580
2013	$17,167	$12,876
2014	$17,726	$13,295

TR320

YEARS MFRD 2018-2018
ENGINE . . . . KUBOTA D1105
CYLINDERS. 3
ENGINE HP 24.8
FUEL . . . . D
STANDARD DECK . . . . 72"
WEIGHT . . . . 1,646 LBS.

TR330

YEARS MFRD 2018-2018
ENGINE . . . . KUBOTA D1105
CYLINDERS. 3
ENGINE HP 24.8
FUEL . . . . D
STANDARD DECK . . . . 72"
WEIGHT . . . . 1,664 LBS.

TRI-KING

YEARS MFRD 2008-2014
ENGINE . . . . KUBOTA
CYLINDERS. 3
CID 40.03
ENGINE HP 19
COOLING . . . . LIQUID
FUEL . . . . D
SPEEDS . . . . VARIABLE
TRANSMISSION . . . . .HYDRO
STEERING. . . . . ZERO
WEIGHT . . . . 1,594 LBS.

TURFCAT

YEARS MFRD 2016-2016
ENGINE . . . . . . KUBOTA D1105 E4B
CYLINDERS. 3
CID 68.5
ENGINE HP 24.8
COOLING . . . . LIQUID
FUEL . . . . D
SPEEDS . . . . VARIABLE
TRANSMISSION . . . . .HYDRO
STEERING. . . . . ZERO
DRIVE TYPE 2WD
STANDARD DECK . . . . 60"
WEIGHT . . . . 1,640 LBS.

OPTIONS

4WD
63"DECK, 72"DECK

TURFCAT

YEARS MFRD 2010-2014
SERIES. . . . . 600 SERIES
ENGINE . . . . KUBOTA D1305-EB
CYLINDERS. 3
CID 68.5
ENGINE HP 29.1
COOLING . . . . LIQUID
FUEL . . . . D
SPEEDS . . . . VARIABLE
TRANSMISSION . . . . .HYDRO
STEERING. . . . . ZERO
BLADE CLUTCH . . . . ELECTRIC
DRIVE TYPE 2WD
WEIGHT . . . . 1,310 LBS.

OPTIONS

4WD

JACOBSEN

WZT PRO

YEARS MFRD 2017-2017
ENGINE .... B&S PRO
ENGINE HP 15
COOLING .... AIR
FUEL .... G
SPEEDS .... VARIABLE
TRANSMISSION .... HYDRO
STEERING .... ZERO
STANDARD DECK .... 36"

OPTIONS

DUAL HYDRO

Z FASTCAT ES

YEARS MFRD 2003-2004
ENGINE .... B&S ELS
ENGINE HP 17.5
COOLING .... AIR
FUEL .... G
SPEEDS .... VARIABLE
TRANSMISSION .... HYDRO
STEERING .... ZERO

OPTIONS

B&S INTEK 18HP
B&S INTEK 25HP

ZT400 2248

YEARS MFRD 2017-2018
SERIES .... ZT400 SERIES
ENGINE .... KAWASAKI
ENGINE HP 22
COOLING .... AIR
TRANSMISSION .... HYDRO
STEERING .... ZERO
STANDARD DECK .... 48"
MSRP $7,949

RETAIL PRICING

YEAR	HIGH	LOW
2017	$4,562	$3,421
2018	$5,068	$3,801

ZT400 2454

YEARS MFRD 2017-2018
SERIES .... ZT400 SERIES
ENGINE .... KAWASAKI
ENGINE HP 24
COOLING .... AIR
FUEL .... G
TRANSMISSION .... HYDRO
STEERING .... ZERO
STANDARD DECK .... 54"
MSRP $8,449

RETAIL PRICING

YEAR	HIGH	LOW
2017	$4,848	$3,636
2018	$5,387	$4,040

ZT400 2460

YEARS MFRD 2017-2018
SERIES .... ZT400 SERIES
ENGINE .... KAWASAKI
ENGINE HP 24
COOLING .... AIR
FUEL .... G
TRANSMISSION .... HYDRO
STEERING .... ZERO
STANDARD DECK .... 54"
MSRP $8,449

RETAIL PRICING

YEAR	HIGH	LOW
2017	$4,848	$3,636
2018	$5,381	$4,036

ZT400 2554

YEARS MFRD 2017-2017
SERIES .... ZT400 SERIES
ENGINE .... B&S
ENGINE HP 25
COOLING .... AIR
TRANSMISSION .... HYDRO
STEERING .... ZERO
STANDARD DECK .... 54"
MSRP $7,499

RETAIL PRICING

YEAR	HIGH	LOW
2017	$4,577	$3,433

ZT400 2560

YEARS MFRD 2017-2017
SERIES .... ZT400 SERIES
ENGINE .... B&S
ENGINE HP 25
COOLING .... AIR
TRANSMISSION .... HYDRO
STEERING .... ZERO
STANDARD DECK .... 60"
MSRP $7,699

RETAIL PRICING

YEAR	HIGH	LOW
2017	$4,701	$3,525

ZT600 2248

YEARS MFRD 2017-2018
SERIES .... ZT600 SERIES
ENGINE .... KAWASAKI
ENGINE HP 22
COOLING .... AIR
FUEL .... G
TRANSMISSION .... HYDRO
STEERING .... ZERO
STANDARD DECK .... 48"
MSRP $9,049

RETAIL PRICING

YEAR	HIGH	LOW
2017	$5,192	$3,894
2018	$5,755	$4,316

ZT600 2454

YEARS MFRD 2017-2018
SERIES .... ZT600 SERIES
ENGINE .... KAWASAKI
ENGINE HP 24
COOLING .... AIR
FUEL .... G
TRANSMISSION .... HYDRO
STEERING .... ZERO
STANDARD DECK .... 54"
MSRP $9,399

RETAIL PRICING

YEAR	HIGH	LOW
2017	$5,393	$4,045
2018	$6,025	$4,519

ZT600 2460

YEARS MFRD 2017-2018
SERIES .... ZT600 SERIES
ENGINE .... KAWASAKI
ENGINE HP 24
COOLING .... AIR
FUEL .... G
TRANSMISSION .... HYDRO
STEERING .... ZERO
STANDARD DECK .... 60"
MSRP $9,649

RETAIL PRICING

YEAR	HIGH	LOW
2017	$5,537	$4,152
2018	$6,117	$4,588

ZT600 2548

YEARS MFRD 2017-2018
SERIES .... ZT600 SERIES
ENGINE .... KOHLER EFI
ENGINE HP 25
COOLING .... AIR
FUEL .... G
TRANSMISSION .... HYDRO
STEERING .... ZERO
STANDARD DECK .... 48"
MSRP $8,899

RETAIL PRICING

YEAR	HIGH	LOW
2017	$5,106	$3,830
2018	$5,604	$4,203

ZT600 2554

YEARS MFRD 2017-2018
SERIES .... ZT600 SERIES
ENGINE .... KOHLER EFI
ENGINE HP 25
COOLING .... AIR
FUEL .... G
TRANSMISSION .... HYDRO
STEERING .... ZERO
STANDARD DECK .... 54"
MSRP $9,399

RETAIL PRICING

YEAR	HIGH	LOW
2017	$5,393	$4,045
2018	$5,948	$4,461

ZT600 2560

YEARS MFRD 2017-2018
SERIES .... ZT600 SERIES
ENGINE .... KOHLER EFI
ENGINE HP 25
COOLING .... AIR
FUEL .... G
TRANSMISSION .... HYDRO
STEERING .... ZERO
STANDARD DECK .... 60"
MSRP $9,499

RETAIL PRICING

YEAR	HIGH	LOW
2017	$5,450	$4,088
2018	$6,016	$4,512

ZT900 2754

YEARS MFRD 2018-2018
SERIES .... ZT900 SERIES
ENGINE .... KAWASAKI
ENGINE HP 27
COOLING .... AIR
TRANSMISSION .... HYDRO
STEERING .... ZERO
STANDARD DECK .... 54"

OPTIONS

27HP KOHLER EFI

ZT900 2760

YEARS MFRD 2018-2018
SERIES .... ZT900 SERIES
ENGINE .... KAWASAKI
ENGINE HP 27
COOLING .... AIR
TRANSMISSION .... HYDRO
STEERING .... ZERO
STANDARD DECK .... 60"

OPTIONS

27HP KOHLER EFI

ZT1000 2960

YEARS MFRD 2018-2018
SERIES .... ZT1000 SERIES
ENGINE .... KOHLER LP EFI
ENGINE HP 29
COOLING .... AIR
TRANSMISSION .... HYDRO
STEERING .... ZERO
STANDARD DECK .... 60"

ZT1000 2972

YEARS MFRD 2018-2018
SERIES .... ZT1000 SERIES
ENGINE .... KOHLER LP EFI
ENGINE HP 29
COOLING .... AIR
TRANSMISSION .... HYDRO
STEERING .... ZERO
STANDARD DECK .... 72"

ZT1000 3160

YEARS MFRD 2018-2018
SERIES . . . . ZT1000 SERIES
ENGINE . . . . KAWASAKI
ENGINE HP 31
COOLING . . . . AIR
TRANSMISSION . . . . HYDRO
STEERING . . . . ZERO
STANDARD DECK . . . . 60"

OPTIONS

31HP KOHLER EFI

ZT1000 3366

YEARS MFRD 2018-2018
SERIES . . . . ZT1000 SERIES
ENGINE . . . . KOHLER EFI
ENGINE HP 33
COOLING . . . . AIR
TRANSMISSION . . . . HYDRO
STEERING . . . . ZERO
STANDARD DECK . . . . 66"

ZT1000 3372

YEARS MFRD 2018-2018
SERIES . . . . ZT1000 SERIES
ENGINE . . . . KOHLER EFI
ENGINE HP 33
COOLING . . . . AIR
TRANSMISSION . . . . HYDRO
STEERING . . . . ZERO
STANDARD DECK . . . . 72"

ZT1000 3566

YEARS MFRD 2018-2018
SERIES . . . . ZT1000 SERIES
ENGINE . . . . KAWASAKI
ENGINE HP 35
COOLING . . . . AIR
TRANSMISSION . . . . HYDRO
STEERING . . . . ZERO
STANDARD DECK . . . . 66"

ZT1000 3572

YEARS MFRD 2018-2018
SERIES . . . . ZT1000 SERIES
ENGINE . . . . KAWASAKI
ENGINE HP 35
COOLING . . . . AIR
TRANSMISSION . . . . HYDRO
STEERING . . . . ZERO
STANDARD DECK . . . . 72"

ZT 400

YEARS MFRD 2017-2017
ENGINE . . . . KAWASAKI
ENGINE HP 22
COOLING . . . . AIR
FUEL . . . . G
SPEEDS . . . . VARIABLE
TRANSMISSION . . . . HYDRO
STEERING . . . . ZERO
STANDARD DECK . . . . 48"

OPTIONS

54" DECK
60" DECK

ZT 600

YEARS MFRD 2017-2017
ENGINE . . . . KAWASAKI
ENGINE HP 22
COOLING . . . . AIR
FUEL . . . . G
SPEEDS . . . . VARIABLE
TRANSMISSION . . . . HYDRO
STEERING . . . . ZERO
STANDARD DECK . . . . 48"

OPTIONS

54" DECK
60" DECK

623

YEARS MFRD 2002-2002
ENGINE . . . . KUBOTA
ENGINE HP 23
FUEL . . . . D
TRANSMISSION . . . . HYDRO
STEERING . . . . STANDARD
DRIVE TYPE 2WD

623D

YEARS MFRD 2003-2007
SERIES . . . . . . TURFCAT 600 SERIES
ENGINE . . . . KUBOTA D905-EB
CYLINDERS 3
ENGINE HP 23
COOLING . . . . LIQUID
FUEL . . . . D
SPEEDS . . . . VARIABLE
TRANSMISSION . . . . HYDRO
STEERING . . . . ZERO
HYDRAULIC . . . . YES
PTO . . . . YES
WEIGHT . . . . 1,310 LBS.

628

YEARS MFRD 2001-2004
SERIES . . . . TURFCAT SERIES
ENGINE . . . . KUBOTA
ENGINE HP 26
FUEL . . . . G
SPEEDS . . . . VARIABLE
TRANSMISSION . . . . HYDRO
STEERING . . . . STANDARD
DRIVE TYPE 2WD
MSRP $15,230

OPTIONS

4WD

RETAIL PRICING

YEAR	HIGH	LOW
2003	$7,413	$5,560
2004	$7,892	$5,919

628D

YEARS MFRD 2003-2007
SERIES . . . . . . TURFCAT 600 SERIES
ENGINE . . . . KUBOTA D1105-EB
CYLINDERS 3
ENGINE HP 26
COOLING . . . . LIQUID
FUEL . . . . D
SPEEDS . . . . VARIABLE
TRANSMISSION . . . . HYDRO
STEERING . . . . ZERO
HYDRAULIC . . . . YES
PTO . . . . YES
DRIVE TYPE 4WD
ROPS/CAB . . . . ROPS
WEIGHT . . . . 1,559 LBS.

1800D

YEARS MFRD 1997-1998
ENGINE . . . . B&S
ENGINE HP 18
FUEL . . . . G
TRANSMISSION . . . . HYDRO
STEERING . . . . STANDARD
STANDARD DECK . . . . 84"
MSRP $7,270

RETAIL PRICING

YEAR	HIGH	LOW
1997	$2,353	$1,765
1998	$2,723	$2,042

1800G

YEARS MFRD 1997-2004
SERIES . . . . TRI-KING SERIES
ENGINE . . . B&S VANGUARD V-TWIN
CYLINDERS 2
CID 34.8
ENGINE HP 18
COOLING . . . . AIR
FUEL . . . . G
SPEEDS . . . . VARIABLE
TRANSMISSION . . . . HYDRO
STEERING . . . . ZERO
HYDRAULIC . . . . YES
STANDARD DECK . . . . 72"
WEIGHT . . . . 1,528 LBS.
MSRP $20,775

OPTIONS

84" DECK

RETAIL PRICING

YEAR	HIGH	LOW
2003	$10,111	$7,583
2004	$10,764	$8,073

1900D

YEARS MFRD 1997-2007
SERIES . . . . TRI-KING SERIES
ENGINE . . . . KUBOTA D662
CYLINDERS 3
CID 40.3
ENGINE HP 19
COOLING . . . . LIQUID
FUEL . . . . D
SPEEDS . . . . VARIABLE
TRANSMISSION . . . . HYDRO
STEERING . . . . ZERO
HYDRAULIC . . . . YES
STANDARD DECK . . . . 72"
WEIGHT . . . . 1,594 LBS.
MSRP $27,297

OPTIONS

84" DECK

RETAIL PRICING

YEAR	HIGH	LOW
2003	$12,004	$9,003
2004	$12,780	$9,585
2005	$15,001	$11,251
2006	$15,860	$11,895

2750 EFI

YEARS MFRD 2015-2015
ENGINE . . . . KOHLER EFI
ENGINE HP 27
COOLING . . . . AIR
FUEL . . . . G
SPEEDS . . . . VARIABLE
TRANSMISSION . . . . HYDRO
STEERING . . . . ZERO
BLADE CLUTCH . . . . ELECTRIC
STANDARD DECK . . . . 50"

2760 EFI

YEARS MFRD 2015-2015
ENGINE . . . . KOHLER EFI
ENGINE HP 27
COOLING . . . . AIR
FUEL . . . . G
SPEEDS . . . . VARIABLE
TRANSMISSION . . . . HYDRO
STEERING . . . . ZERO
BLADE CLUTCH . . . . ELECTRIC
STANDARD DECK . . . . 60"

4300 MULTI-USE

YEARS MFRD 2004-2004
SERIES . . GARDEN TRACTOR SERIES
ENGINE . . . . KUBOTA D722
ENGINE HP 21
COOLING . . . . LIQUID
FUEL . . . . D
SPEEDS . . . . VARIABLE
TRANSMISSION . . . . GEAR
STEERING . . . . STANDARD
HYDRAULIC . . . . YES
PTO . . . . YES
WEIGHT . . . . 1,760 LBS.
MSRP $14,995

OPTIONS

KOHLER COMMAND 25HP
KUBOTA WG752 25HP
LINAMAR LX90 20HP

RETAIL PRICING

YEAR	HIGH	LOW
2004	$7,769	$5,827

66014

YEARS MFRD 1988-1994
SERIES . . . . TURFCAT X420G SERIES
ENGINE . . . . KUBOTA
ENGINE HP 21
FUEL . . . . G
TRANSMISSION . . . . HYDRO

STEERING............STANDARD
STANDARD DECK........... 50"
MSRP...............$8,275

RETAIL PRICING

YEAR	HIGH	LOW
1988	$1,965	$1,473
1989	$2,059	$1,544
1990	$2,144	$1,608
1991	$2,330	$1,748

JCB

D20-50

YEARS MFRD........2008-2008
CYLINDERS.................2
ENGINE HP................20
COOLING..................AIR
FUEL........................D
SPEEDS............VARIABLE
TRANSMISSION..........HYDRO
STEERING.................ZERO
BLADE CLUTCH........ELECTRIC

FM30

YEARS MFRD........2009-2009
ENGINE...............YANMAR
CYLINDERS.................3
ENGINE HP................30
COOLING...............LIQUID
FUEL........................D
SPEEDS............VARIABLE
TRANSMISSION..........HYDRO
STEERING.................ZERO
BLADE CLUTCH........ELECTRIC

JCB 323

YEARS MFRD........2007-2012
CYLINDERS.................3
ENGINE HP................23
COOLING...............LIQUID
FUEL........................D
SPEEDS............VARIABLE
TRANSMISSION..........HYDRO
STEERING...........STANDARD
HITCH...................CAT. II

JCB 327

YEARS MFRD........2007-2012
CYLINDERS.................3
ENGINE HP................27
COOLING..................AIR
FUEL........................D
SPEEDS............VARIABLE
TRANSMISSION..........HYDRO
STEERING...........STANDARD
HITCH...................CAT. II

JCB 331

YEARS MFRD........2007-2010
CYLINDERS.................3
ENGINE HP................31
COOLING...............LIQUID
FUEL........................D
SPEEDS............VARIABLE
TRANSMISSION..........HYDRO
STEERING...........STANDARD
HITCH...................CAT. II

JCB 335

YEARS MFRD........2007-2010
CYLINDERS.................3
ENGINE HP................35
COOLING...............LIQUID
FUEL........................D
SPEEDS............VARIABLE
TRANSMISSION..........HYDRO
STEERING...........STANDARD
HITCH...................CAT. II

ZT20D

YEARS MFRD........2008-2011
ENGINE HP................20
FUEL........................D
SPEEDS............VARIABLE
TRANSMISSION..........HYDRO
STEERING.................ZERO
BLADE CLUTCH........ELECTRIC

354

YEARS MFRD........2010-2011
CYLINDERS.................4
ENGINE HP................54
COOLING...............LIQUID
FUEL........................D
SPEEDS..................24/24
TRANSMISSION...SHUTTLE SHIFT
STEERING...........STANDARD

JOHN DEERE

D100

YEARS MFRD........2011-2012
SERIES............100 SERIES
ENGINE....................B&S
CYLINDERS.................1
CID......................30.6
ENGINE HP..............17.5
COOLING..................AIR
FUEL........................G
SPEEDS............VARIABLE
TRANSMISSION..........HYDRO
STEERING...........STANDARD
BLADE CLUTCH..........MANUAL
STANDARD DECK........... 42"
WEIGHT..............442 LBS.
MSRP...............$1,499

OPTIONS

46" BLADE
BAGGER

SERIAL NUMBERS

YEAR	BEGINNING NO.
2011	B00001
2012	C300001

RETAIL PRICING

YEAR	HIGH	LOW
2011	$747	$560
2012	$818	$614

D105

YEARS MFRD........2013-2017
ENGINE....................B&S
ENGINE HP..............17.5
COOLING..................AIR
FUEL........................G
SPEEDS............VARIABLE
TRANSMISSION..............CVT
STEERING...........STANDARD
STANDARD DECK........... 42"
MSRP...............$1,499

OPTIONS

46" BLADE
6.5 BU BAG
SNOCAB
SPRAYER

SERIAL NUMBERS

YEAR	BEGINNING NO.
2013	400001
2014	500001
2015	600001
2016	700001
2017	800001

RETAIL PRICING

YEAR	HIGH	LOW
2013	$800	$600
2014	$865	$649
2015	$951	$713
2016	$1,039	$780
2017	$1,127	$845

D110

YEARS MFRD........2011-2017
SERIES............100 SERIES
ENGINE....................B&S
CYLINDERS.................1
CID......................30.6
ENGINE HP..............19.5
COOLING..................AIR
FUEL........................G
SPEEDS............VARIABLE
TRANSMISSION..........HYDRO
STEERING...........STANDARD
BLADE CLUTCH..........MANUAL
STANDARD DECK........... 42"
WEIGHT..............450 LBS.
MSRP...............$1,699

OPTIONS

46" BLADE
6.5BU BAG
SNOCAB

SERIAL NUMBERS

YEAR	BEGINNING NO.
2011	B100001
2012	C300001
2013	D400001
2014	E500001
2015	F600001
2016	700001
2017	800001

RETAIL PRICING

YEAR	HIGH	LOW
2011	$767	$575
2012	$826	$620
2013	$897	$672
2014	$980	$735
2015	$1,084	$813
2016	$1,199	$899
2017	$1,279	$959

D120

YEARS MFRD........2011-2017
SERIES............100 SERIES
ENGINE....................B&S
CYLINDERS.................1
CID.......................33
ENGINE HP................21
COOLING..................AIR
FUEL........................G
SPEEDS............VARIABLE
TRANSMISSION..........HYDRO
STEERING...........STANDARD
BLADE CLUTCH..........MANUAL
STANDARD DECK........... 42"
WEIGHT..............452 LBS.
MSRP...............$1,799

OPTIONS

46" BLADE
6.5 BU BAG
SNOCAB

SERIAL NUMBERS

YEAR	BEGINNING NO.
2011	B100001
2012	C300001
2013	D400001
2014	500001
2015	600001
2016	700001
2017	800001

RETAIL PRICING

YEAR	HIGH	LOW
2011	$796	$597
2012	$859	$644
2013	$941	$706
2014	$1,026	$770
2015	$1,125	$844
2016	$1,234	$926
2017	$1,354	$1,015

D125

YEARS MFRD........2014-2017
ENGINE....................B&S
ENGINE HP................20
COOLING..................AIR
FUEL........................G
SPEEDS............VARIABLE
TRANSMISSION..........HYDRO

STEERING. . . . . .STANDARD
STANDARD DECK . . . . 42"
MSRP. $1,799

OPTIONS

46" BLADE
6.5 BU BAG
SNOCAB

SERIAL NUMBERS

YEAR	BEGINNING NO.
2014	E500001
2015	F600001
2016	700001
2017	800001

RETAIL PRICING

YEAR	HIGH	LOW
2014	$1,028	$771
2015	$1,137	$853
2016	$1,240	$930
2017	$1,354	$1,015

D130

YEARS MFRD 2011-2017
SERIES. . . . . 100 SERIES
ENGINE . . . . B&S
CYLINDERS. 2
CID 40
ENGINE HP 22
COOLING . . . . AIR
FUEL . . . . G
SPEEDS . . . . VARIABLE
TRANSMISSION . . . . HYDRO
STEERING. . . . . .STANDARD
BLADE CLUTCH . . . . MANUAL
STANDARD DECK . . . . 42"
WEIGHT . . . . 478 LBS.
MSRP. $1,899

OPTIONS

46" BLADE
6.5 BU BAG
SNOCAB

SERIAL NUMBERS

YEAR	BEGINNING NO.
2011	B100001
2012	C300001
2013	D400001
2014	E500001
2015	F600001
2016	700001
2017	800001

RETAIL PRICING

YEAR	HIGH	LOW
2011	$855	$641
2012	$953	$715
2013	$1,006	$754
2014	$1,099	$824
2015	$1,213	$910
2016	$1,346	$1,010
2017	$1,429	$1,072

AVG. AUCTION PRICING

LOW	HIGH	AVG
$1,339	$1,929	$1,560

D140

YEARS MFRD 2011-2017
SERIES. . . . . 100 SERIES
ENGINE . . . . B&S
CYLINDERS. 2
CID 40
ENGINE HP 22
COOLING . . . . AIR
FUEL . . . . G
SPEEDS . . . . VARIABLE
TRANSMISSION . . . . HYDRO
STEERING. . . . . .STANDARD
BLADE CLUTCH . . . . ELECTRIC
STANDARD DECK . . . . 48"
WEIGHT . . . . 491 LBS.
MSRP. $1,999

OPTIONS

46" BLADE
6.5 BU BAG
SNOCAB

SERIAL NUMBERS

YEAR	BEGINNING NO.
2011	B100001
2012	C300001
2013	D400001
2014	E500001
2015	F600001
2016	700001
2017	800001

RETAIL PRICING

YEAR	HIGH	LOW
2011	$890	$668
2012	$975	$731
2013	$1,075	$806
2014	$1,177	$883
2015	$1,286	$965
2016	$1,405	$1,053
2017	$1,503	$1,128

D150

YEARS MFRD 2011-2011
SERIES. . . . . 100 SERIES
ENGINE . . . . B&S
CYLINDERS. 2
CID 40
ENGINE HP 22
COOLING . . . . AIR
FUEL . . . . G
SPEEDS . . . . VARIABLE
TRANSMISSION . . . . HYDRO
STEERING. . . . . .STANDARD
BLADE CLUTCH . . . . ELECTRIC
STANDARD DECK . . . . 48"
WEIGHT . . . . 520 LBS.
MSRP. $2,299

OPTIONS

46" BLADE
BAGGER

SERIAL NUMBERS

YEAR	BEGINNING NO.
2011	B100001

RETAIL PRICING

YEAR	HIGH	LOW
2011	$1,213	$910

D155

YEARS MFRD 2015-2017
ENGINE . . . . B&S
ENGINE HP 24
COOLING . . . . AIR
FUEL . . . . G
SPEEDS . . . . VARIABLE
TRANSMISSION . . . . HYDRO
STEERING. . . . . .STANDARD
STANDARD DECK . . . . 48"
MSRP. $2,199

OPTIONS

46" BLADE
BAGGER
CAB

SERIAL NUMBERS

YEAR	BEGINNING NO.
2015	600001
2016	700001
2017	800001

RETAIL PRICING

YEAR	HIGH	LOW
2015	$1,406	$1,054
2016	$1,547	$1,161
2017	$1,654	$1,241

D160

YEARS MFRD 2011-2017
SERIES. . . . . 100 SERIES
ENGINE . . . . B&S
CYLINDERS. 2
CID 44.2
ENGINE HP 24
COOLING . . . . AIR
FUEL . . . . G
SPEEDS . . . . VARIABLE
TRANSMISSION . . . . HYDRO
STEERING. . . . . .STANDARD
BLADE CLUTCH . . . . ELECTRIC
STANDARD DECK . . . . 48"
WEIGHT . . . . 528 LBS.
MSRP. $2,349

OPTIONS

46" BLADE
6.5 BU BAG
SNOCAB

SERIAL NUMBERS

YEAR	BEGINNING NO.
2011	B100001
2012	C300001
2013	D400001
2014	E500001
2015	F600001
2016	700001
2017	800001

RETAIL PRICING

YEAR	HIGH	LOW
2011	$1,019	$764
2012	$1,120	$840
2013	$1,230	$923
2014	$1,349	$1,012
2015	$1,494	$1,121
2016	$1,644	$1,233
2017	$1,767	$1,325

D170

YEARS MFRD 2011-2017
SERIES. . . . . 100 SERIES
ENGINE . . . . B&S
CYLINDERS. 2
CID 44.2
ENGINE HP 25
COOLING . . . . AIR
FUEL . . . . G
SPEEDS . . . . VARIABLE
TRANSMISSION . . . . HYDRO
STEERING. . . . . .STANDARD
BLADE CLUTCH . . . . ELECTRIC
STANDARD DECK . . . . 54"
WEIGHT . . . . 552 LBS.
MSRP. $2,799

OPTIONS

46" BLADE
6.5 BU BAG
SNOCAB

SERIAL NUMBERS

YEAR	BEGINNING NO.
2011	B100001
2012	C300001
2013	D400001
2014	E500001
2015	F600001
2016	700001
2017	800001

RETAIL PRICING

YEAR	HIGH	LOW
2011	$1,255	$941
2012	$1,342	$1,007
2013	$1,484	$1,113
2014	$1,640	$1,230
2015	$1,799	$1,349
2016	$1,952	$1,464
2017	$2,105	$1,579

E100

YEARS MFRD 2018-2020
SERIES. . . . . 100 SERIES
CYLINDERS. 1
CID 30.5
ENGINE HP 17.5
COOLING . . . . AIR
FUEL . . . . G
SPEEDS . . . . VARIABLE
TRANSMISSION . . . . CVT
STEERING. . . . . .STANDARD
BLADE CLUTCH . . . . MANUAL
STANDARD DECK . . . . 42"
WEIGHT . . . . 427 LBS.
MSRP. $1,599

OPTIONS

44" SNOW BLOWER $1,519

E110

YEARS MFRD 2018-2020
SERIES. . . . . 100 SERIES
CYLINDERS. 1
CID 33
ENGINE HP 19
COOLING . . . . AIR
FUEL . . . . G
SPEEDS . . . . VARIABLE
TRANSMISSION . . . . HYDRO
STEERING. . . . . .STANDARD
BLADE CLUTCH . . . . MANUAL
STANDARD DECK . . . . 42"
WEIGHT . . . . 386 LBS.
MSRP. $1,799

OPTIONS

44" SNOW BLOWER $1,519

JOHN DEERE

E120

YEARS MFRD 2018-2020
SERIES. . . . . 100 SERIES
CID 40
ENGINE HP 20
COOLING . . . . .AIR
FUEL . . . . G
SPEEDS . . . . VARIABLE
TRANSMISSION . . . . .HYDRO
STEERING. . . . . .STANDARD
BLADE CLUTCH . . . . MANUAL
STANDARD DECK . . . . 42"
WEIGHT . . . . 420 LBS.
MSRP. $1,899

OPTIONS

44" SNOW BLOWER $1,519

E130

YEARS MFRD 2018-2020
SERIES. . . . . 100 SERIES
CID 44
ENGINE HP 22
COOLING . . . . .AIR
FUEL . . . . G
SPEEDS . . . . VARIABLE
TRANSMISSION . . . . .HYDRO
STEERING. . . . . .STANDARD
BLADE CLUTCH . . . . MANUAL
STANDARD DECK . . . . 42"
WEIGHT . . . . 438 LBS.
MSRP. $1,999

OPTIONS

44" SNOW BLOWER $1,519

E140

YEARS MFRD 2018-2020
SERIES. . . . . 100 SERIES
CID 44
ENGINE HP 22
COOLING . . . . .AIR
FUEL . . . . G
SPEEDS . . . . VARIABLE
TRANSMISSION . . . . .HYDRO
STEERING. . . . . .STANDARD
BLADE CLUTCH . . . . .ELECTRIC
STANDARD DECK . . . . 48"
WEIGHT . . . . 475 LBS.
MSRP. $2,099

OPTIONS

44" SNOW BLOWER $1,519

E150

YEARS MFRD 2018-2020
SERIES. . . . . 100 SERIES
CID 44
ENGINE HP 22
COOLING . . . . .AIR
FUEL . . . . G
SPEEDS . . . . VARIABLE
TRANSMISSION . . . . .HYDRO
STEERING. . . . . .STANDARD
BLADE CLUTCH . . . . .ELECTRIC
STANDARD DECK . . . . 48"
WEIGHT . . . . 483 LBS.
MSRP. $2,199

OPTIONS

44" SNOW BLOWER $1,519

E160

YEARS MFRD 2018-2020
SERIES. . . . . 100 SERIES
CID 44
ENGINE HP 24
COOLING . . . . .AIR
FUEL . . . . G
SPEEDS . . . . VARIABLE
TRANSMISSION . . . . .HYDRO
STEERING. . . . . .STANDARD
BLADE CLUTCH . . . . .ELECTRIC
STANDARD DECK . . . . 48"
WEIGHT . . . . 492 LBS.
MSRP. $2,349

OPTIONS

44" SNOW BLOWER $1,519

E170

YEARS MFRD 2018-2020
SERIES. . . . . 100 SERIES
CID 44
ENGINE HP 25
COOLING . . . . .AIR
FUEL . . . . G
SPEEDS . . . . VARIABLE
TRANSMISSION . . . . .HYDRO
STEERING. . . . . .STANDARD
BLADE CLUTCH . . . . .ELECTRIC
STANDARD DECK . . . . 48"
WEIGHT . . . . 512 LBS.
MSRP. $2,449

OPTIONS

44" SNOW BLOWER $1,519

E180

YEARS MFRD 2018-2020
SERIES. . . . . 100 SERIES
CID 44
ENGINE HP 25
COOLING . . . . .AIR
FUEL . . . . G
SPEEDS . . . . VARIABLE
TRANSMISSION . . . . .HYDRO
STEERING. . . . . .STANDARD
BLADE CLUTCH . . . . .ELECTRIC
STANDARD DECK . . . . 54"
WEIGHT . . . . 531 LBS.
MSRP. $2,799

OPTIONS

44" SNOW BLOWER $1,519

F510

YEARS MFRD 1989-2002
SERIES. . . . .FRONT MOWER SERIES
ENGINE . . . . KAWASAKI
ENGINE HP 14
COOLING . . . . .AIR
FUEL . . . . G
SPEEDS . . . . VARIABLE
TRANSMISSION . . . . .HYDRO
STEERING. . . . . ZERO
BLADE CLUTCH . . . . .ELECTRIC
STANDARD DECK . . . . 38"
WEIGHT . . . . 868 LBS.
MSRP. $5,049

OPTIONS

2 BAG
38" SNOW THROWER
BAG & FAN

SERIAL NUMBERS

YEAR	BEGINNING NO.
1989	595001
1990	010001
1991	100001
1992	110001
1993	120001
1994	130001
1995	140001
1996	150001
1997	160001
1998	170001
1999	180001
2000	190001
2001	200001
2002	200002
2003	220001

RETAIL PRICING

YEAR	HIGH	LOW
1994	$662	$496
1995	$734	$551
1996	$821	$616
1997	$906	$679
1998	$1,003	$752
1999	$1,112	$834
2000	$1,234	$926
2001	$1,371	$1,028
2002	$1,519	$1,139

F525

YEARS MFRD 1989-2003
SERIES. . . . .FRONT MOWER SERIES
ENGINE . . . . KAWASAKI
ENGINE HP 17
COOLING . . . . .AIR
FUEL . . . . G
SPEEDS . . . . VARIABLE
TRANSMISSION . . . . .HYDRO
STEERING. . . . . ZERO
BLADE CLUTCH . . . . .ELECTRIC
STANDARD DECK . . . . 48"
WEIGHT . . . . 913 LBS.
MSRP. $5,849

OPTIONS

2 BAG
38" SNOW THROWER
BAG & FAN

SERIAL NUMBERS

YEAR	BEGINNING NO.
1989	595001
1990	010001
1991	100001
1992	110001
1993	120001
1994	130001
1995	140001
1996	150001
1997	160001
1998	170001
1999	180001
2000	190001
2001	195001
2002	205001
2003	215001

RETAIL PRICING

YEAR	HIGH	LOW
1995	$1,122	$842
1996	$1,234	$926
1997	$1,364	$1,023
1998	$1,519	$1,139
1999	$1,653	$1,240
2000	$1,886	$1,414
2001	$2,056	$1,542
2002	$2,274	$1,705
2003	$2,548	$1,911

F620

YEARS MFRD 1998-1999
SERIES. . . . . .Z-TRAK SERIES
ENGINE . . . . KOHLER
ENGINE HP 20
COOLING . . . . .AIR
FUEL . . . . G
SPEEDS . . . . VARIABLE
TRANSMISSION . . . . .HYDRO
STEERING. . . . . ZERO
STANDARD DECK . . . . 48"
MSRP. $8,665

OPTIONS

60" DECK
BAGGER

SERIAL NUMBERS

YEAR	BEGINNING NO.
1998	010001

RETAIL PRICING

YEAR	HIGH	LOW
1998	$2,253	$1,690
1999	$2,532	$1,899

F625

YEARS MFRD 1998-1998
SERIES. . . . . .Z-TRAK SERIES
ENGINE . . . . KOHLER
ENGINE HP 25
COOLING . . . . .AIR
FUEL . . . . G
SPEEDS . . . . VARIABLE
TRANSMISSION . . . . .HYDRO
STEERING. . . . . ZERO
STANDARD DECK . . . . 48"
MSRP. $9,125

OPTIONS

60" DECK

SERIAL NUMBERS

YEAR	BEGINNING NO.
1998	010001

RETAIL PRICING

YEAR	HIGH	LOW
1998	$2,408	$1,806

AVG. AUCTION PRICING

LOW	HIGH	AVG
$765	$1,887	$1,190

F680

YEARS MFRD . . . 2000-2002
SERIES . . . Z-TRAK SERIES
ENGINE . . . KOHLER
ENGINE HP . . . 20
COOLING . . . AIR
FUEL . . . G
SPEEDS . . . VARIABLE
TRANSMISSION . . . HYDRO
STEERING . . . ZERO
STANDARD DECK . . . 48"
WEIGHT . . . 1,247 LBS.
MSRP . . . $9,079

OPTIONS

54" DECK
60" DECK
BAGGER

SERIAL NUMBERS

YEAR	BEGINNING NO.
2000	TCF680X010001
2001	TCF680X020001
2002	TCF680X030001

RETAIL PRICING

YEAR	HIGH	LOW
2000	$2,229	$1,672
2001	$2,480	$1,860
2002	$2,708	$2,031

F687

YEARS MFRD . . . 2003-2008
SERIES . . . FRONT Z-TRAK SERIES
ENGINE . . . KOHLER
CYLINDERS . . . 2
CID . . . 38
ENGINE HP . . . 23
COOLING . . . AIR
FUEL . . . G
SPEEDS . . . VARIABLE
TRANSMISSION . . . HYDRO
STEERING . . . ZERO
STANDARD DECK . . . 48"
WEIGHT . . . 1,223 LBS.
MSRP . . . $10,349

OPTIONS

54" DECK
60" DECK
BAG & FAN

SERIAL NUMBERS

YEAR	BEGINNING NO.
2003	X020001
2004	X030001
2005	X040001
2006	X050001
2007	X060001
2008	X070001

RETAIL PRICING

YEAR	HIGH	LOW
2003	$3,604	$2,703
2004	$4,036	$3,027
2005	$4,456	$3,342
2006	$4,891	$3,668
2007	$5,448	$4,086
2008	$6,001	$4,500

F710

YEARS MFRD . . . 1990-1997
SERIES . . . FRONT MOWER SERIES
ENGINE . . . KAWASAKI
ENGINE HP . . . 17.5
COOLING . . . AIR
FUEL . . . G
SPEEDS . . . VARIABLE
TRANSMISSION . . . HYDRO
STEERING . . . STANDARD
BLADE CLUTCH . . . ELECTRIC
STANDARD DECK . . . 48"
WEIGHT . . . 975 LBS.
MSRP . . . $9,046

OPTIONS

46" SNOW THROWER
BAGGER

SERIAL NUMBERS

YEAR	BEGINNING NO.
1991	010001
1992	020001
1993	030001
1994	040001
1995	050001
1996	060001
1997	070001

RETAIL PRICING

YEAR	HIGH	LOW
1990	$872	$654
1991	$986	$740
1992	$1,075	$806
1993	$1,194	$896
1994	$1,323	$992
1995	$1,467	$1,100
1996	$1,633	$1,225
1997	$1,809	$1,357

F725

YEARS MFRD . . . 1990-2006
SERIES . . . FRONT MOWER SERIES
ENGINE . . . KAWASAKI
CYLINDERS . . . 2
ENGINE HP . . . 20
COOLING . . . LIQUID
FUEL . . . G
SPEEDS . . . VARIABLE
TRANSMISSION . . . HYDRO
STEERING . . . ZERO
BLADE CLUTCH . . . ELECTRIC
STANDARD DECK . . . 54"
WEIGHT . . . 1,089 LBS.
MSRP . . . $9,729

OPTIONS

46" SNOW THROWER
BAG & FAN
BAGGER

SERIAL NUMBERS

YEAR	BEGINNING NO.
1991	010001
1992	020001
1993	030001
1994	040001
1995	050001
1996	060001
1997	070001
1998	080001
1999	090001
2000	100001
2001	110001
2002	120001
2005	150001
2006	160001

RETAIL PRICING

YEAR	HIGH	LOW
1998	$2,113	$1,585
1999	$2,378	$1,783
2000	$2,657	$1,993
2001	$2,939	$2,204
2002	$3,197	$2,398
2003	$3,554	$2,665
2004	$3,915	$2,936
2005	$4,374	$3,280
2006	$4,723	$3,542

AVG. AUCTION PRICING

LOW	HIGH	AVG
$1,179	$2,680	$2,063

F735

YEARS MFRD . . . 1998-2005
SERIES . . . FRONT MOWER SERIES
ENGINE . . . YANMAR
CYLINDERS . . . 2
ENGINE HP . . . 20.5
COOLING . . . LIQUID
FUEL . . . D
SPEEDS . . . VARIABLE
TRANSMISSION . . . HYDRO
STEERING . . . STANDARD
BLADE CLUTCH . . . ELECTRIC
STANDARD DECK . . . 54"
WEIGHT . . . 1,109 LBS.
MSRP . . . $11,459

OPTIONS

46" SNOW THROWER
60" DECK
BAG & FAN
BAGGER

SERIAL NUMBERS

YEAR	BEGINNING NO.
1998	010001
2000	015001
2001	020001
2002	030001
2003	040001
2004	050001
2005	060001

RETAIL PRICING

YEAR	HIGH	LOW
1998	$2,537	$1,903
1999	$2,848	$2,136
2000	$3,107	$2,330
2001	$3,483	$2,612
2002	$3,829	$2,872
2003	$4,247	$3,185
2004	$4,805	$3,604
2005	$5,287	$3,965

F910

YEARS MFRD . . . 1984-1990
SERIES . . . FRONT MOWER SERIES
ENGINE . . . ONAN
ENGINE HP . . . 20
COOLING . . . AIR
FUEL . . . G
SPEEDS . . . VARIABLE
TRANSMISSION . . . HYDRO
STEERING . . . STANDARD
STANDARD DECK . . . 60"
WEIGHT . . . 1,702 LBS.
MSRP . . . $11,386

OPTIONS

CANOPY

SERIAL NUMBERS

YEAR	BEGINNING NO.
1984	X285001
1985	X315001
1986	X360001
1987	X420001
1988	X475001
1989	X595001
1990	X010001

RETAIL PRICING

YEAR	HIGH	LOW
1984	$724	$543
1985	$802	$601
1986	$888	$666
1987	$986	$740
1988	$1,094	$821
1989	$1,230	$923
1990	$1,343	$1,008

F911

YEARS MFRD . . . 1991-2001
SERIES . . . FRONT MOWER SERIES
ENGINE . . . KAWASAKI
ENGINE HP . . . 22
COOLING . . . LIQUID
FUEL . . . G
SPEEDS . . . VARIABLE
TRANSMISSION . . . HYDRO
STEERING . . . STANDARD
STANDARD DECK . . . 60"
WEIGHT . . . 2,103 LBS.
MSRP . . . $14,550

OPTIONS

3 BAG & FAN
4 ROPS
54" BLADE
72" DECK

SERIAL NUMBERS

YEAR	BEGINNING NO.
1991	100001
1992	110001
1993	120001
1994	130001
1995	140001
1996	150001
1997	160001
1998	170001
2000	185001

RETAIL PRICING

YEAR	HIGH	LOW
1993	$1,942	$1,457
1994	$2,140	$1,605
1995	$2,440	$1,830

1996	$2,676	$2,007
1997	$3,027	$2,271
1998	$3,282	$2,462
1999	$3,622	$2,717
2000	$4,016	$3,012
2001	$4,486	$3,364

F912

YEARS MFRD 1987-1991
SERIES. . . . .FRONT MOWER SERIES
ENGINE . . . . .YANMAR
ENGINE HP 20
COOLING . . . . LIQUID
FUEL . . . . G
SPEEDS . . . . .VARIABLE
TRANSMISSION . . . . .HYDRO
STEERING. . . . . .STANDARD
STANDARD DECK . . . . 60"
WEIGHT . . . . .2,264 LBS.
MSRP. $12,883

OPTIONS

CANOPY

SERIAL NUMBERS

YEAR	BEGINNING NO.
1987	420001
1988	460001
1989	595001
1990	010001
1991	100001

RETAIL PRICING

YEAR	HIGH	LOW
1987	$1,188	$891
1988	$1,333	$1,000
1989	$1,463	$1,097
1990	$1,622	$1,216
1991	$1,804	$1,353

F915

YEARS MFRD 1986-1993
SERIES. . . . .FRONT MOWER SERIES
ENGINE . . . . .YANMAR
ENGINE HP 17
COOLING . . . . LIQUID
FUEL . . . . D
SPEEDS . . . . .VARIABLE
TRANSMISSION . . . . .HYDRO
STEERING. . . . . .STANDARD
STANDARD DECK . . . . 60"
WEIGHT . . . . .2,136 LBS.
MSRP. $13,978

OPTIONS

46" SNOW THROWER

SERIAL NUMBERS

YEAR	BEGINNING NO.
1986	360001
1987	420001
1988	460001
1989	595001
1990	010001
1991	100001
1992	110001
1993	120001

RETAIL PRICING

YEAR	HIGH	LOW
1986	$895	$671
1987	$992	$744
1988	$1,101	$825
1989	$1,225	$919
1990	$1,359	$1,019
1991	$1,508	$1,131
1992	$1,669	$1,252
1993	$1,855	$1,392

F925

YEARS MFRD 1993-2001
SERIES. . . . .FRONT MOWER SERIES
ENGINE . . . . .YANMAR
ENGINE HP 22
COOLING . . . . LIQUID
FUEL . . . . D
SPEEDS . . . . .VARIABLE
TRANSMISSION . . . . .HYDRO
STEERING. . . . . .STANDARD
STANDARD DECK . . . . 60"
WEIGHT . . . . .2,080 LBS.
MSRP. $16,970

OPTIONS

3 BAG & FAN
54" BLADE
72" DECK

SERIAL NUMBERS

YEAR	BEGINNING NO.
1993	120001
1994	130001
1995	140001
1996	150001
1997	160001
1998	170001
1999	180001
2000	185001

RETAIL PRICING

YEAR	HIGH	LOW
1993	$2,036	$1,527
1994	$2,257	$1,693
1995	$2,497	$1,873
1996	$2,842	$2,131
1997	$3,086	$2,314
1998	$3,437	$2,578
1999	$3,798	$2,849
2000	$4,257	$3,193
2001	$4,672	$3,504

F930

YEARS MFRD 1987-1991
SERIES. . . . .FRONT MOWER SERIES
ENGINE . . . . .ONAN
ENGINE HP 24
COOLING . . . . AIR
FUEL . . . . G
SPEEDS . . . . .VARIABLE
TRANSMISSION . . . . .HYDRO
STEERING. . . . . .STANDARD
STANDARD DECK . . . . 72"
WEIGHT . . . . .1,994 LBS.
MSRP. $12,947

OPTIONS

CANOPY

SERIAL NUMBERS

YEAR	BEGINNING NO.
1987	420001
1988	460001
1989	595001
1990	010001
1991	100001

RETAIL PRICING

YEAR	HIGH	LOW
1987	$1,013	$760
1988	$1,112	$834
1989	$1,230	$923
1990	$1,371	$1,028
1991	$1,540	$1,155

F932

YEARS MFRD 1988-2001
SERIES. . . . .FRONT MOWER SERIES
ENGINE . . . . .YANMAR
ENGINE HP 28
COOLING . . . . LIQUID
FUEL . . . . G
SPEEDS . . . . .VARIABLE
TRANSMISSION . . . . .HYDRO
STEERING. . . . . .STANDARD
STANDARD DECK . . . . 72"
WEIGHT . . . . .2,291 LBS.
MSRP. $17,825

OPTIONS

54" BLADE
60" DECK
CANOPY

SERIAL NUMBERS

YEAR	BEGINNING NO.
1988	460001
1989	595001
1990	010001
1991	100001
1992	110001
1993	120001
1994	130001
1995	140001
1996	150001
1997	160001
1998	170001
1999	180001
2000	185001

RETAIL PRICING

YEAR	HIGH	LOW
1993	$2,140	$1,605
1994	$2,372	$1,779
1995	$2,635	$1,976
1996	$2,920	$2,190
1997	$3,220	$2,415
1998	$3,612	$2,709
1999	$4,039	$3,029
2000	$4,424	$3,318
2001	$4,909	$3,682

F935

YEARS MFRD 1986-2001
SERIES. . . . .FRONT MOWER SERIES
ENGINE . . . . .YANMAR
ENGINE HP 22
COOLING . . . . LIQUID
FUEL . . . . D
SPEEDS . . . . .VARIABLE
TRANSMISSION . . . . .HYDRO
STEERING. . . . . .STANDARD
STANDARD DECK . . . . 72"
WEIGHT . . . . .1,501 LBS.
MSRP. $18,170

OPTIONS

54" BLADE
60" DECK
CANOPY

SERIAL NUMBERS

YEAR	BEGINNING NO.
1986	360001
1987	420001
1988	460001
1989	595001
1990	010001
1991	100001
1992	110001
1993	120001
1994	130001
1995	140001
1996	150001
1997	160001
1998	170001
1999	180001
2000	185001

RETAIL PRICING

YEAR	HIGH	LOW
1993	$2,403	$1,802
1994	$2,656	$1,992
1995	$2,914	$2,186
1996	$3,272	$2,454
1997	$3,582	$2,687
1998	$3,980	$2,985
1999	$4,474	$3,355
2000	$4,974	$3,730
2001	$5,427	$4,071

AVG. AUCTION PRICING

LOW	HIGH	AVG
$918	$3,672	$2,210

F1145

YEARS MFRD 1992-2001
SERIES. . . . .FRONT MOWER SERIES
ENGINE . . . . .YANMAR
ENGINE HP 28
COOLING . . . . LIQUID
FUEL . . . . D
SPEEDS . . . . .VARIABLE
TRANSMISSION . . . . .HYDRO
STEERING. . . . . .STANDARD
BLADE CLUTCH . . . . .ELECTRIC
DRIVE TYPE 4WD
STANDARD DECK . . . . 72"
WEIGHT . . . . .2,584 LBS.
MSRP. $22,170

OPTIONS

54" BLADE
60" DECK
CANOPY

SERIAL NUMBERS

YEAR	BEGINNING NO.
1992	010001
1993	020001
1994	130001
1995	140001
1996	150001
1997	160001
1998	170001
1999	180001
2000	185001
2001	M01145A

RETAIL PRICING

YEAR	HIGH	LOW
1993	$3,162	$2,372
1994	$3,507	$2,630
1995	$3,891	$2,918
1996	$4,321	$3,241
1997	$4,749	$3,562
1998	$5,317	$3,988
1999	$5,891	$4,418
2000	$6,593	$4,945
2001	$7,249	$5,437

G100

YEARS MFRD 2003-2004
SERIES .... G100 SERIES
ENGINE .... KOHLER
ENGINE HP 25
COOLING .... AIR
FUEL .... G
SPEEDS .... VARIABLE
TRANSMISSION .... HYDRO
STEERING .... STANDARD
BLADE CLUTCH .... MANUAL
STANDARD DECK .... 54"
MSRP $4,299

OPTIONS

46" BLADE
BAGGER

SERIAL NUMBERS

YEAR	BEGINNING NO.
2003	A010000
2004	A020000

RETAIL PRICING

YEAR	HIGH	LOW
2003	$1,417	$1,063
2004	$1,505	$1,128

G110

YEARS MFRD 2004-2005
ENGINE .... KOHLER
ENGINE HP 17.5
COOLING .... AIR
FUEL .... G
SPEEDS .... VARIABLE
TRANSMISSION .... HYDRO
STEERING .... STANDARD
STANDARD DECK .... 54"
WEIGHT .... 629 LBS.
MSRP $3,699

OPTIONS

46" BLADE
BAGGER

SERIAL NUMBERS

YEAR	BEGINNING NO.
2004	10001
2005	30001

RETAIL PRICING

YEAR	HIGH	LOW
2004	$1,163	$872
2005	$1,282	$962

AVG. AUCTION PRICING

LOW	HIGH	AVG
$434	$1,158	$868

GT225

YEARS MFRD 1999-2003
SERIES .... GT SERIES
ENGINE .... KOHLER
CYLINDERS 1
ENGINE HP 16
COOLING .... AIR
FUEL .... G
SPEEDS .... VARIABLE
TRANSMISSION .... HYDRO
STEERING .... STANDARD
STANDARD DECK .... 42"
WEIGHT .... 892 LBS.
MSRP $4,299

OPTIONS

30" TILLER
42" SNOW THROWER
48" BLADE
BAGGER

SERIAL NUMBERS

YEAR	BEGINNING NO.
1999	A010001
2000	A025001
2001	A040001
2002	A060001
2003	A070001

RETAIL PRICING

YEAR	HIGH	LOW
1999	$954	$715
2000	$1,051	$788
2001	$1,164	$873
2002	$1,275	$956
2003	$1,409	$1,056

GT235

YEARS MFRD 1999-2005
SERIES .... GT SERIES
ENGINE .... KAWASAKI
CYLINDERS 2
ENGINE HP 18
COOLING .... AIR
FUEL .... G
SPEEDS .... VARIABLE
TRANSMISSION .... HYDRO
STEERING .... STANDARD
STANDARD DECK .... 48"
WEIGHT .... 893 LBS.
MSRP $5,299

OPTIONS

42" SNOW THROWER
48" BLADE
54" DECK
BAGGER

SERIAL NUMBERS

YEAR	BEGINNING NO.
1999	A010001-48
1999	B010001-54
2000	A025001-48
2000	B025001-54
2001	A040001-48
2001	B040001-54
2002	A060001-48
2003	070001
2004	110001
2005	130001

RETAIL PRICING

YEAR	HIGH	LOW
1999	$1,082	$812
2000	$1,195	$897
2001	$1,288	$966
2002	$1,423	$1,067
2003	$1,572	$1,179
2004	$1,739	$1,304
2005	$1,899	$1,424

AVG. AUCTION PRICING

LOW	HIGH	AVG
$663	$1,122	$880

GT242

YEARS MFRD 1993-1998
SERIES .... GT SERIES
ENGINE .... JD K SERIES
ENGINE HP 14
COOLING .... AIR
FUEL .... G
SPEEDS 6/1
TRANSMISSION .... GEAR
STEERING .... STANDARD
STANDARD DECK .... 38"
WEIGHT .... 640 LBS.
MSRP $3,999

OPTIONS

38" SNOW THROWER
42" BLADE
48" DECK
BAGGER

SERIAL NUMBERS

YEAR	BEGINNING NO.
1993	025001
1994	035001
1995	045001
1996	055001
1997	070001
1998	A090001-38
1998	B090001-LM
1998	D090001-48

RETAIL PRICING

YEAR	HIGH	LOW
1993	$487	$365
1994	$537	$402
1995	$593	$444
1996	$655	$491
1997	$722	$542
1998	$798	$598

GT245

YEARS MFRD 1999-2005
SERIES .... GT SERIES
ENGINE .... KAWASAKI
ENGINE HP 20
COOLING .... AIR
FUEL .... G
SPEEDS .... VARIABLE
TRANSMISSION .... HYDRO
STEERING .... STANDARD
STANDARD DECK .... 54"
WEIGHT .... 912 LBS.
MSRP $6,029

SERIAL NUMBERS

YEAR	BEGINNING NO.
2002	D060001
2002	E060001
2002	B060001
2003	B070001
2003	E070001
2003	D070001
2004	110001
2005	130001

RETAIL PRICING

YEAR	HIGH	LOW
1999	$1,118	$838
2000	$1,233	$925
2001	$1,362	$1,021
2002	$1,548	$1,161
2003	$1,685	$1,264
2004	$1,892	$1,419
2005	$2,066	$1,549

GT262

YEARS MFRD 1992-1998
SERIES .... GT SERIES
ENGINE .... JD K-SERIES
ENGINE HP 17
COOLING .... AIR
FUEL .... G
SPEEDS 6
TRANSMISSION .... GEAR
STEERING .... STANDARD
STANDARD DECK .... 44"
WEIGHT .... 700 LBS.
MSRP $4,649

OPTIONS

2 BAG
30" TILLER
38" SNOW THROWER
42" BLADE
48" DECK

SERIAL NUMBERS

YEAR	BEGINNING NO.
1992	010001
1993	025001
1994	035001
1994	A090001-44
1994	A090001-44
1994	A090001-44
1995	045001
1996	055001
1997	070001
1998	B090001-LM
1998	A090001-44
1998	X090001-48

RETAIL PRICING

YEAR	HIGH	LOW
1992	$527	$396
1993	$581	$436
1994	$641	$480
1995	$707	$530
1996	$784	$588
1997	$863	$647
1998	$952	$714

GT275

YEARS MFRD 1995-1998
SERIES .... GT SERIES
ENGINE .... JD K-SERIES
ENGINE HP 17
COOLING .... AIR
FUEL .... G

SPEEDS	VARIABLE
TRANSMISSION	HYDRO
STEERING	STANDARD
STANDARD DECK	48"
WEIGHT	700 LBS.
MSRP	$4,999

OPTIONS

2 BAG
30" TILLER
38" SNOW THROWER
42" BLADE

SERIAL NUMBERS

YEAR	BEGINNING NO.
1995	045001
1996	055001
1997	070001
1998	C090001-44
1998	B090001-48
1998	D090001-LM

RETAIL PRICING

YEAR	HIGH	LOW
1995	$762	$571
1996	$865	$649
1997	$939	$705
1998	$1,024	$768

GX70

YEARS MFRD	1991-1992
SERIES	GX SERIES
ENGINE	KAWASAKI
ENGINE HP	9
COOLING	AIR
FUEL	G
SPEEDS	5
TRANSMISSION	GEAR
STEERING	STANDARD
STANDARD DECK	30"
MSRP	$1,569

OPTIONS

BAGGER

SERIAL NUMBERS

YEAR	BEGINNING NO.
1991	010001
1992	025001

RETAIL PRICING

YEAR	HIGH	LOW
1991	$411	$308
1992	$419	$314

GX75

YEARS MFRD	1991-1997
SERIES	GX SERIES
ENGINE	JD K SERIES
ENGINE HP	9
COOLING	AIR
FUEL	G
SPEEDS	5
TRANSMISSION	GEAR
STEERING	STANDARD
STANDARD DECK	30"
WEIGHT	448 LBS.
MSRP	$1,899

OPTIONS

BAGGER

SERIAL NUMBERS

YEAR	BEGINNING NO.
1991	010001
1992	025001
1993	045001
1994	055001
1995	065001
1996	075001
1997	085001

RETAIL PRICING

YEAR	HIGH	LOW
1991	$450	$337
1992	$487	$365
1993	$502	$376
1994	$547	$410
1995	$560	$420
1996	$590	$442
1997	$633	$475

GX85

YEARS MFRD	1997-2003
SERIES	GX SERIES
ENGINE	B&S
ENGINE HP	13
COOLING	AIR
FUEL	G
SPEEDS	5/1
TRANSMISSION	GEAR
STEERING	STANDARD
STANDARD DECK	30"
WEIGHT	530 LBS.
MSRP	$2,159

OPTIONS

BAGGER

SERIAL NUMBERS

YEAR	BEGINNING NO.
1997	085001
1998	095001
1999	105001
2000	120001
2001	130001
2002	140001
2003	145001

RETAIL PRICING

YEAR	HIGH	LOW
1997	$204	$153
1998	$224	$168
1999	$250	$187
2000	$276	$207
2001	$312	$234
2002	$340	$255
2003	$376	$282

GX95

YEARS MFRD	1991-1997
SERIES	GX SERIES
ENGINE	JD K SERIES
ENGINE HP	12.5
COOLING	AIR
FUEL	G
SPEEDS	1-5
TRANSMISSION	GEAR
STEERING	STANDARD
STANDARD DECK	30"
WEIGHT	370 LBS.
MSRP	$2,199

OPTIONS

BAGGER

SERIAL NUMBERS

YEAR	BEGINNING NO.
1991	01001
1992	025001
1993	045001
1994	055001
1995	065001
1996	075001
1997	085001

RETAIL PRICING

YEAR	HIGH	LOW
1991	$532	$399
1992	$551	$413
1993	$584	$438
1994	$635	$477
1995	$653	$490
1996	$681	$511
1997	$699	$524

GX255

YEARS MFRD	2004-2005
SERIES	GX SERIES
ENGINE	KAWASAKI V TWIN
CYLINDERS	2
ENGINE HP	20
COOLING	AIR
FUEL	G
SPEEDS	VARIABLE
TRANSMISSION	HYDRO
STEERING	STANDARD
STANDARD DECK	48"
MSRP	$6,419

OPTIONS

42" SNOW THROWER
44" BLADE
54" DECK
BAG & FAN

SERIAL NUMBERS

YEAR	BEGINNING NO.
2004	A120001-48
2004	B120001-54
2005	A140001-54
2005	A140001-48

RETAIL PRICING

YEAR	HIGH	LOW
2004	$2,032	$1,524
2005	$2,222	$1,666

GX325

YEARS MFRD	2002-2003
SERIES	GX SERIES
ENGINE	KAWASAKI
CYLINDERS	2
ENGINE HP	18
COOLING	AIR
FUEL	G
SPEEDS	VARIABLE
TRANSMISSION	HYDRO
STEERING	STANDARD
HITCH	SLEEVE
STANDARD DECK	48"
WEIGHT	964 LBS.
MSRP	$5,749

OPTIONS

42" SNOW THROWER
42" TILLER
48" BLADE
BAG & FAN

SERIAL NUMBERS

YEAR	BEGINNING NO.
2002	D105001
2002	B105001
2003	B110001
2003	D110001

RETAIL PRICING

YEAR	HIGH	LOW
2002	$1,747	$1,310
2003	$1,917	$1,437

GX335

YEARS MFRD	2002-2005
SERIES	GX SERIES
ENGINE	KAWASAKI
CYLINDERS	2
ENGINE HP	20
COOLING	AIR
FUEL	G
SPEEDS	VARIABLE
TRANSMISSION	HYDRO
STEERING	STANDARD
HITCH	SLEEVE
HYDRAULIC	YES
STANDARD DECK	48"
WEIGHT	985 LBS.
MSRP	$7,679

OPTIONS

42" SNOW BLOWER
42" TILLER
48" BLADE
54" DECK
BAG & FAN

SERIAL NUMBERS

YEAR	BEGINNING NO.
2002	A105001
2002	C105001
2002	B105001
2003	A110001
2003	B110001
2003	C110001
2004	D120001
2004	E120001
2005	E140001
2005	C140001
2005	D140001

RETAIL PRICING

YEAR	HIGH	LOW
2002	$2,017	$1,512
2003	$2,235	$1,676
2004	$2,459	$1,844
2005	$2,720	$2,040

AVG. AUCTION PRICING

LOW	HIGH	AVG
$1,020	$1,836	$1,428

GX345

YEARS MFRD	2002-2005
SERIES	GX SERIES
ENGINE	KAWASAKI

CYLINDERS.....2
ENGINE HP.....20
COOLING.....LIQUID
FUEL.....G
SPEEDS.....VARIABLE
TRANSMISSION.....HYDRO
STEERING.....STANDARD
HITCH.....SLEEVE
STANDARD DECK.....48"
WEIGHT.....1,000 LBS.
MSRP.....$8,199

OPTIONS

42" SNOW THROWER
42" TILLER
48" BLADE
54" DECK
BAG & FAN

SERIAL NUMBERS

YEAR	BEGINNING NO.
2002	A105001
2002	C105001
2002	B105001
2003	A110001
2003	B110001
2003	C110001
2004	F120001
2004	D120001
2004	E120001
2005	F140001
2005	D140001
2005	E140001

RETAIL PRICING

YEAR	HIGH	LOW
2002	$2,176	$1,632
2003	$2,461	$1,846
2004	$2,650	$1,987
2005	$2,936	$2,202

AVG. AUCTION PRICING

LOW	HIGH	AVG
$1,020	$3,162	$1,591

GX355

YEARS MFRD.....2002-2005
SERIES.....GX SERIES
ENGINE.....YANMAR
CYLINDERS.....2
ENGINE HP.....18
COOLING.....LIQUID
FUEL.....D
SPEEDS.....VARIABLE
TRANSMISSION.....HYDRO
STEERING.....STANDARD
HITCH.....SLEEVE
STANDARD DECK.....48"
WEIGHT.....1,095 LBS.
MSRP.....$8,959

OPTIONS

42" SNOW THROWER
48" BLADE
54" DECK
BAG & FAN

SERIAL NUMBERS

YEAR	BEGINNING NO.
2002	105001
2003	A110001-48
2003	B110001-54
2004	120001
2005	140001

RETAIL PRICING

YEAR	HIGH	LOW
2002	$2,295	$1,721
2003	$2,530	$1,897
2004	$2,793	$2,095
2005	$3,082	$2,312

L100

YEARS MFRD.....2003-2005
SERIES.....100 SERIES
ENGINE.....B&S
CYLINDERS.....2
ENGINE HP.....17
COOLING.....AIR
FUEL.....G
SPEEDS.....5
TRANSMISSION.....GEAR
STEERING.....STANDARD
BLADE CLUTCH.....MANUAL
STANDARD DECK.....42"
WEIGHT.....638 LBS.
MSRP.....$1,499

OPTIONS

BAGGER

SERIAL NUMBERS

YEAR	BEGINNING NO.
2003	B010001
2003	A010001
2004	B15001
2004	A080001
2005	B30001
2005	A140001

RETAIL PRICING

YEAR	HIGH	LOW
2003	$393	$295
2004	$430	$323
2005	$476	$357

L108

YEARS MFRD.....2005-2005
SERIES.....100 SERIES
ENGINE.....KOHLER
CYLINDERS.....2
ENGINE HP.....18.5
COOLING.....AIR
FUEL.....G
SPEEDS.....VARIABLE
TRANSMISSION.....HYDRO
STEERING.....STANDARD
STANDARD DECK.....42"
MSRP.....$1,599

OPTIONS

BAGGER

RETAIL PRICING

YEAR	HIGH	LOW
2005	$506	$379

L110

YEARS MFRD.....2003-2004
SERIES.....100 SERIES
ENGINE.....KOHLER
CYLINDERS.....2
ENGINE HP.....17.5
COOLING.....AIR
FUEL.....G
SPEEDS.....VARIABLE
TRANSMISSION.....HYDRO
STEERING.....STANDARD
STANDARD DECK.....42"
WEIGHT.....629 LBS.
MSRP.....$1,799

OPTIONS

BAGGER

SERIAL NUMBERS

YEAR	BEGINNING NO.
2003	B010001
2003	A010001
2004	B140001 CANADIAN
2004	A140001

RETAIL PRICING

YEAR	HIGH	LOW
2003	$459	$344
2004	$485	$363

AVG. AUCTION PRICING

LOW	HIGH	AVG
$607	$695	$665

L111

YEARS MFRD.....2005-2005
SERIES.....100 SERIES
ENGINE.....B&S
CYLINDERS.....2
ENGINE HP.....20
COOLING.....AIR
FUEL.....G
SPEEDS.....VARIABLE
TRANSMISSION.....HYDRO
STEERING.....STANDARD
BLADE CLUTCH.....MANUAL
STANDARD DECK.....42"
MSRP.....$1,799

OPTIONS

BAGGER

SERIAL NUMBERS

YEAR	BEGINNING NO.
2005	10001

RETAIL PRICING

YEAR	HIGH	LOW
2005	$591	$443

L118

YEARS MFRD.....2004-2005
SERIES.....100 SERIES
ENGINE.....B&S
ENGINE HP.....20
COOLING.....AIR
FUEL.....G
SPEEDS.....VARIABLE
TRANSMISSION.....HYDRO
STEERING.....STANDARD
STANDARD DECK.....42"
MSRP.....$1,999

OPTIONS

BAGGER

SERIAL NUMBERS

YEAR	BEGINNING NO.
2004	A010001
2005	B050001

RETAIL PRICING

YEAR	HIGH	LOW
2004	$580	$435
2005	$639	$479

L120

YEARS MFRD.....2003-2005
SERIES.....100 SERIES
ENGINE.....B&S
CYLINDERS.....2
ENGINE HP.....20
COOLING.....AIR
FUEL.....G
SPEEDS.....VARIABLE
TRANSMISSION.....HYDRO
STEERING.....STANDARD
BLADE CLUTCH.....ELECTRIC
STANDARD DECK.....48"
WEIGHT.....699 LBS.
MSRP.....$2,299

OPTIONS

BAGGER

SERIAL NUMBERS

YEAR	BEGINNING NO.
2003	A010001
2003	B010001
2003	C010001
2004	B080001-EXPORT
2004	A080001
2004	C080001-CANADA
2005	D150001
2005	E020001-EXPORT

RETAIL PRICING

YEAR	HIGH	LOW
2003	$632	$474
2004	$689	$516
2005	$744	$558

AVG. AUCTION PRICING

LOW	HIGH	AVG
$536	$714	$638

L130

YEARS MFRD.....2003-2005
SERIES.....100 SERIES
ENGINE.....KOHLER
CYLINDERS.....2
ENGINE HP.....23
COOLING.....AIR
FUEL.....G
SPEEDS.....VARIABLE
TRANSMISSION.....HYDRO
STEERING.....STANDARD
BLADE CLUTCH.....ELECTRIC
STANDARD DECK.....48"
WEIGHT.....699 LBS.
MSRP.....$2,599

OPTIONS

BAGGER

SERIAL NUMBERS

YEAR	BEGINNING NO.
2003	A010001
2003	B010001
2004	A060001
2004	B060001-CANADA
2005	B020001-CANADA
2005	A130001

JOHN DEERE

RETAIL PRICING

YEAR	HIGH	LOW
2003	$700	$525
2004	$754	$565
2005	$818	$614

AVG. AUCTION PRICING

LOW	HIGH	AVG
$375	$965	$621

LA100

YEARS MFRD	2007-2007
SERIES	100 SERIES
ENGINE	B&S
CYLINDERS	1
CID	30.6
ENGINE HP	18.5
COOLING	AIR
FUEL	G
SPEEDS	5/1
TRANSMISSION	GEAR
STEERING	STANDARD
BLADE CLUTCH	ELECTRIC
STANDARD DECK	42"
MSRP	$1,499

OPTIONS

44" SNOW BLOWER
46" BLADE
BAGGER

RETAIL PRICING

YEAR	HIGH	LOW
2007	$605	$454

LA105

YEARS MFRD	2008-2010
SERIES	100 SERIES
ENGINE	B&S
CYLINDERS	1
CID	30.6
ENGINE HP	19.5
COOLING	AIR
FUEL	G
SPEEDS	5/1
TRANSMISSION	GEAR
STEERING	STANDARD
BLADE CLUTCH	MANUAL
STANDARD DECK	42"
MSRP	$1,499

OPTIONS

44" SNOW BLOWER
46" BLADE
BAGGER

SERIAL NUMBERS

YEAR	BEGINNING NO.
2008	A050001
2009	A200001
2010	A300001

RETAIL PRICING

YEAR	HIGH	LOW
2008	$581	$436
2009	$634	$476
2010	$697	$522

AVG. AUCTION PRICING

LOW	HIGH	AVG
$318	$925	$589

LA110

YEARS MFRD	2007-2007
SERIES	100 SERIES
ENGINE	B&S
CYLINDERS	1
CID	30.6
ENGINE HP	19.5
COOLING	AIR
FUEL	G
SPEEDS	VARIABLE
TRANSMISSION	HYDRO
STEERING	STANDARD
BLADE CLUTCH	MANUAL
STANDARD DECK	42"
MSRP	$1,649

OPTIONS

44" SNOW BLOWER
46" BLADE
BAGGER

RETAIL PRICING

YEAR	HIGH	LOW
2007	$666	$500

LA115

YEARS MFRD	2008-2010
SERIES	100 SERIES
ENGINE	B&S
CYLINDERS	1
CID	30.6
ENGINE HP	19.5
COOLING	AIR
FUEL	G
SPEEDS	VARIABLE
TRANSMISSION	HYDRO
STEERING	STANDARD
BLADE CLUTCH	MANUAL
STANDARD DECK	42"
MSRP	$1,699

OPTIONS

44" SNOW BLOWER
46" BLADE
BAGGER

SERIAL NUMBERS

YEAR	BEGINNING NO.
2008	A050001
2009	A200001
2010	A300001

RETAIL PRICING

YEAR	HIGH	LOW
2008	$662	$496
2009	$727	$545
2010	$803	$602

LA120

YEARS MFRD	2007-2007
SERIES	100 SERIES
ENGINE	B&S
CYLINDERS	2
CID	44.2
ENGINE HP	21
COOLING	AIR
FUEL	G
SPEEDS	VARIABLE
TRANSMISSION	HYDRO
STEERING	STANDARD
BLADE CLUTCH	MANUAL
STANDARD DECK	42"
MSRP	$1,849

OPTIONS

44" SNOW BLOWER
46" BLADE
BAGGER

RETAIL PRICING

YEAR	HIGH	LOW
2007	$755	$566

LA125

YEARS MFRD	2008-2010
SERIES	100 SERIES
ENGINE	B&S
CYLINDERS	1
CID	33
ENGINE HP	21
COOLING	AIR
FUEL	G
SPEEDS	VARIABLE
TRANSMISSION	HYDRO
STEERING	STANDARD
BLADE CLUTCH	MANUAL
STANDARD DECK	42"
MSRP	$1,799

OPTIONS

44" SNOW BLOWER
46" BLADE
BAGGER

SERIAL NUMBERS

YEAR	BEGINNING NO.
2008	A050001
2009	A200001
2010	A300001

RETAIL PRICING

YEAR	HIGH	LOW
2008	$702	$526
2009	$765	$574
2010	$847	$635

LA130

YEARS MFRD	2007-2007
SERIES	100 SERIES
ENGINE	B&S
CYLINDERS	2
CID	44.2
ENGINE HP	21
COOLING	AIR
FUEL	G
SPEEDS	VARIABLE
TRANSMISSION	HYDRO
STEERING	STANDARD
BLADE CLUTCH	ELECTRIC
STANDARD DECK	48"
MSRP	$1,999

OPTIONS

44" SNOW BLOWER
46" BLADE
BAGGER

RETAIL PRICING

YEAR	HIGH	LOW
2007	$809	$607

LA135

YEARS MFRD	2008-2010
SERIES	100 SERIES
ENGINE	B&S
CYLINDERS	2
CID	40
ENGINE HP	22
COOLING	AIR
FUEL	G
SPEEDS	VARIABLE
TRANSMISSION	HYDRO
STEERING	STANDARD
BLADE CLUTCH	MANUAL
STANDARD DECK	42"
MSRP	$1,899

OPTIONS

44" SNOW BLOWER
46" BLADE
BAGGER

SERIAL NUMBERS

YEAR	BEGINNING NO.
2008	A050001
2009	A200001
2010	A300001

RETAIL PRICING

YEAR	HIGH	LOW
2008	$743	$557
2009	$818	$614
2010	$889	$667

LA140

YEARS MFRD	2007-2007
SERIES	100 SERIES
ENGINE	B&S
CYLINDERS	2
CID	44.2
ENGINE HP	23
COOLING	AIR
FUEL	G
SPEEDS	VARIABLE
TRANSMISSION	HYDRO
STEERING	STANDARD
BLADE CLUTCH	ELECTRIC
STANDARD DECK	48"
MSRP	$2,299

OPTIONS

44" SNOW BLOWER
46" BLADE
BAGGER

RETAIL PRICING

YEAR	HIGH	LOW
2007	$924	$693

AVG. AUCTION PRICING

LOW	HIGH	AVG
$590	$1,179	$840

LA145

YEARS MFRD	2008-2010
SERIES	100 SERIES
ENGINE	B&S
CYLINDERS	2
CID	40
ENGINE HP	22
COOLING	AIR
FUEL	G

SPEEDS............VARIABLE
TRANSMISSION..........HYDRO
STEERING............STANDARD
BLADE CLUTCH........MANUAL
STANDARD DECK............48"
MSRP..................$1,999

OPTIONS

44" SNOW BLOWER
46" BLADE
BAGGER

SERIAL NUMBERS

YEAR	BEGINNING NO.
2008	A050001
2009	A200001
2010	A300001

RETAIL PRICING

YEAR	HIGH	LOW
2008	$783	$588
2009	$854	$640
2010	$933	$700

LA150

YEARS MFRD........2007-2007
SERIES.............100 SERIES
ENGINE..................B&S
CYLINDERS....................2
CID........................44.2
ENGINE HP....................26
COOLING....................AIR
FUEL..........................G
SPEEDS..............VARIABLE
TRANSMISSION..........HYDRO
STEERING............STANDARD
BLADE CLUTCH........ELECTRIC
STANDARD DECK...........54"
MSRP..................$2,799

OPTIONS

44" SNOW BLOWER
46" BLADE

RETAIL PRICING

YEAR	HIGH	LOW
2007	$1,121	$841

LA155

YEARS MFRD........2009-2010
SERIES.............100 SERIES
ENGINE..................B&S
CYLINDERS....................2
CID..........................40
ENGINE HP....................22
COOLING....................AIR
FUEL..........................G
SPEEDS..............VARIABLE
TRANSMISSION..........HYDRO
STEERING............STANDARD
BLADE CLUTCH........ELECTRIC
STANDARD DECK...........48"
MSRP..................$2,349

OPTIONS

44" SNOW BLOWER
46" BLADE
BAGGER

SERIAL NUMBERS

YEAR	BEGINNING NO.
2009	A200001
2010	A300001

RETAIL PRICING

YEAR	HIGH	LOW
2009	$996	$747
2010	$1,092	$819

LA165

YEARS MFRD........2008-2010
SERIES.............100 SERIES
ENGINE..................B&S
CYLINDERS....................2
CID........................44.2
ENGINE HP....................24
COOLING....................AIR
FUEL..........................G
SPEEDS..............VARIABLE
TRANSMISSION..........HYDRO
STEERING............STANDARD
BLADE CLUTCH........ELECTRIC
STANDARD DECK...........48"
MSRP..................$2,549

OPTIONS

44" SNOW BLOWER
46" BLADE
BAGGER

SERIAL NUMBERS

YEAR	BEGINNING NO.
2008	A050001
2009	A200001
2010	A300001

RETAIL PRICING

YEAR	HIGH	LOW
2008	$984	$738
2009	$1,076	$807
2010	$1,183	$887

LA175

YEARS MFRD........2008-2010
SERIES.............100 SERIES
ENGINE..................B&S
CYLINDERS....................2
ENGINE HP....................26
COOLING....................AIR
FUEL..........................G
SPEEDS..............VARIABLE
TRANSMISSION..........HYDRO
STEERING............STANDARD
BLADE CLUTCH........ELECTRIC
STANDARD DECK...........54"
MSRP..................$2,749

OPTIONS

44" SNOW BLOWER
46" BLADE
BAGGER

SERIAL NUMBERS

YEAR	BEGINNING NO.
2008	A050001
2009	A200001
2010	A300001

RETAIL PRICING

YEAR	HIGH	LOW
2008	$1,064	$798
2009	$1,164	$873
2010	$1,284	$963

LT133

YEARS MFRD........1998-2001
SERIES...............LT SERIES
ENGINE................KOHLER
ENGINE HP....................13
COOLING....................AIR
FUEL..........................G
SPEEDS........................5
TRANSMISSION..........GEAR
STEERING............STANDARD
STANDARD DECK...........38"
WEIGHT..............640 LBS.
MSRP..................$1,999

OPTIONS

42" BLADE
BAGGER

SERIAL NUMBERS

YEAR	BEGINNING NO.
1998	A010001
1999	A045001
2000	A085001
2001	A125001

RETAIL PRICING

YEAR	HIGH	LOW
1998	$282	$211
1999	$307	$230
2000	$336	$252
2001	$369	$277

LT150

YEARS MFRD........2002-2005
SERIES...............LT SERIES
ENGINE................KOHLER
CYLINDERS....................1
ENGINE HP....................15
COOLING....................AIR
FUEL..........................G
SPEEDS......................5/1
TRANSMISSION..........GEAR
STEERING............STANDARD
STANDARD DECK...........38"
WEIGHT..............648 LBS.
MSRP..................$2,559

OPTIONS

BAGGER
HYDRO

SERIAL NUMBERS

YEAR	BEGINNING NO.
2002	B010001
2002	A010001
2003	B035001
2004	B500001
2005	B530001

RETAIL PRICING

YEAR	HIGH	LOW
2002	$644	$483
2003	$692	$519
2004	$760	$570
2005	$835	$627

AVG. AUCTION PRICING

LOW	HIGH	AVG
$242	$750	$620

LT155

YEARS MFRD........1998-2001
SERIES...............LT SERIES
ENGINE................KOHLER
CYLINDERS....................1
ENGINE HP....................15
COOLING....................AIR
FUEL..........................G
SPEEDS..............VARIABLE
TRANSMISSION..........HYDRO
STEERING............STANDARD
STANDARD DECK...........38"
WEIGHT..............655 LBS.
MSRP..................$2,499

OPTIONS

42" BLADE
42" DECK
BAGGER

SERIAL NUMBERS

YEAR	BEGINNING NO.
1998	B010001-38
1998	C010001-42
1999	B045001-38
1999	C045001-42
2000	B085001-38
2000	C085001-42
2001	B125001-38
2001	C125001-42

RETAIL PRICING

YEAR	HIGH	LOW
1998	$375	$282
1999	$414	$311
2000	$453	$340
2001	$511	$383

LT160

YEARS MFRD........2002-2005
SERIES...............LT SERIES
ENGINE................KOHLER
CYLINDERS....................1
ENGINE HP....................16
COOLING....................AIR
FUEL..........................G
SPEEDS..............VARIABLE
TRANSMISSION..........HYDRO
STEERING............STANDARD
STANDARD DECK...........42"
WEIGHT..............677 LBS.
MSRP..................$2,779

OPTIONS

44" BLADE
BAGGER

SERIAL NUMBERS

YEAR	BEGINNING NO.
2002	H010001
2002	D010001
2002	G010001
2002	C010001
2003	H035001
2003	D035001
2003	D035001
2003	C035001
2004	D500001-42C
2004	C500001-42M
2004	G500001-38
2005	530001

RETAIL PRICING

YEAR	HIGH	LOW
2002	$704	$528
2003	$766	$575
2004	$836	$627
2005	$913	$685

AVG. AUCTION PRICING

LOW	HIGH	AVG
$386	$1,346	$961

LT166

YEARS MFRD	1998-2001
SERIES	LT SERIES
ENGINE	VANGUARD
CYLINDERS	1
ENGINE HP	16
COOLING	AIR
FUEL	G
SPEEDS	VARIABLE
TRANSMISSION	HYDRO
STEERING	STANDARD
STANDARD DECK	38"
WEIGHT	650 LBS.
MSRP	$3,299

OPTIONS

2 BAG
42" BLADE
48" DECK
BAGGER

SERIAL NUMBERS

YEAR	BEGINNING NO.
1998	E010001-42
1998	D010001-46
1999	G045001-38
1999	E045001-42
1999	D045001-46
2000	G085001-38
2000	J085001-48
2000	E085001-42
2001	G125001-38
2001	E125001-42
2001	J125001-48

RETAIL PRICING

YEAR	HIGH	LOW
1998	$495	$371
1999	$547	$410
2000	$598	$448
2001	$647	$485

LT170

YEARS MFRD	2002-2003
SERIES	LT SERIES
ENGINE	VANGUARD
CYLINDERS	2
ENGINE HP	16
COOLING	AIR
FUEL	G
SPEEDS	VARIABLE
TRANSMISSION	HYDRO
STEERING	STANDARD
STANDARD DECK	42"
WEIGHT	678 LBS.
MSRP	$3,099

OPTIONS

44" BLADE
BAGGER

SERIAL NUMBERS

YEAR	BEGINNING NO.
2002	E010001
2003	E035001

RETAIL PRICING

YEAR	HIGH	LOW
2002	$638	$478
2003	$666	$500

LT180

YEARS MFRD	2002-2005
SERIES	LT SERIES
ENGINE	KAWASAKI
CYLINDERS	2
ENGINE HP	17
COOLING	AIR
FUEL	G
SPEEDS	VARIABLE
TRANSMISSION	HYDRO
STEERING	STANDARD
STANDARD DECK	48"
WEIGHT	693 LBS.
MSRP	$3,639

OPTIONS

44" BLADE
BAG & FAN
BAGGER

SERIAL NUMBERS

YEAR	BEGINNING NO.
2002	J010001
2002	F010001
2003	K035001
2003	L035001
2003	F035001
2003	J035001
2004	L500001-42M
2004	K500001-42C
2004	F500001 NO DECK
2004	J500001-48C
2005	530001

RETAIL PRICING

YEAR	HIGH	LOW
2002	$902	$676
2003	$993	$745
2004	$1,083	$812
2005	$1,188	$891

AVG. AUCTION PRICING

LOW	HIGH	AVG
$482	$965	$707

LT190

YEARS MFRD	2004-2005
SERIES	LT SERIES
ENGINE	KAWASAKI
CYLINDERS	2
ENGINE HP	18
COOLING	AIR
FUEL	G
SPEEDS	VARIABLE
TRANSMISSION	HYDRO
STEERING	STANDARD
STANDARD DECK	48"
WEIGHT	693 LBS.
MSRP	$3,939

OPTIONS

42" SNOW BLOWER
44" BLADE

SERIAL NUMBERS

YEAR	BEGINNING NO.
2004	N500001
2005	530001

RETAIL PRICING

YEAR	HIGH	LOW
2004	$1,200	$900
2005	$1,315	$986

LTR166

YEARS MFRD	1999-2001
SERIES	LT SERIES
ENGINE	JD VANGUARD
CYLINDERS	1
ENGINE HP	16
COOLING	AIR
FUEL	G
SPEEDS	VARIABLE
TRANSMISSION	HYDRO
STEERING	STANDARD
STANDARD DECK	42"
WEIGHT	555 LBS.
MSRP	$3,799

OPTIONS

42" BLADE
HOPPER

SERIAL NUMBERS

YEAR	BEGINNING NO.
1999	10001
2000	20001
2001	30001

RETAIL PRICING

YEAR	HIGH	LOW
1999	$617	$463
2000	$676	$507
2001	$743	$557

LTR180

YEARS MFRD	2002-2006
SERIES	LT SERIES
ENGINE	KAWASAKI
CYLINDERS	2
ENGINE HP	17
COOLING	AIR
FUEL	G
SPEEDS	VARIABLE
TRANSMISSION	HYDRO
STEERING	STANDARD
STANDARD DECK	42"
WEIGHT	790 LBS.
MSRP	$4,169

OPTIONS

44" BLADE
CADDY
HOPPER

SERIAL NUMBERS

YEAR	BEGINNING NO.
2002	R010001
2003	R035001
2004	R500001-42
2005	530001
2006	540001-EXPORT

RETAIL PRICING

YEAR	HIGH	LOW
2002	$968	$726
2003	$1,058	$793
2004	$1,160	$870
2005	$1,271	$953
2006	$1,395	$1,047

LX172

YEARS MFRD	1991-1997
SERIES	LX SERIES
ENGINE	JD K SERIES
ENGINE HP	14
COOLING	AIR
FUEL	G
SPEEDS	5/1
TRANSMISSION	GEAR
STEERING	STANDARD
STANDARD DECK	44"
WEIGHT	590 LBS.
MSRP	$3,545

OPTIONS

2 BAG
38" SNOW THROWER
42" BLADE

SERIAL NUMBERS

YEAR	BEGINNING NO.
1991	010001
1992	040001
1993	070001
1994	090001
1995	110001
1996	130001
1997	160001

RETAIL PRICING

YEAR	HIGH	LOW
1991	$267	$200
1992	$293	$220
1993	$322	$242
1994	$352	$264
1995	$386	$289
1996	$424	$318
1997	$463	$347

LX173

YEARS MFRD	1996-1998
SERIES	LX SERIES
ENGINE	KOHLER
CYLINDERS	1
ENGINE HP	15
COOLING	AIR
FUEL	G
SPEEDS	5/1
TRANSMISSION	GEAR
STEERING	STANDARD
STANDARD DECK	38"
WEIGHT	570 LBS.
MSRP	$3,395

OPTIONS

38" SNOW THROWER
42" BLADE
48" DECK
BAGGER

SERIAL NUMBERS

YEAR	BEGINNING NO.
1996	150001
1997	160001

1998 . . . . A180001-LM
1998 . . . . B180001-48
1998 . . . . X180001-38
1998 . . . . C180001-44

RETAIL PRICING

YEAR	HIGH	LOW
1996	$493	$369
1997	$544	$408
1998	$590	$442

LX176

YEARS MFRD 1991-1998
SERIES . . . . LX SERIES
ENGINE . . . . JD K SERIES
ENGINE HP 14
COOLING . . . . AIR
FUEL . . . . G
SPEEDS . . . . VARIABLE
TRANSMISSION . . . . HYDRO
STEERING . . . . STANDARD
STANDARD DECK . . . . 38"
WEIGHT . . . . 622 LBS.
MSRP $3,945

OPTIONS

38" SNOW THROWER
42" BLADE
48" DECK
BAGGER

SERIAL NUMBERS

YEAR	BEGINNING NO.
1991	010001
1992	040001
1993	070001
1994	090001
1995	110001
1996	130001
1997	160001
1998	A180001 48
1998	B180001 LM
1998	C180001 44
1998	X180001 38

RETAIL PRICING

YEAR	HIGH	LOW
1991	$360	$270
1992	$395	$296
1993	$431	$324
1994	$477	$358
1995	$521	$391
1996	$570	$428
1997	$625	$469
1998	$689	$516

LX178

YEARS MFRD 1991-1998
SERIES . . . . LX SERIES
ENGINE . . . . JD K-SERIES
CYLINDERS 1
ENGINE HP 15
COOLING . . . . LIQUID
FUEL . . . . G
SPEEDS . . . . VARIABLE
TRANSMISSION . . . . HYDRO
STEERING . . . . STANDARD
STANDARD DECK . . . . 38"
WEIGHT . . . . 620 LBS.
MSRP $4,445

OPTIONS

38" SNOW THROWER
42" BLADE
44" DECK
BAGGER

SERIAL NUMBERS

YEAR	BEGINNING NO.
1991	010001
1992	040001
1993	070001
1994	090001
1995	110001
1996	130001
1997	160001
1998	X180001-38
1998	A180001-44
1998	B180001-LM

RETAIL PRICING

YEAR	HIGH	LOW
1991	$406	$304
1992	$444	$333
1993	$492	$369
1994	$540	$405
1995	$590	$442
1996	$646	$484
1997	$704	$528
1998	$774	$581

AVG. AUCTION PRICING

LOW	HIGH	AVG
$295	$590	$468

LX186

YEARS MFRD 1991-1992
SERIES . . . . LX SERIES
ENGINE . . . . JD K-SERIES
CYLINDERS 2
ENGINE HP 17
COOLING . . . . AIR
FUEL . . . . G
SPEEDS . . . . VARIABLE
TRANSMISSION . . . . HYDRO
STEERING . . . . STANDARD
STANDARD DECK . . . . 48"
WEIGHT . . . . 644 LBS.
MSRP $4,595

OPTIONS

2 BAG
42" BLADE

SERIAL NUMBERS

YEAR	BEGINNING NO.
1991	010001
1992	40001

RETAIL PRICING

YEAR	HIGH	LOW
1991	$454	$340
1992	$546	$409

LX188

YEARS MFRD 1992-1998
SERIES . . . . LX SERIES
ENGINE . . . . JD K-SERIES
CYLINDERS 2
ENGINE HP 17
COOLING . . . . LIQUID
FUEL . . . . G
SPEEDS . . . . VARIABLE
TRANSMISSION . . . . HYDRO
STEERING . . . . STANDARD
STANDARD DECK . . . . 48"
WEIGHT . . . . 630 LBS.
MSRP $4,945

OPTIONS

2 BAG
38" SNOW THROWER
42" BLADE

SERIAL NUMBERS

YEAR	BEGINNING NO.
1992	040001
1993	070001
1994	090001
1995	110001
1996	130001
1997	160001
1998	A180001-44
1998	X180001-48
1998	B180001-LM

RETAIL PRICING

YEAR	HIGH	LOW
1992	$497	$373
1993	$544	$408
1994	$597	$448
1995	$655	$491
1996	$716	$537
1997	$789	$592
1998	$867	$650

LX255

YEARS MFRD 1999-2001
SERIES . . . . LX SERIES
ENGINE . . . . KHI
CYLINDERS 1
ENGINE HP 15
COOLING . . . . AIR
FUEL . . . . G
SPEEDS . . . . VARIABLE
TRANSMISSION . . . . HYDRO
STEERING . . . . STANDARD
STANDARD DECK . . . . 42"
WEIGHT . . . . 759 LBS.
MSRP $3,649

OPTIONS

42" BLADE
42" SNOW THROWER
BAGGER

SERIAL NUMBERS

YEAR	BEGINNING NO.
1999	B010101-C
1999	A010101-M
2000	A020001-M
2000	B020001-C
2001	A040001-M
2001	B040001-C

RETAIL PRICING

YEAR	HIGH	LOW
1999	$617	$463
2000	$673	$505
2001	$735	$552

AVG. AUCTION PRICING

LOW	HIGH	AVG
$463	$724	$527

LX266

YEARS MFRD 2002-2003
SERIES . . . . LX SERIES
ENGINE . . . . KOHLER
CYLINDERS 1
ENGINE HP 16
COOLING . . . . AIR
FUEL . . . . G
SPEEDS . . . . VARIABLE
TRANSMISSION . . . . HYDRO
STEERING . . . . STANDARD
STANDARD DECK . . . . 42"
WEIGHT . . . . 760 LBS.
MSRP $3,699

OPTIONS

42" SNOW THROWER
44" DECK
7 BU BAG

SERIAL NUMBERS

YEAR	BEGINNING NO.
2002	B060001
2002	A060001
2002	C060001
2003	C070001
2003	A070001
2003	B070001

RETAIL PRICING

YEAR	HIGH	LOW
2002	$781	$586
2003	$848	$636

LX277

YEARS MFRD 1999-2003
SERIES . . . . LX SERIES
ENGINE . . . . KAWASAKI
CYLINDERS 2
ENGINE HP 17
COOLING . . . . AIR
FUEL . . . . G
SPEEDS . . . . VARIABLE
TRANSMISSION . . . . HYDRO
STEERING . . . . STANDARD
STANDARD DECK . . . . 42"
WEIGHT . . . . 794 LBS.
MSRP $4,299

OPTIONS

42" SNOW THROWER
44" BLADE
48" DECK
AWS
BAGGER

SERIAL NUMBERS

YEAR	BEGINNING NO.
1999	C010101-48
1999	A010101-42
1999	H010101-42C
2000	H020001-42
2000	C020001-48
2000	H020001-42C
2001	A040001-42
2001	H040001-42C
2001	C040001-48
2002	A060001-42
2002	H060001-42C
2002	C060001-48
2003	C070001-48

RETAIL PRICING

YEAR	HIGH	LOW
1999	$759	$569
2000	$848	$636
2001	$932	$699
2002	$1,016	$762
2003	$1,120	$840

AVG. AUCTION PRICING

LOW	HIGH	AVG
$521	$1,459	$923

LX279

YEARS MFRD 1999-2003
SERIES .... LX SERIES
ENGINE .... KAWASAKI
CYLINDERS 2
ENGINE HP 17
COOLING .... LIQUID
FUEL .... G
SPEEDS .... VARIABLE
TRANSMISSION .... HYDRO
STEERING .... STANDARD
STANDARD DECK .... 42"
WEIGHT .... 769 LBS.
MSRP $5,049

OPTIONS

42" SNOW THROWER
44" BLADE
48" DECK
BAGGER

SERIAL NUMBERS

YEAR	BEGINNING NO.
1999	B010101-48
1999	F010101-42
2000	A02001-42
2000	C010101-48
2001	A040001-42
2001	B040001-48
2001	F040001-42C
2002	A060001-42
2002	B060001-48
2002	F060001-42C
2003	A070001-42
2003	B070001-48

RETAIL PRICING

YEAR	HIGH	LOW
1999	$889	$667
2000	$980	$735
2001	$1,078	$809
2002	$1,182	$887
2003	$1,293	$970

LX280

YEARS MFRD 2004-2005
SERIES .... LX SERIES
ENGINE .... KAWASAKI TWIN V
CYLINDERS 2
ENGINE HP 18
COOLING .... AIR
FUEL .... G
SPEEDS .... VARIABLE
TRANSMISSION .... HYDRO
STEERING .... STANDARD
STANDARD DECK .... 42"
MSRP $4,389

OPTIONS

44" BLADE
48" DECK
54" DECK
AWS
BAGGER

SERIAL NUMBERS

YEAR	BEGINNING NO.
2004	A100001-42C
2004	B100001-48C
2004	C100001-54C
2005	120001

RETAIL PRICING

YEAR	HIGH	LOW
2004	$1,215	$911
2005	$1,302	$976

AVG. AUCTION PRICING

LOW	HIGH	AVG
$643	$1,929	$1,129

LX288

YEARS MFRD 1999-2003
SERIES .... LX SERIES
ENGINE .... KAWASAKI
CYLINDERS 2
ENGINE HP 18
COOLING .... AIR
FUEL .... G
SPEEDS .... VARIABLE
TRANSMISSION .... HYDRO
STEERING .... STANDARD
STANDARD DECK .... 48"
WEIGHT .... 794 LBS.
MSRP $4,949

OPTIONS

42" SNOW THROWER
44" BLADE
54" DECK
BAGGER

SERIAL NUMBERS

YEAR	BEGINNING NO.
1999	B010001-54
1999	A010001-48
2000	A020001-48
2000	B020001-54
2001	B040001-54
2001	A040001-48
2002	A060001-48
2002	B060001-54
2003	F090001-54
2003	G090001-48

RETAIL PRICING

YEAR	HIGH	LOW
1999	$843	$632
2000	$915	$686
2001	$1,004	$753
2002	$1,100	$825
2003	$1,207	$905

LX289

YEARS MFRD 2004-2005
SERIES .... LX SERIES
ENGINE .... KAWASAKI
CYLINDERS 2
ENGINE HP 17
COOLING .... LIQUID
FUEL .... G
SPEEDS .... VARIABLE
TRANSMISSION .... HYDRO
STEERING .... STANDARD
STANDARD DECK .... 48"
MSRP $5,549

OPTIONS

42" SNOW THROWER
44" BLADE
54" DECK
BAGGER

SERIAL NUMBERS

YEAR	BEGINNING NO.
2004	100001
2005	120001

RETAIL PRICING

YEAR	HIGH	LOW
2004	$1,704	$1,278
2005	$1,854	$1,391

M653

YEARS MFRD 2000-2002
SERIES .... Z-TRAK SERIES
ENGINE .... KOHLER COMMAND
CYLINDERS 2
CID 41
ENGINE HP 23
COOLING .... AIR
FUEL .... G
SPEEDS .... VARIABLE
TRANSMISSION .... HYDRO
STEERING .... ZERO
STANDARD DECK .... 54"
WEIGHT .... 1,200 LBS.
MSRP $8,599

OPTIONS

BAG & FAN

SERIAL NUMBERS

YEAR	BEGINNING NO.
2000	TCM653X010001
2001	TCM653X020001
2002	TCM653X020001

RETAIL PRICING

YEAR	HIGH	LOW
2000	$2,056	$1,542
2001	$2,284	$1,713
2002	$2,562	$1,922

M655

YEARS MFRD 2000-2002
SERIES .... Z-TRAK SERIES
ENGINE .... KOHLER COMMAND
CYLINDERS 2
CID 44
ENGINE HP 25
COOLING .... AIR
FUEL .... G
SPEEDS .... VARIABLE
TRANSMISSION .... HYDRO
STEERING .... ZERO
STANDARD DECK .... 54"
WEIGHT .... 1,200 LBS.
MSRP $8,999

OPTIONS

BAG & FAN

SERIAL NUMBERS

YEAR	BEGINNING NO.
2000	TCM655X010001
2001	TCM655X020001
2002	TCM655X020001

RETAIL PRICING

YEAR	HIGH	LOW
2000	$2,300	$1,725
2001	$2,559	$1,919
2002	$2,869	$2,152

M665

YEARS MFRD 2000-2002
SERIES .... Z-TRAK SERIES
ENGINE .... KOHLER COMMAND
CYLINDERS 2
CID 44
ENGINE HP 25
COOLING .... AIR
FUEL .... G
SPEEDS .... VARIABLE
TRANSMISSION .... HYDRO
STEERING .... ZERO
STANDARD DECK .... 60"
WEIGHT .... 1,225 LBS.
MSRP $9,449

OPTIONS

BAG & FAN

SERIAL NUMBERS

YEAR	BEGINNING NO.
2000	TCM665X010001
2001	TCM665X020001
2002	TCM665X020001

RETAIL PRICING

YEAR	HIGH	LOW
2000	$2,418	$1,814
2001	$2,682	$2,011
2002	$3,018	$2,264

RX63

YEARS MFRD 1988-1990
ENGINE .... KAWASAKI
ENGINE HP 6
COOLING .... AIR
FUEL .... G
SPEEDS .... VARIABLE
TRANSMISSION .... GEAR
STEERING .... STANDARD
STANDARD DECK .... 26"
WEIGHT .... 366 LBS.
MSRP $1,200

SERIAL NUMBERS

YEAR	BEGINNING NO.
1988	475001
1989	595001
1990	010001

RETAIL PRICING

YEAR	HIGH	LOW
1988	$322	$242
1989	$349	$262
1990	$375	$282

RX73

YEARS MFRD 1987-1990
ENGINE . . . . KAWASAKI
ENGINE HP 9
COOLING . . . . AIR
FUEL . . . . G
SPEEDS 7
TRANSMISSION . . . . GEAR
STEERING. . . . . STANDARD
STANDARD DECK . . . . 30"
MSRP. $1,549

OPTIONS

BAGGER

SERIAL NUMBERS

YEAR	BEGINNING NO.
1987	420001
1988	475001
1989	595001
1990	010001

RETAIL PRICING

YEAR	HIGH	LOW
1987	$292	$219
1988	$321	$241
1989	$354	$265
1990	$396	$297

RX75

YEARS MFRD 1987-1990
ENGINE . . . . KAWASAKI
ENGINE HP 9
COOLING . . . . AIR
FUEL . . . . G
SPEEDS . . . . VARIABLE
TRANSMISSION . . . . GEAR
STEERING. . . . . STANDARD
STANDARD DECK . . . . 30"
WEIGHT . . . . 448 LBS.
MSRP. $1,749

OPTIONS

BAGGER

SERIAL NUMBERS

YEAR	BEGINNING NO.
1987	420001
1988	475001
1989	595001
1990	010001

RETAIL PRICING

YEAR	HIGH	LOW
1987	$336	$252
1988	$368	$276
1989	$395	$296
1990	$449	$337

RX95

YEARS MFRD 1987-1990
ENGINE . . . . KAWASAKI
ENGINE HP 12.5
COOLING . . . . AIR
FUEL . . . . G
SPEEDS . . . . VARIABLE
TRANSMISSION . . . . GEAR
STEERING. . . . . STANDARD
STANDARD DECK . . . . 30"
WEIGHT . . . . 473 LBS.
MSRP. $2,019

OPTIONS

BAGGER

SERIAL NUMBERS

YEAR	BEGINNING NO.
1987	420001
1988	475001
1989	595001
1990	010001

RETAIL PRICING

YEAR	HIGH	LOW
1987	$393	$295
1988	$425	$319
1989	$459	$344
1990	$518	$389

S240

YEARS MFRD 2015-2020
ENGINE FS600V
CID 36.8
ENGINE HP 18.5
COOLING . . . . AIR
FUEL . . . . G
SPEEDS . . . . VARIABLE
TRANSMISSION . . . . HYDRO
STEERING. . . . . STANDARD
STANDARD DECK . . . . 42"
WEIGHT . . . . 458 LBS.
MSRP. $2,599

OPTIONS

48" DECK. $300
6.5 BU BAG

SERIAL NUMBERS

YEAR	BEGINNING NO.
2015	600001
2016	700001
2017	800001

RETAIL PRICING

YEAR	HIGH	LOW
2015	$1,661	$1,246
2016	$1,819	$1,365
2017	$1,933	$1,450
2018	$2,117	$1,653
2019	$2,321	$1,834
2020	$2,522	$1,946

SRX75

YEARS MFRD 1991-1997
ENGINE . . . . JD K SERIES
ENGINE HP 9
COOLING . . . . AIR
FUEL . . . . G
SPEEDS . . . . VARIABLE
TRANSMISSION . . . . GEAR
STEERING. . . . . STANDARD
STANDARD DECK . . . . 30"
MSRP. $2,229

OPTIONS

BAGGER

SERIAL NUMBERS

YEAR	BEGINNING NO.
1991	010001
1992	025001
1993	045001
1994	055001
1995	065001
1996	075001
1997	085001

RETAIL PRICING

YEAR	HIGH	LOW
1991	$523	$392
1992	$569	$427
1993	$600	$450
1994	$630	$473
1995	$670	$503
1996	$691	$518
1997	$738	$554

SRX95

YEARS MFRD 1991-1994
ENGINE . . . . JD K SERIES
ENGINE HP 12.5
COOLING . . . . AIR
FUEL . . . . G
SPEEDS 12.5
TRANSMISSION . . . . GEAR
STEERING. . . . . STANDARD
STANDARD DECK . . . . 38"
WEIGHT . . . . 419 LBS.
MSRP. $2,629

OPTIONS

BAGGER

SERIAL NUMBERS

YEAR	BEGINNING NO.
1991	010001
1992	025001
1993	045001
1994	055001

RETAIL PRICING

YEAR	HIGH	LOW
1991	$628	$471
1992	$679	$509
1993	$711	$533
1994	$773	$580

SST15

YEARS MFRD 2002-2004
SERIES. . . . . SST SERIES
ENGINE . . . . . . KOHLER COMMAND
CYLINDERS. 1
ENGINE HP 15
COOLING . . . . AIR
FUEL . . . . G
SPEEDS . . . . VARIABLE
TRANSMISSION . . . . HYDRO
STEERING. . . . . ZERO
BLADE CLUTCH . . . . ELECTRIC
STANDARD DECK . . . . 42"
WEIGHT . . . . 840 LBS.
MSRP. $2,749

OPTIONS

44" BLADE
7 BU BAG

SERIAL NUMBERS

YEAR	BEGINNING NO.
2002	A040001
2003	A050001
2004	A060001

RETAIL PRICING

YEAR	HIGH	LOW
2002	$636	$477
2003	$699	$524
2004	$875	$656

SST16

YEARS MFRD 2001-2003
SERIES. . . . . SST SERIES
ENGINE . . . . VANGUARD
CYLINDERS. 1
ENGINE HP 16
COOLING . . . . AIR
FUEL . . . . G
SPEEDS . . . . VARIABLE
TRANSMISSION . . . . HYDRO
STEERING. . . . . ZERO
BLADE CLUTCH . . . . ELECTRIC
STANDARD DECK . . . . 42"
WEIGHT . . . . 850 LBS.
MSRP. $3,299

OPTIONS

44" BLADE
BAGGER
MULCHER

SERIAL NUMBERS

YEAR	BEGINNING NO.
2001	A010001
2001	B010001
2002	040001
2003	B050001
2003	A050001

RETAIL PRICING

YEAR	HIGH	LOW
2001	$702	$526
2002	$764	$573
2003	$838	$629

SST18

YEARS MFRD 2001-2003
SERIES. . . . . SST SERIES
ENGINE . . . . VANGUARD
CYLINDERS. 2
ENGINE HP 18
COOLING . . . . AIR
FUEL . . . . G
SPEEDS . . . . VARIABLE
TRANSMISSION . . . . HYDRO
STEERING. . . . . ZERO
BLADE CLUTCH . . . . ELECTRIC
STANDARD DECK . . . . 48"
WEIGHT . . . . 885 LBS.
MSRP. $3,999

OPTIONS

44" BLADE
BAGGER

SERIAL NUMBERS

YEAR	BEGINNING NO.
2001	C010001
2002	C040001
2003	C050001

RETAIL PRICING

YEAR	HIGH	LOW
2001	$847	$635
2002	$925	$694
2003	$1,016	$762

STX30

YEARS MFRD 1989-1993
ENGINE . . . . KOHLER
ENGINE HP 9

COOLING................AIR
FUEL..................G
SPEEDS.............1.35-5.3
TRANSMISSION..........GEAR
STEERING...........STANDARD
STANDARD DECK..........30"
WEIGHT............508 LBS.
MSRP................$1,799

OPTIONS

BAGGER

SERIAL NUMBERS

YEAR	BEGINNING NO.
1989	595001
1990	010001
1991	100001
1992	135001
1993	160001

RETAIL PRICING

YEAR	HIGH	LOW
1989	$216	$162
1990	$337	$252
1991	$366	$275
1992	$400	$300
1993	$504	$378

STX38

YEARS MFRD........1989-1998
ENGINE..............KOHLER
ENGINE HP..............12.5
COOLING................AIR
FUEL..................G
SPEEDS..................5/1
TRANSMISSION..........GEAR
STEERING...........STANDARD
STANDARD DECK..........38"
WEIGHT............410 LBS.
MSRP................$1,999

OPTIONS

38" SNOW THROWER
BAGGER
HYDRO

SERIAL NUMBERS

YEAR	BEGINNING NO.
1989	595001
1990	010001
1991	100001
1992	135001
1993	160001
1994	210001
1995	240001
1996	270001
1997	290001

RETAIL PRICING

YEAR	HIGH	LOW
1990	$154	$116
1991	$169	$127
1992	$186	$139
1993	$204	$153
1994	$222	$167
1995	$246	$184
1996	$270	$203
1997	$299	$224
1998	$332	$249

STX46

YEARS MFRD........1995-1998
ENGINE..............KOHLER
CYLINDERS.................1
ENGINE HP.................15
COOLING................AIR
FUEL..................G
SPEEDS..................5/1
TRANSMISSION..........GEAR
STEERING...........STANDARD
STANDARD DECK..........46"
WEIGHT............450 LBS.
MSRP................$2,499

OPTIONS

2 BAG
38" SNOW THROWER
HYDRO

SERIAL NUMBERS

YEAR	BEGINNING NO.
1995	240001
1996	270001
1997	290001

RETAIL PRICING

YEAR	HIGH	LOW
1995	$306	$230
1996	$335	$251
1997	$368	$276
1998	$427	$321

SX75

YEARS MFRD........1987-1990
ENGINE............KAWASAKI
ENGINE HP.................9
COOLING................AIR
FUEL..................G
SPEEDS..................7
TRANSMISSION..........GEAR
STEERING...........STANDARD
STANDARD DECK..........30"
WEIGHT............399 LBS.
MSRP................$2,039

OPTIONS

BAGGER

SERIAL NUMBERS

YEAR	BEGINNING NO.
1987	420001
1988	475001
1989	595001
1990	010001

RETAIL PRICING

YEAR	HIGH	LOW
1987	$393	$295
1988	$426	$320
1989	$462	$347
1990	$524	$393

SX85

YEARS MFRD........1997-2003
ENGINE..................B&S
ENGINE HP..............12.5
COOLING................AIR
FUEL..................G
SPEEDS............VARIABLE
TRANSMISSION..........GEAR
STEERING...........STANDARD
STANDARD DECK..........30"
WEIGHT............545 LBS.
MSRP................$2,429

OPTIONS

BAGGER

SERIAL NUMBERS

YEAR	BEGINNING NO.
1997	085001
1998	095001
1999	105001
2000	110001
2001	115001
2002	120001
2003	125001

RETAIL PRICING

YEAR	HIGH	LOW
1997	$356	$267
1998	$390	$292
1999	$427	$321
2000	$468	$351
2001	$515	$386
2002	$566	$425
2003	$622	$467

SX95

YEARS MFRD........1987-1990
ENGINE............KAWASAKI
ENGINE HP..............12.5
COOLING................AIR
FUEL..................G
SPEEDS..................7
TRANSMISSION..........GEAR
STEERING...........STANDARD
STANDARD DECK..........38"
WEIGHT............422 LBS.
MSRP................$2,419

OPTIONS

BAGGER

SERIAL NUMBERS

YEAR	BEGINNING NO.
1987	420001
1988	475001
1989	595001
1990	010001

RETAIL PRICING

YEAR	HIGH	LOW
1987	$470	$353
1988	$512	$384
1989	$551	$413
1990	$621	$466

X300

YEARS MFRD........2006-2015
SERIES......X300 SELECT SERIES
ENGINE............KAWASAKI
CYLINDERS.................2
CID....................28.8
ENGINE HP.................17
COOLING................AIR
FUEL..................G
SPEEDS............VARIABLE
TRANSMISSION.........HYDRO
STEERING...........STANDARD
BLADE CLUTCH........ELECTRIC
STANDARD DECK..........42"
MSRP................$2,999

OPTIONS

44" BLADE
44" SNOW BLOWER
48" DECK
7 BU BAG

SERIAL NUMBERS

YEAR	BEGINNING NO.
2006	10001
2007	40001
2008	85001
2009	120001
2010	150001
2011	180001
2012	220001
2013	250001
2014	280001
2015	310001

RETAIL PRICING

YEAR	HIGH	LOW
2006	$1,129	$847
2007	$1,192	$894
2008	$1,272	$954
2009	$1,408	$1,056
2010	$1,487	$1,115
2011	$1,719	$1,289
2012	$1,814	$1,360
2013	$1,966	$1,474
2014	$2,134	$1,600
2015	$2,260	$1,695

AVG. AUCTION PRICING

LOW	HIGH	AVG
$600	$1,600	$867

X300R

YEARS MFRD........2007-2015
SERIES......X300 SELECT SERIES
ENGINE............KAWASAKI
CYLINDERS.................2
CID....................28.8
ENGINE HP..............18.5
COOLING................AIR
FUEL..................G
SPEEDS............VARIABLE
TRANSMISSION.........HYDRO
STEERING...........STANDARD
BLADE CLUTCH........ELECTRIC
STANDARD DECK..........42"
MSRP................$4,199

OPTIONS

44" BLADE
44" SNOW BLOWER
7 BU BAG

SERIAL NUMBERS

YEAR	BEGINNING NO.
2007	40001
2008	085001
2009	120001
2010	150001
2011	180001
2012	220001
2013	250001
2014	280001
2015	310001

RETAIL PRICING

YEAR	HIGH	LOW
2007	$1,410	$1,057
2008	$1,556	$1,167
2009	$1,706	$1,280

YEAR	HIGH	LOW
2010	$1,864	$1,398
2011	$2,054	$1,541
2012	$2,242	$1,681
2013	$2,450	$1,838
2014	$2,699	$2,024
2015	$2,952	$2,214

X304

YEARS MFRD 2006-2015
SERIES...... X300 SELECT SERIES
ENGINE .... KAWASAKI
CYLINDERS.................. 2
CID 28.8
ENGINE HP 18.5
COOLING .... AIR
FUEL .... G
SPEEDS .... VARIABLE
TRANSMISSION .... HYDRO
STEERING........... ALL WHEEL
BLADE CLUTCH .... ELECTRIC
STANDARD DECK .... 42"
MSRP................. $3,799

OPTIONS

44" BLADE
44" SNOW BLOWER
48" DECK
7 BU BAG

SERIAL NUMBERS

YEAR	BEGINNING NO.
2006	10001
2007	40001
2008	85001
2009	120001
2010	150001
2011	180001
2012	220001
2013	250001
2014	280001
2015	310001

RETAIL PRICING

YEAR	HIGH	LOW
2006	$1,180	$885
2007	$1,326	$995
2008	$1,431	$1,073
2009	$1,576	$1,182
2010	$1,766	$1,324
2011	$1,857	$1,393
2012	$2,034	$1,525
2013	$2,248	$1,686
2014	$2,494	$1,870
2015	$2,748	$2,061

AVG. AUCTION PRICING

LOW	HIGH	AVG
$1,020	$1,428	$1,212

X310

YEARS MFRD 2012-2015
ENGINE .... KAWASAKI
ENGINE HP 18.5
COOLING .... AIR
FUEL .... G
SPEEDS .... VARIABLE
TRANSMISSION .... HYDRO
STEERING............ STANDARD
STANDARD DECK .... 42"
MSRP................. $3,999

OPTIONS

44" BLADE
44" SNOW BLOWER
7 BU BAG
ENCLOSURE

SERIAL NUMBERS

YEAR	BEGINNING NO.
2012	220001
2013	250001
2014	280001
2015	310001

RETAIL PRICING

YEAR	HIGH	LOW
2012	$2,203	$1,652
2013	$2,334	$1,750
2014	$2,531	$1,898
2015	$2,861	$2,146

X320

YEARS MFRD 2006-2015
SERIES...... X300 SELECT SERIES
ENGINE .... KAWASAKI
CYLINDERS.................. 2
CID 41.2
ENGINE HP 22
COOLING .... AIR
FUEL .... G
SPEEDS .... VARIABLE
TRANSMISSION .... HYDRO
STEERING............ STANDARD
BLADE CLUTCH .... ELECTRIC
STANDARD DECK .... 48"
MSRP................. $4,299

OPTIONS

44" BLADE
44" SNOW BLOWER
54" DECK
7 BU BAG
BAG & FAN

SERIAL NUMBERS

YEAR	BEGINNING NO.
2006	10001
2007	40001
2008	85001
2009	120001
2010	150001
2011	180001
2012	220001
2013	250001
2014	280001
2015	310001

RETAIL PRICING

YEAR	HIGH	LOW
2006	$1,506	$1,129
2007	$1,672	$1,254
2008	$1,869	$1,401
2009	$1,993	$1,495
2010	$2,209	$1,657
2011	$2,418	$1,814
2012	$2,578	$1,933
2013	$2,836	$2,127
2014	$3,063	$2,297
2015	$3,466	$2,599

AVG. AUCTION PRICING

LOW	HIGH	AVG
$950	$2,700	$1,783

X324

YEARS MFRD 2006-2015
SERIES...... X300 SELECT SERIES
ENGINE .... KAWASAKI
CYLINDERS.................. 2
CID 41.2
ENGINE HP 22
COOLING .... AIR
FUEL .... G
SPEEDS .... VARIABLE
TRANSMISSION .... HYDRO
STEERING........... ALL WHEEL
BLADE CLUTCH .... ELECTRIC
STANDARD DECK .... 48"
MSRP................. $4,799

OPTIONS

44" BLADE
44" SNOW BLOWER
7 BU BAG
BAG & FAN

SERIAL NUMBERS

YEAR	BEGINNING NO.
2006	10001
2007	40001
2008	85001
2009	120001
2010	150001
2011	180001
2012	220001
2013	250001
2014	280001
2015	310001

RETAIL PRICING

YEAR	HIGH	LOW
2006	$1,517	$1,138
2007	$1,640	$1,230
2008	$1,794	$1,346
2009	$1,982	$1,486
2010	$2,240	$1,680
2011	$2,386	$1,789
2012	$2,580	$1,935
2013	$2,844	$2,133
2014	$3,112	$2,334
2015	$3,458	$2,593

AVG. AUCTION PRICING

LOW	HIGH	AVG
$918	$2,550	$1,598

X330

YEARS MFRD 2016-2020
SERIES...... X300 SELECT SERIES
ENGINE .... 44J6 CYCLONIC
CYLINDERS.................. 2
CID 724CC
ENGINE HP 20
COOLING .... AIR
FUEL .... G
SPEEDS .... VARIABLE
TRANSMISSION .... HYDRO
STEERING............ STANDARD
BLADE CLUTCH .... ELECTRIC
STANDARD DECK .... 42"
WEIGHT .... 542 LBS.
MSRP................. $2,999

OPTIONS

44" FRT BLADE............ $589
44" SNOW BLOWER $1,639
48" DECK................. $400

SERIAL NUMBERS

YEAR	BEGINNING NO.
2016	10001
2017	20001
2018	50001

RETAIL PRICING

YEAR	HIGH	LOW
2016	$2,179	$1,634
2017	$2,320	$1,740
2018	$2,547	$1,990
2019	$2,792	$2,222
2020	$2,995	$2,312

X340

YEARS MFRD 2006-2011
SERIES...... X300 SELECT SERIES
ENGINE .... KAWASAKI
CYLINDERS.................. 2
CID 41.2
ENGINE HP 25
COOLING .... AIR
FUEL .... G
SPEEDS .... VARIABLE
TRANSMISSION .... HYDRO
STEERING............ STANDARD
BLADE CLUTCH .... ELECTRIC
STANDARD DECK .... 54"
MSRP................. $4,749

OPTIONS

44" BLADE
44" SNOW BLOWER
BAG & FAN

SERIAL NUMBERS

YEAR	BEGINNING NO.
2006	10001
2007	45000
2009	120001
2010	150001
2011	180001

RETAIL PRICING

YEAR	HIGH	LOW
2006	$1,645	$1,234
2007	$1,775	$1,331
2008	$1,935	$1,451
2009	$2,132	$1,599
2010	$2,317	$1,738
2011	$2,522	$1,892

X350

YEARS MFRD 2016-2020
SERIES...... X300 SELECT SERIES
CYLINDERS.................. 2
CID 36.8
ENGINE HP 18.5
COOLING .... AIR
FUEL .... G
SPEEDS .... VARIABLE
TRANSMISSION .... HYDRO
STEERING............ STANDARD
STANDARD DECK .... 42"
WEIGHT .... 607 LBS.
MSRP................. $3,299

OPTIONS

44" FRT BLADE............ $589
44" SNOW BLOWER $1,639
48" DECK................. $400

JOHN DEERE

SERIAL NUMBERS

YEAR	BEGINNING NO.
2016	10001
2017	20001
2018	50001

RETAIL PRICING

YEAR	HIGH	LOW
2016	$2,378	$1,783
2017	$2,481	$1,862
2018	$2,731	$2,136
2019	$3,009	$2,354
2020	$3,252	$2,513

X350R

YEARS MFRD	2016-2020
SERIES	X300 SELECT SERIES
CID	36.8
ENGINE HP	18.5
COOLING	AIR
FUEL	G
SPEEDS	VARIABLE
TRANSMISSION	HYDRO
STEERING	STANDARD
STANDARD DECK	42"
WEIGHT	646 LBS.
MSRP	$4,599

OPTIONS

44" FRT BLADE	$589
44" SNOW BLOWER	$1,639

SERIAL NUMBERS

YEAR	BEGINNING NO.
2016	10001
2017	20001
2018	50001

RETAIL PRICING

YEAR	HIGH	LOW
2016	$3,104	$2,328
2017	$3,404	$2,552
2018	$3,758	$2,935
2019	$4,141	$3,239
2020	$4,486	$3,463

X354

YEARS MFRD	2016-2020
SERIES	X300 SELECT SERIES
CID	36.8
ENGINE HP	18.5
COOLING	AIR
FUEL	G
SPEEDS	VARIABLE
TRANSMISSION	HYDRO
STEERING	STANDARD
STANDARD DECK	42"
WEIGHT	623 LBS.
MSRP	$3,999

OPTIONS

44" FRT BLADE	$589
44" SNOW BLOWER	$1,639

SERIAL NUMBERS

YEAR	BEGINNING NO.
2016	10001
2017	20001
2018	50001

RETAIL PRICING

YEAR	HIGH	LOW
2016	$2,752	$2,064
2017	$2,939	$2,204
2018	$3,222	$2,520
2019	$3,546	$2,748
2020	$3,902	$2,977

X360

YEARS MFRD	2008-2015
ENGINE	KAWASAKI
CYLINDERS	2
CID	41.2
ENGINE HP	22
COOLING	AIR
FUEL	G
SPEEDS	VARIABLE
TRANSMISSION	HYDRO
STEERING	STANDARD
BLADE CLUTCH	ELECTRIC
STANDARD DECK	48"
MSRP	$5,299

OPTIONS

44" BLADE
44" SNOW BLOWER
BAG & FAN
ENCLOSURE

SERIAL NUMBERS

YEAR	BEGINNING NO.
2008	085001
2009	120001
2010	150001
2011	180001
2012	220001
2013	250001
2014	280001
2015	310001

RETAIL PRICING

YEAR	HIGH	LOW
2008	$2,056	$1,542
2009	$2,207	$1,655
2010	$2,464	$1,848
2011	$2,678	$2,008
2012	$2,948	$2,211
2013	$3,269	$2,452
2014	$3,498	$2,623
2015	$3,775	$2,831

AVG. AUCTION PRICING

LOW	HIGH	AVG
$1,326	$2,142	$1,785

X370

YEARS MFRD	2016-2020
SERIES	X300 SELECT SERIES
ENGINE	FS600V
CYLINDERS	2
CID	603CC
ENGINE HP	18.5
COOLING	AIR
FUEL	G
SPEEDS	VARIABLE
TRANSMISSION	HYDRO
STEERING	STANDARD
STANDARD DECK	42"
WEIGHT	570 LBS.
MSRP	$4,199

OPTIONS

44" FRT BLADE	$589
44" SNOW BLOWER	$1,639

SERIAL NUMBERS

YEAR	BEGINNING NO.
2016	10001
2017	20001
2018	50001

RETAIL PRICING

YEAR	HIGH	LOW
2016	$2,899	$2,175
2017	$3,094	$2,320
2018	$3,409	$2,667
2019	$3,729	$2,918
2020	$4,125	$3,155

X380

YEARS MFRD	2016-2020
SERIES	X300 SELECT SERIES
ENGINE	FS651V
CYLINDERS	2
CID	44.3
ENGINE HP	22
COOLING	AIR
FUEL	G
SPEEDS	VARIABLE
TRANSMISSION	HYDRO
STEERING	STANDARD
STANDARD DECK	48"
WEIGHT	651 LBS.
MSRP	$4,699

OPTIONS

44" FRT BLADE	$589
44" SNOW BLOWER	$1,639
54" DECK	$300

SERIAL NUMBERS

YEAR	BEGINNING NO.
2016	10001
2017	20001
2018	50001

RETAIL PRICING

YEAR	HIGH	LOW
2016	$3,302	$2,476
2017	$3,404	$2,552
2018	$3,751	$2,921
2019	$4,129	$3,238
2020	$4,575	$3,488

X384

YEARS MFRD	2016-2020
SERIES	X300 SELECT SERIES
ENGINE	FS651V
CYLINDERS	2
CID	44.3
ENGINE HP	22
COOLING	AIR
FUEL	G
SPEEDS	VARIABLE
TRANSMISSION	HYDRO
STEERING	STANDARD
STANDARD DECK	48"
WEIGHT	700 LBS.
MSRP	$5,399

OPTIONS

44" FRT BLADE	$589
44" SNOW BLOWER	$1,639

SERIAL NUMBERS

YEAR	BEGINNING NO.
2016	10001
2017	20001
2018	50001

RETAIL PRICING

YEAR	HIGH	LOW
2016	$3,703	$2,778
2017	$3,946	$2,959
2018	$4,379	$3,413
2019	$4,820	$3,768
2020	$5,310	$4,067

X390

YEARS MFRD	2016-2020
SERIES	X300 SELECT SERIES
ENGINE	FS651V
CYLINDERS	2
CID	44.3
ENGINE HP	22
COOLING	AIR
FUEL	G
SPEEDS	VARIABLE
TRANSMISSION	HYDRO
STEERING	STANDARD
BLADE CLUTCH	ELECTRIC
STANDARD DECK	48"
WEIGHT	678 LBS.
MSRP	$5,699

OPTIONS

44" FRT BLADE	$589
44" SNOW BLOWER	$1,639
54" DECK	$300

SERIAL NUMBERS

YEAR	BEGINNING NO.
2016	10001
2017	20001
2018	50001

RETAIL PRICING

YEAR	HIGH	LOW
2016	$4,011	$3,007
2017	$3,935	$3,134
2018	$4,340	$3,397
2019	$4,797	$3,761
2020	$5,312	$4,075

X394

YEARS MFRD	2016-2020
SERIES	X300 SELECT SERIES
ENGINE	FS651V
CYLINDERS	2
CID	44.3
ENGINE HP	22
COOLING	AIR
FUEL	G
SPEEDS	VARIABLE
TRANSMISSION	HYDRO
STEERING	STANDARD
BLADE CLUTCH	ELECTRIC
STANDARD DECK	48"
WEIGHT	755 LBS.
MSRP	$6,399

OPTIONS

44" FRT BLADE	$589
44" SNOW BLOWER	$1,639

SERIAL NUMBERS

YEAR	BEGINNING NO.
2016	10001
2017	20001
2018	50001

RETAIL PRICING

YEAR	HIGH	LOW
2016	$4,343	$3,254
2017	$4,719	$3,540
2018	$5,206	$3,964
2019	$5,757	$4,515
2020	$6,354	$4,873

X465

YEARS MFRD	2002-2005
SERIES	X SERIES
ENGINE	KAWASAKI
CYLINDERS	2
ENGINE HP	21
COOLING	AIR
FUEL	G
SPEEDS	VARIABLE
TRANSMISSION	HYDRO
STEERING	ALL WHEEL
HITCH	CAT. I
HYDRAULIC	YES
PTO	YES
STANDARD DECK	48"
WEIGHT	1,035 LBS.
MSRP	$8,699

OPTIONS

42" TILLER
47" SNOW BLOWER
54" DECK
AWS
BAG & FAN

SERIAL NUMBERS

YEAR	BEGINNING NO.
2002	A010001-2WS
2002	B010001-AWS
2003	B020001-AWS
2003	A020001-2WS
2004	030001
2005	040001

RETAIL PRICING

YEAR	HIGH	LOW
2002	$2,240	$1,680
2003	$2,485	$1,864
2004	$2,711	$2,033
2005	$2,992	$2,244

X475

YEARS MFRD	2002-2005
SERIES	X SERIES
ENGINE	KAWASAKI
CYLINDERS	2
ENGINE HP	23
COOLING	LIQUID
FUEL	G
SPEEDS	VARIABLE
TRANSMISSION	HYDRO
STEERING	ALL WHEEL
HITCH	CAT. I
HYDRAULIC	YES
PTO	YES
STANDARD DECK	48"
WEIGHT	1,055 LBS.
MSRP	$10,039

OPTIONS

54" BLADE
62" DECK
AWS
BAG & FAN

SERIAL NUMBERS

YEAR	BEGINNING NO.
2002	A010001-2WS
2002	B010001-AWS
2003	B020002-AWS
2003	A020001-2WS
2004	030001
2005	040001

RETAIL PRICING

YEAR	HIGH	LOW
2002	$2,915	$2,186
2003	$3,265	$2,449
2004	$3,458	$2,593
2005	$3,819	$2,864

AVG. AUCTION PRICING

LOW	HIGH	AVG
$1,900	$3,750	$2,629

X485

YEARS MFRD	2002-2005
SERIES	X SERIES
ENGINE	KAWASAKI
CYLINDERS	2
ENGINE HP	25
COOLING	LIQUID
FUEL	G
SPEEDS	VARIABLE
TRANSMISSION	HYDRO
STEERING	STANDARD
HITCH	CAT. I
HYDRAULIC	YES
PTO	YES
STANDARD DECK	54"
WEIGHT	1,065 LBS.
MSRP	$10,529

OPTIONS

47" SNOW BLOWER
54" BLADE
62" DECK
AWS

SERIAL NUMBERS

YEAR	BEGINNING NO.
2002	A010001-2WS
2002	B010001-AWS
2003	A020001-2WS
2003	B010001-AWS
2004	030001
2005	040001

RETAIL PRICING

YEAR	HIGH	LOW
2002	$3,233	$2,425
2003	$3,548	$2,661
2004	$3,852	$2,889
2005	$4,222	$3,166

AVG. AUCTION PRICING

LOW	HIGH	AVG
$2,300	$6,500	$3,790

X485SE

YEARS MFRD	2004-2005
SERIES	X SERIES
ENGINE	KAWASAKI
CYLINDERS	2
ENGINE HP	25
COOLING	AIR
FUEL	G
SPEEDS	VARIABLE
TRANSMISSION	HYDRO
STEERING	STANDARD
HITCH	CAT. I
HYDRAULIC	YES
PTO	YES
STANDARD DECK	54"
MSRP	$11,579

OPTIONS

AWS

SERIAL NUMBERS

YEAR	BEGINNING NO.
2004	E030001
2005	E040001

RETAIL PRICING

YEAR	HIGH	LOW
2004	$5,216	$3,912
2005	$5,428	$4,071

X495

YEARS MFRD	2002-2005
SERIES	X SERIES
ENGINE	YANMAR
CYLINDERS	3
ENGINE HP	24
COOLING	LIQUID
FUEL	D
SPEEDS	VARIABLE
TRANSMISSION	HYDRO
STEERING	STANDARD
HITCH	CAT. I
HYDRAULIC	YES
PTO	YES
STANDARD DECK	54"
WEIGHT	1,215 LBS.
MSRP	$12,179

OPTIONS

47" SNOW BLOWER
54" BLADE
62" DECK
AWS

SERIAL NUMBERS

YEAR	BEGINNING NO.
2002	A010001-2WS
2003	D010001-2WS
2003	A020001-2WS
2003	C010001-AWS
2004	030001-2WS
2005	040001

RETAIL PRICING

YEAR	HIGH	LOW
2002	$3,459	$2,594
2003	$3,836	$2,877
2004	$4,121	$3,091
2005	$4,577	$3,433

AVG. AUCTION PRICING

LOW	HIGH	AVG
$2,550	$4,488	$3,641

X500

YEARS MFRD	2006-2015
SERIES	X500 SERIES
ENGINE	KAWASAKI
CYLINDERS	2
CID	41.2
ENGINE HP	25
COOLING	AIR
FUEL	G
SPEEDS	VARIABLE
TRANSMISSION	HYDRO
STEERING	STANDARD
BLADE CLUTCH	ELECTRIC
STANDARD DECK	54"
MSRP	$6,199

OPTIONS

14 BU BAG
30" TILLER
48" BLADE
48" DECK
7 BU BAG

SERIAL NUMBERS

YEAR	BEGINNING NO.
2006	10001
2007	20001
2008	30001
2009	40001
2010	50001
2011	60001
2012	70001
2013	80001
2014	90001
2015	100001

RETAIL PRICING

YEAR	HIGH	LOW
2006	$1,918	$1,438
2007	$2,103	$1,577
2008	$2,400	$1,800
2009	$2,635	$1,976
2010	$2,918	$2,189
2011	$3,254	$2,440
2012	$3,467	$2,600
2013	$3,746	$2,810
2014	$4,144	$3,108
2015	$4,612	$3,459

AVG. AUCTION PRICING

LOW	HIGH	AVG
$1,734	$3,468	$2,427

X520

YEARS MFRD	2006-2009
SERIES	X500 SERIES
ENGINE	KAWASAKI
CYLINDERS	2
CID	41.2
ENGINE HP	26
COOLING	LIQUID
FUEL	G
SPEEDS	VARIABLE
TRANSMISSION	HYDRO
STEERING	STANDARD
BLADE CLUTCH	ELECTRIC
STANDARD DECK	54"
MSRP	$6,659

JOHN DEERE

OPTIONS

14 BU BAG
30" TILLER
48" BLADE
7 BU BAG

SERIAL NUMBERS

YEAR	BEGINNING NO.
2006	10001
2007	20001
2008	30001
2009	40001

RETAIL PRICING

YEAR	HIGH	LOW
2006	$2,615	$1,961
2007	$2,869	$2,152
2008	$3,152	$2,364
2009	$3,475	$2,606

X530

YEARS MFRD	2010-2015
SERIES	X500 SELECT SERIES
ENGINE	KAWASAKI
CYLINDERS	2
CID	41.2
ENGINE HP	25
COOLING	AIR
FUEL	G
SPEEDS	VARIABLE
TRANSMISSION	HYDRO
STEERING	STANDARD
STANDARD DECK	54"
MSRP	$6,999

OPTIONS

14 BU BAG
30" TILLER
48" BLADE
7 BU BAG

SERIAL NUMBERS

YEAR	BEGINNING NO.
2010	50001
2011	60001
2012	70001
2013	80001
2014	90001
2015	100001

RETAIL PRICING

YEAR	HIGH	LOW
2010	$3,354	$2,515
2011	$3,515	$2,636
2012	$3,791	$2,844
2013	$4,194	$3,146
2014	$4,604	$3,453
2015	$5,051	$3,788

X534 4WS

YEARS MFRD	2006-2015
SERIES	X500 SERIES
ENGINE	KAWASAKI
CYLINDERS	2
CID	41.2
ENGINE HP	25
COOLING	AIR
FUEL	G
SPEEDS	VARIABLE
TRANSMISSION	HYDRO
STEERING	ALL WHEEL
BLADE CLUTCH	ELECTRIC
STANDARD DECK	54"
MSRP	$7,799

OPTIONS

14 BU BAG
48" BLADE
48" DECK
7 BU BAG

SERIAL NUMBERS

YEAR	BEGINNING NO.
2006	10001
2007	20001
2008	30001
2009	40001
2010	50001
2011	60001
2012	70001
2013	80001
2014	90001
2015	100001

RETAIL PRICING

YEAR	HIGH	LOW
2006	$2,396	$1,797
2007	$2,567	$1,926
2008	$2,919	$2,189
2009	$3,214	$2,411
2010	$3,543	$2,658
2011	$3,889	$2,917
2012	$4,303	$3,228
2013	$4,672	$3,504
2014	$5,178	$3,883
2015	$5,706	$4,279

X540

YEARS MFRD	2006-2015
SERIES	X500 SERIES
ENGINE	KAWASAKI
CYLINDERS	2
CID	41.2
ENGINE HP	23.5
COOLING	LIQUID
FUEL	G
SPEEDS	VARIABLE
TRANSMISSION	HYDRO
STEERING	STANDARD
BLADE CLUTCH	ELECTRIC
STANDARD DECK	54"
MSRP	$7,799

OPTIONS

14 BU BAG
30" TILLER
48" BLADE
48" DECK
7 BU BAG

SERIAL NUMBERS

YEAR	BEGINNING NO.
2006	10001
2007	20001
2008	30001
2009	40001
2010	50001
2011	60001
2012	70001
2013	80001
2014	90001
2015	100001

RETAIL PRICING

YEAR	HIGH	LOW
2006	$2,530	$1,897
2007	$2,853	$2,140
2008	$3,352	$2,514
2009	$3,567	$2,675
2010	$3,714	$2,785
2011	$4,130	$3,097
2012	$4,568	$3,426
2013	$4,834	$3,625
2014	$5,307	$3,980
2015	$5,591	$4,193

AVG. AUCTION PRICING

LOW	HIGH	AVG
$1,500	$5,000	$2,675

X570

YEARS MFRD	2016-2020
SERIES	X500 SELECT SERIES
ENGINE	KAWASAKI
CYLINDERS	2
ENGINE HP	24
COOLING	AIR
FUEL	G
SPEEDS	VARIABLE
TRANSMISSION	HYDRO
STEERING	STANDARD
BLADE CLUTCH	ELECTRIC
STANDARD DECK	48"
WEIGHT	748 LBS.
MSRP	$6,399

OPTIONS

30" TILLER	$1,859
44" SNOW BLOWER	$1,639
48" FRT BLADE	$829
54" DECK	$300

SERIAL NUMBERS

YEAR	BEGINNING NO.
2016	110001
2017	120001
2018	130001

RETAIL PRICING

YEAR	HIGH	LOW
2016	$4,569	$3,427
2017	$4,474	$3,739
2018	$5,257	$4,115
2019	$5,786	$4,627
2020	$6,317	$5,032

X575

YEARS MFRD	2002-2005
SERIES	X SERIES
ENGINE	KAWASAKI
CYLINDERS	2
ENGINE HP	23
COOLING	LIQUID
FUEL	G
SPEEDS	VARIABLE
TRANSMISSION	HYDRO
STEERING	STANDARD
HITCH	CAT. I
HYDRAULIC	YES
PTO	YES
DRIVE TYPE	4WD
STANDARD DECK	54"
WEIGHT	1,215 LBS.
MSRP	$11,499

OPTIONS

47" SNOW BLOWER
54" BLADE
62" DECK
BAG & FAN

SERIAL NUMBERS

YEAR	BEGINNING NO.
2002	C010001
2003	C020001
2004	C030001
2005	040001

RETAIL PRICING

YEAR	HIGH	LOW
2002	$2,942	$2,206
2003	$3,248	$2,436
2004	$3,583	$2,687
2005	$3,987	$2,990

X580

YEARS MFRD	2016-2020
SERIES	X500 SELECT SERIES
ENGINE	KAWASAKI
CYLINDERS	2
CID	44.3
ENGINE HP	24
COOLING	AIR
FUEL	G
SPEEDS	VARIABLE
TRANSMISSION	HYDRO
STEERING	STANDARD
STANDARD DECK	54"
WEIGHT	787 LBS.
MSRP	$7,699

OPTIONS

30" TILLER	$1,859
42" HYD TILLER	$2,689
47" SNOW BLOWER	$1,849
48" FRT BLADE	$829

SERIAL NUMBERS

YEAR	BEGINNING NO.
2016	110001
2017	120001
2018	130001

RETAIL PRICING

YEAR	HIGH	LOW
2016	$5,333	$3,999
2017	$5,570	$4,176
2018	$6,152	$4,721
2019	$6,803	$5,321
2020	$7,453	$5,686

X584

YEARS MFRD	2016-2018
SERIES	X500 SELECT SERIES
ENGINE	KAWASAKI
CYLINDERS	2
CID	44.3
ENGINE HP	24
COOLING	AIR
FUEL	G
SPEEDS	VARIABLE
TRANSMISSION	HYDRO
STEERING	STANDARD
STANDARD DECK	48"
WEIGHT	837 LBS.
MSRP	$7,699

OPTIONS
38" THATCHER
40" SHOVEL
GROOMER
TOW SPRAYER

SERIAL NUMBERS

YEAR	BEGINNING NO.
2016	110001
2017	120001
2018	130001

RETAIL PRICING

YEAR	HIGH	LOW
2016	$5,387	$4,040
2017	$5,705	$4,279
2018	$6,300	$4,725

X585

YEARS MFRD 2002-2005
SERIES .... X SERIES
ENGINE .... KAWASAKI
CYLINDERS 2
ENGINE HP 25
COOLING .... LIQUID
FUEL .... G
SPEEDS .... VARIABLE
TRANSMISSION .... HYDRO
STEERING .... STANDARD
HITCH .... CAT. I
HYDRAULIC .... YES
PTO .... YES
DRIVE TYPE 4WD
STANDARD DECK .... 48"
WEIGHT .... 1,216 LBS.
MSRP $12,499

OPTIONS
42" TILLER
46" SNOW THROWER
47" SNOW BLOWER
54" BLADE
54" DECK

SERIAL NUMBERS

YEAR	BEGINNING NO.
2002	C010001
2003	C020001
2004	C030001
2005	C040001

RETAIL PRICING

YEAR	HIGH	LOW
2002	$3,207	$2,405
2003	$3,609	$2,707
2004	$3,981	$2,986
2005	$4,450	$3,338

X585SE

YEARS MFRD 2004-2006
SERIES .... X SERIES
ENGINE .... KAWASAKI
CYLINDERS 2
ENGINE HP 25
COOLING .... LIQUID
FUEL .... G
SPEEDS .... VARIABLE
TRANSMISSION .... HYDRO
STEERING .... STANDARD
HITCH .... CAT. I
HYDRAULIC .... YES
PTO .... YES
DRIVE TYPE 4WD
STANDARD DECK .... 54"
MSRP $13,449

SERIAL NUMBERS

YEAR	BEGINNING NO.
2004	E030001
2005	E040001
2006	E050001

RETAIL PRICING

YEAR	HIGH	LOW
2004	$5,962	$4,471
2005	$6,295	$4,722
2006	$6,639	$4,979

X590

YEARS MFRD 2015-2020
SERIES .... X500 SELECT SERIES
ENGINE .... KAWASAKI
CYLINDERS 2
CID 44.3
ENGINE HP 25.5
COOLING .... LIQUID
FUEL .... G
SPEEDS .... VARIABLE
TRANSMISSION .... HYDRO
STEERING .... STANDARD
BLADE CLUTCH .... ELECTRIC
STANDARD DECK .... 48"
WEIGHT .... 805 LBS.
MSRP $8,099

OPTIONS
30" TILLER $1,859
42" HYD TILLER $2,689
47" SNOW BLOWER $1,849
48" FRT BLADE $829
54" DECK $300

SERIAL NUMBERS

YEAR	BEGINNING NO.
2015	100001
2016	110001
2017	120001
2018	130001

RETAIL PRICING

YEAR	HIGH	LOW
2015	$5,417	$4,063
2016	$5,699	$4,275
2017	$6,028	$4,622
2018	$6,601	$5,139
2019	$7,196	$5,668
2020	$7,879	$6,082

AVG. AUCTION PRICING

LOW	HIGH	AVG
$4,600	$5,250	$4,830

X595

YEARS MFRD 2002-2005
SERIES .... X SERIES
ENGINE .... YANMAR
CYLINDERS 3
ENGINE HP 24
COOLING .... LIQUID
FUEL .... D
SPEEDS .... VARIABLE
TRANSMISSION .... HYDRO
STEERING .... STANDARD
HITCH .... CAT. I
HYDRAULIC .... YES
PTO .... YES
DRIVE TYPE 4WD
STANDARD DECK .... 48"
WEIGHT .... 1,310 LBS.
MSRP $13,649

OPTIONS
47" SNOW BLOWER
54" BLADE
54" DECK
62" DECK
BAG & FAN

SERIAL NUMBERS

YEAR	BEGINNING NO.
2002	C010001
2003	D020001
2003	C020001
2004	C030001
2005	C040001

RETAIL PRICING

YEAR	HIGH	LOW
2002	$3,501	$2,625
2003	$3,997	$2,998
2004	$4,291	$3,218
2005	$4,811	$3,609

X595SE

YEARS MFRD 2004-2005
SERIES .... X SERIES
ENGINE .... YANMAR
CYLINDERS 3
ENGINE HP 24
COOLING .... LIQUID
FUEL .... D
SPEEDS .... VARIABLE
TRANSMISSION .... HYDRO
STEERING .... STANDARD
HITCH .... CAT. I
HYDRAULIC .... YES
PTO .... YES
DRIVE TYPE 4WD
STANDARD DECK .... 62"
MSRP $13,999

SERIAL NUMBERS

YEAR	BEGINNING NO.
2004	G030001
2005	G040001

RETAIL PRICING

YEAR	HIGH	LOW
2004	$5,962	$4,471
2005	$6,619	$4,964

X700

YEARS MFRD 2006-2012
SERIES .... X700 SERIES
ENGINE .... KAWASAKI
CYLINDERS 2
ENGINE HP 23
COOLING .... LIQUID
FUEL .... G
SPEEDS .... VARIABLE
TRANSMISSION .... HYDRO
STEERING .... STANDARD
HITCH .... CAT. I
HYDRAULIC .... YES
PTO .... YES
STANDARD DECK .... 54"
WEIGHT .... 1,064 LBS.
MSRP $9,699

OPTIONS
47" SNOW BLOWER
54" BLADE
7 BU BAG
SOFT ROPS

SERIAL NUMBERS

YEAR	BEGINNING NO.
2006	10001
2007	20001
2008	30001
2009	40001
2010	50001
2011	60001
2012	70001

RETAIL PRICING

YEAR	HIGH	LOW
2006	$3,051	$2,288
2007	$3,368	$2,526
2008	$3,742	$2,807
2009	$4,147	$3,110
2010	$4,504	$3,378
2011	$4,964	$3,723
2012	$5,468	$4,101

X700 ULTIMATE

YEARS MFRD 2009-2009
ENGINE .... KAWASAKI
CYLINDERS 2
CID 45.5
ENGINE HP 23
COOLING .... AIR
FUEL .... G
SPEEDS .... VARIABLE
TRANSMISSION .... HYDRO
STEERING .... STANDARD
BLADE CLUTCH .... ELECTRIC
STANDARD DECK .... 48"
MSRP $9,599

OPTIONS
54" DECK
62" DECK

SERIAL NUMBERS

YEAR	BEGINNING NO.
2009	40001

RETAIL PRICING

YEAR	HIGH	LOW
2009	$5,529	$4,147

X710

YEARS MFRD 2013-2018
ENGINE .... KAWASAKI
CYLINDERS 2
CID 45.5
ENGINE HP 22
COOLING .... LIQUID
FUEL .... G
SPEEDS .... VARIABLE
TRANSMISSION .... HYDRO
STEERING .... STANDARD

BLADE CLUTCH .... ELECTRIC
STANDARD DECK .... 54"
WEIGHT .... 1,083 LBS.
MSRP $10,459

OPTIONS

60" DECK

SERIAL NUMBERS

YEAR	BEGINNING NO.
2013	10001
2014	20001
2015	30001
2016	40001
2017	50001
2018	60001

RETAIL PRICING

YEAR	HIGH	LOW
2013	$5,319	$3,989
2014	$5,801	$4,351
2015	$6,457	$4,842
2016	$7,145	$5,359
2017	$7,800	$5,850
2018	$8,631	$6,473

X720

YEARS MFRD 2006-2012
SERIES .... X700 SERIES
ENGINE .... KAWASAKI
CYLINDERS 2
CID 45.5
ENGINE HP 25.5
COOLING .... LIQUID
FUEL .... G
SPEEDS .... VARIABLE
TRANSMISSION .... HYDRO
STEERING .... STANDARD
DRIVE TYPE 2WD
ROPS/CAB .... ROPS
STANDARD DECK .... 54"
WEIGHT .... 1,099 LBS.
MSRP $10,199

OPTIONS

47" SNOW BLOWER
54" BLADE
7 BU BAG

SERIAL NUMBERS

YEAR	BEGINNING NO.
2006	10001
2007	20001
2008	30001
2009	40001
2010	50001
2011	60001
2012	70001

RETAIL PRICING

YEAR	HIGH	LOW
2006	$3,693	$2,770
2007	$3,885	$2,914
2008	$4,438	$3,329
2009	$5,015	$3,762
2010	$5,479	$4,110
2011	$5,967	$4,475
2012	$6,562	$4,921

AVG. AUCTION PRICING

LOW	HIGH	AVG
$2,750	$5,800	$3,657

X720SE

YEARS MFRD 2006-2012
SERIES .... X700 SERIES
ENGINE .... KAWASAKI
CYLINDERS 2
CID 45.5
ENGINE HP 27
COOLING .... LIQUID
FUEL .... G
SPEEDS .... VARIABLE
TRANSMISSION .... HYDRO
STEERING .... STANDARD
STANDARD DECK .... 54"
MSRP $10,499

RETAIL PRICING

YEAR	HIGH	LOW
2006	$5,248	$3,936
2007	$5,765	$4,324
2008	$6,786	$5,090
2009	$7,323	$5,492
2010	$7,831	$5,873
2011	$8,241	$6,180
2012	$8,578	$6,434

X724

YEARS MFRD 2006-2012
SERIES .... X700 SERIES
ENGINE .... KAWASAKI
CYLINDERS 2
CID 45.5
ENGINE HP 25.5
COOLING .... LIQUID
FUEL .... G
SPEEDS .... VARIABLE
TRANSMISSION .... HYDRO
STEERING .... ALL WHEEL
BLADE CLUTCH .... ELECTRIC
DRIVE TYPE 2WD
ROPS/CAB .... ROPS
STANDARD DECK .... 62"
MSRP $11,599

OPTIONS

47" SNOW BLOWER
54" BLADE
7 BU BAG
SOFT ROPS

SERIAL NUMBERS

YEAR	BEGINNING NO.
2006	10001
2007	20001
2008	30001
2009	40001
2010	50001
2011	60001
2012	70001

RETAIL PRICING

YEAR	HIGH	LOW
2006	$3,903	$2,927
2007	$4,474	$3,355
2008	$4,788	$3,591
2009	$5,440	$4,080
2010	$5,881	$4,411
2011	$6,476	$4,857
2012	$7,112	$5,334

AVG. AUCTION PRICING

LOW	HIGH	AVG
$4,335	$6,528	$5,090

X728

YEARS MFRD 2006-2012
SERIES .... X700 SERIES
ENGINE .... KAWASAKI
CYLINDERS 2
CID 45.5
ENGINE HP 25.5
COOLING .... LIQUID
FUEL .... G
SPEEDS .... VARIABLE
TRANSMISSION .... HYDRO
STEERING .... STANDARD
BLADE CLUTCH .... ELECTRIC
DRIVE TYPE 4WD
STANDARD DECK .... 62"
MSRP $12,199

OPTIONS

47" SNOW BLOWER
54" BLADE
7 BU BAG

SERIAL NUMBERS

YEAR	BEGINNING NO.
2006	10001
2007	20001
2008	30001
2009	40001
2010	50001
2011	60001
2012	70001

RETAIL PRICING

YEAR	HIGH	LOW
2006	$4,042	$3,032
2007	$4,461	$3,346
2008	$4,998	$3,749
2009	$5,561	$4,171
2010	$6,049	$4,536
2011	$6,799	$5,099
2012	$7,542	$5,656

AVG. AUCTION PRICING

LOW	HIGH	AVG
$4,488	$6,885	$5,649

X728SE

YEARS MFRD 2006-2012
SERIES .... X700 SERIES
ENGINE .... KAWASAKI
CYLINDERS 2
CID 45.5
ENGINE HP 27
COOLING .... LIQUID
FUEL .... G
SPEEDS .... VARIABLE
TRANSMISSION .... HYDRO
STEERING .... STANDARD
DRIVE TYPE 4WD
STANDARD DECK .... 62"
WEIGHT .... 1,224 LBS.
MSRP $12,499

RETAIL PRICING

YEAR	HIGH	LOW
2006	$5,490	$4,117
2007	$6,142	$4,607
2008	$6,860	$5,145
2009	$7,377	$5,532
2010	$8,367	$6,275
2011	$9,347	$7,010
2012	$10,001	$7,501

X729

YEARS MFRD 2008-2012
ENGINE .... KAWASAKI
CYLINDERS 2
CID 45.5
ENGINE HP 25.5
COOLING .... LIQUID
FUEL .... G
SPEEDS .... VARIABLE
TRANSMISSION .... HYDRO
STEERING .... ALL WHEEL
DRIVE TYPE 4WD
STANDARD DECK .... 62"
WEIGHT .... 1,314 LBS.
MSRP $12,999

OPTIONS

47" SNOW BLOWER
54" BLADE
7 BU BAG
SOFT ROPS

SERIAL NUMBERS

YEAR	BEGINNING NO.
2008	30001
2009	40001
2010	50001
2011	60001
2012	70001

RETAIL PRICING

YEAR	HIGH	LOW
2008	$5,182	$3,886
2009	$5,745	$4,308
2010	$6,284	$4,713
2011	$6,966	$5,224
2012	$7,738	$5,803

X730

YEARS MFRD 2013-2020
SERIES .... X700 SERIES
ENGINE .... KAWASAKI
CYLINDERS 2
CID 45.5
ENGINE HP 25.5
COOLING .... LIQUID
FUEL .... G
SPEEDS .... VARIABLE
TRANSMISSION .... HYDRO
STEERING .... STANDARD
BLADE CLUTCH .... ELECTRIC
DRIVE TYPE 2WD
STANDARD DECK .... 54"
WEIGHT .... 1,088 LBS.
MSRP $11,789

OPTIONS

42" HYD TILLER $2,569
47" SNOW BLOWER $2,219
48" DECK .... $-400
60" DECK $400
60" FRT BLADE $929
HARD CAB $5,119

SERIAL NUMBERS

YEAR	BEGINNING NO.
2013	10001
2014	20001
2015	30001
2016	40001
2017	50001
2018	60001

RETAIL PRICING

YEAR	HIGH	LOW
2013	$6,703	$5,027
2014	$7,226	$5,419
2015	$7,645	$5,733
2016	$8,096	$6,072
2017	$8,499	$6,375
2018	$9,385	$7,259
2019	$10,253	$8,040
2020	$11,084	$8,579

AVG. AUCTION PRICING

LOW	HIGH	AVG
$6,000	$7,700	$6,733

X734

YEARS MFRD 2013-2020
SERIES .... X700 SERIES
ENGINE .... KAWASAKI
CYLINDERS 2
CID 45.5
ENGINE HP 25.5
COOLING .... LIQUID
FUEL .... G
SPEEDS .... VARIABLE
TRANSMISSION .... HYDRO
STEERING .... ALL WHEEL
BLADE CLUTCH .... ELECTRIC
STANDARD DECK .... 54"
WEIGHT .... 1,143 LBS.
MSRP $12,799

OPTIONS

42" HYD TILLER $2,569
47" SNOW BLOWER $2,219
48" DECK .... $-400
54" FRT BLADE $539
60" DECK $400

SERIAL NUMBERS

YEAR	BEGINNING NO.
2013	10001
2014	20001
2015	30001
2016	40001
2017	50001
2018	60001

RETAIL PRICING

YEAR	HIGH	LOW
2013	$7,082	$5,312
2014	$7,653	$5,739
2015	$8,399	$6,299
2016	$9,313	$6,984
2017	$9,734	$7,301
2018	$10,774	$8,080
2019	$11,913	$8,935
2020	$12,754	$9,871

AVG. AUCTION PRICING

LOW	HIGH	AVG
$6,375	$9,180	$7,395

X738

YEARS MFRD 2013-2020
SERIES .... X700 SERIES
ENGINE .... KAWASAKI
CYLINDERS 2
CID 45.5
ENGINE HP 25.5
COOLING .... LIQUID
FUEL .... G
SPEEDS .... VARIABLE
TRANSMISSION .... HYDRO
STEERING .... STANDARD
BLADE CLUTCH .... ELECTRIC
DRIVE TYPE 4WD
STANDARD DECK .... 48"
WEIGHT .... 1,178 LBS.
MSRP $13,009

OPTIONS

42" HYD TILLER $2,569
47" SNOW BLOWER $2,219
54" DECK $400
60" DECK $800

SERIAL NUMBERS

YEAR	BEGINNING NO.
2013	10001
2014	20001
2015	30001
2016	40001
2017	50001
2018	60001

RETAIL PRICING

YEAR	HIGH	LOW
2013	$6,770	$5,078
2014	$7,626	$5,720
2015	$8,587	$6,503
2016	$9,422	$7,066
2017	$9,736	$7,812
2018	$10,751	$8,423
2019	$11,775	$9,181
2020	$12,803	$9,832

X739

YEARS MFRD 2013-2020
SERIES .... X700 SERIES
ENGINE .... KAWASAKI
CYLINDERS 2
CID 45.5
ENGINE HP 25.5
COOLING .... LIQUID
FUEL .... G
SPEEDS .... VARIABLE
TRANSMISSION .... HYDRO
STEERING .... ALL WHEEL
BLADE CLUTCH .... ELECTRIC
STANDARD DECK .... 48"
WEIGHT .... 1,265 LBS.
MSRP $13,669

OPTIONS

42" HYD TILLER $2,569
47" SNOW BLOWER $2,219
54" DECK $400
54" FRT BLADE $539
60" DECK $800

SERIAL NUMBERS

YEAR	BEGINNING NO.
2013	010001
2014	020001
2015	30001
2016	40001
2017	50001
2018	60001

RETAIL PRICING

YEAR	HIGH	LOW
2013	$7,474	$5,605
2014	$8,288	$6,215
2015	$8,960	$6,720
2016	$9,864	$7,399
2017	$10,621	$8,068
2018	$11,659	$9,163
2019	$12,565	$10,087
2020	$13,396	$10,730

X740

YEARS MFRD 2006-2012
SERIES .... X700 SERIES
ENGINE .... YANMAR
CYLINDERS 3
CID 68.1
ENGINE HP 24
COOLING .... LIQUID
FUEL .... D
SPEEDS .... VARIABLE
TRANSMISSION .... HYDRO
STEERING .... STANDARD
BLADE CLUTCH .... ELECTRIC
DRIVE TYPE 2WD
STANDARD DECK .... 62"
WEIGHT .... 1,184 LBS.
MSRP $11,699

OPTIONS

47" SNOW BLOWER
54" BLADE
7 BU BAG
SOFT ROPS

SERIAL NUMBERS

YEAR	BEGINNING NO.
2006	10001
2007	20001
2008	30001
2009	40001
2010	50001
2011	60001
2012	70001

RETAIL PRICING

YEAR	HIGH	LOW
2006	$3,622	$2,717
2007	$3,995	$2,997
2008	$4,486	$3,364
2009	$4,962	$3,722
2010	$5,458	$4,094
2011	$6,062	$4,546
2012	$6,674	$5,005

AVG. AUCTION PRICING

LOW	HIGH	AVG
$3,162	$6,018	$4,529

X744

YEARS MFRD 2006-2012
SERIES .... X700 SERIES
ENGINE .... YANMAR
CYLINDERS 3
CID 68.1
ENGINE HP 24
COOLING .... LIQUID
FUEL .... D
SPEEDS .... VARIABLE
TRANSMISSION .... HYDRO
STEERING .... ALL WHEEL
BLADE CLUTCH .... ELECTRIC
DRIVE TYPE 2WD
STANDARD DECK .... 62"
MSRP $12,699

OPTIONS

47" SNOW BLOWER
54" BLADE
7 BU BAG
SOFT ROPS

SERIAL NUMBERS

YEAR	BEGINNING NO.
2006	10001
2007	20001
2008	30001
2009	40001
2010	50001
2011	60001
2012	70001

RETAIL PRICING

YEAR	HIGH	LOW
2006	$3,833	$2,875
2007	$4,243	$3,182
2008	$4,758	$3,569
2009	$5,193	$3,895
2010	$5,685	$4,264
2011	$6,309	$4,732
2012	$6,898	$5,174

X748

YEARS MFRD 2006-2012
SERIES .... X700 SERIES
ENGINE .... YANMAR
CYLINDERS 3
CID 68.1
ENGINE HP 24
COOLING .... LIQUID
FUEL .... D
SPEEDS .... VARIABLE
TRANSMISSION .... HYDRO
STEERING .... STANDARD
BLADE CLUTCH .... ELECTRIC
DRIVE TYPE 4WD
STANDARD DECK .... 62"
WEIGHT .... 1,309 LBS.
MSRP $13,299

OPTIONS

47" SNOW BLOWER
54" BLADE
7 BU BAG

SERIAL NUMBERS

YEAR	BEGINNING NO.
2006	10001
2007	20001
2008	30001
2009	40001
2010	50001
2011	60001
2012	70001

RETAIL PRICING

YEAR	HIGH	LOW
2006	$4,038	$3,029
2007	$4,453	$3,340
2008	$4,934	$3,700
2009	$5,424	$4,068
2010	$6,126	$4,595
2011	$6,892	$5,169
2012	$7,390	$5,542

AVG. AUCTION PRICING

LOW	HIGH	AVG
$6,944	$9,259	$7,947

JOHN DEERE

X748SE

YEARS MFRD 2006-2012
SERIES. . . . . X700 SERIES
ENGINE . . . . YANMAR
CYLINDERS. 3
CID 68.1
ENGINE HP 24
COOLING . . . . LIQUID
FUEL . . . . D
SPEEDS . . . . VARIABLE
TRANSMISSION . . . . HYDRO
STEERING. . . . . STANDARD
DRIVE TYPE 4WD
STANDARD DECK . . . . 62"
WEIGHT . . . . 1,309 LBS.
MSRP. $13,679

RETAIL PRICING

YEAR	HIGH	LOW
2006	$6,175	$4,631
2007	$6,997	$5,248
2008	$7,460	$5,595
2009	$8,325	$6,244
2010	$9,210	$6,907
2011	$10,095	$7,571
2012	$11,349	$8,511

X749

YEARS MFRD 2008-2012
ENGINE . . . . YANMAR
CYLINDERS. 3
CID 68.1
ENGINE HP 24
COOLING . . . . LIQUID
FUEL . . . . D
SPEEDS . . . . VARIABLE
TRANSMISSION . . . . HYDRO
STEERING. . . . . ALL WHEEL
DRIVE TYPE 4WD
STANDARD DECK . . . . 62"
WEIGHT . . . . 1,424 LBS.
MSRP. $14,099

OPTIONS

47" SNOW BLADE
54" BLADE
7 BU BAG
SOFT ROPS

SERIAL NUMBERS

YEAR	BEGINNING NO.
2008	30001
2009	40001
2010	50001
2011	60001
2012	70001

RETAIL PRICING

YEAR	HIGH	LOW
2008	$5,356	$4,017
2009	$5,805	$4,354
2010	$6,346	$4,760
2011	$6,926	$5,194
2012	$7,882	$5,911

X750

YEARS MFRD 2013-2020
SERIES. . . . . X700 SERIES
ENGINE . . . . YANMAR
CYLINDERS. 3
CID 60.6
ENGINE HP 24
COOLING . . . . LIQUID
FUEL . . . . D
SPEEDS . . . . VARIABLE
TRANSMISSION . . . . HYDRO
STEERING. . . . . STANDARD
BLADE CLUTCH . . . . ELECTRIC
DRIVE TYPE 2WD
STANDARD DECK . . . . 48"
WEIGHT . . . . 1,168 LBS.
MSRP. $12,609

OPTIONS

47" SNOW BLOWER $2,219
54" DECK. $400
54" FRT BLADE. $539
60" DECK. $800

SERIAL NUMBERS

YEAR	BEGINNING NO.
2013	10001
2014	20001
2015	30001
2016	40001
2017	50001
2018	60001

RETAIL PRICING

YEAR	HIGH	LOW
2013	$7,024	$5,268
2014	$7,544	$5,657
2015	$8,249	$6,187
2016	$9,296	$6,973
2017	$9,764	$7,323
2018	$10,682	$8,364
2019	$11,626	$9,157
2020	$12,447	$10,032

X754

YEARS MFRD 2013-2020
SERIES. . . . . X700 SERIES
ENGINE . . . . KAWASAKI
CYLINDERS. 3
CID 60.6
ENGINE HP 24
COOLING . . . . LIQUID
FUEL . . . . D
SPEEDS . . . . VARIABLE
TRANSMISSION . . . . HYDRO
STEERING. . . . . ALL WHEEL
BLADE CLUTCH . . . . ELECTRIC
STANDARD DECK . . . . 48"
WEIGHT . . . . 1,215 LBS.
MSRP. $14,229

OPTIONS

42" HYD TILLER $2,569
47" SNOW BLOWER $2,219
54" DECK. $400
54" FRT BLADE. $539
60" DECK. $800

SERIAL NUMBERS

YEAR	BEGINNING NO.
2013	10001
2014	20001
2015	30001
2016	40001
2017	50001
2018	60001

RETAIL PRICING

YEAR	HIGH	LOW
2013	$7,384	$5,538
2014	$8,174	$6,100
2015	$8,698	$6,523
2016	$9,698	$7,273
2017	$10,583	$7,936
2018	$11,600	$8,983
2019	$12,790	$10,009
2020	$13,856	$11,170

X758

YEARS MFRD 2013-2020
SERIES. . . . . X700 SERIES
ENGINE . . . . YANMAR
CYLINDERS. 3
CID 60.6
ENGINE HP 24
COOLING . . . . LIQUID
FUEL . . . . D
SPEEDS . . . . VARIABLE
TRANSMISSION . . . . HYDRO
STEERING. . . . . STANDARD
BLADE CLUTCH . . . . ELECTRIC
DRIVE TYPE 4WD
STANDARD DECK . . . . 48"
WEIGHT . . . . 1,258 LBS.
MSRP. $14,229

OPTIONS

42" HYD TILLER $2,569
47" SNOW BLOWER $2,219
54" DECK. $400
54" FRT BLADE. $539
60" DECK. $800

SERIAL NUMBERS

YEAR	BEGINNING NO.
2013	10001
2014	20001
2015	30001
2016	40001
2017	50001
2018	60001

RETAIL PRICING

YEAR	HIGH	LOW
2013	$7,953	$5,965
2014	$8,523	$6,392
2015	$9,507	$7,130
2016	$10,612	$7,959
2017	$11,048	$8,694
2018	$12,162	$9,522
2019	$13,211	$10,370
2020	$14,184	$11,020

Z225

YEARS MFRD 2007-2012
SERIES. . . . . EZTRAK SERIES
ENGINE . . . . B&S
CYLINDERS. 1
CID 31
ENGINE HP 18.5
COOLING . . . . AIR
FUEL . . . . G
SPEEDS . . . . VARIABLE
TRANSMISSION . . . . HYDRO
STEERING. . . . . ZERO
BLADE CLUTCH . . . . ELECTRIC
STANDARD DECK . . . . 42"
WEIGHT . . . . 550 LBS.
MSRP. $2,899

OPTIONS

BAGGER

SERIAL NUMBERS

YEAR	BEGINNING NO.
2007	10001
2008	40001
2009	080001
2010	090001
2011	100001
2012	110001

RETAIL PRICING

YEAR	HIGH	LOW
2007	$1,455	$1,091
2008	$1,603	$1,203
2009	$1,692	$1,269
2010	$1,940	$1,455
2011	$2,107	$1,580
2012	$2,355	$1,766

AVG. AUCTION PRICING

LOW	HIGH	AVG
$918	$1,530	$1,122

Z235

YEARS MFRD 2013-2015
ENGINE . . . . B&S
ENGINE HP 20
COOLING . . . . AIR
FUEL . . . . G
SPEEDS . . . . VARIABLE
TRANSMISSION . . . . HYDRO
STEERING. . . . . ZERO
STANDARD DECK . . . . 42"
WEIGHT . . . . 545 LBS.
MSRP. $2,499

OPTIONS

6.5 BU BAG

SERIAL NUMBERS

YEAR	BEGINNING NO.
2013	130001
2014	150001
2015	170001

RETAIL PRICING

YEAR	HIGH	LOW
2013	$1,851	$1,388
2014	$1,938	$1,454
2015	$2,045	$1,534

Z245

YEARS MFRD 2008-2012
SERIES. . . . . EZTRAK SERIES
ENGINE . . . . B&S
CYLINDERS. 2
CID 44.2
ENGINE HP 23
COOLING . . . . AIR
FUEL . . . . G
SPEEDS . . . . VARIABLE
TRANSMISSION . . . . HYDRO
STEERING. . . . . ZERO
BLADE CLUTCH . . . . ELECTRIC
STANDARD DECK . . . . 48"
WEIGHT . . . . 590 LBS.
MSRP. $3,599

OPTIONS

BAGGER

SERIAL NUMBERS

YEAR	BEGINNING NO.
2008	040001
2009	060001
2010	080001
2011	100001
2012	120001

RETAIL PRICING

YEAR	HIGH	LOW
2008	$1,726	$1,294
2009	$1,891	$1,418
2010	$2,094	$1,571
2011	$2,332	$1,749
2012	$2,606	$1,955

Z252E

YEARS MFRD 2016-2016
ENGINE HP 22
COOLING . . . . AIR
FUEL . . . . G
SPEEDS . . . . VARIABLE
TRANSMISSION . . . . HYDRO
STEERING . . . . ZERO
STANDARD DECK . . . . 48"

Z255

YEARS MFRD 2013-2015
ENGINE . . . . B&S
ENGINE HP 22
COOLING . . . . AIR
FUEL . . . . G
SPEEDS . . . . VARIABLE
TRANSMISSION . . . . HYDRO
STEERING . . . . ZERO
BLADE CLUTCH . . . . ELECTRIC
STANDARD DECK . . . . 48"
MSRP $2,999

OPTIONS

6.5 BU BAG

SERIAL NUMBERS

YEAR	BEGINNING NO.
2013	130001
2014	150001
2015	170001

RETAIL PRICING

YEAR	HIGH	LOW
2013	$2,215	$1,662
2014	$2,424	$1,818
2015	$2,620	$1,965

Z335E

YEARS MFRD 2016-2020
SERIES . . . . ZTRAK SERIES
ENGINE . . . . B&S INTEK
CID 40
ENGINE HP 20
COOLING . . . . AIR
FUEL . . . . G
SPEEDS . . . . VARIABLE
TRANSMISSION . . . . HYDRO
STEERING . . . . ZERO
STANDARD DECK . . . . 42"
WEIGHT . . . . 491 LBS.
MSRP $2,599

SERIAL NUMBERS

YEAR	BEGINNING NO.
2016	01001
2017	50001

RETAIL PRICING

YEAR	HIGH	LOW
2016	$1,847	$1,384
2017	$1,920	$1,440
2018	$2,039	$1,594
2019	$2,213	$1,717
2020	$2,415	$1,878

Z335M

YEARS MFRD 2017-2020
SERIES . . . . ZTRAK SERIES
ENGINE . . . . B&S INTEK
CID 40
ENGINE HP 20
COOLING . . . . AIR
FUEL . . . . G
SPEEDS . . . . VARIABLE
TRANSMISSION . . . . HYDRO
STEERING . . . . ZERO
STANDARD DECK . . . . 42"
WEIGHT . . . . 496 LBS.
MSRP $2,699

SERIAL NUMBERS

YEAR	BEGINNING NO.
2017	50001

RETAIL PRICING

YEAR	HIGH	LOW
2017	$1,973	$1,479
2018	$2,156	$1,639
2019	$2,325	$1,819
2020	$2,542	$1,964

Z345M

YEARS MFRD 2017-2020
SERIES . . . . ZTRAK SERIES
ENGINE . . . . B&S INTEK
CID 44.2
ENGINE HP 22
COOLING . . . . AIR
FUEL . . . . G
SPEEDS . . . . VARIABLE
TRANSMISSION . . . . HYDRO
STEERING . . . . ZERO
STANDARD DECK . . . . 42"
WEIGHT . . . . 496 LBS.
MSRP $2,799

SERIAL NUMBERS

YEAR	BEGINNING NO.
2017	50001

RETAIL PRICING

YEAR	HIGH	LOW
2017	$2,048	$1,536
2018	$2,243	$1,745
2019	$2,476	$1,918
2020	$2,691	$2,064

Z345R

YEARS MFRD 2017-2020
SERIES . . . . ZTRAK SERIES
ENGINE . . . . B&S INTEK
CID 44.2
ENGINE HP 22
COOLING . . . . AIR
FUEL . . . . G
SPEEDS . . . . VARIABLE
TRANSMISSION . . . . HYDRO
STEERING . . . . ZERO
STANDARD DECK . . . . 42"
WEIGHT . . . . 500 LBS.
MSRP $2,899

OPTIONS

6.5 BU BAG

SERIAL NUMBERS

YEAR	BEGINNING NO.
2017	50001

RETAIL PRICING

YEAR	HIGH	LOW
2017	$2,124	$1,593
2018	$2,345	$1,835
2019	$2,567	$2,015
2020	$2,787	$2,159

Z355E

YEARS MFRD 2016-2020
SERIES . . . . ZTRAK SERIES
ENGINE . . . . B&S INTEK
CID 44.2
ENGINE HP 22
COOLING . . . . AIR
FUEL . . . . G
SPEEDS . . . . VARIABLE
TRANSMISSION . . . . HYDRO
STEERING . . . . ZERO
STANDARD DECK . . . . 48"
WEIGHT . . . . 570 LBS.
MSRP $2,999

OPTIONS

6.5 BU BAG
LIGHTS

SERIAL NUMBERS

YEAR	BEGINNING NO.
2016	01001
2017	50001

RETAIL PRICING

YEAR	HIGH	LOW
2016	$2,065	$1,548
2017	$2,200	$1,650
2018	$2,347	$1,814
2019	$2,588	$2,021
2020	$2,770	$2,135

Z355R

YEARS MFRD 2017-2020
SERIES . . . . ZTRAK SERIES
ENGINE . . . . B&S INTEK
CID 44.2
ENGINE HP 22
COOLING . . . . AIR
FUEL . . . . G
SPEEDS . . . . VARIABLE
TRANSMISSION . . . . HYDRO
STEERING . . . . ZERO
STANDARD DECK . . . . 48"
WEIGHT . . . . 575 LBS.
MSRP $3,199

RETAIL PRICING

YEAR	HIGH	LOW
2017	$2,352	$1,764
2018	$2,588	$2,001
2019	$2,772	$2,279
2020	$3,009	$2,331

Z375R

YEARS MFRD 2017-2020
SERIES . . . . ZTRAK SERIES
ENGINE . . . . B&S ELS
CID 44.2
ENGINE HP 25
COOLING . . . . AIR
FUEL . . . . G
SPEEDS . . . . VARIABLE
TRANSMISSION . . . . HYDRO
STEERING . . . . ZERO
STANDARD DECK . . . . 42"
WEIGHT . . . . 590 LBS.
MSRP $3,499

SERIAL NUMBERS

YEAR	BEGINNING NO.
2017	50001

RETAIL PRICING

YEAR	HIGH	LOW
2017	$2,657	$1,992
2018	$2,934	$2,291
2019	$3,013	$2,508
2020	$3,292	$2,666

Z425

YEARS MFRD 2007-2015
SERIES . . . . EZTRAK SERIES
ENGINE . . . . B&S
CYLINDERS 2
CID 44.2
ENGINE HP 22
COOLING . . . . AIR
FUEL . . . . G
SPEEDS . . . . VARIABLE
TRANSMISSION . . . . HYDRO
STEERING . . . . ZERO
BLADE CLUTCH . . . . ELECTRIC
STANDARD DECK . . . . 48"
WEIGHT . . . . 650 LBS.
MSRP $3,999

OPTIONS

54" DECK
BAG & FAN
BAGGER

SERIAL NUMBERS

YEAR	BEGINNING NO.
2007	10001
2008	40001
2010	080001
2011	100001
2012	120001
2013	130001
2014	150001
2015	170001

RETAIL PRICING

YEAR	HIGH	LOW
2007	$1,805	$1,354
2008	$2,009	$1,507
2009	$2,118	$1,588
2010	$2,274	$1,705
2011	$2,502	$1,877
2012	$2,625	$1,969
2013	$2,961	$2,221
2014	$3,054	$2,290
2015	$3,250	$2,437

AVG. AUCTION PRICING

LOW	HIGH	AVG
$1,200	$2,050	$1,488

Z435

YEARS MFRD	2015-2015
SERIES	EZTRAK SERIES
ENGINE	B&S
CYLINDERS	2
CID	724CC
ENGINE HP	25
COOLING	AIR
FUEL	G
SPEEDS	VARIABLE
TRANSMISSION	HYDRO
STEERING	ZERO
BLADE CLUTCH	ELECTRIC
STANDARD DECK	48"
MSRP	$4,599

Z445

YEARS MFRD	2007-2015
SERIES	EZTRAK SERIES
ENGINE	KAWASAKI
CYLINDERS	2
CID	41.2
ENGINE HP	24
COOLING	AIR
FUEL	G
SPEEDS	VARIABLE
TRANSMISSION	HYDRO
STEERING	ZERO
BLADE CLUTCH	ELECTRIC
STANDARD DECK	54"
WEIGHT	685 LBS.
MSRP	$5,099

OPTIONS

48" DECK
BAG & FAN
BAGGER

SERIAL NUMBERS

YEAR	BEGINNING NO.
2007	010001
2008	040001
2009	060001
2010	080001
2011	100001
2012	120001
2013	130001
2014	150001
2015	170001

RETAIL PRICING

YEAR	HIGH	LOW
2007	$2,488	$1,866
2008	$2,668	$2,001
2009	$2,884	$2,163
2010	$3,211	$2,408
2011	$3,317	$2,488
2012	$3,620	$2,715
2013	$3,699	$2,774
2014	$3,786	$2,840
2015	$4,078	$3,058

AVG. AUCTION PRICING

LOW	HIGH	AVG
$1,224	$4,080	$2,149

Z465

YEARS MFRD	2008-2015
SERIES	EZTRAK SERIES
ENGINE	KAWASAKI
CYLINDERS	2
CID	41.2
ENGINE HP	25
COOLING	AIR
FUEL	G
SPEEDS	VARIABLE
TRANSMISSION	HYDRO
STEERING	ZERO
BLADE CLUTCH	ELECTRIC
STANDARD DECK	62"
WEIGHT	750 LBS.
MSRP	$5,499

OPTIONS

MULCH KIT

SERIAL NUMBERS

YEAR	BEGINNING NO.
2008	040001
2009	060001
2010	080001
2011	100001
2012	120001
2013	130001
2014	150001
2015	170001

RETAIL PRICING

YEAR	HIGH	LOW
2008	$2,503	$1,877
2009	$2,845	$2,134
2010	$3,224	$2,418
2011	$3,683	$2,762
2012	$3,821	$2,866
2013	$4,194	$3,146
2014	$4,405	$3,304
2015	$4,809	$3,607

AVG. AUCTION PRICING

LOW	HIGH	AVG
$2,193	$4,080	$2,831

Z510A

YEARS MFRD	2008-2009
ENGINE	KOHLER SV715S
CYLINDERS	2
CID	44
ENGINE HP	22
COOLING	AIR
FUEL	G
SPEEDS	VARIABLE
TRANSMISSION	HYDRO
STEERING	ZERO
BLADE CLUTCH	ELECTRIC
STANDARD DECK	48"
WEIGHT	1,128 LBS.
MSRP	$6,699

OPTIONS

2 BAG

RETAIL PRICING

YEAR	HIGH	LOW
2008	$3,566	$2,674
2009	$4,047	$3,036

Z520A

YEARS MFRD	2008-2009
ENGINE	KOHLER SV730
CYLINDERS	2
CID	44.2
ENGINE HP	25
COOLING	AIR
FUEL	G
SPEEDS	VARIABLE
TRANSMISSION	DUAL HYDRO
STEERING	ZERO
BLADE CLUTCH	ELECTRIC
STANDARD DECK	54"
WEIGHT	1,153 LBS.
MSRP	$7,319

OPTIONS

2 BAG
60" DECK

RETAIL PRICING

YEAR	HIGH	LOW
2008	$4,191	$3,143
2009	$4,471	$3,353

Z525E

YEARS MFRD	2016-2020
SERIES	ZTRAK SERIES
ENGINE	B&S ELS
CID	44.2
ENGINE HP	22
COOLING	AIR
FUEL	G
SPEEDS	VARIABLE
TRANSMISSION	HYDRO
STEERING	ZERO
STANDARD DECK	48"
WEIGHT	615 LBS.
MSRP	$3,899

OPTIONS

54" DECK	$100

SERIAL NUMBERS

YEAR	BEGINNING NO.
2016	01001
2017	50001

RETAIL PRICING

YEAR	HIGH	LOW
2016	$3,957	$2,162
2017	$2,960	$2,301
2018	$3,164	$2,462
2019	$3,359	$2,626
2020	$3,683	$2,835

Z535M

YEARS MFRD	2016-2020
SERIES	ZTRAK SERIES
ENGINE	B&S CYCLONIC
CID	44.2
ENGINE HP	25
COOLING	AIR
FUEL	G
SPEEDS	VARIABLE
TRANSMISSION	HYDRO
STEERING	ZERO
STANDARD DECK	48"
WEIGHT	615 LBS.
MSRP	$4,399

OPTIONS

54" DECK	$200
62" DECK	$300

SERIAL NUMBERS

YEAR	BEGINNING NO.
2016	01001
2017	50001

RETAIL PRICING

YEAR	HIGH	LOW
2016	$3,183	$2,387
2017	$3,388	$2,539
2018	$3,633	$2,819
2019	$3,902	$3,025
2020	$4,213	$3,269

Z535R

YEARS MFRD	2016-2020
SERIES	ZTRAK SERIES
ENGINE	B&S CYCLONIC
CYLINDERS	2
CID	44.2
ENGINE HP	25
COOLING	AIR
FUEL	G
SPEEDS	VARIABLE
TRANSMISSION	HYDRO
STEERING	ZERO
STANDARD DECK	54"
WEIGHT	710 LBS.
MSRP	$5,399

SERIAL NUMBERS

YEAR	BEGINNING NO.
2016	01001
2017	50001

RETAIL PRICING

YEAR	HIGH	LOW
2016	$4,013	$3,009
2017	$4,404	$3,301
2018	$4,695	$3,620
2019	$5,005	$3,859
2020	$5,307	$4,071

Z540M

YEARS MFRD	2016-2020
SERIES	ZTRAK SERIES
ENGINE	KAWASAKI FS730V
CID	44.3
ENGINE HP	24
COOLING	AIR
FUEL	G
SPEEDS	VARIABLE
TRANSMISSION	HYDRO
STEERING	ZERO
STANDARD DECK	48"
WEIGHT	638 LBS.
MSRP	$4,799

OPTIONS

54" DECK $300
62" DECK $600

SERIAL NUMBERS

YEAR	BEGINNING NO.
2016	01001
2017	50001

RETAIL PRICING

YEAR	HIGH	LOW
2016	$3,919	$2,939
2017	$4,032	$3,131
2018	$4,260	$3,369
2019	$4,464	$3,512
2020	$4,689	$3,674

Z540R

YEARS MFRD 2016-2020
SERIES . . . . ZTRAK SERIES
ENGINE . . . . . . KAWASAKI FS730V
CYLINDERS 2
CID 44.3
ENGINE HP 24
COOLING . . . . AIR
FUEL . . . . G
SPEEDS . . . . VARIABLE
TRANSMISSION . . . . HYDRO
STEERING . . . . ZERO
STANDARD DECK . . . . 48"
WEIGHT . . . . 697 LBS.
MSRP $5,499

OPTIONS

54" DECK $300
60" DECK $600

SERIAL NUMBERS

YEAR	BEGINNING NO.
2016	01001
2017	50001

RETAIL PRICING

YEAR	HIGH	LOW
2016	$4,525	$3,395
2017	$4,743	$3,556
2018	$4,875	$3,873
2019	$5,041	$4,026
2020	$5,408	$4,180

Z625

YEARS MFRD 2015-2015
SERIES . . . . EZTRAK SERIES
ENGINE . . . . KAWASAKI
CYLINDERS 2
CID 724CC
ENGINE HP 25
COOLING . . . . AIR
FUEL . . . . G
STEERING . . . . ZERO
STANDARD DECK . . . . 54"
WEIGHT . . . . 738 LBS.
MSRP $5,799

Z645

YEARS MFRD 2012-2015
SERIES . . . . EZTRAK SERIES
CYLINDERS 2
CID 44.2
ENGINE HP 27
COOLING . . . . AIR
FUEL . . . . G
SPEEDS . . . . VARIABLE
TRANSMISSION . . . . HYDRO
STEERING . . . . ZERO
BLADE CLUTCH . . . . ELECTRIC
STANDARD DECK . . . . 48"
WEIGHT . . . . 750 LBS.
MSRP $6,099

OPTIONS

15 GAL
6.5 BU BAG
MULCH KIT

SERIAL NUMBERS

YEAR	BEGINNING NO.
2012	120001
2013	130001
2014	150001
2015	170001

RETAIL PRICING

YEAR	HIGH	LOW
2012	$4,052	$3,039
2013	$4,355	$3,267
2014	$4,797	$3,598
2015	$5,436	$4,077

Z655

YEARS MFRD 2011-2015
SERIES . . . . EZTRAK SERIES
ENGINE . . . . KAWASAKI
CYLINDERS 2
CID 44.2
ENGINE HP 24
COOLING . . . . AIR
FUEL . . . . G
SPEEDS . . . . VARIABLE
TRANSMISSION . . . . HYDRO
STEERING . . . . ZERO
BLADE CLUTCH . . . . ELECTRIC
STANDARD DECK . . . . 54"
WEIGHT . . . . 750 LBS.
MSRP $6,299

OPTIONS

15 GAL
6.5 BU BAG
MULCH KIT

SERIAL NUMBERS

YEAR	BEGINNING NO.
2011	100001
2012	120001
2013	130001
2014	150001
2015	170001

RETAIL PRICING

YEAR	HIGH	LOW
2012	$4,589	$3,442
2013	$4,879	$3,659
2014	$4,984	$3,738
2015	$6,017	$4,513

AVG. AUCTION PRICING

LOW	HIGH	AVG
$2,040	$4,590	$3,050

Z665

YEARS MFRD 2012-2015
ENGINE . . . . JD
ENGINE HP 27
COOLING . . . . AIR
FUEL . . . . G
SPEEDS . . . . VARIABLE
TRANSMISSION . . . . HYDRO
STEERING . . . . ZERO
BLADE CLUTCH . . . . ELECTRIC
STANDARD DECK . . . . 60"
MSRP $6,499

OPTIONS

15 GAL
MULCH KIT

SERIAL NUMBERS

YEAR	BEGINNING NO.
2012	120001
2013	130001
2014	150001
2015	170001

RETAIL PRICING

YEAR	HIGH	LOW
2012	$4,562	$3,422
2013	$4,863	$3,648
2014	$5,053	$3,790
2015	$5,963	$4,472

Z710A

YEARS MFRD 2011-2012
ENGINE . . . . KOHLER
ENGINE HP 23
COOLING . . . . AIR
FUEL . . . . G
SPEEDS . . . . VARIABLE
TRANSMISSION . . . . HYDRO
STEERING . . . . ZERO
STANDARD DECK . . . . 48"
MSRP $7,780

OPTIONS

54" DECK
8BU BAG

RETAIL PRICING

YEAR	HIGH	LOW
2011	$5,486	$4,114
2012	$6,001	$4,500

Z720A

YEARS MFRD 2011-2013
ENGINE . . . . KOHLER
ENGINE HP 25
COOLING . . . . AIR
FUEL . . . . G
SPEEDS . . . . VARIABLE
TRANSMISSION . . . . HYDRO
STEERING . . . . ZERO
BLADE CLUTCH . . . . ELECTRIC
STANDARD DECK . . . . 60"
MSRP $8,655

OPTIONS

8 BU BAG

RETAIL PRICING

YEAR	HIGH	LOW
2011	$5,891	$4,418
2012	$6,471	$4,853
2013	$7,024	$5,268

Z720E

YEARS MFRD 2019-2020
SERIES . . . . Z700 SERIES
ENGINE . . . . . . KAWASAKI FR691V
CYLINDERS 2
CID 44.3
ENGINE HP 23
COOLING . . . . AIR
FUEL . . . . G
SPEEDS . . . . VARIABLE
TRANSMISSION . . . . . DUAL HYDRO
STEERING . . . . ZERO
STANDARD DECK . . . . 48"
WEIGHT . . . . 950 LBS.
MSRP $6,449

OPTIONS

54" DECK $300
60" DECK $600

Z730M

YEARS MFRD 2019-2020
SERIES . . . . Z700 SERIES
ENGINE . . . . . . KAWASAKI FS730V
CYLINDERS 2
CID 44.3
ENGINE HP 24
COOLING . . . . AIR
FUEL . . . . G
SPEEDS . . . . VARIABLE
TRANSMISSION . . . . . DUAL HYDRO
STEERING . . . . ZERO
STANDARD DECK . . . . 54"
WEIGHT . . . . 965 LBS.
MSRP $7,649

OPTIONS

60" DECK $300

Z735E

YEARS MFRD 2019-2020
SERIES . . . . Z700 SERIES
ENGINE . . . . M49-810CC SSC
CYLINDERS 2
CID 49.4
ENGINE HP 25
COOLING . . . . AIR
FUEL . . . . G
SPEEDS . . . . VARIABLE
TRANSMISSION . . . . . DUAL HYDRO
STEERING . . . . ZERO
STANDARD DECK . . . . 60"
WEIGHT . . . . 990 LBS.
MSRP $7,149

Z735M

YEARS MFRD 2019-2020
SERIES . . . . Z700 SERIES
ENGINE . . . . M49-810CC SSC
CYLINDERS 2
CID 49.4
ENGINE HP 25
COOLING . . . . AIR
FUEL . . . . G
SPEEDS . . . . VARIABLE
TRANSMISSION . . . . . DUAL HYDRO
STEERING . . . . ZERO

STANDARD DECK . . . . 48"
WEIGHT . . . . 950 LBS.
MSRP. $7,349

OPTIONS

54" DECK. $300
60" DECK. $600

Z740R

YEARS MFRD 2019-2020
SERIES. . . . . Z700 SERIES
ENGINE . . . . KAWASAKI FX730V
CYLINDERS. 2
CID 44.2
ENGINE HP 23.5
COOLING . . . . AIR
FUEL . . . . G
SPEEDS . . . . VARIABLE
TRANSMISSION . . . . . DUAL HYDRO
STEERING. . . . . ZERO
STANDARD DECK . . . . 48"
WEIGHT . . . . 995 LBS.
MSRP. $8,549

OPTIONS

54" DECK. $300
60" DECK. $600
TWEELS. $1,250

Z810A

YEARS MFRD 2008-2009
ENGINE . . . . KAWASAKI
CYLINDERS. 2
ENGINE HP 22
COOLING . . . . AIR
FUEL . . . . G
SPEEDS . . . . VARIABLE
TRANSMISSION . . . . HYDRO
STEERING. . . . . ZERO
STANDARD DECK . . . . 48"
MSRP. $8,209

OPTIONS

2 BAG
3 BAG
54" DECK

RETAIL PRICING

YEAR	HIGH	LOW
2008	$4,660	$3,495
2009	$5,106	$3,830

Z820A

YEARS MFRD 2008-2009
ENGINE . . . . KAWASAKI
CYLINDERS. 2
ENGINE HP 25
COOLING . . . . AIR
FUEL . . . . G
SPEEDS . . . . VARIABLE
TRANSMISSION . . . . HYDRO
STEERING. . . . . ZERO
STANDARD DECK . . . . 48"
MSRP. $10,109

OPTIONS

2 BAG
3 BAG
54" DECK
60" DECK

RETAIL PRICING

YEAR	HIGH	LOW
2008	$5,654	$4,240
2009	$6,282	$4,712

AVG. AUCTION PRICING

LOW	HIGH	AVG
$3,009	$5,556	$4,167

Z830A

YEARS MFRD 2008-2009
ENGINE . . . . KAWASAKI
CYLINDERS. 2
ENGINE HP 27
COOLING . . . . AIR
FUEL . . . . G
SPEEDS . . . . VARIABLE
TRANSMISSION . . . . HYDRO
STEERING. . . . . ZERO
STANDARD DECK . . . . 54"
MSRP. $11,739

OPTIONS

2 BAG
3 BAG
60" DECK
72" DECK

RETAIL PRICING

YEAR	HIGH	LOW
2008	$6,735	$5,051
2009	$7,446	$5,585

AVG. AUCTION PRICING

LOW	HIGH	AVG
$2,805	$4,845	$3,536

Z840A

YEARS MFRD 2008-2009
ENGINE . . . . KAWASAKI
CYLINDERS. 2
ENGINE HP 26
COOLING . . . . AIR
FUEL . . . . G
SPEEDS . . . . VARIABLE
TRANSMISSION . . . . . DUAL HYDRO
STEERING. . . . . ZERO
STANDARD DECK . . . . 54"
MSRP. $12,029

OPTIONS

2 BAG
3 BAG
60" DECK

RETAIL PRICING

YEAR	HIGH	LOW
2008	$6,696	$5,022
2009	$7,503	$5,627

Z850A

YEARS MFRD 2008-2009
ENGINE . . . . KAWASAKI
CYLINDERS. 2
ENGINE HP 31
COOLING . . . . AIR
FUEL . . . . G
SPEEDS . . . . VARIABLE
TRANSMISSION . . . . . DUAL HYDRO
STEERING. . . . . ZERO
STANDARD DECK . . . . 60"
MSRP. $12,339

OPTIONS

2 BAG
3 BAG
72" DECK

RETAIL PRICING

YEAR	HIGH	LOW
2008	$6,967	$5,225
2009	$7,664	$5,748

Z860A

YEARS MFRD 2009-2009
ENGINE . . . . KAWASAKI
CYLINDERS. 2
ENGINE HP 34
COOLING . . . . AIR
FUEL . . . . G
SPEEDS . . . . VARIABLE
TRANSMISSION . . . . HYDRO
STEERING. . . . . ZERO
STANDARD DECK . . . . 60"
MSRP. $15,339

OPTIONS

72" DECK

RETAIL PRICING

YEAR	HIGH	LOW
2009	$9,519	$7,139

Z910A

YEARS MFRD 2010-2012
ENGINE . . . . KAWASAKI
ENGINE HP 22
COOLING . . . . AIR
FUEL . . . . G
SPEEDS . . . . VARIABLE
TRANSMISSION . . . . HYDRO
STEERING. . . . . ZERO
STANDARD DECK . . . . 48"
MSRP. $9,291

OPTIONS

54" DECK

RETAIL PRICING

YEAR	HIGH	LOW
2010	$5,848	$4,386
2011	$6,348	$4,761
2012	$7,076	$5,307

AVG. AUCTION PRICING

LOW	HIGH	AVG
$1,632	$4,488	$3,545

Z915B

YEARS MFRD 2013-2018
ENGINE . . . . KAWASAKI
ENGINE HP 25
COOLING . . . . AIR
FUEL . . . . G
SPEEDS . . . . VARIABLE
TRANSMISSION . . . . . DUAL HYDRO
STEERING. . . . . ZERO
BLADE CLUTCH . . . . ELECTRIC
STANDARD DECK . . . . 48"
MSRP. $8,459

OPTIONS

54" DECK
60" DECK
DLX SEAT

RETAIL PRICING

YEAR	HIGH	LOW
2013	$4,484	$3,363
2014	$4,983	$3,737
2015	$5,511	$4,133
2016	$6,030	$4,523
2017	$6,455	$4,841
2018	$7,039	$5,279

AVG. AUCTION PRICING

LOW	HIGH	AVG
$2,900	$5,300	$3,586

Z915E

YEARS MFRD 2017-2020
SERIES. . . . . ZTRAK E SERIES
ENGINE . . . . KOHLER CV742
CYLINDERS. 2
CID 747CC
ENGINE HP 25
COOLING . . . . AIR
FUEL . . . . G
SPEEDS . . . . VARIABLE
TRANSMISSION . . . . . DUAL HYDRO
STEERING. . . . . ZERO
STANDARD DECK . . . . 48"
WEIGHT . . . . 1,178 LBS.
MSRP. $9,099

OPTIONS

54" DECK. $270
60" DECK. $540
DLX SEAT. $195
TWEEL. $949

RETAIL PRICING

YEAR	HIGH	LOW
2017	$6,309	$4,731
2018	$6,986	$5,458
2019	$7,751	$6,099
2020	$8,574	$6,627

Z920A

YEARS MFRD 2010-2012
ENGINE . . . . KAWASAKI
ENGINE HP 26
COOLING . . . . AIR
FUEL . . . . G
SPEEDS . . . . VARIABLE
TRANSMISSION . . . . HYDRO
STEERING. . . . . ZERO
STANDARD DECK . . . . 48"
MSRP. $11,003

OPTIONS

54" DECK
60" DECK

RETAIL PRICING

YEAR	HIGH	LOW
2010	$6,640	$4,980
2011	$7,094	$5,321
2012	$7,742	$5,806

AVG. AUCTION PRICING

LOW	HIGH	AVG
$1,500	$4,250	$2,583

Z920M

YEARS MFRD 2013-2020
SERIES . . . . ZTRAK M SERIES
ENGINE . . . . KAWASAKI FX730V
CYLINDERS 2
CID 726CC
ENGINE HP 23.5
COOLING . . . . AIR
FUEL . . . . G
SPEEDS . . . . VARIABLE
TRANSMISSION . . . . . DUAL HYDRO
STEERING . . . . ZERO
BLADE CLUTCH . . . . ELECTRIC
STANDARD DECK . . . . 48"
WEIGHT . . . . 1,283 LBS.
MSRP $10,449

OPTIONS

48" MOD $870
54" DECK $270
60" DECK $540
DLX SEAT $195
TWEEL $949

RETAIL PRICING

YEAR	HIGH	LOW
2013	$5,521	$4,141
2014	$5,929	$4,447
2015	$6,547	$4,910
2016	$7,182	$5,386
2017	$7,733	$5,799
2018	$8,579	$6,435
2019	$9,524	$7,143
2020	$10,140	$7,922

AVG. AUCTION PRICING

LOW	HIGH	AVG
$2,500	$4,500	$3,750

Z920R

YEARS MFRD 2013-2015
ENGINE . . . . KAWASAKI
ENGINE HP 23.5
COOLING . . . . AIR
FUEL . . . . G
SPEEDS . . . . VARIABLE
TRANSMISSION . . . . HYDRO
STEERING . . . . ZERO
BLADE CLUTCH . . . . ELECTRIC
STANDARD DECK . . . . 48"
MSRP $11,439

OPTIONS

3 BAG
54" DECK
DLX SEAT
SUSPENSION SEAT

RETAIL PRICING

YEAR	HIGH	LOW
2013	$8,206	$6,154
2014	$9,033	$6,775
2015	$10,108	$7,581

Z925A

YEARS MFRD 2010-2013
ENGINE . . . . KAWASAKI
ENGINE HP 27
COOLING . . . . AIR
FUEL . . . . G
SPEEDS . . . . VARIABLE
TRANSMISSION . . . . HYDRO
STEERING . . . . ZERO
BLADE CLUTCH . . . . ELECTRIC
STANDARD DECK . . . . 54"
MSRP $11,987

OPTIONS

3 BAG
60" PRO
STRIPER
SUS SEAT

RETAIL PRICING

YEAR	HIGH	LOW
2010	$7,297	$5,473
2011	$7,620	$5,715
2012	$8,171	$6,128
2013	$9,011	$6,758

AVG. AUCTION PRICING

LOW	HIGH	AVG
$3,060	$4,386	$3,762

Z925M EFI

YEARS MFRD 2013-2016
ENGINE . . . . KAWASAKI
ENGINE HP 24.6
COOLING . . . . AIR
FUEL . . . . G
SPEEDS . . . . VARIABLE
TRANSMISSION . . . . . DUAL HYDRO
STEERING . . . . ZERO
BLADE CLUTCH . . . . ELECTRIC
STANDARD DECK . . . . 54"
MSRP $10,529

OPTIONS

3 BAG
60" DECK
SUS SEAT

RETAIL PRICING

YEAR	HIGH	LOW
2013	$7,508	$5,631
2014	$8,262	$6,197
2015	$9,156	$6,867
2016	$10,968	$8,226

Z925M EFI FLEX

YEARS MFRD 2017-2019
SERIES . . . . ZTRAK SERIES
ENGINE . . . . KOHLER FCV740
CYLINDERS 2
CID 45.6
ENGINE HP 25
COOLING . . . . AIR
FUEL . . . . G
SPEEDS . . . . VARIABLE
TRANSMISSION . . . . HYDRO
STEERING . . . . ZERO
STANDARD DECK . . . . 54"
WEIGHT . . . . 1,198 LBS.
MSRP $11,299

OPTIONS

54" MOD
60" DECK
DLX SEAT

Z925M FLEX

YEARS MFRD 2014-2018
SERIES . . . . ZTRAK M SERIES
ENGINE . . . . KAWASAKI
ENGINE HP 25
COOLING . . . . AIR
FUEL . . . . G
SPEEDS . . . . VARIABLE
TRANSMISSION . . . . . DUAL HYDRO
STEERING . . . . ZERO
STANDARD DECK . . . . 54"
MSRP $10,999

OPTIONS

54" MOD
60" DECK
DLX SEAT

RETAIL PRICING

YEAR	HIGH	LOW
2014	$6,118	$4,588
2015	$6,801	$5,101
2016	$7,511	$5,633
2017	$8,323	$6,242
2018	$9,224	$6,918

Z930A

YEARS MFRD 2010-2013
ENGINE . . . . KAWASAKI
ENGINE HP 29
COOLING . . . . AIR
FUEL . . . . G
SPEEDS . . . . VARIABLE
TRANSMISSION . . . . HYDRO
STEERING . . . . ZERO
STANDARD DECK . . . . 60"
MSRP $13,901

OPTIONS

3 BAG
STRIPER
SUS SEAT

RETAIL PRICING

YEAR	HIGH	LOW
2010	$7,782	$5,836
2011	$8,596	$6,447
2012	$9,338	$7,004
2013	$10,450	$7,837

AVG. AUCTION PRICING

LOW	HIGH	AVG
$2,856	$5,610	$4,325

Z930M

YEARS MFRD 2013-2020
SERIES . . . . ZTRAK M SERIES
ENGINE . . . . KAWASAKI
CYLINDERS 2
CID 852CC
ENGINE HP 25.5
COOLING . . . . AIR
FUEL . . . . G
SPEEDS . . . . VARIABLE
TRANSMISSION . . . . . DUAL HYDRO
STEERING . . . . ZERO
BLADE CLUTCH . . . . ELECTRIC
STANDARD DECK . . . . 60"
WEIGHT . . . . 1,365 LBS.
MSRP $11,399

OPTIONS

54" DECK . . . . $-270
54" MOD $600
60" MOD $870
DLX SEAT $195
TWEEL $949

RETAIL PRICING

YEAR	HIGH	LOW
2013	$6,078	$4,559
2014	$6,711	$5,033
2015	$7,483	$5,612
2016	$8,002	$6,001
2017	$8,492	$6,369
2018	$9,277	$6,957
2019	$10,162	$7,621
2020	$11,054	$8,676

AVG. AUCTION PRICING

LOW	HIGH	AVG
$1,300	$5,500	$3,021

Z930R

YEARS MFRD 2013-2020
SERIES . . . . ZTRAK R SERIES
ENGINE . . . . KAWASAKI
CYLINDERS 2
CID 852CC
ENGINE HP 25.5
COOLING . . . . AIR
FUEL . . . . G
SPEEDS . . . . VARIABLE
TRANSMISSION . . . . . DUAL HYDRO
STEERING . . . . ZERO
BLADE CLUTCH . . . . ELECTRIC
STANDARD DECK . . . . 54"
MSRP $13,699

OPTIONS

54" MOD $870
60" DECK $270
DLX SEAT . . . . $-300
TWEEL $949

RETAIL PRICING

YEAR	HIGH	LOW
2013	$6,435	$4,826
2014	$7,107	$5,329
2015	$8,070	$6,052
2016	$8,615	$6,460
2017	$9,351	$7,013
2018	$10,347	$8,006
2019	$11,443	$9,074
2020	$12,456	$10,114

Z945M EFI

YEARS MFRD 2018-2020
SERIES . . . . ZTRAK M SERIES
ENGINE . . . . KOHLER ECV850
CYLINDERS 2
CID 50.3
ENGINE HP 27
COOLING . . . . AIR
FUEL . . . . G
SPEEDS . . . . VARIABLE
TRANSMISSION . . . . . DUAL HYDRO
STEERING . . . . ZERO
STANDARD DECK . . . . 60"
WEIGHT . . . . 1,275 LBS.
MSRP $12,199

JOHN DEERE

OPTIONS

60" MOD . . . $870
SUS SEAT . . . $495
TWEEL . . . $949

Z950A

YEARS MFRD . . . 2010-2012
ENGINE . . . KAWASAKI
ENGINE HP . . . 29
COOLING . . . AIR
FUEL . . . G
SPEEDS . . . VARIABLE
TRANSMISSION . . . HYDRO
STEERING . . . ZERO
STANDARD DECK . . . 60"
MSRP . . . $14,384

OPTIONS

3 BAG
72" DECK
SUS SEAT

RETAIL PRICING

YEAR	HIGH	LOW
2010	$8,313	$6,235
2011	$8,986	$6,740
2012	$10,171	$7,629

AVG. AUCTION PRICING

LOW	HIGH	AVG
$2,856	$6,885	$4,807

Z950M

YEARS MFRD . . . 2014-2020
SERIES . . . ZTRAK M SERIES
ENGINE . . . KAWASAKI
CYLINDERS . . . 2
CID . . . 747CC
ENGINE HP . . . 27
COOLING . . . AIR
FUEL . . . G
SPEEDS . . . VARIABLE
TRANSMISSION . . . DUAL HYDRO
STEERING . . . ZERO
STANDARD DECK . . . 60"
WEIGHT . . . 1,340 LBS.
MSRP . . . $11,829

OPTIONS

60" MOD . . . $870
72" DECK . . . $540
SUS SEAT . . . $495
TWEEL . . . $949

RETAIL PRICING

YEAR	HIGH	LOW
2014	$6,888	$5,166
2015	$7,749	$5,812
2016	$8,646	$6,484
2017	$9,250	$6,938
2018	$10,238	$7,678
2019	$11,174	$8,379
2020	$11,779	$8,480

AVG. AUCTION PRICING

LOW	HIGH	AVG
$2,040	$7,395	$4,675

Z950R

YEARS MFRD . . . 2013-2020
SERIES . . . ZTRAK R SERIES
ENGINE . . . KAWASAKI
CYLINDERS . . . 2
CID . . . 852CC
ENGINE HP . . . 27
COOLING . . . AIR
FUEL . . . G
SPEEDS . . . VARIABLE
TRANSMISSION . . . DUAL HYDRO
STEERING . . . ZERO
BLADE CLUTCH . . . ELECTRIC
STANDARD DECK . . . 60"
WEIGHT . . . 1,340 LBS.
MSRP . . . $14,399

OPTIONS

60" MOD . . . $870
72" DECK . . . $540
DLX SEAT . . . $-300
TWEEL . . . $949

SERIAL NUMBERS

YEAR	BEGINNING NO.
2016	30001

RETAIL PRICING

YEAR	HIGH	LOW
2013	$7,166	$5,375
2014	$7,807	$5,855
2015	$8,509	$6,382
2016	$9,557	$7,167
2017	$10,293	$7,821
2018	$11,266	$8,866
2019	$12,438	$9,869
2020	$13,431	$10,785

AVG. AUCTION PRICING

LOW	HIGH	AVG
$2,000	$6,000	$4,320

Z955M EFI

YEARS MFRD . . . 2018-2020
SERIES . . . ZTRAK SERIES
ENGINE . . . KOHLER ECV860J
CYLINDERS . . . 2
CID . . . 50.3
ENGINE HP . . . 29
COOLING . . . AIR
FUEL . . . G
TRANSMISSION . . . DUAL HYDRO
STEERING . . . ZERO
STANDARD DECK . . . 60"
WEIGHT . . . 1,275 LBS.
MSRP . . . $12,619

OPTIONS

60" MOD . . . $870
72" DECK . . . $540
DLX SEAT . . . $195
SUS SEAT . . . $495
TWEEL . . . $949

Z955R EFI

YEARS MFRD . . . 2020-2020
SERIES . . . ZTRAK SERIES
ENGINE . . . KOHLER ECV860J
CYLINDERS . . . 2
CID . . . 824CC
ENGINE HP . . . 29
COOLING . . . AIR
FUEL . . . G
SPEEDS . . . VARIABLE
TRANSMISSION . . . HYDRO
STEERING . . . ZERO
ROPS/CAB . . . ROPS
STANDARD DECK . . . 60"
WEIGHT . . . 1,275 LBS.
MSRP . . . $15,089

OPTIONS

TWEEL . . . $949

Z960A

YEARS MFRD . . . 2011-2013
ENGINE . . . KAWASAKI
ENGINE HP . . . 34
COOLING . . . AIR
FUEL . . . G
SPEEDS . . . VARIABLE
TRANSMISSION . . . HYDRO
STEERING . . . ZERO
STANDARD DECK . . . 72"
MSRP . . . $14,490

OPTIONS

8 BU BAG
SUS SEAT

RETAIL PRICING

YEAR	HIGH	LOW
2011	$9,235	$6,926
2012	$9,801	$7,351
2013	$10,894	$8,170

AVG. AUCTION PRICING

LOW	HIGH	AVG
$3,715	$6,129	$4,520

Z960M

YEARS MFRD . . . 2016-2020
SERIES . . . ZTRAK M SERIES
ENGINE . . . KAWASAKI FX921V
CYLINDERS . . . 2
CID . . . 999CC
ENGINE HP . . . 31
COOLING . . . AIR
FUEL . . . G
SPEEDS . . . VARIABLE
TRANSMISSION . . . DUAL HYDRO
STEERING . . . ZERO
STANDARD DECK . . . 60"
WEIGHT . . . 1,340 LBS.
MSRP . . . $12,569

OPTIONS

60" MOD . . . $870
72" DECK . . . $540
DLX SEAT . . . $195
SUS SEAT . . . $495
TWEEL . . . $949

RETAIL PRICING

YEAR	HIGH	LOW
2016	$12,757	$6,440
2017	$9,351	$7,013
2018	$10,350	$8,193
2019	$11,329	$9,086
2020	$12,234	$9,823

Z960R

YEARS MFRD . . . 2013-2015
ENGINE . . . KAWASAKI
ENGINE HP . . . 31
COOLING . . . AIR
FUEL . . . G
SPEEDS . . . VARIABLE
TRANSMISSION . . . DUAL HYDRO
STEERING . . . ZERO
BLADE CLUTCH . . . ELECTRIC
STANDARD DECK . . . 60"
MSRP . . . $13,499

OPTIONS

72" DECK
DIX SEAT
SUSPENSION SEAT

RETAIL PRICING

YEAR	HIGH	LOW
2013	$10,137	$7,603
2014	$10,869	$8,152
2015	$12,412	$9,309

AVG. AUCTION PRICING

LOW	HIGH	AVG
$3,060	$8,160	$5,284

Z970A

YEARS MFRD . . . 2011-2013
ENGINE . . . KAWASAKI
ENGINE HP . . . 37
COOLING . . . AIR
FUEL . . . G
SPEEDS . . . VARIABLE
TRANSMISSION . . . HYDRO
STEERING . . . ZERO
BLADE CLUTCH . . . ELECTRIC
STANDARD DECK . . . 72"
MSRP . . . $15,882

OPTIONS

8 BU BAG
STRIPER
SUS SEAT

RETAIL PRICING

YEAR	HIGH	LOW
2011	$10,411	$7,808
2012	$11,628	$8,721
2013	$12,893	$9,670

Z970R

YEARS MFRD . . . 2013-2020
SERIES . . . ZTRAK R SERIES
ENGINE . . . KAWASAKI FX1000V
CYLINDERS . . . 2
CID . . . 999CC
ENGINE HP . . . 35
COOLING . . . AIR
FUEL . . . G
SPEEDS . . . VARIABLE
TRANSMISSION . . . DUAL HYDRO
STEERING . . . ZERO
BLADE CLUTCH . . . ELECTRIC
STANDARD DECK . . . 72"
WEIGHT . . . 1,340 LBS.
MSRP . . . $16,329

OPTIONS

60" DECK . . . $-540
60" MOD . . . $300
DLX SEAT . . . $-300
TWEEL . . . $949

RETAIL PRICING

YEAR	HIGH	LOW
2013	$7,585	$5,689
2014	$8,384	$6,288
2015	$9,287	$6,964
2016	$10,455	$7,841
2017	$11,286	$8,668
2018	$12,538	$9,923
2019	$13,922	$10,919
2020	$15,383	$11,891

Z994R

YEARS MFRD . . . 2019-2020
SERIES . . . ZTRAK DIESEL SERIES
ENGINE . . . 3TNV80F
CID . . . 77.3
ENGINE HP . . . 24.7
COOLING . . . LIQUID
FUEL . . . D
SPEEDS . . . VARIABLE
TRANSMISSION . . . DUAL HYDRO
STEERING . . . ZERO
STANDARD DECK . . . 54"
WEIGHT . . . 1,720 LBS.
MSRP . . . $18,129

OPTIONS

60" DECK SD . . . $270
60" MOD . . . $1,140
72" DECK . . . $810
TWEEL . . . $979

Z997R

YEARS MFRD . . . 2015-2020
SERIES . . . ZTRAK DIESEL SERIES
ENGINE . . . YANMAR
CYLINDERS . . . 3
CID . . . 100.2
ENGINE HP . . . 37.4
COOLING . . . LIQUID
FUEL . . . D
SPEEDS . . . VARIABLE
TRANSMISSION . . . DUAL HYDRO
STEERING . . . ZERO
STANDARD DECK . . . 60"
WEIGHT . . . 1,774 LBS.
MSRP . . . $25,349

OPTIONS

60" MOD . . . $870
60" RD DECK . . . $630
72" DECK . . . $540
TWEEL . . . $979

RETAIL PRICING

YEAR	HIGH	LOW
2015	$15,222	$11,416
2016	$16,642	$12,482
2017	$18,403	$13,802
2018	$20,369	$15,524
2019	$22,517	$17,720
2020	$24,686	$19,673

AVG. AUCTION PRICING

LOW	HIGH	AVG
$5,000	$6,500	$5,833

102

YEARS MFRD . . . 2006-2006
SERIES . . . 100 SERIES
ENGINE . . . B&S
CYLINDERS . . . 1
ENGINE HP . . . 17
COOLING . . . AIR
FUEL . . . G
SPEEDS . . . 5/1
TRANSMISSION . . . GEAR
STEERING . . . STANDARD
STANDARD DECK . . . 42"
MSRP . . . $1,399

SERIAL NUMBERS

YEAR	BEGINNING NO.
2006	10001

RETAIL PRICING

YEAR	HIGH	LOW
2006	$489	$366

110 TLB

YEARS MFRD . . . 2010-2011
ENGINE . . . YANMAR TNV88
CYLINDERS . . . 4
CID . . . 133.6
PTO HP . . . 33
ENGINE HP . . . 43
COOLING . . . LIQUID
FUEL . . . D
SPEEDS . . . VARIABLE
TRANSMISSION . . . HYDRO
STEERING . . . STANDARD
WEIGHT . . . 7,280 LBS.
MSRP . . . $46,821

RETAIL PRICING

YEAR	HIGH	LOW
2010	$44,431	$33,323
2011	$45,785	$34,339

115

YEARS MFRD . . . 2006-2006
SERIES . . . 100 SERIES
ENGINE . . . B&S
CYLINDERS . . . 1
ENGINE HP . . . 19
COOLING . . . AIR
FUEL . . . G
SPEEDS . . . VARIABLE
TRANSMISSION . . . HYDRO
STEERING . . . STANDARD
STANDARD DECK . . . 42"
MSRP . . . $1,599

SERIAL NUMBERS

YEAR	BEGINNING NO.
2006	10001

RETAIL PRICING

YEAR	HIGH	LOW
2006	$567	$425

125

YEARS MFRD . . . 2006-2006
SERIES . . . 100 SERIES
ENGINE . . . B&S
CYLINDERS . . . 2
ENGINE HP . . . 20
COOLING . . . AIR
FUEL . . . G
SPEEDS . . . VARIABLE
TRANSMISSION . . . HYDRO
STEERING . . . STANDARD
STANDARD DECK . . . 42"
MSRP . . . $1,799

SERIAL NUMBERS

YEAR	BEGINNING NO.
2006	10001

RETAIL PRICING

YEAR	HIGH	LOW
2006	$642	$481

135

YEARS MFRD . . . 2006-2006
SERIES . . . 100 SERIES
ENGINE . . . B&S
CYLINDERS . . . 2
ENGINE HP . . . 22
COOLING . . . AIR
FUEL . . . G
SPEEDS . . . VARIABLE
TRANSMISSION . . . HYDRO
STEERING . . . STANDARD
STANDARD DECK . . . 42"
MSRP . . . $1,999

SERIAL NUMBERS

YEAR	BEGINNING NO.
2006	10001

RETAIL PRICING

YEAR	HIGH	LOW
2006	$712	$534

145

YEARS MFRD . . . 2006-2006
SERIES . . . 100 SERIES
ENGINE . . . B&S
CYLINDERS . . . 2
ENGINE HP . . . 22
COOLING . . . AIR
FUEL . . . G
SPEEDS . . . VARIABLE
TRANSMISSION . . . HYDRO
STEERING . . . STANDARD
STANDARD DECK . . . 48"
MSRP . . . $2,299

SERIAL NUMBERS

YEAR	BEGINNING NO.
2006	10001

RETAIL PRICING

YEAR	HIGH	LOW
2006	$812	$609

155C

YEARS MFRD . . . 2006-2006
SERIES . . . 100 SERIES
ENGINE . . . B&S
CYLINDERS . . . 2
ENGINE HP . . . 25
COOLING . . . AIR
FUEL . . . G
SPEEDS . . . VARIABLE
TRANSMISSION . . . HYDRO
STEERING . . . STANDARD
STANDARD DECK . . . 48"
MSRP . . . $2,599

SERIAL NUMBERS

YEAR	BEGINNING NO.
2006	10001

RETAIL PRICING

YEAR	HIGH	LOW
2006	$906	$679

170

YEARS MFRD . . . 1989-1990
ENGINE . . . KAWASAKI
ENGINE HP . . . 14
COOLING . . . AIR
FUEL . . . G
TRANSMISSION . . . GEAR
STEERING . . . STANDARD
STANDARD DECK . . . 38"
WEIGHT . . . 575 LBS.
MSRP . . . $2,829

OPTIONS

BAGGER

SERIAL NUMBERS

YEAR	BEGINNING NO.
1989	595001
1990	010001

RETAIL PRICING

YEAR	HIGH	LOW
1989	$409	$307
1990	$428	$321

175

YEARS MFRD . . . 1987-1990
ENGINE . . . KAWASAKI
ENGINE HP . . . 17
COOLING . . . AIR
FUEL . . . G
SPEEDS . . . VARIABLE
TRANSMISSION . . . HYDRO
STEERING . . . STANDARD
STANDARD DECK . . . 38"
WEIGHT . . . 605 LBS.
MSRP . . . $3,419

OPTIONS

BAGGER

SERIAL NUMBERS

YEAR	BEGINNING NO.
1987	420001
1988	475001
1989	595001
1990	010001

RETAIL PRICING

YEAR	HIGH	LOW
1987	$194	$145
1988	$212	$159
1989	$235	$176
1990	$256	$192

180

YEARS MFRD . . . 1986-1990
SERIES . . . LT SERIES
ENGINE . . . KAWASAKI

ENGINE HP . . . 17
COOLING . . . AIR
FUEL . . . G
TRANSMISSION . . . GEAR
STEERING . . . STANDARD
STANDARD DECK . . . 38"
WEIGHT . . . 580 LBS.
MSRP . . . $3,399

OPTIONS

46" DECK
48" DECK
BAGGER
HYDRO

SERIAL NUMBERS

YEAR	BEGINNING NO.
1986	378001-48H
1986	360001-38G
1986	378001-38H
1986	366001-46G
1987	440001-38H
1987	450001-48H
1987	430001-46G
1987	420001-38G
1988	450001-38G
1988	505001-48H
1988	475001-46G
1988	505001-38H
1989	605001-38H
1989	605001-46G
1989	595001-38G
1989	605110-48H
1990	010001-38G
1990	020001-46G
1990	020001-48H
1990	020001-38H
1989	595001-38
1989	605001-46
1990	010001-38
1990	020001-46

RETAIL PRICING

YEAR	HIGH	LOW
1986	$174	$131
1987	$192	$144
1988	$212	$159
1989	$233	$174
1990	$256	$192

185

YEARS MFRD . . . 1986-1990
SERIES . . . LT SERIES
ENGINE . . . KAWASAKI
ENGINE HP . . . 17
COOLING . . . AIR
FUEL . . . G
SPEEDS . . . VARIABLE
TRANSMISSION . . . HYDRO
STEERING . . . STANDARD
STANDARD DECK . . . 38"
WEIGHT . . . 622 LBS.
MSRP . . . $3,899

OPTIONS

46" DECK
BAGGER

SERIAL NUMBERS

YEAR	BEGINNING NO.
1986	372001-38
1986	378001-46
1987	440001-38
1987	450001-46
1988	495001-38
1988	505001-46

RETAIL PRICING

YEAR	HIGH	LOW
1986	$202	$151
1987	$220	$165
1988	$245	$184
1989	$266	$200
1990	$292	$219

AVG. AUCTION PRICING

LOW	HIGH	AVG
$697	$965	$812

190C

YEARS MFRD . . . 2006-2006
SERIES . . . 100 SERIES
ENGINE . . . B&S
CYLINDERS . . . 2
ENGINE HP . . . 25
COOLING . . . AIR
FUEL . . . G
SPEEDS . . . VARIABLE
TRANSMISSION . . . HYDRO
STEERING . . . STANDARD
STANDARD DECK . . . 54"
MSRP . . . $2,999

SERIAL NUMBERS

YEAR	BEGINNING NO.
2006	10001

RETAIL PRICING

YEAR	HIGH	LOW
2006	$1,051	$788

240

YEARS MFRD . . . 1988-1992
ENGINE . . . KAWASAKI
ENGINE HP . . . 18
COOLING . . . AIR
FUEL . . . G
TRANSMISSION . . . GEAR
STEERING . . . STANDARD
STANDARD DECK . . . 38"
WEIGHT . . . 840 LBS.
MSRP . . . $4,324

OPTIONS

48" DECK
BAGGER

SERIAL NUMBERS

YEAR	BEGINNING NO.
1988	495001-46
1988	475001-38
1989	595001-38
1989	605001-46
1990	010001-38
1990	020001-46
1991	120001-46
1991	100001-38
1992	140001-46
1992	130001-38

RETAIL PRICING

YEAR	HIGH	LOW
1988	$301	$226
1989	$330	$248
1990	$365	$274
1991	$405	$304
1992	$448	$336

245

YEARS MFRD . . . 1993-1994
ENGINE . . . JD K SERIES
ENGINE HP . . . 14
COOLING . . . AIR
FUEL . . . G
SPEEDS . . . VARIABLE
TRANSMISSION . . . HYDRO
STEERING . . . STANDARD
STANDARD DECK . . . 38"
WEIGHT . . . 930 LBS.
MSRP . . . $4,949

OPTIONS

42" SNOW THROWER
48" BLADE
48" DECK
BAGGER

SERIAL NUMBERS

YEAR	BEGINNING NO.
1993	150001
1994	160001

RETAIL PRICING

YEAR	HIGH	LOW
1993	$605	$454
1994	$668	$501

260

YEARS MFRD . . . 1988-1992
SERIES . . . GT SERIES
ENGINE . . . KAWASAKI
ENGINE HP . . . 17
COOLING . . . AIR
FUEL . . . G
TRANSMISSION . . . GEAR
STEERING . . . STANDARD
STANDARD DECK . . . 46"
WEIGHT . . . 890 LBS.
MSRP . . . $4,899

OPTIONS

2 BAG
42" SNOW THROWER
46" BLADE
48" DECK

SERIAL NUMBERS

YEAR	BEGINNING NO.
1988	475001
1989	595001
1990	010001
1991	100001
1992	130001

RETAIL PRICING

YEAR	HIGH	LOW
1988	$341	$256
1989	$375	$282
1990	$414	$311
1991	$457	$343
1992	$504	$378

265

YEARS MFRD . . . 1988-1994
SERIES . . . GT SERIES
ENGINE . . . KAWASAKI
ENGINE HP . . . 17
COOLING . . . AIR
FUEL . . . G
SPEEDS . . . VARIABLE
TRANSMISSION . . . HYDRO
STEERING . . . STANDARD
STANDARD DECK . . . 46"
WEIGHT . . . 980 LBS.
MSRP . . . $5,849

OPTIONS

2 BAG
42" SNOW THROWER
46" BLADE
48" DECK

SERIAL NUMBERS

YEAR	BEGINNING NO.
1988	475001
1989	595001
1990	010001
1991	100001
1992	130001
1993	150001
1994	160001

RETAIL PRICING

YEAR	HIGH	LOW
1988	$439	$329
1989	$482	$362
1990	$532	$399
1991	$591	$443
1992	$649	$487
1993	$716	$537
1994	$794	$595

285

YEARS MFRD . . . 1988-1992
SERIES . . . GT SERIES
ENGINE . . . KAWASAKI
ENGINE HP . . . 18
COOLING . . . LIQUID
FUEL . . . G
SPEEDS . . . VARIABLE
TRANSMISSION . . . HYDRO
STEERING . . . STANDARD
STANDARD DECK . . . 46"
WEIGHT . . . 910 LBS.
MSRP . . . $6,159

OPTIONS

2 BAG
42" SNOW THROWER
48" DECK
50" DECK

SERIAL NUMBERS

YEAR	BEGINNING NO.
1988	475001-46
1988	495001-50
1989	595001-46
1989	605001-50
1990	010001-46
1990	020001-50
1991	100001-48
1992	130001-48

RETAIL PRICING

YEAR	HIGH	LOW
1988	$521	$391
1989	$569	$427
1990	$628	$471

YEAR	HIGH	LOW
1991	$695	$521
1992	$768	$576

301 DIESEL

YEARS MFRD	1974-1975
ENGINE	JD
CYLINDERS	3
CID	152
ENGINE HP	43
COOLING	LIQUID
FUEL	D
SPEEDS	DIRECT DRIVE
TRANSMISSION	GEAR
STEERING	STANDARD
HITCH	CAT. I
BLADE CLUTCH	MANUAL
HYDRAULIC	YES
PTO	YES
WEIGHT	4,057 LBS.
MSRP	$5,250

SERIAL NUMBERS

YEAR	BEGINNING NO.
1974	192104
1975	219951

RETAIL PRICING

YEAR	HIGH	LOW
1975	$1,215	$911

301 GAS

YEARS MFRD	1971-1974
ENGINE	JD
CYLINDERS	3
CID	135
ENGINE HP	43
COOLING	LIQUID
FUEL	G
SPEEDS	DIRECT DRIVE
TRANSMISSION	GEAR
STEERING	STANDARD
HITCH	CAT. I
BLADE CLUTCH	MANUAL
HYDRAULIC	YES
PTO	YES
WEIGHT	3,937 LBS.
MSRP	$4,885

SERIAL NUMBERS

YEAR	BEGINNING NO.
1971	125262
1972	138609
1973	164353
1974	192104

RETAIL PRICING

YEAR	HIGH	LOW
1974	$1,129	$847

301A DIESEL

YEARS MFRD	1974-1981
ENGINE	JD
CYLINDERS	3
CID	152
ENGINE HP	43
COOLING	LIQUID
FUEL	D
SPEEDS	DIRECT DRIVE,8
TRANSMISSION	GEAR
STEERING	STANDARD
HITCH	CAT. I
BLADE CLUTCH	MANUAL
HYDRAULIC	YES
PTO	YES
WEIGHT	4,435 LBS.
MSRP	$16,410

SERIAL NUMBERS

YEAR	BEGINNING NO.
1974	192104
1975	219951
1976	240855
1977	262241
1978	286769
1979	314230
1980	341902
1981	364716

RETAIL PRICING

YEAR	HIGH	LOW
1981	$3,798	$2,849

301A GAS

YEARS MFRD	1974-1979
ENGINE	JD
CYLINDERS	3
CID	135
ENGINE HP	43
COOLING	LIQUID
FUEL	G
SPEEDS	DIRECT DRIVE,8
TRANSMISSION	GEAR
STEERING	STANDARD
HITCH	CAT. I
BLADE CLUTCH	MANUAL
HYDRAULIC	YES
PTO	YES
WEIGHT	4,103 LBS.
MSRP	$9,320

SERIAL NUMBERS

YEAR	BEGINNING NO.
1974	192104
1975	219951
1976	240855
1977	262241
1978	286769
1979	314230

RETAIL PRICING

YEAR	HIGH	LOW
1979	$2,156	$1,617

302

YEARS MFRD	1974-1981
SERIES	INDUSTRIAL SERIES
ENGINE	JD 3-164D
CYLINDERS	3
CID	164
ENGINE HP	50
COOLING	LIQUID
FUEL	D
SPEEDS	DIRECT DRIVE
TRANSMISSION	GEAR
STEERING	STANDARD
HITCH	CAT. I
BLADE CLUTCH	MANUAL
PTO	YES
WEIGHT	4,465 LBS.
MSRP	$10,355

SERIAL NUMBERS

YEAR	BEGINNING NO.
1974	192216
1975	220059
1976	262165
1977	262193
1978	286764
1979	314238
1980	341643
1981	364697

RETAIL PRICING

YEAR	HIGH	LOW
1981	$2,395	$1,796

AVG. AUCTION PRICING

LOW	HIGH	AVG
$3,422	$4,425	$3,894

316

YEARS MFRD	1984-1992
SERIES	GT SERIES
ENGINE	ONAN
CYLINDERS	2
ENGINE HP	18
COOLING	AIR
FUEL	G
SPEEDS	VARIABLE
TRANSMISSION	HYDRO
STEERING	STANDARD
STANDARD DECK	46"
WEIGHT	852 LBS.
MSRP	$6,397

OPTIONS

49" SNOW THROWER
54" BLADE
BAGGER

SERIAL NUMBERS

YEAR	BEGINNING NO.
1984	285001
1985	315001
1986	360001
1987	420001
1988	475001
1989	595001
1990	010001
1991	100001
1992	110001

RETAIL PRICING

YEAR	HIGH	LOW
1984	$361	$271
1985	$399	$299
1986	$440	$330
1987	$486	$364
1988	$538	$403
1989	$592	$444
1990	$655	$491
1991	$720	$540
1992	$802	$601

AVG. AUCTION PRICING

LOW	HIGH	AVG
$321	$2,680	$1,028

318

YEARS MFRD	1983-1992
SERIES	GT SERIES
ENGINE	ONAN
ENGINE HP	18
COOLING	AIR
FUEL	G
SPEEDS	VARIABLE
TRANSMISSION	HYDRO
STEERING	STANDARD
STANDARD DECK	46"
WEIGHT	800 LBS.
MSRP	$7,246

OPTIONS

2 BAG
47" SNOW BLOWER
54" BLADE

SERIAL NUMBERS

YEAR	BEGINNING NO.
1983	222001
1984	285001
1985	315001
1986	360001
1987	420001
1988	475001
1989	595001
1990	010001
1991	100001
1992	110001

RETAIL PRICING

YEAR	HIGH	LOW
1983	$516	$387
1984	$564	$423
1985	$619	$464
1986	$692	$519
1987	$755	$566
1988	$838	$629
1989	$936	$702
1990	$1,031	$773
1991	$1,119	$839
1992	$1,237	$928

AVG. AUCTION PRICING

LOW	HIGH	AVG
$750	$1,000	$925

320

YEARS MFRD	1992-1994
SERIES	GT SERIES
ENGINE	KAWASAKI
ENGINE HP	18
COOLING	LIQUID
FUEL	G
SPEEDS	VARIABLE
TRANSMISSION	HYDRO
STEERING	STANDARD
STANDARD DECK	48"
WEIGHT	985 LBS.
MSRP	$6,849

OPTIONS

2 BAG
46" BLADE
46" SNOW THROWER
47" SNOW BLOWER

SERIAL NUMBERS

YEAR	BEGINNING NO.
1992	130001
1993	150001
1994	160001

RETAIL PRICING

YEAR	HIGH	LOW
1992	$1,001	$750
1993	$1,108	$831
1994	$1,225	$919

JOHN DEERE

322

YEARS MFRD 1988-1992
SERIES . . . . GT SERIES
ENGINE . . . . YANMAR
ENGINE HP 18
COOLING . . . . LIQUID
FUEL . . . . G
SPEEDS . . . . VARIABLE
TRANSMISSION . . . . HYDRO
STEERING. . . . . STANDARD
STANDARD DECK . . . . 46"
WEIGHT . . . . 980 LBS.
MSRP. $8,146

OPTIONS

2 BAG
47" SNOW BLOWER
54" BLADE

SERIAL NUMBERS

YEAR	BEGINNING NO.
1988	475001
1989	595001
1990	010001
1991	100001
1992	110001

RETAIL PRICING

YEAR	HIGH	LOW
1988	$742	$556
1989	$818	$614
1990	$904	$678
1991	$997	$747
1992	$1,102	$826

325

YEARS MFRD 1995-2001
SERIES . . . . GT SERIES
ENGINE . . . . JD K-SERIES
ENGINE HP 18
COOLING . . . . AIR
FUEL . . . . G
SPEEDS . . . . VARIABLE
TRANSMISSION . . . . HYDRO
STEERING. . . . . STANDARD
STANDARD DECK . . . . 48"
WEIGHT . . . . 953 LBS.
MSRP. $6,399

OPTIONS

3 BAG
30" TILLER
42" SNOW THROWER
48" BLADE

SERIAL NUMBERS

YEAR	BEGINNING NO.
1995	010001
1996	020001
1997	040001
1998	A055001-44
1998	B055001-48
1998	C055001-LM
1999	B070001-48
2000	B085001-48
2001	B095001-48

RETAIL PRICING

YEAR	HIGH	LOW
1995	$885	$664
1996	$972	$729
1997	$1,071	$803
1998	$1,180	$885
1999	$1,311	$983
2000	$1,441	$1,081
2001	$1,605	$1,204

AVG. AUCTION PRICING

LOW	HIGH	AVG
$857	$1,688	$1,286

332

YEARS MFRD 1987-1992
SERIES . . . . GT SERIES
ENGINE . . . . YANMAR
ENGINE HP 16
COOLING . . . . LIQUID
FUEL . . . . D
SPEEDS . . . . VARIABLE
TRANSMISSION . . . . HYDRO
STEERING. . . . . STANDARD
STANDARD DECK . . . . 46"
MSRP. $8,266

OPTIONS

2 BAG
47" SNOW BLOWER
54" BLADE

SERIAL NUMBERS

YEAR	BEGINNING NO.
1987	420001
1988	475001
1989	595001
1990	010001
1991	100001
1992	110001

RETAIL PRICING

YEAR	HIGH	LOW
1987	$685	$514
1988	$752	$564
1989	$831	$623
1990	$916	$687
1991	$1,014	$760
1992	$1,117	$838

335

YEARS MFRD 1999-2001
SERIES . . . . GT SERIES
ENGINE . . . . JD K-SERIES
ENGINE HP 20
COOLING . . . . AIR
FUEL . . . . G
SPEEDS . . . . VARIABLE
TRANSMISSION . . . . HYDRO
STEERING. . . . . STANDARD
STANDARD DECK . . . . 48"
WEIGHT . . . . 987 LBS.
MSRP. $7,199

OPTIONS

3 BAG & FAN
42" SNOW THROWER
48" BLADE
54" DECK
BAGGER

SERIAL NUMBERS

YEAR	BEGINNING NO.
1999	A070001-48
1999	B070001-54
2000	A085001-48
2000	B085001-54
2001	A095001-48
2001	B095001-54

RETAIL PRICING

YEAR	HIGH	LOW
1999	$1,306	$979
2000	$1,445	$1,084
2001	$1,626	$1,219

345

YEARS MFRD 1995-2001
SERIES . . . . GT SERIES
ENGINE . . . . JD K-SERIES
ENGINE HP 20
COOLING . . . . LIQUID
FUEL . . . . G
SPEEDS . . . . VARIABLE
TRANSMISSION . . . . HYDRO
STEERING. . . . . STANDARD
STANDARD DECK . . . . 48"
WEIGHT . . . . 960 LBS.
MSRP. $7,749

OPTIONS

3 BAG & FAN
30" TILLER
42" SNOW THROWER
48" BLADE
54" DECK

SERIAL NUMBERS

YEAR	BEGINNING NO.
1995	010001
1996	020001
1997	040001
1998	D055001-44
1998	A055001-48
1998	B055001-54
1998	C055001-LM
1999	A070001-48
1999	B070001-54
2000	B085001-54
2000	A085001-48
2001	C095001-LM
2001	B095001-54
2001	A095001-48

RETAIL PRICING

YEAR	HIGH	LOW
1995	$988	$741
1996	$1,119	$839
1997	$1,217	$913
1998	$1,345	$1,009
1999	$1,518	$1,138
2000	$1,679	$1,259
2001	$2,076	$1,557

AVG. AUCTION PRICING

LOW	HIGH	AVG
$663	$2,652	$1,464

355D

YEARS MFRD 1999-2001
SERIES . . . . GT SERIES
ENGINE . . . . YANMAR
ENGINE HP 18
COOLING . . . . LIQUID
FUEL . . . . D
SPEEDS . . . . VARIABLE
TRANSMISSION . . . . HYDRO
STEERING. . . . . STANDARD
STANDARD DECK . . . . 48"
WEIGHT . . . . 1,007 LBS.
MSRP. $8,449

OPTIONS

3 BAG & FAN
30" TILLER
42" SNOW THROWER
48" BLADE
54" DECK

SERIAL NUMBERS

YEAR	BEGINNING NO.
1999	B070001-54
1999	A070001-48
2000	A085001-48
2000	B085001-54
2001	A095001-48
2001	B095001-54

RETAIL PRICING

YEAR	HIGH	LOW
1999	$1,532	$1,149
2000	$1,691	$1,268
2001	$1,865	$1,398

420

YEARS MFRD 1983-1992
SERIES . . . . GT SERIES
ENGINE . . . . ONAN
ENGINE HP 20
COOLING . . . . AIR
FUEL . . . . G
SPEEDS . . . . VARIABLE
TRANSMISSION . . . . HYDRO
STEERING. . . . . STANDARD
STANDARD DECK . . . . 50"
WEIGHT . . . . 1,013 LBS.
MSRP. $8,984

OPTIONS

2 BAG
47" SNOW BLOWER
54" BLADE

SERIAL NUMBERS

YEAR	BEGINNING NO.
1983	222001
1984	285001
1985	315001
1987	420001
1988	475001
1989	595001
1990	010001
1991	100001
1992	110001

RETAIL PRICING

YEAR	HIGH	LOW
1983	$531	$399
1984	$606	$454
1985	$672	$504
1986	$738	$554
1987	$815	$611
1988	$903	$677
1989	$993	$745
1990	$1,095	$822
1991	$1,210	$907
1992	$1,352	$1,014

AVG. AUCTION PRICING

LOW	HIGH	AVG
$1,020	$1,887	$1,397

425

YEARS MFRD	1993-2001
SERIES	GT SERIES
ENGINE	JD K-SERIES
ENGINE HP	20
COOLING	LIQUID
FUEL	G
SPEEDS	VARIABLE
TRANSMISSION	HYDRO
STEERING	STANDARD
DRIVE TYPE	2WD
STANDARD DECK	54"
WEIGHT	944 LBS.
MSRP	$9,199

OPTIONS

3 BAG
47" SNOW BLOWER
60" DECK
AWS

SERIAL NUMBERS

YEAR	BEGINNING NO.
1993	010001
1994	020001
1995	030001
1996	040001
1997	050001
1998	A060001-2WS
1998	B060001-AWS
1999	A070001-2WS
1999	B070001-AWS
2000	B080001-AWS
2000	A080001-2WS
2001	B090001-AWS
2001	A090001-2WS

RETAIL PRICING

YEAR	HIGH	LOW
1993	$1,153	$864
1994	$1,212	$909
1995	$1,340	$1,005
1996	$1,500	$1,125
1997	$1,656	$1,242
1998	$1,836	$1,377
1999	$2,002	$1,502
2000	$2,183	$1,637
2001	$2,446	$1,834

AVG. AUCTION PRICING

LOW	HIGH	AVG
$1,000	$2,700	$1,800

430

YEARS MFRD	1984-1992
SERIES	GT SERIES
ENGINE	YANMAR
ENGINE HP	20
COOLING	LIQUID
FUEL	D
SPEEDS	VARIABLE
TRANSMISSION	HYDRO
STEERING	STANDARD
STANDARD DECK	50"
WEIGHT	1,246 LBS.
MSRP	$10,764

OPTIONS

2 BAG
47" SNOW BLOWER
54" BLADE

SERIAL NUMBERS

YEAR	BEGINNING NO.
1984	285001
1985	315001
1987	420001
1988	475001
1989	595001
1990	010001
1991	100001
1992	110001

RETAIL PRICING

YEAR	HIGH	LOW
1984	$713	$535
1985	$786	$590
1986	$868	$651
1987	$958	$718
1988	$1,061	$796
1989	$1,167	$875
1990	$1,288	$966
1991	$1,422	$1,066
1992	$1,572	$1,179

AVG. AUCTION PRICING

LOW	HIGH	AVG
$1,000	$3,000	$1,950

445

YEARS MFRD	1993-2001
SERIES	GT SERIES
ENGINE	JD K-SERIES
ENGINE HP	22
COOLING	LIQUID
FUEL	G
SPEEDS	VARIABLE
TRANSMISSION	HYDRO
STEERING	STANDARD
STANDARD DECK	54"
WEIGHT	1,041 LBS.
MSRP	$9,999

OPTIONS

47" SNOW BLOWER
60" DECK
AWS
BAG

SERIAL NUMBERS

YEAR	BEGINNING NO.
1993	010001
1994	020001
1995	030001
1996	040001
1997	050001
1998	060001
1999	D070001-AWS
1999	C070001-2WS
2000	D080001-AWS
2000	C080001-2WS
2001	D090001-AWS
2001	C090001-2WS

RETAIL PRICING

YEAR	HIGH	LOW
1993	$1,158	$868
1994	$1,281	$961
1995	$1,409	$1,056
1996	$1,577	$1,183
1997	$1,717	$1,287
1998	$1,915	$1,436
1999	$2,211	$1,659
2000	$2,400	$1,800
2001	$2,785	$2,088

AVG. AUCTION PRICING

LOW	HIGH	AVG
$850	$4,000	$1,893

455

YEARS MFRD	1993-2001
SERIES	GT SERIES
ENGINE	YANMAR
ENGINE HP	22
COOLING	LIQUID
FUEL	D
SPEEDS	VARIABLE
TRANSMISSION	HYDRO
STEERING	STANDARD
DRIVE TYPE	2WD
STANDARD DECK	54"
WEIGHT	1,177 LBS.
MSRP	$11,299

OPTIONS

3 BAG
47" SNOW BLOWER
60" DECK
AWS

SERIAL NUMBERS

YEAR	BEGINNING NO.
1993	010001
1994	020001
1995	030001
1996	040001
1997	050001
1998	C060001-2WS
1998	D060001-AWS
1999	C070001-2WS
1999	D070001-AWS
2000	D080001-AWS
2000	C080001-2WS
2001	C090001-2WS
2001	D090001-AWS

RETAIL PRICING

YEAR	HIGH	LOW
1993	$1,399	$1,050
1994	$1,532	$1,149
1995	$1,693	$1,270
1996	$1,880	$1,410
1997	$2,088	$1,566
1998	$2,289	$1,717
1999	$2,515	$1,886
2000	$2,807	$2,105
2001	$3,091	$2,318

AVG. AUCTION PRICING

LOW	HIGH	AVG
$1,020	$4,080	$2,474

636M

YEARS MFRD	2015-2020
SERIES	QUIKTRAK SERIES
ENGINE	KAWASAKI FS600V
CYLINDERS	2
CID	603CC
ENGINE HP	18.5
COOLING	AIR
FUEL	G
SPEEDS	VARIABLE
TRANSMISSION	HYDRO
STEERING	ZERO
STANDARD DECK	36"
WEIGHT	731 LBS.
MSRP	$8,659

647A

YEARS MFRD	2002-2008
SERIES	QUIK-TRAK SERIES
ENGINE	KAWASAKI
CYLINDERS	2
CID	41.2
ENGINE HP	19
COOLING	AIR
FUEL	G
SPEEDS	VARIABLE
TRANSMISSION	HYDRO
STEERING	ZERO
BLADE CLUTCH	ELECTRIC
STANDARD DECK	48"
WEIGHT	885 LBS.
MSRP	$6,939

SERIAL NUMBERS

YEAR	BEGINNING NO.
2002	X010001
2003	X020001
2006	30001
2007	40001

RETAIL PRICING

YEAR	HIGH	LOW
2002	$4,169	$3,127
2003	$4,686	$3,514
2004	$5,077	$3,807
2005	$5,797	$4,347

648M

YEARS MFRD	2015-2020
SERIES	QUIKTRAK SERIES
ENGINE	KAWASAKI FX691V
CYLINDERS	2
CID	726CC
ENGINE HP	22
COOLING	AIR
FUEL	G
SPEEDS	VARIABLE
TRANSMISSION	HYDRO
STEERING	ZERO
STANDARD DECK	48"
WEIGHT	820 LBS.
MSRP	$9,389

648R

YEARS MFRD	2013-2020
SERIES	QUIKTRAK SERIES
ENGINE	KAWASAKI FX691V
CYLINDERS	2
CID	726CC
ENGINE HP	22
COOLING	AIR
FUEL	G
SPEEDS	VARIABLE
TRANSMISSION	HYDRO
STEERING	ZERO
STANDARD DECK	48"
WEIGHT	910 LBS.
MSRP	$9,799

JOHN DEERE

650
YEARS MFRD 1981-1989
ENGINE .... YANMAR
CYLINDERS.................. 2
CID 52
PTO HP 14.5
ENGINE HP 17
COOLING .... LIQUID
FUEL .... D
SPEEDS 8/2
TRANSMISSION .... GEAR
STEERING............ STANDARD
HITCH .... CAT. I
BLADE CLUTCH .... MANUAL
HYDRAULIC .... YES
PTO .... YES
DRIVE TYPE 2WD
ROPS/CAB .... ROPS
WEIGHT .... 1,420 LBS.
MSRP.................. $8,408

OPTIONS

2 HYD
4WD
60"DECK
LDR

SERIAL NUMBERS

LEFT SIDE OF ENGINE BLOCK

YEAR	BEGINNING NO.
1981	1000
1982	3539
1983	6250
1984	10543
1985	15001
1986	19001
1987	22501
1988	24298

RETAIL PRICING

YEAR	HIGH	LOW
1981	$1,305	$978
1982	$1,465	$1,099
1983	$1,648	$1,236
1984	$1,833	$1,375
1985	$1,983	$1,487
1986	$2,151	$1,613
1987	$2,338	$1,753
1988	$2,526	$1,894
1989	$2,732	$2,049

AVG. AUCTION PRICING

LOW	HIGH	AVG
$1,938	$3,315	$2,691

652E
YEARS MFRD 2017-2020
SERIES......... QUIKTRAK SERIES
ENGINE .... KAWASAKI FX691V
CYLINDERS.................. 2
CID 726CC
ENGINE HP 22
COOLING .... AIR
FUEL .... G
SPEEDS .... VARIABLE
TRANSMISSION .... HYDRO
STEERING.................. ZERO
STANDARD DECK .... 52"
WEIGHT .... 927 LBS.
MSRP.................. $9,149

652M
YEARS MFRD 2015-2020
SERIES......... QUIKTRAK SERIES
ENGINE .... KAWASAKI FX691V
CYLINDERS.................. 2
CID 726CC
ENGINE HP 22
COOLING .... AIR
FUEL .... G
SPEEDS .... VARIABLE
TRANSMISSION .... HYDRO
STEERING.................. ZERO
STANDARD DECK .... 52"
WEIGHT .... 828 LBS.
MSRP.................. $9,709

652R
YEARS MFRD 2013-2020
SERIES......... QUIKTRAK SERIES
ENGINE .... KAWASAKI FX730V
CYLINDERS.................. 2
CID 726CC
ENGINE HP 23.5
COOLING .... AIR
SPEEDS .... VARIABLE
TRANSMISSION .... HYDRO
STEERING.................. ZERO
STANDARD DECK .... 52"
WEIGHT .... 927 LBS.
MSRP.................. $10,219

652R EFI
YEARS MFRD 2014-2020
SERIES......... QUIKTRAK SERIES
ENGINE .... KOHLER ECV740
CYLINDERS.................. 2
CID 747CC
ENGINE HP 20
COOLING .... AIR
FUEL .... G
SPEEDS .... VARIABLE
TRANSMISSION .... HYDRO
STEERING.................. ZERO
STANDARD DECK .... 52"
WEIGHT .... 927 LBS.
MSRP.................. $10,749

655
YEARS MFRD 1986-1990
ENGINE .... YANMAR
CYLINDERS.................. 3
CID 40.1
PTO HP 10.6
ENGINE HP 16
COOLING .... LIQUID
FUEL .... D
SPEEDS .... VARIABLE
TRANSMISSION .... HYDRO
STEERING............ STANDARD
HITCH .... CAT. I
BLADE CLUTCH .... MANUAL
HYDRAULIC .... YES
PTO .... YES
DRIVE TYPE 2WD
ROPS/CAB .... ROPS
WEIGHT .... 1,415 LBS.
MSRP.................. $9,624

OPTIONS

2 HYD
4WD
60"DECK
LDR

SERIAL NUMBERS

PLATE LOCATED BELOW REAR PTO SHAFT

YEAR	BEGINNING NO.
1986	M0360001
1986	364001 4WD
1986	360001
1986	362001
1987	420001
1987	430001 4WD
1987	425001
1987	M0420001
1988	485001 4WD
1988	475001
1988	480001
1988	M0475001
1989	615001
1989	M0615001
1989	600001
1989	605001 4WD

RETAIL PRICING

YEAR	HIGH	LOW
1986	$2,054	$1,541
1987	$2,230	$1,672
1988	$2,464	$1,848
1989	$2,634	$1,975
1990	$2,840	$2,130

AVG. AUCTION PRICING

LOW	HIGH	AVG
$2,622	$7,102	$5,041

657A
YEARS MFRD 2002-2008
SERIES....... QUIK-TRAK SERIES
ENGINE .... KAWASAKI
CYLINDERS.................. 2
CID 41.2
ENGINE HP 23
COOLING .... AIR
FUEL .... G
SPEEDS .... VARIABLE
TRANSMISSION .... HYDRO
STEERING.................. ZERO
STANDARD DECK .... 54"
WEIGHT .... 900 LBS.
MSRP.................. $7,649

SERIAL NUMBERS

YEAR	BEGINNING NO.
2002	X010101

RETAIL PRICING

YEAR	HIGH	LOW
2002	$3,596	$2,697
2003	$4,201	$3,151
2004	$4,618	$3,463
2005	$5,529	$4,147

661R
YEARS MFRD 2013-2020
SERIES......... QUIKTRAK SERIES
ENGINE .... KAWASAKI FX730V
CYLINDERS.................. 2
CID 726CC
ENGINE HP 23.5
COOLING .... AIR
FUEL .... G
SPEEDS .... VARIABLE
TRANSMISSION .... HYDRO
STEERING.................. ZERO
STANDARD DECK .... 61"
WEIGHT .... 998 LBS.
MSRP.................. $10,849

661R EFI
YEARS MFRD 2014-2020
SERIES......... QUIKTRAK SERIES
ENGINE .... KOHLER ECV740
CYLINDERS.................. 2
CID 747C
ENGINE HP 25
COOLING .... AIR
FUEL .... G
SPEEDS .... VARIABLE
TRANSMISSION .... HYDRO
STEERING.................. ZERO
STANDARD DECK .... 61"
WEIGHT .... 998 LBS.
MSRP.................. $11,379

667A
YEARS MFRD 2002-2008
SERIES....... QUIK-TRAK SERIES
ENGINE .... KAWASAKI
CYLINDERS.................. 2
CID 41.2
ENGINE HP 23
COOLING .... AIR
FUEL .... G
SPEEDS .... VARIABLE
TRANSMISSION .... HYDRO
STEERING.................. ZERO
BLADE CLUTCH ...... ELECTRIC
STANDARD DECK .... 60"
WEIGHT .... 925 LBS.
MSRP.................. $7,859

SERIAL NUMBERS

YEAR	BEGINNING NO.
2002	X010101

RETAIL PRICING

YEAR	HIGH	LOW
2002	$3,749	$2,811
2003	$4,371	$3,278
2004	$4,919	$3,690
2005	$5,770	$4,328
2006	$6,456	$4,842

670
YEARS MFRD 1989-1998
ENGINE .... YANMAR
CYLINDERS.................. 3
CID 53.6

PTO HP . . . 16
ENGINE HP . . . 18.5
COOLING . . . LIQUID
FUEL . . . D
SPEEDS . . . 8/2
TRANSMISSION . . . GEAR
STEERING . . . STANDARD
HITCH . . . CAT. I
BLADE CLUTCH . . . MANUAL
HYDRAULIC . . . YES
PTO . . . YES
DRIVE TYPE . . . 2WD
ROPS/CAB . . . ROPS
WEIGHT . . . 1,730 LBS.
MSRP . . . $11,796

OPTIONS

2 HYD
4WD
60"DECK
LDR

SERIAL NUMBERS

YEAR	BEGINNING NO.
1989	1001
1990	2889
1991	100001
1992	110001
1993	120001
1994	130001
1995	140001
1996	150001
1997	160001
1998	170001

RETAIL PRICING

YEAR	HIGH	LOW
1990	$1,797	$1,348
1991	$2,030	$1,522
1992	$2,268	$1,701
1993	$2,512	$1,884
1994	$2,796	$2,097
1995	$3,035	$2,276
1996	$3,377	$2,533
1997	$3,738	$2,804
1998	$4,110	$3,082

AVG. AUCTION PRICING

LOW	HIGH	AVG
$4,400	$4,700	$4,600

717A

YEARS MFRD . . . 2004-2008
ENGINE . . . KAWASAKI
ENGINE HP . . . 19
COOLING . . . AIR
FUEL . . . G
SPEEDS . . . VARIABLE
TRANSMISSION . . . DUAL HYDRO
STEERING . . . ZERO
STANDARD DECK . . . 48"
MSRP . . . $7,819

OPTIONS

BAG & FAN

SERIAL NUMBERS

YEAR	BEGINNING NO.
2005	20001
2006	30001
2007	40001

RETAIL PRICING

YEAR	HIGH	LOW
2004	$3,229	$2,422
2005	$3,552	$2,664
2006	$3,906	$2,929
2007	$4,311	$3,233
2008	$4,779	$3,584

AVG. AUCTION PRICING

LOW	HIGH	AVG
$2,404	$2,841	$1,584

717A

YEARS MFRD . . . 2002-2003
SERIES . . . Z-TRAK SERIES
ENGINE . . . KAWASAKI
CYLINDERS . . . 2
CID . . . 41.2
ENGINE HP . . . 19
COOLING . . . AIR
FUEL . . . G
SPEEDS . . . VARIABLE
TRANSMISSION . . . HYDRO
STEERING . . . ZERO
STANDARD DECK . . . 48"
WEIGHT . . . 1,160 LBS.
MSRP . . . $7,399

OPTIONS

2BAG

SERIAL NUMBERS

YEAR	BEGINNING NO.
2002	X010001
2003	X020001

RETAIL PRICING

YEAR	HIGH	LOW
2002	$2,161	$1,621
2003	$2,410	$1,808

AVG. AUCTION PRICING

LOW	HIGH	AVG
$1,428	$2,652	$2,244

727

YEARS MFRD . . . 2002-2003
ENGINE . . . KAWASAKI
ENGINE HP . . . 23
COOLING . . . AIR
FUEL . . . G
SPEEDS . . . VARIABLE
TRANSMISSION . . . HYDRO
STEERING . . . ZERO
STANDARD DECK . . . 54"
MSRP . . . $8,099

OPTIONS

2 BAG

RETAIL PRICING

YEAR	HIGH	LOW
2002	$2,497	$1,873
2003	$2,761	$2,071

727A

YEARS MFRD . . . 2004-2008
SERIES . . . Z-TRAK SERIES
ENGINE . . . KAWASAKI FH680V
CYLINDERS . . . 2
CID . . . 41.2
ENGINE HP . . . 23
COOLING . . . AIR
FUEL . . . G
SPEEDS . . . VARIABLE
TRANSMISSION . . . HYDRO
STEERING . . . ZERO
BLADE CLUTCH . . . ELECTRIC
STANDARD DECK . . . 54"
WEIGHT . . . 1,284 LBS.
MSRP . . . $9,009

OPTIONS

2 BAG & FAN

SERIAL NUMBERS

YEAR	BEGINNING NO.
2004	10001
2005	20001
2006	30001
2007	40001
2008	50001

RETAIL PRICING

YEAR	HIGH	LOW
2004	$3,411	$2,558
2005	$3,798	$2,849
2006	$4,212	$3,159
2007	$4,629	$3,472
2008	$5,121	$3,841

737

YEARS MFRD . . . 2003-2008
SERIES . . . Z-TRAK SERIES
ENGINE . . . KAWASAKI
CYLINDERS . . . 2
CID . . . 41.5
ENGINE HP . . . 23
COOLING . . . AIR
FUEL . . . G
SPEEDS . . . VARIABLE
TRANSMISSION . . . DUAL HYDRO
STEERING . . . ZERO
STANDARD DECK . . . 54"
WEIGHT . . . 1,308 LBS.
MSRP . . . $9,599

OPTIONS

2 BAG & FAN
3 BAG & FAN
60" DECK

SERIAL NUMBERS

YEAR	BEGINNING NO.
2003	B020001
2003	A020001
2005	40001
2006	50001
2007	60001
2008	70001

RETAIL PRICING

YEAR	HIGH	LOW
2003	$3,151	$2,363
2004	$3,513	$2,635
2005	$3,953	$2,964
2006	$4,298	$3,224
2007	$4,679	$3,509
2008	$5,166	$3,875

AVG. AUCTION PRICING

LOW	HIGH	AVG
$1,300	$3,500	$2,060

750

YEARS MFRD . . . 1981-1989
ENGINE . . . YANMAR
CYLINDERS . . . 3
CID . . . 78
PTO HP . . . 18.5
ENGINE HP . . . 20
COOLING . . . LIQUID
FUEL . . . D
SPEEDS . . . 8/2
TRANSMISSION . . . GEAR
STEERING . . . STANDARD
HITCH . . . CAT. I
BLADE CLUTCH . . . MANUAL
HYDRAULIC . . . YES
PTO . . . YES
DRIVE TYPE . . . 2WD
ROPS/CAB . . . ROPS
WEIGHT . . . 1,760 LBS.
MSRP . . . $9,424

OPTIONS

2 HYD
4WD
60"DECK
LDR

SERIAL NUMBERS

REAR OF TRANSMISSION CASE BELOW PTO

YEAR	BEGINNING NO.
1981	1000
1982	3448
1983	5613
1984	8597
1985	13001
1986	18501
1987	22601
1988	26450

RETAIL PRICING

YEAR	HIGH	LOW
1981	$1,694	$1,271
1982	$1,833	$1,375
1983	$2,024	$1,518
1984	$2,301	$1,726
1985	$2,356	$1,767
1986	$2,558	$1,919
1987	$2,722	$2,042
1988	$2,917	$2,188
1989	$3,139	$2,354

AVG. AUCTION PRICING

LOW	HIGH	AVG
$1,900	$4,000	$3,300

755

YEARS MFRD . . . 1986-1998
ENGINE . . . YANMAR
CYLINDERS . . . 3
CID . . . 53.6
PTO HP . . . 15
ENGINE HP . . . 20
COOLING . . . LIQUID
FUEL . . . D
SPEEDS . . . VARIABLE
TRANSMISSION . . . HYDRO
STEERING . . . STANDARD
HITCH . . . CAT. I
BLADE CLUTCH . . . MANUAL
HYDRAULIC . . . YES

JOHN DEERE

PTO ... YES
DRIVE TYPE ... 2WD
ROPS/CAB ... ROPS
WEIGHT ... 1,700 LBS.
MSRP ... $14,378

OPTIONS

2 HYD
4WD
60"DECK
LDR

SERIAL NUMBERS

PLATE LOCATED BELOW REAR PTO SHAFT

YEAR	BEGINNING NO.
1986	M0360001
1987	M0420001
1988	M0475001
1989	M0600001
1990	M010001
1991	M0100001
1992	LV100700
1993	LV130000
1994	LV165001
1995	LVA165180
1996	LVE190001
1997	LVE200001
1998	300001

RETAIL PRICING

YEAR	HIGH	LOW
1990	$2,809	$2,107
1991	$3,020	$2,265
1992	$3,234	$2,426
1993	$3,467	$2,600
1994	$3,691	$2,769
1995	$3,924	$2,943
1996	$4,232	$3,174
1997	$4,550	$3,413
1998	$4,828	$3,621

AVG. AUCTION PRICING

LOW	HIGH	AVG
$2,900	$6,900	$4,429

757

YEARS MFRD ... 2003-2008
SERIES ... Z-TRAK SERIES
ENGINE ... KAWASAKI
CYLINDERS ... 2
CID ... 41.2
ENGINE HP ... 25
COOLING ... AIR
FUEL ... G
SPEEDS ... VARIABLE
TRANSMISSION ... DUAL HYDRO
STEERING ... ZERO
STANDARD DECK ... 54"
WEIGHT ... 1,308 LBS.
MSRP ... $10,079

OPTIONS

2 BAG & FAN
3 BAG & FAN
60" DECK

SERIAL NUMBERS

YEAR	BEGINNING NO.
2003	B020001
2003	A020001
2004	30001
2005	40001
2006	50001
2007	60001
2008	70001

RETAIL PRICING

YEAR	HIGH	LOW
2003	$3,392	$2,544
2004	$3,942	$2,957
2005	$4,308	$3,231
2006	$4,884	$3,663
2007	$5,133	$3,849
2008	$5,409	$4,057

AVG. AUCTION PRICING

LOW	HIGH	AVG
$1,000	$3,800	$2,219

770

YEARS MFRD ... 1989-1998
ENGINE ... YANMAR
CYLINDERS ... 3
CID ... 83.1
PTO HP ... 20
ENGINE HP ... 23
COOLING ... LIQUID
FUEL ... D
SPEEDS ... 8/2
TRANSMISSION ... GEAR
STEERING ... STANDARD
HITCH ... CAT. I
BLADE CLUTCH ... MANUAL
HYDRAULIC ... YES
PTO ... YES
DRIVE TYPE ... 2WD
ROPS/CAB ... ROPS
WEIGHT ... 1,930 LBS.
MSRP ... $12,739

OPTIONS

2 HYD
4WD
60"DECK
LDR

SERIAL NUMBERS

YEAR	BEGINNING NO.
1989	1001
1990	4111
1991	100001
1992	115001
1993	120001
1994	130001
1995	140001
1996	150001
1997	160001
1998	170001

RETAIL PRICING

YEAR	HIGH	LOW
1990	$3,302	$2,476
1991	$3,523	$2,642
1992	$3,749	$2,811
1993	$3,985	$2,989
1994	$4,237	$3,178
1995	$4,469	$3,351
1996	$4,791	$3,593
1997	$5,119	$3,840
1998	$5,459	$4,094

AVG. AUCTION PRICING

LOW	HIGH	AVG
$4,750	$5,600	$5,283

777

YEARS MFRD ... 2003-2008
SERIES ... Z-TRAK SERIES
ENGINE ... KAWASAKI
CYLINDERS ... 2
CID ... 45.5
ENGINE HP ... 27
COOLING ... LIQUID
FUEL ... G
SPEEDS ... VARIABLE
TRANSMISSION ... DUAL HYDRO
STEERING ... ZERO
STANDARD DECK ... 60"
WEIGHT ... 1,420 LBS.
MSRP ... $11,739

OPTIONS

72" DECK
BAG & FAN

SERIAL NUMBERS

YEAR	BEGINNING NO.
2003	C010001
2003	B010001
2004	20001
2005	30001
2006	40001
2007	50001
2008	60001

RETAIL PRICING

YEAR	HIGH	LOW
2003	$3,806	$2,854
2004	$4,196	$3,147
2005	$4,839	$3,629
2006	$5,138	$3,853
2007	$5,688	$4,266
2008	$6,308	$4,731

AVG. AUCTION PRICING

LOW	HIGH	AVG
$2,244	$3,570	$3,142

790

YEARS MFRD ... 2000-2008
SERIES ... 90 SERIES
ENGINE ... YANMAR 3TNE84
CYLINDERS ... 3
CID ... 81.2
PTO HP ... 24
ENGINE HP ... 27
COOLING ... LIQUID
FUEL ... D
SPEEDS ... 8/2
TRANSMISSION ... GEAR
STEERING ... STANDARD
HITCH ... CAT. I
BLADE CLUTCH ... MANUAL
HYDRAULIC ... YES
PTO ... YES
DRIVE TYPE ... 2WD
ROPS/CAB ... ROPS
WEIGHT ... 1,930 LBS.
MSRP ... $9,639

OPTIONS

2 HYD
4WD
60" DECK
LDR

SERIAL NUMBERS

YEAR	BEGINNING NO.
2000	390001
2001	470001
2002	570001
2003	670001
2004	790001
2005	890001
2006	900001
2007	190001

RETAIL PRICING

YEAR	HIGH	LOW
2000	$3,523	$2,642
2001	$4,077	$3,058
2002	$4,426	$3,319
2003	$4,842	$3,631
2004	$5,371	$4,028
2005	$5,834	$4,376
2006	$6,424	$4,818
2007	$6,994	$5,246
2008	$7,431	$5,573

AVG. AUCTION PRICING

LOW	HIGH	AVG
$4,750	$11,000	$8,050

797

YEARS MFRD ... 2003-2008
SERIES ... Z-TRAK SERIES
ENGINE ... KAWASAKI
CYLINDERS ... 2
CID ... 45.5
ENGINE HP ... 29
COOLING ... LIQUID
FUEL ... G
SPEEDS ... VARIABLE
TRANSMISSION ... DUAL HYDRO
STEERING ... ZERO
STANDARD DECK ... 60"
WEIGHT ... 1,420 LBS.
MSRP ... $13,039

OPTIONS

72" DECK
BAG & FAN

SERIAL NUMBERS

YEAR	BEGINNING NO.
2003	C010001
2003	B010001
2005	30001
2006	40001
2007	50001

RETAIL PRICING

YEAR	HIGH	LOW
2003	$4,453	$3,340
2004	$4,884	$3,663
2005	$5,400	$4,050
2006	$6,041	$4,531
2007	$6,718	$5,038
2008	$7,416	$5,562

AVG. AUCTION PRICING

LOW	HIGH	AVG
$1,800	$2,000	$1,933

850

YEARS MFRD ... 1978-1988
ENGINE ... YANMAR
CYLINDERS ... 3

CID ... 78
PTO HP ... 22.2
ENGINE HP ... 25
COOLING ... LIQUID
FUEL ... D
SPEEDS ... 8/2
TRANSMISSION ... GEAR
STEERING ... STANDARD
HITCH ... CAT. I
BLADE CLUTCH ... MANUAL
HYDRAULIC ... YES
PTO ... YES
DRIVE TYPE ... 2WD
ROPS/CAB ... ROPS
WEIGHT ... 2,537 LBS.
MSRP ... $10,157

OPTIONS

2 HYD
4WD
60"DECK
72"DECK
LDR

SERIAL NUMBERS

ON DIFFERENTIAL HOUSING AT REAR OF THE TRACTOR,REAR OF TRANSMISSON CASE BELOW PTO

YEAR	BEGINNING NO.
1978	1024
1979	3859
1980	7389
1981	11338
1982	12481
1983	14183
1984	16006
1985	18001
1986	22001
1987	25501
1988	28337

RETAIL PRICING

YEAR	HIGH	LOW
1980	$1,396	$1,047
1981	$1,562	$1,171
1982	$1,711	$1,283
1983	$1,900	$1,425
1984	$2,080	$1,560
1985	$2,265	$1,699
1986	$2,456	$1,842
1987	$2,650	$1,987
1988	$2,886	$2,164

AVG. AUCTION PRICING

LOW	HIGH	AVG
$2,550	$3,825	$3,254

855

YEARS MFRD ... 1986-1998
ENGINE ... YANMAR
CYLINDERS ... 3
CID ... 60.7
PTO HP ... 19
ENGINE HP ... 24
COOLING ... LIQUID
FUEL ... D
SPEEDS ... VARIABLE
TRANSMISSION ... HYDRO
STEERING ... STANDARD
HITCH ... CAT. I
HYDRAULIC ... YES
PTO ... YES
DRIVE TYPE ... 2WD
ROPS/CAB ... ROPS
WEIGHT ... 1,790 LBS.
MSRP ... $15,332

OPTIONS

2 HYD
4WD
60" DECK
72" DECK
LDR

SERIAL NUMBERS

PLATE LOCATED BELOW REAR PTO SHAFT

YEAR	BEGINNING NO.
1986	M0364001
1986	M0360001
1987	M0420001
1987	M0430001
1988	M0475001
1988	M0485001
1989	M0615001
1989	M0605001
1990	M010001
1991	M0100001
1992	LV100700
1993	LV130000
1994	LV165001
1995	LVB170123
1996	LVE190001
1997	LVE200001
1998	LVE300001

RETAIL PRICING

YEAR	HIGH	LOW
1990	$3,281	$2,461
1991	$3,553	$2,664
1992	$3,810	$2,857
1993	$4,129	$3,097
1994	$4,432	$3,324
1995	$4,751	$3,563
1996	$5,259	$3,944
1997	$5,572	$4,179
1998	$5,987	$4,491

AVG. AUCTION PRICING

LOW	HIGH	AVG
$4,500	$7,100	$5,757

870

YEARS MFRD ... 1989-1998
ENGINE ... YANMAR
CYLINDERS ... 3
CID ... 87.3
PTO HP ... 25
ENGINE HP ... 28
COOLING ... LIQUID
FUEL ... D
SPEEDS ... 9/3
TRANSMISSION ... GEAR
STEERING ... STANDARD
HITCH ... CAT. I
BLADE CLUTCH ... MANUAL
HYDRAULIC ... YES
PTO ... YES
DRIVE TYPE ... 2WD
ROPS/CAB ... ROPS
WEIGHT ... 2,515 LBS.
MSRP ... $13,994

OPTIONS

2 HYD
4WD
60" DECK
72" DECK
LDR
MID PTO

SERIAL NUMBERS

YEAR	BEGINNING NO.
1989	1001
1989	1001 PS
1990	1625
1990	2746 PS
1991	100001
1991	100001 PS
1992	110001
1992	110001 PS
1993	120001
1994	130001
1995	140001
1996	150001
1997	160001
1998	170001

RETAIL PRICING

YEAR	HIGH	LOW
1990	$3,687	$2,765
1991	$3,924	$2,943
1992	$4,170	$3,127
1993	$4,422	$3,316
1994	$4,679	$3,509
1995	$4,997	$3,748
1996	$5,244	$3,933
1997	$5,576	$4,182
1998	$6,009	$4,507

AVG. AUCTION PRICING

LOW	HIGH	AVG
$3,672	$10,200	$7,426

900HC

YEARS MFRD ... 1986-1990
ENGINE ... YANMAR
CYLINDERS ... 3
CID ... 78.2
PTO HP ... 22
ENGINE HP ... 25
COOLING ... LIQUID
FUEL ... D
SPEEDS ... 8/2
TRANSMISSION ... GEAR
STEERING ... STANDARD
HITCH ... CAT. I
BLADE CLUTCH ... MANUAL
HYDRAULIC ... YES
PTO ... YES
WEIGHT ... 2,780 LBS.
MSRP ... $12,301

SERIAL NUMBERS

YEAR	BEGINNING NO.
1986	1001
1987	1701
1988	2127

RETAIL PRICING

YEAR	HIGH	LOW
1988	$3,678	$2,759
1989	$4,170	$3,127
1990	$4,528	$3,396

AVG. AUCTION PRICING

LOW	HIGH	AVG
$8,925	$12,750	$10,625

950

YEARS MFRD ... 1978-1988
ENGINE ... YANMAR
CYLINDERS ... 3
CID ... 105
PTO HP ... 27.3
ENGINE HP ... 31
COOLING ... LIQUID
FUEL ... D
SPEEDS ... 8/2
TRANSMISSION ... GEAR
STEERING ... STANDARD
HITCH ... CAT. I
BLADE CLUTCH ... MANUAL
HYDRAULIC ... YES
PTO ... YES
DRIVE TYPE ... 2WD
ROPS/CAB ... ROPS
WEIGHT ... 2,600 LBS.
MSRP ... $11,598

OPTIONS

2 HYD
4WD
60"DECK
72"DECK
LDR

SERIAL NUMBERS

ON DIFFERENTIAL HOUSING AT REAR OF THE TRACTOR

YEAR	BEGINNING NO.
1978	1024
1979	5229
1980	10453
1981	14893
1982	16204
1983	18204
1984	20007
1985	23001
1986	26001
1987	28501
1988	30082

RETAIL PRICING

YEAR	HIGH	LOW
1980	$1,073	$805
1981	$1,237	$928
1982	$1,438	$1,079
1983	$1,586	$1,190
1984	$1,773	$1,330
1985	$1,961	$1,471
1986	$2,166	$1,625
1987	$2,368	$1,776
1988	$2,646	$1,984

AVG. AUCTION PRICING

LOW	HIGH	AVG
$3,060	$4,947	$3,944

955

YEARS MFRD ... 1989-1998
ENGINE ... YANMAR
CYLINDERS ... 3
CID ... 87.3
PTO HP ... 27
ENGINE HP ... 33
COOLING ... LIQUID
FUEL ... D
SPEEDS ... VARIABLE
TRANSMISSION ... HYDRO

STEERING .... STANDARD
HITCH .... CAT. I
BLADE CLUTCH .... MANUAL
HYDRAULIC .... YES
PTO .... YES
DRIVE TYPE 4WD
ROPS/CAB .... ROPS
WEIGHT .... 1,835 LBS.
MSRP $17,945

OPTIONS

2 HYD
60" DECK
72" DECK
LDR

SERIAL NUMBERS

PLATE LOCATED BELOW REAR PTO SHAFT

YEAR	BEGINNING NO.
1990	M010001
1991	M0100001
1992	LV100700
1993	LV130000
1994	LV165001
1995	LVC175320
1996	LVE190000
1997	LVE200001
1998	LVE300001

RETAIL PRICING

YEAR	HIGH	LOW
1990	$3,332	$2,499
1991	$3,682	$2,762
1992	$4,072	$3,054
1993	$4,469	$3,351
1994	$4,802	$3,602
1995	$5,274	$3,956
1996	$5,649	$4,237
1997	$6,069	$4,552
1998	$6,532	$4,899

AVG. AUCTION PRICING

LOW	HIGH	AVG
$3,876	$9,282	$6,911

970

YEARS MFRD 1989-1998
ENGINE .... YANMAR
CYLINDERS 4
CID 110.8
PTO HP 30
ENGINE HP 33
COOLING .... LIQUID
FUEL .... D
SPEEDS 9/3
TRANSMISSION .... GEAR
STEERING .... STANDARD
HITCH .... CAT. I
BLADE CLUTCH .... MANUAL
HYDRAULIC .... YES
PTO .... YES
DRIVE TYPE 2WD
ROPS/CAB .... ROPS
WEIGHT .... 2,670 LBS.
MSRP $16,193

OPTIONS

2 HYD
4WD
60" DECK
72" DECK
LDR
MID PTO

SERIAL NUMBERS

YEAR	BEGINNING NO.
1989	001001
1990	001338 W/OUT PS
1990	2242 W/ PS
1991	100001
1992	110001
1993	120001
1994	130001
1995	140001
1996	150001
1997	160001
1998	170001

RETAIL PRICING

YEAR	HIGH	LOW
1990	$3,122	$2,342
1991	$3,359	$2,519
1992	$3,605	$2,704
1993	$3,861	$2,896
1994	$4,134	$3,101
1995	$4,396	$3,297
1996	$4,679	$3,509
1997	$4,971	$3,729
1998	$5,284	$3,963

AVG. AUCTION PRICING

LOW	HIGH	AVG
$4,600	$8,700	$7,025

990

YEARS MFRD 2000-2008
SERIES .... 90 SERIES
ENGINE .... YANMAR 4TNE84
CYLINDERS 4
CID 121.7
PTO HP 35
ENGINE HP 40.4
COOLING .... LIQUID
FUEL .... D
SPEEDS 9/3
TRANSMISSION .... GEAR
STEERING .... STANDARD
HITCH .... CAT. I
BLADE CLUTCH .... MANUAL
HYDRAULIC .... YES
PTO .... YES
DRIVE TYPE 2WD
ROPS/CAB .... ROPS
WEIGHT .... 2,954 LBS.
MSRP $13,499

OPTIONS

2 HYD
4WD
LDR

SERIAL NUMBERS

YEAR	BEGINNING NO.
2000	G190001
2001	290002
2002	291001
2003	391001
2004	590001
2005	690001
2006	790001
2007	890001
2008	990001

RETAIL PRICING

YEAR	HIGH	LOW
2000	$5,434	$4,075
2001	$5,943	$4,457
2002	$6,462	$4,846
2003	$6,999	$5,249
2004	$7,524	$5,643
2005	$8,140	$6,105
2006	$8,745	$6,559
2007	$9,373	$7,030
2008	$10,143	$7,607

AVG. AUCTION PRICING

LOW	HIGH	AVG
$6,120	$15,402	$9,568

997

YEARS MFRD 2005-2015
ENGINE .... YANMAR 3TNV82A
CYLINDERS 3
CID 81
ENGINE HP 31
COOLING .... LIQUID
FUEL .... D
SPEEDS .... VARIABLE
TRANSMISSION .... HYDRO
STEERING .... ZERO
BLADE CLUTCH .... ELECTRIC
STANDARD DECK .... 60"
WEIGHT .... 1,774 LBS.
MSRP $20,329

OPTIONS

72" DECK

RETAIL PRICING

YEAR	HIGH	LOW
2006	$6,869	$5,152
2007	$7,562	$5,672
2008	$8,303	$6,227
2009	$9,094	$6,821
2010	$10,171	$7,629
2011	$11,509	$8,631
2012	$12,694	$9,520
2013	$13,982	$10,487
2014	$14,898	$11,174
2015	$16,470	$12,352

AVG. AUCTION PRICING

LOW	HIGH	AVG
$2,750	$7,500	$3,930

1023E

YEARS MFRD 2011-2020
ENGINE .... YANMAR
CYLINDERS 3
CID 60.6
PTO HP 15.3
ENGINE HP 22.4
COOLING .... LIQUID
FUEL .... D
SPEEDS .... VARIABLE
TRANSMISSION .... HYDRO
STEERING .... STANDARD
HITCH .... CAT. I
DRIVE TYPE 4WD
ROPS/CAB .... ROPS
WEIGHT .... 1,345 LBS.
MSRP $12,672

OPTIONS

54" DECK $1,926
54" FRT BLADE $539
60" DECK $2,374
IMATCH QUICK HITCH $306
LDR W/BKT $4,265

SERIAL NUMBERS

YEAR	BEGINNING NO.
2011	110001
2012	210001
2013	310001
2014	410001
2015	510001

RETAIL PRICING

YEAR	HIGH	LOW
2011	$6,581	$4,935
2012	$7,033	$5,275
2013	$7,485	$5,614
2014	$8,150	$6,113
2015	$9,015	$6,761
2016	$9,951	$7,463
2017	$10,764	$8,073
2018	$11,215	$9,006
2019	$11,867	$9,739
2020	$12,605	$10,336

AVG. AUCTION PRICING

LOW	HIGH	AVG
$5,850	$13,000	$10,389

1025R

YEARS MFRD 2013-2020
ENGINE .... YANMAR 3TNV80
CYLINDERS 3
CID 68
PTO HP 18
ENGINE HP 24.2
COOLING .... LIQUID
FUEL .... D
SPEEDS .... VARIABLE
TRANSMISSION .... HYDRO
STEERING .... STANDARD
HITCH .... CAT. I
HYDRAULIC .... YES
PTO .... YES
DRIVE TYPE 4WD
ROPS/CAB .... ROPS
WEIGHT .... 1,444 LBS.
MSRP $14,587

OPTIONS

54" DECK $1,926
60" DECK $2,374
BACKHOE W/BKT $6,706
CAB/HEAT $6,566
IMATCH QUICK HITCH $306
LOADER W/BKT $4,265

SERIAL NUMBERS

YEAR	BEGINNING NO.
2013	110001
2014	210001
2015	310001

RETAIL PRICING

YEAR	HIGH	LOW
2013	$9,354	$7,015
2014	$10,326	$7,744
2015	$10,799	$8,100
2016	$11,750	$8,812
2017	$12,107	$9,334
2018	$12,696	$10,258
2019	$13,299	$11,330
2020	$14,439	$12,172

AVG. AUCTION PRICING

LOW	HIGH	AVG
$6,600	$15,000	$9,888

1026R

YEARS MFRD ... 2011-2013
ENGINE ... YANMAR
CYLINDERS ... 3
PTO HP ... 18
ENGINE HP ... 25.2
COOLING ... LIQUID
FUEL ... D
SPEEDS ... VARIABLE
TRANSMISSION ... HYDRO
STEERING ... STANDARD
MSRP ... $12,847

OPTIONS

3 HYD
54" DECK
60" DECK
LDR

SERIAL NUMBERS

YEAR	BEGINNING NO.
2011	110001
2012	210001
2013	310001

RETAIL PRICING

YEAR	HIGH	LOW
2011	$11,180	$8,385
2012	$11,542	$8,657
2013	$12,120	$9,090

AVG. AUCTION PRICING

LOW	HIGH	AVG
$8,000	$12,750	$9,636

1050

YEARS MFRD ... 1980-1988
ENGINE ... YANMAR
CYLINDERS ... 3
CID ... 105
PTO HP ... 33.4
ENGINE HP ... 37
COOLING ... LIQUID
FUEL ... D
SPEEDS ... 8/2
TRANSMISSION ... GEAR
STEERING ... STANDARD
HITCH ... CAT. I
BLADE CLUTCH ... MANUAL
HYDRAULIC ... YES
PTO ... YES
DRIVE TYPE ... 2WD
ROPS/CAB ... ROPS
WEIGHT ... 2,800 LBS.
MSRP ... $13,390

OPTIONS

2 HYD
4WD
72"DECK
LDR

SERIAL NUMBERS

LEFT SIDE OF ENGINE BLOCK,REAR OF TRANSMISSION CASE BELOW PTO

YEAR	BEGINNING NO.
1980	1000
1981	5280
1982	6572
1983	9001
1984	11006
1985	14001
1986	17001
1987	19501
1988	21479

RETAIL PRICING

YEAR	HIGH	LOW
1980	$1,931	$1,448
1981	$2,012	$1,509
1982	$2,105	$1,579
1983	$2,198	$1,649
1984	$2,347	$1,760
1985	$2,507	$1,880
1986	$2,675	$2,007
1987	$2,835	$2,126
1988	$3,030	$2,273

AVG. AUCTION PRICING

LOW	HIGH	AVG
$3,264	$8,262	$4,349

1070

YEARS MFRD ... 1989-1998
ENGINE ... YANMAR
CYLINDERS ... 4
CID ... 116.3
PTO HP ... 35
ENGINE HP ... 39
COOLING ... LIQUID
FUEL ... D
SPEEDS ... 9/3
TRANSMISSION ... GEAR
STEERING ... STANDARD
HITCH ... CAT. I
BLADE CLUTCH ... MANUAL
HYDRAULIC ... YES
PTO ... YES
DRIVE TYPE ... 2WD
ROPS/CAB ... ROPS
WEIGHT ... 1,876 LBS.
MSRP ... $18,071

OPTIONS

2 HYD
4WD
72"DECK
LDR
MID PTO

SERIAL NUMBERS

YEAR	BEGINNING NO.
1989	1001
1990	1338
1991	100001
1992	115001
1993	120001
1994	130001
1995	140001
1996	150001
1997	160001
1998	170001

RETAIL PRICING

YEAR	HIGH	LOW
1990	$3,993	$2,995
1991	$4,222	$3,166
1992	$4,547	$3,410
1993	$4,874	$3,655
1994	$5,196	$3,897
1995	$5,557	$4,168
1996	$5,918	$4,439
1997	$6,295	$4,722
1998	$6,688	$5,016

AVG. AUCTION PRICING

LOW	HIGH	AVG
$3,876	$8,160	$6,758

1250

YEARS MFRD ... 1982-1988
ENGINE ... YANMAR
CYLINDERS ... 3
CID ... 142.7
PTO HP ... 40.7
COOLING ... LIQUID
FUEL ... D
SPEEDS ... 9/2
TRANSMISSION ... GEAR
STEERING ... STANDARD
HITCH ... CAT. I
BLADE CLUTCH ... MANUAL
HYDRAULIC ... YES
PTO ... YES
DRIVE TYPE ... 2WD
ROPS/CAB ... ROPS
WEIGHT ... 4,800 LBS.
MSRP ... $18,720

OPTIONS

2 HYD
4WD
72"MOWER
LDR

SERIAL NUMBERS

LEFT SIDE OF ENGINE BLOCK,REAR OF TRANSMISSION CASE BELOW PTO

YEAR	BEGINNING NO.
1982	1001
1983	1256
1984	3001
1985	4001
1986	5001
1987	5501
1988	5785

RETAIL PRICING

YEAR	HIGH	LOW
1982	$2,790	$2,092
1983	$3,079	$2,310
1984	$3,377	$2,533
1985	$3,683	$2,762
1986	$3,998	$2,999
1987	$4,320	$3,240
1988	$4,648	$3,486

AVG. AUCTION PRICING

LOW	HIGH	AVG
$3,570	$7,140	$5,610

1420

YEARS MFRD ... 2001-2014
SERIES ... 1400 SERIES II
ENGINE ... YANMAR
CYLINDERS ... 3
ENGINE HP ... 28
COOLING ... LIQUID
FUEL ... G
SPEEDS ... VARIABLE
TRANSMISSION ... HYDRO
STEERING ... STANDARD
HYDRAULIC ... YES
DRIVE TYPE ... 2WD
ROPS/CAB ... ROPS
STANDARD DECK ... 62"
WEIGHT ... 1,860 LBS.
MSRP ... $22,510

OPTIONS

47" SNOW BLOWER
4WD
60" BLADE
72" DECK

SERIAL NUMBERS

YEAR	BEGINNING NO.
2001	G010001-4WD
2002	G020001-4WD
2002	G020001-2WD
2005	50001
2006	60001
2007	70001
2008	80001

RETAIL PRICING

YEAR	HIGH	LOW
2002	$5,560	$4,170
2003	$6,690	$5,018
2004	$7,210	$5,408
2005	$7,428	$5,571
2006	$8,240	$6,180
2007	$9,136	$6,852
2008	$10,414	$7,811
2009	$11,184	$8,388
2010	$12,474	$9,355
2011	$13,900	$10,425
2012	$15,347	$11,510
2013	$17,024	$12,768
2014	$19,965	$14,974

1435

YEARS MFRD ... 2001-2014
SERIES ... 1400 SERIES
ENGINE ... YANMAR
CYLINDERS ... 3
ENGINE HP ... 26
COOLING ... LIQUID
FUEL ... D
SPEEDS ... VARIABLE
TRANSMISSION ... HYDRO
STEERING ... ZERO
PTO ... YES
DRIVE TYPE ... 2WD
ROPS/CAB ... ROPS
STANDARD DECK ... 62"
WEIGHT ... 1,860 LBS.
MSRP ... $22,650

OPTIONS

47" SNOW BLOWER
4WD
60" BLADE
72" DECK

SERIAL NUMBERS

YEAR	BEGINNING NO.
2001	D010001-4WD
2001	D010001-4WD
2002	D020001-2WD
2002	D020001-4WD
2005	50001
2006	60001
2007	70001
2008	80001

JOHN DEERE

RETAIL PRICING

YEAR	HIGH	LOW
2002	$5,250	$3,937
2003	$5,629	$4,222
2004	$5,979	$4,484
2005	$6,139	$4,605
2006	$6,777	$5,083
2007	$7,626	$5,719
2008	$8,770	$6,577
2009	$9,289	$6,967
2010	$10,094	$7,570
2011	$11,448	$8,586
2012	$12,412	$9,309
2013	$13,805	$10,354
2014	$14,425	$10,819

AVG. AUCTION PRICING

LOW	HIGH	AVG
$2,448	$10,200	$4,998

1445

YEARS MFRD 2001-2014
SERIES . . . . 1400 SERIES II
ENGINE . . . . YANMAR
CYLINDERS 3
ENGINE HP 31.1
COOLING . . . . LIQUID
FUEL . . . . D
SPEEDS . . . . VARIABLE
TRANSMISSION . . . . HYDRO
STEERING . . . . ZERO
PTO . . . . YES
DRIVE TYPE 2WD
ROPS/CAB . . . . ROPS
STANDARD DECK . . . . 72"
WEIGHT . . . . 1,860 LBS.
MSRP $25,752

OPTIONS

4WD
60" BLADE
BAGGER
SOFT CAB

SERIAL NUMBERS

YEAR	BEGINNING NO.
2001	D010001-2WD
2001	D010001-4WD
2002	D020001-4WD
2002	D020001-2WD
2005	50001
2006	60001
2007	70001
2008	80001

RETAIL PRICING

YEAR	HIGH	LOW
2001	$3,513	$2,635
2002	$4,228	$3,171
2003	$5,377	$4,033
2004	$6,255	$4,691
2005	$6,693	$5,020
2006	$7,436	$5,577
2007	$7,993	$5,995
2008	$9,150	$6,863
2009	$9,806	$7,355
2010	$10,624	$7,968
2011	$12,437	$9,328
2012	$13,392	$10,044
2013	$14,805	$11,104
2014	$17,477	$13,108

AVG. AUCTION PRICING

LOW	HIGH	AVG
$4,488	$13,515	$7,642

1545

YEARS MFRD 2003-2014
SERIES . . . SERIES II FRONT MOWER
ENGINE . . . . YANMAR
CYLINDERS 3
CID 73.5
ENGINE HP 31
COOLING . . . . LIQUID
FUEL . . . . D
SPEEDS . . . . VARIABLE
TRANSMISSION . . . . HYDRO
STEERING . . . . ZERO
BLADE CLUTCH . . . . ELECTRIC
HYDRAULIC . . . . YES
PTO . . . . YES
STANDARD DECK . . . . 72"
WEIGHT . . . . 1,860 LBS.
MSRP $30,414

OPTIONS

60" BLADE
AIR SUSPENSION
BAGGER
ROPS/CANOPY

SERIAL NUMBERS

YEAR	BEGINNING NO.
2005	50001
2006	60001
2007	70001

RETAIL PRICING

YEAR	HIGH	LOW
2003	$8,906	$6,679
2004	$9,049	$6,787
2005	$9,869	$7,401
2006	$10,989	$8,242
2007	$12,222	$9,166
2008	$13,498	$10,123
2009	$14,899	$11,174
2010	$16,780	$12,585
2011	$18,333	$13,750
2012	$20,628	$15,471
2013	$22,558	$16,919
2014	$25,619	$19,215

1550

YEARS MFRD 2015-2020
SERIES . . . . . . TERRAINCUT SERIES
ENGINE 3TNV80F
CYLINDERS 3
CID 77
ENGINE HP 24.2
COOLING . . . . LIQUID
FUEL . . . . D
SPEEDS . . . . VARIABLE
TRANSMISSION . . . . HYDRO
STEERING . . . . ZERO
STANDARD DECK . . . . 0"
WEIGHT . . . . 1,675 LBS.
MSRP $19,899

OPTIONS

4WD $2,913
60" DECK SD
62" DECK RD
72" DECK RD
72" DECK SD
AIR SEAT $680
COMFORT SEAT $390

RETAIL PRICING

YEAR	HIGH	LOW
2015	$14,580	$10,881
2016	$15,782	$11,836
2017	$17,097	$12,899
2018	$17,934	$13,916
2019	$18,655	$15,275
2020	$19,740	$16,697

1565

YEARS MFRD 2003-2014
SERIES . . . SERIES II FRONT MOWER
ENGINE . . . . YANMAR
CYLINDERS 3
CID 102.8
ENGINE HP 36
COOLING . . . . LIQUID
FUEL . . . . D
SPEEDS . . . . VARIABLE
TRANSMISSION . . . . HYDRO
STEERING . . . . ZERO
BLADE CLUTCH . . . . ELECTRIC
HYDRAULIC . . . . YES
PTO . . . . YES
STANDARD DECK . . . . 72"
WEIGHT . . . . 1,860 LBS.
MSRP $32,555

OPTIONS

60" BLADE
60" SNOW BLOWER
62" DECK
BAGGER

SERIAL NUMBERS

YEAR	BEGINNING NO.
2004	40001
2005	50001
2006	60001

RETAIL PRICING

YEAR	HIGH	LOW
2003	$8,874	$6,656
2004	$9,545	$7,159
2005	$10,535	$7,901
2006	$11,750	$8,813
2007	$12,958	$9,719
2008	$14,378	$10,783
2009	$15,949	$11,962
2010	$17,748	$13,311
2011	$19,535	$14,651
2012	$22,103	$16,578
2013	$24,149	$18,111
2014	$27,596	$20,697

1570

YEARS MFRD 2015-2020
SERIES . . . . . . TERRAINCUT SERIES
ENGINE 3TNV88C
CYLINDERS 3
CID 100.2
ENGINE HP 37.4
COOLING . . . . LIQUID
FUEL . . . . D
SPEEDS . . . . VARIABLE
TRANSMISSION . . . . HYDRO
STEERING . . . . ZERO
STANDARD DECK . . . . 72"
WEIGHT . . . . 1,800 LBS.
MSRP $27,949

OPTIONS

4WD $2,913
60" DECK SD
62" DECK RD
72" DECK RD
72" DECK SD
AIR SEAT $680
COMFORT SEAT $390

RETAIL PRICING

YEAR	HIGH	LOW
2015	$19,599	$14,699
2016	$21,987	$16,491
2017	$23,314	$17,485
2018	$24,260	$18,612
2019	$25,187	$19,499
2020	$26,617	$21,677

1575

YEARS MFRD 2015-2020
SERIES . . . . . . TERRAINCUT SERIES
ENGINE 3TNV88C
CYLINDERS 3
CID 100.2
ENGINE HP 37.4
COOLING . . . . LIQUID
FUEL . . . . D
SPEEDS . . . . VARIABLE
TRANSMISSION . . . . HYDRO
STEERING . . . . ZERO
STANDARD DECK . . . . 72"
MSRP $41,599

OPTIONS

62" DECK RD
72" DECK RD
72" DECK SD

RETAIL PRICING

YEAR	HIGH	LOW
2015	$28,128	$21,097
2016	$29,813	$22,360
2017	$32,907	$24,680
2018	$34,529	$26,473
2019	$36,170	$28,042
2020	$38,154	$31,095

1580

YEARS MFRD 2015-2020
SERIES . . . . . . TERRAINCUT SERIES
ENGINE 3TNV88C
CYLINDERS 3
CID 100.2
ENGINE HP 37.4
COOLING . . . . LIQUID
FUEL . . . . D
SPEEDS . . . . VARIABLE
TRANSMISSION . . . . HYDRO
STEERING . . . . ZERO
STANDARD DECK . . . . 72"
WEIGHT . . . . 2,120 LBS.
MSRP $33,649

OPTIONS

60" DECK SD
62" DECK RD
72" DECK RD
72" DECK SD
AIR SEAT $680
COMFORT SEAT $390

RETAIL PRICING

YEAR	HIGH	LOW
2015	$22,450	$16,837
2016	$24,780	$18,584
2017	$27,350	$20,512
2018	$28,686	$22,266
2019	$30,082	$23,097
2020	$31,878	$25,618

1585

YEARS MFRD 2015-2020
SERIES TERRAINCUT SERIES
ENGINE 3TNV88C
CYLINDERS 3
CID 100.2
ENGINE HP 37.4
COOLING LIQUID
FUEL D
SPEEDS VARIABLE
TRANSMISSION HYDRO
STEERING ZERO
STANDARD DECK 72"
WEIGHT 2,593 LBS.
MSRP $44,149

OPTIONS

60" BLADE
60" DECK SD
62" DECK RD
72" DECK RD
72" DECK SD

RETAIL PRICING

YEAR	HIGH	LOW
2015	$29,312	$21,983
2016	$31,466	$23,599
2017	$34,731	$26,048
2018	$36,417	$27,760
2019	$38,224	$29,104
2020	$40,168	$31,673

1600

YEARS MFRD 1997-2017
SERIES SERIES II TURBO
ENGINE YANMAR
CYLINDERS 4
CID 122
ENGINE HP 57.3
COOLING LIQUID
FUEL D
SPEEDS VARIABLE
TRANSMISSION HYDRO
STEERING ZERO
BLADE CLUTCH ELECTRIC
STANDARD DECK 62"
WEIGHT 3,950 LBS.
MSRP $66,960

OPTIONS

4 ROPS
LIGHTS

RETAIL PRICING

YEAR	HIGH	LOW
2006	$17,414	$13,061
2007	$18,678	$14,009
2008	$21,895	$16,421
2009	$23,652	$17,739
2010	$26,106	$19,579
2011	$28,815	$21,611
2012	$34,961	$26,220
2013	$35,103	$26,327
2014	$40,585	$30,439
2015	$42,766	$32,074
2016	$47,203	$35,402
2017	$52,100	$39,075

AVG. AUCTION PRICING

LOW	HIGH	AVG
$7,500	$11,000	$9,100

1600

YEARS MFRD 2018-2020
SERIES SERIES III TURBO
ENGINE 4TNV86CT
CYLINDERS 4
CID 127.6
ENGINE HP 60
COOLING LIQUID
FUEL D
TRANSMISSION HYDRO
STEERING STANDARD
STANDARD DECK 62"
WEIGHT 3,264 LBS.
MSRP $73,599

OPTIONS

4 ROPS/CAN
LIGHTS

1905

YEARS MFRD 2007-2007
ENGINE YANMAR
CYLINDERS 4
ENGINE HP 41.5
COOLING LIQUID
FUEL D
SPEEDS VARIABLE
TRANSMISSION HYDRO
STEERING STANDARD
WEIGHT 3,938 LBS.
MSRP $72,420

RETAIL PRICING

YEAR	HIGH	LOW
2007	$75,525	$56,644

1905 WIDE AREA

YEARS MFRD 2008-2008
ENGINE YANMAR TURBO
CYLINDERS 4
ENGINE HP 57
COOLING LIQUID
FUEL D
SPEEDS VARIABLE
TRANSMISSION HYDRO
STEERING ZERO
MSRP $72,720

RETAIL PRICING

YEAR	HIGH	LOW
2008	$75,860	$56,895

2025R

YEARS MFRD 2013-2020
ENGINE YANMAR
CYLINDERS 3
CID 68
PTO HP 18
ENGINE HP 24.2
COOLING LIQUID
FUEL D
SPEEDS VARIABLE
TRANSMISSION HYDRO
STEERING STANDARD
HITCH CAT. I
DRIVE TYPE 4WD
ROPS/CAB ROPS
WEIGHT 1,793 LBS.
MSRP $17,043

OPTIONS

47" SNOW BLOWER $2,219
54" BLADE $539
BACKHOE W/BKT $6,706
CAB/HEAT $6,567
IMATCH QUICK HITCH $306
LDR W/BKT $4,265

SERIAL NUMBERS

RIGHT SIDE OF TRACTOR FRAME ABOVE AND BEHIND THE FRONT AXLE

YEAR	BEGINNING NO.
2013	110001
2014	111414
2015	115072

RETAIL PRICING

YEAR	HIGH	LOW
2013	$10,640	$7,980
2014	$11,804	$8,853
2015	$13,484	$10,113
2016	$13,652	$10,239
2017	$14,239	$10,679
2018	$14,940	$11,428
2019	$15,749	$12,241
2020	$17,002	$13,125

AVG. AUCTION PRICING

LOW	HIGH	AVG
$7,548	$15,300	$12,036

2032R

YEARS MFRD 2013-2020
ENGINE YANMAR
CYLINDERS 3
CID 100.2
PTO HP 23.5
ENGINE HP 31.7
COOLING LIQUID
FUEL D
SPEEDS VARIABLE
TRANSMISSION HYDRO
STEERING STANDARD
HITCH CAT. I
DRIVE TYPE 4WD
ROPS/CAB ROPS
WEIGHT 2,436 LBS.
MSRP $23,214

OPTIONS

60" DECK
BACKHOE
FRT BLADE
IMATCH QUICK HITCH $306
LDR W/BKT $4,798

SERIAL NUMBERS

RIGHT SIDE OF TRACTOR FRAME ABOVE AND BEHIND THE FRONT AXLE

YEAR	BEGINNING NO.
2013	110001
2014	111913

RETAIL PRICING

YEAR	HIGH	LOW
2013	$13,665	$10,249
2014	$14,985	$11,239
2015	$16,537	$12,403
2016	$16,912	$12,685
2017	$17,624	$13,219
2018	$18,689	$14,413
2019	$19,728	$15,278
2020	$21,774	$16,613

AVG. AUCTION PRICING

LOW	HIGH	AVG
$9,435	$20,400	$13,209

2038R

YEARS MFRD 2017-2020
ENGINE YANMAR
CYLINDERS 3
CID 1.568L
PTO HP 30.4
ENGINE HP 37.3
COOLING LIQUID
FUEL D
SPEEDS VARIABLE
TRANSMISSION HYDRO
STEERING STANDARD
HITCH CAT. I
ROPS/CAB ROPS
WEIGHT 2,436 LBS.
MSRP $25,171

OPTIONS

60" DECK
BACKHOE
IMATCH QUICK HITCH $306
LOADER W/BKT $4,798

SERIAL NUMBERS

YEAR	BEGINNING NO.
2017	100392
2018	103000

RETAIL PRICING

YEAR	HIGH	LOW
2017	$18,645	$13,983
2018	$19,793	$15,101
2019	$20,757	$16,055
2020	$23,009	$17,498

2040

YEARS MFRD 1976-1982
ENGINE JD
CYLINDERS 3
CID 179
PTO HP 41.2
COOLING LIQUID

FUEL . . . . . D
SPEEDS 8/4
TRANSMISSION . . . . . GEAR
STEERING. . . . . STANDARD
PTO . . . . . YES
DRIVE TYPE 2WD
ROPS/CAB . . . . . ROPS
WEIGHT . . . . . 4,376 LBS.
MSRP. $13,970

OPTIONS

2 HYD
4WD
LDR

SERIAL NUMBERS

ON DIFFERENTIAL HOUSING

YEAR	BEGINNING NO.
1976	179963
1977	221555
1978	266057
1979	304165
1980	336935
1981	392026
1982	419145

RETAIL PRICING

YEAR	HIGH	LOW
1979	$6,177	$4,633
1980	$5,650	$4,237
1981	$6,445	$4,834
1982	$6,674	$5,005

AVG. AUCTION PRICING

LOW	HIGH	AVG
$3,570	$6,528	$4,973

2155

YEARS MFRD 1987-1992
ENGINE . . . . . JD
CYLINDERS. 3
CID 179
PTO HP 45.6
FUEL . . . . . D
SPEEDS 8/4-16/8
TRANSMISSION . . . . . GEAR
STEERING. . . . . STANDARD
PTO . . . . . YES
DRIVE TYPE 2WD
ROPS/CAB . . . . . ROPS
WEIGHT . . . . . 4,970 LBS.
MSRP. $17,840

OPTIONS

2 HYD
4WD
CAB W/A/H
LDR
LDR SL

SERIAL NUMBERS

RIGHT SIDE OF TRACTOR FRAME

YEAR	BEGINNING NO.
1987	600000
1988	624800
1989	652073
1990	686146
1991	720721
1992	747375

RETAIL PRICING

YEAR	HIGH	LOW
1987	$5,354	$4,015
1988	$5,791	$4,343
1989	$6,010	$4,507
1990	$6,337	$4,753
1991	$6,665	$4,999
1992	$7,102	$5,327

AVG. AUCTION PRICING

LOW	HIGH	AVG
$3,900	$8,000	$6,333

2210

YEARS MFRD 2003-2005
SERIES. . . . . 2000 SERIES
ENGINE . . . . . YANMAR 3TNE74
CYLINDERS. 3
CID 61
PTO HP 17.7
ENGINE HP 23
COOLING . . . . . LIQUID
FUEL . . . . . D
SPEEDS . . . . . VARIABLE
TRANSMISSION . . . . . HYDRO
STEERING. . . . . STANDARD
HITCH . . . . . CAT. I
BLADE CLUTCH . . . . . ELECTRIC
PTO . . . . . YES
DRIVE TYPE 4WD
ROPS/CAB . . . . . ROPS
WEIGHT . . . . . 1,400 LBS.
MSRP. $10,709

OPTIONS

2 HYD
54"DECK
62"DECK
LDR

SERIAL NUMBERS

YEAR	BEGINNING NO.
2003	H210001-HYDRO
2004	H310001-HYDRO
2005	H431001-HYDRO

RETAIL PRICING

YEAR	HIGH	LOW
2003	$4,474	$3,355
2004	$5,233	$3,924
2005	$5,402	$4,051

AVG. AUCTION PRICING

LOW	HIGH	AVG
$3,950	$7,800	$6,298

2305

YEARS MFRD 2006-2010
SERIES. . . . . 2000 SERIES
ENGINE . . . . . YANMAR
CYLINDERS. 3
CID 68
ENGINE HP 24
COOLING . . . . . AIR
FUEL . . . . . D
SPEEDS . . . . . VARIABLE
TRANSMISSION . . . . . HYDRO
STEERING. . . . . STANDARD
HITCH . . . . . CAT. I
WEIGHT . . . . . 1,125 LBS.
MSRP. $11,069

OPTIONS

54" DECK
62" DECK
LDR

SERIAL NUMBERS

YEAR	BEGINNING NO.
2006	120001
2007	320001
2008	420001
2009	520001
2010	620001

RETAIL PRICING

YEAR	HIGH	LOW
2006	$5,884	$4,413
2007	$6,337	$4,753
2008	$6,872	$5,154
2009	$7,543	$5,657
2010	$8,211	$6,158

AVG. AUCTION PRICING

LOW	HIGH	AVG
$4,000	$9,000	$6,581

2320

YEARS MFRD 2006-2013
SERIES. . . . . 2000 SERIES
ENGINE . . . . . YANMAR
CYLINDERS. 3
CID 68
PTO HP 18
ENGINE HP 24
COOLING . . . . . LIQUID
FUEL . . . . . D
SPEEDS . . . . . VARIABLE
TRANSMISSION . . . . . HYDRO
STEERING. . . . . STANDARD
BLADE CLUTCH . . . . . ELECTRIC
WEIGHT . . . . . 1,660 LBS.
MSRP. $13,877

OPTIONS

54" DECK
62" DECK
LDR

SERIAL NUMBERS

YEAR	BEGINNING NO.
2006	102001
2007	202001
2008	302001-H
2008	382001-HR
2009	402001
2010	502001
2011	602001
2012	710001

RETAIL PRICING

YEAR	HIGH	LOW
2006	$7,272	$5,454
2007	$8,238	$6,178
2008	$8,679	$6,509
2009	$9,150	$6,863
2010	$9,896	$7,422
2011	$10,624	$7,968
2012	$11,426	$8,570
2013	$11,949	$8,962

AVG. AUCTION PRICING

LOW	HIGH	AVG
$4,300	$12,100	$7,490

2500A

YEARS MFRD 2007-2007
ENGINE . . . . . KAWASAKI FD 620D
CYLINDERS. 2
ENGINE HP 19.9
COOLING . . . . . LIQUID
FUEL . . . . . G
SPEEDS . . . . . VARIABLE
TRANSMISSION . . . . . HYDRO
STEERING. . . . . STANDARD
DRIVE TYPE 2WD
ROPS/CAB . . . . . ROPS
STANDARD DECK . . . . . 62"
MSRP. $27,390

OPTIONS

4WD

RETAIL PRICING

YEAR	HIGH	LOW
2007	$23,749	$17,811

2500E

YEARS MFRD 2007-2007
ENGINE . . . . . JD
CYLINDERS. 2
ENGINE HP 19.9
COOLING . . . . . LIQUID
FUEL . . . . . D
SPEEDS . . . . . VARIABLE
TRANSMISSION . . . . . HYDRO
STEERING. . . . . STANDARD
MSRP. $33,710

RETAIL PRICING

YEAR	HIGH	LOW
2007	$23,674	$17,756

AVG. AUCTION PRICING

LOW	HIGH	AVG
$1,530	$6,885	$3,733

2520

YEARS MFRD 2006-2013
SERIES. . . . . TWENTY SERIES
ENGINE . . . . . YANMAR
CYLINDERS. 3
CID 81.2
PTO HP 20
ENGINE HP 26.5
COOLING . . . . . LIQUID
FUEL . . . . . D
SPEEDS . . . . . VARIABLE
TRANSMISSION . . . . . HYDRO
STEERING. . . . . STANDARD
HITCH . . . . . CAT. I
DRIVE TYPE 4WD
ROPS/CAB . . . . . ROPS
WEIGHT . . . . . 1,865 LBS.
MSRP. $16,363

OPTIONS

62" DECK
72" DECK

SERIAL NUMBERS

YEAR	BEGINNING NO.
2006	107001
2007	306001
2008	406007-H
2008	486003-HR
2009	506001
2010	606001
2011	710001
2012	810001

RETAIL PRICING

YEAR	HIGH	LOW
2006	$8,483	$6,363
2007	$9,186	$6,890
2008	$9,977	$7,482
2009	$10,391	$7,793
2010	$11,264	$8,448
2011	$12,071	$9,053
2012	$12,627	$9,470
2013	$13,304	$9,978

AVG. AUCTION PRICING

LOW	HIGH	AVG
$4,850	$15,000	$9,750

2653A

YEARS MFRD	2007-2007
ENGINE	JD SERIES 220
CYLINDERS	3
CID	47.8
COOLING	LIQUID
FUEL	D
SPEEDS	VARIABLE
TRANSMISSION	HYDRO
STEERING	ZERO
MSRP	$26,681

RETAIL PRICING

YEAR	HIGH	LOW
2007	$22,680	$17,010

2720

YEARS MFRD	2008-2013
ENGINE	YANMAR 3TNV88
CYLINDERS	3
CID	100.2
PTO HP	23.5
ENGINE HP	31.4
COOLING	LIQUID
FUEL	D
SPEEDS	VARIABLE
TRANSMISSION	HYDRO
STEERING	STANDARD
BLADE CLUTCH	ELECTRIC
HYDRAULIC	YES
PTO	YES
WEIGHT	1,973 LBS.
MSRP	$18,141

OPTIONS

62" DECK
72" DECK

SERIAL NUMBERS

YEAR	BEGINNING NO.
2008	E186003-HR2
2008	H106005-H
2009	206001
2010	306001
2011	410001
2012	510001

RETAIL PRICING

YEAR	HIGH	LOW
2008	$11,845	$8,884
2009	$12,677	$9,507
2010	$13,347	$10,010
2011	$14,469	$10,852
2012	$15,036	$11,277
2013	$15,891	$11,918

3005

YEARS MFRD	2008-2013
ENGINE	YANMAR 3TNV82A
CYLINDERS	3
CID	81.2
PTO HP	23.5
ENGINE HP	27.5
COOLING	LIQUID
FUEL	D
SPEEDS	12/12
TRANSMISSION	SHUTTLE SHIFT
STEERING	STANDARD
HYDRAULIC	YES
PTO	YES
DRIVE TYPE	2WD
ROPS/CAB	ROPS
WEIGHT	1,930 LBS.
MSRP	$11,683

OPTIONS

2 HYD
4WD
60" DECK
LDR
MID PTO

SERIAL NUMBERS

YEAR	BEGINNING NO.
2008	G000100
2009	200001
2010	300001
2011	410001
2012	510001
2013	510477

RETAIL PRICING

YEAR	HIGH	LOW
2008	$8,053	$6,040
2009	$8,752	$6,564
2010	$9,468	$7,101
2011	$10,028	$7,521
2012	$10,710	$8,033
2013	$11,458	$8,593

3025D

YEARS MFRD	2019-2020
SERIES	3D SERIES
ENGINE	YANMAR 3TNV88F
CYLINDERS	3
CID	100.2
PTO HP	20
ENGINE HP	24.4
COOLING	LIQUID
FUEL	D
SPEEDS	8/8
STEERING	STANDARD
HITCH	CAT. I
DRIVE TYPE	4WD
ROPS/CAB	ROPS
WEIGHT	2,778 LBS.
MSRP	$17,023

OPTIONS

IMATCH QUICK HITCH	$306
LDR W/BKT.	$5,247

3025E

YEARS MFRD	2017-2020
ENGINE	YANMAR
CYLINDERS	3
CID	97.6
PTO HP	17.4
ENGINE HP	24.7
COOLING	LIQUID
FUEL	D
SPEEDS	VARIABLE
TRANSMISSION	HYDRO
STEERING	STANDARD
HITCH	CAT. I
DRIVE TYPE	4WD
ROPS/CAB	ROPS
WEIGHT	2,222 LBS.
MSRP	$18,330

OPTIONS

BACKHOE	$8,395
IMATCH QUICK HITCH	$306
LOADER W/BKT	$5,247

SERIAL NUMBERS

YEAR	BEGINNING NO.
2017	102206
2018	121000

RETAIL PRICING

YEAR	HIGH	LOW
2017	$12,297	$9,223
2018	$13,367	$10,372
2019	$14,435	$11,195
2020	$15,950	$12,185

AVG. AUCTION PRICING

LOW	HIGH	AVG
$13,500	$15,250	$14,583

3032E

YEARS MFRD	2009-2020
ENGINE	YANMAR 3TNV88
CYLINDERS	3
CID	97.6
PTO HP	25
ENGINE HP	31.4
COOLING	LIQUID
FUEL	D
SPEEDS	VARIABLE
TRANSMISSION	HYDRO
STEERING	STANDARD
HITCH	CAT. I
DRIVE TYPE	4WD
ROPS/CAB	ROPS
WEIGHT	2,222 LBS.
MSRP	$20,719

OPTIONS

BACKHOE	$8,395
LOADER W/BKT	$5,247

SERIAL NUMBERS

YEAR	BEGINNING NO.
2009	110001-HST/LDR
2009	140001-HST
2010	240001-HST
2010	210001-HST/LDR
2011	310001
2012	410001
2013	510001
2014	610000
2015	711402

RETAIL PRICING

YEAR	HIGH	LOW
2009	$8,105	$6,079
2010	$8,945	$6,709
2011	$9,462	$7,096
2012	$10,177	$7,633
2013	$10,948	$8,211
2014	$11,997	$8,997
2015	$13,270	$9,953
2016	$14,509	$10,881
2017	$15,508	$11,630
2018	$16,830	$12,772
2019	$18,591	$14,228
2020	$20,340	$15,682

AVG. AUCTION PRICING

LOW	HIGH	AVG
$11,750	$16,100	$13,892

3033R

YEARS MFRD	2015-2020
ENGINE	YANMAR
CYLINDERS	3
CID	100
PTO HP	24.8
ENGINE HP	32.2
COOLING	LIQUID
FUEL	D
SPEEDS	VARIABLE
TRANSMISSION	HYDRO
STEERING	STANDARD
HITCH	CAT. I
DRIVE TYPE	4WD
ROPS/CAB	ROPS
WEIGHT	2,900 LBS.
MSRP	$24,642

OPTIONS

BACKHOE	$9,946
CAB	$8,709
EHYDRO	$1,393
LOADER W/BKT	$6,143
MID PTO	$757

SERIAL NUMBERS

YEAR	BEGINNING NO.
2017	101601
2018	103230 OPN STN
2018	401150 CAB

RETAIL PRICING

YEAR	HIGH	LOW
2015	$17,741	$13,304
2016	$18,982	$14,237
2017	$20,128	$15,299
2018	$22,031	$16,634
2019	$23,360	$17,821
2020	$24,441	$18,892

3035D

YEARS MFRD	2019-2020
SERIES	3D SERIES
ENGINE	YANMAR 3TNV88C
CYLINDERS	3
CID	100.2
PTO HP	30.8
ENGINE HP	34.7
COOLING	LIQUID
FUEL	D
SPEEDS	8/8
STEERING	STANDARD
HITCH	CAT. I
DRIVE TYPE	4WD
ROPS/CAB	ROPS
WEIGHT	2,811 LBS.
MSRP	$21,008

JOHN DEERE

OPTIONS

IMATCH QUICK HITCH....... $306
LDR W/BKT............ $5,247

3038E

YEARS MFRD........ 2009-2020
ENGINE....... YANMAR 3TNV84T
CYLINDERS.................. 3
CID........................ 95.7
PTO HP..................... 30
ENGINE HP.............. 36.7
COOLING.............. LIQUID
FUEL....................... D
SPEEDS.............. VARIABLE
TRANSMISSION.......... HYDRO
STEERING........... STANDARD
HITCH.................. CAT. I
HYDRAULIC.............. YES
PTO...................... YES
DRIVE TYPE............. 4WD
ROPS/CAB............... ROPS
WEIGHT............. 2,087 LBS.
MSRP................ $23,108

OPTIONS

BACKHOE............ $8,395
IMATCH QUICK HITCH....... $306
LOADER W/BKT......... $5,247

SERIAL NUMBERS

YEAR........... BEGINNING NO.
2009.............. 140001-HST
2009.......... 110001-HST/LDR
2010.......... 210001-HST/LDR
2010.............. 240001-HST
2011.................. 310001
2012.................. 410001
2013.................. 510001
2014.................. 610000
2015.................. 711402

RETAIL PRICING

YEAR	HIGH	LOW
2009	$9,630	$7,222
2010	$10,211	$7,658
2011	$10,790	$8,093
2012	$11,501	$8,626
2013	$12,413	$9,309
2014	$14,064	$10,548
2015	$15,388	$11,541
2016	$16,519	$12,389
2017	$17,129	$13,049
2018	$18,531	$13,940
2019	$20,042	$15,244
2020	$22,003	$16,887

AVG. AUCTION PRICING

LOW	HIGH	AVG
$7,000	$13,500	$11,114

3039R

YEARS MFRD........ 2015-2020
ENGINE.............. YANMAR
CYLINDERS.................. 3
CID........................ 91
PTO HP..................... 31.6
ENGINE HP.............. 38.7
COOLING.............. LIQUID
FUEL....................... D
SPEEDS.................. 12/12
TRANSMISSION..... POWER SHIFT
STEERING........... STANDARD
HITCH.................. CAT. I
DRIVE TYPE............. 4WD
ROPS/CAB............... ROPS
WEIGHT............. 2,900 LBS.
MSRP................ $27,222

OPTIONS

BACKHOE............ $9,946
CAB................. $8,709
DLX CAB............. $9,630
EHYDRO.............. $1,393
LDR W/BKT........... $6,143
MID PTO.............. $757

SERIAL NUMBERS

YEAR........... BEGINNING NO.
2017.................. 101201
2018.......... 102201 OPN STN
2018.............. 402200 CAB

RETAIL PRICING

YEAR	HIGH	LOW
2015	$20,147	$15,110
2016	$21,284	$15,963
2017	$22,166	$16,624
2018	$24,014	$18,370
2019	$25,846	$20,064
2020	$26,939	$21,631

3043D

YEARS MFRD........ 2019-2020
SERIES.............. 3D SERIES
ENGINE...... YANMAR 3TNV86CT
CYLINDERS.................. 3
CID........................ 95.8
PTO HP..................... 36.3
ENGINE HP.............. 42.2
COOLING.............. LIQUID
FUEL....................... D
SPEEDS..................... 8/8
STEERING........... STANDARD
HITCH.................. CAT. I
DRIVE TYPE............. 4WD
ROPS/CAB............... ROPS
WEIGHT............. 2,840 LBS.
MSRP................ $24,195

OPTIONS

IMATCH QUICK HITCH....... $306
LDR W/BKT............ $5,247

3046R

YEARS MFRD........ 2015-2020
ENGINE.............. YANMAR
CYLINDERS.................. 3
CID........................ 95
PTO HP..................... 36.6
ENGINE HP.............. 45.3
COOLING.............. LIQUID
FUEL....................... D
SPEEDS.............. VARIABLE
TRANSMISSION.......... HYDRO
STEERING........... STANDARD
HITCH.................. CAT. I
DRIVE TYPE............. 4WD
ROPS/CAB............... ROPS
WEIGHT............. 2,900 LBS.
MSRP................ $31,622

OPTIONS

AIR RIDE SEAT............ $520
CAB................. $8,709
DLX CAB............. $9,630
IMATCH QUICK HITCH....... $306
LDR W/BKT........... $6,143
MID PTO.............. $757

SERIAL NUMBERS

YEAR........... BEGINNING NO.
2017.................. 100701
2018.......... 101370 OPN STN
2018.............. 402300 CAB

RETAIL PRICING

YEAR	HIGH	LOW
2015	$23,437	$18,664
2016	$25,119	$18,839
2017	$26,167	$19,626
2018	$27,769	$21,223
2019	$28,974	$22,965
2020	$31,021	$24,041

AVG. AUCTION PRICING

LOW	HIGH	AVG
$15,810	$32,640	$24,608

3120

YEARS MFRD........ 2005-2008
SERIES..... 4000 TWENTY SERIES
ENGINE.............. YANMAR
CYLINDERS.................. 3
CID........................ 91
PTO HP..................... 22
ENGINE HP.............. 29.5
COOLING.............. LIQUID
FUEL....................... D
SPEEDS.............. VARIABLE
TRANSMISSION.......... HYDRO
STEERING........... STANDARD
HITCH.................. CAT. I
HYDRAULIC.............. YES
PTO...................... YES
WEIGHT............. 2,900 LBS.
MSRP................ $17,159

OPTIONS

LDR

SERIAL NUMBERS

YEAR........... BEGINNING NO.
2005.............. 110001-H
2005.............. 116001-PR
2006.............. 220001-PR
2006.............. 210001-H
2007.............. 310001-H
2008.............. 410001-H

RETAIL PRICING

YEAR	HIGH	LOW
2005	$10,632	$7,974
2006	$11,170	$8,378
2007	$12,056	$9,042
2008	$12,761	$9,571

3203

YEARS MFRD........ 2006-2008
SERIES.............. 3000 SERIES
ENGINE......... YANMAR 3TNV84
CYLINDERS.................. 3
CID........................ 91.5
PTO HP..................... 24
ENGINE HP.............. 32
COOLING.............. LIQUID
FUEL....................... D
SPEEDS.............. VARIABLE
TRANSMISSION.......... HYDRO
STEERING........... STANDARD
HITCH.................. CAT. I
HYDRAULIC.............. YES
PTO...................... YES
DRIVE TYPE............. 4WD
ROPS/CAB............... ROPS
WEIGHT............. 2,700 LBS.
MSRP................ $15,499

OPTIONS

LDR

SERIAL NUMBERS

YEAR........... BEGINNING NO.
2006.................. 294001
2007.................. 394001
2008.................. 496001

RETAIL PRICING

YEAR	HIGH	LOW
2006	$9,289	$6,967
2007	$9,825	$7,368
2008	$10,553	$7,915

AVG. AUCTION PRICING

LOW	HIGH	AVG
$7,446	$13,260	$10,180

3225C

YEARS MFRD........ 2007-2007
SERIES.............. C SERIES
ENGINE.... JD SERIES 220 TURBO
CYLINDERS.................. 3
CID........................ 91.3
ENGINE HP.............. 32
COOLING.............. LIQUID
FUEL....................... D
SPEEDS.............. VARIABLE
TRANSMISSION.......... HYDRO
STEERING................ ZERO
BLADE CLUTCH........ ELECTRIC
WEIGHT............. 3,260 LBS.
MSRP................ $42,500

RETAIL PRICING

YEAR	HIGH	LOW
2007	$33,739	$25,304

3235C

YEARS MFRD........ 2007-2007
SERIES.............. C SERIES
ENGINE.... JD SERIES 220 TURBO
CYLINDERS.................. 3
CID........................ 91.3
ENGINE HP.............. 41
COOLING.............. LIQUID
FUEL....................... D
SPEEDS.............. VARIABLE
TRANSMISSION.......... HYDRO
STEERING................ ZERO
BLADE CLUTCH........ ELECTRIC
WEIGHT............. 3,324 LBS.
MSRP................ $46,090

RETAIL PRICING

YEAR	HIGH	LOW
2007	$35,216	$26,412

3245C

YEARS MFRD . . . 2007-2007
ENGINE . . . JD SERIES 220 TURBO
CYLINDERS . . . 3
CID . . . 91.3
ENGINE HP . . . 48.5
COOLING . . . LIQUID
FUEL . . . D
SPEEDS . . . VARIABLE
TRANSMISSION . . . HYDRO
STEERING . . . ZERO
WEIGHT . . . 3,026 LBS.
MSRP . . . $50,200

RETAIL PRICING

YEAR	HIGH	LOW
2007	$44,610	$33,457

3320

YEARS MFRD . . . 2005-2014
SERIES . . . 4000 TWENTY SERIES
ENGINE . . . YANMAR 3TNV88
CYLINDERS . . . 3
CID . . . 100
PTO HP . . . 25
ENGINE HP . . . 32.5
COOLING . . . AIR
FUEL . . . D
SPEEDS . . . 12/12
TRANSMISSION . . . SHUTTLE SHIFT
STEERING . . . STANDARD
HITCH . . . CAT. I
HYDRAULIC . . . YES
PTO . . . YES
DRIVE TYPE . . . 2WD
ROPS/CAB . . . CAB
STANDARD DECK . . . 60"
WEIGHT . . . 2,900 LBS.
MSRP . . . $21,166

OPTIONS

60" DECK
72"DECK
CAB
HYDRO
LDR

SERIAL NUMBERS

YEAR	BEGINNING NO.
2005	138001-HR
2005	139001-PRR
2005	130001-H
2005	136001-PR
2006	245001-HR
2006	240001-PR
2006	230001-H
2006	250001-PRR
2007	330001-H
2007	350001-PRR
2007	345001-HR
2007	340001-PR
2008	420001
2009	500001
2010	600001
2011	710001
2012	810001
2013	910001

RETAIL PRICING

YEAR	HIGH	LOW
2005	$11,209	$8,407
2006	$11,925	$8,944
2007	$12,620	$9,465
2008	$13,520	$10,140
2009	$14,377	$10,783
2010	$15,298	$11,473
2011	$16,188	$12,141
2012	$17,362	$13,022
2013	$17,928	$13,446
2014	$19,707	$14,781

AVG. AUCTION PRICING

LOW	HIGH	AVG
$5,600	$12,400	$9,350

3520

YEARS MFRD . . . 2005-2014
SERIES . . . 4000 TWENTY SERIES
ENGINE . YANMAR 3TNV84T TURBO
CYLINDERS . . . 3
CID . . . 91.5
PTO HP . . . 30
ENGINE HP . . . 37
COOLING . . . LIQUID
FUEL . . . D
SPEEDS . . . 12/12
TRANSMISSION . . . SHUTTLE SHIFT
STEERING . . . STANDARD
HITCH . . . CAT. I
HYDRAULIC . . . YES
PTO . . . YES
DRIVE TYPE . . . 4WD
ROPS/CAB . . . ROPS
WEIGHT . . . 2,900 LBS.
MSRP . . . $23,395

OPTIONS

60"DECK
72"DECK
CAB
HYDRO
LDR
MID PTO

SERIAL NUMBERS

YEAR	BEGINNING NO.
2005	150001-H
2005	159001-PRR
2005	158001-HR
2005	156001-PR
2006	275001-PRR
2006	270001-HR
2006	266001-PR
2006	258001-H
2007	370001-HR
2007	375001-PRR
2007	366001-PR
2007	358001-H
2008	450001
2009	512001
2010	612001
2011	710001
2012	810001
2013	910001

RETAIL PRICING

YEAR	HIGH	LOW
2005	$12,351	$9,263
2006	$13,173	$9,880
2007	$14,041	$10,531
2008	$15,097	$11,323
2009	$15,936	$11,952
2010	$16,768	$12,576
2011	$18,052	$13,539
2012	$18,679	$14,009
2013	$19,703	$14,778
2014	$21,702	$16,276

AVG. AUCTION PRICING

LOW	HIGH	AVG
$7,000	$20,000	$14,375

3720

YEARS MFRD . . . 2005-2014
SERIES . . . 4000 TWENTY SERIES
ENGINE YANMAR 3TNV84HT TURBO
CYLINDERS . . . 3
CID . . . 91.5
PTO HP . . . 35
ENGINE HP . . . 44
COOLING . . . AIR
FUEL . . . D
SPEEDS . . . VARIABLE
TRANSMISSION . . . HYDRO
STEERING . . . STANDARD
HITCH . . . CAT. I
HYDRAULIC . . . YES
PTO . . . YES
DRIVE TYPE . . . 4WD
ROPS/CAB . . . ROPS
WEIGHT . . . 2,900 LBS.
MSRP . . . $27,088

OPTIONS

60" DECK
72" DECK
CAB
LDR
MID PTO

SERIAL NUMBERS

YEAR	BEGINNING NO.
2005	170001-H
2005	178001-HR
2006	290001-HR
2006	280001-H
2007	390001-HR
2007	380001-H
2008	480001
2009	522001
2010	622001
2011	710001
2012	810001
2013	910001

RETAIL PRICING

YEAR	HIGH	LOW
2005	$15,524	$11,643
2006	$16,503	$12,377
2007	$17,344	$13,008
2008	$18,219	$13,664
2009	$19,369	$14,527
2010	$20,362	$15,272
2011	$21,530	$16,148
2012	$22,018	$16,513
2013	$23,105	$17,329
2014	$25,779	$19,335

AVG. AUCTION PRICING

LOW	HIGH	AVG
$15,045	$28,560	$20,166

4005

YEARS MFRD . . . 2008-2012
ENGINE . . . YANMAR 4TNV84
CYLINDERS . . . 4
CID . . . 121.7
PTO HP . . . 35
ENGINE HP . . . 41.5
COOLING . . . LIQUID
FUEL . . . D
SPEEDS . . . 9/3
TRANSMISSION . . . GEAR
STEERING . . . STANDARD
DRIVE TYPE . . . 2WD
ROPS/CAB . . . ROPS
WEIGHT . . . 2,954 LBS.
MSRP . . . $16,215

OPTIONS

2 HYD
4WD
CANOPY
LDR

SERIAL NUMBERS

YEAR	BEGINNING NO.
2008	G000100
2009	210001
2010	310001
2011	410001
2012	510001

RETAIL PRICING

YEAR	HIGH	LOW
2008	$11,559	$8,669
2009	$12,306	$9,230
2010	$13,084	$9,813
2011	$13,838	$10,379
2012	$14,763	$11,073

4010

YEARS MFRD . . . 2002-2005
SERIES . . . 4000 TEN SERIES
ENGINE . . . YANMAR 3TNE68
CYLINDERS . . . 3
CID . . . 47.84
PTO HP . . . 14
ENGINE HP . . . 18.5
COOLING . . . LIQUID
FUEL . . . D
SPEEDS . . . VARIABLE
TRANSMISSION . . . HYDRO
STEERING . . . STANDARD
HITCH . . . CAT. I
BLADE CLUTCH . . . ELECTRIC
HYDRAULIC . . . YES
PTO . . . YES
DRIVE TYPE . . . 4WD
ROPS/CAB . . . ROPS
WEIGHT . . . 1,420 LBS.
MSRP . . . $12,202

OPTIONS

60" DECK
LDR

SERIAL NUMBERS

YEAR	BEGINNING NO.
2002	100001
2003	210001
2004	310001
2005	401001

JOHN DEERE

RETAIL PRICING

YEAR	HIGH	LOW
2002	$5,553	$4,165
2003	$5,995	$4,496
2004	$6,435	$4,826
2005	$6,942	$5,207

AVG. AUCTION PRICING

LOW	HIGH	AVG
$5,900	$7,400	$6,513

4044M

YEARS MFRD	2015-2020
ENGINE	YANMAR
CYLINDERS	4
CID	133.5
PTO HP	33
ENGINE HP	43.1
COOLING	LIQUID
FUEL	D
SPEEDS	12/12
TRANSMISSION	SHUTTLE SHIFT
STEERING	STANDARD
HITCH	CAT. I
DRIVE TYPE	4WD
ROPS/CAB	ROPS
WEIGHT	3,770 LBS.
MSRP	$28,443

OPTIONS

BACKHOE	$11,423
EHYDRO	$1,162
IMATCH QUICK HITCH	$306
LDR W/BKT	$6,291

SERIAL NUMBERS

YEAR	BEGINNING NO.
2017	101401
2018	103600

RETAIL PRICING

YEAR	HIGH	LOW
2015	$17,808	$13,356
2016	$19,379	$14,534
2017	$20,583	$15,438
2018	$22,447	$17,313
2019	$24,272	$18,467
2020	$26,938	$20,526

4044R

YEARS MFRD	2015-2020
ENGINE	YANMAR
CYLINDERS	4
CID	133.5
PTO HP	34.5
ENGINE HP	43.1
COOLING	LIQUID
FUEL	D
SPEEDS	VARIABLE
TRANSMISSION	HYDRO
STEERING	STANDARD
HITCH	CAT. I
DRIVE TYPE	4WD
ROPS/CAB	ROPS
WEIGHT	3,770 LBS.
MSRP	$32,648

OPTIONS

12/12 PR	$-1,162
CAB	$8,709
IMATCH QUICK HITCH	$306
LOADER W/BKT	$7,024

SERIAL NUMBERS

YEAR	BEGINNING NO.
2017	100551
2018	101000 OPN STN
2018	400800 CAB

RETAIL PRICING

YEAR	HIGH	LOW
2015	$22,589	$17,196
2016	$23,934	$17,951
2017	$25,647	$19,236
2018	$27,782	$21,426
2019	$29,723	$22,722
2020	$32,245	$24,570

4052M

YEARS MFRD	2015-2020
ENGINE	YANMAR
CYLINDERS	4
CID	127.6
PTO HP	39.9
ENGINE HP	51.5
FUEL	D
SPEEDS	12/12
TRANSMISSION	SHUTTLE SHIFT
STEERING	STANDARD
HITCH	CAT. I
DRIVE TYPE	4WD
ROPS/CAB	ROPS
WEIGHT	3,770 LBS.
MSRP	$31,396

OPTIONS

BACKHOE	$11,423
EHYDRO	$1,162
IMATCH QUICK HITCH	$306
LDR W/BKT	$6,291

SERIAL NUMBERS

YEAR	BEGINNING NO.
2017	100901
2018	102280

RETAIL PRICING

YEAR	HIGH	LOW
2015	$21,080	$15,810
2016	$22,244	$16,683
2017	$23,671	$17,753
2018	$25,682	$19,436
2019	$27,664	$21,083
2020	$30,703	$23,457

AVG. AUCTION PRICING

LOW	HIGH	AVG
$18,360	$21,420	$20,400

4052M HD

YEARS MFRD	2020-2020
ENGINE	YANMAR 4TNV86CT-MJT
CYLINDERS	4
CID	127.6
PTO HP	40.9
ENGINE HP	51.5
COOLING	LIQUID
FUEL	D
SPEEDS	VARIABLE
TRANSMISSION	HYDRO
STEERING	STANDARD
ROPS/CAB	ROPS
WEIGHT	4,255 LBS.
MSRP	$37,096

OPTIONS

LDR W/BKT	$7,452

4052R

YEARS MFRD	2015-2020
ENGINE	YANMAR
CYLINDERS	4
CID	127.6
PTO HP	39.9
ENGINE HP	51.5
FUEL	D
SPEEDS	VARIABLE
TRANSMISSION	HYDRO
STEERING	STANDARD
HITCH	CAT. I
DRIVE TYPE	4WD
ROPS/CAB	ROPS
MSRP	$35,630

OPTIONS

12/12 PR	$-1,162
CAB	$8,709
IMATCH QUICK HITCH	$306
LDR W/BKT	$7,024

SERIAL NUMBERS

YEAR	BEGINNING NO.
2017	101001
2018	101800 OPEN
2018	401750 CAB

RETAIL PRICING

YEAR	HIGH	LOW
2015	$24,824	$18,618
2016	$26,566	$19,924
2017	$28,074	$21,056
2018	$29,214	$22,036
2019	$31,628	$23,566
2020	$34,668	$26,258

4066M

YEARS MFRD	2015-2020
ENGINE	YANMAR
CYLINDERS	4
CID	127.6
PTO HP	54
ENGINE HP	65.9
COOLING	LIQUID
FUEL	G
SPEEDS	12/12
TRANSMISSION	SHUTTLE SHIFT
STEERING	STANDARD
HITCH	CAT. I
DRIVE TYPE	4WD
ROPS/CAB	ROPS
WEIGHT	3,770 LBS.
MSRP	$37,152

OPTIONS

BACKHOE	$11,423
EHYDRO	$1,162
IMATCH QUICK HITCH	$306
LDR W/BKT	$6,291

SERIAL NUMBERS

YEAR	BEGINNING NO.
2017	100651
2018	101380

RETAIL PRICING

YEAR	HIGH	LOW
2015	$23,118	$17,338
2016	$24,987	$18,738
2017	$26,077	$19,558
2018	$27,845	$21,142
2019	$29,562	$22,313
2020	$32,564	$24,846

4066M HD

YEARS MFRD	2020-2020
ENGINE	YANMAR 4TNV86CT-MJT
CYLINDERS	4
CID	127.6
PTO HP	52
ENGINE HP	65.9
COOLING	LIQUID
FUEL	D
SPEEDS	VARIABLE
TRANSMISSION	HYDRO
STEERING	STANDARD
ROPS/CAB	ROPS
WEIGHT	4,255 LBS.
MSRP	$42,881

OPTIONS

LDR W/BKT	$7,452

4066R

YEARS MFRD	2015-2020
ENGINE	YANMAR
CYLINDERS	4
CID	127.6
PTO HP	52
ENGINE HP	65.9
COOLING	LIQUID
FUEL	D
SPEEDS	VARIABLE
TRANSMISSION	HYDRO
STEERING	STANDARD
HITCH	CAT. I
DRIVE TYPE	4WD
ROPS/CAB	ROPS
MSRP	$41,415

OPTIONS

12/12 PR	$-1,162
BACKHOE	$11,423
CAB	$9,630
IMATCH QUICK HITCH	$306
LDR W/BKT	$7,024

SERIAL NUMBERS

YEAR	BEGINNING NO.
2017	100901
2018	101450 OPEN
2018	403450 CAB

RETAIL PRICING

YEAR	HIGH	LOW
2015	$29,598	$22,199
2016	$31,341	$23,505
2017	$32,645	$24,483
2018	$34,516	$26,031
2019	$36,408	$27,280
2020	$39,921	$30,219

4100

YEARS MFRD 1998-2001
ENGINE . . . . YANMAR
CYLINDERS. 3
CID 61.4
PTO HP 17
ENGINE HP 20
COOLING . . . . LIQUID
FUEL . . . . D
SPEEDS 8/4
TRANSMISSION . . . . GEAR
STEERING. . . . . STANDARD
HITCH . . . . CAT. I
BLADE CLUTCH . . . . MANUAL
HYDRAULIC . . . . YES
PTO . . . . YES
DRIVE TYPE 4WD
ROPS/CAB . . . . ROPS
WEIGHT . . . . 1,710 LBS.
MSRP. $12,500

OPTIONS

2 HYD
54"DECK
60"DECK
HYDRO
LDR

SERIAL NUMBERS

RH SIDE IMMEDIATELY UP FROM FRONT AXLE ON MAIN FRAME

YEAR	BEGINNING NO.
1998	110000
1998	LV4100H110134
1998	LV4100G110031
1999	220001
2000	310001
2001	410001

RETAIL PRICING

YEAR	HIGH	LOW
1998	$3,976	$2,982
1999	$4,180	$3,135
2000	$4,791	$3,593
2001	$5,007	$3,755

AVG. AUCTION PRICING

LOW	HIGH	AVG
$3,500	$7,900	$5,680

4100 NARROW

YEARS MFRD 2001-2003
ENGINE . . . . YANMAR
CYLINDERS. 3
CID 61.4
PTO HP 16
ENGINE HP 20
COOLING . . . . LIQUID
FUEL . . . . D
SPEEDS 8/2
TRANSMISSION . . . . GEAR
STEERING. . . . . STANDARD
HITCH . . . . CAT. I
BLADE CLUTCH . . . . MANUAL
HYDRAULIC . . . . YES
PTO . . . . YES
DRIVE TYPE 2WD
ROPS/CAB . . . . ROPS
WEIGHT . . . . 1,700 LBS.
MSRP. $13,850

RETAIL PRICING

YEAR	HIGH	LOW
2001	$9,811	$7,359
2002	$10,683	$8,013
2003	$11,736	$8,802

4105

YEARS MFRD 2008-2016
SERIES. . . . . 4000 SERIES
ENGINE . . . . YANMAR 3TNV84T-KJT
CYLINDERS. 3
CID 91.5
PTO HP 32.5
ENGINE HP 40.2
COOLING . . . . LIQUID
FUEL . . . . D
SPEEDS . . . . VARIABLE
TRANSMISSION . . . . HYDRO
STEERING. . . . . STANDARD
HITCH . . . . CAT. I
HYDRAULIC . . . . YES
PTO . . . . YES
DRIVE TYPE 4WD
ROPS/CAB . . . . ROPS
WEIGHT . . . . 2,987 LBS.
MSRP. $23,634

OPTIONS

CANOPY
LDR

SERIAL NUMBERS

YEAR	BEGINNING NO.
2008	H100001
2009	210001
2010	310001
2011	410001
2012	510001
2013	610001
2014	710001
2015	810001

RETAIL PRICING

YEAR	HIGH	LOW
2008	$12,040	$9,030
2009	$12,831	$9,623
2010	$13,827	$10,370
2011	$14,981	$11,236
2012	$16,146	$12,109
2013	$17,484	$13,113
2014	$18,860	$14,145
2015	$20,613	$15,460
2016	$22,471	$16,853

AVG. AUCTION PRICING

LOW	HIGH	AVG
$10,098	$18,870	$14,873

4110

YEARS MFRD 2002-2006
SERIES. . . . . 4000 TEN SERIES
ENGINE . . . . YANMAR 3YNR74
CYLINDERS. 3
CID 91
PTO HP 17
ENGINE HP 20
COOLING . . . . LIQUID
FUEL . . . . D
SPEEDS 8/4
TRANSMISSION . . . . GEAR
STEERING. . . . . STANDARD
HITCH . . . . CAT. I
BLADE CLUTCH . . . . ELECTRIC
HYDRAULIC . . . . YES
PTO . . . . YES
DRIVE TYPE 4WD
ROPS/CAB . . . . ROPS
WEIGHT . . . . 1,517 LBS.
MSRP. $15,042

OPTIONS

54" DECK
60"DECK
HYDRO
LDR

SERIAL NUMBERS

YEAR	BEGINNING NO.
2002	113501G
2002	110001H
2003	210001
2004	310001
2005	410001
2006	510001

RETAIL PRICING

YEAR	HIGH	LOW
2002	$6,311	$4,733
2003	$6,866	$5,149
2004	$7,353	$5,515
2005	$7,893	$5,920
2006	$8,500	$6,375

AVG. AUCTION PRICING

LOW	HIGH	AVG
$7,430	$9,287	$8,413

4115

YEARS MFRD 2002-2005
SERIES. . . . . 4000 TEN SERIES
ENGINE . . . . YANMAR 3TNE78A
CYLINDERS. 3
CID 73.22
PTO HP 19.9
ENGINE HP 24
COOLING . . . . LIQUID
FUEL . . . . D
SPEEDS . . . . VARIABLE
TRANSMISSION . . . . HYDRO
STEERING. . . . . STANDARD
HITCH . . . . CAT. I
BLADE CLUTCH . . . . ELECTRIC
HYDRAULIC . . . . YES
PTO . . . . YES
DRIVE TYPE 4WD
ROPS/CAB . . . . ROPS
WEIGHT . . . . 1,771 LBS.
MSRP. $17,492

OPTIONS

60" DECK
LDR

SERIAL NUMBERS

YEAR	BEGINNING NO.
2002	H115001
2003	210001
2004	310001
2005	421001

RETAIL PRICING

YEAR	HIGH	LOW
2002	$7,783	$5,837
2003	$8,277	$6,208
2004	$8,953	$6,714
2005	$9,599	$7,199

4120

YEARS MFRD 2005-2014
SERIES. . . . . 4000 TWENTY SERIES
ENGINE . . . . JD 4024T TURBO
CYLINDERS. 4
CID 148.9
PTO HP 35.5
ENGINE HP 43
FUEL . . . . D
SPEEDS 12/12
TRANSMISSION . . . SHUTTLE SHIFT
STEERING. . . . . STANDARD
HITCH . . . . CAT. I
DRIVE TYPE 4WD
ROPS/CAB . . . . ROPS
WEIGHT . . . . 3,700 LBS.
MSRP. $28,880

OPTIONS

72" DECK
HYDRO
LDR
MID PTO

SERIAL NUMBERS

YEAR	BEGINNING NO.
2005	P122001-POWER REV
2005	H120101-HYDRO
2006	317001-PR
2006	310001-H
2007	417001-PR
2007	410001-H
2008	510001
2009	610001
2010	710001
2011	810001
2012	910001
2013	916001

RETAIL PRICING

YEAR	HIGH	LOW
2005	$15,091	$11,318
2006	$16,276	$12,207
2007	$17,440	$13,080
2008	$18,944	$14,208
2009	$20,031	$15,023
2010	$21,315	$15,986
2011	$23,006	$17,255
2012	$24,542	$18,407
2013	$26,136	$19,602
2014	$28,502	$21,376

AVG. AUCTION PRICING

LOW	HIGH	AVG
$12,240	$16,830	$14,395

4200

YEARS MFRD 1998-2001
ENGINE . . . . YANMAR
CYLINDERS. 3
CID 73.5
PTO HP 21.5
ENGINE HP 26.3
COOLING . . . . LIQUID
FUEL . . . . D
SPEEDS 9/3
TRANSMISSION . . . . GEAR

JOHN DEERE

STEERING............STANDARD
HITCH..................CAT. I
BLADE CLUTCH........MANUAL
PTO.....................YES
DRIVE TYPE..............2WD
ROPS/CAB................ROPS
WEIGHT............2,375 LBS.
MSRP................$13,575

OPTIONS

2 HYD
4WD
60" DECK
HYDRO
LDR
MID PTO

SERIAL NUMBERS

YEAR	BEGINNING NO.
1998	120000
1999	220001
2000	320001
2001	420001

RETAIL PRICING

YEAR	HIGH	LOW
1998	$4,304	$3,228
1999	$4,889	$3,667
2000	$5,320	$3,990
2001	$5,793	$4,344

AVG. AUCTION PRICING

LOW	HIGH	AVG
$6,000	$11,000	$8,225

4210

YEARS MFRD........2002-2004
SERIES.........4000 TEN SERIES
ENGINE.......YANMAR 3TNE82A
CYLINDERS..................3
CID...................81.16
PTO HP....................23
ENGINE HP.................28
COOLING...............LIQUID
FUEL.......................D
SPEEDS.............VARIABLE
TRANSMISSION..........HYDRO
STEERING............STANDARD
HITCH..................CAT. I
BLADE CLUTCH........ELECTRIC
HYDRAULIC.................YES
PTO.......................YES
DRIVE TYPE................4WD
ROPS/CAB..................ROPS
WEIGHT............2,375 LBS.
MSRP................$18,593

OPTIONS

60" DECK
9/3 SYNC SHIFT
LDR
MID PTO

SERIAL NUMBERS

YEAR	BEGINNING NO.
2002	128001-S
2002	120001-H
2003	220001-H
2003	228001-S
2004	320001-H

RETAIL PRICING

YEAR	HIGH	LOW
2002	$7,559	$5,669
2003	$8,222	$6,167
2004	$8,838	$6,629

AVG. AUCTION PRICING

LOW	HIGH	AVG
$5,354	$12,019	$9,260

4300

YEARS MFRD........1998-2001
ENGINE...............YANMAR
CYLINDERS..................3
CID.....................91.3
PTO HP....................27
ENGINE HP.................32
COOLING...............LIQUID
FUEL.......................D
SPEEDS...................9/3
TRANSMISSION............GEAR
STEERING............STANDARD
HITCH..................CAT. I
BLADE CLUTCH........MANUAL
HYDRAULIC.................YES
PTO.......................YES
DRIVE TYPE................2WD
ROPS/CAB..................ROPS
WEIGHT............2,600 LBS.
MSRP................$15,050

OPTIONS

2 HYD
4WD
60" DECK
72" DECK
HYDRO
LDR
MID PTO

SERIAL NUMBERS

YEAR	BEGINNING NO.
1999	H130001-HYDRO
1999	S130001-SYNC REV
1999	C130001-GEAR
1999	E239001-EXPORT
2000	H330001-HYDRO
2000	C335001-SYNC SHIFT
2000	S336001-SYNC REV
2000	E339501-EXPORT
2001	E430001-EXPORT
2001	S436001-SYNC REV
2001	C435001-SYNC SHIFT
2001	H430001-HYDRO

RETAIL PRICING

YEAR	HIGH	LOW
1998	$5,114	$3,836
1999	$5,618	$4,214
2000	$6,256	$4,692
2001	$6,825	$5,119

AVG. AUCTION PRICING

LOW	HIGH	AVG
$5,500	$8,500	$7,850

4310

YEARS MFRD........2002-2004
SERIES.........4000 TEN SERIES
ENGINE........YANMAR 3TNE84
CYLINDERS..................3
CID.......................92
PTO HP....................27
ENGINE HP.................32
COOLING...............LIQUID
FUEL.......................D
SPEEDS...................9/3
TRANSMISSION............GEAR
STEERING............STANDARD
HITCH..................CAT. I
BLADE CLUTCH........ELECTRIC
HYDRAULIC.................YES
PTO.......................YES
DRIVE TYPE................4WD
ROPS/CAB..................ROPS
WEIGHT............2,610 LBS.
MSRP................$18,739

OPTIONS

60" DECK
72" DECK
HYDRO
LDR
MID PTO

SERIAL NUMBERS

YEAR	BEGINNING NO.
2002	P135001
2002	E139001
2002	H130001
2003	S238001
2003	E239001
2003	P235001
2003	H230001
2004	R339001
2004	P335001
2004	H330001

RETAIL PRICING

YEAR	HIGH	LOW
2002	$7,975	$5,982
2003	$8,567	$6,425
2004	$9,265	$6,948

AVG. AUCTION PRICING

LOW	HIGH	AVG
$5,500	$15,500	$9,970

4320

YEARS MFRD........2005-2014
SERIES.....4000 TWENTY SERIES
ENGINE..............JD 4024T
CYLINDERS..................4
CID....................148.9
PTO HP....................43
ENGINE HP.................48
COOLING..................AIR
FUEL.......................D
SPEEDS.................12/12
TRANSMISSION...SHUTTLE SHIFT
STEERING............STANDARD
HITCH..................CAT. I
HYDRAULIC.................YES
PTO.......................YES
DRIVE TYPE................4WD
ROPS/CAB..................ROPS
WEIGHT............3,700 LBS.
MSRP................$29,700

OPTIONS

72" DECK
CAB
HYDRO
LDR
MID PTO

SERIAL NUMBERS

YEAR	BEGINNING NO.
2005	230001-H
2005	235001-PR
2005	239001-PRR
2005	238001-HR
2006	339001-PRR
2006	338001-HR
2006	330001-PR
2006	320001-H
2007	438001-HR
2007	439001-PRR
2007	430001-PR
2007	420001-H
2008	520001
2009	620001
2010	720001
2011	810001
2012	910001
2013	916001

RETAIL PRICING

YEAR	HIGH	LOW
2005	$14,515	$10,886
2006	$15,903	$11,927
2007	$16,690	$12,518
2008	$17,937	$13,453
2009	$19,144	$14,358
2010	$20,520	$15,390
2011	$21,882	$16,412
2012	$23,547	$17,660
2013	$24,957	$18,718
2014	$27,512	$20,634

AVG. AUCTION PRICING

LOW	HIGH	AVG
$8,500	$23,500	$13,567

4400

YEARS MFRD........1998-2001
ENGINE...............YANMAR
CYLINDERS..................3
CID......................101
PTO HP....................30
ENGINE HP...............35.7
COOLING...............LIQUID
FUEL.......................D
SPEEDS.................12/12
TRANSMISSION...SHUTTLE SHIFT
STEERING............STANDARD
HITCH..................CAT. I
BLADE CLUTCH........MANUAL
PTO.......................YES
DRIVE TYPE................4WD
ROPS/CAB..................ROPS
WEIGHT............2,850 LBS.
MSRP................$18,775

OPTIONS

2 HYD
60" DECK
72" DECK
HYDRO
LDR
MID PTO

SERIAL NUMBERS

RH SIDE IMMEDIATELY UP FROM FRONT AXLE ON MAIN FRAME

YEAR	BEGINNING NO.
1999	S140001-SYNC
1999	H140001-HYDRO
2000	S336001-SYNC
2000	H340001-HYDRO
2001	H440001-HYDRO
2001	S445001-SYNC

RETAIL PRICING

YEAR	HIGH	LOW
1998	$6,918	$5,188
1999	$7,370	$5,527
2000	$7,872	$5,904
2001	$8,627	$6,470

AVG. AUCTION PRICING

LOW	HIGH	AVG
$7,648	$12,019	$10,096

4410

YEARS MFRD	2002-2004
SERIES	4000 TEN SERIES
ENGINE	YANMAR 3TNE88
CYLINDERS	3
CID	101
PTO HP	29
ENGINE HP	35
COOLING	LIQUID
FUEL	D
SPEEDS	12/12
TRANSMISSION	SHUTTLE SHIFT
STEERING	STANDARD
HITCH	CAT. I
BLADE CLUTCH	ELECTRIC
HYDRAULIC	YES
PTO	YES
DRIVE TYPE	4WD
ROPS/CAB	ROPS
WEIGHT	2,830 LBS.
MSRP	$20,463

OPTIONS

60" DECK
72" DECK
HYDRO
LDR
MID PTO

SERIAL NUMBERS

YEAR	BEGINNING NO.
2002	145001-P
2002	140001-H
2002	149001-R
2003	240001-H
2003	245001-P
2003	249001-R
2004	340001-H
2004	345001-P
2004	349001-R

RETAIL PRICING

YEAR	HIGH	LOW
2002	$9,527	$7,145
2003	$10,349	$7,762
2004	$10,806	$8,104

AVG. AUCTION PRICING

LOW	HIGH	AVG
$10,107	$15,624	$12,328

4500

YEARS MFRD	1998-2001
ENGINE	YANMAR
CYLINDERS	4
CID	121.7
PTO HP	33
ENGINE HP	39
COOLING	LIQUID
FUEL	D
SPEEDS	9/3
TRANSMISSION	GEAR
STEERING	STANDARD
HITCH	CAT. I
BLADE CLUTCH	MANUAL
HYDRAULIC	YES
PTO	YES
DRIVE TYPE	2WD
ROPS/CAB	ROPS
WEIGHT	3,150 LBS.
MSRP	$17,325

OPTIONS

2 HYD
4WD
72" DECK
LDR
MID PTO

SERIAL NUMBERS

YEAR	BEGINNING NO.
1998	150000
1999	250001
2000	350001
2001	450001

RETAIL PRICING

YEAR	HIGH	LOW
1998	$6,713	$5,034
1999	$7,308	$5,481
2000	$7,754	$5,816
2001	$8,370	$6,278

AVG. AUCTION PRICING

LOW	HIGH	AVG
$4,182	$13,005	$8,122

4510

YEARS MFRD	2002-2004
SERIES	4000 TEN SERIES
ENGINE	YANMAR 4TNE84
CYLINDERS	4
CID	121
PTO HP	33
ENGINE HP	39
COOLING	LIQUID
FUEL	D
SPEEDS	9/3
TRANSMISSION	GEAR
STEERING	STANDARD
HITCH	CAT. I
BLADE CLUTCH	ELECTRIC
HYDRAULIC	YES
PTO	YES
DRIVE TYPE	2WD
ROPS/CAB	ROPS
WEIGHT	3,420 LBS.
MSRP	$22,164

OPTIONS

4WD
72" DECK
LDR
MID PTO

SERIAL NUMBERS

YEAR	BEGINNING NO.
2002	S154001
2002	P155001
2003	C254001
2003	P255001
2004	P355001

RETAIL PRICING

YEAR	HIGH	LOW
2002	$12,030	$9,022
2003	$12,840	$9,630
2004	$13,922	$10,441

4520

YEARS MFRD	2005-2014
SERIES	4000 TWENTY SERIES
ENGINE	JD 4024T
CYLINDERS	4
CID	148.9
PTO HP	45
ENGINE HP	53
COOLING	AIR
FUEL	D
SPEEDS	9/3-12/12
TRANSMISSION	GEAR
STEERING	STANDARD
HITCH	CAT. I
HYDRAULIC	YES
PTO	YES
DRIVE TYPE	4WD
ROPS/CAB	ROPS
WEIGHT	3,700 LBS.
MSRP	$31,667

OPTIONS

72" DECK
CAB
HYDRO
LDR
MID PTO

SERIAL NUMBERS

YEAR	BEGINNING NO.
2005	250001-H
2005	255001-PR
2005	259001-PRR
2005	258001-HR
2006	360001-PRR
2006	347001-PR
2006	358001-HR
2006	340001-H
2007	458001-HR
2007	460001-PRR
2007	447001-PR
2007	440001-H
2008	550001
2009	650001
2010	750001
2011	810001
2012	910001
2013	916001

RETAIL PRICING

YEAR	HIGH	LOW
2005	$16,053	$12,040
2006	$17,225	$12,919
2007	$18,273	$13,705
2008	$19,472	$14,604
2009	$20,726	$15,545
2010	$22,101	$16,576
2011	$23,767	$17,825
2012	$25,183	$18,887
2013	$26,938	$20,204
2014	$30,365	$22,774

AVG. AUCTION PRICING

LOW	HIGH	AVG
$7,100	$15,250	$11,117

4600

YEARS MFRD	1998-2001
ENGINE	YANMAR
CYLINDERS	4
CID	121
PTO HP	36
ENGINE HP	43
COOLING	LIQUID
FUEL	D
SPEEDS	9/3
TRANSMISSION	GEAR
STEERING	STANDARD
HITCH	CAT. I
BLADE CLUTCH	MANUAL
HYDRAULIC	YES
PTO	YES
DRIVE TYPE	2WD
ROPS/CAB	ROPS
WEIGHT	3,150 LBS.
MSRP	$18,725

OPTIONS

2 HYD
4WD
72" DECK
HYDRO
LDR
MID PTO

SERIAL NUMBERS

YEAR	BEGINNING NO.
1998	160000
1999	260001
2000	360001
2001	460001

RETAIL PRICING

YEAR	HIGH	LOW
1998	$7,062	$5,297
1999	$7,549	$5,662
2000	$8,174	$6,131
2001	$9,017	$6,763

AVG. AUCTION PRICING

LOW	HIGH	AVG
$5,000	$11,000	$8,333

4610

YEARS MFRD	2002-2004
SERIES	4000 TEN SERIES
ENGINE	YANMAR 4TNE84
CYLINDERS	4
CID	121
PTO HP	37
ENGINE HP	44
COOLING	LIQUID
FUEL	D
SPEEDS	12/12
TRANSMISSION	SHUTTLE SHIFT
STEERING	STANDARD
HITCH	CAT. I
BLADE CLUTCH	ELECTRIC

HYDRAULIC . . . . YES
PTO . . . . YES
DRIVE TYPE 4WD
ROPS/CAB . . . . ROPS
WEIGHT . . . . 3,425 LBS.
MSRP $23,649

OPTIONS

4WD
72" DECK
9/3 SYNC SHIFT
HYDRO
LDR
MID PTO

SERIAL NUMBERS

YEAR	BEGINNING NO.
2002	S164001-SYNC SHIFT
2002	H160001-HYDRO
2002	P165001-POWER REV
2003	P265001-POWER REV
2003	E269001-EXPORT
2003	H260001-HYDRO
2003	S264001-SYNC SHIFT
2004	E369001-EXPORT
2004	H360001-HYDRO
2004	P365001-POWER REV

RETAIL PRICING

YEAR	HIGH	LOW
2002	$11,969	$8,977
2003	$12,802	$9,602
2004	$13,817	$10,363

4700

YEARS MFRD 2000-2001
ENGINE . . . . YANMAR
CYLINDERS 4
CID 134
PTO HP 41.5
ENGINE HP 48
COOLING . . . . LIQUID
FUEL . . . . D
SPEEDS 12/12-24/24
TRANSMISSION . . . . . POWER SHIFT
STEERING . . . . STANDARD
HITCH . . . . CAT. I
BLADE CLUTCH . . . . MANUAL
HYDRAULIC . . . . YES
PTO . . . . YES
DRIVE TYPE 4WD
ROPS/CAB . . . . ROPS
WEIGHT . . . . 3,360 LBS.
MSRP $23,800

OPTIONS

2 HYD
72" DECK
HYDRO
LDR

SERIAL NUMBERS

YEAR	BEGINNING NO.
2000	P170001-POWER REV
2000	H175001-HYDRO
2000	E179001-EXPORT
2001	H270001-HYDRO
2001	E279001-EXPORT
2001	P275001-POWER REV

RETAIL PRICING

YEAR	HIGH	LOW
2000	$11,696	$8,772
2001	$12,495	$9,371

4710

YEARS MFRD 2002-2004
SERIES . . . . 4000 TEN SERIES
ENGINE . . . . YANMAR 4TNE88
CYLINDERS 4
CID 133.6
PTO HP 40
ENGINE HP 48
COOLING . . . . LIQUID
FUEL . . . . D
SPEEDS 12/12
TRANSMISSION . . . . HYDRO
STEERING . . . . STANDARD
HITCH . . . . CAT. I
HYDRAULIC . . . . YES
PTO . . . . YES
DRIVE TYPE 4WD
ROPS/CAB . . . . ROPS
WEIGHT . . . . 3,467 LBS.
MSRP $25,409

OPTIONS

72" DECK
HYDRO
LDR

SERIAL NUMBERS

YEAR	BEGINNING NO.
2002	H170001
2002	P175001
2002	R179001
2003	H270001
2003	P275001
2003	R279001
2004	H370001
2004	P375001
2004	R379001

RETAIL PRICING

YEAR	HIGH	LOW
2002	$13,350	$10,012
2003	$14,402	$10,802
2004	$15,452	$11,589

AVG. AUCTION PRICING

LOW	HIGH	AVG
$11,016	$17,340	$14,382

4720

YEARS MFRD 2005-2014
SERIES . . . . . 4000 TWENTY SERIES
ENGINE . . . . JD 4024T TURBO
CYLINDERS 4
CID 148.9
PTO HP 51
ENGINE HP 58
COOLING . . . . LIQUID
FUEL . . . . D
SPEEDS . . . . VARIABLE
TRANSMISSION . . . . HYDRO
STEERING . . . . STANDARD
HITCH . . . . CAT. I
HYDRAULIC . . . . YES
PTO . . . . YES
DRIVE TYPE 4WD
ROPS/CAB . . . . ROPS
WEIGHT . . . . 3,700 LBS.
MSRP $35,633

OPTIONS

72" DECK
CAB
LDR
MID PTO

SERIAL NUMBERS

YEAR	BEGINNING NO.
2005	270001
2006	370001
2007	480001-HR
2007	470001-H
2008	570001-H
2008	580001-HR
2009	670001-H
2009	680001-HR
2010	770001-H
2010	780001-HR
2011	810001
2012	910001
2013	916001

RETAIL PRICING

YEAR	HIGH	LOW
2005	$18,224	$13,668
2006	$19,304	$14,478
2007	$20,493	$15,370
2008	$22,096	$16,572
2009	$23,243	$17,432
2010	$24,757	$18,568
2011	$27,015	$20,261
2012	$28,214	$21,161
2013	$29,891	$22,418
2014	$33,766	$25,325

AVG. AUCTION PRICING

LOW	HIGH	AVG
$14,280	$30,090	$21,391

5045D

YEARS MFRD 2009-2015
ENGINE . . . . JD POWETECH
CYLINDERS 3
CID 179
PTO HP 37
ENGINE HP 45
COOLING . . . . LIQUID
FUEL . . . . D
SPEEDS 8/4
TRANSMISSION . . . . GEAR
STEERING . . . . STANDARD
DRIVE TYPE 4WD
ROPS/CAB . . . . ROPS
WEIGHT . . . . 4,189 LBS.
MSRP $17,233

OPTIONS

LDR

SERIAL NUMBERS

YEAR	BEGINNING NO.
2009	B000001
2010	1113
2011	2809
2012	4708
2013	8775

RETAIL PRICING

YEAR	HIGH	LOW
2009	$10,543	$7,907
2010	$11,288	$8,466
2011	$12,334	$9,250
2012	$13,143	$9,857
2013	$14,056	$10,542
2014	$15,295	$11,471
2015	$16,051	$12,038

AVG. AUCTION PRICING

LOW	HIGH	AVG
$6,200	$7,500	$6,900

5045E

YEARS MFRD 2009-2019
ENGINE . . . . JD POWERTECH
CYLINDERS 3
CID 179
PTO HP 37
ENGINE HP 50
COOLING . . . . LIQUID
FUEL . . . . D
SPEEDS 9/3
TRANSMISSION . . . SHUTTLE SHIFT
STEERING . . . . STANDARD
HITCH . . . . CAT. I
HYDRAULIC . . . . YES
PTO . . . . YES
DRIVE TYPE 2WD
ROPS/CAB . . . . ROPS
MSRP $20,543

OPTIONS

MFWD

SERIAL NUMBERS

YEAR	BEGINNING NO.
2009	U000001
2010	0431
2011	1520
2012	2261
2013	3194
2014	4154

RETAIL PRICING

YEAR	HIGH	LOW
2009	$12,254	$9,191
2010	$13,070	$9,803
2011	$13,960	$10,470
2012	$14,836	$11,127
2013	$15,693	$11,770
2014	$16,409	$12,307
2015	$17,262	$12,947
2016	$17,927	$13,445
2017	$18,870	$14,153
2018	$19,436	$14,577
2019	$19,732	$14,799

AVG. AUCTION PRICING

LOW	HIGH	AVG
$9,100	$20,600	$14,867

5055D

YEARS MFRD 2009-2015
ENGINE . . . . JD TURBO
CYLINDERS 3
CID 179
PTO HP 45
ENGINE HP 55

COOLING . . . . LIQUID
FUEL . . . . D
SPEEDS 8/4
TRANSMISSION . . . . GEAR
STEERING. . . . . .STANDARD
HITCH . . . . CAT. I
HYDRAULIC . . . . YES
PTO . . . . YES
DRIVE TYPE 2WD
ROPS/CAB . . . . ROPS
MSRP. $18,754

OPTIONS

LDR

SERIAL NUMBERS

YEAR	BEGINNING NO.
2009	B000001
2010	0947
2011	2454
2012	4097
2013	5386
2014	4154

RETAIL PRICING

YEAR	HIGH	LOW
2009	$11,079	$8,309
2010	$12,079	$9,059
2011	$12,881	$9,660
2012	$13,900	$10,425
2013	$15,051	$11,288
2014	$16,271	$12,203
2015	$17,137	$12,853

AVG. AUCTION PRICING

LOW	HIGH	AVG
$9,180	$14,535	$11,480

5055E

YEARS MFRD 2009-2019
ENGINE . . . . JD TURBO
CYLINDERS. 3
CID 179
PTO HP 41
ENGINE HP 59
COOLING . . . . LIQUID
FUEL . . . . D
SPEEDS 9/3
TRANSMISSION . . . SHUTTLE SHIFT
STEERING. . . . . .STANDARD
HITCH . . . . CAT. I
HYDRAULIC . . . . YES
PTO . . . . YES
DRIVE TYPE 4WD
ROPS/CAB . . . . ROPS
MSRP. $23,599

OPTIONS

12/12 SHUTTLE SHIFT
2 HYD
CAB W/A/H (2013)
MFWD

SERIAL NUMBERS

YEAR	BEGINNING NO.
2009	U000001
2010	0983
2011	2507
2012	7677
2013	14571
2013	140001-CAB
2014	1231-CAB
2014	21655

RETAIL PRICING

YEAR	HIGH	LOW
2009	$13,989	$10,492
2010	$14,929	$11,197
2011	$15,888	$11,916
2012	$16,606	$12,454
2013	$17,341	$13,006
2014	$18,024	$13,518
2015	$18,898	$14,173
2016	$19,768	$14,826
2017	$20,592	$15,444
2018	$21,608	$16,206
2019	$22,939	$17,204

AVG. AUCTION PRICING

LOW	HIGH	AVG
$7,140	$36,720	$18,211

5103

YEARS MFRD 2003-2008
SERIES. . . . . 03 SERIES
ENGINE . . . . JD
CYLINDERS. 3
CID 179
PTO HP 38
ENGINE HP 45
COOLING . . . . LIQUID
FUEL . . . . D
SPEEDS 9/3
TRANSMISSION . . . . GEAR
STEERING. . . . . .STANDARD
HITCH . . . . CAT. I
BLADE CLUTCH . . . . MANUAL
HYDRAULIC . . . . YES
PTO . . . . YES
DRIVE TYPE 2WD
ROPS/CAB . . . . ROPS
WEIGHT . . . . 4,475 LBS.
MSRP. $14,886

OPTIONS

4WD
LDR

SERIAL NUMBERS

YEAR	BEGINNING NO.
2003	U000001
2004	U001282
2005	U003847
2006	U011780
2008	U015563

RETAIL PRICING

YEAR	HIGH	LOW
2003	$9,716	$7,287
2004	$10,618	$7,964
2005	$11,304	$8,478
2006	$12,165	$9,123
2007	$12,947	$9,710
2008	$13,840	$10,380

AVG. AUCTION PRICING

LOW	HIGH	AVG
$6,000	$8,200	$7,261

5105

YEARS MFRD 2000-2007
SERIES. . . . . 05 SERIES
ENGINE . . . . JD
CYLINDERS. 3
CID 179
PTO HP 40
ENGINE HP 45.6
COOLING . . . . LIQUID
FUEL . . . . D
SPEEDS 8/4
TRANSMISSION . . . SHUTTLE SHIFT
STEERING. . . . . .STANDARD
HITCH . . . . CAT. I
BLADE CLUTCH . . . . MANUAL
HYDRAULIC . . . . YES
PTO . . . . YES
DRIVE TYPE 2WD
ROPS/CAB . . . . ROPS
WEIGHT . . . . 3,850 LBS.
MSRP. $21,997

OPTIONS

2 HYD
4WD
LDR
LDR S-L

SERIAL NUMBERS

YEAR	BEGINNING NO.
2000	110001
2001	210001
2002	310001
2003	410001
2004	510001
2005	610001
2006	710001
2007	810001

RETAIL PRICING

YEAR	HIGH	LOW
2000	$7,689	$5,767
2001	$7,948	$5,961
2002	$8,157	$6,118
2003	$8,622	$6,467
2004	$10,006	$7,505
2005	$10,662	$7,997
2006	$10,631	$7,974
2007	$12,263	$9,198

AVG. AUCTION PRICING

LOW	HIGH	AVG
$4,080	$18,870	$12,438

5200

YEARS MFRD 1992-1997
ENGINE . . . . JD
CYLINDERS. 3
CID 179
PTO HP 40
ENGINE HP 45.6
FUEL . . . . D
SPEEDS 9/3
TRANSMISSION . . . . GEAR
STEERING. . . . . .STANDARD
PTO . . . . YES
DRIVE TYPE 2WD
ROPS/CAB . . . . ROPS
WEIGHT . . . . 4,250 LBS.
MSRP. $19,986

OPTIONS

12/12 SS
4WD
C/A/H
LDR
LDR SL

SERIAL NUMBERS

RIGHT SIDE OF TRACTOR FRAME

YEAR	BEGINNING NO.
1992	110001
1993	111583
1994	221268
1995	420141
1996	520001
1997	620000

RETAIL PRICING

YEAR	HIGH	LOW
1992	$5,948	$4,461
1993	$6,291	$4,719
1994	$6,784	$5,088
1995	$7,169	$5,376
1996	$7,661	$5,746
1997	$8,104	$6,078

AVG. AUCTION PRICING

LOW	HIGH	AVG
$5,200	$12,000	$7,950

5203

YEARS MFRD 2003-2008
SERIES. . . . . 03 SERIES
ENGINE . . . . JD POWERTECH
CYLINDERS. 3
CID 179
PTO HP 44
ENGINE HP 53
COOLING . . . . LIQUID
FUEL . . . . D
SPEEDS 9/3
TRANSMISSION . . . . GEAR
STEERING. . . . . .STANDARD
HITCH . . . . CAT. I
DRIVE TYPE 2WD
ROPS/CAB . . . . ROPS
WEIGHT . . . . 4,498 LBS.
MSRP. $16,155

OPTIONS

4WD
LDR

SERIAL NUMBERS

YEAR	BEGINNING NO.
2003	U000001
2004	U001018
2005	U002908
2008	U006731

RETAIL PRICING

YEAR	HIGH	LOW
2003	$7,965	$5,974
2004	$8,679	$6,509
2005	$9,382	$7,036
2006	$10,210	$7,658
2007	$11,005	$8,254
2008	$11,837	$8,878

AVG. AUCTION PRICING

LOW	HIGH	AVG
$6,000	$7,300	$6,529

5210

YEARS MFRD 1998-2001
ENGINE . . . . JD
CYLINDERS. 3
CID 179

PTO HP 45
FUEL . . . . D
SPEEDS 9/3
TRANSMISSION . . . . GEAR
STEERING. . . . STANDARD
PTO . . . . YES
DRIVE TYPE 2WD
ROPS/CAB . . . . ROPS
WEIGHT . . . . 5,270 LBS.
MSRP. . . . $20,185

OPTIONS

12/12 SS
4WD
C/A/H
LDR
LDR SL

SERIAL NUMBERS

YEAR	BEGINNING NO.
1998	120000
1999	220001
2000	320000
2001	420000

RETAIL PRICING

YEAR	HIGH	LOW
1998	$8,771	$6,578
1999	$9,280	$6,960
2000	$9,711	$7,284
2001	$10,353	$7,765

AVG. AUCTION PRICING

LOW	HIGH	AVG
$6,600	$11,500	$8,938

5220

YEARS MFRD 2002-2004
ENGINE . . . . JD PWRTECH 3029D
CYLINDERS. . . . 3
CID 179
PTO HP 45
ENGINE HP 53
FUEL . . . . D
SPEEDS 9/3
TRANSMISSION . . . . GEAR
STEERING. . . . STANDARD
PTO . . . . YES
WEIGHT . . . . 4,370 LBS.
MSRP. . . . $21,689

OPTIONS

12/12 SS
4WD
C/A/H
LDR S-L

SERIAL NUMBERS

YEAR	BEGINNING NO.
2002	220001
2003	320001
2004	420001

RETAIL PRICING

YEAR	HIGH	LOW
2002	$11,990	$8,993
2003	$12,662	$9,497
2004	$13,389	$10,041

AVG. AUCTION PRICING

LOW	HIGH	AVG
$9,834	$18,138	$13,789

5225

YEARS MFRD 2005-2008
ENGINE . . . . JD
CYLINDERS. . . . 5
CID 184
PTO HP 45
ENGINE HP 56
COOLING . . . . LIQUID
FUEL . . . . D
SPEEDS 9/3
STEERING. . . . STANDARD
DRIVE TYPE 2WD
ROPS/CAB . . . . ROPS

OPTIONS

12/12 SS
4WD
CAB W/A/H
LDR
LDR SL

SERIAL NUMBERS

YEAR	BEGINNING NO.
2005	120001
2006	220001
2007	320001
2008	420001

RETAIL PRICING

YEAR	HIGH	LOW
2005	$14,633	$10,975
2006	$15,222	$11,417
2007	$16,402	$12,301
2008	$17,229	$12,922

AVG. AUCTION PRICING

LOW	HIGH	AVG
$9,435	$29,580	$16,405

KIOTI

CK20

YEARS MFRD 2003-2003
ENGINE 3C093A
CYLINDERS 3
CID 56.6
PTO HP 16.5
ENGINE HP 21
FUEL .... D
SPEEDS 6/2
TRANSMISSION .... GEAR
STEERING .... STANDARD
PTO .... YES
WEIGHT .... 1,962 LBS.
MSRP $10,990

OPTIONS

1 HYD
HYDRO

RETAIL PRICING

YEAR	HIGH	LOW
2003	$4,836	$3,627

CK20S

YEARS MFRD 2009-2016
ENGINE 3C100A
CYLINDERS 3
CID 61.45
ENGINE HP 22
COOLING .... LIQUID
FUEL .... D
SPEEDS 6/2
TRANSMISSION ... SHUTTLE SHIFT
STEERING .... STANDARD
HITCH .... CAT. I
HYDRAULIC .... YES
PTO .... YES
DRIVE TYPE 4WD
ROPS/CAB .... ROPS
WEIGHT .... 2,125 LBS.
MSRP $13,954

OPTIONS

HYDRO

RETAIL PRICING

YEAR	HIGH	LOW
2009	$5,281	$3,960
2010	$5,831	$4,373
2011	$6,419	$4,814
2012	$7,008	$5,256
2013	$7,097	$5,323
2014	$7,191	$5,393
2015	$8,103	$6,077
2016	$9,081	$6,811

CK25

YEARS MFRD 2006-2008
SERIES .... CK SERIES
ENGINE .... KIOTI TD1300A
CYLINDERS 3
CID 79.3
ENGINE HP 25
COOLING .... LIQUID
FUEL .... D
SPEEDS 8/8
TRANSMISSION ..... POWER SHIFT
STEERING .... STANDARD
HYDRAULIC .... YES
PTO .... YES
DRIVE TYPE 4WD
ROPS/CAB .... ROPS
WEIGHT .... 3,042 LBS.
MSRP $13,763

OPTIONS

HYDRO

RETAIL PRICING

YEAR	HIGH	LOW
2006	$6,288	$4,716
2007	$6,850	$5,137
2008	$7,151	$5,363

CK27

YEARS MFRD 2009-2016
ENGINE .... DAEDONG 3A139LWM
CYLINDERS 3
ENGINE HP 28
COOLING .... LIQUID
FUEL .... D
SPEEDS 8/8
TRANSMISSION ... SHUTTLE SHIFT
STEERING .... STANDARD
HYDRAULIC .... YES
DRIVE TYPE 4WD
ROPS/CAB .... ROPS
WEIGHT .... 3,161 LBS.
MSRP $16,344

OPTIONS

HYDRO

RETAIL PRICING

YEAR	HIGH	LOW
2009	$6,567	$4,925
2010	$7,265	$5,449
2011	$8,001	$6,001
2012	$9,286	$6,964
2013	$10,153	$7,615
2014	$10,528	$7,896
2015	$10,866	$8,149
2016	$11,967	$8,975

CK30

YEARS MFRD 2006-2016
SERIES .... CK SERIES
ENGINE .... KIOTI 3A150D
CYLINDERS 3
CID 91.5
ENGINE HP 30
COOLING .... LIQUID
FUEL .... D
SPEEDS 8/8
TRANSMISSION ..... POWER SHIFT
STEERING .... STANDARD
PTO .... YES
DRIVE TYPE 4WD
ROPS/CAB .... ROPS
WEIGHT .... 3,042 LBS.
MSRP $17,323

OPTIONS

HYDRO

RETAIL PRICING

YEAR	HIGH	LOW
2006	$4,839	$3,629
2007	$5,612	$4,209
2008	$6,089	$4,567
2009	$6,897	$5,173
2010	$7,668	$5,751
2011	$8,404	$6,303
2012	$10,094	$7,571
2013	$10,840	$8,130
2014	$11,586	$8,689
2015	$11,751	$8,813
2016	$13,243	$9,932

AVG. AUCTION PRICING

LOW	HIGH	AVG
$4,925	$8,865	$7,338

CK35

YEARS MFRD 2006-2016
ENGINE ..... DAEDONG 3A165LXD
CYLINDERS 3
CID 100.5
ENGINE HP 34
COOLING .... LIQUID
FUEL .... D
SPEEDS 8/8
TRANSMISSION ... SHUTTLE SHIFT
STEERING .... STANDARD
HITCH .... CAT. I
DRIVE TYPE 4WD
ROPS/CAB .... ROPS
WEIGHT .... 3,151 LBS.
MSRP $18,339

OPTIONS

HYDRO

RETAIL PRICING

YEAR	HIGH	LOW
2006	$5,318	$3,989
2007	$5,979	$4,484
2008	$6,494	$4,871
2009	$7,338	$5,504
2010	$8,147	$6,110
2011	$8,918	$6,689
2012	$10,831	$8,123
2013	$11,490	$8,618
2014	$12,152	$9,114
2015	$12,532	$9,399
2016	$14,087	$10,566

CK2510

YEARS MFRD 2013-2020
ENGINE .... DAEDONG TIER 4
CYLINDERS 3
PTO HP 20
ENGINE HP 24.5
COOLING .... LIQUID
FUEL .... D
SPEEDS 6/2
TRANSMISSION .... GEAR
STEERING .... STANDARD
HITCH .... CAT. I
HYDRAULIC .... YES
PTO .... YES
DRIVE TYPE 4WD
ROPS/CAB .... ROPS
WEIGHT .... 2,260 LBS.

OPTIONS

BACKHOE
HYDRO
LDR

RETAIL PRICING

YEAR	HIGH	LOW
2014	$7,401	$5,550
2015	$8,218	$6,164
2016	$9,911	$7,433
2017	$10,680	$8,010
2018	$11,906	$8,930
2019	$13,222	$9,916
2020	$14,156	$10,900

AVG. AUCTION PRICING

LOW	HIGH	AVG
$7,634	$13,298	$9,538

CK2610

YEARS MFRD 2017-2020
ENGINE 3A165LWM-U
CYLINDERS 3
CID 100.5
PTO HP 21.7
ENGINE HP 24.5
COOLING .... LIQUID
FUEL .... D
SPEEDS 9/3
TRANSMISSION .... GEAR
STEERING .... STANDARD
HITCH .... CAT. I
DRIVE TYPE 4WD
ROPS/CAB .... ROPS
WEIGHT .... 2,646 LBS.

OPTIONS

HYDRO

CK2610SE

YEARS MFRD 2020-2020
ENGINE 3H-TM4B
CYLINDERS 3
CID 100.5
PTO HP 18.6
ENGINE HP 24.5
FUEL .... D
SPEEDS .... VARIABLE
TRANSMISSION .... HYDRO
STEERING .... STANDARD
HITCH .... CAT. I
ROPS/CAB .... CAB
WEIGHT .... 3,397 LBS.

CK3510

YEARS MFRD 2017-2020
ENGINE 3F-YM4-U
CYLINDERS 3
CID 111.4
PTO HP 30.8
ENGINE HP 34.9
COOLING .... LIQUID
FUEL .... D
SPEEDS 9/3
TRANSMISSION .... GEAR
STEERING .... STANDARD
HITCH .... CAT. I
DRIVE TYPE 4WD

KIOTI

ROPS/CAB ... ROPS
WEIGHT ... 2,679 LBS.

OPTIONS

HYDRO

CK3510SE

YEARS MFRD ... 2018-2020
ENGINE ... 3F-TM4-U
CYLINDERS ... 3
CID ... 111.4
PTO HP ... 30.8
ENGINE HP ... 34.9
FUEL ... D
SPEEDS ... 12/12
TRANSMISSION ... SHUTTLE SHIFT
STEERING ... STANDARD
HITCH ... CAT. I
ROPS/CAB ... ROPS
WEIGHT ... 2,906 LBS.

CK3510SE HC

YEARS MFRD ... 2017-2020
ENGINE ... 3F-TH4-U
CYLINDERS ... 3
CID ... 111.44
PTO HP ... 29.4
ENGINE HP ... 34.9
FUEL ... D
TRANSMISSION ... HYDRO
STEERING ... STANDARD
HITCH ... CAT. I
ROPS/CAB ... CAB
WEIGHT ... 3,307 LBS.

CK3510SE HST

YEARS MFRD ... 2018-2020
ENGINE ... 3F-TH4-U
CYLINDERS ... 3
CID ... 111.4
PTO HP ... 28
ENGINE HP ... 34.9
FUEL ... D
TRANSMISSION ... HYDRO
STEERING ... STANDARD
HITCH ... CAT. I
ROPS/CAB ... ROPS
WEIGHT ... 2,921 LBS.

CK4010

YEARS MFRD ... 2017-2020
ENGINE ... 3F-TM4-U
CYLINDERS ... 3
CID ... 111.4
ENGINE HP ... 39.6
COOLING ... LIQUID
FUEL ... D
SPEEDS ... 9/3
TRANSMISSION ... GEAR
STEERING ... STANDARD
HITCH ... CAT. I
DRIVE TYPE ... 4WD
ROPS/CAB ... ROPS
WEIGHT ... 2,679 LBS.

OPTIONS

HYDRO

CK4010SE

YEARS MFRD ... 2018-2020
ENGINE ... 3F-TM4-U
CYLINDERS ... 3
CID ... 111.4
PTO HP ... 34.9
ENGINE HP ... 39.6
FUEL ... D
SPEEDS ... 12/12
STEERING ... STANDARD
HITCH ... CAT. I
ROPS/CAB ... ROPS
WEIGHT ... 2,906 LBS.

CK4010SE HC

YEARS MFRD ... 2017-2020
ENGINE ... 3F-TH4-U
CYLINDERS ... 3
CID ... 111.4
PTO HP ... 31.9
ENGINE HP ... 39.6
FUEL ... D
TRANSMISSION ... HYDRO
STEERING ... STANDARD
HITCH ... CAT. I
ROPS/CAB ... CAB
WEIGHT ... 3,307 LBS.

CK4010SE HST

YEARS MFRD ... 2018-2020
ENGINE ... 3F-TH4-U
CYLINDERS ... 3
CID ... 111.4
PTO HP ... 33.5
ENGINE HP ... 39.6
FUEL ... D
TRANSMISSION ... HYDRO
STEERING ... STANDARD
HITCH ... CAT. I
ROPS/CAB ... ROPS
WEIGHT ... 2,921 LBS.

CS2210

YEARS MFRD ... 2016-2020
ENGINE ... S773L-F21
CYLINDERS ... 3
CID ... 69
PTO HP ... 18.7
ENGINE HP ... 21.1
COOLING ... LIQUID
FUEL ... D
SPEEDS ... VARIABLE
TRANSMISSION ... HYDRO
STEERING ... STANDARD
HITCH ... CAT. I
DRIVE TYPE ... 4WD
ROPS/CAB ... ROPS
WEIGHT ... 1,485 LBS.

CS2410

YEARS MFRD ... 2013-2017
ENGINE ... DAEDONG S773L
CYLINDERS ... 3
CID ... 69
PTO HP ... 19.4
ENGINE HP ... 24.5
COOLING ... LIQUID
FUEL ... D
SPEEDS ... VARIABLE
TRANSMISSION ... HYDRO
STEERING ... STANDARD
HITCH ... CAT. I
HYDRAULIC ... YES
PTO ... YES
WEIGHT ... 1,485 LBS.
MSRP ... $12,295

RETAIL PRICING

YEAR	HIGH	LOW
2015	$7,403	$5,552
2016	$8,402	$6,302
2017	$9,168	$6,876

AVG. AUCTION PRICING

LOW	HIGH	AVG
$6,698	$8,373	$7,461

CS2510

YEARS MFRD ... 2016-2020
ENGINE ... S773L
CYLINDERS ... 3
CID ... 69
PTO HP ... 19.4
ENGINE HP ... 24.5
COOLING ... LIQUID
FUEL ... D
SPEEDS ... VARIABLE
TRANSMISSION ... HYDRO
STEERING ... STANDARD
HITCH ... CAT. I
DRIVE TYPE ... 4WD
ROPS/CAB ... ROPS
WEIGHT ... 1,485 LBS.

CX2510

YEARS MFRD ... 2020-2020
ENGINE ... 3A165LWH-U
CYLINDERS ... 3
CID ... 87
PTO HP ... 19.3
ENGINE HP ... 24.5
FUEL ... D
SPEEDS ... 6/2
TRANSMISSION ... GEAR
STEERING ... STANDARD
HITCH ... CAT. I
ROPS/CAB ... ROPS
WEIGHT ... 2,260 LBS.

OPTIONS

HYDRO

DK35

YEARS MFRD ... 2000-2003
SERIES ... DK SERIES
ENGINE ... KIOTI
CYLINDERS ... 3
CID ... 98
PTO HP ... 28.3
ENGINE HP ... 35
COOLING ... LIQUID
FUEL ... D
SPEEDS ... 8/8
TRANSMISSION ... SHUTTLE SHIFT
STEERING ... STANDARD
HITCH ... CAT. I
PTO ... YES
WEIGHT ... 3,615 LBS.
MSRP ... $16,850

OPTIONS

CRT

RETAIL PRICING

YEAR	HIGH	LOW
2000	$5,877	$4,407
2001	$6,285	$4,714
2002	$6,723	$5,042
2003	$7,421	$5,566

DK35SE

YEARS MFRD ... 2007-2013
ENGINE ... 3B183LXM
CYLINDERS ... 3
CID ... 111.43
ENGINE HP ... 38
COOLING ... LIQUID
FUEL ... D
SPEEDS ... 8/8
TRANSMISSION ... SHUTTLE SHIFT
STEERING ... STANDARD
HITCH ... CAT. I
DRIVE TYPE ... 4WD
ROPS/CAB ... ROPS
WEIGHT ... 3,666 LBS.
MSRP ... $19,370

OPTIONS

HYDRO

RETAIL PRICING

YEAR	HIGH	LOW
2007	$6,176	$4,632
2008	$6,703	$5,027
2009	$7,720	$5,790
2010	$8,563	$6,422
2011	$10,072	$7,554
2012	$11,896	$8,922
2013	$12,317	$9,238

AVG. AUCTION PRICING

LOW	HIGH	AVG
$4,003	$8,695	$5,955

DK35SE HST

YEARS MFRD ... 2007-2013
ENGINE ... 3B183LXH
CYLINDERS ... 3
CID ... 111.43
ENGINE HP ... 38
COOLING ... LIQUID
FUEL ... D
SPEEDS ... VARIABLE
TRANSMISSION ... HYDRO
STEERING ... STANDARD
HITCH ... CAT. I
MSRP ... $21,205

RETAIL PRICING

YEAR	HIGH	LOW
2007	$6,468	$4,851
2008	$6,978	$5,233
2009	$8,204	$6,153

YEAR	HIGH	LOW
2010	$9,088	$6,816
2011	$11,063	$8,297
2012	$12,493	$9,370

DK40

YEARS MFRD 2000-2003
SERIES .... DK SERIES
ENGINE .... KIOTI 4A200
CYLINDERS 4
CID 119
PTO HP 33.4
ENGINE HP 40
COOLING .... LIQUID
FUEL .... D
SPEEDS .... 8/8~16/16
TRANSMISSION ... SHUTTLE SHIFT
STEERING .... STANDARD
HITCH .... CAT. I
PTO .... YES
WEIGHT .... 3,836 LBS.
MSRP $18,700

OPTIONS

CRT

RETAIL PRICING

YEAR	HIGH	LOW
2000	$6,523	$4,892
2001	$6,977	$5,233
2002	$7,460	$5,595
2003	$7,979	$5,985

DK40SE

YEARS MFRD 2007-2016
ENGINE 4A200LXM
CYLINDERS 4
CID 121.98
ENGINE HP 41
COOLING .... LIQUID
FUEL .... D
SPEEDS 12/12
TRANSMISSION ... SHUTTLE SHIFT
STEERING .... STANDARD
HITCH .... CAT. I
PTO .... YES
DRIVE TYPE 4WD
ROPS/CAB .... ROPS
WEIGHT .... 4,202 LBS.
MSRP $22,072

OPTIONS

CAB
HYDRO

RETAIL PRICING

YEAR	HIGH	LOW
2007	$6,934	$5,201
2008	$7,522	$5,642
2009	$8,771	$6,579
2010	$9,727	$7,295
2011	$11,061	$8,295
2012	$12,886	$9,664
2013	$14,393	$10,795
2014	$15,239	$11,429
2015	$15,389	$11,541
2016	$16,535	$12,401

DK45

YEARS MFRD 1999-2003
SERIES .... DK SERIES
ENGINE .... KIOTI 4A220
CYLINDERS 4
CID 132
PTO HP 38
ENGINE HP 45
FUEL .... D
SPEEDS 12/12
TRANSMISSION ... SHUTTLE SHIFT
STEERING .... STANDARD
HITCH .... CAT. I
PTO .... YES
WEIGHT .... 3,792 LBS.
MSRP $20,365

OPTIONS

2HYD

RETAIL PRICING

YEAR	HIGH	LOW
1999	$6,642	$4,981
2000	$7,105	$5,329
2001	$7,598	$5,699
2002	$8,127	$6,095
2003	$8,699	$6,524

DK45S

YEARS MFRD 2006-2012
ENGINE 4A220LXB
CYLINDERS 4
CID 134.1
ENGINE HP 45
COOLING .... LIQUID
FUEL .... D
SPEEDS 12/12
TRANSMISSION ... SHUTTLE SHIFT
STEERING .... STANDARD
HITCH .... CAT. I
HYDRAULIC .... YES
PTO .... YES
WEIGHT .... 4,299 LBS.
MSRP $22,940

RETAIL PRICING

YEAR	HIGH	LOW
2006	$6,670	$5,003
2007	$7,076	$5,307
2008	$7,653	$5,740
2009	$8,873	$6,655
2010	$9,786	$7,339
2011	$10,734	$8,050
2012	$12,834	$9,625

AVG. AUCTION PRICING

LOW	HIGH	AVG
$11,622	$12,569	$12,074

DK45SE

YEARS MFRD 2009-2016
ENGINE 4A220LWH
CYLINDERS 4
CID 134.06
ENGINE HP 45
COOLING .... LIQUID
FUEL .... D
SPEEDS 12/12
TRANSMISSION ... SHUTTLE SHIFT
STEERING .... STANDARD
HITCH .... CAT. I
DRIVE TYPE 4WD
ROPS/CAB .... ROPS
WEIGHT .... 4,189 LBS.
MSRP $25,367

OPTIONS

CAB
HYDRO

RETAIL PRICING

YEAR	HIGH	LOW
2009	$10,205	$7,653
2010	$11,233	$8,425
2011	$12,336	$9,252
2012	$14,610	$10,957
2013	$15,994	$11,996
2014	$16,928	$12,696
2015	$17,627	$13,220
2016	$19,104	$14,328

DK50

YEARS MFRD 2001-2002
SERIES .... DK SERIES
ENGINE 4A200T
CYLINDERS 4
CID 120
PTO HP 41.5
ENGINE HP 49
COOLING .... LIQUID
FUEL .... D
SPEEDS 12/12
TRANSMISSION ... SHUTTLE SHIFT
STEERING .... STANDARD
HYDRAULIC .... YES
PTO .... YES
DRIVE TYPE 4WD
ROPS/CAB .... ROPS
WEIGHT .... 4,107 LBS.
MSRP $21,500

OPTIONS

CAB

RETAIL PRICING

YEAR	HIGH	LOW
2001	$8,699	$6,524
2002	$9,458	$7,093

DK50SE

YEARS MFRD 2012-2016
ENGINE .... DAEDONG
CYLINDERS 4
CID 148
PTO HP 41.7
COOLING .... LIQUID
FUEL .... D
SPEEDS 12/12
TRANSMISSION .... GEAR
STEERING .... STANDARD
DRIVE TYPE 4WD
ROPS/CAB .... ROPS
MSRP $27,229

OPTIONS

CAB
HYDRO

RETAIL PRICING

YEAR	HIGH	LOW
2012	$12,510	$9,383
2013	$13,732	$10,299
2014	$17,810	$13,357
2015	$18,408	$13,806
2016	$20,597	$15,448

DK55

YEARS MFRD 2003-2016
SERIES .... DK SERIES
ENGINE .... KIOTI 4A220TLWB
CYLINDERS 4
CID 134.1
PTO HP 42.2
ENGINE HP 55
COOLING .... LIQUID
FUEL .... D
SPEEDS 12/12
TRANSMISSION ..... POWER SHIFT
STEERING .... STANDARD
HITCH .... CAT. II
HYDRAULIC .... YES
PTO .... YES
DRIVE TYPE 4WD
ROPS/CAB .... ROPS
WEIGHT .... 5,105 LBS.
MSRP $30,004

OPTIONS

CAB

RETAIL PRICING

YEAR	HIGH	LOW
2003	$7,140	$5,355
2004	$7,348	$5,511
2005	$7,558	$5,668
2006	$8,267	$6,200
2007	$8,810	$6,607
2008	$9,227	$6,921
2009	$10,146	$7,610
2010	$10,522	$7,891
2011	$10,982	$8,236
2012	$11,984	$8,988
2013	$14,238	$10,679
2014	$15,783	$11,837
2015	$18,371	$13,778
2016	$23,758	$17,819

AVG. AUCTION PRICING

LOW	HIGH	AVG
$12,313	$19,208	$14,857

DK55C

YEARS MFRD 2009-2016
ENGINE .... DAEDONG
CID 134D
PTO HP 44.4
FUEL .... D
SPEEDS 12/12
STEERING .... STANDARD
DRIVE TYPE 4WD
ROPS/CAB .... CAB
WEIGHT .... 5,205 LBS.
MSRP $36,356

RETAIL PRICING

YEAR	HIGH	LOW
2009	$11,691	$8,768
2010	$12,109	$9,081
2011	$12,609	$9,457

KIOTI

YEAR	HIGH	LOW
2012	$14,907	$11,180
2013	$17,452	$13,089
2014	$19,289	$14,467
2015	$22,255	$16,691
2016	$25,787	$19,340

AVG. AUCTION PRICING

LOW	HIGH	AVG
$10,589	$11,574	$11,229

DK65

YEARS MFRD 2001-2003
SERIES .... DK SERIES
ENGINE .... PERKINS 903.27T
CYLINDERS 3
CID 164.8
PTO HP 55
ENGINE HP 65
FUEL .... D
SPEEDS 12/12
TRANSMISSION .... GEAR
STEERING .... STANDARD
HITCH .... CAT. II
HYDRAULIC .... YES
PTO .... YES
DRIVE TYPE 4WD
ROPS/CAB .... ROPS
WEIGHT .... 6,925 LBS.
MSRP $25,990

OPTIONS

CAB

RETAIL PRICING

YEAR	HIGH	LOW
2001	$10,094	$7,571
2002	$10,702	$8,027
2003	$11,603	$8,702

DK65S

YEARS MFRD 2005-2007
SERIES .... DK SERIES
ENGINE 1103C-33T
CYLINDERS 3
CID 201.4
ENGINE HP 64
FUEL .... D
SPEEDS 12/12
TRANSMISSION ...... POWER SHIFT
STEERING .... STANDARD
HITCH .... CAT. II
HYDRAULIC .... YES
PTO .... YES
WEIGHT .... 6,503 LBS.

DK4210SE HST

YEARS MFRD 2018-2020
SERIES .... DK10SE SERIES
ENGINE .... DAEDONG
CYLINDERS 3
CID 111.4
PTO HP 29.1
ENGINE HP 39.6
FUEL .... D
TRANSMISSION .... HYDRO
STEERING .... STANDARD
HITCH .... CAT. I
DRIVE TYPE 4WD
ROPS/CAB .... ROPS
WEIGHT .... 3,523 LBS.

OPTIONS

CAB HC MODEL

DK4510

YEARS MFRD 2015-2020
ENGINE 3F1863T-45
CYLINDERS 3
CID 111.4
PTO HP 41.6
ENGINE HP 45
COOLING .... LIQUID
FUEL .... D
SPEEDS 8/8
TRANSMISSION .... GEAR
STEERING .... STANDARD
WEIGHT .... 3,390 LBS.

OPTIONS

HYD SHUTTLE

DK4710SE HST

YEARS MFRD 2018-2020
SERIES .... DK10SE SERIES
ENGINE .... DAEDONG
CYLINDERS 3
CID 111.4
PTO HP 33.4
ENGINE HP 44.9
FUEL .... D
TRANSMISSION .... HYDRO
STEERING .... STANDARD
HITCH .... CAT. I
DRIVE TYPE 4WD
ROPS/CAB .... ROPS
WEIGHT .... 3,523 LBS.

OPTIONS

CAB HC MODEL

DK5310SE HST

YEARS MFRD 2018-2020
SERIES .... DK10SE SERIES
ENGINE .... DAEDONG
CYLINDERS 3
CID 111.4
PTO HP 39.3
ENGINE HP 50.3
FUEL .... D
TRANSMISSION .... HYDRO
STEERING .... STANDARD
HITCH .... CAT. I
DRIVE TYPE 4WD
ROPS/CAB .... ROPS
WEIGHT .... 3,523 LBS.

OPTIONS

CAB HC MODEL

DS3510

YEARS MFRD 2011-2016
ENGINE .... DAEDONG
CYLINDERS 3
CID 100
PTO HP 27.6
COOLING .... AIR
FUEL .... D
SPEEDS 8/8
TRANSMISSION .... GEAR
STEERING .... STANDARD
DRIVE TYPE 4WD
ROPS/CAB .... ROPS
WEIGHT .... 2,897 LBS.
MSRP $15,085

RETAIL PRICING

YEAR	HIGH	LOW
2011	$6,972	$5,229
2012	$7,376	$5,532
2013	$8,074	$6,056
2014	$10,058	$7,543
2015	$10,472	$7,854
2016	$11,391	$8,543

DS4110

YEARS MFRD 2011-2016
SERIES .... DS SERIES
ENGINE .... DAEDONG 4A200LWM
CYLINDERS 4
CID 121.9
ENGINE HP 41
COOLING .... LIQUID
FUEL .... D
SPEEDS 8/8
TRANSMISSION ... SHUTTLE SHIFT
STEERING .... STANDARD
HITCH .... CAT. I
HYDRAULIC .... YES
PTO .... YES
DRIVE TYPE 4WD
ROPS/CAB .... ROPS
WEIGHT .... 3,527 LBS.
MSRP $17,721

RETAIL PRICING

YEAR	HIGH	LOW
2011	$7,474	$5,606
2012	$8,110	$6,083
2013	$9,916	$7,437
2014	$10,608	$7,956
2015	$11,432	$8,574
2016	$12,516	$9,387

DS4110HS

YEARS MFRD 2012-2016
SERIES .... DS SERIES
ENGINE .... DAEDONG 4A220LWM
CYLINDERS 4
CID 121.99
ENGINE HP 41
COOLING .... LIQUID
FUEL .... D
SPEEDS 8/8
TRANSMISSION ... SHUTTLE SHIFT
STEERING .... STANDARD
HITCH .... CAT. I
HYDRAULIC .... YES
PTO .... YES
DRIVE TYPE 4WD
ROPS/CAB .... ROPS
WEIGHT .... 3,527 LBS.
MSRP $18,425

RETAIL PRICING

YEAR	HIGH	LOW
2012	$9,066	$6,799
2013	$10,278	$7,709
2014	$11,527	$8,646
2015	$12,007	$9,005
2016	$13,335	$10,001

DS4510

YEARS MFRD 2011-2016
SERIES .... DS SERIES
ENGINE .... DAEDONG 4A220LWM
CYLINDERS 4
CID 134.07
ENGINE HP 45
COOLING .... LIQUID
FUEL .... D
SPEEDS 8/8
TRANSMISSION ... SHUTTLE SHIFT
STEERING .... STANDARD
HITCH .... CAT. I
HYDRAULIC .... YES
PTO .... YES
DRIVE TYPE 4WD
ROPS/CAB .... ROPS
WEIGHT .... 3,538 LBS.
MSRP $18,650

RETAIL PRICING

YEAR	HIGH	LOW
2011	$7,852	$5,889
2012	$9,506	$7,130
2013	$10,424	$7,818
2014	$11,527	$8,646
2015	$12,090	$9,067
2016	$14,080	$10,560

DS4510HS

YEARS MFRD 2012-2016
SERIES .... DS SERIES
ENGINE .... DAEDONG 4A220LWM
CYLINDERS 4
CID 134.07
ENGINE HP 45
COOLING .... LIQUID
FUEL .... D
SPEEDS 8/8
TRANSMISSION ... SHUTTLE SHIFT
STEERING .... STANDARD
HITCH .... CAT. I
HYDRAULIC .... YES
PTO .... YES
DRIVE TYPE 4WD
ROPS/CAB .... ROPS
WEIGHT .... 3,538 LBS.
MSRP $19,414

RETAIL PRICING

YEAR	HIGH	LOW
2012	$9,837	$7,378
2013	$11,527	$8,646
2014	$13,005	$9,754
2015	$13,942	$10,456
2016	$14,917	$11,188

LB1714

YEARS MFRD 1988-1993
ENGINE .... DAEDONG
CYLINDERS.................3
CID 56.6
PTO HP 14.5
ENGINE HP 17
FUEL ....D
SPEEDS 8/8
WEIGHT ....1,900 LBS.
MSRP................ $7,495

SERIAL NUMBERS

FORWARD OF CLUTCH PEDAL ON TRANSMISSION

YEAR	BEGINNING NO.
1988	400001
1989	500001
1990	600001
1991	700001
1992	800001
1993	900001

RETAIL PRICING

YEAR	HIGH	LOW
1988	$1,823	$1,367
1989	$1,991	$1,493
1990	$2,073	$1,555

LB1914

YEARS MFRD 1995-2003
SERIES.............. LB SERIES
ENGINE ....KIOTI 3C093
CYLINDERS.................3
CID 56.6
PTO HP 17.5
ENGINE HP 20.5
COOLING ....AIR
FUEL ....D
SPEEDS 8/8
TRANSMISSION ......POWER SHIFT
STEERING............STANDARD
PTO.......................YES
DRIVE TYPE 4WD
ROPS/CAB ....ROPS
WEIGHT ....2,132 LBS.
MSRP................ $10,300

SERIAL NUMBERS

FORWARD OF THE CLUTCH PEDAL ON THE TRANSMISSION HOUSING

RETAIL PRICING

YEAR	HIGH	LOW
1995	$2,568	$1,926
1996	$2,748	$2,061
1997	$2,935	$2,201
1998	$3,138	$2,354
1999	$3,358	$2,518
2000	$3,559	$2,669
2001	$3,842	$2,881
2002	$4,108	$3,081
2003	$4,395	$3,296

AVG. AUCTION PRICING

LOW	HIGH	AVG
$2,463	$2,857	$2,692

LB2202

YEARS MFRD 1989-1989
ENGINE ....KIOTI
CYLINDERS.................3
CID 68.3
PTO HP 19
ENGINE HP 22
FUEL ....D
SPEEDS 8/2
TRANSMISSION ....GEAR
STEERING............STANDARD
WEIGHT ....2,070 LBS.
MSRP................ $7,195

SERIAL NUMBERS

FORWARD OF THE CLUTCH PEDAL ON THE TRANSMISSION HOUSING

YEAR	BEGINNING NO.
1989	500001

RETAIL PRICING

YEAR	HIGH	LOW
1989	$1,648	$1,236

LB2204

YEARS MFRD 1986-1988
ENGINE ....KIOTI
CYLINDERS.................3
CID 68
PTO HP 19
ENGINE HP 22
FUEL ....D
SPEEDS 8/2
TRANSMISSION ....GEAR
STEERING............STANDARD
DRIVE TYPE 4WD
ROPS/CAB ....ROPS
WEIGHT ....2,290 LBS.
MSRP................ $8,995

SERIAL NUMBERS

FORWARD OF CLUTCH PEDAL ON TRANSMISSION

YEAR	BEGINNING NO.
1986	200001
1987	300001
1988	400001

RETAIL PRICING

YEAR	HIGH	LOW
1986	$1,690	$1,268
1987	$1,809	$1,357
1988	$1,934	$1,450

LB2214

YEARS MFRD 1988-1992
ENGINE ....KIOTI TD1101-D
CYLINDERS.................3
CID 68.3
PTO HP 19
ENGINE HP 22
FUEL ....D
SPEEDS 8/8
TRANSMISSION ....GEAR
STEERING............STANDARD
PTO.......................YES
DRIVE TYPE 4WD
ROPS/CAB ....CAB
WEIGHT ....2,286 LBS.
MSRP................ $10,195

SERIAL NUMBERS

FORWARD OF THE CLUTCH PEDAL ON THE TRANSMISSION HOUSING

YEAR	BEGINNING NO.
1990	600001
1991	700001
1992	800001

RETAIL PRICING

YEAR	HIGH	LOW
1988	$2,181	$1,636
1989	$2,331	$1,748
1990	$2,494	$1,871
1991	$2,669	$2,002
1992	$2,917	$2,187

LB2614

YEARS MFRD 1988-1993
ENGINE ....KIOTI TD1300-D
CYLINDERS.................3
CID 79.6
PTO HP 22
ENGINE HP 26
FUEL ....D
TRANSMISSION ....GEAR
STEERING............STANDARD
PTO.......................YES
DRIVE TYPE 4WD
ROPS/CAB ....CAB
WEIGHT ....2,314 LBS.
MSRP................ $11,195

SERIAL NUMBERS

FORWARD OF THE CLUTCH PEDAL ON THE TRANSMISSION HOUSING

YEAR	BEGINNING NO.
1990	600001
1991	700001
1992	800001
1993	900001

RETAIL PRICING

YEAR	HIGH	LOW
1988	$2,356	$1,767
1989	$2,520	$1,890
1990	$2,695	$2,021
1991	$2,880	$2,160
1992	$3,080	$2,310
1993	$3,295	$2,471

LK30

YEARS MFRD 2009-2012
ENGINE .... DAEDONG TD1400B-1
CYLINDERS.................3
CID 85.13
ENGINE HP 28
COOLING ....LIQUID
FUEL ....D
SPEEDS 8/8
TRANSMISSION ... SHUTTLE SHIFT
STEERING............STANDARD
HITCH ....CAT. I
HYDRAULIC ....YES
PTO.......................YES
WEIGHT ....2,974 LBS.
MSRP................ $13,795

RETAIL PRICING

YEAR	HIGH	LOW
2009	$5,157	$3,868
2010	$5,717	$4,288
2011	$6,242	$4,681
2012	$7,423	$5,567

LK2552

YEARS MFRD 1998-2001
ENGINE ....KIOTI TD1300F-1
CYLINDERS.................3
CID 79.3
PTO HP 20
ENGINE HP 26
FUEL ....D
TRANSMISSION ....BELT
STEERING............STANDARD
DRIVE TYPE 4WD
ROPS/CAB ....ROPS
WEIGHT ....2,648 LBS.
MSRP................ $11,100

RETAIL PRICING

YEAR	HIGH	LOW
1998	$3,065	$2,299
1999	$3,280	$2,460
2000	$3,510	$2,632
2001	$3,753	$2,815

LK2554

YEARS MFRD 1994-1999
SERIES.............. LK SERIES
ENGINE ....KIOTI TD1300F-1
CYLINDERS.................3
CID 79.3
PTO HP 22
ENGINE HP 25.5
COOLING ....LIQUID
FUEL ....D
SPEEDS 8/2
TRANSMISSION ....GEAR
STEERING............STANDARD
HITCH ....CAT. I
PTO.......................YES
DRIVE TYPE 4WD
ROPS/CAB ....ROPS
WEIGHT ....2,648 LBS.
MSRP................ $11,780

OPTIONS

RETAIL PRICING

YEAR	HIGH	LOW
1994	$2,599	$1,950
1995	$2,782	$2,086
1996	$2,975	$2,231
1997	$3,182	$2,386
1998	$3,403	$2,552
1999	$3,641	$2,730

LK3052

YEARS MFRD 1993-1998
ENGINE TD1400
CYLINDERS.................3
CID 85.1
PTO HP 23
ENGINE HP 30.5
COOLING ....LIQUID
FUEL ....D
SPEEDS 8/8
TRANSMISSION ....GEAR

STEERING............STANDARD
DRIVE TYPE 4WD
ROPS/CAB ....ROPS
WEIGHT ....2,574 LBS.
MSRP................$12,775

RETAIL PRICING

YEAR	HIGH	LOW
1993	$2,687	$2,015
1994	$2,873	$2,155
1995	$3,072	$2,304
1996	$3,287	$2,465
1997	$3,516	$2,637
1998	$3,761	$2,821

LK3054

YEARS MFRD 1993-2003
ENGINE ....KIOTI TD1400
CYLINDERS.....................3
CID 85.1
PTO HP 24
ENGINE HP 30.5
FUEL ....G
TRANSMISSION ....GEAR
STEERING............STANDARD
DRIVE TYPE 4WD
ROPS/CAB ....ROPS
WEIGHT ....2,974 LBS.
MSRP................$13,360

OPTIONS

RETAIL PRICING

YEAR	HIGH	LOW
1995	$3,434	$2,575
1996	$3,669	$2,752
1997	$3,927	$2,945
1998	$4,280	$3,210
1999	$4,492	$3,369
2000	$4,804	$3,603
2001	$5,154	$3,865
2002	$5,493	$4,120
2003	$6,040	$4,530

LK3054XS

YEARS MFRD 2004-2007
SERIES..............LK SERIES
ENGINE ....KIOTI TD14008B1
CYLINDERS.....................3
CID 85.13
ENGINE HP 30.5
COOLING ....LIQUID
FUEL ....D
SPEEDS 8/8
TRANSMISSION .....POWER SHIFT
STEERING............STANDARD
HITCH ....CAT. I
PTO............................YES
WEIGHT ....2,974 LBS.

LK3504

YEARS MFRD 1998-2000
ENGINE 3A165
CYLINDERS.....................3
CID 101
PTO HP 29
ENGINE HP 35

FUEL ....D
SPEEDS 8/8
WEIGHT ....3,170 LBS.
MSRP................$14,515

RETAIL PRICING

YEAR	HIGH	LOW
1998	$4,250	$3,188
1999	$4,589	$3,442
2000	$4,864	$3,648

NX4510

YEARS MFRD 2014-2020
ENGINE ....DAEDONG 3F183T
CYLINDERS.....................4
PTO HP 37.6
ENGINE HP 45
COOLING ....LIQUID
FUEL ....D
SPEEDS 24/24
TRANSMISSION ....GEAR
STEERING............STANDARD
HITCH ....CAT. I
HYDRAULIC ....YES
PTO............................YES
DRIVE TYPE 4WD
ROPS/CAB ....ROPS
WEIGHT ....4,065 LBS.

OPTIONS

CAB
HYDRO
HYDRO/CAB
LDR

RETAIL PRICING

YEAR	HIGH	LOW
2014	$17,167	$12,914
2015	$19,177	$14,383
2016	$20,985	$15,739
2017	$24,273	$18,204
2018	$27,074	$20,305
2019	$30,535	$22,902
2020	$32,149	$24,747

NX5010

YEARS MFRD 2014-2020
ENGINE ....DAEDONG
CYLINDERS.....................3
CID 111D
PTO HP 38.9
COOLING ....LIQUID
FUEL ....D
SPEEDS 24/24
TRANSMISSION ....GEAR
STEERING............STANDARD
DRIVE TYPE 4WD
ROPS/CAB ....CAB
WEIGHT ....4,424 LBS.

OPTIONS

CAB
HYDRO
HYDRO/CAB
LDR

RETAIL PRICING

YEAR	HIGH	LOW
2014	$18,155	$13,616
2015	$20,155	$15,119
2016	$23,436	$17,577
2017	$25,491	$19,118
2018	$27,607	$20,705
2019	$29,706	$22,279
2020	$31,335	$24,005

NX5510

YEARS MFRD 2014-2020
ENGINE ....DAEDONG
CYLINDERS.....................3
CID 111D
PTO HP 43.1
FUEL ....D
SPEEDS 24/24
TRANSMISSION ....GEAR
STEERING............STANDARD
WEIGHT ....4,620 LBS.

OPTIONS

CAB
HYDRO
HYDRO/CAB
LDR

RETAIL PRICING

YEAR	HIGH	LOW
2014	$22,684	$17,012
2015	$24,922	$18,692
2016	$26,670	$20,003
2017	$28,581	$21,436
2018	$30,212	$22,779
2019	$31,372	$23,623
2020	$32,526	$24,547

NX6010

YEARS MFRD 2014-2020
ENGINE ....DAEDONG
CYLINDERS.....................3
CID 111D
PTO HP 43.1
FUEL ....D
SPEEDS ....VARIABLE
TRANSMISSION ....HYDRO
STEERING............STANDARD
DRIVE TYPE 4WD
ROPS/CAB ....ROPS
WEIGHT ....4,620 LBS.

OPTIONS

CAB
LDR

RETAIL PRICING

YEAR	HIGH	LOW
2014	$18,500	$13,875
2015	$20,556	$15,417
2016	$24,737	$18,552
2017	$26,440	$19,830
2018	$27,714	$20,868
2019	$29,145	$21,928
2020	$30,540	$22,977

ZXC48

YEARS MFRD 2019-2020
SERIES.............ZXC SERIES
ENGINE ....B&S
CID 44.18
ENGINE HP 23
FUEL ....G
SPEEDS ....VARIABLE
TRANSMISSION ....HYDRO
STEERING....................ZERO
STANDARD DECK ....48"
WEIGHT ....922 LBS.

ZXC48 SE

YEARS MFRD 2019-2020
SERIES...........ZXC SE SERIES
ENGINE .. KOHLER COMMAND PRO
CID 42.35
ENGINE HP 22.5
FUEL ....G
SPEEDS ....VARIABLE
TRANSMISSION ....HYDRO
STEERING....................ZERO
STANDARD DECK ....48"
WEIGHT ....939 LBS.

ZXC54

YEARS MFRD 2019-2020
SERIES.............ZXC SERIES
ENGINE ....B&S
CID 44.18
ENGINE HP 25
FUEL ....G
SPEEDS ....VARIABLE
TRANSMISSION ....HYDRO
STEERING....................ZERO
STANDARD DECK ....54"
WEIGHT ....939 LBS.

ZXC54 SE

YEARS MFRD 2019-2020
SERIES...........ZXC SE SERIES
ENGINE .. KOHLER COMMAND PRO
CID 42.35
ENGINE HP 23.5
FUEL ....G
SPEEDS ....VARIABLE
TRANSMISSION ....HYDRO
STEERING....................ZERO
STANDARD DECK ....54"
WEIGHT ....957 LBS.

ZXC60

YEARS MFRD 2019-2020
SERIES.............ZXC SERIES
ENGINE ....B&S
CID 49.42
ENGINE HP 27
FUEL ....G
SPEEDS ....VARIABLE
TRANSMISSION ....HYDRO
STEERING....................ZERO
STANDARD DECK ....60"
WEIGHT ....950 LBS.

ZXC60 SE

YEARS MFRD 2019-2020
SERIES...........ZXC SE SERIES
ENGINE .. KOHLER COMMAND PRO
CID 45.58

ENGINE HP 25
FUEL . . . . G
SPEEDS . . . . VARIABLE
TRANSMISSION . . . . HYDRO
STEERING. . . . . ZERO
STANDARD DECK . . . . 60"
WEIGHT . . . . 992 LBS.

ZXR48

YEARS MFRD 2019-2020
SERIES. . . . . ZXR SERIES
ENGINE . . . . B&S
CID 44.18
ENGINE HP 22
FUEL . . . . G
SPEEDS . . . . VARIABLE
TRANSMISSION . . . . HYDRO
STEERING. . . . . ZERO
STANDARD DECK . . . . 48"
WEIGHT . . . . 893 LBS.

ZXR48 SE

YEARS MFRD 2019-2020
SERIES. . . . . ZXR SE SERIES
ENGINE . . . . . .KOHLER CONFIDANT
CID 44.24
ENGINE HP 21
FUEL . . . . G
SPEEDS . . . . VARIABLE
TRANSMISSION . . . . HYDRO
STEERING. . . . . ZERO
STANDARD DECK . . . . 48"
WEIGHT . . . . 970 LBS.

ZXR54

YEARS MFRD 2019-2020
SERIES. . . . . ZXR SERIES
ENGINE . . . . B&S
CID 44.18
ENGINE HP 24
FUEL . . . . G
SPEEDS . . . . VARIABLE
TRANSMISSION . . . . HYDRO
STEERING. . . . . ZERO
STANDARD DECK . . . . 54"
WEIGHT . . . . 910 LBS.

ZXR54 SE

YEARS MFRD 2019-2020
SERIES. . . . . ZXR SE SERIES
ENGINE . . . . . .KOHLER CONFIDANT
CID 45.58
ENGINE HP 23
FUEL . . . . G
SPEEDS . . . . VARIABLE
TRANSMISSION . . . . HYDRO
STEERING. . . . . ZERO
STANDARD DECK . . . . 54"
WEIGHT . . . . 988 LBS.

ZXR60

YEARS MFRD 2019-2020
SERIES. . . . . ZXR SERIES
ENGINE . . . . B&S
CID 49.42
ENGINE HP 27
FUEL . . . . G
SPEEDS . . . . VARIABLE
TRANSMISSION . . . . HYDRO
STEERING. . . . . ZERO
STANDARD DECK . . . . 60"
WEIGHT . . . . 948 LBS.

ZXR60 SE

YEARS MFRD 2019-2020
SERIES. . . . . ZXR SE SERIES
ENGINE . . . . . .KOHLER CONFIDANT
CID 45.58
ENGINE HP 25
FUEL . . . . G
SPEEDS . . . . VARIABLE
TRANSMISSION . . . . HYDRO
STEERING. . . . . ZERO
STANDARD DECK . . . . 60"
WEIGHT . . . . 999 LBS.

NOTES

KUBOTA MODELS Suffix Identification

Code	Description	Code	Description
DT	MFWD (Dual Traction) Std Trans	HDT-W	MFWD Hyd Shuttle Wet Clutch
DT-1	MFWD Shuttle Trans (M7580/M9580)	HF	2WD Hyd Shuttle
DTC	MFWD No Cab	HSD	MFWD Hydrostatic Trans
DTCA	MFWD Cab	HSD-1	MFWD Hydro Trans Bi-Speed Turn
DTL	MFWD Low Profile	HSDB	MFWD Hydro Trans Bi-Speed Turn
DTM	MFWD Std Trans Mudder	HSD-T	MFWD Hydro Trans Tow Tractor
DTN	MFWD Narrow Tread	HSE	2WD Hydrostatic Trans
DTN-B	MFWD Narrow Tread BI-Speed Turn	L	Low Profile
DTS	MFWD Power Steering	MDT	MFWD Mech Shuttle
DTSC	MFWD Power Steering Live PTO	MDTL	MFWD Mech Shuttle Low Profile
DT-W	MFWD Wet Clutch	MF	2WD Mech Shuttle
E	2WD Standard Trans	ML	Mech Shuttle Low Profile
F	2WD	OC	Orchard Model
F-1	2WD Two Pump Hydraulics (M-Series)	S	2WD Partial Synchro Trans
FC	2WD (Live PTO No Cab on B&L Series) Cab on M Series	SD	MFWD Partial Synchro Trans
F-CS	2WD Creep Speed	SCS	2WD Partial Synchro Trans Creep Speed
FSC	2WD Power Steering Live PTO	SS	Shuttle Shift
FST	Fully Sychronized Trans	SU	Special Utility
FGST	2WD Glide Shift	SUMDT	MFWD Utility Special Mech Shuttle
GST	Glide Shift Trans	SUDT	MFWD Utility Special
GSTC	MFWD Glide Shift Trans, Cab	TL	Tractor Loader
HC	High Clearance	TLB	Tractor Loader Backhoe
HDT	MFWD Hyd Shuttle	W	Wide Tread

KUBOTA

B20TL

YEARS MFRD........ 1990-1995
SERIES............... B SERIES
ENGINE............... KUBOTA
CYLINDERS.................. 3
CID..................... 56.6
PTO HP................. 13.5
ENGINE HP................. 20
COOLING.............. LIQUID
FUEL........................ D
SPEEDS............. VARIABLE
TRANSMISSION.......... HYDRO
STEERING........... STANDARD
HITCH.................. CAT. I
HYDRAULIC............... YES
PTO...................... YES
DRIVE TYPE.............. 4WD
ROPS/CAB................ ROPS
WEIGHT............ 2,050 LBS.
MSRP................ $20,485

SERIAL NUMBERS

YEAR	BEGINNING NO.
1990	50617
1991	51298
1992	51771

RETAIL PRICING

YEAR	HIGH	LOW
1995	$5,123	$3,842

B20TLB

YEARS MFRD........ 1990-1995
SERIES............... B SERIES
ENGINE............... KUBOTA
CYLINDERS.................. 3
CID..................... 56.6
PTO HP................. 13.5
ENGINE HP................. 20
COOLING.............. LIQUID
FUEL........................ D
SPEEDS............. VARIABLE
TRANSMISSION.......... HYDRO
STEERING........... STANDARD
HITCH.................. CAT. I
HYDRAULIC............... YES
PTO...................... YES
DRIVE TYPE.............. 4WD
ROPS/CAB................ ROPS
WEIGHT............ 2,050 LBS.
MSRP................ $27,914

SERIAL NUMBERS

YEAR	BEGINNING NO.
1990	50617
1991	51298
1992	51771

RETAIL PRICING

YEAR	HIGH	LOW
1995	$7,003	$5,252

AVG. AUCTION PRICING

LOW	HIGH	AVG
$7,416	$9,013	$8,356

B21TLB

YEARS MFRD........ 1998-2009
ENGINE............... KUBOTA
CYLINDERS.................. 3
CID..................... 61.1
ENGINE HP................. 21
FUEL........................ D
SPEEDS............. VARIABLE
TRANSMISSION.......... HYDRO
STEERING........... STANDARD
HITCH................. CAT. II
HYDRAULIC............... YES
PTO...................... YES
WEIGHT............ 3,836 LBS.
MSRP................ $40,035

RETAIL PRICING

YEAR	HIGH	LOW
2001	$13,398	$10,049
2002	$14,484	$10,863
2003	$15,656	$11,742
2004	$16,923	$12,692
2005	$18,427	$13,820
2006	$19,782	$14,837
2007	$21,386	$16,039
2008	$23,119	$17,340
2009	$24,823	$18,617

B26TLB

YEARS MFRD........ 2010-2019
ENGINE............... KUBOTA
CYLINDERS.................. 3
CID....................... 68
PTO HP................. 19.5
ENGINE HP................. 26
COOLING.............. LIQUID
FUEL........................ D
SPEEDS............. VARIABLE
TRANSMISSION.......... HYDRO
STEERING........... STANDARD
HITCH.................. CAT. I
HYDRAULIC............... YES
PTO...................... YES
DRIVE TYPE.............. 4WD
ROPS/CAB................ ROPS
WEIGHT............ 4,000 LBS.
MSRP................ $36,587

OPTIONS

REMOTE VALVE KIT

RETAIL PRICING

YEAR	HIGH	LOW
2010	$20,794	$15,595
2011	$22,580	$16,935
2012	$24,127	$18,095
2013	$26,272	$19,704
2014	$27,525	$20,644
2015	$29,009	$21,757
2016	$31,704	$23,778
2017	$34,584	$25,938
2018	$37,757	$28,318
2019	$38,684	$29,013

B1550DT

YEARS MFRD........ 1988-1996
SERIES............. B50 SERIES
ENGINE............... KUBOTA
CYLINDERS.................. 3
CID..................... 52.2
PTO HP................... 14
ENGINE HP................. 17
COOLING.............. LIQUID
FUEL........................ D
SPEEDS.................. 6/2
TRANSMISSION............ GEAR
STEERING........... STANDARD
HITCH.................. CAT. I
HYDRAULIC............... YES
PTO...................... YES
DRIVE TYPE.............. 4WD
ROPS/CAB................ ROPS
WEIGHT............ 1,345 LBS.
MSRP................ $10,000

SERIAL NUMBERS

RH SIDE OF CLUTCH HOUSING/TRANS CASE

YEAR	BEGINNING NO.
1988	50162
1989	50785
1992	52349

RETAIL PRICING

YEAR	HIGH	LOW
1988	$1,114	$836
1989	$1,378	$1,034
1990	$1,651	$1,238
1991	$1,931	$1,448
1992	$2,218	$1,663
1993	$2,516	$1,887
1994	$2,820	$2,115
1995	$3,128	$2,346
1996	$3,448	$2,586

B1550E

YEARS MFRD........ 1988-1996
SERIES............. B50 SERIES
ENGINE............... KUBOTA
CYLINDERS.................. 3
CID..................... 52.2
PTO HP................... 14
ENGINE HP................. 17
COOLING.............. LIQUID
FUEL........................ D
SPEEDS.................. 6/2
TRANSMISSION............ GEAR
STEERING........... STANDARD
HITCH.................. CAT. I
HYDRAULIC............... YES
PTO...................... YES
DRIVE TYPE.............. 2WD
ROPS/CAB................ ROPS
WEIGHT............ 1,224 LBS.
MSRP................ $10,000

RETAIL PRICING

YEAR	HIGH	LOW
1990	$2,754	$2,066
1991	$2,804	$2,103
1992	$3,016	$2,262
1993	$3,280	$2,460
1994	$3,600	$2,700
1995	$3,696	$2,772
1996	$3,796	$2,847

B1550HSD

YEARS MFRD........ 1988-1996
SERIES............. B50 SERIES
ENGINE............... KUBOTA
CYLINDERS.................. 3
CID..................... 52.2
PTO HP................... 13
ENGINE HP................. 17
COOLING.............. LIQUID
FUEL........................ D
SPEEDS............. VARIABLE
TRANSMISSION.......... HYDRO
STEERING........... STANDARD
HITCH.................. CAT. I
PTO...................... YES
DRIVE TYPE.............. 4WD
ROPS/CAB................ ROPS
WEIGHT............ 1,378 LBS.
MSRP................ $13,000

SERIAL NUMBERS

RIGHT SIDE OF CLUTCH HOUSING CASE

YEAR	BEGINNING NO.
1988	50001
1989	60080
1990	61456
1991	61798
1993	62001
1994	63217

RETAIL PRICING

YEAR	HIGH	LOW
1990	$3,601	$2,701
1991	$3,669	$2,752
1992	$3,943	$2,957
1993	$4,239	$3,180
1994	$4,681	$3,511
1995	$4,805	$3,604
1996	$4,935	$3,701

B1550HSE

YEARS MFRD........ 1988-1996
SERIES............. B50 SERIES
ENGINE............... KUBOTA
CYLINDERS.................. 3
CID..................... 52.2
PTO HP................... 13
ENGINE HP................. 17
COOLING.............. LIQUID
FUEL........................ D
SPEEDS............. VARIABLE
TRANSMISSION.......... HYDRO
STEERING........... STANDARD
HITCH.................. CAT. I
HYDRAULIC............... YES
PTO...................... YES
DRIVE TYPE.............. 2WD
ROPS/CAB................ ROPS
WEIGHT............ 1,190 LBS.
MSRP................ $11,500

SERIAL NUMBERS

YEAR	BEGINNING NO.
1988	50001
1989	60080

RETAIL PRICING

YEAR	HIGH	LOW
1990	$3,194	$2,396
1991	$3,252	$2,439
1992	$3,497	$2,623
1993	$3,760	$2,820

1994	$4,142	$3,106
1995	$4,251	$3,188
1996	$4,365	$3,274

B1700DT

YEARS MFRD	1995-1999
SERIES	B SERIES
ENGINE	KUBOTA
CYLINDERS	3
CID	54.8
PTO HP	14
ENGINE HP	17
COOLING	LIQUID
FUEL	D
SPEEDS	6/2
TRANSMISSION	GEAR
STEERING	STANDARD
HITCH	CAT. I
HYDRAULIC	YES
PTO	YES
DRIVE TYPE	4WD
ROPS/CAB	ROPS
WEIGHT	1,265 LBS.
MSRP	$10,490

RETAIL PRICING

YEAR	HIGH	LOW
1995	$3,139	$2,355
1996	$3,472	$2,604
1997	$3,870	$2,902
1998	$4,247	$3,185
1999	$4,703	$3,527

AVG. AUCTION PRICING

LOW	HIGH	AVG
$2,165	$7,700	$4,331

B1700E

YEARS MFRD	1995-2000
SERIES	B SERIES
ENGINE	KUBOTA
CYLINDERS	3
CID	54.8
PTO HP	14
ENGINE HP	17
COOLING	LIQUID
FUEL	D
SPEEDS	6/2
TRANSMISSION	GEAR
STEERING	STANDARD
HITCH	CAT. I
HYDRAULIC	YES
PTO	YES
DRIVE TYPE	2WD
ROPS/CAB	ROPS
WEIGHT	1,268 LBS.
MSRP	$10,490

RETAIL PRICING

YEAR	HIGH	LOW
1997	$4,085	$3,064
1998	$4,660	$3,495
1999	$5,210	$3,907
2000	$5,775	$4,331

B1700HSD

YEARS MFRD	1995-2000
SERIES	B SERIES
ENGINE	KUBOTA
CYLINDERS	3
CID	54.8
PTO HP	13
ENGINE HP	17
COOLING	LIQUID
FUEL	D
SPEEDS	VARIABLE
TRANSMISSION	HYDRO
STEERING	STANDARD
HITCH	CAT. I
HYDRAULIC	YES
PTO	YES
DRIVE TYPE	4WD
ROPS/CAB	ROPS
WEIGHT	1,268 LBS.
MSRP	$13,190

RETAIL PRICING

YEAR	HIGH	LOW
1997	$4,669	$3,502
1998	$5,326	$3,995
1999	$5,958	$4,468
2000	$6,600	$4,950

AVG. AUCTION PRICING

LOW	HIGH	AVG
$2,533	$7,369	$4,145

B1700HSDB

YEARS MFRD	1995-2000
SERIES	B SERIES
ENGINE	KUBOTA
CYLINDERS	3
CID	54.8
PTO HP	13
ENGINE HP	17
COOLING	LIQUID
FUEL	D
SPEEDS	BI-SPEED
TRANSMISSION	HYDRO
STEERING	STANDARD
HITCH	CAT. I
HYDRAULIC	YES
PTO	YES
DRIVE TYPE	4WD
ROPS/CAB	ROPS
WEIGHT	1,268 LBS.
MSRP	$13,590

RETAIL PRICING

YEAR	HIGH	LOW
1997	$5,291	$3,968
1998	$6,038	$4,528
1999	$6,751	$5,063
2000	$7,392	$5,544

B1750DT

YEARS MFRD	1988-1996
SERIES	B50 SERIES
ENGINE	KUBOTA
CYLINDERS	3
CID	56.6
PTO HP	15
ENGINE HP	20
COOLING	LIQUID
FUEL	D
SPEEDS	6/2
TRANSMISSION	GEAR
STEERING	STANDARD
HITCH	CAT. I
HYDRAULIC	YES
PTO	YES
DRIVE TYPE	4WD
ROPS/CAB	ROPS
WEIGHT	1,384 LBS.
MSRP	$11,100

OPTIONS

HYDRO

SERIAL NUMBERS

RH SIDE OF CLUTCH HOUSING/TRANS CASE

YEAR	BEGINNING NO.
1988	50246
1989	50699
1991	52476
1992	52632
1994	53727

RETAIL PRICING

YEAR	HIGH	LOW
1988	$1,797	$1,348
1989	$2,066	$1,550
1990	$2,334	$1,750
1991	$2,625	$1,969
1992	$2,929	$2,197
1993	$3,221	$2,416
1994	$3,530	$2,647
1995	$3,851	$2,888
1996	$4,230	$3,173

B1750E

YEARS MFRD	1988-1996
SERIES	B50 SERIES
ENGINE	KUBOTA
CYLINDERS	3
CID	56.6
PTO HP	15
ENGINE HP	20
COOLING	LIQUID
FUEL	D
SPEEDS	6/2
TRANSMISSION	GEAR
STEERING	STANDARD
HITCH	CAT. I
HYDRAULIC	YES
PTO	YES
DRIVE TYPE	2WD
ROPS/CAB	ROPS
WEIGHT	1,257 LBS.
MSRP	$11,100

SERIAL NUMBERS

YEAR	BEGINNING NO.
1988	50246
1989	50699
1991	52476
1992	52632
1994	53727

RETAIL PRICING

YEAR	HIGH	LOW
1990	$3,076	$2,307
1991	$3,131	$2,348
1992	$3,607	$2,705
1993	$3,658	$2,743
1994	$3,998	$2,999
1995	$4,102	$3,077
1996	$4,213	$3,160

B1750HSD

YEARS MFRD	1988-1996
SERIES	B50 SERIES
ENGINE	KUBOTA
CYLINDERS	3
CID	56.6
PTO HP	15
ENGINE HP	20
COOLING	LIQUID
FUEL	D
SPEEDS	VARIABLE
TRANSMISSION	HYDRO
STEERING	STANDARD
HITCH	CAT. I
HYDRAULIC	YES
PTO	YES
DRIVE TYPE	4WD
ROPS/CAB	ROPS
WEIGHT	1,367 LBS.
MSRP	$14,200

SERIAL NUMBERS

YEAR	BEGINNING NO.
1988	50431
1989	60057
1990	61712
1991	62445
1992	63730
1993	65134
1994	66107

RETAIL PRICING

YEAR	HIGH	LOW
1990	$3,923	$2,942
1991	$3,992	$2,994
1992	$4,294	$3,221
1993	$4,613	$3,460
1994	$5,114	$3,835
1995	$5,247	$3,935
1996	$5,391	$4,043

B1750HSE

YEARS MFRD	1989-1996
SERIES	B50 SERIES
ENGINE	KUBOTA
CYLINDERS	3
CID	56.6
PTO HP	15.5
ENGINE HP	20
COOLING	LIQUID
FUEL	D
SPEEDS	VARIABLE
TRANSMISSION	HYDRO
STEERING	STANDARD
HITCH	CAT. I
HYDRAULIC	YES
PTO	YES
DRIVE TYPE	2WD
ROPS/CAB	ROPS
WEIGHT	1,224 LBS.
MSRP	$12,700

SERIAL NUMBERS

YEAR	BEGINNING NO.
1989	60057

RETAIL PRICING

YEAR	HIGH	LOW
1990	$3,514	$2,636
1991	$3,578	$2,684
1992	$3,841	$2,881

1993 $4,139 $3,104
1994 $4,574 $3,431
1995 $4,695 $3,521
1996 $4,820 $3,615

B2100DT

YEARS MFRD 1995-1999
SERIES B100 SERIES
ENGINE KUBOTA
CYLINDERS 3
CID 61.1
PTO HP 17
ENGINE HP 21
COOLING LIQUID
FUEL D
SPEEDS 6/2
TRANSMISSION GEAR
STEERING STANDARD
HITCH CAT. I
HYDRAULIC YES
PTO YES
DRIVE TYPE 4WD
ROPS/CAB ROPS
WEIGHT 1,310 LBS.
MSRP $12,890

OPTIONS

HYDRO

RETAIL PRICING

YEAR	HIGH	LOW
1995	$2,924	$2,193
1996	$3,332	$2,499
1997	$3,746	$2,810
1998	$4,190	$3,143
1999	$4,738	$3,554

B2100HSD

YEARS MFRD 1997-2000
SERIES B100 SERIES
ENGINE KUBOTA
CYLINDERS 3
CID 61.1
PTO HP 16
ENGINE HP 21
COOLING LIQUID
FUEL D
SPEEDS VARIABLE
TRANSMISSION HYDRO
STEERING STANDARD
HITCH CAT. I
HYDRAULIC YES
PTO YES
DRIVE TYPE 4WD
ROPS/CAB ROPS
WEIGHT 1,310 LBS.
MSRP $14,490

RETAIL PRICING

YEAR	HIGH	LOW
1997	$5,642	$4,232
1998	$6,434	$4,826
1999	$7,198	$5,398
2000	$7,977	$5,983

B2100HSDB

YEARS MFRD 1997-1999
SERIES B100 SERIES
ENGINE KUBOTA
CYLINDERS 3
CID 61.1
PTO HP 16
ENGINE HP 21
COOLING LIQUID
FUEL D
SPEEDS VARIABLE
TRANSMISSION HYDRO
STEERING STANDARD
HITCH CAT. I
HYDRAULIC YES
PTO YES
DRIVE TYPE 4WD
ROPS/CAB ROPS
WEIGHT 1,310 LBS.
MSRP $14,890

RETAIL PRICING

YEAR	HIGH	LOW
1997	$5,798	$4,348
1998	$6,614	$4,960
1999	$7,398	$5,549

B2150DT

YEARS MFRD 1988-1999
SERIES B50 SERIES
ENGINE KUBOTA
CYLINDERS 4
CID 75.4
PTO HP 18
ENGINE HP 24
COOLING LIQUID
FUEL D
SPEEDS 9/3
TRANSMISSION GEAR
STEERING STANDARD
HITCH CAT. I
HYDRAULIC YES
PTO YES
DRIVE TYPE 4WD
ROPS/CAB ROPS
WEIGHT 1,850 LBS.
MSRP $12,000

OPTIONS

HYDRO

SERIAL NUMBERS

RH SIDE OF CLUTCH HOUSING/TRANS CASE

YEAR	BEGINNING NO.
1988	50156
1989	50564

RETAIL PRICING

YEAR	HIGH	LOW
1991	$2,773	$2,080
1992	$3,104	$2,328
1993	$3,448	$2,586
1994	$3,811	$2,858
1995	$4,178	$3,133
1996	$4,563	$3,422
1997	$4,962	$3,721
1998	$5,451	$4,088
1999	$5,900	$4,425

AVG. AUCTION PRICING

LOW	HIGH	AVG
$1,925	$10,228	$4,774

B2150E

YEARS MFRD 1988-1996
SERIES B50 SERIES
ENGINE KUBOTA
CYLINDERS 4
CID 75.4
PTO HP 20
ENGINE HP 24
COOLING LIQUID
FUEL D
SPEEDS 9/3
TRANSMISSION GEAR
STEERING STANDARD
HITCH CAT. I
HYDRAULIC YES
PTO YES
DRIVE TYPE 2WD
ROPS/CAB ROPS
WEIGHT 1,725 LBS.
MSRP $12,000

SERIAL NUMBERS

YEAR	BEGINNING NO.
1988	50156
1989	50564

RETAIL PRICING

YEAR	HIGH	LOW
1990	$3,358	$2,518
1991	$3,421	$2,565
1992	$3,673	$2,755
1993	$4,102	$3,077
1994	$4,320	$3,240
1995	$4,435	$3,326
1996	$4,555	$3,416

B2150HSD

YEARS MFRD 1988-1999
SERIES B50 SERIES
ENGINE KUBOTA
CYLINDERS 4
CID 75.4
PTO HP 18
ENGINE HP 24
COOLING LIQUID
FUEL D
SPEEDS VARIABLE
TRANSMISSION HYDRO
STEERING STANDARD
HITCH CAT. I
HYDRAULIC YES
PTO YES
DRIVE TYPE 4WD
ROPS/CAB ROPS
WEIGHT 1,861 LBS.
MSRP $15,490

SERIAL NUMBERS

YEAR	BEGINNING NO.
1988	50001
1989	50848
1990	52062
1991	53511

RETAIL PRICING

YEAR	HIGH	LOW
1990	$3,856	$2,892
1991	$3,926	$2,945
1992	$4,218	$3,163
1994	$5,011	$3,758
1995	$5,142	$3,856
1996	$5,278	$3,958
1997	$5,483	$4,112
1998	$6,256	$4,692
1999	$6,996	$5,247

AVG. AUCTION PRICING

LOW	HIGH	AVG
$2,072	$8,636	$4,342

B2150HSE

YEARS MFRD 1988-1996
SERIES B50 SERIES
ENGINE KUBOTA
CYLINDERS 4
CID 75.4
PTO HP 18
ENGINE HP 24
COOLING LIQUID
FUEL D
SPEEDS VARIABLE
TRANSMISSION HYDRO
STEERING STANDARD
HITCH CAT. I
HYDRAULIC YES
PTO YES
DRIVE TYPE 2WD
ROPS/CAB ROPS
WEIGHT 1,736 LBS.
MSRP $13,700

SERIAL NUMBERS

YEAR	BEGINNING NO.
1988	50001
1989	50848

RETAIL PRICING

YEAR	HIGH	LOW
1990	$3,833	$2,874
1991	$3,902	$2,926
1992	$4,179	$3,134
1993	$4,477	$3,358
1994	$4,934	$3,700
1995	$5,065	$3,798
1996	$5,199	$3,900

B2301

YEARS MFRD 2015-2018
ENGINE KUBOTA
CYLINDERS 3
CID 61.1
PTO HP 17.5
ENGINE HP 22
COOLING LIQUID
FUEL D
SPEEDS VARIABLE
TRANSMISSION HYDRO
STEERING STANDARD
HITCH CAT. I
DRIVE TYPE 2WD
ROPS/CAB ROPS
MSRP $14,690

OPTIONS

54" DECK
60" DECK
LDR

See Kubota Model Suffix Identification on page 415

RETAIL PRICING

YEAR	HIGH	LOW
2015	$13,275	$9,956
2016	$14,048	$10,536
2017	$14,739	$11,054
2018	$15,249	$11,437

B2301 HSD

YEARS MFRD	2019-2020
SERIES	B01 SERIES
ENGINE	KUBOTA D1005
CYLINDERS	3
CID	61.1
PTO HP	17.5
ENGINE HP	20.9
COOLING	LIQUID
FUEL	D
TRANSMISSION	HYDRO
STEERING	STANDARD
HITCH	CAT. I
DRIVE TYPE	4WD
ROPS/CAB	ROPS
WEIGHT	1,566 LBS.
MSRP	$14,884

OPTIONS

54" MM MOWER	$2,162
LDR PKG	$3,031

B2320DT

YEARS MFRD	2008-2020
ENGINE	KUBOTA
CYLINDERS	3
CID	61.1
PTO HP	18
ENGINE HP	20.9
COOLING	AIR
FUEL	D
SPEEDS	9/3
TRANSMISSION	GEAR
STEERING	STANDARD
HITCH	CAT. I
DRIVE TYPE	4WD
ROPS/CAB	ROPS
WEIGHT	1,433 LBS.
MSRP	$11,999

OPTIONS

BACKHOE	$6,886
LDR PKG	$2,810

RETAIL PRICING

YEAR	HIGH	LOW
2008	$6,636	$4,977
2009	$7,137	$5,352
2010	$7,653	$5,740
2011	$8,184	$6,138
2012	$8,730	$6,548
2013	$9,246	$6,934
2014	$9,856	$7,393
2015	$10,264	$7,698
2016	$10,903	$8,178
2017	$11,187	$8,390
2018	$11,551	$8,663
2019	$11,923	$8,943
2020	$12,384	$9,411

AVG. AUCTION PRICING

LOW	HIGH	AVG
$9,210	$12,089	$10,554

B2320DTN

YEARS MFRD	2010-2014
ENGINE	KUBOTA
CYLINDERS	3
CID	61
PTO HP	17.2
ENGINE HP	23
COOLING	LIQUID
FUEL	D
SPEEDS	VARIABLE
TRANSMISSION	HYDRO
STEERING	STANDARD
HYDRAULIC	YES
PTO	YES
DRIVE TYPE	2WD
ROPS/CAB	ROPS
WEIGHT	1,433 LBS.
MSRP	$12,909

RETAIL PRICING

YEAR	HIGH	LOW
2010	$6,597	$4,948
2011	$7,210	$5,408
2012	$8,078	$6,059
2013	$9,102	$6,827
2014	$10,176	$7,632

B2320DTN-1

YEARS MFRD	2019-2020
ENGINE	KUBOTA D1005 E-TVCS
CYLINDERS	3
CID	61.1
PTO HP	18
ENGINE HP	20.9
COOLING	LIQUID
FUEL	D
SPEEDS	9/3
TRANSMISSION	GEAR
STEERING	STANDARD
HITCH	CAT. I
DRIVE TYPE	4WD
ROPS/CAB	ROPS
WEIGHT	1,334 LBS.
MSRP	$12,586

B2320HSD

YEARS MFRD	2008-2014
SERIES	B SERIES
ENGINE	KUBOTA D1005
CYLINDERS	3
CID	61.1
PTO HP	17
ENGINE HP	23
COOLING	LIQUID
FUEL	D
SPEEDS	VARIABLE
TRANSMISSION	HYDRO
STEERING	STANDARD
HITCH	CAT. I
HYDRAULIC	YES
PTO	YES
DRIVE TYPE	4WD
ROPS/CAB	ROPS
WEIGHT	1,433 LBS.
MSRP	$13,499

OPTIONS

LDR

RETAIL PRICING

YEAR	HIGH	LOW
2008	$5,779	$4,334
2009	$6,392	$4,794
2010	$6,904	$5,178
2011	$7,569	$5,677
2012	$8,437	$6,328
2013	$9,511	$7,133
2014	$10,636	$7,977

B2400HSD

YEARS MFRD	1995-1999
SERIES	B SERIES
ENGINE	KUBOTA
CYLINDERS	3
CID	68.5
PTO HP	18
ENGINE HP	24
COOLING	LIQUID
FUEL	D
SPEEDS	VARIABLE
TRANSMISSION	HYDRO
STEERING	STANDARD
HITCH	CAT. I
HYDRAULIC	YES
PTO	YES
DRIVE TYPE	4WD
ROPS/CAB	ROPS
WEIGHT	1,461 LBS.
MSRP	$13,690

RETAIL PRICING

YEAR	HIGH	LOW
1995	$2,988	$2,241
1996	$3,343	$2,508
1997	$3,717	$2,788
1998	$4,178	$3,133
1999	$4,937	$3,703

AVG. AUCTION PRICING

LOW	HIGH	AVG
$2,369	$7,313	$4,987

B2400HSDB

YEARS MFRD	1995-1999
SERIES	B SERIES
ENGINE	KUBOTA
CYLINDERS	3
CID	68.5
PTO HP	18
ENGINE HP	24
COOLING	LIQUID
FUEL	D
TRANSMISSION	HYDRO
STEERING	STANDARD
HITCH	CAT. I
HYDRAULIC	YES
PTO	YES
DRIVE TYPE	4WD
ROPS/CAB	ROPS
WEIGHT	1,461 LBS.
MSRP	$15,390

RETAIL PRICING

YEAR	HIGH	LOW
1997	$5,993	$4,494
1998	$6,836	$5,127
1999	$7,646	$5,734

B2400HSE

YEARS MFRD	1995-2000
SERIES	B SERIES
ENGINE	KUBOTA
CYLINDERS	3
CID	68.5
PTO HP	18
ENGINE HP	24
COOLING	LIQUID
FUEL	D
SPEEDS	VARIABLE
TRANSMISSION	HYDRO
STEERING	STANDARD
HITCH	CAT. I
HYDRAULIC	YES
PTO	YES
DRIVE TYPE	2WD
ROPS/CAB	ROPS
WEIGHT	1,325 LBS.
MSRP	$13,690

RETAIL PRICING

YEAR	HIGH	LOW
1997	$5,330	$3,998
1998	$6,080	$4,560
1999	$6,799	$5,099
2000	$7,535	$5,652

B2401DT

YEARS MFRD	2020-2020
SERIES	B01 SERIES
ENGINE	KUBOTA D1105
CYLINDERS	3
CID	68.5
PTO HP	19.2
ENGINE HP	21.9
COOLING	LIQUID
FUEL	D
SPEEDS	9/3
TRANSMISSION	GEAR
STEERING	STANDARD
HITCH	CAT. I
PTO	YES
DRIVE TYPE	4WD
ROPS/CAB	ROPS
WEIGHT	1,521 LBS.
MSRP	$11,895

OPTIONS

54" MM MOWER	$2,162
LDR PKG	$3,031

B2401DTN

YEARS MFRD	2020-2020
SERIES	B01 SERIES
ENGINE	KUBOTA D1105
CYLINDERS	3
CID	68.5
PTO HP	19.2
ENGINE HP	21.9
COOLING	LIQUID
FUEL	D
SPEEDS	9/3
TRANSMISSION	GEAR
STEERING	STANDARD
HITCH	CAT. I
PTO	YES
DRIVE TYPE	4WD

ROPS/CAB . . . . . ROPS
WEIGHT . . . . . 1,334 LBS.
MSRP. $13,240

OPTIONS

SUNSHADE. $444

B2410HSD

YEARS MFRD 2000-2005
SERIES. . . . . B DELUXE SERIES
ENGINE . . . . . KUBOTA
CYLINDERS. 3
CID 68.5
PTO HP 18
ENGINE HP. 24
COOLING . . . . . LIQUID
FUEL . . . . . D
SPEEDS . . . . . VARIABLE
TRANSMISSION . . . . . HYDRO
STEERING. . . . . STANDARD
HITCH . . . . . CAT. I
HYDRAULIC . . . . . YES
PTO . . . . . YES
DRIVE TYPE 4WD
ROPS/CAB . . . . . ROPS
WEIGHT . . . . . 1,477 LBS.
MSRP. $14,280

RETAIL PRICING

YEAR	HIGH	LOW
2000	$5,532	$4,149
2001	$5,685	$4,263
2002	$6,196	$4,647
2003	$6,792	$5,094
2004	$7,650	$5,737
2005	$8,356	$6,267

B2410HSDB

YEARS MFRD 2001-2005
SERIES. . . . . B DELUXE SERIES
ENGINE . . . . . KUBOTA E TVCS
CYLINDERS. 3
CID 68.5
PTO HP 18
ENGINE HP. 24
COOLING . . . . . LIQUID
FUEL . . . . . D
SPEEDS . . . . . VARIABLE
TRANSMISSION . . . . . HYDRO
STEERING. . . . . STANDARD
HITCH . . . . . CAT. I
PTO . . . . . YES
DRIVE TYPE 4WD
ROPS/CAB . . . . . ROPS
WEIGHT . . . . . 1,500 LBS.
MSRP. $14,680

RETAIL PRICING

YEAR	HIGH	LOW
2001	$8,869	$6,652
2002	$9,658	$7,244
2003	$10,469	$7,852
2004	$11,557	$8,667
2005	$12,507	$9,380

B2410HSE

YEARS MFRD 2000-2006
SERIES. . . . . B DELUXE SERIES
ENGINE . . . . . KUBOTA E TVCS
CYLINDERS. 3
CID 68.5
PTO HP 18
ENGINE HP. 24
COOLING . . . . . LIQUID
FUEL . . . . . D
SPEEDS . . . . . VARIABLE
TRANSMISSION . . . . . HYDRO
STEERING. . . . . STANDARD
HITCH . . . . . CAT. I
HYDRAULIC . . . . . YES
PTO . . . . . YES
DRIVE TYPE 2WD
ROPS/CAB . . . . . ROPS
WEIGHT . . . . . 1,367 LBS.
MSRP. $12,680

RETAIL PRICING

YEAR	HIGH	LOW
2000	$6,851	$5,138
2001	$6,966	$5,224
2002	$7,583	$5,687
2003	$8,332	$6,249
2004	$8,809	$6,606
2005	$8,929	$6,697
2006	$9,550	$7,163

AVG. AUCTION PRICING

LOW	HIGH	AVG
$4,605	$11,283	$8,251

B2410SDB

YEARS MFRD 2004-2004
SERIES. . . . . B SERIES
ENGINE . . . . . KUBOTA E TVCS
CYLINDERS. 3
CID 81.5
PTO HP 20
ENGINE HP. 27
COOLING . . . . . LIQUID
FUEL . . . . . D
SPEEDS . . . . . 3 RANGE
TRANSMISSION . . . . . GEAR
STEERING. . . . . STANDARD
HITCH . . . . . CAT. I
PTO . . . . . YES
DRIVE TYPE 4WD
ROPS/CAB . . . . . ROPS
MSRP. $13,680

RETAIL PRICING

YEAR	HIGH	LOW
2004	$10,769	$8,076

AVG. AUCTION PRICING

LOW	HIGH	AVG
$4,812	$11,790	$8,623

B2601 HSD

YEARS MFRD 2019-2020
SERIES. . . . . B01 SERIES
ENGINE . . . . . KUBOTA D1105
CYLINDERS. 3
CID 68.5
PTO HP 19.5
ENGINE HP. 24.3
COOLING . . . . . LIQUID
FUEL . . . . . D
TRANSMISSION . . . . . HYDRO
STEERING. . . . . STANDARD
HITCH . . . . . CAT. I
DRIVE TYPE 4WD
ROPS/CAB . . . . . ROPS
WEIGHT . . . . . 1,632 LBS.
MSRP. $15,893

OPTIONS

54" MM MOWER $2,162
LDR PKG $3,031

B2601DT

YEARS MFRD 2015-2018
ENGINE . . . . . KUBOTA
CYLINDERS. 3
CID 68.5
PTO HP 19.5
ENGINE HP. 25.5
COOLING . . . . . LIQUID
FUEL . . . . . D
SPEEDS . . . . . VARIABLE
TRANSMISSION . . . . . HYDRO
STEERING. . . . . STANDARD
HITCH . . . . . CAT. I
DRIVE TYPE 4WD
ROPS/CAB . . . . . ROPS
WEIGHT . . . . . 1,632 LBS.
MSRP. $15,680

OPTIONS

54"DECK
60"DECK
BACKHOE
LDR

RETAIL PRICING

YEAR	HIGH	LOW
2015	$13,340	$10,005
2016	$14,452	$10,839
2017	$15,817	$11,863
2018	$16,607	$12,455

B2620HSD

YEARS MFRD 2008-2016
SERIES. . . . . B SERIES
ENGINE . . . . . KUBOTA D1105
CYLINDERS. 3
CID 68.5
PTO HP 19
ENGINE HP. 26
COOLING . . . . . LIQUID
FUEL . . . . . D
SPEEDS . . . . . VARIABLE
TRANSMISSION . . . . . HYDRO
STEERING. . . . . STANDARD
HITCH . . . . . CAT. I
HYDRAULIC . . . . . YES
PTO . . . . . YES
DRIVE TYPE 4WD
ROPS/CAB . . . . . ROPS
WEIGHT . . . . . 1,554 LBS.
MSRP. $14,648

OPTIONS

54"DECK
60"DECK
LDR

RETAIL PRICING

YEAR	HIGH	LOW
2008	$8,865	$6,649
2009	$9,672	$7,254
2010	$10,362	$7,771
2011	$11,053	$8,290
2012	$11,974	$8,980
2013	$12,780	$9,585
2014	$13,701	$10,276
2015	$14,392	$10,794
2016	$14,967	$11,225

AVG. AUCTION PRICING

LOW	HIGH	AVG
$8,636	$14,392	$10,554

B2630HSD

YEARS MFRD 2005-2012
ENGINE . . . KUBOTA D1105-E2-D21
CYLINDERS. 3
CID 68.5
PTO HP 19.5
ENGINE HP. 26
COOLING . . . . . LIQUID
FUEL . . . . . D
SPEEDS . . . . . VARIABLE
TRANSMISSION . . . . . HYDRO
STEERING. . . . . STANDARD
HITCH . . . . . CAT. I
HYDRAULIC . . . . . YES
PTO . . . . . YES
DRIVE TYPE 4WD
ROPS/CAB . . . . . ROPS
WEIGHT . . . . . 1,786 LBS.
MSRP. $17,403

OPTIONS

60"DECK
72"DECK
LDR

RETAIL PRICING

YEAR	HIGH	LOW
2005	$9,460	$7,095
2006	$10,191	$7,643
2007	$10,848	$8,136
2008	$11,750	$8,813
2009	$12,579	$9,435
2010	$13,439	$10,080
2011	$14,386	$10,790
2012	$15,423	$11,567

B2650HSDC

YEARS MFRD 2013-2020
SERIES. . . . . B50 SERIES
ENGINE . . . . . KUBOTA
CYLINDERS. 3
CID 77
PTO HP 19.5
ENGINE HP. 26
COOLING . . . . . LIQUID
FUEL . . . . . D
SPEEDS . . . . . VARIABLE
TRANSMISSION . . . . . HYDRO
STEERING. . . . . STANDARD
DRIVE TYPE 4WD
ROPS/CAB . . . . . CAB
WEIGHT . . . . . 2,293 LBS.
MSRP. $24,435

OPTIONS

60"DECK $2,839
72"DECK $3,574
BACKHOE. $8,004
LDR PKG $3,322
ROPS. . . . . $-7,707

RETAIL PRICING

YEAR	HIGH	LOW
2013	$19,706	$14,779
2014	$20,178	$15,133
2015	$21,292	$15,969
2016	$22,280	$16,710
2017	$23,823	$17,867
2018	$24,618	$18,463
2019	$25,276	$18,957
2020	$25,957	$19,622

B2710HSD

YEARS MFRD 2000-2005
SERIES . . . . B PREMIER SERIES
ENGINE . . . . KUBOTA
CYLINDERS 4
CID 81.5
PTO HP 20
ENGINE HP 27
COOLING . . . . LIQUID
FUEL . . . . D
SPEEDS . . . . VARIABLE
TRANSMISSION . . . . HYDRO
STEERING . . . . STANDARD
HITCH . . . . CAT. I
HYDRAULIC . . . . YES
PTO . . . . YES
DRIVE TYPE 4WD
ROPS/CAB . . . . ROPS
WEIGHT . . . . 1,741 LBS.
MSRP $15,500

OPTIONS

60"DECK
72"DECK
LDR

SERIAL NUMBERS

YEAR	BEGINNING NO.
2000	50907

RETAIL PRICING

YEAR	HIGH	LOW
2000	$6,966	$5,224
2001	$7,126	$5,344
2002	$7,284	$5,463
2003	$7,899	$5,924
2004	$8,538	$6,403
2005	$9,201	$6,901

AVG. AUCTION PRICING

LOW	HIGH	AVG
$7,519	$8,446	$8,068

B2910HSD

YEARS MFRD 2000-2005
SERIES . . . . B PREMIER SERIES
ENGINE . . . . KUBOTA
CYLINDERS 4
CID 91.5
PTO HP 22
ENGINE HP 30
COOLING . . . . LIQUID
FUEL . . . . D
SPEEDS . . . . VARIABLE
TRANSMISSION . . . . HYDRO
STEERING . . . . STANDARD
HITCH . . . . CAT. I
HYDRAULIC . . . . YES
PTO . . . . YES
DRIVE TYPE 4WD
ROPS/CAB . . . . ROPS
WEIGHT . . . . 1,763 LBS.
MSRP $16,580

OPTIONS

60"DECK
72"DECK
LDR

RETAIL PRICING

YEAR	HIGH	LOW
2000	$7,008	$5,256
2001	$7,597	$5,698
2002	$8,249	$6,187
2003	$8,852	$6,639
2004	$9,514	$7,136
2005	$10,387	$7,790

AVG. AUCTION PRICING

LOW	HIGH	AVG
$5,383	$10,511	$7,494

B2920HSD

YEARS MFRD 2008-2013
SERIES . . . . B SERIES
ENGINE . . . . KUBOTA D1305
CYLINDERS 3
PTO HP 21
ENGINE HP 29
COOLING . . . . LIQUID
FUEL . . . . D
SPEEDS . . . . VARIABLE
TRANSMISSION . . . . HYDRO
STEERING . . . . STANDARD
HITCH . . . . CAT. I
HYDRAULIC . . . . YES
PTO . . . . YES
DRIVE TYPE 4WD
ROPS/CAB . . . . ROPS
WEIGHT . . . . 1,554 LBS.
MSRP $15,539

OPTIONS

60"DECK
LDR

RETAIL PRICING

YEAR	HIGH	LOW
2008	$11,246	$8,434
2009	$12,089	$9,067
2010	$13,090	$9,818
2011	$14,067	$10,550
2012	$14,845	$11,134
2013	$15,946	$11,960

B3000HSDC

YEARS MFRD 2012-2014
ENGINE . . . . KUBOTA
CYLINDERS 4
CID 91
PTO HP 23
COOLING . . . . LIQUID
FUEL . . . . D
SPEEDS . . . . VARIABLE
TRANSMISSION . . . . HYDRO
STEERING . . . . STANDARD
DRIVE TYPE 4WD
ROPS/CAB . . . . ROPS
WEIGHT . . . . 2,271 LBS.
MSRP $23,007

OPTIONS

2 HYD
60" DECK
72" DECK
CAB W/A/H
LDR

RETAIL PRICING

YEAR	HIGH	LOW
2012	$15,126	$11,344
2013	$17,117	$12,837
2014	$19,055	$14,291

B3030HSD

YEARS MFRD 2005-2012
ENGINE . . . . KUBOTA
CYLINDERS 4
CID 91.5
PTO HP 23
ENGINE HP 30
COOLING . . . . LIQUID
FUEL . . . . D
SPEEDS . . . . VARIABLE
TRANSMISSION . . . . HYDRO
STEERING . . . . STANDARD
HITCH . . . . CAT. I
HYDRAULIC . . . . YES
PTO . . . . YES
DRIVE TYPE 4WD
ROPS/CAB . . . . ROPS
WEIGHT . . . . 1,852 LBS.
MSRP $18,903

OPTIONS

60" DECK
72" DECK
CAB W/A/H
LDR

RETAIL PRICING

YEAR	HIGH	LOW
2005	$10,793	$8,095
2006	$11,470	$8,603
2007	$12,106	$9,079
2008	$13,236	$9,927
2009	$14,184	$10,638
2010	$14,652	$10,989
2011	$15,502	$11,626
2012	$16,411	$12,308

AVG. AUCTION PRICING

LOW	HIGH	AVG
$5,150	$12,875	$8,729

B3200HSD

YEARS MFRD 2009-2013
ENGINE . . . . KUBOTA V1505-E3D24
CYLINDERS 4
CID 91.5
PTO HP 23.9
ENGINE HP 32
COOLING . . . . LIQUID
FUEL . . . . D
SPEEDS . . . . VARIABLE
TRANSMISSION . . . . HYDRO
STEERING . . . . STANDARD
HITCH . . . . CAT. I
HYDRAULIC . . . . YES
PTO . . . . YES
DRIVE TYPE 4WD
ROPS/CAB . . . . ROPS
WEIGHT . . . . 1,764 LBS.
MSRP $15,874

OPTIONS

60"DECK
72"DECK
LDR

RETAIL PRICING

YEAR	HIGH	LOW
2009	$11,108	$8,331
2010	$11,849	$8,887
2011	$12,938	$9,703
2012	$14,093	$10,570
2013	$14,798	$11,099

AVG. AUCTION PRICING

LOW	HIGH	AVG
$10,300	$13,287	$11,673

B3300SUHSDP

YEARS MFRD 2010-2014
ENGINE . . . . KUBOTA
CYLINDERS 4
CID 91.4
PTO HP 25
ENGINE HP 33
COOLING . . . . LIQUID
FUEL . . . . D
SPEEDS . . . . VARIABLE
TRANSMISSION . . . . HYDRO
STEERING . . . . STANDARD
HITCH . . . . CAT. I
HYDRAULIC . . . . YES
PTO . . . . YES
DRIVE TYPE 4WD
ROPS/CAB . . . . ROPS
MSRP $18,704

OPTIONS

2 HYD
LDR

RETAIL PRICING

YEAR	HIGH	LOW
2010	$8,289	$6,217
2011	$11,627	$8,720
2012	$12,380	$9,285
2013	$13,887	$10,416
2014	$15,502	$11,626

B3350HSDC

YEARS MFRD 2013-2020
SERIES . . . . B50 SERIES
ENGINE . . . . KUBOTA
CYLINDERS 4
CID 91
PTO HP 27
FUEL . . . . D
SPEEDS . . . . VARIABLE
TRANSMISSION . . . . HYDRO
STEERING . . . . STANDARD
DRIVE TYPE 4WD
ROPS/CAB . . . . CAB
WEIGHT . . . . 2,447 LBS.
MSRP $28,130

OPTIONS

60"DECK $2,839
72"DECK $3,574
BACKHOE $8,004
LDR PKG $3,322
ROPS . . . . $-7,425

KUBOTA See Kubota Model Suffix Identification on page 415

RETAIL PRICING

YEAR	HIGH	LOW
2013	$21,311	$15,983
2014	$22,039	$16,529
2015	$23,168	$17,376
2016	$25,430	$19,072
2017	$27,730	$20,797
2018	$28,701	$21,526
2019	$29,212	$21,908
2020	$29,961	$23,668

B3350SUHSD

YEARS MFRD	2015-2019
SERIES	50SU SERIES
ENGINE	KUBOTA V1505
CYLINDERS	4
CID	91.5
PTO HP	27
ENGINE HP	30.8
COOLING	LIQUID
FUEL	D
TRANSMISSION	HYDRO
STEERING	STANDARD
DRIVE TYPE	4WD
ROPS/CAB	ROPS
WEIGHT	1,874 LBS.
MSRP	$18,454

OPTIONS

BACKHOE
LDR PKG

B4200DT

YEARS MFRD	1987-1996
SERIES	B200 SERIES
ENGINE	KUBOTA
CYLINDERS	2
CID	34.8
PTO HP	10
ENGINE HP	12.5
COOLING	LIQUID
FUEL	D
SPEEDS	6/2
TRANSMISSION	GEAR
STEERING	STANDARD
HITCH	CAT. I
HYDRAULIC	YES
PTO	YES
DRIVE TYPE	4WD
ROPS/CAB	ROPS
WEIGHT	926 LBS.
MSRP	$8,300

OPTIONS

44"DECK
LDR

SERIAL NUMBERS

RH SIDE OF CLUTCH HOUSING/TRANS CASE

YEAR	BEGINNING NO.
1987	10003
1988	10619
1989	30014
1990	44409
1991	58806
1992	73203
1993	55750
1994	55906

RETAIL PRICING

YEAR	HIGH	LOW
1988	$1,726	$1,295
1989	$1,959	$1,469
1990	$2,192	$1,644
1991	$2,438	$1,829
1992	$2,697	$2,022
1993	$2,954	$2,216
1994	$3,225	$2,419
1995	$3,582	$2,687
1996	$3,950	$2,963

B5100DT

YEARS MFRD	1976-1986
SERIES	B100 SERIES
ENGINE	KUBOTA
CYLINDERS	2
CID	31
PTO HP	9.5
ENGINE HP	12
COOLING	LIQUID
FUEL	D
SPEEDS	6/2
TRANSMISSION	GEAR
STEERING	STANDARD
HITCH	CAT. I
DRIVE TYPE	4WD
ROPS/CAB	ROPS
WEIGHT	882 LBS.
MSRP	$4,400

SERIAL NUMBERS

RIGHT SIDE OF CLUTCH HOUSING

YEAR	BEGINNING NO.
1976	10001
1977	11031
1978	14661
1979	16477
1980	17225
1981	18360
1982	50001
1983	50880
1984	51639
1985	52156
1986	52859

RETAIL PRICING

YEAR	HIGH	LOW
1978	$832	$624
1979	$921	$691
1980	$925	$694
1981	$977	$733
1982	$1,036	$777
1983	$1,122	$841
1984	$1,256	$942
1985	$1,392	$1,044
1986	$1,530	$1,147

B5200DT

YEARS MFRD	1983-1996
SERIES	B200 SERIES
ENGINE	KUBOTA
CYLINDERS	3
CID	45.5
PTO HP	11.5
ENGINE HP	13
COOLING	LIQUID
FUEL	D
SPEEDS	6/2
TRANSMISSION	GEAR
STEERING	STANDARD
HITCH	CAT. I
DRIVE TYPE	2WD
ROPS/CAB	ROPS
WEIGHT	1,254 LBS.
MSRP	$8,200

OPTIONS

4WD
54"DECK
LDR

SERIAL NUMBERS

YEAR	BEGINNING NO.
1983	10003
1984	11800
1985	30003
1986	48516
1987	66409
1988	74602
1989	82795
1990	90488
1991	97681
1992	104372

RETAIL PRICING

YEAR	HIGH	LOW
1988	$1,787	$1,340
1989	$2,015	$1,511
1990	$2,255	$1,691
1991	$2,500	$1,875
1992	$2,751	$2,063
1993	$3,090	$2,318
1994	$3,440	$2,580
1995	$3,797	$2,847
1996	$4,164	$3,123

B6100DT

YEARS MFRD	1976-1984
SERIES	B100 SERIES
ENGINE	KUBOTA
CYLINDERS	3
CID	41.2
PTO HP	11
ENGINE HP	14
COOLING	LIQUID
FUEL	D
SPEEDS	6/2
TRANSMISSION	GEAR
STEERING	STANDARD
HITCH	CAT. I
DRIVE TYPE	4WD
ROPS/CAB	ROPS
WEIGHT	1,030 LBS.
MSRP	$5,200

SERIAL NUMBERS

LEFT SIDE OF CLUTCH HOUSING

YEAR	BEGINNING NO.
1976	10001
1977	13181
1978	22029
1979	25699
1980	30108
1981	32873
1982	51152
1984	51844
1985	52075

RETAIL PRICING

YEAR	HIGH	LOW
1978	$899	$674
1979	$1,070	$803
1980	$1,242	$932
1981	$1,430	$1,072
1982	$1,616	$1,212
1983	$1,873	$1,404
1984	$2,072	$1,554
1985	$2,155	$1,616

B6100E

YEARS MFRD	1976-1985
SERIES	B100 SERIES
ENGINE	KUBOTA
CYLINDERS	3
CID	41.2
PTO HP	11
ENGINE HP	14
COOLING	LIQUID
FUEL	D
SPEEDS	6/2
TRANSMISSION	GEAR
STEERING	STANDARD
HITCH	CAT. I
DRIVE TYPE	2WD
ROPS/CAB	ROPS
WEIGHT	945 LBS.
MSRP	$5,290

SERIAL NUMBERS

LEFT SIDE OF CLUTCH HOUSING

YEAR	BEGINNING NO.
1976	10001
1977	10051
1978	10801
1979	12987
1980	13582
1981	16911
1982	17923
1983	18815
1984	18823

RETAIL PRICING

YEAR	HIGH	LOW
1978	$717	$538
1979	$799	$599
1980	$850	$637
1981	$926	$694
1982	$1,002	$752
1983	$1,085	$813
1984	$1,143	$857
1985	$1,281	$961

B6100HSD

YEARS MFRD	1980-1986
SERIES	B100 SERIES
ENGINE	KUBOTA
CYLINDERS	3
CID	41.2
PTO HP	11
ENGINE HP	14
COOLING	LIQUID
FUEL	D
SPEEDS	VARIABLE
TRANSMISSION	HYDRO
STEERING	STANDARD
HITCH	CAT. I

DRIVE TYPE 4WD
ROPS/CAB . . . . . ROPS
WEIGHT . . . . . 1,155 LBS.
MSRP $6,925

SERIAL NUMBERS

LEFT SIDE OF CLUTCH HOUSING

YEAR	BEGINNING NO.
1980	10002
1981	30001
1982	50001
1983	51127
1984	52253
1985	52853
1986	53456

RETAIL PRICING

YEAR	HIGH	LOW
1981	$1,154	$865
1982	$1,248	$936
1983	$1,349	$1,012
1984	$1,422	$1,067
1985	$1,643	$1,232
1986	$1,832	$1,374

B6100HSE

YEARS MFRD 1981-1986
SERIES . . . . . B100 SERIES
ENGINE . . . . . KUBOTA
CYLINDERS 3
CID 41.2
PTO HP 11
ENGINE HP 14
COOLING . . . . . LIQUID
FUEL . . . . . D
SPEEDS . . . . . VARIABLE
TRANSMISSION . . . . . HYDRO
STEERING . . . . . STANDARD
HITCH . . . . . CAT. I
DRIVE TYPE 2WD
ROPS/CAB . . . . . ROPS
WEIGHT . . . . . 1,089 LBS.
MSRP $6,445

SERIAL NUMBERS

LEFT SIDE OF CLUTCH HOUSING

YEAR	BEGINNING NO.
1981	10002
1982	10886
1983	11140
1984	11396
1985	11650
1986	11904

RETAIL PRICING

YEAR	HIGH	LOW
1981	$1,052	$789
1982	$1,138	$854
1983	$1,231	$923
1984	$1,297	$973
1985	$1,515	$1,136
1986	$1,705	$1,278

B6200DT

YEARS MFRD 1983-1995
SERIES . . . . . B200 SERIES
ENGINE . . . . . KUBOTA
CYLINDERS 3
CID 52.2
PTO HP 12.5
ENGINE HP 15
COOLING . . . . . LIQUID
FUEL . . . . . D
SPEEDS 6/2
TRANSMISSION . . . . . GEAR
STEERING . . . . . STANDARD
HITCH . . . . . CAT. I
HYDRAULIC . . . . . YES
PTO . . . . . YES
DRIVE TYPE 4WD
ROPS/CAB . . . . . ROPS
WEIGHT . . . . . 1,179 LBS.
MSRP $8,300

SERIAL NUMBERS

YEAR	BEGINNING NO.
1983	10001
1984	11022
1984	38505
1985	20183
1986	29344
1987	38505
1988	49666
1989	19666
1990	59827
1991	68687
1992	78848
1993	88001
1994	98151
1995	108301

RETAIL PRICING

YEAR	HIGH	LOW
1986	$2,766	$2,074
1987	$2,993	$2,245
1988	$3,227	$2,420
1989	$3,467	$2,600
1990	$3,782	$2,837
1991	$4,107	$3,080
1992	$4,447	$3,335
1993	$4,791	$3,593
1994	$5,153	$3,865
1995	$5,381	$4,036

B6200E

YEARS MFRD 1983-1996
SERIES . . . . . B200 SERIES
ENGINE . . . . . KUBOTA
CYLINDERS 3
CID 52.2
PTO HP 12.5
ENGINE HP 15
COOLING . . . . . LIQUID
FUEL . . . . . D
SPEEDS 6/2
TRANSMISSION . . . . . GEAR
STEERING . . . . . STANDARD
HITCH . . . . . CAT. I
HYDRAULIC . . . . . YES
PTO . . . . . YES
DRIVE TYPE 2WD
ROPS/CAB . . . . . ROPS
WEIGHT . . . . . 1,130 LBS.
MSRP $8,300

SERIAL NUMBERS

YEAR	BEGINNING NO.
1983	10001
1984	11022
1985	20183
1986	29344
1987	38505
1988	49666
1989	59827
1990	68687
1991	78848
1992	88001
1993	98151
1994	108301

RETAIL PRICING

YEAR	HIGH	LOW
1984	$1,258	$943
1985	$1,427	$1,070
1986	$1,668	$1,251
1987	$1,864	$1,398
1988	$1,997	$1,498
1989	$2,073	$1,555
1990	$2,492	$1,869
1991	$2,535	$1,901
1992	$2,723	$2,042
1993	$2,837	$2,127
1994	$2,990	$2,243
1995	$3,067	$2,301
1996	$3,149	$2,362

B6200HSD

YEARS MFRD 1983-1996
SERIES . . . . . B200 SERIES
ENGINE . . . . . KUBOTA
CYLINDERS 3
CID 52.2
PTO HP 12.5
ENGINE HP 15
COOLING . . . . . LIQUID
FUEL . . . . . D
SPEEDS . . . . . VARIABLE
TRANSMISSION . . . . . HYDRO
STEERING . . . . . STANDARD
HITCH . . . . . CAT. I
HYDRAULIC . . . . . YES
PTO . . . . . YES
DRIVE TYPE 4WD
ROPS/CAB . . . . . ROPS
WEIGHT . . . . . 1,150 LBS.
MSRP $10,600

SERIAL NUMBERS

YEAR	BEGINNING NO.
1983	50001
1984	50972
1985	51943
1986	52916
1987	53886
1988	54856

RETAIL PRICING

YEAR	HIGH	LOW
1985	$1,775	$1,331
1986	$2,102	$1,577
1987	$2,421	$1,815
1988	$2,594	$1,945
1989	$2,693	$2,020
1990	$3,213	$2,409
1991	$3,269	$2,452
1992	$3,515	$2,637
1993	$3,623	$2,717
1994	$3,818	$2,864
1995	$3,917	$2,938
1996	$4,025	$3,019

B6200HSE

YEARS MFRD 1983-1996
SERIES . . . . . B200 SERIES
ENGINE . . . . . KUBOTA
CYLINDERS 3
CID 52.2
PTO HP 12.5
ENGINE HP 15
COOLING . . . . . LIQUID
FUEL . . . . . D
SPEEDS . . . . . VARIABLE
TRANSMISSION . . . . . HYDRO
STEERING . . . . . STANDARD
HITCH . . . . . CAT. I
HYDRAULIC . . . . . YES
PTO . . . . . YES
DRIVE TYPE 2WD
ROPS/CAB . . . . . ROPS
WEIGHT . . . . . 1,100 LBS.
MSRP $9,600

SERIAL NUMBERS

YEAR	BEGINNING NO.
1987	29344
1988	38505
1989	49666
1990	59827
1991	68687
1992	78848

RETAIL PRICING

YEAR	HIGH	LOW
1985	$1,632	$1,224
1986	$1,904	$1,428
1987	$2,153	$1,615
1988	$2,307	$1,730
1989	$2,396	$1,797
1990	$2,900	$2,175
1991	$2,950	$2,212
1992	$3,167	$2,375
1993	$3,280	$2,460
1994	$3,458	$2,593
1995	$3,550	$2,663
1996	$3,644	$2,733

B7100

YEARS MFRD 1977-1997
ENGINE . . . . . KUBOTA
CYLINDERS 3
CID 46.5
PTO HP 13
ENGINE HP 16
COOLING . . . . . LIQUID
FUEL . . . . . D
SPEEDS 6/2
TRANSMISSION . . . . . GEAR
STEERING . . . . . STANDARD
HITCH . . . . . CAT. I
HYDRAULIC . . . . . YES
PTO . . . . . YES
DRIVE TYPE 2WD
ROPS/CAB . . . . . ROPS
WEIGHT . . . . . 1,040 LBS.

OPTIONS

48"DECK
54"DECK
60"DECK
HYDRO
LDR

 See Kubota Model Suffix Identification on page 415

AVG. AUCTION PRICING

LOW	HIGH	AVG
$1,300	$3,100	$2,067

B7100DT

YEARS MFRD 1976-1985
SERIES B100 SERIES
ENGINE KUBOTA
CYLINDERS 3
CID 46.5
PTO HP 13
ENGINE HP 16
COOLING LIQUID
FUEL D
SPEEDS 6/2
TRANSMISSION GEAR
STEERING STANDARD
HITCH CAT. I
HYDRAULIC YES
PTO YES
DRIVE TYPE 4WD
ROPS/CAB ROPS
WEIGHT 1,135 LBS.
MSRP $6,195

SERIAL NUMBERS
LEFT SIDE OF CLUTCH HOUSING

YEAR	BEGINNING NO.
1976	10001
1977	13931
1978	36646
1979	54221
1980	64448
1981	70678
1982	74217
1983	76009
1984	77309
1985	78435

RETAIL PRICING

YEAR	HIGH	LOW
1977	$700	$525
1978	$849	$637
1979	$958	$718
1980	$1,025	$769
1981	$1,120	$840
1982	$1,198	$898
1983	$1,296	$972
1984	$1,367	$1,025
1985	$2,765	$2,073

B7100E

YEARS MFRD 1976-1985
SERIES B100 SERIES
ENGINE KUBOTA
CYLINDERS 3
CID 46.5
PTO HP 13
ENGINE HP 16
COOLING LIQUID
FUEL D
SPEEDS 6/2
TRANSMISSION GEAR
STEERING STANDARD
HITCH CAT. I
DRIVE TYPE 2WD
ROPS/CAB ROPS
WEIGHT 985 LBS.
MSRP $5,300

SERIAL NUMBERS
LEFT SIDE OF CLUTCH HOUSING

YEAR	BEGINNING NO.
1976	10001
1977	13931
1978	36646
1979	54221
1980	64448
1981	70678
1982	74217
1983	76009
1984	77309
1985	78435

RETAIL PRICING

YEAR	HIGH	LOW
1985	$1,285	$964

B7100HSD

YEARS MFRD 1977-1997
SERIES B100 SERIES
ENGINE KUBOTA
CYLINDERS 3
CID 46.5
PTO HP 13
ENGINE HP 16
COOLING LIQUID
FUEL D
SPEEDS VARIABLE
TRANSMISSION HYDRO
STEERING STANDARD
HITCH CAT. I
PTO YES
DRIVE TYPE 4WD
ROPS/CAB ROPS
WEIGHT 1,257 LBS.
MSRP $10,040

SERIAL NUMBERS
LEFT SIDE OF CLUTCH HOUSING

YEAR	BEGINNING NO.
1980	10001
1981	10890
1982	50001
1983	51993
1984	53662
1985	54897
1986	56132
1990	RE-INTRODUCED
1991	63844
1992	65176
1993	68005
1994	71302

RETAIL PRICING

YEAR	HIGH	LOW
1989	$1,815	$1,361
1990	$2,095	$1,571
1991	$2,357	$1,767
1992	$2,644	$1,983
1993	$2,895	$2,171
1994	$3,192	$2,394
1995	$3,549	$2,662
1996	$3,874	$2,905
1997	$4,183	$3,137

AVG. AUCTION PRICING

LOW	HIGH	AVG
$1,030	$3,863	$2,747

B7100HSE

YEARS MFRD 1980-1999
SERIES B100 SERIES
ENGINE KUBOTA
CYLINDERS 3
CID 46.5
PTO HP 13
ENGINE HP 16
COOLING LIQUID
FUEL D
SPEEDS VARIABLE
TRANSMISSION HYDRO
STEERING STANDARD
HITCH CAT. I
HYDRAULIC YES
PTO YES
DRIVE TYPE 2WD
ROPS/CAB ROPS
WEIGHT 1,257 LBS.
MSRP $6,416

SERIAL NUMBERS
LEFT SIDE OF CLUTCH HOUSING

YEAR	BEGINNING NO.
1980	10001
1981	10890
1982	50001
1983	51993
1984	53662
1985	54897
1986	56132
1990	RE-INTRODUCED

RETAIL PRICING

YEAR	HIGH	LOW
1980	$2,411	$1,808
1981	$2,657	$1,993
1982	$2,825	$2,119
1983	$2,952	$2,214
1984	$3,051	$2,288

B7200DT

YEARS MFRD 1983-1990
SERIES B200 SERIES
ENGINE KUBOTA
CYLINDERS 3
CID 56.6
PTO HP 14
ENGINE HP 17
COOLING LIQUID
FUEL D
SPEEDS 6/2
TRANSMISSION GEAR
STEERING STANDARD
HITCH CAT. I
HYDRAULIC YES
PTO YES
DRIVE TYPE 4WD
ROPS/CAB ROPS
WEIGHT 1,320 LBS.
MSRP $8,200

SERIAL NUMBERS
LEFT SIDE OF CLUTCH HOUSING

YEAR	BEGINNING NO.
1983	50001
1984	51740
1985	61210
1986	62548
1987	64737
1988	65307

RETAIL PRICING

YEAR	HIGH	LOW
1983	$980	$735
1984	$1,231	$923
1985	$1,495	$1,121
1986	$1,786	$1,340
1987	$2,048	$1,536
1988	$2,334	$1,750
1989	$2,637	$1,978
1990	$2,948	$2,211

B7200E

YEARS MFRD 1983-1995
SERIES B200 SERIES
ENGINE KUBOTA
CYLINDERS 3
CID 56.6
PTO HP 14
ENGINE HP 17
COOLING LIQUID
FUEL D
SPEEDS 6/2
TRANSMISSION GEAR
STEERING STANDARD
HITCH CAT. I
PTO YES
DRIVE TYPE 2WD
ROPS/CAB ROPS
WEIGHT 1,215 LBS.
MSRP $8,200

SERIAL NUMBERS
LEFT SIDE OF CLUTCH HOUSING

YEAR	BEGINNING NO.
1983	50001
1984	51740
1985	61210

RETAIL PRICING

YEAR	HIGH	LOW
1984	$1,382	$1,037
1985	$1,527	$1,146
1986	$1,772	$1,329
1987	$1,971	$1,479
1988	$2,110	$1,583
1989	$2,192	$1,644
1990	$2,379	$1,784
1991	$2,622	$1,967

B7200HSD

YEARS MFRD 1983-1995
SERIES B200 SERIES
ENGINE KUBOTA
CYLINDERS 3
CID 56.6
PTO HP 14
ENGINE HP 17
COOLING LIQUID
FUEL D
SPEEDS VARIABLE
TRANSMISSION HYDRO
STEERING STANDARD
HITCH CAT. I
HYDRAULIC YES
PTO YES
DRIVE TYPE 4WD
ROPS/CAB ROPS
WEIGHT 1,275 LBS.
MSRP $10,500

SERIAL NUMBERS

LEFT SIDE OF CLUTCH HOUSING

YEAR	BEGINNING NO.
1984	50001
1985	50867
1986	50975

RETAIL PRICING

YEAR	HIGH	LOW
1985	$1,886	$1,414
1986	$2,248	$1,686
1987	$2,563	$1,922
1988	$2,745	$2,059
1989	$2,852	$2,139
1990	$3,296	$2,472
1991	$3,357	$2,518

B7200HSE

YEARS MFRD 1983-1995
SERIES B200 SERIES
ENGINE KUBOTA
CYLINDERS 3
CID 56.6
PTO HP 14
ENGINE HP 17
COOLING LIQUID
FUEL D
SPEEDS VARIABLE
TRANSMISSION HYDRO
STEERING STANDARD
HITCH CAT. I
HYDRAULIC YES
PTO YES
DRIVE TYPE 2WD
ROPS/CAB ROPS
WEIGHT 1,225 LBS.
MSRP $9,450

SERIAL NUMBERS

LEFT SIDE OF CLUTCH HOUSING

YEAR	BEGINNING NO.
1984	10001
1985	10619

RETAIL PRICING

YEAR	HIGH	LOW
1985	$1,740	$1,305
1986	$2,037	$1,528
1987	$2,301	$1,726
1988	$2,465	$1,849
1989	$2,559	$1,919
1990	$2,966	$2,225
1991	$3,022	$2,267

B7300HSD

YEARS MFRD 1998-1999
SERIES B SERIES
ENGINE KUBOTA
CYLINDERS 3
CID 43.4
PTO HP 12.5
ENGINE HP 16
COOLING LIQUID
FUEL D
SPEEDS VARIABLE
TRANSMISSION HYDRO
STEERING STANDARD
HITCH CAT. I
HYDRAULIC YES
PTO YES
DRIVE TYPE 4WD
ROPS/CAB ROPS
WEIGHT 1,312 LBS.
MSRP $10,300

OPTIONS

48"DECK
54"DECK
60"DECK
LDR

RETAIL PRICING

YEAR	HIGH	LOW
1998	$4,141	$3,105
1999	$4,581	$3,436

AVG. AUCTION PRICING

LOW	HIGH	AVG
$3,673	$4,305	$3,926

B7400HSD

YEARS MFRD 2000-2003
SERIES B SERIES
ENGINE KUBOTA
CYLINDERS 3
CID 43.9
PTO HP 12.5
ENGINE HP 16
COOLING LIQUID
FUEL D
SPEEDS VARIABLE
TRANSMISSION HYDRO
STEERING STANDARD
HITCH CAT. I
HYDRAULIC YES
PTO YES
DRIVE TYPE 4WD
ROPS/CAB ROPS
WEIGHT 1,290 LBS.
MSRP $10,300

OPTIONS

54"DECK
60"DECK
LDR
POWER STEERING

SERIAL NUMBERS

YEAR	BEGINNING NO.
2000	50754

RETAIL PRICING

YEAR	HIGH	LOW
2000	$5,264	$3,948
2001	$5,744	$4,308
2002	$6,235	$4,676
2003	$6,737	$5,053

B7410DT

YEARS MFRD 2004-2007
SERIES B SERIES
ENGINE KUBOTA D782-E-D20
CYLINDERS 3
CID 47.5
PTO HP 15
ENGINE HP 18
COOLING LIQUID
FUEL G
SPEEDS 6/2
TRANSMISSION GEAR
STEERING STANDARD
HITCH CAT. I
PTO YES
WEIGHT 1,246 LBS.
MSRP $9,066

RETAIL PRICING

YEAR	HIGH	LOW
2007	$6,302	$4,726

B7410HSD

YEARS MFRD 2004-2007
SERIES B SERIES
ENGINE KUBOTA
CYLINDERS 3
CID 44
ENGINE HP 12.5
COOLING AIR
FUEL D
SPEEDS VARIABLE
TRANSMISSION HYDRO
STEERING STANDARD
WEIGHT 1,270 LBS.
MSRP $8,847

OPTIONS

LDR

RETAIL PRICING

YEAR	HIGH	LOW
2004	$5,374	$4,030
2005	$5,864	$4,398
2006	$6,365	$4,774
2007	$6,886	$5,164

B7500DT

YEARS MFRD 2000-2003
SERIES B SERIES
ENGINE KUBOTA
CYLINDERS 3
CID 61.1
PTO HP 17
ENGINE HP 21
COOLING LIQUID
FUEL D
SPEEDS 6/2
TRANSMISSION GEAR
STEERING STANDARD
HITCH CAT. I
HYDRAULIC YES
PTO YES
DRIVE TYPE 4WD
ROPS/CAB ROPS
WEIGHT 1,323 LBS.
MSRP $10,130

RETAIL PRICING

YEAR	HIGH	LOW
2000	$3,899	$2,924
2001	$4,499	$3,374
2002	$4,977	$3,733
2003	$5,696	$4,272

AVG. AUCTION PRICING

LOW	HIGH	AVG
$4,305	$6,711	$5,622

B7500DTN

YEARS MFRD 2001-2003
SERIES B SERIES
ENGINE KUBOTA
CYLINDERS 3
CID 61.1
PTO HP 17
ENGINE HP 21
COOLING LIQUID
FUEL D
SPEEDS 6/2
TRANSMISSION GEAR
STEERING STANDARD
HITCH CAT. I
HYDRAULIC YES
PTO YES
DRIVE TYPE 4WD
ROPS/CAB ROPS
WEIGHT 1,323 LBS.
MSRP $10,630

RETAIL PRICING

YEAR	HIGH	LOW
2001	$6,422	$4,817
2002	$6,993	$5,245
2003	$7,213	$5,410

B7500HSD

YEARS MFRD 2001-2003
SERIES B SERIES
ENGINE KUBOTA
CYLINDERS 3
CID 61.1
PTO HP 16
ENGINE HP 21
COOLING LIQUID
FUEL D
SPEEDS VARIABLE
TRANSMISSION HYDRO
STEERING STANDARD
HITCH CAT. I
HYDRAULIC YES
PTO YES
DRIVE TYPE 4WD
ROPS/CAB ROPS
WEIGHT 1,367 LBS.
MSRP $11,730

RETAIL PRICING

YEAR	HIGH	LOW
2001	$7,087	$5,316
2002	$7,716	$5,787
2003	$7,821	$5,866

AVG. AUCTION PRICING

LOW	HIGH	AVG
$3,914	$8,034	$6,032

B7510DT

YEARS MFRD 2004-2007
SERIES B SERIES
ENGINE KUBOTA E TVCS
CYLINDERS 3
CID 61.1
PTO HP 17
ENGINE HP 21
COOLING LIQUID
FUEL D
SPEEDS 6/2

TRANSMISSION .... GEAR
STEERING .... STANDARD
HITCH .... CAT. I
PTO .... YES
WEIGHT .... 1,367 LBS.
MSRP $11,108

RETAIL PRICING

YEAR	HIGH	LOW
2004	$5,771	$4,328
2005	$6,291	$4,718
2006	$6,827	$5,120
2007	$7,423	$5,567

AVG. AUCTION PRICING

LOW	HIGH	AVG
$1,139	$11,398	$6,739

B7510DTN (NARROW)

YEARS MFRD 2004-2008
SERIES .... B SERIES
ENGINE .... KUBOTA D1005-E-D16
CYLINDERS 3
CID 61.1
PTO HP 17
ENGINE HP 21
COOLING .... LIQUID
FUEL .... D
SPEEDS 6/2
TRANSMISSION .... GEAR
STEERING .... STANDARD
HITCH .... CAT. I
PTO .... YES
WEIGHT .... 1,323 LBS.
MSRP $11,056

RETAIL PRICING

YEAR	HIGH	LOW
2004	$7,114	$5,336
2005	$7,332	$5,499
2006	$7,548	$5,661
2007	$7,756	$5,817
2008	$8,049	$6,037

B7510HSD

YEARS MFRD 2004-2008
SERIES .... B SERIES
ENGINE .... KUBOTA D1005-E-D16
CYLINDERS 3
CID 61.1
PTO HP 16
ENGINE HP 21
COOLING .... LIQUID
FUEL .... D
SPEEDS .... 2 RANGE
TRANSMISSION .... HYDRO
STEERING .... STANDARD
HITCH .... CAT. I
PTO .... YES
WEIGHT .... 1,367 LBS.
MSRP $12,322

RETAIL PRICING

YEAR	HIGH	LOW
2004	$8,301	$6,226
2005	$8,537	$6,402
2006	$8,777	$6,582
2007	$9,135	$6,851
2008	$9,811	$7,358

B7610HSD

YEARS MFRD 2004-2007
SERIES .... B SERIES
ENGINE .... KUBOTA E TVCS
CYLINDERS 3
CID 68.5
PTO HP 18
ENGINE HP 24
COOLING .... LIQUID
FUEL .... D
SPEEDS .... 2 RANGE
TRANSMISSION .... HYDRO
STEERING .... STANDARD
HITCH .... CAT. I
PTO .... YES
WEIGHT .... 1,367 LBS.
MSRP $11,876

OPTIONS

54"DECK
60"DECK
LDR

RETAIL PRICING

YEAR	HIGH	LOW
2004	$6,941	$5,206
2005	$7,603	$5,703
2006	$8,293	$6,219
2007	$8,943	$6,708

AVG. AUCTION PRICING

LOW	HIGH	AVG
$5,066	$7,916	$6,801

B7800

YEARS MFRD 2003-2004
SERIES .... B SERIES
ENGINE .... KUBOTA
CYLINDERS 4
CID 91.5
PTO HP 22
ENGINE HP 30
COOLING .... LIQUID
FUEL .... D
SPEEDS .... VARIABLE
TRANSMISSION .... HYDRO
STEERING .... STANDARD
HITCH .... CAT. I
HYDRAULIC .... YES
PTO .... YES
WEIGHT .... 1,741 LBS.
MSRP $13,999

RETAIL PRICING

YEAR	HIGH	LOW
2003	$6,560	$4,920
2004	$6,876	$5,157

B7800HSD

YEARS MFRD 2003-2009
SERIES .... B SERIES
ENGINE .... KUBOTA E TVCS
CYLINDERS 4
CID 91.5
PTO HP 22
ENGINE HP 30
COOLING .... LIQUID
FUEL .... D
SPEEDS .... VARIABLE
TRANSMISSION .... HYDRO
STEERING .... STANDARD
HITCH .... CAT. I
PTO .... YES
DRIVE TYPE 4WD
ROPS/CAB .... ROPS
WEIGHT .... 1,770 LBS.
MSRP $14,370

OPTIONS

60"DECK
72"DECK
LDR

RETAIL PRICING

YEAR	HIGH	LOW
2003	$7,119	$5,340
2004	$7,715	$5,786
2005	$8,409	$6,307
2006	$9,060	$6,795
2007	$9,754	$7,316
2008	$10,411	$7,808
2009	$11,222	$8,416

B8200DT

YEARS MFRD 1981-1990
SERIES .... B200 SERIES
ENGINE .... KUBOTA
CYLINDERS 3
CID 56.6
PTO HP 16
ENGINE HP 19
COOLING .... LIQUID
FUEL .... D
SPEEDS 9/3
TRANSMISSION .... GEAR
STEERING .... STANDARD
HITCH .... CAT. I
HYDRAULIC .... YES
PTO .... YES
DRIVE TYPE 4WD
ROPS/CAB .... ROPS
WEIGHT .... 1,525 LBS.
MSRP $7,200

SERIAL NUMBERS

RH SIDE OF CLUTCH HOUSING

YEAR	BEGINNING NO.
1981	10001
1982	50001
1983	51644
1984	53823
1985	56002
1986	58081
1987	60056
1988	65072

RETAIL PRICING

YEAR	HIGH	LOW
1981	$947	$710
1982	$1,103	$827
1983	$1,353	$1,015
1984	$1,611	$1,208
1985	$1,880	$1,410
1986	$2,160	$1,620
1987	$2,444	$1,833
1988	$2,744	$2,058
1989	$3,052	$2,289
1990	$3,332	$2,499

B8200DT 2

YEARS MFRD 1981-1995
SERIES .... B200 SERIES
ENGINE .... KUBOTA
CYLINDERS 3
CID 56.6
PTO HP 16
ENGINE HP 19
COOLING .... LIQUID
FUEL .... D
SPEEDS 9/3
TRANSMISSION .... GEAR
STEERING .... STANDARD
HITCH .... CAT. I
HYDRAULIC .... YES
PTO .... YES
DRIVE TYPE 4WD
ROPS/CAB .... ROPS
WEIGHT .... 1,525 LBS.
MSRP $10,100

SERIAL NUMBERS

YEAR	BEGINNING NO.
1981	10001
1982	50001
1983	51644
1984	53823
1985	56002
1986	58081
1987	60056

RETAIL PRICING

YEAR	HIGH	LOW
1985	$1,865	$1,399
1986	$2,128	$1,596
1987	$2,424	$1,818
1988	$2,597	$1,947
1989	$2,697	$2,022
1990	$3,174	$2,381

B8200E

YEARS MFRD 1981-1995
SERIES .... B200 SERIES
ENGINE .... KUBOTA
CYLINDERS 3
CID 56.6
PTO HP 16
ENGINE HP 19
COOLING .... LIQUID
FUEL .... D
SPEEDS 9/3
TRANSMISSION .... GEAR
STEERING .... STANDARD
HITCH .... CAT. I
HYDRAULIC .... YES
PTO .... YES
DRIVE TYPE 2WD
ROPS/CAB .... ROPS
WEIGHT .... 1,420 LBS.
MSRP $9,000

SERIAL NUMBERS

YEAR	BEGINNING NO.
1981	10001
1982	10483
1983	11070
1984	12025
1985	20329
1986	28631
1987	36432

YEAR	BEGINNING NO.
1988	43216
1989	50001
1990	51645
1991	53828
1992	56001
1993	58080
1994	60160
1995	62245

RETAIL PRICING

YEAR	HIGH	LOW
1982	$1,191	$893
1983	$1,289	$966
1984	$1,358	$1,018
1985	$1,673	$1,255
1986	$1,904	$1,428
1987	$2,150	$1,612
1988	$2,302	$1,727
1989	$2,390	$1,792
1990	$2,826	$2,120
1991	$2,877	$2,158

B8200E 2

YEARS MFRD........ 1981-1995
SERIES............ B200 SERIES
ENGINE............ KUBOTA
CYLINDERS........... 3
CID............ 56.6
PTO HP............ 16
ENGINE HP............ 19
COOLING............ LIQUID
FUEL............ D
SPEEDS............ 9/3
TRANSMISSION............ GEAR
STEERING............ STANDARD
HITCH............ CAT. I
HYDRAULIC............ YES
PTO............ YES
DRIVE TYPE............ 2WD
ROPS/CAB............ ROPS
WEIGHT............ 1,405 LBS.
MSRP............ $8,800

SERIAL NUMBERS

YEAR	BEGINNING NO.
1981	10001
1982	10483
1983	11070
1984	12025
1985	20329
1986	28631
1987	36432
1988	43216
1989	50001
1990	51645
1991	53828
1992	56001
1993	58080
1994	60160
1995	62245

RETAIL PRICING

YEAR	HIGH	LOW
1990	$2,261	$1,696
1991	$2,399	$1,799
1992	$2,631	$1,973
1993	$2,735	$2,051
1994	$3,097	$2,323
1995	$3,252	$2,439

B8200HSD

YEARS MFRD........ 1983-1995
SERIES............ B200 SERIES
ENGINE............ KUBOTA
CYLINDERS............ 3
CID............ 56.6
PTO HP............ 14.5
ENGINE HP............ 19
COOLING............ LIQUID
FUEL............ D
SPEEDS............ VARIABLE
TRANSMISSION............ HYDRO
STEERING............ STANDARD
HITCH............ CAT. I
HYDRAULIC............ YES
PTO............ YES
DRIVE TYPE............ 4WD
ROPS/CAB............ ROPS
WEIGHT............ 1,525 LBS.
MSRP............ $11,400

SERIAL NUMBERS

YEAR	BEGINNING NO.
1983	50297

RETAIL PRICING

YEAR	HIGH	LOW
1983	$1,591	$1,194
1984	$1,673	$1,255
1985	$2,084	$1,563
1986	$2,418	$1,814
1987	$2,782	$2,087
1988	$2,983	$2,237
1989	$3,097	$2,323
1990	$3,384	$2,538
1991	$3,645	$2,734
1992	$3,911	$2,933
1993	$4,145	$3,109
1994	$4,399	$3,299
1995	$4,536	$3,402

B8200HSE

YEARS MFRD........ 1983-1995
SERIES............ B200 SERIES
ENGINE............ KUBOTA
CYLINDERS............ 3
CID............ 56.6
PTO HP............ 14.5
ENGINE HP............ 19
COOLING............ LIQUID
FUEL............ D
SPEEDS............ VARIABLE
TRANSMISSION............ HYDRO
STEERING............ STANDARD
HITCH............ CAT. I
HYDRAULIC............ YES
PTO............ YES
DRIVE TYPE............ 2WD
ROPS/CAB............ ROPS
WEIGHT............ 1,408 LBS.
MSRP............ $10,350

SERIAL NUMBERS

YEAR	BEGINNING NO.
1983	50297

RETAIL PRICING

YEAR	HIGH	LOW
1984	$1,512	$1,134
1985	$1,889	$1,417
1986	$2,194	$1,645
1987	$2,479	$1,859
1988	$2,650	$1,988
1989	$2,752	$2,064
1990	$3,251	$2,438
1991	$3,309	$2,482

B9200DT

YEARS MFRD........ 1987-1990
SERIES............ B200 SERIES
ENGINE............ KUBOTA
CYLINDERS............ 4
CID............ 75.4
PTO HP............ 18.5
ENGINE HP............ 22.5
COOLING............ LIQUID
FUEL............ D
SPEEDS............ 9/3
TRANSMISSION............ GEAR
STEERING............ STANDARD
HITCH............ CAT. I
HYDRAULIC............ YES
PTO............ YES
DRIVE TYPE............ 4WD
ROPS/CAB............ ROPS
WEIGHT............ 1,709 LBS.
MSRP............ $9,900

RETAIL PRICING

YEAR	HIGH	LOW
1987	$3,027	$2,270
1988	$3,343	$2,508
1989	$3,671	$2,753
1990	$4,010	$3,007

B9200E

YEARS MFRD........ 1987-1995
SERIES............ B200 SERIES
ENGINE............ KUBOTA
CYLINDERS............ 4
CID............ 75.4
PTO HP............ 18.5
ENGINE HP............ 22.5
COOLING............ LIQUID
FUEL............ D
SPEEDS............ 9/3
TRANSMISSION............ GEAR
STEERING............ STANDARD
HITCH............ CAT. I
HYDRAULIC............ YES
PTO............ YES
DRIVE TYPE............ 2WD
ROPS/CAB............ ROPS
WEIGHT............ 1,555 LBS.
MSRP............ $9,900

RETAIL PRICING

YEAR	HIGH	LOW
1987	$2,288	$1,716
1988	$2,450	$1,838
1989	$2,546	$1,910
1990	$3,110	$2,332
1991	$3,165	$2,374

B9200HSD

YEARS MFRD........ 1987-1995
SERIES............ B200 SERIES
ENGINE............ KUBOTA
CYLINDERS............ 4
CID............ 75.4
PTO HP............ 16
ENGINE HP............ 22.5
FUEL............ D
SPEEDS............ VARIABLE
TRANSMISSION............ HYDRO
STEERING............ STANDARD
HYDRAULIC............ YES
PTO............ YES
DRIVE TYPE............ 4WD
ROPS/CAB............ ROPS
WEIGHT............ 1,720 LBS.
MSRP............ $12,300

RETAIL PRICING

YEAR	HIGH	LOW
1987	$2,659	$1,995
1988	$3,039	$2,279
1989	$3,247	$2,435
1990	$3,863	$2,897
1991	$3,934	$2,950

B9200HSE

YEARS MFRD........ 1987-1995
SERIES............ B200 SERIES
ENGINE............ KUBOTA
CYLINDERS............ 4
CID............ 75.4
PTO HP............ 16
ENGINE HP............ 22.5
COOLING............ LIQUID
FUEL............ D
SPEEDS............ VARIABLE
TRANSMISSION............ HYDRO
STEERING............ STANDARD
HITCH............ CAT. I
HYDRAULIC............ YES
PTO............ YES
DRIVE TYPE............ 2WD
ROPS/CAB............ ROPS
WEIGHT............ 1,603 LBS.
MSRP............ $11,250

RETAIL PRICING

YEAR	HIGH	LOW
1987	$2,618	$1,964
1988	$2,804	$2,103
1989	$2,911	$2,183
1990	$3,535	$2,651
1991	$3,597	$2,698

BX22

YEARS MFRD........ 2002-2003
SERIES............ BX SERIES
ENGINE............ KUBOTA
CYLINDERS............ 3
CID............ 54.8
PTO HP............ 16.7
ENGINE HP............ 22
COOLING............ LIQUID
FUEL............ D
SPEEDS............ VARIABLE
TRANSMISSION............ HYDRO
STEERING............ STANDARD
HITCH............ CAT. I
HYDRAULIC............ YES
PTO............ YES
MSRP............ $16,990

RETAIL PRICING

YEAR	HIGH	LOW
2002	$10,368	$7,776
2003	$11,308	$8,481

BX23

YEARS MFRD . . . 2004-2005
SERIES . . . BX SERIES
ENGINE . . . KUBOTA D905-E-BX
CYLINDERS . . . 3
CID . . . 54.8
PTO HP . . . 16.7
ENGINE HP . . . 22
COOLING . . . LIQUID
FUEL . . . D
SPEEDS . . . VARIABLE
TRANSMISSION . . . HYDRO
STEERING . . . STANDARD
HITCH . . . CAT. I
HYDRAULIC . . . YES
PTO . . . YES
WEIGHT . . . 1,520 LBS.
MSRP . . . $17,690

RETAIL PRICING

YEAR	HIGH	LOW
2004	$12,371	$9,278
2005	$13,242	$9,931

BX23S

YEARS MFRD . . . 2017-2020
ENGINE . . . KUBOTA D902
CYLINDERS . . . 3
CID . . . 54.8
PTO HP . . . 17.7
ENGINE HP . . . 23
COOLING . . . LIQUID
FUEL . . . D
TRANSMISSION . . . HYDRO
HITCH . . . CAT. I
DRIVE TYPE . . . 4WD
WEIGHT . . . 1,570 LBS.
MSRP . . . $20,683

OPTIONS

CAB . . . $5,071

RETAIL PRICING

YEAR	HIGH	LOW
2017	$18,219	$13,664
2018	$18,918	$14,189
2019	$19,851	$14,889
2020	$20,730	$15,998

BX24

YEARS MFRD . . . 2006-2008
ENGINE . . . KUBOTA 902
CYLINDERS . . . 3
CID . . . 54.8
PTO HP . . . 17.7
ENGINE HP . . . 23
COOLING . . . LIQUID
FUEL . . . D
SPEEDS . . . VARIABLE
TRANSMISSION . . . HYDRO
STEERING . . . STANDARD
HITCH . . . CAT. I
HYDRAULIC . . . YES
PTO . . . YES
WEIGHT . . . 1,542 LBS.
MSRP . . . $16,941

OPTIONS

60" DECK
BLADE

RETAIL PRICING

YEAR	HIGH	LOW
2006	$11,414	$8,561
2007	$12,826	$9,619
2008	$14,210	$10,657

BX25D

YEARS MFRD . . . 2013-2017
ENGINE . . . KUBOTA
CYLINDERS . . . 3
CID . . . 54.8
PTO HP . . . 17.5
ENGINE HP . . . 23
FUEL . . . D
SPEEDS . . . VARIABLE
TRANSMISSION . . . HYDRO
STEERING . . . STANDARD
WEIGHT . . . 1,587 LBS.
MSRP . . . $20,336

RETAIL PRICING

YEAR	HIGH	LOW
2013	$14,928	$11,196
2014	$16,720	$12,540
2015	$17,816	$13,362
2016	$18,993	$14,245
2017	$20,365	$15,274

AVG. AUCTION PRICING

LOW	HIGH	AVG
$9,500	$10,500	$10,100

BX25LB-T8

YEARS MFRD . . . 2008-2012
SERIES . . . BX SERIES
ENGINE . . . KUBOTA D902
CYLINDERS . . . 3
CID . . . 54
PTO HP . . . 17.7
ENGINE HP . . . 23
COOLING . . . LIQUID
FUEL . . . D
SPEEDS . . . VARIABLE
TRANSMISSION . . . HYDRO
STEERING . . . STANDARD
HITCH . . . CAT. I
HYDRAULIC . . . YES
PTO . . . YES
WEIGHT . . . 1,542 LBS.
MSRP . . . $19,160

RETAIL PRICING

YEAR	HIGH	LOW
2008	$14,257	$10,693
2009	$15,347	$11,510
2010	$16,519	$12,389
2011	$17,891	$13,418
2012	$18,510	$13,883

BX1500-D

YEARS MFRD . . . 2003-2005
SERIES . . . BX SERIES
ENGINE . . . KUBOTA Z602-E
CYLINDERS . . . 2
CID . . . 36.6
PTO HP . . . 10.5
ENGINE HP . . . 15
COOLING . . . LIQUID
FUEL . . . D
SPEEDS . . . VARIABLE
TRANSMISSION . . . HYDRO
STEERING . . . STANDARD
HITCH . . . CAT. I
HYDRAULIC . . . YES
PTO . . . YES
WEIGHT . . . 1,213 LBS.
MSRP . . . $8,085

OPTIONS

37" TILLER
48" DECK
50" SNOWBLOWER
54" DECK
LDR

RETAIL PRICING

YEAR	HIGH	LOW
2003	$3,747	$2,810
2004	$4,244	$3,183
2005	$4,741	$3,556

AVG. AUCTION PRICING

LOW	HIGH	AVG
$5,066	$6,649	$5,920

BX1800-D

YEARS MFRD . . . 2000-2003
SERIES . . . BX SERIES
ENGINE . . . KUBOTA
CYLINDERS . . . 3
CID . . . 43.9
PTO HP . . . 13.7
ENGINE HP . . . 18
COOLING . . . LIQUID
FUEL . . . D
SPEEDS . . . VARIABLE
TRANSMISSION . . . HYDRO
STEERING . . . STANDARD
HITCH . . . CAT. I
HYDRAULIC . . . YES
PTO . . . YES
MSRP . . . $9,385

OPTIONS

37" TILLER
48" DECK
50" SNOWBLOWER
54" DECK
LDR

RETAIL PRICING

YEAR	HIGH	LOW
2000	$3,102	$2,327
2001	$3,563	$2,672
2002	$4,042	$3,031
2003	$4,538	$3,404

AVG. AUCTION PRICING

LOW	HIGH	AVG
$3,545	$6,839	$4,458

BX1830-D

YEARS MFRD . . . 2004-2005
SERIES . . . BZ SERIES
ENGINE . . . KUBOTA D722
CYLINDERS . . . 3
CID . . . 43.9
PTO HP . . . 14
ENGINE HP . . . 18
COOLING . . . LIQUID
FUEL . . . D
SPEEDS . . . VARIABLE
TRANSMISSION . . . HYDRO
STEERING . . . STANDARD
HITCH . . . CAT. I
HYDRAULIC . . . YES
PTO . . . YES
WEIGHT . . . 1,255 LBS.
MSRP . . . $9,685

OPTIONS

37" TILLER
50" SNOWBLOWER
54" DECK
60" DECK
LDR

RETAIL PRICING

YEAR	HIGH	LOW
2004	$5,147	$3,860
2005	$5,674	$4,256

BX1850

YEARS MFRD . . . 2006-2008
ENGINE . . . KUBOTA D722
CYLINDERS . . . 3
CID . . . 43.9
PTO HP . . . 13.7
ENGINE HP . . . 18
COOLING . . . LIQUID
FUEL . . . D
SPEEDS . . . VARIABLE
TRANSMISSION . . . HYDRO
STEERING . . . STANDARD
HITCH . . . CAT. I
HYDRAULIC . . . YES
PTO . . . YES
WEIGHT . . . 1,255 LBS.
MSRP . . . $8,231

OPTIONS

37" TILLER
48" DECK
50" SNOWBLOWER
54" DECK
LDR

RETAIL PRICING

YEAR	HIGH	LOW
2006	$5,395	$4,046
2007	$6,073	$4,555
2008	$6,498	$4,874

BX1860-B

YEARS MFRD . . . 2008-2012
SERIES . . . BX SERIES
ENGINE . . . KUBOTA D722
CYLINDERS . . . 3
CID . . . 43.9
PTO HP . . . 13.7
ENGINE HP . . . 18

COOLING .... LIQUID
FUEL .... D
SPEEDS .... VARIABLE
TRANSMISSION .... HYDRO
STEERING .... STANDARD
HITCH .... CAT. I
HYDRAULIC .... YES
PTO .... YES
WEIGHT .... 1,355 LBS.
MSRP $9,606

OPTIONS
48"DECK
54"DECK
LDR
MID PTO
SNOWBLOWER

RETAIL PRICING
YEAR	HIGH	LOW
2008	$7,150	$5,363
2009	$7,733	$5,800
2010	$8,286	$6,215
2011	$9,054	$6,790
2012	$9,595	$7,197

AVG. AUCTION PRICING
LOW	HIGH	AVG
$5,768	$8,240	$6,747

BX1870
YEARS MFRD 2013-2017
ENGINE .... KUBOTA
CYLINDERS 3
CID 43.9
PTO HP 13.7
ENGINE HP 18
COOLING .... AIR
FUEL .... D
SPEEDS .... VARIABLE
TRANSMISSION .... HYDRO
STEERING .... STANDARD
WEIGHT .... 1,345 LBS.
MSRP $10,150

OPTIONS
48" DECK
54" DECK
LDR
SNOW BLOWER

RETAIL PRICING
YEAR	HIGH	LOW
2013	$7,804	$5,853
2014	$8,444	$6,333
2015	$9,058	$6,793
2016	$9,744	$7,308
2017	$10,795	$8,097

AVG. AUCTION PRICING
LOW	HIGH	AVG
$4,841	$7,365	$6,360

BX1880
YEARS MFRD 2017-2020
SERIES .... BX80 SERIES
ENGINE .... KUBOTA
CYLINDERS 3
CID 43.9
PTO HP 13.7
ENGINE HP 18
COOLING .... LIQUID
FUEL .... D
TRANSMISSION .... HYDRO
STEERING .... STANDARD
HITCH .... CAT. I
DRIVE TYPE 4WD
ROPS/CAB .... ROPS
WEIGHT .... 1,336 LBS.
MSRP $9,891

OPTIONS
48" DECK $1,565
51" SNOW BLOWER $2,867
CAB $4,726
LDR W/BKT $3,390

BX2200-D
YEARS MFRD 2000-2003
SERIES .... BX SERIES
ENGINE .... KUBOTA
CYLINDERS 3
CID 54.8
PTO HP 16.7
ENGINE HP 22
FUEL .... D
SPEEDS .... VARIABLE
TRANSMISSION .... HYDRO
STEERING .... STANDARD
PTO .... YES
WEIGHT .... 1,540 LBS.
MSRP $9,885

OPTIONS
37" TILLER
50" SNOWBLOWER
54" DECK
60" DECK
LDR

RETAIL PRICING
YEAR	HIGH	LOW
2000	$3,661	$2,745
2001	$4,111	$3,083
2002	$4,668	$3,501
2003	$5,240	$3,930

AVG. AUCTION PRICING
LOW	HIGH	AVG
$2,500	$6,000	$3,750

BX2230-D
YEARS MFRD 2004-2005
SERIES .... BX SERIES
ENGINE .... KUBOTA D902-E-BX
CYLINDERS 3
CID 54.8
PTO HP 16.7
ENGINE HP 22
COOLING .... LIQUID
FUEL .... D
SPEEDS .... VARIABLE
TRANSMISSION .... HYDRO
STEERING .... STANDARD
HITCH .... CAT. I
HYDRAULIC .... YES
PTO .... YES
WEIGHT .... 1,290 LBS.
MSRP $10,185

OPTIONS
37" TILLER
50" SNOWBLOWER
54" DECK
60" DECK
LDR

RETAIL PRICING
YEAR	HIGH	LOW
2004	$5,215	$3,911
2005	$5,678	$4,259

AVG. AUCTION PRICING
LOW	HIGH	AVG
$3,863	$7,828	$5,943

BX2350
YEARS MFRD 2006-2008
ENGINE .... KUBOTA D902
CYLINDERS 3
CID 54.8
PTO HP 17.7
ENGINE HP 23
COOLING .... LIQUID
FUEL .... D
SPEEDS .... VARIABLE
TRANSMISSION .... HYDRO
STEERING .... STANDARD
HITCH .... CAT. I
HYDRAULIC .... YES
PTO .... YES
WEIGHT .... 1,322 LBS.
MSRP $9,779

OPTIONS
37" TILLER
50" SNOWBLOWER
54" DECK
60" DECK
LDR

RETAIL PRICING
YEAR	HIGH	LOW
2006	$7,033	$5,275
2007	$7,574	$5,680
2008	$8,015	$6,012

AVG. AUCTION PRICING
LOW	HIGH	AVG
$4,500	$6,800	$5,850

BX2360-B
YEARS MFRD 2008-2012
SERIES .... BX SERIES
ENGINE .... KUBOTA D902
CYLINDERS 3
PTO HP 17.7
ENGINE HP 23
COOLING .... LIQUID
FUEL .... D
SPEEDS .... VARIABLE
TRANSMISSION .... HYDRO
STEERING .... STANDARD
HITCH .... CAT. I
HYDRAULIC .... YES
PTO .... YES
WEIGHT .... 1,322 LBS.
MSRP $11,135

OPTIONS
50" SNOWBLOWER
54" DECK
60" DECK
LDR
MID PTO

RETAIL PRICING
YEAR	HIGH	LOW
2008	$8,458	$6,344
2009	$9,182	$6,887
2010	$9,497	$7,122
2011	$10,263	$7,697
2012	$10,927	$8,195

AVG. AUCTION PRICING
LOW	HIGH	AVG
$3,250	$7,500	$6,013

BX2370
YEARS MFRD 2013-2017
ENGINE .... KUBOTA
CYLINDERS 3
CID 54
PTO HP 17.7
ENGINE HP 23
COOLING .... AIR
FUEL .... D
SPEEDS .... VARIABLE
TRANSMISSION .... HYDRO
STEERING .... STANDARD
DRIVE TYPE 2WD
ROPS/CAB .... ROPS
WEIGHT .... 1,411 LBS.
MSRP $11,760

OPTIONS
50" SNOWBLOWER
54" DECK
60" DECK
LDR

RETAIL PRICING
YEAR	HIGH	LOW
2013	$9,250	$6,938
2014	$9,741	$7,306
2015	$10,527	$7,895
2016	$11,336	$8,502
2017	$11,547	$8,660

AVG. AUCTION PRICING
LOW	HIGH	AVG
$5,250	$10,500	$8,605

BX2380
YEARS MFRD 2017-2020
SERIES .... BX80 SERIES
ENGINE .... KUBOTA
CYLINDERS 3
CID 54.8
PTO HP 17.7
ENGINE HP 23
COOLING .... LIQUID
FUEL .... D
TRANSMISSION .... HYDRO
STEERING .... STANDARD
HITCH .... CAT. I
DRIVE TYPE 4WD
ROPS/CAB .... ROPS
WEIGHT .... 1,443 LBS.
MSRP $12,170

OPTIONS

54" MM MOWER $2,357
60" MM MOWER $2,581
CAB $4,726
LDR W/BKT. $3,390

BX2660-B

YEARS MFRD 2008-2012
SERIES............. BX SERIES
ENGINE .... KUBOTA D1005
CYLINDERS..................3
CID 61
PTO HP 19.5
ENGINE HP 25.5
COOLING .... LIQUID
FUEL ....D
SPEEDS .... VARIABLE
TRANSMISSION .... HYDRO
STEERING............ STANDARD
HITCH .... CAT. I
HYDRAULIC .... YES
PTO .... YES
WEIGHT .... 1,389 LBS.
MSRP................ $12,482

OPTIONS

37" TILLER
54" DECK
60" DECK
LDR
MID PTO

RETAIL PRICING

YEAR	HIGH	LOW
2008	$8,582	$6,436
2009	$9,326	$6,994
2010	$9,878	$7,408
2011	$10,604	$7,953
2012	$11,542	$8,657

AVG. AUCTION PRICING

LOW	HIGH	AVG
$8,343	$9,579	$9,064

BX2670

YEARS MFRD 2013-2017
ENGINE .... KUBOTA
CYLINDERS..................3
CID 61
PTO HP 19.5
ENGINE HP 25
COOLING .... AIR
FUEL ....D
SPEEDS .... VARIABLE
TRANSMISSION .... HYDRO
STEERING............ STANDARD
DRIVE TYPE 2WD
ROPS/CAB .... ROPS
WEIGHT .... 1,466 LBS.
MSRP................ $13,060

OPTIONS

54"DECK
60"DECK
LDR

RETAIL PRICING

YEAR	HIGH	LOW
2013	$10,201	$7,651
2014	$10,973	$8,229
2015	$11,845	$8,884
2016	$12,604	$9,453
2017	$13,828	$10,371

AVG. AUCTION PRICING

LOW	HIGH	AVG
$9,373	$13,390	$10,815

BX2680

YEARS MFRD 2017-2020
SERIES............ BX80 SERIES
ENGINE .... KUBOTA
CYLINDERS..................3
CID 61.1
COOLING .... LIQUID
FUEL ....D
TRANSMISSION .... HYDRO
HITCH .... CAT. I
DRIVE TYPE 4WD
ROPS/CAB .... ROPS
WEIGHT .... 1,521 LBS.
MSRP................ $13,619

OPTIONS

54" MM MOWER $2,357
60" MM MOWER $2,581
CAB $4,726
LDR W/BKT. $3,390

F2000

YEARS MFRD 1986-1994
SERIES.............. F SERIES
ENGINE .... KUBOTA
ENGINE HP 20
COOLING .... LIQUID
FUEL ....D
SPEEDS .... VARIABLE
TRANSMISSION .... HYDRO
STEERING.................ZERO
BLADE CLUTCH .... MANUAL
DRIVE TYPE 4WD
ROPS/CAB .... ROPS
STANDARD DECK .... 60"
MSRP................ $13,300

OPTIONS

52" SNOW BLOWER
60" BLADE
BAGGER

SERIAL NUMBERS

YEAR	BEGINNING NO.
1986	10046
1987	10541
1988	12083

RETAIL PRICING

YEAR	HIGH	LOW
1986	$1,062	$796
1987	$1,181	$886
1988	$1,309	$982
1989	$1,454	$1,091
1990	$1,612	$1,209
1991	$1,787	$1,340
1992	$1,984	$1,488
1993	$2,202	$1,652
1994	$2,445	$1,834

F2100

YEARS MFRD 1989-1997
SERIES.............. F SERIES
ENGINE .... KUBOTA
ENGINE HP 21
COOLING .... LIQUID
FUEL ....D
SPEEDS .... VARIABLE
TRANSMISSION .... HYDRO
STEERING............ STANDARD
HITCH .... CAT. I
BLADE CLUTCH .... MANUAL
HYDRAULIC .... YES
PTO .... YES
DRIVE TYPE 4WD
ROPS/CAB .... ROPS
STANDARD DECK .... 60"
WEIGHT .... 1,380 LBS.
MSRP................ $18,083

OPTIONS

4 ROPS
50" SNOW BLOWER
60" BLADE
72" DECK

SERIAL NUMBERS

YEAR	BEGINNING NO.
1990	10024
1991	10806
1992	10830
1993	11077
1994	11446

RETAIL PRICING

YEAR	HIGH	LOW
1989	$1,320	$990
1990	$1,467	$1,100
1991	$1,632	$1,224
1992	$1,809	$1,357
1993	$2,004	$1,503
1994	$2,226	$1,669
1995	$2,467	$1,850
1996	$2,737	$2,053
1997	$3,034	$2,276

F2100E

YEARS MFRD 1990-1994
SERIES.............. F SERIES
ENGINE .... KUBOTA
ENGINE HP 20
COOLING .... LIQUID
FUEL ....D
SPEEDS .... VARIABLE
TRANSMISSION .... HYDRO
STEERING.................ZERO
HITCH .... CAT. I
BLADE CLUTCH .... MANUAL
HYDRAULIC .... YES
PTO .... YES
DRIVE TYPE 2WD
ROPS/CAB .... ROPS
STANDARD DECK .... 60"
WEIGHT .... 1,380 LBS.
MSRP................ $15,883

SERIAL NUMBERS

YEAR	BEGINNING NO.
1990	10024
1991	10806
1992	10830
1993	11077
1994	11446

RETAIL PRICING

YEAR	HIGH	LOW
1990	$2,252	$1,689
1991	$2,464	$1,848
1992	$2,733	$2,049
1993	$3,027	$2,270
1994	$3,361	$2,521

F2260

YEARS MFRD 1996-2005
SERIES.............. F SERIES
ENGINE .... KUBOTA
CYLINDERS..................3
CID 61.1
ENGINE HP 22
COOLING .... LIQUID
FUEL ....D
SPEEDS .... VARIABLE
TRANSMISSION .... HYDRO
STEERING.................ZERO
BLADE CLUTCH .... MANUAL
HYDRAULIC .... YES
PTO .... YES
DRIVE TYPE 4WD
ROPS/CAB .... ROPS
STANDARD DECK .... 72"
WEIGHT .... 1,290 LBS.
MSRP................ $18,708

OPTIONS

51" SNOW BLOWER
BAGGER

RETAIL PRICING

YEAR	HIGH	LOW
1996	$3,607	$2,705
1997	$3,866	$2,899
1998	$4,289	$3,217
1999	$4,754	$3,566
2000	$5,276	$3,957
2001	$5,850	$4,388
2002	$6,490	$4,868
2004	$7,985	$5,988
2005	$8,862	$6,647

F2400

YEARS MFRD 1988-1994
SERIES.............. F SERIES
ENGINE .... KUBOTA
ENGINE HP 24
COOLING .... LIQUID
FUEL ....D
SPEEDS .... VARIABLE
TRANSMISSION .... HYDRO
STEERING............ STANDARD
HITCH .... CAT. I
BLADE CLUTCH .... MANUAL
HYDRAULIC .... YES
PTO .... YES
DRIVE TYPE 4WD
ROPS/CAB .... ROPS
STANDARD DECK .... 60"
MSRP................ $19,183

SERIAL NUMBERS

YEAR	BEGINNING NO.
1988	10005
1989	11095
1990	11924

1991 13024
1992 13809
1993 15165
1994 16817

RETAIL PRICING

YEAR	HIGH	LOW
1991	$2,718	$2,039
1992	$3,041	$2,280
1993	$3,356	$2,517
1994	$3,757	$2,818

F2560E

YEARS MFRD 1996-2005
SERIES .... F SERIES
ENGINE .... KUBOTA
CYLINDERS 3
CID 68.6
ENGINE HP 25
COOLING .... LIQUID
FUEL .... D
SPEEDS .... VARIABLE
TRANSMISSION .... HYDRO
STEERING .... STANDARD
BLADE CLUTCH .... MANUAL
DRIVE TYPE 2WD
ROPS/CAB .... ROPS
STANDARD DECK .... 72"
WEIGHT .... 1,500 LBS.
MSRP $16,772

OPTIONS

51" SNOW BLOWER
BAGGER

RETAIL PRICING

YEAR	HIGH	LOW
1997	$3,463	$2,597
1998	$3,843	$2,882
1999	$4,265	$3,199
2000	$4,727	$3,545
2001	$5,243	$3,932
2002	$5,943	$4,457
2003	$6,433	$4,825
2004	$7,166	$5,374
2005	$8,046	$6,035

F2560R

YEARS MFRD 1997-2005
SERIES .... F SERIES
ENGINE .... KUBOTA
CYLINDERS 3
CID 68.6
ENGINE HP 25
COOLING .... LIQUID
FUEL .... D
SPEEDS .... VARIABLE
TRANSMISSION .... HYDRO
STEERING .... ZERO
BLADE CLUTCH .... MANUAL
HYDRAULIC .... YES
PTO .... YES
DRIVE TYPE 4WD
ROPS/CAB .... ROPS
STANDARD DECK .... 72"
WEIGHT .... 1,290 LBS.
MSRP $16,196

RETAIL PRICING

YEAR	HIGH	LOW
1997	$6,304	$4,728
1998	$7,191	$5,394
1999	$8,043	$6,032
2000	$8,917	$6,688
2001	$9,785	$7,339
2002	$10,655	$7,992
2003	$11,704	$8,778
2004	$12,752	$9,564
2005	$13,800	$10,350

F2680

YEARS MFRD 2008-2013
ENGINE .... KUBOTA D1105
CYLINDERS 3
ENGINE HP 25.5
COOLING .... LIQUID
FUEL .... D
SPEEDS .... VARIABLE
TRANSMISSION .... HYDRO
STEERING .... STANDARD
STANDARD DECK .... 60"
WEIGHT .... 1,594 LBS.
MSRP $19,683

OPTIONS

51" SNOW BLOWER
60" BLADE
BAGGER
HARD CAB

RETAIL PRICING

YEAR	HIGH	LOW
2008	$10,289	$7,717
2009	$11,418	$8,563
2010	$12,666	$9,499
2011	$14,217	$10,663
2012	$15,583	$11,687
2013	$17,284	$12,963

F2690

YEARS MFRD 2013-2020
SERIES .... F90 SERIES
ENGINE .... KUBOTA D1105
CYLINDERS 3
CID 68.6
ENGINE HP 25.5
COOLING .... LIQUID
FUEL .... D
TRANSMISSION .... HYDRO
DRIVE TYPE 4WD
STANDARD DECK .... 72"
WEIGHT .... 1,606 LBS.
MSRP $24,521

OPTIONS

51" SNOW BLOWER $3,829
60" DECK .... $-958
72" DECK RD .... $-143
HARD CAB $5,799

RETAIL PRICING

YEAR	HIGH	LOW
2013	$14,772	$11,154
2014	$16,462	$12,422
2015	$17,994	$13,571
2016	$20,133	$15,175
2017	$21,974	$16,555
2018	$23,307	$17,556
2019	$24,534	$18,626
2020	$25,083	$19,198

F2690E

YEARS MFRD 2013-2020
SERIES .... F90 SERIES
ENGINE .... KUBOTA D1105
CYLINDERS 3
CID 68.6
ENGINE HP 25.5
COOLING .... LIQUID
FUEL .... D
TRANSMISSION .... HYDRO
DRIVE TYPE 2WD
STANDARD DECK .... 72"
WEIGHT .... 1,594 LBS.
MSRP $21,829

OPTIONS

51" SNOW BLOWER $3,829
60" DECK .... $-958
72" DECK RD .... $-143
HARD CAB $5,799

RETAIL PRICING

YEAR	HIGH	LOW
2013	$13,112	$9,909
2014	$14,481	$10,936
2015	$15,997	$12,072
2016	$17,666	$13,325
2017	$19,510	$14,708
2018	$20,477	$15,433
2019	$21,596	$16,279
2020	$22,325	$17,018

F2880E

YEARS MFRD 2006-2007
ENGINE D1105
CYLINDERS 3
CID 68.6
ENGINE HP 28
COOLING .... AIR
FUEL .... D
SPEEDS .... VARIABLE
TRANSMISSION .... HYDRO
STEERING .... STANDARD
HITCH .... CAT. I
STANDARD DECK .... 60"
WEIGHT .... 1,488 LBS.
MSRP $15,994

OPTIONS

51" SNOW BLOWER
60" BLADE
72" DECK
BAGGER

RETAIL PRICING

YEAR	HIGH	LOW
2006	$7,924	$5,943
2007	$8,553	$6,415

F3060

YEARS MFRD 1996-2005
SERIES .... F SERIES
ENGINE .... KUBOTA
CYLINDERS 4
CID 81.5
ENGINE HP 30
COOLING .... LIQUID
FUEL .... D
SPEEDS .... VARIABLE
TRANSMISSION .... HYDRO
STEERING .... ZERO
BLADE CLUTCH .... MANUAL
HYDRAULIC .... YES
PTO .... YES
DRIVE TYPE 4WD
ROPS/CAB .... ROPS
STANDARD DECK .... 72"
WEIGHT .... 1,340 LBS.
MSRP $20,708

OPTIONS

51" SNOW BLOWER
BAGGER

RETAIL PRICING

YEAR	HIGH	LOW
1996	$3,833	$2,874
1997	$4,299	$3,224
1998	$4,805	$3,604
1999	$5,265	$3,949
2000	$5,839	$4,379
2001	$6,447	$4,835
2002	$7,148	$5,361
2003	$7,967	$5,975
2004	$8,839	$6,630
2005	$9,952	$7,464

F3080

YEARS MFRD 2008-2013
ENGINE .... KUBOTA D1305
CYLINDERS 3
ENGINE HP 30
COOLING .... LIQUID
FUEL .... D
SPEEDS .... VARIABLE
TRANSMISSION .... HYDRO
STEERING .... STANDARD
DRIVE TYPE 4WD
STANDARD DECK .... 72"
WEIGHT .... 1,656 LBS.
MSRP $24,359

OPTIONS

51" SNOW BLOWER
60" BLADE
BAGGER
HARD CAB

RETAIL PRICING

YEAR	HIGH	LOW
2008	$12,739	$9,554
2009	$14,048	$10,536
2010	$15,734	$11,801
2011	$17,386	$13,040
2012	$19,436	$14,577
2013	$21,392	$16,044

F3680F

YEARS MFRD 2006-2013
ENGINE V1505
CYLINDERS 4
CID 91.5
ENGINE HP 36
COOLING .... LIQUID
FUEL .... D
SPEEDS .... VARIABLE
TRANSMISSION .... HYDRO
STEERING .... STANDARD
DRIVE TYPE 4WD

 See Kubota Model Suffix Identification on page 415

STANDARD DECK . . . . 72"
WEIGHT . . . . 1,581 LBS.
MSRP $25,241

OPTIONS

51" SNOW BLOWER
60" BLADE
BAGGER

RETAIL PRICING

YEAR	HIGH	LOW
2006	$10,766	$8,074
2007	$12,003	$9,002
2008	$13,198	$9,899
2009	$14,778	$11,084
2010	$16,240	$12,180
2011	$18,071	$13,554
2012	$20,173	$15,129
2013	$22,168	$16,626

F3990

YEARS MFRD 2013-2020
SERIES . . . . F90 SERIES
ENGINE . . . . KUBOTA V1505T
CYLINDERS 4
CID 91.4
ENGINE HP 39
COOLING . . . . LIQUID
FUEL . . . . D
TRANSMISSION . . . . HYDRO
DRIVE TYPE 4WD
STANDARD DECK . . . . 72"
WEIGHT . . . . 1,716 LBS.
MSRP $29,121

OPTIONS

51" SNOW BLOWER $3,829
60" DECK . . . . $-958
72" DECK RD . . . . $-143
HARD CAB $5,799

RETAIL PRICING

YEAR	HIGH	LOW
2013	$17,307	$13,056
2014	$19,184	$14,463
2015	$21,106	$15,904
2016	$23,306	$17,555
2017	$25,736	$19,376
2018	$26,992	$20,319
2019	$28,110	$21,232
2020	$28,850	$22,048

FZ2100

YEARS MFRD 1994-1997
SERIES . . . . FZ SERIES
ENGINE . . . . KUBOTA
ENGINE HP 20
COOLING . . . . LIQUID
FUEL . . . . D
SPEEDS . . . . VARIABLE
TRANSMISSION . . . . HYDRO
STEERING . . . . ZERO
BLADE CLUTCH . . . . MANUAL
DRIVE TYPE 4WD
ROPS/CAB . . . . ROPS
STANDARD DECK . . . . 60"
WEIGHT . . . . 1,595 LBS.
MSRP $18,056

OPTIONS

50" SNOW BLOWER
60" BLADE
72" DECK

RETAIL PRICING

YEAR	HIGH	LOW
1994	$2,698	$2,023
1995	$2,989	$2,242
1996	$3,317	$2,487
1997	$3,681	$2,761

FZ2400

YEARS MFRD 1994-1997
SERIES . . . . FZ SERIES
ENGINE . . . . KUBOTA
ENGINE HP 24
COOLING . . . . LIQUID
FUEL . . . . D
SPEEDS . . . . VARIABLE
TRANSMISSION . . . . HYDRO
STEERING . . . . ZERO
BLADE CLUTCH . . . . MANUAL
DRIVE TYPE 4WD
ROPS/CAB . . . . ROPS
STANDARD DECK . . . . 72"
WEIGHT . . . . 1,587 LBS.
MSRP $20,981

OPTIONS

50" SNOW BLOWER
60" BLADE

SERIAL NUMBERS

YEAR	BEGINNING NO.
1994	10114
1995	10379
1996	10439

RETAIL PRICING

YEAR	HIGH	LOW
1994	$3,135	$2,351
1995	$3,477	$2,608
1996	$3,855	$2,891
1997	$4,276	$3,207

G1800

YEARS MFRD 1989-2000
SERIES . . . . G SERIES
ENGINE . . . . KUBOTA
CID 40
ENGINE HP 16
COOLING . . . . LIQUID
FUEL . . . . D
SPEEDS . . . . VARIABLE
TRANSMISSION . . . . HYDRO
STEERING . . . . STANDARD
HITCH . . . . CAT. I
BLADE CLUTCH . . . . MANUAL
HYDRAULIC . . . . YES
PTO . . . . YES
STANDARD DECK . . . . 48"
WEIGHT . . . . 705 LBS.
MSRP $9,016

OPTIONS

3 BAG
40" TILLER
42" SNOW BLOWER
54" DECK

RETAIL PRICING

YEAR	HIGH	LOW
1992	$864	$648
1993	$957	$718
1994	$1,059	$794
1995	$1,170	$878
1996	$1,296	$972
1997	$1,433	$1,075
1998	$1,584	$1,188
1999	$1,763	$1,323
2000	$1,943	$1,457

AVG. AUCTION PRICING

LOW	HIGH	AVG
$1,000	$1,200	$1,050

G1800S

YEARS MFRD 1988-2000
SERIES . . . . G SERIES
ENGINE . . . . KUBOTA
CID 40
ENGINE HP 16
COOLING . . . . LIQUID
FUEL . . . . D
SPEEDS . . . . VARIABLE
TRANSMISSION . . . . HYDRO
STEERING . . . . ALL WHEEL
HITCH . . . . CAT. I
BLADE CLUTCH . . . . MANUAL
HYDRAULIC . . . . YES
PTO . . . . YES
STANDARD DECK . . . . 48"
WEIGHT . . . . 750 LBS.
MSRP $9,616

OPTIONS

3 BAG
40" TILLER
42" SNOW BLOWER
54" DECK

SERIAL NUMBERS

YEAR	BEGINNING NO.
1988	10001
1989	10036
1990	11570
1991	12686
1992	13278
1993	14292
1994	14663

RETAIL PRICING

YEAR	HIGH	LOW
1992	$922	$691
1993	$1,020	$765
1994	$1,129	$847
1995	$1,248	$936
1996	$1,381	$1,036
1997	$1,527	$1,146
1998	$1,691	$1,268
1999	$1,868	$1,401
2000	$2,069	$1,552

G1900

YEARS MFRD 1989-2000
SERIES . . . . G SERIES
ENGINE . . . . KUBOTA
CID 43.9
ENGINE HP 18
COOLING . . . . LIQUID
FUEL . . . . D
SPEEDS . . . . VARIABLE
TRANSMISSION . . . . HYDRO
STEERING . . . . STANDARD
HITCH . . . . CAT. I
BLADE CLUTCH . . . . MANUAL
HYDRAULIC . . . . YES
PTO . . . . YES
STANDARD DECK . . . . 54"
WEIGHT . . . . 706 LBS.
MSRP $10,083

OPTIONS

3 BAG
40" TILLER
42" SNOW BLOWER
60" DECK

RETAIL PRICING

YEAR	HIGH	LOW
1992	$1,004	$753
1993	$1,110	$833
1994	$1,229	$922
1995	$1,360	$1,020
1996	$1,503	$1,127
1997	$1,664	$1,248
1998	$1,841	$1,380
1999	$2,035	$1,526
2000	$2,252	$1,689

AVG. AUCTION PRICING

LOW	HIGH	AVG
$2,027	$3,166	$2,681

G1900S

YEARS MFRD 1989-2000
SERIES . . . . G SERIES
ENGINE . . . . KUBOTA
CID 43.9
ENGINE HP 18
COOLING . . . . LIQUID
FUEL . . . . D
SPEEDS . . . . VARIABLE
TRANSMISSION . . . . HYDRO
STEERING . . . . ALL WHEEL
HITCH . . . . CAT. I
BLADE CLUTCH . . . . MANUAL
PTO . . . . YES
STANDARD DECK . . . . 54"
WEIGHT . . . . 750 LBS.
MSRP $10,683

OPTIONS

3 BAG
40" TILLER
42" SNOW BLOWER
60" DECK

RETAIL PRICING

YEAR	HIGH	LOW
1992	$1,025	$769
1993	$1,134	$851
1994	$1,254	$940
1995	$1,387	$1,041
1996	$1,534	$1,150
1997	$1,697	$1,273
1998	$1,879	$1,409
1999	$2,078	$1,558
2000	$2,298	$1,723

G2000

YEARS MFRD 1989-1997
SERIES .... G SERIES
ENGINE .... KUBOTA
CID 46
ENGINE HP 21
COOLING .... LIQUID
FUEL .... G
SPEEDS .... VARIABLE
TRANSMISSION .... HYDRO
STEERING .... STANDARD
HITCH .... CAT. I
BLADE CLUTCH .... MANUAL
HYDRAULIC .... YES
PTO .... YES
STANDARD DECK .... 60"
WEIGHT .... 706 LBS.
MSRP $9,870

OPTIONS

3 BAG
40" TILLER
42" SNOW BLOWER
48" BLADE

RETAIL PRICING

YEAR	HIGH	LOW
1989	$702	$527
1990	$778	$583
1991	$860	$645
1992	$951	$713
1993	$1,053	$789
1994	$1,164	$873
1995	$1,286	$965
1996	$1,424	$1,068
1997	$1,576	$1,182

G2000S

YEARS MFRD 1989-1997
SERIES .... G SERIES
ENGINE .... KUBOTA
CID 46
ENGINE HP 21
COOLING .... LIQUID
FUEL .... G
SPEEDS .... VARIABLE
TRANSMISSION .... HYDRO
STEERING .... ALL WHEEL
HITCH .... CAT. I
BLADE CLUTCH .... MANUAL
HYDRAULIC .... YES
PTO .... YES
STANDARD DECK .... 60"
MSRP $10,470

OPTIONS

3 BAG
40" TILLER
42" SNOW BLOWER
48" BLADE

SERIAL NUMBERS

YEAR	BEGINNING NO.
1992	10913
1993	11059
1994	11133

RETAIL PRICING

YEAR	HIGH	LOW
1989	$745	$559
1990	$826	$620
1991	$913	$684
1992	$1,008	$756
1993	$1,117	$837
1994	$1,236	$927
1995	$1,366	$1,024
1996	$1,512	$1,134
1997	$1,672	$1,254

G2160

YEARS MFRD 2001-2008
SERIES .... G SERIES
ENGINE .... KUBOTA E TVCS
CYLINDERS 3
CID 47.5
ENGINE HP 21
COOLING .... LIQUID
FUEL .... D
SPEEDS .... VARIABLE
TRANSMISSION .... HYDRO
STEERING .... STANDARD
BLADE CLUTCH .... ELECTRIC
HYDRAULIC .... YES
PTO .... YES
STANDARD DECK .... 54"
WEIGHT .... 1,080 LBS.
MSRP $8,800

OPTIONS

3 BAG
48" BLADE
50" SNOW BLOWER
60" DECK

RETAIL PRICING

YEAR	HIGH	LOW
2001	$1,872	$1,404
2002	$2,068	$1,551
2003	$2,288	$1,716
2004	$2,531	$1,898
2005	$2,799	$2,099
2006	$3,102	$2,327
2007	$3,431	$2,573
2008	$3,788	$2,841

AVG. AUCTION PRICING

LOW	HIGH	AVG
$1,854	$2,833	$2,284

G2160 R48S

YEARS MFRD 2001-2008
SERIES .... G SERIES
ENGINE .... KUBOTA E TVCS
CYLINDERS 3
CID 47.5
ENGINE HP 21
COOLING .... LIQUID
FUEL .... D
SPEEDS .... VARIABLE
TRANSMISSION .... HYDRO
STEERING .... STANDARD
BLADE CLUTCH .... ELECTRIC
HYDRAULIC .... YES
PTO .... YES
STANDARD DECK .... 48"
WEIGHT .... 1,240 LBS.
MSRP $9,700

OPTIONS

47" SWEEPER
48" BLADE
50" SNOW BLOWER
54" BLADE

RETAIL PRICING

YEAR	HIGH	LOW
2001	$1,985	$1,489
2002	$2,195	$1,646
2003	$2,429	$1,822
2004	$2,686	$2,015
2005	$2,972	$2,229
2006	$3,288	$2,466
2007	$3,636	$2,727
2008	$4,043	$3,032

G2460G

YEARS MFRD 2001-2007
SERIES .... G SERIES
ENGINE .... KUBOTA
CYLINDERS 3
CID 45.3
ENGINE HP 24
COOLING .... LIQUID
FUEL .... G
SPEEDS .... VARIABLE
TRANSMISSION .... HYDRO
STEERING .... STANDARD
STANDARD DECK .... 54"
WEIGHT .... 1,080 LBS.
MSRP $8,788

OPTIONS

3 BAG
48" BLADE
50" SNOW BLOWER
60" DECK

RETAIL PRICING

YEAR	HIGH	LOW
2001	$1,829	$1,372
2002	$2,023	$1,517
2003	$2,239	$1,679
2004	$2,475	$1,856
2005	$2,750	$2,063
2006	$3,029	$2,272
2007	$3,352	$2,514

G3200G

YEARS MFRD 1983-1988
SERIES .... G SERIES
ENGINE .... KUBOTA
ENGINE HP 12
COOLING .... LIQUID
FUEL .... D
SPEEDS 8/8
TRANSMISSION .... GEAR
STEERING .... STANDARD
BLADE CLUTCH .... MANUAL
STANDARD DECK .... 40"
WEIGHT .... 675 LBS.
MSRP $5,065

OPTIONS

36" TILLER
38" SNOW BLOWER
46" BLADE

SERIAL NUMBERS

YEAR	BEGINNING NO.
1984	10546
1985	30001
1986	40217
1987	40333

RETAIL PRICING

YEAR	HIGH	LOW
1983	$217	$163
1984	$240	$180
1985	$266	$199
1986	$295	$221
1987	$325	$244
1988	$359	$270

G4200G

YEARS MFRD 1983-1990
SERIES .... G SERIES
ENGINE .... KUBOTA
ENGINE HP 12
COOLING .... LIQUID
FUEL .... D
SPEEDS 8/8
TRANSMISSION .... GEAR
STEERING .... STANDARD
BLADE CLUTCH .... MANUAL
STANDARD DECK .... 44"
WEIGHT .... 675 LBS.
MSRP $5,475

OPTIONS

36" TILLER
38" SNOW BLOWER
46" BLADE

SERIAL NUMBERS

YEAR	BEGINNING NO.
1984	10622
1985	30001
1986	30516
1987	32391
1988	32862

RETAIL PRICING

YEAR	HIGH	LOW
1983	$221	$166
1984	$245	$184
1985	$272	$204
1986	$301	$226
1987	$332	$249
1988	$367	$275
1989	$406	$304
1990	$449	$337

G4200H

YEARS MFRD 1984-1990
SERIES .... G SERIES
ENGINE .... KUBOTA
ENGINE HP 12
COOLING .... LIQUID
FUEL .... D
SPEEDS .... VARIABLE
TRANSMISSION .... HYDRO
STEERING .... STANDARD
BLADE CLUTCH .... MANUAL
STANDARD DECK .... 44"
WEIGHT .... 685 LBS.
MSRP $6,300

OPTIONS

36" TILLER
38" SNOW BLOWER
46" BLADE

KUBOTA See Kubota Model Suffix Identification on page 415

SERIAL NUMBERS

YEAR	BEGINNING NO.
1984	11834
1985	30001
1986	31874
1987	32390
1988	32862

RETAIL PRICING

YEAR	HIGH	LOW
1984	$302	$226
1985	$333	$250
1986	$368	$276
1987	$408	$306
1988	$451	$338
1989	$499	$374
1990	$552	$414

G5200H

YEARS MFRD	1984-1990
SERIES	G SERIES
ENGINE	KUBOTA
ENGINE HP	14
COOLING	LIQUID
FUEL	D
SPEEDS	VARIABLE
TRANSMISSION	HYDRO
STEERING	STANDARD
BLADE CLUTCH	MANUAL
STANDARD DECK	44"
WEIGHT	710 LBS.
MSRP	$6,800

OPTIONS

36" TILLER
38" SNOW BLOWER
46" BLADE

SERIAL NUMBERS

YEAR	BEGINNING NO.
1984	12140
1985	30001
1986	30516
1987	36042
1988	37274

RETAIL PRICING

YEAR	HIGH	LOW
1984	$325	$244
1985	$359	$270
1986	$398	$298
1987	$440	$330
1988	$488	$366
1989	$539	$404
1990	$595	$447

G6200H

YEARS MFRD	1986-1990
SERIES	G SERIES
ENGINE	KUBOTA
ENGINE HP	16
COOLING	LIQUID
FUEL	D
SPEEDS	VARIABLE
TRANSMISSION	HYDRO
STEERING	STANDARD
BLADE CLUTCH	MANUAL
STANDARD DECK	48"
WEIGHT	739 LBS.
MSRP	$7,480

OPTIONS

36" TILLER
38" SNOW BLOWER
46" BLADE

RETAIL PRICING

YEAR	HIGH	LOW
1986	$438	$328
1987	$484	$363
1988	$536	$402
1989	$591	$443
1990	$656	$492

GF1800

YEARS MFRD	1994-2003
SERIES	GF SERIES
ENGINE	KUBOTA
CYLINDERS	3
CID	43.9
ENGINE HP	18
COOLING	LIQUID
FUEL	D
SPEEDS	VARIABLE
TRANSMISSION	HYDRO
STEERING	ZERO
BLADE CLUTCH	MANUAL
HYDRAULIC	YES
PTO	YES
DRIVE TYPE	4WD
STANDARD DECK	54"
WEIGHT	963 LBS.
MSRP	$13,213

OPTIONS

3 BAG
42" SNOW BLOWER
60" DECK

SERIAL NUMBERS

YEAR	BEGINNING NO.
1994	10031

RETAIL PRICING

YEAR	HIGH	LOW
1995	$2,194	$1,645
1996	$2,433	$1,825
1997	$2,703	$2,027
1998	$2,993	$2,245
1999	$3,321	$2,491
2000	$3,676	$2,757
2001	$4,090	$3,068
2002	$4,534	$3,401
2003	$5,107	$3,830

AVG. AUCTION PRICING

LOW	HIGH	AVG
$1,236	$3,090	$1,880

GF1800E

YEARS MFRD	1994-2003
SERIES	GF SERIES
ENGINE	KUBOTA
CYLINDERS	3
CID	43.9
ENGINE HP	18
COOLING	LIQUID
FUEL	D
SPEEDS	VARIABLE
TRANSMISSION	HYDRO
STEERING	STANDARD
BLADE CLUTCH	MANUAL
HYDRAULIC	YES
PTO	YES
DRIVE TYPE	2WD
STANDARD DECK	54"
WEIGHT	885 LBS.
MSRP	$11,763

OPTIONS

3 BAG
42" SNOW BLOWER
60" DECK

SERIAL NUMBERS

YEAR	BEGINNING NO.
1994	10031

RETAIL PRICING

YEAR	HIGH	LOW
1995	$1,883	$1,412
1996	$2,084	$1,563
1997	$2,315	$1,737
1998	$2,568	$1,926
1999	$2,850	$2,138
2000	$3,159	$2,369
2001	$3,507	$2,630
2002	$3,888	$2,916
2003	$4,317	$3,238

GR2000G

YEARS MFRD	2005-2007
SERIES	GR SERIES
ENGINE	KUBOTA GH630
CYLINDERS	2
CID	38.1
ENGINE HP	20
COOLING	AIR
FUEL	G
SPEEDS	VARIABLE
TRANSMISSION	HYDRO
STEERING	STANDARD
STANDARD DECK	48"
WEIGHT	881 LBS.
MSRP	$7,163

OPTIONS

46" SNOW BLOWER
48" BLADE
BAGGER

RETAIL PRICING

YEAR	HIGH	LOW
2005	$2,556	$1,917
2006	$2,842	$2,131
2007	$3,129	$2,347

GR2010G

YEARS MFRD	2008-2010
SERIES	GR SERIES
ENGINE	KUBOTA GH630
CYLINDERS	2
ENGINE HP	20
COOLING	AIR
FUEL	G
SPEEDS	VARIABLE
TRANSMISSION	HYDRO
STEERING	STANDARD
STANDARD DECK	48"
WEIGHT	881 LBS.
MSRP	$8,212

OPTIONS

46" SNOW BLOWER
48" BLADE
BAGGER

RETAIL PRICING

YEAR	HIGH	LOW
2008	$4,703	$3,527
2009	$5,210	$3,907
2010	$5,795	$4,346

GR2020G

YEARS MFRD	2011-2018
SERIES	GR SERIES
ENGINE	KOHLER GH631
ENGINE HP	20
COOLING	AIR
FUEL	G
SPEEDS	VARIABLE
TRANSMISSION	HYDRO
STEERING	STANDARD
STANDARD DECK	48"
WEIGHT	882 LBS.
MSRP	$11,505

OPTIONS

46" SNOW BLOWER
48" BLADE

RETAIL PRICING

YEAR	HIGH	LOW
2011	$4,277	$3,207
2012	$4,732	$3,549
2013	$5,246	$3,934
2014	$5,790	$4,342
2015	$6,415	$4,811
2016	$7,118	$5,339
2017	$7,836	$5,877
2018	$8,306	$6,229

GR2100

YEARS MFRD	2005-2007
ENGINE	KUBOTA D782
CYLINDERS	3
CID	47.7
ENGINE HP	21
COOLING	LIQUID
FUEL	D
SPEEDS	VARIABLE
TRANSMISSION	HYDRO
STEERING	STANDARD
STANDARD DECK	54"
WEIGHT	948 LBS.
MSRP	$8,124

OPTIONS

46" SNOW BLOWER
48" BLADE
BAGGER

RETAIL PRICING

YEAR	HIGH	LOW
2005	$3,006	$2,254
2006	$3,349	$2,511
2007	$3,722	$2,792

AVG. AUCTION PRICING

LOW	HIGH	AVG
$1,950	$3,000	$2,500

GR2110

YEARS MFRD	2008-2010
SERIES	GR SERIES
ENGINE	KUBOTA D782

CYLINDERS	3
ENGINE HP	21
COOLING	LIQUID
FUEL	D
SPEEDS	VARIABLE
TRANSMISSION	HYDRO
STEERING	STANDARD
STANDARD DECK	54"
WEIGHT	948 LBS.
MSRP	$9,217

OPTIONS

46" SNOW BLOWER
48" BLADE
BAGGER

RETAIL PRICING

YEAR	HIGH	LOW
2008	$3,541	$2,656
2009	$3,967	$2,975
2010	$4,398	$3,299

GR2120

YEARS MFRD	2011-2020
SERIES	GR SERIES
ENGINE	KUBOTA D782
CYLINDERS	3
ENGINE HP	21
COOLING	LIQUID
FUEL	D
SPEEDS	VARIABLE
TRANSMISSION	HYDRO
STEERING	STANDARD
STANDARD DECK	48"
WEIGHT	959 LBS.
MSRP	$9,640

OPTIONS

46" SNOW BLOWER	$1,539
48" BLADE	$449
54" DECK	$145

RETAIL PRICING

YEAR	HIGH	LOW
2011	$4,594	$3,520
2012	$5,095	$3,897
2013	$5,709	$4,357
2014	$6,235	$4,751
2015	$6,938	$5,278
2016	$7,682	$5,837
2017	$8,474	$6,431
2018	$8,794	$6,670
2019	$9,097	$6,898
2020	$9,445	$7,210

L35TLB

YEARS MFRD	1994-1994
ENGINE	KUBOTA
CYLINDERS	3
CID	100.5
ENGINE HP	35
COOLING	LIQUID
FUEL	D
SPEEDS	8/8
TRANSMISSION	GEAR
STEERING	STANDARD
HITCH	CAT. I
HYDRAULIC	YES
PTO	YES
DRIVE TYPE	4WD
ROPS/CAB	ROPS
WEIGHT	5,997 LBS.
MSRP	$35,061

RETAIL PRICING

YEAR	HIGH	LOW
1994	$10,631	$7,973

AVG. AUCTION PRICING

LOW	HIGH	AVG
$10,815	$15,450	$13,411

L39TL

YEARS MFRD	2005-2014
SERIES	L SERIES
ENGINE	KUBOTA
CYLINDERS	3
CID	111
PTO HP	39
COOLING	LIQUID
FUEL	D
SPEEDS	12/8
TRANSMISSION	GEAR
STEERING	STANDARD
HITCH	CAT. I
DRIVE TYPE	4WD
ROPS/CAB	ROPS
WEIGHT	4,605 LBS.
MSRP	$31,941

RETAIL PRICING

YEAR	HIGH	LOW
2005	$12,136	$9,102
2006	$12,839	$9,629
2007	$13,830	$10,372
2008	$14,822	$11,116
2009	$16,223	$12,167
2010	$17,972	$13,479
2011	$19,666	$14,749
2012	$22,000	$16,500
2013	$25,268	$18,951
2014	$28,358	$21,268

L39TLB

YEARS MFRD	2006-2013
ENGINE	KUBOTA
CYLINDERS	3
CID	111.4
ENGINE HP	39
FUEL	D
SPEEDS	VARIABLE
TRANSMISSION	SHUTTLE SHIFT
STEERING	STANDARD
HITCH	CAT. II
HYDRAULIC	YES
PTO	YES
DRIVE TYPE	4WD
ROPS/CAB	ROPS
MSRP	$45,031

RETAIL PRICING

YEAR	HIGH	LOW
2006	$25,367	$19,025
2007	$27,174	$20,381
2008	$29,636	$22,227
2009	$31,056	$23,292
2010	$33,395	$25,046
2011	$35,905	$26,929
2012	$38,401	$28,801
2013	$41,512	$31,134

L45TLB

YEARS MFRD	2009-2013
ENGINE	KUBOTA
CYLINDERS	4
CID	134
PTO HP	32
ENGINE HP	45
COOLING	LIQUID
FUEL	D
SPEEDS	VARIABLE
TRANSMISSION	HYDRO
STEERING	STANDARD
HITCH	CAT. I
HYDRAULIC	YES
PTO	YES
DRIVE TYPE	4WD
ROPS/CAB	ROPS
WEIGHT	7,173 LBS.
MSRP	$48,702

RETAIL PRICING

YEAR	HIGH	LOW
2009	$33,856	$25,392
2010	$36,115	$27,086
2011	$38,833	$29,125
2012	$42,307	$31,730
2013	$44,903	$33,677

L47TLB

YEARS MFRD	2016-2019
ENGINE	TIER 4
CYLINDERS	4
CID	148.5
PTO HP	33
ENGINE HP	44.7
FUEL	D
TRANSMISSION	HYDRO
STEERING	STANDARD
DRIVE TYPE	4WD
ROPS/CAB	ROPS
WEIGHT	7,205 LBS.
MSRP	$51,962

OPTIONS

REMOTE VALVE KIT

L48

YEARS MFRD	2000-2007
ENGINE	KUBOTA E-TVCS
CYLINDERS	4
CID	148.5
ENGINE HP	48
FUEL	D
SPEEDS	VARIABLE
TRANSMISSION	HYDRO
STEERING	STANDARD
HITCH	CAT. I
HYDRAULIC	YES
PTO	YES
MSRP	$41,579

RETAIL PRICING

YEAR	HIGH	LOW
2000	$16,713	$12,535
2001	$17,932	$13,449
2002	$19,094	$14,321
2003	$20,684	$15,513
2004	$22,611	$16,958
2005	$23,919	$17,939
2006	$25,967	$19,475
2007	$27,892	$20,919

L48TL

YEARS MFRD	2001-2008
ENGINE	KUBOTA
CYLINDERS	4
CID	148.5
PTO HP	37.5
ENGINE HP	48
COOLING	LIQUID
FUEL	D
SPEEDS	VARIABLE
TRANSMISSION	HYDRO
STEERING	STANDARD
HITCH	CAT. I
HYDRAULIC	YES
PTO	YES
DRIVE TYPE	4WD
ROPS/CAB	ROPS
WEIGHT	5,790 LBS.
MSRP	$32,675

RETAIL PRICING

YEAR	HIGH	LOW
2001	$18,257	$13,693
2002	$18,894	$14,171
2003	$19,530	$14,647
2004	$20,177	$15,133
2005	$20,814	$15,611
2006	$21,774	$16,331
2007	$22,734	$17,051
2008	$22,834	$17,126

L48TL SG

YEARS MFRD	2004-2004
ENGINE	KUBOTA E TVCS
CYLINDERS	4
CID	148.5
ENGINE HP	48
COOLING	LIQUID
FUEL	D
SPEEDS	VARIABLE
TRANSMISSION	HYDRO
STEERING	STANDARD
HITCH	CAT. I
HYDRAULIC	YES
PTO	YES
WEIGHT	5,790 LBS.
MSRP	$5,790

RETAIL PRICING

YEAR	HIGH	LOW
2004	$4,560	$3,420

L48TLB

YEARS MFRD	1997-2003
ENGINE	KUBOTA
CYLINDERS	4
CID	148.5
PTO HP	37.5
ENGINE HP	48
COOLING	LIQUID
FUEL	D
SPEEDS	VARIABLE
TRANSMISSION	HYDRO
STEERING	STANDARD
HITCH	CAT. I
HYDRAULIC	YES
PTO	YES
WEIGHT	5,790 LBS.
MSRP	$43,450

RETAIL PRICING

YEAR	HIGH	LOW
2001	$26,253	$19,689
2002	$28,587	$21,440
2003	$31,396	$23,547

L48TLB SG

YEARS MFRD 2004-2004
ENGINE KUBOTA E TVCS
CYLINDERS 4
CID 148.5
ENGINE HP 48
COOLING LIQUID
FUEL D
SPEEDS VARIABLE
TRANSMISSION HYDRO
STEERING STANDARD
HITCH CAT. I
HYDRAULIC YES
PTO YES
WEIGHT 7,260 LBS.
MSRP $43,450

RETAIL PRICING

YEAR	HIGH	LOW
2004	$34,206	$25,655

L185DT

YEARS MFRD 1977-1982
SERIES L SERIES
ENGINE KUBOTA
CYLINDERS 2
CID 45.3
PTO HP 15.4
ENGINE HP 17
COOLING LIQUID
FUEL D
SPEEDS 8/2
TRANSMISSION GEAR
STEERING STANDARD
HITCH CAT. I
HYDRAULIC YES
PTO YES
DRIVE TYPE 4WD
ROPS/CAB ROPS
WEIGHT 1,734 LBS.
MSRP $6,290

OPTIONS

1 HYD
4WD

SERIAL NUMBERS

LEFT SIDE OF CLUTCH HOUSING

YEAR	BEGINNING NO.
1977	10366
1978	10916
1979	10979
1980	11042
1981	11105
1982	11186

RETAIL PRICING

YEAR	HIGH	LOW
1977	$1,198	$898
1978	$1,273	$955
1979	$1,359	$1,019
1980	$1,442	$1,082
1981	$1,527	$1,146
1982	$1,635	$1,226

AVG. AUCTION PRICING

LOW	HIGH	AVG
$1,152	$2,211	$1,731

L185DT2

YEARS MFRD 1977-1983
ENGINE KUBOTA
CYLINDERS 2
CID 45.3
PTO HP 15.4
ENGINE HP 17
COOLING LIQUID
FUEL D
SPEEDS 8/2
TRANSMISSION GEAR
STEERING STANDARD
HITCH CAT. I
HYDRAULIC YES
PTO YES
DRIVE TYPE 4WD
ROPS/CAB ROPS
MSRP $5,780

SERIAL NUMBERS

LEFT SIDE OF CLUTCH HOUSING

YEAR	BEGINNING NO.
1977	50001
1978	50619
1979	51656
1980	53004
1981	55139
1982	70001
1983	70062

RETAIL PRICING

YEAR	HIGH	LOW
1983	$1,211	$908

L185F

YEARS MFRD 1976-1982
SERIES L SERIES
ENGINE KUBOTA
CYLINDERS 2
CID 45.3
PTO HP 15.3
ENGINE HP 17
COOLING LIQUID
FUEL D
SPEEDS 8/2
TRANSMISSION GEAR
STEERING STANDARD
HITCH CAT. I
HYDRAULIC YES
PTO YES
DRIVE TYPE 2WD
ROPS/CAB ROPS
WEIGHT 1,595 LBS.
MSRP $5,730

SERIAL NUMBERS

LEFT SIDE OF CLUTCH HOUSING

YEAR	BEGINNING NO.
1976	10001
1977	10606
1978	12446
1979	12506
1980	12842
1981	13177
1982	13511

RETAIL PRICING

YEAR	HIGH	LOW
1977	$709	$531
1978	$858	$643
1979	$964	$723
1980	$1,025	$769
1981	$1,074	$806
1982	$1,128	$846

L185F2

YEARS MFRD 1977-1983
ENGINE KUBOTA
CYLINDERS 2
CID 45.3
PTO HP 15.4
ENGINE HP 17
COOLING LIQUID
FUEL D
SPEEDS 8/2
TRANSMISSION GEAR
STEERING STANDARD
HITCH CAT. I
HYDRAULIC YES
PTO YES
DRIVE TYPE 2WD
ROPS/CAB ROPS
WEIGHT 1,727 LBS.
MSRP $5,270

SERIAL NUMBERS

LEFT SIDE OF CLUTCH HOUSING

YEAR	BEGINNING NO.
1977	50001
1978	51640
1979	53700
1980	55139
1981	56061
1982	56491
1983	56691

RETAIL PRICING

YEAR	HIGH	LOW
1983	$1,105	$829

L185T

YEARS MFRD 1978-1982
SERIES L SERIES
ENGINE KUBOTA
CYLINDERS 2
CID 45.3
PTO HP 15
ENGINE HP 17
COOLING LIQUID
FUEL D
SPEEDS 8/2
TRANSMISSION GEAR
STEERING STANDARD
HITCH CAT. I
HYDRAULIC YES
PTO YES
DRIVE TYPE 2WD
ROPS/CAB ROPS
WEIGHT 1,780 LBS.
MSRP $5,780

SERIAL NUMBERS

LEFT SIDE OF CLUTCH HOUSING

YEAR	BEGINNING NO.
1978	50349

RETAIL PRICING

YEAR	HIGH	LOW
1982	$1,139	$854

L235DT

YEARS MFRD 1981-1985
SERIES L SERIES
ENGINE KUBOTA
CYLINDERS 3
CID 68
PTO HP 19.5
ENGINE HP 23.5
COOLING LIQUID
FUEL D
SPEEDS 8/7
TRANSMISSION GEAR
STEERING STANDARD
HITCH CAT. I
HYDRAULIC YES
PTO YES
DRIVE TYPE 4WD
ROPS/CAB ROPS
WEIGHT 2,211 LBS.
MSRP $7,500

SERIAL NUMBERS

YEAR	BEGINNING NO.
1981	10167
1982	10642
1983	50204
1984	51307

RETAIL PRICING

YEAR	HIGH	LOW
1981	$1,780	$1,335
1982	$1,873	$1,404
1983	$1,997	$1,498
1984	$2,078	$1,558
1985	$2,189	$1,642

L235F

YEARS MFRD 1981-1986
ENGINE KUBOTA
CYLINDERS 3
CID 68
PTO HP 19.5
ENGINE HP 23.5
COOLING LIQUID
FUEL D
SPEEDS 8/7
TRANSMISSION GEAR
STEERING STANDARD
HITCH CAT. I
HYDRAULIC YES
PTO YES
DRIVE TYPE 2WD
ROPS/CAB ROPS
WEIGHT 1,950 LBS.
MSRP $7,300

SERIAL NUMBERS

YEAR	BEGINNING NO.
1981	10162

RETAIL PRICING

YEAR	HIGH	LOW
1982	$1,271	$953
1983	$1,378	$1,034
1984	$1,452	$1,089
1985	$1,771	$1,328

L245HC

YEARS MFRD 1976-1995
SERIES . . . . L SERIES
ENGINE . . . . KUBOTA
CYLINDERS 3
CID 68
PTO HP 22.3
ENGINE HP 25
COOLING . . . . LIQUID
FUEL . . . . D
SPEEDS . . . . VARIABLE
TRANSMISSION . . . . HYDRO
HITCH . . . . CAT. I
HYDRAULIC . . . . YES
PTO . . . . YES
DRIVE TYPE 4WD
ROPS/CAB . . . . ROPS
WEIGHT . . . . 2,322 LBS.
MSRP $11,900

SERIAL NUMBERS

YEAR	BEGINNING NO.
1976	10001
1977	10436
1978	13666
1979	13764
1980	13876
1981	13976
1982	14061
1983	14126
1984	14191
1985	14296
1986	14496
1987	14721
1988	14946
1989	15170
1990	15393
1991	15616
1992	15836

RETAIL PRICING

YEAR	HIGH	LOW
1978	$1,241	$931
1979	$1,408	$1,056
1980	$1,479	$1,109
1981	$1,501	$1,126
1982	$1,522	$1,142
1983	$1,646	$1,234
1984	$1,736	$1,302
1985	$2,088	$1,566
1986	$2,453	$1,840
1987	$2,673	$2,005
1988	$2,860	$2,145
1989	$2,974	$2,230
1990	$3,296	$2,472
1991	$3,581	$2,686
1992	$3,943	$2,957
1993	$3,999	$3,000
1994	$4,286	$3,214
1995	$4,398	$3,299

L275DT

YEARS MFRD 1981-1985
ENGINE . . . . KUBOTA
CYLINDERS 3
CID 79.3
PTO HP 23.4
ENGINE HP 27.5
COOLING . . . . LIQUID
FUEL . . . . D
SPEEDS 8/7
TRANSMISSION . . . . GEAR
STEERING . . . . STANDARD
HITCH . . . . CAT. I
HYDRAULIC . . . . YES
PTO . . . . YES
DRIVE TYPE 4WD
ROPS/CAB . . . . ROPS
WEIGHT . . . . 2,365 LBS.
MSRP $8,150

SERIAL NUMBERS

YEAR	BEGINNING NO.
1981	10168
1982	10780
1983	51007
1984	51965

RETAIL PRICING

YEAR	HIGH	LOW
1981	$1,780	$1,335
1982	$1,873	$1,404
1983	$1,972	$1,479
1984	$2,078	$1,558
1985	$2,194	$1,645

L275DTS

YEARS MFRD 1984-1986
SERIES . . . . L SERIES
ENGINE . . . . KUBOTA
CYLINDERS 3
CID 79.3
PTO HP 23.4
ENGINE HP 27.5
COOLING . . . . LIQUID
FUEL . . . . D
SPEEDS 8/7
TRANSMISSION . . . . GEAR
STEERING . . . . STANDARD
HITCH . . . . CAT. I
HYDRAULIC . . . . YES
PTO . . . . YES
DRIVE TYPE 4WD
ROPS/CAB . . . . ROPS
WEIGHT . . . . 2,365 LBS.

L275F

YEARS MFRD 1981-1986
ENGINE . . . . KUBOTA
CYLINDERS 3
CID 79.3
PTO HP 23.4
ENGINE HP 27.5
COOLING . . . . LIQUID
FUEL . . . . D
SPEEDS 8/7
TRANSMISSION . . . . GEAR
STEERING . . . . STANDARD
HITCH . . . . CAT. I
HYDRAULIC . . . . YES
PTO . . . . YES
DRIVE TYPE 2WD
ROPS/CAB . . . . ROPS
WEIGHT . . . . 2,150 LBS.
MSRP $8,150

RETAIL PRICING

YEAR	HIGH	LOW
1982	$1,456	$1,092
1983	$1,578	$1,183
1984	$1,659	$1,244
1985	$1,977	$1,482

L285DT

YEARS MFRD 1975-1981
ENGINE . . . . KUBOTA
CYLINDERS 4
CID 91
PTO HP 26.4
ENGINE HP 30
COOLING . . . . LIQUID
FUEL . . . . D
SPEEDS 8/2
TRANSMISSION . . . . GEAR
STEERING . . . . STANDARD
HITCH . . . . CAT. I
HYDRAULIC . . . . YES
PTO . . . . YES
DRIVE TYPE 4WD
ROPS/CAB . . . . ROPS
WEIGHT . . . . 2,550 LBS.
MSRP $6,675

SERIAL NUMBERS

LEFT SIDE OF CLUTCH HOUSING

YEAR	BEGINNING NO.
1977	10001
1978	10013
1979	11758
1980	13503
1981	15243

RETAIL PRICING

YEAR	HIGH	LOW
1975	$1,430	$1,072
1976	$1,505	$1,129
1977	$1,581	$1,186
1978	$1,670	$1,252
1979	$1,757	$1,318
1980	$1,849	$1,387
1981	$1,943	$1,457

L285F

YEARS MFRD 1975-1982
SERIES . . . . L SERIES
ENGINE . . . . KUBOTA
CYLINDERS 4
CID 91
PTO HP 26.4
ENGINE HP 30
COOLING . . . . LIQUID
FUEL . . . . D
SPEEDS 8/2
TRANSMISSION . . . . GEAR
STEERING . . . . STANDARD
HITCH . . . . CAT. I
HYDRAULIC . . . . YES
PTO . . . . YES
DRIVE TYPE 2WD
ROPS/CAB . . . . ROPS
WEIGHT . . . . 2,230 LBS.
MSRP $6,675

SERIAL NUMBERS

LEFT SIDE OF CLUTCH HOUSING

YEAR	BEGINNING NO.
1975	10001
1976	10151
1977	12701
1978	20301
1979	27901
1980	35401
1981	42001
1982	48101

RETAIL PRICING

YEAR	HIGH	LOW
1977	$985	$739
1978	$1,240	$930
1979	$1,252	$939
1980	$1,273	$955
1981	$1,296	$972
1982	$1,318	$989

L305DT

YEARS MFRD 1980-1985
ENGINE . . . . KUBOTA
CYLINDERS 3
CID 79.3
PTO HP 26.2
ENGINE HP 30
COOLING . . . . LIQUID
FUEL . . . . D
SPEEDS 8/2
TRANSMISSION . . . . GEAR
STEERING . . . . STANDARD
HITCH . . . . CAT. I
HYDRAULIC . . . . YES
PTO . . . . YES
DRIVE TYPE 4WD
ROPS/CAB . . . . ROPS
WEIGHT . . . . 2,985 LBS.
MSRP $8,800

SERIAL NUMBERS

LEFT SIDE OF CLUTCH HOUSING

YEAR	BEGINNING NO.
1980	10001
1981	10565
1982	50001
1983	50602
1984	50645
1985	50735

RETAIL PRICING

YEAR	HIGH	LOW
1980	$1,659	$1,244
1981	$1,745	$1,309
1982	$1,841	$1,380
1983	$1,937	$1,453
1984	$2,037	$1,528
1985	$2,142	$1,607

AVG. AUCTION PRICING

LOW	HIGH	AVG
$2,648	$3,339	$2,955

L305F

YEARS MFRD 1980-1986
ENGINE . . . . KUBOTA
CYLINDERS 3
CID 79.3
PTO HP 26.2

See Kubota Model Suffix Identification on page 415

ENGINE HP . . . 30
COOLING . . . LIQUID
FUEL . . . D
SPEEDS . . . 8/2
TRANSMISSION . . . GEAR
STEERING . . . STANDARD
HITCH . . . CAT. I
HYDRAULIC . . . YES
PTO . . . YES
DRIVE TYPE . . . 2WD
ROPS/CAB . . . ROPS
WEIGHT . . . 2,555 LBS.
MSRP . . . $8,805

SERIAL NUMBERS

LEFT SIDE OF CLUTCH HOUSING

YEAR	BEGINNING NO.
1980	10001
1981	10327
1982	10521
1983	10715
1984	10940
1985	11176
1986	11412

RETAIL PRICING

YEAR	HIGH	LOW
1980	$1,501	$1,126
1981	$1,607	$1,205
1982	$1,702	$1,276
1983	$1,841	$1,380
1984	$1,941	$1,455
1985	$2,134	$1,601
1986	$2,328	$1,746

L345DT

YEARS MFRD . . . 1979-1986
ENGINE . . . KUBOTA
CYLINDERS . . . 4
CID . . . 91
PTO HP . . . 28
COOLING . . . LIQUID
FUEL . . . D
SPEEDS . . . 8/2
TRANSMISSION . . . GEAR
STEERING . . . STANDARD
HITCH . . . CAT. I
HYDRAULIC . . . YES
PTO . . . YES
DRIVE TYPE . . . 4WD
ROPS/CAB . . . ROPS
WEIGHT . . . 3,155 LBS.
MSRP . . . $10,330

SERIAL NUMBERS

LEFT SIDE OF CLUTCH HOUSING

YEAR	BEGINNING NO.
1979	10001
1980	11121
1981	11914
1982	50001
1983	50602
1984	50645
1985	50735
1986	50841

RETAIL PRICING

YEAR	HIGH	LOW
1979	$2,271	$1,703
1980	$2,394	$1,795
1981	$2,516	$1,887
1982	$2,649	$1,987
1983	$2,789	$2,092
1984	$2,959	$2,219
1985	$3,093	$2,320
1986	$3,251	$2,438

L355DTSS

YEARS MFRD . . . 1982-1987
ENGINE . . . KUBOTA
CYLINDERS . . . 4
CID . . . 105.6
PTO HP . . . 29
ENGINE HP . . . 36
COOLING . . . LIQUID
FUEL . . . D
SPEEDS . . . 8/8
TRANSMISSION . . . GEAR
STEERING . . . STANDARD
HITCH . . . CAT. I
HYDRAULIC . . . YES
PTO . . . YES
DRIVE TYPE . . . 4WD
ROPS/CAB . . . ROPS
WEIGHT . . . 2,684 LBS.
MSRP . . . $13,950

SERIAL NUMBERS

YEAR	BEGINNING NO.
1982	50063
1983	51058

RETAIL PRICING

YEAR	HIGH	LOW
1982	$3,397	$2,548
1983	$3,575	$2,681
1984	$3,765	$2,823
1985	$3,961	$2,971
1986	$4,174	$3,130
1987	$4,393	$3,295

L2050DT

YEARS MFRD . . . 1989-1990
SERIES . . . L1 SERIES
ENGINE . . . KUBOTA
CYLINDERS . . . 3
CID . . . 68
PTO HP . . . 20
ENGINE HP . . . 25
COOLING . . . LIQUID
FUEL . . . D
SPEEDS . . . 8/2
TRANSMISSION . . . GEAR
STEERING . . . STANDARD
HITCH . . . CAT. I
HYDRAULIC . . . YES
PTO . . . YES
DRIVE TYPE . . . 4WD
ROPS/CAB . . . ROPS
WEIGHT . . . 2,093 LBS.
MSRP . . . $8,700

OPTIONS

2 HYD
60" DECK
72" DECK
LDR

RETAIL PRICING

YEAR	HIGH	LOW
1989	$3,059	$2,294
1990	$3,459	$2,594

L2050F

YEARS MFRD . . . 1989-1995
SERIES . . . L1 SERIES
ENGINE . . . KUBOTA
CYLINDERS . . . 3
CID . . . 68
PTO HP . . . 20
ENGINE HP . . . 25
COOLING . . . LIQUID
FUEL . . . D
SPEEDS . . . 8/2
TRANSMISSION . . . GEAR
STEERING . . . STANDARD
HITCH . . . CAT. I
HYDRAULIC . . . YES
PTO . . . YES
DRIVE TYPE . . . 2WD
ROPS/CAB . . . ROPS
WEIGHT . . . 1,781 LBS.
MSRP . . . $8,920

RETAIL PRICING

YEAR	HIGH	LOW
1990	$2,608	$1,956
1991	$2,718	$2,039
1992	$2,865	$2,149
1993	$2,975	$2,231
1994	$3,133	$2,350
1995	$3,296	$2,472

L2250DT

YEARS MFRD . . . 1985-1990
SERIES . . . L1 SERIES
ENGINE . . . KUBOTA
CYLINDERS . . . 3
CID . . . 79.3
PTO HP . . . 21.15
ENGINE HP . . . 26.5
COOLING . . . LIQUID
FUEL . . . D
SPEEDS . . . 8/7
TRANSMISSION . . . GEAR
STEERING . . . STANDARD
HITCH . . . CAT. I
HYDRAULIC . . . YES
PTO . . . YES
DRIVE TYPE . . . 4WD
ROPS/CAB . . . ROPS
WEIGHT . . . 2,380 LBS.
MSRP . . . $9,700

OPTIONS

2 HYD
60" DECK
72" DECK
LDR

SERIAL NUMBERS

YEAR	BEGINNING NO.
1985	50348
1986	52176
1987	54592
1988	55815
1989	56680
1990	57375

RETAIL PRICING

YEAR	HIGH	LOW
1985	$2,593	$1,944
1986	$2,869	$2,151
1987	$3,157	$2,368
1988	$3,453	$2,589
1989	$3,752	$2,814
1990	$4,164	$3,123

L2250F

YEARS MFRD . . . 1986-1991
SERIES . . . L1 SERIES
ENGINE . . . KUBOTA
CYLINDERS . . . 3
CID . . . 79.3
PTO HP . . . 21.1
ENGINE HP . . . 26.5
COOLING . . . LIQUID
FUEL . . . D
SPEEDS . . . 8/7
TRANSMISSION . . . GEAR
STEERING . . . STANDARD
HITCH . . . CAT. I
HYDRAULIC . . . YES
PTO . . . YES
DRIVE TYPE . . . 2WD
ROPS/CAB . . . ROPS
WEIGHT . . . 2,170 LBS.
MSRP . . . $9,920

RETAIL PRICING

YEAR	HIGH	LOW
1986	$3,179	$2,384
1987	$3,512	$2,634
1988	$3,699	$2,774
1989	$3,788	$2,841
1990	$4,488	$3,366
1991	$4,586	$3,439

L2250GST

YEARS MFRD . . . 1986-1995
SERIES . . . L1 SERIES
ENGINE . . . KUBOTA
CYLINDERS . . . 3
CID . . . 79.3
PTO HP . . . 23.5
ENGINE HP . . . 26.5
COOLING . . . LIQUID
FUEL . . . D
SPEEDS . . . 8/7
TRANSMISSION . . . GEAR
STEERING . . . STANDARD
HITCH . . . CAT. I
HYDRAULIC . . . YES
PTO . . . YES
DRIVE TYPE . . . 4WD
ROPS/CAB . . . ROPS
WEIGHT . . . 2,380 LBS.
MSRP . . . $12,520

RETAIL PRICING

YEAR	HIGH	LOW
1990	$3,930	$2,948
1991	$4,003	$3,002

L2350DT

YEARS MFRD . . . 1991-1997
SERIES . . . L1 SERIES
ENGINE . . . KUBOTA
CYLINDERS . . . 3
CID . . . 68.0
PTO HP . . . 20.5

ENGINE HP . . . 25
COOLING . . . LIQUID
FUEL . . . D
SPEEDS . . . 8/2
TRANSMISSION . . . GEAR
STEERING . . . STANDARD
HITCH . . . CAT. I
HYDRAULIC . . . YES
PTO . . . YES
DRIVE TYPE . . . 4WD
ROPS/CAB . . . ROPS
WEIGHT . . . 2,093 LBS.
MSRP . . . $11,070

OPTIONS

2 HYD
60"DECK
72"DECK
LDR

SERIAL NUMBERS

YEAR	BEGINNING NO.
1992	51460
1993	52900
1994	55760

RETAIL PRICING

YEAR	HIGH	LOW
1991	$3,378	$2,534
1992	$3,674	$2,756
1993	$3,976	$2,982
1994	$4,300	$3,225
1995	$4,586	$3,439
1996	$4,886	$3,665
1997	$5,277	$3,958

AVG. AUCTION PRICING

LOW	HIGH	AVG
$3,914	$9,579	$7,107

L2350F

YEARS MFRD . . . 1991-1997
SERIES . . . L1 SERIES
ENGINE . . . KUBOTA
CYLINDERS . . . 3
CID . . . 68.0
PTO HP . . . 20.5
ENGINE HP . . . 25
COOLING . . . LIQUID
FUEL . . . D
SPEEDS . . . 8/2
TRANSMISSION . . . GEAR
STEERING . . . STANDARD
HITCH . . . CAT. I
HYDRAULIC . . . YES
PTO . . . YES
DRIVE TYPE . . . 2WD
ROPS/CAB . . . ROPS
WEIGHT . . . 1,781 LBS.
MSRP . . . $11,070

RETAIL PRICING

YEAR	HIGH	LOW
1991	$3,322	$2,491
1992	$3,408	$2,556
1993	$3,514	$2,636
1994	$3,597	$2,698
1995	$3,695	$2,771
1996	$3,790	$2,843
1997	$4,312	$3,234

L2500DT

YEARS MFRD . . . 1998-1999
SERIES . . . L SERIES
ENGINE . . . KUBOTA
CYLINDERS . . . 3
CID . . . 85
PTO HP . . . 22.5
ENGINE HP . . . 27
COOLING . . . LIQUID
FUEL . . . D
SPEEDS . . . 8/2
TRANSMISSION . . . GEAR
STEERING . . . STANDARD
HITCH . . . CAT. I
HYDRAULIC . . . YES
PTO . . . YES
DRIVE TYPE . . . 4WD
ROPS/CAB . . . ROPS
WEIGHT . . . 2,205 LBS.
MSRP . . . $11,392

RETAIL PRICING

YEAR	HIGH	LOW
1998	$3,818	$2,864
1999	$4,414	$3,310

AVG. AUCTION PRICING

LOW	HIGH	AVG
$3,502	$6,695	$5,219

L2500F

YEARS MFRD . . . 1997-2000
SERIES . . . L SERIES
ENGINE . . . KUBOTA
CYLINDERS . . . 3
CID . . . 85
PTO HP . . . 22.5
ENGINE HP . . . 27
COOLING . . . LIQUID
FUEL . . . D
SPEEDS . . . 8/2
TRANSMISSION . . . GEAR
STEERING . . . STANDARD
HITCH . . . CAT. I
HYDRAULIC . . . YES
PTO . . . YES
DRIVE TYPE . . . 2WD
ROPS/CAB . . . ROPS
WEIGHT . . . 2,116 LBS.
MSRP . . . $11,400

RETAIL PRICING

YEAR	HIGH	LOW
1999	$5,662	$4,246
2000	$6,276	$4,707

L2501

YEARS MFRD . . . 2014-2020
ENGINE . . . KUBOTA
CYLINDERS . . . 3
CID . . . 100.47
PTO HP . . . 19
ENGINE HP . . . 24.8
COOLING . . . LIQUID
FUEL . . . D
SPEEDS . . . VARIABLE
TRANSMISSION . . . HYDRO
STEERING . . . STANDARD
DRIVE TYPE . . . 4WD
ROPS/CAB . . . ROPS
MSRP . . . $16,813

OPTIONS

2WD/GEAR . . . $-3,161
BACKHOE . . . $7,816
LDR PKG . . . $4,466

RETAIL PRICING

YEAR	HIGH	LOW
2014	$12,761	$9,570
2015	$13,260	$9,945
2016	$15,031	$11,274
2017	$15,658	$11,743
2018	$16,481	$12,361
2019	$17,097	$12,822
2020	$17,921	$14,095

AVG. AUCTION PRICING

LOW	HIGH	AVG
$12,000	$13,400	$16,200

L2550DT

YEARS MFRD . . . 1985-1990
ENGINE . . . KUBOTA
CYLINDERS . . . 3
CID . . . 85.2
PTO HP . . . 23.5
ENGINE HP . . . 26.5
COOLING . . . LIQUID
FUEL . . . D
SPEEDS . . . 8/7
TRANSMISSION . . . GEAR
STEERING . . . STANDARD
HITCH . . . CAT. I
HYDRAULIC . . . YES
PTO . . . YES
DRIVE TYPE . . . 4WD
ROPS/CAB . . . ROPS
WEIGHT . . . 2,485 LBS.
MSRP . . . $11,800

OPTIONS

2 HYD
60"DECK
72"DECK
LDR

SERIAL NUMBERS

YEAR	BEGINNING NO.
1985	50006
1986	52410
1987	55111
1988	56242
1989	57159

RETAIL PRICING

YEAR	HIGH	LOW
1985	$2,804	$2,103
1986	$3,066	$2,300
1987	$3,328	$2,496
1988	$3,601	$2,701
1989	$3,887	$2,915
1990	$4,176	$3,132

AVG. AUCTION PRICING

LOW	HIGH	AVG
$1,727	$5,181	$3,845

L2550F

YEARS MFRD . . . 1972-1995
SERIES . . . L SERIES
ENGINE . . . KUBOTA
CYLINDERS . . . 3
CID . . . 85.2
PTO HP . . . 23.5
ENGINE HP . . . 29.5
COOLING . . . LIQUID
FUEL . . . D
SPEEDS . . . 8/7
TRANSMISSION . . . GEAR
STEERING . . . STANDARD
HITCH . . . CAT. I
HYDRAULIC . . . YES
PTO . . . YES
DRIVE TYPE . . . 2WD
ROPS/CAB . . . ROPS
WEIGHT . . . 2,305 LBS.
MSRP . . . $12,300

RETAIL PRICING

YEAR	HIGH	LOW
1990	$3,707	$2,780
1991	$3,872	$2,904
1992	$4,047	$3,035
1993	$4,102	$3,077
1994	$4,429	$3,322
1995	$4,547	$3,411

L2550GST

YEARS MFRD . . . 1985-1991
ENGINE . . . KUBOTA
CYLINDERS . . . 3
CID . . . 85.2
PTO HP . . . 23.5
ENGINE HP . . . 29.5
COOLING . . . LIQUID
FUEL . . . D
SPEEDS . . GLIDE W/ SHUTTLE SHIFT
TRANSMISSION . . . GEAR
STEERING . . . STANDARD
HITCH . . . CAT. I
HYDRAULIC . . . YES
PTO . . . YES
DRIVE TYPE . . . 4WD
ROPS/CAB . . . ROPS
WEIGHT . . . 2,490 LBS.
MSRP . . . $15,000

SERIAL NUMBERS

YEAR	BEGINNING NO.
1988	80011
1989	81885

RETAIL PRICING

YEAR	HIGH	LOW
1990	$4,711	$3,533
1991	$4,798	$3,598

L2600DT

YEARS MFRD . . . 2000-2003
SERIES . . . L SERIES
ENGINE . . . KUBOTA
CYLINDERS . . . 3
CID . . . 85
PTO HP . . . 22.5
ENGINE HP . . . 27
COOLING . . . LIQUID
FUEL . . . D
SPEEDS . . . 8/2
TRANSMISSION . . . GEAR
STEERING . . . STANDARD
HITCH . . . CAT. I

HYDRAULIC . . . YES
PTO . . . YES
DRIVE TYPE . . . 4WD
ROPS/CAB . . . ROPS
WEIGHT . . . 2,359 LBS.
MSRP . . . $13,110

OPTIONS

2HYD
LDR

RETAIL PRICING

YEAR	HIGH	LOW
2000	$5,804	$4,353
2001	$6,364	$4,773
2002	$6,947	$5,211
2003	$7,560	$5,670

AVG. AUCTION PRICING

LOW	HIGH	AVG
$5,572	$11,145	$8,581

L2600F

YEARS MFRD . . . 2001-2003
SERIES . . . L SERIES
ENGINE . . . KUBOTA
CYLINDERS . . . 3
CID . . . 85
PTO HP . . . 22.5
ENGINE HP . . . 27
COOLING . . . LIQUID
FUEL . . . D
SPEEDS . . . 8/2
TRANSMISSION . . . GEAR
STEERING . . . STANDARD
HITCH . . . CAT. I
HYDRAULIC . . . YES
PTO . . . YES
DRIVE TYPE . . . 2WD
ROPS/CAB . . . ROPS
WEIGHT . . . 1,975 LBS.
MSRP . . . $11,070

OPTIONS

2HYD
LDR

RETAIL PRICING

YEAR	HIGH	LOW
2001	$6,650	$4,987
2002	$6,879	$5,160
2003	$7,106	$5,329

L2601DT

ENGINE . . . D1801
CYLINDERS . . . 3
ENGINE HP . . . 26
COOLING . . . LIQUID
FUEL . . . D
TRANSMISSION . . . DISC
STEERING . . . STANDARD

L2650DT

YEARS MFRD . . . 1990-1996
SERIES . . . L1 SERIES
ENGINE . . . KUBOTA
CYLINDERS . . . 3
CID . . . 85
PTO HP . . . 23.5
ENGINE HP . . . 28.5
COOLING . . . LIQUID
FUEL . . . D
SPEEDS . . . 8/16
TRANSMISSION . . . GEAR
STEERING . . . STANDARD
HITCH . . . CAT. I
HYDRAULIC . . . YES
PTO . . . YES
DRIVE TYPE . . . 4WD
ROPS/CAB . . . ROPS
WEIGHT . . . 2,385 LBS.
MSRP . . . $14,135

SERIAL NUMBERS

YEAR	BEGINNING NO.
1991	50149
1992	50975

RETAIL PRICING

YEAR	HIGH	LOW
1990	$3,117	$2,338
1991	$3,454	$2,590
1992	$3,804	$2,853
1993	$4,167	$3,126
1994	$4,545	$3,409
1995	$4,931	$3,698
1996	$5,340	$4,005

L2650DT W

YEARS MFRD . . . 1990-1996
SERIES . . . L1 SERIES
ENGINE . . . KUBOTA
CYLINDERS . . . 3
CID . . . 85.1
PTO HP . . . 23.5
ENGINE HP . . . 28.5
COOLING . . . LIQUID
FUEL . . . D
SPEEDS . . . 8/7
TRANSMISSION . . . GEAR
STEERING . . . STANDARD
HITCH . . . CAT. I
HYDRAULIC . . . YES
PTO . . . YES
DRIVE TYPE . . . 4WD
ROPS/CAB . . . ROPS
WEIGHT . . . 2,480 LBS.
MSRP . . . $15,240

RETAIL PRICING

YEAR	HIGH	LOW
1990	$4,208	$3,156
1991	$4,286	$3,214
1992	$4,606	$3,455
1993	$5,092	$3,819
1994	$5,486	$4,114
1995	$5,632	$4,224
1996	$5,784	$4,338

L2650F

YEARS MFRD . . . 1991-1996
SERIES . . . L1 SERIES
ENGINE . . . KUBOTA
CYLINDERS . . . 3
CID . . . 85
PTO HP . . . 23.5
ENGINE HP . . . 28.5
COOLING . . . LIQUID
FUEL . . . D
SPEEDS . . . 8/16
TRANSMISSION . . . GEAR
STEERING . . . STANDARD
HITCH . . . CAT. I
HYDRAULIC . . . YES
PTO . . . YES
DRIVE TYPE . . . 2WD
ROPS/CAB . . . ROPS
WEIGHT . . . 2,650 LBS.
MSRP . . . $12,300

SERIAL NUMBERS

YEAR	BEGINNING NO.
1991	10001

RETAIL PRICING

YEAR	HIGH	LOW
1991	$3,934	$2,950
1992	$4,146	$3,109
1993	$4,203	$3,153

L2650GST

YEARS MFRD . . . 1991-1996
SERIES . . . L1 SERIES
ENGINE . . . KUBOTA
CYLINDERS . . . 3
CID . . . 85
PTO HP . . . 23.5
ENGINE HP . . . 28.5
COOLING . . . LIQUID
FUEL . . . D
SPEEDS . . . 8/16 SHUTTLE
TRANSMISSION . . . GEAR
STEERING . . . STANDARD
HITCH . . . CAT. I
HYDRAULIC . . . YES
PTO . . . YES
DRIVE TYPE . . . 4WD
ROPS/CAB . . . ROPS
WEIGHT . . . 2,655 LBS.
MSRP . . . $16,055

RETAIL PRICING

YEAR	HIGH	LOW
1991	$5,134	$3,850
1992	$5,413	$4,059
1993	$5,486	$4,114

L2800

YEARS MFRD . . . 2004-2011
SERIES . . . L SERIES
ENGINE . . . KUBOTA
CYLINDERS . . . 3
CID . . . 85
PTO HP . . . 22.5
ENGINE HP . . . 29
COOLING . . . LIQUID
FUEL . . . D
SPEEDS . . . 8/4
TRANSMISSION . . . GEAR
STEERING . . . STANDARD
HITCH . . . CAT. I
DRIVE TYPE . . . 2WD
ROPS/CAB . . . ROPS
WEIGHT . . . 2,600 LBS.
MSRP . . . $12,213

OPTIONS

2 HYD
4WD
HYDRO
LDR

RETAIL PRICING

YEAR	HIGH	LOW
2004	$6,013	$4,510
2005	$6,517	$4,888
2006	$7,153	$5,365
2007	$7,751	$5,813
2008	$8,371	$6,278
2009	$9,107	$6,830
2010	$9,734	$7,300
2011	$10,519	$7,890

AVG. AUCTION PRICING

LOW	HIGH	AVG
$3,200	$11,000	$8,240

L2850DT

YEARS MFRD . . . 1985-1990
SERIES . . . L1 SERIES
ENGINE . . . KUBOTA
CYLINDERS . . . 4
CID . . . 105.7
PTO HP . . . 27.51
ENGINE HP . . . 34
COOLING . . . LIQUID
FUEL . . . D
SPEEDS . . . 8/7
TRANSMISSION . . . GEAR
STEERING . . . STANDARD
HITCH . . . CAT. I
HYDRAULIC . . . YES
PTO . . . YES
DRIVE TYPE . . . 4WD
ROPS/CAB . . . ROPS
WEIGHT . . . 2,680 LBS.
MSRP . . . $13,500

OPTIONS

2 HYD
LDR

SERIAL NUMBERS

YEAR	BEGINNING NO.
1985	50005
1986	51786
1987	53807
1988	55931
1989	57212
1990	58326

RETAIL PRICING

YEAR	HIGH	LOW
1985	$460	$345
1986	$767	$576
1987	$1,093	$820
1988	$1,426	$1,069
1989	$1,770	$1,327
1990	$2,119	$1,589

L2850F

YEARS MFRD . . . 1985-1990
SERIES . . . L1 SERIES
ENGINE . . . KUBOTA
CYLINDERS . . . 4
CID . . . 105.7

PTO HP 27.5
ENGINE HP 34
COOLING . . . . . LIQUID
FUEL . . . . . D
SPEEDS 8/7
TRANSMISSION . . . . . GEAR
HITCH . . . . . CAT. I
HYDRAULIC . . . . . YES
PTO . . . . . YES
DRIVE TYPE 2WD
ROPS/CAB . . . . . ROPS
WEIGHT . . . . . 2,480 LBS.
MSRP $10,250

RETAIL PRICING

YEAR	HIGH	LOW
1986	$2,446	$1,835
1987	$2,740	$2,055
1988	$2,937	$2,202
1989	$3,051	$2,288

L2850GST

YEARS MFRD 1989-1995
SERIES . . . . . L1 SERIES
ENGINE . . . . . KUBOTA
CYLINDERS 4
CID 105.7
PTO HP 27.5
ENGINE HP 34
COOLING . . . . . LIQUID
FUEL . . . . . D
SPEEDS . . . . . CLUTCHLESS
TRANSMISSION . . . . . GEAR
STEERING . . . . . STANDARD
HITCH . . . . . CAT. I
HYDRAULIC . . . . . YES
PTO . . . . . YES
DRIVE TYPE 4WD
ROPS/CAB . . . . . ROPS
WEIGHT . . . . . 2,800 LBS.
MSRP $16,900

SERIAL NUMBERS

YEAR	BEGINNING NO.
1988	80001
1989	80100

RETAIL PRICING

YEAR	HIGH	LOW
1990	$5,308	$3,981
1991	$5,402	$4,052

L2900DT

YEARS MFRD 1994-1999
SERIES . . . . . GRAND L SERIES
ENGINE . . . . . KUBOTA
CYLINDERS 3
CID 91.5
PTO HP 25
ENGINE HP 32.1
COOLING . . . . . LIQUID
FUEL . . . . . D
SPEEDS 8/8
TRANSMISSION . . . SHUTTLE SHIFT
STEERING . . . . . STANDARD
HITCH . . . . . CAT. I
HYDRAULIC . . . . . YES
PTO . . . . . YES
DRIVE TYPE 4WD
ROPS/CAB . . . . . ROPS
WEIGHT . . . . . 2,800 LBS.
MSRP $15,080

OPTIONS

2 HYD
LDR

SERIAL NUMBERS

YEAR	BEGINNING NO.
1994	50005

RETAIL PRICING

YEAR	HIGH	LOW
1994	$4,658	$3,493
1995	$5,165	$3,874
1996	$5,652	$4,239
1997	$6,131	$4,598
1998	$6,646	$4,984
1999	$7,271	$5,453

AVG. AUCTION PRICING

LOW	HIGH	AVG
$4,720	$8,116	$6,827

L2900F

YEARS MFRD 1994-1998
SERIES . . . . . GRAND L SERIES
ENGINE . . . . . KUBOTA
CYLINDERS 3
CID 91.5
PTO HP 25
ENGINE HP 32.1
COOLING . . . . . LIQUID
FUEL . . . . . D
SPEEDS . . . . . 8/8 FST
TRANSMISSION . . . . . GEAR
STEERING . . . . . STANDARD
HITCH . . . . . CAT. I
HYDRAULIC . . . . . YES
PTO . . . . . YES
DRIVE TYPE 2WD
ROPS/CAB . . . . . ROPS
WEIGHT . . . . . 2,645 LBS.
MSRP $15,080

OPTIONS

CAB

RETAIL PRICING

YEAR	HIGH	LOW
1994	$5,114	$3,835
1995	$5,247	$3,935
1996	$5,391	$4,043
1997	$5,872	$4,404
1998	$6,697	$5,023

L2900GST

YEARS MFRD 1994-1998
SERIES . . . . . GRAND L SERIES
ENGINE . . . . . KUBOTA
CYLINDERS 3
CID 91.5
PTO HP 25
ENGINE HP 32.1
COOLING . . . . . LIQUID
FUEL . . . . . D
SPEEDS 8/8
TRANSMISSION . . . . . GEAR
STEERING . . . . . STANDARD
HITCH . . . . . CAT. I
HYDRAULIC . . . . . YES
PTO . . . . . YES
DRIVE TYPE 4WD
ROPS/CAB . . . . . ROPS
WEIGHT . . . . . 2,610 LBS.
MSRP $17,580

SERIAL NUMBERS

YEAR	BEGINNING NO.
1994	50002
1995	54654
1996	56282
1997	58445

RETAIL PRICING

YEAR	HIGH	LOW
1994	$5,961	$4,470
1995	$6,117	$4,588
1996	$6,281	$4,711
1997	$6,847	$5,136
1998	$7,809	$5,857

L2950DT

YEARS MFRD 1990-1993
SERIES . . . . . L1 SERIES
ENGINE . . . . . KUBOTA
CYLINDERS 3
CID 89.2
PTO HP 26
ENGINE HP 31.7
COOLING . . . . . LIQUID
FUEL . . . . . D
SPEEDS 8/8
TRANSMISSION . . . SHUTTLE SHIFT
STEERING . . . . . STANDARD
HITCH . . . . . CAT. I
HYDRAULIC . . . . . YES
PTO . . . . . YES
DRIVE TYPE 4WD
ROPS/CAB . . . . . ROPS
WEIGHT . . . . . 2,905 LBS.
MSRP $13,000

OPTIONS

2 HYD
LDR

SERIAL NUMBERS

YEAR	BEGINNING NO.
1990	50001
1991	50207
1992	50754
1993	51630

RETAIL PRICING

YEAR	HIGH	LOW
1990	$3,526	$2,644
1991	$3,736	$2,802
1992	$4,054	$3,041
1993	$4,392	$3,294

L2950DT W

YEARS MFRD 1990-1995
SERIES . . . . . L1 SERIES
ENGINE . . . . . KUBOTA
CYLINDERS 3
CID 89.2
PTO HP 26
ENGINE HP 31.7
COOLING . . . . . LIQUID
FUEL . . . . . D
SPEEDS 8/8
TRANSMISSION . . . . . GEAR
STEERING . . . . . STANDARD
HITCH . . . . . CAT. I
HYDRAULIC . . . . . YES
PTO . . . . . YES
DRIVE TYPE 4WD
ROPS/CAB . . . . . CAB
WEIGHT . . . . . 2,735 LBS.
MSRP $15,820

SERIAL NUMBERS

YEAR	BEGINNING NO.
1990	50001
1991	50207

RETAIL PRICING

YEAR	HIGH	LOW
1990	$4,687	$3,515
1991	$4,868	$3,651
1992	$5,233	$3,925
1993	$5,409	$4,056

L2950F

YEARS MFRD 1990-1995
SERIES . . . . . L1 SERIES
ENGINE . . . . . KUBOTA
CYLINDERS 4
CID 89.2
PTO HP 26
ENGINE HP 31.7
COOLING . . . . . LIQUID
FUEL . . . . . D
SPEEDS 8/16
TRANSMISSION . . . . . GEAR
STEERING . . . . . STANDARD
HITCH . . . . . CAT. I
HYDRAULIC . . . . . YES
PTO . . . . . YES
DRIVE TYPE 2WD
ROPS/CAB . . . . . ROPS
WEIGHT . . . . . 2,725 LBS.
MSRP $13,000

RETAIL PRICING

YEAR	HIGH	LOW
1991	$4,155	$3,116
1992	$4,382	$3,286
1993	$4,543	$3,407

L2950GST

YEARS MFRD 1990-1995
SERIES . . . . . L1 SERIES
ENGINE . . . . . KUBOTA
CYLINDERS 4
CID 89.2
PTO HP 26
ENGINE HP 31.7
COOLING . . . . . LIQUID
FUEL . . . . . D
SPEEDS 8/16
TRANSMISSION . . . . . GEAR
STEERING . . . . . STANDARD
HITCH . . . . . CAT. I
HYDRAULIC . . . . . YES
PTO . . . . . YES
DRIVE TYPE 4WD
ROPS/CAB . . . . . ROPS
WEIGHT . . . . . 2,720 LBS.
MSRP $16,955

KUBOTA See Kubota Model Suffix Identification on page 415

SERIAL NUMBERS

YEAR	BEGINNING NO.
1990	80000
1991	80006

RETAIL PRICING

YEAR	HIGH	LOW
1991	$5,422	$4,066
1992	$5,717	$4,287
1993	$5,796	$4,347

L3000DT

YEARS MFRD . . . 2000-2003
SERIES . . . L SERIES
ENGINE . . . KUBOTA
CYLINDERS . . . 3
CID . . . 91.5
PTO HP . . . 27.5
ENGINE HP . . . 32.1
COOLING . . . LIQUID
FUEL . . . D
SPEEDS . . . 8/2
TRANSMISSION . . . GEAR
STEERING . . . STANDARD
HITCH . . . CAT. I
HYDRAULIC . . . YES
PTO . . . YES
DRIVE TYPE . . . 4WD
ROPS/CAB . . . ROPS
WEIGHT . . . 2,425 LBS.
MSRP . . . $14,130

OPTIONS

2WD
LDR

RETAIL PRICING

YEAR	HIGH	LOW
2000	$6,487	$4,865
2001	$7,082	$5,312
2002	$7,702	$5,777
2003	$8,317	$6,238

L3000F

YEARS MFRD . . . 2000-2003
SERIES . . . L SERIES
ENGINE . . . KUBOTA
CYLINDERS . . . 3
CID . . . 91.5
PTO HP . . . 27.5
ENGINE HP . . . 32.1
COOLING . . . LIQUID
FUEL . . . D
SPEEDS . . . 8/2
TRANSMISSION . . . GEAR
STEERING . . . STANDARD
HITCH . . . CAT. I
HYDRAULIC . . . YES
PTO . . . YES
DRIVE TYPE . . . 2WD
ROPS/CAB . . . ROPS
WEIGHT . . . 2,183 LBS.
MSRP . . . $12,600

RETAIL PRICING

YEAR	HIGH	LOW
2000	$6,937	$5,203
2001	$7,613	$5,710
2002	$8,290	$6,218
2003	$9,105	$6,829

L3010DT

YEARS MFRD . . . 1999-2002
SERIES . . . GRAND L TEN SERIES
ENGINE . . . KUBOTA
CYLINDERS . . . 3
CID . . . 91.5
PTO HP . . . 25.5
ENGINE HP . . . 32.1
COOLING . . . LIQUID
FUEL . . . D
SPEEDS . . . 8/8
TRANSMISSION . . . SHUTTLE SHIFT
STEERING . . . STANDARD
HITCH . . . CAT. I
HYDRAULIC . . . YES
PTO . . . YES
DRIVE TYPE . . . 4WD
ROPS/CAB . . . ROPS
WEIGHT . . . 2,710 LBS.
MSRP . . . $14,444

OPTIONS

2 HYD
HYDRO
LDR

RETAIL PRICING

YEAR	HIGH	LOW
1999	$7,577	$5,683
2000	$8,159	$6,119
2001	$8,717	$6,538
2002	$9,252	$6,939

AVG. AUCTION PRICING

LOW	HIGH	AVG
$4,490	$11,801	$8,683

L3010F

YEARS MFRD . . . 1999-2002
SERIES . . . GRAND L TEN SERIES
ENGINE . . . KUBOTA
CYLINDERS . . . 3
CID . . . 91.5
PTO HP . . . 25.5
ENGINE HP . . . 32
COOLING . . . LIQUID
FUEL . . . D
SPEEDS . . . 8/8
TRANSMISSION . . . GEAR
STEERING . . . STANDARD
HITCH . . . CAT. I
HYDRAULIC . . . YES
PTO . . . YES
DRIVE TYPE . . . 2WD
ROPS/CAB . . . ROPS
WEIGHT . . . 2,560 LBS.
MSRP . . . $14,144

RETAIL PRICING

YEAR	HIGH	LOW
1999	$6,955	$5,216
2000	$7,709	$5,781
2001	$8,485	$6,364
2002	$9,306	$6,980

L3010GST

YEARS MFRD . . . 1999-2002
SERIES . . . GRAND L TEN SERIES
ENGINE . . . KUBOTA
CYLINDERS . . . 3
CID . . . 91.5
PTO HP . . . 25.5
ENGINE HP . . . 32.1
COOLING . . . LIQUID
FUEL . . . D
SPEEDS . . . 8/8
TRANSMISSION . . . GEAR
STEERING . . . STANDARD
HITCH . . . CAT. I
HYDRAULIC . . . YES
PTO . . . YES
DRIVE TYPE . . . 4WD
ROPS/CAB . . . ROPS
WEIGHT . . . 2,720 LBS.
MSRP . . . $16,816

RETAIL PRICING

YEAR	HIGH	LOW
1999	$8,272	$6,204
2000	$9,167	$6,875
2001	$10,099	$7,574
2002	$11,063	$8,297

L3010HST

YEARS MFRD . . . 1999-2002
SERIES . . . GRAND L TEN SERIES
ENGINE . . . KUBOTA
CYLINDERS . . . 3
CID . . . 91.5
PTO HP . . . 24
ENGINE HP . . . 32.1
COOLING . . . LIQUID
FUEL . . . D
SPEEDS . . . VARIABLE
TRANSMISSION . . . HYDRO
STEERING . . . STANDARD
HITCH . . . CAT. I
HYDRAULIC . . . YES
PTO . . . YES
DRIVE TYPE . . . 4WD
ROPS/CAB . . . ROPS
WEIGHT . . . 2,745 LBS.
MSRP . . . $17,316

RETAIL PRICING

YEAR	HIGH	LOW
1999	$8,520	$6,390
2000	$9,443	$7,082
2001	$10,401	$7,801
2002	$11,393	$8,545

L3130DT

YEARS MFRD . . . 2003-2006
SERIES . . . GRAND L30 SERIES
ENGINE . . . KUBOTA E TVCS
CYLINDERS . . . 3
CID . . . 91.5
PTO HP . . . 25.5
ENGINE HP . . . 32.1
COOLING . . . LIQUID
FUEL . . . D
SPEEDS . . . 8/8
TRANSMISSION . . . SHUTTLE SHIFT
STEERING . . . STANDARD
HITCH . . . CAT. I
HYDRAULIC . . . YES
PTO . . . YES
DRIVE TYPE . . . 4WD
ROPS/CAB . . . ROPS
WEIGHT . . . 3,220 LBS.
MSRP . . . $15,920

OPTIONS

2 HYD
HYDRO
LDR

RETAIL PRICING

YEAR	HIGH	LOW
2003	$9,460	$7,095
2004	$10,090	$7,567
2005	$10,654	$7,991
2006	$11,369	$8,527

AVG. AUCTION PRICING

LOW	HIGH	AVG
$5,469	$16,118	$10,554

L3130F

YEARS MFRD . . . 2003-2008
SERIES . . . GRAND L30 SERIES
ENGINE . . . KUBOTA
CYLINDERS . . . 3
CID . . . 91.5
PTO HP . . . 25.5
ENGINE HP . . . 32.1
COOLING . . . LIQUID
FUEL . . . D
SPEEDS . . . 12/8
TRANSMISSION . . . GEAR
STEERING . . . STANDARD
HITCH . . . CAT. I
HYDRAULIC . . . YES
PTO . . . YES
DRIVE TYPE . . . 2WD
ROPS/CAB . . . ROPS
WEIGHT . . . 3,120 LBS.
MSRP . . . $12,900

RETAIL PRICING

YEAR	HIGH	LOW
2004	$10,156	$7,617
2005	$10,691	$8,019
2008	$12,222	$9,166

L3130GST

YEARS MFRD . . . 2003-2008
SERIES . . . GRAND L30 SERIES
ENGINE . . . KUBOTA
CYLINDERS . . . 3
CID . . . 91.5
PTO HP . . . 25.5
ENGINE HP . . . 32.1
COOLING . . . LIQUID
FUEL . . . D
SPEEDS . . . 12/8
TRANSMISSION . . . SHUTTLE SHIFT
STEERING . . . STANDARD
HITCH . . . CAT. I
HYDRAULIC . . . YES
PTO . . . YES
DRIVE TYPE . . . 4WD
ROPS/CAB . . . ROPS
WEIGHT . . . 3,260 LBS.
MSRP . . . $15,870

RETAIL PRICING

YEAR	HIGH	LOW
2003	$9,486	$7,115
2004	$9,801	$7,351
2005	$10,115	$7,586
2006	$10,575	$7,931
2007	$11,044	$8,283
2008	$11,662	$8,746

L3130HST

YEARS MFRD 2003-2008
SERIES .... GRAND L30 SERIES
ENGINE .... KUBOTA
CYLINDERS 3
CID 91.5
PTO HP 24
ENGINE HP 32.1
COOLING .... LIQUID
FUEL .... D
SPEEDS .... VARIABLE
TRANSMISSION .... HYDRO
STEERING .... STANDARD
HITCH .... CAT. I
HYDRAULIC .... YES
PTO .... YES
DRIVE TYPE 4WD
ROPS/CAB .... ROPS
WEIGHT .... 3,305 LBS.
MSRP $16,370

RETAIL PRICING

YEAR	HIGH	LOW
2003	$9,789	$7,342
2004	$10,104	$7,578
2005	$10,428	$7,821
2006	$10,907	$8,180
2007	$11,388	$8,541
2008	$12,033	$9,025

AVG. AUCTION PRICING

LOW	HIGH	AVG
$8,549	$12,360	$10,165

L3200DT

YEARS MFRD 2011-2014
ENGINE .... KUBOTA
CYLINDERS 3
CID 91
PTO HP 26.7
FUEL .... D
SPEEDS .... VARIABLE
TRANSMISSION .... HYDRO
STEERING .... STANDARD
DRIVE TYPE 4WD
ROPS/CAB .... ROPS
WEIGHT .... 2,601 LBS.
MSRP $15,994

OPTIONS

LDR

RETAIL PRICING

YEAR	HIGH	LOW
2011	$13,586	$10,189
2012	$15,082	$11,312
2013	$16,003	$12,002
2014	$16,181	$12,136

AVG. AUCTION PRICING

LOW	HIGH	AVG
$6,000	$12,800	$8,267

L3200F

YEARS MFRD 2011-2014
ENGINE .... KUBOTA
CYLINDERS 3
CID 91
PTO HP 26.7
FUEL .... D
SPEEDS 8/4
TRANSMISSION .... GEAR
STEERING .... STANDARD
DRIVE TYPE 2WD
ROPS/CAB .... ROPS
WEIGHT .... 2,425 LBS.
MSRP $13,795

OPTIONS

LDR

RETAIL PRICING

YEAR	HIGH	LOW
2011	$11,667	$8,750
2012	$12,854	$9,641
2013	$13,809	$10,357
2014	$13,944	$10,458

L3200HST

YEARS MFRD 2011-2014
ENGINE .... KUBOTA
CYLINDERS 3
CID 91
PTO HP 25.2
FUEL .... D
SPEEDS .... VARIABLE
TRANSMISSION .... HYDRO
STEERING .... STANDARD
DRIVE TYPE 4WD
ROPS/CAB .... ROPS
WEIGHT .... 2,623 LBS.
MSRP $17,290

OPTIONS

LDR

RETAIL PRICING

YEAR	HIGH	LOW
2011	$13,970	$10,477
2012	$15,616	$11,712
2013	$16,628	$12,471
2014	$18,118	$13,588

AVG. AUCTION PRICING

LOW	HIGH	AVG
$5,562	$22,660	$13,678

L3240

YEARS MFRD 2007-2012
ENGINE .... KUBOTA
CYLINDERS 3
CID 100.5
PTO HP 26.5
ENGINE HP 34
FUEL .... D
SPEEDS 8/8
TRANSMISSION ... SHUTTLE SHIFT
STEERING .... STANDARD
HITCH .... CAT. I
HYDRAULIC .... YES
PTO .... YES
DRIVE TYPE 4WD
ROPS/CAB .... ROPS
WEIGHT .... 3,395 LBS.
MSRP $19,948

OPTIONS

2 HYD
4WD
CAB
HYDRO
LDR

RETAIL PRICING

YEAR	HIGH	LOW
2007	$12,515	$9,386
2008	$13,262	$9,947
2009	$14,033	$10,525
2010	$14,910	$11,183
2011	$16,263	$12,197
2012	$17,266	$12,949

AVG. AUCTION PRICING

LOW	HIGH	AVG
$8,636	$21,875	$13,432

L3250DT

YEARS MFRD 1989-1990
SERIES .... L1 SERIES
ENGINE .... KUBOTA
CYLINDERS 4
CID 113.6
PTO HP 32.6
ENGINE HP 40
COOLING .... LIQUID
FUEL .... D
SPEEDS 8/7
TRANSMISSION .... GEAR
STEERING .... STANDARD
HITCH .... CAT. I
HYDRAULIC .... YES
PTO .... YES
DRIVE TYPE 4WD
ROPS/CAB .... ROPS
WEIGHT .... 2,740 LBS.
MSRP $14,100

OPTIONS

2 HYD
LDR

RETAIL PRICING

YEAR	HIGH	LOW
1989	$1,873	$1,404
1990	$2,227	$1,670

L3250F

YEARS MFRD 1989-1995
SERIES .... L1 SERIES
ENGINE .... KUBOTA
CYLINDERS 4
CID 113.6
PTO HP 32.6
ENGINE HP 40
COOLING .... LIQUID
FUEL .... D
SPEEDS 8/7
TRANSMISSION .... GEAR
STEERING .... STANDARD
HITCH .... CAT. I
HYDRAULIC .... YES
PTO .... YES
DRIVE TYPE 2WD
ROPS/CAB .... ROPS
WEIGHT .... 2,530 LBS.
MSRP $14,590

RETAIL PRICING

YEAR	HIGH	LOW
1989	$4,346	$3,259
1990	$4,581	$3,436
1991	$4,665	$3,499
1992	$4,921	$3,691
1993	$4,986	$3,740
1994	$5,255	$3,941
1995	$5,393	$4,045

L3300DT

YEARS MFRD 1994-1999
SERIES .... GRAND L SERIES
ENGINE .... KUBOTA
CYLINDERS 3
CID 100.5
PTO HP 28
ENGINE HP 32.1
COOLING .... LIQUID
FUEL .... D
SPEEDS 8/8FST, 8/8GST
TRANSMISSION .... GEAR
STEERING .... STANDARD
HITCH .... CAT. I
HYDRAULIC .... YES
PTO .... YES
DRIVE TYPE 4WD
ROPS/CAB .... ROPS
WEIGHT .... 2,690 LBS.
MSRP $15,880

OPTIONS

2 HYD
LDR

SERIAL NUMBERS

YEAR	BEGINNING NO.
1994	50006
1995	51708
1997	53952

RETAIL PRICING

YEAR	HIGH	LOW
1994	$3,814	$2,861
1995	$4,214	$3,160
1996	$4,620	$3,465
1997	$5,037	$3,778
1998	$5,468	$4,101
1999	$5,903	$4,427

L3300F

YEARS MFRD 1994-1998
SERIES .... GRAND L SERIES
ENGINE .... KUBOTA
CYLINDERS 3
CID 100.5
PTO HP 28
ENGINE HP 35.1
COOLING .... LIQUID
FUEL .... D
SPEEDS 8/8
TRANSMISSION .... GEAR
STEERING .... STANDARD
HITCH .... CAT. I
PTO .... YES
DRIVE TYPE 2WD
ROPS/CAB .... ROPS
WEIGHT .... 2,645 LBS.
MSRP $15,880

SERIAL NUMBERS

YEAR	BEGINNING NO.
1994	10098
1997	10505

RETAIL PRICING

YEAR	HIGH	LOW
1994	$5,402	$4,052
1995	$5,544	$4,158
1996	$5,691	$4,268
1997	$6,184	$4,638
1998	$7,053	$5,290

L3300GST

YEARS MFRD	1994-1998
SERIES	GRAND L SERIES
ENGINE	KUBOTA
CYLINDERS	3
CID	100.5
PTO HP	28
ENGINE HP	32.1
COOLING	LIQUID
FUEL	D
SPEEDS	8/8
TRANSMISSION	GEAR
STEERING	STANDARD
HITCH	CAT. I
HYDRAULIC	YES
PTO	YES
DRIVE TYPE	4WD
ROPS/CAB	ROPS
WEIGHT	2,690 LBS.
MSRP	$19,130

SERIAL NUMBERS

YEAR	BEGINNING NO.
1994	50016
1995	51756

RETAIL PRICING

YEAR	HIGH	LOW
1994	$6,505	$4,879
1995	$6,675	$5,007
1996	$6,852	$5,139
1997	$7,450	$5,587
1998	$8,496	$6,372

L3301

YEARS MFRD	2014-2020
ENGINE	KUBOTA
CYLINDERS	3
CID	111.4
PTO HP	26.2
ENGINE HP	31.4
COOLING	LIQUID
FUEL	D
SPEEDS	VARIABLE
TRANSMISSION	HYDRO
STEERING	STANDARD
DRIVE TYPE	4WD
ROPS/CAB	ROPS
WEIGHT	2,410 LBS.
MSRP	$20,177

OPTIONS

2WD/GEAR	$-2,705
BACKHOE	$7,816
LDR PKG	$4,466

RETAIL PRICING

YEAR	HIGH	LOW
2014	$16,088	$12,066
2015	$17,206	$12,905
2016	$18,345	$13,759
2017	$19,135	$14,351
2018	$19,870	$14,903
2019	$20,358	$15,269
2020	$20,896	$15,985

AVG. AUCTION PRICING

LOW	HIGH	AVG
$8,500	$15,500	$11,833

L3350DT

YEARS MFRD	1985-1990
SERIES	L3 SERIES
ENGINE	KUBOTA
CYLINDERS	4
CID	113.6
PTO HP	32.86
ENGINE HP	40
COOLING	LIQUID
FUEL	D
SPEEDS	8/8
TRANSMISSION	GEAR
STEERING	STANDARD
HITCH	CAT. I
HYDRAULIC	YES
PTO	YES
DRIVE TYPE	4WD
ROPS/CAB	ROPS
WEIGHT	3,770 LBS.
MSRP	$18,500

OPTIONS

2 HYD
LDR

SERIAL NUMBERS

YEAR	BEGINNING NO.
1985	50323
1986	50475
1987	50950
1988	60092
1989	60417
1990	60099

RETAIL PRICING

YEAR	HIGH	LOW
1985	$2,833	$2,124
1986	$3,194	$2,396
1987	$3,574	$2,681
1988	$3,961	$2,971
1989	$4,366	$3,275
1990	$4,784	$3,588

L3350F

YEARS MFRD	1985-1991
SERIES	L3 SERIES
ENGINE	KUBOTA
CYLINDERS	4
CID	113.6
PTO HP	32.8
ENGINE HP	40
COOLING	LIQUID
FUEL	D
SPEEDS	8/8
TRANSMISSION	GEAR
STEERING	STANDARD
HITCH	CAT. I
HYDRAULIC	YES
PTO	YES
DRIVE TYPE	2WD
ROPS/CAB	ROPS
WEIGHT	3,500 LBS.
MSRP	$16,590

SERIAL NUMBERS

YEAR	BEGINNING NO.
1985	50001
1986	50475
1987	50950

RETAIL PRICING

YEAR	HIGH	LOW
1990	$5,210	$3,907
1991	$5,306	$3,979

L3350HDT

YEARS MFRD	1985-1995
SERIES	L3 SERIES
ENGINE	KUBOTA
CYLINDERS	4
CID	113.6
PTO HP	32.8
ENGINE HP	40
COOLING	LIQUID
FUEL	D
SPEEDS	8/8
TRANSMISSION	GEAR
STEERING	STANDARD
HITCH	CAT. I
HYDRAULIC	YES
PTO	YES
DRIVE TYPE	4WD
ROPS/CAB	ROPS
WEIGHT	3,770 LBS.
MSRP	$18,999

SERIAL NUMBERS

YEAR	BEGINNING NO.
1986	50475
1987	50950

RETAIL PRICING

YEAR	HIGH	LOW
1986	$4,101	$3,076
1987	$4,683	$3,513
1988	$5,015	$3,761
1989	$5,210	$3,907
1990	$5,654	$4,240
1991	$5,757	$4,318
1992	$6,203	$4,652
1993	$6,291	$4,718
1994	$6,841	$5,131
1995	$7,019	$5,265

L3350MDT

YEARS MFRD	1985-1995
SERIES	L3 SERIES
ENGINE	KUBOTA
CYLINDERS	4
CID	113.6
PTO HP	32.8
ENGINE HP	40
COOLING	LIQUID
FUEL	D
SPEEDS	8/8
TRANSMISSION	SHUTTLE SHIFT
STEERING	STANDARD
HITCH	CAT. I
DRIVE TYPE	4WD
ROPS/CAB	ROPS
WEIGHT	3,790 LBS.
MSRP	$19,200

SERIAL NUMBERS

YEAR	BEGINNING NO.
1985	50001
1986	50475
1987	50950

RETAIL PRICING

YEAR	HIGH	LOW
1990	$5,810	$4,358
1991	$5,915	$4,436
1992	$6,399	$4,800
1993	$6,491	$4,868
1994	$6,914	$5,186
1995	$7,096	$5,322

L3400

YEARS MFRD	2005-2012
ENGINE	KUBOTA
CYLINDERS	3
CID	101
PTO HP	29
ENGINE HP	34.7
COOLING	LIQUID
FUEL	D
SPEEDS	VARIABLE
TRANSMISSION	HYDRO
STEERING	STANDARD
HITCH	CAT. I
HYDRAULIC	YES
PTO	YES
DRIVE TYPE	2WD
ROPS/CAB	ROPS
WEIGHT	2,580 LBS.
MSRP	$14,724

OPTIONS

4WD

RETAIL PRICING

YEAR	HIGH	LOW
2005	$7,199	$5,399
2006	$7,790	$5,842
2007	$8,373	$6,280
2008	$9,016	$6,762
2009	$9,820	$7,365
2010	$10,644	$7,983
2011	$11,523	$8,642
2012	$12,611	$9,458

AVG. AUCTION PRICING

LOW	HIGH	AVG
$7,622	$13,133	$11,155

L3400DT

YEARS MFRD	2004-2011
ENGINE	KUBOTA
CYLINDERS	3
CID	101
PTO HP	29
COOLING	LIQUID
FUEL	D
SPEEDS	8/4
TRANSMISSION	GEAR
STEERING	STANDARD

HYDRAULIC .... YES
DRIVE TYPE 4WD
ROPS/CAB .... ROPS
WEIGHT .... 2,110 LBS.
MSRP $15,744

OPTIONS

2 HYD
2WD
HYDRO
LDR

RETAIL PRICING

YEAR	HIGH	LOW
2004	$8,267	$6,200
2005	$8,937	$6,703
2006	$9,625	$7,219
2007	$10,368	$7,776
2008	$10,957	$8,218
2009	$11,868	$8,901
2010	$12,721	$9,540
2011	$14,158	$10,619

L3400F

YEARS MFRD 2004-2008
ENGINE .... KUBOTA
CYLINDERS 3
CID 101
PTO HP 29.5
FUEL .... D
SPEEDS 8/4
TRANSMISSION .... GEAR
STEERING .... STANDARD
WEIGHT .... 2,210 LBS.
MSRP $13,160

RETAIL PRICING

YEAR	HIGH	LOW
2004	$5,031	$3,773
2005	$5,397	$4,048
2006	$6,078	$4,559
2007	$6,498	$4,874
2008	$7,180	$5,385

L3410DT

YEARS MFRD 1999-2002
SERIES .... GRAND L TEN SERIES
ENGINE .... KUBOTA
CYLINDERS 3
CID 100.5
PTO HP 28.5
ENGINE HP 35.1
COOLING .... LIQUID
FUEL .... D
SPEEDS 8/8
TRANSMISSION .... SHUTTLE SHIFT
STEERING .... STANDARD
HITCH .... CAT. I
HYDRAULIC .... YES
PTO .... YES
DRIVE TYPE 4WD
ROPS/CAB .... ROPS
WEIGHT .... 2,765 LBS.
MSRP $17,766

OPTIONS

2 HYD
HYDRO
LDR

RETAIL PRICING

YEAR	HIGH	LOW
1999	$9,466	$7,099
2000	$10,221	$7,666
2001	$10,896	$8,172
2002	$11,598	$8,698

L3410GST

YEARS MFRD 1999-2002
SERIES .... GRAND L TEN SERIES
ENGINE .... KUBOTA
CYLINDERS 3
CID 100.5
PTO HP 28.5
ENGINE HP 35.1
COOLING .... LIQUID
FUEL .... D
SPEEDS 8/8
TRANSMISSION .... GEAR
STEERING .... STANDARD
HITCH .... CAT. I
HYDRAULIC .... YES
PTO .... YES
DRIVE TYPE 4WD
ROPS/CAB .... ROPS
WEIGHT .... 2,775 LBS.
MSRP $18,316

RETAIL PRICING

YEAR	HIGH	LOW
1999	$9,018	$6,763
2000	$9,992	$7,494
2001	$11,007	$8,255
2002	$12,048	$9,036

L3410HST

YEARS MFRD 1998-2002
SERIES .... GRAND L TEN SERIES
ENGINE .... KUBOTA
CYLINDERS 3
CID 100.5
PTO HP 28.5
ENGINE HP 35.1
COOLING .... LIQUID
FUEL .... D
SPEEDS .... VARIABLE
TRANSMISSION .... HYDRO
STEERING .... STANDARD
HITCH .... CAT. I
HYDRAULIC .... YES
PTO .... YES
DRIVE TYPE 4WD
ROPS/CAB .... ROPS
WEIGHT .... 2,800 LBS.
MSRP $18,816

RETAIL PRICING

YEAR	HIGH	LOW
1999	$9,265	$6,949
2000	$10,266	$7,700
2001	$11,307	$8,481
2002	$12,380	$9,285

L3430DT

YEARS MFRD 2003-2006
SERIES .... GRAND L30 SERIES
ENGINE .... KUBOTA
CYLINDERS 3
CID 100.5
PTO HP 28.5
ENGINE HP 35.1
COOLING .... LIQUID
FUEL .... D
SPEEDS 8/8
TRANSMISSION .... SHUTTLE SHIFT
STEERING .... STANDARD
HITCH .... CAT. I
HYDRAULIC .... YES
PTO .... YES
DRIVE TYPE 4WD
ROPS/CAB .... ROPS
WEIGHT .... 3,220 LBS.
MSRP $17,170

OPTIONS

2 HYD
CAB W/A/H
HYDRO
LDR

RETAIL PRICING

YEAR	HIGH	LOW
2003	$11,868	$8,901
2004	$12,855	$9,642
2005	$13,599	$10,199
2006	$14,250	$10,688

L3430GST

YEARS MFRD 2003-2008
SERIES .... GRAND L30 SERIES
ENGINE .... KUBOTA
CYLINDERS 3
CID 100.5
PTO HP 28.5
ENGINE HP 35.1
COOLING .... LIQUID
FUEL .... D
SPEEDS 12/8
TRANSMISSION .... SHUTTLE SHIFT
STEERING .... STANDARD
HITCH .... CAT. I
HYDRAULIC .... YES
PTO .... YES
DRIVE TYPE 4WD
ROPS/CAB .... ROPS
WEIGHT .... 3,260 LBS.
MSRP $16,275

RETAIL PRICING

YEAR	HIGH	LOW
2003	$9,930	$7,448
2004	$10,256	$7,692
2005	$10,570	$7,927
2006	$10,894	$8,171
2007	$11,374	$8,531
2008	$11,849	$8,887

L3430HST

YEARS MFRD 2003-2008
SERIES .... GRAND L30 SERIES
ENGINE .... KUBOTA
CYLINDERS 3
CID 100.5
PTO HP 27
ENGINE HP 35.1
COOLING .... LIQUID
FUEL .... D
SPEEDS .... VARIABLE
TRANSMISSION .... HYDRO
STEERING .... STANDARD
HITCH .... CAT. I
HYDRAULIC .... YES
PTO .... YES
DRIVE TYPE 4WD
ROPS/CAB .... ROPS
WEIGHT .... 3,305 LBS.
MSRP $16,825

OPTIONS

CAB

RETAIL PRICING

YEAR	HIGH	LOW
2003	$10,055	$7,541
2004	$10,387	$7,790
2005	$10,721	$8,041
2006	$11,211	$8,408
2007	$11,710	$8,783
2008	$12,367	$9,275

L3450DT

YEARS MFRD 1990-1993
SERIES .... L1 SERIES
ENGINE .... KUBOTA
CYLINDERS 4
CID 113.6
PTO HP 30
ENGINE HP 36.7
COOLING .... LIQUID
FUEL .... D
SPEEDS 8/8
TRANSMISSION .... SHUTTLE SHIFT
STEERING .... STANDARD
HITCH .... CAT. I
HYDRAULIC .... YES
PTO .... YES
DRIVE TYPE 4WD
ROPS/CAB .... ROPS
WEIGHT .... 2,845 LBS.
MSRP $15,100

OPTIONS

2 HYD
LDR

SERIAL NUMBERS

YEAR	BEGINNING NO.
1991	50211
1992	50664
1993	51052

RETAIL PRICING

YEAR	HIGH	LOW
1990	$2,278	$1,709
1991	$2,643	$1,982
1992	$3,011	$2,258
1993	$3,391	$2,543

L3450DT W

YEARS MFRD 1990-1996
SERIES .... L1 SERIES
ENGINE .... KUBOTA
CYLINDERS 4
CID 113.6
PTO HP 30
ENGINE HP 36.7
COOLING .... LIQUID

 See Kubota Model Suffix Identification on page 415

FUEL ... D
SPEEDS ... 8/8
TRANSMISSION ... GEAR
STEERING ... STANDARD
HITCH ... CAT. I
HYDRAULIC ... YES
PTO ... YES
DRIVE TYPE ... 4WD
ROPS/CAB ... ROPS
WEIGHT ... 2,866 LBS.
MSRP ... $15,900

RETAIL PRICING

YEAR	HIGH	LOW
1990	$4,837	$3,628
1991	$4,923	$3,693
1992	$5,292	$3,969
1993	$5,366	$4,025
1994	$5,726	$4,294
1995	$5,876	$4,407
1996	$6,035	$4,526

L3450F

YEARS MFRD ... 1991-1995
SERIES ... L1 SERIES
ENGINE ... KUBOTA
CYLINDERS ... 4
CID ... 113.6
PTO HP ... 30
ENGINE HP ... 36.7
COOLING ... LIQUID
FUEL ... D
SPEEDS ... 8/16
TRANSMISSION ... GEAR
STEERING ... STANDARD
HITCH ... CAT. I
HYDRAULIC ... YES
PTO ... YES
DRIVE TYPE ... 2WD
ROPS/CAB ... ROPS
WEIGHT ... 2,425 LBS.
MSRP ... $15,100

RETAIL PRICING

YEAR	HIGH	LOW
1993	$5,163	$3,873

L3450GST

YEARS MFRD ... 1991-1993
SERIES ... L1 SERIES
ENGINE ... KUBOTA
CYLINDERS ... 4
CID ... 113.6
PTO HP ... 30
ENGINE HP ... 36.7
COOLING ... LIQUID
FUEL ... D
SPEEDS ... 8/16
TRANSMISSION ... GEAR
STEERING ... STANDARD
HITCH ... CAT. I
HYDRAULIC ... YES
PTO ... YES
WEIGHT ... 2,900 LBS.
MSRP ... $18,355

SERIAL NUMBERS

YEAR	BEGINNING NO.
1992	80206
1993	80419

RETAIL PRICING

YEAR	HIGH	LOW
1991	$5,869	$4,402
1992	$6,188	$4,641
1993	$6,274	$4,705

L3500

ENGINE ... DS1900
CYLINDERS ... 4
ENGINE HP ... 35
COOLING ... LIQUID
FUEL ... D
TRANSMISSION ... GEAR
STEERING ... STANDARD
WEIGHT ... 1,285 LBS.

L3540

YEARS MFRD ... 2007-2012
ENGINE ... L3540
CYLINDERS ... 3
CID ... 100.5
PTO HP ... 28
ENGINE HP ... 37
FUEL ... D
SPEEDS ... 12/8
TRANSMISSION ... SHUTTLE SHIFT
STEERING ... STANDARD
HITCH ... CAT. I
HYDRAULIC ... YES
PTO ... YES
DRIVE TYPE ... 4WD
ROPS/CAB ... ROPS
WEIGHT ... 3,748 LBS.
MSRP ... $22,410

OPTIONS

2 HYD
CAB W/A/H
HYDRO
LDR

RETAIL PRICING

YEAR	HIGH	LOW
2007	$14,283	$10,712
2008	$15,077	$11,308
2009	$15,898	$11,924
2010	$16,763	$12,572
2011	$18,728	$14,046
2012	$19,544	$14,658

AVG. AUCTION PRICING

LOW	HIGH	AVG
$12,089	$29,071	$20,781

L3560DT

YEARS MFRD ... 2013-2020
ENGINE ... KUBOTA
CYLINDERS ... 3
CID ... 111
PTO HP ... 29.5
ENGINE HP ... 37
COOLING ... LIQUID
FUEL ... D
SPEEDS ... 8/8
TRANSMISSION ... SHUTTLE SHIFT
STEERING ... STANDARD
HITCH ... CAT. I
DRIVE TYPE ... 4WD
ROPS/CAB ... ROPS
WEIGHT ... 3,483 LBS.
MSRP ... $23,462

OPTIONS

BACKHOE ... $8,309
LDR PKG ... $3,886

RETAIL PRICING

YEAR	HIGH	LOW
2013	$18,428	$13,896
2014	$19,595	$14,771
2015	$20,490	$15,443
2016	$21,775	$16,331
2017	$23,515	$17,711
2018	$24,062	$18,121
2019	$24,404	$18,378
2020	$24,796	$18,968

L3560GST

YEARS MFRD ... 2014-2020
ENGINE ... KUBOTA
CYLINDERS ... 3
CID ... 111
PTO HP ... 29.5
ENGINE HP ... 37
COOLING ... LIQUID
FUEL ... D
SPEEDS ... 12/8
TRANSMISSION ... GEAR
STEERING ... STANDARD
HITCH ... CAT. I
DRIVE TYPE ... 4WD
ROPS/CAB ... ROPS
WEIGHT ... 3,494 LBS.
MSRP ... $24,619

OPTIONS

BACKHOE ... $8,309
LDR PKG ... $3,886

RETAIL PRICING

YEAR	HIGH	LOW
2014	$18,317	$13,812
2015	$19,633	$14,799
2016	$20,539	$15,479
2017	$22,072	$16,629
2018	$24,732	$18,625
2019	$25,291	$19,043
2020	$25,804	$19,670

L3560HST

YEARS MFRD ... 2014-2020
ENGINE ... KUBOTA
CYLINDERS ... 3
CID ... 111
PTO HP ... 28
COOLING ... LIQUID
FUEL ... D
SPEEDS ... VARIABLE
TRANSMISSION ... HYDRO
STEERING ... STANDARD
HITCH ... CAT. I
DRIVE TYPE ... 4WD
ROPS/CAB ... ROPS
WEIGHT ... 3,905 LBS.
MSRP ... $24,974

OPTIONS

CAB ... $8,310
LDR PKG ... $3,886

RETAIL PRICING

YEAR	HIGH	LOW
2014	$18,714	$14,110
2015	$20,046	$15,109
2016	$21,868	$16,476
2017	$23,741	$17,881
2018	$25,491	$19,193
2019	$25,864	$19,472
2020	$26,363	$19,938

AVG. AUCTION PRICING

LOW	HIGH	AVG
$18,283	$29,870	$21,244

L3560HSTC LE

YEARS MFRD ... 2020-2020
ENGINE ... KUBOTA
CYLINDERS ... 3
CID ... 111.4
PTO HP ... 28
ENGINE HP ... 35
COOLING ... LIQUID
FUEL ... D
SPEEDS ... VARIABLE
TRANSMISSION ... HYDRO
STEERING ... STANDARD
PTO ... YES
DRIVE TYPE ... 4WD
ROPS/CAB ... CAB
WEIGHT ... 3,880 LBS.
MSRP ... $30,508

OPTIONS

LDR PKG ... $3,886

L3600DT

YEARS MFRD ... 1994-1999
SERIES ... GRAND L SERIES
ENGINE ... KUBOTA
CYLINDERS ... 4
CID ... 113.3
PTO HP ... 31
ENGINE HP ... 38.5
COOLING ... LIQUID
FUEL ... D
SPEEDS ... 8/8
TRANSMISSION ... SHUTTLE SHIFT
STEERING ... STANDARD
HITCH ... CAT. I
HYDRAULIC ... YES
PTO ... YES
DRIVE TYPE ... 4WD
ROPS/CAB ... ROPS
WEIGHT ... 3,030 LBS.
MSRP ... $20,230

OPTIONS

2 HYD
CAB W/A/H
LDR

SERIAL NUMBERS

YEAR	BEGINNING NO.
1994	50008
1997	55766

RETAIL PRICING

YEAR	HIGH	LOW
1994	$5,182	$3,886
1995	$5,746	$4,310

YEAR	HIGH	LOW
1996	$6,171	$4,628
1997	$6,695	$5,021
1998	$7,238	$5,428
1999	$7,862	$5,896

AVG. AUCTION PRICING

LOW	HIGH	AVG
$6,332	$10,938	$7,944

L3600GST

YEARS MFRD 1994-1998
SERIES .... GRAND L SERIES
ENGINE .... KUBOTA
CYLINDERS 4
CID 113.3
PTO HP 31
ENGINE HP 38.5
COOLING .... LIQUID
FUEL .... D
SPEEDS 8/8
TRANSMISSION .... GEAR
STEERING .... STANDARD
HITCH .... CAT. I
HYDRAULIC .... YES
PTO .... YES
DRIVE TYPE 4WD
ROPS/CAB .... ROPS
WEIGHT .... 3,075 LBS.
MSRP $20,230

SERIAL NUMBERS

YEAR	BEGINNING NO.
1994	50101
1995	52217
1997	55761

RETAIL PRICING

YEAR	HIGH	LOW
1994	$6,906	$5,180
1995	$7,089	$5,317
1996	$7,278	$5,458
1997	$7,878	$5,909
1998	$8,986	$6,739

L3600GSTCA

YEARS MFRD 1996-1998
SERIES .... GRAND L SERIES
ENGINE .... KUBOTA
CYLINDERS 4
CID 113.3
PTO HP 31
ENGINE HP 38.5
COOLING .... LIQUID
FUEL .... D
SPEEDS 16/16
TRANSMISSION .... GEAR
STEERING .... STANDARD
HITCH .... CAT. I
HYDRAULIC .... YES
PTO .... YES
DRIVE TYPE 4WD
ROPS/CAB .... CAB
WEIGHT .... 3,495 LBS.
MSRP $28,680

RETAIL PRICING

YEAR	HIGH	LOW
1997	$11,167	$8,375
1998	$12,739	$9,554

L3650DT

YEARS MFRD 1990-1993
SERIES .... L1 SERIES
ENGINE .... KUBOTA
CYLINDERS 4
CID 113.6
PTO HP 33
ENGINE HP 40.5
COOLING .... LIQUID
FUEL .... D
SPEEDS 8/8
TRANSMISSION .... GEAR
STEERING .... STANDARD
HITCH .... CAT. I
HYDRAULIC .... YES
PTO .... YES
DRIVE TYPE 4WD
ROPS/CAB .... ROPS
MSRP $18,010

OPTIONS

2 HYD
LDR

RETAIL PRICING

YEAR	HIGH	LOW
1990	$4,969	$3,727
1991	$5,405	$4,054
1992	$5,853	$4,390
1993	$6,315	$4,736

L3650DT W

YEARS MFRD 1990-1995
SERIES .... L1 SERIES
ENGINE .... KUBOTA
CYLINDERS 4
CID 113.6
PTO HP 33
ENGINE HP 40.5
COOLING .... AIR
FUEL .... D
SPEEDS 8/8
TRANSMISSION .... GEAR
STEERING .... STANDARD
HITCH .... CAT. I
HYDRAULIC .... YES
PTO .... YES
DRIVE TYPE 4WD
ROPS/CAB .... ROPS
WEIGHT .... 2,911 LBS.
MSRP $18,299

RETAIL PRICING

YEAR	HIGH	LOW
1990	$5,089	$3,817
1991	$5,340	$4,005
1992	$5,798	$4,348
1993	$6,155	$4,616
1994	$6,486	$4,864
1995	$6,763	$5,072

L3650F

YEARS MFRD 1991-1995
SERIES .... L1 SERIES
ENGINE .... KUBOTA
CYLINDERS 4
CID 113.6
PTO HP 33
ENGINE HP 40.5
COOLING .... LIQUID
FUEL .... D
SPEEDS 8/8
TRANSMISSION .... GEAR
STEERING .... STANDARD
HITCH .... CAT. I
HYDRAULIC .... YES
PTO .... YES
DRIVE TYPE 2WD
ROPS/CAB .... ROPS
WEIGHT .... 2,470 LBS.
MSRP $15,890

RETAIL PRICING

YEAR	HIGH	LOW
1991	$5,081	$3,811
1992	$5,257	$3,943
1993	$5,430	$4,073
1994	$5,624	$4,218
1995	$5,874	$4,406

L3650GST

YEARS MFRD 1990-1996
SERIES .... L1 SERIES
ENGINE .... KUBOTA
CYLINDERS 4
CID 113.6
PTO HP 33
ENGINE HP 40.5
FUEL .... D
SPEEDS 8/8
TRANSMISSION .... GEAR
STEERING .... STANDARD
HYDRAULIC .... YES
PTO .... YES
DRIVE TYPE 4WD
ROPS/CAB .... ROPS
WEIGHT .... 2,910 LBS.
MSRP $19,200

RETAIL PRICING

YEAR	HIGH	LOW
1990	$5,939	$4,454
1991	$6,045	$4,534
1992	$6,373	$4,779
1993	$6,663	$4,997
1994	$6,816	$5,112
1995	$6,998	$5,248
1996	$7,286	$5,465

L3700

YEARS MFRD 2012-2012
ENGINE .... KUBOTA
CYLINDERS 3
CID 111.4
PTO HP 30
ENGINE HP 37.4
COOLING .... LIQUID
FUEL .... D
SPEEDS 3SP
TRANSMISSION .... HYDRO
STEERING .... STANDARD
HITCH .... CAT. I
DRIVE TYPE 2WD
ROPS/CAB .... ROPS
WEIGHT .... 2,568 LBS.

OPTIONS

LDR

RETAIL PRICING

YEAR	HIGH	LOW
2012	$1,507	$1,130

L3710DT

YEARS MFRD 1999-2002
SERIES ...... GRAND L TEN SERIES
ENGINE .... KUBOTA
CYLINDERS 4
CID 113.3
PTO HP 31.5
ENGINE HP 38.5
COOLING .... LIQUID
FUEL .... D
SPEEDS 8/8
TRANSMISSION .... SHUTTLE SHIFT
STEERING .... STANDARD
HITCH .... CAT. I
HYDRAULIC .... YES
PTO .... YES
DRIVE TYPE 4WD
ROPS/CAB .... ROPS
WEIGHT .... 2,955 LBS.
MSRP $18,800

OPTIONS

2 HYD
CAB W/A/H
HYDRO
LDR

RETAIL PRICING

YEAR	HIGH	LOW
1999	$8,778	$6,583
2000	$9,583	$7,187
2001	$10,263	$7,697
2002	$11,129	$8,347

AVG. AUCTION PRICING

LOW	HIGH	AVG
$4,939	$9,752	$7,598

L3710GST

YEARS MFRD 1999-2002
SERIES ...... GRAND L TEN SERIES
ENGINE .... KUBOTA
CYLINDERS 4
CID 113.3
PTO HP 31.5
ENGINE HP 38.5
COOLING .... LIQUID
FUEL .... D
SPEEDS 8/8
TRANSMISSION .... GEAR
STEERING .... STANDARD
HITCH .... CAT. I
HYDRAULIC .... YES
PTO .... YES
DRIVE TYPE 4WD
ROPS/CAB .... ROPS
WEIGHT .... 2,965 LBS.
MSRP $19,450

RETAIL PRICING

YEAR	HIGH	LOW
1999	$9,613	$7,210
2000	$10,652	$7,989
2001	$11,691	$8,768
2002	$12,796	$9,597

KUBOTA See Kubota Model Suffix Identification on page 415

L3710HST

YEARS MFRD........ 1999-2002
SERIES...... GRAND L TEN SERIES
ENGINE............... KUBOTA
CYLINDERS................ 4
CID.................. 113.3
PTO HP.................. 30
ENGINE HP.............. 38.5
COOLING............... LIQUID
FUEL...................... D
SPEEDS............... VARIABLE
TRANSMISSION.......... HYDRO
STEERING............ STANDARD
HITCH................. CAT. I
HYDRAULIC............... YES
PTO..................... YES
DRIVE TYPE.............. 4WD
ROPS/CAB............... ROPS
WEIGHT............. 2,990 LBS.
MSRP................ $20,150

OPTIONS

CAB

RETAIL PRICING

YEAR	HIGH	LOW
1999	$11,203	$8,402
2000	$11,338	$8,504
2001	$12,116	$9,087
2002	$13,257	$9,943

L3750DT

YEARS MFRD........ 1984-1990
SERIES............. L3 SERIES
ENGINE............... KUBOTA
CYLINDERS................ 5
CID..................... 142
PTO HP.................. 36.96
ENGINE HP................ 45
COOLING............... LIQUID
FUEL...................... D
SPEEDS.................. 8/8
TRANSMISSION........... GEAR
STEERING............ STANDARD
HITCH................. CAT. I
HYDRAULIC............... YES
PTO..................... YES
DRIVE TYPE.............. 4WD
ROPS/CAB............... ROPS
WEIGHT............. 3,860 LBS.
MSRP................ $16,000

OPTIONS

2 HYD
LDR

RETAIL PRICING

YEAR	HIGH	LOW
1984	$2,549	$1,912
1985	$2,905	$2,178
1986	$3,275	$2,457
1987	$3,649	$2,737
1988	$4,042	$3,031
1989	$4,447	$3,335
1990	$4,865	$3,649

L3750F

YEARS MFRD........ 1984-1995
SERIES............. L3 SERIES
ENGINE............... KUBOTA
CYLINDERS................ 5
CID..................... 142
PTO HP.................. 36.9
ENGINE HP................ 45
COOLING............... LIQUID
FUEL...................... D
SPEEDS.................. 8/8
TRANSMISSION........... GEAR
STEERING............ STANDARD
HITCH................. CAT. I
HYDRAULIC............... YES
PTO..................... YES
DRIVE TYPE.............. 2WD
ROPS/CAB............... ROPS
WEIGHT............. 3,640 LBS.
MSRP................ $16,900

SERIAL NUMBERS

RETAIL PRICING

YEAR	HIGH	LOW
1985	$3,529	$2,647
1986	$3,969	$2,976
1987	$4,133	$3,100
1988	$4,428	$3,321
1989	$4,798	$3,598
1990	$4,926	$3,695
1991	$5,115	$3,836
1992	$5,481	$4,110
1993	$5,657	$4,243
1994	$5,887	$4,416
1995	$6,247	$4,685

L3750HDT

YEARS MFRD........ 1984-1995
SERIES............. L3 SERIES
ENGINE............... KUBOTA
CYLINDERS................ 5
CID..................... 142
PTO HP.................. 36.9
ENGINE HP................ 45
COOLING............... LIQUID
FUEL...................... D
SPEEDS.................. 8/8
TRANSMISSION........... GEAR
STEERING............ STANDARD
HITCH................. CAT. I
HYDRAULIC............... YES
PTO..................... YES
DRIVE TYPE.............. 4WD
ROPS/CAB............... ROPS
WEIGHT............. 3,860 LBS.
MSRP................ $20,500

RETAIL PRICING

YEAR	HIGH	LOW
1986	$4,631	$3,473
1987	$5,235	$3,927
1988	$5,610	$4,208
1989	$5,826	$4,369
1990	$6,050	$4,538
1991	$6,362	$4,772
1992	$6,710	$5,033
1993	$7,006	$5,255
1994	$7,380	$5,535
1995	$7,577	$5,683

L3800DT

YEARS MFRD........ 2011-2013
ENGINE............... KUBOTA
CYLINDERS................ 3
CID..................... 111
PTO HP.................. 31.5
FUEL...................... D
SPEEDS.................. 8/4
TRANSMISSION........... GEAR
STEERING............ STANDARD
DRIVE TYPE.............. 4WD
ROPS/CAB............... ROPS
WEIGHT............. 2,657 LBS.
MSRP................ $17,244

OPTIONS

2WD
BACKHOE
HYDRO
LDR

RETAIL PRICING

YEAR	HIGH	LOW
2011	$13,312	$9,984
2012	$14,389	$10,792
2013	$15,517	$11,638

AVG. AUCTION PRICING

LOW	HIGH	AVG
$13,528	$18,997	$16,445

L3800F

YEARS MFRD........ 2011-2014
ENGINE............... KUBOTA
CYLINDERS................ 3
CID..................... 100
PTO HP.................. 31.5
COOLING............... LIQUID
FUEL...................... D
SPEEDS.................. 8/8
TRANSMISSION........... GEAR
STEERING............ STANDARD
HITCH................. CAT. I
DRIVE TYPE.............. 2WD
ROPS/CAB............... ROPS
WEIGHT............. 3,252 LBS.
MSRP................ $16,000

OPTIONS

LDR

RETAIL PRICING

YEAR	HIGH	LOW
2011	$8,642	$6,481
2012	$9,409	$7,057
2013	$10,790	$8,093
2014	$12,578	$9,434

L3800HST

YEARS MFRD........ 2011-2014
ENGINE............... KUBOTA
CYLINDERS................ 3
CID..................... 100
PTO HP.................. 31.5
COOLING............... LIQUID
FUEL...................... D
SPEEDS.................. 8/8
TRANSMISSION........... GEAR
STEERING............ STANDARD
DRIVE TYPE.............. 4WD
ROPS/CAB............... ROPS
WEIGHT............. 3,252 LBS.
MSRP................ $19,335

OPTIONS

LDR

RETAIL PRICING

YEAR	HIGH	LOW
2011	$10,278	$7,709
2012	$11,148	$8,361
2013	$13,040	$9,780
2014	$15,238	$11,428

AVG. AUCTION PRICING

LOW	HIGH	AVG
$6,386	$17,510	$13,223

L3830DT

YEARS MFRD........ 2003-2006
SERIES....... GRAND L30 SERIES
ENGINE............... KUBOTA
CYLINDERS................ 3
CID.................... 111.5
PTO HP.................. 32
ENGINE HP................ 39
COOLING............... LIQUID
FUEL...................... D
SPEEDS.................. 12/8
TRANSMISSION... SHUTTLE SHIFT
STEERING............ STANDARD
HITCH................. CAT. I
HYDRAULIC............... YES
PTO..................... YES
DRIVE TYPE.............. 4WD
ROPS/CAB............... ROPS
WEIGHT............. 3,260 LBS.
MSRP................ $20,604

OPTIONS

2 HYD
2WD
8/8 GEAR
LDR

RETAIL PRICING

YEAR	HIGH	LOW
2003	$12,083	$9,062
2004	$12,880	$9,660
2005	$13,637	$10,228
2006	$14,490	$10,868

L3830F

YEARS MFRD........ 2003-2008
SERIES....... GRAND L30 SERIES
ENGINE............... KUBOTA
CYLINDERS................ 3
CID.................... 111.5
PTO HP.................. 32
ENGINE HP................ 39
COOLING............... LIQUID
FUEL...................... D
SPEEDS.................. 12/8
TRANSMISSION... SHUTTLE SHIFT
STEERING............ STANDARD
HITCH................. CAT. I
HYDRAULIC............... YES
PTO..................... YES
DRIVE TYPE.............. 2WD
ROPS/CAB............... ROPS

WEIGHT . . . . .3,150 LBS.
MSRP. $15,020

RETAIL PRICING

YEAR	HIGH	LOW
2003	$8,977	$6,733
2004	$9,270	$6,953
2005	$9,566	$7,174
2006	$10,004	$7,503
2007	$10,447	$7,835
2008	$11,044	$8,283

L3830GST

YEARS MFRD 2003-2008
SERIES. . . . . . . GRAND L30 SERIES
ENGINE . . . . KUBOTA
CYLINDERS. 3
CID 111.5
PTO HP 32
ENGINE HP 39
COOLING . . . . LIQUID
FUEL . . . . D
SPEEDS 12/8
TRANSMISSION . . . SHUTTLE SHIFT
STEERING. . . . . STANDARD
HITCH . . . . CAT. I
HYDRAULIC . . . . YES
PTO . . . . YES
DRIVE TYPE 4WD
ROPS/CAB . . . . ROPS
WEIGHT . . . . .3,275 LBS.
MSRP. $17,450

RETAIL PRICING

YEAR	HIGH	LOW
2003	$10,436	$7,827
2004	$10,769	$8,076
2005	$11,112	$8,334
2006	$11,631	$8,723
2007	$12,143	$9,107
2008	$12,828	$9,621

L3830HST

YEARS MFRD 2003-2008
SERIES. . . . . . . GRAND L30 SERIES
ENGINE . . . . KUBOTA
CYLINDERS. 3
CID 111.5
PTO HP 30.5
ENGINE HP 39
COOLING . . . . LIQUID
FUEL . . . . D
SPEEDS . . . . VARIABLE
TRANSMISSION . . . . HYDRO
STEERING. . . . . STANDARD
HITCH . . . . CAT. I
HYDRAULIC . . . . YES
PTO . . . . YES
DRIVE TYPE 4WD
ROPS/CAB . . . . ROPS
WEIGHT . . . . .3,340 LBS.
MSRP. $17,990

RETAIL PRICING

YEAR	HIGH	LOW
2003	$9,773	$7,329
2004	$10,094	$7,571
2005	$10,414	$7,811
2006	$10,895	$8,172
2007	$11,375	$8,531
2008	$12,019	$9,014

AVG. AUCTION PRICING

LOW	HIGH	AVG
$5,296	$21,012	$11,600

L3901

YEARS MFRD 2014-2020
ENGINE . . . . KUBOTA
CYLINDERS. 3
CID 111.4
PTO HP 30.6
ENGINE HP 36.3
COOLING . . . . LIQUID
FUEL . . . . D
SPEEDS . . . . VARIABLE
TRANSMISSION . . . . HYDRO
STEERING. . . . . STANDARD
HITCH . . . . CAT. I
DRIVE TYPE 4WD
ROPS/CAB . . . . ROPS
WEIGHT . . . . .2,778 LBS.
MSRP. $22,232

OPTIONS

2WD/GEAR. . . . . $-3,755
BACKHOE. $7,816
LDR PKG $4,466

RETAIL PRICING

YEAR	HIGH	LOW
2014	$18,347	$13,761
2015	$19,682	$14,762
2016	$20,135	$15,101
2017	$21,053	$15,790
2018	$22,028	$16,520
2019	$22,569	$16,926
2020	$23,023	$17,496

AVG. AUCTION PRICING

LOW	HIGH	AVG
$6,000	$16,000	$12,920

L3940HST

YEARS MFRD 2007-2012
ENGINE . . . . KUBOTA
CYLINDERS. 4
CID 122
PTO HP 33
ENGINE HP 40.5
FUEL . . . . D
SPEEDS . . . . VARIABLE
TRANSMISSION . . . . HYDRO
STEERING. . . . . STANDARD
HITCH . . . . CAT. I
HYDRAULIC . . . . YES
PTO . . . . YES
DRIVE TYPE 4WD
ROPS/CAB . . . . ROPS
WEIGHT . . . . .3,527 LBS.
MSRP. $25,078

OPTIONS

2 HYD
CAB W/A/H
LDR

RETAIL PRICING

YEAR	HIGH	LOW
2007	$15,596	$11,697
2008	$16,406	$12,304
2009	$17,478	$13,109
2010	$18,355	$13,766
2011	$20,196	$15,147
2012	$21,281	$15,961

AVG. AUCTION PRICING

LOW	HIGH	AVG
$14,935	$22,660	$19,635

L4060DT

YEARS MFRD 2013-2020
ENGINE . . . . KUBOTA
CYLINDERS. 4
CID 148
PTO HP 34
ENGINE HP 40
COOLING . . . . LIQUID
FUEL . . . . D
SPEEDS . . . . VARIABLE
TRANSMISSION . . . . GEAR
STEERING. . . . . STANDARD
DRIVE TYPE 4WD
ROPS/CAB . . . . ROPS
WEIGHT . . . . .3,737 LBS.
MSRP. $26,780

OPTIONS

12/8 GEAR. $1,156
BACKHOE. $9,295
HYDRO. $1,539
HYDRO/CAB $9,849
LDR $4,645

RETAIL PRICING

YEAR	HIGH	LOW
2013	$20,932	$15,774
2014	$22,025	$16,593
2015	$23,204	$17,479
2016	$24,353	$18,339
2017	$26,423	$19,892
2018	$27,075	$20,380
2019	$27,663	$20,616
2020	$28,072	$21,038

L4060GST

YEARS MFRD 2014-2014
ENGINE . . . . KUBOTA
CYLINDERS. 4
CID 148
PTO HP 34
COOLING . . . . LIQUID
FUEL . . . . D
SPEEDS 12/8
TRANSMISSION . . . . GEAR
STEERING. . . . . STANDARD
DRIVE TYPE 2WD
ROPS/CAB . . . . ROPS
WEIGHT . . . . .3,748 LBS.
MSRP. $27,119

RETAIL PRICING

YEAR	HIGH	LOW
2014	$21,375	$16,031

L4060HST

YEARS MFRD 2014-2014
ENGINE . . . . KUBOTA
CYLINDERS. 4
CID 148
PTO HP 32.5
COOLING . . . . LIQUID
FUEL . . . . D
SPEEDS . . . . VARIABLE
TRANSMISSION . . . . HYDRO
STEERING. . . . . STANDARD
DRIVE TYPE 2WD
ROPS/CAB . . . . ROPS
WEIGHT . . . . .3,759 LBS.
MSRP. $27,599

RETAIL PRICING

YEAR	HIGH	LOW
2014	$21,733	$16,300

L4150DT REG SHIFT

YEARS MFRD 1984-1995
SERIES. . . . . L3 SERIES
ENGINE . . . . KUBOTA
CYLINDERS. 5
CID 142
PTO HP 40.64
ENGINE HP 50
COOLING . . . . LIQUID
FUEL . . . . D
SPEEDS 8/8
TRANSMISSION . . . . GEAR
STEERING. . . . . STANDARD
HITCH . . . . CAT. I
HYDRAULIC . . . . YES
PTO . . . . YES
DRIVE TYPE 4WD
ROPS/CAB . . . . ROPS
WEIGHT . . . . .4,080 LBS.
MSRP. $22,900

SERIAL NUMBERS

YEAR	BEGINNING NO.
1985	60001
1986	60138
1987	60276
1988	60462
1989	60555

RETAIL PRICING

YEAR	HIGH	LOW
1985	$4,402	$3,302
1986	$5,079	$3,809
1987	$5,647	$4,236
1988	$6,049	$4,537
1989	$6,283	$4,712
1990	$6,909	$5,182
1991	$7,034	$5,275
1992	$7,584	$5,688
1993	$7,689	$5,767
1994	$8,246	$6,185
1995	$8,465	$6,348

L4150DT SHUTTLE

YEARS MFRD 1984-1990
ENGINE . . . . KUBOTA
CYLINDERS. 5
CID 142
PTO HP 40.64
ENGINE HP 50
FUEL . . . . D
SPEEDS 8/8

TRANSMISSION . . . SHUTTLE SHIFT
STEERING . . . STANDARD
PTO . . . YES
DRIVE TYPE . . . 4WD
ROPS/CAB . . . ROPS
WEIGHT . . . 3,750 LBS.
MSRP . . . $22,000

OPTIONS

2 HYD
LDR

RETAIL PRICING

YEAR	HIGH	LOW
1984	$4,053	$3,040
1985	$4,433	$3,325
1986	$4,812	$3,609
1987	$5,320	$3,990
1988	$5,826	$4,369
1989	$6,332	$4,749
1990	$6,839	$5,129

L4150DTM

YEARS MFRD . . . 1985-1995
ENGINE . . . KUBOTA
CYLINDERS . . . 5
CID . . . 142
PTO HP . . . 40.6
ENGINE HP . . . 50
FUEL . . . D
SPEEDS . . . 8/8
TRANSMISSION . . . HYDRO
STEERING . . . STANDARD
PTO . . . YES
DRIVE TYPE . . . 4WD
ROPS/CAB . . . ROPS
WEIGHT . . . 4,080 LBS.
MSRP . . . $22,050

SERIAL NUMBERS

YEAR	BEGINNING NO.
1985	60001
1986	60138
1987	60276
1988	60462
1989	60555

RETAIL PRICING

YEAR	HIGH	LOW
1995	$8,150	$6,113

L4150DTN

YEARS MFRD . . . 1986-1995
ENGINE . . . KUBOTA
CYLINDERS . . . 5
CID . . . 142
PTO HP . . . 40.6
ENGINE HP . . . 50
FUEL . . . D
SPEEDS . . . 8/8
TRANSMISSION . . . HYDRO
STEERING . . . STANDARD
PTO . . . YES
DRIVE TYPE . . . 4WD
ROPS/CAB . . . ROPS
WEIGHT . . . 3,990 LBS.
MSRP . . . $21,900

SERIAL NUMBERS

YEAR	BEGINNING NO.
1986	50022
1987	50057
1989	60082

RETAIL PRICING

YEAR	HIGH	LOW
1987	$5,538	$4,154
1988	$5,934	$4,450
1989	$6,161	$4,621
1990	$6,596	$4,947
1991	$6,715	$5,036
1992	$7,245	$5,434
1993	$7,349	$5,512
1994	$7,886	$5,914
1995	$8,097	$6,073

L4150F

YEARS MFRD . . . 1984-1990
SERIES . . . L3 SERIES
ENGINE . . . KUBOTA
CYLINDERS . . . 5
CID . . . 142
PTO HP . . . 40.6
ENGINE HP . . . 50
COOLING . . . LIQUID
FUEL . . . D
SPEEDS . . . 8/8
TRANSMISSION . . . GEAR
STEERING . . . STANDARD
HITCH . . . CAT. I
DRIVE TYPE . . . 2WD
ROPS/CAB . . . ROPS
WEIGHT . . . 3,750 LBS.
MSRP . . . $17,200

SERIAL NUMBERS

YEAR	BEGINNING NO.
1985	10396
1986	10084
1987	40543

RETAIL PRICING

YEAR	HIGH	LOW
1984	$3,968	$2,976
1985	$4,371	$3,278
1986	$4,784	$3,588
1987	$5,210	$3,907
1988	$5,661	$4,246
1989	$6,121	$4,591
1990	$6,606	$4,955

L4150FM

YEARS MFRD . . . 1985-1995
ENGINE . . . KUBOTA
CYLINDERS . . . 5
CID . . . 142
PTO HP . . . 40.6
ENGINE HP . . . 50
FUEL . . . D
SPEEDS . . . 8/8
TRANSMISSION . . . HYDRO
STEERING . . . STANDARD
PTO . . . YES
DRIVE TYPE . . . 2WD
ROPS/CAB . . . ROPS
WEIGHT . . . 3,750 LBS.
MSRP . . . $17,200

RETAIL PRICING

YEAR	HIGH	LOW
1995	$6,358	$4,769

L4150H F

YEARS MFRD . . . 1985-1995
ENGINE . . . KUBOTA
CYLINDERS . . . 5
CID . . . 142
PTO HP . . . 40.6
ENGINE HP . . . 50
FUEL . . . D
SPEEDS . . . 8/8
TRANSMISSION . . . HYDRO
STEERING . . . STANDARD
PTO . . . YES
DRIVE TYPE . . . 2WD
ROPS/CAB . . . ROPS
WEIGHT . . . 3,750 LBS.
MSRP . . . $18,200

RETAIL PRICING

YEAR	HIGH	LOW
1995	$6,726	$5,044

L4150HDT

YEARS MFRD . . . 1984-1995
ENGINE . . . KUBOTA
CYLINDERS . . . 5
CID . . . 142
PTO HP . . . 40.6
ENGINE HP . . . 50
FUEL . . . D
SPEEDS . . . 8/8
TRANSMISSION . . . HYDRO
STEERING . . . STANDARD
PTO . . . YES
DRIVE TYPE . . . 4WD
ROPS/CAB . . . ROPS
WEIGHT . . . 4,080 LBS.
MSRP . . . $23,000

SERIAL NUMBERS

YEAR	BEGINNING NO.
1984	50356

RETAIL PRICING

YEAR	HIGH	LOW
1995	$8,502	$6,376

L4200DT

YEARS MFRD . . . 1994-1999
SERIES . . . GRAND L SERIES
ENGINE . . . KUBOTA
CYLINDERS . . . 4
CID . . . 134.1
PTO HP . . . 37
ENGINE HP . . . 45.3
COOLING . . . LIQUID
FUEL . . . D
SPEEDS . . . 8/8
TRANSMISSION . . . GEAR
STEERING . . . STANDARD
HITCH . . . CAT. I
HYDRAULIC . . . YES
PTO . . . YES
DRIVE TYPE . . . 4WD
ROPS/CAB . . . ROPS
WEIGHT . . . 3,030 LBS.
MSRP . . . $18,780

OPTIONS

2 HYD
CAB W/A
LDR

SERIAL NUMBERS

YEAR	BEGINNING NO.
1994	50051
1996	53968
1997	54370
1998	57727

RETAIL PRICING

YEAR	HIGH	LOW
1994	$5,898	$4,423
1995	$6,375	$4,781
1996	$6,874	$5,156
1997	$7,383	$5,537
1998	$7,912	$5,934
1999	$8,451	$6,338

AVG. AUCTION PRICING

LOW	HIGH	AVG
$5,066	$10,132	$7,916

L4200F

YEARS MFRD . . . 1994-1998
SERIES . . . GRAND L SERIES
ENGINE . . . KUBOTA
CYLINDERS . . . 4
CID . . . 134.1
PTO HP . . . 37
ENGINE HP . . . 45.3
COOLING . . . LIQUID
FUEL . . . D
SPEEDS . . . 8/8
TRANSMISSION . . . GEAR
STEERING . . . STANDARD
HITCH . . . CAT. I
HYDRAULIC . . . YES
PTO . . . YES
DRIVE TYPE . . . 2WD
ROPS/CAB . . . ROPS
WEIGHT . . . 2,875 LBS.
MSRP . . . $18,780

SERIAL NUMBERS

YEAR	BEGINNING NO.
1994	10001
1996	10003
1997	10479
1998	10540

RETAIL PRICING

YEAR	HIGH	LOW
1994	$6,408	$4,806
1995	$6,581	$4,936
1996	$6,754	$5,065
1997	$7,312	$5,484
1998	$8,342	$6,256

L4200FGST

YEARS MFRD . . . 1994-1998
SERIES . . . GRAND L SERIES
ENGINE . . . KUBOTA
CYLINDERS . . . 4
CID . . . 134.1
PTO HP . . . 37
ENGINE HP . . . 45.3
COOLING . . . LIQUID
FUEL . . . D

SPEEDS	8/8
TRANSMISSION	GEAR
STEERING	STANDARD
HITCH	CAT. I
HYDRAULIC	YES
PTO	YES
DRIVE TYPE	2WD
ROPS/CAB	ROPS
WEIGHT	2,875 LBS.
MSRP	$19,080

RETAIL PRICING

YEAR	HIGH	LOW
1994	$6,521	$4,891
1995	$6,695	$5,021
1996	$6,874	$5,156
1997	$7,428	$5,571
1998	$8,474	$6,355

L4200GST

YEARS MFRD	1994-1998
SERIES	GRAND L SERIES
ENGINE	KUBOTA
CYLINDERS	4
CID	134.1
PTO HP	37
ENGINE HP	45.3
COOLING	LIQUID
FUEL	D
SPEEDS	8/8
TRANSMISSION	GEAR
STEERING	STANDARD
HITCH	CAT. I
HYDRAULIC	YES
PTO	YES
DRIVE TYPE	4WD
ROPS/CAB	ROPS
WEIGHT	3,055 LBS.
MSRP	$22,580

SERIAL NUMBERS

YEAR	BEGINNING NO.
1994	50043
1995	51660

RETAIL PRICING

YEAR	HIGH	LOW
1994	$7,701	$5,776
1995	$7,905	$5,929
1996	$8,114	$6,086
1997	$8,792	$6,594
1998	$10,030	$7,523

L4200GSTCA

YEARS MFRD	1994-1998
SERIES	GRAND L SERIES
ENGINE	KUBOTA
CYLINDERS	4
CID	134.1
PTO HP	37
ENGINE HP	45.3
COOLING	LIQUID
FUEL	D
SPEEDS	16/16
TRANSMISSION	GEAR
STEERING	STANDARD
HITCH	CAT. I
HYDRAULIC	YES
PTO	YES
DRIVE TYPE	4WD
ROPS/CAB	ROPS
WEIGHT	3,495 LBS.
MSRP	$30,180

SERIAL NUMBERS

YEAR	BEGINNING NO.
1994	50902
1995	53228
1996	55474
1997	55478

RETAIL PRICING

YEAR	HIGH	LOW
1997	$11,753	$8,815
1998	$13,403	$10,053

L4240

YEARS MFRD	2007-2012
ENGINE	KUBOTA
CYLINDERS	4
CID	134.1
PTO HP	36.5
ENGINE HP	44
FUEL	D
SPEEDS	8/8
TRANSMISSION	SHUTTLE SHIFT
STEERING	STANDARD
HITCH	CAT. I
HYDRAULIC	YES
PTO	YES
DRIVE TYPE	4WD
ROPS/CAB	ROPS
WEIGHT	3,671 LBS.
MSRP	$26,428

OPTIONS

2 HYD
CAB W/A/H
HYDRO
LDR

RETAIL PRICING

YEAR	HIGH	LOW
2007	$18,329	$13,747
2008	$19,429	$14,572
2009	$20,363	$15,272
2010	$21,512	$16,134
2011	$23,477	$17,608
2012	$24,938	$18,704

AVG. AUCTION PRICING

LOW	HIGH	AVG
$10,250	$18,500	$15,683

L4300DT

YEARS MFRD	2001-2005
SERIES	L SERIES
ENGINE	KUBOTA
CYLINDERS	4
CID	134.1
PTO HP	37.5
ENGINE HP	45.3
COOLING	LIQUID
FUEL	D
SPEEDS	8/2
TRANSMISSION	GEAR
STEERING	STANDARD
HITCH	CAT. I
HYDRAULIC	YES
PTO	YES
DRIVE TYPE	4WD
ROPS/CAB	ROPS
WEIGHT	3,290 LBS.
MSRP	$18,000

OPTIONS

2 HYD
2WD
LDR

RETAIL PRICING

YEAR	HIGH	LOW
2001	$9,539	$7,154
2002	$10,228	$7,671
2003	$10,946	$8,209
2004	$11,689	$8,767
2005	$12,458	$9,343

L4300F

YEARS MFRD	2001-2003
SERIES	L SERIES
ENGINE	KUBOTA
CYLINDERS	4
CID	134.1
PTO HP	37.5
ENGINE HP	45.3
COOLING	LIQUID
FUEL	D
SPEEDS	8/2
TRANSMISSION	GEAR
STEERING	STANDARD
HITCH	CAT. I
HYDRAULIC	YES
PTO	YES
DRIVE TYPE	2WD
ROPS/CAB	ROPS
WEIGHT	2,822 LBS.
MSRP	$15,490

RETAIL PRICING

YEAR	HIGH	LOW
2001	$9,358	$7,018
2002	$10,192	$7,644
2003	$11,194	$8,396

L4310DT

YEARS MFRD	1999-2002
SERIES	GRAND L TEN SERIES
ENGINE	KUBOTA
CYLINDERS	4
CID	134.1
PTO HP	37.5
ENGINE HP	45.3
COOLING	LIQUID
FUEL	D
SPEEDS	8/8
TRANSMISSION	GEAR
STEERING	STANDARD
HITCH	CAT. I
HYDRAULIC	YES
PTO	YES
DRIVE TYPE	4WD
ROPS/CAB	ROPS
WEIGHT	3,030 LBS.
MSRP	$16,500

OPTIONS

2 HYD
CAB W/A
HYDRO
LDR

RETAIL PRICING

YEAR	HIGH	LOW
1999	$8,071	$6,053
2000	$8,661	$6,496
2001	$9,324	$6,993
2002	$10,300	$7,725

AVG. AUCTION PRICING

LOW	HIGH	AVG
$5,572	$20,010	$10,670

L4310F

YEARS MFRD	1999-2003
SERIES	GRAND L TEN SERIES
ENGINE	KUBOTA
CYLINDERS	4
CID	134.1
PTO HP	37.5
ENGINE HP	45.3
COOLING	LIQUID
FUEL	D
SPEEDS	8/8
TRANSMISSION	GEAR
STEERING	STANDARD
HITCH	CAT. I
HYDRAULIC	YES
PTO	YES
DRIVE TYPE	2WD
ROPS/CAB	ROPS
WEIGHT	2,875 LBS.
MSRP	$17,250

RETAIL PRICING

YEAR	HIGH	LOW
1999	$8,197	$6,148
2000	$9,084	$6,813
2001	$9,970	$7,478
2002	$11,348	$8,511
2003	$12,464	$9,348

L4310GST

YEARS MFRD	1999-2003
SERIES	GRAND L TEN SERIES
ENGINE	KUBOTA
CYLINDERS	4
CID	134.1
PTO HP	37.5
ENGINE HP	45.3
COOLING	LIQUID
FUEL	D
SPEEDS	8/8
TRANSMISSION	GEAR
STEERING	STANDARD
HITCH	CAT. I
HYDRAULIC	YES
PTO	YES
DRIVE TYPE	4WD
ROPS/CAB	ROPS
WEIGHT	3,040 LBS.
MSRP	$22,750

RETAIL PRICING

YEAR	HIGH	LOW
1999	$11,253	$8,440
2000	$12,468	$9,351
2001	$13,687	$10,265
2002	$14,968	$11,226
2003	$16,441	$12,331

 See Kubota Model Suffix Identification on page 415

L4310GSTC

YEARS MFRD 1999-2003
SERIES. . . . . . GRAND L TEN SERIES
ENGINE . . . . KUBOTA
CYLINDERS. 4
CID 134.1
PTO HP 37.5
ENGINE HP 45.3
COOLING . . . . LIQUID
FUEL . . . . D
SPEEDS 16/16
TRANSMISSION . . . . GEAR
STEERING. . . . . STANDARD
HITCH . . . . CAT. I
HYDRAULIC . . . . YES
PTO . . . . YES
DRIVE TYPE 4WD
ROPS/CAB . . . . CAB
WEIGHT . . . . 3,520 LBS.
MSRP. $29,450

RETAIL PRICING

YEAR	HIGH	LOW
2001	$17,732	$13,299
2002	$19,376	$14,532
2003	$21,282	$15,961

L4310HST

YEARS MFRD 1999-2003
SERIES. . . . . . GRAND L TEN SERIES
ENGINE . . . . KUBOTA
CYLINDERS. 4
CID 134.1
PTO HP 37.5
ENGINE HP 45.3
COOLING . . . . LIQUID
FUEL . . . . D
SPEEDS . . . . VARIABLE
TRANSMISSION . . . . HYDRO
STEERING. . . . . STANDARD
HITCH . . . . CAT. I
HYDRAULIC . . . . YES
PTO . . . . YES
DRIVE TYPE 4WD
ROPS/CAB . . . . ROPS
WEIGHT . . . . 3,060 LBS.
MSRP. $22,650

RETAIL PRICING

YEAR	HIGH	LOW
1999	$11,203	$8,402
2000	$12,415	$9,311
2001	$13,625	$10,219
2002	$14,903	$11,177
2003	$16,366	$12,274

L4310HSTC

YEARS MFRD 1999-2003
SERIES. . . . . . GRAND L TEN SERIES
ENGINE . . . . KUBOTA
CYLINDERS. 4
CID 134.1
PTO HP 37.5
ENGINE HP 45.3
COOLING . . . . LIQUID
FUEL . . . . D
SPEEDS . . . . VARIABLE
TRANSMISSION . . . . HYDRO
STEERING. . . . . STANDARD
HITCH . . . . CAT. I
HYDRAULIC . . . . YES
PTO . . . . YES
DRIVE TYPE 4WD
ROPS/CAB . . . . CAB
WEIGHT . . . . 3,520 LBS.
MSRP. $29,050

RETAIL PRICING

YEAR	HIGH	LOW
1999	$14,382	$10,786
2000	$15,936	$11,952
2001	$17,491	$13,119
2002	$19,114	$14,335
2003	$20,993	$15,745

L4330DT

YEARS MFRD 2003-2006
SERIES. . . . . . . GRAND L30 SERIES
ENGINE . . . . KUBOTA
CYLINDERS. 4
CID 134.1
PTO HP 36
ENGINE HP 43.2
COOLING . . . . LIQUID
FUEL . . . . D
SPEEDS 8/8
TRANSMISSION . . . SHUTTLE SHIFT
STEERING. . . . . STANDARD
HITCH . . . . CAT. I
HYDRAULIC . . . . YES
PTO . . . . YES
DRIVE TYPE 4WD
ROPS/CAB . . . . ROPS
WEIGHT . . . . 3,440 LBS.
MSRP. $22,000

OPTIONS

CAB W/A/H
HYDRO
LDR

RETAIL PRICING

YEAR	HIGH	LOW
2003	$13,918	$10,439
2004	$14,675	$11,007
2005	$15,553	$11,665
2006	$16,475	$12,356

AVG. AUCTION PRICING

LOW	HIGH	AVG
$6,649	$23,936	$15,831

L4330GST

YEARS MFRD 2003-2008
SERIES. . . . . . . GRAND L30 SERIES
ENGINE . . . . KUBOTA
CYLINDERS. 4
CID 134.4
PTO HP 36
ENGINE HP 43.2
COOLING . . . . LIQUID
FUEL . . . . D
SPEEDS 12/8
TRANSMISSION . . . SHUTTLE SHIFT
STEERING. . . . . STANDARD
HITCH . . . . CAT. I
HYDRAULIC . . . . YES
PTO . . . . YES
DRIVE TYPE 4WD
ROPS/CAB . . . . ROPS
WEIGHT . . . . 3,470 LBS.
MSRP. $19,175

RETAIL PRICING

YEAR	HIGH	LOW
2003	$11,466	$8,599
2004	$11,840	$8,880
2005	$12,210	$9,157
2006	$12,779	$9,584
2007	$13,337	$10,003
2008	$14,091	$10,569

L4330HST

YEARS MFRD 2003-2008
SERIES. . . . . . . GRAND L30 SERIES
ENGINE . . . . KUBOTA
CYLINDERS. 4
CID 134.1
PTO HP 34.5
ENGINE HP 43.2
COOLING . . . . LIQUID
FUEL . . . . D
SPEEDS . . . . VARIABLE
TRANSMISSION . . . . HYDRO
STEERING. . . . . STANDARD
HITCH . . . . CAT. I
HYDRAULIC . . . . YES
PTO . . . . YES
DRIVE TYPE 4WD
ROPS/CAB . . . . ROPS
WEIGHT . . . . 3,515 LBS.
MSRP. $19,625

RETAIL PRICING

YEAR	HIGH	LOW
2003	$11,731	$8,798
2004	$12,113	$9,085
2005	$12,505	$9,379
2006	$13,081	$9,811
2007	$13,653	$10,239
2008	$14,425	$10,819

L4330HSTC

YEARS MFRD 2003-2008
SERIES. . . . . . . GRAND L30 SERIES
ENGINE . . . . KUBOTA
CYLINDERS. 4
CID 134.1
PTO HP 34.5
ENGINE HP 43.2
COOLING . . . . LIQUID
FUEL . . . . D
SPEEDS . . . . VARIABLE
TRANSMISSION . . . . HYDRO
STEERING. . . . . STANDARD
HITCH . . . . CAT. I
HYDRAULIC . . . . YES
PTO . . . . YES
DRIVE TYPE 4WD
ROPS/CAB . . . . CAB
WEIGHT . . . . 3,860 LBS.
MSRP. $24,125

RETAIL PRICING

YEAR	HIGH	LOW
2003	$14,425	$10,819
2004	$14,895	$11,171
2005	$15,365	$11,523
2006	$16,080	$12,060
2007	$16,787	$12,590
2008	$17,727	$13,295

L4350

YEARS MFRD 1990-1997
ENGINE . . . . KUBOTA V2203-DI
CID 134.1
PTO HP 38
ENGINE HP 47.5
FUEL . . . . D
SPEEDS 8/8
TRANSMISSION . . . SHUTTLE SHIFT
STEERING. . . . . STANDARD
PTO . . . . YES
DRIVE TYPE 4WD
ROPS/CAB . . . . ROPS
WEIGHT . . . . 4,190 LBS.
MSRP. $24,580

OPTIONS

2 HYD
LDR

SERIAL NUMBERS

YEAR	BEGINNING NO.
1990	60005

RETAIL PRICING

YEAR	HIGH	LOW
1990	$7,248	$5,436
1991	$7,784	$5,838
1992	$8,335	$6,251
1993	$8,913	$6,684
1994	$9,509	$7,132
1995	$10,130	$7,598
1996	$10,775	$8,081
1997	$11,438	$8,579

L4350HDT

YEARS MFRD 1990-1998
SERIES. . . . . L3 SERIES
ENGINE . . . . KUBOTA
CYLINDERS. 4
CID 134.1
PTO HP 38
ENGINE HP 47.5
COOLING . . . . LIQUID
FUEL . . . . D
SPEEDS 8/8
TRANSMISSION . . . . GEAR
STEERING. . . . . STANDARD
HITCH . . . . CAT. I
HYDRAULIC . . . . YES
PTO . . . . YES
DRIVE TYPE 4WD
ROPS/CAB . . . . ROPS
WEIGHT . . . . 3,860 LBS.
MSRP. $25,780

SERIAL NUMBERS

YEAR	BEGINNING NO.
1990	60005

RETAIL PRICING

YEAR	HIGH	LOW
1990	$6,878	$5,159
1991	$7,003	$5,252
1992	$7,525	$5,644

1993	$7,929	$5,947
1994	$8,823	$6,617
1995	$9,055	$6,791
1996	$9,298	$6,973
1997	$10,040	$7,530
1998	$11,451	$8,588

L4350HDT W

- YEARS MFRD 1990-1998
- SERIES L3 SERIES
- ENGINE KUBOTA
- CYLINDERS 4
- CID 134.1
- PTO HP 38
- ENGINE HP 47.5
- COOLING LIQUID
- FUEL D
- SPEEDS 8/8
- TRANSMISSION GEAR
- STEERING STANDARD
- HITCH CAT. I
- HYDRAULIC YES
- PTO YES
- DRIVE TYPE 4WD
- ROPS/CAB ROPS
- WEIGHT 3,860 LBS.
- MSRP $26,480

SERIAL NUMBERS

YEAR	BEGINNING NO.
1990	60005
1992	60494

RETAIL PRICING

YEAR	HIGH	LOW
1990	$7,097	$5,323
1991	$7,223	$5,418
1992	$7,770	$5,828
1993	$8,320	$6,240
1994	$9,075	$6,806
1995	$9,315	$6,986
1996	$9,563	$7,172
1997	$10,309	$7,732
1998	$11,761	$8,820

L4350MDT

- YEARS MFRD 1990-1998
- SERIES L3 SERIES
- ENGINE KUBOTA
- CYLINDERS 4
- CID 134.1
- PTO HP 38
- ENGINE HP 47.5
- COOLING LIQUID
- FUEL D
- SPEEDS 8/8
- TRANSMISSION GEAR
- STEERING STANDARD
- HITCH CAT. I
- HYDRAULIC YES
- PTO YES
- DRIVE TYPE 4WD
- ROPS/CAB ROPS
- WEIGHT 3,860 LBS.
- MSRP $24,580

SERIAL NUMBERS

YEAR	BEGINNING NO.
1990	60005

RETAIL PRICING

YEAR	HIGH	LOW
1990	$6,563	$4,922
1991	$6,684	$5,013
1992	$7,181	$5,386
1993	$7,621	$5,716
1994	$8,425	$6,319
1995	$8,649	$6,487
1996	$8,881	$6,660
1997	$9,570	$7,177
1998	$10,918	$8,189

L4400

- YEARS MFRD 2005-2011
- ENGINE KUBOTA
- CYLINDERS 4
- CID 134.1
- PTO HP 37.5
- ENGINE HP 45.3
- COOLING LIQUID
- FUEL D
- SPEEDS 8/4
- TRANSMISSION SHUTTLE SHIFT
- STEERING STANDARD
- HITCH CAT. II
- HYDRAULIC YES
- PTO YES
- DRIVE TYPE 4WD
- ROPS/CAB ROPS
- WEIGHT 3,153 LBS.
- MSRP $19,980

OPTIONS

- 2 HYD
- 2WD
- HYDRO
- LDR

RETAIL PRICING

YEAR	HIGH	LOW
2005	$10,699	$8,024
2006	$11,503	$8,627
2007	$12,218	$9,163
2008	$13,127	$9,846
2009	$13,977	$10,483
2010	$14,965	$11,224
2011	$16,568	$12,426

AVG. AUCTION PRICING

LOW	HIGH	AVG
$8,034	$18,025	$13,570

L4600DT

- YEARS MFRD 2012-2013
- ENGINE KUBOTA
- CYLINDERS 4
- CID 134.1
- PTO HP 36.8
- ENGINE HP 43.8
- COOLING AIR
- FUEL D
- SPEEDS VARIABLE
- TRANSMISSION HYDRO
- STEERING STANDARD
- DRIVE TYPE 4WD
- ROPS/CAB ROPS
- MSRP $23,430

OPTIONS

- 2 HYD
- 2WD
- 8/8 GEAR
- BACKHOE
- LDR

RETAIL PRICING

YEAR	HIGH	LOW
2012	$21,641	$16,231
2013	$23,028	$17,271

L4600F

- YEARS MFRD 2013-2014
- ENGINE KUBOTA
- CYLINDERS 4
- CID 134
- PTO HP 38.3
- COOLING LIQUID
- FUEL D
- SPEEDS 8/8
- TRANSMISSION GEAR
- STEERING STANDARD
- DRIVE TYPE 2WD
- ROPS/CAB ROPS
- WEIGHT 3,109 LBS.
- MSRP $16,328

OPTIONS

- LDR

RETAIL PRICING

YEAR	HIGH	LOW
2013	$11,045	$8,284
2014	$12,836	$9,627

L4600HST

- YEARS MFRD 2013-2014
- ENGINE KUBOTA
- CYLINDERS 4
- CID 134
- PTO HP 36.8
- FUEL D
- SPEEDS VARIABLE
- TRANSMISSION HYDRO
- STEERING STANDARD
- DRIVE TYPE 4WD
- ROPS/CAB ROPS
- WEIGHT 3,197 LBS.
- MSRP $24,514

OPTIONS

- LDR

RETAIL PRICING

YEAR	HIGH	LOW
2013	$16,517	$12,388
2014	$19,329	$14,497

L4610GST/HST

- YEARS MFRD 2000-2002
- ENGINE KUBOTA E-TVCS
- CYLINDERS 4
- CID 134.1
- PTO HP 39
- ENGINE HP 40.5
- FUEL D
- SPEEDS 8/8
- TRANSMISSION SHUTTLE SHIFT
- STEERING STANDARD
- PTO YES
- DRIVE TYPE 2WD
- ROPS/CAB ROPS
- WEIGHT 3,190 LBS.
- MSRP $24,090

OPTIONS

- 2 HYD
- 3 HYD
- CAB W/A
- LDR

RETAIL PRICING

YEAR	HIGH	LOW
2000	$13,366	$10,025
2001	$14,129	$10,596
2002	$14,927	$11,195

L4630DT

- YEARS MFRD 2003-2006
- SERIES GRAND L30 SERIES
- ENGINE KUBOTA
- CYLINDERS 4
- CID 134.1
- PTO HP 39.5
- ENGINE HP 47.2
- COOLING LIQUID
- FUEL D
- SPEEDS 8/8
- TRANSMISSION SHUTTLE SHIFT
- STEERING STANDARD
- HITCH CAT. I
- HYDRAULIC YES
- PTO YES
- DRIVE TYPE 4WD
- ROPS/CAB ROPS
- WEIGHT 3,440 LBS.
- MSRP $22,544

OPTIONS

- 2 HYD
- CAB W/A
- GST
- HYDRO
- LDR

RETAIL PRICING

YEAR	HIGH	LOW
2003	$15,123	$11,343
2004	$15,749	$11,812
2005	$16,823	$12,617
2006	$17,720	$13,290

L4630GST

- YEARS MFRD 2003-2008
- SERIES GRAND L30 SERIES
- ENGINE KUBOTA
- CYLINDERS 4
- CID 134.1
- PTO HP 38
- ENGINE HP 47.2
- COOLING LIQUID
- FUEL D
- SPEEDS 12/8
- TRANSMISSION SHUTTLE SHIFT
- STEERING STANDARD
- HITCH CAT. I
- HYDRAULIC YES
- PTO YES

DRIVE TYPE 4WD
ROPS/CAB .... ROPS
WEIGHT .... 3,515 LBS.
MSRP................ $20,230

OPTIONS

CAB

RETAIL PRICING

YEAR	HIGH	LOW
2003	$15,460	$11,595
2004	$16,842	$12,631
2005	$17,237	$12,928
2008	$19,168	$14,376

L4630HST

YEARS MFRD 2003-2008
SERIES....... GRAND L30 SERIES
ENGINE .... KUBOTA
CYLINDERS.................. 4
CID 134.1
PTO HP 38
ENGINE HP 47.2
COOLING .... LIQUID
FUEL .... D
SPEEDS .... VARIABLE
TRANSMISSION .... HYDRO
STEERING............ STANDARD
HITCH .... CAT. I
HYDRAULIC .... YES
PTO .... YES
DRIVE TYPE 4WD
ROPS/CAB .... ROPS
WEIGHT .... 3,515 LBS.
MSRP................ $20,570

RETAIL PRICING

YEAR	HIGH	LOW
2003	$12,548	$9,411
2004	$12,958	$9,719
2005	$13,365	$10,024
2006	$13,769	$10,327
2007	$14,378	$10,783
2008	$14,979	$11,234

L4701

YEARS MFRD 2014-2020
ENGINE .... KUBOTA
CYLINDERS.................. 4
CID 148.5
PTO HP 37.8
ENGINE HP 44.8
COOLING .... LIQUID
FUEL .... D
SPEEDS .... VARIABLE
TRANSMISSION .... HYDRO
STEERING............ STANDARD
HITCH .... CAT. I
DRIVE TYPE 4WD
ROPS/CAB .... ROPS
WEIGHT .... 3,307 LBS.
MSRP................ $26,922

OPTIONS

2WD/GEAR.............. $-7,228
BACKHOE.............. $9,125
LDR PKG $5,117

RETAIL PRICING

YEAR	HIGH	LOW
2014	$22,687	$17,016
2015	$24,022	$18,016
2016	$25,245	$18,933
2017	$25,957	$19,468
2018	$26,438	$19,829
2019	$27,032	$20,275
2020	$27,688	$20,866

AVG. AUCTION PRICING

LOW	HIGH	AVG
$14,935	$19,313	$17,994

L4740

YEARS MFRD 2007-2012
ENGINE .... KUBOTA
CYLINDERS.................. 4
CID 148.5
PTO HP 41.5
ENGINE HP 49
COOLING .... LIQUID
FUEL .... D
SPEEDS .... VARIABLE
TRANSMISSION .... HYDRO
STEERING............ STANDARD
HITCH .... CAT. I
HYDRAULIC .... YES
PTO .... YES
DRIVE TYPE 4WD
ROPS/CAB .... ROPS
WEIGHT .... 3,671 LBS.
MSRP................ $29,188

OPTIONS

2 HYD
CAB W/A
LDR

RETAIL PRICING

YEAR	HIGH	LOW
2007	$19,496	$14,622
2008	$20,578	$15,434
2009	$21,664	$16,248
2010	$23,015	$17,262
2011	$25,154	$18,865
2012	$26,645	$19,984

AVG. AUCTION PRICING

LOW	HIGH	AVG
$12,360	$19,570	$16,480

L4760GST

YEARS MFRD 2013-2020
ENGINE .... KUBOTA
CYLINDERS.................. 4
CID 148.5
PTO HP 41
ENGINE HP 47
COOLING .... LIQUID
FUEL .... D
SPEEDS 12/8
TRANSMISSION .... GEAR
STEERING............ STANDARD
HITCH .... CAT. I
DRIVE TYPE 4WD
ROPS/CAB .... ROPS
WEIGHT .... 3,836 LBS.
MSRP................ $33,105

OPTIONS

LDR PKG $5,071

L4760HST

YEARS MFRD 2013-2020
ENGINE .... KUBOTA
CYLINDERS.................. 4
CID 148.5
PTO HP 39.5
ENGINE HP 47
COOLING .... LIQUID
FUEL .... D
SPEEDS .... VARIABLE
TRANSMISSION .... HYDRO
STEERING............ STANDARD
HITCH .... CAT. I
DRIVE TYPE 4WD
ROPS/CAB .... ROPS
WEIGHT .... 3,847 LBS.
MSRP................ $33,475

OPTIONS

CAB W/A $8,310
LDR PKG $5,071

RETAIL PRICING

YEAR	HIGH	LOW
2013	$29,827	$22,445
2014	$31,653	$23,814
2015	$32,822	$24,692
2016	$33,774	$25,405
2017	$34,286	$25,790
2018	$34,807	$26,180
2019	$35,170	$26,452
2020	$35,563	$26,985

L4850

YEARS MFRD 1990-1997
ENGINE .... KUBOTA F2503-DI
CID 152.5
PTO HP 43
ENGINE HP 53
FUEL .... D
SPEEDS 8/8
TRANSMISSION .... HYDRO
STEERING............ STANDARD
PTO .... YES
DRIVE TYPE 4WD
ROPS/CAB .... ROPS
WEIGHT .... 4,380 LBS.
MSRP................ $27,980

OPTIONS

2 HYD
LDR
MUDDER

SERIAL NUMBERS

YEAR	BEGINNING NO.
1990	60001
1991	60279

RETAIL PRICING

YEAR	HIGH	LOW
1990	$7,470	$5,602
1991	$8,008	$6,006
1992	$8,576	$6,432
1993	$9,154	$6,865
1994	$9,760	$7,320
1995	$10,387	$7,790
1996	$11,032	$8,274
1997	$11,706	$8,779

L4850HDT W

YEARS MFRD 1990-1998
SERIES.............. L3 SERIES
ENGINE .... KUBOTA
CYLINDERS.................. 4
CID 152.5
PTO HP 43
ENGINE HP 53
COOLING .... LIQUID
FUEL .... D
SPEEDS 8/8
TRANSMISSION .... GEAR
STEERING............ STANDARD
HITCH .... CAT. I
HYDRAULIC .... YES
PTO .... YES
DRIVE TYPE 4WD
ROPS/CAB .... ROPS
WEIGHT .... 4,080 LBS.
MSRP................ $23,800

SERIAL NUMBERS

YEAR	BEGINNING NO.
1990	60001
1991	60279

RETAIL PRICING

YEAR	HIGH	LOW
1990	$7,475	$5,606
1991	$7,611	$5,708

L5030GST

YEARS MFRD 2003-2006
SERIES....... GRAND L30 SERIES
ENGINE .... KUBOTA E-TVCS
CYLINDERS.................. 4
CID 148.6
PTO HP 44
ENGINE HP 52.2
COOLING .... LIQUID
FUEL .... D
SPEEDS 12/8
TRANSMISSION ... SHUTTLE SHIFT
STEERING............ STANDARD
HITCH .... CAT. I
HYDRAULIC .... YES
PTO .... YES
DRIVE TYPE 4WD
ROPS/CAB .... ROPS
WEIGHT .... 3,705 LBS.
MSRP................ $25,344

OPTIONS

2 HYD
HYDRO

RETAIL PRICING

YEAR	HIGH	LOW
2003	$15,371	$11,528
2004	$15,966	$11,975
2005	$16,902	$12,677
2006	$18,370	$13,778

See Kubota Model Suffix Identification on page 415

L5030HST

YEARS MFRD 2003-2008
SERIES GRAND L30 SERIES
ENGINE KUBOTA
CYLINDERS 4
CID 148.6
PTO HP 42.5
ENGINE HP 52.2
COOLING LIQUID
FUEL D
SPEEDS VARIABLE
TRANSMISSION HYDRO
STEERING STANDARD
HITCH CAT. I
HYDRAULIC YES
PTO YES
DRIVE TYPE 4WD
ROPS/CAB ROPS
WEIGHT 3,745 LBS.
MSRP $22,150

OPTIONS

2 HYD
CAB W/A
HYDRO
LDR

RETAIL PRICING

YEAR	HIGH	LOW
2003	$13,936	$10,452
2004	$14,400	$10,800
2005	$14,854	$11,140
2006	$15,534	$11,651
2007	$16,226	$12,169
2008	$17,132	$12,849

AVG. AUCTION PRICING

LOW	HIGH	AVG
$8,755	$17,510	$13,630

L5040

YEARS MFRD 2007-2012
ENGINE KUBOTA
CYLINDERS 4
CID 148.5
PTO HP 44
ENGINE HP 52
FUEL D
SPEEDS 12/8
TRANSMISSION SHUTTLE SHIFT
STEERING STANDARD
HITCH CAT. I
HYDRAULIC YES
PTO YES
DRIVE TYPE 4WD
ROPS/CAB ROPS
WEIGHT 3,902 LBS.
MSRP $30,357

OPTIONS

2 HYD
LDR

RETAIL PRICING

YEAR	HIGH	LOW
2007	$20,332	$15,249
2008	$21,438	$16,079
2009	$22,628	$16,971
2010	$23,919	$17,939
2011	$26,389	$19,791
2012	$27,905	$20,929

L5060GST

YEARS MFRD 2013-2020
ENGINE KUBOTA
CYLINDERS 4
CID 148
PTO HP 44
ENGINE HP 50
COOLING LIQUID
FUEL D
SPEEDS 12/8
TRANSMISSION GEAR
STEERING STANDARD
HITCH CAT. I
DRIVE TYPE 2WD
ROPS/CAB ROPS
WEIGHT 3,579 LBS.
MSRP $35,332

OPTIONS

BACKHOE $9,295
LDR PKG $5,071

RETAIL PRICING

YEAR	HIGH	LOW
2013	$25,989	$19,491
2014	$27,057	$20,292
2015	$28,480	$21,360
2016	$30,006	$22,503
2017	$31,995	$23,996
2018	$33,713	$25,285
2019	$35,164	$26,447
2020	$36,042	$27,364

L5240

YEARS MFRD 2007-2012
ENGINE E-TVCS INDIRECT INJ
CYLINDERS 4
CID 148.5
PTO HP 45
ENGINE HP 54
COOLING AIR
FUEL D
SPEEDS VARIABLE
TRANSMISSION HYDRO
STEERING STANDARD
HITCH CAT. I
HYDRAULIC YES
PTO YES
DRIVE TYPE 4WD
ROPS/CAB ROPS
WEIGHT 3,902 LBS.
MSRP $31,274

OPTIONS

2 HYD
CAB W/A
LDR

RETAIL PRICING

YEAR	HIGH	LOW
2007	$21,522	$16,141
2008	$22,978	$17,234
2009	$24,109	$18,082
2010	$25,577	$19,183
2011	$27,660	$20,745
2012	$29,202	$21,901

L5450DT

YEARS MFRD 1991-1997
ENGINE KUBOTA
CYLINDERS 5
CID 167.6
PTO HP 49
ENGINE HP 59.5
COOLING LIQUID
FUEL D
SPEEDS 8/8
TRANSMISSION SHUTTLE SHIFT
STEERING STANDARD
DRIVE TYPE 4WD
ROPS/CAB ROPS
WEIGHT 3,980 LBS.

L5450HDT W

YEARS MFRD 1990-1998
SERIES L3 SERIES
ENGINE KUBOTA
CYLINDERS 5
CID 167.6
PTO HP 49
ENGINE HP 59.5
COOLING LIQUID
FUEL D
SPEEDS 8/8
TRANSMISSION GEAR
STEERING STANDARD
HITCH CAT. I
HYDRAULIC YES
PTO YES
DRIVE TYPE 4WD
ROPS/CAB ROPS
WEIGHT 4,410 LBS.
MSRP $25,850

SERIAL NUMBERS

YEAR	BEGINNING NO.
1990	60348
1991	60546
1992	60595
1993	60851
1994	61071

RETAIL PRICING

YEAR	HIGH	LOW
1990	$7,817	$5,863
1991	$7,960	$5,970

L5460HST

YEARS MFRD 2013-2019
ENGINE KUBOTA
CYLINDERS 4
CID 148
PTO HP 46.5
ENGINE HP 54
COOLING LIQUID
FUEL D
SPEEDS VARIABLE
TRANSMISSION HYDRO
STEERING STANDARD
HITCH CAT. I
DRIVE TYPE 4WD
ROPS/CAB ROPS
WEIGHT 3,990 LBS.
MSRP $35,457

OPTIONS

BACKHOE
CAB W/A
LDR PKG

RETAIL PRICING

YEAR	HIGH	LOW
2013	$27,471	$20,603
2014	$28,839	$21,629
2015	$30,494	$22,871
2016	$32,167	$24,125
2017	$33,775	$25,331
2018	$35,626	$26,719
2019	$36,826	$27,619

L5740

YEARS MFRD 2007-2012
ENGINE E-TVCS INDIRECT INJ
CYLINDERS 4
PTO HP 50
ENGINE HP 57
COOLING LIQUID
FUEL D
SPEEDS VARIABLE
TRANSMISSION HYDRO
STEERING STANDARD
HITCH CAT. I
HYDRAULIC YES
PTO YES
DRIVE TYPE 4WD
ROPS/CAB ROPS
WEIGHT 3,930 LBS.
MSRP $32,520

OPTIONS

2 HYD
CAB W/A
LDR

RETAIL PRICING

YEAR	HIGH	LOW
2007	$20,839	$15,629
2008	$22,018	$16,514
2009	$23,169	$17,377
2010	$24,591	$18,443
2011	$26,446	$19,835
2012	$27,462	$20,596

AVG. AUCTION PRICING

LOW	HIGH	AVG
$15,708	$27,089	$22,163

LX2610HSD

YEARS MFRD 2020-2020
ENGINE KUBOTA D1305
CYLINDERS 3
CID 77
PTO HP 19.5
ENGINE HP 24.8
COOLING LIQUID
FUEL D
SPEEDS VARIABLE
TRANSMISSION HYDRO
STEERING STANDARD
DRIVE TYPE 4WD
ROPS/CAB ROPS
WEIGHT 1,786 LBS.
MSRP $17,175

OPTIONS

CAB $7,648

KUBOTA

See Kubota Model Suffix Identification on page 415

LX2610SU

YEARS MFRD	2020-2020
ENGINE	KUBOTA D1305
CYLINDERS	3
CID	77
PTO HP	19.5
ENGINE HP	24.8
COOLING	LIQUID
FUEL	D
SPEEDS	VARIABLE
TRANSMISSION	HYDRO
STEERING	STANDARD
PTO	YES
DRIVE TYPE	4WD
ROPS/CAB	ROPS
WEIGHT	1,786 LBS.
MSRP	$16,183

LX3310HSD

YEARS MFRD	2020-2020
ENGINE	KUBOTA V1505
CYLINDERS	4
CID	91.5
PTO HP	27
ENGINE HP	30.8
COOLING	LIQUID
FUEL	D
SPEEDS	VARIABLE
TRANSMISSION	HYDRO
STEERING	STANDARD
DRIVE TYPE	4WD
ROPS/CAB	ROPS
WEIGHT	1,918 LBS.
MSRP	$21,845

OPTIONS

CAB	$7,043

M4N-071HDC12

YEARS MFRD	2017-2017
SERIES	M NARROW SERIES
ENGINE	V3800-TE4
CYLINDERS	4
PTO HP	61
ENGINE HP	70.4
FUEL	D
SPEEDS	12/12
TRANSMISSION	SHUTTLE SHIFT
STEERING	STANDARD
HITCH	CAT. II
DRIVE TYPE	4WD
ROPS/CAB	CAB
WEIGHT	5,291 LBS.

M5L-111-SN

YEARS MFRD	2017-2017
SERIES	M5 SERIES
ENGINE	V3800-TIEF4
CYLINDERS	4
PTO HP	89
ENGINE HP	100
COOLING	LIQUID
FUEL	D
SPEEDS	12/12
TRANSMISSION	SYNCHRO SHUTTLE
STEERING	STANDARD
HITCH	CAT. II
DRIVE TYPE	4WD
ROPS/CAB	ROPS
WEIGHT	5,904 LBS.

M5N-091HDC12

YEARS MFRD	2017-2017
SERIES	M NARROW SERIES
ENGINE	V3800-TIEF4
CYLINDERS	4
PTO HP	78
ENGINE HP	87.5
FUEL	D
SPEEDS	12/12
TRANSMISSION	SYNCHRO SHUTTLE
STEERING	STANDARD
HITCH	CAT. II
WEIGHT	5,622 LBS.

M5N-111HDC12

YEARS MFRD	2017-2017
SERIES	M NARROW SERIES
ENGINE	V3800-TIEF4
CYLINDERS	4
PTO HP	91
ENGINE HP	100.7
COOLING	LIQUID
FUEL	D
SPEEDS	12/12
TRANSMISSION	SYNCHRO SHUTTLE
STEERING	STANDARD
HITCH	CAT. II
DRIVE TYPE	4WD
ROPS/CAB	CAB
WEIGHT	5,622 LBS.

M6S-111SDSC

YEARS MFRD	2017-2017
SERIES	M6 SERIES
ENGINE	V-3800-CR-TIEF4
CYLINDERS	4
PTO HP	95
ENGINE HP	105
COOLING	LIQUID
FUEL	D
SPEEDS	32/32
TRANSMISSION	SYNCHRO SHUTTLE
STEERING	STANDARD
HITCH	CAT. II
DRIVE TYPE	4WD
ROPS/CAB	CAB
WEIGHT	8,973 LBS.

M6S-111SHC

YEARS MFRD	2017-2017
SERIES	M6 SERIES
ENGINE	V-3800-CR-TIEF4
CYLINDERS	4
PTO HP	95
ENGINE HP	105
COOLING	LIQUID
FUEL	D
SPEEDS	16/16
TRANSMISSION	SYNCHRO SHUTTLE
STEERING	STANDARD
HITCH	CAT. II
DRIVE TYPE	2WD
ROPS/CAB	CAB
WEIGHT	7,341 LBS.

M6S-111SHDC

YEARS MFRD	2017-2017
SERIES	M6 SERIES
ENGINE	V-3800-CR-TIEF4
CYLINDERS	4
PTO HP	95
ENGINE HP	105
COOLING	LIQUID
FUEL	D
SPEEDS	16/16
STEERING	STANDARD
HITCH	CAT. II
DRIVE TYPE	4WD
ROPS/CAB	CAB
WEIGHT	8,973 LBS.

M59TLB

YEARS MFRD	2008-2013
ENGINE	KUBOTA
CYLINDERS	4
CID	148
PTO HP	50
COOLING	LIQUID
FUEL	D
SPEEDS	VARIABLE
TRANSMISSION	HYDRO
STEERING	STANDARD
DRIVE TYPE	4WD
ROPS/CAB	ROPS
WEIGHT	5,790 LBS.
MSRP	$59,879

RETAIL PRICING

YEAR	HIGH	LOW
2008	$39,084	$29,313
2009	$41,296	$30,972
2010	$44,407	$33,306
2011	$47,746	$35,809
2012	$51,164	$38,373
2013	$55,202	$41,401

M4000

YEARS MFRD	1978-1981
ENGINE	KUBOTA
CYLINDERS	6
CID	136
PTO HP	40.5
ENGINE HP	47.5
COOLING	LIQUID
FUEL	D
SPEEDS	16/4
TRANSMISSION	GEAR
STEERING	STANDARD
PTO	YES
DRIVE TYPE	2WD
ROPS/CAB	ROPS
WEIGHT	4,257 LBS.
MSRP	$9,785

SERIAL NUMBERS

RH SIDE OF TRANSMISSION HOUSING

YEAR	BEGINNING NO.
1978	11071
1979	10124
1980	10164
1981	11204

RETAIL PRICING

YEAR	HIGH	LOW
1978	$3,534	$2,650
1979	$3,612	$2,709
1980	$3,661	$2,745
1981	$3,711	$2,783

M4030

YEARS MFRD	1985-1998
ENGINE	KUBOTA
CYLINDERS	6
CID	158.5
PTO HP	44.1
ENGINE HP	51
COOLING	LIQUID
FUEL	D
SPEEDS	8/2
TRANSMISSION	GEAR
STEERING	STANDARD
HITCH	CAT. I
PTO	YES
DRIVE TYPE	4WD
ROPS/CAB	ROPS
WEIGHT	4,562 LBS.
MSRP	$18,100

OPTIONS

2 HYD
4WD
LDR

SERIAL NUMBERS

YEAR	BEGINNING NO.
1985	50001

RETAIL PRICING

YEAR	HIGH	LOW
1986	$2,406	$1,805
1987	$2,786	$2,090
1988	$3,166	$2,375
1989	$3,673	$2,755
1990	$4,053	$3,040
1991	$4,560	$3,420
1992	$5,066	$3,799
1993	$5,572	$4,179
1994	$6,079	$4,559
1995	$6,586	$4,939
1996	$7,093	$5,319
1997	$7,726	$5,795
1998	$8,358	$6,269

M4030SU UTILITY SPECIAL

YEARS MFRD	1986-1994
ENGINE	KUBOTA
CYLINDERS	6
CID	158.5
PTO HP	44.1
ENGINE HP	51
COOLING	LIQUID

FUEL . . . . . . D
SPEEDS 8/2
TRANSMISSION . . . . . . GEAR
STEERING. . . . . . STANDARD
PTO . . . . . . YES
DRIVE TYPE 2WD
ROPS/CAB . . . . . . ROPS
WEIGHT . . . . . . 4,562 LBS.
MSRP. $18,100

RETAIL PRICING

YEAR	HIGH	LOW
1994	$6,518	$4,888

M4050DT

YEARS MFRD 1981-1988
ENGINE . . . . . . KUBOTA
CYLINDERS. 6
CID 158.5
PTO HP 42
ENGINE HP 48
COOLING . . . . . . LIQUID
FUEL . . . . . . D
SPEEDS 8/2
TRANSMISSION . . . . . . GEAR
STEERING. . . . . . STANDARD
PTO . . . . . . YES
DRIVE TYPE 4WD
ROPS/CAB . . . . . . ROPS
WEIGHT . . . . . . 4,600 LBS.
MSRP. $18,890

SERIAL NUMBERS

YEAR	BEGINNING NO.
1981	50002
1982	50104
1983	50297
1984	50500
1985	50648
1986	50798
1987	50948
1988	51088

RETAIL PRICING

YEAR	HIGH	LOW
1988	$5,417	$4,063

M4050F

YEARS MFRD 1981-1988
ENGINE . . . . . . KUBOTA
CYLINDERS. 6
CID 158.5
PTO HP 42
ENGINE HP 48
COOLING . . . . . . LIQUID
FUEL . . . . . . D
SPEEDS 8/2
TRANSMISSION . . . . . . GEAR
STEERING. . . . . . STANDARD
PTO . . . . . . YES
DRIVE TYPE 2WD
ROPS/CAB . . . . . . ROPS
WEIGHT . . . . . . 4,080 LBS.
MSRP. $15,000

SERIAL NUMBERS

YEAR	BEGINNING NO.
1981	10001
1982	10103
1983	10547
1984	10792
1985	11192
1986	11592
1987	11992
1988	12392

RETAIL PRICING

YEAR	HIGH	LOW
1988	$4,301	$3,226

M4700

YEARS MFRD 1995-1999
ENGINE . . . . . . KUBOTA F2803-LA
CYLINDERS. 5
CID 168.6
PTO HP 42
ENGINE HP 47
FUEL . . . . . . D
SPEEDS 8/4
TRANSMISSION . . . . . . GEAR
STEERING. . . . . . STANDARD
PTO . . . . . . YES
DRIVE TYPE 2WD
ROPS/CAB . . . . . . ROPS
WEIGHT . . . . . . 3,748 LBS.
MSRP. $18,790

OPTIONS

2 HYD
4WD
LDR

RETAIL PRICING

YEAR	HIGH	LOW
1995	$5,526	$4,144
1996	$6,102	$4,576
1997	$6,562	$4,922
1998	$7,138	$5,353
1999	$7,598	$5,699

AVG. AUCTION PRICING

LOW	HIGH	AVG
$4,635	$13,648	$8,807

M4800SU

YEARS MFRD 2006-2010
ENGINE . . . . . . KUBOTA
CYLINDERS. 4
CID 148.5
PTO HP 43
ENGINE HP 51
COOLING . . . . . . LIQUID
FUEL . . . . . . D
SPEEDS 8/4
TRANSMISSION . . . . . . GEAR
STEERING. . . . . . STANDARD
HITCH . . . . . . CAT. I
DRIVE TYPE 2WD
ROPS/CAB . . . . . . ROPS
WEIGHT . . . . . . 3,747 LBS.
MSRP. $18,221

OPTIONS

2HYD
CAB
LDR

RETAIL PRICING

YEAR	HIGH	LOW
2006	$12,618	$9,463
2007	$12,980	$9,735
2008	$13,488	$10,116
2009	$14,534	$10,901
2010	$15,126	$11,344

AVG. AUCTION PRICING

LOW	HIGH	AVG
$5,150	$18,283	$12,746

M4900

YEARS MFRD 2001-2008
ENGINE . . . . . . KUBOTA E-TVCS
CYLINDERS. 5
CID 167.6
PTO HP 45
ENGINE HP 49.5
COOLING . . . . . . LIQUID
FUEL . . . . . . D
SPEEDS 8/8
TRANSMISSION . . . . . . POWER SHIFT
STEERING. . . . . . STANDARD
HITCH . . . . . . CAT. I
PTO . . . . . . YES
DRIVE TYPE 2WD
ROPS/CAB . . . . . . ROPS
WEIGHT . . . . . . 3,750 LBS.
MSRP. $19,490

OPTIONS

2 HYD
4WD
CAB
LDR

RETAIL PRICING

YEAR	HIGH	LOW
2001	$11,705	$8,779
2002	$12,110	$9,082
2003	$12,515	$9,386
2004	$12,918	$9,689
2005	$13,322	$9,992
2006	$13,727	$10,295
2007	$14,337	$10,752
2008	$14,938	$11,204

AVG. AUCTION PRICING

LOW	HIGH	AVG
$4,000	$12,500	$7,000

M4900SUD

YEARS MFRD 2006-2008
ENGINE . . . . . . KUBOTA E-TVCS
CYLINDERS. 5
CID 167.6
PTO HP 45
ENGINE HP 54
COOLING . . . . . . LIQUID
SPEEDS 8/4
TRANSMISSION . . . SHUTTLE SHIFT
STEERING. . . . . . STANDARD
HITCH . . . . . . CAT. I
DRIVE TYPE 4WD
ROPS/CAB . . . . . . ROPS
WEIGHT . . . . . . 3,968 LBS.

M5040

YEARS MFRD 2006-2011
ENGINE . . . . . . KUBOTA
CYLINDERS. 4
CID 184
PTO HP 45
ENGINE HP 50
COOLING . . . . . . LIQUID
FUEL . . . . . . D
SPEEDS 12/8
TRANSMISSION . . . SHUTTLE SHIFT
STEERING. . . . . . STANDARD
DRIVE TYPE 4WD
ROPS/CAB . . . . . . ROPS
WEIGHT . . . . . . 4,333 LBS.
MSRP. $25,861

OPTIONS

2 HYD
2WD
CAB
LDR

RETAIL PRICING

YEAR	HIGH	LOW
2006	$16,156	$12,117
2007	$17,345	$13,009
2008	$18,158	$13,618
2009	$19,300	$14,475
2010	$21,044	$15,783
2011	$22,014	$16,511

AVG. AUCTION PRICING

LOW	HIGH	AVG
$6,180	$21,630	$13,830

MX4700

YEARS MFRD 2009-2013
ENGINE . . . . . . KUBOTA
CYLINDERS. 4
CID 148.5
PTO HP 39.5
ENGINE HP 46
COOLING . . . . . . AIR
FUEL . . . . . . D
SPEEDS 8/8
TRANSMISSION . . . SHUTTLE SHIFT
STEERING. . . . . . STANDARD
DRIVE TYPE 2WD
ROPS/CAB . . . . . . ROPS
MSRP. $22,597

OPTIONS

4WD
LDR

RETAIL PRICING

YEAR	HIGH	LOW
2009	$18,052	$13,539
2010	$19,158	$14,369
2011	$20,393	$15,295
2012	$22,168	$16,626
2013	$23,599	$17,700

AVG. AUCTION PRICING

LOW	HIGH	AVG
$9,528	$18,798	$12,703

MX4800

YEARS MFRD 2014-2020
ENGINE . . . . . . KUBOTA
CYLINDERS. 4
CID 148.6
PTO HP 40.5
ENGINE HP 46.9
COOLING . . . . . . LIQUID
FUEL . . . . . . D

SPEEDS 8/8
TRANSMISSION ... SHUTTLE SHIFT
STEERING .... STANDARD
HITCH .... CAT. I
DRIVE TYPE 4WD
ROPS/CAB .... ROPS
WEIGHT .... 3,712 LBS.
MSRP $26,533

OPTIONS

2WD .... $-5,145
BACKHOE $9,255
HYDRO $1,556
LDR PKG $4,930

RETAIL PRICING

YEAR	HIGH	LOW
2014	$25,196	$18,971
2015	$25,818	$19,438
2016	$26,454	$19,916
2017	$27,146	$20,435
2018	$27,836	$20,952
2019	$28,051	$21,188
2020	$28,531	$21,766

AVG. AUCTION PRICING

LOW	HIGH	AVG
$14,214	$19,879	$16,171

MX5000

YEARS MFRD 2002-2008
ENGINE .... KUBOTA V2403
CYLINDERS 4
CID 148.5
PTO HP 44
ENGINE HP 52.2
COOLING .... LIQUID
SPEEDS 8/4
TRANSMISSION .... GEAR
STEERING .... STANDARD
HITCH .... CAT. I
HYDRAULIC .... YES
PTO .... YES
DRIVE TYPE 4WD
ROPS/CAB .... ROPS
WEIGHT .... 3,285 LBS.

OPTIONS

2HYD
2WD
LDR

RETAIL PRICING

YEAR	HIGH	LOW
2002	$11,525	$8,644
2003	$12,410	$9,308
2004	$12,918	$9,689
2005	$13,931	$10,448
2006	$14,819	$11,114
2007	$15,704	$11,778
2008	$16,591	$12,443

AVG. AUCTION PRICING

LOW	HIGH	AVG
$11,073	$18,952	$13,481

SZ19-36

YEARS MFRD 2019-2020
SERIES .... SZ SERIES
ENGINE .... KAWASAKI FX600V
CYLINDERS 2
CID 36.8
ENGINE HP 19
COOLING .... AIR
FUEL .... G
SPEEDS .... VARIABLE
TRANSMISSION .... HYDRO
STEERING .... ZERO
BLADE CLUTCH .... ELECTRIC
STANDARD DECK .... 36"
WEIGHT .... 831 LBS.
MSRP $7,899

OPTIONS

MULCHER $177

SZ22-48

YEARS MFRD 2019-2020
SERIES .... SZ SERIES
ENGINE .... KAWASAKI FX691V
CYLINDERS 2
CID 44.3
ENGINE HP 22
COOLING .... AIR
FUEL .... G
SPEEDS .... VARIABLE
TRANSMISSION .... HYDRO
STEERING .... ZERO
BLADE CLUTCH .... ELECTRIC
STANDARD DECK .... 48"
WEIGHT .... 965 LBS.
MSRP $8,699

OPTIONS

MULCHER $250

SZ26-52

YEARS MFRD 2019-2020
SERIES .... SZ SERIES
ENGINE .... KAWASAKI FT730V EFI
CYLINDERS 2
CID 44.3
ENGINE HP 26
COOLING .... AIR
FUEL .... G
SPEEDS .... VARIABLE
TRANSMISSION .... HYDRO
STEERING .... ZERO
BLADE CLUTCH .... ELECTRIC
STANDARD DECK .... 52"
WEIGHT .... 997 LBS.
MSRP $9,299

OPTIONS

MULCHER $250

SZ26-61

YEARS MFRD 2020-2020
SERIES .... SZ SERIES
ENGINE .... KAWASAKI FT730V EFI
ENGINE HP 26
FUEL .... G
SPEEDS .... VARIABLE
TRANSMISSION .... HYDRO
STEERING .... ZERO
BLADE CLUTCH .... ELECTRIC
STANDARD DECK .... 61"
WEIGHT .... 1,034 LBS.
MSRP $9,899

OPTIONS

MULCHER $250

T1400H

YEARS MFRD 1987-1995
SERIES .... T SERIES
ENGINE .... KUBOTA
ENGINE HP 13.5
COOLING .... AIR
FUEL .... G
SPEEDS .... VARIABLE
TRANSMISSION .... HYDRO
STEERING .... STANDARD
BLADE CLUTCH .... MANUAL
STANDARD DECK .... 40"
WEIGHT .... 507 LBS.
MSRP $3,870

OPTIONS

2 BAG
42" BLADE
42" SNOW BLOWER

SERIAL NUMBERS

YEAR	BEGINNING NO.
1988	17591
1989	31831
1990	35300
1991	39996
1992	41678
1993	42456

RETAIL PRICING

YEAR	HIGH	LOW
1987	$177	$133
1988	$195	$146
1989	$216	$162
1990	$239	$179
1991	$263	$197
1992	$290	$218
1993	$321	$241
1994	$354	$266
1995	$390	$293

T1460

YEARS MFRD 1994-1998
SERIES .... T SERIES
ENGINE .... KUBOTA
CID 25.8
ENGINE HP 12.5
COOLING .... AIR
FUEL .... G
SPEEDS .... VARIABLE
TRANSMISSION .... HYDRO
STEERING .... STANDARD
BLADE CLUTCH .... MANUAL
STANDARD DECK .... 40"
WEIGHT .... 528 LBS.
MSRP $3,120

OPTIONS

2 BAG
38" SNOW BLOWER
42" BLADE

SERIAL NUMBERS

YEAR	BEGINNING NO.
1995	10005
1996	21805
1997	23103
1998	35067

RETAIL PRICING

YEAR	HIGH	LOW
1994	$329	$246
1995	$363	$272
1996	$400	$300
1997	$443	$332
1998	$490	$368

T1460B

YEARS MFRD 2002-2002
SERIES .... T SERIES
ENGINE .... KUBOTA
CID 25.8
ENGINE HP 12.5
COOLING .... AIR
FUEL .... G
SPEEDS .... VARIABLE
TRANSMISSION .... HYDRO
STEERING .... STANDARD
BLADE CLUTCH .... MANUAL
STANDARD DECK .... 40"
WEIGHT .... 528 LBS.
MSRP $3,160

OPTIONS

2 BAG
38" SNOW BLOWER
42" BLADE

RETAIL PRICING

YEAR	HIGH	LOW
2002	$616	$462

T1560

YEARS MFRD 1994-1998
SERIES .... T SERIES
ENGINE .... KUBOTA
CID 25.8
ENGINE HP 14
COOLING .... AIR
FUEL .... G
SPEEDS .... VARIABLE
TRANSMISSION .... HYDRO
STEERING .... STANDARD
BLADE CLUTCH .... MANUAL
STANDARD DECK .... 40"
WEIGHT .... 528 LBS.
MSRP $3,670

OPTIONS

2 BAG
38" SNOW BLOWER
42" BLADE
44" DECK

SERIAL NUMBERS

YEAR	BEGINNING NO.
1995	10001
1995	10326-40
1995	11729-44
1996	20493-44
1997	23648-40
1997	23656-44
1998	35352-40
1998	35141-44

See Kubota Model Suffix Identification on page 415

RETAIL PRICING

YEAR	HIGH	LOW
1994	$389	$292
1995	$426	$320
1996	$471	$353
1997	$520	$390
1998	$576	$432

T1560B

YEARS MFRD 2002-2002
SERIES T SERIES
ENGINE KUBOTA
CID 25.8
ENGINE HP 14
COOLING AIR
FUEL G
SPEEDS VARIABLE
TRANSMISSION HYDRO
STEERING STANDARD
BLADE CLUTCH MANUAL
STANDARD DECK 40"
WEIGHT 528 LBS.
MSRP $3,720

OPTIONS

2 BAG
38" SNOW BLOWER
42" BLADE
44" DECK

RETAIL PRICING

YEAR	HIGH	LOW
2002	$726	$545

T1570

YEARS MFRD 2002-2003
SERIES T SERIES
ENGINE KOHLER CV15
CYLINDERS 1
CID 26
ENGINE HP 15
COOLING AIR
FUEL G
SPEEDS VARIABLE
TRANSMISSION HYDRO
STEERING STANDARD
BLADE CLUTCH MANUAL
STANDARD DECK 40"
WEIGHT 550 LBS.
MSRP $2,899

OPTIONS

2 BAG
40" SNOW BLOWER
42" BLADE

RETAIL PRICING

YEAR	HIGH	LOW
2002	$543	$407
2003	$604	$453

T1570A

YEARS MFRD 2005-2007
SERIES T SERIES
ENGINE KOHLER
ENGINE HP 15
COOLING AIR
FUEL G
SPEEDS VARIABLE
TRANSMISSION HYDRO
STEERING STANDARD
STANDARD DECK 40"
MSRP $2,862

OPTIONS

2 BAG
40" SNOW BLOWER
44" BLADE

RETAIL PRICING

YEAR	HIGH	LOW
2005	$1,155	$866
2006	$1,283	$963
2007	$1,423	$1,068

T1600H

YEARS MFRD 1988-1997
SERIES T SERIES
ENGINE KUBOTA
ENGINE HP 13.5
COOLING LIQUID
FUEL D
SPEEDS VARIABLE
TRANSMISSION HYDRO
STEERING STANDARD
BLADE CLUTCH MANUAL
STANDARD DECK 44"
WEIGHT 661 LBS.
MSRP $6,230

OPTIONS

2 BAG
42" SNOW BLOWER
48" BLADE

SERIAL NUMBERS

YEAR	BEGINNING NO.
1988	10007
1989	10152
1990	11489
1991	12984
1992	14537
1993	16036
1994	16919

RETAIL PRICING

YEAR	HIGH	LOW
1990	$453	$340
1991	$500	$375
1992	$552	$414
1993	$610	$457
1994	$673	$504
1995	$743	$557
1996	$820	$615
1997	$905	$679

T1670

YEARS MFRD 2002-2003
SERIES T SERIES
ENGINE KOHLER OHV CV15
CYLINDERS 1
CID 26
ENGINE HP 15
COOLING AIR
FUEL G
SPEEDS VARIABLE
TRANSMISSION HYDRO
STEERING STANDARD
BLADE CLUTCH MANUAL
STANDARD DECK 40"
WEIGHT 559 LBS.
MSRP $3,199

OPTIONS

2 BAG
40" SNOW BLOWER
42" BLADE
44" DECK

RETAIL PRICING

YEAR	HIGH	LOW
2002	$694	$521
2003	$766	$575

T1670A

YEARS MFRD 2005-2007
SERIES T SERIES
ENGINE KOHLER
ENGINE HP 15
COOLING AIR
FUEL G
SPEEDS VARIABLE
TRANSMISSION HYDRO
STANDARD DECK 40"
MSRP $3,199

OPTIONS

2 BAG
40" SNOW BLOWER
44" BLADE
44" DECK

RETAIL PRICING

YEAR	HIGH	LOW
2005	$853	$640
2006	$939	$705
2007	$1,036	$777

T1700HX

YEARS MFRD 1991-1997
SERIES T SERIES
ENGINE KUBOTA
ENGINE HP 17
COOLING AIR
FUEL G
SPEEDS VARIABLE
TRANSMISSION HYDRO
STEERING STANDARD
BLADE CLUTCH MANUAL
STANDARD DECK 48"
WEIGHT 792 LBS.
MSRP $5,175

OPTIONS

2 BAG
42" SNOW BLOWER
48" BLADE

SERIAL NUMBERS

YEAR	BEGINNING NO.
1991	10077
1992	11367
1993	11790
1994	50151

RETAIL PRICING

YEAR	HIGH	LOW
1991	$410	$307
1992	$441	$331
1993	$487	$365
1994	$538	$403
1995	$592	$444
1996	$656	$492
1997	$724	$543

T1760

YEARS MFRD 1995-1998
SERIES T SERIES
ENGINE KUBOTA
CID 26.7
ENGINE HP 17
COOLING LIQUID
FUEL G
SPEEDS VARIABLE
TRANSMISSION HYDRO
STEERING STANDARD
BLADE CLUTCH MANUAL
STANDARD DECK 48"
WEIGHT 606 LBS.
MSRP $5,120

OPTIONS

2 BAG
38" SNOW BLOWER
42" BLADE

SERIAL NUMBERS

YEAR	BEGINNING NO.
1995	10006
1996	10108
1997	11727
1998	35407

RETAIL PRICING

YEAR	HIGH	LOW
1995	$575	$431
1996	$634	$476
1997	$699	$525
1998	$771	$579

T1760A

YEARS MFRD 1999-2001
SERIES T SERIES
ENGINE KUBOTA
CID 26.7
ENGINE HP 17
COOLING LIQUID
FUEL G
SPEEDS VARIABLE
TRANSMISSION HYDRO
STEERING STANDARD
BLADE CLUTCH MANUAL
STANDARD DECK 48"
WEIGHT 606 LBS.
MSRP $5,140

OPTIONS

2 BAG
38" SNOW THROWER
42" BLADE

RETAIL PRICING

YEAR	HIGH	LOW
1999	$805	$604
2000	$890	$667
2001	$982	$736

T1760B

YEARS MFRD 2002-2002
SERIES T SERIES
ENGINE KUBOTA
CID 26.7
ENGINE HP 17
COOLING LIQUID
FUEL G

SPEEDS .... VARIABLE
TRANSMISSION .... HYDRO
STEERING............ STANDARD
BLADE CLUTCH .... MANUAL
STANDARD DECK .... 48"
WEIGHT .... 606 LBS.
MSRP................. $5,140

OPTIONS

38" SNOW BLOWER
42" BLADE
BAGGER

RETAIL PRICING

YEAR	HIGH	LOW
2002	$1,060	$795

T1770

YEARS MFRD 2002-2003
SERIES................ T SERIES
ENGINE .... KOHLER GH570V
CYLINDERS.................. 2
CID 30.1
ENGINE HP.................. 17
COOLING .... AIR
FUEL .... G
SPEEDS .... VARIABLE
TRANSMISSION .... HYDRO
STEERING............ STANDARD
BLADE CLUTCH .... MANUAL
STANDARD DECK .... 44"
WEIGHT .... 562 LBS.
MSRP................. $3,999

OPTIONS

2 BAG
40" SNOW BLOWER
42" BLADE

RETAIL PRICING

YEAR	HIGH	LOW
2002	$827	$620
2003	$921	$691

T1770A

YEARS MFRD 2005-2007
SERIES................ T SERIES
ENGINE .... KOHLER
ENGINE HP.................. 17
COOLING .... AIR
FUEL .... G
SPEEDS .... VARIABLE
TRANSMISSION .... HYDRO
STEERING............ STANDARD
STANDARD DECK .... 44"
MSRP................. $3,948

OPTIONS

2 BAG
40" SNOW BLOWER
44" BLADE

RETAIL PRICING

YEAR	HIGH	LOW
2005	$1,063	$797
2006	$1,174	$881
2007	$1,297	$973

T1870

YEARS MFRD 2002-2003
SERIES................ T SERIES
ENGINE .... KOHLER GH630V
CYLINDERS.................. 2
CID 38
ENGINE HP.................. 19
COOLING .... AIR
FUEL .... G
SPEEDS .... VARIABLE
TRANSMISSION .... HYDRO
STEERING............ STANDARD
BLADE CLUTCH .... MANUAL
STANDARD DECK .... 48"
WEIGHT .... 636 LBS.
MSRP................. $4,399

OPTIONS

2 BAG
40" SNOW BLOWER
42" BLADE

RETAIL PRICING

YEAR	HIGH	LOW
2002	$913	$684
2003	$1,004	$753

T1870A

YEARS MFRD 2005-2007
SERIES................ T SERIES
ENGINE .... KOHLER
ENGINE HP.................. 19
COOLING .... AIR
FUEL .... G
SPEEDS .... VARIABLE
TRANSMISSION .... HYDRO
STEERING............ STANDARD
STANDARD DECK .... 48"
MSRP................. $4,343

OPTIONS

2 BAG
40" SNOW BLOWER
44" BLADE

RETAIL PRICING

YEAR	HIGH	LOW
2005	$1,169	$877
2006	$1,292	$969
2007	$1,426	$1,069

T1880

YEARS MFRD 2008-2013
ENGINE .... KOHLER
CYLINDERS.................. 1
CID 32.6
ENGINE HP.................. 18
COOLING .... AIR
FUEL .... G
SPEEDS .... VARIABLE
TRANSMISSION .... HYDRO
STEERING............ STANDARD
STANDARD DECK .... 42"
WEIGHT .... 617 LBS.
MSRP................. $3,598

OPTIONS

2 BAG
46" SNOW BLOWER
48" BLADE

RETAIL PRICING

YEAR	HIGH	LOW
2008	$1,931	$1,448
2009	$2,149	$1,611
2010	$2,380	$1,785
2011	$2,637	$1,978
2012	$2,918	$2,188
2013	$3,233	$2,425

T1880A2

YEARS MFRD 2016-2020
SERIES............ T80 SERIES
ENGINE GH541V
CYLINDERS.................. 1
CID 36.4
ENGINE HP.................. 18
COOLING .... AIR
FUEL .... G
SPEEDS .... VARIABLE
TRANSMISSION .... HYDRO
STEERING............ STANDARD
BLADE CLUTCH .... ELECTRIC
STANDARD DECK .... 42"
WEIGHT .... 639 LBS.
MSRP................. $3,699

OPTIONS

2 BAG $628
48" BLADE $689

T2080

YEARS MFRD 2008-2013
ENGINE .... KOHLER
CYLINDERS.................. 2
ENGINE HP.................. 20
COOLING .... AIR
FUEL .... G
SPEEDS .... VARIABLE
TRANSMISSION .... HYDRO
STEERING............ STANDARD
STANDARD DECK .... 42"
WEIGHT .... 617 LBS.
MSRP................. $4,248

OPTIONS

2 BAG
46" SNOW BLOWER
48" BLADE

RETAIL PRICING

YEAR	HIGH	LOW
2008	$2,305	$1,729
2009	$2,533	$1,900
2010	$2,802	$2,101
2011	$3,111	$2,333
2012	$3,482	$2,612
2013	$3,829	$2,871

T2080A2

YEARS MFRD 2016-2020
SERIES............ T80 SERIES
ENGINE GH737V
CYLINDERS.................. 2
CID 44.2
ENGINE HP.................. 20
COOLING .... AIR
FUEL .... G
SPEEDS .... VARIABLE
TRANSMISSION .... HYDRO
STEERING............ STANDARD
BLADE CLUTCH .... ELECTRIC
STANDARD DECK .... 42"
WEIGHT .... 650 LBS.
MSRP................. $4,399

OPTIONS

2 BAG $628
48" BLADE $689

T2090

YEARS MFRD 2018-2020
SERIES............ T90 SERIES
ENGINE .... B&S
CYLINDERS.................. 2
CID 40
ENGINE HP.................. 20
COOLING .... AIR
FUEL .... G
TRANSMISSION .... HYDRO
STEERING............ STANDARD
STANDARD DECK .... 42"
WEIGHT .... 595 LBS.
MSRP................. $3,889

OPTIONS

46" SNOW BLOWER $1,989
GRASS CATCHER $679

T2290

YEARS MFRD 2018-2020
SERIES............ T90 SERIES
ENGINE .... KAWASAKI
CYLINDERS.................. 2
CID 44.3
ENGINE HP................ 21.5
COOLING .... AIR
FUEL .... G
TRANSMISSION .... HYDRO
STEERING............ STANDARD
STANDARD DECK .... 42"
WEIGHT .... 622 LBS.
MSRP................. $4,489

OPTIONS

46" SNOW BLOWER $1,989
48" DECK................ $680
GRASS CATCHER $679

T2380

YEARS MFRD 2008-2013
ENGINE .... KOHLER
CYLINDERS.................. 2
ENGINE HP.................. 23
COOLING .... AIR
FUEL .... G
SPEEDS .... VARIABLE
TRANSMISSION .... HYDRO
STEERING............ STANDARD
STANDARD DECK .... 48"
WEIGHT .... 628 LBS.
MSRP................. $4,998

OPTIONS

2 BAG
46" SNOW BLOWER
48" BLADE

RETAIL PRICING

YEAR	HIGH	LOW
2008	$2,683	$2,012
2009	$3,017	$2,263
2010	$3,303	$2,477
2011	$3,659	$2,744
2012	$4,074	$3,055
2013	$4,499	$3,374

T2380A2

YEARS MFRD 2016-2020
SERIES . . . . T80 SERIES
ENGINE GH738V
CYLINDERS 2
CID 44.2
ENGINE HP 22
COOLING . . . . AIR
FUEL . . . . G
SPEEDS . . . . VARIABLE
TRANSMISSION . . . . HYDRO
STEERING . . . . STANDARD
BLADE CLUTCH . . . . ELECTRIC
STANDARD DECK . . . . 48"
WEIGHT . . . . 661 LBS.
MSRP $4,999

OPTIONS

2 BAG $628
BLADE $569

TG1860

YEARS MFRD 1997-2001
SERIES . . . . TG SERIES
ENGINE . . . . KUBOTA
CYLINDERS 3
CID 43.9
ENGINE HP 18
COOLING . . . . LIQUID
FUEL . . . . D
SPEEDS . . . . VARIABLE
TRANSMISSION . . . . HYDRO
STEERING . . . . STANDARD
BLADE CLUTCH . . . . MANUAL
PTO . . . . YES
STANDARD DECK . . . . 48"
WEIGHT . . . . 959 LBS.
MSRP $7,399

OPTIONS

3 BAG
46" SNOW BLOWER
48" BLADE
54" DECK

SERIAL NUMBERS

YEAR	BEGINNING NO.
1997	15021-54
1998	15875-54

RETAIL PRICING

YEAR	HIGH	LOW
1997	$1,228	$921
1998	$1,244	$933
1999	$1,368	$1,026
2000	$1,513	$1,135
2001	$1,673	$1,255

TG1860A

YEARS MFRD 2002-2003
SERIES . . . . TG SERIES
ENGINE . . . . KUBOTA
CID 43.9
ENGINE HP 18
COOLING . . . . LIQUID
FUEL . . . . G
SPEEDS . . . . VARIABLE
TRANSMISSION . . . . HYDRO
STEERING . . . . STANDARD
BLADE CLUTCH . . . . MANUAL
PTO . . . . YES
STANDARD DECK . . . . 48"
WEIGHT . . . . 980 LBS.
MSRP $7,399

OPTIONS

3 BAG
46" SNOW BLOWER
48" BLADE
54" DECK

RETAIL PRICING

YEAR	HIGH	LOW
2002	$1,661	$1,246
2003	$1,836	$1,377

TG1860G

YEARS MFRD 1998-2001
SERIES . . . . TG SERIES
ENGINE . . . . KUBOTA OHV
CYLINDERS 2
CID 35.7
ENGINE HP 18
COOLING . . . . LIQUID
FUEL . . . . G
SPEEDS . . . . VARIABLE
TRANSMISSION . . . . HYDRO
STEERING . . . . STANDARD
BLADE CLUTCH . . . . MANUAL
PTO . . . . YES
STANDARD DECK . . . . 48"
WEIGHT . . . . 859 LBS.
MSRP $6,399

OPTIONS

3 BAG
46" SNOW BLOWER
48" BLADE
54" DECK

SERIAL NUMBERS

YEAR	BEGINNING NO.
1998	15040-54

RETAIL PRICING

YEAR	HIGH	LOW
1998	$1,069	$802
1999	$1,185	$888
2000	$1,308	$981
2001	$1,454	$1,091

TG1860GA

YEARS MFRD 2002-2003
SERIES . . . . TG SERIES
ENGINE . . . . KUBOTA
CID 43.9
ENGINE HP 18
COOLING . . . . LIQUID
FUEL . . . . D
SPEEDS . . . . VARIABLE
TRANSMISSION . . . . HYDRO
STEERING . . . . STANDARD
BLADE CLUTCH . . . . MANUAL
STANDARD DECK . . . . 48"
WEIGHT . . . . 880 LBS.
MSRP $6,399

OPTIONS

3 BAG
46" SNOW BLOWER
48" BLADE
54" DECK

RETAIL PRICING

YEAR	HIGH	LOW
2002	$1,437	$1,078
2003	$1,588	$1,191

Z121S

YEARS MFRD 2014-2020
SERIES . . . . . KOMMANDER SERIES
ENGINE . . . . KOHLER
CYLINDERS 2
CID 747CC
ENGINE HP 21
COOLING . . . . AIR
FUEL . . . . G
TRANSMISSION . . . . HYDRO
STEERING . . . . ZERO
STANDARD DECK . . . . 48"
WEIGHT . . . . 749 LBS.
MSRP $5,601

OPTIONS

2 BAG $789

RETAIL PRICING

YEAR	HIGH	LOW
2014	$3,224	$2,493
2015	$3,581	$2,761
2016	$4,001	$3,076
2017	$4,384	$3,363
2018	$4,547	$3,484
2019	$4,729	$3,621
2020	$5,014	$3,842

Z122E

YEARS MFRD 2014-2020
SERIES . . . . . KOMMANDER SERIES
ENGINE . . . . B&S
CYLINDERS 2
CID 724CC
ENGINE HP 22
COOLING . . . . AIR
FUEL . . . . G
TRANSMISSION . . . . HYDRO
STEERING . . . . ZERO
BLADE CLUTCH . . . . ELECTRIC
STANDARD DECK . . . . 48"
WEIGHT . . . . 737 LBS.
MSRP $5,118

OPTIONS

2 BAG $789
SUS SEAT $249

RETAIL PRICING

YEAR	HIGH	LOW
2014	$2,997	$2,285
2015	$3,336	$2,540
2016	$3,675	$2,794
2017	$4,048	$3,074
2018	$4,266	$3,237
2019	$4,552	$3,421
2020	$4,776	$3,645

Z122R

YEARS MFRD 2015-2020
SERIES . . . . . KOMMANDER SERIES
ENGINE . . . . KAWASAKI
CYLINDERS 2
CID 726CC
ENGINE HP 21.5
FUEL . . . . G
TRANSMISSION . . . . HYDRO
STEERING . . . . ZERO
BLADE CLUTCH . . . . ELECTRIC
STANDARD DECK . . . . 42"
WEIGHT . . . . 621 LBS.
MSRP $4,442

OPTIONS

GRASS CATCHER $669
MULCH KIT $149

RETAIL PRICING

YEAR	HIGH	LOW
2015	$2,849	$2,211
2016	$3,136	$2,427
2017	$3,457	$2,668
2018	$3,691	$2,843
2019	$3,924	$3,018
2020	$4,189	$3,207

Z125E

YEARS MFRD 2014-2020
SERIES . . . . . KOMMANDER SERIES
ENGINE . . . . B&S
CYLINDERS 2
CID 724CC
ENGINE HP 25
COOLING . . . . AIR
FUEL . . . . G
TRANSMISSION . . . . HYDRO
STEERING . . . . ZERO
BLADE CLUTCH . . . . ELECTRIC
STANDARD DECK . . . . 54"
WEIGHT . . . . 749 LBS.
MSRP $5,976

OPTIONS

2 BAG $789
SUS SEAT $249

RETAIL PRICING

YEAR	HIGH	LOW
2014	$3,390	$2,580
2015	$3,727	$2,833
2016	$4,119	$3,126
2017	$4,551	$3,451
2018	$4,814	$3,648
2019	$5,092	$3,857
2020	$5,379	$4,110

Z125S

YEARS MFRD 2014-2020
SERIES . . . . . KOMMANDER SERIES
ENGINE . . . . KOHLER
CYLINDERS 2
CID 747CC

 See Kubota Model Suffix Identification on page 415

ENGINE HP . . . 25
COOLING . . . AIR
FUEL . . . G
TRANSMISSION . . . HYDRO
STEERING. . . . ZERO
BLADE CLUTCH . . . ELECTRIC
STANDARD DECK . . . 54"
WEIGHT . . . 771 LBS.
MSRP. . . . $6,459

OPTIONS

2 BAG . . . $789
MULCH KIT. . . . $209

RETAIL PRICING

YEAR	HIGH	LOW
2014	$3,683	$2,800
2015	$4,032	$3,061
2016	$4,479	$3,396
2017	$4,922	$3,729
2018	$5,197	$3,935
2019	$5,491	$4,156
2020	$5,807	$4,434

Z231BR-48

YEARS MFRD . . . 2020-2020
SERIES. . . . Z200 RES SERIES
ENGINE . . . BRIGGS & STRATTON
CID . . . 44.2
ENGINE HP . . . 22
COOLING . . . AIR
FUEL . . . G
SPEEDS . . . VARIABLE
TRANSMISSION . . . HYDRO
STEERING. . . . ZERO
STANDARD DECK . . . 48"
WEIGHT . . . 737 LBS.
MSRP. . . . $5,218

Z231KH-48

YEARS MFRD . . . 2020-2020
SERIES. . . . Z200 RES SERIES
ENGINE . . . KOHLER
CID . . . 45.6
ENGINE HP . . . 21
COOLING . . . AIR
FUEL . . . G
SPEEDS . . . VARIABLE
TRANSMISSION . . . HYDRO
STEERING. . . . ZERO
STANDARD DECK . . . 48"
WEIGHT . . . 749 LBS.
MSRP. . . . $5,701

Z231KW-42

YEARS MFRD . . . 2020-2020
SERIES. . . . Z200 RES SERIES
ENGINE . . . KAWASAKI
CID . . . 44.3
ENGINE HP . . . 21.5
COOLING . . . AIR
FUEL . . . G
SPEEDS . . . VARIABLE
TRANSMISSION . . . HYDRO
STEERING. . . . ZERO
STANDARD DECK . . . 42"
WEIGHT . . . 621 LBS.
MSRP. . . . $4,442

Z251BR-54

YEARS MFRD . . . 2020-2020
SERIES. . . . Z200 RES SERIES
ENGINE . . . BRIGGS & STRATTON
CID . . . 44.2
ENGINE HP . . . 25
COOLING . . . AIR
SPEEDS . . . VARIABLE
TRANSMISSION . . . HYDRO
STEERING. . . . ZERO
STANDARD DECK . . . 54"
WEIGHT . . . 749 LBS.
MSRP. . . . $6,076

Z251KH-54

YEARS MFRD . . . 2020-2020
SERIES. . . . Z200 RES SERIES
ENGINE . . . KOHLER
CID . . . 45.6
ENGINE HP . . . 25
COOLING . . . AIR
FUEL . . . G
SPEEDS . . . VARIABLE
TRANSMISSION . . . HYDRO
STEERING. . . . ZERO
STANDARD DECK . . . 54"
WEIGHT . . . 771 LBS.
MSRP. . . . $6,559

Z411KW

YEARS MFRD . . . 2017-2020
SERIES. . . KOMMANDERPRO SERIES
ENGINE . . . GH7302V
CYLINDERS. . . . 2
CID . . . 44.3
ENGINE HP . . . 22
COOLING . . . AIR
FUEL . . . G
SPEEDS . . . VARIABLE
TRANSMISSION . . . DUAL HYDRO
STEERING. . . . ZERO
BLADE CLUTCH . . . ELECTRIC
STANDARD DECK . . . 48"
MSRP. . . . $6,691

OPTIONS

CATCHER/BAGGER . . . $1,329
SUS SEAT. . . . $309

RETAIL PRICING

YEAR	HIGH	LOW
2017	$5,592	$4,194
2018	$5,908	$4,431
2019	$6,234	$4,675
2020	$6,526	$4,915

Z421KW

YEARS MFRD . . . 2017-2020
SERIES. . . KOMMANDERPRO SERIES
ENGINE . . . GH7301V
CYLINDERS. . . . 2
CID . . . 44.3
ENGINE HP . . . 24
COOLING . . . AIR
FUEL . . . G
SPEEDS . . . VARIABLE
TRANSMISSION . . . DUAL HYDRO
STEERING. . . . ZERO
BLADE CLUTCH . . . ELECTRIC
STANDARD DECK . . . 54"
WEIGHT . . . 870 LBS.
MSRP. . . . $7,227

OPTIONS

CATCHER/BAGGER . . . $1,329
SUS SEAT. . . . $309

RETAIL PRICING

YEAR	HIGH	LOW
2017	$6,040	$4,529
2018	$6,385	$4,788
2019	$6,745	$5,058
2020	$7,038	$5,363

Z421KWT

YEARS MFRD . . . 2017-2020
SERIES. . . KOMMANDERPRO SERIES
ENGINE . . . KAWASAKI
CYLINDERS. . . . 2
CID . . . 44.3
ENGINE HP . . . 24
COOLING . . . AIR
FUEL . . . G
TRANSMISSION . . . HYDRO
STEERING. . . . ZERO
STANDARD DECK . . . 60"
WEIGHT . . . 904 LBS.
MSRP. . . . $7,770

OPTIONS

CATCHER/BAGGER . . . $1,329
SUS SEAT. . . . $309

RETAIL PRICING

YEAR	HIGH	LOW
2017	$6,493	$4,870
2018	$6,843	$5,131
2019	$7,185	$5,389
2020	$7,501	$5,753

Z723

YEARS MFRD . . . 2013-2020
SERIES. . . . Z700 SERIES
ENGINE . . . KOHLER
CYLINDERS. . . . 2
CID . . . 42
ENGINE HP . . . 22.5
COOLING . . . AIR
FUEL . . . G
TRANSMISSION . . . HYDRO
STEERING. . . . ZERO
STANDARD DECK . . . 48"
WEIGHT . . . 1,212 LBS.
MSRP. . . . $8,979

OPTIONS

CANOPY. . . . $269
GRASS CATCHER . . . $2,419
LESS SEAT SUSP . . . $-680

RETAIL PRICING

YEAR	HIGH	LOW
2013	$4,767	$3,575
2014	$5,260	$3,945
2015	$5,806	$4,355
2016	$6,410	$4,808
2017	$7,074	$5,305
2018	$7,602	$5,702
2019	$8,042	$6,032
2020	$8,495	$6,498

Z724

YEARS MFRD . . . 2013-2020
SERIES. . . . Z700 SERIES
ENGINE . . . KOHLER
CYLINDERS. . . . 2
CID . . . 42
ENGINE HP . . . 23.5
COOLING . . . AIR
FUEL . . . G
TRANSMISSION . . . HYDRO
STEERING. . . . ZERO
STANDARD DECK . . . 54"
WEIGHT . . . 1,225 LBS.
MSRP. . . . $9,492

OPTIONS

CANOPY. . . . $269
GRASS CATCHER . . . $2,429
LESS SEAT SUSP . . . $-693

RETAIL PRICING

YEAR	HIGH	LOW
2013	$5,052	$3,790
2014	$5,606	$4,205
2015	$6,190	$4,642
2016	$6,829	$5,121
2017	$7,536	$5,652
2018	$8,124	$6,093
2019	$8,735	$6,551
2020	$9,278	$6,974

Z724X

YEARS MFRD . . . 2016-2020
ENGINE . . . KAWASAKI
CYLINDERS. . . . 2
CID . . . 44
ENGINE HP . . . 23.5
COOLING . . . AIR
FUEL . . . G
SPEEDS . . . VARIABLE
TRANSMISSION . . . HYDRO
STEERING. . . . ZERO
STANDARD DECK . . . 48"
WEIGHT . . . 1,207 LBS.
MSRP. . . . $9,384

OPTIONS

54" DECK. . . . $360
CANOPY. . . . $269
GRASS CATCHER . . . $2,419
LESS SEAT SUSP . . . $-685

RETAIL PRICING

YEAR	HIGH	LOW
2016	$6,751	$5,063
2017	$7,450	$5,587
2018	$8,019	$6,014
2019	$8,614	$6,460
2020	$9,137	$6,949

Z725

YEARS MFRD . . . 2013-2020
SERIES. . . . Z700 SERIES
ENGINE . . . KOHLER

CYLINDERS. 2
CID 46
ENGINE HP 25
COOLING . . . . . AIR
FUEL . . . . . G
TRANSMISSION . . . . . HYDRO
STEERING. . . . . ZERO
STANDARD DECK . . . . . 60"
WEIGHT . . . . . 1,256 LBS.
MSRP. $10,005

OPTIONS

CANOPY. $269
GRASS CATCHER $2,529
LESS SEAT SUSP . . . . . $-706

RETAIL PRICING

YEAR	HIGH	LOW
2013	$5,367	$4,025
2014	$5,944	$4,458
2015	$6,539	$4,904
2016	$7,221	$5,416
2017	$7,964	$5,974
2018	$8,628	$6,471
2019	$9,389	$7,042
2020	$9,829	$7,518

Z726X

YEARS MFRD 2016-2020
SERIES. . . . . Z700 SERIES
ENGINE . . . . . KAWASAKI
CYLINDERS. 2
CID 52
ENGINE HP 25.5
COOLING . . . . . AIR
FUEL . . . . . G
TRANSMISSION . . . . . HYDRO
STEERING. . . . . ZERO
STANDARD DECK . . . . . 60"
WEIGHT . . . . . 1,276 LBS.
MSRP. $10,366

OPTIONS

CANOPY. $269
GRASS CATCHER $2,529
LESS SEAT SUSP . . . . . $-707

RETAIL PRICING

YEAR	HIGH	LOW
2016	$7,473	$5,604
2017	$8,248	$6,186
2018	$8,957	$6,718
2019	$9,796	$7,347
2020	$10,165	$7,833

Z751 EFI

YEARS MFRD 2019-2020
SERIES. . . . . Z700 EFI SERIES
ENGINE . . . . . KAWASAKI GH7303V-F
CYLINDERS. 2
CID 44.3
ENGINE HP 25.5
COOLING . . . . . AIR
FUEL . . . . . G
SPEEDS . . . . . VARIABLE
TRANSMISSION . . . . . HYDRO
STEERING. . . . . ZERO
STANDARD DECK . . . . . 48"
WEIGHT . . . . . 1,215 LBS.
MSRP. $10,550

OPTIONS

CANOPY. $498
GRASS CATCHER $2,419

Z781 EFI

YEARS MFRD 2019-2020
SERIES. . . . . Z700 EFI SERIES
ENGINE . . . . . KAWASAKI GH860V-F
CYLINDERS. 2
CID 52
ENGINE HP 29.5
COOLING . . . . . AIR
FUEL . . . . . G
SPEEDS . . . . . VARIABLE
TRANSMISSION . . . . . HYDRO
STEERING. . . . . ZERO
STANDARD DECK . . . . . 54"
WEIGHT . . . . . 1,254 LBS.
MSRP. $11,297

OPTIONS

60" DECK. $520
CANOPY. $498
GRASS CATCHER $2,529

ZD18F

YEARS MFRD 2002-2006
SERIES. . . . . ZD SERIES
ENGINE . . . . . KUBOTA E TVCS
CYLINDERS. 3
CID 43.9
ENGINE HP 18
COOLING . . . . . LIQUID
FUEL . . . . . D
SPEEDS . . . . . VARIABLE
TRANSMISSION . . . . . HYDRO
STEERING. . . . . ZERO
BLADE CLUTCH . . . . . ELECTRIC
HYDRAULIC . . . . . YES
PTO . . . . . YES
STANDARD DECK . . . . . 54"
WEIGHT . . . . . 1,349 LBS.
MSRP. $10,810

OPTIONS

3 BAG

RETAIL PRICING

YEAR	HIGH	LOW
2002	$3,695	$2,771
2003	$4,104	$3,078
2004	$4,559	$3,419
2005	$5,060	$3,795
2006	$5,643	$4,233

AVG. AUCTION PRICING

LOW	HIGH	AVG
$2,627	$5,150	$3,387

ZD21

YEARS MFRD 2001-2001
SERIES. . . . . ZD SERIES
ENGINE . . . . . KUBOTA
ENGINE HP 21
COOLING . . . . . LIQUID
FUEL . . . . . D
SPEEDS . . . . . VARIABLE
TRANSMISSION . . . . . HYDRO
STEERING. . . . . ZERO
BLADE CLUTCH . . . . . MANUAL
STANDARD DECK . . . . . 60"
MSRP. $10,580

OPTIONS

BAGGER

RETAIL PRICING

YEAR	HIGH	LOW
2001	$5,060	$3,795

AVG. AUCTION PRICING

LOW	HIGH	AVG
$1,100	$4,750	$2,825

ZD21F

YEARS MFRD 2002-2006
SERIES. . . . . ZD SERIES
ENGINE . . . . . KUBOTA E TVCS
CYLINDERS. 3
CID 47.5
ENGINE HP 21
COOLING . . . . . LIQUID
FUEL . . . . . D
SPEEDS . . . . . VARIABLE
TRANSMISSION . . . . . HYDRO
STEERING. . . . . ZERO
BLADE CLUTCH . . . . . ELECTRIC
HYDRAULIC . . . . . YES
PTO . . . . . YES
STANDARD DECK . . . . . 60"
WEIGHT . . . . . 1,430 LBS.
MSRP. $11,910

OPTIONS

2 BAG
3 BAG

RETAIL PRICING

YEAR	HIGH	LOW
2002	$3,916	$2,937
2003	$4,338	$3,254
2004	$4,815	$3,611
2005	$5,327	$3,995
2006	$6,069	$4,552

ZD25F

YEARS MFRD 2005-2006
SERIES. . . . . ZD SERIES
ENGINE . . . . . KUBOTA
CYLINDERS. 3
CID 61.08
ENGINE HP 25
COOLING . . . . . LIQUID
FUEL . . . . . D
SPEEDS . . . . . VARIABLE
TRANSMISSION . . . . . HYDRO
STEERING. . . . . ZERO
BLADE CLUTCH . . . . . ELECTRIC
STANDARD DECK . . . . . 60"
WEIGHT . . . . . 1,660 LBS.
MSRP. $12,510

OPTIONS

2 BAG
3 BAG

RETAIL PRICING

YEAR	HIGH	LOW
2005	$6,407	$4,805
2006	$7,026	$5,269

AVG. AUCTION PRICING

LOW	HIGH	AVG
$3,090	$5,150	$3,880

ZD28F

YEARS MFRD 2003-2006
SERIES. . . . . ZD SERIES
ENGINE . . . . . KUBOTA E TVCS
CYLINDERS. 3
CID 68.5
ENGINE HP 28
COOLING . . . . . LIQUID
FUEL . . . . . D
SPEEDS . . . . . VARIABLE
TRANSMISSION . . . . . HYDRO
STEERING. . . . . ZERO
BLADE CLUTCH . . . . . ELECTRIC
HYDRAULIC . . . . . YES
PTO . . . . . YES
STANDARD DECK . . . . . 72"
WEIGHT . . . . . 1,627 LBS.
MSRP. $13,810

OPTIONS

2 BAG
3 BAG

RETAIL PRICING

YEAR	HIGH	LOW
2003	$4,638	$3,479
2004	$5,215	$3,911
2005	$5,818	$4,364
2006	$6,395	$4,796

AVG. AUCTION PRICING

LOW	HIGH	AVG
$2,772	$8,315	$5,116

ZD28FP

YEARS MFRD 2002-2002
SERIES. . . . . ZD SERIES
ENGINE . . . . . KUBOTA
ENGINE HP 28
COOLING . . . . . LIQUID
FUEL . . . . . D
SPEEDS . . . . . VARIABLE
TRANSMISSION . . . . . HYDRO
STEERING. . . . . ZERO
BLADE CLUTCH . . . . . MANUAL
STANDARD DECK . . . . . 60"
MSRP. $12,380

OPTIONS

72" DECK

RETAIL PRICING

YEAR	HIGH	LOW
2002	$7,032	$5,274

ZD221

YEARS MFRD 2009-2015
ENGINE . . . . . KUBOTA D782
CYLINDERS. 3
CID 47.5
ENGINE HP 21
COOLING . . . . . LIQUID
FUEL . . . . . D
SPEEDS . . . . . VARIABLE
TRANSMISSION . . . . . HYDRO

STEERING................ZERO
BLADE CLUTCH ....ELECTRIC
STANDARD DECK .... 48"
WEIGHT ....1,224 LBS.
MSRP............... $11,659

OPTIONS

54" DECK
CANOPY

RETAIL PRICING

YEAR	HIGH	LOW
2009	$5,016	$3,762
2010	$5,588	$4,191
2011	$6,151	$4,613
2012	$6,765	$5,074
2013	$7,505	$5,628
2014	$8,217	$6,163
2015	$9,070	$6,803

ZD321

YEARS MFRD 2007-2011
SERIES...........ZD 300 SERIES
ENGINE .... KUBOTA D782
CYLINDERS.................3
CID 47.48
ENGINE HP.................21
COOLING ....LIQUID
FUEL ....D
SPEEDS ....VARIABLE
TRANSMISSION ....HYDRO
STEERING................ZERO
STANDARD DECK .... 54"
WEIGHT ....1,671 LBS.
MSRP............... $12,640

OPTIONS

2 BAG
64" BLADE
SHADE

RETAIL PRICING

YEAR	HIGH	LOW
2007	$5,710	$4,283
2008	$6,375	$4,781
2009	$7,013	$5,260
2010	$7,795	$5,846
2011	$8,714	$6,535

AVG. AUCTION PRICING

LOW	HIGH	AVG
$3,437	$3,991	$3,798

ZD323

YEARS MFRD 2009-2013
ENGINE .... KUBOTA D902
CYLINDERS.................3
CID 54.8
ENGINE HP.................23
COOLING ....LIQUID
FUEL ....D
SPEEDS ....VARIABLE
TRANSMISSION ....HYDRO
STEERING................ZERO
BLADE CLUTCH ....ELECTRIC
STANDARD DECK .... 60"
WEIGHT ....1,645 LBS.
MSRP............... $13,872

OPTIONS

64" BLADE
SHADE

RETAIL PRICING

YEAR	HIGH	LOW
2009	$8,308	$6,231
2010	$9,225	$6,919
2011	$10,137	$7,603
2012	$11,166	$8,375
2013	$12,391	$9,293

ZD326

YEARS MFRD 2007-2013
SERIES...........ZD 300 SERIES
ENGINE .... KUBOTA D1005
CYLINDERS.................3
CID 61.08
ENGINE HP.................26
COOLING ....LIQUID
FUEL ....D
SPEEDS ....VARIABLE
TRANSMISSION ....HYDRO
STEERING................ZERO
STANDARD DECK .... 60"
WEIGHT ....1,757 LBS.
MSRP............... $14,892

OPTIONS

2 BAG
64" BLADE
SHADE

RETAIL PRICING

YEAR	HIGH	LOW
2007	$6,598	$4,949
2008	$7,550	$5,662
2009	$8,237	$6,178
2010	$8,720	$6,540
2011	$9,830	$7,373
2012	$10,721	$8,041
2013	$11,856	$8,892

AVG. AUCTION PRICING

LOW	HIGH	AVG
$3,000	$6,700	$4,713

ZD331

YEARS MFRD 2007-2013
SERIES...........ZD 300 SERIES
ENGINE .... KUBOTA D1305
CYLINDERS.................3
CID 76.98
ENGINE HP.................31
COOLING ....LIQUID
FUEL ....D
SPEEDS ....VARIABLE
TRANSMISSION ....HYDRO
STEERING................ZERO
STANDARD DECK .... 60"
WEIGHT ....1,812 LBS.
MSRP............... $16,167

OPTIONS

2 BAG
72" DECK
BLADE
SHADE

RETAIL PRICING

YEAR	HIGH	LOW
2007	$8,071	$6,053
2008	$9,108	$6,831
2009	$9,446	$7,085
2010	$10,409	$7,807
2011	$11,664	$8,748
2012	$12,604	$9,453
2013	$14,157	$10,618

AVG. AUCTION PRICING

LOW	HIGH	AVG
$3,500	$6,700	$4,833

ZD1011

YEARS MFRD 2016-2020
SERIES.......... ZD1000 SERIES
ENGINE ....KUBOTA
CYLINDERS.................3
CID 47.5
ENGINE HP................ 19.3
COOLING ....LIQUID
FUEL ....D
TRANSMISSION ....HYDRO
STEERING................ZERO
STANDARD DECK .... 48"
WEIGHT ....1,296 LBS.
MSRP............... $12,699

OPTIONS

54" DECK................$300
DELX CANOPY $528

RETAIL PRICING

YEAR	HIGH	LOW
2016	$9,617	$7,287
2017	$10,584	$8,013
2018	$11,364	$8,598
2019	$12,112	$9,234
2020	$12,635	$9,766

ZD1021

YEARS MFRD 2016-2020
SERIES.......... ZD1000 SERIES
ENGINE ....KUBOTA
CYLINDERS.................3
CID 54.8
ENGINE HP................ 21.6
COOLING ....LIQUID
FUEL ....D
TRANSMISSION ....HYDRO
STEERING................ZERO
STANDARD DECK .... 60"
WEIGHT ....1,389 LBS.
MSRP............... $14,599

OPTIONS

DELX CANOPY $528
GRASS CATCHER $2,529

RETAIL PRICING

YEAR	HIGH	LOW
2016	$10,998	$8,323
2017	$12,150	$9,187
2018	$13,015	$9,836
2019	$13,966	$10,549
2020	$14,486	$11,016

ZD1211

YEARS MFRD 2016-2020
SERIES.......... ZD1200 SERIES
ENGINE ....KUBOTA
CYLINDERS.................3
CID 68.53
ENGINE HP................ 24.8
COOLING ....LIQUID
FUEL ....D
TRANSMISSION ....HYDRO
STEERING................ZERO
STANDARD DECK .... 60"
WEIGHT ....1,676 LBS.
MSRP............... $16,199

OPTIONS

60" DECK RD $300
72" DECK $800
72" DECK RD $1,100

RETAIL PRICING

YEAR	HIGH	LOW
2016	$12,232	$9,174
2017	$13,469	$10,101
2018	$14,411	$10,808
2019	$15,316	$11,487
2020	$15,939	$12,129

ZD1511LF

YEARS MFRD 2017-2020
SERIES.......... ZD1500 SERIES
ENGINE ..... KUBOTA V1505-T-E4
CYLINDERS.................4
CID 91.41
ENGINE HP................ 30.8
COOLING ....LIQUID
FUEL ....D
SPEEDS ....VARIABLE
TRANSMISSION ..... DUAL HYDRO
STEERING................ZERO
BLADE CLUTCH ....ELECTRIC
STANDARD DECK .... 72"
MSRP............... $22,099

OPTIONS

CANOPY..................$498
MULCH KIT...............$299

ZD1511RL

YEARS MFRD 2017-2020
SERIES.......... ZD1500 SERIES
ENGINE ..... KUBOTA V1505-T-E4
CYLINDERS.................4
CID 91.41
ENGINE HP................ 30.8
COOLING ....LIQUID
FUEL ....D
SPEEDS ....VARIABLE
TRANSMISSION ..... DUAL HYDRO
STEERING................ZERO
BLADE CLUTCH ....ELECTRIC
STANDARD DECK .... 60"
MSRP............... $21,099

OPTIONS

72" DECK.............. $1,500
DELX CANOPY $528

RETAIL PRICING

YEAR	HIGH	LOW
2017	$17,696	$13,272
2018	$18,921	$14,191
2019	$20,212	$15,160
2020	$20,979	$16,034

ZG20

YEARS MFRD 2004-2007
SERIES. . . . . ZG SERIES
ENGINE . . . . KUBOTA OHV
CYLINDERS. 2
CID 38.1
ENGINE HP 20
COOLING . . . . AIR
FUEL . . . . G
SPEEDS . . . . VARIABLE
TRANSMISSION . . . . .HYDRO
STEERING. . . . . ZERO
STANDARD DECK . . . . 48"
WEIGHT . . . . 1,058 LBS.
MSRP. $7,211

OPTIONS

BAGGER
SHADE

RETAIL PRICING

YEAR	HIGH	LOW
2004	$2,843	$2,132
2005	$3,159	$2,369
2006	$3,529	$2,647
2007	$3,923	$2,942

ZG23

YEARS MFRD 2004-2007
SERIES. . . . . ZG SERIES
ENGINE . . . . KUBOTA OHV
CYLINDERS. 2
CID 41.1
ENGINE HP 23
COOLING . . . . AIR
FUEL . . . . G
SPEEDS . . . . VARIABLE
TRANSMISSION . . . . .HYDRO
STEERING. . . . . ZERO
STANDARD DECK . . . . 54"
WEIGHT . . . . 1,102 LBS.
MSRP. $7,980

OPTIONS

BAGGER
SHADE

RETAIL PRICING

YEAR	HIGH	LOW
2004	$3,101	$2,326
2005	$3,439	$2,579
2006	$3,800	$2,850
2007	$4,226	$3,170

ZG123S

YEARS MFRD 2013-2013
ENGINE . . . . KUBOTA
ENGINE HP 23
COOLING . . . . AIR
FUEL . . . . G
SPEEDS . . . . VARIABLE
TRANSMISSION . . . . .HYDRO
STEERING. . . . . ZERO
STANDARD DECK . . . . 48"
MSRP. $5,458

OPTIONS

2 BAG
SUS SEAT

RETAIL PRICING

YEAR	HIGH	LOW
2013	$5,286	$3,964

ZG124E

YEARS MFRD 2013-2013
ENGINE . . . . B&S
ENGINE HP 24
COOLING . . . . AIR
FUEL . . . . G
SPEEDS . . . . VARIABLE
TRANSMISSION . . . . .HYDRO
STEERING. . . . . ZERO
STANDARD DECK . . . . 48"
MSRP. $4,985

OPTIONS

2 BAG
SUS SEAT

RETAIL PRICING

YEAR	HIGH	LOW
2013	$4,833	$3,625

ZG127E

YEARS MFRD 2013-2013
ENGINE . . . . B&S
ENGINE HP 27
COOLING . . . . AIR
FUEL . . . . G
SPEEDS . . . . VARIABLE
TRANSMISSION . . . . .HYDRO
STEERING. . . . . ZERO
STANDARD DECK . . . . 54"
MSRP. $5,827

OPTIONS

2 BAG
SUS SEAT

RETAIL PRICING

YEAR	HIGH	LOW
2013	$5,643	$4,233

ZG222

YEARS MFRD 2008-2013
ENGINE . . .KUBOTA KGZ770-E2-M3
CYLINDERS. 2
CID 46.87
ENGINE HP 22
COOLING . . . . AIR
FUEL . . . . G
SPEEDS . . . . VARIABLE
TRANSMISSION . . . . .HYDRO
STEERING. . . . . ZERO
BLADE CLUTCH . . . . ELECTRIC
STANDARD DECK . . . . 48"
WEIGHT . . . . 1,098 LBS.
MSRP. $8,568

OPTIONS

2 BAG
CANOPY

RETAIL PRICING

YEAR	HIGH	LOW
2008	$4,530	$3,397
2009	$4,931	$3,698
2010	$5,508	$4,131
2011	$6,156	$4,617
2012	$6,827	$5,120
2013	$7,504	$5,628

AVG. AUCTION PRICING

LOW	HIGH	AVG
$2,575	$5,150	$3,948

ZG222A

YEARS MFRD 2013-2020
ENGINE . . . . KUBOTA
CYLINDERS. 2
CID 46.9
ENGINE HP 22
COOLING . . . . AIR
FUEL . . . . G
SPEEDS . . . . VARIABLE
TRANSMISSION . . . . .HYDRO
STEERING. . . . . ZERO
STANDARD DECK . . . . 48"
WEIGHT . . . . 1,102 LBS.
MSRP. $8,160

OPTIONS

48" FAB DECK $639
DELX CANOPY $528

RETAIL PRICING

YEAR	HIGH	LOW
2013	$5,419	$4,064
2014	$6,268	$4,701

ZG227

YEARS MFRD 2008-2013
ENGINE . . .KUBOTA KGZ770-E2-M2
CYLINDERS. 2
ENGINE HP 27
COOLING . . . . AIR
FUEL . . . . G
SPEEDS . . . . VARIABLE
TRANSMISSION . . . . .HYDRO
STEERING. . . . . ZERO
BLADE CLUTCH . . . . ELECTRIC
STANDARD DECK . . . . 54"
WEIGHT . . . . 1,199 LBS.
MSRP. $9,894

OPTIONS

2 BAG
60" DECK
CANOPY

RETAIL PRICING

YEAR	HIGH	LOW
2008	$5,107	$3,830
2009	$5,829	$4,372
2010	$6,356	$4,767
2011	$7,063	$5,297
2012	$7,766	$5,825
2013	$8,664	$6,498

AVG. AUCTION PRICING

LOW	HIGH	AVG
$3,800	$3,926	$3,841

ZG227A

YEARS MFRD 2013-2020
ENGINE . . . . KUBOTA
CYLINDERS. 2
CID 46.9
ENGINE HP 27
COOLING . . . . AIR
FUEL . . . . G
SPEEDS . . . . VARIABLE
TRANSMISSION . . . . .HYDRO
STEERING. . . . . ZERO
STANDARD DECK . . . . 54"
WEIGHT . . . . 1,190 LBS.
MSRP. $9,999

OPTIONS

60" DECK. $500
DELX CANOPY $528

RETAIL PRICING

YEAR	HIGH	LOW
2013	$6,571	$4,927
2014	$7,597	$5,698

ZG327

YEARS MFRD 2008-2013
ENGINE . . . . . .KUBOTA ZG327P-60
CYLINDERS. 2
ENGINE HP 27
COOLING . . . . AIR
FUEL . . . . G
SPEEDS . . . . VARIABLE
TRANSMISSION . . . . .HYDRO
STEERING. . . . . ZERO
BLADE CLUTCH . . . . ELECTRIC
STANDARD DECK . . . . 60"
WEIGHT . . . . 1,473 LBS.
MSRP. $11,394

OPTIONS

2 BAG
BLADE
CANOPY

RETAIL PRICING

YEAR	HIGH	LOW
2008	$5,958	$4,468
2009	$6,558	$4,919
2010	$7,306	$5,479
2011	$8,204	$6,153
2012	$9,005	$6,754
2013	$9,979	$7,484

AVG. AUCTION PRICING

LOW	HIGH	AVG
$2,627	$3,708	$3,348

ZG327PA

YEARS MFRD 2015-2020
ENGINE . . . . KUBOTA KGZ770
CYLINDERS. 2
CID 46.9
ENGINE HP 27
COOLING . . . . AIR
FUEL . . . . G
TRANSMISSION . . . . .HYDRO
STEERING. . . . . ZERO
STANDARD DECK . . . . 60"
WEIGHT . . . . 1,565 LBS.
MSRP. $11,699

OPTIONS

60" DECK RD $300

ZG332

YEARS MFRD 2011-2017
ENGINE . . . . KUBOTA
CYLINDERS. 3
CID 58.7
ENGINE HP 32
COOLING . . . . AIR
FUEL . . . . G
SPEEDS . . . . VARIABLE
TRANSMISSION . . . . HYDRO
STEERING. . . . . ZERO
STANDARD DECK . . . . 60"
WEIGHT . . . . 1,651 LBS.
MSRP. $14,168

RETAIL PRICING

YEAR	HIGH	LOW
2011	$10,059	$7,544
2012	$11,174	$8,381
2013	$12,408	$9,306

ZP330

YEARS MFRD 2012-2017
ENGINE . . . . KUBOTA
CYLINDERS. 3
CID 58.7
ENGINE HP 31
COOLING . . . . LIQUID
FUEL . . . . D
SPEEDS . . . . VARIABLE
TRANSMISSION . . . . HYDRO
STEERING. . . . . ZERO
STANDARD DECK . . . . 60"
WEIGHT . . . . 1,876 LBS.
MSRP. $15,861

RETAIL PRICING

YEAR	HIGH	LOW
2012	$12,505	$9,379
2013	$13,889	$10,416

LAND PRIDE

LPZ52
YEARS MFRD 2004-2005
SERIES........... ACCU Z SERIES
ENGINE .... KAWASAKI
ENGINE HP 23
COOLING .... AIR
FUEL .... G
SPEEDS .... VARIABLE
TRANSMISSION .... HYDRO
STEERING................ ZERO
STANDARD DECK .... 52"

LPZ60
YEARS MFRD 2006-2006
SERIES........... ACCU Z SERIES
ENGINE .... KAWASAKI
ENGINE HP 23
COOLING .... AIR
FUEL .... G
SPEEDS .... VARIABLE
TRANSMISSION .... HYDRO
STEERING................ ZERO
STANDARD DECK .... 60"
MSRP............... $10,049

OPTIONS
HONDA 24HP

RETAIL PRICING

YEAR	HIGH	LOW
2006	$3,416	$2,562

LPZ72
YEARS MFRD 2006-2006
SERIES.......... ACCU-Z SERIES
ENGINE .... KAWASAKI
ENGINE HP 25
COOLING .... AIR
FUEL .... G
SPEEDS .... VARIABLE
TRANSMISSION ..... DUAL HYDRO
STEERING................ ZERO
STANDARD DECK .... 72"
MSRP............... $11,049

OPTIONS
HONDA 24HP

RETAIL PRICING

YEAR	HIGH	LOW
2006	$3,756	$2,817

LPZ
YEARS MFRD 2001-2002
SERIES.......... ACCU-Z SERIES
ENGINE .... KAWASAKI
ENGINE HP 23
FUEL .... G
TRANSMISSION .... HYDRO
STEERING................ ZERO
STANDARD DECK .... 52"
MSRP................ $8,999

OPTIONS
60" DECK

RETAIL PRICING

YEAR	HIGH	LOW
2001	$4,456	$3,342
2002	$4,581	$3,435

Z44
YEARS MFRD 2006-2008
SERIES.......... ACCU-Z RAZOR
ENGINE .... HONDA
CYLINDERS.................. 2
CID 32.5
ENGINE HP 18
COOLING .... AIR
FUEL .... G
SPEEDS .... VARIABLE
TRANSMISSION .... HYDRO
STEERING................ ZERO
BLADE CLUTCH .... ELECTRIC
STANDARD DECK .... 44"
WEIGHT .... 740 LBS.
MSRP................ $5,299

OPTIONS
B&S 20HP

RETAIL PRICING

YEAR	HIGH	LOW
2006	$1,705	$1,279
2007	$1,893	$1,420
2008	$2,098	$1,574

Z48
YEARS MFRD 2010-2014
ENGINE .... KAWASAKI
ENGINE HP 20
COOLING .... AIR
FUEL .... G
SPEEDS .... VARIABLE
TRANSMISSION .... HYDRO
STEERING................ ZERO
STANDARD DECK .... 48"
WEIGHT .... 835 LBS.

OPTIONS
B&S 22HP

Z52
YEARS MFRD 2006-2010
SERIES.......... ACCU-Z RAZOR
ENGINE .... HONDA
CYLINDERS.................. 2
CID 32.5
ENGINE HP 18
COOLING .... AIR
FUEL .... G
SPEEDS .... VARIABLE
TRANSMISSION .... HYDRO
STEERING................ ZERO
BLADE CLUTCH .... ELECTRIC
STANDARD DECK .... 52"
WEIGHT .... 755 LBS.

OPTIONS
HONDA 20HP
HONDA 25HP

Z54
YEARS MFRD 2010-2014
ENGINE .... KAWASAKI
CID 44.3
ENGINE HP 24
COOLING .... AIR
FUEL .... G
SPEEDS .... VARAIBLE
TRANSMISSION .... HYDRO
STEERING................ ZERO
STANDARD DECK .... 54"

OPTIONS
B&S 26HP

ZR44
YEARS MFRD 2003-2005
SERIES........... RAZOR SERIES
ENGINE .... HONDA
PTO HP 16
ENGINE HP 18
COOLING .... AIR
FUEL .... G
SPEEDS .... VARIABLE
TRANSMISSION .... HYDRO
STEERING................ ZERO
STANDARD DECK .... 44"

ZR52
YEARS MFRD 2003-2006
SERIES........... RAZOR SERIES
ENGINE .... HONDA
ENGINE HP 20
COOLING .... AIR
FUEL .... G
SPEEDS .... VARIABLE
TRANSMISSION .... HYDRO
STEERING................ ZERO
STANDARD DECK .... 52"
MSRP................ $5,023

OPTIONS
HONDA 18HP

RETAIL PRICING

YEAR	HIGH	LOW
2003	$3,157	$2,367
2004	$3,214	$2,411
2005	$3,264	$2,448
2006	$3,332	$2,499

ZRP44
YEARS MFRD 2003-2004
SERIES....... RAZOR PRO SERIES
ENGINE .... HONDA
CYLINDERS.................. 2
ENGINE HP 19
SPEEDS .... VARIABLE
TRANSMISSION .... GEAR
STEERING................ ZERO
STANDARD DECK .... 44"
WEIGHT .... 985 LBS.
MSRP................ $8,200

RETAIL PRICING

YEAR	HIGH	LOW
2003	$4,526	$3,394
2004	$4,819	$3,614

ZRP52
YEARS MFRD 2003-2004
SERIES....... RAZOR PRO SERIES
ENGINE .... KAWASAKI
CYLINDERS.................. 2
ENGINE HP 23
SPEEDS .... VARIABLE
TRANSMISSION .... HYDRO
STEERING................ ZERO
STANDARD DECK .... 52"
WEIGHT .... 985 LBS.
MSRP................ $8,600

OPTIONS
HONDA 24HP

RETAIL PRICING

YEAR	HIGH	LOW
2003	$4,745	$3,559
2004	$5,053	$3,790

ZSR54
YEARS MFRD 2010-2017
ENGINE .... KAWASAKI
CID 44.3
ENGINE HP 24
COOLING .... AIR
FUEL .... G
SPEEDS .... VARIABLE
TRANSMISSION .... HYDRO
STEERING................ ZERO
STANDARD DECK .... 54"

OPTIONS
B&S 26HP
KAWASAKI 26HP

ZSR60
YEARS MFRD 2010-2017
ENGINE .... KAWASAKI
ENGINE HP 24
COOLING .... AIR
FUEL .... G
SPEEDS .... VARIABLE
TRANSMISSION .... HYDRO
STEERING................ ZERO
STANDARD DECK .... 60"

OPTIONS
B&S 26HP
KAWASAKI 26HP

ZST40
YEARS MFRD 2012-2017
ENGINE .... KAWASAKI FR541V
CYLINDERS.................. 2
CID 603CC
ENGINE HP 15
COOLING .... AIR
FUEL .... G
SPEEDS .... VARIABLE
TRANSMISSION .... HYDRO
STEERING................ ZERO
BLADE CLUTCH .... ELECTRIC
STANDARD DECK .... 40"
WEIGHT .... 595 LBS.

OPTIONS
B&S 17.5

LAND PRIDE

ZST48

YEARS MFRD 2012-2017
ENGINE . . . . KAWASAKI FR600V
CYLINDERS. 2
CID 603CC
ENGINE HP 18
COOLING . . . . AIR
FUEL . . . . G
SPEEDS . . . . VARIABLE
TRANSMISSION . . . . HYDRO
STEERING. . . . . ZERO
BLADE CLUTCH . . . . ELECTRIC
STANDARD DECK . . . . 48"
WEIGHT . . . . 610 LBS.

OPTIONS

B&S 21HP

ZT60-0224

YEARS MFRD 2007-2008
SERIES. . . . . ACCU-Z SERIES
ENGINE . . . . HONDA
ENGINE HP 24
COOLING . . . . AIR
FUEL . . . . G
SPEEDS . . . . VARIABLE
TRANSMISSION . . . . HYDRO
STEERING. . . . . ZERO
BLADE CLUTCH . . . . ELECTRIC
STANDARD DECK . . . . 60"
WEIGHT . . . . 1,140 LBS.
MSRP. $8,549

RETAIL PRICING

YEAR	HIGH	LOW
2007	$3,058	$2,293
2008	$3,408	$2,556

ZT60-0225

YEARS MFRD 2007-2008
SERIES. . . . . ACCU-Z SERIES
ENGINE . . . . KAWASAKI
ENGINE HP 25
COOLING . . . . AIR
FUEL . . . . G
SPEEDS . . . . VARIABLE
TRANSMISSION . . . . HYDRO
STEERING. . . . . ZERO
BLADE CLUTCH . . . . ELECTRIC
STANDARD DECK . . . . 60"
WEIGHT . . . . 1,140 LBS.
MSRP. $8,549

RETAIL PRICING

YEAR	HIGH	LOW
2007	$3,058	$2,293
2008	$3,397	$2,548

ZT60-0227

YEARS MFRD 2008-2008
SERIES. . . . . ACCU-Z SERIES
ENGINE . . . . KOHLER
ENGINE HP 27
COOLING . . . . AIR
FUEL . . . . G
SPEEDS . . . . VARIABLE
TRANSMISSION . . . . . DUAL HYDRO
STEERING. . . . . ZERO
BLADE CLUTCH . . . . ELECTRIC
STANDARD DECK . . . . 60"
WEIGHT . . . . 1,120 LBS.
MSRP. $8,699

RETAIL PRICING

YEAR	HIGH	LOW
2008	$3,455	$2,591

ZT60-0230

YEARS MFRD 2008-2008
SERIES. . . . . ACCU-Z
ENGINE . . . . KOHLER
ENGINE HP 30
COOLING . . . . AIR
FUEL . . . . G
SPEEDS . . . . VARIABLE
TRANSMISSION . . . . . DUAL HYDRO
STEERING. . . . . ZERO
BLADE CLUTCH . . . . ELECTRIC
STANDARD DECK . . . . 60"
WEIGHT . . . . 1,120 LBS.
MSRP. $8,849

RETAIL PRICING

YEAR	HIGH	LOW
2008	$3,515	$2,636

ZT60I

YEARS MFRD 2010-2012
ENGINE . . . . KAWASAKI FX730V
CID 44.3
ENGINE HP 26
COOLING . . . . AIR
FUEL . . . . G
SPEEDS . . . . VARIABLE
TRANSMISSION . . . . HYDRO
STEERING. . . . . ZERO

OPTIONS

KAWASAKI FX850V 31HP

ZT72-0225

YEARS MFRD 2007-2008
SERIES. . . . . ACCU-Z SERIES
ENGINE . . . . KAWASAKI
ENGINE HP 25
COOLING . . . . AIR
FUEL . . . . G
SPEEDS . . . . VARIABLE
TRANSMISSION . . . . . DUAL HYDRO
STEERING. . . . . ZERO
BLADE CLUTCH . . . . ELECTRIC
STANDARD DECK . . . . 72"
WEIGHT . . . . 1,250 LBS.
MSRP. $9,249

RETAIL PRICING

YEAR	HIGH	LOW
2007	$3,308	$2,481
2008	$3,673	$2,755

ZT72-0227

YEARS MFRD 2008-2008
SERIES. . . . . ACCU-Z SERIES
ENGINE . . . . KOHLER
ENGINE HP 27
COOLING . . . . AIR
FUEL . . . . G
SPEEDS . . . . VARIABLE
TRANSMISSION . . . . . DUAL HYDRO
STEERING. . . . . ZERO
BLADE CLUTCH . . . . ELECTRIC
STANDARD DECK . . . . 72"
WEIGHT . . . . 1,250 LBS.
MSRP. $9,399

RETAIL PRICING

YEAR	HIGH	LOW
2008	$3,733	$2,800

ZT72-0230

YEARS MFRD 2008-2008
SERIES. . . . . ACCU-Z SERIES
ENGINE . . . . KOHLER
ENGINE HP 30
COOLING . . . . AIR
FUEL . . . . G
SPEEDS . . . . VARIABLE
TRANSMISSION . . . . . DUAL HYDRO
STEERING. . . . . ZERO
BLADE CLUTCH . . . . ELECTRIC
STANDARD DECK . . . . 72"
WEIGHT . . . . 1,250 LBS.
MSRP. $9,549

RETAIL PRICING

YEAR	HIGH	LOW
2008	$3,795	$2,846

ZT72I

YEARS MFRD 2010-2011
ENGINE . . . . KAWASAKI
CID 52
ENGINE HP 31
COOLING . . . . AIR
FUEL . . . . G
SPEEDS . . . . VARIABLE
TRANSMISSION . . . . HYDRO
STEERING. . . . . ZERO
WEIGHT . . . . 1,230 LBS.

ZT360

YEARS MFRD 2014-2016
ENGINE . . . . KAWASAKI
COOLING . . . . AIR
FUEL . . . . G
SPEEDS . . . . VARIABLE
TRANSMISSION . . . . HYDRO
STEERING. . . . . ZERO
BLADE CLUTCH . . . . ELECTRIC
STANDARD DECK . . . . 60"

ZT372

YEARS MFRD 2014-2016
ENGINE . . . . KAWASAKI
COOLING . . . . AIR
FUEL . . . . G
SPEEDS . . . . VARIABLE
TRANSMISSION . . . . HYDRO
STEERING. . . . . ZERO
BLADE CLUTCH . . . . ELECTRIC
STANDARD DECK . . . . 72"

ZXT54

YEARS MFRD 2009-2012
ENGINE . . . . HONDA
CYLINDERS. 2
ENGINE HP 24
COOLING . . . . AIR
FUEL . . . . G
SPEEDS . . . . VARIABLE
TRANSMISSION . . . . HYDRO
STEERING. . . . . ZERO
HITCH . . . . CAT. I
STANDARD DECK . . . . 54"

OPTIONS

B&S 26HP
KAWASAKI 25HP
KAWASAKI 31HP

ZXT60

YEARS MFRD 2009-2012
ENGINE . . . . HONDA
CYLINDERS. 2
ENGINE HP 24
COOLING . . . . AIR
FUEL . . . . G
SPEEDS . . . . VARIABLE
TRANSMISSION . . . . HYDRO
STEERING. . . . . ZERO

LENAR

JL254

YEARS MFRD 2003-2009
ENGINE NJ358B
CYLINDERS. 3
CID 98.7
PTO HP 22
ENGINE HP 25
COOLING . . . . LIQUID
FUEL . . . . D
SPEEDS 8/1
TRANSMISSION . . . . GEAR
STEERING. . . . . STANDARD
HITCH . . . . CAT. I
HYDRAULIC . . . . YES
PTO . . . . YES
WEIGHT . . . . 3,400 LBS.

LE200

YEARS MFRD 2005-2006
SERIES. . . . . SERIES 1
ENGINE . . . . YANG DONG
CYLINDERS. 3
ENGINE HP 20
COOLING . . . . LIQUID
FUEL . . . . D
SPEEDS 8/1
TRANSMISSION . . . . GEAR
STEERING. . . . . STANDARD
HITCH . . . . CAT. I
HYDRAULIC . . . . YES
PTO . . . . YES

LE204D
YEARS MFRD 2007-2011
SERIES . . . . SERIES 1
ENGINE . . . . YANG DONG
CYLINDERS 3
ENGINE HP 20
COOLING . . . . LIQUID
FUEL . . . . D
SPEEDS 8/1
TRANSMISSION . . . . GEAR
STEERING . . . . STANDARD
HITCH . . . . CAT. I

LE254
YEARS MFRD 2005-2010
SERIES . . . . SERIES 11
ENGINE . . . JIANGLING MOTORS CO
CYLINDERS 3
ENGINE HP 25
COOLING . . . . LIQUID
FUEL . . . . D
SPEEDS . . . . VARIABLE
TRANSMISSION . . . SHUTTLE SHIFT
STEERING . . . . STANDARD
HITCH . . . . CAT. I

LE274
YEARS MFRD 2005-2006
SERIES . . . . SERIES 1
ENGINE . . . JIANGLING MOTORS CO
CYLINDERS 3
ENGINE HP 28
COOLING . . . . LIQUID
FUEL . . . . D
SPEEDS 8/2
TRANSMISSION . . . . GEAR
STEERING . . . . STANDARD
HITCH . . . . CAT. I

LE284
YEARS MFRD 2002-2002
ENGINE NJ385
CYLINDERS 3
CID 1.617L
PTO HP 24
ENGINE HP 28.6
FUEL . . . . G
TRANSMISSION . . . . GEAR
STEERING . . . . STANDARD
HITCH . . . . CAT. I
PTO . . . . YES
WEIGHT . . . . 3,330 LBS.

LE304A
YEARS MFRD 2007-2011
CYLINDERS 3
ENGINE HP 30
COOLING . . . . LIQUID
FUEL . . . . D
SPEEDS 8/2
TRANSMISSION . . . . GEAR
STEERING . . . . STANDARD
HITCH . . . . CAT. I

LE354
YEARS MFRD 2005-2010
SERIES . . . . SERIES 1
ENGINE . . JIANGDONG MOTORS CO
CYLINDERS 3
ENGINE HP 35
COOLING . . . . LIQUID
FUEL . . . . D
SPEEDS 8/2
TRANSMISSION . . . . GEAR
STEERING . . . . STANDARD
HITCH . . . . CAT. I
HYDRAULIC . . . . YES
PTO . . . . YES

LE404
YEARS MFRD 2007-2011
CYLINDERS 4
ENGINE HP 40
COOLING . . . . LIQUID
FUEL . . . . D
SPEEDS 8/2
TRANSMISSION . . . . GEAR
STEERING . . . . STANDARD
HITCH . . . . CAT. I
HYDRAULIC . . . . YES
PTO . . . . YES

LE FS274-1
YEARS MFRD 2002-2005
ENGINE NJ385
CYLINDERS 3
CID 98
PTO HP 24
ENGINE HP 28.6
COOLING . . . . LIQUID
FUEL . . . . D
SPEEDS 8/2
TRANSMISSION . . . . GEAR
STEERING . . . . STANDARD
HITCH . . . . CAT. I
HYDRAULIC . . . . YES
PTO . . . . YES
WEIGHT . . . . 3,330 LBS.

LONG

FT45
YEARS MFRD 2004-2005
SERIES . . . . FARMTRAC SERIES
CYLINDERS 3
CID 175
PTO HP 36.9
ENGINE HP 42
COOLING . . . . LIQUID
FUEL . . . . D
SPEEDS 8/2
TRANSMISSION . . . . GEAR
HITCH . . . . CAT. II
HYDRAULIC . . . . YES
PTO . . . . YES

FT60
YEARS MFRD 2005-2005
SERIES . . . . FARMTRAC SERIES
ENGINE . . . . LONG
CYLINDERS 3
CID 192
ENGINE HP 50
COOLING . . . . LIQUID
FUEL . . . . D
SPEEDS 8/2
TRANSMISSION . . . . GEAR
STEERING . . . . STANDARD
HITCH . . . . CAT. II
HYDRAULIC . . . . YES
PTO . . . . YES

LG320
YEARS MFRD 1999-2005
SERIES . . . . LONGTRAC SERIES
ENGINE . . . . UNIVERSAL
CYLINDERS 2
CID 109.7
PTO HP 28
ENGINE HP 33
FUEL . . . . D
SPEEDS 8/2
TRANSMISSION . . . . GEAR
STEERING . . . . STANDARD
DRIVE TYPE 2WD
ROPS/CAB . . . . ROPS
WEIGHT . . . . 3,700 LBS.

LT300DTC
YEARS MFRD 2004-2005
SERIES . . . . LANDTRAC SERIES
CYLINDERS 4
CID 91.5
PTO HP 26
ENGINE HP 30
COOLING . . . . LIQUID
FUEL . . . . D
SPEEDS 12/6
TRANSMISSION . . . . GEAR
STEERING . . . . STANDARD
HITCH . . . . CAT. I
HYDRAULIC . . . . YES
PTO . . . . YES

LT360DTC
YEARS MFRD 2004-2005
SERIES . . . . LANDTRAC SERIES
CYLINDERS 4
CID 107.3
PTO HP 33
ENGINE HP 39
COOLING . . . . LIQUID
FUEL . . . . D
SPEEDS 12/12
TRANSMISSION . . . . POWER SHIFT
STEERING . . . . STANDARD
HYDRAULIC . . . . YES
PTO . . . . YES

LT450
YEARS MFRD 2004-2005
SERIES . . . . LANDTRAC SERIES
CYLINDERS 4
CID 141
PTO HP 36
ENGINE HP 45
COOLING . . . . LIQUID
FUEL . . . . D
SPEEDS 8/8
TRANSMISSION . . . . POWER SHIFT
STEERING . . . . STANDARD
HITCH . . . . CAT. I
HYDRAULIC . . . . YES
PTO . . . . YES

LT450DTC
YEARS MFRD 2005-2005
SERIES . . . . LANDTRAC SERIES
CYLINDERS 4
CID 141
PTO HP 38
ENGINE HP 45
COOLING . . . . LIQUID
FUEL . . . . D
SPEEDS 8/8
TRANSMISSION . . . . POWER SHIFT
STEERING . . . . STANDARD
HITCH . . . . CAT. II
HYDRAULIC . . . . YES
PTO . . . . YES

25
YEARS MFRD 1998-1999
SERIES . . . . LANDTRAC SERIES
ENGINE . . . . MITSUBISHI
CYLINDERS 4
CID 91.5
PTO HP 26
ENGINE HP 28
FUEL . . . . D
SPEEDS 12/6
WEIGHT . . . . 3,050 LBS.

30
YEARS MFRD 1998-1999
SERIES . . . . LANDTRAC SERIES
ENGINE . . . . MITSUBISHI
CYLINDERS 4
CID 107.3
PTO HP 33
ENGINE HP 36
FUEL . . . . D
SPEEDS 12/6
WEIGHT . . . . 3,050 LBS.

35
YEARS MFRD 2004-2004
SERIES . . . . FARMTRAC SERIES
ENGINE E3.215
CYLINDERS 3
CID 131
PTO HP 31
ENGINE HP 35

COOLING....LIQUID
FUEL....D
SPEEDS....8/2
TRANSMISSION....GEAR
STEERING....STANDARD
HITCH....CAT. I
HYDRAULIC....YES
PTO....YES
WEIGHT....4,220 LBS.

45

YEARS MFRD....2002-2003
SERIES....FARMTRAC SERIES
ENGINE....FORD
CYLINDERS....3
CID....175
PTO HP....35
ENGINE HP....42
FUEL....D
SPEEDS....8/2
WEIGHT....4,158 LBS.
MSRP....$13,686

RETAIL PRICING

YEAR	HIGH	LOW
2002	$5,069	$3,801
2003	$5,340	$4,005

260

YEARS MFRD....1980-1986
ENGINE....UTB
CID....95
PTO HP....24
FUEL....D
SPEEDS....6/2
TRANSMISSION....GEAR
STEERING....STANDARD
PTO....YES
WEIGHT....3,700 LBS.
MSRP....$8,630

RETAIL PRICING

YEAR	HIGH	LOW
1986	$2,213	$1,660

260C

YEARS MFRD....1980-1986
ENGINE....UTB
CID....95
PTO HP....24
FUEL....D
SPEEDS....6/2
TRANSMISSION....GEAR
STEERING....STANDARD
PTO....YES
WEIGHT....3,195 LBS.
MSRP....$8,620

RETAIL PRICING

YEAR	HIGH	LOW
1986	$2,209	$1,657

270DTC

YEARS MFRD....2005-2005
SERIES....FARMTRAC SERIES
ENGINE....LONG
CYLINDERS....3
CID....85
PTO HP....23.8
ENGINE HP....27
COOLING....LIQUID
FUEL....D
SPEEDS....8/8
TRANSMISSION....SHUTTLE SHIFT
STEERING....STANDARD
HITCH....CAT. I
HYDRAULIC....YES
PTO....YES
WEIGHT....2,600 LBS.
MSRP....$12,727

RETAIL PRICING

YEAR	HIGH	LOW
2005	$5,249	$3,937

280

YEARS MFRD....1998-2000
SERIES....LANDTRAC SERIES
ENGINE....MITSUBISHI
CYLINDERS....4
CID....91.5
PTO HP....27
ENGINE HP....28
FUEL....D
SPEEDS....12/6
WEIGHT....3,050 LBS.
MSRP....$15,450

RETAIL PRICING

YEAR	HIGH	LOW
1998	$6,227	$4,670
1999	$6,641	$4,981
2000	$6,963	$5,222

300DTC

YEARS MFRD....2004-2005
SERIES....FARMTRAC SERIES
ENGINE....MITSUBISHI
CYLINDERS....4
CID....91.5
PTO HP....27
ENGINE HP....30
COOLING....LIQUID
FUEL....D
SPEEDS....12/12
TRANSMISSION....SHUTTLE SHIFT
STEERING....STANDARD
HITCH....CAT. I
HYDRAULIC....YES
PTO....YES
DRIVE TYPE....4WD
ROPS/CAB....ROPS
WEIGHT....3,050 LBS.
MSRP....$14,805

RETAIL PRICING

YEAR	HIGH	LOW
2004	$5,902	$4,426
2005	$6,109	$4,582

310

YEARS MFRD....1980-1990
ENGINE....UTB
CID....109.7
PTO HP....28
FUEL....D
SPEEDS....8/2
TRANSMISSION....GEAR
STEERING....STANDARD
WEIGHT....3,270 LBS.
MSRP....$8,515

RETAIL PRICING

YEAR	HIGH	LOW
1990	$2,419	$1,814

310C

YEARS MFRD....1981-1984
ENGINE....UTB
CID....109.7
PTO HP....28
FUEL....D
SPEEDS....6/2
TRANSMISSION....GEAR
STEERING....STANDARD
PTO....YES
WEIGHT....3,195 LBS.
MSRP....$8,735

RETAIL PRICING

YEAR	HIGH	LOW
1984	$1,997	$1,498

310DTC

YEARS MFRD....1980-1994
ENGINE....UTB
CID....109.7
PTO HP....28
FUEL....D
SPEEDS....8/2
TRANSMISSION....GEAR
STEERING....STANDARD
PTO....YES
WEIGHT....4,430 LBS.
MSRP....$11,465

RETAIL PRICING

YEAR	HIGH	LOW
1990	$3,088	$2,316
1991	$3,356	$2,517
1992	$3,493	$2,620
1993	$3,732	$2,799
1994	$3,943	$2,957

320DTC

YEARS MFRD....2004-2005
SERIES....FARMTRAC SERIES
ENGINE....LONG
CYLINDERS....3
CID....100.5
PTO HP....28.5
ENGINE HP....32
COOLING....LIQUID
FUEL....D
SPEEDS....8/8
TRANSMISSION....SHUTTLE SHIFT
STEERING....STANDARD
HITCH....CAT. I
HYDRAULIC....YES
PTO....YES
WEIGHT....2,660 LBS.
MSRP....$13,766

RETAIL PRICING

YEAR	HIGH	LOW
2004	$5,488	$4,116
2005	$5,677	$4,258

330HST

YEARS MFRD....2002-2006
SERIES....FARMTRAC SERIES
ENGINE....DAEDONG 3A165LG
CYLINDERS....3
CID....100.5
PTO HP....30
ENGINE HP....35
COOLING....LIQUID
FUEL....D
SPEEDS....VARIABLE
TRANSMISSION....HYDRO
STEERING....STANDARD
HYDRAULIC....YES
PTO....YES
WEIGHT....3,087 LBS.

350

YEARS MFRD....1974-1976
ENGINE....UTB
CID....143
PTO HP....32
FUEL....D
SPEEDS....6/2
TRANSMISSION....GEAR
STEERING....STANDARD
PTO....YES
WEIGHT....3,700 LBS.
MSRP....$4,554

RETAIL PRICING

YEAR	HIGH	LOW
1976	$791	$593

360

YEARS MFRD....1977-1994
ENGINE....UTB
CID....142.8
PTO HP....35
FUEL....D
SPEEDS....8/2
TRANSMISSION....GEAR
STEERING....STANDARD
PTO....YES
WEIGHT....3,900 LBS.
MSRP....$8,995

RETAIL PRICING

YEAR	HIGH	LOW
1994	$3,094	$2,320

360DTC

YEARS MFRD....2004-2005
SERIES....FARMTRAC SERIES
ENGINE....MITSUBISHI
CYLINDERS....4
CID....107.3
PTO HP....33
ENGINE HP....39
COOLING....LIQUID
FUEL....D

SPEEDS 12/12
TRANSMISSION ... SHUTTLE SHIFT
STEERING .... STANDARD
HITCH .... CAT. I
HYDRAULIC .... YES
PTO .... YES
WEIGHT .... 3,050 LBS.
MSRP $16,757

OPTIONS

UTB 35PTO HP

RETAIL PRICING

YEAR	HIGH	LOW
2004	$6,676	$5,007
2005	$6,915	$5,186

360DTC

YEARS MFRD 1980-1994
ENGINE .... UTB
CID 142.8
PTO HP 35
FUEL .... D
SPEEDS 8/2
TRANSMISSION .... GEAR
STEERING .... STANDARD
PTO .... YES
WEIGHT .... 4,300 LBS.
MSRP $12,140

RETAIL PRICING

YEAR	HIGH	LOW
1994	$4,174	$3,130

360DTC

YEARS MFRD 1998-2003
SERIES .... LANDTRAC SERIES
ENGINE .... MITSUBISHI
CYLINDERS 4
CID 107.3
PTO HP 33
ENGINE HP 39
FUEL .... D
SPEEDS 12/6
WEIGHT .... 3,050 LBS.
MSRP $17,309

OPTIONS

UTB 35PTO HP

RETAIL PRICING

YEAR	HIGH	LOW
2003	$7,114	$5,335

390HST

YEARS MFRD 2004-2005
SERIES .... FARMTRAC SERIES
ENGINE .... LONG
CYLINDERS 4
CID 107.3
PTO HP 33
ENGINE HP 39
COOLING .... LIQUID
FUEL .... D
SPEEDS .... VARIABLE
TRANSMISSION .... HYDRO
STEERING .... STANDARD
HITCH .... CAT. I
HYDRAULIC .... YES
PTO .... YES
WEIGHT .... 3,090 LBS.
MSRP $18,961

RETAIL PRICING

YEAR	HIGH	LOW
2004	$7,558	$5,668
2005	$7,822	$5,867

390ST

YEARS MFRD 2002-2002
SERIES .... LANDTRAC SERIES
ENGINE .... MITSUBISHI S4L2
CID 107.3
PTO HP 33
ENGINE HP 39
FUEL .... D
SPEEDS .... HYDRO
WEIGHT .... 3,087 LBS.

410

YEARS MFRD 1997-2000
SERIES .... LANDTRAC SERIES
ENGINE .... MITSUBISHI
CYLINDERS 4
CID 141
PTO HP 35
ENGINE HP 41
FUEL .... D
SPEEDS 16/16, 8/8
WEIGHT .... 4,440 LBS.
MSRP $18,895

RETAIL PRICING

YEAR	HIGH	LOW
1997	$5,948	$4,461
1998	$6,312	$4,734
1999	$6,822	$5,116
2000	$7,214	$5,410

435

YEARS MFRD 2005-2007
SERIES .... FARMTRAC SERIES
ENGINE .... LONG
CYLINDERS 3
CID 131
PTO HP 31
ENGINE HP 35
COOLING .... LIQUID
FUEL .... D
SPEEDS 8/2
TRANSMISSION .... GEAR
STEERING .... STANDARD
HITCH .... CAT. I
HYDRAULIC .... YES
PTO .... YES
WEIGHT .... 4,220 LBS.

445

YEARS MFRD 1972-1976
ENGINE .... UTB
CYLINDERS 3
CID 143
PTO HP 41
FUEL .... D
SPEEDS 6/2
TRANSMISSION .... GEAR
STEERING .... STANDARD
PTO .... YES
WEIGHT .... 4,100 LBS.
MSRP $3,665

RETAIL PRICING

YEAR	HIGH	LOW
1976	$638	$478

445DTC

YEARS MFRD 1972-1976
ENGINE .... UTB
CYLINDERS 3
CID 143
PTO HP 41
FUEL .... D
SPEEDS 6/2
TRANSMISSION .... GEAR
STEERING .... STANDARD
PTO .... YES
WEIGHT .... 4,540 LBS.
MSRP $5,825

RETAIL PRICING

YEAR	HIGH	LOW
1976	$1,012	$759

450

YEARS MFRD 2000-2002
SERIES .... LANDTRAC SERIES
ENGINE .... MITSUBISHI
CYLINDERS 4
CID 141
PTO HP 36
ENGINE HP 45
COOLING .... LIQUID
FUEL .... D
SPEEDS 8/8
TRANSMISSION .... GEAR
HYDRAULIC .... YES
WEIGHT .... 4,610 LBS.

450DTC

YEARS MFRD 2005-2005
SERIES .... FARMTRAC SERIES
ENGINE .... LONG
CYLINDERS 4
CID 141
PTO HP 36
ENGINE HP 45
COOLING .... LIQUID
FUEL .... D
SPEEDS 8/8
TRANSMISSION ..... POWER SHIFT
STEERING .... STANDARD
HITCH .... CAT. II
HYDRAULIC .... YES
PTO .... YES
WEIGHT .... 4,440 LBS.

450DTC

YEARS MFRD 2000-2003
SERIES .... LANDTRAC SERIES
ENGINE .... MITSUBISHI
CYLINDERS 4
CID 141
PTO HP 36
ENGINE HP 45
FUEL .... D
SPEEDS 8/8
MSRP $19,228

RETAIL PRICING

YEAR	HIGH	LOW
2003	$8,769	$6,577

460

YEARS MFRD 1977-1994
ENGINE .... UTB
CYLINDERS 3
CID 142.8
PTO HP 41.9
FUEL .... D
SPEEDS 8/2
TRANSMISSION .... GEAR
STEERING .... STANDARD
PTO .... YES
DRIVE TYPE 2WD
ROPS/CAB .... ROPS
WEIGHT .... 4,010 LBS.
MSRP $9,610

RETAIL PRICING

YEAR	HIGH	LOW
1994	$3,305	$2,478

460 V

YEARS MFRD 1980-1986
ENGINE .... UTB
CID 142.8
PTO HP 41.9
FUEL .... D
SPEEDS 8/2
TRANSMISSION .... GEAR
STEERING .... STANDARD
PTO .... YES
WEIGHT .... 3,820 LBS.
MSRP $10,885

RETAIL PRICING

YEAR	HIGH	LOW
1986	$2,790	$2,093

460DTC

YEARS MFRD 1978-1994
ENGINE .... UTB
CYLINDERS 3
CID 142.8
PTO HP 41.9
FUEL .... D
SPEEDS 8/2
TRANSMISSION .... GEAR
STEERING .... STANDARD
PTO .... YES
WEIGHT .... 5,263 LBS.
MSRP $12,765

RETAIL PRICING

YEAR	HIGH	LOW
1994	$4,388	$3,291

LONG

460SD

YEARS MFRD 1988-1994
ENGINE .... UTB
CID 143
PTO HP 41.9
FUEL .... D
SPEEDS 8/8-8/2
STEERING............ STANDARD
PTO .... YES
DRIVE TYPE 4WD
ROPS/CAB .... ROPS
WEIGHT .... 4,653 LBS.
MSRP.................. $13,645

RETAIL PRICING

YEAR	HIGH	LOW
1994	$4,693	$3,520

470DTC

YEARS MFRD 1997-2003
SERIES........ LANDTRAC SERIES
ENGINE .... MITSUBISHI
CYLINDERS.................... 4
CID 153
PTO HP 41
ENGINE HP 50
FUEL .... D
SPEEDS 8/8
WEIGHT .... 4,540 LBS.
MSRP.................. $20,222

RETAIL PRICING

YEAR	HIGH	LOW
2003	$9,289	$6,967

480

YEARS MFRD 1999-2003
SERIES........ LONGTRAC SERIES
ENGINE .... UTB
CYLINDERS.................... 3
CID 172
PTO HP 42
ENGINE HP 48
FUEL .... D
SPEEDS 8/2
TRANSMISSION .... GEAR
STEERING............ STANDARD
PTO .... YES

480DTC

YEARS MFRD 1999-2003
SERIES........ LONGTRAC SERIES
ENGINE .... UTB
CYLINDERS.................... 3
CID 172
PTO HP 42
ENGINE HP 49
FUEL .... D
SPEEDS 8/8
TRANSMISSION .... HYDRO
STEERING............ STANDARD
PTO .... YES

510

YEARS MFRD 1979-1990
ENGINE .... UTB/UNIVERSAL
CYLINDERS.................... 3
PTO HP 49.3
COOLING .... LIQUID
FUEL .... D
SPEEDS 8/2
TRANSMISSION .... GEAR
STEERING............ STANDARD
WEIGHT .... 4,285 LBS.

535

YEARS MFRD 2005-2007
SERIES........ FARMTRAC SERIES
ENGINE .... LONG
CYLINDERS.................... 3
CID 131
PTO HP 30
ENGINE HP 35
COOLING .... LIQUID
FUEL .... D
SPEEDS 8/2
TRANSMISSION .... GEAR
STEERING............ STANDARD
HITCH .... CAT. I
HYDRAULIC .... YES
PTO .... YES
WEIGHT .... 4,220 LBS.

545

YEARS MFRD 2005-2007
SERIES........ FARMTRAC SERIES
ENGINE .... LONG
CYLINDERS.................... 3
CID 175
PTO HP 37
ENGINE HP 42
COOLING .... LIQUID
FUEL .... D
SPEEDS 8/2
TRANSMISSION .... GEAR
STEERING............ STANDARD
HITCH .... CAT. I
HYDRAULIC .... YES
PTO .... YES
WEIGHT .... 4,160 LBS.

545DTC

YEARS MFRD 2005-2007
SERIES........ FARMTRAC SERIES
ENGINE .... LONG
CYLINDERS.................... 3
CID 175
PTO HP 37
ENGINE HP 42
COOLING .... LIQUID
FUEL .... D
SPEEDS 8/2
TRANSMISSION .... GEAR
STEERING............ STANDARD
HITCH .... CAT. I
HYDRAULIC .... YES
PTO .... YES
WEIGHT .... 4,600 LBS.

2260

YEARS MFRD 1993-1995
ENGINE .... UNIVERSAL
CYLINDERS.................... 2
CID 95.15
PTO HP 24
FUEL .... D
TRANSMISSION .... GEAR
STEERING............ STANDARD
PTO .... YES
MSRP.................... $7,830

RETAIL PRICING

YEAR	HIGH	LOW
1993	$2,520	$1,890
1994	$2,692	$2,019
1995	$2,796	$2,097

2260 COMPACT

YEARS MFRD 1994-1996
ENGINE .... UTB
CYLINDERS.................... 2
CID 95.15
PTO HP 24
FUEL .... D
SPEEDS .... 6/2 SYNC
TRANSMISSION .... GEAR
STEERING............ STANDARD
PTO .... YES
WEIGHT .... 3,120 LBS.
MSRP.................. $10,180

RETAIL PRICING

YEAR	HIGH	LOW
1994	$3,432	$2,574
1995	$3,634	$2,725
1996	$3,766	$2,825

2310

YEARS MFRD 1995-1999
ENGINE .... UNIVERSAL
CYLINDERS.................... 2
CID 109.7
PTO HP 28
ENGINE HP 32
FUEL .... D
SPEEDS 8/4,6/2
TRANSMISSION .... GEAR
STEERING............ STANDARD
MSRP.................... $9,195

RETAIL PRICING

YEAR	HIGH	LOW
1995	$3,217	$2,413
1996	$3,403	$2,552
1997	$3,529	$2,647
1998	$3,706	$2,780
1999	$3,952	$2,964

2360

YEARS MFRD 1990-2001
ENGINE .... UTB
CYLINDERS.................... 3
CID 142.8
PTO HP 35
FUEL .... D
SPEEDS 8/2
WEIGHT .... 4,220 LBS.
MSRP.................. $12,900

RETAIL PRICING

YEAR	HIGH	LOW
1990	$3,524	$2,643
1991	$3,759	$2,819
1992	$3,977	$2,983
1993	$4,102	$3,077
1994	$4,402	$3,302
1995	$4,568	$3,426
1996	$4,845	$3,634
1997	$5,025	$3,769
1998	$5,159	$3,869
1999	$5,502	$4,126
2000	$5,814	$4,361
2001	$6,062	$4,547

2360DTC

YEARS MFRD 1990-2001
SERIES........ LONGTRAC SERIES
ENGINE .... UTB
CYLINDERS.................... 3
CID 142.8
PTO HP 35
FUEL .... D
SPEEDS 8/2
WEIGHT .... 4,760 LBS.
MSRP.................. $17,100

RETAIL PRICING

YEAR	HIGH	LOW
1990	$4,830	$3,623
1991	$5,156	$3,867
1992	$5,428	$4,071
1993	$5,599	$4,199
1994	$5,949	$4,461
1995	$6,178	$4,633
1996	$6,511	$4,883
1997	$6,754	$5,066
1998	$6,972	$5,229
1999	$7,439	$5,579
2000	$7,707	$5,780
2001	$8,037	$6,028

2460

YEARS MFRD 1990-2001
ENGINE .... UNIVERSAL
CYLINDERS.................... 3
CID 109.7
PTO HP 41.9
FUEL .... D
SPEEDS 8/2
TRANSMISSION .... GEAR
STEERING............ STANDARD
PTO .... YES
WEIGHT .... 4,220 LBS.
MSRP.................. $13,531

RETAIL PRICING

YEAR	HIGH	LOW
2001	$6,555	$4,916

AVG. AUCTION PRICING

LOW	HIGH	AVG
$2,695	$6,125	$4,736

2460DTC

YEARS MFRD 1990-2002
ENGINE UNIVERSAL
CYLINDERS 3
CID 109.7
PTO HP 41.9
FUEL D
SPEEDS 8/2
TRANSMISSION GEAR
STEERING STANDARD
PTO YES
WEIGHT 4,760 LBS.
MSRP $17,496

RETAIL PRICING

YEAR	HIGH	LOW
2002	$8,452	$6,339

2460DTC-SD

YEARS MFRD 1990-1996
ENGINE UTB
CYLINDERS 3
CID 142.8
PTO HP 41.9
FUEL D
SPEEDS 8/2
TRANSMISSION GEAR
STEERING STANDARD
PTO YES
DRIVE TYPE 4WD
ROPS/CAB ROPS
WEIGHT 4,760 LBS.
MSRP $14,905

RETAIL PRICING

YEAR	HIGH	LOW
1996	$5,513	$4,135

2460SD

YEARS MFRD 1990-1996
ENGINE UTB
CYLINDERS 3
CID 142.8
PTO HP 41.9
FUEL D
SPEEDS 8/8
TRANSMISSION HYDRO
STEERING STANDARD
PTO YES
DRIVE TYPE 2WD
ROPS/CAB ROPS
WEIGHT 4,220 LBS.
MSRP $11,575

RETAIL PRICING

YEAR	HIGH	LOW
1996	$4,283	$3,212

LS TRACTOR USA

C3030

YEARS MFRD 2010-2011
ENGINE MITSUBISHI
CYLINDERS 4
CID 91
PTO HP 23
COOLING LIQUID
FUEL D
SPEEDS 12/12
TRANSMISSION SHUTTLE SHIFT
STEERING STANDARD
HITCH CAT. I
HYDRAULIC YES
PTO YES
MSRP $15,495

RETAIL PRICING

YEAR	HIGH	LOW
2010	$8,754	$6,566
2011	$8,865	$6,649

G3033

YEARS MFRD 2011-2016
ENGINE L3BL
CYLINDERS 3
CID 116.9
PTO HP 27
ENGINE HP 33
COOLING LIQUID
FUEL D
SPEEDS 12/12
TRANSMISSION SHUTTLE SHIFT
STEERING STANDARD
HITCH CAT. I
HYDRAULIC YES
PTO YES
DRIVE TYPE 2WD
ROPS/CAB ROPS
WEIGHT 2,590 LBS.
MSRP $17,990

OPTIONS

HYDRO

RETAIL PRICING

YEAR	HIGH	LOW
2011	$6,089	$4,567
2012	$6,745	$5,059
2013	$9,769	$7,326
2014	$11,039	$8,279
2015	$11,608	$8,706
2016	$13,034	$9,776

G3038

YEARS MFRD 2011-2016
ENGINE L3AL
CYLINDERS 3
CID 122.2
PTO HP 32
ENGINE HP 38
COOLING LIQUID
FUEL D
SPEEDS 12/12
TRANSMISSION SHUTTLE SHIFT
STEERING STANDARD
HITCH CAT. I
HYDRAULIC YES
PTO YES
DRIVE TYPE 2WD
ROPS/CAB ROPS
WEIGHT 2,690 LBS.
MSRP $15,425

OPTIONS

4WD
HYDRO

RETAIL PRICING

YEAR	HIGH	LOW
2011	$6,571	$4,928
2012	$7,316	$5,487
2013	$10,294	$7,720
2014	$10,776	$8,082
2015	$11,390	$8,542
2016	$12,372	$9,279

I3030

YEARS MFRD 2009-2012
ENGINE MITSUBISHI S4L
CYLINDERS 4
CID 91.5
PTO HP 23
ENGINE HP 28.5
COOLING LIQUID
FUEL D
SPEEDS 12/12
TRANSMISSION GEAR
STEERING STANDARD
HITCH CAT. I
HYDRAULIC YES
PTO YES
WEIGHT 2,780 LBS.
MSRP $18,260

RETAIL PRICING

YEAR	HIGH	LOW
2009	$5,824	$4,368
2010	$6,650	$4,988
2011	$8,305	$6,228
2012	$10,959	$8,220

I3030H

YEARS MFRD 2009-2012
ENGINE MITSUBISHI S4L
CYLINDERS 4
CID 91.5
PTO HP 22.5
ENGINE HP 28.5
COOLING LIQUID
FUEL D
SPEEDS VARIABLE
TRANSMISSION HYDRO
STEERING STANDARD
HYDRAULIC YES
PTO YES
WEIGHT 2,780 LBS.
MSRP $17,395

RETAIL PRICING

YEAR	HIGH	LOW
2009	$6,100	$4,575
2010	$6,962	$5,221
2011	$8,787	$6,590
2012	$10,511	$7,883

I3040

YEARS MFRD 2009-2012
ENGINE MITSUBISHI S4L2
CYLINDERS 4
CID 107.3
PTO HP 31
ENGINE HP 38.5
COOLING LIQUID
FUEL D
SPEEDS 12/12
TRANSMISSION GEAR
STEERING STANDARD
HITCH CAT. I
HYDRAULIC YES
PTO YES
WEIGHT 2,780 LBS.
MSRP $17,895

RETAIL PRICING

YEAR	HIGH	LOW
2009	$6,306	$4,730
2010	$7,169	$5,377
2011	$9,064	$6,798
2012	$10,235	$7,676

I3040H

YEARS MFRD 2009-2012
ENGINE MITSUBISHI S4L2
CYLINDERS 4
CID 107.3
PTO HP 29
ENGINE HP 38.5
COOLING LIQUID
FUEL D
SPEEDS VARIABLE
TRANSMISSION HYDRO
STEERING STANDARD
HITCH CAT. I
HYDRAULIC YES
PTO YES
WEIGHT 2,780 LBS.
MSRP $19,195

RETAIL PRICING

YEAR	HIGH	LOW
2009	$6,755	$5,066
2010	$7,685	$5,764
2011	$9,787	$7,340
2012	$11,958	$8,968

J2020H

YEARS MFRD 2009-2015
ENGINE MITSUBISHI S3L
CYLINDERS 3
CID 68.7
PTO HP 17.5
ENGINE HP 23
COOLING LIQUID
FUEL D
SPEEDS VARIABLE
TRANSMISSION HYDRO
STEERING STANDARD
HITCH CAT. I
HYDRAULIC YES
PTO YES
DRIVE TYPE 2WD
ROPS/CAB ROPS
WEIGHT 1,565 LBS.
MSRP $17,610

RETAIL PRICING

YEAR	HIGH	LOW
2009	$4,034	$3,025
2010	$4,663	$3,497
2011	$4,885	$3,664

LS TRACTOR USA

2012	$5,292	$3,969
2013	$8,067	$6,051
2014	$8,882	$6,661
2015	$10,688	$8,016

J2023

YEARS MFRD 2015-2015
ENGINE . . . . MITSUBISHI S3L
CYLINDERS. 3
CID 68.7
PTO HP 17.5
ENGINE HP 23
COOLING . . . . LIQUID
FUEL . . . . D
SPEEDS 12/12
TRANSMISSION . . . SHUTTLE SHIFT
STEERING. . . . . STANDARD
HITCH . . . . CAT. I
DRIVE TYPE 2WD
ROPS/CAB . . . . ROPS
WEIGHT . . . . 1,565 LBS.

J2030H

YEARS MFRD 2009-2015
ENGINE . . . . MITSUBISHI S3L2
CYLINDERS. 3
CID 80.1
PTO HP 20.5
ENGINE HP 27
COOLING . . . . LIQUID
FUEL . . . . D
SPEEDS . . . . VARIABLE
TRANSMISSION . . . . HYDRO
STEERING. . . . . STANDARD
HITCH . . . . CAT. I
HYDRAULIC . . . . YES
PTO . . . . YES
DRIVE TYPE 2WD
ROPS/CAB . . . . ROPS
WEIGHT . . . . 1,587 LBS.
MSRP. $18,830

RETAIL PRICING

YEAR	HIGH	LOW
2009	$4,330	$3,247
2010	$4,958	$3,718
2011	$5,329	$3,997
2012	$5,810	$4,358
2013	$8,659	$6,494
2014	$9,473	$7,105
2015	$11,100	$8,325

K5047

YEARS MFRD 2015-2016
ENGINE . . . . MITSUBISHI
CYLINDERS. 4
CID 152D
PTO HP 38
COOLING . . . . LIQUID
FUEL . . . . D
SPEEDS 8/8
TRANSMISSION . . . SHUTTLE SHIFT
STEERING. . . . . STANDARD
DRIVE TYPE 4WD
ROPS/CAB . . . . ROPS
WEIGHT . . . . 4,492 LBS.
MSRP. $23,780

RETAIL PRICING

YEAR	HIGH	LOW
2015	$14,148	$10,611
2016	$17,329	$12,997

K5055

YEARS MFRD 2015-2016
ENGINE . . . . MITSUBISHI
CYLINDERS. 4
CID 203D
PTO HP 46
COOLING . . . . LIQUID
FUEL . . . . D
SPEEDS 8/8
TRANSMISSION . . . SHUTTLE SHIFT
DRIVE TYPE 2WD
ROPS/CAB . . . . ROPS
WEIGHT . . . . 4,453 LBS.
MSRP. $22,415

OPTIONS

4WD

RETAIL PRICING

YEAR	HIGH	LOW
2015	$13,360	$10,020
2016	$17,398	$13,048

MT122

YEARS MFRD 2017-2020
ENGINE . . . . YANMAR
CYLINDERS. 3
CID 68
PTO HP 15
ENGINE HP 21.5
COOLING . . . . LIQUID
FUEL . . . . D
SPEEDS . . . . VARIABLE
TRANSMISSION . . . . HYDRO
STEERING. . . . . STANDARD
HITCH . . . . CAT. I
DRIVE TYPE 2WD
ROPS/CAB . . . . ROPS
WEIGHT . . . . 1,433 LBS.

MT125

YEARS MFRD 2017-2020
ENGINE . . . . YANMAR 3TNV80F
CYLINDERS. 3
CID 77.3
PTO HP 17.2
ENGINE HP 24.7
COOLING . . . . LIQUID
FUEL . . . . D
SPEEDS . . . . VARIABLE
TRANSMISSION . . . . HYDRO
STEERING. . . . . STANDARD
HITCH . . . . CAT. I
DRIVE TYPE 2WD
ROPS/CAB . . . . ROPS
WEIGHT . . . . 1,444 LBS.

MT225E

YEARS MFRD 2019-2020
SERIES. . . . . MT2E SERIES
ENGINE S3L2
CYLINDERS. 3
CID 80.4
PTO HP 19.2
ENGINE HP 24.6
COOLING . . . . LIQUID
FUEL . . . . D
SPEEDS 12/12
TRANSMISSION SYNCHRO SHUTTLE
STEERING. . . . . STANDARD
HITCH . . . . CAT. I
ROPS/CAB . . . . ROPS
WEIGHT . . . . 2,434 LBS.

MT225HE

YEARS MFRD 2019-2020
SERIES. . . . . MT2E SERIES
ENGINE S3LA
CYLINDERS. 3
CID 80.4
PTO HP 17.2
ENGINE HP 24.6
COOLING . . . . LIQUID
FUEL . . . . D
SPEEDS . . . . VARIABLE
TRANSMISSION . . . . HYDRO
STEERING. . . . . STANDARD
HITCH . . . . CAT. I
ROPS/CAB . . . . ROPS
WEIGHT . . . . 2,469 LBS.

MT230E

YEARS MFRD 2019-2020
SERIES. . . . . MT2E SERIES
ENGINE L3C19-D3
CYLINDERS. 3
CID 114.7
PTO HP 25.5
ENGINE HP 30
COOLING . . . . LIQUID
FUEL . . . . D
SPEEDS 12/12
TRANSMISSION SYNCHRO SHUTTLE
STEERING. . . . . STANDARD
HITCH . . . . CAT. I
ROPS/CAB . . . . ROPS
WEIGHT . . . . 2,866 LBS.

MT235E

YEARS MFRD 2019-2020
SERIES. . . . . MT2E SERIES
ENGINE L3C19-D2
CYLINDERS. 3
CID 114.7
PTO HP 29.7
ENGINE HP 35
COOLING . . . . LIQUID
FUEL . . . . D
SPEEDS 12/12
TRANSMISSION SYNCHRO SHUTTLE
STEERING. . . . . STANDARD
HITCH . . . . CAT. I
ROPS/CAB . . . . ROPS
WEIGHT . . . . 2,866 LBS.

MT235HE

YEARS MFRD 2019-2020
SERIES. . . . . MT2E SERIES
ENGINE L3C19-D2
CYLINDERS. 3
CID 114.7
PTO HP 28
ENGINE HP 35
COOLING . . . . LIQUID
FUEL . . . . D
SPEEDS . . . . VARIABLE
TRANSMISSION . . . . HYDRO
STEERING. . . . . STANDARD
HITCH . . . . CAT. I
ROPS/CAB . . . . ROPS
WEIGHT . . . . 2,870 LBS.

MT240E

YEARS MFRD 2019-2020
SERIES. . . . . MT2E SERIES
ENGINE L3C19-T
CYLINDERS. 3
CID 114.7
PTO HP 34.4
ENGINE HP 40
COOLING . . . . LIQUID
FUEL . . . . D
SPEEDS 12/12
TRANSMISSION SYNCHRO SHUTTLE
STEERING. . . . . STANDARD
HITCH . . . . CAT. I
ROPS/CAB . . . . ROPS
WEIGHT . . . . 2,881 LBS.

MT240HE

YEARS MFRD 2019-2020
SERIES. . . . . MT2E SERIES
ENGINE L3C19-T
CYLINDERS. 3
CID 114.7
PTO HP 32
ENGINE HP 40
COOLING . . . . LIQUID
FUEL . . . . D
SPEEDS . . . . VARIABLE
TRANSMISSION . . . . HYDRO
STEERING. . . . . STANDARD
HITCH . . . . CAT. I
ROPS/CAB . . . . ROPS
WEIGHT . . . . 2,884 LBS.

MT345E

YEARS MFRD 2018-2020
ENGINE L3C19T
CYLINDERS. 3
CID 114.7
PTO HP 38.2
ENGINE HP 45
COOLING . . . . LIQUID
FUEL . . . . D
SPEEDS 8/8
STEERING. . . . . STANDARD
DRIVE TYPE 4WD
ROPS/CAB . . . . ROPS
WEIGHT . . . . 3,724 LBS.

OPTIONS

HYDRO

MT350E

YEARS MFRD 2018-2020
ENGINE L3C19T
CYLINDERS 3
CID 114.7
PTO HP 42.5
ENGINE HP 50
COOLING .... LIQUID
FUEL .... D
SPEEDS 8/8
STEERING .... STANDARD
DRIVE TYPE 4WD
ROPS/CAB .... ROPS
WEIGHT .... 3,724 LBS.

OPTIONS

HYDRO

R3037C

YEARS MFRD 2013-2014
ENGINE .... SHIBAURA
CYLINDERS 3
CID 91
PTO HP 30.3
COOLING .... LIQUID
FUEL .... D
SPEEDS 12/12
TRANSMISSION .... GEAR
STEERING .... STANDARD
DRIVE TYPE 2WD
ROPS/CAB .... CAB
WEIGHT .... 3,567 LBS.
MSRP $31,715

OPTIONS

HYDRO

RETAIL PRICING

YEAR	HIGH	LOW
2013	$15,950	$11,962
2014	$17,837	$13,378

R3039

YEARS MFRD 2011-2015
ENGINE .... MITSUBISHI S4L2
CYLINDERS 4
CID 107.3
PTO HP 31
ENGINE HP 38.5
COOLING .... LIQUID
FUEL .... D
SPEEDS 12/12
TRANSMISSION ... SHUTTLE SHIFT
STEERING .... STANDARD
HITCH .... CAT. I
HYDRAULIC .... YES
PTO .... YES
DRIVE TYPE 2WD
ROPS/CAB .... ROPS
WEIGHT .... 2,780 LBS.
MSRP $25,405

OPTIONS

HYDRO

RETAIL PRICING

YEAR	HIGH	LOW
2011	$7,845	$5,884
2012	$8,511	$6,383
2013	$11,657	$8,743
2014	$12,805	$9,604
2015	$15,814	$11,861

R4010

YEARS MFRD 2009-2012
ENGINE .... MITSUBISHI S4QL
CYLINDERS 4
CID 152.9
PTO HP 35
ENGINE HP 41
COOLING .... LIQUID
FUEL .... D
SPEEDS 16/16
TRANSMISSION ... SHUTTLE SHIFT
STEERING .... STANDARD
HITCH .... CAT. I
HYDRAULIC .... YES
PTO .... YES
WEIGHT .... 3,813 LBS.
MSRP $19,795

RETAIL PRICING

YEAR	HIGH	LOW
2009	$6,962	$5,221
2010	$7,927	$5,945
2011	$9,581	$7,186
2012	$11,647	$8,735

R4010H

YEARS MFRD 2009-2012
ENGINE .... MITSUBISHI S4QS
CYLINDERS 4
CID 152.9
PTO HP 33
ENGINE HP 41
COOLING .... LIQUID
FUEL .... D
SPEEDS .... VARIABLE
TRANSMISSION .... HYDRO
STEERING .... STANDARD
HITCH .... CAT. I
HYDRAULIC .... YES
PTO .... YES
WEIGHT .... 3,813 LBS.
MSRP $21,595

RETAIL PRICING

YEAR	HIGH	LOW
2009	$7,580	$5,685
2010	$8,650	$6,488
2011	$10,545	$7,909
2012	$12,716	$9,537

R4020

YEARS MFRD 2009-2012
ENGINE .... MITSUBISHI S4QL
CYLINDERS 4
CID 152.9
PTO HP 41
ENGINE HP 47
COOLING .... LIQUID
FUEL .... D
SPEEDS 16/16
TRANSMISSION ... SHUTTLE SHIFT
STEERING .... STANDARD
HITCH .... CAT. I
WEIGHT .... 3,813 LBS.
MSRP $21,795

RETAIL PRICING

YEAR	HIGH	LOW
2009	$7,651	$5,738
2010	$8,717	$6,538
2011	$10,097	$7,573
2012	$13,061	$9,796

R4020H

YEARS MFRD 2009-2012
ENGINE .... MITSUBISHI S4QL
CYLINDERS 4
CID 152.9
PTO HP 38
ENGINE HP 47
COOLING .... LIQUID
FUEL .... D
SPEEDS .... VARIABLE
TRANSMISSION .... HYDRO
STEERING .... STANDARD
HITCH .... CAT. I
HYDRAULIC .... YES
PTO .... YES
WEIGHT .... 3,813 LBS.
MSRP $23,195

RETAIL PRICING

YEAR	HIGH	LOW
2009	$8,167	$6,125
2010	$9,270	$6,952
2011	$11,269	$8,452
2012	$14,164	$10,623

R4040

YEARS MFRD 2013-2014
ENGINE .... SHIBAURA
CYLINDERS 4
CID 135
PTO HP 33
COOLING .... LIQUID
FUEL .... D
SPEEDS 16/16
TRANSMISSION ... SHUTTLE SHIFT
STEERING .... STANDARD
DRIVE TYPE 2WD
ROPS/CAB .... CAB
WEIGHT .... 4,334 LBS.
MSRP $34,615

OPTIONS

HYDRO

RETAIL PRICING

YEAR	HIGH	LOW
2013	$17,429	$13,072
2014	$19,464	$14,598

R4041

YEARS MFRD 2011-2015
ENGINE .... MITSUBISHI S4QL
CYLINDERS 4
CID 152.9
PTO HP 35
ENGINE HP 41
COOLING .... LIQUID
FUEL .... D
SPEEDS 16/16
TRANSMISSION ... SHUTTLE SHIFT
STEERING .... STANDARD
HITCH .... CAT. I
HYDRAULIC .... YES
PTO .... YES
DRIVE TYPE 2WD
ROPS/CAB .... ROPS
WEIGHT .... 3,813 LBS.
MSRP $28,005

OPTIONS

HYDRO

RETAIL PRICING

YEAR	HIGH	LOW
2011	$8,400	$6,300
2012	$9,139	$6,855
2013	$12,840	$9,630
2014	$14,099	$10,574
2015	$17,508	$13,131

R4041EZ

YEARS MFRD 2011-2014
ENGINE .... MITSUBISHI S4QL-D
CYLINDERS 4
CID 152.9
PTO HP 35
ENGINE HP 41
COOLING .... LIQUID
FUEL .... D
SPEEDS 16/16
TRANSMISSION ... SHUTTLE SHIFT
STEERING .... STANDARD
HITCH .... CAT. I
HYDRAULIC .... YES
PTO .... YES
DRIVE TYPE 2WD
ROPS/CAB .... ROPS
WEIGHT .... 3,813 LBS.
MSRP $28,845

RETAIL PRICING

YEAR	HIGH	LOW
2011	$9,511	$7,133
2012	$10,288	$7,716
2013	$14,506	$10,879
2014	$16,948	$12,711

R4046

YEARS MFRD 2013-2014
ENGINE .... SHIBAURA
CYLINDERS 4
CID 135
PTO HP 37.6
COOLING .... LIQUID
FUEL .... D
SPEEDS 16/16
TRANSMISSION ... SHUTTLE SHIFT
STEERING .... STANDARD
DRIVE TYPE 2WD
ROPS/CAB .... CAB
WEIGHT .... 4,334 LBS.
MSRP $36,255

OPTIONS

HYDRO

LS TRACTOR USA

RETAIL PRICING

YEAR	HIGH	LOW
2013	$18,243	$13,682
2014	$20,390	$15,292

R4047

YEARS MFRD 2011-2015
ENGINE . . . . MITSUBISHI S4QL
CYLINDERS. 4
CID 152.9
PTO HP 41
ENGINE HP 47
COOLING . . . . LIQUID
FUEL . . . . D
SPEEDS 16/16
TRANSMISSION . . . SHUTTLE SHIFT
STEERING. . . . . STANDARD
HITCH . . . . CAT. I
HYDRAULIC . . . . YES
PTO . . . . YES
DRIVE TYPE 2WD
ROPS/CAB . . . . ROPS
WEIGHT . . . . 3,813 LBS.
MSRP. $29,495

OPTIONS

HYDRO

RETAIL PRICING

YEAR	HIGH	LOW
2011	$9,214	$6,910
2012	$9,991	$7,493
2013	$13,544	$10,158
2014	$15,580	$11,685
2015	$18,346	$13,759

R4047EZ

YEARS MFRD 2011-2014
ENGINE . . . . MITSUBISHI S4QL
CYLINDERS. 4
CID 152.9
PTO HP 41
ENGINE HP 47
COOLING . . . . LIQUID
FUEL . . . . D
SPEEDS 16/16
TRANSMISSION . . . SHUTTLE SHIFT
STEERING. . . . . STANDARD
HITCH . . . . CAT. I
HYDRAULIC . . . . YES
PTO . . . . YES
DRIVE TYPE 2WD
ROPS/CAB . . . . ROPS
WEIGHT . . . . 3,813 LBS.
MSRP. $30,345

RETAIL PRICING

YEAR	HIGH	LOW
2011	$10,436	$7,827
2012	$11,250	$8,438
2013	$15,283	$11,462
2014	$17,060	$12,795

S3010

YEARS MFRD 2009-2013
ENGINE . . . . MITSUBISHI S4L
CYLINDERS. 4
CID 91.5
PTO HP 24
ENGINE HP 28.5
COOLING . . . . LIQUID
FUEL . . . . D
SPEEDS 8/8
TRANSMISSION . . . SHUTTLE SHIFT
STEERING. . . . . STANDARD
HITCH . . . . CAT. I
HYDRAULIC . . . . YES
PTO . . . . YES
WEIGHT . . . . 2,769 LBS.
MSRP. $15,915

RETAIL PRICING

YEAR	HIGH	LOW
2009	$4,964	$3,723
2010	$5,607	$4,205
2011	$6,892	$5,169
2012	$7,713	$5,784
2013	$9,371	$7,028

U5020

YEARS MFRD 2010-2011
ENGINE . . . . MITSUBISHI S4QL
CYLINDERS. 4
CID 152.9
PTO HP 42
ENGINE HP 47
COOLING . . . . LIQUID
FUEL . . . . D
SPEEDS 16/16
TRANSMISSION . . . SHUTTLE SHIFT
STEERING. . . . . STANDARD
HITCH . . . . CAT. I
HYDRAULIC . . . . YES
PTO . . . . YES
WEIGHT . . . . 4,280 LBS.
MSRP. $26,995

RETAIL PRICING

YEAR	HIGH	LOW
2010	$15,253	$11,440
2011	$15,443	$11,582

XG3025

YEARS MFRD 2016-2019
ENGINE . . . . MHI S3L2
CYLINDERS. 3
CID 80.4
PTO HP 19.2
ENGINE HP 24.4
COOLING . . . . LIQUID
SPEEDS 12/12
STEERING. . . . . STANDARD
HITCH . . . . CAT. I
DRIVE TYPE 2WD
ROPS/CAB . . . . ROPS
WEIGHT . . . . 2,434 LBS.

OPTIONS

HYDRO

XG3032

YEARS MFRD 2015-2019
ENGINE . . . . SHIBAURA
CYLINDERS. 3
CID 91.3
PTO HP 27.4
ENGINE HP 32.2
COOLING . . . . LIQUID
FUEL . . . . D
SPEEDS 12/12
TRANSMISSION . . . . GEAR
STEERING. . . . . STANDARD
HITCH . . . . CAT. I
DRIVE TYPE 4WD
ROPS/CAB . . . . ROPS
WEIGHT . . . . 2,822 LBS.

OPTIONS

HYDRO

RETAIL PRICING

YEAR	HIGH	LOW
2015	$10,273	$7,705
2016	$13,673	$10,255
2017	$15,407	$11,555
2018	$18,026	$13,520
2019	$20,258	$15,193

XG3037

YEARS MFRD 2015-2019
ENGINE . . . . SHIBAURA
CYLINDERS. 3
CID 91.3
PTO HP 30.8
ENGINE HP 36.2
COOLING . . . . LIQUID
FUEL . . . . D
SPEEDS 12/12
TRANSMISSION . . . SHUTTLE SHIFT
STEERING. . . . . STANDARD
HITCH . . . . CAT. I
DRIVE TYPE 4WD
ROPS/CAB . . . . ROPS
WEIGHT . . . . 2,822 LBS.

OPTIONS

HYDRO

RETAIL PRICING

YEAR	HIGH	LOW
2015	$11,718	$8,788
2016	$13,677	$10,258
2017	$16,279	$12,209
2018	$18,166	$13,625
2019	$20,556	$15,417

XG3135

YEARS MFRD 2016-2019
ENGINE L3C19-T
CYLINDERS. 3
CID 114.7
PTO HP 30.1
ENGINE HP 35
COOLING . . . . LIQUID
FUEL . . . . D
SPEEDS 12/12
STEERING. . . . . STANDARD
HITCH . . . . CAT. I
DRIVE TYPE 2WD
ROPS/CAB . . . . ROPS
WEIGHT . . . . 2,881 LBS.

OPTIONS

HYDRO

XG3140

YEARS MFRD 2016-2019
ENGINE L3C19-T
CYLINDERS. 3
CID 114.7
PTO HP 34.4
ENGINE HP 40
COOLING . . . . LIQUID
FUEL . . . . D
SPEEDS 12/12
STEERING. . . . . STANDARD
HITCH . . . . CAT. I
DRIVE TYPE 2WD
ROPS/CAB . . . . ROPS
WEIGHT . . . . 2,881 LBS.

OPTIONS

HYDRO

XJ2025

YEARS MFRD 2015-2020
ENGINE . . . . MITSUBISHI S3L2
CYLINDERS. 3
CID 80.4
PTO HP 19.5
ENGINE HP 24.4
COOLING . . . . LIQUID
FUEL . . . . D
SPEEDS 6/2
TRANSMISSION . . . . GEAR
STEERING. . . . . STANDARD
HITCH . . . . CAT. I
DRIVE TYPE 2WD
ROPS/CAB . . . . ROPS
WEIGHT . . . . 1,785 LBS.

OPTIONS

HYDRO

RETAIL PRICING

YEAR	HIGH	LOW
2015	$8,366	$6,274
2016	$9,439	$7,079
2017	$10,473	$7,854
2018	$11,620	$8,715
2019	$12,735	$9,551
2020	$13,524	$10,332

XR3032

YEARS MFRD 2015-2015
ENGINE N843T-F
CYLINDERS. 3
CID 91.3
PTO HP 26.4
ENGINE HP 32.2
COOLING . . . . LIQUID
FUEL . . . . D
SPEEDS 12/12
TRANSMISSION . . . SHUTTLE SHIFT
STEERING. . . . . STANDARD
HITCH . . . . CAT. I
WEIGHT . . . . 3,220 LBS.

OPTIONS

HYDRO

XR3037

YEARS MFRD 2015-2018
ENGINE N843T-F
CYLINDERS. 3
CID 91.3
PTO HP 30.3
ENGINE HP 36.5
COOLING . . . . LIQUID
FUEL . . . . D
SPEEDS 12/12
TRANSMISSION . . . SHUTTLE SHIFT
STEERING. . . . . STANDARD
HITCH . . . . CAT. I
DRIVE TYPE 2WD
ROPS/CAB . . . . ROPS
WEIGHT . . . . 3,220 LBS.

OPTIONS

CAB
HYDRO

RETAIL PRICING

YEAR	HIGH	LOW
2015	$12,918	$9,689
2016	$14,722	$11,041
2017	$16,456	$12,342
2018	$18,042	$13,531

XR3135

YEARS MFRD 2015-2020
ENGINE . . . . SHIBAURA
CYLINDERS. 3
CID 114D
PTO HP 30.1
ENGINE HP 35
COOLING . . . . LIQUID
FUEL . . . . D
SPEEDS 12/12
TRANSMISSION . . . SHUTTLE SHIFT
STEERING. . . . . STANDARD
DRIVE TYPE 2WD
ROPS/CAB . . . . ROPS
WEIGHT . . . . 3,689 LBS.

OPTIONS

CAB
HYDRO

RETAIL PRICING

YEAR	HIGH	LOW
2015	$10,534	$7,900
2016	$13,976	$10,482
2017	$16,503	$12,377
2018	$18,141	$13,606
2019	$19,892	$14,919
2020	$20,443	$15,624

XR4040

YEARS MFRD 2015-2018
ENGINE N844L-F
CYLINDERS. 4
CID 135.2
PTO HP 32.4
ENGINE HP 40
COOLING . . . . LIQUID
FUEL . . . . D
SPEEDS 16/16
TRANSMISSION . . . SHUTTLE SHIFT
STEERING. . . . . STANDARD
HITCH . . . . CAT. I
DRIVE TYPE 2WD
ROPS/CAB . . . . ROPS
WEIGHT . . . . 3,870 LBS.

OPTIONS

HYDRO

RETAIL PRICING

YEAR	HIGH	LOW
2015	$14,212	$10,659
2016	$17,236	$12,927
2017	$18,876	$14,157
2018	$20,768	$15,576

XR4040C

YEARS MFRD 2015-2018
ENGINE N844L-F
CYLINDERS. 4
CID 135.2
PTO HP 32.4
ENGINE HP 40
COOLING . . . . LIQUID
FUEL . . . . D
SPEEDS 16/16
TRANSMISSION . . . SHUTTLE SHIFT
STEERING. . . . . STANDARD
HITCH . . . . CAT. I
DRIVE TYPE 2WD
ROPS/CAB . . . . CAB
WEIGHT . . . . 4,330 LBS.

OPTIONS

HYDRO

RETAIL PRICING

YEAR	HIGH	LOW
2015	$17,601	$13,201
2016	$20,497	$15,373
2017	$23,098	$17,323
2018	$25,296	$18,972

XR4046

YEARS MFRD 2015-2018
ENGINE N844L-F
CYLINDERS. 4
CID 135.2
PTO HP 37.3
ENGINE HP 46
COOLING . . . . LIQUID
FUEL . . . . D
SPEEDS 16/16
TRANSMISSION . . . SHUTTLE SHIFT
STEERING. . . . . STANDARD
HITCH . . . . CAT. I
DRIVE TYPE 2WD
ROPS/CAB . . . . ROPS
WEIGHT . . . . 3,870 LBS.

OPTIONS

HYDRO

RETAIL PRICING

YEAR	HIGH	LOW
2015	$14,219	$10,664
2016	$17,687	$13,265
2017	$20,288	$15,216
2018	$22,166	$16,624

XR4046C

YEARS MFRD 2015-2018
ENGINE N844L-F
CYLINDERS. 4
CID 135.2
PTO HP 37.3
ENGINE HP 46
COOLING . . . . LIQUID
FUEL . . . . D
SPEEDS 16/16
TRANSMISSION . . . SHUTTLE SHIFT
STEERING. . . . . STANDARD
DRIVE TYPE 2WD
ROPS/CAB . . . . CAB
WEIGHT . . . . 4,330 LBS.

OPTIONS

HYDRO

RETAIL PRICING

YEAR	HIGH	LOW
2015	$17,687	$13,265
2016	$21,988	$16,491
2017	$23,722	$17,791
2018	$26,270	$19,702

XR4140C

YEARS MFRD 2015-2020
ENGINE . . . . SHIBAURA
CYLINDERS. 3
CID 114D
PTO HP 34.4
ENGINE HP 40
COOLING . . . . LIQUID
FUEL . . . . D
SPEEDS 16/16
TRANSMISSION . . . SHUTTLE SHIFT
STEERING. . . . . STANDARD
DRIVE TYPE 2WD
ROPS/CAB . . . . CAB
WEIGHT . . . . 4,480 LBS.

OPTIONS

HYDRO
ROPS

RETAIL PRICING

YEAR	HIGH	LOW
2015	$16,039	$12,029
2016	$18,883	$14,162
2017	$22,466	$16,850
2018	$24,486	$18,364
2019	$26,869	$20,151
2020	$27,414	$20,958

XR4145

YEARS MFRD 2015-2020
ENGINE . . . . SHIBAURA
CYLINDERS. 3
CID 114D
PTO HP 38.7
ENGINE HP 45
COOLING . . . . LIQUID
FUEL . . . . D
SPEEDS 16/16
STEERING. . . . . STANDARD
HITCH . . . . CAT. I
DRIVE TYPE 2WD
ROPS/CAB . . . . ROPS
WEIGHT . . . . 3,970 LBS.

OPTIONS

CAB
HYDRO

RETAIL PRICING

YEAR	HIGH	LOW
2015	$14,349	$10,761
2016	$17,886	$13,415
2017	$21,355	$16,016
2018	$23,376	$17,533
2019	$25,132	$18,849
2020	$26,270	$20,057

XR4150

YEARS MFRD 2015-2020
ENGINE . . . . SHIBAURA
CYLINDERS. 3
CID 114D
PTO HP 43
ENGINE HP 50
COOLING . . . . LIQUID
FUEL . . . . D
SPEEDS 16/16
TRANSMISSION . . . SHUTTLE SHIFT
STEERING. . . . . STANDARD
HITCH . . . . CAT. I
DRIVE TYPE 2WD
ROPS/CAB . . . . ROPS
WEIGHT . . . . 3,970 LBS.

OPTIONS

CAB
HYDRO

RETAIL PRICING

YEAR	HIGH	LOW
2015	$15,129	$11,346
2016	$19,734	$14,800
2017	$22,334	$16,751
2018	$24,356	$18,268
2019	$25,609	$19,207
2020	$26,581	$20,223

NOTES

MAHINDRA

C27
YEARS MFRD 2003-2006
ENGINE .... MDI 1895COM
CYLINDERS 3
CID 115
ENGINE HP 27
COOLING .... LIQUID
FUEL .... D
SPEEDS 8/2
TRANSMISSION .... GEAR
STEERING .... STANDARD
HITCH .... CAT. I
HYDRAULIC .... YES
PTO .... YES
WEIGHT .... 3,630 LBS.

C35
YEARS MFRD 2003-2006
ENGINE .... MDI 1895E
CYLINDERS 3
CID 115
PTO HP 28
ENGINE HP 35
COOLING .... LIQUID
FUEL .... D
SPEEDS 8/2
TRANSMISSION .... GEAR
STEERING .... STANDARD
HITCH .... CAT. I
HYDRAULIC .... YES
PTO .... YES
WEIGHT .... 3,630 LBS.

C4005 DI
YEARS MFRD 1999-2001
ENGINE .... MDI 2385E
CYLINDERS 4
CID 145
PTO HP 31.5
ENGINE HP 39.5
FUEL .... D
SPEEDS 8/2
WEIGHT .... 4,015 LBS.

E40 DI
YEARS MFRD 1999-1999
ENGINE .... MDI 1895A
CYLINDERS 3
CID 115
ENGINE HP 39
FUEL .... D
SPEEDS 8/2
WEIGHT .... 3,900 LBS.

E350 DI
YEARS MFRD 2000-2004
ENGINE .... MDI 1895E
CYLINDERS 3
CID 115
PTO HP 31
ENGINE HP 35
COOLING .... LIQUID
FUEL .... D
SPEEDS 8/2
TRANSMISSION .... GEAR
STEERING .... STANDARD
HITCH .... CAT. I
HYDRAULIC .... YES
PTO .... YES
DRIVE TYPE 2WD
ROPS/CAB .... ROPS
WEIGHT .... 3,900 LBS.

AVG. AUCTION PRICING

LOW	HIGH	AVG
$2,205	$4,655	$3,594

EMAX 20S
YEARS MFRD 2018-2020
CYLINDERS 3
CID 60.6
PTO HP 14.2
ENGINE HP 19.4
COOLING .... LIQUID
FUEL .... D
TRANSMISSION .... HYDRO
STEERING .... STANDARD
HITCH .... CAT. I
DRIVE TYPE 4WD
ROPS/CAB .... ROPS
WEIGHT .... 1,499 LBS.
MSRP $10,969

OPTIONS

54" MM MOWER $2,810
LOADER $3,746
SOFT CAB $4,214

EMAX 22
YEARS MFRD 2014-2016
CYLINDERS 3
CID 61.5
PTO HP 16.9
ENGINE HP 22
COOLING .... LIQUID
FUEL .... D
SPEEDS 6/2
TRANSMISSION .... GEAR
STEERING .... STANDARD
HITCH .... CAT. I
WEIGHT .... 1,540 LBS.

OPTIONS

BACKHOE
HYDRO
LDR

SERIAL NUMBERS

YEAR	BEGINNING NO.
2014	22GRH00001-GEAR
2014	22HRH00001-HYDRO
2015	22HRH01036-HYDRO
2015	22GRJ00815-GEAR
2016	22HRJ01875-HYDRO
2016	22GRJ00839-GEAR

RETAIL PRICING

YEAR	HIGH	LOW
2014	$6,891	$5,169
2015	$7,532	$5,649
2016	$8,247	$6,185

EMAX 22L
YEARS MFRD 2019-2020
ENGINE .... FOUR STROKE
CYLINDERS 3
CID 71.7
PTO HP 15.9
ENGINE HP 22
COOLING .... LIQUID
FUEL .... D
SPEEDS 6/2
STEERING .... STANDARD
HITCH .... CAT. I
DRIVE TYPE 4WD
ROPS/CAB .... ROPS
WEIGHT .... 1,610 LBS.
MSRP $13,090

OPTIONS

HYDRO $555
LOADER $4,830

EMAX 22S
YEARS MFRD 2017-2019
ENGINE .... FOUR STROKE
CYLINDERS 3
CID 61.5
PTO HP 15.9
ENGINE HP 22
COOLING .... LIQUID
FUEL .... D
SPEEDS 6/2
TRANSMISSION SYNCHRO SHUTTLE
STEERING .... STANDARD
HITCH .... CAT. I
DRIVE TYPE 4WD
ROPS/CAB .... ROPS
WEIGHT .... 1,540 LBS.
MSRP $12,670

OPTIONS

HYDRO

EMAX 25
YEARS MFRD 2014-2016
CYLINDERS 3
PTO HP 19.3
ENGINE HP 24
FUEL .... D
SPEEDS .... VARIABLE
TRANSMISSION .... HYDRO
STEERING .... STANDARD
HITCH .... CAT. I
DRIVE TYPE 4WD
ROPS/CAB .... ROPS
WEIGHT .... 1,640 LBS.

OPTIONS

BACKHOE
CAB
LDR

SERIAL NUMBERS

YEAR	BEGINNING NO.
2014	25HRH00001
2015	25HRJ00938
2016	25HRJ01775

RETAIL PRICING

YEAR	HIGH	LOW
2014	$7,955	$5,966
2015	$8,674	$6,505
2016	$9,469	$7,102

EMAX 25L
YEARS MFRD 2018-2020
ENGINE .... FOUR STROKE
CYLINDERS 3
CID 71.7
PTO HP 16.9
ENGINE HP 24
COOLING .... LIQUID
FUEL .... D
SPEEDS .... VARIABLE
TRANSMISSION .... HYDRO
STEERING .... STANDARD
HITCH .... CAT. I
DRIVE TYPE 4WD
ROPS/CAB .... ROPS
WEIGHT .... 1,638 LBS.
MSRP $14,982

OPTIONS

CAB $4,147
LOADER $4,615

EMAX 25S
YEARS MFRD 2017-2019
ENGINE .... FOUR STROKE
CYLINDERS 3
CID 61.5
PTO HP 16.9
ENGINE HP 24
COOLING .... LIQUID
FUEL .... D
SPEEDS .... VARIABLE
TRANSMISSION .... HYDRO
STEERING .... STANDARD
HITCH .... CAT. I
DRIVE TYPE 4WD
ROPS/CAB .... ROPS
WEIGHT .... 1,540 LBS.
MSRP $14,630

OPTIONS

CAB

ES25
CYLINDERS 3
ENGINE HP 25
COOLING .... LIQUID
FUEL .... D
DRIVE TYPE 4WD
ROPS/CAB .... ROPS

MAX25XL
YEARS MFRD 2019-2020
ENGINE .... FOUR STROKE
CYLINDERS 3
CID 80.4
PTO HP 20
ENGINE HP 24
COOLING .... LIQUID
FUEL .... D

MAHINDRA

SPEEDS . . . . . VARIABLE
TRANSMISSION . . . . . HYDRO
STEERING. . . . . STANDARD
HITCH . . . . . CAT. I
DRIVE TYPE 4WD
ROPS/CAB . . . . . ROPS
WEIGHT . . . . . 1,715 LBS.
MSRP. $15,986

OPTIONS

62" MM MOWER $3,360
BACKHOE. $6,489
LOADER $4,615

MAX26XLT

YEARS MFRD 2019-2020
ENGINE . . . . . FOUR STROKE
CYLINDERS. 3
CID 80.4
PTO HP 21.7
ENGINE HP 25.9
COOLING . . . . . LIQUID
FUEL . . . . . D
SPEEDS 8/8
STEERING. . . . . STANDARD
HITCH . . . . . CAT. I
DRIVE TYPE 4WD
ROPS/CAB . . . . . ROPS
WEIGHT . . . . . 1,896 LBS.
MSRP. $16,721

OPTIONS

HYDRO. $1,137
LOADER $4,749

MAX 22

YEARS MFRD 2011-2014
ENGINE . . . . . MAHINDRA
CYLINDERS. 3
CID 68
PTO HP 16
COOLING . . . . . AIR
FUEL . . . . . D
SPEEDS . . . . . VARIABLE
TRANSMISSION . . . . . HYDRO
STEERING. . . . . STANDARD
DRIVE TYPE 4WD
ROPS/CAB . . . . . ROPS
WEIGHT . . . . . 1,693 LBS.
MSRP. $12,690

OPTIONS

60" DECK
BACKHOE
LDR

RETAIL PRICING

YEAR	HIGH	LOW
2011	$6,581	$4,936
2012	$7,183	$5,388
2013	$7,816	$5,862
2014	$8,519	$6,389

MAX 24

YEARS MFRD 2014-2019
CID 80.4
PTO HP 19.5
ENGINE HP 24.4
FUEL . . . . . D
SPEEDS . . . . . VARIABLE
TRANSMISSION . . . . . HYDRO
STEERING. . . . . STANDARD
HITCH . . . . . CAT. I
DRIVE TYPE 4WD
ROPS/CAB . . . . . ROPS
WEIGHT . . . . . 1,693 LBS.
MSRP. $15,680

OPTIONS

60" DECK
BACKHOE
LOADER

SERIAL NUMBERS

YEAR	BEGINNING NO.
2014	80115
2015	81519

RETAIL PRICING

YEAR	HIGH	LOW
2014	$8,376	$6,282
2015	$9,052	$6,789
2016	$9,796	$7,347
2017	$10,791	$8,093
2018	$11,690	$8,768
2019	$12,688	$9,516

MAX 25

YEARS MFRD 2011-2014
ENGINE . . . . . MAHINDRA
CYLINDERS. 3
CID 80
PTO HP 20
COOLING . . . . . LIQUID
FUEL . . . . . D
SPEEDS . . . . . VARIABLE
TRANSMISSION . . . . . HYDRO
STEERING. . . . . STANDARD
DRIVE TYPE 4WD
ROPS/CAB . . . . . ROPS
WEIGHT . . . . . 1,693 LBS.
MSRP. $13,440

OPTIONS

60" DECK
BACKHOE
LDR

RETAIL PRICING

YEAR	HIGH	LOW
2011	$7,005	$5,254
2012	$7,611	$5,708
2013	$8,283	$6,212
2014	$9,028	$6,771

MAX 26

YEARS MFRD 2014-2017
CYLINDERS. 4
PTO HP 21.5
ENGINE HP 25.6
FUEL . . . . . D
TRANSMISSION . . . . . GEAR
STEERING. . . . . STANDARD
DRIVE TYPE 4WD
ROPS/CAB . . . . . ROPS
MSRP. $15,960

OPTIONS

60" DECK
BACKHOE

SERIAL NUMBERS

YEAR	BEGINNING NO.
2014	70011
2015	70971

RETAIL PRICING

YEAR	HIGH	LOW
2014	$9,083	$6,812
2015	$9,988	$7,491
2016	$10,678	$8,009
2017	$12,066	$9,049

MAX 26XL

YEARS MFRD 2016-2019
CYLINDERS. 3
CID 80.4
PTO HP 20
ENGINE HP 25.6
COOLING . . . . . LIQUID
FUEL . . . . . D
SPEEDS . . . . . VARIABLE
TRANSMISSION . . . . . HYDRO
STEERING. . . . . STANDARD
DRIVE TYPE 4WD
ROPS/CAB . . . . . ROPS
WEIGHT . . . . . 1,863 LBS.
MSRP. $17,570

OPTIONS

LOADER
SHUTTLE

RETAIL PRICING

YEAR	HIGH	LOW
2016	$11,638	$8,728
2017	$12,956	$9,717
2018	$13,973	$10,480
2019	$15,254	$11,440

MAX 28

YEARS MFRD 2011-2013
ENGINE . . . . . MAHINDRA
CYLINDERS. 3
CID 80.4
PTO HP 23.5
COOLING . . . . . LIQUID
FUEL . . . . . D
SPEEDS 8/8
TRANSMISSION . . . SHUTTLE SHIFT
STEERING. . . . . STANDARD
DRIVE TYPE 4WD
ROPS/CAB . . . . . ROPS
WEIGHT . . . . . 1,819 LBS.
MSRP. $13,440

OPTIONS

60" DECK
BACKHOE
HYDRO
LDR

SERIAL NUMBERS

YEAR	BEGINNING NO.
2011	28MH60011
2012	28MH60255

RETAIL PRICING

YEAR	HIGH	LOW
2011	$7,754	$5,815
2012	$8,450	$6,337
2013	$9,214	$6,910

350

YEARS MFRD 1988-1996
ENGINE . . . . . OWN
CID 144
PTO HP 29.9
FUEL . . . . . D
SPEEDS 8/2
TRANSMISSION . . . . . GEAR
STEERING. . . . . STANDARD
WEIGHT . . . . . 3,638 LBS.
MSRP. $8,075

SERIAL NUMBERS

YEAR	BEGINNING NO.
1988	EX501
1989	EX1157
1990	EX1394
1991	EX1631
1992	EX1870
1993	EX2107

RETAIL PRICING

YEAR	HIGH	LOW
1996	$3,328	$2,496

450 SUPER

YEARS MFRD 1988-1996
ENGINE . . . . . OWN
CYLINDERS. 4
CID 154
PTO HP 36.8
ENGINE HP 45
FUEL . . . . . D
SPEEDS 8/2
WEIGHT . . . . . 3,850 LBS.

SERIAL NUMBERS

YEAR	BEGINNING NO.
1988	EX501
1989	EX1157
1990	EX1394
1991	EX1631
1992	EX1870
1993	EX2107

475 DI

YEARS MFRD 1996-1998
ENGINE . . . . MAHINDRA MDI 1895
CID 115
ENGINE HP 39
FUEL . . . . . D
SPEEDS 8/2
WEIGHT . . . . . 3,894 LBS.
MSRP. $9,000

RETAIL PRICING

YEAR	HIGH	LOW
1996	$3,710	$2,783

AVG. AUCTION PRICING

LOW	HIGH	AVG
$1,388	$2,168	$1,892

485 DI

YEARS MFRD 1996-1998
ENGINE . . . . MAHINDRA MDI 2385
CYLINDERS. 4
CID 145.5
ENGINE HP 45

FUEL . . . D
SPEEDS . . . 8/2
WEIGHT . . . 4,092 LBS.
MSRP . . . $10,800

RETAIL PRICING

YEAR	HIGH	LOW
1996	$4,453	$3,340

AVG. AUCTION PRICING

LOW	HIGH	AVG
$4,335	$6,068	$5,168

1526

YEARS MFRD . . . 2015-2019
ENGINE . . . TIER 4
CYLINDERS . . . 3
CID . . . 80.4
PTO HP . . . 19
ENGINE HP . . . 25.6
COOLING . . . LIQUID
FUEL . . . D
SPEEDS . . . 8/8
TRANSMISSION . . . SHUTTLE SHIFT
STEERING . . . STANDARD
HITCH . . . CAT. I
WEIGHT . . . 2,437 LBS.
MSRP . . . $17,850

OPTIONS

HYDRO
LOADER

SERIAL NUMBERS

YEAR	BEGINNING NO.
2015	10011
2016	10427
2017	113083

RETAIL PRICING

YEAR	HIGH	LOW
2016	$10,732	$8,049
2017	$12,913	$9,685
2018	$14,429	$10,821
2019	$15,381	$11,536

1533

YEARS MFRD . . . 2014-2019
ENGINE . . . MAHINDRA
CYLINDERS . . . 4
CID . . . 166.7
PTO HP . . . 25.2
ENGINE HP . . . 32.8
FUEL . . . D
SPEEDS . . . 8/8
TRANSMISSION . . . SHUTTLE SHIFT
STEERING . . . STANDARD
HITCH . . . CAT. I
DRIVE TYPE . . . 4WD
ROPS/CAB . . . ROPS
WEIGHT . . . 3,175 LBS.
MSRP . . . $22,190

OPTIONS

HYDRO
LOADER

SERIAL NUMBERS

YEAR	BEGINNING NO.
2014	10011-GEAR
2014	20011-HYDRO
2015	20113-HYDRO
2015	10333-GEAR
2016	12389-GEAR
2016	21223-HYDRO
2017	21673-HYDRO
2017	12869-GEAR

RETAIL PRICING

YEAR	HIGH	LOW
2014	$11,761	$8,821
2015	$12,668	$9,501
2016	$13,657	$10,243
2017	$15,469	$11,602
2018	$16,906	$12,679
2019	$18,549	$13,912

1538

YEARS MFRD . . . 2014-2019
ENGINE . . . MAHINDRA
CYLINDERS . . . 4
CID . . . 166.7
PTO HP . . . 29.9
ENGINE HP . . . 36.9
FUEL . . . D
SPEEDS . . . 8/8
TRANSMISSION . . . SHUTTLE SHIFT
STEERING . . . STANDARD
HITCH . . . CAT. I
DRIVE TYPE . . . 4WD
ROPS/CAB . . . ROPS
WEIGHT . . . 3,186 LBS.
MSRP . . . $25,130

OPTIONS

CAB
HYDRO
LOADER

SERIAL NUMBERS

YEAR	BEGINNING NO.
2014	40011-GEAR
2014	70011-CAB
2014	60011-HYDRO
2015	40087-GEAR
2015	70053-CAB
2015	60087-HYDRO
2016	60995-HYDRO
2016	40844-GEAR
2016	70431-CAB
2017	41009-GEAR

RETAIL PRICING

YEAR	HIGH	LOW
2014	$13,408	$10,056
2015	$14,376	$10,782
2016	$15,424	$11,568
2017	$17,077	$12,807
2018	$18,643	$13,982
2019	$20,342	$15,256

1626

YEARS MFRD . . . 2018-2020
CYLINDERS . . . 3
CID . . . 80.4
PTO HP . . . 19
ENGINE HP . . . 25.9
FUEL . . . D
SPEEDS . . . 8/8
STEERING . . . STANDARD
DRIVE TYPE . . . 4WD
ROPS/CAB . . . ROPS
WEIGHT . . . 2,437 LBS.
MSRP . . . $18,126

OPTIONS

HYDRO . . . $1,137
LOADER . . . $5,017

1635

YEARS MFRD . . . 2018-2020
CYLINDERS . . . 3
CID . . . 125
PTO HP . . . 27
ENGINE HP . . . 36.2
FUEL . . . D
SPEEDS . . . 8/8
TRANSMISSION . . . SHUTTLE SHIFT
STEERING . . . STANDARD
DRIVE TYPE . . . 4WD
ROPS/CAB . . . ROPS
WEIGHT . . . 3,086 LBS.
MSRP . . . $19,865

OPTIONS

BACKHOE . . . $7,920
HYDRO . . . $1,337
HYDRO CAB . . . $8,628
LOADER . . . $5,150

1640

YEARS MFRD . . . 2018-2020
CYLINDERS . . . 4
CID . . . 166.7
PTO HP . . . 27.7
ENGINE HP . . . 38.7
TRANSMISSION . . . HYDRO
STEERING . . . STANDARD
DRIVE TYPE . . . 4WD
ROPS/CAB . . . ROPS
WEIGHT . . . 3,175 LBS.
MSRP . . . $23,410

OPTIONS

CAB . . . $7,624
LOADER . . . $5,284
SHUTTLE . . . $-1,338

1815

YEARS MFRD . . . 2006-2008
SERIES . . . 15 SERIES
CYLINDERS . . . 3
CID . . . 58.1
ENGINE HP . . . 18
COOLING . . . LIQUID
FUEL . . . D
SPEEDS . . . VARIABLE
TRANSMISSION . . . HYDRO
STEERING . . . STANDARD
DRIVE TYPE . . . 4WD
ROPS/CAB . . . ROPS
WEIGHT . . . 1,515 LBS.
MSRP . . . $10,660

OPTIONS

52" DECK
BACKHOE
LDR

SERIAL NUMBERS

YEAR	BEGINNING NO.
2006	10021
2007	10158

RETAIL PRICING

YEAR	HIGH	LOW
2007	$4,647	$3,485
2008	$5,170	$3,877

1816

YEARS MFRD . . . 2008-2010
SERIES . . . 16 SERIES
ENGINE . . . MAHINDRA
CYLINDERS . . . 3
CID . . . 58.1
ENGINE HP . . . 18
COOLING . . . LIQUID
FUEL . . . D
SPEEDS . . . VARIABLE
TRANSMISSION . . . HYDRO
STEERING . . . STANDARD
HITCH . . . CAT. I
HYDRAULIC . . . YES
PTO . . . YES
DRIVE TYPE . . . 2WD
ROPS/CAB . . . ROPS
WEIGHT . . . 1,515 LBS.
MSRP . . . $11,700

OPTIONS

60" DECK
BACKHOE
LDR
MID PTO

SERIAL NUMBERS

YEAR	BEGINNING NO.
2008	20021
2009	20201
2010	20221

RETAIL PRICING

YEAR	HIGH	LOW
2008	$5,349	$4,012
2009	$5,905	$4,429
2010	$6,491	$4,868

2015

YEARS MFRD . . . 2004-2007
SERIES . . . 15 SERIES
ENGINE . . . MITSUBISHI S3L
CYLINDERS . . . 3
CID . . . 68.6
PTO HP . . . 17.5
ENGINE HP . . . 20
COOLING . . . LIQUID
FUEL . . . D
SPEEDS . . . 6/2
TRANSMISSION . . . GEAR
STEERING . . . STANDARD
HITCH . . . CAT. I
HYDRAULIC . . . YES
PTO . . . YES
DRIVE TYPE . . . 4WD
ROPS/CAB . . . ROPS
WEIGHT . . . 1,819 LBS.
MSRP . . . $11,960

OPTIONS

60" DECK
BACKHOE
LDR

MAHINDRA

SERIAL NUMBERS

YEAR .... BEGINNING NO.
2004 .... 30511-GEAR
2005 .... 31820-GEAR
2006 .... 31820-GEAR
2007 .... 32158-GEAR

RETAIL PRICING

YEAR	HIGH	LOW
2004	$2,774	$2,081
2005	$3,120	$2,340
2006	$3,554	$2,666
2007	$4,075	$3,056

2015 HST

YEARS MFRD 2003-2008
ENGINE .... MITSUBISHI
CYLINDERS 3
CID 68.6
PTO HP 16
ENGINE HP 20
COOLING .... LIQUID
FUEL .... D
SPEEDS .... VARIABLE
TRANSMISSION .... HYDRO
STEERING .... STANDARD
HITCH .... CAT. I
DRIVE TYPE 4WD
ROPS/CAB .... ROPS
WEIGHT .... 1,973 LBS.
MSRP $14,110

OPTIONS

60" DECK
BACKHOE
LDR

SERIAL NUMBERS

YEAR .... BEGINNING NO.
2003 10511
2004 10827
2005 11502
2007 11989
2008 12159

RETAIL PRICING

YEAR	HIGH	LOW
2004	$3,208	$2,406
2005	$3,641	$2,731
2006	$4,075	$3,056
2007	$4,594	$3,446
2008	$5,028	$3,771

2216

YEARS MFRD 2008-2011
SERIES .... 16 SERIES
ENGINE .... MAHINDRA
CYLINDERS 3
CID 68.6
PTO HP 17.5
ENGINE HP 22
COOLING .... LIQUID
FUEL .... D
SPEEDS 6/2
TRANSMISSION .... GEAR
STEERING .... STANDARD
HITCH .... CAT. I
HYDRAULIC .... YES
PTO .... YES
DRIVE TYPE 2WD
ROPS/CAB .... ROPS
WEIGHT .... 1,819 LBS.
MSRP $11,960

OPTIONS

60" DECK
BACKHOE
LDR

SERIAL NUMBERS

YEAR .... BEGINNING NO.
2008 40551
2009 40837
2010 40913
2011 40963

RETAIL PRICING

YEAR	HIGH	LOW
2008	$5,272	$3,954
2009	$5,820	$4,365
2010	$6,395	$4,796
2011	$6,992	$5,244

2216 HST

YEARS MFRD 2008-2009
ENGINE .... MAHINDRA
CYLINDERS 3
CID 68
PTO HP 16
COOLING .... AIR
FUEL .... D
SPEEDS .... VARIABLE
TRANSMISSION .... HYDRO
STEERING .... STANDARD
HITCH .... CAT. I
WEIGHT .... 1,973 LBS.
MSRP $12,599

OPTIONS

60" DECK
BACKHOE
LDR

SERIAL NUMBERS

YEAR .... BEGINNING NO.
2008 20511
2009 20681

RETAIL PRICING

YEAR	HIGH	LOW
2008	$5,884	$4,413
2009	$6,452	$4,839

2310

YEARS MFRD 2004-2005
SERIES .... 10 SERIES
ENGINE TD1300
CYLINDERS 3
CID 79
PTO HP 20
ENGINE HP 25
COOLING .... LIQUID
FUEL .... D
SPEEDS 12/12
TRANSMISSION ... SHUTTLE SHIFT
STEERING .... STANDARD
HITCH .... CAT. I
HYDRAULIC .... YES
PTO .... YES
DRIVE TYPE 4WD
ROPS/CAB .... ROPS
WEIGHT .... 3,064 LBS.
MSRP $12,450

OPTIONS

LDR

SERIAL NUMBERS

YEAR .... BEGINNING NO.
2004 .... V120176
2005 .... 2310W110241

RETAIL PRICING

YEAR	HIGH	LOW
2004	$4,100	$3,075
2005	$4,550	$3,413

2310 HST

YEARS MFRD 2003-2004
SERIES .... 10 SERIES
ENGINE TD1300-DY1
CYLINDERS 3
CID 79
PTO HP 20
ENGINE HP 25
COOLING .... LIQUID
FUEL .... D
SPEEDS .... VARIABLE
TRANSMISSION .... HYDRO
STEERING .... STANDARD
HITCH .... CAT. I
HYDRAULIC .... YES
PTO .... YES
DRIVE TYPE 4WD
ROPS/CAB .... ROPS
WEIGHT .... 3,064 LBS.
MSRP $13,700

OPTIONS

LDR

SERIAL NUMBERS

YEAR .... BEGINNING NO.
2003 .... V120002
2004 .... 2310W040007

RETAIL PRICING

YEAR	HIGH	LOW
2003	$4,023	$3,017
2004	$4,494	$3,371

2415

YEARS MFRD 2006-2007
CYLINDERS 3
CID 80.4
ENGINE HP 24
COOLING .... LIQUID
FUEL .... D
SPEEDS 8/8
TRANSMISSION ... SHUTTLE SHIFT
STEERING .... STANDARD
HYDRAULIC .... YES
PTO .... YES
WEIGHT .... 1,819 LBS.
MSRP $11,570

OPTIONS

60" DECK
BACKHOE
HYDRO
LDR

SERIAL NUMBERS

YEAR .... BEGINNING NO.
2006 .... 10511-GEAR
2006 .... 30511-HYDRO
2007 .... 10647-GEAR
2007 .... 30641-HYDRO

RETAIL PRICING

YEAR	HIGH	LOW
2006	$4,787	$3,590
2007	$5,315	$3,986

2516

YEARS MFRD 2008-2011
SERIES .... 16 SERIES
ENGINE .... MAHINDRA
CYLINDERS 3
CID 80.4
ENGINE HP 22
COOLING .... LIQUID
FUEL .... D
SPEEDS 8/8
TRANSMISSION ... SHUTTLE SHIFT
STEERING .... STANDARD
HITCH .... CAT. I
HYDRAULIC .... YES
PTO .... YES
DRIVE TYPE 4WD
ROPS/CAB .... ROPS
WEIGHT .... 1,819 LBS.
MSRP $13,975

OPTIONS

60" DECK
BACKHOE
HYDRO
LDR

SERIAL NUMBERS

YEAR .... BEGINNING NO.
2008 .... 25H40511-HYDRO
2008 .... 25G20511-GEAR
2009 .... 25H40595-HYDRO
2009 .... 25G20623-GEAR
2010 .... 25H40789-HYDRO
2010 .... 25G20805-GEAR
2011 .... 25H40869-HYDRO
2011 .... 25G20829-GEAR

RETAIL PRICING

YEAR	HIGH	LOW
2008	$6,300	$4,725
2009	$6,894	$5,171
2010	$7,519	$5,639
2011	$8,173	$6,130

2525

YEARS MFRD 2008-2009
SERIES .... 25 SERIES
CYLINDERS 3
CID 98.7
PTO HP 20
ENGINE HP 25
COOLING .... LIQUID
FUEL .... D
SPEEDS 8/8
TRANSMISSION ... SHUTTLE SHIFT
STEERING .... STANDARD
HITCH .... CAT. I
DRIVE TYPE 4WD

ROPS/CAB . . . . ROPS
WEIGHT . . . . 3,445 LBS.
MSRP $9,615

OPTIONS

LDR

SERIAL NUMBERS

YEAR . . . . BEGINNING NO.
2008 2135
2009 2602

RETAIL PRICING

YEAR	HIGH	LOW
2008	$4,568	$3,426
2009	$5,060	$3,795

2538

YEARS MFRD 2015-2018
CYLINDERS 4
CID 167
PTO HP 29.5
ENGINE HP 37.4
COOLING . . . . LIQUID
FUEL . . . . D
SPEEDS . . . . VARIABLE
TRANSMISSION . . . . HYDRO
STEERING . . . . STANDARD
HITCH . . . . CAT. I
DRIVE TYPE 2WD
ROPS/CAB . . . . ROPS
WEIGHT . . . . 3,351 LBS.
MSRP $22,820

OPTIONS

CAB
LOADER

SERIAL NUMBERS

YEAR . . . . BEGINNING NO.
2015 . . . . 38HRJ00393-CAB
2015 . . . . 38HRH00001
2016 . . . . 38HRJ00614-CAB
2016 . . . . 38HCK00001
2017 . . . . 38HCK00792-CAB
2017 . . . . 38HRK02972

RETAIL PRICING

YEAR	HIGH	LOW
2016	$13,408	$10,056
2017	$14,971	$11,229
2018	$16,611	$12,458

2540

YEARS MFRD 2014-2019
ENGINE . . . . MAHINDRA
CYLINDERS 4
CID 166.7
PTO HP 35
ENGINE HP 40
FUEL . . . . D
SPEEDS 12/12
TRANSMISSION . . . SHUTTLE SHIFT
STEERING . . . . STANDARD
HITCH . . . . CAT. I
DRIVE TYPE 4WD
ROPS/CAB . . . . ROPS
WEIGHT . . . . 3,285 LBS.
MSRP $24,430

OPTIONS

LOADER

SERIAL NUMBERS

YEAR . . . . BEGINNING NO.
2014 . . . . 40GRH00456
2015 . . . . 40GRH00536
2016 . . . . 40GRJ01092
2017 . . . . 40GRK01375

RETAIL PRICING

YEAR	HIGH	LOW
2015	$14,147	$10,610
2016	$15,218	$11,414
2017	$16,319	$12,239
2018	$17,842	$13,381
2019	$19,486	$14,615

2545

YEARS MFRD 2017-2019
CYLINDERS 4
CID 166.7
PTO HP 39
ENGINE HP 44
FUEL . . . . D
SPEEDS 12/12
STEERING . . . . STANDARD
HITCH . . . . CAT. I
DRIVE TYPE 4WD
ROPS/CAB . . . . ROPS
WEIGHT . . . . 3,285 LBS.
MSRP $25,410

OPTIONS

CAB
LOADER

SERIAL NUMBERS

YEAR . . . . BEGINNING NO.
2017 . . . . 45GRK00029-OPEN
2017 . . . . 45GCL00011-CAB

2555

YEARS MFRD 2014-2019
ENGINE . . . . MAHINDRA
CYLINDERS 3
CID 161.5
PTO HP 44.5
ENGINE HP 55
FUEL . . . . D
SPEEDS . . . . VARIABLE
TRANSMISSION . . . . HYDRO
STEERING . . . . STANDARD
HITCH . . . . CAT. I
DRIVE TYPE 4WD
ROPS/CAB . . . . ROPS
WEIGHT . . . . 4,299 LBS.
MSRP $30,870

OPTIONS

CAB
LOADER
SYNC SHUTTLE

SERIAL NUMBERS

YEAR . . . . BEGINNING NO.
2014 . . . . 55GCH00001-SC
2014 . . . . 55GRH00001-S
2014 . . . . 55HRH00001-H
2014 . . . . 55HCH00001-HSTC
2015 . . . . 55HCH00058-HSTC
2015 . . . . 55HRH00079-H
2015 . . . . 55GCJ00025-SC
2015 . . . . 55GRH00240-S
2016 . . . . 55GRJ00538-S
2016 . . . . 55GCJ00391-SC
2016 . . . . 55HCJ0040-HSTC
2016 . . . . 55HRK00457-H
2017 . . . . 55HRK00758-H
2017 . . . . 55HCK01062-HSTC
2017 . . . . 55GRK01120-S
2017 . . . . 55GCK00683-SC

RETAIL PRICING

YEAR	HIGH	LOW
2015	$16,727	$12,545
2016	$17,609	$13,206
2017	$19,240	$14,430
2018	$21,330	$15,997
2019	$23,946	$17,960

2565

YEARS MFRD 2014-2017
CYLINDERS 3
CID 161.5
PTO HP 50
ENGINE HP 55
COOLING . . . . LIQUID
FUEL . . . . D
SPEEDS . . . . VARIABLE
TRANSMISSION . . . . HYDRO
STEERING . . . . STANDARD
HITCH . . . . CAT. I
DRIVE TYPE 4WD
ROPS/CAB . . . . ROPS
WEIGHT . . . . 5,070 LBS.
MSRP $41,230

OPTIONS

CAB

SERIAL NUMBERS

YEAR . . . . BEGINNING NO.
2014 . . . . 65GCH00001
2015 . . . . 65GCH00033
2016 . . . . 65GCJ00829
2017 . . . . 65GCL01397

RETAIL PRICING

YEAR	HIGH	LOW
2014	$23,303	$17,478
2015	$24,682	$18,512
2016	$26,164	$19,623
2017	$29,377	$22,033

2615

YEARS MFRD 2004-2008
SERIES . . . . 15 SERIES
ENGINE . . . . MITSUBISHI S3L2
CYLINDERS 3
CID 80
PTO HP 21
ENGINE HP 26
COOLING . . . . LIQUID
FUEL . . . . D
SPEEDS 9/3
TRANSMISSION . . . . GEAR
STEERING . . . . STANDARD
HITCH . . . . CAT. I
HYDRAULIC . . . . YES
PTO . . . . YES
WEIGHT . . . . 2,458 LBS.
MSRP $12,839

OPTIONS

60" DECK
72" DECK
HYDRO
LDR

SERIAL NUMBERS

YEAR . . . . BEGINNING NO.
2004 . . . . 70511-GEAR
2004 . . . . 30511-HYDRO
2005 . . . . 70651-GEAR
2005 . . . . 30812-HYDRO
2006 . . . . 26G71505-GEAR
2006 . . . . 26H31536-HYDRO
2007 . . . . 26G72290-GEAR
2007 . . . . 26H31826-HYDRO
2008 . . . . 26G73850-GEAR
2008 . . . . 26H32192-HYDRO

RETAIL PRICING

YEAR	HIGH	LOW
2004	$3,950	$2,963
2005	$4,432	$3,324
2006	$4,931	$3,699
2007	$5,464	$4,098
2008	$6,020	$4,515

2638

YEARS MFRD 2018-2020
CYLINDERS 4
CID 166.7
PTO HP 31
ENGINE HP 37.4
FUEL . . . . D
TRANSMISSION . . . . HYDRO
STEERING . . . . STANDARD
HITCH . . . . CAT. I
DRIVE TYPE 4WD
ROPS/CAB . . . . ROPS
WEIGHT . . . . 3,130 LBS.
MSRP $23,008

OPTIONS

CAB $8,160
LOADER $5,552

2645

YEARS MFRD 2018-2020
CYLINDERS 4
CID 166.7
PTO HP 35
ENGINE HP 44
FUEL . . . . D
SPEEDS 12/12
TRANSMISSION . . . SHUTTLE SHIFT
STEERING . . . . STANDARD
HITCH . . . . CAT. I
DRIVE TYPE 4WD
ROPS/CAB . . . . ROPS
WEIGHT . . . . 3,285 LBS.
MSRP $25,215

OPTIONS

CAB $8,829
LOADER $6,689

MAHINDRA

2655

YEARS MFRD 2018-2019
CYLINDERS.................3
CID 161.5
PTO HP 44.5
ENGINE HP 55
FUEL ....D
SPEEDS 12/12
STEERING............STANDARD
HITCH ....CAT. I
DRIVE TYPE 4WD
ROPS/CAB ....ROPS
WEIGHT ....4,056 LBS.
MSRP................ $28,470

OPTIONS

CAB
HYDRO
LOADER

2660

YEARS MFRD 2020-2020
ENGINE .... 4 STROKE
CYLINDERS.................3
CID 161.7
PTO HP 48.5
ENGINE HP 60
COOLING ....LIQUID
FUEL ....D
SPEEDS 12/12
TRANSMISSION ... SHUTTLE SHIFT
STEERING............STANDARD
HITCH ....CAT. I
ROPS/CAB ....ROPS
WEIGHT ....4,145 LBS.

OPTIONS

CAB
HYDRO
HYDRO CAB

2810

YEARS MFRD 2003-2006
ENGINE .... DAEDONG 3A139
CYLINDERS.................3
CID 85
PTO HP 23
ENGINE HP 28
COOLING ....LIQUID
FUEL ....D
SPEEDS 12/12
TRANSMISSION ... SHUTTLE SHIFT
STEERING............STANDARD
HITCH ....CAT. I
HYDRAULIC ....YES
PTO ....YES
DRIVE TYPE 4WD
ROPS/CAB ....ROPS
WEIGHT ....3,064 LBS.
MSRP................ $14,300

OPTIONS

HYDRO
LDR

SERIAL NUMBERS

YEAR	BEGINNING NO.
2003	W010009-HYDRO
2004	W030156-HYDRO
2004	V120391-GEAR
2005	W040188-GEAR
2006	W040236-GEAR

RETAIL PRICING

YEAR	HIGH	LOW
2004	$4,800	$3,600
2005	$5,310	$3,982
2006	$5,845	$4,384

2815

YEARS MFRD 2005-2008
SERIES.............. 15 SERIES
ENGINE S3L3
CYLINDERS.................3
CID 91.3
PTO HP 22
ENGINE HP 28
COOLING ....LIQUID
FUEL ....D
SPEEDS ....VARIABLE
TRANSMISSION ....HYDRO
STEERING............STANDARD
HITCH ....CAT. I
DRIVE TYPE 2WD
ROPS/CAB ....ROPS
WEIGHT ....2,555 LBS.
MSRP................ $15,275

OPTIONS

72" DECK
BACKHOE
LDR

SERIAL NUMBERS

YEAR	BEGINNING NO.
2005	30511
2006	30568
2008	30839

RETAIL PRICING

YEAR	HIGH	LOW
2006	$6,045	$4,533
2007	$6,614	$4,961
2008	$7,213	$5,410

2816

YEARS MFRD 2008-2011
SERIES.............. 16 SERIES
ENGINE .... MAHINDRA
CYLINDERS.................3
ENGINE HP 28
COOLING ....LIQUID
FUEL ....D
SPEEDS 9/3
TRANSMISSION ....GEAR
STEERING............STANDARD
HITCH ....CAT. I
HYDRAULIC ....YES
PTO ....YES
WEIGHT ....2,315 LBS.
MSRP................ $13,615

OPTIONS

72" DECK
BACKHOE
HYDRO
LDR

SERIAL NUMBERS

YEAR	BEGINNING NO.
2008	28G40511-GEAR
2008	28H20511-HYDRO
2009	28G40921-GEAR
2009	28H20671-HYDRO
2010	28G42813-GEAR
2010	28H20903-HYDRO
2011	28G43441-GEAR
2011	28H20943-HYDRO

RETAIL PRICING

YEAR	HIGH	LOW
2008	$6,253	$4,690
2009	$6,934	$5,200
2010	$7,557	$5,668
2011	$8,216	$6,162

3015

YEARS MFRD 2004-2008
SERIES.............. 15 SERIES
ENGINE .... MITSUBISHI K3M-D
CYLINDERS.................3
CID 91
PTO HP 24
ENGINE HP 30
COOLING ....LIQUID
FUEL ....D
SPEEDS ....VARIABLE
TRANSMISSION ....HYDRO
STEERING........... ALL WHEEL
HITCH ....CAT. I
HYDRAULIC ....YES
PTO ....YES
WEIGHT ....2,601 LBS.
MSRP................ $15,440

OPTIONS

72" DECK
LDR

SERIAL NUMBERS

YEAR	BEGINNING NO.
2004	51511
2005	50752
2006	30H50944
2007	30H51176
2008	30H51244

RETAIL PRICING

YEAR	HIGH	LOW
2004	$4,966	$3,724
2005	$5,450	$4,087
2006	$5,955	$4,467
2007	$6,491	$4,868
2008	$7,081	$5,311

3016

YEARS MFRD 2010-2014
ENGINE .... MAHINDRA
CYLINDERS.................3
CID 80.4
PTO HP 23
ENGINE HP 28
COOLING ....LIQUID
FUEL ....D
SPEEDS 8/8
TRANSMISSION ... SHUTTLE SHIFT
STEERING............STANDARD
HITCH ....CAT. I
HYDRAULIC ....YES
PTO ....YES
DRIVE TYPE 4WD
ROPS/CAB ....ROPS
WEIGHT ....2,437 LBS.
MSRP................ $16,810

OPTIONS

72" DECK
BACKHOE
HYDRO
LDR

SERIAL NUMBERS

YEAR	BEGINNING NO.
2010	10011-SHUTTLE
2011	10434-SHUTTLE
2011	20011-HST
2012	20161-HST
2012	11674-SHUTTLE
2013	13258-SHUTTLE
2013	20417-HST

RETAIL PRICING

YEAR	HIGH	LOW
2011	$9,818	$7,363
2012	$10,603	$7,952
2013	$11,465	$8,599

3215

YEARS MFRD 2005-2008
SERIES.............. 15 SERIES
ENGINE .... S3L3 TURBO
CYLINDERS.................3
CID 91.3
ENGINE HP 32
COOLING ....LIQUID
FUEL ....D
SPEEDS 8/8
TRANSMISSION ... SHUTTLE SHIFT
STEERING............STANDARD
HITCH ....CAT. I
DRIVE TYPE 4WD
ROPS/CAB ....ROPS
WEIGHT ....2,544 LBS.
MSRP................ $15,665

OPTIONS

72" DECK
BACKHOE
HYDRO
LDR

SERIAL NUMBERS

YEAR	BEGINNING NO.
2005	50511-GEAR
2005	70511-HYDRO
2006	50598-GEAR
2006	70573-HYDRO
2007	51171-GEAR
2007	70899-HYDRO

RETAIL PRICING

YEAR	HIGH	LOW
2006	$6,395	$4,796
2007	$6,976	$5,232
2008	$7,590	$5,693

3316

YEARS MFRD 2008-2011
SERIES.............. 16 SERIES
ENGINE .... MAHINDRA

CYLINDERS	3
CID	91.3
ENGINE HP	33
COOLING	LIQUID
FUEL	D
SPEEDS	8/8
TRANSMISSION	SHUTTLE SHIFT
STEERING	STANDARD
HITCH	CAT. I
HYDRAULIC	YES
PTO	YES
DRIVE TYPE	4WD
ROPS/CAB	ROPS
WEIGHT	2,544 LBS.
MSRP	$17,355

OPTIONS

72" DECK
BACKHOE
HYDRO
LDR

SERIAL NUMBERS

YEAR	BEGINNING NO.
2008	40511-HYDRO
2008	20511-SHUTTLE
2009	40667-HYDRO
2009	20829-SHUTTLE
2010	40717-HYDRO
2010	20919-SHUTTLE
2011	40747-HYDRO
2011	21013-SHUTTLE

RETAIL PRICING

YEAR	HIGH	LOW
2008	$8,453	$6,340
2009	$9,125	$6,844
2010	$9,869	$7,401
2011	$10,688	$8,016

3325

YEARS MFRD	2005-2008
CID	115
PTO HP	30
ENGINE HP	35
COOLING	LIQUID
FUEL	D
SPEEDS	8/2
TRANSMISSION	GEAR
STEERING	STANDARD
HITCH	CAT. I
HYDRAULIC	YES
PTO	YES
DRIVE TYPE	2WD
ROPS/CAB	ROPS
WEIGHT	3,990 LBS.
MSRP	$10,820

SERIAL NUMBERS

YEAR	BEGINNING NO.
2005	101
2006	526
2007	1062
2008	1443

RETAIL PRICING

YEAR	HIGH	LOW
2005	$4,214	$3,161
2006	$4,716	$3,537
2007	$5,239	$3,929
2008	$5,795	$4,346

AVG. AUCTION PRICING

LOW	HIGH	AVG
$1,908	$5,808	$3,323

3505 DI

YEARS MFRD	1999-2004
ENGINE	MDI 1895E
CYLINDERS	3
CID	115
PTO HP	27
ENGINE HP	35
COOLING	LIQUID
FUEL	D
SPEEDS	8/2
TRANSMISSION	GEAR
STEERING	STANDARD
HITCH	CAT. I
HYDRAULIC	YES
PTO	YES
DRIVE TYPE	2WD
ROPS/CAB	ROPS
WEIGHT	3,900 LBS.

3510

YEARS MFRD	2003-2009
ENGINE	DAEDONG 3A165
CYLINDERS	3
CID	100
PTO HP	28.7
ENGINE HP	35
COOLING	LIQUID
FUEL	D
SPEEDS	12/12
TRANSMISSION	SHUTTLE SHIFT
STEERING	STANDARD
HITCH	CAT. I
PTO	YES
DRIVE TYPE	4WD
ROPS/CAB	ROPS
WEIGHT	3,881 LBS.
MSRP	$18,330

OPTIONS

2 HYD
CANOPY
LDR

SERIAL NUMBERS

YEAR	BEGINNING NO.
2003	W010007
2004	W030241
2005	3510X100544
2006	3510Y1001101
2007	3510A0101413
2008	3510A1101509
2009	3510B0301582

RETAIL PRICING

YEAR	HIGH	LOW
2003	$5,764	$4,323
2004	$6,279	$4,709
2005	$6,819	$5,114
2006	$7,383	$5,537
2007	$7,978	$5,984
2008	$8,602	$6,452
2009	$9,252	$6,939

AVG. AUCTION PRICING

LOW	HIGH	AVG
$2,774	$7,803	$5,635

3510 HST

YEARS MFRD	2004-2006
SERIES	10 SERIES
ENGINE	3A165C-DY1
CYLINDERS	3
CID	100.3
PTO HP	28
ENGINE HP	34
COOLING	LIQUID
FUEL	D
SPEEDS	VARIABLE
TRANSMISSION	HYDRO
STEERING	STANDARD
HITCH	CAT. I
HYDRAULIC	YES
PTO	YES
DRIVE TYPE	4WD
ROPS/CAB	ROPS
WEIGHT	3,064 LBS.
MSRP	$18,330

OPTIONS

CANOPY
LDR

SERIAL NUMBERS

YEAR	BEGINNING NO.
2005	351HY0400150

RETAIL PRICING

YEAR	HIGH	LOW
2004	$7,077	$5,307
2005	$7,646	$5,734
2006	$8,246	$6,184

3525

YEARS MFRD	2005-2008
ENGINE	MAHINDRA
CYLINDERS	3
CID	115
ENGINE HP	35
COOLING	LIQUID
FUEL	D
SPEEDS	8/2
TRANSMISSION	GEAR
STEERING	STANDARD
HITCH	CAT. I
HYDRAULIC	YES
PTO	YES
DRIVE TYPE	2WD
ROPS/CAB	ROPS
WEIGHT	4,387 LBS.
MSRP	$12,415

OPTIONS

LDR

SERIAL NUMBERS

YEAR	BEGINNING NO.
2005	101
2006	766
2007	2084
2008	3805

RETAIL PRICING

YEAR	HIGH	LOW
2005	$4,550	$3,413
2006	$5,060	$3,795
2007	$5,595	$4,196
2008	$6,151	$4,614

3535

YEARS MFRD	2009-2014
ENGINE	CE35
CYLINDERS	3
CID	115.4
ENGINE HP	35
COOLING	LIQUID
FUEL	D
SPEEDS	12/12
TRANSMISSION	SHUTTLE SHIFT
STEERING	STANDARD
HYDRAULIC	YES
PTO	YES
DRIVE TYPE	4WD
ROPS/CAB	ROPS
WEIGHT	4,125 LBS.
MSRP	$19,875

OPTIONS

1 HYD
BACKHOE
LDR

SERIAL NUMBERS

YEAR	BEGINNING NO.
2009	1001
2010	1037
2011	1242
2012	1361
2013	1466
2014	1520

RETAIL PRICING

YEAR	HIGH	LOW
2009	$10,760	$8,070
2010	$11,576	$8,682
2011	$12,469	$9,351
2012	$13,441	$10,081
2013	$13,891	$10,418
2014	$14,583	$10,938

3540

YEARS MFRD	2014-2019
CYLINDERS	4
CID	166.7
PTO HP	31
ENGINE HP	40
COOLING	LIQUID
FUEL	D
SPEEDS	12/12
TRANSMISSION	SHUTTLE SHIFT
STEERING	STANDARD
DRIVE TYPE	4WD
ROPS/CAB	ROPS
WEIGHT	4,939 LBS.
MSRP	$28,190

OPTIONS

CAB
HYDRO
LOADER

SERIAL NUMBERS

YEAR	BEGINNING NO.
2014	1001-HST
2014	1002-PST
2014	1003-HST CAB
2014	1002-PST CAB
2015	1018-PST CAB
2015	1007-HST CAB
2015	1006-HST

2015 .... 1005-PST
2016 .... 1704-HST
2016 .... 1396-PST

RETAIL PRICING

YEAR	HIGH	LOW
2014	$16,692	$12,519
2015	$17,773	$13,330
2016	$18,942	$14,207
2017	$20,472	$15,354
2018	$22,336	$16,752
2019	$24,447	$18,335

3550

YEARS MFRD 2014-2019
CYLINDERS 4
CID 166.7
PTO HP 40
ENGINE HP 49
COOLING .... LIQUID
FUEL .... D
SPEEDS 12/12
TRANSMISSION ... SHUTTLE SHIFT
STEERING .... STANDARD
HITCH .... CAT. I
DRIVE TYPE 4WD
ROPS/CAB .... ROPS
WEIGHT .... 4,620 LBS.
MSRP $31,820

OPTIONS

CAB
HYDRO
LOADER

SERIAL NUMBERS

YEAR	BEGINNING NO.
2014	1006-HST CAB
2014	1004-HST
2014	1002-PST
2014	1003-PST CAB
2015	1043-PST CAB
2015	1262-HST
2015	1280-PST
2015	1035-HST CAB
2016	1701-PST
2016	1239-PST CAB
2016	1155-HST CAB
2016	1397-HST

RETAIL PRICING

YEAR	HIGH	LOW
2014	$19,228	$14,421
2015	$20,399	$15,299
2016	$21,660	$16,245
2017	$22,893	$17,170
2018	$24,937	$18,703
2019	$27,078	$20,309

AVG. AUCTION PRICING

LOW	HIGH	AVG
$16,415	$26,460	$21,969

3616

YEARS MFRD 2010-2013
ENGINE .... MAHINDRA
CYLINDERS 3
CID 101.4
PTO HP 30
ENGINE HP 36.2
COOLING .... LIQUID
FUEL .... D
SPEEDS 8/8
TRANSMISSION ... SHUTTLE SHIFT
STEERING .... STANDARD
HITCH .... CAT. I
HYDRAULIC .... YES
PTO .... YES
DRIVE TYPE 4WD
ROPS/CAB .... ROPS
WEIGHT .... 2,560 LBS.
MSRP $25,750

OPTIONS

72"DECK
BACKHOE
CAB
HYDRO
LDR
MID PTO

SERIAL NUMBERS

YEAR	BEGINNING NO.
2010	30011-SHUTTLE
2010	70011-HST CAB
2010	40011-HST
2010	60011-SHUTTLE CAB
2011	70142-HST CAB
2011	30177-SHUTTLE
2011	40135-HST
2011	60195-SHUTTLE CAB
2012	40351-HST
2012	70366-HST CAB
2012	30577-SHUTTLE
2013	40599-HST
2013	70452-HST CAB
2013	30889-SHUTTLE
2013	60439-SHUTTLE CAB

RETAIL PRICING

YEAR	HIGH	LOW
2011	$15,060	$11,295
2012	$16,117	$12,088
2013	$17,261	$12,946

AVG. AUCTION PRICING

LOW	HIGH	AVG
$13,600	$18,250	$15,950

3640

YEARS MFRD 2018-2020
ENGINE .... FOUR STROKE
CYLINDERS 4
CID 166.7
PTO HP 31
ENGINE HP 40
COOLING .... LIQUID
FUEL .... D
SPEEDS 12/12
TRANSMISSION ... SHUTTLE SHIFT
STEERING .... STANDARD
HITCH .... CAT. II
DRIVE TYPE 4WD
ROPS/CAB .... ROPS
WEIGHT .... 4,367 LBS.
MSRP $26,754

OPTIONS

HYDRO $1,337
LOADER $7,692

3650

YEARS MFRD 2018-2020
ENGINE .... FOUR STROKE
CYLINDERS 4
CID 166.7
PTO HP 40
ENGINE HP 49
COOLING .... LIQUID
FUEL .... D
SPEEDS .... 12/12 PS
STEERING .... STANDARD
DRIVE TYPE 4WD
ROPS/CAB .... ROPS
WEIGHT .... 4,620 LBS.
MSRP $30,633

OPTIONS

CAB $9,899
HYDRO $1,338
HYDRO CAB $11,236
LOADER $7,692

3825

YEARS MFRD 2008-2009
SERIES .... 25 SERIES
ENGINE .... MAHINDRA
CYLINDERS 4
ENGINE HP 41
COOLING .... LIQUID
FUEL .... D
SPEEDS 8/8
TRANSMISSION ... SHUTTLE SHIFT
STEERING .... STANDARD
HITCH .... CAT. I
HYDRAULIC .... YES
PTO .... YES
WEIGHT .... 4,081 LBS.
MSRP $11,869

SERIAL NUMBERS

YEAR	BEGINNING NO.
2008	101
2009	102

RETAIL PRICING

YEAR	HIGH	LOW
2008	$5,731	$4,298

4010

YEARS MFRD 2011-2013
ENGINE .... MAHINDRA
CYLINDERS 3
CID 111.4
PTO HP 31
ENGINE HP 38
COOLING .... LIQUID
FUEL .... D
SPEEDS 9/3
TRANSMISSION .... GEAR
STEERING .... STANDARD
DRIVE TYPE 4WD
ROPS/CAB .... ROPS
WEIGHT .... 3,065 LBS.
MSRP $19,810

OPTIONS

1 HYD
2 HYD
BACKHOE
HYDRO
LDR

SERIAL NUMBERS

YEAR	BEGINNING NO.
2011	40GRE1280001-GEAR
2011	40HRE1280001-HY
2012	40HRF0001-HY
2012	40GRF00001-GEAR
2013	40GRF00390-GEAR

RETAIL PRICING

YEAR	HIGH	LOW
2012	$12,163	$9,122
2013	$13,177	$9,883

4025

YEARS MFRD 2008-2015
SERIES .... 25 SERIES
ENGINE .... MAHINDRA
CYLINDERS 4
ENGINE HP 41
COOLING .... LIQUID
FUEL .... D
SPEEDS 8/2
TRANSMISSION ..... POWER SHIFT
STEERING .... STANDARD
HITCH .... CAT. I
HYDRAULIC .... YES
PTO .... YES
DRIVE TYPE 2WD
ROPS/CAB .... ROPS
WEIGHT .... 4,191 LBS.
MSRP $15,125

OPTIONS

4WD-2012/2015
BACKHOE
LDR

SERIAL NUMBERS

YEAR	BEGINNING NO.
2008	101-2WD
2009	364-2WD
2010	1206-2WD
2011	2158-2WD
2012	3020-2WD
2012	102-4WD
2013	4332-2WD
2013	1677-4WD
2014	2391-4WD
2014	7001-2WD
2015	3703-4WD
2015	7606-2WD

RETAIL PRICING

YEAR	HIGH	LOW
2008	$6,410	$4,808
2009	$7,013	$5,260
2010	$7,684	$5,763
2011	$8,428	$6,321
2012	$9,247	$6,935
2013	$9,567	$7,175
2014	$10,772	$8,079

4035

YEARS MFRD 2009-2015
ENGINE CE40
CYLINDERS 3
CID 115.4
ENGINE HP 40

COOLING .... LIQUID
FUEL .... D
SPEEDS 12/12
TRANSMISSION ... SHUTTLE SHIFT
STEERING............ STANDARD
DRIVE TYPE 4WD
ROPS/CAB .... ROPS
WEIGHT .... 4,367 LBS.
MSRP $23,720

OPTIONS

12/12 PS 2010-2013
2 HYD
BACKHOE
HYDRO
LDR

SERIAL NUMBERS

YEAR	BEGINNING NO.
2009	1001-HST
2009	1001-SHUTTLE
2010	1004-HST
2010	1145-SHUTTLE
2011	1006-HST
2011	1001-PST
2011	1579-SHUTTLE
2012	1218-HST
2012	1985-SHUTTLE
2012	1255-PST
2013	1283-HST
2013	1475-PST
2013	2126-SHUTTLE
2014	1674-PST
2014	1461-HST
2014	2237-SHUTTLE
2015	1537-HST
2015	1750-PST

RETAIL PRICING

YEAR	HIGH	LOW
2009	$12,982	$9,737
2010	$13,920	$10,440
2011	$14,902	$11,176
2012	$15,972	$11,979
2013	$17,127	$12,846
2014	$17,927	$13,445

4110

YEARS MFRD 2003-2010
ENGINE 4A200
CYLINDERS...................4
CID 122
PTO HP 33.6
ENGINE HP 41
COOLING .... LIQUID
FUEL .... D
SPEEDS 12/12
TRANSMISSION ... SHUTTLE SHIFT
STEERING............ STANDARD
HITCH .... CAT. I
HYDRAULIC .... YES
PTO .... YES
DRIVE TYPE 4WD
ROPS/CAB .... ROPS
WEIGHT .... 3,969 LBS.
MSRP $19,339

OPTIONS

2 HYD
CANOPY
LDR

SERIAL NUMBERS

YEAR	BEGINNING NO.
2003	W010012
2004	W040380
2005	4110X030162
2006	4110Y0301022
2007	4110Z0401844
2008	4110A0302245
2009	4110B0302668
2010	4110C0402738

RETAIL PRICING

YEAR	HIGH	LOW
2003	$7,018	$5,263
2004	$7,566	$5,674
2005	$8,144	$6,108
2006	$8,747	$6,560
2007	$9,379	$7,034
2008	$10,076	$7,557
2009	$10,804	$8,103
2010	$11,606	$8,705

AVG. AUCTION PRICING

LOW	HIGH	AVG
$8,134	$10,290	$8,999

4500

YEARS MFRD 2005-2008
ENGINE NE-342
CYLINDERS...................3
CID 146
PTO HP 35
ENGINE HP 42
COOLING .... LIQUID
FUEL .... D
SPEEDS 8/2
TRANSMISSION .... GEAR
STEERING............ STANDARD
HITCH .... CAT. II
HYDRAULIC .... YES
PTO .... YES
DRIVE TYPE 2WD
ROPS/CAB .... ROPS
WEIGHT .... 4,752 LBS.
MSRP $13,819

OPTIONS

2 HYD
LDR

SERIAL NUMBERS

YEAR	BEGINNING NO.
2005	2853
2006	3360
2007	3835
2008	3966

RETAIL PRICING

YEAR	HIGH	LOW
2005	$4,962	$3,721
2006	$5,484	$4,113
2007	$6,037	$4,528
2008	$6,555	$4,916

4505 DI

YEARS MFRD 1999-2000
ENGINE .... MDI 2500
CYLINDERS...................4
CID 154
PTO HP 35.5
ENGINE HP 43
FUEL .... D
SPEEDS 8/2
WEIGHT .... 4,070 LBS.

4510

YEARS MFRD 2004-2011
CYLINDERS...................4
CID 133.7
ENGINE HP 44
COOLING .... LIQUID
FUEL .... D
SPEEDS 16/16
TRANSMISSION ... SHUTTLE SHIFT
STEERING............ STANDARD
DRIVE TYPE 2WD
ROPS/CAB .... CAB
WEIGHT .... 4,737 LBS.
MSRP $27,560

OPTIONS

LDR

SERIAL NUMBERS

YEAR	BEGINNING NO.
2004	4510X030004
2005	4510X030020
2006	4510Y0400328
2007	4510Z0400382
2008	4510A0400488
2009	4510B0400602
2010	4510D0100672
2011	4510D1200747

RETAIL PRICING

YEAR	HIGH	LOW
2004	$10,009	$7,507
2005	$10,706	$8,029
2006	$11,441	$8,580
2007	$12,206	$9,154
2008	$13,004	$9,753
2009	$13,841	$10,380
2010	$14,754	$11,065
2011	$15,743	$11,807

4525

YEARS MFRD 2008-2014
SERIES .... 25 SERIES
ENGINE .... MAHINDRA
CYLINDERS...................4
CID 167
ENGINE HP 46
COOLING .... LIQUID
FUEL .... D
SPEEDS 8/2
TRANSMISSION .... GEAR
STEERING............ STANDARD
HITCH .... CAT. I
HYDRAULIC .... YES
PTO .... YES
DRIVE TYPE 2WD
ROPS/CAB .... ROPS
WEIGHT .... 4,246 LBS.
MSRP $15,730

OPTIONS

LDR

SERIAL NUMBERS

YEAR	BEGINNING NO.
2008	101
2009	102
2010	171
2011	241
2012	489
2013	552
2014	611

RETAIL PRICING

YEAR	HIGH	LOW
2008	$6,730	$5,047
2009	$7,340	$5,505
2010	$8,016	$6,012
2011	$8,764	$6,573
2012	$9,582	$7,187
2013	$10,357	$7,767
2014	$11,062	$8,297

4530 T2

YEARS MFRD 2005-2008
SERIES .... 30 SERIES
ENGINE NE342R
CYLINDERS...................3
CID 152
PTO HP 34
ENGINE HP 42.5
COOLING .... LIQUID
FUEL .... D
SPEEDS 8/8
TRANSMISSION ... SHUTTLE SHIFT
STEERING............ STANDARD
HITCH .... CAT. II
HYDRAULIC .... YES
PTO .... YES
DRIVE TYPE 4WD
ROPS/CAB .... ROPS
WEIGHT .... 5,720 LBS.
MSRP $19,149

OPTIONS

LDR

SERIAL NUMBERS

YEAR	BEGINNING NO.
2005	1007
2006	1272
2007	1943
2008	2361

RETAIL PRICING

YEAR	HIGH	LOW
2005	$8,503	$6,378
2006	$9,158	$6,869
2007	$9,844	$7,383
2008	$10,564	$7,923

4530 T4

YEARS MFRD 2010-2015
ENGINE .... MAHINDRA
CYLINDERS...................3
CID 152.4
PTO HP 35
ENGINE HP 44
COOLING .... LIQUID
FUEL .... D
SPEEDS 8/8
TRANSMISSION ... SHUTTLE SHIFT
STEERING............ STANDARD
DRIVE TYPE 4WD
ROPS/CAB .... ROPS
WEIGHT .... 5,567 LBS.
MSRP $22,250

OPTIONS

2 HYD
BACKHOE
LDR

SERIAL NUMBERS

YEAR	BEGINNING NO.
2010	1001
2011	1428
2012	1917
2013	2379
2014	3102
2015	4444

RETAIL PRICING

YEAR	HIGH	LOW
2010	$12,306	$9,229
2011	$13,228	$9,921
2012	$14,232	$10,674
2013	$15,323	$11,492
2014	$17,642	$13,231

AVG. AUCTION PRICING

LOW	HIGH	AVG
$9,438	$13,630	$11,073

4540

YEARS MFRD	2014-2020
ENGINE	MAHINDRA
CYLINDERS	4
CID	166.7
PTO HP	31
ENGINE HP	41
SPEEDS	12/12
TRANSMISSION	SHUTTLE SHIFT
STEERING	STANDARD
HITCH	CAT. I
DRIVE TYPE	2WD
ROPS/CAB	ROPS
WEIGHT	4,191 LBS.
MSRP	$19,263

OPTIONS

4WD	$3,010
LOADER	$6,622

SERIAL NUMBERS

YEAR	BEGINNING NO.
2014	1002-4WD
2014	1001-2WD
2015	1535-4WD
2015	1606-2WD
2016	2843-4WD
2016	2137-2WD

RETAIL PRICING

YEAR	HIGH	LOW
2015	$10,865	$8,148
2016	$11,879	$8,910
2017	$13,030	$9,772
2018	$13,992	$10,493
2019	$15,215	$11,411
2020	$16,683	$12,650

AVG. AUCTION PRICING

LOW	HIGH	AVG
$9,000	$15,500	$13,167

4550

YEARS MFRD	2014-2020
ENGINE	MAHINDRA
CYLINDERS	4
CID	166.7
PTO HP	38
ENGINE HP	48
COOLING	LIQUID
FUEL	D
SPEEDS	8/2
TRANSMISSION	SHUTTLE SHIFT
STEERING	STANDARD
HITCH	CAT. I
DRIVE TYPE	4WD
ROPS/CAB	ROPS
WEIGHT	5,192 LBS.
MSRP	$24,680

OPTIONS

2WD THROUGH 2019

LDR	$6,622

SERIAL NUMBERS

YEAR	BEGINNING NO.
2014	1001
2015	1350-4WD
2015	1502-2WD
2016	1747-4WD

RETAIL PRICING

YEAR	HIGH	LOW
2014	$11,225	$8,419
2015	$12,203	$9,152
2016	$13,267	$9,949
2017	$13,957	$10,468
2018	$15,287	$11,465
2019	$16,652	$12,489
2020	$21,858	$16,657

4565

YEARS MFRD	2013-2017
CYLINDERS	3
CID	161.5
PTO HP	52
ENGINE HP	62
COOLING	LIQUID
FUEL	D
SPEEDS	8/2
TRANSMISSION	GEAR
STEERING	STANDARD
HITCH	CAT. I
DRIVE TYPE	2WD
ROPS/CAB	ROPS
WEIGHT	4,928 LBS.
MSRP	$22,030

OPTIONS

LDR

SERIAL NUMBERS

YEAR	BEGINNING NO.
2013	1002
2014	1005
2015	2101
2016	2305

RETAIL PRICING

YEAR	HIGH	LOW
2014	$13,348	$10,011
2015	$14,431	$10,824
2016	$15,608	$11,706
2017	$16,678	$12,508

5005 DI

YEARS MFRD	1999-2002
ENGINE	MDI 3000E
CYLINDERS	4
CID	154
PTO HP	42
ENGINE HP	51
FUEL	D
SPEEDS	8/2
TRANSMISSION	GEAR
STEERING	STANDARD
PTO	YES
WEIGHT	4,576 LBS.
MSRP	$14,225

RETAIL PRICING

YEAR	HIGH	LOW
2002	$7,657	$5,743

5010

YEARS MFRD	2010-2013
ENGINE	MAHINDRA
CYLINDERS	4
CID	148
PTO HP	41.5
COOLING	LIQUID
FUEL	D
SPEEDS	9/3
TRANSMISSION	GEAR
STEERING	STANDARD
HITCH	CAT. I
DRIVE TYPE	4WD
ROPS/CAB	ROPS
WEIGHT	3,836 LBS.
MSRP	$21,560

OPTIONS

2 HYD
BACKHOE
CAB
HYDRO
LDR

SERIAL NUMBERS

YEAR	BEGINNING NO.
2010	50NCD1200001-GEAR
2010	50SHD1200001-HY CAB
2011	5010E0100001-GEAR
2011	5010E0100026-GEAR CA
2011	5010E0100036-HY CAB
2012	50GRE0900499-GEAR
2012	50HCE1000469-HY CAB
2012	50GCE1000504-GEAR CA
2013	50GCF00763-GEAR CAB
2013	50GRF00836-GEAR
2013	50HCG00950-HY CAB

RETAIL PRICING

YEAR	HIGH	LOW
2011	$12,285	$9,214
2012	$13,279	$9,959
2013	$14,358	$10,768

AVG. AUCTION PRICING

LOW	HIGH	AVG
$13,611	$14,088	$13,857

5035

YEARS MFRD	2009-2014
ENGINE	MAHINDRA
CYLINDERS	4
CID	153
PTO HP	43
COOLING	LIQUID
FUEL	D
SPEEDS	12/12
TRANSMISSION	SHUTTLE SHIFT
STEERING	STANDARD
DRIVE TYPE	4WD
ROPS/CAB	ROPS
WEIGHT	4,939 LBS.
MSRP	$27,250

OPTIONS

12/12PS-2010-2012
2 HYD
BACKHOE
HYDRO
LDR

SERIAL NUMBERS

YEAR	BEGINNING NO.
2009	1001-HYDRO
2009	1001-GEAR
2010	1005-HYDRO
2010	1013-GEAR
2011	1007-HYDRO
2011	1001-PS
2011	1237-GEAR
2012	1111-HYDRO
2012	1297-GEAR
2012	1125-PS
2013	1170-HYDRO
2013	1235-PS
2013	1431-GEAR
2014	1416-PS
2014	1257-HYDRO
2014	1581-GEAR

RETAIL PRICING

YEAR	HIGH	LOW
2009	$13,883	$10,412
2010	$14,830	$11,123
2011	$15,857	$11,893
2012	$16,975	$12,731
2013	$18,177	$13,633
2014	$19,478	$14,608

5500

YEARS MFRD	2005-2008
ENGINE	NE452
CYLINDERS	4
CID	186
PTO HP	44
ENGINE HP	54
COOLING	LIQUID
FUEL	D
SPEEDS	8/2
TRANSMISSION	GEAR
STEERING	STANDARD
PTO	YES
DRIVE TYPE	2WD
ROPS/CAB	ROPS
WEIGHT	4,966 LBS.
MSRP	$15,930

OPTIONS

4WD
CANOPY
LDR

SERIAL NUMBERS

YEAR	BEGINNING NO.
2005	907-2WD
2005	1361-4WD
2006	1183-2WD
2006	1634-4WD
2007	1810-2WD
2007	2017-4WD
2008	2225-2WD
2008	2203-4WD

RETAIL PRICING

YEAR	HIGH	LOW
2005	$6,661	$4,996
2006	$7,247	$5,435
2007	$7,864	$5,898
2008	$8,543	$6,407

AVG. AUCTION PRICING

LOW	HIGH	AVG
$3,295	$13,438	$6,043

5525

YEARS MFRD	2007-2014
ENGINE	MAHINDRA
CYLINDERS	4
CID	186
PTO HP	44
ENGINE HP	54
COOLING	LIQUID
FUEL	D
SPEEDS	8/2
TRANSMISSION	GEAR
STEERING	STANDARD
WEIGHT	5,370 LBS.
MSRP	$14,165

OPTIONS

2 HYD
LDR

SERIAL NUMBERS

YEAR	BEGINNING NO.
2007	1001-T2
2008	1001-T3
2008	1135-T2
2009	1085-T3
2009	1651-T2
2010	1262-T3
2011	1364-T3
2012	1676-T3
2013	1734-T3
2014	1825-T3

RETAIL PRICING

YEAR	HIGH	LOW
2008	$6,181	$4,636
2009	$6,843	$5,133
2010	$7,574	$5,681
2011	$8,382	$6,286
2012	$8,959	$6,719
2013	$9,448	$7,086
2014	$10,246	$7,684

5530

YEARS MFRD	2008-2014
ENGINE	MAHINDRA
CYLINDERS	3
CID	152.4
PTO HP	45
ENGINE HP	55
COOLING	LIQUID
FUEL	D
SPEEDS	8/8
TRANSMISSION	SHUTTLE SHIFT
STEERING	STANDARD
DRIVE TYPE	4WD
ROPS/CAB	ROPS
MSRP	$24,975

OPTIONS

1 HYD
2 HYD
2WD
LDR

SERIAL NUMBERS

YEAR	BEGINNING NO.
2008	1001-4WD
2008	1001-2WD GEAR
2009	1042-4WD
2009	1064-2WD GEAR
2010	1136-4WD
2010	1180-2WD GEAR
2011	1001-2WD SHUTTLE
2011	1311-4WD
2012	1424-4WD
2012	1080-2WD SHUTTLE
2013	1166-2WD SHUTTLE
2013	1562-4WD
2014	1838-4WD

RETAIL PRICING

YEAR	HIGH	LOW
2008	$12,591	$9,443
2009	$13,491	$10,118
2010	$14,470	$10,852
2011	$15,533	$11,650
2012	$16,684	$12,513
2013	$17,929	$13,447
2014	$19,435	$14,577

5545

YEARS MFRD	2015-2020
ENGINE	MAHINDRA
CYLINDERS	3
CID	161.7
PTO HP	34
ENGINE HP	43
FUEL	D
SPEEDS	12/12
TRANSMISSION	SHUTTLE SHIFT
STEERING	STANDARD
HITCH	CAT. I
DRIVE TYPE	4WD
ROPS/CAB	ROPS
WEIGHT	5,567 LBS.
MSRP	$28,025

OPTIONS

LOADER	$7,090

SERIAL NUMBERS

YEAR	BEGINNING NO.
2015	1501
2016	1985

RETAIL PRICING

YEAR	HIGH	LOW
2015	$16,452	$12,339
2016	$17,631	$13,223
2017	$19,997	$14,998
2018	$21,759	$16,319
2019	$23,634	$17,726
2020	$26,055	$19,890

5555

YEARS MFRD	2013-2020
ENGINE	MAHINDRA
CYLINDERS	3
CID	161.7
PTO HP	45
ENGINE HP	55
COOLING	LIQUID
FUEL	D
SPEEDS	8/8
TRANSMISSION	SHUTTLE SHIFT
STEERING	STANDARD
HITCH	CAT. I
DRIVE TYPE	2WD
ROPS/CAB	ROPS
WEIGHT	6,039 LBS.
MSRP	$33,442

OPTIONS

2WD THROUGH 2019

LDR	$8,026

SERIAL NUMBERS

YEAR	BEGINNING NO.
2013	1002-4WD
2013	1001-2WD
2014	1004-2WD
2014	1007-4WD
2015	1056-2WD
2015	1501-4WD
2016	1120-2WD
2016	1833-4WD

RETAIL PRICING

YEAR	HIGH	LOW
2014	$17,228	$12,921
2015	$17,984	$13,488
2016	$18,573	$13,930
2017	$20,275	$15,206
2018	$21,754	$16,316
2019	$23,117	$17,338
2020	$29,994	$22,864

5570

YEARS MFRD	2014-2017
CYLINDERS	3
CID	161.5
PTO HP	61
ENGINE HP	70
COOLING	LIQUID
FUEL	D
SPEEDS	8/2
TRANSMISSION	GEAR
STEERING	STANDARD
HITCH	CAT. I
DRIVE TYPE	2WD
ROPS/CAB	ROPS
WEIGHT	5,657 LBS.
MSRP	$26,440

OPTIONS

4WD

SERIAL NUMBERS

YEAR	BEGINNING NO.
2014	1001-4WD
2015	2001-2WD
2015	1006-4WD
2016	2214-2WD
2016	2155-4WD

RETAIL PRICING

YEAR	HIGH	LOW
2015	$18,393	$13,794
2016	$19,733	$14,800
2017	$21,557	$16,168

6000

YEARS MFRD	2003-2008
CYLINDERS	4
ENGINE HP	59
FUEL	D
SPEEDS	8/8
TRANSMISSION	SHUTTLE SHIFT
STEERING	STANDARD
HITCH	CAT. I
DRIVE TYPE	2WD
ROPS/CAB	ROPS
WEIGHT	6,250 LBS.
MSRP	$17,123

OPTIONS

4WD
LDR

SERIAL NUMBERS

YEAR	BEGINNING NO.
2005	1783
2006	1961
2007	2053

RETAIL PRICING

YEAR	HIGH	LOW
2003	$4,855	$3,641
2004	$5,374	$4,031
2005	$5,895	$4,421
2006	$6,502	$4,877
2007	$7,109	$5,332
2008	$7,717	$5,787

AVG. AUCTION PRICING

LOW	HIGH	AVG
$5,096	$8,085	$6,248

6500

YEARS MFRD	2005-2008
SERIES	00 SERIES
ENGINE	NE465
CYLINDERS	4
CID	216
PTO HP	57
ENGINE HP	65
COOLING	LIQUID
FUEL	D
SPEEDS	8/8
TRANSMISSION	SHUTTLE SHIFT
STEERING	STANDARD
HITCH	CAT. II
HYDRAULIC	YES
PTO	YES
DRIVE TYPE	2WD
ROPS/CAB	ROPS
WEIGHT	6,280 LBS.
MSRP	$18,559

OPTIONS

4WD
BACKHOE
LDR
SNOWBLOWER

MAHINDRA

SERIAL NUMBERS

YEAR	BEGINNING NO.
2005	1001-2WD
2005	1574-4WD
2006	1002-2WD
2006	2075-4WD
2007	1320-2WD
2007	2414-4WD
2008	1556-2WD
2008	2658-4WD

RETAIL PRICING

YEAR	HIGH	LOW
2005	$7,629	$5,722
2006	$8,236	$6,177
2007	$8,929	$6,697
2008	$9,623	$7,217

MASSEY FERGUSON

FC23

YEARS MFRD	2002-2003
ENGINE HP	22.9
FUEL	D
SPEEDS	VARIABLE
TRANSMISSION	HYDRO
STEERING	STANDARD
DRIVE TYPE	4WD
ROPS/CAB	ROPS
STANDARD DECK	60"
MSRP	$17,460

RETAIL PRICING

YEAR	HIGH	LOW
2002	$4,549	$3,412
2003	$5,048	$3,786

FC33

YEARS MFRD	2002-2003
ENGINE HP	33
FUEL	D
SPEEDS	VARIABLE
TRANSMISSION	HYDRO
STEERING	STANDARD
DRIVE TYPE	4WD
ROPS/CAB	ROPS
STANDARD DECK	72"
MSRP	$20,360

RETAIL PRICING

YEAR	HIGH	LOW
2002	$5,304	$3,978
2003	$5,885	$4,414

GC1705

YEARS MFRD	2013-2019
ENGINE	MF TIER 4
CYLINDERS	3
CID	68.5
PTO HP	18.7
ENGINE HP	22.5
COOLING	LIQUID
FUEL	D
SPEEDS	VARIABLE
TRANSMISSION	HYDRO
STEERING	STANDARD
HYDRAULIC	YES
PTO	YES
DRIVE TYPE	4WD
ROPS/CAB	ROPS
WEIGHT	1,433 LBS.
MSRP	$10,498

OPTIONS

BACKHOE
LDR

SERIAL NUMBERS

YEAR	BEGINNING NO.
2013	D
2014	E
2015	F
2016	G
2017	H

RETAIL PRICING

YEAR	HIGH	LOW
2013	$6,387	$4,791
2014	$6,786	$5,090
2015	$7,747	$5,811
2016	$8,394	$6,296
2017	$9,251	$6,938
2018	$10,022	$7,517
2019	$10,653	$7,990

GC1710

YEARS MFRD	2013-2019
ENGINE	ISEKI
CYLINDERS	3
CID	68.5
PTO HP	18.7
ENGINE HP	22.5
COOLING	LIQUID
FUEL	D
SPEEDS	VARIABLE
TRANSMISSION	HYDRO
STEERING	STANDARD
DRIVE TYPE	4WD
ROPS/CAB	ROPS
MSRP	$18,845

OPTIONS

LDR/BKH STD

SERIAL NUMBERS

YEAR	BEGINNING NO.
2013	D
2014	E
2015	F
2016	G
2017	H

RETAIL PRICING

YEAR	HIGH	LOW
2013	$12,238	$9,178
2014	$13,018	$9,764
2015	$13,829	$10,372
2016	$15,105	$11,329
2017	$16,090	$12,067
2018	$17,407	$13,055
2019	$18,530	$13,897

GC1715

YEARS MFRD	2013-2019
ENGINE	MF TIER 4
CYLINDERS	3
CID	68.5
PTO HP	19.6
ENGINE HP	25
COOLING	LIQUID
FUEL	D
SPEEDS	VARIABLE
TRANSMISSION	HYDRO
STEERING	STANDARD
HITCH	CAT. I
HYDRAULIC	YES
PTO	YES
DRIVE TYPE	4WD
ROPS/CAB	ROPS
WEIGHT	1,433 LBS.
MSRP	$11,798

OPTIONS

LOADER

SERIAL NUMBERS

YEAR	BEGINNING NO.
2013	D
2014	E
2015	F
2016	G
2017	H

RETAIL PRICING

YEAR	HIGH	LOW
2013	$7,389	$5,542
2014	$8,113	$6,085
2015	$8,835	$6,626
2016	$9,669	$7,252
2017	$10,588	$7,941
2018	$11,046	$8,285
2019	$11,472	$8,604

GC1720TLB

YEARS MFRD	2013-2019
ENGINE	MF TIER 4
CYLINDERS	3
CID	68.5
PTO HP	19.6
ENGINE HP	25
COOLING	LIQUID
FUEL	D
SPEEDS	VARIABLE
TRANSMISSION	HYDRO
STEERING	STANDARD
HITCH	CAT. I
HYDRAULIC	YES
PTO	YES
DRIVE TYPE	4WD
ROPS/CAB	ROPS
WEIGHT	2,670 LBS.
MSRP	$20,645

SERIAL NUMBERS

YEAR	BEGINNING NO.
2013	D
2014	E
2015	F
2016	G
2017	H

RETAIL PRICING

YEAR	HIGH	LOW
2013	$13,279	$9,959
2014	$14,075	$10,556
2015	$14,944	$11,208
2016	$16,312	$12,234
2017	$17,355	$13,017
2018	$18,404	$13,803
2019	$19,557	$14,668

GC1723E

YEARS MFRD	2019-2020
SERIES	GC SERIES
ENGINE	ISEKI
CYLINDERS	3
PTO HP	18.7
ENGINE HP	22.5
COOLING	LIQUID
FUEL	D
TRANSMISSION	HYDRO
STEERING	STANDARD
ROPS/CAB	ROPS
MSRP	$11,156

OPTIONS

BACKHOE	$8,921
LOADER	$3,346

SERIAL NUMBERS

YEAR	BEGINNING NO.
2019	JKR04302

GC1725M

YEARS MFRD	2019-2020
SERIES	GC SERIES
ENGINE	ISEKI
CYLINDERS	3
PTO HP	19.6
ENGINE HP	24.5
COOLING	LIQUID
FUEL	D
TRANSMISSION	HYDRO
STEERING	STANDARD
HITCH	CAT. I
ROPS/CAB	ROPS
MSRP	$12,645

OPTIONS

BACKHOE	$8,929
LOADER	$3,346

SERIAL NUMBERS

YEAR	BEGINNING NO.
2019	JKR24302

GC2300

YEARS MFRD	2002-2007
ENGINE	ISEKI E3112-G01
CYLINDERS	3
CID	68.5
PTO HP	18.7
ENGINE HP	22.5
COOLING	LIQUID
FUEL	D
SPEEDS	VARIABLE
TRANSMISSION	HYDRO
STANDARD DECK	60"
WEIGHT	1,367 LBS.
MSRP	$12,414

OPTIONS

2 HYD
60" DECK
LDR

SERIAL NUMBERS

YEAR	BEGINNING NO.
2002	LT
2003	MT
2004	NT
2005	JP
2006	JR
2007	JS

RETAIL PRICING

YEAR	HIGH	LOW
2003	$3,796	$2,847
2004	$4,205	$3,154
2005	$4,663	$3,497
2006	$5,193	$3,895

AVG. AUCTION PRICING

LOW	HIGH	AVG
$3,350	$5,836	$4,415

GC2310TLB

YEARS MFRD 2002-2008
ENGINE .... ISEKI E3112-G01
CYLINDERS 3
CID 68.5
PTO HP 18.7
ENGINE HP 22.5
COOLING .... LIQUID
FUEL .... D
SPEEDS .... VARIABLE
TRANSMISSION .... HYDRO
STEERING .... STANDARD
HITCH .... CAT. I
WEIGHT .... 2,597 LBS.
MSRP $19,310

OPTIONS

10" BUCKET
12" BUCKET
2 HYD
LDR

RETAIL PRICING

YEAR	HIGH	LOW
2002	$6,066	$4,549
2003	$6,628	$4,971
2004	$7,226	$5,419
2005	$7,848	$5,886
2006	$8,617	$6,463
2007	$9,197	$6,898
2008	$9,920	$7,440

GC2400

YEARS MFRD 2009-2012
ENGINE .... PERKINS
CYLINDERS 3
PTO HP 18.7
ENGINE HP 22.5
COOLING .... LIQUID
FUEL .... D
SPEEDS .... VARIABLE
TRANSMISSION .... HYDRO
STEERING .... STANDARD
WEIGHT .... 1,433 LBS.
MSRP $10,955

OPTIONS

2 HYD
60" DECK
LDR

SERIAL NUMBERS

YEAR	BEGINNING NO.
2009	JU
2010	JV
2011	JW
2012	JX

RETAIL PRICING

YEAR	HIGH	LOW
2009	$6,514	$4,886
2010	$7,238	$5,428
2011	$7,940	$5,955
2012	$8,880	$6,660

AVG. AUCTION PRICING

LOW	HIGH	AVG
$5,900	$8,900	$6,933

GC2410TLB

YEARS MFRD 2009-2012
ENGINE .... PERKINS
CYLINDERS 3
PTO HP 18.7
ENGINE HP 22.5
COOLING .... LIQUID
FUEL .... D
SPEEDS .... VARIABLE
TRANSMISSION .... HYDRO
STEERING .... STANDARD
WEIGHT .... 2,670 LBS.
MSRP $19,265

OPTIONS

10" BUCKET
12" BUCKET

SERIAL NUMBERS

YEAR	BEGINNING NO.
2009	JU
2010	JV
2011	JW
2012	JX

RETAIL PRICING

YEAR	HIGH	LOW
2009	$11,023	$8,267
2010	$11,840	$8,880
2011	$12,690	$9,517
2012	$13,621	$10,216

GC2600

YEARS MFRD 2009-2012
ENGINE .... PERKINS
CYLINDERS 3
PTO HP 19.6
ENGINE HP 25
COOLING .... LIQUID
FUEL .... D
SPEEDS .... VARIABLE
TRANSMISSION .... HYDRO
STEERING .... STANDARD
WEIGHT .... 1,433 LBS.
MSRP $12,255

OPTIONS

2 HYD
50" SNOWBLOWER
54" DECK
60" DECK
LDR

SERIAL NUMBERS

YEAR	BEGINNING NO.
2009	JU
2010	JV
2011	JW
2012	JX

RETAIL PRICING

YEAR	HIGH	LOW
2009	$7,454	$5,591
2010	$8,195	$6,146
2011	$9,040	$6,780
2012	$9,811	$7,358

GC2610TLB

YEARS MFRD 2009-2012
ENGINE .... PERKINS
CYLINDERS 3
PTO HP 19.6
ENGINE HP 25
COOLING .... LIQUID
FUEL .... D
SPEEDS .... VARIABLE
TRANSMISSION .... HYDRO
STEERING .... STANDARD
WEIGHT .... 2,670 LBS.
MSRP $20,360

OPTIONS

10" BUCKET
12" BUCKET

SERIAL NUMBERS

YEAR	BEGINNING NO.
2009	JU
2010	JV
2011	JW
2012	JX

RETAIL PRICING

YEAR	HIGH	LOW
2009	$11,805	$8,854
2010	$12,622	$9,466
2011	$13,515	$10,136
2012	$14,490	$10,868

TW2061

YEARS MFRD 2001-2001
SERIES .... DERBY SERIES
ENGINE .... B&S
ENGINE HP 20
FUEL .... G
TRANSMISSION .... HYDRO
STEERING .... ZERO
STANDARD DECK .... 61"
MSRP $6,099

OPTIONS

50" SNOW BLOWER
60" BLADE
60" BROOM

RETAIL PRICING

YEAR	HIGH	LOW
2001	$1,261	$945

ZT24

YEARS MFRD 2008-2011
ENGINE .... B&S
ENGINE HP 24
COOLING .... AIR
FUEL .... G
SPEEDS .... VARIABLE
TRANSMISSION .... HYDRO
STEERING .... ZERO
BLADE CLUTCH .... ELECTRIC
STANDARD DECK .... 52"
MSRP $4,600

OPTIONS

3 BAG

RETAIL PRICING

YEAR	HIGH	LOW
2008	$1,920	$1,440
2009	$2,130	$1,598
2010	$2,367	$1,775
2011	$2,629	$1,972

ZT29

YEARS MFRD 2005-2013
ENGINE .... ISEKI
CYLINDERS 3
CID 89.3
ENGINE HP 28.4
COOLING .... AIR
FUEL .... D
SPEEDS .... VARIABLE
TRANSMISSION .... HYDRO
STEERING .... ZERO
BLADE CLUTCH .... ELECTRIC
STANDARD DECK .... 60"
WEIGHT .... 1,367 LBS.
MSRP $12,186

RETAIL PRICING

YEAR	HIGH	LOW
2005	$3,414	$2,561
2006	$3,793	$2,845
2007	$4,215	$3,161
2008	$4,678	$3,509
2009	$5,199	$3,899
2010	$5,769	$4,327
2011	$6,410	$4,807
2012	$7,152	$5,364
2013	$7,904	$5,928

ZT33

YEARS MFRD 2005-2013
ENGINE .... ISEKI
CYLINDERS 3
CID 91.4
ENGINE HP 33
COOLING .... AIR
FUEL .... D
SPEEDS .... VARIABLE
TRANSMISSION .... HYDRO
STEERING .... ZERO
BLADE CLUTCH .... ELECTRIC
STANDARD DECK .... 72"
WEIGHT .... 1,367 LBS.
MSRP $13,646

RETAIL PRICING

YEAR	HIGH	LOW
2005	$3,824	$2,868
2006	$4,245	$3,184
2007	$4,713	$3,534

YEAR	HIGH	LOW
2008	$5,232	$3,924
2009	$5,814	$4,360
2010	$6,455	$4,842
2011	$7,170	$5,377
2012	$7,961	$5,970
2013	$8,841	$6,630

ZT1638

YEARS MFRD 2002-2003
SERIES .... ZT SERIES
ENGINE .... KOHLER
ENGINE HP 16
FUEL .... G
TRANSMISSION .... HYDRO
STEERING .... ZERO
STANDARD DECK .... 38"
MSRP $3,675

OPTIONS

BAGGER

RETAIL PRICING

YEAR	HIGH	LOW
2002	$953	$715
2003	$1,057	$792

ZT1644

YEARS MFRD 1998-2003
SERIES .... ZT SERIES
ENGINE .... KOHLER
ENGINE HP 16
COOLING .... AIR
FUEL .... G
TRANSMISSION .... HYDRO
STEERING .... ZERO
STANDARD DECK .... 44"
MSRP $4,075

OPTIONS

2 BAG
4 BAG

RETAIL PRICING

YEAR	HIGH	LOW
1998	$696	$522
1999	$769	$577
2000	$855	$641
2001	$949	$712
2002	$1,057	$792
2003	$1,173	$880

ZT1844

YEARS MFRD 2005-2007
ENGINE .... KOHLER
ENGINE HP 18
COOLING .... AIR
FUEL .... G
SPEEDS .... VARIABLE
TRANSMISSION .... HYDRO
STEERING .... ZERO
STANDARD DECK .... 44"
MSRP $4,299

OPTIONS

2 BAG
3 BAG

RETAIL PRICING

YEAR	HIGH	LOW
2005	$1,409	$1,057
2006	$1,563	$1,172
2007	$1,736	$1,302

ZT1850

YEARS MFRD 1999-2003
SERIES .... ZT SERIES
ENGINE .... B&S
ENGINE HP 18
COOLING .... AIR
FUEL .... G
SPEEDS .... VARIABLE
TRANSMISSION ..... DUAL HYDRO
STEERING .... ZERO
STANDARD DECK .... 50"
MSRP $5,125

OPTIONS

2 BAG
4 BAG

RETAIL PRICING

YEAR	HIGH	LOW
1999	$971	$729
2000	$1,078	$808
2001	$1,195	$896
2002	$1,328	$996
2003	$1,473	$1,105

ZT2050

YEARS MFRD 2005-2007
ENGINE .... VANGUARD
ENGINE HP 20
COOLING .... AIR
FUEL .... G
SPEEDS .... VARIABLE
TRANSMISSION .... HYDRO
STEERING .... ZERO
STANDARD DECK .... 50"
MSRP $4,999

OPTIONS

2 BAG
3 BAG

RETAIL PRICING

YEAR	HIGH	LOW
2005	$1,637	$1,228
2006	$1,817	$1,363
2007	$2,020	$1,515

ZT2148

YEARS MFRD 2002-2003
SERIES .... DERBY SERIES
ENGINE .... KOHLER
ENGINE HP 21
FUEL .... G
SPEEDS .... VARIABLE
TRANSMISSION .... HYDRO
STEERING .... ZERO
STANDARD DECK .... 48"
MSRP $6,299

OPTIONS

3 BAG

RETAIL PRICING

YEAR	HIGH	LOW
2002	$1,633	$1,225
2003	$1,814	$1,360

ZT2321

YEARS MFRD 2013-2014
ENGINE .... B&S
ENGINE HP 21
COOLING .... AIR
FUEL .... G
SPEEDS .... VARIABLE
TRANSMISSION .... HYDRO
STEERING .... ZERO
STANDARD DECK .... 42"
MSRP $2,599

RETAIL PRICING

YEAR	HIGH	LOW
2013	$1,294	$971
2014	$1,669	$1,251

ZT2324

YEARS MFRD 2013-2014
ENGINE .... B&S
ENGINE HP 24
COOLING .... AIR
FUEL .... G
SPEEDS .... VARIABLE
TRANSMISSION .... HYDRO
STEERING .... ZERO
STANDARD DECK .... 46"
MSRP $2,999

RETAIL PRICING

YEAR	HIGH	LOW
2013	$1,490	$1,118
2014	$1,921	$1,441

ZT2326

YEARS MFRD 2013-2014
ENGINE .... B&S
ENGINE HP 26
COOLING .... AIR
FUEL .... G
SPEEDS .... VARIABLE
TRANSMISSION .... HYDRO
STEERING .... ZERO
STANDARD DECK .... 52"
MSRP $3,299

RETAIL PRICING

YEAR	HIGH	LOW
2013	$1,636	$1,227
2014	$2,245	$1,684

ZT2352

YEARS MFRD 2002-2003
SERIES .... DERBY SERIES
ENGINE .... KOHLER
ENGINE HP 23
FUEL .... G
SPEEDS .... VARIABLE
TRANSMISSION .... HYDRO
STEERING .... ZERO
STANDARD DECK .... 52"
MSRP $6,699

OPTIONS

3 BAG

RETAIL PRICING

YEAR	HIGH	LOW
2002	$1,736	$1,302
2003	$1,929	$1,446

ZT2354

YEARS MFRD 2001-2002
SERIES .... DERBY SERIES
ENGINE .... KOHLER
ENGINE HP 23
FUEL .... G
SPEEDS .... VARIABLE
TRANSMISSION ..... DUAL HYDRO
STEERING .... ZERO
STANDARD DECK .... 54"
MSRP $7,299

OPTIONS

3 BAG

RETAIL PRICING

YEAR	HIGH	LOW
2001	$1,637	$1,228
2002	$1,821	$1,366

ZT2450

YEARS MFRD 2009-2009
ENGINE .... B&S
CYLINDERS 2
ENGINE HP 24
COOLING .... AIR
FUEL .... G
SPEEDS .... VARIABLE
TRANSMISSION .... HYDRO
STEERING .... ZERO
BLADE CLUTCH .... ELECTRIC

ZT2561

YEARS MFRD 2001-2003
SERIES .... DERBY SERIES
ENGINE .... KOHLER
ENGINE HP 25
FUEL .... G
SPEEDS .... VARIABLE
TRANSMISSION ..... DUAL HYDRO
STEERING .... ZERO
STANDARD DECK .... 61"
MSRP $7,999

OPTIONS

3 BAG

RETAIL PRICING

YEAR	HIGH	LOW
2001	$1,814	$1,360
2002	$2,015	$1,511
2003	$2,234	$1,676

ZT2927

YEARS MFRD 2012-2014
ENGINE .... B&S
ENGINE HP 27
COOLING .... AIR
FUEL .... G
SPEEDS .... VARIABLE
TRANSMISSION .... HYDRO
STEERING .... ZERO
STANDARD DECK .... 48"
MSRP $4,499

RETAIL PRICING

YEAR	HIGH	LOW
2012	$1,866	$1,399
2013	$2,230	$1,672
2014	$3,109	$2,332

ZT3022

YEARS MFRD 2012-2014
ENGINE .... KAWASAKI
ENGINE HP 22
COOLING ....AIR
FUEL .... G
SPEEDS .... VARIABLE
TRANSMISSION .... HYDRO
STEERING................ ZERO
STANDARD DECK .... 52"
MSRP................ $6,699

RETAIL PRICING

YEAR	HIGH	LOW
2012	$2,784	$2,088
2013	$3,330	$2,498
2014	$4,858	$3,643

ZT3928

YEARS MFRD 2012-2014
ENGINE .... B&S
ENGINE HP 28
COOLING ....AIR
FUEL .... G
SPEEDS .... VARIABLE
TRANSMISSION .... HYDRO
STEERING................ ZERO
STANDARD DECK .... 61"
MSRP................ $7,999

RETAIL PRICING

YEAR	HIGH	LOW
2012	$3,321	$2,491
2013	$4,054	$3,040
2014	$5,363	$4,022

15.5

YEARS MFRD 2001-2001
SERIES........ EXPRESS SERIES
ENGINE .... B&S
ENGINE HP 15.5
COOLING ....AIR
FUEL .... G
TRANSMISSION .... HYDRO
STEERING........... STANDARD
STANDARD DECK .... 38"
MSRP................ $1,899

RETAIL PRICING

YEAR	HIGH	LOW
2001	$344	$258

17

YEARS MFRD 2001-2001
SERIES........ EXPRESS SERIES
ENGINE .... B&S
ENGINE HP 17
COOLING ....AIR
FUEL .... G
TRANSMISSION .... HYDRO
STEERING........... STANDARD
STANDARD DECK .... 44"
MSRP................ $2,299

OPTIONS

42" BLADE
SNOCAB

RETAIL PRICING

YEAR	HIGH	LOW
2001	$309	$231

18H

YEARS MFRD 2001-2001
SERIES.......... BARON SERIES
ENGINE .... B&S
ENGINE HP 18
COOLING ....AIR
FUEL .... G
TRANSMISSION .... HYDRO
STEERING........... STANDARD
STANDARD DECK .... 40"
MSRP................ $4,849

OPTIONS

36" SNOW THROWER
40" SNOW BLOWER
42" BLADE

RETAIL PRICING

YEAR	HIGH	LOW
2001	$651	$488

20 INDUSTRIAL

YEARS MFRD 1966-1976
ENGINE .... PERKINS
CID 152/153
ENGINE HP 42
SPEEDS 6/2,6/6
WEIGHT .... 3,291 LBS.

SERIAL NUMBERS

YEAR	BEGINNING NO.
1966	800708
1967	801397
1968	802274
1969	802987
1970	803826
1971	804546
1972	805202
1973	805919
1974	806579
1975	807208
1976	808002

20 INDUSTRIAL (REINTRODUCED)

YEARS MFRD 1983-1992
ENGINE .... PERKINS
CID 153
ENGINE HP 42
FUEL .... D
SPEEDS 8
WEIGHT .... 4,025 LBS.

SERIAL NUMBERS

YEAR	BEGINNING NO.
1983	810003
1984	810320
1985	810726
1986	810985
1987	2996V03158
1988	2996N10001
1989	2996P1260
1990	2996R1450
1991	2996S1705
1992	2996T1955

20C INDUSTRIAL

YEARS MFRD 1976-1982
ENGINE .... PERKINS
CID 152/153
ENGINE HP 42
SPEEDS 8
WEIGHT .... 3,576 LBS.

SERIAL NUMBERS

YEAR	BEGINNING NO.
1976	9A250640
1977	9A257837
1978	9A280301
1979	9A300200
1980	9A326169
1981	9A339334
1982	9A350584

20C TURF

YEARS MFRD 1975-1976
ENGINE .... PERKINS
CID 153
ENGINE HP 42
FUEL .... D
SPEEDS 8
WEIGHT .... 4,042 LBS.

20E INDUSTRIAL

YEARS MFRD 1983-1986
ENGINE .... PERKINS
CID 153
ENGINE HP 42
FUEL .... D
SPEEDS 8
WEIGHT .... 4,155 LBS.

SERIAL NUMBERS

YEAR	BEGINNING NO.
1983	850001
1984	850719
1985	850839
1986	850974

20F UTILITY

YEARS MFRD 1984-1990
ENGINE .... PERKINS
CID 153
ENGINE HP 42
FUEL .... D
SPEEDS 8
WEIGHT .... 4,100 LBS.

SERIAL NUMBERS

YEAR	BEGINNING NO.
1985	5101Y0001
1986	5101A0001
1987	5101B0231
1988	5101C0426
1989	5101D0621
1990	5101E0811

30B INDUSTRIAL

YEARS MFRD 1976-1982
ENGINE .... PERKINS,CONT
CID 212,162
ENGINE HP 35
SPEEDS 6,SHUTTLE
WEIGHT .... 4,336 LBS.

OPTIONS

PERKINS 44.4HP

SERIAL NUMBERS

YEAR	BEGINNING NO.
1976	9A250640
1977	9A257837
1978	9A280301
1979	9A300200
1980	9A326169
1981	9A339334
1982	9A350584

30E INDUSTRIAL

YEARS MFRD 1983-1992
ENGINE .... CONT
CID 162
PTO HP 27.2
FUEL .... G
SPEEDS 5/1
WEIGHT .... 3,560 LBS.
MSRP................ $2,140

SERIAL NUMBERS

YEAR	BEGINNING NO.
1983	900001
1984	900637
1985	901222
1985	5102Y0001
1986	5102A0524
1987	5102B0773
1988	5102C0984
1989	5102D1194
1990	5102E1402
1991	5102F1607
1992	5102G1812

RETAIL PRICING

YEAR	HIGH	LOW
1990	$520	$390
1991	$529	$397
1992	$557	$418

30E UTILITY

YEARS MFRD 1984-1987
ENGINE .... PERKINS
CID 212
ENGINE HP 44.4
FUEL .... D
SPEEDS 8
WEIGHT .... 4,320 LBS.

40 (2203-2205)

YEARS MFRD 1956-1984
ENGINE .... CONT.
CYLINDERS.................. 4

MASSEY FERGUSON

CID....................134
PTO HP.................32.8
FUEL...................G
SPEEDS.................6/1
TRANSMISSION...........GEAR
STEERING...............STANDARD
WEIGHT.................3,200 LBS.

SERIAL NUMBERS

YEAR	BEGINNING NO.
1956	400001
1957	405671
1966	831475
1967	832975
1968	835550
1969	836912
1970	838138
1971	839413
1972	840280
1973	841073
1975	842272

40 INDUSTRIAL

YEARS MFRD.............1969-1975
ENGINE.................PERKINS
CID....................152
ENGINE HP..............42
SPEEDS.................MANUAL
WEIGHT.................5,600 LBS.

40B INDUSTRIAL

YEARS MFRD.............1976-1982
ENGINE.................PERKINS
CID....................153
ENGINE HP..............42
FUEL...................D
SPEEDS.................8
WEIGHT.................4,875 LBS.

SERIAL NUMBERS

YEAR	BEGINNING NO.
1976	9A250640
1977	9A257837
1978	9A280301
1979	9A300200
1980	9A326169
1981	9A339334
1982	9A350584

40E INDUSTRIAL

YEARS MFRD.............1987-1989
ENGINE.................PERKINS
ENGINE HP..............42
SPEEDS.................6/1
WEIGHT.................5,675 LBS.

SERIAL NUMBERS

YEAR	BEGINNING NO.
1987	5218B0006
1988	5218C0172
1989	5218D0359

50E 2WD

YEARS MFRD.............1983-1988
ENGINE.................CONT.
CID....................134
PTO HP.................33
FUEL...................G
SPEEDS.................6/2
TRANSMISSION...........GEAR
STEERING...............STANDARD
WEIGHT.................3,490 LBS.

SERIAL NUMBERS

YEAR	BEGINNING NO.
1983	870001
1984	877849
1985	5103X0001
1986	5103Y0528
1987	5157B0249
1988	5103C1412

50E 2WD UTILITY

YEARS MFRD.............1988-1992
ENGINE.................PERKINS
CYLINDERS..............3
CID....................152.7
PTO HP.................38.33
FUEL...................D
SPEEDS.................8/1
TRANSMISSION...........GEAR
STEERING...............STANDARD
PTO....................YES
WEIGHT.................3,490 LBS.

50E INDUSTRIAL

YEARS MFRD.............1987-1989
ENGINE.................PERKINS
CYLINDERS..............3
CID....................184
ENGINE HP..............38
FUEL...................D
SPEEDS.................6/1
DRIVE TYPE.............4WD
ROPS/CAB...............ROPS
WEIGHT.................5,695 LBS.

SERIAL NUMBERS

YEAR	BEGINNING NO.
1987	5157B0249
1988	5157C0577
1989	5157D0904

50F 2WD

YEARS MFRD.............NA-1986

SERIAL NUMBERS

YEAR	BEGINNING NO.
1983	2882W0001
1984	2882W0925
1985	2882W2114
1986	2882X3041

50F 4WD

YEARS MFRD.............1983-1987
ENGINE.................PERKINS
CYLINDERS..............3
CID....................153
PTO HP.................38.33
FUEL...................D
SPEEDS.................6/2
TRANSMISSION...........GEAR
STEERING...............STANDARD
PTO....................YES
WEIGHT.................3,490 LBS.

SERIAL NUMBERS

YEAR	BEGINNING NO.
1983	2915W0001
1984	2915W0201
1985	2915W0377
1986	2915W0915
1987	2915W1115

116LTX

YEARS MFRD.............1992-1994
ENGINE.................B&S
ENGINE HP..............16
COOLING................AIR
FUEL...................G
TRANSMISSION...........HYDRO
STEERING...............STANDARD
STANDARD DECK..........44"
MSRP...................$3,746

SERIAL NUMBERS

YEAR	BEGINNING NO.
1992	A01001
1993	B01001
1994	C01001

RETAIL PRICING

YEAR	HIGH	LOW
1992	$977	$733
1993	$990	$742
1994	$1,044	$783

154-2

YEARS MFRD.............1980-1984
ENGINE.................PERKINS
CYLINDERS..............3
CID....................153
PTO HP.................42.5
FUEL...................D
SPEEDS.................12/4
TRANSMISSION...........GEAR
STEERING...............STANDARD
WEIGHT.................4,685 LBS.

SERIAL NUMBERS

LOWER LEFT OF INSTRUMENT PANEL

YEAR	BEGINNING NO.
1980	2226706
1981	2227212
1982	2229282
1983	2229927
1984	22210485

154-4

YEARS MFRD.............1980-1984
ENGINE.................PERKINS
CYLINDERS..............3
CID....................153
PTO HP.................42.52
FUEL...................D
SPEEDS.................12/4
TRANSMISSION...........GEAR
STEERING...............STANDARD
PTO....................YES
DRIVE TYPE.............4WD
ROPS/CAB...............ROPS
WEIGHT.................5,100 LBS.

SERIAL NUMBERS

LOWER LEFT OF INSTRUMENT PANEL

YEAR	BEGINNING NO.
1980	2226706
1981	2227212
1982	2229282
1983	2229927
1984	22210485

154S

YEARS MFRD.............1986-1989
ENGINE.................PERKINS
CYLINDERS..............3
CID....................152
PTO HP.................42
FUEL...................D
SPEEDS.................12/4
TRANSMISSION...........GEAR
STEERING...............STANDARD
PTO....................YES
WEIGHT.................4,520 LBS.

SERIAL NUMBERS

ON DASH PANEL

YEAR	BEGINNING NO.
1986	13300288
1987	133A00489
1988	133C00645
1989	133C00791

154S 4WD

YEARS MFRD.............1986-1989
ENGINE.................PERKINS
CYLINDERS..............3
CID....................153
PTO HP.................42
FUEL...................D
SPEEDS.................12/4
TRANSMISSION...........GEAR
STEERING...............STANDARD
PTO....................YES
WEIGHT.................4,935 LBS.

SERIAL NUMBERS

YEAR	BEGINNING NO.
1986	23300755
1987	233A01012
1988	233C01304
1989	233C01511

202

YEARS MFRD.............1978-1984
ENGINE.................TOYOSHA
CYLINDERS..............2
CID....................65.2
PTO HP.................16.34

ENGINE HP 20
FUEL . . . . . D
SPEEDS 6/2
DRIVE TYPE 2WD
ROPS/CAB . . . . . ROPS
WEIGHT . . . . . 1,740 LBS.

SERIAL NUMBERS

BELOW CENTER OF INSTRUMENT PANEL

YEAR	BEGINNING NO.
1978	101
1979	315
1980	683
1981	1512
1982	1966
1983	2159
1984	2337

205

YEARS MFRD 1978-1984
ENGINE . . . . . TOYOSHA
CYLINDERS 2
CID 65.2
PTO HP 16.4
ENGINE HP 20
FUEL . . . . . D
SPEEDS 6/2
TRANSMISSION . . . . . GEAR
DRIVE TYPE 2WD
ROPS/CAB . . . . . ROPS
WEIGHT . . . . . 1,850 LBS.
MSRP $6,210

OPTIONS

4WD

SERIAL NUMBERS

BELOW CENTER OF INSTRUMENT PANEL

YEAR	BEGINNING NO.
1979	101-4WD
1979	315
1980	677-4WD
1980	683
1981	916-4WD
1981	1512
1982	1390-4WD
1982	1966
1983	1440-4WD
1983	2159
1984	1516-4WD
1984	2337

RETAIL PRICING

YEAR	HIGH	LOW
1979	$845	$634
1980	$859	$644
1981	$934	$700
1982	$948	$711
1983	$1,006	$754
1984	$1,059	$794

210

YEARS MFRD 1978-1984
ENGINE . . . . . TOYOSHA
CYLINDERS 2
CID 77.1
PTO HP 21.96
ENGINE HP 25
FUEL . . . . . D
SPEEDS 12/3
TRANSMISSION . . . . . GEAR
DRIVE TYPE 2WD
ROPS/CAB . . . . . ROPS
WEIGHT . . . . . 2,210 LBS.
MSRP $7,765

OPTIONS

4WD
HYDRO

SERIAL NUMBERS

BELOW CENTER OF INSTRUMENT PANEL

YEAR	BEGINNING NO.
1978	101-2WD
1979	101-4WD
1979	961-2WD
1980	1711-2WD
1980	711-4WD
1981	2700-2WD
1981	764-4WD
1982	1594-4WD
1982	3892-2WD
1983	1915-4WD
1983	4231-2WD
1984	2209-4WD
1984	4902-2WD

RETAIL PRICING

YEAR	HIGH	LOW
1978	$489	$367
1979	$542	$407
1980	$593	$445
1981	$653	$489
1982	$718	$538
1983	$787	$590
1984	$864	$648

216GTX

YEARS MFRD 1991-1994
ENGINE . . . . . KOHLER
ENGINE HP 16
COOLING . . . . . AIR
FUEL . . . . . G
TRANSMISSION . . . . . HYDRO
STEERING . . . . . STANDARD
STANDARD DECK . . . . . 38"
MSRP $5,253

SERIAL NUMBERS

YEAR	BEGINNING NO.
1991	S01001
1992	A01001
1993	B01001
1994	C01001

RETAIL PRICING

YEAR	HIGH	LOW
1991	$393	$295
1992	$436	$327
1993	$482	$362
1994	$533	$400

218GT

YEARS MFRD 1992-1994
ENGINE . . . . . KOHLER
ENGINE HP 18
FUEL . . . . . G
TRANSMISSION . . . . . HYDRO
STEERING . . . . . STANDARD
MSRP $5,680

RETAIL PRICING

YEAR	HIGH	LOW
1992	$1,482	$1,111
1993	$1,503	$1,127
1994	$1,582	$1,187

218GTX

YEARS MFRD 1991-1994
ENGINE . . . . . KOHLER
ENGINE HP 18
COOLING . . . . . AIR
FUEL . . . . . G
TRANSMISSION . . . . . HYDRO
STEERING . . . . . STANDARD
STANDARD DECK . . . . . 48"
MSRP $6,533

SERIAL NUMBERS

YEAR	BEGINNING NO.
1991	S01001
1992	A01001
1993	B01001
1994	C01001

RETAIL PRICING

YEAR	HIGH	LOW
1991	$489	$367
1992	$542	$407
1993	$599	$449
1994	$663	$497

220

YEARS MFRD 1978-1984
ENGINE . . . . . TOYOSHA
CYLINDERS 2
CID 90.3
PTO HP 26.37
ENGINE HP 30
FUEL . . . . . D
SPEEDS 12/3
TRANSMISSION . . . . . GEAR
DRIVE TYPE 2WD
ROPS/CAB . . . . . ROPS
WEIGHT . . . . . 2,390 LBS.
MSRP $8,486

OPTIONS

2 HYD
4WD

SERIAL NUMBERS

BELOW CENTER OF INSTRUMENT PANEL

YEAR	BEGINNING NO.
1978	101-2WD
1979	300-2WD
1979	101-4WD
1980	552-2WD
1980	520-4WD
1981	868-4WD
1981	750-2WD
1982	1673-4WD
1982	1339-2WD
1983	1981-4WD
1983	1458-2WD
1984	2163-4WD
1984	1708-2WD

RETAIL PRICING

YEAR	HIGH	LOW
1978	$538	$403
1979	$589	$442
1980	$648	$486
1981	$713	$534
1982	$782	$586
1983	$860	$645
1984	$949	$712

230

YEARS MFRD 1976-1983
ENGINE . . . . . PERKINS
CYLINDERS 3
CID 153
PTO HP 34.53
FUEL . . . . . D
SPEEDS 6/2
TRANSMISSION . . . . . GEAR
STEERING . . . . . STANDARD
HITCH . . . . . CAT. I
PTO . . . . . YES
DRIVE TYPE 2WD
ROPS/CAB . . . . . ROPS
WEIGHT . . . . . 4,000 LBS.
MSRP $11,995

OPTIONS

2 HYD
LDR

SERIAL NUMBERS

ON DASH PANEL

YEAR	BEGINNING NO.
1976	9A232539
1977	9A257837
1978	9A280301
1979	9A300200
1980	9A326169
1981	9A339343
1982	9A350584
1983	9A354679

RETAIL PRICING

YEAR	HIGH	LOW
1976	$618	$464
1977	$623	$467
1978	$803	$602
1979	$984	$738
1980	$1,168	$876
1981	$1,388	$1,041
1982	$1,558	$1,169
1983	$1,757	$1,318

AVG. AUCTION PRICING

LOW	HIGH	AVG
$1,537	$5,686	$3,215

231

YEARS MFRD 1989-1999
ENGINE . . . . . PERKINS AD3.152
CYLINDERS 3
CID 153
PTO HP 34
ENGINE HP 38
FUEL . . . . . D
SPEEDS 8/2
TRANSMISSION . . . . . GEAR
STEERING . . . . . STANDARD
HITCH . . . . . CAT. I
DRIVE TYPE 2WD
ROPS/CAB . . . . . ROPS
WEIGHT . . . . . 4,065 LBS.
MSRP $13,045

MASSEY FERGUSON

OPTIONS

2 HYD
LDR

SERIAL NUMBERS

RH SIDE OF INSTRUMENT CONSOLE

YEAR	BEGINNING NO.
1989	P17001
1990	R08001
1990	Q01001
1991	S01001
1992	A01001
1993	B01001
1994	C01001
1995	D01001
1996	E01001
1997	F01001
1998	G01001
1999	H01001

RETAIL PRICING

YEAR	HIGH	LOW
1989	$2,562	$1,921
1990	$2,868	$2,151
1991	$3,176	$2,382
1992	$3,483	$2,613
1993	$3,791	$2,843
1994	$4,201	$3,151
1995	$4,508	$3,381
1996	$4,918	$3,688
1997	$5,328	$3,996
1998	$5,635	$4,226
1999	$6,249	$4,687

AVG. AUCTION PRICING

LOW	HIGH	AVG
$2,000	$5,900	$3,936

231S

YEARS MFRD	1999-2004
ENGINE	PERKINS 903.27
CYLINDERS	3
CID	165
PTO HP	42
ENGINE HP	45
FUEL	D
SPEEDS	8/2
TRANSMISSION	GEAR
WEIGHT	4,120 LBS.
MSRP	$16,856

OPTIONS

2 HYD
LDR

SERIAL NUMBERS

LEFT SIDE OF INSTRUMENT PANEL

YEAR	BEGINNING NO.
1999	H01001
2000	J01001
2001	K01001
2002	L01001
2003	M00000

RETAIL PRICING

YEAR	HIGH	LOW
1999	$5,991	$4,493
2000	$8,443	$6,332
2001	$8,602	$6,452
2002	$8,734	$6,551
2003	$10,436	$7,827
2004	$10,886	$8,164

AVG. AUCTION PRICING

LOW	HIGH	AVG
$5,075	$6,902	$5,887

240

YEARS MFRD	1983-1998
ENGINE	PERKINS AD3.152
CYLINDERS	3
CID	153
PTO HP	34
ENGINE HP	41
FUEL	D
SPEEDS	8/2
DRIVE TYPE	2WD
ROPS/CAB	ROPS
WEIGHT	4,015 LBS.
MSRP	$19,165

OPTIONS

4WD
LDR

SERIAL NUMBERS

RIGHT SIDE OF CONSOLE

YEAR	BEGINNING NO.
1983	524172
1984	552016
1985	557882
1986	562389
1987	V01001
1988	N01001
1989	P01001
1990	R01001
1991	S01001
1992	A01001
1993	B01001
1994	C01001
1995	D01001
1996	E01001
1997	F01001
1998	G01001

RETAIL PRICING

YEAR	HIGH	LOW
1990	$5,084	$3,813
1991	$5,204	$3,903
1992	$5,516	$4,137
1993	$5,592	$4,194
1994	$5,900	$4,425
1995	$6,091	$4,568
1996	$6,319	$4,740
1997	$6,542	$4,906
1998	$7,462	$5,597

AVG. AUCTION PRICING

LOW	HIGH	AVG
$4,314	$12,485	$6,300

240S

YEARS MFRD	1996-1998
ENGINE	PERKINS AD3.152
CID	153
PTO HP	34
ENGINE HP	41
FUEL	D
SPEEDS	8/2
TRANSMISSION	GEAR
STEERING	STANDARD
PTO	YES
DRIVE TYPE	2WD
ROPS/CAB	ROPS
WEIGHT	3,812 LBS.

OPTIONS

4WD
LDR

241

YEARS MFRD	1999-2002
ENGINE	PERKINS 903.27
CYLINDERS	3
CID	165
PTO HP	45
ENGINE HP	48
FUEL	D
SPEEDS	8/2
TRANSMISSION	GEAR
STEERING	STANDARD
HITCH	CAT. I
PTO	YES
DRIVE TYPE	2WD
ROPS/CAB	ROPS
WEIGHT	4,160 LBS.

OPTIONS

2 HYD
LDR
TURF TIRES

SERIAL NUMBERS

YEAR	BEGINNING NO.
1999	H01001
2000	J01001
2001	K01001
2002	L01001

RETAIL PRICING

YEAR	HIGH	LOW
1999	$5,167	$3,876
2000	$5,665	$4,249
2001	$6,262	$4,696
2002	$6,857	$5,143

245

YEARS MFRD	1976-1983
ENGINE	CONT. 4CYL
CID	145
PTO HP	41
FUEL	D
SPEEDS	6/2
TRANSMISSION	GEAR
STEERING	STANDARD
PTO	YES
WEIGHT	3,640 LBS.

OPTIONS

PERKINS 3CYL

SERIAL NUMBERS

LEFT OF STEERING COLUMN BELOW INSTRUMENT PANEL

YEAR	BEGINNING NO.
1976	9A242489
1977	9A257837
1978	9A280301
1979	9A300200
1980	9A326169
1981	9A339343
1982	9A350584
1983	9A354679

AVG. AUCTION PRICING

LOW	HIGH	AVG
$3,073	$5,533	$4,278

250

YEARS MFRD	1983-1986
ENGINE	PERKINS
CYLINDERS	3
CID	152
PTO HP	37
FUEL	D
SPEEDS	8/2
TRANSMISSION	GEAR
STEERING	STANDARD
HITCH	CAT. I
PTO	YES
DRIVE TYPE	2WD
ROPS/CAB	ROPS
WEIGHT	4,360 LBS.

OPTIONS

2 HYD
LDR

SERIAL NUMBERS

RIGHT SIDE OF CONSOLE

YEAR	BEGINNING NO.
1983	621838
1984	624021
1985	627250
1986	629926

RETAIL PRICING

YEAR	HIGH	LOW
1983	$2,087	$1,565
1984	$2,384	$1,788
1985	$2,584	$1,938
1986	$2,883	$2,162

AVG. AUCTION PRICING

LOW	HIGH	AVG
$5,366	$5,864	$5,665

251XE

YEARS MFRD	2001-2002
ENGINE	PERKINS 903.27
CID	165
PTO HP	45
ENGINE HP	48
FUEL	D
SPEEDS	8/2
TRANSMISSION	GEAR
STEERING	STANDARD
HITCH	CAT. I
PTO	YES
DRIVE TYPE	2WD
ROPS/CAB	ROPS
WEIGHT	4,738 LBS.
MSRP	$15,890

OPTIONS

4WD
LDR

SERIAL NUMBERS

YEAR	BEGINNING NO.
2001	K01001
2002	BL01001

RETAIL PRICING

YEAR	HIGH	LOW
2001	$6,992	$5,244
2002	$7,620	$5,715

253

YEARS MFRD........1988-1998
ENGINE..........PERKINS TURBO
CYLINDERS..................3
CID..................152.7
PTO HP..................45
ENGINE HP..................48
COOLING..............LIQUID
FUEL......................D
SPEEDS..................8/2
TRANSMISSION............GEAR
STEERING............STANDARD
PTO......................YES
DRIVE TYPE..............2WD
ROPS/CAB................ROPS
WEIGHT............4,265 LBS.
MSRP..................$19,970

OPTIONS

2 HYD
4WD
LDR

SERIAL NUMBERS

YEAR	BEGINNING NO.
1988	N01001
1989	P01001
1990	R01001
1991	S01001
1992	A01001
1993	B01001
1994	C01001
1995	D01001
1996	E01001
1997	F01001
1998	G01001

RETAIL PRICING

YEAR	HIGH	LOW
1988	$3,180	$2,385
1989	$3,478	$2,609
1990	$3,776	$2,832
1991	$4,074	$3,056
1992	$4,373	$3,279
1993	$4,771	$3,578
1994	$5,068	$3,801
1995	$5,366	$4,025
1996	$5,763	$4,322
1997	$6,162	$4,622
1998	$6,459	$4,845

254

YEARS MFRD........1982-1987
ENGINE..................PERKINS
CYLINDERS..................3
CID......................153
PTO HP..................43.3
FUEL......................D
SPEEDS..................12/4
TRANSMISSION............GEAR
STEERING............STANDARD
HITCH..................CAT. I
PTO......................YES
DRIVE TYPE..............4WD
ROPS/CAB................ROPS
WEIGHT............5,200 LBS.

OPTIONS

2 HYD
LDR

SERIAL NUMBERS

LOWER LEFT OF INSTRUMENT PANEL

YEAR	BEGINNING NO.
1982	2229280
1983	2229927
1984	22210485
1985	22201750
1986	22202733
1987	22203556

RETAIL PRICING

YEAR	HIGH	LOW
1982	$1,392	$1,044
1983	$1,591	$1,193
1984	$1,888	$1,416
1985	$2,186	$1,640
1986	$2,485	$1,864
1987	$2,684	$2,013

316GTX

YEARS MFRD........1991-1994
ENGINE..................KOHLER
ENGINE HP..................16
COOLING....................AIR
FUEL......................G
TRANSMISSION............HYDRO
STEERING............STANDARD
STANDARD DECK............60"
MSRP..................$6,574

SERIAL NUMBERS

YEAR	BEGINNING NO.
1991	S01001
1992	A01001

RETAIL PRICING

YEAR	HIGH	LOW
1991	$393	$295
1992	$434	$326
1993	$481	$361
1994	$532	$399

318GTX

YEARS MFRD........1991-1994
ENGINE..................KOHLER
ENGINE HP..................18
COOLING....................AIR
FUEL......................G
TRANSMISSION............HYDRO
STEERING............STANDARD
STANDARD DECK............60"
MSRP..................$7,480

SERIAL NUMBERS

YEAR	BEGINNING NO.
1991	S01001
1992	A01001
1993	B01001
1994	C01001

RETAIL PRICING

YEAR	HIGH	LOW
1991	$448	$336
1992	$494	$371
1993	$547	$410
1994	$605	$454

320GTX

YEARS MFRD........1991-1994
ENGINE..................KOHLER
ENGINE HP..................20
COOLING....................AIR
FUEL......................G
TRANSMISSION............HYDRO
STEERING............STANDARD
STANDARD DECK............60"
MSRP..................$7,814

SERIAL NUMBERS

YEAR	BEGINNING NO.
1991	S01001
1992	A01001
1993	B01001
1994	C01001

RETAIL PRICING

YEAR	HIGH	LOW
1991	$467	$350
1992	$517	$387
1993	$571	$429
1994	$632	$474

350

YEARS MFRD........1986-1990
ENGINE..................PERKINS
CID......................152
PTO HP..................43
FUEL......................D
SPEEDS..................8/2
TRANSMISSION............GEAR
STEERING............STANDARD
PTO......................YES
WEIGHT............6,300 LBS.

354 ALL MODELS

YEARS MFRD..........NA-1999

SERIAL NUMBERS

YEAR	BEGINNING NO.
1994	C01001
1995	D01001
1996	E01001
1997	F01001
1998	G01001
1999	H01001

354GE 4WD

YEARS MFRD........1994-1999
ENGINE............PERKINS AD3
CID......................152
PTO HP..................42
FUEL......................D
SPEEDS..................12/4
TRANSMISSION............GEAR
STEERING............STANDARD
PTO......................YES
WEIGHT............5,020 LBS.

354S

YEARS MFRD........1994-1999
ENGINE............PERKINS AD3
CID......................152
PTO HP..................42
FUEL......................D
SPEEDS..................12/4
TRANSMISSION............GEAR
STEERING............STANDARD
PTO......................YES
WEIGHT............4,760 LBS.

OPTIONS

4WD

354V

YEARS MFRD........1998-1999
ENGINE............PERKINS AD3
CID......................152
PTO HP..................42
FUEL......................D
SPEEDS..................12/12
TRANSMISSION............GEAR
STEERING............STANDARD
PTO......................YES
DRIVE TYPE..............2WD
ROPS/CAB................ROPS
WEIGHT............5,290 LBS.

OPTIONS

4WD

415

YEARS MFRD........2004-2004
ENGINE........PERKINS AD3.152
CYLINDERS..................3
CID......................152
PTO HP..................39.7
ENGINE HP..................46
FUEL......................D
SPEEDS..................8/2
TRANSMISSION............GEAR
STEERING............STANDARD
PTO......................YES
WEIGHT............4,475 LBS.

OPTIONS

4WD

431

YEARS MFRD........2004-2005
SERIES..............400 SERIES
ENGINE..................PERKINS
CYLINDERS..................3
CID......................202
PTO HP..................44
ENGINE HP..................50
COOLING..............LIQUID
FUEL......................D
SPEEDS..................8/2
TRANSMISSION............GEAR
STEERING............STANDARD
HITCH..................CAT. I
HYDRAULIC..............YES
PTO......................YES
DRIVE TYPE..............2WD
ROPS/CAB................ROPS
WEIGHT............4,321 LBS.

OPTIONS

LDR

MASSEY FERGUSON

SERIAL NUMBERS

YEAR	BEGINNING NO.
2004	EN
2005	EP

RETAIL PRICING

YEAR	HIGH	LOW
2004	$8,149	$6,112
2005	$8,745	$6,559

451

YEARS MFRD	2002-2006
ENGINE	PERKINS 903.27
CYLINDERS	3
CID	202
PTO HP	45
ENGINE HP	48
COOLING	LIQUID
FUEL	D
SPEEDS	8/2
TRANSMISSION	GEAR
STEERING	STANDARD
HITCH	CAT. I
HYDRAULIC	YES
PTO	YES
DRIVE TYPE	2WD
ROPS/CAB	ROPS
WEIGHT	4,738 LBS.
MSRP	$20,346

OPTIONS

4WD
LDR

SERIAL NUMBERS

LEFT SIDE OF DASH

YEAR	BEGINNING NO.
2002	BL
2003	BM
2004	BN
2005	BP

RETAIL PRICING

YEAR	HIGH	LOW
2002	$8,001	$6,001
2003	$8,534	$6,401
2004	$9,088	$6,816
2005	$9,658	$7,243
2006	$10,248	$7,686

533

YEARS MFRD	2006-2008
SERIES	500 SERIES
ENGINE	1103C-33
CYLINDERS	3
CID	202
PTO HP	44
ENGINE HP	52
FUEL	D
SPEEDS	8/2
TRANSMISSION	GEAR
STEERING	STANDARD
HITCH	CAT. I
HYDRAULIC	YES
PTO	YES
DRIVE TYPE	2WD
ROPS/CAB	ROPS
WEIGHT	4,321 LBS.
MSRP	$16,586

OPTIONS

LDR

SERIAL NUMBERS

YEAR	BEGINNING NO.
2006	ER
2007	ES
2008	ET

RETAIL PRICING

YEAR	HIGH	LOW
2006	$10,701	$8,026
2007	$11,544	$8,658
2008	$12,219	$9,164

543

YEARS MFRD	2006-2008
SERIES	500 SERIES
ENGINE	1103C-33
CYLINDERS	3
CID	202
PTO HP	45
ENGINE HP	52
COOLING	LIQUID
FUEL	D
SPEEDS	8/2
TRANSMISSION	GEAR
STEERING	STANDARD
HITCH	CAT. I
HYDRAULIC	YES
PTO	YES
DRIVE TYPE	2WD
ROPS/CAB	ROPS
WEIGHT	4,962 LBS.
MSRP	$20,455

OPTIONS

4WD
LDR

SERIAL NUMBERS

YEAR	BEGINNING NO.
2006	ER
2007	ES
2008	ET

RETAIL PRICING

YEAR	HIGH	LOW
2006	$12,225	$9,168
2007	$12,739	$9,554
2008	$13,448	$10,086

1010

YEARS MFRD	1982-1994
ENGINE	TOYOSHA
CYLINDERS	3
CID	52.8
PTO HP	13.5
ENGINE HP	16
FUEL	D
SPEEDS	6/2
TRANSMISSION	GEAR
STEERING	STANDARD
HITCH	CAT. I
DRIVE TYPE	2WD
ROPS/CAB	ROPS
WEIGHT	1,580 LBS.
MSRP	$8,199

OPTIONS

2 HYD
4WD
54"DECK
HYDRO
LDR

SERIAL NUMBERS

STEERING COVER BELOW DASH

YEAR	BEGINNING NO.
1982	40101-4WD
1982	00101-2WD
1983	00613-2WD
1983	40607-4WD
1984	40809-4WD
1984	10901-2WD
1985	41491-4WD
1985	11727-2WD
1986	12075-2WD
1986	42317-4WD
1987	13953-2H
1987	13902-2WD
1987	43683-4WD
1987	43640-4H
1988	14433-2WD
1988	144552H
1988	44498-4WD
1988	44370-4H
1989	44696-4WD
1989	44696-4H
1989	14549-2H
1990	44886-4WD
1990	14600-2H
1990	14549-2WD
1990	449074H
1991	14840-2WD
1991	14879-2H
1991	45211-4WD
1991	45226-4H
1992	14937-2WD
1992	45362-4WD

RETAIL PRICING

YEAR	HIGH	LOW
1986	$1,518	$1,139
1987	$1,538	$1,153
1988	$1,558	$1,169
1989	$1,576	$1,182
1990	$1,602	$1,201
1991	$1,785	$1,339
1992	$1,980	$1,485
1993	$2,185	$1,639
1994	$2,389	$1,792

AVG. AUCTION PRICING

LOW	HIGH	AVG
$513	$2,459	$1,895

1010H

YEARS MFRD	1987-1994
ENGINE	TOYOSHA
CYLINDERS	3
CID	52.8
PTO HP	12
ENGINE HP	16
FUEL	D
TRANSMISSION	HYDRO
STEERING	STANDARD
DRIVE TYPE	2WD
ROPS/CAB	ROPS
WEIGHT	1,772 LBS.
MSRP	$8,499

OPTIONS

4WD

SERIAL NUMBERS

STEERING COVER BELOW DASH

YEAR	BEGINNING NO.
1987	13953
1988	14455
1989	14549
1990	14600
1991	14836
1992	15158

RETAIL PRICING

YEAR	HIGH	LOW
1987	$1,614	$1,210
1988	$1,633	$1,225
1989	$1,649	$1,237
1990	$1,672	$1,254
1991	$1,834	$1,376
1992	$2,006	$1,504
1993	$2,186	$1,640
1994	$2,367	$1,775

1020

YEARS MFRD	1983-1994
ENGINE	TOYOSHA
CYLINDERS	3
CID	68.7
PTO HP	17
ENGINE HP	21
FUEL	D
SPEEDS	12/4
TRANSMISSION	GEAR
STEERING	STANDARD
PTO	YES
DRIVE TYPE	2WD
ROPS/CAB	ROPS
WEIGHT	1,750 LBS.
MSRP	$9,681

OPTIONS

4WD

SERIAL NUMBERS

BELOW CENTER OF INSTRUMENT

YEAR	BEGINNING NO.
1983	40101-4WD
1983	00101-2WD
1984	00411-2WD
1984	40395-4WD
1985	405494WD
1985	00809-2WD
1986	41002-4WD
1986	01548-2WD
1987	02394-2WD
1987	41709-4H
1987	41787-4WD
1987	02319-2H
1988	42343-4H
1988	42273—4WD
1988	02707-2WD
1988	02707-2H
1989	42532-4WD
1989	02768-2H
1989	02768-2WD
1989	42641-4H
1990	02913-2WD
1990	02933-2H
1990	43016-4H
1990	42963-4WD

YEAR	BEGINNING NO.
1991	03157-2H
1991	03159-2WD
1991	43326-4WD
1991	43355-4H
1992	03262-2WD
1992	43647-4WD

RETAIL PRICING

YEAR	HIGH	LOW
1986	$938	$703
1987	$949	$712
1988	$962	$722
1989	$1,211	$908
1990	$1,470	$1,102
1991	$1,736	$1,302
1992	$2,015	$1,511
1993	$2,298	$1,723
1994	$2,625	$1,969

1020H

YEARS MFRD 1987-1994
ENGINE .... TOYOSHA
CYLINDERS 3
CID 68.7
PTO HP 14.5
ENGINE HP 21
FUEL .... D
TRANSMISSION .... HYDRO
STEERING .... STANDARD
DRIVE TYPE 2WD
ROPS/CAB .... ROPS
WEIGHT .... 1,950 LBS.
MSRP $10,181

OPTIONS

4WD

SERIAL NUMBERS

STEERING COVER BELOW DASH

YEAR	BEGINNING NO.
1987	41709
1988	42343
1989	42641
1990	43016
1991	43264
1992	43694

RETAIL PRICING

YEAR	HIGH	LOW
1987	$1,379	$1,035
1988	$1,392	$1,044
1989	$1,641	$1,231
1990	$1,900	$1,425
1991	$2,166	$1,625
1992	$2,444	$1,833
1993	$2,728	$2,046
1994	$3,054	$2,291

1030

YEARS MFRD 1984-1991
ENGINE .... TOYOSHA
CYLINDERS 3
CID 87
PTO HP 23.35
ENGINE HP 26
FUEL .... D
SPEEDS 12/3
TRANSMISSION .... GEAR
STEERING .... STANDARD
HITCH .... CAT. I
PTO .... YES
DRIVE TYPE 2WD
ROPS/CAB .... ROPS
WEIGHT .... 2,990 LBS.
MSRP $11,508

OPTIONS

2 HYD
4WD
60" DECK
72" DECK
HYDRO
LDR

SERIAL NUMBERS

BELOW CENTER OF INSTRUMENT PANEL

YEAR	BEGINNING NO.
1984	40101-4WD
1984	00101-2WD
1985	00820-2WD
1985	40600-4WD
1986	01501-2WD
1986	41245-4WD
1987	02391-2WD
1987	41959-4WD
1988	03139-2WD
1988	42594-4WD
1989	03285-4WD
1989	42953-2WD
1990	03430-2WD
1990	43310-4WD
1991	03774-4WD
1991	43667-2WD

RETAIL PRICING

YEAR	HIGH	LOW
1984	$581	$435
1985	$586	$439
1986	$841	$631
1987	$1,105	$829
1988	$1,373	$1,030
1989	$1,652	$1,239
1990	$1,940	$1,455
1991	$2,237	$1,678

1030L

YEARS MFRD 1986-1994
ENGINE .... TOYOSHA
CYLINDERS 3
CID 87
PTO HP 23.35
ENGINE HP 26
FUEL .... D
SPEEDS 12/4
TRANSMISSION .... GEAR
DRIVE TYPE 2WD
ROPS/CAB .... ROPS
WEIGHT .... 2,620 LBS.
MSRP $10,635

OPTIONS

4WD

SERIAL NUMBERS

YEAR	BEGINNING NO.
1986	02067-2WD
1986	41713-4WD
1987	02542-2WD
1987	42167-4WD
1988	42594-4WD
1988	03139-2WD
1989	42953-4WD
1989	03285-2WD
1990	03308-2WD
1990	43251-4WD
1991	03713-2WD
1991	43549-4WD
1992	43846-4WD
1992	44119-2WD
1993	44141-2WD
1994	44431-4WD

RETAIL PRICING

YEAR	HIGH	LOW
1990	$2,477	$1,857
1991	$2,530	$1,898
1992	$2,698	$2,023
1993	$2,761	$2,071
1994	$2,965	$2,224

1035

YEARS MFRD 1986-1991
ENGINE .... TOYOSHA
CYLINDERS 3
CID 91.8
PTO HP 26
ENGINE HP 31
FUEL .... D
SPEEDS 12/4
TRANSMISSION .... GEAR
STEERING .... STANDARD
HITCH .... CAT. I
PTO .... YES
DRIVE TYPE 2WD
ROPS/CAB .... ROPS
WEIGHT .... 2,801 LBS.
MSRP $12,369

OPTIONS

2 HYD
4WD
LDR

SERIAL NUMBERS

LEFT SIDE OF CLUTCH HOUSING

YEAR	BEGINNING NO.
1986	00100
1986	40100
1987	00315
1987	40377
1988	00415
1988	40691
1989	00540
1989	40936
1990	00585
1990	41058
1991	00729
1991	41252

RETAIL PRICING

YEAR	HIGH	LOW
1986	$2,049	$1,537
1987	$2,246	$1,685
1988	$2,454	$1,841
1989	$2,667	$2,001
1990	$2,890	$2,167
1991	$3,220	$2,415

AVG. AUCTION PRICING

LOW	HIGH	AVG
$3,147	$5,938	$4,682

1040

YEARS MFRD 1984-1986
ENGINE .... TOYOSHA
CID 121.7
PTO HP 27.7
COOLING .... LIQUID
FUEL .... D
SPEEDS 12/4
TRANSMISSION .... GEAR
STEERING .... STANDARD
DRIVE TYPE 2WD
ROPS/CAB .... ROPS
WEIGHT .... 3,490 LBS.
MSRP $10,525

OPTIONS

2 HYD
4WD

SERIAL NUMBERS

BELOW CENTER OF INSTRUMENT PANEL

YEAR	BEGINNING NO.
1984	101-2WD
1984	40101-4WD
1985	155-2WD
1985	40351-4WD
1986	552-2WD
1986	40562-4WD

RETAIL PRICING

YEAR	HIGH	LOW
1984	$1,546	$1,159
1985	$1,672	$1,254
1986	$1,809	$1,357

1045

YEARS MFRD 1986-1990
ENGINE .... TOYOSHA
CYLINDERS 3
CID 122
PTO HP 30
ENGINE HP 35
FUEL .... D
SPEEDS 9/3
TRANSMISSION .... GEAR
STEERING .... STANDARD
HITCH .... CAT. I
PTO .... YES
DRIVE TYPE 2WD
ROPS/CAB .... ROPS
WEIGHT .... 3,527 LBS.
MSRP $12,950

OPTIONS

2 HYD
4WD
LDR

SERIAL NUMBERS

YEAR	BEGINNING NO.
1986	00100
1986	40100
1987	00234
1987	40275
1988	00267
1988	40566
1989	40757
1989	00301
1990	41144
1990	00334

MASSEY FERGUSON

RETAIL PRICING

YEAR	HIGH	LOW
1986	$1,784	$1,338
1987	$1,977	$1,483
1988	$2,176	$1,632
1989	$2,383	$1,787
1990	$2,600	$1,950

1120

YEARS MFRD	1993-1996
ENGINE	ISUZU
CYLINDERS	3
CID	52
PTO HP	14
ENGINE HP	16
FUEL	D
SPEEDS	6/2
TRANSMISSION	GEAR
STEERING	STANDARD
HITCH	CAT. I
PTO	YES
DRIVE TYPE	4WD
ROPS/CAB	ROPS
WEIGHT	1,360 LBS.
MSRP	$9,584

OPTIONS

2 HYD
54"DECK
HYDRO
LDR
TURF TIRES

SERIAL NUMBERS

YEAR	BEGINNING NO.
1993	B00101
1994	C00101
1995	D00101
1996	E00101

RETAIL PRICING

YEAR	HIGH	LOW
1993	$2,082	$1,561
1994	$2,336	$1,752
1995	$2,606	$1,954
1996	$2,881	$2,160

1125

YEARS MFRD	1992-1992
ENGINE	ISEKI
CYLINDERS	3
CID	87.2
PTO HP	22.5
ENGINE HP	25
FUEL	D
SPEEDS	16/16
TRANSMISSION	GEAR
STEERING	STANDARD
PTO	YES
DRIVE TYPE	2WD
ROPS/CAB	ROPS
WEIGHT	2,524 LBS.
MSRP	$11,800

OPTIONS

2 HYD
4WD
60" DECK
72" DECK
HYDRO
LDR

SERIAL NUMBERS

YEAR	BEGINNING NO.
1992	A40101
1993	B40101

RETAIL PRICING

YEAR	HIGH	LOW
1992	$2,125	$1,594

1140

YEARS MFRD	1991-1992
ENGINE	ISEKI
CYLINDERS	3
CID	91.4
PTO HP	26.2
ENGINE HP	30
FUEL	D
SPEEDS	16/16
TRANSMISSION	GEAR
STEERING	STANDARD
PTO	YES
DRIVE TYPE	2WD
ROPS/CAB	ROPS
WEIGHT	2,590 LBS.
MSRP	$13,185

OPTIONS

2 HYD
4WD

SERIAL NUMBERS

YEAR	BEGINNING NO.
1991	S201001-2W
1991	S401001-4W
1992	A50101-2W
1992	A50101-4W

RETAIL PRICING

YEAR	HIGH	LOW
1991	$2,990	$2,243
1992	$3,281	$2,461

1145

YEARS MFRD	1991-1992
ENGINE	ISEKI
CYLINDERS	3
CID	91.4
PTO HP	31
ENGINE HP	35
FUEL	D
SPEEDS	16/16
TRANSMISSION	GEAR
STEERING	STANDARD
HITCH	CAT. I
PTO	YES
DRIVE TYPE	2WD
ROPS/CAB	ROPS
WEIGHT	2,889 LBS.
MSRP	$15,950

OPTIONS

2 HYD
72" DECK
LDR

SERIAL NUMBERS

YEAR	BEGINNING NO.
1991	S401001
1992	A601001

RETAIL PRICING

YEAR	HIGH	LOW
1991	$3,743	$2,807
1992	$3,998	$2,999

1160

YEARS MFRD	1992-1999
ENGINE	ISUZU 4JC1
CYLINDERS	4
CID	137
PTO HP	37
ENGINE HP	41
FUEL	D
SPEEDS	16/16
TRANSMISSION	GEAR
STEERING	STANDARD
HITCH	CAT. I
DRIVE TYPE	4WD
ROPS/CAB	ROPS
WEIGHT	3,848 LBS.
MSRP	$24,600

OPTIONS

2 HYD
LDR
ROPS

SERIAL NUMBERS

ON PANEL, THE SEAT BELOW

YEAR	BEGINNING NO.
1992	A01001
1993	B01001
1994	C01001
1995	D01001
1996	E01001
1997	FJ01001
1998	GJ01001

RETAIL PRICING

YEAR	HIGH	LOW
1992	$4,894	$3,671
1993	$5,350	$4,013
1994	$5,815	$4,361
1995	$6,307	$4,730
1996	$6,822	$5,116
1997	$7,359	$5,519
1998	$7,921	$5,941
1999	$8,507	$6,380

1165

YEARS MFRD	1999-2003
ENGINE	ISUZU
CYLINDERS	4
CID	134
PTO HP	37
ENGINE HP	44.2
FUEL	D
SPEEDS	16/16
TRANSMISSION	GEAR
HITCH	CAT. I
DRIVE TYPE	4WD
ROPS/CAB	ROPS
WEIGHT	4,275 LBS.
MSRP	$26,210

OPTIONS

2 HYD
HYDRO
LDR

SERIAL NUMBERS

YEAR	BEGINNING NO.
1999	HN01001
2000	JN01001
2001	KN01001
2002	LN01001

RETAIL PRICING

YEAR	HIGH	LOW
1999	$10,770	$8,078
2000	$12,246	$9,184
2001	$13,466	$10,100
2002	$14,665	$10,999
2003	$16,105	$12,079

1180

YEARS MFRD	1992-1996
ENGINE	TOYOSHA
CYLINDERS	4
CID	169
PTO HP	46
FUEL	D
SPEEDS	16/16
TRANSMISSION	GEAR
STEERING	STANDARD
HITCH	CAT. I
DRIVE TYPE	4WD
ROPS/CAB	ROPS
WEIGHT	4,775 LBS.
MSRP	$25,980

OPTIONS

2 HYD
LDR

RETAIL PRICING

YEAR	HIGH	LOW
1992	$6,464	$4,848
1993	$6,554	$4,915
1994	$7,576	$5,682
1995	$8,166	$6,124
1996	$8,385	$6,289

1180 4WD

YEARS MFRD	1992-1999
ENGINE	ISUZU
CYLINDERS	4
CID	169
PTO HP	46
ENGINE HP	52
FUEL	D
SPEEDS	16/16
TRANSMISSION	HYDRO
STEERING	STANDARD
PTO	YES
DRIVE TYPE	4WD
ROPS/CAB	ROPS
WEIGHT	4,354 LBS.
MSRP	$26,760

SERIAL NUMBERS

YEAR	BEGINNING NO.
1992	A80101
1993	B80101
1994	C01001
1995	D01001
1996	E01001
1997	FJ01001
1998	GK01001
1999	HL01001

RETAIL PRICING

YEAR	HIGH	LOW
1999	$10,286	$7,715

1205

YEARS MFRD........1996-2001
SERIES............1200 SERIES
ENGINE.................ISEKI
CYLINDERS..................3
CID.......................61
PTO HP..................13.5
ENGINE HP...............16.6
COOLING...............LIQUID
FUEL.......................D
SPEEDS...................6/2
TRANSMISSION............GEAR
STEERING............STANDARD
HITCH..................CAT. I
PTO......................YES
DRIVE TYPE...............4WD
ROPS/CAB................ROPS
WEIGHT............1,668 LBS.
MSRP..................$11,019

OPTIONS

2 HYD
54" DECK
HYDRO
LDR
TURF TIRES

SERIAL NUMBERS

YEAR	BEGINNING NO.
1996	E00101
1997	FA0101
1998	GA01001
1999	HA01001
2000	JA01001
2001	KA01001

RETAIL PRICING

YEAR	HIGH	LOW
1996	$3,225	$2,418
1997	$3,574	$2,680
1998	$3,932	$2,949
1999	$4,306	$3,229
2000	$4,716	$3,537
2001	$5,180	$3,885

1210

YEARS MFRD........1993-1996
ENGINE.................ISEKI
CYLINDERS..................3
CID.....................61.6
PTO HP....................15
ENGINE HP.................18
FUEL.......................D
SPEEDS...................6/2
TRANSMISSION............GEAR
STEERING............STANDARD
HITCH..................CAT. I
PTO......................YES
DRIVE TYPE...............2WD
ROPS/CAB................ROPS
WEIGHT............1,984 LBS.
MSRP..................$10,285

OPTIONS

2 HYD
4WD
54" DECK
60" DECK
HYDRO
LDR
TURF TIRES

SERIAL NUMBERS

ON PANEL, THE SEAT BELOW

YEAR	BEGINNING NO.
1993	B10101
1994	C10101
1995	D10101
1996	E10101

RETAIL PRICING

YEAR	HIGH	LOW
1993	$1,794	$1,345
1994	$2,110	$1,583
1995	$2,417	$1,813
1996	$2,729	$2,047

1215

YEARS MFRD........1996-2001
SERIES............1200 SERIES
ENGINE.................ISEKI
CYLINDERS..................3
CID.....................61.6
PTO HP....................15
ENGINE HP...............18.5
COOLING...............LIQUID
FUEL.......................D
SPEEDS..............VARIABLE
TRANSMISSION...........HYDRO
STEERING............STANDARD
PTO......................YES
DRIVE TYPE...............2WD
ROPS/CAB................ROPS
WEIGHT............1,460 LBS.
MSRP..................$12,240

OPTIONS

2 HYD
4WD
54" DECK
HYDRO
LDR
TURF TIRES

SERIAL NUMBERS

YEAR	BEGINNING NO.
1996	E10101
1997	FB0101
1998	GB01001
1999	HB01001
2000	JB01001
2001	KB01001

RETAIL PRICING

YEAR	HIGH	LOW
1996	$3,568	$2,676
1997	$3,923	$2,942
1998	$4,286	$3,215
1999	$4,659	$3,494
2000	$5,047	$3,785
2001	$5,449	$4,086

1220

YEARS MFRD........1993-1998
ENGINE.................ISEKI
CYLINDERS..................3
CID.....................68.5
PTO HP..................17.2
ENGINE HP.................20
SPEEDS...................6/2
TRANSMISSION............GEAR
STEERING............STANDARD
PTO......................YES
DRIVE TYPE...............2WD
ROPS/CAB................ROPS
WEIGHT............2,403 LBS.
MSRP..................$12,300

OPTIONS

2 HYD
4WD
60" DECK
HYDRO
LDR
TURF TIRES

SERIAL NUMBERS

YEAR	BEGINNING NO.
1993	B20101
1994	C20101
1995	D20101
1996	E20101
1997	FC0101
1998	GC1001

RETAIL PRICING

YEAR	HIGH	LOW
1993	$1,316	$987
1994	$1,700	$1,275
1995	$1,912	$1,434
1996	$2,220	$1,665
1997	$2,535	$1,902
1998	$2,861	$2,146

1225

YEARS MFRD........1998-2001
SERIES............1200 SERIES
ENGINE.................ISEKI
CYLINDERS..................3
CID.......................68
PTO HP....................19
FUEL.......................G
SPEEDS...................6/2
TRANSMISSION............GEAR
STEERING............STANDARD
DRIVE TYPE...............2WD
ROPS/CAB................ROPS
WEIGHT............1,874 LBS.
MSRP..................$11,905

OPTIONS

2 HYD
4WD
60" DECK
HYDRO
LDR
TURF TIRES

SERIAL NUMBERS

YEAR	BEGINNING NO.
1999	HM01001
2000	JM01001
2001	KM01001

RETAIL PRICING

YEAR	HIGH	LOW
1998	$2,869	$2,152
1999	$3,204	$2,403
2000	$3,545	$2,659
2001	$3,866	$2,900

1230

YEARS MFRD........1993-2001
SERIES............1200 SERIES
ENGINE.................ISEKI
CYLINDERS..................3
CID.....................87.2
PTO HP..................20.5
ENGINE HP.................25
FUEL.......................D
SPEEDS...................9/3
TRANSMISSION............GEAR
STEERING............STANDARD
PTO......................YES
DRIVE TYPE...............2WD
ROPS/CAB................ROPS
WEIGHT............1,860 LBS.
MSRP..................$14,205

OPTIONS

2 HYD
4WD
60" DECK
72" DECK
HYDRO
LDR

SERIAL NUMBERS

YEAR	BEGINNING NO.
1993	B30101
1994	C30101
1995	D30101
1996	E30101
1997	FC0101
1998	GD01001
1999	HD01001
2000	JD01001
2001	KD01001

RETAIL PRICING

YEAR	HIGH	LOW
1993	$2,544	$1,908
1994	$2,869	$2,152
1995	$3,204	$2,403
1996	$3,550	$2,663
1997	$3,909	$2,932
1998	$4,278	$3,209
1999	$4,659	$3,494
2000	$5,055	$3,791
2001	$5,462	$4,096

1233

YEARS MFRD........2000-2001
SERIES............1200 SERIES
ENGINE.................ISEKI
CYLINDERS..................3
CID.......................89
PTO HP..................22.9
ENGINE HP...............27.6
FUEL.......................D
SPEEDS...................9/3
TRANSMISSION............GEAR
STEERING............STANDARD
DRIVE TYPE...............2WD
ROPS/CAB................ROPS
WEIGHT............1,548 LBS.
MSRP..................$10,525

OPTIONS

4WD
60" DECK
72" DECK
LDR

MASSEY FERGUSON

SERIAL NUMBERS

YEAR	BEGINNING NO.
2000	JP
2001	KP

RETAIL PRICING

YEAR	HIGH	LOW
2000	$4,216	$3,162
2001	$4,607	$3,455

1235

YEARS MFRD	1997-2002
CYLINDERS	3
CID	91.4
PTO HP	24
ENGINE HP	30
FUEL	D
SPEEDS	VARIABLE
TRANSMISSION	HYDRO
STEERING	STANDARD
PTO	YES
DRIVE TYPE	4WD
ROPS/CAB	ROPS
MSRP	$18,445

OPTIONS

1 HYD
2 HYD
60" DECK
72" DECK
LDR

SERIAL NUMBERS

YEAR	BEGINNING NO.
1997	FE0101
1998	GE01001
1999	HE01001
2000	JE01001
2001	KE01001
2002	LE01001

RETAIL PRICING

YEAR	HIGH	LOW
1997	$5,164	$3,873
1998	$5,609	$4,207
1999	$6,071	$4,553
2000	$6,547	$4,910
2001	$7,043	$5,282
2002	$7,558	$5,668

1240

YEARS MFRD	1992-2001
SERIES	1200 SERIES
ENGINE	ISEKI
CYLINDERS	3
CID	89.3
PTO HP	22.8
ENGINE HP	28
FUEL	D
SPEEDS	16/16
TRANSMISSION	GEAR
STEERING	STANDARD
HITCH	CAT. I
PTO	YES
DRIVE TYPE	2WD
ROPS/CAB	ROPS
WEIGHT	2,634 LBS.
MSRP	$15,125

OPTIONS

2 HYD
4WD
60" DECK
LDR

SERIAL NUMBERS

YEAR	BEGINNING NO.
1992	A44401
1993	B40101
1994	C40101
1995	D40101
1996	E40101
1997	FF0101
1998	GF01001
1999	HF01001
2000	JF01001
2001	KF01001

RETAIL PRICING

YEAR	HIGH	LOW
1992	$1,950	$1,462
1993	$2,096	$1,572
1994	$2,412	$1,809
1995	$2,743	$2,057
1996	$3,077	$2,308
1997	$3,428	$2,571
1998	$3,791	$2,843
1999	$4,164	$3,123
2000	$4,545	$3,409
2001	$5,085	$3,814

1250

YEARS MFRD	1992-2002
SERIES	1200 SERIES
ENGINE	ISEKI
CYLINDERS	3
CID	91.4
PTO HP	27
ENGINE HP	33
FUEL	D
SPEEDS	16/16
TRANSMISSION	GEAR
STEERING	STANDARD
HITCH	CAT. I
PTO	YES
DRIVE TYPE	2WD
ROPS/CAB	ROPS
WEIGHT	2,745 LBS.
MSRP	$16,300

OPTIONS

2 HYD
4WD
72" DECK
HYDRO
LDR

SERIAL NUMBERS

ON PANEL, THE SEAT BELOW

YEAR	BEGINNING NO.
1992	A54401
1993	B50101
1994	C50101
1995	D50101
1996	E50101
1997	FG0101
1998	GG01001
1999	HG01001
2000	JG01001
2001	KG01001
2002	LG01001

RETAIL PRICING

YEAR	HIGH	LOW
1994	$3,725	$2,794
1995	$4,027	$3,020
1996	$4,367	$3,275
1997	$4,783	$3,587
1998	$5,164	$3,873
1999	$5,665	$4,249
2000	$6,199	$4,649
2001	$6,623	$4,967
2002	$7,129	$5,347

1260

YEARS MFRD	1992-2002
SERIES	1200 SERIES
ENGINE	ISEKI TURBO
CYLINDERS	3
CID	91.4
PTO HP	31.7
ENGINE HP	40
FUEL	D
SPEEDS	16/16
TRANSMISSION	GEAR
STEERING	STANDARD
HITCH	CAT. I
PTO	YES
DRIVE TYPE	4WD
ROPS/CAB	ROPS
WEIGHT	3,155 LBS.
MSRP	$21,250

OPTIONS

2 HYD
72" DECK
HYDRO
LDR

SERIAL NUMBERS

YEAR	BEGINNING NO.
1992	A64401
1993	B60101
1994	C60101
1995	D60101
1996	E60101
1997	FH0101
1998	GH01001
1999	HH01001
2000	JH01001
2001	KH01001
2002	LH01001

RETAIL PRICING

YEAR	HIGH	LOW
1994	$5,065	$3,799
1995	$5,418	$4,064
1996	$5,788	$4,341
1997	$6,166	$4,625
1998	$6,594	$4,946
1999	$6,968	$5,226
2000	$7,355	$5,516
2001	$7,832	$5,874
2002	$8,284	$6,213

1325

YEARS MFRD	2003-2003
ENGINE	MITSUBISHI
CYLINDERS	3
ENGINE HP	27
SPEEDS	12/12
WEIGHT	1,005 LBS.

1335

YEARS MFRD	2003-2003
ENGINE	MITSUBISHI
CYLINDERS	4
ENGINE HP	35
SPEEDS	12/12
WEIGHT	1,140 LBS.

1345

YEARS MFRD	2003-2003
ENGINE	MITSUBISHI
CYLINDERS	4
ENGINE HP	42
SPEEDS	12/12
WEIGHT	1,010 LBS.

1417

YEARS MFRD	2002-2004
SERIES	1400 SERIES
CYLINDERS	3
CID	56.6
PTO HP	13.3
ENGINE HP	16.6
FUEL	D
SPEEDS	6/2
TRANSMISSION	GEAR
STEERING	STANDARD
HITCH	CAT. I
DRIVE TYPE	4WD
ROPS/CAB	ROPS
WEIGHT	1,335 LBS.
MSRP	$10,943

OPTIONS

2 HYD
54" DECK
HYDRO
LDR
TURF TIRES

SERIAL NUMBERS

YEAR	BEGINNING NO.
2002	LA
2003	MA
2004	NA

RETAIL PRICING

YEAR	HIGH	LOW
2002	$5,367	$4,025
2003	$5,782	$4,337
2004	$6,212	$4,659

1417-4

YEARS MFRD	2005-2006
SERIES	1400 SERIES
ENGINE	PERKINS
CYLINDERS	3
CID	56.6
PTO HP	13.3
ENGINE HP	16.6
COOLING	LIQUID
FUEL	D
SPEEDS	6/2
TRANSMISSION	GEAR
STEERING	STANDARD
HITCH	CAT. I
WEIGHT	1,422 LBS.

1423

YEARS MFRD 2002-2004
SERIES............ 1400 SERIES
ENGINE .... ISEKI
CYLINDERS.................. 3
CID 68.5
PTO HP 19.5
ENGINE HP 23.5
COOLING .... LIQUID
FUEL .... D
SPEEDS 6/2
TRANSMISSION .... GEAR
STEERING............ STANDARD
HITCH .... CAT. I
DRIVE TYPE 4WD
ROPS/CAB .... ROPS
WEIGHT .... 3,086 LBS.
MSRP................. $13,267

OPTIONS

2 HYD
60" DECK
HYDRO
LDR
TURF TIRES

SERIAL NUMBERS

YEAR	BEGINNING NO.
2002	LM
2003	MM
2004	NM

RETAIL PRICING

YEAR	HIGH	LOW
2002	$4,103	$3,077
2003	$4,532	$3,399
2004	$4,977	$3,732

1423-4

YEARS MFRD 2005-2006
SERIES............ 1400 SERIES
ENGINE .... PERKINS
CYLINDERS.................. 3
CID 68.5
PTO HP 19.5
ENGINE HP 23.3
COOLING .... LIQUID
FUEL .... D
SPEEDS 6/2
TRANSMISSION .... GEAR
STEERING............ STANDARD
HITCH .... CAT. I
HYDRAULIC .... YES
PTO .... YES
DRIVE TYPE 4WD
ROPS/CAB .... ROPS
WEIGHT .... 1,498 LBS.

OPTIONS

HYDRO

1428V

YEARS MFRD 2002-2004
SERIES............ 1400 SERIES
CYLINDERS.................. 3
CID 89.3
PTO HP 24.5
ENGINE HP 28.4
FUEL .... D
SPEEDS 9/3
TRANSMISSION .... GEAR
STEERING............ STANDARD
DRIVE TYPE 4WD
ROPS/CAB .... ROPS
WEIGHT .... 1,995 LBS.
MSRP................. $13,636

OPTIONS

2WD
60" DECK
HYDRO
LDR

SERIAL NUMBERS

OPERATORS PLATFORM BELOW THE SEAT

YEAR	BEGINNING NO.
2002	LP
2003	MP
2004	NP

RETAIL PRICING

YEAR	HIGH	LOW
2002	$5,118	$3,838
2003	$5,543	$4,157
2004	$5,977	$4,483

1428V-2/4

YEARS MFRD 2005-2006
SERIES............ 1400 SERIES
ENGINE .... PERKINS
CYLINDERS.................. 3
CID 89.3
PTO HP 24.5
ENGINE HP 28.4
COOLING .... LIQUID
FUEL .... D
SPEEDS 9/3
TRANSMISSION .... GEAR
STEERING............ STANDARD
HITCH .... CAT. I
HYDRAULIC .... YES
PTO .... YES
WEIGHT .... 2,013 LBS.

OPTIONS

HYDRO

1429

YEARS MFRD 2002-2004
SERIES............ 1400 SERIES
CYLINDERS.................. 3
CID 89.3
PTO HP 23
ENGINE HP 28.4
FUEL .... D
SPEEDS 8/8
TRANSMISSION ... SHUTTLE SHIFT
STEERING............ STANDARD
DRIVE TYPE 4WD
ROPS/CAB .... ROPS
WEIGHT .... 2,766 LBS.
MSRP................. $16,923

OPTIONS

2 HYD
72" DECK
LDR
TURF

SERIAL NUMBERS

OPERATORS PLATFORM BELOW THE SEAT

YEAR	BEGINNING NO.
2002	LF
2003	MF
2004	NF

RETAIL PRICING

YEAR	HIGH	LOW
2002	$5,443	$4,083
2003	$5,962	$4,472
2004	$6,506	$4,880

1431

YEARS MFRD 2004-2004
SERIES............ 1400 SERIES
ENGINE .... PERKINS
CYLINDERS.................. 3
CID 91.4
PTO HP 25.9
ENGINE HP 33
COOLING .... LIQUID
FUEL .... D
SPEEDS .... VARIABLE
TRANSMISSION .... HYDRO
STEERING............ STANDARD
HITCH .... CAT. I
HYDRAULIC .... YES
PTO .... YES
DRIVE TYPE 4WD
ROPS/CAB .... ROPS
WEIGHT .... 2,356 LBS.
MSRP................. $16,958

OPTIONS

2 HYD
LDR
SOFT CAB

RETAIL PRICING

YEAR	HIGH	LOW
2004	$7,762	$5,821

1433

YEARS MFRD 2002-2003
SERIES............ 1400 SERIES
CYLINDERS.................. 3
CID 91.4
PTO HP 27
ENGINE HP 33
FUEL .... D
SPEEDS 16/16
TRANSMISSION .... GEAR
STEERING............ STANDARD
DRIVE TYPE 4WD
ROPS/CAB .... ROPS
WEIGHT .... 2,800 LBS.

SERIAL NUMBERS

OPERATORS PLATFORM BELOW THE SEAT

YEAR	BEGINNING NO.
2002	LG01001
2003	MG0201

1433-4

YEARS MFRD 2005-2006
SERIES............ 1400 SERIES
ENGINE .... PERKINS
CYLINDERS.................. 3
CID 91.4
PTO HP 27
ENGINE HP 33
COOLING .... LIQUID
FUEL .... D
SPEEDS 16/16
TRANSMISSION ..... POWER SHIFT
STEERING............ STANDARD
HITCH .... CAT. I
HYDRAULIC .... YES
PTO .... YES
WEIGHT .... 2,810 LBS.

1433V

YEARS MFRD 2001-2004
SERIES............ 1400 SERIES
ENGINE .... ISEKI
CYLINDERS.................. 3
CID 91.4
PTO HP 27
ENGINE HP 33
FUEL .... D
SPEEDS 8/8
TRANSMISSION .... GEAR
STEERING............ STANDARD
DRIVE TYPE 4WD
ROPS/CAB .... ROPS
WEIGHT .... 2,744 LBS.
MSRP................. $16,590

OPTIONS

2 HYD
LDR

SERIAL NUMBERS

OPERATORS PLATFORM BELOW THE SEAT

YEAR	BEGINNING NO.
2001	KR
2002	LR
2003	MR
2004	NR

RETAIL PRICING

YEAR	HIGH	LOW
2001	$6,199	$4,649
2002	$6,694	$5,020
2003	$7,208	$5,406
2004	$7,741	$5,806

AVG. AUCTION PRICING

LOW	HIGH	AVG
$5,516	$10,933	$7,504

1433V-4

YEARS MFRD 2005-2006
SERIES............ 1400 SERIES
ENGINE .... PERKINS
CYLINDERS.................. 3
CID 91.4
PTO HP 27
ENGINE HP 33
COOLING .... LIQUID
FUEL .... D
SPEEDS 8/8
TRANSMISSION ..... POWER SHIFT
STEERING............ STANDARD
HITCH .... CAT. I

HYDRAULIC . . . . YES
PTO . . . . YES
WEIGHT . . . . 2,788 LBS.

1440

YEARS MFRD 2002-2003
SERIES . . . . 1400 SERIES
CYLINDERS 3
CID 91.4
PTO HP 32.4
ENGINE HP 40.1
FUEL . . . . D
SPEEDS 16/16
TRANSMISSION . . . . HYDRO
STEERING . . . . STANDARD
DRIVE TYPE 4WD
ROPS/CAB . . . . ROPS
WEIGHT . . . . 2,843 LBS.

SERIAL NUMBERS

OPERATORS PLATFORM
BELOW THE SEAT

YEAR	BEGINNING NO.
2002	LH
2003	MH

1440-4

YEARS MFRD 2005-2006
SERIES . . . . 1400 SERIES
ENGINE . . . . PERKINS
CYLINDERS 3
CID 91.4
PTO HP 32.4
ENGINE HP 40.1
COOLING . . . . LIQUID
FUEL . . . . D
SPEEDS 16/16
TRANSMISSION . . . . . POWER SHIFT
STEERING . . . . STANDARD
HITCH . . . . CAT. I
HYDRAULIC . . . . YES
PTO . . . . YES
WEIGHT . . . . 3,001 LBS.

1440V

YEARS MFRD 2001-2004
SERIES . . . . 1400 SERIES
ENGINE . . . . ISEKI
CYLINDERS 3
CID 91.4
PTO HP 32.4
ENGINE HP 40.1
FUEL . . . . D
SPEEDS 8/8
TRANSMISSION . . . . GEAR
STEERING . . . . STANDARD
DRIVE TYPE 4WD
ROPS/CAB . . . . ROPS
WEIGHT . . . . 2,788 LBS.
MSRP $19,014

OPTIONS

2 HYD
LDR

SERIAL NUMBERS

OPERATORS PLATFORM
BELOW THE SEAT

YEAR	BEGINNING NO.
2001	KS
2002	LS
2003	MS
2004	NS

RETAIL PRICING

YEAR	HIGH	LOW
2001	$6,552	$4,914
2002	$7,175	$5,381
2003	$7,836	$5,877
2004	$8,610	$6,458

1440V-4

YEARS MFRD 2005-2006
SERIES . . . . 1400 SERIES
ENGINE . . . . PERKINS
CYLINDERS 3
CID 91.4
PTO HP 32.4
ENGINE HP 40.1
COOLING . . . . LIQUID
FUEL . . . . D
SPEEDS 8/8
TRANSMISSION . . . . . POWER SHIFT
STEERING . . . . STANDARD
HITCH . . . . CAT. I
HYDRAULIC . . . . YES
PTO . . . . YES
WEIGHT . . . . 2,935 LBS.

1445

YEARS MFRD 2003-2004
SERIES . . . . 1400 SERIES
ENGINE . . . . PERKINS
CYLINDERS 4
CID 134.1
PTO HP 37
ENGINE HP 44.2
COOLING . . . . LIQUID
FUEL . . . . D
SPEEDS 16/16
TRANSMISSION . . . . . POWER SHIFT
STEERING . . . . STANDARD
HITCH . . . . CAT. I
HYDRAULIC . . . . YES
PTO . . . . YES
DRIVE TYPE 4WD
ROPS/CAB . . . . ROPS
WEIGHT . . . . 4,331 LBS.
MSRP $26,420

OPTIONS

2 HYD
HYDRO
LDR

SERIAL NUMBERS

OPERATORS PLATFORM
BELOW THE SEAT

YEAR	BEGINNING NO.
2003	MN
2004	NN

RETAIL PRICING

YEAR	HIGH	LOW
2003	$11,725	$8,794
2004	$12,473	$9,355

1455

YEARS MFRD 2002-2004
SERIES . . . . 1400 SERIES
ENGINE . . . . PERKINS
CYLINDERS 4
CID 173
PTO HP 45.6
ENGINE HP 55.3
COOLING . . . . LIQUID
FUEL . . . . D
SPEEDS 16/16
TRANSMISSION . . . . . POWER SHIFT
STEERING . . . . STANDARD
HITCH . . . . CAT. I
DRIVE TYPE 4WD
ROPS/CAB . . . . ROPS
WEIGHT . . . . 3,791 LBS.
MSRP $27,500

OPTIONS

2 HYD
LDR

SERIAL NUMBERS

OPERATORS PLATFORM
BELOW THE SEAT

YEAR	BEGINNING NO.
2002	LY
2003	MW
2004	NW

RETAIL PRICING

YEAR	HIGH	LOW
2002	$10,731	$8,048
2003	$11,512	$8,634
2004	$12,335	$9,251

1455V-2/4

YEARS MFRD 2003-2004
SERIES . . . . 1400 SERIES
ENGINE . . . . PERKINS
CYLINDERS 4
CID 173
PTO HP 45.6
ENGINE HP 55.3
COOLING . . . . LIQUID
FUEL . . . . D
SPEEDS 12/12
TRANSMISSION . . . . . POWER SHIFT
STEERING . . . . STANDARD
HITCH . . . . CAT. I
HYDRAULIC . . . . YES
PTO . . . . YES
DRIVE TYPE 4WD
ROPS/CAB . . . . ROPS
WEIGHT . . . . 3,560 LBS.

OPTIONS

2WD
LDR

SERIAL NUMBERS

OPERATORS PLATFORM
BELOW THE SEAT

YEAR	BEGINNING NO.
2003	MX
2004	NX

RETAIL PRICING

YEAR	HIGH	LOW
2003	$10,534	$7,900
2004	$11,429	$8,572

1523

YEARS MFRD 2005-2010
SERIES . . . . 1500 SERIES
ENGINE . . . . PERKINS
CYLINDERS 3
CID 68.5
PTO HP 18.7
ENGINE HP 22.5
COOLING . . . . LIQUID
FUEL . . . . D
SPEEDS 6/2
TRANSMISSION . . . . GEAR
STEERING . . . . STANDARD
HITCH . . . . CAT. I
HYDRAULIC . . . . YES
PTO . . . . YES
DRIVE TYPE 4WD
ROPS/CAB . . . . ROPS
WEIGHT . . . . 1,632 LBS.
MSRP $11,442

OPTIONS

HYDRO
LDR

SERIAL NUMBERS

YEAR	BEGINNING NO.
2005	JP
2006	JR
2007	JS
2008	JT
2009	JU
2010	JV

RETAIL PRICING

YEAR	HIGH	LOW
2005	$5,665	$4,249
2006	$6,146	$4,609
2007	$6,646	$4,985
2008	$7,162	$5,371
2009	$7,700	$5,775
2010	$8,252	$6,189

1525H

ENGINE . . . . AGCO SISU E3112
CYLINDERS 3
ENGINE HP 25
SPEEDS . . . . VARIABLE
TRANSMISSION . . . . HYDRO
STEERING . . . . STANDARD
HYDRAULIC . . . . YES
PTO . . . . YES
DRIVE TYPE 4WD
ROPS/CAB . . . . ROPS

1526

YEARS MFRD 2011-2020
ENGINE . . . . ISEKI
CYLINDERS 3
CID 91.4
PTO HP 20.1
ENGINE HP 24.8
COOLING . . . . LIQUID
FUEL . . . . D
SPEEDS . . . . VARIABLE
TRANSMISSION . . . . HYDRO
STEERING . . . . STANDARD
HITCH . . . . CAT. I

DRIVE TYPE 4WD
ROPS/CAB . . . . ROPS
WEIGHT . . . . 1,873 LBS.
MSRP. $15,908

OPTIONS

LDR $3,729

SERIAL NUMBERS

YEAR	BEGINNING NO.
2012	C
2013	D
2014	E
2015	F
2016	G
2017	H
2018	HJG84403

RETAIL PRICING

YEAR	HIGH	LOW
2011	$9,403	$7,052
2012	$9,939	$7,454
2013	$10,491	$7,868
2014	$11,057	$8,292
2015	$11,685	$8,763
2016	$12,616	$9,462
2017	$13,706	$10,279
2018	$14,233	$10,674
2019	$15,044	$11,283
2020	$15,897	$12,045

1528

YEARS MFRD 2005-2010
SERIES. . . . . 1500 SERIES
ENGINE . . . . ISEKI
CYLINDERS. 3
CID 89.3
PTO HP 24.5
ENGINE HP. 28.4
COOLING . . . . LIQUID
FUEL . . . . D
SPEEDS . . . . VARIABLE
TRANSMISSION . . . . HYDRO
STEERING. . . . . STANDARD
HITCH . . . . CAT. I
HYDRAULIC . . . . YES
PTO . . . . YES
DRIVE TYPE 4WD
ROPS/CAB . . . . ROPS
WEIGHT . . . . 2,423 LBS.
MSRP. $15,100

OPTIONS

LDR

SERIAL NUMBERS

YEAR	BEGINNING NO.
2005	JP
2006	JR
2007	JS
2008	JT
2009	JU HYDRO
2010	JV HYDRO

RETAIL PRICING

YEAR	HIGH	LOW
2005	$8,039	$6,029
2006	$8,544	$6,408
2007	$9,045	$6,783
2008	$9,558	$7,169
2009	$10,087	$7,565
2010	$10,635	$7,976

1529

YEARS MFRD 2007-2014
SERIES. . . . . 1500 SERIES
ENGINE . . . . PERKINS
CYLINDERS. 3
PTO HP 23.2
ENGINE HP. 28.4
COOLING . . . . LIQUID
FUEL . . . . D
SPEEDS 8/8
TRANSMISSION . . . SHUTTLE SHIFT
STEERING. . . . . STANDARD
HITCH . . . . CAT. I
HYDRAULIC . . . . YES
PTO . . . . YES
DRIVE TYPE 2WD
ROPS/CAB . . . . ROPS
WEIGHT . . . . 2,579 LBS.
MSRP. $15,681

OPTIONS

HYDRO
LDR

SERIAL NUMBERS

YEAR	BEGINNING NO.
2007	JS
2008	JT
2009	JU
2010	JV
2011	JW
2012	JX
2013	D

RETAIL PRICING

YEAR	HIGH	LOW
2007	$8,087	$6,065
2008	$8,705	$6,528
2009	$9,349	$7,012
2010	$9,950	$7,463
2011	$10,774	$8,081
2012	$11,571	$8,678
2013	$12,457	$9,343
2014	$13,237	$9,927

1531

YEARS MFRD 2005-2010
SERIES. . . . . 1500 SERIES
ENGINE . . . . PERKINS
CYLINDERS. 3
CID 91.4
PTO HP 24.5
ENGINE HP. 33
COOLING . . . . LIQUID
FUEL . . . . D
SPEEDS . . . . VARIABLE
TRANSMISSION . . . . HYDRO
STEERING. . . . . STANDARD
HITCH . . . . CAT. I
HYDRAULIC . . . . YES
PTO . . . . YES
DRIVE TYPE 4WD
ROPS/CAB . . . . ROPS
WEIGHT . . . . 2,423 LBS.
MSRP. $16,348

OPTIONS

LDR

SERIAL NUMBERS

YEAR	BEGINNING NO.
2005	JP
2006	JR
2007	JS
2008	JT
2009	JU
2010	JV

RETAIL PRICING

YEAR	HIGH	LOW
2005	$8,367	$6,275
2006	$8,997	$6,748
2007	$9,655	$7,241
2008	$10,343	$7,757
2009	$11,055	$8,292
2010	$11,807	$8,856

1532

YEARS MFRD 2007-2014
SERIES. . . . . 1500 SERIES
ENGINE . . . . PERKINS
CYLINDERS. 3
PTO HP 26.5
ENGINE HP. 33
COOLING . . . . LIQUID
FUEL . . . . D
SPEEDS . . . . VARIABLE
TRANSMISSION . . . . HYDRO
STEERING. . . . . STANDARD
HITCH . . . . CAT. I
HYDRAULIC . . . . YES
PTO . . . . YES
DRIVE TYPE 4WD
ROPS/CAB . . . . ROPS
WEIGHT . . . . 2,590 LBS.
MSRP. $18,846

OPTIONS

9/3 GEAR
LDR

SERIAL NUMBERS

YEAR	BEGINNING NO.
2007	JS
2008	JT
2009	JU
2010	JV
2011	JW
2012	JX
2013	D

RETAIL PRICING

YEAR	HIGH	LOW
2007	$10,166	$7,625
2008	$10,847	$8,135
2009	$11,482	$8,611
2010	$12,299	$9,224
2011	$13,117	$9,838
2012	$13,597	$10,198
2013	$14,953	$11,215
2014	$15,812	$11,859

1533

YEARS MFRD 2005-2013
SERIES. . . . . 1500 SERIES
ENGINE . . . . PERKINS
CYLINDERS. 3
CID 91.4
PTO HP 26
ENGINE HP 33
COOLING . . . . LIQUID
FUEL . . . . D
SPEEDS 8/8
TRANSMISSION . . . SHUTTLE SHIFT
STEERING. . . . . STANDARD
HITCH . . . . CAT. I
HYDRAULIC . . . . YES
PTO . . . . YES
DRIVE TYPE 4WD
ROPS/CAB . . . . ROPS
WEIGHT . . . . 2,844 LBS.
MSRP. $19,782

OPTIONS

12/12 PS
2 HYD
72" DECK
CAB
HYDRO
LDR

SERIAL NUMBERS

YEAR	BEGINNING NO.
2005	JP
2006	JR
2007	JS
2008	JT
2009	JU
2010	JV
2011	JW
2012	JX
2013	D

RETAIL PRICING

YEAR	HIGH	LOW
2005	$8,921	$6,691
2006	$9,553	$7,165
2007	$10,375	$7,781
2008	$11,243	$8,432
2009	$12,127	$9,095
2010	$13,101	$9,825
2011	$14,171	$10,629
2012	$15,267	$11,450
2013	$16,590	$12,443

AVG. AUCTION PRICING

LOW	HIGH	AVG
$5,075	$15,225	$10,693

1540

YEARS MFRD 2005-2013
SERIES. . . . . 1500 SERIES
ENGINE . . . . PERKINS
CYLINDERS. 3
CID 91.4
PTO HP 31
ENGINE HP. 40
COOLING . . . . LIQUID
FUEL . . . . D
SPEEDS 8/8
TRANSMISSION . . . SHUTTLE SHIFT
STEERING. . . . . STANDARD
HITCH . . . . CAT. I
HYDRAULIC . . . . YES
PTO . . . . YES
DRIVE TYPE 4WD
ROPS/CAB . . . . ROPS
WEIGHT . . . . 2,888 LBS.
MSRP. $22,719

OPTIONS

12/12 PS
2 HYD
72" DECK
HYDRO
LDR

SERIAL NUMBERS

YEAR	BEGINNING NO.
2005	JP
2006	JR
2007	JS
2008	JT
2009	JU
2010	JV
2011	JW
2012	JX
2013	JY

RETAIL PRICING

YEAR	HIGH	LOW
2005	$9,738	$7,303
2006	$10,626	$7,970
2007	$11,566	$8,674
2008	$12,568	$9,426
2009	$13,624	$10,218
2010	$14,747	$11,060
2011	$15,974	$11,981
2012	$17,325	$12,994
2013	$18,793	$14,095

1547

YEARS MFRD	2005-2009
SERIES	1500 SERIES
ENGINE	PERKINS
CYLINDERS	4
CID	134
PTO HP	38
ENGINE HP	47
COOLING	LIQUID
FUEL	D
SPEEDS	8/8
TRANSMISSION	SHUTTLE SHIFT
STEERING	STANDARD
HITCH	CAT. I
HYDRAULIC	YES
PTO	YES
DRIVE TYPE	2WD
ROPS/CAB	ROPS
WEIGHT	3,494 LBS.
MSRP	$21,084

OPTIONS

4WD
CAB
HYDRO
LDR

SERIAL NUMBERS

YEAR	BEGINNING NO.
2005	JP
2006	JR
2007	JS
2008	JT
2009	JU

RETAIL PRICING

YEAR	HIGH	LOW
2005	$11,844	$8,883
2006	$12,386	$9,290
2007	$13,406	$10,055
2008	$14,243	$10,683
2009	$15,149	$11,362

1552

YEARS MFRD	2005-2009
SERIES	1500 SERIES
ENGINE	PERKINS
CYLINDERS	4
CID	180
PTO HP	41
ENGINE HP	52
COOLING	LIQUID
FUEL	D
SPEEDS	8/8
TRANSMISSION	SHUTTLE SHIFT
STEERING	STANDARD
HITCH	CAT. I
HYDRAULIC	YES
PTO	YES
DRIVE TYPE	2WD
ROPS/CAB	ROPS
WEIGHT	3,694 LBS.
MSRP	$21,775

OPTIONS

4WD
CAB
LDR

SERIAL NUMBERS

YEAR	BEGINNING NO.
2005	JP
2006	JR
2007	JS
2008	JT
2009	JU

RETAIL PRICING

YEAR	HIGH	LOW
2005	$11,116	$8,337
2006	$11,939	$8,955
2007	$12,802	$9,602
2008	$13,746	$10,310
2009	$14,776	$11,082

1560

YEARS MFRD	2006-2009
ENGINE	PERKINS
CYLINDERS	4
PTO HP	46.4
ENGINE HP	59.1
COOLING	LIQUID
FUEL	D
SPEEDS	12/12
TRANSMISSION	SHUTTLE SHIFT
STEERING	STANDARD
HITCH	CAT. I
DRIVE TYPE	4WD
ROPS/CAB	ROPS
WEIGHT	4,078 LBS.
MSRP	$29,562

OPTIONS

CAB
LDR

SERIAL NUMBERS

YEAR	BEGINNING NO.
2006	JR
2007	JS

RETAIL PRICING

YEAR	HIGH	LOW
2006	$17,301	$12,976
2007	$18,226	$13,670
2008	$19,228	$14,421
2009	$20,309	$15,232

1635

YEARS MFRD	2009-2013
SERIES	1600 SERIES
ENGINE	ISEKI
CYLINDERS	3
CID	100.5
PTO HP	27.1
ENGINE HP	35.7
COOLING	LIQUID
FUEL	D
SPEEDS	12/12
TRANSMISSION	POWER SHIFT
STEERING	STANDARD
HITCH	CAT. I
HYDRAULIC	YES
PTO	YES
DRIVE TYPE	2WD
ROPS/CAB	ROPS
WEIGHT	3,527 LBS.
MSRP	$22,262

OPTIONS

CAB
HYDRO
LDR

SERIAL NUMBERS

YEAR	BEGINNING NO.
2009	U
2010	V

RETAIL PRICING

YEAR	HIGH	LOW
2009	$13,425	$10,069
2010	$14,430	$10,823
2011	$15,532	$11,649
2012	$16,971	$12,728
2013	$18,039	$13,529

1643

YEARS MFRD	2009-2013
SERIES	1600 SERIES
ENGINE	ISEKI
CYLINDERS	4
CID	134.1
PTO HP	34.3
ENGINE HP	43.5
COOLING	LIQUID
FUEL	D
SPEEDS	8/8
TRANSMISSION	SHUTTLE SHIFT
STEERING	STANDARD
HITCH	CAT. I
HYDRAULIC	YES
PTO	YES
DRIVE TYPE	2WD
ROPS/CAB	ROPS
WEIGHT	3,384 LBS.
MSRP	$24,485

OPTIONS

12/12 PS
CAB
HYDRO
LDR

SERIAL NUMBERS

YEAR	BEGINNING NO.
2009	U
2010	V

RETAIL PRICING

YEAR	HIGH	LOW
2009	$14,626	$10,970
2010	$15,956	$11,967
2011	$17,258	$12,944
2012	$18,684	$14,013
2013	$20,083	$15,062

1648

YEARS MFRD	2009-2013
ENGINE	ISEKI
CYLINDERS	4
CID	134.1
PTO HP	38
ENGINE HP	47.1
COOLING	LIQUID
FUEL	D
SPEEDS	12/12
TRANSMISSION	SHUTTLE SHIFT
STEERING	STANDARD
HITCH	CAT. I
DRIVE TYPE	2WD
ROPS/CAB	ROPS
WEIGHT	3,715 LBS.
MSRP	$27,035

OPTIONS

CAB
HYDRO
LDR

SERIAL NUMBERS

YEAR	BEGINNING NO.
2009	U
2010	V

RETAIL PRICING

YEAR	HIGH	LOW
2009	$17,358	$13,018
2010	$18,420	$13,815
2011	$19,561	$14,671
2012	$20,799	$15,600
2013	$22,135	$16,601

1652

YEARS MFRD	2009-2013
ENGINE	ISEKI
CYLINDERS	4
CID	180.4
PTO HP	41
ENGINE HP	52.2
COOLING	LIQUID
FUEL	D
SPEEDS	12/12
TRANSMISSION	SHUTTLE SHIFT
STEERING	STANDARD
HITCH	CAT. I
HYDRAULIC	YES
PTO	YES
DRIVE TYPE	2WD
ROPS/CAB	ROPS
WEIGHT	3,780 LBS.
MSRP	$29,560

OPTIONS

CAB
HYDRO
LDR

SERIAL NUMBERS

YEAR	BEGINNING NO.
2009	U
2010	V

RETAIL PRICING

YEAR	HIGH	LOW
2009	$18,297	$13,723
2010	$19,557	$14,668
2011	$20,921	$15,691
2012	$22,395	$16,796
2013	$23,985	$17,989

1655

YEARS MFRD . . . 2009-2013
ENGINE . . . ISEKI
CYLINDERS . . . 4
CID . . . 180.4
PTO HP . . . 43
ENGINE HP . . . 55.4
COOLING . . . LIQUID
FUEL . . . D
SPEEDS . . . 8/8
TRANSMISSION . . . SHUTTLE SHIFT
STEERING . . . STANDARD
HITCH . . . CAT. I
DRIVE TYPE . . . 2WD
ROPS/CAB . . . ROPS
WEIGHT . . . 3,770 LBS.
MSRP . . . $29,755

OPTIONS

CAB
LDR

SERIAL NUMBERS

YEAR	BEGINNING NO.
2009	U
2010	V

RETAIL PRICING

YEAR	HIGH	LOW
2009	$19,737	$14,803
2010	$20,884	$15,663
2011	$22,116	$16,587
2012	$23,442	$17,582
2013	$24,869	$18,651

1660

YEARS MFRD . . . 2009-2013
ENGINE . . . ISEKI
CYLINDERS . . . 4
CID . . . 180.4
PTO HP . . . 46.4
ENGINE HP . . . 60
COOLING . . . LIQUID
FUEL . . . D
SPEEDS . . . 12/12
TRANSMISSION . . . SHUTTLE SHIFT
STEERING . . . STANDARD
HITCH . . . CAT. I
DRIVE TYPE . . . 4WD
ROPS/CAB . . . ROPS
WEIGHT . . . 4,079 LBS.
MSRP . . . $31,826

OPTIONS

CAB
LDR

SERIAL NUMBERS

YEAR	BEGINNING NO.
2009	U
2010	V

RETAIL PRICING

YEAR	HIGH	LOW
2009	$21,204	$15,903
2010	$22,612	$16,959
2011	$24,122	$18,092
2012	$25,043	$18,782
2013	$26,529	$19,897

1726E

YEARS MFRD . . . 2014-2020
ENGINE . . . SHIBAURA
CYLINDERS . . . 3
CID . . . 91.4
ENGINE HP . . . 24
FUEL . . . D
SPEEDS . . . 9/3
TRANSMISSION . . . GEAR
STEERING . . . STANDARD
HITCH . . . CAT. I
DRIVE TYPE . . . 4WD
ROPS/CAB . . . ROPS
WEIGHT . . . 2,657 LBS.
MSRP . . . $15,111

OPTIONS

HYDRO . . . $1,288
LDR . . . $5,225

SERIAL NUMBERS

YEAR	BEGINNING NO.
2014	E
2015	F
2016	G
2017	H

RETAIL PRICING

YEAR	HIGH	LOW
2014	$10,520	$7,890
2015	$11,141	$8,355
2016	$12,070	$9,052
2017	$13,227	$9,920
2018	$13,840	$10,380
2019	$14,381	$10,786
2020	$15,035	$11,279

1734E

YEARS MFRD . . . 2014-2020
ENGINE . . . SHIBAURA
CYLINDERS . . . 3
CID . . . 91.4
PTO HP . . . 29
ENGINE HP . . . 34
COOLING . . . LIQUID
FUEL . . . D
SPEEDS . . . 9/3
TRANSMISSION . . . GEAR
STEERING . . . STANDARD
DRIVE TYPE . . . 4WD
ROPS/CAB . . . ROPS
MSRP . . . $17,542

OPTIONS

HYDRO . . . $1,301
LDR . . . $5,225

SERIAL NUMBERS

YEAR	BEGINNING NO.
2014	E
2015	F
2016	G
2017	H

RETAIL PRICING

YEAR	HIGH	LOW
2014	$11,434	$8,576
2015	$12,278	$9,208
2016	$13,485	$10,113
2017	$14,970	$11,228
2018	$16,011	$12,008
2019	$17,015	$12,761
2020	$17,724	$13,446

1735E

YEARS MFRD . . . 2020-2020
ENGINE . . . SHIBAURA 1.5LTR
CYLINDERS . . . 3
PTO HP . . . 29
ENGINE HP . . . 34.1
COOLING . . . LIQUID
FUEL . . . D
SPEEDS . . . 8/8
TRANSMISSION SYNCHRO SHUTTLE
STEERING . . . STANDARD
HITCH . . . CAT. I
DRIVE TYPE . . . 4WD
ROPS/CAB . . . ROPS
WEIGHT . . . 2,734 LBS.
MSRP . . . $18,107

OPTIONS

HYDRO . . . $861
LDR . . . $5,225

1735M

YEARS MFRD . . . 2018-2020
ENGINE . . . SHIBAURA 1.7L
CYLINDERS . . . 3
PTO HP . . . 27.5
ENGINE HP . . . 36.2
FUEL . . . D
SPEEDS . . . 12/12 PS
STEERING . . . STANDARD
DRIVE TYPE . . . 4WD
ROPS/CAB . . . ROPS
WEIGHT . . . 3,362 LBS.
MSRP . . . $23,620

OPTIONS

CAB . . . $8,082
HYDRO . . . $670
LOADER . . . $4,647

1736

YEARS MFRD . . . 2014-2018
ENGINE . . . MITSUBISHI
CYLINDERS . . . 3
CID . . . 101
PTO HP . . . 27.5
ENGINE HP . . . 36.2
FUEL . . . D
SPEEDS . . . 12/12
TRANSMISSION . . . SHUTTLE SHIFT
STEERING . . . STANDARD
HITCH . . . CAT. I
DRIVE TYPE . . . 4WD
ROPS/CAB . . . ROPS
MSRP . . . $23,468

OPTIONS

CAB
HYDRO
LDR

SERIAL NUMBERS

YEAR	BEGINNING NO.
2014	E
2015	F
2016	G
2017	H

RETAIL PRICING

YEAR	HIGH	LOW
2014	$15,359	$11,519
2015	$16,933	$12,700
2016	$18,594	$13,945
2017	$20,335	$15,251
2018	$21,951	$16,464

1739E

YEARS MFRD . . . 2014-2020
ENGINE . . . SHIBAURA
CYLINDERS . . . 3
CID . . . 91.4
PTO HP . . . 30.8
ENGINE HP . . . 39.5
COOLING . . . LIQUID
FUEL . . . D
SPEEDS . . . 9/3
TRANSMISSION . . . GEAR
STEERING . . . STANDARD
HITCH . . . CAT. I
DRIVE TYPE . . . 4WD
ROPS/CAB . . . ROPS
MSRP . . . $19,623

OPTIONS

HYDRO . . . $1,301
LDR . . . $5,225

SERIAL NUMBERS

YEAR	BEGINNING NO.
2014	E
2015	F
2016	G
2017	H

RETAIL PRICING

YEAR	HIGH	LOW
2014	$12,016	$9,011
2015	$13,092	$9,819
2016	$14,640	$10,980
2017	$16,500	$12,375
2018	$17,838	$13,378
2019	$19,315	$14,486
2020	$20,030	$15,334

1740E

YEARS MFRD . . . 2020-2020
ENGINE . . . SHIBAURA 1.5LTR
CYLINDERS . . . 3
PTO HP . . . 32.7

MASSEY FERGUSON

ENGINE HP . . . 38.5
COOLING . . . LIQUID
FUEL . . . D
SPEEDS . . . 8/8
TRANSMISSION SYNCHRO SHUTTLE
STEERING . . . STANDARD
HITCH . . . CAT. I
DRIVE TYPE . . . 4WD
ROPS/CAB . . . ROPS
WEIGHT . . . 2,756 LBS.
MSRP . . . $20,188

OPTIONS

HYDRO . . . $861
LDR . . . $5,225

1740M

YEARS MFRD . . . 2018-2020
ENGINE . . . SHIBAURA 1.7L
CYLINDERS . . . 3
PTO HP . . . 31.2
ENGINE HP . . . 40
FUEL . . . D
SPEEDS . . . 12/12 PS
STEERING . . . STANDARD
DRIVE TYPE . . . 4WD
ROPS/CAB . . . ROPS
WEIGHT . . . 3,638 LBS.
MSRP . . . $26,510

OPTIONS

CAB . . . $7,790
HYDRO . . . $670
LOADER . . . $4,647

1742

YEARS MFRD . . . 2014-2018
ENGINE . . . MITSUBISHI
CYLINDERS . . . 3
CID . . . 101
PTO HP . . . 32.8
ENGINE HP . . . 41.6
COOLING . . . LIQUID
FUEL . . . D
SPEEDS . . . 12/12
TRANSMISSION . . . SHUTTLE SHIFT
STEERING . . . STANDARD
DRIVE TYPE . . . 4WD
ROPS/CAB . . . ROPS
MSRP . . . $26,358

OPTIONS

CAB
LDR

SERIAL NUMBERS

YEAR	BEGINNING NO.
2014	E
2015	F
2016	G
2017	H

RETAIL PRICING

YEAR	HIGH	LOW
2014	$17,441	$13,081
2015	$19,384	$14,538
2016	$20,954	$15,715
2017	$22,730	$17,047
2018	$24,232	$18,174

1749

YEARS MFRD . . . 2014-2018
ENGINE . . . MITSUBISHI
CYLINDERS . . . 3
CID . . . 101
PTO HP . . . 39
ENGINE HP . . . 48.3
COOLING . . . LIQUID
FUEL . . . D
SPEEDS . . . 12/12
TRANSMISSION . . . SHUTTLE SHIFT
STEERING . . . STANDARD
DRIVE TYPE . . . 4WD
ROPS/CAB . . . CAB
MSRP . . . $39,115

OPTIONS

LDR
ROPS

SERIAL NUMBERS

YEAR	BEGINNING NO.
2014	E
2015	F
2016	G
2017	H

RETAIL PRICING

YEAR	HIGH	LOW
2014	$20,224	$15,168
2015	$22,096	$16,572
2016	$24,328	$18,246
2017	$26,684	$20,013
2018	$28,539	$21,404

1750M

YEARS MFRD . . . 2018-2020
ENGINE . . . SHIBAURA 2.2L
CYLINDERS . . . 4
PTO HP . . . 38.1
ENGINE HP . . . 48.8
FUEL . . . D
SPEEDS . . . 12/12 PS
STEERING . . . STANDARD
DRIVE TYPE . . . 4WD
ROPS/CAB . . . ROPS
WEIGHT . . . 3,913 LBS.
MSRP . . . $31,730

OPTIONS

CAB . . . $7,610
HYDRO . . . $660
LOADER . . . $5,482

SERIAL NUMBERS

YEAR	BEGINNING NO.
2019	JJ

1754

YEARS MFRD . . . 2014-2018
ENGINE . . . MITSUBISHI
CYLINDERS . . . 4
CID . . . 135
PTO HP . . . 42.1
ENGINE HP . . . 53.6
COOLING . . . LIQUID
FUEL . . . D
SPEEDS . . . 12/12
TRANSMISSION . . . SHUTTLE SHIFT
STEERING . . . STANDARD
HITCH . . . CAT. I
DRIVE TYPE . . . 4WD
ROPS/CAB . . . ROPS
MSRP . . . $32,835

OPTIONS

CAB
HYDRO
LDR

SERIAL NUMBERS

YEAR	BEGINNING NO.
2014	E
2015	F
2016	G
2017	H
2018	HJJ74058

RETAIL PRICING

YEAR	HIGH	LOW
2014	$20,977	$15,733
2015	$22,712	$17,034
2016	$25,126	$18,845
2017	$27,636	$20,727
2018	$29,545	$22,158

1755M

YEARS MFRD . . . 2018-2020
ENGINE . . . SHIBAURA 2.2L
CYLINDERS . . . 4
PTO HP . . . 41.3
ENGINE HP . . . 53.9
FUEL . . . D
SPEEDS . . . 12/12 PS
STEERING . . . STANDARD
DRIVE TYPE . . . 4WD
ROPS/CAB . . . ROPS
WEIGHT . . . 4,145 LBS.
MSRP . . . $32,885

OPTIONS

CAB . . . $7,610
HYDRO CAB . . . $8,260

SERIAL NUMBERS

YEAR	BEGINNING NO.
2019	JJ

1758

YEARS MFRD . . . 2014-2018
ENGINE . . . MITSUBISHI
CYLINDERS . . . 4
CID . . . 135
PTO HP . . . 44.4
ENGINE HP . . . 59
COOLING . . . LIQUID
FUEL . . . D
SPEEDS . . . VARIABLE
TRANSMISSION . . . HYDRO
STEERING . . . STANDARD
DRIVE TYPE . . . 4WD
ROPS/CAB . . . ROPS
MSRP . . . $35,115

OPTIONS

CAB
LDR

SERIAL NUMBERS

YEAR	BEGINNING NO.
2014	E
2015	F
2016	G
2017	H
2018	HJJ34634

RETAIL PRICING

YEAR	HIGH	LOW
2014	$22,541	$16,906
2015	$24,325	$18,244
2016	$26,858	$20,143
2017	$29,486	$22,114
2018	$31,337	$23,503

1759

YEARS MFRD . . . 2014-2018
ENGINE . . . MITSUBISHI
CYLINDERS . . . 4
CID . . . 135
PTO HP . . . 45.6
ENGINE HP . . . 59
COOLING . . . LIQUID
FUEL . . . D
SPEEDS . . . 12/12
TRANSMISSION . . . SHUTTLE SHIFT
STEERING . . . STANDARD
HITCH . . . CAT. I
DRIVE TYPE . . . 4WD
ROPS/CAB . . . ROPS
MSRP . . . $35,608

OPTIONS

CAB
LDR

SERIAL NUMBERS

YEAR	BEGINNING NO.
2014	E
2015	F
2016	G
2017	H
2018	JJJ80104

RETAIL PRICING

YEAR	HIGH	LOW
2014	$22,835	$17,127
2015	$24,667	$18,500
2016	$27,225	$20,419
2017	$29,880	$22,410
2018	$31,719	$23,789

1825E

YEARS MFRD . . . 2020-2020
ENGINE . . . ISEKI 1.5LTR
CYLINDERS . . . 3
PTO HP . . . 20.4
ENGINE HP . . . 24
COOLING . . . LIQUID
FUEL . . . D
SPEEDS . . . 8/8
TRANSMISSION SYNCHRO SHUTTLE
STEERING . . . STANDARD
HITCH . . . CAT. I
ROPS/CAB . . . ROPS
WEIGHT . . . 2,667 LBS.
MSRP . . . $15,991

OPTIONS

HYDRO . . . $848

2020

YEARS MFRD 2013-2014
ENGINE .... B&S
ENGINE HP 20
COOLING .... AIR
FUEL .... G
SPEEDS .... VARIABLE
TRANSMISSION .... HYDRO
STEERING .... ZERO
STANDARD DECK .... 42"
MSRP $1,799

RETAIL PRICING

YEAR	HIGH	LOW
2013	$896	$672
2014	$1,107	$831

2021

YEARS MFRD 2013-2014
ENGINE .... B&S
ENGINE HP 21
COOLING .... AIR
FUEL .... G
SPEEDS .... VARIABLE
TRANSMISSION .... HYDRO
STEERING .... ZERO
STANDARD DECK .... 42"
MSRP $1,899

RETAIL PRICING

YEAR	HIGH	LOW
2013	$945	$709
2014	$1,107	$831

2316H

YEARS MFRD 1995-1997
ENGINE .... B&S
ENGINE HP 16
COOLING .... AIR
FUEL .... G
TRANSMISSION .... HYDRO
STEERING .... ZERO
STANDARD DECK .... 42"
MSRP $4,850

RETAIL PRICING

YEAR	HIGH	LOW
1995	$581	$435
1996	$646	$484
1997	$713	$534

2413H

YEARS MFRD 1996-2006
SERIES .... 2400 SERIES
ENGINE .... B&S
CYLINDERS 1
ENGINE HP 13
COOLING .... AIR
FUEL .... G
SPEEDS .... VARIABLE
TRANSMISSION .... HYDRO
STEERING .... STANDARD
BLADE CLUTCH .... ELECTRIC
STANDARD DECK .... 30"
WEIGHT .... 415 LBS.
MSRP $2,199

OPTIONS

BAGGER
CART
DETHATCHER

RETAIL PRICING

YEAR	HIGH	LOW
1998	$231	$174
1999	$255	$191
2000	$282	$212
2001	$314	$235
2002	$347	$260
2003	$385	$289
2004	$426	$320
2005	$473	$355
2006	$524	$393

2515G

YEARS MFRD 2002-2004
SERIES .... 2500 SERIES
ENGINE .... B&S
CYLINDERS 2
ENGINE HP 16
COOLING .... AIR
FUEL .... G
SPEEDS 5/1
TRANSMISSION .... GEAR
STEERING .... STANDARD
STANDARD DECK .... 38"
WEIGHT .... 455 LBS.
MSRP $1,999

RETAIL PRICING

YEAR	HIGH	LOW
2002	$917	$687
2003	$1,006	$754
2004	$1,218	$914

2515H

YEARS MFRD 2000-2004
SERIES .... 2500 SERIES
ENGINE .... B&S
CYLINDERS 1
ENGINE HP 15
COOLING .... AIR
FUEL .... G
TRANSMISSION .... HYDRO
STEERING .... STANDARD
STANDARD DECK .... 38"
WEIGHT .... 455 LBS.
MSRP $1,999

OPTIONS

2 BAG
36" SWEEPER
42" BLADE
42" SNOW THROWER

RETAIL PRICING

YEAR	HIGH	LOW
2000	$271	$203
2001	$298	$224
2002	$330	$247
2003	$363	$273
2004	$402	$301

2516H

YEARS MFRD 1997-2004
SERIES .... 2500 SERIES
ENGINE .... KOHLER
CYLINDERS 1
ENGINE HP 16
COOLING .... AIR
FUEL .... G
SPEEDS .... VARIABLE
TRANSMISSION .... HYDRO
STEERING .... STANDARD
STANDARD DECK .... 44"
WEIGHT .... 463 LBS.
MSRP $2,799

OPTIONS

36" SNOW THROWER
42" BLADE
42" SNOW THROWER
BAGGER

RETAIL PRICING

YEAR	HIGH	LOW
1997	$282	$212
1998	$311	$233
1999	$343	$257
2000	$380	$285
2001	$418	$314
2002	$461	$346
2003	$510	$382
2004	$562	$422

2517H

YEARS MFRD 2000-2002
SERIES .... 2500 SERIES
ENGINE .... B&S
ENGINE HP 17
COOLING .... AIR
FUEL .... G
SPEEDS .... VARIABLE
TRANSMISSION .... HYDRO
STEERING .... STANDARD
STANDARD DECK .... 40"
MSRP $2,899

OPTIONS

36" SNOW THROWER
42" BLADE
42" SNOW BLOWER
SNOCAB

RETAIL PRICING

YEAR	HIGH	LOW
2000	$333	$250
2001	$366	$275
2002	$404	$303

2518

YEARS MFRD 2005-2005
SERIES .... 2500 SERIES
ENGINE .... B&S
CYLINDERS 1
ENGINE HP 18
COOLING .... AIR
FUEL .... G
SPEEDS .... VARIABLE
TRANSMISSION .... HYDRO
STEERING .... STANDARD
STANDARD DECK .... 38"
WEIGHT .... 463 LBS.
MSRP $2,799

OPTIONS

2 BAG
42" BLADE
42" SNOW THROWER
44" DECK

RETAIL PRICING

YEAR	HIGH	LOW
2005	$620	$465

2518G

YEARS MFRD 2005-2005
SERIES .... 2500 SERIES
ENGINE .... B&S
ENGINE HP 18
COOLING .... AIR
FUEL .... G
SPEEDS 5/1
TRANSMISSION .... GEAR
STEERING .... STANDARD
STANDARD DECK .... 38"
MSRP $1,899

OPTIONS

2 BAG
42" BLADE
42" SNOW THROWER
SNOCAB

RETAIL PRICING

YEAR	HIGH	LOW
2005	$420	$315

2518H

YEARS MFRD 2005-2011
SERIES .... 2500 SERIES
ENGINE .... B&S
CYLINDERS 1
ENGINE HP 18
COOLING .... AIR
FUEL .... G
SPEEDS .... VARIABLE
TRANSMISSION .... HYDRO
STEERING .... ZERO
STANDARD DECK .... 38"
WEIGHT .... 463 LBS.
MSRP $2,250

OPTIONS

2 BAG
42" BLADE
42" SNOW THROWER
SNOCAB

RETAIL PRICING

YEAR	HIGH	LOW
2005	$531	$398
2006	$586	$439
2007	$647	$485
2008	$713	$534
2009	$788	$591
2010	$869	$652
2011	$959	$719

2519

YEARS MFRD 2012-2014
ENGINE .... B&S
ENGINE HP 19.5
COOLING .... AIR

MASSEY FERGUSON

FUEL . . . . G
SPEEDS . . . . VARIABLE
TRANSMISSION . . . . . HYDRO
STEERING. . . . . . . STANDARD
STANDARD DECK . . . . . . 38"
MSRP. $2,199

RETAIL PRICING

YEAR	HIGH	LOW
2012	$910	$683
2013	$1,090	$818
2014	$1,416	$1,062

2520H

YEARS MFRD 2006-2011
ENGINE . . . . B&S
ENGINE HP 20
COOLING . . . . AIR
FUEL . . . . G
SPEEDS . . . . VARIABLE
TRANSMISSION . . . . . HYDRO
STEERING. . . . . . . STANDARD
STANDARD DECK . . . . . . 38"
MSRP. $2,600

OPTIONS

3 BAG
42" BLADE
42" SNOW THROWER
SNOCAB

RETAIL PRICING

YEAR	HIGH	LOW
2006	$869	$652
2007	$962	$722
2008	$1,066	$799
2009	$1,180	$885
2010	$1,310	$983
2011	$1,457	$1,092

2522

YEARS MFRD 2006-2011
ENGINE . . . . B&S
ENGINE HP 22
COOLING . . . . AIR
FUEL . . . . G
SPEEDS . . . . VARIABLE
TRANSMISSION . . . . . HYDRO
STEERING. . . . . . . STANDARD
STANDARD DECK . . . . . . 44"
MSRP. $2,799

OPTIONS

3 BAG & FAN
42" BLADE
42" SNOW THROWER
SNOCAB

RETAIL PRICING

YEAR	HIGH	LOW
2006	$729	$547
2007	$804	$603
2008	$887	$665
2009	$979	$735
2010	$1,081	$811
2011	$1,193	$894

2523

YEARS MFRD 2013-2014
ENGINE . . . . KOHLER
ENGINE HP 23
COOLING . . . . AIR
FUEL . . . . G
SPEEDS . . . . VARIABLE
TRANSMISSION . . . . . HYDRO
STEERING. . . . . . . STANDARD
STANDARD DECK . . . . . . 46"
MSRP. $2,899

RETAIL PRICING

YEAR	HIGH	LOW
2013	$1,441	$1,081
2014	$1,855	$1,392

2524H

YEARS MFRD 2006-2011
SERIES. . . . . 2500 SERIES
ENGINE . . . . B&S
ENGINE HP 24
COOLING . . . . AIR
FUEL . . . . G
SPEEDS . . . . VARIABLE
TRANSMISSION . . . . . HYDRO
STEERING. . . . . . . STANDARD
STANDARD DECK . . . . . . 50"
MSRP. $3,250

OPTIONS

3 BAG & FAN
42" BLADE
42" SNOW THROWER
SNOCAB

RETAIL PRICING

YEAR	HIGH	LOW
2006	$1,087	$815
2007	$1,204	$903
2008	$1,336	$1,002
2009	$1,477	$1,108
2010	$1,641	$1,231
2011	$1,817	$1,363

2526

YEARS MFRD 2003-2004
SERIES. . . . . 2500 SERIES
ENGINE . . . . HONDA
CYLINDERS. 2
ENGINE HP 16
COOLING . . . . AIR
FUEL . . . . G
SPEEDS . . . . VARIABLE
TRANSMISSION . . . . . HYDRO
STEERING. . . . . . . STANDARD
STANDARD DECK . . . . . . 38"
WEIGHT . . . . 463 LBS.
MSRP. $3,299

OPTIONS

2 BAG
42" BLADE
42" SNOW THROWER
44" DECK

RETAIL PRICING

YEAR	HIGH	LOW
2003	$600	$450
2004	$663	$497

2542H

YEARS MFRD 2007-2007
SERIES. . . . . 2500 SERIES
ENGINE . . . . B&S OHV
CYLINDERS. 2
ENGINE HP 24
COOLING . . . . AIR
FUEL . . . . G
SPEEDS . . . . VARIABLE
TRANSMISSION . . . . . HYDRO
STEERING. . . . . . . STANDARD
BLADE CLUTCH . . . . . . MANUAL
WEIGHT . . . . 585 LBS.

2604H

YEARS MFRD 2016-2019
SERIES. . . . . . . 2600H SERIES
ENGINE . . . . SIMPSON
CYLINDERS. 3
PTO HP 38
ENGINE HP 45
FUEL . . . . D
TRANSMISSION . . . . . . GEAR
STEERING. . . . . . . STANDARD
HITCH . . . . CAT. I
DRIVE TYPE 2WD
ROPS/CAB . . . . ROPS
WEIGHT . . . . 4,597 LBS.
MSRP. $18,771

OPTIONS

4WD
LOADER

SERIAL NUMBERS

YEAR	BEGINNING NO.
2016	G
2017	H
2018	H1163838
2019	J1203227

2605

YEARS MFRD 2008-2014
SERIES. . . . . 2600 SERIES
ENGINE . . . . . . S325.3 TIER 11
CYLINDERS. 3
CID 152.6
PTO HP 32
ENGINE HP 38.5
COOLING . . . . LIQUID
SPEEDS 8/2
TRANSMISSION . . . . . . GEAR
STEERING. . . . . . . STANDARD
HITCH . . . . CAT. I
HYDRAULIC . . . . YES
PTO . . . . YES
DRIVE TYPE 2WD
ROPS/CAB . . . . ROPS
WEIGHT . . . . 4,080 LBS.
MSRP. $15,150

OPTIONS

4WD
LDR

SERIAL NUMBERS

YEAR	BEGINNING NO.
2008	FT
2009	FU
2010	FV
2011	FW
2012	FX
2013	FY

RETAIL PRICING

YEAR	HIGH	LOW
2008	$8,094	$6,070
2009	$8,914	$6,685
2010	$9,835	$7,377
2011	$10,758	$8,068
2012	$11,372	$8,529
2013	$12,602	$9,452
2014	$13,934	$10,450

AVG. AUCTION PRICING

LOW	HIGH	AVG
$9,425	$13,576	$11,782

2606

YEARS MFRD 2003-2004
SERIES. . . . . 2600 SERIES
ENGINE . . . . KOHLER
CYLINDERS. 1
ENGINE HP 16
COOLING . . . . AIR
FUEL . . . . G
SPEEDS . . . . VARIABLE
TRANSMISSION . . . . . HYDRO
STEERING. . . . . . . STANDARD
STANDARD DECK . . . . . . 44"
WEIGHT . . . . 618 LBS.
MSRP. $3,550

OPTIONS

3 BAG
42" BLADE
42" SNOW BLOWER
SNOCAB

RETAIL PRICING

YEAR	HIGH	LOW
2003	$646	$484
2004	$713	$534

2615

YEARS MFRD 2008-2014
SERIES. . . . . 2600 SERIES
ENGINE SJ327E TIER11
CYLINDERS. 3
CID 164.8
PTO HP 31.3
ENGINE HP 36.5
COOLING . . . . LIQUID
SPEEDS 8/2
TRANSMISSION . . . . . . GEAR
STEERING. . . . . . . STANDARD
HITCH . . . . CAT. I
HYDRAULIC . . . . YES
PTO . . . . YES
DRIVE TYPE 2WD
ROPS/CAB . . . . ROPS
WEIGHT . . . . 4,365 LBS.
MSRP. $19,340

OPTIONS

4WD
8/8 PS
LDR

SERIAL NUMBERS

YEAR	BEGINNING NO.
2008	FT
2009	FU
2010	FV
2011	FW
2012	FX
2013	FY

RETAIL PRICING

YEAR	HIGH	LOW
2008	$11,716	$8,787
2009	$12,522	$9,392
2010	$13,416	$10,062
2011	$14,312	$10,734
2012	$15,294	$11,471
2013	$16,279	$12,209
2014	$16,771	$12,578

AVG. AUCTION PRICING

LOW	HIGH	AVG
$8,881	$18,016	$13,170

2615H

YEARS MFRD 1997-2002
SERIES .... 2600 SERIES
ENGINE .... KOHLER
ENGINE HP 16
COOLING .... AIR
FUEL .... G
SPEEDS .... VARIABLE
TRANSMISSION .... HYDRO
STEERING .... STANDARD
STANDARD DECK .... 44"
MSRP $3,099

OPTIONS

2 BAG
40" SNOW BLOWER
42" BLADE

RETAIL PRICING

YEAR	HIGH	LOW
1997	$264	$198
1998	$290	$218
1999	$321	$241
2000	$354	$266
2001	$391	$293
2002	$431	$324

2615HC

YEARS MFRD 2001-2001
SERIES .... 2600 SERIES
ENGINE .... KOHLER
ENGINE HP 16
FUEL .... G
TRANSMISSION .... HYDRO
STEERING .... STANDARD
STANDARD DECK .... 44"
MSRP $3,525

RETAIL PRICING

YEAR	HIGH	LOW
2001	$1,648	$1,236

2616

YEARS MFRD 2004-2004
SERIES .... 2600 SERIES
ENGINE .... B&S
CYLINDERS 2
ENGINE HP 16
COOLING .... AIR
FUEL .... G
SPEEDS .... VARIABLE
TRANSMISSION .... HYDRO
STEERING .... STANDARD
STANDARD DECK .... 38"
WEIGHT .... 618 LBS.
MSRP $3,850

RETAIL PRICING

YEAR	HIGH	LOW
2004	$2,345	$1,758

2616H

YEARS MFRD 1995-2004
SERIES .... 2600 SERIES
ENGINE .... B&S
ENGINE HP 16
COOLING .... AIR
FUEL .... G
SPEEDS .... VARIABLE
TRANSMISSION .... HYDRO
STEERING .... STANDARD
STANDARD DECK .... 44"
MSRP $3,850

OPTIONS

2 BAG
38" DECK
40" SNOW BLOWER
42" BLADE

RETAIL PRICING

YEAR	HIGH	LOW
1995	$282	$212
1996	$351	$263
1997	$387	$290
1998	$427	$320
1999	$473	$355
2000	$521	$391
2001	$576	$432
2002	$634	$476
2003	$700	$525
2004	$773	$580

2616HV

YEARS MFRD 2001-2003
SERIES .... 2600 SERIES
ENGINE .... B&S
ENGINE HP 16
COOLING .... AIR
FUEL .... G
SPEEDS .... VARIABLE
TRANSMISSION .... HYDRO
STEERING .... STANDARD
STANDARD DECK .... 38"
MSRP $3,525

OPTIONS

44" DECK

RETAIL PRICING

YEAR	HIGH	LOW
2001	$1,404	$1,053
2002	$1,576	$1,182
2003	$1,972	$1,479

2617HC

YEARS MFRD 2000-2000
SERIES .... 2600 SERIES
ENGINE .... B&S
ENGINE HP 17
FUEL .... G
TRANSMISSION .... HYDRO
STEERING .... STANDARD
STANDARD DECK .... 44"
MSRP $3,525

OPTIONS

2 BAG
40" SNOW BLOWER
42" BLADE
SNOCAB

RETAIL PRICING

YEAR	HIGH	LOW
2000	$1,187	$890

2618H

YEARS MFRD 1999-2001
SERIES .... 2600 SERIES
ENGINE .... B&S
CYLINDERS 2
ENGINE HP 18
COOLING .... AIR
FUEL .... G
SPEEDS .... VARIABLE
TRANSMISSION .... HYDRO
STEERING .... STANDARD
STANDARD DECK .... 50"
WEIGHT .... 618 LBS.
MSRP $5,225

OPTIONS

3 BAG
40" SNOW BLOWER
42" BLADE

RETAIL PRICING

YEAR	HIGH	LOW
1999	$597	$448
2000	$660	$495
2001	$729	$547

2620

YEARS MFRD 2005-2011
SERIES .... 2600 SERIES
ENGINE .... B&S
CYLINDERS 2
ENGINE HP 20
COOLING .... AIR
FUEL .... G
SPEEDS .... VARIABLE
TRANSMISSION .... HYDRO
STEERING .... STANDARD
STANDARD DECK .... 44"
WEIGHT .... 690 LBS.
MSRP $4,650

OPTIONS

3 BAG & FAN
42" BLADE
42" SNOW BLOWER
50" DECK

RETAIL PRICING

YEAR	HIGH	LOW
2005	$901	$676
2006	$1,210	$907
2007	$1,335	$1,001
2008	$1,474	$1,105
2009	$1,627	$1,220
2010	$1,797	$1,347
2011	$1,981	$1,486

2622

YEARS MFRD 2012-2014
ENGINE .... B&S
ENGINE HP 22
COOLING .... AIR
FUEL .... G
SPEEDS .... VARIABLE
TRANSMISSION .... HYDRO
STEERING .... STANDARD
STANDARD DECK .... 44"
MSRP $3,599

RETAIL PRICING

YEAR	HIGH	LOW
2012	$1,498	$1,124
2013	$1,790	$1,343
2014	$2,427	$1,820

2625

YEARS MFRD 2008-2010
SERIES .... 2600 SERIES
ENGINE .... SJ436E TIER 11
CYLINDERS 4
CID 220
PTO HP 54
ENGINE HP 63
COOLING .... LIQUID
SPEEDS 8/2
TRANSMISSION .... GEAR
STEERING .... STANDARD
HITCH .... CAT. I
HYDRAULIC .... YES
PTO .... YES
DRIVE TYPE 2WD
ROPS/CAB .... ROPS
WEIGHT .... 5,250 LBS.
MSRP $18,872

OPTIONS

4WD
LDR

SERIAL NUMBERS

YEAR	BEGINNING NO.
2008	FT
2009	FU
2010	FV

RETAIL PRICING

YEAR	HIGH	LOW
2008	$8,100	$6,075
2009	$8,494	$6,370

AVG. AUCTION PRICING

LOW	HIGH	AVG
$11,165	$11,926	$11,588

2626

YEARS MFRD 2003-2004
SERIES .... 2600 SERIES
ENGINE .... HONDA
CYLINDERS 2
ENGINE HP 16

COOLING . . . AIR
FUEL . . . G
SPEEDS . . . VARIABLE
TRANSMISSION . . . HYDRO
STEERING . . . STANDARD
STANDARD DECK . . . 44"
WEIGHT . . . 618 LBS.
MSRP . . . $4,175

OPTIONS

3 BAG
42" BLADE
42" SNOW BLOWER

RETAIL PRICING

YEAR	HIGH	LOW
2003	$759	$569
2004	$838	$629

2705E

YEARS MFRD . . . 2015-2019
ENGINE . . . SHIBAURA
CYLINDERS . . . 4
CID . . . 135
PTO HP . . . 36.8
ENGINE HP . . . 48.8
COOLING . . . LIQUID
FUEL . . . D
SPEEDS . . . 8/8
TRANSMISSION . . . SHUTTLE SHIFT
STEERING . . . STANDARD
HITCH . . . CAT. I
DRIVE TYPE . . . 4WD
ROPS/CAB . . . ROPS
MSRP . . . $25,508

OPTIONS

HYDRO
LDR

SERIAL NUMBERS

YEAR	BEGINNING NO.
2015	F
2016	G
2017	H
2018	HKM24405

RETAIL PRICING

YEAR	HIGH	LOW
2015	$16,994	$12,746
2016	$18,984	$14,238
2017	$21,074	$15,806
2018	$22,550	$16,913
2019	$24,112	$18,084

2706E

YEARS MFRD . . . 2015-2019
ENGINE . . . SHIBAURA
CYLINDERS . . . 4
CID . . . 135
PTO HP . . . 48
ENGINE HP . . . 57.3
COOLING . . . LIQUID
FUEL . . . D
SPEEDS . . . 8/8
TRANSMISSION . . . SHUTTLE SHIFT
STEERING . . . STANDARD
HITCH . . . CAT. I
DRIVE TYPE . . . 4WD
ROPS/CAB . . . ROPS
MSRP . . . $27,661

OPTIONS

HYDRO
LDR

SERIAL NUMBERS

YEAR	BEGINNING NO.
2015	F
2016	G
2017	H
2018	HKM34405

RETAIL PRICING

YEAR	HIGH	LOW
2015	$18,477	$13,858
2016	$20,607	$15,455
2017	$22,777	$17,082
2018	$24,338	$18,253
2019	$25,940	$19,455

2716H

YEARS MFRD . . . 2002-2003
SERIES . . . 2700 SERIES
ENGINE HP . . . 16
FUEL . . . G
TRANSMISSION . . . HYDRO
STEERING . . . STANDARD
STANDARD DECK . . . 44"
MSRP . . . $4,399

OPTIONS

4 BAG
40" SNOW BLOWER
42" BLADE
42" SNOW THROWER

RETAIL PRICING

YEAR	HIGH	LOW
2002	$912	$684
2003	$1,009	$757

2717H

YEARS MFRD . . . 1997-1999
SERIES . . . 2700 SERIES
ENGINE . . . KAWASAKI
ENGINE HP . . . 17
COOLING . . . LIQUID
FUEL . . . G
TRANSMISSION . . . HYDRO
STEERING . . . STANDARD
STANDARD DECK . . . 50"
MSRP . . . $6,700

OPTIONS

36" TILLER
40" SNOW BLOWER
42" BLADE
BAGGER

RETAIL PRICING

YEAR	HIGH	LOW
1997	$752	$564
1998	$832	$624
1999	$920	$690

2718H

YEARS MFRD . . . 1995-2004
SERIES . . . 2700 SERIES
ENGINE . . . B&S
CYLINDERS . . . 2
ENGINE HP . . . 18
COOLING . . . AIR
FUEL . . . G
SPEEDS . . . VARIABLE
TRANSMISSION . . . HYDRO
STEERING . . . STANDARD
STANDARD DECK . . . 44"
WEIGHT . . . 698 LBS.
MSRP . . . $4,799

OPTIONS

2 BAG
40" SNOW BLOWER
42" BLADE

RETAIL PRICING

YEAR	HIGH	LOW
1995	$501	$376
1996	$514	$385
1997	$567	$426
1998	$628	$471
1999	$694	$521
2000	$768	$576
2001	$850	$637
2002	$941	$706
2003	$1,040	$780
2004	$1,153	$865

2720H

YEARS MFRD . . . 1999-2005
SERIES . . . 2700 SERIES
ENGINE . . . B&S
CYLINDERS . . . 2
ENGINE HP . . . 20
COOLING . . . AIR
FUEL . . . G
SPEEDS . . . VARIABLE
TRANSMISSION . . . HYDRO
STEERING . . . STANDARD
STANDARD DECK . . . 50"
WEIGHT . . . 778 LBS.
MSRP . . . $4,695

OPTIONS

3 BAG
36" TILLER
4 BAG
42" SNOW BLOWER
54" DECK

RETAIL PRICING

YEAR	HIGH	LOW
1999	$667	$500
2000	$738	$553
2001	$817	$613
2002	$902	$677
2003	$1,000	$750
2004	$1,104	$828
2005	$1,222	$917

2721H

YEARS MFRD . . . 2006-2006
ENGINE . . . VANGUARD
ENGINE HP . . . 21
COOLING . . . AIR
FUEL . . . G
SPEEDS . . . VARIABLE
TRANSMISSION . . . HYDRO
STEERING . . . STANDARD
STANDARD DECK . . . 44"
MSRP . . . $4,825

OPTIONS

3 BAG & FAN
42" BLADE
42" SNOW BLOWER
42" SNOW THROWER

RETAIL PRICING

YEAR	HIGH	LOW
2006	$1,454	$1,091

2722

YEARS MFRD . . . 2005-2005
SERIES . . . 2700 SERIES
ENGINE . . . B&S
CYLINDERS . . . 2
ENGINE HP . . . 22
COOLING . . . AIR
FUEL . . . G
SPEEDS . . . VARIABLE
TRANSMISSION . . . HYDRO
STEERING . . . STANDARD
STANDARD DECK . . . 50"
WEIGHT . . . 778 LBS.
MSRP . . . $5,125

OPTIONS

3 BAG
42" BLADE
42" SNOW BLOWER
54" DECK

RETAIL PRICING

YEAR	HIGH	LOW
2005	$1,334	$1,000

2723H

YEARS MFRD . . . 2001-2001
SERIES . . . 2700 SERIES
ENGINE . . . KOHLER
ENGINE HP . . . 23
COOLING . . . AIR
FUEL . . . G
SPEEDS . . . VARIABLE
TRANSMISSION . . . HYDRO
STEERING . . . STANDARD
STANDARD DECK . . . 54"
MSRP . . . $7,099

OPTIONS

3 BAG
36" TILLER
42" BLADE
42" SNOW BLOWER

RETAIL PRICING

YEAR	HIGH	LOW
2001	$1,265	$949

2723H-PS

YEARS MFRD . . . 2006-2011
ENGINE . . . B&S VANGUARD
CYLINDERS . . . 2
ENGINE HP . . . 23
COOLING . . . AIR
FUEL . . . G
SPEEDS . . . VARIABLE
TRANSMISSION . . . HYDRO
STEERING . . . STANDARD
STANDARD DECK . . . 50"
MSRP . . . $5,900

OPTIONS

3 BAG & FAN
42" BLADE
42" SNOW BLOWER
P/S

RETAIL PRICING

YEAR	HIGH	LOW
2006	$2,024	$1,518
2007	$2,242	$1,682
2008	$2,487	$1,865
2009	$2,754	$2,065
2010	$3,050	$2,288
2011	$3,381	$2,536

2724

YEARS MFRD 2012-2014
ENGINE .... B&S
ENGINE HP 24
COOLING .... AIR
FUEL .... G
SPEEDS .... VARIABLE
TRANSMISSION .... HYDRO
STEERING .... STANDARD
STANDARD DECK .... 52"
MSRP $5,799

OPTIONS

POWER STEERING

RETAIL PRICING

YEAR	HIGH	LOW
2012	$2,409	$1,806
2013	$2,963	$2,222
2014	$3,713	$2,785

2818-PS

YEARS MFRD 1995-1999
SERIES .... 2800 SERIES
ENGINE .... KOHLER
ENGINE HP 18
COOLING .... AIR
FUEL .... G
TRANSMISSION .... HYDRO
STEERING .... STANDARD
STANDARD DECK .... 48"
MSRP $7,275

OPTIONS

36" TILLER
42" BLADE
42" SNOW BLOWER
BAGGER

RETAIL PRICING

YEAR	HIGH	LOW
1995	$718	$538
1996	$794	$595
1997	$877	$658
1998	$970	$728
1999	$1,074	$805

2818H

YEARS MFRD 1995-1999
SERIES .... 2800 SERIES
ENGINE .... KOHLER
ENGINE HP 18
FUEL .... G
TRANSMISSION .... HYDRO
STEERING .... STANDARD
STANDARD DECK .... 48"
MSRP $7,050

RETAIL PRICING

YEAR	HIGH	LOW
1995	$1,731	$1,298
1996	$1,819	$1,364
1997	$2,018	$1,513
1998	$2,364	$1,773
1999	$2,709	$2,032

2820H

YEARS MFRD 2002-2004
SERIES .... 2800 SERIES
ENGINE .... KOHLER
CYLINDERS 2
ENGINE HP 20
COOLING .... AIR
FUEL .... G
SPEEDS .... VARIABLE
TRANSMISSION .... HYDRO
STEERING .... STANDARD
STANDARD DECK .... 50"
WEIGHT .... 791 LBS.
MSRP $5,725

OPTIONS

2 BAG
40" SNOW BLOWER
42" BLADE
P/S

RETAIL PRICING

YEAR	HIGH	LOW
2002	$1,122	$841
2003	$1,241	$931
2004	$1,372	$1,029

2823

YEARS MFRD 2002-2006
SERIES .... 2800 SERIES
ENGINE .... KOHLER
CYLINDERS 2
ENGINE HP 23
COOLING .... AIR
FUEL .... G
SPEEDS .... VARIABLE
TRANSMISSION .... HYDRO
STEERING .... STANDARD
STANDARD DECK .... 54"
WEIGHT .... 858 LBS.
MSRP $6,795

OPTIONS

3 BAG
40" SNOW BLOWER
42" BLADE
SNOCAB

RETAIL PRICING

YEAR	HIGH	LOW
2002	$1,653	$1,240
2003	$1,834	$1,376
2004	$2,032	$1,524
2005	$2,251	$1,688
2006	$2,501	$1,876

2825H

YEARS MFRD 2007-2009
SERIES .... 2800 SERIES
ENGINE ...... KOHLER COMMAND
CYLINDERS 2
ENGINE HP 25
COOLING .... AIR
FUEL .... G
SPEEDS .... VARIABLE
TRANSMISSION .... HYDRO
STEERING .... STANDARD
STANDARD DECK .... 50"
WEIGHT .... 791 LBS.
MSRP $7,550

OPTIONS

3 BAG
36" TILLER
42" BLADE
42" SNOW BLOWER

RETAIL PRICING

YEAR	HIGH	LOW
2007	$2,942	$2,207
2008	$3,264	$2,448
2009	$3,617	$2,713

2827

YEARS MFRD 2007-2011
SERIES .... 2800 SERIES
ENGINE ...... KOHLER COMMAND
CYLINDERS 2
ENGINE HP 27
COOLING .... AIR
FUEL .... G
SPEEDS .... VARIABLE
TRANSMISSION .... HYDRO
STEERING .... STANDARD
STANDARD DECK .... 54"
WEIGHT .... 858 LBS.
MSRP $7,799

OPTIONS

3 BAG
36" TILLER
42" BLADE
42" SNOW BLOWER

RETAIL PRICING

YEAR	HIGH	LOW
2007	$2,156	$1,617
2008	$2,384	$1,788
2009	$2,639	$1,979
2010	$2,918	$2,189
2011	$3,229	$2,422

2830

YEARS MFRD 2013-2014
ENGINE .... B&S
ENGINE HP 30
COOLING .... AIR
FUEL .... G
SPEEDS .... VARIABLE
TRANSMISSION .... HYDRO
STEERING .... STANDARD
STANDARD DECK .... 54"
MSRP $6,599

RETAIL PRICING

YEAR	HIGH	LOW
2013	$3,280	$2,460
2014	$4,296	$3,222

2918H

YEARS MFRD 1995-1997
SERIES .... 2900 SERIES
ENGINE .... B&S
ENGINE HP 18
COOLING .... AIR
FUEL .... G
TRANSMISSION .... HYDRO
STEERING .... STANDARD
STANDARD DECK .... 48"
MSRP $7,950

OPTIONS

38" TILLER
46" BLADE
47" SNOW BLOWER
BAGGER

RETAIL PRICING

YEAR	HIGH	LOW
1995	$692	$519
1996	$765	$574
1997	$847	$635

2920H

YEARS MFRD 1995-2002
SERIES .... 2900 SERIES
ENGINE .... KOHLER
ENGINE HP 20
COOLING .... AIR
FUEL .... G
TRANSMISSION .... HYDRO
STEERING .... STANDARD
STANDARD DECK .... 48"
MSRP $8,250

OPTIONS

3 BAG
54" DECK
60" BLADE

RETAIL PRICING

YEAR	HIGH	LOW
1995	$767	$576
1996	$848	$636
1997	$939	$704
1998	$1,039	$780
1999	$1,149	$862
2000	$1,271	$953
2001	$1,406	$1,054
2002	$1,556	$1,167

2920LC

YEARS MFRD 1995-2002
SERIES .... 2900 SERIES
ENGINE .... KAWASAKI
ENGINE HP 20
COOLING .... LIQUID
FUEL .... G
SPEEDS .... VARIABLE
TRANSMISSION .... HYDRO
STEERING .... STANDARD
STANDARD DECK .... 54"
MSRP $9,799

OPTIONS

3 BAG
47" SNOW BLOWER
50" TILLER
60" BLADE

MASSEY FERGUSON

RETAIL PRICING

YEAR	HIGH	LOW
1995	$911	$684
1996	$1,008	$756
1997	$1,115	$837
1998	$1,233	$925
1999	$1,364	$1,023
2000	$1,509	$1,132
2001	$1,670	$1,252
2002	$1,847	$1,385

2923H

YEARS MFRD 2001-2003
SERIES . . . . 2900 SERIES
ENGINE . . . . KOHLER
CYLINDERS 2
ENGINE HP 23
COOLING . . . . AIR
FUEL . . . . G
SPEEDS . . . . VARIABLE
TRANSMISSION . . . . HYDRO
STEERING . . . . STANDARD
HYDRAULIC . . . . YES
STANDARD DECK . . . . 54"
WEIGHT . . . . 1,085 LBS.
MSRP $9,075

OPTIONS

3 BAG
47" SNOW BLOWER
50" TILLER
60" BLADE

RETAIL PRICING

YEAR	HIGH	LOW
2001	$1,626	$1,220
2002	$1,800	$1,350
2003	$1,989	$1,492

2924D

YEARS MFRD 1999-2002
SERIES . . . . 2900 SERIES
ENGINE . . . . B&S
ENGINE HP 24.5
COOLING . . . . LIQUID
FUEL . . . . D
TRANSMISSION . . . . HYDRO
STEERING . . . . STANDARD
STANDARD DECK . . . . 54"
MSRP $11,550

OPTIONS

3 BAG
47" SNOW BLOWER
50" TILLER
60" BLADE

RETAIL PRICING

YEAR	HIGH	LOW
1999	$1,609	$1,207
2000	$1,779	$1,334
2001	$1,968	$1,476
2002	$2,177	$1,633

2925FH

YEARS MFRD 2000-2000
SERIES . . . . 2900 SERIES
ENGINE . . . . KOHLER
CYLINDERS 2
ENGINE HP 25
COOLING . . . . AIR
FUEL . . . . G
SPEEDS . . . . VARIABLE
TRANSMISSION . . . . HYDRO
STEERING . . . . STANDARD
HYDRAULIC . . . . YES
STANDARD DECK . . . . 60"
WEIGHT . . . . 1,125 LBS.
MSRP $10,550

OPTIONS

3 BAG
46" SNOW THROWER
47" SNOW BLOWER
60" BLADE

RETAIL PRICING

YEAR	HIGH	LOW
2000	$1,557	$1,168

2925H

YEARS MFRD 1998-2003
SERIES . . . . 2900 SERIES
ENGINE . . . . KOHLER
ENGINE HP 25
COOLING . . . . AIR
FUEL . . . . G
TRANSMISSION . . . . HYDRO
STEERING . . . . STANDARD
STANDARD DECK . . . . 60"
MSRP $9,750

OPTIONS

3 BAG
47" SNOW BLOWER
50" TILLER
60" BLADE

RETAIL PRICING

YEAR	HIGH	LOW
1998	$1,291	$968
1999	$1,427	$1,070
2000	$1,578	$1,184
2001	$1,747	$1,310
2002	$1,932	$1,449
2003	$2,138	$1,603

2927-2WD

YEARS MFRD 2006-2006
SERIES . . . . 2900 SERIES
ENGINE . . . . KOHLER
CYLINDERS 2
CID 725
ENGINE HP 27
COOLING . . . . AIR
FUEL . . . . G
SPEEDS . . . . VARIABLE
TRANSMISSION . . . . HYDRO
STEERING . . . . STANDARD
HITCH . . . . CAT. I
HYDRAULIC . . . . YES
PTO . . . . YES
STANDARD DECK . . . . 60"
WEIGHT . . . . 830 LBS.
MSRP $8,650

OPTIONS

3 BAG
46" SNOW THROWER
47" SNOW BLOWER
50" TILLER
54" DECK
60" DECK

RETAIL PRICING

YEAR	HIGH	LOW
2006	$3,716	$2,787

2927-4WD

YEARS MFRD 2006-2006
SERIES . . . . 2900 SERIES
ENGINE . . . . KAWASAKI
CYLINDERS 2
ENGINE HP 27
COOLING . . . . LIQUID
FUEL . . . . D
SPEEDS . . . . VARIABLE
TRANSMISSION . . . . HYDRO
STEERING . . . . STANDARD
DRIVE TYPE 4WD
ROPS/CAB . . . . ROPS
STANDARD DECK . . . . 60"
WEIGHT . . . . 1,280 LBS.
MSRP $10,750

OPTIONS

3 BAG
46" SNOW THROWER
47" SNOW BLOWER
50" TILLER
54" DECK
60" DECK

RETAIL PRICING

YEAR	HIGH	LOW
2006	$4,618	$3,464

4417

YEARS MFRD 2003-2005
SERIES . . . . 4400 SERIES
ENGINE . . . . B&S
CYLINDERS 1
ENGINE HP 17
COOLING . . . . AIR
FUEL . . . . G
SPEEDS . . . . VARIABLE
TRANSMISSION . . . . HYDRO
STEERING . . . . ZERO
STANDARD DECK . . . . 44"
MSRP $3,895

RETAIL PRICING

YEAR	HIGH	LOW
2003	$1,160	$870
2004	$1,284	$963
2005	$1,426	$1,070

MC CORMICK

C60 MAX

YEARS MFRD 2005-2008
ENGINE . . . . PERKINS
CID 201
ENGINE HP 58.5
COOLING . . . . LIQUID
FUEL . . . . D
SPEEDS 12/12
TRANSMISSION . . . SHUTTLE SHIFT
STEERING . . . . STANDARD
HITCH . . . . CAT. I
DRIVE TYPE 2WD
ROPS/CAB . . . . ROPS
MSRP $28,620

OPTIONS

4WD

RETAIL PRICING

YEAR	HIGH	LOW
2005	$15,549	$11,662
2008	$16,319	$12,239

C75 MAX

YEARS MFRD 2005-2008
ENGINE . . . . PERKINS
CYLINDERS 4
CID 268
ENGINE HP 62.4
COOLING . . . . LIQUID
FUEL . . . . D
SPEEDS 12/12
TRANSMISSION . . . SHUTTLE SHIFT
STEERING . . . . STANDARD
HITCH . . . . CAT. I
DRIVE TYPE 2WD
ROPS/CAB . . . . ROPS
MSRP $37,735

OPTIONS

4WD

RETAIL PRICING

YEAR	HIGH	LOW
2005	$13,958	$10,469
2006	$15,113	$11,334
2007	$16,191	$12,143
2008	$17,639	$13,230

CT28

YEARS MFRD 2008-2010
SERIES . . . . CT SERIES
ENGINE . . . . MITSUBISHI
CYLINDERS 4
CID 92
ENGINE HP 28
COOLING . . . . LIQUID
FUEL . . . . D
SPEEDS 12/12
TRANSMISSION . . . . GEAR
STEERING . . . . STANDARD
HITCH . . . . CAT. I
HYDRAULIC . . . . YES
PTO . . . . YES
WEIGHT . . . . 2,645 LBS.
MSRP $16,410

OPTIONS

66" DECK
BACKHOE
HYDRO
LDR
MID MOUNT PTO

RETAIL PRICING

YEAR	HIGH	LOW
2008	$8,520	$6,390
2009	$9,300	$6,975
2010	$10,211	$7,658

CT28HST

YEARS MFRD 2008-2011
SERIES .... CT SERIES
ENGINE .... MITSUBISHI
CYLINDERS 4
ENGINE HP 28
COOLING .... LIQUID
FUEL .... D
SPEEDS .... VARIABLE
TRANSMISSION .... HYDRO
STEERING .... STANDARD
HYDRAULIC .... YES
PTO .... YES
WEIGHT .... 2,645 LBS.
MSRP $17,090

RETAIL PRICING

YEAR	HIGH	LOW
2008	$8,604	$6,453
2009	$9,353	$7,015
2010	$9,603	$7,202
2011	$10,314	$7,736

CT36

YEARS MFRD 2008-2010
SERIES .... CT SERIES
ENGINE .... MITSUBISHI
CYLINDERS 4
ENGINE HP 38.5
COOLING .... LIQUID
FUEL .... D
SPEEDS 12/12
TRANSMISSION .... GEAR
STEERING .... STANDARD
HITCH .... CAT. I
HYDRAULIC .... YES
PTO .... YES
WEIGHT .... 2,711 LBS.
MSRP $18,890

OPTIONS

66" DECK
72" DECK
BACKHOE
HYDRO
LDR

RETAIL PRICING

YEAR	HIGH	LOW
2008	$10,016	$7,512
2009	$10,861	$8,146
2010	$11,186	$8,390

CT41

YEARS MFRD 2008-2010
SERIES .... CT SERIES
ENGINE .... MITSUBISHI
CYLINDERS 4
PTO HP 36
ENGINE HP 41
COOLING .... LIQUID
FUEL .... D
SPEEDS 16/16
TRANSMISSION .... GEAR
STEERING .... STANDARD
HITCH .... CAT. I
HYDRAULIC .... YES
PTO .... YES
WEIGHT .... 3,583 LBS.
MSRP $20,240

OPTIONS

66" DECK
72" DECK
BACKHOE
HYDRO
LDR

RETAIL PRICING

YEAR	HIGH	LOW
2008	$10,861	$8,146
2009	$11,706	$8,779
2010	$12,033	$9,025

CT41HST

YEARS MFRD 2008-2011
ENGINE .... MITSUBISHI
CYLINDERS 4
ENGINE HP 41
COOLING .... LIQUID
FUEL .... D
SPEEDS .... VARIABLE
TRANSMISSION .... HYDRO
STEERING .... STANDARD
HITCH .... CAT. I
HYDRAULIC .... YES
PTO .... YES
WEIGHT .... 3,583 LBS.
MSRP $21,140

RETAIL PRICING

YEAR	HIGH	LOW
2008	$10,988	$8,241
2009	$11,801	$8,851
2010	$12,113	$9,085
2011	$13,085	$9,814

CT47

YEARS MFRD 2008-2010
SERIES .... CT SERIES
ENGINE .... MITSUBISHI
CYLINDERS 4
ENGINE HP 47
COOLING .... LIQUID
FUEL .... D
SPEEDS 16/16
TRANSMISSION ... SHUTTLE SHIFT
STEERING .... STANDARD
HITCH .... CAT. I
HYDRAULIC .... YES
PTO .... YES
WEIGHT .... 3,583 LBS.
MSRP $21,500

OPTIONS

66" DECK
72" DECK
BACKHOE
HYDRO
LDR

RETAIL PRICING

YEAR	HIGH	LOW
2008	$11,512	$8,634
2009	$12,553	$9,415
2010	$12,878	$9,658

CTJ23

YEARS MFRD 2009-2010
ENGINE .... MITSUBISHI S3L
CYLINDERS 3
CID 68.6
PTO HP 16.5
ENGINE HP 23
COOLING .... LIQUID
FUEL .... D
SPEEDS .... VARIABLE
TRANSMISSION .... HYDRO
STEERING .... STANDARD
HITCH .... CAT. I
DRIVE TYPE 2WD
ROPS/CAB .... ROPS
WEIGHT .... 1,587 LBS.
MSRP $12,950

RETAIL PRICING

YEAR	HIGH	LOW
2009	$7,349	$5,512
2010	$7,544	$5,658

CTJ27

YEARS MFRD 2009-2011
ENGINE .... MITSUBISHI
CYLINDERS 3
CID 80.4
PTO HP 21.5
ENGINE HP 27
COOLING .... LIQUID
FUEL .... D
SPEEDS .... VARIABLE
TRANSMISSION .... HYDRO
STEERING .... STANDARD
HITCH .... CAT. I
DRIVE TYPE 2WD
ROPS/CAB .... ROPS
WEIGHT .... 1,609 LBS.
MSRP $13,900

RETAIL PRICING

YEAR	HIGH	LOW
2009	$6,952	$5,214
2010	$7,589	$5,692
2011	$7,679	$5,760

CTV28

YEARS MFRD 2009-2010
ENGINE .... MITSUBISHI S4L
CYLINDERS 4
CID 1.5L
ENGINE HP 28
COOLING .... LIQUID
FUEL .... D
SPEEDS 8/8
TRANSMISSION ... SHUTTLE SHIFT
STEERING .... STANDARD
HITCH .... CAT. I
HYDRAULIC .... YES
PTO .... YES
WEIGHT .... 2,645 LBS.
MSRP $14,630

OPTIONS

BACKHOE
LDR
MID MOUNT PTO

RETAIL PRICING

YEAR	HIGH	LOW
2009	$8,194	$6,145
2010	$8,391	$6,294

G25

YEARS MFRD 2006-2006
ENGINE .... KUBOTA D722-E
CYLINDERS 3
ENGINE HP 21
COOLING .... LIQUID
FUEL .... D
SPEEDS .... VARIABLE
TRANSMISSION .... HYDRO
STEERING .... STANDARD
HITCH .... CAT. I
HYDRAULIC .... YES
PTO .... YES
WEIGHT .... 1,323 LBS.

G30R

YEARS MFRD 2006-2006
ENGINE .... PERKINS 103.10
CYLINDERS 3
ENGINE HP 23.5
COOLING .... LIQUID
FUEL .... D
SPEEDS .... VARIABLE
TRANSMISSION .... HYDRO
STEERING .... STANDARD
HITCH .... CAT. I
HYDRAULIC .... YES
PTO .... YES
WEIGHT .... 1,587 LBS.

GM40

YEARS MFRD 2015-2016
ENGINE .... YANMAR
CYLINDERS 3
PTO HP 32
ENGINE HP 35
COOLING .... LIQUID
FUEL .... D
SPEEDS 12/12
TRANSMISSION ... SHUTTLE SHIFT
STEERING .... STANDARD
HITCH .... CAT. I

GM45

YEARS MFRD 2015-2016
ENGINE ... YANMAR 4TNV84-KLAN
CYLINDERS 4
PTO HP 40
ENGINE HP 44
COOLING .... LIQUID
FUEL .... D
SPEEDS 12/12
TRANSMISSION ... SHUTTLE SHIFT
STEERING .... STANDARD
HITCH .... CAT. I

MC CORMICK

GM50

YEARS MFRD 2015-2016
ENGINE ... YANMAR 4TNV88-KLAN
CYLINDERS.................4
PTO HP 43
ENGINE HP.................47
COOLING ....LIQUID
FUEL ....D
SPEEDS 12/12
TRANSMISSION ... SHUTTLE SHIFT
STEERING............STANDARD
HITCH ....CAT. I

GM55

YEARS MFRD 2015-2016
ENGINE . YANMAR 4TNV84T-2XLAN
CYLINDERS.................4
PTO HP 50
ENGINE HP.................54
COOLING ....LIQUID
FUEL ....D
SPEEDS 12/12
TRANSMISSION ... SHUTTLE SHIFT
STEERING............STANDARD
HITCH ....CAT. I

GX40

YEARS MFRD 2001-2005
SERIES..............GX SERIES
ENGINE .... YANMAR 3TNE88
CYLINDERS.................3
CID 100
ENGINE HP...............37.5
COOLING ....LIQUID
FUEL ....D
SPEEDS 12/12
TRANSMISSION .....POWER SHIFT
STEERING............STANDARD
HITCH ....CAT. I
HYDRAULIC ....YES
PTO ....YES
DRIVE TYPE 4WD
ROPS/CAB ....ROPS
WEIGHT ....3,351 LBS.
MSRP................ $18,684

OPTIONS

2WD
HYDRO
LDR
MID PTO

RETAIL PRICING

YEAR	HIGH	LOW
2001	$4,934	$3,701
2002	$5,428	$4,071
2003	$6,003	$4,502
2004	$6,580	$4,935
2005	$7,156	$5,367

GX40H

YEARS MFRD 2004-2005
SERIES..............GX SERIES
ENGINE .... YANMAR 3TNE88
CYLINDERS.................3
CID 100
ENGINE HP...............37.5
FUEL ....D
SPEEDS ....VARIABLE
TRANSMISSION ....HYDRO
STEERING............STANDARD
HITCH ....CAT. I
HYDRAULIC ....YES
PTO ....YES
DRIVE TYPE 2WD
ROPS/CAB ....ROPS
WEIGHT ....3,351 LBS.
MSRP................ $21,376

OPTIONS

4WD

RETAIL PRICING

YEAR	HIGH	LOW
2004	$8,167	$6,126
2005	$8,400	$6,300

GX45

YEARS MFRD 2004-2007
SERIES..............GX SERIES
ENGINE .... YANMAR 4TNE84
CYLINDERS.................4
CID 122
ENGINE HP.................44
FUEL ....D
SPEEDS 12/12
TRANSMISSION .....POWER SHIFT
STEERING............STANDARD
HITCH ....CAT. I
HYDRAULIC ....YES
PTO ....YES
DRIVE TYPE 4WD
ROPS/CAB ....ROPS
WEIGHT ....3,373 LBS.
MSRP................ $22,227

OPTIONS

2WD
HYDRO
LDR

RETAIL PRICING

YEAR	HIGH	LOW
2004	$8,591	$6,443
2005	$8,890	$6,668
2006	$9,470	$7,103
2007	$9,938	$7,453

GX50

YEARS MFRD 2001-2006
SERIES..............GX SERIES
ENGINE .... YANMAR 4TNE88
CYLINDERS.................4
CID 134
ENGINE HP...............49.5
FUEL ....D
SPEEDS 12/12
TRANSMISSION .....POWER SHIFT
STEERING............STANDARD
HITCH ....CAT. I
HYDRAULIC ....YES
PTO ....YES
DRIVE TYPE 4WD
ROPS/CAB ....ROPS
WEIGHT ....3,373 LBS.
MSRP................ $23,441

OPTIONS

2WD
HYDRO
LDR

RETAIL PRICING

YEAR	HIGH	LOW
2001	$5,721	$4,291
2002	$6,257	$4,693
2003	$6,794	$5,095
2004	$7,330	$5,498
2005	$7,956	$5,967
2006	$8,582	$6,436

X1.25

YEARS MFRD 2014-2020
CYLINDERS.................3
CID 1.2L
PTO HP 21
ENGINE HP.................24
FUEL ....D
SPEEDS 6/2
TRANSMISSION ....GEAR
STEERING............STANDARD
HITCH ....CAT. I
DRIVE TYPE 2WD
ROPS/CAB ....ROPS
WEIGHT ....1,810 LBS.

OPTIONS

60" DECK
HYDRO
LDR

RETAIL PRICING

YEAR	HIGH	LOW
2014	$9,095	$6,822
2015	$9,868	$7,402
2016	$10,813	$8,110
2017	$11,911	$8,933
2018	$12,807	$9,605
2019	$13,921	$10,441
2020	$14,433	$11,021

X1.35

YEARS MFRD 2014-2020
CYLINDERS.................3
CID 1.7L
PTO HP 29
ENGINE HP.................35
FUEL ....D
SPEEDS 12/12
TRANSMISSION ... SHUTTLE SHIFT
STEERING............STANDARD
HITCH ....CAT. I
WEIGHT ....4,053 LBS.

OPTIONS

LDR

RETAIL PRICING

YEAR	HIGH	LOW
2014	$12,700	$9,525
2015	$13,730	$10,297
2016	$14,760	$11,070
2017	$16,200	$12,151
2018	$17,382	$13,036
2019	$18,679	$14,008
2020	$19,587	$14,944

X1.37C

YEARS MFRD 2019-2020
ENGINE ....KUKJE
CYLINDERS.................4
CID 127.1
PTO HP 33
ENGINE HP.................37
FUEL ....D
SPEEDS 12/12
STEERING............STANDARD
HITCH ....CAT. I
DRIVE TYPE 4WD
ROPS/CAB ....CAB
WEIGHT ....4,211 LBS.

OPTIONS

HYDRO

X1.45

YEARS MFRD 2014-2020
CYLINDERS.................4
CID 2.3L
PTO HP 42
ENGINE HP.................47
FUEL ....D
SPEEDS 12/12
TRANSMISSION ... SHUTTLE SHIFT
STEERING............STANDARD
HITCH ....CAT. I
WEIGHT ....4,118 LBS.

OPTIONS

CAB
HYDRO CAB
LDR

RETAIL PRICING

YEAR	HIGH	LOW
2014	$16,734	$12,550
2015	$18,021	$13,515
2016	$19,395	$14,546
2017	$21,367	$16,025
2018	$22,955	$17,216
2019	$24,655	$18,491
2020	$25,591	$19,513

X1.55C

YEARS MFRD 2017-2020
CYLINDERS.................4
CID 2.3L
PTO HP 47
ENGINE HP.................55
COOLING ....LIQUID
FUEL ....D
SPEEDS ....VARIABLE
TRANSMISSION ....HYDRO
STEERING............STANDARD
HITCH ....CAT. I
DRIVE TYPE 2WD
ROPS/CAB ....CAB

OPTIONS

HYDRO
LDR

X10.25H

YEARS MFRD 2011-2013
ENGINE ....DAEDONG

CYLINDERS................3
PTO HP................16.2
ENGINE HP................22
COOLING................LIQUID
FUEL................D
SPEEDS................VARIABLE
TRANSMISSION................HYDRO
STEERING................STANDARD
HITCH................CAT. I
DRIVE TYPE................2WD
ROPS/CAB................ROPS
WEIGHT................2,138 LBS.
MSRP................$15,590

OPTIONS

1 HYD OUTLET
MID PTO

RETAIL PRICING

YEAR	HIGH	LOW
2011	$8,684	$6,513
2012	$9,482	$7,111
2013	$10,349	$7,762

X10.30H

YEARS MFRD................2011-2014
ENGINE................DAEDONG
CYLINDERS................3
PTO HP................21
ENGINE HP................28
COOLING................LIQUID
FUEL................D
SPEEDS................VARIABLE
TRANSMISSION................HYDRO
STEERING................STANDARD
HITCH................CAT. I
DRIVE TYPE................2WD
ROPS/CAB................ROPS
WEIGHT................3,117 LBS.
MSRP................$18,860

OPTIONS

1 HYD OUTLET
2 HYD OUTLET
MID PTO

RETAIL PRICING

YEAR	HIGH	LOW
2011	$10,783	$8,088
2012	$11,653	$8,739
2013	$12,594	$9,445
2014	$12,955	$9,716

X10.35H

YEARS MFRD................2011-2014
ENGINE................DAEDONG
CYLINDERS................3
PTO HP................27
ENGINE HP................34
COOLING................LIQUID
FUEL................D
SPEEDS................VARIABLE
TRANSMISSION................HYDRO
STEERING................STANDARD
HITCH................CAT. I
DRIVE TYPE................2WD
ROPS/CAB................ROPS
WEIGHT................3,114 LBS.
MSRP................$20,340

OPTIONS

1 HYD OUTLET
2 HYD OUTLET
MID PTO

RETAIL PRICING

YEAR	HIGH	LOW
2011	$10,977	$8,233
2012	$11,951	$8,964
2013	$12,923	$9,692
2014	$13,549	$10,162

X10.35M

YEARS MFRD................2011-2014
ENGINE................DAEDONG
CYLINDERS................3
PTO HP................28
ENGINE HP................34
COOLING................LIQUID
FUEL................D
SPEEDS................8/8
TRANSMISSION................SHUTTLE SHIFT
STEERING................STANDARD
HITCH................CAT. I
DRIVE TYPE................2WD
ROPS/CAB................ROPS
WEIGHT................3,151 LBS.
MSRP................$19,240

OPTIONS

1 HYD OUTLET
2 HYD OUTLET
MID PTO

RETAIL PRICING

YEAR	HIGH	LOW
2011	$10,283	$7,712
2012	$11,256	$8,442
2013	$12,229	$9,172
2014	$12,576	$9,432

X10.40H

YEARS MFRD................2011-2014
ENGINE................DAEDONG
CYLINDERS................4
PTO HP................33
ENGINE HP................41
COOLING................LIQUID
FUEL................D
SPEEDS................VARIABLE
TRANSMISSION................HYDRO
STEERING................STANDARD
HITCH................CAT. I
DRIVE TYPE................2WD
ROPS/CAB................ROPS
WEIGHT................3,950 LBS.
MSRP................$23,190

OPTIONS

2 HYD OUTLET
CAB
MID PTO

RETAIL PRICING

YEAR	HIGH	LOW
2011	$12,715	$9,536
2012	$13,757	$10,317
2013	$14,869	$11,152
2014	$15,494	$11,620

X10.40M

YEARS MFRD................2011-2014
ENGINE................DAEDONG
CYLINDERS................4
PTO HP................34
ENGINE HP................41
COOLING................LIQUID
FUEL................D
SPEEDS................12/12
TRANSMISSION................SHUTTLE SHIFT
STEERING................STANDARD
HITCH................CAT. I
DRIVE TYPE................2WD
ROPS/CAB................ROPS
WEIGHT................3,924 LBS.
MSRP................$22,090

OPTIONS

2 HYD OUTLET
CAB
MID PTO

RETAIL PRICING

YEAR	HIGH	LOW
2011	$12,020	$9,015
2012	$13,062	$9,797
2013	$14,174	$10,630
2014	$14,798	$11,099

X10.50

YEARS MFRD................2011-2014
ENGINE................DAEDONG
CYLINDERS................4
CID................148.59
PTO HP................41.7
ENGINE HP................49
COOLING................LIQUID
FUEL................D
SPEEDS................12/12
TRANSMISSION................SHUTTLE SHIFT
STEERING................STANDARD
DRIVE TYPE................2WD
ROPS/CAB................ROPS
MSRP................$25,670

OPTIONS

2 HYD
CAB
HYDRO
MID PTO

RETAIL PRICING

YEAR	HIGH	LOW
2011	$14,837	$11,128
2012	$15,994	$11,996
2013	$17,224	$12,918
2014	$18,022	$13,516

4630ARM

YEARS MFRD................2015-2016
ENGINE................YANMAR 3TNV76-XVA
CYLINDERS................3
PTO HP................16.7
ENGINE HP................23
COOLING................LIQUID
FUEL................D
SPEEDS................8/4
TRANSMISSION................GEAR
STEERING................STANDARD
HITCH................CAT. I
DRIVE TYPE................4WD
ROPS/CAB................ROPS

4630ISM

YEARS MFRD................2015-2016
ENGINE................YANMAR 3TNV76-XVA
CYLINDERS................3
PTO HP................16.7
ENGINE HP................23
COOLING................LIQUID
FUEL................D
SPEEDS................8/4
TRANSMISSION................GEAR
STEERING................STANDARD
HITCH................CAT. I
DRIVE TYPE................4WD
ROPS/CAB................ROPS

4645ARM

YEARS MFRD................2015-2016
ENGINE................YANMAR 3TNV88-BKVA
CYLINDERS................3
PTO HP................26
ENGINE HP................35.4
COOLING................LIQUID
FUEL................D
SPEEDS................8/4
TRANSMISSION................GEAR
STEERING................STANDARD
HITCH................CAT. I

4645ISM-VRM

YEARS MFRD................2015-2016
ENGINE................YANMAR
CYLINDERS................3
PTO HP................26
ENGINE HP................35.4
COOLING................LIQUID
FUEL................D
SPEEDS................8/4
TRANSMISSION................GEAR
STEERING................STANDARD
HITCH................CAT. I
DRIVE TYPE................4WD
ROPS/CAB................ROPS

4655ARM

YEARS MFRD................2015-2016
ENGINE................YANMAR 4TNV88-BKVA
CYLINDERS................4
PTO HP................34.8
ENGINE HP................47.3
COOLING................LIQUID
FUEL................D
SPEEDS................8/4
TRANSMISSION................GEAR
STEERING................STANDARD
HITCH................CAT. I
DRIVE TYPE................4WD
ROPS/CAB................ROPS

MC CORMICK

4655ISM-VRM

YEARS MFRD 2015-2016
ENGINE . . . YANMAR 4TNV88-BKVA
CYLINDERS. 4
PTO HP 34.8
ENGINE HP 47.3
COOLING . . . . LIQUID
FUEL . . . . D
SPEEDS 8/4
TRANSMISSION . . . . GEAR
STEERING. . . . . STANDARD
HITCH . . . . CAT. I
DRIVE TYPE 4WD
ROPS/CAB . . . . ROPS

MONTANA

MZT 2548

YEARS MFRD 2005-2010
SERIES. . . . . MZT SERIES
ENGINE . . . . B&S INTEK
ENGINE HP 25
COOLING . . . . AIR
FUEL . . . . G
SPEEDS . . . . VARIABLE
TRANSMISSION . . . . HYDRO
STEERING. . . . . ZERO

MZT 2560

YEARS MFRD 2005-2010
SERIES. . . . . MZT SERIES
ENGINE . . . . B&S
CYLINDERS. 2
ENGINE HP 25
COOLING . . . . AIR
FUEL . . . . G
SPEEDS . . . . VARIABLE
TRANSMISSION . . . . HYDRO
STEERING. . . . . ZERO

MZT 2636P

YEARS MFRD 2008-2010
ENGINE . . . . B&S INTEK ELS
CYLINDERS. 2
ENGINE HP 26
COOLING . . . . AIR
FUEL . . . . G
SPEEDS . . . . VARIABLE
TRANSMISSION . . . . HYDRO
STEERING. . . . . ZERO
BLADE CLUTCH . . . . ELECTRIC

MZT 2648A

YEARS MFRD 2008-2010
ENGINE . . . . B&S
CYLINDERS. 2
ENGINE HP 27
COOLING . . . . AIR
FUEL . . . . G
SPEEDS . . . . VARIABLE
TRANSMISSION . . . . HYDRO
STEERING. . . . . STANDARD
BLADE CLUTCH . . . . ELECTRIC

MZT 2650P

YEARS MFRD 2008-2010
ENGINE . . . . B&S INTEK ELS
CYLINDERS. 2
ENGINE HP 26
COOLING . . . . AIR
FUEL . . . . G
SPEEDS . . . . VARIABLE
TRANSMISSION . . . . HYDRO
STEERING. . . . . ZERO
BLADE CLUTCH . . . . ELECTRIC

MZT 2660

YEARS MFRD 2005-2010
SERIES. . . . . MZT SERIES
ENGINE . . . . KAWASAKI
CYLINDERS. 2
ENGINE HP 26
COOLING . . . . LIQUID
FUEL . . . . G
SPEEDS . . . . VARIABLE
TRANSMISSION . . . . HYDRO
STEERING. . . . . ZERO

MZT 2660A

YEARS MFRD 2008-2010
ENGINE . . . . B&S
CYLINDERS. 2
ENGINE HP 27
COOLING . . . . AIR
FUEL . . . . G
SPEEDS . . . . VARIABLE
TRANSMISSION . . . . HYDRO
STEERING. . . . . ZERO
BLADE CLUTCH . . . . ELECTRIC

MZT 2660P

YEARS MFRD 2008-2010
ENGINE . . . . B&S INTEK ELS
CYLINDERS. 2
ENGINE HP 26
COOLING . . . . AIR
FUEL . . . . G
SPEEDS . . . . VARIABLE
TRANSMISSION . . . . HYDRO
STEERING. . . . . ZERO
BLADE CLUTCH . . . . ELECTRIC

MZT 2672

YEARS MFRD 2005-2010
SERIES. . . . . MZT SERIES
ENGINE . . . . KAWASAKI
CYLINDERS. 2
ENGINE HP 26
COOLING . . . . LIQUID
FUEL . . . . G
SPEEDS . . . . VARIABLE
TRANSMISSION . . . . HYDRO
STEERING. . . . . ZERO

MZT 2860

YEARS MFRD 2005-2010
SERIES. . . . . MZT SERIES
ENGINE . . . . CAT
CYLINDERS. 3
ENGINE HP 28
COOLING . . . . LIQUID
FUEL . . . . D
SPEEDS . . . . VARIABLE
TRANSMISSION . . . . HYDRO
STEERING. . . . . ZERO

MZT 3560

YEARS MFRD 2005-2006
SERIES. . . . . MZT SERIES
ENGINE . . . . VANGUARD
CYLINDERS. 2
ENGINE HP 35
COOLING . . . . AIR
FUEL . . . . G
SPEEDS . . . . VARIABLE
TRANSMISSION . . . . HYDRO
STEERING. . . . . ZERO

MZT 3572

YEARS MFRD 2005-2006
SERIES. . . . . MZT SERIES
ENGINE . . . . VANGUARD
CYLINDERS. 2
ENGINE HP 35
COOLING . . . . AIR
FUEL . . . . G
SPEEDS . . . . VARIABLE
TRANSMISSION . . . . HYDRO
STEERING. . . . . ZERO

R2844

YEARS MFRD 2008-2009
SERIES. . . . . R SERIES
ENGINE S4L
CYLINDERS. 4
CID 91.5
PTO HP 23
ENGINE HP 28
COOLING . . . . LIQUID
FUEL . . . . G
SPEEDS 12/12
TRANSMISSION . . . SHUTTLE SHIFT
STEERING. . . . . STANDARD
HITCH . . . . CAT. I
HYDRAULIC . . . . YES
PTO . . . . YES
WEIGHT . . . . 2,645 LBS.

R3644

YEARS MFRD 2008-2009
SERIES. . . . . R SERIES
ENGINE 54L2
CYLINDERS. 4
CID 107.3
PTO HP 31
ENGINE HP 38.5
COOLING . . . . LIQUID
FUEL . . . . G
SPEEDS 12/12
TRANSMISSION . . . SHUTTLE SHIFT
STEERING. . . . . STANDARD
HITCH . . . . CAT. I
HYDRAULIC . . . . YES
PTO . . . . YES
WEIGHT . . . . 2,712 LBS.

R3644HST

YEARS MFRD 2008-2008
SERIES. . . . . R SERIES
ENGINE 54L2
CYLINDERS. 4
CID 107
PTO HP 29
ENGINE HP 38.5
COOLING . . . . LIQUID
FUEL . . . . G
SPEEDS . . . . VARIABLE
TRANSMISSION . . . . HYDRO
STEERING. . . . . STANDARD
HITCH . . . . CAT. I
HYDRAULIC . . . . YES
PTO . . . . YES
WEIGHT . . . . 2,712 LBS.

R4344

YEARS MFRD 2008-2009
SERIES. . . . . R SERIES
ENGINE S4QS
CYLINDERS. 4
CID 141
PTO HP 36
ENGINE HP 41
COOLING . . . . LIQUID
FUEL . . . . G
SPEEDS 16/16
TRANSMISSION . . . SHUTTLE SHIFT
STEERING. . . . . STANDARD
HYDRAULIC . . . . YES
PTO . . . . YES
WEIGHT . . . . 3,582 LBS.

T300DTC

YEARS MFRD 2009-2011
ENGINE . . . . MITSUBISHI
CYLINDERS. 4
CID 91.5
PTO HP 26
ENGINE HP 30
COOLING . . . . LIQUID
FUEL . . . . D
SPEEDS 12/12
TRANSMISSION . . . SHUTTLE SHIFT
STEERING. . . . . STANDARD
HYDRAULIC . . . . YES
PTO . . . . YES
WEIGHT . . . . 3,050 LBS.

T2334

YEARS MFRD	2007-2008
SERIES	30 SERIES
ENGINE	MITSUBISHI
CYLINDERS	3
ENGINE HP	23
FUEL	D
SPEEDS	VARIABLE
TRANSMISSION	HYDRO
STEERING	STANDARD
HITCH	CAT. I
HYDRAULIC	YES
PTO	YES
WEIGHT	1,984 LBS.
MSRP	$12,187

RETAIL PRICING

YEAR	HIGH	LOW
2008	$7,481	$5,610

T2734

YEARS MFRD	2007-2008
SERIES	30 SERIES
ENGINE	MITSUBISHI S3L2
CYLINDERS	3
ENGINE HP	27
FUEL	D
SPEEDS	VARIABLE
TRANSMISSION	HYDRO
STEERING	STANDARD
HITCH	CAT. I
HYDRAULIC	YES
PTO	YES
WEIGHT	1,984 LBS.
MSRP	$14,375

RETAIL PRICING

YEAR	HIGH	LOW
2007	$7,290	$5,467
2008	$8,824	$6,618

U4384

YEARS MFRD	2009-2009
ENGINE	LS S4QS
CYLINDERS	4
ENGINE HP	41
COOLING	LIQUID
FUEL	D
SPEEDS	16/16
TRANSMISSION	SHUTTLE SHIFT
STEERING	STANDARD
HYDRAULIC	YES
PTO	YES
WEIGHT	4,442 LBS.

U4384C

YEARS MFRD	2009-2009
ENGINE	LS S4QS
CYLINDERS	4
ENGINE HP	41
COOLING	LIQUID
FUEL	D
SPEEDS	16/16
TRANSMISSION	SHUTTLE SHIFT
STEERING	STANDARD
HYDRAULIC	YES
PTO	YES
WEIGHT	5,004 LBS.

270DTC

YEARS MFRD	2010-2011
ENGINE	MITSUBISHI
CYLINDERS	3
CID	85
PTO HP	23.8
ENGINE HP	27
COOLING	LIQUID
FUEL	D
SPEEDS	8/8
TRANSMISSION	SHUTTLE SHIFT
STEERING	STANDARD
HITCH	CAT. I
HYDRAULIC	YES
PTO	YES

320DTC

YEARS MFRD	2010-2011
ENGINE	MITSUBISHI
CYLINDERS	3
CID	100.5
PTO HP	28.5
ENGINE HP	32
COOLING	LIQUID
FUEL	D
SPEEDS	8/8
TRANSMISSION	SHUTTLE SHIFT
STEERING	STANDARD
HITCH	CAT. I

435

YEARS MFRD	2010-2011
ENGINE	MITSUBISHI
CYLINDERS	3
CID	131
PTO HP	31
ENGINE HP	35
COOLING	LIQUID
FUEL	D
SPEEDS	8/2
TRANSMISSION	GEAR
STEERING	STANDARD
HITCH	CAT. I
HYDRAULIC	YES
PTO	YES
WEIGHT	4,220 LBS.

535

YEARS MFRD	2010-2011
ENGINE	MITSUBISHI
CYLINDERS	3
CID	131
PTO HP	30
ENGINE HP	35
COOLING	LIQUID
FUEL	D
SPEEDS	8/2
TRANSMISSION	GEAR
STEERING	STANDARD
HITCH	CAT. I
HYDRAULIC	YES
PTO	YES
WEIGHT	4,220 LBS.

545/545DTC

YEARS MFRD	2010-2011
ENGINE	MITSUBISHI
CYLINDERS	3
CID	175
PTO HP	37
ENGINE HP	42
COOLING	LIQUID
FUEL	D
SPEEDS	8/2
TRANSMISSION	GEAR
STEERING	STANDARD
HITCH	CAT. I
HYDRAULIC	YES
PTO	YES
DRIVE TYPE	2WD
ROPS/CAB	ROPS
WEIGHT	4,160 LBS.

OPTIONS

4WD

555DTC

YEARS MFRD	2005-2009
CYLINDERS	3
CID	192
PTO HP	44.7
ENGINE HP	50
COOLING	LIQUID
FUEL	D
SPEEDS	8/2
TRANSMISSION	GEAR
STEERING	STANDARD
HITCH	CAT. I
HYDRAULIC	YES
PTO	YES
DRIVE TYPE	2WD
ROPS/CAB	ROPS
WEIGHT	4,950 LBS.

OPTIONS

4WD

2740

YEARS MFRD	2007-2008
ENGINE	DAEDONG
CYLINDERS	3
CID	85.43
ENGINE HP	27
COOLING	LIQUID
FUEL	D
SPEEDS	8/8
TRANSMISSION	SHUTTLE SHIFT
STEERING	STANDARD
HITCH	CAT. I
HYDRAULIC	YES
PTO	YES
WEIGHT	2,600 LBS.
MSRP	$12,487

RETAIL PRICING

YEAR	HIGH	LOW
2007	$7,016	$5,262
2008	$7,664	$5,748

2840

YEARS MFRD	2008-2010
ENGINE	DAEDONG S4L
CYLINDERS	4
CID	91.5
PTO HP	23.8
ENGINE HP	28
COOLING	LIQUID
FUEL	D
SPEEDS	8/8
TRANSMISSION	SHUTTLE SHIFT
STEERING	STANDARD
HITCH	CAT. I
HYDRAULIC	YES
PTO	YES
WEIGHT	2,600 LBS.

3040

YEARS MFRD	2007-2009
ENGINE	MITSUBISHI S4L
CYLINDERS	4
CID	91
ENGINE HP	30
COOLING	LIQUID
FUEL	D
SPEEDS	12/12
TRANSMISSION	SHUTTLE SHIFT
STEERING	STANDARD
HITCH	CAT. I
HYDRAULIC	YES
PTO	YES
WEIGHT	3,418 LBS.
MSRP	$14,789

RETAIL PRICING

YEAR	HIGH	LOW
2007	$8,156	$6,117
2008	$8,248	$6,186
2009	$8,294	$6,221

3130DT/3130DTH

YEARS MFRD	2010-2011
ENGINE	MITSUBISHI
CYLINDERS	4
CID	91.5
PTO HP	23
ENGINE HP	28
COOLING	LIQUID
FUEL	D
SPEEDS	12/12
TRANSMISSION	SHUTTLE SHIFT
STEERING	STANDARD
HITCH	CAT. I
HYDRAULIC	YES
PTO	YES
WEIGHT	2,811 LBS.

OPTIONS

HYDRO

3140DT/3140

YEARS MFRD	2010-2011
ENGINE	MITSUBISHI
CYLINDERS	4
CID	107.3

PTO HP 31
ENGINE HP 38.5
COOLING ..... LIQUID
FUEL ..... D
SPEEDS 12/12
TRANSMISSION ... SHUTTLE SHIFT
STEERING ..... STANDARD
HITCH ..... CAT. I
HYDRAULIC ..... YES
PTO ..... YES
WEIGHT ..... 2,855 LBS.

OPTIONS

HYDRO

3240

YEARS MFRD 2007-2008
ENGINE ..... DAEDONG 3A165LG-2
CYLINDERS 3
CID 103
ENGINE HP 32
COOLING ..... LIQUID
FUEL ..... D
SPEEDS 8/8
TRANSMISSION ... SHUTTLE SHIFT
STEERING ..... STANDARD
HITCH ..... CAT. I
HYDRAULIC ..... YES
PTO ..... YES
WEIGHT ..... 2,659 LBS.
MSRP $13,618

RETAIL PRICING

YEAR	HIGH	LOW
2007	$7,651	$5,739
2008	$8,359	$6,270

3440

YEARS MFRD 2007-2008
ENGINE ..... DAEDONG 3A165LG
CYLINDERS 3
CID 103
ENGINE HP 34
COOLING ..... LIQUID
FUEL ..... D
SPEEDS ..... VARIABLE
TRANSMISSION ..... HYDRO
STEERING ..... STANDARD
HITCH ..... CAT. I
HYDRAULIC ..... YES
PTO ..... YES
WEIGHT ..... 2,696 LBS.
MSRP $16,852

RETAIL PRICING

YEAR	HIGH	LOW
2007	$9,469	$7,102
2008	$10,343	$7,757

3840

YEARS MFRD 2007-2008
ENGINE ..... MITSUBISHI
CYLINDERS 4
CID 109
ENGINE HP 38
COOLING ..... LIQUID
FUEL ..... D
SPEEDS 12/12
TRANSMISSION ..... HYDRO
STEERING ..... STANDARD
HITCH ..... CAT. I
HYDRAULIC ..... YES
PTO ..... YES
WEIGHT ..... 3,418 LBS.
MSRP $15,972

RETAIL PRICING

YEAR	HIGH	LOW
2007	$8,974	$6,731
2008	$9,804	$7,353

3940

YEARS MFRD 2005-2008
ENGINE ..... MITSUBISHI S4L2
CYLINDERS 4
ENGINE HP 39
COOLING ..... LIQUID
FUEL ..... D
SPEEDS ..... VARIABLE
TRANSMISSION ..... HYDRO
STEERING ..... STANDARD
HITCH ..... CAT. I
HYDRAULIC ..... YES
PTO ..... YES
WEIGHT ..... 2,955 LBS.
MSRP $18,083

RETAIL PRICING

YEAR	HIGH	LOW
2007	$10,160	$7,620
2008	$11,099	$8,324

4320

YEARS MFRD 2005-2006
ENGINE ..... MITSUBISHI
CYLINDERS 4
CID 141.03
ENGINE HP 43
COOLING ..... LIQUID
FUEL ..... D
SPEEDS 16/16
TRANSMISSION ... SHUTTLE SHIFT
STEERING ..... STANDARD
HITCH ..... CAT. I
HYDRAULIC ..... YES
PTO ..... YES
WEIGHT ..... 5,063 LBS.

4340C

YEARS MFRD 2006-2009
ENGINE ..... MITSUBISHI S4QS
CYLINDERS 4
CID 141.35
ENGINE HP 45
COOLING ..... LIQUID
FUEL ..... G
SPEEDS 12/12
TRANSMISSION ... SHUTTLE SHIFT
STEERING ..... STANDARD
HITCH ..... CAT. I
HYDRAULIC ..... YES
PTO ..... YES
WEIGHT ..... 3,815 LBS.

4540

YEARS MFRD 2005-2010
ENGINE ..... MITSUBISHI S4QS
CYLINDERS 4
CID 141
ENGINE HP 45
COOLING ..... LIQUID
FUEL ..... D
SPEEDS 12/12
TRANSMISSION ..... POWER SHIFT
STEERING ..... STANDARD
HITCH ..... CAT. I
HYDRAULIC ..... YES
PTO ..... YES
WEIGHT ..... 3,815 LBS.

4920C

YEARS MFRD 2009-2009
ENGINE ..... MITSUBISHI S4QL
CYLINDERS 4
ENGINE HP 49
COOLING ..... LIQUID
FUEL ..... D
SPEEDS 16/16
TRANSMISSION ... SHUTTLE SHIFT
STEERING ..... STANDARD
HYDRAULIC ..... YES
PTO ..... YES
WEIGHT ..... 5,202 LBS.

4940

YEARS MFRD 2009-2009
ENGINE ..... MITSUBISHI S4QL
CYLINDERS 4
ENGINE HP 49
COOLING ..... LIQUID
FUEL ..... D
SPEEDS 16/16
TRANSMISSION ... SHUTTLE SHIFT
STEERING ..... STANDARD
HYDRAULIC ..... YES
PTO ..... YES
WEIGHT ..... 4,321 LBS.

4940C

YEARS MFRD 2009-2009
ENGINE ..... MITSUBISHI S4QL
CYLINDERS 4
ENGINE HP 49
COOLING ..... LIQUID
FUEL ..... D
SPEEDS 16/16
TRANSMISSION ... SHUTTLE SHIFT
STEERING ..... STANDARD
HYDRAULIC ..... YES
PTO ..... YES
WEIGHT ..... 5,202 LBS.

MTD YARD MACHINES

BH660F

YEARS MFRD 2002-2002
ENGINE ..... B&S
ENGINE HP 13
COOLING ..... AIR
FUEL ..... G
TRANSMISSION ..... GEAR
STEERING ..... STANDARD
STANDARD DECK ..... 38"
MSRP $1,099

RETAIL PRICING

YEAR	HIGH	LOW
2002	$552	$414

C650F

YEARS MFRD 2004-2004
ENGINE ..... B&S
ENGINE HP 13
COOLING ..... AIR
FUEL ..... G
SPEEDS 5
TRANSMISSION ..... GEAR
STEERING ..... STANDARD
BLADE CLUTCH ..... MANUAL

E451F

YEARS MFRD 1997-1998
SERIES ..... 400 SERIES
ENGINE ..... TECUMSEH
ENGINE HP 12.5
COOLING ..... AIR
FUEL ..... G
TRANSMISSION ..... GEAR
STEERING ..... STANDARD
STANDARD DECK ..... 38"
MSRP $899

RETAIL PRICING

YEAR	HIGH	LOW
1997	$360	$270
1998	$378	$284

F673G

YEARS MFRD 2002-2002
ENGINE ..... B&S
ENGINE HP 16.5
FUEL ..... G
TRANSMISSION ..... GEAR
STEERING ..... STANDARD
STANDARD DECK ..... 42"
MSRP $1,299

RETAIL PRICING

YEAR	HIGH	LOW
2002	$655	$491

F695G

YEARS MFRD	2002-2002
ENGINE	B&S
ENGINE HP	16.5
FUEL	G
TRANSMISSION	HYDRO
STEERING	STANDARD
STANDARD DECK	42"
MSRP	$1,399

RETAIL PRICING

YEAR	HIGH	LOW
2002	$705	$528

G688H722

YEARS MFRD	2004-2004
SERIES	YARD TRACTOR SERIES
ENGINE	B&S INTEK
CYLINDERS	2
ENGINE HP	22
FUEL	G
SPEEDS	8/1
TRANSMISSION	HYDRO
STEERING	STANDARD

H660F

YEARS MFRD	2000-2003
ENGINE	B&S
ENGINE HP	12.5
COOLING	AIR
FUEL	G
TRANSMISSION	GEAR
STEERING	STANDARD
STANDARD DECK	38"
MSRP	$999

RETAIL PRICING

YEAR	HIGH	LOW
2000	$469	$352
2001	$491	$368
2002	$504	$378
2003	$545	$409

H661F

YEARS MFRD	1997-1998
SERIES	600 SERIES
ENGINE	B&S
ENGINE HP	12.5
COOLING	AIR
FUEL	G
TRANSMISSION	GEAR
STEERING	STANDARD
STANDARD DECK	38"
MSRP	$949

RETAIL PRICING

YEAR	HIGH	LOW
1997	$380	$285
1998	$399	$299

L450C

YEARS MFRD	1997-1997
ENGINE	B&S
ENGINE HP	12.5
COOLING	AIR
FUEL	G
TRANSMISSION	GEAR
STEERING	STANDARD
STANDARD DECK	30"
MSRP	$1,399

RETAIL PRICING

YEAR	HIGH	LOW
1997	$560	$420

L660F

YEARS MFRD	1997-1997
ENGINE	B7S
ENGINE HP	12.5
COOLING	AIR
FUEL	G
TRANSMISSION	GEAR
STEERING	STANDARD
STANDARD DECK	38"
MSRP	$1,099

RETAIL PRICING

YEAR	HIGH	LOW
1997	$440	$330

L670G

YEARS MFRD	2002-2002
ENGINE	B&S
ENGINE HP	15.5
FUEL	G
TRANSMISSION	GEAR
STEERING	STANDARD
STANDARD DECK	42"
MSRP	$1,199

RETAIL PRICING

YEAR	HIGH	LOW
2002	$605	$453

M660F

YEARS MFRD	2003-2004
ENGINE	B&S
ENGINE HP	15
COOLING	AIR
FUEL	G
SPEEDS	6/1
TRANSMISSION	GEAR
STEERING	STANDARD
BLADE CLUTCH	MANUAL
STANDARD DECK	38"
MSRP	$1,099

RETAIL PRICING

YEAR	HIGH	LOW
2003	$601	$451
2004	$639	$479

M660G

YEARS MFRD	2004-2004
SERIES	LAWN TRACTOR SERIES
ENGINE	B&S
ENGINE HP	15
FUEL	G
SPEEDS	6
STEERING	STANDARD
BLADE CLUTCH	MANUAL

M675G

YEARS MFRD	2000-2002
ENGINE	B&S
ENGINE HP	14.5
FUEL	G
TRANSMISSION	GEAR
STEERING	STANDARD
STANDARD DECK	42"
MSRP	$1,099

RETAIL PRICING

YEAR	HIGH	LOW
2000	$516	$387
2001	$539	$404
2002	$552	$414

M685G

YEARS MFRD	2003-2004
SERIES	LAWN TRACTOR SERIES
ENGINE	B&S
ENGINE HP	14.5
FUEL	G
SPEEDS	8/1
TRANSMISSION	GEAR
STEERING	STANDARD
BLADE CLUTCH	MANUAL
STANDARD DECK	42"
MSRP	$1,099

RETAIL PRICING

YEAR	HIGH	LOW
2003	$601	$451
2004	$639	$479

N665G

YEARS MFRD	2003-2003
ENGINE	B&S
ENGINE HP	16
COOLING	AIR
FUEL	G
TRANSMISSION	GEAR
STEERING	STANDARD
STANDARD DECK	42"
MSRP	$1,199

RETAIL PRICING

YEAR	HIGH	LOW
2003	$655	$491

Q507N

YEARS MFRD	2003-2003
ENGINE	B&S
ENGINE HP	18
FUEL	G
TRANSMISSION	HYDRO
STEERING	STANDARD
STANDARD DECK	41"
MSRP	$2,099

RETAIL PRICING

YEAR	HIGH	LOW
2003	$1,148	$861

Q807H

YEARS MFRD	2003-2003
ENGINE	B&S
ENGINE HP	18.5
FUEL	G
SPEEDS	VARIABLE
TRANSMISSION	HYDRO
STEERING	STANDARD
STANDARD DECK	46"
MSRP	$1,999

RETAIL PRICING

YEAR	HIGH	LOW
2003	$1,093	$820

S845H

YEARS MFRD	2002-2002
ENGINE	B&S
ENGINE HP	18.5
FUEL	G
TRANSMISSION	GEAR
STEERING	STANDARD
STANDARD DECK	46"
MSRP	$1,999

RETAIL PRICING

YEAR	HIGH	LOW
2002	$1,007	$756

T808H722

YEARS MFRD	2004-2004
SERIES	GARDEN TRACTOR SERIES
ENGINE	B&S INTEK V-TWIN
ENGINE HP	22
COOLING	AIR
FUEL	G
SPEEDS	VARIABLE
TRANSMISSION	HYDRO
STEERING	STANDARD
BLADE CLUTCH	MANUAL

13A2775S000

YEARS MFRD	2015-2017
ENGINE	POWERMORE OHV
CYLINDERS	1
CID	420CC
COOLING	AIR
FUEL	G
SPEEDS	7/1
TRANSMISSION	GEAR
STEERING	STANDARD
STANDARD DECK	42"
MSRP	$1,199

RETAIL PRICING

YEAR	HIGH	LOW
2015	$662	$496
2016	$793	$595
2017	$911	$684

13A2775S029

YEARS MFRD	2018-2018
ENGINE	OHV
CYLINDERS	1
CID	420CC
FUEL	G
SPEEDS	7/1
TRANSMISSION	GEAR
STEERING	STANDARD
STANDARD DECK	42"

MTD YARD MACHINES

13A326JC700
YEARS MFRD 2015-2017
ENGINE .... B&S
CYLINDERS 1
CID 190CC
COOLING .... AIR
FUEL .... G
SPEEDS 6/1
TRANSMISSION .... GEAR
STEERING .... STANDARD
STANDARD DECK .... 24"
MSRP $859

RETAIL PRICING

YEAR	HIGH	LOW
2015	$427	$320
2016	$546	$409
2017	$591	$443

13A6665H
YEARS MFRD 1998-1998
ENGINE .... B&S
ENGINE HP 17
FUEL .... G
TRANSMISSION .... GEAR
STEERING .... STANDARD
STANDARD DECK .... 46"
MSRP $1,399

RETAIL PRICING

YEAR	HIGH	LOW
1998	$588	$441

13A6695H
YEARS MFRD 1999-1999
ENGINE .... TECUMSEH
ENGINE HP 17.5
FUEL .... G
TRANSMISSION .... HYDRO
STEERING .... STANDARD
STANDARD DECK .... 46"
MSRP $1,500

RETAIL PRICING

YEAR	HIGH	LOW
1999	$673	$505

13A726JD029
YEARS MFRD 2018-2018
ENGINE .... OHV
CYLINDERS 1
CID 382CC
FUEL .... G
SPEEDS 6/1
TRANSMISSION .... GEAR
STEERING .... STANDARD

13AB775S000
YEARS MFRD 2019-2020
ENGINE .... POWERMORE OHV
CYLINDERS 1
CID 439CC
FUEL .... G
SPEEDS 7/1
TRANSMISSION .... GEAR
STEERING .... STANDARD
STANDARD DECK .... 42"

13AC26JD000
YEARS MFRD 2017-2017
ENGINE .... B&S
CID 344CC
ENGINE HP 10.5
FUEL .... G
SPEEDS 6/1
STEERING .... STANDARD
STANDARD DECK .... 30"

13AC762F000
YEARS MFRD 2011-2016
ENGINE .... B&S
ENGINE HP 12.5
COOLING .... AIR
FUEL .... G
SPEEDS 6/1
TRANSMISSION .... GEAR
STEERING .... STANDARD
BLADE CLUTCH .... MANUAL
STANDARD DECK .... 38"
MSRP $999

RETAIL PRICING

YEAR	HIGH	LOW
2011	$210	$157
2012	$305	$229
2013	$382	$287
2014	$462	$346
2015	$560	$420
2016	$688	$516

13AC762F020
YEARS MFRD 2011-2012
ENGINE .... B&S
ENGINE HP 13.5
COOLING .... AIR
FUEL .... G
SPEEDS 6/1
TRANSMISSION .... GEAR
STEERING .... STANDARD
BLADE CLUTCH .... MANUAL
STANDARD DECK .... 38"
MSRP $899

RETAIL PRICING

YEAR	HIGH	LOW
2011	$343	$257
2012	$408	$306

13AG695G
YEARS MFRD 1997-1997
ENGINE .... TECUMSEH
ENGINE HP 16
FUEL .... G
TRANSMISSION .... HYDRO
STEERING .... STANDARD
STANDARD DECK .... 42"
MSRP $1,299

RETAIL PRICING

YEAR	HIGH	LOW
1997	$519	$390

13AL795S004
YEARS MFRD 2016-2016
ENGINE .... B&S
ENGINE HP 19
COOLING .... AIR
FUEL .... G
SPEEDS .... VARIABLE
TRANSMISSION .... HYDRO
STEERING .... STANDARD
STANDARD DECK .... 42"
MSRP $1,299

RETAIL PRICING

YEAR	HIGH	LOW
2016	$883	$662

13AM772S000
YEARS MFRD 2011-2014
ENGINE .... B&S
ENGINE HP 14.5
COOLING .... AIR
FUEL .... G
SPEEDS 7/1
TRANSMISSION .... GEAR
STEERING .... STANDARD
BLADE CLUTCH .... MANUAL
STANDARD DECK .... 42"
MSRP $1,049

RETAIL PRICING

YEAR	HIGH	LOW
2011	$303	$227
2012	$401	$301
2013	$475	$356
2014	$597	$448

13AM775S000
YEARS MFRD 2015-2018
ENGINE .... B&S OHV
CYLINDERS 1
ENGINE HP 15.5
COOLING .... AIR
FUEL .... G
SPEEDS 7/1
TRANSMISSION .... GEAR
STEERING .... STANDARD
STANDARD DECK .... 42"
MSRP $1,099

RETAIL PRICING

YEAR	HIGH	LOW
2015	$539	$404
2016	$761	$571
2017	$817	$613
2018	$874	$656

13AN695G
YEARS MFRD 1998-2003
SERIES .... 600 SERIES
ENGINE .... B&S
ENGINE HP 16.5
COOLING .... AIR
FUEL .... G
TRANSMISSION .... HYDRO
STEERING .... STANDARD
STANDARD DECK .... 42"
MSRP $1,399

RETAIL PRICING

YEAR	HIGH	LOW
1998	$588	$441
1999	$627	$470
2000	$657	$492
2001	$703	$527
2002	$714	$536
2003	$764	$573

13AN775S000
YEARS MFRD 2013-2014
ENGINE .... B&S
ENGINE HP 16.5
COOLING .... AIR
FUEL .... G
SPEEDS 7/1
TRANSMISSION .... GEAR
STEERING .... STANDARD
BLADE CLUTCH .... MANUAL
STANDARD DECK .... 42"
MSRP $1,099

RETAIL PRICING

YEAR	HIGH	LOW
2013	$499	$374
2014	$597	$448

13AN775S200
YEARS MFRD 2017-2017
ENGINE .... B&S INTEX
ENGINE HP 16.5
COOLING .... AIR
FUEL .... G
SPEEDS 7/1
TRANSMISSION .... GEAR
STEERING .... STANDARD
BLADE CLUTCH .... MANUAL
STANDARD DECK .... 42"

13AQ607H
YEARS MFRD 2000-2003
ENGINE .... B&S
ENGINE HP 18
FUEL .... G
TRANSMISSION .... HYDRO
STEERING .... STANDARD
STANDARD DECK .... 46"
MSRP $1,699

RETAIL PRICING

YEAR	HIGH	LOW
2000	$704	$528
2001	$784	$588
2002	$856	$642
2003	$928	$696

13AQ665H
YEARS MFRD 1997-1997
ENGINE .... B&S
ENGINE HP 18
FUEL .... G
TRANSMISSION .... GEAR
STEERING .... STANDARD
STANDARD DECK .... 46"
MSRP $1,499

RETAIL PRICING

YEAR	HIGH	LOW
1997	$601	$451

13AX795S004

YEARS MFRD 2015-2017
ENGINE .... KOHLER COURAGE
CYLINDERS 1
ENGINE HP 20
FUEL .... G
SPEEDS .... VARIABLE
TRANSMISSION .... HYDRO
STEERING .... STANDARD
STANDARD DECK .... 42"
MSRP $1,399

RETAIL PRICING

YEAR	HIGH	LOW
2015	$811	$609
2016	$980	$735
2017	$1,093	$820

13B2775S000

YEARS MFRD 2016-2017
ENGINE .... POWERMORE OHV
CYLINDERS 1
CID 420CC
COOLING .... AIR
FUEL .... G
SPEEDS 7/1
TRANSMISSION .... GEAR
STEERING .... STANDARD
STANDARD DECK .... 42"
MSRP $1,099

RETAIL PRICING

YEAR	HIGH	LOW
2016	$735	$551

13BC762F000

YEARS MFRD 2015-2017
ENGINE .... B&S
CYLINDERS 1
ENGINE HP 10.5
COOLING .... AIR
FUEL .... G
SPEEDS 6/1
TRANSMISSION .... GEAR
STEERING .... STANDARD
STANDARD DECK .... 38"
MSRP $999

RETAIL PRICING

YEAR	HIGH	LOW
2015	$560	$420
2016	$704	$528

13C2775S000

YEARS MFRD 2018-2019
ENGINE .... POWERMORE OHV
CYLINDERS 1
CID 420CC
FUEL .... G
SPEEDS 7/1
TRANSMISSION .... GEAR
STEERING .... STANDARD
BLADE CLUTCH .... MANUAL
STANDARD DECK .... 42"

14AJ825P

YEARS MFRD 1998-1998
ENGINE .... B&S
ENGINE HP 20
FUEL .... G
TRANSMISSION .... GEAR
STEERING .... STANDARD
STANDARD DECK .... 50"
MSRP $1,899

RETAIL PRICING

YEAR	HIGH	LOW
1998	$798	$598

14AS825H

YEARS MFRD 1997-2001
ENGINE .... B&S
ENGINE HP 18.5
FUEL .... G
TRANSMISSION .... GEAR
STEERING .... STANDARD
STANDARD DECK .... 46"
MSRP $1,899

RETAIL PRICING

YEAR	HIGH	LOW
1997	$720	$540
1998	$757	$567
1999	$852	$639
2000	$872	$654
2001	$999	$749

17AF2ACK004 RZT

YEARS MFRD 2011-2011
ENGINE .... KOHLER
ENGINE HP 22
COOLING .... AIR
FUEL .... G
SPEEDS .... VARIABLE
TRANSMISSION .... HYDRO
STEERING .... ZERO
STANDARD DECK .... 54"
MSRP $3,199

RETAIL PRICING

YEAR	HIGH	LOW
2011	$1,210	$908

17AF2ACP004 RZT

YEARS MFRD 2011-2011
ENGINE .... KOHLER
ENGINE HP 22
COOLING .... AIR
FUEL .... G
SPEEDS .... VARIABLE
TRANSMISSION .... HYDRO
STEERING .... ZERO
STANDARD DECK .... 50"
MSRP $2,899

RETAIL PRICING

YEAR	HIGH	LOW
2011	$1,101	$825

17AF2ACS004 RZT

YEARS MFRD 2011-2011
ENGINE .... KOHLER
ENGINE HP 22
COOLING .... AIR
FUEL .... G
SPEEDS .... VARIABLE
TRANSMISSION .... HYDRO
STEERING .... ZERO
MSRP $2,399

RETAIL PRICING

YEAR	HIGH	LOW
2011	$910	$683

17AQNA-MU029

YEARS MFRD 2018-2018
CYLINDERS 1
CID 452CC
FUEL .... G
TRANSMISSION ..... DUAL HYDRO
STEERING .... ZERO
BLADE CLUTCH .... MANUAL
STANDARD DECK .... 34"

132G665G

YEARS MFRD 1992-1992
ENGINE .... TECUMSEH
ENGINE HP 16
FUEL .... G
TRANSMISSION ...... TRANSAXLE
STEERING .... STANDARD

1320695G

YEARS MFRD 1992-1992
ENGINE .... B&S
ENGINE HP 16
FUEL .... G
TRANSMISSION .... HYDRO
STEERING .... STANDARD

132P668H

YEARS MFRD 1992-1992
ENGINE .... B&S
ENGINE HP 18
FUEL .... G
TRANSMISSION ...... TRANSAXLE
STEERING .... STANDARD

132P828H

YEARS MFRD 1992-1992
ENGINE .... B&S
ENGINE HP 18
FUEL .... G
TRANSMISSION ...... TRANSAXLE
STEERING .... STANDARD

133G665G

YEARS MFRD 1993-1993
ENGINE .... TECUMSEH
ENGINE HP 16
FUEL .... G
TRANSMISSION ...... TRANSAXLE
STEERING .... STANDARD

1330695G

YEARS MFRD 1993-1993
ENGINE .... B&S
ENGINE HP 16
FUEL .... G
TRANSMISSION .... HYDRO
STEERING .... STANDARD

133P338H

YEARS MFRD 1993-1993
ENGINE .... B&S
ENGINE HP 18
FUEL .... G
TRANSMISSION ...... TRANSAXLE
STEERING .... STANDARD

133P828H

YEARS MFRD 1993-1993
ENGINE .... B&S
ENGINE HP 18
FUEL .... G
TRANSMISSION ...... TRANSAXLE
STEERING .... STANDARD

134G665G

YEARS MFRD 1994-1994
ENGINE .... TECUMSEH
ENGINE HP 16
FUEL .... G
STEERING .... STANDARD

1340695G

YEARS MFRD 1994-1994
ENGINE .... B&S
ENGINE HP 16
FUEL .... G
TRANSMISSION .... HYDRO
STEERING .... STANDARD

134P668H

YEARS MFRD 1994-1994
ENGINE .... B&S
ENGINE HP 18
FUEL .... G
TRANSMISSION ...... TRANSAXLE
STEERING .... STANDARD

134P828H

YEARS MFRD 1994-1994
ENGINE .... B&S
ENGINE HP 18
FUEL .... G
TRANSMISSION ...... TRANSAXLE
STEERING .... STANDARD

MTD YARD MACHINES

1350660G
YEARS MFRD 1995-1995
ENGINE . . . . B&S
ENGINE HP 16
FUEL . . . . G
TRANSMISSION . . . . GEAR
STEERING. . . . . STANDARD

1350675G
YEARS MFRD 1995-1995
ENGINE . . . . B&S
ENGINE HP 16
FUEL . . . . G
TRANSMISSION . . . . GEAR
STEERING. . . . . STANDARD

135P670G
YEARS MFRD 1995-1995
ENGINE . . . . B&S
ENGINE HP 18
FUEL . . . . G
TRANSMISSION . . . . GEAR
STEERING. . . . . STANDARD

135Q699G
YEARS MFRD 1995-1995
ENGINE . . . . B&S
ENGINE HP 18
FUEL . . . . G
TRANSMISSION . . . . HYDRO
STEERING. . . . . STANDARD

135Q699H
YEARS MFRD 1995-1995
ENGINE . . . . B&S
ENGINE HP 18
FUEL . . . . G
TRANSMISSION . . . . HYDRO
STEERING. . . . . STANDARD

135V694H
YEARS MFRD 1995-1995
ENGINE . . . . B&S
ENGINE HP 19
FUEL . . . . G
TRANSMISSION . . . . HYDRO
STEERING. . . . . STANDARD

136G765N
YEARS MFRD 1996-1996
ENGINE . . . . TECUMSEH
ENGINE HP 16
FUEL . . . . G
TRANSMISSION . . . . GEAR
STEERING. . . . . STANDARD

1360695G
YEARS MFRD 1996-1996
ENGINE . . . . B&S
ENGINE HP 16
FUEL . . . . G
TRANSMISSION . . . . HYDRO
STEERING. . . . . STANDARD

136P665H
YEARS MFRD 1996-1997
ENGINE . . . . B&S
ENGINE HP 18
COOLING . . . . AIR
FUEL . . . . G
TRANSMISSION . . . . GEAR
STEERING. . . . . STANDARD
STANDARD DECK . . . . 46"
MSRP. $1,599

RETAIL PRICING

YEAR	HIGH	LOW
1996	$613	$460
1997	$664	$498

140-812
YEARS MFRD 1990-1990
ENGINE . . . . B&S
ENGINE HP 18
FUEL . . . . G
TRANSMISSION . . . . . . TRANSAXLE
STEERING. . . . . STANDARD

140-852
YEARS MFRD 1990-1990
ENGINE . . . . B&S
ENGINE HP 18
FUEL . . . . G
TRANSMISSION . . . . HYDRO
STEERING. . . . . STANDARD

141-812
YEARS MFRD 1991-1991
ENGINE . . . . B&S
ENGINE HP 18
FUEL . . . . G
TRANSMISSION . . . . . . TRANSAXLE
STEERING. . . . . STANDARD

141-852
YEARS MFRD 1991-1991
ENGINE . . . . B&S
ENGINE HP 18
FUEL . . . . G
TRANSMISSION . . . . HYDRO
STEERING. . . . . STANDARD

145S845H
YEARS MFRD 1995-1995
ENGINE . . . . B&S
ENGINE HP 18.5
FUEL . . . . G
TRANSMISSION . . . . GEAR
STEERING. . . . . STANDARD

145V848H
YEARS MFRD 1995-1995
ENGINE . . . . B&S
ENGINE HP 18
FUEL . . . . G
TRANSMISSION . . . . GEAR
STEERING. . . . . STANDARD

146K828H
YEARS MFRD 1996-1997
ENGINE . . . . B&S
ENGINE HP 18.5
FUEL . . . . G
TRANSMISSION . . . . GEAR
STEERING. . . . . STANDARD
STANDARD DECK . . . . 46"
MSRP. $1,899

RETAIL PRICING

YEAR	HIGH	LOW
1996	$733	$550
1997	$760	$570

1660F
YEARS MFRD 2003-2004
SERIES. . . . LAWN TRACTOR SERIES
ENGINE . . . . TECUMSEH
ENGINE HP 13.5
FUEL . . . . G
SPEEDS 6/1
TRANSMISSION . . . . GEAR
STEERING. . . . . STANDARD
BLADE CLUTCH . . . . MANUAL
STANDARD DECK . . . . 38"
MSRP. $999

RETAIL PRICING

YEAR	HIGH	LOW
2003	$576	$432
2004	$580	$435

3665G
YEARS MFRD 2004-2004
SERIES. . . . LAWN TRACTOR SERIES
ENGINE . . . . TECUMSEH
ENGINE HP 17.5
FUEL . . . . G
SPEEDS 6/1
STEERING. . . . . STANDARD
BLADE CLUTCH . . . . MANUAL

3668G
YEARS MFRD 2003-2003
ENGINE . . . . TECUMSEH
ENGINE HP 17.5
COOLING . . . . AIR
FUEL . . . . G
TRANSMISSION . . . . GEAR
STEERING. . . . . STANDARD
STANDARD DECK . . . . 42"
MSRP. $1,199

RETAIL PRICING

YEAR	HIGH	LOW
2003	$655	$491

4065
YEARS MFRD 2004-2004
SERIES. . . . LAWN TRACTOR SERIES
ENGINE . . . . B&S OHV
ENGINE HP 6.75
FUEL . . . . G
SPEEDS . . . . VARIABLE
TRANSMISSION . . . . HYDRO
STEERING. . . . . STANDARD
BLADE CLUTCH . . . . ELECTRIC

MURRAY

DYNAMARK 40
YEARS MFRD 2004-2004
ENGINE . . . . B&S
ENGINE HP 14
COOLING . . . . AIR
FUEL . . . . G
SPEEDS 5/1
TRANSMISSION . . . . GEAR
STEERING. . . . . STANDARD

DYNAMARK 42
YEARS MFRD 2004-2004
ENGINE . . . . B&S
CYLINDERS. 2
ENGINE HP 18
COOLING . . . . AIR
FUEL . . . . G
SPEEDS . . . . VARIABLE
TRANSMISSION . . . . HYDRO
STEERING. . . . . STANDARD

F431607MP
YEARS MFRD 1995-1995
SERIES. . . . . MURRAY SERIES
ENGINE . . . . B&S
ENGINE HP 16
COOLING . . . . AIR
FUEL . . . . G
SPEEDS . . . . VARIABLE
TRANSMISSION . . . . HYDRO
STEERING. . . . . STANDARD
STANDARD DECK . . . . 43"
MSRP. $1,699

RETAIL PRICING

YEAR	HIGH	LOW
1995	$601	$451

MRD100
YEARS MFRD 2017-2017
COOLING . . . . AIR
FUEL . . . . G
SPEEDS . . . . VARIABLE
TRANSMISSION . . . . HYDRO
STEERING. . . . . STANDARD
BLADE CLUTCH . . . . MANUAL

MRD200
YEARS MFRD 2017-2017
COOLING . . . . AIR
FUEL . . . . G
SPEEDS . . . . VARIABLE
TRANSMISSION . . . . HYDRO
STEERING. . . . . STANDARD
BLADE CLUTCH . . . . MANUAL

MRD300
YEARS MFRD 2017-2017
COOLING . . . . AIR
FUEL . . . . G
SPEEDS . . . . VARIABLE
TRANSMISSION . . . . HYDRO
STEERING. . . . . STANDARD
BLADE CLUTCH . . . . MANUAL

MSD100
YEARS MFRD 2017-2017
ENGINE . . . . B&S INTEK
COOLING . . . . AIR
FUEL . . . . G
SPEEDS . . . . VARIABLE
TRANSMISSION . . . . HYDRO
STEERING. . . . . STANDARD
BLADE CLUTCH . . . . MANUAL

MSD200
YEARS MFRD 2017-2017
ENGINE . . . . B&S INTEK
COOLING . . . . AIR
FUEL . . . . G
SPEEDS 6/1
TRANSMISSION . . . . DISC
STEERING. . . . . STANDARD
BLADE CLUTCH . . . . MANUAL

MURRAY 10
YEARS MFRD 2004-2004
ENGINE . . . . TECUMSEH
CYLINDERS. 1
ENGINE HP 10
COOLING . . . . AIR
FUEL . . . . G
SPEEDS 5/1
TRANSMISSION . . . . GEAR
STEERING. . . . . STANDARD

MURRAY 11
YEARS MFRD 2004-2004
CYLINDERS. 1
ENGINE HP 11
COOLING . . . . AIR
FUEL . . . . G
SPEEDS 5/1
TRANSMISSION . . . . GEAR
STEERING. . . . . STANDARD

MURRAY 12
YEARS MFRD 2004-2004
ENGINE . . . . B&S
CYLINDERS. 1
ENGINE HP 12
COOLING . . . . AIR
FUEL . . . . G
SPEEDS 5/1
TRANSMISSION . . . . GEAR
STEERING. . . . . STANDARD

MURRAY 12.5
YEARS MFRD 2004-2004
ENGINE . . . . B&S
CYLINDERS. 1
ENGINE HP 12.5
COOLING . . . . AIR
FUEL . . . . G
SPEEDS 5/1
TRANSMISSION . . . . GEAR
STEERING. . . . . STANDARD

MURRAY 13.5
YEARS MFRD 2004-2004
ENGINE . . . . TECUMSEH
CYLINDERS. 1
ENGINE HP 13.5
COOLING . . . . AIR
FUEL . . . . G
SPEEDS 5/1
TRANSMISSION . . . . GEAR
STEERING. . . . . STANDARD

MURRAY 15.5
YEARS MFRD 2004-2004
ENGINE . . . . B&S
ENGINE HP 15.5
COOLING . . . . AIR
FUEL . . . . G
SPEEDS . . . . VARIABLE
TRANSMISSION . . . . DISC
STEERING. . . . . STANDARD

MURRAY 17.5
YEARS MFRD 2004-2004
ENGINE . . . . B&S
ENGINE HP 17.5
COOLING . . . . AIR
FUEL . . . . G
SPEEDS 6/1
TRANSMISSION . . . . GEAR
STEERING. . . . . STANDARD

MURRAY 18
YEARS MFRD 2004-2004
ENGINE . . . . B&S
ENGINE HP 18
COOLING . . . . AIR
FUEL . . . . G
SPEEDS . . . . VARIABLE
TRANSMISSION . . . . HYDRO
STEERING. . . . . STANDARD

MURRAY 18.5
YEARS MFRD 2004-2004
ENGINE . . . . B&S
ENGINE HP 18.5
COOLING . . . . AIR
FUEL . . . . G
SPEEDS . . . . VARIABLE
TRANSMISSION . . . . HYDRO
STEERING. . . . . STANDARD

MURRAY 20
YEARS MFRD 2004-2004
ENGINE . . . . TECUMSEH
ENGINE HP 20
COOLING . . . . AIR
FUEL . . . . G
SPEEDS . . . . VARIABLE
TRANSMISSION . . . . HYDRO
STEERING. . . . . STANDARD

MURRAY 22
YEARS MFRD 2004-2004
ENGINE . . . . B&S
ENGINE HP 22
COOLING . . . . AIR
FUEL . . . . G
SPEEDS . . . . VARIABLE
TRANSMISSION . . . . HYDRO
STEERING. . . . . STANDARD

MURRAY 25
YEARS MFRD 2004-2004
ENGINE . . . . B&S
CYLINDERS. 2
ENGINE HP 25
COOLING . . . . AIR
FUEL . . . . G
SPEEDS . . . . VARIABLE
TRANSMISSION . . . . HYDRO
STEERING. . . . . STANDARD

TURF MASTER
YEARS MFRD 2004-2004
ENGINE . . . . B&S
CYLINDERS. 2
ENGINE HP 18
COOLING . . . . AIR
FUEL . . . . G
SPEEDS . . . . VARIABLE
TRANSMISSION . . . . HYDRO
STEERING. . . . . STANDARD

YARD KING
YEARS MFRD 2004-2004
ENGINE . . . . KOHLER
CYLINDERS. 2
ENGINE HP 18
COOLING . . . . AIR
FUEL . . . . G
SPEEDS . . . . VARIABLE
TRANSMISSION . . . . HYDRO
STEERING. . . . . STANDARD

4625X92
YEARS MFRD 1995-1995
SERIES. . . . . MURRAY SERIES
ENGINE . . . . B&S
ENGINE HP 18
COOLING . . . . AIR
FUEL . . . . G
SPEEDS . . . . VARIABLE
TRANSMISSION . . . . HYDRO
STEERING. . . . . STANDARD
STANDARD DECK . . . . 46"
MSRP. $1,599

RETAIL PRICING

YEAR	HIGH	LOW
1995	$565	$423

25501
YEARS MFRD 1982-1991
SERIES. . . . . MURRAY SERIES
ENGINE . . . . B&S
CYLINDERS. 1
ENGINE HP 5
COOLING . . . . AIR
FUEL . . . . G
SPEEDS 3
TRANSMISSION . . . . BELT
STEERING. . . . . STANDARD
STANDARD DECK . . . . 25"
WEIGHT . . . . 265 LBS.
MSRP. $899

RETAIL PRICING

YEAR	HIGH	LOW
1982	$123	$92
1983	$153	$115
1984	$167	$125
1987	$204	$153
1988	$212	$159
1989	$236	$177
1990	$237	$178
1991	$269	$202

30500X92
YEARS MFRD 1999-1999
SERIES. . . . . MURRAY SERIES
ENGINE . . . . B&S
CYLINDERS. 1
ENGINE HP 10
COOLING . . . . AIR
FUEL . . . . G
SPEEDS 5/1
TRANSMISSION . . . . GEAR
STEERING. . . . . STANDARD
STANDARD DECK . . . . 30"
MSRP. $767

RETAIL PRICING

YEAR	HIGH	LOW
1999	$325	$244

30502
YEARS MFRD 1982-1991
SERIES. . . . . MURRAY SERIES
ENGINE . . . . B&S
CYLINDERS. 1
ENGINE HP 8

COOLING . . . . AIR
FUEL . . . . G
TRANSMISSION . . . . BELT
STEERING. . . . STANDARD
STANDARD DECK . . . . 30"
WEIGHT . . . . 305 LBS.
MSRP. . . . $1,149

RETAIL PRICING

YEAR	HIGH	LOW
1982	$168	$126
1983	$205	$154
1984	$225	$169
1987	$266	$199
1989	$305	$228
1990	$307	$231
1991	$344	$258

30544X92

YEARS MFRD 1995-1995
SERIES. . . . MURRAY SERIES
ENGINE . . . . TECUMSEH
CYLINDERS. . . . 1
ENGINE HP 8
COOLING . . . . AIR
FUEL . . . . G
SPEEDS 5/1
TRANSMISSION . . . . GEAR
STEERING. . . . STANDARD
STANDARD DECK . . . . 30"
MSRP. . . . $699

RETAIL PRICING

YEAR	HIGH	LOW
1995	$248	$186

30544X92D

YEARS MFRD 1996-1996
SERIES. . . . MURRAY SERIES
ENGINE . . . . TECUMSEH
CYLINDERS. . . . 1
ENGINE HP 8
COOLING . . . . AIR
FUEL . . . . G
SPEEDS 5/1
TRANSMISSION . . . . GEAR
STEERING. . . . STANDARD
STANDARD DECK . . . . 30"
MSRP. . . . $759

RETAIL PRICING

YEAR	HIGH	LOW
1996	$277	$208

30550

YEARS MFRD 1993-1994
SERIES. . . . MURRAY SERIES
ENGINE . . . . TECUMSEH
CYLINDERS. . . . 1
ENGINE HP 10
COOLING . . . . AIR
FUEL . . . . G
SPEEDS 5/1
TRANSMISSION . . . . GEAR
STEERING. . . . STANDARD
STANDARD DECK . . . . 30"
WEIGHT . . . . 340 LBS.
MSRP. . . . $879

RETAIL PRICING

YEAR	HIGH	LOW
1993	$280	$210
1994	$299	$224

30560

YEARS MFRD 1993-1994
SERIES. . . . MURRAY SERIES
ENGINE . . . . B&S
CYLINDERS. . . . 1
ENGINE HP 10
COOLING . . . . AIR
FUEL . . . . G
SPEEDS 5/1
TRANSMISSION . . . . GEAR
STEERING. . . . STANDARD
STANDARD DECK . . . . 30"
WEIGHT . . . . 340 LBS.
MSRP. . . . $899

RETAIL PRICING

YEAR	HIGH	LOW
1993	$286	$215
1994	$307	$230

30577X

YEARS MFRD 1998-1998
SERIES. . . . MURRAY SERIES
ENGINE . . . . B&S
CYLINDERS. . . . 1
ENGINE HP 12
COOLING . . . . AIR
FUEL . . . . G
TRANSMISSION . . . . GEAR
STEERING. . . . STANDARD
STANDARD DECK . . . . 30"
MSRP. . . . $899

RETAIL PRICING

YEAR	HIGH	LOW
1998	$360	$270

30577X92

YEARS MFRD 2000-2000
SERIES. . . . MURRAY SERIES
ENGINE . . . . B&S
CYLINDERS. . . . 1
ENGINE HP 12
COOLING . . . . AIR
FUEL . . . . G
SPEEDS 5/1
TRANSMISSION . . . . GEAR
STEERING. . . . STANDARD
STANDARD DECK . . . . 30"
MSRP. . . . $895

RETAIL PRICING

YEAR	HIGH	LOW
2000	$399	$299

31515

YEARS MFRD 1987-1991
SERIES. . . . MURRAY SERIES
ENGINE . . . . B&S
CYLINDERS. . . . 1
ENGINE HP 8
COOLING . . . . AIR
FUEL . . . . G
TRANSMISSION . . . . GEAR
STEERING. . . . STANDARD
STANDARD DECK . . . . 30"
WEIGHT . . . . 399 LBS.
MSRP. . . . $1,174

RETAIL PRICING

YEAR	HIGH	LOW
1987	$307	$230
1988	$315	$236
1989	$327	$245
1990	$331	$248
1991	$354	$266

35500

YEARS MFRD 1987-1991
SERIES. . . . MURRAY SERIES
ENGINE . . . . B&S
CYLINDERS. . . . 1
ENGINE HP 10
COOLING . . . . AIR
FUEL . . . . G
SPEEDS 5
TRANSMISSION . . . . BELT
STEERING. . . . STANDARD
STANDARD DECK . . . . 36"
WEIGHT . . . . 350 LBS.
MSRP. . . . $1,299

RETAIL PRICING

YEAR	HIGH	LOW
1987	$277	$208
1989	$348	$261
1990	$351	$263
1991	$391	$293

36506

YEARS MFRD 1984-1991
SERIES. . . . MURRAY SERIES
ENGINE . . . . B&S
CYLINDERS. . . . 1
ENGINE HP 11
COOLING . . . . AIR
FUEL . . . . G
TRANSMISSION . . . . GEAR
STEERING. . . . STANDARD
STANDARD DECK . . . . 36"
WEIGHT . . . . 442 LBS.
MSRP. . . . $1,270

RETAIL PRICING

YEAR	HIGH	LOW
1984	$276	$207
1987	$332	$249
1988	$341	$256
1989	$355	$266
1990	$357	$268
1991	$380	$285

36508

YEARS MFRD 1983-1991
SERIES. . . . MURRAY SERIES
ENGINE . . . . B&S
CYLINDERS. . . . 1
ENGINE HP 11
COOLING . . . . AIR
FUEL . . . . G
TRANSMISSION . . . . GEAR
STEERING. . . . STANDARD
STANDARD DECK . . . . 36"
WEIGHT . . . . 442 LBS.
MSRP. . . . $1,291

RETAIL PRICING

YEAR	HIGH	LOW
1983	$259	$194
1984	$286	$215
1987	$337	$252
1988	$345	$259
1989	$360	$270
1990	$363	$272
1991	$387	$290

36557

YEARS MFRD 1987-1991
SERIES. . . . MURRAY SERIES
ENGINE . . . . B&S
CYLINDERS. . . . 1
ENGINE HP 12
COOLING . . . . AIR
FUEL . . . . G
TRANSMISSION . . . . GEAR
STEERING. . . . STANDARD
STANDARD DECK . . . . 36"
WEIGHT . . . . 445 LBS.
MSRP. . . . $1,393

RETAIL PRICING

YEAR	HIGH	LOW
1987	$363	$272
1988	$374	$281
1989	$389	$292
1990	$392	$294
1991	$417	$313

36560

YEARS MFRD 1987-1991
SERIES. . . . MURRAY SERIES
ENGINE . . . . B&S
CYLINDERS. . . . 1
ENGINE HP 12
COOLING . . . . AIR
FUEL . . . . G
TRANSMISSION . . . . GEAR
STEERING. . . . STANDARD
STANDARD DECK . . . . 36"
WEIGHT . . . . 450 LBS.
MSRP. . . . $1,318

RETAIL PRICING

YEAR	HIGH	LOW
1987	$343	$258
1988	$354	$266
1989	$368	$276
1990	$372	$279
1991	$397	$298

38211

YEARS MFRD 1987-1991
SERIES. . . . MURRAY SERIES
ENGINE . . . . B&S
CYLINDERS. . . . 1
ENGINE HP 14
COOLING . . . . AIR

FUEL ..... G
TRANSMISSION ..... GEAR
STEERING ..... STANDARD
STANDARD DECK ..... 38"
WEIGHT ..... 585 LBS.
MSRP $1,897

RETAIL PRICING

YEAR	HIGH	LOW
1987	$495	$371
1988	$507	$380
1989	$529	$396
1990	$534	$401
1991	$569	$427

38219

YEARS MFRD 1987-1991
SERIES ..... MURRAY SERIES
ENGINE ..... B&S
CYLINDERS 1
ENGINE HP 12
COOLING ..... AIR
FUEL ..... G
TRANSMISSION ..... GEAR
STEERING ..... STANDARD
STANDARD DECK ..... 38"
WEIGHT ..... 560 LBS.
MSRP $1,645

RETAIL PRICING

YEAR	HIGH	LOW
1987	$430	$322
1988	$440	$330
1989	$459	$344
1990	$465	$348
1991	$494	$370

38618

YEARS MFRD 1994-1994
SERIES ..... MURRAY SERIES
ENGINE ..... B&S
CYLINDERS 1
ENGINE HP 11
COOLING ..... AIR
FUEL ..... G
SPEEDS 4/1
TRANSMISSION ..... GEAR
STEERING ..... STANDARD
STANDARD DECK ..... 38"
MSRP $1,119

RETAIL PRICING

YEAR	HIGH	LOW
1994	$380	$285

38618X92

YEARS MFRD 1995-1995
SERIES ..... MURRAY SERIES
ENGINE ..... B&S
CYLINDERS 1
ENGINE HP 11
COOLING ..... AIR
FUEL ..... G
SPEEDS 4/1
TRANSMISSION ..... GEAR
STEERING ..... STANDARD
STANDARD DECK ..... 38"
MSRP $799

RETAIL PRICING

YEAR	HIGH	LOW
1995	$283	$212

38633X92B

YEARS MFRD 1996-1996
SERIES ..... MURRAY SERIES
ENGINE ..... B&S
CYLINDERS 1
ENGINE HP 12
COOLING ..... AIR
FUEL ..... G
SPEEDS 4/1
TRANSMISSION ..... GEAR
STEERING ..... STANDARD
STANDARD DECK ..... 38"
MSRP $795

RETAIL PRICING

YEAR	HIGH	LOW
1996	$291	$218

38701

YEARS MFRD 1993-1994
SERIES ..... MURRAY SERIES
ENGINE ..... TECUMSEH
CYLINDERS 1
ENGINE HP 12
COOLING ..... AIR
FUEL ..... G
SPEEDS 5/1
TRANSMISSION ..... GEAR
STEERING ..... STANDARD
STANDARD DECK ..... 38"
WEIGHT ..... 415 LBS.
MSRP $1,049

RETAIL PRICING

YEAR	HIGH	LOW
1993	$328	$246
1994	$357	$268

38701X92

YEARS MFRD 1995-1995
SERIES ..... MURRAY SERIES
ENGINE ..... TECUMSEH
CYLINDERS 1
ENGINE HP 12
COOLING ..... AIR
FUEL ..... G
SPEEDS 5/1
TRANSMISSION ..... GEAR
STEERING ..... STANDARD
STANDARD DECK ..... 38"
MSRP $799

RETAIL PRICING

YEAR	HIGH	LOW
1995	$283	$212

38702

YEARS MFRD 1993-1994
SERIES ..... MURRAY SERIES
ENGINE ..... B&S
CYLINDERS 1
ENGINE HP 12
COOLING ..... AIR
FUEL ..... G
SPEEDS 5/1
TRANSMISSION ..... GEAR
STEERING ..... STANDARD
STANDARD DECK ..... 38"
WEIGHT ..... 422 LBS.
MSRP $1,079

RETAIL PRICING

YEAR	HIGH	LOW
1993	$339	$254
1994	$368	$276

39004

YEARS MFRD 1982-1991
SERIES ..... MURRAY SERIES
ENGINE ..... B&S
CYLINDERS 1
ENGINE HP 10
COOLING ..... AIR
FUEL ..... G
TRANSMISSION ..... GEAR
STEERING ..... STANDARD
STANDARD DECK ..... 40"
WEIGHT ..... 658 LBS.
MSRP $2,199

RETAIL PRICING

YEAR	HIGH	LOW
1982	$340	$255
1983	$411	$308
1984	$453	$340
1987	$573	$430
1988	$588	$441
1989	$614	$461
1990	$619	$464
1991	$660	$495

40504X92

YEARS MFRD 1999-1999
SERIES ..... MURRAY SERIES
ENGINE ..... B&S
CYLINDERS 1
ENGINE HP 12.5
COOLING ..... AIR
FUEL ..... G
SPEEDS 6/1
TRANSMISSION ..... GEAR
STEERING ..... STANDARD
STANDARD DECK ..... 40"
MSRP $799

RETAIL PRICING

YEAR	HIGH	LOW
1999	$341	$256

40507X92

YEARS MFRD 2000-2000
SERIES ..... MURRAY SERIES
ENGINE ..... B&S
CYLINDERS 1
ENGINE HP 12.5
COOLING ..... AIR
FUEL ..... G
SPEEDS 8/1
TRANSMISSION ..... GEAR
STEERING ..... STANDARD
STANDARD DECK ..... 40"
MSRP $799

RETAIL PRICING

YEAR	HIGH	LOW
2000	$357	$268

40530X92

YEARS MFRD 1997-1997
SERIES ..... MURRAY SERIES
ENGINE ..... B&S
CYLINDERS 1
ENGINE HP 14.5
COOLING ..... AIR
FUEL ..... G
SPEEDS 6/1
TRANSMISSION ..... GEAR
STEERING ..... STANDARD
STANDARD DECK ..... 40"
MSRP $937

RETAIL PRICING

YEAR	HIGH	LOW
1997	$356	$267

40607

YEARS MFRD 1993-1993
SERIES ..... MURRAY SERIES
ENGINE ..... B&S
CYLINDERS 1
ENGINE HP 12.5
COOLING ..... AIR
FUEL ..... G
SPEEDS 6/1
TRANSMISSION ..... GEAR
STEERING ..... STANDARD
STANDARD DECK ..... 40"
WEIGHT ..... 450 LBS.
MSRP $1,095

RETAIL PRICING

YEAR	HIGH	LOW
1993	$354	$266

40702

YEARS MFRD 1994-1994
SERIES ..... MURRAY SERIES
ENGINE ..... B&S
CYLINDERS 1
ENGINE HP 12.5
COOLING ..... AIR
FUEL ..... G
SPEEDS 5/1
TRANSMISSION ..... GEAR
STEERING ..... STANDARD
STANDARD DECK ..... 40"
MSRP $1,179

RETAIL PRICING

YEAR	HIGH	LOW
1994	$402	$301

40702X92

YEARS MFRD 1995-1995
SERIES ..... MURRAY SERIES
ENGINE ..... B&S
CYLINDERS 1
ENGINE HP 12.5
COOLING ..... AIR
FUEL ..... G

SPEEDS 5/1
TRANSMISSION . . . . . GEAR
STEERING. . . . . STANDARD
STANDARD DECK . . . . . 40"
MSRP. $899

RETAIL PRICING

YEAR	HIGH	LOW
1995	$318	$239

40708X92B

YEARS MFRD 1996-1996
SERIES. . . . . MURRAY SERIES
ENGINE . . . . . B&S
CYLINDERS. 1
ENGINE HP 12.5
COOLING . . . . . AIR
FUEL . . . . . G
SPEEDS 6/1
TRANSMISSION . . . . . GEAR
STEERING. . . . . STANDARD
STANDARD DECK . . . . . 40"
MSRP. $899

RETAIL PRICING

YEAR	HIGH	LOW
1996	$329	$247

40713

YEARS MFRD 1987-1991
SERIES. . . . . MURRAY SERIES
ENGINE . . . . . B&S
CYLINDERS. 1
ENGINE HP 12
COOLING . . . . . AIR
FUEL . . . . . G
TRANSMISSION . . . . . GEAR
STEERING. . . . . STANDARD
STANDARD DECK . . . . . 40"
WEIGHT . . . . . 470 LBS.
MSRP. $1,510

RETAIL PRICING

YEAR	HIGH	LOW
1987	$395	$296
1988	$405	$304
1989	$421	$316
1990	$426	$319
1991	$453	$340

42170

YEARS MFRD 1994-1994
SERIES. . . . . MURRAY SERIES
ENGINE . . . . . B&S
ENGINE HP 18
COOLING . . . . . AIR
FUEL . . . . . G
SPEEDS 5/1
TRANSMISSION . . . . . GEAR
STEERING. . . . . STANDARD
STANDARD DECK . . . . . 42"
MSRP. $1,599

RETAIL PRICING

YEAR	HIGH	LOW
1994	$544	$408

42514X92

YEARS MFRD 2000-2000
SERIES. . . . . MURRAY SERIES
ENGINE . . . . . B&S
CYLINDERS. 1
ENGINE HP 14.5
COOLING . . . . . AIR
FUEL . . . . . G
SPEEDS 8/1
TRANSMISSION . . . . . GEAR
STEERING. . . . . STANDARD
STANDARD DECK . . . . . 42"
MSRP. $999

RETAIL PRICING

YEAR	HIGH	LOW
2000	$446	$335

42544X

YEARS MFRD 1998-1998
SERIES. . . . . MURRAY SERIES
ENGINE . . . . . B&S
ENGINE HP 16.5
COOLING . . . . . AIR
FUEL . . . . . G
SPEEDS 6/1
TRANSMISSION . . . . . GEAR
STEERING. . . . . STANDARD
STANDARD DECK . . . . . 42"
MSRP. $1,099

RETAIL PRICING

YEAR	HIGH	LOW
1998	$438	$329

42544X92

YEARS MFRD 2000-2000
SERIES. . . . . MURRAY SERIES
ENGINE . . . . . B&S
ENGINE HP 16.5
COOLING . . . . . AIR
FUEL . . . . . G
SPEEDS 6/1
TRANSMISSION . . . . . GEAR
STEERING. . . . . STANDARD
STANDARD DECK . . . . . 42"
MSRP. $1,099

RETAIL PRICING

YEAR	HIGH	LOW
2000	$490	$367

42560X92

YEARS MFRD 1997-1997
SERIES. . . . . MURRAY SERIES
ENGINE . . . . . B&S
CYLINDERS. 1
ENGINE HP 14.5
COOLING . . . . . AIR
FUEL . . . . . G
SPEEDS . . . . . VARIABLE
TRANSMISSION . . . . . HYDRO
STEERING. . . . . STANDARD
STANDARD DECK . . . . . 42"
MSRP. $1,053

RETAIL PRICING

YEAR	HIGH	LOW
1997	$400	$300

42572X92

YEARS MFRD 2000-2000
SERIES. . . . . MURRAY SERIES
ENGINE . . . . . B&S
ENGINE HP 20
COOLING . . . . . AIR
FUEL . . . . . G
SPEEDS . . . . . VARIABLE
TRANSMISSION . . . . . HYDRO
STEERING. . . . . STANDARD
STANDARD DECK . . . . . 42"
MSRP. $1,398

RETAIL PRICING

YEAR	HIGH	LOW
2000	$623	$467

42583X

YEARS MFRD 1998-1998
SERIES. . . . . MURRAY SERIES
ENGINE . . . . . B&S
ENGINE HP 16.5
COOLING . . . . . AIR
FUEL . . . . . G
SPEEDS . . . . . VARIABLE
TRANSMISSION . . . . . HYDRO
STEERING. . . . . STANDARD
STANDARD DECK . . . . . 42"
MSRP. $1,199

RETAIL PRICING

YEAR	HIGH	LOW
1998	$479	$359

42586X

YEARS MFRD 1998-1998
SERIES. . . . . MURRAY SERIES
ENGINE . . . . . B&S
ENGINE HP 18.5
COOLING . . . . . AIR
FUEL . . . . . G
SPEEDS . . . . . VARIABLE
TRANSMISSION . . . . . HYDRO
STEERING. . . . . STANDARD
STANDARD DECK . . . . . 42"
MSRP. $1,449

RETAIL PRICING

YEAR	HIGH	LOW
1998	$581	$436

42591X92

YEARS MFRD 2000-2000
SERIES. . . . . MURRAY SERIES
ENGINE . . . . . B&S
ENGINE HP 17
COOLING . . . . . AIR
FUEL . . . . . G
SPEEDS . . . . . VARIABLE
TRANSMISSION . . . . . HYDRO
STEERING. . . . . STANDARD
STANDARD DECK . . . . . 42"
MSRP. $1,199

RETAIL PRICING

YEAR	HIGH	LOW
2000	$534	$401

42598X92

YEARS MFRD 1999-1999
SERIES. . . . . MURRAY SERIES
ENGINE . . . . . B&S
CYLINDERS. 1
ENGINE HP 14.5
COOLING . . . . . AIR
FUEL . . . . . G
SPEEDS . . . . . VARIABLE
TRANSMISSION . . . . . HYDRO
STEERING. . . . . STANDARD
STANDARD DECK . . . . . 42"
MSRP. $1,053

RETAIL PRICING

YEAR	HIGH	LOW
1999	$448	$336

42614

YEARS MFRD 1993-1993
SERIES. . . . . MURRAY SERIES
ENGINE . . . . . B&S
ENGINE HP 14
COOLING . . . . . AIR
FUEL . . . . . G
SPEEDS 6/1
TRANSMISSION . . . . . GEAR
STEERING. . . . . STANDARD
STANDARD DECK . . . . . 42"
WEIGHT . . . . . 480 LBS.
MSRP. $1,230

RETAIL PRICING

YEAR	HIGH	LOW
1993	$397	$298

42802A

YEARS MFRD 1994-1994
SERIES. . . . . MURRAY SERIES
ENGINE . . . . . B&S
CYLINDERS. 1
ENGINE HP 12.5
COOLING . . . . . AIR
FUEL . . . . . G
SPEEDS 6/1
TRANSMISSION . . . . . GEAR
STEERING. . . . . STANDARD
STANDARD DECK . . . . . 42"
WEIGHT . . . . . 450 LBS.
MSRP. $1,169

RETAIL PRICING

YEAR	HIGH	LOW
1994	$397	$298

42816

YEARS MFRD 1994-1994
SERIES. . . . . MURRAY SERIES
ENGINE . . . . . B&S
ENGINE HP 16
COOLING . . . . . AIR
FUEL . . . . . G
SPEEDS 6/1
TRANSMISSION . . . . . GEAR
STEERING. . . . . STANDARD
STANDARD DECK . . . . . 42"
WEIGHT . . . . . 480 LBS.
MSRP. $1,249

RETAIL PRICING

YEAR	HIGH	LOW
1994	$426	$319

42819X92

YEARS MFRD 1995-1995
SERIES MURRAY SERIES
ENGINE B&S
CYLINDERS 1
ENGINE HP 14.5
COOLING AIR
FUEL G
SPEEDS 6/1
TRANSMISSION GEAR
STEERING STANDARD
STANDARD DECK 42"
MSRP $988

RETAIL PRICING

YEAR	HIGH	LOW
1995	$350	$263

42819X92A

YEARS MFRD 1996-1996
SERIES MURRAY SERIES
ENGINE B&S
CYLINDERS 1
ENGINE HP 14.5
COOLING AIR
FUEL G
SPEEDS 6/1
TRANSMISSION GEAR
STEERING STANDARD
STANDARD DECK 42"
MSRP $999

RETAIL PRICING

YEAR	HIGH	LOW
1996	$366	$274

42910X92

YEARS MFRD 1995-1995
SERIES MURRAY SERIES
ENGINE B&S
CYLINDERS 1
ENGINE HP 14.5
COOLING AIR
FUEL G
SPEEDS VARIABLE
TRANSMISSION BELT
STEERING STANDARD
STANDARD DECK 42"
MSRP $999

RETAIL PRICING

YEAR	HIGH	LOW
1995	$354	$266

42910X92A

YEARS MFRD 1996-1996
SERIES MURRAY SERIES
ENGINE B&S
CYLINDERS 1
ENGINE HP 14.5
COOLING AIR
FUEL G
SPEEDS VARIABLE
TRANSMISSION HYDRO
STEERING STANDARD
STANDARD DECK 42"
MSRP $999

RETAIL PRICING

YEAR	HIGH	LOW
1996	$366	$274

46100

YEARS MFRD 1993-1993
SERIES MURRAY SERIES
ENGINE B&S
ENGINE HP 18
COOLING AIR
FUEL G
SPEEDS 5/1
TRANSMISSION GEAR
STEERING STANDARD
STANDARD DECK 46"
WEIGHT 554 LBS.
MSRP $1,665

RETAIL PRICING

YEAR	HIGH	LOW
1993	$537	$403

46103X92

YEARS MFRD 1999-1999
SERIES MURRAY SERIES
ENGINE B&S
ENGINE HP 18.5
COOLING AIR
FUEL G
SPEEDS 5/1
TRANSMISSION GEAR
STEERING STANDARD
STANDARD DECK 46"
MSRP $1,699

RETAIL PRICING

YEAR	HIGH	LOW
1999	$724	$543

46104X92

YEARS MFRD 2000-2000
SERIES MURRAY SERIES
ENGINE B&S
ENGINE HP 20
COOLING AIR
FUEL G
SPEEDS 5/1
TRANSMISSION GEAR
STEERING STANDARD
STANDARD DECK 46"
MSRP $1,699

RETAIL PRICING

YEAR	HIGH	LOW
2000	$760	$570

46253

YEARS MFRD 1994-1994
SERIES MURRAY SERIES
ENGINE B&S
ENGINE HP 18
COOLING AIR
FUEL G
SPEEDS 5/1
TRANSMISSION GEAR
STEERING STANDARD
STANDARD DECK 46"
WEIGHT 554 LBS.
MSRP $1,699

RETAIL PRICING

YEAR	HIGH	LOW
1994	$581	$436

46300

YEARS MFRD 1993-1994
SERIES MURRAY SERIES
ENGINE B&S
ENGINE HP 18
COOLING AIR
FUEL G
SPEEDS 5/1
TRANSMISSION GEAR
STEERING STANDARD
STANDARD DECK 46"
WEIGHT 647 LBS.
MSRP $1,699

RETAIL PRICING

YEAR	HIGH	LOW
1993	$577	$433
1994	$581	$436

46371X92

YEARS MFRD 1995-1995
SERIES MURRAY SERIES
ENGINE B&S
ENGINE HP 18
COOLING AIR
FUEL G
SPEEDS 5/1
TRANSMISSION GEAR
STEERING STANDARD
STANDARD DECK 46"
MSRP $1,597

RETAIL PRICING

YEAR	HIGH	LOW
1995	$564	$423

46379X92A

YEARS MFRD 1996-1997
SERIES MURRAY SERIES
ENGINE B&S
ENGINE HP 18.5
COOLING AIR
FUEL G
SPEEDS 5/1
TRANSMISSION GEAR
STEERING STANDARD
STANDARD DECK 46"
MSRP $1,594

RETAIL PRICING

YEAR	HIGH	LOW
1996	$582	$437
1997	$605	$454

46430X

YEARS MFRD 1998-1998
SERIES MURRAY SERIES
ENGINE B&S
ENGINE HP 20
COOLING AIR
FUEL G
SPEEDS 5/1
TRANSMISSION GEAR
STEERING STANDARD
STANDARD DECK 46"
MSRP $1,698

RETAIL PRICING

YEAR	HIGH	LOW
1998	$678	$509

46560X92

YEARS MFRD 1997-1997
SERIES MURRAY SERIES
ENGINE B&S
ENGINE HP 17
COOLING AIR
FUEL G
SPEEDS VARIABLE
TRANSMISSION HYDRO
STEERING STANDARD
STANDARD DECK 46"
MSRP $1,194

RETAIL PRICING

YEAR	HIGH	LOW
1997	$453	$340

46569X

YEARS MFRD 1998-1998
SERIES MURRAY SERIES
ENGINE B&S
ENGINE HP 20
COOLING AIR
FUEL G
SPEEDS VARIABLE
TRANSMISSION HYDRO
STEERING STANDARD
STANDARD DECK 46"
MSRP $1,699

RETAIL PRICING

YEAR	HIGH	LOW
1998	$678	$509

46570X

YEARS MFRD 1998-1998
SERIES MURRAY SERIES
ENGINE B&S
ENGINE HP 18.5
COOLING AIR
FUEL G
SPEEDS VARIABLE
TRANSMISSION HYDRO
STEERING STANDARD
STANDARD DECK 46"
MSRP $1,399

RETAIL PRICING

YEAR	HIGH	LOW
1998	$559	$419

MURRAY

46576X92
YEARS MFRD 1999-1999
SERIES.......... MURRAY SERIES
ENGINE ....B&S
ENGINE HP................17.5
COOLING..................AIR
FUEL ....G
SPEEDS...............VARIABLE
TRANSMISSION ....HYDRO
STEERING............STANDARD
STANDARD DECK ....46"
MSRP.................$1,299

RETAIL PRICING

YEAR	HIGH	LOW
1999	$552	$414

46577X92
YEARS MFRD 1999-2000
SERIES.......... MURRAY SERIES
ENGINE ....TECUMSEH
ENGINE HP..................17
COOLING..................AIR
FUEL ....G
TRANSMISSION ....GEAR
STEERING............STANDARD
STANDARD DECK ....46"
MSRP.................$1,199

RETAIL PRICING

YEAR	HIGH	LOW
1999	$509	$382
2000	$534	$401

46621
YEARS MFRD 1993-1994
SERIES.......... MURRAY SERIES
ENGINE ....B&S
ENGINE HP..................18
COOLING..................AIR
FUEL ....G
SPEEDS....................6/1
TRANSMISSION ....GEAR
STEERING............STANDARD
STANDARD DECK ....46"
WEIGHT...............500 LBS.
MSRP.................$1,499

RETAIL PRICING

YEAR	HIGH	LOW
1993	$477	$358
1994	$509	$382

46901X92
YEARS MFRD 1995-1995
SERIES.......... MURRAY SERIES
ENGINE ....B&S
ENGINE HP..................16
COOLING..................AIR
FUEL ....G
SPEEDS...............VARIABLE
TRANSMISSION ....HYDRO
STEERING............STANDARD
STANDARD DECK ....46"
MSRP.................$1,197

RETAIL PRICING

YEAR	HIGH	LOW
1995	$423	$317

46901X92B
YEARS MFRD 1996-1996
SERIES.......... MURRAY SERIES
ENGINE ....B&S
ENGINE HP..................16
COOLING..................AIR
FUEL ....G
SPEEDS...............VARIABLE
TRANSMISSION ....HYDRO
STEERING............STANDARD
STANDARD DECK ....46"
MSRP.................$1,194

RETAIL PRICING

YEAR	HIGH	LOW
1996	$438	$329

46904X92A
YEARS MFRD 1996-1996
SERIES.......... MURRAY SERIES
ENGINE ....B&S
ENGINE HP..................18
COOLING..................AIR
FUEL ....G
SPEEDS...............VARIABLE
TRANSMISSION ....HYDRO
STEERING............STANDARD
STANDARD DECK ....46"
MSRP.................$1,394

RETAIL PRICING

YEAR	HIGH	LOW
1996	$509	$382

48560X92
YEARS MFRD 1997-1997
SERIES.......... MURRAY SERIES
ENGINE ....B&S
ENGINE HP................18.5
COOLING..................AIR
FUEL ....G
SPEEDS...............VARIABLE
TRANSMISSION ....HYDRO
STEERING............STANDARD
STANDARD DECK ....48"
MSRP.................$1,394

RETAIL PRICING

YEAR	HIGH	LOW
1997	$529	$396

52100X92
YEARS MFRD 1999-1999
SERIES.......... MURRAY SERIES
ENGINE ....B&S
ENGINE HP..................20
COOLING..................AIR
FUEL ....G
SPEEDS....................5/1
TRANSMISSION ....GEAR
STEERING............STANDARD
STANDARD DECK ....52"
MSRP.................$1,899

RETAIL PRICING

YEAR	HIGH	LOW
1999	$808	$606

52370X92
YEARS MFRD 1997-1997
SERIES.......... MURRAY SERIES
ENGINE ....B&S
ENGINE HP..................20
COOLING..................AIR
FUEL ....G
SPEEDS....................5/1
TRANSMISSION ....GEAR
STEERING............STANDARD
STANDARD DECK ....52"
MSRP.................$1,999

RETAIL PRICING

YEAR	HIGH	LOW
1997	$761	$571

309002
YEARS MFRD 2006-2006
SERIES..... TURF MASTER SERIES
ENGINE ....B&S
CYLINDERS...................1
ENGINE HP................12.5
COOLING..................AIR
FUEL ....G
SPEEDS....................5/1
TRANSMISSION ....GEAR
STEERING............STANDARD

309002X24
YEARS MFRD 2008-2008
SERIES..... TURF MASTER SERIES
ENGINE ....B&S
CYLINDERS...................1
ENGINE HP................12.5
FUEL ....G
SPEEDS....................5/1
TRANSMISSION ....GEAR
STEERING............STANDARD
BLADE CLUTCH ....MANUAL

309007X8
YEARS MFRD 2006-2009
SERIES.... MURRAY SELECT SERIES
ENGINE ....B&S
CYLINDERS...................1
ENGINE HP................12.5
COOLING..................AIR
FUEL ....G
SPEEDS....................5/1
TRANSMISSION ....GEAR
STEERING............STANDARD

309008X99
YEARS MFRD 2006-2009
SERIES.......... MURRAY SERIES
ENGINE ....B&S
CYLINDERS...................1
ENGINE HP................10.5
COOLING..................AIR
FUEL ....G
SPEEDS....................5/1
TRANSMISSION ....GEAR
STEERING............STANDARD

309009
YEARS MFRD 2006-2006
SERIES..... TURF MASTER SERIES
ENGINE ....B&S
CYLINDERS...................1
ENGINE HP................11.5
COOLING..................AIR
FUEL ....G
SPEEDS....................5/1
TRANSMISSION ....GEAR
STEERING............STANDARD

309009
YEARS MFRD 2006-2006
SERIES.......... MURRAY SERIES
ENGINE ....B&S
CYLINDERS...................1
ENGINE HP..................10
COOLING..................AIR
FUEL ....G
SPEEDS....................5/1
TRANSMISSION ....GEAR
STEERING............STANDARD

309009X18
YEARS MFRD 2008-2008
SERIES..... TURF MASTER SERIES
ENGINE ....B&S
ENGINE HP................11.5
COOLING..................AIR
FUEL ....G
SPEEDS....................5/1
TRANSMISSION ....GEAR
STEERING............STANDARD
BLADE CLUTCH ....MANUAL

309009X92
YEARS MFRD 2007-2009
ENGINE ....B&S
CYLINDERS...................1
ENGINE HP..................10
COOLING..................AIR
FUEL ....G
SPEEDS....................5/1
TRANSMISSION ....GEAR
STEERING............STANDARD

387002X92
YEARS MFRD 2007-2009
ENGINE ....B&S
CYLINDERS...................1
ENGINE HP................12.5
COOLING..................AIR
FUEL ....G
SPEEDS....................5/1
TRANSMISSION ....GEAR
STEERING............STANDARD

405000X8
YEARS MFRD 2006-2009
SERIES.... MURRAY SELECT SERIES
ENGINE ....B&S

ENGINE HP 13.5
COOLING . . . . .AIR
FUEL . . . . .G
SPEEDS 5/1
TRANSMISSION . . . . .GEAR
STEERING. . . . . .STANDARD

405004X99
YEARS MFRD 2006-2009
SERIES. . . . . .MURRAY SERIES
ENGINE . . . . .B&S
CYLINDERS. 1
ENGINE HP 12.5
COOLING . . . . .AIR
FUEL . . . . .G
SPEEDS 5/1
TRANSMISSION . . . . .GEAR
STEERING. . . . . .STANDARD

405011X48
YEARS MFRD 2006-2009
SERIES. . . . . .MURRAY SERIES
ENGINE . . . . .B&S
CYLINDERS. 1
ENGINE HP 13
COOLING . . . . .AIR
FUEL . . . . .G
SPEEDS 5/1
TRANSMISSION . . . . .GEAR
STEERING. . . . . .STANDARD

425001X8
YEARS MFRD 2006-2009
SERIES. . . .MURRAY SELECT SERIES
ENGINE . . . . .B&S
ENGINE HP 17.5
COOLING . . . . .AIR
FUEL . . . . .G
SPEEDS 6/1
TRANSMISSION . . . . .GEAR
STEERING. . . . . .STANDARD

425001X99
YEARS MFRD 2006-2009
SERIES. . . . . .MURRAY SERIES
ENGINE . . . . .B&S
CYLINDERS. 1
ENGINE HP 17.5
COOLING . . . . .AIR
FUEL . . . . .G
SPEEDS 6/1
TRANSMISSION . . . . .GEAR
STEERING. . . . . .STANDARD

425014
YEARS MFRD 2006-2006
SERIES. . . . . .MURRAY SERIES
ENGINE . . . . .B&S
CYLINDERS. 1
ENGINE HP 15.5
COOLING . . . . .AIR
FUEL . . . . .G
SPEEDS 5/1
TRANSMISSION . . . . .GEAR
STEERING. . . . . .STANDARD

425014X92
YEARS MFRD 2007-2009
ENGINE . . . . .B&S
CYLINDERS. 1
ENGINE HP 15.5
COOLING . . . . .AIR
FUEL . . . . .G
SPEEDS 5/1
TRANSMISSION . . . . .GEAR
STEERING. . . . . .STANDARD

425016X48
YEARS MFRD 2007-2009
ENGINE . . . . .B&S IC
ENGINE HP 18
COOLING . . . . .AIR
FUEL . . . . .G
SPEEDS 6/1
TRANSMISSION . . . . .GEAR
STEERING. . . . . .STANDARD

425017
YEARS MFRD 2006-2006
SERIES. . . . . TURF MASTER SERIES
ENGINE . . . . .B&S
CYLINDERS. 1
ENGINE HP 16.5
COOLING . . . . .AIR
FUEL . . . . .G
SPEEDS 6/1
TRANSMISSION . . . . .GEAR
STEERING. . . . . .STANDARD

425600X48
YEARS MFRD 2006-2009
SERIES. . . . .
. . .MURRAY PERFORMANCE SERIES
ENGINE . . . . .B&S
ENGINE HP 18
COOLING . . . . .AIR
FUEL . . . . .G
SPEEDS . . . . .VARIABLE
TRANSMISSION . . . . .HYDRO
STEERING. . . . . .STANDARD

425604X99
YEARS MFRD 2007-2009
SERIES. . . . .
. . .MURRAY PERFORMANCE SERIES
ENGINE . . . . B&S OHV
CYLINDERS. 2
ENGINE HP 20
COOLING . . . . .AIR
FUEL . . . . .G
SPEEDS . . . . .VARIABLE
TRANSMISSION . . . . .HYDRO
STEERING. . . . . .STANDARD

425615X99
YEARS MFRD 2006-2009
SERIES. . . . .
. . .MURRAY PERFORMANCE SERIES
ENGINE . . . . .B&S
ENGINE HP 18.5
COOLING . . . . .AIR
FUEL . . . . .G
SPEEDS . . . . .VARIABLE
TRANSMISSION . . . . .HYDRO
STEERING. . . . . .STANDARD

425624X18
YEARS MFRD 2006-2008
SERIES. . . . . TURF MASTER SERIES
ENGINE . . . . .B&S
CYLINDERS. 1
ENGINE HP 16.5
COOLING . . . . .AIR
FUEL . . . . .G
SPEEDS 6/1
TRANSMISSION . . . . .GEAR
STEERING. . . . . .STANDARD

461004X92
YEARS MFRD 2006-2009
SERIES. . . . .
. . .MURRAY PERFORMANCE SERIES
ENGINE . . . . .B&S
CYLINDERS. 2
ENGINE HP 21
COOLING . . . . .AIR
FUEL . . . . .G
SPEEDS 5/1
TRANSMISSION . . . . .GEAR
STEERING. . . . . .STANDARD

461605X99
YEARS MFRD 2006-2009
SERIES. . . . .
. . .MURRAY PERFORMANCE SERIES
ENGINE . . . . .B&S
CYLINDERS. 2
ENGINE HP 22
COOLING . . . . .AIR
FUEL . . . . .G
SPEEDS . . . . .VARIABLE
TRANSMISSION . . . . .HYDRO
STEERING. . . . . .STANDARD

465306X8
YEARS MFRD 2006-2009
SERIES. . . .MURRAY SELECT SERIES
ENGINE . . . . .B&S
ENGINE HP 21
COOLING . . . . .AIR
FUEL . . . . .G
SPEEDS . . . . .VARIABLE
TRANSMISSION . . . . .HYDRO
STEERING. . . . . .STANDARD

465600X48
YEARS MFRD 2006-2009
SERIES. . . . .
. . .MURRAY PERFORMANCE SERIES
ENGINE . . . . .B&S
CYLINDERS. 2
ENGINE HP 20
COOLING . . . . .AIR
FUEL . . . . .G
SPEEDS . . . . .VARIABLE
TRANSMISSION . . . . .HYDRO
STEERING. . . . . .STANDARD

NOTES

NEW HOLLAND

BOOMER 8N

YEARS MFRD	2009-2011
ENGINE	SHIBAURA
CYLINDERS	4
CID	135.2
PTO HP	40
ENGINE HP	50
COOLING	LIQUID
FUEL	D
SPEEDS	VARIABLE
TRANSMISSION	CVT
STEERING	STANDARD
HITCH	CAT. I
DRIVE TYPE	4WD
ROPS/CAB	ROPS
WEIGHT	3,564 LBS.
MSRP	$32,958

OPTIONS

BACKHOE
LDR
ROPS

SERIAL NUMBERS

YEAR	BEGINNING NO.
2009	Z9D8N0101
2010	Z9D8N0525

RETAIL PRICING

YEAR	HIGH	LOW
2009	$22,268	$16,701
2010	$24,006	$18,004
2011	$25,628	$19,221

BOOMER 20

YEARS MFRD	2012-2013
ENGINE	MITSUBISHI
CYLINDERS	3
CID	68.7
PTO HP	16.5
ENGINE HP	23
COOLING	LIQUID
FUEL	D
SPEEDS	VARIABLE
TRANSMISSION	HYDRO
STEERING	STANDARD
HITCH	CAT. I
DRIVE TYPE	4WD
ROPS/CAB	ROPS
MSRP	$12,601

OPTIONS

60"DECK
LDR

SERIAL NUMBERS

YEAR	BEGINNING NO.
2012	2197010636
2013	2197011517

RETAIL PRICING

YEAR	HIGH	LOW
2012	$10,470	$7,853
2013	$11,438	$8,579

BOOMER 24

YEARS MFRD	2014-2018
ENGINE	MITSUBISHI
CYLINDERS	3
CID	80.4
PTO HP	18.5
ENGINE HP	24.4
COOLING	LIQUID
FUEL	D
SPEEDS	VARIABLE
TRANSMISSION	HYDRO
STEERING	STANDARD
HITCH	CAT. I
DRIVE TYPE	4WD
ROPS/CAB	ROPS
WEIGHT	1,708 LBS.
MSRP	$15,374

OPTIONS

LDR

SERIAL NUMBERS

YEAR	BEGINNING NO.
2014	2248000001
2015	2250000630
2016	2250000986

RETAIL PRICING

YEAR	HIGH	LOW
2014	$10,868	$8,151
2015	$11,650	$8,738
2016	$13,000	$9,750
2017	$13,943	$10,458
2018	$14,779	$11,084

BOOMER 25

YEARS MFRD	2012-2013
ENGINE	MITSUBISHI
CYLINDERS	3
PTO HP	19.9
ENGINE HP	27
COOLING	LIQUID
FUEL	D
SPEEDS	VARIABLE
TRANSMISSION	HYDRO
STEERING	STANDARD
HITCH	CAT. I
DRIVE TYPE	4WD
ROPS/CAB	ROPS
MSRP	$14,510

OPTIONS

60"DECK
LDR

SERIAL NUMBERS

YEAR	BEGINNING NO.
2012	2199010642
2013	2199011839

RETAIL PRICING

YEAR	HIGH	LOW
2012	$12,003	$9,003
2013	$13,021	$9,766

BOOMER 30

YEARS MFRD	2010-2013
ENGINE	MITSUBISHI
CYLINDERS	4
CID	92
PTO HP	23.9
ENGINE HP	28
COOLING	LIQUID
FUEL	D
SPEEDS	12/12
TRANSMISSION	SHUTTLE SHIFT
STEERING	STANDARD
HITCH	CAT. I
HYDRAULIC	YES
PTO	YES
DRIVE TYPE	2WD
ROPS/CAB	ROPS
WEIGHT	2,913 LBS.
MSRP	$17,573

OPTIONS

4WD
66"DECK
HYDRO
LDR

SERIAL NUMBERS

YEAR	BEGINNING NO.
2010	2107012151
2011	2107012083
2012	2107013446
2013	2107014520

RETAIL PRICING

YEAR	HIGH	LOW
2010	$11,860	$8,895
2011	$12,690	$9,517
2012	$13,609	$10,207
2013	$14,660	$10,995

AVG. AUCTION PRICING

LOW	HIGH	AVG
$5,610	$14,076	$8,935

BOOMER 33

YEARS MFRD	2014-2016
ENGINE	ISM
CYLINDERS	3
CID	92
PTO HP	26
ENGINE HP	33
COOLING	LIQUID
FUEL	D
SPEEDS	12/12
TRANSMISSION	SHUTTLE SHIFT
STEERING	STANDARD
HITCH	CAT. I
DRIVE TYPE	4WD
ROPS/CAB	ROPS
MSRP	$22,192

OPTIONS

2 HYD
HYDRO
LDR

SERIAL NUMBERS

YEAR	BEGINNING NO.
2014	2242010006
2015	2242010540
2016	2242011010

RETAIL PRICING

YEAR	HIGH	LOW
2014	$17,919	$13,440
2015	$19,721	$14,791
2016	$21,131	$15,849

BOOMER 35

YEARS MFRD	2010-2013
ENGINE	MITSUBISHI
CYLINDERS	4
CID	107
PTO HP	30.3
ENGINE HP	38
COOLING	LIQUID
FUEL	D
SPEEDS	VARIABLE
TRANSMISSION	HYDRO
STEERING	STANDARD
HITCH	CAT. I
HYDRAULIC	YES
PTO	YES
DRIVE TYPE	4WD
ROPS/CAB	ROPS
WEIGHT	2,913 LBS.
MSRP	$22,307

OPTIONS

12/12 SYNCHRO
72"DECK
LDR

SERIAL NUMBERS

YEAR	BEGINNING NO.
2010	2109012634
2011	2109012515
2012	2109013914
2013	2109015307

RETAIL PRICING

YEAR	HIGH	LOW
2010	$15,473	$11,605
2011	$16,420	$12,315
2012	$17,439	$13,079
2013	$18,558	$13,918

BOOMER 35 T4B

YEARS MFRD	2017-2020
ENGINE	L3C19T
CYLINDERS	3
CID	1.9L
PTO HP	29.7
ENGINE HP	35
FUEL	D
SPEEDS	12/12
TRANSMISSION	SHUTTLE SHIFT
STEERING	STANDARD
HITCH	CAT. I
DRIVE TYPE	4WD
ROPS/CAB	ROPS
WEIGHT	2,804 LBS.
MSRP	$22,622

OPTIONS

HYDRO	$1,835
LOADER	
MID PTO	$406

RETAIL PRICING

YEAR	HIGH	LOW
2017	$19,590	$14,692
2018	$20,725	$15,544
2019	$21,988	$16,491
2020	$22,742	$17,336

NEW HOLLAND

BOOMER 37

YEARS MFRD 2014-2016
ENGINE . . . . ISM
CYLINDERS. 3
CID 92
PTO HP 29.6
ENGINE HP 37
COOLING . . . . LIQUID
FUEL . . . . D
SPEEDS 12/12
TRANSMISSION . . . SHUTTLE SHIFT
STEERING. . . . . STANDARD
HITCH . . . . CAT. I
DRIVE TYPE 2WD
ROPS/CAB . . . . ROPS
MSRP. $23,943

OPTIONS

2 HYD
HYDRO
LDR

SERIAL NUMBERS

YEAR . . . . BEGINNING NO.
2014 2230010308
2015 2230011356
2016 2230011980

RETAIL PRICING

YEAR	HIGH	LOW
2014	$19,611	$14,708
2015	$21,259	$15,944
2016	$22,836	$17,127

BOOMER 40

YEARS MFRD 2010-2013
ENGINE . . . . MITSUBISHI
CYLINDERS. 4
CID 153
PTO HP 34.3
ENGINE HP 41
COOLING . . . . LIQUID
FUEL . . . . D
SPEEDS 12/12
TRANSMISSION . . . SHUTTLE SHIFT
STEERING. . . . . STANDARD
HITCH . . . . CAT. I
HYDRAULIC . . . . YES
PTO . . . . YES
DRIVE TYPE 4WD
ROPS/CAB . . . . ROPS
WEIGHT . . . . 3,449 LBS.
MSRP. $23,534

OPTIONS

CAB W/A
HYDRO
LDR

SERIAL NUMBERS

YEAR . . . . BEGINNING NO.
2010 2103011711
2011 2103011629
2012 2103012442
2013 2103014115

RETAIL PRICING

YEAR	HIGH	LOW
2010	$15,374	$11,531
2011	$16,477	$12,358
2012	$18,015	$13,511
2013	$19,283	$14,462

BOOMER 40 T4B

YEARS MFRD 2017-2020
CYLINDERS. 3
CID 1.9L
PTO HP 34
ENGINE HP 40
COOLING . . . . LIQUID
FUEL . . . . D
SPEEDS 12/12
TRANSMISSION . . . SHUTTLE SHIFT
STEERING. . . . . STANDARD
HITCH . . . . CAT. I
DRIVE TYPE 4WD
ROPS/CAB . . . . ROPS
WEIGHT . . . . 2,804 LBS.
MSRP. $24,486

OPTIONS

CAB. $5,597
HYDRO. $1,835
LOADER
MID PTO. $406

RETAIL PRICING

YEAR	HIGH	LOW
2017	$21,281	$16,036
2018	$22,589	$17,017
2019	$24,038	$18,103
2020	$24,927	$18,877

BOOMER 41

YEARS MFRD 2014-2016
ENGINE . . . . ISM
CYLINDERS. 4
CID 135
PTO HP 32.4
ENGINE HP 41
COOLING . . . . LIQUID
FUEL . . . . D
SPEEDS 16/16
TRANSMISSION . . . SHUTTLE SHIFT
STEERING. . . . . STANDARD
HITCH . . . . CAT. I
DRIVE TYPE 4WD
ROPS/CAB . . . . ROPS
MSRP. $26,510

OPTIONS

2 HYD
HYDRO
LDR

SERIAL NUMBERS

YEAR . . . . BEGINNING NO.
2014 2231010257
2015 2231011773
2016 2231012263

RETAIL PRICING

YEAR	HIGH	LOW
2014	$21,897	$16,423
2015	$23,773	$17,830
2016	$25,904	$19,428

BOOMER 45 T4B

YEARS MFRD 2017-2020
CYLINDERS. 3
CID 1.9L
PTO HP 38.2
ENGINE HP 45
FUEL . . . . D
SPEEDS 16/16
TRANSMISSION . . . SHUTTLE SHIFT
STEERING. . . . . STANDARD
HITCH . . . . CAT. I
DRIVE TYPE 4WD
ROPS/CAB . . . . ROPS
WEIGHT . . . . 3,424 LBS.
MSRP. $27,612

OPTIONS

CAB. $5,427
HYDRO. $1,835
LOADER
MID PTO. $406

RETAIL PRICING

YEAR	HIGH	LOW
2017	$24,063	$18,047
2018	$25,636	$19,227
2019	$27,100	$20,325
2020	$28,042	$21,530

BOOMER 46D

YEARS MFRD 2015-2018
ENGINE . . . . FPT
CYLINDERS. 3
CID 135.9
PTO HP 36
ENGINE HP 45.1
FUEL . . . . D
SPEEDS . . . . VARIABLE
TRANSMISSION . . . . CVT
STEERING. . . . . STANDARD
HITCH . . . . CAT. I
DRIVE TYPE 4WD
ROPS/CAB . . . . ROPS
WEIGHT . . . . 4,190 LBS.
MSRP. $32,802

OPTIONS

CAB W/A
LDR

SERIAL NUMBERS

YEAR . . . . BEGINNING NO.
2015 . . . . ZEMCB1001
2016 . . . . ZFMCB1226

RETAIL PRICING

YEAR	HIGH	LOW
2015	$22,741	$17,056
2016	$25,365	$19,024
2017	$27,676	$20,757
2018	$30,098	$22,574

BOOMER 47

YEARS MFRD 2014-2016
ENGINE . . . . ISM
CYLINDERS. 4
CID 135
PTO HP 37.3
ENGINE HP 47
COOLING . . . . LIQUID
FUEL . . . . D
SPEEDS 16/16
TRANSMISSION . . . SHUTTLE SHIFT
STEERING. . . . . STANDARD
HITCH . . . . CAT. I
DRIVE TYPE 4WD
ROPS/CAB . . . . ROPS
MSRP. $28,990

OPTIONS

2 HYD
HYDRO
LDR

SERIAL NUMBERS

YEAR . . . . BEGINNING NO.
2014 2229010260
2015 2229012243
2016 2229012778

RETAIL PRICING

YEAR	HIGH	LOW
2014	$24,170	$18,127
2015	$26,652	$19,989
2016	$27,948	$20,961

BOOMER 50

YEARS MFRD 2010-2013
ENGINE . . . . MITSUBISHI
CYLINDERS. 4
CID 153
PTO HP 37.1
ENGINE HP 47
COOLING . . . . LIQUID
FUEL . . . . D
SPEEDS . . . . VARIABLE
TRANSMISSION . . . . HYDRO
STEERING. . . . . STANDARD
HITCH . . . . CAT. I
HYDRAULIC . . . . YES
PTO . . . . YES
DRIVE TYPE 4WD
ROPS/CAB . . . . ROPS
WEIGHT . . . . 3,549 LBS.
MSRP. $27,092

OPTIONS

LDR

SERIAL NUMBERS

YEAR . . . . BEGINNING NO.
2010 2105011502
2011 2105011325
2012 2105012065
2013 2105013195

RETAIL PRICING

YEAR	HIGH	LOW
2010	$18,105	$13,579
2011	$19,288	$14,466
2012	$20,642	$15,481
2013	$22,147	$16,610

BOOMER 50 T4B

YEARS MFRD 2017-2020
CYLINDERS. 3
CID 1.9L
PTO HP 42.5
ENGINE HP 50
FUEL . . . . D
SPEEDS 16/16
TRANSMISSION . . . SHUTTLE SHIFT
STEERING. . . . . STANDARD

HITCH . . . . . CAT. I
DRIVE TYPE 4WD
ROPS/CAB . . . . . ROPS
WEIGHT . . . . . 3,424 LBS.
MSRP. $30,792

OPTIONS

CAB $5,541
HYDRO. $1,835
LOADER
MID PTO. $406

RETAIL PRICING

YEAR	HIGH	LOW
2017	$26,298	$19,723
2018	$27,781	$20,836
2019	$29,321	$21,991
2020	$30,531	$23,310

BOOMER 54D

YEARS MFRD 2015-2018
ENGINE . . . . . FPT
CYLINDERS. 3
CID 135.9
PTO HP 43
ENGINE HP 53
FUEL . . . . . D
SPEEDS . . . . . VARIABLE
TRANSMISSION . . . . . CVT
STEERING. . . . . STANDARD
HITCH . . . . . CAT. I
DRIVE TYPE 4WD
ROPS/CAB . . . . . ROPS
WEIGHT . . . . . 4,190 LBS.
MSRP. $35,899

OPTIONS

CAB W/A
LDR

SERIAL NUMBERS

YEAR	BEGINNING NO.
2015	ZEMCB1001
2016	ZFMCB1226

RETAIL PRICING

YEAR	HIGH	LOW
2015	$24,666	$18,499
2016	$27,411	$20,559
2017	$29,857	$22,393
2018	$32,609	$24,457

BOOMER 55 T4B

YEARS MFRD 2017-2020
CYLINDERS. 3
CID 1.9L
PTO HP 46.7
ENGINE HP 55
FUEL . . . . . D
SPEEDS 16/16
TRANSMISSION . . . SHUTTLE SHIFT
STEERING. . . . . STANDARD
HITCH . . . . . CAT. I
DRIVE TYPE 4WD
ROPS/CAB . . . . . ROPS
WEIGHT . . . . . 3,424 LBS.
MSRP. $33,862

OPTIONS

CAB $5,541
HYDRO. $1,835
LOADER $6,475
MID PTO. $406

RETAIL PRICING

YEAR	HIGH	LOW
2017	$28,718	$21,538
2018	$30,311	$22,733
2019	$32,879	$24,659
2020	$33,996	$25,756

BOOMER 1020

YEARS MFRD 2008-2011
SERIES. . . . . 1000 SERIES
CYLINDERS. 3
PTO HP 15.5
ENGINE HP 20
COOLING . . . . . LIQUID
FUEL . . . . . D
SPEEDS . . . . . VARIABLE
TRANSMISSION . . . . . HYDRO
STEERING. . . . . STANDARD
HITCH . . . . . CAT. I
HYDRAULIC . . . . . YES
PTO. . . . . YES
DRIVE TYPE 4WD
ROPS/CAB . . . . . ROPS
WEIGHT . . . . . 1,455 LBS.
MSRP. $11,556

OPTIONS

60"DECK
LDR

SERIAL NUMBERS

YEAR	BEGINNING NO.
2009	Z8NXK1041
2010	Z9NXK1066
2011	ZANXK1079

RETAIL PRICING

YEAR	HIGH	LOW
2008	$7,153	$5,365
2009	$7,866	$5,900
2010	$8,612	$6,459
2011	$9,388	$7,041

BOOMER 1025

YEARS MFRD 2008-2011
SERIES. . . . . 1000 SERIES
ENGINE . . . . . SHIBAURA
CYLINDERS. 3
CID 69
PTO HP 19.7
ENGINE HP 26
COOLING . . . . . LIQUID
FUEL . . . . . D
SPEEDS . . . . . VARIABLE
TRANSMISSION . . . . . HYDRO
STEERING. . . . . STANDARD
HITCH . . . . . CAT. I
HYDRAULIC . . . . . YES
PTO. . . . . YES
DRIVE TYPE 4WD
ROPS/CAB . . . . . ROPS
WEIGHT . . . . . 1,455 LBS.
MSRP. $12,350

OPTIONS

60"DECK
LDR

SERIAL NUMBERS

YEAR	BEGINNING NO.
2009	Z7DB05182
2010	Z9NXL1285
2011	ZANXL1226

RETAIL PRICING

YEAR	HIGH	LOW
2008	$7,808	$5,856
2009	$8,537	$6,403
2010	$9,309	$6,981
2011	$10,111	$7,583

BOOMER 1030

YEARS MFRD 2008-2011
ENGINE . . . . . SHIBAURA
CYLINDERS. 3
PTO HP 20.5
ENGINE HP 28
COOLING . . . . . AIR
FUEL . . . . . D
SPEEDS . . . . . VARIABLE
TRANSMISSION . . . . . HYDRO
STEERING. . . . . STANDARD
HITCH . . . . . CAT. I
HYDRAULIC . . . . . YES
PTO. . . . . YES
DRIVE TYPE 4WD
ROPS/CAB . . . . . ROPS
WEIGHT . . . . . 1,492 LBS.
MSRP. $14,055

OPTIONS

60"DECK
LDR

SERIAL NUMBERS

YEAR	BEGINNING NO.
2008	Z8NXM1093
2009	Z8NXL1029
2010	Z9NXL1285
2011	ZANXM1214

RETAIL PRICING

YEAR	HIGH	LOW
2008	$9,531	$7,148
2009	$10,134	$7,600
2010	$10,762	$8,072
2011	$11,453	$8,589

BOOMER 2030

YEARS MFRD 2008-2011
SERIES. . . . . 2000 SERIES
ENGINE . . . . . SHIBAURA
CYLINDERS. 3
PTO HP 26.5
ENGINE HP 31
COOLING . . . . . LIQUID
FUEL . . . . . D
SPEEDS 9/3
TRANSMISSION . . . . . GEAR
STEERING. . . . . STANDARD
HITCH . . . . . CAT. I
HYDRAULIC . . . . . YES
PTO. . . . . YES
DRIVE TYPE 4WD
ROPS/CAB . . . . . ROPS
WEIGHT . . . . . 2,605 LBS.
MSRP. $18,525

OPTIONS

2 HYD
HYDRO
LDR

SERIAL NUMBERS

YEAR	BEGINNING NO.
2009	Z8DA09510
2011	Z9DA06634

RETAIL PRICING

YEAR	HIGH	LOW
2008	$13,074	$9,806
2009	$13,931	$10,448
2010	$14,825	$11,119
2011	$15,752	$11,814

BOOMER 2035

YEARS MFRD 2008-2011
SERIES. . . . . 2000 SERIES
ENGINE . . . . . SHIBAURA
CYLINDERS. 3
CID 101
PTO HP 28.9
ENGINE HP 35
COOLING . . . . . LIQUID
FUEL . . . . . D
SPEEDS . . . . . VARIABLE
TRANSMISSION . . . . . HYDRO
STEERING. . . . . STANDARD
HITCH . . . . . CAT. I
HYDRAULIC . . . . . YES
PTO. . . . . YES
WEIGHT . . . . . 2,620 LBS.
MSRP. $20,974

OPTIONS

72"DECK
LDR

SERIAL NUMBERS

YEAR	BEGINNING NO.
2009	Z8DA09507
2011	Z9DA06636

RETAIL PRICING

YEAR	HIGH	LOW
2008	$15,765	$11,824
2009	$16,799	$12,600
2010	$17,729	$13,296
2011	$18,733	$14,050

BOOMER 3040

YEARS MFRD 2008-2011
SERIES. . . . . 3000 SERIES
ENGINE . . . . . SHIBAURA
CYLINDERS. 4
CID 121
PTO HP 35
ENGINE HP 40
COOLING . . . . . LIQUID
FUEL . . . . . D
SPEEDS 12/12
TRANSMISSION . . . SHUTTLE SHIFT
STEERING. . . . . STANDARD
HITCH . . . . . CAT. I
HYDRAULIC . . . . . YES
PTO. . . . . YES
DRIVE TYPE 2WD
ROPS/CAB . . . . . ROPS
WEIGHT . . . . . 2,860 LBS.
MSRP. $22,955

OPTIONS

4WD
CAB W/A/H
HYDRO
LDR

SERIAL NUMBERS

YEAR	BEGINNING NO.
2009	Z8DB02510
2011	Z9DB12137

RETAIL PRICING

YEAR	HIGH	LOW
2008	$14,865	$11,149
2009	$15,980	$11,985
2010	$17,053	$12,790
2011	$18,215	$13,661

BOOMER 3040 CVT

YEARS MFRD 2013-2014
ENGINE . . . . SHIBAURA N844
CYLINDERS. 4
CID 121.7
PTO HP 32
ENGINE HP 40
COOLING . . . . LIQUID
FUEL . . . . D
SPEEDS . . . . VARIABLE
TRANSMISSION . . . . CVT
STEERING. . . . . STANDARD
HITCH . . . . CAT. I
HYDRAULIC . . . . YES
PTO . . . . YES
DRIVE TYPE 4WD
ROPS/CAB . . . . CAB
MSRP. $36,027

OPTIONS

MID PTO

SERIAL NUMBERS

YEAR	BEGINNING NO.
2013	ZCMB11138
2014	ZDMB11990

RETAIL PRICING

YEAR	HIGH	LOW
2013	$26,847	$20,136
2014	$28,622	$21,467

BOOMER 3045

YEARS MFRD 2008-2011
SERIES. . . . . 3000 SERIES
ENGINE . . . . SHIBAURA
CYLINDERS. 4
CID 135
PTO HP 39.6
ENGINE HP 45
COOLING . . . . LIQUID
FUEL . . . . D
SPEEDS . . . . VARIABLE
TRANSMISSION . . . . HYDRO
STEERING. . . . . STANDARD
HITCH . . . . CAT. I
HYDRAULIC . . . . YES
PTO . . . . YES
DRIVE TYPE 4WD
ROPS/CAB . . . . ROPS
WEIGHT . . . . 2,881 LBS.
MSRP. $27,705

OPTIONS

2 HYD
C/A/H

RETAIL PRICING

YEAR	HIGH	LOW
2008	$17,813	$13,360
2009	$18,971	$14,228
2010	$20,245	$15,184
2011	$21,544	$16,158

AVG. AUCTION PRICING

LOW	HIGH	AVG
$13,918	$26,415	$19,408

BOOMER 3045CVT

YEARS MFRD 2013-2014
SERIES. . . . . 3000 SERIES
ENGINE . . . . SHIBAURA N844L
CYLINDERS. 4
CID 135.2
PTO HP 36
ENGINE HP 45
COOLING . . . . LIQUID
FUEL . . . . D
SPEEDS . . . . VARIABLE
TRANSMISSION . . . . CVT
STEERING. . . . . STANDARD
HITCH . . . . CAT. I
HYDRAULIC . . . . YES
PTO . . . . YES
DRIVE TYPE 4WD
ROPS/CAB . . . . CAB
WEIGHT . . . . 4,136 LBS.
MSRP. $38,309

OPTIONS

MID PTO

SERIAL NUMBERS

YEAR	BEGINNING NO.
2013	ZCMB11138
2014	ZDMB11990

RETAIL PRICING

YEAR	HIGH	LOW
2013	$29,030	$21,773
2014	$30,308	$22,731

BOOMER 3050

YEARS MFRD 2008-2011
SERIES. . . . . 3000 SERIES
ENGINE . . . . SHIBAURA
CYLINDERS. 4
CID 135
PTO HP 43
ENGINE HP 50
COOLING . . . . LIQUID
FUEL . . . . D
SPEEDS 12/12
TRANSMISSION . . . SHUTTLE SHIFT
STEERING. . . . . STANDARD
HITCH . . . . CAT. I
HYDRAULIC . . . . YES
PTO . . . . YES
DRIVE TYPE 4WD
ROPS/CAB . . . . CAB
WEIGHT . . . . 3,497 LBS.
MSRP. $26,702

OPTIONS

LDR
MID PTO
SUPER STEER

SERIAL NUMBERS

YEAR	BEGINNING NO.
2008	Z7DG11425
2009	Z8DB02569
2010	Z9DB12125
2011	ZADB12729

RETAIL PRICING

YEAR	HIGH	LOW
2008	$17,354	$13,016
2009	$18,459	$13,844
2010	$19,653	$14,740
2011	$20,943	$15,707

BOOMER 3050CVT

YEARS MFRD 2013-2014
SERIES. . . . . 3000 SERIES
ENGINE . . . . SHIBAURA N844L
CYLINDERS. 4
CID 135.2
PTO HP 40
ENGINE HP 50
COOLING . . . . LIQUID
FUEL . . . . D
SPEEDS . . . . VARIABLE
TRANSMISSION . . . . CVT
STEERING. . . . . STANDARD
HITCH . . . . CAT. I
HYDRAULIC . . . . YES
PTO . . . . YES
DRIVE TYPE 4WD
ROPS/CAB . . . . CAB
WEIGHT . . . . 4,136 LBS.
MSRP. $40,745

OPTIONS

MID PTO

SERIAL NUMBERS

YEAR	BEGINNING NO.
2013	ZCMB11138
2014	ZDMB11990

RETAIL PRICING

YEAR	HIGH	LOW
2013	$30,895	$23,171
2014	$32,348	$24,261

CM222

YEARS MFRD 1993-2000
ENGINE . . . . ISM
ENGINE HP 22
COOLING . . . . LIQUID
FUEL . . . . D
SPEEDS . . . . VARIABLE
TRANSMISSION . . . . HYDRO
STEERING. . . . . ZERO
STANDARD DECK . . . . 60"
MSRP. $17,308

OPTIONS

60" BLADE
72" DECK

SERIAL NUMBERS

YEAR	BEGINNING NO.
1994	TA11717
1995	TA11989
1996	TA12235
1997	TA12249
1998	TA12422
1999	TA12590

RETAIL PRICING

YEAR	HIGH	LOW
1993	$2,044	$1,533
1994	$2,268	$1,701
1995	$2,515	$1,886
1996	$2,788	$2,091
1997	$3,096	$2,322
1998	$3,430	$2,573
1999	$3,807	$2,855
2000	$4,222	$3,166

CM224

YEARS MFRD 1990-2000
ENGINE . . . . ISM
ENGINE HP 22
COOLING . . . . LIQUID
FUEL . . . . D
TRANSMISSION . . . . HYDRO
STEERING. . . . . ZERO
DRIVE TYPE 4WD
STANDARD DECK . . . . 60"
MSRP. $18,691

OPTIONS

60" BLADE
72" DECK

SERIAL NUMBERS

YEAR	BEGINNING NO.
1994	TA11717
1995	TA11989
1996	TA12235
1997	TA12252
1998	TA12547
1999	TA12590

RETAIL PRICING

YEAR	HIGH	LOW
1992	$1,990	$1,493
1993	$2,208	$1,656
1994	$2,445	$1,834
1995	$2,713	$2,035
1996	$3,011	$2,258
1997	$3,342	$2,506
1998	$3,704	$2,778
1999	$4,110	$3,082
2000	$4,599	$3,449

CM272

YEARS MFRD 1992-2000
ENGINE . . . . ISM
ENGINE HP 27
COOLING . . . . LIQUID
FUEL . . . . D
TRANSMISSION . . . . HYDRO
STEERING. . . . . ZERO
STANDARD DECK . . . . 60"
MSRP. $18,502

OPTIONS

60" BLADE
72" DECK

SERIAL NUMBERS

YEAR	BEGINNING NO.
1994	TB11580
1995	TB12112
1996	TB12545
1997	TB12732
1998	TB13122
1999	TB13593

RETAIL PRICING

YEAR	HIGH	LOW
1992	$1,926	$1,444
1993	$2,139	$1,604
1994	$2,373	$1,779
1995	$2,635	$1,976
1996	$2,920	$2,190
1997	$3,237	$2,428
1998	$3,594	$2,696
1999	$3,985	$2,989
2000	$4,421	$3,316

CM274

YEARS MFRD 1990-2000
ENGINE .... ISM
ENGINE HP 27
COOLING .... LIQUID
FUEL .... D
TRANSMISSION .... HYDRO
STEERING .... ZERO
DRIVE TYPE 4WD
STANDARD DECK .... 60"
MSRP $20,074

OPTIONS

60" BLADE
72" DECK

SERIAL NUMBERS

YEAR	BEGINNING NO.
1994	TB11580
1995	TB12112
1996	TB12545
1997	TB12732
1998	TB13122
1999	TB13593

RETAIL PRICING

YEAR	HIGH	LOW
1992	$2,134	$1,600
1993	$2,365	$1,774
1994	$2,630	$1,972
1995	$2,915	$2,186
1996	$3,268	$2,451
1997	$3,588	$2,691
1998	$4,040	$3,030
1999	$4,417	$3,312
2000	$4,937	$3,703

G4010

YEARS MFRD 2007-2009
SERIES .... G SERIES
ENGINE . . KOHLER COURAGE SV590
CYLINDERS 1
ENGINE HP 19
COOLING .... AIR
FUEL .... G
SPEEDS .... VARIABLE
TRANSMISSION ..... DUAL HYDRO
STEERING .... ZERO
STANDARD DECK .... 42"
WEIGHT .... 500 LBS.
MSRP $3,251

OPTIONS

BAGGER

RETAIL PRICING

YEAR	HIGH	LOW
2007	$1,446	$1,085
2008	$1,610	$1,207
2009	$1,787	$1,340

G4020

YEARS MFRD 2007-2008
SERIES .... G SERIES
ENGINE . . KOHLER COURAGE SV610
CYLINDERS 1
ENGINE HP 21
COOLING .... AIR
FUEL .... G
SPEEDS .... VARIABLE
TRANSMISSION ..... DUAL HYDRO
STEERING .... ZERO
STANDARD DECK .... 50"
WEIGHT .... 552 LBS.
MSRP $3,420

OPTIONS

BAGGER

RETAIL PRICING

YEAR	HIGH	LOW
2007	$1,575	$1,181
2008	$1,763	$1,322

G4030

YEARS MFRD 2007-2008
SERIES .... G SERIES
ENGINE . . KOHLER COURAGE SV720
CYLINDERS 2
ENGINE HP 23
COOLING .... AIR
FUEL .... G
SPEEDS .... VARIABLE
TRANSMISSION ..... DUAL HYDRO
STEERING .... ZERO
STANDARD DECK .... 50"
WEIGHT .... 565 LBS.
MSRP $3,794

OPTIONS

BAGGER

RETAIL PRICING

YEAR	HIGH	LOW
2007	$1,757	$1,318
2008	$1,971	$1,478

G4035

YEARS MFRD 2009-2009
ENGINE ... KOHLER COURAGE PRO
CYLINDERS 2
ENGINE HP 25
COOLING .... AIR
FUEL .... G
SPEEDS .... VARIABLE
TRANSMISSION .... HYDRO
STEERING .... ZERO
STANDARD DECK .... 50"
WEIGHT .... 649 LBS.
MSRP $4,175

OPTIONS

BAGGER

RETAIL PRICING

YEAR	HIGH	LOW
2009	$2,293	$1,720

G4050

YEARS MFRD 2008-2011
SERIES .... G SERIES
ENGINE ... KOHLER COURAGE PRO
CYLINDERS 2
ENGINE HP 25
COOLING .... AIR
FUEL .... G
SPEEDS .... VARIABLE
TRANSMISSION ..... DUAL HYDRO
STEERING .... ZERO
STANDARD DECK .... 52"
WEIGHT .... 649 LBS.
MSRP $6,456

OPTIONS

BAGGER

RETAIL PRICING

YEAR	HIGH	LOW
2008	$3,128	$2,346
2009	$3,474	$2,606
2010	$3,856	$2,892
2011	$4,281	$3,211

G5030

YEARS MFRD 2009-2011
ENGINE .... KAWASAKI FX751V
CYLINDERS 2
ENGINE HP 27
COOLING .... AIR
FUEL .... G
SPEEDS .... VARIABLE
TRANSMISSION .... HYDRO
STEERING .... ZERO
STANDARD DECK .... 54"
WEIGHT .... 974 LBS.
MSRP $10,439

OPTIONS

60" DECK

RETAIL PRICING

YEAR	HIGH	LOW
2009	$5,620	$4,215
2010	$6,238	$4,679
2011	$8,827	$6,620

G5035

YEARS MFRD 2009-2011
ENGINE .... KAWASAKI FX850V
CYLINDERS 2
ENGINE HP 31
COOLING .... AIR
FUEL .... G
SPEEDS .... VARIABLE
TRANSMISSION .... HYDRO
STEERING .... ZERO
STANDARD DECK .... 66"
WEIGHT .... 974 LBS.
MSRP $11,636

RETAIL PRICING

YEAR	HIGH	LOW
2009	$6,416	$4,812
2010	$7,126	$5,344
2011	$7,912	$5,934

G6030

YEARS MFRD 2009-2011
CYLINDERS 3
CID 101.4
ENGINE HP 30
COOLING .... LIQUID
FUEL .... D
SPEEDS .... VARIABLE
TRANSMISSION .... HYDRO
STEERING .... ZERO
STANDARD DECK .... 60"
MSRP $23,855

OPTIONS

52" SNOW BLOWER
60" BLADE
84" DECK

RETAIL PRICING

YEAR	HIGH	LOW
2009	$12,699	$9,524
2010	$14,085	$10,564
2011	$15,624	$11,718

G6035

YEARS MFRD 2009-2011
CYLINDERS 3
CID 101.4
ENGINE HP 36
COOLING .... LIQUID
FUEL .... D
SPEEDS .... VARIABLE
TRANSMISSION .... HYDRO
STEERING .... STANDARD
STANDARD DECK .... 60"
MSRP $25,602

OPTIONS

52" SNOW BLOWER
60" BLADE
84" DECK

RETAIL PRICING

YEAR	HIGH	LOW
2009	$13,624	$10,218
2010	$15,114	$11,336
2011	$16,769	$12,577

GT18

YEARS MFRD 1998-2003
ENGINE .... KOHLER
ENGINE HP 18
COOLING .... AIR
FUEL .... G
SPEEDS .... VARIABLE
TRANSMISSION .... HYDRO
STEERING .... STANDARD
STANDARD DECK .... 44"
WEIGHT .... 1,008 LBS.
MSRP $6,822

NEW HOLLAND

OPTIONS
44" SNOW BLOWER
48" BLADE
52" DECK
BAGGER

SERIAL NUMBERS

YEAR	BEGINNING NO.
1998	T8AA0001
1999	T9AA0001
2000	T0AA0001
2002	T2AA0001
2003	T3AA0001

RETAIL PRICING

YEAR	HIGH	LOW
1998	$984	$738
1999	$1,089	$817
2000	$1,204	$903
2001	$1,335	$1,001
2002	$1,473	$1,105
2003	$1,629	$1,222

GT20

YEARS MFRD 1998-2004
ENGINE .... KAWASAKI
ENGINE HP 20
COOLING .... LIQUID
FUEL .... G
SPEEDS .... VARIABLE
TRANSMISSION .... HYDRO
STEERING .... STANDARD
STANDARD DECK .... 52"
WEIGHT .... 1,018 LBS.
MSRP $8,987

OPTIONS
44" SNOW BLOWER
48" BLADE
60" DECK
BAGGER

SERIAL NUMBERS

YEAR	BEGINNING NO.
1998	T8AB0001
1999	T9AB0001
2000	T0AB0001
2002	T2AB0001
2003	T3AB0001
2004	T04AF0001

RETAIL PRICING

YEAR	HIGH	LOW
1998	$1,592	$1,194
1999	$1,757	$1,318
2000	$1,942	$1,457
2001	$2,146	$1,610
2002	$2,373	$1,779
2003	$2,620	$1,965
2004	$2,897	$2,173

AVG. AUCTION PRICING

LOW	HIGH	AVG
$893	$1,428	$1,097

GT20A

YEARS MFRD 2004-2006
ENGINE .... KOHLER COMMAND
ENGINE HP 20
COOLING .... AIR
FUEL .... G
SPEEDS .... VARIABLE
TRANSMISSION .... HYDRO
STEERING .... STANDARD
BLADE CLUTCH .... ELECTRIC
HYDRAULIC .... YES
STANDARD DECK .... 52"
WEIGHT .... 1,008 LBS.
MSRP $7,737

OPTIONS
2 BAG
36" TILLER
44" SNOW BLOWER
60" DECK

SERIAL NUMBERS

YEAR	BEGINNING NO.
2004	T04AF0001
2005	T05AF0001
2006	T06AF0001

RETAIL PRICING

YEAR	HIGH	LOW
2004	$2,332	$1,749
2005	$2,577	$1,932
2006	$2,847	$2,135

GT22

YEARS MFRD 1998-2004
ENGINE .... KOHLER
ENGINE HP 22
COOLING .... AIR
FUEL .... G
SPEEDS .... VARIABLE
TRANSMISSION .... HYDRO
STEERING .... STANDARD
STANDARD DECK .... 60"
WEIGHT .... 1,017 LBS.
MSRP $8,819

OPTIONS
44" SNOW BLOWER
52" DECK
BAGGER
P/S

SERIAL NUMBERS

YEAR	BEGINNING NO.
1998	T8AD0001
1999	T9AE0001
2000	T0AE0001
2002	T2AE0026
2003	T3AE0001
2004	T04AG0001

RETAIL PRICING

YEAR	HIGH	LOW
1998	$1,524	$1,143
1999	$1,683	$1,262
2000	$1,862	$1,396
2001	$2,056	$1,542
2002	$2,273	$1,704
2003	$2,510	$1,883
2004	$2,774	$2,081

GT22A

YEARS MFRD 2004-2006
ENGINE .... KOHLER COMMAND
ENGINE HP 22
COOLING .... AIR
FUEL .... G
SPEEDS .... VARIABLE
TRANSMISSION .... HYDRO
STEERING .... STANDARD
BLADE CLUTCH .... ELECTRIC
HYDRAULIC .... YES
STANDARD DECK .... 60"
WEIGHT .... 1,017 LBS.
MSRP $9,231

OPTIONS
36" TILLER
42" SNOW THROWER
44" SNOW BLOWER
52" DECK

SERIAL NUMBERS

YEAR	BEGINNING NO.
2004	T04AG0001
2005	T05AG0001
2006	T06AG0001

RETAIL PRICING

YEAR	HIGH	LOW
2004	$2,781	$2,085
2005	$3,073	$2,305
2006	$3,397	$2,547

GT75

YEARS MFRD 1992-1998
ENGINE .... ISM
ENGINE HP 16
COOLING .... LIQUID
FUEL .... D
TRANSMISSION .... HYDRO
STEERING .... STANDARD
STANDARD DECK .... 48"
MSRP $10,790

OPTIONS
42" SNOW BLOWER
60" DECK
BAGGER
P/S

SERIAL NUMBERS

YEAR	BEGINNING NO.
1992	T700001
1993	T700589
1994	T700903
1995	T701268
1996	T701461
1997	T701550
1998	T701756

RETAIL PRICING

YEAR	HIGH	LOW
1992	$935	$702
1993	$1,033	$775
1994	$1,142	$857
1995	$1,263	$947
1996	$1,395	$1,047
1997	$1,541	$1,156
1998	$1,703	$1,278

GT85

YEARS MFRD 1992-1997
ENGINE .... KOHLER
ENGINE HP 18
COOLING .... AIR
FUEL .... G
TRANSMISSION .... HYDRO
STEERING .... STANDARD
STANDARD DECK .... 48"
MSRP $9,406

OPTIONS
42" SNOW BLOWER
60" DECK
BAGGER
P/S

SERIAL NUMBERS

YEAR	BEGINNING NO.
1992	T800001
1993	T800784
1994	T801221
1995	T801614
1996	T801877
1997	T801920

RETAIL PRICING

YEAR	HIGH	LOW
1992	$901	$675
1993	$996	$747
1994	$1,101	$825
1995	$1,216	$912
1996	$1,344	$1,008
1997	$1,485	$1,114

GT95

YEARS MFRD 1992-1997
ENGINE .... KOHLER
ENGINE HP 20
COOLING .... AIR
FUEL .... G
TRANSMISSION .... HYDRO
STEERING .... STANDARD
STANDARD DECK .... 60"
MSRP $10,684

OPTIONS
42" SNOW BLOWER
48" DECK
BAGGER
P/S

SERIAL NUMBERS

YEAR	BEGINNING NO.
1992	T900001
1993	T900319
1994	T900414
1995	T900557
1996	T900683
1997	T900708

RETAIL PRICING

YEAR	HIGH	LOW
1992	$963	$722
1993	$1,062	$796
1994	$1,175	$881
1995	$1,296	$972
1996	$1,434	$1,076
1997	$1,583	$1,187

LGT16D

YEARS MFRD 1988-1991
ENGINE .... ISM
ENGINE HP 16
COOLING .... LIQUID
FUEL .... D
TRANSMISSION .... HYDRO
STEERING .... STANDARD

STANDARD DECK	48"
MSRP	$7,795

SERIAL NUMBERS

YEAR	BEGINNING NO.
1988	T100001
1989	T100263
1990	T100862
1991	T101040

RETAIL PRICING

YEAR	HIGH	LOW
1988	$329	$247
1989	$366	$275
1990	$406	$304
1991	$452	$339

LGT18H

YEARS MFRD	1988-1991
ENGINE	KOHLER
ENGINE HP	18
COOLING	AIR
FUEL	G
TRANSMISSION	HYDRO
STEERING	STANDARD
STANDARD DECK	48"
MSRP	$6,000

SERIAL NUMBERS

YEAR	BEGINNING NO.
1988	L8L
1989	L9L
1990	L0L
1991	L1L

RETAIL PRICING

YEAR	HIGH	LOW
1988	$1,043	$783
1989	$1,106	$829
1990	$1,404	$1,053
1991	$1,538	$1,154

LS35

YEARS MFRD	1994-2003
ENGINE	KOHLER
ENGINE HP	15
COOLING	AIR
FUEL	G
SPEEDS	VARIABLE
TRANSMISSION	HYDRO
STEERING	STANDARD
STANDARD DECK	42"
MSRP	$3,977

OPTIONS

36" TILLER
42" SNOW BLOWER
BAGGER
HYD LIFT

SERIAL NUMBERS

YEAR	BEGINNING NO.
1994	T4B
1995	T5B
1996	T6B0001
1997	T7B0001
1998	T8B0001
1999	T9B0001
2000	T0B0001
2001	T1B0001
2002	T2B0001
2003	T3B0001

RETAIL PRICING

YEAR	HIGH	LOW
1995	$349	$262
1996	$385	$288
1997	$424	$318
1998	$468	$351
1999	$518	$389
2000	$570	$428
2001	$630	$473
2002	$695	$521
2003	$768	$576

LS45G

YEARS MFRD	1994-1998
ENGINE	KOHLER
ENGINE HP	16
FUEL	G
TRANSMISSION	GEAR
STEERING	STANDARD
STANDARD DECK	48"
MSRP	$4,389

SERIAL NUMBERS

YEAR	BEGINNING NO.
1994	T4C
1995	T5C
1996	T6C
1997	T7C
1998	T8C

RETAIL PRICING

YEAR	HIGH	LOW
1994	$1,150	$862
1995	$1,206	$904
1996	$1,276	$957
1997	$1,369	$1,027
1998	$1,563	$1,172

LS45H

YEARS MFRD	1994-2003
ENGINE	KOHLER
ENGINE HP	18
COOLING	AIR
FUEL	G
SPEEDS	VARIABLE
TRANSMISSION	HYDRO
STEERING	STANDARD
STANDARD DECK	42"
MSRP	$4,699

OPTIONS

36" TILLER
42" SNOW BLOWER
52" DECK
BAGGER

SERIAL NUMBERS

YEAR	BEGINNING NO.
1994	T4D
1995	T5D
1996	T6D
1997	T7D
1998	T8D
1999	T9D
2000	T0D
2001	T1D
2002	T2D
2003	T3D

RETAIL PRICING

YEAR	HIGH	LOW
1994	$563	$422
1995	$609	$457
1996	$674	$506
1997	$746	$559
1998	$827	$620
1999	$922	$692
2000	$1,021	$766
2001	$1,132	$849
2002	$1,258	$943
2003	$1,395	$1,047

LS55H

YEARS MFRD	1994-2003
ENGINE	KOHLER
ENGINE HP	20
COOLING	AIR
FUEL	G
SPEEDS	VARIABLE
TRANSMISSION	HYDRO
STEERING	STANDARD
STANDARD DECK	48"
MSRP	$5,512

OPTIONS

36" TILLER
42" SNOW BLOWER
52" DECK
BAGGER

SERIAL NUMBERS

YEAR	BEGINNING NO.
1994	T4E0001
1995	T5E0001
1996	T6E0001
1997	T7E0001
1998	T8E0001
1999	T9E0001
2000	T0E0001
2001	T1E0001
2002	T2E0174
2003	T3E0001

RETAIL PRICING

YEAR	HIGH	LOW
1994	$649	$487
1995	$716	$537
1996	$791	$593
1997	$877	$658
1998	$974	$731
1999	$1,079	$809
2000	$1,196	$897
2001	$1,329	$997
2002	$1,471	$1,103
2003	$1,632	$1,224

MC22

YEARS MFRD	2000-2008
ENGINE	NH
CYLINDERS	3
CID	61.3
ENGINE HP	22
FUEL	D
SPEEDS	VARIABLE
TRANSMISSION	HYDRO
STEERING	STANDARD
HYDRAULIC	YES
PTO	YES
DRIVE TYPE	2WD
ROPS/CAB	ROPS
STANDARD DECK	60"
WEIGHT	1,550 LBS.
MSRP	$15,944

OPTIONS

4WD
52" SNOW BLOWER
72" DECK
BAGGER

SERIAL NUMBERS

YEAR	BEGINNING NO.
2000	TD00001
2002	TD00223
2003	TD00367
2004	TD00368
2006	TD20015
2007	TD20052
2008	TD20067
2009	TD20084

RETAIL PRICING

YEAR	HIGH	LOW
2000	$3,693	$2,770
2001	$4,095	$3,071
2002	$4,545	$3,409
2003	$5,041	$3,781
2004	$5,596	$4,197
2005	$6,203	$4,652
2006	$6,881	$5,161
2007	$7,634	$5,725
2008	$8,466	$6,350

MC28

YEARS MFRD	2000-2008
ENGINE	ISM
CYLINDERS	3
ENGINE HP	28
FUEL	D
SPEEDS	VARIABLE
TRANSMISSION	HYDRO
STEERING	STANDARD
DRIVE TYPE	2WD
ROPS/CAB	ROPS
STANDARD DECK	72"
MSRP	$17,793

OPTIONS

4WD
52" SNOW BLOWER
84" DECK
BAGGER

SERIAL NUMBERS

YEAR	BEGINNING NO.
2000	TE00001
2002	TE00648
2003	TE00956
2004	TE01057
2005	TE20001
2006	TE20236
2007	TE20443
2008	TE20504

RETAIL PRICING

YEAR	HIGH	LOW
2000	$4,237	$3,178
2001	$4,778	$3,583
2002	$5,200	$3,900
2003	$5,783	$4,338
2004	$6,415	$4,811

NEW HOLLAND

2005...........$7,105 .... $5,329
2006...........$7,897 .... $5,923
2007...........$8,833 .... $6,625
2008...........$9,847 .... $7,385

MC35

YEARS MFRD 2000-2008
ENGINE .... ISM
CYLINDERS.................. 3
CID 101.4
ENGINE HP 35
FUEL .... D
SPEEDS 2
TRANSMISSION .... HYDRO
STEERING............ STANDARD
HYDRAULIC .... YES
PTO .... YES
DRIVE TYPE 4WD
ROPS/CAB .... ROPS
STANDARD DECK .... 72"
MSRP................ $22,481

OPTIONS

52" SNOW BLOWER
60" BLADE
84" DECK
BAGGER

SERIAL NUMBERS

YEAR .... BEGINNING NO.
2000 .... TF00001
2002 .... TF00441
2003 .... TF00694
2004 .... TF00810
2005 .... TF20001
2006 .... TF20273
2007 .... TF20421
2008 .... TF20472

RETAIL PRICING

YEAR	HIGH	LOW
2000	$5,446	$4,084
2001	$5,940	$4,455
2002	$6,589	$4,942
2003	$7,306	$5,480
2004	$8,133	$6,100
2005	$8,990	$6,743
2006	$10,036	$7,527
2007	$11,065	$8,299
2008	$12,401	$9,301

MC222F

YEARS MFRD 2000-2006
ENGINE .... ISM
ENGINE HP 22
FUEL .... D
SPEEDS .... VARIABLE
TRANSMISSION .... HYDRO
STEERING............ STANDARD
WEIGHT .... 1,480 LBS.
MSRP................ $13,045

RETAIL PRICING

YEAR	HIGH	LOW
2000	$5,886	$4,415
2001	$6,353	$4,764
2002	$7,054	$5,291
2003	$7,885	$5,913
2004	$8,588	$6,441
2005	$8,907	$6,680
2006	$9,581	$7,186

MC224F 4WD

YEARS MFRD 2001-2006
ENGINE .... ISM
ENGINE HP 22
COOLING .... AIR
FUEL .... D
SPEEDS .... VARIABLE
TRANSMISSION .... HYDRO
STEERING............ STANDARD
WEIGHT .... 1,560 LBS.
MSRP................ $15,305

RETAIL PRICING

YEAR	HIGH	LOW
2001	$7,403	$5,552
2002	$8,223	$6,167
2003	$9,169	$6,877
2004	$9,988	$7,491
2005	$10,448	$7,836
2006	$11,241	$8,431

MC282F

YEARS MFRD 2001-2006
ENGINE .... ISM
ENGINE HP 28
COOLING .... AIR
FUEL .... D
SPEEDS .... VARIABLE
TRANSMISSION .... HYDRO
STEERING............ STANDARD
WEIGHT .... 1,500 LBS.
MSRP................ $14,622

RETAIL PRICING

YEAR	HIGH	LOW
2001	$6,785	$5,089
2002	$7,536	$5,652
2003	$8,413	$6,310
2004	$9,166	$6,874
2005	$9,892	$7,419
2006	$10,739	$8,054

MC284F

YEARS MFRD 2000-2006
ENGINE .... ISM
ENGINE HP 28
COOLING .... AIR
FUEL .... D
SPEEDS .... VARIABLE
TRANSMISSION .... HYDRO
STEERING............ STANDARD
WEIGHT .... 1,580 LBS.
MSRP................ $17,704

RETAIL PRICING

YEAR	HIGH	LOW
2000	$7,585	$5,689
2001	$8,096	$6,072
2002	$8,991	$6,743
2003	$10,010	$7,508
2004	$10,906	$8,179
2005	$11,995	$8,996
2006	$13,003	$9,752

MC354F 4WD

YEARS MFRD 2000-2006
ENGINE .... ISM
ENGINE HP 35
COOLING .... AIR
FUEL .... D
SPEEDS .... VARIABLE
TRANSMISSION .... HYDRO
STEERING............ STANDARD
WEIGHT .... 1,580 LBS.
MSRP................ $19,310

RETAIL PRICING

YEAR	HIGH	LOW
2000	$8,123	$6,092
2001	$8,685	$6,514
2002	$9,644	$7,233
2003	$10,730	$8,048
2004	$11,690	$8,768
2005	$13,091	$9,818
2006	$14,183	$10,637

MCH38

YEARS MFRD 2004-2004
ENGINE .... NH
CYLINDERS.................. 3
CID 81.1
ENGINE HP 28
FUEL .... D
SPEEDS 2
TRANSMISSION .... HYDRO
STEERING............ STANDARD
HYDRAULIC .... YES
PTO .... YES
DRIVE TYPE 4WD
ROPS/CAB .... ROPS
WEIGHT .... 1,570 LBS.

MY16

YEARS MFRD 2004-2006
ENGINE ...... KOHLER COMMAND
CYLINDERS.................. 1
ENGINE HP 16
FUEL .... G
SPEEDS .... VARIABLE
TRANSMISSION .... HYDRO
STEERING............ STANDARD
BLADE CLUTCH .... ELECTRIC
STANDARD DECK .... 48"
WEIGHT .... 614 LBS.
MSRP................. $4,705

OPTIONS

42" SNOW BLOWER
48" BLADE
52" DECK
BAGGER

SERIAL NUMBERS

YEAR .... BEGINNING NO.
2004 .... T04MA0001
2005 .... T05MA0001
2006 .... T06MA0001

RETAIL PRICING

YEAR	HIGH	LOW
2004	$1,013	$760
2005	$1,119	$839
2006	$1,234	$926

MY17

YEARS MFRD 2004-2006
ENGINE .... KAWASAKI
CYLINDERS.................. 2
ENGINE HP 17
COOLING .... AIR
FUEL .... G
SPEEDS .... VARIABLE
TRANSMISSION .... HYDRO
STEERING............ STANDARD
BLADE CLUTCH .... ELECTRIC
STANDARD DECK .... 52"
WEIGHT .... 664 LBS.
MSRP................. $5,719

OPTIONS

36" TILLER
42" SNOW BLOWER
48" BLADE
BAGGER

SERIAL NUMBERS

YEAR .... BEGINNING NO.
2004 .... T04MB0001
2005 .... T05MB0001
2006 .... T06MB0001

RETAIL PRICING

YEAR	HIGH	LOW
2004	$1,232	$924
2005	$1,360	$1,020
2006	$1,500	$1,125

MY19

YEARS MFRD 2004-2006
ENGINE .... KAWASAKI
CYLINDERS.................. 2
ENGINE HP 19
FUEL .... G
SPEEDS .... VARIABLE
TRANSMISSION .... HYDRO
STEERING............ STANDARD
BLADE CLUTCH .... ELECTRIC
STANDARD DECK .... 52"
WEIGHT .... 664 LBS.
MSRP................. $6,366

OPTIONS

36" TILLER
42" SNOW BLOWER
48" BLADE
BAGGER

SERIAL NUMBERS

YEAR .... BEGINNING NO.
2004 .... T04MC0001
2005 .... T05MC0001
2006 .... T06MC0001

RETAIL PRICING

YEAR	HIGH	LOW
2004	$1,370	$1,027
2005	$1,513	$1,134
2006	$1,670	$1,252

MZ14H

YEARS MFRD 2004-2005
SERIES .... MZH SERIES
ENGINE .... B&S
CYLINDERS.................. 1
ENGINE HP 14
COOLING .... AIR
FUEL .... G
SPEEDS .... VARIABLE

TRANSMISSION ... HYDRO
STEERING ... ZERO
STANDARD DECK ... 38"
WEIGHT ... 664 LBS.
MSRP ... $2,829

OPTIONS

2 BAG
48" BLADE

SERIAL NUMBERS

YEAR	BEGINNING NO.
2004	T04ZA0001
2005	T05ZA0001

RETAIL PRICING

YEAR	HIGH	LOW
2004	$1,046	$784
2005	$1,163	$872

MZ16H

YEARS MFRD ... 2004-2006
SERIES ... MZH SERIES
ENGINE ... B&S
CYLINDERS ... 1
ENGINE HP ... 16
COOLING ... AIR
FUEL ... G
SPEEDS ... VARIABLE
TRANSMISSION ... DUAL HYDRO
STEERING ... ZERO
STANDARD DECK ... 42"
WEIGHT ... 645 LBS.
MSRP ... $2,705

OPTIONS

2 BAG
48" BLADE

SERIAL NUMBERS

YEAR	BEGINNING NO.
2004	T04ZB0001
2005	T05ZB0001
2006	T06ZB0001

RETAIL PRICING

YEAR	HIGH	LOW
2004	$1,016	$762
2005	$1,134	$851
2006	$1,267	$950

MZ17H

YEARS MFRD ... 2006-2006
ENGINE ... KOHLER
ENGINE HP ... 18
COOLING ... AIR
FUEL ... G
SPEEDS ... VARIABLE
TRANSMISSION ... HYDRO
STEERING ... ZERO
STANDARD DECK ... 44"
WEIGHT ... 680 LBS.
MSRP ... $4,370

OPTIONS

56" BLADE
BAGGER

RETAIL PRICING

YEAR	HIGH	LOW
2006	$2,035	$1,526

MZ18H

YEARS MFRD ... 2004-2006
ENGINE ... B&S
CYLINDERS ... 2
ENGINE HP ... 18
COOLING ... AIR
FUEL ... G
SPEEDS ... VARIABLE
TRANSMISSION ... DUAL HYDRO
STEERING ... ZERO
STANDARD DECK ... 48"
WEIGHT ... 670 LBS.
MSRP ... $3,536

OPTIONS

2 BAG
48" BLADE

SERIAL NUMBERS

YEAR	BEGINNING NO.
2004	T04ZC0001
2005	T05ZC0001
2006	T06ZE0101

RETAIL PRICING

YEAR	HIGH	LOW
2004	$1,332	$999
2005	$1,491	$1,118
2006	$1,660	$1,245

MZ19H

YEARS MFRD ... 2004-2007
SERIES ... MZH SERIES
ENGINE ... KAWASAKI
CYLINDERS ... 2
ENGINE HP ... 19
COOLING ... AIR
FUEL ... G
SPEEDS ... VARIABLE
TRANSMISSION ... DUAL HYDRO
STEERING ... ZERO
STANDARD DECK ... 52"
WEIGHT ... 680 LBS.
MSRP ... $5,241

OPTIONS

56" BLADE

SERIAL NUMBERS

YEAR	BEGINNING NO.
2004	T04ZD0001
2005	T05ZD0001
2006	T06ZF0101
2007	T07ZF0101

RETAIL PRICING

YEAR	HIGH	LOW
2004	$1,787	$1,340
2005	$1,986	$1,489
2006	$2,198	$1,649
2007	$2,440	$1,830

T3.60F

YEARS MFRD ... 2019-2019
SERIES ... T3F COMPACT SERIES
ENGINE ... S8000
CYLINDERS ... 3
CID ... 179
PTO HP ... 40
ENGINE HP ... 54
FUEL ... D
SPEEDS ... 12/12
TRANSMISSION ... SHUTTLE SHIFT
STEERING ... STANDARD
DRIVE TYPE ... 4WD
ROPS/CAB ... ROPS
WEIGHT ... 5,000 LBS.
MSRP ... $37,260

OPTIONS

20/20 CREEPER

T1010

YEARS MFRD ... 2008-2008
SERIES ... T1000 SERIES
CYLINDERS ... 3
PTO HP ... 15.5
ENGINE HP ... 20
COOLING ... LIQUID
FUEL ... D
SPEEDS ... VARIABLE
TRANSMISSION ... HYDRO
STEERING ... STANDARD
HITCH ... CAT. I
HYDRAULIC ... YES
PTO ... YES
DRIVE TYPE ... 4WD
ROPS/CAB ... ROPS
WEIGHT ... 1,455 LBS.
MSRP ... $9,869

OPTIONS

60" DECK
LDR

RETAIL PRICING

YEAR	HIGH	LOW
2008	$6,471	$4,853

T1030

YEARS MFRD ... 2008-2008
SERIES ... T1000 SERIES
CYLINDERS ... 3
PTO HP ... 19.7
ENGINE HP ... 26
COOLING ... LIQUID
FUEL ... D
SPEEDS ... VARIABLE
TRANSMISSION ... HYDRO
STEERING ... STANDARD
HITCH ... CAT. I
HYDRAULIC ... YES
PTO ... YES
DRIVE TYPE ... 4WD
ROPS/CAB ... ROPS
WEIGHT ... 1,455 LBS.
MSRP ... $10,547

OPTIONS

1 HYD
60" DECK
LDR

RETAIL PRICING

YEAR	HIGH	LOW
2008	$7,233	$5,425

T1110

YEARS MFRD ... 2008-2008
CYLINDERS ... 3
PTO HP ... 20.5
ENGINE HP ... 28
COOLING ... AIR
FUEL ... D
SPEEDS ... VARIABLE
TRANSMISSION ... HYDRO
STEERING ... STANDARD
HITCH ... CAT. I
HYDRAULIC ... YES
PTO ... YES
WEIGHT ... 1,492 LBS.
MSRP ... $12,002

OPTIONS

1 HYD
60" DECK
LDR

RETAIL PRICING

YEAR	HIGH	LOW
2008	$9,208	$6,906

T1510

YEARS MFRD ... 2008-2012
CYLINDERS ... 3
CID ... 91
PTO HP ... 25.5
ENGINE HP ... 30
COOLING ... LIQUID
FUEL ... D
SPEEDS ... 9/3
TRANSMISSION ... GEAR
STEERING ... STANDARD
HITCH ... CAT. I
HYDRAULIC ... YES
PTO ... YES
DRIVE TYPE ... 2WD
ROPS/CAB ... ROPS
WEIGHT ... 2,385 LBS.
MSRP ... $14,788

OPTIONS

4WD
HYDRO
LDR

SERIAL NUMBERS

YEAR	BEGINNING NO.
2008	Z7NGH1082-4WD
2008	Z7NGJ1051-4H
2008	Z7NGG1001-2WD
2009	Z8NGG1177-2WD
2009	Z8NGJ1871-4H
2009	Z8NGH2342-4WD
2010	Z9NGG1001-2WD
2010	Z9NGH1474-4WD
2010	Z9NGJ1372-4H
2011	ZANGH1844-4WD
2011	ZANGJ1293-4H
2011	ZANGG1019-2WD
2012	ZBNGG1014-2WD
2012	ZBNGH1516-4WD
2012	ZBNGJ1241-4H

RETAIL PRICING

YEAR	HIGH	LOW
2008	$7,899	$5,924
2009	$8,690	$6,518
2010	$9,335	$7,001
2011	$10,053	$7,540
2012	$11,011	$8,258

AVG. AUCTION PRICING

LOW	HIGH	AVG
$4,700	$9,250	$6,425

NEW HOLLAND

T1520

YEARS MFRD 2007-2012
ENGINE .... SHIBAURA
CYLINDERS.................. 3
CID 101
PTO HP 29.5
ENGINE HP 35
COOLING .... LIQUID
FUEL .... D
SPEEDS 9/3
TRANSMISSION .... GEAR
STEERING.......... STANDARD
HITCH .... CAT. I
HYDRAULIC .... YES
PTO .... YES
DRIVE TYPE 4WD
ROPS/CAB .... ROPS
WEIGHT .... 2,306 LBS.
MSRP.................. $17,469

OPTIONS

1 HYD
60"DECK
72"DECK
HYDRO
LDR

SERIAL NUMBERS

YEAR	BEGINNING NO.
2008	Z7NGL1498-H
2008	Z7NGK1926-G
2009	Z8NGL1426-G
2009	Z8NGL1456-H
2010	Z9NGK1312-G
2010	Z9NGL1421-H
2011	ZANGL1210-H
2011	ZANGK1185-G
2012	ZBNGK1135-G
2012	ZBNGL1171-H

RETAIL PRICING

YEAR	HIGH	LOW
2007	$9,484	$7,113
2008	$10,144	$7,608
2009	$10,693	$8,019
2010	$11,369	$8,527
2011	$12,207	$9,156
2012	$13,019	$9,764

AVG. AUCTION PRICING

LOW	HIGH	AVG
$6,500	$13,000	$9,013

T1530

YEARS MFRD 2009-2012
ENGINE .... SHIBAURA
CYLINDERS.................. 4
CID 135.2
PTO HP 38
ENGINE HP 45
COOLING .... LIQUID
FUEL .... D
SPEEDS .... VARIABLE
TRANSMISSION .... HYDRO
STEERING.......... STANDARD
DRIVE TYPE 4WD
ROPS/CAB .... ROPS
WEIGHT .... 3,311 LBS.
MSRP.................. $25,027

OPTIONS

HYDRO

SERIAL NUMBERS

YEAR	BEGINNING NO.
2009	Z9NBA1001-G
2009	Z9NBB1001-H
2010	ZANBA1001-G
2010	Z9NBB1201-H
2011	ZANBA1174-G
2011	ZANBB1231-H
2012	ZBNBB1092-H
2012	ZBNBA1183-G

RETAIL PRICING

YEAR	HIGH	LOW
2009	$15,753	$11,815
2010	$16,535	$12,401
2011	$17,393	$13,045
2012	$18,323	$13,742

AVG. AUCTION PRICING

LOW	HIGH	AVG
$15,841	$16,933	$16,386

T2210

YEARS MFRD 2008-2008
SERIES............ 2200 SERIES
CYLINDERS.................. 3
PTO HP 26.5
ENGINE HP 31
COOLING .... LIQUID
FUEL .... D
SPEEDS 9/3
TRANSMISSION .... GEAR
STEERING.......... STANDARD
HITCH .... CAT. I
HYDRAULIC .... YES
PTO .... YES
DRIVE TYPE 4WD
ROPS/CAB .... ROPS
WEIGHT .... 2,605 LBS.
MSRP.................. $17,276

OPTIONS

HYDRO
LDR

SERIAL NUMBERS

YEAR	BEGINNING NO.
2008	Z7DA04325

RETAIL PRICING

YEAR	HIGH	LOW
2008	$11,933	$8,950

T2220

YEARS MFRD 2008-2008
SERIES.......... T2200 SERIES
CYLINDERS.................. 3
PTO HP 28.9
ENGINE HP 35
COOLING .... LIQUID
FUEL .... D
SPEEDS .... VARIABLE
TRANSMISSION .... HYDRO
STEERING.......... STANDARD
HYDRAULIC .... YES
PTO .... YES
DRIVE TYPE 2WD
ROPS/CAB .... ROPS
WEIGHT .... 2,620 LBS.
MSRP.................. $17,930

OPTIONS

72"DECK
LDR

RETAIL PRICING

YEAR	HIGH	LOW
2008	$14,566	$10,924

T2310

YEARS MFRD 2008-2008
SERIES.......... T2300 SERIES
CYLINDERS.................. 4
PTO HP 33.2
ENGINE HP 40
COOLING .... LIQUID
FUEL .... D
SPEEDS .... VARIABLE
TRANSMISSION .... HYDRO
STEERING.......... STANDARD
HITCH .... CAT. I
HYDRAULIC .... YES
PTO .... YES
DRIVE TYPE 4WD
ROPS/CAB .... ROPS
MSRP.................. $21,425

OPTIONS

2 HYD
CAB W/A
LDR

RETAIL PRICING

YEAR	HIGH	LOW
2008	$14,120	$10,590

T2320

YEARS MFRD 2008-2008
SERIES.......... T2300 SERIES
CYLINDERS.................. 4
PTO HP 37.8
ENGINE HP 45
COOLING .... LIQUID
FUEL .... D
SPEEDS .... VARIABLE
TRANSMISSION .... HYDRO
STEERING.......... STANDARD
HYDRAULIC .... YES
PTO .... YES
WEIGHT .... 4,115 LBS.
MSRP.................. $23,261

RETAIL PRICING

YEAR	HIGH	LOW
2008	$16,291	$12,219

T2330

YEARS MFRD 2008-2008
SERIES.......... T2300 SERIES
CYLINDERS.................. 4
PTO HP 43
ENGINE HP 50
COOLING .... LIQUID
FUEL .... D
SPEEDS 12/12
TRANSMISSION ... SHUTTLE SHIFT
STEERING.......... STANDARD
HYDRAULIC .... YES
PTO .... YES
DRIVE TYPE 4WD
ROPS/CAB .... ROPS
WEIGHT .... 3,497 LBS.
MSRP.................. $22,403

OPTIONS

1 HYD
2 HYD
LDR

RETAIL PRICING

YEAR	HIGH	LOW
2008	$16,468	$12,351

TC18

YEARS MFRD 1998-2003
SERIES......... BOOMER SERIES
CYLINDERS.................. 3
CID 58.2
PTO HP 15
ENGINE HP 17
FUEL .... D
SPEEDS 6/2
TRANSMISSION .... GEAR
STEERING.......... STANDARD
HITCH .... CAT. I
PTO .... YES
DRIVE TYPE 2WD
ROPS/CAB .... ROPS
WEIGHT .... 1,438 LBS.
MSRP.................. $8,279

OPTIONS

4WD
54"DECK
60"DECK
HYDRO
LDR
POWER STEERING

SERIAL NUMBERS

LEFT SIDE OF TRANS HOUSING

YEAR	BEGINNING NO.
1998	G003207
1999	UD30385
2000	UD31116
2001	UD32035
2002	UD32984
2003	UD33681

RETAIL PRICING

YEAR	HIGH	LOW
1998	$3,131	$2,349
1999	$3,424	$2,568
2000	$3,752	$2,814
2001	$4,121	$3,091
2002	$4,432	$3,324
2003	$4,834	$3,625

TC21

YEARS MFRD 1998-2003
SERIES......... BOOMER SERIES
CYLINDERS.................. 3
CID 61.3
PTO HP 17
ENGINE HP 20
FUEL .... D
SPEEDS 9/3
TRANSMISSION .... GEAR
STEERING.......... STANDARD

HITCH . . . . CAT. I
DRIVE TYPE 4WD
ROPS/CAB . . . . ROPS
MSRP $12,837

OPTIONS

2 HYD
HYDRO
LDR

SERIAL NUMBERS

LEFT SIDE OF TRANS HOUSING

YEAR	BEGINNING NO.
1998	G003207-G
1998	G003207-H
1999	G009604-H
1999	UF30352-G
2000	UF31353-G
2000	UF31353-H
2001	UF32159-G
2001	UF32159-H
2002	UF32870-G
2002	UF32655-H
2003	UF30957-H
2003	UF33269-G

RETAIL PRICING

YEAR	HIGH	LOW
1998	$4,115	$3,086
1999	$4,476	$3,357
2000	$4,820	$3,615
2001	$5,188	$3,891
2002	$5,568	$4,176
2003	$6,013	$4,510

TC21DA

YEARS MFRD 2004-2005
SERIES . . . . BOOMER SERIES
ENGINE . . . . NH
CYLINDERS 3
CID 61.3
PTO HP 17
ENGINE HP 21
SPEEDS 9/3
TRANSMISSION . . . . GEAR
STEERING . . . . STANDARD
HYDRAULIC . . . . YES
PTO . . . . YES
DRIVE TYPE 4WD
ROPS/CAB . . . . ROPS
MSRP $14,204

OPTIONS

60"DECK
HYDRO
LDR
MID PTO

SERIAL NUMBERS

YEAR	BEGINNING NO.
2004	HF10001
2005	HF10161

RETAIL PRICING

YEAR	HIGH	LOW
2004	$6,509	$4,881
2005	$6,941	$5,206

TC23DA

YEARS MFRD 2005-2007
SERIES . . . . BOOMER SERIES
ENGINE . . . . NH
CYLINDERS 3
CID 61.3
PTO HP 18.5
ENGINE HP 23
FUEL . . . . D
SPEEDS 9/3
TRANSMISSION . . . . GEAR
STEERING . . . . STANDARD
HITCH . . . . CAT. I
HYDRAULIC . . . . YES
PTO . . . . YES
WEIGHT . . . . 1,592 LBS.
MSRP $12,582

OPTIONS

60" DECK
HYDRO
LDR
MID PTO

SERIAL NUMBERS

YEAR	BEGINNING NO.
2006	HF20062
2007	Z6NUF1042

RETAIL PRICING

YEAR	HIGH	LOW
2005	$6,699	$5,025
2006	$7,217	$5,412
2007	$7,755	$5,816

TC24D

YEARS MFRD 2002-2003
SERIES . . . . BOOMER SERIES
ENGINE . . . . SHIBAURA
CYLINDERS 3
CID 69
PTO HP 18.5
ENGINE HP 24
FUEL . . . . D
SPEEDS 9/3
TRANSMISSION . . . . GEAR
STEERING . . . . STANDARD
DRIVE TYPE 2WD
ROPS/CAB . . . . ROPS
WEIGHT . . . . 1,723 LBS.
MSRP $13,118

OPTIONS

2 HYD
4WD
HYDRO

RETAIL PRICING

YEAR	HIGH	LOW
2002	$4,773	$3,579
2003	$5,264	$3,948

AVG. AUCTION PRICING

LOW	HIGH	AVG
$4,000	$8,200	$6,317

TC24DA

YEARS MFRD 2004-2005
SERIES . . . . BOOMER SERIES
ENGINE . . . . SHIBAURA
CYLINDERS 3
CID 69
PTO HP 19.5
ENGINE HP 24
FUEL . . . . D
SPEEDS 9/3
TRANSMISSION . . . . GEAR
STEERING . . . . STANDARD
HITCH . . . . CAT. I
HYDRAULIC . . . . YES
PTO . . . . YES
DRIVE TYPE 2WD
ROPS/CAB . . . . ROPS
WEIGHT . . . . 1,308 LBS.
MSRP $14,484

OPTIONS

4WD
60"DECK
HYDRO
LDR

SERIAL NUMBERS

YEAR	BEGINNING NO.
2004	HG10001
2005	HG11722

RETAIL PRICING

YEAR	HIGH	LOW
2004	$6,090	$4,568
2005	$6,593	$4,945

TC25

YEARS MFRD 1998-2002
SERIES . . . . BOOMER SERIES
ENGINE . . . . SHIBAURA
CYLINDERS 3
CID 81.2
PTO HP 22
ENGINE HP 25
FUEL . . . . D
SPEEDS 9/3
TRANSMISSION . . . . GEAR
STEERING . . . . STANDARD
HITCH . . . . CAT. I
DRIVE TYPE 2WD
ROPS/CAB . . . . ROPS
WEIGHT . . . . 2,334 LBS.
MSRP $11,808

OPTIONS

4WD
72"DECK
HYDRO
LDR

SERIAL NUMBERS

YEAR	BEGINNING NO.
1998	G003207
1999	G009604
2000	G017662
2001	G026689
2002	G035084

RETAIL PRICING

YEAR	HIGH	LOW
1998	$5,224	$3,918
1999	$5,577	$4,183
2000	$5,875	$4,406
2001	$6,297	$4,723
2002	$6,905	$5,179

TC25D HYDRO SUPERSTEER

YEARS MFRD 2001-2002
ENGINE . . . . SHIBAURA
CYLINDERS 3
CID 81
PTO HP 20.3
FUEL . . . . G
SPEEDS . . . . VARIABLE
TRANSMISSION . . . . HYDRO
STEERING . . . . STANDARD
DRIVE TYPE 4WD
ROPS/CAB . . . . ROPS
MSRP $16,922

RETAIL PRICING

YEAR	HIGH	LOW
2001	$7,864	$5,898
2002	$8,675	$6,506

TC25DA

YEARS MFRD 2004-2004
SERIES . . . . BOOMER SERIES
ENGINE . . . . NH
CYLINDERS 3
CID 101.1
PTO HP 29.1
ENGINE HP 35
SPEEDS 4
TRANSMISSION . . . . GEAR
STEERING . . . . STANDARD
HYDRAULIC . . . . YES
PTO . . . . YES

TC26DA

YEARS MFRD 2005-2007
SERIES . . . . BOOMER SERIES
ENGINE . . . . NH
CYLINDERS 3
CID 69
PTO HP 20.5
ENGINE HP 26
FUEL . . . . D
SPEEDS 2
TRANSMISSION . . . . HYDRO
STEERING . . . . STANDARD
HITCH . . . . CAT. I
HYDRAULIC . . . . YES
PTO . . . . YES
DRIVE TYPE 4WD
ROPS/CAB . . . . ROPS
WEIGHT . . . . 1,600 LBS.
MSRP $14,362

OPTIONS

60" DECK
LDR

SERIAL NUMBERS

YEAR	BEGINNING NO.
2006	HG20164
2007	Z6NUG1204

RETAIL PRICING

YEAR	HIGH	LOW
2005	$7,544	$5,658
2006	$8,084	$6,063
2007	$8,637	$6,478

TC29

YEARS MFRD 1998-2003
SERIES . . . . BOOMER SERIES
ENGINE . . . . CUMMINS
CYLINDERS 3

CID 81.2
PTO HP 25
ENGINE HP 29
FUEL .... D
SPEEDS 9/3
TRANSMISSION .... GEAR
STEERING .... STANDARD
HITCH .... CAT. I
DRIVE TYPE 2WD
ROPS/CAB .... ROPS
WEIGHT .... 2,334 LBS.
MSRP $15,234

OPTIONS

4WD
60"DECK
72"DECK
HYDRO
LDR

SERIAL NUMBERS

LEFT SIDE OF TRANS HOUSING

YEAR	BEGINNING NO.
1998	G003207
1999	G010466
2000	G017579
2001	G026722
2002	G035036
2003	G039479

RETAIL PRICING

YEAR	HIGH	LOW
1998	$3,393	$2,544
1999	$3,851	$2,888
2000	$4,323	$3,242
2001	$4,827	$3,620
2002	$6,223	$4,667
2003	$7,046	$5,285

AVG. AUCTION PRICING

LOW	HIGH	AVG
$5,355	$7,956	$6,919

TC29D HYDRO SUPERSTEER

YEARS MFRD 2001-2002
ENGINE .... SHIBAURA
CYLINDERS 3
CID 81
PTO HP 23.5
FUEL .... G
SPEEDS .... VARIABLE
TRANSMISSION .... HYDRO
STEERING .... STANDARD
DRIVE TYPE 4WD
ROPS/CAB .... ROPS
MSRP $18,690

RETAIL PRICING

YEAR	HIGH	LOW
2001	$8,187	$6,140
2002	$9,214	$6,910

AVG. AUCTION PRICING

LOW	HIGH	AVG
$5,735	$10,379	$7,702

TC29DA

YEARS MFRD 2004-2006
SERIES .... BOOMER SERIES
ENGINE .... NH
CYLINDERS 3
CID 81.2
PTO HP 25
ENGINE HP 29
FUEL .... D
SPEEDS 9/3
TRANSMISSION .... GEAR
STEERING .... STANDARD
HITCH .... CAT. I
HYDRAULIC .... YES
PTO .... YES
WEIGHT .... 2,474 LBS.
MSRP $15,836

OPTIONS

60"DECK
72"DECK
HYDRO
LDR

SERIAL NUMBERS

YEAR	BEGINNING NO.
2004	G100001
2005	G103054
2006	G105497

RETAIL PRICING

YEAR	HIGH	LOW
2004	$7,871	$5,904
2005	$8,648	$6,486
2006	$9,324	$6,993

TC30

YEARS MFRD 2002-2007
SERIES .... BOOMER SERIES
ENGINE .... NH
CYLINDERS 3
CID 91.3
PTO HP 25
ENGINE HP 29
FUEL .... D
SPEEDS 9/3
TRANSMISSION .... GEAR
STEERING .... STANDARD
HITCH .... CAT. I
PTO .... YES
DRIVE TYPE 2WD
ROPS/CAB .... ROPS
WEIGHT .... 2,193 LBS.
MSRP $10,215

OPTIONS

4WD
60"DECK
72"DECK
HYDRO
LDR

SERIAL NUMBERS

YEAR	BEGINNING NO.
2002	UD3010001
2003	HK19542
2004	HK30001
2005	HK34333
2006	HK38930
2007	Z6NGB3283

RETAIL PRICING

YEAR	HIGH	LOW
2002	$4,517	$3,387
2003	$4,872	$3,654
2004	$5,313	$3,985
2005	$5,775	$4,331
2006	$6,416	$4,812
2007	$7,086	$5,314

AVG. AUCTION PRICING

LOW	HIGH	AVG
$5,750	$12,500	$7,917

TC31DA

YEARS MFRD 2006-2007
ENGINE .... NEW HOLLAND
CYLINDERS 3
CID 91
PTO HP 26.5
ENGINE HP 31
FUEL .... D
SPEEDS 9/3
TRANSMISSION .... GEAR
STEERING .... STANDARD
HITCH .... CAT. I
DRIVE TYPE 4WD
ROPS/CAB .... ROPS
WEIGHT .... 2,511 LBS.
MSRP $15,140

OPTIONS

66"DECK
72"DECK
HYDRO
LDR

SERIAL NUMBERS

YEAR	BEGINNING NO.
2006	Z6DA03340
2007	Z7DA04325

RETAIL PRICING

YEAR	HIGH	LOW
2006	$10,095	$7,571
2007	$10,841	$8,130

TC33

YEARS MFRD 1998-2003
SERIES .... BOOMER SERIES
ENGINE .... SHIBAURA
CYLINDERS 3
CID 91
PTO HP 29
ENGINE HP 33
FUEL .... D
SPEEDS 9/3
TRANSMISSION .... GEAR
STEERING .... STANDARD
HITCH .... CAT. I
DRIVE TYPE 2WD
ROPS/CAB .... ROPS
WEIGHT .... 2,206 LBS.
MSRP $15,883

OPTIONS

4WD
72"DECK
HYDRO
LDR

SERIAL NUMBERS

LEFT SIDE OF TRANS HOUSING

YEAR	BEGINNING NO.
1998	G003207
1999	G010499
2000	G017605
2001	G026729
2002	G035134
2003	G039436

RETAIL PRICING

YEAR	HIGH	LOW
1998	$4,760	$3,570
1999	$5,345	$4,009
2000	$5,745	$4,308
2001	$6,274	$4,706
2002	$7,827	$5,871
2003	$8,423	$6,317

AVG. AUCTION PRICING

LOW	HIGH	AVG
$1,836	$7,242	$4,828

TC33DA

YEARS MFRD 2004-2006
SERIES .... BOOMER SERIES
ENGINE .... NH
CYLINDERS 3
CID 91.3
PTO HP 25.1
ENGINE HP 33
FUEL .... D
SPEEDS 9/3
TRANSMISSION .... GEAR
HITCH .... CAT. I
HYDRAULIC .... YES
PTO .... YES
DRIVE TYPE 4WD
ROPS/CAB .... ROPS
WEIGHT .... 2,474 LBS.
MSRP $16,505

OPTIONS

72"DECK
HYDRO
LDR
SUPER STEER

SERIAL NUMBERS

YEAR	BEGINNING NO.
2004	G100001
2005	G103054
2006	G105490

RETAIL PRICING

YEAR	HIGH	LOW
2004	$9,346	$7,010
2005	$10,111	$7,583
2006	$11,401	$8,550

AVG. AUCTION PRICING

LOW	HIGH	AVG
$6,800	$10,000	$7,912

TC34DA

YEARS MFRD 2006-2007
ENGINE .... NEW HOLLAND
CYLINDERS 3
CID 101
PTO HP 28.9
ENGINE HP 35
FUEL .... D
SPEEDS .... VARIABLE
TRANSMISSION .... HYDRO
STEERING .... STANDARD
HITCH .... CAT. I
DRIVE TYPE 4WD

ROPS/CAB . . . . ROPS
WEIGHT . . . . 2,515 LBS.
MSRP $17,150

OPTIONS

72"DECK
LDR
SUPER STEER

RETAIL PRICING

YEAR	HIGH	LOW
2006	$11,950	$8,963
2007	$12,721	$9,541

TC35

YEARS MFRD 2000-2003
SERIES . . . . BOOMER SERIES
CYLINDERS 3
CID 101
PTO HP 30
ENGINE HP 33
FUEL . . . . D
SPEEDS 12/12
TRANSMISSION . . . SHUTTLE SHIFT
STEERING . . . . STANDARD
HITCH . . . . CAT. I
PTO . . . . YES
DRIVE TYPE 2WD
ROPS/CAB . . . . ROPS
WEIGHT . . . . 3,096 LBS.
MSRP $13,814

OPTIONS

4WD
HYDRO
LDR

SERIAL NUMBERS

YEAR	BEGINNING NO.
2002	G510698
2003	G517021

RETAIL PRICING

YEAR	HIGH	LOW
2000	$6,066	$4,549
2001	$6,523	$4,892
2002	$6,994	$5,246
2003	$7,635	$5,726

AVG. AUCTION PRICING

LOW	HIGH	AVG
$6,630	$10,710	$8,160

TC35A

YEARS MFRD 2004-2007
SERIES . . . . BOOMER SERIES
ENGINE . . . . NH
CYLINDERS 3
CID 101.1
PTO HP 29.6
ENGINE HP 35
SPEEDS 12/12
TRANSMISSION . . . SHUTTLE SHIFT
STEERING . . . . STANDARD
HITCH . . . . CAT. I
HYDRAULIC . . . . YES
PTO . . . . YES
DRIVE TYPE 4WD
ROPS/CAB . . . . ROPS
WEIGHT . . . . 3,231 LBS.
MSRP $16,664

OPTIONS

HYDRO
LDR
MID PTO
SUPER STEER

SERIAL NUMBERS

YEAR	BEGINNING NO.
2004	G600001
2005	G103054
2006	G612341
2007	Z6DB01043

RETAIL PRICING

YEAR	HIGH	LOW
2004	$9,769	$7,326
2005	$10,316	$7,737
2006	$10,876	$8,157
2007	$11,460	$8,595

AVG. AUCTION PRICING

LOW	HIGH	AVG
$6,991	$15,567	$10,094

TC35DA

YEARS MFRD 2004-2008
SERIES . . . . BOOMER SERIES
ENGINE . . . . NH
CYLINDERS 3
CID 101.1
PTO HP 29.1
ENGINE HP 35
FUEL . . . . D
SPEEDS . . . . VARIABLE
TRANSMISSION . . . . HYDRO
STEERING . . . . STANDARD
HITCH . . . . CAT. I
HYDRAULIC . . . . YES
PTO . . . . YES
DRIVE TYPE 4WD
ROPS/CAB . . . . ROPS
WEIGHT . . . . 3,357 LBS.
MSRP $18,978

OPTIONS

LDR
MID PTO
SUPER STEER

SERIAL NUMBERS

YEAR	BEGINNING NO.
2004	G100009
2005	G103054
2006	G612341
2007	Z6DB01043
2008	Z7DB05219

RETAIL PRICING

YEAR	HIGH	LOW
2004	$11,433	$8,575
2005	$12,288	$9,216
2006	$12,896	$9,672
2007	$13,800	$10,350
2008	$14,174	$10,630

AVG. AUCTION PRICING

LOW	HIGH	AVG
$7,140	$17,085	$11,450

TC35S

YEARS MFRD 2001-2002
ENGINE . . . . SHIBAURA
CYLINDERS 3
CID 122
PTO HP 29.6
FUEL . . . . G
TRANSMISSION . . . . HYDRO
STEERING . . . . STANDARD
DRIVE TYPE 4WD
ROPS/CAB . . . . ROPS
MSRP $19,571

RETAIL PRICING

YEAR	HIGH	LOW
2001	$9,033	$6,775
2002	$10,033	$7,525

TC40

YEARS MFRD 2000-2003
SERIES . . . . BOOMER SERIES
CYLINDERS 4
CID 121.7
PTO HP 35
ENGINE HP 38
FUEL . . . . D
SPEEDS 12/12
TRANSMISSION . . . SHUTTLE SHIFT
STEERING . . . . STANDARD
HITCH . . . . CAT. I
DRIVE TYPE 2WD
ROPS/CAB . . . . ROPS
WEIGHT . . . . 3,147 LBS.
MSRP $15,438

OPTIONS

4WD
HYDRO
LDR
SUPER STEER

SERIAL NUMBERS

YEAR	BEGINNING NO.
2002	G510674
2003	G517016

RETAIL PRICING

YEAR	HIGH	LOW
2000	$6,151	$4,613
2001	$6,704	$5,028
2002	$7,211	$5,409
2003	$7,977	$5,983

AVG. AUCTION PRICING

LOW	HIGH	AVG
$4,800	$11,000	$8,683

TC40A

YEARS MFRD 2004-2007
SERIES . . . . BOOMER SERIES
ENGINE . . . . NH
CYLINDERS 4
CID 121.7
PTO HP 35
ENGINE HP 40
COOLING . . . . LIQUID
SPEEDS 12/12
TRANSMISSION . . . SHUTTLE SHIFT
STEERING . . . . STANDARD
HITCH . . . . CAT. I
HYDRAULIC . . . . YES
PTO . . . . YES
DRIVE TYPE 2WD
ROPS/CAB . . . . ROPS
WEIGHT . . . . 3,405 LBS.
MSRP $15,496

OPTIONS

4WD
HYDRO
LDR

SERIAL NUMBERS

YEAR	BEGINNING NO.
2004	G600008
2005	G606713
2006	G612294
2007	G616959

RETAIL PRICING

YEAR	HIGH	LOW
2004	$8,690	$6,518
2005	$9,298	$6,974
2006	$9,953	$7,465
2007	$10,603	$7,952

AVG. AUCTION PRICING

LOW	HIGH	AVG
$6,500	$11,100	$9,533

TC40DA

YEARS MFRD 2004-2008
SERIES . . . . BOOMER SERIES
ENGINE . . . . NH
CYLINDERS 4
CID 121.7
PTO HP 33.2
ENGINE HP 40
SPEEDS . . . . VARIABLE
TRANSMISSION . . . . HYDRO
STEERING . . . . STANDARD
HITCH . . . . CAT. I
HYDRAULIC . . . . YES
PTO . . . . YES
DRIVE TYPE 4WD
ROPS/CAB . . . . ROPS
WEIGHT . . . . 3,433 LBS.
MSRP $20,602

OPTIONS

CAB
LDR
SUPER STEER

SERIAL NUMBERS

YEAR	BEGINNING NO.
2004	G600008
2005	G606713
2006	G612294
2007	G616959
2008	Z7DB05182

RETAIL PRICING

YEAR	HIGH	LOW
2004	$11,712	$8,784
2005	$12,721	$9,541
2006	$13,403	$10,052
2007	$14,042	$10,532
2008	$15,067	$11,301

AVG. AUCTION PRICING

LOW	HIGH	AVG
$11,645	$15,338	$13,046

TC45

YEARS MFRD 2000-2003
SERIES . . . . BOOMER SERIES
ENGINE . . . . SHIBAURA
CYLINDERS 4

- CID 135.2
- PTO HP 39.6
- ENGINE HP 43
- FUEL G
- SPEEDS 12/12
- TRANSMISSION SHUTTLE SHIFT
- STEERING STANDARD
- HITCH CAT. I
- DRIVE TYPE 2WD
- ROPS/CAB ROPS
- WEIGHT 3,349 LBS.
- MSRP $17,516

OPTIONS

4WD
HYDRO
LDR

SERIAL NUMBERS

YEAR	BEGINNING NO.
2002	G510642
2003	G517031

RETAIL PRICING

YEAR	HIGH	LOW
2000	$7,914	$5,936
2001	$8,376	$6,282
2002	$9,037	$6,778
2003	$9,331	$6,998

AVG. AUCTION PRICING

LOW	HIGH	AVG
$5,244	$17,479	$12,837

TC45A

- YEARS MFRD 2004-2007
- SERIES BOOMER SERIES
- ENGINE NH
- CYLINDERS 4
- CID 135.2
- PTO HP 39.6
- ENGINE HP 45
- COOLING LIQUID
- SPEEDS 12/12
- TRANSMISSION SHUTTLE SHIFT
- STEERING STANDARD
- HITCH CAT. I
- HYDRAULIC YES
- PTO YES
- DRIVE TYPE 2WD
- ROPS/CAB ROPS
- WEIGHT 3,454 LBS.
- MSRP $19,755

OPTIONS

4WD
HYDRO
LDR

SERIAL NUMBERS

YEAR	BEGINNING NO.
2004	G600001
2005	G606713
2006	G612321
2007	G616755

RETAIL PRICING

YEAR	HIGH	LOW
2004	$11,015	$8,261
2005	$11,707	$8,780
2006	$12,420	$9,315
2007	$13,159	$9,869

TC45DA

- YEARS MFRD 2004-2008
- SERIES BOOMER SERIES
- ENGINE NH
- CYLINDERS 4
- CID 135.2
- PTO HP 37.8
- ENGINE HP 45
- COOLING LIQUID
- FUEL D
- SPEEDS VARIABLE
- TRANSMISSION HYDRO
- STEERING STANDARD
- HITCH CAT. I
- HYDRAULIC YES
- PTO YES
- DRIVE TYPE 4WD
- ROPS/CAB ROPS
- WEIGHT 3,738 LBS.
- MSRP $22,367

OPTIONS

CAB W/A
LDR
SUPER STEER

SERIAL NUMBERS

YEAR	BEGINNING NO.
2004	G600008
2005	G606713
2006	G612321
2007	G616755
2008	Z7DB15180

RETAIL PRICING

YEAR	HIGH	LOW
2004	$12,468	$9,351
2005	$13,313	$9,985
2006	$13,963	$10,472
2007	$14,920	$11,190
2008	$15,890	$11,917

AVG. AUCTION PRICING

LOW	HIGH	AVG
$6,200	$20,000	$11,600

TC48DA

- YEARS MFRD 2004-2007
- SERIES BOOMER SERIES
- ENGINE ISM-N844L
- CID 135.2
- PTO HP 40
- ENGINE HP 48
- FUEL D
- SPEEDS 12/12
- TRANSMISSION SHUTTLE SHIFT
- STEERING STANDARD
- HITCH CAT. I
- PTO YES
- DRIVE TYPE 2WD
- ROPS/CAB ROPS
- WEIGHT 4,158 LBS.
- MSRP $22,410

OPTIONS

4WD
LDR

SERIAL NUMBERS

YEAR	BEGINNING NO.
2004	HV10001
2005	HV11258
2006	HV11347
2007	Z6NCA1225

RETAIL PRICING

YEAR	HIGH	LOW
2004	$11,302	$8,476
2005	$12,039	$9,029
2006	$12,934	$9,700
2007	$13,988	$10,491

AVG. AUCTION PRICING

LOW	HIGH	AVG
$8,521	$22,941	$13,218

TC55DA

- YEARS MFRD 2004-2008
- ENGINE NEW HOLLAND
- CYLINDERS 4
- CID 135
- PTO HP 45
- FUEL D
- SPEEDS VARIABLE
- TRANSMISSION HYDRO
- STEERING STANDARD
- HITCH CAT. I
- HYDRAULIC YES
- PTO YES
- DRIVE TYPE 2WD
- ROPS/CAB ROPS
- MSRP $23,650

OPTIONS

4WD
LDR

SERIAL NUMBERS

YEAR	BEGINNING NO.
2004	HX10001
2005	HX11615
2006	HX12946
2007	Z6NCB1063
2008	Z7DG11425

RETAIL PRICING

YEAR	HIGH	LOW
2004	$12,353	$9,265
2005	$12,612	$9,459
2006	$13,567	$10,175
2007	$14,368	$10,776
2008	$15,349	$11,512

AVG. AUCTION PRICING

LOW	HIGH	AVG
$10,200	$19,992	$15,861

TN55D

- YEARS MFRD 1998-2004
- ENGINE IVECO
- CYLINDERS 3
- CID 179
- PTO HP 42
- FUEL D
- SPEEDS 8/8-16/16
- TRANSMISSION HYDRO
- STEERING STANDARD
- PTO YES
- DRIVE TYPE 2WD
- ROPS/CAB ROPS

OPTIONS

4WD

SERIAL NUMBERS

YEAR	BEGINNING NO.
1998	1128584
1999	1157784
2000	1184720
2001	1219443
2002	1252974
2003	1287178
2004	1317364

TN55S

- YEARS MFRD 1998-2004
- ENGINE IVECO
- CYLINDERS 3
- CID 179
- PTO HP 42
- FUEL D
- SPEEDS 16/16
- TRANSMISSION SHUTTLE SHIFT
- STEERING STANDARD
- HITCH CAT. I
- PTO YES
- DRIVE TYPE 2WD
- ROPS/CAB ROPS

OPTIONS

4WD
CAB W/A
LDR

SERIAL NUMBERS

YEAR	BEGINNING NO.
1998	1128584
1999	1157784
2000	1184720
2001	1219443
2002	1252974
2003	1287178
2004	1317364

RETAIL PRICING

YEAR	HIGH	LOW
1998	$10,379	$7,784
1999	$10,924	$8,193
2000	$11,798	$8,849
2001	$12,235	$9,176
2002	$12,891	$9,668
2003	$13,546	$10,159
2004	$14,311	$10,733

AVG. AUCTION PRICING

LOW	HIGH	AVG
$5,750	$8,670	$7,473

TN60A ECONOMY

- YEARS MFRD 2004-2004
- ENGINE IVECO
- CYLINDERS 3
- CID 179
- PTO HP 45
- ENGINE HP 57
- FUEL D
- SPEEDS 8/8-12/12-16/16
- TRANSMISSION GEAR
- STEERING STANDARD
- PTO YES
- DRIVE TYPE 2WD
- ROPS/CAB ROPS
- WEIGHT 5,180 LBS.

OPTIONS

4WD

TN60A STANDARD

YEARS MFRD 2004-2008
ENGINE .... IVECO
CYLINDERS................ 3
CID 179
PTO HP 45
ENGINE HP 57
FUEL .... D
SPEEDS 12/12
TRANSMISSION ... SHUTTLE SHIFT
STEERING............ STANDARD
HITCH .... CAT. I
PTO .... YES
DRIVE TYPE 4WD
ROPS/CAB .... ROPS
WEIGHT .... 5,180 LBS.

OPTIONS

16/16SS
2WD
CAB W/A
LDR

SERIAL NUMBERS

RIGHT SIDE OF FRONT AXLE SUPPORT

YEAR	BEGINNING NO.
2004	HJE000001
2005	HJE015646
2006	HJE044200
2007	HJE073937
2008	HJE102906

RETAIL PRICING

YEAR	HIGH	LOW
2004	$15,338	$11,503
2005	$16,247	$12,185
2006	$17,269	$12,951
2007	$18,177	$13,633
2008	$19,314	$14,485

TN60DA

YEARS MFRD 2004-2008
ENGINE .... IVECO
CYLINDERS................ 3
CID 179
PTO HP 45
ENGINE HP 57
FUEL .... D
SPEEDS 8/8-12/12-16/16
TRANSMISSION .... GEAR
STEERING............ STANDARD
PTO .... YES
DRIVE TYPE 2WD
ROPS/CAB .... CAB
WEIGHT .... 5,180 LBS.

OPTIONS

4WD

SERIAL NUMBERS

RIGHT SIDE OF FRONT AXLE SUPPORT

YEAR	BEGINNING NO.
2004	HJE000001
2005	HJE015646
2006	HJE044200
2007	HJE073937
2008	HJE102906

AVG. AUCTION PRICING

LOW	HIGH	AVG
$10,404	$19,890	$16,439

TN60SA

YEARS MFRD 2004-2008
ENGINE .... IVECO
CYLINDERS................ 3
CID 179
PTO HP 45
ENGINE HP 57
FUEL .... D
SPEEDS 8/8-12/12-16/16
TRANSMISSION .... GEAR
STEERING............ STANDARD
PTO .... YES
DRIVE TYPE 4WD
ROPS/CAB .... ROPS
WEIGHT .... 5,180 LBS.

OPTIONS

CAB

SERIAL NUMBERS

RIGHT SIDE OF FRONT AXLE SUPPORT

YEAR	BEGINNING NO.
2004	HJE000001
2005	HJE015646
2006	HJE044200
2007	HJE073937
2008	HJE102906

TT45A

YEARS MFRD 2007-2011
ENGINE .... NH
CYLINDERS................ 4
CID 121.7
ENGINE HP 40
COOLING .... LIQUID
FUEL .... D
SPEEDS 8/2
TRANSMISSION .... GEAR
STEERING............ STANDARD
HITCH .... CAT. I
DRIVE TYPE 2WD
ROPS/CAB .... ROPS
WEIGHT .... 3,600 LBS.
MSRP $16,350

OPTIONS

LDR

RETAIL PRICING

YEAR	HIGH	LOW
2007	$8,219	$6,164
2008	$9,029	$6,772
2009	$9,922	$7,441
2010	$10,905	$8,179
2011	$11,987	$8,990

TT55

YEARS MFRD 2004-2006
SERIES.............. TT SERIES
ENGINE .... OWN
CYLINDERS................ 3
CID 165
PTO HP 47
ENGINE HP 56
FUEL .... D
SPEEDS 8/2
TRANSMISSION .... GEAR
STEERING............ STANDARD
HITCH .... CAT. I
HYDRAULIC .... YES
PTO .... YES
DRIVE TYPE 2WD
ROPS/CAB .... ROPS
WEIGHT .... 4,895 LBS.

OPTIONS

4WD
LDR

SERIAL NUMBERS

YEAR	BEGINNING NO.
2004	T00001M
2005	T00301M
2006	T00768M

RETAIL PRICING

YEAR	HIGH	LOW
2004	$8,294	$6,220
2005	$9,089	$6,817
2006	$9,625	$7,219

TT75

YEARS MFRD 2004-2006
SERIES.............. TT SERIES
ENGINE .... OWN
CYLINDERS................ 4
CID 220
PTO HP 59
FUEL .... D
SPEEDS 8/2
TRANSMISSION .... GEAR
STEERING............ STANDARD
HITCH .... CAT. II
HYDRAULIC .... YES
PTO .... YES
DRIVE TYPE 2WD
ROPS/CAB .... ROPS
WEIGHT .... 5,470 LBS.

OPTIONS

4WD

SERIAL NUMBERS

YEAR	BEGINNING NO.
2004	T40001M
2005	T40615M
2006	T41078M

AVG. AUCTION PRICING

LOW	HIGH	AVG
$4,600	$15,500	$9,450

TZ18DA

YEARS MFRD 2004-2008
SERIES.......... BOOMER SERIES
ENGINE .... NH
CYLINDERS................ 3
CID 58.2
PTO HP 13.7
ENGINE HP 18
FUEL .... D
SPEEDS .... VARIABLE
TRANSMISSION .... HYDRO
STEERING............ STANDARD
HITCH .... CAT. I
PTO .... YES
DRIVE TYPE 4WD
ROPS/CAB .... ROPS
WEIGHT .... 1,444 LBS.
MSRP $9,247

OPTIONS

54" DECK
60" DECK
LDR

SERIAL NUMBERS

YEAR	BEGINNING NO.
2004	HB10001
2005	HB11024
2006	HB20439
2007	NO PRODUCTION
2008	Z7NXC1209

RETAIL PRICING

YEAR	HIGH	LOW
2004	$4,010	$3,007
2005	$4,400	$3,300
2006	$4,850	$3,638
2007	$5,347	$4,010
2008	$5,599	$4,199

TZ22DA

YEARS MFRD 2006-2008
SERIES.......... BOOMER SERIES
ENGINE .... NH
CYLINDERS................ 3
CID 58.2
PTO HP 17
ENGINE HP 22
FUEL .... D
SPEEDS .... VARIABLE
TRANSMISSION .... HYDRO
STEERING............ STANDARD
HITCH .... CAT. I
PTO .... YES
DRIVE TYPE 4WD
ROPS/CAB .... ROPS
WEIGHT .... 1,320 LBS.
MSRP $9,728

OPTIONS

54" DECK
60" DECK
LDR

SERIAL NUMBERS

YEAR	BEGINNING NO.
2006	HB20706
2007	Z6NXD1598
2008	Z7NXD1004

RETAIL PRICING

YEAR	HIGH	LOW
2006	$4,771	$3,578
2007	$5,199	$3,899
2008	$5,817	$4,363

TZ24DA

YEARS MFRD 2004-2005
SERIES.......... BOOMER SERIES
ENGINE .... NH
CYLINDERS................ 3
CID 61
PTO HP 18
ENGINE HP 24
FUEL .... D

NEW HOLLAND

SPEEDS .... VARIABLE
TRANSMISSION .... HYDRO
STEERING .... STANDARD
HITCH .... CAT. I
PTO .... YES
DRIVE TYPE 4WD
ROPS/CAB .... ROPS
WEIGHT .... 1,455 LBS.
MSRP $10,100

OPTIONS

54" DECK
60" DECK
LDR

SERIAL NUMBERS

YEAR	BEGINNING NO.
2004	HC10001
2005	HC12233

RETAIL PRICING

YEAR	HIGH	LOW
2004	$4,158	$3,118
2005	$4,696	$3,522

TZ25DA

YEARS MFRD 2006-2008
SERIES .... BOOMER SERIES
ENGINE .... NH
CYLINDERS 3
CID 61.3
PTO HP 19
ENGINE HP 25
SPEEDS .... VARIABLE
TRANSMISSION .... HYDRO
STEERING .... STANDARD
HITCH .... CAT. I
PTO .... YES
DRIVE TYPE 4WD
ROPS/CAB .... ROPS
WEIGHT .... 1,455 LBS.
MSRP $11,088

OPTIONS

60" DECK
LDR

SERIAL NUMBERS

YEAR	BEGINNING NO.
2006	Z6NXE2757
2007	Z6NXE27502
2008	Z7NXE1017

RETAIL PRICING

YEAR	HIGH	LOW
2006	$5,151	$3,863
2007	$5,649	$4,237
2008	$6,282	$4,712

WORKMASTER 25 T4B

YEARS MFRD 2018-2020
ENGINE .... MITSUBISHI
CYLINDERS 3
CID 1.3L
PTO HP 19.2
ENGINE HP 24.4
FUEL .... D
SPEEDS 12/12
TRANSMISSION ... SHUTTLE SHIFT
STEERING .... STANDARD
HITCH .... CAT. I
DRIVE TYPE 4WD
ROPS/CAB .... ROPS
WEIGHT .... 2,469 LBS.
MSRP $15,259

OPTIONS

HYDRO $1,331
MID PTO $324

WORKMASTER 25S

YEARS MFRD 2018-2020
ENGINE .... YANMAR
CYLINDERS 3
CID 1.26L
PTO HP 17.2
ENGINE HP 24.7
FUEL .... D
TRANSMISSION .... HYDRO
STEERING .... STANDARD
DRIVE TYPE 4WD
ROPS/CAB .... ROPS
MSRP $16,604

OPTIONS

LDR $2,911

WORKMASTER 33

YEARS MFRD 2015-2016
ENGINE .... SHIBAURA
CYLINDERS 3
CID 1.5L
PTO HP 26
ENGINE HP 32.2
COOLING .... LIQUID
FUEL .... D
SPEEDS 12/12
TRANSMISSION ... SHUTTLE SHIFT
STEERING .... STANDARD
HITCH .... CAT. I
DRIVE TYPE 4WD
ROPS/CAB .... ROPS
MSRP $20,689

OPTIONS

HYDRO
LDR

SERIAL NUMBERS

YEAR	BEGINNING NO.
2015	2270000001
2016	2271111719

RETAIL PRICING

YEAR	HIGH	LOW
2015	$18,307	$13,730
2016	$20,859	$15,644

WORKMASTER 35

YEARS MFRD 2013-2015
ENGINE .... NH
CYLINDERS 3
CID 122
PTO HP 28.4
ENGINE HP 33
COOLING .... LIQUID
FUEL .... D
SPEEDS 12/12
TRANSMISSION ... SHUTTLE SHIFT
STEERING .... STANDARD
HITCH .... CAT. I
DRIVE TYPE 4WD
ROPS/CAB .... ROPS
STANDARD DECK .... 3,220"
MSRP $16,414

OPTIONS

1 HYD
HYDRO

SERIAL NUMBERS

YEAR	BEGINNING NO.
2013	2211011338
2014	2211013682
2015	2211016035

RETAIL PRICING

YEAR	HIGH	LOW
2013	$12,974	$9,731
2014	$14,010	$10,507
2015	$15,279	$11,459

AVG. AUCTION PRICING

LOW	HIGH	AVG
$11,000	$15,000	$12,867

WORKMASTER 35 T4B

YEARS MFRD 2017-2020
CYLINDERS 3
CID 1.9L
PTO HP 29.7
ENGINE HP 35
FUEL .... D
SPEEDS 12/12
STEERING .... STANDARD
HITCH .... CAT. I
DRIVE TYPE 4WD
WEIGHT .... 3,067 LBS.
MSRP $19,858

OPTIONS

HYDRO $1,331
LOADER $5,284
MID PTO $324

RETAIL PRICING

YEAR	HIGH	LOW
2017	$17,573	$13,180
2018	$18,498	$13,874
2019	$19,248	$14,436
2020	$20,063	$15,340

WORKMASTER 37

YEARS MFRD 2015-2016
ENGINE .... SHIBAURA
CYLINDERS 3
CID 1.5L
PTO HP 29.6
ENGINE HP 36.2
COOLING .... LIQUID
FUEL .... D
SPEEDS 12/12
TRANSMISSION ... SHUTTLE SHIFT
STEERING .... STANDARD
DRIVE TYPE 4WD
ROPS/CAB .... ROPS
MSRP $22,289

OPTIONS

HYDRO
LDR

SERIAL NUMBERS

YEAR	BEGINNING NO.
2015	2271000001
2016	2271001259

RETAIL PRICING

YEAR	HIGH	LOW
2015	$19,620	$14,715
2016	$22,369	$16,776

WORKMASTER 40

YEARS MFRD 2013-2015
ENGINE .... NH
CYLINDERS 3
CID 122
PTO HP 33.4
ENGINE HP 38
COOLING .... LIQUID
FUEL .... D
SPEEDS 12/12
TRANSMISSION ... SHUTTLE SHIFT
STEERING .... STANDARD
HITCH .... CAT. I
DRIVE TYPE 4WD
ROPS/CAB .... ROPS
WEIGHT .... 3,120 LBS.
MSRP $18,398

OPTIONS

1 HYD
HYDRO

SERIAL NUMBERS

YEAR	BEGINNING NO.
2013	2210011036
2014	2210012212
2015	2210013991

RETAIL PRICING

YEAR	HIGH	LOW
2013	$14,566	$10,924
2014	$15,648	$11,736
2015	$16,546	$12,410

WORKMASTER 40 T4B

YEARS MFRD 2017-2020
ENGINE N843T-F-24
CYLINDERS 3
CID 1.9L
PTO HP 34
ENGINE HP 40
FUEL .... D
SPEEDS 12/12
STEERING .... STANDARD
HITCH .... CAT. I
DRIVE TYPE 4WD
ROPS/CAB .... ROPS

WEIGHT ....3,067 LBS.
MSRP................ $21,496

OPTIONS

HYDRO................ $1,331
LOADER............... $5,284
MID PTO.................$324

RETAIL PRICING

YEAR	HIGH	LOW
2017	$18,059	$14,097
2018	$19,661	$14,746
2019	$20,452	$15,338
2020	$21,424	$16,125

WORKMASTER 45

YEARS MFRD 2010-2014
ENGINE ....NH
CYLINDERS..................4
CID 135.2
PTO HP 39
ENGINE HP.................45
COOLING ....LIQUID
FUEL ....D
SPEEDS 8/8
TRANSMISSION ... SHUTTLE SHIFT
STEERING............STANDARD
HITCH ....CAT. I
HYDRAULIC ....YES
PTO.......................YES
DRIVE TYPE 2WD
ROPS/CAB ....ROPS
WEIGHT ....3,527 LBS.
MSRP................ $17,601

OPTIONS

4WD
LDR

SERIAL NUMBERS

YEAR	BEGINNING NO.
2010	6128170
2011	6148605
2012	6189207
2013	6231807
2014	NH6271829

RETAIL PRICING

YEAR	HIGH	LOW
2010	$10,088	$7,566
2011	$10,918	$8,189
2012	$12,086	$9,064
2013	$13,231	$9,924
2014	$14,441	$10,831

WORKMASTER 50

YEARS MFRD 2015-2020
CYLINDERS..................3
CID 136
PTO HP 45
ENGINE HP.................53
FUEL ....D
SPEEDS 8/8
TRANSMISSION ... SHUTTLE SHIFT
STEERING............STANDARD
HITCH ....CAT. I
DRIVE TYPE 2WD
ROPS/CAB ....ROPS
MSRP................ $28,973

OPTIONS

2 HYD OUTLETS
LDR READY
MFWD $3,523

SERIAL NUMBERS

YEAR	BEGINNING NO.
2015	NH5319311
2016	NH5326877

RETAIL PRICING

YEAR	HIGH	LOW
2015	$15,650	$11,738
2016	$18,197	$13,648
2017	$20,197	$15,148
2018	$21,930	$16,447
2019	$23,755	$17,816
2020	$27,002	$20,623

YT16

YEARS MFRD 1985-1993
ENGINE ....KOHLER
ENGINE HP.................16
COOLING ....AIR
FUEL ....G
TRANSMISSION ....GEAR
STEERING............STANDARD
STANDARD DECK .... 42"
MSRP................ $3,900

OPTIONS

48" DECK

SERIAL NUMBERS

YEAR	BEGINNING NO.
1989	L9H
1990	L0H
1991	L1H
1992	L2H
1993	L3H

RETAIL PRICING

YEAR	HIGH	LOW
1988	$565	$424
1989	$614	$461
1990	$908	$681
1991	$971	$728
1992	$1,053	$789
1993	$1,068	$801

YT16H

YEARS MFRD 1986-1993
ENGINE ....KOHLER
ENGINE HP.................16
COOLING ....AIR
FUEL ....G
TRANSMISSION ....HYDRO
STEERING............STANDARD
STANDARD DECK .... 42"
MSRP................ $4,400

OPTIONS

48" DECK

SERIAL NUMBERS

YEAR	BEGINNING NO.
1989	L9J
1990	L0J
1991	L1J
1992	L2J
1993	L3J

RETAIL PRICING

YEAR	HIGH	LOW
1988	$664	$498
1989	$741	$555
1990	$1,020	$765
1991	$1,101	$825
1992	$1,189	$892
1993	$1,204	$903

YT18H

YEARS MFRD 1989-1993
ENGINE ....KOHLER
ENGINE HP.................18
COOLING ....AIR
FUEL ....G
SPEEDS ....VARIABLE
TRANSMISSION ....HYDRO
STEERING............STANDARD
STANDARD DECK .... 48"
MSRP................ $4,675

RETAIL PRICING

YEAR	HIGH	LOW
1989	$259	$194
1990	$284	$213
1991	$313	$235
1992	$350	$262
1993	$392	$294

NOTES

POULAN

BB24H42YT
YEARS MFRD 2005-2006
SERIES...... POULAN PRO SERIES
ENGINE .... B&S
ENGINE HP 24
COOLING .... AIR
FUEL .... G
SPEEDS .... VARIABLE
TRANSMISSION .... HYDRO
STEERING............ STANDARD

BB185H42LT
YEARS MFRD 2005-2006
SERIES...... POULAN PRO SERIES
ENGINE .... B&S
ENGINE HP 18.5
COOLING .... AIR
FUEL .... G
SPEEDS .... VARIABLE
TRANSMISSION .... HYDRO
STEERING............ STANDARD

BB185H42YT
YEARS MFRD 2005-2006
SERIES...... POULAN PRO SERIES
ENGINE .... B&S
ENGINE HP 18.5
COOLING .... AIR
FUEL .... G
SPEEDS .... VARIABLE
TRANSMISSION .... HYDRO
STEERING............ STANDARD
BLADE CLUTCH .... MANUAL

BB18542LT
YEARS MFRD 2005-2006
SERIES...... POULAN PRO SERIES
ENGINE .... B&S
ENGINE HP 18.5
COOLING .... AIR
FUEL .... G
SPEEDS 6/1
TRANSMISSION .... GEAR
STEERING............ STANDARD

BD18542YT
YEARS MFRD 2005-2005
ENGINE .... B&S
ENGINE HP 18.5
COOLING .... AIR
FUEL .... G
SPEEDS 6/1
TRANSMISSION .... GEAR
STEERING............ STANDARD
BLADE CLUTCH .... ELECTRIC

DB24H42YT
YEARS MFRD 2005-2006
ENGINE .... B&S
ENGINE HP 24
COOLING .... AIR
FUEL .... G
SPEEDS .... VARIABLE
TRANSMISSION .... HYDRO
STEERING............ STANDARD
BLADE CLUTCH .... ELECTRIC

DB24H48YT
YEARS MFRD 2005-2006
ENGINE .... B&S INTEK
CYLINDERS.................. 2
ENGINE HP 24
COOLING .... AIR
FUEL .... G
SPEEDS .... VARIABLE
TRANSMISSION .... HYDRO
STEERING............ STANDARD
BLADE CLUTCH .... ELECTRIC

DB27H48YT
YEARS MFRD 2005-2006
ENGINE .... B&S ELS
CYLINDERS.................. 2
ENGINE HP 27
COOLING .... AIR
FUEL .... G
SPEEDS .... VARIABLE
TRANSMISSION .... HYDRO
STEERING............ STANDARD
BLADE CLUTCH .... ELECTRIC

DB185H42YT
YEARS MFRD 2005-2006
ENGINE .... B&S
ENGINE HP 18.5
COOLING .... AIR
FUEL .... G
SPEEDS .... VARIABLE
TRANSMISSION .... HYDRO
STEERING............ STANDARD
BLADE CLUTCH .... ELECTRIC

DB18542YT
YEARS MFRD 2006-2006
SERIES............ PRO SERIES
ENGINE .... B&S
ENGINE HP 18.5
COOLING .... AIR
FUEL .... G
SPEEDS 6/1
TRANSMISSION .... GEAR
STEERING............ STANDARD

P46ZX
YEARS MFRD 2015-2016
ENGINE .... B&S
CYLINDERS.................. 1
CID 540CC
ENGINE HP 22
COOLING .... AIR
FUEL .... G
SPEEDS .... VARIABLE
TRANSMISSION .... HYDRO
STEERING................ ZERO
STANDARD DECK .... 46"

P54ZX
YEARS MFRD 2015-2016
ENGINE .... B&S
CYLINDERS.................. 2
ENGINE HP 24
COOLING .... AIR
FUEL .... G
SPEEDS .... VARIABLE
TRANSMISSION .... HYDRO
STEERING................ ZERO
STANDARD DECK .... 54"

OPTIONS

KOHLER

P54ZXT
YEARS MFRD 2015-2016
ENGINE .... KOHLER
CYLINDERS.................. 2
ENGINE HP 26
COOLING .... AIR
FUEL .... G
SPEEDS .... VARIABLE
TRANSMISSION .... HYDRO
STEERING................ ZERO
STANDARD DECK .... 54"

PO12530LT
YEARS MFRD 2010-2011
ENGINE .... B&S
CYLINDERS.................. 1
ENGINE HP 12.5
COOLING .... AIR
FUEL .... G
SPEEDS 3/1
TRANSMISSION .... GEAR
STEERING............ STANDARD
BLADE CLUTCH .... MANUAL

PO17542LT
YEARS MFRD 2010-2012
ENGINE .... B&S
CYLINDERS.................. 1
ENGINE HP 17.5
COOLING .... AIR
FUEL .... G
SPEEDS 6/1
TRANSMISSION .... GEAR
STEERING............ STANDARD
BLADE CLUTCH .... MANUAL

PB18VA46
YEARS MFRD 2015-2015
ENGINE .... B&S
CYLINDERS.................. 2
ENGINE HP 18
COOLING .... AIR
FUEL .... G
SPEEDS .... VARIABLE
TRANSMISSION .... CVT
STEERING............ STANDARD
BLADE CLUTCH .... MANUAL
STANDARD DECK .... 46"
WEIGHT .... 411 LBS.

PB20A46
YEARS MFRD 2015-2015
ENGINE .... KOHLER
CYLINDERS.................. 1
ENGINE HP 20
COOLING .... AIR
FUEL .... G
SPEEDS .... VARIABLE
TRANSMISSION .... CVT
STEERING............ STANDARD
BLADE CLUTCH .... MANUAL
STANDARD DECK .... 46"
WEIGHT .... 411 LBS.

PB20H42YT
YEARS MFRD 2013-2013
ENGINE .... B&S INTEK 40
CYLINDERS.................. 2
CID 656CC
ENGINE HP 20
COOLING .... AIR
FUEL .... G
SPEEDS .... VARIABLE
STEERING................ ZERO
BLADE CLUTCH .... MANUAL
WEIGHT .... 434 LBS.

PB20H46LT 960420042
YEARS MFRD 2007-2007
ENGINE .... B&S
ENGINE HP 20
COOLING .... AIR
FUEL .... G
SPEEDS .... VARIABLE
TRANSMISSION .... HYDRO
STEERING................ ZERO

PB20H46YT 960420037
YEARS MFRD 2007-2007
ENGINE .... B&S
ENGINE HP 20
COOLING .... AIR
FUEL .... G
SPEEDS .... VARIABLE
TRANSMISSION .... HYDRO
STEERING................ ZERO

PB20VA46
YEARS MFRD 2015-2015
ENGINE .... B&S
CYLINDERS.................. 2
ENGINE HP 20

POULAN

COOLING . . . . . AIR
FUEL . . . . . G
SPEEDS . . . . . VARIABLE
TRANSMISSION . . . . . CVT
STEERING . . . . . STANDARD
BLADE CLUTCH . . . . . MANUAL
STANDARD DECK . . . . . 46"
WEIGHT . . . . . 411 LBS.

PB22H42YT 960420041

YEARS MFRD 2007-2011
ENGINE . . . . . B&S
CYLINDERS 2
ENGINE HP 22
COOLING . . . . . AIR
FUEL . . . . . G
SPEEDS . . . . . VARIABLE
TRANSMISSION . . . . . HYDRO
STEERING . . . . . ZERO

PB22H46YT 960420038

YEARS MFRD 2007-2013
SERIES . . . . . 500 SERIES
ENGINE . . . . . B&S INTEK 40
CYLINDERS 2
CID 656CC
ENGINE HP 22
COOLING . . . . . AIR
FUEL . . . . . G
SPEEDS . . . . . VARIABLE
TRANSMISSION . . . . . HYDRO
STEERING . . . . . STANDARD
BLADE CLUTCH . . . . . MANUAL
WEIGHT . . . . . 439 LBS.

PB22H54BF

YEARS MFRD 2010-2010
ENGINE . . . . . B&S INTEK
CYLINDERS 2
CID 300CC
ENGINE HP 22
COOLING . . . . . AIR
FUEL . . . . . G
SPEEDS . . . . . VARIABLE
TRANSMISSION . . . . . HYDRO
STEERING . . . . . STANDARD
BLADE CLUTCH . . . . . ELECTRIC

PB22H54YT 960420060

YEARS MFRD 2008-2009
SERIES . . . . . 700 SERIES
ENGINE . . . . . B&S INTEK
CYLINDERS 2
ENGINE HP 22
COOLING . . . . . AIR
FUEL . . . . . G
SPEEDS . . . . . VARIABLE
TRANSMISSION . . . . . HYDRO
STEERING . . . . . STANDARD
BLADE CLUTCH . . . . . ELECTRIC

PB22VA48

YEARS MFRD 2015-2015
ENGINE . . . . . B&S
CYLINDERS 2
ENGINE HP 22
COOLING . . . . . AIR
FUEL . . . . . G
SPEEDS . . . . . VARIABLE
TRANSMISSION . . . . . CVT
STEERING . . . . . STANDARD
BLADE CLUTCH . . . . . ELECTRIC
STANDARD DECK . . . . . 48"
WEIGHT . . . . . 474 LBS.

PB23H48YT

YEARS MFRD 2013-2013
ENGINE . . . . . B&S INTEK 44
CYLINDERS 2
CID 724CC
ENGINE HP 23
COOLING . . . . . AIR
FUEL . . . . . G
SPEEDS . . . . . VARIABLE
TRANSMISSION . . . . . HYDRO
STEERING . . . . . ZERO
BLADE CLUTCH . . . . . ELECTRIC
WEIGHT . . . . . 480 LBS.

PB24H54YT 960420039

YEARS MFRD 2007-2007
ENGINE . . . . . B&S
CYLINDERS 2
ENGINE HP 24
COOLING . . . . . AIR
FUEL . . . . . G
SPEEDS . . . . . VARIABLE
TRANSMISSION . . . . . HYDRO
STEERING . . . . . ZERO

PB24VA54

YEARS MFRD 2015-2015
ENGINE . . . . . B&S
CYLINDERS 2
ENGINE HP 24
COOLING . . . . . AIR
FUEL . . . . . G
SPEEDS . . . . . VARIABLE
TRANSMISSION . . . . . CVT
STEERING . . . . . STANDARD
BLADE CLUTCH . . . . . ELECTRIC
STANDARD DECK . . . . . 54"
WEIGHT . . . . . 497 LBS.

PB26H54YT

YEARS MFRD 2013-2013
ENGINE . . . . . B&S INTEK 44
CYLINDERS 2
CID 724CC
ENGINE HP 26
COOLING . . . . . AIR
FUEL . . . . . G
SPEEDS . . . . . VARIABLE

TRANSMISSION . . . . . HYDRO
STEERING . . . . . ZERO
BLADE CLUTCH . . . . . ELECTRIC
WEIGHT . . . . . 574 LBS.

PB145G42

YEARS MFRD 2015-2015
ENGINE . . . . . B&S
CYLINDERS 1
ENGINE HP 14.5
COOLING . . . . . AIR
FUEL . . . . . G
SPEEDS 6/1
TRANSMISSION . . . . . GEAR
STEERING . . . . . STANDARD
BLADE CLUTCH . . . . . MANUAL
STANDARD DECK . . . . . 42"
WEIGHT . . . . . 393 LBS.

PB175G42

YEARS MFRD 2015-2015
ENGINE . . . . . B&S
CYLINDERS 1
ENGINE HP 17.5
COOLING . . . . . AIR
FUEL . . . . . G
SPEEDS 6/1
TRANSMISSION . . . . . GEAR
STEERING . . . . . STANDARD
BLADE CLUTCH . . . . . MANUAL
STANDARD DECK . . . . . 42"
WEIGHT . . . . . 393 LBS.

PB185A42

YEARS MFRD 2015-2015
ENGINE . . . . . B&S
CYLINDERS 1
ENGINE HP 18
COOLING . . . . . AIR
FUEL . . . . . G
SPEEDS . . . . . VARIABLE
TRANSMISSION . . . . . DISC
STEERING . . . . . STANDARD
BLADE CLUTCH . . . . . MANUAL
STANDARD DECK . . . . . 42"
WEIGHT . . . . . 405 LBS.

PB185H42LT

YEARS MFRD 2005-2006
ENGINE . . . . . B&S INTEK
ENGINE HP 18.5
COOLING . . . . . AIR
FUEL . . . . . G
SPEEDS . . . . . VARIABLE
TRANSMISSION . . . . . HYDRO
STEERING . . . . . STANDARD

PB195H42LT 960420036

YEARS MFRD 2007-2013
SERIES 300SERIES
ENGINE . . . . . B&S INTEK

CYLINDERS 1
CID 500CC
ENGINE HP 19.5
COOLING . . . . . AIR
FUEL . . . . . G
SPEEDS . . . . . VARIABLE
TRANSMISSION . . . . . HYDRO
STEERING . . . . . STANDARD
BLADE CLUTCH . . . . . MANUAL
WEIGHT . . . . . 405 LBS.

PB195H46YT 960420059

YEARS MFRD 2008-2010
SERIES . . . . . 500 SERIES
ENGINE . . . . . B&S
CYLINDERS 1
ENGINE HP 19.5
COOLING . . . . . AIR
FUEL . . . . . G
SPEEDS . . . . . VARIABLE
TRANSMISSION . . . . . HYDRO
STEERING . . . . . STANDARD

PB301

YEARS MFRD 2015-2016
ENGINE . . . . . B&S
CYLINDERS 1
ENGINE HP 11.5
COOLING . . . . . AIR
FUEL . . . . . G
SPEEDS 4/1
TRANSMISSION . . . . . GEAR
STEERING . . . . . STANDARD
BLADE CLUTCH . . . . . MANUAL
STANDARD DECK . . . . . 30"
WEIGHT . . . . . 307 LBS.

PB18542LT

YEARS MFRD 2005-2006
ENGINE . . . . . B&S INTEK
ENGINE HP 18.5
COOLING . . . . . AIR
FUEL . . . . . G
SPEEDS 6/1
TRANSMISSION . . . . . GEAR
STEERING . . . . . STANDARD
BLADE CLUTCH . . . . . MANUAL

PB19542LT 960420034

YEARS MFRD 2007-2007
ENGINE . . . . . B&S
ENGINE HP 19.5
COOLING . . . . . AIR
FUEL . . . . . G
SPEEDS . . . . . VARIABLE
TRANSMISSION . . . . . HYDRO
STEERING . . . . . ZERO

PB19546LT 960420035
YEARS MFRD 2007-2010
SERIES............. 300 SERIES
ENGINE .... B&S
ENGINE HP 19.5
COOLING ....AIR
FUEL ....G
SPEEDS 5/1
TRANSMISSION ....GEAR
STEERING............STANDARD

PBGT26H54 960420040
YEARS MFRD 2007-2013
ENGINE .... B&S INTEK
CYLINDERS.................. 2
CID 724CC
ENGINE HP 26
COOLING ....AIR
FUEL ....G
SPEEDS ....VARIABLE
TRANSMISSION ....HYDRO
STEERING................ZERO
BLADE CLUTCH ....ELECTRIC

PBGT27H54
YEARS MFRD 2005-2006
ENGINE ....B&S ELS
CYLINDERS.................. 2
ENGINE HP 27
COOLING ....AIR
FUEL ....G
SPEEDS ....VARIABLE
TRANSMISSION ....HYDRO
STEERING............STANDARD
BLADE CLUTCH ....ELECTRIC

PBGT2254
YEARS MFRD 2005-2006
ENGINE ....B&S ELS
CYLINDERS.................. 2
ENGINE HP 22
COOLING ....AIR
FUEL ....G
SPEEDS 6/1
TRANSMISSION ....GEAR
STEERING............STANDARD
BLADE CLUTCH ....ELECTRIC

PBGT2654
YEARS MFRD 2015-2015
ENGINE ....KOHLER
CYLINDERS.................. 2
ENGINE HP 26
COOLING ....AIR
FUEL ....G
SPEEDS ....VARIABLE
TRANSMISSION ....HYDRO
STEERING............STANDARD
BLADE CLUTCH ....ELECTRIC
STANDARD DECK .... 54"
WEIGHT .... 598 LBS.

PBLGT2654
YEARS MFRD 2015-2015
ENGINE ....KOHLER
CYLINDERS.................. 2
ENGINE HP 26
COOLING ....AIR
FUEL ....G
SPEEDS ....VARIABLE
TRANSMISSION ....HYDRO
STEERING............STANDARD
BLADE CLUTCH ....ELECTRIC
STANDARD DECK .... 54"
WEIGHT .... 564 LBS.

PD18H42ST
YEARS MFRD 2004-2004
ENGINE ...... KOHLER COMMAND
CYLINDERS.................. 2
ENGINE HP 18
COOLING ....AIR
FUEL ....G
SPEEDS ....VARIABLE
TRANSMISSION ....HYDRO
STEERING............STANDARD
WEIGHT .... 465 LBS.

PD20H42ST
YEARS MFRD 2004-2004
ENGINE ... B&S INTEK V-TWIN OHV
CYLINDERS.................. 2
ENGINE HP 20
COOLING ....AIR
FUEL ....G
SPEEDS ....VARIABLE
TRANSMISSION ....HYDRO
STEERING............STANDARD
WEIGHT .... 560 LBS.

PD20PH48ST
YEARS MFRD 2004-2004
ENGINE .... KOHLER V-TWIN
CYLINDERS.................. 2
ENGINE HP 20
COOLING ....AIR
FUEL ....G
SPEEDS ....VARIABLE
TRANSMISSION ....HYDRO
STEERING............STANDARD
WEIGHT .... 580 LBS.

PD25PH48ST
YEARS MFRD 2004-2004
ENGINE ... B&S INTEK V-TWIN OHV
CYLINDERS.................. 2
ENGINE HP 25
COOLING ....AIR
FUEL ....G
SPEEDS ....VARIABLE
TRANSMISSION ....HYDRO
STEERING............STANDARD
WEIGHT .... 580 LBS.

PD1842ST
YEARS MFRD 2004-2004
ENGINE ...... KOHLER COMMAND
CYLINDERS.................. 1
ENGINE HP 18
COOLING ....AIR
FUEL ....G
SPEEDS 6/1
TRANSMISSION ....GEAR
STEERING............STANDARD
WEIGHT .... 550 LBS.

PD2042ST
YEARS MFRD 2004-2004
ENGINE .... B&S INTEK V-TWIN
CYLINDERS.................. 2
ENGINE HP 20
COOLING ....AIR
SPEEDS 6/1
TRANSMISSION ....GEAR
STEERING............STANDARD
WEIGHT .... 550 LBS.

PD15538LT
YEARS MFRD 2005-2006
SERIES....... POULAN STL SERIES
ENGINE .... B&S I/C
ENGINE HP 15.5
COOLING ....AIR
FUEL ....G
SPEEDS 5/1
TRANSMISSION ....GEAR
STEERING............STANDARD
BLADE CLUTCH .... MANUAL

PD17542LT
YEARS MFRD 2005-2006
ENGINE .... B&S I/C
ENGINE HP 17.5
COOLING ....AIR
FUEL ....G
SPEEDS 6/1
TRANSMISSION ....GEAR
STEERING............STANDARD
BLADE CLUTCH .... MANUAL

PDGT26H48
YEARS MFRD 2004-2004
ENGINE .... B&S INTEK V-TWIN
CYLINDERS.................. 2
ENGINE HP 26
COOLING ....AIR
FUEL ....G
SPEEDS ....VARIABLE
TRANSMISSION ....HYDRO
STEERING............STANDARD
WEIGHT .... 700 LBS.

PK19H42LT
YEARS MFRD 2005-2006
SERIES...... POULAN PRO SERIES
ENGINE .... KOHLER COURAGE
ENGINE HP 19
COOLING ....AIR
FUEL ....G
SPEEDS ....VARIABLE
TRANSMISSION ....HYDRO
STEERING............STANDARD

PK19H42YT
YEARS MFRD 2005-2006
SERIES...... POULAN PRO SERIES
ENGINE .... KOHLER COURAGE
ENGINE HP 19
COOLING ....AIR
FUEL ....G
SPEEDS 6/1
TRANSMISSION ....GEAR
STEERING............STANDARD

PK20H42YT
YEARS MFRD 2005-2006
SERIES...... POULAN PRO SERIES
ENGINE .... KOHLER COURAGE
ENGINE HP 20
COOLING ....AIR
FUEL ....G
SPEEDS ....VARIABLE
TRANSMISSION ....HYDRO
STEERING............STANDARD

PK20H48YT
YEARS MFRD 2005-2006
SERIES...... POULAN PRO SERIES
ENGINE .... KOHLER COURAGE
ENGINE HP 20
COOLING ....AIR
FUEL ....G
SPEEDS ....VARIABLE
TRANSMISSION ....HYDRO
STEERING............STANDARD

PK23H48YT
YEARS MFRD 2005-2006
SERIES...... POULAN PRO SERIES
ENGINE ...... KOHLER COMMAND
CYLINDERS.................. 2
ENGINE HP 23
COOLING ....AIR
FUEL ....G
SPEEDS ....VARIABLE
TRANSMISSION ....HYDRO
STEERING............STANDARD

PK1942LT
YEARS MFRD 2005-2006
SERIES...... POULAN PRO SERIES
ENGINE .... KOHLER COURAGE
ENGINE HP 19
COOLING ....AIR
FUEL ....G
SPEEDS 6/1
TRANSMISSION ....GEAR
STEERING............STANDARD

POULAN

PK1942YT
YEARS MFRD 2005-2006
SERIES...... POULAN PRO SERIES
ENGINE .... KOHLER COURAGE
ENGINE HP 19
COOLING .... AIR
FUEL .... G
SPEEDS 6/1
TRANSMISSION .... GEAR
STEERING............ STANDARD

PKGT25H54
YEARS MFRD 2005-2006
SERIES...... POULAN PRO SERIES
ENGINE ...... KOHLER COMMAND
CYLINDERS.................... 2
ENGINE HP 25
COOLING .... AIR
FUEL .... G
SPEEDS .... VARIABLE
TRANSMISSION .... HYDRO
STEERING............ STANDARD
HYDRAULIC .... YES

PO1538
YEARS MFRD 2004-2004
ENGINE .... B&S OHV
CYLINDERS.................... 1
ENGINE HP 15
COOLING .... AIR
FUEL .... G
SPEEDS 5/1
TRANSMISSION .... GEAR
STEERING............ STANDARD

PO1742ST
YEARS MFRD 2004-2004
ENGINE .... B&S OHV
CYLINDERS.................... 1
ENGINE HP 17
COOLING .... AIR
FUEL .... G
SPEEDS 6/1
TRANSMISSION .... GEAR
STEERING............ STANDARD
WEIGHT .... 465 LBS.

PO14542LT
YEARS MFRD 2012-2015
ENGINE .... B&S
CYLINDERS.................... 1
CID 500CC
ENGINE HP 14.5
COOLING .... AIR
FUEL .... G
SPEEDS 6/1
TRANSMISSION .... GEAR
STEERING............ STANDARD
WEIGHT .... 385 LBS.

PO16542
YEARS MFRD 2010-2010
ENGINE .... B&S I/C
CYLINDERS.................... 1
ENGINE HP 16.5
COOLING .... AIR
FUEL .... G
SPEEDS 6/1
TRANSMISSION .... GEAR
STEERING............ STANDARD

PO17542LT
YEARS MFRD 2013-2015
ENGINE .... B&S
CYLINDERS.................... 1
CID 500CC
ENGINE HP 17.5
COOLING .... AIR
FUEL .... G
SPEEDS 6/1
TRANSMISSION .... GEAR
STEERING............ STANDARD
STANDARD DECK .... 42"
WEIGHT .... 385 LBS.

PO18542LT
YEARS MFRD 2010-2011
ENGINE .... B&S
CYLINDERS.................... 1
ENGINE HP 18.5
COOLING .... AIR
FUEL .... G
SPEEDS 6/1
TRANSMISSION .... GEAR
STEERING............ STANDARD

PO19542LT
YEARS MFRD 2012-2015
ENGINE .... B&S
CYLINDERS.................... 1
CID 500CC
ENGINE HP 19.5
COOLING .... AIR
FUEL .... G
SPEEDS 6/1
TRANSMISSION .... GEAR
STEERING............ STANDARD
WEIGHT .... 387 LBS.

POGT20H48ST
YEARS MFRD 2004-2004
ENGINE ... B&S INTEK V-TWIN OHV
CYLINDERS.................... 2
ENGINE HP 20
COOLING .... AIR
FUEL .... G
SPEEDS .... VARIABLE
TRANSMISSION .... HYDRO
STEERING............ STANDARD
WEIGHT .... 580 LBS.

PP19A42
YEARS MFRD 2016-2017
ENGINE .... B&S
CID 540CC
ENGINE HP 19
COOLING .... AIR
FUEL .... G
SPEEDS .... VARIABLE
TRANSMISSION .... HYDRO
STEERING............ STANDARD
BLADE CLUTCH .... MANUAL
STANDARD DECK .... 42"
WEIGHT .... 408 LBS.

PP20VA46
YEARS MFRD 2016-2017
ENGINE .... B&S INTEK
CYLINDERS.................... 2
CID 656CC
ENGINE HP 20
COOLING .... AIR
FUEL .... G
SPEEDS .... VARIABLE
TRANSMISSION .... HYDRO
STEERING............ STANDARD
BLADE CLUTCH .... MANUAL
STANDARD DECK .... 46"
WEIGHT .... 426 LBS.

PP22VA48
YEARS MFRD 2017-2017
ENGINE .... B&S INTEK
CYLINDERS.................... 2
ENGINE HP 22
FUEL .... G
SPEEDS .... VARIABLE
TRANSMISSION .... CVT
STEERING............ STANDARD
BLADE CLUTCH .... ELECTRIC
STANDARD DECK .... 48"

PP24VA54
YEARS MFRD 2016-2016
ENGINE .... B&S 05 SERIES
CYLINDERS.................... 2
CID 725CC
ENGINE HP 24
COOLING .... AIR
FUEL .... G
SPEEDS .... VARIABLE
TRANSMISSION .... HYDRO
STEERING............ STANDARD
BLADE CLUTCH .... ELECTRIC
STANDARD DECK .... 54"
WEIGHT .... 488 LBS.

PP105G30
YEARS MFRD 2017-2017
ENGINE .... B&S INTEK
ENGINE HP 10.5
COOLING .... AIR
FUEL .... G
TRANSMISSION .... GEAR
STEERING............ STANDARD
BLADE CLUTCH .... MANUAL
STANDARD DECK .... 30"

PP155G42
YEARS MFRD 2017-2017
ENGINE .... B&S
ENGINE HP 15.5
COOLING .... AIR
FUEL .... G
SPEEDS 6/1
TRANSMISSION .... GEAR
STEERING............ STANDARD
BLADE CLUTCH .... MANUAL
STANDARD DECK .... 42"

PP175G42
YEARS MFRD 2016-2017
ENGINE .... B&S
CYLINDERS.................... 1
CID 500CC
ENGINE HP 17.5
COOLING .... AIR
FUEL .... G
SPEEDS 6/1
TRANSMISSION .... GEAR
STEERING............ STANDARD
BLADE CLUTCH .... MANUAL
STANDARD DECK .... 42"
WEIGHT .... 393 LBS.

301ZX
YEARS MFRD 2011-2013
SERIES.............. PRO SERIES
ENGINE .... B&S
CYLINDERS.................... 1
ENGINE HP 16.5
COOLING .... AIR
FUEL .... G
SPEEDS .... VARIABLE
TRANSMISSION .... HYDRO
STEERING.................. ZERO
STANDARD DECK .... 30"
WEIGHT .... 395 LBS.
MSRP.................. $2,326

RETAIL PRICING

YEAR	HIGH	LOW
2011	$1,214	$911
2012	$1,296	$972
2013	$1,447	$1,085

461ZX
YEARS MFRD 2011-2013
SERIES.............. PRO SERIES
ENGINE .... B&S
CYLINDERS.................... 1
ENGINE HP 19.5
COOLING .... AIR
FUEL .... G
SPEEDS .... VARIABLE
TRANSMISSION .... HYDRO
STEERING.................. ZERO
STANDARD DECK .... 46"
WEIGHT .... 430 LBS.
MSRP.................. $2,819

RETAIL PRICING

YEAR	HIGH	LOW
2011	$1,278	$959
2012	$1,528	$1,146
2013	$1,765	$1,324

541ZX

YEARS MFRD . . . 2011-2013
SERIES . . . PRO SERIES
ENGINE . . . B&S
CYLINDERS . . . 1
ENGINE HP . . . 22
COOLING . . . AIR
FUEL . . . G
SPEEDS . . . VARIABLE
TRANSMISSION . . . HYDRO
STEERING . . . ZERO
STANDARD DECK . . . 54"
WEIGHT . . . 640 LBS.
MSRP . . . $2,799

RETAIL PRICING

YEAR	HIGH	LOW
2011	$1,271	$953
2012	$1,514	$1,136
2013	$1,735	$1,301

925ZX 968999516

YEARS MFRD . . . 2007-2010
ENGINE . . . B&S
CYLINDERS . . . 2
ENGINE HP . . . 24
COOLING . . . AIR
FUEL . . . G
SPEEDS . . . VARIABLE
TRANSMISSION . . . HYDRO
STEERING . . . ZERO

950ZX

YEARS MFRD . . . 2007-2010
SERIES . . . ZTR SERIES
ENGINE . . . B&S ELS
CYLINDERS . . . 2
ENGINE HP . . . 26
COOLING . . . AIR
FUEL . . . G
SPEEDS . . . VARIABLE
TRANSMISSION . . . HYDRO
STEERING . . . ZERO

27119

YEARS MFRD . . . 2004-2004
ENGINE . . . B&S
CYLINDERS . . . 1
CID . . . 28
ENGINE HP . . . 15.5
COOLING . . . AIR
FUEL . . . G
SPEEDS . . . 5/1
TRANSMISSION . . . GEAR
STEERING . . . STANDARD
STANDARD DECK . . . 38"
WEIGHT . . . 478 LBS.
MSRP . . . $849

RETAIL PRICING

YEAR	HIGH	LOW
2004	$494	$370

27937

YEARS MFRD . . . 2004-2004
ENGINE . . . B&S
CYLINDERS . . . 1
CID . . . 30
ENGINE HP . . . 18
COOLING . . . AIR
FUEL . . . G
SPEEDS . . . 6/1
TRANSMISSION . . . GEAR
STEERING . . . STANDARD
STANDARD DECK . . . 42"
WEIGHT . . . 518 LBS.
MSRP . . . $1,399

RETAIL PRICING

YEAR	HIGH	LOW
2004	$815	$611

POWER TRAC

PT180

YEARS MFRD . . . 2004-2016
SERIES . . . H CLASS
ENGINE HP . . . 18
FUEL . . . G
SPEEDS . . . VARIABLE
TRANSMISSION . . . HYDRO
STEERING . . . ALL WHEEL
HYDRAULIC . . . YES
STANDARD DECK . . . 42"
WEIGHT . . . 1,260 LBS.
MSRP . . . $6,500

RETAIL PRICING

YEAR	HIGH	LOW
2004	$822	$617
2005	$986	$739
2006	$1,078	$809
2007	$1,187	$890
2008	$1,406	$1,055
2009	$1,643	$1,233
2010	$2,018	$1,513
2011	$2,255	$1,691
2012	$2,557	$1,918
2013	$2,848	$2,136
2014	$3,205	$2,403
2015	$3,743	$2,807
2016	$4,546	$3,410

PT184

YEARS MFRD . . . 1983-1996
ENGINE . . . B&S
CID . . . 42.33
ENGINE HP . . . 18
FUEL . . . G
TRANSMISSION . . . HYDRO
STEERING . . . STANDARD
DRIVE TYPE . . . 4WD
ROPS/CAB . . . ROPS
WEIGHT . . . 900 LBS.
MSRP . . . $7,495

OPTIONS

KOHLER COMMAND 18HP

RETAIL PRICING

YEAR	HIGH	LOW
1990	$2,115	$1,586
1991	$2,258	$1,693
1992	$2,384	$1,788
1993	$2,493	$1,870
1994	$2,670	$2,002
1995	$2,812	$2,109
1996	$2,952	$2,214

PT418

YEARS MFRD . . . 1999-2000
SERIES . . . 400 SERIES
ENGINE . . . ROBIN
ENGINE HP . . . 18
FUEL . . . G
TRANSMISSION . . . HYDRO
STEERING . . . ZERO
DRIVE TYPE . . . 4WD
ROPS/CAB . . . ROPS
STANDARD DECK . . . 48"
WEIGHT . . . 2,560 LBS.
MSRP . . . $5,794

RETAIL PRICING

YEAR	HIGH	LOW
1999	$1,021	$766
2000	$1,138	$853

PT420

YEARS MFRD . . . 1984-1994
SERIES . . . 400 SERIES
ENGINE . . . KOHLER
ENGINE HP . . . 20
FUEL . . . G
TRANSMISSION . . . HYDRO
DRIVE TYPE . . . 4WD
ROPS/CAB . . . ROPS
WEIGHT . . . 1,000 LBS.
MSRP . . . $7,550

RETAIL PRICING

YEAR	HIGH	LOW
1990	$2,192	$1,644
1991	$2,339	$1,754
1992	$2,472	$1,854
1993	$2,582	$1,937
1994	$2,764	$2,073

PT422

YEARS MFRD . . . 2000-2016
SERIES . . . 400 SERIES
ENGINE . . . ROBIN
ENGINE HP . . . 22
FUEL . . . G
SPEEDS . . . VARIABLE
TRANSMISSION . . . HYDRO
STEERING . . . ZERO
DRIVE TYPE . . . 4WD
ROPS/CAB . . . ROPS
STANDARD DECK . . . 60"
WEIGHT . . . 1,344 LBS.
MSRP . . . $8,500

RETAIL PRICING

YEAR	HIGH	LOW
2000	$977	$733
2001	$1,013	$760
2002	$1,068	$801
2003	$1,132	$849
2004	$1,187	$890
2005	$1,406	$1,055
2006	$1,534	$1,150
2007	$1,707	$1,280
2008	$1,917	$1,438
2009	$2,190	$1,643
2010	$2,638	$1,979
2011	$2,949	$2,212
2012	$3,341	$2,506
2013	$3,725	$2,794
2014	$4,190	$3,143
2015	$4,893	$3,670
2016	$5,853	$4,389

PT422S

YEARS MFRD . . . 1984-1994
SERIES . . . 400 SERIES
ENGINE . . . KUBOTA
ENGINE HP . . . 22
FUEL . . . D
TRANSMISSION . . . HYDRO
DRIVE TYPE . . . 4WD
ROPS/CAB . . . ROPS
WEIGHT . . . 900 LBS.
MSRP . . . $9,795

RETAIL PRICING

YEAR	HIGH	LOW
1990	$2,873	$2,155
1991	$3,063	$2,298
1992	$3,224	$2,418
1993	$3,359	$2,520
1994	$3,586	$2,689

PT423

YEARS MFRD . . . 1984-1994
SERIES . . . 400 SERIES
ENGINE . . . KOHLER
ENGINE HP . . . 23
FUEL . . . G
TRANSMISSION . . . HYDRO
DRIVE TYPE . . . 4WD
ROPS/CAB . . . ROPS
WEIGHT . . . 1,300 LBS.
MSRP . . . $9,795

RETAIL PRICING

YEAR	HIGH	LOW
1990	$2,873	$2,155
1991	$3,063	$2,298
1992	$3,224	$2,418
1993	$3,359	$2,520
1994	$3,586	$2,689

PT425

YEARS MFRD . . . 1999-2000
SERIES . . . 400 SERIES
ENGINE . . . KOHLER
ENGINE HP . . . 25

POWER TRAC

FUEL . . . . . G
SPEEDS . . . . . VARIABLE
TRANSMISSION . . . . . HYDRO
STEERING . . . . . ZERO
HYDRAULIC . . . . . YES
DRIVE TYPE 4WD
ROPS/CAB . . . . . ROPS
STANDARD DECK . . . . . 60"
WEIGHT . . . . . 1,387 LBS.
MSRP $7,994

RETAIL PRICING

YEAR	HIGH	LOW
1999	$1,412	$1,059
2000	$1,566	$1,175

PT430

YEARS MFRD 1984-1994
SERIES . . . . . 400 SERIES
ENGINE . . . . . KUBOTA
ENGINE HP 30
FUEL . . . . . D
TRANSMISSION . . . . . HYDRO
DRIVE TYPE 4WD
ROPS/CAB . . . . . ROPS
WEIGHT . . . . . 1,600 LBS.
MSRP $12,995

RETAIL PRICING

YEAR	HIGH	LOW
1990	$3,780	$2,835
1991	$4,033	$3,025
1992	$4,233	$3,174
1993	$4,468	$3,351
1994	$4,759	$3,569

PT445

YEARS MFRD 1984-1994
ENGINE . . . . . FORD
PTO HP 45
FUEL . . . . . G
SPEEDS . . . . . VARIABLE
TRANSMISSION . . . . . HYDRO
STEERING . . . . . STANDARD
PTO . . . . . YES
DRIVE TYPE 4WD
ROPS/CAB . . . . . ROPS
WEIGHT . . . . . 1,600 LBS.
MSRP $11,995

RETAIL PRICING

YEAR	HIGH	LOW
1994	$4,394	$3,296

PT1418 2WD

YEARS MFRD 1984-1994
SERIES . . . . . 1400 SERIES
ENGINE . . . . . LISTER-PETTER
CID 44.3
ENGINE HP 18
FUEL . . . . . D
TRANSMISSION . . . . . HYDRO
DRIVE TYPE 2WD
ROPS/CAB . . . . . ROPS
WEIGHT . . . . . 900 LBS.
MSRP $13,900

OPTIONS

B&S 18HP
KOHLER 18HP

RETAIL PRICING

YEAR	HIGH	LOW
1990	$4,024	$3,018
1991	$4,358	$3,269
1992	$4,604	$3,453
1993	$4,782	$3,587
1994	$5,090	$3,818

PT1418 4WD

YEARS MFRD 1984-1994
ENGINE . . . . . B&S
ENGINE HP 18
FUEL . . . . . G
SPEEDS . . . . . VARIABLE
TRANSMISSION . . . . . HYDRO
DRIVE TYPE 4WD
ROPS/CAB . . . . . ROPS
WEIGHT . . . . . 900 LBS.

OPTIONS

KOHLER 18HP

PT1422

YEARS MFRD 1984-1994
SERIES . . . . . 1400 SERIES
ENGINE . . . . . KOHLER-COMMANDO
CID 38
ENGINE HP 22
FUEL . . . . . G
TRANSMISSION . . . . . HYDRO
DRIVE TYPE 4WD
ROPS/CAB . . . . . ROPS
WEIGHT . . . . . 900 LBS.
MSRP $11,795

RETAIL PRICING

YEAR	HIGH	LOW
1990	$3,327	$2,495
1991	$3,613	$2,710
1992	$3,829	$2,872
1993	$4,019	$3,014
1994	$4,320	$3,240

PT1422L

YEARS MFRD 1984-1994
SERIES . . . . . 1400 SERIES
ENGINE . . . . . KUBOTA
PTO HP 22
FUEL . . . . . D
TRANSMISSION . . . . . HYDRO
STEERING . . . . . STANDARD
DRIVE TYPE 4WD
ROPS/CAB . . . . . ROPS
WEIGHT . . . . . 1,300 LBS.
MSRP $14,595

RETAIL PRICING

YEAR	HIGH	LOW
1990	$4,235	$3,176
1991	$4,519	$3,389
1992	$4,772	$3,579
1993	$4,988	$3,741
1994	$5,344	$4,008

PT1422S

YEARS MFRD 1984-1994
SERIES . . . . . 1400 SERIES
ENGINE . . . . . KUBOTA
PTO HP 22
FUEL . . . . . D
TRANSMISSION . . . . . HYDRO
STEERING . . . . . STANDARD
DRIVE TYPE 4WD
ROPS/CAB . . . . . ROPS
WEIGHT . . . . . 900 LBS.
MSRP $11,995

RETAIL PRICING

YEAR	HIGH	LOW
1990	$3,477	$2,608
1991	$3,711	$2,783
1992	$3,930	$2,947
1993	$4,122	$3,091
1994	$4,394	$3,296

PT1423

YEARS MFRD 1984-1994
SERIES . . . . . 1400 SERIES
ENGINE . . . . . KOHLER
PTO HP 23
FUEL . . . . . G
TRANSMISSION . . . . . HYDRO
STEERING . . . . . STANDARD
DRIVE TYPE 4WD
ROPS/CAB . . . . . ROPS
WEIGHT . . . . . 1,300 LBS.
MSRP $11,595

RETAIL PRICING

YEAR	HIGH	LOW
1990	$3,327	$2,495
1991	$3,549	$2,661
1992	$3,762	$2,822
1993	$3,949	$2,962
1994	$4,246	$3,185

PT1425

YEARS MFRD 1983-1995
SERIES . . . . . 1400 SERIES
ENGINE . . . . . KOHLER-COMMANDO
CID 44
ENGINE HP 25
FUEL . . . . . G
TRANSMISSION . . . . . HYDRO
DRIVE TYPE 4WD
ROPS/CAB . . . . . ROPS
WEIGHT . . . . . 900 LBS.
MSRP $12,295

RETAIL PRICING

YEAR	HIGH	LOW
1990	$3,568	$2,676
1991	$3,807	$2,855
1992	$4,030	$3,022
1993	$4,226	$3,169
1994	$4,502	$3,377
1995	$4,674	$3,505

PT1425 LARGE FRAME

YEARS MFRD 1984-1994
SERIES . . . . . 1400 SERIES
ENGINE . . . . . KOHLER-COMMANDO
CID 44
ENGINE HP 25
FUEL . . . . . G
TRANSMISSION . . . . . HYDRO
WEIGHT . . . . . 1,500 LBS.
MSRP $13,940

RETAIL PRICING

YEAR	HIGH	LOW
1990	$4,036	$3,027
1991	$4,306	$3,230
1992	$4,549	$3,412
1993	$4,763	$3,572
1994	$5,104	$3,828

PT1430

YEARS MFRD 1999-2000
SERIES . . . 1400 SERIES T12 CLASS
ENGINE . . . . . DUETZ
CID 85
ENGINE HP 30
FUEL . . . . . D
SPEEDS . . . . . VARIABLE
TRANSMISSION . . . . . HYDRO
STEERING . . . . . ALL WHEEL
HYDRAULIC . . . . . YES
DRIVE TYPE 2WD
ROPS/CAB . . . . . ROPS
STANDARD DECK . . . . . 72"
WEIGHT . . . . . 2,560 LBS.
MSRP $15,099

RETAIL PRICING

YEAR	HIGH	LOW
1999	$2,668	$2,001
2000	$2,962	$2,221

PT1445

YEARS MFRD 2004-2011
SERIES . . . . . T18 CLASS
ENGINE HP 45
FUEL . . . . . D
SPEEDS . . . . . VARIABLE
TRANSMISSION . . . . . HYDRO
STEERING . . . . . ALL WHEEL
HYDRAULIC . . . . . YES
PTO . . . . . YES
WEIGHT . . . . . 3,920 LBS.

PT1445 4WD

YEARS MFRD 1983-2005
SERIES . . . . . T18 CLASS
ENGINE . . . . . FORD
CID 79.33
PTO HP 45
FUEL . . . . . D
SPEEDS . . . . . VARIABLE
TRANSMISSION . . . . . HYDRO
STEERING . . . . . STANDARD
HYDRAULIC . . . . . YES
PTO . . . . . YES

DRIVE TYPE	4WD
ROPS/CAB	ROPS
WEIGHT	3,920 LBS.

PT1460

YEARS MFRD	2003-2010
SERIES	1400 SERIES T24 CLASS
ENGINE	DEUTZ
ENGINE HP	60
FUEL	D
SPEEDS	VARIABLE
TRANSMISSION	HYDRO
STEERING	ALL WHEEL
HYDRAULIC	YES
PTO	YES
DRIVE TYPE	4WD
ROPS/CAB	ROPS
WEIGHT	5,620 LBS.
MSRP	$25,000

RETAIL PRICING

YEAR	HIGH	LOW
2003	$10,595	$7,946
2004	$12,763	$9,572
2005	$13,852	$10,389
2006	$13,992	$10,494
2007	$14,232	$10,674
2008	$14,560	$10,920
2009	$14,990	$11,243
2010	$15,910	$11,933

PT1845

YEARS MFRD	2006-2009
ENGINE HP	45
COOLING	LIQUID
FUEL	D
SPEEDS	VARIABLE
TRANSMISSION	HYDRO
STEERING	ZERO
BLADE CLUTCH	ELECTRIC
STANDARD DECK	70"
WEIGHT	3,463 LBS.
MSRP	$31,000

RETAIL PRICING

YEAR	HIGH	LOW
2006	$13,896	$10,422
2007	$14,599	$10,949
2008	$15,883	$11,912
2009	$19,430	$14,573

PT1850 4WD

YEARS MFRD	1984-2009
ENGINE	ISUZU
CID	134.08
ENGINE HP	65
FUEL	D
SPEEDS	VARIABLE
TRANSMISSION	HYDRO
STEERING	STANDARD
PTO	YES
DRIVE TYPE	4WD
ROPS/CAB	ROPS
STANDARD DECK	84"
WEIGHT	3,848 LBS.
MSRP	$32,000

RETAIL PRICING

YEAR	HIGH	LOW
1994	$7,320	$5,490
2006	$16,556	$12,417
2007	$16,917	$12,688
2008	$17,723	$13,292
2009	$20,059	$15,044

PT2422

YEARS MFRD	2003-2003
SERIES	2400 SERIES
ENGINE	DEUTZ
ENGINE HP	22
FUEL	G
STEERING	STANDARD

PT2425

YEARS MFRD	2004-2011
SERIES	CLASS T8
ENGINE HP	25
FUEL	G
SPEEDS	VARIABLE
TRANSMISSION	HYDRO
STEERING	ALL WHEEL
HYDRAULIC	YES
WEIGHT	1,725 LBS.
MSRP	$14,000

RETAIL PRICING

YEAR	HIGH	LOW
2004	$7,255	$5,441
2005	$7,694	$5,770
2006	$7,767	$5,826
2007	$8,377	$6,283
2008	$8,521	$6,391
2009	$8,937	$6,702
2010	$9,072	$6,804
2011	$8,243	$6,182

PT2430

YEARS MFRD	2004-2011
SERIES	T12 CLASS
ENGINE HP	30
FUEL	D
SPEEDS	VARIABLE
TRANSMISSION	HYDRO
STEERING	ALL WHEEL
HYDRAULIC	YES
WEIGHT	2,560 LBS.
MSRP	$20,000

RETAIL PRICING

YEAR	HIGH	LOW
2004	$10,275	$7,706
2005	$10,899	$8,174
2006	$11,139	$8,354
2007	$11,610	$8,708
2008	$12,248	$9,186
2009	$12,766	$9,575
2010	$12,961	$9,720
2011	$13,161	$9,871

PT2445

YEARS MFRD	2003-2010
SERIES	2400 SERIES T18 CLASS
ENGINE	DEUTZ
ENGINE HP	45
FUEL	D
SPEEDS	VARIABLE
TRANSMISSION	HYDRO
STEERING	ALL WHEEL
HYDRAULIC	YES
PTO	YES
DRIVE TYPE	4WD
ROPS/CAB	ROPS
WEIGHT	4,260 LBS.
MSRP	$25,000

RETAIL PRICING

YEAR	HIGH	LOW
2003	$10,595	$7,946
2004	$11,239	$8,429
2005	$13,852	$10,389
2006	$14,075	$10,556
2007	$14,640	$10,980
2008	$15,191	$11,393
2009	$15,671	$11,753
2010	$15,910	$11,933

PT2456 4WD

YEARS MFRD	1983-1995
ENGINE	ISUZU
CID	146.5
FUEL	D
SPEEDS	VARIABLE
TRANSMISSION	HYDRO
STEERING	STANDARD
WEIGHT	4,500 LBS.
MSRP	$31,600

RETAIL PRICING

YEAR	HIGH	LOW
1995	$12,010	$9,007

PT2460

YEARS MFRD	2004-2010
SERIES	T24 CLASS
ENGINE	DEUTZ
ENGINE HP	60
FUEL	D
SPEEDS	VARIABLE
TRANSMISSION	HYDRO
STEERING	ALL WHEEL
HYDRAULIC	YES
PTO	YES
WEIGHT	5,980 LBS.
MSRP	$28,000

RETAIL PRICING

YEAR	HIGH	LOW
2004	$15,435	$11,576
2005	$16,367	$12,275
2006	$16,456	$12,342
2007	$16,759	$12,569
2008	$17,042	$12,782
2009	$18,232	$13,674
2010	$18,363	$13,772

PT2488 4WD

YEARS MFRD	1983-1995
ENGINE	ISUZU
CID	146.5
ENGINE HP	88
FUEL	D
SPEEDS	VARIABLE
TRANSMISSION	HYDRO
STEERING	STANDARD
WEIGHT	4,800 LBS.
MSRP	$44,900

RETAIL PRICING

YEAR	HIGH	LOW
1995	$17,066	$12,799

NOTES

SCAG

MAG6128KBD

YEARS MFRD 1997-1999
SERIES. . . . . . . MAGNUM III SERIES
ENGINE . . . . KUBOTA
ENGINE HP 28
FUEL . . . . D
SPEEDS . . . . VARIABLE
TRANSMISSION . . . . .HYDRO
STEERING. . . . . ZERO
STANDARD DECK . . . . 61"
MSRP. $9,999

OPTIONS

72" DECK

RETAIL PRICING

YEAR	HIGH	LOW
1997	$1,052	$789
1998	$1,170	$877
1999	$1,299	$974

MAG7228KBD

YEARS MFRD 1996-1999
SERIES. . . . . . . MAGNUM III SERIES
ENGINE . . . . KUBOTA
ENGINE HP 28
FUEL . . . . D
SPEEDS . . . . VARIABLE
TRANSMISSION . . . . .HYDRO
STEERING. . . . . .STANDARD
STANDARD DECK . . . . 72"
MSRP. $11,000

RETAIL PRICING

YEAR	HIGH	LOW
1996	$4,967	$3,725
1997	$5,116	$3,837
1998	$5,376	$4,032
1999	$5,690	$4,268

SABRE TOOTH TIGER

YEARS MFRD 2006-2008
ENGINE . . . . BRIGGS DAIHATSU
CYLINDERS. 3
ENGINE HP 31
COOLING . . . . LIQUID
FUEL . . . . D
SPEEDS . . . . VARIABLE
TRANSMISSION . . . . .HYDRO
STEERING. . . . . ZERO
BLADE CLUTCH . . . . ELECTRIC
WEIGHT . . . . 1,710 LBS.
MSRP. $19,671

RETAIL PRICING

YEAR	HIGH	LOW
2008	$12,395	$9,296

SCR48A25CH

YEARS MFRD 2000-2000
SERIES. . . . . SCR SERIES
ENGINE . . . . KOHLER
ENGINE HP 25
FUEL . . . . G
SPEEDS . . . . VARIABLE
TRANSMISSION . . . . .HYDRO
STEERING. . . . . STANDARD
STANDARD DECK . . . . 48"
MSRP. $9,575

RETAIL PRICING

YEAR	HIGH	LOW
2000	$4,573	$3,430

SCR48A M25CH (UTILITY)

YEARS MFRD 2004-2005
SERIES. . . . . COUGAR SERIES
ENGINE . . . . . . KOHLER COMMAND
ENGINE HP 25
COOLING . . . . AIR
FUEL . . . . G
SPEEDS . . . . VARIABLE
TRANSMISSION . . . . .HYDRO
STEERING. . . . . ZERO
BLADE CLUTCH . . . . MANUAL
WEIGHT . . . . 1,150 LBS.

SCR52A 25CH

YEARS MFRD 2002-2002
SERIES. . . . . SCR SERIES
ENGINE . . . . KOHLER
ENGINE HP 25
FUEL . . . . G
SPEEDS . . . . VARIABLE
TRANSMISSION . . . . .HYDRO
STEERING. . . . . STANDARD
STANDARD DECK . . . . 52"
MSRP. $10,093

RETAIL PRICING

YEAR	HIGH	LOW
2002	$5,167	$3,875

SCR52A M25CH

YEARS MFRD 2002-2005
SERIES. . . . . SCR SERIES
ENGINE . . . . KOHLER
ENGINE HP 25
COOLING . . . . AIR
FUEL . . . . G
SPEEDS . . . . VARIABLE
TRANSMISSION . . . . .HYDRO
STEERING. . . . . ZERO
STANDARD DECK . . . . 52"
MSRP. $10,350

RETAIL PRICING

YEAR	HIGH	LOW
2002	$5,137	$3,853
2003	$5,569	$4,177
2004	$5,930	$4,447
2005	$6,487	$4,865

SCR4224CH

YEARS MFRD 2004-2005
SERIES. . . . . COUGAR SERIES
ENGINE . . . . . . KOHLER COMMAND
ENGINE HP 25
COOLING . . . . AIR
FUEL . . . . G
SPEEDS . . . . VARIABLE
TRANSMISSION . . . . .HYDRO
STEERING. . . . . ZERO
BLADE CLUTCH . . . . MANUAL
WEIGHT . . . . 1,285 LBS.

SCR4225CH

YEARS MFRD 2001-2001
SERIES. . . . . SCR SERIES
ENGINE . . . . KOHLER
ENGINE HP 25
FUEL . . . . G
SPEEDS . . . . VARIABLE
TRANSMISSION . . . . .HYDRO
STEERING. . . . . ZERO
STANDARD DECK . . . . 42"
MSRP. $10,199

SERIAL NUMBERS

YEAR	BEGINNING NO.
2001	6430001

RETAIL PRICING

YEAR	HIGH	LOW
2001	$2,010	$1,507

SCR4825CH

YEARS MFRD 2000-2001
SERIES. . . . . SCR SERIES
ENGINE . . . . KOHLER
ENGINE HP 25
FUEL . . . . G
SPEEDS . . . . VARIABLE
TRANSMISSION . . . . .HYDRO
STEERING. . . . . ZERO
STANDARD DECK . . . . 48"
MSRP. $10,499

SERIAL NUMBERS

YEAR	BEGINNING NO.
2000	5590001
2001	6430001

RETAIL PRICING

YEAR	HIGH	LOW
2000	$1,865	$1,399
2001	$2,072	$1,554

SCR4827KA

YEARS MFRD 2001-2001
SERIES. . . . . SCR SERIES
ENGINE . . . . KAWASAKI
ENGINE HP 27
FUEL . . . . G
SPEEDS . . . . VARIABLE
TRANSMISSION . . . . .HYDRO
STEERING. . . . . ZERO
STANDARD DECK . . . . 48"
MSRP. $10,799

SERIAL NUMBERS

YEAR	BEGINNING NO.
2001	6430001

RETAIL PRICING

YEAR	HIGH	LOW
2001	$2,131	$1,598

SCR5225CH

YEARS MFRD 2001-2001
SERIES. . . . . SCR SERIES
ENGINE . . . . KOHLER
ENGINE HP 25
FUEL . . . . G
SPEEDS . . . . VARIABLE
TRANSMISSION . . . . .HYDRO
STEERING. . . . . ZERO
STANDARD DECK . . . . 52"
MSRP. $10,799

SERIAL NUMBERS

YEAR	BEGINNING NO.
2001	6430001

RETAIL PRICING

YEAR	HIGH	LOW
2001	$2,131	$1,598

SCR5227KA

YEARS MFRD 2001-2001
SERIES. . . . . SCR SERIES
ENGINE . . . . KAWASAKI
ENGINE HP 27
FUEL . . . . G
SPEEDS . . . . VARIABLE
TRANSMISSION . . . . .HYDRO
STEERING. . . . . ZERO
STANDARD DECK . . . . 52"
MSRP. $10,999

SERIAL NUMBERS

YEAR	BEGINNING NO.
2001	6430001

RETAIL PRICING

YEAR	HIGH	LOW
2001	$2,170	$1,628

SCZ48V-22FX

YEARS MFRD 2016-2019
SERIES. . . . . CHEETAH SERIES
ENGINE . . . . KAWASAKI 691FX
ENGINE HP 22
COOLING . . . . AIR
FUEL . . . . G
SPEEDS . . . . VARIABLE
TRANSMISSION . . . . .HYDRO
STEERING. . . . . ZERO
STANDARD DECK . . . . 48"
WEIGHT . . . . 1,075 LBS.

SCZ48V-23CV-EFI

YEARS MFRD 2016-2019
SERIES. . . . . CHEETAH SERIES
ENGINE . . . . KOHLER EFI
ENGINE HP 23
COOLING . . . . AIR
FUEL . . . . G
SPEEDS . . . . VARIABLE
TRANSMISSION . . . . .HYDRO

STEERING . . . . ZERO
STANDARD DECK . . . . 48"
WEIGHT . . . . 1,075 LBS.
MSRP $10,844

SCZ48V-28BS

YEARS MFRD 2016-2017
SERIES . . . . CHEETAH SERIES
ENGINE . . . . B&S CYCLONIC
ENGINE HP 28
COOLING . . . . AIR
FUEL . . . . G
SPEEDS . . . . VARIABLE
TRANSMISSION . . . . HYDRO
STEERING . . . . ZERO
STANDARD DECK . . . . 48"
WEIGHT . . . . 1,075 LBS.

SCZ48V 23CVEFI

YEARS MFRD 2014-2014
SERIES . . . . CHEETAH SERIES
ENGINE . . . . KOHLER
ENGINE HP 23
COOLING . . . . AIR
FUEL . . . . G
SPEEDS . . . . VARIABLE
TRANSMISSION . . . . HYDRO
STEERING . . . . ZERO
STANDARD DECK . . . . 48"
MSRP $10,775

RETAIL PRICING

YEAR	HIGH	LOW
2014	$7,388	$5,541

SCZ48V 691FX

YEARS MFRD 2013-2014
SERIES . . . . SCZ SERIES
ENGINE . . . . KAWASAKI
CID 691CC
COOLING . . . . AIR
FUEL . . . . G
SPEEDS . . . . VARIABLE
TRANSMISSION . . . . HYDRO
STEERING . . . . ZERO
BLADE CLUTCH . . . . ELECTRIC
STANDARD DECK . . . . 48"
MSRP $10,467

RETAIL PRICING

YEAR	HIGH	LOW
2013	$6,011	$4,508
2014	$7,328	$5,496

SCZ52V-23FX

YEARS MFRD 2016-2019
SERIES . . . . CHEETAH SERIES
ENGINE . . . . KAWASAKI 730FX
ENGINE HP 23
COOLING . . . . AIR
FUEL . . . . G
SPEEDS . . . . VARIABLE
TRANSMISSION . . . . HYDRO
STEERING . . . . ZERO
STANDARD DECK . . . . 52"
WEIGHT . . . . 1,080 LBS.
MSRP $10,960

SCZ52V-25CV-EFI

YEARS MFRD 2016-2019
SERIES . . . . CHEETAH SERIES
ENGINE . . . . KOHLER EFI
ENGINE HP 25
COOLING . . . . AIR
FUEL . . . . G
SPEEDS . . . . VARIABLE
TRANSMISSION . . . . HYDRO
STEERING . . . . ZERO
STANDARD DECK . . . . 52"
WEIGHT . . . . 1,080 LBS.
MSRP $11,252

SCZ52V 25CVEFI

YEARS MFRD 2014-2014
SERIES . . . . CHEETAH SERIES
ENGINE . . . . KOHLER
ENGINE HP 25
COOLING . . . . AIR
FUEL . . . . G
SPEEDS . . . . VARIABLE
TRANSMISSION . . . . HYDRO
STEERING . . . . ZERO
STANDARD DECK . . . . 52"
MSRP $10,975

RETAIL PRICING

YEAR	HIGH	LOW
2014	$7,484	$5,613

SCZ52V 730FX

YEARS MFRD 2013-2014
SERIES . . . . CHEETAH SERIES
ENGINE . . . . KAWASAKI
CID 730CC
COOLING . . . . AIR
FUEL . . . . G
SPEEDS . . . . VARIABLE
TRANSMISSION . . . . HYDRO
STEERING . . . . ZERO
BLADE CLUTCH . . . . ELECTRIC
STANDARD DECK . . . . 52"
MSRP $10,692

RETAIL PRICING

YEAR	HIGH	LOW
2013	$6,139	$4,604
2014	$7,440	$5,580

SCZ61RD-31FX

YEARS MFRD 2017-2019
SERIES . . . . CHEETAH SERIES
ENGINE . . . . KAWASAKI FX921V
ENGINE HP 31
COOLING . . . . AIR
FUEL . . . . G
TRANSMISSION . . . . . DUAL HYDRO
STEERING . . . . ZERO
BLADE CLUTCH . . . . ELECTRIC
STANDARD DECK . . . . 61"
WEIGHT . . . . 1,365 LBS.
MSRP $13,446

SCZ61RD 921FX

YEARS MFRD 2013-2014
SERIES . . . . CHEETAH SERIES
ENGINE . . . . KAWASAKI
CID 921CC
COOLING . . . . AIR
FUEL . . . . G
SPEEDS . . . . VARIABLE
TRANSMISSION . . . . HYDRO
STEERING . . . . ZERO
BLADE CLUTCH . . . . ELECTRIC
STANDARD DECK . . . . 61"
MSRP $12,858

RETAIL PRICING

YEAR	HIGH	LOW
2013	$7,384	$5,538
2014	$9,015	$6,761

SCZ61V-27FX

YEARS MFRD 2016-2019
SERIES . . . . CHEETAH SERIES
ENGINE . . . . KAWASAKI FX850V
ENGINE HP 27
COOLING . . . . AIR
FUEL . . . . G
TRANSMISSION . . . . . DUAL HYDRO
STEERING . . . . ZERO
BLADE CLUTCH . . . . ELECTRIC
STANDARD DECK . . . . 61"
WEIGHT . . . . 1,365 LBS.
MSRP $11,748

SCZ61V-31CV-EFI

YEARS MFRD 2018-2020
SERIES . . . . CHEETAH SERIES
ENGINE . . . . KOHLER
ENGINE HP 31
COOLING . . . . AIR
FUEL . . . . G
TRANSMISSION . . . . . DUAL HYDRO
STEERING . . . . ZERO
BLADE CLUTCH . . . . ELECTRIC
STANDARD DECK . . . . 61"
WEIGHT . . . . 1,365 LBS.

SCZ61V-31FX

YEARS MFRD 2016-2020
SERIES . . . . CHEETAH SERIES
ENGINE . . . . KAWASAKI FX921
CYLINDERS 2
ENGINE HP 31
COOLING . . . . AIR
FUEL . . . . G
SPEEDS . . . . VARIABLE
TRANSMISSION . . . . HYDRO
STEERING . . . . ZERO
STANDARD DECK . . . . 61"

SCZ61V-37BV-EFI

YEARS MFRD 2018-2020
SERIES . . . . CHEETAH SERIES
ENGINE . . . . VANGUARD
CYLINDERS 2
ENGINE HP 37
COOLING . . . . AIR
FUEL . . . . G
SPEEDS . . . . VARIABLE
TRANSMISSION . . . . . DUAL HYDRO
STEERING . . . . ZERO
STANDARD DECK . . . . 61"

SCZ61V31FX

YEARS MFRD 2011-2012
SERIES . . . . CHEETAH SERIES
ENGINE . . . . KAWASAKI
CYLINDERS 2
ENGINE HP 31
COOLING . . . . AIR
FUEL . . . . G
SPEEDS . . . . VARIABLE
TRANSMISSION . . . . HYDRO
STEERING . . . . ZERO
BLADE CLUTCH . . . . ELECTRIC
STANDARD DECK . . . . 61"
WEIGHT . . . . 1,350 LBS.
MSRP $11,329

RETAIL PRICING

YEAR	HIGH	LOW
2011	$5,925	$4,443
2012	$6,560	$4,920

SCZ61V32BV

YEARS MFRD 2011-2012
SERIES . . . . CHEETAH SERIES
ENGINE . . . . B&S
CYLINDERS 2
ENGINE HP 32
COOLING . . . . AIR
FUEL . . . . G
SPEEDS . . . . VARIABLE
TRANSMISSION . . . . HYDRO
STEERING . . . . ZERO
BLADE CLUTCH . . . . ELECTRIC
STANDARD DECK . . . . 61"
WEIGHT . . . . 1,361 LBS.
MSRP $11,329

RETAIL PRICING

YEAR	HIGH	LOW
2011	$5,910	$4,432
2012	$6,560	$4,920

SCZ61V34KH
YEARS MFRD 2012-2013
ENGINE .... KOHLER
ENGINE HP 34
COOLING .... AIR
FUEL .... G
SPEEDS .... VARIABLE
TRANSMISSION .... HYDRO
STEERING .... ZERO
MSRP $12,550

RETAIL PRICING

YEAR	HIGH	LOW
2012	$6,954	$5,215
2013	$8,891	$6,668

SCZ61V34KH
YEARS MFRD 2012-2013
SERIES .... CHEETAH SERIES
ENGINE .... KOHLER
ENGINE HP 34
COOLING .... AIR
FUEL .... G
SPEEDS .... VARIABLE
TRANSMISSION .... HYDRO
STEERING .... ZERO
STANDARD DECK .... 61"
MSRP $12,550

RETAIL PRICING

YEAR	HIGH	LOW
2012	$6,998	$5,249
2013	$7,774	$5,830

SCZ61V35CV-EFI
YEARS MFRD 2017-2018
SERIES .... CHEETAH SERIES
ENGINE .... KOHLER
ENGINE HP 35
COOLING .... AIR
FUEL .... G
TRANSMISSION ..... DUAL HYDRO
STEERING .... ZERO
STANDARD DECK .... 61"
WEIGHT .... 1,350 LBS.

SCZ61V36BV
YEARS MFRD 2012-2014
ENGINE .... B&S
ENGINE HP 36
COOLING .... AIR
FUEL .... G
SPEEDS .... VARIABLE
TRANSMISSION .... HYDRO
STEERING .... ZERO
STANDARD DECK .... 61"
MSRP $12,642

RETAIL PRICING

YEAR	HIGH	LOW
2012	$6,538	$4,903
2013	$7,260	$5,445
2014	$8,809	$6,607

SCZ61V850FX
YEARS MFRD 2012-2014
ENGINE .... KAWASAKI
CID 850CC
COOLING .... AIR
FUEL .... G
SPEEDS .... VARIABLE
TRANSMISSION .... HYDRO
STEERING .... ZERO
STANDARD DECK .... 61"
MSRP $11,915

RETAIL PRICING

YEAR	HIGH	LOW
2012	$6,161	$4,621
2013	$6,842	$5,131
2014	$8,438	$6,328

SCZ61V921FX
YEARS MFRD 2012-2014
ENGINE .... KAWASAKI
CID 921CC
COOLING .... AIR
FUEL .... G
SPEEDS .... VARIABLE
TRANSMISSION .... HYDRO
STEERING .... ZERO
BLADE CLUTCH .... ELECTRIC
STANDARD DECK .... 61"
MSRP $12,692

RETAIL PRICING

YEAR	HIGH	LOW
2012	$6,562	$4,921
2013	$7,288	$5,466
2014	$8,898	$6,674

SCZ72V-31FX
YEARS MFRD 2016-2020
SERIES .... CHEETAH SERIES
ENGINE .... KAWASAKI FX921V
ENGINE HP 31
COOLING .... AIR
FUEL .... G
TRANSMISSION ..... DUAL HYDRO
STEERING .... ZERO
BLADE CLUTCH .... ELECTRIC
STANDARD DECK .... 72"
WEIGHT .... 1,365 LBS.

SCZ72V-35CV-EFI
YEARS MFRD 2017-2020
SERIES .... CHEETAH SERIES
ENGINE .... KOHLER
ENGINE HP 35
COOLING .... AIR
FUEL .... G
TRANSMISSION ..... DUAL HYDRO
STEERING .... ZERO
BLADE CLUTCH .... ELECTRIC
STANDARD DECK .... 72"
WEIGHT .... 1,350 LBS.

SCZ72V-37BV-EFI
YEARS MFRD 2018-2019
SERIES .... CHEETAH SERIES
ENGINE .... VANGUARD
CYLINDERS 2
ENGINE HP 37
COOLING .... AIR
FUEL .... G
SPEEDS .... VARIABLE
TRANSMISSION ..... DUAL HYDRO
STEERING .... ZERO
STANDARD DECK .... 72"
MSRP $14,009

SCZ72V 34CVEFI
YEARS MFRD 2014-2014
SERIES .... CHEETAH SERIES
ENGINE .... KOHLER EFI
ENGINE HP 34
COOLING .... AIR
FUEL .... G
SPEEDS .... VARIABLE
TRANSMISSION .... HYDRO
STEERING .... ZERO
STANDARD DECK .... 72"
MSRP $13,350

RETAIL PRICING

YEAR	HIGH	LOW
2014	$9,307	$6,980

SCZ72V34FX
YEARS MFRD 2011-2011
SERIES .... CHEETAH SERIES
ENGINE .... KAWASAKI
CYLINDERS 2
ENGINE HP 34
COOLING .... AIR
FUEL .... G
SPEEDS .... VARIABLE
TRANSMISSION .... HYDRO
STEERING .... ZERO
BLADE CLUTCH .... ELECTRIC
STANDARD DECK .... 72"
WEIGHT .... 1,400 LBS.
MSRP $11,844

RETAIL PRICING

YEAR	HIGH	LOW
2011	$6,382	$4,787

SCZ72V34KH
YEARS MFRD 2012-2013
ENGINE .... KOHLER
ENGINE HP 34
COOLING .... AIR
FUEL .... G
SPEEDS .... VARIABLE
TRANSMISSION .... HYDRO
STEERING .... ZERO
BLADE CLUTCH .... ELECTRIC
STANDARD DECK .... 72"
MSRP $12,900

RETAIL PRICING

YEAR	HIGH	LOW
2012	$7,196	$5,397
2013	$7,986	$5,990

SCZ72V36BV
YEARS MFRD 2012-2013
SERIES .... CHEETAH SERIES
ENGINE .... B&S
ENGINE HP 36
COOLING .... AIR
FUEL .... G
SPEEDS .... VARIABLE
TRANSMISSION .... HYDRO
STEERING .... ZERO
BLADE CLUTCH .... ELECTRIC
STANDARD DECK .... 72"
MSRP $12,983

RETAIL PRICING

YEAR	HIGH	LOW
2012	$7,239	$5,429
2013	$8,040	$6,030

SCZ72V921FX
YEARS MFRD 2012-2014
SERIES .... CHEETAH SERIES
ENGINE .... KAWASAKI
CID 921CC
COOLING .... AIR
FUEL .... G
SPEEDS .... VARIABLE
TRANSMISSION .... HYDRO
STEERING .... ZERO
BLADE CLUTCH .... ELECTRIC
STANDARD DECK .... 72"
MSRP $13,033

RETAIL PRICING

YEAR	HIGH	LOW
2012	$6,334	$4,750
2013	$7,034	$5,275
2014	$9,127	$6,846

SCZII-61RD-31FX
YEARS MFRD 2020-2020
SERIES .... CHEETAH II SERIES
ENGINE .... KAWASAKI FX921
ENGINE HP 31
COOLING .... AIR
FUEL .... G
SPEEDS .... VARIABLE
TRANSMISSION .... HYDRO
STEERING .... ZERO
ROPS/CAB .... ROPS
STANDARD DECK .... 61"
MSRP $13,834

SCZII-61V-31FX
YEARS MFRD 2020-2020
SERIES .... CHEETAH II SERIES
ENGINE .... KAWASAKI FX921

ENGINE HP 31
COOLING . . . . . AIR
FUEL . . . . . G
SPEEDS . . . . . VARIABLE
TRANSMISSION . . . . . HYDRO
STEERING . . . . . ZERO
ROPS/CAB . . . . . ROPS
STANDARD DECK . . . . . 61"
MSRP $13,000

SCZII-61V-37BV-EFI

YEARS MFRD 2020-2020
SERIES . . . . . CHEETAH II SERIES
ENGINE . . . . . BRIGGS VANGUARD
ENGINE HP 37
COOLING . . . . . AIR
FUEL . . . . . G
SPEEDS . . . . . VARIABLE
TRANSMISSION . . . . . HYDRO
STEERING . . . . . ZERO
ROPS/CAB . . . . . ROPS
STANDARD DECK . . . . . 61"
MSRP $13,750

SCZII-72V-31FX

YEARS MFRD 2020-2020
SERIES . . . . . CHEETAH II SERIES
ENGINE . . . . . KAWASAKI FX921
ENGINE HP 31
COOLING . . . . . AIR
FUEL . . . . . G
SPEEDS . . . . . VARIABLE
TRANSMISSION . . . . . HYDRO
STEERING . . . . . ZERO
ROPS/CAB . . . . . ROPS
STANDARD DECK . . . . . 72"
MSRP $13,917

SCZII-72V-37BV-EFI

YEARS MFRD 2020-2020
SERIES . . . . . CHEETAH II SERIES
ENGINE . . . . . BRIGGS VANGUARD
ENGINE HP 37
COOLING . . . . . AIR
FUEL . . . . . G
SPEEDS . . . . . VARIABLE
TRANSMISSION . . . . . HYDRO
STEERING . . . . . ZERO
ROPS/CAB . . . . . ROPS
STANDARD DECK . . . . . 72"
MSRP $14,417

SFZ48-22KT

YEARS MFRD 2016-2020
SERIES . . . . . FREEDOM Z SERIES
ENGINE . . . . . KOHLER 7000 SERIES
CYLINDERS 2
ENGINE HP 22
COOLING . . . . . AIR
FUEL . . . . . G
SPEEDS . . . . . VARIABLE
TRANSMISSION . . . . . HYDRO
STEERING . . . . . ZERO
STANDARD DECK . . . . . 48"
WEIGHT . . . . . 745 LBS.
MSRP $5,800

SFZ52-24KT

YEARS MFRD 2016-2020
SERIES . . . . . FREEDOM Z SERIES
ENGINE . . . . . KOHLER 7000 SERIES
CYLINDERS 2
ENGINE HP 24
COOLING . . . . . AIR
FUEL . . . . . G
SPEEDS . . . . . VARIABLE
TRANSMISSION . . . . . HYDRO
STEERING . . . . . ZERO
STANDARD DECK . . . . . 52"
WEIGHT . . . . . 765 LBS.
MSRP $5,954

SFZ52-27BS

YEARS MFRD 2013-2013
SERIES . . . . . FREEDOM SERIES
ENGINE . . . . . B&S
ENGINE HP 27
COOLING . . . . . AIR
FUEL . . . . . G
SPEEDS . . . . . VARIABLE
TRANSMISSION . . . . . HYDRO
STEERING . . . . . ZERO
BLADE CLUTCH . . . . . ELECTRIC
STANDARD DECK . . . . . 52"
MSRP $6,731

RETAIL PRICING

YEAR	HIGH	LOW
2013	$4,599	$3,449

SFZ3617KA

YEARS MFRD 2008-2010
SERIES . . . . . FREEDOM SERIES
ENGINE . . . . . KAWASAKI
CYLINDERS 2
ENGINE HP 17
COOLING . . . . . AIR
FUEL . . . . . G
SPEEDS . . . . . VARIABLE
TRANSMISSION . . . . . DUAL HYDRO
STEERING . . . . . ZERO
BLADE CLUTCH . . . . . ELECTRIC
STANDARD DECK . . . . . 36"
WEIGHT . . . . . 740 LBS.
MSRP $5,770

RETAIL PRICING

YEAR	HIGH	LOW
2008	$2,336	$1,752
2009	$2,589	$1,941
2010	$2,879	$2,159

SFZ3618FS

YEARS MFRD 2011-2011
SERIES . . . . . FREEDOM SERIES
ENGINE . . . . . KAWASAKI
CYLINDERS 2
ENGINE HP 18
COOLING . . . . . AIR
FUEL . . . . . G
SPEEDS . . . . . VARIABLE
TRANSMISSION . . . . . DUAL HYDRO
STEERING . . . . . ZERO
BLADE CLUTCH . . . . . ELECTRIC
STANDARD DECK . . . . . 36"
WEIGHT . . . . . 775 LBS.
MSRP $5,870

RETAIL PRICING

YEAR	HIGH	LOW
2011	$3,163	$2,372

SFZ3620BS

YEARS MFRD 2008-2011
SERIES . . . . . FREEDOM SERIES
ENGINE . . . . . B&S
CYLINDERS 2
ENGINE HP 20
COOLING . . . . . AIR
FUEL . . . . . G
SPEEDS . . . . . VARIABLE
TRANSMISSION . . . . . DUAL HYDRO
STEERING . . . . . ZERO
BLADE CLUTCH . . . . . ELECTRIC
STANDARD DECK . . . . . 36"
MSRP $5,664

RETAIL PRICING

YEAR	HIGH	LOW
2008	$2,226	$1,670
2009	$2,476	$1,857
2010	$2,748	$2,061
2011	$3,051	$2,288

SFZ4819FS

YEARS MFRD 2014-2015
SERIES . . . . . FREEDOM Z SERIES
ENGINE . . . . . KAWASAKI
ENGINE HP 19
COOLING . . . . . AIR
FUEL . . . . . G
SPEEDS . . . . . VARIABLE
TRANSMISSION . . . . . DUAL HYDRO
STEERING . . . . . ZERO
STANDARD DECK . . . . . 48"
MSRP $6,123

RETAIL PRICING

YEAR	HIGH	LOW
2014	$3,717	$2,788
2015	$4,474	$3,356

SFZ4819KA

YEARS MFRD 2007-2010
SERIES . . . . . FREEDOM SERIES
ENGINE . . . . . KAWASAKI
CYLINDERS 2
ENGINE HP 19
COOLING . . . . . AIR
FUEL . . . . . G
SPEEDS . . . . . VARIABLE
TRANSMISSION . . . . . DUAL HYDRO
STEERING . . . . . ZERO
BLADE CLUTCH . . . . . ELECTRIC
STANDARD DECK . . . . . 48"
MSRP $5,975

RETAIL PRICING

YEAR	HIGH	LOW
2007	$2,138	$1,604
2008	$2,376	$1,782
2009	$2,642	$1,982
2010	$2,931	$2,198

SFZ4820KA

YEARS MFRD 2011-2011
SERIES . . . . . FREEDOM SERIES
ENGINE . . . . . KAWASAKI
CYLINDERS 2
ENGINE HP 20
COOLING . . . . . AIR
FUEL . . . . . G
SPEEDS . . . . . VARIABLE
TRANSMISSION . . . . . HYDRO
STEERING . . . . . ZERO
BLADE CLUTCH . . . . . ELECTRIC
MSRP $6,358

RETAIL PRICING

YEAR	HIGH	LOW
2011	$3,274	$2,456

SFZ4824BS

YEARS MFRD 2014-2015
SERIES . . . . . FREEDOM SERIES
ENGINE . . . . . B&S
ENGINE HP 24
COOLING . . . . . AIR
FUEL . . . . . G
SPEEDS . . . . . VARIABLE
TRANSMISSION . . . . . DUAL HYDRO
STEERING . . . . . ZERO
STANDARD DECK . . . . . 48"
MSRP $6,085

RETAIL PRICING

YEAR	HIGH	LOW
2014	$3,694	$2,770
2015	$4,366	$3,275

SFZ4826BS

YEARS MFRD 2007-2013
SERIES . . . . . FREEDOM SERIES
ENGINE . . . . . B&S
CYLINDERS 2
ENGINE HP 26
COOLING . . . . . AIR
FUEL . . . . . G
SPEEDS . . . . . VARIABLE
TRANSMISSION . . . . . DUAL HYDRO
STEERING . . . . . ZERO
BLADE CLUTCH . . . . . ELECTRIC
STANDARD DECK . . . . . 48"
MSRP $6,000

RETAIL PRICING

YEAR	HIGH	LOW
2007	$2,006	$1,504
2008	$2,226	$1,670
2009	$2,472	$1,854
2010	$2,748	$2,061

2011............$3,051 .... $2,288
2012............$3,389 .... $2,541
2013............$3,761 .... $2,821

SFZ48600FS

YEARS MFRD 2012-2013
SERIES....... FREEDOM Z SERIES
ENGINE .... KAWASAKI
CID 600CC
COOLING .... AIR
FUEL .... G
SPEEDS .... VARIABLE
TRANSMISSION ..... DUAL HYDRO
STEERING................ ZERO
BLADE CLUTCH .... ELECTRIC
STANDARD DECK .... 48"
MSRP.................. $6,123

RETAIL PRICING

YEAR	HIGH	LOW
2012	$3,457	$2,593
2013	$3,839	$2,879

SFZ5219KA

YEARS MFRD 2007-2010
SERIES......... FREEDOM SERIES
ENGINE .... KAWASAKI
ENGINE HP 19
COOLING .... AIR
FUEL .... G
SPEEDS .... VARIABLE
TRANSMISSION ..... DUAL HYDRO
STEERING................ ZERO
BLADE CLUTCH .... ELECTRIC
STANDARD DECK .... 52"
MSRP.................. $6,180

RETAIL PRICING

YEAR	HIGH	LOW
2007	$2,214	$1,660
2008	$2,455	$1,841
2009	$2,744	$2,058
2010	$3,031	$2,273

SFZ5220FS

YEARS MFRD 2011-2011
SERIES......... FREEDOM SERIES
ENGINE .... KAWASAKI
CYLINDERS.................. 2
ENGINE HP 20
COOLING .... AIR
FUEL .... G
SPEEDS .... VARAIBLE
TRANSMISSION .... HYDRO
STEERING................ ZERO
BLADE CLUTCH .... ELECTRIC
STANDARD DECK .... 52"
MSRP.................. $6,179

RETAIL PRICING

YEAR	HIGH	LOW
2011	$3,329	$2,497

SFZ5223FS

YEARS MFRD 2014-2015
SERIES....... FREEDOM Z SERIES
ENGINE .... KAWASAKI
ENGINE HP 23
COOLING .... AIR
FUEL .... G
SPEEDS .... VARIABLE
TRANSMISSION .... HYDRO
STEERING................ ZERO
STANDARD DECK .... 52"
MSRP.................. $7,123

RETAIL PRICING

YEAR	HIGH	LOW
2014	$4,325	$3,244
2015	$5,032	$3,774

SFZ5225BS

YEARS MFRD 2014-2015
SERIES....... FREEDOM Z SERIES
ENGINE .... B&S
ENGINE HP 25
COOLING .... AIR
FUEL .... G
SPEEDS .... VARIABLE
TRANSMISSION ..... DUAL HYDRO
STEERING................ ZERO
STANDARD DECK .... 52"
MSRP.................. $6,731

RETAIL PRICING

YEAR	HIGH	LOW
2014	$4,088	$3,066
2015	$4,724	$3,543

SFZ5226BS

YEARS MFRD 2007-2012
SERIES......... FREEDOM SERIES
ENGINE .... B&S
CYLINDERS.................. 2
ENGINE HP 26
COOLING .... AIR
FUEL .... G
SPEEDS .... VARIABLE
TRANSMISSION ..... DUAL HYDRO
STEERING................ ZERO
BLADE CLUTCH .... ELECTRIC
STANDARD DECK .... 52"
MSRP.................. $6,179

RETAIL PRICING

YEAR	HIGH	LOW
2007	$2,117	$1,588
2008	$2,351	$1,763
2009	$2,613	$1,960
2010	$2,901	$2,176
2011	$3,219	$2,414
2012	$3,578	$2,684

SFZ6124FS

YEARS MFRD 2014-2015
SERIES....... FREEDOM Z SERIES
ENGINE .... KAWASAKI
ENGINE HP 24
COOLING .... AIR
FUEL .... G
SPEEDS .... VARAIBLE
TRANSMISSION ..... DUAL HYDRO
STEERING................ ZERO
STANDARD DECK .... 61"
MSRP.................. $7,845

RETAIL PRICING

YEAR	HIGH	LOW
2014	$4,763	$3,572
2015	$5,595	$4,197

SFZ6127BS

YEARS MFRD 2014-2015
SERIES....... FREEDOM Z SERIES
ENGINE .... B&S
ENGINE HP 27
COOLING .... AIR
FUEL .... G
SPEEDS .... VARIABLE
TRANSMISSION ..... DUAL HYDRO
STEERING................ ZERO
STANDARD DECK .... 61"
MSRP.................. $7,485

RETAIL PRICING

YEAR	HIGH	LOW
2014	$4,546	$3,410
2015	$5,431	$4,073

SFZ6128BS

YEARS MFRD 2010-2012
SERIES......... FREEDOM SERIES
ENGINE .... B&S
CYLINDERS.................. 2
ENGINE HP 28
COOLING .... AIR
FUEL .... G
SPEEDS .... VARIABLE
TRANSMISSION .... HYDRO
STEERING................ ZERO
BLADE CLUTCH .... ELECTRIC
STANDARD DECK .... 61"
MSRP.................. $6,179

RETAIL PRICING

YEAR	HIGH	LOW
2010	$2,901	$2,176
2011	$3,219	$2,414
2012	$3,606	$2,704

SFZ6130BS

YEARS MFRD 2012-2013
SERIES....... FREEDOM Z SERIES
ENGINE .... B&S
ENGINE HP 30
COOLING .... AIR
FUEL .... G
SPEEDS .... VARIABLE
TRANSMISSION ..... DUAL HYDRO
STEERING................ ZERO
STANDARD DECK .... 61"
MSRP.................. $7,485

RETAIL PRICING

YEAR	HIGH	LOW
2012	$4,172	$3,129
2013	$4,634	$3,475

SFZ52600FS

YEARS MFRD 2012-2012
ENGINE .... KAWASAKI
CID 600CC
COOLING .... AIR
FUEL .... G
SPEEDS .... VARIABLE
TRANSMISSION .... HYDRO
STEERING................ ZERO
STANDARD DECK .... 52"
MSRP.................. $6,282

RETAIL PRICING

YEAR	HIGH	LOW
2012	$4,159	$3,119

SFZ52691FS

YEARS MFRD 2013-2013
SERIES....... FREEDOM Z SERIES
ENGINE .... KAWASAKI
CID 691CC
COOLING .... AIR
FUEL .... G
SPEEDS .... VARIABLE
TRANSMISSION .... HYDRO
STEERING................ ZERO
BLADE CLUTCH .... ELECTRIC
STANDARD DECK .... 52"
MSRP.................. $7,123

RETAIL PRICING

YEAR	HIGH	LOW
2013	$4,869	$3,652

SFZ61730FS

YEARS MFRD 2012-2013
SERIES....... FREEDOM Z SERIES
ENGINE .... KAWASAKI
CID 730CC
COOLING .... AIR
FUEL .... G
SPEEDS .... VARIABLE
TRANSMISSION ..... DUAL HYDRO
STEERING................ ZERO
BLADE CLUTCH .... ELECTRIC
STANDARD DECK .... 61"
MSRP.................. $7,845

RETAIL PRICING

YEAR	HIGH	LOW
2012	$4,374	$3,281
2013	$4,860	$3,645

SPZ52-22FX

YEARS MFRD 2016-2020
SERIES.......... PATRIOT SERIES
ENGINE .... KAWASAKI FX691
ENGINE HP 22
COOLING .... AIR
FUEL .... G
SPEEDS .... VARIABLE
TRANSMISSION .... HYDRO
STEERING................ ZERO
STANDARD DECK .... 52"
WEIGHT .... 805 LBS.
MSRP.................. $7,583

SPZ52-23CV

YEARS MFRD 2019-2020
SERIES.......... PATRIOT SERIES
ENGINE .... KOHLER
CYLINDERS.................. 2

ENGINE HP 23
COOLING . . . . AIR
FUEL . . . . G
SPEEDS . . . . VARIABLE
TRANSMISSION . . . . HYDRO
STEERING. . . . . ZERO
BLADE CLUTCH . . . . ELECTRIC
STANDARD DECK . . . . 52"
WEIGHT . . . . 907 LBS.
MSRP. $7,199

SPZ61-23FX

YEARS MFRD 2016-2020
SERIES. . . . . PATRIOT SERIES
ENGINE . . . . KAWASAKI FX730
ENGINE HP. 23
COOLING . . . . AIR
FUEL . . . . G
SPEEDS . . . . VARIABLE
TRANSMISSION . . . . HYDRO
STEERING. . . . . ZERO
STANDARD DECK . . . . 61"
WEIGHT . . . . 875 LBS.
MSRP. $8,219

SPZ61-25CV

YEARS MFRD 2019-2020
SERIES. . . . . PATRIOT SERIES
ENGINE . . . . KOHLER
CYLINDERS. 2
ENGINE HP. 25
COOLING . . . . AIR
FUEL . . . . G
SPEEDS . . . . VARIABLE
TRANSMISSION . . . . HYDRO
STEERING. . . . . ZERO
BLADE CLUTCH . . . . ELECTRIC
STANDARD DECK . . . . 61"
WEIGHT . . . . 952 LBS.
MSRP. $7,734

SST61V25KBD

YEARS MFRD 2014-2014
ENGINE . . . . KUBOTA
ENGINE HP. 25
COOLING . . . . LIQUID
FUEL . . . . D
SPEEDS . . . . VARIABLE
TRANSMISSION . . . . . DUAL HYDRO
STEERING. . . . . ZERO
STANDARD DECK . . . . 61"
MSRP. $18,675

RETAIL PRICING

YEAR	HIGH	LOW
2014	$13,143	$9,857

SSZ18CVLT

YEARS MFRD 1998-1998
SERIES. . . . . SSZ SERIES
ENGINE . . . . KOHLER
ENGINE HP. 18
FUEL . . . . G
SPEEDS . . . . VARIABLE
TRANSMISSION . . . . HYDRO
STEERING. . . . . STANDARD
STANDARD DECK . . . . 48"
MSRP. $6,450

RETAIL PRICING

YEAR	HIGH	LOW
1998	$2,754	$2,066

SSZ20CV

YEARS MFRD 1994-1997
SERIES. . . . . SSZ SERIES
ENGINE . . . . KOHLER
ENGINE HP. 20
FUEL . . . . G
SPEEDS . . . . VARIABLE
TRANSMISSION . . . . HYDRO
STEERING. . . . . STANDARD
STANDARD DECK . . . . 52"
WEIGHT . . . . 1,100 LBS.
MSRP. $8,235

OPTIONS

61" DECK

RETAIL PRICING

YEAR	HIGH	LOW
1994	$2,587	$1,940
1995	$2,892	$2,169
1996	$3,149	$2,362
1997	$3,349	$2,512

SSZ22CV

YEARS MFRD 1994-1997
SERIES. . . . . SSZ SERIES
ENGINE . . . . KOHLER
ENGINE HP. 22
FUEL . . . . G
SPEEDS . . . . VARIABLE
TRANSMISSION . . . . HYDRO
STEERING. . . . . STANDARD
STANDARD DECK . . . . 52"
WEIGHT . . . . 1,100 LBS.
MSRP. $8,545

OPTIONS

61" DECK

RETAIL PRICING

YEAR	HIGH	LOW
1994	$2,695	$2,021
1995	$3,007	$2,255
1996	$3,273	$2,455
1997	$3,475	$2,607

SSZ4216BV

YEARS MFRD 1993-1993
SERIES. . . . . SSZ SERIES
ENGINE . . . . B&S
ENGINE HP. 16
COOLING . . . . AIR
FUEL . . . . G
SPEEDS . . . . VARIABLE
TRANSMISSION . . . . HYDRO
STEERING. . . . . ZERO
STANDARD DECK . . . . 42"
MSRP. $5,100

RETAIL PRICING

YEAR	HIGH	LOW
1993	$329	$247

SSZ4816BV

YEARS MFRD 1993-1995
SERIES. . . . . SSZ SERIES
ENGINE . . . . B&S
ENGINE HP. 16
COOLING . . . . AIR
FUEL . . . . G
SPEEDS . . . . VARIABLE
TRANSMISSION . . . . HYDRO
STEERING. . . . . ZERO
STANDARD DECK . . . . 48"
WEIGHT . . . . 980 LBS.
MSRP. $6,740

OPTIONS

BAGGER

RETAIL PRICING

YEAR	HIGH	LOW
1993	$483	$362
1994	$538	$404
1995	$599	$449

SSZ4818BV

YEARS MFRD 1993-1995
SERIES. . . . . SSZ SERIES
ENGINE . . . . B&S
ENGINE HP. 18
FUEL . . . . G
TRANSMISSION . . . . HYDRO
STEERING. . . . . STANDARD
STANDARD DECK . . . . 48"
MSRP. $6,840

RETAIL PRICING

YEAR	HIGH	LOW
1993	$2,192	$1,644
1994	$2,440	$1,830
1995	$2,589	$1,941

SSZ4818CV

YEARS MFRD 1993-1999
SERIES. . . . . SSZ SERIES
ENGINE . . . . KOHLER
ENGINE HP. 18
COOLING . . . . AIR
FUEL . . . . G
SPEEDS . . . . VARIABLE
TRANSMISSION . . . . HYDRO
STEERING. . . . . ZERO
STANDARD DECK . . . . 48"
MSRP. $6,299

OPTIONS

BAGGER

SERIAL NUMBERS

YEAR	BEGINNING NO.
1994	4XXXX
1995	5XXXX
1996	6XXXX
1997	7XXXX
1998	8XXXX
1999	9XXXX

RETAIL PRICING

YEAR	HIGH	LOW
1993	$675	$506
1994	$748	$561
1995	$831	$623
1996	$925	$694
1997	$1,029	$772
1998	$1,141	$856
1999	$1,267	$950

SSZ4818KH

YEARS MFRD 1993-1993
SERIES. . . . . SSZ SERIES
ENGINE . . . . KOHLER
ENGINE HP. 18
FUEL . . . . G
SPEEDS . . . . VARIABLE
TRANSMISSION . . . . HYDRO
STEERING. . . . . STANDARD
STANDARD DECK . . . . 48"
WEIGHT . . . . 1,045 LBS.
MSRP. $6,350

RETAIL PRICING

YEAR	HIGH	LOW
1993	$2,192	$1,644

SSZ5220CV

YEARS MFRD 1993-1997
SERIES. . . . . SSZ SERIES
ENGINE . . . . KOHLER
ENGINE HP. 20
COOLING . . . . AIR
FUEL . . . . G
SPEEDS . . . . VARIABLE
TRANSMISSION . . . . HYDRO
STEERING. . . . . ZERO
STANDARD DECK . . . . 52"
WEIGHT . . . . 1,100 LBS.
MSRP. $8,125

OPTIONS

BAGGER

RETAIL PRICING

YEAR	HIGH	LOW
1993	$707	$530
1994	$788	$591
1995	$876	$657
1996	$973	$729
1997	$1,082	$811

SSZ5222CV

YEARS MFRD 1993-1999
SERIES. . . . . SSZ SERIES
ENGINE . . . . KOHLER
ENGINE HP. 22
COOLING . . . . AIR
FUEL . . . . G
SPEEDS . . . . VARIABLE
TRANSMISSION . . . . . DUAL HYDRO
STEERING. . . . . ZERO
STANDARD DECK . . . . 52"
WEIGHT . . . . 1,100 LBS.
MSRP. $7,399

OPTIONS

BAGGER

RETAIL PRICING

YEAR	HIGH	LOW
1993	$587	$440
1994	$651	$489
1995	$723	$542
1996	$803	$602
1997	$893	$670

YEAR	HIGH	LOW
1998	$993	$745
1999	$1,101	$826

SSZ5222CVLT

YEARS MFRD........ 1998-1998
SERIES............. SSZ SERIES
ENGINE .... KOHLER
ENGINE HP................. 22
FUEL .... G
SPEEDS .... VARIABLE
TRANSMISSION .... HYDRO
STEERING............ STANDARD
STANDARD DECK............ 52"
MSRP.................. $7,260

RETAIL PRICING

YEAR	HIGH	LOW
1998	$3,101	$2,326

SSZ6120CV

YEARS MFRD........ 1993-1997
SERIES............. SSZ SERIES
ENGINE .... KOHLER
ENGINE HP................. 20
COOLING .... AIR
FUEL .... G
SPEEDS .... VARIABLE
TRANSMISSION ..... DUAL HYDRO
STEERING................. ZERO
STANDARD DECK............ 61"
WEIGHT .... 1,175 LBS.
MSRP.................. $8,450

OPTIONS

BAGGER

RETAIL PRICING

YEAR	HIGH	LOW
1993	$646	$485
1994	$719	$539
1995	$801	$601
1996	$889	$667
1997	$985	$739

SSZ6122CV

YEARS MFRD........ 1993-1999
SERIES............. SSZ SERIES
ENGINE .... KOHLER
ENGINE HP................. 22
COOLING .... AIR
FUEL .... G
SPEEDS .... VARIABLE
TRANSMISSION ..... DUAL HYDRO
STEERING................. ZERO
STANDARD DECK............ 61"
WEIGHT .... 1,175 LBS.
MSRP.................. $7,499

OPTIONS

BAGGER

RETAIL PRICING

YEAR	HIGH	LOW
1993	$563	$422
1994	$622	$467
1995	$696	$522
1996	$771	$578
1997	$856	$642
1998	$953	$715
1999	$1,056	$792

SSZ6122CVLT

YEARS MFRD........ 1998-1998
SERIES............. SSZ SERIES
ENGINE .... KOHLER
ENGINE HP................. 22
FUEL .... G
SPEEDS .... VARIABLE
TRANSMISSION .... HYDRO
STEERING............ STANDARD
STANDARD DECK............ 61"
MSRP.................. $7,540

RETAIL PRICING

YEAR	HIGH	LOW
1998	$3,220	$2,415

STC48A19KA

YEARS MFRD........ 2000-2001
SERIES............. STC SERIES
ENGINE .... KAWASAKI
ENGINE HP................. 19
COOLING .... AIR
FUEL .... G
SPEEDS .... VARIABLE
TRANSMISSION .... HYDRO
STEERING................. ZERO
STANDARD DECK............ 48"
WEIGHT .... 975 LBS.
MSRP.................. $6,999

OPTIONS

BAGGER
SEAT

SERIAL NUMBERS

YEAR	BEGINNING NO.
2000	5810001
2001	6570001

RETAIL PRICING

YEAR	HIGH	LOW
2000	$1,267	$950
2001	$1,408	$1,056

STC48A20CV

YEARS MFRD........ 2000-2001
SERIES........ TIGER CUB SERIES
ENGINE ...... KOHLER COMMAND
ENGINE HP................. 20
COOLING .... AIR
FUEL .... G
SPEEDS .... VARIABLE
TRANSMISSION .... HYDRO
STEERING................. ZERO
STANDARD DECK............ 48"
WEIGHT .... 975 LBS.
MSRP.................. $6,999

OPTIONS

BAGGER
SEAT

SERIAL NUMBERS

YEAR	BEGINNING NO.
2000	5810001
2001	6570001

RETAIL PRICING

YEAR	HIGH	LOW
2000	$1,267	$950
2001	$1,408	$1,056

STC48A21KA

YEARS MFRD........ 2000-2001
SERIES........ TIGER CUB SERIES
ENGINE .... KAWASAKI
ENGINE HP................. 21
COOLING .... AIR
FUEL .... G
SPEEDS .... VARIABLE
TRANSMISSION .... HYDRO
STEERING................. ZERO
STANDARD DECK............ 48"
WEIGHT .... 975 LBS.
MSRP.................. $7,199

OPTIONS

52" DECK
BAGGER

SERIAL NUMBERS

YEAR	BEGINNING NO.
2000	5810001
2001	6570001

RETAIL PRICING

YEAR	HIGH	LOW
2000	$1,302	$976
2001	$1,451	$1,089

STC48V-22FS

YEARS MFRD........ 2016-2017
SERIES........ TIGER CAT SERIES
ENGINE .... KAWASAKI 651FS
ENGINE HP................. 22
COOLING .... AIR
FUEL .... G
SPEEDS .... VARIABLE
TRANSMISSION .... HYDRO
STEERING................. ZERO
STANDARD DECK............ 48"
WEIGHT .... 1,030 LBS.

STC48V-23CV

YEARS MFRD........ 2016-2017
SERIES........ TIGER CAT SERIES
ENGINE .... KOHLER
ENGINE HP................. 23
COOLING .... AIR
FUEL .... G
SPEEDS .... VARIABLE
TRANSMISSION .... HYDRO
STEERING................. ZERO
STANDARD DECK............ 48"
WEIGHT .... 1,040 LBS.

STC48V-27BS

YEARS MFRD........ 2016-2016
SERIES........ TIGER CAT SERIES
ENGINE .... B&S
ENGINE HP................. 27
COOLING .... AIR
FUEL .... G
SPEEDS .... VARIABLE
TRANSMISSION .... HYDRO
STEERING................. ZERO
STANDARD DECK............ 48"
WEIGHT .... 1,050 LBS.

STC48V19KAI

YEARS MFRD........ 2006-2010
SERIES........ TIGER CUB SERIES
ENGINE .... KAWASAKI
ENGINE HP................. 19
COOLING .... AIR
FUEL .... G
SPEEDS .... VARIABLE
TRANSMISSION .... HYDRO
STEERING................. ZERO
STANDARD DECK............ 48"
MSRP.................. $8,140

OPTIONS

FROPS
ROPS
SOFT SEAT

RETAIL PRICING

YEAR	HIGH	LOW
2006	$2,625	$1,969
2007	$2,914	$2,185
2008	$3,241	$2,431
2009	$3,598	$2,698
2010	$4,000	$3,000

STC48V22FS

YEARS MFRD........ 2014-2014
SERIES........ TIGER CAT SERIES
ENGINE .... KAWASAKI
ENGINE HP................. 22
COOLING .... AIR
FUEL .... G
SPEEDS .... VARIABLE
TRANSMISSION .... HYDRO
STEERING................. ZERO
STANDARD DECK............ 48"
MSRP.................. $8,831

RETAIL PRICING

YEAR	HIGH	LOW
2014	$6,353	$4,765

STC48V22FS

YEARS MFRD........ 2011-2012
SERIES........ TIGER CAT SERIES
ENGINE .... KAWASAKI
CYLINDERS.................. 2
ENGINE HP................. 22
COOLING .... AIR
FUEL .... G
SPEEDS .... VARIABLE
TRANSMISSION .... HYDRO
STEERING................. ZERO
BLADE CLUTCH .... ELECTRIC
STANDARD DECK............ 48"
MSRP.................. $7,724

RETAIL PRICING

YEAR	HIGH	LOW
2011	$4,029	$3,022
2012	$4,474	$3,356

STC48V23CV

YEARS MFRD........ 2006-2008
SERIES........ TIGER CUB SERIES
ENGINE .... KOHLER
ENGINE HP................. 23

COOLING . . . . AIR
FUEL . . . . G
SPEEDS . . . . VARIABLE
TRANSMISSION . . . . .HYDRO
STEERING. . . . . ZERO
STANDARD DECK . . . . 48"
MSRP. $8,239

OPTIONS

FROPS
ROPS
SOFT SEAT

RETAIL PRICING

YEAR	HIGH	LOW
2006	$2,742	$2,057
2007	$3,043	$2,282
2008	$3,379	$2,535

STC48V23CV

YEARS MFRD 2014-2014
SERIES. . . . . TIGER CAT SERIES
ENGINE . . . . .KOHLER
ENGINE HP 23
COOLING . . . . AIR
FUEL . . . . G
SPEEDS . . . . VARIABLE
TRANSMISSION . . . . .HYDRO
STEERING. . . . . ZERO
STANDARD DECK . . . . 48"
MSRP. $9,223

RETAIL PRICING

YEAR	HIGH	LOW
2014	$6,711	$5,034

STC48V24BS

YEARS MFRD 2006-2006
SERIES. . . . . TIGER CUB SERIES
ENGINE . . . . .B&S
ENGINE HP 24
COOLING . . . . AIR
FUEL . . . . G
SPEEDS . . . . VARIABLE
TRANSMISSION . . . . .HYDRO
STEERING. . . . . ZERO
STANDARD DECK . . . . 48"
MSRP. $6,649

RETAIL PRICING

YEAR	HIGH	LOW
2006	$2,351	$1,763

STC48V 25CVSS

YEARS MFRD 2010-2012
SERIES. . . . . TIGER CAT SERIES
ENGINE . . . . .KOHLER
CYLINDERS. 2
ENGINE HP 25
COOLING . . . . AIR
FUEL . . . . G
SPEEDS . . . . VARIABLE
TRANSMISSION . . . . . DUAL HYDRO
STEERING. . . . . ZERO
BLADE CLUTCH . . . . .ELECTRIC
STANDARD DECK . . . . 48"
MSRP. $8,754

RETAIL PRICING

YEAR	HIGH	LOW
2010	$4,112	$3,084
2011	$4,566	$3,425
2012	$5,072	$3,804

STC48V26BS

YEARS MFRD 2007-2012
SERIES. . . . . TURF CAT SERIES
ENGINE . . . . .B&S
CYLINDERS. 2
ENGINE HP 26
COOLING . . . . AIR
FUEL . . . . G
SPEEDS . . . . VARIABLE
TRANSMISSION . . . . .HYDRO
STEERING. . . . . ZERO
BLADE CLUTCH . . . . .ELECTRIC
STANDARD DECK . . . . 48"
MSRP. $7,724

RETAIL PRICING

YEAR	HIGH	LOW
2007	$2,649	$1,987
2008	$2,938	$2,204
2009	$3,256	$2,442
2010	$3,634	$2,725
2011	$4,029	$3,022
2012	$4,474	$3,356

STC48V26BV

YEARS MFRD 2008-2010
SERIES. . . . . TIGER CAT SERIES
ENGINE . . . . .VANGUARD
CYLINDERS. 2
ENGINE HP 26
COOLING . . . . AIR
FUEL . . . . G
SPEEDS . . . . VARIABLE
TRANSMISSION . . . . .HYDRO
STEERING. . . . . ZERO
BLADE CLUTCH . . . . .ELECTRIC
STANDARD DECK . . . . 48"
MSRP. $7,595

RETAIL PRICING

YEAR	HIGH	LOW
2008	$2,446	$1,835
2009	$2,933	$2,200
2010	$3,424	$2,568

STC48V27BS

YEARS MFRD 2013-2013
SERIES. . . . . STC SERIES
ENGINE . . . . .B&S
ENGINE HP 27
COOLING . . . . AIR
FUEL . . . . G
SPEEDS . . . . VARIABLE
TRANSMISSION . . . . .HYDRO
STEERING. . . . . ZERO
BLADE CLUTCH . . . . .ELECTRIC
STANDARD DECK . . . . 48"
MSRP. $8,231

RETAIL PRICING

YEAR	HIGH	LOW
2013	$5,096	$3,822

STC48V651FS

YEARS MFRD 2012-2013
SERIES. . . . . STC SERIES
ENGINE . . . . .KAWASAKI
CID 651CC
COOLING . . . . AIR
FUEL . . . . G
SPEEDS . . . . VARIABLE
TRANSMISSION . . . . . DUAL HYDRO
STEERING. . . . . ZERO
BLADE CLUTCH . . . . .ELECTRIC
STANDARD DECK . . . . 48"
MSRP. $8,831

RETAIL PRICING

YEAR	HIGH	LOW
2012	$4,924	$3,693
2013	$5,467	$4,100

STC52A21KA

YEARS MFRD 2000-2004
SERIES. . . . . TIGER CUB SERIES
ENGINE . . . . .KAWASAKI
ENGINE HP 21
COOLING . . . . AIR
FUEL . . . . G
SPEEDS . . . . VARIABLE
TRANSMISSION . . . . .HYDRO
STEERING. . . . . ZERO
STANDARD DECK . . . . 52"
WEIGHT . . . . 980 LBS.
MSRP. $8,305

RETAIL PRICING

YEAR	HIGH	LOW
2000	$3,630	$2,722
2001	$3,915	$2,936
2002	$4,083	$3,063
2003	$4,527	$3,395
2004	$4,909	$3,681

STC52A23KA

YEARS MFRD 2000-2001
SERIES. . . . . TIGER CUB SERIES
ENGINE . . . . .KAWASAKI
ENGINE HP 23
COOLING . . . . AIR
FUEL . . . . G
SPEEDS . . . . VARIABLE
TRANSMISSION . . . . .HYDRO
STEERING. . . . . ZERO
STANDARD DECK . . . . 52"
WEIGHT . . . . 980 LBS.
MSRP. $7,599

OPTIONS

BAGGER
SEAT

SERIAL NUMBERS

YEAR	BEGINNING NO.
2000	5810001
2001	6570001

RETAIL PRICING

YEAR	HIGH	LOW
2000	$1,322	$992
2001	$1,467	$1,100

STC52A23LV

YEARS MFRD 2001-2001
SERIES. . . . . STC SERIES
ENGINE . . . . .KOHLER
ENGINE HP 23
COOLING . . . . LIQUID
FUEL . . . . G
SPEEDS . . . . VARIABLE
TRANSMISSION . . . . .HYDRO
STEERING. . . . . ZERO
STANDARD DECK . . . . 52"
MSRP. $7,999

OPTIONS

BAGGER
SEAT

SERIAL NUMBERS

YEAR	BEGINNING NO.
2001	6570001

RETAIL PRICING

YEAR	HIGH	LOW
2001	$1,544	$1,158

STC52A24HN

YEARS MFRD 2004-2005
SERIES. . . . . TIGER CUB SERIES
ENGINE . . . . HONDA
ENGINE HP 24
COOLING . . . . AIR
FUEL . . . . G
SPEEDS . . . . VARIABLE
TRANSMISSION . . . . .HYDRO
STEERING. . . . . ZERO
BLADE CLUTCH . . . . .ELECTRIC
PTO . . . . YES
STANDARD DECK . . . . 52"
WEIGHT . . . . 980 LBS.
MSRP. $9,050

RETAIL PRICING

YEAR	HIGH	LOW
2004	$4,927	$3,695
2005	$5,670	$4,253

STC52V-22FX

YEARS MFRD 2016-2017
SERIES. . . . . TIGER CAT SERIES
ENGINE . . . . KAWASAKI 691FX
ENGINE HP 22
COOLING . . . . AIR
FUEL . . . . G
SPEEDS . . . . VARIABLE
TRANSMISSION . . . . .HYDRO
STEERING. . . . . ZERO
STANDARD DECK . . . . 52"
WEIGHT . . . . 1,100 LBS.

STC52V-25CV-EFI

YEARS MFRD 2016-2017
SERIES. . . . . TIGER CAT SERIES
ENGINE . . . . KOHLER EFI
ENGINE HP 27
COOLING . . . . AIR
FUEL . . . . G

SPEEDS . . . . VARIABLE
TRANSMISSION . . . . HYDRO
STEERING. . . . . ZERO
STANDARD DECK . . . . 52"
WEIGHT . . . . 1,100 LBS.

STC52V-27CV

YEARS MFRD 2016-2016
SERIES. . . . . TIGER CAT SERIES
ENGINE . . . . KOHLER
ENGINE HP 27
COOLING . . . . AIR
FUEL . . . . G
SPEEDS . . . . VARIABLE
TRANSMISSION . . . . HYDRO
STEERING. . . . . ZERO
STANDARD DECK . . . . 52"
WEIGHT . . . . 1,100 LBS.

STC52V22FX

YEARS MFRD 2014-2014
SERIES. . . . . TIGER CAT SERIES
ENGINE . . . . KAWASAKI
ENGINE HP 22
COOLING . . . . AIR
FUEL . . . . G
SPEEDS . . . . VARIABLE
TRANSMISSION . . . . HYDRO
STEERING. . . . . ZERO
STANDARD DECK . . . . 52"
MSRP. $9,062

RETAIL PRICING

YEAR	HIGH	LOW
2014	$6,537	$4,903

STC52V23KA

YEARS MFRD 2006-2007
SERIES. . . . . TIGER CUB SERIES
ENGINE . . . . KAWASAKI
ENGINE HP 23
COOLING . . . . AIR
FUEL . . . . G
SPEEDS . . . . VARIABLE
TRANSMISSION . . . . HYDRO
STEERING. . . . . ZERO
STANDARD DECK . . . . 52"
MSRP. $8,999

OPTIONS

FROPS
ROPS
SOFT SEAT

RETAIL PRICING

YEAR	HIGH	LOW
2006	$2,998	$2,248
2007	$3,329	$2,497

STC52V24FX

YEARS MFRD 2011-2011
SERIES. . . . . TIGER CAT SERIES
ENGINE . . . . KAWASAKI
CYLINDERS. 2
ENGINE HP 24
COOLING . . . . AIR
FUEL . . . . G
SPEEDS . . . . VARIABLE
TRANSMISSION . . . . . DUAL HYDRO
STEERING. . . . . ZERO
BLADE CLUTCH . . . . ELECTRIC
STANDARD DECK . . . . 52"
MSRP. $8,600

RETAIL PRICING

YEAR	HIGH	LOW
2011	$4,634	$3,475

STC52V24HN

YEARS MFRD 2006-2008
SERIES. . . . . TIGER CUB SERIES
ENGINE . . . . HONDA
ENGINE HP 24
COOLING . . . . AIR
FUEL . . . . G
SPEEDS . . . . VARIABLE
TRANSMISSION . . . . HYDRO
STEERING. . . . . ZERO
STANDARD DECK . . . . 52"
MSRP. $9,269

OPTIONS

FROPS
ROPS
SOFT SEAT

RETAIL PRICING

YEAR	HIGH	LOW
2006	$3,083	$2,312
2007	$3,424	$2,568
2008	$3,804	$2,853

STC52V 25CVEFI

YEARS MFRD 2014-2014
ENGINE . . . . KOHLER EFI
ENGINE HP 25
COOLING . . . . AIR
FUEL . . . . G
SPEEDS . . . . VARIABLE
TRANSMISSION . . . . HYDRO
STEERING. . . . . ZERO
STANDARD DECK . . . . 52"
MSRP. $9,831

RETAIL PRICING

YEAR	HIGH	LOW
2014	$7,152	$5,364

STC52V 27CVSS

YEARS MFRD 2010-2013
SERIES. . . . . TIGER CAT SERIES
ENGINE . . . . KOHLER
CYLINDERS. 2
ENGINE HP 27
COOLING . . . . AIR
FUEL . . . . G
SPEEDS . . . . VARIABLE
TRANSMISSION . . . . . DUAL HYDRO
STEERING. . . . . ZERO
BLADE CLUTCH . . . . ELECTRIC
STANDARD DECK . . . . 52"
MSRP. $9,415

RETAIL PRICING

YEAR	HIGH	LOW
2010	$4,256	$3,192
2011	$4,727	$3,545
2012	$5,251	$3,938
2013	$5,829	$4,372

STC52V 691FXSS

YEARS MFRD 2012-2015
SERIES. . . . . TIGER CAT SERIES
ENGINE . . . . KAWASAKI
CID 691CC
COOLING . . . . AIR
FUEL . . . . G
SPEEDS . . . . VARIABLE
TRANSMISSION . . . . . DUAL HYDRO
STEERING. . . . . ZERO
STANDARD DECK . . . . 52"
MSRP. $9,014

RETAIL PRICING

YEAR	HIGH	LOW
2012	$4,899	$3,674
2013	$5,383	$4,037
2014	$6,087	$4,565
2015	$7,643	$5,732

STC61A25KA

YEARS MFRD 2004-2004
SERIES. . . . . TIGER CUB SERIES
ENGINE . . . . KAWASAKI
ENGINE HP 25
COOLING . . . . AIR
FUEL . . . . G
SPEEDS . . . . VARIABLE
TRANSMISSION . . . . HYDRO
STEERING. . . . . ZERO
BLADE CLUTCH . . . . ELECTRIC
PTO . . . . YES
WEIGHT . . . . 1,160 LBS.

STC61V-23FX

YEARS MFRD 2016-2017
SERIES. . . . . TIGER CAT SERIES
ENGINE . . . . KAWASAKI 730FX
ENGINE HP 23
COOLING . . . . AIR
FUEL . . . . G
SPEEDS . . . . VARIABLE
TRANSMISSION . . . . HYDRO
STEERING. . . . . ZERO
STANDARD DECK . . . . 61"
WEIGHT . . . . 1,150 LBS.

STC61V-26CV-EFI

YEARS MFRD 2016-2017
SERIES. . . . . TIGER CAT SERIES
ENGINE . . . . KOHLER EFI
ENGINE HP 26
COOLING . . . . AIR
FUEL . . . . G
SPEEDS . . . . VARIABLE
TRANSMISSION . . . . HYDRO
STEERING. . . . . ZERO
STANDARD DECK . . . . 61"
WEIGHT . . . . 1,150 LBS.

STC61V-27BS

YEARS MFRD 2016-2016
SERIES. . . . . TIGER CAT SERIES
ENGINE . . . . B&S
ENGINE HP 27
COOLING . . . . AIR
FUEL . . . . G
SPEEDS . . . . VARIABLE
TRANSMISSION . . . . HYDRO
STEERING. . . . . ZERO
STANDARD DECK . . . . 61"
WEIGHT . . . . 1,150 LBS.

STC61V-27CV

YEARS MFRD 2016-2016
SERIES. . . . . TIGER CAT SERIES
ENGINE . . . . KOHLER
ENGINE HP 27
COOLING . . . . AIR
FUEL . . . . G
SPEEDS . . . . VARIABLE
TRANSMISSION . . . . HYDRO
STEERING. . . . . ZERO
STANDARD DECK . . . . 61"
WEIGHT . . . . 1,150 LBS.

STC61V23FX

YEARS MFRD 2014-2014
SERIES. . . . . TIGER CAT SERIES
ENGINE . . . . KAWASAKI
ENGINE HP 23
COOLING . . . . AIR
FUEL . . . . G
SPEEDS . . . . VARIABLE
TRANSMISSION . . . . HYDRO
STEERING. . . . . ZERO
STANDARD DECK . . . . 61"
MSRP. $9,508

RETAIL PRICING

YEAR	HIGH	LOW
2014	$6,925	$5,193

STC61V25CV

YEARS MFRD 2008-2010
SERIES. . . . . TIGER CAT SERIES
ENGINE . . . . KOHLER
CYLINDERS. 2
ENGINE HP 25
COOLING . . . . AIR
FUEL . . . . G
SPEEDS . . . . VARIABLE
TRANSMISSION . . . . HYDRO
STEERING. . . . . ZERO
BLADE CLUTCH . . . . ELECTRIC
STANDARD DECK . . . . 61"
MSRP. $8,550

RETAIL PRICING

YEAR	HIGH	LOW
2008	$3,625	$2,719
2009	$4,024	$3,018
2010	$4,470	$3,353

SCAG

STC61V 26CVEFI

YEARS MFRD........2014-2014
ENGINE............KOHLER EFI
ENGINE HP..................26
COOLING...................AIR
FUEL.........................G
SPEEDS.............VARIABLE
TRANSMISSION..........HYDRO
STEERING.................ZERO
STANDARD DECK............61"
MSRP..................$10,139

RETAIL PRICING

YEAR	HIGH	LOW
2014	$7,304	$5,478

STC61V27BS

YEARS MFRD........2014-2014
SERIES........TIGER CAT SERIES
ENGINE....................B&S
ENGINE HP..................27
COOLING...................AIR
FUEL.........................G
SPEEDS.............VARIABLE
TRANSMISSION..........HYDRO
STEERING.................ZERO
STANDARD DECK............61"
MSRP..................$10,139

RETAIL PRICING

YEAR	HIGH	LOW
2014	$7,304	$5,478

STC61V 27CVSS

YEARS MFRD........2010-2013
SERIES........TIGER CAT SERIES
ENGINE.................KOHLER
CYLINDERS...................2
ENGINE HP..................27
COOLING...................AIR
FUEL.........................G
SPEEDS.............VARIABLE
TRANSMISSION.....DUAL HYDRO
STEERING.................ZERO
BLADE CLUTCH.........ELECTRIC
STANDARD DECK............61"
MSRP....................$8,857

RETAIL PRICING

YEAR	HIGH	LOW
2010	$4,003	$3,002
2011	$4,445	$3,334
2012	$4,940	$3,705
2013	$5,482	$4,112

STC61V 730FXSS

YEARS MFRD........2012-2013
SERIES........TIGER CAT SERIES
ENGINE..............KAWASAKI
CID......................730CC
COOLING...................AIR
FUEL.........................G
SPEEDS.............VARIABLE
TRANSMISSION.....DUAL HYDRO
STEERING.................ZERO
STANDARD DECK............61"
MSRP....................$9,460

RETAIL PRICING

YEAR	HIGH	LOW
2012	$5,272	$3,954
2013	$5,857	$4,393

STC4017KA

YEARS MFRD........2000-2001
SERIES................STC SERIES
ENGINE..............KAWASAKI
ENGINE HP..................17
FUEL.........................G
SPEEDS.............VARIABLE
TRANSMISSION..........HYDRO
STEERING.................ZERO
STANDARD DECK............40"
MSRP....................$6,799

OPTIONS

BAGGER
SEAT

SERIAL NUMBERS

YEAR	BEGINNING NO.
2000	5810001
2001	6570001

RETAIL PRICING

YEAR	HIGH	LOW
2000	$3,246	$2,435
2001	$3,447	$2,585

STC4819KA

YEARS MFRD........2000-2001
SERIES................STC SERIES
ENGINE..............KAWASAKI
ENGINE HP..................19
FUEL.........................G
SPEEDS.............VARIABLE
TRANSMISSION..........HYDRO
STEERING............STANDARD
STANDARD DECK............48"
MSRP....................$6,999

RETAIL PRICING

YEAR	HIGH	LOW
2000	$3,391	$2,543
2001	$3,486	$2,614

STC4820CV

YEARS MFRD........2000-2000
SERIES................STC SERIES
ENGINE.................KOHLER
ENGINE HP..................20
FUEL.........................G
SPEEDS.............VARIABLE
TRANSMISSION..........HYDRO
STEERING............STANDARD
STANDARD DECK............48"
MSRP....................$7,099

RETAIL PRICING

YEAR	HIGH	LOW
2000	$3,391	$2,543

STC4821KA

YEARS MFRD........2000-2000
SERIES................STC SERIES
ENGINE..............KAWASAKI
ENGINE HP..................21
FUEL.........................G
SPEEDS.............VARIABLE
TRANSMISSION..........HYDRO
STEERING............STANDARD
STANDARD DECK............48"
MSRP....................$7,299

RETAIL PRICING

YEAR	HIGH	LOW
2000	$3,486	$2,614

STCII-48V-22FS

YEARS MFRD........2016-2017
SERIES.......TIGER CAT II SERIES
ENGINE........KAWASAKI 651FS
ENGINE HP..................22
COOLING...................AIR
FUEL.........................G
SPEEDS.............VARIABLE
TRANSMISSION..........HYDRO
STEERING.................ZERO
STANDARD DECK............48"
WEIGHT.............1,160 LBS.

STCII-48V-22FX

YEARS MFRD........2018-2020
SERIES.......TIGER CAT II SERIES
ENGINE......KAWASAKI FX691FX
ENGINE HP..................22
COOLING...................AIR
FUEL.........................G
TRANSMISSION..........HYDRO
STEERING.................ZERO
BLADE CLUTCH.........ELECTRIC
STANDARD DECK............48"
WEIGHT.............1,171 LBS.
MSRP..................$10,515

STCII-48V-23CV

YEARS MFRD........2016-2019
SERIES.......TIGER CAT II SERIES
ENGINE.................KOHLER
ENGINE HP..................23
COOLING...................AIR
FUEL.........................G
SPEEDS.............VARIABLE
TRANSMISSION..........HYDRO
STEERING.................ZERO
STANDARD DECK............48"
WEIGHT.............1,175 LBS.
MSRP..................$10,913

STCII-52V-22FX

YEARS MFRD........2016-2019
SERIES.......TIGER CAT II SERIES
ENGINE........KAWASAKI 691FX
ENGINE HP..................22
COOLING...................AIR
FUEL.........................G
SPEEDS.............VARIABLE
TRANSMISSION..........HYDRO
STEERING.................ZERO
STANDARD DECK............52"
WEIGHT.............1,175 LBS.
MSRP..................$10,412

STCII-52V-25CV-EFI

YEARS MFRD........2016-2020
SERIES.......TIGER CAT II SERIES
ENGINE............KOHLER EFI
ENGINE HP..................25
COOLING...................AIR
FUEL.........................G
SPEEDS.............VARIABLE
TRANSMISSION..........HYDRO
STEERING.................ZERO
STANDARD DECK............52"
WEIGHT.............1,180 LBS.
MSRP..................$11,739

STCII-52V-26FT-EFI

YEARS MFRD........2020-2020
SERIES.......TIGER CAT II SERIES
ENGINE........KAWASAKI 730FT
ENGINE HP..................26
COOLING...................AIR
FUEL.........................G
SPEEDS.............VARIABLE
TRANSMISSION..........HYDRO
STEERING.................ZERO
ROPS/CAB.................ROPS
STANDARD DECK............52"

STCII-61V-23FX

YEARS MFRD........2016-2019
SERIES.......TIGER CAT II SERIES
ENGINE........KAWASAKI 730FX
ENGINE HP..................23
COOLING...................AIR
FUEL.........................G
SPEEDS.............VARIABLE
TRANSMISSION..........HYDRO
STEERING.................ZERO
STANDARD DECK............61"
WEIGHT.............1,255 LBS.
MSRP..................$11,817

STCII-61V-26CV-EFI

YEARS MFRD 2016-2017
SERIES. . . . . . . TIGER CAT II SERIES
ENGINE . . . . KOHLER EFI
ENGINE HP 26
COOLING . . . . AIR
FUEL . . . . G
SPEEDS . . . . VARIABLE
TRANSMISSION . . . . HYDRO
STEERING. . . . . ZERO
STANDARD DECK . . . . 61"
WEIGHT . . . . 1,260 LBS.

STCII-61V-26FT-EFI

YEARS MFRD 2018-2020
SERIES. . . . . . . TIGER CAT II SERIES
ENGINE . . . . KAWASAKI FT730
CYLINDERS. 2
ENGINE HP. 26
COOLING . . . . AIR
FUEL . . . . G
SPEEDS . . . . VARIABLE
TRANSMISSION . . . . . DUAL HYDRO
STEERING. . . . . ZERO
BLADE CLUTCH . . . . ELECTRIC
STANDARD DECK . . . . 61"
WEIGHT . . . . 1,255 LBS.

STCII-61V-29CV-EFI

YEARS MFRD 2018-2019
SERIES. . . . . . . TIGER CAT II SERIES
ENGINE . . . . KOHLER
ENGINE HP. 29
COOLING . . . . AIR
FUEL . . . . G
TRANSMISSION . . . . HYDRO
STEERING. . . . . ZERO
STANDARD DECK . . . . 61"
WEIGHT . . . . 1,255 LBS.
MSRP. $11,407

STCII-61V-32BV

YEARS MFRD 2020-2020
SERIES. . . . . . . TIGER CAT II SERIES
ENGINE . . . . . . BRIGGS VANGUARD
ENGINE HP 32
COOLING . . . . AIR
FUEL . . . . G
SPEEDS . . . . VARIABLE
TRANSMISSION . . . . HYDRO
STEERING. . . . . ZERO
ROPS/CAB . . . . ROPS
STANDARD DECK . . . . 61"
MSRP. $11,902

STG4013KA

YEARS MFRD 1987-1992
SERIES. . . . . STG SERIES
ENGINE . . . . KAWASAKI
CYLINDERS. 1
ENGINE HP 12.5
COOLING . . . . AIR
FUEL . . . . G
TRANSMISSION . . . . GEAR
STEERING. . . . . STANDARD
STANDARD DECK . . . . 40"
MSRP. $4,991

RETAIL PRICING

YEAR	HIGH	LOW
1992	$1,669	$1,251

STG4014KH

YEARS MFRD 1990-1992
SERIES. . . . . STG SERIES
ENGINE . . . . KOHLER
CYLINDERS. 1
ENGINE HP 14
COOLING . . . . AIR
FUEL . . . . G
TRANSMISSION . . . . GEAR
STEERING. . . . . STANDARD
STANDARD DECK . . . . 40"
WEIGHT . . . . 565 LBS.
MSRP. $4,991

RETAIL PRICING

YEAR	HIGH	LOW
1992	$1,669	$1,251

STG4813KA

YEARS MFRD 1987-1992
SERIES. . . . . STG SERIES
ENGINE . . . . B&S
CYLINDERS. 1
ENGINE HP 12.5
COOLING . . . . AIR
FUEL . . . . G
TRANSMISSION . . . . GEAR
STEERING. . . . . STANDARD
STANDARD DECK . . . . 48"
MSRP. $5,150

RETAIL PRICING

YEAR	HIGH	LOW
1987	$173	$130
1988	$193	$145
1989	$217	$163
1990	$236	$177
1991	$267	$200
1992	$294	$220

STG4817KA

YEARS MFRD 1987-1990
SERIES. . . . . STG SERIES
ENGINE . . . . KAWASAKI
ENGINE HP 17
FUEL . . . . G
SPEEDS 5/0
TRANSMISSION . . . . GEAR
STEERING. . . . . STANDARD
STANDARD DECK . . . . 48"
WEIGHT . . . . 610 LBS.
MSRP. $5,290

RETAIL PRICING

YEAR	HIGH	LOW
1987	$1,478	$1,108
1988	$1,516	$1,137
1989	$1,581	$1,185
1990	$1,594	$1,195

STG4818KH

YEARS MFRD 1987-1990
SERIES. . . . . STG SERIES
ENGINE . . . . KOHLER
ENGINE HP 18
FUEL . . . . G
SPEEDS 5/0
TRANSMISSION . . . . GEAR
STEERING. . . . . STANDARD
STANDARD DECK . . . . 48"
WEIGHT . . . . 650 LBS.
MSRP. $5,295

RETAIL PRICING

YEAR	HIGH	LOW
1990	$1,594	$1,195

STG6118KH

YEARS MFRD 1987-1994
SERIES. . . . . STG SERIES
ENGINE . . . . KOHLER
ENGINE HP 18
COOLING . . . . AIR
FUEL . . . . G
SPEEDS 5/0
TRANSMISSION . . . . GEAR
STEERING. . . . . ZERO
STANDARD DECK . . . . 61"
WEIGHT . . . . 565 LBS.
MSRP. $6,295

RETAIL PRICING

YEAR	HIGH	LOW
1987	$148	$111
1988	$166	$124
1989	$185	$139
1990	$205	$154
1991	$224	$168
1992	$254	$190
1993	$277	$208
1994	$310	$233

STH4014BV

YEARS MFRD 1989-1990
SERIES. . . . . STH SERIES
ENGINE . . . . B&S
CYLINDERS. 1
ENGINE HP 14
COOLING . . . . AIR
FUEL . . . . G
SPEEDS . . . . VARIABLE
TRANSMISSION . . . . HYDRO
STEERING. . . . . STANDARD
STANDARD DECK . . . . 40"
MSRP. $4,810

RETAIL PRICING

YEAR	HIGH	LOW
1990	$1,450	$1,088

STH4814BV

YEARS MFRD 1989-1990
SERIES. . . . . STH SERIES
ENGINE . . . . KOHLER
CYLINDERS. 1
ENGINE HP 14
COOLING . . . . AIR
FUEL . . . . G
SPEEDS . . . . VARIABLE
TRANSMISSION . . . . HYDRO
STEERING. . . . . ZERO
STANDARD DECK . . . . 48"
MSRP. $4,990

RETAIL PRICING

YEAR	HIGH	LOW
1990	$1,502	$1,126

STH5218KH

YEARS MFRD 1989-1990
SERIES. . . . . STH SERIES
ENGINE . . . . KOHLER
ENGINE HP 18
COOLING . . . . AIR
FUEL . . . . G
SPEEDS . . . . VARIABLE
TRANSMISSION . . . . HYDRO
STEERING. . . . . ZERO
STANDARD DECK . . . . 52"
WEIGHT . . . . 695 LBS.
MSRP. $6,440

RETAIL PRICING

YEAR	HIGH	LOW
1990	$1,939	$1,454

STHM23CVSM52

YEARS MFRD 2000-2000
SERIES. . . . . STHM SERIES
ENGINE . . . . KOHLER
ENGINE HP 23
COOLING . . . . AIR
FUEL . . . . G
STEERING. . . . . ZERO
STANDARD DECK . . . . 52"
MSRP. $8,249

RETAIL PRICING

YEAR	HIGH	LOW
2000	$1,602	$1,201

STHM61A23CV

YEARS MFRD 2000-2001
SERIES. . . . . STHM SERIES
ENGINE . . . . KOHLER
ENGINE HP 23
COOLING . . . . LIQUID
FUEL . . . . G
SPEEDS . . . . VARIABLE
TRANSMISSION . . . . HYDRO
STEERING. . . . . ZERO
BLADE CLUTCH . . . . ELECTRIC
STANDARD DECK . . . . 61"
WEIGHT . . . . 950 LBS.
MSRP. $8,465

RETAIL PRICING

YEAR	HIGH	LOW
2000	$1,697	$1,273
2001	$1,882	$1,411

STHM61V-23CV

YEARS MFRD 2005-2011
ENGINE .... KOHLER
ENGINE HP 23
COOLING .... AIR
FUEL .... G
SPEEDS .... VARIABLE
TRANSMISSION .... HYDRO
STEERING .... ZERO
STANDARD DECK .... 61"
WEIGHT .... 950 LBS.
MSRP $10,505

RETAIL PRICING

YEAR	HIGH	LOW
2005	$2,998	$2,248
2006	$3,324	$2,493
2007	$3,690	$2,767
2008	$4,093	$3,069
2009	$4,537	$3,403
2010	$5,036	$3,777
2011	$5,583	$4,187

STHM72A23CV

YEARS MFRD 2000-2011
SERIES .... STHM SERIES
ENGINE .... KOHLER
ENGINE HP 23
COOLING .... LIQUID
FUEL .... G
SPEEDS .... VARIABLE
TRANSMISSION .... HYDRO
STEERING .... ZERO
BLADE CLUTCH .... ELECTRIC
STANDARD DECK .... 72"
WEIGHT .... 980 LBS.
MSRP $10,299

OPTIONS

BAGGER
E LIFT

RETAIL PRICING

YEAR	HIGH	LOW
2003	$2,371	$1,779
2004	$2,629	$1,972
2005	$2,914	$2,185
2006	$3,236	$2,427
2007	$3,590	$2,692
2008	$3,980	$2,985
2009	$4,418	$3,313
2010	$4,901	$3,675
2011	$5,434	$4,075

STHM5218KH

YEARS MFRD 1989-1990
SERIES .... STHM SERIES
ENGINE .... KOHLER
ENGINE HP 18
COOLING .... AIR
FUEL .... G
SPEEDS .... VARIABLE
TRANSMISSION .... HYDRO
STEERING .... ZERO
STANDARD DECK .... 52"
MSRP $6,440

RETAIL PRICING

YEAR	HIGH	LOW
1990	$1,939	$1,454

STHM5220CV

YEARS MFRD 1989-1997
SERIES .... STHM SERIES
ENGINE .... KOHLER
ENGINE HP 20
COOLING .... AIR
FUEL .... G
SPEEDS .... VARIABLE
TRANSMISSION .... HYDRO
STEERING .... ZERO
STANDARD DECK .... 52"
WEIGHT .... 1,160 LBS.
MSRP $8,750

RETAIL PRICING

YEAR	HIGH	LOW
1990	$2,477	$1,857
1991	$2,666	$2,000
1992	$2,803	$2,102
1993	$2,915	$2,186
1994	$3,106	$2,329
1995	$3,254	$2,441
1996	$3,402	$2,551
1997	$3,559	$2,669

STHM5220KH

YEARS MFRD 1991-1994
SERIES .... STHM SERIES
ENGINE .... KOHLER
ENGINE HP 20
FUEL .... G
SPEEDS .... VARIABLE
TRANSMISSION .... HYDRO
STEERING .... STANDARD
STANDARD DECK .... 52"
WEIGHT .... 1,160 LBS.
MSRP $8,115

RETAIL PRICING

YEAR	HIGH	LOW
1991	$2,305	$1,729
1992	$2,601	$1,951
1993	$2,664	$1,998
1994	$2,957	$2,218

STHM5222CV

YEARS MFRD 1995-1999
SERIES .... STHM SERIES
ENGINE .... KOHLER
ENGINE HP 22
COOLING .... AIR
FUEL .... G
SPEEDS .... VARIABLE
TRANSMISSION .... HYDRO
STEERING .... ZERO
STANDARD DECK .... 52"
WEIGHT .... 1,175 LBS.
MSRP $8,249

RETAIL PRICING

YEAR	HIGH	LOW
1995	$3,008	$2,256
1996	$3,155	$2,366
1997	$3,314	$2,485
1998	$3,524	$2,643
1999	$3,758	$2,819

STHM5223CV

YEARS MFRD 2000-2000
SERIES .... STHM SERIES
ENGINE .... KOHLER
ENGINE HP 23
FUEL .... G
SPEEDS .... VARIABLE
TRANSMISSION .... HYDRO
STEERING .... STANDARD
STANDARD DECK .... 52"
MSRP $8,870

RETAIL PRICING

YEAR	HIGH	LOW
2000	$4,236	$3,177

STHM6118KH

YEARS MFRD 1989-1990
SERIES .... STHM SERIES
ENGINE .... KOHLER
ENGINE HP 18
COOLING .... AIR
SPEEDS .... VARIABLE
TRANSMISSION .... HYDRO
STEERING .... ZERO
STANDARD DECK .... 61"
MSRP $6,535

RETAIL PRICING

YEAR	HIGH	LOW
1990	$1,967	$1,476

STHM6120CV

YEARS MFRD 1995-1999
SERIES .... STHM SERIES
ENGINE .... KOHLER
ENGINE HP 20
COOLING .... AIR
FUEL .... G
SPEEDS .... VARIABLE
TRANSMISSION .... HYDRO
STEERING .... STANDARD
STANDARD DECK .... 61"
WEIGHT .... 1,205 LBS.
MSRP $8,980

RETAIL PRICING

YEAR	HIGH	LOW
1995	$3,294	$2,470
1996	$3,437	$2,578
1997	$3,578	$2,684
1998	$3,756	$2,817
1999	$4,093	$3,069

STHM6120KH

YEARS MFRD 1991-1994
SERIES .... STHM SERIES
ENGINE .... KOHLER
ENGINE HP 20
FUEL .... G
SPEEDS .... VARIABLE
TRANSMISSION .... HYDRO
STEERING .... STANDARD
STANDARD DECK .... 61"
WEIGHT .... 1,175 LBS.
MSRP $8,235

RETAIL PRICING

YEAR	HIGH	LOW
1991	$2,343	$1,757
1992	$2,640	$1,980
1993	$2,704	$2,028
1994	$3,001	$2,251

STHM6122CV

YEARS MFRD 1993-1999
SERIES .... STHM SERIES
ENGINE .... KOHLER
ENGINE HP 22
COOLING .... AIR
FUEL .... G
SPEEDS .... VARIABLE
TRANSMISSION .... HYDRO
STEERING .... ZERO
STANDARD DECK .... 61"
WEIGHT .... 1,250 LBS.
MSRP $8,349

RETAIL PRICING

YEAR	HIGH	LOW
1993	$2,759	$2,069
1994	$2,933	$2,200
1995	$3,063	$2,297
1996	$3,195	$2,396
1997	$3,335	$2,501
1998	$3,524	$2,643
1999	$3,805	$2,854

STHM6123CV

YEARS MFRD 2000-2000
SERIES .... STHM SERIES
ENGINE .... KOHLER
ENGINE HP 23
FUEL .... G
SPEEDS .... VARIABLE
TRANSMISSION .... HYDRO
STEERING .... STANDARD
STANDARD DECK .... 61"
MSRP $9,036

RETAIL PRICING

YEAR	HIGH	LOW
2000	$4,315	$3,236

STHM7218KH

YEARS MFRD 1989-1990
SERIES .... STHM SERIES
ENGINE .... KOHLER
ENGINE HP 18
COOLING .... AIR
FUEL .... G
SPEEDS .... VARIABLE
TRANSMISSION .... HYDRO
STEERING .... ZERO
STANDARD DECK .... 72"
MSRP $6,695

RETAIL PRICING

YEAR	HIGH	LOW
1990	$2,015	$1,511
1997	$828	$621
1998	$916	$687
1999	$1,017	$763

STHM7220CV

YEARS MFRD: 1997-1997
SERIES: STHM SERIES
ENGINE: KOHLER
ENGINE HP: 20
FUEL: G
SPEEDS: VARIABLE
TRANSMISSION: HYDRO
STEERING: ZERO
STANDARD DECK: 72"
WEIGHT: 1,280 LBS.
MSRP: $9,120

OPTIONS

BAGGER

RETAIL PRICING

YEAR	HIGH	LOW
1997	$640	$480

STHM7220KH

YEARS MFRD: 1989-1994
SERIES: STHM SERIES
ENGINE: KOHLER
ENGINE HP: 20
COOLING: AIR
FUEL: G
SPEEDS: VARIABLE
TRANSMISSION: HYDRO
STEERING: STANDARD
STANDARD DECK: 72"
WEIGHT: 1,280 LBS.
MSRP: $8,020

RETAIL PRICING

YEAR	HIGH	LOW
1989	$224	$168
1990	$249	$187
1991	$277	$208
1992	$305	$229
1993	$341	$256
1994	$377	$283

STHM7222CV

YEARS MFRD: 1993-1999
SERIES: STHM SERIES
ENGINE: KOHLER
ENGINE HP: 22
COOLING: AIR
FUEL: G
SPEEDS: VARIABLE
TRANSMISSION: HYDRO
STEERING: STANDARD
STANDARD DECK: 72"
WEIGHT: 1,275 LBS.
MSRP: $8,449

OPTIONS

BAGGER

RETAIL PRICING

YEAR	HIGH	LOW
1993	$547	$411
1994	$607	$455
1995	$671	$503
1996	$743	$558

STHM7223CV

YEARS MFRD: 2000-2000
SERIES: STHM SERIES
ENGINE: KOHLER
ENGINE HP: 23
FUEL: G
SPEEDS: VARIABLE
TRANSMISSION: HYDRO
STEERING: STANDARD
STANDARD DECK: 72"
MSRP: $9,239

RETAIL PRICING

YEAR	HIGH	LOW
2000	$4,414	$3,310

STR4820CH

YEARS MFRD: 1997-1997
SERIES: TURF RUNNER SERIES
ENGINE: KOHLER
ENGINE HP: 20
FUEL: G
SPEEDS: VARIABLE
TRANSMISSION: HYDRO
STEERING: ZERO
STANDARD DECK: 48"
MSRP: $9,000

RETAIL PRICING

YEAR	HIGH	LOW
1997	$1,153	$865

STR4822CH

YEARS MFRD: 1997-1999
SERIES: TURF RUNNER SERIES
ENGINE: KOHLER
ENGINE HP: 22
FUEL: G
SPEEDS: VARIABLE
TRANSMISSION: HYDRO
STEERING: ZERO
STANDARD DECK: 48"
MSRP: $5,999

RETAIL PRICING

YEAR	HIGH	LOW
1997	$868	$651
1998	$961	$720
1999	$1,065	$798

STT52A22KA

YEARS MFRD: 2001-2001
SERIES: STT SERIES
ENGINE: KAWASAKI
ENGINE HP: 22
FUEL: G
SPEEDS: VARIABLE
TRANSMISSION: HYDRO
STEERING: STANDARD
STANDARD DECK: 52"
MSRP: $8,922

RETAIL PRICING

YEAR	HIGH	LOW
2001	$4,443	$3,332

STT52A23CH

YEARS MFRD: 2000-2001
SERIES: STT SERIES
ENGINE: KOHLER
ENGINE HP: 23
FUEL: G
SPEEDS: VARIABLE
TRANSMISSION: HYDRO
STEERING: ZERO
STANDARD DECK: 52"
MSRP: $8,099

OPTIONS

BAGGER
ROPS
SEAT

SERIAL NUMBERS

YEAR	BEGINNING NO.
2000	5380001
2001	6670001

RETAIL PRICING

YEAR	HIGH	LOW
2000	$1,467	$1,100
2001	$1,627	$1,220

STT52A23KA

YEARS MFRD: 2002-2004
SERIES: STT SERIES
ENGINE: KAWASAKI
ENGINE HP: 23
COOLING: LIQUID
FUEL: G
SPEEDS: VARIABLE
TRANSMISSION: HYDRO
STEERING: ZERO
STANDARD DECK: 52"
WEIGHT: 1,200 LBS.
MSRP: $9,424

RETAIL PRICING

YEAR	HIGH	LOW
2002	$4,660	$3,495
2003	$5,155	$3,866
2004	$5,567	$4,175

STT52A25CH

YEARS MFRD: 2000-2004
SERIES: STT SERIES
ENGINE: KOHLER COMMAND
ENGINE HP: 25
COOLING: AIR
FUEL: G
SPEEDS: VARIABLE
TRANSMISSION: HYDRO
STEERING: ZERO
STANDARD DECK: 52"
WEIGHT: 1,200 LBS.
MSRP: $9,065

SERIAL NUMBERS

YEAR	BEGINNING NO.
2000	5380001
2001	6670001

RETAIL PRICING

YEAR	HIGH	LOW
2000	$4,059	$3,044
2001	$4,234	$3,175
2002	$4,549	$3,412
2003	$5,032	$3,774
2004	$5,357	$4,018

STT52A27CH

YEARS MFRD: 2004-2005
SERIES: TURF TIGER SERIES
ENGINE: KOHLER COMMAND
ENGINE HP: 27
COOLING: AIR
FUEL: G
SPEEDS: VARIABLE
TRANSMISSION: HYDRO
STEERING: ZERO
STANDARD DECK: 52"
WEIGHT: 1,200 LBS.
MSRP: $10,010

RETAIL PRICING

YEAR	HIGH	LOW
2004	$5,409	$4,056
2005	$6,274	$4,706

STT52V-26CH-EFI

YEARS MFRD: 2016-2016
SERIES: TURF TIGER SERIES
ENGINE: KOHLER EFI
ENGINE HP: 26
COOLING: AIR
FUEL: G
SPEEDS: VARIABLE
TRANSMISSION: HYDRO
STEERING: ZERO
STANDARD DECK: 52"
WEIGHT: 1,250 LBS.

STT52V 25CHLP

YEARS MFRD: 2010-2014
SERIES: TURF TIGER SERIES
ENGINE: KOHLER
CYLINDERS: 2
ENGINE HP: 25
COOLING: AIR
SPEEDS: VARIABLE
TRANSMISSION: HYDRO
STEERING: ZERO
BLADE CLUTCH: ELECTRIC
STANDARD DECK: 52"
MSRP: $13,417

RETAIL PRICING

YEAR	HIGH	LOW
2010	$5,626	$4,219
2011	$6,247	$4,685
2012	$6,939	$5,204
2013	$7,703	$5,777
2014	$9,204	$6,903

STT52V 26CHEFI

YEARS MFRD: 2014-2014
ENGINE: KOHLER EFI
ENGINE HP: 26
COOLING: AIR
FUEL: G
SPEEDS: VARIABLE

TRANSMISSION . . . . HYDRO
STEERING . . . . ZERO
STANDARD DECK . . . . 52"
MSRP $12,292

RETAIL PRICING

YEAR	HIGH	LOW
2014	$9,034	$6,776

STT52V27CH

YEARS MFRD 2006-2012
SERIES . . . . TURF TIGER SERIES
ENGINE . . . . KOHLER
ENGINE HP 27
COOLING . . . . AIR
FUEL . . . . G
SPEEDS . . . . VARIABLE
TRANSMISSION . . . . HYDRO
STEERING . . . . ZERO
STANDARD DECK . . . . 52"
MSRP $12,153

OPTIONS

FROPS
ROPS
SUS SEAT

RETAIL PRICING

YEAR	HIGH	LOW
2006	$3,750	$2,813
2007	$4,168	$3,126
2008	$4,627	$3,470
2009	$5,137	$3,853
2010	$5,708	$4,281
2011	$6,339	$4,754
2012	$7,039	$5,279

STT52V 29CHEFI

YEARS MFRD 2013-2013
SERIES . . . . TURF TIGER SERIES
ENGINE . . . . KOHLER
ENGINE HP 29
COOLING . . . . AIR
FUEL . . . . G
SPEEDS . . . . VARIABLE
TRANSMISSION . . . . . DUAL HYDRO
STEERING . . . . ZERO
BLADE CLUTCH . . . . ELECTRIC
STANDARD DECK . . . . 52"
MSRP $12,292

RETAIL PRICING

YEAR	HIGH	LOW
2013	$7,709	$5,782

STT61A22KA

YEARS MFRD 2001-2001
SERIES . . . . STT SERIES
ENGINE . . . . KAWASAKI
ENGINE HP 22
FUEL . . . . G
SPEEDS . . . . VARIABLE
TRANSMISSION . . . . HYDRO
STEERING . . . . STANDARD
STANDARD DECK . . . . 61"
MSRP $9,134

RETAIL PRICING

YEAR	HIGH	LOW
2001	$4,548	$3,411

STT61A23CH

YEARS MFRD 2001-2001
SERIES . . . . STT SERIES
ENGINE . . . . KOHLER
ENGINE HP 23
FUEL . . . . G
SPEEDS . . . . VARIABLE
TRANSMISSION . . . . HYDRO
STEERING . . . . STANDARD
STANDARD DECK . . . . 61"
MSRP $8,858

RETAIL PRICING

YEAR	HIGH	LOW
2001	$4,413	$3,310

STT61A23KA

YEARS MFRD 2002-2004
SERIES . . . . TURF TIGER SERIES
ENGINE . . . . KAWASAKI
ENGINE HP 23
COOLING . . . . LIQUID
FUEL . . . . G
SPEEDS . . . . VARIABLE
TRANSMISSION . . . . HYDRO
STEERING . . . . ZERO
STANDARD DECK . . . . 61"
WEIGHT . . . . 1,298 LBS.
MSRP $9,500

RETAIL PRICING

YEAR	HIGH	LOW
2002	$4,771	$3,578
2003	$5,272	$3,954
2004	$5,614	$4,210

STT61A25CH

YEARS MFRD 2001-2004
SERIES . . . . TURF TIGER SERIES
ENGINE . . . . . . KOHLER COMMAND
ENGINE HP 25
COOLING . . . . AIR
FUEL . . . . G
SPEEDS . . . . VARIABLE
TRANSMISSION . . . . HYDRO
STEERING . . . . ZERO
STANDARD DECK . . . . 61"
WEIGHT . . . . 1,298 LBS.
MSRP $9,195

RETAIL PRICING

YEAR	HIGH	LOW
2001	$4,444	$3,333
2002	$4,616	$3,462
2003	$5,105	$3,828
2004	$5,433	$4,075

STT61A27CH

YEARS MFRD 2004-2005
SERIES . . . . TURF TIGER SERIES
ENGINE . . . . . . KOHLER COMMAND
ENGINE HP 27
COOLING . . . . AIR
FUEL . . . . G
SPEEDS . . . . VARIABLE
TRANSMISSION . . . . HYDRO
STEERING . . . . ZERO
STANDARD DECK . . . . 61"
WEIGHT . . . . 1,298 LBS.
MSRP $10,150

RETAIL PRICING

YEAR	HIGH	LOW
2004	$5,484	$4,113
2005	$6,360	$4,770

STT61A27KA

YEARS MFRD 2001-2001
SERIES . . . . TURF TIGER SERIES
ENGINE . . . . KAWASAKI
ENGINE HP 27
COOLING . . . . LIQUID
FUEL . . . . G
SPEEDS . . . . VARIABLE
TRANSMISSION . . . . HYDRO
STEERING . . . . ZERO
STANDARD DECK . . . . 61"
WEIGHT . . . . 1,298 LBS.
MSRP $8,999

RETAIL PRICING

YEAR	HIGH	LOW
2001	$2,002	$1,501

STT61A29KA

YEARS MFRD 2005-2005
SERIES . . . . TURF TIGER SERIES
ENGINE . . . . KAWASAKI
ENGINE HP 29
COOLING . . . . LIQUID
FUEL . . . . G
SPEEDS . . . . VARIABLE
TRANSMISSION . . . . HYDRO
STEERING . . . . ZERO
STANDARD DECK . . . . 61"
MSRP $11,907

RETAIL PRICING

YEAR	HIGH	LOW
2005	$7,462	$5,596

STT61A31BSD

YEARS MFRD 2004-2005
SERIES . . . . STT SERIES
ENGINE . . . . B&S VANGUARD
CYLINDERS 3
ENGINE HP 31
COOLING . . . . LIQUID
FUEL . . . . D
SPEEDS . . . . VARIABLE
TRANSMISSION . . . . HYDRO
STEERING . . . . ZERO
HYDRAULIC . . . . YES
STANDARD DECK . . . . 61"
WEIGHT . . . . 1,635 LBS.
MSRP $18,856

RETAIL PRICING

YEAR	HIGH	LOW
2004	$10,050	$7,537
2005	$11,817	$8,863

STT61A31BSG

YEARS MFRD 2000-2001
SERIES . . . . STT SERIES
ENGINE . . . . B&S VANGUARD
CYLINDERS 3
CID 22
ENGINE HP 31
COOLING . . . . LIQUID
FUEL . . . . G
SPEEDS . . . . VARIABLE
TRANSMISSION . . . . HYDRO
STEERING . . . . ZERO
BLADE CLUTCH . . . . ELECTRIC
PTO . . . . YES
STANDARD DECK . . . . 61"
WEIGHT . . . . 1,600 LBS.
MSRP $12,999

OPTIONS

72" DECK
BAGGER
DIESEL

SERIAL NUMBERS

YEAR	BEGINNING NO.
2000	5540001
2001	6830001

RETAIL PRICING

YEAR	HIGH	LOW
2000	$2,545	$1,909
2001	$2,826	$2,119

STT61A31BV

YEARS MFRD 2004-2005
SERIES . . . . STT SERIES
ENGINE . . . . B&S
ENGINE HP 31
FUEL . . . . G
SPEEDS . . . . VARIABLE
TRANSMISSION . . . . HYDRO
STEERING . . . . ZERO
STANDARD DECK . . . . 61"
MSRP $11,907

RETAIL PRICING

YEAR	HIGH	LOW
2004	$6,298	$4,724
2005	$7,462	$5,596

STT61A 35BVSS

YEARS MFRD 2005-2005
SERIES . . . . STT SERIES
ENGINE . . . . B&S VANGUARD
ENGINE HP 35
COOLING . . . . LIQUID
FUEL . . . . G
SPEEDS . . . . VARIABLE
TRANSMISSION . . . . HYDRO
STEERING . . . . ZERO
STANDARD DECK . . . . 61"
MSRP $12,175

RETAIL PRICING

YEAR	HIGH	LOW
2005	$7,631	$5,723

STT61A39KA DFI

YEARS MFRD 2003-2004
SERIES. . . . . . . .TURF TIGER SERIES
ENGINE . . .KAWASAKI DIGITAL FUEL INJECTION
ENGINE HP 39
COOLING . . . . .AIR
FUEL . . . . G
SPEEDS . . . . .VARIABLE
TRANSMISSION . . . . .HYDRO
STEERING. . . . . ZERO
STANDARD DECK . . . . 61"
WEIGHT . . . . .1,298 LBS.
MSRP. $10,658

RETAIL PRICING

YEAR	HIGH	LOW
2003	$5,916	$4,437
2004	$6,298	$4,724

STT61V-25KA

YEARS MFRD 2016-2017
SERIES. . . . . . . .TURF TIGER SERIES
ENGINE . . . . . . KAWASAKI FD750D
ENGINE HP 25
COOLING . . . . .LIQUID
FUEL . . . . G
SPEEDS . . . . .VARIABLE
TRANSMISSION . . . . .HYDRO
STEERING. . . . . ZERO
STANDARD DECK . . . . 61"
WEIGHT . . . . .1,450 LBS.

STT61V-25KBD

YEARS MFRD 2016-2017
SERIES. . . . . . . .TURF TIGER SERIES
ENGINE . . . . KUBOTA
ENGINE HP 25
COOLING . . . . .LIQUID
FUEL . . . . D
SPEEDS . . . . .VARIABLE
TRANSMISSION . . . . .HYDRO
STEERING. . . . . ZERO
STANDARD DECK . . . . 61"
WEIGHT . . . . .1,350 LBS.

STT61V-26CH-EFI

YEARS MFRD 2016-2017
SERIES. . . . . . . .TURF TIGER SERIES
ENGINE . . . . KOHLER EFI
ENGINE HP 26
COOLING . . . . .AIR
FUEL . . . . G
SPEEDS . . . . .VARIABLE
TRANSMISSION . . . . .HYDRO
STEERING. . . . . ZERO
STANDARD DECK . . . . 61"
WEIGHT . . . . .1,550 LBS.

STT61V-26DFI

YEARS MFRD 2016-2017
SERIES. . . . . . . .TURF TIGER SERIES
ENGINE . . . . .KAWASAKI FD791
ENGINE HP 61
COOLING . . . . .LIQUID
FUEL . . . . G
SPEEDS . . . . .VARIABLE
TRANSMISSION . . . . .HYDRO
STEERING. . . . . ZERO
STANDARD DECK . . . . 61"
WEIGHT . . . . .1,650 LBS.

STT61V-35BVAC

YEARS MFRD 2016-2017
SERIES. . . . . . . .TURF TIGER SERIES
ENGINE . . . . B&S VANGUARD
ENGINE HP 35
COOLING . . . . .AIR
FUEL . . . . G
SPEEDS . . . . .VARIABLE
TRANSMISSION . . . . .HYDRO
STEERING. . . . . ZERO
STANDARD DECK . . . . 61"
WEIGHT . . . . .1,700 LBS.

STT61V 25CHLP

YEARS MFRD 2010-2014
SERIES. . . . . . . .TURF TIGER SERIES
ENGINE . . . . KOHLER
CYLINDERS. 2
ENGINE HP 25
COOLING . . . . .AIR
SPEEDS . . . . .VARIABLE
TRANSMISSION . . . . .HYDRO
STEERING. . . . . ZERO
BLADE CLUTCH . . . . .ELECTRIC
STANDARD DECK . . . . 61"
MSRP. $13,600

RETAIL PRICING

YEAR	HIGH	LOW
2010	$5,701	$4,276
2011	$6,333	$4,750
2012	$7,033	$5,274
2013	$7,808	$5,856
2014	$9,597	$7,198

STT61V25KBD

YEARS MFRD 2007-2011
SERIES. . . . . . . .TURF TIGER SERIES
ENGINE . . . . KUBOTA
CYLINDERS. 2
ENGINE HP 25
COOLING . . . . .LIQUID
FUEL . . . . D
SPEEDS . . . . .VARIABLE
TRANSMISSION . . . . .HYDRO
STEERING. . . . . ZERO
BLADE CLUTCH . . . . .ELECTRIC
STANDARD DECK . . . . 61"
MSRP. $15,965

RETAIL PRICING

YEAR	HIGH	LOW
2007	$5,616	$4,212
2008	$6,234	$4,675
2009	$6,925	$5,193
2010	$7,689	$5,767
2011	$8,542	$6,406

STT61V 26CHEFI

YEARS MFRD 2014-2014
ENGINE . . . . KOHLER EFI
ENGINE HP 26
COOLING . . . . .AIR
FUEL . . . . G
SPEEDS . . . . .VARIABLE
TRANSMISSION . . . . .HYDRO
STEERING. . . . . ZERO
STANDARD DECK . . . . 61"
MSRP. $12,467

RETAIL PRICING

YEAR	HIGH	LOW
2014	$8,581	$6,436

STT61V27CH

YEARS MFRD 2006-2012
SERIES. . . . . . . .TURF TIGER SERIES
ENGINE . . . . KOHLER
ENGINE HP 27
COOLING . . . . .AIR
FUEL . . . . G
SPEEDS . . . . .VARIABLE
TRANSMISSION . . . . .HYDRO
STEERING. . . . . ZERO
STANDARD DECK . . . . 61"
MSRP. $12,359

OPTIONS

FROPS
ROPS
SUS SEAT

RETAIL PRICING

YEAR	HIGH	LOW
2006	$3,814	$2,860
2007	$4,236	$3,177
2008	$4,708	$3,531
2009	$5,225	$3,919
2010	$5,804	$4,353
2011	$6,444	$4,833
2012	$7,158	$5,368

STT61V27KA

YEARS MFRD 2006-2010
SERIES. . . . . . . .TURF TIGER SERIES
ENGINE . . . . KAWASAKI
ENGINE HP 27
COOLING . . . . .LIQUID
FUEL . . . . G
SPEEDS . . . . .VARIABLE
TRANSMISSION . . . . .HYDRO
STEERING. . . . . ZERO
STANDARD DECK . . . . 61"
MSRP. $12,874

OPTIONS

FROPS
ROPS
SUS SEAT

RETAIL PRICING

YEAR	HIGH	LOW
2006	$4,141	$3,106
2007	$4,611	$3,458
2008	$5,121	$3,841
2009	$5,688	$4,266
2010	$6,319	$4,739

STT61V28CAT

YEARS MFRD 2008-2013
SERIES. . . . . . . .TURF TIGER SERIES
ENGINE . . . . CAT
CYLINDERS. 2
ENGINE HP 28
COOLING . . . . .LIQUID
FUEL . . . . D
SPEEDS . . . . .VARIABLE
TRANSMISSION . . . . .HYDRO
STEERING. . . . . ZERO
BLADE CLUTCH . . . . .ELECTRIC
STANDARD DECK . . . . 61"
MSRP. $18,783

RETAIL PRICING

YEAR	HIGH	LOW
2008	$6,889	$5,167
2009	$7,648	$5,736
2010	$8,493	$6,370
2011	$9,405	$7,054
2012	$10,418	$7,814
2013	$11,632	$8,724

STT61V 29CHEFI

YEARS MFRD 2013-2013
SERIES. . . . . . . .TURF TIGER SERIES
ENGINE . . . . KOHLER
ENGINE HP 29
COOLING . . . . .AIR
FUEL . . . . G
SPEEDS . . . . .VARIABLE
TRANSMISSION . . . . . DUAL HYDRO
STEERING. . . . . ZERO
BLADE CLUTCH . . . . .ELECTRIC
STANDARD DECK . . . . 61"
MSRP. $12,225

RETAIL PRICING

YEAR	HIGH	LOW
2013	$7,569	$5,677

STT61V29KA-DFI

YEARS MFRD 2006-2011
SERIES. . . . . . . .TURF TIGER SERIES
ENGINE . . . . KAWASAKI
CYLINDERS. 2
ENGINE HP 27
COOLING . . . . .LIQUID
FUEL . . . . G
SPEEDS . . . . .VARIABLE

TRANSMISSION .... HYDRO
STEERING................ ZERO
BLADE CLUTCH .... ELECTRIC
STANDARD DECK .... 61"
MSRP................ $13,390

OPTIONS

FROPS
LIGHTS
ROPS

RETAIL PRICING

YEAR	HIGH	LOW
2006	$4,241	$3,181
2007	$4,711	$3,533
2008	$5,228	$3,921
2009	$5,809	$4,356
2010	$6,447	$4,835
2011	$7,214	$5,411

STT61V29KB-DF

YEARS MFRD 2010-2011
SERIES....... TURF TIGER SERIES
ENGINE .... KUBOTA
CYLINDERS.................. 2
ENGINE HP 29
COOLING .... LIQUID
SPEEDS .... VARIABLE
TRANSMISSION .... HYDRO
STEERING................ ZERO
BLADE CLUTCH .... ELECTRIC
STANDARD DECK .... 61"
MSRP................ $18,425

RETAIL PRICING

YEAR	HIGH	LOW
2010	$8,300	$6,225
2011	$9,487	$7,115

STT61V31BSD

YEARS MFRD 2006-2007
SERIES............. STT SERIES
ENGINE .... DAIHATSU
ENGINE HP 31
COOLING .... LIQUID
FUEL .... D
SPEEDS .... VARIABLE
TRANSMISSION .... HYDRO
STEERING................ ZERO
STANDARD DECK .... 61"
MSRP................ $18,299

RETAIL PRICING

YEAR	HIGH	LOW
2006	$6,231	$4,673
2007	$6,921	$5,190

STT61V31EFI

YEARS MFRD 2008-2012
SERIES....... TURF TIGER SERIES
ENGINE .... KOHLER
CYLINDERS.................. 2
ENGINE HP 31
COOLING .... LIQUID
FUEL .... G
SPEEDS .... VARIABLE
TRANSMISSION .... HYDRO
STEERING................ ZERO
BLADE CLUTCH .... ELECTRIC
STANDARD DECK .... 61"
MSRP................ $12,874

RETAIL PRICING

YEAR	HIGH	LOW
2008	$4,901	$3,675
2009	$5,434	$4,075
2010	$6,047	$4,535
2011	$6,713	$5,035
2012	$7,477	$5,608

STT61V31KB-DF

YEARS MFRD 2010-2014
SERIES....... TURF TIGER SERIES
ENGINE .... KUBOTA
CYLINDERS.................. 2
ENGINE HP 31
COOLING .... AIR
FUEL .... D
SPEEDS .... VARIABLE
TRANSMISSION .... HYDRO
STEERING................ ZERO
BLADE CLUTCH .... ELECTRIC
STANDARD DECK .... 61"
MSRP................ $18,608

RETAIL PRICING

YEAR	HIGH	LOW
2010	$6,957	$5,218
2011	$7,727	$5,795
2012	$8,579	$6,434
2013	$9,527	$7,145
2014	$12,530	$9,398

STT61V 35BVAC

YEARS MFRD 2012-2012
SERIES....... TURF TIGER SERIES
ENGINE .... B&S
CYLINDERS.................. 2
ENGINE HP 35
COOLING .... AIR
FUEL .... G
SPEEDS .... VARIABLE
TRANSMISSION .... HYDRO
STEERING................ ZERO
BLADE CLUTCH .... ELECTRIC
STANDARD DECK .... 61"
MSRP................ $11,638

RETAIL PRICING

YEAR	HIGH	LOW
2012	$6,741	$5,056

STT61V 35BVAC

YEARS MFRD 2014-2014
ENGINE .... B&S
ENGINE HP 35
COOLING .... AIR
FUEL .... G
SPEEDS .... VARIABLE
TRANSMISSION .... HYDRO
STEERING................ ZERO
STANDARD DECK .... 61"
MSRP................ $12,767

RETAIL PRICING

YEAR	HIGH	LOW
2012	$8,566	$6,424

STT61V 750KASS

YEARS MFRD 2012-2014
SERIES....... TURF TIGER SERIES
ENGINE .... KAWASAKI
CID 750CC
COOLING .... AIR
FUEL .... G
SPEEDS .... VARIABLE
TRANSMISSION .... HYDRO
STEERING................ ZERO
STANDARD DECK .... 61"
MSRP................ $13,375

RETAIL PRICING

YEAR	HIGH	LOW
2012	$6,915	$5,187
2013	$7,681	$5,761
2014	$9,398	$7,049

STT61V 791DFISS

YEARS MFRD 2012-2014
ENGINE .... KAWASAKI
CID 791CC
COOLING .... AIR
FUEL .... G
SPEEDS .... VARIABLE
TRANSMISSION .... HYDRO
STEERING................ ZERO
STANDARD DECK .... 61"
MSRP................ $14,417

RETAIL PRICING

YEAR	HIGH	LOW
2012	$7,454	$5,590
2013	$8,278	$6,208
2014	$9,740	$7,305

STT72A27KA

YEARS MFRD 2001-2004
SERIES............. STT SERIES
ENGINE .... KAWASAKI
ENGINE HP 27
FUEL .... G
SPEEDS .... VARIABLE
TRANSMISSION .... HYDRO
STEERING............ STANDARD
STANDARD DECK .... 72"
MSRP................ $10,594

RETAIL PRICING

YEAR	HIGH	LOW
2001	$4,957	$3,718
2002	$5,239	$3,929
2003	$5,792	$4,344
2004	$6,261	$4,696

STT72A29KA

YEARS MFRD 2004-2005
SERIES....... TURF TIGER SERIES
ENGINE ... KAWASAKI DIGITAL FUEL INJECTION
ENGINE HP 29
COOLING .... AIR
FUEL .... G
SPEEDS .... VARIABLE
TRANSMISSION .... HYDRO
STEERING................ ZERO
STANDARD DECK .... 72"
WEIGHT .... 1,348 LBS.
MSRP................ $12,607

RETAIL PRICING

YEAR	HIGH	LOW
2004	$6,676	$5,007
2005	$7,900	$5,925

STT72A29KA DFI

YEARS MFRD 2003-2006
SERIES............. STT SERIES
ENGINE .... KAWASAKI
ENGINE HP 29
COOLING .... AIR
FUEL .... G
SPEEDS .... VARIABLE
TRANSMISSION .... HYDRO
STEERING................ ZERO
STANDARD DECK .... 72"
WEIGHT .... 1,348 LBS.
MSRP................ $11,299

RETAIL PRICING

YEAR	HIGH	LOW
2004	$2,167	$1,626
2005	$2,324	$1,743
2006	$2,480	$1,860

STT72A29KA-DFI

YEARS MFRD 2006-2008
SERIES....... TURF TIGER SERIES
ENGINE .... KAWASAKI
CYLINDERS.................. 2
ENGINE HP 29
COOLING .... LIQUID
FUEL .... G
SPEEDS .... VARIABLE
TRANSMISSION .... HYDRO
STEERING................ ZERO
BLADE CLUTCH .... ELECTRIC
STANDARD DECK .... 72"
MSRP................ $13,080

OPTIONS

FROPS
LIGHTS
ROPS

RETAIL PRICING

YEAR	HIGH	LOW
2006	$4,011	$3,008
2007	$4,454	$3,341
2008	$4,960	$3,720

STT72A31BSD

YEARS MFRD 2006-2007
SERIES. . . . . STT SERIES
ENGINE . . . . DAIHATSU
ENGINE HP 31
COOLING . . . . LIQUID
FUEL . . . . D
SPEEDS . . . . VARIABLE
TRANSMISSION . . . . HYDRO
STEERING. . . . . STANDARD
STANDARD DECK . . . . 72"
MSRP. $18,599

RETAIL PRICING

YEAR	HIGH	LOW
2006	$6,334	$4,750
2007	$7,035	$5,276

STT72A31BSG

YEARS MFRD 2000-2003
SERIES. . . . . STT SERIES
ENGINE . . . . B&S
ENGINE HP 31
FUEL . . . . G
SPEEDS . . . . VARIABLE
TRANSMISSION . . . . HYDRO
STEERING. . . . . STANDARD
STANDARD DECK . . . . 72"
MSRP. $14,900

RETAIL PRICING

YEAR	HIGH	LOW
2000	$6,839	$5,129
2001	$7,280	$5,460
2002	$7,482	$5,612
2003	$8,270	$6,202

STT72A31BV

YEARS MFRD 2004-2005
SERIES. . . . . STT SERIES
ENGINE . . . . B&S
ENGINE HP 31
COOLING . . . . AIR
FUEL . . . . G
SPEEDS . . . . VARIABLE
TRANSMISSION . . . . HYDRO
STEERING. . . . . ZERO
STANDARD DECK . . . . 72"
MSRP. $12,607

RETAIL PRICING

YEAR	HIGH	LOW
2004	$6,676	$5,007
2005	$7,900	$5,925

STT72A31EFI

YEARS MFRD 2008-2011
SERIES. . . . . TURF TIGER SERIES
ENGINE . . . . KOHLER
CYLINDERS. 2
ENGINE HP 31
COOLING . . . . LIQUID
FUEL . . . . G
SPEEDS . . . . VARIABLE
TRANSMISSION . . . . HYDRO
STEERING. . . . . ZERO
BLADE CLUTCH . . . . ELECTRIC
STANDARD DECK . . . . 61"
MSRP. $14,647

RETAIL PRICING

YEAR	HIGH	LOW
2008	$4,712	$3,534
2009	$5,656	$4,242
2010	$6,600	$4,950
2011	$7,543	$5,657

STT72A35BV

YEARS MFRD 2006-2008
SERIES. . . . . STT SERIES
ENGINE . . . . B&S VANGUARD
ENGINE HP 35
COOLING . . . . LIQUID
FUEL . . . . G
SPEEDS . . . . VARIABLE
TRANSMISSION . . . . HYDRO
STEERING. . . . . ZERO
STANDARD DECK . . . . 72"
MSRP. $13,389

OPTIONS

FROPS
LIGHTS
ROPS

RETAIL PRICING

YEAR	HIGH	LOW
2006	$4,103	$3,077
2007	$4,558	$3,419
2008	$5,066	$3,800

STT72V-25KBD

YEARS MFRD 2016-2017
SERIES. . . . . TURF TIGER SERIES
ENGINE . . . . KUBOTA
ENGINE HP 25
COOLING . . . . LIQUID
FUEL . . . . D
SPEEDS . . . . VARIABLE
TRANSMISSION . . . . HYDRO
STEERING. . . . . ZERO
STANDARD DECK . . . . 72"
WEIGHT . . . . 1,500 LBS.

STT72V-26CH-EFI

YEARS MFRD 2016-2017
SERIES. . . . . TURF TIGER SERIES
ENGINE . . . . KOHLER EFI
ENGINE HP 26
COOLING . . . . AIR
FUEL . . . . G
SPEEDS . . . . VARIABLE
TRANSMISSION . . . . HYDRO
STEERING. . . . . ZERO
STANDARD DECK . . . . 72"
WEIGHT . . . . 1,400 LBS.

STT72V-26DFI

YEARS MFRD 2016-2017
SERIES. . . . . TURF TIGER
ENGINE . . . . KAWASAKI FD791
ENGINE HP 26
COOLING . . . . LIQUID
SPEEDS . . . . VARIABLE
TRANSMISSION . . . . HYDRO
STEERING. . . . . ZERO
STANDARD DECK . . . . 72"
WEIGHT . . . . 1,600 LBS.

STT72V-35BVAC

YEARS MFRD 2016-2017
SERIES. . . . . TURF TIGER SERIES
ENGINE . . . . B&S VANGUARD
ENGINE HP 35
COOLING . . . . AIR
FUEL . . . . G
SPEEDS . . . . VARIABLE
TRANSMISSION . . . . HYDRO
STEERING. . . . . ZERO
STANDARD DECK . . . . 72"
WEIGHT . . . . 1,750 LBS.

STT72V25KBD

YEARS MFRD 2014-2014
ENGINE . . . . KUBOTA
ENGINE HP 25
COOLING . . . . LIQUID
FUEL . . . . D
SPEEDS . . . . VARIABLE
TRANSMISSION . . . . . DUAL HYDRO
STEERING. . . . . ZERO
STANDARD DECK . . . . 72"
MSRP. $18,675

RETAIL PRICING

YEAR	HIGH	LOW
2014	$13,495	$10,121

STT72V28CAT

YEARS MFRD 2008-2013
SERIES. . . . . TURF TIGER SERIES
ENGINE . . . . CAT
CYLINDERS. 2
ENGINE HP 28
COOLING . . . . LIQUID
FUEL . . . . D
SPEEDS . . . . VARIABLE
TRANSMISSION . . . . HYDRO
STEERING. . . . . ZERO
BLADE CLUTCH . . . . ELECTRIC
STANDARD DECK . . . . 72"
MSRP. $18,024

RETAIL PRICING

YEAR	HIGH	LOW
2008	$6,607	$4,956
2009	$7,341	$5,506
2010	$8,152	$6,114
2011	$9,051	$6,788
2012	$10,053	$7,539
2013	$11,163	$8,372

STT72V35VAC

YEARS MFRD 2011-2011
SERIES. . . . . TURF TIGER SERIES
ENGINE . . . . B&S
CYLINDERS. 2
ENGINE HP 35
COOLING . . . . AIR
FUEL . . . . G
SPEEDS . . . . VARIABLE
TRANSMISSION . . . . HYDRO
STEERING. . . . . ZERO
BLADE CLUTCH . . . . ELECTRIC
STANDARD DECK . . . . 72"
MSRP. $11,903

RETAIL PRICING

YEAR	HIGH	LOW
2011	$6,129	$4,597

STT72VS26 CHEFI

YEARS MFRD 2014-2014
ENGINE . . . . KOHLER EFI
ENGINE HP 26
COOLING . . . . AIR
FUEL . . . . G
SPEEDS . . . . VARIABLE
TRANSMISSION . . . . . DUAL HYDRO
STEERING. . . . . ZERO
STANDARD DECK . . . . 72"
MSRP. $13,234

RETAIL PRICING

YEAR	HIGH	LOW
2014	$9,609	$7,207

STT72VS29 CHEFI

YEARS MFRD 2013-2013
SERIES. . . . . TURF TIGER SERIES
ENGINE . . . . KAWASAKI
ENGINE HP 29
COOLING . . . . AIR
FUEL . . . . G
SPEEDS . . . . VARIABLE
TRANSMISSION . . . . . DUAL HYDRO
STEERING. . . . . ZERO
BLADE CLUTCH . . . . ELECTRIC
STANDARD DECK . . . . 72"
MSRP. $13,233

RETAIL PRICING

YEAR	HIGH	LOW
2013	$8,196	$6,147

STT72VS31EFI

YEARS MFRD 2010-2012
ENGINE . . . . KOHLER
ENGINE HP 31
COOLING . . . . AIR
FUEL . . . . G
SPEEDS . . . . VARIABLE
TRANSMISSION . . . . . DUAL HYDRO
STEERING. . . . . ZERO
STANDARD DECK . . . . 72"
MSRP. $14,419

RETAIL PRICING

YEAR	HIGH	LOW
2010	$6,768	$5,076
2011	$7,520	$5,640
2012	$8,349	$6,261

SCAG

STT72VS35 BVAC

YEARS MFRD 2012-2014
SERIES . . . . TURF TIGER
ENGINE . . . . B&S
ENGINE HP 35
COOLING . . . . AIR
FUEL . . . . G
SPEEDS . . . . VARIABLE
TRANSMISSION . . . . HYDRO
STEERING . . . . ZERO
STANDARD DECK . . . . 72"
MSRP $13,483

RETAIL PRICING

YEAR	HIGH	LOW
2012	$6,971	$5,228
2013	$7,742	$5,806
2014	$9,606	$7,205

STT72VS791 DFISS

YEARS MFRD 2012-2014
SERIES . . . . TURF TIGER
ENGINE . . . . KAWASAKI
CID 791CC
COOLING . . . . LIQUID
FUEL . . . . G
SPEEDS . . . . VARIABLE
TRANSMISSION . . . . HYDRO
STEERING . . . . ZERO
BLADE CLUTCH . . . . ELECTRIC
STANDARD DECK . . . . 72"
MSRP $15,241

RETAIL PRICING

YEAR	HIGH	LOW
2012	$7,882	$5,912
2013	$8,752	$6,564
2014	$11,025	$8,269

STT5222CH

YEARS MFRD 1999-1999
SERIES . . . . TURF TIGER SERIES
ENGINE . . . . KOHLER
ENGINE HP 22
FUEL . . . . G
SPEEDS . . . . VARIABLE
TRANSMISSION . . . . HYDRO
STEERING . . . . ZERO
STANDARD DECK . . . . 52"
MSRP $7,859

RETAIL PRICING

YEAR	HIGH	LOW
1999	$1,182	$886

STT5222KA

YEARS MFRD 1998-2001
SERIES . . . . . . TURF TRACER SERIES
ENGINE . . . . KAWASAKI
ENGINE HP 22
COOLING . . . . LIQUID
FUEL . . . . G
SPEEDS . . . . VARIABLE
TRANSMISSION . . . . HYDRO
STEERING . . . . ZERO
STANDARD DECK . . . . 52"
MSRP $9,122

SERIAL NUMBERS

YEAR	BEGINNING NO.
1999	4260001
2000	5380001
2001	6670001

RETAIL PRICING

YEAR	HIGH	LOW
1998	$3,631	$2,723
1999	$4,066	$3,050
2000	$4,261	$3,196
2001	$4,543	$3,407

STT5223CH

YEARS MFRD 2000-2000
SERIES . . . . STT SERIES
ENGINE . . . . KOHLER
ENGINE HP 23
FUEL . . . . G
SPEEDS . . . . VARIABLE
TRANSMISSION . . . . HYDRO
STEERING . . . . STANDARD
STANDARD DECK . . . . 52"
MSRP $8,294

RETAIL PRICING

YEAR	HIGH	LOW
2000	$3,962	$2,972

STT5225CH

YEARS MFRD 1998-2000
SERIES . . . . TURF TIGER SERIES
ENGINE . . . . KOHLER
ENGINE HP 25
FUEL . . . . G
SPEEDS . . . . VARIABLE
TRANSMISSION . . . . HYDRO
STEERING . . . . ZERO
STANDARD DECK . . . . 52"
MSRP $8,714

RETAIL PRICING

YEAR	HIGH	LOW
1998	$3,544	$2,658
1999	$3,971	$2,978
2000	$4,161	$3,121

STT6122CH

YEARS MFRD 1998-1998
SERIES . . . . STT SERIES
ENGINE . . . . KOHLER
ENGINE HP 22
FUEL . . . . G
SPEEDS . . . . VARIABLE
TRANSMISSION . . . . HYDRO
STEERING . . . . STANDARD
STANDARD DECK . . . . 61"
MSRP $8,099

RETAIL PRICING

YEAR	HIGH	LOW
1998	$3,460	$2,595

STT6122KA

YEARS MFRD 1998-2001
SERIES . . . . . . TURF TRACER SERIES
ENGINE . . . . KAWASAKI
ENGINE HP 22
COOLING . . . . LIQUID
FUEL . . . . G
TRANSMISSION . . . . HYDRO
STEERING . . . . ZERO
STANDARD DECK . . . . 61"
MSRP $9,200

SERIAL NUMBERS

YEAR	BEGINNING NO.
1999	4260001
2000	5380001
2001	6670001

RETAIL PRICING

YEAR	HIGH	LOW
1998	$3,715	$2,786
1999	$4,162	$3,122
2000	$4,364	$3,273
2001	$4,583	$3,438

STT6123CH

YEARS MFRD 2000-2000
SERIES . . . . STT SERIES
ENGINE . . . . KOHLER
ENGINE HP 23
FUEL . . . . G
SPEEDS . . . . VARIABLE
TRANSMISSION . . . . HYDRO
STEERING . . . . STANDARD
STANDARD DECK . . . . 61"
MSRP $8,858

RETAIL PRICING

YEAR	HIGH	LOW
2000	$4,232	$3,174

STT6125CH

YEARS MFRD 1998-2001
SERIES . . . . . . TURF TRACER SERIES
ENGINE . . . . KOHLER
ENGINE HP 25
FUEL . . . . G
SPEEDS . . . . VARIABLE
TRANSMISSION . . . . HYDRO
STEERING . . . . ZERO
STANDARD DECK . . . . 61"
MSRP $9,225

SERIAL NUMBERS

YEAR	BEGINNING NO.
1999	4260001
2000	5380001
2001	6670001

RETAIL PRICING

YEAR	HIGH	LOW
1998	$3,631	$2,723
1999	$4,067	$3,050
2000	$4,263	$3,197
2001	$4,594	$3,446

STT6131BSG

YEARS MFRD 2000-2000
SERIES . . . . STT SERIES
ENGINE . . . . B&S
ENGINE HP 31
FUEL . . . . G
SPEEDS . . . . VARIABLE
TRANSMISSION . . . . HYDRO
STEERING . . . . STANDARD
STANDARD DECK . . . . 61"
MSRP $13,995

RETAIL PRICING

YEAR	HIGH	LOW
2000	$6,684	$5,013

STT7231BSG

YEARS MFRD 2000-2000
SERIES . . . . STT SERIES
ENGINE . . . . B&S
ENGINE HP 31
FUEL . . . . G
SPEEDS . . . . VARIABLE
TRANSMISSION . . . . HYDRO
STEERING . . . . STANDARD
STANDARD DECK . . . . 72"
MSRP $14,295

RETAIL PRICING

YEAR	HIGH	LOW
2000	$6,827	$5,120

STTII-52V-25CH-LP-EFI

YEARS MFRD 2020-2020
SERIES . . . . . TURF TIGER II SERIES
ENGINE . . KOHLER COMMAND PRO
ENGINE HP 25
SPEEDS . . . . VARIABLE
TRANSMISSION . . . . HYDRO
ROPS/CAB . . . . ROPS
STANDARD DECK . . . . 52"
MSRP $15,442

STTII-52V-26CH-EFI

YEARS MFRD 2016-2019
SERIES . . . . . TURF TIGER II SERIES
ENGINE . . . . KOHLER EFI
ENGINE HP 26
COOLING . . . . AIR
FUEL . . . . G
SPEEDS . . . . VARIABLE
TRANSMISSION . . . . HYDRO
STEERING . . . . ZERO
STANDARD DECK . . . . 52"
WEIGHT . . . . 1,420 LBS.
MSRP $13,359

STTII-52V-31BV

YEARS MFRD 2020-2020
SERIES...... TURF TIGER II SERIES
ENGINE ...... BRIGGS VANGUARD
ENGINE HP 31
COOLING .... AIR
FUEL .... G
SPEEDS .... VARIABLE
TRANSMISSION .... HYDRO
STEERING................ ZERO
ROPS/CAB .... ROPS
STANDARD DECK .... 52"
MSRP................ $14,004

STTII-61V-25CH-LP-EFI

YEARS MFRD 2020-2020
SERIES...... TURF TIGER II SERIES
ENGINE .. KOHLER COMMAND PRO
ENGINE HP 25
SPEEDS .... VARIABLE
TRANSMISSION .... HYDRO
STEERING................ ZERO
ROPS/CAB .... ROPS
STANDARD DECK .... 61"
MSRP................ $15,762

STTII-61V-25KA

YEARS MFRD 2016-2018
SERIES...... TURF TIGER II SERIES
ENGINE ...... KAWASAKI FD750D
ENGINE HP 25
COOLING .... LIQUID
FUEL .... G
SPEEDS .... VARIABLE
TRANSMISSION .... HYDRO
STEERING................ ZERO
STANDARD DECK .... 61"
WEIGHT .... 1,510 LBS.

STTII-61V-25KBD

YEARS MFRD 2017-2020
SERIES...... TURF TIGER II SERIES
ENGINE .... KUBOTA
ENGINE HP 25
COOLING .... LIQUID
FUEL .... D
STEERING................ ZERO
BLADE CLUTCH .... ELECTRIC
STANDARD DECK .... 61"
WEIGHT .... 1,728 LBS.
MSRP................ $19,847

STTII-61V-26CH-EFI

YEARS MFRD 2016-2019
SERIES...... TURF TIGER II SERIES
ENGINE .... KOHLER EFI
ENGINE HP 26
COOLING .... AIR
FUEL .... G
SPEEDS .... VARIABLE
TRANSMISSION .... HYDRO
STEERING................ ZERO
STANDARD DECK .... 61"
WEIGHT .... 1,530 LBS.
MSRP................ $13,542

STTII-61V-26DFI

YEARS MFRD 2016-2018
SERIES...... TURF TIGER II SERIES
ENGINE .... KAWASAKI FD791
ENGINE HP 26
COOLING .... LIQUID
FUEL .... G
SPEEDS .... VARIABLE
TRANSMISSION .... HYDRO
STEERING................ ZERO
STANDARD DECK .... 61"
WEIGHT .... 1,520 LBS.

STTII-61V-31BV

YEARS MFRD 2020-2020
SERIES....... TURF TIGER II SRIES
ENGINE ...... BRIGGS VANGUARD
ENGINE HP 31
COOLING .... AIR
FUEL .... G
SPEEDS .... VARIABLE
TRANSMISSION .... HYDRO
STEERING................ ZERO
ROPS/CAB .... ROPS
STANDARD DECK .... 61"
MSRP................ $14,135

STTII-61V-31DFI

YEARS MFRD 2016-2020
SERIES...... TURF TIGER II SERIES
ENGINE ...... KAWASAKI FD851D
ENGINE HP 31
COOLING .... LIQUID
FUEL .... G
SPEEDS .... VARIABLE
TRANSMISSION .... HYDRO
STEERING................ ZERO
STANDARD DECK .... 61"
WEIGHT .... 1,540 LBS.
MSRP................ $17,079

STTII-61V-35BV

YEARS MFRD 2017-2020
SERIES...... TURF TIGER II SERIES
ENGINE .... B&S VANGUARD
ENGINE HP 35
COOLING .... AIR
FUEL .... G
STEERING................ ZERO
STANDARD DECK .... 61"
MSRP................ $14,519

STTII-61V-35BVAC

YEARS MFRD 2016-2016
SERIES...... TURF TIGER II SERIES
ENGINE .... B&S VANGUARD
ENGINE HP 35
COOLING .... AIR
FUEL .... G
SPEEDS .... VARIABLE
TRANSMISSION .... HYDRO
STEERING................ ZERO
STANDARD DECK .... 61"
WEIGHT .... 1,555 LBS.

STTII-61V-37BV-EFI

YEARS MFRD 2018-2020
SERIES............ TURF TIGER II
ENGINE .... B&S VANGUARD
ENGINE HP 37
COOLING .... AIR
FUEL .... G
STEERING................ ZERO
BLADE CLUTCH .... ELECTRIC
STANDARD DECK .... 61"
WEIGHT .... 1,515 LBS.
MSRP................ $15,314

STTII-72V-25KBD

YEARS MFRD 2017-2020
SERIES...... TURF TIGER II SERIES
ENGINE .... KUBOTA
ENGINE HP 25
COOLING .... LIQUID
FUEL .... D
STEERING................ ZERO
BLADE CLUTCH .... ELECTRIC
STANDARD DECK .... 72"
WEIGHT .... 1,758 LBS.
MSRP................ $20,957

STTII-72V-26CH-EFI

YEARS MFRD 2016-2019
SERIES...... TURF TIGER II SERIES
ENGINE .... KOHLER EFI
ENGINE HP 26
COOLING .... AIR
FUEL .... G
SPEEDS .... VARIABLE
TRANSMISSION .... HYDRO
STEERING................ ZERO
STANDARD DECK .... 72"
WEIGHT .... 1,580 LBS.
MSRP................ $13,399

STTII-72V-26DFI

YEARS MFRD 2016-2018
SERIES...... TURF TIGER II SERIES
ENGINE .... KAWASAKI FD791
ENGINE HP 26
COOLING .... LIQUID
FUEL .... G
SPEEDS .... VARIABLE
TRANSMISSION .... HYDRO
STEERING................ ZERO
STANDARD DECK .... 72"
WEIGHT .... 1,570 LBS.

STTII-72V-31DFI

YEARS MFRD 2016-2020
SERIES...... TURF TIGER II SERIES
ENGINE ...... KAWASAKI FD851D
ENGINE HP 31
COOLING .... LIQUID
FUEL .... G
SPEEDS .... VARIABLE
TRANSMISSION .... HYDRO
STEERING................ ZERO
STANDARD DECK .... 72"
WEIGHT .... 1,590 LBS.
MSRP................ $17,992

STTII-72V-35BVAC

YEARS MFRD 2016-2019
SERIES...... TURF TIGER II SERIES
ENGINE .... B&S VANGUARD
ENGINE HP 35
COOLING .... AIR
FUEL .... G
SPEEDS .... VARIABLE
TRANSMISSION .... HYDRO
STEERING................ ZERO
STANDARD DECK .... 72"
WEIGHT .... 1,600 LBS.
MSRP................ $14,613

STTII-72V-37BV-EFI

YEARS MFRD 2018-2020
SERIES...... TURF TIGER II SERIES
ENGINE .... B&S VANGUARD
ENGINE HP 37
COOLING .... AIR
FUEL .... G

STEERING. . . . . ZERO
BLADE CLUTCH . . . . ELECTRIC
STANDARD DECK . . . . 72"
WEIGHT . . . . 1,575 LBS.
MSRP. $16,139

STWC48V25CV

YEARS MFRD 2010-2010
ENGINE . . . . KOHLER
CYLINDERS. 2
ENGINE HP 25
COOLING . . . . AIR
FUEL . . . . G
SPEEDS . . . . VARIABLE
TRANSMISSION . . . . . DUAL HYDRO
STEERING. . . . . ZERO
BLADE CLUTCH . . . . ELECTRIC
STANDARD DECK . . . . 48"
MSRP. $9,270

RETAIL PRICING

YEAR	HIGH	LOW
2010	$4,546	$3,410

STWC48V26 KALC

YEARS MFRD 2010-2010
ENGINE . . . . KAWASAKI
CYLINDERS. 2
ENGINE HP 26
COOLING . . . . AIR
FUEL . . . . G
SPEEDS . . . . VARIABLE
TRANSMISSION . . . . . DUAL HYDRO
STEERING. . . . . ZERO
BLADE CLUTCH . . . . ELECTRIC
STANDARD DECK . . . . 48"
MSRP. $9,785

RETAIL PRICING

YEAR	HIGH	LOW
2010	$4,799	$3,599

STWC52A 25KA

YEARS MFRD 2005-2005
SERIES. . . . . WILDCAT SERIES
ENGINE . . . . KAWASAKI
ENGINE HP 25
COOLING . . . . AIR
FUEL . . . . G
SPEEDS . . . . VARIABLE
TRANSMISSION . . . . HYDRO
STEERING. . . . . ZERO
STANDARD DECK . . . . 52"
MSRP. $9,228

RETAIL PRICING

YEAR	HIGH	LOW
2005	$5,785	$4,339

STWC52V 25KA

YEARS MFRD 2006-2010
SERIES. . . . . WILDCAT SERIES
ENGINE . . . . KAWASAKI
ENGINE HP 25
COOLING . . . . AIR
FUEL . . . . G
SPEEDS . . . . VARIABLE
TRANSMISSION . . . . HYDRO
STEERING. . . . . ZERO
STANDARD DECK . . . . 52"
MSRP. $9,990

OPTIONS

FROPS
LIGHTS
ROPS

RETAIL PRICING

YEAR	HIGH	LOW
2006	$3,224	$2,418
2007	$3,598	$2,698
2008	$3,975	$2,982
2009	$4,414	$3,310
2010	$4,901	$3,675

STWC52V 26FX

YEARS MFRD 2011-2011
ENGINE . . . . KAWASAKI
CYLINDERS. 2
ENGINE HP 26
COOLING . . . . AIR
FUEL . . . . G
SPEEDS . . . . VARIABLE
TRANSMISSION . . . . HYDRO
STEERING. . . . . ZERO
BLADE CLUTCH . . . . ELECTRIC
STANDARD DECK . . . . 52"
WEIGHT . . . . 1,120 LBS.
MSRP. $10,788

RETAIL PRICING

YEAR	HIGH	LOW
2011	$5,556	$4,167

STWC52V26 KALC

YEARS MFRD 2006-2011
SERIES. . . . . WILDCAT SERIES
ENGINE . . . . KAWASAKI
ENGINE HP 26
COOLING . . . . AIR
FUEL . . . . G
SPEEDS . . . . VARIABLE
TRANSMISSION . . . . HYDRO
STEERING. . . . . ZERO
STANDARD DECK . . . . 52"
MSRP. $10,853

RETAIL PRICING

YEAR	HIGH	LOW
2006	$2,111	$1,583
2007	$2,603	$1,952
2008	$3,474	$2,606
2009	$4,188	$3,141
2010	$4,576	$3,432
2011	$4,890	$3,668

STWC61A 27CV

YEARS MFRD 2006-2006
SERIES. . . . . WILDCAT SERIES
ENGINE . . . . KOHLER
CYLINDERS. 2
ENGINE HP 27
COOLING . . . . AIR
FUEL . . . . G
SPEEDS . . . . VARIABLE
TRANSMISSION . . . . GEAR
STEERING. . . . . ZERO
STANDARD DECK . . . . 61"
WEIGHT . . . . 1,160 LBS.
MSRP. $7,499

RETAIL PRICING

YEAR	HIGH	LOW
2006	$2,857	$2,143

STWC61V26 KALC

YEARS MFRD 2006-2011
SERIES. . . . . WILDCAT SERIES
ENGINE . . . . KAWASAKI
ENGINE HP 25
COOLING . . . . AIR
FUEL . . . . G
SPEEDS . . . . VARIABLE
TRANSMISSION . . . . HYDRO
STEERING. . . . . ZERO
STANDARD DECK . . . . 61"
MSRP. $9,269

OPTIONS

FROPS
LIGHTS
ROPS

RETAIL PRICING

YEAR	HIGH	LOW
2006	$2,958	$2,219
2007	$3,285	$2,463
2008	$3,646	$2,735
2009	$4,052	$3,039
2010	$4,499	$3,374
2011	$4,996	$3,747

STWC61V 27CV

YEARS MFRD 2006-2010
ENGINE . . . . KOHLER
CYLINDERS. 2
ENGINE HP 27
COOLING . . . . AIR
FUEL . . . . G
SPEEDS . . . . VARIABLE
TRANSMISSION . . . . HYDRO
STEERING. . . . . ZERO
BLADE CLUTCH . . . . ELECTRIC
STANDARD DECK . . . . 61"
MSRP. $10,300

OPTIONS

FROPS
LIGHTS
ROPS

RETAIL PRICING

YEAR	HIGH	LOW
2006	$3,324	$2,493
2007	$3,690	$2,767
2008	$4,097	$3,072
2009	$4,550	$3,413
2010	$5,053	$3,790

STZ5220KH

YEARS MFRD 1992-1993
SERIES. . . . . STZ SERIES
ENGINE . . . . KOHLER
ENGINE HP 20
FUEL . . . . G
SPEEDS . . . . VARIABLE
TRANSMISSION . . . . HYDRO
STEERING. . . . . STANDARD
STANDARD DECK . . . . 52"
WEIGHT . . . . 1,265 LBS.
MSRP. $7,795

RETAIL PRICING

YEAR	HIGH	LOW
1992	$2,690	$2,017
1993	$2,756	$2,067

STZ5220KHE

YEARS MFRD 1992-1993
SERIES. . . . . STZ SERIES
ENGINE . . . . KOHLER
ENGINE HP 20
COOLING . . . . AIR
FUEL . . . . G
SPEEDS . . . . VARIABLE
TRANSMISSION . . . . HYDRO
STEERING. . . . . ZERO
STANDARD DECK . . . . 52"
WEIGHT . . . . 1,150 LBS.
MSRP. $7,795

RETAIL PRICING

YEAR	HIGH	LOW
1992	$483	$362
1993	$534	$401

STZ6120KH

YEARS MFRD 1993-1993
SERIES. . . . . STZ SERIES
ENGINE . . . . KOHLER
ENGINE HP 20
FUEL . . . . G
SPEEDS . . . . VARIABLE
TRANSMISSION . . . . HYDRO
STEERING. . . . . STANDARD
STANDARD DECK . . . . 61"
MSRP. $7,995

RETAIL PRICING

YEAR	HIGH	LOW
1993	$547	$411

SVR36V20FK

YEARS MFRD 2010-2011
ENGINE . . . . KAWASAKI FX
CYLINDERS. 2
ENGINE HP 20
COOLING . . . . AIR
FUEL . . . . G
SPEEDS . . . . VARIABLE
TRANSMISSION . . . . HYDRO
STEERING. . . . . ZERO
STANDARD DECK . . . . 36"
WEIGHT . . . . 775 LBS.
MSRP. $7,486
COOLING . . . . AIR
FUEL . . . . G
SPEEDS . . . . VARIABLE
TRANSMISSION . . . . HYDRO
STEERING. . . . . ZERO
BLADE CLUTCH . . . . ELECTRIC
STANDARD DECK . . . . 61"
MSRP. $8,933

RETAIL PRICING

YEAR	HIGH	LOW
2011	$4,597	$3,447

OPTIONS

KAWASAKI 24HP
KAWASAKI 26HP

RETAIL PRICING

YEAR	HIGH	LOW
2010	$2,945	$2,209
2011	$3,853	$2,890

SVR48V24FK

YEARS MFRD 2010-2011
ENGINE . . . . KAWASAKI
CYLINDERS. 2
ENGINE HP 24
COOLING . . . . AIR
FUEL . . . . G
SPEEDS . . . . VARIABLE
TRANSMISSION . . . . HYDRO
STEERING. . . . . ZERO
BLADE CLUTCH . . . . ELECTRIC
STANDARD DECK . . . . 48"
WEIGHT . . . . 860 LBS.
MSRP. $8,332

RETAIL PRICING

YEAR	HIGH	LOW
2010	$3,281	$2,461
2011	$4,289	$3,217

SVR52V26FK

YEARS MFRD 2010-2011
ENGINE . . . . KAWASAKI
CYLINDERS. 2
ENGINE HP 26
COOLING . . . . AIR
FUEL . . . . G
SPEEDS . . . . VARIABLE
TRANSMISSION . . . . HYDRO
STEERING. . . . . ZERO
BLADE CLUTCH . . . . ELECTRIC
STANDARD DECK . . . . 52"
WEIGHT . . . . 860 LBS.
MSRP. $8,498

RETAIL PRICING

YEAR	HIGH	LOW
2010	$3,345	$2,509
2011	$4,376	$3,282

SVR61V29FX

YEARS MFRD 2011-2011
ENGINE . . . . KAWASAKI
CYLINDERS. 2
ENGINE HP 29

SVRII-32A-16FX

YEARS MFRD 2020-2020
SERIES. . . . . V-RIDE II SERIES
ENGINE . . . . KAWASAKI FX541
CYLINDERS. 2
ENGINE HP 16
COOLING . . . . AIR
FUEL . . . . G
SPEEDS . . . . VARIABLE
TRANSMISSION . . . . HYDRO
STEERING. . . . . ZERO
STANDARD DECK . . . . 32"
WEIGHT . . . . 818 LBS.
MSRP. $8,253

SVRII-36A-15FS

YEARS MFRD 2018-2019
SERIES. . . . . V-RIDE II SERIES
ENGINE . . . . KAWASAKI FS541V
CYLINDERS. 2
ENGINE HP 15
COOLING . . . . AIR
FUEL . . . . G
SPEEDS . . . . VARIABLE
TRANSMISSION . . . . . DUAL HYDRO
STEERING. . . . . ZERO
STANDARD DECK . . . . 36"
MSRP. $7,407

SVRII-36A-19FX

YEARS MFRD 2018-2020
SERIES. . . . . V-RIDE II SERIES
ENGINE . . . . KAWASAKI FX600V
CYLINDERS. 2
ENGINE HP 19
COOLING . . . . AIR
FUEL . . . . G
SPEEDS . . . . VARIABLE
TRANSMISSION . . . . . DUAL HYDRO
STEERING. . . . . ZERO
STANDARD DECK . . . . 36"
MSRP. $8,554

SVRII-48V-22FX

YEARS MFRD 2018-2020
SERIES. . . . . V-RIDE II SERIES
ENGINE . . . . . . KAWASAKI FX691V
CYLINDERS. 2
ENGINE HP 22
COOLING . . . . AIR
FUEL . . . . G
SPEEDS . . . . VARIABLE
TRANSMISSION . . . . . DUAL HYDRO
STEERING. . . . . ZERO
STANDARD DECK . . . . 48"
MSRP. $9,512

SVRII-52V-23FX

YEARS MFRD 2018-2020
SERIES. . . . . V-RIDE II SERIES
ENGINE . . . . . . KAWASAKI FX730V
CYLINDERS. 2
ENGINE HP 23
COOLING . . . . AIR
FUEL . . . . G
SPEEDS . . . . VARIABLE
TRANSMISSION . . . . . DUAL HYDRO
STEERING. . . . . ZERO
STANDARD DECK . . . . 52"
MSRP. $9,777

SVRII-52V-25CV-EFI

YEARS MFRD 2018-2020
SERIES. . . . . V-RIDE II SERIES
ENGINE . . KOHLER COMMAND PRO
CYLINDERS. 2
ENGINE HP 25
COOLING . . . . AIR
FUEL . . . . G
SPEEDS . . . . VARIABLE
TRANSMISSION . . . . . DUAL HYDRO
STEERING. . . . . ZERO
STANDARD DECK . . . . 52"
MSRP. $9,997

SVRII-61V-25FX

YEARS MFRD 2018-2020
SERIES. . . . . V-RIDE II SERIES
ENGINE . . . . KAWASAKI FX801V
CYLINDERS. 2
ENGINE HP 25
COOLING . . . . AIR
FUEL . . . . G
SPEEDS . . . . VARIABLE
TRANSMISSION . . . . . DUAL HYDRO
STEERING. . . . . ZERO
STANDARD DECK . . . . 61"
MSRP. $10,199

SVRII-61V-29CV-EFI

YEARS MFRD 2018-2020
SERIES. . . . . V-RIDE II SERIES
ENGINE . . . KOHLER COMMAND PRO
CYLINDERS. 2
ENGINE HP 29
COOLING . . . . AIR
FUEL . . . . G
SPEEDS . . . . VARIABLE
TRANSMISSION . . . . . DUAL HYDRO
STEERING. . . . . ZERO
STANDARD DECK . . . . 61"
MSRP. $10,465

SVRII-61V-37BV-EFI

YEARS MFRD 2020-2020
SERIES. . . . . V-RIDE II SERIES
ENGINE . . . . . . BRIGGS VANGUARD
ENGINE HP 37
COOLING . . . . AIR
FUEL . . . . G
SPEEDS . . . . VARIABLE
TRANSMISSION . . . . HYDRO
STEERING. . . . . ZERO
STANDARD DECK . . . . 61"
WEIGHT . . . . 1,145 LBS.
MSRP. $11,547

SW36A14KA

YEARS MFRD 2000-2001
SERIES. . . . . SW SERIES
ENGINE . . . . KAWASAKI
CYLINDERS. 1
ENGINE HP 14
COOLING . . . . AIR
FUEL . . . . G
TRANSMISSION . . . . GEAR
STEERING. . . . . STANDARD
STANDARD DECK . . . . 36"
MSRP. $2,839

RETAIL PRICING

YEAR	HIGH	LOW
2001	$1,413	$1,060

SW48A14KA

YEARS MFRD 2000-2001
SERIES. . . . . SW SERIES
ENGINE . . . . KAWASAKI
CYLINDERS. 1
ENGINE HP 14
COOLING . . . . AIR
FUEL . . . . G
TRANSMISSION . . . . GEAR
STEERING. . . . . ZERO
STANDARD DECK . . . . 48"
MSRP. $2,999

RETAIL PRICING

YEAR	HIGH	LOW
2001	$1,493	$1,120

SCAG

SW52A17KA

YEARS MFRD 2000-2001
SERIES. . . . . SW SERIES
ENGINE . . . . KAWASAKI
ENGINE HP 17
FUEL . . . . G
TRANSMISSION . . . . GEAR
STEERING. . . . . ZERO
STANDARD DECK . . . . 52"
MSRP. $3,499

RETAIL PRICING

YEAR	HIGH	LOW
2000	$1,651	$1,239
2001	$1,744	$1,308

SW3213KA

YEARS MFRD 1992-2001
SERIES. . . . . SW SERIES
ENGINE . . . . KAWASAKI
ENGINE HP 12.5
COOLING . . . . AIR
FUEL . . . . G
TRANSMISSION . . . . GEAR
STEERING. . . . . ZERO
STANDARD DECK . . . . 32"
MSRP. $2,699

RETAIL PRICING

YEAR	HIGH	LOW
1993	$929	$697
1994	$985	$739
1995	$1,021	$766
1996	$1,057	$793
1997	$1,097	$823
1998	$1,154	$866
1999	$1,231	$923
2000	$1,289	$967
2001	$1,343	$1,007

SW3613KA

YEARS MFRD 1987-2001
SERIES. . . . . SW SERIES
ENGINE . . . . KAWASAKI
ENGINE HP 12.5
COOLING . . . . AIR
FUEL . . . . G
TRANSMISSION . . . . GEAR
STEERING. . . . . ZERO
STANDARD DECK . . . . 36"
MSRP. $2,699

RETAIL PRICING

YEAR	HIGH	LOW
2001	$1,343	$1,007

SW3614KH

YEARS MFRD 1989-1991
SERIES. . . . . SW SERIES
ENGINE . . . . KOHLER
CYLINDERS. 1
ENGINE HP 14
COOLING . . . . AIR
FUEL . . . . G
TRANSMISSION . . . . BELT
STEERING. . . . . STANDARD
STANDARD DECK . . . . 36"
MSRP. $3,070

RETAIL PRICING

YEAR	HIGH	LOW
1991	$987	$740

SW4813KA

YEARS MFRD 1986-1990
SERIES. . . . . SW SERIES
ENGINE . . . . KAWASAKI
CYLINDERS. 1
ENGINE HP 12.5
COOLING . . . . AIR
FUEL . . . . G
TRANSMISSION . . . . GEAR
STEERING. . . . . ZERO
STANDARD DECK . . . . 48"
MSRP. $2,975

RETAIL PRICING

YEAR	HIGH	LOW
1990	$896	$672

SW4814KA

YEARS MFRD 1989-1997
SERIES. . . . . SW SERIES
ENGINE . . . . KAWASAKI
CYLINDERS. 1
ENGINE HP 14
COOLING . . . . AIR
FUEL . . . . G
TRANSMISSION . . . . GEAR
STEERING. . . . . ZERO
STANDARD DECK . . . . 48"
MSRP. $2,899

RETAIL PRICING

YEAR	HIGH	LOW
1997	$1,179	$884

SW4815KH

YEARS MFRD 1999-2001
SERIES. . . . . SW SERIES
ENGINE . . . . KOHLER
ENGINE HP 15
FUEL . . . . G
TRANSMISSION . . . . BELT
STEERING. . . . . ZERO
STANDARD DECK . . . . 48"
MSRP. $2,999

RETAIL PRICING

YEAR	HIGH	LOW
1999	$1,492	$1,119
2000	$1,581	$1,185
2001	$1,629	$1,222

SW4817KA

YEARS MFRD 1998-2001
SERIES. . . . . SW SERIES
ENGINE . . . . KAWASAKI
ENGINE HP 17
FUEL . . . . G
TRANSMISSION . . . . BELT
STEERING. . . . . ZERO
STANDARD DECK . . . . 48"
MSRP. $3,299

RETAIL PRICING

YEAR	HIGH	LOW
1998	$1,450	$1,088
1999	$1,584	$1,188
2000	$1,677	$1,257
2001	$1,683	$1,262

SW5214KA

YEARS MFRD 1991-1996
SERIES. . . . . SW SERIES
ENGINE . . . . KAWASAKI
CYLINDERS. 1
ENGINE HP 14
COOLING . . . . AIR
FUEL . . . . G
TRANSMISSION . . . . GEAR
STEERING. . . . . ZERO
STANDARD DECK . . . . 52"
MSRP. $3,940

RETAIL PRICING

YEAR	HIGH	LOW
1996	$1,546	$1,160

SW5216BV

YEARS MFRD 1993-1997
SERIES. . . . . SW SERIES
ENGINE . . . . B&S
ENGINE HP 16
COOLING . . . . AIR
FUEL . . . . G
TRANSMISSION . . . . BELT
STEERING. . . . . ZERO
STANDARD DECK . . . . 52"
WEIGHT . . . . 605 LBS.
MSRP. $4,080

RETAIL PRICING

YEAR	HIGH	LOW
1993	$1,338	$1,004
1994	$1,432	$1,074
1995	$1,508	$1,131
1996	$1,581	$1,185
1997	$1,659	$1,245

SW5218CVE

YEARS MFRD 1996-1997
SERIES. . . . . SW SERIES
ENGINE . . . . KOHLER
ENGINE HP 18
FUEL . . . . G
TRANSMISSION . . . . BELT
STEERING. . . . . ZERO
STANDARD DECK . . . . 52"
MSRP. $4,575

RETAIL PRICING

YEAR	HIGH	LOW
1996	$1,753	$1,315
1997	$1,862	$1,397

SW5220KHE

YEARS MFRD 1988-1991
SERIES. . . . . SW SERIES
ENGINE . . . . KOHLER
ENGINE HP 20
COOLING . . . . AIR
FUEL . . . . G
TRANSMISSION . . . . BELT
STEERING. . . . . ZERO
STANDARD DECK . . . . 52"
MSRP. $4,270

RETAIL PRICING

YEAR	HIGH	LOW
1990	$1,268	$951
1991	$1,373	$1,029

SW6116BV

YEARS MFRD 1995-1997
SERIES. . . . . SW SERIES
ENGINE . . . . B&S
ENGINE HP 16
COOLING . . . . AIR
FUEL . . . . G
TRANSMISSION . . . . BELT
STEERING. . . . . ZERO
STANDARD DECK . . . . 61"
MSRP. $4,325

RETAIL PRICING

YEAR	HIGH	LOW
1995	$1,617	$1,213
1996	$1,715	$1,286
1997	$1,758	$1,319

SW6118BV

YEARS MFRD 1995-1997
SERIES. . . . . SW SERIES
ENGINE . . . . B&S
ENGINE HP 18
COOLING . . . . AIR
FUEL . . . . G
TRANSMISSION . . . . BELT
STEERING. . . . . ZERO
STANDARD DECK . . . . 61"
MSRP. $4,660

RETAIL PRICING

YEAR	HIGH	LOW
1995	$1,717	$1,288
1996	$1,805	$1,354
1997	$1,897	$1,423

SW6118CVE

YEARS MFRD 1997-1997
SERIES. . . . . SW SERIES
ENGINE . . . . KOHLER
ENGINE HP 18
FUEL . . . . G
TRANSMISSION . . . . BELT
STEERING. . . . . ZERO
STANDARD DECK . . . . 61"
MSRP. $4,870

RETAIL PRICING

YEAR	HIGH	LOW
1997	$1,980	$1,485

SW6120KHE

YEARS MFRD 1988-1991
SERIES. . . . . SW SERIES
ENGINE . . . . KOHLER

ENGINE HP 20
COOLING . . . . . AIR
FUEL . . . . . G
TRANSMISSION . . . . . BELT
STEERING . . . . . ZERO
STANDARD DECK . . . . . 61"
WEIGHT . . . . . 705 LBS.
MSRP $4,500

RETAIL PRICING

YEAR	HIGH	LOW
1990	$1,324	$993
1991	$1,447	$1,085

SW7218CVE

YEARS MFRD 1989-1997
SERIES . . . . . SW SERIES
ENGINE . . . . . KOHLER
ENGINE HP 18
COOLING . . . . . AIR
FUEL . . . . . G
TRANSMISSION . . . . . BELT
STEERING . . . . . ZERO
STANDARD DECK . . . . . 72"
MSRP $5,035

RETAIL PRICING

YEAR	HIGH	LOW
1997	$2,047	$1,535

SW7220KHE

YEARS MFRD 1988-1991
SERIES . . . . . SW SERIES
ENGINE . . . . . KOHLER
ENGINE HP 20
COOLING . . . . . AIR
FUEL . . . . . G
TRANSMISSION . . . . . BELT
STEERING . . . . . ZERO
STANDARD DECK . . . . . 72"
MSRP $4,670

RETAIL PRICING

YEAR	HIGH	LOW
1991	$1,502	$1,126

SWU36A15KA

YEARS MFRD 2000-2001
SERIES . . . . . SWU SERIES
ENGINE . . . . . KAWASAKI
ENGINE HP 15
FUEL . . . . . G
TRANSMISSION . . . . . BELT
STEERING . . . . . ZERO
STANDARD DECK . . . . . 36"
MSRP $3,350

RETAIL PRICING

YEAR	HIGH	LOW
2000	$1,528	$1,146
2001	$1,668	$1,251

SWU48A17KA

YEARS MFRD 2000-2001
SERIES . . . . . SWU SERIES
ENGINE . . . . . KAWASAKI
CYLINDERS 1
ENGINE HP 17
COOLING . . . . . LIQUID
FUEL . . . . . G
TRANSMISSION . . . . . GEAR
STEERING . . . . . ZERO
STANDARD DECK . . . . . 48"
MSRP $3,599

RETAIL PRICING

YEAR	HIGH	LOW
2001	$1,793	$1,345

SWU3615KH

YEARS MFRD 1999-2000
SERIES . . . . . SWU SERIES
ENGINE . . . . . KOHLER
ENGINE HP 15
FUEL . . . . . G
TRANSMISSION . . . . . GEAR
STEERING . . . . . ZERO
STANDARD DECK . . . . . 36"
MSRP $3,199

RETAIL PRICING

YEAR	HIGH	LOW
2000	$1,528	$1,146

SWZ20CVE52A

YEARS MFRD 2000-2000
SERIES . . . . . SWZ SERIES
ENGINE . . . . . KOHLER
ENGINE HP 20
COOLING . . . . . AIR
FUEL . . . . . G
STEERING . . . . . ZERO
STANDARD DECK . . . . . 52"
MSRP $6,049

RETAIL PRICING

YEAR	HIGH	LOW
2000	$2,890	$2,167

SWZ21KAE 52A

YEARS MFRD 2000-2000
SERIES . . . . . SWZ SERIES
ENGINE . . . . . KAWASAKI
ENGINE HP 21
COOLING . . . . . AIR
FUEL . . . . . G
STEERING . . . . . ZERO
STANDARD DECK . . . . . 52"
MSRP $6,139

RETAIL PRICING

YEAR	HIGH	LOW
2000	$2,933	$2,200

SWZ52A17KA

YEARS MFRD 2000-2001
SERIES . . . . . SWZ SERIES
ENGINE . . . . . KAWASAKI
ENGINE HP 17
FUEL . . . . . G
STEERING . . . . . ZERO
STANDARD DECK . . . . . 52"
MSRP $5,189

RETAIL PRICING

YEAR	HIGH	LOW
2000	$2,453	$1,840
2001	$2,586	$1,939

SWZ52A20CVE

YEARS MFRD 2000-2000
SERIES . . . . . SWZ SERIES
ENGINE . . . . . KOHLER
ENGINE HP 20
FUEL . . . . . G
STEERING . . . . . ZERO
STANDARD DECK . . . . . 52"
MSRP $6,049

RETAIL PRICING

YEAR	HIGH	LOW
2000	$2,890	$2,167

SWZ52A21 KAE

YEARS MFRD 2000-2001
SERIES . . . . . SWZ SERIES
ENGINE . . . . . KAWASAKI
ENGINE HP 21
FUEL . . . . . G
STEERING . . . . . ZERO
STANDARD DECK . . . . . 52"
MSRP $6,189

RETAIL PRICING

YEAR	HIGH	LOW
2000	$2,933	$2,200
2001	$3,083	$2,312

SWZ3213KA

YEARS MFRD 1993-1995
SERIES . . . . . SWZ SERIES
ENGINE . . . . . KAWASAKI
ENGINE HP 13
COOLING . . . . . AIR
FUEL . . . . . G
SPEEDS . . . . . VARIABLE
TRANSMISSION . . . . . HYDRO
STEERING . . . . . ZERO
STANDARD DECK . . . . . 32"
MSRP $3,890

RETAIL PRICING

YEAR	HIGH	LOW
1993	$1,341	$1,006
1994	$1,417	$1,063
1995	$1,472	$1,104

SWZ3614KA

YEARS MFRD 1990-2001
SERIES . . . . . SWZ SERIES
ENGINE . . . . . KAWASAKI
ENGINE HP 14
COOLING . . . . . AIR
FUEL . . . . . G
SPEEDS . . . . . VARIABLE
TRANSMISSION . . . . . HYDRO
STEERING . . . . . STANDARD
STANDARD DECK . . . . . 36"
MSRP $4,529

RETAIL PRICING

YEAR	HIGH	LOW
2001	$2,255	$1,691

SWZ3615KA

YEARS MFRD 1999-1999
SERIES . . . . . SWZ SERIES
ENGINE . . . . . KAWASAKI
ENGINE HP 15
FUEL . . . . . G
STEERING . . . . . ZERO
STANDARD DECK . . . . . 36"
MSRP $4,479

RETAIL PRICING

YEAR	HIGH	LOW
1999	$2,041	$1,531

SWZ3615KH

YEARS MFRD 1999-2000
SERIES . . . . . SWZ SERIES
ENGINE . . . . . KOHLER
ENGINE HP 15
FUEL . . . . . G
STEERING . . . . . ZERO
STANDARD DECK . . . . . 36"
MSRP $4,529

RETAIL PRICING

YEAR	HIGH	LOW
1999	$2,180	$1,635
2000	$2,231	$1,673

SWZ4814KA

YEARS MFRD 1990-2000
SERIES . . . . . SWZ SERIES
ENGINE . . . . . KAWASAKI
CYLINDERS 1
ENGINE HP 14
COOLING . . . . . AIR
FUEL . . . . . G
SPEEDS . . . . . VARIABLE
TRANSMISSION . . . . . HYDRO
STEERING . . . . . ZERO
STANDARD DECK . . . . . 48"
MSRP $4,669

RETAIL PRICING

YEAR	HIGH	LOW
2000	$2,231	$1,673

SWZ4815KH

YEARS MFRD 1999-2000
SERIES . . . . . SWZ SERIES
ENGINE . . . . . KOHLER
ENGINE HP 15
FUEL . . . . . G
STEERING . . . . . ZERO
STANDARD DECK . . . . . 48"
MSRP $4,669

RETAIL PRICING

YEAR	HIGH	LOW
1999	$2,127	$1,595
2000	$2,231	$1,673

SCAG

SWZ4816BV

YEARS MFRD	1997-1998
SERIES	SWZ SERIES
ENGINE	B&S
ENGINE HP	16
FUEL	G
STEERING	ZERO
STANDARD DECK	48"
MSRP	$4,945

RETAIL PRICING

YEAR	HIGH	LOW
1997	$2,031	$1,523
1998	$2,111	$1,583

SWZ4817KA

YEARS MFRD	1998-2001
SERIES	SWZ SERIES
ENGINE	KAWASAKI
ENGINE HP	17
FUEL	G
STEERING	ZERO
STANDARD DECK	48"
MSRP	$4,799

RETAIL PRICING

YEAR	HIGH	LOW
1998	$2,134	$1,601
1999	$2,310	$1,732
2000	$2,446	$1,835
2001	$2,457	$1,843

SWZ5214KA

YEARS MFRD	1990-1997
SERIES	SWZ SERIES
ENGINE	KAWASAKI
CYLINDERS	1
ENGINE HP	14
COOLING	AIR
FUEL	G
SPEEDS	VARAIBLE
TRANSMISSION	HYDRO
STEERING	ZERO
STANDARD DECK	52"
MSRP	$4,930

RETAIL PRICING

YEAR	HIGH	LOW
1997	$2,005	$1,504

SWZ5216BV

YEARS MFRD	1993-1997
SERIES	SWZ SERIES
ENGINE	B&S
ENGINE HP	16
COOLING	AIR
FUEL	G
STEERING	ZERO
STANDARD DECK	52"
WEIGHT	705 LBS.
MSRP	$5,160

RETAIL PRICING

YEAR	HIGH	LOW
1993	$1,619	$1,214
1994	$1,747	$1,310
1995	$1,891	$1,418
1996	$2,022	$1,517
1997	$2,099	$1,574

SWZ5217KA

YEARS MFRD	1999-2001
SERIES	SWZ SERIES
ENGINE	KAWASAKI
ENGINE HP	17
FUEL	G
STEERING	ZERO
STANDARD DECK	52"
MSRP	$4,989

RETAIL PRICING

YEAR	HIGH	LOW
1999	$2,229	$1,672
2000	$2,288	$1,716
2001	$2,486	$1,864

SWZ5218BV

YEARS MFRD	1996-1998
SERIES	SWZ SERIES
ENGINE	B&S
ENGINE HP	18
COOLING	AIR
FUEL	G
STEERING	ZERO
STANDARD DECK	52"
MSRP	$5,560

RETAIL PRICING

YEAR	HIGH	LOW
1996	$2,141	$1,606
1997	$2,241	$1,681
1998	$2,376	$1,782

SWZ5218KH

YEARS MFRD	1989-1992
SERIES	SWZ SERIES
ENGINE	KOHLER
ENGINE HP	18
COOLING	AIR
FUEL	G
TRANSMISSION	HYDRO
STEERING	ZERO
STANDARD DECK	52"
WEIGHT	790 LBS.
MSRP	$4,699

RETAIL PRICING

YEAR	HIGH	LOW
1990	$1,385	$1,039
1991	$1,493	$1,120
1992	$1,573	$1,179

SWZ5220CVE

YEARS MFRD	1989-1999
SERIES	SWZ SERIES
ENGINE	KOHLER
ENGINE HP	20
COOLING	AIR
FUEL	G
TRANSMISSION	HYDRO
STEERING	ZERO
STANDARD DECK	52"
MSRP	$5,950

RETAIL PRICING

YEAR	HIGH	LOW
1990	$1,656	$1,242
1991	$1,800	$1,350
1992	$1,891	$1,418
1993	$1,964	$1,473
1994	$2,096	$1,572
1995	$2,197	$1,648
1996	$2,296	$1,722
1997	$2,380	$1,785
1998	$2,521	$1,891
1999	$2,711	$2,033

SWZ6116BV

YEARS MFRD	1993-1994
SERIES	SWZ SERIES
ENGINE	B&S
ENGINE HP	16
COOLING	AIR
FUEL	G
STEERING	ZERO
STANDARD DECK	61"
MSRP	$4,825

RETAIL PRICING

YEAR	HIGH	LOW
1993	$1,629	$1,222
1994	$1,758	$1,319

SWZ6118BV

YEARS MFRD	1995-1997
SERIES	SWZ SERIES
ENGINE	B&S
ENGINE HP	18
COOLING	AIR
FUEL	G
STEERING	ZERO
STANDARD DECK	61"
MSRP	$5,805

RETAIL PRICING

YEAR	HIGH	LOW
1995	$2,121	$1,591
1996	$2,237	$1,678
1997	$2,359	$1,770

SWZ6118KH

YEARS MFRD	1989-1992
SERIES	SWZ SERIES
ENGINE	KOHLER
ENGINE HP	18
COOLING	AIR
FUEL	G
STEERING	ZERO
STANDARD DECK	61"
WEIGHT	810 LBS.
MSRP	$4,955

RETAIL PRICING

YEAR	HIGH	LOW
1990	$1,460	$1,095
1991	$1,577	$1,182
1992	$1,658	$1,244

SWZ6120CVE

YEARS MFRD	1989-1999
SERIES	SWZ SERIES
ENGINE	KOHLER
ENGINE HP	20
COOLING	AIR
FUEL	G
STEERING	ZERO
STANDARD DECK	61"
MSRP	$6,150

RETAIL PRICING

YEAR	HIGH	LOW
1990	$1,717	$1,288
1991	$1,849	$1,387
1992	$1,940	$1,455
1993	$2,019	$1,514
1994	$2,150	$1,613
1995	$2,252	$1,689
1996	$2,352	$1,764
1997	$2,460	$1,845
1998	$2,607	$1,955
1999	$2,803	$2,102

SWZ7218KH

YEARS MFRD	1989-1992
SERIES	SWZ SERIES
ENGINE	KOHLER
ENGINE HP	18
COOLING	AIR
FUEL	G
STEERING	ZERO
STANDARD DECK	72"
MSRP	$5,125

RETAIL PRICING

YEAR	HIGH	LOW
1990	$1,508	$1,131
1991	$1,630	$1,223
1992	$1,714	$1,285

SWZ7220CVE

YEARS MFRD	1995-1999
SERIES	SWZ SERIES
ENGINE	KOHLER
ENGINE HP	20
COOLING	AIR
FUEL	G
STEERING	ZERO
STANDARD DECK	72"
MSRP	$6,349

RETAIL PRICING

YEAR	HIGH	LOW
1999	$2,893	$2,169

SWZL52A17KA

YEARS MFRD	2001-2001
SERIES	SWZL SERIES
ENGINE	KAWASAKI
CYLINDERS	1
ENGINE HP	17
COOLING	AIR
FUEL	G
SPEEDS	VARIABLE
TRANSMISSION	HYDRO
STEERING	ZERO
STANDARD DECK	52"
MSRP	$5,139

RETAIL PRICING

YEAR	HIGH	LOW
2001	$2,559	$1,920

SWZU21KAE 52

YEARS MFRD 2000-2000
SERIES .... SWZ SERIES
ENGINE .... KAWASAKI
ENGINE HP 21
COOLING .... AIR
FUEL .... G
STEERING .... ZERO
STANDARD DECK .... 52"
MSRP $6,719

RETAIL PRICING

YEAR	HIGH	LOW
2000	$3,209	$2,407

SWZU48A 17KA

YEARS MFRD 2000-2001
SERIES .... SWZU SERIES
ENGINE .... KAWASAKI
ENGINE HP 17
FUEL .... G
STEERING .... ZERO
STANDARD DECK .... 48"
MSRP $4,999

RETAIL PRICING

YEAR	HIGH	LOW
2000	$2,293	$1,720
2001	$2,491	$1,868

SWZU52A 17KA

YEARS MFRD 2001-2001
SERIES .... SWZU SERIES
ENGINE .... KAWASAKI
ENGINE HP 17
FUEL .... G
STEERING .... ZERO
STANDARD DECK .... 52"
MSRP $5,139

RETAIL PRICING

YEAR	HIGH	LOW
2001	$2,559	$1,920

SWZU52A 21KA

YEARS MFRD 2001-2001
SERIES .... SWZU SERIES
ENGINE .... KAWASAKI
ENGINE HP 21
FUEL .... G
TRANSMISSION .... HYDRO
STEERING .... ZERO
STANDARD DECK .... 52"
MSRP $6,719

RETAIL PRICING

YEAR	HIGH	LOW
2001	$3,346	$2,510

SWZU3615KH

YEARS MFRD 1999-2000
SERIES .... SWZU SERIES
ENGINE .... KOHLER
ENGINE HP 15
FUEL .... G
STEERING .... ZERO
STANDARD DECK .... 36"
MSRP $4,799

RETAIL PRICING

YEAR	HIGH	LOW
1999	$2,189	$1,642
2000	$2,293	$1,720

SWZU5221 KAE

YEARS MFRD 2000-2000
SERIES .... SWZU SERIES
ENGINE .... KAWASAKI
ENGINE HP 21
FUEL .... G
STEERING .... ZERO
STANDARD DECK .... 52"
MSRP $6,719

RETAIL PRICING

YEAR	HIGH	LOW
2000	$3,209	$2,407

SYG4814KH

YEARS MFRD 1990-1992
SERIES .... SYG SERIES
ENGINE .... KOHLER
CYLINDERS 1
ENGINE HP 14
COOLING .... AIR
FUEL .... G
TRANSMISSION .... GEAR
STEERING .... STANDARD
STANDARD DECK .... 48"
MSRP $5,150

RETAIL PRICING

YEAR	HIGH	LOW
1992	$1,722	$1,292

SZC36A16HN

YEARS MFRD 2006-2006
SERIES .... Z-CAT SERIES
ENGINE .... HONDA
ENGINE HP 16
COOLING .... AIR
FUEL .... G
SPEEDS .... VARIABLE
TRANSMISSION .... HYDRO
STEERING .... ZERO
STANDARD DECK .... 36"
MSRP $5,899

OPTIONS

FROPS
LIGHTS

RETAIL PRICING

YEAR	HIGH	LOW
2006	$2,018	$1,513

SZC36A17KA

YEARS MFRD 2005-2006
SERIES .... Z-CAT SERIES
ENGINE .... KAWASAKI
CYLINDERS 2
ENGINE HP 17
COOLING .... AIR
FUEL .... G
SPEEDS .... VARIABLE
TRANSMISSION .... HYDRO
STEERING .... ZERO
STANDARD DECK .... 36"
WEIGHT .... 883 LBS.
MSRP $5,899

RETAIL PRICING

YEAR	HIGH	LOW
2005	$1,937	$1,453
2006	$2,154	$1,616

SZC36A19KA

YEARS MFRD 2005-2007
SERIES .... Z-CAT SERIES
ENGINE .... KAWASAKI
ENGINE HP 19
COOLING .... AIR
FUEL .... G
SPEEDS .... VARIABLE
TRANSMISSION .... HYDRO
STEERING .... ZERO
STANDARD DECK .... 36"
MSRP $6,299

OPTIONS

FROPS
LIGHTS

RETAIL PRICING

YEAR	HIGH	LOW
2005	$1,961	$1,471
2006	$2,180	$1,635
2007	$2,420	$1,815

SZC42A19KA

YEARS MFRD 2005-2006
SERIES .... Z-CAT SERIES
ENGINE .... KAWASAKI
CYLINDERS 2
ENGINE HP 19
COOLING .... AIR
FUEL .... G
SPEEDS .... VARIABLE
TRANSMISSION .... HYDRO
STEERING .... ZERO
BLADE CLUTCH .... ELECTRIC
STANDARD DECK .... 42"
MSRP $6,648

RETAIL PRICING

YEAR	HIGH	LOW
2005	$4,043	$3,032
2006	$4,405	$3,303

SZL36-18FR

YEARS MFRD 2017-2020
SERIES .... LIBERTY Z SERIES
ENGINE .... KAWASAKI FR600
CID 603CC
ENGINE HP 18
COOLING .... AIR
FUEL .... G
TRANSMISSION .... HYDRO
STEERING .... ZERO
STANDARD DECK .... 36"
WEIGHT .... 555 LBS.
MSRP $4,783

SZL48-18FR

YEARS MFRD 2017-2018
SERIES .... LIBERTY Z SERIES
ENGINE .... KAWASAKI FR600
CID 603CC
ENGINE HP 18
COOLING .... AIR
FUEL .... G
TRANSMISSION .... HYDRO
STEERING .... ZERO
STANDARD DECK .... 48"

SZL48-21FR

YEARS MFRD 2018-2020
SERIES .... LIBERTY Z SERIES
ENGINE .... KAWASAKI FR651
CID 726CC
ENGINE HP 21
COOLING .... AIR
FUEL .... G
TRANSMISSION .... HYDRO
STEERING .... ZERO
STANDARD DECK .... 48"
MSRP $5,042

SZL48-22KT

YEARS MFRD 2016-2017
SERIES .... LIBERTY Z SERIES
ENGINE . KOHLER 7000 SERIES PRO
CID 725CC
COOLING .... AIR
FUEL .... G
SPEEDS .... VARIABLE
TRANSMISSION .... HYDRO
STEERING .... ZERO
WEIGHT .... 610 LBS.

SZL52-21FR

YEARS MFRD 2017-2018
SERIES .... LIBERTY Z SERIES
ENGINE .... KAWASAKI FR651
CID 726CC
ENGINE HP 21
COOLING .... AIR
FUEL .... G
TRANSMISSION .... HYDRO
STEERING .... ZERO
STANDARD DECK .... 52"

SZL52-23FR

YEARS MFRD 2018-2020
SERIES .... LIBERTY Z SERIES
ENGINE .... KAWASAKI FR691
CID 726CC

SCAG

ENGINE HP 23
COOLING .... AIR
FUEL .... G
TRANSMISSION .... HYDRO
STEERING .... ZERO
STANDARD DECK .... 52"
MSRP $5,249

SZL52-24KT

YEARS MFRD 2016-2017
SERIES .... LIBERTY Z SERIES
ENGINE . KOHLER 7000 SERIES PRO
CID 725CC
COOLING .... AIR
FUEL .... G
SPEEDS .... VARIABLE
TRANSMISSION .... HYDRO
STEERING .... ZERO
WEIGHT .... 640 LBS.

SZL61-26KT

YEARS MFRD 2018-2020
SERIES .... LIBERTY Z SERIES
ENGINE .... KOHLER
CYLINDERS 2
ENGINE HP 26
COOLING .... AIR
FUEL .... G
SPEEDS .... VARIABLE
TRANSMISSION .... HYDRO
STEERING .... ZERO
BLADE CLUTCH .... ELECTRIC
STANDARD DECK .... 61"
MSRP $5,923

TIGER CAT

YEARS MFRD 2009-2010
ENGINE .... KAWASAKI
CYLINDERS 2
ENGINE HP 19
COOLING .... AIR
FUEL .... G
SPEEDS .... VARIABLE
TRANSMISSION .... HYDRO
STEERING .... ZERO
BLADE CLUTCH .... ELECTRIC
WEIGHT .... 1,100 LBS.
MSRP $7,595

OPTIONS

B&S 26HP
KOHLER 23HP
KOHLER 25HP

RETAIL PRICING

YEAR	HIGH	LOW
2009	$4,303	$3,227
2010	$4,812	$3,609

AVG. AUCTION PRICING

LOW	HIGH	AVG
$1,616	$3,636	$3,018

TIGER CUB

YEARS MFRD 2006-2008
ENGINE .... KAWASAKI
CYLINDERS 2
ENGINE HP 19
COOLING .... AIR
FUEL .... G
SPEEDS .... VARIABLE
TRANSMISSION .... HYDRO
STEERING .... ZERO
BLADE CLUTCH .... ELECTRIC
WEIGHT .... 1,038 LBS.

OPTIONS

B&S 26HP
KOHLER 23HP
KOHLER 25HP

AVG. AUCTION PRICING

LOW	HIGH	AVG
$1,100	$2,650	$2,010

TURF TIGER

YEARS MFRD 2006-2010
ENGINE .... KUBOTA
CYLINDERS 3
ENGINE HP 25
COOLING .... LIQUID
FUEL .... D
SPEEDS .... VARIABLE
TRANSMISSION .... HYDRO
STEERING .... ZERO
BLADE CLUTCH .... ELECTRIC
WEIGHT .... 1,275 LBS.
MSRP $10,840

OPTIONS

CAT 28HP LIQUID
KAWASAKI 27HP LIQUID
KAWASAKI 29HP LIQUID
KOHLER 27HP AIR
KOHLER 31HP LIQUID

RETAIL PRICING

YEAR	HIGH	LOW
2008	$6,898	$5,174
2009	$6,965	$5,224
2010	$7,080	$5,310

AVG. AUCTION PRICING

LOW	HIGH	AVG
$1,818	$3,333	$2,769

TURF TIGER

YEARS MFRD 2009-2009
SERIES .... DUAL FUEL SERIES
ENGINE .... KUBOTA
CYLINDERS 3
ENGINE HP 29
FUEL .... G
SPEEDS .... VARIABLE
TRANSMISSION .... HYDRO
STEERING .... ZERO
BLADE CLUTCH .... ELECTRIC
WEIGHT .... 1,540 LBS.

WILDCAT

YEARS MFRD 2006-2010
ENGINE .... KAWASAKI
CYLINDERS 2
ENGINE HP 25
COOLING .... AIR
FUEL .... G
SPEEDS .... VARIABLE
TRANSMISSION .... HYDRO
STEERING .... ZERO
BLADE CLUTCH .... ELECTRIC
WEIGHT .... 52 LBS.
MSRP $10,625

OPTIONS

KAWASAKI 26HP
KOHLER 27HP
KOHLER 30HP

RETAIL PRICING

YEAR	HIGH	LOW
2008	$5,608	$4,206
2009	$6,169	$4,627
2010	$6,731	$5,048

Z CAT

YEARS MFRD 2007-2008
ENGINE .... HONDA
CYLINDERS 2
ENGINE HP 16
COOLING .... AIR
FUEL .... G
SPEEDS .... VARIABLE
TRANSMISSION .... HYDRO
STEERING .... ZERO
BLADE CLUTCH .... ELECTRIC
STANDARD DECK .... 36"
WEIGHT .... 850 LBS.
MSRP $6,423

OPTIONS

42" DECK
KAWASAKI 17HP
KAWASAKI 19HP

RETAIL PRICING

YEAR	HIGH	LOW
2008	$4,047	$3,035

SCHWEISS

ZF2101DKU

YEARS MFRD 2004-2004
SERIES ..... TURF CRUISER SERIES
ENGINE .... KUBOTA
CYLINDERS 3
ENGINE HP 20.9
COOLING .... LIQUID
FUEL .... D
SPEEDS .... VARIABLE
TRANSMISSION .... HYDRO
STEERING .... ZERO

ZF2301GKU

YEARS MFRD 2004-2004
SERIES ..... TURF CRUISER SERIES
ENGINE .... KUBOTA
CYLINDERS 3
ENGINE HP 23
COOLING .... LIQUID
FUEL .... G
SPEEDS .... VARIABLE
TRANSMISSION .... HYDRO
STEERING .... ZERO

ZF2501KH

YEARS MFRD 2004-2004
SERIES ..... TURF CRUISER SERIES
ENGINE .... KOHLER
CYLINDERS 2
ENGINE HP 25
COOLING .... AIR
FUEL .... G
SPEEDS .... VARIABLE
TRANSMISSION .... HYDRO
STEERING .... ZERO

ZT18440KH

YEARS MFRD 2004-2004
SERIES .... FAST CUT SERIES
ENGINE ...... KOHLER COMMAND
CYLINDERS 1
ENGINE HP 18
COOLING .... LIQUID
FUEL .... G
SPEEDS .... VARIABLE
TRANSMISSION .... HYDRO
STEERING .... ZERO
STANDARD DECK .... 44"
MSRP $4,099

RETAIL PRICING

YEAR	HIGH	LOW
2004	$2,286	$1,715

ZT20500BV

YEARS MFRD 2004-2004
SERIES .... FAST CUT SERIES
ENGINE .... B&S
CYLINDERS 2
ENGINE HP 20
COOLING .... AIR
FUEL .... G
SPEEDS .... VARIABLE
TRANSMISSION .... HYDRO
STEERING .... ZERO
STANDARD DECK .... 50"
MSRP $4,699

RETAIL PRICING

YEAR	HIGH	LOW
2004	$2,622	$1,966

50

YEARS MFRD 1992-2001
ENGINE .... LISTER
ENGINE HP 18
FUEL .... D
TRANSMISSION .... HYDRO
STEERING .... STANDARD
STANDARD DECK .... 50"
MSRP $13,550

SERIAL NUMBERS

YEAR	BEGINNING NO.
1996	6W11125

RETAIL PRICING

YEAR	HIGH	LOW
1992	$3,585	$2,689
1993	$3,697	$2,772
1994	$3,903	$2,928
1995	$4,054	$3,041
1996	$4,516	$3,387
1997	$4,741	$3,556
1998	$5,019	$3,764
1999	$5,355	$4,016
2000	$5,680	$4,260
2001	$6,372	$4,779

50FM

YEARS MFRD 1995-2001
ENGINE . . . . LISTER
ENGINE HP 18
FUEL . . . . D
TRANSMISSION . . . . HYDRO
STEERING. . . . . STANDARD
STANDARD DECK . . . . 50"
MSRP. $14,075

SERIAL NUMBERS

YEAR	BEGINNING NO.
1996	6W11125

RETAIL PRICING

YEAR	HIGH	LOW
1995	$3,994	$2,996
1996	$4,708	$3,531
1997	$4,944	$3,708
1998	$5,232	$3,924
1999	$5,581	$4,186
2000	$5,916	$4,437
2001	$6,618	$4,963

60

YEARS MFRD 1992-2001
ENGINE . . . . LISTER
ENGINE HP 18
FUEL . . . . D
TRANSMISSION . . . . HYDRO
STEERING. . . . . STANDARD
STANDARD DECK . . . . 60"
MSRP. $13,750

SERIAL NUMBERS

YEAR	BEGINNING NO.
1996	6W11125

RETAIL PRICING

YEAR	HIGH	LOW
1992	$3,615	$2,711
1993	$3,730	$2,797
1994	$3,939	$2,954
1995	$4,090	$3,067
1996	$4,589	$3,442
1997	$4,818	$3,613
1998	$5,101	$3,826
1999	$5,442	$4,081
2000	$5,771	$4,328
2001	$6,466	$4,850

60FM

YEARS MFRD 1995-2001
ENGINE . . . . LISTER
ENGINE HP 18
FUEL . . . . D
TRANSMISSION . . . . HYDRO
STEERING. . . . . STANDARD
STANDARD DECK . . . . 60"
MSRP. $14,275

RETAIL PRICING

YEAR	HIGH	LOW
1995	$4,269	$3,202
1996	$4,784	$3,588
1997	$5,019	$3,764
1998	$5,313	$3,984
1999	$5,668	$4,251
2000	$5,963	$4,472
2001	$6,711	$5,033

72

YEARS MFRD 1991-2001
SERIES. . . . . MAGNUM SERIES
ENGINE . . . . LISTER
ENGINE HP 24
FUEL . . . . D
TRANSMISSION . . . . HYDRO
STEERING. . . . . STANDARD
STANDARD DECK . . . . 72"
MSRP. $13,950

SERIAL NUMBERS

YEAR	BEGINNING NO.
1996	6W11125

RETAIL PRICING

YEAR	HIGH	LOW
1991	$3,504	$2,628
1992	$3,678	$2,758
1993	$3,794	$2,845
1994	$4,007	$3,005
1995	$4,162	$3,122
1996	$4,663	$3,497
1997	$4,894	$3,671
1998	$5,180	$3,885
1999	$5,526	$4,145
2000	$5,861	$4,396
2001	$6,558	$4,919

72FM

YEARS MFRD 1995-2001
ENGINE . . . . LISTER
ENGINE HP 18
FUEL . . . . D
TRANSMISSION . . . . HYDRO
STEERING. . . . . STANDARD
STANDARD DECK . . . . 72"
MSRP. $14,475

RETAIL PRICING

YEAR	HIGH	LOW
1995	$4,339	$3,255
1996	$4,856	$3,642
1997	$5,097	$3,823
1998	$5,392	$4,044
1999	$5,754	$4,315
2000	$6,098	$4,573
2001	$6,805	$5,104

520Z

YEARS MFRD 2003-2005
ENGINE . . . . KOHLER
ENGINE HP 20
FUEL . . . . G
SPEEDS . . . . VARIABLE
TRANSMISSION . . . . HYDRO
STEERING. . . . . ZERO
STANDARD DECK . . . . 50"
WEIGHT . . . . 1,100 LBS.
MSRP. $9,799

RETAIL PRICING

YEAR	HIGH	LOW
2005	$5,797	$4,348

525Z

YEARS MFRD 2003-2006
ENGINE . . . . KOHLER
ENGINE HP 25
COOLING . . . . AIR
FUEL . . . . G
SPEEDS . . . . VARIABLE
TRANSMISSION . . . . HYDRO
STEERING. . . . . ZERO
STANDARD DECK . . . . 50"
MSRP. $9,699

RETAIL PRICING

YEAR	HIGH	LOW
2003	$4,951	$3,713
2004	$5,271	$3,954
2005	$5,739	$4,304
2006	$6,064	$4,548

625Z

YEARS MFRD 2003-2006
ENGINE . . . . KOHLER
CYLINDERS. 2
ENGINE HP 25
COOLING . . . . AIR
FUEL . . . . G
SPEEDS . . . . VARIABLE
TRANSMISSION . . . . HYDRO
STEERING. . . . . ZERO
STANDARD DECK . . . . 60"
MSRP. $10,199

RETAIL PRICING

YEAR	HIGH	LOW
2003	$5,333	$4,000
2004	$5,674	$4,256
2005	$6,035	$4,526
2006	$6,378	$4,783

725Z

YEARS MFRD 2003-2006
ENGINE . . . . KOHLER
CYLINDERS. 2
ENGINE HP 25
COOLING . . . . AIR
FUEL . . . . G
SPEEDS . . . . VARIABLE
TRANSMISSION . . . . HYDRO
STEERING. . . . . ZERO
STANDARD DECK . . . . 70"
MSRP. $10,699

RETAIL PRICING

YEAR	HIGH	LOW
2003	$5,438	$4,079
2004	$5,788	$4,341
2005	$6,330	$4,747
2006	$6,692	$5,019

1840

YEARS MFRD 1989-1993
SERIES. . . . . MAGNUM SERIES
ENGINE . . . . KOHLER
ENGINE HP 18
FUEL . . . . G
TRANSMISSION . . . . HYDRO
STEERING. . . . . STANDARD
STANDARD DECK . . . . 40"
MSRP. $7,000

RETAIL PRICING

YEAR	HIGH	LOW
1989	$1,439	$1,079
1990	$1,522	$1,141
1991	$1,821	$1,366
1992	$2,210	$1,657
1993	$2,279	$1,710

1850

YEARS MFRD 1989-1993
SERIES. . . . . MAGNUM I SERIES
ENGINE . . . . KOHLER
ENGINE HP 18
FUEL . . . . G
TRANSMISSION . . . . HYDRO
STEERING. . . . . STANDARD
STANDARD DECK . . . . 50"
MSRP. $7,100

RETAIL PRICING

YEAR	HIGH	LOW
1989	$1,664	$1,248
1990	$1,760	$1,320
1991	$2,093	$1,570
1992	$2,243	$1,682
1993	$2,312	$1,734

2040

YEARS MFRD 1990-1993
SERIES. . . . . MAGNUM SERIES
ENGINE . . . . KOHLER
ENGINE HP 20
FUEL . . . . G
TRANSMISSION . . . . HYDRO
STEERING. . . . . STANDARD
STANDARD DECK . . . . 40"
MSRP. $7,150

RETAIL PRICING

YEAR	HIGH	LOW
1990	$1,611	$1,208
1991	$1,892	$1,419
1992	$2,256	$1,692
1993	$2,328	$1,746

2050

YEARS MFRD 1989-1993
SERIES. . . . . MAGNUM I SERIES
ENGINE . . . . KOHLER
ENGINE HP 20
FUEL . . . . G
TRANSMISSION . . . . HYDRO
STEERING. . . . . STANDARD
STANDARD DECK . . . . 50"
MSRP. $7,250

SCHWEISS

RETAIL PRICING

YEAR	HIGH	LOW
1989	$1,748	$1,311
1990	$1,850	$1,388
1991	$2,168	$1,626
1992	$2,289	$1,717
1993	$2,362	$1,771

2350

- YEARS MFRD 1989-1995
- SERIES .... MAGNUM I SERIES
- ENGINE .... KOHLER
- ENGINE HP 23
- FUEL .... G
- SPEEDS .... VARIABLE
- TRANSMISSION .... HYDRO
- STEERING .... STANDARD
- STANDARD DECK .... 50"
- MSRP $7,900

OPTIONS

KUBOTA 19.8HP

RETAIL PRICING

YEAR	HIGH	LOW
1989	$1,900	$1,425
1990	$2,009	$1,507
1991	$2,335	$1,752
1992	$2,496	$1,872
1993	$2,573	$1,930
1994	$2,718	$2,038
1995	$2,821	$2,116

2350FM

- YEARS MFRD 1995-1996
- ENGINE .... KOHLER
- ENGINE HP 23
- FUEL .... G
- TRANSMISSION .... HYDRO
- STEERING .... STANDARD
- STANDARD DECK .... 50"
- MSRP $8,400

SERIAL NUMBERS

YEAR	BEGINNING NO.
1996	6W11125

RETAIL PRICING

YEAR	HIGH	LOW
1995	$3,000	$2,250

2360

- YEARS MFRD 1989-1995
- SERIES .... MAGNUM II SERIES
- ENGINE .... KOHLER
- ENGINE HP 23
- FUEL .... G
- TRANSMISSION .... HYDRO
- STEERING .... STANDARD
- STANDARD DECK .... 60"
- MSRP $8,000

OPTIONS

KUBOTA 23HP

RETAIL PRICING

YEAR	HIGH	LOW
1989	$1,902	$1,427
1990	$2,015	$1,511
1991	$2,366	$1,774
1992	$2,526	$1,895
1993	$2,605	$1,954
1994	$2,752	$2,064
1995	$2,858	$2,143

2360FM

- YEARS MFRD 1995-1996
- ENGINE .... KOHLER
- ENGINE HP 23
- FUEL .... G
- TRANSMISSION .... HYDRO
- STEERING .... STANDARD
- STANDARD DECK .... 60"
- MSRP $8,500

SERIAL NUMBERS

YEAR	BEGINNING NO.
1996	6W11125

RETAIL PRICING

YEAR	HIGH	LOW
1995	$3,037	$2,278

2372

- YEARS MFRD 1991-1995
- SERIES .... MAGNUM SERIES
- ENGINE .... KOHLER
- ENGINE HP 23
- FUEL .... G
- TRANSMISSION .... HYDRO
- STEERING .... STANDARD
- STANDARD DECK .... 72"
- MSRP $8,200

RETAIL PRICING

YEAR	HIGH	LOW
1991	$2,428	$1,821
1992	$2,589	$1,942
1993	$2,671	$2,004
1994	$2,821	$2,116
1995	$2,930	$2,198

2372FM

- YEARS MFRD 1995-1996
- ENGINE .... KOHLER
- ENGINE HP 23
- FUEL .... G
- TRANSMISSION .... HYDRO
- STEERING .... STANDARD
- STANDARD DECK .... 72"
- MSRP $8,700

SERIAL NUMBERS

YEAR	BEGINNING NO.
1996	6W11125

RETAIL PRICING

YEAR	HIGH	LOW
1995	$3,107	$2,330

2450

- YEARS MFRD 1989-1999
- SERIES .... MAGNUM I SERIES
- ENGINE .... ONAN
- ENGINE HP 24
- FUEL .... G
- TRANSMISSION .... HYDRO
- STEERING .... STANDARD
- STANDARD DECK .... 50"
- MSRP $9,100

SERIAL NUMBERS

YEAR	BEGINNING NO.
1996	6W11125
1997	7W11225
1997	7S11250
1998	8S11280

RETAIL PRICING

YEAR	HIGH	LOW
1989	$1,900	$1,425
1990	$2,009	$1,507
1991	$2,486	$1,865
1992	$2,621	$1,965
1993	$2,703	$2,027
1994	$2,857	$2,143
1995	$2,965	$2,223
1996	$3,331	$2,498
1997	$3,455	$2,591
1998	$3,670	$2,753
1999	$3,914	$2,936

2450FM

- YEARS MFRD 1995-1999
- ENGINE .... ONAN
- ENGINE HP 24
- FUEL .... G
- TRANSMISSION .... HYDRO
- STEERING .... STANDARD
- STANDARD DECK .... 50"
- MSRP $9,625

SERIAL NUMBERS

YEAR	BEGINNING NO.
1996	6W11125
1997	7W11225
1997	7S11250
1998	8S11280

RETAIL PRICING

YEAR	HIGH	LOW
1995	$3,143	$2,357
1996	$3,525	$2,644
1997	$3,656	$2,742
1998	$3,882	$2,911
1999	$4,141	$3,105

2460

- YEARS MFRD 1989-1999
- SERIES .... MAGNUM II SERIES
- ENGINE .... ONAN
- ENGINE HP 24
- FUEL .... G
- TRANSMISSION .... HYDRO
- STEERING .... STANDARD
- STANDARD DECK .... 60"
- MSRP $9,300

SERIAL NUMBERS

YEAR	BEGINNING NO.
1996	6W11125
1997	7W11225
1997	7S11250
1998	8S11280

RETAIL PRICING

YEAR	HIGH	LOW
1989	$1,902	$1,427
1990	$2,015	$1,511
1991	$2,518	$1,888
1992	$2,651	$1,988
1993	$2,734	$2,051
1994	$2,891	$2,168
1995	$3,000	$2,250
1996	$3,406	$2,554
1997	$3,531	$2,648
1998	$3,667	$2,750
1999	$4,001	$3,001

2460FM

- YEARS MFRD 1995-1999
- ENGINE .... ONAN
- ENGINE HP 24
- FUEL .... G
- TRANSMISSION .... HYDRO
- STEERING .... STANDARD
- STANDARD DECK .... 60"
- MSRP $9,825

SERIAL NUMBERS

YEAR	BEGINNING NO.
1996	6W11125
1997	7W11225
1997	7S11250
1998	8S11280

RETAIL PRICING

YEAR	HIGH	LOW
1995	$3,179	$2,384
1996	$3,601	$2,700
1997	$3,734	$2,800
1998	$3,962	$2,972
1999	$4,226	$3,169

2472

- YEARS MFRD 1991-1999
- SERIES .... MAGNUM SERIES
- ENGINE .... ONAN
- ENGINE HP 24
- FUEL .... G
- TRANSMISSION .... HYDRO
- STEERING .... STANDARD
- STANDARD DECK .... 72"
- MSRP $9,500

SERIAL NUMBERS

YEAR	BEGINNING NO.
1996	6W11125
1997	7W11225
1997	7S11250
1998	8S11280

RETAIL PRICING

YEAR	HIGH	LOW
1991	$2,577	$1,933
1992	$2,716	$2,037
1993	$2,801	$2,101
1994	$2,960	$2,220
1995	$3,072	$2,304
1996	$3,478	$2,609
1997	$3,608	$2,706
1998	$3,830	$2,872
1999	$4,087	$3,065

2472FM

- YEARS MFRD 1995-1999
- ENGINE .... ONAN
- ENGINE HP 24

FUEL . . . . . G
TRANSMISSION . . . . . HYDRO
STEERING . . . . . STANDARD
STANDARD DECK . . . . . 72"
MSRP $10,025

SERIAL NUMBERS

YEAR	BEGINNING NO.
1996	6W11125
1997	7W11225
1997	7S11250
1998	8S11280

RETAIL PRICING

YEAR	HIGH	LOW
1995	$3,250	$2,437
1996	$3,674	$2,756
1997	$3,809	$2,857
1998	$4,043	$3,032
1999	$4,311	$3,233

5020

YEARS MFRD 1994-2002
ENGINE . . . . . KOHLER
ENGINE HP 20
FUEL . . . . . G
TRANSMISSION . . . . . HYDRO
STEERING . . . . . STANDARD
STANDARD DECK . . . . . 50"
MSRP $9,175

SERIAL NUMBERS

YEAR	BEGINNING NO.
1996	6W11125
1997	7W11225
1997	7S11250
1998	8S11280

RETAIL PRICING

YEAR	HIGH	LOW
1994	$2,528	$1,896
1995	$2,625	$1,969
1996	$2,999	$2,249
1997	$3,167	$2,376
1998	$3,366	$2,525
1999	$3,591	$2,693
2000	$3,832	$2,874
2001	$4,313	$3,235
2002	$4,434	$3,325

5020FM

YEARS MFRD 1994-2001
ENGINE . . . . . KOHLER
ENGINE HP 20
FUEL . . . . . G
TRANSMISSION . . . . . HYDRO
STEERING . . . . . STANDARD
STANDARD DECK . . . . . 50"
MSRP $9,775

SERIAL NUMBERS

YEAR	BEGINNING NO.
1996	6W11125
1997	7W11225
1997	7S11250
1998	8S11280

RETAIL PRICING

YEAR	HIGH	LOW
1994	$2,702	$2,026
1995	$2,804	$2,103
1996	$3,192	$2,394
1997	$3,367	$2,525
1998	$3,579	$2,684
1999	$3,818	$2,864
2000	$4,068	$3,051
2001	$4,596	$3,447

5025

YEARS MFRD 1995-2001
ENGINE . . . . . KOHLER
ENGINE HP 25
FUEL . . . . . G
TRANSMISSION . . . . . HYDRO
STEERING . . . . . STANDARD
STANDARD DECK . . . . . 50"
MSRP $9,675

SERIAL NUMBERS

YEAR	BEGINNING NO.
1996	6W11125
1997	7W11225
1997	7S11250
1998	8S11280

RETAIL PRICING

YEAR	HIGH	LOW
1995	$2,821	$2,116
1996	$3,182	$2,387
1997	$3,360	$2,520
1998	$3,567	$2,675
1999	$3,807	$2,855
2000	$4,059	$3,044
2001	$4,549	$3,412

5025FM

YEARS MFRD 1995-2001
ENGINE . . . . . KOHLER
ENGINE HP 25
FUEL . . . . . G
TRANSMISSION . . . . . HYDRO
STEERING . . . . . STANDARD
STANDARD DECK . . . . . 50"
MSRP $10,275

SERIAL NUMBERS

YEAR	BEGINNING NO.
1996	6W11125
1997	7W11225
1997	7S11250
1998	8S11280

RETAIL PRICING

YEAR	HIGH	LOW
1995	$3,000	$2,250
1996	$3,378	$2,534
1997	$3,561	$2,671
1998	$3,781	$2,836
1999	$4,032	$3,024
2000	$4,292	$3,219
2001	$4,830	$3,623

6020

YEARS MFRD 1994-2001
ENGINE . . . . . KOHLER
ENGINE HP 20
FUEL . . . . . G
TRANSMISSION . . . . . HYDRO
STEERING . . . . . STANDARD
STANDARD DECK . . . . . 60"
MSRP $9,375

SERIAL NUMBERS

YEAR	BEGINNING NO.
1996	6W11125
1997	7W11225
1997	7S11250
1998	8S11280

RETAIL PRICING

YEAR	HIGH	LOW
1994	$2,563	$1,922
1995	$2,661	$1,996
1996	$3,071	$2,303
1997	$3,246	$2,434
1998	$3,448	$2,586
1999	$3,677	$2,758
2000	$3,922	$2,941
2001	$4,406	$3,305

6020FM

YEARS MFRD 1994-2001
ENGINE . . . . . KOHLER
ENGINE HP 20
FUEL . . . . . G
TRANSMISSION . . . . . HYDRO
STEERING . . . . . STANDARD
STANDARD DECK . . . . . 60"
MSRP $9,975

SERIAL NUMBERS

YEAR	BEGINNING NO.
1996	6W11125
1997	7W11225
1997	7S11250
1998	8S11280

RETAIL PRICING

YEAR	HIGH	LOW
1994	$2,734	$2,051
1995	$2,840	$2,130
1996	$3,266	$2,450
1997	$3,446	$2,584
1998	$3,658	$2,744
1999	$3,903	$2,928
2000	$4,160	$3,120
2001	$4,689	$3,517

6025

YEARS MFRD 1995-2001
ENGINE . . . . . KOHLER
ENGINE HP 25
FUEL . . . . . G
TRANSMISSION . . . . . HYDRO
STEERING . . . . . STANDARD
STANDARD DECK . . . . . 60"
MSRP $9,875

SERIAL NUMBERS

YEAR	BEGINNING NO.
1996	6W11125
1997	7W11225
1997	7S11250
1998	8S11280

RETAIL PRICING

YEAR	HIGH	LOW
1995	$2,858	$2,143
1996	$3,257	$2,442
1997	$3,436	$2,577
1998	$3,649	$2,736
1999	$3,893	$2,919
2000	$4,147	$3,111
2001	$4,644	$3,483

6025FM

YEARS MFRD 1995-2001
ENGINE . . . . . KOHLER
ENGINE HP 25
FUEL . . . . . G
TRANSMISSION . . . . . HYDRO
STEERING . . . . . STANDARD
STANDARD DECK . . . . . 60"
MSRP $10,475

SERIAL NUMBERS

YEAR	BEGINNING NO.
1996	6W11125
1997	7W11225
1997	7S11250
1998	8S11280

RETAIL PRICING

YEAR	HIGH	LOW
1995	$3,037	$2,278
1996	$3,452	$2,589
1997	$3,638	$2,728
1998	$3,862	$2,897
1999	$4,119	$3,089
2000	$4,386	$3,289
2001	$4,925	$3,694

6252

YEARS MFRD 2002-2002
ENGINE . . . . . KOHLER
ENGINE HP 25
FUEL . . . . . G
TRANSMISSION . . . . . HYDRO
STEERING . . . . . STANDARD
STANDARD DECK . . . . . 62"
MSRP $9,875

RETAIL PRICING

YEAR	HIGH	LOW
2002	$4,773	$3,579

7220

YEARS MFRD 1994-2000
ENGINE . . . . . KOHLER
ENGINE HP 20
FUEL . . . . . G
TRANSMISSION . . . . . HYDRO
STEERING . . . . . STANDARD
STANDARD DECK . . . . . 72"
MSRP $8,900

SERIAL NUMBERS

YEAR	BEGINNING NO.
1996	6W11125
1997	7W11225
1997	7S11250
1998	8S11280

RETAIL PRICING

YEAR	HIGH	LOW
1994	$2,632	$1,974
1995	$2,732	$2,049
1996	$3,146	$2,359
1997	$3,322	$2,492
1998	$3,529	$2,647
1999	$3,764	$2,823
2000	$4,012	$3,009

SCHWEISS

7220FM

YEARS MFRD 1994-2000
ENGINE . . . . KOHLER
ENGINE HP 20
FUEL . . . . G
TRANSMISSION . . . . HYDRO
STEERING. . . . . STANDARD
STANDARD DECK . . . . 72"
MSRP. $9,425

SERIAL NUMBERS

YEAR	BEGINNING NO.
1996	6W11125
1997	7W11225
1997	7S11250
1998	8S11280

RETAIL PRICING

YEAR	HIGH	LOW
1994	$2,805	$2,104
1995	$2,911	$2,183
1996	$3,341	$2,506
1997	$3,522	$2,642
1998	$3,740	$2,805
1999	$3,990	$2,992
2000	$4,249	$3,187

7225

YEARS MFRD 1995-2002
ENGINE . . . . KOHLER
ENGINE HP 25
FUEL . . . . G
TRANSMISSION . . . . HYDRO
STEERING. . . . . STANDARD
STANDARD DECK . . . . 72"
MSRP. $10,075

SERIAL NUMBERS

YEAR	BEGINNING NO.
1996	6W11125

RETAIL PRICING

YEAR	HIGH	LOW
1995	$2,930	$2,198
1996	$3,331	$2,498
1997	$3,511	$2,634
1998	$3,731	$2,798
1999	$3,979	$2,984
2000	$4,237	$3,177
2001	$4,737	$3,553
2002	$4,870	$3,652

7225FM

YEARS MFRD 1995-2002
ENGINE . . . . KOHLER
ENGINE HP 25
FUEL . . . . G
TRANSMISSION . . . . HYDRO
STEERING. . . . . STANDARD
STANDARD DECK . . . . 72"
MSRP. $10,675

SERIAL NUMBERS

YEAR	BEGINNING NO.
1996	6W11125
1997	7W11225
1997	7S11250
1998	8S11280

RETAIL PRICING

YEAR	HIGH	LOW
1995	$3,107	$2,330
1996	$3,156	$2,367
1997	$3,713	$2,785
1998	$3,942	$2,956
1999	$4,205	$3,154
2000	$4,476	$3,357
2001	$4,700	$3,525
2002	$4,997	$3,748

SHIBAURA

CM214

YEARS MFRD 2005-2018
ENGINE . . . . SHIBAURA S773
CYLINDERS. 3
CID 1005CC
ENGINE HP 21
FUEL . . . . D
SPEEDS . . . . VARIABLE
TRANSMISSION . . . . HYDRO
STEERING. . . . . ZERO
ROPS/CAB . . . . ROPS
WEIGHT . . . . 1,168 LBS.

CM284

YEARS MFRD 2005-2010
ENGINE . . . . SHIBAURA J843
CYLINDERS. 3
ENGINE HP 28
FUEL . . . . D
SPEEDS . . . . VARIABLE
TRANSMISSION . . . . HYDRO
STEERING. . . . . ZERO

CM314

YEARS MFRD 2010-2018
ENGINE N843
CYLINDERS. 3
CID 1496
ENGINE HP 33.9
COOLING . . . . LIQUID
FUEL . . . . D
SPEEDS . . . . VARIABLE
TRANSMISSION . . . . HYDRO
STEERING. . . . . STANDARD
HITCH . . . . CAT. I
ROPS/CAB . . . . ROPS
WEIGHT . . . . 1,664 LBS.

CM364

YEARS MFRD 2005-2010
ENGINE . . . . SHIBAURA N843-L
CYLINDERS. 3
ENGINE HP 35
FUEL . . . . D
SPEEDS . . . . VARIABLE
TRANSMISSION . . . . HYDRO
STEERING. . . . . ZERO

CM374

YEARS MFRD 2010-2018
ENGINE N843-L
CYLINDERS. 3
CID 1662
ENGINE HP 40
COOLING . . . . LIQUID
FUEL . . . . D
SPEEDS . . . . VARIABLE
TRANSMISSION . . . . HYDRO
STEERING. . . . . STANDARD
HITCH . . . . CAT. I
HYDRAULIC . . . . YES
PTO . . . . YES
ROPS/CAB . . . . ROPS
WEIGHT . . . . 1,697 LBS.

GT141

YEARS MFRD 2007-2010
ENGINE . . . . SHIBAURA E643
CYLINDERS. 3
COOLING . . . . LIQUID
FUEL . . . . D
SPEEDS . . . . VARIABLE
TRANSMISSION . . . . HYDRO
STEERING. . . . . STANDARD
HITCH . . . . CAT. I

GT161

YEARS MFRD 2005-2018
ENGINE . . . . SHIBAURA E673
CYLINDERS. 3
CID 676CC
ENGINE HP 17
COOLING . . . . LIQUID
FUEL . . . . D
SPEEDS . . . . VARIABLE
TRANSMISSION . . . . HYDRO
STEERING. . . . . STANDARD
WEIGHT . . . . 842 LBS.

GT181

YEARS MFRD 2007-2010
ENGINE . . . . SHIBAURA M18QS
CYLINDERS. 2
COOLING . . . . AIR
FUEL . . . . G
SPEEDS . . . . VARIABLE
TRANSMISSION . . . . HYDRO
STEERING. . . . . STANDARD
HITCH . . . . CAT. I

GT201

YEARS MFRD 2007-2010
ENGINE . . . . SHIBAURA M20QS
CYLINDERS. 2
COOLING . . . . AIR
FUEL . . . . G
SPEEDS . . . . VARIABLE
TRANSMISSION . . . . HYDRO
STEERING. . . . . STANDARD
HITCH . . . . CAT. I

SG280

YEARS MFRD 2012-2014
ENGINE . . . . SHIBAURA N843
CYLINDERS. 3
CID 1496CC
ENGINE HP 28
COOLING . . . . LIQUID
FUEL . . . . D
SPEEDS . . . . VARIABLE
TRANSMISSION . . . . HYDRO
STEERING. . . . . STANDARD
WEIGHT . . . . 1,962 LBS.

ST318

YEARS MFRD 2005-2018
SERIES. . . . . ST SERIES
ENGINE . . . . SHIBAURA S753
CYLINDERS. 3
CID 58.2
PTO HP 15
ENGINE HP 18.5
FUEL . . . . D
SPEEDS . . . . VARIABLE
TRANSMISSION . . . . HYDRO
STEERING. . . . . STANDARD
PTO . . . . YES
DRIVE TYPE 4WD
ROPS/CAB . . . . ROPS
WEIGHT . . . . 1,636 LBS.

ST321

YEARS MFRD 2005-2018
SERIES. . . . . ST SERIES
ENGINE . . . . SHIBAURA
CYLINDERS. 3
CID 61.3
PTO HP 17
ENGINE HP 21
FUEL . . . . D
SPEEDS . . . . VARIABLE
TRANSMISSION . . . . HYDRO
STEERING. . . . . STANDARD
HITCH . . . . CAT. I
PTO . . . . YES
DRIVE TYPE 4WD
ROPS/CAB . . . . ROPS
WEIGHT . . . . 1,666 LBS.

ST324

YEARS MFRD 2005-2018
SERIES. . . . . ST SERIES
ENGINE . . . . SHIBAURA
CYLINDERS. 3
CID 69
PTO HP 19
ENGINE HP 24
FUEL . . . . D
SPEEDS . . . . VARIABLE
TRANSMISSION . . . . HYDRO
STEERING. . . . . STANDARD
HITCH . . . . CAT. I
PTO . . . . YES
DRIVE TYPE 4WD
ROPS/CAB . . . . ROPS
WEIGHT . . . . 1,680 LBS.

ST329

YEARS MFRD 2005-2010
ENGINE .... SHIBAURA
CYLINDERS................... 3
ENGINE HP 29
FUEL .... D
SPEEDS .... VARIABLE
TRANSMISSION .... HYDRO
STEERING............ STANDARD
HITCH .... CAT. I
PTO .... YES
WEIGHT .... 1,075 LBS.

ST330

YEARS MFRD 2009-2018
SERIES............... ST SERIES
ENGINE .... SHIBAURA N843
CYLINDERS................... 3
CID 91.2
PTO HP 23.7
ENGINE HP 30
FUEL .... D
SPEEDS .... VARIABLE
TRANSMISSION .... HYDRO
STEERING............ STANDARD
DRIVE TYPE 4WD
ROPS/CAB .... ROPS
WEIGHT .... 2,461 LBS.

ST333

YEARS MFRD 2005-2018
ENGINE .... SHIBAURA
CYLINDERS................... 3
CID 91.2
PTO HP 26
ENGINE HP 33
FUEL .... D
SPEEDS .... VARIABLE
TRANSMISSION .... HYDRO
STEERING............ STANDARD
HITCH .... CAT. I
PTO .... YES
DRIVE TYPE 4WD
ROPS/CAB .... ROPS
WEIGHT .... 2,461 LBS.

ST440

YEARS MFRD 2008-2018
ENGINE N844
CYLINDERS................... 4
CID 1995CC
PTO HP 34
ENGINE HP 40
COOLING .... LIQUID
FUEL .... D
SPEEDS 12/12
TRANSMISSION ... SHUTTLE SHIFT
STEERING............ STANDARD
HITCH .... CAT. I
HYDRAULIC .... YES
PTO .... YES
DRIVE TYPE 4WD
ROPS/CAB .... ROPS
WEIGHT .... 3,219 LBS.

ST445

YEARS MFRD 2008-2018
ENGINE N844L
CYLINDERS................... 4
CID 2216CC
PTO HP 38
ENGINE HP 45
COOLING .... LIQUID
FUEL .... D
SPEEDS 12/12
TRANSMISSION ... SHUTTLE SHIFT
STEERING............ STANDARD
HITCH .... CAT. I
HYDRAULIC .... YES
PTO .... YES
DRIVE TYPE 4WD
ROPS/CAB .... ROPS
WEIGHT .... 3,329 LBS.

SX21

YEARS MFRD 2007-2018
ENGINE .... SHIBAURA S753
CYLINDERS................... 3
CID 954CC
ENGINE HP 21
COOLING .... AIR
FUEL .... D
SPEEDS .... VARIABLE
TRANSMISSION .... HYDRO
STEERING............ STANDARD
HITCH .... CAT. I
DRIVE TYPE 4WD
ROPS/CAB .... ROPS
WEIGHT .... 1,530 LBS.

SX24

YEARS MFRD 2007-2018
ENGINE .... SHIBAURA S773
CYLINDERS................... 3
CID 1005CC
ENGINE HP 24
COOLING .... AIR
FUEL .... D
SPEEDS .... VARIABLE
TRANSMISSION .... HYDRO
STEERING............ STANDARD
HITCH .... CAT. I
DRIVE TYPE 4WD
ROPS/CAB .... ROPS
WEIGHT .... 1,534 LBS.

SIMPLICITY

COURIER 23/42

YEARS MFRD 2016-2019
SERIES.......... COURIER SERIES
ENGINE .... B&S
CYLINDERS................... 2
CID 724CC
ENGINE HP 23
FUEL .... G
SPEEDS .... VARIABLE
TRANSMISSION .... HYDRO
STEERING................ ZERO
STANDARD DECK .... 42"
MSRP $3,149

OPTIONS

2 BAG
CARGO BED

RETAIL PRICING

YEAR	HIGH	LOW
2016	$1,677	$1,258
2017	$1,852	$1,389
2018	$2,046	$1,534
2019	$2,258	$1,694

COURIER 23/44

YEARS MFRD 2016-2020
SERIES.......... COURIER SERIES
ENGINE .... B&S
CYLINDERS................... 2
CID 724CC
ENGINE HP 23
FUEL .... G
SPEEDS .... VARIABLE
TRANSMISSION .... HYDRO
STEERING................ ZERO
STANDARD DECK .... 44"
MSRP $2,849

RETAIL PRICING

YEAR	HIGH	LOW
2016	$1,900	$1,425
2017	$2,098	$1,573
2018	$2,328	$1,746
2019	$2,577	$1,933
2020	$2,712	$2,072

LEGACY XL 31

YEARS MFRD 2017-2019
ENGINE .... VANGUARD
CYLINDERS................... 2
CID 885CC
ENGINE HP 31
COOLING .... AIR
FUEL .... G
SPEEDS .... VARIABLE
TRANSMISSION .... HYDRO
STEERING............ STANDARD
BLADE CLUTCH .... ELECTRIC
STANDARD DECK .... 61"
MSRP $11,798

OPTIONS

47" SNOW THROWER
50" TILLER
52" DECK
60" BLADE

RETAIL PRICING

YEAR	HIGH	LOW
2017	$7,251	$5,438
2018	$7,950	$5,963
2019	$8,798	$6,598

LEGACY XL 33

YEARS MFRD 2017-2019
ENGINE .... VANGUARD
CYLINDERS................... 2
CID 885
ENGINE HP 33
COOLING .... AIR
FUEL .... G
SPEEDS .... VARIABLE
TRANSMISSION .... HYDRO
STEERING............ STANDARD
BLADE CLUTCH .... ELECTRIC
STANDARD DECK .... 61"
MSRP $14,298

OPTIONS

47" SNOW THROWER
50" TILLER
52" DECK
540 RR PTO
60" BLADE

RETAIL PRICING

YEAR	HIGH	LOW
2017	$8,787	$6,590
2018	$10,017	$7,513
2019	$11,084	$8,313

SCS 23/48

YEARS MFRD 2016-2019
SERIES.......... COURIER SERIES
ENGINE .... B&S
ENGINE HP 23
COOLING .... AIR
FUEL .... G
SPEEDS .... VARIABLE
TRANSMISSION .... HYDRO
STEERING................ ZERO
STANDARD DECK .... 48"
MSRP $3,899

OPTIONS

2 BAG
CARGO BED

RETAIL PRICING

YEAR	HIGH	LOW
2016	$2,069	$1,552
2017	$2,283	$1,713
2018	$2,518	$1,889
2019	$2,783	$2,087

SCS 25/52

YEARS MFRD 2016-2019
SERIES.......... COURIER SERIES
ENGINE .... B&S
CYLINDERS................... 2
CID 724CC
ENGINE HP 25
FUEL .... G
SPEEDS .... VARIABLE
TRANSMISSION .... HYDRO
STEERING................ ZERO
STANDARD DECK .... 52"
MSRP $4,449

OPTIONS

2 BAG & FAN
CARGO BED

SIMPLICITY

RETAIL PRICING

YEAR	HIGH	LOW
2016	$2,348	$1,761
2017	$2,593	$1,945
2018	$2,860	$2,145
2019	$3,154	$2,366

SS16HO

YEARS MFRD........1988-1990
SERIES.........SUNSTAR SERIES
ENGINE...............KOHLER
ENGINE HP................16
FUEL......................G
SPEEDS..............HYDRO
WEIGHT.............955 LBS.
MSRP................$4,840

RETAIL PRICING

YEAR	HIGH	LOW
1990	$1,348	$1,011

SS16HW

YEARS MFRD........1989-1990
SERIES.........SUNSTAR SERIES
ENGINE...............KOHLER
ENGINE HP................16
FUEL......................G
TRANSMISSION..........HYDRO
STEERING...........STANDARD
STANDARD DECK...........48"
MSRP................$6,249

RETAIL PRICING

YEAR	HIGH	LOW
1989	$1,644	$1,233
1990	$1,741	$1,306

SS18HO

YEARS MFRD........1988-1990
SERIES.........SUNSTAR SERIES
ENGINE...............KOHLER
ENGINE HP................18
FUEL......................G
SPEEDS..............HYDRO
WEIGHT.............955 LBS.
MSRP................$5,220

RETAIL PRICING

YEAR	HIGH	LOW
1990	$1,455	$1,091

SS18HOPS

YEARS MFRD........1988-1990
SERIES.........SUNSTAR SERIES
ENGINE...............KOHLER
ENGINE HP................18
FUEL......................G
SPEEDS..............HYDRO
WEIGHT.............955 LBS.
MSRP................$5,520

RETAIL PRICING

YEAR	HIGH	LOW
1990	$1,537	$1,153

SS18HWPS

YEARS MFRD........1990-1990
SERIES.........SUNSTAR SERIES
ENGINE...............KOHLER
ENGINE HP................18
FUEL......................G
TRANSMISSION..........HYDRO
STEERING...........STANDARD
STANDARD DECK...........48"
MSRP................$6,949

RETAIL PRICING

YEAR	HIGH	LOW
1990	$1,936	$1,452

SS20

YEARS MFRD........1990-1990
SERIES.........SUNSTAR SERIES
ENGINE...............KOHLER
ENGINE HP................20
FUEL......................G
TRANSMISSION..........HYDRO
STEERING...........STANDARD
PTO.....................YES
STANDARD DECK...........48"
MSRP................$7,049

RETAIL PRICING

YEAR	HIGH	LOW
1990	$1,963	$1,472

SS20HO

YEARS MFRD........1988-1990
SERIES.........SUNSTAR SERIES
ENGINE...............KOHLER
ENGINE HP................20
FUEL......................G
SPEEDS..............HYDRO
WEIGHT...........1,003 LBS.
MSRP................$5,950

RETAIL PRICING

YEAR	HIGH	LOW
1990	$1,658	$1,243

SS20HW

YEARS MFRD........1989-1990
SERIES.........SUNSTAR SERIES
ENGINE...............KOHLER
ENGINE HP................20
FUEL......................G
TRANSMISSION..........HYDRO
STEERING...........STANDARD
STANDARD DECK...........48"
MSRP................$7,449

RETAIL PRICING

YEAR	HIGH	LOW
1989	$1,947	$1,460
1990	$2,075	$1,556

TW2061

YEARS MFRD........2004-2005
SERIES....DERBY MORGAN SERIES
ENGINE..................B&S
CYLINDERS.................2
ENGINE HP................20
COOLING.................AIR
FUEL......................G
SPEEDS.............VARIABLE
TRANSMISSION..........HYDRO
STEERING...............ZERO
STANDARD DECK...........61"
MSRP................$6,999

OPTIONS

CAB

RETAIL PRICING

YEAR	HIGH	LOW
2004	$1,730	$1,298
2005	$1,921	$1,440

XL27 4WD

YEARS MFRD........2007-2007
SERIES..........LEGACY SERIES
ENGINE...........KAWASAKI LC
CYLINDERS.................2
ENGINE HP................27
COOLING.................AIR
FUEL......................G
SPEEDS.............VARIABLE
TRANSMISSION..........HYDRO
STEERING...........STANDARD
BLADE CLUTCH.......ELECTRIC
WEIGHT...........1,030 LBS.
MSRP...............$10,395

RETAIL PRICING

YEAR	HIGH	LOW
2007	$5,546	$4,160

ZT18H

YEARS MFRD........2006-2006
SERIES......CONSUMER Z SERIES
ENGINE...............KOHLER
CYLINDERS.................1
ENGINE HP................18
COOLING.................AIR
FUEL......................G
SPEEDS.............VARIABLE
TRANSMISSION..........HYDRO
STEERING...............ZERO
STANDARD DECK...........44"
WEIGHT.............712 LBS.
MSRP................$4,625

RETAIL PRICING

YEAR	HIGH	LOW
2006	$2,834	$2,126

ZT20H

YEARS MFRD........2006-2006
SERIES...........CONSUMER Z
ENGINE..................B&S
CYLINDERS.................2
ENGINE HP................20
COOLING.................AIR
FUEL......................G
SPEEDS.............VARIABLE
TRANSMISSION..........HYDRO
STEERING...............ZERO
STANDARD DECK...........50"
WEIGHT.............723 LBS.
MSRP................$5,295

RETAIL PRICING

YEAR	HIGH	LOW
2006	$3,246	$2,434

ZT1438

YEARS MFRD........1998-2001
SERIES...............ZT SERIES
ENGINE...............KOHLER
ENGINE HP................14
COOLING.................AIR
FUEL......................G
SPEEDS.............VARIABLE
TRANSMISSION..........HYDRO
STEERING...............ZERO
STANDARD DECK...........38"
MSRP................$3,799

OPTIONS

BAG & FAN
BAGGER

RETAIL PRICING

YEAR	HIGH	LOW
2001	$1,751	$1,313

ZT1500 18

YEARS MFRD........2013-2014
SERIES...............ZT SERIES
ENGINE.............KAWASAKI
ENGINE HP................18
COOLING.................AIR
FUEL......................G
SPEEDS.............VARIABLE
TRANSMISSION..........HYDRO
STEERING...............ZERO
BLADE CLUTCH.......ELECTRIC
STANDARD DECK...........42"
MSRP................$3,049

OPTIONS

2 BAG

RETAIL PRICING

YEAR	HIGH	LOW
2013	$1,618	$1,213
2014	$1,819	$1,364

ZT1500 20

YEARS MFRD........2013-2013
SERIES...............ZT SERIES
ENGINE..................B&S
ENGINE HP................20
COOLING.................AIR
FUEL......................G
SPEEDS.............VARIABLE
TRANSMISSION..........HYDRO
STEERING...............ZERO
BLADE CLUTCH.......ELECTRIC
STANDARD DECK...........42"
MSRP................$2,899

OPTIONS

2 BAG

RETAIL PRICING

YEAR	HIGH	LOW
2013	$1,583	$1,187

ZT1500 21.5

YEARS MFRD 2013-2014
SERIES. . . . . ZT SERIES
ENGINE . . . . KAWASAKI
ENGINE HP 21.5
COOLING . . . . AIR
FUEL . . . . G
SPEEDS . . . . VARIABLE
TRANSMISSION . . . . HYDRO
STEERING. . . . . ZERO
BLADE CLUTCH . . . . ELECTRIC
STANDARD DECK . . . . 46"
MSRP. $3,399

OPTIONS

3 BAG

RETAIL PRICING

YEAR	HIGH	LOW
2013	$1,805	$1,354
2014	$2,108	$1,581

ZT1500 22

YEARS MFRD 2014-2015
ENGINE . . . . B&S
ENGINE HP 22
COOLING . . . . AIR
FUEL . . . . G
SPEEDS . . . . VARIABLE
TRANSMISSION . . . . HYDRO
STEERING. . . . . ZERO
STANDARD DECK . . . . 42"
MSRP. $2,899

OPTIONS

2 BAG
46" DECK

RETAIL PRICING

YEAR	HIGH	LOW
2014	$1,555	$1,166
2015	$1,782	$1,336

ZT1500 23

YEARS MFRD 2015-2015
ENGINE . . . . B&S
ENGINE HP 24
COOLING . . . . AIR
FUEL . . . . G
SPEEDS . . . . VARIABLE
TRANSMISSION . . . . HYDRO
STEERING. . . . . ZERO
STANDARD DECK . . . . 46"
MSRP. $2,999

RETAIL PRICING

YEAR	HIGH	LOW
2015	$1,722	$1,291

ZT1500 24

YEARS MFRD 2014-2014
ENGINE . . . . B&S
ENGINE HP 24
COOLING . . . . AIR
FUEL . . . . G
SPEEDS . . . . VARIABLE
TRANSMISSION . . . . HYDRO
STEERING. . . . . ZERO
STANDARD DECK . . . . 52"
MSRP. $3,399

OPTIONS

3 BAG

RETAIL PRICING

YEAR	HIGH	LOW
2014	$2,068	$1,551

ZT1500 25

YEARS MFRD 2015-2015
ENGINE . . . . B&S
ENGINE HP 25
FUEL . . . . G
SPEEDS . . . . VARIABLE
TRANSMISSION . . . . HYDRO
STEERING. . . . . ZERO
STANDARD DECK . . . . 52"
MSRP. $3,199

RETAIL PRICING

YEAR	HIGH	LOW
2015	$1,919	$1,439

ZT1638

YEARS MFRD 2002-2003
SERIES. . . . . ZT SERIES
ENGINE HP 16
FUEL . . . . G
TRANSMISSION . . . . HYDRO
STEERING. . . . . ZERO
STANDARD DECK . . . . 38"
MSRP. $3,675

OPTIONS

2 BAG

RETAIL PRICING

YEAR	HIGH	LOW
2002	$764	$573
2003	$849	$637

ZT1644

YEARS MFRD 1998-2003
SERIES. . . . . ZT SERIES
ENGINE . . . . KOHLER
ENGINE HP 16
COOLING . . . . AIR
FUEL . . . . G
STEERING. . . . . ZERO
STANDARD DECK . . . . 44"
WEIGHT . . . . 581 LBS.
MSRP. $4,075

OPTIONS

BAG & FAN

RETAIL PRICING

YEAR	HIGH	LOW
1998	$558	$418
1999	$617	$463
2000	$685	$514
2001	$764	$573
2002	$846	$634
2003	$941	$706

ZT1844

YEARS MFRD 2004-2005
SERIES. . . . . . CONSUMER Z SERIES
ENGINE . . . . KOHLER
CYLINDERS. 1
ENGINE HP 18
COOLING . . . . AIR
FUEL . . . . G
SPEEDS . . . . VARIABLE
TRANSMISSION . . . . HYDRO
STEERING. . . . . ZERO
STANDARD DECK . . . . 44"
WEIGHT . . . . 957 LBS.
MSRP. $4,525

OPTIONS

2 BAG
3 BAG

RETAIL PRICING

YEAR	HIGH	LOW
2004	$1,158	$869
2005	$1,285	$964

ZT1850

YEARS MFRD 1999-2003
SERIES. . . . . ZT SERIES
ENGINE . . . . B&S
ENGINE HP 18
COOLING . . . . AIR
FUEL . . . . G
TRANSMISSION . . . . HYDRO
STEERING. . . . . ZERO
STANDARD DECK . . . . 50"
WEIGHT . . . . 612 LBS.
MSRP. $5,125

OPTIONS

BAG & FAN

RETAIL PRICING

YEAR	HIGH	LOW
1999	$778	$583
2000	$863	$647
2001	$959	$719
2002	$1,065	$799
2003	$1,182	$887

ZT2000 26/52

YEARS MFRD 2011-2013
ENGINE . . . . B&S
CYLINDERS. 2
ENGINE HP 26
COOLING . . . . AIR
FUEL . . . . G
SPEEDS . . . . VARIABLE
TRANSMISSION . . . . HYDRO
STEERING. . . . . ZERO
BLADE CLUTCH . . . . ELECTRIC
STANDARD DECK . . . . 52"
WEIGHT . . . . 554 LBS.
MSRP. $3,499

OPTIONS

3 BAG

RETAIL PRICING

YEAR	HIGH	LOW
2011	$1,551	$1,163
2012	$1,722	$1,291
2013	$1,914	$1,435

ZT2000 27/46

YEARS MFRD 2011-2012
ENGINE . . . . B&S PRO
CYLINDERS. 2
ENGINE HP 27
COOLING . . . . AIR
FUEL . . . . G
SPEEDS . . . . VARIABLE
TRANSMISSION . . . . HYDRO
STEERING. . . . . ZERO
BLADE CLUTCH . . . . ELECTRIC
STANDARD DECK . . . . 46"
WEIGHT . . . . 604 LBS.
MSRP. $3,800

OPTIONS

3 BAG

RETAIL PRICING

YEAR	HIGH	LOW
2011	$1,751	$1,313
2012	$1,943	$1,457

ZT2044

YEARS MFRD 2006-2007
SERIES. . . . . . . ZERO TURN SERIES
ENGINE . . . . B&S
ENGINE HP 20
COOLING . . . . AIR
FUEL . . . . G
SPEEDS . . . . VARIABLE
TRANSMISSION . . . . HYDRO
STEERING. . . . . ZERO
STANDARD DECK . . . . 44"
MSRP. $4,950

OPTIONS

2 BAG & FAN
3 BAG & FAN

RETAIL PRICING

YEAR	HIGH	LOW
2006	$1,488	$1,116
2007	$1,651	$1,238

ZT2050

YEARS MFRD 2004-2007
SERIES. . . . . CONSUMER Z SERIES
ENGINE . . . . B&S
CYLINDERS. 2
ENGINE HP 20
COOLING . . . . AIR
FUEL . . . . G
SPEEDS . . . . VARIABLE
TRANSMISSION . . . . HYDRO
STEERING. . . . . ZERO
STANDARD DECK . . . . 50"
WEIGHT . . . . 977 LBS.
MSRP. $5,595

OPTIONS

2 BAG & FAN
3 BAG & FAN

RETAIL PRICING

YEAR	HIGH	LOW
2004	$1,031	$773
2005	$1,140	$855
2006	$1,611	$1,208
2007	$1,791	$1,343

SIMPLICITY

ZT2148

YEARS MFRD 2002-2005
SERIES. . . . . CITATION SERIES
ENGINE . . . . B&S
CYLINDERS. 2
ENGINE HP 21
COOLING . . . . AIR
FUEL . . . . G
SPEEDS . . . . VARIABLE
TRANSMISSION . . . . HYDRO
STEERING. . . . . ZERO
BLADE CLUTCH . . . . ELECTRIC
STANDARD DECK . . . . 48"
WEIGHT . . . . 970 LBS.
MSRP. $5,695

OPTIONS

3 BAG

RETAIL PRICING

YEAR	HIGH	LOW
2002	$918	$688
2003	$1,016	$762
2004	$1,129	$847
2005	$1,253	$940

ZT2148

YEARS MFRD 2002-2003
SERIES. . . . . DERBY SERIES
ENGINE . . . . KOHLER
ENGINE HP 21
COOLING . . . . AIR
FUEL . . . . G
SPEEDS . . . . VARIABLE
TRANSMISSION . . . . HYDRO
STEERING. . . . . ZERO
STANDARD DECK . . . . 48"
MSRP. $6,299

RETAIL PRICING

YEAR	HIGH	LOW
2003	$3,234	$2,425

ZT2348T

YEARS MFRD 2004-2004
SERIES. . . . . . . DERBY COLT SERIES
ENGINE . . . . KOHLER
ENGINE HP 23
COOLING . . . . AIR
FUEL . . . . G
SPEEDS . . . . VARIABLE
TRANSMISSION . . . . HYDRO
STEERING. . . . . ZERO
STANDARD DECK . . . . 48"
MSRP. $6,699

RETAIL PRICING

YEAR	HIGH	LOW
2004	$1,810	$1,358

ZT2352

YEARS MFRD 2002-2005
SERIES. . . . . DERBY SERIES
ENGINE . . . . KOHLER
ENGINE HP 23
COOLING . . . . AIR
FUEL . . . . G
SPEEDS . . . . VARIABLE
TRANSMISSION . . . . HYDRO
STEERING. . . . . ZERO
STANDARD DECK . . . . 52"
MSRP. $6,395

OPTIONS

3 BAG

RETAIL PRICING

YEAR	HIGH	LOW
2002	$1,031	$773
2003	$1,144	$858
2004	$1,269	$952
2005	$1,416	$1,062

ZT2352

YEARS MFRD 2005-2006
SERIES. . . . . CITATION SERIES
ENGINE . . . . B&S
CYLINDERS. 2
ENGINE HP 23
COOLING . . . . AIR
FUEL . . . . G
SPEEDS . . . . VARIABLE
TRANSMISSION . . . . HYDRO
STEERING. . . . . ZERO
BLADE CLUTCH . . . . ELECTRIC
STANDARD DECK . . . . 52"
WEIGHT . . . . 1,000 LBS.
MSRP. $6,495

RETAIL PRICING

YEAR	HIGH	LOW
2005	$3,767	$2,825
2006	$3,982	$2,986

ZT2354

YEARS MFRD 2001-2002
SERIES. . . . . DERBY SERIES
ENGINE . . . . KOHLER
ENGINE HP 23
COOLING . . . . AIR
FUEL . . . . G
SPEEDS . . . . VARIABLE
TRANSMISSION . . . . . DUAL HYDRO
STEERING. . . . . ZERO
STANDARD DECK . . . . 54"
MSRP. $7,299

OPTIONS

3 BAG
ROPS

RETAIL PRICING

YEAR	HIGH	LOW
2001	$1,307	$980
2002	$1,453	$1,090

ZT2500 24

YEARS MFRD 2013-2014
SERIES. . . . . ZT SERIES
ENGINE . . . . B&S
ENGINE HP 24
COOLING . . . . AIR
FUEL . . . . G
SPEEDS . . . . VARIABLE
TRANSMISSION . . . . HYDRO
STEERING. . . . . ZERO
BLADE CLUTCH . . . . ELECTRIC
STANDARD DECK . . . . 48"
MSRP. $4,099

OPTIONS

3 BAG & FAN

RETAIL PRICING

YEAR	HIGH	LOW
2013	$2,177	$1,633
2014	$2,514	$1,886

ZT2500 25

YEARS MFRD 2015-2015
ENGINE . . . . B&S
ENGINE HP 25
COOLING . . . . AIR
FUEL . . . . G
SPEEDS . . . . VARIABLE
TRANSMISSION . . . . . DUAL HYDRO
STEERING. . . . . ZERO
STANDARD DECK . . . . 48"
MSRP. $3,799

RETAIL PRICING

YEAR	HIGH	LOW
2015	$2,291	$1,718

ZT2500 27

YEARS MFRD 2013-2013
SERIES. . . . . ZT SERIES
ENGINE . . . . B&S
CYLINDERS. 2
ENGINE HP 27
COOLING . . . . AIR
FUEL . . . . G
SPEEDS . . . . VARIABLE
TRANSMISSION . . . . HYDRO
STEERING. . . . . ZERO
BLADE CLUTCH . . . . ELECTRIC
STANDARD DECK . . . . 46"
MSRP. $4,099

OPTIONS

3 BAG & FAN

RETAIL PRICING

YEAR	HIGH	LOW
2013	$2,241	$1,681

ZT2561

YEARS MFRD 2001-2003
SERIES. . . . . DERBY SERIES
ENGINE . . . . B&S
ENGINE HP 25
COOLING . . . . AIR
FUEL . . . . G
SPEEDS . . . . VARIABLE
TRANSMISSION . . . . . DUAL HYDRO
STEERING. . . . . ZERO
STANDARD DECK . . . . 61"
MSRP. $7,999

OPTIONS

3 BAG
ROPS

RETAIL PRICING

YEAR	HIGH	LOW
2001	$1,474	$1,106
2002	$1,638	$1,229
2003	$1,819	$1,364

ZT2561F

YEARS MFRD 2005-2006
SERIES. . . . . STALLION SERIES
ENGINE . . . . KOHLER
CYLINDERS. 2
ENGINE HP 25
COOLING . . . . AIR
FUEL . . . . G
SPEEDS . . . . VARIABLE
TRANSMISSION . . . . HYDRO
STEERING. . . . . ZERO
BLADE CLUTCH . . . . ELECTRIC
STANDARD DECK . . . . 61"
WEIGHT . . . . 1,223 LBS.
MSRP. $10,395

RETAIL PRICING

YEAR	HIGH	LOW
2005	$6,027	$4,520
2006	$6,053	$4,540

ZT2761F

YEARS MFRD 2004-2004
SERIES. . . DERBY STALLION SERIES
ENGINE . . . . KOHLER
ENGINE HP 27
COOLING . . . . AIR
FUEL . . . . G
SPEEDS . . . . VARIABLE
TRANSMISSION . . . . HYDRO
STEERING. . . . . ZERO
STANDARD DECK . . . . 61"
MSRP. $8,299

OPTIONS

BAG & FAN
ROPS

RETAIL PRICING

YEAR	HIGH	LOW
2004	$2,074	$1,555

ZT3000 24/46

YEARS MFRD 2008-2012
ENGINE . . . . B&S EXTENDED
CYLINDERS. 2
ENGINE HP 24
COOLING . . . . AIR
FUEL . . . . G
SPEEDS . . . . VARIABLE
TRANSMISSION . . . . HYDRO
STEERING. . . . . ZERO
BLADE CLUTCH . . . . ELECTRIC
STANDARD DECK . . . . 46"
WEIGHT . . . . 712 LBS.
MSRP. $4,400

OPTIONS

3 BAG & FAN
50" DECK

RETAIL PRICING

YEAR	HIGH	LOW
2008	$1,480	$1,110
2009	$1,659	$1,244
2010	$1,826	$1,369
2011	$2,028	$1,521
2012	$2,251	$1,689

ZT3500 25

YEARS MFRD 2014-2015
ENGINE . . . . B&S
ENGINE HP 25
COOLING . . . . AIR
FUEL . . . . G
SPEEDS . . . . VARIABLE
TRANSMISSION . . . . . DUAL HYDRO
STEERING. . . . . ZERO
STANDARD DECK . . . . 48"
MSRP. $4,799

OPTIONS

FASTVAC

RETAIL PRICING

YEAR	HIGH	LOW
2014	$2,574	$1,931
2015	$2,937	$2,203

ZT3500 27

YEARS MFRD 2013-2013
SERIES. . . . . ZT SERIES
ENGINE . . . . B&S
ENGINE HP 27
COOLING . . . . AIR
FUEL . . . . G
SPEEDS . . . . VARIABLE
TRANSMISSION . . . . . DUAL HYDRO
STEERING. . . . . ZERO
BLADE CLUTCH . . . . ELECTRIC
STANDARD DECK . . . . 48"
MSRP. $4,799

OPTIONS

FAST VAC

RETAIL PRICING

YEAR	HIGH	LOW
2013	$2,624	$1,968

ZT4000 26/48

YEARS MFRD 2010-2012
ENGINE . . . . B&S
CYLINDERS. 2
ENGINE HP 26
COOLING . . . . AIR
FUEL . . . . G
SPEEDS . . . . VARIABLE
TRANSMISSION . . . . HYDRO
STEERING. . . . . ZERO
BLADE CLUTCH . . . . ELECTRIC
STANDARD DECK . . . . 48"
MSRP. $5,600

OPTIONS

2 BAG

RETAIL PRICING

YEAR	HIGH	LOW
2010	$2,322	$1,742
2011	$2,577	$1,933
2012	$2,866	$2,150

12.5FCH42

YEARS MFRD 1992-1994
SERIES. . . . . FRONT CUTTER SERIES
ENGINE . . . . B&S
CYLINDERS. 1
ENGINE HP 12.5
COOLING . . . . AIR
FUEL . . . . G
SPEEDS . . . . VARIABLE
TRANSMISSION . . . . HYDRO
STEERING. . . . . ZERO
STANDARD DECK . . . . 42"
MSRP. $3,790

RETAIL PRICING

YEAR	HIGH	LOW
1992	$221	$166
1993	$244	$183
1994	$274	$205

12.5H

YEARS MFRD 1993-1993
SERIES. . . . . FRONT CUTTER SERIES
ENGINE . . . . B&S
CYLINDERS. 1
ENGINE HP 12.5
COOLING . . . . AIR
FUEL . . . . G
SPEEDS . . . . VARIABLE
TRANSMISSION . . . . HYDRO
STEERING. . . . . ZERO
STANDARD DECK . . . . 42"
MSRP. $3,950

RETAIL PRICING

YEAR	HIGH	LOW
1993	$1,261	$946

12FCG42

YEARS MFRD 1990-1991
SERIES. . . . . FRONT CUTTER SERIES
ENGINE . . . . B&S
CYLINDERS. 1
ENGINE HP 12
COOLING . . . . AIR
FUEL . . . . G
TRANSMISSION . . . . GEAR
STEERING. . . . . ZERO
STANDARD DECK . . . . 42"
MSRP. $3,200

RETAIL PRICING

YEAR	HIGH	LOW
1991	$951	$713

12FCH42

YEARS MFRD 1990-1991
SERIES. . . . . FRONT CUTTER SERIES
ENGINE . . . . B&S
CYLINDERS. 1
ENGINE HP 12
COOLING . . . . AIR
FUEL . . . . G
SPEEDS . . . . VARIABLE
TRANSMISSION . . . . HYDRO
STEERING. . . . . ZERO
MSRP. $3,600

RETAIL PRICING

YEAR	HIGH	LOW
1991	$1,070	$802

13.5/30

YEARS MFRD 2009-2011
SERIES. . . . . CORONET SERIES
ENGINE . . . . B&S INTEK
CYLINDERS. 1
ENGINE HP 13.5
COOLING . . . . AIR
FUEL . . . . G
SPEEDS . . . . VARIABLE
TRANSMISSION . . . . HYDRO
STEERING. . . . . STANDARD
STANDARD DECK . . . . 30"
WEIGHT . . . . 415 LBS.
MSRP. $2,450

RETAIL PRICING

YEAR	HIGH	LOW
2009	$1,313	$985
2010	$1,399	$1,049
2011	$1,460	$1,095

13/30

YEARS MFRD 2007-2008
SERIES. . . . . CORONET SERIES
ENGINE . . . . B&S OHV
CYLINDERS. 1
ENGINE HP 13
COOLING . . . . AIR
FUEL . . . . G
SPEEDS . . . . VARIABLE
TRANSMISSION . . . . HYDRO
STEERING. . . . . STANDARD
STANDARD DECK . . . . 30"
WEIGHT . . . . 415 LBS.
MSRP. $2,249

RETAIL PRICING

YEAR	HIGH	LOW
2007	$1,200	$900
2008	$1,310	$983

13H

YEARS MFRD 1995-2012
SERIES. . . . . CORONET SERIES
ENGINE . . . . B&S
CYLINDERS. 1
ENGINE HP 13.5
COOLING . . . . AIR
FUEL . . . . G
SPEEDS . . . . VARIABLE
TRANSMISSION . . . . HYDRO
STEERING. . . . . ZERO
BLADE CLUTCH . . . . ELECTRIC
STANDARD DECK . . . . 30"
WEIGHT . . . . 531 LBS.
MSRP. $2,550

OPTIONS

2 BAG
CART

RETAIL PRICING

YEAR	HIGH	LOW
2003	$403	$302
2004	$449	$337
2005	$498	$373
2006	$551	$413
2007	$611	$458
2008	$677	$508
2009	$749	$562
2010	$829	$622
2011	$920	$690
2012	$1,019	$764

14.5

YEARS MFRD 2013-2013
ENGINE . . . . B&S
ENGINE HP 14.5
COOLING . . . . AIR
FUEL . . . . G
SPEEDS . . . . VARIABLE
TRANSMISSION . . . . HYDRO
STEERING. . . . . STANDARD
STANDARD DECK . . . . 33"
MSRP. $2,099

OPTIONS

2 BAG
BAGGER

RETAIL PRICING

YEAR	HIGH	LOW
2013	$877	$658

15.5

YEARS MFRD 2014-2014
ENGINE . . . . B&S
ENGINE HP 15.5
COOLING . . . . AIR
FUEL . . . . G
SPEEDS . . . . VARIABLE
TRANSMISSION . . . . HYDRO
STEERING. . . . . STANDARD
STANDARD DECK . . . . 33"
MSRP. $2,099

OPTIONS

2 BAG
BAGGER

RETAIL PRICING

YEAR	HIGH	LOW
2014	$919	$689

15.5H

YEARS MFRD 2000-2001
SERIES. . . . . EXPRESS SERIES
ENGINE . . . . B&S
ENGINE HP 15.5
FUEL . . . . G
TRANSMISSION . . . . HYDRO
STEERING. . . . . STANDARD
STANDARD DECK . . . . 38"
MSRP. $1,899

RETAIL PRICING

YEAR	HIGH	LOW
2000	$281	$211
2001	$313	$235

15G

YEARS MFRD 1994-1995
SERIES. . . . . . BROADMOOR SERIES
ENGINE . . . . B&S
ENGINE HP 15
COOLING . . . . AIR
FUEL . . . . G

SIMPLICITY

TRANSMISSION ... GEAR
STEERING ... STANDARD
STANDARD DECK ... 44"
MSRP ... $3,250

RETAIL PRICING

YEAR	HIGH	LOW
1994	$235	$176
1995	$259	$194

15H

YEARS MFRD ... 2000-2004
SERIES ... REGENT SERIES
ENGINE ... B&S
ENGINE HP ... 15
COOLING ... AIR
FUEL ... G
SPEEDS ... VARIABLE
TRANSMISSION ... HYDRO
STEERING ... STANDARD
STANDARD DECK ... 38"
WEIGHT ... 455 LBS.
MSRP ... $1,999

OPTIONS

2 BAG
36" SNOW THROWER
42" BLADE
GEAR

RETAIL PRICING

YEAR	HIGH	LOW
2000	$211	$159
2001	$235	$176
2002	$260	$195
2003	$288	$216
2004	$319	$239

15H

YEARS MFRD ... 1995-1997
SERIES ... BROADMOOR SERIES
ENGINE ... KOHLER
ENGINE HP ... 15
COOLING ... AIR
FUEL ... G
TRANSMISSION ... HYDRO
STEERING ... STANDARD
STANDARD DECK ... 44"
MSRP ... $3,500

OPTIONS

2 BAG
36" SNOW THROWER
42" BLADE

RETAIL PRICING

YEAR	HIGH	LOW
1995	$262	$196
1996	$289	$217
1997	$319	$239

16/34

YEARS MFRD ... 2007-2010
SERIES ... CORONET SERIES
ENGINE ... KOHLER COMMAND
CYLINDERS ... 1
ENGINE HP ... 16
COOLING ... AIR
FUEL ... G
SPEEDS ... VARIABLE
TRANSMISSION ... HYDRO
STEERING ... STANDARD
STANDARD DECK ... 34"
WEIGHT ... 446 LBS.
MSRP ... $2,850

RETAIL PRICING

YEAR	HIGH	LOW
2007	$1,413	$1,060
2008	$1,544	$1,158
2009	$1,582	$1,187
2010	$1,670	$1,253

16CFC

YEARS MFRD ... 1991-1994
SERIES ... FRONT CUTTER SERIES
ENGINE ... B&S
ENGINE HP ... 16
COOLING ... AIR
FUEL ... G
TRANSMISSION ... HYDRO
STEERING ... ZERO
STANDARD DECK ... 46"
MSRP ... $6,900

RETAIL PRICING

YEAR	HIGH	LOW
1991	$1,899	$1,424
1992	$2,008	$1,506
1993	$2,169	$1,627
1994	$2,327	$1,745

16CFC46

YEARS MFRD ... 1991-1994
SERIES ... FRONT CUTTER SERIES
ENGINE ... B&S
ENGINE HP ... 16
COOLING ... AIR
FUEL ... G
SPEEDS ... VARIABLE
TRANSMISSION ... HYDRO
STEERING ... ZERO
STANDARD DECK ... 46"
MSRP ... $6,900

OPTIONS

2 BAG & FAN
4 BAG & FAN

RETAIL PRICING

YEAR	HIGH	LOW
1991	$362	$271
1992	$402	$301
1993	$448	$336
1994	$498	$373

16CFCL

YEARS MFRD ... 1991-1992
SERIES ... FRONT CUTTER SERIES
ENGINE ... B&S
ENGINE HP ... 16
COOLING ... AIR
FUEL ... G
TRANSMISSION ... HYDRO
STEERING ... ZERO
STANDARD DECK ... 46"
MSRP ... $6,290

RETAIL PRICING

YEAR	HIGH	LOW
1991	$1,710	$1,283
1992	$1,947	$1,460

16CFCL46

YEARS MFRD ... 1991-1992
SERIES ... FRONT CUTTER SERIES
ENGINE ... B&S
ENGINE HP ... 16
COOLING ... AIR
FUEL ... G
SPEEDS ... VARIABLE
TRANSMISSION ... HYDRO
STEERING ... ZERO
STANDARD DECK ... 46"
MSRP ... $6,275

OPTIONS

2 BAG & FAN
4 BAG & FAN

RETAIL PRICING

YEAR	HIGH	LOW
1991	$284	$213
1992	$316	$237

16CFCS

YEARS MFRD ... 1991-1991
ENGINE ... B&S
ENGINE HP ... 16
FUEL ... G
TRANSMISSION ... HYDRO
STEERING ... STANDARD
STANDARD DECK ... 46"
MSRP ... $5,950

RETAIL PRICING

YEAR	HIGH	LOW
1991	$1,768	$1,326

16FCH

YEARS MFRD ... 1990-1997
SERIES ... FRONT CUTTER SERIES
ENGINE ... B&S
ENGINE HP ... 16
FUEL ... G
TRANSMISSION ... HYDRO
STEERING ... ZERO
STANDARD DECK ... 48"
MSRP ... $4,850

RETAIL PRICING

YEAR	HIGH	LOW
1990	$1,142	$856
1991	$1,248	$936
1992	$1,362	$1,021
1997	$1,825	$1,368

16FCH42

YEARS MFRD ... 1997-1997
SERIES ... FRONT CUTTER SERIES
ENGINE ... B&S
ENGINE HP ... 16
COOLING ... AIR
FUEL ... G
SPEEDS ... VARIABLE
TRANSMISSION ... HYDRO
STEERING ... ZERO
STANDARD DECK ... 42"
MSRP ... $4,850

OPTIONS

2 BAG & FAN
4 BAG & FAN

RETAIL PRICING

YEAR	HIGH	LOW
1997	$554	$415

16FCH48

YEARS MFRD ... 1990-1997
SERIES ... FRONT CUTTER SERIES
ENGINE ... B&S
ENGINE HP ... 16
COOLING ... AIR
FUEL ... G
SPEEDS ... VARIABLE
TRANSMISSION ... HYDRO
STEERING ... ZERO
STANDARD DECK ... 48"
MSRP ... $5,050

OPTIONS

2 BAG & FAN
4 BAG & FAN

RETAIL PRICING

YEAR	HIGH	LOW
1990	$281	$211
1991	$310	$233
1992	$344	$258
1993	$380	$285
1994	$422	$316
1995	$469	$351
1996	$524	$393
1997	$579	$434

16G

YEARS MFRD ... 1997-1998
SERIES ... REGENT SERIES
ENGINE ... B&S
ENGINE HP ... 16
COOLING ... AIR
FUEL ... G
TRANSMISSION ... GEAR
STEERING ... STANDARD
STANDARD DECK ... 44"
MSRP ... $2,950

OPTIONS

2 BAG
36" SNOW THROWER
42" BLADE

RETAIL PRICING

YEAR	HIGH	LOW
1997	$244	$183
1998	$272	$204

16G

YEARS MFRD ... 1993-1996
SERIES ... LANDLORD SERIES
ENGINE ... B&S
ENGINE HP ... 16
COOLING ... AIR
FUEL ... G

TRANSMISSION .... GEAR
STEERING .... STANDARD
STANDARD DECK .... 50"
MSRP $4,900

OPTIONS

36" TILLER
42" BLADE
42" SNOW THROWER
BAG & FAN

RETAIL PRICING

YEAR	HIGH	LOW
1993	$243	$182
1994	$268	$201
1995	$296	$222
1996	$328	$246

16GTH

YEARS MFRD 1992-1992
SERIES .... GT SERIES
ENGINE .... B&S
ENGINE HP 16
COOLING .... AIR
FUEL .... G
TRANSMISSION .... HYDRO
STEERING .... STANDARD
STANDARD DECK .... 50"
MSRP $5,190

RETAIL PRICING

YEAR	HIGH	LOW
1992	$267	$200

16H

YEARS MFRD 1993-2004
SERIES ...... BROADMOOR SERIES
ENGINE .... KOHLER
ENGINE HP 16
COOLING .... AIR
FUEL .... G
SPEEDS .... VARIABLE
TRANSMISSION .... HYDRO
STEERING .... STANDARD
STANDARD DECK .... 44"
WEIGHT .... 690 LBS.
MSRP $3,550

OPTIONS

2 BAG
36" SNOW THROWER
42" BLADE
SOFTCAB

RETAIL PRICING

YEAR	HIGH	LOW
1996	$271	$203
1997	$300	$225
1998	$330	$247
1999	$364	$273
2000	$403	$302
2001	$443	$332
2002	$490	$367
2003	$540	$405
2004	$597	$447

16H

YEARS MFRD 1996-1996
SERIES .... FRONT CUTTER SERIES
ENGINE .... B&S
ENGINE HP 16
COOLING .... AIR
FUEL .... G
TRANSMISSION .... HYDRO
STEERING .... ZERO
STANDARD DECK .... 48"
MSRP $4,700

OPTIONS

2 BAG & FAN
4 BAG & FAN

RETAIL PRICING

YEAR	HIGH	LOW
1996	$471	$354

16H

YEARS MFRD 1993-1998
SERIES .... LANDLORD SERIES
ENGINE .... B&S
ENGINE HP 16
COOLING .... AIR
FUEL .... G
TRANSMISSION .... HYDRO
STEERING .... STANDARD
STANDARD DECK .... 44"
MSRP $5,850

OPTIONS

36" TILLER
42" BLADE
42" SNOW THROWER
BAG & FAN

RETAIL PRICING

YEAR	HIGH	LOW
1993	$1,173	$880
1994	$1,263	$947
1995	$1,347	$1,010
1996	$1,397	$1,048
1997	$1,488	$1,116
1998	$1,618	$1,213

16H

YEARS MFRD 1997-2004
SERIES .... REGENT SERIES
ENGINE .... B&S
CYLINDERS 2
ENGINE HP 16
COOLING .... AIR
FUEL .... G
SPEEDS .... VARIABLE
TRANSMISSION .... HYDRO
STEERING .... STANDARD
STANDARD DECK .... 44"
WEIGHT .... 463 LBS.
MSRP $2,799

OPTIONS

36" SNOW THROWER
42" BLADE
BAG & FAN
KOHLER 16HP

RETAIL PRICING

YEAR	HIGH	LOW
1997	$218	$164
1998	$242	$181
1999	$268	$201
2000	$296	$222
2001	$329	$247
2002	$364	$273
2003	$404	$303
2004	$447	$335

16H

YEARS MFRD 2002-2010
SERIES .... CORONET SERIES
ENGINE ...... KOHLER COMMAND
CYLINDERS 1
ENGINE HP 16
COOLING .... AIR
FUEL .... G
SPEEDS .... VARIABLE
TRANSMISSION .... HYDRO
STEERING .... STANDARD
BLADE CLUTCH .... ELECTRIC
STANDARD DECK .... 34"
WEIGHT .... 446 LBS.
MSRP $2,850

OPTIONS

2 BAG
CART

RETAIL PRICING

YEAR	HIGH	LOW
2002	$400	$300
2003	$442	$332
2004	$491	$368
2005	$544	$408
2006	$601	$451
2007	$666	$500
2008	$738	$554
2009	$820	$615
2010	$908	$681

16H

YEARS MFRD 2002-2003
SERIES .... CONQUEST SERIES
ENGINE .... B&S
ENGINE HP 16
COOLING .... AIR
FUEL .... G
TRANSMISSION .... HYDRO
STEERING .... STANDARD
STANDARD DECK .... 44"
WEIGHT .... 698 LBS.
MSRP $4,399

OPTIONS

3 BAG
36" TILLER
40" SNOW BLOWER
42" BLADE

RETAIL PRICING

YEAR	HIGH	LOW
2002	$736	$552
2003	$810	$607

16HW

YEARS MFRD 1988-1990
SERIES .... SUNSTAR SERIES
ENGINE .... KOHLER
ENGINE HP 16
COOLING .... AIR
FUEL .... G
TRANSMISSION .... HYDRO
STEERING .... STANDARD
STANDARD DECK .... 48"
MSRP $6,349

RETAIL PRICING

YEAR	HIGH	LOW
1988	$209	$156
1989	$230	$172
1990	$259	$194

16LTH

YEARS MFRD 1990-1992
SERIES .... LT SERIES
ENGINE .... B&S
ENGINE HP 16
COOLING .... AIR
FUEL .... G
TRANSMISSION .... HYDRO
STEERING .... STANDARD
STANDARD DECK .... 44"
MSRP $3,990

RETAIL PRICING

YEAR	HIGH	LOW
1990	$1,031	$773
1991	$1,159	$869
1992	$1,235	$926

16VH

YEARS MFRD 1999-2004
SERIES ...... BROADMOOR SERIES
ENGINE .... B&S VANGUARD
CYLINDERS 2
ENGINE HP 16
COOLING .... AIR
FUEL .... G
SPEEDS .... VARIABLE
TRANSMISSION .... HYDRO
STEERING .... STANDARD
STANDARD DECK .... 44"
WEIGHT .... 700 LBS.
MSRP $3,850

OPTIONS

42" BLADE
42" SNOW THROWER
BAG & FAN
CAB

RETAIL PRICING

YEAR	HIGH	LOW
1999	$395	$296
2000	$436	$327
2001	$481	$361
2002	$531	$398
2003	$587	$440
2004	$653	$490

17GTH

YEARS MFRD 1991-1992
SERIES .... GT SERIES
ENGINE .... KOHLER
ENGINE HP 17
COOLING .... AIR
FUEL .... G
TRANSMISSION .... HYDRO
STEERING .... STANDARD
STANDARD DECK .... 48"
MSRP $5,170

SIMPLICITY

RETAIL PRICING

YEAR	HIGH	LOW
1991	$238	$178
1992	$267	$200

17H

YEARS MFRD 2003-2005
SERIES . . . . LANCER SERIES
ENGINE . . . . B&S
CYLINDERS 1
ENGINE HP 17
COOLING . . . . AIR
FUEL . . . . G
SPEEDS . . . . VARIABLE
TRANSMISSION . . . . HYDRO
STEERING . . . . ZERO
STANDARD DECK . . . . 44"
WEIGHT . . . . 635 LBS.
MSRP $3,895

RETAIL PRICING

YEAR	HIGH	LOW
2003	$866	$650
2004	$962	$722
2005	$1,069	$802

17H

YEARS MFRD 2000-2001
SERIES . . . . . . BROADMOOR SERIES
ENGINE . . . . B&S
ENGINE HP 17
COOLING . . . . LIQUID
FUEL . . . . G
TRANSMISSION . . . . HYDRO
STEERING . . . . STANDARD
STANDARD DECK . . . . 44"
MSRP $3,525

OPTIONS

2 BAG
36" SNOW THROWER
42" BLADE
SNOCAB

RETAIL PRICING

YEAR	HIGH	LOW
2000	$530	$397
2001	$587	$440

17H

YEARS MFRD 2000-2004
SERIES . . . . REGENT SERIES
ENGINE . . . . B&S
CYLINDERS 1
ENGINE HP 17
COOLING . . . . AIR
FUEL . . . . G
SPEEDS . . . . VARIABLE
TRANSMISSION . . . . HYDRO
STEERING . . . . STANDARD
STANDARD DECK . . . . 40"
WEIGHT . . . . 463 LBS.
MSRP $2,899

OPTIONS

36" SNOW THROWER
42" BLADE
42" SNOW BLOWER
SNOCAB

RETAIL PRICING

YEAR	HIGH	LOW
2000	$307	$231
2001	$340	$255
2002	$376	$282
2003	$418	$314
2004	$464	$348

17H

YEARS MFRD 2000-2001
SERIES . . . . EXPRESS SERIES
ENGINE . . . . B&S
ENGINE HP 17
COOLING . . . . AIR
FUEL . . . . G
TRANSMISSION . . . . HYDRO
STEERING . . . . STANDARD
STANDARD DECK . . . . 44"
MSRP $2,299

OPTIONS

2 BAG
42" BLADE
SNOCAB

RETAIL PRICING

YEAR	HIGH	LOW
2000	$266	$199
2001	$294	$220

17H

YEARS MFRD 1996-2000
SERIES . . . . LANDLORD SERIES
ENGINE . . . . KAWASAKI
ENGINE HP 17
COOLING . . . . LIQUID
FUEL . . . . G
TRANSMISSION . . . . HYDRO
STEERING . . . . STANDARD
STANDARD DECK . . . . 50"
MSRP $6,800

OPTIONS

3 BAG
36" TILLER
42" BLADE
42" SNOW THROWER

RETAIL PRICING

YEAR	HIGH	LOW
1996	$591	$443
1997	$653	$490
1998	$723	$542
1999	$799	$599
2000	$885	$663

18-HP HYDRO

YEARS MFRD 2005-2005
SERIES . . . . . . BROADMOOR SERIES
ENGINE . . . . B&S VANGUARD
CYLINDERS 2
ENGINE HP 18
COOLING . . . . AIR
FUEL . . . . G
SPEEDS . . . . VARIABLE
TRANSMISSION . . . . HYDRO
STEERING . . . . STANDARD
STANDARD DECK . . . . 38"
WEIGHT . . . . 690 LBS.
MSRP $3,755

OPTIONS

44" DECK
KOHLER 18HP

RETAIL PRICING

YEAR	HIGH	LOW
2005	$2,164	$1,623

18.5 AXION

YEARS MFRD 2009-2014
SERIES . . . . AXION SERIES
ENGINE . . . . B&S
CYLINDERS 1
ENGINE HP 18.5
COOLING . . . . AIR
FUEL . . . . G
SPEEDS . . . . VARIABLE
TRANSMISSION . . . . HYDRO
STEERING . . . . ZERO
BLADE CLUTCH . . . . ELECTRIC
STANDARD DECK . . . . 33"
MSRP $2,699

OPTIONS

2 BAG
CART

RETAIL PRICING

YEAR	HIGH	LOW
2009	$943	$707
2010	$1,046	$784
2011	$1,162	$872
2012	$1,291	$968
2013	$1,433	$1,075
2014	$1,618	$1,213

18/36 2691520

YEARS MFRD 2019-2020
SERIES . . . . COURIER SERIES
ENGINE . . . . KAWASAKI FR600V
CYLINDERS 2
CID 603
ENGINE HP 18
FUEL . . . . G
TRANSMISSION . . . . HYDRO
STEERING . . . . ZERO
BLADE CLUTCH . . . . ELECTRIC
STANDARD DECK . . . . 36"
MSRP $3,049

18/38

YEARS MFRD 2007-2010
SERIES . . . . . . BROADMOOR SERIES
ENGINE . . . . B&S VANGUARD
CYLINDERS 2
ENGINE HP 18
COOLING . . . . AIR
FUEL . . . . G
SPEEDS . . . . VARIABLE
TRANSMISSION . . . . HYDRO
STEERING . . . . STANDARD
STANDARD DECK . . . . 38"
WEIGHT . . . . 570 LBS.
MSRP $4,369

RETAIL PRICING

YEAR	HIGH	LOW
2007	$2,239	$1,679
2008	$2,322	$1,742
2009	$2,420	$1,815
2010	$2,561	$1,921

18CFC

YEARS MFRD 1993-1993
SERIES . . . . SUNSTAR SERIES
ENGINE . . . . KOHLER
ENGINE HP 18
FUEL . . . . G
TRANSMISSION . . . . HYDRO
STEERING . . . . STANDARD
STANDARD DECK . . . . 54"
MSRP $7,700

RETAIL PRICING

YEAR	HIGH	LOW
1993	$2,456	$1,842

18CFCL

YEARS MFRD 1991-1992
SERIES . . . . . FRONT CUTTER SERIES
ENGINE . . . . KOHLER
ENGINE HP 18
COOLING . . . . AIR
FUEL . . . . G
TRANSMISSION . . . . HYDRO
STEERING . . . . ZERO
STANDARD DECK . . . . 54"
MSRP $7,290

RETAIL PRICING

YEAR	HIGH	LOW
1991	$1,963	$1,472
1992	$2,255	$1,691

18CFCL54

YEARS MFRD 1991-1992
SERIES . . . . . FRONT CUTTER SERIES
ENGINE . . . . KOHLER
ENGINE HP 18
COOLING . . . . AIR
FUEL . . . . G
SPEEDS . . . . VARIABLE
TRANSMISSION . . . . HYDRO
STEERING . . . . ZERO
STANDARD DECK . . . . 54"
MSRP $7,195

OPTIONS

BAG & FAN

RETAIL PRICING

YEAR	HIGH	LOW
1991	$373	$280
1992	$415	$311

18CFCS

YEARS MFRD 1991-1992
SERIES . . . . . FRONT CUTTER SERIES
ENGINE . . . . KOHLER
ENGINE HP 18
COOLING . . . . AIR
FUEL . . . . G

TRANSMISSION . . . . HYDRO
STEERING . . . . ZERO
STANDARD DECK . . . . 54"
MSRP $7,490

RETAIL PRICING

YEAR	HIGH	LOW
1991	$2,021	$1,516
1992	$2,318	$1,739

18CFCS54

YEARS MFRD 1991-1993
SERIES . . . . . FRONT CUTTER SERIES
ENGINE . . . . KOHLER
ENGINE HP 18
COOLING . . . . AIR
FUEL . . . . G
SPEEDS . . . . VARIABLE
TRANSMISSION . . . . HYDRO
STEERING . . . . ZERO
STANDARD DECK . . . . 54"
MSRP $7,395

OPTIONS

BAG & FAN

RETAIL PRICING

YEAR	HIGH	LOW
1991	$391	$293
1992	$434	$325
1993	$479	$359

18G

YEARS MFRD 2005-2005
SERIES . . . . REGENT SERIES
ENGINE . . . . B&S
CYLINDERS 2
ENGINE HP 18
COOLING . . . . AIR
FUEL . . . . G
TRANSMISSION . . . . GEAR
STEERING . . . . STANDARD
BLADE CLUTCH . . . . ELECTRIC
STANDARD DECK . . . . 38"
WEIGHT . . . . 445 LBS.
MSRP $1,899

OPTIONS

2 BAG
42" BLADE
42" SNOW THROWER
SNOCAB

RETAIL PRICING

YEAR	HIGH	LOW
2005	$381	$286

18GTH

YEARS MFRD 1992-1992
SERIES . . . . GT SERIES
ENGINE . . . . KOHLER
ENGINE HP 18
COOLING . . . . AIR
FUEL . . . . G
TRANSMISSION . . . . HYDRO
STEERING . . . . STANDARD
STANDARD DECK . . . . 48"
MSRP $7,750

OPTIONS

36" TILLER
42" BLADE
42" SNOW THROWER
BAG & FAN

RETAIL PRICING

YEAR	HIGH	LOW
1992	$308	$231

18H

YEARS MFRD 1993-2001
SERIES . . . . LANDLORD SERIES
ENGINE . . . . B&S
ENGINE HP 18
COOLING . . . . AIR
FUEL . . . . G
SPEEDS . . . . VARIABLE
TRANSMISSION . . . . HYDRO
STEERING . . . . STANDARD
STANDARD DECK . . . . 50"
MSRP $6,399

OPTIONS

3 BAG
42" BLADE
42" SNOW THROWER
44" DECK

RETAIL PRICING

YEAR	HIGH	LOW
1993	$409	$307
1994	$454	$340
1995	$501	$375
1996	$555	$416
1997	$614	$461
1998	$679	$509
1999	$751	$563
2000	$830	$623
2001	$919	$689

18H

YEARS MFRD 2004-2006
SERIES . . . . . BROADMOOR SERIES
ENGINE . . . . B&S
ENGINE HP 18
FUEL . . . . G
SPEEDS . . . . VARIABLE
TRANSMISSION . . . . HYDRO
STEERING . . . . STANDARD
STANDARD DECK . . . . 44"
WEIGHT . . . . 783 LBS.
MSRP $3,850

OPTIONS

3 BAG
42" BLADE
42" SNOW BLOWER
46" SNOW THROWER
KOHLER 18HP

RETAIL PRICING

YEAR	HIGH	LOW
2004	$676	$507
2005	$743	$557
2006	$822	$616

18H

YEARS MFRD 1993-1997
SERIES . . . . SUNSTAR SERIES
ENGINE . . . . B&S
ENGINE HP 18
COOLING . . . . AIR
FUEL . . . . G
TRANSMISSION . . . . HYDRO
STEERING . . . . STANDARD
STANDARD DECK . . . . 48"
MSRP $7,950

OPTIONS

38" TILLER
47" SNOW BLOWER
BAG F&C
LDR

RETAIL PRICING

YEAR	HIGH	LOW
1993	$547	$410
1994	$605	$454
1995	$669	$502
1996	$739	$554
1997	$819	$614

18H

YEARS MFRD 2002-2004
SERIES . . . . CONQUEST SERIES
ENGINE . . . . B&S
CYLINDERS 2
ENGINE HP 18
COOLING . . . . AIR
FUEL . . . . G
SPEEDS . . . . VARIABLE
TRANSMISSION . . . . HYDRO
STEERING . . . . STANDARD
STANDARD DECK . . . . 44"
WEIGHT . . . . 711 LBS.
MSRP $4,525

OPTIONS

3 BAG
36" TILLER
40" SNOW BLOWER
42" BLADE

RETAIL PRICING

YEAR	HIGH	LOW
2002	$749	$562
2003	$827	$621
2004	$917	$687

18H

YEARS MFRD 2005-2005
SERIES . . . . . . CONSUMER Z SERIES
ENGINE . . . . KOHLER
CYLINDERS 1
ENGINE HP 18
COOLING . . . . AIR
FUEL . . . . G
SPEEDS . . . . VARIABLE
TRANSMISSION . . . . HYDRO
STEERING . . . . ZERO
BLADE CLUTCH . . . . ELECTRIC
STANDARD DECK . . . . 44"
WEIGHT . . . . 723 LBS.
MSRP $4,625

RETAIL PRICING

YEAR	HIGH	LOW
2005	$2,682	$2,012

18H

YEARS MFRD 2000-2001
SERIES . . . . BARON SERIES
ENGINE . . . . B&S
ENGINE HP 18
COOLING . . . . AIR
FUEL . . . . G
SPEEDS . . . . VARIABLE
TRANSMISSION . . . . HYDRO
STEERING . . . . STANDARD
STANDARD DECK . . . . 40"
MSRP $4,849

OPTIONS

36" SNOW THROWER
40" SNOW BLOWER
42" BLADE

RETAIL PRICING

YEAR	HIGH	LOW
2000	$501	$375
2001	$552	$414

18H

YEARS MFRD 1993-2000
SERIES . . . . SOVEREIGN SERIES
ENGINE . . . . KOHLER
ENGINE HP 18
COOLING . . . . AIR
FUEL . . . . G
TRANSMISSION . . . . HYDRO
STEERING . . . . STANDARD
STANDARD DECK . . . . 48"
MSRP $6,925

OPTIONS

42" SNOW BLOWER
42" SNOW THROWER
BAG & FAN
P/S

RETAIL PRICING

YEAR	HIGH	LOW
1993	$475	$356
1994	$526	$394
1995	$582	$437
1996	$643	$482
1997	$711	$533
1998	$788	$591
1999	$871	$653
2000	$963	$722

18H

YEARS MFRD 2006-2009
SERIES . . . . REGENT SERIES
ENGINE . . . . KOHLER COURAGE
CYLINDERS 1
ENGINE HP 18
COOLING . . . . AIR
FUEL . . . . G
SPEEDS . . . . VARIABLE
TRANSMISSION . . . . HYDRO
STEERING . . . . STANDARD
STANDARD DECK . . . . 38"
WEIGHT . . . . 502 LBS.
MSRP $2,285

SIMPLICITY

OPTIONS

2 BAG & FAN
42" BLADE
42" SNOW THROWER
SNOCAB

RETAIL PRICING

YEAR	HIGH	LOW
2006	$496	$372
2007	$549	$412
2008	$609	$457
2009	$675	$506

18H48

YEARS MFRD 1987-1990
SERIES SUNSTAR SERIES
ENGINE KOHLER
ENGINE HP 18
COOLING AIR
FUEL G
TRANSMISSION HYDRO
STEERING STANDARD
STANDARD DECK 48"
MSRP $6,949

RETAIL PRICING

YEAR	HIGH	LOW
1987	$207	$155
1988	$230	$172
1989	$256	$192
1990	$284	$213

18HPS

YEARS MFRD 1997-2000
SERIES SOVEREIGN SERIES
ENGINE KOHLER
ENGINE HP 18
FUEL G
TRANSMISSION HYDRO
STEERING STANDARD
STANDARD DECK 48"
MSRP $7,425

RETAIL PRICING

YEAR	HIGH	LOW
1997	$2,596	$1,947
1998	$2,815	$2,111
1999	$3,066	$2,300
2000	$3,280	$2,460

18VH GT

YEARS MFRD 2005-2009
SERIES BROADMOOR SERIES
ENGINE B&S
CYLINDERS 2
ENGINE HP 18
COOLING AIR
FUEL G
SPEEDS VARIABLE
TRANSMISSION HYDRO
STEERING STANDARD
STANDARD DECK 38"
WEIGHT 783 LBS.
MSRP $4,300

OPTIONS

2 BAG
42" BLADE
42" SNOW BLOWER
46" SNOW THROWER

RETAIL PRICING

YEAR	HIGH	LOW
2005	$853	$639
2006	$942	$706
2007	$1,039	$779
2008	$1,148	$861
2009	$1,267	$950

19.5

YEARS MFRD 2011-2012
SERIES REGENT SERIES
ENGINE B&S INTEK
CYLINDERS 1
ENGINE HP 19.5
COOLING AIR
FUEL G
SPEEDS VARIABLE
TRANSMISSION HYDRO
STEERING STANDARD
BLADE CLUTCH ELECTRIC
STANDARD DECK 38"
WEIGHT 502 LBS.
MSRP $2,399

OPTIONS

2 BAG
36" TILLER
42" BLADE
42" SNOW THROWER

RETAIL PRICING

YEAR	HIGH	LOW
2011	$889	$666
2012	$979	$734

19/36 2691501

YEARS MFRD 2019-2020
SERIES COURIER SERIES
ENGINE B&S
CYLINDERS 1
CID 500
ENGINE HP 19
FUEL G
TRANSMISSION HYDRO
STEERING ZERO
BLADE CLUTCH ELECTRIC
STANDARD DECK 36"
MSRP $2,649

20

YEARS MFRD 2011-2012
SERIES BROADMOOR SERIES
ENGINE B&S VANGUARD
CYLINDERS 2
ENGINE HP 20
COOLING AIR
FUEL G
SPEEDS VARIABLE
TRANSMISSION HYDRO
STEERING STANDARD
STANDARD DECK 46"
WEIGHT 701 LBS.
MSRP $4,300

OPTIONS

3 BAG & FAN
42" BLADE
42" SNOW BLOWER
50" TILLER

RETAIL PRICING

YEAR	HIGH	LOW
2011	$1,548	$1,161
2012	$1,720	$1,290

20

YEARS MFRD 2013-2013
SERIES REGENT EX
ENGINE B&S
ENGINE HP 20
COOLING AIR
FUEL G
SPEEDS VARIABLE
TRANSMISSION HYDRO
STEERING STANDARD
STANDARD DECK 38"
MSRP $2,599

OPTIONS

2 BAG & FAN
36" TILLER
42" BLADE
42" SNOW THROWER

RETAIL PRICING

YEAR	HIGH	LOW
2013	$1,225	$919

20

YEARS MFRD 2013-2013
SERIES REGENT SERIES
ENGINE B&S
ENGINE HP 20
COOLING AIR
FUEL G
SPEEDS VARIABLE
TRANSMISSION HYDRO
STEERING STANDARD
STANDARD DECK 42"
MSRP $2,299

OPTIONS

2 BAG
36"TILLER
42" BLADE
42" SNOW THROWER

RETAIL PRICING

YEAR	HIGH	LOW
2013	$1,083	$813

20 AXION

YEARS MFRD 2008-2009
SERIES AXION SERIES
ENGINE B&S ELS
CYLINDERS 1
ENGINE HP 20
COOLING AIR
SPEEDS VARIABLE
TRANSMISSION HYDRO
STEERING ZERO
STANDARD DECK 42"
MSRP $2,700

OPTIONS

2 BAG

RETAIL PRICING

YEAR	HIGH	LOW
2008	$959	$719
2009	$1,065	$799

20-HP HYDRO

YEARS MFRD 2005-2005
SERIES CONQUEST SERIES
ENGINE B&S VANGUARD
CYLINDERS 2
ENGINE HP 20
COOLING AIR
FUEL G
SPEEDS VARIABLE
TRANSMISSION HYDRO
STEERING STANDARD
STANDARD DECK 44"
WEIGHT 700 LBS.
MSRP $4,695

RETAIL PRICING

YEAR	HIGH	LOW
2005	$2,724	$2,043

20/38

YEARS MFRD 2007-2009
SERIES JAVELIN SERIES
ENGINE KOHLER COURAGE
CYLINDERS 1
ENGINE HP 20
COOLING AIR
FUEL G
SPEEDS VARIABLE
TRANSMISSION HYDRO
STEERING ZERO
STANDARD DECK 38"
WEIGHT 520 LBS.
MSRP $3,399

RETAIL PRICING

YEAR	HIGH	LOW
2007	$1,813	$1,360
2008	$1,981	$1,486
2009	$2,272	$1,704

20/44

YEARS MFRD 2007-2010
SERIES REGENT SERIES
ENGINE KOHLER COURAGE
CYLINDERS 1
ENGINE HP 20
COOLING AIR
FUEL G
SPEEDS VARIABLE
TRANSMISSION HYDRO
STEERING STANDARD
STANDARD DECK 44"
WEIGHT 502 LBS.
MSRP $2,879

RETAIL PRICING

YEAR	HIGH	LOW
2007	$1,385	$1,039
2008	$1,516	$1,137
2009	$1,616	$1,212
2010	$1,688	$1,266

20/44

YEARS MFRD........ 2007-2010
SERIES...... BROADMOOR SERIES
ENGINE......... B&S VANGUARD
CYLINDERS................ 2
ENGINE HP................ 20
COOLING................. AIR
FUEL..................... G
SPEEDS............ VARIABLE
TRANSMISSION.......... HYDRO
STEERING............ STANDARD
BLADE CLUTCH........ ELECTRIC
STANDARD DECK............ 44"
WEIGHT............. 580 LBS.
MSRP................ $4,695

RETAIL PRICING

YEAR	HIGH	LOW
2007	$2,292	$1,719
2008	$2,506	$1,879
2009	$2,685	$2,014
2010	$2,752	$2,064

20/44

YEARS MFRD........ 2007-2008
SERIES.......... JAVELIN SERIES
ENGINE......... B&S INTEK OHV
CYLINDERS................ 2
ENGINE HP................ 20
COOLING................. AIR
FUEL..................... G
SPEEDS............ VARIABLE
TRANSMISSION.......... HYDRO
STEERING................ ZERO
STANDARD DECK............ 44"
WEIGHT............. 575 LBS.
MSRP................ $3,799

OPTIONS

2 BAG

RETAIL PRICING

YEAR	HIGH	LOW
2007	$1,240	$930
2008	$1,374	$1,031

20/44

YEARS MFRD........ 2007-2007
SERIES........ CHAMPION SERIES
ENGINE....... KOHLER COURAGE
CYLINDERS................ 1
ENGINE HP................ 20
COOLING................. AIR
FUEL..................... G
SPEEDS............ VARIABLE
TRANSMISSION.......... HYDRO
STEERING................ ZERO
STANDARD DECK............ 44"
WEIGHT............. 712 LBS.
MSRP................ $4,950

RETAIL PRICING

YEAR	HIGH	LOW
2007	$2,641	$1,981

20/46

YEARS MFRD........ 2011-2012
SERIES...... BROADMOOR SERIES
ENGINE............... B&S PRO
CYLINDERS................ 2
ENGINE HP................ 20
COOLING................. AIR
FUEL..................... G
SPEEDS............ VARIABLE
TRANSMISSION.......... HYDRO
STEERING............ STANDARD
BLADE CLUTCH........ ELECTRIC
STANDARD DECK............ 46"
WEIGHT............. 580 LBS.
MSRP................ $4,300

RETAIL PRICING

YEAR	HIGH	LOW
2011	$2,134	$1,601
2012	$2,564	$1,923

20/50

YEARS MFRD........ 2007-2010
SERIES...... BROADMOOR SERIES
ENGINE......... B&S VANGUARD
CYLINDERS................ 2
ENGINE HP................ 20
COOLING................. AIR
FUEL..................... G
SPEEDS............ VARIABLE
TRANSMISSION.......... HYDRO
STEERING............ STANDARD
BLADE CLUTCH........ ELECTRIC
STANDARD DECK............ 50"
WEIGHT............. 591 LBS.
MSRP................ $4,999

RETAIL PRICING

YEAR	HIGH	LOW
2007	$2,453	$1,840
2008	$2,681	$2,011
2009	$2,856	$2,142
2010	$2,928	$2,196

20/50

YEARS MFRD........ 2007-2007
SERIES........ CHAMPION SERIES
ENGINE......... B&S VANGUARD
CYLINDERS................ 2
ENGINE HP................ 20
COOLING................. AIR
FUEL..................... G
SPEEDS............ VARIABLE
TRANSMISSION.......... HYDRO
STEERING................ ZERO
STANDARD DECK............ 50"
WEIGHT............. 723 LBS.
MSRP................ $5,595

RETAIL PRICING

YEAR	HIGH	LOW
2007	$2,987	$2,240

20/50

YEARS MFRD........ 2007-2007
SERIES.......... JAVELIN SERIES
ENGINE......... B&S INTEK OHV
CYLINDERS................ 2
ENGINE HP................ 22
COOLING................. AIR
FUEL..................... G
SPEEDS............ VARIABLE
TRANSMISSION.......... HYDRO
STEERING................ ZERO
STANDARD DECK............ 50"
WEIGHT............. 590 LBS.
MSRP................ $3,999

RETAIL PRICING

YEAR	HIGH	LOW
2007	$2,133	$1,600

20/52

YEARS MFRD........ 2011-2011
SERIES...... BROADMOOR SERIES
ENGINE......... B&S VANGUARD
CYLINDERS................ 2
ENGINE HP................ 20
COOLING................. AIR
FUEL..................... G
SPEEDS............ VARIABLE
TRANSMISSION.......... HYDRO
STEERING............ STANDARD
BLADE CLUTCH........ ELECTRIC
STANDARD DECK............ 52"
WEIGHT............. 595 LBS.
MSRP................ $4,700

RETAIL PRICING

YEAR	HIGH	LOW
2011	$2,548	$1,911

20CFC

YEARS MFRD........ 1993-1994
SERIES..... FRONT CUTTER SERIES
ENGINE.............. KOHLER
ENGINE HP................ 20
COOLING................. AIR
FUEL..................... G
TRANSMISSION.......... HYDRO
STEERING................ ZERO
STANDARD DECK............ 60"
MSRP................ $8,100

RETAIL PRICING

YEAR	HIGH	LOW
1993	$2,549	$1,912
1994	$2,732	$2,049

20CFC60

YEARS MFRD........ 1991-1994
SERIES..... FRONT CUTTER SERIES
ENGINE.............. KOHLER
ENGINE HP................ 20
COOLING................. AIR
FUEL..................... G
SPEEDS............ VARIABLE
TRANSMISSION.......... HYDRO
STEERING................ ZERO
STANDARD DECK............ 60"
MSRP................ $7,975

OPTIONS

BAG & FAN

RETAIL PRICING

YEAR	HIGH	LOW
1991	$463	$347
1992	$512	$384
1993	$568	$426
1994	$629	$471

20CFCL

YEARS MFRD........ 1991-1992
SERIES..... FRONT CUTTER SERIES
ENGINE.............. KOHLER
ENGINE HP................ 20
COOLING................. AIR
FUEL..................... G
TRANSMISSION.......... HYDRO
STEERING................ ZERO
STANDARD DECK............ 60"
MSRP................ $7,590

RETAIL PRICING

YEAR	HIGH	LOW
1991	$2,052	$1,539
1992	$2,349	$1,762

20CFCL60

YEARS MFRD........ 1991-1992
SERIES..... FRONT CUTTER SERIES
ENGINE.............. KOHLER
ENGINE HP................ 20
COOLING................. AIR
FUEL..................... G
SPEEDS............ VARIABLE
TRANSMISSION.......... HYDRO
STEERING................ ZERO
STANDARD DECK............ 60"
MSRP................ $7,495

OPTIONS

BAG & FAN

RETAIL PRICING

YEAR	HIGH	LOW
1991	$411	$308
1992	$458	$343

20CFCS

YEARS MFRD........ 1991-1992
ENGINE.............. KOHLER
ENGINE HP................ 20
FUEL..................... G
TRANSMISSION.......... HYDRO
STEERING............ STANDARD
STANDARD DECK............ 60"
MSRP................ $7,790

RETAIL PRICING

YEAR	HIGH	LOW
1991	$2,109	$1,582
1992	$2,410	$1,808

20GTH

YEARS MFRD........ 1991-1992
SERIES............. GT SERIES
ENGINE.............. KOHLER
ENGINE HP................ 20
COOLING................. AIR
FUEL..................... G
TRANSMISSION.......... HYDRO
STEERING............ STANDARD
STANDARD DECK............ 48"
MSRP................ $8,250

OPTIONS

36" TILLER
40" SNOW BLOWER
60" DECK
BAG & FAN

SIMPLICITY

RETAIL PRICING

YEAR	HIGH	LOW
1991	$296	$222
1992	$328	$246

20H

YEARS MFRD 2006-2009
SERIES .... REGENT SERIES
ENGINE .... B&S
CYLINDERS 2
ENGINE HP 20
COOLING .... AIR
FUEL .... G
SPEEDS .... VARIABLE
TRANSMISSION .... HYDRO
STEERING .... STANDARD
STANDARD DECK .... 38"
WEIGHT .... 520 LBS.
MSRP $2,600

OPTIONS

2 BAG & FAN
42" BLADE
42" SNOW THROWER
SNOCAB

RETAIL PRICING

YEAR	HIGH	LOW
2006	$571	$428
2007	$634	$476
2008	$704	$528
2009	$784	$588

20H

YEARS MFRD 2002-2005
SERIES .... CONQUEST SERIES
ENGINE .... KOHLER
CYLINDERS 2
ENGINE HP 20
COOLING .... AIR
FUEL .... G
SPEEDS .... VARIABLE
TRANSMISSION .... HYDRO
STEERING .... STANDARD
STANDARD DECK .... 44"
WEIGHT .... 867 LBS.
MSRP $4,695

OPTIONS

3 BAG
42" BLADE
42" SNOW BLOWER

RETAIL PRICING

YEAR	HIGH	LOW
2002	$764	$573
2003	$846	$634
2004	$936	$702
2005	$1,036	$777

20H

YEARS MFRD 1999-2001
SERIES .... LANDLORD SERIES
ENGINE .... B&S
ENGINE HP 20
COOLING .... AIR
FUEL .... G
TRANSMISSION .... HYDRO
STEERING .... STANDARD
STANDARD DECK .... 50"
MSRP $6,799

OPTIONS

3 BAG
36" TILLER
42" BLADE
42" SNOW THROWER

RETAIL PRICING

YEAR	HIGH	LOW
1999	$798	$599
2000	$883	$662
2001	$977	$733

20H

YEARS MFRD 1998-2003
SERIES .... LEGACY SERIES
ENGINE .... KOHLER
CYLINDERS 2
ENGINE HP 20
COOLING .... AIR
FUEL .... G
SPEEDS .... VARIABLE
TRANSMISSION .... HYDRO
STEERING .... STANDARD
STANDARD DECK .... 48"
WEIGHT .... 1,050 LBS.
MSRP $8,525

OPTIONS

3 BAG
47" SNOW BLOWER
50" TILLER
54" DECK

RETAIL PRICING

YEAR	HIGH	LOW
1998	$949	$711
1999	$1,049	$786
2000	$1,160	$870
2001	$1,283	$962
2002	$1,425	$1,069
2003	$1,571	$1,179

20H

YEARS MFRD 2002-2004
SERIES .... PRESTIGE SERIES
ENGINE .... KOHLER
ENGINE HP 20
COOLING .... AIR
FUEL .... G
TRANSMISSION .... HYDRO
STEERING .... STANDARD
STANDARD DECK .... 50"
WEIGHT .... 791 LBS.
MSRP $5,725

OPTIONS

3 BAG
40" SNOW BLOWER
P/S

RETAIL PRICING

YEAR	HIGH	LOW
2002	$1,010	$757
2003	$1,117	$838
2004	$1,236	$927

20H

YEARS MFRD 1993-1997
SERIES .... SUNSTAR SERIES
ENGINE .... KOHLER
ENGINE HP 20
COOLING .... AIR
FUEL .... G
TRANSMISSION .... HYDRO
STEERING .... STANDARD
STANDARD DECK .... 48"
MSRP $8,250

OPTIONS

38" TILLER
42" SNOW THROWER
60" DECK
BAG & FAN

RETAIL PRICING

YEAR	HIGH	LOW
1993	$568	$426
1994	$628	$471
1995	$695	$521
1996	$768	$576
1997	$850	$637

20H

YEARS MFRD 2005-2005
SERIES ...... CONSUMER Z SERIES
ENGINE .... B&S
CYLINDERS 2
ENGINE HP 20
COOLING .... AIR
FUEL .... G
SPEEDS .... VARIABLE
TRANSMISSION .... HYDRO
STEERING .... ZERO
BLADE CLUTCH .... ELECTRIC
STANDARD DECK .... 50"
WEIGHT .... 712 LBS.
MSRP $5,295

RETAIL PRICING

YEAR	HIGH	LOW
2005	$3,070	$2,303

20HPS

YEARS MFRD 2002-2004
SERIES .... PRESTIGE SERIES
ENGINE .... KOHLER
CYLINDERS 2
ENGINE HP 20
FUEL .... G
SPEEDS .... VARIABLE
TRANSMISSION .... HYDRO
STEERING .... STANDARD
STANDARD DECK .... 50"
WEIGHT .... 791 LBS.
MSRP $6,079

RETAIL PRICING

YEAR	HIGH	LOW
2002	$2,878	$2,158
2003	$3,121	$2,341
2004	$3,322	$2,492

20HW

YEARS MFRD 1988-1990
SERIES .... SUNSTAR SERIES
ENGINE .... KOHLER
ENGINE HP 20
COOLING .... AIR
FUEL .... G
TRANSMISSION .... HYDRO
STEERING .... STANDARD
STANDARD DECK .... 48"
MSRP $7,545

RETAIL PRICING

YEAR	HIGH	LOW
1988	$249	$187
1989	$277	$208
1990	$306	$229

20LC

YEARS MFRD 1998-2002
SERIES .... LEGACY SERIES
ENGINE .... KAWASAKI
ENGINE HP 20
COOLING .... LIQUID
FUEL .... D
TRANSMISSION .... HYDRO
STEERING .... STANDARD
STANDARD DECK .... 54"
WEIGHT .... 1,050 LBS.
MSRP $9,799

OPTIONS

3 BAG
47" SNOW BLOWER
50" TILLER
60" BLADE

RETAIL PRICING

YEAR	HIGH	LOW
1998	$1,087	$816
1999	$1,203	$902
2000	$1,331	$998
2001	$1,472	$1,104
2002	$1,629	$1,221

21

YEARS MFRD 2013-2013
SERIES ...... BROADMOOR SERIES
ENGINE .... VANGUARD
ENGINE HP 21
COOLING .... AIR
FUEL .... G
SPEEDS .... VARIABLE
TRANSMISSION .... HYDRO
STEERING .... STANDARD
STANDARD DECK .... 44"
MSRP $4,399

OPTIONS

3 BAG & FAN
36" TILLER
42" BLADE
42" SNOW BLOWER

RETAIL PRICING

YEAR	HIGH	LOW
2013	$1,994	$1,496

21 AXION

YEARS MFRD 2010-2012
SERIES . . . . AXION SERIES
ENGINE . . . . B&S
ENGINE HP 21
COOLING . . . . AIR
FUEL . . . . G
SPEEDS . . . . VARIABLE
TRANSMISSION . . . . HYDRO
STEERING . . . . ZERO
STANDARD DECK . . . . 42"
MSRP $2,700

OPTIONS

2 BAG
CART

RETAIL PRICING

YEAR	HIGH	LOW
2010	$1,119	$840
2011	$1,245	$933
2012	$1,382	$1,037

21 CITATION

YEARS MFRD 2007-2009
SERIES . . . . CITATION SERIES
ENGINE . . . . B&S VANGUARD
CYLINDERS 2
ENGINE HP 21
COOLING . . . . AIR
FUEL . . . . G
SPEEDS . . . . VARIABLE
TRANSMISSION . . . . HYDRO
STEERING . . . . ZERO
STANDARD DECK . . . . 48"
WEIGHT . . . . 970 LBS.
MSRP $6,900

OPTIONS

3 BAG & FAN
ROPS

RETAIL PRICING

YEAR	HIGH	LOW
2007	$2,226	$1,670
2008	$2,452	$1,839
2009	$2,735	$2,052

21.5/42

YEARS MFRD 2018-2019
SERIES . . . . COURIER SERIES
ENGINE . . . . KAWASAKI FR651
CYLINDERS 2
CID 726CC
ENGINE HP 21.5
FUEL . . . . G
TRANSMISSION . . . . HYDRO
STEERING . . . . ZERO
STANDARD DECK . . . . 42"
MSRP $3,399

21.5/42 2691658

YEARS MFRD 2020-2020
SERIES . . . . COURIER SERIES
ENGINE . . . . KAWASAKI FR651
CYLINDERS 2
CID 726CC
ENGINE HP 21.5
FUEL . . . . G
SPEEDS . . . . VARIABLE
TRANSMISSION . . . . HYDRO
STEERING . . . . ZERO
BLADE CLUTCH . . . . ELECTRIC
STANDARD DECK . . . . 42"
MSRP $3,399

21.5/48

YEARS MFRD 2018-2019
SERIES . . . . COURIER SERIES
ENGINE . . . . KAWASAKI FR651
CYLINDERS 2
CID 726CC
ENGINE HP 21.5
FUEL . . . . G
TRANSMISSION . . . . HYDRO
STEERING . . . . ZERO
STANDARD DECK . . . . 48"
MSRP $4,099

21.5/48 2691660

YEARS MFRD 2020-2020
SERIES . . . . COURIER SERIES
ENGINE . . . . KAWASAKI FR651
CYLINDERS 2
CID 726CC
ENGINE HP 21.5
FUEL . . . . G
SPEEDS . . . . VARIABLE
TRANSMISSION . . . . HYDRO
STEERING . . . . ZERO
BLADE CLUTCH . . . . ELECTRIC
STANDARD DECK . . . . 48"
MSRP $4,199

21.5/52

YEARS MFRD 2018-2019
SERIES . . . . COURIER SERIES
ENGINE . . . . KAWASAKI FR651
CYLINDERS 2
CID 726CC
ENGINE HP 21.5
FUEL . . . . G
TRANSMISSION . . . . HYDRO
STEERING . . . . ZERO
STANDARD DECK . . . . 52"
MSRP $4,649

21.5/52 2691662

YEARS MFRD 2020-2020
SERIES . . . . COURIER SERIES
ENGINE . . . . KAWASAKI FR651
CYLINDERS 2
CID 726CC
ENGINE HP 21.5
FUEL . . . . G
SPEEDS . . . . VARIABLE
TRANSMISSION . . . . HYDRO
STEERING . . . . ZERO
BLADE CLUTCH . . . . ELECTRIC
STANDARD DECK . . . . 52"
MSRP $5,949

22

YEARS MFRD 2014-2017
SERIES . . . . REGENT EX SERIES
ENGINE . . . . B&S
ENGINE HP 22
COOLING . . . . AIR
FUEL . . . . G
SPEEDS . . . . VARIABLE
TRANSMISSION . . . . HYDRO
STEERING . . . . STANDARD
STANDARD DECK . . . . 38"
MSRP $2,399

OPTIONS

2 BAG
36" TILLER
42" BLADE
42" SNOW THROWER

RETAIL PRICING

YEAR	HIGH	LOW
2014	$1,100	$825
2015	$1,220	$915
2016	$1,352	$1,014
2017	$1,500	$1,125

22

YEARS MFRD 2011-2012
SERIES . . . . REGENT SERIES
ENGINE . . . . B&S
ENGINE HP 22
COOLING . . . . AIR
FUEL . . . . G
SPEEDS . . . . VARIABLE
TRANSMISSION . . . . HYDRO
STEERING . . . . STANDARD
STANDARD DECK . . . . 44"
MSRP $2,899

OPTIONS

2 BAG
36" TILLER
42" BLADE
42" SNOW THROWER

RETAIL PRICING

YEAR	HIGH	LOW
2011	$1,305	$978
2012	$1,445	$1,084

22

YEARS MFRD 2011-2017
SERIES . . . . . BROADMOOR SERIES
ENGINE . . . . B&S PRO
CYLINDERS 2
ENGINE HP 22
COOLING . . . . AIR
FUEL . . . . G
SPEEDS . . . . VARIABLE
TRANSMISSION . . . . HYDRO
STEERING . . . . STANDARD
BLADE CLUTCH . . . . ELECTRIC
STANDARD DECK . . . . 44"
WEIGHT . . . . 570 LBS.
MSRP $3,899

OPTIONS

3 BAG & FAN
36" TILLER
42" BLADE
42" SNOW BLOWER

RETAIL PRICING

YEAR	HIGH	LOW
2011	$1,252	$939
2012	$1,392	$1,044
2013	$1,539	$1,155
2014	$1,706	$1,280
2015	$1,892	$1,419
2016	$2,097	$1,573
2017	$2,326	$1,745

22 B&S

YEARS MFRD 2014-2015
SERIES . . . . REGENT SERIES
ENGINE . . . . B&S
ENGINE HP 22
COOLING . . . . AIR
FUEL . . . . G
SPEEDS . . . . VARIABLE
TRANSMISSION . . . . HYDRO
STEERING . . . . STANDARD
STANDARD DECK . . . . 42"
MSRP $2,299

OPTIONS

2 BAG
36" TILLER
42" BLADE
42" SNOW BLOWER

RETAIL PRICING

YEAR	HIGH	LOW
2014	$1,224	$918
2015	$1,356	$1,017

22/48 2691671

YEARS MFRD 2020-2020
SERIES . . . . . . BROADMOOR SERIES
ENGINE . . . . . BRIGGS & STRATTON
CYLINDERS 2
CID 724CC
ENGINE HP 22
SPEEDS . . . . VARIABLE
TRANSMISSION . . . . HYDRO
STEERING . . . . STANDARD
BLADE CLUTCH . . . . ELECTRIC
STANDARD DECK . . . . 48"
MSRP $3,999

22/50

YEARS MFRD 2007-2008
SERIES . . . . JAVELIN
ENGINE . . . . B&S
CYLINDERS 2
ENGINE HP 22
COOLING . . . . AIR
FUEL . . . . G
SPEEDS . . . . VARIABLE
TRANSMISSION . . . . HYDRO
STEERING . . . . ZERO
BLADE CLUTCH . . . . ELECTRIC

STANDARD DECK . . . . 50"
WEIGHT . . . . 590 LBS.
MSRP. $3,999

OPTIONS

3 BAG

RETAIL PRICING

YEAR	HIGH	LOW
2007	$1,305	$978
2008	$1,449	$1,087

22H

YEARS MFRD 2005-2005
SERIES. . . . . CONQUEST SERIES
ENGINE . . . . .VANGUARD
CYLINDERS. 2
ENGINE HP 22
COOLING . . . . .AIR
FUEL . . . . G
SPEEDS . . . . VARIABLE
TRANSMISSION . . . . .HYDRO
STEERING. . . . . .STANDARD
STANDARD DECK . . . . 50"
WEIGHT . . . . 778 LBS.
MSRP. $5,125

OPTIONS

3 BAG
36" TILLER
42" SNOW BLOWER
54" DECK

RETAIL PRICING

YEAR	HIGH	LOW
2005	$1,131	$848

22H

YEARS MFRD 2006-2009
SERIES. . . . . REGENT SERIES
ENGINE . . . . B&S
CYLINDERS. 2
ENGINE HP 22
COOLING . . . . .AIR
FUEL . . . . G
SPEEDS . . . . VARIABLE
TRANSMISSION . . . . .HYDRO
STEERING. . . . . .STANDARD
STANDARD DECK . . . . 44"
WEIGHT . . . . 552 LBS.
MSRP. $2,900

OPTIONS

3 BAG & FAN
42" BLADE
42" SNOW THROWER
SNOCAB

RETAIL PRICING

YEAR	HIGH	LOW
2006	$639	$479
2007	$708	$531
2008	$784	$588
2009	$870	$653

23

YEARS MFRD 2014-2019
SERIES. . . . . . BROADMOOR SERIES
ENGINE . . . . B&S
ENGINE HP 23
COOLING . . . . .AIR
FUEL . . . . G
SPEEDS . . . . VARIABLE
TRANSMISSION . . . . .HYDRO
STEERING. . . . . .STANDARD
STANDARD DECK . . . . 50"
MSRP. $4,349

OPTIONS

36" TILLER
42" SNOW THROWER
48" BLADE

RETAIL PRICING

YEAR	HIGH	LOW
2014	$1,839	$1,379
2015	$2,038	$1,528
2016	$2,261	$1,696
2017	$2,506	$1,879
2018	$2,767	$2,076
2019	$3,051	$2,288

23

YEARS MFRD 2011-2012
SERIES. . . . . CONQUEST SERIES
ENGINE . . . . KOHLER COURAGE
CYLINDERS. 2
ENGINE HP 23
COOLING . . . . .AIR
FUEL . . . . G
SPEEDS . . . . VARIABLE
TRANSMISSION . . . . .HYDRO
STEERING. . . . . .STANDARD
BLADE CLUTCH . . . . .ELECTRIC
STANDARD DECK . . . . 46"
WEIGHT . . . . 700 LBS.
MSRP. $5,799

OPTIONS

3 BAG & FAN
42" BLADE
42" SNOW BLOWER
42" SNOW THROWER

RETAIL PRICING

YEAR	HIGH	LOW
2011	$2,214	$1,660
2012	$2,448	$1,836

23

YEARS MFRD 2013-2017
SERIES. . . . . REGENT EX SERIES
ENGINE . . . . B&S
ENGINE HP 23
COOLING . . . . .AIR
FUEL . . . . G
SPEEDS . . . . VARIABLE
TRANSMISSION . . . . .HYDRO
STEERING. . . . . .STANDARD
STANDARD DECK . . . . 42"
MSRP. $2,799

OPTIONS

3 BAG & FAN
36" TILLER
42" BLADE
42" SNOW BLOWER

RETAIL PRICING

YEAR	HIGH	LOW
2013	$1,099	$824
2014	$1,215	$912
2015	$1,347	$1,010
2016	$1,494	$1,120
2017	$1,656	$1,242

23 CITATION

YEARS MFRD 2007-2009
SERIES. . . . . CITATION SERIES
ENGINE . . . . B&S VANGUARD
CYLINDERS. 2
ENGINE HP 23
COOLING . . . . .AIR
FUEL . . . . G
SPEEDS . . . . VARIABLE
TRANSMISSION . . . . .HYDRO
STEERING. . . . . ZERO
STANDARD DECK . . . . 52"
WEIGHT . . . . 1,000 LBS.
MSRP. $7,700

OPTIONS

3 BAG & FAN
ROPS

RETAIL PRICING

YEAR	HIGH	LOW
2007	$2,460	$1,845
2008	$2,744	$2,058
2009	$3,037	$2,278

23 CITATION XT

YEARS MFRD 2014-2015
ENGINE . . . . KAWASAKI
ENGINE HP 23
COOLING . . . . .AIR
FUEL . . . . G
SPEEDS . . . . VARIABLE
TRANSMISSION . . . . .HYDRO
STEERING. . . . . ZERO
STANDARD DECK . . . . 52"
MSRP. $7,199

OPTIONS

FASTVAC

RETAIL PRICING

YEAR	HIGH	LOW
2014	$3,864	$2,898
2015	$4,539	$3,404

23 KOH

YEARS MFRD 2007-2008
SERIES. . . . . CONQUEST SERIES
ENGINE . . . . KOHLER COURAGE
CYLINDERS. 2
ENGINE HP 23
COOLING . . . . .AIR
FUEL . . . . G
SPEEDS . . . . VARIABLE
TRANSMISSION . . . . .HYDRO
STEERING. . . . . .STANDARD
BLADE CLUTCH . . . . .ELECTRIC
STANDARD DECK . . . . 44"
WEIGHT . . . . 700 LBS.
MSRP. $5,024

OPTIONS

3 BAG & FAN
42" BLADE
42" SNOW BLOWER
42" SNOW THROWER

RETAIL PRICING

YEAR	HIGH	LOW
2007	$1,330	$997
2008	$1,471	$1,103

23/36 2691519

YEARS MFRD 2019-2020
SERIES. . . . . COURIER SERIES
ENGINE . . . . B&S
CYLINDERS. 2
CID 724
ENGINE HP 23
FUEL . . . . G
TRANSMISSION . . . . .HYDRO
STEERING. . . . . ZERO
BLADE CLUTCH . . . . .ELECTRIC
STANDARD DECK . . . . 36"
MSRP. $2,949

23/38 2691454

YEARS MFRD 2018-2020
SERIES. . . . . REGENT SERIES
ENGINE . . . . B&S
CYLINDERS. 2
CID 724CC
ENGINE HP 23
TRANSMISSION . . . . .HYDRO
STEERING. . . . . .STANDARD
STANDARD DECK . . . . 38"
MSRP. $2,549

23/42 2691455

YEARS MFRD 2018-2020
SERIES. . . . . REGENT SERIES
ENGINE . . . . B&S
CYLINDERS. 2
CID 724CC
ENGINE HP 23
TRANSMISSION . . . . .HYDRO
STEERING. . . . . .STANDARD
STANDARD DECK . . . . 42"
MSRP. $2,749

23/42 2691657

YEARS MFRD 2020-2020
SERIES. . . . . COURIER SERIES
ENGINE . . . . . BRIGGS & STRATTON
CYLINDERS. 2
CID 724CC
ENGINE HP 23
FUEL . . . . G
SPEEDS . . . . VARIABLE
TRANSMISSION . . . . .HYDRO
STEERING. . . . . ZERO
BLADE CLUTCH . . . . .ELECTRIC

STANDARD DECK .... 42"
MSRP $3,149

23/44 2691467

YEARS MFRD 2018-2019
SERIES ...... BROADMOOR SERIES
ENGINE .... B&S
CYLINDERS 2
CID 724CC
ENGINE HP 23
FUEL .... G
TRANSMISSION .... HYDRO
STEERING .... STANDARD
BLADE CLUTCH .... ELECTRIC
STANDARD DECK .... 44"
MSRP $3,899

23/44 2691670

YEARS MFRD 2020-2020
SERIES ...... BROADMOOR SERIES
ENGINE .... BRIGGS & STRATTON
CYLINDERS 2
CID 724CC
ENGINE HP 23
SPEEDS .... VARIABLE
TRANSMISSION .... HYDRO
STEERING .... STANDARD
BLADE CLUTCH .... ELECTRIC
STANDARD DECK .... 44"
MSRP $3,899

23/46

YEARS MFRD 2011-2012
SERIES .... REGENT SERIES
ENGINE .... KOHLER COURAGE
CYLINDERS 2
ENGINE HP 23
COOLING .... AIR
FUEL .... G
SPEEDS .... VARIABLE
TRANSMISSION .... HYDRO
STEERING .... STANDARD
BLADE CLUTCH .... ELECTRIC
STANDARD DECK .... 46"
WEIGHT .... 585 LBS.
MSRP $3,199

OPTIONS

2 BAG
36" TILLER
42" BLADE
42" SNOW THROWER

RETAIL PRICING

YEAR	HIGH	LOW
2011	$1,178	$883
2012	$1,310	$983

23/48 2691659

YEARS MFRD 2020-2020
SERIES .... COURIER SERIES
ENGINE ..... BRIGGS & STRATTON
CYLINDERS 2
CID 724CC
ENGINE HP 23
FUEL .... G
SPEEDS .... VARIABLE
TRANSMISSION .... HYDRO
STEERING .... ZERO
BLADE CLUTCH .... ELECTRIC
STANDARD DECK .... 48"
MSRP $3,999

23/50

YEARS MFRD 2007-2010
SERIES .... CONQUEST SERIES
ENGINE .... B&S VANGUARD
CYLINDERS 2
ENGINE HP 23
COOLING .... AIR
FUEL .... G
SPEEDS .... VARIABLE
TRANSMISSION .... HYDRO
STEERING .... STANDARD
BLADE CLUTCH .... ELECTRIC
STANDARD DECK .... 50"
WEIGHT .... 711 LBS.
MSRP $5,959

RETAIL PRICING

YEAR	HIGH	LOW
2007	$2,854	$2,140
2008	$3,163	$2,372
2009	$3,406	$2,554
2010	$3,492	$2,619

23/50 4WD

YEARS MFRD 2007-2010
SERIES .... CONQUEST SERIES
ENGINE .... B&S VANGUARD
CYLINDERS 2
ENGINE HP 23
COOLING .... AIR
FUEL .... G
SPEEDS .... VARIABLE
TRANSMISSION .... HYDRO
STEERING .... STANDARD
BLADE CLUTCH .... ELECTRIC
STANDARD DECK .... 50"
WEIGHT .... 778 LBS.
MSRP $7,129

RETAIL PRICING

YEAR	HIGH	LOW
2007	$3,762	$2,821
2008	$3,992	$2,994
2009	$4,070	$3,053
2010	$4,178	$3,133

23/50 PS

YEARS MFRD 2007-2010
SERIES .... CONQUEST SERIES
ENGINE .... B&S VANGUARD
CYLINDERS 2
ENGINE HP 23
COOLING .... AIR
FUEL .... G
SPEEDS .... VARIABLE
TRANSMISSION .... HYDRO
STEERING .... STANDARD
BLADE CLUTCH .... ELECTRIC
STANDARD DECK .... 50"
WEIGHT .... 711 LBS.
MSRP $6,289

RETAIL PRICING

YEAR	HIGH	LOW
2007	$3,121	$2,341
2008	$3,468	$2,601
2009	$3,606	$2,705
2010	$3,687	$2,765

23/54

YEARS MFRD 2007-2010
SERIES .... CONQUEST SERIES
ENGINE .... B&S VANGUARD
CYLINDERS 2
ENGINE HP 23
COOLING .... AIR
FUEL .... G
SPEEDS .... VARIABLE
TRANSMISSION .... HYDRO
STEERING .... STANDARD
BLADE CLUTCH .... ELECTRIC
STANDARD DECK .... 54"
WEIGHT .... 778 LBS.
MSRP $6,199

RETAIL PRICING

YEAR	HIGH	LOW
2007	$3,015	$2,261
2008	$3,353	$2,515
2009	$3,550	$2,663
2010	$3,633	$2,724

23H

YEARS MFRD 2001-2003
SERIES .... LEGACY SERIES
ENGINE .... KOHLER
CYLINDERS 2
ENGINE HP 23
COOLING .... AIR
FUEL .... G
SPEEDS .... VARIABLE
TRANSMISSION .... HYDRO
STEERING .... STANDARD
STANDARD DECK .... 54"
WEIGHT .... 1,085 LBS.
MSRP $9,075

OPTIONS

3 BAG
47" SNOW BLOWER
50" TILLER
60" BLADE

RETAIL PRICING

YEAR	HIGH	LOW
2001	$1,367	$1,025
2002	$1,512	$1,134
2003	$1,671	$1,253

23H

YEARS MFRD 2001-2001
SERIES .... LANDLORD SERIES
ENGINE .... KOHLER
ENGINE HP 23
FUEL .... G
TRANSMISSION .... HYDRO
STEERING .... STANDARD
STANDARD DECK .... 54"
MSRP $8,999

OPTIONS

3 BAG
36" TILLER
42" BLADE
42" SNOW BLOWER

RETAIL PRICING

YEAR	HIGH	LOW
2001	$947	$710

23H

YEARS MFRD 2002-2006
SERIES .... PRESTIGE SERIES
ENGINE .... KOHLER
CYLINDERS 2
ENGINE HP 23
COOLING .... AIR
FUEL .... G
SPEEDS .... VARIABLE
TRANSMISSION .... HYDRO
STEERING .... STANDARD
STANDARD DECK .... 54"
WEIGHT .... 858 LBS.
MSRP $6,695

OPTIONS

3 BAG
40" SNOW BLOWER
42" BLADE
50" DECK

RETAIL PRICING

YEAR	HIGH	LOW
2002	$1,108	$831
2003	$1,223	$917
2004	$1,354	$1,016
2005	$1,502	$1,126
2006	$1,664	$1,248

24

YEARS MFRD 2016-2017
SERIES ...... BROADMOOR SERIES
ENGINE .... B&S
ENGINE HP 25
COOLING .... AIR
FUEL .... G
SPEEDS .... VARIABLE
TRANSMISSION .... HYDRO
STEERING .... STANDARD
STANDARD DECK .... 48"
MSRP $5,000

OPTIONS

3 BAG AND FAN
36" TILLER
42"BLADE
42"SNOW BLOWER

RETAIL PRICING

YEAR	HIGH	LOW
2016	$2,899	$2,174
2017	$3,230	$2,423

SIMPLICITY

24 AXION

YEARS MFRD 2008-2009
SERIES . . . . AXION SERIES
ENGINE . . . . B&S ELS
CYLINDERS 2
ENGINE HP 24
COOLING . . . . AIR
FUEL . . . . G
SPEEDS . . . . VARIABLE
TRANSMISSION . . . . HYDRO
STEERING . . . . STANDARD
STANDARD DECK . . . . 50"
MSRP $3,200

OPTIONS

2 BAG

RETAIL PRICING

YEAR	HIGH	LOW
2008	$1,136	$852
2009	$1,261	$946

24 CITATION XT

YEARS MFRD 2013-2013
SERIES . . . . CITATION XT SERIES
ENGINE . . . . KAWASAKI
CYLINDERS 2
ENGINE HP 24
COOLING . . . . AIR
FUEL . . . . G
SPEEDS . . . . VARIABLE
TRANSMISSION . . . . HYDRO
STEERING . . . . ZERO
BLADE CLUTCH . . . . ELECTRIC
STANDARD DECK . . . . 52"
MSRP $7,199

OPTIONS

FAST VAC

RETAIL PRICING

YEAR	HIGH	LOW
2013	$3,938	$2,954

24 GT

YEARS MFRD 2011-2012
SERIES . . . . CONQUEST SERIES
ENGINE . . . . B&S PRO
CYLINDERS 2
ENGINE HP 24
COOLING . . . . AIR
FUEL . . . . G
SPEEDS . . . . VARIABLE
TRANSMISSION . . . . HYDRO
STEERING . . . . STANDARD
BLADE CLUTCH . . . . ELECTRIC
STANDARD DECK . . . . 52"
WEIGHT . . . . 711 LBS.
MSRP $6,100

OPTIONS

3 BAG & FAN
42" BLADE
42" SNOW BLOWER
42" SNOW THROWER

RETAIL PRICING

YEAR	HIGH	LOW
2011	$2,410	$1,808
2012	$2,667	$2,000

24.5H

YEARS MFRD 1999-2003
SERIES . . . . LEGACY SERIES
ENGINE . . . . B&S
CYLINDERS 2
ENGINE HP 24.5
COOLING . . . . LIQUID
FUEL . . . . D
SPEEDS . . . . VARIABLE
TRANSMISSION . . . . HYDRO
STEERING . . . . STANDARD
STANDARD DECK . . . . 54"
WEIGHT . . . . 1,285 LBS.
MSRP $11,550

OPTIONS

3 BAG
47" SNOW BLOWER
50" TILLER
60" DECK

RETAIL PRICING

YEAR	HIGH	LOW
1999	$1,422	$1,067
2000	$1,572	$1,179
2001	$1,739	$1,304
2002	$1,924	$1,443
2003	$2,128	$1,596

24/44

YEARS MFRD 2008-2010
SERIES ZT3000
ENGINE . . . . B&S
CYLINDERS 1
ENGINE HP 24
COOLING . . . . AIR
FUEL . . . . G
SPEEDS . . . . VARIABLE
TRANSMISSION . . . . HYDRO
STEERING . . . . ZERO
BLADE CLUTCH . . . . ELECTRIC
STANDARD DECK . . . . 44"
WEIGHT . . . . 712 LBS.
MSRP $4,499

RETAIL PRICING

YEAR	HIGH	LOW
2009	$2,570	$1,927
2010	$2,635	$1,976

24/44

YEARS MFRD 2008-2009
SERIES ZT4000
ENGINE . . . . B&S ELS
CYLINDERS 1
ENGINE HP 24
COOLING . . . . AIR
FUEL . . . . G
SPEEDS . . . . VARIABLE
TRANSMISSION . . . . HYDRO
STEERING . . . . ZERO
BLADE CLUTCH . . . . ELECTRIC
STANDARD DECK . . . . 44"
WEIGHT . . . . 712 LBS.
MSRP $5,700

RETAIL PRICING

YEAR	HIGH	LOW
2009	$3,292	$2,469

24/50

YEARS MFRD 2008-2010
SERIES ZT3000
ENGINE . . . . B&S
CYLINDERS 2
ENGINE HP 24
COOLING . . . . AIR
FUEL . . . . G
SPEEDS . . . . VARIABLE
TRANSMISSION . . . . HYDRO
STEERING . . . . ZERO
BLADE CLUTCH . . . . ELECTRIC
STANDARD DECK . . . . 50"
WEIGHT . . . . 723 LBS.
MSRP $4,799

RETAIL PRICING

YEAR	HIGH	LOW
2009	$2,742	$2,057
2010	$2,812	$2,109

24H

YEARS MFRD 2006-2009
SERIES . . . . REGENT SERIES
ENGINE . . . . B&S
CYLINDERS 2
ENGINE HP 24
COOLING . . . . AIR
FUEL . . . . G
SPEEDS . . . . VARIABLE
TRANSMISSION . . . . HYDRO
STEERING . . . . STANDARD
STANDARD DECK . . . . 50"
WEIGHT . . . . 585 LBS.
MSRP $3,250

OPTIONS

2 BAG & FAN
42" BLADE
42" SNOW THROWER
SNOCAB

RETAIL PRICING

YEAR	HIGH	LOW
2006	$715	$536
2007	$793	$595
2008	$879	$659
2009	$975	$731

25

YEARS MFRD 2014-2019
SERIES . . . . . . BROADMOOR SERIES
ENGINE . . . . B&S
ENGINE HP 25
COOLING . . . . AIR
FUEL . . . . G
SPEEDS . . . . VARIABLE
TRANSMISSION . . . . HYDRO
STEERING . . . . STANDARD
STANDARD DECK . . . . 48"
MSRP $5,249

OPTIONS

36" TILLER
42" SNOW THROWER
48" BLADE
52" DECK

RETAIL PRICING

YEAR	HIGH	LOW
2014	$2,199	$1,649
2015	$2,437	$1,827
2016	$2,704	$2,028
2017	$2,995	$2,247
2018	$3,301	$2,476
2019	$3,642	$2,732

25

YEARS MFRD 2007-2009
SERIES . . . . PRESTIGE SERIES
ENGINE . . . . . . KOHLER COMMAND
CYLINDERS 2
ENGINE HP 25
COOLING . . . . AIR
FUEL . . . . G
SPEEDS . . . . VARIABLE
TRANSMISSION . . . . HYDRO
STEERING . . . . STANDARD
BLADE CLUTCH . . . . ELECTRIC
STANDARD DECK . . . . 44"
WEIGHT . . . . 779 LBS.
MSRP $7,500

OPTIONS

3 BAG
42" SNOW THROWER
50" DECK
SNOCAB

RETAIL PRICING

YEAR	HIGH	LOW
2007	$2,072	$1,554
2008	$2,291	$1,718
2009	$2,534	$1,900

25

YEARS MFRD 2014-2019
SERIES . . . . CONQUEST SERIES
ENGINE . . . . B&S
CYLINDERS 2
ENGINE HP 25
COOLING . . . . AIR
FUEL . . . . G
SPEEDS . . . . VARIABLE
TRANSMISSION . . . . HYDRO
STEERING . . . . STANDARD
STANDARD DECK . . . . 50"
MSRP $6,199

OPTIONS

36" TILLER
42" SNOW THROWER
48" BLADE
52" DECK

RETAIL PRICING

YEAR	HIGH	LOW
2014	$2,645	$1,984
2015	$2,912	$2,184
2016	$3,221	$2,416
2017	$3,564	$2,673
2018	$3,931	$2,949
2019	$4,317	$3,237

25
YEARS MFRD 2014-2017
SERIES. . . . . REGENT EX SERIES
ENGINE . . . . B&S
ENGINE HP 25
COOLING . . . . AIR
FUEL . . . . G
SPEEDS . . . . VARIABLE
TRANSMISSION . . . . HYDRO
STEERING. . . . . STANDARD
STANDARD DECK . . . . 48"
MSRP. $2,999

OPTIONS
2 BAG
36" TILLER
42" BLADE
42" SNOW BLOWER

RETAIL PRICING

YEAR	HIGH	LOW
2014	$1,310	$982
2015	$1,451	$1,088
2016	$1,614	$1,211
2017	$1,783	$1,337

25 CHAMPION
YEARS MFRD 2014-2015
ENGINE . . . . B&S
ENGINE HP 25
COOLING . . . . AIR
FUEL . . . . G
SPEEDS . . . . VARIABLE
TRANSMISSION . . . . HYDRO
STEERING. . . . . ZERO
STANDARD DECK . . . . 50"
MSRP. $5,399

OPTIONS
3 BAG

RETAIL PRICING

YEAR	HIGH	LOW
2014	$2,898	$2,174
2015	$3,434	$2,575

25 CHAMPION XT
YEARS MFRD 2014-2020
SERIES. . . . . CHAMPION SERIES
ENGINE . . . . B&S
CYLINDERS. 2
CID 724
ENGINE HP 25
COOLING . . . . AIR
FUEL . . . . G
SPEEDS . . . . VARIABLE
TRANSMISSION . . . . HYDRO
STEERING. . . . . ZERO
ROPS/CAB . . . . ROPS
STANDARD DECK . . . . 48"
MSRP. $5,799

RETAIL PRICING

YEAR	HIGH	LOW
2014	$2,661	$1,996
2015	$2,939	$2,203
2016	$3,243	$2,432
2017	$3,580	$2,684
2018	$3,945	$2,959
2019	$4,355	$3,265
2020	$4,711	$3,596

25 CITATION
YEARS MFRD 2010-2012
SERIES. . . . . CITATION SERIES
ENGINE . . . . KAWASAKI
CYLINDERS. 2
ENGINE HP 25
COOLING . . . . AIR
FUEL . . . . G
SPEEDS . . . . VARIABLE
TRANSMISSION . . . . HYDRO
STEERING. . . . . ZERO
BLADE CLUTCH . . . . ELECTRIC
STANDARD DECK . . . . 52"
MSRP. $7,800

OPTIONS
3 BAG & FAN
ROPS

RETAIL PRICING

YEAR	HIGH	LOW
2010	$3,235	$2,426
2011	$3,600	$2,700
2012	$3,993	$2,994

25 KOH
YEARS MFRD 2015-2015
SERIES. . . . . LEGACY SERIES
ENGINE . . . . KOHLER
ENGINE HP 25
COOLING . . . . AIR
FUEL . . . . G
SPEEDS . . . . VARIABLE
TRANSMISSION . . . . HYDRO
STEERING. . . . . STANDARD
STANDARD DECK . . . . 54"
MSRP. $10,368

OPTIONS
4WD
61" DECK

RETAIL PRICING

YEAR	HIGH	LOW
2015	$5,026	$3,769

25/44 2691457
YEARS MFRD 2018-2019
SERIES. . . . . REGENT SERIES
ENGINE . . . . B&S
CYLINDERS. 2
CID 724CC
ENGINE HP 25
TRANSMISSION . . . . HYDRO
STEERING. . . . . STANDARD
STANDARD DECK . . . . 44"
MSRP. $3,149

25/44 2691668
YEARS MFRD 2020-2020
SERIES. . . . . REGENT SERIES
ENGINE . . . . . BRIGGS & STRATTON
CYLINDERS. 2
CID 724CC
ENGINE HP 25
FUEL . . . . G
SPEEDS . . . . VARIABLE
TRANSMISSION . . . . HYDRO
STEERING. . . . . STANDARD
BLADE CLUTCH . . . . ELECTRIC
STANDARD DECK . . . . 44"
MSRP. $3,149

25/48 2691456
YEARS MFRD 2018-2020
SERIES. . . . . REGENT SERIES
ENGINE . . . . B&S
CYLINDERS. 2
CID 724CC
ENGINE HP 25
TRANSMISSION . . . . HYDRO
STEERING. . . . . STANDARD
STANDARD DECK . . . . 48"
MSRP. $2,949

OPTIONS
RR SUSP

25/48 2691669
YEARS MFRD 2020-2020
SERIES. . . . . REGENT SERIES
ENGINE . . . . . BRIGGS & STRATTON
CYLINDERS. 2
CID 724CC
ENGINE HP 25
FUEL . . . . G
SPEEDS . . . . VARIABLE
TRANSMISSION . . . . HYDRO
STEERING. . . . . STANDARD
BLADE CLUTCH . . . . ELECTRIC
STANDARD DECK . . . . 48"
MSRP. $3,399

25/48 2691673
YEARS MFRD 2020-2020
SERIES. . . . . . BROADMOOR SERIES
ENGINE . . . . . BRIGGS & STRATTON
CYLINDERS. 2
CID 724CC
ENGINE HP 25
SPEEDS . . . . VARIABLE
TRANSMISSION . . . . HYDRO
STEERING. . . . . STANDARD
BLADE CLUTCH . . . . ELECTRIC
STANDARD DECK . . . . 48"
MSRP. $4,999

25/50 2691672
YEARS MFRD 2020-2020
SERIES. . . . . . BROADMOOR SERIES
ENGINE . . . . . BRIGGS & STRATTON
CYLINDERS. 2
CID 724CC
ENGINE HP 25
SPEEDS . . . . VARIABLE
TRANSMISSION . . . . HYDRO
STEERING. . . . . STANDARD
BLADE CLUTCH . . . . ELECTRIC
STANDARD DECK . . . . 50"
MSRP. $4,499

25/50 2691675
YEARS MFRD 2020-2020
SERIES. . . . . CONQUEST SERIES
ENGINE . . . . . BRIGGS & STRATTON
CYLINDERS. 2
CID 724CC
ENGINE HP 25
FUEL . . . . G
SPEEDS . . . . VARIABLE
TRANSMISSION . . . . HYDRO
STEERING. . . . . STANDARD
BLADE CLUTCH . . . . ELECTRIC
STANDARD DECK . . . . 50"
MSRP. $6,849

25/52
YEARS MFRD 2016-2020
SERIES. . . . . . . CONTENDER SERIES
ENGINE . . . . B&S
ENGINE HP 25
FUEL . . . . G
SPEEDS . . . . VARIABLE
TRANSMISSION . . . . HYDRO
STEERING. . . . . ZERO
STANDARD DECK . . . . 52"
MSRP. $6,099

OPTIONS
48" DECK. . . . . $-100

RETAIL PRICING

YEAR	HIGH	LOW
2016	$2,907	$2,180
2017	$3,209	$2,407
2018	$3,542	$2,656
2019	$3,913	$2,935
2020	$4,288	$3,276

25/52 2691661
YEARS MFRD 2020-2020
SERIES. . . . . COURIER SERIES
ENGINE . . . . . BRIGGS & STRATTON
CYLINDERS. 2
CID 724CC
ENGINE HP 25
FUEL . . . . G
SPEEDS . . . . VARIABLE

TRANSMISSION . . . HYDRO
STEERING . . . ZERO
BLADE CLUTCH . . . ELECTRIC
STANDARD DECK . . . 52"
MSRP . . . $5,699

25/52 2691674

YEARS MFRD . . . 2020-2020
SERIES . . . BROADMOOR SERIES
ENGINE . . . BRIGGS & STRATTON
CYLINDERS . . . 2
CID . . . 724CC
ENGINE HP . . . 25
FUEL . . . G
SPEEDS . . . VARIABLE
TRANSMISSION . . . HYDRO
STEERING . . . STANDARD
BLADE CLUTCH . . . ELECTRIC
STANDARD DECK . . . 52"
MSRP . . . $5,799

25/52 2691676

YEARS MFRD . . . 2020-2020
SERIES . . . CONQUEST SERIES
ENGINE . . . BRIGGS & STRATTON
CYLINDERS . . . 2
CID . . . 724CC
ENGINE HP . . . 25
FUEL . . . G
SPEEDS . . . VARIABLE
TRANSMISSION . . . HYDRO
STEERING . . . STANDARD
BLADE CLUTCH . . . ELECTRIC
STANDARD DECK . . . 52"
MSRP . . . $7,349

25/61

YEARS MFRD . . . 2016-2020
SERIES . . . CONTENDER SERIES
ENGINE . . . B&S
CYLINDERS . . . 2
ENGINE HP . . . 25
COOLING . . . AIR
FUEL . . . G
SPEEDS . . . VARIABLE
TRANSMISSION . . . HYDRO
STEERING . . . ZERO
STANDARD DECK . . . 61"
MSRP . . . $7,149

RETAIL PRICING

YEAR	HIGH	LOW
2016	$2,964	$2,223
2017	$3,271	$2,454
2018	$3,704	$2,778
2019	$4,270	$3,202
2020	$5,023	$3,832

25FH

YEARS MFRD . . . 2000-2000
SERIES . . . LEGACY SERIES
ENGINE . . . KOHLER
ENGINE HP . . . 25
COOLING . . . AIR
FUEL . . . G
SPEEDS . . . VARIABLE
TRANSMISSION . . . HYDRO
STEERING . . . STANDARD
STANDARD DECK . . . 60"
MSRP . . . $10,550

OPTIONS

3 BAG
47" SNOW BLOWER
50" TILLER
54" DECK

RETAIL PRICING

YEAR	HIGH	LOW
2000	$1,468	$1,101

25H

YEARS MFRD . . . 1998-2003
SERIES . . . LEGACY SERIES
ENGINE . . . KOHLER
CYLINDERS . . . 2
ENGINE HP . . . 25
COOLING . . . AIR
FUEL . . . G
SPEEDS . . . VARIABLE
TRANSMISSION . . . HYDRO
STEERING . . . STANDARD
STANDARD DECK . . . 60"
WEIGHT . . . 1,125 LBS.
MSRP . . . $9,750

OPTIONS

3 BAG
47" SNOW BLOWER
50" TILLER
60" BLADE

RETAIL PRICING

YEAR	HIGH	LOW
1998	$1,084	$813
1999	$1,199	$899
2000	$1,327	$995
2001	$1,468	$1,101
2002	$1,624	$1,218
2003	$1,804	$1,353

25HP KOHLER/ COMMAND

YEARS MFRD . . . 2009-2009
SERIES . . . PRESTIGE
ENGINE . . . KOHLER COMMAND
CYLINDERS . . . 2
ENGINE HP . . . 25
COOLING . . . AIR
FUEL . . . G
SPEEDS . . . VARIABLE
TRANSMISSION . . . HYDRO
STEERING . . . STANDARD
BLADE CLUTCH . . . ELECTRIC
WEIGHT . . . 791 LBS.
MSRP . . . $6,400

RETAIL PRICING

YEAR	HIGH	LOW
2009	$3,694	$2,770

26

YEARS MFRD . . . 2013-2013
SERIES . . . BROADMOOR SERIES
ENGINE . . . VANGUARD
ENGINE HP . . . 26
COOLING . . . AIR
FUEL . . . G
SPEEDS . . . VARIABLE
TRANSMISSION . . . HYDRO
STEERING . . . STANDARD
STANDARD DECK . . . 50"
MSRP . . . $4,399

OPTIONS

3 BAG & FAN
36" TILLER
42" BLADE
42" SNOW BLOWER

RETAIL PRICING

YEAR	HIGH	LOW
2013	$1,994	$1,496

26

YEARS MFRD . . . 2013-2013
SERIES . . . REGENT EX SERIES
ENGINE . . . B&S
ENGINE HP . . . 26
COOLING . . . AIR
FUEL . . . G
SPEEDS . . . VARIABLE
TRANSMISSION . . . HYDRO
STEERING . . . STANDARD
STANDARD DECK . . . 52"
MSRP . . . $3,299

OPTIONS

3 BAG & FAN
36" TILLER
42" BLADE
42" SNOW THROWER

RETAIL PRICING

YEAR	HIGH	LOW
2013	$1,555	$1,166

26 CHAMPION

YEARS MFRD . . . 2008-2012
ENGINE . . . B&S
ENGINE HP . . . 26
COOLING . . . AIR
FUEL . . . G
SPEEDS . . . VARIABLE
TRANSMISSION . . . HYDRO
STEERING . . . ZERO
STANDARD DECK . . . 52"
MSRP . . . $4,800

OPTIONS

3 BAG

RETAIL PRICING

YEAR	HIGH	LOW
2008	$1,611	$1,208
2009	$1,794	$1,345
2010	$1,989	$1,492
2011	$2,219	$1,665
2012	$2,475	$1,857

26 COBALT

YEARS MFRD . . . 2015-2020
SERIES . . . COBALT SERIES
ENGINE . . . B&S
CYLINDERS . . . 2
CID . . . 810CC
ENGINE HP . . . 26
COOLING . . . AIR
FUEL . . . G
SPEEDS . . . VARIABLE
TRANSMISSION . . . HYDRO
STEERING . . . ZERO
BLADE CLUTCH . . . ELECTRIC
ROPS/CAB . . . ROPS
STANDARD DECK . . . 61"
MSRP . . . $10,399

RETAIL PRICING

YEAR	HIGH	LOW
2015	$4,611	$3,458
2016	$5,089	$3,817
2017	$5,619	$4,213
2018	$6,233	$4,675
2019	$6,789	$5,145
2020	$7,476	$5,705

26/48

YEARS MFRD . . . 2010-2010
SERIES . . . ZT4000
ENGINE . . . B&S
CYLINDERS . . . 2
ENGINE HP . . . 26
COOLING . . . AIR
FUEL . . . G
SPEEDS . . . VARIABLE
TRANSMISSION . . . HYDRO
STEERING . . . ZERO
BLADE CLUTCH . . . ELECTRIC
STANDARD DECK . . . 48"
MSRP . . . $5,700

RETAIL PRICING

YEAR	HIGH	LOW
2010	$3,341	$2,506

26/52

YEARS MFRD . . . 2008-2011
SERIES . . . CHAMPION
ENGINE . . . B&S
CYLINDERS . . . 2
ENGINE HP . . . 26
COOLING . . . AIR
FUEL . . . G
SPEEDS . . . VARIABLE
TRANSMISSION . . . HYDRO
STEERING . . . ZERO
BLADE CLUTCH . . . ELECTRIC
STANDARD DECK . . . 52"
WEIGHT . . . 723 LBS.
MSRP . . . $4,800

RETAIL PRICING

YEAR	HIGH	LOW
2008	$1,820	$1,365
2009	$2,018	$1,513
2010	$2,244	$1,683
2011	$2,603	$1,953

27

YEARS MFRD 2013-2013
SERIES. . . . . CONQUEST SERIES
ENGINE . . . . B&S
ENGINE HP. 27
COOLING . . . . AIR
FUEL . . . . G
SPEEDS . . . . VARIABLE
TRANSMISSION . . . . HYDRO
STEERING. . . . . STANDARD
STANDARD DECK . . . . 50"
MSRP. $5,899

OPTIONS

3 BAG & FAN
42" BLADE
42" SNOW BLOWER
42" SNOW THROWER

RETAIL PRICING

YEAR	HIGH	LOW
2013	$2,792	$2,094

27

YEARS MFRD 2013-2013
SERIES. . . . . . BROADMOOR SERIES
ENGINE . . . . VANGUARD
ENGINE HP. 27
COOLING . . . . AIR
FUEL . . . . G
SPEEDS . . . . VARIABLE
TRANSMISSION . . . . HYDRO
STEERING. . . . . STANDARD
STANDARD DECK . . . . 50"
MSRP. $5,099

OPTIONS

3 BAG & FAN
36" TILLER
42" BLADE
42" SNOW BLOWER

RETAIL PRICING

YEAR	HIGH	LOW
2013	$2,326	$1,745

27

YEARS MFRD 2007-2012
SERIES. . . . . PRESTIGE SERIES
ENGINE . . . . KOHLER COURAGE
CYLINDERS. 2
ENGINE HP. 27
COOLING . . . . AIR
FUEL . . . . G
SPEEDS . . . . VARIABLE
TRANSMISSION . . . . HYDRO
STEERING. . . . . STANDARD
BLADE CLUTCH . . . . ELECTRIC
STANDARD DECK . . . . 54"
WEIGHT . . . . 858 LBS.
MSRP. $8,148

OPTIONS

3 BAG
36" TILLER
4WD
SNOCAB

RETAIL PRICING

YEAR	HIGH	LOW
2007	$2,240	$1,680
2008	$2,478	$1,859
2009	$2,740	$2,055
2010	$3,031	$2,273
2011	$3,353	$2,515
2012	$3,730	$2,797

27 2WD

YEARS MFRD 2007-2011
SERIES. . . . . LEGACY SERIES
ENGINE . . . . . KOHLER COMMAND
CYLINDERS. 2
ENGINE HP. 27
COOLING . . . . AIR
FUEL . . . . G
SPEEDS . . . . VARIABLE
TRANSMISSION . . . . HYDRO
STEERING. . . . . STANDARD
BLADE CLUTCH . . . . ELECTRIC
WEIGHT . . . . 830 LBS.
MSRP. $10,210

OPTIONS

KAWASAKI LC 27HP

RETAIL PRICING

YEAR	HIGH	LOW
2007	$4,345	$3,258
2008	$4,805	$3,604
2009	$5,140	$3,855
2010	$5,281	$3,961
2011	$5,491	$4,118

27 4WD

YEARS MFRD 2007-2011
SERIES. . . . . LEGACY SERIES
ENGINE . . . . . KOHLER COMMAND
CYLINDERS. 2
ENGINE HP. 27
COOLING . . . . AIR
FUEL . . . . G
SPEEDS . . . . VARIABLE
TRANSMISSION . . . . HYDRO
STEERING. . . . . STANDARD
BLADE CLUTCH . . . . ELECTRIC
WEIGHT . . . . 980 LBS.
MSRP. $10,200

OPTIONS

DAIHATSU DIESEL 27HP
KAWASAKI LC 27HP

RETAIL PRICING

YEAR	HIGH	LOW
2007	$4,996	$3,747
2008	$5,516	$4,137
2009	$5,903	$4,428
2010	$6,027	$4,520
2011	$6,069	$4,552

27 B&S

YEARS MFRD 2014-2019
SERIES. . . . . PRESTIGE SERIES
ENGINE . . . . B&S
CYLINDERS. 2
CID 810
ENGINE HP. 27
COOLING . . . . AIR
FUEL . . . . G
SPEEDS . . . . VARIABLE
TRANSMISSION . . . . HYDRO
STEERING. . . . . STANDARD
STANDARD DECK . . . . 50"
MSRP. $8,749

OPTIONS

36" TILLER
42" SNOW THROWER
4WD
52" DECK

RETAIL PRICING

YEAR	HIGH	LOW
2014	$3,731	$2,798
2015	$4,127	$3,096
2016	$4,554	$3,416
2017	$5,039	$3,779
2018	$5,705	$4,278
2019	$6,492	$4,869

27 CHAMPION

YEARS MFRD 2013-2013
SERIES. . . . . CHAMPION SERIES
ENGINE . . . . B&S
CYLINDERS. 2
ENGINE HP. 27
COOLING . . . . AIR
FUEL . . . . G
SPEEDS . . . . VARIABLE
TRANSMISSION . . . . HYDRO
STEERING. . . . . ZERO
BLADE CLUTCH . . . . ELECTRIC
STANDARD DECK . . . . 50"
MSRP. $5,399

OPTIONS

3 BAG & FAN

RETAIL PRICING

YEAR	HIGH	LOW
2013	$2,956	$2,217

27 CHAMPION XT

YEARS MFRD 2013-2013
SERIES. . . . . CHAMPION SERIES
ENGINE . . . . B&S
CYLINDERS. 2
ENGINE HP. 27
COOLING . . . . AIR
FUEL . . . . G
SPEEDS . . . . VARIABLE
TRANSMISSION . . . . HYDRO
STEERING. . . . . ZERO
BLADE CLUTCH . . . . ELECTRIC
STANDARD DECK . . . . 48"
MSRP. $6,099

OPTIONS

FAST VAC

RETAIL PRICING

YEAR	HIGH	LOW
2013	$3,335	$2,501

27 CITATION XT

YEARS MFRD 2014-2018
SERIES. . . . . CITATIONXT SERIES
ENGINE . . . . KAWASAKI
ENGINE HP. 27
COOLING . . . . AIR
FUEL . . . . G
SPEEDS . . . . VARIABLE
TRANSMISSION . . . . HYDRO
STEERING. . . . . ZERO
STANDARD DECK . . . . 52"
MSRP. $6,399

OPTIONS

3BAG
61" DECK

RETAIL PRICING

YEAR	HIGH	LOW
2014	$2,938	$2,204
2015	$3,243	$2,432
2016	$3,582	$2,687
2017	$3,951	$2,963
2018	$4,361	$3,271

27 CITATION XT B&S

YEARS MFRD 2019-2020
SERIES. . . . . . . CITATION XT SERIES
ENGINE . . . . B&S COMMERCIAL
CYLINDERS. 2
CID 810
ENGINE HP. 27
FUEL . . . . G
SPEEDS . . . . VARIABLE
TRANSMISSION . . . . HYDRO
STEERING. . . . . ZERO
BLADE CLUTCH . . . . ELECTRIC
ROPS/CAB . . . . ROPS
STANDARD DECK . . . . 52"
MSRP. $7,799

OPTIONS

61" DECK. $500

27 COBALT

YEARS MFRD 2007-2009
SERIES. . . . . COBALT SERIES
ENGINE . . . . . KOHLER COMMAND
CYLINDERS. 2
ENGINE HP. 27
COOLING . . . . AIR
FUEL . . . . G
SPEEDS . . . . VARIABLE
TRANSMISSION . . . . HYDRO
STEERING. . . . . ZERO
STANDARD DECK . . . . 61"
WEIGHT . . . . 1,150 LBS.
MSRP. $9,400

OPTIONS

3 BAG & FAN

RETAIL PRICING

YEAR	HIGH	LOW
2007	$3,004	$2,253
2008	$3,356	$2,517
2009	$3,708	$2,781

27 DAI

YEARS MFRD 2005-2015
SERIES. . . . . LEGACY XL SERIES
ENGINE . . . . B&S DAIHATSU
CYLINDERS. 3

SIMPLICITY

ENGINE HP ... 27
COOLING ... AIR
FUEL ... D
SPEEDS ... VARIABLE
TRANSMISSION ... HYDRO
STEERING ... STANDARD
STANDARD DECK ... 60"
WEIGHT ... 1,431 LBS.
MSRP ... $16,548

OPTIONS

3 BAG
46" SNOW THROWER
4WD
50" TILLER

RETAIL PRICING

YEAR	HIGH	LOW
2006	$3,602	$2,701
2007	$3,973	$2,980
2008	$4,391	$3,293
2009	$4,841	$3,631
2010	$5,360	$4,020
2011	$5,930	$4,447
2012	$6,559	$4,919
2013	$7,256	$5,442
2014	$8,062	$6,046
2015	$8,879	$6,660

27 KAW

YEARS MFRD ... 2005-2016
SERIES ... LEGACY XL SERIES
ENGINE ... KAWASAKI
ENGINE HP ... 27
COOLING ... LIQUID
FUEL ... G
SPEEDS ... VARIABLE
TRANSMISSION ... HYDRO
STEERING ... STANDARD
STANDARD DECK ... 61"
MSRP ... $13,998

OPTIONS

3 BAG
46" SNOW THROWER
60" BLADE

RETAIL PRICING

YEAR	HIGH	LOW
2005	$2,980	$2,235
2006	$3,143	$2,357
2007	$3,397	$2,548
2008	$3,769	$2,827
2009	$4,165	$3,124
2010	$4,582	$3,437
2011	$5,068	$3,801
2012	$5,607	$4,205
2013	$6,203	$4,652
2014	$6,863	$5,147
2015	$7,589	$5,692
2016	$8,395	$6,297

27 KOH

YEARS MFRD ... 2005-2014
SERIES ... LEGACY XL SERIES
ENGINE ... KOHLER
ENGINE HP ... 27
COOLING ... AIR
FUEL ... G
SPEEDS ... VARIABLE
TRANSMISSION ... HYDRO
STEERING ... STANDARD
STANDARD DECK ... 60"
MSRP ... $11,248

OPTIONS

3 BAG
46" SNOW THROWER
4WD
60" BLADE

RETAIL PRICING

YEAR	HIGH	LOW
2005	$2,272	$1,704
2006	$2,510	$1,883
2007	$2,777	$2,083
2008	$3,072	$2,304
2009	$3,398	$2,548
2010	$3,768	$2,826
2011	$4,180	$3,135
2012	$4,608	$3,456
2013	$5,088	$3,816
2014	$5,628	$4,221

27/50 2691677

YEARS MFRD ... 2020-2020
SERIES ... PRESTIGE SERIES
ENGINE ... BRIGGS & STRATTON
CYLINDERS ... 2
CID ... 810CC
ENGINE HP ... 27
FUEL ... G
SPEEDS ... VARIABLE
TRANSMISSION ... HYDRO
STEERING ... STANDARD
BLADE CLUTCH ... ELECTRIC
STANDARD DECK ... 50"
MSRP ... $8,849

27/50 4WD

YEARS MFRD ... 2007-2011
SERIES ... PRESTIGE SERIES
ENGINE ... KOHLER COMMAND
CYLINDERS ... 2
ENGINE HP ... 27
COOLING ... AIR
FUEL ... G
SPEEDS ... VARIABLE
TRANSMISSION ... HYDRO
STEERING ... STANDARD
BLADE CLUTCH ... ELECTRIC
STANDARD DECK ... 50"
WEIGHT ... 858 LBS.
MSRP ... $8,075

RETAIL PRICING

YEAR	HIGH	LOW
2007	$4,318	$3,239
2008	$4,327	$3,245
2009	$4,348	$3,261
2010	$4,820	$3,615
2011	$5,027	$3,770

27/50 4WD 2691678

YEARS MFRD ... 2020-2020
SERIES ... PRESTIGE SERIES
ENGINE ... BRIGGS & STRATTON
CYLINDERS ... 2
CID ... 810CC
ENGINE HP ... 27
FUEL ... G
SPEEDS ... VARIABLE
TRANSMISSION ... HYDRO
STEERING ... STANDARD
BLADE CLUTCH ... ELECTRIC
STANDARD DECK ... 50"
MSRP ... $8,949

27HP KOHLER COMMAND

YEARS MFRD ... 2009-2009
ENGINE ... KOHLER COMMAND
CYLINDERS ... 2
ENGINE HP ... 27
COOLING ... AIR
FUEL ... G
SPEEDS ... VARIABLE
TRANSMISSION ... HYDRO
STEERING ... STANDARD
BLADE CLUTCH ... ELECTRIC
WEIGHT ... 858 LBS.
MSRP ... $6,650

RETAIL PRICING

YEAR	HIGH	LOW
2009	$3,839	$2,879

28 CITATION

YEARS MFRD ... 2010-2012
SERIES ... CITATION SERIES
ENGINE ... B&S VANGUARD
CYLINDERS ... 2
ENGINE HP ... 28
COOLING ... AIR
FUEL ... G
SPEEDS ... VARIABLE
TRANSMISSION ... HYDRO
STEERING ... ZERO
BLADE CLUTCH ... ELECTRIC
STANDARD DECK ... 61"
MSRP ... $8,300

OPTIONS

3 BAG & FAN
ROPS

RETAIL PRICING

YEAR	HIGH	LOW
2010	$3,438	$2,578
2011	$3,826	$2,869
2012	$4,248	$3,186

28 CITATION XT

YEARS MFRD ... 2013-2013
SERIES ... CITATION XT SERIES
ENGINE ... B&S
CYLINDERS ... 2
ENGINE HP ... 28
COOLING ... AIR
FUEL ... G
SPEEDS ... VARIABLE
TRANSMISSION ... HYDRO
STEERING ... ZERO
BLADE CLUTCH ... ELECTRIC
STANDARD DECK ... 52"
MSRP ... $6,699

OPTIONS

61" DECK
FAST VAC

RETAIL PRICING

YEAR	HIGH	LOW
2013	$3,421	$2,566

28 COBALT

YEARS MFRD ... 2016-2020
SERIES ... COBALT SERIES
ENGINE ... B&S
CYLINDERS ... 2
CID ... 810CC
ENGINE HP ... 28
COOLING ... AIR
FUEL ... G
SPEEDS ... VARIABLE
TRANSMISSION ... HYDRO
STEERING ... ZERO
BLADE CLUTCH ... ELECTRIC
ROPS/CAB ... ROPS
STANDARD DECK ... 61"

RETAIL PRICING

YEAR	HIGH	LOW
2016	$5,426	$4,069
2017	$5,989	$4,492
2018	$6,896	$5,172
2019	$8,042	$6,031
2020	$9,009	$6,888

30

YEARS MFRD ... 2013-2013
SERIES ... PRESTIGE SERIES
ENGINE ... B&S
ENGINE HP ... 30
COOLING ... AIR
FUEL ... G
SPEEDS ... VARIABLE
TRANSMISSION ... HYDRO
STEERING ... STANDARD
STANDARD DECK ... 54"
MSRP ... $8,668

OPTIONS

3 BAG
36" TILLER
4WD
SNOCAB

RETAIL PRICING

YEAR	HIGH	LOW
2013	$4,105	$3,079

30 COBALT

YEARS MFRD ... 2009-2014
SERIES ... COBALT SERIES
ENGINE ... B&S VANGUARD

CYLINDERS....2
ENGINE HP....30
COOLING....AIR
FUEL....G
SPEEDS....VARIABLE
TRANSMISSION....HYDRO
STEERING....ZERO
BLADE CLUTCH....ELECTRIC
STANDARD DECK....61"
WEIGHT....1,150 LBS.
MSRP....$9,499

OPTIONS

3 BAG & FAN

RETAIL PRICING

YEAR	HIGH	LOW
2009	$3,338	$2,503
2010	$3,692	$2,769
2011	$4,085	$3,064
2012	$4,535	$3,401
2013	$5,042	$3,782
2014	$5,529	$4,147

31 2WD 2691522

YEARS MFRD....2020-2020
SERIES....LEGACY XL SERIES
ENGINE....BRIGGS VANGUARD
CYLINDERS....2
CID....885CC
ENGINE HP....31
FUEL....G
SPEEDS....VARIABLE
TRANSMISSION....HYDRO
STEERING....STANDARD
MSRP....$9,699

OPTIONS

52" DECK
61" DECK

32 COBALT

YEARS MFRD....2013-2015
SERIES....COBALT SERIES
ENGINE....B&S
CYLINDERS....2
ENGINE HP....32
COOLING....AIR
FUEL....G
SPEEDS....VARIABLE
TRANSMISSION....HYDRO
STEERING....ZERO
BLADE CLUTCH....ELECTRIC
STANDARD DECK....61"
MSRP....$11,199

OPTIONS

3 BAG & FAN

RETAIL PRICING

YEAR	HIGH	LOW
2013	$5,436	$4,077
2014	$6,026	$4,519
2015	$6,811	$5,109

33 4WD 2691523

YEARS MFRD....2020-2020
SERIES....LEGACY XL SERIES
ENGINE....BRIGGS VANGUARD
CYLINDERS....2
CID....885CC
ENGINE HP....33
SPEEDS....VARIABLE
TRANSMISSION....HYDRO
STEERING....STANDARD
MSRP....$12,299

OPTIONS

52" DECK
540 RR PTO....$950
61" DECK

37/61 5901798

YEARS MFRD....2019-2020
SERIES....COBALT LE SERIES
ENGINE....BRIGGS VANGUARD
CYLINDERS....2
CID....993CC
ENGINE HP....37
FUEL....G
SPEEDS....VARIABLE
TRANSMISSION....HYDRO
STEERING....ZERO
BLADE CLUTCH....ELECTRIC
ROPS/CAB....ROPS
STANDARD DECK....61"
MSRP....$14,099

37/72 5901799

YEARS MFRD....2019-2020
SERIES....COBALT LE SERIES
ENGINE....BRIGGS VANGUARD
CYLINDERS....2
CID....993CC
ENGINE HP....37
FUEL....G
SPEEDS....VARIABLE
TRANSMISSION....HYDRO
STEERING....ZERO
BLADE CLUTCH....ELECTRIC
ROPS/CAB....ROPS
STANDARD DECK....72"
MSRP....$14,849

550Z 25

YEARS MFRD....2015-2015
ENGINE....B&S
ENGINE HP....25
FUEL....D
SPEEDS....VARIABLE
TRANSMISSION....HYDRO
STEERING....ZERO
STANDARD DECK....52"
MSRP....$4,899

OPTIONS

61" DECK

RETAIL PRICING

YEAR	HIGH	LOW
2015	$3,000	$2,250

2048HW

YEARS MFRD....1987-1990
SERIES....SUNSTAR SERIES
ENGINE....KOHLER
ENGINE HP....20
COOLING....AIR
FUEL....G
TRANSMISSION....HYDRO
STEERING....STANDARD
STANDARD DECK....48"
MSRP....$7,449

RETAIL PRICING

YEAR	HIGH	LOW
1987	$223	$167
1988	$244	$183
1989	$274	$205
1990	$302	$226

5216HW

YEARS MFRD....1990-1990
SERIES....LT SERIES
ENGINE....B&S
ENGINE HP....16
FUEL....G
TRANSMISSION....HYDRO
STEERING....STANDARD
STANDARD DECK....48"
MSRP....$3,799

RETAIL PRICING

YEAR	HIGH	LOW
1990	$1,059	$794

6216

YEARS MFRD....1986-1990
ENGINE....B&S
ENGINE HP....16
FUEL....G
SPEEDS....4/1
WEIGHT....605 LBS.
MSRP....$3,130

RETAIL PRICING

YEAR	HIGH	LOW
1990	$872	$654

6516HO

YEARS MFRD....1988-1990
ENGINE....B&S
ENGINE HP....16
FUEL....G
SPEEDS....0-5.5
WEIGHT....605 LBS.
MSRP....$3,280

RETAIL PRICING

YEAR	HIGH	LOW
1990	$915	$686

7116G

YEARS MFRD....1979-1990
ENGINE....B&S
ENGINE HP....16
FUEL....G
TRANSMISSION....GEAR
WEIGHT....644 LBS.
MSRP....$4,800

RETAIL PRICING

YEAR	HIGH	LOW
1990	$1,339	$1,004

7116H

YEARS MFRD....1979-1990
ENGINE....B&S
ENGINE HP....16
FUEL....G
SPEEDS....HYDRO
WEIGHT....816 LBS.
MSRP....$4,800

RETAIL PRICING

YEAR	HIGH	LOW
1990	$1,339	$1,004

7116HO

YEARS MFRD....1986-1990
ENGINE....B&S
ENGINE HP....16
FUEL....G
SPEEDS....9-5.1
WEIGHT....816 LBS.

7116S

YEARS MFRD....1985-1991
ENGINE....B&S
ENGINE HP....16
FUEL....G
SPEEDS....HYDRO
WEIGHT....816 LBS.
MSRP....$5,795

RETAIL PRICING

YEAR	HIGH	LOW
1990	$1,559	$1,169
1991	$1,724	$1,293

7117HW

YEARS MFRD....1981-1990
SERIES....GT SERIES
ENGINE....KOHLER
ENGINE HP....17
FUEL....G
TRANSMISSION....HYDRO
STEERING....STANDARD
STANDARD DECK....48"
MSRP....$5,499

RETAIL PRICING

YEAR	HIGH	LOW
1981	$711	$533
1982	$837	$628
1983	$1,064	$798
1984	$1,216	$912
1985	$1,349	$1,012
1986	$1,458	$1,093

1987...........$1,517...........$1,138
1988...........$1,568...........$1,176
1989...........$1,597...........$1,197
1990...........$1,657...........$1,243

7790

YEARS MFRD 1984-1990
ENGINE . . . . B&S
ENGINE HP 18.5
FUEL . . . . D
SPEEDS . . . . HYDRO
WEIGHT . . . . 814 LBS.
MSRP. $5,600

RETAIL PRICING

YEAR	HIGH	LOW
1990	$1,559	$1,169

7790HO

YEARS MFRD 1984-1990
ENGINE . . . . B&S
ENGINE HP 18.5
FUEL . . . . G
SPEEDS . . . . HYDRO
WEIGHT . . . . 925 LBS.
MSRP. $5,600

RETAIL PRICING

YEAR	HIGH	LOW
1990	$1,559	$1,169

1691017

YEARS MFRD 1986-1991
ENGINE . . . . KOHLER TWIN
ENGINE HP 18
FUEL . . . . G
SPEEDS . . . . HYDRO
WEIGHT . . . . 955 LBS.
MSRP. $5,125

RETAIL PRICING

YEAR	HIGH	LOW
1990	$1,430	$1,072
1991	$1,522	$1,141

1691018

YEARS MFRD 1986-1990
ENGINE . . . . KOHLER TWIN
ENGINE HP 20
FUEL . . . . G
SPEEDS . . . . VARIABLE
TRANSMISSION . . . . HYDRO
WEIGHT . . . . 1,003 LBS.
MSRP. $5,825

RETAIL PRICING

YEAR	HIGH	LOW
1990	$1,622	$1,216

SNAPPER

ALL MODELS

SERIAL NUMBERS

FIRST NUMBER OF SERIAL NUMBER IS YEAR MANUFACTURED

CZT1948 KWV

YEARS MFRD 2005-2006
ENGINE . . . . KAWASAKI
CYLINDERS. 2
ENGINE HP 19
COOLING . . . . AIR
FUEL . . . . G
SPEEDS . . . . VARIABLE
TRANSMISSION . . . . . DUAL HYDRO
STEERING. . . . . ZERO
STANDARD DECK . . . . 48"
WEIGHT . . . . 892 LBS.
MSRP. $6,099

OPTIONS

2 BAG & FAN

RETAIL PRICING

YEAR	HIGH	LOW
2005	$1,687	$1,265
2006	$1,872	$1,404

GT180H335K

YEARS MFRD 1992-1994
ENGINE . . . . KOHLER
ENGINE HP 18
FUEL . . . . G
TRANSMISSION . . . . HYDRO
STEERING. . . . . STANDARD
STANDARD DECK . . . . 33"
MSRP. $4,299

RETAIL PRICING

YEAR	HIGH	LOW
1992	$1,355	$1,016
1993	$1,397	$1,048
1994	$1,510	$1,133

GT180H425K

YEARS MFRD 1992-1998
ENGINE . . . . KOHLER
ENGINE HP 18
FUEL . . . . G
TRANSMISSION . . . . HYDRO
STEERING. . . . . STANDARD
STANDARD DECK . . . . 42"
MSRP. $4,399

RETAIL PRICING

YEAR	HIGH	LOW
1992	$1,419	$1,064
1993	$1,463	$1,097
1994	$1,583	$1,187
1995	$1,660	$1,245
1997	$1,725	$1,293
1998	$1,811	$1,358

GT180H42K

YEARS MFRD 1996-1996
ENGINE . . . . KOHLER
ENGINE HP 18
FUEL . . . . G
TRANSMISSION . . . . HYDRO
STEERING. . . . . STANDARD
STANDARD DECK . . . . 42"
MSRP. $4,399

RETAIL PRICING

YEAR	HIGH	LOW
1996	$1,663	$1,247

GT180H485K

YEARS MFRD 1992-1998
ENGINE . . . . KOHLER
ENGINE HP 18
FUEL . . . . G
TRANSMISSION . . . . HYDRO
STEERING. . . . . STANDARD
STANDARD DECK . . . . 48"
MSRP. $4,699

RETAIL PRICING

YEAR	HIGH	LOW
1992	$1,483	$1,112
1993	$1,530	$1,147
1994	$1,650	$1,237
1995	$1,750	$1,312
1996	$1,815	$1,361
1997	$1,841	$1,381
1998	$1,934	$1,451

GT180H48K

YEARS MFRD 1996-1996
ENGINE . . . . KOHLER
ENGINE HP 18
FUEL . . . . G
TRANSMISSION . . . . HYDRO
STEERING. . . . . STANDARD
STANDARD DECK . . . . 48"
MSRP. $4,699

RETAIL PRICING

YEAR	HIGH	LOW
1996	$1,776	$1,332

GT1848H

YEARS MFRD 1996-1997
ENGINE . . . . KOHLER
ENGINE HP 18
FUEL . . . . G
TRANSMISSION . . . . HYDRO
STEERING. . . . . STANDARD
STANDARD DECK . . . . 48"
MSRP. $6,769

RETAIL PRICING

YEAR	HIGH	LOW
1996	$2,558	$1,918
1997	$2,653	$1,990

GT2048H

YEARS MFRD 1997-1998
ENGINE . . . . KOHLER
ENGINE HP 20
FUEL . . . . G
TRANSMISSION . . . . HYDRO
STEERING. . . . . STANDARD
STANDARD DECK . . . . 48"
MSRP. $7,384

OPTIONS

42" SNOW THROWER
46" TILLER
48" BLADE
CAB

SERIAL NUMBERS

YEAR	BEGINNING NO.
1997	971013001

RETAIL PRICING

YEAR	HIGH	LOW
1997	$737	$553
1998	$827	$621

GT2554

YEARS MFRD 2007-2008
SERIES. . . . . GT500 SERIES
ENGINE . . . . . KOHLER COMMAND
CYLINDERS. 2
ENGINE HP 25
COOLING . . . . AIR
FUEL . . . . G
SPEEDS . . . . VARIABLE
TRANSMISSION . . . . HYDRO
STEERING. . . . . STANDARD
STANDARD DECK . . . . 54"
WEIGHT . . . . 858 LBS.
MSRP. $6,950

RETAIL PRICING

YEAR	HIGH	LOW
2007	$3,724	$2,793
2008	$4,221	$3,166

GT2754

YEARS MFRD 2010-2010
SERIES. . . . . GT600 SERIES
ENGINE . . . . B&S VANGUARD
CYLINDERS. 3
ENGINE HP 27
COOLING . . . . AIR
FUEL . . . . D
SPEEDS . . . . VARIABLE
TRANSMISSION . . . . HYDRO
STEERING. . . . . STANDARD
DRIVE TYPE 4WD
STANDARD DECK . . . . 54"
WEIGHT . . . . 1,131 LBS.
MSRP. $13,995

RETAIL PRICING

YEAR	HIGH	LOW
2010	$5,107	$3,830

GT2760

YEARS MFRD 2010-2010
SERIES. . . . . GT600 SERIES
ENGINE . . . . B&S VANGUARD
CYLINDERS. 3
ENGINE HP 27
COOLING . . . . AIR
FUEL . . . . D

SPEEDS . . . . VARIABLE
TRANSMISSION . . . . HYDRO
STEERING. . . . . STANDARD
STANDARD DECK . . . . 60"
WEIGHT . . . . 1,131 LBS.
MSRP. $14,150

RETAIL PRICING

YEAR	HIGH	LOW
2010	$5,163	$3,872

GT2772

YEARS MFRD 2008-2008
SERIES. . . . . GT600 SERIES
ENGINE . . . . B&S VANGUARD
CYLINDERS. 3
ENGINE HP 27
COOLING . . . . AIR
FUEL . . . . D
SPEEDS . . . . VARIABLE
TRANSMISSION . . . . HYDRO
STEERING. . . . . STANDARD
STANDARD DECK . . . . 72"
WEIGHT . . . . 1,131 LBS.
MSRP. $12,899

RETAIL PRICING

YEAR	HIGH	LOW
2008	$7,836	$5,877

GT23540

YEARS MFRD 2005-2006
ENGINE . . . . KOHLER
CYLINDERS. 2
ENGINE HP 23
COOLING . . . . AIR
FUEL . . . . G
SPEEDS . . . . VARIABLE
TRANSMISSION . . . . HYDRO
STEERING. . . . . STANDARD
STANDARD DECK . . . . 54"
MSRP. $6,699

OPTIONS

3 BAG
36" TILLER
42" BLADE
42" SNOW THROWER

RETAIL PRICING

YEAR	HIGH	LOW
2005	$1,499	$1,124
2006	$1,659	$1,244

GT25540

YEARS MFRD 2010-2010
SERIES. . . . . GT500 SERIES
ENGINE . . . . KOHLER COMMAND
CYLINDERS. 2
ENGINE HP 25
COOLING . . . . AIR
FUEL . . . . G
SPEEDS . . . . VARIABLE
TRANSMISSION . . . . HYDRO
STEERING. . . . . STANDARD
STANDARD DECK . . . . 54"
WEIGHT . . . . 858 LBS.
MSRP. $7,600

RETAIL PRICING

YEAR	HIGH	LOW
2010	$2,773	$2,080

HZ14330BVE

YEARS MFRD 1997-1997
SERIES. . . . . YARD CRUISER SERIES
ENGINE . . . . B&S
CYLINDERS. 1
ENGINE HP 14
COOLING . . . . AIR
FUEL . . . . G
SPEEDS . . . . VARIABLE
TRANSMISSION . . . . HYDRO
STEERING. . . . . ZERO
STANDARD DECK . . . . 33"
MSRP. $3,499

OPTIONS

1 BAG
2 BAG

RETAIL PRICING

YEAR	HIGH	LOW
1997	$399	$299

HZ14380BVE

YEARS MFRD 1997-1997
SERIES. . . . . YARD CRUISER SERIES
ENGINE . . . . B&S
ENGINE HP 14
COOLING . . . . AIR
FUEL . . . . G
SPEEDS . . . . VARIABLE
TRANSMISSION . . . . HYDRO
STEERING. . . . . ZERO
STANDARD DECK . . . . 38"
MSRP. $3,599

OPTIONS

1 BAG
2 BAG

RETAIL PRICING

YEAR	HIGH	LOW
1997	$415	$311

HZ15420KVE

YEARS MFRD 1997-1997
SERIES. . . . . YARD CRUISER SERIES
ENGINE . . . . KOHLER
ENGINE HP 15
COOLING . . . . AIR
FUEL . . . . G
SPEEDS . . . . VARIABLE
TRANSMISSION . . . . HYDRO
STEERING. . . . . ZERO
STANDARD DECK . . . . 42"
MSRP. $3,799

OPTIONS

1 BAG
2 BAG

RETAIL PRICING

YEAR	HIGH	LOW
1997	$437	$327

HZS14381BVE

YEARS MFRD 1998-1998
SERIES. . . . . YARD CRUISER SERIES
ENGINE . . . . B&S
CYLINDERS. 1
ENGINE HP 14
COOLING . . . . AIR
FUEL . . . . G
SPEEDS . . . . VARIABLE
TRANSMISSION . . . . HYDRO
STEERING. . . . . ZERO
STANDARD DECK . . . . 38"
MSRP. $3,899

OPTIONS

1 BAG
2 BAG

RETAIL PRICING

YEAR	HIGH	LOW
1998	$503	$378

HZS15420KVE

YEARS MFRD 1997-1997
SERIES. . . . . YARD CRUISER SERIES
ENGINE . . . . KOHLER
ENGINE HP 15
FUEL . . . . G
STEERING. . . . . ZERO
STANDARD DECK . . . . 42"
MSRP. $3,799

RETAIL PRICING

YEAR	HIGH	LOW
1997	$1,490	$1,117

HZS15421KVE

YEARS MFRD 1998-1998
SERIES. . . . . YARD CRUISER SERIES
ENGINE . . . . KOHLER
ENGINE HP 15
FUEL . . . . G
TRANSMISSION . . . . HYDRO
STEERING. . . . . ZERO
STANDARD DECK . . . . 42"
MSRP. $3,799

OPTIONS

1 BAG

RETAIL PRICING

YEAR	HIGH	LOW
1998	$492	$369

HZS15422KVE

YEARS MFRD 1999-2002
SERIES. . . . . YARD CRUISER SERIES
ENGINE . . . . KOHLER
ENGINE HP 15
FUEL . . . . G
TRANSMISSION . . . . HYDRO
STEERING. . . . . ZERO
STANDARD DECK . . . . 42"
MSRP. $3,599

OPTIONS

2 BAG
36" SWEEPER

RETAIL PRICING

YEAR	HIGH	LOW
1999	$534	$400
2000	$593	$445
2001	$659	$494
2002	$733	$550

HZS15423KVE

YEARS MFRD 2003-2003
SERIES. . . . . YARD CRUISER SERIES
ENGINE . . . . KOHLER
ENGINE HP 15
FUEL . . . . G
TRANSMISSION . . . . HYDRO
STEERING. . . . . STANDARD
STANDARD DECK . . . . 42"
MSRP. $3,499

OPTIONS

1 BAG

RETAIL PRICING

YEAR	HIGH	LOW
2003	$830	$623

HZS18482BVE

YEARS MFRD 1999-2002
SERIES. . . . . YARD CRUISER SERIES
ENGINE . . . . B&S
ENGINE HP 18
FUEL . . . . G
TRANSMISSION . . . . HYDRO
STEERING. . . . . ZERO
STANDARD DECK . . . . 48"
MSRP. $4,049

OPTIONS

36" SWEEPER

RETAIL PRICING

YEAR	HIGH	LOW
1999	$602	$452
2000	$669	$502
2001	$744	$558
2002	$830	$623

HZS18483BVE

YEARS MFRD 2003-2003
SERIES. . . . . YARD CRUISER SERIES
ENGINE . . . . B&S
ENGINE HP 18
FUEL . . . . G
TRANSMISSION . . . . . . DUAL HYDRO
STEERING. . . . . ZERO
STANDARD DECK . . . . 48"
MSRP. $3,999

RETAIL PRICING

YEAR	HIGH	LOW
2003	$948	$711

HZT21480BV

YEARS MFRD 2006-2006
SERIES. . . . . FAST CUT SERIES
ENGINE . . . . B&S
CYLINDERS. 2
ENGINE HP 21
COOLING . . . . AIR

SNAPPER

FUEL . . . . . G
SPEEDS . . . . . VARIABLE
TRANSMISSION . . . . . HYDRO
STEERING. . . . . ZERO
STANDARD DECK . . . . . 48"
WEIGHT . . . . . 832 LBS.
MSRP. $5,299

RETAIL PRICING

YEAR	HIGH	LOW
2006	$3,384	$2,538

HZT21481BV

YEARS MFRD 2005-2007
ENGINE . . . . . B&S
ENGINE HP 21
COOLING . . . . . AIR
FUEL . . . . . G
SPEEDS . . . . . VARIABLE
TRANSMISSION . . . . . HYDRO
STEERING. . . . . ZERO
STANDARD DECK . . . . . 48"
MSRP. $5,599

RETAIL PRICING

YEAR	HIGH	LOW
2005	$1,581	$1,186
2006	$1,755	$1,316
2007	$1,946	$1,459

LT125/2342

YEARS MFRD 2010-2013
ENGINE . . . . . B&S
ENGINE HP 23
COOLING . . . . . AIR
FUEL . . . . . G
SPEEDS . . . . . VARIABLE
TRANSMISSION . . . . . HYDRO
STEERING. . . . . STANDARD
STANDARD DECK . . . . . 46"
MSRP. $1,799

RETAIL PRICING

YEAR	HIGH	LOW
2010	$643	$482
2011	$771	$578
2012	$806	$605
2013	$964	$723

LT125/2446

YEARS MFRD 2010-2013
ENGINE . . . . . B&S
ENGINE HP 24
COOLING . . . . . AIR
FUEL . . . . . G
SPEEDS . . . . . VARIABLE
TRANSMISSION . . . . . HYDRO
STEERING. . . . . STANDARD
STANDARD DECK . . . . . 52"
MSRP. $1,999

RETAIL PRICING

YEAR	HIGH	LOW
2010	$706	$530
2011	$850	$637
2012	$899	$674
2013	$1,028	$771

LT130 AWS2346

YEARS MFRD 2012-2012
ENGINE . . . . . B&S
ENGINE HP 23
COOLING . . . . . AIR
FUEL . . . . . G
SPEEDS . . . . . VARIABLE
TRANSMISSION . . . . . HYDRO
STEERING. . . . . STANDARD
STANDARD DECK . . . . . 46"
MSRP. $2,699

RETAIL PRICING

YEAR	HIGH	LOW
2012	$1,336	$1,002

LT150H331BV

YEARS MFRD 2005-2005
ENGINE . . . . . B&S
CYLINDERS. 1
ENGINE HP 15
COOLING . . . . . AIR
FUEL . . . . . G
SPEEDS . . . . . VARIABLE
TRANSMISSION . . . . . HYDRO
STEERING. . . . . STANDARD
WEIGHT . . . . . 512 LBS.

LT150H381BV

YEARS MFRD 2005-2005
ENGINE . . . . . B&S
CYLINDERS. 1
ENGINE HP 15
COOLING . . . . . AIR
FUEL . . . . . G
SPEEDS . . . . . VARIABLE
TRANSMISSION . . . . . HYDRO
STEERING. . . . . STANDARD
BLADE CLUTCH . . . . . MANUAL
WEIGHT . . . . . 507 LBS.

LT150H38BBV

YEARS MFRD 1995-1995
ENGINE . . . . . B&S
ENGINE HP 15
FUEL . . . . . G
TRANSMISSION . . . . . HYDRO
STEERING. . . . . STANDARD
STANDARD DECK . . . . . 38"
MSRP. $2,549

RETAIL PRICING

YEAR	HIGH	LOW
1995	$928	$696

LT150H38GKV

YEARS MFRD 2005-2005
ENGINE . . . . . B&S
CYLINDERS. 1
ENGINE HP 15
COOLING . . . . . AIR
FUEL . . . . . G
SPEEDS . . . . . VARIABLE
TRANSMISSION . . . . . HYDRO
STEERING. . . . . STANDARD
BLADE CLUTCH . . . . . MANUAL
WEIGHT . . . . . 558 LBS.

LT150H 38GKV2

YEARS MFRD 2001-2001
ENGINE . . . . . KOHLER
ENGINE HP 15
FUEL . . . . . G
TRANSMISSION . . . . . HYDRO
STEERING. . . . . STANDARD
STANDARD DECK . . . . . 38"
MSRP. $2,500

RETAIL PRICING

YEAR	HIGH	LOW
2001	$1,200	$900

LT150H38HKV

YEARS MFRD 2002-2002
ENGINE . . . . . KOHLER
ENGINE HP 15
FUEL . . . . . G
TRANSMISSION . . . . . HYDRO
STEERING. . . . . STANDARD
STANDARD DECK . . . . . 38"
MSRP. $2,300

RETAIL PRICING

YEAR	HIGH	LOW
2002	$1,135	$851

LT150H422KV

YEARS MFRD 1995-1995
ENGINE . . . . . KOHLER
ENGINE HP 15
FUEL . . . . . G
TRANSMISSION . . . . . HYDRO
STEERING. . . . . STANDARD
STANDARD DECK . . . . . 42"
MSRP. $3,499

RETAIL PRICING

YEAR	HIGH	LOW
1995	$1,276	$957

LT155H42BBV

YEARS MFRD 1995-1995
ENGINE . . . . . B&S
ENGINE HP 15.5
FUEL . . . . . G
TRANSMISSION . . . . . HYDRO
STEERING. . . . . STANDARD
STANDARD DECK . . . . . 42"
MSRP. $2,699

RETAIL PRICING

YEAR	HIGH	LOW
1995	$985	$738

LT160H42CBV

YEARS MFRD 1996-1996
ENGINE . . . . . B&S
ENGINE HP 16
FUEL . . . . . G
TRANSMISSION . . . . . HYDRO
STEERING. . . . . STANDARD
STANDARD DECK . . . . . 42"
WEIGHT . . . . . 583 LBS.
MSRP. $2,599

RETAIL PRICING

YEAR	HIGH	LOW
1996	$983	$737

LT160H42DBV

YEARS MFRD 1997-1999
ENGINE . . . . . B&S
ENGINE HP 16
FUEL . . . . . G
TRANSMISSION . . . . . HYDRO
STEERING. . . . . STANDARD
STANDARD DECK . . . . . 42"
WEIGHT . . . . . 558 LBS.
MSRP. $2,699

RETAIL PRICING

YEAR	HIGH	LOW
1997	$1,019	$765
1998	$1,071	$803
1999	$1,186	$890

LT160H42FBV

YEARS MFRD 2000-2000
ENGINE . . . . . B&S
ENGINE HP 16
FUEL . . . . . G
TRANSMISSION . . . . . HYDRO
STEERING. . . . . STANDARD
STANDARD DECK . . . . . 42"
MSRP. $2,999

RETAIL PRICING

YEAR	HIGH	LOW
2000	$1,381	$1,036

LT160H42GBV

YEARS MFRD 2001-2001
ENGINE . . . . . B&S
ENGINE HP 16
FUEL . . . . . G
TRANSMISSION . . . . . HYDRO
STEERING. . . . . STANDARD
STANDARD DECK . . . . . 42"
MSRP. $2,999

RETAIL PRICING

YEAR	HIGH	LOW
2001	$1,440	$1,080

LT160H42HBV

YEARS MFRD 2002-2005
ENGINE . . . . . B&S
CYLINDERS. 2
ENGINE HP 16
COOLING . . . . . AIR
FUEL . . . . . G
SPEEDS . . . . . VARIABLE
TRANSMISSION . . . . . HYDRO
STEERING. . . . . STANDARD
BLADE CLUTCH . . . . . ELECTRIC

STANDARD DECK . . . . 42"
WEIGHT . . . . 558 LBS.
MSRP. $3,000

RETAIL PRICING

YEAR	HIGH	LOW
2002	$1,383	$1,037
2003	$1,606	$1,205
2004	$1,822	$1,366
2005	$1,896	$1,422

LT160H482BV

YEARS MFRD 1992-1994
ENGINE . . . . KOHLER
ENGINE HP 16
FUEL . . . . G
TRANSMISSION . . . . GEAR
STEERING. . . . . STANDARD
STANDARD DECK . . . . 48"
MSRP. $3,699

RETAIL PRICING

YEAR	HIGH	LOW
1992	$1,162	$872
1993	$1,196	$897
1994	$1,300	$975

LT160H482KV

YEARS MFRD 1995-1995
ENGINE . . . . B&S
ENGINE HP 16
FUEL . . . . G
TRANSMISSION . . . . HYDRO
STEERING. . . . . STANDARD
STANDARD DECK . . . . 48"
MSRP. $3,899

RETAIL PRICING

YEAR	HIGH	LOW
1995	$1,422	$1,067

LT180H331BV

YEARS MFRD 2006-2006
ENGINE . . . . B&S INTEK
CYLINDERS. 1
ENGINE HP 18
COOLING . . . . AIR
FUEL . . . . G
SPEEDS . . . . VARIABLE
TRANSMISSION . . . . HYDRO
STEERING. . . . . ZERO
STANDARD DECK . . . . 33"
WEIGHT . . . . 407 LBS.
MSRP. $2,199

RETAIL PRICING

YEAR	HIGH	LOW
2006	$1,405	$1,053

LT180H381BV

YEARS MFRD 2006-2006
ENGINE . . . . B&S
CYLINDERS. 1
ENGINE HP 18
COOLING . . . . AIR
FUEL . . . . G
SPEEDS . . . . VARIABLE
TRANSMISSION . . . . HYDRO
STEERING. . . . . ZERO
STANDARD DECK . . . . 38"
WEIGHT . . . . 410 LBS.
MSRP. $2,299

RETAIL PRICING

YEAR	HIGH	LOW
2006	$1,469	$1,101

LT180H 421BV2

YEARS MFRD 2005-2005
ENGINE . . . . B&S
CYLINDERS. 2
ENGINE HP 18
COOLING . . . . AIR
FUEL . . . . G
SPEEDS . . . . VARIABLE
TRANSMISSION . . . . HYDRO
STEERING. . . . . STANDARD
BLADE CLUTCH . . . . ELECTRIC
WEIGHT . . . . 620 LBS.

LT180H 42HBV

YEARS MFRD 2006-2006
ENGINE . . . . B&S INTEK
CYLINDERS. 1
ENGINE HP 18
COOLING . . . . AIR
FUEL . . . . G
SPEEDS . . . . VARIABLE
TRANSMISSION . . . . HYDRO
STEERING. . . . . STANDARD
STANDARD DECK . . . . 42"
WEIGHT . . . . 455 LBS.
MSRP. $2,299

RETAIL PRICING

YEAR	HIGH	LOW
2006	$1,469	$1,101

LT180H 48DBV2

YEARS MFRD 1999-1999
ENGINE . . . . B&S
ENGINE HP 18
FUEL . . . . G
TRANSMISSION . . . . HYDRO
STEERING. . . . . STANDARD
STANDARD DECK . . . . 48"
MSRP. $3,699

RETAIL PRICING

YEAR	HIGH	LOW
1999	$1,625	$1,219

LT180H 48FBV2

YEARS MFRD 2000-2001
ENGINE . . . . B&S
ENGINE HP 18
FUEL . . . . G
TRANSMISSION . . . . HYDRO
STEERING. . . . . STANDARD
STANDARD DECK . . . . 48"
MSRP. $3,500

RETAIL PRICING

YEAR	HIGH	LOW
2000	$1,611	$1,208
2001	$1,681	$1,261

LT180H 48HBV2

YEARS MFRD 2002-2003
ENGINE . . . . B&S
ENGINE HP 18
FUEL . . . . G
TRANSMISSION . . . . HYDRO
STEERING. . . . . STANDARD
STANDARD DECK . . . . 48"
MSRP. $4,000

RETAIL PRICING

YEAR	HIGH	LOW
2002	$1,974	$1,480
2003	$2,140	$1,605

LT200H 421BV2

YEARS MFRD 2006-2006
ENGINE . . . . B&S INTEK
CYLINDERS. 2
ENGINE HP 20
COOLING . . . . AIR
FUEL . . . . G
SPEEDS . . . . VARIABLE
TRANSMISSION . . . . HYDRO
STEERING. . . . . STANDARD
STANDARD DECK . . . . 42"
WEIGHT . . . . 455 LBS.
MSRP. $2,999

RETAIL PRICING

YEAR	HIGH	LOW
2006	$1,915	$1,436

LT200H 481BV2

YEARS MFRD 2005-2006
ENGINE . . . . B&S
CYLINDERS. 2
ENGINE HP 20
COOLING . . . . AIR
FUEL . . . . G
SPEEDS . . . . VARIABLE
TRANSMISSION . . . . HYDRO
STEERING. . . . . STANDARD
BLADE CLUTCH . . . . ELECTRIC
STANDARD DECK . . . . 48"
WEIGHT . . . . 620 LBS.
MSRP. $3,699

RETAIL PRICING

YEAR	HIGH	LOW
2006	$2,363	$1,772

LT300 2246

YEARS MFRD 2013-2015
ENGINE . . . . B&S
ENGINE HP 23
COOLING . . . . AIR
FUEL . . . . G
SPEEDS . . . . VARIABLE
TRANSMISSION . . . . HYDRO
STEERING. . . . . STANDARD
STANDARD DECK . . . . 46"
MSRP. $3,999

RETAIL PRICING

YEAR	HIGH	LOW
2013	$1,518	$1,139
2014	$2,014	$1,510
2015	$2,576	$1,932

LT2042

YEARS MFRD 2006-2010
ENGINE . . . . B&S
ENGINE HP 20
COOLING . . . . AIR
FUEL . . . . G
SPEEDS . . . . VARIABLE
TRANSMISSION . . . . HYDRO
STEERING. . . . . STANDARD
STANDARD DECK . . . . 42"
MSRP. $2,400

OPTIONS

2 BAG & FAN
3 BAG & FAN
42" BLADE
42" SNOW THROWER

RETAIL PRICING

YEAR	HIGH	LOW
2006	$534	$400
2007	$592	$444
2008	$656	$492
2009	$728	$546
2010	$806	$605

LT2044

YEARS MFRD 2006-2010
ENGINE . . . . B&S
CYLINDERS. 2
ENGINE HP 20
COOLING . . . . AIR
FUEL . . . . G
SPEEDS . . . . VARIABLE
TRANSMISSION . . . . HYDRO
STEERING. . . . . STANDARD
STANDARD DECK . . . . 44"
MSRP. $4,450

OPTIONS

2 BAG & FAN
3 BAG & FAN
42" BLADE
42" SNOW THROWER

RETAIL PRICING

YEAR	HIGH	LOW
2006	$989	$742
2007	$1,097	$823
2008	$1,216	$912
2009	$1,348	$1,011
2010	$1,495	$1,121

SNAPPER

LT2250

YEARS MFRD 2006-2010
ENGINE . . . . B&S
CYLINDERS. 2
ENGINE HP 22
COOLING . . . . AIR
FUEL . . . . G
SPEEDS . . . . VARIABLE
TRANSMISSION . . . . HYDRO
STEERING. . . . . STANDARD
STANDARD DECK . . . . 50"
MSRP. $2,950

OPTIONS

2 BAG & FAN
3 BAG & FAN
42" BLADE
42" SNOW THROWER

RETAIL PRICING

YEAR	HIGH	LOW
2006	$656	$492
2007	$728	$546
2008	$806	$605
2009	$894	$671
2010	$990	$743

LT2342

YEARS MFRD 2010-2010
SERIES. . . . . .LT125 SERIES
ENGINE . . . . B&S
CYLINDERS. 2
ENGINE HP 23
COOLING . . . . AIR
FUEL . . . . G
SPEEDS . . . . VARIABLE
TRANSMISSION . . . . HYDRO
STEERING. . . . . STANDARD
STANDARD DECK . . . . 42"
WEIGHT . . . . 532 LBS.
MSRP. $1,999

RETAIL PRICING

YEAR	HIGH	LOW
2010	$672	$504

LT2346

YEARS MFRD 2010-2010
ENGINE . . . . B&S
CYLINDERS. 2
ENGINE HP 23
COOLING . . . . AIR
FUEL . . . . G
SPEEDS . . . . VARIABLE
TRANSMISSION . . . . HYDRO
STEERING. . . . . ALL WHEEL
STANDARD DECK . . . . 46"
WEIGHT . . . . 490 LBS.
MSRP. $1,999

RETAIL PRICING

YEAR	HIGH	LOW
2010	$673	$505

LT2446

YEARS MFRD 2010-2010
SERIES. . . . . .LT125 SERIES
ENGINE . . . . B&S
CYLINDERS. 2
ENGINE HP 24
COOLING . . . . AIR
FUEL . . . . G
SPEEDS . . . . VARIABLE
TRANSMISSION . . . . HYDRO
STEERING. . . . . STANDARD
STANDARD DECK . . . . 46"
WEIGHT . . . . 560 LBS.
MSRP. $2,199

RETAIL PRICING

YEAR	HIGH	LOW
2010	$738	$554

LT2452

YEARS MFRD 2010-2010
ENGINE . . . . B&S
CYLINDERS. 2
ENGINE HP 24
COOLING . . . . AIR
FUEL . . . . G
SPEEDS . . . . VARIABLE
TRANSMISSION . . . . HYDRO
STEERING. . . . . STANDARD
STANDARD DECK . . . . 46"
WEIGHT . . . . 515 LBS.
MSRP. $2,199

RETAIL PRICING

YEAR	HIGH	LOW
2010	$738	$554

LT18538

YEARS MFRD 2006-2010
ENGINE . . . . B&S
CYLINDERS. 1
ENGINE HP 18.5
COOLING . . . . AIR
FUEL . . . . G
SPEEDS . . . . VARIABLE
TRANSMISSION . . . . HYDRO
STEERING. . . . . STANDARD
STANDARD DECK . . . . 38"
MSRP. $2,200

OPTIONS

2 BAG & FAN
3 BAG & FAN
42" BLADE
42" SNOW THROWER

RETAIL PRICING

YEAR	HIGH	LOW
2006	$489	$367
2007	$543	$407
2008	$601	$451
2009	$666	$500
2010	$738	$554

LT20440

YEARS MFRD 2005-2007
SERIES. . . . . LT 200 SERIES
ENGINE . . . . B&S VANGUARD
CYLINDERS. 2
ENGINE HP 20
COOLING . . . . AIR
FUEL . . . . G
SPEEDS . . . . VARIABLE
TRANSMISSION . . . . HYDRO
STEERING. . . . . STANDARD
STANDARD DECK . . . . 44"
MSRP. $2,649

OPTIONS

2 BAG
42" BLADE
42" SNOW BLOWER
42" SNOW THROWER

RETAIL PRICING

YEAR	HIGH	LOW
2005	$510	$383
2006	$566	$424
2007	$627	$470

LT22500

YEARS MFRD 2006-2006
ENGINE . . . . B&S
CYLINDERS. 2
ENGINE HP 22
COOLING . . . . AIR
FUEL . . . . G
SPEEDS . . . . VARIABLE
TRANSMISSION . . . . HYDRO
STEERING. . . . . STANDARD
STANDARD DECK . . . . 50"
MSRP. $5,099

RETAIL PRICING

YEAR	HIGH	LOW
2006	$3,256	$2,442

MGT1800G

YEARS MFRD 1996-1997
ENGINE . . . . KOHLER
ENGINE HP 18
FUEL . . . . G
TRANSMISSION . . . . GEAR
STEERING. . . . . STANDARD
STANDARD DECK . . . . 60"
MSRP. $8,903

RETAIL PRICING

YEAR	HIGH	LOW
1996	$3,263	$2,447
1997	$3,490	$2,618

MGT2000G

YEARS MFRD 1997-1998
ENGINE . . . . KOHLER
ENGINE HP 20
FUEL . . . . G
TRANSMISSION . . . . GEAR
STEERING. . . . . STANDARD
STANDARD DECK . . . . 48"
MSRP. $8,503

OPTIONS

46" TILLER
47" SNOW BLOWER
54" BLADE
60" DECK

SERIAL NUMBERS

YEAR . . . . BEGINNING NO.
1997 971014001

RETAIL PRICING

YEAR	HIGH	LOW
1997	$894	$671
1998	$953	$714

MGT2000H

YEARS MFRD 1996-1997
ENGINE . . . . KOHLER
ENGINE HP 20
FUEL . . . . G
TRANSMISSION . . . . HYDRO
STEERING. . . . . STANDARD
STANDARD DECK . . . . 60"
MSRP. $9,703

RETAIL PRICING

YEAR	HIGH	LOW
1996	$3,661	$2,746
1997	$3,805	$2,854

MGT2200H

YEARS MFRD 1997-1998
ENGINE . . . . KOHLER
ENGINE HP 22
FUEL . . . . G
TRANSMISSION . . . . HYDRO
STEERING. . . . . STANDARD
STANDARD DECK . . . . 60"
MSRP. $9,590

OPTIONS

46" TILLER
47" SNOW BLOWER
54" BLADE

SERIAL NUMBERS

YEAR . . . . BEGINNING NO.
1998 971015001

RETAIL PRICING

YEAR	HIGH	LOW
1997	$1,011	$758
1998	$1,074	$805

MZM2200KH

YEARS MFRD 1999-2000
SERIES. . . . . . PRO CRUISER SERIES
ENGINE . . . . KOHLER PRO
ENGINE HP 22
FUEL . . . . G
TRANSMISSION . . . . HYDRO
STEERING. . . . . ZERO
STANDARD DECK . . . . 61"
MSRP. $6,999

OPTIONS

BAGGER
ROPS

RETAIL PRICING

YEAR	HIGH	LOW
1999	$1,166	$874
2000	$1,296	$972

MZM2300KH

YEARS MFRD 2001-2003
SERIES. . . . . . PRO CRUISER SERIES
ENGINE . . . . KOHLER
ENGINE HP 23

COOLING . . . . . AIR
FUEL . . . . . G
SPEEDS . . . . . VARIABLE
TRANSMISSION . . . . . DUAL HYDRO
STEERING. . . . . ZERO
STANDARD DECK . . . . . 52"
MSRP. $6,999

OPTIONS

61" DECK
CATCHER
ROPS

RETAIL PRICING

YEAR	HIGH	LOW
2001	$1,343	$1,008
2002	$1,496	$1,122
2003	$1,654	$1,240

NXT2242

YEARS MFRD 2013-2015
ENGINE . . . . . B&S
ENGINE HP 22
COOLING . . . . . AIR
FUEL . . . . . G
SPEEDS . . . . . VARIABLE
TRANSMISSION . . . . . HYDRO
STEERING. . . . . STANDARD
STANDARD DECK . . . . . 42"
MSRP. $2,599

RETAIL PRICING

YEAR	HIGH	LOW
2013	$1,037	$778
2014	$1,213	$909
2015	$1,547	$1,160

NXT2346

YEARS MFRD 2012-2015
ENGINE . . . . . B&S
ENGINE HP 23
COOLING . . . . . AIR
FUEL . . . . . G
SPEEDS . . . . . VARIABLE
TRANSMISSION . . . . . HYDRO
STEERING. . . . . STANDARD
STANDARD DECK . . . . . 46"
MSRP. $2,799

RETAIL PRICING

YEAR	HIGH	LOW
2012	$925	$694
2013	$1,117	$838
2014	$1,302	$976
2015	$1,732	$1,299

NXT2652

YEARS MFRD 2013-2015
ENGINE . . . . . B&S
ENGINE HP 26
COOLING . . . . . AIR
FUEL . . . . . G
SPEEDS . . . . . VARIABLE
TRANSMISSION . . . . . HYDRO
STEERING. . . . . STANDARD
STANDARD DECK . . . . . 52"
MSRP. $2,999

RETAIL PRICING

YEAR	HIGH	LOW
2013	$1,237	$928
2014	$1,398	$1,048
2015	$1,872	$1,404

NXT2752

YEARS MFRD 2012-2012
ENGINE . . . . . B&S
ENGINE HP 27
COOLING . . . . . AIR
FUEL . . . . . G
SPEEDS . . . . . VARIABLE
TRANSMISSION . . . . . HYDRO
STEERING. . . . . STANDARD
STANDARD DECK . . . . . 52"
MSRP. $2,999

RETAIL PRICING

YEAR	HIGH	LOW
2012	$1,489	$1,117

NXT19542

YEARS MFRD 2012-2012
ENGINE . . . . . B&S
ENGINE HP 19.5
COOLING . . . . . AIR
FUEL . . . . . G
SPEEDS . . . . . VARIABLE
TRANSMISSION . . . . . HYDRO
STEERING. . . . . STANDARD
STANDARD DECK . . . . . 42"
MSRP. $2,299

RETAIL PRICING

YEAR	HIGH	LOW
2012	$1,145	$858

NZM19480 KWV

YEARS MFRD 2003-2006
SERIES. . . . . FASTBACK SERIES
ENGINE . . . . . KAWASAKI
CYLINDERS. 2
ENGINE HP 19
COOLING . . . . . AIR
FUEL . . . . . G
SPEEDS . . . . . VARIABLE
TRANSMISSION . . . . . HYDRO
STEERING. . . . . ZERO
STANDARD DECK . . . . . 48"
MSRP. $7,199

OPTIONS

ROPS
SUS SEAT
Z VAC

RETAIL PRICING

YEAR	HIGH	LOW
2003	$1,654	$1,240
2004	$1,835	$1,376
2005	$2,039	$1,529
2006	$2,265	$1,699

NZM21520 KWV

YEARS MFRD 2003-2006
SERIES. . . . . FASTBACK SERIES
ENGINE . . . . . KAWASAKI
CYLINDERS. 2
ENGINE HP 21
COOLING . . . . . AIR
FUEL . . . . . G
SPEEDS . . . . . VARIABLE
TRANSMISSION . . . . . HYDRO
STEERING. . . . . ZERO
STANDARD DECK . . . . . 52"
MSRP. $7,599

OPTIONS

ROPS
SUS SEAT
Z VAC

RETAIL PRICING

YEAR	HIGH	LOW
2003	$1,747	$1,310
2004	$1,940	$1,455
2005	$2,154	$1,616
2006	$2,390	$1,793

NZM25523 KWV

YEARS MFRD 2006-2006
ENGINE . . . . . KAWASAKI
CYLINDERS. 2
ENGINE HP 25
COOLING . . . . . AIR
FUEL . . . . . G
SPEEDS . . . . . VARIABLE
TRANSMISSION . . . . . HYDRO
STEERING. . . . . STANDARD
STANDARD DECK . . . . . 52"
WEIGHT . . . . . 1,092 LBS.
MSRP. $7,999

OPTIONS

ROPS
SUS SEAT
Z VAC

RETAIL PRICING

YEAR	HIGH	LOW
2006	$2,517	$1,888

NZM25611 KWV

YEARS MFRD 2004-2006
SERIES. . . . . FASTBACK SERIES
ENGINE . . . . . KAWASAKI
CYLINDERS. 2
ENGINE HP 25
COOLING . . . . . AIR
FUEL . . . . . G
SPEEDS . . . . . VARIABLE
TRANSMISSION . . . . . HYDRO
STEERING. . . . . ZERO
STANDARD DECK . . . . . 61"
MSRP. $8,299

OPTIONS

ROPS
SUS SEAT
Z VAC

RETAIL PRICING

YEAR	HIGH	LOW
2004	$2,118	$1,588
2005	$2,353	$1,765
2006	$2,613	$1,960

NZM27613KH

YEARS MFRD 2005-2006
ENGINE . . . . . KOHLER
CYLINDERS. 2
ENGINE HP 27
COOLING . . . . . AIR
FUEL . . . . . G
SPEEDS . . . . . VARIABLE
TRANSMISSION . . . . . HYDRO
STEERING. . . . . ZERO
STANDARD DECK . . . . . 61"
WEIGHT . . . . . 1,188 LBS.
MSRP. $8,699

OPTIONS

ROPS
SUS SEAT
Z VAC

RETAIL PRICING

YEAR	HIGH	LOW
2005	$2,465	$1,849
2006	$2,739	$2,054

NZMJ25

YEARS MFRD 2004-2004
SERIES. . . . . FASTBACK SERIES
ENGINE . . . . . KOHLER
CYLINDERS. 2
ENGINE HP 25
FUEL . . . . . G
SPEEDS . . . . . VARIABLE
TRANSMISSION . . . . . HYDRO
STEERING. . . . . ZERO
STANDARD DECK . . . . . 61"
MSRP. $7,099

RETAIL PRICING

YEAR	HIGH	LOW
2004	$4,045	$3,034

NZMJ23521 KH

YEARS MFRD 2004-2006
SERIES. . . . . FASTBACK SERIES
ENGINE . . . . . KOHLER
CYLINDERS. 2
ENGINE HP 23
COOLING . . . . . AIR
FUEL . . . . . G
SPEEDS . . . . . VARIABLE
TRANSMISSION . . . . . HYDRO
STEERING. . . . . ZERO
STANDARD DECK . . . . . 52"
MSRP. $7,699

OPTIONS

BLOWER
ROPS
Z VAC

SNAPPER

RETAIL PRICING

YEAR	HIGH	LOW
2004	$1,965	$1,474
2005	$2,183	$1,637
2006	$2,425	$1,819

NZMJ25611 KH

YEARS MFRD 2004-2006
ENGINE . . . . KOHLER
ENGINE HP 25
COOLING . . . . AIR
FUEL . . . . G
SPEEDS . . . . VARIABLE
TRANSMISSION . . . . HYDRO
STEERING . . . . ZERO
STANDARD DECK . . . . 61"
MSRP $8,199

OPTIONS

BLOWER
ROPS
Z VAC

RETAIL PRICING

YEAR	HIGH	LOW
2004	$2,090	$1,568
2005	$2,323	$1,742
2006	$2,580	$1,935

RE100

YEARS MFRD 2016-2017
ENGINE . . . . B&S
ENGINE HP 10
COOLING . . . . AIR
FUEL . . . . G
SPEEDS 5/1
TRANSMISSION . . . . DISC
STEERING . . . . STANDARD
STANDARD DECK . . . . 28"
MSRP $1,299

RETAIL PRICING

YEAR	HIGH	LOW
2016	$705	$529
2017	$849	$637

RE110

YEARS MFRD 2016-2018
ENGINE . . . . B&S
ENGINE HP 11.5
COOLING . . . . AIR
FUEL . . . . G
SPEEDS 5/1
TRANSMISSION . . . . DISC
STEERING . . . . STANDARD
STANDARD DECK . . . . 28"
MSRP $1,599

RETAIL PRICING

YEAR	HIGH	LOW
2016	$789	$591
2017	$946	$709
2018	$1,113	$834

RE200

YEARS MFRD 2013-2013
ENGINE . . . . B&S
ENGINE HP 14.5
COOLING . . . . AIR
FUEL . . . . G
SPEEDS . . . . VARIABLE
TRANSMISSION . . . . HYDRO
STEERING . . . . STANDARD
STANDARD DECK . . . . 30"
MSRP $2,399

RETAIL PRICING

YEAR	HIGH	LOW
2013	$1,236	$927

RE200/13530

YEARS MFRD 2012-2012
ENGINE . . . . B&S
ENGINE HP 13.5
COOLING . . . . AIR
FUEL . . . . G
SPEEDS . . . . VARIABLE
TRANSMISSION . . . . HYDRO
STEERING . . . . STANDARD
STANDARD DECK . . . . 30"
MSRP $2,299

RETAIL PRICING

YEAR	HIGH	LOW
2012	$1,365	$1,024

RE1330

YEARS MFRD 2008-2008
ENGINE . . . . B&S I/C OHV AVS
CYLINDERS 1
ENGINE HP 13
COOLING . . . . AIR
FUEL . . . . G
SPEEDS . . . . VARIABLE
TRANSMISSION . . . . HYDRO
STEERING . . . . STANDARD
STANDARD DECK . . . . 30"
WEIGHT . . . . 415 LBS.
MSRP $2,270

RETAIL PRICING

YEAR	HIGH	LOW
2008	$1,378	$1,034

RE13530

YEARS MFRD 2010-2010
ENGINE . . . . B&S INTEK
CYLINDERS 1
ENGINE HP 13.5
COOLING . . . . AIR
FUEL . . . . G
SPEEDS . . . . VARIABLE
TRANSMISSION . . . . HYDRO
STEERING . . . . STANDARD
STANDARD DECK . . . . 30"
WEIGHT . . . . 415 LBS.
MSRP $2,449

RETAIL PRICING

YEAR	HIGH	LOW
2010	$956	$717

RER11.5/28

YEARS MFRD 2012-2015
ENGINE . . . . B&S
ENGINE HP 11.5
COOLING . . . . AIR
FUEL . . . . G
SPEEDS 5/1
TRANSMISSION . . . . DISC
STEERING . . . . STANDARD
STANDARD DECK . . . . 28"
MSRP $1,299

RETAIL PRICING

YEAR	HIGH	LOW
2012	$370	$277
2013	$466	$349
2014	$577	$433
2015	$725	$543

RER12.5/28

YEARS MFRD 2012-2015
ENGINE . . . . B&S
ENGINE HP 12.5
COOLING . . . . AIR
FUEL . . . . G
SPEEDS 5/1
TRANSMISSION . . . . DISC
STEERING . . . . STANDARD
BLADE CLUTCH . . . . MANUAL
STANDARD DECK . . . . 28"
MSRP $1,449

RETAIL PRICING

YEAR	HIGH	LOW
2012	$429	$322
2013	$540	$405
2014	$643	$482
2015	$756	$567

RER13.5/30

YEARS MFRD 2012-2012
ENGINE . . . . B&S
ENGINE HP 13.5
COOLING . . . . AIR
FUEL . . . . G
SPEEDS 5/1
TRANSMISSION . . . . DISC
STEERING . . . . STANDARD
STANDARD DECK . . . . 30"
MSRP $1,799

RETAIL PRICING

YEAR	HIGH	LOW
2012	$930	$698

RER14.5/30

YEARS MFRD 2013-2015
ENGINE . . . . B&S
ENGINE HP 14.5
COOLING . . . . AIR
FUEL . . . . G
SPEEDS 5/1
TRANSMISSION . . . . DISC
STEERING . . . . STANDARD
STANDARD DECK . . . . 30"
MSRP $1,599

RETAIL PRICING

YEAR	HIGH	LOW
2013	$666	$500
2014	$711	$533
2015	$842	$631

RER17.5/33

YEARS MFRD 2012-2015
ENGINE . . . . B&S
ENGINE HP 17.5
COOLING . . . . AIR
FUEL . . . . G
SPEEDS 5/1
TRANSMISSION . . . . DISC
STEERING . . . . STANDARD
BLADE CLUTCH . . . . MANUAL
STANDARD DECK . . . . 33"
MSRP $1,899

RETAIL PRICING

YEAR	HIGH	LOW
2012	$607	$455
2013	$762	$572
2014	$844	$633
2015	$1,147	$860

RYT16D334K

YEARS MFRD 1991-1991
ENGINE . . . . KOHLER
ENGINE HP 16
COOLING . . . . AIR
FUEL . . . . G
TRANSMISSION . . . . GEAR
STEERING . . . . STANDARD
STANDARD DECK . . . . 33"
MSRP $3,299

RETAIL PRICING

YEAR	HIGH	LOW
1991	$1,021	$766

RZT20420BVE

YEARS MFRD 2006-2007
ENGINE . . . . B&S
CYLINDERS 2
ENGINE HP 20
COOLING . . . . AIR
FUEL . . . . G
SPEEDS . . . . VARIABLE
TRANSMISSION . . . . HYDRO
STEERING . . . . ZERO
STANDARD DECK . . . . 42"
MSRP $3,599

RETAIL PRICING

YEAR	HIGH	LOW
2006	$1,128	$846
2007	$1,251	$938

RZT22500 BVE2

YEARS MFRD 2006-2007
ENGINE . . . . B&S
CYLINDERS 2
ENGINE HP 22
COOLING . . . . AIR

FUEL . . . . G
SPEEDS . . . . VARIABLE
TRANSMISSION . . . . HYDRO
STEERING. . . . . ZERO
STANDARD DECK . . . . 50"
MSRP. $3,899

RETAIL PRICING

YEAR	HIGH	LOW
2006	$1,221	$916
2007	$1,355	$1,016

RZT185380 BVE

YEARS MFRD 2006-2007
ENGINE . . . . B&S
CYLINDERS. 1
ENGINE HP 18.5
COOLING . . . . AIR
FUEL . . . . G
SPEEDS . . . . VARIABLE
TRANSMISSION . . . . HYDRO
STEERING. . . . . ZERO
STANDARD DECK . . . . 38"
MSRP. $3,299

RETAIL PRICING

YEAR	HIGH	LOW
2006	$1,033	$775
2007	$1,147	$860

SGT27540D

YEARS MFRD 2007-2007
SERIES. . . . . GT600 SERIES
ENGINE . . . . B&S VANGUARD
CYLINDERS. 3
ENGINE HP 27
COOLING . . . . AIR
FUEL . . . . D
SPEEDS . . . . VARIABLE
TRANSMISSION . . . . HYDRO
STEERING. . . . . STANDARD
STANDARD DECK . . . . 54"
MSRP. $12,329

RETAIL PRICING

YEAR	HIGH	LOW
2007	$6,855	$5,141

SPX2042

YEARS MFRD 2014-2015
ENGINE . . . . B&S
ENGINE HP 20
COOLING . . . . AIR
FUEL . . . . G
SPEEDS . . . . VARIABLE
TRANSMISSION . . . . HYDRO
STEERING. . . . . STANDARD
STANDARD DECK . . . . 42"
MSRP. $1,799

RETAIL PRICING

YEAR	HIGH	LOW
2014	$835	$626
2015	$1,095	$821

SPX2146

YEARS MFRD 2012-2012
ENGINE . . . . B&S
ENGINE HP 21
COOLING . . . . AIR
FUEL . . . . G
SPEEDS . . . . VARIABLE
TRANSMISSION . . . . HYDRO
STEERING. . . . . STANDARD
STANDARD DECK . . . . 46"
MSRP. $2,299

RETAIL PRICING

YEAR	HIGH	LOW
2012	$1,145	$858

SPX2242

YEARS MFRD 2016-2017
ENGINE . . . . B&S
ENGINE HP 22
COOLING . . . . AIR
FUEL . . . . G
SPEEDS . . . . VARIABLE
TRANSMISSION . . . . HYDRO
STEERING. . . . . STANDARD
STANDARD DECK . . . . 42"
MSRP. $1,799

RETAIL PRICING

YEAR	HIGH	LOW
2016	$1,020	$765
2017	$1,175	$881

SPX2246

YEARS MFRD 2013-2017
ENGINE . . . . B&S
ENGINE HP 22
COOLING . . . . AIR
FUEL . . . . G
SPEEDS . . . . VARIABLE
TRANSMISSION . . . . HYDRO
STEERING. . . . . STANDARD
STANDARD DECK . . . . 46"
MSRP. $1,999

RETAIL PRICING

YEAR	HIGH	LOW
2013	$777	$583
2014	$976	$732
2015	$1,139	$854
2016	$1,301	$976
2017	$1,365	$1,024

SPX2342

YEARS MFRD 2016-2020
SERIES. . . . . SPX SERIES
ENGINE . . . . B&S
CYLINDERS. 2
ENGINE HP 23
COOLING . . . . AIR
FUEL . . . . G
SPEEDS . . . . VARIABLE
TRANSMISSION . . . . HYDRO
STEERING. . . . . STANDARD
BLADE CLUTCH . . . . ELECTRIC
STANDARD DECK . . . . 42"
MSRP. $2,099

RETAIL PRICING

YEAR	HIGH	LOW
2016	$1,374	$1,031
2017	$1,577	$1,182
2018	$1,755	$1,317
2019	$1,874	$1,405
2020	$1,967	$1,501

SPX2346

YEARS MFRD 2017-2020
SERIES. . . . . SPX SERIES
ENGINE . . . . B&S INTEK
CYLINDERS. 2
ENGINE HP 23
FUEL . . . . G
TRANSMISSION . . . . HYDRO
STEERING. . . . . STANDARD
BLADE CLUTCH . . . . ELECTRIC
STANDARD DECK . . . . 46"
MSRP. $2,249

SPX2352

YEARS MFRD 2013-2015
ENGINE . . . . B&S
ENGINE HP 23
COOLING . . . . AIR
FUEL . . . . G
SPEEDS . . . . VARIABLE
TRANSMISSION . . . . HYDRO
STEERING. . . . . STANDARD
STANDARD DECK . . . . 52"
MSRP. $2,499

RETAIL PRICING

YEAR	HIGH	LOW
2013	$800	$600
2014	$1,163	$872
2015	$1,533	$1,149

SPX2452

YEARS MFRD 2012-2012
ENGINE . . . . B&S
ENGINE HP 24
COOLING . . . . AIR
FUEL . . . . G
SPEEDS . . . . VARIABLE
TRANSMISSION . . . . HYDRO
STEERING. . . . . STANDARD
STANDARD DECK . . . . 52"
MSRP. $2,499

RETAIL PRICING

YEAR	HIGH	LOW
2012	$1,241	$930

SPX2542

YEARS MFRD 2018-2020
SERIES. . . . . SPX SERIES
ENGINE . . . . . B&S PROFESSIONAL
CYLINDERS. 2
ENGINE HP 25
FUEL . . . . G
TRANSMISSION . . . . HYDRO
STEERING. . . . . STANDARD
BLADE CLUTCH . . . . ELECTRIC
STANDARD DECK . . . . 42"
MSRP. $2,649

SPX2548

YEARS MFRD 2017-2020
SERIES. . . . . SPX SERIES
ENGINE . . . . . B&S PROFESSIONAL
CYLINDERS. 2
ENGINE HP 25
FUEL . . . . G
TRANSMISSION . . . . HYDRO
STEERING. . . . . STANDARD
BLADE CLUTCH . . . . ELECTRIC
STANDARD DECK . . . . 48"
MSRP. $2,849

ST1842

YEARS MFRD 2016-2016
ENGINE . . . . B&S
ENGINE HP 18.5
COOLING . . . . AIR
FUEL . . . . G
SPEEDS . . . . VARIABLE
TRANSMISSION . . . . HYDRO
STEERING. . . . . STANDARD
STANDARD DECK . . . . 42"
MSRP. $1,399

RETAIL PRICING

YEAR	HIGH	LOW
2016	$886	$664

ST1942

YEARS MFRD 2019-2020
SERIES. . . . . ST SERIES
ENGINE . . . . B&S INTEK
CYLINDERS. 1
ENGINE HP 19
FUEL . . . . G
TRANSMISSION . . . . HYDRO
STEERING. . . . . STANDARD
BLADE CLUTCH . . . . MANUAL
STANDARD DECK . . . . 42"

ST1946

YEARS MFRD 2017-2018
SERIES. . . . . ST SERIES
ENGINE . . . . B&S INTEK
CYLINDERS. 1
ENGINE HP 19
FUEL . . . . G
TRANSMISSION . . . . HYDRO
STEERING. . . . . STANDARD
STANDARD DECK . . . . 46"

ST2046

YEARS MFRD 2016-2016
ENGINE . . . . B&S
ENGINE HP 20
COOLING . . . . AIR
FUEL . . . . G
SPEEDS . . . . VARIABLE
TRANSMISSION . . . . HYDRO
STEERING. . . . . STANDARD
STANDARD DECK . . . . 46"
MSRP. $1,599

SNAPPER

RETAIL PRICING

YEAR	HIGH	LOW
2016	$1,008	$756

ST2446

YEARS MFRD . . . 2017-2020
SERIES . . . ST SERIES
ENGINE . . . B&S INTEK
CYLINDERS . . . 2
ENGINE HP . . . 20
FUEL . . . G
TRANSMISSION . . . HYDRO
STEERING . . . STANDARD
STANDARD DECK . . . 46"

SZ2246

YEARS MFRD . . . 2018-2020
SERIES . . . SZ SERIES
ENGINE . . . B&S INTEK
CYLINDERS . . . 2
CID . . . 724CC
ENGINE HP . . . 22
FUEL . . . G
TRANSMISSION . . . HYDRO
STEERING . . . ZERO
BLADE CLUTCH . . . ELECTRIC
STANDARD DECK . . . 46"

SZ2454

YEARS MFRD . . . 2017-2020
SERIES . . . SZ SERIES
ENGINE . . . KOHLER KT7000
CYLINDERS . . . 2
CID . . . 724CC
ENGINE HP . . . 24
FUEL . . . G
TRANSMISSION . . . HYDRO
STEERING . . . ZERO
BLADE CLUTCH . . . ELECTRIC
STANDARD DECK . . . 54"

UGT2060H

YEARS MFRD . . . 1996-1997
ENGINE . . . KOHLER
ENGINE HP . . . 20
FUEL . . . G
TRANSMISSION . . . HYDRO
STEERING . . . STANDARD
STANDARD DECK . . . 60"
MSRP . . . $11,222

RETAIL PRICING

YEAR	HIGH	LOW
1996	$4,234	$3,176
1997	$4,400	$3,300

UGT2260H

YEARS MFRD . . . 1997-1998
ENGINE . . . KOHLER
ENGINE HP . . . 22
FUEL . . . G
TRANSMISSION . . . HYDRO
STEERING . . . STANDARD
STANDARD DECK . . . 60"
MSRP . . . $10,863

OPTIONS

46" TILLER
47" SNOW BLOWER
54" BLADE

SERIAL NUMBERS

YEAR	BEGINNING NO.
1997	971016001

RETAIL PRICING

YEAR	HIGH	LOW
1997	$1,090	$818
1998	$1,216	$912

YT16D334B

YEARS MFRD . . . 1990-1991
ENGINE . . . B&S
ENGINE HP . . . 16
COOLING . . . AIR
FUEL . . . G
TRANSMISSION . . . GEAR
STEERING . . . STANDARD
STANDARD DECK . . . 33"
MSRP . . . $3,199

RETAIL PRICING

YEAR	HIGH	LOW
1990	$899	$674
1991	$990	$743

YT16D334K

YEARS MFRD . . . 1991-1991
ENGINE . . . KOHLER
ENGINE HP . . . 16
FUEL . . . G
TRANSMISSION . . . GEAR
STEERING . . . STANDARD
STANDARD DECK . . . 33"
MSRP . . . $3,299

RETAIL PRICING

YEAR	HIGH	LOW
1991	$1,021	$766

YT16D414B

YEARS MFRD . . . 1990-1991
ENGINE . . . B&S
ENGINE HP . . . 16
COOLING . . . AIR
FUEL . . . G
TRANSMISSION . . . GEAR
STEERING . . . STANDARD
STANDARD DECK . . . 41"
MSRP . . . $3,299

RETAIL PRICING

YEAR	HIGH	LOW
1990	$928	$696
1991	$1,021	$766

YT16D414K

YEARS MFRD . . . 1991-1991
ENGINE . . . KOHLER
ENGINE HP . . . 16
FUEL . . . G
TRANSMISSION . . . GEAR
STEERING . . . STANDARD
STANDARD DECK . . . 41"
MSRP . . . $3,399

RETAIL PRICING

YEAR	HIGH	LOW
1991	$1,052	$789

YT16D484B

YEARS MFRD . . . 1990-1994
ENGINE . . . B&S
ENGINE HP . . . 16
COOLING . . . AIR
FUEL . . . G
TRANSMISSION . . . GEAR
STEERING . . . STANDARD
STANDARD DECK . . . 48"
MSRP . . . $3,499

RETAIL PRICING

YEAR	HIGH	LOW
1990	$987	$741
1991	$1,083	$813

YT16D484K

YEARS MFRD . . . 1991-1991
ENGINE . . . KOHLER
ENGINE HP . . . 16
FUEL . . . G
TRANSMISSION . . . GEAR
STEERING . . . STANDARD
STANDARD DECK . . . 48"
MSRP . . . $3,599

RETAIL PRICING

YEAR	HIGH	LOW
1991	$1,115	$836

YT18H334K

YEARS MFRD . . . 1990-1991
ENGINE . . . KOHLER
ENGINE HP . . . 18
COOLING . . . AIR
FUEL . . . G
TRANSMISSION . . . HYDRO
STEERING . . . STANDARD
STANDARD DECK . . . 33"
MSRP . . . $3,999

RETAIL PRICING

YEAR	HIGH	LOW
1990	$1,090	$818
1991	$1,239	$929

YT18H414K

YEARS MFRD . . . 1990-1991
ENGINE . . . KOHLER
ENGINE HP . . . 18
COOLING . . . AIR
FUEL . . . G
TRANSMISSION . . . HYDRO
STEERING . . . STANDARD
STANDARD DECK . . . 41"
MSRP . . . $4,099

RETAIL PRICING

YEAR	HIGH	LOW
1990	$1,117	$838
1991	$1,271	$953

YT18H484K

YEARS MFRD . . . 1990-1991
ENGINE . . . KOHLER
ENGINE HP . . . 18
FUEL . . . G
TRANSMISSION . . . HYDRO
STEERING . . . STANDARD
STANDARD DECK . . . 48"
MSRP . . . $4,299

RETAIL PRICING

YEAR	HIGH	LOW
1990	$1,176	$882
1991	$1,331	$998

YT180H334K

YEARS MFRD . . . 1991-1992
ENGINE . . . KOHLER
ENGINE HP . . . 18
COOLING . . . AIR
FUEL . . . G
TRANSMISSION . . . HYDRO
STEERING . . . STANDARD
STANDARD DECK . . . 33"
MSRP . . . $3,600

RETAIL PRICING

YEAR	HIGH	LOW
1992	$1,162	$872

YT400

YEARS MFRD . . . 2013-2015
ENGINE . . . B&S
COOLING . . . AIR
FUEL . . . G
SPEEDS . . . VARIABLE
TRANSMISSION . . . HYDRO
STEERING . . . STANDARD
STANDARD DECK . . . 52"
MSRP . . . $5,499

RETAIL PRICING

YEAR	HIGH	LOW
2013	$2,199	$1,649
2014	$2,561	$1,921
2015	$3,545	$2,659

YT2350

YEARS MFRD . . . 2006-2008
ENGINE . . . B&S
CYLINDERS . . . 2
ENGINE HP . . . 23
COOLING . . . AIR
FUEL . . . G
SPEEDS . . . VARIABLE
TRANSMISSION . . . HYDRO
STEERING . . . STANDARD
STANDARD DECK . . . 50"
MSRP . . . $5,350

RETAIL PRICING

YEAR	HIGH	LOW
2006	$2,922	$2,191
2007	$3,023	$2,268
2008	$3,314	$2,486

YT16333

YEARS MFRD........1987-1990
ENGINE..................B&S
ENGINE HP.................16
COOLING.................AIR
FUEL........................G
TRANSMISSION...........GEAR
STEERING............STANDARD
STANDARD DECK............33"
MSRP................$3,048

RETAIL PRICING

YEAR	HIGH	LOW
1990	$886	$664

YT16413

YEARS MFRD........1987-1991
ENGINE..................B&S
ENGINE HP.................16
COOLING.................AIR
TRANSMISSION...........GEAR
STEERING............STANDARD
STANDARD DECK............41"
WEIGHT.............656 LBS.
MSRP................$3,125

RETAIL PRICING

YEAR	HIGH	LOW
1990	$907	$680
1991	$967	$725

YT16483

YEARS MFRD........1987-1990
ENGINE..................B&S
ENGINE HP.................16
COOLING.................AIR
FUEL........................G
TRANSMISSION...........GEAR
STEERING............STANDARD
STANDARD DECK............48"
MSRP................$3,220

RETAIL PRICING

YEAR	HIGH	LOW
1990	$935	$701

YT20440

YEARS MFRD........2005-2005
ENGINE.........B&S VANGUARD
CYLINDERS...................2
ENGINE HP.................20
COOLING.................AIR
FUEL........................G
SPEEDS...............VARIABLE
TRANSMISSION..........HYDRO
STEERING............STANDARD
STANDARD DECK............44"
MSRP................$4,699

OPTIONS

2 BAG
36" TILLER
42" BLADE
42" SNOW THROWER

RETAIL PRICING

YEAR	HIGH	LOW
2005	$815	$611

YT21440

YEARS MFRD........2006-2006
ENGINE..................B&S
ENGINE HP.................21
COOLING.................AIR
FUEL........................G
SPEEDS...............VARIABLE
TRANSMISSION..........HYDRO
STEERING............STANDARD
STANDARD DECK............44"
MSRP................$4,799

OPTIONS

2 BAG & FAN
3 BAG & FAN
42" SNOW BLOWER
46" SNOW THROWER

RETAIL PRICING

YEAR	HIGH	LOW
2006	$896	$672

YT23500

YEARS MFRD........2005-2010
SERIES...........YT400 SERIES
ENGINE.........B&S VANGUARD
CYLINDERS...................2
ENGINE HP.................23
COOLING.................AIR
FUEL........................G
SPEEDS...............VARIABLE
TRANSMISSION..........HYDRO
STEERING............STANDARD
STANDARD DECK............50"
WEIGHT.............711 LBS.
MSRP................$5,800

OPTIONS

2 BAG
36" TILLER
42" BLADE
42" SNOW THROWER

RETAIL PRICING

YEAR	HIGH	LOW
2005	$1,163	$872
2006	$1,290	$968
2007	$1,430	$1,072
2008	$1,585	$1,189
2009	$1,758	$1,318
2010	$1,950	$1,462

YZ13331BE

YEARS MFRD........1998-1999
SERIES.....YARD CRUISER SERIES
ENGINE..................B&S
CYLINDERS...................1
ENGINE HP.................13
COOLING.................AIR
FUEL........................G
SPEEDS...............VARIABLE
TRANSMISSION..........HYDRO
STEERING................ZERO
STANDARD DECK............33"
MSRP................$2,699

OPTIONS

1 BAG
2 BAG

RETAIL PRICING

YEAR	HIGH	LOW
1998	$360	$270
1999	$399	$299

YZ13381BE

YEARS MFRD........1998-2000
SERIES.....YARD CRUISER SERIES
ENGINE..................B&S
CYLINDERS...................1
ENGINE HP.................13
COOLING.................AIR
FUEL........................G
SPEEDS...............VARIABLE
TRANSMISSION..........HYDRO
STEERING................ZERO
STANDARD DECK............38"
MSRP................$2,749

OPTIONS

2 BAG
SWEEPER

RETAIL PRICING

YEAR	HIGH	LOW
1998	$395	$296
1999	$440	$330
2000	$488	$366

YZ15334BVE

YEARS MFRD........2003-2003
SERIES.......SCRAMBLER SERIES
ENGINE..................B&S
CYLINDERS...................1
ENGINE HP.................15
COOLING.................AIR
FUEL........................G
SPEEDS...............VARIABLE
TRANSMISSION.....DUAL HYDRO
STEERING................ZERO
BLADE CLUTCH.........ELECTRIC
STANDARD DECK............33"
WEIGHT.............542 LBS.
MSRP................$2,699

OPTIONS

1 BAG
2 BAG

RETAIL PRICING

YEAR	HIGH	LOW
2003	$598	$449

YZ15384BVE

YEARS MFRD........2003-2003
SERIES.......SCRAMBLER SERIES
ENGINE..................B&S
CYLINDERS...................1
ENGINE HP.................15
COOLING.................AIR
FUEL........................G
SPEEDS...............VARIABLE
TRANSMISSION..........HYDRO
STEERING................ZERO
STANDARD DECK............38"
WEIGHT.............538 LBS.
MSRP................$2,799

OPTIONS

1 BAG
2 BAG

RETAIL PRICING

YEAR	HIGH	LOW
2003	$621	$466

YZ16335BVE

YEARS MFRD........2004-2004
SERIES.......SCRAMBLER SERIES
ENGINE..................B&S
ENGINE HP.................16
COOLING.................AIR
FUEL........................G
SPEEDS...............VARIABLE
TRANSMISSION.....DUAL HYDRO
STEERING................ZERO
STANDARD DECK............33"
MSRP................$2,899

OPTIONS

1 BAG
2 BAG

RETAIL PRICING

YEAR	HIGH	LOW
2004	$751	$563

YZ16336BVE

YEARS MFRD........2006-2006
ENGINE..................B&S
CYLINDERS...................1
ENGINE HP.................18
COOLING.................AIR
FUEL........................G
SPEEDS...............VARIABLE
TRANSMISSION..........HYDRO
STEERING............STANDARD
STANDARD DECK............33"
WEIGHT.............532 LBS.
MSRP................$3,099

RETAIL PRICING

YEAR	HIGH	LOW
2006	$1,979	$1,484

YZ16385BVE

YEARS MFRD........2004-2004
SERIES.......SCRAMBLER SERIES
ENGINE..................B&S
ENGINE HP.................16
COOLING.................AIR
FUEL........................G
SPEEDS...............VARIABLE
TRANSMISSION.....DUAL HYDRO
STEERING................ZERO
STANDARD DECK............38"
MSRP................$3,199

OPTIONS

1 BAG
2 BAG

RETAIL PRICING

YEAR	HIGH	LOW
2004	$830	$623

SNAPPER

YZ16386BVE

- YEARS MFRD: 2006-2006
- ENGINE: B&S
- CYLINDERS: 1
- ENGINE HP: 18
- COOLING: AIR
- FUEL: G
- SPEEDS: VARIABLE
- TRANSMISSION: HYDRO
- STEERING: STANDARD
- STANDARD DECK: 38"
- WEIGHT: 538 LBS.
- MSRP: $3,199

RETAIL PRICING

YEAR	HIGH	LOW
2006	$2,044	$1,533

YZ16424BVE

- YEARS MFRD: 2003-2003
- ENGINE: B&S
- ENGINE HP: 16
- COOLING: AIR
- FUEL: G
- SPEEDS: VARIABLE
- TRANSMISSION: DUAL HYDRO
- STEERING: ZERO
- STANDARD DECK: 42"
- MSRP: $3,499

OPTIONS

1 BAG

RETAIL PRICING

YEAR	HIGH	LOW
2003	$777	$583

YZ18425

- YEARS MFRD: 2004-2004
- SERIES: SCRAMBLER SERIES
- ENGINE: B&S
- ENGINE HP: 16
- COOLING: AIR
- FUEL: G
- SPEEDS: VARIABLE
- TRANSMISSION: HYDRO
- STEERING: ZERO
- STANDARD DECK: 44"
- MSRP: $3,699

RETAIL PRICING

YEAR	HIGH	LOW
2004	$2,108	$1,581

YZ18426BVE

- YEARS MFRD: 2004-2005
- ENGINE: B&S
- CYLINDERS: 1
- ENGINE HP: 18
- COOLING: AIR
- FUEL: G
- SPEEDS: VARIABLE
- TRANSMISSION: HYDRO
- STEERING: ZERO
- STANDARD DECK: 42"
- WEIGHT: 562 LBS.
- MSRP: $3,699

OPTIONS

1 BAG
2 BAG

RETAIL PRICING

YEAR	HIGH	LOW
2004	$961	$721
2005	$1,066	$800

YZ20484BVE

- YEARS MFRD: 2003-2005
- SERIES: SCRAMBLER SERIES
- ENGINE: B&S
- CYLINDERS: 2
- ENGINE HP: 20
- COOLING: AIR
- FUEL: G
- SPEEDS: VARIABLE
- TRANSMISSION: HYDRO
- STEERING: ZERO
- STANDARD DECK: 48"
- WEIGHT: 624 LBS.
- MSRP: $4,199

OPTIONS

1 BAG

RETAIL PRICING

YEAR	HIGH	LOW
2003	$984	$738
2004	$1,092	$819
2005	$1,213	$909

YZ145332BVE

- YEARS MFRD: 2001-2002
- ENGINE: B&S
- ENGINE HP: 14.5
- COOLING: AIR
- FUEL: G
- SPEEDS: VARIABLE
- TRANSMISSION: DUAL HYDRO
- STEERING: ZERO
- STANDARD DECK: 33"
- MSRP: $2,699

OPTIONS

2 BAG
36" SWEEP
BAGGER

SERIAL NUMBERS

YEAR	BEGINNING NO.
2002	2XXXXXX

RETAIL PRICING

YEAR	HIGH	LOW
2001	$478	$359
2002	$530	$397

YZ145333BVE

- YEARS MFRD: 2003-2003
- ENGINE: B&S
- CYLINDERS: 1
- ENGINE HP: 14.5
- COOLING: AIR
- FUEL: G
- SPEEDS: VARIABLE
- TRANSMISSION: HYDRO
- STEERING: ZERO
- STANDARD DECK: 33"
- MSRP: $2,699

OPTIONS

1 BAG
2 BAG

RETAIL PRICING

YEAR	HIGH	LOW
2003	$598	$449

YZ145382BVE

- YEARS MFRD: 2001-2002
- SERIES: YARD CRUISER SERIES
- ENGINE: B&S
- ENGINE HP: 14.5
- COOLING: AIR
- FUEL: G
- SPEEDS: VARIABLE
- TRANSMISSION: DUAL HYDRO
- STEERING: ZERO
- STANDARD DECK: 38"
- MSRP: $2,799

OPTIONS

2 BAG
36" SWEEPER
BAGGER

SERIAL NUMBERS

YEAR	BEGINNING NO.
2002	2XXXXXX

RETAIL PRICING

YEAR	HIGH	LOW
2001	$485	$364
2002	$536	$402

YZ145383BVE

- YEARS MFRD: 2003-2003
- ENGINE: B&S
- CYLINDERS: 1
- ENGINE HP: 14.5
- COOLING: AIR
- FUEL: G
- SPEEDS: VARIABLE
- TRANSMISSION: DUAL HYDRO
- STEERING: ZERO
- STANDARD DECK: 38"
- MSRP: $2,799

OPTIONS

1 BAG
2 BAG

RETAIL PRICING

YEAR	HIGH	LOW
2003	$621	$466

Z120T

- YEARS MFRD: 1990-1990
- ENGINE: B&S
- ENGINE HP: 12
- COOLING: AIR
- FUEL: G
- SPEEDS: VARIABLE
- TRANSMISSION: HYDRO
- STEERING: ZERO
- STANDARD DECK: 42"
- MSRP: $3,698

RETAIL PRICING

YEAR	HIGH	LOW
1990	$1,073	$805

Z140T

- YEARS MFRD: 1990-1990
- ENGINE: B&S
- ENGINE HP: 14
- COOLING: AIR
- FUEL: G
- SPEEDS: VARIABLE
- TRANSMISSION: HYDRO
- STEERING: ZERO
- STANDARD DECK: 42"
- MSRP: $4,100

RETAIL PRICING

YEAR	HIGH	LOW
1990	$1,190	$893

Z160T

- YEARS MFRD: 1990-1990
- ENGINE: B&S
- ENGINE HP: 16
- COOLING: AIR
- FUEL: G
- TRANSMISSION: HYDRO
- STEERING: ZERO
- STANDARD DECK: 42"
- MSRP: $4,300

RETAIL PRICING

YEAR	HIGH	LOW
1990	$1,249	$937

Z180T

- YEARS MFRD: 1990-1990
- ENGINE: B&S
- ENGINE HP: 18
- COOLING: AIR
- FUEL: G
- TRANSMISSION: HYDRO
- STEERING: ZERO
- STANDARD DECK: 42"
- MSRP: $4,512

RETAIL PRICING

YEAR	HIGH	LOW
1990	$1,310	$982

Z1202B

- YEARS MFRD: 1991-1994
- ENGINE: B&S
- CYLINDERS: 1
- ENGINE HP: 12
- COOLING: AIR
- FUEL: G
- SPEEDS: VARIABLE
- TRANSMISSION: HYDRO
- STEERING: ZERO
- STANDARD DECK: 41"
- MSRP: $4,999

RETAIL PRICING

YEAR	HIGH	LOW
1991	$297	$223
1992	$330	$247
1993	$367	$275
1994	$407	$306

Z1203B

YEARS MFRD 1995-1995
ENGINE .... B&S
CYLINDERS.................. 1
ENGINE HP 12
COOLING .... AIR
FUEL .... G
SPEEDS .... VARIABLE
TRANSMISSION .... HYDRO
STEERING................ ZERO
STANDARD DECK .... 41"
MSRP................ $4,706

RETAIL PRICING

YEAR	HIGH	LOW
1995	$386	$290

Z1401K

YEARS MFRD 1990-1990
ENGINE .... KOHLER
CYLINDERS.................. 1
ENGINE HP 14
COOLING .... AIR
FUEL .... G
SPEEDS .... VARIABLE
TRANSMISSION .... HYDRO
STEERING................ ZERO
STANDARD DECK .... 42"
MSRP................ $4,175

RETAIL PRICING

YEAR	HIGH	LOW
1990	$1,212	$909

Z1402B

YEARS MFRD 1992-1992
ENGINE .... B&S
CYLINDERS.................. 1
ENGINE HP 14
COOLING .... AIR
FUEL .... G
SPEEDS .... VARIABLE
TRANSMISSION .... HYDRO
STEERING................ ZERO
MSRP................ $5,125

RETAIL PRICING

YEAR	HIGH	LOW
1992	$267	$200

Z1402K

YEARS MFRD 1991-1994
ENGINE .... KOHLER
CYLINDERS.................. 1
ENGINE HP 14
COOLING .... AIR
FUEL .... G
SPEEDS .... VARIABLE
TRANSMISSION .... HYDRO
STEERING................ ZERO
STANDARD DECK .... 42"
MSRP................ $5,300

OPTIONS

2 BAG

RETAIL PRICING

YEAR	HIGH	LOW
1991	$260	$195
1992	$284	$213
1993	$318	$239
1994	$355	$266

Z1404K

YEARS MFRD 1995-1995
ENGINE .... KOHLER
CYLINDERS.................. 1
ENGINE HP 14
COOLING .... AIR
FUEL .... G
SPEEDS .... VARIABLE
TRANSMISSION .... HYDRO
STEERING................ ZERO
STANDARD DECK .... 42"
MSRP................ $5,320

RETAIL PRICING

YEAR	HIGH	LOW
1995	$433	$324

Z1800S

YEARS MFRD 1990-1990
ENGINE .... B&S
ENGINE HP 18
COOLING .... AIR
FUEL .... G
TRANSMISSION .... HYDRO
STEERING................ ZERO
STANDARD DECK .... 42"
MSRP................ $5,000

RETAIL PRICING

YEAR	HIGH	LOW
1990	$1,453	$1,090

Z1801K

YEARS MFRD 1990-1990
ENGINE .... KOHLER
ENGINE HP 18
COOLING .... AIR
FUEL .... G
TRANSMISSION .... HYDRO
STEERING................ ZERO
STANDARD DECK .... 42"
MSRP................ $4,600

RETAIL PRICING

YEAR	HIGH	LOW
1990	$1,335	$1,001

Z1802K

YEARS MFRD 1991-1995
ENGINE .... KOHLER
ENGINE HP 18
COOLING .... AIR
FUEL .... G
TRANSMISSION .... HYDRO
STEERING................ ZERO
STANDARD DECK .... 42"
MSRP................ $5,100

OPTIONS

2 BAG
48" DECK

RETAIL PRICING

YEAR	HIGH	LOW
1991	$275	$206
1992	$305	$228
1993	$336	$252
1994	$372	$279
1995	$415	$311

Z1804K

YEARS MFRD 1995-1995
ENGINE .... KOHLER
ENGINE HP 18
COOLING .... AIR
FUEL .... G
TRANSMISSION .... HYDRO
STEERING................ ZERO
STANDARD DECK .... 44"
MSRP................ $5,674

OPTIONS

48" DECK

RETAIL PRICING

YEAR	HIGH	LOW
1995	$463	$347

Z1805K

YEARS MFRD 1996-1997
ENGINE .... KOHLER
ENGINE HP 18
FUEL .... G
TRANSMISSION .... HYDRO
STEERING............ STANDARD
STANDARD DECK .... 48"
MSRP................ $6,299

OPTIONS

60" DECK

RETAIL PRICING

YEAR	HIGH	LOW
1996	$2,381	$1,786
1997	$2,471	$1,853

Z1805KV

YEARS MFRD 1997-1997
ENGINE .... KOHLER
ENGINE HP 18
FUEL .... G
TRANSMISSION .... HYDRO
STEERING................ ZERO
STANDARD DECK .... 48"
MSRP................ $6,299

OPTIONS

2 BAG
60" DECK

RETAIL PRICING

YEAR	HIGH	LOW
1997	$558	$418

Z2001K

YEARS MFRD 1990-1990
ENGINE .... KOHLER
ENGINE HP 20
COOLING .... AIR
FUEL .... G
TRANSMISSION .... HYDRO
STEERING................ ZERO
STANDARD DECK .... 42"
MSRP................ $4,800

RETAIL PRICING

YEAR	HIGH	LOW
1990	$1,395	$1,046

Z2002K

YEARS MFRD 1991-1994
ENGINE .... KOHLER
ENGINE HP 20
COOLING .... AIR
FUEL .... G
TRANSMISSION .... HYDRO
STEERING................ ZERO
STANDARD DECK .... 48"
MSRP................ $5,900

OPTIONS

2 BAG
60" DECK

RETAIL PRICING

YEAR	HIGH	LOW
1991	$351	$263
1992	$390	$292
1993	$433	$324
1994	$482	$362

Z2004K

YEARS MFRD 1995-1995
ENGINE .... KOHLER
ENGINE HP 20
COOLING .... AIR
FUEL .... G
TRANSMISSION .... HYDRO
STEERING................ ZERO
STANDARD DECK .... 42"
MSRP................ $5,874

RETAIL PRICING

YEAR	HIGH	LOW
1995	$478	$359

Z2010K

YEARS MFRD 1990-1990
ENGINE .... KOHLER
ENGINE HP 20
COOLING .... AIR
FUEL .... G
TRANSMISSION .... HYDRO
STEERING................ ZERO
STANDARD DECK .... 60"
MSRP................ $5,700

RETAIL PRICING

YEAR	HIGH	LOW
1990	$1,655	$1,241

Z2205K

YEARS MFRD 1996-1997
ENGINE .... KOHLER
ENGINE HP 20
FUEL .... G
TRANSMISSION .... HYDRO
STEERING............ STANDARD
STANDARD DECK .... 48"
MSRP................ $6,649

OPTIONS

60" DECK

SNAPPER

RETAIL PRICING

YEAR	HIGH	LOW
1996	$2,513	$1,885
1997	$2,606	$1,955

Z2205KV

YEARS MFRD . . . 1997-1997
ENGINE . . . KOHLER
ENGINE HP . . . 22
FUEL . . . G
TRANSMISSION . . . HYDRO
STEERING . . . ZERO
STANDARD DECK . . . 60"
MSRP . . . $6,899

OPTIONS

2 BAG

RETAIL PRICING

YEAR	HIGH	LOW
1997	$792	$594

ZF2100DKU

YEARS MFRD . . . 1998-2000
SERIES . . . TURF CRUISER SERIES
ENGINE . . . KUBOTA
ENGINE HP . . . 21
COOLING . . . LIQUID
FUEL . . . D
TRANSMISSION . . . HYDRO
STEERING . . . ZERO
STANDARD DECK . . . 61"
MSRP . . . $10,855

OPTIONS

50" SNOW THROWER
54" BLADE
73" DECK

RETAIL PRICING

YEAR	HIGH	LOW
1998	$1,335	$1,001
1999	$1,483	$1,112
2000	$1,650	$1,237

ZF2100GKU

YEARS MFRD . . . 1999-1999
SERIES . . . TURF CRUISER SERIES
ENGINE . . . KUBOTA
ENGINE HP . . . 21
FUEL . . . D
TRANSMISSION . . . HYDRO
STEERING . . . STANDARD
STANDARD DECK . . . 60"
MSRP . . . $9,099

RETAIL PRICING

YEAR	HIGH	LOW
1999	$3,996	$2,997

ZF2101DKU

YEARS MFRD . . . 2001-2005
SERIES . . . TURF CRUISER SERIES
ENGINE . . . KUBOTA
ENGINE HP . . . 21
COOLING . . . LIQUID
FUEL . . . D
STEERING . . . ZERO
STANDARD DECK . . . 61"
MSRP . . . $11,699

OPTIONS

47" BROOM
50" SNOW BLOWER
CATCHER

SERIAL NUMBERS

YEAR	BEGINNING NO.
2002	2XXXXXX
2004	4XXXXXX

RETAIL PRICING

YEAR	HIGH	LOW
2001	$2,220	$1,665
2002	$2,472	$1,854
2003	$2,743	$2,057
2004	$3,042	$2,281
2005	$3,378	$2,533

ZF2200K

YEARS MFRD . . . 1997-1997
SERIES . . . TURF CRUISER SERIES
ENGINE . . . KOHLER
ENGINE HP . . . 22
FUEL . . . G
TRANSMISSION . . . HYDRO
STEERING . . . ZERO
STANDARD DECK . . . 61"
MSRP . . . $8,624

OPTIONS

ROPS

RETAIL PRICING

YEAR	HIGH	LOW
1997	$999	$749

ZF2300GKU

YEARS MFRD . . . 1999-2000
SERIES . . . TURF CRUISER SERIES
ENGINE . . . KUBOTA
ENGINE HP . . . 23
COOLING . . . LIQUID
FUEL . . . G
TRANSMISSION . . . HYDRO
STEERING . . . ZERO
STANDARD DECK . . . 61"
MSRP . . . $10,658

OPTIONS

50" SNOW BLOWER
73" DECK
BAGGER

RETAIL PRICING

YEAR	HIGH	LOW
1999	$1,636	$1,227
2000	$1,818	$1,363

ZF2301GKU

YEARS MFRD . . . 2001-2005
SERIES . . . TURF CRUISER SERIES
ENGINE . . . KUBOTA
ENGINE HP . . . 23
COOLING . . . LIQUID
FUEL . . . G
TRANSMISSION . . . DUAL HYDRO
STEERING . . . ZERO
STANDARD DECK . . . 61"
MSRP . . . $11,499

OPTIONS

46" BLADE
50" SNOW BLOWER
73" DECK
CATCHER

SERIAL NUMBERS

YEAR	BEGINNING NO.
2002	2XXXXX
2004	4XXXXX

RETAIL PRICING

YEAR	HIGH	LOW
2001	$2,183	$1,637
2002	$2,425	$1,819
2003	$2,695	$2,021
2004	$2,991	$2,244
2005	$3,323	$2,492

ZF2500K

YEARS MFRD . . . 1998-1998
SERIES . . . TURF CRUISER SERIES
ENGINE . . . KOHLER
ENGINE HP . . . 25
FUEL . . . G
TRANSMISSION . . . HYDRO
STEERING . . . STANDARD
STANDARD DECK . . . 52"
MSRP . . . $8,659

OPTIONS

61" DECK

RETAIL PRICING

YEAR	HIGH	LOW
1998	$3,566	$2,674

ZF2500KH

YEARS MFRD . . . 1998-2000
SERIES . . . TURF CRUISER SERIES
ENGINE . . . KOHLER
ENGINE HP . . . 25
FUEL . . . G
SPEEDS . . . VARIABLE
TRANSMISSION . . . HYDRO
STEERING . . . ZERO
STANDARD DECK . . . 61"
MSRP . . . $8,758

OPTIONS

50" SNOW BLOWER
73" DECK
BAGGER

RETAIL PRICING

YEAR	HIGH	LOW
1998	$1,314	$986
1999	$1,461	$1,096
2000	$1,621	$1,216

ZF2501KH

YEARS MFRD . . . 2003-2005
SERIES . . . TURF CRUISER SERIES
ENGINE . . . KOHLER
ENGINE HP . . . 25
FUEL . . . G
SPEEDS . . . VARIABLE
TRANSMISSION . . . DUAL HYDRO
STEERING . . . STANDARD
STANDARD DECK . . . 61"
MSRP . . . $9,599

OPTIONS

50" SNOW THROWER
73" DECK
BAGGER
CAB

SERIAL NUMBERS

YEAR	BEGINNING NO.
2004	4XXXXX

RETAIL PRICING

YEAR	HIGH	LOW
2003	$2,258	$1,694
2004	$2,497	$1,873
2005	$2,772	$2,079

ZM2200K

YEARS MFRD . . . 1998-1998
ENGINE . . . KOHLER
ENGINE HP . . . 22
FUEL . . . G
TRANSMISSION . . . HYDRO
STEERING . . . STANDARD
STANDARD DECK . . . 52"
MSRP . . . $7,499

OPTIONS

61" DECK

RETAIL PRICING

YEAR	HIGH	LOW
1998	$3,088	$2,316

ZM2200KH

YEARS MFRD . . . 1998-1998
SERIES . . . PRO CRUISER SERIES
ENGINE . . . KOHLER
ENGINE HP . . . 22
COOLING . . . AIR
FUEL . . . G
TRANSMISSION . . . HYDRO
STEERING . . . ZERO
STANDARD DECK . . . 61"
MSRP . . . $7,549

OPTIONS

2 BAG
ROPS

RETAIL PRICING

YEAR	HIGH	LOW
1998	$1,398	$1,048

ZM2500K

YEARS MFRD . . . 1998-1998
ENGINE . . . KOHLER
ENGINE HP . . . 25
FUEL . . . G
TRANSMISSION . . . HYDRO
STEERING . . . STANDARD
STANDARD DECK . . . 52"
MSRP . . . $7,699

OPTIONS

61" DECK

RETAIL PRICING

YEAR	HIGH	LOW
1998	$3,171	$2,378

ZM2500KH
YEARS MFRD 1998-2000
SERIES...... PRO CRUISER SERIES
ENGINE .... KOHLER
ENGINE HP 25
COOLING .... AIR
FUEL .... G
TRANSMISSION .... HYDRO
STEERING................ ZERO
STANDARD DECK .... 61"
MSRP................. $7,799

OPTIONS

2 BAG
ROPS

RETAIL PRICING

YEAR	HIGH	LOW
1998	$1,169	$877
1999	$1,299	$974
2000	$1,446	$1,085

ZM2501KGH
YEARS MFRD 2001-2002
SERIES...... PRO CRUISER SERIES
ENGINE .... KOHLER
ENGINE HP 25
COOLING .... AIR
FUEL .... G
STEERING................ ZERO
STANDARD DECK .... 61"
MSRP................. $7,999

RETAIL PRICING

YEAR	HIGH	LOW
2001	$3,841	$2,881
2002	$3,948	$2,961

ZM2501KH
YEARS MFRD 2001-2003
SERIES...... PRO CRUISER SERIES
ENGINE .... KOHLER
ENGINE HP 25
COOLING .... AIR
FUEL .... G
TRANSMISSION ..... DUAL HYDRO
STEERING................ ZERO
STANDARD DECK .... 61"
MSRP................. $7,999

OPTIONS

BAGGER
ROPS

RETAIL PRICING

YEAR	HIGH	LOW
2001	$1,563	$1,172
2002	$1,736	$1,302
2003	$1,924	$1,443

ZMT2500KH
YEARS MFRD 1999-2003
SERIES...... PRO CRUISER SERIES
ENGINE .... KOHLER
ENGINE HP 25
FUEL .... G
SPEEDS .... VARIABLE
TRANSMISSION ..... DUAL HYDRO
STEERING................ ZERO
STANDARD DECK .... 61"
MSRP................. $7,999

OPTIONS

BAGGER
ROPS

RETAIL PRICING

YEAR	HIGH	LOW
1999	$1,267	$950
2000	$1,407	$1,055
2001	$1,563	$1,172
2002	$1,736	$1,302
2003	$1,924	$1,443

ZMT2501KH
YEARS MFRD 2000-2002
SERIES...... PRO CRUISER SERIES
ENGINE .... KOHLER
ENGINE HP 25
FUEL .... G
TRANSMISSION .... HYDRO
STEERING............ STANDARD
STANDARD DECK .... 61"
MSRP................. $6,649

RETAIL PRICING

YEAR	HIGH	LOW
2000	$3,038	$2,279
2001	$3,193	$2,395
2002	$3,282	$2,461

ZT18440KH
YEARS MFRD 2004-2005
SERIES......... FAST CUT SERIES
ENGINE .... KOHLER
CYLINDERS................. 1
ENGINE HP 18
COOLING .... AIR
FUEL .... G
SPEEDS .... VARIABLE
TRANSMISSION .... HYDRO
STEERING................ ZERO
BLADE CLUTCH .... ELECTRIC
STANDARD DECK .... 44"
WEIGHT .... 670 LBS.
MSRP................. $4,299

OPTIONS

2 BAG
3 BAG

SERIAL NUMBERS

YEAR	BEGINNING NO.
2004	4XXXXX

RETAIL PRICING

YEAR	HIGH	LOW
2004	$1,117	$838
2005	$1,240	$930

ZT18441KHC
YEARS MFRD 2006-2007
ENGINE .. KOHLER COURAGE T OHV
ENGINE HP 18
COOLING .... AIR
FUEL .... G
SPEEDS .... VARIABLE
TRANSMISSION .... HYDRO
STEERING................ ZERO
STANDARD DECK .... 44"
MSRP................. $4,499

OPTIONS

2 BAG & FAN
3 BAG & FAN

RETAIL PRICING

YEAR	HIGH	LOW
2006	$1,396	$1,047
2007	$1,547	$1,160

ZT19441KWV
YEARS MFRD 2006-2007
ENGINE .... KAWASAKI
CYLINDERS................. 2
ENGINE HP 19
COOLING .... AIR
FUEL .... G
SPEEDS .... VARIABLE
TRANSMISSION .... HYDRO
STEERING................ ZERO
STANDARD DECK .... 44"
MSRP................. $4,799

OPTIONS

2 BAG & FAN
3 BAG & FAN

RETAIL PRICING

YEAR	HIGH	LOW
2006	$1,488	$1,116
2007	$1,650	$1,237

ZT20500BV
YEARS MFRD 2004-2006
SERIES......... FAST CUT SERIES
ENGINE .... B&S
CYLINDERS................. 2
ENGINE HP 20
COOLING .... AIR
FUEL .... G
SPEEDS .... VARIABLE
TRANSMISSION .... HYDRO
STEERING................ ZERO
BLADE CLUTCH .... ELECTRIC
STANDARD DECK .... 50"
WEIGHT .... 690 LBS.
MSRP................. $4,899

RETAIL PRICING

YEAR	HIGH	LOW
2004	$2,677	$2,008
2005	$2,840	$2,130
2006	$3,128	$2,346

ZT20501BV
YEARS MFRD 2006-2007
ENGINE .... B&S
CYLINDERS................. 2
ENGINE HP 20
COOLING .... AIR
FUEL .... G
SPEEDS .... VARIABLE
TRANSMISSION .... HYDRO
STEERING................ ZERO
STANDARD DECK .... 50"
MSRP................. $5,099

RETAIL PRICING

YEAR	HIGH	LOW
2006	$2,737	$2,053
2007	$2,835	$2,126

ZU2003K
YEARS MFRD 1991-1994
ENGINE .... KOHLER
ENGINE HP 20
COOLING .... AIR
FUEL .... G
TRANSMISSION .... HYDRO
STEERING................ ZERO
STANDARD DECK .... 48"
MSRP................. $7,385

OPTIONS

2 BAG
60" DECK

RETAIL PRICING

YEAR	HIGH	LOW
1991	$399	$299
1992	$444	$333
1993	$492	$369
1994	$548	$411

ZU2013K
YEARS MFRD 1991-1994
ENGINE .... KOHLER
ENGINE HP 20
COOLING .... AIR
FUEL .... G
TRANSMISSION .... HYDRO
STEERING................ ZERO
STANDARD DECK .... 48"
MSRP................. $7,399

OPTIONS

2 BAG
60" DECK

RETAIL PRICING

YEAR	HIGH	LOW
1991	$399	$299
1992	$444	$333
1993	$496	$372
1994	$548	$411

ZU2014K
YEARS MFRD 1992-1995
ENGINE .... KOHLER
ENGINE HP 20
COOLING .... AIR
FUEL .... G
TRANSMISSION .... HYDRO
STEERING................ ZERO
STANDARD DECK .... 48"
MSRP................. $8,599

OPTIONS

60" DECK

RETAIL PRICING

YEAR	HIGH	LOW
1992	$558	$418
1993	$621	$466
1994	$688	$516
1995	$767	$575

SNAPPER

16HP HYDRO
YEARS MFRD 2005-2005
ENGINE . . . . B&S VANGUARD
CYLINDERS. 2
ENGINE HP 16
COOLING . . . . AIR
FUEL . . . . G
SPEEDS . . . . VARIABLE
TRANSMISSION . . . . HYDRO
STEERING. . . . . STANDARD
BLADE CLUTCH . . . . ELECTRIC
COOLING . . . . AIR
FUEL . . . . G
TRANSMISSION . . . . HYDRO
STEERING. . . . . STANDARD
STANDARD DECK . . . . 48"
MSRP. $4,095

RETAIL PRICING

YEAR	HIGH	LOW
1990	$1,188	$891
1991	$1,270	$952

18.5/33
YEARS MFRD 2010-2010
SERIES. . . . . 150Z SERIES
ENGINE . . . . B&S INTEK
CYLINDERS. 1
ENGINE HP 18.5
COOLING . . . . AIR
FUEL . . . . G
SPEEDS . . . . VARIABLE
TRANSMISSION . . . . HYDRO
STEERING. . . . . ZERO
STANDARD DECK . . . . 33"
WEIGHT . . . . 500 LBS.
MSRP. $2,600

RETAIL PRICING

YEAR	HIGH	LOW
2010	$1,174	$880

18H334K
YEARS MFRD 1990-1991
ENGINE . . . . KOHLER
ENGINE HP 18
COOLING . . . . AIR
FUEL . . . . G
TRANSMISSION . . . . HYDRO
STEERING. . . . . STANDARD
STANDARD DECK . . . . 33"
MSRP. $3,999

RETAIL PRICING

YEAR	HIGH	LOW
1990	$1,162	$872
1991	$1,239	$929

18H414K
YEARS MFRD 1990-1991
ENGINE . . . . KOHLER
ENGINE HP 18
FUEL . . . . G
TRANSMISSION . . . . HYDRO
STEERING. . . . . STANDARD
STANDARD DECK . . . . 41"
MSRP. $4,099

RETAIL PRICING

YEAR	HIGH	LOW
1990	$1,189	$892
1991	$1,271	$953

18H484K
YEARS MFRD 1990-1991
ENGINE . . . . KOHLER
ENGINE HP 18

18HP HYDRO
YEARS MFRD 2005-2005
ENGINE . . . . B&S VANGUARD
CYLINDERS. 2
ENGINE HP 18
COOLING . . . . AIR
FUEL . . . . G
SPEEDS . . . . VARIABLE
TRANSMISSION . . . . HYDRO
STEERING. . . . . STANDARD
BLADE CLUTCH . . . . ELECTRIC

20/42
YEARS MFRD 2010-2010
SERIES. . . . . 150Z SERIES
ENGINE . . . . B&S
CYLINDERS. 1
ENGINE HP 20
COOLING . . . . AIR
FUEL . . . . G
SPEEDS . . . . HYDRO
TRANSMISSION . . . . HYDRO
STEERING. . . . . ZERO
STANDARD DECK . . . . 42"
WEIGHT . . . . 500 LBS.
MSRP. $2,700

RETAIL PRICING

YEAR	HIGH	LOW
2010	$1,217	$913

20HP HYDRO
YEARS MFRD 2005-2005
ENGINE . . . . B&S VANGUARD
CYLINDERS. 2
ENGINE HP 20
COOLING . . . . AIR
FUEL . . . . G
SPEEDS . . . . VARIABLE
TRANSMISSION . . . . HYDRO
STEERING. . . . . STANDARD
BLADE CLUTCH . . . . ELECTRIC

21/42
YEARS MFRD 2011-2011
SERIES. . . . . 150Z SERIES
ENGINE . . . . B&S EXTENDED
CYLINDERS. 1
ENGINE HP 21
COOLING . . . . AIR
FUEL . . . . G
SPEEDS . . . . VARIABLE
TRANSMISSION . . . . HYDRO
STEERING. . . . . ZERO
BLADE CLUTCH . . . . ELECTRIC
STANDARD DECK . . . . 42"
WEIGHT . . . . 500 LBS.
MSRP. $2,700

RETAIL PRICING

YEAR	HIGH	LOW
2011	$1,526	$1,144

23HP HYDRO
YEARS MFRD 2005-2005
ENGINE . . . . B&S VANGUARD
CYLINDERS. 2
ENGINE HP 23
COOLING . . . . AIR
FUEL . . . . G
SPEEDS . . . . VARIBLE
TRANSMISSION . . . . HYDRO
STEERING. . . . . STANDARD
BLADE CLUTCH . . . . ELECTRIC

24/44
YEARS MFRD 2010-2010
SERIES. . . . . 355Z SERIES
ENGINE . . . . B&S
CYLINDERS. 2
ENGINE HP 24
COOLING . . . . AIR
FUEL . . . . G
SPEEDS . . . . VARIABLE
TRANSMISSION . . . . HYDRO
STEERING. . . . . ZERO
STANDARD DECK . . . . 44"
MSRP. $4,300

OPTIONS

50" DECK

RETAIL PRICING

YEAR	HIGH	LOW
2010	$1,943	$1,457

24/46
YEARS MFRD 2010-2011
SERIES. . . . . 355Z SERIES
ENGINE . . . . B&S
CYLINDERS. 2
ENGINE HP 24
COOLING . . . . AIR
FUEL . . . . G
SPEEDS . . . . VARIABLE
TRANSMISSION . . . . HYDRO
STEERING. . . . . ZERO
STANDARD DECK . . . . 46"
WEIGHT . . . . 712 LBS.
MSRP. $4,300

RETAIL PRICING

YEAR	HIGH	LOW
2010	$2,177	$1,633
2011	$2,430	$1,822

24/50
YEARS MFRD 2010-2010
SERIES. . . . . 400Z SERIES
ENGINE . . . . B&S
CYLINDERS. 2
ENGINE HP 24
COOLING . . . . AIR
FUEL . . . . G
SPEEDS . . . . VARIABLE
TRANSMISSION . . . . HYDRO
STEERING. . . . . ZERO
STANDARD DECK . . . . 50"
WEIGHT . . . . 670 LBS.
MSRP. $4,799

RETAIL PRICING

YEAR	HIGH	LOW
2010	$2,931	$2,199

24/50
YEARS MFRD 2010-2010
SERIES. . . . . 150Z SERIES
ENGINE . . . . B&S
CYLINDERS. 2
ENGINE HP 24
COOLING . . . . AIR
FUEL . . . . G
SPEEDS . . . . VARIABLE
TRANSMISSION . . . . HYDRO
STEERING. . . . . ZERO
STANDARD DECK . . . . 50"
WEIGHT . . . . 500 LBS.
MSRP. $3,200

RETAIL PRICING

YEAR	HIGH	LOW
2010	$1,443	$1,083

26/48
YEARS MFRD 2010-2010
SERIES. . . . . 500Z SERIES
ENGINE . . . . B&S
CYLINDERS. 2
ENGINE HP 26
COOLING . . . . AIR
FUEL . . . . G
SPEEDS . . . . VARIABLE
TRANSMISSION . . . . HYDRO
STEERING. . . . . ZERO
STANDARD DECK . . . . 48"
WEIGHT . . . . 724 LBS.
MSRP. $4,999

RETAIL PRICING

YEAR	HIGH	LOW
2010	$2,258	$1,694

26/50
YEARS MFRD 2011-2011
SERIES. . . . . 150Z SERIES
ENGINE . . . . B&S EXTENDED
CYLINDERS. 2
ENGINE HP 26
COOLING . . . . AIR
FUEL . . . . G
SPEEDS . . . . VARIABLE
TRANSMISSION . . . . HYDRO
STEERING. . . . . ZERO
BLADE CLUTCH . . . . ELECTRIC
STANDARD DECK . . . . 50"
WEIGHT . . . . 500 LBS.
MSRP. $3,200

RETAIL PRICING

YEAR	HIGH	LOW
2011	$1,807	$1,355

26/54

YEARS MFRD 2010-2010
SERIES .... 355Z SERIES
ENGINE .... B&S
CYLINDERS 2
ENGINE HP 26
COOLING .... AIR
FUEL .... G
SPEEDS .... VARIABLE
TRANSMISSION .... HYDRO
STEERING .... ZERO
BLADE CLUTCH .... ELECTRIC
STANDARD DECK .... 54"
WEIGHT .... 723 LBS.
MSRP $4,500

RETAIL PRICING

YEAR	HIGH	LOW
2010	$2,031	$1,523

150H33BBV

YEARS MFRD 1995-1995
ENGINE .... B&S
ENGINE HP 15
COOLING .... AIR
FUEL .... G
TRANSMISSION .... HYDRO
STEERING .... STANDARD
STANDARD DECK .... 33"
MSRP $2,550

RETAIL PRICING

YEAR	HIGH	LOW
1995	$929	$697

150H38GKV

YEARS MFRD 2001-2003
ENGINE .... KOHLER
ENGINE HP 15
COOLING .... AIR
FUEL .... G
SPEEDS .... VARIABLE
TRANSMISSION .... HYDRO
STEERING .... STANDARD
STANDARD DECK .... 38"
MSRP $2,299

OPTIONS

2 BAG
40" SNOW THROWER
42" BLADE
BAGGER

SERIAL NUMBERS

YEAR	BEGINNING NO.
2002	2XXXXXX

RETAIL PRICING

YEAR	HIGH	LOW
2001	$291	$218
2002	$323	$242
2003	$357	$268

150H422KV

YEARS MFRD 1995-1995
ENGINE .... KOHLER
ENGINE HP 15
COOLING .... AIR
FUEL .... G
TRANSMISSION .... HYDRO
STEERING .... STANDARD
STANDARD DECK .... 42"
MSRP $3,500

RETAIL PRICING

YEAR	HIGH	LOW
1995	$1,276	$957

150Z

YEARS MFRD 2007-2008
ENGINE .... B&S
CYLINDERS 2
ENGINE HP 20
COOLING .... AIR
FUEL .... G
SPEEDS .... VARIABLE
TRANSMISSION .... HYDRO
STEERING .... ZERO
BLADE CLUTCH .... ELECTRIC
STANDARD DECK .... 42"
MSRP $2,699

OPTIONS

50" DECK
B&S 24HP

RETAIL PRICING

YEAR	HIGH	LOW
2007	$1,502	$1,126
2008	$1,640	$1,230

150Z/ZT18533

YEARS MFRD 2012-2015
ENGINE .... B&S
ENGINE HP 18.5
COOLING .... AIR
FUEL .... G
SPEEDS .... VARIABLE
TRANSMISSION .... HYDRO
STEERING .... STANDARD
STANDARD DECK .... 33"
MSRP $2,499

RETAIL PRICING

YEAR	HIGH	LOW
2012	$889	$667
2013	$999	$749
2014	$1,163	$872
2015	$1,503	$1,127

150Z/ZT2142

YEARS MFRD 2012-2013
ENGINE .... B&S
ENGINE HP 21
COOLING .... AIR
FUEL .... G
SPEEDS .... VARIABLE
TRANSMISSION .... HYDRO
STEERING .... STANDARD
STANDARD DECK .... 42"
MSRP $2,599

RETAIL PRICING

YEAR	HIGH	LOW
2012	$1,172	$879
2013	$1,421	$1,066

155H42BBV

YEARS MFRD 1995-1995
ENGINE .... B&S
ENGINE HP 15.5
COOLING .... AIR
FUEL .... G
TRANSMISSION .... HYDRO
STEERING .... STANDARD
STANDARD DECK .... 42"
MSRP $2,682

RETAIL PRICING

YEAR	HIGH	LOW
1995	$979	$734

160H42DBV

YEARS MFRD 1997-2000
ENGINE .... B&S
ENGINE HP 16
COOLING .... AIR
FUEL .... G
SPEEDS .... VARIABLE
TRANSMISSION .... HYDRO
STEERING .... STANDARD
STANDARD DECK .... 42"
MSRP $2,599

OPTIONS

1 BAG
2 CYL
40" SNOW BLOWER
44" BLADE

SERIAL NUMBERS

YEAR	BEGINNING NO.
1998	8XXXXXX
1999	9XXXXXX
2000	01XXXXX

RETAIL PRICING

YEAR	HIGH	LOW
1997	$210	$158
1998	$234	$175
1999	$259	$194
2000	$286	$215

160H42GBV

YEARS MFRD 2001-2002
ENGINE .... B&S
ENGINE HP 16
FUEL .... G
TRANSMISSION .... HYDRO
STEERING .... STANDARD
STANDARD DECK .... 42"
MSRP $2,499

OPTIONS

40" SNOW THROWER
42" BLADE
44" BLADE
BAGGER

SERIAL NUMBERS

YEAR	BEGINNING NO.
2002	2XXXXXX

RETAIL PRICING

YEAR	HIGH	LOW
2001	$320	$240
2002	$354	$266

160H42GBV2

YEARS MFRD 2001-2002
ENGINE .... B&S
ENGINE HP 16
COOLING .... AIR
FUEL .... G
SPEEDS .... VARIABLE
TRANSMISSION .... HYDRO
STEERING .... STANDARD
STANDARD DECK .... 42"
MSRP $2,799

OPTIONS

40" SNOW THROWER
42" BLADE
44" BLADE
BAGGER

SERIAL NUMBERS

YEAR	BEGINNING NO.
2002	2XXXXXX

RETAIL PRICING

YEAR	HIGH	LOW
2001	$358	$268
2002	$396	$297

160H482BV

YEARS MFRD 1992-1994
ENGINE .... KOHLER
ENGINE HP 16
COOLING .... AIR
FUEL .... G
TRANSMISSION .... GEAR
STEERING .... STANDARD
STANDARD DECK .... 48"
MSRP $3,800

RETAIL PRICING

YEAR	HIGH	LOW
1992	$1,226	$920
1993	$1,265	$949
1994	$1,335	$1,001

160H482KV

YEARS MFRD 1995-1995
ENGINE .... B&S
ENGINE HP 16
COOLING .... AIR
FUEL .... G
TRANSMISSION .... HYDRO
STEERING .... STANDARD
STANDARD DECK .... 48"
MSRP $3,900

RETAIL PRICING

YEAR	HIGH	LOW
1995	$1,422	$1,067

180H335K

YEARS MFRD 1992-1994
ENGINE .... KOHLER
ENGINE HP 18

COOLING . . . AIR
FUEL . . . G
TRANSMISSION . . . HYDRO
STEERING . . . STANDARD
STANDARD DECK . . . 33"
MSRP . . . $4,304

OPTIONS

1 BAG

RETAIL PRICING

YEAR	HIGH	LOW
1992	$251	$188
1993	$277	$208
1994	$307	$230

180H425K

YEARS MFRD . . . 1992-1998
ENGINE . . . KOHLER
ENGINE HP . . . 18
COOLING . . . AIR
FUEL . . . G
TRANSMISSION . . . HYDRO
STEERING . . . STANDARD
STANDARD DECK . . . 42"
MSRP . . . $4,399

OPTIONS

1 BAG
42" BLADE
44" SNOW THROWER

SERIAL NUMBERS

YEAR	BEGINNING NO.
1998	8XXXXXXX

RETAIL PRICING

YEAR	HIGH	LOW
1992	$269	$202
1993	$298	$223
1994	$329	$247
1995	$364	$273
1996	$403	$302
1997	$445	$334
1998	$492	$369

180H485K

YEARS MFRD . . . 1992-1998
ENGINE . . . KOHLER
ENGINE HP . . . 18
COOLING . . . AIR
FUEL . . . G
TRANSMISSION . . . HYDRO
STEERING . . . STANDARD
STANDARD DECK . . . 48"
MSRP . . . $4,699

OPTIONS

42" BLADE
44" SNOW THROWER

SERIAL NUMBERS

YEAR	BEGINNING NO.
1998	8XXXXXXX

RETAIL PRICING

YEAR	HIGH	LOW
1992	$287	$215
1993	$318	$239
1994	$351	$263
1995	$389	$292
1996	$430	$322
1997	$476	$357
1998	$527	$395

180H48DBV2

YEARS MFRD . . . 1999-2000
ENGINE . . . B&S
ENGINE HP . . . 18
FUEL . . . G
TRANSMISSION . . . HYDRO
STEERING . . . STANDARD
STANDARD DECK . . . 48"
MSRP . . . $3,499

OPTIONS

40" SNOW THROWER
44" BLADE
CAB

SERIAL NUMBERS

YEAR	BEGINNING NO.
1999	9XXXXXX
2000	01XXXXX

RETAIL PRICING

YEAR	HIGH	LOW
1999	$362	$271
2000	$401	$300

180H48GBV2

YEARS MFRD . . . 2001-2002
ENGINE . . . B&S
ENGINE HP . . . 18
FUEL . . . G
TRANSMISSION . . . HYDRO
STEERING . . . STANDARD
STANDARD DECK . . . 48"
MSRP . . . $3,499

OPTIONS

42" BLADE

SERIAL NUMBERS

YEAR	BEGINNING NO.
2002	2XXXXXX

RETAIL PRICING

YEAR	HIGH	LOW
2001	$421	$316
2002	$467	$350

200Z/2242

YEARS MFRD . . . 2016-2017
ENGINE . . . B&S
ENGINE HP . . . 22
COOLING . . . AIR
FUEL . . . G
SPEEDS . . . VARIABLE
TRANSMISSION . . . HYDRO
STEERING . . . ZERO
STANDARD DECK . . . 42"
MSRP . . . $2,599

RETAIL PRICING

YEAR	HIGH	LOW
2016	$1,481	$1,111
2017	$1,689	$1,267

200Z/2346

YEARS MFRD . . . 2016-2017
ENGINE . . . B&S
ENGINE HP . . . 23
COOLING . . . AIR
FUEL . . . G
SPEEDS . . . VARIABLE
TRANSMISSION . . . HYDRO
STEERING . . . ZERO
STANDARD DECK . . . 46"
MSRP . . . $2,999

RETAIL PRICING

YEAR	HIGH	LOW
2016	$1,707	$1,280
2017	$1,952	$1,464

200Z/ZT1842

YEARS MFRD . . . 2014-2015
ENGINE . . . KAWASAKI
ENGINE HP . . . 23
COOLING . . . AIR
FUEL . . . G
SPEEDS . . . VARIABLE
TRANSMISSION . . . HYDRO
STEERING . . . ZERO
STANDARD DECK . . . 42"
MSRP . . . $2,799

RETAIL PRICING

YEAR	HIGH	LOW
2014	$1,302	$976
2015	$1,828	$1,371

200Z/ZT2042

YEARS MFRD . . . 2014-2015
ENGINE . . . B&S
ENGINE HP . . . 20
COOLING . . . AIR
FUEL . . . G
SPEEDS . . . VARIABLE
TRANSMISSION . . . HYDRO
STEERING . . . ZERO
STANDARD DECK . . . 42"
MSRP . . . $2,649

RETAIL PRICING

YEAR	HIGH	LOW
2014	$1,302	$976
2015	$1,584	$1,188

200Z/ ZT21.546

YEARS MFRD . . . 2014-2015
ENGINE . . . KAWASAKI
ENGINE HP . . . 21.5
COOLING . . . AIR
FUEL . . . G
SPEEDS . . . VARIABLE
TRANSMISSION . . . HYDRO
STEERING . . . ZERO
STANDARD DECK . . . 46"
MSRP . . . $3,049

RETAIL PRICING

YEAR	HIGH	LOW
2014	$1,421	$1,066
2015	$1,903	$1,427

200Z/ZT2142

YEARS MFRD . . . 2013-2013
ENGINE . . . B&S
ENGINE HP . . . 21
COOLING . . . AIR
FUEL . . . G
SPEEDS . . . VARIABLE
TRANSMISSION . . . HYDRO
STEERING . . . ZERO
STANDARD DECK . . . 42"
MSRP . . . $2,599

RETAIL PRICING

YEAR	HIGH	LOW
2013	$1,335	$1,001

200Z/ZT2246

YEARS MFRD . . . 2013-2013
ENGINE . . . B&S
ENGINE HP . . . 22
COOLING . . . AIR
FUEL . . . G
SPEEDS . . . VARIABLE
TRANSMISSION . . . HYDRO
STEERING . . . ZERO
STANDARD DECK . . . 46"
MSRP . . . $2,799

RETAIL PRICING

YEAR	HIGH	LOW
2013	$1,442	$1,082

250Z

YEARS MFRD . . . 2008-2008
ENGINE . . . B&S INTEK OHV
CYLINDERS . . . 1
ENGINE HP . . . 18.5
COOLING . . . AIR
FUEL . . . G
SPEEDS . . . VARIABLE
TRANSMISSION . . . HYDRO
STEERING . . . ZERO
STANDARD DECK . . . 38"
WEIGHT . . . 530 LBS.
MSRP . . . $3,300

OPTIONS

42" DECK
50" DECK
B&S INTEK 22HP

RETAIL PRICING

YEAR	HIGH	LOW
2008	$2,005	$1,504

285Z/2552

YEARS MFRD . . . 2016-2017
ENGINE . . . B&S
ENGINE HP . . . 25
COOLING . . . AIR
FUEL . . . G
SPEEDS . . . VARIABLE
TRANSMISSION . . . HYDRO
STEERING . . . ZERO
STANDARD DECK . . . 52"
MSRP . . . $3,199

RETAIL PRICING

YEAR	HIGH	LOW
2016	$1,825	$1,368
2017	$2,078	$1,558

285Z/ZT2652

YEARS MFRD 2013-2013
ENGINE .... B&S
ENGINE HP 26
COOLING .... AIR
FUEL .... G
SPEEDS .... VARIABLE
TRANSMISSION .... HYDRO
STEERING .... ZERO
STANDARD DECK .... 52"
MSRP $3,499

RETAIL PRICING

YEAR	HIGH	LOW
2013	$1,799	$1,350

285Z/ZT2746

YEARS MFRD 2011-2012
ENGINE .... B&S PRO
CYLINDERS 2
ENGINE HP 26
COOLING .... AIR
FUEL .... G
SPEEDS .... VARIABLE
TRANSMISSION .... HYDRO
STEERING .... ZERO
BLADE CLUTCH .... ELECTRIC
STANDARD DECK .... 52"
MSRP $3,499

RETAIL PRICING

YEAR	HIGH	LOW
2011	$1,392	$1,044
2012	$1,737	$1,303

300Z/2548

YEARS MFRD 2016-2017
ENGINE .... B&S
ENGINE HP 25
COOLING .... AIR
FUEL .... G
SPEEDS .... VARIABLE
TRANSMISSION .... HYDRO
STEERING .... ZERO
STANDARD DECK .... 48"
MSRP $3,699

RETAIL PRICING

YEAR	HIGH	LOW
2016	$2,105	$1,579
2017	$2,403	$1,802

300Z/ZT2446

YEARS MFRD 2013-2013
ENGINE .... B&S
ENGINE HP 24
COOLING .... AIR
FUEL .... G
SPEEDS .... VARIABLE
TRANSMISSION .... HYDRO
STEERING .... ZERO
STANDARD DECK .... 46"
MSRP $3,699

RETAIL PRICING

YEAR	HIGH	LOW
2013	$1,900	$1,425

300Z/ZT2752

YEARS MFRD 2013-2015
ENGINE .... B&S
ENGINE HP 27
COOLING .... AIR
FUEL .... G
SPEEDS .... VARIABLE
TRANSMISSION .... HYDRO
STEERING .... ZERO
STANDARD DECK .... 52"
MSRP $3,999

RETAIL PRICING

YEAR	HIGH	LOW
2013	$1,680	$1,260
2014	$2,014	$1,510
2015	$2,576	$1,932

355Z/ZT2446

YEARS MFRD 2012-2012
ENGINE .... B&S
ENGINE HP 24
COOLING .... AIR
FUEL .... G
SPEEDS .... VARIABLE
TRANSMISSION .... HYDRO
STEERING .... STANDARD
STANDARD DECK .... 46"
MSRP $4,199

RETAIL PRICING

YEAR	HIGH	LOW
2012	$2,083	$1,562

355Z/ZT2654

YEARS MFRD 2012-2012
ENGINE .... B&S
ENGINE HP 26
COOLING .... AIR
FUEL .... G
SPEEDS .... VARIABLE
TRANSMISSION .... HYDRO
STEERING .... STANDARD
STANDARD DECK .... 54"
MSRP $4,299

RETAIL PRICING

YEAR	HIGH	LOW
2012	$2,137	$1,603

360Z 18/36

YEARS MFRD 2019-2020
SERIES .... 360Z SERIES
ENGINE .... KAWASAKI FR651V
CYLINDERS 2
CID 603
ENGINE HP 18
FUEL .... G
SPEEDS .... VARIABLE
TRANSMISSION .... HYDRO
STEERING .... ZERO
BLADE CLUTCH .... ELECTRIC
STANDARD DECK .... 36"
MSRP $2,749

360Z 19/36

YEARS MFRD 2019-2020
SERIES .... 360Z SERIES
ENGINE B&S PROFESSIONAL SERIES
CYLINDERS 1
CID 500
ENGINE HP 19
FUEL .... G
SPEEDS .... VARIABLE
TRANSMISSION .... HYDRO
STEERING .... ZERO
BLADE CLUTCH .... ELECTRIC
STANDARD DECK .... 36"
MSRP $2,549

360Z 21.5/42

YEARS MFRD 2017-2020
SERIES .... 360Z SERIES
ENGINE .... KAWASAKI FR651V
CYLINDERS 2
CID 726CC
ENGINE HP 21.5
FUEL .... G
TRANSMISSION .... HYDRO
STEERING .... ZERO
BLADE CLUTCH .... ELECTRIC
STANDARD DECK .... 42"
MSRP $3,149

360Z 21.5/48

YEARS MFRD 2016-2020
SERIES .... 360Z SERIES
ENGINE .... KAWASAKI FR651
CYLINDERS 2
CID 726CC
ENGINE HP 21.5
COOLING .... AIR
FUEL .... G
SPEEDS .... VARIABLE
TRANSMISSION .... HYDRO
STEERING .... ZERO
BLADE CLUTCH .... ELECTRIC
STANDARD DECK .... 48"
MSRP $3,599

OPTIONS

52" DECK $750

RETAIL PRICING

YEAR	HIGH	LOW
2016	$1,769	$1,326
2017	$2,014	$1,511
2018	$2,235	$1,677
2019	$2,485	$1,863
2020	$2,790	$2,132

360Z 22/46

YEARS MFRD 2016-2018
SERIES .... 360Z SERIES
ENGINE .... B&S
CYLINDERS 2
CID 724CC
ENGINE HP 22
COOLING .... AIR
FUEL .... G
SPEEDS .... VARIABLE
TRANSMISSION .... HYDRO
STEERING .... ZERO
BLADE CLUTCH .... ELECTRIC
STANDARD DECK .... 46"
MSRP $2,599

RETAIL PRICING

YEAR	HIGH	LOW
2016	$1,481	$1,111
2017	$1,689	$1,267
2018	$1,892	$1,419

360Z 23/42

YEARS MFRD 2016-2020
SERIES .... 360Z SERIES
ENGINE .... B&S
CYLINDERS 2
CID 724CC
ENGINE HP 23
COOLING .... AIR
FUEL .... G
SPEEDS .... VARIABLE
TRANSMISSION .... HYDRO
STEERING .... ZERO
BLADE CLUTCH .... ELECTRIC
STANDARD DECK .... 42"
MSRP $2,949

RETAIL PRICING

YEAR	HIGH	LOW
2016	$1,542	$1,156
2017	$1,769	$1,326
2018	$1,960	$1,470
2019	$2,174	$1,630
2020	$2,424	$1,799

360Z 23/46

YEARS MFRD 2019-2020
SERIES .... 360Z SERIES
ENGINE B&S PROFESSIONAL SERIES
CYLINDERS 2
CID 724
ENGINE HP 23
FUEL .... G
SPEEDS .... VARIABLE
TRANSMISSION .... HYDRO
STEERING .... ZERO
BLADE CLUTCH .... ELECTRIC
STANDARD DECK .... 46"
MSRP $2,649

360Z 23/48

YEARS MFRD 2016-2020
SERIES .... 360Z SERIES
ENGINE .... B&S
CYLINDERS 2
CID 724CC
ENGINE HP 23
COOLING .... AIR
FUEL .... G
SPEEDS .... VARIABLE
TRANSMISSION .... HYDRO
STEERING .... ZERO
BLADE CLUTCH .... ELECTRIC
STANDARD DECK .... 48"
MSRP $3,399

SNAPPER

RETAIL PRICING

YEAR	HIGH	LOW
2016	$1,769	$1,326
2017	$2,014	$1,511
2018	$2,227	$1,670
2019	$2,555	$1,917
2020	$2,766	$2,114

360Z 25/52

YEARS MFRD 2016-2020
SERIES . . . . 360Z SERIES
ENGINE . . . . B&S
CYLINDERS 2
CID 724CC
ENGINE HP 25
COOLING . . . . AIR
FUEL . . . . G
SPEEDS . . . . VARIABLE
TRANSMISSION . . . . HYDRO
STEERING . . . . ZERO
BLADE CLUTCH . . . . ELECTRIC
STANDARD DECK . . . . 52"
MSRP $3,899

RETAIL PRICING

YEAR	HIGH	LOW
2016	$2,040	$1,530
2017	$2,330	$1,747
2018	$2,584	$1,938
2019	$2,859	$2,144
2020	$3,142	$2,402

400Z

YEARS MFRD 2010-2010
SERIES . . . . 400 Z SERIES
ENGINE . . . . B&S
CYLINDERS 2
ENGINE HP 24
COOLING . . . . AIR
FUEL . . . . G
SPEEDS . . . . VARIABLE
TRANSMISSION . . . . HYDRO
STEERING . . . . ZERO
STANDARD DECK . . . . 50"
WEIGHT . . . . 670 LBS.
MSRP $4,500

RETAIL PRICING

YEAR	HIGH	LOW
2010	$2,031	$1,523

400Z/21.548

YEARS MFRD 2016-2017
ENGINE . . . . KAWASAKI
ENGINE HP 21.5
COOLING . . . . AIR
FUEL . . . . G
SPEEDS . . . . VARIABLE
TRANSMISSION . . . . HYDRO
STEERING . . . . ZERO
STANDARD DECK . . . . 48"
MSRP $4,299

RETAIL PRICING

YEAR	HIGH	LOW
2016	$2,448	$1,836
2017	$2,800	$2,100

400Z/2548

YEARS MFRD 2016-2017
ENGINE . . . . B&S
ENGINE HP 25
COOLING . . . . AIR
FUEL . . . . G
SPEEDS . . . . VARIABLE
TRANSMISSION . . . . HYDRO
STEERING . . . . ZERO
STANDARD DECK . . . . 48"
MSRP $4,299

RETAIL PRICING

YEAR	HIGH	LOW
2016	$2,448	$1,836
2017	$2,800	$2,100

400Z/ZT2748

YEARS MFRD 2013-2015
ENGINE . . . . B&S
ENGINE HP 27
COOLING . . . . AIR
FUEL . . . . G
SPEEDS . . . . VARIABLE
TRANSMISSION . . . . HYDRO
STEERING . . . . ZERO
STANDARD DECK . . . . 48"
MSRP $4,499

RETAIL PRICING

YEAR	HIGH	LOW
2013	$1,797	$1,348
2014	$2,093	$1,570
2015	$2,932	$2,199

460Z 21.5/48

YEARS MFRD 2018-2019
SERIES . . . . 460Z SERIES
ENGINE . . . . KAWASAKI FR651
CYLINDERS 2
CID 726CC
ENGINE HP 21.5
FUEL . . . . G
TRANSMISSION . . . . HYDRO
STEERING . . . . ZERO
BLADE CLUTCH . . . . ELECTRIC
STANDARD DECK . . . . 48"
MSRP $4,949

460Z 25/48

YEARS MFRD 2018-2019
SERIES . . . . 460Z SERIES
ENGINE . . . . B&S
CYLINDERS 2
CID 724CC
ENGINE HP 25
FUEL . . . . G
TRANSMISSION . . . . HYDRO
STEERING . . . . ZERO
BLADE CLUTCH . . . . ELECTRIC
STANDARD DECK . . . . 48"
MSRP $4,749

500Z/2648

YEARS MFRD 2010-2011
ENGINE . . . . B&S
CYLINDERS 2
ENGINE HP 26
COOLING . . . . AIR
FUEL . . . . G
SPEEDS . . . . VARIABLE
TRANSMISSION . . . . HYDRO
STEERING . . . . ZERO
STANDARD DECK . . . . 48"
WEIGHT . . . . 724 LBS.
MSRP $4,999

RETAIL PRICING

YEAR	HIGH	LOW
2010	$1,407	$1,055
2011	$1,592	$1,194

500Z/ZT2648

YEARS MFRD 2012-2015
ENGINE . . . . B&S
ENGINE HP 26
COOLING . . . . AIR
FUEL . . . . G
SPEEDS . . . . VARIABLE
TRANSMISSION . . . . HYDRO
STEERING . . . . ZERO
STANDARD DECK . . . . 48"
MSRP $5,199

RETAIL PRICING

YEAR	HIGH	LOW
2012	$1,851	$1,388
2013	$2,154	$1,616
2014	$2,650	$1,988
2015	$3,471	$2,603

550Z/2452

YEARS MFRD 2016-2017
ENGINE . . . . KAWASAKI
ENGINE HP 24
COOLING . . . . AIR
FUEL . . . . G
SPEEDS . . . . VARIABLE
TRANSMISSION . . . . HYDRO
STEERING . . . . ZERO
STANDARD DECK . . . . 52"
MSRP $5,099

RETAIL PRICING

YEAR	HIGH	LOW
2016	$2,900	$2,175
2017	$3,314	$2,486

550Z/2461

YEARS MFRD 2016-2017
ENGINE . . . . KAWASAKI
ENGINE HP 24
COOLING . . . . AIR
FUEL . . . . G
SPEEDS . . . . VARIABLE
TRANSMISSION . . . . HYDRO
STEERING . . . . ZERO
STANDARD DECK . . . . 61"
MSRP $5,199

RETAIL PRICING

YEAR	HIGH	LOW
2016	$2,963	$2,223
2017	$3,378	$2,533

550Z/2552

YEARS MFRD 2016-2017
ENGINE . . . . B&S
ENGINE HP 25
COOLING . . . . AIR
FUEL . . . . G
SPEEDS . . . . VARIABLE
TRANSMISSION . . . . HYDRO
STEERING . . . . ZERO
STANDARD DECK . . . . 52"
MSRP $4,899

RETAIL PRICING

YEAR	HIGH	LOW
2016	$2,791	$2,093
2017	$3,188	$2,391

550Z/2561

YEARS MFRD 2016-2017
ENGINE . . . . B&S
ENGINE HP 25
COOLING . . . . AIR
FUEL . . . . G
SPEEDS . . . . VARIABLE
TRANSMISSION . . . . HYDRO
STEERING . . . . ZERO
STANDARD DECK . . . . 61"
MSRP $4,999

RETAIL PRICING

YEAR	HIGH	LOW
2016	$2,845	$2,134
2017	$3,251	$2,439

560Z 24/52

YEARS MFRD 2017-2019
SERIES . . . . 560Z SERIES
ENGINE . . . . . . KAWASAKI FR730V
CYLINDERS 2
CID 726CC
ENGINE HP 24
FUEL . . . . G
TRANSMISSION . . . . HYDRO
STEERING . . . . ZERO
BLADE CLUTCH . . . . ELECTRIC
STANDARD DECK . . . . 52"
MSRP $5,699

560Z 24/61

YEARS MFRD 2017-2019
SERIES . . . . 560Z SERIES
ENGINE . . . . . . KAWASAKI FR730V
CYLINDERS 2
CID 726CC
ENGINE HP 24
FUEL . . . . G
TRANSMISSION . . . . HYDRO
STEERING . . . . ZERO
BLADE CLUTCH . . . . ELECTRIC
STANDARD DECK . . . . 61"
MSRP $5,799

OPTIONS

CARGO BED

560Z 25/52

YEARS MFRD 2017-2019
SERIES . . . . 560Z SERIES
ENGINE . . . . B&S COMMERCIAL
CYLINDERS 2
CID 724CC
ENGINE HP 25
TRANSMISSION . . . . HYDRO
STEERING . . . . ZERO
BLADE CLUTCH . . . . ELECTRIC
STANDARD DECK . . . . 52"
MSRP $5,249

560Z 25/61

YEARS MFRD 2017-2019
SERIES . . . . 560Z SERIES
ENGINE . . . . B&S COMMERCIAL
CYLINDERS 2
CID 724CC
ENGINE HP 25
FUEL . . . . G
TRANSMISSION . . . . HYDRO
STEERING . . . . ZERO
BLADE CLUTCH . . . . ELECTRIC
STANDARD DECK . . . . 61"
MSRP $5,399

OPTIONS

CARGO BED

1848H

YEARS MFRD 1997-1997
ENGINE . . . . KOHLER
ENGINE HP 18
FUEL . . . . G
SPEEDS . . . . VARIABLE
TRANSMISSION . . . . HYDRO
STEERING . . . . ZERO
STANDARD DECK . . . . 48"
MSRP $6,769

OPTIONS

44" SNOW THROWER

RETAIL PRICING

YEAR	HIGH	LOW
1997	$1,858	$1,393

3317BVE

YEARS MFRD 2006-2008
ENGINE . . . . B&S
CYLINDERS 1
ENGINE HP 17
COOLING . . . . AIR
FUEL . . . . G
SPEEDS 5/1
TRANSMISSION . . . . DISC
STEERING . . . . STANDARD
STANDARD DECK . . . . 33"
WEIGHT . . . . 365 LBS.
MSRP $2,169

RETAIL PRICING

YEAR	HIGH	LOW
2006	$1,208	$906
2007	$1,262	$946
2008	$1,317	$988

28115BV

YEARS MFRD 2006-2010
ENGINE . . . . B&S
CYLINDERS 1
ENGINE HP 11.5
COOLING . . . . AIR
FUEL . . . . G
SPEEDS 5/1
TRANSMISSION . . . . DISC
STEERING . . . . STANDARD
STANDARD DECK . . . . 28"
WEIGHT . . . . 300 LBS.
MSRP $1,399

RETAIL PRICING

YEAR	HIGH	LOW
2006	$667	$501
2007	$723	$542
2008	$801	$601
2009	$807	$605
2010	$855	$641

28125BVE

YEARS MFRD 2006-2010
ENGINE . . . . KUBOTA
CYLINDERS 1
ENGINE HP 12.5
COOLING . . . . AIR
FUEL . . . . G
SPEEDS 5/1
TRANSMISSION . . . . DISC
STEERING . . . . STANDARD
STANDARD DECK . . . . 28"
WEIGHT . . . . 314 LBS.
MSRP $1,799

RETAIL PRICING

YEAR	HIGH	LOW
2006	$826	$620
2007	$852	$639
2008	$871	$653
2009	$935	$701
2010	$1,098	$824

30115BV

YEARS MFRD 2006-2010
ENGINE . . . . B&S
CYLINDERS 1
ENGINE HP 11.5
COOLING . . . . AIR
FUEL . . . . G
SPEEDS 5/1
TRANSMISSION . . . . DISC
STEERING . . . . STANDARD
STANDARD DECK . . . . 30"
WEIGHT . . . . 308 LBS.
MSRP $1,399

RETAIL PRICING

YEAR	HIGH	LOW
2006	$700	$525
2007	$750	$562
2008	$821	$615
2009	$835	$626
2010	$855	$641

30125BV

YEARS MFRD 2009-2009
SERIES . . . . . . REAR ENGINE SERIES
ENGINE . . . . B&S
CYLINDERS 1
ENGINE HP 12.5
COOLING . . . . AIR
FUEL . . . . G
SPEEDS 4/1
TRANSMISSION . . . . DISC
STEERING . . . . STANDARD
STANDARD DECK . . . . 30"
WEIGHT . . . . 324 LBS.
MSRP $1,899

RETAIL PRICING

YEAR	HIGH	LOW
2009	$1,144	$858

30125BVE

YEARS MFRD 2006-2011
ENGINE . . . . B&S
CYLINDERS 1
ENGINE HP 12.5
COOLING . . . . AIR
FUEL . . . . G
SPEEDS 5/1
TRANSMISSION . . . . DISC
STEERING . . . . STANDARD
STANDARD DECK . . . . 30"
WEIGHT . . . . 324 LBS.
MSRP $1,899

RETAIL PRICING

YEAR	HIGH	LOW
2006	$774	$581
2007	$857	$643
2008	$885	$663
2009	$1,015	$761
2010	$1,114	$835
2011	$1,192	$894

33175BVE

YEARS MFRD 2010-2011
ENGINE . . . . B&S INTEK
CYLINDERS 1
ENGINE HP 17.5
COOLING . . . . AIR
FUEL . . . . G
SPEEDS 5/1
TRANSMISSION . . . . DISC
STEERING . . . . STANDARD
STANDARD DECK . . . . 33"
WEIGHT . . . . 365 LBS.
MSRP $2,249

RETAIL PRICING

YEAR	HIGH	LOW
2010	$1,096	$822
2011	$1,271	$953

281123BVE

YEARS MFRD 2003-2003
SERIES . . . . HI-VAC SERIES
ENGINE . . . . B&S
CYLINDERS 1
ENGINE HP 11
COOLING . . . . AIR
FUEL . . . . G
SPEEDS 5/1
TRANSMISSION . . . . DISC
STEERING . . . . STANDARD
BLADE CLUTCH . . . . MANUAL
STANDARD DECK . . . . 28"
WEIGHT . . . . 314 LBS.
MSRP $1,199

RETAIL PRICING

YEAR	HIGH	LOW
2003	$272	$204

281123HVE

YEARS MFRD 2003-2005
SERIES . . . . HI-VAC SERIES
ENGINE . . . . HONDA
CYLINDERS 1
ENGINE HP 11
COOLING . . . . AIR
FUEL . . . . G
SPEEDS 5/1
TRANSMISSION . . . . DISC
STEERING . . . . STANDARD
BLADE CLUTCH . . . . MANUAL
STANDARD DECK . . . . 28"
WEIGHT . . . . 332 LBS.
MSRP $2,003

OPTIONS

1 BAG
2 BAG
36" BLADE
BAGGER

RETAIL PRICING

YEAR	HIGH	LOW
2003	$269	$202
2004	$298	$223
2005	$330	$247

281223BVE

YEARS MFRD 2004-2005
SERIES . . . . HI-VAC SERIES
ENGINE . . . . B&S
CYLINDERS 1
ENGINE HP 12
COOLING . . . . AIR
FUEL . . . . G
SPEEDS 5/1
TRANSMISSION . . . . DISC
STEERING . . . . STANDARD
BLADE CLUTCH . . . . MANUAL
STANDARD DECK . . . . 28"
WEIGHT . . . . 314 LBS.
MSRP $1,599

OPTIONS

1 BAG
2 BAG
36" BLADE
BAGGER

SNAPPER

SERIAL NUMBERS

YEAR	BEGINNING NO.
2004	4XXXXX

RETAIL PRICING

YEAR	HIGH	LOW
2004	$237	$178
2005	$264	$198

300922B

YEARS MFRD 2003-2003
SERIES .... SIDE DISC SERIES
ENGINE .... B&S
CYLINDERS 1
ENGINE HP 9
COOLING .... AIR
FUEL .... G
SPEEDS 5
TRANSMISSION .... DISC
STEERING .... STANDARD
BLADE CLUTCH .... MANUAL
STANDARD DECK .... 30"
WEIGHT .... 308 LBS.
MSRP $999

RETAIL PRICING

YEAR	HIGH	LOW
2003	$192	$144

301123BVE

YEARS MFRD 2003-2003
SERIES .... SIDE DISC SERIES
ENGINE .... B&S
CYLINDERS 1
ENGINE HP 11
COOLING .... AIR
FUEL .... G
SPEEDS 5
TRANSMISSION .... DISC
STEERING .... STANDARD
BLADE CLUTCH .... MANUAL
STANDARD DECK .... 30"
WEIGHT .... 324 LBS.
MSRP $1,399

RETAIL PRICING

YEAR	HIGH	LOW
2003	$270	$202

301223BVE

YEARS MFRD 2004-2005
SERIES .... SIDE DISCHARGE SERIES
ENGINE .... B&S
CYLINDERS 1
ENGINE HP 12
COOLING .... AIR
FUEL .... G
SPEEDS 5/1
TRANSMISSION .... GEAR
STEERING .... STANDARD
STANDARD DECK .... 30"
WEIGHT .... 324 LBS.
MSRP $1,699

OPTIONS

1 BAG
36" BLADE

SERIAL NUMBERS

YEAR	BEGINNING NO.
2004	4XXXXX

RETAIL PRICING

YEAR	HIGH	LOW
2004	$253	$190
2005	$280	$210

301323BVE

YEARS MFRD 2003-2004
SERIES .... SIDE DISC SERIES
ENGINE .... B&S
CYLINDERS 1
ENGINE HP 13
COOLING .... AIR
FUEL .... G
SPEEDS 5
TRANSMISSION .... DISC
STEERING .... STANDARD
BLADE CLUTCH .... MANUAL
STANDARD DECK .... 30"
WEIGHT .... 354 LBS.
MSRP $1,799

OPTIONS

1 BAG
36" BLADE

SERIAL NUMBERS

YEAR	BEGINNING NO.
2004	4XXXXX

RETAIL PRICING

YEAR	HIGH	LOW
2003	$267	$200
2004	$297	$223

331323HVE

YEARS MFRD 2003-2005
SERIES .... HI-VAC SERIES
ENGINE .... HONDA
CYLINDERS 1
ENGINE HP 13
COOLING .... AIR
FUEL .... G
SPEEDS 5
TRANSMISSION .... DISC
STEERING .... STANDARD
BLADE CLUTCH .... MANUAL
STANDARD DECK .... 33"
WEIGHT .... 382 LBS.
MSRP $2,599

OPTIONS

1 BAG
2 BAG
36" BLADE

SERIAL NUMBERS

YEAR	BEGINNING NO.
2004	4XXXXX

RETAIL PRICING

YEAR	HIGH	LOW
2003	$349	$262
2004	$387	$290
2005	$428	$321

331518KVE

YEARS MFRD 1999-2000
ENGINE .... KOHLER
ENGINE HP 15
FUEL .... G
TRANSMISSION .... HYDRO
STEERING .... STANDARD
STANDARD DECK .... 33"
MSRP $2,199

RETAIL PRICING

YEAR	HIGH	LOW
1999	$281	$211
2000	$310	$233

331520KVE

YEARS MFRD 2001-2002
ENGINE .... KOHLER
ENGINE HP 15
COOLING .... AIR
FUEL .... G
TRANSMISSION .... HYDRO
STEERING .... STANDARD
STANDARD DECK .... 33"
MSRP $2,249

SERIAL NUMBERS

YEAR	BEGINNING NO.
2002	2XXXXXXX

RETAIL PRICING

YEAR	HIGH	LOW
2001	$333	$250
2002	$370	$277

331522KVE

YEARS MFRD 2003-2003
ENGINE .... KOHLER
ENGINE HP 15
COOLING .... AIR
FUEL .... G
TRANSMISSION .... DISC
STEERING .... STANDARD
STANDARD DECK .... 33"
MSRP $2,249

OPTIONS

1 BAG
2 BAG
36" BLADE

RETAIL PRICING

YEAR	HIGH	LOW
2003	$330	$247

331523KVE

YEARS MFRD 2004-2007
SERIES .... HI-VAC SERIES
ENGINE .... KOHLER
CYLINDERS 1
ENGINE HP 15
COOLING .... AIR
FUEL .... G
SPEEDS 5
TRANSMISSION .... DISC
STEERING .... STANDARD
BLADE CLUTCH .... MANUAL
STANDARD DECK .... 33"
WEIGHT .... 385 LBS.
MSRP $2,399

OPTIONS

1 BAG
2 BAG
36" BLADE
BAGGER

SERIAL NUMBERS

YEAR	BEGINNING NO.
2004	4XXXXX

RETAIL PRICING

YEAR	HIGH	LOW
2004	$385	$289
2005	$428	$321
2006	$474	$356
2007	$526	$394

331623BVE

YEARS MFRD 2004-2005
SERIES .... HI-VAC SERIES
ENGINE .... B&S
CYLINDERS 1
ENGINE HP 16
COOLING .... AIR
FUEL .... G
SPEEDS 5/1
TRANSMISSION .... DISC
STEERING .... STANDARD
BLADE CLUTCH .... MANUAL
STANDARD DECK .... 33"
WEIGHT .... 365 LBS.
MSRP $2,299

OPTIONS

1 BAG
2 BAG
36" BLADE
BAGGER

SERIAL NUMBERS

YEAR	BEGINNING NO.
2004	4XXXXX

RETAIL PRICING

YEAR	HIGH	LOW
2004	$398	$298
2005	$441	$331

381451HBVE

YEARS MFRD 2001-2004
ENGINE .... B&S
CYLINDERS 1
ENGINE HP 14.5
COOLING .... AIR
FUEL .... G
SPEEDS .... VARIABLE
TRANSMISSION .... HYDRO
STEERING .... STANDARD
STANDARD DECK .... 38"
WEIGHT .... 450 LBS.
MSRP $2,099

OPTIONS

2 BAG
36" SWEEP
7 CU BAG
BAGGER

SERIAL NUMBERS

YEAR	BEGINNING NO.
2002	2XXXXXXX

RETAIL PRICING

YEAR	HIGH	LOW
2001	$255	$191
2002	$282	$212
2003	$312	$234
2004	$346	$260

411611BE

YEARS MFRD 1992-1993
SERIES .... DELUXE SERIES
ENGINE .... B&S
ENGINE HP 16
COOLING .... AIR
FUEL .... G
TRANSMISSION .... GEAR
STEERING .... STANDARD
STANDARD DECK .... 41"
MSRP $2,200

RETAIL PRICING

YEAR	HIGH	LOW
1992	$709	$532
1993	$732	$549

421613BVE

YEARS MFRD 1992-1994
ENGINE .... B&S
ENGINE HP 16
COOLING .... AIR
FUEL .... G
TRANSMISSION .... GEAR
STEERING .... STANDARD
STANDARD DECK .... 42"
MSRP $2,699

RETAIL PRICING

YEAR	HIGH	LOW
1992	$805	$604
1993	$864	$648
1994	$950	$712

421614BVE

YEARS MFRD 1995-1995
ENGINE .... B&S
ENGINE HP 16
COOLING .... AIR
FUEL .... G
TRANSMISSION .... HYDRO
STEERING .... STANDARD
STANDARD DECK .... 42"
MSRP $2,809

RETAIL PRICING

YEAR	HIGH	LOW
1995	$1,025	$769

421616BVE

YEARS MFRD 1997-1998
ENGINE .... B&S
ENGINE HP 16
FUEL .... G
TRANSMISSION .... HYDRO
STEERING .... STANDARD
STANDARD DECK .... 42"
MSRP $2,699

RETAIL PRICING

YEAR	HIGH	LOW
1997	$237	$178
1998	$263	$197

421618BVE

YEARS MFRD 1999-2000
ENGINE .... B&S
ENGINE HP 16
FUEL .... G
TRANSMISSION .... HYDRO
STEERING .... STANDARD
STANDARD DECK .... 42"
MSRP $2,599

RETAIL PRICING

YEAR	HIGH	LOW
1999	$351	$263
2000	$390	$292

421620BVE

YEARS MFRD 2001-2002
ENGINE .... B&S
CYLINDERS 2
ENGINE HP 16
FUEL .... G
TRANSMISSION .... DISC
STEERING .... STANDARD
STANDARD DECK .... 42"
MSRP $2,599

OPTIONS

36" BLADE
36" SWEEPER
BAGGER

SERIAL NUMBERS

YEAR	BEGINNING NO.
2002	2XXXXXX

RETAIL PRICING

YEAR	HIGH	LOW
2001	$281	$211
2002	$310	$233

421622BVE

YEARS MFRD 2003-2003
ENGINE .... B&S
ENGINE HP 16
COOLING .... AIR
FUEL .... G
TRANSMISSION .... DISC
STEERING .... STANDARD
STANDARD DECK .... 42"
MSRP $2,599

OPTIONS

1 BAG
36" BLADE

RETAIL PRICING

YEAR	HIGH	LOW
2003	$381	$286

421823BVE

YEARS MFRD 2003-2005
SERIES ... SIDE DISCHARGE SERIES
ENGINE .... B&S
CYLINDERS 2
ENGINE HP 18
COOLING .... AIR
FUEL .... G
SPEEDS 5
TRANSMISSION .... DISC
STEERING .... STANDARD
BLADE CLUTCH .... MANUAL
STANDARD DECK .... 42"
WEIGHT .... 432 LBS.
MSRP $2,899

OPTIONS

1 BAG
36" BLADE

SERIAL NUMBERS

YEAR	BEGINNING NO.
2004	4XXXXX

RETAIL PRICING

YEAR	HIGH	LOW
2003	$454	$340
2004	$502	$377
2005	$556	$417

422023BVE

YEARS MFRD 2006-2007
SERIES ... SIDE DISCHARGE SERIES
ENGINE .... B&S
CYLINDERS 2
ENGINE HP 20
COOLING .... AIR
FUEL .... G
SPEEDS 5/1
TRANSMISSION .... DISC
STEERING .... STANDARD
STANDARD DECK .... 42"
WEIGHT .... 415 LBS.
MSRP $2,799

OPTIONS

1 BAG
36" BLADE

RETAIL PRICING

YEAR	HIGH	LOW
2006	$553	$415
2007	$613	$460

780009

YEARS MFRD 2009-2009
SERIES .... 250Z SERIES
ENGINE .... B&S INTEK
CYLINDERS 1
ENGINE HP 18.5
COOLING .... AIR
FUEL .... G
SPEEDS .... VARIABLE
TRANSMISSION .... HYDRO
STEERING .... ZERO
STANDARD DECK .... 38"
WEIGHT .... 530 LBS.
MSRP $3,300

RETAIL PRICING

YEAR	HIGH	LOW
2009	$1,986	$1,489

2690249

YEARS MFRD 2009-2009
SERIES .... RE200 SERIES
ENGINE .... B&S INTEK
CYLINDERS 1
ENGINE HP 13.5
COOLING .... AIR
FUEL .... G
SPEEDS .... VARIABLE
TRANSMISSION .... HYDRO
STEERING .... STANDARD
STANDARD DECK .... 30"
WEIGHT .... 415 LBS.
MSRP $2,449

RETAIL PRICING

YEAR	HIGH	LOW
2009	$1,473	$1,105

2690577

YEARS MFRD 2009-2009
SERIES .... LT200 SERIES
ENGINE .... B&S INTEK
CYLINDERS 1
ENGINE HP 18.5
COOLING .... AIR
FUEL .... G
SPEEDS .... VARIABLE
TRANSMISSION .... HYDRO
STEERING .... STANDARD
STANDARD DECK .... 38"
WEIGHT .... 460 LBS.
MSRP $2,200

RETAIL PRICING

YEAR	HIGH	LOW
2009	$1,323	$992

2690578

YEARS MFRD 2009-2009
SERIES .... LT200 SERIES
ENGINE .... B&S INTEK
CYLINDERS 2
ENGINE HP 20
COOLING .... AIR
FUEL .... G
SPEEDS .... VARIABLE
TRANSMISSION .... HYDRO
STEERING .... STANDARD
STANDARD DECK .... 42"
WEIGHT .... 494 LBS.
MSRP $2,400

RETAIL PRICING

YEAR	HIGH	LOW
2009	$1,443	$1,083

2690579

YEARS MFRD 2009-2009
SERIES .... LT200 SERIES
ENGINE .... B&S INTEK
CYLINDERS 2
ENGINE HP 20
COOLING .... AIR
FUEL .... G
SPEEDS .... VARIABLE
TRANSMISSION .... HYDRO

SNAPPER

STEERING. . . . . .STANDARD
STANDARD DECK . . . . 44"
WEIGHT . . . . 532 LBS.
MSRP. $2,750

RETAIL PRICING

YEAR	HIGH	LOW
2009	$1,653	$1,240

2690580

YEARS MFRD 2009-2009
SERIES. . . . . .LT200 SERIES
ENGINE . . . . B&S INTEK
CYLINDERS. 2
ENGINE HP 22
COOLING . . . . .AIR
FUEL . . . . G
SPEEDS . . . . .VARIABLE
TRANSMISSION . . . . .HYDRO
STEERING. . . . . .STANDARD
STANDARD DECK . . . . 50"
WEIGHT . . . . 560 LBS.
MSRP. $2,950

RETAIL PRICING

YEAR	HIGH	LOW
2009	$1,774	$1,331

2690645

YEARS MFRD 2009-2009
SERIES. . . . . 150Z SERIES
ENGINE . . . . .B&S
CYLINDERS. 1
ENGINE HP 20
COOLING . . . . .AIR
FUEL . . . . G
SPEEDS . . . . .VARIABLE
TRANSMISSION . . . . .HYDRO
STEERING. . . . . .ZERO
STANDARD DECK . . . . 42"
WEIGHT . . . . 500 LBS.
MSRP. $2,900

RETAIL PRICING

YEAR	HIGH	LOW
2009	$1,744	$1,308

2690647

YEARS MFRD 2009-2009
SERIES. . . . . 355Z SERIES
ENGINE . . . . .B&S
CYLINDERS. 2
ENGINE HP 24
COOLING . . . . .AIR
FUEL . . . . G
SPEEDS . . . . .VARIABLE
TRANSMISSION . . . . .HYDRO
STEERING. . . . . .ZERO
BLADE CLUTCH . . . . .ELECTRIC
STANDARD DECK . . . . 50"
WEIGHT . . . . 670 LBS.
MSRP. $4,500

RETAIL PRICING

YEAR	HIGH	LOW
2009	$2,706	$2,030

2690752

YEARS MFRD 2009-2009
SERIES. YT400
ENGINE . . . . .B&S
CYLINDERS. 2
ENGINE HP 23
COOLING . . . . .AIR
FUEL . . . . G
SPEEDS . . . . .VARIABLE
TRANSMISSION . . . . .HYDRO
STEERING. . . . . .STANDARD
STANDARD DECK . . . . 50"
WEIGHT . . . . 700 LBS.
MSRP. $5,800

RETAIL PRICING

YEAR	HIGH	LOW
2009	$3,489	$2,617

2690759

YEARS MFRD 2009-2009
SERIES. . . . . .LT300 SERIES
ENGINE . . . . B&S VANGUARD
CYLINDERS. 2
ENGINE HP 20
COOLING . . . . .AIR
FUEL . . . . G
SPEEDS . . . . .VARIABLE
TRANSMISSION . . . . .HYDRO
STEERING. . . . . .STANDARD
STANDARD DECK . . . . 44"
WEIGHT . . . . 580 LBS.
MSRP. $4,450

RETAIL PRICING

YEAR	HIGH	LOW
2009	$2,676	$2,007

2690826

YEARS MFRD 2009-2009
SERIES. . . . . .LT100 SERIES
ENGINE . . . . .B&S
CYLINDERS. 2
ENGINE HP 23
COOLING . . . . .AIR
FUEL . . . . G
SPEEDS . . . . .VARIABLE
TRANSMISSION . . . . .HYDRO
STEERING. . . . . .STANDARD
WEIGHT . . . . 532 LBS.

2811525BVE

YEARS MFRD 2019-2020
SERIES . . . . . CLASSIC REAR ENGINE SERIES
ENGINE . . . . B&S INTEK
CYLINDERS. 1
ENGINE HP 11.5
FUEL . . . . G
TRANSMISSION . . . . DISC
STEERING. . . . . .STANDARD
BLADE CLUTCH . . . . MANUAL
STANDARD DECK . . . . 28"
MSRP. $2,249

2813523BVE

YEARS MFRD 2005-2007
ENGINE . . . . .B&S
CYLINDERS. 1
ENGINE HP 13.5
COOLING . . . . .AIR
FUEL . . . . G
SPEEDS 5/1
TRANSMISSION . . . . DISC
STEERING. . . . . .STANDARD
STANDARD DECK . . . . 28"
WEIGHT . . . . 332 LBS.
MSRP. $1,799

OPTIONS

1 BAG
2 BAG
36" BLADE
BAGGER

RETAIL PRICING

YEAR	HIGH	LOW
2005	$307	$231
2006	$340	$255
2007	$377	$283

3013523BVE

YEARS MFRD 2005-2007
SERIES. . . .SIDE DISCHARGE SERIES
ENGINE . . . . .B&S
CYLINDERS. 1
ENGINE HP 13.5
COOLING . . . . .AIR
FUEL . . . . G
SPEEDS 5/1
TRANSMISSION . . . . DISC
STEERING. . . . . .STANDARD
STANDARD DECK . . . . 30"
WEIGHT . . . . 354 LBS.
MSRP. $1,899

OPTIONS

1 BAG
36" BLADE

RETAIL PRICING

YEAR	HIGH	LOW
2005	$326	$244
2006	$360	$270
2007	$399	$299

3315525BVE

YEARS MFRD 2019-2020
SERIES . . . . . CLASSIC REAR ENGINE SERIES
ENGINE . . . . B&S INTEK
CYLINDERS. 1
ENGINE HP 15.5
FUEL . . . . G
TRANSMISSION . . . . DISC
STEERING. . . . . .STANDARD
BLADE CLUTCH . . . . MANUAL
STANDARD DECK . . . . 33"
MSRP. $2,349

5900681

YEARS MFRD 2009-2009
SERIES. . . . . 355Z SERIES
ENGINE . . . . .B&S
CYLINDERS. 2
ENGINE HP 24
COOLING . . . . .AIR
FUEL . . . . G
SPEEDS . . . . .VARIABLE
TRANSMISSION . . . . .HYDRO
STEERING. . . . . .ZERO
BLADE CLUTCH . . . . .ELECTRIC
STANDARD DECK . . . . 44"
WEIGHT . . . . 655 LBS.
MSRP. $4,300

RETAIL PRICING

YEAR	HIGH	LOW
2009	$2,587	$1,940

5900682

YEARS MFRD 2009-2009
SERIES. . . . . 150Z SERIES
ENGINE . . . . .B&S
CYLINDERS. 2
ENGINE HP 24
COOLING . . . . .AIR
FUEL . . . . G
SPEEDS . . . . .VARIABLE
TRANSMISSION . . . . .HYDRO
STEERING. . . . . .ZERO
STANDARD DECK . . . . 50"
WEIGHT . . . . 785 LBS.
MSRP. $3,300

RETAIL PRICING

YEAR	HIGH	LOW
2009	$1,986	$1,489

5900706

YEARS MFRD 2009-2009
SERIES. . . . . 400Z SERIES
ENGINE . . . . .B&S
CYLINDERS. 2
ENGINE HP 24
COOLING . . . . .AIR
FUEL . . . . G
SPEEDS . . . . .VARIABLE
TRANSMISSION . . . . .HYDRO
STEERING. . . . . .ZERO
BLADE CLUTCH . . . . .ELECTRIC
STANDARD DECK . . . . 50"
WEIGHT . . . . 670 LBS.
MSRP. $4,799

RETAIL PRICING

YEAR	HIGH	LOW
2009	$2,887	$2,165

5900731

YEARS MFRD 2009-2009
SERIES. . . . . 500Z SERIES
ENGINE . . . . .B&S
CYLINDERS. 2
ENGINE HP 26
COOLING . . . . .AIR
FUEL . . . . G
SPEEDS . . . . .VARIABLE
TRANSMISSION . . . . .HYDRO
STEERING. . . . . .ZERO
BLADE CLUTCH . . . . .ELECTRIC
STANDARD DECK . . . . 48"
WEIGHT . . . . 724 LBS.
MSRP. $4,999

RETAIL PRICING

YEAR	HIGH	LOW
2009	$3,007	$2,255

7800010

YEARS MFRD . . . 2009-2009
SERIES . . . 250Z SERIES
ENGINE . . . B&S
CYLINDERS . . . 2
ENGINE HP . . . 20
COOLING . . . AIR
FUEL . . . G
SPEEDS . . . VARIABLE
TRANSMISSION . . . HYDRO
STEERING . . . ZERO
STANDARD DECK . . . 42"
WEIGHT . . . 570 LBS.
MSRP . . . $3,600

RETAIL PRICING

YEAR	HIGH	LOW
2009	$2,166	$1,625

7800011

YEARS MFRD . . . 2009-2009
SERIES . . . 250Z SERIES
ENGINE . . . B&S
CYLINDERS . . . 2
ENGINE HP . . . 22
COOLING . . . AIR
FUEL . . . G
SPEEDS . . . VARIABLE
TRANSMISSION . . . HYDRO
STEERING . . . ZERO
STANDARD DECK . . . 50"
WEIGHT . . . 600 LBS.
MSRP . . . $3,900

RETAIL PRICING

YEAR	HIGH	LOW
2009	$2,346	$1,760

7800102

YEARS MFRD . . . 2009-2009
SERIES . . . REAR ENGINE SERIES
ENGINE . . . B&S
CYLINDERS . . . 1
ENGINE HP . . . 11.5
COOLING . . . AIR
FUEL . . . G
SPEEDS . . . 4/1
TRANSMISSION . . . DISC
STEERING . . . STANDARD
STANDARD DECK . . . 28"
WEIGHT . . . 300 LBS.
MSRP . . . $1,399

RETAIL PRICING

YEAR	HIGH	LOW
2009	$842	$631

7800103

YEARS MFRD . . . 2009-2009
SERIES . . . REAR ENGINE SERIES
ENGINE . . . B&S
CYLINDERS . . . 1
ENGINE HP . . . 11.5
COOLING . . . AIR
FUEL . . . G
SPEEDS . . . 4/1
TRANSMISSION . . . DISC
STEERING . . . STANDARD
STANDARD DECK . . . 30"
WEIGHT . . . 308 LBS.
MSRP . . . $1,449

RETAIL PRICING

YEAR	HIGH	LOW
2009	$871	$653

7800104

YEARS MFRD . . . 2009-2009
SERIES . . . REAR ENGINE SERIES
ENGINE . . . B&S
CYLINDERS . . . 1
ENGINE HP . . . 12.5
COOLING . . . AIR
FUEL . . . G
SPEEDS . . . 4/1
TRANSMISSION . . . DISC
STEERING . . . STANDARD
STANDARD DECK . . . 28"
WEIGHT . . . 314 LBS.
MSRP . . . $1,799

RETAIL PRICING

YEAR	HIGH	LOW
2009	$1,083	$812

7800107

YEARS MFRD . . . 2009-2009
SERIES . . . REAR ENGINE SERIES
ENGINE . . . B&S
CYLINDERS . . . 1
ENGINE HP . . . 17
COOLING . . . AIR
FUEL . . . G
SPEEDS . . . 4/1
TRANSMISSION . . . DISC
STEERING . . . STANDARD
STANDARD DECK . . . 33"
WEIGHT . . . 365 LBS.
MSRP . . . $2,299

RETAIL PRICING

YEAR	HIGH	LOW
2009	$1,383	$1,037

7800207

YEARS MFRD . . . 2009-2009
SERIES . . . LT100 SERIES
ENGINE . . . B&S
CYLINDERS . . . 2
ENGINE HP . . . 23
COOLING . . . AIR
FUEL . . . G
SPEEDS . . . VARIABLE
TRANSMISSION . . . HYDRO
STEERING . . . STANDARD
STANDARD DECK . . . 46"
WEIGHT . . . 490 LBS.
MSRP . . . $1,999

RETAIL PRICING

YEAR	HIGH	LOW
2009	$1,203	$902

7800212

YEARS MFRD . . . 2009-2009
SERIES . . . LT100 SERIES
ENGINE . . . B&S
CYLINDERS . . . 2
ENGINE HP . . . 23
COOLING . . . AIR
FUEL . . . G
SPEEDS . . . VARIABLE
TRANSMISSION . . . HYDRO
STEERING . . . STANDARD
STANDARD DECK . . . 52"
WEIGHT . . . 515 LBS.
MSRP . . . $2,199

RETAIL PRICING

YEAR	HIGH	LOW
2009	$1,323	$992

7800545

YEARS MFRD . . . 2009-2009
SERIES . . . LT100 SERIES
ENGINE . . . B&S
CYLINDERS . . . 2
ENGINE HP . . . 23
COOLING . . . AIR
FUEL . . . G
SPEEDS . . . VARIABLE
TRANSMISSION . . . HYDRO
STEERING . . . STANDARD
WEIGHT . . . 532 LBS.

STEINER

ZTM320

YEARS MFRD . . . 2001-2001
SERIES . . . MID-MOUNT SERIES
ENGINE . . . KOHLER COMMAND
ENGINE HP . . . 20
COOLING . . . AIR
FUEL . . . G
TRANSMISSION . . . HYDRO
STEERING . . . ZERO
STANDARD DECK . . . 52"
WEIGHT . . . 1,078 LBS.
MSRP . . . $6,495

RETAIL PRICING

YEAR	HIGH	LOW
2001	$3,184	$2,388

ZTM322

YEARS MFRD . . . 2003-2003
ENGINE . . . ROBIN USA
ENGINE HP . . . 22
COOLING . . . AIR
TRANSMISSION . . . HYDRO
WEIGHT . . . 1,078 LBS.

ZTM325

YEARS MFRD . . . 2001-2001
ENGINE . . . KOHLER COMMAND
ENGINE HP . . . 25
COOLING . . . AIR
FUEL . . . G
TRANSMISSION . . . HYDRO
STEERING . . . ZERO
STANDARD DECK . . . 61"
WEIGHT . . . 1,136 LBS.
MSRP . . . $8,195

RETAIL PRICING

YEAR	HIGH	LOW
2001	$4,016	$3,012

25TH ANNIVERSARY

YEARS MFRD . . . 2000-2001
ENGINE . . . ONAN
ENGINE HP . . . 20
COOLING . . . AIR
FUEL . . . G
STEERING . . . ZERO
STANDARD DECK . . . 60"
MSRP . . . $14,245

OPTIONS

72" DECK

RETAIL PRICING

YEAR	HIGH	LOW
2000	$2,440	$1,830
2001	$2,704	$2,028

75-60010

YEARS MFRD . . . 2004-2007
SERIES . . . 415 SERIES
ENGINE . . . KOHLER
ENGINE HP . . . 23
FUEL . . . G
SPEEDS . . . VARIABLE
TRANSMISSION . . . HYDRO
STEERING . . . ALL WHEEL
HYDRAULIC . . . YES
MSRP . . . $10,500

RETAIL PRICING

YEAR	HIGH	LOW
2004	$3,890	$2,917
2005	$5,018	$3,763
2006	$5,386	$4,040
2007	$5,917	$4,438

75-70005

YEARS MFRD . . . 2004-2006
SERIES . . . 430 MAX SERIES
ENGINE . . . KOHLER
ENGINE HP . . . 27
FUEL . . . G
SPEEDS . . . VARIABLE
TRANSMISSION . . . HYDRO
STEERING . . . ALL WHEEL
HITCH . . . CAT. I
HYDRAULIC . . . YES
MSRP . . . $13,349

STEINER

RETAIL PRICING

YEAR	HIGH	LOW
2004	$6,859	$5,144
2005	$7,599	$5,699
2006	$8,704	$6,528

75-70006

YEARS MFRD 2004-2006
SERIES .... 430 MAX SERIES
ENGINE .... KUBOTA
ENGINE HP 25
FUEL .... G
SPEEDS .... VARIABLE
TRANSMISSION .... HYDRO
STEERING .... STANDARD
HITCH .... CAT. I
MSRP $15,083

RETAIL PRICING

YEAR	HIGH	LOW
2004	$8,081	$6,061
2005	$8,952	$6,714
2006	$9,836	$7,377

75-70008

YEARS MFRD 2004-2006
SERIES .... 430 MAX SERIES
ENGINE .... KUBOTA
ENGINE HP 21
FUEL .... D
SPEEDS .... VARIABLE
TRANSMISSION .... HYDRO
STEERING .... STANDARD
HITCH .... CAT. I
MSRP $16,424

RETAIL PRICING

YEAR	HIGH	LOW
2004	$8,720	$6,540
2005	$9,659	$7,244
2006	$10,710	$8,032

75-70040

YEARS MFRD 1994-2007
SERIES .... 525 SERIES
ENGINE .... KUBOTA D1105
ENGINE HP 28
COOLING .... LIQUID
FUEL .... D
SPEEDS .... VARIABLE
TRANSMISSION .... HYDRO
STEERING .... ALL WHEEL
HYDRAULIC .... YES
WEIGHT .... 1,520 LBS.
MSRP $21,086

SERIAL NUMBERS

YEAR	BEGINNING NO.
1994	1001
1995	1004
1996	1087

RETAIL PRICING

YEAR	HIGH	LOW
1994	$4,957	$3,718
1995	$5,938	$4,454
1996	$6,558	$4,919
1997	$7,002	$5,252
1998	$7,355	$5,516
1999	$7,845	$5,884
2000	$8,223	$6,167
2004	$11,046	$8,285
2005	$12,303	$9,227
2006	$13,083	$9,813
2007	$14,664	$10,998

75-70134

YEARS MFRD 2004-2004
SERIES .... UM 428 SERIES
ENGINE .... DAIHATSU
ENGINE HP 31
COOLING .... LIQUID
FUEL .... G
SPEEDS .... VARIABLE
TRANSMISSION .... HYDRO
STEERING .... STANDARD
STANDARD DECK .... 60"
MSRP $17,499

RETAIL PRICING

YEAR	HIGH	LOW
2004	$10,177	$7,633

75-70136

YEARS MFRD 2004-2004
SERIES .... UM 428 SERIES
ENGINE .... VANGUARD
ENGINE HP 34
COOLING .... LIQUID
FUEL .... D
SPEEDS .... VARIABLE
TRANSMISSION .... HYDRO
STEERING .... STANDARD
STANDARD DECK .... 60"
WEIGHT .... 1,760 LBS.
MSRP $18,499

RETAIL PRICING

YEAR	HIGH	LOW
2004	$10,758	$8,069

75-70256

YEARS MFRD 2004-2007
SERIES .... 230 SERIES
ENGINE .... KOHLER
CYLINDERS 2
ENGINE HP 27
COOLING .... AIR
FUEL .... G
SPEEDS .... VARIABLE
TRANSMISSION .... HYDRO
STEERING .... STANDARD
MSRP $11,437

RETAIL PRICING

YEAR	HIGH	LOW
2004	$5,521	$4,141
2005	$7,054	$5,290
2006	$7,458	$5,594
2007	$8,637	$6,478

75-70258

YEARS MFRD 2004-2006
SERIES .... 230 SERIES
ENGINE .... KUBOTA
ENGINE HP 25
COOLING .... LIQUID
FUEL .... G
SPEEDS .... VARIABLE
TRANSMISSION .... HYDRO
STEERING .... STANDARD
MSRP $12,380

RETAIL PRICING

YEAR	HIGH	LOW
2004	$6,859	$5,144
2005	$7,635	$5,726
2006	$8,073	$6,055

75-70265

YEARS MFRD 2004-2007
SERIES .... 230 SERIES
ENGINE .... KUBOTA
ENGINE HP 28
COOLING .... LIQUID
FUEL .... D
SPEEDS .... VARIABLE
TRANSMISSION .... HYDRO
STEERING .... STANDARD
MSRP $14,712

RETAIL PRICING

YEAR	HIGH	LOW
2004	$7,440	$5,580
2005	$9,074	$6,806
2006	$9,593	$7,195
2007	$10,882	$8,162

202

YEARS MFRD 1990-2000
ENGINE .... ONAN
ENGINE HP 20
COOLING .... AIR
FUEL .... G
SPEEDS .... VARIABLE
TRANSMISSION .... HYDRO
STEERING .... ZERO
STANDARD DECK .... 50"
MSRP $6,995

SERIAL NUMBERS

YEAR	BEGINNING NO.
1990	1214
1991	1360
1992	1460
1993	1495
1994	2100
1995	2124
1996	2166

RETAIL PRICING

YEAR	HIGH	LOW
1992	$589	$442
1993	$654	$490
1994	$726	$544
1995	$805	$604
1996	$895	$671
1997	$993	$745
1998	$1,099	$824
1999	$1,220	$915
2000	$1,353	$1,015

220

YEARS MFRD 1989-1998
ENGINE .... ONAN
ENGINE HP 20
COOLING .... AIR
FUEL .... G
TRANSMISSION .... HYDRO
STEERING .... STANDARD
STANDARD DECK .... 60"
MSRP $11,045

OPTIONS

KUBOTA 16.5
KUBOTA D600B 16.5HP
KUBOTA WG600B 21HP
ONAN P220 20HP

SERIAL NUMBERS

YEAR	BEGINNING NO.
1989	1169
1990	1429
1991	1496
1992	1567
1993	1619
1994	1684
1995	1782
1996	1958

RETAIL PRICING

YEAR	HIGH	LOW
1990	$696	$522
1991	$770	$578
1992	$857	$643
1993	$948	$711
1994	$1,054	$791
1995	$1,172	$879
1996	$1,297	$973
1997	$1,439	$1,080
1998	$1,598	$1,198

230

YEARS MFRD 1999-2002
ENGINE .... KOHLER
ENGINE HP 27
COOLING .... AIR
FUEL .... G
TRANSMISSION .... HYDRO
STEERING .... ZERO
STANDARD DECK .... 60"
MSRP $11,845

OPTIONS

72" DECK
KUBOTA 25HP
KUBOTA 28HP

RETAIL PRICING

YEAR	HIGH	LOW
1999	$1,878	$1,408
2000	$2,082	$1,561
2001	$2,308	$1,731
2002	$2,561	$1,921

AVG. AUCTION PRICING

LOW	HIGH	AVG
$894	$2,326	$1,402

235 75-70282

YEARS MFRD 2012-2020
ENGINE KUBOTA D1105-E3B TIER IV
CYLINDERS 3

CID 1123CC
ENGINE HP 24.8
COOLING . . . . LIQUID
FUEL . . . . D
SPEEDS . . . . VARIABLE
TRANSMISSION . . . . HYDRO
STEERING . . . . STANDARD
HITCH . . . . CAT. I
DRIVE TYPE 2WD
ROPS/CAB . . . . ROPS
WEIGHT . . . . 1,420 LBS.
MSRP $19,730

RETAIL PRICING

YEAR	HIGH	LOW
2012	$6,745	$5,058
2013	$8,004	$6,003
2014	$9,413	$7,060
2015	$10,317	$7,738
2016	$11,737	$8,802
2017	$12,630	$9,473
2018	$13,818	$10,364
2019	$15,152	$11,364
2020	$16,853	$12,813

235 75-70283

YEARS MFRD 2012-2019
ENGINE . . . . B&S
CID 992CC
ENGINE HP 35
COOLING . . . . AIR
FUEL . . . . G
SPEEDS . . . . VARIABLE
TRANSMISSION . . . . HYDRO
STEERING . . . . STANDARD
DRIVE TYPE 2WD
ROPS/CAB . . . . ROPS
WEIGHT . . . . 1,420 LBS.

RETAIL PRICING

YEAR	HIGH	LOW
2012	$5,769	$4,326
2013	$6,871	$5,153
2014	$8,099	$6,074
2015	$9,028	$6,771
2016	$11,060	$8,295
2017	$11,955	$8,966
2018	$12,727	$9,546
2019	$14,095	$10,571

320

YEARS MFRD 2001-2002
SERIES . . . . MID MOUNT SERIES
ENGINE . . . . KOHLER
ENGINE HP 20
COOLING . . . . AIR
FUEL . . . . G
SPEEDS . . . . VARIABLE
TRANSMISSION . . . . HYDRO
STEERING . . . . ZERO
STANDARD DECK . . . . 52"
MSRP $6,495

OPTIONS

BAGGER

RETAIL PRICING

YEAR	HIGH	LOW
2001	$1,267	$950
2002	$1,407	$1,055

322

YEARS MFRD 2002-2002
SERIES . . . . MID MOUNT SERIES
ENGINE . . . . ROBIN
ENGINE HP 22
STANDARD DECK . . . . 61"
MSRP $7,495

RETAIL PRICING

YEAR	HIGH	LOW
2002	$1,621	$1,216

323

YEARS MFRD 2003-2003
ENGINE . . . . KOHLER
ENGINE HP 23
FUEL . . . . G
STANDARD DECK . . . . 52"
MSRP $6,995

OPTIONS

61" DECK
BAGGER

RETAIL PRICING

YEAR	HIGH	LOW
2003	$1,670	$1,253

325

YEARS MFRD 1999-2001
ENGINE . . . . KOHLER
ENGINE HP 27
COOLING . . . . AIR
FUEL . . . . G
SPEEDS . . . . VARIABLE
TRANSMISSION . . . . HYDRO
STEERING . . . . STANDARD
STANDARD DECK . . . . 61"
MSRP $8,495

RETAIL PRICING

YEAR	HIGH	LOW
1999	$1,232	$924
2000	$1,367	$1,025
2001	$1,514	$1,136

410

YEARS MFRD 1992-2002
ENGINE . . . . ONAN
ENGINE HP 20
COOLING . . . . AIR
FUEL . . . . G
TRANSMISSION . . . . HYDRO
STEERING . . . . ZERO
DRIVE TYPE 4WD
ROPS/CAB . . . . ROPS
STANDARD DECK . . . . 48"
WEIGHT . . . . 950 LBS.
MSRP $10,895

SERIAL NUMBERS

YEAR	BEGINNING NO.
1992	1008
1993	1068
1994	1164
1995	1260
1996	1356

RETAIL PRICING

YEAR	HIGH	LOW
1994	$1,009	$757
1995	$1,118	$839
1996	$1,243	$932
1997	$1,379	$1,035
1998	$1,531	$1,148
1999	$1,697	$1,272
2000	$1,881	$1,411
2001	$2,089	$1,567
2002	$2,315	$1,737

415

YEARS MFRD 2003-2003
ENGINE . . . . KOHLER
ENGINE HP 23
COOLING . . . . AIR
FUEL . . . . G
SPEEDS . . . . VARIABLE
TRANSMISSION . . . . HYDRO
STEERING . . . . STANDARD
STANDARD DECK . . . . 61"
WEIGHT . . . . 950 LBS.
MSRP $11,345

RETAIL PRICING

YEAR	HIGH	LOW
2003	$2,668	$2,001

420

YEARS MFRD 1989-1996
ENGINE . . . . ONAN
ENGINE HP 20
COOLING . . . . AIR
TRANSMISSION . . . . HYDRO
STEERING . . . . ZERO
DRIVE TYPE 4WD
ROPS/CAB . . . . ROPS
STANDARD DECK . . . . 60"
MSRP $12,690

OPTIONS

KUBOTA 16.5HP
KUBOTA 21HP
KUBOTA D600B 16.5HP
KUBOTA WG600B 21HP

SERIAL NUMBERS

YEAR	BEGINNING NO.
1989	1207
1990	1741
1991	2511
1992	2746
1993	3478
1994	3907
1995	4473
1996	5154

RETAIL PRICING

YEAR	HIGH	LOW
1989	$642	$482
1990	$710	$533
1991	$791	$593
1992	$877	$658
1993	$971	$728
1994	$1,078	$808
1995	$1,193	$895
1996	$1,326	$994

425

YEARS MFRD 1989-1996
ENGINE . . . . ONAN
ENGINE HP 24
FUEL . . . . G
TRANSMISSION . . . . HYDRO
STEERING . . . . STANDARD
DRIVE TYPE 4WD
ROPS/CAB . . . . ROPS
MSRP $11,295

OPTIONS

KUBOTA 21.5HP DIESEL
KUBOTA D950B 21.5HP DSL
ONAN P224 24HP GAS

SERIAL NUMBERS

YEAR	BEGINNING NO.
1989	1147
1990	1515
1991	1642
1992	3002
1993	3070
1994	3099

RETAIL PRICING

YEAR	HIGH	LOW
1989	$3,186	$2,390
1990	$3,259	$2,444
1991	$3,476	$2,607
1992	$3,620	$2,715
1993	$3,801	$2,851
1994	$4,015	$3,011
1995	$4,206	$3,154
1996	$4,356	$3,267

430

YEARS MFRD 1997-2003
ENGINE . . . . KOHLER WG752
ENGINE HP 27
COOLING . . . . LIQUID
FUEL . . . . G
TRANSMISSION . . . . HYDRO
STEERING . . . . ZERO
DRIVE TYPE 4WD
ROPS/CAB . . . . ROPS
STANDARD DECK . . . . 60"
MSRP $13,845

OPTIONS

KUBOTA 25HP DIESEL
ONAN 20HP

RETAIL PRICING

YEAR	HIGH	LOW
1997	$1,833	$1,375
1998	$2,032	$1,524
1999	$2,255	$1,691
2000	$2,501	$1,875
2001	$2,774	$2,081
2002	$3,080	$2,310
2003	$3,495	$2,621

430-21D

YEARS MFRD 2008-2012
ENGINE . . . . KUBOTA D722
ENGINE HP 21
COOLING . . . . LIQUID
FUEL . . . . D
SPEEDS . . . . VARIABLE

TRANSMISSION . . . . HYDRO
STEERING. . . . . STANDARD
WEIGHT . . . . .1,000 LBS.

430-25G

YEARS MFRD 2008-2012
ENGINE . . . . KUBOTA WG750
ENGINE HP 25
COOLING . . . . LIQUID
FUEL . . . . G
SPEEDS . . . . VARIABLE
TRANSMISSION . . . . HYDRO
STEERING. . . . . STANDARD
WEIGHT . . . . .1,100 LBS.

430-33G

YEARS MFRD 2008-2012
ENGINE . . . . GENERAC
CYLINDERS. 2
ENGINE HP 33
COOLING . . . . AIR
FUEL . . . . G
SPEEDS . . . . VARIABLE
TRANSMISSION . . . . HYDRO
STEERING. . . . . STANDARD
WEIGHT . . . . .1,000 LBS.

440 75-72010

YEARS MFRD 2012-2017
ENGINE . . . . KUBOTA D902
CYLINDERS. 3
CID 54.8
ENGINE HP 25
COOLING . . . . AIR
FUEL . . . . D
SPEEDS . . . . VARIABLE
TRANSMISSION . . . . HYDRO
STEERING. . . . . STANDARD
BLADE CLUTCH . . . . ELECTRIC
DRIVE TYPE 4WD
ROPS/CAB . . . . ROPS
WEIGHT . . . . .1,517 LBS.
MSRP. $21,000

RETAIL PRICING

YEAR	HIGH	LOW
2012	$8,358	$6,269
2013	$9,891	$7,418
2014	$11,595	$8,697
2015	$12,953	$9,715
2016	$15,556	$11,667
2017	$16,478	$12,359

440 75-72011

YEARS MFRD 2012-2017
ENGINE . . . . KUBOTA WG972
CYLINDERS. 3
CID 58.7
ENGINE HP 32
COOLING . . . . LIQUID
FUEL . . . . G
SPEEDS . . . . VARIABLE
TRANSMISSION . . . . HYDRO
STEERING. . . . . STANDARD
DRIVE TYPE 4WD
ROPS/CAB . . . . ROPS
WEIGHT . . . . .1,517 LBS.
MSRP. $21,900

RETAIL PRICING

YEAR	HIGH	LOW
2012	$17,985	$13,489
2013	$10,363	$7,772
2014	$12,140	$9,105
2015	$13,121	$9,841
2016	$15,657	$11,743
2017	$16,578	$12,434

440 75-72012

YEARS MFRD 2012-2017
ENGINE . . KOHLER COMMAND PRO CH904
CYLINDERS. 2
CID 61
ENGINE HP 34
COOLING . . . . AIR
FUEL . . . . G
SPEEDS . . . . VARIABLE
TRANSMISSION . . . . HYDRO
STEERING. . . . . STANDARD
BLADE CLUTCH . . . . ELECTRIC
DRIVE TYPE 4WD
ROPS/CAB . . . . ROPS
WEIGHT . . . . .1,489 LBS.
MSRP. $18,300

RETAIL PRICING

YEAR	HIGH	LOW
2012	$7,158	$5,368
2013	$8,488	$6,366
2014	$9,973	$7,479
2015	$11,128	$8,346
2016	$13,555	$10,166
2017	$14,476	$10,857

440 75-72013

YEARS MFRD 2012-2017
ENGINE . . KOHLER COMMAND PRO CH1000
CYLINDERS. 2
CID 61
ENGINE HP 40
COOLING . . . . AIR
FUEL . . . . G
SPEEDS . . . . VARIABLE
TRANSMISSION . . . . HYDRO
STEERING. . . . . STANDARD
DRIVE TYPE 4WD
ROPS/CAB . . . . ROPS
WEIGHT . . . . .1,489 LBS.
MSRP. $18,800

RETAIL PRICING

YEAR	HIGH	LOW
2012	$7,468	$5,601
2013	$8,746	$6,560
2014	$10,272	$7,704
2015	$10,954	$8,216
2016	$13,726	$10,295
2017	$14,649	$10,987

450 75-75025

YEARS MFRD 2017-2020
ENGINE . . . . KUBOTA D902
CYLINDERS. 3
CID 898CC
ENGINE HP 25
COOLING . . . . LIQUID
FUEL . . . . D
SPEEDS . . . . VARIABLE
STEERING. . . . . STANDARD
ROPS/CAB . . . . ROPS
WEIGHT . . . . .1,665 LBS.
MSRP. $23,540

450 75-75032

YEARS MFRD 2017-2020
ENGINE . . . . KUBOTA WG972
CYLINDERS. 3
CID 962CC
ENGINE HP 32.5
COOLING . . . . LIQUID
FUEL . . . . G
STEERING. . . . . STANDARD
ROPS/CAB . . . . ROPS
WEIGHT . . . . .1,660 LBS.
MSRP. $23,820

450 75-75037

YEARS MFRD 2017-2020
ENGINE . . B&S VANGUARD M61 EFI
CYLINDERS. 2
CID 993CC
ENGINE HP 37
COOLING . . . . AIR
FUEL . . . . G
STEERING. . . . . STANDARD
ROPS/CAB . . . . ROPS
WEIGHT . . . . .1,575 LBS.
MSRP. $21,420

450DX 75-75125FT

YEARS MFRD 2019-2020
SERIES. . . . . 450DX SERIES
ENGINE . . . . VANGUARD M54
ENGINE HP 25
COOLING . . . . AIR
FUEL . . . . G
SPEEDS . . . . VARIABLE
STEERING. . . . . STANDARD
DRIVE TYPE 4WD
ROPS/CAB . . . . ROPS
WEIGHT . . . . .1,531 LBS.
MSRP. $18,758

523

YEARS MFRD 1992-1996
ENGINE . . . . KUBOTA
ENGINE HP 23
FUEL . . . . D
SPEEDS . . . . VARIABLE
TRANSMISSION . . . . HYDRO
WEIGHT . . . . .1,800 LBS.
MSRP. $18,895

SERIAL NUMBERS

YEAR	BEGINNING NO.
1992	1001
1993	1021

RETAIL PRICING

YEAR	HIGH	LOW
1992	$6,089	$4,567
1993	$6,279	$4,709
1994	$6,706	$5,029
1995	$6,962	$5,221
1996	$7,290	$5,467

525

YEARS MFRD 1994-2003
ENGINE . . . . KUBOTA D1105
ENGINE HP 28
COOLING . . . . LIQUID
FUEL . . . . D
SPEEDS . . . . VARIABLE
TRANSMISSION . . . . HYDRO
STEERING. . . . . STANDARD
STANDARD DECK . . . . 72"
WEIGHT . . . . .1,520 LBS.
MSRP. $21,145

RETAIL PRICING

YEAR	HIGH	LOW
1995	$2,275	$1,706
1996	$2,523	$1,892
1997	$2,799	$2,100
1998	$3,106	$2,329
1999	$3,444	$2,583
2000	$3,819	$2,864
2001	$4,240	$3,180
2002	$4,700	$3,525
2003	$5,214	$3,910

720

YEARS MFRD 1989-1991
SERIES. . . . . . MOWPACKER SERIES
ENGINE . . . . KUBOTA
ENGINE HP 21
FUEL . . . . G
TRANSMISSION . . . . HYDRO
STEERING. . . . . STANDARD
WEIGHT . . . . .1,620 LBS.
MSRP. $11,995

RETAIL PRICING

YEAR	HIGH	LOW
1990	$3,436	$2,577
1991	$3,794	$2,845

442211

YEARS MFRD 2004-2005
SERIES. . . . . ZTM 200 SERIES
ENGINE . . . . B&S
ENGINE HP 18
COOLING . . . . AIR
FUEL . . . . G
SPEEDS . . . . VARIABLE
TRANSMISSION . . . . HYDRO
STEERING. . . . . ZERO
STANDARD DECK . . . . 52"
MSRP. $7,728

RETAIL PRICING		
YEAR	HIGH	LOW
2004	$4,187	$3,141
2005	$4,765	$3,573

442212

YEARS MFRD 2004-2005
SERIES. . . . . ZTM 200 SERIES
ENGINE . . . . B&S 226C INTEK
CYLINDERS. 2
ENGINE HP 26
COOLING . . . . AIR
FUEL . . . . G
SPEEDS . . . . VARIABLE
TRANSMISSION . . . . HYDRO
STEERING. . . . . ZERO
STANDARD DECK . . . . 61"
MSRP. $8,471

RETAIL PRICING		
YEAR	HIGH	LOW
2004	$4,650	$3,488
2005	$5,225	$3,919

442214

YEARS MFRD 2005-2005
SERIES. . . . . ZTM 200 SERIES
ENGINE . . . . B&S
CYLINDERS. 2
ENGINE HP 20
COOLING . . . . AIR
FUEL . . . . G
SPEEDS . . . . VARIABLE
TRANSMISSION . . . . HYDRO
STEERING. . . . . ZERO
BLADE CLUTCH . . . . ELECTRIC

442221

YEARS MFRD 2004-2005
SERIES. . . . . ZTM 200 SERIES
ENGINE . . . . KAWASAKI
ENGINE HP 19
COOLING . . . . AIR
FUEL . . . . G
SPEEDS . . . . VARIABLE
TRANSMISSION . . . . HYDRO
STEERING. . . . . ZERO
STANDARD DECK . . . . 52"
MSRP. $8,359

RETAIL PRICING		
YEAR	HIGH	LOW
2004	$4,650	$3,488
2005	$5,157	$3,867

442233

YEARS MFRD 2004-2005
SERIES. . . . . ZTM 200 SERIES
ENGINE . . . . KAWASAKI
ENGINE HP 25
COOLING . . . . AIR
FUEL . . . . G
SPEEDS . . . . VARIABLE
TRANSMISSION . . . . HYDRO
STEERING. . . . . ZERO
STANDARD DECK . . . . 61"
MSRP. $10,264

RETAIL PRICING		
YEAR	HIGH	LOW
2004	$5,684	$4,263
2005	$6,332	$4,749

442237

YEARS MFRD 2005-2005
SERIES. . . . . ZTM 200 SERIES
ENGINE . . . . KOHLER
CYLINDERS. 2
ENGINE HP 27
COOLING . . . . AIR
FUEL . . . . G
SPEEDS . . . . VARIABLE
TRANSMISSION . . . . HYDRO
STEERING. . . . . ZERO
STANDARD DECK . . . . 61"
MSRP. $9,873

RETAIL PRICING		
YEAR	HIGH	LOW
2005	$6,091	$4,568

442280

YEARS MFRD 2004-2005
SERIES. . . . . ZTM 200 SERIES
ENGINE . . . . B&S
ENGINE HP 17.5
COOLING . . . . AIR
FUEL . . . . G
SPEEDS . . . . VARIABLE
TRANSMISSION . . . . HYDRO
STEERING. . . . . ZERO
STANDARD DECK . . . . 48"
MSRP. $5,192

RETAIL PRICING		
YEAR	HIGH	LOW
2004	$2,907	$2,180
2005	$3,204	$2,403

442281

YEARS MFRD 2004-2005
SERIES. . . . . ZTM 200 SERIES
ENGINE . . . . B&S
CYLINDERS. 2
ENGINE HP 18
COOLING . . . . AIR
FUEL . . . . G
SPEEDS . . . . VARIABLE
TRANSMISSION . . . . HYDRO
STEERING. . . . . ZERO
STANDARD DECK . . . . 52"
MSRP. $5,711

RETAIL PRICING		
YEAR	HIGH	LOW
2004	$3,198	$2,399
2005	$3,524	$2,643

442282

YEARS MFRD 2004-2005
SERIES. . . . . ZTM 200 SERIES
ENGINE . . . . B&S
CYLINDERS. 2
ENGINE HP 25
COOLING . . . . AIR
FUEL . . . . G
SPEEDS . . . . VARIABLE
TRANSMISSION . . . . HYDRO
STEERING. . . . . ZERO
STANDARD DECK . . . . 52"
MSRP. $6,023

RETAIL PRICING		
YEAR	HIGH	LOW
2004	$3,372	$2,529
2005	$3,715	$2,786

442283

YEARS MFRD 2005-2005
SERIES. . . . . ZTM 200 SERIES
ENGINE . . . . B&S
CYLINDERS. 1
ENGINE HP 17.5
COOLING . . . . AIR
FUEL . . . . G
SPEEDS . . . . VARIABLE
TRANSMISSION . . . . HYDRO
STEERING. . . . . ZERO
BLADE CLUTCH . . . . ELECTRIC
STANDARD DECK . . . . 48"
MSRP. $5,195

RETAIL PRICING		
YEAR	HIGH	LOW
2005	$3,205	$2,404

442285

YEARS MFRD 2005-2005
SERIES. . . . . ZTM 200 SERIES
ENGINE . . . . B&S
CYLINDERS. 2
ENGINE HP 25
COOLING . . . . AIR
FUEL . . . . G
SPEEDS . . . . VARIABLE
TRANSMISSION . . . . HYDRO
STEERING. . . . . ZERO
STANDARD DECK . . . . 52"
MSRP. $6,029

RETAIL PRICING		
YEAR	HIGH	LOW
2005	$3,718	$2,789

442286

YEARS MFRD 2005-2005
SERIES. . . . . ZTM 200 SERIES
ENGINE . . . . B&S
CYLINDERS. 2
ENGINE HP 20
COOLING . . . . AIR
FUEL . . . . G
SPEEDS . . . . VARIABLE
TRANSMISSION . . . . HYDRO
STEERING. . . . . ZERO
BLADE CLUTCH . . . . ELECTRIC
STANDARD DECK . . . . 52"
MSRP. $5,710

RETAIL PRICING		
YEAR	HIGH	LOW
2005	$3,524	$2,643

SWISHER

Z2460CPKA

YEARS MFRD 2017-2019
ENGINE . . . . KAWASAKI
CID 726CC
ENGINE HP 24
FUEL . . . . G
SPEEDS . . . . VARIABLE
TRANSMISSION . . . . HYDRO
STEERING. . . . . ZERO
BLADE CLUTCH . . . . ELECTRIC
STANDARD DECK . . . . 60"
MSRP. $7,299

Z2466CPKA

YEARS MFRD 2017-2019
ENGINE . . . . KAWASAKI
CID 726CC
ENGINE HP 24
FUEL . . . . G
SPEEDS . . . . VARIABLE
TRANSMISSION . . . . HYDRO
STEERING. . . . . ZERO
BLADE CLUTCH . . . . ELECTRIC
STANDARD DECK . . . . 66"
MSRP. $7,799

Z3151CPKA

YEARS MFRD 2019-2020
SERIES. . . . . BIG MOW SERIES
ENGINE . . . . KAWASAKI
CID 9999
ENGINE HP 31
FUEL . . . . G
TRANSMISSION . . . . HYDRO
STEERING. . . . . ZERO
ROPS/CAB . . . . ROPS
STANDARD DECK . . . . 51"
MSRP. $13,399

Z3166CPKA

YEARS MFRD 2017-2020
ENGINE . . . . KAWASAKI
CID 999CC
ENGINE HP 31
FUEL . . . . G
SPEEDS . . . . VARIABLE
TRANSMISSION . . . . HYDRO
STEERING. . . . . ZERO
BLADE CLUTCH . . . . ELECTRIC
STANDARD DECK . . . . 66"
MSRP. $13,399

Z21554CPHO

YEARS MFRD 2017-2019
ENGINE . . . . HONDA
CID 688CC
ENGINE HP 21.5

SWISHER

FUEL	G
SPEEDS	VARIABLE
TRANSMISSION	HYDRO
STEERING	ZERO
BLADE CLUTCH	ELECTRIC
STANDARD DECK	54"
MSRP	$5,019

Z21560CPHO

YEARS MFRD	2017-2019
ENGINE	HONDA
CID	688CC
ENGINE HP	21.5
FUEL	G
SPEEDS	VARIABLE
TRANSMISSION	HYDRO
STEERING	ZERO
BLADE CLUTCH	ELECTRIC
STANDARD DECK	60"
MSRP	$7,499

Z-MAX

YEARS MFRD	2008-2008
ENGINE	B&S
CYLINDERS	2
ENGINE HP	26
COOLING	AIR
FUEL	G
SPEEDS	VARIABLE
TRANSMISSION	HYDRO
STEERING	ZERO
BLADE CLUTCH	ELECTRIC
WEIGHT	910 LBS.

Z-MAX XZT60

YEARS MFRD	2005-2006
ENGINE	B&S
CYLINDERS	2
ENGINE HP	24
COOLING	AIR
FUEL	G
SPEEDS	VARIABLE
TRANSMISSION	HYDRO
STEERING	ZERO
STANDARD DECK	60"
MSRP	$3,999

RETAIL PRICING

YEAR	HIGH	LOW
2005	$2,416	$1,812
2006	$2,619	$1,964

ZT1436

YEARS MFRD	2003-2003
ENGINE	B&S INTEK
ENGINE HP	14.5
COOLING	AIR
FUEL	G
SPEEDS	VARIABLE
TRANSMISSION	HYDRO
STEERING	ZERO
STANDARD DECK	36"
MSRP	$2,699

RETAIL PRICING

YEAR	HIGH	LOW
2003	$629	$471

ZT2052

YEARS MFRD	2007-2008
SERIES	RIDE KING
ENGINE	B&S
CYLINDERS	2
ENGINE HP	20
COOLING	AIR
FUEL	G
SPEEDS	VARIABLE
TRANSMISSION	HYDRO
STEERING	ZERO
BLADE CLUTCH	ELECTRIC
STANDARD DECK	52"
WEIGHT	875 LBS.
MSRP	$2,999

RETAIL PRICING

YEAR	HIGH	LOW
2007	$1,667	$1,251
2008	$1,823	$1,367

ZT2250

YEARS MFRD	2005-2006
ENGINE	B&S
ENGINE HP	22
COOLING	AIR
FUEL	G
SPEEDS	VARIABLE
TRANSMISSION	HYDRO
STEERING	ZERO
STANDARD DECK	50"
MSRP	$3,599

RETAIL PRICING

YEAR	HIGH	LOW
2005	$2,176	$1,632
2006	$2,378	$1,784

ZT2350A

YEARS MFRD	2007-2008
SERIES	ZT SERIES
ENGINE	B&S
CYLINDERS	2
ENGINE HP	23
COOLING	AIR
FUEL	G
SPEEDS	VARIABLE
TRANSMISSION	HYDRO
STEERING	ZERO
BLADE CLUTCH	ELECTRIC
STANDARD DECK	50"
WEIGHT	875 LBS.
MSRP	$3,199

RETAIL PRICING

YEAR	HIGH	LOW
2007	$1,780	$1,335
2008	$1,943	$1,457

ZT2450A

YEARS MFRD	2009-2012
ENGINE	B&S ELS
CYLINDERS	2
ENGINE HP	24
COOLING	AIR
FUEL	G
SPEEDS	VARIABLE
TRANSMISSION	HYDRO
STEERING	ZERO
BLADE CLUTCH	ELECTRIC
STANDARD DECK	50"
WEIGHT	875 LBS.
MSRP	$3,733

RETAIL PRICING

YEAR	HIGH	LOW
2009	$841	$631
2010	$1,040	$780
2011	$1,242	$931
2012	$1,751	$1,313

ZT2452

YEARS MFRD	2010-2012
SERIES	RIDE KING SERIES
ENGINE	B&S ELS
CYLINDERS	2
ENGINE HP	24
COOLING	AIR
FUEL	G
SPEEDS	VARIABLE
TRANSMISSION	HYDRO
STEERING	ZERO
BLADE CLUTCH	ELECTRIC
STANDARD DECK	52"
WEIGHT	860 LBS.
MSRP	$3,789

RETAIL PRICING

YEAR	HIGH	LOW
2010	$1,075	$806
2011	$1,281	$961
2012	$1,971	$1,478

ZT2454

YEARS MFRD	2009-2011
ENGINE	B&S ELS
CYLINDERS	2
ENGINE HP	24
COOLING	AIR
FUEL	G
SPEEDS	VARIABLE
TRANSMISSION	HYDRO
STEERING	ZERO
BLADE CLUTCH	ELECTRIC
WEIGHT	900 LBS.

ZT2460

YEARS MFRD	2005-2006
ENGINE	B&S INTEK
ENGINE HP	24
COOLING	AIR
FUEL	G
SPEEDS	VARIABLE
TRANSMISSION	HYDRO
STEERING	ZERO
BLADE CLUTCH	ELECTRIC
STANDARD DECK	60"
MSRP	$3,999

RETAIL PRICING

YEAR	HIGH	LOW
2005	$2,416	$1,812
2006	$2,619	$1,964

ZT2560

YEARS MFRD	2007-2007
SERIES	ZT SERIES
ENGINE	B&S
CYLINDERS	2
ENGINE HP	25
COOLING	AIR
FUEL	G
SPEEDS	VARIABLE
TRANSMISSION	HYDRO
STEERING	ZERO
BLADE CLUTCH	ELECTRIC
STANDARD DECK	60"
WEIGHT	910 LBS.
MSRP	$4,099

RETAIL PRICING

YEAR	HIGH	LOW
2007	$2,280	$1,710

ZT2660B

YEARS MFRD	2009-2012
SERIES	Z MAX SERIES
ENGINE	B&G ELS
CYLINDERS	2
ENGINE HP	26
COOLING	AIR
FUEL	G
SPEEDS	VARIABLE
TRANSMISSION	HYDRO
STEERING	ZERO
BLADE CLUTCH	ELECTRIC
STANDARD DECK	60"
WEIGHT	900 LBS.
MSRP	$4,660

RETAIL PRICING

YEAR	HIGH	LOW
2009	$1,103	$827
2010	$1,365	$1,024
2011	$1,833	$1,375
2012	$2,495	$1,871

ZT2760

YEARS MFRD	2010-2012
ENGINE	B&S
ENGINE HP	27
COOLING	AIR
FUEL	G
SPEEDS	VARIABLE
TRANSMISSION	HYDRO
STEERING	ZERO
STANDARD DECK	60"
MSRP	$4,899

RETAIL PRICING

YEAR	HIGH	LOW
2010	$1,434	$1,075
2011	$1,916	$1,437
2012	$2,626	$1,969

ZT2766

YEARS MFRD	2006-2012
ENGINE	B&S ELS
CYLINDERS	2
ENGINE HP	27
COOLING	AIR

FUEL ... G
SPEEDS ... VARIABLE
TRANSMISSION ... HYDRO
STEERING ... ZERO
BLADE CLUTCH ... ELECTRIC
STANDARD DECK ... 66"
WEIGHT ... 950 LBS.
MSRP ... $5,266

RETAIL PRICING

YEAR	HIGH	LOW
2006	$917	$687
2007	$1,013	$760
2008	$1,173	$880
2009	$1,303	$977
2010	$1,613	$1,210
2011	$2,060	$1,545
2012	$2,750	$2,062

ZT2766KP

YEARS MFRD ... 2009-2012
ENGINE ... KOHLER COURAGE
CYLINDERS ... 2
ENGINE HP ... 27
COOLING ... AIR
FUEL ... G
SPEEDS ... VARIABLE
TRANSMISSION ... HYDRO
STEERING ... ZERO
BLADE CLUTCH ... ELECTRIC
STANDARD DECK ... 66"
WEIGHT ... 1,010 LBS.
MSRP ... $6,266

RETAIL PRICING

YEAR	HIGH	LOW
2009	$1,709	$1,282
2010	$2,048	$1,536
2011	$2,730	$2,047
2012	$3,438	$2,578

ZT18542

YEARS MFRD ... 2005-2008
ENGINE ... B&S INTEK OHV
ENGINE HP ... 18.5
COOLING ... AIR
FUEL ... G
SPEEDS ... VARIABLE
TRANSMISSION ... HYDRO
STEERING ... ZERO
STANDARD DECK ... 42"
WEIGHT ... 680 LBS.
MSRP ... $2,799

RETAIL PRICING

YEAR	HIGH	LOW
2005	$1,546	$1,160
2006	$1,588	$1,191
2007	$1,689	$1,267
2008	$1,856	$1,392

ZT18542A

YEARS MFRD ... 2010-2011
ENGINE ... B&S
CYLINDERS ... 1
ENGINE HP ... 18.5
COOLING ... AIR
FUEL ... G
SPEEDS ... VARIABLE
TRANSMISSION ... HYDRO
STEERING ... ZERO
BLADE CLUTCH ... ELECTRIC
STANDARD DECK ... 42"
MSRP ... $2,799

RETAIL PRICING

YEAR	HIGH	LOW
2010	$1,408	$1,056
2011	$1,582	$1,187

ZTR2354KA

YEARS MFRD ... 2017-2018
ENGINE ... KAWASAKI
CID ... 726CC
ENGINE HP ... 23
FUEL ... G
SPEEDS ... VARIABLE
TRANSMISSION ... HYDRO
STEERING ... ZERO
BLADE CLUTCH ... ELECTRIC
STANDARD DECK ... 54"
MSRP ... $6,199

RETAIL PRICING

YEAR	HIGH	LOW
2017	$4,951	$3,713
2018	$5,437	$4,078

ZTR2360KA

YEARS MFRD ... 2017-2019
ENGINE ... KAWASAKI
CID ... 726CC
ENGINE HP ... 23
FUEL ... G
SPEEDS ... VARIABLE
TRANSMISSION ... HYDRO
STEERING ... ZERO
BLADE CLUTCH ... ELECTRIC
STANDARD DECK ... 60"

RETAIL PRICING

YEAR	HIGH	LOW
2017	$5,051	$3,788

ZTR2366KA

YEARS MFRD ... 2017-2019
ENGINE ... KAWASAKI
CID ... 726CC
ENGINE HP ... 23
FUEL ... G
SPEEDS ... VARIABLE
TRANSMISSION ... HYDRO
STEERING ... ZERO
BLADE CLUTCH ... ELECTRIC
STANDARD DECK ... 66"

RETAIL PRICING

YEAR	HIGH	LOW
2017	$5,073	$3,805

ZTR2454BS

YEARS MFRD ... 2013-2019
ENGINE ... B&S
CYLINDERS ... 2
ENGINE HP ... 24
COOLING ... AIR
FUEL ... G
SPEEDS ... VARIABLE
TRANSMISSION ... HYDRO
STEERING ... ZERO
STANDARD DECK ... 54"

RETAIL PRICING

YEAR	HIGH	LOW
2013	$1,782	$1,336
2014	$2,553	$1,915
2015	$3,238	$2,428
2016	$3,780	$2,835
2017	$4,151	$3,113

ZTR2454KA

YEARS MFRD ... 2013-2016
ENGINE ... KAWASAKI
CYLINDERS ... 2
ENGINE HP ... 24
COOLING ... AIR
FUEL ... G
SPEEDS ... VARIABLE
TRANSMISSION ... HYDRO
STEERING ... ZERO
STANDARD DECK ... 54"
MSRP ... $5,899

RETAIL PRICING

YEAR	HIGH	LOW
2013	$2,043	$1,532
2014	$2,976	$2,232
2015	$3,770	$2,828
2016	$4,324	$3,243

ZTR2460BS

YEARS MFRD ... 2013-2014
ENGINE ... B&S
CYLINDERS ... 2
ENGINE HP ... 24
COOLING ... AIR
FUEL ... G
SPEEDS ... VARIABLE
TRANSMISSION ... HYDRO
STEERING ... ZERO
STANDARD DECK ... 60"
MSRP ... $5,299

RETAIL PRICING

YEAR	HIGH	LOW
2013	$2,161	$1,621
2014	$2,945	$2,209

ZTR2460KA

YEARS MFRD ... 2013-2016
ENGINE ... KAWASAKI
CYLINDERS ... 2
ENGINE HP ... 24
COOLING ... AIR
FUEL ... G
SPEEDS ... VARIABLE
TRANSMISSION ... HYDRO
STEERING ... ZERO
STANDARD DECK ... 60"
MSRP ... $6,149

RETAIL PRICING

YEAR	HIGH	LOW
2013	$2,375	$1,781
2014	$2,815	$2,111
2015	$3,508	$2,631
2016	$4,439	$3,329

ZTR2760B

YEARS MFRD ... 2013-2014
ENGINE ... B&S
ENGINE HP ... 27
COOLING ... AIR
FUEL ... G
SPEEDS ... VARIABLE
TRANSMISSION ... HYDRO
STEERING ... ZERO
STANDARD DECK ... 60"
MSRP ... $4,999

RETAIL PRICING

YEAR	HIGH	LOW
2013	$2,205	$1,654
2014	$2,954	$2,215

ZTR2760BS

YEARS MFRD ... 2013-2016
ENGINE ... B&S
CYLINDERS ... 2
ENGINE HP ... 27
COOLING ... AIR
FUEL ... G
SPEEDS ... VARIABLE
TRANSMISSION ... HYDRO
STEERING ... ZERO
STANDARD DECK ... 60"
MSRP ... $6,199

RETAIL PRICING

YEAR	HIGH	LOW
2013	$2,198	$1,649
2014	$2,991	$2,244
2015	$3,732	$2,799
2016	$4,478	$3,358

ZTR2766BS

YEARS MFRD ... 2016-2016
ENGINE ... B&S
ENGINE HP ... 27
COOLING ... AIR
FUEL ... G
SPEEDS ... VARIABLE
TRANSMISSION ... HYDRO
STEERING ... ZERO
BLADE CLUTCH ... ELECTRIC
STANDARD DECK ... 66"
MSRP ... $6,599

RETAIL PRICING

YEAR	HIGH	LOW
2016	$5,260	$3,945

ZTR2766CP

YEARS MFRD ... 2016-2016
ENGINE ... B&S
ENGINE HP ... 27
COOLING ... AIR
FUEL ... G
SPEEDS ... VARIABLE
TRANSMISSION ... HYDRO
STEERING ... ZERO
BLADE CLUTCH ... ELECTRIC
STANDARD DECK ... 66"
MSRP ... $7,399

SWISHER

RETAIL PRICING

YEAR	HIGH	LOW
2016	$5,617	$4,213

ZTR2866BM

YEARS MFRD 2016-2017
ENGINE . . . . B&S
ENGINE HP 28
COOLING . . . . AIR
FUEL . . . . G
SPEEDS . . . . VARIABLE
TRANSMISSION . . . . HYDRO
STEERING. . . . . ZERO
BLADE CLUTCH . . . . ELECTRIC
STANDARD DECK . . . . 66"
MSRP. $12,249

RETAIL PRICING

YEAR	HIGH	LOW
2016	$8,183	$6,137
2017	$10,004	$7,503

ZTR2866BS

YEARS MFRD 2013-2015
ENGINE . . . . B&S
CYLINDERS. 2
ENGINE HP 28
COOLING . . . . AIR
FUEL . . . . G
SPEEDS . . . . VARIABLE
TRANSMISSION . . . . HYDRO
STEERING. . . . . ZERO
STANDARD DECK . . . . 66"
MSRP. $6,599

RETAIL PRICING

YEAR	HIGH	LOW
2013	$1,887	$1,415
2014	$3,323	$2,492
2015	$4,056	$3,042

ZTR3166KA

YEARS MFRD 2015-2015
ENGINE . . . . KAWASAKI
ENGINE HP 31
FUEL . . . . G
SPEEDS . . . . VARIABLE
TRANSMISSION . . . . HYDRO
STEERING. . . . . ZERO
STANDARD DECK . . . . 66"
MSRP. $12,499

RETAIL PRICING

YEAR	HIGH	LOW
2015	$7,319	$5,489

TORO

ALL MODELS

YEARS MFRD 1994-2016

SERIAL NUMBERS

FIRST NUMBER OF SERIAL NUMBER INDICATES YEAR OF MANUFACTURE.

YEAR	BEGINNING NO.
1994	4
1995	5
1996	6
1997	7
1998	8
1999	9
2000	20
2001	21
2002	22
2003	23
2004	24
2005	25
2006	26
2007	27
2008	28
2009	29
2010	30
2011	31
2012	32
2013	33
2014	34
2015	35
2016	36

GM120

YEARS MFRD 1994-2004
SERIES . . GROUNDSMASTER SERIES
ENGINE . . . . KOHLER
ENGINE HP 20
COOLING . . . . AIR
FUEL . . . . G
TRANSMISSION . . . . HYDRO
STEERING. . . . . ZERO
STANDARD DECK . . . . 44"
MSRP. $9,355

OPTIONS

52" DECK
BAGGER
SNOW THROWER

RETAIL PRICING

YEAR	HIGH	LOW
1996	$1,132	$849
1997	$1,258	$943
1998	$1,395	$1,046
1999	$1,545	$1,159
2000	$1,716	$1,287
2001	$1,901	$1,426
2002	$2,111	$1,583
2003	$2,341	$1,755
2004	$2,597	$1,948

GM220

YEARS MFRD 1992-1997
SERIES . . GROUNDSMASTER SERIES
ENGINE . . . . ONAN
ENGINE HP 20
COOLING . . . . AIR
FUEL . . . . G
TRANSMISSION . . . . HYDRO
STEERING. . . . . ZERO
STANDARD DECK . . . . 52"
MSRP. $10,779

OPTIONS

62" DECK

RETAIL PRICING

YEAR	HIGH	LOW
1992	$870	$652
1993	$965	$724
1994	$1,067	$800
1995	$1,186	$889
1996	$1,316	$987
1997	$1,460	$1,095

GM223D

YEARS MFRD 1996-1998
SERIES . . GROUNDSMASTER SERIES
ENGINE . . . . MITSUBISHI
CID 58.09
ENGINE HP 23
COOLING . . . . LIQUID
FUEL . . . . D
SPEEDS . . . . VARIABLE
TRANSMISSION . . . . HYDRO
STEERING. . . . . ZERO
STANDARD DECK . . . . 52"
WEIGHT . . . . 1,120 LBS.
MSRP. $16,078

OPTIONS

4WD
62" DECK
72" DECK
BAGGER

RETAIL PRICING

YEAR	HIGH	LOW
1996	$1,924	$1,443
1997	$2,136	$1,602
1998	$2,369	$1,777

GM224

YEARS MFRD 1996-1998
SERIES . . GROUNDSMASTER SERIES
ENGINE . . . . MITSUBISHI
ENGINE HP 24
COOLING . . . . LIQUID
FUEL . . . . G
TRANSMISSION . . . . HYDRO
STEERING. . . . . ZERO
DRIVE TYPE 2WD
ROPS/CAB . . . . ROPS
STANDARD DECK . . . . 52"
MSRP. $15,282

OPTIONS

62" DECK
72" DECK

RETAIL PRICING

YEAR	HIGH	LOW
1996	$1,830	$1,373
1997	$2,028	$1,521
1998	$2,253	$1,690

GM225

YEARS MFRD 2003-2003
SERIES . . GROUNDSMASTER SERIES
ENGINE . . . . B&S
ENGINE HP 24.9
COOLING . . . . LIQUID
FUEL . . . . G
TRANSMISSION . . . . HYDRO
STEERING. . . . . STANDARD
DRIVE TYPE 2WD
ROPS/CAB . . . . ROPS
WEIGHT . . . . 1,120 LBS.

OPTIONS

DAIHATSU 24HP

GM325D

YEARS MFRD 1996-1998
SERIES . . GROUNDSMASTER SERIES
ENGINE . . . . MITSUBISHI
CID 59.7
ENGINE HP 25
COOLING . . . . LIQUID
FUEL . . . . D
TRANSMISSION . . . . HYDRO
STEERING. . . . . ZERO
DRIVE TYPE 2WD
ROPS/CAB . . . . ROPS
STANDARD DECK . . . . 72"
WEIGHT . . . . 1,250 LBS.
MSRP. $19,126

OPTIONS

4WD

RETAIL PRICING

YEAR	HIGH	LOW
1996	$2,290	$1,717
1997	$2,543	$1,907
1998	$2,820	$2,115

GM345

YEARS MFRD 1996-1998
SERIES. . . . .
. . . . 300 GROUNDSMASTER SERIES
ENGINE . . . . FORD
CYLINDERS. 4
CID 79
ENGINE HP 45
COOLING . . . . LIQUID
FUEL . . . . G
SPEEDS . . . . VARIABLE
TRANSMISSION . . . . HYDRO
STEERING. . . . . ZERO
STANDARD DECK . . . . 72"
WEIGHT . . . . 1,300 LBS.
MSRP. $17,967

OPTIONS

SNOW BLOWER

RETAIL PRICING

YEAR	HIGH	LOW
1996	$2,150	$1,612
1997	$2,388	$1,791
1998	$2,648	$1,986

GM1000L

YEARS MFRD 1997-1998
SERIES . . GROUNDSMASTER SERIES
ENGINE . . . . KAWASAKI
ENGINE HP 20
COOLING . . . . LIQUID
FUEL . . . . G
TRANSMISSION . . . . HYDRO
STEERING. . . . . ZERO
STANDARD DECK . . . . 52"
MSRP. $12,563

OPTIONS

62" DECK
72" DECK

RETAIL PRICING

YEAR	HIGH	LOW
1997	$1,669	$1,251
1998	$1,851	$1,389

GM3000D

YEARS MFRD 2003-2003
SERIES. . . . .
. . . GROUNDSMASTER 3000 SERIES
ENGINE . . . . PEUGEOT
ENGINE HP 36
COOLING . . . . LIQUID
FUEL . . . . D
TRANSMISSION . . . . HYDRO
STEERING. . . . . STANDARD
DRIVE TYPE 2WD
ROPS/CAB . . . . ROPS
WEIGHT . . . . 1,895 LBS.

OPTIONS

4WD

GM3500D

YEARS MFRD 2003-2011
SERIES. . . . .
. . . GROUNDSMASTER 3500 SERIES
ENGINE . . . . KUBOTA
CYLINDERS. 3
ENGINE HP 35
COOLING . . . . LIQUID
FUEL . . . . D
SPEEDS . . . . VARIABLE
TRANSMISSION . . . . HYDRO
STEERING. . . . . ZERO
STANDARD DECK . . . . 68"
WEIGHT . . . . 2,200 LBS.
MSRP. $29,025

RETAIL PRICING

YEAR	HIGH	LOW
2003	$3,553	$2,664
2004	$3,570	$2,677
2005	$3,638	$2,728
2006	$5,606	$4,204
2007	$7,532	$5,649
2008	$9,167	$6,876
2009	$11,530	$8,648
2010	$13,495	$10,122
2011	$17,518	$13,138

AVG. AUCTION PRICING

LOW	HIGH	AVG
$1,827	$8,628	$4,403

TORO

GM3505D

YEARS MFRD 2005-2005
SERIES. . . . .
. . . GROUNDSMASTER 3500 SERIES
ENGINE . . . . KUBOTA
CYLINDERS. 3
CID 67.1
ENGINE HP 35
COOLING . . . . LIQUID
FUEL . . . . D
SPEEDS . . . . VARIABLE
TRANSMISSION . . . . HYDRO
STEERING. . . . . ZERO
WEIGHT . . . . 2,100 LBS.

GM4500D

YEARS MFRD 2004-2011
SERIES. . GROUNDSMASTER SERIES
ENGINE . . . . KUBOTA
CYLINDERS. 4
CID 122
ENGINE HP 60
COOLING . . . . LIQUID
FUEL . . . . D
SPEEDS . . . . VARIABLE
TRANSMISSION . . . . HYDRO
STEERING. . . . . ZERO
STANDARD DECK . . . . 109"
WEIGHT . . . . 4,273 LBS.
MSRP. $51,700

RETAIL PRICING

YEAR	HIGH	LOW
2004	$9,805	$7,354
2005	$10,147	$7,610
2006	$10,822	$8,116
2007	$12,776	$9,582
2008	$15,540	$11,655
2009	$20,477	$15,357
2010	$23,937	$17,953
2011	$31,206	$23,405

GM4700D

YEARS MFRD 2004-2009
SERIES. . GROUNDSMASTER SERIES
ENGINE . . . . KUBOTA
CYLINDERS. 4
CID 122
ENGINE HP 60
COOLING . . . . LIQUID
FUEL . . . . D
SPEEDS . . . . VARIABLE
TRANSMISSION . . . . HYDRO
STEERING. . . . . STANDARD
WEIGHT . . . . 4,824 LBS.
MSRP. $61,320

RETAIL PRICING

YEAR	HIGH	LOW
2005	$34,610	$25,958
2006	$35,681	$26,761
2007	$36,900	$27,675
2008	$37,778	$28,334
2009	$41,495	$31,121

GM5900

YEARS MFRD 2009-2011
SERIES. . GROUNDSMASTER SERIES
ENGINE . . . . CUMMINS
CYLINDERS. 4
ENGINE HP 99
COOLING . . . . LIQUID
FUEL . . . . D
SPEEDS . . . . VARIABLE
TRANSMISSION . . . . HYDRO
STEERING. . . . . ZERO
BLADE CLUTCH . . . . ELECTRIC

RETAIL PRICING

YEAR	HIGH	LOW
2009	$31,175	$23,381
2010	$36,416	$27,312

GM5910

YEARS MFRD 2009-2011
SERIES. . GROUNDSMASTER SERIES
ENGINE . . . . CUMMINS
CYLINDERS. 4
ENGINE HP 99
COOLING . . . . LIQUID
FUEL . . . . D
SPEEDS . . . . VARIABLE
TRANSMISSION . . . . HYDRO
STEERING. . . . . ZERO
BLADE CLUTCH . . . . ELECTRIC

RETAIL PRICING

YEAR	HIGH	LOW
2009	$32,404	$24,303
2010	$37,853	$28,390

GREENSMASTER 3150

YEARS MFRD 2007-2007
SERIES. . . . .
. . . RIDING GREENSMASTER SERIES
ENGINE . . . . B&S VANGUARD
ENGINE HP 18
FUEL . . . . G
SPEEDS . . . . VARIABLE
TRANSMISSION . . . . HYDRO
STEERING. . . . . ZERO
STANDARD DECK . . . . 59"
WEIGHT . . . . 970 LBS.
MSRP. $27,450

RETAIL PRICING

YEAR	HIGH	LOW
2007	$17,670	$13,253

GT410/416XT

YEARS MFRD 2007-2007
SERIES. . . . . 400XT SERIES
ENGINE . . KOHLER COMMAND OHV
ENGINE HP 16
FUEL . . . . G
SPEEDS . . . . VARIABLE
TRANSMISSION . . . . HYDRO
STEERING. . . . . STANDARD
BLADE CLUTCH . . . . ELECTRIC
STANDARD DECK . . . . 36"
MSRP. $3,819

RETAIL PRICING

YEAR	HIGH	LOW
2007	$2,458	$1,844

GT420/417XT

YEARS MFRD 2006-2007
SERIES. . . . . 400XT SERIES
ENGINE . . . . KAWASAKI
CYLINDERS. 2
ENGINE HP 17
COOLING . . . . AIR
FUEL . . . . G
SPEEDS . . . . VARIABLE
TRANSMISSION . . . . HYDRO
STEERING. . . . . STANDARD
BLADE CLUTCH . . . . ELECTRIC
MSRP. $5,539

RETAIL PRICING

YEAR	HIGH	LOW
2006	$2,949	$2,211
2007	$3,062	$2,297

GT430/419XT

YEARS MFRD 2006-2007
SERIES. . . . . 400XT SERIES
ENGINE . . . . KAWASAKI
CYLINDERS. 2
ENGINE HP 19
COOLING . . . . AIR
FUEL . . . . G
SPEEDS . . . . VARIABLE
TRANSMISSION . . . . HYDRO
STEERING. . . . . STANDARD
BLADE CLUTCH . . . . ELECTRIC
MSRP. $6,159

RETAIL PRICING

YEAR	HIGH	LOW
2006	$3,551	$2,664
2007	$4,019	$3,015

GT550/522XI

YEARS MFRD 2007-2007
SERIES. . . . . 5XI SERIES
ENGINE . . . . . KOHLER COMMAND
CYLINDERS. 2
ENGINE HP 22
FUEL . . . . G
SPEEDS . . . . VARIABLE
TRANSMISSION . . . . HYDRO
BLADE CLUTCH . . . . ELECTRIC
WEIGHT . . . . 1,022 LBS.
MSRP. $7,469

RETAIL PRICING

YEAR	HIGH	LOW
2007	$4,807	$3,605

GT2100

YEARS MFRD 2007-2008
SERIES. . . . . GT2000 SERIES
ENGINE . . . . KOHLER COURAGE
CYLINDERS. 2
ENGINE HP 23
FUEL . . . . G
SPEEDS . . . . VARIABLE
TRANSMISSION . . . . BELT
STEERING. . . . . STANDARD
BLADE CLUTCH . . . . ELECTRIC
STANDARD DECK . . . . 50"
WEIGHT . . . . 575 LBS.
MSRP. $2,499

RETAIL PRICING

YEAR	HIGH	LOW
2007	$1,609	$1,207
2008	$1,657	$1,243

GT2200

YEARS MFRD 2006-2015
SERIES. . . . . GT2000 SERIES
ENGINE . . . . KOHLER COURAGE
CYLINDERS. 2
ENGINE HP 25
COOLING . . . . AIR
FUEL . . . . G
SPEEDS . . . . VARIABLE
TRANSMISSION . . . . HYDRO
STEERING. . . . . STANDARD
BLADE CLUTCH . . . . ELECTRIC
STANDARD DECK . . . . 50"
WEIGHT . . . . 575 LBS.
MSRP. $3,099

RETAIL PRICING

YEAR	HIGH	LOW
2006	$594	$445
2007	$410	$308
2008	$688	$516
2009	$783	$587
2010	$901	$676
2011	$949	$712
2012	$1,099	$824
2013	$1,241	$931
2014	$1,526	$1,144
2015	$1,882	$1,411

GT2300

YEARS MFRD 2007-2007
SERIES. . . . . GT2000 SERIES
ENGINE . . . . KOHLER COURAGE
CYLINDERS. 2
ENGINE HP 26
FUEL . . . . G
SPEEDS . . . . VARIABLE
TRANSMISSION . . . . HYDRO
STEERING. . . . . STANDARD
BLADE CLUTCH . . . . ELECTRIC
STANDARD DECK . . . . 50"
WEIGHT . . . . 675 LBS.
MSRP. $3,299

RETAIL PRICING

YEAR	HIGH	LOW
2007	$2,123	$1,593

GT/315-8

YEARS MFRD 2006-2008
SERIES. . . . . 300 SERIES
ENGINE . . . . . . KOHLER COMMAND
ENGINE HP 15
COOLING . . . . AIR
FUEL . . . . G

SPEEDS . . . . VARIABLE
TRANSMISSION . . . . HYDRO
STEERING. . . . . STANDARD
WEIGHT . . . . 624 LBS.
MSRP. $5,339

RETAIL PRICING

YEAR	HIGH	LOW
2006	$3,254	$2,441
2008	$3,296	$2,472

LX423

YEARS MFRD 2009-2015
SERIES. . . . . LX SERIES
ENGINE . . . . KOHLER COURAGE
CYLINDERS. 2
ENGINE HP 20
COOLING . . . . AIR
FUEL . . . . G
SPEEDS . . . . VARIABLE
TRANSMISSION . . . . CVT
STEERING. . . . . STANDARD
BLADE CLUTCH . . . . MANUAL
STANDARD DECK . . . . 42"
MSRP. $1,899

RETAIL PRICING

YEAR	HIGH	LOW
2009	$340	$255
2010	$388	$291
2011	$418	$314
2012	$570	$428
2013	$711	$533
2014	$933	$700
2015	$1,076	$807

LX425

YEARS MFRD 2007-2008
SERIES. . . . . LX SERIES
ENGINE . . . . KOHLER COURAGE
CYLINDERS. 2
ENGINE HP 20
FUEL . . . . G
SPEEDS . . . . VARIABLE
TRANSMISSION . . . . BELT
STEERING. . . . . STANDARD
BLADE CLUTCH . . . . MANUAL
STANDARD DECK . . . . 42"
MSRP. $1,699

RETAIL PRICING

YEAR	HIGH	LOW
2007	$1,029	$772
2008	$1,127	$845

LX426

YEARS MFRD 2008-2008
SERIES. . . . . LX SERIES
ENGINE . . . . B&S INTEK
ENGINE HP 20
COOLING . . . . AIR
FUEL . . . . G
SPEEDS . . . . VARIABLE
TRANSMISSION . . . . HYDRO
STEERING. . . . . STANDARD
BLADE CLUTCH . . . . MANUAL
STANDARD DECK . . . . 42"
MSRP. $1,699

RETAIL PRICING

YEAR	HIGH	LOW
2008	$1,127	$845

LX427

YEARS MFRD 2009-2015
SERIES. . . . . LX SERIES
ENGINE . . . . KOHLER COURAGE
CYLINDERS. 2
ENGINE HP 20
COOLING . . . . AIR
FUEL . . . . G
SPEEDS . . . . VARIABLE
TRANSMISSION . . . . HYDRO
STEERING. . . . . STANDARD
BLADE CLUTCH . . . . MANUAL
STANDARD DECK . . . . 42"
MSRP. $1,999

RETAIL PRICING

YEAR	HIGH	LOW
2009	$379	$284
2010	$435	$327
2011	$466	$349
2012	$602	$451
2013	$751	$563
2014	$901	$676
2015	$1,241	$931

LX465

YEARS MFRD 2007-2008
SERIES. . . . . LX SERIES
ENGINE . . . . KOHLER COURAGE
CYLINDERS. 2
ENGINE HP 2
FUEL . . . . G
SPEEDS . . . . VARIABLE
TRANSMISSION . . . . HYDRO
STEERING. . . . . STANDARD
BLADE CLUTCH . . . . MANUAL
STANDARD DECK . . . . 46"
MSRP. $1,799

RETAIL PRICING

YEAR	HIGH	LOW
2007	$1,158	$869
2008	$1,193	$894

LX466

YEARS MFRD 2008-2008
SERIES. . . . . LX SERIES
ENGINE . . . . B&S INTEK
CYLINDERS. 2
ENGINE HP 22
COOLING . . . . AIR
FUEL . . . . G
SPEEDS . . . . VARIABLE
TRANSMISSION . . . . HYDRO
STEERING. . . . . STANDARD
BLADE CLUTCH . . . . MANUAL
STANDARD DECK . . . . 46"
MSRP. $1,799

RETAIL PRICING

YEAR	HIGH	LOW
2008	$1,193	$894

LX468

YEARS MFRD 2009-2015
SERIES. . . . . LX SERIES
ENGINE . . . . KOHLER COURAGE
CYLINDERS. 2
ENGINE HP 22
COOLING . . . . AIR
FUEL . . . . G
SPEEDS . . . . VARIABLE
TRANSMISSION . . . . HYDRO
STEERING. . . . . ZERO
STANDARD DECK . . . . 46"
MSRP. $2,299

RETAIL PRICING

YEAR	HIGH	LOW
2009	$435	$327
2010	$506	$380
2011	$546	$410
2012	$696	$522
2013	$870	$652
2014	$1,124	$843
2015	$1,447	$1,086

LX500

YEARS MFRD 2007-2008
SERIES. . . . . LX SERIES
ENGINE . . . . KOHLER COURAGE
CYLINDERS. 2
ENGINE HP 22
FUEL . . . . G
SPEEDS . . . . VARIABLE
TRANSMISSION . . . . BELT
STEERING. . . . . STANDARD
BLADE CLUTCH . . . . ELECTRIC
STANDARD DECK . . . . 50"
MSRP. $1,899

RETAIL PRICING

YEAR	HIGH	LOW
2007	$1,223	$917
2008	$1,261	$945

MX3450

YEARS MFRD 2015-2019
SERIES. . . . TIMECUTTER MX SERIES
ENGINE . . . . TORO
CYLINDERS. 1
CID 452CC
COOLING . . . . AIR
FUEL . . . . G
SPEEDS . . . . VARIABLE
TRANSMISSION . . . . HYDRO
STEERING. . . . . ZERO
STANDARD DECK . . . . 34"
MSRP. $3,599

RETAIL PRICING

YEAR	HIGH	LOW
2015	$1,768	$1,326
2016	$2,058	$1,544
2017	$2,358	$1,768
2018	$2,645	$1,984
2019	$3,013	$2,259

MX4200

YEARS MFRD 2017-2019
SERIES. . . . TIMECUTTER MX SERIES
ENGINE . . . . TORO
CID 708CC
ENGINE HP 22.5
FUEL . . . . G
SPEEDS . . . . VARIABLE
TRANSMISSION . . . . HYDRO
STEERING. . . . . ZERO
STANDARD DECK . . . . 42"
MSRP. $3,099

RETAIL PRICING

YEAR	HIGH	LOW
2017	$2,021	$1,516
2018	$2,307	$1,730
2019	$2,576	$1,932

MX4250

YEARS MFRD 2015-2019
SERIES. . . . TIMECUTTER MX SERIES
ENGINE . . . . TORO
CID 708CC
ENGINE HP 24.5
COOLING . . . . AIR
FUEL . . . . G
SPEEDS . . . . VARIABLE
TRANSMISSION . . . . HYDRO
STEERING. . . . . ZERO
STANDARD DECK . . . . 42"
MSRP. $3,899

RETAIL PRICING

YEAR	HIGH	LOW
2015	$1,918	$1,439
2016	$2,236	$1,677
2017	$2,564	$1,923
2018	$2,975	$2,231
2019	$3,407	$2,556

MX4260

YEARS MFRD 2012-2015
SERIES. . . . . . . TIMECUTTER SERIES
ENGINE . . . . KAWASAKI
ENGINE HP 23
COOLING . . . . AIR
FUEL . . . . G
SPEEDS . . . . VARIABLE
TRANSMISSION . . . . HYDRO
STEERING. . . . . ZERO
STANDARD DECK . . . . 42"
MSRP. $3,799

RETAIL PRICING

YEAR	HIGH	LOW
2012	$1,407	$1,055
2013	$1,740	$1,305
2014	$2,111	$1,583
2015	$2,499	$1,874

MX4800

YEARS MFRD 2015-2017
SERIES. . . . . TITAN SERIES
ENGINE . . . . KOHLER
ENGINE HP 21
COOLING . . . . AIR
FUEL . . . . G
SPEEDS . . . . VARIABLE
TRANSMISSION . . . . HYDRO
STEERING. . . . . ZERO
STANDARD DECK . . . . 48"
MSRP. $5,499

TORO

RETAIL PRICING

YEAR	HIGH	LOW
2015	$2,866	$2,150
2016	$3,647	$2,735
2017	$4,169	$3,126

MX4880

YEARS MFRD	2011-2014
SERIES	TITAN SERIES
ENGINE	KAWASAKI
CYLINDERS	2
CID	726CC
ENGINE HP	22
COOLING	AIR
FUEL	G
SPEEDS	VARIABLE
TRANSMISSION	HYDRO
STEERING	ZERO
BLADE CLUTCH	ELECTRIC
STANDARD DECK	48"
MSRP	$5,999

RETAIL PRICING

YEAR	HIGH	LOW
2011	$2,016	$1,512
2012	$2,419	$1,814
2013	$3,114	$2,336
2014	$3,922	$2,941

MX5000

YEARS MFRD	2017-2019
SERIES	TIMECUTTER MX SERIES
ENGINE	TORO
CID	708CC
ENGINE HP	24.5
FUEL	G
SPEEDS	VARIABLE
TRANSMISSION	HYDRO
STEERING	ZERO
STANDARD DECK	50"
MSRP	$3,399

RETAIL PRICING

YEAR	HIGH	LOW
2017	$2,292	$1,719
2018	$2,620	$1,965
2019	$2,888	$2,166

MX5000 74773

YEARS MFRD	2019-2019
SERIES	TIMECUTTER SERIES
ENGINE	KOHLER
CID	725CC
ENGINE HP	24
FUEL	G
SPEEDS	VARIABLE
TRANSMISSION	DUAL HYDRO
STEERING	ZERO
STANDARD DECK	50"
MSRP	$3,199

MX5025

YEARS MFRD	2017-2019
SERIES	TIMECUTTER MX SERIES
ENGINE	KAWASAKI
CID	726CC
ENGINE HP	23
FUEL	G
SPEEDS	VARIABLE
TRANSMISSION	HYDRO
STEERING	ZERO
STANDARD DECK	50"
MSRP	$3,799

RETAIL PRICING

YEAR	HIGH	LOW
2017	$2,489	$1,867
2018	$2,809	$2,106
2019	$3,153	$2,364

MX5050

YEARS MFRD	2015-2018
SERIES	TIMECUTTER SERIES
ENGINE	KOHLER
ENGINE HP	24
COOLING	AIR
FUEL	G
SPEEDS	VARIABLE
TRANSMISSION	HYDRO
STEERING	ZERO
STANDARD DECK	50"
MSRP	$4,199

RETAIL PRICING

YEAR	HIGH	LOW
2015	$2,190	$1,643
2016	$2,557	$1,918
2017	$2,914	$2,186
2018	$3,266	$2,450

MX5050 74774

YEARS MFRD	2019-2019
SERIES	TIMECUTTER SERIES
ENGINE	TORO
CID	708CC
ENGINE HP	24.5
FUEL	G
SPEEDS	VARIABLE
TRANSMISSION	DUAL HYDRO
STEERING	ZERO
STANDARD DECK	50"
MSRP	$3,699

MX5060

YEARS MFRD	2012-2015
ENGINE	KAWASAKI
CYLINDERS	2
ENGINE HP	23
COOLING	AIR
FUEL	G
SPEEDS	VARIABLE
TRANSMISSION	HYDRO
STEERING	ZERO
STANDARD DECK	50"
MSRP	$4,199

RETAIL PRICING

YEAR	HIGH	LOW
2012	$1,559	$1,169
2013	$1,906	$1,430
2014	$2,482	$1,861
2015	$2,980	$2,235

MX5060

YEARS MFRD	2016-2016
SERIES	TIMECUTTER SERIES
ENGINE	KAWASAKI
ENGINE HP	23
COOLING	AIR
FUEL	G
SPEEDS	VARIABLE
TRANSMISSION	HYDRO
STEERING	ZERO
STANDARD DECK	50"
MSRP	$4,199

RETAIL PRICING

YEAR	HIGH	LOW
2016	$2,919	$2,189

MX5075

YEARS MFRD	2018-2019
SERIES	TIMECUTTER MX SERIES
ENGINE	TORO
CID	708CC
ENGINE HP	24.5
FUEL	G
TRANSMISSION	DUAL HYDRO
STEERING	ZERO
STANDARD DECK	50"
MSRP	$4,399

MX5400

YEARS MFRD	2015-2017
SERIES	TITAN SERIES
ENGINE	KOHLER
ENGINE HP	23
COOLING	AIR
FUEL	G
SPEEDS	VARIABLE
TRANSMISSION	HYDRO
STEERING	ZERO
STANDARD DECK	54"
MSRP	$6,299

RETAIL PRICING

YEAR	HIGH	LOW
2015	$3,174	$2,380
2016	$3,705	$2,779
2017	$4,381	$3,286

MX5480

YEARS MFRD	2011-2014
SERIES	TITAN SERIES
ENGINE	KAWASAKI
CYLINDERS	2
CID	726CC
ENGINE HP	24
COOLING	AIR
FUEL	G
SPEEDS	VARIABLE
TRANSMISSION	HYDRO
STEERING	ZERO
BLADE CLUTCH	ELECTRIC
STANDARD DECK	54"
MSRP	$6,299

RETAIL PRICING

YEAR	HIGH	LOW
2011	$2,118	$1,589
2012	$2,539	$1,904
2013	$3,178	$2,383
2014	$3,945	$2,959

MX6000

YEARS MFRD	2015-2017
SERIES	TITAN SERIES
ENGINE	KAWASAKI
ENGINE HP	24
COOLING	AIR
FUEL	G
SPEEDS	VARIABLE
TRANSMISSION	HYDRO
STEERING	ZERO
STANDARD DECK	60"
MSRP	$6,599

OPTIONS

KOHLER 25HP

RETAIL PRICING

YEAR	HIGH	LOW
2015	$3,541	$2,656
2016	$4,014	$3,011
2017	$4,583	$3,437

MX6050

YEARS MFRD	2018-2019
SERIES	TIMECUTTER MX SERIES
ENGINE	TORO
CID	708CC
ENGINE HP	24.5
FUEL	G
TRANSMISSION	DUAL HYDRO
STEERING	ZERO
STANDARD DECK	60"
MSRP	$4,599

MX6080

YEARS MFRD	2012-2014
ENGINE	KAWASAKI
CYLINDERS	2
CID	726CC
ENGINE HP	24
COOLING	AIR
FUEL	G
SPEEDS	VARIABLE
TRANSMISSION	HYDRO
STEERING	ZERO
STANDARD DECK	60"
MSRP	$5,099

RETAIL PRICING

YEAR	HIGH	LOW
2012	$2,214	$1,660
2013	$2,601	$1,951
2014	$3,209	$2,407

RM2000D

YEARS MFRD	2004-2011
SERIES	REELMASTER SERIES
ENGINE	DAIHATSU
CYLINDERS	3
CID	51
ENGINE HP	19
COOLING	LIQUID
FUEL	D

SPEEDS ... VARIABLE
TRANSMISSION ... HYDRO
STEERING ... STANDARD
DRIVE TYPE ... 2WD
ROPS/CAB ... ROPS
STANDARD DECK ... 72"
WEIGHT ... 1,860 LBS.
MSRP ... $24,740

OPTIONS

3WD

RETAIL PRICING

YEAR	HIGH	LOW
2005	$3,390	$2,543
2006	$4,406	$3,305
2007	$5,528	$4,146
2008	$7,035	$5,276
2009	$9,144	$6,858
2010	$11,347	$8,510
2011	$14,932	$11,199

RM4000D

YEARS MFRD ... 2000-2011
SERIES REELMASTER 4000D SERIES
ENGINE ... KUBOTA
CYLINDERS ... 4
CID ... 134
ENGINE HP ... 49
COOLING ... LIQUID
FUEL ... D
SPEEDS ... VARIABLE
TRANSMISSION ... HYDRO
STEERING ... ZERO
DRIVE TYPE ... 2WD
ROPS/CAB ... ROPS
STANDARD DECK ... 137"
WEIGHT ... 4,360 LBS.
MSRP ... $64,350

OPTIONS

4WD

RETAIL PRICING

YEAR	HIGH	LOW
2000	$7,311	$5,483
2001	$7,597	$5,698
2002	$8,078	$6,059
2003	$10,381	$7,786
2004	$11,155	$8,366
2005	$11,539	$8,654
2006	$12,533	$9,400
2007	$14,756	$11,067
2008	$17,948	$13,461
2009	$24,349	$18,262
2010	$28,874	$21,655
2011	$38,841	$29,131

RM5200D

YEARS MFRD ... 2003-2004
SERIES . .REELMASTER 5200 SERIES
ENGINE ... KUBOTA
CID ... 68.5
ENGINE HP ... 28
COOLING ... LIQUID
FUEL ... D
TRANSMISSION ... HYDRO
STEERING ... STANDARD
DRIVE TYPE ... 2WD
ROPS/CAB ... ROPS
WEIGHT ... 2,320 LBS.

OPTIONS

4WD P/S

RM5210

YEARS MFRD ... 2009-2009
SERIES ... REELMASTER SERIES
ENGINE ... KUBOTA
CYLINDERS ... 3
ENGINE HP ... 28
COOLING ... LIQUID
FUEL ... D
SPEEDS ... VARIABLE
TRANSMISSION ... HYDRO
STEERING ... ZERO
BLADE CLUTCH ... ELECTRIC
WEIGHT ... 2,396 LBS.

RM5400D

YEARS MFRD ... 2003-2004
SERIES . .REELMASTER 5400 SERIES
ENGINE ... KUBOTA
CID ... 68.5
ENGINE HP ... 35
COOLING ... LIQUID
FUEL ... D
TRANSMISSION ... HYDRO
STEERING ... STANDARD
DRIVE TYPE ... 2WD
ROPS/CAB ... ROPS
WEIGHT ... 2,330 LBS.

OPTIONS

4WD P/S

RM5500D

YEARS MFRD ... 2003-2003
SERIES . .REELMASTER 5500 SERIES
ENGINE ... KUBOTA
CID ... 68.5
ENGINE HP ... 35
COOLING ... LIQUID
FUEL ... D
TRANSMISSION ... HYDRO
STEERING ... STANDARD
DRIVE TYPE ... 2WD
ROPS/CAB ... ROPS
WEIGHT ... 2,962 LBS.

OPTIONS

4WD P/S

RM5510

YEARS MFRD ... 2009-2010
SERIES ... REELMASTER SERIES
ENGINE ... KUBOTA
CYLINDERS ... 4
ENGINE HP ... 35.5
COOLING ... LIQUID
FUEL ... D
SPEEDS ... VARIABLE
TRANSMISSION ... HYDRO
STEERING ... ZERO
BLADE CLUTCH ... ELECTRIC
WEIGHT ... 2,693 LBS.

RM5610

YEARS MFRD ... 2009-2010
SERIES ... REELMASTER SERIES
ENGINE ... KUBOTA
CYLINDERS ... 4
ENGINE HP ... 44.2
COOLING ... LIQUID
FUEL ... D
SPEEDS ... VARIABLE
TRANSMISSION ... HYDRO
STEERING ... ZERO
BLADE CLUTCH ... ELECTRIC
WEIGHT ... 2,813 LBS.

RM6500D

YEARS MFRD ... 2002-2011
SERIES ... REELMASTER SERIES
ENGINE ... KUBOTA
CYLINDERS ... 4
ENGINE HP ... 38
COOLING ... LIQUID
FUEL ... D
SPEEDS ... VARIABLE
TRANSMISSION ... HYDRO
STEERING ... STANDARD
BLADE CLUTCH ... ELECTRIC
DRIVE TYPE ... 2WD
ROPS/CAB ... ROPS
STANDARD DECK ... 96"
WEIGHT ... 3,200 LBS.
MSRP ... $47,950

OPTIONS

4WD

RETAIL PRICING

YEAR	HIGH	LOW
2002	$6,267	$4,700
2003	$8,057	$6,043
2004	$8,655	$6,491
2005	$8,950	$6,713
2006	$9,734	$7,300
2007	$11,567	$8,675
2008	$14,068	$10,551
2009	$18,780	$14,085
2010	$21,912	$16,434
2011	$28,942	$21,706

RM6700D

YEARS MFRD ... 2002-2011
SERIES ... REELMASTER SERIES
ENGINE ... KUBOTA
CYLINDERS ... 4
ENGINE HP ... 46
COOLING ... LIQUID
FUEL ... D
SPEEDS ... VARIABLE
TRANSMISSION ... HYDRO
STEERING ... ZERO
STANDARD DECK ... 133"
WEIGHT ... 3,950 LBS.
MSRP ... $60,500

OPTIONS

4WD

RETAIL PRICING

YEAR	HIGH	LOW
2002	$7,873	$5,905
2003	$10,119	$7,589
2004	$10,872	$8,154
2005	$11,246	$8,435
2006	$11,994	$8,996
2007	$14,396	$10,797
2008	$17,509	$13,132
2009	$24,275	$18,206
2010	$28,413	$21,310
2011	$36,516	$27,387

SS3200

YEARS MFRD ... 2011-2015
SERIES ... TIMECUTTER SERIES
ENGINE ... KOHLER
CYLINDERS ... 1
ENGINE HP ... 15
COOLING ... AIR
FUEL ... G
SPEEDS ... VARIABLE
TRANSMISSION ... HYDRO
STEERING ... ZERO
STANDARD DECK ... 32"
MSRP ... $2,499

RETAIL PRICING

YEAR	HIGH	LOW
2011	$783	$587
2012	$870	$652
2013	$980	$735
2014	$1,226	$920
2015	$1,573	$1,180

SS3216

YEARS MFRD ... 2015-2015
SERIES ... TIMECUTTER SERIES
ENGINE ... TORO
CID ... 452CC
ENGINE HP ... 16
COOLING ... AIR
FUEL ... G
SPEEDS ... VARIABLE
TRANSMISSION ... DUAL HYDRO
STEERING ... ZERO
STANDARD DECK ... 32"
MSRP ... $2,599

RETAIL PRICING

YEAR	HIGH	LOW
2015	$1,598	$1,198

SS3225

YEARS MFRD ... 2016-2020
SERIES ... TIMECUTTER SERIES
ENGINE ... TORO
CID ... 452CC
ENGINE HP ... 16
COOLING ... AIR
FUEL ... G
SPEEDS ... VARIABLE
TRANSMISSION ... HYDRO
STEERING ... ZERO
STANDARD DECK ... 32"
MSRP ... $2,699

RETAIL PRICING

YEAR	HIGH	LOW
2016	$1,533	$1,149
2017	$1,750	$1,312
2018	$1,940	$1,455
2019	$2,126	$1,594
2020	$2,314	$1,766

TORO

SS4200

YEARS MFRD 2011-2017
SERIES. . . . . . . TIMECUTTER SERIES
ENGINE . . . . KOHLER
CYLINDERS. 1
ENGINE HP 19
COOLING . . . . AIR
FUEL . . . . G
SPEEDS . . . . VARIABLE
TRANSMISSION . . . . HYDRO
STEERING. . . . . ZERO
STANDARD DECK . . . . 42"
MSRP. $2,599

RETAIL PRICING

YEAR	HIGH	LOW
2011	$792	$594
2012	$917	$687
2013	$1,081	$811
2014	$1,197	$898
2015	$1,302	$977
2016	$1,515	$1,137
2017	$1,737	$1,302

SS4200 74711

YEARS MFRD 2018-2019
SERIES. . . . TIMECUTTER SS SERIES
ENGINE . . . . TORO
CID 452CC
ENGINE HP 16
TRANSMISSION . . . . . DUAL HYDRO
STEERING. . . . . ZERO
STANDARD DECK . . . . 42"
MSRP. $2,599

SS4216

YEARS MFRD 2015-2015
SERIES. . . . . . . TIMECUTTER SERIES
ENGINE . . . . TORO
CID 452CC
ENGINE HP 16
COOLING . . . . AIR
FUEL . . . . G
SPEEDS . . . . VARIABLE
TRANSMISSION . . . . . DUAL HYDRO
STEERING. . . . . ZERO
STANDARD DECK . . . . 42"
MSRP. $2,499

RETAIL PRICING

YEAR	HIGH	LOW
2015	$1,573	$1,180

SS4225

YEARS MFRD 2015-2017
SERIES. . . . . . . TIMECUTTER SERIES
ENGINE . . . . KOHLER
CYLINDERS. 2
CID 725CC
ENGINE HP 22
COOLING . . . . AIR
FUEL . . . . G
SPEEDS . . . . VARIABLE
TRANSMISSION . . . . HYDRO
STEERING. . . . . ZERO
STANDARD DECK . . . . 42"
MSRP. $2,799

RETAIL PRICING

YEAR	HIGH	LOW
2015	$1,331	$998
2016	$1,698	$1,274
2017	$1,950	$1,462

SS4225 74726

YEARS MFRD 2018-2019
SERIES. . . . TIMECUTTER SS SERIES
ENGINE . . . . TORO
CYLINDERS. 2
CID 708CC
ENGINE HP 22.5
TRANSMISSION . . . . . DUAL HYDRO
STEERING. . . . . ZERO
STANDARD DECK . . . . 42"
MSRP. $2,799

SS4235

YEARS MFRD 2011-2015
SERIES. . . . . . . TIMECUTTER SERIES
ENGINE . . . . KAWASAKI
CYLINDERS. 2
ENGINE HP 16
COOLING . . . . AIR
FUEL . . . . G
SPEEDS . . . . VARIABLE
TRANSMISSION . . . . HYDRO
STEERING. . . . . ZERO
STANDARD DECK . . . . 42"
MSRP. $2,899

OPTIONS

KOHLER 22HP

RETAIL PRICING

YEAR	HIGH	LOW
2011	$887	$665
2012	$989	$741
2013	$1,155	$866
2014	$1,344	$1,008
2015	$1,787	$1,341

SS4250

YEARS MFRD 2015-2017
SERIES. . . . . . . TIMECUTTER SERIES
ENGINE . . . . TORO
CYLINDERS. 2
CID 708CC
ENGINE HP 24.5
COOLING . . . . AIR
FUEL . . . . G
SPEEDS . . . . VARIABLE
TRANSMISSION . . . . HYDRO
STEERING. . . . . ZERO
STANDARD DECK . . . . 42"
MSRP. $3,199

RETAIL PRICING

YEAR	HIGH	LOW
2015	$1,669	$1,251
2016	$1,950	$1,462
2017	$2,219	$1,664

SS4260

YEARS MFRD 2011-2015
SERIES. . . . . . . TIMECUTTER SERIES
ENGINE . . . . KAWASAKI
CYLINDERS. 2
ENGINE HP 22
COOLING . . . . AIR
FUEL . . . . G
SPEEDS . . . . VARIABLE
TRANSMISSION . . . . HYDRO
STEERING. . . . . ZERO
STANDARD DECK . . . . 42"
MSRP. $3,199

RETAIL PRICING

YEAR	HIGH	LOW
2011	$989	$741
2012	$1,138	$853
2013	$1,281	$961
2014	$1,550	$1,162
2015	$2,048	$1,536

SS5000

YEARS MFRD 2011-2017
SERIES. . . . . . . TIMECUTTER SERIES
ENGINE . . . . KAWASAKI
CYLINDERS. 2
ENGINE HP 22
COOLING . . . . AIR
FUEL . . . . G
SPEEDS . . . . VARIABLE
TRANSMISSION . . . . HYDRO
STEERING. . . . . ZERO
STANDARD DECK . . . . 50"
MSRP. $3,199

OPTIONS

TORO 24.5HP

RETAIL PRICING

YEAR	HIGH	LOW
2011	$985	$738
2012	$1,099	$824
2013	$1,244	$933
2014	$1,390	$1,042
2015	$1,563	$1,172
2016	$1,950	$1,462
2017	$2,219	$1,664

SS5000 74731

YEARS MFRD 2015-2019
SERIES. . . . TIMECUTTER SS SERIES
ENGINE . . . . TORO
CYLINDERS. 2
CID 708CC
ENGINE HP 24.5
FUEL . . . . G
SPEEDS . . . . VARIABLE
TRANSMISSION . . . . . DUAL HYDRO
STEERING. . . . . ZERO
STANDARD DECK . . . . 50"
MSRP. $2,999

SS5060

YEARS MFRD 2011-2015
SERIES. . . . . . . TIMECUTTER SERIES
ENGINE . . . . KAWASAKI
CYLINDERS. 2
ENGINE HP 24
COOLING . . . . AIR
FUEL . . . . G
SPEEDS . . . . VARIABLE
TRANSMISSION . . . . HYDRO
STEERING. . . . . ZERO
STANDARD DECK . . . . 50"
MSRP. $3,599

RETAIL PRICING

YEAR	HIGH	LOW
2011	$1,124	$843
2012	$1,559	$1,169
2013	$1,748	$1,311
2014	$2,009	$1,507
2015	$2,436	$1,827

SS5425

YEARS MFRD 2015-2017
SERIES. . . . . . . TIMECUTTER SERIES
ENGINE . . . . KOHLER
CYLINDERS. 2
CID 725CC
ENGINE HP 24
COOLING . . . . AIR
FUEL . . . . G
SPEEDS . . . . VARIABLE
TRANSMISSION . . . . HYDRO
STEERING. . . . . ZERO
STANDARD DECK . . . . 54"
MSRP. $3,599

RETAIL PRICING

YEAR	HIGH	LOW
2015	$1,930	$1,447
2016	$2,190	$1,643
2017	$2,499	$1,874

SW3200

YEARS MFRD 2015-2019
SERIES. . . . . . . TIMECUTTER SERIES
ENGINE . . . . TORO
CID 452CC
ENGINE HP 16
FUEL . . . . G
TRANSMISSION . . . . . DUAL HYDRO
STEERING. . . . . ZERO
STANDARD DECK . . . . 32"
MSRP. $3,199

SW4200

YEARS MFRD 2016-2019
SERIES. . . . . . . TIMECUTTER SERIES
ENGINE . . . . TORO
CYLINDERS. 2
CID 708CC
ENGINE HP 24.5
COOLING . . . . AIR
FUEL . . . . G
SPEEDS . . . . VARIABLE
TRANSMISSION . . . . HYDRO
STEERING. . . . . ZERO
STANDARD DECK . . . . 42"
MSRP. $3,399

OPTIONS

22HP TORO

RETAIL PRICING

YEAR	HIGH	LOW
2016	$1,890	$1,417
2017	$2,152	$1,614
2018	$2,377	$1,783
2019	$2,610	$1,957

SW5000

YEARS MFRD 2015-2019
SERIES .... TIMECUTTER SERIES
ENGINE .... TORO
CYLINDERS 2
ENGINE HP 24.5
COOLING .... AIR
FUEL .... G
SPEEDS .... VARIABLE
TRANSMISSION .... HYDRO
STEERING .... ZERO
STANDARD DECK .... 50"
MSRP $3,499

RETAIL PRICING

YEAR	HIGH	LOW
2015	$1,619	$1,214
2016	$2,004	$1,503
2017	$2,292	$1,719
2018	$2,566	$1,924
2019	$2,816	$2,112

SWX4250

YEARS MFRD 2016-2017
SERIES .... TIMECUTTER SERIES
ENGINE .... TORO
ENGINE HP 24.5
COOLING .... AIR
FUEL .... G
SPEEDS .... VARIABLE
TRANSMISSION .... HYDRO
STEERING .... ZERO
STANDARD DECK .... 42"
MSRP $4,499

RETAIL PRICING

YEAR	HIGH	LOW
2016	$2,730	$2,048
2017	$3,126	$2,345

SWX5000

YEARS MFRD 2017-2019
SERIES .... TIMECUTTER SERIES
ENGINE .... TORO
CYLINDERS 2
CID 708CC
ENGINE HP 24.5
FUEL .... G
TRANSMISSION ..... DUAL HYDRO
STEERING .... ZERO
STANDARD DECK .... 50"
MSRP $3,799

SWX5050

YEARS MFRD 2016-2019
SERIES .... TIMECUTTER SERIES
ENGINE .... TORO
CYLINDERS 2
ENGINE HP 24.5
COOLING .... AIR
FUEL .... G
SPEEDS .... VARIABLE
TRANSMISSION .... HYDRO
STEERING .... ZERO
STANDARD DECK .... 50"
MSRP $4,899

OPTIONS

KOHLER 22HP

RETAIL PRICING

YEAR	HIGH	LOW
2016	$2,892	$2,169
2017	$3,303	$2,477
2018	$3,642	$2,731
2019	$4,031	$3,023

TITAN HD 1500

YEARS MFRD 2017-2019
ENGINE .... TORO
ENGINE HP 24.5
FUEL .... G
SPEEDS .... VARIABLE
TRANSMISSION .... HYDRO
STEERING .... ZERO
STANDARD DECK .... 48"
MSRP $6,110

OPTIONS

52" DECK
60" DECK

RETAIL PRICING

YEAR	HIGH	LOW
2017	$4,118	$3,088
2018	$4,521	$3,391
2019	$4,983	$3,737

TITAN HD 2000

YEARS MFRD 2017-2019
ENGINE .... KOHLER
ENGINE HP 21
COOLING .... AIR
FUEL .... G
SPEEDS .... VARIABLE
TRANSMISSION .... HYDRO
STEERING .... ZERO
STANDARD DECK .... 48"
MSRP $7,332

OPTIONS

52" DECK
60" DECK

RETAIL PRICING

YEAR	HIGH	LOW
2017	$4,940	$3,705
2018	$5,483	$4,112
2019	$6,077	$4,558

TITAN HD 2500

YEARS MFRD 2017-2017
ENGINE .... KAWASAKI
ENGINE HP 20.5
FUEL .... G
SPEEDS .... VARIABLE
TRANSMISSION .... HYDRO
STEERING .... ZERO
STANDARD DECK .... 48"
MSRP $8,443

OPTIONS

52" DECK
60" DECK

RETAIL PRICING

YEAR	HIGH	LOW
2017	$5,866	$4,399

XL320/12-32XL

YEARS MFRD 2004-2007
SERIES .... XL SERIES
ENGINE .... B&S
ENGINE HP 12.5
COOLING .... AIR
FUEL .... G
SPEEDS 5/1
TRANSMISSION .... GEAR
STEERING .... STANDARD
STANDARD DECK .... 32"
WEIGHT .... 480 LBS.
MSRP $1,799

RETAIL PRICING

YEAR	HIGH	LOW
2004	$919	$689
2005	$993	$745
2006	$1,073	$805
2007	$1,158	$869

XL380/16-38XL

YEARS MFRD 2000-2007
SERIES .... XL SERIES
ENGINE .... B&S
ENGINE HP 16
COOLING .... AIR
FUEL .... G
SPEEDS 5/1
TRANSMISSION .... GEAR
STEERING .... STANDARD
STANDARD DECK .... 38"
WEIGHT .... 465 LBS.
MSRP $2,159

RETAIL PRICING

YEAR	HIGH	LOW
2000	$706	$530
2001	$872	$654
2002	$949	$712
2003	$1,041	$781
2004	$1,135	$851
2005	$1,230	$923
2006	$1,322	$991
2007	$1,394	$1,045

XL380H16-38HXL

YEARS MFRD 2000-2007
SERIES .... XL SERIES
ENGINE .... B&S
ENGINE HP 16
COOLING .... AIR
FUEL .... G
SPEEDS .... VARIABLE
TRANSMISSION .... HYDRO
STEERING .... STANDARD
STANDARD DECK .... 38"
WEIGHT .... 485 LBS.
MSRP $2,399

RETAIL PRICING

YEAR	HIGH	LOW
2000	$788	$591
2001	$953	$715
2002	$1,038	$779
2003	$1,190	$892
2004	$1,296	$972
2005	$1,405	$1,054
2006	$1,512	$1,134
2007	$1,683	$1,262

XL440H/17-44HXL

YEARS MFRD 1999-2007
SERIES .... XL SERIES
ENGINE .... B&S
ENGINE HP 17
COOLING .... AIR
FUEL .... G
SPEEDS .... VARIABLE
TRANSMISSION .... HYDRO
STEERING .... STANDARD
STANDARD DECK .... 44"
WEIGHT .... 550 LBS.
MSRP $2,899

RETAIL PRICING

YEAR	HIGH	LOW
1999	$904	$678
2000	$1,001	$751
2001	$1,182	$887
2002	$1,289	$967
2003	$1,439	$1,079
2004	$1,568	$1,176
2005	$1,696	$1,272
2006	$1,767	$1,325
2007	$1,866	$1,399

Z16

YEARS MFRD 2001-2002
SERIES ..... TIMECUTTER Z SERIES
ENGINE .... B&S
ENGINE HP 16.5
FUEL .... G
TRANSMISSION .... HYDRO
STEERING .... STANDARD
STANDARD DECK .... 44"
MSRP $4,599

RETAIL PRICING

YEAR	HIGH	LOW
2001	$1,908	$1,431
2002	$2,079	$1,559

Z17

YEARS MFRD 2001-2002
SERIES ..... TIMECUTTER Z SERIES
ENGINE .... KOHLER
ENGINE HP 17
FUEL .... G
TRANSMISSION .... HYDRO
STEERING .... STANDARD
STANDARD DECK .... 44"
MSRP $4,899

TORO

OPTIONS

52" DECK

RETAIL PRICING

YEAR	HIGH	LOW
2001	$2,033	$1,525
2002	$2,213	$1,660

Z18

YEARS MFRD 2003-2003
SERIES. . . . . TIMECUTTER Z SERIES
ENGINE . . . . KAWASAKI
ENGINE HP 18
COOLING . . . . AIR
FUEL . . . . G
TRANSMISSION . . . . . HYDRO DUAL
STEERING. . . . . STANDARD

Z117

YEARS MFRD 2000-2000
SERIES. . . . . Z MASTER 100 SERIES
ENGINE . . . . KAWASAKI
ENGINE HP 17
FUEL . . . . G
SPEEDS . . . . VARIABLE
TRANSMISSION . . . . HYDRO
STEERING. . . . . STANDARD

Z118

YEARS MFRD 1997-1998
SERIES. . . . . Z MASTER 100 SERIES
ENGINE . . . . KOHLER
ENGINE HP 18
COOLING . . . . AIR
FUEL . . . . G
SPEEDS . . . . VARIABLE
STEERING. . . . . ZERO
STANDARD DECK . . . . 42"
WEIGHT . . . . 720 LBS.
MSRP. $5,581

OPTIONS

52" DECK

RETAIL PRICING

YEAR	HIGH	LOW
1997	$696	$522
1998	$771	$579

Z119

YEARS MFRD 2000-2000
SERIES. . . . . Z MASTER 100 SERIES
ENGINE . . . . KAWASAKI
ENGINE HP 19
FUEL . . . . G
SPEEDS . . . . VARIABLE
TRANSMISSION . . . . HYDRO
STEERING. . . . . STANDARD

Z120

YEARS MFRD 2000-2000
SERIES. . . . . Z MASTER 100 SERIES
ENGINE . . . . KOHLER
ENGINE HP 20
FUEL . . . . G
SPEEDS . . . . VARIABLE
TRANSMISSION . . . . HYDRO
STEERING. . . . . STANDARD

Z147

YEARS MFRD 1999-2004
SERIES. . . . . Z MASTER 100 SERIES
ENGINE . . . . KAWASAKI
ENGINE HP 17
COOLING . . . . AIR
FUEL . . . . G
SPEEDS . . . . VARIABLE
TRANSMISSION . . . . HYDRO
STEERING. . . . . ZERO
STANDARD DECK . . . . 44"
MSRP. $7,766

OPTIONS

2 BAG
BAG

SERIAL NUMBERS

YEAR	BEGINNING NO.
2001	210000

RETAIL PRICING

YEAR	HIGH	LOW
1999	$1,273	$955
2000	$1,416	$1,062
2001	$1,569	$1,177
2002	$1,743	$1,307
2003	$1,938	$1,453
2004	$2,150	$1,612

Z149

YEARS MFRD 1999-2006
SERIES. . . . . Z MASTER 100 SERIES
ENGINE . . . . KAWASAKI
ENGINE HP 19
COOLING . . . . AIR
FUEL . . . . G
SPEEDS . . . . VARIABLE
TRANSMISSION . . . . HYDRO
STEERING. . . . . ZERO
STANDARD DECK . . . . 44"
MSRP. $7,579

OPTIONS

2 BAG
BAG
ROPS

SERIAL NUMBERS

YEAR	BEGINNING NO.
2001	210000

RETAIL PRICING

YEAR	HIGH	LOW
1999	$1,223	$917
2000	$1,360	$1,020
2001	$1,511	$1,134
2002	$1,676	$1,257
2003	$1,860	$1,395
2004	$2,068	$1,551
2005	$2,293	$1,720
2006	$2,549	$1,911

Z150

YEARS MFRD 1999-2004
SERIES. . . . . Z MASTER 100 SERIES
ENGINE . . . . KOHLER
ENGINE HP 20
COOLING . . . . AIR
FUEL . . . . G
SPEEDS . . . . VARIABLE
TRANSMISSION . . . . HYDRO
STEERING. . . . . ZERO
STANDARD DECK . . . . 52"
MSRP. $8,782

OPTIONS

2 BAG
ROPS

SERIAL NUMBERS

YEAR	BEGINNING NO.
2001	210000

RETAIL PRICING

YEAR	HIGH	LOW
1999	$1,439	$1,079
2000	$1,598	$1,198
2001	$1,775	$1,331
2002	$1,973	$1,480
2003	$2,190	$1,643
2004	$2,432	$1,824

Z153

YEARS MFRD 2000-2004
SERIES. . . . . Z MASTER 100 SERIES
ENGINE . . . . KOHLER
ENGINE HP 23
COOLING . . . . AIR
FUEL . . . . G
SPEEDS . . . . VARIABLE
TRANSMISSION . . . . HYDRO
STEERING. . . . . ZERO
STANDARD DECK . . . . 52"
MSRP. $9,140

OPTIONS

2 BAG
BAG
KAWASAKI 23HP

SERIAL NUMBERS

YEAR	BEGINNING NO.
2001	210000

RETAIL PRICING

YEAR	HIGH	LOW
2000	$1,665	$1,248
2001	$1,847	$1,385
2002	$2,051	$1,538
2003	$2,281	$1,711
2004	$2,530	$1,898

Z222

YEARS MFRD 1997-1997
SERIES. . . . . Z MASTER SERIES
ENGINE . . . . KOHLER
ENGINE HP 22
COOLING . . . . AIR
FUEL . . . . G
SPEEDS . . . . VARIABLE
TRANSMISSION . . . . HYDRO
STEERING. . . . . ZERO
STANDARD DECK . . . . 52"
WEIGHT . . . . 900 LBS.
MSRP. $7,599

OPTIONS

60" DECK

RETAIL PRICING

YEAR	HIGH	LOW
1997	$901	$676

Z244

YEARS MFRD 2002-2002
SERIES. . . . . Z MASTER SERIES
ENGINE . . . . KAWASAKI
ENGINE HP 25
COOLING . . . . AIR
FUEL . . . . G
TRANSMISSION . . . . HYDRO
STEERING. . . . . ZERO
STANDARD DECK . . . . 62"
MSRP. $8,699

RETAIL PRICING

YEAR	HIGH	LOW
2002	$1,894	$1,420

Z252

YEARS MFRD 1998-1999
SERIES. . . . . Z MASTER 200 SERIES
ENGINE . . . . KOHLER
ENGINE HP 22
COOLING . . . . AIR
FUEL . . . . G
SPEEDS . . . . VARIABLE
TRANSMISSION . . . . . DUAL HYDRO
STEERING. . . . . ZERO
STANDARD DECK . . . . 52"
WEIGHT . . . . 1,000 LBS.
MSRP. $7,749

RETAIL PRICING

YEAR	HIGH	LOW
1998	$1,051	$788
1999	$1,166	$875

Z252L

YEARS MFRD 1999-2000
SERIES. . . . . Z MASTER 200 SERIES
ENGINE . . . . KAWASAKI
ENGINE HP 22
COOLING . . . . LIQUID
FUEL . . . . G
TRANSMISSION . . . . HYDRO
STEERING. . . . . ZERO
STANDARD DECK . . . . 52"
MSRP. $8,689

OPTIONS

62" DECK
ROPS

RETAIL PRICING

YEAR	HIGH	LOW
1999	$1,550	$1,162
2000	$1,719	$1,290

Z253

YEARS MFRD 2000-2003
SERIES. . . . . Z MASTER 200 SERIES
ENGINE . . . . KOHLER
ENGINE HP 23
COOLING . . . . AIR
FUEL . . . . G

TRANSMISSION ....HYDRO
STEERING..................ZERO
STANDARD DECK .... 62"
MSRP.................. $8,329

OPTIONS

ROPS
SUS SEAT

SERIAL NUMBERS

YEAR	BEGINNING NO.
2001	210000

RETAIL PRICING

YEAR	HIGH	LOW
2000	$1,565	$1,174
2001	$1,736	$1,302
2002	$1,929	$1,446
2003	$2,144	$1,608

Z255

YEARS MFRD 1998-2003
SERIES..... Z MASTER 200 SERIES
ENGINE ....KOHLER
ENGINE HP..................25
COOLING ....AIR
FUEL.........................G
TRANSMISSION ..... DUAL HYDRO
STEERING..................ZERO
STANDARD DECK .... 62"
MSRP.................. $8,899

OPTIONS

72" DECK

SERIAL NUMBERS

YEAR	BEGINNING NO.
2001	210000

RETAIL PRICING

YEAR	HIGH	LOW
1998	$1,357	$1,018
1999	$1,506	$1,130
2000	$1,672	$1,254
2001	$1,854	$1,391
2002	$2,058	$1,544
2003	$2,328	$1,746

Z256E

YEARS MFRD 2000-2000
SERIES..... Z MASTER 200 SERIES
ENGINE ....KOHLER
ENGINE HP..................26
FUEL.........................G
TRANSMISSION ....HYDRO
STEERING..................ZERO
STANDARD DECK .... 62"
MSRP.................. $9,633

OPTIONS

72" DECK
ROPS

RETAIL PRICING

YEAR	HIGH	LOW
2000	$1,640	$1,230

Z283L

YEARS MFRD 2001-2001
SERIES........ Z MASTER SERIES
ENGINE .... KAWASAKI
ENGINE HP..................23
COOLING .... LIQUID
FUEL.........................G
TRANSMISSION ....HYDRO
STEERING..................ZERO
STANDARD DECK .... 62"
MSRP.................. $7,299

OPTIONS

ROPS

RETAIL PRICING

YEAR	HIGH	LOW
2001	$1,328	$996

Z286E

YEARS MFRD 2001-2003
SERIES........ Z MASTER SERIES
ENGINE ....KOHLER
ENGINE HP..................26
FUEL.........................G
TRANSMISSION ....HYDRO
STEERING..................ZERO
STANDARD DECK .... 62"
MSRP.................. $10,209

OPTIONS

72" DECK
ROPS

SERIAL NUMBERS

YEAR	BEGINNING NO.
2001	210000

RETAIL PRICING

YEAR	HIGH	LOW
2001	$2,132	$1,599
2002	$2,626	$1,969
2003	$2,626	$1,969

Z287L

YEARS MFRD 2001-2003
SERIES........ Z MASTER SERIES
ENGINE .... KAWASAKI
ENGINE HP..................27
COOLING .... LIQUID
FUEL.........................G
TRANSMISSION ....HYDRO
STEERING..................ZERO
STANDARD DECK .... 62"
MSRP.................. $10,279

OPTIONS

72" DECK
ROPS

SERIAL NUMBERS

YEAR	BEGINNING NO.
2001	210000

RETAIL PRICING

YEAR	HIGH	LOW
2001	$2,144	$1,608
2002	$2,380	$1,785
2003	$2,644	$1,983

Z320

YEARS MFRD 1998-2000
SERIES..... Z MASTER 300 SERIES
ENGINE ....KOHLER
ENGINE HP..................20
COOLING ....AIR
FUEL.........................G
SPEEDS ....VARIABLE
TRANSMISSION ..... DUAL HYDRO
STEERING..................ZERO
STANDARD DECK .... 48"
MSRP.................. $9,519

OPTIONS

BAGGER

RETAIL PRICING

YEAR	HIGH	LOW
1998	$1,463	$1,097
1999	$1,628	$1,221
2000	$1,808	$1,356

Z325

YEARS MFRD 1998-2000
SERIES..... Z MASTER 300 SERIES
ENGINE ....KOHLER
ENGINE HP..................25
COOLING ....AIR
FUEL.........................G
SPEEDS ....VARIABLE
TRANSMISSION ..... DUAL HYDRO
STEERING..................ZERO
STANDARD DECK .... 60"
MSRP.................. $10,019

OPTIONS

BAGGER

RETAIL PRICING

YEAR	HIGH	LOW
1998	$1,542	$1,156
1999	$1,716	$1,287
2000	$1,906	$1,430

Z350

YEARS MFRD 2001-2001
SERIES..... Z MASTER 300 SERIES
ENGINE ....KOHLER
ENGINE HP..................25
FUEL.........................G
SPEEDS ....VARIABLE
TRANSMISSION ....HYDRO
STEERING............STANDARD

Z355

YEARS MFRD 2001-2004
SERIES..... Z MASTER 300 SERIES
ENGINE ....KOHLER
ENGINE HP..................25
COOLING ....AIR
FUEL.........................G
SPEEDS ....VARIABLE
TRANSMISSION ..... DUAL HYDRO
STEERING..................ZERO
STANDARD DECK .... 48"
MSRP.................. $11,719

SERIAL NUMBERS

YEAR	BEGINNING NO.
2001	210000

RETAIL PRICING

YEAR	HIGH	LOW
2001	$2,369	$1,777
2002	$2,633	$1,975
2003	$2,921	$2,191
2004	$3,246	$2,434

Z380/14-38Z

YEARS MFRD 2004-2006
SERIES....... TIMECUTTER SERIES
ENGINE ....B&S
ENGINE HP..................14
COOLING ....AIR
FUEL.........................G
SPEEDS ....VARIABLE
TRANSMISSION ....HYDRO
STEERING..................ZERO
BLADE CLUTCH ....ELECTRIC
STANDARD DECK .... 38"
MSRP.................. $2,899

RETAIL PRICING

YEAR	HIGH	LOW
2004	$1,568	$1,176
2005	$1,696	$1,272
2006	$1,824	$1,368

Z420/16-42Z

YEARS MFRD 2004-2006
SERIES....... TIMECUTTER SERIES
ENGINE ....B&S
ENGINE HP..................16
COOLING ....AIR
FUEL.........................G
SPEEDS ....VARIABLE
TRANSMISSION ....HYDRO
STEERING..................ZERO
BLADE CLUTCH ....ELECTRIC
STANDARD DECK .... 42"
MSRP.................. $3,199

RETAIL PRICING

YEAR	HIGH	LOW
2004	$1,731	$1,298
2005	$1,873	$1,405
2006	$2,014	$1,510

Z480

YEARS MFRD 2006-2006
SERIES..... TIMECUTTER Z SERIES
ENGINE ....B&S
ENGINE HP..................16
COOLING ....AIR
FUEL.........................G
SPEEDS ....VARIABLE
TRANSMISSION ....HYDRO
STEERING..................ZERO
STANDARD DECK .... 48"
MSRP.................. $3,799

RETAIL PRICING

YEAR	HIGH	LOW
2006	$2,390	$1,793

Z500

YEARS MFRD 2004-2006
SERIES........ Z MASTER SERIES
ENGINE ....KOHLER
ENGINE HP..................20
COOLING ....AIR
FUEL.........................G
SPEEDS ....VARIABLE
TRANSMISSION ....HYDRO
STEERING..................ZERO
STANDARD DECK .... 52"
MSRP.................. $8,797

TORO

OPTIONS

2 BAG
3 BAG
BAG

RETAIL PRICING

YEAR	HIGH	LOW
2004	$2,539	$1,904
2005	$2,820	$2,115
2006	$3,123	$2,342

Z553

YEARS MFRD 2004-2005
SERIES . . . . Z MASTER SERIES
ENGINE . . . . KOHLER
ENGINE HP 23
COOLING . . . . AIR
FUEL . . . . G
SPEEDS . . . . VARIABLE
TRANSMISSION . . . . HYDRO
STEERING . . . . ZERO
STANDARD DECK . . . . 60"
MSRP $9,896

OPTIONS

2 BAG
3 BAG
BAG

RETAIL PRICING

YEAR	HIGH	LOW
2004	$2,752	$2,064
2005	$3,052	$2,289

Z555

YEARS MFRD 2004-2005
SERIES . . . . Z MASTER SERIES
ENGINE . . . . KAWASAKI
ENGINE HP 25
COOLING . . . . AIR
FUEL . . . . G
SPEEDS . . . . VARIABLE
TRANSMISSION . . . . HYDRO
STEERING . . . . ZERO
STANDARD DECK . . . . 60"
MSRP $10,580

OPTIONS

2 BAG
3 BAG
BAG

RETAIL PRICING

YEAR	HIGH	LOW
2004	$2,941	$2,206
2005	$3,265	$2,449

Z557

YEARS MFRD 2004-2005
SERIES . . . . Z MASTER SERIES
ENGINE . . . . KOHLER
ENGINE HP 27
COOLING . . . . AIR
FUEL . . . . G
SPEEDS . . . . VARIABLE
TRANSMISSION . . . . HYDRO
STEERING . . . . ZERO
STANDARD DECK . . . . 52"
MSRP $10,204

OPTIONS

2 BAG
60" DECK
72" DECK
BAG

RETAIL PRICING

YEAR	HIGH	LOW
2004	$2,835	$2,126
2005	$3,152	$2,364

Z587L

YEARS MFRD 2004-2006
SERIES . . . . Z MASTER SERIES
ENGINE . . . . KAWASAKI
ENGINE HP 27
COOLING . . . . LIQUID
FUEL . . . . G
SPEEDS . . . . VARIABLE
TRANSMISSION . . . . HYDRO
STEERING . . . . ZERO
STANDARD DECK . . . . 60"
MSRP $12,335

OPTIONS

72" DECK
BAG

RETAIL PRICING

YEAR	HIGH	LOW
2004	$3,336	$2,502
2005	$3,704	$2,778
2006	$4,116	$3,087

Z588E

YEARS MFRD 2004-2006
SERIES . . . . Z MASTER SERIES
ENGINE . . . . KOHLER
ENGINE HP 28
COOLING . . . . LIQUID
FUEL . . . . G
SPEEDS . . . . VARIABLE
TRANSMISSION . . . . HYDRO
STEERING . . . . ZERO
STANDARD DECK . . . . 60"
MSRP $12,220

OPTIONS

72" DECK
BAG

RETAIL PRICING

YEAR	HIGH	LOW
2004	$3,332	$2,499
2005	$3,699	$2,774
2006	$4,112	$3,084

Z4200

YEARS MFRD 2010-2010
SERIES . . . . . TIMECUTTER Z SERIES
ENGINE . . . . KOHLER
CYLINDERS 2
ENGINE HP 19
COOLING . . . . AIR
FUEL . . . . G
SPEEDS . . . . VARIABLE
TRANSMISSION . . . . HYDRO
STEERING . . . . ZERO
BLADE CLUTCH . . . . ELECTRIC
STANDARD DECK . . . . 42"
MSRP $2,349

RETAIL PRICING

YEAR	HIGH	LOW
2010	$1,451	$1,089

Z4235

YEARS MFRD 2010-2010
SERIES . . . . . TIMECUTTER Z SERIES
ENGINE . . . . KAWASAKI
CYLINDERS 2
ENGINE HP 22
COOLING . . . . AIR
FUEL . . . . G
SPEEDS . . . . VARIABLE
TRANSMISSION . . . . HYDRO
STEERING . . . . ZERO
STANDARD DECK . . . . 42"
MSRP $2,799

RETAIL PRICING

YEAR	HIGH	LOW
2010	$1,860	$1,395

Z5030

YEARS MFRD 2010-2010
SERIES . . . . . TIMECUTTER Z SERIES
ENGINE . . . . KOHLER
CYLINDERS 2
ENGINE HP 23
COOLING . . . . AIR
FUEL . . . . G
SPEEDS . . . . VARIABLE
TRANSMISSION . . . . HYDRO
STEERING . . . . ZERO
STANDARD DECK . . . . 50"
MSRP $3,199

RETAIL PRICING

YEAR	HIGH	LOW
2010	$2,127	$1,596

Z5035

YEARS MFRD 2010-2010
SERIES . . . . . TIMECUTTER Z SERIES
ENGINE . . . . KAWASAKI
CYLINDERS 2
ENGINE HP 24
COOLING . . . . AIR
FUEL . . . . G
SPEEDS . . . . VARIABLE
TRANSMISSION . . . . HYDRO
STEERING . . . . ZERO
STANDARD DECK . . . . 50"
MSRP $2,799

RETAIL PRICING

YEAR	HIGH	LOW
2010	$1,348	$1,011

Z5060

YEARS MFRD 2010-2010
SERIES . . . . . TIMECUTTER Z SERIES
ENGINE . . . . KOHLER
CYLINDERS 2
ENGINE HP 25
COOLING . . . . AIR
FUEL . . . . G
SPEEDS . . . . VARIABLE
TRANSMISSION . . . . HYDRO
STEERING . . . . ZERO
STANDARD DECK . . . . 50"
MSRP $3,499

RETAIL PRICING

YEAR	HIGH	LOW
2010	$2,326	$1,745

ZX525/19-52ZX

YEARS MFRD 2006-2006
SERIES . . . . . . TIMECUTTER SERIES
ENGINE . . . . KAWASAKI
CYLINDERS 2
ENGINE HP 19
COOLING . . . . AIR
FUEL . . . . G
SPEEDS . . . . VARIABLE
TRANSMISSION . . . . HYDRO
STEERING . . . . ZERO
BLADE CLUTCH . . . . ELECTRIC
STANDARD DECK . . . . 52"
MSRP $5,299

RETAIL PRICING

YEAR	HIGH	LOW
2006	$3,336	$2,502

ZX4800

YEARS MFRD 2015-2017
SERIES . . . . TITAN SERIES
ENGINE . . . . KOHLER PRO
ENGINE HP 21
COOLING . . . . AIR
FUEL . . . . G
SPEEDS . . . . VARIABLE
TRANSMISSION . . . . HYDRO
STEERING . . . . ZERO
STANDARD DECK . . . . 48"
MSRP $4,899

OPTIONS

2 BAG

RETAIL PRICING

YEAR	HIGH	LOW
2015	$2,557	$1,918
2016	$3,280	$2,460
2017	$3,753	$2,815

ZX4820

YEARS MFRD 2011-2014
SERIES . . . . TITAN SERIES
ENGINE . . . . KAWASAKI
CYLINDERS 2
CID 726CC
ENGINE HP 22
COOLING . . . . AIR
FUEL . . . . G
SPEEDS . . . . VARIABLE
TRANSMISSION . . . . HYDRO
STEERING . . . . ZERO
BLADE CLUTCH . . . . ELECTRIC
STANDARD DECK . . . . 48"
MSRP $4,899

RETAIL PRICING

YEAR	HIGH	LOW
2011	$1,708	$1,281
2012	$1,898	$1,424
2013	$2,585	$1,939
2014	$3,258	$2,444

ZX5000

YEARS MFRD 2010-2010
SERIES .... TITAN SERIES
ENGINE .... B&S
ENGINE HP 22
COOLING .... AIR
FUEL .... G
SPEEDS .... VARIABLE
TRANSMISSION .... HYDRO
STEERING .... ZERO
STANDARD DECK .... 50"
MSRP $3,669

OPTIONS

2 BAG

RETAIL PRICING

YEAR	HIGH	LOW
2010	$1,770	$1,328

ZX5020

YEARS MFRD 2011-2014
SERIES .... TITAN SERIES
ENGINE ... KOHLER COURAGE PRO
CID 725CC
ENGINE HP 23
COOLING .... AIR
FUEL .... G
SPEEDS .... VARIABLE
TRANSMISSION .... HYDRO
STEERING .... ZERO
BLADE CLUTCH .... ELECTRIC
STANDARD DECK .... 50"
MSRP $4,699

RETAIL PRICING

YEAR	HIGH	LOW
2011	$1,534	$1,150
2012	$1,810	$1,357
2013	$2,324	$1,743
2014	$3,061	$2,296

ZX5400

YEARS MFRD 2015-2017
SERIES .... TITAN SERIES
ENGINE .... KOHLER
ENGINE HP 23
COOLING .... AIR
FUEL .... G
SPEEDS .... VARIABLE
TRANSMISSION .... HYDRO
STEERING .... ZERO
STANDARD DECK .... 54"
MSRP $5,699

RETAIL PRICING

YEAR	HIGH	LOW
2015	$2,760	$2,070
2016	$3,223	$2,417
2017	$3,955	$2,967

ZX5420

YEARS MFRD 2011-2014
SERIES .... TITAN SERIES
ENGINE .... KAWASAKI
CYLINDERS 2
CID 726CC
ENGINE HP 24
COOLING .... AIR
FUEL .... G
SPEEDS .... VARIABLE
TRANSMISSION .... HYDRO
STEERING .... ZERO
BLADE CLUTCH .... ELECTRIC
STANDARD DECK .... 54"
MSRP $5,499

RETAIL PRICING

YEAR	HIGH	LOW
2011	$1,842	$1,382
2012	$2,214	$1,660
2013	$2,973	$2,230
2014	$3,549	$2,662

ZX5450

YEARS MFRD 2010-2010
SERIES .... TITAN SERIES
ENGINE .... KOHLER PRO
ENGINE HP 25
COOLING .... AIR
FUEL .... G
SPEEDS .... VARIABLE
TRANSMISSION .... HYDRO
STEERING .... ZERO
STANDARD DECK .... 54"
MSRP $5,299

RETAIL PRICING

YEAR	HIGH	LOW
2010	$3,525	$2,644

ZX6000

YEARS MFRD 2015-2017
SERIES .... TITAN SERIES
ENGINE .... KOHLER
ENGINE HP 26
COOLING .... AIR
FUEL .... G
SPEEDS .... VARIABLE
TRANSMISSION .... HYDRO
STEERING .... ZERO
STANDARD DECK .... 60"
MSRP $5,999

RETAIL PRICING

YEAR	HIGH	LOW
2015	$3,020	$2,265
2016	$3,522	$2,642
2017	$4,169	$3,126

ZX6020

YEARS MFRD 2011-2014
SERIES .... TITAN SERIES
ENGINE .... KAWASAKI
CYLINDERS 2
CID 726CC
ENGINE HP 26
COOLING .... AIR
FUEL .... G
SPEEDS .... VARIABLE
TRANSMISSION .... HYDRO
STEERING .... ZERO
BLADE CLUTCH .... ELECTRIC
STANDARD DECK .... 60"
MSRP $5,899

RETAIL PRICING

YEAR	HIGH	LOW
2011	$1,985	$1,489
2012	$2,419	$1,814
2013	$3,114	$2,336
2014	$3,819	$2,865

ZX6030

YEARS MFRD 2010-2010
SERIES .... TITAN SERIES
ENGINE .... KOHLER PRO
ENGINE HP 27
COOLING .... AIR
FUEL .... G
SPEEDS .... VARIABLE
TRANSMISSION .... HYDRO
STEERING .... ZERO
STANDARD DECK .... 60"
MSRP $5,699

RETAIL PRICING

YEAR	HIGH	LOW
2010	$3,791	$2,843

ZX6050

YEARS MFRD 2010-2010
SERIES .... TITAN SERIES
ENGINE .... KAWASAKI FS
ENGINE HP 26
COOLING .... AIR
FUEL .... G
SPEEDS .... VARIABLE
TRANSMISSION .... HYDRO
STEERING .... ZERO
STANDARD DECK .... 60"
MSRP $5,899

RETAIL PRICING

YEAR	HIGH	LOW
2010	$3,924	$2,943

8-25

YEARS MFRD 1991-2000
ENGINE .... B&S
ENGINE HP 8
COOLING .... AIR
FUEL .... G
SPEEDS 5/1
TRANSMISSION .... GEAR
STEERING .... STANDARD
WEIGHT .... 330 LBS.

15-38HXL

YEARS MFRD 1999-1999
SERIES .... XL SERIES
ENGINE .... B&S
ENGINE HP 15.5
FUEL .... G
TRANSMISSION .... HYDRO
STEERING .... STANDARD
STANDARD DECK .... 38"
MSRP $1,999

RETAIL PRICING

YEAR	HIGH	LOW
1999	$352	$264

15-44HXL

YEARS MFRD 1995-1995
SERIES .... XL SERIES
ENGINE .... B&S
ENGINE HP 15.5
COOLING .... AIR
FUEL .... G
TRANSMISSION .... HYDRO
STEERING .... STANDARD
STANDARD DECK .... 44"
MSRP $2,599

RETAIL PRICING

YEAR	HIGH	LOW
1995	$661	$496

16-44HXL

YEARS MFRD 1996-1998
SERIES .... XL SERIES
ENGINE .... B&S
ENGINE HP 16
COOLING .... AIR
FUEL .... G
TRANSMISSION .... HYDRO
STEERING .... STANDARD
STANDARD DECK .... 44"
MSRP $2,499

RETAIL PRICING

YEAR	HIGH	LOW
1996	$651	$488
1997	$669	$502
1998	$762	$572

17-42Z

YEARS MFRD 2004-2005
SERIES .... TIMECUTTER SERIES
ENGINE .... B&S
ENGINE HP 17
COOLING .... AIR
FUEL .... G
SPEEDS .... VARIABLE
TRANSMISSION .... HYDRO
STEERING .... ZERO
BLADE CLUTCH .... ELECTRIC
STANDARD DECK .... 42"
MSRP $3,599

RETAIL PRICING

YEAR	HIGH	LOW
2004	$1,948	$1,461
2005	$2,105	$1,579

17-44ZX

YEARS MFRD 2004-2004
SERIES .... TIMECUTTER SERIES
ENGINE .... B&S
ENGINE HP 17
COOLING .... AIR

TORO

FUEL .... G
SPEEDS .... VARIABLE
TRANSMISSION .... HYDRO
STEERING .... ZERO
BLADE CLUTCH .... ELECTRIC

17-52ZX

YEARS MFRD 2004-2004
SERIES .... TIMECUTTER SERIES
ENGINE .... KOHLER COMMAND
ENGINE HP 17
COOLING .... AIR
FUEL .... G
SPEEDS .... VARIABLE
TRANSMISSION .... HYDRO
STEERING .... ZERO
BLADE CLUTCH .... ELECTRIC

17K-44ZX

YEARS MFRD 2004-2004
SERIES .... TIMECUTTER SERIES
ENGINE .... KOHLER
ENGINE HP 17
COOLING .... AIR
FUEL .... G
SPEEDS .... VARIABLE
TRANSMISSION .... HYDRO
STEERING .... ZERO
BLADE CLUTCH .... ELECTRIC

18-44Z

YEARS MFRD 2004-2005
SERIES .... TIMECUTTER SERIES
ENGINE .... B&S
ENGINE HP 18
COOLING .... AIR
FUEL .... G
SPEEDS .... VARIABLE
TRANSMISSION .... HYDRO
STEERING .... ZERO
STANDARD DECK .... 44"
MSRP $3,999

RETAIL PRICING

YEAR	HIGH	LOW
2004	$2,162	$1,621
2005	$2,342	$1,756

18-44ZX

YEARS MFRD 2004-2006
SERIES .... TIMECUTTER SERIES
ENGINE .... B&S
CYLINDERS 2
ENGINE HP 18
COOLING .... AIR
FUEL .... G
SPEEDS .... VARIABLE
TRANSMISSION .... HYDRO
STEERING .... ZERO
BLADE CLUTCH .... ELECTRIC
STANDARD DECK .... 44"
MSRP $5,299

RETAIL PRICING

YEAR	HIGH	LOW
2004	$2,486	$1,864
2005	$2,692	$2,019
2006	$3,336	$2,502

18-52ZX

YEARS MFRD 2004-2006
SERIES .... TIMECUTTER SERIES
ENGINE .... KAWASAKI
CYLINDERS 2
ENGINE HP 18
COOLING .... AIR
FUEL .... G
SPEEDS .... VARIABLE
TRANSMISSION .... HYDRO
STEERING .... ZERO
BLADE CLUTCH .... ELECTRIC
STANDARD DECK .... 52"
MSRP $4,899

RETAIL PRICING

YEAR	HIGH	LOW
2004	$2,648	$1,986
2005	$2,867	$2,151
2006	$3,085	$2,313

19-52ZX

YEARS MFRD 2004-2005
SERIES .... TIMECUTTER SERIES
ENGINE .... KAWASAKI
CYLINDERS 2
ENGINE HP 19
COOLING .... AIR
FUEL .... G
SPEEDS .... VARIABLE
TRANSMISSION .... HYDRO
STEERING .... ZERO
STANDARD DECK .... 52"
MSRP $5,299

RETAIL PRICING

YEAR	HIGH	LOW
2004	$2,866	$2,150
2005	$3,101	$2,326

118

YEARS MFRD 1992-1994
SERIES .... PROLINE SERIES
ENGINE .... TORO
ENGINE HP 18
COOLING .... AIR
FUEL .... G
TRANSMISSION .... HYDRO
STEERING .... ZERO
STANDARD DECK .... 44"
MSRP $5,880

RETAIL PRICING

YEAR	HIGH	LOW
1992	$526	$394
1993	$581	$435
1994	$649	$486

120

YEARS MFRD 1990-2002
SERIES .. GROUNDSMASTER SERIES
ENGINE .... KOHLER
ENGINE HP 20
FUEL .... G
SPEEDS .... VARIABLE
TRANSMISSION .... HYDRO
STEERING .... STANDARD
STANDARD DECK .... 44"
MSRP $7,399

OPTIONS

52" DECK

RETAIL PRICING

YEAR	HIGH	LOW
1990	$1,359	$1,019
1991	$1,382	$1,037
1992	$1,482	$1,111
1993	$1,502	$1,127
1994	$1,608	$1,206
1995	$1,649	$1,237
1996	$1,719	$1,290
1997	$1,763	$1,322
1998	$2,075	$1,556
1999	$2,387	$1,790
2000	$2,724	$2,043
2001	$2,988	$2,241
2002	$3,344	$2,508

216H

YEARS MFRD 1990-1991
ENGINE .... TORO
ENGINE HP 16
COOLING .... AIR
FUEL .... G
TRANSMISSION .... HYDRO
STEERING .... STANDARD
STANDARD DECK .... 36"
MSRP $3,249

RETAIL PRICING

YEAR	HIGH	LOW
1990	$702	$527
1991	$784	$588

220

YEARS MFRD 1990-1997
SERIES .. GROUNDSMASTER SERIES
ENGINE .... ONAN
ENGINE HP 20
FUEL .... G
TRANSMISSION .... HYDRO
STEERING .... STANDARD
STANDARD DECK .... 52"
MSRP $10,999

OPTIONS

62" DECK

RETAIL PRICING

YEAR	HIGH	LOW
1990	$2,244	$1,683
1991	$2,305	$1,729
1992	$2,431	$1,823
1993	$2,487	$1,865
1994	$2,647	$1,985
1995	$2,716	$2,037
1996	$2,815	$2,111
1997	$2,941	$2,206

220D

YEARS MFRD 1990-1991
SERIES .. GROUNDSMASTER SERIES
ENGINE .... MITSUBISHI
ENGINE HP 20.5
FUEL .... D
TRANSMISSION .... HYDRO
STEERING .... STANDARD

223D

YEARS MFRD 1992-2001
SERIES .. GROUNDSMASTER SERIES
ENGINE .... MITSUBISHI
ENGINE HP 23
FUEL .... D
TRANSMISSION .... HYDRO
STEERING .... STANDARD

OPTIONS

4WD

224

YEARS MFRD 1990-1997
SERIES .. GROUNDSMASTER SERIES
ENGINE .... MITSUBISHI
ENGINE HP 20.5
FUEL .... G
TRANSMISSION .... HYDRO
STEERING .... STANDARD

225

YEARS MFRD 1998-2002
SERIES .. GROUNDSMASTER SERIES
ENGINE .... MITSUBISHI
ENGINE HP 24
FUEL .... G
TRANSMISSION .... HYDRO
STEERING .... STANDARD

228D

YEARS MFRD 2002-2002
SERIES .. GROUNDSMASTER SERIES
ENGINE .... KUBOTA
CYLINDERS 3
CID 68.5
ENGINE HP 28
COOLING .... LIQUID
FUEL .... D
SPEEDS .... VARIABLE
TRANSMISSION .... HYDRO
STEERING .... STANDARD
WEIGHT .... 1,120 LBS.

OPTIONS

4WD

246H

YEARS MFRD 1992-1993
ENGINE .... TORO
ENGINE HP 16
COOLING .... AIR
FUEL .... G
TRANSMISSION .... HYDRO
STEERING .... STANDARD
STANDARD DECK .... 38"
MSRP $3,599

RETAIL PRICING

YEAR	HIGH	LOW
1992	$834	$626
1993	$844	$633

257H
YEARS MFRD 1988-1990
ENGINE .... KAWASAKI
ENGINE HP 17
TRANSMISSION .... HYDRO
WEIGHT .... 559 LBS.
MSRP $2,700

RETAIL PRICING

YEAR	HIGH	LOW
1990	$581	$435

265-6
YEARS MFRD 1995-2000
SERIES .... 260 SERIES
ENGINE .... KOHLER
ENGINE HP 15
COOLING .... AIR
FUEL .... G
TRANSMISSION .... GEAR
STEERING .... STANDARD
STANDARD DECK .... 38"
MSRP $2,999

OPTIONS

42" SNOW THROWER
48" BLADE
48" DECK
BAGGER

RETAIL PRICING

YEAR	HIGH	LOW
1995	$236	$177
1996	$263	$197
1997	$291	$218
1998	$322	$241
1999	$358	$269
2000	$398	$298

265H
YEARS MFRD 1994-2000
SERIES .... 260 SERIES
ENGINE .... KOHLER
ENGINE HP 15
COOLING .... AIR
FUEL .... G
SPEEDS .... VARIABLE
TRANSMISSION .... HYDRO
STEERING .... STANDARD
STANDARD DECK .... 38"
MSRP $3,639

OPTIONS

42" SNOW THROWER
48" BLADE
48" DECK
BAGGER

RETAIL PRICING

YEAR	HIGH	LOW
1994	$259	$194
1995	$287	$215
1996	$318	$238
1997	$353	$265
1998	$392	$294
1999	$434	$326
2000	$481	$361

266H
YEARS MFRD 1994-2003
SERIES .... 260 SERIES
ENGINE .... KOHLER
ENGINE HP 16
FUEL .... G
STEERING .... STANDARD
MSRP $3,319

RETAIL PRICING

YEAR	HIGH	LOW
1994	$787	$590
1995	$794	$595
1996	$814	$611
1997	$842	$632
1998	$960	$720
1999	$1,091	$818
2000	$1,227	$920
2001	$1,353	$1,015
2002	$1,499	$1,124

267H
YEARS MFRD 1996-1998
SERIES .... 260 SERIES
ENGINE .... KOHLER
ENGINE HP 17
COOLING .... AIR
FUEL .... G
TRANSMISSION .... HYDRO
STEERING .... STANDARD
STANDARD DECK .... 42"
MSRP $3,989

OPTIONS

36" TILLER
48" DECK
BAGGER

RETAIL PRICING

YEAR	HIGH	LOW
1996	$319	$239
1997	$354	$266
1998	$393	$295

268H
YEARS MFRD 1999-2000
SERIES .... 260 SERIES
ENGINE .... KOHLER
ENGINE HP 18
COOLING .... AIR
FUEL .... G
TRANSMISSION .... HYDRO
STEERING .... STANDARD
STANDARD DECK .... 48"
MSRP $4,329

OPTIONS

42" SNOW THROWER
48" BLADE
52" DECK
BAGGER

RETAIL PRICING

YEAR	HIGH	LOW
1999	$497	$373
2000	$551	$413

269H
YEARS MFRD 1996-1998
SERIES .... 260 SERIES
ENGINE .... KOHLER
ENGINE HP 19
COOLING .... AIR
FUEL .... G
TRANSMISSION .... HYDRO
STEERING .... STANDARD
STANDARD DECK .... 48"
MSRP $4,809

OPTIONS

36" TILLER
42" SNOW THROWER
52" DECK
BAGGER

RETAIL PRICING

YEAR	HIGH	LOW
1996	$385	$289
1997	$426	$320
1998	$474	$356

270H
YEARS MFRD 1999-2000
SERIES .... 260 SERIES
ENGINE .... KOHLER
ENGINE HP 20
COOLING .... AIR
FUEL .... G
TRANSMISSION .... HYDRO
STEERING .... STANDARD
STANDARD DECK .... 48"
MSRP $4,809

OPTIONS

42" SNOW THROWER
48" BLADE
52" DECK
BAGGER

RETAIL PRICING

YEAR	HIGH	LOW
1999	$553	$415
2000	$612	$459

315-8
YEARS MFRD 2003-2005
SERIES .... 300 SERIES
ENGINE .... KOHLER
ENGINE HP 15
COOLING .... AIR
FUEL .... G
SPEEDS 8/1
TRANSMISSION .... GEAR
STEERING .... STANDARD
WEIGHT .... 624 LBS.
MSRP $3,969

RETAIL PRICING

YEAR	HIGH	LOW
2003	$1,969	$1,477
2004	$2,147	$1,610
2005	$2,323	$1,743

322D
YEARS MFRD 1990-1991
SERIES . . GROUNDSMASTER SERIES
ENGINE .... MITSUBISHI
ENGINE HP 22
FUEL .... D
TRANSMISSION .... HYDRO
STEERING .... STANDARD

325D
YEARS MFRD 1992-2001
SERIES . . GROUNDSMASTER SERIES
ENGINE .... MITSUBISHI
ENGINE HP 25
FUEL .... D
TRANSMISSION .... HYDRO
STEERING .... STANDARD

OPTIONS

4WD

AVG. AUCTION PRICING

LOW	HIGH	AVG
$1,030	$2,341	$1,467

327
YEARS MFRD 1990-1991
SERIES . . GROUNDSMASTER SERIES
ENGINE .... CONTINENTAL
ENGINE HP 27
FUEL .... G
TRANSMISSION .... HYDRO
STEERING .... STANDARD

328D
YEARS MFRD 2002-2011
SERIES . . GROUNDSMASTER SERIES
ENGINE .... KUBOTA
CYLINDERS 3
CID 68.5
ENGINE HP 28
FUEL .... D
SPEEDS .... VARIABLE
TRANSMISSION .... HYDRO
STEERING .... STANDARD
DRIVE TYPE 2WD
ROPS/CAB .... ROPS
STANDARD DECK .... 72"
WEIGHT .... 1,665 LBS.
MSRP $20,470

OPTIONS

4WD

RETAIL PRICING

YEAR	HIGH	LOW
2002	$2,718	$2,039
2003	$3,496	$2,622
2004	$3,750	$2,813
2005	$3,882	$2,912
2006	$4,138	$3,104
2007	$5,326	$3,994
2008	$6,483	$4,862
2009	$8,093	$6,069
2010	$9,807	$7,355
2011	$12,737	$9,553

AVG. AUCTION PRICING

LOW	HIGH	AVG
$2,284	$6,090	$4,737

TORO

360 QUAD STEER

YEARS MFRD........2011-2011
SERIES.. GROUNDSMASTER SERIES
ENGINE..........KUBOTA 1505
CYLINDERS..................4
ENGINE HP.................36
COOLING...............LIQUID
FUEL.......................D
SPEEDS..............VARIABLE
TRANSMISSION..........HYDRO
STEERING.................ZERO
WEIGHT............2,562 LBS.

416-8

YEARS MFRD........1985-1997
ENGINE..................ONAN
ENGINE HP.................16
COOLING....................AIR
FUEL.......................G
TRANSMISSION...........GEAR
STEERING............STANDARD
STANDARD DECK...........42"
MSRP..................$4,729

OPTIONS

36" TILLER
44" SNOW BLOWER
48" BLADE
BAGGER

RETAIL PRICING

YEAR	HIGH	LOW
1989	$216	$162
1990	$242	$181
1991	$266	$199
1992	$295	$222
1993	$327	$245
1994	$362	$272
1995	$403	$302
1996	$448	$336
1997	$495	$371

416H

YEARS MFRD........1990-1997
SERIES.............400 SERIES
ENGINE..................ONAN
ENGINE HP.................16
COOLING....................AIR
FUEL.......................G
TRANSMISSION..........HYDRO
STEERING............STANDARD
STANDARD DECK...........36"
MSRP..................$5,379

OPTIONS

36" TILLER
44" SNOW BLOWER
48" BLADE
BAGGER

RETAIL PRICING

YEAR	HIGH	LOW
1990	$273	$205
1991	$302	$227
1992	$338	$253
1993	$375	$281
1994	$411	$308
1995	$459	$344
1996	$509	$381
1997	$561	$421

416XT

YEARS MFRD........2004-2006
SERIES...........400XT SERIES
ENGINE.................KOHLER
ENGINE HP.................16
COOLING....................AIR
FUEL.......................G
SPEEDS..............VARIABLE
TRANSMISSION..........HYDRO
STEERING............STANDARD
BLADE CLUTCH........ELECTRIC
WEIGHT.................631 LBS.
MSRP..................$3,719

RETAIL PRICING

YEAR	HIGH	LOW
2004	$2,011	$1,508
2005	$2,176	$1,632

417XT

YEARS MFRD........2004-2005
SERIES...........400XT SERIES
ENGINE.............KAWASAKI
CYLINDERS..................2
ENGINE HP.................17
COOLING....................AIR
FUEL.......................G
SPEEDS..............VARIABLE
TRANSMISSION..........HYDRO
STEERING............STANDARD
BLADE CLUTCH........ELECTRIC
STANDARD DECK...........42"
WEIGHT.................657 LBS.
MSRP..................$4,419

RETAIL PRICING

YEAR	HIGH	LOW
2004	$2,388	$1,791
2005	$2,585	$1,939

419XT

YEARS MFRD........2004-2005
SERIES...........400XT SERIES
ENGINE.............KAWASAKI
CYLINDERS..................2
ENGINE HP.................19
COOLING....................AIR
FUEL.......................G
SPEEDS..............VARIABLE
TRANSMISSION..........HYDRO
STEERING............STANDARD
BLADE CLUTCH........ELECTRIC
WEIGHT.................657 LBS.
MSRP..................$5,019

RETAIL PRICING

YEAR	HIGH	LOW
2004	$2,714	$2,036
2005	$2,936	$2,202

518XI

YEARS MFRD........1998-2000
SERIES..............5XI SERIES
ENGINE.................KOHLER
ENGINE HP.................18
COOLING....................AIR
FUEL.......................G
SPEEDS..............VARIABLE
TRANSMISSION..........HYDRO
STEERING............STANDARD
STANDARD DECK...........44"
MSRP..................$6,299

OPTIONS

42" SNOW THROWER
48" BLADE
52" DECK
BAGGER

RETAIL PRICING

YEAR	HIGH	LOW
1998	$914	$685
1999	$1,011	$758
2000	$1,119	$839

520-8

YEARS MFRD........1990-1991
SERIES..............5XI SERIES
ENGINE..................TORO
ENGINE HP.................20
FUEL.......................G
TRANSMISSION...........GEAR
STEERING............STANDARD
STANDARD DECK...........48"
MSRP..................$5,249

RETAIL PRICING

YEAR	HIGH	LOW
1990	$1,124	$843
1991	$1,152	$864

520H

YEARS MFRD........1988-1997
SERIES..........41-200E SERIES
ENGINE..................ONAN
ENGINE HP.................20
COOLING....................AIR
FUEL.......................G
TRANSMISSION..........HYDRO
STEERING............STANDARD
STANDARD DECK...........48"
MSRP..................$6,189

OPTIONS

36" TILLER
44" SNOW BLOWER
48" BLADE
BAGGER

RETAIL PRICING

YEAR	HIGH	LOW
1988	$284	$213
1989	$305	$228
1990	$336	$252
1991	$371	$279
1992	$410	$308
1993	$455	$341
1994	$503	$378
1995	$556	$417
1996	$615	$461
1997	$683	$512

520LXI

YEARS MFRD........1998-2000
SERIES..............5XI SERIES
ENGINE.............KAWASAKI
ENGINE HP.................20
COOLING...............LIQUID
FUEL.......................G
TRANSMISSION..........HYDRO
STEERING............STANDARD
STANDARD DECK...........48"
MSRP..................$8,179

OPTIONS

44" SNOW THROWER
48" BLADE
52" DECK
BAGGER

RETAIL PRICING

YEAR	HIGH	LOW
1998	$1,187	$890
1999	$1,312	$984
2000	$1,452	$1,089

520XI

YEARS MFRD........1998-2000
SERIES..............5XI SERIES
ENGINE.................KOHLER
CYLINDERS..................2
ENGINE HP.................20
COOLING....................AIR
FUEL.......................G
SPEEDS..............VARIABLE
TRANSMISSION..........HYDRO
STEERING............STANDARD
STANDARD DECK...........48"
WEIGHT..............1,014 LBS.
MSRP..................$6,939

OPTIONS

42" SNOW THROWER
48" BLADE
52" DECK
BAGGER

RETAIL PRICING

YEAR	HIGH	LOW
1998	$1,006	$754
1999	$1,113	$835
2000	$1,231	$923

522XI

YEARS MFRD........1998-2000
SERIES..............5XI SERIES
ENGINE.................KOHLER
CYLINDERS..................2
ENGINE HP.................22
COOLING....................AIR
FUEL.......................G
SPEEDS..............VARIABLE
TRANSMISSION..........HYDRO
STEERING............STANDARD
STANDARD DECK...........52"
WEIGHT..............1,022 LBS.
MSRP..................$7,929

OPTIONS

44" SNOW THROWER
48" BLADE
60" DECK
BAGGER

RETAIL PRICING

YEAR	HIGH	LOW
1998	$1,150	$862
1999	$1,273	$955
2000	$1,410	$1,057

523DXI

YEARS MFRD 1998-2000
SERIES . . . . 5XI SERIES
ENGINE . . . . B&S
ENGINE HP 23
COOLING . . . . LIQUID
FUEL . . . . D
SPEEDS . . . . VARIABLE
TRANSMISSION . . . . HYDRO
STEERING. . . . . STANDARD
STANDARD DECK . . . . 60"
MSRP. $9,849

OPTIONS

44" SNOW THROWER
48" BLADE
52" DECK
BAGGER

RETAIL PRICING

YEAR	HIGH	LOW
1998	$1,428	$1,071
1999	$1,580	$1,185
2000	$1,756	$1,317

580D

YEARS MFRD 2007-2007
SERIES . . GROUNDSMASTER SERIES
ENGINE . . . . MITSUBISHI
ENGINE HP 80
FUEL . . . . D
SPEEDS . . . . VARIABLE
TRANSMISSION . . . . HYDRO
STEERING. . . . . ZERO
STANDARD DECK . . . . 95"
WEIGHT . . . . 6,540 LBS.
MSRP. $76,400

RETAIL PRICING

YEAR	HIGH	LOW
2007	$49,179	$36,884

616

YEARS MFRD 1990-1996
SERIES . . . . PROLINE SERIES
ENGINE . . . . ONAN
ENGINE HP 16
COOLING . . . . AIR
FUEL . . . . G
TRANSMISSION . . . . HYDRO
STEERING. . . . . ZERO
STANDARD DECK . . . . 38"
MSRP. $4,959

OPTIONS

52" DECK
BAG & FAN

RETAIL PRICING

YEAR	HIGH	LOW
1990	$273	$205
1991	$300	$225
1992	$336	$252
1993	$371	$279
1994	$415	$311
1995	$459	$344
1996	$510	$382

616Z

YEARS MFRD 1990-1993
SERIES . . . . Y1-120E SERIES
ENGINE . . . . TORO
ENGINE HP 16
FUEL . . . . G
TRANSMISSION . . . . HYDRO
STEERING. . . . . STANDARD
STANDARD DECK . . . . 42"
WEIGHT . . . . 720 LBS.
MSRP. $4,399

OPTIONS

52" DECK

RETAIL PRICING

YEAR	HIGH	LOW
1990	$841	$631
1991	$910	$683
1992	$989	$741
1993	$1,033	$775

620

YEARS MFRD 1990-1996
SERIES . . . . PROLINE SERIES
ENGINE . . . . ONAN
ENGINE HP 20
COOLING . . . . AIR
FUEL . . . . G
TRANSMISSION . . . . HYDRO
STEERING. . . . . ZERO
STANDARD DECK . . . . 38"
MSRP. $5,379

OPTIONS

52" DECK
BAG & FAN

RETAIL PRICING

YEAR	HIGH	LOW
1990	$293	$220
1991	$328	$246
1992	$363	$273
1993	$404	$303
1994	$447	$335
1995	$498	$374
1996	$553	$415

620Z

YEARS MFRD 1990-1993
SERIES . . . . Y1-200E SERIES
ENGINE . . . . TORO
ENGINE HP 20
FUEL . . . . G
SPEEDS . . . . VARIABLE
TRANSMISSION . . . . HYDRO
STEERING. . . . . STANDARD
STANDARD DECK . . . . 52"
WEIGHT . . . . 720 LBS.
MSRP. $4,799

RETAIL PRICING

YEAR	HIGH	LOW
1990	$927	$695
1991	$1,000	$750
1992	$1,081	$811
1993	$1,127	$845

724

YEARS MFRD 1990-1996
SERIES . . . . PROLINE SERIES
ENGINE . . . . ONAN
ENGINE HP 24
COOLING . . . . AIR
FUEL . . . . G
TRANSMISSION . . . . HYDRO
STEERING. . . . . ZERO
STANDARD DECK . . . . 50"
MSRP. $6,699

OPTIONS

60" DECK

RETAIL PRICING

YEAR	HIGH	LOW
1990	$367	$276
1991	$408	$306
1992	$455	$341
1993	$503	$378
1994	$556	$417
1995	$620	$465
1996	$688	$516

1000L

YEARS MFRD 1996-2001
SERIES . . GROUNDSMASTER SERIES
ENGINE . . . . KAWASAKI
ENGINE HP 20
FUEL . . . . G
TRANSMISSION . . . . HYDRO
STEERING. . . . . STANDARD
MSRP. $10,450

RETAIL PRICING

YEAR	HIGH	LOW
1996	$2,569	$1,927
1997	$2,635	$1,976
1998	$3,036	$2,277
1999	$3,462	$2,597
2000	$3,890	$2,918
2001	$4,337	$3,253

1600HMR

YEARS MFRD 1988-1990
ENGINE . . . . KOHLER
ENGINE HP 16
COOLING . . . . AIR
FUEL . . . . G
STEERING. . . . . STANDARD
STANDARD DECK . . . . 44"
MSRP. $4,199

RETAIL PRICING

YEAR	HIGH	LOW
1990	$905	$679

2000

YEARS MFRD 2000-2001
SERIES . . . . . GROUNDS PRO SERIES
ENGINE . . . . VANGUARD
ENGINE HP 16
FUEL . . . . G
TRANSMISSION . . . . HYDRO
STEERING. . . . . STANDARD

2300D

YEARS MFRD 1998-2002
SERIES . . . . . . REELMASTER SERIES
ENGINE . . . . PERKINS
ENGINE HP 18
FUEL . . . . D
TRANSMISSION . . . . HYDRO
STEERING. . . . . STANDARD

2600D

YEARS MFRD 1998-2002
SERIES . . . . . . REELMASTER SERIES
ENGINE . . . . PERKINS
ENGINE HP 18
FUEL . . . . D
TRANSMISSION . . . . HYDRO
STEERING. . . . . STANDARD

3000

YEARS MFRD 1996-2002
SERIES . . GROUNDSMASTER SERIES
ENGINE . . . . PEUGEOT
ENGINE HP 33
FUEL . . . . D
TRANSMISSION . . . . HYDRO
STEERING. . . . . STANDARD

3000D

YEARS MFRD 1998-2002
SERIES . . GROUNDSMASTER SERIES
ENGINE . . . . PEUGEOT
ENGINE HP 33
FUEL . . . . D
TRANSMISSION . . . . HYDRO
STEERING. . . . . STANDARD
DRIVE TYPE 4WD
ROPS/CAB . . . . ROPS

3050

YEARS MFRD 2000-2010
SERIES . . . . GREENSMASTER SERIES
ENGINE . . . . VANGUARD V-TWIN
CID 29.3
ENGINE HP 16
COOLING . . . . AIR
FUEL . . . . G
SPEEDS . . . . VARAIBLE
TRANSMISSION . . . . HYDRO
STEERING. . . . . STANDARD
STANDARD DECK . . . . 59"
WEIGHT . . . . 940 LBS.
MSRP. $23,750

OPTIONS

KOHLER 16HP

RETAIL PRICING

YEAR	HIGH	LOW
2005	$13,462	$10,096
2006	$14,025	$10,519
2007	$14,554	$10,916
2008	$15,210	$11,407
2009	$15,258	$11,444
2010	$15,802	$11,851

TORO

3100

YEARS MFRD 2000-2010
SERIES. . . . GREENSMASTER SERIES
ENGINE . . . . .VANGUARD
ENGINE HP. 18
COOLING . . . . .AIR
FUEL . . . . G
SPEEDS . . . . .VARIABLE
TRANSMISSION . . . . .HYDRO
STEERING. . . . . ZERO
DRIVE TYPE 2WD
ROPS/CAB . . . . .ROPS
STANDARD DECK . . . . 70"
WEIGHT . . . . .1,021 LBS.
MSRP. $25,450

RETAIL PRICING

YEAR	HIGH	LOW
2005	$14,688	$11,016
2006	$15,314	$11,486
2007	$15,836	$11,877
2008	$16,497	$12,373
2009	$16,663	$12,497
2010	$16,930	$12,698

3100D

YEARS MFRD 2000-2011
SERIES. . . . . . REELMASTER SERIES
ENGINE . . . . KUBOTA
ENGINE HP. 21.5
FUEL . . . . D
SPEEDS . . . . .VARIABLE
TRANSMISSION . . . . .HYDRO
STEERING. . . . . ZERO
STANDARD DECK . . . . 72"
WEIGHT . . . . .1,860 LBS.
MSRP. $26,515

OPTIONS

85" DECK

RETAIL PRICING

YEAR	HIGH	LOW
2000	$3,084	$2,313
2001	$3,247	$2,435
2002	$3,402	$2,552
2003	$4,576	$3,432
2004	$4,916	$3,687
2005	$5,088	$3,816
2006	$5,428	$4,071
2007	$6,537	$4,902
2008	$7,949	$5,962
2009	$10,167	$7,625
2010	$11,908	$8,931

3150-Q

YEARS MFRD 2009-2010
SERIES. . . . GREENSMASTER SERIES
ENGINE . . . . .VANGUARD
ENGINE HP. 18
FUEL . . . . G
SPEEDS . . . . .VARIABLE
TRANSMISSION . . . . .HYDRO
STEERING. . . . . ZERO
BLADE CLUTCH . . . . .ELECTRIC
WEIGHT . . . . 970 LBS.

3250D

YEARS MFRD 2003-2010
SERIES. . . . GREENSMASTER SERIES
ENGINE . . . . B&S
CID 51.9
ENGINE HP. 21
COOLING . . . . LIQUID
FUEL . . . . D
TRANSMISSION . . . . .HYDRO
STEERING. . . . . .STANDARD
STANDARD DECK . . . . 59"
WEIGHT . . . . .1,338 LBS.
MSRP. $30,799

OPTIONS

DAIHATSU 21HP
PERKINS 15HP

RETAIL PRICING

YEAR	HIGH	LOW
2008	$18,454	$13,840
2009	$19,348	$14,511
2010	$20,490	$15,367

3280D

YEARS MFRD 2005-2011
SERIES. . GROUNDSMASTER SERIES
ENGINE . . . . KUBOTA
ENGINE HP. 28
COOLING . . . . .AIR
FUEL . . . . D
SPEEDS . . . . .VARIABLE
TRANSMISSION . . . . .HYDRO
STEERING. . . . . ZERO
STANDARD DECK . . . . 72"
MSRP. $20,030

RETAIL PRICING

YEAR	HIGH	LOW
2005	$3,638	$2,728
2006	$4,014	$3,011
2007	$4,903	$3,678
2008	$5,967	$4,475
2009	$7,546	$5,659
2010	$8,817	$6,613
2011	$12,089	$9,066

3320

YEARS MFRD 2005-2011
SERIES. . GROUNDSMASTER SERIES
ENGINE . . . . .B&S/DAIHATSU
ENGINE HP. 32
COOLING . . . . .AIR
FUEL . . . . G
SPEEDS . . . . .VARIABLE
TRANSMISSION . . . . .HYDRO
STEERING. . . . . ZERO
STANDARD DECK . . . . 72"
MSRP. $19,200

RETAIL PRICING

YEAR	HIGH	LOW
2005	$2,508	$1,881
2006	$3,260	$2,445
2007	$4,377	$3,283
2008	$5,570	$4,178
2009	$7,261	$5,446
2010	$8,676	$6,507
2011	$11,588	$8,691

03543

YEARS MFRD 2004-2004
SERIES. . . . .
. . . . .REELMASTER 5400-D SERIES
ENGINE . . . . KUBOTA
CYLINDERS. 3
CID 68.5
ENGINE HP. 35
COOLING . . . . LIQUID
FUEL . . . . D
SPEEDS . . . . .VARIABLE
TRANSMISSION . . . . .HYDRO
STEERING. . . . . .STANDARD
WEIGHT . . . . .2,330 LBS.

4000-D

YEARS MFRD 2004-2011
SERIES. . GROUNDSMASTER SERIES
ENGINE . . . . KUBOTA 2003-T
CYLINDERS. 4
CID 122
ENGINE HP. 60
COOLING . . . . LIQUID
FUEL . . . . D
SPEEDS . . . . .VARIABLE
TRANSMISSION . . . . .HYDRO
STEERING. . . . . .STANDARD
STANDARD DECK . . . . 132"
WEIGHT . . . . .3,860 LBS.
MSRP. $55,195

RETAIL PRICING

YEAR	HIGH	LOW
2004	$9,608	$7,206
2005	$9,593	$7,195
2006	$10,459	$7,844
2007	$12,357	$9,267
2008	$15,028	$11,271
2009	$20,832	$15,624
2010	$24,349	$18,262
2011	$33,314	$24,986

4100D

YEARS MFRD 2005-2011
SERIES. . GROUNDSMASTER SERIES
ENGINE . . . . KUBOTA 2003-T
CYLINDERS. 4
CID 122
ENGINE HP. 60
COOLING . . . . LIQUID
FUEL . . . . D
SPEEDS . . . . .VARIABLE
TRANSMISSION . . . . .HYDRO
STEERING. . . . . ZERO
STANDARD DECK . . . . 124"
WEIGHT . . . . .3,905 LBS.
MSRP. $53,950

RETAIL PRICING

YEAR	HIGH	LOW
2005	$10,744	$8,058
2006	$11,062	$8,297
2007	$13,314	$9,985
2008	$16,199	$12,150
2009	$20,505	$15,379
2010	$24,121	$18,091
2011	$32,563	$24,422

4700D

YEARS MFRD 2007-2011
SERIES. . GROUNDSMASTER SERIES
ENGINE . . . . KUBOTA
CYLINDERS. 4
ENGINE HP. 60
FUEL . . . . D
SPEEDS . . . . .VARIABLE
TRANSMISSION . . . . .HYDRO
STEERING. . . . . ZERO
STANDARD DECK . . . . 150"
WEIGHT . . . . .4,824 LBS.
MSRP. $61,999

RETAIL PRICING

YEAR	HIGH	LOW
2007	$14,715	$11,037
2008	$17,897	$13,423
2009	$23,511	$17,634
2010	$27,482	$20,612
2011	$37,421	$28,066

5100D

YEARS MFRD 1998-1998
SERIES. . . . . . REELMASTER SERIES
ENGINE . . . . MITSUBISHI
ENGINE HP. 23
FUEL . . . . D
TRANSMISSION . . . . .HYDRO
STEERING. . . . . .STANDARD

5200D

YEARS MFRD 1998-2005
SERIES. . . . . . REELMASTER SERIES
ENGINE . . . . KUBOTA
ENGINE HP. 28
FUEL . . . . D
TRANSMISSION . . . . .HYDRO
STEERING. . . . . .STANDARD
DRIVE TYPE 2WD
ROPS/CAB . . . . .ROPS
STANDARD DECK . . . . 95"
MSRP. $37,700

OPTIONS

4WD

RETAIL PRICING

YEAR	HIGH	LOW
2005	$22,061	$16,546

5210

YEARS MFRD 2007-2008
SERIES. .REELMASTER 5010 SERIES
ENGINE . . . . KUBOTA
CYLINDERS. 3
ENGINE HP. 28
FUEL . . . . D
SPEEDS . . . . .VARIABLE
TRANSMISSION . . . . .HYDRO
STEERING. . . . . ZERO
WEIGHT . . . . .2,506 LBS.

5300D

YEARS MFRD 1998-1998
SERIES. . . . . . REELMASTER SERIES
ENGINE . . . . MITSUBISHI

ENGINE HP 32
FUEL . . . . . D
TRANSMISSION . . . . . HYDRO
STEERING . . . . . STANDARD

5400D

YEARS MFRD 1999-2005
SERIES . . . . . REELMASTER SERIES
ENGINE . . . . . MITSUBISHI
ENGINE HP 32
FUEL . . . . . D
TRANSMISSION . . . . . HYDRO
STEERING . . . . . STANDARD
DRIVE TYPE 2WD
ROPS/CAB . . . . . ROPS
STANDARD DECK . . . . . 95"
MSRP $40,100

OPTIONS

4WD

RETAIL PRICING

YEAR	HIGH	LOW
2005	$23,467	$17,600

5410

YEARS MFRD 2007-2008
SERIES . . REELMASTER 5010 SERIES
ENGINE . . . . . KUBOTA
CYLINDERS 4
ENGINE HP 35.5
FUEL . . . . . D
SPEEDS . . . . . VARIABLE
TRANSMISSION . . . . . HYDRO
STEERING . . . . . ZERO
DRIVE TYPE 4WD
ROPS/CAB . . . . . ROPS
WEIGHT . . . . . 2,505 LBS.

5500D

YEARS MFRD 2000-2005
SERIES . . . . . REELMASTER SERIES
ENGINE . . . . . MITSUBISHI
ENGINE HP 32
FUEL . . . . . D
TRANSMISSION . . . . . HYDRO
STEERING . . . . . STANDARD
DRIVE TYPE 2WD
ROPS/CAB . . . . . ROPS
STANDARD DECK . . . . . 100"
MSRP $43,820

OPTIONS

4WD

RETAIL PRICING

YEAR	HIGH	LOW
2005	$25,642	$19,231

5510

YEARS MFRD 2007-2008
SERIES . . REELMASTER 5010 SERIES
ENGINE . . . . . KUBOTA
CYLINDERS 4
ENGINE HP 35.5
FUEL . . . . . D
SPEEDS . . . . . VARIABLE
TRANSMISSION . . . . . HYDRO
STEERING . . . . . ZERO
DRIVE TYPE 4WD
ROPS/CAB . . . . . ROPS
WEIGHT . . . . . 2,693 LBS.

5610

YEARS MFRD 2007-2008
SERIES . . REELMASTER 5010 SERIES
ENGINE . . . . . KUBOTA TURBO
CYLINDERS 4
ENGINE HP 44.2
FUEL . . . . . D
SPEEDS . . . . . VARIABLE
TRANSMISSION . . . . . HYDRO
STEERING . . . . . ZERO
DRIVE TYPE 4WD
ROPS/CAB . . . . . ROPS
WEIGHT . . . . . 2,813 LBS.

7200

YEARS MFRD 2011-2011
SERIES . . GROUNDSMASTER SERIES
ENGINE . . . . . KUBOTA
ENGINE HP 28
COOLING . . . . . LIQUID
FUEL . . . . . D
SPEEDS . . . . . VARIABLE
TRANSMISSION . . . . . HYDRO
STEERING . . . . . ZERO
WEIGHT . . . . . 1,900 LBS.

AVG. AUCTION PRICING

LOW	HIGH	AVG
$1,421	$2,436	$2,063

7210

YEARS MFRD 2011-2011
SERIES . . GROUNDSMASTER SERIES
ENGINE . . . . . KUBOTA
ENGINE HP 35
COOLING . . . . . LIQUID
FUEL . . . . . D
SPEEDS . . . . . VARIABLE
TRANSMISSION . . . . . HYDRO
STEERING . . . . . ZERO
WEIGHT . . . . . 1,900 LBS.

30410

YEARS MFRD 2005-2005
SERIES . . . . .
. . GROUNDSMASTER 4000D SERIES
ENGINE . . . . . KUBOTA
CYLINDERS 4
CID 122
ENGINE HP 60
COOLING . . . . . LIQUID
FUEL . . . . . D
SPEEDS . . . . . VARIABLE
TRANSMISSION . . . . . HYDRO
STEERING . . . . . ZERO
WEIGHT . . . . . 3,860 LBS.

30582

YEARS MFRD 2004-2005
SERIES . . . . .
. . . GROUNDSMASTER 580D SERIES
ENGINE . . . . . MITSUBISHI
CYLINDERS 4
CID 203
ENGINE HP 80
COOLING . . . . . LIQUID
FUEL . . . . . D
SPEEDS . . . . . VARIABLE
TRANSMISSION . . . . . HYDRO
STEERING . . . . . ZERO
WEIGHT . . . . . 6,540 LBS.

30627

YEARS MFRD 2005-2005
SERIES . . . . .
. . . GROUNDSMASTER 328D SERIES
ENGINE . . . . . KUBOTA
CYLINDERS 3
CID 68.5
ENGINE HP 28
FUEL . . . . . D
SPEEDS . . . . . VARIABLE
TRANSMISSION . . . . . HYDRO
STEERING . . . . . ZERO
WEIGHT . . . . . 1,665 LBS.

72266

YEARS MFRD 2020-2020
SERIES . . Z MASTER 7000 D SERIES
ENGINE . . . . . KUBOTA
CID 898CC
ENGINE HP 25
FUEL . . . . . D
STEERING . . . . . ZERO
ROPS/CAB . . . . . ROPS
STANDARD DECK . . . . . 52"
WEIGHT . . . . . 1,443 LBS.

72267

YEARS MFRD 2020-2020
SERIES . . Z MASTER 7000 D SERIES
ENGINE . . . . . KUBOTA
CID 898CC
ENGINE HP 25
FUEL . . . . . D
STEERING . . . . . ZERO
ROPS/CAB . . . . . ROPS
STANDARD DECK . . . . . 60"
WEIGHT . . . . . 1,484 LBS.

72274

YEARS MFRD 2020-2020
SERIES . . Z MASTER 7000 D SERIES
ENGINE . . . . . KUBOTA
CID 898CC
ENGINE HP 25
FUEL . . . . . D
STEERING . . . . . ZERO
ROPS/CAB . . . . . ROPS
STANDARD DECK . . . . . 72"
WEIGHT . . . . . 1,543 LBS.

72904

YEARS MFRD 2020-2020
SERIES . . . . Z MASTER 5000 SERIES
ENGINE . . KOHLER COMMAND PRO
CID 747CC
ENGINE HP 23
FUEL . . . . . G
STEERING . . . . . ZERO
ROPS/CAB . . . . . ROPS
STANDARD DECK . . . . . 48"
WEIGHT . . . . . 1,120 LBS.

72906

YEARS MFRD 2020-2020
SERIES . . . . Z MASTER 5000 SERIES
ENGINE . . KOHLER COMMAND PRO
CID 747CC
ENGINE HP 25
FUEL . . . . . G
STEERING . . . . . ZERO
ROPS/CAB . . . . . ROPS
STANDARD DECK . . . . . 52"
WEIGHT . . . . . 1,168 LBS.

72915

YEARS MFRD 2020-2020
SERIES . . . . Z MASTER 5000 SERIES
ENGINE . . KOHLER COMMAND PRO
CID 747CC
ENGINE HP 25
FUEL . . . . . G
STEERING . . . . . ZERO
ROPS/CAB . . . . . ROPS
STANDARD DECK . . . . . 60"
WEIGHT . . . . . 1,216 LBS.

72918

YEARS MFRD 2020-2020
SERIES . . . . Z MASTER 5000 SERIES
ENGINE KOHLER COMMAND PRO EFI
CID 747CC
ENGINE HP 26.5
FUEL . . . . . G
STEERING . . . . . ZERO
ROPS/CAB . . . . . ROPS
STANDARD DECK . . . . . 72"
WEIGHT . . . . . 1,296 LBS.

72926

YEARS MFRD 2020-2020
SERIES . . . . Z MASTER 6000 SERIES
ENGINE KOHLER COMMAND PRO EFI
CID 747CC
ENGINE HP 26.5
FUEL . . . . . G
STEERING . . . . . ZERO
ROPS/CAB . . . . . ROPS
STANDARD DECK . . . . . 60"
WEIGHT . . . . . 1,254 LBS.

TORO

72928
YEARS MFRD 2020-2020
SERIES.... Z MASTER 6000 SERIES
ENGINE KOHLER COMMAND PRO EFI
CID 747CC
ENGINE HP 26.5
FUEL ....G
STEERING.................ZERO
ROPS/CAB ....ROPS
STANDARD DECK .... 72"
WEIGHT ....1,350 LBS.

72930
YEARS MFRD 2020-2020
SERIES.... Z MASTER 5000 SERIES
ENGINE KOHLER COMMAND PRO EFI
CID 747CC
ENGINE HP 25
FUEL ....G
STEERING.................ZERO
ROPS/CAB ....ROPS
STANDARD DECK .... 60"
WEIGHT ....1,255 LBS.

72932
YEARS MFRD 2020-2020
SERIES.......................
.. Z MASTER 3000 MYRIDE SERIES
ENGINE ....KAWASAKI FX
CID 852CC
ENGINE HP 24.5
FUEL ....G
STEERING.................ZERO
ROPS/CAB ....ROPS
STANDARD DECK .... 52"
WEIGHT ....1,185 LBS.
MSRP................ $12,026

72936
YEARS MFRD 2020-2020
SERIES.......................
.. Z MASTER 3000 MYRIDE SERIES
ENGINE ....KAWASAKI FX
CID 852CC
ENGINE HP 25.5
FUEL ....G
STEERING.................ZERO
ROPS/CAB ....ROPS
STANDARD DECK .... 60"
WEIGHT ....1,185 LBS.
MSRP................ $12,599

72943
YEARS MFRD 2020-2020
SERIES. Z MASTER 5000 RD SERIES
ENGINE KOHLER COMMAND PRO EFI
CID 747CC
ENGINE HP 25
FUEL ....G
STEERING.................ZERO
ROPS/CAB ....ROPS
STANDARD DECK .... 60"
WEIGHT ....1,271 LBS.

72945
YEARS MFRD 2020-2020
SERIES. Z MASTER 5000 RD SERIES
ENGINE KOHLER COMMAND PRO EFI
CID 747CC
ENGINE HP 26.5
FUEL ....G
STEERING.................ZERO
ROPS/CAB ....ROPS
STANDARD DECK .... 72"
WEIGHT ....1,335 LBS.

72946
YEARS MFRD 2020-2020
SERIES.... Z MASTER 6000 SERIES
ENGINE ....
KOHLER COMMAND PRO HOR TECH
CID 999CC
ENGINE HP 38
FUEL ....G
STEERING.................ZERO
ROPS/CAB ....ROPS
STANDARD DECK .... 60"
WEIGHT ....1,289 LBS.

72947
YEARS MFRD 2020-2020
SERIES.... Z MASTER 6000 SERIES
ENGINE ....
KOHLER COMMAND PRO HOR TECH
CID 999CC
ENGINE HP 38
FUEL ....G
STEERING.................ZERO
ROPS/CAB ....ROPS
STANDARD DECK .... 72"
WEIGHT ....1,369 LBS.

72949
YEARS MFRD 2020-2020
SERIES.... Z MASTER 3000 SERIES
ENGINE ....KAWASAKI FX
CID 852CC
ENGINE HP 24.5
FUEL ....G
STEERING.................ZERO
ROPS/CAB ....ROPS
STANDARD DECK .... 52"
WEIGHT ....1,085 LBS.
MSRP................ $11,215

72950
YEARS MFRD 2020-2020
SERIES.... Z MASTER 3000 SERIES
ENGINE ....KAWASAKI FX
CID 852CC
ENGINE HP 25.5
FUEL ....G
STEERING.................ZERO
ROPS/CAB ....ROPS
STANDARD DECK .... 60"
WEIGHT ....1,165 LBS.
MSRP................ $11,805

72951
YEARS MFRD 2020-2020
SERIES.......................
.. Z MASTER 5000 MYRIDE SERIES
ENGINE KOHLER COMMAND PRO EFI
CID 747CC
ENGINE HP 25
FUEL ....G
STEERING.................ZERO
ROPS/CAB ....ROPS
STANDARD DECK .... 60"
WEIGHT ....1,304 LBS.

72952
YEARS MFRD 2020-2020
SERIES.... Z MASTER 3000 SERIES
ENGINE ....KAWASAKI FX
CID 726CC
ENGINE HP 20.5
FUEL ....G
STEERING.................ZERO
ROPS/CAB ....ROPS
STANDARD DECK .... 48"
WEIGHT ....1,048 LBS.
MSRP................ $10,625

72955
YEARS MFRD 2020-2020
SERIES.......................
.. Z MASTER 5000 MYRIDE SERIES
ENGINE KOHLER COMMAND PRO EFI
CID 747CC
ENGINE HP 25
FUEL ....G
STEERING.................ZERO
ROPS/CAB ....ROPS
STANDARD DECK .... 52"
WEIGHT ....1,259 LBS.

72958
YEARS MFRD 2020-2020
SERIES.... Z MASTER 3000 SERIES
ENGINE .. KOHLER COMMAND PRO
CID 747CC
ENGINE HP 25
FUEL ....G
STEERING.................ZERO
ROPS/CAB ....ROPS
STANDARD DECK .... 60"
WEIGHT ....1,185 LBS.
MSRP................ $12,485

72959
YEARS MFRD 2020-2020
SERIES.... Z MASTER 3000 SERIES
ENGINE .. KOHLER COMMAND PRO
CID 747CC
ENGINE HP 25
FUEL ....G
STEERING.................ZERO
ROPS/CAB ....ROPS
STANDARD DECK .... 72"
WEIGHT ....1,255 LBS.
MSRP................ $12,599

72960
YEARS MFRD 2020-2020
SERIES.... Z MASTER 6000 SERIES
ENGINE ....KAWASAKI FX
CID 999CC
ENGINE HP 31
FUEL ....G
STEERING.................ZERO
ROPS/CAB ....ROPS
STANDARD DECK .... 60"
WEIGHT ....1,254 LBS.

72961
YEARS MFRD 2020-2020
SERIES.... Z MASTER 6000 SERIES
ENGINE ....KAWASAKI FX
CID 999CC
ENGINE HP 31
FUEL ....G
STEERING.................ZERO
ROPS/CAB ....ROPS
STANDARD DECK .... 72"
WEIGHT ....1,334 LBS.

72967
YEARS MFRD 2020-2020
SERIES.......................
.. Z MASTER 6000 MYRIDE SERIES
ENGINE ....KAWASAKI FX
CID 999CC
ENGINE HP 31
FUEL ....G
STEERING.................ZERO
ROPS/CAB ....ROPS
STANDARD DECK .... 60"
WEIGHT ....1,370 LBS.

72968
YEARS MFRD 2020-2020
SERIES.......................
.. Z MASTER 6000 MYRIDE SERIES
ENGINE ....KAWASAKI FX
CID 999CC
ENGINE HP 31
FUEL ....G
STEERING.................ZERO
ROPS/CAB ....ROPS
STANDARD DECK .... 72"
WEIGHT ....1,440 LBS.

72969
YEARS MFRD 2020-2020
SERIES.... Z MASTER 6000 SERIES
ENGINE ..KAWASAKI FX HOR TECH
CID 852CC
ENGINE HP 29.5
FUEL ....G
STEERING.................ZERO
ROPS/CAB ....ROPS
STANDARD DECK .... 60"
WEIGHT ....1,290 LBS.

74028
YEARS MFRD 2020-2020
SERIES.. Z MASTER 7500 D SERIES
ENGINE .... YANMAR
CID 1267CC
ENGINE HP 25
FUEL .... D
SPEEDS .... VARIABLE
TRANSMISSION .... HYDRO
STEERING................ ZERO
ROPS/CAB .... ROPS
STANDARD DECK .... 60"
WEIGHT .... 2,136 LBS.

74029
YEARS MFRD 2020-2020
SERIES.. Z MASTER 7500 D SERIES
ENGINE .... YANMAR
CID 1267CC
ENGINE HP 25
FUEL .... D
STEERING................ ZERO
ROPS/CAB .... ROPS
STANDARD DECK .... 72"
WEIGHT .... 2,143 LBS.

74060
YEARS MFRD 2018-2020
SERIES........... 7500 D SERIES
ENGINE .... YANMAR
CYLINDERS.................... 4
CID 1642CC
ENGINE HP 37
FUEL .... D
STEERING................ ZERO
STANDARD DECK .... 60"

74064
YEARS MFRD 2018-2020
SERIES........ 7500 D SERIES RD
ENGINE .... YANMAR
CYLINDERS.................... 4
CID 1642CC
ENGINE HP 37
FUEL .... D
STEERING................ ZERO
STANDARD DECK .... 60"

74072
YEARS MFRD 2018-2020
SERIES........... 7500 D SERIES
ENGINE .... YANMAR
CYLINDERS.................... 4
CID 1642CC
ENGINE HP 37
FUEL .... D
STEERING................ ZERO
STANDARD DECK .... 72"

74074
YEARS MFRD 2018-2020
SERIES........ 7500 D SERIES RD
ENGINE .... YANMAR
CYLINDERS.................... 4
CID 1642CC
ENGINE HP 37
FUEL .... D
STEERING................ ZERO
STANDARD DECK .... 72"

74090
YEARS MFRD 2020-2020
SERIES.. Z MASTER 7500 G SERIES
ENGINE .... KOHLER EFI
ENGINE HP 38
FUEL .... G
STEERING................ ZERO
ROPS/CAB .... ROPS
STANDARD DECK .... 96"
WEIGHT .... 2,584 LBS.

74096
YEARS MFRD 2018-2020
SERIES........ 7500 D SERIES RD
ENGINE .... YANMAR
CYLINDERS.................... 4
CID 1642CC
ENGINE HP 37
FUEL .... D
STEERING................ ZERO
STANDARD DECK .... 96"

74176
YEARS MFRD 2002-2002
SERIES............ Z100 SERIES
ENGINE .... KAWASAKI
ENGINE HP 17
FUEL .... G
TRANSMISSION .... HYDRO
STEERING............ STANDARD

74178
YEARS MFRD 2002-2002
SERIES............ Z100 SERIES
ENGINE .... KOHLER
ENGINE HP 20
FUEL .... G
TRANSMISSION .... HYDRO
STEERING............ STANDARD

74179
YEARS MFRD 2002-2002
SERIES............ Z100 SERIES
ENGINE .... KAWASAKI
ENGINE HP 19
FUEL .... G
TRANSMISSION .... HYDRO
STEERING............ STANDARD

74197
YEARS MFRD 2002-2002
SERIES............ Z100 SERIES
ENGINE .... KOHLER
ENGINE HP 23
FUEL .... G
TRANSMISSION .... HYDRO
STEERING............ STANDARD

74198
YEARS MFRD 2002-2002
SERIES............ Z100 SERIES
ENGINE .... KAWASAKI
ENGINE HP 23
FUEL .... G
TRANSMISSION .... HYDRO
STEERING............ STANDARD

74213
YEARS MFRD 2002-2002
SERIES............ Z280 SERIES
ENGINE .... KAWASAKI
ENGINE HP 27
FUEL .... G
TRANSMISSION .... HYDRO
STEERING............ STANDARD

74214
YEARS MFRD 2002-2002
SERIES............ Z280 SERIES
ENGINE .... KAWASAKI
ENGINE HP 27
FUEL .... G
TRANSMISSION .... HYDRO
STEERING............ STANDARD

74225
YEARS MFRD 2002-2002
SERIES............ Z250 SERIES
ENGINE .... KOHLER
ENGINE HP 23
FUEL .... G
TRANSMISSION .... HYDRO
STEERING............ STANDARD

74226
YEARS MFRD 2002-2002
SERIES............ Z250 SERIES
ENGINE .... KOHLER
ENGINE HP 25
FUEL .... G
TRANSMISSION .... HYDRO
STEERING............ STANDARD

74227
YEARS MFRD 2002-2002
SERIES............ Z250 SERIES
ENGINE .... KOHLER
ENGINE HP 25
FUEL .... G
TRANSMISSION .... HYDRO
STEERING............ STANDARD

74228
YEARS MFRD 2002-2002
SERIES............ Z250 SERIES
ENGINE .... KOHLER
ENGINE HP 25
FUEL .... G
TRANSMISSION .... HYDRO
STEERING............ STANDARD

74239
YEARS MFRD 2005-2005
SERIES............ Z500 SERIES
ENGINE .... KOHLER
CYLINDERS.................... 2
ENGINE HP 23
FUEL .... G
SPEEDS .... VARIABLE
TRANSMISSION .... HYDRO
STEERING................ ZERO
STANDARD DECK .... 52"
MSRP................. $9,680

RETAIL PRICING

YEAR	HIGH	LOW
2005	$5,663	$4,247

74240E
YEARS MFRD 2002-2002
SERIES............ Z280 SERIES
ENGINE .... KOHLER
ENGINE HP 26
FUEL .... G
TRANSMISSION .... HYDRO
STEERING............ STANDARD

74241
YEARS MFRD 2002-2002
SERIES............ Z280 SERIES
ENGINE .... KOHLER
ENGINE HP 26
FUEL .... G
TRANSMISSION .... HYDRO
STEERING............ STANDARD

74242
YEARS MFRD 2004-2004
SERIES..... Z MASTER 500 SERIES
ENGINE .... KOHLER
ENGINE HP 20
COOLING .... AIR
FUEL .... G
SPEEDS .... VARIABLE
TRANSMISSION .... HYDRO
WEIGHT .... 1,140 LBS.

74243
YEARS MFRD 2004-2005
SERIES..... Z MASTER 500 SERIES
ENGINE .... KOHLER
CYLINDERS.................... 2
ENGINE HP 27
COOLING .... AIR
FUEL .... G
SPEEDS .... VARIABLE
TRANSMISSION .... HYDRO
STEERING................ ZERO
STANDARD DECK .... 52"
WEIGHT .... 1,176 LBS.
MSRP................ $10,204

TORO

RETAIL PRICING

YEAR	HIGH	LOW
2004	$5,729	$4,296
2005	$5,972	$4,479

74244

YEARS MFRD 2004-2005
SERIES ..... Z MASTER 500 SERIES
ENGINE .... KOHLER
CYLINDERS 2
ENGINE HP 23
COOLING .... AIR
FUEL .... G
SPEEDS .... VARIABLE
TRANSMISSION .... HYDRO
STEERING .... ZERO
STANDARD DECK .... 60"
WEIGHT .... 1,215 LBS.
MSRP $9,896

RETAIL PRICING

YEAR	HIGH	LOW
2004	$5,563	$4,172
2005	$5,791	$4,343

74245

YEARS MFRD 2004-2005
SERIES ..... Z MASTER 500 SERIES
ENGINE .... KAWASAKI
CYLINDERS 2
ENGINE HP 25
COOLING .... AIR
FUEL .... G
SPEEDS .... VARIABLE
TRANSMISSION .... HYDRO
STEERING .... ZERO
STANDARD DECK .... 60"
WEIGHT .... 1,215 LBS.
MSRP $10,580

RETAIL PRICING

YEAR	HIGH	LOW
2004	$6,038	$4,529
2005	$6,190	$4,643

74246

YEARS MFRD 2004-2005
SERIES ..... Z MASTER 500 SERIES
ENGINE .... KOHLER
CYLINDERS 2
ENGINE HP 27
COOLING .... AIR
FUEL .... G
SPEEDS .... VARIABLE
TRANSMISSION .... HYDRO
STEERING .... ZERO
STANDARD DECK .... 60"
WEIGHT .... 1,215 LBS.
MSRP $10,580

RETAIL PRICING

YEAR	HIGH	LOW
2004	$6,038	$4,529
2005	$6,190	$4,643

74247

YEARS MFRD 2004-2005
SERIES ..... Z MASTER 500 SERIES
ENGINE .... KOHLER
CYLINDERS 2
ENGINE HP 27
COOLING .... AIR
FUEL .... G
SPEEDS .... VARIABLE
TRANSMISSION .... HYDRO
STEERING .... ZERO
STANDARD DECK .... 72"
WEIGHT .... 1,280 LBS.
MSRP $11,354

RETAIL PRICING

YEAR	HIGH	LOW
2004	$6,186	$4,640
2005	$6,644	$4,983

74251

YEARS MFRD 2004-2005
SERIES ..... Z MASTER 580 SERIES
ENGINE .... KAWASAKI
ENGINE HP 27
COOLING .... LIQUID
FUEL .... G
SPEEDS .... VARIABLE
TRANSMISSION .... HYDRO
STEERING .... ZERO
STANDARD DECK .... 60"
WEIGHT .... 1,330 LBS.
MSRP $12,379

RETAIL PRICING

YEAR	HIGH	LOW
2004	$6,940	$5,205
2005	$7,244	$5,433

74252

YEARS MFRD 2004-2005
SERIES ..... Z MASTER 580 SERIES
ENGINE .... KAWASAKI
ENGINE HP 27
COOLING .... LIQUID
FUEL .... G
SPEEDS .... VARIABLE
TRANSMISSION .... HYDRO
STEERING .... ZERO
STANDARD DECK .... 72"
WEIGHT .... 1,395 LBS.
MSRP $12,833

RETAIL PRICING

YEAR	HIGH	LOW
2004	$7,127	$5,345
2005	$7,508	$5,631

74253

YEARS MFRD 2008-2010
SERIES .... Z580 SERIES
ENGINE .... KAWASAKI DFI
ENGINE HP 29
COOLING .... LIQUID
FUEL .... D
SPEEDS .... VARIABLE
TRANSMISSION .... HYDRO
STEERING .... ZERO
BLADE CLUTCH .... ELECTRIC
STANDARD DECK .... 60"
MSRP $12,799

RETAIL PRICING

YEAR	HIGH	LOW
2008	$7,644	$5,733
2009	$7,954	$5,965
2010	$8,516	$6,387

74254

YEARS MFRD 2008-2010
SERIES .... Z580 SERIES
ENGINE .... KAWASAKI DFI
ENGINE HP 29
COOLING .... LIQUID
FUEL .... D
SPEEDS .... VARIABLE
TRANSMISSION .... HYDRO
STEERING .... ZERO

74255

YEARS MFRD 2004-2005
SERIES ..... Z MASTER 580 SERIES
ENGINE .. KOHLER COMMAND PRO
ENGINE HP 28
COOLING .... LIQUID
FUEL .... G
SPEEDS .... VARIABLE
TRANSMISSION .... HYDRO
STEERING .... ZERO
STANDARD DECK .... 60"
WEIGHT .... 1,254 LBS.
MSRP $12,265

RETAIL PRICING

YEAR	HIGH	LOW
2004	$6,489	$4,867
2005	$7,176	$5,382

74256

YEARS MFRD 2004-2005
SERIES ..... Z MASTER 580 SERIES
ENGINE .. KOHLER COMMAND PRO
ENGINE HP 28
COOLING .... LIQUID
FUEL .... G
SPEEDS .... VARIABLE
TRANSMISSION .... HYDRO
STEERING .... ZERO
STANDARD DECK .... 72"
WEIGHT .... 1,319 LBS.
MSRP $12,812

RETAIL PRICING

YEAR	HIGH	LOW
2004	$6,886	$5,164
2005	$7,498	$5,623

74266

YEARS MFRD 2014-2019
SERIES .... Z MASTER 7000 SERIES
ENGINE .... KUBOTA
CID 898CC
ENGINE HP 25
FUEL .... D
SPEEDS .... VARIABLE
TRANSMISSION .... HYDRO
STEERING .... ZERO
STANDARD DECK .... 52"
MSRP $17,999

74266

YEARS MFRD 2007-2011
SERIES .... Z580-D SERIES
ENGINE .... KUBOTA
CYLINDERS 3
ENGINE HP 25
COOLING .... LIQUID
FUEL .... D
SPEEDS .... VARIABLE
TRANSMISSION .... HYDRO
STEERING .... ZERO
STANDARD DECK .... 52"
MSRP $13,250

RETAIL PRICING

YEAR	HIGH	LOW
2007	$3,418	$2,563
2008	$4,155	$3,117
2009	$5,180	$3,885
2010	$6,310	$4,733
2011	$7,997	$5,998

74267

YEARS MFRD 2014-2019
SERIES .... Z MASTER 7000 SERIES
ENGINE .... KUBOTA
CID 898CC
ENGINE HP 25
FUEL .... D
SPEEDS .... VARIABLE
TRANSMISSION .... HYDRO
STEERING .... ZERO
STANDARD DECK .... 60"
MSRP $18,554

74267

YEARS MFRD 2009-2011
SERIES .... Z580-D SERIES
ENGINE .... KUBOTA
CYLINDERS 3
ENGINE HP 25
COOLING .... LIQUID
FUEL .... D
SPEEDS .... VARIABLE
TRANSMISSION .... HYDRO
STEERING .... ZERO
STANDARD DECK .... 60"
MSRP $13,299

RETAIL PRICING

YEAR	HIGH	LOW
2009	$5,331	$3,998
2010	$6,267	$4,700
2011	$9,009	$6,757

74268

YEARS MFRD 2005-2011
SERIES .... Z MASTER 590D SERIES
ENGINE .... DAIHATSU

CYLINDERS . . . 3
ENGINE HP . . . 27
COOLING . . . LIQUID
FUEL . . . D
SPEEDS . . . VARIABLE
TRANSMISSION . . . HYDRO
STEERING . . . ZERO
STANDARD DECK . . . 60"
WEIGHT . . . 1,630 LBS.
MSRP . . . $15,259

RETAIL PRICING

YEAR	HIGH	LOW
2005	$2,160	$1,620
2006	$2,806	$2,105
2007	$3,561	$2,670
2008	$4,534	$3,401
2009	$5,911	$4,434
2010	$7,162	$5,371
2011	$9,210	$6,908

74269

YEARS MFRD . . . 2005-2011
SERIES . . . Z MASTER 590D SERIES
ENGINE . . . DAIHATSU
CYLINDERS . . . 3
ENGINE HP . . . 27
COOLING . . . AIR
FUEL . . . D
SPEEDS . . . VARIABLE
TRANSMISSION . . . HYDRO
STANDARD DECK . . . 72"
WEIGHT . . . 1,695 LBS.
MSRP . . . $15,649

RETAIL PRICING

YEAR	HIGH	LOW
2005	$2,217	$1,663
2006	$2,877	$2,157
2007	$3,651	$2,738
2008	$4,647	$3,485
2009	$6,097	$4,573
2010	$7,381	$5,536
2011	$9,445	$7,083

74271

YEARS MFRD . . . 2008-2010
SERIES . . . Z558 SERIES
ENGINE . . . KAWASAKI
CYLINDERS . . . 2
ENGINE HP . . . 28
COOLING . . . AIR
FUEL . . . G
SPEEDS . . . VARIABLE
TRANSMISSION . . . HYDRO
STEERING . . . ZERO
BLADE CLUTCH . . . ELECTRIC

74272

YEARS MFRD . . . 2008-2010
SERIES . . . Z558 SERIES
ENGINE . . . KAWASAKI
CYLINDERS . . . 2
ENGINE HP . . . 28
FUEL . . . G
SPEEDS . . . VARIABLE
TRANSMISSION . . . HYDRO
STEERING . . . ZERO
BLADE CLUTCH . . . ELECTRIC

74273

YEARS MFRD . . . 2008-2010
SERIES . . . Z558 SERIES
ENGINE . . . KAWASAKI
CYLINDERS . . . 2
ENGINE HP . . . 28
COOLING . . . AIR
FUEL . . . G
SPEEDS . . . VARIABLE
TRANSMISSION . . . HYDRO
STEERING . . . ZERO
BLADE CLUTCH . . . ELECTRIC

74274

YEARS MFRD . . . 2014-2019
SERIES . . . Z MASTER 7000 SERIES
ENGINE . . . KUBOTA
CID . . . 898CC
ENGINE HP . . . 25
FUEL . . . D
SPEEDS . . . VARIABLE
TRANSMISSION . . . HYDRO
STEERING . . . ZERO
STANDARD DECK . . . 72"
MSRP . . . $19,110

74274

YEARS MFRD . . . 2008-2011
SERIES . . . Z580-D SERIES
ENGINE . . . KUBOTA
CYLINDERS . . . 3
ENGINE HP . . . 25
COOLING . . . LIQUID
FUEL . . . D
SPEEDS . . . VARIABLE
TRANSMISSION . . . HYDRO
STEERING . . . ZERO
BLADE CLUTCH . . . ELECTRIC
STANDARD DECK . . . 72"
MSRP . . . $13,989

RETAIL PRICING

YEAR	HIGH	LOW
2008	$4,391	$3,293
2009	$5,450	$4,087
2010	$6,402	$4,801
2011	$8,444	$6,333

74282

YEARS MFRD . . . 2008-2010
SERIES . . . Z550 SERIES
ENGINE . . . KOHLER COMMAND
ENGINE HP . . . 27
COOLING . . . AIR
FUEL . . . G
SPEEDS . . . VARIABLE
TRANSMISSION . . . HYDRO
STEERING . . . ZERO
BLADE CLUTCH . . . ELECTRIC

74283

YEARS MFRD . . . 2008-2010
SERIES . . . Z550 SERIES
ENGINE . . . KOHLER COMMAND
ENGINE HP . . . 27
COOLING . . . AIR
FUEL . . . G
SPEEDS . . . VARIABLE
TRANSMISSION . . . HYDRO
STEERING . . . ZERO
BLADE CLUTCH . . . ELECTRIC

74284

YEARS MFRD . . . 2008-2010
SERIES . . . Z550 SERIES
ENGINE . . . KOHLER COMMAND
ENGINE HP . . . 27
COOLING . . . AIR
FUEL . . . G
SPEEDS . . . VARIABLE
TRANSMISSION . . . HYDRO
STEERING . . . ZERO
BLADE CLUTCH . . . ELECTRIC

74291

YEARS MFRD . . . 2008-2010
SERIES . . . Z500 SERIES
ENGINE . . KOHLER COMMAND PRO
ENGINE HP . . . 27
COOLING . . . AIR
FUEL . . . G
SPEEDS . . . VARIABLE
TRANSMISSION . . . HYDRO
STEERING . . . ZERO
BLADE CLUTCH . . . ELECTRIC
STANDARD DECK . . . 52"
MSRP . . . $10,688

RETAIL PRICING

YEAR	HIGH	LOW
2008	$6,169	$4,627
2009	$6,726	$5,045
2010	$7,111	$5,333

74292

YEARS MFRD . . . 2008-2010
SERIES . . . Z500 SERIES
ENGINE . . KOHLER COMMAND PRO
ENGINE HP . . . 27
COOLING . . . AIR
FUEL . . . G
SPEEDS . . . VARIABLE
TRANSMISSION . . . HYDRO
STEERING . . . ZERO
BLADE CLUTCH . . . ELECTRIC
STANDARD DECK . . . 60"
MSRP . . . $11,259

RETAIL PRICING

YEAR	HIGH	LOW
2008	$6,388	$4,791
2009	$7,080	$5,310
2010	$7,491	$5,618

74295

YEARS MFRD . . . 2010-2011
SERIES . . . Z500 SERIES
ENGINE . . KOHLER COMMAND PRO
ENGINE HP . . . 27
COOLING . . . AIR
FUEL . . . G
SPEEDS . . . VARIABLE
TRANSMISSION . . . HYDRO
STEERING . . . ZERO
STANDARD DECK . . . 52"
MSRP . . . $9,370

RETAIL PRICING

YEAR	HIGH	LOW
2010	$5,021	$3,766
2011	$5,657	$4,242

74296

YEARS MFRD . . . 2010-2011
SERIES . . . Z500 SERIES
ENGINE . . KOHLER COMMAND PRO
ENGINE HP . . . 27
COOLING . . . AIR
FUEL . . . G
SPEEDS . . . VARIABLE
TRANSMISSION . . . HYDRO
STEERING . . . ZERO
STANDARD DECK . . . 60"
MSRP . . . $9,740

RETAIL PRICING

YEAR	HIGH	LOW
2010	$5,155	$3,866
2011	$5,879	$4,409

74297

YEARS MFRD . . . 2010-2011
SERIES . . . Z500 SERIES
ENGINE . . KOHLER COMMAND PRO
ENGINE HP . . . 27
COOLING . . . AIR
FUEL . . . G
SPEEDS . . . VARIABLE
TRANSMISSION . . . HYDRO
STEERING . . . ZERO
STANDARD DECK . . . 72"
MSRP . . . $7,999

RETAIL PRICING

YEAR	HIGH	LOW
2010	$4,779	$3,584
2011	$4,828	$3,621

74301

YEARS MFRD . . . 2007-2007
SERIES . . . TIMECUTTER Z SERIES
ENGINE . . . B&S IC OHV
ENGINE HP . . . 14
FUEL . . . G
SPEEDS . . . VARIABLE
TRANSMISSION . . . HYDRO
STEERING . . . ZERO
BLADE CLUTCH . . . ELECTRIC
STANDARD DECK . . . 38"
MSRP . . . $2,699

RETAIL PRICING
YEAR HIGH LOW
2007 $1,736 $1,302

74312
YEARS MFRD 2014-2020
SERIES 8000 DIRECT COLLECT Z
ENGINE KOHLER COMMAND PRO
CID 747CC
ENGINE HP 23
FUEL G
SPEEDS VARIABLE
TRANSMISSION HYDRO
STEERING ZERO
STANDARD DECK 48"

74313
YEARS MFRD 2017-2020
SERIES 8000 DIRECT COLLECT Z
ENGINE KOHLER COMMAND PRO
CID 725CC
ENGINE HP 25
FUEL G
SPEEDS VARIABLE
TRANSMISSION HYDRO
STEERING ZERO
STANDARD DECK 48"

74315
YEARS MFRD 2017-2020
SERIES 8000 DIRECT COLLECT Z
ENGINE KOHLER COMMAND PRO
CID 725CC
ENGINE HP 25
FUEL G
SPEEDS VARIABLE
STEERING ZERO
STANDARD DECK 42"
WEIGHT 1,140 LBS.

74360
YEARS MFRD 2008-2008
SERIES TIMECUTTER Z4200 SERIES
ENGINE KOHLER OHV
CYLINDERS 2
ENGINE HP 19
COOLING AIR
FUEL G
SPEEDS VARIABLE
TRANSMISSION HYDRO
STEERING ZERO
STANDARD DECK 42"
MSRP $2,699

RETAIL PRICING
YEAR HIGH LOW
2008 $1,789 $1,342

74363
YEARS MFRD 2008-2008
SERIES TIMECUTTER Z4220 SERIES
ENGINE KOHLER COURAGE
CYLINDERS 2
ENGINE HP 21
COOLING AIR
FUEL G
SPEEDS VARIABLE
TRANSMISSION HYDRO
STEERING ZERO
STANDARD DECK 42"
MSRP $2,899

RETAIL PRICING
YEAR HIGH LOW
2008 $1,920 $1,440

74370
YEARS MFRD 2007-2008
SERIES TIMECUTTER Z SERIES
ENGINE KOHLER OHV
CYLINDERS 2
ENGINE HP 21
FUEL G
SPEEDS VARIABLE
TRANSMISSION HYDRO
STEERING ZERO
BLADE CLUTCH ELECTRIC
STANDARD DECK 50"
MSRP $2,999

RETAIL PRICING
YEAR HIGH LOW
2007 $1,532 $1,149
2008 $1,988 $1,491

74372
YEARS MFRD 2007-2008
SERIES TIMECUTTER Z SERIES
ENGINE KOHLER COURAGE
CYLINDERS 2
ENGINE HP 23
FUEL G
SPEEDS VARIABLE
TRANSMISSION HYDRO
STEERING ZERO
BLADE CLUTCH ELECTRIC
STANDARD DECK 50"
MSRP $3,499

RETAIL PRICING
YEAR HIGH LOW
2007 $1,940 $1,455
2008 $2,321 $1,741

74374
YEARS MFRD 2007-2008
SERIES TIMECUTTER Z SERIES
ENGINE KAWASAKI OHV
CYLINDERS 2
ENGINE HP 21
FUEL G
SPEEDS VARIABLE
TRANSMISSION HYDRO
STEERING ZERO
BLADE CLUTCH ELECTRIC
STANDARD DECK 50"
MSRP $3,699

RETAIL PRICING
YEAR HIGH LOW
2007 $1,919 $1,440
2008 $2,452 $1,839

74375
YEARS MFRD 2008-2008
SERIES TIMECUTTER Z5060 SERIES
ENGINE KOHLER COURAGE
CYLINDERS 2
ENGINE HP 25
COOLING AIR
FUEL G
SPEEDS VARIABLE
TRANSMISSION HYDRO
STEERING ZERO
STANDARD DECK 50"
MSRP $3,699

RETAIL PRICING
YEAR HIGH LOW
2008 $2,452 $1,839

74408
YEARS MFRD 2008-2009
SERIES Z300 SERIES
ENGINE KAWASAKI
ENGINE HP 19
COOLING AIR
FUEL G
SPEEDS VARIABLE
TRANSMISSION HYDRO
STEERING ZERO
BLADE CLUTCH ELECTRIC

74409
YEARS MFRD 2008-2009
SERIES Z300 SERIES
ENGINE KAWASAKI
ENGINE HP 19
COOLING AIR
FUEL G
SPEEDS VARIABLE
TRANSMISSION HYDRO
STEERING ZERO
BLADE CLUTCH ELECTRIC

74411
YEARS MFRD 2005-2005
SERIES Z100 SERIES
ENGINE KAWASAKI FH601V
CYLINDERS 2
ENGINE HP 18
COOLING AIR
FUEL G
SPEEDS VARIABLE
TRANSMISSION HYDRO
STEERING ZERO
WEIGHT 924 LBS.

74412
YEARS MFRD 2005-2005
SERIES Z400 ESTATE SERIES
ENGINE KOHLER
ENGINE HP 18
COOLING AIR
FUEL G
SPEEDS VARIABLE
TRANSMISSION HYDRO
STEERING ZERO
STANDARD DECK 48"
WEIGHT 899 LBS.
MSRP $6,499

RETAIL PRICING
YEAR HIGH LOW
2005 $3,804 $2,853

74413
YEARS MFRD 2005-2005
SERIES Z440 PRO SERIES
ENGINE KAWASAKI
CYLINDERS 2
ENGINE HP 19
COOLING AIR
FUEL G
SPEEDS VARIABLE
TRANSMISSION HYDRO
STEERING ZERO
STANDARD DECK 48"
MSRP $7,800

RETAIL PRICING
YEAR HIGH LOW
2005 $4,564 $3,423

74414
YEARS MFRD 2005-2005
SERIES Z450 PRO SERIES
ENGINE KOHLER
CYLINDERS 2
ENGINE HP 20
COOLING AIR
FUEL G
SPEEDS VARIABLE
TRANSMISSION HYDRO
STEERING ZERO
STANDARD DECK 52"
MSRP $8,785

RETAIL PRICING
YEAR HIGH LOW
2005 $5,141 $3,856

74415
YEARS MFRD 2005-2005
SERIES Z440 PRO SERIES
ENGINE KAWASAKI
CYLINDERS 2
ENGINE HP 19
COOLING AIR
FUEL G
SPEEDS VARIABLE
TRANSMISSION HYDRO
STEERING ZERO
STANDARD DECK 52"
MSRP $8,387

RETAIL PRICING
YEAR HIGH LOW
2005 $4,908 $3,681

74416
YEARS MFRD 2008-2010
SERIES Z450 SERIES
ENGINE KAWASAKI

CYLINDERS. . . . 2
ENGINE HP 23
COOLING . . . . AIR
FUEL . . . . G
SPEEDS . . . . VARIABLE
TRANSMISSION . . . . HYDRO
STEERING. . . . ZERO
BLADE CLUTCH . . . . ELECTRIC
STANDARD DECK . . . . 52"
MSRP. . . . $9,229

RETAIL PRICING

YEAR	HIGH	LOW
2008	$6,067	$4,550
2009	$6,096	$4,572
2010	$6,141	$4,606

74417

YEARS MFRD 2005-2010
SERIES. . . . Z450 PRO SERIES
ENGINE . . . . KAWASAKI
CYLINDERS. . . . 2
ENGINE HP 23
COOLING . . . . AIR
FUEL . . . . G
SPEEDS . . . . VARIABLE
TRANSMISSION . . . . HYDRO
STEERING. . . . ZERO
BLADE CLUTCH . . . . ELECTRIC
STANDARD DECK . . . . 48"
MSRP. . . . $8,628

RETAIL PRICING

YEAR	HIGH	LOW
2005	$4,977	$3,732
2008	$5,268	$3,951
2009	$5,437	$4,078
2010	$5,740	$4,305

74448

YEARS MFRD 2008-2009
SERIES. . . . Z400 SERIES
ENGINE . . . . KAWASAKI
CYLINDERS. . . . 2
ENGINE HP 21
COOLING . . . . AIR
FUEL . . . . G
SPEEDS . . . . VARIABLE
TRANSMISSION . . . . HYDRO
STEERING. . . . ZERO
BLADE CLUTCH . . . . ELECTRIC
STANDARD DECK . . . . 48"
MSRP. . . . $7,649

RETAIL PRICING

YEAR	HIGH	LOW
2008	$4,309	$3,232
2009	$4,511	$3,383

74449

YEARS MFRD 2008-2010
SERIES. . . . Z400 SERIES
ENGINE . . . . KAWASAKI OHV
CYLINDERS. . . . 2
ENGINE HP 21
COOLING . . . . AIR
FUEL . . . . G
SPEEDS . . . . VARIABLE
TRANSMISSION . . . . HYDRO
STEERING. . . . ZERO
BLADE CLUTCH . . . . ELECTRIC
STANDARD DECK . . . . 52"
MSRP. . . . $7,969

RETAIL PRICING

YEAR	HIGH	LOW
2008	$4,889	$3,667
2009	$5,020	$3,765
2010	$5,300	$3,975

74453

YEARS MFRD 2019-2019
SERIES. . . . TITAN HD 1500 SERIES
ENGINE . . . . TORO
CID 708CC
ENGINE HP 24.5
FUEL . . . . G
SPEEDS . . . . VARIABLE
TRANSMISSION . . . . HYDRO
STEERING. . . . ZERO
ROPS/CAB . . . . ROPS
STANDARD DECK . . . . 48"
WEIGHT . . . . 849 LBS.
MSRP. . . . $6,332

74454

YEARS MFRD 2019-2019
SERIES. . . . TITAN HD 1500 SERIES
ENGINE . . . . TORO
CID 708CC
ENGINE HP 24.5
FUEL . . . . G
SPEEDS . . . . VARIABLE
TRANSMISSION . . . . HYDRO
STEERING. . . . ZERO
ROPS/CAB . . . . ROPS
STANDARD DECK . . . . 52"
WEIGHT . . . . 862 LBS.
MSRP. . . . $6,888

74463

YEARS MFRD 2017-2019
SERIES. . TITAN HD 2000 RD SERIES
ENGINE . . . . KOHLER
CID 747CC
ENGINE HP 25
FUEL . . . . G
SPEEDS . . . . VARIABLE
TRANSMISSION . . . . HYDRO
STEERING. . . . ZERO
ROPS/CAB . . . . ROPS
STANDARD DECK . . . . 60"
MSRP. . . . $9,443

74465

YEARS MFRD 2018-2019
SERIES. . . . TITAN HD 2000 SERIES
ENGINE . . . . TORO V-TWIN
CID 708CC
ENGINE HP 24.5
FUEL . . . . G
SPEEDS . . . . VARIABLE
TRANSMISSION . . . . HYDRO
STEERING. . . . ZERO
ROPS/CAB . . . . ROPS
STANDARD DECK . . . . 48"
MSRP. . . . $7,777

74466

YEARS MFRD 2018-2019
SERIES. . . . TITAN HD 2000 SERIES
ENGINE . . . . TORO V-TWIN
CID 708CC
ENGINE HP 24.5
FUEL . . . . G
SPEEDS . . . . VARIABLE
TRANSMISSION . . . . HYDRO
STEERING. . . . ZERO
ROPS/CAB . . . . ROPS
STANDARD DECK . . . . 52"
MSRP. . . . $8,332

74467

YEARS MFRD 2018-2019
SERIES. . . . TITAN HD 2000 SERIES
ENGINE . . . . TORO V-TWIN
CID 708CC
ENGINE HP 24.5
FUEL . . . . G
SPEEDS . . . . VARIABLE
TRANSMISSION . . . . HYDRO
STEERING. . . . ZERO
ROPS/CAB . . . . ROPS
STANDARD DECK . . . . 60"
MSRP. . . . $8,888

74470

YEARS MFRD 2017-2019
SERIES. . . . TITAN HD 2500 SERIES
ENGINE . . . . KAWASAKI FX
CID 726CC
ENGINE HP 20.5
FUEL . . . . G
TRANSMISSION . . . . HYDRO
STEERING. . . . ZERO
STANDARD DECK . . . . 48"
MSRP. . . . $8,332

74471

YEARS MFRD 2017-2019
SERIES. . . . TITAN HD 2500 SERIES
ENGINE . . . . KAWASAKI FX
CID 726CC
ENGINE HP 22
FUEL . . . . G
TRANSMISSION . . . . HYDRO
STEERING. . . . ZERO
STANDARD DECK . . . . 52"
MSRP. . . . $9,129

74472

YEARS MFRD 2017-2019
SERIES. . . . TITAN HD 2500
ENGINE . . . . KAWASAKI FX
CID 726CC
ENGINE HP 23.5
FUEL . . . . G
TRANSMISSION . . . . HYDRO
STEERING. . . . ZERO
STANDARD DECK . . . . 60"
MSRP. . . . $9,568

74480

YEARS MFRD 2019-2019
SERIES. . . . TITAN HD 2000 SERIES
ENGINE . . . . KAWASAKI FX730V
ENGINE HP 23.5
FUEL . . . . G
SPEEDS . . . . VARIABLE
TRANSMISSION . . . . HYDRO
STEERING. . . . ZERO
ROPS/CAB . . . . ROPS
STANDARD DECK . . . . 60"
MSRP. . . . $9,999

74490

YEARS MFRD 2020-2020
SERIES. . . . Z MASTER 2000 SERIES
ENGINE . . . . TORO
CYLINDERS. . . . 2
CID 708CC
ENGINE HP 24.5
FUEL . . . . G
SPEEDS . . . . VARIABLE
TRANSMISSION . . . . HYDRO
STEERING. . . . ZERO
ROPS/CAB . . . . ROPS
STANDARD DECK . . . . 48"
WEIGHT . . . . 870 LBS.
MSRP. . . . $7,083

74491

YEARS MFRD 2020-2020
SERIES. . . . Z MASTER 2000 SERIES
ENGINE . . . . TORO
CYLINDERS. . . . 2
CID 708CC
ENGINE HP 24.5
FUEL . . . . G
SPEEDS . . . . VARIABLE
TRANSMISSION . . . . HYDRO
STEERING. . . . ZERO
ROPS/CAB . . . . ROPS
STANDARD DECK . . . . 52"
WEIGHT . . . . 890 LBS.
MSRP. . . . $7,673

74492

YEARS MFRD 2020-2020
SERIES. . . . Z MASTER 2000 SERIES
ENGINE . . . . TORO
CYLINDERS. . . . 2
CID 708CC
ENGINE HP 24.5
FUEL . . . . G
SPEEDS . . . . VARIABLE
TRANSMISSION . . . . HYDRO
STEERING. . . . ZERO
ROPS/CAB . . . . ROPS
STANDARD DECK . . . . 60"
WEIGHT . . . . 920 LBS.
MSRP. . . . $8,263

TORO

74493
YEARS MFRD 2020-2020
SERIES Z MASTER 2000 HDX SERIES
ENGINE .... TORO
CYLINDERS................ 2
CID 708CC
ENGINE HP 24.5
FUEL .... G
SPEEDS .... VARIABLE
TRANSMISSION .... HYDRO
STEERING............. ZERO
ROPS/CAB .... ROPS
STANDARD DECK .... 52"
WEIGHT .... 1,012 LBS.
MSRP............... $9,163

74494
YEARS MFRD 2020-2020
SERIES Z MASTER 2000 HDX SERIES
ENGINE .... TORO
CYLINDERS................ 2
CID 708CC
ENGINE HP 24.5
FUEL .... G
SPEEDS .... VARIABLE
TRANSMISSION .... HYDRO
STEERING............. ZERO
ROPS/CAB .... ROPS
STANDARD DECK .... 60"
WEIGHT .... 1,036 LBS.
MSRP............... $9,735

74497 CARB
YEARS MFRD 2020-2020
SERIES Z MASTER 2000 HDX SERIES
ENGINE .... KAWASAKI FX730V
CID 726CC
ENGINE HP 23.5
FUEL .... G
SPEEDS .... VARIABLE
TRANSMISSION .... HYDRO
STEERING............. ZERO
ROPS/CAB .... ROPS
STANDARD DECK .... 60"
WEIGHT .... 1,036 LBS.
MSRP............... $11,454

74538
YEARS MFRD 2011-2011
SERIES...... GRANDSTAND SERIES
ENGINE .... KAWASAKI
ENGINE HP 20
COOLING .... AIR
FUEL .... G
SPEEDS .... VARIABLE
TRANSMISSION .... HYDRO
STEERING............. ZERO

74539
YEARS MFRD 2011-2011
SERIES...... GRANDSTAND SERIES
ENGINE .... KAWASAKI
ENGINE HP 20
COOLING .... AIR
FUEL .... G
SPEEDS .... VARIABLE
TRANSMISSION .... HYDRO
STEERING............. ZERO

74558
YEARS MFRD 2009-2009
SERIES...... GRANDSTAND SERIES
ENGINE .... KAWASAKI
ENGINE HP 19
COOLING .... AIR
FUEL .... G
SPEEDS .... VARIABLE
TRANSMISSION .... HYDRO
STEERING............. ZERO

74559
YEARS MFRD 2009-2009
SERIES...... GRANDSTAND SERIES
ENGINE .... KAWASAKI
ENGINE HP 19
COOLING .... LIQUID
FUEL .... G
SPEEDS .... VARIABLE
TRANSMISSION .... HYDRO
STEERING............. ZERO

74568
YEARS MFRD 2009-2009
SERIES...... GRANDSTAND SERIES
ENGINE .... KAWASAKI
ENGINE HP 23
COOLING .... AIR
FUEL .... G
SPEEDS .... VARIABLE
TRANSMISSION .... HYDRO
STEERING............. ZERO

74569
YEARS MFRD 2009-2009
SERIES...... GRANDSTAND SERIES
ENGINE .... KAWASAKI
ENGINE HP 23
COOLING .... AIR
FUEL .... G
SPEEDS .... VARIABLE
TRANSMISSION .... HYDRO
STEERING............. ZERO

74603
YEARS MFRD 2008-2008
SERIES. TIMECUTTER ZX440 SERIES
ENGINE .. KOHLER COMMAND OHV
ENGINE HP 18
COOLING .... AIR
FUEL .... G
SPEEDS .... VARIABLE
TRANSMISSION .... HYDRO
STEERING............. ZERO
STANDARD DECK .... 44"
MSRP............... $4,399

RETAIL PRICING

YEAR	HIGH	LOW
2008	$2,916	$2,187

74704
YEARS MFRD 2006-2008
SERIES. TIMECUTTER ZX480 SERIES
ENGINE .... B&S
CYLINDERS................ 2
ENGINE HP 20
COOLING .... AIR
FUEL .... G
SPEEDS .... VARIABLE
TRANSMISSION .... HYDRO
STEERING............. ZERO
BLADE CLUTCH .... ELECTRIC
STANDARD DECK .... 48"
MSRP............... $4,699

RETAIL PRICING

YEAR	HIGH	LOW
2006	$2,958	$2,218
2007	$2,983	$2,237
2008	$3,115	$2,336

74805
YEARS MFRD 2002-2002
SERIES........... Z350 SERIES
ENGINE .... KOHLER
ENGINE HP 25
FUEL .... G
TRANSMISSION .... HYDRO
STEERING........... STANDARD

74812
YEARS MFRD 2007-2008
SERIES...... TITAN Z4800 SERIES
ENGINE .... B&S ELS
CYLINDERS................ 2
ENGINE HP 22
FUEL .... G
SPEEDS .... VARIABLE
TRANSMISSION .... HYDRO
STEERING............. ZERO
BLADE CLUTCH .... ELECTRIC
STANDARD DECK .... 48"
MSRP............... $4,599

RETAIL PRICING

YEAR	HIGH	LOW
2007	$2,602	$1,952
2008	$3,049	$2,287

74814
YEARS MFRD 2008-2008
SERIES...... TITAN Z5200 SERIES
ENGINE .... B&S ELS OHV
CYLINDERS................ 2
ENGINE HP 24
COOLING .... AIR
FUEL .... G
SPEEDS .... VARIABLE
TRANSMISSION .... HYDRO
STEERING............. ZERO
STANDARD DECK .... 52"
MSRP............... $5,399

RETAIL PRICING

YEAR	HIGH	LOW
2008	$3,582	$2,686

74816
YEARS MFRD 2008-2008
SERIES..... TITAN Z4800K SERIES
ENGINE ... KOHLER COURAGE PRO
CYLINDERS................ 2
ENGINE HP 23
COOLING .... AIR
FUEL .... G
SPEEDS .... VARIABLE
TRANSMISSION .... HYDRO
STEERING............. ZERO
STANDARD DECK .... 48"
MSRP............... $4,999

RETAIL PRICING

YEAR	HIGH	LOW
2008	$3,314	$2,485

74818
YEARS MFRD 2007-2008
SERIES...... TITAN Z5200 SERIES
ENGINE .... B&S ELS
CYLINDERS................ 2
ENGINE HP 24
FUEL .... G
SPEEDS .... VARIABLE
TRANSMISSION .... HYDRO
STEERING............. ZERO
BLADE CLUTCH .... ELECTRIC
STANDARD DECK .... 52"
MSRP............... $5,399

RETAIL PRICING

YEAR	HIGH	LOW
2007	$3,061	$2,296
2008	$3,582	$2,686

74901
YEARS MFRD 2009-2011
SERIES......... Z MASTER SERIES
ENGINE ...... KOHLER COMMAND
ENGINE HP 23
COOLING .... AIR
FUEL .... G
SPEEDS .... VARIABLE
TRANSMISSION .... HYDRO
STEERING............. ZERO

74903
YEARS MFRD 2009-2011
SERIES......... Z MASTER SERIES
ENGINE ...... KOHLER COMMAND
ENGINE HP 25
COOLING .... AIR
FUEL .... G
SPEEDS .... VARIABLE
TRANSMISSION .... HYDRO
STEERING............. ZERO

74904
YEARS MFRD 2016-2019
SERIES.... Z MASTER 5000 SERIES
ENGINE .. KOHLER COMMAND PRO
CID 747CC
ENGINE HP 23

FUEL . . . . G
STEERING. . . . . ZERO
STANDARD DECK . . . . 48"
MSRP. $12,221

74906
YEARS MFRD 2014-2019
SERIES. . . . Z MASTER 5000 SERIES
ENGINE . . KOHLER COMMAND PRO
CID 747CC
ENGINE HP 25
FUEL . . . . G
STEERING. . . . . ZERO
STANDARD DECK . . . . 52"
MSRP. $12,777

74915
YEARS MFRD 2009-2011
SERIES. . . . . Z MASTER SERIES
ENGINE . . KOHLER COMMAND PRO
ENGINE HP 27
COOLING . . . . AIR
FUEL . . . . G
SPEEDS . . . . VARIABLE
TRANSMISSION . . . . HYDRO
STEERING. . . . . ZERO

74915
YEARS MFRD 2014-2019
SERIES. . . . Z MASTER 5000 SERIES
ENGINE . . KOHLER COMMAND PRO
CID 747CC
ENGINE HP 25
FUEL . . . . G
STEERING. . . . . ZERO
STANDARD DECK . . . . 60"
MSRP. $12,888

74918
YEARS MFRD 2014-2019
SERIES. . . . Z MASTER 5000 SERIES
ENGINE . . KOHLER COMMAND PRO
CID 747CC
ENGINE HP 26.5
FUEL . . . . G
STEERING. . . . . ZERO
STANDARD DECK . . . . 72"
MSRP. $14,110

74921
YEARS MFRD 2009-2010
SERIES. . . . . Z MASTER SERIES
ENGINE . . . . KAWASAKI
ENGINE HP 23
COOLING . . . . AIR
FUEL . . . . G
SPEEDS . . . . VARIABLE
TRANSMISSION . . . . HYDRO
STEERING. . . . . ZERO

74923
YEARS MFRD 2009-2010
SERIES. . . . . Z MASTER SERIES
ENGINE . . . . KAWASAKI
ENGINE HP 27
COOLING . . . . AIR
FUEL . . . . G
SPEEDS . . . . VARIABLE
TRANSMISSION . . . . HYDRO
STEERING. . . . . ZERO

74925
YEARS MFRD 2009-2011
SERIES. . . . . Z MASTER SERIES
ENGINE . . . . KAWASAKI FX801V
ENGINE HP 29
COOLING . . . . AIR
FUEL . . . . G
SPEEDS . . . . VARIABLE
TRANSMISSION . . . . HYDRO
STEERING. . . . . ZERO

74926
YEARS MFRD 2014-2018
SERIES. . . . Z MASTER 6000 SERIES
ENGINE . . KOHLER COMMAND PRO
CID 747CC
ENGINE HP 26.5
FUEL . . . . G
SPEEDS . . . . VARIABLE
TRANSMISSION . . . . HYDRO
STEERING. . . . . ZERO
STANDARD DECK . . . . 60"

74927
YEARS MFRD 2009-2011
SERIES. . . . . Z MASTER SERIES
ENGINE . . . . KAWASAKI FX801V
ENGINE HP 29
COOLING . . . . AIR
FUEL . . . . G
SPEEDS . . . . VARIABLE
TRANSMISSION . . . . HYDRO
STEERING. . . . . ZERO

74928
YEARS MFRD 2011-2011
SERIES. . . . . G3 SERIES
ENGINE . . . . KOHLER EFI
ENGINE HP 29
COOLING . . . . AIR
FUEL . . . . G
SPEEDS . . . . VARIABLE
TRANSMISSION . . . . HYDRO
STEERING. . . . . ZERO
BLADE CLUTCH . . . . ELECTRIC

74930
YEARS MFRD 2014-2019
SERIES. . . . Z MASTER 5000 SERIES
ENGINE . . KOHLER COMMAND PRO
CYLINDERS. 2
CID 747CC
ENGINE HP 25
FUEL . . . . G
STEERING. . . . . ZERO
STANDARD DECK . . . . 60"
MSRP. $13,666

74933
YEARS MFRD 2014-2019
SERIES. . . . Z MASTER 5000 SERIES
ENGINE KOHLER COMMAND PRO LP
STEERING. . . . . ZERO
STANDARD DECK . . . . 60"
MSRP. $16,443

74934
YEARS MFRD 2014-2019
SERIES. . . . Z MASTER 5000 SERIES
ENGINE KOHLER COMMAND PRO LP
STEERING. . . . . ZERO
STANDARD DECK . . . . 72"
MSRP. $16,888

74935
YEARS MFRD 2009-2010
SERIES. . . . . Z MASTER SERIES
ENGINE . . . . KAWASAKI FX921V
ENGINE HP 34
COOLING . . . . AIR
FUEL . . . . G
SPEEDS . . . . VARIABLE
TRANSMISSION . . . . HYDRO
STEERING. . . . . ZERO

74936
YEARS MFRD 2011-2011
SERIES. . . . . G3 SERIES
ENGINE . . . . . . KOHLER COMMAND
ENGINE HP 34
COOLING . . . . AIR
FUEL . . . . G
SPEEDS . . . . VARIABLE
TRANSMISSION . . . . HYDRO
STEERING. . . . . ZERO
BLADE CLUTCH . . . . ELECTRIC

74937
YEARS MFRD 2009-2010
SERIES. . . . . Z MASTER SERIES
ENGINE . . . . KAWASAKI FX921V
ENGINE HP 34
FUEL . . . . G
SPEEDS . . . . VARIABLE
TRANSMISSION . . . . HYDRO
STEERING. . . . . ZERO

74938
YEARS MFRD 2011-2011
SERIES. . . . . G3 SERIES
ENGINE . . . . . . KOHLER COMMAND
ENGINE HP 34
COOLING . . . . AIR
FUEL . . . . G
SPEEDS . . . . VARIABLE
TRANSMISSION . . . . HYDRO
STEERING. . . . . ZERO

74943
YEARS MFRD 2017-2019
SERIES. Z MASTER 5000 SERIES RD
ENGINE . . KOHLER COMMAND PRO
CID 747CC
ENGINE HP 25
FUEL . . . . G
STEERING. . . . . ZERO
STANDARD DECK . . . . 60"
MSRP. $14,221

74945
YEARS MFRD 2017-2019
SERIES. Z MASTER 5000 SERIES RD
ENGINE . . KOHLER COMMAND PRO
CID 747CC
ENGINE HP 26.5
FUEL . . . . G
STEERING. . . . . ZERO
STANDARD DECK . . . . 72"
MSRP. $14,666

74946
YEARS MFRD 2014-2019
SERIES. . . . Z MASTER 6000 SERIES
ENGINE . . KOHLER COMMAND PRO
CID 999CC
ENGINE HP 34
FUEL . . . . G
SPEEDS . . . . VARIABLE
TRANSMISSION . . . . HYDRO
STEERING. . . . . ZERO
STANDARD DECK . . . . 60"
MSRP. $16,888

74947
YEARS MFRD 2014-2019
SERIES. . . . Z MASTER 6000 SERIES
ENGINE . . KOHLER COMMAND PRO
CID 999CC
ENGINE HP 34
FUEL . . . . G
SPEEDS . . . . VARIABLE
TRANSMISSION . . . . HYDRO
STEERING. . . . . ZERO
STANDARD DECK . . . . 72"
MSRP. $17,666

74949
YEARS MFRD 2018-2019
SERIES. . . . Z MASTER 3000 SERIES
ENGINE . . . . KAWASAKI FX
CID 852CC
ENGINE HP 24.5
FUEL . . . . G
STEERING. . . . . ZERO
STANDARD DECK . . . . 52"
MSRP. $11,438

TORO

74950
YEARS MFRD 2017-2019
SERIES. . . . Z MASTER 3000 SERIES
ENGINE . . . . KAWASAKI FX
CID 852CC
ENGINE HP. 25.5
FUEL . . . . G
STEERING. . . . . ZERO
STANDARD DECK . . . . 60"
MSRP. $11,989

74951
YEARS MFRD 2011-2011
SERIES. . . . . G3 SERIES
ENGINE . . . . KAWASAKI
ENGINE HP. 20
COOLING . . . . AIR
FUEL . . . . G
SPEEDS . . . . VARIABLE
TRANSMISSION . . . . HYDRO
STEERING. . . . . ZERO

74952
YEARS MFRD 2011-2011
SERIES. . . . . G3 SERIES
ENGINE . . . . KAWASAKI
ENGINE HP. 22
COOLING . . . . AIR
FUEL . . . . G
SPEEDS . . . . VARIABLE
TRANSMISSION . . . . HYDRO
STEERING. . . . . ZERO

74952
YEARS MFRD 2014-2019
SERIES. . . . Z MASTER 3000 SERIES
ENGINE . . . . KAWASAKI FX
CID 726CC
ENGINE HP. 20.5
FUEL . . . . G
STEERING. . . . . ZERO
STANDARD DECK . . . . 48"
MSRP. $10,443

74953
YEARS MFRD 2011-2011
SERIES. . . . . G3 SERIES
ENGINE . . . . KAWASAKI
ENGINE HP. 24
COOLING . . . . AIR
FUEL . . . . G
SPEEDS . . . . VARIABLE
TRANSMISSION . . . . HYDRO
STEERING. . . . . ZERO

74958
YEARS MFRD 2014-2019
SERIES. . . . Z MASTER 3000 SERIES
ENGINE . . KOHLER COMMAND PRO
CID 747CC
ENGINE HP. 25
FUEL . . . . G
STEERING. . . . . ZERO
STANDARD DECK . . . . 60"
MSRP. $11,888

74959
YEARS MFRD 2014-2019
SERIES. . . . Z MASTER 3000 SERIES
ENGINE . . KOHLER COMMAND PRO
CID 747CC
ENGINE HP. 25
FUEL . . . . G
STEERING. . . . . ZERO
STANDARD DECK . . . . 72"
MSRP. $12,110

74960
YEARS MFRD 2017-2019
SERIES. . . . Z MASTER 6000 SERIES
ENGINE . . . . KAWASAKI FX
CID 999CC
ENGINE HP. 31
FUEL . . . . G
SPEEDS . . . . VARIABLE
TRANSMISSION . . . . HYDRO
STEERING. . . . . ZERO
STANDARD DECK . . . . 60"
MSRP. $15,332

74961
YEARS MFRD 2017-2019
SERIES. . . . Z MASTER 6000 SERIES
ENGINE . . . . KAWASAKI FX
CID 999CC
ENGINE HP. 31
FUEL . . . . G
SPEEDS . . . . VARIABLE
TRANSMISSION . . . . HYDRO
STEERING. . . . . ZERO
STANDARD DECK . . . . 72"
MSRP. $15,888

74969
YEARS MFRD 2018-2019
SERIES. . . . Z MASTER 6000 SERIES
ENGINE . . . . KAWASAKI FX
CID 852CC
ENGINE HP. 29
FUEL . . . . G
STEERING. . . . . ZERO
STANDARD DECK . . . . 60"
MSRP. $16,110

74975
YEARS MFRD 2011-2011
SERIES. . . . . G3 SERIES
ENGINE . . . KAWASAKI FX PROPANE
ENGINE HP. 29
COOLING . . . . AIR
SPEEDS . . . . VARIABLE
TRANSMISSION . . . . HYDRO
STEERING. . . . . ZERO

74977
YEARS MFRD 2011-2011
SERIES. . . . . G3 SERIES
ENGINE . . . KAWASAKI FX PROPANE
ENGINE HP. 29
COOLING . . . . AIR
SPEEDS . . . . VARIABLE
TRANSMISSION . . . . HYDRO
STEERING. . . . . ZERO

75201
YEARS MFRD 2017-2019
SERIES. . . . TIMECUTTER HD SERIES
ENGINE . . . . TORO
CYLINDERS. 2
ENGINE HP. 22.5
FUEL . . . . G
TRANSMISSION . . . . . DUAL HYDRO
STEERING. . . . . ZERO
STANDARD DECK . . . . 48"
MSRP. $5,399

75202
YEARS MFRD 2017-2019
SERIES. . . . TIMECUTTER HD SERIES
ENGINE . . . . TORO
CYLINDERS. 2
CID 708CC
ENGINE HP. 24.5
FUEL . . . . G
TRANSMISSION . . . . . DUAL HYDRO
STEERING. . . . . ZERO
STANDARD DECK . . . . 54"
MSRP. $5,699

75211
YEARS MFRD 2017-2019
SERIES. . . . TIMECUTTER HD SERIES
ENGINE . . . . TORO
CYLINDERS. 2
ENGINE HP. 22.5
FUEL . . . . G
SPEEDS . . . . VARIABLE
TRANSMISSION . . . . . DUAL HYDRO
STEERING. . . . . ZERO
STANDARD DECK . . . . 48"
MSRP. $75,211

75212
YEARS MFRD 2017-2019
SERIES. . . . TIMECUTTER HD SERIES
ENGINE . . . . TORO
CYLINDERS. 2
CID 708CC
ENGINE HP. 24.5
FUEL . . . . G
SPEEDS . . . . VARIABLE
TRANSMISSION . . . . . DUAL HYDRO
STEERING. . . . . ZERO
STANDARD DECK . . . . 54"
MSRP. $6,199

75213
YEARS MFRD 2017-2019
SERIES. . . . TIMECUTTER HD SERIES
ENGINE . . . . TORO
CYLINDERS. 2
CID 708CC
ENGINE HP. 24.5
FUEL . . . . G
SPEEDS . . . . VARIABLE
TRANSMISSION . . . . . DUAL HYDRO
STEERING. . . . . ZERO
STANDARD DECK . . . . 60"
MSRP. $6,299

75301
YEARS MFRD 2020-2020
SERIES. . . . . TITAN SERIES
ENGINE . . . . TORO
CID 708CC
ENGINE HP. 24.5
FUEL . . . . G
SPEEDS . . . . VARIABLE
TRANSMISSION . . . . . DUAL HYDRO
STEERING. . . . . ZERO
STANDARD DECK . . . . 48"
MSRP. $5,099

75302
YEARS MFRD 2020-2020
SERIES. . . . . TITAN SERIES
ENGINE . . . . TORO
CID 708CC
ENGINE HP. 24.5
FUEL . . . . G
SPEEDS . . . . VARIABLE
TRANSMISSION . . . . . DUAL HYDRO
STEERING. . . . . ZERO
STANDARD DECK . . . . 54"
MSRP. $5,299

75303
YEARS MFRD 2020-2020
SERIES. . . . . TITAN SERIES
ENGINE . . . . TORO
CID 708CC
ENGINE HP. 24.5
FUEL . . . . G
SPEEDS . . . . VARIABLE
TRANSMISSION . . . . . DUAL HYDRO
STEERING. . . . . ZERO
STANDARD DECK . . . . 60"
MSRP. $5,599

75311
YEARS MFRD 2020-2020
SERIES. . . . . . TITAN MYRIDE SERIES
ENGINE . . . . TORO
CID 708CC
ENGINE HP. 24.5
FUEL . . . . G
SPEEDS . . . . VARIABLE
TRANSMISSION . . . . . DUAL HYDRO
STEERING. . . . . ZERO
STANDARD DECK . . . . 48"
MSRP. $5,799

75312
YEARS MFRD 2020-2020
SERIES...... TITAN MYRIDE SERIES
ENGINE .... TORO
CID 708CC
ENGINE HP 24.5
FUEL .... G
SPEEDS .... VARIABLE
TRANSMISSION ..... DUAL HYDRO
STEERING.............. ZERO
STANDARD DECK .... 54"
MSRP.................. $5,999

75313
YEARS MFRD 2020-2020
SERIES...... TITAN MYRIDE SERIES
ENGINE .... TORO
CID 708CC
ENGINE HP 24.5
FUEL .... G
SPEEDS .... VARIABLE
TRANSMISSION ..... DUAL HYDRO
STEERING.............. ZERO
STANDARD DECK .... 60"
MSRP.................. $6,199

75740
YEARS MFRD 2020-2020
SERIES....... TIMECUTTER SERIES
ENGINE .... TORO
CID 452CC
FUEL .... G
SPEEDS .... VARIABLE
TRANSMISSION ..... DUAL HYDRO
STEERING.............. ZERO
STANDARD DECK .... 42"
MSRP.................. $2,599

75742
YEARS MFRD 2020-2020
SERIES....... TIMECUTTER SERIES
ENGINE .... TORO
CID 708CC
ENGINE HP 22.5
FUEL .... G
SPEEDS .... VARIABLE
TRANSMISSION ..... DUAL HYDRO
STEERING.............. ZERO
STANDARD DECK .... 42"
MSRP.................. $2,799

75744 FAB
YEARS MFRD 2020-2020
SERIES....... TIMECUTTER SERIES
ENGINE .... TORO
CID 708CC
ENGINE HP 22.5
FUEL .... G
SPEEDS .... VARIABLE
TRANSMISSION ..... DUAL HYDRO
STEERING.............. ZERO
STANDARD DECK .... 42"
MSRP.................. $3,099

75745
YEARS MFRD 2020-2020
SERIES TIMECUTTER MYRIDE SERIES
ENGINE .... TORO
CID 708CC
ENGINE HP 24.5
FUEL .... G
SPEEDS .... VARIABLE
TRANSMISSION ..... DUAL HYDRO
STEERING.............. ZERO
STANDARD DECK .... 42"
MSRP.................. $3,699

75750
YEARS MFRD 2020-2020
SERIES....... TIMECUTTER SERIES
ENGINE .... KAWASAKI
CID 726CC
ENGINE HP 23
FUEL .... G
SPEEDS .... VARIABLE
TRANSMISSION ..... DUAL HYDRO
STEERING.............. ZERO
STANDARD DECK .... 50"
MSRP.................. $3,299

75751
YEARS MFRD 2020-2020
SERIES....... TIMECUTTER SERIES
ENGINE .... KOHLER
CID 725CC
ENGINE HP 24
FUEL .... G
SPEEDS .... VARIABLE
TRANSMISSION ..... DUAL HYDRO
STEERING.............. ZERO
STANDARD DECK .... 50"
MSRP.................. $3,199

75754
YEARS MFRD 2020-2020
SERIES TIMECUTTER MYRIDE SERIES
ENGINE .... TORO
CID 708CC
ENGINE HP 24.5
FUEL .... G
SPEEDS .... VARIABLE
TRANSMISSION ..... DUAL HYDRO
STEERING.............. ZERO
STANDARD DECK .... 54"
MSRP.................. $4,099

75755
YEARS MFRD 2020-2020
SERIES TIMECUTTER MYRIDE SERIES
ENGINE .... TORO
CID 708CC
ENGINE HP 24.5
FUEL .... G
SPEEDS .... VARIABLE
TRANSMISSION ..... DUAL HYDRO
STEERING.............. ZERO
STANDARD DECK .... 50"
MSRP.................. $3,899

75759
YEARS MFRD 2020-2020
SERIES TIMECUTTER MYRIDE SERIES
ENGINE .... KAWASAKI
CID 726CC
ENGINE HP 23
FUEL .... G
SPEEDS .... VARIABLE
TRANSMISSION ..... DUAL HYDRO
STEERING.............. ZERO
STANDARD DECK .... 50"
MSRP.................. $4,099

75760
YEARS MFRD 2020-2020
SERIES....... TIMECUTTER SERIES
ENGINE .... TORO
CID 708CC
ENGINE HP 24.5
FUEL .... G
SPEEDS .... VARIABLE
TRANSMISSION ..... DUAL HYDRO
STEERING.............. ZERO
STANDARD DECK .... 60"
MSRP.................. $4,199

75932
YEARS MFRD 2018-2019
SERIES.... Z MASTER 3000 SERIES
ENGINE .... KAWASAKI FX
CID 852CC
ENGINE HP 24.5
FUEL .... G
STEERING.............. ZERO
STANDARD DECK .... 52"
MSRP.................. $12,538

75936
YEARS MFRD 2017-2019
SERIES.... Z MASTER 3000 SERIES
ENGINE .... KAWASAKI FX
CID 852CC
ENGINE HP 25.5
FUEL .... G
STEERING.............. ZERO
STANDARD DECK .... 60"
MSRP.................. $13,088

75951
YEARS MFRD 2017-2019
SERIES.... Z MASTER 5000 SERIES
ENGINE .. KOHLER COMMAND PRO
CID 747CC
ENGINE HP 25
FUEL .... G
STEERING.............. ZERO
STANDARD DECK .... 60"
MSRP.................. $14,777

75955
YEARS MFRD 2017-2019
SERIES.... Z MASTER 5000 SERIES
ENGINE .. KOHLER COMMAND PRO
CID 747CC
ENGINE HP 25
FUEL .... G
STEERING.............. ZERO
STANDARD DECK .... 52"
MSRP.................. $13,888

75967
YEARS MFRD 2017-2019
SERIES.... Z MASTER 6000 SERIES
ENGINE .... KAWASAKI FX
CID 999CC
ENGINE HP 31
FUEL .... G
STEERING.............. ZERO
STANDARD DECK .... 60"
MSRP.................. $16,443

75968
YEARS MFRD 2017-2019
SERIES.... Z MASTER 6000 SERIES
ENGINE .... KAWASAKI FX
CID 999CC
ENGINE HP 31
FUEL .... G
STEERING.............. ZERO
STANDARD DECK .... 72"
MSRP.................. $16,999

78472 (CARB)
YEARS MFRD 2018-2019
SERIES..... TITAN HD 2500 SERIES
ENGINE .... KAWASAKI FX
CID 726CC
ENGINE HP 23.5
FUEL .... G
TRANSMISSION .... HYDRO
STEERING.............. ZERO
STANDARD DECK .... 60"

TROY-BILT

BIG RED
YEARS MFRD 2004-2004
ENGINE .... B&S
CYLINDERS.................. 2
ENGINE HP 24
FUEL .... G
SPEEDS .... VARIABLE
TRANSMISSION .... HYDRO
STEERING........... STANDARD
BLADE CLUTCH .... ELECTRIC
STANDARD DECK .... 54"
MSRP.................. $2,999

RETAIL PRICING

YEAR	HIGH	LOW
2004	$1,519	$1,139

TROY-BILT

BIG RED HORSE 50GT

YEARS MFRD 2007-2011
ENGINE . . . . B&S INTEK
CYLINDERS. 2
ENGINE HP 23
COOLING . . . . AIR
FUEL . . . . G
SPEEDS . . . . VARIABLE
TRANSMISSION . . . . HYDRO
STEERING. . . . . STANDARD
STANDARD DECK . . . . 50"
WEIGHT . . . . 720 LBS.
MSRP. $2,299

RETAIL PRICING

YEAR	HIGH	LOW
2007	$741	$556
2008	$822	$617
2009	$910	$683
2010	$1,006	$755
2011	$1,117	$838

BIG RED LT

YEARS MFRD 2011-2011
ENGINE . . . . KOHLER
CYLINDERS. 2
ENGINE HP 24
COOLING . . . . AIR
FUEL . . . . G
SPEEDS . . . . VARIABLE
TRANSMISSION . . . . HYDRO
STEERING. . . . . STANDARD
BLADE CLUTCH . . . . ELECTRIC
STANDARD DECK . . . . 50"
WEIGHT . . . . 660 LBS.
MSRP. $1,999

RETAIL PRICING

YEAR	HIGH	LOW
2011	$1,130	$847

BRONCO 42

YEARS MFRD 2018-2020
ENGINE . . . . B&S INTEK
ENGINE HP 19
FUEL . . . . G
TRANSMISSION . . . . CVT
STEERING. . . . . STANDARD
BLADE CLUTCH . . . . MANUAL
STANDARD DECK . . . . 42"
WEIGHT . . . . 495 LBS.
MSRP. $1,449

BRONCO 42X

YEARS MFRD 2020-2020
ENGINE . . . . TROYBILT OHV
CYLINDERS. 1
CID 547CC
FUEL . . . . G
SPEEDS . . . . AUTOMATIC
STEERING. . . . . STANDARD
BLADE CLUTCH . . . . ELECTRIC
STANDARD DECK . . . . 42"
WEIGHT . . . . 520 LBS.
MSRP. $1,449

OPTIONS

46" DECK. $50

BRONCO 46

YEARS MFRD 2018-2019
ENGINE . . . . B&S
ENGINE HP 19
TRANSMISSION . . . . CVT
STEERING. . . . . STANDARD
BLADE CLUTCH . . . . MANUAL
STANDARD DECK . . . . 46"
WEIGHT . . . . 500 LBS.
MSRP. $1,599

BRONCO 46T

YEARS MFRD 2019-2020
ENGINE . . . . TROYBILT
CYLINDERS. 2
CID 679CC
FUEL . . . . G
TRANSMISSION . . . . CVT
STEERING. . . . . STANDARD
BLADE CLUTCH . . . . MANUAL
STANDARD DECK . . . . 46"
WEIGHT . . . . 500 LBS.
MSRP. $1,599

BRONCO

YEARS MFRD 2009-2017
ENGINE . . . . KOHLER COURAGE
CYLINDERS. 1
ENGINE HP 20
COOLING . . . . AIR
FUEL . . . . G
SPEEDS . . . . VARIABLE
TRANSMISSION . . . . CVT
STEERING. . . . . STANDARD
BLADE CLUTCH . . . . MANUAL
STANDARD DECK . . . . 42"
WEIGHT . . . . 615 LBS.
MSRP. $1,199

OPTIONS

2 BAG
42" SNOW BLOWER
46" BLADE

RETAIL PRICING

YEAR	HIGH	LOW
2009	$307	$230
2010	$325	$244
2011	$370	$278
2012	$434	$326
2013	$469	$352
2014	$524	$393
2015	$587	$440
2016	$687	$515
2017	$777	$583

COLT XP

YEARS MFRD 2011-2013
ENGINE . . . . KOHLER COURAGE
CYLINDERS. 2
ENGINE HP 20
COOLING . . . . AIR
FUEL . . . . G
SPEEDS . . . . VARIABLE
TRANSMISSION . . . . . DUAL HYDRO
STEERING. . . . . ZERO
BLADE CLUTCH . . . . ELECTRIC
STANDARD DECK . . . . 42"
MSRP. $2,299

OPTIONS

2 BAG

RETAIL PRICING

YEAR	HIGH	LOW
2011	$1,062	$797
2012	$1,182	$886
2013	$1,310	$983

HORSE

YEARS MFRD 2004-2004
ENGINE . . . . B&S
CYLINDERS. 2
ENGINE HP 21
FUEL . . . . G
SPEEDS . . . . VARIABLE
TRANSMISSION . . . . HYDRO
STEERING. . . . . STANDARD
STANDARD DECK . . . . 46"
MSRP. $1,999

RETAIL PRICING

YEAR	HIGH	LOW
2004	$1,011	$759

HORSE XP

YEARS MFRD 2013-2019
ENGINE . . . . KOHLER
CYLINDERS. 1
ENGINE HP 22
COOLING . . . . AIR
FUEL . . . . G
SPEEDS . . . . VARIABLE
TRANSMISSION . . . . HYDRO
STEERING. . . . . STANDARD
BLADE CLUTCH . . . . ELECTRIC
STANDARD DECK . . . . 46"
WEIGHT . . . . 720 LBS.
MSRP. $1,599

OPTIONS

46" BLADE
BAGGER

RETAIL PRICING

YEAR	HIGH	LOW
2013	$519	$390
2014	$580	$435
2015	$659	$494
2016	$763	$573
2017	$876	$657
2018	$972	$729
2019	$1,068	$801

J609G

YEARS MFRD 2004-2006
SERIES. . . . . BRONCO SERIES
ENGINE . . . . B&S
ENGINE HP 18.5
COOLING . . . . AIR
FUEL . . . . G
SPEEDS . . . . VARIABLE
TRANSMISSION . . . . HYDRO
STEERING. . . . . STANDARD
STANDARD DECK . . . . 42"
MSRP. $1,299

RETAIL PRICING

YEAR	HIGH	LOW
2004	$658	$493
2005	$712	$534
2006	$765	$574

MUSTANG 42 XP

YEARS MFRD 2013-2019
ENGINE . . . . KOHLER
ENGINE HP 22
COOLING . . . . AIR
FUEL . . . . G
SPEEDS . . . . VARIABLE
TRANSMISSION . . . . HYDRO
STEERING. . . . . ZERO
STANDARD DECK . . . . 42"
MSRP. $2,499

RETAIL PRICING

YEAR	HIGH	LOW
2013	$858	$644
2014	$953	$714
2015	$1,074	$806
2016	$1,257	$943
2017	$1,440	$1,080
2018	$1,596	$1,197
2019	$1,752	$1,314

MUSTANG 46 XP

YEARS MFRD 2013-2019
ENGINE . . . . B&S
ENGINE HP 24
COOLING . . . . AIR
FUEL . . . . G
SPEEDS . . . . VARIABLE
TRANSMISSION . . . . HYDRO
STEERING. . . . . ZERO
STANDARD DECK . . . . 46"
MSRP. $2,799

RETAIL PRICING

YEAR	HIGH	LOW
2013	$971	$728
2014	$1,084	$813
2015	$1,213	$910
2016	$1,422	$1,066
2017	$1,621	$1,216
2018	$1,789	$1,341
2019	$1,975	$1,481

MUSTANG 50 XP

YEARS MFRD 2013-2019
ENGINE . . . . KOHLER
ENGINE HP 25
FUEL . . . . G
SPEEDS . . . . VARIABLE
TRANSMISSION . . . . HYDRO

STEERING ... ZERO
STANDARD DECK ... 50"
MSRP ... $2,999

RETAIL PRICING

YEAR	HIGH	LOW
2013	$1,005	$754
2014	$1,127	$845
2015	$1,309	$982
2016	$1,526	$1,144
2017	$1,751	$1,313
2018	$1,930	$1,447
2019	$2,129	$1,596

MUSTANG 54 XP

YEARS MFRD ... 2013-2019
ENGINE ... B&S
ENGINE HP ... 26
SPEEDS ... VARIABLE
TRANSMISSION ... HYDRO
STEERING ... ZERO
STANDARD DECK ... 54"
MSRP ... $3,099

OPTIONS

54" FAB DECK

RETAIL PRICING

YEAR	HIGH	LOW
2013	$1,117	$838
2014	$1,248	$936
2015	$1,403	$1,053
2016	$1,638	$1,228
2017	$1,873	$1,405
2018	$2,049	$1,537
2019	$2,263	$1,697

MUSTANG 60 XP

YEARS MFRD ... 2016-2019
ENGINE ... B&S
ENGINE HP ... 25
FUEL ... G
SPEEDS ... VARIABLE
TRANSMISSION ... DUAL HYDRO
STEERING ... ZERO
BLADE CLUTCH ... ELECTRIC
STANDARD DECK ... 60"
WEIGHT ... 875 LBS.
MSRP ... $4,299

MUSTANG FIT 34

YEARS MFRD ... 2017-2019
ENGINE ... TROYBILT
CID ... 452CC
FUEL ... G
SPEEDS ... VARIABLE
TRANSMISSION ... DUAL HYDRO
STEERING ... ZERO
BLADE CLUTCH ... MANUAL
STANDARD DECK ... 34"
WEIGHT ... 530 LBS.
MSRP ... $2,399

MUSTANG PIVOT S46

YEARS MFRD ... 2015-2019
ENGINE ... KOHLER
CYLINDERS ... 2
ENGINE HP ... 22
COOLING ... AIR
FUEL ... G
SPEEDS ... VARIABLE
TRANSMISSION ... HYDRO
STEERING ... ZERO
STANDARD DECK ... 46"
WEIGHT ... 690 LBS.
MSRP ... $2,999

RETAIL PRICING

YEAR	HIGH	LOW
2015	$1,360	$1,020
2016	$1,587	$1,190
2017	$1,811	$1,358
2018	$1,981	$1,485
2019	$2,151	$1,613

MUSTANG PIVOT S54

YEARS MFRD ... 2015-2018
ENGINE ... KOHLER
CYLINDERS ... 2
ENGINE HP ... 25
COOLING ... AIR
FUEL ... G
SPEEDS ... VARIABLE
TRANSMISSION ... HYDRO
STEERING ... ZERO
BLADE CLUTCH ... ELECTRIC
STANDARD DECK ... 54"
WEIGHT ... 829 LBS.
MSRP ... $3,299

RETAIL PRICING

YEAR	HIGH	LOW
2015	$1,638	$1,228
2016	$1,917	$1,438
2017	$2,063	$1,547
2018	$2,259	$1,694

MUSTANG XP

YEARS MFRD ... 2011-2014
ENGINE ... KOHLER COURAGE
CYLINDERS ... 2
ENGINE HP ... 22
COOLING ... AIR
FUEL ... G
SPEEDS ... VARIABLE
TRANSMISSION ... HYDRO
STEERING ... ZERO
BLADE CLUTCH ... ELECTRIC
STANDARD DECK ... 50"
MSRP ... $2,799

OPTIONS

42" DECK
46" DECK
54" DECK
B&S 24HP
B&S 26HP
KOHLER 25HP

RETAIL PRICING

YEAR	HIGH	LOW
2011	$1,299	$974
2012	$1,438	$1,078
2013	$1,595	$1,197
2014	$1,751	$1,313

MUSTANG Z42

YEARS MFRD ... 2019-2020
ENGINE ... TROYBILT
CYLINDERS ... 2
CID ... 679CC
FUEL ... G
SPEEDS ... VARIABLE
TRANSMISSION ... DUAL HYDRO
STEERING ... ZERO
BLADE CLUTCH ... ELECTRIC
STANDARD DECK ... 42"
WEIGHT ... 600 LBS.
MSRP ... $2,599

OPTIONS

46" DECK ... $100
50" DECK ... $300

MUSTANG Z54

YEARS MFRD ... 2020-2020
ENGINE ... BRIGGS & STRATTON
CYLINDERS ... 2
CID ... 724CC
ENGINE HP ... 24
FUEL ... G
TRANSMISSION ... HYDRO
STEERING ... ZERO
BLADE CLUTCH ... ELECTRIC
STANDARD DECK ... 54"
WEIGHT ... 800 LBS.
MSRP ... $3,099

OPTIONS

2 BAG ... $550

PONY 42

YEARS MFRD ... 2020-2020
ENGINE ... TROYBILT
CYLINDERS ... 1
CID ... 439CC
FUEL ... G
SPEEDS ... 7 SPD
STEERING ... STANDARD
STANDARD DECK ... 42"
MSRP ... $1,349

OPTIONS

36" DECK ... $-50

PONY 42T

YEARS MFRD ... 2018-2020
ENGINE ... TROYBILT
CID ... 420CC
FUEL ... G
SPEEDS ... 7 SPD
TRANSMISSION ... GEAR
STEERING ... STANDARD
BLADE CLUTCH ... MANUAL
STANDARD DECK ... 42"
WEIGHT ... 520 LBS.

PONY 42X

YEARS MFRD ... 2018-2020
ENGINE ... TROYBILT
CYLINDERS ... 1
CID ... 547CC
FUEL ... G
SPEEDS ... 7 SPD
STEERING ... STANDARD
STANDARD DECK ... 42"
MSRP ... $1,399

PONY

YEARS MFRD ... 2007-2019
ENGINE ... B&S IC
CYLINDERS ... 1
ENGINE HP ... 17.5
COOLING ... AIR
FUEL ... G
SPEEDS ... 7/1
TRANSMISSION ... GEAR
STEERING ... STANDARD
STANDARD DECK ... 42"
WEIGHT ... 520 LBS.
MSRP ... $1,299

OPTIONS

42" SNOW BLOWER
46" BLADE
BAGGER

RETAIL PRICING

YEAR	HIGH	LOW
2007	$208	$156
2008	$225	$169
2009	$243	$182
2010	$286	$215
2011	$319	$240
2012	$329	$247
2013	$389	$292
2014	$433	$325
2015	$467	$351
2016	$546	$409
2017	$623	$467
2018	$681	$511
2019	$762	$572

RANGE RIDER LT

YEARS MFRD ... 2007-2007
ENGINE ... KOHLER
CYLINDERS ... 1
ENGINE HP ... 20
COOLING ... AIR
FUEL ... G
SPEEDS ... VARIABLE
TRANSMISSION ... HYDRO
STEERING ... STANDARD
BLADE CLUTCH ... MANUAL
STANDARD DECK ... 46"
WEIGHT ... 580 LBS.
MSRP ... $1,699

RETAIL PRICING

YEAR	HIGH	LOW
2007	$356	$267

TROY-BILT

RZT42

YEARS MFRD 2007-2007
ENGINE . . . . B&S
ENGINE HP 19
COOLING . . . . AIR
FUEL . . . . G
SPEEDS . . . . VARIABLE
TRANSMISSION . . . . . DUAL HYDRO
STEERING. . . . . STANDARD
BLADE CLUTCH . . . . ELECTRIC
STANDARD DECK . . . . 42"
MSRP. $2,899

RETAIL PRICING

YEAR	HIGH	LOW
2007	$997	$747

RZT50

YEARS MFRD 2007-2007
SERIES. . . . . MUSTANG SERIES
ENGINE . . . . KOHLER COURAGE
CYLINDERS. 2
ENGINE HP 22
COOLING . . . . AIR
FUEL . . . . G
SPEEDS . . . . VARIABLE
TRANSMISSION . . . . . DUAL HYDRO
STEERING. . . . . ZERO
BLADE CLUTCH . . . . ELECTRIC
STANDARD DECK . . . . 50"
MSRP. $3,299

RETAIL PRICING

YEAR	HIGH	LOW
2007	$1,132	$849

SUPER BRONCO

YEARS MFRD 2014-2020
ENGINE . . . . TROY BILT
ENGINE HP 20
COOLING . . . . AIR
FUEL . . . . G
SPEEDS . . . . VARIABLE
TRANSMISSION . . . . HYDRO
STEERING. . . . . STANDARD
STANDARD DECK . . . . 42"
MSRP. $1,699

OPTIONS

46" DECK. $400

RETAIL PRICING

YEAR	HIGH	LOW
2014	$537	$402
2015	$606	$454
2016	$710	$533
2017	$813	$610
2018	$890	$668
2019	$976	$732
2020	$1,147	$854

SUPER BRONCO LT

YEARS MFRD 2007-2009
ENGINE . . . . KOHLER
ENGINE HP 19
COOLING . . . . AIR
FUEL . . . . G
SPEEDS . . . . VARIABLE
TRANSMISSION . . . . CVT
STEERING. . . . . STANDARD
BLADE CLUTCH . . . . ELECTRIC
STANDARD DECK . . . . 42"
WEIGHT . . . . 615 LBS.
MSRP. $1,729

OPTIONS

2 BAG
42" SNOW THROWER
46" BLADE

RETAIL PRICING

YEAR	HIGH	LOW
2007	$421	$316
2008	$467	$351
2009	$518	$389

SUPER BRONCO XP

YEARS MFRD 2014-2020
ENGINE . . . . KOHLER
ENGINE HP 24
FUEL . . . . G
SPEEDS . . . . VARIABLE
TRANSMISSION . . . . HYDRO
STEERING. . . . . STANDARD
STANDARD DECK . . . . 50"
MSRP. $2,199

OPTIONS

54" DECK. $100
54" FAB DECK

RETAIL PRICING

YEAR	HIGH	LOW
2014	$788	$591
2015	$892	$669
2016	$1,039	$780
2017	$1,187	$890
2018	$1,308	$981
2019	$1,430	$1,073
2020	$1,643	$1,254

T609G

YEARS MFRD 2004-2005
SERIES. . . . SUPER BRONCO SERIES
ENGINE . . . . B&S
CYLINDERS. 2
ENGINE HP 21
COOLING . . . . AIR
FUEL . . . . G
SPEEDS . . . . VARIABLE
TRANSMISSION . . . . HYDRO
STEERING. . . . . STANDARD
STANDARD DECK . . . . 42"
MSRP. $1,299

RETAIL PRICING

YEAR	HIGH	LOW
2004	$369	$277
2005	$408	$306

TB30R

YEARS MFRD 2013-2020
ENGINE . . . . B&S
CYLINDERS. 1
CID 382CC
ENGINE HP 11.5
COOLING . . . . AIR
FUEL . . . . G
SPEEDS 6/1
TRANSMISSION . . . . GEAR
STEERING. . . . . STANDARD
BLADE CLUTCH . . . . MANUAL
STANDARD DECK . . . . 30"
WEIGHT . . . . 340 LBS.
MSRP. $1,199

OPTIONS

BAGGER. $250
HYDRO

RETAIL PRICING

YEAR	HIGH	LOW
2013	$389	$292
2014	$415	$311
2015	$467	$350
2016	$545	$409
2017	$623	$467
2018	$708	$531
2019	$785	$588
2020	$869	$654

TB42

YEARS MFRD 2014-2017
ENGINE . . . . TROY BILT
CYLINDERS. 1
CID 420CC
COOLING . . . . AIR
FUEL . . . . G
SPEEDS . . . . VARIABLE
TRANSMISSION . . . . CVT
STEERING. . . . . STANDARD
STANDARD DECK . . . . 42"
WEIGHT . . . . 495 LBS.
MSRP. $1,199

RETAIL PRICING

YEAR	HIGH	LOW
2014	$524	$393
2015	$587	$440
2016	$687	$515
2017	$777	$583

TB46

YEARS MFRD 2014-2017
ENGINE . . . . B&S
CYLINDERS. 1
ENGINE HP 19
COOLING . . . . AIR
FUEL . . . . G
SPEEDS . . . . VARIABLE
TRANSMISSION . . . . CVT
STEERING. . . . . STANDARD
STANDARD DECK . . . . 46"
WEIGHT . . . . 500 LBS.
MSRP. $1,299

RETAIL PRICING

YEAR	HIGH	LOW
2014	$560	$420
2015	$687	$515
2016	$795	$596
2017	$912	$684

TB1942

YEARS MFRD 2014-2017
ENGINE . . . . B&S
CYLINDERS. 1
ENGINE HP 19
COOLING . . . . AIR
FUEL . . . . G
SPEEDS . . . . VARIABLE
TRANSMISSION . . . . HYDRO
STEERING. . . . . STANDARD
STANDARD DECK . . . . 42"
WEIGHT . . . . 505 LBS.
MSRP. $1,499

RETAIL PRICING

YEAR	HIGH	LOW
2014	$650	$487
2015	$732	$549
2016	$858	$644
2017	$976	$732

TB2246

YEARS MFRD 2014-2017
ENGINE . . . . B&S
CYLINDERS. 2
ENGINE HP 22
COOLING . . . . AIR
FUEL . . . . G
SPEEDS . . . . VARIABLE
TRANSMISSION . . . . HYDRO
STEERING. . . . . STANDARD
STANDARD DECK . . . . 46"
WEIGHT . . . . 600 LBS.
MSRP. $1,699

RETAIL PRICING

YEAR	HIGH	LOW
2014	$741	$556
2015	$831	$623
2016	$966	$725
2017	$1,102	$826

TB2654

YEARS MFRD 2014-2017
ENGINE . . . . B&S
ENGINE HP 26
COOLING . . . . AIR
FUEL . . . . G
SPEEDS . . . . VARIABLE
TRANSMISSION . . . . BELT
STEERING. . . . . STANDARD
STANDARD DECK . . . . 54"
MSRP. $2,899

RETAIL PRICING

YEAR	HIGH	LOW
2014	$1,255	$942
2015	$1,418	$1,064
2016	$1,653	$1,240
2017	$1,887	$1,416

THOROUGHBRED

YEARS MFRD 2010-2011
ENGINE . . . . KOHLER COURAGE
CYLINDERS. 1
ENGINE HP 22
COOLING . . . . AIR
FUEL . . . . G

SPEEDS .... VARIABLE
TRANSMISSION .... DISC
STEERING .... STANDARD
BLADE CLUTCH .... MANUAL
STANDARD DECK .... 46"
MSRP $1,499

OPTIONS

2 BAG
42" SNOW THROWER
46" BLADE

RETAIL PRICING

YEAR	HIGH	LOW
2010	$491	$368
2011	$545	$409

TUFFY

YEARS MFRD 2004-2004
ENGINE .... B&S
ENGINE HP 18.5
FUEL .... G
SPEEDS 8/1
TRANSMISSION .... GEAR
STEERING .... STANDARD
STANDARD DECK .... 42"
MSRP $1,099

RETAIL PRICING

YEAR	HIGH	LOW
2004	$557	$417

TUFFY LT

YEARS MFRD 2010-2011
ENGINE .... KOHLER COURAGE
CYLINDERS 1
ENGINE HP 17
COOLING .... AIR
FUEL .... G
SPEEDS .... VARIABLE
TRANSMISSION .... CVT
STEERING .... STANDARD
BLADE CLUTCH .... MANUAL
STANDARD DECK .... 38"
MSRP $1,250

OPTIONS

2 BAG
42" SNOW THROWER
46" BLADE

RETAIL PRICING

YEAR	HIGH	LOW
2010	$410	$307
2011	$455	$341

16H

YEARS MFRD 2000-2001
SERIES .... LT SERIES
ENGINE .... KOHLER
ENGINE HP 16
FUEL .... G
TRANSMISSION .... HYDRO
STEERING .... STANDARD
STANDARD DECK .... 42"
MSRP $1,899

RETAIL PRICING

YEAR	HIGH	LOW
2000	$671	$503
2001	$739	$554

17H

YEARS MFRD 2000-2000
SERIES .... LT SERIES
ENGINE .... B&S
ENGINE HP 17
FUEL .... G
TRANSMISSION .... HYDRO
STEERING .... STANDARD
STANDARD DECK .... 42"
MSRP $1,799

RETAIL PRICING

YEAR	HIGH	LOW
2000	$637	$478

18H

YEARS MFRD 2001-2001
SERIES .... LT SERIES
ENGINE .... B&S
ENGINE HP 18
FUEL .... G
TRANSMISSION .... HYDRO
STEERING .... STANDARD
STANDARD DECK .... 42"
MSRP $1,799

RETAIL PRICING

YEAR	HIGH	LOW
2001	$700	$525

20H

YEARS MFRD 2000-2001
SERIES .... LT SERIES
ENGINE .... B&S
ENGINE HP 20
FUEL .... G
TRANSMISSION .... HYDRO
STEERING .... STANDARD
STANDARD DECK .... 46"
MSRP $2,299

RETAIL PRICING

YEAR	HIGH	LOW
2000	$813	$610
2001	$892	$669

22H

YEARS MFRD 2000-2001
SERIES .... GT SERIES
ENGINE .... B&S
ENGINE HP 22
FUEL .... G
TRANSMISSION .... HYDRO
STEERING .... STANDARD
STANDARD DECK .... 46"
MSRP $2,699

RETAIL PRICING

YEAR	HIGH	LOW
2000	$955	$716
2001	$1,050	$787

23H

YEARS MFRD 2001-2001
SERIES .... GT SERIES
ENGINE .... KOHLER
ENGINE HP 23
FUEL .... G
TRANSMISSION .... HYDRO
STEERING .... STANDARD
STANDARD DECK .... 46"
MSRP $3,199

RETAIL PRICING

YEAR	HIGH	LOW
2001	$1,243	$932

25H

YEARS MFRD 2000-2001
SERIES .... LT SERIES
ENGINE .... B&S
ENGINE HP 25
FUEL .... G
TRANSMISSION .... HYDRO
STEERING .... STANDARD
STANDARD DECK .... 46"
MSRP $2,899

RETAIL PRICING

YEAR	HIGH	LOW
2000	$1,027	$770
2001	$1,126	$845

779G

YEARS MFRD 2004-2005
SERIES .... PONY SERIES
ENGINE .... B&S
ENGINE HP 17.5
COOLING .... AIR
FUEL .... G
SPEEDS 7/1
TRANSMISSION .... DISC
STEERING .... STANDARD
STANDARD DECK .... 42"
MSRP $999

RETAIL PRICING

YEAR	HIGH	LOW
2004	$229	$172
2005	$256	$192

1842

YEARS MFRD 2003-2003
SERIES .... LTX SERIES
ENGINE .... B&S
ENGINE HP 18
FUEL .... G
TRANSMISSION .... HYDRO
STEERING .... STANDARD
STANDARD DECK .... 42"
MSRP $1,598

RETAIL PRICING

YEAR	HIGH	LOW
2003	$743	$557

2046

YEARS MFRD 2003-2003
ENGINE .... B&S
ENGINE HP 20
FUEL .... G
TRANSMISSION .... HYDRO
STEERING .... STANDARD

2146

YEARS MFRD 2003-2003
SERIES .... LTX SERIES
ENGINE .... B&S
ENGINE HP 21
COOLING .... AIR
FUEL .... G
TRANSMISSION .... HYDRO
STANDARD DECK .... 46"
MSRP $1,898

RETAIL PRICING

YEAR	HIGH	LOW
2003	$882	$662

2246

YEARS MFRD 2002-2002
ENGINE .... B&S
ENGINE HP 20
FUEL .... G
TRANSMISSION .... GEAR
STEERING .... STANDARD
STANDARD DECK .... 46"
MSRP $2,700

RETAIL PRICING

YEAR	HIGH	LOW
2002	$1,143	$857

2554

YEARS MFRD 2003-2003
ENGINE .... B&S
ENGINE HP 25
FUEL .... G
TRANSMISSION .... GEAR
STEERING .... STANDARD

3016HR

YEARS MFRD 1990-1990
ENGINE .... B&S
ENGINE HP 16
COOLING .... AIR
FUEL .... G
TRANSMISSION .... HYDRO
STEERING .... STANDARD
STANDARD DECK .... 36"
MSRP $3,279

RETAIL PRICING

YEAR	HIGH	LOW
1990	$662	$497

13025

YEARS MFRD 1992-1994
ENGINE .... KOHLER
ENGINE HP 12.5
COOLING .... AIR
FUEL .... G
TRANSMISSION .... GEAR
STEERING .... STANDARD
STANDARD DECK .... 36"
MSRP $2,310

RETAIL PRICING

YEAR	HIGH	LOW
1994	$535	$401

TROY-BILT

13027

YEARS MFRD 1992-1992
ENGINE .... KOHLER
CYLINDERS................. 1
ENGINE HP 14
COOLING .... AIR
FUEL .... G
SPEEDS .... VARIABLE
TRANSMISSION .... HYDRO
STEERING........... STANDARD
STANDARD DECK .... 42"
MSRP................. $3,305

RETAIL PRICING

YEAR	HIGH	LOW
1992	$716	$537

13034

YEARS MFRD 1995-1995
ENGINE .... B&S
CYLINDERS................. 1
ENGINE HP 13
COOLING .... AIR
FUEL .... G
TRANSMISSION .... GEAR
STEERING........... STANDARD
STANDARD DECK .... 38"
MSRP................. $2,119

RETAIL PRICING

YEAR	HIGH	LOW
1995	$504	$378

13035

YEARS MFRD 1995-1995
ENGINE .... B&S
CYLINDERS................. 1
ENGINE HP 13
COOLING .... AIR
FUEL .... G
SPEEDS .... VARIABLE
TRANSMISSION .... HYDRO
STEERING........... STANDARD
STANDARD DECK .... 38"
MSRP................. $2,645

RETAIL PRICING

YEAR	HIGH	LOW
1995	$628	$471

13036

YEARS MFRD 1994-1996
ENGINE .... B&S
ENGINE HP 15
COOLING .... AIR
FUEL .... G
TRANSMISSION .... HYDRO
STEERING........... STANDARD
STANDARD DECK .... 42"
MSRP................. $3,189

RETAIL PRICING

YEAR	HIGH	LOW
1994	$764	$573
1995	$785	$589
1996	$778	$584

13037

YEARS MFRD 1995-1995
ENGINE .... B&S
ENGINE HP 16
COOLING .... AIR
FUEL .... G
TRANSMISSION .... HYDRO
STEERING........... STANDARD
STANDARD DECK .... 48"
MSRP................. $3,999

RETAIL PRICING

YEAR	HIGH	LOW
1995	$270	$203

13039

YEARS MFRD 1994-1995
ENGINE .... B&S
ENGINE HP 16
COOLING .... AIR
FUEL .... G
TRANSMISSION .... HYDRO
STEERING........... STANDARD
STANDARD DECK .... 48"
MSRP................. $4,705

OPTIONS

2 BAG
30" TILLER
42" BLADE

RETAIL PRICING

YEAR	HIGH	LOW
1994	$342	$257
1995	$378	$284

13040

YEARS MFRD 1994-1995
ENGINE .... B&S
ENGINE HP 18
COOLING .... AIR
FUEL .... G
TRANSMISSION .... HYDRO
STEERING........... STANDARD
STANDARD DECK .... 48"
MSRP................. $5,110

OPTIONS

2 BAG
30" TILLER
42" BLADE

RETAIL PRICING

YEAR	HIGH	LOW
1994	$371	$279
1995	$412	$309

13053

YEARS MFRD 1994-1995
ENGINE .... B&S
ENGINE HP 15
COOLING .... AIR
FUEL .... G
SPEEDS 0-6
TRANSMISSION .... GEAR
STEERING........... STANDARD
STANDARD DECK .... 42"
WEIGHT .... 466 LBS.
MSRP................. $3,599

OPTIONS

2 BAG
30" TILLER
42" BLADE

RETAIL PRICING

YEAR	HIGH	LOW
1994	$262	$196
1995	$289	$217

13060

YEARS MFRD 1994-1995
ENGINE .... KOHLER
ENGINE HP 18
COOLING .... AIR
FUEL .... G
TRANSMISSION .... HYDRO
STEERING........... STANDARD
STANDARD DECK .... 60"
MSRP................. $6,699

OPTIONS

2 BAG
30" TILLER
42" BLADE

RETAIL PRICING

YEAR	HIGH	LOW
1994	$486	$365
1995	$538	$404

13062

YEARS MFRD 1994-1995
ENGINE .... KOHLER
ENGINE HP 20
COOLING .... AIR
FUEL .... G
SPEEDS 0-9
TRANSMISSION .... HYDRO
STEERING........... STANDARD
STANDARD DECK .... 60"
WEIGHT .... 830 LBS.
MSRP................. $7,699

OPTIONS

2 BAG
30" TILLER
42" BLADE

RETAIL PRICING

YEAR	HIGH	LOW
1994	$559	$419
1995	$619	$465

13074

YEARS MFRD 1996-2001
SERIES............ GTX SERIES
ENGINE .... KOHLER
ENGINE HP 18
COOLING .... AIR
FUEL .... G
SPEEDS 0-7
TRANSMISSION .... HYDRO
STEERING........... STANDARD
STANDARD DECK .... 42"
WEIGHT .... 1,130 LBS.
MSRP................. $6,599

OPTIONS

54" BLADE
BAG & FAN

SERIAL NUMBERS

YEAR	BEGINNING NO.
1996	0100486
1997	0100651
1998	1200101

RETAIL PRICING

YEAR	HIGH	LOW
1996	$590	$442
1997	$653	$490
1998	$722	$542
1999	$799	$599
2000	$883	$662
2001	$977	$733

13076

YEARS MFRD 1996-2001
SERIES............ GTX SERIES
ENGINE .... KOHLER
ENGINE HP 20
COOLING .... AIR
FUEL .... G
TRANSMISSION .... HYDRO
STEERING........... STANDARD
STANDARD DECK .... 42"
MSRP................. $6,999

OPTIONS

46" SNOW THROWER
54" BLADE
BAG & FAN
LOADER

SERIAL NUMBERS

YEAR	BEGINNING NO.
1996	0100859
1997	0101323
1998	1200101

RETAIL PRICING

YEAR	HIGH	LOW
1996	$625	$469
1997	$693	$520
1998	$765	$574
1999	$847	$635
2000	$937	$703
2001	$1,037	$778

13095

YEARS MFRD 1996-1998
SERIES............ LTX SERIES
ENGINE .... B&S
CYLINDERS................. 1
ENGINE HP 13
COOLING .... AIR
FUEL .... G
TRANSMISSION .... GEAR
STEERING........... STANDARD
STANDARD DECK .... 38"
MSRP................. $1,899

SERIAL NUMBERS

YEAR	BEGINNING NO.
1996	0100111

RETAIL PRICING

YEAR	HIGH	LOW
1998	$540	$405

13097

YEARS MFRD 1996-1998
SERIES. . . . . .LTX SERIES
ENGINE . . . . B&S
ENGINE HP 15.5
COOLING . . . . .AIR
FUEL . . . . .G
TRANSMISSION . . . . .HYDRO
STEERING. . . . . .STANDARD
STANDARD DECK . . . . 38"
MSRP. $2,499

OPTIONS

42" DECK

SERIAL NUMBERS

YEAR	BEGINNING NO.
1996	0100103

RETAIL PRICING

YEAR	HIGH	LOW
1996	$212	$159
1997	$237	$178
1998	$263	$197

13099

YEARS MFRD 1996-1998
SERIES. . . . . .LTX SERIES
ENGINE . . . . B&S
ENGINE HP 16
COOLING . . . . .AIR
FUEL . . . . .G
TRANSMISSION . . . . .HYDRO
STEERING. . . . . .STANDARD
STANDARD DECK . . . . 48"
MSRP. $3,499

SERIAL NUMBERS

YEAR	BEGINNING NO.
1996	0100103

RETAIL PRICING

YEAR	HIGH	LOW
1996	$296	$222
1997	$329	$247
1998	$367	$275

13101

YEARS MFRD 1996-2001
SERIES. . . . . GTX SERIES
ENGINE . . . . B&S
ENGINE HP 16
COOLING . . . . .AIR
FUEL . . . . .G
TRANSMISSION . . . . .HYDRO
STEERING. . . . . .STANDARD
STANDARD DECK . . . . 42"
MSRP. $6,299

OPTIONS

46" SNOW THROWER
54" BLADE
BAG & FAN
LOADER

SERIAL NUMBERS

YEAR	BEGINNING NO.
1996	0100110
1997	0101060
1998	1200101

RETAIL PRICING

YEAR	HIGH	LOW
1996	$564	$423
1997	$623	$467
1998	$689	$517
1999	$762	$572
2000	$844	$633
2001	$933	$700

13102

YEARS MFRD 1997-2001
SERIES. . . . . .LTX SERIES
ENGINE . . . . B&S
CYLINDERS. 1
ENGINE HP 13
COOLING . . . . .AIR
FUEL . . . . .G
TRANSMISSION . . . . GEAR
STEERING. . . . . .STANDARD
STANDARD DECK . . . . 38"
MSRP. $1,999

SERIAL NUMBERS

YEAR	BEGINNING NO.
1997	0100108
1998	1200101

RETAIL PRICING

YEAR	HIGH	LOW
1997	$196	$147
1998	$220	$165
1999	$241	$181
2000	$267	$200
2001	$296	$222

13104

YEARS MFRD 1997-2001
SERIES. . . . . .LTX SERIES
ENGINE . . . . B&S
ENGINE HP 15.5
COOLING . . . . .AIR
FUEL . . . . .G
TRANSMISSION . . . . .HYDRO
STEERING. . . . . .STANDARD
STANDARD DECK . . . . 42"
MSRP. $2,799

OPTIONS

2 BAG
38" SNOW THROWER
54" BLADE

SERIAL NUMBERS

YEAR	BEGINNING NO.
1997	0100108
1998	1200101

RETAIL PRICING

YEAR	HIGH	LOW
1997	$229	$172
1998	$254	$190
1999	$282	$212
2000	$313	$234
2001	$346	$259

13105

YEARS MFRD 1997-2001
SERIES. . . . . .LTX SERIES
ENGINE . . . . B&S
ENGINE HP 16
COOLING . . . . .AIR
FUEL . . . . .G
TRANSMISSION . . . . .HYDRO
STEERING. . . . . .STANDARD
STANDARD DECK . . . . 48"
MSRP. $3,899

OPTIONS

2 BAG
38" SNOW THROWER
54" BLADE

SERIAL NUMBERS

YEAR	BEGINNING NO.
1997	0100108
1998	1200146

RETAIL PRICING

YEAR	HIGH	LOW
1997	$319	$240
1998	$354	$265
1999	$393	$295
2000	$435	$326
2001	$482	$362

13123

YEARS MFRD 1998-2001
SERIES. . . . . .LTX SERIES
ENGINE . . . . B&S
ENGINE HP 14
COOLING . . . . .AIR
FUEL . . . . .G
TRANSMISSION . . . . .HYDRO
STANDARD DECK . . . . 38"
MSRP. $2,399

OPTIONS

2 BAG
54" BLADE

SERIAL NUMBERS

YEAR	BEGINNING NO.
1998	1200281

RETAIL PRICING

YEAR	HIGH	LOW
1998	$218	$163
1999	$241	$181
2000	$268	$201
2001	$297	$223

13126

YEARS MFRD 2001-2001
SERIES. . . . . .LT SERIES
ENGINE . . . . KOHLER
ENGINE HP 16
COOLING . . . . .AIR
FUEL . . . . .G
TRANSMISSION . . . . GEAR
STANDARD DECK . . . . 42"
MSRP. $1,799

RETAIL PRICING

YEAR	HIGH	LOW
2001	$293	$220

13145

YEARS MFRD 2001-2001
SERIES. . . . . .LT SERIES
ENGINE . . . . B&S
ENGINE HP 19
COOLING . . . . .AIR
FUEL . . . . .G
TRANSMISSION . . . . GEAR
STANDARD DECK . . . . 42"
MSRP. $1,999

RETAIL PRICING

YEAR	HIGH	LOW
2001	$326	$245

13146

YEARS MFRD 2001-2001
SERIES. . . . . .LT SERIES
ENGINE . . . . B&S
ENGINE HP 21
COOLING . . . . .AIR
FUEL . . . . .G
TRANSMISSION . . . . .HYDRO
STANDARD DECK . . . . 46"
MSRP. $2,299

OPTIONS

2 BAG
42" SNOW THROWER
46" BLADE

RETAIL PRICING

YEAR	HIGH	LOW
2001	$284	$213

TYM AMERICA

T194

YEARS MFRD 2017-2020
ENGINE . . . . YANMAR
CYLINDERS. 3
CID 60.9
ENGINE HP 19
COOLING . . . . LIQUID
FUEL . . . . .D
TRANSMISSION . . . . .HYDRO
STEERING. . . . . .STANDARD
HITCH . . . . CAT. I
ROPS/CAB . . . . .ROPS
WEIGHT . . . . 1,433 LBS.

T224

YEARS MFRD 2020-2020
ENGINE . . . . YANMAR 3TNM74F
CYLINDERS. 3
CID 60.9
ENGINE HP 21.5
FUEL . . . . .D
SPEEDS . . . . 2 RANGE
TRANSMISSION . . . . .HYDRO
STEERING. . . . . .STANDARD
HITCH . . . . CAT. I
ROPS/CAB . . . . .ROPS
WEIGHT . . . . 1,433 LBS.

TYM AMERICA

T233 HST

YEARS MFRD 2006-2015
ENGINE . . . . MITSUBISHI S3L
CYLINDERS. 3
CID 68.6
PTO HP 19.5
ENGINE HP 23
COOLING . . . . LIQUID
FUEL . . . . D
SPEEDS . . . . VARIABLE
TRANSMISSION . . . . HYDRO
STEERING. . . . . STANDARD
HITCH . . . . CAT. I
HYDRAULIC . . . . YES
PTO . . . . YES
DRIVE TYPE 2WD
ROPS/CAB . . . . ROPS
WEIGHT . . . . 1,962 LBS.
MSRP. $13,995

OPTIONS

LDR

RETAIL PRICING

YEAR	HIGH	LOW
2006	$3,555	$2,666
2007	$3,680	$2,760
2008	$3,950	$2,962
2009	$4,372	$3,279
2010	$4,664	$3,498
2011	$5,027	$3,770
2012	$5,502	$4,126
2013	$6,092	$4,569
2014	$7,016	$5,262
2015	$8,252	$6,189

T234

YEARS MFRD 2015-2018
ENGINE . . . . MITSUBISHI S3L2
CYLINDERS. 3
CID 80.4
PTO HP 18.3
ENGINE HP 24.4
FUEL . . . . D
SPEEDS . . . . VARIABLE
TRANSMISSION . . . . HYDRO
STEERING. . . . . STANDARD
HITCH . . . . CAT. I
ROPS/CAB . . . . ROPS
WEIGHT . . . . 1,907 LBS.

T254

YEARS MFRD 2014-2020
ENGINE . . . . YANMAR
CYLINDERS. 3
CID 77.3
PTO HP 18.6
ENGINE HP 25
FUEL . . . . D
SPEEDS 6/2
TRANSMISSION . . . . GEAR
STEERING. . . . . STANDARD
ROPS/CAB . . . . ROPS
WEIGHT . . . . 1,610 LBS.

OPTIONS

HYDRO
LDR

RETAIL PRICING

YEAR	HIGH	LOW
2014	$6,832	$5,124
2015	$7,772	$5,829
2016	$8,886	$6,665
2017	$9,740	$7,304
2018	$10,629	$7,971
2019	$11,636	$8,727
2020	$12,706	$9,699

T264

YEARS MFRD 2019-2020
ENGINE . . . . KUKJE A1100N2
CYLINDERS. 3
CID 71.7
PTO HP 18.3
ENGINE HP 24.1
FUEL . . . . D
SPEEDS . . . . INFINITE/2 RANGE
TRANSMISSION . . . . HYDRO
STEERING. . . . . STANDARD
HITCH . . . . CAT. I
ROPS/CAB . . . . ROPS
WEIGHT . . . . 1,881 LBS.

T273 HST

YEARS MFRD 2010-2015
ENGINE . . . . MITSUBISHI S3L2
CYLINDERS. 3
CID 80.4
PTO HP 20.7
ENGINE HP 27
COOLING . . . . LIQUID
FUEL . . . . D
SPEEDS . . . . VARIABLE
TRANSMISSION . . . . HYDRO
STEERING. . . . . STANDARD
HITCH . . . . CAT. I
HYDRAULIC . . . . YES
PTO . . . . YES
DRIVE TYPE 2WD
ROPS/CAB . . . . ROPS
MSRP. $15,114

OPTIONS

CAB
LDR

RETAIL PRICING

YEAR	HIGH	LOW
2010	$5,136	$3,852
2011	$5,682	$4,262
2012	$6,266	$4,700
2013	$6,813	$5,110
2014	$7,505	$5,628
2015	$8,890	$6,668

AVG. AUCTION PRICING

LOW	HIGH	AVG
$2,438	$5,363	$3,900

T293 HST

YEARS MFRD 2010-2015
ENGINE . . . . MITSUBISHI S3L2
CYLINDERS. 3
CID 80.4
PTO HP 21.8
ENGINE HP 29
COOLING . . . . LIQUID
FUEL . . . . G
SPEEDS . . . . VARIABLE
TRANSMISSION . . . . HYDRO
STEERING. . . . . STANDARD
HYDRAULIC . . . . YES
PTO . . . . YES
WEIGHT . . . . 1,980 LBS.
MSRP. $16,641

OPTIONS

CAB
LDR

RETAIL PRICING

YEAR	HIGH	LOW
2010	$5,829	$4,371
2011	$6,448	$4,836
2012	$6,923	$5,192
2013	$7,505	$5,628
2014	$8,234	$6,175
2015	$9,385	$7,039

T300

YEARS MFRD 2010-2015
ENGINE . . . . MITSUBISHI S4L
CYLINDERS. 4
CID 91.5
PTO HP 24
ENGINE HP 30
COOLING . . . . LIQUID
FUEL . . . . G
SPEEDS 9/3
TRANSMISSION . . . . GEAR
STEERING. . . . . STANDARD
HITCH . . . . CAT. I
HYDRAULIC . . . . YES
PTO . . . . YES
DRIVE TYPE 2WD
ROPS/CAB . . . . ROPS
WEIGHT . . . . 3,065 LBS.
MSRP. $16,872

OPTIONS

LDR

RETAIL PRICING

YEAR	HIGH	LOW
2010	$6,521	$4,891
2011	$6,726	$5,044
2012	$6,960	$5,220
2013	$7,578	$5,683
2014	$8,343	$6,257
2015	$9,224	$6,918

T330

YEARS MFRD 2007-2009
ENGINE . . . . KUBOTA D-1503
CYLINDERS. 3
PTO HP 26.5
ENGINE HP 33.5
COOLING . . . . LIQUID
FUEL . . . . D
SPEEDS 12/12
TRANSMISSION . . . SHUTTLE SHIFT
STEERING. . . . . STANDARD
HITCH . . . . CAT. I
HYDRAULIC . . . . YES
PTO . . . . YES
DRIVE TYPE 4WD
ROPS/CAB . . . . ROPS
WEIGHT . . . . 3,064 LBS.
MSRP. $17,150

OPTIONS

HYDRO

RETAIL PRICING

YEAR	HIGH	LOW
2007	$4,762	$3,571
2008	$5,231	$3,923
2009	$5,558	$4,169

T350

YEARS MFRD 2010-2015
ENGINE . . . . MITSUBISHI S4L2
CYLINDERS. 4
CID 107.3
PTO HP 29
ENGINE HP 35
COOLING . . . . LIQUID
FUEL . . . . G
SPEEDS 9/3
TRANSMISSION . . . . GEAR
STEERING. . . . . STANDARD
HYDRAULIC . . . . YES
PTO . . . . YES
WEIGHT . . . . 3,065 LBS.
MSRP. $16,184

OPTIONS

LDR

RETAIL PRICING

YEAR	HIGH	LOW
2010	$6,849	$5,137
2011	$7,214	$5,411
2012	$7,543	$5,657
2013	$8,234	$6,175
2014	$8,816	$6,612
2015	$9,692	$7,269

T353

YEARS MFRD 2008-2015
ENGINE . . . . MITSUBISHI S4L2
CYLINDERS. 4
CID 107.3
PTO HP 29
ENGINE HP 35
COOLING . . . . LIQUID
FUEL . . . . D
SPEEDS 12/12
TRANSMISSION . . . SHUTTLE SHIFT
STEERING. . . . . STANDARD
HITCH . . . . CAT. I
HYDRAULIC . . . . YES
PTO . . . . YES
WEIGHT . . . . 3,065 LBS.
MSRP. $19,442

OPTIONS

HYDRO
LDR

RETAIL PRICING

YEAR	HIGH	LOW
2008	$6,923	$5,192
2009	$7,266	$5,449
2010	$7,543	$5,657
2011	$7,760	$5,820
2012	$8,088	$6,066

2013	$8,781	$6,586
2014	$9,617	$7,213
2015	$11,534	$8,651

T354

YEARS MFRD 2014-2020
ENGINE .... YANMAR
CYLINDERS 3
CID 100.2
PTO HP 28.1
ENGINE HP 34.2
FUEL .... D
SPEEDS 12/12
TRANSMISSION .... GEAR
STEERING .... STANDARD
HITCH .... CAT. I
DRIVE TYPE 4WD
ROPS/CAB .... ROPS
WEIGHT .... 3,065 LBS.

OPTIONS

HYDRO
LDR

RETAIL PRICING

YEAR	HIGH	LOW
2014	$11,106	$8,330
2015	$14,096	$10,571
2016	$15,262	$11,446
2017	$16,115	$12,087
2018	$17,613	$13,210
2019	$19,411	$14,558
2020	$20,747	$15,603

T394

YEARS MFRD 2017-2020
ENGINE .... YANMAR
CYLINDERS 3
CID 100.2
PTO HP 28.8
ENGINE HP 37.4
COOLING .... LIQUID
FUEL .... D
SPEEDS .... VARIABLE
TRANSMISSION .... GEAR
STEERING .... STANDARD
HITCH .... CAT. I
ROPS/CAB .... ROPS
WEIGHT .... 3,020 LBS.

T400

YEARS MFRD 2006-2009
ENGINE .... KUBOTA V1903
CYLINDERS 4
PTO HP 36.5
ENGINE HP 43
COOLING .... LIQUID
FUEL .... D
SPEEDS 12/12
TRANSMISSION ... SHUTTLE SHIFT
STEERING .... STANDARD
HITCH .... CAT. I
HYDRAULIC .... YES
PTO .... YES
DRIVE TYPE 4WD
ROPS/CAB .... ROPS
WEIGHT .... 3,960 LBS.

T433

YEARS MFRD 2008-2015
ENGINE .... CATERPILLAR C2.2
CYLINDERS 4
CID 135.2
PTO HP 32.8
ENGINE HP 42.7
COOLING .... LIQUID
FUEL .... D
SPEEDS 16/16
TRANSMISSION ... SHUTTLE SHIFT
STEERING .... STANDARD
HITCH .... CAT. I
HYDRAULIC .... YES
PTO .... YES
DRIVE TYPE 2WD
ROPS/CAB .... ROPS
WEIGHT .... 4,188 LBS.
MSRP $23,442

OPTIONS

CAB

RETAIL PRICING

YEAR	HIGH	LOW
2008	$6,631	$4,973
2009	$7,885	$5,914
2010	$8,489	$6,367
2011	$9,399	$7,049
2012	$9,728	$7,296
2013	$10,421	$7,816
2014	$11,622	$8,717
2015	$13,516	$10,137

T450

YEARS MFRD 2007-2009
ENGINE .... KUBOTA V2203
CYLINDERS 4
CID 134
PTO HP 38
ENGINE HP 45.3
COOLING .... LIQUID
FUEL .... D
SPEEDS 16/16
TRANSMISSION ... SHUTTLE SHIFT
STEERING .... STANDARD
HITCH .... CAT. I
DRIVE TYPE 4WD
ROPS/CAB .... ROPS
WEIGHT .... 3,960 LBS.
MSRP $21,435

RETAIL PRICING

YEAR	HIGH	LOW
2008	$13,282	$9,962
2009	$13,600	$10,200

T451

YEARS MFRD 2006-2009
ENGINE .... KUBOTA V2203
CYLINDERS 4
ENGINE HP 45.3
COOLING .... LIQUID
FUEL .... D
SPEEDS 16/16
TRANSMISSION ... SHUTTLE SHIFT
STEERING .... STANDARD
HITCH .... CAT. I
HYDRAULIC .... YES
PTO .... YES
DRIVE TYPE 4WD
ROPS/CAB .... CAB
WEIGHT .... 4,369 LBS.
MSRP $27,875

RETAIL PRICING

YEAR	HIGH	LOW
2008	$16,669	$12,501
2009	$16,976	$12,732

T454

YEARS MFRD 2014-2020
ENGINE .... YANMAR
CYLINDERS 4
CID 133.6
PTO HP 36.7
ENGINE HP 46
COOLING .... LIQUID
FUEL .... D
SPEEDS 16/16
TRANSMISSION ... SHUTTLE SHIFT
STEERING .... STANDARD
HITCH .... CAT. I
DRIVE TYPE 4WD
ROPS/CAB .... ROPS
WEIGHT .... 3,814 LBS.

OPTIONS

CAB
HYDRO

RETAIL PRICING

YEAR	HIGH	LOW
2014	$14,037	$10,528
2015	$17,642	$13,231
2016	$19,129	$14,347
2017	$20,837	$15,628
2018	$22,515	$16,887
2019	$24,685	$18,514
2020	$26,423	$20,158

T474

YEARS MFRD 2019-2020
ENGINE .... KUKJE A2300N2
CYLINDERS 4
CID 139.5
PTO HP 35.9
ENGINE HP 48.3
FUEL .... D
SPEEDS 12/12
STEERING .... STANDARD
HITCH .... CAT. I
WEIGHT .... 3,289 LBS.

T494

YEARS MFRD 2019-2020
ENGINE .... KUKJE A2300N2
CYLINDERS 4
CID 139.5
PTO HP 37.2
ENGINE HP 48.3
FUEL .... D
SPEEDS 8.8
HITCH .... CAT. I
WEIGHT .... 3,871 LBS.

OPTIONS

HYDRO

T500

YEARS MFRD 2014-2015
ENGINE .... PERKINS
CYLINDERS 4
CID 135
PTO HP 39.8
COOLING .... LIQUID
FUEL .... D
SPEEDS 9/3
TRANSMISSION .... GEAR
STEERING .... STANDARD
WEIGHT .... 4,536 LBS.
MSRP $22,611

RETAIL PRICING

YEAR	HIGH	LOW
2014	$11,221	$8,416
2015	$13,553	$10,165

T503

YEARS MFRD 2010-2017
ENGINE .... PERKINS 404D-22
CYLINDERS 4
CID 135.2
PTO HP 39.8
ENGINE HP 50.7
COOLING .... LIQUID
FUEL .... D
SPEEDS 16/16
TRANSMISSION ... SHUTTLE SHIFT
STEERING .... STANDARD
HYDRAULIC .... YES
PTO .... YES
DRIVE TYPE 2WD
ROPS/CAB .... ROPS
WEIGHT .... 4,140 LBS.
MSRP $25,846

OPTIONS

CAB
HYDRO

RETAIL PRICING

YEAR	HIGH	LOW
2010	$10,066	$7,549
2011	$10,591	$7,944
2012	$11,080	$8,310
2013	$12,057	$9,043
2014	$13,221	$9,916
2015	$14,259	$10,695
2016	$16,104	$12,078
2017	$18,110	$13,582

T554

YEARS MFRD 2014-2020
ENGINE .... YANMAR
CYLINDERS 4
CID 127.6
PTO HP 44.9
ENGINE HP 55.1
COOLING .... LIQUID
FUEL .... D
SPEEDS 16/16
TRANSMISSION ... SHUTTLE SHIFT
STEERING .... STANDARD
HITCH .... CAT. I
DRIVE TYPE 4WD
ROPS/CAB .... ROPS
WEIGHT .... 3,924 LBS.

TYM AMERICA

OPTIONS

CAB
HYDRO

RETAIL PRICING

YEAR	HIGH	LOW
2014	$14,862	$11,147
2015	$18,603	$13,952
2016	$20,171	$15,129
2017	$22,733	$17,049
2018	$24,560	$18,420
2019	$26,450	$19,837
2020	$28,150	$21,196

T574

YEARS MFRD	2019-2020
ENGINE	KUKJE A2300T3
CYLINDERS	4
CID	139.5
PTO HP	44.7
ENGINE HP	55
FUEL	D
SPEEDS	8/8
STEERING	STANDARD
HITCH	CAT. I
ROPS/CAB	ROPS
WEIGHT	3,887 LBS.

OPTIONS

HYDRO

T4500

YEARS MFRD	2006-2006
ENGINE	KUBOTA V2203
CYLINDERS	4
ENGINE HP	45.3
COOLING	LIQUID
FUEL	D
SPEEDS	16/16
TRANSMISSION	SHUTTLE SHIFT
STEERING	STANDARD
HITCH	CAT. I
HYDRAULIC	YES
PTO	YES
WEIGHT	3,960 LBS.

VENTRAC

RT7200

YEARS MFRD 2008-2010
ENGINE . . . . VANGUARD DM950DT
CID 953CC
ENGINE HP 31
COOLING . . . . LIQUID
FUEL . . . . D
SPEEDS . . . . VARIABLE
TRANSMISSION . . . . HYDRO
STEERING. . . . . STANDARD
WEIGHT . . . . .1,820 LBS.

300

YEARS MFRD 2005-2007
ENGINE . . . . KAWASAKI
CYLINDERS. 1
ENGINE HP 6.5
COOLING . . . . AIR
FUEL . . . . G
SPEEDS . . . . VARIABLE
TRANSMISSION . . . . HYDRO
STEERING. . . . . STANDARD
WEIGHT . . . . 320 LBS.

3000

YEARS MFRD 2005-2006
ENGINE . . . . KAWASAKI FH641V
CYLINDERS. 2
ENGINE HP 21
COOLING . . . . AIR
FUEL . . . . G
SPEEDS . . . . VARIABLE
TRANSMISSION . . . . HYDRO
STEERING. . . . . STANDARD
WEIGHT . . . . 710 LBS.

3100

YEARS MFRD 2007-2011
ENGINE . . . . B&S VANGUARD
CYLINDERS. 2
ENGINE HP 21
COOLING . . . . AIR
FUEL . . . . G
SPEEDS . . . . VARIABLE
TRANSMISSION . . . . HYDRO
STEERING. . . . . STANDARD
BLADE CLUTCH . . . . ELECTRIC
WEIGHT . . . . 850 LBS.

3121

YEARS MFRD 2010-2015
ENGINE . . . . VANGUARD
ENGINE HP 21
COOLING . . . . AIR
FUEL . . . . G
SPEEDS . . . . VARIABLE
TRANSMISSION . . . . HYDRO
STEERING. . . . . STANDARD
MSRP. $10,995

RETAIL PRICING

YEAR	HIGH	LOW
2010	$3,063	$2,297
2011	$3,501	$2,626
2012	$3,907	$2,930
2013	$4,396	$3,297
2014	$5,128	$3,846
2015	$6,424	$4,818

3200

YEARS MFRD 2007-2011
ENGINE . . . . B&S VANGUARD
CYLINDERS. 3
ENGINE HP 23.6
COOLING . . . . LIQUID
FUEL . . . . G
SPEEDS . . . . VARIABLE
TRANSMISSION . . . . HYDRO
STEERING. . . . . STANDARD
WEIGHT . . . . .1,050 LBS.

3223D

YEARS MFRD 2010-2015
ENGINE . . . . DAIHATSU
ENGINE HP 23.6
FUEL . . . . D
SPEEDS . . . . VARIABLE
TRANSMISSION . . . . HYDRO
STEERING. . . . . STANDARD
WEIGHT . . . . .1,050 LBS.
MSRP. $13,495

RETAIL PRICING

YEAR	HIGH	LOW
2010	$3,767	$2,826
2011	$4,293	$3,220
2012	$4,797	$3,597
2013	$5,395	$4,046
2014	$6,291	$4,719
2015	$7,010	$5,258

3400L

YEARS MFRD 2016-2020
SERIES. . . . . 3000 SERIES
ENGINE . . . . B&S VANGUARD
CYLINDERS. 2
CID 627CC
ENGINE HP 20
COOLING . . . . AIR
FUEL . . . . G
SPEEDS . . . . VARIABLE
TRANSMISSION . . . . HYDRO
STEERING. . . . . STANDARD
ROPS/CAB . . . . ROPS
WEIGHT . . . . .1,000 LBS.
MSRP. $15,245

3400Y

YEARS MFRD 2016-2020
SERIES. . . . . 3000 SERIES
ENGINE . . . . KUBOTA D902
CYLINDERS. 3
CID 898
ENGINE HP 22
COOLING . . . . LIQUID
FUEL . . . . D
SPEEDS . . . . VARIABLE
TRANSMISSION . . . . HYDRO
STEERING. . . . . STANDARD
ROPS/CAB . . . . ROPS
WEIGHT . . . . .1,200 LBS.
MSRP. $18,180

4100

YEARS MFRD 2005-2011
ENGINE . . . . B&S VANGUAARD
CYLINDERS. 2
ENGINE HP 31
COOLING . . . . AIR
FUEL . . . . G
SPEEDS . . . . VARIABLE
TRANSMISSION . . . . HYDRO
STEERING. . . . . STANDARD
WEIGHT . . . . .1,250 LBS.

4131

YEARS MFRD 2010-2013
SERIES. . . . . 4000 SERIES
ENGINE . . . . B&S VANGUARD
CYLINDERS. 2
CID 895CC
ENGINE HP 31
COOLING . . . . AIR
FUEL . . . . G
SPEEDS . . . . VARIABLE
TRANSMISSION . . . . HYDRO
STEERING. . . . . STANDARD
WEIGHT . . . . .1,290 LBS.
MSRP. $16,445

RETAIL PRICING

YEAR	HIGH	LOW
2010	$5,272	$3,954
2011	$6,343	$4,757
2012	$7,399	$5,549
2013	$9,043	$6,782

4200VXD

YEARS MFRD 2005-2011
ENGINE . . . . . . KAWASAKI FD750D
CYLINDERS. 2
ENGINE HP 27
COOLING . . . . LIQUID
FUEL . . . . G
SPEEDS . . . . VARIABLE
TRANSMISSION . . . . HYDRO
STEERING. . . . . STANDARD
BLADE CLUTCH . . . . ELECTRIC
WEIGHT . . . . .1,699 LBS.

OPTIONS

VANGUARD 26.5HP DIESEL
VANGUARD 31HP DIESEL
VANGUARD 31HP GAS

4226D

YEARS MFRD 2010-2013
SERIES. . . . . 4000 SERIES
ENGINE . . . . B&S DAIHATSU
CYLINDERS. 3
CID 953CC
ENGINE HP 26.5
COOLING . . . . LIQUID
FUEL . . . . D
SPEEDS . . . . VARIABLE
TRANSMISSION . . . . HYDRO
STEERING. . . . . STANDARD
WEIGHT . . . . .1,560 LBS.
MSRP. $20,950

RETAIL PRICING

YEAR	HIGH	LOW
2010	$6,685	$5,014
2011	$8,077	$6,058
2012	$9,427	$7,071
2013	$12,928	$9,696

4227

YEARS MFRD 2010-2013
SERIES. . . . . 4000 SERIES
ENGINE . . . . KAWASAKI
CYLINDERS. 2
CID 746CC
ENGINE HP 27
COOLING . . . . LIQUID
FUEL . . . . G
SPEEDS . . . . VARIABLE
TRANSMISSION . . . . HYDRO
STEERING. . . . . STANDARD
WEIGHT . . . . .1,500 LBS.
MSRP. $17,445

RETAIL PRICING

YEAR	HIGH	LOW
2010	$5,593	$4,195
2011	$6,728	$5,046
2012	$7,849	$5,887
2013	$9,464	$7,098

4231TD

YEARS MFRD 2010-2013
SERIES. . . . . 4000 SERIES
ENGINE . . . . B&S DAIHATSU TURBO
CYLINDERS. 3
CID 953CC
ENGINE HP 31
COOLING . . . . LIQUID
FUEL . . . . D
SPEEDS . . . . VARIABLE
TRANSMISSION . . . . HYDRO
STEERING. . . . . STANDARD
WEIGHT . . . . .1,630 LBS.
MSRP. $21,990

RETAIL PRICING

YEAR	HIGH	LOW
2010	$7,034	$5,276
2011	$8,484	$6,363
2012	$9,893	$7,420
2013	$13,428	$10,071

4500K

YEARS MFRD 2013-2020
ENGINE . . . . VANGUARD
CYLINDERS. 2
CID 896CC
ENGINE HP 31

VENTRAC

COOLING .... AIR
FUEL .... G
SPEEDS .... VARIABLE
TRANSMISSION .... HYDRO
STEERING............. STANDARD
ROPS/CAB .... ROPS
WEIGHT .... 1,340 LBS.
MSRP.................. $19,960

RETAIL PRICING

YEAR	HIGH	LOW
2013	$7,635	$5,726
2014	$8,651	$6,488
2015	$12,118	$9,088
2016	$13,241	$9,930
2017	$14,145	$10,607
2018	$15,680	$11,510
2019	$17,356	$12,765
2020	$18,914	$14,253

4500P

YEARS MFRD 2013-2020
ENGINE .... KAWASAKI
CYLINDERS..................... 2
CID 824CC
ENGINE HP.................... 31
COOLING .... LIQUID
FUEL .... G
SPEEDS .... VARIABLE
TRANSMISSION .... HYDRO
STEERING............. STANDARD
ROPS/CAB .... ROPS
WEIGHT .... 1,575 LBS.
MSRP.................. $22,920

RETAIL PRICING

YEAR	HIGH	LOW
2013	$8,923	$6,692
2014	$10,840	$8,129
2015	$14,457	$10,843
2016	$16,827	$12,620
2017	$17,730	$13,297
2018	$18,468	$14,409
2019	$20,032	$15,722
2020	$21,692	$16,566

4500Y

YEARS MFRD 2014-2020
ENGINE .... KUBOTA
CYLINDERS..................... 3
CID 898CC
ENGINE HP.................... 25
COOLING .... LIQUID
FUEL .... D
SPEEDS .... VARIABLE
TRANSMISSION .... HYDRO
STEERING............. STANDARD
ROPS/CAB .... ROPS
WEIGHT .... 1,655 LBS.
MSRP.................. $23,950

RETAIL PRICING

YEAR	HIGH	LOW
2014	$11,506	$8,629
2015	$14,603	$10,952
2016	$16,588	$12,442
2017	$18,395	$13,797
2018	$19,560	$15,386
2019	$21,031	$16,492
2020	$22,553	$17,237

4500Z

YEARS MFRD 2013-2020
ENGINE .... KUBOTA
CYLINDERS..................... 3
CID 962CC
ENGINE HP.................. 32.5
COOLING .... LIQUID
FUEL .... G
SPEEDS .... VARIABLE
TRANSMISSION .... HYDRO
STEERING............. STANDARD
WEIGHT .... 1,655 LBS.
MSRP.................. $23,950

RETAIL PRICING

YEAR	HIGH	LOW
2013	$9,699	$7,275
2014	$11,506	$8,629
2015	$14,783	$11,088
2016	$16,588	$12,442
2017	$18,395	$13,797
2018	$19,553	$14,941
2019	$20,934	$16,404
2020	$22,408	$17,206

WALKER

ALL MODELS

YEARS MFRD NA-1993

SERIAL NUMBERS

FIRST TWO NUMBERS OF SERIAL NUMBER INDICATE YEAR OF MANUFACTURE.

MB18

YEARS MFRD 2017-2020
ENGINE .... B&S
CYLINDERS.................. 2
CID 34.8
ENGINE HP.................. 18
COOLING .... AIR
FUEL .... G
SPEEDS .... VARIABLE
TRANSMISSION .... HYDRO
STEERING................ ZERO
STANDARD DECK .... 42"
WEIGHT .... 910 LBS.
MSRP................. $9,735

OPTIONS

48" BLADE
52" DECK
56" DECK
SUS SEAT

SERIAL NUMBERS

YEAR	BEGINNING NO.
2017	142383
2018	148381

RETAIL PRICING

YEAR	HIGH	LOW
2017	$5,835	$4,376
2018	$6,455	$5,105
2019	$7,144	$5,693
2020	$8,178	$6,362

MB19

YEARS MFRD 2017-2020
ENGINE .... KOHLER
CYLINDERS.................. 2
CID 39.1
ENGINE HP.................. 19
COOLING .... AIR
FUEL .... G
SPEEDS .... VARIABLE
TRANSMISSION .... HYDRO
STEERING................ ZERO
STANDARD DECK .... 42"
WEIGHT .... 835 LBS.
MSRP................. $9,935

OPTIONS

48" BLADE
52" DECK
56" DECK

SERIAL NUMBERS

YEAR	BEGINNING NO.
2017	142383
2018	148381

RETAIL PRICING

YEAR	HIGH	LOW
2017	$5,950	$4,462
2018	$6,572	$5,167
2019	$7,266	$5,698
2020	$8,251	$6,408

MB23I

YEARS MFRD 2017-2020
ENGINE .... KOHLER
CYLINDERS.................. 2
CID 45
ENGINE HP.................. 23
COOLING .... AIR
FUEL .... G
SPEEDS .... VARIABLE
TRANSMISSION .... HYDRO
STEERING................ ZERO
STANDARD DECK .... 42"
WEIGHT .... 940 LBS.
MSRP................. $10,825

OPTIONS

48" DECK
52" DECK
56" DECK
62" DECK

SERIAL NUMBERS

YEAR	BEGINNING NO.
2017	142383
2018	148381

RETAIL PRICING

YEAR	HIGH	LOW
2017	$6,600	$4,949
2018	$7,299	$5,717
2019	$8,072	$6,344
2020	$9,244	$7,188

MB25P

YEARS MFRD 2015-2019
ENGINE .... KOHLER LP
CID 45.6
ENGINE HP.................. 25
COOLING .... AIR
SPEEDS .... VARIABLE
TRANSMISSION .... HYDRO
STEERING................ ZERO
STANDARD DECK .... 48"

OPTIONS

36" SNOW BLOWER
48" BLADE
52" DECK
56" DECK

SERIAL NUMBERS

YEAR	BEGINNING NO.
2015	130551
2016	136524
2017	142383
2018	148381

RETAIL PRICING

YEAR	HIGH	LOW
2015	$5,993	$4,495
2016	$6,628	$4,971
2017	$7,332	$5,499
2018	$8,101	$6,076
2019	$8,941	$6,705

MB27I

YEARS MFRD 2020-2020
ENGINE .... KOHLER ECH749
CID 45.6
ENGINE HP.................. 26.5
COOLING .... AIR
FUEL .... G
STEERING................ ZERO
STANDARD DECK .... 42"
WEIGHT .... 610 LBS.
MSRP................. $11,135

OPTIONS

48" DECK................ $155
52" DECK................ $305

MB42

YEARS MFRD 2005-2009
ENGINE .... B&S VANGUARD
CYLINDERS.................. 2
CID 34.7
ENGINE HP.................. 18
COOLING .... AIR
FUEL .... G
SPEEDS .... VARIABLE
TRANSMISSION .... HYDRO
STEERING................ ZERO
STANDARD DECK .... 42"
WEIGHT .... 764 LBS.
MSRP................. $7,110

RETAIL PRICING

YEAR	HIGH	LOW
2005	$1,194	$895
2006	$1,364	$1,023
2007	$1,626	$1,219
2008	$2,032	$1,524
2009	$2,752	$2,064

MB48

YEARS MFRD 2005-2016
ENGINE .... B&S
ENGINE HP.................. 18
COOLING .... AIR
FUEL .... G
SPEEDS .... VARIABLE
TRANSMISSION .... HYDRO
STEERING................ ZERO
STANDARD DECK .... 48"
MSRP................. $8,806

OPTIONS

56" DECK
AERATOR

SERIAL NUMBERS

YEAR	BEGINNING NO.
2005	2005-71500
2006	2006-78692
2007	07-85128
2008	08-92037
2010	10-103389
2011	11-107968
2012	12-113766
2013	13-119135
2014	14-124782
2015	130551
2016	136524

RETAIL PRICING

YEAR	HIGH	LOW
2006	$2,350	$1,763
2007	$2,625	$1,969
2008	$2,905	$2,179
2009	$3,212	$2,409
2010	$3,553	$2,665
2011	$3,931	$2,948
2012	$4,348	$3,261
2013	$4,810	$3,607
2014	$5,321	$3,991
2015	$5,886	$4,414
2016	$6,998	$5,249

MB56

YEARS MFRD 2005-2009
ENGINE .... B&S
CYLINDERS.................. 2
CID 34.7
ENGINE HP.................. 18
COOLING .... AIR
FUEL .... G
SPEEDS .... VARIABLE
TRANSMISSION .... HYDRO
STEERING................ ZERO
STANDARD DECK .... 56"
WEIGHT .... 764 LBS.
MSRP................. $7,795

RETAIL PRICING

YEAR	HIGH	LOW
2005	$1,326	$994
2006	$1,557	$1,168
2007	$1,783	$1,337
2008	$2,145	$1,609
2009	$2,912	$2,184

MBK23

YEARS MFRD 2013-2016
ENGINE .... KOHLER
ENGINE HP.................. 23
COOLING .... AIR
FUEL .... G
SPEEDS .... VARIABLE
TRANSMISSION .... HYDRO
STEERING................ ZERO
BLADE CLUTCH .... ELECTRIC
STANDARD DECK .... 56"
MSRP................. $10,455

OPTIONS

36" SNOW BLOWER
48" BLADE

SERIAL NUMBERS

YEAR	BEGINNING NO.
2013	13-119135
2014	14-124782
2015	130551
2016	136524

RETAIL PRICING

YEAR	HIGH	LOW
2013	$5,710	$4,283
2014	$6,317	$4,738
2015	$6,988	$5,241
2016	$8,207	$6,155

WALKER

MBK42

YEARS MFRD 2010-2011
ENGINE .... KOHLER
CYLINDERS................1
ENGINE HP 18
COOLING ....AIR
FUEL ....G
SPEEDS ....VARIABLE
TRANSMISSION ....HYDRO
STEERING................ZERO
STANDARD DECK .... 42"
WEIGHT .... 835 LBS.
MSRP................ $7,840

RETAIL PRICING

YEAR	HIGH	LOW
2010	$3,209	$2,406
2011	$3,873	$2,905

MBK56

YEARS MFRD 2010-2011
ENGINE .... KOHLER
ENGINE HP 18
COOLING ....AIR
FUEL ....G
SPEEDS ....VARIABLE
TRANSMISSION ....HYDRO
STEERING................ZERO
STANDARD DECK .... 56"
WEIGHT .... 910 LBS.
MSRP................ $7,890

RETAIL PRICING

YEAR	HIGH	LOW
2010	$3,296	$2,472
2011	$3,969	$2,977

MBK

YEARS MFRD 2010-2016
ENGINE .... KOHLER
ENGINE HP 19
COOLING ....AIR
FUEL ....G
SPEEDS ....VARIABLE
TRANSMISSION ....HYDRO
STEERING................ZERO
BLADE CLUTCH ....ELECTRIC
STANDARD DECK .... 48"
MSRP................ $8,896

OPTIONS

56" DECK
AERATOR

SERIAL NUMBERS

YEAR	BEGINNING NO.
2010	10-103389
2011	11-107968
2012	12-113766
2013	13-119135
2014	14-124782
2015	130551
2016	136524

RETAIL PRICING

YEAR	HIGH	LOW
2010	$3,590	$2,692
2011	$3,971	$2,978
2012	$4,392	$3,294
2013	$4,860	$3,645
2014	$5,375	$4,031
2015	$5,946	$4,459
2016	$7,169	$5,377

MBS26

YEARS MFRD 2010-2012
ENGINE .... KOHLER
ENGINE HP 26
COOLING ....AIR
FUEL ....D
SPEEDS ....VARIABLE
TRANSMISSION ..... DUAL HYDRO
STEERING................ZERO
STANDARD DECK .... 60"
WEIGHT .... 1,230 LBS.
MSRP................ $12,475

OPTIONS

ROPS

SERIAL NUMBERS

YEAR	BEGINNING NO.
2010	10-103389
2011	11-107968
2012	12-113766

RETAIL PRICING

YEAR	HIGH	LOW
2010	$5,872	$4,404
2011	$6,516	$4,887

MBS29

YEARS MFRD 2012-2013
ENGINE .... KOHLER
ENGINE HP 29
COOLING ....AIR
FUEL ....G
SPEEDS ....VARIABLE
TRANSMISSION ....HYDRO
STEERING................ZERO
BLADE CLUTCH ....ELECTRIC
STANDARD DECK .... 60"
MSRP................ $12,310

OPTIONS

50" SNOW BLOWER
60" BLADE
ROPS

SERIAL NUMBERS

YEAR	BEGINNING NO.
2012	12-113766
2013	13-119135

RETAIL PRICING

YEAR	HIGH	LOW
2012	$6,762	$5,072
2013	$7,499	$5,624

MBS60

YEARS MFRD 2008-2013
ENGINE .... KOHLER
ENGINE HP 27
COOLING ....AIR
FUEL ....D
SPEEDS ....VARIABLE
TRANSMISSION ..... DUAL HYDRO
STEERING................ZERO
STANDARD DECK .... 60"
WEIGHT .... 1,225 LBS.
MSRP................ $11,665

OPTIONS

50" SNOW BLOWER
60" BLADE
ROPS

SERIAL NUMBERS

YEAR	BEGINNING NO.
2010	10-103389
2011	11-107968
2012	12-113766
2013	13-119135

RETAIL PRICING

YEAR	HIGH	LOW
2008	$4,297	$3,223
2009	$4,695	$3,521
2010	$5,206	$3,904
2011	$5,774	$4,331
2012	$6,406	$4,805
2013	$7,109	$5,332

MBSY

YEARS MFRD 2011-2013
ENGINE .... YANMAR
ENGINE HP 23.6
COOLING ....AIR
FUEL ....D
SPEEDS ....VARIABLE
TRANSMISSION ..... DUAL HYDRO
STEERING................ZERO
BLADE CLUTCH ....ELECTRIC
STANDARD DECK .... 60"
MSRP................ $17,050

OPTIONS

50" SNOW BLOWER
60" BLADE
ROPS

SERIAL NUMBERS

YEAR	BEGINNING NO.
2012	12-113766
2013	13-119135

RETAIL PRICING

YEAR	HIGH	LOW
2011	$8,444	$6,333
2012	$9,364	$7,023
2013	$10,386	$7,790

MBV42

YEARS MFRD 2010-2011
ENGINE .... B&S
CYLINDERS................2
ENGINE HP 18
COOLING ....AIR
FUEL ....G
SPEEDS ....VARIABLE
TRANSMISSION ....HYDRO
STEERING................ZERO
STANDARD DECK .... 42"
WEIGHT .... 835 LBS.
MSRP................ $7,645

RETAIL PRICING

YEAR	HIGH	LOW
2010	$3,188	$2,391
2011	$3,846	$2,884

MBV56

YEARS MFRD 2010-2011
ENGINE .... B&S
CYLINDERS................2
ENGINE HP 18
COOLING ....AIR
FUEL ....G
SPEEDS ....VARIABLE
TRANSMISSION ....HYDRO
STEERING................ZERO
STANDARD DECK .... 56"
WEIGHT .... 910 LBS.
MSRP................ $8,325

RETAIL PRICING

YEAR	HIGH	LOW
2010	$3,466	$2,600
2011	$4,187	$3,140

MC19

YEARS MFRD 2014-2020
ENGINE .... KOHLER
CID 41.1
ENGINE HP 19
COOLING ....AIR
FUEL ....G
SPEEDS ....VARIABLE
TRANSMISSION ....HYDRO
STEERING................ZERO
STANDARD DECK .... 42"
WEIGHT .... 925 LBS.
MSRP................ $12,865

OPTIONS

42" SNOW BLOWER
48" DECK
52" DECK
CAB

SERIAL NUMBERS

YEAR	BEGINNING NO.
2014	14-124782
2015	130551
2016	136524
2017	142383
2018	148381

RETAIL PRICING

YEAR	HIGH	LOW
2014	$5,764	$4,323
2015	$6,542	$4,906
2016	$7,055	$5,291
2017	$7,802	$5,852
2018	$8,620	$6,699
2019	$9,534	$7,518
2020	$10,333	$8,293

MC19I

YEARS MFRD 2015-2020
ENGINE .... KOHLER EFI
CID 42.4
ENGINE HP 19
COOLING ....AIR
FUEL ....G
SPEEDS ....VARIABLE
TRANSMISSION ....HYDRO
STEERING................ZERO
STANDARD DECK .... 42"
WEIGHT .... 930 LBS.
MSRP................ $13,575

OPTIONS
48" DECK ... $150
SUS SEAT

SERIAL NUMBERS
YEAR	BEGINNING NO.
2015	130551
2016	136524
2017	142383
2018	148381

RETAIL PRICING
YEAR	HIGH	LOW
2015	$6,721	$5,041
2016	$7,436	$5,576
2017	$8,226	$6,169
2018	$9,087	$7,089
2019	$10,040	$7,900
2020	$11,255	$8,801

MC36GHS
YEARS MFRD ... 1988-2011
ENGINE ... KOHLER CH20
CYLINDERS ... 2
CID ... 38
ENGINE HP ... 16
COOLING ... AIR
FUEL ... G
SPEEDS ... VARIABLE
TRANSMISSION ... HYDRO
STEERING ... STANDARD
BLADE CLUTCH ... MANUAL
STANDARD DECK ... 36"
WEIGHT ... 954 LBS.
MSRP ... $10,945

OPTIONS
KOHLER 18HP
KOHLER 20HP

RETAIL PRICING
YEAR	HIGH	LOW
1988	$498	$373
1989	$506	$379
1990	$512	$384
1991	$525	$394
1992	$537	$403
1993	$557	$417
1994	$616	$462
1995	$663	$498
1996	$741	$556
1997	$795	$596
1998	$906	$679
1999	$990	$742
2000	$1,043	$782
2001	$1,148	$861
2002	$1,293	$969
2003	$1,456	$1,092
2004	$1,653	$1,240
2005	$1,941	$1,456
2006	$2,210	$1,657
2007	$2,675	$2,007
2008	$3,195	$2,396
2009	$4,190	$3,143
2010	$4,658	$3,493
2011	$5,456	$4,092

MC42GHS
YEARS MFRD ... 1988-2006
ENGINE ... KOHLER
CYLINDERS ... 2
ENGINE HP ... 16
COOLING ... AIR
FUEL ... G
SPEEDS ... VARIABLE
TRANSMISSION ... HYDRO
STEERING ... ZERO
STANDARD DECK ... 42"
WEIGHT ... 965 LBS.
MSRP ... $8,870

OPTIONS
42" SNOW BLOWER
46" BLADE
47" BROOM
CAB

SERIAL NUMBERS
YEAR	BEGINNING NO.
1998	98
1999	99
2000	2000-43710
2001	2001-49578
2002	2002-55282
2003	2003-60533
2004	2004-65790
2005	2005-71500
2006	2006-78732

RETAIL PRICING
YEAR	HIGH	LOW
1998	$1,303	$978
1999	$1,446	$1,085
2000	$1,604	$1,203
2001	$1,777	$1,333
2002	$1,971	$1,478
2003	$2,187	$1,641
2004	$2,426	$1,819
2005	$2,693	$2,020
2006	$2,986	$2,240

MC42SD
YEARS MFRD ... 1988-2013
ENGINE ... KOHLER
ENGINE HP ... 20
COOLING ... AIR
FUEL ... G
SPEEDS ... VARIABLE
TRANSMISSION ... HYDRO
STEERING ... ZERO
BLADE CLUTCH ... ELECTRIC
STANDARD DECK ... 42"
WEIGHT ... 890 LBS.
MSRP ... $10,275

OPTIONS
42" SNOW BLOWER
46" BLADE
47" BROOM
CAB

SERIAL NUMBERS
YEAR	BEGINNING NO.
1998	98
1999	99
2000	2000-43710
2001	2001-49578
2002	2002-55282
2003	2003-60533
2004	2004-65790
2005	2005-71500
2006	2006-78732
2007	2007-85128
2008	2008-92037
2010	10-103389
2011	11-107968
2012	12-113766
2013	13-119135

RETAIL PRICING
YEAR	HIGH	LOW
2005	$2,729	$2,047
2006	$3,028	$2,271
2007	$3,361	$2,521
2008	$3,728	$2,796
2009	$4,135	$3,101
2010	$4,585	$3,439
2011	$5,088	$3,816
2012	$5,644	$4,233
2013	$6,260	$4,695

MC54SD
YEARS MFRD ... 1988-2001
ENGINE ... KOHLER
ENGINE HP ... 16
FUEL ... G
TRANSMISSION ... HYDRO
STEERING ... STANDARD
STANDARD DECK ... 54"
WEIGHT ... 875 LBS.
MSRP ... $7,525

RETAIL PRICING
YEAR	HIGH	LOW
1988	$1,635	$1,226
1989	$1,726	$1,294
1990	$1,758	$1,319
1991	$1,932	$1,449
1992	$2,034	$1,526
1993	$2,074	$1,555
1994	$2,244	$1,683
1995	$2,351	$1,763
1996	$2,533	$1,900
1997	$2,657	$1,993
1998	$2,993	$2,245
1999	$3,290	$2,467
2000	$3,416	$2,562
2001	$3,563	$2,672

MC56SD
YEARS MFRD ... 2002-2011
ENGINE ... KOHLER
ENGINE HP ... 16
COOLING ... AIR
FUEL ... G
TRANSMISSION ... HYDRO
STEERING ... STANDARD
STANDARD DECK ... 56"
MSRP ... $10,570

OPTIONS
KOHLER 18HP
KOHLER 20HP

RETAIL PRICING
YEAR	HIGH	LOW
2002	$1,227	$920
2003	$1,385	$1,039
2004	$1,567	$1,175
2005	$1,863	$1,397
2006	$2,171	$1,628
2007	$2,597	$1,948
2008	$3,096	$2,322
2009	$4,086	$3,064
2010	$4,656	$3,492
2011	$5,457	$4,092

MC565D
YEARS MFRD ... 2006-2006
ENGINE ... KOHLER
ENGINE HP ... 18
COOLING ... AIR
FUEL ... G
SPEEDS ... VARIABLE
TRANSMISSION ... HYDRO
STEERING ... ZERO
STANDARD DECK ... 56"
WEIGHT ... 965 LBS.
MSRP ... $8,720

RETAIL PRICING
YEAR	HIGH	LOW
2006	$5,492	$4,119

MCGHSA
YEARS MFRD ... 2007-2012
ENGINE ... KOHLER
ENGINE HP ... 20
COOLING ... AIR
FUEL ... G
SPEEDS ... VARIABLE
TRANSMISSION ... HYDRO
STEERING ... ZERO
STANDARD DECK ... 48"
MSRP ... $11,480

OPTIONS
42" SNOW BLOWER
46" BLADE
56" DECK

SERIAL NUMBERS
YEAR	BEGINNING NO.
2007	07-85128
2008	08-92037
2010	10-103389
2011	11-107968
2012	12-113766

RETAIL PRICING
YEAR	HIGH	LOW
2007	$3,867	$2,900
2008	$4,289	$3,217
2009	$4,759	$3,569
2010	$5,280	$3,960
2011	$5,857	$4,393
2012	$6,497	$4,873

MD21D
YEARS MFRD ... 2014-2020
ENGINE ... KUBOTA
CYLINDERS ... 3
CID ... 43.9
ENGINE HP ... 20.9
COOLING ... AIR
FUEL ... D
SPEEDS ... VARIABLE
TRANSMISSION ... HYDRO
STEERING ... ZERO
STANDARD DECK ... 52"
WEIGHT ... 1,178 LBS.
MSRP ... $20,115

WALKER

OPTIONS
42" SNOW BLOWER
52" DECK RD $810
56" DECK SD $305
62" DECK SD $1,090

SERIAL NUMBERS

YEAR	BEGINNING NO.
2014	14-124782
2015	130551
2016	136524
2017	142383
2018	148381

RETAIL PRICING

YEAR	HIGH	LOW
2014	$8,960	$6,719
2015	$9,910	$7,432
2016	$10,963	$8,223
2017	$12,119	$9,096
2018	$13,425	$10,360
2019	$14,847	$11,462
2020	$16,814	$13,165

MD42

YEARS MFRD 2006-2007
ENGINE . . . . KUBOTA D722
CID 44
ENGINE HP 20.9
COOLING . . . . LIQUID
FUEL . . . . D
SPEEDS . . . . VARIABLE
TRANSMISSION . . . . HYDRO
STEERING. . . . . ZERO
WEIGHT . . . . 1,020 LBS.
MSRP. $14,095

RETAIL PRICING

YEAR	HIGH	LOW
2006	$6,784	$5,088
2007	$7,727	$5,795

MDD42GHS

YEARS MFRD 1992-2006
ENGINE . . . . KUBOTA
CYLINDERS. 3
ENGINE HP 20.9
COOLING . . . . LIQUID
FUEL . . . . D
SPEEDS . . . . VARIABLE
TRANSMISSION . . . . HYDRO
STEERING. . . . . ZERO
STANDARD DECK . . . . 42"
WEIGHT . . . . 1,100 LBS.
MSRP. $13,200

OPTIONS
42" SNOW BLOWER
47" BROOM
CAB

SERIAL NUMBERS

YEAR	BEGINNING NO.
1997	97
1998	98
1999	99
2000	2000-43710
2001	2001-49578
2002	2002-55282
2003	2003-60533
2004	2004-65790
2005	2005-71500
2006	2006-79108

RETAIL PRICING

YEAR	HIGH	LOW
1998	$1,940	$1,455
1999	$2,148	$1,611
2000	$2,384	$1,788
2001	$2,646	$1,985
2002	$2,935	$2,201
2003	$3,258	$2,443
2004	$3,613	$2,710
2005	$4,009	$3,007
2006	$4,447	$3,335

MDD52SD

YEARS MFRD 2002-2016
ENGINE . . . . KUBOTA
ENGINE HP 20.9
COOLING . . . . LIQUID
FUEL . . . . D
SPEEDS . . . . VARIABLE
TRANSMISSION . . . . HYDRO
STEERING. . . . . ZERO
BLADE CLUTCH . . . . ELECTRIC
STANDARD DECK . . . . 52"
MSRP. $18,303

OPTIONS
42" SNOW BLOWER
47" BROOM
CAB
HITCH

SERIAL NUMBERS

YEAR	BEGINNING NO.
2002	2002-55282
2003	2003-60533
2004	2004-65790
2005	2005-71500
2006	2006-79108
2007	07-85128
2008	08-92037
2010	10-103389
2011	11-107968
2012	12-113766
2013	13-119135
2014	14-124782
2015	130551

RETAIL PRICING

YEAR	HIGH	LOW
2006	$4,928	$3,696
2007	$5,456	$4,092
2008	$6,036	$4,527
2009	$6,677	$5,008
2010	$7,386	$5,540
2011	$8,170	$6,128
2012	$9,039	$6,779
2013	$9,998	$7,498
2014	$11,059	$8,294
2015	$12,234	$9,176
2016	$14,308	$10,731

MDD54SD

YEARS MFRD 1992-2001
ENGINE . . . . KUBOTA
ENGINE HP 20.9
COOLING . . . . LIQUID
FUEL . . . . D
SPEEDS 0-5
TRANSMISSION . . . . HYDRO
STEERING. . . . . ZERO
STANDARD DECK . . . . 54"
WEIGHT . . . . 1,025 LBS.
MSRP. $11,400

OPTIONS
42" SNOW BLOWER
62" DECK
CAB

SERIAL NUMBERS

YEAR	BEGINNING NO.
1992	92-11756
2000	2000-43710
2001	2001-49578

RETAIL PRICING

YEAR	HIGH	LOW
1992	$809	$607
1993	$1,007	$756
1994	$1,117	$838
1995	$1,240	$930
1996	$1,375	$1,031
1997	$1,524	$1,143
1998	$1,691	$1,268
1999	$1,876	$1,407
2000	$2,082	$1,561
2001	$2,306	$1,729

MDD56SD

YEARS MFRD 1992-2002
ENGINE . . . . KUBOTA
ENGINE HP 20.9
COOLING . . . . LIQUID
FUEL . . . . D
SPEEDS . . . . VARIABLE
TRANSMISSION . . . . HYDRO
STEERING. . . . . ZERO
STANDARD DECK . . . . 56"
MSRP. $11,660

OPTIONS
42" SNOW BLOWER
62" DECK
CAB

SERIAL NUMBERS

YEAR	BEGINNING NO.
1992	92-11756

RETAIL PRICING

YEAR	HIGH	LOW
1994	$1,092	$819
1995	$1,209	$907
1996	$1,339	$1,004
1997	$1,489	$1,116
1998	$1,651	$1,238
1999	$1,828	$1,371
2000	$2,030	$1,522
2001	$2,251	$1,688
2002	$2,496	$1,872

MDD62SD

YEARS MFRD 1994-2011
ENGINE . . . . KUBOTA
ENGINE HP 20.9
FUEL . . . . D
SPEEDS . . . . VARIABLE
TRANSMISSION . . . . HYDRO
STEERING. . . . . STANDARD
STANDARD DECK . . . . 62"
WEIGHT . . . . 1,285 LBS.
MSRP. $16,775

RETAIL PRICING

YEAR	HIGH	LOW
1994	$906	$679
1995	$998	$748
1996	$1,117	$838
1997	$1,285	$964
1998	$1,385	$1,039
1999	$1,470	$1,103
2000	$1,588	$1,191
2001	$1,751	$1,313
2002	$1,948	$1,461
2003	$2,190	$1,643
2004	$2,484	$1,863
2005	$2,958	$2,218
2006	$3,376	$2,532
2007	$4,144	$3,108
2008	$4,951	$3,713
2009	$6,532	$4,899
2010	$7,427	$5,571
2011	$8,664	$6,498

MDD565D

YEARS MFRD 2006-2006
ENGINE . . . . KUBOTA
ENGINE HP 20.9
FUEL . . . . D
SPEEDS . . . . VARIABLE
TRANSMISSION . . . . HYDRO
STEERING. . . . . ZERO
STANDARD DECK . . . . 56"
WEIGHT . . . . 1,065 LBS.
MSRP. $12,975

RETAIL PRICING

YEAR	HIGH	LOW
2006	$8,171	$6,128

MDDGHSA

YEARS MFRD 2007-2012
ENGINE . . . . KUBOTA
ENGINE HP 20.9
COOLING . . . . LIQUID
FUEL . . . . D
SPEEDS . . . . VARIABLE
TRANSMISSION . . . . . DUAL HYDRO
STEERING. . . . . ZERO
STANDARD DECK . . . . 62"
MSRP. $18,465

OPTIONS
42" SNOW BLOWER
46" BLADE

SERIAL NUMBERS

YEAR	BEGINNING NO.
2007	07-85128
2008	08-92037
2010	10-103389
2011	11-107968
2012	12-113766

RETAIL PRICING

YEAR	HIGH	LOW
2007	$6,265	$4,699
2008	$6,946	$5,210
2009	$7,709	$5,782

2010	$8,550	$6,412
2011	$9,486	$7,115
2012	$10,521	$7,891

MDG42GHS

YEARS MFRD 1992-2001
ENGINE . . . . KUBOTA
ENGINE HP 24.5
FUEL . . . . G
SPEEDS . . . . VARIABLE
TRANSMISSION . . . . HYDRO
STEERING. . . . . STANDARD
STANDARD DECK . . . . 42"
WEIGHT . . . . 1,080 LBS.
MSRP. $11,330

SERIAL NUMBERS

YEAR	BEGINNING NO.
1992	92-11756

RETAIL PRICING

YEAR	HIGH	LOW
1992	$2,861	$2,145
1993	$2,975	$2,231
1994	$3,207	$2,405
1995	$3,427	$2,570
1996	$3,710	$2,783
1997	$4,223	$3,167
1998	$4,567	$3,425
1999	$4,907	$3,680
2000	$5,142	$3,857
2001	$5,364	$4,023

MDG48GHS

YEARS MFRD 1992-2001
ENGINE . . . . KUBOTA
ENGINE HP 24.5
COOLING . . . . LIQUID
FUEL . . . . G
TRANSMISSION . . . . HYDRO
STEERING. . . . . ZERO
STANDARD DECK . . . . 48"
MSRP. $11,400

OPTIONS

42" SNOW BLOWER
46" BLADE
CAB

SERIAL NUMBERS

YEAR	BEGINNING NO.
1992	92-11756
1998	98-XXXX
1999	99-XXXX
2000	00-XXXX
2001	01-XXXX

RETAIL PRICING

YEAR	HIGH	LOW
1992	$854	$640
1993	$1,007	$756
1994	$1,117	$838
1995	$1,240	$930
1996	$1,375	$1,031
1997	$1,524	$1,143
1998	$1,691	$1,268
1999	$1,876	$1,407
2000	$2,082	$1,561
2001	$2,306	$1,729

MDG54SD

YEARS MFRD 1992-2001
ENGINE . . . . KUBOTA
ENGINE HP 21
FUEL . . . . G
TRANSMISSION . . . . HYDRO
STEERING. . . . . STANDARD
STANDARD DECK . . . . 54"
MSRP. $10,850

SERIAL NUMBERS

YEAR	BEGINNING NO.
1992	92-11756

RETAIL PRICING

YEAR	HIGH	LOW
1992	$2,726	$2,045
1993	$2,894	$2,170
1994	$3,110	$2,332
1995	$3,327	$2,495
1996	$3,568	$2,676
1997	$4,030	$3,022
1998	$4,335	$3,251
1999	$4,699	$3,524
2000	$4,924	$3,693
2001	$5,136	$3,852

MDG62SD

YEARS MFRD 1992-2001
ENGINE . . . . KUBOTA
ENGINE HP 24.5
COOLING . . . . LIQUID
FUEL . . . . G
TRANSMISSION . . . . HYDRO
STEERING. . . . . ZERO
STANDARD DECK . . . . 62"
MSRP. $11,585

OPTIONS

42" SNOW BLOWER
CAB

SERIAL NUMBERS

YEAR	BEGINNING NO.
1992	92-11756
1998	98-XXXX
1999	99-XXXX
2000	00-XXXX
2001	01-XXXX

RETAIL PRICING

YEAR	HIGH	LOW
1992	$845	$634
1993	$1,023	$767
1994	$1,134	$850
1995	$1,259	$944
1996	$1,395	$1,046
1997	$1,547	$1,161
1998	$1,718	$1,288
1999	$1,908	$1,431
2000	$2,113	$1,585
2001	$2,345	$1,759

MH24D

YEARS MFRD 2014-2015
ENGINE . . . . YANMAR
ENGINE HP 23.6
COOLING . . . . AIR
FUEL . . . . D
SPEEDS . . . . VARIABLE
TRANSMISSION . . . . HYDRO
STEERING. . . . . ZERO
STANDARD DECK . . . . 60"
MSRP. $17,710

OPTIONS

50" SNOW BLOWER
52" DECK
60" BROOM
HITCH

SERIAL NUMBERS

YEAR	BEGINNING NO.
2014	14-124782
2015	130551

RETAIL PRICING

YEAR	HIGH	LOW
2014	$10,545	$7,909
2015	$12,345	$9,259

MH24D KOH

YEARS MFRD 2017-2020
ENGINE . . . . KOHLER
CID 62.7
ENGINE HP 23.6
COOLING . . . . AIR
FUEL . . . . D
SPEEDS . . . . VARIABLE
TRANSMISSION . . . . HYDRO
STEERING. . . . . ZERO
STANDARD DECK . . . . 61"
MSRP. $19,380

OPTIONS

42" SNOW BLOWER
48" BLADE
60" BROOM
HITCH

SERIAL NUMBERS

YEAR	BEGINNING NO.
2017	142383
2018	148381

RETAIL PRICING

YEAR	HIGH	LOW
2017	$12,274	$9,206
2018	$13,577	$10,567
2019	$15,015	$11,687
2020	$17,195	$13,370

MH25

YEARS MFRD 2014-2018
ENGINE . . . . KOHLER CH740
CYLINDERS. 2
CID 725CC
ENGINE HP 25
COOLING . . . . AIR
FUEL . . . . G
SPEEDS . . . . VARIABLE
TRANSMISSION . . . . HYDRO
STEERING. . . . . ZERO
STANDARD DECK . . . . 60"
WEIGHT . . . . 752 LBS.
MSRP. $12,675

OPTIONS

50" SNOW BLOWER
52" DECK
60" BROOM
HARD CAB
HITCH

SERIAL NUMBERS

YEAR	BEGINNING NO.
2014	14-124782
2015	130551
2016	136524
2017	142383

RETAIL PRICING

YEAR	HIGH	LOW
2014	$7,053	$5,290
2015	$7,802	$5,851
2016	$8,631	$6,473
2017	$9,614	$7,210
2018	$10,628	$7,971

MH27I

YEARS MFRD 2014-2020
ENGINE . . . . KOHLER EFI
CYLINDERS. 2
CID 45
ENGINE HP 27
COOLING . . . . AIR
FUEL . . . . G
SPEEDS . . . . VARIABLE
TRANSMISSION . . . . HYDRO
STEERING. . . . . ZERO
STANDARD DECK . . . . 61"
WEIGHT . . . . 1,198 LBS.
MSRP. $14,490

OPTIONS

50" SNOW BLOWER
52" DECK RD
HARD CAB
HITCH
ROPS

SERIAL NUMBERS

YEAR	BEGINNING NO.
2014	14-124782
2015	150331
2016	136524
2017	142383
2018	148381

RETAIL PRICING

YEAR	HIGH	LOW
2014	$6,665	$4,998
2015	$7,373	$5,530
2016	$8,157	$6,117
2017	$9,022	$6,767
2018	$9,975	$7,749
2019	$11,021	$8,559
2020	$12,818	$10,027

MH37I

YEARS MFRD 2018-2020
ENGINE . . . . VANGUARD
CID 60.6
ENGINE HP 37
COOLING . . . . AIR
FUEL . . . . G
SPEEDS . . . . VARIABLE
TRANSMISSION . . . . . DUAL HYDRO
STEERING. . . . . ZERO
WEIGHT . . . . 778 LBS.
MSRP. $15,860

WALKER

MH38I

YEARS MFRD 2017-2019
ENGINE . . . . KOHLER EFI
CID 61
ENGINE HP 38
COOLING . . . . AIR
FUEL . . . . G
SPEEDS . . . . VARIABLE
TRANSMISSION . . . . .HYDRO
STEERING. . . . . ZERO
STANDARD DECK . . . . 60"
WEIGHT . . . . 1,264 LBS.

OPTIONS

52" DECK RD
HARD CAB
HITCH
ROPS

SERIAL NUMBERS

YEAR	BEGINNING NO.
2017	142383
2018	148381

RETAIL PRICING

YEAR	HIGH	LOW
2017	$9,609	$7,207
2018	$10,620	$7,965
2019	$11,733	$8,799

MODEL B

YEARS MFRD 2010-2010
ENGINE . . . . KOHLER
ENGINE HP 20
COOLING . . . . AIR
FUEL . . . . G
SPEEDS . . . . VARIABLE
TRANSMISSION . . . . .HYDRO
STEERING. . . . . ZERO
BLADE CLUTCH . . . . MANUAL

MODEL C

YEARS MFRD 2003-2010
ENGINE . . . . KOHLER CH20
CYLINDERS. 2
CID 624CC
ENGINE HP 20
COOLING . . . . AIR
FUEL . . . . G
SPEEDS . . . . VARIABLE
TRANSMISSION . . . . .HYDRO
STEERING. . . . . ZERO
WEIGHT . . . . 850 LBS.

MODEL D

YEARS MFRD 2003-2010
ENGINE . . . . .KUBOTA D722-B
CYLINDERS. 3
ENGINE HP 20.9
COOLING . . . . LIQUID
FUEL . . . . D
SPEEDS . . . . VARIABLE
TRANSMISSION . . . . .HYDRO
STEERING. . . . . ZERO
WEIGHT . . . . 1,045 LBS.

MODEL S

YEARS MFRD 2003-2010
ENGINE . . . . .KAWASAKI FE400
CYLINDERS. 1
CID 21.4
ENGINE HP 13
COOLING . . . . AIR
FUEL . . . . G
SPEEDS . . . . VARIABLE
TRANSMISSION . . . . .HYDRO
STEERING. . . . . ZERO
WEIGHT . . . . 735 LBS.

MODEL T

YEARS MFRD 2003-2010
ENGINE . . . . KOHLER CH20
CYLINDERS. 2
ENGINE HP 20
COOLING . . . . AIR
FUEL . . . . G
SPEEDS . . . . VARIABLE
TRANSMISSION . . . . .HYDRO
STEERING. . . . . ZERO
WEIGHT . . . . 930 LBS.

MR21

YEARS MFRD 2020-2020
ENGINE . . . . KOHLER KT620
CID 660CC
ENGINE HP 21
FUEL . . . . G
SPEEDS . . . . VARIABLE
TRANSMISSION . . . . . DUAL HYDRO
STEERING. . . . . ZERO
BLADE CLUTCH . . . . ELECTRIC
STANDARD DECK . . . . 42"
WEIGHT . . . . 575 LBS.
MSRP. $5,910

OPTIONS

48" DECK. $100

MS14

YEARS MFRD 2013-2018
ENGINE . . . . SUBARU-ROBIN
CYLINDERS. 1
CID 24.65
ENGINE HP 14
COOLING . . . . AIR
FUEL . . . . G
SPEEDS . . . . VARIABLE
TRANSMISSION . . . . .HYDRO
STEERING. . . . . ZERO
STANDARD DECK . . . . 36"
WEIGHT . . . . 788 LBS.
MSRP. $9,371

OPTIONS

36"SNOW BLOWER
42" DECK
48" DECK
52" DECK

SERIAL NUMBERS

YEAR	BEGINNING NO.
2013	13-119135
2014	14-124782
2015	130551
2016	136524
2017	142383
2018	148381

RETAIL PRICING

YEAR	HIGH	LOW
2013	$3,977	$2,983
2014	$4,432	$3,324
2015	$4,902	$3,676
2016	$5,422	$4,067
2017	$5,998	$4,498
2018	$6,638	$4,978

MS14I

YEARS MFRD 2018-2020
ENGINE . . . . KOHLER ECH440
CID 24.7
ENGINE HP 14
COOLING . . . . AIR
FUEL . . . . G
SPEEDS . . . . VARIABLE
TRANSMISSION . . . . .HYDRO
STEERING. . . . . ZERO
STANDARD DECK . . . . 42"
WEIGHT . . . . 596 LBS.
MSRP. $9,910

OPTIONS

48" DECK. $25

MS18

YEARS MFRD 2018-2020
ENGINE . . . . B&S
CID 34.8
ENGINE HP 18
COOLING . . . . AIR
FUEL . . . . G
SPEEDS . . . . VARIABLE
TRANSMISSION . . . . .HYDRO
STEERING. . . . . ZERO
STANDARD DECK . . . . 42"
WEIGHT . . . . 827 LBS.
MSRP. $11,005

MS36GHS

YEARS MFRD 1994-2011
ENGINE . . . . .KAWASAKI FE400
CYLINDERS. 1
CID 24.5
ENGINE HP 13
COOLING . . . . AIR
FUEL . . . . G
SPEEDS . . . . VARIABLE
TRANSMISSION . . . . .HYDRO
STEERING. . . . . ZERO
STANDARD DECK . . . . 36"
WEIGHT . . . . 735 LBS.
MSRP. $9,325

OPTIONS

36" SNOW BLOWER
SUS SEAT

SERIAL NUMBERS

YEAR	BEGINNING NO.
1998	98
1999	99
2000	2000-43710
2001	2001-49578
2002	2002-55282
2003	2003-60533
2004	2004-65790
2005	2005-71500
2006	2006-78964
2007	07-85128
2008	08-92037
2010	10-103389
2011	11-107968

RETAIL PRICING

YEAR	HIGH	LOW
2003	$2,126	$1,594
2004	$2,358	$1,768
2005	$2,614	$1,960
2006	$2,899	$2,174
2007	$3,214	$2,411
2008	$3,566	$2,675
2009	$3,957	$2,968
2010	$4,391	$3,294
2011	$4,945	$3,709

MS42GHS

YEARS MFRD 2005-2011
ENGINE . . . . KAWASAKI
CYLINDERS. 1
ENGINE HP 13
COOLING . . . . AIR
FUEL . . . . G
SPEEDS . . . . VARIABLE
TRANSMISSION . . . . .HYDRO
STEERING. . . . . ZERO
STANDARD DECK . . . . 42"
WEIGHT . . . . 830 LBS.
MSRP. $9,410

RETAIL PRICING

YEAR	HIGH	LOW
2005	$1,699	$1,274
2006	$1,921	$1,441
2007	$2,290	$1,718
2008	$2,746	$2,059
2009	$3,647	$2,735
2010	$4,145	$3,109
2011	$4,860	$3,645

MS42SD

YEARS MFRD 1998-2011
ENGINE . . . . KAWASAKI
CYLINDERS. 1
ENGINE HP 11
COOLING . . . . AIR
FUEL . . . . G
SPEEDS . . . . VARIABLE
TRANSMISSION . . . . .HYDRO
STEERING. . . . . ZERO
STANDARD DECK . . . . 42"
WEIGHT . . . . 750 LBS.
MSRP. $8,565

OPTIONS

KAWASAKI 11.5HP
KAWASAKI 13HP

RETAIL PRICING

YEAR	HIGH	LOW
1998	$700	$525
1999	$748	$561
2000	$813	$610

YEAR	HIGH	LOW
2001	$898	$673
2002	$998	$748
2003	$1,136	$852
2004	$1,272	$954
2005	$1,527	$1,145
2006	$1,732	$1,299
2007	$2,066	$1,549
2008	$2,484	$1,863
2009	$3,285	$2,464
2010	$3,764	$2,823
2011	$4,425	$3,319

MT23

YEARS MFRD	2014-2020
ENGINE	KOHLER
CYLINDERS	2
CID	41.1
ENGINE HP	23
COOLING	AIR
FUEL	G
SPEEDS	VARIABLE
TRANSMISSION	DUAL HYDRO
STEERING	ZERO
STANDARD DECK	62"
WEIGHT	1,014 LBS.
MSRP	$14,615

OPTIONS

10 BU COLL
48" DECK SD $125
HI DUMP
POWER DUMP

SERIAL NUMBERS

YEAR	BEGINNING NO.
2017	142383
2018	148381

RETAIL PRICING

YEAR	HIGH	LOW
2014	$6,617	$4,962
2015	$7,320	$5,489
2016	$8,123	$6,091
2017	$8,958	$6,718
2018	$9,898	$7,705
2019	$10,941	$8,520
2020	$12,390	$9,669

MT23-11

YEARS MFRD	2014-2014
ENGINE	KOHLER
ENGINE HP	23
COOLING	AIR
FUEL	G
SPEEDS	VARIABLE
TRANSMISSION	HYDRO
STEERING	ZERO
STANDARD DECK	42"
WEIGHT	1,030 LBS.
MSRP	$13,050

OPTIONS

48" DECK

RETAIL PRICING

YEAR	HIGH	LOW
2014	$7,238	$5,429

MT25I

YEARS MFRD	2014-2019
ENGINE	KOHLER EFI
CYLINDERS	2
CID	45
ENGINE HP	25
COOLING	AIR
FUEL	G
SPEEDS	VARIABLE
TRANSMISSION	HYDRO
STEERING	ZERO
STANDARD DECK	62"
WEIGHT	1,018 LBS.

OPTIONS

10 BU COLL
42" SNOW BLOWER
48" BLADE
48" DECK SD
CAB
HI DUMP
POWER DUMP

SERIAL NUMBERS

YEAR	BEGINNING NO.
2014	14-124782
2015	130551
2016	142383
2017	148381

RETAIL PRICING

YEAR	HIGH	LOW
2014	$7,016	$5,262
2015	$7,762	$5,821
2016	$8,586	$6,439
2017	$9,497	$7,123
2018	$10,502	$7,876
2019	$11,610	$8,708

MT25IGHS

YEARS MFRD	2014-2016
ENGINE	KOHLER EFI
ENGINE HP	25
COOLING	AIR
FUEL	G
SPEEDS	VARIABLE
TRANSMISSION	HYDRO
STEERING	ZERO
STANDARD DECK	52"
MSRP	$14,485

OPTIONS

10 BU BAG
42" SNOW BLOWER
48" BLADE
HITCH

SERIAL NUMBERS

YEAR	BEGINNING NO.
2014	14-124782
2015	130551
2016	136524

RETAIL PRICING

YEAR	HIGH	LOW
2014	$8,752	$6,564
2015	$9,681	$7,261
2016	$11,617	$8,713

MT27I

YEARS MFRD	2020-2020
ENGINE	KOHLER COMMAND PRO EFI
CID	45.6
ENGINE HP	26.5
FUEL	G
STEERING	ZERO
STANDARD DECK	48"
WEIGHT	1,006 LBS.
MSRP	$15,535

OPTIONS

52" DECK $360

MT30I

YEARS MFRD	2014-2019
ENGINE	KOHLER EFI
CYLINDERS	2
CID	45.6
ENGINE HP	30
COOLING	AIR
FUEL	G
SPEEDS	VARIABLE
TRANSMISSION	HYDRO
STEERING	ZERO
STANDARD DECK	52"
WEIGHT	1,117 LBS.

OPTIONS

10 BU BAG
42" SNOW BLOWER
48" BLADE
48" DECK SD
HI DUMP
HITCH
POWER DUMP

SERIAL NUMBERS

YEAR	BEGINNING NO.
2014	14-124782
2015	130551
2016	136524
2017	142383
2018	148381

RETAIL PRICING

YEAR	HIGH	LOW
2014	$8,960	$6,720
2015	$9,911	$7,433
2016	$10,963	$8,222
2017	$12,128	$9,096
2018	$13,400	$10,050
2019	$14,709	$11,032

MT42GHS-26

YEARS MFRD	2004-2011
ENGINE	KOHLER
ENGINE HP	26
COOLING	AIR
FUEL	G
SPEEDS	VARIABLE
TRANSMISSION	HYDRO
STEERING	ZERO
STANDARD DECK	42"
WEIGHT	1,058 LBS.
MSRP	$13,090

RETAIL PRICING

YEAR	HIGH	LOW
2004	$2,127	$1,595
2005	$2,508	$1,881
2006	$2,881	$2,161
2007	$3,418	$2,564
2008	$4,077	$3,058
2009	$5,301	$3,976
2010	$5,804	$4,353
2011	$6,762	$5,072

MT48GHS-20

YEARS MFRD	1992-2006
ENGINE	KOHLER
ENGINE HP	20
COOLING	AIR
FUEL	G
SPEEDS	VARIABLE
TRANSMISSION	HYDRO
STEERING	ZERO
STANDARD DECK	48"
WEIGHT	1,030 LBS.
MSRP	$9,910

OPTIONS

42" SNOW BLOWER
CAB
KOHLER 25HP

SERIAL NUMBERS

YEAR	BEGINNING NO.
1998	98
1999	99
2000	2000-43710
2001	2001-49578
2002	2002-55282
2003	2003-60533
2004	2004-65790
2005	2005-71500
2006	2006-78572

RETAIL PRICING

YEAR	HIGH	LOW
1998	$1,422	$1,066
1999	$1,575	$1,181
2000	$1,750	$1,313
2001	$1,940	$1,455
2002	$2,152	$1,614
2003	$2,384	$1,788
2004	$2,646	$1,985
2005	$2,938	$2,204
2006	$3,258	$2,443

MT48GHS-26

YEARS MFRD	2000-2006
ENGINE	KOHLER
ENGINE HP	26
COOLING	AIR
FUEL	G
SPEEDS	VARIABLE
TRANSMISSION	BELT
STEERING	ZERO
STANDARD DECK	48"
WEIGHT	1,035 LBS.
MSRP	$11,125

OPTIONS

42" SNOW BLOWER
46" BLADE
47" BROOM
CAB

RETAIL PRICING

YEAR	HIGH	LOW
2000	$1,963	$1,472
2001	$2,176	$1,632
2002	$2,417	$1,813

WALKER

YEAR	HIGH	LOW
2003	$2,681	$2,011
2004	$2,974	$2,231
2005	$3,298	$2,473
2006	$3,657	$2,743

MT52GHS-26

YEARS MFRD 2008-2011
ENGINE .... KOHLER
ENGINE HP 26
COOLING .... AIR
FUEL .... G
SPEEDS .... VARIABLE
TRANSMISSION .... HYDRO
STEERING................ ZERO
STANDARD DECK .... 52"
WEIGHT .... 1,070 LBS.
MSRP................ $13,445

RETAIL PRICING

YEAR	HIGH	LOW
2008	$4,187	$3,140
2009	$5,444	$4,083
2010	$5,952	$4,464
2011	$6,944	$5,208

MT52SD

YEARS MFRD 1998-2011
ENGINE .... KOHLER
ENGINE HP 20
FUEL .... G
SPEEDS .... VARIABLE
TRANSMISSION .... HYDRO
STEERING............ STANDARD
STANDARD DECK .... 52"
WEIGHT .... 1,060 LBS.
MSRP................ $12,195

RETAIL PRICING

YEAR	HIGH	LOW
1998	$1,016	$762
1999	$1,082	$811
2000	$1,187	$890
2001	$1,305	$979
2002	$1,448	$1,086
2003	$1,634	$1,225
2004	$1,856	$1,392
2005	$2,203	$1,652
2006	$2,525	$1,894
2007	$3,017	$2,263
2008	$3,593	$2,695
2009	$4,716	$3,537
2010	$5,368	$4,026
2011	$6,299	$4,725

MT54SD

YEARS MFRD 1993-2001
ENGINE .... KOHLER
ENGINE HP 20
FUEL .... G
SPEEDS 0-5
TRANSMISSION .... HYDRO
STEERING............ STANDARD
STANDARD DECK .... 54"
WEIGHT .... 965 LBS.
MSRP.................. $8,450

RETAIL PRICING

YEAR	HIGH	LOW
1993	$2,402	$1,801
1994	$2,607	$1,955
1995	$2,787	$2,090
1996	$2,971	$2,229
1997	$3,140	$2,355
1998	$3,359	$2,520
1999	$3,660	$2,745
2000	$3,837	$2,878
2001	$4,000	$3,000

MT56SD

YEARS MFRD 2002-2009
ENGINE .... KOHLER
ENGINE HP 20
FUEL .... G
SPEEDS .... VARIABLE
TRANSMISSION .... HYDRO
STEERING............ STANDARD
STANDARD DECK .... 56"
WEIGHT .... 965 LBS.
MSRP................ $11,190

RETAIL PRICING

YEAR	HIGH	LOW
2002	$4,215	$3,161
2003	$4,591	$3,443
2004	$4,988	$3,741
2005	$5,534	$4,151
2006	$6,089	$4,567
2007	$6,305	$4,729
2008	$6,493	$4,869
2009	$6,637	$4,977

MT62SD-20

YEARS MFRD 1992-2006
ENGINE .... KOHLER
ENGINE HP 20
COOLING .... AIR
FUEL .... G
SPEEDS .... VARIABLE
TRANSMISSION .... HYDRO
STEERING................ ZERO
STANDARD DECK .... 62"
WEIGHT .... 1,065 LBS.
MSRP................ $10,235

OPTIONS

42" SNOW BLOWER
46" BLADE
CAB
KOHLER 25HP

SERIAL NUMBERS

YEAR	BEGINNING NO.
2000	2000-43710
2001	2001-49578
2002	2002-55282
2003	2003-60533
2004	2004-65790
2005	2005-71500
2006	2006-78572

RETAIL PRICING

YEAR	HIGH	LOW
1998	$1,470	$1,103
1999	$1,627	$1,220
2000	$1,804	$1,353
2001	$2,001	$1,501
2002	$2,224	$1,668
2003	$2,465	$1,849
2004	$2,732	$2,049
2005	$3,033	$2,275
2006	$3,365	$2,524

MT62SD-26

YEARS MFRD 2000-2013
ENGINE .... KOHLER
ENGINE HP 26
COOLING .... AIR
FUEL .... G
SPEEDS .... VARIABLE
TRANSMISSION ..... DUAL HYDRO
STEERING................ ZERO
BLADE CLUTCH .... ELECTRIC
STANDARD DECK .... 62"
MSRP................ $13,760

OPTIONS

42" SNOW BLOWER
46" BLADE
CAB
SUS SEAT

SERIAL NUMBERS

YEAR	BEGINNING NO.
2000	2000-43710
2001	2001-49578
2002	2002-55282
2003	2003-60533
2004	2004-65790
2005	2005-71500
2006	2006-78572
2007	07-85128
2008	08-92037
2010	10-103389
2011	11-107968
2012	12-113766
2013	13-119135

RETAIL PRICING

YEAR	HIGH	LOW
2005	$3,657	$2,743
2006	$4,056	$3,042
2007	$4,498	$3,374
2008	$4,992	$3,744
2009	$5,537	$4,153
2010	$6,176	$4,632
2011	$6,812	$5,109
2012	$7,559	$5,669
2013	$8,385	$6,289

MT68SD

YEARS MFRD 1994-1994
ENGINE .... KOHLER
ENGINE HP 20
FUEL .... G
TRANSMISSION .... HYDRO
STEERING............ STANDARD
STANDARD DECK .... 62"
MSRP.................. $7,895

RETAIL PRICING

YEAR	HIGH	LOW
1994	$2,735	$2,051

MTGHS23A

YEARS MFRD 2007-2016
ENGINE .... KOHLER
ENGINE HP 23
COOLING .... AIR
FUEL .... G
SPEEDS .... VARIABLE
TRANSMISSION ..... DUAL HYDRO
STEERING................ ZERO
STANDARD DECK .... 62"
MSRP................ $13,633

OPTIONS

10 BU BAG
42" SNOW BLOWER
48" BLADE
HITCH

SERIAL NUMBERS

YEAR	BEGINNING NO.
2007	07-85128
2008	08-92037
2010	10-103389
2011	11-107968
2012	12-113766
2013	13-119135
2014	14-124782
2015	130551
2016	136524

RETAIL PRICING

YEAR	HIGH	LOW
2007	$4,064	$3,048
2008	$4,496	$3,372
2009	$5,009	$3,757
2010	$5,502	$4,126
2011	$6,086	$4,564
2012	$6,783	$5,087
2013	$7,511	$5,633
2014	$8,238	$6,178
2015	$9,113	$6,835
2016	$10,300	$7,725

MTGHS26A

YEARS MFRD 2007-2012
ENGINE .... KOHLER
ENGINE HP 26
COOLING .... AIR
FUEL .... G
SPEEDS .... VARIABLE
TRANSMISSION ..... DUAL HYDRO
STEERING................ ZERO
STANDARD DECK .... 62"
MSRP................ $15,040

OPTIONS

42" SNOW BLOWER
46" BLADE

SERIAL NUMBERS

YEAR	BEGINNING NO.
2007	07-85128
2008	08-92037
2010	10-103389
2011	11-107968
2012	12-113766

RETAIL PRICING

YEAR	HIGH	LOW
2007	$5,102	$3,826
2008	$5,659	$4,244
2009	$6,280	$4,710

2010 ... $6,964 ... $5,223
2011 ... $7,725 ... $5,794
2012 ... $8,570 ... $6,428

MTL42GHS

YEARS MFRD ... 2002-2009
ENGINE ... KOHLER
ENGINE HP ... 25
FUEL ... G
SPEEDS ... VARIABLE
TRANSMISSION ... HYDRO
STEERING ... STANDARD
STANDARD DECK ... 42"
WEIGHT ... 1,058 LBS.
MSRP ... $13,790

OPTIONS

KOHLER 26HP

RETAIL PRICING

YEAR	HIGH	LOW
2002	$4,981	$3,736
2003	$5,535	$4,151
2004	$5,987	$4,490
2005	$6,591	$4,943
2006	$7,170	$5,377
2007	$7,393	$5,545
2008	$7,777	$5,833
2009	$8,179	$6,134

MTL48GHS

YEARS MFRD ... 2003-2005
ENGINE ... KOHLER
ENGINE HP ... 25
COOLING ... AIR
FUEL ... G
SPEEDS ... VARIABLE
TRANSMISSION ... HYDRO
STEERING ... ZERO
STANDARD DECK ... 48"
WEIGHT ... 1,088 LBS.
MSRP ... $11,090

OPTIONS

42" SNOW BLOWER
46" BLADE
47" BROOM
CAB

SERIAL NUMBERS

YEAR	BEGINNING NO.
2003	2003-60533
2004	2004-65790
2005	2005-71500

RETAIL PRICING

YEAR	HIGH	LOW
2003	$2,749	$2,062
2004	$3,049	$2,287
2005	$3,384	$2,538

MTL52GHS-31

YEARS MFRD ... 2008-2011
ENGINE ... KOHLER
ENGINE HP ... 31
COOLING ... LIQUID
FUEL ... G
SPEEDS ... VARIABLE
TRANSMISSION ... HYDRO
STEERING ... ZERO
BLADE CLUTCH ... ELECTRIC
STANDARD DECK ... 52"
WEIGHT ... 1,123 LBS.
MSRP ... $15,870

RETAIL PRICING

YEAR	HIGH	LOW
2008	$4,879	$3,660
2009	$6,354	$4,766
2010	$7,040	$5,280
2011	$8,196	$6,147

MTL56SD

YEARS MFRD ... 2002-2009
ENGINE ... KOHLER
ENGINE HP ... 25
FUEL ... G
SPEEDS ... VARIABLE
TRANSMISSION ... HYDRO
STEERING ... STANDARD
STANDARD DECK ... 56"
WEIGHT ... 1,065 LBS.
MSRP ... $13,395

RETAIL PRICING

YEAR	HIGH	LOW
2002	$4,798	$3,599
2003	$5,276	$3,957
2004	$5,702	$4,276
2005	$6,326	$4,744
2006	$6,960	$5,220
2007	$7,326	$5,495
2008	$7,707	$5,780
2009	$7,944	$5,958

MTL62SD

YEARS MFRD ... 2002-2006
ENGINE ... KOHLER
ENGINE HP ... 25
COOLING ... AIR
FUEL ... G
TRANSMISSION ... HYDRO
STEERING ... ZERO
STANDARD DECK ... 62"
MSRP ... $11,615

OPTIONS

42" SNOW BLOWER
46" BLADE
CAB

SERIAL NUMBERS

YEAR	BEGINNING NO.
2002	2002-55282
2003	2003-60533
2004	2004-65790
2005	2005-71500
2006	2006-78988

RETAIL PRICING

YEAR	HIGH	LOW
2002	$2,524	$1,893
2003	$2,796	$2,097
2004	$3,105	$2,328
2005	$3,444	$2,583
2006	$3,819	$2,864

MTL74SD

YEARS MFRD ... 2003-2011
ENGINE ... KOHLER
ENGINE HP ... 29
FUEL ... G
SPEEDS ... VARIABLE
TRANSMISSION ... HYDRO
STEERING ... ZERO
STANDARD DECK ... 74"
WEIGHT ... 1,160 LBS.
MSRP ... $15,900

OPTIONS

KOHLER 31HP

RETAIL PRICING

YEAR	HIGH	LOW
2003	$2,099	$1,574
2004	$2,375	$1,781
2005	$2,819	$2,115
2006	$3,213	$2,410
2007	$4,111	$3,083
2008	$4,907	$3,680
2009	$6,409	$4,807
2010	$7,033	$5,275
2011	$8,209	$6,157

MTLGHS31A

YEARS MFRD ... 2007-2012
ENGINE ... KOHLER
ENGINE HP ... 31
COOLING ... LIQUID
FUEL ... D
SPEEDS ... VARIABLE
TRANSMISSION ... DUAL HYDRO
STEERING ... ZERO
STANDARD DECK ... 62"
MSRP ... $17,465

OPTIONS

42" SNOW BLOWER
46" BLADE

SERIAL NUMBERS

YEAR	BEGINNING NO.
2007	07-85128
2008	08-92037
2010	10-103389
2011	11-107968
2012	12-113766

RETAIL PRICING

YEAR	HIGH	LOW
2007	$5,924	$4,443
2008	$6,694	$5,021
2009	$7,290	$5,468
2010	$8,089	$6,067
2011	$8,973	$6,730
2012	$9,952	$7,464

MTSD23

YEARS MFRD ... 2007-2016
ENGINE ... KOHLER
ENGINE HP ... 23
COOLING ... AIR
FUEL ... G
SPEEDS ... VARIABLE
TRANSMISSION ... DUAL HYDRO
STEERING ... ZERO
BLADE CLUTCH ... ELECTRIC
STANDARD DECK ... 62"
MSRP ... $13,607

OPTIONS

42" SNOW BLOWER
48" BLADE
CAB

SERIAL NUMBERS

YEAR	BEGINNING NO.
2007	07-85128
2008	08-92037
2010	10-103389
2011	11-107968
2012	12-113766
2013	13-119135
2014	14-124782
2015	130551
2016	136524

RETAIL PRICING

YEAR	HIGH	LOW
2007	$4,056	$3,042
2008	$4,486	$3,365
2009	$4,976	$3,732
2010	$5,492	$4,119
2011	$6,173	$4,630
2012	$6,719	$5,039
2013	$7,432	$5,574
2014	$8,221	$6,166
2015	$9,095	$6,822
2016	$10,233	$7,675

MW36

YEARS MFRD ... 2003-2012
ENGINE ... KAWASAKI
ENGINE HP ... 15
COOLING ... AIR
FUEL ... G
SPEEDS ... VARIABLE
TRANSMISSION ... DUAL HYDRO
STEERING ... ZERO
STANDARD DECK ... 36"
MSRP ... $6,810

OPTIONS

48" DECK
56" DECK
SULKY

SERIAL NUMBERS

YEAR	BEGINNING NO.
2003	2003-60533
2004	2004-65790
2005	2005-71500
2007	07-85128
2008	08-92037
2010	10-103389
2011	11-107968
2012	12-113766

RETAIL PRICING

YEAR	HIGH	LOW
2003	$1,508	$1,131
2004	$1,691	$1,268
2005	$1,876	$1,407
2006	$2,082	$1,561
2007	$2,311	$1,733
2008	$2,563	$1,922
2009	$2,844	$2,133
2010	$3,152	$2,364
2011	$3,495	$2,621
2012	$3,878	$2,908

WALKER

SUPER B

YEARS MFRD 2008-2010
ENGINE ...... KOHLER COMMAND
CYLINDERS.................. 2
CID 44
ENGINE HP 27
COOLING .... AIR
FUEL .... G
SPEEDS .... VARIABLE
TRANSMISSION .... HYDRO
STEERING................ ZERO

RETAIL PRICING

YEAR	HIGH	LOW
1987	$1,573	$1,180
1988	$1,637	$1,228
1989	$1,699	$1,274

WHITE

FB16

YEARS MFRD 1986-1989
ENGINE .... MITSUBISHI
CYLINDERS.................. 3
CID 51.8
PTO HP 14
ENGINE HP 16
FUEL .... D
SPEEDS 6/2
DRIVE TYPE 2WD
ROPS/CAB .... ROPS
WEIGHT .... 1,103 LBS.
MSRP................... $7,300

OPTIONS

4WD

SERIAL NUMBERS

LEFT FRONT OF FRAME

YEAR	BEGINNING NO.
1986	014422-4WD
1986	002314-2WD
1987	014660-4WD
1987	002393-2WD

RETAIL PRICING

YEAR	HIGH	LOW
1986	$1,360	$1,020
1987	$1,417	$1,063
1988	$1,474	$1,105
1989	$1,532	$1,149

FB16H

YEARS MFRD 1987-1989
ENGINE .... MITSUBISHI
CYLINDERS.................. 3
CID 51.8
PTO HP 14
ENGINE HP 16
FUEL .... D
SPEEDS .... HYDRO
DRIVE TYPE 2WD
ROPS/CAB .... ROPS
WEIGHT .... 1,320 LBS.
MSRP................... $8,100

OPTIONS

4WD

SERIAL NUMBERS

YEAR	BEGINNING NO.
1987	002690
1988	016528

FB21

YEARS MFRD 1986-1989
ENGINE .... ISEKI
CYLINDERS.................. 3
CID 71.4
PTO HP 19
ENGINE HP 21
FUEL .... D
SPEEDS 12/4
DRIVE TYPE 2WD
ROPS/CAB .... ROPS
WEIGHT .... 1,588 LBS.
MSRP................... $9,070

OPTIONS

4WD

SERIAL NUMBERS

LEFT FRONT OF FRAME

YEAR	BEGINNING NO.
1986	595-2WD
1986	2879-4WD
1987	3079-4WD
1987	652-2WD
1988	4003-4WD
1988	967-2WD

RETAIL PRICING

YEAR	HIGH	LOW
1986	$1,588	$1,191
1987	$1,655	$1,241
1988	$1,721	$1,291
1989	$1,788	$1,341

FB31

YEARS MFRD 1986-1988
ENGINE .... ISEKI
CYLINDERS.................. 3
CID 91.4
PTO HP 25
ENGINE HP 30
FUEL .... D
SPEEDS 12/4
STEERING............ STANDARD
DRIVE TYPE 2WD
ROPS/CAB .... ROPS
WEIGHT .... 1,676 LBS.
MSRP................... $8,950

OPTIONS

2 HYD
4WD

SERIAL NUMBERS

LEFT FRONT OF FRAME

YEAR	BEGINNING NO.
1986	126-2WD
1986	28-4WD
1987	163-2WD
1987	175-4WD
1988	568-4WD
1988	276-2WD

RETAIL PRICING

YEAR	HIGH	LOW
1986	$1,901	$1,426
1987	$2,041	$1,531
1988	$2,182	$1,637

FB37

YEARS MFRD 1986-1988
ENGINE .... ISUZU
CYLINDERS.................. 4
CID 110.8
PTO HP 30
FUEL .... D
SPEEDS 18/6
TRANSMISSION .... GEAR
STEERING............ STANDARD
DRIVE TYPE 2WD
ROPS/CAB .... ROPS
WEIGHT .... 2,915 LBS.
MSRP.................. $10,950

OPTIONS

2 HYD
4WD

SERIAL NUMBERS

LEFT FRONT OF FRAME

YEAR	BEGINNING NO.
1986	00084-2WD
1986	00679-4WD
1987	00713-4WD
1987	00117-2WD
1988	01025-4WD
1988	00221-2WD

RETAIL PRICING

YEAR	HIGH	LOW
1986	$2,508	$1,881
1987	$2,653	$1,990
1988	$2,806	$2,105

FB43

YEARS MFRD 1986-1988
ENGINE .... ISUZU
CYLINDERS.................. 4
CID 144.6
PTO HP 39
FUEL .... D
SPEEDS 12/4
TRANSMISSION .... GEAR
STEERING............ STANDARD
PTO .... YES
DRIVE TYPE 2WD
ROPS/CAB .... ROPS
WEIGHT .... 3,748 LBS.
MSRP.................. $15,700

OPTIONS

4WD

SERIAL NUMBERS

LEFT FRONT OF FRAME

YEAR	BEGINNING NO.
1986	00322-4WD
1986	00060-2WD
1987	00068-2WD
1987	00329-4WD
1988	00077-2WD
1988	00337-4WD

RETAIL PRICING

YEAR	HIGH	LOW
1988	$2,982	$2,236

2-30

YEARS MFRD 1979-1984
ENGINE .... ISUZU
CYLINDERS.................. 3
CID 91.4
PTO HP 28.33
COOLING .... LIQUID
FUEL .... D
SPEEDS 8/2
TRANSMISSION .... GEAR
STEERING............ STANDARD
DRIVE TYPE 2WD
ROPS/CAB .... ROPS
WEIGHT .... 2,624 LBS.
MSRP................... $9,095

OPTIONS

4WD

SERIAL NUMBERS

LEFT SIDE OF TRACTOR FRAME NEAR FRONT OF TRACTOR

YEAR	BEGINNING NO.
1979	001417-4WD
1979	100337-2WD
1980	100712-2WD
1980	002645-4WD
1981	100925-2WD
1981	003873-4WD
1982	101275-2WD
1982	005102-4WD
1983	006331-4WD
1983	101412-2WD
1984	006401-4WD
1984	101420-2WD

RETAIL PRICING

YEAR	HIGH	LOW
1979	$604	$453
1980	$710	$533
1981	$854	$641
1982	$1,004	$753
1983	$1,158	$868
1984	$1,316	$987

2-32

YEARS MFRD 1984-1986
ENGINE .... ISUZU
CYLINDERS.................. 4
CID 90.7
PTO HP 28
COOLING .... LIQUID
FUEL .... D
SPEEDS 18/6
TRANSMISSION .... GEAR
STEERING............ STANDARD
DRIVE TYPE 2WD
ROPS/CAB .... ROPS
WEIGHT .... 2,915 LBS.
MSRP................... $9,776

OPTIONS

4WD

SERIAL NUMBERS

LEFT SIDE OF TRACTOR FRAME NEAR FRONT OF TRACTOR

YEAR	BEGINNING NO.
1984	6100175-4WD
1984	6100071-2WD
1985	00007-2WD
1985	00245-4WD
1986	00245-2WD
1986	00226-4WD

RETAIL PRICING

YEAR	HIGH	LOW
1984	$1,483	$1,112
1985	$1,646	$1,235
1986	$1,820	$1,365

2-35

YEARS MFRD	1979-1984
ENGINE	ISUZU
CYLINDERS	3
CID	108.4
PTO HP	32.84
FUEL	D
SPEEDS	8/2
TRANSMISSION	GEAR
STEERING	STANDARD
PTO	YES
DRIVE TYPE	2WD
ROPS/CAB	ROPS
WEIGHT	2,756 LBS.
MSRP	$9,555

OPTIONS

4WD

SERIAL NUMBERS

LEFT SIDE OF TRACTOR FRAME NEAR FRONT OF TRACTOR

YEAR	BEGINNING NO.
1979	004001
1980	004394
1981	004786
1982	005177
1983	005570
1984	005960

RETAIL PRICING

YEAR	HIGH	LOW
1979	$1,976	$1,482
1980	$2,164	$1,623
1981	$2,363	$1,772
1982	$2,566	$1,925
1983	$2,776	$2,082
1984	$2,990	$2,243

2-45

YEARS MFRD	1979-1981
ENGINE	ISUZU
CYLINDERS	4
CID	169.3
PTO HP	43.73
FUEL	D
SPEEDS	20/4
TRANSMISSION	GEAR
STEERING	STANDARD
PTO	YES
DRIVE TYPE	2WD
ROPS/CAB	ROPS
WEIGHT	5,015 LBS.
MSRP	$14,370

OPTIONS

4WD

SERIAL NUMBERS

LEFT SIDE OF TRACTOR FRAME NEAR FRONT OF TRACTOR

YEAR	BEGINNING NO.
1980	T5000E00001-2WD
1980	T5000EF00001-4WD
1981	T5000E00548-2WD
1981	T5000EF00405-4WD

RETAIL PRICING

YEAR	HIGH	LOW
1981	$1,998	$1,498

6045

YEARS MFRD	1995-2002
ENGINE	SLH 1000
CYLINDERS	3
CID	183
PTO HP	45
COOLING	LIQUID
SPEEDS	12/12-16/8
TRANSMISSION	GEAR
STEERING	STANDARD
DRIVE TYPE	2WD
ROPS/CAB	ROPS
WEIGHT	4,200 LBS.
MSRP	$23,776

OPTIONS

4WD

RETAIL PRICING

YEAR	HIGH	LOW
2002	$11,025	$8,268

WHITE OUTDOOR

ALL MODELS

SERIAL NUMBERS

5TH DIGIT IN SERIAL NUMBER IS YEAR MFG

FR12

YEARS MFRD	1987-1991
ENGINE	B&S
ENGINE HP	12.5
COOLING	AIR
FUEL	G
SPEEDS	VARIABLE
TRANSMISSION	HYDRO
STEERING	STANDARD
WEIGHT	550 LBS.

FR16

YEARS MFRD	1994-1995
ENGINE	B&S
ENGINE HP	16
COOLING	AIR
FUEL	G
TRANSMISSION	HYDRO
STEERING	ZERO
STANDARD DECK	46"
MSRP	$5,650

RETAIL PRICING

YEAR	HIGH	LOW
1994	$412	$309
1995	$458	$343

FR18

YEARS MFRD	1987-1996
ENGINE	B&S
ENGINE HP	18
COOLING	AIR
FUEL	G
TRANSMISSION	HYDRO
STEERING	ZERO
STANDARD DECK	52"
MSRP	$6,890

RETAIL PRICING

YEAR	HIGH	LOW
1988	$290	$218
1989	$320	$240
1990	$356	$267
1991	$393	$295
1992	$439	$329
1993	$485	$364
1994	$538	$404
1995	$600	$450
1996	$664	$498

FR20

YEARS MFRD	1987-1994
ENGINE	B&S
ENGINE HP	20
COOLING	AIR
FUEL	G
TRANSMISSION	HYDRO
STEERING	ZERO
STANDARD DECK	62"
MSRP	$8,555

RETAIL PRICING

YEAR	HIGH	LOW
1987	$270	$203
1988	$302	$226
1989	$336	$252
1990	$370	$278
1991	$412	$309
1992	$458	$343
1993	$508	$381
1994	$564	$423

FR180

YEARS MFRD	1994-1995
ENGINE	B&S
ENGINE HP	18
COOLING	AIR
FUEL	G
TRANSMISSION	HYDRO
STEERING	ZERO
STANDARD DECK	52"
MSRP	$8,040

RETAIL PRICING

YEAR	HIGH	LOW
1994	$641	$481
1995	$713	$535

FR180C

YEARS MFRD	1994-1995
ENGINE	B&S
ENGINE HP	18
COOLING	AIR
FUEL	G
TRANSMISSION	HYDRO
STEERING	ZERO
STANDARD DECK	52"
MSRP	$8,540

RETAIL PRICING

YEAR	HIGH	LOW
1994	$683	$512
1995	$760	$570

FR200

YEARS MFRD	1996-1997
ENGINE	B&S
ENGINE HP	20
COOLING	AIR
FUEL	G
STEERING	ZERO
STANDARD DECK	62"
MSRP	$8,374

RETAIL PRICING

YEAR	HIGH	LOW
1996	$801	$600
1997	$889	$667

FR1800

YEARS MFRD	1989-1992
ENGINE	B&S
ENGINE HP	18
COOLING	AIR
FUEL	G
TRANSMISSION	HYDRO
STEERING	ZERO
STANDARD DECK	52"
MSRP	$6,340

RETAIL PRICING

YEAR	HIGH	LOW
1989	$252	$189
1990	$278	$209
1991	$310	$232
1992	$344	$258

FR1800D

YEARS MFRD	1995-1995
ENGINE	PERKINS
ENGINE HP	18
FUEL	D
TRANSMISSION	HYDRO
STEERING	ZERO
STANDARD DECK	52"
MSRP	$14,340

RETAIL PRICING

YEAR	HIGH	LOW
1995	$1,275	$956

WHITE OUTDOOR

FR2000C

YEARS MFRD: 1989-1992
ENGINE: ONAN
ENGINE HP: 20
COOLING: AIR
FUEL: G
TRANSMISSION: HYDRO
STEERING: ZERO
STANDARD DECK: 62"
MSRP: $8,625

RETAIL PRICING

YEAR	HIGH	LOW
1989	$344	$258
1990	$381	$286
1991	$422	$317
1992	$468	$351

FST5

YEARS MFRD: 1994-1995
ENGINE: B&S
ENGINE HP: 15
FUEL: G
STEERING: STANDARD
STANDARD DECK: 42"
MSRP: $2,199

RETAIL PRICING

YEAR	HIGH	LOW
1994	$797	$598
1995	$828	$621

FST15

YEARS MFRD: 1994-1995
ENGINE: B&S
ENGINE HP: 15
COOLING: AIR
FUEL: G
TRANSMISSION: GEAR
STEERING: ZERO
STANDARD DECK: 42"
MSRP: $2,199

RETAIL PRICING

YEAR	HIGH	LOW
1994	$760	$570
1995	$828	$621

FST16

YEARS MFRD: 1996-1998
ENGINE: B&S
ENGINE HP: 16
COOLING: AIR
FUEL: G
STEERING: ZERO
STANDARD DECK: 42"
MSRP: $2,099

RETAIL PRICING

YEAR	HIGH	LOW
1996	$818	$614
1997	$830	$623
1998	$891	$668

GT180

YEARS MFRD: 1987-1993
ENGINE: B&S
ENGINE HP: 18
COOLING: AIR
FUEL: G
TRANSMISSION: GEAR
STEERING: STANDARD
STANDARD DECK: 46"
MSRP: $2,999

RETAIL PRICING

YEAR	HIGH	LOW
1989	$789	$592
1990	$868	$651
1991	$925	$694
1992	$997	$747
1993	$1,030	$772

GT185

YEARS MFRD: 1992-1997
ENGINE: B&S
ENGINE HP: 18
COOLING: AIR
FUEL: G
TRANSMISSION: HYDRO
STEERING: STANDARD
STANDARD DECK: 46"
MSRP: $2,999

RETAIL PRICING

YEAR	HIGH	LOW
1992	$202	$151
1993	$221	$166
1994	$249	$187
1995	$274	$206
1996	$302	$226
1997	$336	$252

GT205

YEARS MFRD: 1994-1999
SERIES: GT SERIES
ENGINE: B&S
ENGINE HP: 20
COOLING: AIR
FUEL: G
TRANSMISSION: HYDRO
STEERING: STANDARD
STANDARD DECK: 46"
MSRP: $2,799

RETAIL PRICING

YEAR	HIGH	LOW
1994	$270	$203
1995	$302	$226
1996	$332	$249
1997	$366	$274
1998	$409	$306
1999	$455	$341

GT225

YEARS MFRD: 1998-1999
SERIES: GT SERIES
ENGINE: B&S
ENGINE HP: 22
FUEL: G
TRANSMISSION: HYDRO
STEERING: STANDARD
STANDARD DECK: 50"
MSRP: $3,299

RETAIL PRICING

YEAR	HIGH	LOW
1998	$481	$361
1999	$534	$401

GT945H

YEARS MFRD: 2007-2007
CYLINDERS: 2
ENGINE HP: 26
FUEL: G
SPEEDS: VARIABLE
TRANSMISSION: HYDRO
STEERING: STANDARD
BLADE CLUTCH: ELECTRIC
STANDARD DECK: 54"
WEIGHT: 745 LBS.
MSRP: $2,899

RETAIL PRICING

YEAR	HIGH	LOW
2007	$1,661	$1,246

GT950H

YEARS MFRD: 2005-2005
ENGINE: TECUMSEH
CYLINDERS: 2
ENGINE HP: 24
COOLING: AIR
FUEL: G
SPEEDS: VARIABLE
TRANSMISSION: HYDRO
STEERING: STANDARD
BLADE CLUTCH: ELECTRIC
STANDARD DECK: 50"
MSRP: $2,799

RETAIL PRICING

YEAR	HIGH	LOW
2005	$793	$595

GT954H

YEARS MFRD: 2006-2007
ENGINE: B&S
ENGINE HP: 26
COOLING: AIR
FUEL: G
SPEEDS: VARIABLE
TRANSMISSION: HYDRO
STEERING: STANDARD
STANDARD DECK: 54"
MSRP: $2,899

OPTIONS

3BAG
42" SNOW THROWER
46" BLADE

RETAIL PRICING

YEAR	HIGH	LOW
2006	$900	$675
2007	$1,001	$750

GT1855

YEARS MFRD: 1983-1995
ENGINE: B&S
ENGINE HP: 18
COOLING: AIR
FUEL: G
TRANSMISSION: HYDRO
STEERING: STANDARD
STANDARD DECK: 50"
MSRP: $4,506

RETAIL PRICING

YEAR	HIGH	LOW
1987	$174	$131
1988	$195	$146
1989	$218	$163
1990	$240	$180
1991	$267	$200
1992	$294	$221
1993	$327	$245
1994	$362	$271
1995	$402	$301

GT2055

YEARS MFRD: 1996-2000
ENGINE: B&S
ENGINE HP: 20
COOLING: AIR
FUEL: G
TRANSMISSION: HYDRO
STEERING: STANDARD
STANDARD DECK: 50"
MSRP: $4,998

RETAIL PRICING

YEAR	HIGH	LOW
1996	$626	$470
1997	$691	$518
1998	$767	$576
1999	$852	$639
2000	$944	$708

GT2150

YEARS MFRD: 2000-2003
SERIES: GT SERIES
ENGINE: B&S
ENGINE HP: 21
COOLING: AIR
FUEL: G
TRANSMISSION: HYDRO
STEERING: STANDARD
STANDARD DECK: 46"
MSRP: $3,099

RETAIL PRICING

YEAR	HIGH	LOW
2000	$543	$407
2001	$600	$450
2002	$664	$498
2003	$737	$553

GT2550

YEARS MFRD: 2000-2004
SERIES: GT SERIES
ENGINE: B&S
ENGINE HP: 25
COOLING: AIR
FUEL: G
SPEEDS: VARIABLE
TRANSMISSION: HYDRO
STEERING: STANDARD
STANDARD DECK: 54"
MSRP: $3,399

RETAIL PRICING

YEAR	HIGH	LOW
2000	$588	$441
2001	$652	$489
2002	$722	$542
2003	$801	$600
2004	$886	$664

LGT160

YEARS MFRD 1983-1994
ENGINE .... B&S
ENGINE HP 16
COOLING .... AIR
FUEL .... G
TRANSMISSION .... GEAR
STEERING. .... STANDARD
STANDARD DECK .... 44"
MSRP. $2,650

RETAIL PRICING

YEAR	HIGH	LOW
1989	$712	$534
1994	$959	$720

LGT165

YEARS MFRD 1989-1992
ENGINE .... B&S
ENGINE HP 16
COOLING .... AIR
FUEL .... G
TRANSMISSION .... HYDRO
STEERING. .... STANDARD
STANDARD DECK .... 44"
MSRP. $2,900

RETAIL PRICING

YEAR	HIGH	LOW
1989	$789	$592
1990	$869	$652
1991	$926	$695
1992	$965	$724

LR927

YEARS MFRD 2003-2004
ENGINE .... B&S
ENGINE HP 9
COOLING .... AIR
FUEL .... G
SPEEDS .... VARIABLE
TRANSMISSION .... DISC
STEERING. .... STANDARD
STANDARD DECK .... 27"
MSRP. $1,499

RETAIL PRICING

YEAR	HIGH	LOW
2003	$179	$135
2004	$200	$150

LT15

YEARS MFRD 1994-2003
ENGINE .... B&S
ENGINE HP 15
COOLING .... AIR
FUEL .... G
TRANSMISSION .... GEAR
STEERING. .... STANDARD
STANDARD DECK .... 42"
MSRP. $1,199

RETAIL PRICING

YEAR	HIGH	LOW
1994	$96	$72
1995	$115	$86
1996	$125	$94
1997	$140	$105
1998	$157	$118
1999	$171	$128
2000	$191	$143
2001	$214	$160
2002	$236	$177
2003	$260	$195

LT16

YEARS MFRD 1995-1998
ENGINE .... B&S
ENGINE HP 16
COOLING .... AIR
FUEL .... G
TRANSMISSION .... GEAR
STEERING. .... STANDARD
STANDARD DECK .... 42"
MSRP. $1,599

RETAIL PRICING

YEAR	HIGH	LOW
1995	$134	$101
1996	$149	$112
1998	$183	$137

LT17

YEARS MFRD 1999-1999
SERIES .... LT SERIES
ENGINE .... B&S
ENGINE HP 17
FUEL .... G
STEERING. .... STANDARD
STANDARD DECK .... 38"
MSRP. $1,599

RETAIL PRICING

YEAR	HIGH	LOW
1999	$725	$544

LT18

YEARS MFRD 1999-1999
ENGINE .... B&S
ENGINE HP 18
FUEL .... G
STEERING. .... STANDARD
STANDARD DECK .... 46"
MSRP. $1,999

RETAIL PRICING

YEAR	HIGH	LOW
1999	$906	$679

LT46

YEARS MFRD 2008-2009
ENGINE .... KOHLER COURAGE
CYLINDERS. 1
ENGINE HP 20
COOLING .... AIR
FUEL .... G
SPEEDS .... VARIABLE
TRANSMISSION .... HYDRO
STEERING. .... STANDARD
BLADE CLUTCH .... MANUAL
STANDARD DECK .... 46"
MSRP. $1,399

RETAIL PRICING

YEAR	HIGH	LOW
2008	$598	$448
2009	$868	$651

LT50

YEARS MFRD 2008-2009
ENGINE .... KOHLER COURAGE
CYLINDERS. 2
ENGINE HP 22
COOLING .... AIR
FUEL .... G
SPEEDS .... VARIABLE
TRANSMISSION .... HYDRO
STEERING. .... STANDARD
BLADE CLUTCH .... ELECTRIC
STANDARD DECK .... 50"
MSRP. $1,699

RETAIL PRICING

YEAR	HIGH	LOW
2008	$763	$573
2009	$1,054	$790

LT54

YEARS MFRD 2008-2008
ENGINE .... KOHLER COURAGE
CYLINDERS. 2
ENGINE HP 23
COOLING .... AIR
FUEL .... G
SPEEDS .... VARIABLE
TRANSMISSION .... HYDRO

LT140

YEARS MFRD 1987-1991
ENGINE .... KOHLER
CYLINDERS. 2
ENGINE HP 14
COOLING .... AIR
FUEL .... G
SPEEDS 7/7
TRANSMISSION .... DISC
STEERING. .... STANDARD
WEIGHT .... 585 LBS.

LT155

YEARS MFRD 1996-1997
ENGINE .... B&S
ENGINE HP 15.5
COOLING .... AIR
FUEL .... G
TRANSMISSION .... HYDRO
STEERING. .... STANDARD
STANDARD DECK .... 42"
MSRP. $1,799

RETAIL PRICING

YEAR	HIGH	LOW
1996	$701	$526
1997	$728	$546

LT165

YEARS MFRD 1994-2003
ENGINE .... B&S
ENGINE HP 16
COOLING .... AIR
FUEL .... G
STEERING. .... STANDARD
STANDARD DECK .... 42"
MSRP. $1,499

RETAIL PRICING

YEAR	HIGH	LOW
1994	$130	$98
1995	$140	$105
1996	$157	$118
1997	$174	$131
1998	$195	$146
1999	$218	$163
2000	$240	$180
2001	$267	$200
2002	$294	$221
2003	$327	$245

LT175

YEARS MFRD 2004-2004
SERIES .... LT SERIES
ENGINE .... B&S
ENGINE HP 17.5
COOLING .... AIR
FUEL .... G
SPEEDS 8/1
TRANSMISSION .... DISC
STEERING. .... STANDARD
STANDARD DECK .... 42"
MSRP. $1,199

RETAIL PRICING

YEAR	HIGH	LOW
2004	$278	$209

LT185

YEARS MFRD 1998-1999
SERIES .... LT SERIES
ENGINE .... B&S
ENGINE HP 18
FUEL .... G
TRANSMISSION .... HYDRO
STEERING. .... STANDARD
STANDARD DECK .... 46"
MSRP. $2,099

RETAIL PRICING

YEAR	HIGH	LOW
1998	$232	$174
1999	$260	$195

LT542G

YEARS MFRD 2005-2007
ENGINE .... TECUMSEH
CYLINDERS. 1
ENGINE HP 17.5
COOLING .... AIR
FUEL .... G
SPEEDS .... VARIABLE
TRANSMISSION .... HYDRO
STEERING. .... STANDARD
BLADE CLUTCH .... MANUAL
STANDARD DECK .... 42"
WEIGHT .... 520 LBS.
MSRP. $1,299

WHITE OUTDOOR

OPTIONS

2 BAG
42" SNOW THROWER

RETAIL PRICING

YEAR	HIGH	LOW
2005	$336	$252
2006	$370	$278
2007	$412	$309

LT542H

YEARS MFRD 2005-2007
ENGINE . . . . .TECUMSEH
CYLINDERS. 1
ENGINE HP 18.5
COOLING . . . . .AIR
FUEL . . . . G
SPEEDS . . . . .VARIABLE
TRANSMISSION . . . . .HYDRO
STEERING. . . . . .STANDARD
HYDRAULIC . . . . YES
PTO . . . . YES
STANDARD DECK . . . . 42"
WEIGHT . . . . 545 LBS.
MSRP. $1,599

OPTIONS

2 BAG
42" SNOW THROWER

RETAIL PRICING

YEAR	HIGH	LOW
2005	$412	$309
2006	$458	$343
2007	$508	$381

LT546G

YEARS MFRD 2007-2007
ENGINE . . . . .B&S
CYLINDERS. 1
ENGINE HP 19.5
FUEL . . . . G
SPEEDS 7/1
TRANSMISSION . . . . BELT
STEERING. . . . . .STANDARD
STANDARD DECK . . . . 46"
WEIGHT . . . . 575 LBS.
MSRP. $1,399

RETAIL PRICING

YEAR	HIGH	LOW
2007	$443	$332

LT546H

YEARS MFRD 2007-2007
ENGINE . . . . .B&S
CYLINDERS. 1
ENGINE HP 20
COOLING . . . . .AIR
FUEL . . . . G
SPEEDS . . . . .VARIABLE
TRANSMISSION . . . . .HYDRO
STEERING. . . . . .STANDARD
BLADE CLUTCH . . . . MANUAL
STANDARD DECK . . . . 46"
WEIGHT . . . . 600 LBS.
MSRP. $1,699

OPTIONS

2 BAG
42" SNOW THROWER

RETAIL PRICING

YEAR	HIGH	LOW
2007	$538	$404

LT942H

YEARS MFRD 2005-2005
ENGINE . . . . .TECUMSEH
CYLINDERS. 2
ENGINE HP 22
COOLING . . . . .AIR
FUEL . . . . G
SPEEDS . . . . .VARIABLE
TRANSMISSION . . . . .HYDRO
STEERING. . . . . .STANDARD
BLADE CLUTCH . . . . MANUAL
STANDARD DECK . . . . 42"
MSRP. $1,799

RETAIL PRICING

YEAR	HIGH	LOW
2005	$458	$343

LT946G

YEARS MFRD 2006-2006
ENGINE . . . . .KOHLER
CYLINDERS. 2
ENGINE HP 23
COOLING . . . . .AIR
FUEL . . . . G
TRANSMISSION . . . . BELT
STEERING. . . . . .STANDARD
BLADE CLUTCH . . . . MANUAL
STANDARD DECK . . . . 46"
WEIGHT . . . . 620 LBS.
MSRP. $1,799

RETAIL PRICING

YEAR	HIGH	LOW
2006	$497	$373

LT946H

YEARS MFRD 2005-2005
ENGINE . . . . .TECUMSEH
CYLINDERS. 2
ENGINE HP 22
COOLING . . . . .AIR
FUEL . . . . G
SPEEDS . . . . .VARIABLE
TRANSMISSION . . . . .HYDRO
STEERING. . . . . .STANDARD
BLADE CLUTCH . . . . MANUAL
STANDARD DECK . . . . 46"
MSRP. $1,899

OPTIONS

2 BAG

RETAIL PRICING

YEAR	HIGH	LOW
2005	$481	$361

LT950H

YEARS MFRD 2006-2006
ENGINE . . . . .KOHLER
CYLINDERS. 2
ENGINE HP 23
COOLING . . . . .AIR
FUEL . . . . G
SPEEDS . . . . .VARIABLE
TRANSMISSION . . . . .HYDRO
STEERING. . . . . .STANDARD
BLADE CLUTCH . . . . .ELECTRIC
STANDARD DECK . . . . 50"
WEIGHT . . . . 625 LBS.
MSRP. $1,999

RETAIL PRICING

YEAR	HIGH	LOW
2006	$551	$413

LT1500

YEARS MFRD 2000-2003
SERIES. . . . . .LT SERIES
ENGINE . . . . .B&S
ENGINE HP 15.5
COOLING . . . . .AIR
FUEL . . . . G
TRANSMISSION . . . . GEAR
STEERING. . . . . .STANDARD
STANDARD DECK . . . . 42"
MSRP. $1,699

OPTIONS

2 BAG
40" SNOW THROWER
42" BLADE

RETAIL PRICING

YEAR	HIGH	LOW
2000	$270	$203
2001	$302	$226
2002	$336	$252
2003	$370	$278

LT1650

YEARS MFRD 2000-2003
SERIES. . . . . .LT SERIES
ENGINE . . . . .B&S
ENGINE HP 16.5
COOLING . . . . .AIR
FUEL . . . . G
SPEEDS . . . . .VARIABLE
TRANSMISSION . . . . .HYDRO
STEERING. . . . . .STANDARD
STANDARD DECK . . . . 42"
MSRP. $1,999

OPTIONS

42" BLADE
42" SNOW BLOWER
BAGGER

RETAIL PRICING

YEAR	HIGH	LOW
2000	$320	$240
2001	$356	$267
2002	$398	$298
2003	$439	$329

LT1700

YEARS MFRD 2010-2010
ENGINE . . . . .KOHLER
ENGINE HP 17
COOLING . . . . .AIR
SPEEDS 7/1
TRANSMISSION . . . . GEAR
STEERING. . . . . .STANDARD
STANDARD DECK . . . . 38"
MSRP. $1,215

OPTIONS

2 BAG
42" SNOW BLOWER

RETAIL PRICING

YEAR	HIGH	LOW
2010	$538	$404

LT1800

YEARS MFRD 2004-2004
SERIES. . . . . .LT SERIES
ENGINE . . . . .B&S
ENGINE HP 18
COOLING . . . . .AIR
FUEL . . . . G
SPEEDS . . . . .VARIABLE
TRANSMISSION . . . . DISC
STEERING. . . . . .STANDARD
STANDARD DECK . . . . 42"
MSRP. $1,399

OPTIONS

2 BAG
42" SNOW BLOWER
46" BLADE

RETAIL PRICING

YEAR	HIGH	LOW
2004	$149	$112

LT1850

YEARS MFRD 2000-2003
SERIES. . . . . .LT SERIES
ENGINE . . . . .B&S
ENGINE HP 18
COOLING . . . . .AIR
FUEL . . . . G
SPEEDS . . . . .VARIABLE
TRANSMISSION . . . . .HYDRO
STEERING. . . . . .STANDARD
STANDARD DECK . . . . 46"
MSRP. $2,299

OPTIONS

42" SNOW BLOWER
46" BLADE
BAGGER

RETAIL PRICING

YEAR	HIGH	LOW
2000	$366	$274
2001	$409	$306
2002	$455	$341
2003	$505	$379

LT1855

YEARS MFRD 2004-2004
ENGINE . . . . .B&S
ENGINE HP 18.5
COOLING . . . . .AIR
FUEL . . . . G
SPEEDS . . . . .VARIABLE
TRANSMISSION . . . . DISC
STEERING. . . . . .STANDARD
STANDARD DECK . . . . 42"
MSRP. $1,599

OPTIONS

2 BAG
42" SNOW BLOWER
46" BLADE

RETAIL PRICING

YEAR	HIGH	LOW
2004	$344	$258

LT1855H

YEARS MFRD	2004-2004
ENGINE	B&S
ENGINE HP	18.5
COOLING	AIR
FUEL	G
SPEEDS	VARIABLE
TRANSMISSION	HYDRO
STEERING	STANDARD
STANDARD DECK	42"
MSRP	$1,799

OPTIONS

2 BAG
42" SNOW BLOWER
46" BLADE

RETAIL PRICING

YEAR	HIGH	LOW
2004	$385	$289

LT2000

YEARS MFRD	2010-2010
ENGINE	KOHLER
ENGINE HP	17
COOLING	AIR
FUEL	G
SPEEDS	7/1
TRANSMISSION	GEAR
STEERING	STANDARD
STANDARD DECK	38"
MSRP	$1,390

OPTIONS

2 BAG
42" SNOW BLOWER

RETAIL PRICING

YEAR	HIGH	LOW
2010	$626	$470

LT2150

YEARS MFRD	2000-2000
SERIES	LT SERIES
ENGINE	B&S
ENGINE HP	21
COOLING	AIR
FUEL	G
SPEEDS	VARIABLE
TRANSMISSION	HYDRO
STEERING	STANDARD
STANDARD DECK	46"
MSRP	$2,399

RETAIL PRICING

YEAR	HIGH	LOW
2000	$332	$249

LT2200

YEARS MFRD	2004-2004
ENGINE	WHITE OHV
CYLINDERS	2
ENGINE HP	22
COOLING	AIR
FUEL	G
SPEEDS	VARIABLE
TRANSMISSION	DISC
STEERING	STANDARD
BLADE CLUTCH	ELECTRIC
STANDARD DECK	46"
MSRP	$1,899

OPTIONS

2 BAG
42" SNOW BLOWER
46" BLADE

RETAIL PRICING

YEAR	HIGH	LOW
2004	$488	$366

RD1750

YEARS MFRD	2003-2004
ENGINE	B&S
CYLINDERS	2
ENGINE HP	18
COOLING	AIR
FUEL	G
SPEEDS	VARIABLE
TRANSMISSION	HYDRO
STEERING	STANDARD
STANDARD DECK	41"
MSRP	$3,199

OPTIONS

42" SNOW BLOWER
46" BLADE

RETAIL PRICING

YEAR	HIGH	LOW
2003	$706	$529
2004	$787	$590

Z16

YEARS MFRD	1997-1999
SERIES	Z SERIES
ENGINE	B&S
ENGINE HP	16
COOLING	AIR
FUEL	G
TRANSMISSION	DUAL HYDRO
STEERING	ZERO
STANDARD DECK	42"
MSRP	$3,799

RETAIL PRICING

YEAR	HIGH	LOW
1997	$468	$351
1998	$523	$392
1999	$580	$435

Z180

YEARS MFRD	1997-1997
ENGINE	B&S
ENGINE HP	18
FUEL	G
STEERING	ZERO
STANDARD DECK	48"
MSRP	$4,699

RETAIL PRICING

YEAR	HIGH	LOW
1997	$592	$444

Z180L

YEARS MFRD	1997-1998
ENGINE	KAWASAKI
ENGINE HP	18
COOLING	LIQUID
FUEL	G
TRANSMISSION	DUAL HYDRO
STEERING	ZERO
STANDARD DECK	54"
MSRP	$5,599

RETAIL PRICING

YEAR	HIGH	LOW
1997	$713	$535
1998	$792	$594

Z200

YEARS MFRD	1997-1999
SERIES	Z SERIES
ENGINE	B&S
ENGINE HP	20
FUEL	G
TRANSMISSION	DUAL HYDRO
STEERING	ZERO
STANDARD DECK	48"
MSRP	$4,899

RETAIL PRICING

YEAR	HIGH	LOW
1997	$638	$478
1998	$706	$529
1999	$787	$590

Z220

YEARS MFRD	1998-1999
SERIES	Z SERIES
ENGINE	B&S
ENGINE HP	22
FUEL	G
TRANSMISSION	HYDRO
STEERING	ZERO
STANDARD DECK	54"
MSRP	$5,099

RETAIL PRICING

YEAR	HIGH	LOW
1998	$717	$538
1999	$798	$598

Z1800L

YEARS MFRD	1997-1998
ENGINE	KAWASAKI
ENGINE HP	18
COOLING	LIQUID
FUEL	G
STEERING	STANDARD
STANDARD DECK	54"
MSRP	$5,599

RETAIL PRICING

YEAR	HIGH	LOW
1997	$2,265	$1,699
1998	$2,377	$1,782

ZT17

YEARS MFRD	2004-2004
ENGINE	B&S
ENGINE HP	17
COOLING	AIR
FUEL	G
SPEEDS	VARIABLE
TRANSMISSION	HYDRO
STEERING	ZERO
BLADE CLUTCH	ELECTRIC
STANDARD DECK	42"
MSRP	$2,899

RETAIL PRICING

YEAR	HIGH	LOW
2004	$1,702	$1,277

ZT22

YEARS MFRD	2004-2004
ENGINE	B&S
CYLINDERS	2
ENGINE HP	22
COOLING	AIR
FUEL	G
SPEEDS	VARIABLE
TRANSMISSION	HYDRO
STEERING	ZERO
BLADE CLUTCH	ELECTRIC
STANDARD DECK	50"
MSRP	$3,299

RETAIL PRICING

YEAR	HIGH	LOW
2004	$1,939	$1,455

ZT42

YEARS MFRD	2005-2008
ENGINE	B&S INTEK
CYLINDERS	1
ENGINE HP	18
COOLING	AIR
FUEL	G
SPEEDS	VARIABLE
TRANSMISSION	HYDRO
STEERING	ZERO
BLADE CLUTCH	ELECTRIC
STANDARD DECK	42"
WEIGHT	480 LBS.
MSRP	$2,499

OPTIONS

2 BAG

RETAIL PRICING

YEAR	HIGH	LOW
2005	$709	$531
2006	$787	$590
2007	$875	$656
2008	$974	$731

ZT50

YEARS MFRD	2005-2008
ENGINE	B&S INTEK
CYLINDERS	2
ENGINE HP	23
COOLING	AIR
FUEL	G
SPEEDS	VARIABLE

TRANSMISSION .... HYDRO
STEERING .... ZERO
BLADE CLUTCH .... ELECTRIC
STANDARD DECK .... 50"
WEIGHT .... 527 LBS.
MSRP $3,299

OPTIONS

2 BAG

RETAIL PRICING

YEAR	HIGH	LOW
2005	$939	$704
2006	$1,041	$781
2007	$1,157	$868
2008	$1,282	$961

ZT54

YEARS MFRD 2008-2008
ENGINE .... B&S ELS
CYLINDERS 2
ENGINE HP 26
COOLING .... AIR
FUEL .... G
SPEEDS .... VARIABLE
TRANSMISSION .... HYDRO
STEERING .... ZERO
BLADE CLUTCH .... ELECTRIC
STANDARD DECK .... 54"
MSRP $3,499

OPTIONS

2 BAG

RETAIL PRICING

YEAR	HIGH	LOW
2008	$1,363	$1,022

ZT1850

YEARS MFRD 2000-2000
SERIES .... ZT SERIES
ENGINE .... B&S
ENGINE HP 18
FUEL .... G
TRANSMISSION ..... DUAL HYDRO
STEERING .... ZERO
STANDARD DECK .... 44"
MSRP $4,399

RETAIL PRICING

YEAR	HIGH	LOW
2000	$706	$529

ZT2150

YEARS MFRD 2000-2000
SERIES .... ZT SERIES
ENGINE .... B&S
ENGINE HP 21
FUEL .... G
TRANSMISSION ..... DUAL HYDRO
STEERING .... ZERO
STANDARD DECK .... 48"
MSRP $4,999

RETAIL PRICING

YEAR	HIGH	LOW
2000	$801	$600

ZT2250

YEARS MFRD 2000-2000
SERIES .... ZT SERIES
ENGINE .... B&S
ENGINE HP 22
FUEL .... G
TRANSMISSION ..... DUAL HYDRO
STEERING .... ZERO
STANDARD DECK .... 54"
MSRP $5,399

RETAIL PRICING

YEAR	HIGH	LOW
2000	$866	$650

ZTT1850

YEARS MFRD 2001-2003
ENGINE .... B&S
ENGINE HP 18
FUEL .... G
TRANSMISSION .... HYDRO
STEERING .... ZERO
STANDARD DECK .... 42"
MSRP $3,599

RETAIL PRICING

YEAR	HIGH	LOW
2001	$1,783	$1,337
2002	$1,833	$1,374
2003	$1,986	$1,490

ZTT2150

YEARS MFRD 2001-2003
ENGINE .... B&S
ENGINE HP 21
FUEL .... G
TRANSMISSION .... HYDRO
STEERING .... ZERO
STANDARD DECK .... 46"
MSRP $3,999

RETAIL PRICING

YEAR	HIGH	LOW
2001	$1,981	$1,485
2002	$2,034	$1,526
2003	$2,206	$1,654

WOODS

CZ1736K

YEARS MFRD 2007-2011
ENGINE .... KAWASAKI KAI
CYLINDERS 2
CID 585CC
ENGINE HP 17
COOLING .... AIR
FUEL .... G
SPEEDS .... VARIABLE
TRANSMISSION .... HYDRO
STEERING .... ZERO
BLADE CLUTCH .... ELECTRIC
STANDARD DECK .... 36"
WEIGHT .... 705 LBS.
MSRP $5,759

RETAIL PRICING

YEAR	HIGH	LOW
2007	$3,222	$2,417
2008	$3,834	$2,875
2009	$3,946	$2,960
2010	$4,037	$3,027
2011	$4,118	$3,088

CZ1942K

YEARS MFRD 2007-2011
ENGINE .... KAWASAKI KAI
CYLINDERS 2
CID 585CC
ENGINE HP 19
COOLING .... AIR
FUEL .... G
SPEEDS .... VARIABLE
TRANSMISSION .... HYDRO
STEERING .... ZERO
BLADE CLUTCH .... ELECTRIC
STANDARD DECK .... 42"
WEIGHT .... 733 LBS.
MSRP $5,899

RETAIL PRICING

YEAR	HIGH	LOW
2007	$3,389	$2,542
2008	$3,824	$2,868
2009	$3,980	$2,985
2010	$4,136	$3,102
2011	$4,207	$3,155

CZ1948K

YEARS MFRD 2007-2011
ENGINE .... KAWASAKI KAI
CYLINDERS 2
CID 585CC
ENGINE HP 19
COOLING .... AIR
FUEL .... G
SPEEDS .... VARIABLE
TRANSMISSION .... HYDRO
STEERING .... ZERO
BLADE CLUTCH .... ELECTRIC
STANDARD DECK .... 48"
MSRP $6,179

RETAIL PRICING

YEAR	HIGH	LOW
2007	$3,638	$2,728
2008	$4,161	$3,121
2009	$4,198	$3,149
2010	$4,331	$3,248
2011	$4,384	$3,288

CZ1952K

YEARS MFRD 2007-2011
ENGINE .... KAWASAKI FH601V
CYLINDERS 2
ENGINE HP 19
COOLING .... AIR
FUEL .... G
SPEEDS .... VARIABLE
TRANSMISSION .... HYDRO
STEERING .... ZERO
BLADE CLUTCH .... ELECTRIC
STANDARD DECK .... 52"
WEIGHT .... 585 LBS.
MSRP $6,650

RETAIL PRICING

YEAR	HIGH	LOW
2007	$4,147	$3,111
2008	$4,563	$3,422
2009	$4,586	$3,440
2010	$4,661	$3,496
2011	$4,760	$3,570

CZ2048K

YEARS MFRD 2012-2012
ENGINE .... KAWASAKI
ENGINE HP 20
COOLING .... AIR
FUEL .... G
SPEEDS .... VARIABLE
TRANSMISSION ..... DUAL HYDRO
STEERING .... ZERO
STANDARD DECK .... 48"
MSRP $7,133

OPTIONS

8 BU BAG
ROPS
SUS SEAT

RETAIL PRICING

YEAR	HIGH	LOW
2012	$4,284	$3,213

CZ2136B

YEARS MFRD 2007-2007
ENGINE .... B&S INTEK
CYLINDERS 2
ENGINE HP 21
COOLING .... AIR
FUEL .... G
SPEEDS .... VARIABLE
TRANSMISSION .... HYDRO
STEERING .... ZERO
STANDARD DECK .... 36"
MSRP $4,649

RETAIL PRICING

YEAR	HIGH	LOW
2007	$2,913	$2,184

CZ2252K

YEARS MFRD 2012-2012
ENGINE .... KAWASAKI
ENGINE HP 22
COOLING .... AIR
FUEL .... G
SPEEDS .... VARIABLE
TRANSMISSION ..... DUAL HYDRO
STEERING .... ZERO
STANDARD DECK .... 52"
MSRP $7,483

OPTIONS

8 BU BAG
ROPS
SUS SEAT

RETAIL PRICING

YEAR	HIGH	LOW
2012	$4,495	$3,371

CZ2361V

YEARS MFRD 2012-2012
ENGINE . . . . KAWASAKI
ENGINE HP 23
COOLING . . . . AIR
FUEL . . . . G
SPEEDS . . . . VARIABLE
TRANSMISSION . . . . HYDRO
STEERING . . . . ZERO
STANDARD DECK . . . . 61"
MSRP $8,521

OPTIONS

8 BU BAG
ROPS
SUS SEAT

RETAIL PRICING

YEAR	HIGH	LOW
2012	$5,118	$3,838

CZ2461K

YEARS MFRD 2012-2012
ENGINE . . . . KAWASAKI
ENGINE HP 24
COOLING . . . . AIR
FUEL . . . . G
SPEEDS . . . . VARIABLE
TRANSMISSION . . . . . DUAL HYDRO
STEERING . . . . ZERO
STANDARD DECK . . . . 61"
MSRP $8,861

OPTIONS

8 BU BAG
ROPS
SUS SEAT

RETAIL PRICING

YEAR	HIGH	LOW
2012	$5,321	$3,991

CZR1942B

YEARS MFRD 2009-2009
SERIES . . . . CZR SERIES
ENGINE . . . . BRIGGS ELS
CYLINDERS 2
ENGINE HP 22
COOLING . . . . AIR
FUEL . . . . G
SPEEDS . . . . VARIABLE
TRANSMISSION . . . . HYDRO
STEERING . . . . ZERO
BLADE CLUTCH . . . . ELECTRIC
WEIGHT . . . . 733 LBS.

CZR1952B

YEARS MFRD 2009-2009
SERIES . . . . CZR SERIES
ENGINE . . . . BRIGGS ELS
CYLINDERS 2
ENGINE HP 26
COOLING . . . . AIR
FUEL . . . . G
SPEEDS . . . . VARIABLE
TRANSMISSION . . . . HYDRO
STEERING . . . . ZERO
BLADE CLUTCH . . . . ELECTRIC
WEIGHT . . . . 840 LBS.

CZR2242B

YEARS MFRD 2012-2012
ENGINE . . . . B&S ELS
CYLINDERS 2
CID 721CC
ENGINE HP 22
COOLING . . . . AIR
FUEL . . . . G
SPEEDS . . . . VARIABLE
TRANSMISSION . . . . . DUAL HYDRO
STEERING . . . . ZERO
BLADE CLUTCH . . . . ELECTRIC
STANDARD DECK . . . . 42"
WEIGHT . . . . 733 LBS.
MSRP $6,095

OPTIONS

8 BU BAG
ROPS
SUS SEAT

RETAIL PRICING

YEAR	HIGH	LOW
2012	$3,660	$2,745

CZR2652B

YEARS MFRD 2012-2012
ENGINE . . . . B&S ELS
CYLINDERS 2
ENGINE HP 26
COOLING . . . . AIR
FUEL . . . . G
SPEEDS . . . . VARIABLE
TRANSMISSION . . . . . DUAL HYDRO
STEERING . . . . ZERO
BLADE CLUTCH . . . . ELECTRIC
STANDARD DECK . . . . 52"
WEIGHT . . . . 840 LBS.
MSRP $6,445

OPTIONS

8 BU BAG
ROPS
SUS SEAT

RETAIL PRICING

YEAR	HIGH	LOW
2012	$3,871	$2,903

F21D

YEARS MFRD 2002-2003
SERIES . . . . F SERIES
ENGINE . . . . KUBOTA
ENGINE HP 21
COOLING . . . . LIQUID
FUEL . . . . D
SPEEDS . . . . VARIABLE
TRANSMISSION . . . . HYDRO
STEERING . . . . ZERO
STANDARD DECK . . . . 52"
WEIGHT . . . . 1,000 LBS.
MSRP $12,613

OPTIONS

50" SNOW THROWER
72" DECK
BAGGER

RETAIL PRICING

YEAR	HIGH	LOW
2002	$3,191	$2,393
2003	$3,537	$2,653

F23

YEARS MFRD 2002-2003
SERIES . . . . F SERIES
ENGINE . . . . B&S
CYLINDERS 2
ENGINE HP 23
COOLING . . . . AIR
FUEL . . . . G
SPEEDS . . . . VARIABLE
TRANSMISSION . . . . HYDRO
STEERING . . . . ZERO
STANDARD DECK . . . . 52"
WEIGHT . . . . 950 LBS.
MSRP $9,985

OPTIONS

50" SNOW THROWER
72" DECK
BAGGER

RETAIL PRICING

YEAR	HIGH	LOW
2002	$2,374	$1,780
2003	$2,709	$2,032

F25

YEARS MFRD 2002-2003
SERIES . . . . F SERIES
ENGINE . . . . KOHLER
CYLINDERS 2
ENGINE HP 25
COOLING . . . . AIR
FUEL . . . . G
SPEEDS . . . . VARIABLE
TRANSMISSION . . . . HYDRO
STEERING . . . . ZERO
STANDARD DECK . . . . 52"
WEIGHT . . . . 950 LBS.
MSRP $10,491

OPTIONS

50" SNOW THROWER
72" DECK
BAGGER

RETAIL PRICING

YEAR	HIGH	LOW
2002	$2,494	$1,871
2003	$2,799	$2,099

F25L

YEARS MFRD 2002-2003
SERIES . . . . F SERIES
ENGINE . . . . KUBOTA
ENGINE HP 25
COOLING . . . . LIQUID
FUEL . . . . G
SPEEDS . . . . VARIABLE
TRANSMISSION . . . . HYDRO
STEERING . . . . ZERO
STANDARD DECK . . . . 52"
WEIGHT . . . . 1,000 LBS.
MSRP $12,489

OPTIONS

50" SNOW THROWER
72" DECK
BAGGER

RETAIL PRICING

YEAR	HIGH	LOW
2002	$2,969	$2,227
2003	$3,295	$2,471

FE21B

YEARS MFRD 2007-2011
ENGINE . . . . VANGUARD OHV
CYLINDERS 2
ENGINE HP 21
FUEL . . . . G
SPEEDS . . . . VARIABLE
TRANSMISSION . . . . HYDRO
STEERING . . . . ZERO
STANDARD DECK . . . . 52"
MSRP $9,199

RETAIL PRICING

YEAR	HIGH	LOW
2007	$5,487	$4,115
2008	$6,344	$4,758
2009	$6,398	$4,799
2010	$6,448	$4,836
2011	$6,607	$4,955

FZ21D

YEARS MFRD 2007-2007
ENGINE . . . . KUBOTA
CYLINDERS 3
ENGINE HP 21
FUEL . . . . D
SPEEDS . . . . VARIABLE
TRANSMISSION . . . . HYDRO
STEERING . . . . ZERO
STANDARD DECK . . . . 61"
MSRP $11,918

RETAIL PRICING

YEAR	HIGH	LOW
2007	$7,470	$5,602

FZ22-2

YEARS MFRD 2017-2020
ENGINE . . . . KAWASAKI OHV
CYLINDERS 2
ENGINE HP 22
FUEL . . . . G
TRANSMISSION . . . . HYDRO
STEERING . . . . ZERO
STANDARD DECK . . . . 54"

FZ22K

YEARS MFRD 2013-2018
ENGINE . . . . KAWASAKI FS651V
CYLINDERS 2
ENGINE HP 22
COOLING . . . . AIR
FUEL . . . . G
SPEEDS . . . . VARIABLE
TRANSMISSION . . . . HYDRO
STEERING . . . . ZERO
STANDARD DECK . . . . 54"
MSRP $12,195

RETAIL PRICING

YEAR	HIGH	LOW
2013	$4,801	$3,601
2014	$6,265	$4,699
2015	$6,843	$5,133
2016	$7,775	$5,831
2017	$9,201	$6,901
2018	$10,195	$7,646

WOODS

FZ23B

YEARS MFRD 2006-2015
ENGINE . . . . VANGUARD OHV
CYLINDERS. 2
ENGINE HP 23
COOLING . . . . AIR
FUEL . . . . G
SPEEDS . . . . VARIABLE
TRANSMISSION . . . . HYDRO
STEERING. . . . . ZERO
STANDARD DECK . . . . 54"
MSRP. $11,995

RETAIL PRICING

YEAR	HIGH	LOW
2006	$1,694	$1,271
2007	$1,768	$1,326
2008	$1,902	$1,427
2009	$2,303	$1,727
2010	$2,736	$2,052
2011	$3,305	$2,478
2012	$4,004	$3,003
2013	$5,172	$3,879
2014	$7,198	$5,399
2015	$8,425	$6,319

FZ23BT

YEARS MFRD 2012-2012
ENGINE . . . . VANGUARD
ENGINE HP 23
COOLING . . . . AIR
FUEL . . . . G
SPEEDS . . . . VARIABLE
TRANSMISSION . . . . HYDRO
STEERING. . . . . ZERO
STANDARD DECK . . . . 54"
MSRP. $12,000

OPTIONS

61" DECK

RETAIL PRICING

YEAR	HIGH	LOW
2012	$7,220	$5,415

FZ25D

YEARS MFRD 2008-2020
ENGINE . . . . KUBOTA
CYLINDERS. 3
ENGINE HP 25
COOLING . . . . LIQUID
FUEL . . . . D
SPEEDS . . . . VARIABLE
TRANSMISSION . . . . HYDRO
STEERING. . . . . ZERO
STANDARD DECK . . . . 61"

RETAIL PRICING

YEAR	HIGH	LOW
2008	$1,182	$1,787
2009	$2,692	$2,018
2010	$3,092	$2,318
2011	$3,934	$2,950
2012	$4,769	$3,577
2013	$5,980	$4,485
2014	$7,224	$5,418
2015	$8,341	$6,256
2016	$8,514	$6,385
2017	$10,587	$7,940
2018	$12,017	$9,016
2019	$13,608	$9,887
2020	$14,733	$10,955

FZ27

YEARS MFRD 2019-2020
ENGINE . . . . KOHLER OHV
ENGINE HP 27
COOLING . . . . AIR
FUEL . . . . G
TRANSMISSION . . . . . DUAL HYDRO
STEERING. . . . . ZERO
STANDARD DECK . . . . 61"
WEIGHT . . . . 1,704 LBS.

OPTIONS

54" DECK

FZ28K

YEARS MFRD 2006-2018
ENGINE . . . . KAWASAKI OHV
CYLINDERS. 2
ENGINE HP 28
FUEL . . . . G
SPEEDS . . . . VARIABLE
TRANSMISSION . . . . HYDRO
STEERING. . . . . ZERO
STANDARD DECK . . . . 61"
MSRP. $13,295

RETAIL PRICING

YEAR	HIGH	LOW
2006	$1,700	$1,275
2007	$1,779	$1,334
2008	$1,944	$1,458
2009	$2,306	$1,729
2010	$2,708	$2,031
2011	$3,432	$2,574
2012	$4,164	$3,123
2013	$5,234	$3,926
2014	$6,949	$5,212
2015	$8,146	$6,109
2016	$8,627	$6,470
2017	$10,042	$7,532
2018	$11,082	$8,311

M1950K

YEARS MFRD 2003-2003
SERIES. . . . . M SERIES
ENGINE . . . . KAWASAKI V-TWIN
CYLINDERS. 2
ENGINE HP 19
COOLING . . . . AIR
FUEL . . . . G
SPEEDS . . . . VARIABLE
TRANSMISSION . . . . HYDRO
STEERING. . . . . ZERO
STANDARD DECK . . . . 50"
WEIGHT . . . . 1,080 LBS.
MSRP. $8,235

OPTIONS

BAGGER
ROPS

RETAIL PRICING

YEAR	HIGH	LOW
2003	$2,193	$1,645

M1952K

YEARS MFRD 2006-2006
SERIES. . . . . M-SERIES
ENGINE . . . . KAWASAKI
CYLINDERS. 2
ENGINE HP 19
COOLING . . . . AIR
FUEL . . . . G
SPEEDS . . . . VARIABLE
TRANSMISSION . . . . HYDRO
STEERING. . . . . ZERO
BLADE CLUTCH . . . . ELECTRIC
WEIGHT . . . . 1,080 LBS.

M2050

YEARS MFRD 2002-2003
SERIES. . . . . M SERIES
ENGINE . . . . B&S
ENGINE HP 20
COOLING . . . . AIR
FUEL . . . . G
SPEEDS . . . . VARIABLE
TRANSMISSION . . . . HYDRO
STEERING. . . . . ZERO
STANDARD DECK . . . . 50"
WEIGHT . . . . 997 LBS.
MSRP. $8,235

OPTIONS

BAGGER
ROPS

RETAIL PRICING

YEAR	HIGH	LOW
2002	$1,979	$1,484
2003	$2,193	$1,645

M2250

YEARS MFRD 2000-2001
SERIES. . . . . M SERIES
ENGINE . . . . KOHLER
ENGINE HP 22
FUEL . . . . G
SPEEDS 0-9
TRANSMISSION . . . . HYDRO
STEERING. . . . . ZERO
STANDARD DECK . . . . 50"
WEIGHT . . . . 1,100 LBS.
MSRP. $9,152

OPTIONS

BAGGER
ROPS

RETAIL PRICING

YEAR	HIGH	LOW
2000	$1,694	$1,271
2001	$1,882	$1,411

M2560

YEARS MFRD 2000-2003
SERIES. . . . . M SERIES
ENGINE . . KOHLER COMMAND PRO
ENGINE HP 25
COOLING . . . . AIR
FUEL . . . . G
SPEEDS . . . . VARIABLE
TRANSMISSION . . . . HYDRO
STEERING. . . . . ZERO
STANDARD DECK . . . . 60"
WEIGHT . . . . 1,125 LBS.
MSRP. $9,568

OPTIONS

BAGGER
ROPS

RETAIL PRICING

YEAR	HIGH	LOW
2000	$1,869	$1,402
2001	$2,070	$1,552
2002	$2,298	$1,724
2003	$2,548	$1,911

M2560K

YEARS MFRD 2002-2003
SERIES. . . . . M SERIES
ENGINE . . . . . . KAWASAKI V-TWIN
CYLINDERS. 2
ENGINE HP 25
COOLING . . . . AIR
FUEL . . . . G
SPEEDS . . . . VARIABLE
TRANSMISSION . . . . HYDRO
STEERING. . . . . ZERO
STANDARD DECK . . . . 60"
WEIGHT . . . . 1,125 LBS.
MSRP. $9,568

OPTIONS

BAGGER
ROPS

RETAIL PRICING

YEAR	HIGH	LOW
2002	$2,298	$1,724
2003	$2,536	$1,902

M2760

YEARS MFRD 2002-2003
SERIES. . . . . M SERIES
ENGINE . . KOHLER COMMAND PRO
ENGINE HP 27
COOLING . . . . AIR
FUEL . . . . G
SPEEDS . . . . VARIABLE
TRANSMISSION . . . . HYDRO
STEERING. . . . . ZERO
STANDARD DECK . . . . 60"
WEIGHT . . . . 1,125 LBS.
MSRP. $9,855

OPTIONS

BAGGER
ROPS

RETAIL PRICING

YEAR	HIGH	LOW
2002	$2,365	$1,774
2003	$2,623	$1,968

M2760K

YEARS MFRD 2006-2006
ENGINE . . KOHLER COMMAND PRO
CYLINDERS. 2
ENGINE HP 27
COOLING . . . . AIR
FUEL . . . . G

SPEEDS	VARIABLE
TRANSMISSION	HYDRO
STEERING	ZERO
BLADE CLUTCH	ELECTRIC
WEIGHT	1,125 LBS.

ME1952K

YEARS MFRD	2008-2011
SERIES	ME SERIES
ENGINE	KAWASAKI
CYLINDERS	2
ENGINE HP	19
COOLING	AIR
FUEL	G
SPEEDS	VARIABLE
TRANSMISSION	HYDRO
STEERING	ZERO
BLADE CLUTCH	ELECTRIC
STANDARD DECK	52"
WEIGHT	1,038 LBS.
MSRP	$9,100

RETAIL PRICING

YEAR	HIGH	LOW
2008	$3,356	$2,517
2009	$3,457	$2,593
2010	$4,055	$3,041
2011	$5,795	$4,346

ME2052B

YEARS MFRD	2006-2008
ENGINE	B&S VANGUARD
CYLINDERS	2
ENGINE HP	20
COOLING	AIR
FUEL	G
SPEEDS	VARIABLE
TRANSMISSION	HYDRO
STEERING	ZERO
STANDARD DECK	52"
WEIGHT	1,357 LBS.
MSRP	$8,383

RETAIL PRICING

YEAR	HIGH	LOW
2007	$5,004	$3,753
2008	$5,740	$4,305

ME2661B

YEARS MFRD	2009-2011
SERIES	ME SERIES
ENGINE	BRIGGS ELS
CYLINDERS	2
ENGINE HP	26
COOLING	AIR
FUEL	G
SPEEDS	VARIABLE
TRANSMISSION	HYDRO
STEERING	ZERO
BLADE CLUTCH	ELECTRIC
WEIGHT	1,102 LBS.

MZ1952K

YEARS MFRD	2009-2009
SERIES	MZ SERIES
ENGINE	KAWASAKI
CYLINDERS	2
ENGINE HP	25
COOLING	AIR
FUEL	G
SPEEDS	VARIABLE
TRANSMISSION	HYDRO
STEERING	ZERO
BLADE CLUTCH	ELECTRIC
WEIGHT	1,045 LBS.

MZ1952K

YEARS MFRD	2006-2011
ENGINE	KAWASAKI OHV
CYLINDERS	2
ENGINE HP	19
COOLING	AIR
FUEL	G
SPEEDS	VARIABLE
TRANSMISSION	HYDRO
STEERING	ZERO
BLADE CLUTCH	ELECTRIC
STANDARD DECK	52"
WEIGHT	1,405 LBS.
MSRP	$9,089

RETAIL PRICING

YEAR	HIGH	LOW
2007	$5,635	$4,226
2008	$5,642	$4,231
2009	$5,660	$4,245
2010	$6,371	$4,778
2011	$6,539	$4,904

MZ2061YD

YEARS MFRD	2006-2007
ENGINE	YANMAR
CYLINDERS	2
ENGINE HP	20
COOLING	AIR
FUEL	G
SPEEDS	VARIABLE
TRANSMISSION	HYDRO
STEERING	ZERO
BLADE CLUTCH	ELECTRIC
STANDARD DECK	61"
WEIGHT	1,630 LBS.
MSRP	$13,454

RETAIL PRICING

YEAR	HIGH	LOW
2007	$8,430	$6,322

MZ2252K

YEARS MFRD	2012-2012
ENGINE	KAWASAKI
ENGINE HP	22
COOLING	AIR
FUEL	G
SPEEDS	VARIABLE
TRANSMISSION	DUAL HYDRO
STEERING	ZERO
STANDARD DECK	52"
MSRP	$11,214

OPTIONS

12 BU BAG
DUMP BOX
ROPS

RETAIL PRICING

YEAR	HIGH	LOW
2012	$6,740	$5,055

MZ2552K

YEARS MFRD	2011-2014
SERIES	MZ SERIES
ENGINE	KAWASAKI
CYLINDERS	2
ENGINE HP	25
COOLING	AIR
FUEL	G
SPEEDS	VARIABLE
TRANSMISSION	HYDRO
STEERING	ZERO
STANDARD DECK	52"
WEIGHT	1,045 LBS.
MSRP	$11,295

RETAIL PRICING

YEAR	HIGH	LOW
2011	$3,747	$2,810
2012	$4,680	$3,510
2013	$5,657	$4,242
2014	$7,142	$5,357

MZ2561K

YEARS MFRD	2007-2011
ENGINE	KAWASAKI
CYLINDERS	2
ENGINE HP	25
FUEL	G
SPEEDS	VARIABLE
TRANSMISSION	HYDRO
STEERING	ZERO
STANDARD DECK	61"
WEIGHT	1,438 LBS.
MSRP	$10,499

RETAIL PRICING

YEAR	HIGH	LOW
2007	$6,453	$4,840
2008	$6,638	$4,978
2009	$6,743	$5,058
2010	$7,359	$5,519
2011	$7,435	$5,576

MZ2652G

YEARS MFRD	2006-2010
ENGINE	GENERAC GARDIAN
CYLINDERS	2
ENGINE HP	26
COOLING	AIR
FUEL	G
SPEEDS	VARIABLE
TRANSMISSION	HYDRO
STEERING	ZERO
BLADE CLUTCH	ELECTRIC
STANDARD DECK	52"
WEIGHT	1,371 LBS.
MSRP	$10,599

RETAIL PRICING

YEAR	HIGH	LOW
2007	$5,808	$4,356
2008	$6,385	$4,789
2009	$6,419	$4,814
2010	$7,295	$5,471

MZ2661K

YEARS MFRD	2011-2014
ENGINE	KAWASAKI
ENGINE HP	26
COOLING	AIR
FUEL	G
SPEEDS	VARIABLE
TRANSMISSION	HYDRO
STEERING	ZERO
STANDARD DECK	61"
MSRP	$11,956

OPTIONS

12 BU BAG
DUMP BOX
ROPS

RETAIL PRICING

YEAR	HIGH	LOW
2011	$3,987	$2,990
2012	$4,989	$3,742
2013	$6,006	$4,505
2014	$8,142	$6,106

MZ2761

YEARS MFRD	2006-2011
ENGINE	KOHLER
CYLINDERS	2
ENGINE HP	27
COOLING	AIR
FUEL	G
SPEEDS	VARIABLE
TRANSMISSION	HYDRO
STEERING	ZERO
BLADE CLUTCH	ELECTRIC
STANDARD DECK	61"
WEIGHT	1,438 LBS.
MSRP	$11,299

RETAIL PRICING

YEAR	HIGH	LOW
2007	$6,731	$5,048
2009	$7,643	$5,732
2010	$7,920	$5,940
2011	$8,172	$6,129

MZ3361G

YEARS MFRD	2006-2010
ENGINE	GENERAC GUARDIAN
CYLINDERS	2
ENGINE HP	33
COOLING	AIR
FUEL	G
SPEEDS	VARIABLE
TRANSMISSION	HYDRO
STEERING	ZERO
BLADE CLUTCH	ELECTRIC
STANDARD DECK	61"
WEIGHT	1,406 LBS.
MSRP	$11,252

RETAIL PRICING

YEAR	HIGH	LOW
2007	$6,714	$5,035
2008	$7,044	$5,283
2009	$7,115	$5,336
2010	$7,746	$5,809

WOODS

MZ3372G

YEARS MFRD 2007-2010
ENGINE . . . . . GENERAC GUARDIAN
CYLINDERS. 2
ENGINE HP 33
FUEL . . . . G
SPEEDS . . . . VARIABLE
TRANSMISSION . . . . .HYDRO
STEERING. . . . . ZERO
STANDARD DECK . . . . 72"
WEIGHT . . . . 1,517 LBS.
MSRP. $11,899

RETAIL PRICING

YEAR	HIGH	LOW
2007	$7,099	$5,324
2008	$7,685	$5,764
2009	$7,932	$5,949
2010	$8,191	$6,143

MZ3761K

YEARS MFRD 2012-2012
SERIES. . . . . MZ SERIES
ENGINE . . . . KAWASAKI
CYLINDERS. 2
ENGINE HP 37
COOLING . . . . AIR
FUEL . . . . G
SPEEDS . . . . VARIABLE
TRANSMISSION . . . . . DUAL HYDRO
STEERING. . . . . ZERO
BLADE CLUTCH . . . . ELECTRIC
STANDARD DECK . . . . 61"
WEIGHT . . . . 1,148 LBS.
MSRP. $13,845

OPTIONS

12 BU BAG
DUMP BOX
ROPS

RETAIL PRICING

YEAR	HIGH	LOW
2012	$8,317	$6,238

MZ3772K

YEARS MFRD 2012-2012
SERIES. . . . . MZ SERIES
ENGINE . . . . KAWASAKI
CYLINDERS. 2
ENGINE HP 37
COOLING . . . . AIR
FUEL . . . . G
SPEEDS . . . . VARIABLE
TRANSMISSION . . . . .HYDRO
STEERING. . . . . ZERO
BLADE CLUTCH . . . . ELECTRIC
STANDARD DECK . . . . 72"
WEIGHT . . . . 1,386 LBS.
MSRP. $14,445

OPTIONS

12BU BAG
DUMP BOX
ROPS

RETAIL PRICING

YEAR	HIGH	LOW
2012	$8,688	$6,516

R1540

YEARS MFRD 2000-2000
ENGINE . . . . B&S
ENGINE HP 15
FUEL . . . . G
TRANSMISSION . . . . .HYDRO
STEERING. . . . . ZERO
STANDARD DECK . . . . 40"
MSRP. $4,635

OPTIONS

BAGGER

RETAIL PRICING

YEAR	HIGH	LOW
2000	$817	$613

R2048

YEARS MFRD 2001-2003
ENGINE . . . . B&S
ENGINE HP 20
COOLING . . . . AIR
FUEL . . . . G
SPEEDS 0-5.5
TRANSMISSION . . . . .HYDRO
STEERING. . . . . ZERO
STANDARD DECK . . . . 48"
WEIGHT . . . . 625 LBS.
MSRP. $5,183

RETAIL PRICING

YEAR	HIGH	LOW
2001	$1,123	$842
2002	$1,244	$933
2003	$1,380	$1,035

RZ1848B

YEARS MFRD 2006-2006
ENGINE . . . . B&S ELS
CYLINDERS. 1
ENGINE HP 17.5
COOLING . . . . AIR
FUEL . . . . G
SPEEDS . . . . VARIABLE
TRANSMISSION . . . . .HYDRO
STEERING. . . . . ZERO

RZ2052B

YEARS MFRD 2006-2006
ENGINE . . . . B&S INTEK
CYLINDERS. 2
ENGINE HP 20
COOLING . . . . AIR
FUEL . . . . G
SPEEDS . . . . VARIABLE
TRANSMISSION . . . . .HYDRO
STEERING. . . . . ZERO

RZ2552BE

YEARS MFRD 2006-2006
ENGINE . . . . B&S INTEK
CYLINDERS. 2
ENGINE HP 25
COOLING . . . . AIR
FUEL . . . . G
SPEEDS . . . . VARIABLE
TRANSMISSION . . . . .HYDRO
STEERING. . . . . ZERO

1850

YEARS MFRD 1985-1990
ENGINE . . . . B&S
ENGINE HP 18
COOLING . . . . AIR
FUEL . . . . G
TRANSMISSION . . . . .HYDRO
STEERING. . . . . ZERO
STANDARD DECK . . . . 44"
MSRP. $5,160

OPTIONS

52" DECK
61" DECK

RETAIL PRICING

YEAR	HIGH	LOW
1985	$309	$232
1986	$343	$257
1987	$379	$284
1988	$426	$320
1989	$471	$354
1990	$522	$392

2850

YEARS MFRD 1991-1993
ENGINE . . . . B&S
ENGINE HP 18
COOLING . . . . AIR
FUEL . . . . G
TRANSMISSION . . . . .HYDRO
STEERING. . . . . ZERO
STANDARD DECK . . . . 48"
MSRP. $6,275

RETAIL PRICING

YEAR	HIGH	LOW
1991	$583	$437
1992	$647	$485
1993	$718	$539

2855

YEARS MFRD 1991-1993
ENGINE . . . . KOHLER
ENGINE HP 18
COOLING . . . . AIR
FUEL . . . . G
TRANSMISSION . . . . .HYDRO
STEERING. . . . . ZERO
STANDARD DECK . . . . 48"
MSRP. $6,515

RETAIL PRICING

YEAR	HIGH	LOW
1991	$605	$453
1992	$672	$504
1993	$746	$559

2860

YEARS MFRD 1991-1993
ENGINE . . . . KUBOTA
ENGINE HP 16.5
COOLING . . . . LIQUID
FUEL . . . . D
TRANSMISSION . . . . .HYDRO
STEERING. . . . . ZERO
STANDARD DECK . . . . 48"
MSRP. $8,060

RETAIL PRICING

YEAR	HIGH	LOW
1991	$751	$563
1992	$830	$623
1993	$926	$695

3150

YEARS MFRD 1991-1993
ENGINE . . . . KUBOTA
ENGINE HP 21
COOLING . . . . LIQUID
FUEL . . . . G
TRANSMISSION . . . . .HYDRO
STEERING. . . . . ZERO
STANDARD DECK . . . . 48"
MSRP. $7,800

RETAIL PRICING

YEAR	HIGH	LOW
1991	$725	$544
1992	$806	$604
1993	$893	$670

5160

YEARS MFRD 1993-1994
ENGINE . . . . B&S
ENGINE HP 16
COOLING . . . . AIR
FUEL . . . . G
SPEEDS 0-5.5
TRANSMISSION . . . . .HYDRO
STEERING. . . . . ZERO
STANDARD DECK . . . . 52"
WEIGHT . . . . 710 LBS.
MSRP. $4,750

RETAIL PRICING

YEAR	HIGH	LOW
1993	$563	$422
1994	$626	$470

5180

YEARS MFRD 1993-1994
ENGINE . . . . B&S
ENGINE HP 18
COOLING . . . . AIR
FUEL . . . . G
SPEEDS 0-7
TRANSMISSION . . . . .HYDRO
STEERING. . . . . ZERO
STANDARD DECK . . . . 48"
WEIGHT . . . . 810 LBS.
MSRP. $7,110

RETAIL PRICING

YEAR	HIGH	LOW
1993	$846	$634
1994	$938	$703

5182

YEARS MFRD 1993-1994
ENGINE . . . . KOHLER
ENGINE HP 18

FUEL G
SPEEDS 0-7
TRANSMISSION HYDRO
STEERING STANDARD
WEIGHT 795 LBS.
MSRP $6,055

RETAIL PRICING

YEAR	HIGH	LOW
1993	$2,155	$1,616
1994	$2,398	$1,799

5200

YEARS MFRD 1993-1994
ENGINE KOHLER
ENGINE HP 20
COOLING AIR
FUEL G
SPEEDS 0-7
TRANSMISSION HYDRO
STEERING ZERO
STANDARD DECK 48"
WEIGHT 800 LBS.
MSRP $7,560

RETAIL PRICING

YEAR	HIGH	LOW
1993	$902	$676
1994	$1,005	$753

5210

YEARS MFRD 1993-1994
ENGINE KUBOTA
ENGINE HP 21
COOLING LIQUID
FUEL G
SPEEDS 0-7
TRANSMISSION HYDRO
STEERING ZERO
STANDARD DECK 48"
WEIGHT 940 LBS.
MSRP $8,830

RETAIL PRICING

YEAR	HIGH	LOW
1993	$1,052	$789
1994	$1,158	$869

5215

YEARS MFRD 1993-1994
ENGINE KUBOTA
ENGINE HP 21
COOLING LIQUID
FUEL D
SPEEDS 0-7
TRANSMISSION HYDRO
STEERING ZERO
STANDARD DECK 48"
WEIGHT 945 LBS.
MSRP $9,555

RETAIL PRICING

YEAR	HIGH	LOW
1993	$1,139	$854
1994	$1,260	$945

5250

YEARS MFRD 1993-1994
ENGINE KUBOTA
ENGINE HP 24.5
COOLING LIQUID
FUEL G
SPEEDS 0-7
TRANSMISSION HYDRO
STEERING ZERO
STANDARD DECK 48"
WEIGHT 940 LBS.
MSRP $9,275

RETAIL PRICING

YEAR	HIGH	LOW
1993	$1,104	$828
1994	$1,227	$920

6160

YEARS MFRD 1996-2000
ENGINE B&S
ENGINE HP 16
COOLING AIR
FUEL G
TRANSMISSION HYDRO
STEERING ZERO
STANDARD DECK 44"
WEIGHT 710 LBS.
MSRP $7,180

SERIAL NUMBERS

YEAR	BEGINNING NO.
1996	554254
1997	580179

RETAIL PRICING

YEAR	HIGH	LOW
1996	$959	$720
1997	$1,063	$797
1998	$1,172	$879
1999	$1,301	$976
2000	$1,443	$1,082

6170

YEARS MFRD 2000-2003
ENGINE B&S
CYLINDERS 2
ENGINE HP 18
COOLING AIR
FUEL G
SPEEDS VARIABLE
TRANSMISSION HYDRO
STEERING ZERO
STANDARD DECK 48"
WEIGHT 1,064 LBS.
MSRP $7,488

OPTIONS

48" SNOW BLOWER
BAGGER

RETAIL PRICING

YEAR	HIGH	LOW
2000	$1,494	$1,120
2001	$1,656	$1,242
2002	$1,837	$1,377
2003	$2,040	$1,530

6180

YEARS MFRD 1996-2002
ENGINE B&S
ENGINE HP 18
COOLING AIR
FUEL G
SPEEDS 0-7
TRANSMISSION HYDRO
STEERING ZERO
STANDARD DECK 48"
WEIGHT 815 LBS.
MSRP $8,618

SERIAL NUMBERS

YEAR	BEGINNING NO.
1996	554254
1997	580179

RETAIL PRICING

YEAR	HIGH	LOW
1996	$1,104	$828
1997	$1,227	$920
1998	$1,368	$1,026
1999	$1,518	$1,139
2000	$1,672	$1,254
2001	$1,856	$1,392
2002	$2,070	$1,552

6182

YEARS MFRD 1996-2000
ENGINE KOHLER
ENGINE HP 18
COOLING AIR
FUEL G
SPEEDS 0-7
TRANSMISSION HYDRO
STEERING ZERO
STANDARD DECK 48"
WEIGHT 800 LBS.
MSRP $8,650

OPTIONS

BAGGER
CAB

SERIAL NUMBERS

YEAR	BEGINNING NO.
1996	554254
1997	580179

RETAIL PRICING

YEAR	HIGH	LOW
1996	$1,172	$879
1997	$1,301	$976
1998	$1,443	$1,082
1999	$1,601	$1,201
2000	$1,777	$1,333

6200

YEARS MFRD 1996-2002
ENGINE KOHLER
ENGINE HP 20
COOLING AIR
FUEL G
SPEEDS 0-7
TRANSMISSION HYDRO
STEERING ZERO
STANDARD DECK 52"
WEIGHT 800 LBS.
MSRP $9,249

OPTIONS

61" DECK
CAB

SERIAL NUMBERS

YEAR	BEGINNING NO.
1996	554254
1997	580179

RETAIL PRICING

YEAR	HIGH	LOW
1996	$1,205	$904
1997	$1,315	$986
1998	$1,460	$1,095
1999	$1,618	$1,213
2000	$1,793	$1,345
2001	$1,989	$1,492
2002	$2,232	$1,674

6210

YEARS MFRD 1996-2002
ENGINE KAWASAKI
ENGINE HP 20
COOLING LIQUID
FUEL G
SPEEDS 0-7
TRANSMISSION HYDRO
STEERING ZERO
STANDARD DECK 52"
WEIGHT 800 LBS.
MSRP $10,142

OPTIONS

61" DECK
BAGGER
CAB

SERIAL NUMBERS

YEAR	BEGINNING NO.
1996	554254
1997	580179

RETAIL PRICING

YEAR	HIGH	LOW
1996	$1,301	$976
1997	$1,443	$1,082
1998	$1,598	$1,199
1999	$1,773	$1,330
2000	$1,970	$1,477
2001	$2,181	$1,636
2002	$2,424	$1,818

6215

YEARS MFRD 1996-2002
ENGINE KUBOTA
ENGINE HP 21
COOLING LIQUID
FUEL D
SPEEDS 0-7
TRANSMISSION HYDRO
STEERING ZERO
STANDARD DECK 52"
WEIGHT 945 LBS.
MSRP $11,687

OPTIONS

61" DECK
BAGGER
CAB

SERIAL NUMBERS

YEAR	BEGINNING NO.
1996	554254
1997	580179

WOODS

RETAIL PRICING

YEAR	HIGH	LOW
1996	$1,498	$1,124
1997	$1,660	$1,245
1998	$1,843	$1,383
1999	$2,044	$1,533
2000	$2,306	$1,729
2001	$2,516	$1,887

AVG. AUCTION PRICING

LOW	HIGH	AVG
$1,444	$2,516	$2,142

6225

YEARS MFRD 1998-2002
ENGINE . . . . KOHLER
ENGINE HP 25
FUEL . . . . G
SPEEDS 0-7
TRANSMISSION . . . . .HYDRO
STEERING. . . . . .ZERO
STANDARD DECK . . . . 61"
WEIGHT . . . . 955 LBS.
MSRP. $10,111

OPTIONS

48" SNOW BLOWER
CAB

RETAIL PRICING

YEAR	HIGH	LOW
1998	$1,594	$1,196
1999	$1,768	$1,326
2000	$1,960	$1,470
2001	$2,177	$1,632
2002	$2,416	$1,812

6250

YEARS MFRD 1996-2002
ENGINE . . . . KUBOTA
ENGINE HP 24.5
COOLING . . . . LIQUID
FUEL . . . . G
SPEEDS 0-7
TRANSMISSION . . . . .HYDRO
STEERING. . . . . .ZERO
STANDARD DECK . . . . 61"
WEIGHT . . . . 940 LBS.
MSRP. $11,589

OPTIONS

72" DECK
BAGGER

SERIAL NUMBERS

YEAR	BEGINNING NO.
1996	554254
1997	580179

RETAIL PRICING

YEAR	HIGH	LOW
1996	$1,484	$1,113
1997	$1,647	$1,236
1998	$1,827	$1,370
1999	$2,027	$1,520
2000	$2,249	$1,687
2001	$2,494	$1,871
2002	$2,770	$2,078

WRIGHT

SENTAR 48

YEARS MFRD 2009-2009
SERIES. . . . . SENTAR SERIES
ENGINE . . . . KAWASAKI
CYLINDERS. 2
ENGINE HP 19
COOLING . . . . .AIR
FUEL . . . . G
SPEEDS . . . . .VARIABLE
TRANSMISSION . . . . .HYDRO
STEERING. . . . . .ZERO
BLADE CLUTCH . . . . .ELECTRIC
WEIGHT . . . . 905 LBS.

OPTIONS

KAWASAKI 23HP

SENTAR 52

YEARS MFRD 2009-2009
SERIES. . . . . SENTAR SERIES
ENGINE . . . . KAWASAKI
CYLINDERS. 2
ENGINE HP 23
COOLING . . . . .AIR
FUEL . . . . G
SPEEDS . . . . .VARIABLE
TRANSMISSION . . . . .HYDRO
STEERING. . . . . .ZERO
BLADE CLUTCH . . . . .ELECTRIC
WEIGHT . . . . 905 LBS.

OPTIONS

KAWASAKI 25HP

SENTAR 61

YEARS MFRD 2009-2009
SERIES. . . . . SENTAR SERIES
ENGINE . . . . KAWASAKI
CYLINDERS. 2
ENGINE HP 23
COOLING . . . . .AIR
FUEL . . . . G
SPEEDS . . . . .VARIABLE
TRANSMISSION . . . . .HYDRO
STEERING. . . . . .ZERO
BLADE CLUTCH . . . . .ELECTRIC
WEIGHT . . . . 905 LBS.

OPTIONS

KAWASAKI 25HP

SENTAR SPORT42

YEARS MFRD 2009-2009
SERIES. . . . .SENTAR SPORT SERIES
ENGINE . . . . KAWASAKI
CYLINDERS. 2
ENGINE HP 17
COOLING . . . . .AIR
FUEL . . . . G
SPEEDS . . . . .VARIABLE
TRANSMISSION . . . . .HYDRO
STEERING. . . . . .ZERO
BLADE CLUTCH . . . . .ELECTRIC
WEIGHT . . . . 720 LBS.

OPTIONS

KAWASAKI 19HP

SPORT RH

YEARS MFRD 2013-2015
ENGINE . . . . KAWASAKI
CYLINDERS. 2
ENGINE HP 20
COOLING . . . . .AIR
FUEL . . . . G
SPEEDS . . . . .VARIABLE
TRANSMISSION . . . . .HYDRO
STEERING. . . . . .ZERO
STANDARD DECK . . . . 36"
WEIGHT . . . . 710 LBS.
MSRP. $8,159

OPTIONS

48" DECK
52" DECK

RETAIL PRICING

YEAR	HIGH	LOW
2013	$3,299	$2,474
2014	$3,957	$2,967
2015	$4,397	$3,298

STANDER

YEARS MFRD 2012-2012
ENGINE . . . . KAWASAKI
CYLINDERS. 2
ENGINE HP 18
COOLING . . . . .AIR
FUEL . . . . G
SPEEDS . . . . .VARIABLE
TRANSMISSION . . . . .HYDRO
STEERING. . . . . .STANDARD
WEIGHT . . . . 820 LBS.

OPTIONS

KAWASAKI 20HP
KAWASAKI 24HP

STANDER RH

YEARS MFRD 2010-2011
ENGINE . . . . KAWASAKI
CYLINDERS. 2
ENGINE HP 18
COOLING . . . . .AIR
FUEL . . . . G
SPEEDS . . . . .VARIABLE
TRANSMISSION . . . . .HYDRO
STEERING. . . . . .ZERO
STANDARD DECK . . . . 36"
WEIGHT . . . . 710 LBS.
MSRP. $7,489

OPTIONS

KAWASAKI 20HP

RETAIL PRICING

YEAR	HIGH	LOW
2010	$2,519	$1,889
2011	$3,083	$2,312

STANDER X

YEARS MFRD 2012-2013
ENGINE . . . . KAWASAKI
CYLINDERS. 2
ENGINE HP 24
COOLING . . . . .AIR
FUEL . . . . G
SPEEDS . . . . .VARIABLE
TRANSMISSION . . . . .HYDRO
STEERING. . . . . .ZERO
STANDARD DECK . . . . 48"
WEIGHT . . . . 816 LBS.
MSRP. $9,514

OPTIONS

KAWASAKI 26HP

RETAIL PRICING

YEAR	HIGH	LOW
2012	$4,323	$3,242
2013	$6,076	$4,557

WRIGHT Z

YEARS MFRD 2012-2012
ENGINE . . . . KAWASAKI
CYLINDERS. 2
ENGINE HP 27
COOLING . . . . .AIR
FUEL . . . . G
SPEEDS . . . . .VARIABLE
TRANSMISSION . . . . .HYDRO
STEERING. . . . . .ZERO
WEIGHT . . . . 940 LBS.

OPTIONS

KAWASAKI 31HP

WS32FFS541R

YEARS MFRD 2018-2020
SERIES. . . . STANDER GEN 1 SERIES
ENGINE . . . . . . .KAWASAKI FS541R
CID 603CC
ENGINE HP 15
FUEL . . . . G
SPEEDS . . . . .VARIABLE
TRANSMISSION . . . . .HYDRO
STEERING. . . . . .ZERO
STANDARD DECK . . . . 32"
WEIGHT . . . . 639 LBS.
MSRP. $7,260

WS32FFS600E

YEARS MFRD 2018-2020
SERIES. . . . STANDER GEN 1 SERIES
ENGINE . . . . . . .KAWASAKI FS600E
CID 603CC
ENGINE HP 18.5
FUEL . . . . G
SPEEDS . . . . .VARIABLE
TRANSMISSION . . . . .HYDRO
STEERING. . . . . .ZERO
STANDARD DECK . . . . 32"
WEIGHT . . . . 639 LBS.
MSRP. $7,610

WS32FS541R

YEARS MFRD........ 2013-2019
SERIES......... STANDER SERIES
ENGINE............. KAWASAKI
ENGINE HP................. 18
COOLING.................. AIR
FUEL...................... G
SPEEDS............. VARIABLE
TRANSMISSION.......... HYDRO
STEERING................ ZERO
STANDARD DECK........... 32"
WEIGHT............. 639 LBS.
MSRP................ $6,950

RETAIL PRICING

YEAR	HIGH	LOW
2013	$2,747	$2,060
2014	$3,194	$2,396
2015	$3,641	$2,731
2016	$4,427	$3,320
2017	$5,074	$3,806
2018	$5,865	$4,398
2019	$6,580	$4,935

WS32FS600RE

YEARS MFRD........ 2013-2019
SERIES......... STANDER SERIES
ENGINE............. KAWASAKI
ENGINE HP................. 20
COOLING.................. AIR
FUEL...................... G
SPEEDS............. VARIABLE
TRANSMISSION.......... HYDRO
STEERING................ ZERO
STANDARD DECK........... 32"
WEIGHT............. 639 LBS.
MSRP................ $7,480

RETAIL PRICING

YEAR	HIGH	LOW
2013	$3,086	$2,314
2014	$3,587	$2,690
2015	$4,080	$3,060
2016	$4,846	$3,635
2017	$5,668	$4,251
2018	$6,507	$4,880
2019	$7,174	$5,381

WS32ZT710E

YEARS MFRD........ 2016-2018
SERIES......... STANDER SERIES
ENGINE............... KOHLER
ENGINE HP................. 20
FUEL...................... G
SPEEDS............. VARIABLE
TRANSMISSION.......... HYDRO
STEERING................ ZERO
STANDARD DECK........... 32"
WEIGHT............. 650 LBS.
MSRP................ $7,590

RETAIL PRICING

YEAR	HIGH	LOW
2016	$5,010	$3,758
2017	$5,440	$4,080
2018	$6,004	$4,503

WS36FFS541R

YEARS MFRD........ 2018-2020
SERIES.... STANDER GEN 1 SERIES
ENGINE....... KAWASAKI FS541R
CID.................. 603CC
ENGINE HP................. 15
FUEL...................... G
SPEEDS............. VARIABLE
TRANSMISSION.......... HYDRO
STEERING................ ZERO
STANDARD DECK........... 36"
WEIGHT............. 650 LBS.
MSRP................ $7,380

WS36FFS600E

YEARS MFRD........ 2018-2020
SERIES.... STANDER GEN 1 SERIES
ENGINE....... KAWASAKI FS600E
CID.................. 603CC
ENGINE HP............... 18.5
FUEL...................... G
SPEEDS............. VARIABLE
TRANSMISSION.......... HYDRO
STEERING................ ZERO
STANDARD DECK........... 36"
WEIGHT............. 650 LBS.
MSRP................ $7,730

WS36FS541R

YEARS MFRD........ 2013-2019
SERIES......... STANDER SERIES
ENGINE............. KAWASAKI
ENGINE HP................. 18
COOLING.................. AIR
FUEL...................... G
SPEEDS............. VARIABLE
TRANSMISSION.......... HYDRO
STEERING................ ZERO
STANDARD DECK........... 36"
WEIGHT............. 650 LBS.
MSRP................ $7,020

RETAIL PRICING

YEAR	HIGH	LOW
2013	$2,820	$2,115
2014	$3,277	$2,457
2015	$3,724	$2,793
2016	$4,472	$3,354
2017	$4,938	$3,704
2018	$5,860	$4,395
2019	$6,711	$5,034

WS36FS600RE

YEARS MFRD........ 2013-2019
SERIES......... STANDER SERIES
ENGINE............. KAWASAKI
ENGINE HP................. 20
COOLING.................. AIR
FUEL...................... G
SPEEDS............. VARIABLE
TRANSMISSION.......... HYDRO
STEERING................ ZERO
STANDARD DECK........... 36"
WEIGHT............. 650 LBS.
MSRP................ $7,550

RETAIL PRICING

YEAR	HIGH	LOW
2013	$3,432	$2,574
2014	$3,961	$2,971
2015	$4,336	$3,252
2016	$5,029	$3,772
2017	$5,504	$4,128
2018	$6,363	$4,772
2019	$7,166	$5,375

WS36ZT710E

YEARS MFRD........ 2016-2018
SERIES......... STANDER SERIES
ENGINE............... KOHLER
ENGINE HP................. 20
FUEL...................... G
SPEEDS............. VARIABLE
TRANSMISSION.......... HYDRO
STEERING................ ZERO
STANDARD DECK........... 36"
WEIGHT............. 661 LBS.
MSRP................ $7,660

RETAIL PRICING

YEAR	HIGH	LOW
2016	$5,057	$3,792
2017	$5,504	$4,128
2018	$6,438	$4,828

WS42FS600RE

YEARS MFRD........ 2013-2014
SERIES......... STANDER SERIES
ENGINE............. KAWASAKI
COOLING.................. AIR
FUEL...................... G
SPEEDS............. VARIABLE
TRANSMISSION.......... HYDRO
STEERING................ ZERO
STANDARD DECK........... 42"
MSRP................ $7,674

RETAIL PRICING

YEAR	HIGH	LOW
2013	$3,560	$2,670
2014	$4,248	$3,186

WS48

YEARS MFRD........ 2009-2009
SERIES......... STANDER SERIES
ENGINE............. KAWASAKI
CYLINDERS.................. 2
ENGINE HP................. 17
COOLING.................. AIR
FUEL...................... G
SPEEDS............. VARIABLE
TRANSMISSION.......... HYDRO
STEERING................ ZERO
BLADE CLUTCH........ ELECTRIC

OPTIONS

KAWASAKI 19HP
KAWASAKI 23HP

WS48FS600RE

YEARS MFRD........ 2013-2019
SERIES......... STANDER SERIES
ENGINE............. KAWASAKI
ENGINE HP............... 18.5
COOLING.................. AIR
FUEL...................... G
SPEEDS............. VARIABLE
TRANSMISSION.......... HYDRO
STEERING................ ZERO
STANDARD DECK........... 48"
WEIGHT............. 849 LBS.
MSRP................ $8,770

RETAIL PRICING

YEAR	HIGH	LOW
2013	$3,860	$2,895
2014	$4,462	$3,347
2015	$4,846	$3,635
2016	$5,813	$4,360
2017	$6,608	$4,956
2018	$7,307	$5,480
2019	$8,303	$6,227

WS48FX600RE

YEARS MFRD........ 2013-2019
SERIES......... STANDER SERIES
ENGINE............. KAWASAKI
ENGINE HP................. 19
COOLING.................. AIR
FUEL...................... G
SPEEDS............. VARIABLE
TRANSMISSION.......... HYDRO
STEERING................ ZERO
STANDARD DECK........... 48"
WEIGHT............. 849 LBS.
MSRP................ $9,020

RETAIL PRICING

YEAR	HIGH	LOW
2013	$3,970	$2,978
2014	$4,590	$3,443
2015	$4,983	$3,737
2016	$5,996	$4,497
2017	$6,709	$5,031
2018	$7,606	$5,704
2019	$8,487	$6,365

WS48FX691E

YEARS MFRD........ 2013-2017
SERIES......... STANDER SERIES
ENGINE............. KAWASAKI
ENGINE HP................. 24
COOLING.................. AIR
FUEL...................... G
SPEEDS............. VARIABLE
TRANSMISSION.......... HYDRO
STEERING................ ZERO
STANDARD DECK........... 48"
MSRP................ $8,809

RETAIL PRICING

YEAR	HIGH	LOW
2013	$3,861	$2,895
2014	$4,490	$3,368
2015	$5,065	$3,799
2016	$6,006	$4,505
2017	$6,818	$5,114

WS48FX730E

YEARS MFRD........ 2018-2020
SERIES......... STANDER SERIES
ENGINE............. KAWASAKI

WRIGHT

ENGINE HP 23.5
SPEEDS . . . . VARIABLE
TRANSMISSION . . . . HYDRO
STEERING. . . . . ZERO
STANDARD DECK . . . . 48"
WEIGHT . . . . 849 LBS.
MSRP. $9,640

WS52

YEARS MFRD 2009-2009
SERIES. . . . . STANDER SERIES
ENGINE . . . . KAWASAKI
CYLINDERS. 2
ENGINE HP 17
COOLING . . . . AIR
FUEL . . . . G
SPEEDS . . . . VARIABLE
TRANSMISSION . . . . HYDRO
STEERING. . . . . ZERO
BLADE CLUTCH . . . . ELECTRIC
WEIGHT . . . . 785 LBS.

OPTIONS

KAWASAKI 19HP
KAWASAKI 23HP
KAWASAKI 25HP

WS52FX600E

YEARS MFRD 2013-2017
SERIES. . . . . STANDER SERIES
ENGINE . . . . KAWASAKI
ENGINE HP 20
COOLING . . . . AIR
FUEL . . . . G
SPEEDS . . . . VARIABLE
TRANSMISSION . . . . HYDRO
STEERING. . . . . ZERO
STANDARD DECK . . . . 52"
MSRP. $8,584

RETAIL PRICING

YEAR	HIGH	LOW
2013	$3,998	$2,999
2014	$4,618	$3,464
2015	$5,010	$3,758
2016	$6,069	$4,552
2017	$6,790	$5,093

WS52FX691E

YEARS MFRD 2013-2017
SERIES. . . . . STANDER SERIES
ENGINE . . . . KAWASAKI
ENGINE HP 24
COOLING . . . . AIR
FUEL . . . . G
SPEEDS . . . . VARIABLE
TRANSMISSION . . . . HYDRO
STEERING. . . . . ZERO
STANDARD DECK . . . . 52"
MSRP. $8,849

RETAIL PRICING

YEAR	HIGH	LOW
2013	$4,117	$3,088
2014	$4,755	$3,566
2015	$5,165	$3,874
2016	$6,233	$4,675
2017	$6,790	$5,093

WS52FX730E

YEARS MFRD 2013-2020
SERIES. . . . . STANDER SERIES
ENGINE . . . . KAWASAKI
ENGINE HP 23.5
COOLING . . . . AIR
FUEL . . . . G
SPEEDS . . . . VARIABLE
TRANSMISSION . . . . HYDRO
STEERING. . . . . ZERO
STANDARD DECK . . . . 52"
MSRP. $9,740

RETAIL PRICING

YEAR	HIGH	LOW
2013	$4,298	$3,224
2014	$4,954	$3,716
2015	$5,384	$4,038
2016	$6,270	$4,702
2017	$7,100	$5,325
2018	$7,873	$5,905
2019	$8,644	$6,676
2020	$9,379	$7,159

WS61

YEARS MFRD 2009-2009
SERIES. . . . . STANDER SERIES
ENGINE . . . . KAWASAKI
CYLINDERS. 2
ENGINE HP 23
COOLING . . . . AIR
FUEL . . . . G
SPEEDS . . . . VARIABLE
TRANSMISSION . . . . HYDRO
STEERING. . . . . ZERO
BLADE CLUTCH . . . . ELECTRIC
WEIGHT . . . . 835 LBS.

OPTIONS

KOHLER 25HP

WS61FX691E

YEARS MFRD 2013-2017
SERIES. . . . . STANDER SERIES
ENGINE . . . . KAWASAKI
ENGINE HP 24
COOLING . . . . AIR
FUEL . . . . G
SPEEDS . . . . VARIABLE
TRANSMISSION . . . . HYDRO
STEERING. . . . . ZERO
STANDARD DECK . . . . 61"
MSRP. $9,219

RETAIL PRICING

YEAR	HIGH	LOW
2013	$4,289	$3,217
2014	$4,956	$3,717
2015	$5,384	$4,038
2016	$6,444	$4,833
2017	$7,402	$5,552

WS61FX730E

YEARS MFRD 2013-2020
SERIES. . . . . STANDER SERIES
ENGINE . . . . KAWASAKI
ENGINE HP 23.5
COOLING . . . . AIR
FUEL . . . . G
SPEEDS . . . . VARIABLE
TRANSMISSION . . . . HYDRO
STEERING. . . . . ZERO
STANDARD DECK . . . . 61"
MSRP. $10,040

RETAIL PRICING

YEAR	HIGH	LOW
2013	$4,481	$3,360
2014	$5,165	$3,874
2015	$5,613	$4,208
2016	$6,570	$4,927
2017	$7,446	$5,584
2018	$8,389	$6,292
2019	$9,069	$7,145
2020	$9,927	$7,887

WS3215KAW

YEARS MFRD 2006-2011
SERIES. . . . . STANDER SERIES
ENGINE . . . . KAWASAKI
ENGINE HP 15
COOLING . . . . AIR
FUEL . . . . G
SPEEDS . . . . VARIABLE
TRANSMISSION . . . . HYDRO
STEERING. . . . . ZERO
STANDARD DECK . . . . 32"
MSRP. $5,954

RETAIL PRICING

YEAR	HIGH	LOW
2006	$1,076	$807
2007	$1,297	$973
2008	$1,600	$1,200
2009	$1,995	$1,496
2010	$2,440	$1,830
2011	$2,989	$2,241

WS3217 KAWRE

YEARS MFRD 2006-2011
SERIES. . . . . STANDER SERIES
ENGINE . . . . KAWASAKI
ENGINE HP 17
COOLING . . . . AIR
FUEL . . . . G
SPEEDS . . . . VARIABLE
TRANSMISSION . . . . HYDRO
STEERING. . . . . ZERO
STANDARD DECK . . . . 32"
MSRP. $6,674

RETAIL PRICING

YEAR	HIGH	LOW
2006	$1,203	$902
2007	$1,465	$1,099
2008	$1,795	$1,347
2009	$2,232	$1,674
2010	$2,742	$2,057
2011	$3,349	$2,512

WS3615KAW

YEARS MFRD 2006-2011
SERIES. . . . . STANDER SERIES
ENGINE . . . . KAWASAKI
ENGINE HP 15
COOLING . . . . AIR
FUEL . . . . G
SPEEDS . . . . VARIABLE
TRANSMISSION . . . . HYDRO
STEERING. . . . . ZERO
STANDARD DECK . . . . 36"
MSRP. $6,099

RETAIL PRICING

YEAR	HIGH	LOW
2006	$1,104	$828
2007	$1,337	$1,002
2008	$1,640	$1,230
2009	$2,044	$1,533
2010	$2,500	$1,875
2011	$3,057	$2,293

WS3617 KAWRE

YEARS MFRD 2006-2011
SERIES. . . . . STANDER SERIES
ENGINE . . . . KAWASAKI
ENGINE HP 17
COOLING . . . . AIR
FUEL . . . . G
SPEEDS . . . . VARIABLE
TRANSMISSION . . . . HYDRO
STEERING. . . . . ZERO
STANDARD DECK . . . . 36"
MSRP. $6,989

RETAIL PRICING

YEAR	HIGH	LOW
2006	$1,417	$1,063
2007	$1,640	$1,230
2008	$2,003	$1,502
2009	$2,460	$1,845
2010	$2,964	$2,223
2011	$3,601	$2,700

WS4217 KAWRE

YEARS MFRD 2006-2011
SERIES. . . . . STANDER SERIES
ENGINE . . . . KAWASAKI
ENGINE HP 17
COOLING . . . . AIR
FUEL . . . . G
SPEEDS . . . . VARIABLE
TRANSMISSION . . . . HYDRO
STEERING. . . . . ZERO
STANDARD DECK . . . . 42"
MSRP. $7,044

RETAIL PRICING

YEAR	HIGH	LOW
2006	$1,472	$1,104
2007	$1,727	$1,295
2008	$2,023	$1,518
2009	$2,474	$1,855
2010	$2,991	$2,244
2011	$3,629	$2,722

WS4817KAW

YEARS MFRD 2005-2008
SERIES. . . . . STANDER SERIES
ENGINE . . . . KAWASAKI
ENGINE HP 17
COOLING . . . . AIR
FUEL . . . . G
SPEEDS . . . . VARIABLE
TRANSMISSION . . . . HYDRO
STEERING. . . . . ZERO
STANDARD DECK . . . . 48"
MSRP. $6,849

RETAIL PRICING

YEAR	HIGH	LOW
2005	$1,434	$1,075
2006	$1,560	$1,170
2007	$1,861	$1,396
2008	$2,212	$1,659

WS4817 KAWRE

YEARS MFRD 2006-2011
SERIES. . . . . STANDER SERIES
ENGINE . . . . KAWASAKI
ENGINE HP 17
COOLING . . . . AIR
FUEL . . . . G
SPEEDS . . . . VARIABLE
TRANSMISSION . . . . HYDRO
STEERING. . . . . ZERO
STANDARD DECK . . . . 48"
MSRP. $7,999

RETAIL PRICING

YEAR	HIGH	LOW
2006	$1,573	$1,180
2007	$1,929	$1,447
2008	$2,272	$1,704
2009	$2,776	$2,082
2010	$3,409	$2,556
2011	$4,123	$3,092

WS4819KAWE

YEARS MFRD 2006-2011
SERIES. . . . . STANDER SERIES
ENGINE . . . . KAWASAKI
ENGINE HP 19
COOLING . . . . AIR
FUEL . . . . G
SPEEDS . . . . VARIABLE
TRANSMISSION . . . . HYDRO
STEERING. . . . . ZERO
STANDARD DECK . . . . 48"
MSRP. $8,229

RETAIL PRICING

YEAR	HIGH	LOW
2006	$1,626	$1,219
2007	$1,976	$1,482
2008	$2,339	$1,754
2009	$2,995	$2,247
2010	$3,636	$2,727
2011	$4,241	$3,181

WS4823KAWE

YEARS MFRD 2007-2011
ENGINE . . . . KAWASAKI
ENGINE HP 23
COOLING . . . . AIR
FUEL . . . . G
SPEEDS . . . . VARIABLE
TRANSMISSION . . . . HYDRO
STEERING. . . . . ZERO
STANDARD DECK . . . . 48"
MSRP. $8,494

RETAIL PRICING

YEAR	HIGH	LOW
2007	$1,916	$1,437
2008	$2,346	$1,760
2009	$2,926	$2,194
2010	$3,643	$2,732
2011	$4,262	$3,197

WS5217KAWE

YEARS MFRD 2005-2006
ENGINE . . . . KAWASAKI
ENGINE HP 17
COOLING . . . . AIR
FUEL . . . . G
SPEEDS . . . . VARIABLE
TRANSMISSION . . . . HYDRO
STEERING. . . . . ZERO
STANDARD DECK . . . . 52"
MSRP. $6,609

RETAIL PRICING

YEAR	HIGH	LOW
2006	$4,266	$3,200

WS5219KAWE

YEARS MFRD 2006-2011
ENGINE . . . . KAWASAKI
ENGINE HP 19
COOLING . . . . AIR
FUEL . . . . G
SPEEDS . . . . VARIABLE
TRANSMISSION . . . . HYDRO
STEERING. . . . . ZERO
STANDARD DECK . . . . 52"
MSRP. $8,274

RETAIL PRICING

YEAR	HIGH	LOW
2006	$1,647	$1,235
2007	$1,990	$1,493
2008	$2,438	$1,828
2009	$3,052	$2,289
2010	$3,656	$2,742
2011	$4,262	$3,197

WS5223KAWE

YEARS MFRD 2006-2011
ENGINE . . . . KAWASAKI
ENGINE HP 23
COOLING . . . . AIR
FUEL . . . . G
SPEEDS . . . . VARIABLE
TRANSMISSION . . . . HYDRO
STEERING. . . . . ZERO
STANDARD DECK . . . . 52"
MSRP. $8,529

RETAIL PRICING

YEAR	HIGH	LOW
2006	$1,694	$1,270
2007	$2,052	$1,539
2008	$2,507	$1,881
2009	$3,099	$2,324
2010	$3,767	$2,826
2011	$4,395	$3,296

WS5223KCE

YEARS MFRD 2005-2006
ENGINE . . . . . . KOHLER COMMAND
ENGINE HP 23
COOLING . . . . AIR
FUEL . . . . G
SPEEDS . . . . VARIABLE
TRANSMISSION . . . . HYDRO
STEERING. . . . . ZERO
STANDARD DECK . . . . 52"
MSRP. $7,139

RETAIL PRICING

YEAR	HIGH	LOW
2006	$4,608	$3,456

WS5225KAWE

YEARS MFRD 2006-2011
ENGINE . . . . KAWASAKI
ENGINE HP 25
COOLING . . . . AIR
FUEL . . . . G
SPEEDS . . . . VARIABLE
TRANSMISSION . . . . HYDRO
STEERING. . . . . ZERO
STANDARD DECK . . . . 52"
MSRP. $8,899

RETAIL PRICING

YEAR	HIGH	LOW
2006	$1,801	$1,351
2007	$2,144	$1,608
2008	$2,526	$1,894
2009	$3,119	$2,339
2010	$3,797	$2,847
2011	$4,589	$3,442

WS6123KAWE

YEARS MFRD 2006-2011
ENGINE . . . . KAWASAKI
ENGINE HP 23
COOLING . . . . AIR
FUEL . . . . G
SPEEDS . . . . VARIABLE
TRANSMISSION . . . . HYDRO
STEERING. . . . . ZERO
STANDARD DECK . . . . 61"
MSRP. $8,889

RETAIL PRICING

YEAR	HIGH	LOW
2006	$1,767	$1,326
2007	$2,144	$1,608
2008	$2,619	$1,964
2009	$3,225	$2,419
2010	$3,936	$2,952
2011	$4,583	$3,437

WS6123KCE

YEARS MFRD 2005-2006
ENGINE . . . . . . KOHLER COMMAND
ENGINE HP 23
COOLING . . . . AIR
FUEL . . . . G
SPEEDS . . . . VARIABLE
TRANSMISSION . . . . HYDRO
STEERING. . . . . ZERO
STANDARD DECK . . . . 61"
MSRP. $7,444

RETAIL PRICING

YEAR	HIGH	LOW
2006	$4,805	$3,604

WS6125KAWE

YEARS MFRD 2006-2011
ENGINE . . . . KAWASAKI
ENGINE HP 25
COOLING . . . . AIR
FUEL . . . . G
SPEEDS . . . . VARIABLE
TRANSMISSION . . . . HYDRO
STEERING. . . . . ZERO
STANDARD DECK . . . . 61"
MSRP. $9,269

RETAIL PRICING

YEAR	HIGH	LOW
2006	$1,841	$1,381
2007	$2,232	$1,674
2008	$2,635	$1,976
2009	$3,240	$2,430
2010	$4,111	$3,083
2011	$4,777	$3,583

WSB32S FS600E1B

YEARS MFRD 2020-2020
SERIES. . . . . STANDER B SERIES
ENGINE . . . . KAWASAKI FS600E
ENGINE HP. 18.5
FUEL . . . . G
SPEEDS . . . . VARIABLE
TRANSMISSION . . . . HYDRO
STEERING. . . . . ZERO
STANDARD DECK . . . . 32"
WEIGHT . . . . 703 LBS.
MSRP. $6,500

WSB36S FS600E1B

YEARS MFRD 2020-2020
SERIES. . . . . STANDER B SERIES
ENGINE . . . . KAWASAKI FS600E
ENGINE HP. 18.5
FUEL . . . . G
SPEEDS . . . . VARIABLE
TRANSMISSION . . . . HYDRO
STEERING. . . . . ZERO
STANDARD DECK . . . . 36"
WEIGHT . . . . 713 LBS.
MSRP. $6,600

WRIGHT

WSB48S FS651E1B

YEARS MFRD 2019-2020
SERIES. . . . . . . .STANDER B SERIES
ENGINE . . . . .KAWASAKI FS651
ENGINE HP 22
FUEL . . . . G
SPEEDS . . . . .VARIABLE
TRANSMISSION . . . . .HYDRO
STEERING. . . . . .ZERO
STANDARD DECK . . . . 48"
WEIGHT . . . . 780 LBS.
MSRP. $6,700

RETAIL PRICING

YEAR	HIGH	LOW
2007	$2,333	$1,750
2008	$2,756	$2,067
2009	$3,748	$2,811
2010	$4,478	$3,358
2011	$5,203	$3,902

WSB52S FS651E1B

YEARS MFRD 2019-2020
SERIES. . . . . . . .STANDER B SERIES
ENGINE . . . . .KAWASAKI FS651
ENGINE HP 22
FUEL . . . . G
TRANSMISSION . . . . .HYDRO
STEERING. . . . . .ZERO
STANDARD DECK . . . . 52"
WEIGHT . . . . 800 LBS.
MSRP. $6,800

WSE4819 KAWE

YEARS MFRD 2007-2011
SERIES. . . . . SENTAR SERIES
ENGINE . . . . KAWASAKI
ENGINE HP 19
FUEL . . . . G
SPEEDS . . . . .VARIABLE
TRANSMISSION . . . . .HYDRO
STEERING. . . . . .ZERO
STANDARD DECK . . . . 48"
MSRP. $9,479

RETAIL PRICING

YEAR	HIGH	LOW
2007	$2,178	$1,633
2008	$2,588	$1,941
2009	$3,380	$2,535
2010	$4,053	$3,039
2011	$4,883	$3,662

WSE4823 KAWE

YEARS MFRD 2007-2011
SERIES. . . . . SENTAR SERIES
ENGINE . . . . KAWASAKI
ENGINE HP 23
FUEL . . . . G
SPEEDS . . . . .VARIABLE
TRANSMISSION . . . . .HYDRO
STEERING. . . . . .ZERO
STANDARD DECK . . . . 48"
MSRP. $10,099

WSE5223 KAWE

YEARS MFRD 2007-2011
SERIES. . . . . SENTAR SERIES
ENGINE . . . . KAWASAKI
ENGINE HP 23
FUEL . . . . G
SPEEDS . . . . .VARIABLE
TRANSMISSION . . . . .HYDRO
STEERING. . . . . .ZERO
STANDARD DECK . . . . 52"
MSRP. $10,139

RETAIL PRICING

YEAR	HIGH	LOW
2007	$2,474	$1,855
2008	$2,909	$2,182
2009	$3,811	$2,858
2010	$4,500	$3,375
2011	$5,223	$3,918

WSE5225 KAWE

YEARS MFRD 2007-2011
SERIES. . . . . SENTAR SERIES
ENGINE . . . . KAWASAKI
ENGINE HP 25
FUEL . . . . G
SPEEDS . . . . .VARIABLE
TRANSMISSION . . . . .HYDRO
STEERING. . . . . .ZERO
STANDARD DECK . . . . 52"
MSRP. $10,449

RETAIL PRICING

YEAR	HIGH	LOW
2007	$2,521	$1,891
2008	$2,996	$2,247
2009	$3,791	$2,843
2010	$4,476	$3,357
2011	$5,384	$4,038

WSE6123 KAWE

YEARS MFRD 2007-2007
SERIES. . . . . SENTAR SERIES
ENGINE . . . . KAWASAKI
ENGINE HP 23
FUEL . . . . G
SPEEDS . . . . .VARIABLE
TRANSMISSION . . . . .HYDRO
STEERING. . . . . .ZERO
STANDARD DECK . . . . 61"
MSRP. $8,794

RETAIL PRICING

YEAR	HIGH	LOW
2007	$4,941	$3,706

WSE6125 KAWE

YEARS MFRD 2007-2011
SERIES. . . . . SENTAR SERIES
ENGINE . . . . KAWASAKI
ENGINE HP 25
COOLING . . . . AIR
FUEL . . . . G
SPEEDS . . . . .VARIABLE
TRANSMISSION . . . . .HYDRO
STEERING. . . . . .ZERO
STANDARD DECK . . . . 61"
MSRP. $10,569

RETAIL PRICING

YEAR	HIGH	LOW
2007	$2,574	$1,931
2008	$3,030	$2,273
2009	$3,831	$2,873
2010	$4,530	$3,397
2011	$5,446	$4,084

WSES36 FS600RE

YEARS MFRD 2013-2017
ENGINE . . . . KAWASAKI
ENGINE HP 20
COOLING . . . . AIR
FUEL . . . . G
SPEEDS . . . . .VARIABLE
TRANSMISSION . . . . .HYDRO
STEERING. . . . . .ZERO
BLADE CLUTCH . . . . .ELECTRIC
STANDARD DECK . . . . 36"
MSRP. $8,164

RETAIL PRICING

YEAR	HIGH	LOW
2013	$3,577	$2,683
2014	$4,134	$3,101
2015	$4,691	$3,518
2016	$5,595	$4,196
2017	$6,388	$4,791

WSES36 FX600E

YEARS MFRD 2013-2017
ENGINE . . . . KAWASAKI
ENGINE HP 20
COOLING . . . . AIR
FUEL . . . . G
SPEEDS . . . . .VARIABLE
TRANSMISSION . . . . .HYDRO
STEERING. . . . . .ZERO
STANDARD DECK . . . . 36"
MSRP. $8,639

RETAIL PRICING

YEAR	HIGH	LOW
2013	$3,724	$2,793
2014	$4,308	$3,231
2015	$4,892	$3,669
2016	$5,768	$4,326
2017	$6,635	$4,976

WSES42 FS600RE

YEARS MFRD 2013-2014
ENGINE . . . . KAWASAKI
COOLING . . . . AIR
FUEL . . . . G
SPEEDS . . . . .VARIABLE
TRANSMISSION . . . . .HYDRO
STEERING. . . . . .ZERO
STANDARD DECK . . . . 42"
MSRP. $8,519

RETAIL PRICING

YEAR	HIGH	LOW
2013	$3,777	$2,833
2014	$4,584	$3,438

WSES42 FX600RE

YEARS MFRD 2013-2014
ENGINE . . . . KAWASAKI
COOLING . . . . AIR
FUEL . . . . G
SPEEDS . . . . .VARIABLE
TRANSMISSION . . . . .HYDRO
STEERING. . . . . .ZERO
STANDARD DECK . . . . 42"
MSRP. $8,794

RETAIL PRICING

YEAR	HIGH	LOW
2013	$3,897	$2,923
2014	$4,734	$3,550

WSES48 FX600E

YEARS MFRD 2013-2017
ENGINE . . . . KAWASAKI
ENGINE HP 20
COOLING . . . . AIR
FUEL . . . . G
SPEEDS . . . . .VARIABLE
TRANSMISSION . . . . .HYDRO
STEERING. . . . . .ZERO
STANDARD DECK . . . . 48"
MSRP. $8,909

RETAIL PRICING

YEAR	HIGH	LOW
2013	$3,751	$2,813
2014	$4,344	$3,258
2015	$5,029	$3,772
2016	$5,942	$4,457
2017	$6,991	$5,243

WSES52FX

YEARS MFRD 2013-2014
ENGINE . . . . KAWASAKI
COOLING . . . . AIR
FUEL . . . . G
SPEEDS . . . . .VARIABLE
TRANSMISSION . . . . .HYDRO
STEERING. . . . . .ZERO
STANDARD DECK . . . . 52"
MSRP. $8,844

RETAIL PRICING

YEAR	HIGH	LOW
2013	$3,836	$2,877
2014	$4,765	$3,573

WSES52 FX600E

YEARS MFRD 2013-2017
ENGINE . . . . KAWASAKI
ENGINE HP 20
FUEL . . . . G
SPEEDS . . . . VARIABLE
TRANSMISSION . . . . HYDRO
STEERING. . . . . ZERO
STANDARD DECK . . . . 52"
MSRP. $8,604

RETAIL PRICING

YEAR	HIGH	LOW
2013	$3,687	$2,765
2014	$4,363	$3,272
2015	$4,946	$3,710
2016	$6,051	$4,538
2017	$6,818	$5,114

WSES3617 KAWE

YEARS MFRD 2008-2011
ENGINE . . . . KAWASAKI
CYLINDERS. 2
ENGINE HP 17
COOLING . . . . AIR
FUEL . . . . G
SPEEDS . . . . VARIABLE
TRANSMISSION . . . . HYDRO
STEERING. . . . . ZERO
STANDARD DECK . . . . 36"
WEIGHT . . . . 710 LBS.
MSRP. $7,589

RETAIL PRICING

YEAR	HIGH	LOW
2008	$2,097	$1,573
2009	$2,514	$1,886
2010	$3,173	$2,380
2011	$3,803	$2,853

WSES3619 KAWE

YEARS MFRD 2010-2011
ENGINE . . . . KAWASAKI
ENGINE HP 19
COOLING . . . . AIR
FUEL . . . . G
SPEEDS . . . . VARIABLE
TRANSMISSION . . . . HYDRO
STEERING. . . . . ZERO
BLADE CLUTCH . . . . ELECTRIC
STANDARD DECK . . . . 36"
MSRP. $7,914

RETAIL PRICING

YEAR	HIGH	LOW
2010	$3,427	$2,570
2011	$3,969	$2,977

WSES4217 KAWE

YEARS MFRD 2010-2011
ENGINE . . . . KAWASAKI
ENGINE HP 17
COOLING . . . . AIR
FUEL . . . . G
SPEEDS . . . . VARIABLE
TRANSMISSION . . . . HYDRO
STEERING. . . . . ZERO
BLADE CLUTCH . . . . ELECTRIC
STANDARD DECK . . . . 42"
MSRP. $7,704

RETAIL PRICING

YEAR	HIGH	LOW
2010	$3,179	$2,384
2011	$3,866	$2,900

WSES4219 KAWE

YEARS MFRD 2010-2011
ENGINE . . . . KAWASAKI
ENGINE HP 19
COOLING . . . . AIR
FUEL . . . . G
SPEEDS . . . . VARIABLE
TRANSMISSION . . . . HYDRO
STEERING. . . . . ZERO
BLADE CLUTCH . . . . ELECTRIC
STANDARD DECK . . . . 42"
MSRP. $7,964

RETAIL PRICING

YEAR	HIGH	LOW
2010	$3,407	$2,555
2011	$3,991	$2,993

WSES4819 KAWE

YEARS MFRD 2008-2011
ENGINE . . . . KAWASAKI
CYLINDERS. 2
ENGINE HP 19
COOLING . . . . AIR
FUEL . . . . G
SPEEDS . . . . VARIABLE
TRANSMISSION . . . . HYDRO
STEERING. . . . . ZERO
STANDARD DECK . . . . 48"
WEIGHT . . . . 750 LBS.
MSRP. $8,019

RETAIL PRICING

YEAR	HIGH	LOW
2008	$2,183	$1,638
2009	$2,621	$1,966
2010	$3,313	$2,484
2011	$4,019	$3,014

WSES4823 KAWE

YEARS MFRD 2010-2011
ENGINE . . . . KAWASAKI
CYLINDERS. 2
ENGINE HP 23
COOLING . . . . AIR
FUEL . . . . G
SPEEDS . . . . VARIABLE
TRANSMISSION . . . . HYDRO
STEERING. . . . . ZERO
STANDARD DECK . . . . 48"
MSRP. $8,364

RETAIL PRICING

YEAR	HIGH	LOW
2010	$3,580	$2,685
2011	$4,192	$3,144

WSES5219 KAWE

YEARS MFRD 2008-2011
SERIES. . . . .SENTAR SPORT SERIES
ENGINE . . . . KAWASAKI
CYLINDERS. 2
ENGINE HP 19
COOLING . . . . AIR
FUEL . . . . G
SPEEDS . . . . VARIABLE
TRANSMISSION . . . . HYDRO
STEERING. . . . . ZERO
BLADE CLUTCH . . . . ELECTRIC
STANDARD DECK . . . . 52"
WEIGHT . . . . 790 LBS.
MSRP. $8,069

OPTIONS

KAWASAKI 23HP
KAWASAKI 25HP

RETAIL PRICING

YEAR	HIGH	LOW
2008	$2,204	$1,653
2009	$2,641	$1,981
2010	$3,327	$2,495
2011	$4,048	$3,036

WSES5223 KAWE

YEARS MFRD 2010-2011
ENGINE . . . . KAWASAKI
CYLINDERS. 2
ENGINE HP 23
COOLING . . . . AIR
FUEL . . . . G
SPEEDS . . . . VARIABLE
TRANSMISSION . . . . HYDRO
STEERING. . . . . ZERO
STANDARD DECK . . . . 52"
MSRP. $8,414

RETAIL PRICING

YEAR	HIGH	LOW
2010	$3,607	$2,706
2011	$4,220	$3,165

WSPN36 FS600E

YEARS MFRD 2017-2018
ENGINE . . . . KAWASAKI
ENGINE HP 18.5
TRANSMISSION . . . . HYDRO
STEERING. . . . . ZERO
STANDARD DECK . . . . 36"
WEIGHT . . . . 772 LBS.
MSRP. $8,680

RETAIL PRICING

YEAR	HIGH	LOW
2017	$6,540	$4,905
2018	$7,201	$5,401

WSPN36 FX600E

YEARS MFRD 2017-2020
SERIES. . . . . SPORT I SERIES
ENGINE . . . . KAWASAKI
ENGINE HP 19
TRANSMISSION . . . . HYDRO
STEERING. . . . . ZERO
STANDARD DECK . . . . 36"
WEIGHT . . . . 772 LBS.
MSRP. $9,180

RETAIL PRICING

YEAR	HIGH	LOW
2017	$6,716	$4,986
2018	$7,394	$5,545
2019	$8,191	$6,333
2020	$8,785	$6,814

WSPN36 ZT710E

YEARS MFRD 2017-2018
ENGINE . . . . KOHLER
ENGINE HP 19
TRANSMISSION . . . . HYDRO
STEERING. . . . . ZERO
STANDARD DECK . . . . 36"
WEIGHT . . . . 772 LBS.
MSRP. $8,770

RETAIL PRICING

YEAR	HIGH	LOW
2017	$6,224	$4,668
2018	$7,243	$5,432

WSPN48 FX600E

YEARS MFRD 2017-2018
ENGINE . . . . KAWASAKI
ENGINE HP 19
TRANSMISSION . . . . HYDRO
STEERING. . . . . ZERO
STANDARD DECK . . . . 48"
WEIGHT . . . . 860 LBS.
MSRP. $9,200

RETAIL PRICING

YEAR	HIGH	LOW
2017	$6,657	$4,993
2018	$7,608	$5,706

WRIGHT

WSPN48 FX730E

YEARS MFRD 2017-2019
SERIES . . . . SPORT I SERIES
ENGINE . . . . KAWASAKI
ENGINE HP 23.5
TRANSMISSION . . . . .HYDRO
STEERING . . . . ZERO
STANDARD DECK . . . . 48"
WEIGHT . . . . 860 LBS.
MSRP $9,590

RETAIL PRICING

YEAR	HIGH	LOW
2017	$7,330	$5,498
2018	$7,976	$5,982
2019	$8,829	$6,622

WSPN48 ZT730E

YEARS MFRD 2017-2018
ENGINE . . . . KOHLER
ENGINE HP 23
TRANSMISSION . . . . .HYDRO
STEERING . . . . ZERO
STANDARD DECK . . . . 48"
WEIGHT . . . . 860 LBS.
MSRP $9,100

RETAIL PRICING

YEAR	HIGH	LOW
2017	$6,438	$4,828
2018	$7,549	$5,661

WSPN52 FX600E

YEARS MFRD 2017-2018
ENGINE . . . . KAWASAKI
ENGINE HP 19
TRANSMISSION . . . . .HYDRO
STEERING . . . . ZERO
STANDARD DECK . . . . 52"
WEIGHT . . . . 871 LBS.
MSRP $9,300

RETAIL PRICING

YEAR	HIGH	LOW
2017	$6,633	$4,975
2018	$7,751	$5,813

WSPN52 FX730E

YEARS MFRD 2017-2019
SERIES . . . . SPORT I SERIES
ENGINE . . . . KAWASAKI
ENGINE HP 23.5
TRANSMISSION . . . . .HYDRO
STEERING . . . . ZERO
STANDARD DECK . . . . 52"
WEIGHT . . . . 871 LBS.
MSRP $9,690

RETAIL PRICING

YEAR	HIGH	LOW
2017	$7,059	$5,294
2018	$7,981	$5,986
2019	$8,927	$6,695

WSPN52 ZT730E

YEARS MFRD 2017-2018
ENGINE . . . . KOHLER
ENGINE HP 23
TRANSMISSION . . . . .HYDRO
STEERING . . . . ZERO
STANDARD DECK . . . . 52"
WEIGHT . . . . 871 LBS.
MSRP $9,200

RETAIL PRICING

YEAR	HIGH	LOW
2017	$6,990	$5,242
2018	$7,759	$5,819

WSPX48 FX691E

YEARS MFRD 2013-2017
ENGINE . . . . KAWASAKI
ENGINE HP 24
COOLING . . . . AIR
FUEL . . . . G
SPEEDS . . . . VARIABLE
TRANSMISSION . . . . .HYDRO
STEERING . . . . ZERO
STANDARD DECK . . . . 48"
MSRP $9,409

RETAIL PRICING

YEAR	HIGH	LOW
2013	$4,545	$3,409
2014	$5,229	$3,922
2015	$5,494	$4,121
2016	$6,617	$4,963
2017	$7,338	$5,504

WSPX48 FX730E2A

YEARS MFRD 2018-2020
SERIES . . . . .SPORT X SERIES
ENGINE . . . . KAWASAKI
ENGINE HP 23.5
TRANSMISSION . . . . .HYDRO
STEERING . . . . ZERO
STANDARD DECK . . . . 48"
WEIGHT . . . . 951 LBS.
MSRP $10,220

WSPX52 ECV740E

YEARS MFRD 2013-2017
ENGINE . . . . KOHLER
ENGINE HP 27
COOLING . . . . AIR
FUEL . . . . G
SPEEDS . . . . VARIABLE
TRANSMISSION . . . . .HYDRO
STEERING . . . . ZERO
STANDARD DECK . . . . 52"
MSRP $10,399

RETAIL PRICING

YEAR	HIGH	LOW
2013	$4,929	$3,696
2014	$5,513	$4,134
2015	$6,078	$4,559
2016	$7,082	$5,311
2017	$8,004	$6,003

WSPX52 FX691E

YEARS MFRD 2013-2017
ENGINE . . . . KAWASAKI
ENGINE HP 24
COOLING . . . . AIR
FUEL . . . . G
SPEEDS . . . . VARIABLE
TRANSMISSION . . . . .HYDRO
STEERING . . . . ZERO
STANDARD DECK . . . . 52"
MSRP $9,484

RETAIL PRICING

YEAR	HIGH	LOW
2013	$4,581	$3,436
2014	$5,276	$3,957
2015	$5,540	$4,155
2016	$6,680	$5,010
2017	$7,466	$5,600

WSPX52 FX730E

YEARS MFRD 2013-2017
SERIES . . . . .SPORT X SERIES
ENGINE . . . . KAWASAKI
ENGINE HP 23.5
COOLING . . . . AIR
FUEL . . . . G
SPEEDS . . . . VARIABLE
TRANSMISSION . . . . .HYDRO
STEERING . . . . ZERO
STANDARD DECK . . . . 52"
WEIGHT . . . . 961 LBS.
MSRP $9,869

RETAIL PRICING

YEAR	HIGH	LOW
2013	$4,764	$3,573
2014	$5,485	$4,114
2015	$5,768	$4,326
2016	$6,716	$5,037
2017	$7,683	$5,763

WSPX52 FX730E2A

YEARS MFRD 2018-2020
SERIES . . . . .SPORT X SERIES
ENGINE . . . . .KAWASAKI FX730
ENGINE HP 23.5
FUEL . . . . G
SPEEDS . . . . VARIABLE
TRANSMISSION . . . . .HYDRO
STEERING . . . . ZERO
STANDARD DECK . . . . 52"
WEIGHT . . . . 961 LBS.
MSRP $10,320

WSPX61 ECV740E

YEARS MFRD 2013-2017
ENGINE . . . . KOHLER
ENGINE HP 27
COOLING . . . . AIR
FUEL . . . . G
SPEEDS . . . . VARIABLE
TRANSMISSION . . . . .HYDRO
STEERING . . . . ZERO
STANDARD DECK . . . . 61"
MSRP $10,714

RETAIL PRICING

YEAR	HIGH	LOW
2013	$5,020	$3,765
2014	$5,641	$4,230
2015	$6,253	$4,689
2016	$7,183	$5,387
2017	$8,013	$6,010

WSPX61 FX730E

YEARS MFRD 2013-2017
SERIES . . . . .SPORT X SERIES
ENGINE . . . . KAWASAKI
ENGINE HP 23.5
COOLING . . . . AIR
FUEL . . . . G
SPEEDS . . . . VARIABLE
TRANSMISSION . . . . .HYDRO
STEERING . . . . ZERO
STANDARD DECK . . . . 61"
WEIGHT . . . . 1,031 LBS.
MSRP $10,244

RETAIL PRICING

YEAR	HIGH	LOW
2013	$4,946	$3,710
2014	$5,695	$4,271
2015	$5,987	$4,490
2016	$7,009	$5,257
2017	$8,003	$6,003

WSPX61 FX730E2A

YEARS MFRD 2018-2020
SERIES . . . . .SPORT X SERIES
ENGINE . . . . .KAWASAKI FX730
ENGINE HP 23.5
FUEL . . . . G
TRANSMISSION . . . . .HYDRO
STEERING . . . . ZERO
STANDARD DECK . . . . 61"
WEIGHT . . . . 1,031 LBS.
MSRP $10,620

WSR36 FS600RE

YEARS MFRD 2013-2014
ENGINE . . . . KAWASAKI
COOLING . . . . AIR
FUEL . . . . G
SPEEDS . . . . VARIABLE

TRANSMISSION .... HYDRO
STEERING. .... ZERO
STANDARD DECK .... 36"
MSRP. $8,209

RETAIL PRICING

YEAR	HIGH	LOW
2013	$3,821	$2,866
2014	$4,547	$3,411

WSR36 FX600E

YEARS MFRD 2013-2014
ENGINE .... KAWASAKI
COOLING .... AIR
FUEL .... G
SPEEDS .... VARIABLE
TRANSMISSION .... HYDRO
STEERING. .... ZERO
STANDARD DECK .... 36"
MSRP. $8,564

RETAIL PRICING

YEAR	HIGH	LOW
2013	$3,986	$2,989
2014	$4,741	$3,556

WSR42 FS600RE

YEARS MFRD 2013-2014
ENGINE .... KAWASAKI
COOLING .... AIR
FUEL .... G
SPEEDS .... VARIABLE
TRANSMISSION .... HYDRO
STEERING. .... ZERO
STANDARD DECK .... 42"
MSRP. $8,334

RETAIL PRICING

YEAR	HIGH	LOW
2013	$3,874	$2,906
2014	$4,615	$3,461

WSR42 FX600E

YEARS MFRD 2013-2014
ENGINE .... KAWASAKI
COOLING .... AIR
FUEL .... G
SPEEDS .... VARIABLE
TRANSMISSION .... HYDRO
STEERING. .... ZERO
STANDARD DECK .... 42"
MSRP. $8,609

RETAIL PRICING

YEAR	HIGH	LOW
2013	$4,000	$3,000
2014	$4,765	$3,573

WSR48 FX600E

YEARS MFRD 2013-2014
ENGINE .... KAWASAKI
COOLING .... AIR
FUEL .... G
SPEEDS .... VARIABLE
TRANSMISSION .... HYDRO
STEERING. .... ZERO
STANDARD DECK .... 48"
MSRP. $8,634

RETAIL PRICING

YEAR	HIGH	LOW
2013	$4,017	$3,013
2014	$4,779	$3,584

WSR52 FX600E

YEARS MFRD 2013-2014
ENGINE .... KAWASAKI
COOLING .... AIR
FUEL .... G
SPEEDS .... VARIABLE
TRANSMISSION .... HYDRO
STEERING. .... ZERO
STANDARD DECK .... 52"
MSRP. $8,659

RETAIL PRICING

YEAR	HIGH	LOW
2013	$4,030	$3,023
2014	$4,794	$3,595

WSR3617 KAWE

YEARS MFRD 2010-2011
SERIES......... STANDER SERIES
ENGINE .... KAWASAKI
ENGINE HP 17
COOLING .... AIR
FUEL .... G
SPEEDS .... VARIABLE
TRANSMISSION .... HYDRO
STEERING. .... ZERO
STANDARD DECK .... 36"
MSRP. $7,489

RETAIL PRICING

YEAR	HIGH	LOW
2010	$3,179	$2,384
2011	$3,858	$2,893

WSR3618 KAWE

YEARS MFRD 2012-2013
SERIES....... STANDER RH SERIES
ENGINE .... KAWASAKI
ENGINE HP 18
COOLING .... AIR
FUEL .... G
SPEEDS .... VARIABLE
TRANSMISSION .... HYDRO
STEERING. .... ZERO
STANDARD DECK .... 36"
MSRP. $7,764

RETAIL PRICING

YEAR	HIGH	LOW
2012	$3,644	$2,733
2013	$4,497	$3,373

WSR3619 KAWE

YEARS MFRD 2010-2011
ENGINE .... KAWASAKI
ENGINE HP 19
COOLING .... AIR
FUEL .... G
SPEEDS .... VARIABLE
TRANSMISSION .... HYDRO
STEERING. .... ZERO
BLADE CLUTCH .... ELECTRIC
STANDARD DECK .... 36"
MSRP. $7,814

RETAIL PRICING

YEAR	HIGH	LOW
2010	$3,453	$2,590
2011	$4,027	$3,021

WSR3620 KAWE

YEARS MFRD 2012-2013
SERIES....... STANDER HT SERIES
ENGINE .... KAWASAKI
ENGINE HP 20
COOLING .... AIR
FUEL .... G
SPEEDS .... VARIABLE
TRANSMISSION .... HYDRO
STEERING. .... ZERO
STANDARD DECK .... 36"
MSRP. $9,214

RETAIL PRICING

YEAR	HIGH	LOW
2012	$4,323	$3,242
2013	$5,694	$4,270

WSR4217 KAWE

YEARS MFRD 2010-2011
ENGINE .... KAWASAKI
ENGINE HP 17
COOLING .... AIR
FUEL .... G
SPEEDS .... VARIABLE
TRANSMISSION .... HYDRO
STEERING. .... ZERO
BLADE CLUTCH .... ELECTRIC
STANDARD DECK .... 42"
MSRP. $7,604

RETAIL PRICING

YEAR	HIGH	LOW
2010	$3,349	$2,512
2011	$3,921	$2,941

WSR4218 KAWE

YEARS MFRD 2012-2013
SERIES....... STANDER RH SERIES
ENGINE .... KAWASAKI
ENGINE HP 18
COOLING .... AIR
FUEL .... G
SPEEDS .... VARIABLE
TRANSMISSION .... HYDRO
STEERING. .... ZERO
STANDARD DECK .... 42"
MSRP. $7,884

RETAIL PRICING

YEAR	HIGH	LOW
2012	$3,702	$2,777
2013	$4,894	$3,670

WSR4219 KAWE

YEARS MFRD 2010-2011
ENGINE .... KAWASAKI
ENGINE HP 19
COOLING .... AIR
FUEL .... G
SPEEDS .... VARIABLE
TRANSMISSION .... HYDRO
STEERING. .... ZERO
STANDARD DECK .... 42"
MSRP. $7,864

RETAIL PRICING

YEAR	HIGH	LOW
2010	$3,468	$2,601
2011	$4,054	$3,040

WSR4220 KAWRE

YEARS MFRD 2012-2013
ENGINE .... KAWASAKI
ENGINE HP 20
COOLING .... AIR
FUEL .... G
SPEEDS .... VARIABLE
TRANSMISSION .... HYDRO
STEERING. .... ZERO
STANDARD DECK .... 42"
MSRP. $8,139

RETAIL PRICING

YEAR	HIGH	LOW
2012	$3,818	$2,863
2013	$5,239	$3,929

WSR4819 KAWE

YEARS MFRD 2006-2011
SERIES......... STANDER SERIES
ENGINE .... KAWASAKI
ENGINE HP 19
COOLING .... AIR
FUEL .... G
SPEEDS .... VARIABLE

TRANSMISSION . . . . HYDRO
STEERING. . . . . ZERO
STANDARD DECK . . . . 48"
MSRP. $7,919

RETAIL PRICING

YEAR	HIGH	LOW
2006	$1,605	$1,204
2007	$1,924	$1,443
2008	$2,265	$1,699
2009	$2,830	$2,123
2010	$3,373	$2,530
2011	$4,082	$3,061

WSR4820 KAWE

YEARS MFRD 2012-2013
SERIES. . . . . . STANDER RH SERIES
ENGINE . . . . KAWASAKI
ENGINE HP. 20
COOLING . . . . AIR
FUEL . . . . G
SPEEDS . . . . VARIABLE
TRANSMISSION . . . . HYDRO
STEERING. . . . . ZERO
STANDARD DECK . . . . 48"
MSRP. $8,164

RETAIL PRICING

YEAR	HIGH	LOW
2012	$3,832	$2,874
2013	$5,204	$3,903

WSR4823 KAWRE

YEARS MFRD 2010-2011
ENGINE . . . . KAWASAKI
ENGINE HP. 23
COOLING . . . . AIR
FUEL . . . . G
SPEEDS . . . . VARIABLE
TRANSMISSION . . . . HYDRO
STEERING. . . . . ZERO
STANDARD DECK . . . . 48"
MSRP. $8,264

RETAIL PRICING

YEAR	HIGH	LOW
2010	$3,656	$2,742
2011	$4,262	$3,197

WSR5219 KAWE

YEARS MFRD 2007-2011
ENGINE . . . . KAWASAKI
ENGINE HP. 19
COOLING . . . . AIR
FUEL . . . . G
SPEEDS . . . . VARIABLE
TRANSMISSION . . . . HYDRO
STEERING. . . . . ZERO
STANDARD DECK . . . . 52"
MSRP. $7,969

RETAIL PRICING

YEAR	HIGH	LOW
2007	$1,934	$1,451
2008	$2,284	$1,713
2009	$3,030	$2,273
2010	$3,388	$2,541
2011	$4,111	$3,083

WSR5220 KAWE

YEARS MFRD 2012-2013
SERIES. . . . . . STANDER RH SERIES
ENGINE . . . . KAWASAKI
ENGINE HP. 20
COOLING . . . . AIR
FUEL . . . . G
SPEEDS . . . . VARIABLE
TRANSMISSION . . . . HYDRO
STEERING. . . . . ZERO
STANDARD DECK . . . . 52"
MSRP. $8,189

RETAIL PRICING

YEAR	HIGH	LOW
2012	$3,840	$2,880
2013	$5,183	$3,887

WSR5223 KAWE

YEARS MFRD 2010-2011
ENGINE . . . . KAWASAKI
ENGINE HP. 23
COOLING . . . . AIR
FUEL . . . . G
SPEEDS . . . . VARIABLE
TRANSMISSION . . . . HYDRO
STEERING. . . . . ZERO
STANDARD DECK . . . . 52"
MSRP. $8,314

RETAIL PRICING

YEAR	HIGH	LOW
2010	$3,677	$2,758
2011	$4,283	$3,212

WSRH36

YEARS MFRD 2009-2009
SERIES. . . . . . STANDER RH SERIES
ENGINE . . . . KAWASAKI
CYLINDERS. 2
ENGINE HP. 17
COOLING . . . . AIR
FUEL . . . . G
SPEEDS . . . . VARIABLE
TRANSMISSION . . . . HYDRO
STEERING. . . . . ZERO
BLADE CLUTCH . . . . ELECTRIC
WEIGHT . . . . 710 LBS.

OPTIONS

KAWASAKI 19HP

WSRH42

YEARS MFRD 2009-2009
SERIES. . . . . . STANDER RH SERIES
ENGINE . . . . KAWASAKI
CYLINDERS. 2
ENGINE HP. 17
COOLING . . . . AIR
FUEL . . . . G
SPEEDS . . . . VARIABLE
TRANSMISSION . . . . HYDRO
STEERING. . . . . ZERO
BLADE CLUTCH . . . . ELECTRIC
WEIGHT . . . . 720 LBS.

OPTIONS

KAWASAKI 19HP

WSRH48

YEARS MFRD 2009-2009
SERIES. . . . . . STANDER RH SERIES
ENGINE . . . . KAWASAKI
CYLINDERS. 2
ENGINE HP. 19
COOLING . . . . AIR
FUEL . . . . G
SPEEDS . . . . VARIABLE
TRANSMISSION . . . . HYDRO
STEERING. . . . . ZERO
BLADE CLUTCH . . . . ELECTRIC
WEIGHT . . . . 750 LBS.

OPTIONS

KAWASAKI 23HP
KAWASAKI 25HP

WSRH52

YEARS MFRD 2009-2009
SERIES. . . . . . STANDER RH SERIES
ENGINE . . . . KAWASAKI
CYLINDERS. 2
ENGINE HP. 19
COOLING . . . . AIR
FUEL . . . . G
SPEEDS . . . . VARIABLE
TRANSMISSION . . . . HYDRO
STEERING. . . . . ZERO
BLADE CLUTCH . . . . ELECTRIC
WEIGHT . . . . 790 LBS.

OPTIONS

KAWASAKI 23HP
KAWASAKI 25HP

WSS4819 KAWE

YEARS MFRD 2005-2008
SERIES. . . . . STANDER SERIES
ENGINE . . . . KAWASAKI
ENGINE HP. 19
COOLING . . . . AIR
FUEL . . . . G
SPEEDS . . . . VARIABLE
TRANSMISSION . . . . HYDRO
STEERING. . . . . ZERO
STANDARD DECK . . . . 48"
MSRP. $6,964

RETAIL PRICING

YEAR	HIGH	LOW
2006	$3,792	$2,844
2007	$3,840	$2,880
2008	$4,275	$3,206

WSTN36 FS600E

YEARS MFRD 2015-2018
SERIES. . . . . STANDER I SERIES
ENGINE . . . . KAWASAKI
ENGINE HP. 18.5
FUEL . . . . G
SPEEDS . . . . VARIABLE
TRANSMISSION . . . . HYDRO
STEERING. . . . . ZERO
STANDARD DECK . . . . 36"
WEIGHT . . . . 717 LBS.
MSRP. $8,390

RETAIL PRICING

YEAR	HIGH	LOW
2015	$4,755	$3,566
2016	$5,549	$4,162
2017	$5,987	$4,490
2018	$6,952	$5,214

WSTN36 FX600E

YEARS MFRD 2015-2020
SERIES. . . . . STANDER I SERIES
ENGINE . . . . KAWASAKI
ENGINE HP. 19
FUEL . . . . G
SPEEDS . . . . VARIABLE
TRANSMISSION . . . . HYDRO
STEERING. . . . . ZERO
STANDARD DECK . . . . 36"
WEIGHT . . . . 717 LBS.
MSRP. $8,880

RETAIL PRICING

YEAR	HIGH	LOW
2015	$4,864	$3,648
2016	$5,731	$4,299
2017	$6,489	$4,867
2018	$7,198	$5,399
2019	$7,892	$6,204
2020	$8,504	$6,501

WSTN36 ZT710E

YEARS MFRD 2016-2019
SERIES. . . . . STANDER I SERIES
ENGINE . . . . KOHLER ZT710
ENGINE HP. 20.2
FUEL . . . . G
SPEEDS . . . . VARIABLE
TRANSMISSION . . . . HYDRO
STEERING. . . . . ZERO
STANDARD DECK . . . . 36"
WEIGHT . . . . 728 LBS.
MSRP. $8,540

RETAIL PRICING

YEAR	HIGH	LOW
2016	$5,410	$4,057
2017	$6,187	$4,640
2018	$6,884	$5,163
2019	$7,514	$5,635

WSTN42S FX600E1A

YEARS MFRD 2018-2020
SERIES .... STANDER I SERIES
ENGINE .... KAWASAKI FX600E
ENGINE HP 19
FUEL .... G
SPEEDS .... VARIABLE
TRANSMISSION .... HYDRO
STEERING .... ZERO
STANDARD DECK .... 42"
WEIGHT .... 740 LBS.
MSRP $8,980

WSTN48 FX600E

YEARS MFRD 2015-2018
SERIES .... STANDER I SERIES
ENGINE .... KAWASAKI
ENGINE HP 19
FUEL .... G
SPEEDS .... VARIABLE
TRANSMISSION .... HYDRO
STEERING .... ZERO
STANDARD DECK .... 48"
WEIGHT .... 805 LBS.
MSRP $8,910

RETAIL PRICING

YEAR	HIGH	LOW
2015	$4,763	$3,572
2016	$5,737	$4,302
2017	$6,418	$4,814
2018	$7,257	$5,442

WSTN48 FX691E

YEARS MFRD 2015-2017
ENGINE .... KAWASAKI
ENGINE HP 24
FUEL .... G
SPEEDS .... VARIABLE
TRANSMISSION .... HYDRO
STEERING .... ZERO
STANDARD DECK .... 48"
MSRP $8,679

RETAIL PRICING

YEAR	HIGH	LOW
2015	$5,074	$3,806
2016	$6,069	$4,552
2017	$6,646	$4,985

WSTN48 FX730E

YEARS MFRD 2018-2020
SERIES .... STANDER I SERIES
ENGINE .... KAWASAKI
ENGINE HP 23.5
TRANSMISSION .... HYDRO
STEERING .... ZERO
STANDARD DECK .... 48"
WEIGHT .... 805 LBS.
MSRP $9,550

WSTN48 ZT730E

YEARS MFRD 2016-2019
ENGINE .... KOHLER
ENGINE HP 22.1
FUEL .... G
SPEEDS .... VARIABLE
TRANSMISSION .... HYDRO
STEERING .... ZERO
STANDARD DECK .... 48"
WEIGHT .... 805 LBS.
MSRP $8,870

RETAIL PRICING

YEAR	HIGH	LOW
2016	$5,630	$4,222
2017	$6,383	$4,787
2018	$7,190	$5,392
2019	$7,667	$5,750

WSTN52 FX600E

YEARS MFRD 2015-2018
SERIES .... STANDER I SERIES
ENGINE .... KAWASAKI
ENGINE HP 19
FUEL .... G
SPEEDS .... VARIABLE
TRANSMISSION .... HYDRO
STEERING .... ZERO
STANDARD DECK .... 52"
WEIGHT .... 816 LBS.
MSRP $9,010

RETAIL PRICING

YEAR	HIGH	LOW
2015	$4,771	$3,579
2016	$5,799	$4,349
2017	$6,426	$4,820
2018	$7,305	$5,479

WSTN52 FX691E

YEARS MFRD 2015-2016
ENGINE .... KAWASAKI
ENGINE HP 24
FUEL .... G
SPEEDS .... VARIABLE
TRANSMISSION .... HYDRO
STEERING .... ZERO
STANDARD DECK .... 52"
MSRP $8,704

RETAIL PRICING

YEAR	HIGH	LOW
2015	$4,931	$3,699
2016	$5,967	$4,476

WSTN52 FX730E

YEARS MFRD 2018-2019
ENGINE .... KAWASAKI
ENGINE HP 23.5
TRANSMISSION .... HYDRO
STEERING .... ZERO
STANDARD DECK .... 52"
WEIGHT .... 816 LBS.
MSRP $9,390

WSTN52 ZT730E

YEARS MFRD 2016-2019
ENGINE .... KOHLER
ENGINE HP 22.1
FUEL .... G
SPEEDS .... VARIABLE
TRANSMISSION .... HYDRO
STEERING .... ZERO
STANDARD DECK .... 52"
WEIGHT .... 816 LBS.
MSRP $8,970

RETAIL PRICING

YEAR	HIGH	LOW
2016	$5,692	$4,269
2017	$6,410	$4,807
2018	$7,240	$5,430
2019	$7,630	$5,723

WSTX48 FX691E

YEARS MFRD 2013-2017
SERIES .... STANDER X SERIES
ENGINE .... KAWASAKI
ENGINE HP 24
COOLING .... AIR
FUEL .... G
SPEEDS .... VARIABLE
TRANSMISSION .... HYDRO
STEERING .... ZERO
STANDARD DECK .... 48"
MSRP $9,590

RETAIL PRICING

YEAR	HIGH	LOW
2013	$4,314	$3,235
2014	$4,913	$3,685
2015	$5,258	$3,944
2016	$6,224	$4,668
2017	$6,935	$5,201

WSTX48S FX730E2A

YEARS MFRD 2018-2020
SERIES ... STANDER X GEN 2 SERIES
ENGINE .... KAWASAKI FX730
ENGINE HP 23.5
FUEL .... G
SPEEDS .... VARIABLE
TRANSMISSION .... HYDRO
STEERING .... ZERO
STANDARD DECK .... 48"
WEIGHT .... 900 LBS.
MSRP $9,920

WSTX52 ECV740E

YEARS MFRD 2013-2016
SERIES .... STANDER X SERIES
ENGINE .... KOHLER
ENGINE HP 27
COOLING .... AIR
FUEL .... G
SPEEDS .... VARIABLE
TRANSMISSION .... HYDRO
STEERING .... ZERO
STANDARD DECK .... 52"
MSRP $10,049

RETAIL PRICING

YEAR	HIGH	LOW
2013	$4,524	$3,393
2014	$5,329	$3,997
2015	$5,693	$4,270
2016	$6,498	$4,874

WSTX52 ECV749E

YEARS MFRD 2016-2017
SERIES .... STANDER X SERIES
ENGINE .... KOHLER
ENGINE HP 26.5
TRANSMISSION .... HYDRO
STEERING .... ZERO
STANDARD DECK .... 52"
WEIGHT .... 920 LBS.
MSRP $10,280

WSTX52 FX691E

YEARS MFRD 2013-2017
SERIES .... STANDER X SERIES
ENGINE .... KAWASAKI
ENGINE HP 24
COOLING .... AIR
FUEL .... G
SPEEDS .... VARIABLE
TRANSMISSION .... HYDRO
STEERING .... ZERO
STANDARD DECK .... 52"
MSRP $9,690

RETAIL PRICING

YEAR	HIGH	LOW
2013	$4,312	$3,234
2014	$4,958	$3,718
2015	$5,294	$3,971
2016	$6,294	$4,721
2017	$0	$0

WSTX52 FX730E

YEARS MFRD 2013-2017
SERIES .... STANDER X SERIES
ENGINE .... KAWASAKI
ENGINE HP 23.5
COOLING .... AIR
FUEL .... G
SPEEDS .... VARIABLE

TRANSMISSION .... HYDRO
STEERING .... ZERO
STANDARD DECK .... 52"
WEIGHT .... 920 LBS.
MSRP $9,730

RETAIL PRICING

YEAR	HIGH	LOW
2013	$4,488	$3,366
2014	$5,160	$3,870
2015	$5,515	$4,137
2016	$6,330	$4,748
2017	$7,041	$5,281

WSTX52S49 E8E2B

YEARS MFRD 2018-2020
SERIES .. STANDER X GEN 2 SERIES
ENGINE .... B&S 49E8
ENGINE HP 28
FUEL .... G
SPEEDS .... VARIABLE
TRANSMISSION .... HYDRO
STEERING .... ZERO
STANDARD DECK .... 52"
WEIGHT .... 920 LBS.
MSRP $10,100

OPTIONS

61" DECK $300

WSTX52S ECV749E2A

YEARS MFRD 2018-2020
SERIES .. STANDER X GEN 2 SERIES
ENGINE .... KOHLER ECV749
ENGINE HP 26.5
FUEL .... G
SPEEDS .... VARIABLE
TRANSMISSION .... HYDRO
STEERING .... ZERO
STANDARD DECK .... 52"
WEIGHT .... 920 LBS.
MSRP $10,460

WSTX52S FX730E2A

YEARS MFRD 2018-2020
SERIES .. STANDER X GEN 2 SERIES
ENGINE .... KAWASAKI FX730
ENGINE HP 23.5
FUEL .... G
SPEEDS .... VARIABLE
TRANSMISSION .... HYDRO
STEERING .... ZERO
STANDARD DECK .... 52"
WEIGHT .... 920 LBS.
MSRP $10,020

WSTX61 ECV749E

YEARS MFRD 2017-2017
SERIES .... STANDER X SERIES
ENGINE .... KOHLER
ENGINE HP 26.5
TRANSMISSION .... HYDRO
STEERING .... ZERO
STANDARD DECK .... 61"
WEIGHT .... 980 LBS.
MSRP $10,580

WSTX61 ECX740E

YEARS MFRD 2013-2016
SERIES .... STANDER X SERIES
ENGINE .... KOHER
COOLING .... AIR
FUEL .... G
SPEEDS .... VARIABLE
TRANSMISSION .... HYDRO
STEERING .... ZERO
STANDARD DECK .... 61"
MSRP $10,424

RETAIL PRICING

YEAR	HIGH	LOW
2013	$4,737	$3,552
2014	$5,329	$3,997
2015	$5,817	$4,363
2016	$6,693	$5,020

WSTX61 FX730E

YEARS MFRD 2013-2017
SERIES .... STANDER X SERIES
ENGINE .... KAWASAKI
ENGINE HP 23.5
COOLING .... AIR
FUEL .... G
SPEEDS .... VARIABLE
TRANSMISSION .... HYDRO
STEERING .... ZERO
STANDARD DECK .... 61"
WEIGHT .... 980 LBS.
MSRP $10,080

RETAIL PRICING

YEAR	HIGH	LOW
2013	$4,666	$3,499
2014	$5,365	$4,024
2015	$5,640	$4,230
2016	$6,613	$4,960
2017	$7,410	$5,557

WSTX61S ECV749E2A

YEARS MFRD 2018-2020
SERIES .. STANDER X GEN 2 SERIES
ENGINE .... KOHLER ECV749
ENGINE HP 26.5
FUEL .... G
SPEEDS .... VARIABLE
TRANSMISSION .... HYDRO
STEERING .... ZERO
STANDARD DECK .... 61"
WEIGHT .... 980 LBS.
MSRP $10,760

WSTX61S FX730E2A

YEARS MFRD 2018-2020
SERIES .. STANDER X GEN 2 SERIES
ENGINE .... KAWASAKI FX730
ENGINE HP 23.5
FUEL .... G
SPEEDS .... VARIABLE
TRANSMISSION .... HYDRO
STEERING .... ZERO
STANDARD DECK .... 61"
WEIGHT .... 980 LBS.
MSRP $10,320

WSTX5249E8E

YEARS MFRD 2018-2018
SERIES .... STANDER X SERIES
ENGINE .... B&S
ENGINE HP 28
TRANSMISSION .... HYDRO
STEERING .... ZERO
STANDARD DECK .... 52"
WEIGHT .... 920 LBS.

WSTX5249V6E

YEARS MFRD 2016-2017
ENGINE .... B&S
COOLING .... AIR
FUEL .... G
SPEEDS .... VARIABLE
TRANSMISSION .... HYDRO
STEERING .... ZERO
STANDARD DECK .... 52"
MSRP $9,309

RETAIL PRICING

YEAR	HIGH	LOW
2016	$6,380	$4,785
2017	$6,882	$5,162

WSTZ48 FX730E

YEARS MFRD 2018-2018
SERIES .... STANDER X SERIES
ENGINE .... KAWASAKI
ENGINE HP 23.5
TRANSMISSION .... HYDRO
STEERING .... ZERO
STANDARD DECK .... 48"
WEIGHT .... 900 LBS.

WSZK52

YEARS MFRD 2009-2010
SERIES .... STANDER ZK SERIES
ENGINE .... KAWASAKI
CYLINDERS 2
ENGINE HP 27
COOLING .... AIR
FUEL .... G
SPEEDS .... VARIABLE
TRANSMISSION .... HYDRO
STEERING .... ZERO
BLADE CLUTCH .... ELECTRIC
STANDARD DECK .... 52"
WEIGHT .... 1,200 LBS.
MSRP $10,499

OPTIONS

KAWASAKI 31HP

RETAIL PRICING

YEAR	HIGH	LOW
2009	$5,628	$4,221
2010	$6,478	$4,858

WSZK52 ECV860E

YEARS MFRD 2016-2017
SERIES .... STANDER ZK SERIES
ENGINE .... KOHLER
ENGINE HP 29
FUEL .... G
SPEEDS .... VARIABLE
TRANSMISSION .... HYDRO
STEERING .... ZERO
STANDARD DECK .... 52"
MSRP $11,050

RETAIL PRICING

YEAR	HIGH	LOW
2016	$7,146	$5,359
2017	$7,831	$5,873

WSZK52 FX801E

YEARS MFRD 2013-2017
SERIES .... STANDER ZK SERIES
ENGINE .... KAWASAKI
ENGINE HP 25.5
COOLING .... AIR
FUEL .... G
SPEEDS .... VARIABLE
TRANSMISSION .... HYDRO
STEERING .... ZERO
STANDARD DECK .... 52"
MSRP $10,740

RETAIL PRICING

YEAR	HIGH	LOW
2013	$4,595	$3,446
2014	$5,339	$4,004
2015	$5,666	$4,249
2016	$6,738	$5,053
2017	$7,523	$5,642

WSZK52 FX850E

YEARS MFRD 2013-2017
SERIES .... STANDER ZK SERIES
ENGINE .... KAWASAKI
ENGINE HP 27
COOLING .... AIR
FUEL .... G
SPEEDS .... VARIABLE
TRANSMISSION .... HYDRO
STEERING .... ZERO
STANDARD DECK .... 52"
WEIGHT .... 1,036 LBS.
MSRP $10,790

RETAIL PRICING

YEAR	HIGH	LOW
2013	$4,683	$3,512
2014	$5,445	$4,083
2015	$5,772	$4,329
2016	$6,773	$5,079
2017	$7,830	$5,872

WSZK52S61 E8E2B

YEARS MFRD 2018-2020
SERIES. .STANDER ZK GEN 2 SERIES
ENGINE . . . . B&S 61EB
ENGINE HP 37
FUEL . . . . G
SPEEDS . . . . .VARIABLE
TRANSMISSION . . . . .HYDRO
STEERING. . . . . .ZERO
STANDARD DECK . . . . 52"
WEIGHT . . . . .1,062 LBS.
MSRP. $12,130

WSZK52S ECV860E-49S

YEARS MFRD 2018-2018
SERIES. .STANDER ZK GEN 2 SERIES
ENGINE . . . . KOHLER ECV860
ENGINE HP 29
FUEL . . . . G
SPEEDS . . . . .VARIABLE
TRANSMISSION . . . . .HYDRO
STEERING. . . . . .ZERO
STANDARD DECK . . . . 52"
WEIGHT . . . . .1,036 LBS.
MSRP. $11,210

WSZK52S FX850E-49S

YEARS MFRD 2018-2020
SERIES. .STANDER ZK GEN 2 SERIES
ENGINE . . . . .KAWASAKI FX850
ENGINE HP 27
SPEEDS . . . . .VARIABLE
TRANSMISSION . . . . .HYDRO
STEERING. . . . . .ZERO
STANDARD DECK . . . . 52"
WEIGHT . . . . .1,036 LBS.
MSRP. $11,360

WSZK61

YEARS MFRD 2009-2010
SERIES. . . . . . .STANDER ZK SERIES
ENGINE . . . . KAWASAKI
CYLINDERS. 2
ENGINE HP 31
COOLING . . . . .AIR
FUEL . . . . G
SPEEDS . . . . .VARIABLE
TRANSMISSION . . . . .HYDRO
STEERING. . . . . .ZERO
BLADE CLUTCH . . . . .ELECTRIC
STANDARD DECK . . . . 61"
WEIGHT . . . . .1,240 LBS.
MSRP. $11,444

OPTIONS

KAWASAKI 37HP

RETAIL PRICING

YEAR	HIGH	LOW
2009	$6,196	$4,647
2010	$7,063	$5,297

WSZK61 ECV860E

YEARS MFRD 2016-2017
ENGINE . . . . KOHLER
ENGINE HP 29
FUEL . . . . G
SPEEDS . . . . .VARIABLE
TRANSMISSION . . . . .HYDRO
STEERING. . . . . .ZERO
STANDARD DECK . . . . 61"
WEIGHT . . . . .1,124 LBS.
MSRP. $11,400

RETAIL PRICING

YEAR	HIGH	LOW
2016	$7,375	$5,531
2017	$8,675	$6,506

WSZK61 FX801E

YEARS MFRD 2013-2017
SERIES. . . . . . .STANDER ZK SERIES
ENGINE . . . . KAWASAKI
ENGINE HP 29
COOLING . . . . .AIR
FUEL . . . . G
SPEEDS . . . . .VARIABLE
TRANSMISSION . . . . .HYDRO
STEERING. . . . . .ZERO
STANDARD DECK . . . . 61"
MSRP. $11,090

RETAIL PRICING

YEAR	HIGH	LOW
2013	$4,719	$3,539
2014	$5,480	$4,110
2015	$5,817	$4,363
2016	$6,958	$5,218
2017	$0	$0

WSZK61 FX850E

YEARS MFRD 2015-2017
SERIES. . . . . . .STANDER ZK SERIES
ENGINE . . . . KAWASAKI
ENGINE HP 27
COOLING . . . . .AIR
FUEL . . . . G
SPEEDS . . . . .VARIABLE
TRANSMISSION . . . . .HYDRO
STEERING. . . . . .ZERO
STANDARD DECK . . . . 61"
WEIGHT . . . . .1,124 LBS.
MSRP. $11,140

RETAIL PRICING

YEAR	HIGH	LOW
2015	$6,105	$4,579
2016	$7,119	$5,339
2017	$7,895	$5,921

WSZK61S 61E8E-49S

YEARS MFRD 2018-2020
SERIES. .STANDER ZK GEN 2 SERIES
ENGINE . . . . B&S 61E8
ENGINE HP 37
FUEL . . . . G
SPEEDS . . . . .VARIABLE
TRANSMISSION . . . . .HYDRO
STEERING. . . . . .ZERO
STANDARD DECK . . . . 61"
WEIGHT . . . . .1,124 LBS.
MSRP. $12,480

WSZK61S ECV860E-49S

YEARS MFRD 2018-2018
SERIES. .STANDER ZK GEN 2 SERIES
ENGINE . . . . KOHLER ECV860
ENGINE HP 29
FUEL . . . . G
SPEEDS . . . . .VARIABLE
TRANSMISSION . . . . .HYDRO
STEERING. . . . . .ZERO
STANDARD DECK . . . . 61"
WEIGHT . . . . .1,124 LBS.
MSRP. $11,560

WSZK61S FX850E-49S

YEARS MFRD 2018-2020
SERIES. .STANDER ZK GEN 2 SERIES
ENGINE . . . . .KAWASAKI FX850
ENGINE HP 27
FUEL . . . . G
SPEEDS . . . . .VARIABLE
TRANSMISSION . . . . .HYDRO
STEERING. . . . . .ZERO
STANDARD DECK . . . . 61"
WEIGHT . . . . .1,124 LBS.
MSRP. $11,710

WSZK72 ECV860E

YEARS MFRD 2016-2017
SERIES. . . . . . .STANDER ZK SERIES
ENGINE . . . . KOHLER
ENGINE HP 29
FUEL . . . . G
SPEEDS . . . . .VARIABLE
TRANSMISSION . . . . .HYDRO
STEERING. . . . . .ZERO
STANDARD DECK . . . . 72"
WEIGHT . . . . .1,202 LBS.
MSRP. $11,830

RETAIL PRICING

YEAR	HIGH	LOW
2016	$7,657	$5,743
2017	$8,460	$6,345

WSZK72S 61E8E-49S

YEARS MFRD 2018-2020
SERIES. .STANDER ZK GEN 2 SERIES
ENGINE . . . . B&S 61E8
ENGINE HP 37
FUEL . . . . G
SPEEDS . . . . .VARIABLE
TRANSMISSION . . . . .HYDRO
STEERING. . . . . .ZERO
STANDARD DECK . . . . 61"
WEIGHT . . . . .1,202 LBS.
MSRP. $12,980

WSZK72S ECV860E-49S

YEARS MFRD 2018-2018
SERIES. .STANDER ZK GEN 2 SERIES
ENGINE . . . . KOHLER ECV860
ENGINE HP 29
FUEL . . . . G
SPEEDS . . . . .VARIABLE
TRANSMISSION . . . . .HYDRO
STEERING. . . . . .ZERO
STANDARD DECK . . . . 72"
WEIGHT . . . . .1,202 LBS.
MSRP. $11,990

WSZK5227 KAWE

YEARS MFRD 2010-2011
ENGINE . . . . KAWASAKI
ENGINE HP 27
COOLING . . . . .AIR
FUEL . . . . G
SPEEDS . . . . .VARIABLE
TRANSMISSION . . . . .HYDRO
STEERING. . . . . .ZERO
STANDARD DECK . . . . 52"
MSRP. $10,814

RETAIL PRICING

YEAR	HIGH	LOW
2010	$4,702	$3,526
2011	$5,426	$4,070

WSZK5227 KAWE

YEARS MFRD 2009-2013
SERIES. . . . . . .STANDER ZK SERIES
ENGINE . . . . KAWASAKI
CYLINDERS. 2
ENGINE HP 27
COOLING . . . . .AIR
FUEL . . . . G
SPEEDS . . . . .VARIABLE
TRANSMISSION . . . . .HYDRO

WRIGHT

STEERING . . . . ZERO
STANDARD DECK . . . . 52"
WEIGHT . . . . 1,150 LBS.
MSRP $10,814

OPTIONS

KAWASAKI 31HP

RETAIL PRICING

YEAR	HIGH	LOW
2009	$2,815	$2,111
2010	$3,478	$2,609
2011	$4,216	$3,162
2012	$4,691	$3,518
2013	$6,337	$4,753

WSZK5231 KAWE

YEARS MFRD 2009-2013
SERIES . . . . STANDER ZK SERIES
ENGINE . . . . KAWASAKI
ENGINE HP 31
COOLING . . . . AIR
FUEL . . . . G
SPEEDS . . . . VARIABLE
TRANSMISSION . . . . HYDRO
STEERING . . . . ZERO
STANDARD DECK . . . . 52"
MSRP $10,949

RETAIL PRICING

YEAR	HIGH	LOW
2009	$2,923	$2,192
2010	$3,623	$2,717
2011	$4,424	$3,318
2012	$4,872	$3,654
2013	$6,899	$5,174

WSZK5231 KAWE

YEARS MFRD 2010-2011
ENGINE . . . . KAWASAKI
ENGINE HP 31
COOLING . . . . AIR
FUEL . . . . G
SPEEDS . . . . VARIABLE
TRANSMISSION . . . . HYDRO
STEERING . . . . ZERO
STANDARD DECK . . . . 52"
MSRP $11,359

RETAIL PRICING

YEAR	HIGH	LOW
2010	$4,889	$3,667
2011	$5,698	$4,273

WSZK5261E8E

YEARS MFRD 2018-2018
SERIES . . . . STANDER ZK SERIES
ENGINE . . . . B&S
ENGINE HP 37
TRANSMISSION . . . . HYDRO
STEERING . . . . ZERO
STANDARD DECK . . . . 52"
WEIGHT . . . . 1,062 LBS.

WSZK6131 KAWE

YEARS MFRD 2010-2011
ENGINE . . . . KAWASAKI
ENGINE HP 31
COOLING . . . . AIR
FUEL . . . . G
SPEEDS . . . . VARIABLE
TRANSMISSION . . . . HYDRO
STEERING . . . . ZERO
STANDARD DECK . . . . 61"
MSRP $11,789

RETAIL PRICING

YEAR	HIGH	LOW
2010	$5,085	$3,814
2011	$5,913	$4,435

WSZK6131 KAWE

YEARS MFRD 2009-2013
SERIES . . . . STANDER ZK SERIES
ENGINE . . . . KAWASAKI
ENGINE HP 31
COOLING . . . . AIR
FUEL . . . . G
SPEEDS . . . . VARIABLE
TRANSMISSION . . . . HYDRO
STEERING . . . . ZERO
STANDARD DECK . . . . 61"
MSRP $11,389

RETAIL PRICING

YEAR	HIGH	LOW
2009	$3,038	$2,279
2010	$3,761	$2,821
2011	$4,597	$3,448
2012	$5,002	$3,752
2013	$7,202	$5,402

WSZK6161E8E

YEARS MFRD 2018-2018
SERIES . . . . STANDER ZK SERIES
ENGINE . . . . B&S
ENGINE HP 37
TRANSMISSION . . . . HYDRO
STEERING . . . . ZERO
STANDARD DECK . . . . 61"
WEIGHT . . . . 1,124 LBS.

WSZK7237 KAWE

YEARS MFRD 2011-2011
ENGINE . . . . KAWASAKI
ENGINE HP 37
COOLING . . . . AIR
FUEL . . . . G
SPEEDS . . . . VARIABLE
TRANSMISSION . . . . HYDRO
STEERING . . . . ZERO
BLADE CLUTCH . . . . ELECTRIC
STANDARD DECK . . . . 72"
MSRP $12,709

RETAIL PRICING

YEAR	HIGH	LOW
2011	$6,373	$4,780

WSZK7261E8E

YEARS MFRD 2018-2018
SERIES . . . . STANDER ZK SERIES
ENGINE . . . . B&S
ENGINE HP 37
TRANSMISSION . . . . HYDRO
STEERING . . . . ZERO
STANDARD DECK . . . . 72"
WEIGHT . . . . 1,202 LBS.

WZ48FX801E

YEARS MFRD 2013-2016
SERIES . . . . Z SERIES
ENGINE . . . . KAWASAKI
ENGINE HP 29
COOLING . . . . AIR
FUEL . . . . G
SPEEDS . . . . VARIABLE
TRANSMISSION . . . . HYDRO
STEERING . . . . ZERO
STANDARD DECK . . . . 48"
MSRP $9,404

RETAIL PRICING

YEAR	HIGH	LOW
2013	$4,338	$3,253
2014	$5,010	$3,758
2015	$5,329	$3,997
2016	$6,180	$4,635

WZ52FX801E

YEARS MFRD 2013-2016
SERIES . . . . Z SERIES
ENGINE . . . . KAWASAKI
COOLING . . . . AIR
FUEL . . . . G
SPEEDS . . . . VARIABLE
TRANSMISSION . . . . HYDRO
STEERING . . . . ZERO
STANDARD DECK . . . . 52"
MSRP $9,479

RETAIL PRICING

YEAR	HIGH	LOW
2013	$4,427	$3,320
2014	$5,108	$3,831
2015	$5,702	$4,276
2016	$6,294	$4,721

WZ52FX850E

YEARS MFRD 2013-2020
SERIES . . . . . MID MOUNT Z SERIES
ENGINE . . . . KAWASAKI
ENGINE HP 27
COOLING . . . . AIR
FUEL . . . . G
SPEEDS . . . . VARIABLE
TRANSMISSION . . . . HYDRO
STEERING . . . . ZERO
STANDARD DECK . . . . 52"
WEIGHT . . . . 1,213 LBS.
MSRP $10,160

RETAIL PRICING

YEAR	HIGH	LOW
2013	$4,370	$3,277
2014	$5,049	$3,786
2015	$5,263	$3,947
2016	$6,140	$4,605
2017	$6,906	$5,179
2018	$7,946	$5,959
2019	$8,498	$6,373
2020	$9,317	$7,029

WZ61FX801E

YEARS MFRD 2013-2016
SERIES . . . . Z SERIES
ENGINE . . . . KAWASAKI
ENGINE HP 29
COOLING . . . . AIR
FUEL . . . . G
SPEEDS . . . . VARIABLE
TRANSMISSION . . . . HYDRO
STEERING . . . . ZERO
STANDARD DECK . . . . 61"
MSRP $9,444

RETAIL PRICING

YEAR	HIGH	LOW
2013	$4,444	$3,333
2014	$5,134	$3,851
2015	$5,348	$4,011
2016	$6,463	$4,847

WZ61FX850E

YEARS MFRD 2013-2020
SERIES . . . . . MID MOUNT Z SERIES
ENGINE . . . . KAWASAKI
ENGINE HP 27
COOLING . . . . AIR
FUEL . . . . G
SPEEDS . . . . VARIABLE
TRANSMISSION . . . . HYDRO
STEERING . . . . ZERO
STANDARD DECK . . . . 61"
WEIGHT . . . . 1,235 LBS.
MSRP $10,410

RETAIL PRICING

YEAR	HIGH	LOW
2013	$4,387	$3,290
2014	$5,065	$3,799
2015	$5,281	$3,960
2016	$6,302	$5,019
2017	$7,088	$5,316
2018	$8,157	$6,117
2019	$8,733	$6,550
2020	$9,665	$7,303

WZ4821KAWE

YEARS MFRD 2008-2010
ENGINE . . . . KAWASAKI
CYLINDERS 2
ENGINE HP 21
COOLING . . . . AIR
FUEL . . . . G
SPEEDS . . . . VARIABLE
TRANSMISSION . . . . HYDRO
STEERING . . . . ZERO
STANDARD DECK . . . . 48"

WEIGHT .... 940 LBS.
MSRP.................. $8,794

RETAIL PRICING

YEAR	HIGH	LOW
2008	$4,922	$3,691
2009	$4,982	$3,736
2010	$5,426	$4,070

WZ4827KAWE

YEARS MFRD 2010-2011
ENGINE .... KAWASAKI
ENGINE HP.................. 27
COOLING.................. AIR
FUEL........................ G
SPEEDS .... VARIABLE
TRANSMISSION .... HYDRO
STEERING................ ZERO
BLADE CLUTCH .... ELECTRIC
STANDARD DECK .... 48"
MSRP.................. $8,874

RETAIL PRICING

YEAR	HIGH	LOW
2010	$3,929	$2,946
2011	$4,576	$3,432

WZ5225KAWE

YEARS MFRD 2008-2010
ENGINE .... KAWASAKI
CYLINDERS.................. 2
ENGINE HP.................. 25
COOLING.................. AIR
FUEL........................ G
SPEEDS .... VARIABLE
TRANSMISSION .... HYDRO
STEERING................ ZERO
STANDARD DECK .... 52"
WEIGHT .... 950 LBS.
MSRP.................. $9,699

RETAIL PRICING

YEAR	HIGH	LOW
2008	$5,452	$4,089
2009	$5,769	$4,326
2010	$5,985	$4,489

WZ5227KAWE

YEARS MFRD 2010-2011
ENGINE .... KAWASAKI
ENGINE HP.................. 27
COOLING.................. AIR
FUEL........................ G
SPEEDS .... VARIABLE
TRANSMISSION .... HYDRO
STEERING................ ZERO
STANDARD DECK .... 52"
MSRP.................. $9,564

RETAIL PRICING

YEAR	HIGH	LOW
2010	$4,241	$3,181
2011	$4,931	$3,699

WZ5231KAWE

YEARS MFRD 2010-2011
ENGINE .... KAWASAKI
ENGINE HP.................. 31
COOLING.................. AIR
FUEL........................ G
SPEEDS .... VARIABLE
TRANSMISSION .... HYDRO
STEERING................ ZERO
STANDARD DECK .... 52"
MSRP.................. $9,914

RETAIL PRICING

YEAR	HIGH	LOW
2010	$4,395	$3,296
2011	$5,112	$3,834

WZ6125KAWE

YEARS MFRD 2008-2010
ENGINE .... KAWASAKI
CYLINDERS.................. 2
ENGINE HP.................. 25
COOLING.................. AIR
FUEL........................ G
SPEEDS .... VARIABLE
TRANSMISSION .... HYDRO
STEERING................ ZERO
STANDARD DECK .... 61"
WEIGHT .... 985 LBS.
MSRP.................. $9,879

RETAIL PRICING

YEAR	HIGH	LOW
2008	$4,898	$3,673
2009	$5,223	$3,918
2010	$6,097	$4,573

WZ6131KAWE

YEARS MFRD 2010-2011
ENGINE .... KAWASAKI
ENGINE HP.................. 31
COOLING.................. AIR
FUEL........................ G
SPEEDS .... VARIABLE
TRANSMISSION .... HYDRO
STEERING................ ZERO
STANDARD DECK .... 61"
MSRP.................. $10,269

RETAIL PRICING

YEAR	HIGH	LOW
2010	$4,562	$3,421
2011	$5,293	$3,970

WZ7231

YEARS MFRD 2010-2011
ENGINE .... KAWASAKI
ENGINE HP.................. 31
COOLING.................. AIR
FUEL........................ G
SPEEDS .... VARIABLE
TRANSMISSION .... HYDRO
STEERING................ ZERO
STANDARD DECK .... 72"
MSRP.................. $10,864

RETAIL PRICING

YEAR	HIGH	LOW
2010	$4,826	$3,619
2011	$5,599	$4,199

WZT048 FX691E

YEARS MFRD 2013-2017
SERIES............. ZTO SERIES
ENGINE .... KAWASAKI
ENGINE HP.................. 22
COOLING.................. AIR
FUEL........................ G
SPEEDS .... VARIABLE
TRANSMISSION .... HYDRO
STEERING................ ZERO
STANDARD DECK .... 48"
MSRP.................. $7,964

RETAIL PRICING

YEAR	HIGH	LOW
2013	$3,524	$2,643
2014	$4,072	$3,054
2015	$4,515	$3,387
2016	$4,984	$3,738
2017	$5,468	$4,101

WZT048 FX730E

YEARS MFRD 2018-2020
SERIES............. ZTO SERIES
ENGINE .... KAWASAKI FX730
ENGINE HP................ 23.5
TRANSMISSION .... HYDRO
STEERING................ ZERO
STANDARD DECK .... 48"
WEIGHT .... 1,080 LBS.
MSRP.................. $8,590

WZT052 FX691E

YEARS MFRD 2013-2016
SERIES............. ZTO SERIES
ENGINE .... KAWASAKI
ENGINE HP.................. 24
COOLING.................. AIR
FUEL........................ G
SPEEDS .... VARIABLE
TRANSMISSION .... HYDRO
STEERING................ ZERO
STANDARD DECK .... 52"
MSRP.................. $8,174

RETAIL PRICING

YEAR	HIGH	LOW
2013	$3,621	$2,716
2014	$4,179	$3,134
2015	$4,630	$3,472
2016	$5,472	$4,104

WZT052 FX730E

YEARS MFRD 2014-2020
SERIES............. ZTO SERIES
ENGINE .... KAWASAKI
ENGINE HP................ 23.5
COOLING.................. AIR
FUEL........................ G
SPEEDS .... VARIABLE
TRANSMISSION .... HYDRO
STEERING................ ZERO
STANDARD DECK .... 52"
WEIGHT .... 1,102 LBS.
MSRP.................. $8,770

RETAIL PRICING

YEAR	HIGH	LOW
2014	$4,258	$3,194
2015	$4,718	$3,538
2016	$5,594	$4,196
2017	$6,090	$4,567
2018	$7,024	$5,269
2019	$7,459	$5,594
2020	$8,179	$6,350

WZT061 FX730E

YEARS MFRD 2013-2020
SERIES............. ZTO SERIES
ENGINE .... KAWASAKI
ENGINE HP................ 23.5
COOLING.................. AIR
FUEL........................ G
SPEEDS .... VARIABLE
TRANSMISSION .... HYDRO
STEERING................ ZERO
STANDARD DECK .... 61"
WEIGHT .... 1,157 LBS.
MSRP.................. $9,020

RETAIL PRICING

YEAR	HIGH	LOW
2013	$3,596	$2,697
2014	$4,155	$3,116
2015	$4,601	$3,451
2016	$5,591	$4,193
2017	$6,461	$4,846
2018	$7,381	$5,535
2019	$7,795	$5,847
2020	$8,433	$6,336

WZT0 4824BSE

YEARS MFRD 2013-2014
SERIES............. ZTO SERIES
ENGINE .... B&S
COOLING.................. AIR
FUEL........................ G
SPEEDS .... VARIABLE
TRANSMISSION .... HYDRO
STEERING................ ZERO
STANDARD DECK .... 48"
MSRP.................. $7,589

RETAIL PRICING

YEAR	HIGH	LOW
2013	$3,349	$2,512
2014	$4,085	$3,064

WRIGHT

WZT04844T9E

YEARS MFRD 2015-2017
ENGINE . . . . B&S
ENGINE HP 25
FUEL . . . . G
SPEEDS . . . . VARIABLE
TRANSMISSION . . . . HYDRO
STEERING. . . . . ZERO
STANDARD DECK . . . . 48"
MSRP. $7,549

RETAIL PRICING

YEAR	HIGH	LOW
2015	$4,344	$3,258
2016	$5,020	$3,765
2017	$5,878	$4,409

WZT05224T9E

YEARS MFRD 2015-2015
ENGINE . . . . B&S
ENGINE HP 25
FUEL . . . . G
SPEEDS . . . . VARIABLE
TRANSMISSION . . . . HYDRO
STEERING. . . . . ZERO
STANDARD DECK . . . . 52"
MSRP. $7,699

RETAIL PRICING

YEAR	HIGH	LOW
2015	$4,144	$3,108

WZT05226BSE

YEARS MFRD 2013-2014
SERIES. . . . . ZTO SERIES
ENGINE . . . . B&S
COOLING . . . . AIR
FUEL . . . . G
SPEEDS . . . . VARIABLE
TRANSMISSION . . . . HYDRO
STEERING. . . . . ZERO
STANDARD DECK . . . . 52"
MSRP. $7,799

RETAIL PRICING

YEAR	HIGH	LOW
2013	$3,448	$2,586
2014	$4,204	$3,153

WZT05244T9E

YEARS MFRD 2016-2017
ENGINE . . . . B&S
COOLING . . . . AIR
FUEL . . . . G
SPEEDS . . . . VARIABLE
TRANSMISSION . . . . HYDRO
STEERING. . . . . ZERO
STANDARD DECK . . . . 52"
MSRP. $7,679

RETAIL PRICING

YEAR	HIGH	LOW
2016	$5,047	$3,785
2017	$5,394	$4,046

WZT06144T9E

YEARS MFRD 2015-2017
ENGINE . . . . B&S
ENGINE HP 25
FUEL . . . . G
SPEEDS . . . . VARIABLE
TRANSMISSION . . . . HYDRO
STEERING. . . . . ZERO
STANDARD DECK . . . . 61"
MSRP. $8,379

RETAIL PRICING

YEAR	HIGH	LOW
2015	$4,573	$3,429
2016	$5,448	$4,086
2017	$6,224	$4,668

YANMAR

EX450

YEARS MFRD 2013-2017
ENGINE . . . . YANMAR
CYLINDERS. 4
CID 133
PTO HP 37.5
COOLING . . . . LIQUID
FUEL . . . . D
SPEEDS 9/9
TRANSMISSION . . . SHUTTLE SHIFT
STEERING. . . . . STANDARD
DRIVE TYPE 2WD
ROPS/CAB . . . . ROPS
WEIGHT . . . . 3,464 LBS.
MSRP. $26,770

OPTIONS

BACKHOE
LDR

RETAIL PRICING

YEAR	HIGH	LOW
2013	$12,892	$9,669
2014	$14,118	$10,588
2015	$15,298	$11,473
2016	$17,023	$12,767
2017	$19,429	$14,571

EX2900

YEARS MFRD 2013-2014
ENGINE . . . . YANMAR
CYLINDERS. 3
CID 100
PTO HP 22.7
FUEL . . . . D
SPEEDS . . . . VARIABLE
TRANSMISSION . . . . HYDRO
STEERING. . . . . STANDARD
DRIVE TYPE 2WD
ROPS/CAB . . . . ROPS
WEIGHT . . . . 2,540 LBS.
MSRP. $17,245

OPTIONS

BACKHOE
LDR

RETAIL PRICING

YEAR	HIGH	LOW
2013	$11,547	$8,661
2014	$12,148	$9,111

EX3200

YEARS MFRD 2013-2017
ENGINE . . . . YANMAR
CYLINDERS. 3
CID 100
PTO HP 25.5
COOLING . . . . LIQUID
FUEL . . . . D
SPEEDS . . . . VARIABLE
TRANSMISSION . . . . HYDRO
STEERING. . . . . STANDARD
DRIVE TYPE 2WD
ROPS/CAB . . . . ROPS
WEIGHT . . . . 2,094 LBS.
MSRP. $18,925

OPTIONS

BACKHOE
LDR

RETAIL PRICING

YEAR	HIGH	LOW
2013	$9,124	$6,843
2014	$9,986	$7,490
2015	$10,804	$8,103
2016	$12,030	$9,022
2017	$14,253	$10,690

LX410

YEARS MFRD 2013-2017
ENGINE . . . . YANMAR
CYLINDERS. 4
CID 133
PTO HP 30.4
COOLING . . . . LIQUID
FUEL . . . . D
SPEEDS 12/12
TRANSMISSION . . . SHUTTLE SHIFT
STEERING. . . . . STANDARD
DRIVE TYPE 2WD
ROPS/CAB . . . . ROPS
WEIGHT . . . . 3,585 LBS.
MSRP. $27,250

OPTIONS

BACKHOE
LDR

RETAIL PRICING

YEAR	HIGH	LOW
2013	$13,118	$9,839
2014	$14,344	$10,758
2015	$15,570	$11,678
2016	$17,340	$13,005
2017	$19,383	$14,538

LX450

YEARS MFRD 2013-2017
ENGINE . . . . YANMAR
CYLINDERS. 4
CID 133
PTO HP 34.3
COOLING . . . . LIQUID
FUEL . . . . D
SPEEDS 12/12
TRANSMISSION . . . SHUTTLE SHIFT
STEERING. . . . . STANDARD
DRIVE TYPE 2WD
ROPS/CAB . . . . ROPS
WEIGHT . . . . 3,585 LBS.
MSRP. $29,290

OPTIONS

BACKHOE
LDR

RETAIL PRICING

YEAR	HIGH	LOW
2013	$14,072	$10,554
2014	$15,434	$11,576
2015	$16,750	$12,563
2016	$18,611	$13,958
2017	$20,700	$15,525

LX490

YEARS MFRD 2013-2017
ENGINE . . . . YANMAR
CYLINDERS. 4
CID 121
PTO HP 36.8
COOLING . . . . LIQUID
FUEL . . . . D
SPEEDS 12/12
TRANSMISSION . . . SHUTTLE SHIFT
STEERING. . . . . STANDARD
DRIVE TYPE 2WD
ROPS/CAB . . . . ROPS
WEIGHT . . . . 3,618 LBS.
MSRP. $31,286

OPTIONS

BACKHOE
LDR

RETAIL PRICING

YEAR	HIGH	LOW
2013	$15,070	$11,303
2014	$16,478	$12,358
2015	$17,885	$13,414
2016	$19,882	$14,912
2017	$23,423	$17,567

LX4100

YEARS MFRD 2013-2017
ENGINE . . . . YANMAR
CYLINDERS. 4
CID 133
PTO HP 28.6
COOLING . . . . LIQUID
FUEL . . . . D
SPEEDS . . . . VARIABLE
TRANSMISSION . . . . HYDRO
STEERING. . . . . STANDARD
DRIVE TYPE 2WD
ROPS/CAB . . . . ROPS
WEIGHT . . . . 3,595 LBS.
MSRP. $33,305

OPTIONS

BACKHOE
LDR

RETAIL PRICING

YEAR	HIGH	LOW
2013	$16,024	$12,018
2014	$17,522	$13,142
2015	$19,065	$14,299
2016	$22,062	$16,546
2017	$25,148	$18,861

LX4500

YEARS MFRD 2013-2017
ENGINE . . . . YANMAR
CYLINDERS. 4
CID 133
PTO HP 32.5
FUEL . . . . D
SPEEDS . . . . VARIABLE
TRANSMISSION . . . . HYDRO
STEERING. . . . . STANDARD
DRIVE TYPE 2WD
ROPS/CAB . . . . ROPS
WEIGHT . . . . 3,595 LBS.
MSRP. $34,090

OPTIONS

BACKHOE
LDR

RETAIL PRICING

YEAR	HIGH	LOW
2013	$16,388	$12,291
2014	$17,930	$13,448
2015	$19,520	$14,640
2016	$21,653	$16,240
2017	$24,422	$18,316

LX4900

YEARS MFRD 2013-2017
ENGINE . . . . YANMAR
CYLINDERS. 4
CID 121
PTO HP 35
COOLING . . . . LIQUID
FUEL . . . . D
SPEEDS . . . . VARIABLE
TRANSMISSION . . . . HYDRO
STEERING. . . . . STANDARD
WEIGHT . . . . 3,619 LBS.
MSRP. $35,160

OPTIONS

BACKHOE
LDR

RETAIL PRICING

YEAR	HIGH	LOW
2013	$16,931	$12,699
2014	$18,521	$13,891
2015	$20,110	$15,082
2016	$22,333	$16,750
2017	$26,056	$19,542

SC2400

YEARS MFRD 2013-2014
ENGINE . . . . YANMAR
CYLINDERS. 3
CID 55
PTO HP 16.5
FUEL . . . . D
SPEEDS . . . . VARIABLE
TRANSMISSION . . . . HYDRO
STEERING. . . . . STANDARD
DRIVE TYPE 2WD
ROPS/CAB . . . . ROPS
WEIGHT . . . . 1,280 LBS.
MSRP. $11,865

OPTIONS

60" DECK
BACKHOE
LDR

RETAIL PRICING

YEAR	HIGH	LOW
2013	$7,945	$5,959
2014	$8,147	$6,110

SX3100

YEARS MFRD 2013-2017
ENGINE . . . . YANMAR
CYLINDERS. 3
CID 100
PTO HP 23.5
COOLING . . . . LIQUID

YANMAR

SPEEDS . . . . VARIABLE
TRANSMISSION . . . . HYDRO
STEERING. . . . . STANDARD
DRIVE TYPE 2WD
ROPS/CAB . . . . ROPS
WEIGHT . . . . 2,094 LBS.
MSRP. $20,275

OPTIONS

60" DECK
BACKHOE
LDR

RETAIL PRICING

YEAR	HIGH	LOW
2013	$9,760	$7,320
2014	$10,667	$8,000
2015	$11,576	$8,682
2016	$12,892	$9,669
2017	$14,889	$11,167

TM186

YEARS MFRD 1980-1986
ENGINE . . . . YANMAR
CYLINDERS. 3
CID 53.6
PTO HP 14.5
ENGINE HP 18
FUEL . . . . D
SPEEDS 9/3
DRIVE TYPE 2WD
ROPS/CAB . . . . ROPS
WEIGHT . . . . 1,412 LBS.

TMFX24D

YEARS MFRD 1984-1984
CYLINDERS. 3
ENGINE HP 28
TRANSMISSION . . . . HYDRO
DRIVE TYPE 4WD
ROPS/CAB . . . . ROPS
WEIGHT . . . . 2,623 LBS.

TMG2000D

YEARS MFRD 1988-1988
CYLINDERS. 3
ENGINE HP 23.5
TRANSMISSION . . . . GEAR
DRIVE TYPE 4WD
ROPS/CAB . . . . ROPS
WEIGHT . . . . 1,918 LBS.

YM122

YEARS MFRD 1983-1989
ENGINE . . . . YANMAR
CYLINDERS. 1
CID 32.6
PTO HP 7.8
ENGINE HP 12
FUEL . . . . D
SPEEDS 6/3
DRIVE TYPE 2WD
ROPS/CAB . . . . ROPS
WEIGHT . . . . 822 LBS.
MSRP. $4,295

RETAIL PRICING

YEAR	HIGH	LOW
1983	$908	$681
1984	$1,002	$751
1985	$1,060	$795
1986	$1,121	$841
1987	$1,152	$864
1988	$1,182	$886
1989	$1,243	$932

YM126

YEARS MFRD 1984-1985
ENGINE . . . . YANMAR
CYLINDERS. 1
CID 32.5
PTO HP 7.8
ENGINE HP 12
FUEL . . . . D
SPEEDS 6/3
DRIVE TYPE 2WD
ROPS/CAB . . . . ROPS
WEIGHT . . . . 831 LBS.

YM135

YEARS MFRD 1976-1981
ENGINE . . . . YANMAR
CYLINDERS. 2
CID 38.3
ENGINE HP 13
FUEL . . . . D
SPEEDS 6/2
TRANSMISSION . . . . GEAR
DRIVE TYPE 2WD
WEIGHT . . . . 992 LBS.
MSRP. $4,250

RETAIL PRICING

YEAR	HIGH	LOW
1977	$626	$470
1978	$641	$481
1979	$655	$491
1980	$670	$503
1981	$759	$569

YM135D

YEARS MFRD 1976-1981
ENGINE . . . . YANMAR
CYLINDERS. 2
CID 38.3
ENGINE HP 13
FUEL . . . . D
SPEEDS 6/2
DRIVE TYPE 4WD
WEIGHT . . . . 1,091 LBS.
MSRP. $4,650

RETAIL PRICING

YEAR	HIGH	LOW
1976	$669	$502
1977	$689	$517
1978	$704	$528
1979	$721	$541
1980	$741	$556
1981	$830	$623

YM140-2

YEARS MFRD 1984-1992
ENGINE . . . . YANMAR
CYLINDERS. 2
CID 38.8
PTO HP 10.8
ENGINE HP 14
FUEL . . . . D
SPEEDS 6/3
TRANSMISSION . . . . GEAR
DRIVE TYPE 2WD
ROPS/CAB . . . . ROPS
WEIGHT . . . . 1,266 LBS.
MSRP. $6,550

RETAIL PRICING

YEAR	HIGH	LOW
1984	$1,381	$1,036
1985	$1,465	$1,099
1986	$1,548	$1,161
1987	$1,591	$1,193
1988	$1,633	$1,225
1989	$1,868	$1,401
1990	$1,882	$1,411
1991	$2,024	$1,518
1992	$2,124	$1,593

YM140D-4

YEARS MFRD 1984-1992
ENGINE . . . . YANMAR
CYLINDERS. 2
CID 38.8
ENGINE HP 14
FUEL . . . . D
SPEEDS 6/3
TRANSMISSION . . . . GEAR
DRIVE TYPE 4WD
ROPS/CAB . . . . ROPS
WEIGHT . . . . 1,368 LBS.
MSRP. $6,950

RETAIL PRICING

YEAR	HIGH	LOW
1984	$1,489	$1,116
1985	$1,578	$1,183
1986	$1,669	$1,252
1987	$1,714	$1,286
1988	$1,760	$1,320
1989	$2,011	$1,508
1990	$2,030	$1,522
1991	$2,166	$1,624
1992	$2,252	$1,689

YM142

YEARS MFRD 1984-1985
ENGINE . . . . YANMAR
CYLINDERS. 2
CID 38.8
PTO HP 10.2
ENGINE HP 14
FUEL . . . . D
SPEEDS 6/3
DRIVE TYPE 2WD
WEIGHT . . . . 842 LBS.

YM146

YEARS MFRD 1983-1993
ENGINE . . . . YANMAR
CYLINDERS. 2
CID 38.8
PTO HP 10.2
ENGINE HP 14
FUEL . . . . D
SPEEDS 6/3
TRANSMISSION . . . . GEAR
DRIVE TYPE 2WD
WEIGHT . . . . 836 LBS.
MSRP. $5,250

RETAIL PRICING

YEAR	HIGH	LOW
1983	$1,065	$799
1984	$1,173	$880
1985	$1,242	$931
1986	$1,312	$984
1987	$1,348	$1,011
1988	$1,385	$1,039
1989	$1,519	$1,139
1990	$1,532	$1,149
1991	$1,634	$1,225
1992	$1,701	$1,276
1993	$1,755	$1,316

YM147

YEARS MFRD 1984-1993
ENGINE . . . . YANMAR
CYLINDERS. 2
CID 38.8
PTO HP 10.8
ENGINE HP 14
FUEL . . . . D
SPEEDS 6/3
DRIVE TYPE 2WD
ROPS/CAB . . . . ROPS
WEIGHT . . . . 1,281 LBS.
MSRP. $6,895

RETAIL PRICING

YEAR	HIGH	LOW
1984	$1,474	$1,105
1985	$1,563	$1,172
1986	$1,652	$1,239
1987	$1,697	$1,273
1988	$1,743	$1,308
1989	$1,996	$1,497
1990	$2,012	$1,509
1991	$2,147	$1,610
1992	$2,234	$1,676
1993	$2,304	$1,728

YM147D

YEARS MFRD 1984-1993
ENGINE . . . . YANMAR
CYLINDERS. 2
CID 38.8
PTO HP 10.8
ENGINE HP 14
FUEL . . . . D
SPEEDS 6/3
DRIVE TYPE 4WD
ROPS/CAB . . . . ROPS
WEIGHT . . . . 1,382 LBS.
MSRP. $7,450

RETAIL PRICING

YEAR	HIGH	LOW
1984	$1,596	$1,197
1985	$1,691	$1,269
1986	$1,791	$1,344
1987	$1,839	$1,380
1988	$1,887	$1,416
1989	$2,157	$1,618
1990	$2,174	$1,630
1991	$2,319	$1,739
1992	$2,416	$1,812
1993	$2,491	$1,868

YM150T

ENGINE .... YANMAR
CYLINDERS 2
CID 40.4
ENGINE HP 15
FUEL .... D
SPEEDS 6/2
WEIGHT .... 1,036 LBS.

YM155DT

YEARS MFRD 1976-1980
ENGINE .... YANMAR
CYLINDERS 2
CID 40.4
ENGINE HP 15
FUEL .... D
SPEEDS 6/2
TRANSMISSION .... GEAR
DRIVE TYPE 4WD
WEIGHT .... 1,146 LBS.
MSRP $4,500

RETAIL PRICING

YEAR	HIGH	LOW
1976	$710	$532
1977	$736	$552
1978	$762	$572
1979	$784	$588
1980	$804	$603

YM155T

YEARS MFRD 1976-1980
ENGINE .... YANMAR
CYLINDERS 2
CID 40.4
ENGINE HP 15
FUEL .... D
SPEEDS 6/2
TRANSMISSION .... GEAR
DRIVE TYPE 2WD
WEIGHT .... 1,058 LBS.
MSRP $4,165

RETAIL PRICING

YEAR	HIGH	LOW
1976	$657	$492
1977	$664	$498
1978	$691	$518
1979	$725	$544
1980	$743	$557

YM165

YEARS MFRD 1980-1988
ENGINE .... YANMAR
CYLINDERS 2
CID 40.4
ENGINE HP 16
FUEL .... D
SPEEDS 6/2
TRANSMISSION .... GEAR
DRIVE TYPE 2WD
WEIGHT .... 1,109 LBS.
MSRP $5,810

RETAIL PRICING

YEAR	HIGH	LOW
1980	$809	$606
1981	$874	$656
1982	$981	$736
1983	$1,195	$896
1984	$1,364	$1,023
1985	$1,446	$1,085
1986	$1,531	$1,148
1987	$1,572	$1,179
1988	$1,613	$1,210

YM165D

YEARS MFRD 1980-1988
ENGINE .... YANMAR
CYLINDERS 2
CID 40.4
ENGINE HP 16
FUEL .... D
SPEEDS 6/2
TRANSMISSION .... GEAR
DRIVE TYPE 4WD
WEIGHT .... 1,230 LBS.
MSRP $6,310

RETAIL PRICING

YEAR	HIGH	LOW
1980	$898	$673
1981	$963	$723
1982	$1,070	$803
1983	$1,308	$981
1984	$1,481	$1,111
1985	$1,572	$1,179
1986	$1,661	$1,246
1987	$1,708	$1,281
1988	$1,751	$1,313

YM169

YEARS MFRD 1986-1991
ENGINE .... YANMAR
CYLINDERS 3
CID 53.6
PTO HP 13
ENGINE HP 18
FUEL .... D
SPEEDS 6/2
DRIVE TYPE 2WD
ROPS/CAB .... CAB
WEIGHT .... 1,190 LBS.
MSRP $8,300

RETAIL PRICING

YEAR	HIGH	LOW
1986	$1,870	$1,402
1987	$1,919	$1,439
1988	$1,971	$1,478
1989	$2,074	$1,555
1990	$2,136	$1,602
1991	$2,452	$1,839

YM169 NURSERY SPECIAL

YEARS MFRD 1986-1991
ENGINE .... YANMAR
CYLINDERS 3
CID 53.6
PTO HP 13
ENGINE HP 18
FUEL .... D
SPEEDS 6/2
DRIVE TYPE 2WD
ROPS/CAB .... CAB
WEIGHT .... 1,085 LBS.
MSRP $7,870

RETAIL PRICING

YEAR	HIGH	LOW
1990	$2,063	$1,547
1991	$2,451	$1,838

YM169D

YEARS MFRD 1986-1991
ENGINE .... YANMAR
CYLINDERS 3
CID 53.6
PTO HP 13
ENGINE HP 18
FUEL .... D
SPEEDS 6/2
TRANSMISSION .... GEAR
DRIVE TYPE 4WD
ROPS/CAB .... CAB
WEIGHT .... 1,279 LBS.
MSRP $9,175

RETAIL PRICING

YEAR	HIGH	LOW
1986	$2,080	$1,560
1987	$2,135	$1,602
1988	$2,192	$1,644
1989	$2,633	$1,975
1990	$2,656	$1,992
1991	$2,857	$2,143

YM169D NURSERY SPECIAL

YEARS MFRD 1986-1991
ENGINE .... YANMAR
CYLINDERS 3
CID 53.6
PTO HP 13
ENGINE HP 18
FUEL .... D
SPEEDS 6/2
WEIGHT .... 1,174 LBS.
MSRP $8,530

RETAIL PRICING

YEAR	HIGH	LOW
1986	$2,034	$1,526
1990	$2,256	$1,692
1991	$2,657	$1,993

YM175DT

YEARS MFRD 1976-1979
ENGINE .... YANMAR
CYLINDERS 2
CID 52.14
ENGINE HP 17
FUEL .... D
SPEEDS 8/2
WEIGHT .... 1,520 LBS.

YM175T

YEARS MFRD 1976-1979
ENGINE .... YANMAR
CYLINDERS 2
CID 52.14
ENGINE HP 17
FUEL .... D
SPEEDS 8/2
WEIGHT .... 1,430 LBS.

YM180

YEARS MFRD 1983-1993
ENGINE .... YANMAR
CYLINDERS 3
CID 53.6
PTO HP 14.5
ENGINE HP 18
FUEL .... D
SPEEDS 8/2
TRANSMISSION .... GEAR
DRIVE TYPE 2WD
WEIGHT .... 1,523 LBS.
MSRP $7,440

RETAIL PRICING

YEAR	HIGH	LOW
1990	$1,911	$1,433
1991	$2,039	$1,530
1992	$2,122	$1,591
1993	$2,486	$1,865

YM180-2

YEARS MFRD 1984-1989
ENGINE .... YANMAR
CYLINDERS 3
CID 53.6
PTO HP 14.5
ENGINE HP 18
FUEL .... D
SPEEDS .... 8/2 POWERSHIFT
TRANSMISSION .... GEAR
DRIVE TYPE 2WD
ROPS/CAB .... ROPS
WEIGHT .... 1,643 LBS.
MSRP $7,450

RETAIL PRICING

YEAR	HIGH	LOW
1984	$1,538	$1,153
1985	$1,631	$1,223

YEAR	HIGH	LOW
1986	$1,725	$1,294
1987	$1,771	$1,328
1988	$1,818	$1,363
1989	$2,157	$1,618

YM180D

YEARS MFRD . . . 1984-1993
ENGINE . . . YANMAR
CYLINDERS . . . 3
CID . . . 53.6
PTO HP . . . 14.5
ENGINE HP . . . 18
FUEL . . . D
SPEEDS . . . 8/2
DRIVE TYPE . . . 4WD
ROPS/CAB . . . ROPS
WEIGHT . . . 1,643 LBS.
MSRP . . . $8,165

RETAIL PRICING

YEAR	HIGH	LOW
1990	$2,102	$1,577
1991	$2,244	$1,683
1992	$2,335	$1,752
1993	$2,729	$2,047

YM180D-4

YEARS MFRD . . . 1984-1991
ENGINE . . . YANMAR
CYLINDERS . . . 3
CID . . . 53.6
PTO HP . . . 14.5
ENGINE HP . . . 18
FUEL . . . D
SPEEDS . . . 8/2 POWERSHIFT
TRANSMISSION . . . GEAR
HITCH . . . SLEEVE
DRIVE TYPE . . . 4WD
ROPS/CAB . . . ROPS
WEIGHT . . . 1,793 LBS.
MSRP . . . $8,160

RETAIL PRICING

YEAR	HIGH	LOW
1984	$1,691	$1,268
1985	$1,794	$1,346
1986	$1,895	$1,421
1987	$1,947	$1,460
1988	$1,998	$1,499
1989	$2,359	$1,769
1990	$2,381	$1,786
1991	$2,540	$1,905

YM186-2

YEARS MFRD . . . 1980-1988
ENGINE . . . YANMAR
CYLINDERS . . . 3
CID . . . 53.6
PTO HP . . . 14.5
ENGINE HP . . . 18
FUEL . . . D
SPEEDS . . . 9/3
TRANSMISSION . . . GEAR
DRIVE TYPE . . . 2WD
ROPS/CAB . . . ROPS
WEIGHT . . . 1,412 LBS.
MSRP . . . $6,750

RETAIL PRICING

YEAR	HIGH	LOW
1980	$925	$694
1981	$1,071	$803
1982	$1,141	$856
1983	$1,394	$1,045
1984	$1,584	$1,188
1985	$1,681	$1,261
1986	$1,776	$1,332
1987	$1,827	$1,370
1988	$1,875	$1,406

YM186D-4

YEARS MFRD . . . 1980-1988
ENGINE . . . YANMAR
CYLINDERS . . . 3
CID . . . 53.6
PTO HP . . . 14.5
ENGINE HP . . . 18
FUEL . . . D
SPEEDS . . . 9/3
TRANSMISSION . . . GEAR
DRIVE TYPE . . . 4WD
ROPS/CAB . . . ROPS
WEIGHT . . . 1,538 LBS.
MSRP . . . $7,350

RETAIL PRICING

YEAR	HIGH	LOW
1980	$1,030	$772
1981	$1,143	$857
1982	$1,248	$936
1983	$1,524	$1,143
1984	$1,726	$1,294
1985	$1,831	$1,373
1986	$1,935	$1,451
1987	$1,986	$1,490
1988	$2,040	$1,530

YM187

YEARS MFRD . . . 1985-1990
ENGINE . . . YANMAR
CYLINDERS . . . 3
CID . . . 53.6
PTO HP . . . 14.5
ENGINE HP . . . 18
FUEL . . . D
SPEEDS . . . 9/3
TRANSMISSION . . . GEAR
WEIGHT . . . 1,523 LBS.
MSRP . . . $7,700

RETAIL PRICING

YEAR	HIGH	LOW
1986	$1,999	$1,499
1987	$2,055	$1,541
1988	$2,110	$1,582
1989	$2,228	$1,671
1990	$2,246	$1,685

YM187D

YEARS MFRD . . . 1985-1990
ENGINE . . . YANMAR
CYLINDERS . . . 3
CID . . . 53.6
PTO HP . . . 14.5
ENGINE HP . . . 18
FUEL . . . D
SPEEDS . . . 9/3
DRIVE TYPE . . . 4WD
ROPS/CAB . . . ROPS
WEIGHT . . . 1,652 LBS.
MSRP . . . $7,690

RETAIL PRICING

YEAR	HIGH	LOW
1990	$2,245	$1,684

YM195

YEARS MFRD . . . 1977-1980
ENGINE . . . YANMAR
CYLINDERS . . . 2
CID . . . 60.8
ENGINE HP . . . 19
FUEL . . . D
SPEEDS . . . 6/2
TRANSMISSION . . . GEAR
DRIVE TYPE . . . 2WD
WEIGHT . . . 1,655 LBS.
MSRP . . . $4,985

RETAIL PRICING

YEAR	HIGH	LOW
1977	$797	$598
1978	$814	$611
1979	$868	$651
1980	$890	$667

YM195D

YEARS MFRD . . . 1977-1980
ENGINE . . . YANMAR
CYLINDERS . . . 2
CID . . . 60.8
ENGINE HP . . . 19
FUEL . . . D
SPEEDS . . . 6/2
TRANSMISSION . . . GEAR
DRIVE TYPE . . . 4WD
WEIGHT . . . 1,830 LBS.
MSRP . . . $5,620

RETAIL PRICING

YEAR	HIGH	LOW
1977	$943	$707
1978	$949	$711
1979	$980	$735
1980	$1,004	$753

YM220

YEARS MFRD . . . 1982-1993
ENGINE . . . YANMAR
CYLINDERS . . . 3
CID . . . 68.7
ENGINE HP . . . 22
FUEL . . . D
SPEEDS . . . 8/2
TRANSMISSION . . . GEAR
STEERING . . . STANDARD
PTO . . . YES
DRIVE TYPE . . . 2WD
ROPS/CAB . . . ROPS
WEIGHT . . . 1,874 LBS.
MSRP . . . $8,250

RETAIL PRICING

YEAR	HIGH	LOW
1982	$1,279	$959
1983	$1,532	$1,149
1984	$1,684	$1,263
1985	$1,786	$1,339
1986	$1,887	$1,416
1987	$1,938	$1,454
1988	$1,989	$1,492
1989	$2,075	$1,556
1990	$2,093	$1,570
1991	$2,231	$1,674
1992	$2,325	$1,743
1993	$2,758	$2,068

YM220D

YEARS MFRD . . . 1984-1993
ENGINE . . . YANMAR
CYLINDERS . . . 3
CID . . . 68.7
ENGINE HP . . . 22
FUEL . . . D
SPEEDS . . . 8/2
TRANSMISSION . . . GEAR
DRIVE TYPE . . . 4WD
ROPS/CAB . . . ROPS
WEIGHT . . . 2,178 LBS.
MSRP . . . $9,190

RETAIL PRICING

YEAR	HIGH	LOW
1985	$1,985	$1,488
1986	$2,099	$1,574
1987	$2,156	$1,617
1988	$2,212	$1,659
1989	$2,306	$1,729
1990	$2,327	$1,745
1991	$2,482	$1,862
1992	$2,582	$1,937
1993	$3,072	$2,304

YM220D-4

YEARS MFRD . . . 1984-1993
ENGINE . . . YANMAR
CYLINDERS . . . 3
CID . . . 68.7
ENGINE HP . . . 22
FUEL . . . D
SPEEDS . . . 8/2
TRANSMISSION . . . GEAR
DRIVE TYPE . . . 4WD
ROPS/CAB . . . ROPS
WEIGHT . . . 2,178 LBS.

YM226 2WD

YEARS MFRD . . . 1981-1993
ENGINE . . . YANMAR
CYLINDERS . . . 3
CID . . . 68.7
PTO HP . . . 19
ENGINE HP . . . 22
FUEL . . . D
SPEEDS . . . 9/3 POWERSHIFT
TRANSMISSION . . . GEAR
DRIVE TYPE . . . 2WD
ROPS/CAB . . . ROPS
WEIGHT . . . 1,874 LBS.
MSRP . . . $8,995

RETAIL PRICING

YEAR	HIGH	LOW
1981	$1,336	$1,002
1982	$1,401	$1,051
1983	$1,675	$1,256
1984	$1,843	$1,383
1985	$1,955	$1,466
1986	$2,067	$1,550
1987	$2,124	$1,593
1988	$2,180	$1,635
1989	$2,603	$1,952
1990	$2,625	$1,969
1991	$2,801	$2,101
1992	$2,916	$2,187
1993	$3,008	$2,256

YM226 4WD

YEARS MFRD 1981-1993
ENGINE .... YANMAR
CYLINDERS 3
CID 68.7
PTO HP 19
ENGINE HP 22
FUEL .... D
SPEEDS 9/2
TRANSMISSION .... GEAR
DRIVE TYPE 4WD
ROPS/CAB .... ROPS
WEIGHT .... 1,963 LBS.
MSRP $9,930

RETAIL PRICING

YEAR	HIGH	LOW
1981	$1,478	$1,108
1982	$1,544	$1,158
1983	$1,846	$1,385
1984	$2,032	$1,524
1985	$2,153	$1,615
1986	$2,278	$1,708
1987	$2,339	$1,754
1988	$2,400	$1,800
1989	$2,505	$1,879
1990	$2,898	$2,173
1991	$3,093	$2,320
1992	$3,218	$2,414
1993	$3,318	$2,489

YM226 CAB

YEARS MFRD 1981-1993
ENGINE .... YANMAR
CYLINDERS 3
CID 68.7
PTO HP 19.42
ENGINE HP 22
FUEL .... D
SPEEDS .... 9/3 9/2 PS
TRANSMISSION .... GEAR
DRIVE TYPE 2WD
ROPS/CAB .... CAB
WEIGHT .... 2,300 LBS.
MSRP $8,990

RETAIL PRICING

YEAR	HIGH	LOW
1981	$1,246	$934
1982	$1,310	$983
1983	$1,570	$1,177
1984	$1,726	$1,294
1985	$1,831	$1,373
1986	$1,935	$1,451
1987	$1,986	$1,490
1988	$2,040	$1,530
1989	$2,128	$1,596
1990	$2,143	$1,607
1991	$2,284	$1,713
1992	$2,544	$1,908
1993	$3,006	$2,254

YM240DT

YEARS MFRD 1975-1981
ENGINE .... YANMAR
CYLINDERS 2
CID 70
PTO HP 19.76
ENGINE HP 24
FUEL .... D
SPEEDS 8/2
TRANSMISSION .... GEAR
DRIVE TYPE 4WD
WEIGHT .... 2,000 LBS.
MSRP $7,100

RETAIL PRICING

YEAR	HIGH	LOW
1977	$1,004	$753
1978	$1,023	$767
1979	$1,067	$800
1980	$1,093	$820
1981	$1,266	$950

YM240T

YEARS MFRD 1975-1981
ENGINE .... YANMAR
CYLINDERS 2
CID 69.9
PTO HP 19.76
ENGINE HP 24
FUEL .... D
SPEEDS 8/2
TRANSMISSION .... GEAR
DRIVE TYPE 2WD
WEIGHT .... 1,696 LBS.
MSRP $6,200

RETAIL PRICING

YEAR	HIGH	LOW
1977	$863	$648
1978	$895	$671
1979	$927	$695
1980	$950	$712
1981	$1,106	$830

YM276 2WD

YEARS MFRD 1981-1993
ENGINE .... YANMAR
CYLINDERS 3
CID 86.2
PTO HP 23
ENGINE HP 27
FUEL .... D
SPEEDS .... 12/4 POWERSHIFT
TRANSMISSION .... GEAR
STEERING .... STANDARD
DRIVE TYPE 2WD
ROPS/CAB .... ROPS
WEIGHT .... 2,261 LBS.
MSRP $10,275

RETAIL PRICING

YEAR	HIGH	LOW
1981	$1,603	$1,202
1982	$1,615	$1,211
1983	$1,934	$1,450
1984	$2,128	$1,596
1985	$2,256	$1,692
1986	$2,385	$1,789
1987	$2,450	$1,838
1988	$2,514	$1,885
1989	$2,972	$2,229
1990	$2,999	$2,249
1991	$3,200	$2,400
1992	$3,332	$2,499
1993	$3,435	$2,576

YM276 4WD

YEARS MFRD 1981-1993
ENGINE .... YANMAR
CYLINDERS 3
CID 86.2
PTO HP 23
ENGINE HP 27
FUEL .... D
SPEEDS .... 12/4 POWERSHIFT
TRANSMISSION .... GEAR
STEERING .... STANDARD
DRIVE TYPE 4WD
ROPS/CAB .... ROPS
WEIGHT .... 2,393 LBS.
MSRP $11,470

RETAIL PRICING

YEAR	HIGH	LOW
1981	$1,603	$1,202
1982	$1,649	$1,237
1983	$2,012	$1,509
1984	$2,396	$1,797
1985	$2,543	$1,907
1986	$2,688	$2,016
1987	$2,761	$2,070
1988	$2,834	$2,126
1989	$2,954	$2,215
1990	$2,980	$2,235
1991	$3,179	$2,384
1992	$3,308	$2,481
1993	$3,835	$2,876

YM330

YEARS MFRD 1978-1991
ENGINE .... YANMAR
CYLINDERS 3
CID 91.3
ENGINE HP 33
FUEL .... D
SPEEDS 8/2
TRANSMISSION .... GEAR
STEERING .... STANDARD
DRIVE TYPE 2WD
WEIGHT .... 2,552 LBS.
MSRP $8,165

RETAIL PRICING

YEAR	HIGH	LOW
1978	$1,215	$911
1979	$1,238	$928
1980	$1,285	$964
1981	$1,349	$1,012
1982	$1,416	$1,062
1983	$1,615	$1,211
1984	$1,777	$1,333
1985	$1,932	$1,449
1986	$2,040	$1,530
1987	$2,098	$1,574
1988	$2,151	$1,613
1989	$2,245	$1,684
1990	$2,264	$1,698
1991	$2,543	$1,907

YM330D

YEARS MFRD 1978-1991
ENGINE .... YANMAR
CYLINDERS 3
CID 91.3
ENGINE HP 33
FUEL .... D
SPEEDS 8/2
TRANSMISSION .... GEAR
DRIVE TYPE 4WD
WEIGHT .... 2,888 LBS.
MSRP $9,495

RETAIL PRICING

YEAR	HIGH	LOW
1990	$2,771	$2,079
1991	$2,956	$2,217

YM336 2WD

YEARS MFRD 1981-1993
ENGINE .... YANMAR
CYLINDERS 3
CID 91.3
PTO HP 26.98
ENGINE HP 33
FUEL .... D
SPEEDS 12/4
TRANSMISSION .... GEAR
STEERING .... STANDARD
DRIVE TYPE 2WD
ROPS/CAB .... ROPS
WEIGHT .... 2,855 LBS.
MSRP $12,330

RETAIL PRICING

YEAR	HIGH	LOW
1981	$1,659	$1,244
1982	$1,746	$1,310
1983	$2,132	$1,599
1984	$2,528	$1,896
1985	$2,682	$2,012
1986	$2,834	$2,126
1987	$2,912	$2,184
1988	$2,987	$2,240
1989	$3,117	$2,338
1990	$3,142	$2,356
1991	$3,352	$2,514
1992	$3,629	$2,722
1993	$4,121	$3,091

YM336 4WD

YEARS MFRD 1981-1993
ENGINE .... YANMAR
CYLINDERS 3
CID 91.3
PTO HP 26.98

ENGINE HP . . . 33
FUEL . . . D
SPEEDS . . . 12/4
TRANSMISSION . . . GEAR
STEERING . . . STANDARD
DRIVE TYPE . . . 4WD
ROPS/CAB . . . ROPS
WEIGHT . . . 3,091 LBS.
MSRP . . . $13,905

RETAIL PRICING

YEAR	HIGH	LOW
1981	$1,874	$1,405
1982	$1,997	$1,498
1983	$2,438	$1,829
1984	$2,682	$2,012
1985	$2,843	$2,132
1986	$3,008	$2,256
1987	$3,088	$2,316
1988	$3,169	$2,377
1989	$3,305	$2,478
1990	$3,332	$2,499
1991	$3,555	$2,667
1992	$3,702	$2,777
1993	$4,647	$3,485

YM1100D

YEARS MFRD . . . 1977-1982
CYLINDERS . . . 2
ENGINE HP . . . 14
TRANSMISSION . . . GEAR
DRIVE TYPE . . . 4WD
WEIGHT . . . 948 LBS.

YM1300D

YEARS MFRD . . . 1975-1980
CYLINDERS . . . 2
ENGINE HP . . . 16
TRANSMISSION . . . GEAR
STEERING . . . STANDARD
DRIVE TYPE . . . 4WD
WEIGHT . . . 1,135 LBS.

YM1301

YEARS MFRD . . . 1981-1983
CYLINDERS . . . 3
ENGINE HP . . . 16
TRANSMISSION . . . GEAR
STEERING . . . STANDARD
DRIVE TYPE . . . 2WD
WEIGHT . . . 1,124 LBS.

YM1301D

YEARS MFRD . . . 1981-1983
CYLINDERS . . . 3
ENGINE HP . . . 16
TRANSMISSION . . . GEAR
STEERING . . . STANDARD
DRIVE TYPE . . . 4WD
WEIGHT . . . 1,190 LBS.

YM1401

YEARS MFRD . . . 1979-1981
CYLINDERS . . . 3
ENGINE HP . . . 18
TRANSMISSION . . . GEAR
STEERING . . . STANDARD
DRIVE TYPE . . . 2WD
WEIGHT . . . 1,080 LBS.

YM1401D

YEARS MFRD . . . 1979-1981
CYLINDERS . . . 3
ENGINE HP . . . 19
TRANSMISSION . . . GEAR
STEERING . . . STANDARD
DRIVE TYPE . . . 4WD
WEIGHT . . . 1,168 LBS.

YM1502D

YEARS MFRD . . . 1981-1983
CYLINDERS . . . 3
ENGINE HP . . . 19.5
TRANSMISSION . . . GEAR
STEERING . . . STANDARD
DRIVE TYPE . . . 4WD
WEIGHT . . . 1,510 LBS.

YM1510

YEARS MFRD . . . 1979-1981
CYLINDERS . . . 3
ENGINE HP . . . 19.5
DRIVE TYPE . . . 2WD
WEIGHT . . . 1,235 LBS.

YM1510D

YEARS MFRD . . . 1979-1981
CYLINDERS . . . 3
ENGINE HP . . . 19.5
DRIVE TYPE . . . 4WD
WEIGHT . . . 1,345 LBS.

YM1601

YEARS MFRD . . . 1979-1981
CYLINDERS . . . 3
ENGINE HP . . . 20
TRANSMISSION . . . GEAR
STEERING . . . STANDARD
DRIVE TYPE . . . 4WD
WEIGHT . . . 1,587 LBS.

YM1602D

YEARS MFRD . . . 1982-1983
CYLINDERS . . . 3
ENGINE HP . . . 20
TRANSMISSION . . . GEAR
STEERING . . . STANDARD
DRIVE TYPE . . . 4WD
WEIGHT . . . 1,521 LBS.

YM1610

YEARS MFRD . . . 1979-1981
CYLINDERS . . . 3
ENGINE HP . . . 20
SPEEDS . . . VARIABLE
TRANSMISSION . . . HYDRO
STEERING . . . STANDARD
DRIVE TYPE . . . 2WD
WEIGHT . . . 1,499 LBS.

YM1610D

YEARS MFRD . . . 1979-1981
CYLINDERS . . . 3
ENGINE HP . . . 20
SPEEDS . . . VARIABLE
TRANSMISSION . . . HYDRO
STEERING . . . STANDARD
DRIVE TYPE . . . 4WD
WEIGHT . . . 1,609 LBS.

YM1702D

YEARS MFRD . . . 1982-1983
CYLINDERS . . . 3
ENGINE HP . . . 21
TRANSMISSION . . . GEAR
STEERING . . . STANDARD
DRIVE TYPE . . . 4WD
WEIGHT . . . 2,050 LBS.

YM1720D

YEARS MFRD . . . 1982-1983
CYLINDERS . . . 3
ENGINE HP . . . 21
SPEEDS . . . VARIABLE
TRANSMISSION . . . HYDRO
STEERING . . . STANDARD
DRIVE TYPE . . . 4WD
WEIGHT . . . 2,072 LBS.

YM1802D

YEARS MFRD . . . 1982-1983
CYLINDERS . . . 3
ENGINE HP . . . 21.5
TRANSMISSION . . . GEAR
STEERING . . . STANDARD
DRIVE TYPE . . . 4WD
WEIGHT . . . 2,260 LBS.

YM1810D

YEARS MFRD . . . 1981-1981
CYLINDERS . . . 3
ENGINE HP . . . 21.5
SPEEDS . . . VARIABLE
TRANSMISSION . . . HYDRO
STEERING . . . STANDARD
DRIVE TYPE . . . 4WD
WEIGHT . . . 1,808 LBS.

YM1820D

YEARS MFRD . . . 1982-1983
CYLINDERS . . . 3
ENGINE HP . . . 21.5
SPEEDS . . . VARIABLE
TRANSMISSION . . . HYDRO
STEERING . . . STANDARD
DRIVE TYPE . . . 4WD
WEIGHT . . . 2,314 LBS.

YM2001D

YEARS MFRD . . . 1981-1981
CYLINDERS . . . 3
ENGINE HP . . . 23.5
TRANSMISSION . . . GEAR
STEERING . . . STANDARD
DRIVE TYPE . . . 4WD
WEIGHT . . . 2,039 LBS.

YM2002D

YEARS MFRD . . . 1982-1983
CYLINDERS . . . 3
ENGINE HP . . . 23.5
TRANSMISSION . . . GEAR
STEERING . . . STANDARD
DRIVE TYPE . . . 4WD
WEIGHT . . . 2,314 LBS.

YM2010

YEARS MFRD . . . 1980-1981
CYLINDERS . . . 3
ENGINE HP . . . 23.5
SPEEDS . . . VARIABLE
TRANSMISSION . . . HYDRO
STEERING . . . STANDARD
DRIVE TYPE . . . 2WD
WEIGHT . . . 1,918 LBS.

YM2010D

YEARS MFRD . . . 1980-1981
CYLINDERS . . . 3
ENGINE HP . . . 23.5
SPEEDS . . . VARIABLE
TRANSMISSION . . . HYDRO
STEERING . . . STANDARD
DRIVE TYPE . . . 4WD
WEIGHT . . . 2,061 LBS.

YM2020

YEARS MFRD . . . 1982-1983
CYLINDERS . . . 3
ENGINE HP . . . 23.5
SPEEDS . . . VARIABLE
TRANSMISSION . . . HYDRO
STEERING . . . STANDARD
DRIVE TYPE . . . 2WD
WEIGHT . . . 2,491 LBS.

YM2220D

YEARS MFRD . . . 1982-1983
CYLINDERS . . . 3
ENGINE HP . . . 25
SPEEDS . . . VARIABLE
TRANSMISSION . . . HYDRO
STEERING . . . STANDARD
DRIVE TYPE . . . 4WD
WEIGHT . . . 2,635 LBS.

YM2310

YEARS MFRD . . . 1980-1981
CYLINDERS . . . 3
ENGINE HP . . . 26.5

SPEEDS . . . . VARIABLE
TRANSMISSION . . . . HYDRO
STEERING. . . . . STANDARD
DRIVE TYPE 2WD
WEIGHT . . . . 1,984 LBS.

YM2310D

YEARS MFRD 1980-1981
CYLINDERS. 3
ENGINE HP 26.5
SPEEDS . . . . VARIABLE
TRANSMISSION . . . . HYDRO
STEERING. . . . . STANDARD
DRIVE TYPE 4WD
WEIGHT . . . . 2,127 LBS.

YM2402D

YEARS MFRD 1982-1983
CYLINDERS. 3
ENGINE HP 28
TRANSMISSION . . . . GEAR
STEERING. . . . . STANDARD
DRIVE TYPE 4WD
WEIGHT . . . . 2,711 LBS.

YM2420D

YEARS MFRD 1982-1983
CYLINDERS. 3
ENGINE HP 28
SPEEDS . . . . VARIABLE
TRANSMISSION . . . . HYDRO
STEERING. . . . . STANDARD
DRIVE TYPE 4WD
WEIGHT . . . . 2,723 LBS.

YM2610D

YEARS MFRD 1979-1981
CYLINDERS. 3
ENGINE HP 30
SPEEDS . . . . VARIABLE
TRANSMISSION . . . . HYDRO
STEERING. . . . . STANDARD
DRIVE TYPE 4WD
WEIGHT . . . . 2,712 LBS.

YM2620

YEARS MFRD 1982-1983
CYLINDERS. 3
ENGINE HP 30
SPEEDS . . . . VARIABLE
TRANSMISSION . . . . HYDRO
STEERING. . . . . STANDARD
DRIVE TYPE 2WD
WEIGHT . . . . 3,582 LBS.

YM2620D

YEARS MFRD 1982-1983
CYLINDERS. 3
ENGINE HP 30
SPEEDS . . . . VARIABLE
TRANSMISSION . . . . HYDRO
STEERING. . . . . STANDARD
DRIVE TYPE 4WD
WEIGHT . . . . 3,813 LBS.

YM2820D

YEARS MFRD 1982-1983
CYLINDERS. 3
ENGINE HP 33
SPEEDS . . . . VARIABLE
TRANSMISSION . . . . HYDRO
STEERING. . . . . STANDARD
DRIVE TYPE 4WD
WEIGHT . . . . 3,825 LBS.

YM3110

YEARS MFRD 1979-1981
CYLINDERS. 3
ENGINE HP 35
SPEEDS . . . . VARIABLE
TRANSMISSION . . . . HYDRO
STEERING. . . . . STANDARD
DRIVE TYPE 2WD
WEIGHT . . . . 2,733 LBS.

YM3110D

YEARS MFRD 1979-1981
CYLINDERS. 3
ENGINE HP 35
SPEEDS . . . . VARIABLE
TRANSMISSION . . . . HYDRO
STEERING. . . . . STANDARD
DRIVE TYPE 4WD
WEIGHT . . . . 2,910 LBS.

YM3220D

YEARS MFRD 1982-1983
CYLINDERS. 3
ENGINE HP 35
SPEEDS . . . . VARIABLE
TRANSMISSION . . . . HYDRO
STEERING. . . . . STANDARD
DRIVE TYPE 4WD
WEIGHT . . . . 3,219 LBS.

YM3810D

YEARS MFRD 1979-1981
CYLINDERS. 3
ENGINE HP 42
SPEEDS . . . . VARIABLE
TRANSMISSION . . . . HYDRO
STEERING. . . . . STANDARD
DRIVE TYPE 4WD
WEIGHT . . . . 2,921 LBS.

YM4220D

YEARS MFRD 1982-1983
CYLINDERS. 3
ENGINE HP 45
SPEEDS . . . . VARIABLE
TRANSMISSION . . . . HYDRO
STEERING. . . . . STANDARD
DRIVE TYPE 4WD
WEIGHT . . . . 3,351 LBS.

YMF15D

YEARS MFRD 1983-1986
CYLINDERS. 3
ENGINE HP 19
TRANSMISSION . . . . GEAR
STEERING. . . . . STANDARD
DRIVE TYPE 4WD
WEIGHT . . . . 1,709 LBS.

YMF16D

YEARS MFRD 1983-1986
CYLINDERS. 3
ENGINE HP 20
TRANSMISSION . . . . GEAR
STEERING. . . . . STANDARD
DRIVE TYPE 4WD
WEIGHT . . . . 1,907 LBS.

YMF17D

YEARS MFRD 1984-1984
CYLINDERS. 3
ENGINE HP 21
TRANSMISSION . . . . GEAR
STEERING. . . . . STANDARD
DRIVE TYPE 4WD
WEIGHT . . . . 2,161 LBS.

YMF18D

YEARS MFRD 1984-1984
CYLINDERS. 3
ENGINE HP 21.5
TRANSMISSION . . . . GEAR
STEERING. . . . . STANDARD
DRIVE TYPE 4WD
WEIGHT . . . . 2,183 LBS.

YMF20D

YEARS MFRD 1984-1984
CYLINDERS. 3
ENGINE HP 23.5
TRANSMISSION . . . . GEAR
STEERING. . . . . STANDARD
DRIVE TYPE 4WD
WEIGHT . . . . 2,416 LBS.

YMF22D

YEARS MFRD 1984-1984
CYLINDERS. 3
ENGINE HP 25
TRANSMISSION . . . . GEAR
STEERING. . . . . STANDARD
DRIVE TYPE 4WD
WEIGHT . . . . 2,458 LBS.

YMFX20D

YEARS MFRD 1984-1984
CYLINDERS. 3
ENGINE HP 23.5
SPEEDS . . . . VARIABLE
TRANSMISSION . . . . HYDRO
STEERING. . . . . STANDARD
DRIVE TYPE 4WD
WEIGHT . . . . 2,438 LBS.

YMFX22D

YEARS MFRD 1984-1984
CYLINDERS. 3
ENGINE HP 25
SPEEDS . . . . VARIABLE
TRANSMISSION . . . . HYDRO
STEERING. . . . . STANDARD
DRIVE TYPE 4WD
WEIGHT . . . . 2,480 LBS.

YMFX28D

YEARS MFRD 1984-1984
CYLINDERS. 3
ENGINE HP 33
SPEEDS . . . . VARIABLE
TRANSMISSION . . . . HYDRO
DRIVE TYPE 4WD
WEIGHT . . . . 3,792 LBS.

YMFX42D

YEARS MFRD 1984-1984
CYLINDERS. 3
ENGINE HP 45
SPEEDS . . . . VARIABLE
TRANSMISSION . . . . HYDRO
STEERING. . . . . STANDARD
DRIVE TYPE 4WD
WEIGHT . . . . 3,902 LBS.

YMG1800D

YEARS MFRD 1988-1988
CYLINDERS. 3
ENGINE HP 21.5
TRANSMISSION . . . . GEAR
STEERING. . . . . STANDARD
DRIVE TYPE 4WD
WEIGHT . . . . 1,918 LBS.

YMG2000D

YEARS MFRD 1988-1988
CYLINDERS. 3
ENGINE HP 23.5
TRANSMISSION . . . . GEAR
STEERING. . . . . STANDARD
DRIVE TYPE 4WD
WEIGHT . . . . 1,918 LBS.

YT235

YEARS MFRD 2016-2020
SERIES. . . . . YT2 SERIES
ENGINE . . . . YANMAR
CYLINDERS. 3
CID 100.0
PTO HP 27
ENGINE HP 34.2
COOLING . . . . LIQUID
FUEL . . . . D
TRANSMISSION . . . . HYDRO
STEERING. . . . . STANDARD

YANMAR

HITCH . . . . . . CAT. I
DRIVE TYPE 4WD
ROPS/CAB . . . . . . ROPS
WEIGHT . . . . . . 2,558 LBS.

OPTIONS

60" MOWER
BACKHOE
CAB
LOADER

RETAIL PRICING

YEAR	HIGH	LOW
2016	$17,136	$12,852
2017	$17,744	$13,308
2018	$19,132	$14,349
2019	$20,955	$15,682
2020	$22,700	$17,129

YT347

YEARS MFRD 2016-2020
SERIES . . . . . . YT3 SERIES
ENGINE . . . . . . YANMAR
CYLINDERS 4
CID 133.5
PTO HP 39.5
ENGINE HP 46
COOLING . . . . . . LIQUID
FUEL . . . . . . D
TRANSMISSION . . . . . . HYDRO
STEERING . . . . . . STANDARD
HITCH . . . . . . CAT. I
DRIVE TYPE 4WD
ROPS/CAB . . . . . . ROPS
WEIGHT . . . . . . 3,880 LBS.

OPTIONS

54" SNOW BLOWER
CAB
LOADER

RETAIL PRICING

YEAR	HIGH	LOW
2016	$23,737	$17,803
2017	$26,001	$19,502
2018	$27,742	$20,806
2019	$30,352	$23,553
2020	$32,669	$24,939

221

YEARS MFRD 2014-2020
SERIES . . . . . . SA SERIES
ENGINE . . . . . . YANMAR
CYLINDERS 3
CID 60
PTO HP 15.6
ENGINE HP 19.4
COOLING . . . . . . LIQUID
FUEL . . . . . . D
SPEEDS . . . . . . VARIABLE
TRANSMISSION . . . . . . HYDRO
STEERING . . . . . . STANDARD
HITCH . . . . . . CAT. I
ROPS/CAB . . . . . . ROPS
WEIGHT . . . . . . 1,537 LBS.

OPTIONS

60" DECK
BACKHOE
LDR

RETAIL PRICING

YEAR	HIGH	LOW
2014	$5,945	$4,496
2015	$6,581	$4,936
2016	$7,307	$5,481
2017	$8,142	$6,106
2018	$9,026	$6,770
2019	$9,923	$7,600
2020	$10,522	$8,030

324

YEARS MFRD 2014-2020
SERIES . . . . . . SA SERIES
ENGINE . . . . . . YANMAR
CYLINDERS 3
CID 77
PTO HP 18.1
ENGINE HP 121.7
FUEL . . . . . . D
SPEEDS . . . . . . VARIABLE
TRANSMISSION . . . . . . HYDRO
STEERING . . . . . . STANDARD
HITCH . . . . . . CAT. I
ROPS/CAB . . . . . . ROPS
WEIGHT . . . . . . 1,715 LBS.

OPTIONS

60" DECK
BACKHOE
LDR

RETAIL PRICING

YEAR	HIGH	LOW
2014	$6,899	$5,174
2015	$7,716	$5,786
2016	$8,533	$6,400
2017	$9,377	$7,033
2018	$10,864	$8,148
2019	$11,892	$9,139
2020	$12,759	$9,726

424

YEARS MFRD 2014-2020
SERIES . . . . . . SA SERIES
ENGINE . . . . . . YANMAR
CYLINDERS 3
CID 77
PTO HP 18.1
ENGINE HP 21.7
COOLING . . . . . . LIQUID
FUEL . . . . . . D
SPEEDS . . . . . . VARIABLE
TRANSMISSION . . . . . . HYDRO
STEERING . . . . . . STANDARD
HITCH . . . . . . CAT. I
ROPS/CAB . . . . . . ROPS
WEIGHT . . . . . . 1,830 LBS.

OPTIONS

60" DECK
BACKHOE
LDR

RETAIL PRICING

YEAR	HIGH	LOW
2014	$7,444	$5,583
2015	$8,261	$6,195
2016	$9,213	$6,910
2017	$10,231	$7,673
2018	$11,339	$8,505
2019	$12,419	$9,529
2020	$13,453	$10,252

424DHX

YEARS MFRD 2015-2020
SERIES . . . . . . SA SERIES
ENGINE . . . . . . YANMAR
CYLINDERS 3
CID 77
PTO HP 18.1
ENGINE HP 23.9
COOLING . . . . . . LIQUID
FUEL . . . . . . D
SPEEDS . . . . . . VARIABLE
TRANSMISSION . . . . . . HYDRO
STEERING . . . . . . STANDARD
HITCH . . . . . . CAT. I
DRIVE TYPE 4WD
ROPS/CAB . . . . . . ROPS
WEIGHT . . . . . . 2,041 LBS.

OPTIONS

60" DECK
LDR
SOFT CAB KIT

RETAIL PRICING

YEAR	HIGH	LOW
2015	$9,168	$6,876
2016	$10,213	$7,659
2017	$11,910	$8,932
2018	$13,047	$9,785
2019	$14,289	$10,930
2020	$15,504	$11,802

YARD MACHINES

F673G

YEARS MFRD 2002-2002
ENGINE . . . . . . B&S
ENGINE HP 16.5
COOLING . . . . . . AIR
FUEL . . . . . . G
TRANSMISSION . . . . . . HYDRO
STEERING . . . . . . STANDARD
STANDARD DECK . . . . . . 42"
MSRP $1,299

RETAIL PRICING

YEAR	HIGH	LOW
2002	$237	$178

F695G

YEARS MFRD 2002-2002
ENGINE . . . . . . B&S
ENGINE HP 16.5
COOLING . . . . . . AIR
FUEL . . . . . . G
TRANSMISSION . . . . . . HYDRO
STEERING . . . . . . STANDARD
STANDARD DECK . . . . . . 42"
MSRP $1,399

RETAIL PRICING

YEAR	HIGH	LOW
2002	$148	$111

H762F

YEARS MFRD 2005-2006
ENGINE . . . . . . B&S
CYLINDERS 1
ENGINE HP 12.5
COOLING . . . . . . AIR
FUEL . . . . . . G
SPEEDS 6/1
TRANSMISSION . . . . . . GEAR
STEERING . . . . . . STANDARD
BLADE CLUTCH . . . . . . MANUAL
STANDARD DECK . . . . . . 38"
MSRP $798

RETAIL PRICING

YEAR	HIGH	LOW
2005	$498	$373

H762F752

YEARS MFRD 2006-2006
ENGINE . . . . . . B&S
ENGINE HP 12.5
COOLING . . . . . . AIR
FUEL . . . . . . G
SPEEDS 6/1
TRANSMISSION . . . . . . GEAR
STEERING . . . . . . STANDARD
STANDARD DECK . . . . . . 46"
MSRP $798

RETAIL PRICING

YEAR	HIGH	LOW
2006	$526	$394

J825P

YEARS MFRD 1998-1998
ENGINE HP 20
FUEL . . . . . . G
TRANSMISSION . . . . . . GEAR
STEERING . . . . . . STANDARD
STANDARD DECK . . . . . . 50"
MSRP $1,999

RETAIL PRICING

YEAR	HIGH	LOW
1998	$850	$637

K828H

YEARS MFRD 1997-1997
ENGINE . . . . . . B&S
ENGINE HP 18.5
FUEL . . . . . . G
TRANSMISSION . . . . . . GEAR
STEERING . . . . . . STANDARD
STANDARD DECK . . . . . . 46"
MSRP $1,899

RETAIL PRICING

YEAR	HIGH	LOW
1997	$768	$576

L670G

YEARS MFRD 2002-2002
ENGINE .... B&S
ENGINE HP 15.5
COOLING .... AIR
FUEL .... G
TRANSMISSION .... GEAR
STEERING .... STANDARD
STANDARD DECK .... 42"
MSRP $1,199

RETAIL PRICING

YEAR	HIGH	LOW
2002	$169	$127

M762G

YEARS MFRD 2005-2006
ENGINE .... B&S
CYLINDERS 1
ENGINE HP 15.5
COOLING .... AIR
FUEL .... G
SPEEDS 6/1
TRANSMISSION .... GEAR
STEERING .... STANDARD
BLADE CLUTCH .... MANUAL
STANDARD DECK .... 42"
MSRP $898

RETAIL PRICING

YEAR	HIGH	LOW
2005	$557	$418
2006	$592	$444

Q607H

YEARS MFRD 2003-2003
ENGINE .... B&S
ENGINE HP 18
FUEL .... G
TRANSMISSION ...... AUTOMATIC
STEERING .... STANDARD

S825H

YEARS MFRD 1998-2001
ENGINE .... B&S
ENGINE HP 18.5
COOLING .... AIR
FUEL .... G
TRANSMISSION .... GEAR
STEERING .... STANDARD
STANDARD DECK .... 46"
MSRP $1,899

RETAIL PRICING

YEAR	HIGH	LOW
1998	$226	$170
1999	$249	$187
2001	$309	$232

S845H

YEARS MFRD 2002-2002
ENGINE .... B&S
ENGINE HP 18.5
COOLING .... AIR
FUEL .... G
TRANSMISSION .... DISC
STEERING .... STANDARD
STANDARD DECK .... 46"
MSRP $1,999

RETAIL PRICING

YEAR	HIGH	LOW
2002	$324	$243

13A1762F029

YEARS MFRD 2008-2010
ENGINE .... TECUMSEH
CYLINDERS 1
ENGINE HP 13.5
COOLING .... AIR
FUEL .... G
SPEEDS 6/1
TRANSMISSION .... GEAR
STEERING .... STANDARD

13A1762F700

YEARS MFRD 2007-2007
ENGINE .... TECUMSEH
CYLINDERS 1
ENGINE HP 13.5
FUEL .... G
SPEEDS 6/1
TRANSMISSION .... BELT
STEERING .... STANDARD

13A1762F729

YEARS MFRD 2007-2007
ENGINE .... TECUMSEH
CYLINDERS 1
ENGINE HP 13.5
FUEL .... G
SPEEDS 6/1
TRANSMISSION .... BELT
STEERING .... STANDARD

13A2775S000

YEARS MFRD 2015-2016
ENGINE .... POWERMORE OHV
CYLINDERS 1
CID 420CC
COOLING .... AIR
FUEL .... G
SPEEDS 7/1
TRANSMISSION .... GEAR
STEERING .... STANDARD
STANDARD DECK .... 42"
MSRP $1,099

RETAIL PRICING

YEAR	HIGH	LOW
2015	$596	$447
2016	$714	$535

13A326JC700

YEARS MFRD 2015-2017
ENGINE .... B&S OHV
CYLINDERS 1
CID 190CC
COOLING .... AIR
FUEL .... G
SPEEDS 6/1
TRANSMISSION .... GEAR
STEERING .... STANDARD
STANDARD DECK .... 24"
MSRP $799

RETAIL PRICING

YEAR	HIGH	LOW
2015	$447	$335
2016	$475	$356
2017	$549	$412

13AC762F000

YEARS MFRD 2011-2017
ENGINE .... B&S OHV
CYLINDERS 1
ENGINE HP 12.5
COOLING .... AIR
FUEL .... G
SPEEDS 6/1
TRANSMISSION .... GEAR
STEERING .... STANDARD
BLADE CLUTCH .... MANUAL
STANDARD DECK .... 38"
MSRP $999

RETAIL PRICING

YEAR	HIGH	LOW
2011	$261	$196
2012	$307	$231
2013	$372	$279
2014	$466	$349
2015	$559	$419
2016	$652	$489
2017	$745	$559

13AC762F020

YEARS MFRD 2011-2012
ENGINE .... B&S
CYLINDERS 1
ENGINE HP 13.5
COOLING .... AIR
FUEL .... G
SPEEDS 6/1
TRANSMISSION .... GEAR
STEERING .... STANDARD
BLADE CLUTCH .... MANUAL
STANDARD DECK .... 38"
MSRP $899

RETAIL PRICING

YEAR	HIGH	LOW
2011	$462	$346
2012	$534	$400

13AM762F052

YEARS MFRD 2008-2008
ENGINE .... B&S I/C
CYLINDERS 1
ENGINE HP 15.5
COOLING .... AIR
FUEL .... G
SPEEDS 6/1
TRANSMISSION .... DISC
STEERING .... STANDARD

13AM762F700

YEARS MFRD 2007-2007
ENGINE .... B&S IC
CYLINDERS 1
ENGINE HP 15.5
FUEL .... G
SPEEDS 6/1
TRANSMISSION .... BELT
STEERING .... STANDARD

13AM772F700

YEARS MFRD 2007-2010
ENGINE .... B&S IC
CYLINDERS 1
ENGINE HP 15.5
COOLING .... AIR
FUEL .... G
SPEEDS 6/1
TRANSMISSION .... BELT
STEERING .... STANDARD

13AM772S000

YEARS MFRD 2011-2014
ENGINE .... B&S
ENGINE HP 14.5
COOLING .... AIR
FUEL .... G
SPEEDS 6/1
TRANSMISSION .... GEAR
STEERING .... STANDARD
STANDARD DECK .... 42"
MSRP $1,049

RETAIL PRICING

YEAR	HIGH	LOW
2011	$306	$229
2012	$404	$303
2013	$481	$361
2014	$588	$441

13AM775S000

YEARS MFRD 2015-2017
ENGINE .... B&S
CYLINDERS 1
ENGINE HP 15.5
COOLING .... AIR
FUEL .... G
SPEEDS 7/1
TRANSMISSION .... GEAR
STEERING .... STANDARD
STANDARD DECK .... 42"
MSRP $1,099

RETAIL PRICING

YEAR	HIGH	LOW
2015	$615	$461
2016	$820	$615
2017	$857	$643

13AN771H729

YEARS MFRD 2007-2007
ENGINE .... B&S INTEK
CYLINDERS 1
ENGINE HP 20
FUEL .... G

SPEEDS . . . 7/1
TRANSMISSION . . . BELT
STEERING . . . STANDARD

13AN772G700

YEARS MFRD . . . 2007-2010
ENGINE . . . B&S IC
CYLINDERS . . . 1
ENGINE HP . . . 17.5
COOLING . . . AIR
FUEL . . . G
SPEEDS . . . 7/1
TRANSMISSION . . . BELT
STEERING . . . STANDARD

13AN772G729

YEARS MFRD . . . 2007-2007
ENGINE . . . TECUMSEH
CYLINDERS . . . 1
ENGINE HP . . . 17.5
FUEL . . . G
SPEEDS . . . 7/1
TRANSMISSION . . . BELT
STEERING . . . STANDARD

13AN775S000

YEARS MFRD . . . 2013-2014
ENGINE . . . B&S
ENGINE HP . . . 16.5
COOLING . . . AIR
FUEL . . . G
SPEEDS . . . 6/1
TRANSMISSION . . . GEAR
STEERING . . . STANDARD
MSRP . . . $1,099

RETAIL PRICING

YEAR	HIGH	LOW
2013	$503	$378
2014	$595	$446

13AN775S200

YEARS MFRD . . . 2013-2014
ENGINE . . . B&S
ENGINE HP . . . 16.5
COOLING . . . AIR
FUEL . . . G
SPEEDS . . . 6/1
TRANSMISSION . . . GEAR
STEERING . . . STANDARD
STANDARD DECK . . . 42"
MSRP . . . $1,199

RETAIL PRICING

YEAR	HIGH	LOW
2013	$676	$507
2014	$748	$561

13B2775S000

YEARS MFRD . . . 2017-2017
ENGINE . . . B&S POWERMORE
CYLINDERS . . . 1
CID . . . 420CC
COOLING . . . AIR
FUEL . . . G
SPEEDS . . . 7/1
TRANSMISSION . . . GEAR
STEERING . . . STANDARD
STANDARD DECK . . . 42"
MSRP . . . $1,099

RETAIL PRICING

YEAR	HIGH	LOW
2017	$820	$615

13BC762F000

YEARS MFRD . . . 2015-2017
ENGINE . . . B&S
CYLINDERS . . . 1
ENGINE HP . . . 10.5
COOLING . . . AIR
FUEL . . . G
SPEEDS . . . 6/1
TRANSMISSION . . . GEAR
STEERING . . . STANDARD
STANDARD DECK . . . 38"
MSRP . . . $999

RETAIL PRICING

YEAR	HIGH	LOW
2015	$559	$419
2016	$708	$531
2017	$764	$573

13RC762F729

YEARS MFRD . . . 2009-2010
ENGINE . . . TECUMSEH
CYLINDERS . . . 1
ENGINE HP . . . 13.5
COOLING . . . AIR
FUEL . . . G
SPEEDS . . . 6/1
TRANSMISSION . . . GEAR
STEERING . . . STANDARD

13RL771H029

YEARS MFRD . . . 2008-2008
ENGINE . . . B&S INTEK
CYLINDERS . . . 1
ENGINE HP . . . 20
COOLING . . . AIR
FUEL . . . G
SPEEDS . . . 7/1
TRANSMISSION . . . GEAR
STEERING . . . STANDARD

13RN772G029

YEARS MFRD . . . 2008-2008
ENGINE . . . B&S I/C
CYLINDERS . . . 1
ENGINE HP . . . 17.5
COOLING . . . AIR
FUEL . . . G
SPEEDS . . . 7/1
TRANSMISSION . . . GEAR
STEERING . . . STANDARD

601H729

YEARS MFRD . . . 2006-2006
ENGINE . . . B&S
ENGINE HP . . . 21
COOLING . . . AIR
FUEL . . . G
SPEEDS . . . VARIABLE
TRANSMISSION . . . HYDRO
STEERING . . . STANDARD
STANDARD DECK . . . 60"
MSRP . . . $1,249

RETAIL PRICING

YEAR	HIGH	LOW
2006	$824	$618

762F729

YEARS MFRD . . . 2006-2006
ENGINE . . . B&S
ENGINE HP . . . 13.5
COOLING . . . AIR
FUEL . . . G
SPEEDS . . . 6/1
TRANSMISSION . . . GEAR
STEERING . . . STANDARD
STANDARD DECK . . . 38"
MSRP . . . $829

RETAIL PRICING

YEAR	HIGH	LOW
2006	$545	$409

771GF729

YEARS MFRD . . . 2006-2006
ENGINE . . . B&S
ENGINE HP . . . 17.5
COOLING . . . AIR
FUEL . . . G
SPEEDS . . . 7/1
TRANSMISSION . . . GEAR
STEERING . . . STANDARD
STANDARD DECK . . . 42"
MSRP . . . $1,099

RETAIL PRICING

YEAR	HIGH	LOW
2006	$725	$543

1760F

YEARS MFRD . . . 2005-2006
ENGINE . . . TECUMSEH
CYLINDERS . . . 1
ENGINE HP . . . 13
COOLING . . . AIR
FUEL . . . G
SPEEDS . . . 6/1
TRANSMISSION . . . GEAR
STEERING . . . STANDARD
BLADE CLUTCH . . . MANUAL
STANDARD DECK . . . 38"
MSRP . . . $829

RETAIL PRICING

YEAR	HIGH	LOW
2005	$518	$388
2006	$545	$409

3760F

YEARS MFRD . . . 2005-2006
ENGINE . . . TECUMSEH
CYLINDERS . . . 1
ENGINE HP . . . 15
COOLING . . . AIR
FUEL . . . G
SPEEDS . . . 6/1
TRANSMISSION . . . GEAR
STEERING . . . STANDARD
BLADE CLUTCH . . . MANUAL
STANDARD DECK . . . 38"
MSRP . . . $899

RETAIL PRICING

YEAR	HIGH	LOW
2005	$558	$418
2006	$593	$445

3761G

YEARS MFRD . . . 2005-2006
ENGINE . . . TECUMSEH
CYLINDERS . . . 1
ENGINE HP . . . 15
COOLING . . . AIR
FUEL . . . G
SPEEDS . . . 6/1
TRANSMISSION . . . GEAR
STEERING . . . STANDARD
BLADE CLUTCH . . . MANUAL
STANDARD DECK . . . 42"
MSRP . . . $949

RETAIL PRICING

YEAR	HIGH	LOW
2005	$591	$443
2006	$625	$469

3771G

YEARS MFRD . . . 2005-2006
ENGINE . . . TECUMSEH
CYLINDERS . . . 1
ENGINE HP . . . 17.5
COOLING . . . AIR
FUEL . . . G
SPEEDS . . . 7/1
TRANSMISSION . . . GEAR
STEERING . . . STANDARD
BLADE CLUTCH . . . MANUAL
STANDARD DECK . . . 42"
MSRP . . . $999

RETAIL PRICING

YEAR	HIGH	LOW
2005	$620	$465
2006	$658	$493

3791G

YEARS MFRD . . . 2005-2006
ENGINE . . . TECUMSEH
CYLINDERS . . . 1
ENGINE HP . . . 17.5
COOLING . . . AIR
FUEL . . . G
SPEEDS . . . VARIABLE
TRANSMISSION . . . HYDRO
STEERING . . . STANDARD

BLADE CLUTCH .... MANUAL
STANDARD DECK .... 42"
MSRP................. $1,199

RETAIL PRICING

YEAR	HIGH	LOW
2005	$748	$561
2006	$791	$593

YARDMAN

A1A3G

YEARS MFRD 2000-2000
ENGINE .... B&S
ENGINE HP 17
FUEL .... G
TRANSMISSION ..... DUAL HYDRO
STEERING .... ZERO
STANDARD DECK .... 42"
MSRP $3,999

RETAIL PRICING

YEAR	HIGH	LOW
2000	$613	$460

AX614G

YEARS MFRD 2003-2003
ENGINE .... KOHLER
ENGINE HP 18
COOLING .... AIR
FUEL .... G
TRANSMISSION .... HYDRO
STEERING .... STANDARD
STANDARD DECK .... 42"
MSRP $1,599

RETAIL PRICING

YEAR	HIGH	LOW
2003	$222	$167

BX604G

YEARS MFRD 2001-2001
ENGINE .... KOHLER
ENGINE HP 17
COOLING .... AIR
FUEL .... G
TRANSMISSION .... GEAR
STEERING .... STANDARD
STANDARD DECK .... 42"
MSRP $1,699

RETAIL PRICING

YEAR	HIGH	LOW
2001	$269	$202

D604G

YEARS MFRD 1999-2002
SERIES .... 600 SERIES
ENGINE .... B&S
ENGINE HP 17.5
COOLING .... AIR
FUEL .... G
TRANSMISSION .... GEAR
STEERING .... STANDARD
STANDARD DECK .... 42"
MSRP $1,499

RETAIL PRICING

YEAR	HIGH	LOW
1999	$179	$135
2000	$202	$151
2001	$224	$168
2002	$246	$185

D624G

YEARS MFRD 2001-2002
SERIES ..... REV-O-LUTION SERIES
ENGINE .... B&S
ENGINE HP 17.5
COOLING .... AIR
FUEL .... G
TRANSMISSION ..... DUAL HYDRO
STEERING .... ZERO
PTO .... YES
STANDARD DECK .... 42"
MSRP $2,899

RETAIL PRICING

YEAR	HIGH	LOW
2001	$534	$401
2002	$595	$446

D674G

YEARS MFRD 1998-1999
SERIES .... 600 SERIES
ENGINE .... B&S
ENGINE HP 17
COOLING .... AIR
FUEL .... G
TRANSMISSION .... GEAR
STEERING .... STANDARD
STANDARD DECK .... 42"
MSRP $1,199

RETAIL PRICING

YEAR	HIGH	LOW
1998	$138	$103
1999	$149	$112

I674G

YEARS MFRD 1997-1997
ENGINE .... B&S
ENGINE HP 15.5
FUEL .... G
TRANSMISSION .... GEAR
STEERING .... STANDARD
MSRP $1,199

RETAIL PRICING

YEAR	HIGH	LOW
1997	$475	$356

J693G

YEARS MFRD 2004-2004
ENGINE .... B&S
ENGINE HP 18.5
FUEL .... G
SPEEDS .... VARIABLE
TRANSMISSION .... HYDRO
STEERING .... STANDARD
STANDARD DECK .... 38"
MSRP $1,299

RETAIL PRICING

YEAR	HIGH	LOW
2003	$205	$154
2004	$228	$171

J694H

YEARS MFRD 1997-1997
ENGINE .... B&S
ENGINE HP 20
FUEL .... G
TRANSMISSION .... HYDRO
STEERING .... STANDARD
STANDARD DECK .... 46"
MSRP $1,949

RETAIL PRICING

YEAR	HIGH	LOW
1997	$773	$580

J844H

YEARS MFRD 1997-1997
ENGINE .... B&S
ENGINE HP 20
FUEL .... G
TRANSMISSION .... GEAR
STEERING .... STANDARD
STANDARD DECK .... 46"
MSRP $2,099

RETAIL PRICING

YEAR	HIGH	LOW
1997	$832	$624

P615P

YEARS MFRD 2005-2006
ENGINE .... KOHLER
CYLINDERS 2
ENGINE HP 23
COOLING .... AIR
FUEL .... G
SPEEDS .... VARIABLE
TRANSMISSION .... HYDRO
STEERING .... STANDARD
BLADE CLUTCH .... MANUAL

R814K

YEARS MFRD 2002-2002
ENGINE .... B&S
ENGINE HP 25
COOLING .... AIR
FUEL .... G
SPEEDS .... VARIABLE
TRANSMISSION .... HYDRO
STEERING .... STANDARD
STANDARD DECK .... 54"
MSRP $3,499

RETAIL PRICING

YEAR	HIGH	LOW
2002	$556	$417

T604G

YEARS MFRD 2003-2004
ENGINE .... B&S TWIN INTEK
CYLINDERS 2
ENGINE HP 20
COOLING .... AIR
FUEL .... G
SPEEDS .... VARIABLE
TRANSMISSION .... HYDRO
STEERING .... STANDARD

T604H

YEARS MFRD 2003-2004
ENGINE .... B&S TWIN INTEK
CYLINDERS 2
ENGINE HP 22
COOLING .... AIR
FUEL .... G
SPEEDS .... VARIABLE
TRANSMISSION .... HYDRO
STEERING .... STANDARD
STANDARD DECK .... 38"
MSRP $1,499

RETAIL PRICING

YEAR	HIGH	LOW
2003	$237	$178
2004	$263	$197

T614H

YEARS MFRD 2003-2004
ENGINE .... B&S
ENGINE HP 22
COOLING .... AIR
FUEL .... G
SPEEDS .... VARIABLE
TRANSMISSION .... HYDRO
STEERING .... STANDARD
STANDARD DECK .... 46"
MSRP $1,699

RETAIL PRICING

YEAR	HIGH	LOW
2003	$268	$201
2004	$298	$223

T694G

YEARS MFRD 1998-1998
SERIES .... 600 SERIES
ENGINE .... B&S
ENGINE HP 18
COOLING .... AIR
FUEL .... G
TRANSMISSION .... HYDRO
STEERING .... STANDARD
STANDARD DECK .... 42"
MSRP $1,799

RETAIL PRICING

YEAR	HIGH	LOW
1998	$262	$196

U604H

YEARS MFRD 1999-2002
SERIES .... 600 SERIES
ENGINE .... B&S
ENGINE HP 20
FUEL .... G
STEERING .... STANDARD
STANDARD DECK .... 46"
MSRP $2,099

YARDMAN

RETAIL PRICING

YEAR	HIGH	LOW
1999	$254	$191
2000	$280	$210
2001	$314	$236
2002	$348	$261

U614H

YEARS MFRD........ 2004-2004
ENGINE.................. B&S
CYLINDERS................. 2
ENGINE HP................ 22
FUEL...................... G
SPEEDS............ VARIABLE
TRANSMISSION.......... HYDRO
STEERING........... STANDARD
STANDARD DECK........... 46"
MSRP................ $1,699

RETAIL PRICING

YEAR	HIGH	LOW
2004	$978	$733

U615P

YEARS MFRD........ 2005-2006
ENGINE.................. B&S
CYLINDERS................. 2
ENGINE HP................ 22
COOLING................. AIR
FUEL...................... G
SPEEDS............ VARIABLE
TRANSMISSION.......... HYDRO
BLADE CLUTCH........ MANUAL

U624H

YEARS MFRD........ 2001-2001
SERIES..... REV-O-LUTION SERIES
ENGINE.................. B&S
ENGINE HP................ 20
FUEL...................... G
TRANSMISSION.......... HYDRO
STEERING.................. ZERO
STANDARD DECK........... 46"
MSRP................ $3,299

RETAIL PRICING

YEAR	HIGH	LOW
2001	$617	$463

U694H

YEARS MFRD........ 1998-1998
SERIES............ 600 SERIES
ENGINE.................. B&S
ENGINE HP................ 20
FUEL...................... G
TRANSMISSION.......... HYDRO
STEERING........... STANDARD
STANDARD DECK........... 46"
MSRP................ $2,099

RETAIL PRICING

YEAR	HIGH	LOW
1998	$873	$655

U804H

YEARS MFRD........ 1999-2004
SERIES............ 800 SERIES
ENGINE.................. B&S
ENGINE HP................ 20
COOLING................. AIR
FUEL...................... G
TRANSMISSION.............. CVT
STEERING........... STANDARD
PTO..................... YES
STANDARD DECK........... 46"
MSRP................ $2,299

RETAIL PRICING

YEAR	HIGH	LOW
1999	$297	$223
2000	$328	$246
2001	$362	$271
2002	$402	$301
2003	$443	$332
2004	$491	$368

U844H

YEARS MFRD........ 1998-1999
SERIES............ 800 SERIES
ENGINE.................. B&S
ENGINE HP................ 20
COOLING................. AIR
FUEL...................... G
SPEEDS............ VARIABLE
TRANSMISSION.......... HYDRO
STEERING........... STANDARD
STANDARD DECK........... 46"
MSRP................ $1,999

RETAIL PRICING

YEAR	HIGH	LOW
1998	$243	$183
1999	$273	$204

V694G

YEARS MFRD........ 1997-1997
ENGINE............... KOHLER
ENGINE HP................ 18
FUEL...................... G
TRANSMISSION.......... HYDRO
STEERING........... STANDARD
STANDARD DECK........... 42"
MSRP................ $1,949

RETAIL PRICING

YEAR	HIGH	LOW
1997	$773	$580

V804P

YEARS MFRD........ 1999-2001
SERIES............ 800 SERIES
ENGINE.................. B&S
ENGINE HP................ 22
FUEL...................... G
STEERING........... STANDARD
STANDARD DECK........... 50"
MSRP................ $3,499

RETAIL PRICING

YEAR	HIGH	LOW
1999	$402	$301
2000	$444	$333
2001	$492	$369

V834P

YEARS MFRD........ 1998-1998
ENGINE.................. B&S
ENGINE HP................ 22
FUEL...................... G
TRANSMISSION.......... HYDRO
STEERING........... STANDARD
STANDARD DECK........... 50"
MSRP................ $3,099

RETAIL PRICING

YEAR	HIGH	LOW
1998	$1,288	$966

W804H

YEARS MFRD........ 1999-2002
SERIES............ 800 SERIES
ENGINE............... KOHLER
ENGINE HP................ 20
COOLING................. AIR
FUEL...................... G
SPEEDS............ VARIABLE
TRANSMISSION.......... HYDRO
STEERING........... STANDARD
STANDARD DECK........... 46"
MSRP................ $2,799

RETAIL PRICING

YEAR	HIGH	LOW
1999	$329	$247
2000	$363	$272
2001	$402	$301
2002	$444	$333

W814H

YEARS MFRD........ 2002-2002
ENGINE............... KOHLER
ENGINE HP................ 20
FUEL...................... G
TRANSMISSION.......... HYDRO
STEERING........... STANDARD
STANDARD DECK........... 46"
MSRP................ $2,900

RETAIL PRICING

YEAR	HIGH	LOW
2002	$1,447	$1,085

W834H

YEARS MFRD........ 1997-1999
SERIES............ 800 SERIES
ENGINE............... KOHLER
ENGINE HP................ 20
FUEL...................... G
SPEEDS............ VARIABLE
TRANSMISSION.......... HYDRO
STEERING........... STANDARD
STANDARD DECK........... 46"
MSRP................ $2,699

OPTIONS

28" TILLER
3 BAG

RETAIL PRICING

YEAR	HIGH	LOW
1997	$250	$188
1998	$276	$207
1999	$306	$229

W844H

YEARS MFRD........ 1997-1997
ENGINE............... KOHLER
ENGINE HP................ 20
FUEL...................... G
TRANSMISSION............ GEAR
STEERING........... STANDARD
STANDARD DECK........... 46"
MSRP................ $2,699

RETAIL PRICING

YEAR	HIGH	LOW
1997	$1,070	$802

X604G

YEARS MFRD........ 1999-2001
SERIES............ 600 SERIES
ENGINE............... KOHLER
ENGINE HP................ 16
COOLING................. AIR
FUEL...................... G
TRANSMISSION............ GEAR
STEERING........... STANDARD
STANDARD DECK........... 42"
MSRP................ $1,799

RETAIL PRICING

YEAR	HIGH	LOW
1999	$191	$143
2000	$213	$160
2001	$236	$177

X614G

YEARS MFRD........ 1997-1998
SERIES............ 600 SERIES
ENGINE............... KOHLER
ENGINE HP................ 15
FUEL...................... G
TRANSMISSION............ GEAR
STEERING........... STANDARD
STANDARD DECK........... 42"
MSRP................ $1,879

RETAIL PRICING

YEAR	HIGH	LOW
1997	$752	$564
1998	$782	$586

X674G

YEARS MFRD........ 1997-1997
SERIES............ 600 SERIES
ENGINE............... KOHLER
ENGINE HP................ 15
COOLING................. AIR
FUEL...................... G
TRANSMISSION............ GEAR
STEERING........... STANDARD
STANDARD DECK........... 42"
MSRP................ $1,499

RETAIL PRICING

YEAR	HIGH	LOW
1997	$594	$445

X694G

YEARS MFRD........ 1997-1999
SERIES............ 600 SERIES
ENGINE............... KOHLER

ENGINE HP . . . 15
COOLING . . . AIR
FUEL . . . G
SPEEDS . . . VARIABLE
TRANSMISSION . . . HYDRO
STEERING. . . STANDARD
STANDARD DECK . . . 42"
MSRP. . . $1,599

RETAIL PRICING

YEAR	HIGH	LOW
1997	$149	$112
1998	$168	$126
1999	$187	$140

Y614G

YEARS MFRD . . . 2002-2002
ENGINE . . . B&S
ENGINE HP . . . 17
COOLING . . . AIR
FUEL . . . G
SPEEDS . . . VARIABLE
TRANSMISSION . . . HYDRO
STEERING. . . STANDARD
STANDARD DECK . . . 42"
MSRP. . . $1,599

RETAIL PRICING

YEAR	HIGH	LOW
2002	$259	$194

Y834P

YEARS MFRD . . . 1997-1998
ENGINE . . . KOHLER
ENGINE HP . . . 22
COOLING . . . AIR
FUEL . . . G
SPEEDS . . . VARIABLE
TRANSMISSION . . . HYDRO
STEERING. . . STANDARD
STANDARD DECK . . . 50"
MSRP. . . $3,199

OPTIONS

28" TILLER
3 BAG
B&S

RETAIL PRICING

YEAR	HIGH	LOW
1997	$301	$226
1998	$333	$250

Y844P

YEARS MFRD . . . 1997-1997
ENGINE . . . KOHLER
ENGINE HP . . . 22
COOLING . . . AIR
FUEL . . . G
TRANSMISSION . . . GEAR
STEERING. . . STANDARD
STANDARD DECK . . . 50"
MSRP. . . $2,999

RETAIL PRICING

YEAR	HIGH	LOW
1997	$296	$222

Z614H

YEARS MFRD . . . 2003-2004
ENGINE . . . B&S
ENGINE HP . . . 25
COOLING . . . AIR
FUEL . . . G
SPEEDS . . . VARIABLE
TRANSMISSION . . . HYDRO
STEERING. . . STANDARD
PTO . . . YES
STANDARD DECK . . . 46"
MSRP. . . $2,299

RETAIL PRICING

YEAR	HIGH	LOW
2003	$363	$272
2004	$403	$302

Z804P

YEARS MFRD . . . 1999-2000
SERIES. . . 800 SERIES
ENGINE . . . B&S
ENGINE HP . . . 25
FUEL . . . G
STEERING. . . STANDARD
STANDARD DECK . . . 50"
MSRP. . . $3,499

RETAIL PRICING

YEAR	HIGH	LOW
1999	$387	$290
2000	$428	$321

Z814K

YEARS MFRD . . . 2003-2004
ENGINE . . . B&S TWIN INTEK
CYLINDERS. . . 2
ENGINE HP . . . 25
COOLING . . . AIR
FUEL . . . G
SPEEDS . . . VARIABLE
TRANSMISSION . . . HYDRO
STEERING. . . STANDARD
PTO . . . YES
STANDARD DECK . . . 54"
MSRP. . . $3,699

RETAIL PRICING

YEAR	HIGH	LOW
2003	$654	$490
2004	$723	$542

Z834P

YEARS MFRD . . . 1998-1998
SERIES. . . 800 SERIES
ENGINE . . . KOHLER
ENGINE HP . . . 25
FUEL . . . G
TRANSMISSION . . . HYDRO
STEERING. . . STANDARD
STANDARD DECK . . . 50"
MSRP. . . $3,649

OPTIONS

28" TILLER
BAGGER

RETAIL PRICING

YEAR	HIGH	LOW
1998	$911	$683

13AC760F055

YEARS MFRD . . . 2010-2010
ENGINE . . . B&S
CYLINDERS. . . 1
ENGINE HP . . . 12.5
COOLING . . . AIR
FUEL . . . G
SPEEDS . . . 6/1
TRANSMISSION . . . DISC
STEERING. . . STANDARD
BLADE CLUTCH . . . ELECTRIC

13AC762F755

YEARS MFRD . . . 2007-2007
ENGINE . . . B&S
CYLINDERS. . . 1
ENGINE HP . . . 13.5
COOLING . . . AIR
FUEL . . . G
SPEEDS . . . 6/1
TRANSMISSION . . . BELT
STEERING. . . STANDARD

13AC76LF055

YEARS MFRD . . . 2011-2011
ENGINE . . . B&S
CYLINDERS. . . 1
ENGINE HP . . . 12.5
COOLING . . . AIR
FUEL . . . G
SPEEDS . . . 6/1
TRANSMISSION . . . GEAR
STEERING. . . STANDARD
STANDARD DECK . . . 38"
MSRP. . . $878

RETAIL PRICING

YEAR	HIGH	LOW
2011	$501	$376

13AM772-G755

YEARS MFRD . . . 2007-2007
ENGINE . . . B&S
ENGINE HP . . . 15.5
FUEL . . . G
SPEEDS . . . 7/1
TRANSMISSION . . . BELT
STEERING. . . STANDARD

13AM772-S055

YEARS MFRD . . . 2010-2010
ENGINE . . . B&S
CYLINDERS. . . 1
ENGINE HP . . . 15.5
COOLING . . . AIR
FUEL . . . G
SPEEDS . . . 7/1
TRANSMISSION . . . DISC
STEERING. . . STANDARD
BLADE CLUTCH . . . ELECTRIC

13AN791G755

YEARS MFRD . . . 2005-2006
ENGINE . . . B&S
ENGINE HP . . . 17.5
COOLING . . . AIR
FUEL . . . G
SPEEDS . . . VARIABLE
TRANSMISSION . . . HYDRO
STEERING. . . STANDARD
STANDARD DECK . . . 42"
MSRP. . . $998

RETAIL PRICING

YEAR	HIGH	LOW
2005	$607	$455
2006	$644	$483

13AN795S001

YEARS MFRD . . . 2012-2014
ENGINE . . . B&S
ENGINE HP . . . 17.5
COOLING . . . AIR
FUEL . . . G
SPEEDS . . . 6/1
TRANSMISSION . . . GEAR
STEERING. . . STANDARD
STANDARD DECK . . . 42"
MSRP. . . $1,199

RETAIL PRICING

YEAR	HIGH	LOW
2012	$478	$359
2013	$568	$426
2014	$665	$499

13A0771H055

YEARS MFRD . . . 2008-2009
ENGINE . . . B&S I/C
ENGINE HP . . . 19.5
COOLING . . . AIR
FUEL . . . G
SPEEDS . . . 7/1
TRANSMISSION . . . BELT
STEERING. . . STANDARD

13A0772G055

YEARS MFRD . . . 2008-2009
ENGINE . . . B&S I/C
ENGINE HP . . . 18.5
COOLING . . . AIR
FUEL . . . G
SPEEDS . . . 7/1
TRANSMISSION . . . BELT
STEERING. . . STANDARD

13A0772H755

YEARS MFRD . . . 2007-2007
ENGINE . . . B&S
ENGINE HP . . . 18.5
FUEL . . . G
SPEEDS . . . 7/1
TRANSMISSION . . . BELT
STEERING. . . STANDARD

YARDMAN

13AP615P755

YEARS MFRD 2005-2006
ENGINE . . . . KOHLER
ENGINE HP 23
COOLING . . . . AIR
FUEL . . . . G
SPEEDS . . . . VARIABLE
TRANSMISSION . . . . HYDRO
STEERING. . . . . STANDARD
STANDARD DECK . . . . 50"
MSRP. $1,998

RETAIL PRICING

YEAR	HIGH	LOW
2005	$1,220	$915
2006	$1,289	$967

13AT604H755

YEARS MFRD 2005-2006
ENGINE . . . . B&S
ENGINE HP 22
COOLING . . . . AIR
FUEL . . . . G
SPEEDS . . . . VARIABLE
TRANSMISSION . . . . HYDRO
STEERING. . . . . STANDARD
STANDARD DECK . . . . 46"
MSRP. $1,498

RETAIL PRICING

YEAR	HIGH	LOW
2005	$914	$685
2006	$966	$725

13AT605G755

YEARS MFRD 2005-2006
ENGINE . . . . B&S
ENGINE HP 20
COOLING . . . . AIR
FUEL . . . . G
SPEEDS . . . . VARIABLE
TRANSMISSION . . . . HYDRO
STEERING. . . . . STANDARD
STANDARD DECK . . . . 42"
MSRP. $1,298

RETAIL PRICING

YEAR	HIGH	LOW
2005	$794	$596
2006	$838	$629

13AU615P755

YEARS MFRD 2005-2006
ENGINE . . . . B&S
ENGINE HP 22
COOLING . . . . AIR
FUEL . . . . G
SPEEDS . . . . VARIABLE
TRANSMISSION . . . . HYDRO
STEERING. . . . . STANDARD
STANDARD DECK . . . . 50"
MSRP. $1,698

RETAIL PRICING

YEAR	HIGH	LOW
2005	$1,038	$778
2006	$1,096	$822

13AX615G055

YEARS MFRD 2008-2008
ENGINE . . . . KOHLER COURAGE
ENGINE HP 19
COOLING . . . . AIR
FUEL . . . . G
SPEEDS . . . . VARIABLE
TRANSMISSION . . . . HYDRO
STEERING. . . . . STANDARD

13AX90YT001

YEARS MFRD 2010-2010
ENGINE . . . . KOHLER COURAGE
CYLINDERS. 2
ENGINE HP 22
COOLING . . . . AIR
FUEL . . . . G
SPEEDS . . . . VARIABLE
TRANSMISSION . . . . HYDRO
STEERING. . . . . STANDARD
BLADE CLUTCH . . . . ELECTRIC

13BP605H755

YEARS MFRD 2007-2007
ENGINE . . . . KOHLER
CYLINDERS. 2
ENGINE HP 20
FUEL . . . . G
SPEEDS . . . . VARIABLE
TRANSMISSION . . . . HYDRO
STEERING. . . . . STANDARD

13BX605G755

YEARS MFRD 2007-2007
ENGINE . . . . KOHLER
CYLINDERS. 1
ENGINE HP 19
FUEL . . . . G
SPEEDS . . . . VARIABLE
TRANSMISSION . . . . HYDRO
STEERING. . . . . STANDARD

17AC2ACG055

YEARS MFRD 2010-2010
ENGINE . . . . B&S INTEK
CYLINDERS. 2
ENGINE HP 21
COOLING . . . . AIR
FUEL . . . . G
SPEEDS . . . . VARIABLE
TRANSMISSION . . . . HYDRO
STEERING. . . . . ZERO
BLADE CLUTCH . . . . ELECTRIC

17AC2ACS055

YEARS MFRD 2011-2014
ENGINE . . . . B&S INTEK
ENGINE HP 16
COOLING . . . . AIR
FUEL . . . . G
SPEEDS . . . . VARIABLE
TRANSMISSION . . . . HYDRO
STEERING. . . . . ZERO
STANDARD DECK . . . . 42"
MSRP. $2,198

RETAIL PRICING

YEAR	HIGH	LOW
2011	$777	$583
2012	$943	$707
2013	$1,226	$920
2014	$1,324	$993

17AF2ACK004

YEARS MFRD 2011-2011
SERIES. . . . . MTD GOLD SERIES
ENGINE . . . . KOHLER COURAGE
CYLINDERS. 2
ENGINE HP 26
COOLING . . . . AIR
FUEL . . . . G
SPEEDS . . . . VARIABLE
TRANSMISSION . . . . HYDRO
STEERING. . . . . ZERO
STANDARD DECK . . . . 54"
MSRP. $2,999

RETAIL PRICING

YEAR	HIGH	LOW
2011	$1,712	$1,284

17AF2ACP001

YEARS MFRD 2010-2010
ENGINE . . . . KOHLER COURAGE
CYLINDERS. 2
ENGINE HP 22
COOLING . . . . AIR
FUEL . . . . G
SPEEDS . . . . VARIABLE
TRANSMISSION . . . . HYDRO
STEERING. . . . . ZERO
BLADE CLUTCH . . . . ELECTRIC

17AF2ACP004

YEARS MFRD 2011-2011
SERIES. . . . . MTD GOLD SERIES
ENGINE . . . . KOHLER COURAGE
CYLINDERS. 2
ENGINE HP 25
COOLING . . . . AIR
FUEL . . . . G
SPEEDS . . . . VARIABLE
TRANSMISSION . . . . HYDRO
STEERING. . . . . ZERO
STANDARD DECK . . . . 50"
MSRP. $2,799

RETAIL PRICING

YEAR	HIGH	LOW
2011	$1,599	$1,199

17AF2ACS004

YEARS MFRD 2011-2011
SERIES. . . . . MTD GOLD SERIES
ENGINE . . . . KOHLER COURAGE
CYLINDERS. 2
ENGINE HP 22
COOLING . . . . AIR
FUEL . . . . G
SPEEDS . . . . VARIABLE
TRANSMISSION . . . . HYDRO
STEERING. . . . . ZERO
STANDARD DECK . . . . 42"
MSRP. $2,399

RETAIL PRICING

YEAR	HIGH	LOW
2011	$1,371	$1,028

135D614G

YEARS MFRD 1994-1995
ENGINE . . . . B&S
ENGINE HP 15
COOLING . . . . AIR
FUEL . . . . G
TRANSMISSION . . . . GEAR
STEERING. . . . . STANDARD
STANDARD DECK . . . . 42"
MSRP. $1,699

RETAIL PRICING

YEAR	HIGH	LOW
1994	$639	$479
1995	$646	$485

135V694H

YEARS MFRD 1994-1995
ENGINE . . . . B&S
ENGINE HP 19
COOLING . . . . AIR
FUEL . . . . G
TRANSMISSION . . . . HYDRO
STEERING. . . . . STANDARD
STANDARD DECK . . . . 46"
MSRP. $2,399

RETAIL PRICING

YEAR	HIGH	LOW
1994	$711	$533
1995	$883	$662

135X694G

YEARS MFRD 1994-1995
ENGINE . . . . KOHLER
ENGINE HP 15
COOLING . . . . AIR
FUEL . . . . G
TRANSMISSION . . . . HYDRO
STEERING. . . . . STANDARD
STANDARD DECK . . . . 42"
MSRP. $1,699

RETAIL PRICING

YEAR	HIGH	LOW
1994	$639	$479
1995	$646	$485

136G765N

YEARS MFRD 1996-1996
ENGINE . . . . B&S
ENGINE HP 16
COOLING . . . . AIR
FUEL . . . . G
TRANSMISSION . . . . GEAR
STEERING. . . . . STANDARD

STANDARD DECK .... 40"
MSRP................ $1,699

RETAIL PRICING

YEAR	HIGH	LOW
1996	$648	$486

1360695G

YEARS MFRD 1996-1996
ENGINE .... B&S
ENGINE HP 16
COOLING .... AIR
FUEL .... G
TRANSMISSION .... HYDRO
STEERING............ STANDARD
STANDARD DECK .... 42"
MSRP................ $1,599

RETAIL PRICING

YEAR	HIGH	LOW
1996	$608	$456

136P668H

YEARS MFRD 1996-1996
ENGINE .... B&S
ENGINE HP 18
COOLING .... AIR
FUEL .... G
TRANSMISSION .... GEAR
STEERING............ STANDARD
STANDARD DECK .... 46"
MSRP................ $1,499

RETAIL PRICING

YEAR	HIGH	LOW
1996	$571	$428

136X694G

YEARS MFRD 1996-1996
ENGINE .... KOHLER
ENGINE HP 15
COOLING .... AIR
FUEL .... G
TRANSMISSION .... HYDRO
STEERING............ STANDARD
STANDARD DECK .... 42"
MSRP................ $1,700

RETAIL PRICING

YEAR	HIGH	LOW
1996	$649	$487

145V834H

YEARS MFRD 1994-1995
ENGINE .... B&S
ENGINE HP 19
COOLING .... AIR
FUEL .... G
TRANSMISSION .... HYDRO
STEERING............ STANDARD
STANDARD DECK .... 46"
MSRP................ $2,399

RETAIL PRICING

YEAR	HIGH	LOW
1994	$888	$666
1995	$897	$673

145W834P

YEARS MFRD 1994-1995
ENGINE .... KOHLER
ENGINE HP 20
COOLING .... AIR
FUEL .... G
TRANSMISSION .... HYDRO
STEERING............ STANDARD
STANDARD DECK .... 50"
MSRP................ $2,699

RETAIL PRICING

YEAR	HIGH	LOW
1994	$993	$745
1995	$994	$746

145Y683P

YEARS MFRD 1995-1995
ENGINE .... KOHLER
ENGINE HP 22
COOLING .... AIR
FUEL .... G
TRANSMISSION .... HYDRO
STEERING............ STANDARD
STANDARD DECK .... 50"
MSRP................ $2,999

RETAIL PRICING

YEAR	HIGH	LOW
1995	$1,106	$829

145Y834P

YEARS MFRD 1994-1995
ENGINE .... KOHLER
ENGINE HP 22
COOLING .... AIR
FUEL .... G
TRANSMISSION .... HYDRO
STEERING............ STANDARD
STANDARD DECK .... 50"
MSRP................ $3,399

RETAIL PRICING

YEAR	HIGH	LOW
1994	$1,172	$879
1995	$1,253	$940

146J844H

YEARS MFRD 1996-1996
ENGINE .... B&S
ENGINE HP 20
COOLING .... AIR
FUEL .... G
TRANSMISSION .... GEAR
STEERING............ STANDARD
STANDARD DECK .... 46"
MSRP................ $2,300

RETAIL PRICING

YEAR	HIGH	LOW
1996	$877	$658

146K828H

YEARS MFRD 1996-1996
ENGINE .... B&S
ENGINE HP 18.5
COOLING .... AIR
FUEL .... G
TRANSMISSION .... GEAR
STEERING............ STANDARD
STANDARD DECK .... 46"
MSRP................ $1,999

RETAIL PRICING

YEAR	HIGH	LOW
1996	$763	$573

146W834H

YEARS MFRD 1996-1996
ENGINE .... KOHLER TWIN
ENGINE HP 20
COOLING .... AIR
FUEL .... G
STEERING............ STANDARD
STANDARD DECK .... 46"
MSRP................ $2,700

RETAIL PRICING

YEAR	HIGH	LOW
1996	$1,031	$773

146Y834P

YEARS MFRD 1996-1996
ENGINE .... KOHLER TWIN
ENGINE HP 22
COOLING .... AIR
FUEL .... G
STEERING............ STANDARD
STANDARD DECK .... 50"
MSRP................ $3,199

RETAIL PRICING

YEAR	HIGH	LOW
1996	$280	$210

604H

YEARS MFRD 2005-2006
ENGINE .... B&S
CYLINDERS.................. 2
ENGINE HP 22
COOLING .... AIR
FUEL .... G
SPEEDS .... VARIABLE
TRANSMISSION .... HYDRO
STEERING............ STANDARD
BLADE CLUTCH .... MANUAL

605G

YEARS MFRD 2005-2006
ENGINE .... B&S
CYLINDERS.................. 2
ENGINE HP 20
COOLING .... AIR
FUEL .... G
SPEEDS .... VARIABLE
TRANSMISSION .... HYDRO
STEERING............ STANDARD
BLADE CLUTCH .... MANUAL

791G

YEARS MFRD 2005-2006
ENGINE .... B&S
CYLINDERS.................. 1
ENGINE HP 17.5
COOLING .... AIR
FUEL .... G
SPEEDS .... VARIABLE
TRANSMISSION .... HYDRO
STEERING............ STANDARD
BLADE CLUTCH .... MANUAL

999

YEARS MFRD 1997-1999
ENGINE .... KOHLER
ENGINE HP 22
COOLING .... AIR
FUEL .... G
TRANSMISSION .... HYDRO
STEERING............ STANDARD
STANDARD DECK .... 50"
MSRP................ $5,498

OPTIONS

38" TILLER

RETAIL PRICING

YEAR	HIGH	LOW
1997	$549	$412
1998	$608	$456
1999	$673	$505

1674G

YEARS MFRD 1997-1998
ENGINE .... B&S
ENGINE HP 15.5
FUEL .... G
TRANSMISSION .... GEAR
STEERING............ STANDARD
STANDARD DECK .... 42"
MSRP................ $1,299

RETAIL PRICING

YEAR	HIGH	LOW
1997	$515	$386
1998	$541	$406

130824H

YEARS MFRD 1990-1990
ENGINE .... B&S
ENGINE HP 18
COOLING .... AIR
FUEL .... G
TRANSMISSION .... HYDRO
STEERING............ STANDARD
STANDARD DECK .... 46"
MSRP................ $2,900

RETAIL PRICING

YEAR	HIGH	LOW
1990	$852	$639

131824H

YEARS MFRD 1991-1991
ENGINE .... B&S
ENGINE HP 18
COOLING .... AIR
FUEL .... G
TRANSMISSION .... HYDRO
STEERING............ STANDARD
STANDARD DECK .... 46"
MSRP................ $2,895

YARDMAN

RETAIL PRICING

YEAR	HIGH	LOW
1991	$905	$679

132834H

YEARS MFRD 1992-1992
ENGINE B&S
ENGINE HP 18
COOLING AIR
FUEL G
TRANSMISSION HYDRO
STEERING STANDARD
STANDARD DECK 46"
MSRP $2,835

RETAIL PRICING

YEAR	HIGH	LOW
1992	$925	$694

140844H

YEARS MFRD 1990-1990
ENGINE B&S
ENGINE HP 18
COOLING AIR
FUEL G
TRANSMISSION GEAR
STEERING STANDARD
STANDARD DECK 46"
MSRP $3,000

RETAIL PRICING

YEAR	HIGH	LOW
1990	$880	$660

141844H

YEARS MFRD 1991-1991
ENGINE B&S
ENGINE HP 18
COOLING AIR
FUEL G
TRANSMISSION GEAR
STEERING STANDARD
STANDARD DECK 46"
MSRP $2,999

RETAIL PRICING

YEAR	HIGH	LOW
1991	$938	$703

142854H

YEARS MFRD 1992-1992
ENGINE B&S
ENGINE HP 18
COOLING AIR
FUEL G
TRANSMISSION GEAR
STEERING STANDARD
STANDARD DECK 46"
MSRP $2,735

RETAIL PRICING

YEAR	HIGH	LOW
1992	$892	$669

142995

YEARS MFRD 1992-1992
ENGINE B&S
ENGINE HP 18
COOLING AIR
FUEL G
TRANSMISSION HYDRO
STEERING STANDARD
STANDARD DECK 50"
MSRP $4,440

RETAIL PRICING

YEAR	HIGH	LOW
1992	$1,447	$1,085

145999

YEARS MFRD 1994-1994
ENGINE KOHLER
ENGINE HP 22
COOLING AIR
FUEL G
SPEEDS VARIABLE
TRANSMISSION HYDRO
STEERING STANDARD
STANDARD DECK 50"
MSRP $4,975

RETAIL PRICING

YEAR	HIGH	LOW
1994	$307	$231

146999

YEARS MFRD 1996-1996
ENGINE KOHLER TWIN
CYLINDERS 2
ENGINE HP 22
COOLING AIR
FUEL G
SPEEDS VARIABLE
TRANSMISSION HYDRO
STEERING STANDARD
STANDARD DECK 50"
MSRP $5,498

OPTIONS

EDGE
TILLER

RETAIL PRICING

YEAR	HIGH	LOW
1996	$446	$335

1361614G

YEARS MFRD 1996-1996
ENGINE B&S
ENGINE HP 15.5
COOLING AIR
FUEL G
TRANSMISSION HYDRO
STEERING STANDARD
STANDARD DECK 42"
MSRP $1,800

RETAIL PRICING

YEAR	HIGH	LOW
1996	$687	$515

1362694G

YEARS MFRD 1996-1996
ENGINE B&S
ENGINE HP 17.5
COOLING AIR
FUEL G
TRANSMISSION HYDRO
STEERING STANDARD
STANDARD DECK 42"
MSRP $1,800

RETAIL PRICING

YEAR	HIGH	LOW
1996	$687	$515

1363694H

YEARS MFRD 1996-1996
ENGINE B&S
ENGINE HP 19.5
COOLING AIR
FUEL G
TRANSMISSION HYDRO
STEERING STANDARD
STANDARD DECK 46"
MSRP $2,000

RETAIL PRICING

YEAR	HIGH	LOW
1996	$763	$573

1463834H

YEARS MFRD 1996-1996
ENGINE B&S
ENGINE HP 19.5
COOLING AIR
FUEL G
TRANSMISSION GEAR
STEERING STANDARD
STANDARD DECK 46"
MSRP $2,500

RETAIL PRICING

YEAR	HIGH	LOW
1996	$955	$717

YAZOO/KEES

YHRK18

YEARS MFRD 1992-1992
ENGINE KOHLER
ENGINE HP 18
FUEL G
SPEEDS 0-11
TRANSMISSION HYDRO
STEERING STANDARD
STANDARD DECK 60"
MSRP $5,983

RETAIL PRICING

YEAR	HIGH	LOW
1992	$2,009	$1,507

YHRK20

YEARS MFRD 1997-1997
ENGINE KOHLER
ENGINE HP 20
COOLING AIR
FUEL G
SPEEDS 0-11
TRANSMISSION HYDRO
STEERING ZERO
STANDARD DECK 52"
MSRP $7,398

RETAIL PRICING

YEAR	HIGH	LOW
1997	$778	$584

YHRLD21

YEARS MFRD 1992-1994
ENGINE KUBOTA
ENGINE HP 21
FUEL D
SPEEDS 0-11
TRANSMISSION HYDRO
STEERING STANDARD
STANDARD DECK 60"
MSRP $10,858

RETAIL PRICING

YEAR	HIGH	LOW
1992	$3,471	$2,603
1993	$3,582	$2,686
1994	$3,976	$2,982

YHRLD212

YEARS MFRD 1997-1997
ENGINE KUBOTA
ENGINE HP 21
COOLING LIQUID
FUEL D
SPEEDS 0-11
TRANSMISSION HYDRO
STEERING ZERO
STANDARD DECK 52"
MSRP $11,998

RETAIL PRICING

YEAR	HIGH	LOW
1997	$1,307	$980

YHRLK20

YEARS MFRD 1992-1996
ENGINE KOHLER
ENGINE HP 20
FUEL G
SPEEDS 0-11
TRANSMISSION HYDRO
STEERING STANDARD
STANDARD DECK 60"
MSRP $8,264

RETAIL PRICING

YEAR	HIGH	LOW
1992	$2,060	$1,545
1993	$2,521	$1,890
1994	$2,804	$2,103
1995	$3,083	$2,312
1996	$3,255	$2,441

YHRLK23

YEARS MFRD 1992-1995
ENGINE .... KOHLER
ENGINE HP 23
FUEL .... G
SPEEDS 0-11
TRANSMISSION .... HYDRO
STEERING .... STANDARD
STANDARD DECK .... 60"
MSRP $8,964

RETAIL PRICING

YEAR	HIGH	LOW
1992	$2,721	$2,041
1993	$2,833	$2,125
1994	$3,096	$2,322
1995	$3,407	$2,556

YHRLKI20

YEARS MFRD 1992-1995
ENGINE .... KAWASAKI
ENGINE HP 20
FUEL .... G
SPEEDS 0-11
TRANSMISSION .... HYDRO
STEERING .... STANDARD
STANDARD DECK .... 60"
MSRP $9,095

RETAIL PRICING

YEAR	HIGH	LOW
1992	$2,934	$2,201
1993	$3,028	$2,271
1994	$3,208	$2,406
1995	$3,456	$2,592

YHRLW20

YEARS MFRD 1992-1993
ENGINE .... WISCONSIN
ENGINE HP 20
FUEL .... G
SPEEDS 0-11
TRANSMISSION .... HYDRO
STEERING .... STANDARD
STANDARD DECK .... 60"
MSRP $7,342

RETAIL PRICING

YEAR	HIGH	LOW
1992	$2,514	$1,885
1993	$2,544	$1,908

YHRLWG24.5

YEARS MFRD 1992-1992
ENGINE .... KUBOTA
ENGINE HP 24.5
FUEL .... D
SPEEDS 0-11
TRANSMISSION .... HYDRO
STEERING .... STANDARD
STANDARD DECK .... 60"
MSRP $10,328

RETAIL PRICING

YEAR	HIGH	LOW
1992	$3,471	$2,603

YTBSD265

YEARS MFRD 1999-2000
SERIES .... YT SERIES
ENGINE .... B&S
ENGINE HP 26.5
COOLING .... LIQUID
FUEL .... D
SPEEDS .... VARIABLE
TRANSMISSION .... HYDRO
STEERING .... ZERO
STANDARD DECK .... 72"
MSRP $13,198

RETAIL PRICING

YEAR	HIGH	LOW
1999	$2,080	$1,560
2000	$2,302	$1,727

YTBSV18

YEARS MFRD 1997-2000
SERIES .... YT SERIES
ENGINE .... B&S
ENGINE HP 18
COOLING .... AIR
FUEL .... G
SPEEDS .... VARIABLE
TRANSMISSION .... HYDRO
STEERING .... ZERO
STANDARD DECK .... 50"
MSRP $6,258

OPTIONS

52" DECK

RETAIL PRICING

YEAR	HIGH	LOW
1997	$888	$666
1998	$984	$738
1999	$1,091	$818
2000	$1,211	$908

YTKC22

YEARS MFRD 1997-2000
SERIES .... YT SERIES
ENGINE .... KOHLER
ENGINE HP 22
COOLING .... AIR
FUEL .... G
SPEEDS .... VARIABLE
TRANSMISSION .... HYDRO
STEERING .... ZERO
STANDARD DECK .... 52"
MSRP $7,798

OPTIONS

62" DECK

RETAIL PRICING

YEAR	HIGH	LOW
1997	$1,106	$830
1998	$1,226	$919
1999	$1,361	$1,021
2000	$1,512	$1,134

YTKC25

YEARS MFRD 1997-2000
SERIES .... YT SERIES
ENGINE .... KOHLER
ENGINE HP 25
COOLING .... AIR
FUEL .... G
SPEEDS .... VARIABLE
TRANSMISSION .... HYDRO
STEERING .... ZERO
STANDARD DECK .... 62"
MSRP $9,098

OPTIONS

72" DECK

RETAIL PRICING

YEAR	HIGH	LOW
1997	$1,293	$969
1998	$1,436	$1,077
1999	$1,589	$1,191
2000	$1,763	$1,322

YZTK20

YEARS MFRD 1997-1997
ENGINE .... KOHLER
ENGINE HP 20
FUEL .... G
TRANSMISSION .... HYDRO
STEERING .... ZERO
STANDARD DECK .... 48"
MSRP $6,899

OPTIONS

60" DECK

RETAIL PRICING

YEAR	HIGH	LOW
1997	$852	$639

YZTK22

YEARS MFRD 1997-1997
ENGINE .... KOHLER
ENGINE HP 22
FUEL .... G
TRANSMISSION .... HYDRO
STEERING .... ZERO
STANDARD DECK .... 60"
MSRP $7,599

RETAIL PRICING

YEAR	HIGH	LOW
1997	$941	$706

ZBIQL48812

YEARS MFRD 2002-2003
SERIES .... MINI-MAX SERIES
ENGINE .... B&S
ENGINE HP 18
FUEL .... G
TRANSMISSION .... HYDRO
STANDARD DECK .... 48"
MSRP $6,300

RETAIL PRICING

YEAR	HIGH	LOW
2002	$3,241	$2,431
2003	$3,513	$2,635

ZCBI48180

YEARS MFRD 2005-2006
ENGINE .... B&S INTEK
CYLINDERS 2
ENGINE HP 18
COOLING .... AIR
FUEL .... G
SPEEDS .... VARIABLE
TRANSMISSION .... HYDRO
STEERING .... ZERO
BLADE CLUTCH .... ELECTRIC
STANDARD DECK .... 48"
MSRP $3,999

RETAIL PRICING

YEAR	HIGH	LOW
2005	$1,165	$874
2006	$1,295	$971

ZEKH4220

YEARS MFRD 2010-2011
ENGINE .... KOHLER COURAGE
CYLINDERS 2
ENGINE HP 20
COOLING .... AIR
FUEL .... G
SPEEDS .... VARIABLE
TRANSMISSION .... HYDRO
STEERING .... ZERO
BLADE CLUTCH .... ELECTRIC
STANDARD DECK .... 42"
WEIGHT .... 630 LBS.
MSRP $3,299

RETAIL PRICING

YEAR	HIGH	LOW
2010	$1,535	$1,151
2011	$1,705	$1,279

ZEKH4824

YEARS MFRD 2010-2011
ENGINE .... KOHLER COURAGE
CYLINDERS 2
ENGINE HP 24
COOLING .... AIR
FUEL .... G
SPEEDS .... VARIABLE
TRANSMISSION .... HYDRO
STEERING .... ZERO
BLADE CLUTCH .... ELECTRIC
STANDARD DECK .... 48"
WEIGHT .... 630 LBS.
MSRP $4,199

RETAIL PRICING

YEAR	HIGH	LOW
2010	$1,955	$1,466
2011	$2,172	$1,629

ZEKH5224

YEARS MFRD 2010-2011
ENGINE .... KOHLER COURAGE
CYLINDERS 2
ENGINE HP 24
COOLING .... AIR
FUEL .... G
SPEEDS .... VARIABLE
TRANSMISSION .... HYDRO
STEERING .... ZERO
BLADE CLUTCH .... ELECTRIC
STANDARD DECK .... 52"
WEIGHT .... 665 LBS.
MSRP $4,399

YAZOO/KEES

RETAIL PRICING

YEAR	HIGH	LOW
2010	$2,047	$1,535
2011	$2,276	$1,707

ZEKW42170

YEARS MFRD 2006-2007
ENGINE .... KAWASAKI
CYLINDERS................. 2
ENGINE HP 17
COOLING .... AIR
FUEL .... G
SPEEDS .... VARIABLE
TRANSMISSION .... HYDRO
STEERING .... ZERO
STANDARD DECK .... 42"
WEIGHT .... 630 LBS.
MSRP $5,399

SERIAL NUMBERS

YEAR	BEGINNING NO.
2007	64000000

RETAIL PRICING

YEAR	HIGH	LOW
2006	$1,743	$1,308
2007	$1,936	$1,452

ZEKW48190

YEARS MFRD 2007-2007
ENGINE .... KAWASAKI
ENGINE HP 19
COOLING .... AIR
FUEL .... G
SPEEDS .... VARIABLE
TRANSMISSION .... HYDRO
STEERING .... ZERO
STANDARD DECK .... 48"
WEIGHT .... 630 LBS.
MSRP $4,999

SERIAL NUMBERS

YEAR	BEGINNING NO.
2007	64000000

RETAIL PRICING

YEAR	HIGH	LOW
2007	$1,793	$1,345

ZEKW52210

YEARS MFRD 2007-2007
ENGINE .... KAWASAKI
CYLINDERS................. 2
ENGINE HP 21
COOLING .... AIR
FUEL .... G
SPEEDS .... VARIABLE
TRANSMISSION .... HYDRO
STEERING .... ZERO
STANDARD DECK .... 52"
WEIGHT .... 665 LBS.
MSRP $5,299

SERIAL NUMBERS

YEAR	BEGINNING NO.
2007	64000000

RETAIL PRICING

YEAR	HIGH	LOW
2007	$1,901	$1,426

ZELKH52250

YEARS MFRD 2006-2007
ENGINE ... KOHLER COURAGE PRO
CYLINDERS................. 2
ENGINE HP 25
COOLING .... AIR
FUEL .... G
SPEEDS .... VARIABLE
TRANSMISSION .... HYDRO
STEERING .... ZERO
BLADE CLUTCH .... ELECTRIC
STANDARD DECK .... 52"
WEIGHT .... 760 LBS.
MSRP $5,999

RETAIL PRICING

YEAR	HIGH	LOW
2006	$1,939	$1,455
2007	$2,151	$1,613

ZELKH61250

YEARS MFRD 2006-2007
ENGINE ... KOHLER COURAGE PRO
CYLINDERS................. 2
ENGINE HP 25
COOLING .... AIR
FUEL .... G
SPEEDS .... VARIABLE
TRANSMISSION .... HYDRO
STEERING .... ZERO
BLADE CLUTCH .... ELECTRIC
STANDARD DECK .... 61"
WEIGHT .... 790 LBS.
MSRP $6,299

RETAIL PRICING

YEAR	HIGH	LOW
2006	$2,036	$1,527
2007	$2,260	$1,695

ZELKH61251

YEARS MFRD 2010-2010
ENGINE .... KOHLER
ENGINE HP 25
COOLING .... AIR
FUEL .... G
SPEEDS .... VARIABLE
TRANSMISSION .... HYDRO
STEERING .... ZERO
BLADE CLUTCH .... ELECTRIC
STANDARD DECK .... 61"
MSRP $5,399

RETAIL PRICING

YEAR	HIGH	LOW
2010	$2,793	$2,095

ZELKH72270

YEARS MFRD 2006-2007
ENGINE .... KOHLER COURAGE
CYLINDERS................. 2
ENGINE HP 27
COOLING .... AIR
FUEL .... G
SPEEDS .... VARIABLE
TRANSMISSION .... HYDRO
STEERING .... ZERO
BLADE CLUTCH .... ELECTRIC
STANDARD DECK .... 72"
WEIGHT .... 820 LBS.
MSRP $6,999

RETAIL PRICING

YEAR	HIGH	LOW
2006	$2,260	$1,695
2007	$2,511	$1,883

ZHDD61270

YEARS MFRD 2002-2004
SERIES .... MEGA-MAX SERIES
ENGINE .... DAIHATSU
CYLINDERS................. 3
ENGINE HP 27
FUEL .... D
TRANSMISSION .... HYDRO
STEERING .... ZERO
BLADE CLUTCH .... ELECTRIC
STANDARD DECK .... 61"
MSRP $13,600

RETAIL PRICING

YEAR	HIGH	LOW
2002	$6,993	$5,245
2003	$7,583	$5,687

ZHDD61271

YEARS MFRD 2007-2007
ENGINE ..... VANGUARD DAIHATSU
DM950D
CYLINDERS................. 3
ENGINE HP 27
COOLING .... LIQUID
FUEL .... D
SPEEDS .... VARIABLE
TRANSMISSION ..... DUAL HYDRO
STEERING .... ZERO
BLADE CLUTCH .... ELECTRIC
STANDARD DECK .... 61"
WEIGHT .... 1,540 LBS.
MSRP $13,999

SERIAL NUMBERS

YEAR	BEGINNING NO.
2007	64000000

RETAIL PRICING

YEAR	HIGH	LOW
2007	$5,024	$3,768

ZHDD61340

YEARS MFRD 2002-2004
SERIES .... MEGA-MAX SERIES
ENGINE .... DAIHATSU
CYLINDERS................. 3
ENGINE HP 34
FUEL .... D
TRANSMISSION .... HYDRO
STEERING .... ZERO
BLADE CLUTCH .... ELECTRIC
STANDARD DECK .... 61"
MSRP $15,600

RETAIL PRICING

YEAR	HIGH	LOW
2002	$8,023	$6,017
2003	$8,699	$6,525
2004	$8,797	$6,598

ZHDD72340

YEARS MFRD 2002-2004
SERIES .... MEGA-MAX SERIES
ENGINE .... DAIHATSU
CYLINDERS................. 3
ENGINE HP 34
FUEL .... D
TRANSMISSION .... HYDRO
STEERING .... ZERO
BLADE CLUTCH .... ELECTRIC
STANDARD DECK .... 72"
MSRP $15,900

RETAIL PRICING

YEAR	HIGH	LOW
2002	$8,177	$6,133
2003	$8,866	$6,650
2004	$9,044	$6,783

ZHDD72341

YEARS MFRD 2007-2007
ENGINE ..... VANGUARD DAIHATSU
DM654TD
CYLINDERS................. 3
ENGINE HP 34
COOLING .... LIQUID
FUEL .... D
SPEEDS .... VARIABLE
TRANSMISSION ..... DUAL HYDRO
STEERING .... ZERO
BLADE CLUTCH .... ELECTRIC
STANDARD DECK .... 72"
WEIGHT .... 1,620 LBS.
MSRP $15,999

SERIAL NUMBERS

YEAR	BEGINNING NO.
2007	64000000

RETAIL PRICING

YEAR	HIGH	LOW
2007	$5,742	$4,306

ZHDG61340

YEARS MFRD 2002-2003
SERIES .... MEGA-MAX SERIES
ENGINE .... DAIHATSU
ENGINE HP 34
FUEL .... G
TRANSMISSION .... HYDRO
STANDARD DECK .... 61"
MSRP $14,600

RETAIL PRICING

YEAR	HIGH	LOW
2002	$7,508	$5,631
2003	$8,140	$6,105

ZHDG72340

YEARS MFRD 2002-2003
SERIES .... MEGA-MAX SERIES
ENGINE .... DIAHATSU
ENGINE HP 34
FUEL .... G
TRANSMISSION .... HYDRO
STANDARD DECK .... 72"
MSRP $14,900

RETAIL PRICING

YEAR	HIGH	LOW
2002	$7,662	$5,746
2003	$8,307	$6,231

ZKH52221

YEARS MFRD 1998-1998
SERIES . . . . ZT MAX SERIES
ENGINE . . . . KOHLER
ENGINE HP 22
FUEL . . . . G
SPEEDS 0-9
TRANSMISSION . . . . HYDRO
STEERING. . . . . STANDARD

ZKH52222

YEARS MFRD 1999-1999
SERIES . . . . ZT MAX SERIES
ENGINE . . . . KOHLER
ENGINE HP 22
FUEL . . . . G
SPEEDS 0-9
TRANSMISSION . . . . HYDRO
STEERING. . . . . STANDARD

ZKH52223

YEARS MFRD 1999-2000
SERIES . . . . ZT MAX SERIES
ENGINE . . . . KOHLER
ENGINE HP 22
FUEL . . . . G
TRANSMISSION . . . . HYDRO
STEERING. . . . . ZERO
STANDARD DECK . . . . 52"
MSRP. $8,219

RETAIL PRICING

YEAR	HIGH	LOW
1999	$3,762	$2,822
2000	$3,944	$2,958

ZKH52251

YEARS MFRD 1998-1998
SERIES . . . . ZT MAX SERIES
ENGINE . . . . KOHLER
ENGINE HP 25
FUEL . . . . G
SPEEDS 0-9
TRANSMISSION . . . . HYDRO
STEERING. . . . . STANDARD

ZKH52252

YEARS MFRD 1999-1999
SERIES . . . . ZT MAX SERIES
ENGINE . . . . KOHLER
ENGINE HP 25
FUEL . . . . G
SPEEDS 0-9
TRANSMISSION . . . . HYDRO
STEERING. . . . . STANDARD

ZKH52253

YEARS MFRD 1999-2000
SERIES . . . . ZT MAX SERIES
ENGINE . . . . KOHLER
ENGINE HP 25
FUEL . . . . G
TRANSMISSION . . . . HYDRO
STEERING. . . . . ZERO
STANDARD DECK . . . . 52"
MSRP. $8,769

RETAIL PRICING

YEAR	HIGH	LOW
1999	$1,531	$1,148
2000	$1,700	$1,275

ZKH61251

YEARS MFRD 1998-1999
SERIES . . . . ZT MAX SERIES
ENGINE . . . . KOHLER
ENGINE HP 25
FUEL . . . . G
SPEEDS 0-9
TRANSMISSION . . . . HYDRO
STEERING. . . . . STANDARD

ZKH61253

YEARS MFRD 1999-2000
SERIES . . . . ZT MAX SERIES
ENGINE . . . . KOHLER
ENGINE HP 25
FUEL . . . . G
TRANSMISSION . . . . HYDRO
STEERING. . . . . ZERO
STANDARD DECK . . . . 61"
MSRP. $8,899

RETAIL PRICING

YEAR	HIGH	LOW
1999	$1,554	$1,166
2000	$1,723	$1,292

ZKHP52223

YEARS MFRD 2001-2001
SERIES . . . . ZT MAX SERIES
ENGINE . . . . KOHLER
ENGINE HP 23
FUEL . . . . G
TRANSMISSION . . . . HYDRO
STEERING. . . . . STANDARD
STANDARD DECK . . . . 52"
MSRP. $8,299

RETAIL PRICING

YEAR	HIGH	LOW
2001	$4,153	$3,115

ZKHP52233

YEARS MFRD 2003-2004
SERIES . . . . ZT MAX SERIES
ENGINE . . KOHLER,COMMAND PRO OHV
CYLINDERS. 2
ENGINE HP 23
FUEL . . . . G
SPEEDS 0-9
TRANSMISSION . . . . HYDRO
STEERING. . . . . ZERO
BLADE CLUTCH . . . . ELECTRIC
WEIGHT . . . . 1,045 LBS.

ZKHP52253

YEARS MFRD 2001-2004
SERIES . . . . ZT MAX SERIES
ENGINE . . KOHLER,COMMAND PRO OHV
CYLINDERS. 2
ENGINE HP 25
FUEL . . . . G
SPEEDS 0-9
TRANSMISSION . . . . HYDRO
STEERING. . . . . ZERO
BLADE CLUTCH . . . . ELECTRIC
STANDARD DECK . . . . 52"
WEIGHT . . . . 1,045 LBS.
MSRP. $8,799

RETAIL PRICING

YEAR	HIGH	LOW
2001	$4,402	$3,302
2002	$4,525	$3,393
2003	$4,907	$3,680
2004	$4,924	$3,693

ZKHP61253

YEARS MFRD 2001-2004
SERIES . . . . ZT MAX SERIES
ENGINE . . . . KOHLER
CYLINDERS. 2
ENGINE HP 25
FUEL . . . . G
TRANSMISSION . . . . HYDRO
STEERING. . . . . ZERO
BLADE CLUTCH . . . . ELECTRIC
STANDARD DECK . . . . 61"
MSRP. $8,949

RETAIL PRICING

YEAR	HIGH	LOW
2001	$4,478	$3,358
2002	$4,603	$3,452

ZKW42170

YEARS MFRD 1999-2000
SERIES . . . . ZT MAX SERIES
ENGINE . . . . KAWASAKI
ENGINE HP 17
FUEL . . . . G
TRANSMISSION . . . . HYDRO
STEERING. . . . . ZERO
STANDARD DECK . . . . 42"
MSRP. $6,139

RETAIL PRICING

YEAR	HIGH	LOW
1999	$1,072	$804
2000	$1,188	$891

ZKW42172

YEARS MFRD 2002-2003
SERIES . . . . . ZT MINI-MAX SERIES
ENGINE . . . . KAWASAKI
ENGINE HP 17
FUEL . . . . G
TRANSMISSION . . . . HYDRO
STEERING. . . . . ZERO
BLADE CLUTCH . . . . ELECTRIC
STANDARD DECK . . . . 42"
WEIGHT . . . . 750 LBS.
MSRP. $6,000

RETAIL PRICING

YEAR	HIGH	LOW
2002	$3,085	$2,314
2003	$3,346	$2,509

ZKW48170

YEARS MFRD 1999-2000
SERIES . . . . ZT MAX SERIES
ENGINE . . . . KAWASAKI
ENGINE HP 17
FUEL . . . . G
TRANSMISSION . . . . HYDRO
STEERING. . . . . ZERO
STANDARD DECK . . . . 48"
MSRP. $6,499

RETAIL PRICING

YEAR	HIGH	LOW
1999	$1,134	$850
2000	$1,257	$943

ZKW48190

YEARS MFRD 2000-2000
SERIES . . . . ZT MAX SERIES
ENGINE HP 19
FUEL . . . . G
TRANSMISSION . . . . HYDRO
STEERING. . . . . ZERO
STANDARD DECK . . . . 48"
MSRP. $6,899

RETAIL PRICING

YEAR	HIGH	LOW
2000	$1,339	$1,004

ZKW52233

YEARS MFRD 2001-2004
SERIES . . . . ZT MAX SERIES
ENGINE . . . KAWASAKI,V-TWIN OHV
CYLINDERS. 2
ENGINE HP 23
FUEL . . . . G
SPEEDS 0-9
TRANSMISSION . . . . HYDRO
STEERING. . . . . ZERO
BLADE CLUTCH . . . . ELECTRIC
STANDARD DECK . . . . 52"
WEIGHT . . . . 1,045 LBS.
MSRP. $8,399

RETAIL PRICING

YEAR	HIGH	LOW
2001	$4,201	$3,151
2002	$4,320	$3,240
2003	$4,682	$3,512
2004	$4,759	$3,569

YAZOO/KEES

ZKW61233
YEARS MFRD 2001-2004
SERIES .... ZT MAX SERIES
ENGINE ... KAWASAKI, V-TWIN OHV
CYLINDERS 2
ENGINE HP 23
FUEL .... G
SPEEDS 0-9
TRANSMISSION .... HYDRO
STEERING .... ZERO
BLADE CLUTCH .... ELECTRIC
STANDARD DECK .... 61"
WEIGHT .... 1,065 LBS.
MSRP $8,699

RETAIL PRICING

YEAR	HIGH	LOW
2001	$4,353	$3,265
2002	$4,474	$3,355
2003	$4,851	$3,638
2004	$4,914	$3,685

ZKWQL42171
YEARS MFRD 2001-2001
SERIES ...... ZT MINI-MAX SERIES
ENGINE .... KAWASAKI
ENGINE HP 17
FUEL .... G
TRANSMISSION .... HYDRO
STEERING .... STANDARD
STANDARD DECK .... 42"
MSRP $6,249

RETAIL PRICING

YEAR	HIGH	LOW
2001	$3,126	$2,345

ZKWQL42172
YEARS MFRD 2002-2004
SERIES ...... ZT MINI-MAX SERIES
ENGINE .... KAWASAKI
ENGINE HP 17
FUEL .... G
TRANSMISSION .... HYDRO
STEERING .... ZERO
BLADE CLUTCH .... ELECTRIC
STANDARD DECK .... 42"
WEIGHT .... 750 LBS.
MSRP $6,400

RETAIL PRICING

YEAR	HIGH	LOW
2002	$3,292	$2,469
2003	$3,570	$2,678
2004	$3,584	$2,688

ZKWQL48170
YEARS MFRD 2000-2000
SERIES ...... ZT MINI-MAX SERIES
ENGINE HP 17
FUEL .... G
STEERING .... ZERO
STANDARD DECK .... 48"
MSRP $6,899

RETAIL PRICING

YEAR	HIGH	LOW
2000	$1,339	$1,004

ZKWQL48171
YEARS MFRD 2001-2001
SERIES ...... ZT MINI-MAX SERIES
ENGINE .... KAWASAKI
ENGINE HP 17
FUEL .... G
TRANSMISSION .... HYDRO
STEERING .... STANDARD
STANDARD DECK .... 48"
MSRP $6,599

RETAIL PRICING

YEAR	HIGH	LOW
2001	$3,302	$2,476

ZKWQL48172
YEARS MFRD 2002-2004
SERIES ...... ZT MINI-MAX SERIES
ENGINE .... KAWASAKI
ENGINE HP 17
FUEL .... G
TRANSMISSION .... HYDRO
STEERING .... ZERO
BLADE CLUTCH .... ELECTRIC
STANDARD DECK .... 48"
WEIGHT .... 815 LBS.
MSRP $6,900

OPTIONS

B&S 18HP

RETAIL PRICING

YEAR	HIGH	LOW
2002	$3,548	$2,661
2003	$3,847	$2,885
2004	$3,872	$2,904

ZKWQL48190
YEARS MFRD 2000-2000
SERIES ...... ZT MINI-MAX SERIES
ENGINE HP 19
FUEL .... G
STEERING .... ZERO
STANDARD DECK .... 48"
MSRP $7,299

RETAIL PRICING

YEAR	HIGH	LOW
2000	$1,416	$1,062

ZKWQL48191
YEARS MFRD 2001-2001
SERIES ...... ZT MINI-MAX SERIES
ENGINE .... KAWASAKI
ENGINE HP 19
FUEL .... G
TRANSMISSION .... HYDRO
STEERING .... STANDARD
STANDARD DECK .... 48"
MSRP $6,899

RETAIL PRICING

YEAR	HIGH	LOW
2001	$3,454	$2,590

ZKWQL48192
YEARS MFRD 2002-2004
SERIES ...... ZT MINI-MAX SERIES
ENGINE .... KAWASAKI
ENGINE HP 19
FUEL .... G
TRANSMISSION .... HYDRO
STEERING .... ZERO
BLADE CLUTCH .... ELECTRIC
STANDARD DECK .... 48"
WEIGHT .... 830 LBS.
MSRP $7,300

RETAIL PRICING

YEAR	HIGH	LOW
2002	$3,753	$2,815
2003	$4,071	$3,053
2004	$4,108	$3,081

ZMBI48181
YEARS MFRD 2005-2006
SERIES .... MID MAX SERIES
ENGINE .... B&S INTEK
CYLINDERS 2
ENGINE HP 18
COOLING .... AIR
FUEL .... G
SPEEDS .... VARIABLE
TRANSMISSION .... HYDRO
STEERING .... ZERO
BLADE CLUTCH .... ELECTRIC
WEIGHT .... 870 LBS.

ZMKH52231
YEARS MFRD 2007-2008
SERIES .... MID MAX SERIES
ENGINE .... KOHLER CV23S
CYLINDERS 2
ENGINE HP 23
COOLING .... AIR
FUEL .... G
SPEEDS .... VARIABLE
TRANSMISSION ..... DUAL HYDRO
STEERING .... ZERO
BLADE CLUTCH .... ELECTRIC
STANDARD DECK .... 52"
WEIGHT .... 880 LBS.
MSRP $7,699

SERIAL NUMBERS

YEAR .... BEGINNING NO.
2007 64000000

RETAIL PRICING

YEAR	HIGH	LOW
2007	$2,726	$2,045
2008	$3,031	$2,273

ZMKH52251
YEARS MFRD 2006-2008
SERIES .... MID MAX SERIES
ENGINE .... KOHLER CV730
CYLINDERS 2
ENGINE HP 25
COOLING .... AIR
FUEL .... G
SPEEDS .... VARIABLE
TRANSMISSION ..... DUAL HYDRO
STEERING .... ZERO
STANDARD DECK .... 52"
WEIGHT .... 880 LBS.
MSRP $7,999

SERIAL NUMBERS

YEAR .... BEGINNING NO.
2007 64000000

RETAIL PRICING

YEAR	HIGH	LOW
2006	$2,553	$1,915
2007	$2,835	$2,126
2008	$3,146	$2,359

ZMKH52252
YEARS MFRD 2008-2009
ENGINE .... KOHLER CV730
ENGINE HP 25
COOLING .... AIR
FUEL .... G
SPEEDS .... VARIABLE
TRANSMISSION .... HYDRO
STEERING .... ZERO
BLADE CLUTCH .... ELECTRIC
WEIGHT .... 880 LBS.

ZMKH61251
YEARS MFRD 2006-2008
SERIES .... MID MAX SERIES
ENGINE .... KOHLER CV730
ENGINE HP 25
COOLING .... AIR
FUEL .... G
SPEEDS .... VARIABLE
TRANSMISSION ..... DUAL HYDRO
STEERING .... ZERO
STANDARD DECK .... 61"
WEIGHT .... 920 LBS.
MSRP $8,399

SERIAL NUMBERS

YEAR .... BEGINNING NO.
2007 64000000

RETAIL PRICING

YEAR	HIGH	LOW
2006	$2,680	$2,010
2007	$2,977	$2,233
2008	$3,305	$2,478

ZMKH61252
YEARS MFRD 2008-2009
ENGINE .... KOHLER CV730
ENGINE HP 25
COOLING .... AIR
FUEL .... G
SPEEDS .... VARIABLE
TRANSMISSION .... HYDRO
STEERING .... ZERO
BLADE CLUTCH .... ELECTRIC
WEIGHT .... 920 LBS.

ZMKW5222
YEARS MFRD 2010-2011
ENGINE .... KAWASAKI
ENGINE HP 22

COOLING .... AIR
FUEL .... G
SPEEDS .... VARIABLE
TRANSMISSION .... HYDRO
STEERING .... ZERO
BLADE CLUTCH .... ELECTRIC
STANDARD DECK .... 52"
MSRP $6,299

RETAIL PRICING

YEAR	HIGH	LOW
2010	$2,931	$2,198
2011	$3,255	$2,441

ZMKW6124

YEARS MFRD 2010-2011
ENGINE .... KAWASAKI
ENGINE HP 24
COOLING .... AIR
FUEL .... G
SPEEDS .... VARIABLE
TRANSMISSION .... HYDRO
STEERING .... ZERO
BLADE CLUTCH .... ELECTRIC
STANDARD DECK .... 61"
MSRP $6,699

RETAIL PRICING

YEAR	HIGH	LOW
2010	$3,120	$2,340
2011	$3,462	$2,597

ZMKW48171

YEARS MFRD 2006-2008
SERIES .... MID MAX SERIES
ENGINE .... KAWASAKI
CYLINDERS 2
ENGINE HP 17
COOLING .... AIR
FUEL .... G
SPEEDS .... VARIABLE
TRANSMISSION .... DUAL HYDRO
STEERING .... ZERO
STANDARD DECK .... 48"
WEIGHT .... 832 LBS.
MSRP $6,499

SERIAL NUMBERS

YEAR .... BEGINNING NO.
2007 64000000

RETAIL PRICING

YEAR	HIGH	LOW
2006	$2,075	$1,556
2007	$2,302	$1,727
2008	$2,557	$1,918

ZMKW48172

YEARS MFRD 2008-2009
ENGINE .... KAWASAKI
CYLINDERS 2
ENGINE HP 17
COOLING .... AIR
FUEL .... G
SPEEDS .... VARIABLE
TRANSMISSION .... HYDRO
STEERING .... ZERO
BLADE CLUTCH .... ELECTRIC
WEIGHT .... 832 LBS.

ZMKW48191

YEARS MFRD 2005-2007
SERIES .... MID MAX SERIES
ENGINE .... KAWASAKI FH580V
CYLINDERS 2
ENGINE HP 19
COOLING .... AIR
FUEL .... G
SPEEDS .... VARIABLE
TRANSMISSION .... HYDRO
STEERING .... ZERO
BLADE CLUTCH .... ELECTRIC
STANDARD DECK .... 48"
WEIGHT .... 870 LBS.
MSRP $7,499

RETAIL PRICING

YEAR	HIGH	LOW
2005	$4,723	$3,542

ZMKW48192

YEARS MFRD 2008-2009
ENGINE .... KAWASAKI
CYLINDERS 2
ENGINE HP 19
COOLING .... AIR
FUEL .... G
SPEEDS .... VARIABLE
TRANSMISSION .... HYDRO
STEERING .... ZERO
BLADE CLUTCH .... ELECTRIC
WEIGHT .... 870 LBS.

ZMKW52211

YEARS MFRD 2006-2008
SERIES .... MID MAX SERIES
ENGINE .... KAWASAKI FH641V
CYLINDERS 2
ENGINE HP 21
COOLING .... AIR
FUEL .... G
SPEEDS .... VARIABLE
TRANSMISSION .... DUAL HYDRO
STEERING .... ZERO
BLADE CLUTCH .... ELECTRIC
STANDARD DECK .... 52"
WEIGHT .... 880 LBS.
MSRP $7,699

SERIAL NUMBERS

YEAR .... BEGINNING NO.
2007 64000000

RETAIL PRICING

YEAR	HIGH	LOW
2006	$2,457	$1,843
2007	$2,726	$2,045
2008	$3,031	$2,273

ZMKW52212

YEARS MFRD 2008-2009
ENGINE .... KAWASAKI
CYLINDERS 2
ENGINE HP 21
COOLING .... AIR
FUEL .... G
SPEEDS .... VARIABLE
TRANSMISSION .... HYDRO
STEERING .... ZERO
BLADE CLUTCH .... ELECTRIC
WEIGHT .... 880 LBS.

ZMKW52231

YEARS MFRD 2006-2007
ENGINE .... KAWASAKI FH680V
CYLINDERS 2
ENGINE HP 23
COOLING .... AIR
FUEL .... G
SPEEDS .... VARIABLE
TRANSMISSION .... HYDRO
STEERING .... ZERO
BLADE CLUTCH .... ELECTRIC
WEIGHT .... 880 LBS.
MSRP $7,999

SERIAL NUMBERS

YEAR .... BEGINNING NO.
2007 64000000

RETAIL PRICING

YEAR	HIGH	LOW
2006	$4,475	$3,356
2007	$4,634	$3,476

ZMKW61231

YEARS MFRD 2006-2007
SERIES .... MID MAX SERIES
ENGINE .... KAWASAKI FH680V
CYLINDERS 2
ENGINE HP 23
COOLING .... AIR
FUEL .... G
SPEEDS .... VARIABLE
TRANSMISSION .... DUAL HYDRO
STEERING .... ZERO
BLADE CLUTCH .... ELECTRIC
STANDARD DECK .... 61"
WEIGHT .... 920 LBS.
MSRP $8,199

RETAIL PRICING

YEAR	HIGH	LOW
2006	$2,650	$1,987
2007	$2,942	$2,206

ZMMKW34170

YEARS MFRD 2008-2008
ENGINE .... KAWASAKI
CYLINDERS 2
ENGINE HP 17
COOLING .... AIR
FUEL .... G
SPEEDS .... VARIABLE
TRANSMISSION .... HYDRO
STEERING .... ZERO
BLADE CLUTCH .... ELECTRIC
STANDARD DECK .... 34"
WEIGHT .... 660 LBS.
MSRP $5,599

RETAIL PRICING

YEAR	HIGH	LOW
2008	$2,399	$1,799

ZPKW5426

YEARS MFRD 2010-2011
ENGINE .... KAWASAKI
CYLINDERS 1
ENGINE HP 26
COOLING .... AIR
FUEL .... G
SPEEDS .... VARIABLE
TRANSMISSION .... HYDRO
STEERING .... ZERO
BLADE CLUTCH .... ELECTRIC
STANDARD DECK .... 54"
MSRP $8,899

RETAIL PRICING

YEAR	HIGH	LOW
2010	$4,142	$3,107
2011	$4,600	$3,450

ZPKW6029

YEARS MFRD 2010-2011
ENGINE .... KAWASAKI
ENGINE HP 29
COOLING .... AIR
FUEL .... G
SPEEDS .... VARIABLE
TRANSMISSION .... HYDRO
STEERING .... ZERO
BLADE CLUTCH .... ELECTRIC
STANDARD DECK .... 60"
MSRP $9,599

RETAIL PRICING

YEAR	HIGH	LOW
2010	$4,470	$3,352
2011	$4,964	$3,723

ZVH061241

YEARS MFRD 2004-2004
SERIES .... MAX 2 SERIES
ENGINE .... HONDA
ENGINE HP 24
TRANSMISSION .... HYDRO
STEERING .... ZERO
BLADE CLUTCH .... ELECTRIC

ZVH061242

YEARS MFRD 2006-2007
SERIES .... MAX 2 SERIES
ENGINE .... HONDA GXV670
CYLINDERS 2
ENGINE HP 24
COOLING .... AIR
FUEL .... G
SPEEDS .... VARIABLE
TRANSMISSION .... DUAL HYDRO
STEERING .... ZERO
BLADE CLUTCH .... ELECTRIC
STANDARD DECK .... 61"
WEIGHT .... 1,090 LBS.
MSRP $8,799

SERIAL NUMBERS

YEAR .... BEGINNING NO.
2007 64000000

RETAIL PRICING

YEAR	HIGH	LOW
2006	$2,843	$2,132
2007	$3,159	$2,369

ZVKE61261

YEARS MFRD 2003-2003
SERIES .... MAX 2 SERIES
ENGINE .... KOHLER
ENGINE HP 26
FUEL .... G
SPEEDS .... VARIABLE
TRANSMISSION .... HYDRO
STANDARD DECK .... 61"
MSRP $10,400

RETAIL PRICING

YEAR	HIGH	LOW
2003	$5,799	$4,349

ZVKE72260

YEARS MFRD 2002-2003
SERIES .... MAX 2 SERIES
ENGINE .... KOHLER
ENGINE HP 26
FUEL .... G
SPEEDS .... VARIABLE
TRANSMISSION .... HYDRO
STANDARD DECK .... 72"
MSRP $10,900

RETAIL PRICING

YEAR	HIGH	LOW
2002	$5,606	$4,204
2003	$6,077	$4,558

ZVKH52230

YEARS MFRD 2006-2007
SERIES .... MAX 2 SERIES
ENGINE .... KOHLER PRO CV23
ENGINE HP 23
COOLING .... AIR
FUEL .... G
SPEEDS .... VARIABLE
TRANSMISSION .... HYDRO
STEERING .... ZERO
BLADE CLUTCH .... ELECTRIC
STANDARD DECK .... 52"
WEIGHT .... 1,060 LBS.
MSRP $8,199

RETAIL PRICING

YEAR	HIGH	LOW
2006	$2,650	$1,987
2007	$3,159	$2,369

ZVKH61250

YEARS MFRD 2002-2004
SERIES .... MAX 2 SERIES
ENGINE .... KOHLER PRO
ENGINE HP 25
FUEL .... G
TRANSMISSION .... HYDRO
STEERING .... ZERO
BLADE CLUTCH .... ELECTRIC
STANDARD DECK .... 61"
WEIGHT .... 1,090 LBS.
MSRP $9,300

RETAIL PRICING

YEAR	HIGH	LOW
2002	$4,782	$3,587
2003	$5,186	$3,890
2004	$5,255	$3,941

ZVKH61260

YEARS MFRD 2004-2004
SERIES .... MAX 2 SERIES
ENGINE .... KOHLER PRO EFI
ENGINE HP 26
TRANSMISSION .... HYDRO
STEERING .... ZERO
BLADE CLUTCH .... ELECTRIC

ZVKH61270

YEARS MFRD 2002-2003
SERIES .... MAX 2 SERIES
ENGINE .... KOHLER
ENGINE HP 27
FUEL .... G
TRANSMISSION .... HYDRO
STEERING .... ZERO
STANDARD DECK .... 72"
WEIGHT .... 1,130 LBS.
MSRP $9,800

RETAIL PRICING

YEAR	HIGH	LOW
2002	$5,039	$3,779
2003	$5,464	$4,098

ZVKH61271

YEARS MFRD 2003-2004
SERIES .... MAX 2 SERIES
ENGINE .... KOHLER
ENGINE HP 27
FUEL .... G
TRANSMISSION .... HYDRO
STEERING .... ZERO
BLADE CLUTCH .... ELECTRIC
STANDARD DECK .... 61"
MSRP $9,500

RETAIL PRICING

YEAR	HIGH	LOW
2003	$5,297	$3,973
2004	$5,739	$4,304

ZVKH61272

YEARS MFRD 2005-2008
SERIES .... MAX 2 SERIES
ENGINE ...... KOHLER PRO CV740
CYLINDERS 2
ENGINE HP 27
COOLING .... AIR
FUEL .... G
SPEEDS .... VARIABLE
TRANSMISSION ..... DUAL HYDRO
STEERING .... ZERO
BLADE CLUTCH .... ELECTRIC
STANDARD DECK .... 61"
WEIGHT .... 1,090 LBS.
MSRP $9,299

SERIAL NUMBERS

YEAR .... BEGINNING NO.
2007 64000000

RETAIL PRICING

YEAR	HIGH	LOW
2005	$2,618	$1,963
2006	$2,907	$2,180
2007	$3,232	$2,424
2008	$3,586	$2,689

ZVKH61273

YEARS MFRD 2010-2010
ENGINE ...... KOHLER PRO CV740
CYLINDERS 2
ENGINE HP 27
COOLING .... AIR
FUEL .... G
SPEEDS .... VARIABLE
TRANSMISSION .... HYDRO
STEERING .... ZERO
BLADE CLUTCH .... ELECTRIC
STANDARD DECK .... 61"
WEIGHT .... 1,090 LBS.
MSRP $7,899

RETAIL PRICING

YEAR	HIGH	LOW
2010	$3,718	$2,789

ZVKH61302

YEARS MFRD 2006-2008
ENGINE ...... KOHLER PRO CV750
CYLINDERS 2
ENGINE HP 30
COOLING .... AIR
FUEL .... G
SPEEDS .... VARIABLE
TRANSMISSION ..... DUAL HYDRO
STEERING .... ZERO
STANDARD DECK .... 61"
WEIGHT .... 1,090 LBS.
MSRP $9,599

SERIAL NUMBERS

YEAR .... BEGINNING NO.
2007 64000000

RETAIL PRICING

YEAR	HIGH	LOW
2006	$3,062	$2,296
2007	$3,402	$2,551
2008	$3,780	$2,835

ZVKH61303

YEARS MFRD 2008-2009
ENGINE ...... KOHLER PRO CV750
CYLINDERS 2
ENGINE HP 30
COOLING .... AIR
FUEL .... G
SPEEDS .... VARIABLE
TRANSMISSION .... HYDRO
STEERING .... ZERO
BLADE CLUTCH .... ELECTRIC
WEIGHT .... 1,090 LBS.

ZVKH72260

YEARS MFRD 2004-2004
SERIES .... MAX 2 SERIES
ENGINE .... KOHLER PRO EFI
ENGINE HP 26
TRANSMISSION .... HYDRO
STEERING .... ZERO
BLADE CLUTCH .... ELECTRIC

ZVKH72270

YEARS MFRD 2002-2003
SERIES .... MAX 2 SERIES
ENGINE .... KOHLER
ENGINE HP 27
FUEL .... G
TRANSMISSION .... HYDRO
STEERING .... ZERO
STANDARD DECK .... 72"
WEIGHT .... 1,150 LBS.
MSRP $10,000

RETAIL PRICING

YEAR	HIGH	LOW
2002	$5,099	$3,824
2003	$5,577	$4,183

ZVKH72271

YEARS MFRD 2003-2004
SERIES .... MAX 2 SERIES
ENGINE .... KOHLER
ENGINE HP 27
FUEL .... G
TRANSMISSION .... HYDRO
STEERING .... ZERO
BLADE CLUTCH .... ELECTRIC
STANDARD DECK .... 72"
MSRP $9,700

RETAIL PRICING

YEAR	HIGH	LOW
2003	$5,408	$4,056
2004	$5,470	$4,103

ZVKH72272

YEARS MFRD 2005-2007
SERIES .... MAX 2 SERIES
ENGINE ...... KOHLER PRO CV740
CYLINDERS 2
ENGINE HP 27
FUEL .... G
SPEEDS .... VARIABLE
TRANSMISSION .... HYDRO
STEERING .... ZERO
BLADE CLUTCH .... ELECTRIC
STANDARD DECK .... 72"
WEIGHT .... 1,150 LBS.
MSRP $9,599

RETAIL PRICING

YEAR	HIGH	LOW
2007	$5,562	$4,171

ZVKH72302

YEARS MFRD 2006-2008
ENGINE ...... KOHLER PRO CV750
CYLINDERS 2
ENGINE HP 30
COOLING .... AIR
FUEL .... G
SPEEDS .... VARIABLE
TRANSMISSION ..... DUAL HYDRO
STEERING .... ZERO
STANDARD DECK .... 72"
WEIGHT .... 1,150 LBS.
MSRP $9,999

SERIAL NUMBERS

YEAR .... BEGINNING NO.
2007 64000000

RETAIL PRICING

YEAR	HIGH	LOW
2006	$3,189	$2,392
2007	$3,545	$2,658
2008	$3,933	$2,950

ZVKHL61230

YEARS MFRD 2004-2004
SERIES. . . . . MAX 2 SERIES
ENGINE . . . . KOHLER AEGIS
ENGINE HP 23
COOLING . . . . LIQUID
TRANSMISSION . . . . .HYDRO
STEERING. . . . . ZERO
BLADE CLUTCH . . . . ELECTRIC

ZVKW52230

YEARS MFRD 2004-2004
SERIES. . . . . MAX 2 SERIES
ENGINE . . . . KAWASAKI
ENGINE HP 23
TRANSMISSION . . . . .HYDRO
STEERING. . . . . ZERO
BLADE CLUTCH . . . . ELECTRIC

ZVKW52231

YEARS MFRD 2003-2003
SERIES. . . . . MAX 2 SERIES
ENGINE . . . . KAWASAKI
ENGINE HP 23
FUEL . . . . G
TRANSMISSION . . . . .HYDRO
STANDARD DECK . . . . 52"
MSRP. $8,599

RETAIL PRICING

YEAR	HIGH	LOW
2003	$4,794	$3,596

ZVKW52250

YEARS MFRD 2002-2004
SERIES. . . . . MAX 2 SERIES
ENGINE . . . . KAWASAKI
ENGINE HP 25
FUEL . . . . G
TRANSMISSION . . . . .HYDRO
STEERING. . . . . ZERO
BLADE CLUTCH . . . . ELECTRIC
HYDRAULIC . . . . YES
STANDARD DECK . . . . 52"
WEIGHT . . . . .1,090 LBS.
MSRP. $8,899

RETAIL PRICING

YEAR	HIGH	LOW
2002	$4,525	$3,393
2003	$4,963	$3,722

ZVKW52252

YEARS MFRD 2005-2007
SERIES. . . . . MAX 2 SERIES
ENGINE . . . . . . .KAWASAKI FH721V
CYLINDERS. 2
ENGINE HP 25
FUEL . . . . G
SPEEDS . . . . .VARIABLE
TRANSMISSION . . . . .HYDRO
STEERING. . . . . ZERO
BLADE CLUTCH . . . . ELECTRIC
STANDARD DECK . . . . 52"
WEIGHT . . . . .1,060 LBS.
MSRP. $8,799

SERIAL NUMBERS

YEAR	BEGINNING NO.
2007	64000000

RETAIL PRICING

YEAR	HIGH	LOW
2005	$5,539	$4,154

ZVKW52253

YEARS MFRD 2008-2009
ENGINE . . . . . . .KAWASAKI FH721V
CYLINDERS. 2
ENGINE HP 25
COOLING . . . . AIR
FUEL . . . . G
SPEEDS . . . . .VARIABLE
TRANSMISSION . . . . .HYDRO
STEERING. . . . . ZERO
BLADE CLUTCH . . . . ELECTRIC
WEIGHT . . . . .1,060 LBS.

ZVKW61230

YEARS MFRD 2002-2004
SERIES. . . . . MAX 2 SERIES
ENGINE . . . . KAWASAKI
ENGINE HP 23
FUEL . . . . G
TRANSMISSION . . . . .HYDRO
STEERING. . . . . ZERO
BLADE CLUTCH . . . . ELECTRIC
STANDARD DECK . . . . 61"
WEIGHT . . . . .1,090 LBS.
MSRP. $8,700

RETAIL PRICING

YEAR	HIGH	LOW
2002	$4,476	$3,357
2003	$4,852	$3,639
2004	$4,925	$3,694

ZVKW61230L

YEARS MFRD 2003-2003
SERIES. . . . . MAX 2 SERIES
ENGINE . . . . KOHLER AEGIS
ENGINE HP 23
COOLING . . . . LIQUID
FUEL . . . . G
TRANSMISSION . . . . .HYDRO
STEERING. . . . . ZERO
STANDARD DECK . . . . 61"
WEIGHT . . . . .1,090 LBS.
MSRP. $9,400

RETAIL PRICING

YEAR	HIGH	LOW
2003	$5,242	$3,932

ZVKW61250

YEARS MFRD 2003-2004
SERIES. . . . . MAX 2 SERIES
ENGINE . . . . KAWASAKI
ENGINE HP 25
FUEL . . . . G
TRANSMISSION . . . . .HYDRO
STEERING. . . . . ZERO
BLADE CLUTCH . . . . ELECTRIC
STANDARD DECK . . . . 61"
WEIGHT . . . . .1,090 LBS.
MSRP. $9,400

RETAIL PRICING

YEAR	HIGH	LOW
2003	$5,242	$3,932
2004	$5,293	$3,970

ZVKW61252

YEARS MFRD 2005-2007
SERIES. . . . . MAX 2 SERIES
ENGINE . . . . . . .KAWASAKI FH721V
CYLINDERS. 2
ENGINE HP 25
FUEL . . . . G
SPEEDS . . . . .VARIABLE
TRANSMISSION . . . . .HYDRO
STEERING. . . . . ZERO
BLADE CLUTCH . . . . ELECTRIC
STANDARD DECK . . . . 61"
WEIGHT . . . . .1,090 LBS.
MSRP. $9,199

RETAIL PRICING

YEAR	HIGH	LOW
2005	$5,793	$4,345

4100

YEARS MFRD 2003-2003
SERIES. . . . . 4000 SERIES
CYLINDERS. 3
CID 61.4
ENGINE HP 20
FUEL . . . . D
TRANSMISSION . . . . .HYDRO
STEERING. . . . . .STANDARD
WEIGHT . . . . .1,565 LBS.

4200

YEARS MFRD 2003-2003
SERIES. . . . . 4000 SERIES
CYLINDERS. 3
CID 73.5
ENGINE HP 26.3
FUEL . . . . D
TRANSMISSION . . . . .HYDRO
STEERING. . . . . .STANDARD
WEIGHT . . . . .2,675 LBS.

4300

YEARS MFRD 2003-2003
SERIES. . . . . 4000 SERIES
CYLINDERS. 3
CID 91.3
ENGINE HP 32.2
FUEL . . . . D
TRANSMISSION . . . . .HYDRO
STEERING. . . . . .STANDARD
WEIGHT . . . . .2,900 LBS.

4400

YEARS MFRD 2003-2003
SERIES. . . . . 4000 SERIES
CYLINDERS. 3
CID 100.2
ENGINE HP 35.7
FUEL . . . . D
TRANSMISSION . . . . .HYDRO
STEERING. . . . . .STANDARD
WEIGHT . . . . .2,900 LBS.

NOTES

ZETOR

M22HT
YEARS MFRD........2020-2020
ENGINE..........YANMAR T4F
CYLINDERS..................3
PTO HP..................17.6
ENGINE HP...................22
COOLING...............LIQUID
FUEL.........................D
SPEEDS..............2 RANGE
TRANSMISSION..........HYDRO
STEERING............STANDARD
HITCH....................CAT. I
DRIVE TYPE..............4WD
ROPS/CAB................ROPS

M25HT
YEARS MFRD........2020-2020
ENGINE..........YANMAR T4F
CYLINDERS..................3
PTO HP......................20
ENGINE HP.................25.3
COOLING...............LIQUID
FUEL.........................D
SPEEDS..............2 RANGE
TRANSMISSION..........HYDRO
STEERING............STANDARD
HITCH....................CAT. I
ROPS/CAB................ROPS

M40HT
YEARS MFRD........2020-2020
ENGINE..........YANMAR T4F
CYLINDERS..................3
PTO HP....................29.9
ENGINE HP...................38
COOLING...............LIQUID
FUEL.........................D
SPEEDS..............3 RANGE
TRANSMISSION..........HYDRO
STEERING............STANDARD
HITCH....................CAT. I
DRIVE TYPE..............4WD
ROPS/CAB................ROPS

OPTIONS

CAB

M40SS
YEARS MFRD........2020-2020
ENGINE..........YANMAR T4F
CYLINDERS..................3
PTO HP....................31.8
ENGINE HP...................38
COOLING...............LIQUID
FUEL.........................D
SPEEDS....................12/12
STEERING............STANDARD
HITCH....................CAT. I
DRIVE TYPE..............4WD
ROPS/CAB................ROPS

M50SS
YEARS MFRD........2020-2020
ENGINE..........YANMAR T4F
CYLINDERS..................4
PTO HP....................40.5
ENGINE HP.................47.6
COOLING...............LIQUID
SPEEDS....................16/16
STEERING............STANDARD
HITCH....................CAT. I
DRIVE TYPE..............4WD
ROPS/CAB................ROPS

MAJOR HT45
YEARS MFRD........2017-2019
ENGINE.......YANMAR 4TNV88C
CYLINDERS..................4
CID.......................133.6
PTO HP....................34.6
ENGINE HP...................46
FUEL.........................D
SPEEDS...............VARIABLE
TRANSMISSION..........HYDRO
STEERING............STANDARD
DRIVE TYPE..............4WD
ROPS/CAB..................CAB
WEIGHT.............4,233 LBS.

MAJOR HT55
YEARS MFRD........2017-2019
ENGINE.......YANMAR 4TNV86T
CYLINDERS..................4
CID.......................127.6
PTO HP....................42.2
ENGINE HP.................55.1
COOLING...............LIQUID
FUEL.........................D
SPEEDS...............VARIABLE
TRANSMISSION..........HYDRO
STEERING............STANDARD
DRIVE TYPE..............4WD
ROPS/CAB..................CAB
WEIGHT.............4,233 LBS.

2040
YEARS MFRD........1995-1995
SERIES...........ZEBRA SERIES
ENGINE..................ZETOR
CYLINDERS..................2
CID..........................70
ENGINE HP...................20
FUEL.........................D
TRANSMISSION..........HYDRO
STEERING............STANDARD
PTO.........................YES
MSRP....................$8,500

RETAIL PRICING

YEAR	HIGH	LOW
1995	$3,134	$2,351

2520
YEARS MFRD........1992-1996
SERIES...........ZEBRA SERIES
ENGINE..................ZETOR
CYLINDERS..................2
CID..........................95
PTO HP......................25
FUEL.........................D
SPEEDS.....................10/2
TRANSMISSION............GEAR
STEERING............STANDARD
PTO.........................YES
DRIVE TYPE..............2WD
ROPS/CAB................ROPS
WEIGHT.............3,500 LBS.
MSRP....................$8,570

RETAIL PRICING

YEAR	HIGH	LOW
1995	$3,158	$2,369

2522
YEARS MFRD........1995-1996
SERIES...........ZEBRA SERIES
ENGINE..................ZETOR
CYLINDERS..................2
CID..........................95
PTO HP......................25
FUEL.........................D
SPEEDS.....................10/2
STEERING............STANDARD
PTO.........................YES
DRIVE TYPE..............2WD
ROPS/CAB................ROPS
WEIGHT.............3,570 LBS.
MSRP....................$9,000

RETAIL PRICING

YEAR	HIGH	LOW
1995	$3,317	$2,488
1996	$3,437	$2,578

3320
YEARS MFRD........1993-2004
SERIES.....RANGE 1 STANDARD B SERIES
ENGINE...........ZETOR 5201
CYLINDERS..................3
CID.................164,165
PTO HP......................40
ENGINE HP...................43
COOLING...............LIQUID
FUEL.........................D
SPEEDS.....................10/2
STEERING............STANDARD
HITCH....................CAT. I
HYDRAULIC.................YES
PTO.........................YES
DRIVE TYPE..............2WD
ROPS/CAB................ROPS
WEIGHT.............6,020 LBS.

AVG. AUCTION PRICING

LOW	HIGH	AVG
$3,276	$4,648	$4,085

3321
YEARS MFRD........1997-2004
SERIES....RANGE 1 SUPER SERIES
ENGINE..................ZETOR
CYLINDERS..................3
CID.........................164
PTO HP......................40
ENGINE HP...................43
COOLING...............LIQUID
FUEL.........................D
SPEEDS...............10/2,10/10
TRANSMISSION............GEAR
STEERING............STANDARD
HITCH....................CAT. I
HYDRAULIC.................YES
PTO.........................YES
DRIVE TYPE..............2WD
ROPS/CAB..................CAB
WEIGHT.............6,220 LBS.

OPTIONS

4WD

3340
YEARS MFRD........1993-2004
SERIES.....RANGE 1 STANDARD B SERIES
ENGINE...........ZETOR 5201
CYLINDERS..................3
CID.........................164
PTO HP......................40
ENGINE HP...................43
COOLING...............LIQUID
FUEL.........................D
SPEEDS...............10/2,10/10
TRANSMISSION............GEAR
STEERING............STANDARD
HITCH....................CAT. I
HYDRAULIC.................YES
PTO.........................YES
DRIVE TYPE..............4WD
ROPS/CAB................ROPS
WEIGHT.............6,340 LBS.

3341
YEARS MFRD........2003-2004
SERIES....RANGE 1 SUPER SERIES
CYLINDERS..................3
PTO HP......................42
ENGINE HP...................43
COOLING...............LIQUID
FUEL.........................D
SPEEDS.....................10/2
TRANSMISSION............GEAR
STEERING............STANDARD
HITCH....................CAT. I
HYDRAULIC.................YES
PTO.........................YES
DRIVE TYPE..............4WD
ROPS/CAB................ROPS

3520
YEARS MFRD........1992-1996
SERIES...........ZEBRA SERIES
ENGINE..................ZETOR
CID.........................143
ENGINE HP...................35
FUEL.........................D
SPEEDS.....................10/2
DRIVE TYPE..............2WD
ROPS/CAB................ROPS
WEIGHT.............3,800 LBS.
MSRP....................$9,500

ZETOR

RETAIL PRICING

YEAR	HIGH	LOW
1992	$3,094	$2,321
1993	$3,193	$2,395
1994	$3,372	$2,529
1995	$3,501	$2,626
1996	$3,628	$2,721

3522

YEARS MFRD 1995-1997
SERIES. . . . . ZEBRA SERIES
ENGINE . . . . ZETOR
CYLINDERS. 3
CID 143
ENGINE HP 35
FUEL . . . . D
SPEEDS 10/2
DRIVE TYPE 4WD
ROPS/CAB . . . . ROPS
WEIGHT . . . . 3,870 LBS.
MSRP. $11,845

RETAIL PRICING

YEAR	HIGH	LOW
1995	$4,366	$3,274
1996	$4,524	$3,393
1997	$4,691	$3,518

4522

YEARS MFRD 1995-1997
SERIES. . . . . ZEBRA SERIES
ENGINE . . . . ZETOR
CYLINDERS. 3
CID 152
ENGINE HP 45
FUEL . . . . D
SPEEDS 8/2
DRIVE TYPE 2WD
ROPS/CAB . . . . ROPS
WEIGHT . . . . 4,600 LBS.

5011

YEARS MFRD 1980-1986
ENGINE . . . . ZETOR
CYLINDERS. 3
CID 165
PTO HP 42.5
FUEL . . . . D
SPEEDS 10/2
TRANSMISSION . . . . GEAR
STEERING. . . . . STANDARD
PTO . . . . YES
WEIGHT . . . . 5,611 LBS.
MSRP. $12,550

RETAIL PRICING

YEAR	HIGH	LOW
1986	$3,321	$2,491

5211

YEARS MFRD 1985-1992
ENGINE . . . . ZETOR
CYLINDERS. 3
CID 164.6
PTO HP 42.5
ENGINE HP 52
FUEL . . . . D
SPEEDS 10/2
TRANSMISSION . . . . GEAR
STEERING. . . . . STANDARD
PTO . . . . YES
WEIGHT . . . . 5,550 LBS.
MSRP. $13,580

RETAIL PRICING

YEAR	HIGH	LOW
1992	$4,426	$3,320

AVG. AUCTION PRICING

LOW	HIGH	AVG
$2,522	$3,783	$3,201

5213

YEARS MFRD 1990-1996
ENGINE . . . . ZETOR 5201
CYLINDERS. 3
CID 164.6
PTO HP 42.5
ENGINE HP 52
FUEL . . . . D
SPEEDS 10/2
TRANSMISSION . . . . GEAR
STEERING. . . . . STANDARD
PTO . . . . YES
DRIVE TYPE 2WD
ROPS/CAB . . . . CAB
WEIGHT . . . . 5,700 LBS.
MSRP. $15,445

OPTIONS

4WD

RETAIL PRICING

YEAR	HIGH	LOW
1996	$5,899	$4,424

5213 UTILITY

YEARS MFRD 1990-1996
ENGINE . . . . ZETOR 5201
CYLINDERS. 3
CID 164.6
PTO HP 42.51
ENGINE HP 52
FUEL . . . . D
SPEEDS 10/2
TRANSMISSION . . . . GEAR
STEERING. . . . . STANDARD
PTO . . . . YES
DRIVE TYPE 2WD
ROPS/CAB . . . . CAB
WEIGHT . . . . 4,320 LBS.
MSRP. $12,440

RETAIL PRICING

YEAR	HIGH	LOW
1996	$4,750	$3,563

5243

YEARS MFRD 1990-1996
ENGINE . . . . ZETOR 5201
CYLINDERS. 3
CID 164.6
PTO HP 42.51
FUEL . . . . D
SPEEDS 10/2
TRANSMISSION . . . . GEAR
STEERING. . . . . STANDARD
PTO . . . . YES
DRIVE TYPE 4WD
ROPS/CAB . . . . CAB
WEIGHT . . . . 6,700 LBS.
MSRP. $18,080

RETAIL PRICING

YEAR	HIGH	LOW
1996	$6,904	$5,178

5243 UTILITY

YEARS MFRD 1990-1996
ENGINE . . . . ZETOR 5201
CYLINDERS. 3
CID 164.6
PTO HP 42.51
ENGINE HP 52
FUEL . . . . D
SPEEDS 10/2
TRANSMISSION . . . . GEAR
STEERING. . . . . STANDARD
PTO . . . . YES
DRIVE TYPE 4WD
ROPS/CAB . . . . CAB
WEIGHT . . . . 4,700 LBS.
MSRP. $15,080

RETAIL PRICING

YEAR	HIGH	LOW
1996	$5,759	$4,319

5245 4WD

YEARS MFRD 1985-1996
ENGINE . . . . ZETOR 5201
CYLINDERS. 3
CID 164.6
PTO HP 42.5
ENGINE HP 52
FUEL . . . . D
SPEEDS 10/2
TRANSMISSION . . . . GEAR
STEERING. . . . . STANDARD
PTO . . . . YES
DRIVE TYPE 4WD
ROPS/CAB . . . . ROPS
WEIGHT . . . . 6,200 LBS.
MSRP. $14,180

OPTIONS

CAB

RETAIL PRICING

YEAR	HIGH	LOW
1996	$5,414	$4,060

AVG. AUCTION PRICING

LOW	HIGH	AVG
$3,800	$4,700	$4,333

ZIPPER

C417D

YEARS MFRD 1988-1995
ENGINE . . . . KUBOTA
ENGINE HP 16.5
COOLING . . . . LIQUID
FUEL . . . . D
TRANSMISSION . . . . HYDRO
STEERING. . . . . ZERO
STANDARD DECK . . . . 50"
MSRP. $9,420

RETAIL PRICING

YEAR	HIGH	LOW
1988	$403	$302
1989	$448	$336
1990	$498	$373
1991	$553	$415
1992	$612	$459
1993	$680	$510
1994	$754	$565
1995	$839	$629

LT51895B

YEARS MFRD 1997-1997
ENGINE . . . . B&S
ENGINE HP 18
FUEL . . . . G
TRANSMISSION . . . . HYDRO
STEERING. . . . . ZERO
STANDARD DECK . . . . 44"
MSRP. $5,860

RETAIL PRICING

YEAR	HIGH	LOW
1997	$2,272	$1,704

STS23

YEARS MFRD 2008-2011
ENGINE . . . . KOHLER OHV
CYLINDERS. 2
ENGINE HP 23
COOLING . . . . AIR
FUEL . . . . G
SPEEDS . . . . VARIABLE
TRANSMISSION . . . . HYDRO
STEERING. . . . . ZERO
WEIGHT . . . . 1,400 LBS.

STS27

YEARS MFRD 2008-2008
ENGINE . . . . KOHLER OHV
CYLINDERS. 2
ENGINE HP 27
COOLING . . . . AIR
FUEL . . . . G
SPEEDS . . . . VARIABLE
TRANSMISSION . . . . HYDRO
STEERING. . . . . ZERO
STANDARD DECK . . . . 64"
MSRP. $9,495

OPTIONS

74" DECK

RETAIL PRICING

YEAR	HIGH	LOW
2008	$5,704	$4,278

STS28

YEARS MFRD........2009-2013
ENGINE............KAWASAKI
CYLINDERS..................2
ENGINE HP..................28
COOLING...................AIR
FUEL........................G
SPEEDS...............VARIABLE
TRANSMISSION..........HYDRO
STEERING.................ZERO
BLADE CLUTCH........ELECTRIC

STS28-LP

YEARS MFRD........2009-2013
ENGINE............KAWASAKI
CYLINDERS..................2
ENGINE HP..................28
COOLING...................AIR
SPEEDS...............VARIABLE
TRANSMISSION..........HYDRO
STEERING.................ZERO
BLADE CLUTCH........ELECTRIC
WEIGHT.............1,400 LBS.

STS33

YEARS MFRD........2009-2013
ENGINE...............GENERAC
CYLINDERS..................2
ENGINE HP..................33
COOLING...................AIR
FUEL........................G
SPEEDS...............VARIABLE
TRANSMISSION..........HYDRO
STEERING.................ZERO
BLADE CLUTCH........ELECTRIC
WEIGHT.............1,400 LBS.

TS20K

YEARS MFRD........2001-2001
ENGINE .. KOHLER OHV COMMAND
CYLINDERS..................2
CID........................38
ENGINE HP..................20
COOLING...................AIR
FUEL........................G
SPEEDS...............VARIABLE
TRANSMISSION..........HYDRO
STEERING.................ZERO
STANDARD DECK............54"
MSRP....................$8,185

OPTIONS

64" DECK

RETAIL PRICING

YEAR	HIGH	LOW
2001	$1,504	$1,128

TS22K

YEARS MFRD........2001-2001
ENGINE.................KOHLER
CYLINDERS..................2
CID.......................41.1
ENGINE HP..................22
COOLING...................AIR
FUEL........................G
SPEEDS...............VARIABLE
TRANSMISSION..........HYDRO
STEERING.................ZERO
STANDARD DECK............54"
MSRP....................$8,399

OPTIONS

64" DECK
74" DECK

RETAIL PRICING

YEAR	HIGH	LOW
2001	$1,545	$1,159

TS25K

YEARS MFRD........2001-2007
ENGINE .. KOHLER OHV COMMAND
CYLINDERS..................2
CID........................44
ENGINE HP..................25
COOLING...................AIR
FUEL........................G
SPEEDS...............VARIABLE
TRANSMISSION..........HYDRO
STEERING.................ZERO
STANDARD DECK............54"
MSRP....................$8,805

OPTIONS

64" DECK
74" DECK

RETAIL PRICING

YEAR	HIGH	LOW
2001	$1,617	$1,213

TS950D

YEARS MFRD........2001-2001
ENGINE..............DAIHATSU
CYLINDERS..................3
CID.......................58.1
ENGINE HP................26.5
COOLING................LIQUID
FUEL........................D
SPEEDS...............VARIABLE
TRANSMISSION..........HYDRO
STEERING.................ZERO
STANDARD DECK............64"
MSRP...................$13,023

OPTIONS

74" DECK

RETAIL PRICING

YEAR	HIGH	LOW
2001	$2,397	$1,798

TS950G

YEARS MFRD........2001-2001
ENGINE..............DAIHATSU
CYLINDERS..................3
CID.......................58.1
ENGINE HP..................31
COOLING................LIQUID
FUEL........................G
SPEEDS...................0-10.5
TRANSMISSION..........HYDRO
STEERING.................ZERO
STANDARD DECK............64"
MSRP...................$12,619

OPTIONS

74" DECK

RETAIL PRICING

YEAR	HIGH	LOW
2001	$2,321	$1,740

TS1893B

YEARS MFRD........1995-1997
ENGINE....................B&S
ENGINE HP..................18
COOLING...................AIR
FUEL........................G
SPEEDS...............VARIABLE
TRANSMISSION..........HYDRO
STEERING.................ZERO
STANDARD DECK............54"
WEIGHT.............1,054 LBS.
MSRP....................$6,770

RETAIL PRICING

YEAR	HIGH	LOW
1995	$578	$434
1996	$641	$481
1997	$710	$532

TS1893K

YEARS MFRD........1997-1998
ENGINE.................KOHLER
ENGINE HP..................18
FUEL........................G
SPEEDS.....................0-8
TRANSMISSION..........HYDRO
STEERING.................ZERO
STANDARD DECK............54"
MSRP....................$7,130

OPTIONS

64" DECK

SERIAL NUMBERS

YEAR	BEGINNING NO.
1997	970261

RETAIL PRICING

YEAR	HIGH	LOW
1997	$805	$603
1998	$893	$670

TS2093K

YEARS MFRD........1995-1998
ENGINE.................KOHLER
ENGINE HP..................20
COOLING...................AIR
FUEL........................G
SPEEDS...............VARIABLE
TRANSMISSION..........HYDRO
STEERING.................ZERO
STANDARD DECK............54"
WEIGHT.............1,060 LBS.
MSRP....................$7,180

OPTIONS

64" DECK
74" DECK

SERIAL NUMBERS

YEAR	BEGINNING NO.
1997	970297

RETAIL PRICING

YEAR	HIGH	LOW
1995	$677	$508
1996	$754	$565
1997	$835	$626
1998	$925	$694

TS2293K

YEARS MFRD........1995-1998
ENGINE.................KOHLER
ENGINE HP..................22
COOLING...................AIR
FUEL........................G
SPEEDS...............VARIABLE
TRANSMISSION..........HYDRO
STEERING.................ZERO
STANDARD DECK............54"
WEIGHT.............1,121 LBS.
MSRP....................$7,385

OPTIONS

64" DECK
74" DECK

SERIAL NUMBERS

YEAR	BEGINNING NO.
1997	970210

RETAIL PRICING

YEAR	HIGH	LOW
1995	$677	$508
1996	$750	$562
1997	$835	$626
1998	$925	$694

VR31-50

YEARS MFRD........2009-2016
ENGINE............KAWASAKI
CYLINDERS..................2
ENGINE HP..................31
COOLING...................AIR
FUEL........................G
SPEEDS...............VARIABLE
TRANSMISSION..........HYDRO
STEERING.................ZERO
BLADE CLUTCH........ELECTRIC

VR31-50LP

YEARS MFRD........2011-2016
ENGINE............KAWASAKI
CYLINDERS..................2
CID.....................852CC
ENGINE HP..................31
COOLING...................AIR
SPEEDS...............VARIABLE
TRANSMISSION..........HYDRO
STEERING.................ZERO
BLADE CLUTCH........ELECTRIC

ZIPPER

VR31-60

YEARS MFRD 2009-2016
ENGINE .... KAWASAKI
CYLINDERS.................. 2
ENGINE HP................ 31
COOLING .... AIR
FUEL .... G
SPEEDS .... VARIABLE
TRANSMISSION .... HYDRO
STEERING................ ZERO
BLADE CLUTCH .... ELECTRIC

VR31-60LP

YEARS MFRD 2011-2016
ENGINE .... KAWASAKI
CYLINDERS.................. 2
CID 852CC
ENGINE HP................ 31
COOLING .... AIR
SPEEDS .... VARIABLE
TRANSMISSION .... HYDRO
STEERING................ ZERO
BLADE CLUTCH .... ELECTRIC

455

YEARS MFRD 1993-1998
ENGINE .... YANMAR
ENGINE HP................ 22
COOLING .... LIQUID
FUEL .... G
TRANSMISSION .... HYDRO
STEERING............ STANDARD

1535

YEARS MFRD 1990-1991
ENGINE .... KOHLER
ENGINE HP................ 15
COOLING .... AIR
FUEL .... G
TRANSMISSION .... GEAR
STEERING............ STANDARD
STANDARD DECK .... 44"
MSRP................. $3,999

RETAIL PRICING

YEAR	HIGH	LOW
1990	$1,149	$861
1991	$1,225	$919

NOTES

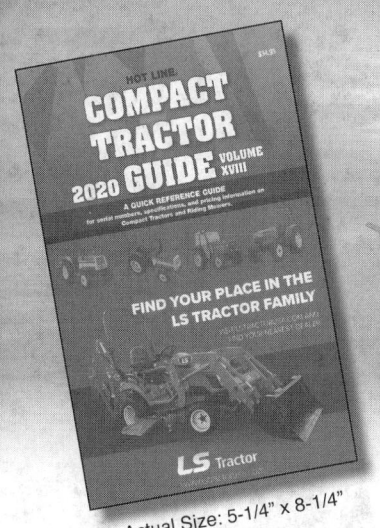

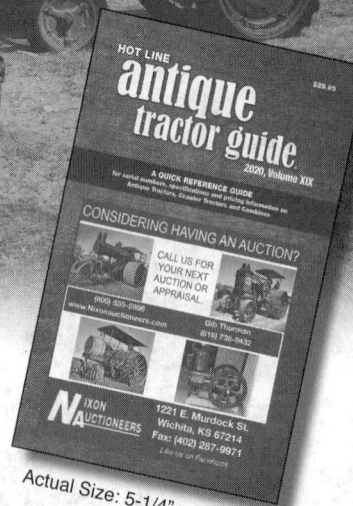